D1402750

GUIDE TO CIVIL WAR PERIODICALS
Volume II

Compiled by Lee W. Merideth

Published by
HISTORICAL INDEXES
Twentynine Palms, California
1997

Previously compiled and published by the author:
CIVIL WAR TIMES and CIVIL WAR TIMES, ILLUSTRATED 30 YEAR COMPREHENSIVE INDEX
GUIDE TO CIVIL WAR PERIODICALS, VOLUME I
Previously compiled for publication:
THE GETTYSBURG MAGAZINE INDEX, ISSUE 1 through 12
MILITARY HISTORY MAGAZINE INDEX: THE FIRST 10 YEARS, 1985-1994

Guide to Civil War Periodicals, Volume II
©1997 by Lee William Merideth

Produced and Published by
Historical Indexes
HCO 1, Box 2083
1638 Hales Road
Twentynine Palms, CA 92277

ISBN: 0-9626237-3-3

Publications and addresses referenced in the **GUIDE TO CIVIL WAR PERIODICALS, VOLUME II**
America's Civil War™, published by Cowles History Group, a division of Cowles Enthusiast Media, Inc., 741 Miller Drive SE, Suite D-2, Leesburg, VA 22075
American History™, published by Cowles History Group, a division of Cowles Enthusiast Media, Inc., 741 Miller Drive SE, Suite D-2, Leesburg, VA 22075
Blue & Gray Magazine™, published by Blue & Gray Enterprises, Inc., P.O. Box 28685, Columbus, Ohio 43228
Civil War: The Magazine of the Civil War Society™, published by Outlook, Inc., P. O. Box 770, Berryville, VA 22611
The Civil War News™, published by Historical Publications, Inc., Rt. 1, Box 36, Tunbridge, VT 05077
Civil War Regiments: A Journal of the American Civil War™, published by Regimental Studies, Inc., 1475 S. Bascom Avenue, Suite 204, Campbell, CA 95008
Civil War Times, Illustrated™, published by Cowles History Group, a division of Cowles Enthusiast Media, Inc., 741 Miller Drive SE, Suite D-2, Leesburg, VA 22075
Gettysburg Magazine™, published by Morningside House, 260 Oak Street, Dayton, OH 45410
Military History™, published by Cowles History Group, a division of Cowles Enthusiast Media, Inc., 741 Miller Drive SE, Suite D-2, Leesburg, VA 22075

Table of Contents

Foreword

The last several decades have been especially good ones for Civil War enthusiasts, historians and the reading public in general. Since the Centennial of the Civil War, the stream of books, articles and magazines pouring off the presses has yet to wane. Indeed, published materials on the conflict have been appearing in ever-increasing numbers—especially during the last half-dozen years. That's the good news.

Unfortunately, it is virtually impossible to keep track of what is available and where you can find it. Even if you merely dabble in the genre you know what I mean. New books are available on almost any given day from any number of presses, both large and small. The number of titles vying for shelf space in your local chain outlet is overwhelming—and yet does not represent even a small percentage of titles in print. The opposite side of the same coin deals with Civil War periodicals, of which there are at least a dozen. This mother lode of information contains thousands of articles and book reviews on virtually every conceivable subject and several you have never considered. How do you determine what article has been recently published on a particular regiment, battle or individual? Where can you find a book review on any of these? Who is reviewing what books and where can I read them?

As an undergraduate student at the University of Northern Iowa, I spent much of my free time digging through bound back issues of Civil War periodicals, absorbing articles on various topics and perusing book reviews. I learned the hard way that without organized record keeping, locating (or relocating) a particular article or review was an exasperating and often unsuccessful task. However, thanks to one researcher/compiler, those days of vexatious hunting are a thing of the past.

Lee Merideth and I became acquainted almost a decade ago. At that time he was climbing the summit of his mammoth project that resulted in the immensely useful *Civil War Times and Civil War Times, Illustrated 30-Year Comprehensive Index*. The success of that reference tool—which unlocked the scholarship trapped inside a collection of magazines that almost everyone owned by no one could effectively utilize—spawned another ground breaking publication: *Guide to Civil War Periodicals, Volume I*. The first volume of the *Guide* boasts over 30,000 cross-referenced listings (including book reviews) from six magazines or periodicals. Many time I have watched Lee smile and nod in appreciation when showered with the words of gratitude by a user of one of his tomes.

Years of additional compiling and research (sandwiched between untold hours of work indexing Savas Publishing titles) has broken new ground once again with the second volume of the *Guide to Civil War Periodicals*. Almost twice as long with 58,000 cross-referenced listings, this installment of the *Guide* includes the same periodicals (published from 1991-1995) covered in the earlier volume, as well as three additional publications *(The Civil War News* book reviews; *Civil War Regiments: A Journal of the American Civil War* and *American History)*. It is now easier than ever to relax in your favorite easy chair and explore your magazine (and local library's) collection in a way never before possible.

It is worth noting that in addition to Lee's triumvirate of indexes, the current outpouring of Civil War titles includes several worthwhile reference works that complement Lee's endeavors. Of recent vintage is David J. Eicher's *The Civil War in Books: An Analytical Bibliography,* a pleasing expansion of the popular but woefully outdated *Civil War Books: A Critical Bibliography,* edited by Allen Nevins, James I. Robertson, Jr., and Bell I. Wiley, and *More Generals in Gray*, by Bruce Allardice. As one who can testify to the rigors of everyday research, all of these books are invaluable additions and worth several times their cover price.

More than half a decade ago I concluded the Foreword to the first volume of Lee's *Guide* with the following observation: "Students and even general readers of the most exciting and defining four years of our existence as a nation will be very excited by the publication of this book. Researchers will be eternally grateful." Having lived with these indexes for some time, I stand behind my closing testimonial.

Theodore P. Savas
Savas Publishing Company

Preface

In January 1990 I completed and published *Civil War Times and Civil War Times, Illustrated 30 Year Comprehensive Index* and in December 1991 I completed the *Guide to Civil War Periodicals, Volume I.* At the time, little did I realize how that innocuous little statement *"Volume I"* would come back to haunt me so many times over the next several years. Had I left it off the title I could easily have ignored any urge to ever publish a *Volume II,* and I wouldn't have set any expectations from the users of that first volume as to the eventual publication of a second volume. Granted, I could have ignored those many, many folks who kept asking when then next volume would be published and gotten on with my life, but the fact is, that isn't what I really wanted to do. That little statement was added to the title because, in all honesty, I really did want to publish a *Volume II.*

What I absolutely did not anticipate was the size of the second volume. My original (and, until fairly recently) projection was a book similar to or even smaller than *Volume I* (at 360 pages) because I figured that this book would only contain five years of the magazines that were in the first volume. Instead of going back to Volume 1, Issue 1 of all of them, I would only be doing those articles published between 1991 and 1995.) I figured that those five years, plus the addition of two new titles, would get me up to about where I was last time. For good measure, I would include in *Volume II* the articles from ten issues of *Civil War Times, Illustrated* that were included in *Volume I* so that those users of *CWTI* wouldn't have to buy all three books to get a complete index of *CWTI.*

Although I was creating my database over the years, it wasn't until late 1996 that I discovered that, instead of around the 30,000 entries in *Volume I, Volume II* would have close to 58,000 entries! I was, to say the least, shocked. Suddenly, my "little" volume was a monster I had to somehow control. The first printed draft came in at 642 pages! So, it became a issue to figure out how to reduce the page count without affecting the usability of the book or deleting any of the listings. By changing the column size and abbreviating some of the military ranks or state names, I was able to drop 114 pages from the first draft, and what you have is a 528 page index. Had I abbreviated all of the ranks and states, I could have reduced another 50-60 pages, but the search-and-replace option on my word processing program wouldn't catch them all, and it became a real mess. So, you'll find some are abbreviated, however most aren't.

Included in the *Guide to Civil War Periodicals, Volume II* are listings for every individual, place, event, military unit, boat and portrait included in the magazines I indexed. Some contemporary photographs (but no drawings, paintings, etc.) are included. Maps and modern photographs were left out this time because my survey of users indicated that very few people ever used them.

Volume II continues where *Volume I* left off: at the beginning of 1991 with all of the same periodicals used in *Volume I: America's Civil War; Civil War, The Magazine of the Civil War Society; Blue and Gray Magazine; Civil War Times, Illustrated; Gettysburg Magazine; Military History.* I have also included two new periodicals: *American Heritage* from May, 1966 and *Civil War Regiments* from Volume 1, Number 1. All of these titles through December 1995 are included. In addition, I've included the ten issues of *Civil War Times, Illustrated* from May 1989 through December 1990. Although these were included in *Volume I,* to make it easier for the folks who only want an index for *CWTI,* I also included them in *Volume II.* Thus, they only have to buy two instead of the three of my current books that contain *CWTI.*

One other thing that is different about *Volume II* is the "mini-index" of the articles in *CWTI.* Because so many people have the first stand-alone index for *CWTI* I had to make a choice to either publish another small index of that magazine for them, or include it in *Volume II* of the *Guide.* The cost of producing such a small index wouldn't justify its publication as a stand alone, so I decided to include it in this volume. It is, basically, an index of articles and book reviews, and not a detailed index as is the rest of the *Guide.* However, note that all of the detailed information not included in the "mini-guide" is included in the main portion of the book.

In the back of the book I've also included the same subsections that were included in *Volume I.* Please, *please* read the section on **"How to Use This Guide"** following this preface. It will provide you with much detail on how to best utilize the book.

Any project of this type takes on a life of its own. Every one of the 58,000+ entries had to be typed into a database, checked, sorted, combined with similar entries, sorted again, cross-referenced, sorted again, text-enhancements added, uploaded from the database to a word processing program and then transferred to a publishing program. To do this, four years ago I bought a new computer that is now not "state of the art" but that has performed flawlessly.

I wish I could say the same about my ability to stay with this and get it done. This volume is about 12 months behind schedule, and if it hadn't been for the rather liberal vacation policy at my real job, it would be another several months late. That, plus having to stop everything whenever a new issue of *Civil War Regiments* or some new book by Savas Publishing needed to be indexed, caused for a lot of lost time.

My original plan was to publish a new index every five years. Due to the size of this one, if and when **Volume III** comes out, it will probably be a three or four year index and not five. So, by adding a *"Volume II"* to the title indicates that maybe, someday soon, I'll actually publish another volume.

There are several people who I want to acknowledge that can be grouped into two categories: those who helped on the book and those who inspired me to do it (many did both).

The "Help" category would include my mother, who checked and proofread listings and continually urged me to get this done with. I've joked through the years about her limited knowledge of the Civil War, but, all joking aside, she is willing to learn about it, and, is a ready worker when called upon. Typical mom, I suppose. Also, in this category I would have to include Ted Savas of Campbell, California, who not only helped on the book, wrote the foreword and provided guidance, but he *sells* a lot of my books which is very handy if I'm going to continue doing them. Then, I would like to thank David Lang of Sunnyvale, California who helped with the proofreading.

The "Inspired" group is extensive: a lot of friends offered suggestions, criticism and condolences (like, *you're crazy for doing this,* or *get a life* or whatever). Maybe I am crazy for spending so much time on this, and maybe now I'll get a life. Anyone out there have an unmarried sister...? Anyway, I want to thank my "team" from work (the job that really pays the bills): Sandra Adame, Kathy Bishop, Laurie Butler, Grace DelVaglio, Lynda Dwyer, Tina Fisher, Gita Patel and Lisa Winterman and my friends Mary Christian, Bill Haley, Michele Hoppe, Michelle McKenzie, Lynda Peterson, Paul Rhilinger, Richard Rollins and Alex and Carol Savas. Finally, I can't ignore my four-legged companion, Ms. Yank who, at this moment, is sound asleep on top of the computer monitor.

Two names sadly missing are my father, Edward, who left us in January, 1994 and my other cat, Ms. Reb, who went down, fighting to the end, late last year.

I hope you find the *Guide to Civil War Periodicals, Volume II* a valuable resource tool. Any errors that have crept into this compilation, and there are going to be some, are regrettable and a result of my oversight alone.

Lee William Merideth
Major, USAR (Ret)
Sunnyvale, California
June 16, 1997

How to Use this Guide

The *GUIDE TO CIVIL WAR PERIODICALS, VOLUME II* (hereafter referred to as the *Guide*) has been organized to allow you to quickly find the source article for any person, place, event, military unit, boat or portrait contained within the *Guide*.

Each article was indexed then combined into one consolidated index which includes over 58,000 listings obtained from the 1,600+ articles included in the index. Next, the listings were organized by topic into categories and sub-categories to make the *Guide* more useful as a researching tool. Finally, the listings were organized in alpha-numeric order, both for the index-at-large and for the category and sub-category listings.

There are a couple notable changes from Volume I. In addition to adding two new titles, there is now a mini-index for *Civil War Times, Illustrated* that lists all of the articles and book reviews from March 1989 through the end of 1995. This was done so that those folks who only use *CWTI* and have the previous stand-alone index (*Civil War Times and Civil War Times, Illustrated 30 Year Comprehensive Index*) would have an easier time finding only those listings relating only to *CWTI*. However, all of the *CWTI* listings are also included in the main consolidated index.

A major change in the organization of the book is the addition of a section called **"SHIPS, BOATS, VESSELS, ETC."** All of the listings for any type of water-craft (Confederate or Federal) are listed in alphabetical order in this section, which reduces the confusion caused by the previous volume where I tried to sort them by type of vessel.

How to use the Guide

The *Guide* is divided into six major sections: *Consolidated Subject Index; Civil War Times, Illustrated Mini-Index; List of Articles, By Author; List of Book Reviews, By Author; List of Book Reviews, By Book Title; Numerical Listings of All Articles, by Magazine Title.* All six sections are inter-related and perform a function as part of the index. As a rule of thumb, three sections are critical to the use of the *Guide*: the *Consolidated Subject Index; List of Book Reviews, By Book Title; Numerical Listings of All Articles.*

The *Consolidated Subject Index* is the heart of the *Guide.* A listing in the *Consolidated Subject Index* consists of:

Subject, e.g. **ANTIETAM, MARYLAND, BATTLE OF**
Categories, e.g. ARTICLES, BOOK REVIEWS, GENERAL LISTINGS, ADDITIONAL LISTINGS etc. are in SMALL TYPE (located primarily in the GENERAL LISTINGS section)
Sub Categories, e.g. *general history, letters to the editor, photos,* etc. are in *italic* type (located primarily in the GENERAL LISTINGS section)

A Category listing for ARTICLES lists all published ARTICLES which relate in a major way to the **SUBJECT.** Each listing includes the title of the article and its location. A Category listing for BOOK REVIEWS lists the **BOOK REVIEWS** pertaining to the **SUBJECT.** A listing here includes only the title of the book because many magazines have reviews for the same book. Thus, you need to look in the major section *BOOK REVIEWS, BY BOOK TITLE* to find all places a book review appeared.

A Category listing for GENERAL LISTINGS contains one or more SUB-CATAGORIES, which consists of specific people, places or events associated with the **SUBJECT.** Thus, under the GENERAL LISTINGS section for **ANTIETAM, MARYLAND, BATTLE OF** you will find the listings *in book review, Iron Brigade, Jackson, letters to the editor, Save Historic Antietam Foundation,* etc., followed by one or more listings for these items. Note that a *SUB-CATAGORY* listing *in book review* means that the subject was mentioned in a book review, but is not the primary subject of that book review.

A Category listing for ADDITIONAL LISTINGS means that the subject was mentioned in an article, but was not a significant subject. Listings appearing here are either too generic to fit into a well-defined category or are so obscure that they are listed only because I have tried to include all references in all articles.

The way I would consider an ADDITIONAL LISTING or a *SUB-CATAGORY* listing is that if I were going to run out and obtain copies of each article for a given subject, I would concentrate on the *SUB-CATAGORY* listing and not on the ADDITIONAL LISTINGS.

There are two types of references to book reviews. The first is a book review devoted to a subject, e.g. **LEE at CHANCELLORSVILLE,** and these are listed under BOOK REVIEWS. The second is a reference contained within a book review that is not a major part of the book, e.g. the mention of **MEADE** in a book review would be listed under *in book review.*

Once you have found the subject and its listings, how do you determine where to find a specific listing? Each listing is contained somewhere within the article referenced. My assumption is that if you are interested enough about a subject to look up the article, you will read the article to find the subject. All references are to the first page the article appears on. How do you interpret the listings? The reference listings are broken into four parts (three if the listing is contained in a BOOK REVIEW). A typical listing would be:

ADAMS, WILLIAM WIRT ACW:MAY/92[47]363

Part 1 is "ACW:", part 2 is "MAY/92", part 3 is [47] and part 4 is "363", defined as follows:

> **ACW** is the abbreviation for the magazine:
> ACW = *America's Civil War*
> AHI = *American History*
> B&G = *Blue & Gray Magazine*
> CWM = *Civil War Magazine*
> CWNEWS = *The Civil War News*
> CWR = *Civil War Regiments*
> CWTI = *Civil War Times, Illustrated*
> GETTY = *Gettysburg Magazine*
> MH = *Military History*
>
> **MAY/92** is the cover date of the magazine
> **[47]** is the page number the article begins on
> **363** is the article number. Each article is numbered sequentially and you can reference this number in the *NUMERICAL LISTING OF ALL ARTICLES, BY MAGAZINE TITLE* section.

(If you check this listing, you will find a listing titled "BRILLIANT CAVALRY EXPLOIT" by Tim DeForest on page 47 of the May 1992 issue of *America's Civil War Magazine.*)

Watercraft and vessels are all listed under **SHIPS, BOATS, VESSELS, ETC.**
Military Rank is the highest rank listed in the sum of the articles.
Military Units are listed by state, United States Troops, United States Colored Troops, United States Sharpshooters (USSS) or Confederate Troops.

The *Civil War Times Mini-Index* follows the same style as the *Consolidated Subject Index.*

The *List of Articles, By Author* and *List of Book Reviews, By Author* allow you to look up an author to find articles or books written by that person.

The *List of Book Reviews, By Book Title* allows you to find all of the reviews about a particular book, the author of the book and the name of the reviewer of the book.

The *Numerical Listing of All Articles, by Magazine Title* is a list of all articles, in numerical sequence. This section is easily identifiable because of the large tab on those pages.

If you do not have access to the magazines listed in the **Guide,** contact your local library or write the publishers directly. Addresses for the publishers are listed on the Legal page (page 2).

If you have any questions or comments, please send them to me. Several suggestions I received from the previous books have been incorporated into this one.

GUIDE TO CIVIL WAR PERIODICALS

Volume II

Containing a complete index of all of the articles, editorials and book reviews included in the following periodicals:

America's Civil War,™ (January 1991 through November 1995), 280 articles
American History,™ (May, 1966 through October 1995), 209 articles
Blue & Gray Magazine,™ (February 1991 through December 1995), 180 articles
Civil War: The Magazine of the Civil War Society,™ (January 1991 through December 1995), 310 articles
The Civil War News,™ (July 1988 through December 1995, book reviews only)
Civil War Regiments: A Journal of the American Civil War,™ (Volume 1, Number 1 through Volume 4, Number 4), 81 articles
Civil War Times, Illustrated,™ (March, 1989 through December, 1995), 384 articles
Gettysburg Magazine,™ (Issue #4, January 1991 through Issue #13, July 1995), 122 articles
Military History,™ (February 1991 through December 1995), 38 articles

A

ABBAY, GEORGE, *Captain, Mississippi Battery;*
ACW:JAN/94[30]450

ABBEVILLE, SOUTH CAROLINA:
ARTICLE: "IN THE LITTLE-KNOWN BURT-STARK HOUSE,
THE DECISION WAS MADE TO END THE
CONFEDERACY," ACW:MAY/92[62]364

ABBEY, FREDERICK, *Lieutenant, 37th Illinois Infantry;*
CWR:VOL1#1[42]105

ABBOTT, EDWARD, *Captain, 2nd Massachusetts Infantry;*
CWR:VOL3#1[31]150, GETTY:6[69]176

ABBOTT, HENRY L., *Colonel, USA;*
BOOK REVIEW: *FALLEN LEAVES: THE CIVIL WAR LETTERS
OF MAJOR HENRY LIVERMORE ABBOTT*
GENERAL LISTINGS: ACW:MAY/92[30]361, ACW:SEP/95[30]545,
CWR:VOL3#1[31]150, *photo;* CWR:VOL3#1[31]150

ABBOTT, JAMES M., *Corporal, 2nd Tennessee Cavalry;*
CWR:VOL4#1[1]163

ABBOTT, JOSEPH C., *Colonel, USA;*
ACW:MAY/92[30]361,B&G:DEC/94[10]585,
CWR:VOL4#3[1]170

ABBOTT, JOSIAH G., *civilian;* CWR:VOL3#1[31]150

ABBOTT, LEMUEL A., *Lieutenant, USA;* B&G:DEC/92[8]503

ABBOTT, OTHMAN, *Private, 95th Illinois Infantry;*
CWTI:JAN/93[20]298

ABERCROMBIE, J.J., *General, USA;* AHI:APR/83[27]233

ABERCROMBIE, JOHN C., *Lieutenant Colonel, 11th Iowa
Infantry;* ACW:JAN/93[10]393

ABERNATHY, MARTHA, BOOK REVIEW: *THE CIVIL WAR
DIARY OF MARTHA ABERNATHY, WIFE OF DR. C.C.
ABERNATHY OF PULASKI, TENNESSEE,*
CWNEWS:APR/95[33]

ABLE, JOHN, *Lieutenant, CSA;* CWTI:JAN/93[12]

ABLES, ZACHARIAH, *Private, 1st Georgia Regulars;*
CWR:VOL2#2[95]135

ABOLITIONISM:
ARTICLES: "BLEEDING KANSAS," AHI:JUL/75[4]160, "METEOR
OF THE WAR," ACW:JUL/91[43]315
BOOK REVIEWS: *THE ABOLITIONIST LEGACY: FROM
RECONSTRUCTION, TO THE NAACP *AHEAD OF HER
TIME: ABBY KELLEY AND THE POLITICS OF
ANTISLAVERY *MOORFIELD STOREY AND THE
ABOLITIONIST TRADITION*
ADDITIONAL LISTINGS: ACW:NOV/94[42]497, ACW:NOV/95[54]558,
CWM:JAN/92[8]399, CWM:JAN/92[21]402,
CWR:VOL3#1[31]150, CWR:VOL3#1[80],
CWTI:MAY/89[21]115, CWTI:SEPT/89[40]130,
CWTI:DEC/89[62]139, CWTI:JUN/90[46]161,
CWTI:DEC/91[48]242, CWTI:JUL/92[20]271,
CWTI:MAY/94[46]385

ABRAHAM, JOSEPH S., *Lieutenant, 164th New York Infantry;*
ACW:JUL/91[50]

ABRAMS, ALEXANDER S., *civilian;* AHI:DEC/77[13]176

ACHESON, DAVID, *Captain, 140th Pennsylvania Infantry;*
BOOK REVIEW: *INSCRIPTION AT GETTYSBURG*

ACKERMAN, ANDREW H., *Captain, 11th New Jersey Infantry;*
GETTY:12[7]241

ACKERMAN, DANIEL, *Pvt., 7th Wisc. Inf.,* GETTY:11[57]233

ACKERMAN, RICHARD, *Private, 5th New York Infantry;*
CWR:VOL1#2[29]112

ACKLEY, GUSTAVUS J., *Private, 154th New York Infantry;*
B&G:OCT/93[36]540

ACTON, THOMAS C., *civilian;* AHI:AUG/77[30]175

ACUFF, JAMES H. and JASPER S., *Private, 2nd Tennessee
Cavalry;* CWR:VOL4#1[1]163

ADAIRE, T.N., *Lt. Col., 4th Mississippi Inf.;* B&G:FEB/94[8]550

ADAMS (MISSISSIPPI) LIGHT GUARD; GETTY:4[7]142

ADAMS, CHARLES F. JR., *Colonel, USA;*
ACW:NOV/91[46]335, ACW:MAY/92[23]360,
B&G:OCT/93[12]537, B&G:OCT/93[21]538,
CWM:MAY/91[26]349, CWM:JUL/93[8]483, GETTY:11[19]232,
GETTY:12[85]248, CWTI:SEP/92[46]284,
CWTI:AUG/95[40]458

ADAMS, CHARLES F. SR.; AHI:JAN/78[34]178,
CWTI:DEC/95[22]476

ADAMS, CHRISTOPHER; AHI:NOV/70[22]130

ADAMS, CICERO, *Private, 22nd South Carolina Infantry;*
ARTICLE: "LEE'S LIEUTENANT: J.E.B. STUART,"
CWM:JUL/92[16]428

ADAMS, DANIEL W., *General, CSA:*
ARTICLE: "TENACITY OF SOLDIERS OF THE DEEP SOUTH AT
MURFREESBORO," CWM:FEB/95[28]560
GENERAL LISTINGS: *buried at,* B&G:AUG/95[8]604, *SIO,*
B&G:JUN/94[38]571
ADDITIONAL LISTINGS: B&G:AUG/95[8]604, CWM:AUG/95[26]604,
CWR:VOL4#3[50]171

ADAMS, G.W., *Pvt., 12th New Jersey Infantry;* GETTY:5[89]162

ADAMS, H.W., *Maj., 7th Kent. Inf. (Union);* B&G:FEB/94[8]550

ADAMS, JOHN, *Capt., 19th Mass. Inf.;* GETTY:10[53]225

ADAMS, JOHN, *General, CSA;* B&G:OCT/91[11]466,
B&G:JUN/93[12]524, B&G:DEC/93[52]548,
B&G:AUG/95[8]604, CWM:OCT/94[8], CWTI:MAR/93[24]309

ADAMS, JOHN, *Lt., 2nd Kentucky Cav.;* CWTI:DEC/94[79]417

ADAMS, JOHN, *Lt. Colonel, 1st Minn. Inf.;* GETTY:5[79]161

ADAMS, JOHN, *Private, Sumter Artillery;* CWR:VOL3#2[1]153

ADAMS, JOSEPH, *Pvt., 51st NC Inf.;* B&G:APR/93[24]520

ADAMS, JULIUS W., *cadet;* B&G:DEC/91[12]469

ADAMS, LEROY, *Capt., 24th Michigan Inf.;* GETTY:5[19]158

ADAMS, MYRON, *Pvt., 126th NY Inf.;* CWR:VOL1#4[7]125

ADAMS, R.J., *Private, 22nd Virginia Inf.;* CWR:VOL1#3[52]122

ADAMS, RICHARD H.T., *Captain, CSA;* GETTY:4[110]152

ADAMS, ROBERT N., *Colonel, USA;* B&G:DEC/95[9]615

ADAMS, SILAS, *Captain, USA;* GETTY:13[50]257

ADAMS, SILAS, *Lieutenant Colonel, 1st Kentucky (Union)
Cavalry;* B&G:DEC/94[22]586

ADAMS, WILLIAM M., *Sergeant, 4th North Carolina Infantry;*
CWM:JUL/92[16]428

ADAMS, WILLIAM WIRT, *General, CSA;*
ACW:NOV/91[22]331, ACW:MAY/92[47]363,
B&G:JUN/93[12]524, B&G:FEB/94[8]550,
B&G:AUG/95[8]604, CWR:VOL2#1[36]132,
CWTI:JUL/94[50]395, MH:JUN/93[82]167, *photo;*
B&G:JUN/93[12]524

ADARE, JOHNNY, *Private, CSA;* MH:JUN/91[20]152

ADDISON-DARNEILLE, HENRIETTA S.; ARTICLE: "FOR
BETTER OR FOR WORSE," CWTI:MAY/92[32]264

ADERHOLD, JACOB W., *Lieutenant Colonel, 1st Confederate
Georgia Infantry;* CWR:VOL1#4[42]126

AERONAUTICS; BOOK REVIEW: *AERONAUTICS IN THE
UNION AND CONFEDERATE ARMIES*

AFTEN, THOMAS D., *Private, 151st Pennsylvania Infantry;*
CWTI:SEP/90[26]174
AGER, WILLIAM; ACW:JUL/93[8]420
AGNEL, HYACINTH R.; B&G:DEC/91[12]469
AGNEW, C.R., *civilian;* CWTI:MAR/93[26]310
AGNEW, SAMUEL A., *Chaplain;* ARTICLE: "A CIVILIAN AT
BRICE'S CROSS ROADS," CWTI:JAN/94[39]362
AGNUS, FELIX, *Lieutenant, 5th New York Infantry;*
CWR:VOL1#2[7]111, CWTI:MAY/94[31]382
AHL, GEORGE, *Captain, USA;* CWTI:JUL/93[20]325
AIKEN, CHARLES G., *Sergeant USA;* GETTY:10[42]224
AIKEN, DAVID W., *Colonel, 7th South Carolina Infantry;*
CWR:VOL1#4[7]125, GETTY:5[35]159, GETTY:5[47]160
AIKEN, HUGH, *Colonel, 5th South Carolina Cavalry;*
B&G:DEC/92[20]504
AIKEN, JOHN, *Surgeon, 71st Pennsylvania Infantry;*
GETTY:10[53]225
AIKEN, STEPHEN, *Private, 125th Pennsylvania Infantry;*
B&G:OCT/95[8]611A
AIKENS, JOHN F., *Captain USA;* CWR:VOL1#4[7]125
"ALABAMA CLAIMS"; AHI:JAN/83[10]232,
CWNEWS:JAN/90[4]
CSS ALABAMA; see listings under **"SHIPS, BOATS,
VESSELS, ETC."**
CSS ALABAMA vs *USS KEARSARGE;* see listings under
**"NAVAL WARFARE" and "SHIPS, BOATS, VESSELS,
ETC."**

ALABAMA TROOPS:
1st Cavalry; CWR:VOL4#1[44]164
1st Infantry; ACW:JAN/94[30]450, CWR:VOL1#4[42]126,
CWR:VOL3#4[68], GETTY:10[102]226, GETTY:13[108]261
1st Infantry (Union); CWTI:NOV/93[65]351
2nd Cavalry; B&G:JUN/93[12]524
3rd Infantry; ACW:SEP/92[38]379, B&G:FEB/95[8]590B,
B&G:APR/95[8]595, CWR:VOL3#3[1]157,
CWTI:DEC/91[26]238, GETTY:4[33]146, GETTY:4[49]147,
GETTY:5[128]167, GETTY:6[94]180, GETTY:10[7]221,
GETTY:12[1]240, GETTY:12[111]250, GETTY:13[33]255
4th Cavalry; B&G:FEB/92[40]479, CWM:DEC/95[48]631
4th Infantry:
ARTICLE: "THE 4TH ALABAMA INFANTRY UNWITTINGLY
HELPED CREATE A CIVIL WAR LEGEND AT MANASSAS,"
ACW:NOV/94[18]495
ADDITIONAL LISTINGS: ACW:JUL/92[30]369, B&G:FEB/91[34]442,
B&G:FEB/94[8]550, CWR:VOL2#4[269]145,
CWTI:JUL/92[8]269, GETTY:6[43]173, GETTY:7[41]189,
GETTY:8[53]203, GETTY:12[1]240, GETTY:12[111]250,
GETTY:13[7]253
5th Infantry; ACW:SEP/93[31]433, ACW:JAN/95[46]507,
B&G:FEB/95[8]590A, B&G:APR/95[8]595,
CWR:VOL1#3[52]122, CWR:VOL3#3[1]157,
CWTI:JUL/93[34]327, GETTY:4[33]146, GETTY:4[49]147,
GETTY:6[7]169, GETTY:4[115]152, ETTY:6[13]170,
GETTY:7[13]186, GETTY:7[83]192, GETTY:9[61]215,
GETTY:10[7]221, GETTY:12[61]245, GETTY:12[123]251,
GETTY:13[33]255
6th Cavalry; B&G:DEC/91[38]471, CWM:JAN/91[40]330
6th Infantry; ACW:JAN/93[8]392, ACW:MAY/93[14]413,
ACW:SEP/93[31]433, ACW:JUL/94[51]480,
ACW:JAN/95[46]507, B&G:APR/95[8]595,
CWR:VOL3#3[1]157, GETTY:4[33]146, GETTY:4[49]147,
GETTY:5[128]167, GETTY:10[7]221, GETTY:12[111]250

7th Cavalry; ACW:MAR/91[38]296
7th Infantry; B&G:AUG/92[40]495
8th Cavalry; CWM:JAN/91[40]330
8th Infantry; CWR:VOL3#1[65]151, CWR:VOL3#3[1]157,
CWTI:JUL/93[42]329, GETTY:9[5]209, GETTY:12[7]241
9th Infantry; CWM:JUL/92[16]428, CWM:JUN/95[29]583,
CWTI:DEC/91[26]238, GETTY:12[111]250
10th Cavalry; B&G:FEB/91[32]441, CWM:JUL/92[16]428,
CWR:VOL3#2[1]153, CWTI:FEB/90[74]149,
CWTI:JUL/93[42]329, GETTY:5[79]161, GETTY:9[5]209,
GETTY:12[7]241, GETTY:12[111]250
11th Infantry; ACW:SEP/92[38]379, CWTI:JUL/93[42]329,
GETTY:12[7]241, GETTY:5[79]161, GETTY:9[5]209
12th Cavalry; B&G:DEC/91[12]469
12th Infantry; ACW:SEP/93[31]433, ACW:JAN/95[46]507,
B&G:DEC/92[8]503, B&G:APR/93[6]517, CWM:SEP/93[8]493,
CWR:VOL3#3[1]157, GETTY:4[33]146, GETTY:4[49]147,
GETTY:5[117]165, GETTY:5[128]167, GETTY:10[7]221
13th Infantry; ACW:JUL/92[30]369, B&G:FEB/95[8]590A,
CWNEWS:NOV/95[29], CWR:VOL1#3[52]122,
CWTI:JUL/93[34]327, GETTY:4[115]152, GETTY:5[4]156,
GETTY:6[7]169, GETTY:6[13]170, GETTY:9[61]215,
GETTY:9[109]218, GETTY:12[61]245, GETTY:12[111]250,
GETTY:12[123]251
14th Infantry; CWR:VOL4#1[1]163, GETTY:5[79]161
15th Infantry:
BOOK REVIEW: *WAR BETWEEN THE UNION AND THE
CONFEDERACY AND ITS LOST OPPORTUNITIES WITH A
HISTORY OF THE 15TH ALABAMA REGIMENT AND THE
FORTY-EIGHT BATTLES IN WHICH IT WAS ENGAGED*
ADDITIONAL LISTINGS: ACW:JAN/92[38]343, ACW:SEP/93[62]436,
ACW:JUL/94[42]479, B&G:AUG/92[11]493,
B&G:JUN/95[8]600, CWM:JUL/92[8]427,
CWM:DEC/94[26]548, CWR:VOL1#3[28]120,
CWR:VOL3#4[68], CWTI:JUL/93[42]329,
CWTI:SEP/93[53]340, CWTI:MAR/94[48]374,
GETTY:5[103]163, GETTY:6[43]173, GETTY:7[13]186,
GETTY:7[41]189, GETTY:8[53]203, GETTY:13[7]253
16th Infantry; ACW:SEP/93[38]434, ACW:NOV/93[34]442,
B&G:FEB/93[12]511, CWTI:SEP/94[40]403
17th Infantry; CWR:VOL1#4[42]126
19th Infantry; B&G:FEB/94[8]550
20th Infantry; B&G:FEB/94[8]550
21st Infantry; ACW:SEP/92[8]374, CWR:VOL4#3[77]174,
CWTI:SEPT/89[20]127
22nd Infantry; CWTI:SEP/92[31]281
23rd Infantry; B&G:APR/92[8]481, B&G:FEB/94[8]550,
B&G:FEB/94[57]555
25th Infantry; ARTICLE: "WRITING HOME TO TALLADEGA,"
CWTI:DEC/90[56]184
26th Infantry; CWR:VOL3#3[1]157, GETTY:4[33]146,
GETTY:4[49]147, GETTY:5[128]167, GETTY:10[7]221
27th Infantry; B&G:FEB/92[10]474, CWR:VOL2#1[36]132
28th Infantry; CWTI:SEP/92[31]281
29th Infantry; B&G:DEC/93[12]545, B&G:DEC/93[52]548
30th Infantry; ACW:NOV/91[22]331, B&G:FEB/94[8]550,
CWR:VOL2#1[19]131
31st Infantry; B&G:FEB/94[8]550
32nd Infantry; CWM:FEB/95[28]560, CWM:AUG/95[26]604
33rd Infantry; AHI:JUL/93[40]312, B&G:AUG/93[6]528,
CWTI:SEP/94[40]403
34th Infantry; CWTI:SEP/92[31]281

ALEXANDER, JAMES H., *Private, Sumter Artillery;*
CWR:VOL3#2[1]153

ALEXANDER, JOHN, *Mosby's Rangers;* ACW:JUL/94[26]477

ALEXANDER, JOSEPH W., *Lieutenant, CSN;*
AHI:OCT/75[30]162

ALEXANDER, SAM, *Mosby's Rangers;* ACW:JUL/94[26]477

ALEXANDER, SAM, *Adjutant, 3rd Georgia Infantry;*
CWTI:DEC/94[32]410

ALEXANDER, WILLIAM, *Lieutenant, 21st Alabama Infantry;*
AHI:OCT/95[16]325, CWR:VOL4#3[77]174,
CWTI:OCT/95[56]471

ALEXANDER, WILLIAM, *Private, 5th New York Infantry;*
CWR:VOL1#2[29]112

ALEXANDER, WILLIAM A., *Lieutenant, 21st Alabama
Infantry;* CWTI:SEPT/89[20]127

ALEXANDER, WILLIAM J., *Captain, 37th North Carolina
Infantry;* GETTY:12[111]250

ALGER, RUSSELL A., *Colonel, 5th Michigan Cavalry;*
ACW:JUL/92[41]370, CWTI:DEC/94[82]418,
GETTY:13[89]260, MH:FEB/93[42]164

ALISON, JOSEPH D., *Doctor, CSA;* ARTICLE: "WITH A
CONFEDERATE SURGEON AT VICKSBURG,"
AHI:JUL/68[31]115A

ALLAN, WILLIAM, *Colonel, CSA;* ACW:JUL/95[26]535,
CWM:JUN/95[53]590, CWM:OCT/95[5]613,
CWTI:JAN/93[40]301

ALLATOONA PASS, GEORGIA, BATTLE OF;
ACW:JAN/95[20]504, CWM:JAN/91[12]326,
CWR:VOL3#3[59]159, CWTI:SUMMER/89[13]120

ALLEGHANY (VIRGINIA) ARTILLERY; B&G:APR/92[8]481,
GETTY:4[49]147, GETTY:10[29]222

ALLEMAN, TILLIE P., *civilian;* GETTY:7[13]186

ALLEN, CHARLES, *Sergeant, 53rd Pennsylvania Infantry;*
GETTY:11[80]235

ALLEN, CHARLES J., *cadet;* B&G:DEC/91[12]469

ALLEN, DANIEL B., *Colonel, 154th New York Infantry;*
ACW:JUL/94[18]476, CWTI:SEP/94[34]402, GETTY:8[17]200,
photo, GETTY:8[17]200

ALLEN, EZRA, *balloonist;* AHI:JUN/84[24]239

ALLEN, FRANK, *Captain, USA;* MH:OCT/92[51]162

ALLEN, GEORGE, *Private, 9th New Hampshire Infantry;*
CWNEWS:MAY/89[4]

ALLEN, HENRY A., *Capt., 9th Virginia Inf.;* GETTY:12[111]250

ALLEN, HENRY W., *Governor, Louisiana;* ACW:NOV/95[8]552,
AHI:JUN/70[30]127, CWNEWS:MAY/90[4],
CWR:VOL4#2[68]167, CWTI:AUG/90[70]171, *photo,*
CWTI:AUG/90[64]170

ALLEN, J.H., *Lt., 14th South Carolina Inf.;* GETTY:13[22]254

ALLEN, JAMES, *balloonist;* AHI:JUN/84[24]239

ALLEN, JAMES, *Private, 15th Massachusetts Infantry;*
AHI:FEB/82[36]225, CWTI:JUL/94[20]390

ALLEN, JOHN H., *Pvt., 2nd Mississippi Inf.;* GETTY:6[77]177

ALLEN, JOHN W., *scout;* ACW:MAR/94[8]456

ALLEN, LAFAYETTE, *Captain, 3rd Arkansas Infantry;*
GETTY:5[117]165

ALLEN, LAWRENCE M., *Colonel, 64th North Carolina
Infantry;* B&G:FEB/91[20]440

ALLEN, NATHANIEL M., *Corporal, 1st Massachusetts
Infantry;* GETTY:12[7]241

ALLEN, RICHARD, *5th North Carolina Cavalry and 65th
North Carolina Infantry;* B&G:APR/92[36]483

ALLEN, ROBERT C., *Major, CSA;* CWTI:JUL/94[44]394

ALLEN, ROBERT T.P., *Colonel, 17th Texas Infantry;*
CWR:VOL3#3[33]158

ALLEN, T.T., *Captain, 7th Ohio Cavalry;* CWTI:JAN/93[49]303

ALLEN, THOMAS M., *Lieutenant, 4th North Carolina Infantry;*
GETTY:12[111]250

ALLEN, WILLIAM B., *Private, Crenshaw's Artillery;*
GETTY:10[107]227

ALLEN, WILLIAM C., *Lieutenant, U.S. Secret Service;*
CWTI:JUN/95[26]445

ALLEN, WILLIAM W., *General, CSA;* ACW:SEP/92[38]379,
B&G:DEC/95[9]615

ALLEY, D.N., *Private, 3rd Texas Cavalry;* ACW:MAR/93[68]409

ALLEY, LEANDER F., *Lieutenant, 20th Massachusetts
Infantry;* CWR:VOL4#4[101]181

ALLIGER, JOHN, *Private, 126th New York Infantry;*
CWR:VOL1#4[7]125

ALLISON, ANDREW B., *Sergeant, 5th New York Infantry;*
CWR:VOL1#2[7]111, CWTI:MAY/94[31]382

ALLISON, CLAY; ACW:MAR/94[6]455

ALLSBROOK, NEWSOM, *Private, 17th North Carolina
Infantry;* ACW:MAR/95[12]513

ALLSTON, BENJAMIN, *Colonel, CSA;* CWR:VOL4#1[1]163

ALLSTON, THOMAS, *Private, 31st USCT;* ACW:SEP/95[38]546

ALSTON, THOMAS P., *Lieutenant Colonel, 1st South Carolina
Infantry;* B&G:APR/93[12]518, GETTY:13[22]254

ALTERNATIVE HISTORY; ARTICLE: "WHAT MIGHT HAVE
BEEN," CWTI:SEP/94[56]405

ALTMAN, WILLIAM, *Surgeon, USA;* GETTY:9[81]216

AMBROSE, J.S., *Captain, CSA;* B&G:OCT/94[11]580

AMBROTYPE; see listings under "PHOTOGRAPHY"

AMELIA COURT HOUSE, VIRGINIA; AHI:SEP/87[40]263

AMENDMENTS, 13TH; CWTI:MAY/94[46]385

AMENDMENTS, 14TH; AHI:JAN/82[16]224,
CWTI:MAY/94[12]379

AMERICA ONLINE; CWTI:OCT/95[40]469

AMERICAN ARMS COMPANY; ACW:JUL/93[8]420

AMERICAN BATTLEFIELD PROTECTION PROGRAM;
see listings under "PRESERVATION"

AMES, ADELBERT, *General, USA;* ACW:JUL/94[42]479,
B&G:DEC/91[12]469, B&G:APR/94[10]558,
B&G:DEC/94[10]585, CWM:JUL/92[8]427,
CWNEWS:APR/90[4], GETTY:4[33]146, GETTY:7[29]188,
GETTY:9[5]209, GETTY:9[17]210, GETTY:11[19]232,
GETTY:12[30]243, *photo,* B&G:DEC/91[12]469

AMES, EDSON D., *Private, 154th New York Infantry;*
GETTY:8[17]200

AMES, HORATIO; CWTI:OCT/95[32]468

AMES, J.F., *Sergeant, CSA;* CWTI:DEC/91[22]237

AMES, LYMAN D., *Chaplain, USA;* GETTY:10[53]225

AMES, NELSON, *Captain, 1st New York Artillery;*
CWR:VOL3#2[1]153, GETTY:5[35]159, GETTY:8[53]203,
GETTY:9[41]212

AMES, OAKES; AHI:JUN/71[10]134

AMES, SARAH; ARTICLE: "MRS. AMES AND MR. LINCOLN:
HOW A SCULPTOR CAPTURED A GREAT AMERICAN'S
SPIRIT IN A STONE AND A PHOTOGRAPH,"
CWTI:APR/89[28]109

AMHERST (VIRGINIA) ARTILLERY; GETTY:7[124]196

AMICI, AUGUSTO, *Corp., 5th NY Inf.;* CWR:VOL1#2[7]111

AMICK, MYRON J., *Sgt., 15th Illinois Cav.;* B&G:FEB/91[8]439

AMMEN, DANIEL; BOOK REVIEW: *THE ATLANTIC COAST*

AMMEN, JACOB; B&G:AUG/91[11]458

AMPEY, THOMAS R., *Private, 54th Massachusetts Infantry;*
CWTI:DEC/89[53]138
AMPUTATION; ARTICLE: "LIMBS MADE AND UNMADE BY
WAR," ACW:SEP/95[38]546
ANACONDA PLAN; ACW:MAR/92[54], ACW:JUL/93[42]425,
B&G:FEB/93[48]515, CWR:VOL2#1[1]130,
CWR:VOL3#3[33]158, CWR:VOL3#3[92]
ANALYSIS OF THE WAR; ARTICLE: "THE WAR WE NEVER
FINISHED," CWTI:DEC/89[62]139
ANDER, GEORGE, *Major, CSA;* ACW:SEP/92[47]380
ANDERSON (WISCONSIN) GUARDS; GETTY:4[16]143
ANDERSON, ADNA, *civilian;* MH:APR/92[18]157
ANDERSON, BEN M., *Colonel, CSA;* MH:JUN/91[20]152
ANDERSON, CHARLES, *Colonel, CSA;* CWTI:MAR/94[20]369
ANDERSON, CHARLES W., *Captain, CSA;* AHI:APR/74[4]154,
CWTI:SEP/93[18]334, CWTI:NOV/93[65]351
ANDERSON, DANIEL W., *Captain, CSA;* B&G:FEB/91[20]440
ANDERSON, E.A., *Colonel, CSA;* B&G:FEB/91[8]339
ANDERSON, E.M., *Midshipman, CSN;* AHI:OCT/88[38]275
ANDERSON, EDWARD, *Chaplain; 37th Illinois Infantry;*
CWR:VOL1#1[42]105
ANDERSON, EDWARD W., *Cadet;* B&G:DEC/91[12]469
ANDERSON, G.L., *Major, USA;* ACW:NOV/94[50]498
ANDERSON, GEORGE, *Major, USA;* B&G:FEB/91[8]439
ANDERSON, GEORGE B., *General, CSA;*
ACW:JAN/95[46]507, CWR:VOL3#2[1]153, GETTY:5[103]163
ANDERSON, GEORGE T., *General, CSA;*
GENERAL LISTINGS: *Antietam;* B&G:OCT/95[8]611C, *Gettysburg;*
GETTY:5[35]159, GETTY:5[107]164, GETTY:8[43]202,
GETTY:8[53]203, GETTY:9[53]214, GETTY:11[19]232,
GETTY:11[80]235, GETTY:11[91]236, GETTY:12[24]242,
GETTY:12[111]250, GETTY:12[123]251, *in order of battle;*
B&G:APR/94[10]558, *list of monuments;*
B&G:OCT/95[8]611A, *Manassas, Second;*
B&G:AUG/92[11]493, *order of battle;* B&G:APR/95[8]595,
Peninsula Campaign; CWM:JUN/95[63]594
ADDITIONAL LISTINGS: ACW:MAR/91[12]292, ACW:MAY/91[23]303,
ACW:MAY/92[30]361, ACW:JAN/93[43]397,
ACW:MAR/94[50]462, ACW:MAY/94[12]466,
B&G:JUN/95[8]600, CWM:AUG/95[38]609,
CWR:VOL2#2[95]135, CWTI:MAR/93[40]312,
CWTI:NOV/93[55]350, CWTI:MAY/94[50]386,
CWTI:DEC/94[32]410
ANDERSON, GEORGE W. JR., *Major, CSA;*
B&G:FEB/91[8]439, CWTI:DEC/94[62]415, *photo;*
CWTI:DEC/94[62]415
ANDERSON, J.K., *Private, CSA;* CWTI:SEP/91[23]228
ANDERSON, JAMES, *Pvt., 6th Wisconsin Inf.;* GETTY:4[16]143
ANDERSON, JAMES B., *Major, CSA;* AHI:DEC/77[46]177
ANDERSON, JAMES PATTON, *General, CSA;*
ACW:JUL/92[12]367, ACW:NOV/93[6]437,
B&G:OCT/91[11]466, CWR:VOL1#4[42]126,
CWR:VOL1#4[64]127, CWR:VOL3#1[65]151,
CWR:VOL4#3[50]171, CWTI:SUMMER/89[50]124,
CWTI:SEP/92[31]281
ANDERSON, JOHN, *Capt., 57th Mass. Inf.;* CWR:VOL1#3[94]
ANDERSON, JOSEPH A., *Private, 19th Indiana Infantry;*
GETTY:11[57]233
ANDERSON, JOSEPH, *Private, USA;* B&G:AUG/91[52]464
ANDERSON, JOSEPH R., *General, CSA:*
ARTICLE: "THE PENINSULA CAMPAIGN OF 1862: THE
BATTLE OF SLASH CHURCH," CWM:JUN/95[43]587

BOOK REVIEW: *IRONMAKER TO THE CONFEDERACY:*
JOSEPH R. ANDERSON AND THE TREDEGAR IRON
WORKS
ADDITIONAL LISTINGS: B&G:DEC/94[10]585, CWM:SEP/91[4]376,
CWM:SEP/91[24]381, CWM:JUN/95[57]592,
CWM:DEC/95[41]630, CWNEWS:JUL/92[4],
CWR:VOL1#1[1]102, CWR:VOL1#3[52]122, *photo;*
CWM:SEP/91[24]381
ANDERSON, MALACHI, *Private, 1st Florida Special Battalion;*
CWR:VOL3#1[65]151
ANDERSON, PETER, *Private, 31st Wisconsin Infantry;*
B&G:DEC/95[9]615
ANDERSON, PEYTON, *Captain, CSA;* B&G:OCT/93[6]536,
CWTI:DEC/91[14]235
ANDERSON, PIERCE B., *Lieutenant, USA;*
B&G:AUG/93[10]529
ANDERSON, R., *Pvt., 22nd Virginia Inf.;* CWR:VOL1#3[52]122
ANDERSON, R.M., *Lieutenant, Richmond Howitzers;*
ACW:SEP/94[38]487
ANDERSON, RICHARD H., *General, CSA:*
GENERAL LISTINGS: *Appomattox Campaign;* CWTI:AUG/90[26]166,
Chancellorsville; ACW:MAY/95[30]525, MH:JUN/92[50]159,
Cold Harbor; ACW:SEP/93[62]436, B&G:APR/94[10]558,
CWR:VOL3#4[1]161, *Crampton's Gap;* ACW:JAN/94[39]451,
Falling Waters; GETTY:9[109]218, *Five Forks,*
B&G:APR/92[8]481, *Fredericksburg;* CWR:VOL4#4[28]178,
Gettysburg; CWTI:SEPT/89[46]132, GETTY:4[7]142,
GETTY:4[101]151, GETTY:4[113]153, GETTY:5[4]156,
GETTY:5[19]158, GETTY:5[35]159, GETTY:5[47]160,
GETTY:5[79]161, GETTY:5[89]162, GETTY:5[103]163,
GETTY:6[7]169, GETTY:7[51]190, GETTY:8[111]206,
GETTY:9[41]212, GETTY:10[107]227, GETTY:10[120]229,
GETTY:11[71]234, GETTY:12[7]241
GENERAL LISTINGS, continued: *Harpers Ferry;* MH:AUG/95[30]185, *in*
order of battle; B&G:APR/92[8]481, B&G:APR/94[10]558,
B&G:APR/95[8]595, *Jericho Mill;* B&G:APR/93[12]518,
Manassas, Second; B&G:AUG/92[11]493, *Mexican War;*
MH:APR/93[39]166, *Overland* Campaign;
B&G:APR/94[10]558, *Peninsula Campaign;*
CWM:JUN/95[34]584, *Sayler's Creek;* ACW:JAN/92[22]341,
ACW:JAN/93[43]397, *Wilderness;* B&G:APR/95[8]595,
B&G:JUN/95[8]600, *Williamsburg;* ACW:MAR/91[47]297,
photos; ACW:JAN/93[43]397, B&G:OCT/95[8]611C,
CWM:DEC/95[34]628
ADDITIONAL LISTINGS: ACW:MAY/92[30]361, ACW:SEP/93[8]429,
ACW:SEP/93[31]433, ACW:MAY/94[35]469,
ACW:JUL/94[42]479, AHI:APR/85[18]250,
B&G:APR/93[12]518, B&G:OCT/95[8]611C,
CWM:OCT/94[17]534, CWM:DEC/95[34]628,
CWR:VOL1#4[v]124, CWR:VOL1#4[7]125,
CWR:VOL1#4[42]126, CWR:VOL2#2[95]135,
CWR:VOL2#3[236]143, CWR:VOL#4[269]145,
CWR:VOL3#2[1]153, CWR:VOL3#2[61]154,
CWR:VOL4#1[61], CWTI:MAR/89[28]103,
CWTI:APR/89[14]107, CWTI:APR/92[49]260,
CWTI:JUL/93[29]326, CWTI:NOV/93[55]350,
CWTI:JUL/94[44]394, CWTI:DEC/94[32]410,
GETTY:13[43]256, GETTY:13[75]259
ANDERSON, ROBERT, *General, USA:*
ARTICLE: "ROBERT ANDERSON: RELUCTANT HERO,"
CWTI:MAY/92[45]266
BOOK REVIEW: *SUMTER: THE FIRST DAY OF THE CIVIL WAR*

GENERAL LISTINGS: *in book review;* ACW:JAN/91[54],
B&G:AUG/91[26], *Fort Sumter;* CWTI:JUL/92[29]272, *letters
to the editor;* CWTI:SEP/92[10]278, *Mexican War;*
MH:APR/93[39]166, *Sherman;* AHI:JAN/67[4]106, *West Point;*
B&G:DEC/91[12]469, *photos;* AHI:MAY/71[3]133A,
CWTI:MAY/92[45]266
ADDITIONAL LISTINGS: ACW:JUL/91[26]313, ACW:JUL/92[22]368,
ACW:JUL/92[30]369, ACW:NOV/92[6]382,
ACW:MAR/93[18]403, ACW:NOV/93[8]438,
ACW:MAY/94[6]464, ACW:SEP/94[46]488,
AHI:MAY/71[3]133A, B&G:FEB/91[8]439,
B&G:FEB/93[12]511, B&G:OCT/93[31]539,
CWM:NOV/92[24]448, CWM:OCT/95[22]614,
CWTI:AUG/91[36]217, CWTI:SEP/92[46]284
ANDERSON, ROBERT, *Lieutenant Colonel, 9th Pennsylvania
Reserves;* AHI:MAY/66[12]101, CWR:VOL4#4[1]177
ANDERSON, ROBERT H., *General, CSA;* B&G:DEC/95[9]61,
GETTY:12[7]241
ANDERSON, SAMUEL R., *General, CSA;* ACW:JAN/92[50]345,
ACW:SEP/94[31]486, B&G:AUG/93[10]529,
B&G:DEC/93[52]548
ANDERSON, THOMAS, *Private, 3rd Georgia Infantry;*
CWTI:SEP/94[26]400
ANDERSON, WILLIAM, "BLOODY BILL":
ARTICLES: "EVEN IN DEATH, GUERRILLA "BLOODY BILL"
ANDERSON REMAINED FEARSOME AND DEFIANT,"
ACW:JAN/93[6]391, "THE MEANEST BUSHWHACKER,"
B&G:JUN/91[32]454
ADDITIONAL LISTINGS: ACW:JAN/93[26]395, ACW:MAR/95[26]515,
B&G:JUN/91[10]452, B&G:OCT/91[6]465,
B&G:OCT/91[11]466, B&G:DEC/92[6]502, B&G:APR/93[6]517,
CWM:JAN/92[8]399, CWM:MAY/92[6]417,
CWNEWS:OCT/93[5], CWTI:MAY/89[44],
CWTI:JAN/94[29]360, CWTI:MAY/94[12]379, *photo;*
ACW:JAN/93[6]391, CWM:JAN/92[8]399,
CWTI:JAN/94[29]360
ANDERSON, WILLIAM T., *Corporal, Sumter Artillery;*
CWR:VOL3#2[1]153
ANDERSONVILLE NATIONAL HISTORIC SITE;
CWTI:JUL/92[8]269
ANDERSONVILLE NATIONAL MILITARY CEMETERY:
ARTICLE: "THE COST OF CAPTURE," CWTI:APR/92[23]255
ADDITIONAL LISTINGS: B&G:AUG/93[18]530
ANDERSONVILLE PRISON; See listings under **"PRISONS,
CONFEDERATE"**
ANDES, JOHN W., *Lieutenant, 2nd Tennessee Cavalry;* BOOK
REVIEW: *LOYAL MOUNTAIN TROOPERS: THE SECOND AND
THIRD TENNESSEE CAVALRY IN THE CIVIL WAR,
REMINISCENCES OF LIEUTENANT JOHN W. ANDES
AND MAJOR WILL A. MCTEER*
ANDRES, WILLIAM H.C., *Captain, 14th New York Cavalry;*
CWR:VOL4#2[26]166
ANDRESS, S.S.; *Louisiana Tigers;* GETTY:5[123]166
ANDREW, JOHN A., *Governor, Massachusetts;*
ACW:NOV/92[51]389, ACW:JUL/95[16]534,
ACW:NOV/95[30]555, AHI:FEB/82[36]225,
AHI:JAN/93[61]309, B&G:FEB/92[6]473, B&G:OCT/93[24],
CWM:NOV/91[12]390, CWR:VOL1#1[76]109,
CWR:VOL3#1[80], CWR:VOL3#1[31]150,
CWNEWS:JUN/91[4], CWTI:MAY/89[21]115,
CWTI:SEPT/89[40]130, CWTI:DEC/89[42]137,
CWTI:SEP/91[42]231, CWTI:MAR/94[38]372,
GETTY:5[47]160, GETTY:8[53]203

ANDREWS' MASSACHUSETTS SHARPSHOOTERS;
GETTY:8[95]205
ANDREWS' RAID; see listings under **"ANDREWS, JAMES J."**
ANDREWS, ALBERT, *Private, 126th New York Infantry;*
GETTY:8[95]205
ANDREWS, CHRISTOPHER C., *General, USA;*
ACW:MAY/91[12]302, CWR:VOL1#1[42]105,
MH:APR/94[54]176
ANDREWS, GARNETT, *Major, CSA;* CWTI:MAR/93[40]312
ANDREWS, GEORGE, *General, USA;* ACW:JAN/94[30]450
ANDREWS, GEORGE L., *Lieutenant Colonel, 1st Missouri
Infantry;* ACW:NOV/93[26]441, CWTI:FEB/92[29]248
ANDREWS, GEORGE W., *Colonel, 6th Ohio Infantry;*
B&G:AUG/93[10]529
ANDREWS, GEORGE W., *Lieutenant Colonel, 71st Ohio
Infantry;* CWTI:JUL/92[42]274
ANDREWS, H.L., *Col., 2nd North Carolina;* GETTY:13[33]255
ANDREWS, J.D., *Private, 9th Georgia Infantry;*
CWR:VOL2#2[95]135
ANDREWS, JAMES J.:
ARTICLES: "AT HOME WITH THE GENERAL"
CWTI:FEB/92[10]246, "AUDACIOUS RAILROAD CHASE,"
ACW:SEP/91[22]321
BOOK REVIEW: *THE GREAT LOCOMOTIVE CHASE: MORE ON
THE ANDREWS RAID AND THE FIRST MEDAL OF HONOR*
ADDITIONAL LISTINGS: ACW:SEP/91[6]317, B&G:JUN/91[42]456,
B&G:AUG/91[40]463, CWTI:FEB/91[18]190,
CWTI:SEP/91[23]228, CWTI:DEC/94[49]413
ANDREWS, JOHN W., *Colonel, USA;* CWR:VOL4#4[28]178
ANDREWS, PETER, *Private, 107th Pennsylvania Infantry;*
GETTY:9[33]211
ANDREWS, R. SNOWDEN, *Lieutenant Colonel, CSA;*
ACW:NOV/92[42]388, CWR:VOL3#3[92], GETTY:10[29]222,
GETTY:12[30]243
ANDREWS, T.P., *Colonel, USA;* ACW:MAR/92[46]354
ANDREWS, W.H., *Sergeant, 1st Georgia Regulars:*
ARTICLES: "THE FIRST GEORGIA REGULARS AT
SHARPSBURG:, RECOLLECTIONS OF THE MARYLAND
CAMPAIGN, 1862," CWR:VOL2#2[95]135
BOOK REVIEW: *FOOTPRINTS OF A REGIMENT: A
RECOLLECTION OF THE FIRST GEORGIA REGULARS
1861-1865*
ADDITIONAL LISTINGS: CWM:AUG/95[38]609, *photo;*
CWR:VOL2#2[95]135
ANDREWS, WILLIAM, *Sgt., 2nd USSS;* CWTI:JUL/93[42]329
ANDRICK, JACOB, *Private, 19th Indiana Infantry;*
CWTI:NOV/93[78]354
ANGELL, JOE, *Private, 4th Alabama Infantry;*
ACW:NOV/94[18]495
ANTHONY, DAN; ACW:JAN/93[26]395, CWM:MAY/92[6]417
ANTHONY, SUSAN B.; ACW:JAN/93[26]395,
CWM:JAN/91[47], CWTI:AUG/90[50]168,
CWTI:DEC/90[50]183, *photo;* CWTI:AUG/90[50]168
ANTI-JEWISH ATTITUDE; CWM:SEP/93[8]493
ANTI-SLAVERY SOCIETY; CWTI:AUG/90[50]168
ANTIQUES; ARTICLE: "COLLECTING LINCOLN,"
CWTI:DEC/95[30]478
ANTIETAM NATIONAL BATTLEFIELD:
ARTICLE: "MASTER PLAN APPROVED FOR PRESERVING
ANTIETAM NATIONAL BATTLEFIELD," AHI:JAN/93[8]306
ADDITIONAL LISTINGS: CWM:MAY/91[31]350, B&G:OCT/95[36]614,
CWM:JAN/92[27]403, CWM:MAY/93[35]478

ANTIETAM NATIONAL CEMETERY; B&G:OCT/95[8]611B, B&G:OCT/95[8]611E

ANTIETAM, MARYLAND, BATTLE AND CAMPAIGN OF:

ARTICLES: "ANTIETAM 'CORNFIELD' DONATED," AHI:NOV/89[11]292, "ATTITUDES OF DEATH," CWTI:JUL/92[36]273, "BLOOD POURED LIKE WATER," ACW:MAR/94[50]462, "CARNAGE IN A CORNFIELD," ACW:JUL/92[30]369, "FIRING THE GAP," ACW:JAN/94[39]451, "THE FIRST GEORGIA REGULARS AT SHARPSBURG: RECOLLECTIONS OF THE MARYLAND CAMPAIGN, 1862," CWR:VOL2#2[95]135, "FORGOTTEN VALOR: OFF THE BEATEN PATH AT ANTIETAM: DEBACLE IN THE WEST WOODS," B&G:OCT/95[8]611A, "FORGOTTEN VALOR: OFF THE BEATEN PATH AT ANTIETAM: ATTACK OF THE TURNVEREIN," B&G:OCT/95[8]611B, "FORGOTTEN VALOR: OFF THE BEATEN PATH AT ANTIETAM: GUNNERS, OF THE 6TH VA. INFY.," B&G:OCT/95[8]611C, "FORGOTTEN VALOR: OFF THE BEATEN PATH AT ANTIETAM: ARTILLERY HELL AND HOT COFFEE," B&G:OCT/95[8]611D, "FORGOTTEN VALOR: OFF THE BEATEN PATH AT ANTIETAM: OLD SIMON," B&G:OCT/95[8]611E, "FORGOTTEN VALOR: OFF THE BEATEN PATH AT ANTIETAM: WHOEVER HEARD OF A DEAD CAVALRYMAN?" B&G:OCT/95[8]611F

ARTICLES, continued: "IN HARM'S WAY," CWTI:MAR/93[26]310, "MASTER PLAN APPROVED FOR PRESERVING ANTIETAM NATIONAL BATTLEFIELD," AHI:JAN/93[8]306, "MEMORIES OF STONEWALL," CWM:APR/94[14]503, "O.T. REILLY, BATTLEFIELD GUIDE," B&G:OCT/95[54]614A, "TO BE HELD AT ALL HAZARDS," CWTI:SEP/93[43]338, "STONEWALL'S FORGOTTEN MASTERPIECE," MH:AUG/95[30]185, "TRAGIC LOSS OF LIFE AT ANTIETAM," CWM:OCT/94[37]539, "WAR COMES TO FREDERICK, ACW:JAN/91[38]287, "WHOEVER LOST ROBERT E. LEE'S "LOST ORDER," A DELIGHTED GEORGE MCCLELLAN FOUND IT," ACW:JAN/94[6]446

BOOK REVIEWS: *THE ANTIETAM AND FREDERICKSBURG * ANTIETAM: ESSAYS ON THE 1862 MARYLAND CAMPAIGN * ANTIETAM: THE AFTERMATH * ANTIETAM: THE SOLDIER'S BATTLE * ARTILLERY HELL: THE EMPLOYMENT OF ARTILLERY AT ANTIETAM * BEFORE ANTIETAM: THE BATTLE FOR SOUTH MOUNTAIN * THE BIVOUACS OF THE DEAD: THE STORY OF THOSE WHO DIED AT ANTIETAM AND SOUTH MOUNTAIN * DEATH IN SEPTEMBER: THE ANTIETAM CAMPAIGN * THE HISTORY OF THE HARPERS FERRY CAVALRY EXPEDITION, SEPTEMBER 14 & 15, 1862 * LANDSCAPE TURNED RED: THE BATTLE OF ANTIETAM * LEE'S TERRIBLE SWIFT SWORD: FROM ANTIETAM TO CHANCELLORSVILLE, AN EYEWITNESS HISTORY * OUT OF THE PAST*

GENERAL LISTINGS: *general history,* AHI:MAY/71[3]133A, *in book review,* ACW:SEP/94[66], ACW:NOV/94[66], ACW:JAN/95[62], CWM:OCT/94[8], CWM:FEB/95[7], CWM:DEC/95[10], CWNEWS:OCT/90[4], CWNEWS:APR/93[4], CWR:VOL1#2[78], CWR:VOL2#2[169], CWR:VOL2#4[346], CWR:VOL3#1[80], *Iron Brigade;* CWTI:MAR/89[28]103, *Jackson,* B&G:JUN/92[8]487, *letters to the editor,* B&G:JUN/93[6]523, B&G:DEC/95[5]614A, CWM:OCT/95[5]613, CWM:DEC/95[5]625, *Save Historic Antietam Foundation;* B&G:FEB/92[40]479, *photos;* CWTI:DEC/95[67]481

ADDITIONAL LISTINGS: ACW:JAN/92[6]337, ACW:MAR/92[10]349, ACW:MAY/92[8]357, ACW:JUL/92[12]367, ACW:MAY/93[14]413, ACW:JUL/93[10]421, ACW:JUL/93[42]425, ACW:SEP/93[31]433, ACW:MAY/94[12]466, ACW:JAN/95[46]507, ACW:MAR/95[42]517, ACW:MAY/95[18]524, ACW:JUL/95[10]533, ACW:SEP/95[54]548, B&G:JUN/94[22]569, B&G:OCT/95[8]611A, CWM:MAR/91[50]340, CWM:JUL/91[24]361, CWM:JUL/91[28]366, CWM:SEP/91[40]385, CWM:MAY/92[8]418, CWM:MAY/92[34]422, CWM:MAY/92[44]423, CWM:JUL/92[18]429, CWM:NOV/92[10]447, CWM:MAR/93[32]468, CWM:SEP/93[24]495, CWM:OCT/94[26]536, CWM:DEC/94[26]548, CWM:AUG/95[17]603, CWM:DEC/95[34]628, CWM:DEC/95[41]630

ADDITIONAL LISTINGS, continued: CWR:VOL1#1[1]102, CWR:VOL1#1[71]107, CWR:VOL1#2[29]112, CWR:VOL1#3[28]120, CWR:VOL1#3[52]122, CWR:VOL1#4[v]124, CWR:VOL1#4[7]125, CWR:VOL1#4[74]128, CWR:VOL2#3[236]143, CWR:VOL2#4[269]145, CWR:VOL3#1[31]150, CWR:VOL3#2[1]153, CWR:VOL3#3[1]157, CWR:VOL4#4[47]179, CWR:VOL4#4[70]180, CWTI:APR/89[14]107, CWTI:DEC/89[34]136, CWTI:FEB/90[74]149, CWTI:AUG/91[52]219, CWTI:SEP/91[31]229, CWTI:FEB/92[36]249, CWTI:APR/92[35]257, CWTI:SEP/92[42]283, CWTI:JUL/93[29]326, CWTI:SEP/93[53]340, CWTI:NOV/93[24]346, CWTI:SEP/94[49]404, CWTI:JAN/95[34]427, CWTI:JUN/95[32]446, CWTI:DEC/95[22]476, CWTI:DEC/95[67]481, GETTY:12[30]243, GETTY:13[43]256, GETTY:13[108]261, MH:JUN/94[8]177, MH:AUG/94[46]178

APACHE CANYON, NEW MEXICO, BATTLE OF; see listings under **"GLORIETA PASS, NEW MEXICO, BATTLE OF"**

APPERSON, GEORGE W., *Private, 2nd Tennessee Cavalry;* CWR:VOL4#1[1]163

APPLER, JESSE J., *Col., 53rd Ohio Inf.;* ACW:JAN/91[22]285

APPOMATTOX COURT HOUSE NATIONAL HISTORIC PARK:

ARTICLES: "APPOMATTOX TODAY," AHI:SEP/87[55]265, "HISTORY COMES HOME," CWTI:MAR/95[20]433

GENERAL LISTINGS: *letters to the editor,* B&G:APR/91[6]444, CWTI:AUG/95[14]454

APPOMATTOX COURT HOUSE, VIRGINIA, BATTLE, CAMPAIGN, AND SURRENDER:

ARTICLES: "AN IROQUOIS AT APPOMATTOX," CWM:SEP/92[19]440, "THE APPOMATTOX SURRENDER TABLE," CWTI:NOV/93[50]349, "APPOMATTOX TODAY," AHI:SEP/87[55]265, "FINAL MARCH TO APPOMATTOX: THE 12TH VIRGINIA INFANTRY, APRIL 2-12, AN EYEWITNESS ACCOUNT," CWR:VOL2#3[236]143, "THE FREDERICKSBURG ARTILLERY AT APPOMATTOX," CWR:VOL1#1[35]104, "I WAS THERE", CWM:JUL/91[8]356, "LAST DAYS OF THE CIVIL WAR: CHAPTER 1: 'SUCCESS WAS, EMINENTLY A HAPPY, A GLORIOUS ONE,'" CWTI:AUG/90[26]166, "LIFE AFTER SURRENDER FOR REBEL WARRIORS," ACW:JUL/95[26]535, "MEETING AT THE MCLEAN HOUSE," AHI:SEP/87[48]264, "WITH LEE AT APPOMATTOX," AHI:SEP/87[40]263

BOOK REVIEWS: *APPOMATTOX COURT HOUSE * THE FINAL BIVOUAC: THE SURRENDER PARADE AT APPOMATTOX*

AND THE DISBANDING OF THE ARMIES, APRIL 10-May 20, 1865 * OUT OF THE STORM: THE END OF THE CIVIL WAR (APRIL-JUNE 1865) * WITH GRANT AND MEADE: FROM THE WILDERNESS TO APPOMATTOX * WITNESS TO APPOMATTOX

GENERAL LISTINGS: *general history,* ACW:SEP/94[66], AHI:MAY/71[3]133A, AHI:FEB/82[9], CWM:AUG/95[45], CWR:VOL1#4[77], CWR:VOL2#3[256], CWR:VOL3#2[105], CWTI:FEB/90[10], CWTI:OCT/95[18], *letters to the editor,,* CWM:SEP/91[6]377, CWTI:JUL/93[10]323

ADDITIONAL LISTINGS: ACW:JAN/93[43]397, ACW:MAY/93[14]413, ACW:JUL/93[66]427, ACW:SEP/93[8]429, ACW:SEP/95[74]550, ACW:NOV/93[10]439, CWM:MAR/91[65]342, CWM:JUL/91[24]360, CWM:JUL/91[46]373, CWM:JUL/92[8]427, CWM:NOV/92[24]448, CWM:MAR/93[4]463, CWM:SEP/93[24]495, CWM:OCT/94[17]534, CWM:OCT/95[22]614, CWM:OCT/95[40]619, CWR:VOL1#1[1]102, CWR:VOL1#1[71]107, CWR:VOL2#3[252]144, CWR:VOL2#4[269]145, CWR:VOL3#2[1]153, CWTI:FEB/90[60]148, CWTI:FEB/91[28]192, CWTI:AUG/91[68]222, CWTI:DEC/91[28]239, CWTI:SEP/92[42]283, CWTI:SEP/94[8]397, CWTI:JAN/95[27]425, CWTI:JAN/95[34]427

ARCHAEOLOGY; BOOK REVIEWS: *ARCHAEOLOGY, HISTORY, AND CUSTER'S LAST BATTLE: THE LITTLE BIG HORN REEXAMINED * LOOK TO THE EARTH: HISTORICAL ARCHAEOLOGY AND THE AMERICAN CIVIL WAR*

ARCHER, FLETCHER, *Major, CSA;* CWNEWS:SEP/90[4]

ARCHER, JAMES J., *General, CSA;*

ARTICLE: "WHAT A DEADLY TRAP WE WERE IN": ARCHER'S BRIGADE ON JULY 1, 1863" GETTY:6[13]170

GENERAL LISTINGS: *Chancellorsville,* MH:JUN/92[50]159, *Fredericksburg,* CWR:VOL4#4[1]177, *Gettysburg,* GETTY:4[22]144, GETTY:5[4]156, GETTY:5[19]158, GETTY:5[103]163, GETTY:5[107]164, GETTY:6[7]169, GETTY:6[94]180, GETTY:7[114]194, GETTY:8[67]204, *Gettysburg, continued:* GETTY:9[61]215, GETTY:10[107]227, GETTY:10[112]228, GETTY:10[120]229, GETTY:11[19]232, GETTY:11[71]234, GETTY:12[123]251, *in book review,* CWR:VOL1#2[78, CWR:VOL2#3[256], *letters to the editor,* *CWTI:DEC/94[12]408, Manassas, Second,* B&G:AUG/92[11]493, *Table, Losses for Archer's brigade at Gettysburg;* GETTY:6[13]170

ADDITIONAL LISTINGS: ACW:NOV/93[66]445, ACW:MAR/95[42]517, ACW:MAY/95[30]525, ACW:JUL/95[44]537, B&G:FEB/95[8]590A, CWM:MAR/91[17]335, CWM:DEC/94[17]547, CWM:OCT/95[38]618, CWM:OCT/95[53]621, CWR:VOL1#1[1]102, CWR:VOL1#1[26]103, CWR:VOL1#3[52]122, CWR:VOL4#4[70]180, CWTI:APR/90[46]153, CWTI:DEC/91[36]240, CWTI:JUL/94[44]394, GETTY:13[75]259, GETTY:13[108]261

ARCHER, W.P., *Private, 42nd Georgia Infantry;* CWTI:DEC/94[49]413

ARCHIBALD, JOHN G., *Sergeant, 15th Alabama Infantry;* ACW:JAN/92[38]343

ARIZONA TROOPS:

4th Cavalry; ACW:JUL/92[46]371

Arizona Battalion; CWR:VOL2#3[212]142, CWR:VOL4#4[129]

ARIZONA, STATE OF;

ARTICLE: "WAR'S WESTERNMOST BATTLE," ACW:JUL/93[27]423

ARKANSAS POST NATIONAL MEMORIAL; CWR:VOL2#1[69]133

ARKANSAS POST, BATTLE OF; ACW:SEP/92[16]376, AHI:MAY/71[3]133A, CWR:VOL1#2[44]114, CWR:VOL1#2[78], CWR:VOL2#1[1]130, CWR:VOL3#3[92], CWTI:MAY/91[16]206, CWTI:MAY/94[16]380

ARKANSAS TROOPS:

1st Cavalry, (Union); B&G:JUN/91[10]452

1st Cavalry:

ARTICLE: "RACKENSACKER RAIDERS: CRAWFORD'S FIRST ARKANSAS CAVALRY," CWR:VOL1#2[44]114

ADDITIONAL LISTINGS: ACW:NOV/93[26]441, CWR:VOL1#2[v]110, CWR:VOL1#2[76]116, CWR:VOL2#1[36]132, CWTI:FEB/92[29]248

1st Infantry:

BOOK REVIEW: *REMINISCENCES OF A PRIVATE: WILLIAM E. BEVENS OF THE FIRST, ARKANSAS INFANTRY, C.S.A.*

ADDITIONAL LISTINGS: ACW:MAY/94[26]468, ACW:MAR/95[26]515, ACW:MAR/95[50]518, AHI:MAR/84[42]238, B&G:JUN/91[10]452, CWTI:APR/92[27]256, CWTI:SEP/94[40]403

1st Mounted Rifles; ACW:SEP/92[38]379, CWTI:FEB/92[29]248

2nd Cavalry; CWR:VOL1#2[44]114

2nd Infantry; ACW:JAN/93[10]393, ACW:MAY/94[26]468, CWR:VOL1#1[1]102, CWR:VOL1#1[42]105, CWTI:FEB/92[42]250, CWTI:SEP/94[40]403, CWTI:JAN/94[82]366

2nd Mounted Rifles; ACW:NOV/93[26]44, CWTI:FEB/92[29]248

3rd Infantry; ACW:MAR/91[12]292, ACW:NOV/93[26]441, B&G:JUN/91[10]452, B&G:AUG/93[10]529, B&G:JUN/95[8]600, CWM:MAY/93[8]474, CWR:VOL1#4[77], CWR:VOL2#3[256], GETTY:5[103]163, GETTY:5[117]165, GETTY:6[7]169, GETTY:8[43]202, GETTY:8[53]203, GETTY:13[7]253

4th Infantry; ACW:NOV/93[26]441, B&G:APR/91[36]448, CWR:VOL1#1[42]105

5th Infantry; ACW:NOV/93[26]441

5th and 13th Infantry (Consolidated); CWTI:SEP/94[40]403

6th Infantry; CWTI:FEB/92[42]250

7th Infantry; ACW:MAR/95[34]516

6th and 7th Infantry (Consolidated); CWTI:SEP/94[40]403

8th Infantry; ACW:JAN/93[10]393

9th Infantry; ACW:SEP/91[46]324, CWR:VOL2#1[36]132

8th and 19th Infantry (Consolidated); CWTI:SEP/94[40]403

10th Infantry; ACW:JAN/94[30]450, CWTI:JAN/95[42]428

11th Infantry:

BOOK REVIEW: *RANKS OF HONOR: A REGIMENTAL HISTORY OF THE ELEVENTH ARKANSAS INFANTRY REGIMENT & POE'S CAVALRY BATTALION C.S.A. 1861*

ADDITIONAL LISTING: CWR:VOL1#2[44]114

12th Infantry; CWM:SEP/93[8]493, B&G:FEB/94[8]550, CWR:VOL3#4[24]162

12th Sharpshooter Battalion; B&G:FEB/94[8]550,
CWR:VOL1#2[44]114, CWR:VOL2#1[19]131,
CWR:VOL2#1[36]132
13th Infantry; ACW:JAN/92[10]339, CWR:VOL3#4[24]162
14th Infantry; CWTI:JUL/94[50]395
15th Infantry; ACW:JAN/94[30]450, ACW:JUL/94[51]480,
AHI:MAR/84[42]238, B&G:FEB/92[10]474,
B&G:FEB/94[8]550, CWM:MAR/91[28]336,
CWM:JUN/94[25]511, CWR:VOL2#1[36]132
15th and 24th Infantry (Consolidated); CWTI:SEP/94[40]403
17th Infantry; CWR:VOL1#3[94], CWTI:JUL/94[50]395
18th Infantry; ACW:JAN/94[30]450, CWR:VOL1#2[44]114
19th Infantry; CWR:VOL1#2[44]114, CWR:VOL2#1[36]132
20th Infantry; CWR:VOL1#2[44]114, CWR:VOL2#1[36]132
21st Infantry; B&G:FEB/94[8]550, CWR:VOL2#1[36]132
25th Infantry; CWTI:SEP/92[31]281
34th Infantry; ACW:MAY/93[22]414, ACW:MAY/94[26]468
McNally's Light Artillery; B&G:AUG/95[8]604
Regiment of Mounted Volunteers; CWR:VOL1#2[44]114
Woodruffs Arkansas Battery; CWM:MAY/93[8]474
ARKANSAS, STATE OF:
ARTICLE: "THE APTLY NAMED TOWN OF WASHINGTON
WAS, FOR A TIME, THE CAPITAL OF CONFEDEREATE
ARKANSAS," ACW:SEP/92[66]381
BOOK REVIEWS: *CIVIL WAR IN THE OZARKS, THE IMPACT OF
THE CIVIL WAR AND RECONSTRUCTION ON ARKANSAS
* RAGGED AND SUBLIME: THE CIVIL WAR IN ARKANSAS*
ARMAMENT; "LINCOLN'S SECRET ARMS RACE,"
CWTI:OCT/95[32]468
ARMANT, LEOPOLD L., *Colonel, 18th Louisiana Consolidated
Infantry;* CWR:VOL3#1[1]14, CWR:VOL4#2[1]165,
CWR:VOL4#2[118]169
ARMISTEAD, FRANK, *Lieutenant, CSA;* CWTI:JUL/93[29]326
ARMISTEAD, W. KEITH, *Lt., CSA;* CWTI:JUL/93[29]326
ARMISTEAD, LEWIS A., *General, CSA:*
ARTICLE: "WHO WILL FOLLOW ME?," CWTI:JUL/93[29]326
BOOK REVIEW: *"TRUST IN GOD AND FEAR NOTHING":
GENERAL LEWIS A. ARMISTEAD, C.S.A.*
GENERAL LISTINGS: *Gettysburg,* ACW:MAR/93[10]402,
GETTY:4[89]150, GETTY:4[113]153, GETTY:5[79]161,
GETTY:5[103]163, GETTY:5[107]164, GETTY:5[117]165,
GETTY:5[123]166, GETTY:6[87]178, GETTY:7[97]193,
GETTY:8[67]204, GETTY:9[61]215, GETTY:10[112]228,
GETTY:11[71]234, GETTY:12[61]245, GETTY:12[111]250,
MH:DEC/91[54]155, *in book review,* B&G:APR/95[30],
CWR:VOL4#3[89], *in list,* CWTI:JUL/93[34]327, *letters to the
editor,* CWTI:NOV/93[12]345, CWTI:JAN/94[8]356,
MH:AUG/92[8]160, *Malvern Hill,* CWM:JUN/95[73]597, *Seven
Pines,* CWTI:APR/89[14]107, *SIO;* B&G:AUG/91[40]463,
B&G:DEC/91[38]471, B&G:APR/92[36]483, *photo,*
CWTI:JUL/93[29]326
ADDITIONAL LISTINGS: ACW:MAY/92[8]357, B&G:JUN/93[40]527,
B&G:DEC/93[30]546, B&G:APR/94[34]561,
B&G:AUG/94[38]578, CWM:OCT/95[22]614,
CWR:VOL2#1[36]132, CWTI:SEP/90[26]174,
CWTI:SEP/93[43]338, CWTI:JUL/94[44]394, GETTY:13[1]252,
GETTY:13[43]256, GETTY:13[64]258, GETTY:13[75]259
ARMOR; ARTICLE: "KNIGHTLY ARMOR, THOUGH
APPEALING TO ROMANTICS, FOUND LITTLE FAVOR
WITH CIVIL WAR VETERANS," ACW:SEP/92[8]374

ARMS AND EQUIPMENT; BOOK REVIEWS: *ARMS AND
EQUIPMENT OF THE CONFEDERACY * ARMS AND
EQUIPMENT OF THE UNION*
ARMSTRONG, EDGAR B., *Sgt., 6th WI. Inf.,* GETTY:11[57]233
ARMSTRONG, FRANK C., *General, CSA:*
ARTICLE: "THE BATTLE OF BRITTON'S LANE: THE CLIMAX
OF ARMSTRONG'S RAID," B&G:APR/93[34]521
GENERAL LISTINGS: *in book review,* CWR:VOL4#3[1]170, *photo,*
B&G:APR/93[34]521,
ADDITIONAL LISTINGS: ACW:SEP/92[38]379, B&G:DEC/93[12]545,
CWM:MAY/93[8]474, CWTI:JUL/94[50]395,
CWTI:MAR/95[46]437
ARMSTRONG, R.F., *Lieutenant, CSN;* AHI:OCT/88[38]275
ARMSTRONG, RICHARD L., *Private, CSA;* GETTY:11[19]232
ARMSTRONG, SAMUEL C., *Captain, 125th New York
Infantry;* GETTY:7[51]190, GETTY:8[95]205
ARMY RAM FLEET; ACW:JUL/93[34]424
ARMY, CONFEDERATE, GENERAL INFORMATION; BOOK
REVIEWS *COMPENDIUM OF THE CONFEDERATE ARMIES
* TWO GREAT REBEL ARMIES*
ARMY, FEDERAL, GENERAL INFORMATION; BOOK
REVIEWS: *THE UNION ARMY, 1861-1865: ORGANIZATIONS
AND OPERATIONS VOL. I: THE EASTERN THEATER *
THE UNION ARMY, 1861-1865: ORGANIZATION AND
OPERATIONS VOL. II: THE WESTERN THEATRE*
ARMY OF GEORGIA; B&G:DEC/95[9]615
ARMY OF KENTUCKY; ACW:MAR/93[10]402,
AHI:NOV/73[18]151
ARMY OF MISSISSIPPI; B&G:JUN/91[10]452,
CWM:JAN/91[12]326, CWR:VOL2#3[212]142,
CWR:VOL4#1[44]164, MH:JUN/93[82]167
ARMY OF NEW MEXICO; B&G:JUN/94[8]568,
CWR:VOL2#2[161]139, CWTI:OCT/95[56]471
ARMY OF NORTHERN VIRGINIA:
ARTICLES: "THE 11TH MISSISSIPPI INFANTRY IN THE ARMY
OF NORTHERN VIRGINIA," CWR:VOL2#4[269]145,
"GETTYSBURG FINALE," ACW:JUL/93[50]426
BOOK REVIEWS: *THE ARMY OF NORTHERN VIRGINIA,
DETAILED MINUTIAE OF SOLDIER LIFE IN THE ARMY
OF NORTHERN VIRGINIA 1861-1865 * THE LONG ARM OF
LEE, OR THE HISTORY OF THE ARTILLERY OF THE
ARMY OF NORTHERN VIRGINIA WITH A BRIEF
ACCOUNT OF THE CONFEDERATE BUREAU OF
ORDNANCE * TWO GREAT REBEL ARMIES*
GENERAL LISTINGS: *Chancellorsville,* MH:JUN/92[50]159, *Fall of
Richmond,* AHI:JAN/74[10]153, *Falling Waters,*
GETTY:9[109]218, *Five Forks,* B&G:APR/92[8]481,
Fredericksburg, AHI:JUN/78[4]180, *general history,*
AHI:MAY/71[3]133A, *Gettysburg,* B&G:APR/91[39]449,
CWTI:SEPT/89[46]132, GETTY:10[29]222, GETTY:11[6]231,
GETTY:11[80]235, GETTY:12[42]244, GETTY:12[61]245,
GETTY:12[111]250, MH:DEC/91[54]155, *Harpers Ferry,*
MH:AUG/95[30]185, *in book review,* ACW:MAY/95[62],
ACW:JUL/93[58], ACW:MAY/94[58], CWM:MAR/92[49],
CWM:OCT/94[8], CWM:FEB/95[7], CWM:APR/95[8],
CWM:APR/95[50], CWM:DEC/95[10], CWNEWS:OCT/89[4],
CWNEWS:NOV/89[4], CWR:VOL1#3[94], CWR:VOL1#4[77],
CWR:VOL2#1[78], CWR:VOL2#3[256], CWR:VOL2#4[346],
CWR:VOL3#1[80], CWR:VOL3#2[105], CWR:VOL3#3[92],
CWR:VOL3#4[68], CWR:VOL4#1[78], CWR:VOL4#4[129],
CWTI:MAR/93[10], *letters to the editor,* CWM:OCT/94[5]533,
Manassas, Second, B&G:AUG/92[11]493, *Overland Campaign,*
B&G:APR/94[10]558, *Wilderness,* B&G:JUN/95[8]600

ADDITIONAL LISTINGS, ACW; ACW:MAR/91[12]292,
  ACW:JUL/91[18]312, ACW:NOV/91[30]332,
  ACW:JAN/92[22]341, ACW:MAR/92[30]352,
  ACW:JUL/92[30]369, ACW:JUL/92[41]370,
  ACW:NOV/92[26]386, ACW:NOV/92[42]388,
  ACW:JAN/93[43]397, ACW:MAR/93[10]402,
  ACW:MAR/93[26]404, ACW:MAY/93[14]413,
  ACW:JUL/93[16]422, ACW:SEP/93[31]433,
  ACW:SEP/93[62]436, ACW:NOV/93[50]444,
  ACW:JAN/94[6]446, ACW:MAR/94[16]458,
  ACW:MAR/94[27]459, ACW:MAR/94[50]462,
  ACW:MAY/94[35]469, ACW:SEP/94[38]487,
  ACW:SEP/94[55]489, ACW:SEP/94[62]490,
  ACW:JAN/95[54]508, ACW:MAR/95[12]513,
  ACW:MAR/95[70]520, ACW:MAY/95[10]523,
  ACW:MAY/95[38]526, ACW:JUL/95[26]535,
  ACW:JUL/95[34]536, ACW:JUL/95[50]538,
  ACW:SEP/95[30]545, ACW:SEP/95[48]547,
  ACW:SEP/95[54]548, ACW:SEP/95[74]55
ADDITIONAL LISTINGS, AHI; AHI:SEP/87[40]263, AHI:SUM/88[12]273
ADDITIONAL LISTINGS, B&G; B&G:APR/91[8]44,
  B&G:AUG/91[30]460, B&G:OCT/91[11]466,
  B&G:DEC/91[34]470, B&G:FEB/93[24]512,
  B&G:OCT/93[12]537, B&G:AUG/94[10]574,
  B&G:DEC/94[10]585, B&G:DEC/94[34]587,
  B&G:FEB/95[8]590C, B&G:OCT/95[8]611A
ADDITIONAL LISTINGS, CWM; CWM:JAN/91[12]326,
  CWM:JAN/91[28]327, CWM:MAR/91[17]335,
  CWM:MAR/91[65]342, CWM:JUL/91[25]363,
  CWM:JUL/91[28]366, CWM:JUL/91[29]367,
  CWM:JUL/91[43]371, CWM:NOV/91[12]390,
  CWM:NOV/91[58]394A, CWM:MAR/92[9]410,
  CWM:MAY/92[8]418, CWM:MAY/92[15]419,
  CWM:MAY/92[20]420, CWM:MAY/92[34]422,
  CWM:MAY/92[44]423, CWM:JAN/93[8]456,
  CWM:JAN/93[16]457, CWM:MAR/93[8]465,
  CWM:SEP/93[24]495, CWM:JUN/94[26]512,
  CWM:JUN/94[27]513, CWM:JUN/94[43]517,
  CWM:AUG/94[8]522, CWM:AUG/94[26]525,
  CWM:AUG/94[30]527, CWM:OCT/94[4]532,
  CWM:OCT/94[34]538, CWM:FEB/95[30]561,
  CWM:APR/95[32]575, CWM:JUN/95[61]593,
  CWM:AUG/95[17]603, CWM:AUG/95[30]606,
  CWM:AUG/95[38]609, CWM:OCT/95[38]618,
  CWM:OCT/95[40]619, CWM:DEC/95[34]628,
  CWM:DEC/95[54]632
ADDITIONAL LISTINGS, CWR; CWR:VOL1#1[1]102,
  CWR:VOL1#1[26]103, CWR:VOL1#1[35]104,
  CWR:VOL1#1[71]107, CWR:VOL1#2[29]112,
  CWR:VOL1#3[52]122, CWR:VOL1#4[v]124,
  CWR:VOL1#4[7]125, CWR:VOL2#1[36]132,
  CWR:VOL2#2[95]135, CWR:VOL2#2[141]137,
  CWR:VOL2#2[156]138, CWR:VOL2#3[212]142,
  CWR:VOL2#4[269]145, CWR:VOL3#1[31]150,
  CWR:VOL3#1[65]151, CWR:VOL3#2[1]153,
  CWR:VOL3#2[70]155, CWR:VOL3#3[1]157,
  CWR:VOL3#4[1]161, CWR:VOL4#4[i]175,
  CWR:VOL4#4[70]180
ADDITIONAL LISTINGS, CWTI; CWTI:APR/89[14]107,
  CWTI:SUMMER/89[13]120, CWTI:DEC/89[34]136,
  CWTI:APR/90[24]152, CWTI:APR/90[46]153,
  CWTI:JUN/90[32]159, CWTI:SEP/90[34]176,
  CWTI:FEB/91[12]189, CWTI:SEP/91[31]229,

CWTI:DEC/91[36]240, CWTI:APR/92[35]257,
  CWTI:APR/92[49]260, CWTI:SEP/92[22]279,
  CWTI:SEP/92[42]283, CWTI:NOV/92[49]292,
  CWTI:JAN/93[40]301, CWTI:MAR/93[26]310,
  CWTI:MAR/93[40]312, CWTI:MAY/93[26]318,
  CWTI:SEP/93[43]338, CWTI:MAY/94[50]386,
  CWTI:JAN/95[34]427, CWTI:JAN/95[48]429,
  CWTI:JUN/95[32]446, CWTI:JUN/95[38]447,
  CWTI:MAR/95[20]433, CWTI:MAR/95[33]435,
  CWTI:MAR/95[60]439
ADDITIONAL LISTINGS, MH; MH:JUN/94[8]177
ARMY OF OBSERVATION; B&G:AUG/95[8]604
ARMY OF RELIEF; B&G:AUG/95[8]604, CWR:VOL2#1[i]129,
  CWR:VOL2#1[36]132, CWR:VOL2#1[78], CWR:VOL3#3[59]159
ARMY OF TENNESSEE:
BOOK REVIEWS: *ARMY OF THE HEARTLAND: THE ARMY OF
  TENNESSEE, 1861-1862 * THE ARMY OF TENNESSEE *
  AUTUMN OF GLORY: THE ARMY OF TENNESSEE,
  1862-1865 * CONFEDERATE HOSPITALS ON THE MOVE:
  SAMUEL H. STOUT AND THE ARMY OF TENNESSEE *
  THE DEATH OF AN ARMY: THE BATTLE OF NASHVILLE
  AND HOOD'S RETREAT * SOLDERING IN THE ARMY OF
  TENNESSEE: A PORTRAIT OF LIFE IN A CONFEDERATE
  ARMY * TWO GREAT REBEL ARMIES*
GENERAL LISTINGS: *Carolina Campaign,* B&G:DEC/95[9]615,
  general history, AHI:MAY/71[3]133A, *in book review,*
  ACW:MAR/91[54], ACW:NOV/95[62], CWM:APR/95[8],
  CWM:AUG/95[45], CWM:OCT/94[8], CWR:VOL1#2[78],
  CWR:VOL1#4[77], CWR:VOL2#2[169], CWR:VOL2#4[346],
  CWR:VOL3#4[68], *Johnston's surrender,*
  CWTI:AUG/90[26]166, *Tullahoma Campaign,*
  B&G:OCT/92[10]496
ADDITIONAL LISTINGS, ACW; ACW:MAY/91[23]303,
  ACW:SEP/91[46]324, ACW:NOV/92[35]387,
  ACW:JAN/93[10]393, ACW:JAN/93[43]397,
  ACW:MAR/93[26]404, ACW:NOV/93[34]442,
  ACW:MAR/94[42]461, ACW:JUL/94[66]481,
  ACW:SEP/94[10]484, ACW:JAN/95[30]505,
  ACW:SEP/95[48]547, ACW:NOV/95[48]557,
  ACW:NOV/95[66]559, ACW:NOV/95[74]560
ADDITIONAL LISTINGS, AHI; AHI:NOV/73[18]151
ADDITIONAL LISTINGS, B&G; B&G:OCT/91[11]466,
  B&G:DEC/91[34]470, B&G:DEC/93[12]545,
  B&G:JUN/94[32]570, B&G:FEB/95[30]591,
  B&G:AUG/95[8]604
ADDITIONAL LISTINGS, B&G; CWM:JAN/91[12]326,
  CWM:JAN/91[28]327, CWM:MAR/91[28]336,
  CWM:MAR/91[50]340, CWM:MAY/91[26]349,
  CWM:NOV/91[50]394, CWM:JAN/93[29]459,
  CWM:MAR/93[16]466, CWM:OCT/94[48]542,
  CWM:APR/95[16]571, CWM:OCT/95[47]620,
  CWM:DEC/95[35]629
ADDITIONAL LISTINGS, CWR: CWR:VOL1#1[71]107,
  CWR:VOL1#3[v]117, CWR:VOL1#3[82]123,
  CWR:VOL1#4[v]124, CWR:VOL1#4[42]126,
  CWR:VOL1#4[64]127, CWR:VOL2#1[36]132,
  CWR:VOL2#3[212]142, CWR:VOL3#2[70]155,
  CWR:VOL3#3[59]159, CWR:VOL4#1[1]163,
  CWR:VOL4#3[65]172
ADDITIONAL LISTINGS, CWTI; CWTI:SUMMER/89[13]120,
  CWTI:SUMMER/89[20]121, CWTI:SEPT/89[30]129,
  CWTI:FEB/90[46]146, CWTI:AUG/91[62]221,
  CWTI:SEP/91[23]228, CWTI:MAY/92[48]267,

ACW:JAN/95[46]507, ACW:JAN/95[54]508,
ACW:MAR/95[42]517, ACW:MAR/95[70]520,
ACW:MAY/95[10]523, ACW:MAY/95[30]525,
ACW:MAY/95[30]525, ACW:JUL/95[34]536,
ACW:JUL/95[50]538, ACW:SEP/95[54]548,
ACW:SEP/95[74]550, ACW:NOV/95[10]553
ADDITIONAL LISTINGS, AHI: AHI:JUN/84[24]239
ADDITIONAL LISTNGS, B&G: B&G:AUG/91[36]462,
B&G:DEC/91[34]470, B&G:FEB/92[22]476,
B&G:APR/92[8]481, B&G:APR/93[12]518,
B&G:AUG/93[30]531, B&G:OCT/93[12]537,
B&G:DEC/94[10]585, B&G:FEB/95[8]590A,
B&G:OCT/95[8]611A, B&G:OCT/95[8]611D
ADDITIONAL LISTNGS, CWM: CWM:MAR/91[35]337,
CWM:MAR/91[56]341, CWM:MAY/91[18]348,
CWM:JUL/91[28]366, CWM:JUL/91[43]371,
CWM:NOV/91[58]394A, CWM:MAY/92[8]418,
CWM:MAY/92[15]419, CWM:MAY/92[20]420,
CWM:MAY/92[44]423, CWM:JUL/92[8]427,
CWM:JUL/92[16]428, CWM:JUL/92[18]429,
CWM:SEP/92[19]440, CWM:SEP/92[24]441,
CWM:JAN/93[16]457, CWM:MAR/93[24]467,
CWM:SEP/93[24]495, CWM:JUN/94[14]509,
CWM:JUN/94[28]514, CWM:DEC/94[40]550,
CWM:JUN/95[24]582, CWM:JUN/95[65]595,
CWM:AUG/95[27]605, CWM:OCT/95[4]612,
CWM:OCT/95[40]619, CWM:DEC/95[54]622
ADDITIONAL LISTNGS, CWR: CWR:VOL1#1[1]102,
CWR:VOL1#2[7]111, CWR:VOL1#3[20]119,
CWR:VOL1#3[28]120, CWR:VOL2#2[118]136,
CWR:VOL2#2[156]138, CWR:VOL2#3[212]142,
CWR:VOL2#4[269]145, CWR:VOL2#4[313]146,
CWR:VOL3#1[31]150, CWR:VOL3#2[70]155,
CWR:VOL3#3[1]157, CWR:VOL3#4[1]161,
CWR:VOL4#4[i]175, CWR:VOL4#4[1]177,
CWR:VOL4#4[28]178, CWR:VOL4#4[47]179,
CWR:VOL4#4[101]181
ADDITIONAL LISTNGS, CWTI: CWTI:MAY/89[36]118,
CWTI:SEPT/89[30]129, CWTI:SEPT/89[40]130,
CWTI:FEB/90[46]146, CWTI:FEB/90[54]147,
CWTI:APR/90[24]152, CWTI:AUG/90[26]166,
CWTI:AUG/90[64]170, CWTI:JUN/90[28]158,
CWTI:JUN/90[32]159, CWTI:FEB/91[24]191,
CWTI:FEB/91[45]194, CWTI:FEB/91[66]196,
CWTI:AUG/91[62]221, CWTI:SEP/91[31]229,
CWTI:SEP/91[42]231, CWTI:SEP/91[54]232,
CWTI:SEP/91[61]233, CWTI:FEB/92[36]249,
CWTI:APR/92[49]260, CWTI:SEP/92[22]279,
CWTI:NOV/92[49]292, CWTI:JAN/93[40]301,
CWTI:MAR/93[20]308, CWTI:MAR/93[26]310,
CWTI:JUL/93[14]324, CWTI:JUL/93[42]329,
CWTI:SEP/93[43]338, CWTI:NOV/93[24]346,
CWTI:JAN/94[20]358, CWTI:JAN/95[34]427,
CWTI:JAN/95[48]429, CWTI:MAR/95[33]435,
CWTI:JUN/95[32]446
ADDITIONAL LISTNGS, GETTY: GETTY:13[7]253, GETTY:13[33]255
ARMY OF THE SHENANDOAH: ACW:MAY/91[38]305,
ACW:NOV/94[18]495, AHI:NOV/80[8]209, B&G:APR/92[8]481,
CWM:JAN/93[24]458, MH:OCT/93[76]173
ARMY OF THE SOUTHWEST: ACW:MAR/94[8]456,
CWR:VOL1#1[42]105, CWR:VOL2#3[212]142

ARMY OF THE TENNESSEE:
GENERAL LISTINGS: *Carolina Campaign*, B&G:DEC/95[9]615,
letters to the editor, CWM:DEC/94[5]546, *Mary Ann
Bickerdyke*, AHI:APR/79[4]186, *Vicksburg*, B&G/95[8]604
ADDITIONAL LISTINGS, ACW: ACW:JAN/91[22]285,
ACW:SEP/91[46]324, ACW:JAN/93[10]393,
ACW:MAY/93[22]414, ACW:JUL/94[66]481,
ACW:JAN/95[30]505, ACW:SEP/95[48]547, ACW:NOV/95[62]
ADDITIONAL LISTINGS, AHI: AHI:NOV/73[18]151, AHI:APR/79[4]186
ADDITIONAL LISTINGS, B&G: B&G:FEB/94[8]550,
B&G:AUG/95[8]604, B&G:DEC/95[9]615
ADDITIONAL LISTINGS, CWM: CWM:JAN/91[12]326,
CWM:JUL/92[18]429, CWM:MAR/93[8]465,
CWM:SEP/93[8]493, CWM:JUN/94[30]515,
CWM:AUG/94[27]526, CWM:DEC/94[5]546,
CWM:DEC/94[46]552, CWM:APR/95[66]579,
CWM:AUG/95[36]608, CWM:DEC/95[35]629
ADDITIONAL LISTINGS, CWR: CWR:VOL1#3[82]123,
CWR:VOL2#1[1]130, CWR:VOL2#1[19]131,
CWR:VOL2#1[69]133, CWR:VOL2#3[212]142,
CWR:VOL2#4[313]146, CWR:VOL3#3[33]158,
CWR:VOL3#3[59]159, CWR:VOL4#2[26]166,
CWR:VOL4#2[104]168
ADDITIONAL LISTINGS, CWTI: CWTI:SUMMER/89[13]120,
CWTI:SUMMER/89[20]121, CWTI:SUMMER/89[40]123,
CWTI:SUMMER/89[50]124, CWTI:SEPT/89[30]129,
CWTI:FEB/90[38]145, CWTI:MAY/91[24]208,
CWTI:SEP/91[23]228, CWTI:SEP/92[28]280,
CWTI:NOV/92[41]291, CWTI:JAN/93[20]298,
CWTI:MAR/93[24]309, CWTI:NOV/93[65]351,
CWTI:MAR/95[40]436
ADDITIONAL LISTINGS, MH: MH:JUN/93[82]167, MH:APR/94[54]176,
MH:DEC/95[58]188
ARMY OF THE TRANS-MISSISSIPPI; ACW:NOV/94[42]497
ARMY OF THE VALLEY; CWM:JAN/93[24]458,
CWM:JAN/93[40]461, CWM:OCT/94[38]540,
CWM:OCT/95[37]617, CWR:VOL2#4[269]145
ARMY OF THE WEST; CWM:SEP/92[38]443,
CWTI:FEB/92[29]248, CWTI:AUG/95[58]461
ARMY OF VIRGINIA:
GENERAL LISTINGS: *in book review*, ACW:JAN/91[54],
CWNEWS:OCT/90[4], CWNEWS:JAN/91[4], CWR:VOL3#1[80]
ADDITIONAL LISTINGS: ACW:JUL/91[18]312, ACW:NOV/92[18]385,
CWM:JUL/91[40]370, CWM:NOV/91[12]390,
CWM:JUL/92[18]429, CWM:JAN/93[16]457,
CWM:MAR/93[32]468, CWM:JUN/95[82]600,
CWR:VOL1#3[52]122, CWR:VOL2#4[269]145,
CWR:VOL3#1[31]150, CWR:VOL3#3[1]157,
CWR:VOL4#2[26]166,
CWTI:APR/89[14]107, CWTI:DEC/89[34]136,
CWTI:DEC/91[36]240, CWTI:NOV/93[55]350,
CWTI:JUN/95[38]447, CWTI:DEC/95[24]477,
MH:AUG/95[30]185
ARMY OF WEST TENNESSEE; AHI:NOV/73[18]151
ARMY OF WEST VIRGINIA; ACW:MAY/91[38]305,
ACW:JUL/94[26]477, CWM:AUG/95[35]607
ARNOLD, ANDREW, *Private, 24th Michigan Infantry;*
GETTY:5[19]158
ARNOLD, FRANK, *Lt., Sumter Artillery;* CWR:VOL3#2[1]153
ARNOLD, JONATHAN; B&G:OCT/94[28]581
ARNOLD, LAURA JACKSON; ARTICLE: "ARNOLD VS.
ARNOLD: THE STRANGE AND HITHERTO UNTOLD

STORY OF THE DIVORCE OF STONEWALL JACKSON'S SISTER," B&G:OCT/94[28]581

ARNOLD, LEWIS G., *Maj., 1st U.S. Arty.;* CWR:VOL1#4[42]126

ARNOLD, RICHARD, *Mayor, Savannah;* ACW:SEP/92[47]380, B&G:FEB/91[8]439

ARNOLD, SAMUEL, *Corporal, 1st Florida Special Battalion;* CWR:VOL3#1[65]151, CWTI:MAY/92[8]261

ARNOLD, WILEY, *Sergeant, 32nd Wisconsin Infantry;* CWR:VOL2#4[313]146

ARNOLD, WILLIAM A., *Captain, 1st Rhode Island Artillery:*
ARTICLE: "ARNOLD'S BATTERY AND THE 26TH NORTH CAROLINA," GETTY:12[61]245
ADDITIONAL LISTINGS: CWR:VOL3#2[1]153, CWR:VOL4#4[28]178, GETTY:4[89]150, GETTY:5[89]162, GETTY:7[51]190, GETTY:7[97]193, GETTY:8[95]205, GETTY:9[61]215, GETTY:13[43]256, *photo*, GETTY:12[61]245

ARP, BENJAMIN, *Pvt., 81st Penn. Inf.;* ACW:SEP/93[22]432

ARRINGTON, J.P., *Adjutant, CSA;* GETTY:4[33]146

ARRINGTON, T.M., *Lt. Col., 31st Ala. Inf.;* B&G:FEB/94[8]550

ARSENALS and ARMORIES, CONFEDERATE:
Ashville, North Carolina; ACW:JAN/94[18]449
Augusta, Georgia; ACW:JAN/94[18]449
Baton Rouge, Louisiana; ACW:JAN/94[18]449
Charleston, South Carolina; ACW:JAN/94[18]449
Columbus, Georgia; ACW:MAR/91[38]296
Fayetteville, North Carolina; ACW:JAN/94[18]449
Greenville, South Carolina; ACW:JAN/94[18]449
Little Rock, Arkansas; ACW:JAN/94[18]449
Macon, Georgia; ACW:JAN/94[18]449
Milledgeville, Georgia; ACW:JAN/94[18]449
Mount Vernon, Louisiana; ACW:JAN/94[18]449
New Orleans, Louisiana; ACW:JAN/94[18]449
Palmetto, (Columbia) South Carolina; ACW:JAN/94[18]449
Richmond, Virginia; ACW:MAY/95[38]526, CWM:SEP/91[8]378
Savannah, Georgia; B&G:FEB/91[8]339
Tredegar:
ARTICLES: "TREDEGAR IRON WORKS: ARSENAL OF THE SOUTH," CWM:SEP/91[24]381, "TREDEGAR," CWM:SEP/91[27]382, "VALENTINE MUSEUM EXPANDS TO TREDEGAR IRON WORKS," AHI:JUL/91[14]296
BOOK REVIEW: *IRONMAKER TO THE CONFEDERACY: JOSEPH R. ANDERSON AND THE TREDEGAR IRON WORKS*
ADDITIONAL LISTINGS: ACW:MAY/94[20]467, ACW:MAY/95[38]526, AHI:NOV/73[18]151, AHI:JAN/74[10]153, CWM:SEP/91[4]376, CWM:JUN/95[43]587, CWR:VOL1#1[1]102, CWTI:JUN/90[28]158, CWTI:JAN/93[49]303, *photos*, CWM:SEP/91[24]381, CWM:JUN/95[24]582

ARSENALS and ARMORIES, FEDERAL:
Harpers Ferry, West Virginia; ACW:JAN/91[8]282
Liberty; CWTI:MAR/91[34]201
Rock Island, Illinois; CWTI:DEC/94[82]418
Springfield, Illinois:
ARTICLE: "MADE IN SPRINGFIELD," CWM:SEP/91[19]380,
ADDITIONAL LISTINGS: ACW:JAN/91[8]282, CWM:SEP/91[4]376, *photo*, CWM:SEP/91[19]380
St. Louis, Missouri; ACW:JUL/94[8]474, CWTI:FEB/92[29]248
Washington, D.C.; ACW:JUL/93[8]420

ARTHUR, CHESTER A.:
ARTICLE: "A PRESIDENTIAL GALLERY," AHI:APR/89[20]282
GENERAL LISTINGS: *President Chester A. Arthur Historic Site;* AHI:APR/89[43]284, *photo*, AHI:FEB/85[10]247, *portrait;* AHI:APR/89[20]282
ADDITIONAL LISTINGS: AHI:APR/89[13]281, AHI:FEB/85[10]247, CWTI:FEB/90[12]141, MH:OCT/91[50]154

ARTILLERY, GENERAL INFORMATION:
ARTICLE: "THE EFFECTS OF ARTILLERY FIRE ON INFANTRY AT GETTYSBURG," GETTY:5[117]165
BOOK REVIEWS: *INTRODUCTION TO FIELD ARTILLERY ORDNANCE 1861-1865: A PICTORIAL STUDY OF CIVIL WAR ARTILLERY PROJECTILES * ARTILLERY HELL: THE EMPLOYMENT OF ARTILLERY AT ANTIETAM * CUSHING OF GETTYSBURG: THE STORY OF A UNION ARTILLERY COMMANDER * THE LONG ARM OF LEE, OR THE HISTORY OF THE ARTILLERY OF THE ARMY OF NORTHERN VIRGINIA*
TABLE: Results of individual artillery shots at Gettysburg causing two or more casualties, GETTY:5[117]165

ARTISTS, CONTEMPORARY and MODERN;
ARTICLES: "THE AMERICAN HERITAGE CENTURY COLLECTION OF CIVIL WAR ART," CWTI:SEP/90[28]175, "THE ARTIST AND THE CIVIL WAR," AHI:NOV/80[28]211, "ENDURING IMAGES OF A NATION DIVIDED: THE GREAT PRINTMAKERS OF THE CIVIL WAR," CWM:NOV/92[24]448, "EYEWITNESS NEWS," CWM:NOV/92[10]447, "MEMOIRS IN OILS," CWM:NOV/92[31]449, "MINE EYES HAVE SEEN THE GLORY," CWTI:SEP/93[30]336
BOOK REVIEWS: *LESLIE'S ILLUSTRATED CIVIL WAR, MINE EYES HAVE SEEN THE GLORY: THE CIVIL WAR IN ART*
Carpenter, Francis B.; ARTICLE: "THE PAINTER AND THE PRESIDENT," CWTI:FEB/92[21]247
Chapman, Conrad Wise; AHI:NOV/80[28]211, CWM:NOV/92[31]449
Elder, John Adams; AHI:NOV/80[28]211
Forbes, Edwin:
BOOK REVIEW: *THIRTY YEARS AFTER: AN ARTIST'S MEMOIR OF THE CIVIL WAR*
ADDITIONAL LISTINGS: AHI:NOV/80[28]211
Homer, Winslow:
BOOK REVIEW: *WINSLOW HOMER: PAINTINGS OF THE CIVIL WAR*
ADDITIONAL LISTINGS: AHI:NOV/80[28]211, CWM:NOV/92[31]449, CWTI:AUG/90[70]171
House, Ned; B&G:FEB/94[24]551
Johnson, Eastman; AHI:NOV/80[28]211
Kuntsler, Mort:
ARTICLE: "A WEARY TROOP OF SOUTHERN CAVALRY RIDES PAST A WARMLY INVITING CHURCH IN MORT KUNSTLER'S 'SOUTHERN STARS,'" ACW:MAY/95[74]530
BOOK REVIEW: *IMAGES OF THE CIVIL WAR*
Neary, Donna J.; ARTICLE: "IN 'EVEN TO HELL ITSELF,' DONNA J. NEARY CAPTURES THE," HUMAN DRAMA OF AN ILL-CONCEIVED UNION ASSAULT," ACW:SEP/95[70]549
Redifer, Rea; ARTICLE: "THE ART OF REA REDIFER: INTERPRETATIONS OF LINCOLN," B&G:OCT/92[55]501

Reeves, Rick; ARTICLE: "RICK REEVES' 'HAND-TO-HAND' CAPTURES A VICIOUS STRUGGLE BETWEEN THE 26TH TENNESSEE AND 78TH PENNSYLVANIA," ACW:NOV/95[66]559

Riddle, Andrew J.; ARTICLE: "THE ANDERSONVILLE ARTIST," B&G:AUG/93[18]530

Rocco, Keith; ARTICLE: "A UNION SOLDIER REFLECTS ON THE DEATH OF A COMRADE IN KEITH ROCCO'S *WHERE THE COLORS STOOD*," ACW:MAR/95[66]519

Scott, Julian:
ARTICLE: "A SOLDIER'S SKETCHBOOK," CWTI:SEP/91[54]232
ADDITIONAL LISTINGS: CWM:NOV/92[31]449

Smith, Xanthus R.; CWM:NOV/92[31]449

Strain, John Paul; ARTICLE: "STONEWALL JACKSON STANDS THE FIRST WATCH IN JOHN PAUL STRAIN'S EVOCATIVE *'DESTINATION MANASSAS,'* ACW:JAN/95[70]509

Taylor, James E.; ACW:SEP/94[55]489

Troiani, Don; ACW:JUL/95[66]539

Walker, James; AHI:NOV/80[28]211

Waud, Alfred R.:
BOOK REVIEW: *OUR SPECIAL ARTIST*
ADDITIONAL LISTINGS: AHI:NOV/80[28]211, B&G:FEB/94[24]551

Wood, Thomas W.; AHI:NOV/80[28]211

ASBOTH, ALEXANDER S., *General, USA;* CWR:VOL1#1[42]105, ACW:MAR/92[46]354, CWTI:DEC/94[82]418

ASBURY, A.E., *Captain, CSA;* CWTI:JAN/95[42]428

ASCHMANN, RUDOLF, *Captain, 1st USSS;* BOOK REVIEW: *MEMOIRS OF A SWISS OFFICER IN THE AMERICAN CIVIL WAR*

ASH, DAVID, *Sgt., 37th Illinois Infantry;* CWR:VOL1#1[42]105

ASHBY, HENRY, *Captain, 2nd Tennessee Cavalry;*
ARTICLE: "DEFENDING THE CONFEDERATE HEARTLAND: COMPANY F OF HENRY ASHBY'S 2ND TENNESSEE CAVALRY," CWR:VOL4#1[1]163
ADDITIONAL LISTINGS: B&G:DEC/95[9]615, *photo,* CWR:VOL4#1[1]163

ASHBY, RICHMOND; CWTI:APR/89[38]111

ASHBY, TURNER, *General, CSA:*
ARTICLE: "TURNER ASHBY'S CAREER AS A SHENANDOAH VALLEY CAVALIER WAS SHORT BUT MEMORABLE," ACW:JAN/92[8]338
BOOK REVIEW: *NINE MEN IN GRAY*
GENERAL LISTINGS: *Harrisburg, Battle of,* GETTY:9[53]214, *in book review,* CWM:APR/95[8], CWM:APR/95[50], *Jackson,* B&G:JUN/92[8]487, B&G:JUN/92[8]487, *shot by,* GETTY:10[120]229, *photo,* ACW:JAN/92[8]338
ADDITIONAL LISTINGS: ACW:JAN/92[16]340, ACW:MAR/92[8]348, ACW:JAN/93[35]396, ACW:MAY/95[10]523, B&G:AUG/92[40]495, B&G:JUN/92[53]491, CWM:JAN/92[27]403, CWM:JUL/92[27]431, CWR:VOL1#3[28]120, CWR:VOL4#1[1]163, CWTI:APR/89[38]111, CWTI:APR/92[35]257, CWTI:MAR/94[29]371

ASHFORD, JOHN, *Col., 38th NC Inf.;* GETTY:8[67]204

ASHLEY, WALTER, *civilian;* ACW:JUL/95[44]537

ASMUSSEN, CHARLES W., *Colonel, USA;* GETTY:4[49]147

ASPINWALL, BILL, *Pvt., 47th Ind. Inf.;* CWTI:MAY/91[24]208

ASSOCIATED PRESS; ACW:NOV/95[54]558

ASSOCIATION FOR THE PRESERVATION OF CIVIL WAR SITES; see listings under "PRESERVATION"

ATCHISON, DAVID R., *Senator, Missouri;* ACW:JAN/93[26]395, AHI:JUL/75[4]160, *photo,* AHI:JUL/75[4]160

ATHENS BATTALION; B&G:FEB/91[8]439

ATHENS, ALABAMA, "SACK OF"; ARTICLE: "A UNION COLONEL WAS THE RUSSIAN CONNECTION IN THE AMERICAN CIVIL WAR," MH:DEC/93[12]174

ATHENS, MISSOURI, BATTLE OF:
ARTICLE: "ATHENS BATTLEFIELD," MH:APR/95[74]184
ADDITIONAL LISTING: CWTI:AUG/95[34]457

ATHERTON, J.B., *Major, 22nd Iowa Infantry;* B&G:FEB/94[8]550, CWR:VOL2#1[19]131

ATKINS, ALFRED, *Corporal, 5th New York Infantry;* CWR:VOL1#2[7]111, CWTI:MAY/94[31]382

ATKINS, ROBERT G., *Captain, Louisiana Tigers;* CWTI:MAR/94[48]374

ATKINS, SMITH D., *Colonel, 98th Illinois Infantry;* B&G:OCT/92[32]499, B&G:APR/93[6]517, B&G:DEC/95[9]615

ATKINSON, B.H., *Adjutant, 1st Georgia Regulars;* CWR:VOL2#2[95]135

ATKINSON, EDMUND N., *General, CSA;* ACW:MAY/91[38]305

ATKINSON, EDWARD; CWNEWS:JUN/93[5]

ATKINSON, JAMES., *Pvt., 33rd NC Inf.;* CWTI:FEB/91[45]194

ATLANTA, GEORGIA, BATTLES AND CAMPAIGNS OF:
ARTICLES: "A DRIVING TOUR OF NORTH GEORGIA TRACES WILLIAM T. SHERMAN'S CAUTIOUS ADVANCE TO ATLANTA," ACW:JUL/94[66]481, "AS THE SHELLS EXPLODED OVER ATLANTA IN 1864, THE OPPOSING GENERALS OPENED A WAR OF WORDS," ACW:JAN/95[6]501, "AT THE BATTLE OF ATLANTA, THE IOWA BRIGADE SACRIFICED ITSELF TO BUY TIME FOR ITS COMRADES," ACW:JAN/93[10]393, "THE ATLANTA CAMPAIGN," CWM:JAN/91[12]326
ADDITIONAL ARTICLES: "THE ATLANTA CAMPAIGN: CHAPTER 1: THE MANEUVERS BEGIN," CWTI:SUMMER/89[13]120, "THE ATLANTA CAMPAIGN: CHAPTER 2: UP AGAINST THE DEFENSES," CWTI:SUMMER/89[20]121, "THE ATLANTA CAMPAIGN: CHAPTER 3: FIGHTING JOHN HOOD," CWTI:SUMMER/89[32]122, "THE ATLANTA CAMPAIGN: CHAPTER 4: THE DEATHS OF FRIENDS AND FOES," CWTI:SUMMER/89[40]123, "THE ATLANTA CAMPAIGN: CHAPTER 5: THE PRIZE I FOUGHT FOR," CWTI:SUMMER/89[50]124
ADDITIONAL ARTICLES: "BATTLE MOST DESPERATE AND BLOODY," ACW:JAN/95[30]505, "THE BATTLE THAT SHOULD NOT HAVE BEEN," CWTI:NOV/92[41]291, "FIGHTING AT ATLANTA," CWM:AUG/94[27]526, "HOW TO LOSE A CITY," CWM:JAN/91[28]327
ADDITIONAL ARTICLES: "JADED MULES, TWISTED RAILS, AND RAZED DEPOTS," CWM:JAN/91[40]330, "KENNESAW MOUNTAIN BATTLEFIELD PARK AND THE ATLANTA CYCLORAMA GIVE VISITORS A GOOD TASTE OF THE ATLANTA CAMPAIGN," ACW:NOV/95[74]560, "REPORT OF THE BATTLE OF ATLANTA," B&G:APR/94[28]559, "SHERMAN MOVES ON ATLANTA," CWM:AUG/95[36]608, "WRECKING ON THE RAILROAD," ACW:SEP/95[48]547
BOOK REVIEWS: *ATLANTA * THE ATLANTA CAMPAIGN: MAY-NOVEMBER, 1864 * THE ATLANTA CAMPAIGN—A CIVIL WAR DRIVING TOUR * THE CAMPAIGN FOR ATLANTA AND SHERMAN'S MARCH TO THE SEA, VOLUMES 1 AND 2 * THE CHATTAHOOCHEE RIVER LINE, AN AMERICAN MAGINOT * DECISION IN THE WEST: THE ATLANTA CAMPAIGN OF 1864 * ECHOES OF*

*BATTLE: THE ATLANTA CAMPAIGN * FIELDS OF GLORY, A HISTORY AND TOUR GUIDE TO THE ATLANTA CAMPAIGN * KENNESAW MOUNTAIN AND THE ATLANTA CAMPAIGN: A TOUR GUIDE * LAST TRAIN FROM ATLANTA * SHROUDS OF GLORY: FROM ATLANTA TO NASHVILLE * TO THE SEA, A HISTORY AND TOUR GUIDE OF SHERMAN'S MARCH*

GENERAL LISTINGS: *Audio/Visual,* B&G:JUN/91[42]456, *general history,* AHI:MAY/71[3]133A, *in book review,* ACW:NOV/93[58], CWM:JUN/94[6], ACW:JUL/94[58], CWM:OCT/94[8], ACW:NOV/94[66], ACW:MAR/95[58], CWM:AUG/95[45], CWM:DEC/95[10], CWR:VOL1#2[78], CWR:VOL2#2[169], CWR:VOL3#2[105], CWR:VOL4#3[89], CWTI:APR/92[30], *letters to the editor,* CWTI:JUL/93[10]323

ADDITIONAL LISTINGS: ACW:MAR/94[27]459, ACW:SEP/94[10]484, ACW:SEP/95[48]547, ACW:NOV/95[74]560, CWM:JAN/91[4]323, CWM:JAN/91[12]326, CWM:JAN/91[40]330, CWM:JAN/91[72]331, CWM:JAN/92[40]405, CWM:JUL/92[18]429, CWM:JUL/92[40]432, CWM:MAR/93[32]468, CWR:VOL1#1[73]108, CWR:VOL1#3[82]123, CWR:VOL1#4[64]127, CWR:VOL2#4[313]146, CWR:VOL4#1[44]164, CWR:VOL4#3[65]172, CWTI:APR/89[32]110, CWTI:SUMMER/89[20]121, CWTI:SUMMER/89[32]122, CWTI:SUMMER/89[40]123, CWTI:SUMMER/89[50]124, CWTI:FEB/90[54]147, CWTI:MAY/91[34]209, CWTI:AUG/91[62]221, CWTI:SEP/92[28]280, CWTI:JAN/93[20]298, CWTI:SEP/93[62]342, CWTI:DEC/94[49]413, CWTI:MAR/95[40]436

ATLANTA CYCLORAMA:
ARTICLE: "ATLANTA'S RESTORED CYCLORAMA," CWTI:FEB/91[18]190
ADDITIONAL LISTING: CWTI:FEB/92[10]246

ATLANTA HISTORICAL SOCIETY; B&G:JUN/93[40]527

ATLANTA, GEORGIA:
ARTICLES: "ATLANTA HISTORY MUSEUM ESTABLISHED," AHI:NOV/93[12]313, "ATLANTA'S RESTORED CYCLORAMA," CWTI:FEB/91[18]190, "FATHER THOMAS O'REILLY: A SAVIOR OF ATLANTA," CWM:JAN/92[40]405
ADDITIONAL LISTING: CWNEWS:SEP/93[5]

ATLANTIC BLOCKADING SQUADRON;
CWM:JUN/95[24]582, CWR:VOL4#3[77]174

ATWATER, DORANCE; CWTI:APR/92[23]255

ATWELL, C.A., *Lieutenant, USA;* ACW:MAY/95[30]525

ATWELL, CHARLES, *Cpt., Penn. Battery;* CWR:VOL3#2[70]155

ATWOOD, SYLVESTER, *Captain, CSA;* ACW:JUL/95[44]537

ATZERODT, GEORGE; AHI:FEB/86[12]257, CWTI:MAY/92[8]261, CWTI:OCT/95[18], CWTI:DEC/95[76]482

ATZRODT, JOHN, *Pvt., 1st LA Inf.;* CWTI:MAR/89[28]10

AUBERNE, AUGUSTUS, *Colonel, USA;* CWTI:DEC/89[62]139

AUDIO REVIEWS:
ARTICLES: "A LEG UP ON JOHN BELL HOOD," B&G:JUN/91[42]456, "STRANGE BEDFELLOWS," B&G:FEB/92[36]478, "THE HORSE SOLDIERS," B&G:JUN/93[36]526
ADDITIONAL LISTINGS: B&G:DEC/91[42]472, B&G:DEC/92[30]505

AUGUR, CHRISTOPHER C., *General, USA;* ACW:JUL/91[50], ACW:JAN/94[30]450, ACW:JUL/94[26]477, B&G:JUN/93[12]524, B&G:AUG/94[10]574

AUGUST, THOMAS P., *Col., 15th VA Inf.;* CWR:VOL4#2[68]167

AUGUSTA (GEORGIA) BATTALION; B&G:FEB/91[8]439

AUGUSTA (GEORGIA) POWDER WORKS:
ARTICLE: "BULWARK OF THE BELEAGUERED CONFEDERACY," CWM:SEP/91[10]379
ADDITIONAL LISTINGS: ACW:MAY/94[20]467, AHI:NOV/73[18]151, CWM:SEP/91[4]376, CWR:VOL3#4[68], *photo,* CWM:SEP/91[10]379

AUGUSTA, KENTUCKY, SKIRMISH AT; ACW:SEP/95[22]544

AUGUSTINE, JACOB M., *Lieutenant Colonel, 55th Illinois Infantry;* CWTI:SEP/92[28]280

AUSTIN, JAMES E., *Captain, 1st Ohio Light Artillery;* CWTI:SEP/91[23]228, GETTY:4[49]147

AUSTIN, JOHN E., *Major, CSA;* CWM:FEB/95[28]560

AUSTIN, JONATHAN M., *Private, 2nd Tennessee Cavalry;* CWR:VOL4#1[1]163

AUTRY, JAMES L., *Lt Col., CSA;* CWR:VOL3#3[33]158

AVANT, WILLIAM R., *Lt., 61st Georgia Inf.;* GETTY:12[111]250

AVERASBORO, NORTH CAROLINA, BATTLE OF:
ARTICLE: "THE BATTLE OF BENTONVILLE, MARCH 19-21, 1865: LAST STAND IN THE CAROLINAS," B&G:DEC/95[9]615
ADDITIONAL LISTINGS: ACW:MAR/95[50]518, CWM:JUL/92[18]429

AVERELL, WILLIAM W., *General, USA:*
ARTICLE: "MELEE ON SAINT PATRICK'S DAY," ACW:NOV/91[30]332
GENERAL LISTINGS: *Droop Mountain,* CWTI:MAR/89[16]101, *Gettysburg,* GETTY:11[19]232, *Saltville,* B&G:AUG/91[11]458, *Stephenson's Depot,* B&G:AUG/94[10]574, *Winchester, Third,* ACW:MAY/91[38]305, *photo,* ACW:NOV/91[30]332, B&G:AUG/94[10]574, CWTI:MAR/89[16]101
ADDITIONAL LISTINGS: ACW:MAR/94[27]459, B&G:JUN/92[46]490, B&G:AUG/94[19]575, B&G:OCT/94[28]581, B&G:APR/95[24]596, B&G:OCT/95[8]611F, CWM:APR/95[32]575, CWTI:MAY/92[48]267, CWTI:JUL/93[38]328

AVERY, CLARK M., *Colonel, 33rd North Carolina Infantry;* GETTY:8[67]204, GETTY:9[109]218, GETTY:13[75]259

AVERY, ISAAC E., *Colonel, CSA;* ACW:NOV/92[42]388, B&G:FEB/95[8]590C, CWTI:SEP/94[34]402, GETTY:4[49]147, GETTY:5[103]163, GETTY:8[17]200, GETTY:9[17]210, GETTY:11[57]233, GETTY:11[126]239, GETTY:12[30]243

AVERY, MATTHEW H., *Maj., 10th NY Cav.;* GETTY:4[65]148

AVERY, WILLIAM, *Lt Col., 95th Ill. Inf.;* ACW:JAN/91[16]284

AYARS, PETER, *Pvt., 99th Pennsylvania Inf.;* GETTY:9[5]209

AYLETT, WILLIAM R., *Colonel, 53rd Virginia Infantry;* B&G:APR/94[10]558, GETTY:13[64]258

AYRES, ROMEYN B., *General, USA:*
GENERAL LISTINGS: *Five Forks,* B&G:APR/92[8]48, B&G:APR/92[8]481, *Gettysburg,* GETTY:5[35]159, GETTY:6[43]173, GETTY:7[29]188, GETTY:8[53]203, GETTY:9[5]209, GETTY:9[41]212, GETTY:9[53]214, GETTY:11[91]236, GETTY:12[24]242, *Wilderness,* B&G:APR/95[8]595ADDITIONAL LISTINGS: ACW:JAN/94[8]447, B&G:APR/92[8]481, B&G:APR/93[12]518, B&G:APR/94[10]558, B&G:APR/95[8]595, CWR:VOL1#3[52]122

AZPELL, THOMAS F., *Surgeon, USA;* CWM:MAY/91[10]347

B

BABB, DANIEL, *Pvt., 9th NH Inf.;* CWR:VOL2#2[118]13
BABCOCK, A.G., *Sergeant, Mosby's Ranger;* CWTI:SEP/90[34]17
BABCOCK, ORVILLE E., *Colonel, USA:*
ARTICLE: "THE BELKNAP SCANDAL," AHI:MAY/69[32]122
ADDITIONAL LISTINGS: AHI:MAY/69[32]122, AHI:SEP/87[48]264,
   B&G:FEB/91[8]439, B&G:DEC/91[12]469,
   CWTI:SEP/92[42]283, CWTI:MAR/95[20]433
BACH, THEODORE, *Private, 24th Michigan Infantry;*
   GETTY:11[57]233
BACHE, GEORGE M., *Lt. Cmdr., USN;* CWTI:MAY/94[16]380
BACHE, THEODORE, *Private, 24th Michigan Infantry;*
   GETTY:9[33]211, GETTY:11[57]233
BACHELDER, JOHN B.:
BOOK REVIEW: *THE BACHELDER PAPERS: GETTYSBURG IN
   THEIR OWN WORDS*
GENERAL LISTINGS: *Gettysburg,* GETTY:4[33]145,
   GETTY:4[65]147, GETTY:4[75]148, GETTY:4[89]149,
   GETTY:4[113]153, GETTY:8[17]200, GETTY:8[53]203,
   GETTY:8[95]205, GETTY:9[61]215, GETTY:9[81]216,
   GETTY:10[112]228, GETTY:12[7]241, GETTY:12[30]243,
   GETTY:12[61]245, GETTY:12[68]246, GETTY:12[97]249, *in
   book review,* CWR:VOL3#3[92]
ADDITIONAL LISTINGS: ACW:MAY/92[8]357, CWNEWS:DEC/95[29],
   CWR:VOL3#3[92], CWTI:JAN/93[35]300, GETTY:5[47]160,
   GETTY:5[79]161, GETTY:6[13]170, GETTY:6[87]178,
   GETTY:7[51]190, GETTY:7[97]193, GETTY:7[114]194,
   GETTY:8[53]203, GETTY:13[22]254, GETTY:13[33]255
BACHELOR'S CREEK, NORTH CAROLINA, BATTLE OF;
   B&G:OCT/95[5]610
BACHMAMN, ALOIS, *Lt. Col., USA;* ACW:JUL/92[30]369
BACON, ALBERT G., *Capt., 3rd KY. Cav.;* ACW:MAR/93[51]407
BACON, EDWARD, *Colonel, 6th Michigan Infantry;* BOOK
   REVIEW: *AMONG THE COTTON THIEVES*
BACON, ELIJAH, *Pvt., 14th Connecticut Inf.;* GETTY:9[61]215
BACOT, ADA W.; BOOK REVIEWS: *A CONFEDERATE NURSE:
   THE DIARY OF ADA W. BACOT, 1860-1863*
BAD OFFICERS; "HOW TO PICK OUT BAD OFFICERS,"
   CWTI:MAR/91[46]203
BADEAU, ADAM, *Colonel, USA;* ACW:JAN/94[47]452,
   AHI:SEP/87[48]264, CWM:SEP/92[19]440,
   CWTI:DEC/95[24]47
BAGBY, ARTHUR P., *Colonel, 7th Texas Cavalry;*
   CWR:VOL2#3[212]14, CWR:VOL3#1[1]149,
   CWR:VOL4#2[68]167, CWR:VOL4#2[118]169
BAGBY, BOB, *Sgt, 3rd Georgia Infantry;* CWTI:DEC/94[32]410
BAGBY, ELBERT R., *Pvt., 22nd VA Inf.;* CWR:VOL1#3[52]122
BAGLEY, JAMES, *Lt. Col., 69th NY Inf.;* CWM:MAR/91[17]335
BAILEY, A., *Lt., 27th Connecticut Infantry;* GETTY:12[24]242
BAILEY, BYRON, *Pvt., 83rd Ohio Inf.;* B&G:AUG/92[40]495
BAILEY, CAULDER A., *Captain, 8th Virginia Cavalry;*
   B&G:AUG/94[10]574
BAILEY, DANIEL J., *Captain, USA;* CWTI:NOV/92[28]29
BAILEY, EDWARD L., *Colonel, 2nd New Hampshire Infantry;*
   GETTY:9[41]212
BAILEY, EZRA H., *Lieutenant, 1st New York Cavalry;*
   CWTI:SEP/90[34]17
BAILEY, GEORGE, *Captain, CSA;* CWTI:DEC/90[29]182
BAILEY, J.M., *Private, CSA;* CWTI:FEB/92[42]250
BAILEY, J. SYD, *Surgeon;* B&G:OCT/94[11]580

BAILEY, JACOB W.; B&G:DEC/91[12]469
BAILEY, JOSEPH, *Colonel, USA;* ACW:MAY/93[12]412,
   CWR:VOL2#3[212]14, CWR:VOL4#2[26]166,
   CWR:VOL4#2[104]168
BAILEY, NELSON, *Private, 14th Connecticut Infantry;*
   GETTY:9[61]215
BAILEY, ROBERT A., *Major, 22nd Virginia Infantry;*
   CWTI:MAR/89[16]101
BAILEY, THEODORUS, *Admiral, USN;* B&G:JUN/92[40]489,
   MH:AUG/93[47]169
BAILEY, W.K., *Col., 99th Illinois Infantry;* B&G:FEB/94[8]550
BAILEY, WILLIAM JR., *Captain, 5th Florida Infantry;*
   GETTY:12[111]250
BAILY, SILAS M., *Major, 8th Pennsylvania Reserves;*
   CWR:VOL4#4[1]177
BAINS, S.C., *Captain, CSA;* CWR:VOL1#2[44]114
BAIRD, ABSALOM, *General, USA;* ACW:JUL/91[26]313,
   B&G:DEC/95[9]615, CWTI:SUMMER/89[50]124,
   CWTI:NOV/92[41]291
BAIRD, EDWARD R., *Captain, CSA;* GETTY:13[75]259
BAIRD, JOHN P., *Colonel, USA;* B&G:OCT/92[10]496
BAIRD, WILLIAM H., *Lieutenant Colonel, 126th New York
   Infantry;* ACW:SEP/94[38]487, CWR:VOL1#4[7]125,
   GETTY:7[51]190
BAKER, AARON, *Pvt., 13th Penna. Res.;* CWR:VOL1#3[28]120
BAKER, ALPHEUS, *General, CSA;* B&G:DEC/95[9]615,
   CWTI:NOV/92[41]291
BAKER, ANDREW, *Sergeant, 11th Mississippi Infantry;*
   ACW:MAR/92[10]349, CWR:VOL2#4[269]14
BAKER, EDWARD D., *Colonel, USA;* ACW:MAY/92[8]357,
   ACW:MAR/93[51]407, AHI:MAY/71[3]133A,
   AHI:FEB/82[36]225, CWM:MAR/91[74], CWR:VOL3#1[78]152,
   CWTI:MAY/89[14]114, CWTI:SEPT/89[24]128,
   CWTI:MAR/91[12]198, CWTI:JUL/94[20]390,
   CWTI:JUN/95[51]449, CWTI:AUG/95[54]460,
   GETTY:7[97]193, *photos,* CWTI:MAY/89[14]114,
   CWTI:AUG/95[54]460
BAKER, HENRY, *Lieutenant, 5th U.S. Cavalry;*
   B&G:OCT/93[12]537
BAKER, ISAAC B., *Captain, CSA;* B&G:OCT/94[11]580
BAKER, JAMES H., *General, USA;* CWTI:AUG/95[58]461,
   GETTY:4[24]145
BAKER, JESSE E., *Pvt., 51st NC Inf.;* B&G:APR/93[24]520
BAKER, JOSEPH, *Pvt., 57th Penna. Inf.;* CWM:MAR/91[17]335
BAKER, JOSEPH F., *Lieutenant, USMC;* CWTI:APR/92[14]254
BAKER, LAFAYETTE C., *General, USA;* AHI:MAY/69[49],
   AHI:MAY/86[4], B&G:APR/91[28], CWTI:MAY/91[48]211,
   CWTI:JUN/95[26]445
BAKER, LAWRENCE S., *Colonel, 1st North Carolina Cavalry;*
   ACW:JUL/92[41]370, CWTI:11[19]232, GETTY:12[68]246
BAKER, LUTHER B., *Lieutenant, USA;* CWTI:MAY/91[48]21
BAKER, PAGE M., *Sergeant, Louisiana Tigers;*
   CWTI:MAR/94[48]374
BAKER, SAMUEL E., *Colonel, 16th Mississippi Infantry;*
   GETTY:4[7]142, GETTY:5[89]162, GETTY:8[111]206
BAKER, THOMAS H., *Captain, CSN;* ARTICLE: "PIRATES OR
   PATRIOTS?" ACW:SEP/94[46]488
BAKERS CREEK, MISSISSIPPI, BATTLE OF; see
   "CHAMPION HILL, BATTLE OF"
BAKERS, LEVI, *Pvt., 9th Massachusetts Arty.;* GETTY:5[47]160
BALCH, WILLIAM L., *Private, 19th Indiana Infantry;*
   GETTY:11[57]233
BALDWIN, AMBROSE, *Cpt, 80th NY Inf.;* B&G:FEB/95[8]590A

BALDWIN, BRISCOE, *Cpt., 56th VA Inf.;* ACW:MAR/93[10]402
BALDWIN, CLARK B., *Lieutenant Colonel, 1st Massachusetts Infantry;* GETTY:12[7]241
BALDWIN, EPHRAIM C., *Lt., USA;* ACW:JUL/93[27]423
BALDWIN, GEORGE, *Pvt., 14th Conn. Inf.;* GETTY:9[61]215
BALDWIN, JAMES, *Sergeant, 3rd Arkansas Infantry (Union):*
ARTICLE: "A FREEDMAN IN THE UNION ARMY," CWTI:JAN/94[82]366
ADDITIONAL LISTING: CWTI:MAY/94[12]379
BALDWIN, JAMES H., *Lieutenant, 35th Massachusetts Infantry;* CWTI:FEB/92[36]249
BALDWIN, WILLIAM E., *General, CSA;* ACW:JUL/94[51]480, B&G:FEB/94[8]550, B&G:FEB/94[57]555, CWM:DEC/94[49]553, CWR:VOL2#1[36]132, *photo,* B&G:FEB/94[8]550
BALL'S BLUFF, BATTLE OF:
ARTICLES: "BALL'S BLUFF ABOVE THE POTOMAC," CWTI:JUL/94[20]390, "THE DEFINITION OF DISASTER," CWTI:MAY/89[14]114, "DISASTER AT BALL'S BLUFF," AHI:FEB/82[36]225
BOOK REVIEW: *FROM BALL'S BLUFF TO GETTYSBURG...AND BEYOND*
ADDITIONAL LISTINGS: AHI:MAY/71[3]133A, AHI:FEB/82[36]225, CWM:DEC/94[49]553, CWR:VOL3#1[31]150, CWR:VOL3#1[78]152, CWR:VOL4#4[129], CWTI:MAY/89[14]114, CWTI:MAY/89[21]115, CWTI:MAY/89[50]119, CWTI:SEPT/89[24]128, CWTI:MAR/91[12]198, CWTI:JUL/94[20]390, CWTI:DEC/94[12]408, CWTI:JUN/95[51]449, GETTY:7[97]193, *poem by Herman Melville;* CWTI:MAY/89[14]114
BALL, CHARLES P., *cadet;* B&G:DEC/91[12]469
BALL, LEWIS A., *Private, 126th New York Infantry;* CWR:VOL1#4[7]125
BALL, WILLIAM H., *Colonel, 122nd Ohio Infantry;* B&G:JUN/95[8]600
BALLANTINE, WILLIAM D., *Captain, 2nd Florida Infantry;* ACW:SEP/93[8]429, GETTY:12[111]250
BALLARD, J.N., *Private, Mosby's Ranger;* CWTI:SEP/90[34]17
BALLING, OLE PETER HANSEN; *Painting:* <u>*Grant with his Generals:*</u> CWTI:FEB/90[20]14
BALLOONS:
ARTICLES: "BALLOONS: AMERICA'S FIRST AIR FORCE," AHI:JUN/84[24]239, "THE CONFEDERATE BALLOON CORPS," B&G:AUG/91[20]459, "FOCUS: CIVIL WAR PHOTOGRAPHY," AHI:JAN/80[29]198,
ADDITIONAL LISTINGS: AHI:JAN/80[29]198, AHI:JUN/84[24]239, B&G:AUG/91[20]459, B&G:OCT/91[6]465, B&G:DEC/91[6]468
BALLOU, SULLIVAN, *Major, USA;* ACW:JAN/91[6]281
BALTHIS, WILLIAM L., *Captain, Staunton Artillery;* CWM:JAN/92[68]407
BALTIMORE RIOTS:
ARTICLES: "FIRST BLOOD IN BALTIMORE," ACW:NOV/95[30]555, "SHADOWS OF CIVIL WAR BALTIMORE," CWTI:OCT/95[24]46
ADDITIONAL LISTING: ACW:NOV/95[30]555
BANCROFT, SAMUEL, *Lt., 38th USCT;* CWM:AUG/94[30]527
BANE, JAMES, *Private, Georgia and Mississippi Regiment;* CWR:VOL1#4[42]126
BANES, CHARLES H., *Captain, USA;* B&G:JUN/95[8]600, GETTY:7[97]193
BANGOR LIGHT INFANTRY; CWR:VOL4#1[78]
BANKER, NATHANIEL B., *General, USA;* CWTI:MAY/93[35]32

BANKHEAD, HENRY C., *Colonel, USA;* AHI:DEC/67[58]114, GETTY:10[7]221
BANKS, JOHN, MRS.; AHI:DEC/73[10]152
BANKS, NATHANIEL P. *General, USA:*
ARTICLES: "CHASING BANKS OUT OF LOUISIANA: PARSON'S TEXAS CAVALRY IN THE RED RIVER CAMPAIGN,"CWR:VOL2#3[212]14, "POUNDING PORT HUDSON," ACW:JAN/94[30]450, "RED RIVER BLUES," CWM:APR/95[39]576, "STONEWALL IN THE VALLEY," ACW:JAN/93[35]396, "PORT HUDSON," MH:AUG/94[82]179, "THE UNION NAVAL EXPEDITION ON THE RED RIVER MARCH 12-MAY 22, 1864," CWR:VOL4#2[26]166
GENERAL LISTINGS: *Cedar Mountain,* CWTI:NOV/93[55]35, *general history,* AHI:MAY/71[3]133A, *Grierson's Raid,* B&G:JUN/93[12]524, *in book review,* ACW:MAY/93[54], CWM:JAN/91[47], CWM:OCT/94[8], CWNEWS:APR/90[4], CWNEWS:MAY/90[4], CWNEWS:MAY/92[4], CWNEWS:JAN/95[25], CWR:VOL2#4[346], *John C. Fremont,* AHI:MAY/70[4]126, *Manassas, Second,* AHI:DEC/66[30]105, B&G:AUG/92[11]493, CWTI:MAR/91[12]19, *Port Hudson,* ACW:MAY/93[12]412, CWM:JAN/92[44]406, CWTI:FEB/90[38]14, *Red River Campaign,* ACW:SEP/92[16]376, ACW:MAR/93[68]409, ACW:MAR/94[27]459, ACW:MAR/95[34]516, ACW:SEP/95[8]542, CWR:VOL4#2[1]165, CWR:VOL4#2[68]167, CWR:VOL4#2[118]16, CWTI:FEB/90[46]14, CWTI:JAN/93[49]30, MH:DEC/95[58]188, *Shenandoah Valley Campaign, 1862, ...* ACW:JAN/92[8]338, ACW:JUL/94[10]475, ACW:MAY/95[10]523, CWTI:JUN/95[18]44, *Thomas J. Jackson,* B&G:JUN/92[8]487, *Winchester,* GETTY:6[69]176
PHOTOS: ACW:MAR/92[40]353, ACW:JUL/92[46]371, ACW:JAN/94[30]450, CWM:APR/95[39]576, CWR:VOL4#2[26]166, CWTI:MAR/94[29]371
ADDITIONAL LISTINGS, ACW: ACW:JUL/91[18]312, ACW:JUL/91[35]314, ACW:SEP/91[16]320, ACW:MAR/92[40]353, ACW:JAN/92[8]338, ACW:JAN/92[10]339, ACW:JUL/92[46]371, ACW:SEP/92[16]376, ACW:JAN/93[35]396, ACW:MAR/93[68]409, ACW:MAY/93[12]412, ACW:MAY/93[54], ACW:JAN/94[30]450, ACW:MAR/94[27]459, ACW:JUL/94[10]475, ACW:NOV/94[50]498, ACW:MAR/95[34]516, ACW:MAY/95[10]523, ACW:JUL/95[26]535, ACW:SEP/95[8]542, ACW:NOV/95[30]555
ADDITIONAL LISTINGS, AHI: AHI:DEC/66[30]105, AHI:MAY/70[4]126, AHI:MAY/71[3]133A, AHI:OCT/88[38]275
ADDITIONAL LISTINGS, B&G: B&G:JUN/92[8]487, B&G:AUG/92[11]493, B&G:JUN/93[12]524, B&G:DEC/94[34]587, B&G:OCT/95[32]613
ADDITIONAL LISTINGS, CWM: CWM:JAN/91[47], CWM:JAN/92[44]406, CWM:MAY/92[8]418, CWM:JUL/92[18]429, CWM:OCT/94[8], CWM:APR/95[39]576, CWM:OCT/95[47]620, CWM:OCT/95[63]623
ADDITIONAL LISTINGS, CWNEWS: CWNEWS:APR/90[4], CWNEWS:MAY/90[4], CWNEWS:MAY/92[4], CWNEWS:JAN/95[25]
ADDITIONAL LISTINGS, CWR: CWR:VOL1#2[78], CWR:VOL1#4[7]125, CWR:VOL2#1[19]131, CWR:VOL2#3[212]14, CWR:VOL2#4[346], CWR:VOL3#1[1]149, CWR:VOL3#1[31]150, CWR:VOL3#3[33]158, CWR:VOL4#2[1]165, CWR:VOL4#2[26]166,

CWR:VOL4#2[68]167, CWR:VOL4#2[104]168,
CWR:VOL4#2[118]169

ADDITIONAL LISTINGS, CWTI: CWTI:FEB/90[38]145,
CWTI:FEB/90[46]146, CWTI:DEC/90[29]182,
CWTI:MAR/91[12]198, CWTI:MAR/91[28]200,
CWTI:MAY/92[32]264, CWTI:MAY/92[48]267,
CWTI:JAN/93[49]303, CWTI:NOV/93[55]350,
CWTI:MAR/94[29]371, CWTI:JUN/95[18]444,
CWTI:DEC/95[67]481

ADDITIONAL LISTINGS, GETTY: GETTY:6[69]176

ADDITIONAL LISTINGS, MH: MH:FEB/91[8]151, MH:APR/94[54]176,
MH:AUG/94[82]179, MH:DEC/95[58]188

BANNAN, BENJAMIN; CWM:MAR/91[56]341
BANNING, HENRY B., *Colonel, USA;* CWR:VOL1#4[7]125
BANNING, PHINEAS, *civilian;* CWTI:SEP/91[18]227,
CWTI:FEB/92[8]245
BANNON, BENJAMIN; CWM:MAR/91[56]341
BANNON, JOHN B., *Chaplain, 1st Missouri Brigade:*
BOOK REVIEWS: *THE CONFEDERACY'S FIGHTING CHAPLAIN:*
*FATHER JOHN B. BANNON * THE FOURTH CAREER OF*
JOHN B. BANNON : ST LOUIS PASTOR, SOUTHERN
CHAPLAIN, CONFEDERATE AGENT, IRISH ORATOR
ADDITIONAL LISTINGS: B&G:AUG/93[24], CWM:OCT/95[10],
CWR:VOL4#1[78], CWR:VOL4#2[136], CWNEWS:JUN/93[5],
CWNEWS:DEC/95[29]
BAPTIST GAP, TENNESSEE, ENGAGEMENT AT;
CWM:SEP/92[8]437
BARBEE, GEORGE, *Sgt., 44th NC Inf.;* CWTI:AUG/90[26]166
BARBER, C.F., *Pvt.,112th Illinois Inf.;* B&G:AUG/93[18]530
BARBER, CHARLES, *Private, 104th New York Infantry;*
BOOK REVIEW: *THE CIVIL WAR LETTERS OF CHARLES*
BARBER, PRIVATE, 104TH NEW YORK VOLUNTEER
INFANTRY
ADDITIONAL LISTING: CWNEWS:NOV/92[4]
BARBER, CHARLES, *Sergeant, 88th Pennsylvania Infantry;*
GETTY:10[7]221
BARBER, FLAVEL C., *Major, 3rd Tennessee Infantry:*
BOOK REVIEW: *HOLDING THE LINE: THE HISTORY OF THE*
THIRD TENNESSEE INFANTRY
ADDITIONAL LISTINGS: CWM:APR/95[8], CWM:AUG/95[45]
BARBER, FREDERICK M., *Private, 7th Wisconsin Infantry,*
GETTY:11[57]233
BARBER, LORENZO, *Chaplain, 2nd USSS;*
CWTI:APR/90[48]154, CWTI:JUL/93[42]329
BARBOUR, ALFRED M., *civilian;* CWTI:APR/89[38]11
BARBOUR, EDWIN, *Lieutenant, CSA;* B&G:APR/91[8]445
BARBOUR, FRED, *Private, 7th Wisconsin Infantry;*
GETTY:9[33]211
BARBOUR, JAMES and JOHN, *civilian;* B&G:APR/91[8]445
BARBOUR, W.M., *Colonel, 37th North Carolina Infantry;*
B&G:FEB/95[8]590A
BARCLAY, ALEXANDER T., *Private, 4th Virginia Infantry:*
BOOK REVIEWS: *TED BARCLAY, LIBERTY HALL VOLUNTEERS:*
LETTERS FROM THE STONEWALL BRIGADE (1861-1864)
ADDITIONAL LISTINGS: CWM:MAY/93[51], CWNEWS:AUG/93[5]
BARCUS, JAMES H., *civilian;* B&G:OCT/94[11]580
BARD, JOHN P., *Captain, 13th Pennsylvania Reserves;*
CWR:VOL1#3[28]120
BARHYDT, GEORGE W., *Private, 7th Wisconsin Infantry;*
GETTY:9[33]211, GETTY:11[57]233
BARKER, AUGUST, *Capt., 5th NY Cav.;* CWTI:DEC/91[22]23
BARKER, CHARLES J., *Private, 18th Louisiana Infantry;*
CWR:VOL4#2[1]165

BARKER, H.L., *Lt., Kansas Militia;* ACW:NOV/94[42]497
BARKER, THOMAS E., *Captain, 12th New Hampshire*
Infantry; ACW:SEP/93[62]436, ACW:SEP/95[74]550
BARKER, WILLIAM C., *Private, 1st Rhode Island Artillery;*
GETTY:12[61]245
BARKSDALE, ANTHONY S., *Private, CSA;*
CWM:MAY/92[34]422
BARKSDALE, WILLIAM E., *General, CSA:*
GENERAL LISTINGS: *buried at,* B&G:AUG/95[8]604, *Crampton's*
Gap, ACW:JAN/94[39]451, *Fredericksburg,*
CWR:VOL4#4[28]178, *Gettysburg,* GETTY:5[35]159,
GETTY:5[47]160, GETTY:5[79]161, GETTY:5[103]163,
GETTY:5[107]164, GETTY:7[51]190, GETTY:7[77]191,
GETTY:7[124]196, GETTY:8[53]203, GETTY:8[95]205,
GETTY:9[41]212, GETTY:9[98]217, GETTY:10[53]225,
GETTY:10[112]228, GETTY:10[120]229, GETTY:11[91]236,
GETTY:12[1]240, GETTY:12[7]241, *Harpers Ferry,*
GETTY:7[51]190, MH:AUG/95[30]185, *Savage's Station,*
CWM:JUN/95[65]595
ADDITIONAL LISTINGS: ACW:SEP/92[30]378, ACW:MAY/93[8]411,
ACW:JAN/94[62], ACW:MAR/94[50]462, ACW:SEP/94[38]487,
B&G:FEB/94[8]550, CWR:VOL1#4[7]125,
CWR:VOL1#4[74]128, CWR:VOL3#1[78]152,
CWR:VOL3#2[1]153, CWR:VOL4#4[i]175,
CWR:VOL4#4[101]181, CWTI:SEPT/89[46]132,
CWTI:SEP/90[26]174, CWTI:DEC/94[32]410, GETTY:13[1]252
BARLETT, ASA, *Captain, 12th New Hampshire Infantry;*
ACW:SEP/93[62]436
BARLOW, FRANCIS C., *General, USA:*
ARTICLE: "FOR TWO FORMER CIVIL WAR FOES, THE NEWS
OF THEIR DEATHS WAS—LIKE MARK
TWAIN'S—GREATLY EXAGGERATED,"
ACW:MAY/93[14]413, "THE GORDON-BARLOW STORY,
WITH SEQUEL," GETTY:8[5]198
GENERAL LISTINGS: *Gettysburg,* GETTY:4[33]146,
GETTY:4[113]153, GETTY:9[17]210, GETTY:11[71]234,
GETTY:12[30]243, *in book review,* CWNEWS:MAY/93[4],
CWR:VOL2#2[169], CWR:VOL4#1[78], *in order of battle,*
B&G:APR/94[10]558, B&G:APR/95[8]595, *Overland*
Campaign, B&G:APR/94[10]558, *Wilderness,*
B&G:APR/95[8]595, *photos,* ACW:MAY/93[14]413,
AHI:MAY/71[3]133A, B&G:APR/94[10]558,
CWTI:SEP/93[43]338, GETTY:8[5]198
ADDITIONAL LISTINGS: ACW:JAN/93[43]397, ACW:MAY/93[14]413,
ACW:MAY/93[31]415, ACW:MAY/95[30]525,
B&G:APR/94[59]565, B&G:FEB/95[8]590C,
CWNEWS:JUL/91[4], CWR:VOL1#3[52]122,
CWR:VOL2#4[269]14, CWR:VOL3#1[65]151,
CWR:VOL3#4[1]161, CWTI:SEP/93[43]338, GETTY:8[5]198
BARLOW-GORDON INCIDENT:
ARTICLE: "THE GORDON-BARLOW STORY, WITH SEQUEL,"
GETTY:8[5]198
ADDITIONAL LISTING: GETTY:4[113]153
BARNARD, GEORGE N.:
BOOK REVIEW: *GEORGE N. BARNARD: PHOTOGRAPHER OF*
SHERMAN'S CAMPAIGNS
ADDITIONAL LISTINGS: B&G:APR/91[28], CWNEWS:MAY/92[4],
CWTI:MAY/91[34]209, CWTI:SEP/91[8]224
BARNARD, JOHN G., *General, USA;* CWM:JUN/95[29]583,
CWTI:OCT/95[32]468
BARNES, ALMONT, *Capt., 1st NY Arty;* GETTY:11[91]236
BARNES, DIXON, *Colonel, 12th South Carolina Infantry;*
B&G:AUG/92[11]493

BARNES, FRANCIS E., *Lt., 56th VA Inf.;* GETTY:12[111]250
BARNES, HENRY, *Pvt., 150th NY Inf.;* GETTY:12[42]244
BARNES, J.T., *Private, 5th Alabama Infantry;* GETTY:6[13]170
BARNES, JAMES, *General, USA;* GENERAL LISTINGS: *Gettysburg,*
 GETTY:4[113]153, GETTY:5[35]159, GETTY:5[47]160,
 GETTY:6[59]174, GETTY:7[29]188, GETTY:7[41]189,
 GETTY:8[31]201, GETTY:8[53]203, GETTY:9[41]212,
 GETTY:9[53]214, GETTY:10[112]228, GETTY:10[120]229,
 GETTY:11[80]235, GETTY:11[91]236, *Second Manassas,*
 AHI:DEC/66[30]105
BARNES, JARED P.; ACW:NOV/94[42]497
BARNES, JOHN C., *Private, 5th South Carolina Cavalry;*
 ACW:MAR/95[50]518
BARNES, JOHN S., *Commander, USN;* CWTI:FEB/91[28]192,
 CWTI:DEC/95[76]482
BARNES, JOHN T.M., *Captain, CSA;* CWR:VOL4#2[118]16
BARNES, JOSEPH K., *Surgeon General, USA;*
 AHI:DEC/66[30]105, AHI:FEB/86[12]257,
 CWM:MAY/91[18]348, CWTI:JUL/92[50]275,
 CWTI:JUN/95[26]445, GETTY:8[121]207, GETTY:10[120]229
BARNES, MYRON S., *Lt. Col., USA;* CWR:VOL1#1[42]105
BARNES, RICHARD, *Private, 12th New Jersey Infantry;*
 GETTY:5[89]162
BARNES, WILLIAM H., *Private, 150th New York Infantry;*
 GETTY:7[119]195, GETTY:12[42]244
BARNETT, JOSEPH W., *Lieutenant, Sumter Artillery;*
 CWR:VOL3#2[1]153, CWR:VOL3#2[61]154
BARNETT, WILLIAM H., *Private, 11th Virginia Infantry;*
 B&G:APR/93[40]522, B&G:AUG/93[36]533
BARNEY, ANDREW, *Major, 24th New York Infantry;*
 ACW:JUL/91[18]312, B&G:AUG/92[11]493
BARNEY, HIRAM; CWTI:FEB/92[21]24
BARNEY, JAMES L., *Pvt., 6th Wisconsin Inf.;* GETTY:11[57]233
BARNEY, WILLIAM; ACW:JUL/94[42]479
BARNUM, HENRY A., *General, USA;* B&G:FEB/91[8]439,
 B&G:DEC/95[9]615, CWTI:SEPT/89[30]129 GETTY:7[83]192,
 GETTY:11[71]234, GETTY:10[36]223
BARNWELL, ROBERT, *Captain, CSA;* ACW:SEP/91[30]322,
 CWTI:MAR/93[24]309
BAROUR, ALFRED, *Quartermaster, CSA;* B&G:APR/91[8]445
BARR, JOHN M., *Pvt., 111th Penna. Inf.;* CWR:VOL3#2[70]155
BARR, JOHN W., *Captain, CSA;* B&G:AUG/91[11]458
BARRAS, SAMUEL A., *Adjutant, 39th New York Infantry;*
 CWR:VOL1#4[7]125, GETTY:7[51]190
BARRETT, EDWIN, *civilian;* ACW:NOV/94[66]
BARRETT, GEORGE C., *Pvt., 4th U.S. Arty;* GETTY:9[33]211
BARRETT, JAMES, *Lieutenant, USA;* ACW:JUL/93[27]423,
 CWTI:SEP/91[18]227
BARRETT, SAMUEL E., *Captain, 1st Illinois Artillery;*
 CWR:VOL2#1[1]130
BARRETT, T.W., *Captain, CSA;* B&G:AUG/91[11]458
BARRETT, THEODORE H., *Colonel, 62nd USCT;*
 ACW:JUL/92[46]371, CWTI:AUG/90[58]169
BARRIER, WILLIAM, *Private, CSA;* GETTY:12[68]246
BARRINGER, RUFUS, *General, CSA:*
GENERAL LISTINGS: *Five Forks,* B&G:APR/92[8]481, *in order of*
 battle, B&G:APR/92[8]481, B&G:APR/94[10]558, *SIO,*
 B&G:AUG/92[40]495
ADDITIONAL LISTINGS: ACW:JUL/92[41]370, CWTI:FEB/91[45]194
BARRON, SAMUEL, *Commodore, CSN;* CWM:JUL/93[8]483
BARRY, ROBERT L., *Captain, Lookout Tennessee Artillery;*
 B&G:AUG/95[8]604

BARRY, WILLIAM A., *Surgeon, 75th Pennsylvania Infantry;*
 GETTY:10[53]225
BARRY, WILLIAM F., *General, USA;* ACW:NOV/94[50]498,
 AHI:JAN/67[4]106, B&G:FEB/91[8]339, CWNEWS:MAY/91[4],
 CWTI:APR/92[14]254, *photo,* AHI:JAN/67[4]106
BARSTOW, HIRAM E., *Captain, 10th Illinois Cavalry;*
 ACW:JUL/94[8]474
BARTEAU, CLARK R., *Colonel, 2nd Tennessee Cavalry;*
 ACW:MAY/92[47]363, ACW:JUL/94[8]474, AHI:APR/74[4]154,
 B&G:JUN/93[12]524, CWTI:NOV/93[65]35
BARTHOLOMEW, WILLIAM, *Private, 2nd Wisconsin Infantry;*
 GETTY:11[57]233
BARTLESS, WILLIAM C., *Colonel, 2nd North Carolina*
 Infantry (Union); B&G:APR/92[28]482
BARTLETT, ASA W., *Captain, 12th New Hampshire Infantry;*
BOOK REVIEW: *HISTORY OF THE TWELFTH REGIMENT, NEW*
 HAMPSHIRE VOLUNTEERS IN THE WAR OF THE
 REBELLION
ADDITIONAL LISTINGS: CWR:VOL4#3[1]170, GETTY:12[7]241
BARTLETT, CHARLES G., *Lieutenant Colonel, 150th New*
 York Infantry; CWR:VOL1#2[7]111, GETTY:12[42]244
BARTLETT, FRANK, *Colonel, 13th Louisiana Cavalry;*
 CWR:VOL3#3[33]158
BARTLETT, HAROLD J., *Private, 1st Michigan Artillery;* BOOK
 REVIEW: *TO THE SOUND OF MUSKETRY AND TAP OF THE*
 DRUM: A HISTORY OF MICHIGAN'S BATTERY D
 THROUGH THE LETTERS OF ARTIFICER HAROLD J.
 BARTLETT, 1861-1864
BARTLETT, JOHN R.; *civilian;* GETTY:12[97]249
BARTLETT, JOSEPH J., *General, USA:*
GENERAL LISTINGS: *Five Forks,* B&G:APR/92[8]481, *in order of*
 battle, B&G:APR/92[8]481, B&G:APR/94[10]558, *Wilderness,*
 B&G:APR/95[8]595
ADDITIONAL LISTINGS: ACW:MAR/92[30]352, ACW:JAN/94[39]451,
 ACW:NOV/94[50]498, B&G:FEB/92[22]476,
 CWR:VOL3#3[1]157, CWTI:MAY/89[36]118
BARTLETT, LEON C., *Lt, 4th Wisc. Inf.;* ACW:MAY/93[12]412
BARTLETT, NAPIER, *Private, CSA;* ACW:JUL/93[50]426
BARTLETT, O.F., *Surgeon, 6th Wisconsin Infantry;*
 GETTY:4[24]145
BARTLETT, WILLIAM F., *General, USA;* B&G:DEC/91[12]469,
 B&G:AUG/95[42]608, CWR:VOL2#2[118]13,
 CWR:VOL3#1[31]150, CWTI:APR/90[24]152,
 CWTI:DEC/94[32]410
BARTON, CLARA:
ARTICLES: "A WOMAN OF VALOR," CWTI:MAR/94[38]37,
 "CLARA BARTON: FOUNDER OF THE AMERICAN RED
 CROSS," AHI:NOV/89[50]288, "CLARA BARTON NATIONAL
 HISTORIC SITE," AHI:NOV/89[65]289
BOOK REVIEW: *A WOMAN OF VALOR: CLARA BARTON AND*
 THE CIVIL WAR
GENERAL LISTINGS: *in book review,* B&G:DEC/94[28],
 B&G:JUN/95[30], CWNEWS:AUG/94[33], *letters to the editor,*
 B&G:APR/95[5]594, CWTI:DEC/94[12]408, *list of monuments,*
 B&G:OCT/95[8]611A
ADDITIONAL LISTINGS: AHI:NOV/89[50]288, AHI:NOV/89[65]289,
 AHI:APR/95[26], B&G:APR/92[36]483, CWM:APR/95[8],
 CWTI:APR/92[23]255, CWTI:MAR/94[38]372,
 CWTI:JAN/95[34]427, *photo,* AHI:NOV/89[50]288
BARTON, FRANCIS S., *Col., 8th GA Inf.;* GETTY:12[111]250
BARTON, GEORGE, *Lieutenant, 57th Massachusetts Infantry;*
 CWR:VOL1#3[94], CWTI:APR/90[24]152, CWTI:JAN/95[34]427

BARTON, HUGH C., *Private, 2nd Kentucky Cavalry;*
CWM:MAR/93[16]466

BARTON, SETH M., *General, CSA;* ACW:NOV/91[22]331,
CWM:SEP/92[16]438, CWR:VOL2#1[36]132,
CWTI:APR/90[46]151, CWTI:MAY/91[24]208, *photos,*
CWTI:MAY/91[24]208, CWTI:JUL/94[10]389

BARTON, WILLIAM B., *Colonel, USA;* B&G:APR/94[10]558,
CWR:VOL3#1[65]151

BARTOW, FRANCIS S., *Colonel, CSA:*
ARTICLE: "THE CIVIL WAR'S FIRST MONUMENT: BARTOW'S
MARKER AT MANASSAS," B&G:APR/91[32]447
ADDITIONAL LISTINGS: ACW:NOV/94[18]495, B&G:FEB/91[8]339,
B&G:APR/91[32]447, CWM:JUN/94[50]518,
CWR:VOL2#4[269]14

BARUCH, SIMON; CWTI:MAY/92[38]26

BARZIZA, DECIMUS ET ULTIMUS, *Captain, 4th Texas
Infantry;* GETTY:7[13]186, GETTY:10[53]225

BASEBALL; ARTICLE: "AN ALL-AMERICAN SPORT IN AN
ALL-AMERICAN WAR," CWM:SEP/93[32]496

BASON, J.D., *Lieutenant, 13th North Carolina Infantry;*
GETTY:8[67]204

BASS, FREDERICK T., *Colonel, Texas Brigade;*
CWM:AUG/94[30]527, CWR:VOL2#3[256]

BASSETT, RICHARD A., *Lieutenant, 126th New York Infantry;*
GETTY:7[51]190, GETTY:8[95]205

BATCHELDER'S CREEK, NORTH CAROLINA,
ENGAGEMENT AT; CWM:SEP/92[16]438,
CWNEWS:JAN/94[5]

BATCHELDER, ALBERT A., *Private, 6th New Hampshire
Infantry;* CWM:MAY/92[44]423

BATCHELLER, O.A., *Ensign, USN;* ACW:MAR/92[40]353

BATE, WILLIAM B., *General, CSA:*
GENERAL LISTINGS: *black soldiers,* ACW:NOV/93[6]437, *Carolina
Campaign,* B&G:DEC/95[9]615, *order of battle,*
B&G:DEC/93[12]545, B&G:DEC/95[9]615, *Tullahoma
Campaign,* B&G:OCT/92[10]496
ADDITIONAL LISTINGS: ACW:JUL/92[12]367, ACW:NOV/95[74]560,
B&G:OCT/92[32]499, B&G:DEC/93[49]547,
B&G:DEC/93[52]548, B&G:DEC/93[12]545,
CWM:OCT/94[48]542, CWM:AUG/95[36]608,
CWR:VOL4#3[65]172, CWTI:SUMMER/89[20]121,
CWTI:SUMMER/89[32]122, CWTI:SUMMER/89[50]124,
CWTI:NOV/92[41]291, CWTI:JAN/95[27]425,
MH:FEB/91[8]151, *photo,* B&G:OCT/92[10]496

BATEMAN, CHARLES, *Private, 70th Ohio Infantry;*
CWTI:DEC/94[62]41

BATES, DAVID H., *civilian;* AHI:NOV/70[22]130,
CWM:NOV/91[58]394, CWTI:AUG/95[46]459,
CWTI:DEC/95[8]474

BATES, EDWARD; ACW:MAR/95[8]512, AHI:NOV/72[10]141,
AHI:JUN/74[12]155, CWM:JAN/91[12]326,
CWM:MAY/93[8]474, CWM:AUG/95[58]611, CWM:DEC/95[10]

BATES, GILBERT, *Sergeant, USA;* ARTICLE: "THAT'S OUR
FLAG, TOO!" AHI:JUL/76[19]170

BATES, JAMES L., *Colonel, USA;* B&G:APR/94[10]558

BATES, WILLIAM S., *Private, CSA;* B&G:JUN/93[12]524

BATES, WILLIAM W., *Lieutenant Colonel, 8th New York Heavy
Artillery;* B&G:APR/94[55]564

BATH, HENRY, *Sgt., 45th New York Inf.;* B&G:OCT/95[5]610

BATH, THEODORE, *Private, 45th New York Infantry;*
B&G:OCT/95[5]610

BATH, WILLIAM L., *Lieutenant, 45th New York Infantry;*
B&G:APR/95[24]596, B&G:OCT/95[5]610

BATMAN, PETER, *Private, 24th Michigan Infantry;*
GETTY:9[33]211, GETTY:11[57]233

BATON ROUGE, LOUISIANA, BATTLE OF;
ACW:SEP/95[48]547, CWM:AUG/94[52]530

BATTERSBY, JAYNES C., *Colonel, 1st New York Cavalry;*
CWR:VOL1#1[35]104

BATTERY GREGG, CHARLESTON, SOUTH CAROLINA;
CWR:VOL2#3[194]14

BATTERY JONES, SAVANNAH, GEORGIA;
B&G:FEB/91[8]439

BATTERY MCBETH, SAVANNAH, GEORGIA;
B&G:FEB/91[8]439

BATTERY WAGNER, CHARLESTON, SOUTH CAROLINA:
ARTICLE: "CARNIVAL OF DEATH," ACW:SEP/91[30]322
BOOK REVIEWS: *A BRAVE BLACK REGIMENT: HISTORY OF
THE 54TH REGIMENT OF MASSACHUSETTS
VOLUNTEER INFANTRY, 1863-1865 * GATE OF HELL,
CAMPAIGN FOR CHARLESTON HARBOR, 1863*
GENERAL LISTINGS: *general history,* AHI:MAY/71[3]133A, *in book
review,* ACW:MAR/93[58], B&G:OCT/93[24], B&G:JUN/95[30],
CWM:APR/95[8], CWM:AUG/95[45], CWNEWS:JUN/92[4],
CWNEWS:MAY/93[4], CWNEWS:APR/95[33],
CWR:VOL3#1[80], CWR:VOL4#3[1], CWR:VOL4#3[37], *letters
to the editor,* CWM:JAN/92[6]398
ADDITIONAL LISTINGS: ACW:MAR/91[8]291, ACW:MAR/91[30]295,
ACW:SEP/91[6]317, ACW:SEP/91[30]322,
ACW:MAY/93[14]413, ACW:SEP/95[38]546,
AHI:MAY/71[3]133A, B&G:AUG/91[32]461,
B&G:OCT/91[11]466, B&G:FEB/94[38]553,
CWM:MAR/92[4]408, CWM:MAR/92[16]411,
CWM:AUG/94[30]527, CWR:VOL1#1[76]109,
CWR:VOL2#3[194]141, CWTI:DEC/89[42]137,
CWTI:DEC/89[53]138, CWTI:DEC/89[62]139,
CWTI:JAN/93[49]303, CWTI:JAN/94[46]364,
CWTI:MAR/94[38]372, CWTI:SEP/94[18], GETTY:12[111]250,
MH:AUG/94[82]179

"BATTLE ABOVE THE CLOUDS"; see listings under
"LOOKOUT MOUNTAIN, BATTLE OF"

BATTLE OF ATHENS STATE HISTORIC SITE;
MH:APR/95[74]184

BATTLE, CULLEN A., *General, CSA;* ACW:MAY/91[38]305,
ACW:SEP/93[31]433, B&G:APR/94[10]558,
B&G:APR/95[8]595, GETTY:4[33]146

BATTLE, JESSE S., *Private, Sumter Artillery;*
CWR:VOL3#2[1]153, CWR:VOL3#2[61]154

BATTLE, JOEL A., *Col., 20th Tenn. Inf.;* B&G:FEB/93[12]511

BATTLE, WESLEY L, *Lieutenant, 37th North Carolina
Infantry;* GETTY:8[67]204

BATTLEFIELD PRESERVATION; see listings under
"PRESERVATION"

BAUGH, JOHN A., *Pvt., 22nd VA Inf.;* CWR:VOL1#3[52]122

BAUSELL, JAMES W., *Captain, CSA;* B&G:OCT/94[6]579

BAUTERIVE, BERNARD D., *Captain, 10th Louisiana
Infantry;* CWR:VOL3#1[1]149

BAXLEY, JOHN W., *Private, 31st North Carolina Infantry;*
B&G:APR/93[24]520

BAXTER SPRINGS, KANSAS, BATTLE OF;
ACW:JAN/93[26]395, B&G:JUN/91[10]452,
CWM:JAN/92[8]399, CWM:SEP/92[38]443

BAXTER, DEWITT C., *Colonel, 72nd Pennsylvania Infantry;*
ACW:MAY/92[8]357, ACW:SEP/94[38]487, GETTY:7[97]193

BAXTER, HENRY, *General, USA:*
ARTICLE: "BRIG. GEN. HENRY BAXTER'S BRIGADE AT
GETTYSBURG, JULY 1," GETTY:10[7]221
GENERAL LISTINGS: *Gettysburg,* GETTY:4[33]146,
GETTY:5[13]157, GETTY:5[117]165, GETTY:5[128]167,
GETTY:6[7]169, GETTY:9[17]210, GETTY:10[7]221,
GETTY:11[19]232, GETTY:11[126]239, GETTY:12[1]240, *in
order of battle,* B&G:APR/92[8]481, *letters to the editor,*
B&G:AUG/95[36]607, *order of battle,* B&G:APR/95[8]595
ADDITIONAL LISTINGS: B&G:FEB/95[8]590B, CWM:MAY/92[15]419,
CWR:VOL4#4[101]18, GETTY:13[1]252, GETTY:13[33]255
BAYARD, GEORGE D., *General, USA;* ACW:JAN/92[8]338,
ACW:MAR/95[42]517, CWM:FEB/95[7], CWR:VOL1#3[28]120,
CWTI:APR/92[35]257, CWTI:JUN/95[38]447,
CWTI:AUG/95[54]460
BAYLOR, GEORGE W., *Colonel, CSA;* CWR:VOL2#3[212]142
BAYLOR, JOHN R., *Colonel, 2nd Texas Mounted Rifles:*
ARTICLE: "COLONEL JOHN R. BAYLOR," ACW:JAN/91[10]283
GENERAL LISTINGS: *editorial,* ACW:JAN/91[6]281, *in book review,*
ACW:NOV/95[62], B&G:OCT/92[30], CWNEWS:APR/92[4],
CWR:VOL4#4[129]
ADDITIONAL LISTINGS: ACW:JAN/91[10]283, ACW:JUL/93[27]423,
B&G:JUN/94[8]568, CWM:MAY/93[16]475,
CWTI:OCT/95[56]471, *photos,* ACW:JAN/91[10]283,
CWM:MAY/93[16]475
BAYLOR, THOMAS G., *Captain, USA;* AHI:JAN/67[4]106
BAYLOR, WILLIAM S., *Colonel, 33rd Virginia Infantry;*
B&G:AUG/92[11]493
BAYNE, GRIFF, *Captain, 12th Arkansas Sharpshooter
Battalion;* B&G:FEB/94[8]550
BAYNES, JOHN T., *Private, 5th Pennsylvania Reserves;*
CWNEWS:JAN/90[4]
BAYOU FORDOCHE, LOUISIANA, ENGAGEMENT AT;
ARTICLE: "BRILLIANT RAID BY GENERAL GREEN,"
CWM:OCT/94[33]537
BAYOU TECHE, LOUISIANA; ACW:SEP/92[16]376
BEACH, AUGUSTUS, *Lieutenant, Ohio Light Artillery;*
B&G:FEB/94[8]550, B&G:AUG/95[8]604
BEADLE'S DIME NOVELS; ARTICLE: "WARTIME READING
RAGE," ACW:SEP/93[46]435
BEADLE, MARCUS, *Lt., 123rd New York Inf.;* GETTY:7[83]192
BEAL, GEORGE L., *Colonel, 10th Maine Infantry;*
ACW:JUL/92[30]369, B&G:OCT/95[32]613
BEALE, GEORGE W., *Lieutenant, 9th Virginia Cavalry:*
BOOK REVIEW: *A LIEUTENANT OF CAVALRY IN LEE'S ARMY*
ADDITIONAL LISTING: GETTY:4[65]148
BEALE, RICHARD L.T., *General, CSA;* B&G:APR/92[8]481,
B&G:OCT/93[12]537, GETTY:13[89]260
BEALL, JOHN A., *Lt., 94th Ohio Infantry;* B&G:APR/94[34]561
BEALL, JOHN YATES; ACW:MAY/92[14]358,
ACW:JUL/95[44]537, B&G:APR/94[34]561,
CWTI:NOV/92[54]293, *photo,* ACW:JUL/95[44]537
BEALL, LLOYD J., *Colonel, CSMC;* ACW:MAR/91[14]293
BEALL, WILLIAM N.R., *General, CSA;* ACW:JUL/95[44]537,
B&G:DEC/93[52]548, CWM:FEB/95[7], GETTY:13[108]261
BEAN, SIDNEY A., *Col., 4th Wisc. Inf.;* ACW:MAY/93[12]412
BEARD, EDWARD, *Private, Consolidated Crescent Regiment;*
CWR:VOL4#2[68]167
BEARD, JAMES H., *Colonel, Consolidated Crescent Regiment:*
ARTICLE: "A DEATH AT MANSFIELD: COL. JAMES HAMILTON
BEARD AND THE CONSOLIDATED CRESCENT
REGIMENT," CWR:VOL4#2[68]167

ADDITIONAL LISTINGS: CWR:VOL4#2[1]165, CWR:VOL4#2[68]167,
CWR:VOL4#2[118]169
BEARD, RICHARD, *Captain, CSA;* CWM:AUG/94[27]526
BEARDSLEE TELEGRAPH; ACW:JAN/95[20]504
BEARID, GEORGE, *Captain, 16th Michigan Infantry;*
CWM:SEP/93[18]494
BEARY, JOHN H., *Private, 5th U.S. Artillery:*
ARTICLE: "A SURGEON'S HANDIWORK," GETTY:12[83]247
ADDITIONAL LISTINGS: GETTY:12[1]240, GETTY:12[83]247
BEATH, R.B., *Lt., 88th Pennsylvania Infantry;* GETTY:10[7]221
BEATTY, ADAM, *Lieutenant, CSA;* CWR:VOL4#2[1]165,
CWR:VOL4#2[118]16
BEATTY, JOHN, *General, USA:*
BOOK REVIEW: *THE CITIZEN SOLDIER; OR MEMOIRS OF A
VOLUNTEER*
ADDITIONAL LISTINGS: ACW:JUL/91[35]314, ACW:NOV/95[66]559,
B&G:AUG/93[10]529, MH:DEC/93[12]174
BEATTY, SAMUEL, *General, USA;* B&G:DEC/93[12]545
BEAUDRY, AMABLE, *Sergeant, 15th Massachusetts Infantry;*
CWM:APR/95[42]577
BEAUFORT, SOUTH CAROLINA; ARTICLE: "FOCUS: CIVIL
WAR PHOTOGRAPHY," AHI:MAY/80[29]202
BEAUREGARD, PIERRE G.T., *General, CSA:*
ARTICLES: "CAPITAL FOLLY," ACW:MAY/93[38]416,
"GUSTAVE," CWTI:JUL/92[29]27
BOOK REVIEWS: *BEAUREGARD * THE BERMUDA HUNDRED
CAMPAIGN * THE MILITARY OPERATIONS OF GENERAL
BEAUREGARD IN THE WAR BETWEEN THE STATES
1861-1865*
GENERAL LISTINGS: *Alexander Stephens,* CWTI:FEB/91[36]193,
balloons, AHI:JUN/84[24]239, *Bermuda Hundred,*
CWTI:MAY/93[29]319, *The "Blackberry" Raid,*
GETTY:11[6]231, *Carolina Campaign,* ACW:MAR/94[42]461,
B&G:DEC/95[9]615, *Corinth,* CWTI:FEB/90[38]14, *Fort
Sumter,* CWTI:MAY/92[45]266, *general history,*
AHI:MAY/71[3]133A, *in book review,* ACW:JAN/91[54],
ACW:MAR/93[58], B&G:OCT/93[24], CWM:AUG/94[9],
CWNEWS:SEP/90[4], CWNEWS:MAY/92[4],
CWNEWS:JUN/92[4], CWR:VOL2#1[78], CWR:VOL4#1[78],
CWTI:SEP/90[12], CWTI:FEB/92[18], CWTI:APR/92[30],
MH:DEC/92[74]
GENERAL LISTINGS, continued: *Jake Thompson,*
CWTI:NOV/92[54]293, *Jefferson Davis,* CWTI:AUG/91[29]216,
Johnston's surrender,
CWTI:AUG/90[26]166, *Manassas,* ACW:JAN/95[20]504,
ACW:JAN/95[46]507, ACW:JUL/92[12]367,
ACW:NOV/94[18]495, CWTI:SEPT/89[24]128,
CWTI:MAR/91[12]198, CWTI:AUG/91[46]218,
CWTI:APR/92[35]257, CWTI:MAR/94[48]374, *Mexican War,*
AHI:MAY/88[38]270, MH:APR/93[34]165, MH:APR/93[39]166,
MH:AUG/91[45]153, *Monuments,* B&G:APR/91[32]447,
Overland Campaign, B&G:APR/94[10]558, *Petersburg,*
MH:APR/95[46]183, *post-war,* ACW:JUL/95[26]535, *relics,*
B&G:JUN/91[38]455, *Rose Greenhow,* AHI:DEC/73[10]152,
Savannah, ACW:SEP/92[47]380, B&G:FEB/91[8]439, *Shiloh,*
ACW:JAN/91[22]285, CWTI:JUL/92[29]272,
CWTI:SEP/93[59]341, *West Point,* B&G:DEC/91[12]469,
Winfield Scott, AHI:FEB/76[14]165, AHI:JUL/81[20]221
PHOTOS: ACW:MAY/92[14]358, ACW:MAY/93[38]416,
AHI:MAY/71[3]133A, B&G:FEB/91[8]439, B&G:DEC/95[9]615,
CWM:JUL/91[48]374, CWM:MAR/92[16]411,
CWTI:JUL/92[29]272

ADDITIONAL LISTINGS, ACW: ACW:SEP/91[30]322,
ACW:NOV/91[41]334, ACW:MAR/92[10]349,
ACW:MAY/92[14]358, ACW:JUL/93[42]425,
ACW:JUL/93[66]427, ACW:SEP/93[10]430,
ACW:MAY/94[35]469, ACW:JUL/94[35]478,
ACW:JUL/95[44]537
ADDITIONAL LISTINGS, AHI: AHI:NOV/73[18]151,
AHI:JAN/85[20]245, AHI:OCT/95[16]325, AHI:OCT/95[24]326,
ADDITIONAL LISTINGS, B&G: B&G:FEB/92[10]474,
B&G:APR/93[12]518, B&G:JUN/93[32]525,
B&G:JUN/94[22]569, B&G:DEC/94[10]585,
B&G:FEB/95[35]592,
ADDITIONAL LISTINGS, CWM: CWM:MAR/91[28]336,
CWM:MAR/91[56]341, CWM:JAN/92[27]403,
CWM:MAR/92[16]411, CWM:JUL/92[16]428,
CWM:JUL/92[40]432, CWM:MAR/93[32]468,
CWM:SEP/93[8]493, CWM:AUG/94[48]529,
CWM:APR/95[16]571, CWM:JUN/95[17]581,
CWM:AUG/95[30]606, CWM:OCT/95[22]614
ADDITIONAL LISTINGS, CWR: CWR:VOL1#2[44]114,
CWR:VOL1#3[7]118, CWR:VOL1#4[42]126,
CWR:VOL2#1[36]132, CWR:VOL2#4[269]14,
CWR:VOL3#1[65]151, CWR:VOL4#1[44]164,
CWR:VOL4#2[68]167, CWR:VOL4#3[77]174,
ADDITIONAL LISTINGS, CWTI: CWTI:APR/89[14]107,
CWTI:APR/89[22]108, CWTI:SEP/90[28]175,
CWTI:AUG/91[36]217, CWTI:AUG/91[46]218,
CWTI:AUG/91[52]219, CWTI:AUG/91[62]221,
CWTI:AUG/91[68]222, CWTI:DEC/91[44]241,
CWTI:FEB/92[42]250, CWTI:MAY/92[38]265,
CWTI:MAR/93[24]309, CWTI:MAR/93[40]312,
CWTI:MAR/93[50]313, CWTI:JUL/93[29]326,
CWTI:JUL/94[44]394, CWTI:DEC/94[73]416,
CWTI:JAN/95[27]425, CWTI:AUG/95[28]456,
CWTI:AUG/95[46]459, CWTI:AUG/95[54]460,
CWTI:DEC/95[67]481
ADDITIONAL LISTINGS, MI: MH:JUN/91[20]152, MH:FEB/94[8]175,
MH:JUN/94[8]177, MH:DEC/95[58]188
BEAUREGARD, RENE, *Captain, CSA;*
BEAUVOIR, (BILOXI) MISSISSIPPI; ARTICLE: "BEAUVOIR,
WHERE THE LEADER OF A LOST REVOLUTION AND
SOME OF HIS TROOPS WAITED OUT THEIR DAYS,"
CWTI:AUG/91[22]215,
ADDITIONAL LISTING: CWTI:AUG/91[68]222
BEAVER DAM CREEK, VIRGINIA, BATTLE OF:
ARTICLE: "THE PENINSULA CAMPAIGN OF 1862: THE
BATTLE OF BEAVER DAM CREEK," CWM:JUN/95[57]592
ADDITIONAL LISTINGS: AHI:JUN/84[24]239, CWM:OCT/94[5]533,
CWR:VOL1#3[28]120, CWR:VOL3#1[80], CWR:VOL3#3[1]157
CWTI:APR/89[14]107, CWTI:JUL/93[42]329
BEAVER, JAMES A., *Colonel, 148th Pennsylvania Infantry;*
CWM:NOV/91[80]396, CWM:OCT/95[55]622,
CWR:VOL2#2[141]13
BEAVERT, VIRGIL A., *Private, 2nd Tennessee Cavalry;*
CWR:VOL4#1[1]163
BECK, FRANKLIN K., *Colonel, 23rd Alabama Infantry;*
B&G:FEB/94[8]550
BECK, MOSES, *Captain, 18th Indiana Battery;*
B&G:AUG/94[22]576
BECKHAM, FONTAINE; CWTI:JAN/95[24]42

BECKHAM, ROBERT F., *Colonel, CSA;*
ARTICLE: "ROBERT F. BECKHAM: THE MAN WHO
COMMANDED STUART'S HORSE ARTILLERY AFTER
PELHAM FELL," B&G:DEC/91[34]470
ADDITIONAL LISTINGS: ACW:JUL/92[41]370, B&G:DEC/91[34]470,
CWTI:JUN/90[32]15, GETTY:11[19]232
BECKWITH, AMOS, *Colonel, USA;* AHI:JAN/67[4]106
BECKWITH, SAMUEL H.; CWTI:AUG/95[46]459
BECNEL, LOUIS, *Lieutenant, 18th Louisiana Infantry;*
CWR:VOL4#2[1]165
BEE, BERNARD E. *General, CSA:*
GENERAL LISTINGS: *in book review,* ACW:NOV/94[66],
CWR:VOL2#2[169], *Manassas,* B&G:APR/91[32]447, *Mexican
War,* MH:APR/93[39]166, *Thomas J. Jackson,*
B&G:JUN/92[8]487, *photo,* B&G:JUN/92[8]487
ADDITIONAL LISTINGS: ACW:MAR/92[10]349, ACW:NOV/94[18]495,
B&G:APR/91[32]447, B&G:AUG/91[40]463,
CWTI:SEPT/89[24]128
BEE, HAMILTON P., *General, CSA;* ACW:JUL/91[58]316,
AHI:JUN/70[30]127, CWR:VOL2#3[212]14,
CWR:VOL4#2[1]165, CWR:VOL4#2[68]167,
CWR:VOL4#2[18]16
BEEBE, THOMAS J., *Lieutenant, Kane County (Illinois)
Cavalry;* B&G:AUG/95[8]604
BEEBY, HENRY E., *Lieutenant, 22nd New York Cavalry;*
B&G:FEB/92[32]477
BEEBY, RICHARD, *Private, 13th Pennsylvania Reserve;*
CWR:VOL1#3[28]120
BEECHAM, HENRY, *Private, 7th Wisconsin Infantry,*
GETTY:11[57]233
BEECHER'S ISLAND, BATTLE OF, (INDIAN WARS);
ARTICLE: "BEECHER'S ISLAND," AHI:DEC/67[4]113
BEECHER, FRED H., *Lieutenant, 16th Maine Infantry;*
GETTY:13[33]255
BEECHER, FREDERICK H., *Lieutenant, 16th Maine Infantry;*
CWM:MAY/92[15]419
BEECHER, FREDERICK, *Lieutenant, USA;* AHI:DEC/67[4]113
BEECHER, HARRIET WARD; CWM:SEP/92[6]436
BEECHER, HENRY WARD; ACW:SEP/93[46]435,
AHI:JUL/75[4]160, AHI:APR/80[21]200,
CWM:MAY/92[15]419, CWNEWS:JUN/92[4],
CWNEWS:NOV/92[4], CWTI:AUG/90[42]16, GETTY:13[33]255
THE "BEEFSTEAK RAID"; MH:JUN/94[8]177
BEEM, DAVID, *Captain, 14th Indiana Infantry;*
GETTY:12[30]243
BEERS, JACOB and LEWIS, *Private, 53rd Pennsylvania
Infantry;* GETTY:11[80]235
BEHEN, EMERY D., *Private, 1st Indiana Cavalry;*
ACW:MAR/95[34]516
BEHN, FERDINAND, *Private, USA;* ACW:JUL/93[27]423
BEINE, CHARLES H., *Lieutenant, 112th Pennsylvania
Infantry;* B&G:APR/95[24]596
BELCHER, SAMUEL C., *Captain, 16th Maine Infantry;*
CWM:MAY/92[15]419, GETTY:13[33]255
BELDEN, SIMEON, *Captain, 10th Louisiana Infantry;*
CWR:VOL3#1[1]149
BELFOUR, EMMA, *civilian;* AHI:DEC/77[13]176
BELGER, JAMES, *Colonel, USA;* GETTY:12[42]244
BELKNAP, CHARLES W., *Private, 125th New York Infantry;*
GETTY:8[95]205, GETTY:10[53]225
BELKNAP, WILLIAM W., *General, USA:*
ARTICLE: "THE BELKNAP SCANDAL," AHI:MAY/69[32]122

ADDITIONAL LISTINGS: CWM:MAR/93[32]468,
  CWM:AUG/95[38]609, CWR:VOL2#2[95]135,
  CWR:VOL3#2[1]153, CWR:VOL3#2[70]155,
  CWTI:DEC/91[36]240, CWTI:MAR/93[40]312,
  CWTI:NOV/93[55]350, CWTI:DEC/94[32]410
BENNYHOFF, AARON, *Corporal, 28th Pennsylvania Infantry;*
  GETTY:9[81]216
BENSINGER, WILLIAM, *Private, USA;* ACW:SEP/91[22]321
BENSON, BERRY, *Sergeant, 1st South Carolina Infantry:*
BOOK REVIEWS: *BERRY BENSON'S CIVIL WAR BOOK:*
  MEMOIRS OF A CONFEDERATE SCOUT AND
  SHARPSHOOTER
ADDITIONAL LISTINGS: CWTI:DEC/91[26]23, GETTY:6[7]169
BENSON, E.S., *journalist;* MH:OCT/91[50]154
BENTEEN, FREDERICK W., *Lieutenant Colonel, 10th*
  Missouri Cavalry:
GENERAL LISTINGS: *in book review,* CWNEWS:JAN/94[5], *Little Big*
  Horn, AHI:JUN/76[4]169, AHI:DEC/84[10]242,
  AHI:DEC/84[18]243, AHI:JAN/85[30]246, MH:AUG/95[82]186,
  photo, AHI:JUN/76[4]169
BENTLEY, JOHN B., *Lieutenant, 22nd Georgia Infantry;*
  GETTY:12[111]250
BENTLEY, W.W., *24th Virginia Infantry;* GETTY:5[123]166
BENTLY, BENJAMIN S., *Private, 154th New York Infantry;*
  GETTY:8[17]200
BENTON, CHARLES, *Private, 150th New York Infantry;*
  GETTY:12[42]244
BENTON, FRANK B., *Lt., 2nd Ill. Arty.;* B&G:AUG/95[8]604
BENTON, JAMES D., *Surgeon, 111th New York Infantry;*
  GETTY:10[63]225
BENTON, S.J., *Captain, USA;* CWTI:DEC/90[18]180
BENTON, THOMAS HART, *Missouri Senator;*
  ACW:MAR/92[46]354, AHI:AUG/66[32]104,
  AHI:AUG/69[5]123, AHI:MAY/70[4]126, AHI:JUL/81[20]221,
  AHI:SEP/87[21]262, MH:APR/93[34]165, *photos,*
  AHI:SEP/87[21]262, AHI:MAY/70[4]126
BENTON, THOMAS O., *Captain, CSA;* CWR:VOL4#2[118]16
BENTON, WILLIAM P., *General, USA;* ACW:JUL/94[51]480,
  B&G:AUG/95[8]604, B&G:FEB/94[8]550
BENTONVILLE BATTLEGROUND HISTORICAL
  ASSOCIATION; B&G:DEC/95[44]617
BENTONVILLE BATTLEGROUND STATE HISTORIC
  SITE; B&G:DEC/95[9]615, CWM:JUL/92[27]431
BENTONVILLE, NORTH CAROLINA, BATTLE OF:
ARTICLES: "A LONG ROAD TO BENTONVILLE: THE FIRST
  CONFEDERATE REGIMENT," CWR:VOL1#4[64]127, "LAST
  STAND IN THE CAROLINAS: THE BATTLE OF
  BENTONVILLE, MARCH 19-21, 1865," B&G:DEC/95[9]615,
  "LAST STAND IN THE CAROLINAS: THE BATTLE OF
  BENTONVILLE: AN INTERVIEW WITH AUTHOR MARK L.
  BRADLEY," CWR:VOL4#3[65]172
GENERAL LISTINGS: *general history,* AHI:MAY/71[3]133A, *in book*
  review, ACW:NOV/93[58], ACW:MAR/94[58],
  CWNEWS:OCT/89[4]
ADDITIONAL LISTINGS: ACW:NOV/93[12]440, ACW:MAR/95[50]518,
  CWM:JUL/92[18]429, CWM:JUL/92[40]432,
  CWR:VOL2#4[313]14
BERARD, ACHILLE, *Captain, 10th Louisiana Infantry;*
  CWR:VOL3#1[1]149
BERAUD, DESIRE, *Captain, 10th Louisiana Infantry;*
  CWR:VOL3#1[1]149

BERDAN'S SHARPSHOOTERS:
ARTICLES: "DEATH AT A DISTANCE," CWTI:APR/90[48]15,
  "THE MOST DANGEROUS SET OF MEN,"
  CWTI:JUL/93[42]329
BOOK REVIEWS: *CIVIL WAR CHIEF OF SHARPSHOOTERS:*
  HIRAM BERDAN, MILITARY COMMANDER AND
  *FIREARMS INVENTOR * THE CIVIL WAR DIARY OF*
  WYMAN WHITE, FIRST SERGEANT OF COMPANY F, 2ND
  UNITED STATES SHARPSHOOTER REGIMENT
ADDITIONAL LISTINGS: ACW:MAY/94[35]469, CWM:DEC/95[59]633,
  CWTI:MAR/89[34]104
BERDAN, HIRAM, *Colonel, USA;*
ARTICLES: "DEATH AT A DISTANCE," CWTI:APR/90[48]15,
  "THE MOST DANGEROUS SET OF MEN,"
  CWTI:JUL/93[42]329
BOOK REVIEWS: *CIVIL WAR CHIEF OF SHARPSHOOTERS:*
  HIRAM BERDAN, MILITARY COMMANDER AND
  *FIREARMS INVENTOR * THE CIVIL WAR DIARY OF*
  WYMAN WHITE, FIRST SERGEANT OF COMPANY F, 2ND
  UNITED STATES SHARPSHOOTER REGIMENT
GENERAL LISTINGS: *Gettysburg,* GETTY:4[113]153,
  GETTY:6[7]169, GETTY:7[29]188, GETTY:8[31]201,
  GETTY:9[5]209, GETTY:12[7]241, *in book review,*
  CWNEWS:MAY/90[4], CWR:VOL2#2[169], CWR:VOL4#3[37],
  CWTI:DEC/89[10]133, MH:DEC/92[74], *letters to the editor,*
  CWTI:NOV/93[12]34, *photos,* CWTI:APR/90[48]15,
  CWTI:JUL/93[42]329
ADDITIONAL LISTINGS: ACW:NOV/92[10]384, ACW:MAY/95[30]525,
  B&G:FEB/95[8]590A, CWM:MAR/92[9]410,
  CWM:JUN/95[8]594, CWR:VOL1#3[20]119,
  CWTI:MAR/89[34]104, CWTI:JUL/93[29]326
BERGE, JACOB, *Private, 53rd Pennsylvania Infantry;*
  GETTY:11[80]235
BERGEN, JAMES, *civilian;* ACW:MAR/92[22]351
BERGER, FRANK, *Private, 2nd Tennessee Cavalry;*
  CWR:VOL4#1[1]163
BERKELEY PLANTATION; ARTICLE: "MCCLELLAN'S
  PLANTATION," CWTI:JAN/94[20]358
BERKELEY, CARTER, *Lieutenant, CSA;* CWM:JUN/94[27]513
BERKELEY, EDMUND, *Major, 8th Virginia Infantry;*
  CWTI:NOV/93[55]350, GETTY:5[107]164
BERKELEY, HENRY R., *Private, CSA;* B&G:FEB/95[8]590B,
  GETTY:10[7]221
BERKLEY, CARTER, *Sergeant, Staunton Artillery;* ARTICLE:
  "LEST WE FORGET," CWM:JAN/92[68]407
BERMUDA HUNDRED CAMPAIGN:
BOOK REVIEWS: *BACK DOOR TO RICHMOND: THE BERMUDA*
  *HUNDRED CAMPAIGN * THE BERMUDA HUNDRED*
  CAMPAIGN
ADDITIONAL LISTINGS: ACW:JUL/91[35]314, ACW:MAY/92[14]358,
  ACW:MAY/92[30]361, ACW:SEP/95[74]550,
  AHI:MAY/71[3]133A, B&G:APR/94[10]558,
  B&G:DEC/94[34]587, CWM:SEP/92[19]440,
  CWNEWS:SEP/90[4], CWR:VOL2#3[236]14,
  CWR:VOL3#2[1]153, CWTI:MAY/93[29]319,
  MH:APR/95[46]183
BERMUDA:
ARTICLES: "BERMUDA IS AN UNLIKELY STARTING POINT
  FOR THOSE TRACING THE MYSTERY OF THE GREAT
  SEAL OF THE CONFEDERACY," ACW:MAY/93[62]418,
  "ISLAND HAVEN FOR A STRUGGLING CONFEDERACY,"
  CWTI:DEC/89[10]133

BINION, J.T., *Private, 10th Georgia Infantry;*
ACW:JUL/95[10]533
BINNEY, HENRY M., *Lieutenant, 10th Maine Infantry;*
CWR:VOL1#4[7]125
BIRD, ALEXANDER, *Lieutenant, 154th New York Infantry;*
GETTY:5[123]166
BIRD, EDGEWORTH; BOOK REVIEW: *THE GRANITE FARM
LETTERS: THE CIVIL WAR CORRESPONDENCE OF
EDGEWORTH AND SALLIE BIRD*
BIRD, FRANCIS W., *Captain, 11th North Carolina Infantry;*
GETTY:13[75]259
BIRD, J.H., *Sergeant, 26th Virginia Infantry;*
B&G:APR/93[24]520
BIRD, JAMES W., *Lieutenant, 154th New York Infantry;*
GETTY:8[17]200
BIRD, JOHN, *Private, 150th Pennsylvania Infantry;*
CWTI:SEP/90[26]17
BIRD, PICKENS, *Major, 9th Florida Infantry;*
CWR:VOL3#4[1]161
BIRD, W.H., *Private, 13th Alabama Infantry;* GETTY:6[13]170
BIRGE'S SHARPSHOOTERS; B&G:FEB/92[10]474
BIRGE, HENRY W., *General, USA;* ACW:MAY/91[38]305,
CWTI:APR/90[48]154
BIRGE, N.A., *Captain, CSA;* ACW:MAR/93[68]409
BIRMINGHAM, THEODORE, *Private, 23rd Michigan
Infantry;* BOOK REVIEW: *YOURS IN LOVE: THE
BIRMINGHAM CIVIL WAR LETTERS*
BIRNEY, DAVID B., *General, USA:*
GENERAL LISTINGS: *Cold Harbor,* B&G:APR/94[10]558, *Gettysburg,*
GETTY:4[113]153, GETTY:5[47]160, GETTY:6[59]174,
GETTY:7[29]188, GETTY:7[51]190, GETTY:8[31]201,
GETTY:8[43]202, GETTY:8[53]203, GETTY:9[5]209,
GETTY:10[42]224, GETTY:10[112]228, GETTY:12[7]241,
GETTY:12[85]248, *in book review,* B&G:APR/94[10],
B&G:JUN/94[34], CWR:VOL4#3[1]170, *in order of battle,*
B&G:APR/95[8]595, *Manassas, Second,* B&G:AUG/92[11]493,
Petersburg, MH:APR/95[46]183, *Wilderness,*
B&G:APR/95[8]595, *photo,* AHI:MAY/71[3]133A,
B&G:APR/94[10]558, B&G:JUN/95[8]600,
CWM:AUG/94[30]527, GETTY:8[5]198
ADDITIONAL LISTINGS: ACW:MAY/92[30]361, ACW:MAY/93[31]415,
ACW:JAN/95[54]508, ACW:MAY/95[30]525,
B&G:FEB/92[22]476, B&G:APR/94[10]558,
B&G:APR/95[8]595, B&G:JUN/95[8]600,
CWM:MAY/92[20]420, CWM:JUL/92[18]429,
CWM:AUG/94[30]527, CWR:VOL1#3[52]122,
CWR:VOL4#1[1]177, CWTI:APR/92[49]260,
CWTI:JUL/93[42]329, MH:APR/95[46]183
BIRNEY, JAMES G., *Lieutenant, 7th Michigan Cavalry;*
GETTY:13[89]260
BIRNEY, WILLIAM, *General, USA;*
ARTICLE: "COSTLY UNION RECONNAISSANCE,"
ACW:JUL/94[42]479
ADDITIONAL LISTINGS: CWM:AUG/94[30]527
BISBEE, Lewis C., *Captain, 16th Maine Infantry;*
CWM:MAY/92[15]419, GETTY:13[33]255
BISHOP, ANDREW, *Private, 7th Wisconsin Infantry,*
GETTY:11[57]233
BISHOP, E.S., *Captain, 25th Virginia Cavalry;*
CWTI:FEB/92[42]25
BISHOP, GEORGE, *Private, 8th Louisiana Infantry;*
CWTI:FEB/91[12]18

BISHOP, JUDSON, *Lieutenant Colonel, 2nd Minnesota
Infantry;* ACW:NOV/94[76]500
BISHOP, LEWIS, *Sergeant, 154th New York Infantry;*
GETTY:8[17]200
BISHOP, WILLIAM, *civilian;* CWTI:AUG/95[34]45
BISHOP, WILLIAM, *Colonel, USA;* MH:APR/95[74]184
BISHOP, WILLIAM P., *Colonel, CSA;* B&G:DEC/95[9]615
BISLAND, LOUISIANA, BATTLE OF; CWR:VOL3#1[78]152
BISSELL, WILLIAM S., *Lieutenant, 2nd South Carolina
Infantry;* GETTY:12[111]250
BIVENS, BARRIEN A., *Private, Sumter Artillery Battalion;*
CWR:VOL3#2[61]154
BIXBY, PHINEUS, *Major, 6th New Hampshire Infantry;*
ACW:MAY/95[18]524
"BLACK CODES"; CWTI:DEC/89[62]139
"BLACK HORSE CAVALRY"; CWTI:APR/89[38]111
BLACK CANADIAN SOLDIERS; CWM:SEP/93[18]494
BLACK CONFEDERATES:
ARTICLES: "ARTICLE BRINGS NOTICE TO A UNIQUE REBEL,"
CWTI:JUN/90[57]163, "BLACK CONFEDERATES AT
GETTYSBURG—1863," GETTY:6[94]180, "THE BLACK
SOLDIERS WHO SERVED IN THE CONFEDERATE ARMY
ARE THE REAL FORGOTTEN MEN OF THE CIVIL WAR,"
ACW:NOV/95[8]552, "EDITOR'S PREFACE TO BLACK
CONFEDERATES AT GETTYSBURG-1863," GETTY:6[93]179
BOOK REVIEWS: *BLACK CONFEDERATES AND
AFRO-YANKEES IN CIVIL WAR VIRGINIA * BLACKS IN
THE BLUE AND GRAY: AFRO-AMERICAN SERVICE IN
THE CIVIL WAR * SOUTHERN NEGROES, 1861-1865*
ADDITIONAL LISTINGS: ACW:NOV/95[8]552, B&G:APR/92[36]483,
CWM:JUL/93[4]482, CWM:AUG/95[45], CWM:OCT/95[10],
CWNEWS:MAY/92[4], CWTI:JUN/90[57]16, GETTY:6[93]179,
GETTY:6[94]180, GETTY:7[124]196, GETTY:10[102]226
BLACK HISTORY:
ARTICLES: "GIVE THE BLACKS TEXAS," CWTI:JUN/90[54]162,
"THE MYTH OF THE UNDERGROUND RAILROAD,"
AHI:JAN/78[34]178, "NOT QUITE FREE: THE FREE NEGRO
BEFORE THE CIVIL WAR," AHI:JUN/74[12]155,
"SLAVERY," AHI:APR/70[11]124, "THIS ONE GREAT EVIL",
AHI:MAY/77[37]174
BOOK REVIEWS: *ALLIES FOR FREEDOM: BLACKS AND JOHN
BROWN * AMERICAN NEGRO SLAVERY: A
DOCUMENTARY HISTORY * THE BLACK INFANTRY IN
THE WEST, 1869-1891 * BLACK SCARE: THE RACIST
RESPONSE TO EMANCIPATION AND RECONSTRUCTION
* THE BLACK WEST: A DOCUMENTARY AND PICTORIAL
* HISTORY EYEWITNESS: THE NEGRO IN AMERICAN
HISTORY * THE FREEDMEN'S BUREAU IN LOUISIANA *
FREEDOM'S LAWMAKERS: A DIRECTORY OF BLACK
OFFICEHOLDERS DURING RECONSTRUCTION *
IMPEACHMENT OF A PRESIDENT: ANDREW JOHNSON
* THE BLACKS AND RECONSTRUCTION IN THE CAGE:
EYEWITNESS ACCOUNTS OF THE FREED NEGRO IN
SOUTHERN SOCIETY, 1877-1929*
BOOK REVIEWS, continued: *MEN AND BROTHERS,
ANGLO-AMERICAN ANTISLAVERY COOPERATION *
MOORFIELD STOREY AND THE ABOLITIONIST
TRADITION * THE NEGRO * NORTH INTO FREEDOM:
THE AUTOBIOGRAPHY OF JOHN MALVIN * FREE
NEGRO, 1795-1880 * THE PROBLEM OF SLAVERY IN THE
AGE OF REVOLUTION, 1770-1823 * ROLL, JORDAN,
ROLL: THE WORLD THE SLAVES MADE * THE SLAVE
COMMUNITY: PLANTATION LIFE IN THE ANTEBELLUM*

*SOUTH * THIS SPECIES OF PROPERTY: SLAVE LIFE AND CULTURE IN THE OLD SOUTH * THE TROUBLE THEY SEEN: BLACK PEOPLE TELL THE STORY OF RECONSTRUCTION * UNDERSTANDING NEGRO HISTORY*
ADDITIONAL LISTINGS: AHI:JUN/68[51], AHI:JUN/69[46], AHI:APR/70[11]124, AHI:AUG/70[50], AHI:NOV/71[48], AHI:DEC/72[49], AHI:JUN/74[12]155, AHI:JUN/74[49], AHI:AUG/75[50], AHI:MAY/76[48], AHI:FEB/77[49], AHI:MAY/77[37]174, AHI:JAN/78[34]178, AHI:JUN/80[6], ACW:NOV/94[8]493

BLACK SOLDIERS: *also, see listings under* **"UNITED STATES COLORED TROOPS"**
ARTICLES: "A BRAVE BLACK REGIMENT—HISTORY OF THE FIFTY-FOURTH REGIMENT OF MASSACHUSETTS VOLUNTEER INFANTRY," CWTI:DEC/89[53]138, "THE BLACK SOLDIERS WHO SERVED IN THE CONFEDERATE ARMY ARE THE REAL FORGOTTEN MEN OF THE CIVIL WAR," ACW:NOV/95[8]552, "CONTROVERSY: WHAT MAKES A MASSACRE?," B&G:AUG/91[52]464, "I WANT YOU TO PROVE YOURSELVES MEN," CWTI:DEC/89[42]132, "LAY THIS LAUREL," CWTI:DEC/89[53]138, "ONE GALLENT RUSH," CWTI:DEC/89[53]138, "PAT CLEBURNE'S MODEST PROPOSAL SENT SHOCKWAVES THROUGH THE CONFEDERATE ARMY AND THE GOVERNMENT," ACW:NOV/93[6]437, "THEY ARE INVINCIBLE: TWO BLACK ARMY CHAPLAINS GET A LOOK AT SHERMAN'S ARMY," CWTI:APR/89[32]110
BOOK REVIEWS: *THE BLACK INFANTRY IN THE WEST, 1869-1891 * BLACK TROOPS, WHITE COMMANDERS, AND FREEDMEN DURING THE CIVIL WAR * BLACKS IN THE BLUE AND GRAY: AFRO-AMERICAN SERVICE IN THE CIVIL WAR * THE BUFFALO SOLDIERS. A NARRATIVE OF THE NEGRO CAVALRY IN THE WEST * FORGED IN BATTLE: THE CIVIL WAR ALLIANCE OF BLACK SOLDIERS AND WHITE OFFICERS * MEN OF COLOR, UNITED STATES COLORED TROOPS 1863-1867*
ADDITIONAL LISTINGS: ACW:NOV/93[6]437, ACW:NOV/95[8]552, AHI:AUG/67[59], AHI:MAY/71[3]133A, AHI:NOV/71[48], B&G:AUG/91[26], B&G:AUG/91[52]464, B&G:FEB/93[36], CWM:JAN/92[6]398, CWM:AUG/95[45], CWNEWS:MAY/89[4], CWNEWS:JUL/90[4], CWNEWS:OCT/90[4], CWNEWS:MAY/92[4], CWNEWS:NOV/94[33], CWR:VOL2#3[256], CWTI:APR/89[32]110, CWTI:DEC/89[42]137, CWTI:APR/90[24]152, CWTI:JUN/90[54]162, CWTI:AUG/91[68]222
BLACK, ALBERT E., *Lieutenant, 111th Pennsylvania Infantry;* CWR:VOL3#2[70]155
BLACK, HENRY M., *Major, USA;* B&G:DEC/91[12]469
BLACK, JAMES, *Private, 7th Wisconsin Infantry;* GETTY:9[33]211
BLACK, JAMES M., *Captain, 10th Maine Infantry;* B&G:OCT/95[32]613
BLACK, JOHN C., *Major, 37th Illinois Infantry;* CWR:VOL1#1[42]105
BLACK, JOHN L., *Colonel, 1st South Carolina Cavalry;* B&G:OCT/93[12]537
BLACK, SAMUEL L., *Major, CSA;* CWTI:SUMMER/89[32]12
BLACK, STEPHEN, *Private, Petersburg Artillery;* B&G:OCT/94[42]583

BLACK, W.T., *Colonel, 5th Georgia Infantry;* CWR:VOL1#4[42]126
BLACK, WILLIAM, *Private, CSA;* ACW:MAR/92[54]
BLACK, WILLIAM P., *Captain, 37th Illinois Infantry;* CWR:VOL1#1[42]105
BLACKBURN, J.K.P., *Captain, Terry's Texas Rangers;* CWM:JUL/92[40]432
BLACKBURN, LEONIDAS, *Sergeant, 53rd Virginia Infantry;* GETTY:13[64]258
BLACKBURN, LUKE, *Surgeon;* CWTI:DEC/89[10]133, CWTI:JAN/93[44]302
BLACKBURN, WILLIAM D., *Lieutenant Colonel, 7th Illinois Cavalry;* B&G:JUN/93[12]524
BLACKFORD, CHARLES M., *Captain, 2nd Virginia Cavalry;* GETTY:13[75]259
BLACKFORD, EUGENE, *Major, 5th Alabama Infantry;* B&G:FEB/95[8]590A, GETTY:4[33]146, GETTY:4[49]147, GETTY:10[7]221
BLACKFORD, LANCELOT M., *Private, CSA;* GETTY:13[1]252, GETTY:13[75]259
BLACKFORD, WILLIAM W., *Captain, CSA:*
BOOK REVIEW: *WAR YEARS WITH JEB STUART*
GENERAL LISTINGS: *Aldie,* GETTY:11[19]232, *Gettysburg,* GETTY:4[65]147, GETTY:4[65]148, *in book review,* CWM:AUG/95[45], CWNEWS:MAY/95[33], *letters to the editor,* B&G:DEC/93[6]544, *Manassas, Second,* B&G:AUG/92[11]493
ADDITIONAL LISTINGS: ACW:NOV/91[35]333, ACW:JAN/93[43]397, ACW:SEP/95[38]546, B&G:OCT/93[49]543, B&G:OCT/95[20]612, CWNEWS:AUG/94[33], CWTI:JUL/92[12]270, CWTI:JUN/95[38]447, GETTY:11[19]232
BLACKLEY, LYMAN W., *Private, 24th Michigan Infantry;* GETTY:11[57]233
BLACKMAN, WILBUR F., *Major, CSA;* CWR:VOL4#2[1]165
BLACKMARR, R.L., *civilian;* B&G:OCT/93[36]540
BLACKNALL, CHARLES C., *Colonel, 23rd North Carolina Infantry;* ACW:MAR/95[50]518, CWTI:MAY/93[26]31, *photos;* ACW:MAR/95[50]518, CWTI:MAY/93[26]31
BLACKNALL, THOMAS H., *Major, 1st Arkansas Infantry;* ACW:MAR/95[50]518
BLACKSHEAR, JAMES A., *Captain, Sumter Artillery;* CWR:VOL3#2[1]153
BLACKWALL, CHARLES C., *Captain, 23rd North Carolina Infantry;* GETTY:5[13]157
BLAIN, DANIEL, *Private, 19th Indiana Infantry;* GETTY:11[57]233
BLAINE, JAMES G., *Governor, Maine;*
GENERAL LISTINGS: *assassination of Garfield,* AHI:FEB/69[12]119, *election of 1876,* AHI:NOV/88[28]277, *James A. Garfield,* AHI:MAY/76[24]167, *Sherman on the Presidency,* AHI:JAN/77[46]173, GETTY:4[65]148
ADDITIONAL LISTINGS: AHI:NOV/89[50]288, B&G:OCT/93[31]539, *photo;* AHI:JAN/77[46]173
BLAIR, AUSTIN, *Governor of Michigan;* GETTY:6[33]172, GETTY:7[7]185
BLAIR, CHARLES W., *Colonel, 2nd Kansas Cavalry;* ACW:NOV/93[26]441, ACW:NOV/94[42]497, B&G:JUN/91[10]452
BLAIR, FRANCIS P., *Private, 7th Wisconsin Infantry,* GETTY:11[57]233
BLAIR, FRANCIS P. JR., *General, USA:*
ARTICLE: "SHERMAN'S FEUDING GENERALS," CWTI:MAR/95[40]436

GENERAL LISTINGS: *Carolina Campaign,* B&G:DEC/95[9]615, *in book review,* B&G:JUN/91[22], CWR:VOL2#1[78], *Jackson, Battle of,* B&G:AUG/95[8]604, *John C. Fremont,* AHI:MAY/70[4]126, *order of battle,* B&G:AUG/95[8]604, B&G:DEC/95[9]615, *Savannah,* B&G:FEB/91[8]439, *photos;* ACW:MAY/91[31]304 CWM:MAY/93[8]474, CWTI:MAR/95[40]436

ADDITIONAL LISTINGS: ACW:MAY/91[31]304, ACW:MAR/91[62]298, ACW:SEP/92[47]380, ACW:NOV/93[26]441, ACW:JUL/94[35]478, ACW:JAN/95[30]505, CWM:MAY/93[8]474, CWM:JUN/94[30]515, CWM:AUG/94[27]526, CWR:VOL2#1[1]130, CWR:VOL2#1[69]133, CWR:VOL3#3[33]158, CWR:VOL4#3[65]172, CWTI:SUMMER/89[13]120, CWTI:SUMMER/89[40]123, CWTI:SUMMER/89[50]124, CWTI:MAR/91[34]201, CWTI:SEP/91[23]228, CWTI:MAR/93[24]309, CWTI:MAR/95[40]436

BLAIR, FRANCIS P. SR.:
BOOK REVIEW: *FRANCIS PRESTON BLAIR*
ADDITIONAL LISTINGS: AHI:MAY/70[4]126, AHI:APR/83[27]233, CWTI:FEB/91[36]193

BLAIR, JOHN A., *Major, 2nd Mississippi Infantry;* GETTY:4[126]154, GETTY:6[29]171, GETTY:6[77]177

BLAIR, MONTGOMERY:
GENERAL LISTINGS: *John C. Fremont,* AHI:MAY/70[4]126, *Lincoln's Gettysburg Address,* GETTY:9[122]220, *Nelson-Davis feud,* AHI:NOV/72[12]142, *photo;* AHI:MAY/70[4]126, *portrait;* AHI:MAY/81[35]218
ADDITIONAL LISTINGS: ACW:MAY/91[31]304, ACW:MAR/92[46]354, AHI:NOV/88[37]278, CWTI:SEP/93[43]338

BLAISDEL, WILLIAM, *Colonel, 11th Massachusetts Infantry;* CWM:MAY/92[20]420, CWNEWS:JUN/95[33]

BLAKE, BENSON, *Colonel, CSA;* CWM:DEC/95[30]627

BLAKE, GEORGE S., *Captain, USN;* ACW:JAN/91[62]289

BLAKE, HENRY M., *Captain, 11th Massachusetts Infantry;* B&G:OCT/94[40], GETTY:12[7]241, *photo;* GETTY:12[7]241

BLAKE, HOMER, *Lieutenant, USN;* ACW:NOV/91[8]328

BLAKE, JOHN R., *civilian;* B&G:JUN/93[12]524

BLAKE, LEVI L., *Captain, 4th Wisconsin Infantry;* ACW:MAY/93[12]412

BLAKELEY, LYMAN W., *Private, 24th Michigan Infantry;* GETTY:9[33]211

BLAKELY, EDWARD, *Corporal, 63rd Ohio Infantry;* ARTICLE: "OVERCOME BY THE SCARS OF WAR," CWTI:JAN/93[82]304

BLALOCK, MRS. L.M.; AHI:DEC/73[10]152

BLANCHARD, ALBERT G., *General, CSA;* ACW:SEP/92[38]379, B&G:DEC/95[9]615, CWR:VOL4#2[68]167, CWTI:SEP/94[26]400

BLANCHARD, WALTER, *Captain, 13th Illinois Infantry;* CWTI:SEP/94[40]403

BLANCHARD, WILLIAM T., *Captain, 1st Pennsylvania Rifles;* CWR:VOL1#3[20]119

BLANCHARD, WILLIAM, *U.S. Consul;* CWM:JUL/93[8]483

BLAND, CHRISTOPHER C., *Private, 36th North Carolina Infantry;* B&G:DEC/94[10]585

BLAND, ELBERT, *Lieutenant Colonel, 50th Georgia Infantry;* GETTY:5[35]159

BLAND, W.H., *Private, 61st Georgia Infantry;* CWTI:JUL/93[20]325

BLANDEN, LEANDER, *Colonel, USA;* B&G:DEC/93[12]545, CWTI:JAN/93[20]298

BLANKENSHIP, WILLIAM, *Lieutenant, 1st Indiana Heavy Artillery;* ACW:JAN/94[30]450

BLANSETT, JOHN, *Private, 126th New York Infantry;* CWR:VOL1#4[7]125

BLAUVELT, ROBERT, *Private, 126th New York Infantry;* CWR:VOL1#4[7]125

BLAZER, RICHARD, *Captain, USA:*
ARTICLE: "A MATCH FOR MOSBY?" ACW:JUL/94[26]477
ADDITIONAL LISTING: ACW:MAY/91[54]

BLEDSOE, A.T., CWTI:MAR/93[24]309

BLEDSOE, HIRAM M., *Captain, Bledsoe's Missouri Artillery;* B&G:AUG/95[8]604

BLEDSOE, MRS. G.B., AHI:DEC/73[10]152

BLEDSOE, W.S., *Captain, CSA;* B&G:FEB/93[12]511

BLENKER, LOUIS, *General, USA;* ACW:JAN/93[35]396, ACW:MAY/95[54]528, CWTI:MAY/94[24]381

BLESSING, WILLIAM, *Major, 23rd Virginia Battalion;* CWTI:MAR/89[16]101

BLESSINGTON, JOHN P., *Private, 16th Texas Infantry;* CWR:VOL2#3[212]142

BLESSINGTON, JOSEPH P., *Private, 16th Texas Infantry:*
BOOK REVIEW: *THE CAMPAIGNS OF WALKER'S TEXAS DIVISION*
ADDITIONAL LISTING: CWR:VOL3#3[33]158

BLICKENSDERFER, MILTON A., *Sergeant, 126th Ohio Infantry:*
ARTICLE: "MEDAL OF HONOR RECIPIENT," CWTI:AUG/95[90]462
ADDITIONAL LISTING: CWTI:DEC/95[8]474

BLIEMEL, EMMERAN, *Chaplain, 10th Tennessee Infantry;* CWM:JUL/91[6]355

BLISS, WILLIAM,, *civilian;* GETTY:4[7]142, GETTY:4[89]150, GETTY:5[89]162, GETTY:7[51]190

BLISS, ZENAS R., *Colonel, USA;* B&G:APR/95[8]595, CWR:VOL2#2[118]136

BLITTERSDORF, AUGUST, *Private, USA;* ACW:NOV/92[8]383

BLOCHER, WILLIAM, *Captain, CSA;* CWR:VOL1#1[42]105

BLOCKADE RUNNERS; see listings under "SHIPS, BOATS, VESSELS, ETC."

BLOCKADE AND BLOCKADE RUNNING:
ARTICLES: "BRAVING THE YANKEE BLOCKADE," ACW:JAN/91[47]288, "THE GREAT GUNBOAT CHASE," CWTI:JUL/94[30]392
BOOK REVIEWS: *THE BLOCKADE RUNNERS: TRUE TALES OF RUNNING THE YANKEE BLOCKADE OF THE CONFEDERATE COAST * BLOCKADERS, REFUGEES & CONTRABANDS—CIVIL WAR ON FLORIDA'S GULF COAST 1861-65 * FROM CAPE CHARLES TO CAPE FEAR: THE NORTH ATLANTIC BLOCKADING SQUADRON DURING THE CIVIL WAR * LIFELINE OF THE CONFEDERACY: BLOCKADE RUNNING DURING THE CIVIL WAR*
ADDITIONAL LISTINGS: CWM:SEP/91[8]378, CWTI:DEC/89[10]133, CWTI:DEC/95[67]481

BLODGETT, WELLS, *Lieutenant, 37th Illinois Infantry;* CWR:VOL1#1[42]105

BLOOM, ENOS, *Private, 13th Pennsylvania Reserves;* CWR:VOL1#3[28]120

BLOOMER, SAMUEL, *Sergeant, 1st Minnesota Infantry;* CWR:VOL2#2[95]135

BLOSS, JOHN M., *Sergeant, 27th Indiana Infantry;* ACW:JAN/94[6]446

BLOUNT, AMBROSE A., *Captain, 17th Ohio Battery;*
  B&G:FEB/94[8]550
BLUCHER, FELIX, *Major, CSA;* ACW:JUL/92[46]371
BLUE SPRINGS, TENNESSEE, BATTLE OF;
  CWTI:JAN/93[49]303
BLUE, JOHN M., *Lieutenant, CSA;* BOOK REVIEWS: *HANGING
  ROCK REBEL; LIEUTENANT JOHN BLUE'S WAR IN
  WEST VIRGINIA & THE SHENANDOAH VALLEY*
BLUNT, GEORGE A., *Private, USA;* ARTICLES: "THE BLUNT
  COLLECTION OF COLD HARBOR PHOTOGRAPHS,"
  B&G:APR/94[47]562A, B&G:APR/94[59]565
BLUNT, JAMES G., *General, USA;* ACW:JAN/91[30]286,
  ACW:JAN/93[26]395, ACW:MAY/94[26]468,
  ACW:NOV/94[42]497, ACW:SEP/94[10]484,
  B&G:JUN/91[10]452, B&G:JUN/92[46]490,
  B&G:OCT/93[38]541, CWM:JAN/92[8]399,
  CWM:SEP/92[38]443, CWR:VOL1#1[42]105,
  CWR:VOL1#2[44]114, CWTI:SEP/90[52]179, *photo;*
  ACW:MAY/94[26]468, B&G:JUN/91[10]452
BLY, ADALBERT, *Lieutenant, 32nd Wisconsin Infantry;*
  CWR:VOL2#4[313]146
BLY, DELL, *Private, 32nd Wisconsin Infantry;*
  CWR:VOL2#4[313]146
BOARDMAN, CALVIN, *Private, 37th Illinois Infantry;*
  CWR:VOL1#1[42]105
BOBB, JOHN H., *civilian;* B&G:OCT/91[11]466
BOBLITZ, EUGENE, *Corporal, 125th Pennsylvania Infantry;*
  B&G:OCT/95[8]611A
BODINE, ROBERT L., *Major, 26th Pennsylvania Infantry;*
  GETTY:12[7]241
BOGGS, CHARLES, *Commander, USN;* MH:AUG/93[47]169
BOGGS, GUS, *Lieutenant, CSA;* ACW:SEP/91[41]323
BOGGS, WILLIAM R., *General, CSA;* CWR:VOL3#1[1]149,
  CWR:VOL4#2[68]167, CWR:VOL4#2[118]169, *photo;*
  CWTI:AUG/90[64]170
BOHLEN, HENRY, *General, USA;* B&G:APR/91[8]445
BOICE, THEODORE A., *Lieutenant Colonel, 5th New York
  Cavalry;* CWM:APR/94[24]505
BOIES, JUSTUS A., *Lieutenant, 13th U.S. Regulars;*
  CWR:VOL2#1[1]130
BOISSEAU, JAMES P., *Surgeon,* B&G:APR/92[8]481
BOLAND, E. T., *Private, 13th Alabama Infantry;*
  GETTY:6[13]170
BOLES, WILLIAM, *Private, CSA;* CWTI:JUL/92[8]269
BOLINGER, HENRY C., *Colonel, 7th Pennsylvania Reserves;*
  CWR:VOL4#4[1]177
BOLTON, WILLIAM, *Captain, 51st Pennsylvania Infantry;*
  CWM:MAY/92[44]423
BOLZA, CHARLES E., *Lieutenant, 6th Michigan Cavalry;*
  GETTY:9[109]218
BOND, DANILE, *Private, 1st Minnesota Infantry;*
  ACW:JAN/94[62]
BONDURANT, J.W., *Captain, CSA;* CWR:VOL3#2[1]153
BONHAM, MILLEDGE L., *General, CSA;* GETTY:13[22]254
BONNER, J.R., *Captain, CSA;* B&G:DEC/95[9]615
BONNEY, USHER P., *Lieutenant, 7th South Carolina Cavalry;*
  CWM:JUL/92[16]428
BONNIN, LEWIS, *Corporal, 88th Pennsylvania Infantry;*
  GETTY:10[7]221
BOOKER, T., *Sergeant, CSA;* CWTI:SEP/90[34]176
BOOMER, GEORGE B., *Colonel, USA;* ACW:NOV/91[22]331,
  CWR:VOL2#1[19]131, CWR:VOL3#3[59]159,
  MH:JUN/93[82]167

BOOMER, L.B., *engineer;* CWM:NOV/91[50]394
BOONE, HAMILTON H., *Major, 13th Texas Cavalry Battalion;*
  CWM:OCT/94[33]537
BOONE, MARK D.L., *57th Virginia Infantry;* GETTY:5[123]166
BOONE, R.M., *Captain, CSA;* ACW:JAN/94[30]450
BOONE, SAM, *Sergeant, 88th Pennsylvania Infantry;*
  GETTY:10[7]221
BOONEVILLE, MISSISSIPPI, BATTLE OF;
  CWM:MAR/93[24]467
BOOTH, EDWIN:
ARTICLES: "EDWIN BOOTH: PRINCE OF TRAGEDY,"
  AHI:OCT/86[22]260, "ON HISTORY'S SLIGHTER SIDE,"
  AHI:JUN/79[19]188
BOOK REVIEW: *AMERICAN GOTHIC: THE STORY OF
  AMERICA'S LEGENDARY THEATRICAL
  FAMILY—JUNIUS, EDWIN AND JOHN WILKES BOOTH*
ADDITIONAL LISTINGS: ACW:JUL/92[62]372, ACW:MAR/93[35]405,
  AHI:FEB/86[12]257, B&G:APR/95[33]597
BOOTH, GEORGE, *Lieutenant, 1st Maryland Cavalry;*
  B&G:AUG/94[10]574
BOOTH, J.B., *Private, 21st Mississippi Infantry;*
  GETTY:7[77]191
BOOTH, JOHN WILKES:
ARTICLES: "A PAPER LINK TO A CONSPIRACY,"
  CWTI:SEP/91[15]225, "BOOTH DERRINGER AUCTIONED,"
  AHI:OCT/94[8]321, "CHILDHOOD HOME OF AN
  AMERICAN ARCH-VILLAIN," CWTI:APR/90[12]150,
  "EYEWITNESSES REMEMBER THE 'FEARFUL NIGHT,'"
  CWTI:MAR/93[12]307, "HERITAGE OR HOAX?"
  CWTI:SEP/94[24]399, "HISTORIANS OPPOSE OPENING OF
  BOOTH GRAVE," CWTI:JUN/95[26]445, "LINCOLN'S
  MURDER: THE SIMPLE CONSPIRACY THEORY,"
  CWTI:DEC/91[28]239, "MORAL VICTORY IN THE
  CRUSADE TO CLEAR MUDD," CWTI:MAY/93[12]316, "ON
  HISTORY'S SLIGHTER SIDE," AHI:JUN/79[19]188,
  "TRAGEDIAN'S GREATEST ROLE," CW:MAR/93[35]405,
  "VISITING THE SITE OF ABRAHAM LINCOLN'S
  ASSASSINATION GIVES HISTORY BUFFS AN EERIE
  SENSE OF STEPPING BACK IN TIME,"
  ACW:MAY/95[68]529, "WHAT REALLY HAPPENED TO THE
  ASSASSIN?" CWTI:JUL/92[50]275, "WHATEVER BECAME
  OF BOSTON CORBETT?" CWTI:MAY/91[48]211
BOOK REVIEWS: *AMERICAN GOTHIC: THE STORY OF
  AMERICA'S LEGENDARY THEATRICAL
  FAMILY—JUNIUS, EDWIN AND JOHN WILKES BOOTH *
  APRIL '65: CONFEDERATE COVERT ACTION IN THE
  AMERICAN CIVIL WAR * THE ASSASSINATION OF
  LINCOLN: HISTORY AND MYTH*
GENERAL LISTINGS: *Harpers Ferry Raid, 1859,*
  AHI:MAR/84[10]236, *in book review,* ACW:JAN/92[54],
  ACW:JAN/95[62], ACW:SEP/95[62], AHI:MAR/82[49],
  AHI:SEP/87[8], B&G:APR/91[28], CWNEWS:MAY/90[4],
  CWNEWS:OCT/94[33], CWTI:NOV/93[14], *in video review,*
  CWTI:NOV/92[10], *Kate Sprague,* AHI:APR/83[27]233, *letters
  to the editor,* AHI:MAY/86[4], CWTI:FEB/92[8]245,
  CWTI:MAY/92[8]261, CWTI:NOV/92[8]288,
  CWTI:JAN/95[16]421, CWTI:OCT/95[14]465, *who's in his
  grave?* B&G:FEB/95[38]593
PHOTOS: ACW:MAR/93[35]405, AHI:FEB/86[20]258,
  B&G:AUG/95[42]608, CWTI:APR/90[12]15,
  CWTI:DEC/91[28]23, CWTI:JUN/95[26]44,
  CWTI:DEC/95[76]48, *photo of handcuff's,* CWTI:SEP/90[22]17,

photo of weapon used to assassinate Lincoln,
CWTI:AUG/90[42]16

ADDITIONAL LISTINGS, ACW: ACW:MAY/92[14]358,
ACW:JUL/92[62]372, ACW:JAN/94[47]452,
ACW:NOV/94[34]496

ADDITIONAL LISTINGS, AHI: AHI:JAN/85[10]244,
AHI:FEB/86[12]257, AHI:FEB/86[20]258, AHI:SEP/87[40]263,
AHI:NOV/88[37]278, AHI:SEP/87[40]263

ADDITIONAL LISTINGS, B&G: B&G:APR/92[36]483,
B&G:DEC/92[40]508, B&G:JUN/93[40]527,
B&G:APR/95[8]595, B&G:AUG/95[42]608

ADDITIONAL LISTINGS, CWM: CWM:JUL/91[4]354,
CWM:MAY/93[32]477

ADDITIONAL LISTINGS, CWTI: CWTI:FEB/90[60]148,
CWTI:AUG/90[8]165, CWTI:AUG/90[26]166,
CWTI:AUG/90[42]167, CWTI:FEB/91[28]192,
CWTI:AUG/91[68]222, CWTI:SEP/91[8]224,
CWTI:DEC/91[8]234, CWTI:JAN/93[8]296,
CWTI:JAN/93[44]302,
CWTI:MAY/93[29]319, CWTI:AUG/95[46]459,
CWTI:OCT/95[24]466, CWTI:DEC/95[76]482,
CWTI:DEC/95[90]483

ADDITIONAL LISTINGS, MH: MH:FEB/94[8]175, MH:JUN/91[20]152

BOOTH, JUNIUS B., ACW:MAR/93[35]405,
CWTI:NOV/92[8]288, *photo,* ACW:MAR/93[35]405

BOOTH, LIONEL F., *Major, 11th U.S. Colored Troops;*
AHI:APR/74[4]154, CWTI:NOV/93[65]351

BORDERS, EZRA, *Sergeant, 37th Illinois Infantry;*
CWR:VOL1#1[42]105

BORROWE, WILLIAM, *Lieutenant, 96th Pennsylvania
Infantry;* CWR:VOL3#3[1]157

BOSANG, JAMES M., *Captain, 4th Virginia Infantry;*
CWTI:JUL/93[20]325

BOSS,GEORGE W., *Private, 126th New York Infantry;*
CWR:VOL1#4[7]125

BOSTON, REUBEN B., *Colonel, CSA;* ACW:JAN/93[43]397,
B&G:APR/92[8]481, B&G:OCT/93[12]537, MH:OCT/92[51]162

BOSTWICK, RICHARD S., *Colonel, 10th Georgia Infantry:*
ARTICLE: "THE 10TH GEORGIA AND 27TH CONNECTICUT IN
THE WHEATFIELD; TWO CAPTURED SWORDS AGAINST
THEIR FORMER OWNERS," GETTY:12[24]242

ADDITIONAL LISTING: GETTY:12[1]240

BOSWELL, JAMES K., *Captain, CSA;* B&G:AUG/92[11]493,
CWM:MAY/92[34]422, MH:JUN/92[50]159

BOTELER, ALEXANDER R., B&G:AUG/94[10]574,
B&G:JUN/92[8]487, B&G:JUN/95[8]600, GETTY:13[108]261

BOTETOURT (VIRGINIA) ARTILLERY;
ACW:NOV/91[22]331, B&G:FEB/94[57]555

BOTSFORD, E.W., *Captain, 16th Ohio Infantry;*
B&G:FEB/94[8]550

BOTSFORD, J.L., *Private, 1st Ohio Artillery;*
B&G:OCT/95[8]611D

BOTTS, JOHN M., B&G:APR/91[8]445

BOTTS, LAWSON, *Colonel, 2nd Virginia Infantry;*
B&G:AUG/92[11]493, CWM:AUG/95[30]606

BOURNS, JOHN F., *Surgeon, USA;* ACW:JUL/94[18]476

BOUTON, EDWARD, *Colonel, USA;* MH:DEC/95[58]188

BOUTWELL, DAN, *Scout, USA;* B&G:JUN/91[10]452

BOUTWELL, GEORGE B.; AHI:DEC/68[28]118,
AHI:JAN/82[16]224

BOWEN, B.A., *Captain, 13th Alabama Infantry;*
GETTY:6[13]170

BOWEN, GEORGE, *Private, 12th New Jersey Infantry;*
B&G:JUN/95[8]600, GETTY:5[89]162, GETTY:11[102]237,
GETTY:12[97]249

BOWEN, JAMES L., *Private, USA;* GETTY:12[97]249

BOWEN, JOHN S., *General, CSA:*
ARTICLE: "GRANT'S BEACHHEAD FOR THE VICKSBURG
CAMPAIGN: THE BATTLE OF PORT GIBSON, MAY 1,
1863," B&G:FEB/94[8]550

GENERAL LISTINGS: *Champion Hill,* CWTI:MAY/91[24]208, *Grand
Gulf, Mississippi,* MH:JUN/93[82]167, *Grierson's Raid,*
B&G:JUN/93[12]524, *in order of battle,* B&G:FEB/94[8]550,
photos; ACW:NOV/91[22]331, B&G:FEB/94[8]550,
CWR:VOL2#1[36]132, CWTI:MAY/91[24]208

ADDITIONAL LISTINGS: ACW:MAY/91[31]304, ACW:SEP/91[50]325,
ACW:NOV/91[22]331, ACW:MAY/92[47]363,
ACW:JUL/94[51]480,
AHI:DEC/77[13]176, B&G:FEB/94[57]555,
CWR:VOL2#1[i]129, CWR:VOL2#1[36]132,
CWR:VOL3#3[33]158

BOWEN, ROBERT E., *Captain, 6th South Carolina Infantry;*
CWR:VOL3#2[70]155

BOWEN, ROLAND E., *Private, 15th Massachusetts Infantry:*
ARTICLE: "'NOTHING BUT COWARDS RUN,'"
CWM:APR/95[42]577

BOOK REVIEWS: *FROM BALL'S BLUFF TO GETTYSBURG...AND
BEYOND: THE CIVIL WAR LETTERS OF PVT. ROLAND E.
BOWEN, 15TH MASS INF 1861-1864*

ADDITIONAL LISTINGS: GETTY:13[43]256, *photo;*
CWM:APR/95[42]577

BOWEN, SAM; ACW:MAY/91[10]301

BOWERMAN, RICHARD N., *Colonel, USA;* B&G:APR/92[8]481

BOWERS, CHARLES, *Private, Petersburg Artillery;*
ACW:MAR/95[12]513

BOWERS, JOSEPH, *Colonel, USA;* CWM:SEP/92[19]440

BOWERS, THEODORE S., *Colonel, USA;* AHI:SEP/87[48]264

BOWERS, W., *Private, 48th North Carolina Infantry;*
B&G:APR/93[24]520

BOWLER, JAMES M., *Corporal, 3rd Minnesota Infantry;*
ACW:MAY/91[12]302

BOWLES, H.H., *Private, 6th Maine Infantry;*
CWTI:SEP/93[43]338

BOWLES, JOHN S. and MATHEW C., *22nd Virginia Infantry;*
CWR:VOL1#3[52]122

BOWLING GREEN, KENTUCKY, BATTLE OF;
CWTI:FEB/90[26]143

BOWMAN, ALEXANDER H., *Colonel, USA;*
B&G:DEC/91[12]469

BOWMAN, DAVE, *Private, 93rd Pennsylvania Infantry;*
GETTY:11[91]236

BOWMAN, HENRY, *Colonel, USA;* B&G:AUG/95[8]604

BOWMAN, PULASKI, *Lieutenant, 150th New York Infantry;*
GETTY:12[42]244

BOWMAN, SAMUEL, *Major, 4th Illinois Cavalry;*
CWR:VOL4#1[44]164

BOWNE, JOHN S.; CWR:VOL3#3[59]159

BOWSER, MARY E.; ACW:JUL/91[8]309, CWTI:DEC/94[12]408

BOYCE, MRS. W.W.; AHI:DEC/73[10]152

BOYD, BELLE; B&G:DEC/92[40]508, B&G:APR/93[40]522,
CWM:SEP/93[18]494, CWM:SEP/93[24]495,

BOYD, CARLILE, *Captain, 5th New York Infantry;*
CWR:VOL1#2[7]111, CWR:VOL1#2[29]112,

BOYD, DAVID F., *Major, CSA;* CWTI:MAR/94[48]374

BOYD, JOSEPH F., *Lieutenant Colonel, USA;*
AHI:NOV/85[38]254

BOYD, SAMUEL H., *Lieutenant Colonel, 45th North Carolina Infantry;* GETTY:4[33]146

BOYD, THOMAS B., *Captain, CSA;* B&G:OCT/94[11]580

BOYDON, G.M., *civilian;* B&G:APR/93[24]520,
CWTI:JAN/95[48]429

BOYDTON PLANK ROAD, VIRGINIA, BATTLE OF; see listings under **"HATCHER'S RUN, VIRGINIA, BATTLE OF"**

BOYER, BENJAMIN M.; CWTI:DEC/95[24]477

BOYER, JOSEPH, *Captain, USA;* ACW:NOV/95[48]557

BOYER, ZACCUR P., *Lieutenant, 96th Pennsylvania Infantry;* CWR:VOL3#3[1]157

BOYLE, J.R., *Lieutenant, 12th South Carolina Infantry;* GETTY:13[22]254

BOYLE, JEREMIAH T., *General, USA;* AHI:NOV/72[12]142,
CWM:NOV/91[58]394A

BOYLE, JOHN A., *Major, 111th Pennsylvania Infantry;*
CWR:VOL3#2[70]155, GETTY:10[120]229

BOYLE, PETER, *Private, 9th Massachusetts Infantry;*
CWTI:JUN/90[28]158

BOYLE, WILLIAM, *Colonel, USA;* B&G:AUG/91[11]458

BRABBLE, EDMUND C., *Colonel, 32nd North Carolina Infantry;* GETTY:4[33]146, GETTY:9[81]216,
GETTY:13[33]255

BRACKEN, PETER, *civilian;* ACW:SEP/91[22]321

BRACKLIN, CHARLES L., *Private, 2nd Kentucky Cavalry;*
CWM:MAR/93[16]466

BRADFORD, C.H., *Lieutenant, USMC;* CWR:VOL2#3[194]141

BRADFORD, J.L., *Captain, 1st Mississippi Artillery;*
ACW:JAN/94[30]450

BRADFORD, LUTHER, *Private, 16th Maine Infantry;*
GETTY:13[33]255

BRADFORD, NERO G., *Captain, 26th North Carolina Infantry;*
GETTY:12[1]240, GETTY:12[111]250

BRADFORD, SILAS P., *Captain, 25th Alabama Infantry;*
CWTI:DEC/90[56]184

BRADFORD, WILLIAM F., *Major, USA;* AHI:APR/74[4]154,
CWTI:NOV/93[65]351

BRADLEY, DAN, *Lieutenant Colonel, 20th Illinois Infantry;*
CWTI:JAN/93[20]298

BRADLEY, EDWIN D., *Colonel, 38th Ohio Infantry;*
B&G:FEB/93[12]511

BRADLEY, HUGH, *Corporal, 69th Pennsylvania Infantry;*
GETTY:4[89]150

BRADLEY, J., *Private, 15th Massachusetts Infantry;*
CWTI:SEP/90[26]174

BRADLEY, JOSEPH, *Captain, 5th New York Infantry;*
CWTI:MAY/94[31]382

BRADLEY, L.D., *Captain, CSA;* CWR:VOL2#1[19]131

BRADWELL, I.G., *Private, CSA;* CWTI:JAN/93[40]301

BRADY, ALLEN, *Major, 17th Connecticut Infantry;*
CWNEWS:JUN/94[5]

BRADY, ANDREW, *Major, 15th Louisiana Infantry;*
CWM:MAR/91[17]335

BRADY, EUGENE, *Lieutenant, 116th Pennsylvania Infantry;*
CWM:MAR/91[17]335

BRADY, JAMES T., *Attorney;* ACW:SEP/94[46]488

BRADY, MATHEW B.:
ARTICLES: "EDITORIAL," ACW:JAN/92[6]337, "GENERAL GRANT IS NEARLY KILLED AT THE BRADY STUDIO,"
B&G:FEB/94[32]552, "MATHEW B. BRADY: A MAN WITH A VISION," B&G:FEB/94[24]551
BOOK REVIEW: *MATHEW BRADY: HIS LIFE AND PHOTOGRAPHS*
GENERAL LISTINGS: *in book review,* ACW:JAN/92[54],
CWM:MAY/91[34], CWNEWS:MAY/92[4], *photos;*
ACW:NOV/95[54]558, AHI:SEP/89[20]286,
B&G:FEB/94[24]551
ADDITIONAL LISTINGS: AHI:SEP/89[20]286, AHI:NOV/69[13]124,
ACW:NOV/95[54]558, B&G:OCT/92[38]500,
CWTI:DEC/89[26]135, CWTI:FEB/90[38]145,
CWTI:AUG/90[42]167, CWTI:MAR/91[22]199,
CWTI:MAY/91[34]209, CWTI:FEB/92[21]247

BRADY, PATRICK, *Private, 5th New York Infantry;*
CWR:VOL1#2[29]112

BRADY, PETER R., *civilian;* ACW:JUL/93[27]423

BRADY, THOMAS M., *Chaplain, 15th Michigan Infantry;*
CWM:MAR/91[50]340

BRAINARD, HENRY C., *Captain, 15th Alabama Infantry;*
ACW:JAN/92[38]343

BRAGG, BRAXTON, *General, CSA:*
ARTICLES: "A CONVERSATION WITH PETER COZZENS, THE LAST HURRAH: BRAGG AND CHATTANOOGA,"
CWM:APR/95[16]571, "A FEW ARE HOLDING OUT UP YONDER," CWTI:SEP/92[31]281, "A WADE IN THE HIGH TIDE AT PERRYVILLE," CWTI:NOV/92[18]289, "CROSSING THE LINE: BRAGG VS MORGAN," CWM:MAR/93[16]466,
"THE DECEPTION OF BRAXTON BRAGG: THE TULLAHOMA CAMPAIGN, JUNE 23 - JULY 4, 1863,"
B&G:OCT/92[10]496, "MIRACLE OF THE RAILS,"
CWTI:SEP/92[22]279, "MOST SPLENDID PIECE OF STRATEGY," CWM:OCT/94[48]542, "TIME LAPSE,"
CWTI:MAR/89[34]104, "TO SAVE AN ARMY,"
CWTI:SEP/94[40]403
BOOK REVIEWS: *BRAXTON BRAGG AND CONFEDERATE DEFEAT, VOLUME II * JEFFERSON DAVIS AND HIS GENERALS: THE FAILURE OF CONFEDERATE COMMAND IN THE WEST * MOUNTAINS TOUCHED BY FIRE: CHATTANOOGA BESIEGED, 1863 * THE SHIPWRECK OF THEIR HOPES: THE BATTLE FOR CHATTANOOGA * THIS TERRIBLE SOUND: THE BATTLE OF CHICKAMAUGA*
GENERAL LISTINGS: *Atlanta Campaign,*
CWTI:SUMMER/89[13]120, *Beauregard,*
CWTI:JUL/92[29]272, *Bentonville,* CWR:VOL4#3[65]172,
Chattanooga, ACW:NOV/95[6]551, *Chickamauga,*
ACW:MAR/94[42]461, CWTI:MAR/93[24]309,
CWTI:SEP/93[53]344, CWTI:NOV/93[33]347, *Cumberland Gap,* ACW:JUL/91[26]313, *Davis,* CWTI:AUG/91[36]217,
CWTI:AUG/91[52]219, CWTI:AUG/91[62]221, *Forrest,*
CWM:DEC/95[48]631, *Fort Pickens,* CWR:VOL1#4[42]126,
general history, AHI:MAY/71[3]133A
GENERAL LISTINGS, continued: *in book review,* ACW:MAR/91[54],
ACW:MAY/93[54], ACW:JUL/94[58], ACW:SEP/94[66],
ACW:NOV/93[58], ACW:MAR/95[58], ACW:SEP/95[62],
B&G:FEB/95[26], B&G:AUG/95[38], B&G:DEC/95[30],
CWM:JAN/91[47], CWM:DEC/94[7], CWM:APR/95[8],
CWM:APR/95[50], CWM:AUG/95[45], CWM:OCT/95[10],
CWNEWS:OCT/89[4], CWNEWS:APR/90[4],
CWNEWS:DEC/93[5], CWR:VOL1#2[78], CWR:VOL1#4[77],
CWR:VOL2#1[78], CWR:VOL2#2[169], CWR:VOL2#4[346],
CWR:VOL3#1[80], CWR:VOL4#1[78], CWR:VOL4#2[136],
CWR:VOL4#3[89], CWR:VOL4#4[129], MH:DEC/92[74]

GENERAL LISTINGS, continued: *Kentucky invasion,*
CWTI:JUL/94[50]395, *Lookout Mountain,*
CWTI:SEPT/89[30]129 *Mexican War,* AHI:OCT/82[28]230,
AHI:MAY/88[38]270, MH:APR/93[39]166, *Morgan,*
CWM:JAN/93[29]459, *order of battle,* B&G:DEC/95[9]615,
Price's 1864 Missouri Campaign, B&G:JUN/91[10]452,
Ringgold Gap, ACW:NOV/93[34]442, *Shiloh,*
ACW:JAN/91[22]285, *West Point,* B&G:DEC/91[12]469
PHOTOS: AHI:MAY/71[3]133A, AHI:NOV/73[18]151,
B&G:OCT/92[10]496, B&G:DEC/94[10]585,
B&G:DEC/95[9]615, CWM:MAR/93[16]466,
CWM:OCT/94[48]542, CWTI:APR/89[14]107
ADDITIONAL LISTINGS, ACW: ACW:MAR/91[14]293,
ACW:MAR/91[30]295, ACW:MAY/91[23]303,
ACW:JUL/91[12]310, ACW:SEP/91[46]324,
ACW:NOV/91[6]327, ACW:MAY/92[47]363,
ACW:MAY/92[62]364, ACW:SEP/92[38]379,
ACW:SEP/93[10]430, ACW:NOV/93[42]443,
ACW:MAY/94[35]469, ACW:JUL/94[66]481,
ACW:SEP/94[74]491, ACW:JAN/95[30]505,
ACW:JUL/95[10]533, ACW:SEP/95[8]542,
ACW:SEP/95[22]544, ACW:NOV/95[66]559
ADDITIONAL LISTINGS, AHI: AHI:NOV/73[18]151,
AHI:OCT/95[24]326
ADDITIONAL LISTINGS, B&G: B&G:AUG/91[32]461,
B&G:OCT/91[11]466, B&G:DEC/91[34]470,
B&G:FEB/93[48]515, B&G:JUN/93[32]525,
B&G:OCT/93[31]539, B&G:DEC/93[12]545,
B&G:OCT/94[11]580, B&G:DEC/94[10]585,
B&G:FEB/95[35]592, B&G:JUN/95[22]601,
B&G:AUG/95[8]604, B&G:DEC/95[25]616
ADDITIONAL LISTINGS, CWM: CWM:JAN/91[28]327,
CWM:JAN/91[40]330, CWM:MAR/91[28]336,
CWM:MAR/91[50]340, CWM:NOV/91[50]394,
CWM:JUL/92[24]430, CWM:JUL/92[40]432,
CWM:MAR/93[8]465, CWM:AUG/94[52]530,
CWM:DEC/94[46]552, CWM:FEB/95[28]560,
CWM:OCT/95[47]620, CWM:DEC/95[35]629
ADDITIONAL LISTINGS, CWR: CWR:VOL1#1[71]107,
CWR:VOL1#2[44]114, CWR:VOL1#4[64]127,
CWR:VOL1#4[74]128, CWR:VOL2#1[1]130,
CWR:VOL2#1[36]132, CWR:VOL2#4[313]14,
CWR:VOL3#2[70]155, CWR:VOL3#3[33]158,
CWR:VOL3#3[59]159, CWR:VOL4#1[1]163,
CWR:VOL4#1[44]164, CWR:VOL4#2[68]167,
CWR:VOL4#3[50]171
ADDITIONAL LISTINGS, CWTI: CWTI:APR/89[14]10,
CWTI:SUMMER/89[20]121 CWTI:FEB/90[38]145,
CWTI:FEB/91[36]193, CWTI:SEP/91[31]229,
CWTI:APR/92[49]260, CWTI:MAY/92[45]266,
CWTI:MAY/92[48]267, CWTI:JUL/92[29]272,
CWTI:MAR/93[24]309, CWTI:MAR/93[40]312,
CWTI:MAR/93[50]313, CWTI:NOV/93[33]347,
CWTI:JAN/94[35]361, CWTI:MAY/94[50]386,
CWTI:JUL/94[44]394, CWTI:JAN/95[27]425,
CWTI:JAN/95[34]427, CWTI:AUG/95[28]456
ADDITIONAL LISTINGS, MH: MH:JUN/91[20]152, MH:JUN/93[82]167,
MH:OCT/94[20]180
BRAGG, MRS. BRAXTON; AHI:DEC/73[10]152
BRAGG, EDWARD, *General, USA;* ACW:JUL/92[30]369,
B&G:APR/93[12]518, B&G:APR/94[10]558,
CWM:FEB/95[30]561
BRAGGON, JOHN, *Colonel, CSA;* B&G:JUN/95[8]600

BRAINERD, THOMAS, *Private, 14th Connecticut Infantry;*
GETTY:9[61]215
BRAINERD, WESLEY, *Captain, 50th New York Engineers;*
ACW:NOV/95[10]553
BRANCH (NORTH CAROLINA) ARTILLERY;
GETTY:5[47]160
BRANCH, DAVID T., *4th Ohio Infantry;* GETTY:10[53]225
BRANCH, JOHN L., *Adjutant, 8th Georgia Infantry;*
B&G:APR/91[32]447
BRANCH, LAWRENCE O'BRYAN, *General, CSA:*
ARTICLE: "THE PENINSULA CAMPAIGN OF 1862: THE
BATTLE OF SLASH CHURCH," CWM:JUN/95[43]587
ADDITIONAL LISTINGS: B&G:AUG/92[11]493, B&G:JUN/93[40]527,
B&G:OCT/95[8]611A, CWR:VOL1#3[52]122, CWR:VOL3#1[80]
BRANCH, SANFORD, *Lieutenant, 8th Georgia Infantry;*
GETTY:12[1]240, GETTY:12[111]250
BRANCH, W.B., *Mayor of Lynchburg, Virginia;*
CWTI:MAY/89[14]11
BRANDER, T.A., *Captain, Letcher Artillery;* GETTY:4[33]146
BRANDES, GEORGE, *Private, USA;* ACW:JUL/93[27]423
BRANDON, LANE, *Lieutenant, 20th Massachusetts Infantry;*
CWR:VOL3#1[31]150, CWR:VOL4#4[101]181
BRANDY STATION, VIRGINIA, BATTLE OF:
ARTICLE: "A NEW BATTLE FLARES AT BRANDY STATION,"
CWTI:JUN/90[43]16, "BATTLE OF BRANDY STATION,"
CWTI:JUN/90[32]15, "DISASTER AT BRANDY STATION,"
B&G:APR/94[35]562, "MORE TROUBLE AT BRANDY
STATION," B&G:DEC/93[31]547, "SHELLS AND SABER
POINTS," MH:OCT/92[51]162
GENERAL LISTINGS: *general history,* AHI:MAY/71[3]133A, *in book
review,* CWR:VOL1#2[78], *letters to the editor,*
B&G:FEB/91[6]438, B&G:JUN/91[6]451
ADDITIONAL LISTINGS: ACW:SEP/94[55]489, B&G:APR/91[8]445,
B&G:DEC/91[34]470, B&G:OCT/92[38]500,
B&G:OCT/93[12]537, B&G:OCT/93[21]538,
B&G:OCT/93[49]543, B&G:DEC/93[30]546,
B&G:FEB/95[8]590A, CWM:MAR/91[80]343,
CWR:VOL3#1[31]150, CWTI:DEC/89[34]13,
CWTI:FEB/91[12]18, CWTI:FEB/91[66]19,
CWTI:APR/92[35]25, CWTI:JAN/94[42]36,
CWTI:MAR/94[67]37, GETTY:11[19]232, GETTY:12[68]246,
MH:OCT/93[6]170
BRANHAM, BENJAMIN F., *Private, 7th Wisconsin Infantry,*
GETTY:11[57]233
BRANNAN, JOHN M., *General, USA;* ACW:NOV/94[58]499,
CWTI:SEPT/89[30]129, CWTI:SEP/92[31]28
BRANNER, BENJAMIN M., *Lieutenant Colonel, 1st Tennessee
Cavalry Battalion;* B&G:FEB/93[12]511, CWR:VOL4#1[1]163
BRANSFORD, J., *Private, 22nd Battalion Virginia Infantry;*
CWR:VOL1#3[52]122
BRANSON, DAVID, *Lieutenant Colonel, 62nd USCT;*
CWTI:AUG/90[58]16
BRANTLEY, WILLIAM F., *General, CSA;*
B&G:DEC/93[12]545, CWTI:SUMMER/89[40]123
BRATTON, JOHN, *General, CSA;* ACW:MAY/92[30]361,
ACW:JUL/94[42]479, B&G:APR/94[10]558,
B&G:JUN/95[8]600, CWM:JUL/92[16]428,
CWM:OCT/94[34]538, CWR:VOL3#2[70]155,
CWR:VOL3#2[102]156
BRAUN, GUSTAVOUS, *Captain, 112th Pennsylvania Infantry;*
B&G:APR/95[24]596

BRAWNER FARM, VIRGINIA, BATTLE OF:
ARTICLE: "STANDOFF AT BRAWNER'S FARM,"
CWM:AUG/95[30]606
ADDITIONAL LISTINGS: ACW:JUL/91[18]312, B&G:AUG/92[11]493,
B&G:OCT/94[42]583, CWM:JAN/93[16]457,
CWR:VOL2#4[269]145, CWTI:DEC/91[36]240,
CWTI:NOV/93[78]354, GETTY:13[119]262
BRAWNER, WILLIAM G., *Captain, 6th Michigan Cavalry;*
CWTI:SEP/90[34]17
BRAXTON, CARTER M., *Lieutenant Colonel, Fredericksburg
Artillery;* B&G:APR/95[8]595, CWR:VOL1#1[1]102,
CWR:VOL4#4[70]180
BRAY, JOHN B., *Captain, CSA;* CWR:VOL1#4[42]126
BRAZIL CONFEDERATES, ARTICLE: "OS CONFEDERADOS,"
CWTI:JAN/93[26]29
BREAD RIOTS, RICHMOND (1863), ACW:MAY/92[39]362,
ACW:JAN/93[18]394
BREAKEY, WILLIAM F., *Surgeon, 16th Michigan Infantry;*
CWR:VOL1#2[29]112
BREATHED, JAMES, *Major, CSA;* ACW:MAY/91[38]305,
ACW:NOV/92[26]386, ACW:JUL/95[34]536,
B&G:DEC/91[34]470, B&G:OCT/93[12]537,
B&G:APR/95[8]595, CWM:JUN/95[50]589,
CWR:VOL4#4[70]180, GETTY:13[89]260
BRECK, GEORGE, *Lieutenant, 1st New York Artillery;*
GETTY:5[117]165, GETTY:12[30]243, GETTY:13[22]254
BRECK, JOHN M., *Mayor, Portland, Oregon;*
CWTI:AUG/95[54]46
BRECKINRIDGE, JAMES, *Captain, 2nd Virginia Cavalry;*
ACW:NOV/91[30]332, B&G:APR/92[8]481
BRECKENRIDGE, JOHN C., *General, CSA:*
ARTICLES: "FORGOTTEN MEN," AHI:DEC/74[12]156, "ORPHAN
BRIGADE," ACW:JUL/91[12]310
BOOK REVIEWS: *BRECKINRIDGE: STATESMAN, SOLDIER,
SYMBOL * THE ORPHAN BRIGADE*
GENERAL LISTINGS: *Confederate exiles,* AHI:JUN/70[30]127, *Davis,*
CWTI:AUG/91[36]217, *escape from Florida,*
ACW:NOV/95[38]556, *general history,* AHI:MAY/71[3]133A, *in
book review,* ACW:MAR/91[54], CWM:NOV/92[55],
CWM:APR/95[50], CWR:VOL4#3[89], *in list,*
B&G:AUG/91[11]458, *Jackson,* B&G:AUG/95[8]604,
Johnston's surrender, CWTI:AUG/90[42]167, *Kernstown, 1864,*
B&G:AUG/94[10]574, *letters to the editor,* B&G:JUN/95[5]599
GENERAL LISTINGS, Continued: *Missionary Ridge,*
CWTI:SEP/94[40]403, *Monocacy,* B&G:DEC/92[8]503, *order of
battle,* B&G:APR/94[10]558, B&G:AUG/95[8]604, *Overland
Campaign,* B&G:APR/94[10]558, *Port Hudson,*
MH:AUG/94[82]179, *Richmond, Fall of,* CWTI:AUG/90[26]166,
Saltville, B&G:AUG/91[52]464, *Shiloh,* ACW:JAN/91[22]285,
Tullahoma Campaign, B&G:OCT/92[10]496, *Vicksburg,*
CWTI:SEPT/89[18]126, *Winchester, Third,*
ACW:MAY/91[38]305, AHI:NOV/80[8]209,
PHOTOS: AHI:JUN/70[30]127, AHI:JUN/73[4]149,
AHI:DEC/74[12]156, AHI:NOV/80[8]209,
B&G:AUG/91[11]458, B&G:DEC/92[8]503,
B&G:AUG/95[8]604, CWM:FEB/95[28]560
ADDITIONAL LISTINGS, ACW: ACW:MAY/92[62]364,
ACW:JUL/92[22]368, ACW:SEP/92[38]379,
ACW:NOV/92[35]387, ACW:JAN/93[43]397,
ACW:MAR/93[55]408, ACW:MAY/93[47]417,
ACW:MAY/93[62]418, ACW:JUL/93[10]421,
ACW:SEP/93[62]436, ACW:NOV/93[50]444,
ACW:MAR/94[27]459, ACW:MAY/94[43]470,

ACW:MAR/95[8]512, ACW:MAY/95[38]526,
ACW:NOV/95[66]559
ADDITIONAL LISTINGS, AHI: AHI:JUN/73[4]149, AHI:NOV/84[18]241
ADDITIONAL LISTINGS, B&G: B&G:AUG/91[11]458,
B&G:APR/93[12]518, B&G:AUG/94[19]575,
B&G:OCT/94[11]580, B&G:DEC/95[9]615
ADDITIONAL LISTINGS, CWM: CWM:MAR/91[56]341,
CWM:NOV/92[41]451, CWM:JAN/93[40]461,
CWM:JUN/94[27]513, CWM:FEB/95[28]560,
CWM:APR/95[16]571
ADDITIONAL LISTINGS, CWR: CWR:VOL1#3[7]118,
CWR:VOL2#1[36]132, CWR:VOL3#1[65]151,
CWR:VOL3#2[1]153, CWR:VOL3#2[61]154,
CWR:VOL3#3[33]158, CWR:VOL3#4[1]161,
CWR:VOL4#1[44]164
ADDITIONAL LISTINGS, CWTI: CWTI:APR/90[20]151,
CWTI:AUG/90[50]168, CWTI:APR/92[49]260,
CWTI:JAN/93[40]301, CWTI:JAN/94[46]364,
CWTI:SEP/94[40]403, CWTI:AUG/95[34]457
BRECKINRIDGE, JOSEPH C.; B&G:JUN/95[36]603
BRECKINRIDGE, LUCY; BOOK REVIEW: *LUCY
BRECKINRIDGE OF GROVE HILL: THE JOURNAL OF A
VIRGINIA GIRL, 1862-1864*
BRECKINRIDGE, ROBERT J., *civilian;* ACW:MAR/93[55]408,
ACW:MAR/95[8]512, B&G:FEB/93[12]511
BRECKINRIDGE, WILLIAM C.P., *Colonel, CSA;*
B&G:AUG/91[11]458, B&G:DEC/95[9]615
BREEDLOVE, JONATHON P., *Lieutenant, 4th Alabama
Infantry;* GETTY:12[1]240, GETTY:12[111]250
BREESE, K. RANDOLPH, *Captain, USN;* B&G:DEC/94[10]585
BREESE, W.B., *Lieutenant, USMC;* CWR:VOL2#3[194]141
BREHM, CHARLES E., *Private, 5th New York Infantry;*
CWR:VOL1#2[29]112
BRENNER, EDWARD F., *Lieutenant, 4th U.S. Infantry;*
B&G:APR/95[24]596
BRENT, GEORGE W., *Colonel, CSA;* CWTI:MAR/93[40]312,
BRENT, JOSEPH L., *Colonel, CSA;* ACW:JUL/93[34]424,
CWR:VOL4#2[118]169
BRESHWOOD, JOHN G., *Lieutenant, USN;*
ACW:MAR/94[35]460
BRETT, DAVID, *Private, 9th Massachusetts Artillery;*
GETTY:5[47]160
BRETT, MARVIN W., *Private, 12th Georgia Infantry;*
ACW:MAR/94[16]458
BREVARD, THEODORE W., *Lieutenant Colonel, 2nd Florida
Battalion;* CWR:VOL3#4[1]161
BREVET PROMOTION SYSTEM; ARTICLE: "A PROBLEM OF
RANK," CWTI:FEB/91[52]195
BREWER, CHARLES, *Surgeon;* ACW:MAY/94[35]469
BREWER, RICHARD H., *Lieutenant Colonel, CSA;*
CWR:VOL4#1[44]164
BREWER, W.S., *Captain, 26th North Carolina Infantry;*
GETTY:5[19]158
BREWSTER, CHARLES H., *Private, 10th Massachusetts
Infantry;* BOOK REVIEWS: *WHEN THIS CRUEL WAR IS OVER:
THE CIVIL WAR LETTERS OF CHARLES HARVEY
BREWSTER*
BREWSTER, WALTER, *Captain, CSA;* CWR:VOL4#4[28]178
BREWSTER, WILLIAM R., *General, USA;*
B&G:APR/94[10]558, B&G:APR/95[8]595,
CWM:MAY/92[20]420, GETTY:8[31]201
BRIANT, CYRUS E., *Lieutenant Colonel, USA;*
B&G:DEC/95[9]615

BRICE'S CROSS ROADS, MISSISSIPPI, BATTLE OF:
ARTICLE: "A CIVILIAN AT BRICE'S CROSS ROADS,"
CWTI:JAN/94[39]362
ADDITIONAL LISTINGS: ACW:JAN/91[16]284, ACW:SEP/92[23]377,
ACW:JUL/95[70]540, AHI:MAY/71[3]133A,
B&G:JUN/91[26]453, B&G:AUG/94[38]578,
CWM:SEP/92[8]437, CWM:OCT/94[8], CWR:VOL2#4[313]146,
CWTI:MAY/93[48]267, CWTI:JAN/94[35]361,
MH:FEB/95[18]182
BRIDEN, D.F., *Private, CSA;* B&G:OCT/91[11]466
BRIDGE BUILDING, ARTICLE: "THE 50TH NEW YORK
ENGINEERS WERE INVALUABLE BRIDGE BUILDERS
DURING THE VARIOUS CAMPAIGNS AGAINST LEE,"
ACW:NOV/95[10]553, "THE DELICATE AND DANGEROUS
WORK OF PLACING PONTOON BRIDGES FELL TO THE
CORPS OF ENGINEERS," ACW:MAY/93[8]411
BRIDGE, N.A., *Captain, 1st Texas Cavalry Battalion;*
ACW:MAR/93[68]409
BRIDGEFORD, DAVID B., *Captain, CSA;*
CWM:MAR/91[65]342
BRIDGEPORT, ALABAMA, CWTI:FEB/90[46]146
BRIDGES, DILLON, *Captain, 13th Indiana Cavalry;*
CWTI:MAR/91[46]203
BRIDGES, R.C., *Private, 11th Mississippi Infantry;*
CWR:VOL2#4[269]145
BRIDGFORD, DAVID B., *Major, 1st Virginia Battalion;*
CWM:MAR/91[65]342
BRIDGMAN, JOHN M., *Captain, 1st Tennessee Cavalry;*
CWR:VOL4#1[1]163
BRIEN, L.T., *Colonel, CSA;* B&G:OCT/92[38]500,
BRIGGS, EPHRAIM; *Lieutenant, USA;* GETTY:4[101]151
BRIGGS, JONATHON, *Private, 24th Michigan Infantry;*
GETTY:9[33]211, GETTY:11[57]233
BRIGGS, LOUISIANA R., *civilian;* B&G:OCT/91[11]466
BRIGGS, R., *Private, 31st North Carolina Infantry;*
B&G:APR/93[24]520
BRIGGS, WELLS, *Private, 95th Illinois Infantry;*
ACW:JAN/91[16]284
BRIGHAM, JOHN A.; ACW:JUL/92[22]368
BRIGHT, J.W., *Sergeant, 26th Virginia Infantry;*
B&G:APR/93[24]520
BRIGHT, JESSE D., *Senator, Indiana;* AHI:JUN/73[4]149,
CWTI:AUG/95[54]460
BRIGHT, ROBERT A., *Captain, CSA;* GETTY:13[75]259
BRIGHTLY, CHARLES H., *Captain, USA;* B&G:DEC/91[12]469
BRIGHURST, W.R., *Private, 71st Ohio Infantry;*
CWTI:JUL/92[42]274
BRINGHURST, GEORGE, *Reverand, U.S. Christian
Commission;* GETTY:10[53]225
BRINGHURST, THOMAS H., *Colonel, 46th Indiana Infantry;*
B&G:FEB/94[8]550
BRINGIER, AMEDEE, *Lieutenant Colonel, 7th Louisiana
Cavalry;* CWR:VOL4#2[118]169
BRINGIER, LOUIS A., *Lieutenant Colonel, 10th Louisiana
Infantry Battalion;* CWR:VOL3#1[1]149
BRINKLEY, W.D.C., *Private, Sumter Artillery;*
WR:VOL3#2[1]153
BRINKMAN, HENRY C., *Lieutenant, 5th Ohio Infantry;*
GETTY:9[81]216
BRINTON, JEREMIAH B., *surgeon;* GETTY:10[53]225
BRINTON, JOHN H., *Major, 27th Illinois Infantry;*
CWM:MAY/91[10]347, CWR:VOL3#4[24]162,

CWTI:APR/92[49]260, CWTI:JUL/92[36]273, *photo;*
CWTI:JUL/92[36]273
BRISBAIN, WILLIAM H., *Chaplain, 2nd Wisconsin Cavalry;*
CWTI:MAY/93[35]320
BRISCOE, F.D.; GETTY:8[43]202
BRISCOE, THOMAS, *Private, 5th New York Infantry;*
CWR:VOL1#2[29]112
BRISCOE, W.S.; ACW:JAN/94[18]449
BRISTOE STATION, VIRGINIA, EVENTS AT:
ARTICLE: "DEATH OF ANOTHER GENERAL,"
CWM:DEC/95[34]628
ADDITIONAL LISTINGS: ACW:JUL/91[18]312, ACW:JUL/92[41]370,
ACW:MAR/93[26]404, ACW:JAN/94[62], ACW:SEP/94[38]487,
ACW:SEP/94[55]489, AHI:DEC/66[30]105,
B&G:AUG/91[30]460, B&G:DEC/91[34]470,
B&G:JUN/92[8]487, B&G:AUG/92[11]493, CWM:OCT/94[8],
CWR:VOL1#1[1]102, CWR:VOL1#3[52]122, CWR:VOL1#4[77],
CWR:VOL3#3[1]157, CWTI:SEP/91[31]229,
CWTI:NOV/93[55]350
BRISTOW, BENJAMIN; AHI:MAY/69[32]122
BRITTON'S LANE, TENNESSEE, BATTLE OF; ARTICLE:
"THE BATTLE OF BRITTON'S LANE: THE CLIMAX OF
ARMSTRONG'S RAID," B&G:APR/93[34]521
BRITTON, WILEY, *Sergeant, CSA;* ACW:JAN/91[30]286
BROADFOOT, CHARLES, *Colonel, CSA;* B&G:DEC/95[9]615
BROADHEAD, SALLIE, *civilian;* GETTY:11[102]237
BROADHEAD, SARAH M., *civilian:*
BOOK REVIEW: *THE DIARY OF A LADY OF GETTYSBURG,
PENNSYLVANIA*
ADDITIONAL LISTINGS: CWM:DEC/95[54]632,GETTY:7[13]186
BROATCH, JOHN, *Captain, 14th Connecticut Infantry;*
GETTY:9[61]215
BROCK, SALLIE; CWTI:AUG/90[26]166
BROCKENBROUGH, JOHN B., *Captain, CSA;*
ACW:MAR/95[42]517, CWR:VOL1#1[1]102,
CWR:VOL4#4[70]180
BROCKENBROUGH, JOHN M., *Colonel, CSA:*
GENERAL LISTINGS: *Falling Waters,* GETTY:9[109]218, *Gettysburg,*
GETTY:5[4]156, GETTY:5[103]163, GETTY:6[13]170,
GETTY:8[67]204, GETTY:8[95]205, GETTY:11[19]232,
GETTY:12[61]245, *in book review,* ACW:JAN/95[62],
CWR:VOL4#2[136], *in list,* CWTI:JUL/93[34]327, *letters to the
editor,* CWTI:DEC/94[12]408, *photo;* CWR:VOL1#3[52]122
ADDITIONAL LISTINGS: CWM:OCT/95[38]618, CWR:VOL1#1[26]103,
CWR:VOL2#4[269]145, CWR:VOL4#2[136],
CWR:VOL4#4[70]180, CWTI:APR/90[46]153,
CWTI:JUL/94[44]394, GETTY:9[109]218, GETTY:13[75]259
BROCKWAY, CHARLES F., *Lt., 1st PA. Arty;* GETTY:12[30]243
BROCKWAY, FRANK, *Private, 1st Pennsylvania Artillery;*
GETTY:12[1]240, GETTY:12[30]243
BROCKWAY, GREEN B., *Private, 1st Ohio Artillery;*
GETTY:4[49]147
BRODRICK, VIRGIL, *Colonel, 1st New Jersey Cavalry;*
B&G:DEC/91[34]470
BROMWELL, WILLIAM J.; ACW:MAY/93[62]418
BROOKE'S VIRGINIA BATTERY; ACW:MAY/95[30]525
BROOKE, JOHN M., *Lieutenant, CSN;* CWM:SEP/91[24]381,
CWM:JUL/93[15]484
BROOKE, JOHN R., *Colonel, 53rd Pennsylvania Infantry:*
GENERAL LISTINGS: *Cold Harbor,* B&G:APR/94[10]558, *Gettysburg,*
GETTY:5[35]159, GETTY:8[53]203, GETTY:10[53]225,
GETTY:11[80]235, GETTY:12[1]240, GETTY:12[24]242, *in*

order of battle, B&G:APR/94[10]558, *order of battle,*
B&G:APR/95[8]595

ADDITIONAL LISTINGS: ACW:MAY/93[31]415, CWTI:AUG/95[24]455

BROOKE-RAWLE, WILLIAM, *Lieutenant, 3rd Pennsylvania
Cavalry:*

ARTICLE: "'GLORY ENOUGH FOR ALL': LIEUTENANT
WILLIAM BROOKE-RAWLE AND THE 3RD
PENNSYLVANIA CAVALRY AT GETTYSBURG,"
GETTY:13[89]260

ADDITIONAL LISTINGS: GETTY:4[75]149, GETTY:12[68]246,
GETTY:13[1]252, *photo;* GETTY:13[89]260

BROOKLYN, NEW YORK; BOOK REVIEW: *PRESIDENT
LINCOLN'S THIRD LARGEST CITY, BROOKLYN AND THE
CIVIL WAR*

BROOKS (SOUTH CAROLINA) ARTILLERY;
GETTY:5[47]160

BROOKS' FOREIGN BATTALION; B&G:FEB/91[8]439

BROOKS, EDWARD J., *Lieutenant, USA;* ACW:JUL/93[27]423

BROOKS, JAMES; AHI:DEC/81[18]223

BROOKS, JAMES M., *Sergeant, 22nd Virginia Infantry;*
CWR:VOL1#3[52]122

BROOKS, JOHN W., *Captain, CSA;* B&G:DEC/95[9]615

BROOKS, NOAH; CWTI:AUG/90[26]166, CWTI:FEB/92[21]247

BROOKS, PRESTON; CWNEWS:SEP/95[33]

BROOKS, T.B., *Major, USA;* CWTI:JAN/93[49]303

BROOKS, ULYSSES R., *Private, 6th South Carolina Cavalry;*
BOOK REVIEWS: *BUTLER AND HIS CAVALRY IN THE WAR
OF SECESSION 1861-1865*

BROOKS, W.H., *Colonel, 34th Arkansas Infantry;*
ACW:MAY/93[22]414

BROOKS, WILLIAM, *Captain, 20th North Carolina Infantry;*
B&G:FEB/95[8]590B

BROOKS, WILLIAM T.H., *General, USA;* ACW:SEP/92[30]378,
ACW:JAN/94[8]447, B&G:APR/94[10]558,
B&G:DEC/95[5]614A, CWM:JUN/95[29]583,
CWM:JUN/95[65]595, CWR:VOL3#3[1]157,
CWTI:MAY/89[36]118, *photos;* ACW:JAN/94[8]447,
B&G:DEC/95[5]614A

BROTHERS AT WAR, ARTICLE: "THE BROTHERS' WAR,"
ACW:MAR/93[55]408

BROUGHTON, E.T., *Captain, CSA;* B&G:DEC/93[12]545

BROUGHTON, GASTON, *Lieutenant, 26th North Carolina
Infantry;* GETTY:8[67]204, GETTY:12[61]245

BROUGHTON, WILLIAM H., *Captain, 16th Maine Infantry;*
CWM:MAY/92[15]419

BROUN, THOMAS L., *Captain, CSA;* B&G:AUG/93[10]529

BROUN, WILLIAM LE ROY, *Colonel, CSA;* ARTICLE: "I WAS
THERE," CWM:SEP/91[8]378

BROUSSARD, T. LAIZER, *Lieutenant, 8th Louisiana Infantry;*
CWTI:FEB/91[12]189

BROUT, DAVID, *Private, 45th Massachusetts Infantry;*
B&G:OCT/93[31]539

BROWDER, GEORGE R., BOOK REVIEWS: *THE HEAVENS ARE
WEEPING: THE DIARIES OF GEORGE RICHARD
BROWDER 1852-1886*

BROWN, AARON, *Colonel, USA;* CWTI:SEP/94[12]398

BROWN, ALBERT H., *Colonel, 96th Ohio Infantry;*
ACW:SEP/92[16]376

BROWN, ALEXANDER C., *Private, 2nd Ohio Infantry;*
B&G:AUG/95[24]605

BROWN, ALLISON, *Colonel, 1st Maryland Infantry;*
ACW:NOV/93[50]444

BROWN, ALLISON L., *Colonel, 149th Ohio Infantry;*
B&G:DEC/92[8]503

BROWN, ALONZO L., *Captain, USA;* ACW:NOV/94[76]500

BROWN, ALSA, *Captain, 38th North Carolina Infantry;*
GETTY:8[67]204

BROWN, ANGUS, *Captain, 1st South Carolina Cavalry;*
B&G:OCT/93[12]537

BROWN, BENJAMIN L., *Lieutenant, 59th Georgia Infantry;*
GETTY:12[111]250

BROWN, BERNARD, *civilian;* ACW:SEP/95[38]546

BROWN, BEZALIEL G., *Captain, 7th Virginia Infantry;*
GETTY:12[111]250

ARTICLE: "GETTYSBURG VIGNETTES #3: AT THE TIME
IMPRACTICABLE. DICK EWELL'S DECISION ON THE
FIRST DAY AT GETTYSBURG," B&G:FEB/95[8]590C

ADDITIONAL LISTINGS: B&G:FEB/95[8]590B, B&G:APR/95[8]595,
B&G:JUN/95[8]600, CWTI:MAR/94[48]374, GETTY:4[33]145,
GETTY:4[33]146, GETTY:4[65]148, GETTY:5[13]157,
GETTY:9[17]210

BROWN, CHARLES, *Lieutenant, 21st Michigan Infantry;*
B&G:DEC/95[9]615

BROWN, CHARLES, *Sergeant, 57th Massachusetts Infantry;*
CWR:VOL1#3[94]

BROWN, CHARLES J., *Captain, 1st Maryland Potomac Home
Brigade;* CWR:VOL1#4[7]125

BROWN, DAVID S., *Sergeant, 2nd Tennessee Cavalry;*
CWR:VOL4#1[1]163

BROWN, EDMUND R., *Corporal, 27th Indiana Infantry;*
CWR:VOL3#2[70]155

BROWN, EGBERT, *General, USA;* B&G:JUN/91[10]452

BROWN, GEORGE, *Lieutenant Commander, USN;*
ACW:JUL/93[34]424

BROWN, GEORGE, *Mayor, Baltimore;* ACW:JAN/92[30]342,
ACW:NOV/95[30]555

BROWN, GEORGE F., *Lieutenant, 16th Massachusetts
Infantry;* GETTY:12[7]241

BROWN, GEORGE M., *Private, CSA;* ACW:JUL/93[27]423

BROWN, GEORGE W., *Major, USA;* CWTI:OCT/95[24]466

BROWN, H.E., *Private, 28th Ohio Infantry;* GETTY:9[81]216

BROWN, HAMILTON A., *Lieutenant Colonel, 1st North
Carolina Infantry;* CWM:MAY/92[20]420, GETTY:7[83]192

BROWN, HARVEY, *Colonel, USA;* CWR:VOL1#4[42]126

BROWN, HENRY, *Private, black Confederate soldier;* ARTICLE:
"ARTICLE BRINGS NOTICE TO A UNIQUE REBEL,"
CWTI:JUN/90[57]163

BROWN, HENRY, *Private, Michigan Infantry;*
GETTY:11[57]233, GETTY:9[33]211

BROWN, HENRY W., *Colonel, USA;* B&G:APR/95[8]595,
B&G:JUN/95[8]600

BROWN, HIRAM, *Colonel, 145th Pennsylvania Infantry;*
GETTY:11[80]235

BROWN, ISAAC N., *Lieutenant, CSA;* CWNEWS:JAN/91[4]

BROWN, J.H., *Captain, 47th Ohio Infantry;*
CWTI:DEC/94[62]415

BROWN, J. SMITH, *Lieutenant, 126th New York Infantry;*
GETTY:7[51]190, GETTY:8[95]205

BROWN, J. THOMPSON, *Colonel, CSA;* CWNEWS:APR/91[4],
CWR:VOL4#4[70]180, GETTY:10[29]222, GETTY:12[30]243

BROWN, JAMES, *Corporal, 9th Indiana Cavalry;* ARTICLE:
"TWO CORPORALS: A TALE OF NATHAN BEDFORD
FORREST'S ATTACK AT SULPHUR BRANCH TRESTLE,
ALABAMA," B&G:JUN/92[32]488

BROWN, JAMES, *Corporal, 169th New York Infantry;*
B&G:JUN/95[36]603A, B&G:OCT/95[36]614
BROWN, JAMES E., *Sergeant, 13th U.S. Regulars;*
CWR:VOL2#1[1]130
BROWN, JERRY Z., *Captain, 148th Pennsylvania Infantry;*
CWR:VOL2#2[141]137
BROWN, JOHN:
ARTICLES: "A VISIT TO JOHN BROWN COUNTRY,"
CWTI:JUL/92[20]271, "METEOR OF THE WAR,"
ACW:JUL/91[43]315
BOOK REVIEWS: *THE OLD MAN: JOHN BROWN AT HARPERS FERRY*
GENERAL LISTINGS: *at Harpers Ferry;* CWTI:DEC/89[34]136, *in book review,* ACW:NOV/94[66], ACW:JUL/95[58], CWM:APR/95[50], CWNEWS:NOV/91[4], *photos;* ACW:MAY/94[43]470, CWTI:SEPT/89[40]130
ADDITIONAL LISTINGS: ACW:MAR/91[14]293, ACW:NOV/91[41]334, ACW:MAY/92[14]358, ACW:JAN/93[26]395, ACW:MAR/93[18]403, ACW:MAY/94[35]469, ACW:MAY/94[43]470, ACW:SEP/94[10]484, ACW:NOV/94[42]497, B&G:DEC/91[12]469, B&G:DEC/91[34]470, B&G:OCT/91[40]467, B&G:JUN/92[8]487, CWM:JUL/91[35]369, CWM:MAY/92[8]418, CWM:SEP/92[8]437, CWM:AUG/95[17]603, CWM:AUG/95[30]606, CWM:NOV/92[10]447, CWR:VOL1#1[1]102, CWTI:SUMMER/89[20]121, CWTI:SUMMER/89[50]124, CWTI:SEP/89[40]130, CWTI:SEP/90[22]173, CWTI:JAN/95[24]424, CWTI:DEC/95[40]479
BROWN, JOHN C., *Captain, 20th Indiana Infantry;*
B&G:APR/93[12]518
BROWN, JOHN C., *General, CSA;* B&G:FEB/92[10]474, CWR:VOL1#3[7]118, CWR:VOL4#3[50]171, CWTI:SEPT/89[30]129
BROWN, JOHN F., *Private, 11th Mississippi Infantry;*
CWR:VOL2#4[269]145
BROWN, JOHN M, *Colonel, CSA;* CWTI:DEC/94[49]413
BROWN, JOSEPH E., *Governor, Georgia:*
ARTICLES "AN ARMY OF HIS OWN," CWTI:DEC/94[49]413, "WOLF AT THE DOOR," ACW:NOV/93[42]443
GENERAL LISTINGS: *in book review,* CWNEWS:JUL/92[4], CWR:VOL3#1[80], *letters to the editor,* CWTI:MAR/95[18]432, *Savannah,* B&G:FEB/91[8]439, *photos;* ACW:NOV/93[42]443, CWTI:AUG/91[52]219, CWTI:DEC/94[49]413
ADDITIONAL LISTINGS: ACW:MAR/91[38]296, CWM:JAN/92[40]405, CWM:AUG/94[8]522, CWR:VOL1#4[42]126, CWTI:SUMMER/89[13]120, CWTI:FEB/91[36]193, CWTI:AUG/91[52]219, CWTI:AUG/91[58]220, CWTI:SEP/91[23]228, CWTI:MAR/93[24]309, CWTI:SEP/94[26]400
BROWN, JOSEPH N., *Colonel, 4th South Carolina Infantry;*
B&G:APR/93[12]518, GETTY:8[9]199, GETTY:13[22]254
BROWN, JOHN NEWTON, *Colonel, 14th South Carolina Infantry;* BOOK REVIEW: *A COLONEL AT GETTYSBURG AND SPOTSYLVANIA: THE LIFE OF COLONEL JOSEPH NEWTON BROWN AND THE BATTLE OF GETTYSBURG AND SPOTSYLVANIA*
BROWN, MORRIS JR., *Captain, 126th New York Infantry;*
CWR:VOL1#4[7]125, GETTY:8[95]205
BROWN, PHILIP P., *Colonel, 157th New York Infantry;*
GETTY:4[49]147, GETTY:12[111]250
BROWN, REUBEN, *Private, 2nd Tennessee Cavalry;*
CWR:VOL4#1[1]163

BROWN, SIMEON, *Lieutenant, 1st Rhode Island Cavalry;*
ACW:NOV/91[30]332
BROWN, T. FREDERICK, *Lieutenant, 1st Rhode Island Artillery;* GETTY:4[89]150, GETTY:5[79]161, GETTY:5[89]162, GETTY:7[97]193, GETTY:12[61]245, GETTY:13[43]256
BROWN, THEODORE, *Private, 5th New York Heavy Artillery;*
B&G:JUN/95[36]603A
BROWN, THOMAS, *Private, 2nd Kentucky Cavalry;*
CWM:MAR/93[16]466
BROWN, THORNSBERRY B., *Private, USA;*
B&G:AUG/93[10]529
BROWN, VAN, *Captain, 2nd North Carolina Battalion;*
GETTY:13[33]255
BROWN, W. HARVEY, *Captain, 14th U.S. Infantry;*
GETTY:10[42]224
BROWN, W.T., *artist;* B&G:AUG/93[18]530
BROWN, WILLIAM, *Private, 8th Ohio Infantry;* GETTY:6[7]169
BROWN, WILLIAM, *Private, Virginia Cavalry;*
ACW:MAR/95[50]518
BROWN, WILLIAM D., *Captain, Chesapeake Artillery;*
GETTY:4[49]147, GETTY:10[29]222
BROWN, WILLIAM H., *Colonel, 45th Virginia Infantry;*
ACW:MAR/94[27]459
BROWN, WILLIAM I., *Adjutant, 9th New Hampshire Infantry;*
CWR:VOL2#2[118]136
BROWN, WILLIAM K., *Corporal, USA;* GETTY:12[7]241
BROWN, WILSON W., *Corporal, USA;* ACW:SEP/91[22]321
BROWN, ZEREMIAH Z., *Captain, 148th Pennsylvania Infantry;* CWR:VOL2#2[141]137
BROWNE, A.G., *civilian;* ACW:SEP/92[47]380, B&G:FEB/91[8]439
BROWNE, JUNIUS H., *reporter;* B&G:APR/92[28]482
BROWNELL, FRANCIS E., *Corporal, USA;*
AHI:DEC/71[30]138
BROWNELL, ROBERT S., *Private, 1st Rhode Island Infantry;*
ACW:JUL/94[58]
BROWNING, ORVILLE H., *Senator, Illinois;*
CWTI:DEC/94[82]418, CWTI:DEC/95[24]477
BROWNLOW, WILLIAM G.: AHI:JAN/80[8]197, B&G:FEB/93[12]511, CWTI:NOV/93[71]352, *photo;* CWTI:NOV/93[71]352
BROWNSON, E.B., *Captain, USA;* GETTY:6[87]178
BROWNSVILLE, TEXAS, BATTLE OF; B&G:DEC/93[30]546, B&G:FEB/94[38]553, CWTI:AUG/90[58]169
BRUCE, GEORGE A., *Lieutenant Colonel, 20th Massachusetts Infantry;* BOOK REVIEW: *THE TWENTIETH REGIMENT OF MASSACHUSETTS VOLUNTEER INFANTRY 1861-1865*
BRUCE, J.W., *Major, CSA;* GETTY:9[17]210
BRUMBY, ARNOLDUS V., *civilian;* B&G:DEC/94[22]586
BRUMFIELD, HENRY A., *Private, 148th Pennsylvania Infantry;* CWR:VOL2#4[361]148
BRUMLEY, OZNIAH R., *Captain, 20th North Carolina Infantry;* GETTY:12[1]240, GETTY:12[111]250
BRUNNER, A.S., *Captain, CSA;* B&G:OCT/94[11]580
BRUNSON'S (SOUTH CAROLINA) BATTERY;
ACW:MAY/95[30]525
BRUNSON, ERVIN B., *Captain, Pee Dee Artillery;*
ACW:MAY/95[30]525, CWR:VOL1#1[26]103, GETTY:10[107]227
BRUNSON, WILLIAM H., *Lieutenant, 14th South Carolina Infantry;* GETTY:13[22]254

BRUNT, ANDREW J., *Private, 7th Wisconsin Infantry,*
GETTY:11[57]233
BRUCKNER, GEORGE D., *Private, Sumter Artillery;*
CWR:VOL3#2[1]153
BRYAN, BENJAMIN F., *Captain, CSA;* B&G:JUN/93[12]524
BRYAN, COUNCIL, *Captain, 5th Florida Infantry;*
CWR:VOL3#4[1]161
BRYAN, GOODE, *General, CSA;* ACW:MAY/91[23]303,
ACW:JUL/95[10]533, B&G:APR/94[10]558,
B&G:APR/95[8]595, CWTI:MAR/93[40]312,
CWTI:MAY/94[50]386
BRYAN, JOHN, *Captain, CSA;* B&G:DEC/91[6]468
BRYAN, JOHN R., *Balloonist;* B&G:AUG/91[20]459
BRYAN, KING, *Captain, 5th Texas Infantry;*
CWTI:DEC/91[36]240
BRYAN, PETER N., *Sergeant, 9th Florida Infantry;*
CWR:VOL3#4[1]161
BRYAN, THOMAS A., *Captain, CSA;* ACW:MAR/94[27]459
BRYAN, WILLIAM JENNINGS; AHI:OCT/68[4]116,
CWNEWS:JUN/92[4]
BRYAND, GEORGE, *Colonel, USA;* ACW:JUL/95[6]531
BRYANT, COLBY M., *Private, 154th New York Infantry;*
GETTY:8[17]200
BRYANT, GEORGE E., *Colonel, USA;* B&G:JUN/93[12]524,
B&G:AUG/95[8]604
BRYANT, TRAVERS, *Private, 51st North Carolina Infantry;*
B&G:APR/93[24]520
BUCHANAN, FRANKLIN; ACW:MAR/91[14]293,
ACW:JUL/94[35]478, AHI:OCT/75[30]162,
B&G:DEC/94[10]585, B&G:JUN/94[34], CWM:JUL/93[24]485,
CWTI:MAR/91[42]202, CWTI:MAR/94[20]369,
CWTI:SEP/94[26]400, *photo;* AHI:OCT/75[30]162
BUCHANAN, JAMES, *President:*
ARTICLES: "A PRESIDENTIAL GALLERY," AHI:APR/89[20]282,
"A PRESIDENTIAL GAZETEER," AHI:APR/89[43]284,
"FIFTEEN PRESIDENTIAL DECISIONS THAT SHAPED
AMERICA," AHI:APR/89[36]283, "THE HEARTBEAT IN THE
WHITE HOUSE," AHI:APR/70[38]125, "MAN ON A
TIGHTROPE," AHI:MAY/66[12]101, "PRESIDENT
FRANKLIN PIERCE LEFT HIS SUCCESSOR, JAMES
BUCHANAN, A SERPENT'S NEST OF TROUBLES,"
ACW:MAR/93[6]400, "WEAK, EAGER-TO-PLEASE JAMES
BUCHANAN WATCHED IN HORROR AS THE AMERICAN
NATION SPLIT INTO WARRING HALVES,"
ACW:MAR/93[18]403
GENERAL LISTINGS: *Bloody Kansas,* AHI:JUL/75[4]160, *Dred Scott,*
AHI:MAY/81[35]218, *Harpers Ferry Raid, 1859,*
AHI:MAR/84[10]236, *in book review,* ACW:SEP/91[54],
AHI:MAY/82[8], *James Buchanan Cabin,* AHI:APR/89[43]284,
John Brown, AHI:AUG/76[34]171, AHI:JAN/86[10]256, *John
C. Fremont,* AHI:MAY/70[4]126, *Mormon confrontation,*
AHI:DEC/72[10]145, *Political Cartoons,* AHI:MAY/66[12]101,
Stephen A. Douglas, AHI:OCT/70[23]129, *Winfield Scott,*
AHI:FEB/76[14]165, *photo of "Wheatland" (home);*
AHI:MAY/66[12]101, *photo;* ACW:MAR/93[18]403, *portraits;*
AHI:MAY/66[12]101, AHI:APR/89[20]282,
ADDITIONAL LISTINGS: ACW:NOV/91[10]329, ACW:MAY/92[14]358,
ACW:MAY/93[47]417, ACW:NOV/93[8]438,
ACW:MAR/94[35]460, ACW:MAY/94[43]470,
ACW:SEP/94[31]486, ACW:NOV/94[8]493,
ACW:NOV/94[42]497, ACW:JAN/95[8]502,
ACW:MAR/95[8]512, ACW:JUL/95[44]537, AHI:OCT/68[4]116,

AHI:DEC/71[30]138, AHI:JUN/73[4]149, AHI:SEP/82[40]229,
AHI:JAN/85[10]244
ADDITIONAL LISTINGS, Continued: CWM:APR/94[32]506,
CWTI:MAY/92[45]266, CWTI:JUL/92[29]272,
CWTI:NOV/92[54]293, CWTI:JAN/93[40]301,
CWTI:JAN/93[44]302, CWTI:SEP/93[59]341,
CWTI:MAY/94[46]385, CWTI:JUL/94[82]396,
CWTI:JAN/95[24]424, MH:AUG/92[26]161, MH:FEB/94[8]175
BUCHANAN, JAMES, *Surgeon, 32nd Ohio Infantry;*
B&G:APR/95[24]596
BUCHANAN, MCKEAN, *Paymaster, USN;* AHI:OCT/75[30]162
BUCHANAN, ROBERT C., *Colonel, USA;*
ACW:NOV/94[50]498, B&G:AUG/92[11]493
BUCHEL, AUGUSTUS, *Colonel, CSA;* CWR:VOL4#2[68]167
BUCK, DANIEL W., *Captain, 8th Illinois Cavalry;*
B&G:FEB/95[8]590A, GETTY:5[4]156,
BUCK, ERASTUS, *Captain, 3rd Vermont Infantry;* BOOK REVIEW:
*BUCK'S BOOK: A VIEW OF THE 3RD VERMONT
INFANTRY REGIMENT*
BUCK, GEORGE, *Private, USA;* CWTI:APR/92[49]260
BUCK, GEORGE W., *Sergeant, 20th Maine Infantry;*
GETTY:6[43]173
BUCK, H.B., *Surgeon, USA;* GETTY:10[53]225
BUCK, IRVING, *Captain, CSA;* ACW:NOV/93[34]442,
CWTI:SEP/94[40]403
BUCK, SAMUEL, *Lieutenant, 13th Virginia Infantry;*
CWM:NOV/92[64]453
BUCKALEW, CHARLES R., *Senator, Pennsylvania;*
GETTY:12[85]248
BUCKINGHAM, PHILO B., *Major, USA;* GETTY:11[102]237
BUCKINGHAM, WILLIAM A., *Governor, Connecticut;*
ACW:JAN/92[16]340, GETTY:9[61]215
BUCKLAND MILLS, VIRGINIA, BATTLE OF:
ARTICLE: "PELL-MELL CAVALRY CHASE," ACW:JUL/92[41]370
ADDITIONAL LISTINGS: ACW:MAR/93[26]404, ACW:JAN/95[10]503,
B&G:AUG/91[36]462, CWM:JUL/92[16]428
BUCKLAND, RALPH P., *Colonel, USA;* CWR:VOL2#4[313]146,
CWR:VOL4#1[44]164
BUCKLES, ABRAM J., *Sergeant, 19th Indiana Infantry;*
B&G:APR/95[8]595
BUCKLEY, JAMES and JOHN, *69th Pennsylvania Infantry;*
GETTY:4[89]150
BUCKLIN, SOPHRONIA, *civilian;* GETTY:10[53]225
BUCKLYN, JOHN, *Lieutenant, 1st Rhode Island Artillery;*
CWM:MAY/92[20]420
BUCKNER, THOMAS R., *Captain, 44th Virginia Infantry;*
GETTY:13[108]261
BUCKNER, SIMON B., *General, CSA:*
ARTICLES: "A CONVERSATION WITH THE PAST,"
CWTI:APR/90[56]155, "FORMULA FOR DISASTER,"
CWM:JAN/92[34]404, "FORTS HENRY & DONELSON:
UNION VICTORY ON THE TWIN RIVERS,"
B&G:FEB/92[10]474, "MAJOR GENERAL SIMON B.
BUCKNER'S UNPUBLISHED AFTER-ACTION REPORT ON
THE BATTLE OF PERRYVILLE," CWR:VOL4#3[50]171,
"U.S. GRANT AND SIMON BUCKNER: FRIENDS,"
AHI:MAR/82[8]227
GENERAL LISTINGS: *Chattanooga,* ACW:MAY/91[23]303,
Chickamauga, CWTI:SEP/92[31]281, *Forts Henry and
Donelson,* B&G:FEB/92[10]474, CWTI:SEP/93[59]341, *Grant,*
AHI:DEC/72[4]144, *Grierson's Raid,* B&G:JUN/93[12]524, *in
book review,* CWR:VOL4#2[136], *letter about Bragg,*
CWTI:APR/89[14]107, *Perryville,* CWTI:NOV/92[18]289

ADDITIONAL LISTINGS: ACW:JUL/91[12]310, ACW:JUL/91[26]313, ACW:JUL/92[22]368, ACW:MAR/93[10]402, B&G:FEB/92[10]474, B&G:OCT/92[32]499, B&G:FEB/93[12]511, B&G:FEB/93[61]516, B&G:FEB/95[35]592, CWM:JAN/92[4]397, CWM:JAN/92[34]404, CWM:JUL/92[24]430, CWM:SEP/92[38]443, CWM:FEB/95[32]562, CWM:OCT/95[22]614, CWR:VOL1#3[7]118, CWR:VOL1#4[42]126, CWR:VOL3#1[1]149, CWTI:FEB/90[26]143, CWTI:APR/90[56]155, CWTI:MAR/93[40]312, CWTI:MAY/94[50]386

BUCKTAIL REGIMENT, see listings under **"PENNSYLVANIA TROOPS, 13TH PENNSYLVANIA INFANTRY"**

BUEHLER, DAVID A. , *civilian;* GETTY:7[114]194

BUEHLER, FANNIE J., *civilian;* ARTICLE: "THREE HEROINES OF GETTYSBURG," GETTY:11[119]238

BUEHLER, L.M., *civilian;* CWTI:DEC/94[42]412

BUEHLER, THEODORE E., *Lieutenant Colonel, 67th Indiana Infantry;* B&G:FEB/94[8]550

BUEL, W.H., *Colonel, USA;* CWTI:DEC/94[57]414

BUELL, AUGUSTUS C., *Private, 4th U.S. Artillery:*
BOOK REVIEW: *THE CANNONEER*
ADDITIONAL LISTINGS: ACW:MAY/92[54], GETTY:4[113]153, GETTY:9[33]211, GETTY:11[57]233, *portrait;* GETTY:9[33]211

BUELL, DON CARLOS, *General, USA:*
ARTICLES: "A WADE IN THE HIGH TIDE AT PERRYVILLE," CWTI:NOV/92[18]289, "AT PERRYVILLE, DON CAROLS BUELL WON A BATTLEFIELD VICTORY, BUT LOST A POLITICAL WAR," ACW:SEP/95[6]541
GENERAL LISTINGS: *general history,* AHI:MAY/71[3]133A, *in book review,* ACW:SEP/95[62], CWNEWS:JUN/91[4], CWTI:MAY/92[18], *letters to the editor,* CWTI:MAR/93[8]306, *Mexican War,* MH:APR/93[39]166, *Nelson-Davis feud,* AHI:NOV/72[12]142, *Shiloh,* CWTI:JUL/92[29]272, GETTY:7[23]187, *William T. Sherman,* AHI:JAN/67[4]106, *photos;* ACW:JUL/91[26]313, ACW:SEP/95[6]541, AHI:NOV/72[12]142, AHI:NOV/73[18]151
ADDITIONAL LISTINGS: ACW:MAR/91[30]295, ACW:MAY/91[12]302, ACW:JUL/91[26]313, ACW:SEP/91[22]321, ACW:SEP/91[46]324, ACW:SEP/93[38]434, AHI:NOV/73[18]151, B&G:FEB/92[10]474, B&G:FEB/93[12]511, B&G:DEC/93[52]548, B&G:FEB/95[30]591, CWM:MAR/91[50]340, CWM:MAY/91[10]347, CWM:JUL/92[24]430, CWM:MAR/93[8]465, CWM:FEB/95[32]562, CWM:APR/95[66]579, CWR:VOL1#3[7]118, CWR:VOL2#1[36]132, CWR:VOL2#4[313]146, CWR:VOL4#1[44]164, CWR:VOL4#3[50]171, CWTI:FEB/90[26]143, CWTI:FEB/90[32]144, CWTI:FEB/90[38]145, CWTI:AUG/91[52]219, CWTI:JUL/92[42]274, CWTI:MAY/93[38]321, CWTI:SEP/93[59]341, CWTI:NOV/93[33]347, CWTI:JUL/94[50]395, CWTI:OCT/95[48]470, CWTI:DEC/95[67]481, MH:DEC/93[12]174

BUELL, GEORGE P., *General, USA;* B&G:DEC/95[9]615, CWTI:NOV/92[41]291

BUFFINGTON ISLAND, OHIO, SKIRMISH AT; B&G:OCT/94[11]580, B&G:OCT/94[42]583

BUFFINGTON, WILLIAM, *Sergeant, CSA;* B&G:JUN/93[12]524

BUFFUM, FRANCIS, *Private, 14th New Hampshire Infantry;* ACW:MAY/91[38]305

BUFFUM, ROBERT, *Private, USA;* ACW:SEP/91[22]321

BUFORD, ABRAHAM, *General, CSA;* ACW:MAR/91[38]296, ACW:NOV/91[22]331, B&G:JUN/93[12]524, B&G:DEC/93[12]545, B&G:FEB/95[8]590A, B&G:AUG/95[8]604, CWR:VOL2#1[36]132, GETTY:11[19]232, *photo;* GETTY:11[19]232

BUFORD, BENJAMIN, *Private, 53rd Pennsylvania Infantry;* GETTY:11[80]235

BUFORD, JOHN, *General, USA:*
ARTICLES: "GETTYSBURG VIGNETTES #1: FIGHT LIKE THE DEVIL TO HOLD YOUR OWN. GENERAL JOHN BUFORD'S CAVALRY AT GETTYSBURG," B&G:FEB/95[8]590A, "JOHN BUFORD AND THE GETTYSBURG CAMPAIGN," GETTY:11[19]232
BOOK REVIEW: *"THE DEVIL'S TO PAY": GENERAL JOHN BUFORD*
GENERAL LISTINGS: *1863 Cavalry Battles,* MH:OCT/92[51]162, *Aldie,* B&G:OCT/93[12]537, GETTY:10[42]224, *Falling Waters,* ACW:JUL/93[50]426, GETTY:9[109]218
GENERAL LISTINGS, continued: *Gettysburg,* AHI:MAY/67[22]107, GETTY:4[24]145, GETTY:4[33]146, GETTY:4[49]147, GETTY:4[75]149, GETTY:4[101]151, GETTY:4[113]153, GETTY:5[4]156, GETTY:5[19]158, GETTY:5[103]163, GETTY:5[123]166, GETTY:6[13]170, GETTY:6[69]176, GETTY:7[23]187, GETTY:7[114]194, GETTY:7[124]196, GETTY:8[31]201, GETTY:8[43]202, GETTY:9[17]210, GETTY:11[6]231, GETTY:11[57]233, GETTY:11[71]234, GETTY:12[7]241, GETTY:12[123]251
GENERAL LISTINGS, continued: *in book review,* CWNEWS:JAN/93[4], review, CWR:VOL1#2[78], *Indian Wars,* AHI:OCT/79[20]194, *letters to the editor,* B&G:APR/95[5]594, CWTI:JUL/92[8]269, CWTI:SEP/92[10]278, *Manassas, 2nd,* B&G:AUG/92[11]493, *SIO,* B&G:AUG/93[36]533, *West Point,* B&G:DEC/91[12]469, *photo;* B&G:OCT/93[12]537, B&G:FEB/95[8]590A, CWTI:JUN/90[32]159, GETTY:11[19]232
ADDITIONAL LISTINGS: ACW:SEP/94[55]489, B&G:DEC/91[34]470, CWR:VOL2#4[269]145, CWTI:JUN/90[32]159, CWTI:APR/92[35]257, CWTI:DEC/94[82]418, GETTY:13[22]254

BUFORD, NAPOLEON B., *General, USA:*
ARTICLE: "NAPOLEON BONAPARTE: THE OTHER BUFORD," CWTI:DEC/94[82]418
ADDITIONAL LISTINGS: ACW:SEP/91[46]324, B&G:FEB/95[8]590A, CWR:VOL3#4[24]162, GETTY:11[19]232, *photos;* CWR:VOL3#4[24]162, CWTI:DEC/94[82]418

BUFORD, THOMAS P., *Private, 11th Mississippi Infantry;* CWR:VOL2#4[269]145

BUGH, WILLIAM A., *Lieutenant Colonel, 32nd Wisconsin Infantry;* CWR:VOL2#4[313]146

BUHL, FREDERICK, *Lieutenant, 24th Michigan Infantry;* GETTY:5[19]158

BUHL, GEORGE, *civilian;* ACW:JAN/91[10]283

BUHOUP, J.W., *Captain, Louisiana Tigers;* CWTI:MAR/94[48]374

BULGER, M.J., *Colonel, 47th Alabama Infantry;* GETTY:6[43]173

BULGER, MICHAEL, *Lieutenant Colonel, 47th Alabama Infantry;* GETTY:7[41]189

BULL RUN, FIRST BATTLE OF, see listings under **"MANASSAS, VIRGINIA, FIRST BATTLE OF"**

BULL RUN, SECOND BATTLE OF, see listings under **"MANASSAS, VIRGINIA, SECOND BATTLE OF"**

BULL, HENRY A., *Private, 8th New York Cavalry;*
CWM:MAY/92[8]418
BULL, JAMES, *Lieutenant Colonel, 126th New York Infantry;*
GETTY:7[51]190, GETTY:8[95]205
BULL, JOHN P., *Lieutenant Colonel, CSA;* B&G:JUN/91[10]452
BULL, RICE C., *Sergeant, 123rd New York Infantry:*
BOOK REVIEW: *SOLDIERING: THE CIVIL WAR DIARY OF RICE C. BULL*
ADDITIONAL LISTINGS: ACW:MAY/91[8]300,
CWTI:SUMMER/89[32]122
BULL, S. OCTAVIUS, *Major, 53rd Pennsylvania Infantry;*
GETTY:11[80]235
BULLARD, IRA, *Corporal, 57th Massachusetts Infantry;*
ACW:SEP/95[70]549
BULLITT, THOMAS W., *Lieutenant, CSA;* B&G:OCT/94[11]580
BULLITT, W.G., *Major, CSA;* B&G:OCT/94[11]580
BULLOCH, I.S., *Lieutenant, CSN;* ACW:MAY/91[46]306
BULLOCH, JAMES D.:
BOOK REVIEW: *THE SECRET SERVICE OF THE CONFEDERATE STATES IN EUROPE*
ADDITIONAL LISTINGS: ACW:MAY/91[46]306, ACW:MAY/92[23]360,
ACW:JAN/93[58]399, ACW:JUL/95[58], AHI:JUN/70[30]127,
AHI:DEC/82[38]231, AHI:OCT/88[38]275, B&G:AUG/92[36],
CWM:JUL/93[30]486, CWNEWS:JUL/92[4],
CWTI:DEC/91[44]241, *portrait;* AHI:DEC/82[38]231
BULLOCK, GEORGE, *Lieutenant, 23rd North Carolina
Infantry;* CWTI:MAY/93[26]318, GETTY:5[13]157
BULLOCK, ROBERT S., *Major, CSA;* B&G:OCT/94[11]580
BUMGARDNER, JAMES, *Captain, 52nd Virginia Infantry;*
B&G:JUN/95[8]600, CWM:NOV/92[64]453
BUNDY, HENRY, *Lieutenant, 13th New York Artillery;*
CWTI:SUMMER/89[32]122
BUNNER, LAFAYETTE *Lieutenant, 7th Missouri Infantry;*
ACW:MAY/94[26]468
BURBANK, SIDNEY, *Colonel USA;* GETTY:8[53]203,
GETTY:9[53]214
BURBRIDGE, STEPHEN G., *General, USA;*
ACW:NOV/91[22]331, ACW:SEP/92[16]376,
ACW:JAN/94[10]448, ACW:JUL/94[51]480,
ACW:NOV/94[76]500, B&G:AUG/91[11]458,
B&G:AUG/91[11]458, B&G:DEC/91[6]468,
B&G:FEB/94[8]550, MH:APR/94[54]176, *photo;*
B&G:AUG/91[11]458
BURCH, NEWELL, *Corporal, 154th New York Infantry;*
GETTY:8[17]200
BURCKMYER, CHARLES, *civilian;* CWM:MAR/92[16]411
BURDICK, AMOS, *Private, USA;* GETTY:9[33]211
BURDSALL, WILLIAM H., *Captain, USA;* B&G:AUG/93[10]529
BUREAU FOR COLORED TROOPS; AHI:MAY/71[3]133A
BUREAU OF CONSCRIPTION; CWTI:SEP/91[23]228
BURFORD, NATHANIEL M., *Colonel, 19th Texas Cavalry;*
CWR:VOL2#3[212]142
BURGESS' MILL, VIRGINIA, BATTLE OF; see listings under
"HATCHER'S RUN, VIRGINIA, BATTLE OF"
BURGESS, THOMAS, *Private, 15th South Carolina Infantry;*
B&G:DEC/95[25]616
BURGHARDT, HENRY, *Private, 2nd Wisconsin Infantry;*
GETTY:11[57]233
BURGIN, JOHN M., *Lieutenant, 22nd North Carolina Infantry;*
GETTY:12[111]250
BURGWYN, HENRY K. JR., *Colonel, 26th North Carolina
Infantry;* CWM:APR/95[50], CWR:VOL4#2[136],
GETTY:5[19]158, GETTY:7[7]185

BURGWYN, WILLIAM H.S., *Captain, 35th North Carolina
Infantry;* BOOK REVIEWS: *A CAPTAIN'S WAR: THE LETTERS
AND DIARIES OF WILLIAM H.S. BURGWYN, 1861-1865*
BURKE, DENIS F., *Lieutenant Colonel, 88th New York
Infantry;* CWM:MAR/91[50]340
BURKE, JESSE, *Colonel, CSA;* ACW:JAN/93[35]396
BURKE, REDMOND, *Captain, CSA;* ACW:JUL/95[34]536
BURKE, ROBERT, *Private, 1st Indiana Cavalry;*
ACW:MAR/95[34]516
BURKE, ROSS E., *Lieutenant Colonel, 2nd Louisiana Infantry;*
CWM:MAR/91[17]335
BURKE, THOMAS, *Private, 97th New York Infantry;*
B&G:FEB/91[34]442
BURKS, JAMES L., *Sergeant, Botetourt Artillery;*
B&G:FEB/94[8]550
BURKS, JESSE, *Colonel, CSA;* B&G:AUG/93[10]529
BURLEY, BENNETT; ACW:JUL/95[44]537
BURLING, GEORGE C., *Colonel, USA;* GETTY:6[59]174,
GETTY:7[29]188, GETTY:8[43]202, GETTY:8[53]203,
GETTY:9[41]212
BURLINGAME, BENJAMIN, *Sergeant, 7th Indiana Infantry;*
B&G:AUG/93[10]529
BURMEISTER, FREDERICK F., *Surgeon, 69th Pennsylvania
Infantry;* GETTY:10[53]225
BURN, WILLIAM J., *Surgeon, 42nd Massachusetts Infantry;*
GETTY:10[53]225
BURNAP, SILAS A., *Captain, Ohio Light Artillery, 7th Battery;*
B&G:AUG/95[8]604
BURNES, LUKE, *Sergeant, 6th Wisconsin Infantry;*
GETTY:4[126]154, GETTY:6[77]177
BURNETT, BARNARD C., *Private, 150th New York Infantry;*
GETTY:12[42]244
BURNETT, H.L., *Colonel USA;* ACW:JUL/92[22]368
BURNETT, HENRY H., *Captain, 5th New York Infantry;*
CWR:VOL1#2[7]111, CWTI:MAY/94[31]382
BURNEY, ADISON, *Private, 11th Mississippi Infantry;*
CWR:VOL2#4[269]145
BURNEY, IVERSON L., *Lieutenant, 49th Georgia Infantry;*
GETTY:12[111]250
BURNEY, TOM, *Private, Terry's Texas Rangers;*
CWM:JUL/92[40]432
BURNHAM, FRANKLIN, *Sergeant, 9th New Hampshire
Infantry;* CWR:VOL2#2[118]136
BURNHAM, HIRAM, *Colonel, 6th Maine Infantry;*
ACW:SEP/92[30]378, B&G:APR/94[10]558,
CWR:VOL3#1[31]150
BURNS, JOHN, *civilian;* GETTY:4[113]153, GETTY:6[13]170,
GETTY:11[19]232
BURNS, PETER, *Private, 2nd U.S. Infantry;*
ACW:NOV/94[50]498
BURNS, W.J., *Sergeant, 1st Georgia Regulars;*
CWR:VOL2#2[95]135
BURNS, WILLIAM W., *General, USA;* CWM:JUN/95[65]595
BURNSIDE, AMBROSE E., *General, USA:*
ARTICLES: "THE BATTLE OF FREDERICKSBURG,"
AHI:JUN/78[4]180, "BURNSIDE'S GEOGRAPHY CLASS,"
CWTI:JAN/95[34]427, "I WAS AN OGRE,"
CWM:OCT/94[60]544, "ICY ASSAULT ROUTED,"
ACW:MAY/91[23]303, "REMNANTS OF CIVIL WAR
KNOXVILLE," CWTI:MAY/94[50]386
BOOK REVIEWS: *ACROSS THE RAPPAHANNOCK: FROM
FREDERICKSBURG TO THE MUD MARCH*

GENERAL LISTINGS: *Antietam,* CWM:JAN/92[44]406,
CWTI:FEB/92[36]249, CWTI:SEP/93[43]338, *Chancellorsville,*
ACW:SEP/95[54]548, *Cold Harbor,* ACW:SEP/93[62]436,
Crater, CWR:VOL2#2[118]136, CWTI:APR/90[24]152,
Cumberland Gap, ACW:JUL/91[26]313, *editorial,*
ACW:MAR/91[6]290, *Fredericksburg,* ACW:MAY/94[12]466,
ACW:JAN/95[20]504, ACW:MAR/95[42]517,
ACW:NOV/95[10]553, B&G:JUN/92[8]487,
CWM:DEC/94[74]555, CWR:VOL4#4[i]175,
CWR:VOL4#4[1]177, CWR:VOL4#4[28]178,
CWR:VOL4#4[70]180, CWR:VOL4#4[101]181,
CWTI:APR/92[35]257, CWTI:JUL/94[44]394, GETTY:8[43]202

GENERAL LISTINGS, Continued: *general history,* AHI:MAY/71[3]133A,
in book review, ACW:JAN/93[58]399, ACW:SEP/94[66],
B&G:AUG/92[36], CWM:DEC/94[7], CWNEWS:MAY/89[4],
CWNEWS:JAN/91[4], CWNEWS:DEC/93[5],
CWNEWS:SEP/94[33], CWNEWS:APR/95[33],
CWNEWS:SEP/95[33], CWR:VOL1#3[94],
CWR:VOL4#3[1]170, MH:DEC/94[70], *in order of battle,*
B&G:APR/94[10]558, B&G:APR/95[8]595, *Knoxville,*
CWTI:MAR/93[40]312, *letters to the editor,*
B&G:DEC/94[6]584, CWM:DEC/95[5]625,
CWTI:JUN/95[14]443, *Manassas, First,* CWTI:MAR/94[48]374,
Mexican War, MH:APR/93[39]166, *Mud March,*
CWTI:MAR/95[26]434, *North Carolina,* ACW:JAN/95[10]503,
ACW:MAY/95[18]524, CWM:FEB/95[49]565, *Overland
Campaign,* B&G:APR/94[10]558, CWTI:APR/92[49]260,
Petersburg, MH:APR/95[46]183, *South Mountain,*
CWTI:SEP/94[49]404, *Wilderness,* ACW:MAY/93[31]415,
B&G:APR/95[8]595, B&G:JUN/95[8]600

PHOTOS: AHI:MAY/71[3]133A, AHI:JUN/78[4]180,
B&G:JUN/95[8]600, CWM:OCT/94[60]544,
CWTI:JAN/95[34]427

ADDITIONAL LISTINGS, ACW: ACW:JAN/91[38]287,
ACW:MAR/91[8]291, ACW:JUL/91[18]312,
ACW:JUL/91[35]314, ACW:NOV/91[30]332,
ACW:JUL/92[12]367, ACW:SEP/93[31]433,
ACW:MAR/95[42]517, ACW:SEP/95[22]544

ADDITIONAL LISTINGS, AHI: AHI:NOV/73[18]151, AHI:APR/85[18]250

ADDITIONAL LISTINGS, B&G: B&G:AUG/91[11]458,
B&G:AUG/91[32]461, B&G:OCT/91[11]466,
B&G:FEB/92[22]476, B&G:APR/92[28]482,
B&G:AUG/92[11]493, B&G:APR/93[12]518,
B&G:JUN/93[40]527, B&G:APR/94[59]565,
B&G:OCT/94[11]580, B&G:AUG/95[8]604,
B&G:OCT/95[8]611D

ADDITIONAL LISTINGS, CWM: CWM:JUL/91[43]371,
CWM:NOV/91[12]390, CWM:NOV/92[10]447,
CWM:MAR/93[16]466, CWM:MAR/93[32]468,
CWM:APR/94[8]502, CWM:APR/95[16]571,
CWM:OCT/95[22]614

ADDITIONAL LISTINGS, CWR: CWR:VOL1#1[1]102,
CWR:VOL1#3[52]122, CWR:VOL1#4[7]125,
CWR:VOL2#2[141]137, CWR:VOL2#3[183]140,
CWR:VOL2#4[269]145, CWR:VOL3#1[31]150,
CWR:VOL3#2[1]153, CWR:VOL3#3[1]157,
CWR:VOL3#4[1]161, CWR:VOL4#1[1]163

ADDITIONAL LISTINGS, CWTI: CWTI:DEC/90[58]185,
CWTI:SEP/91[31]229, CWTI:DEC/91[18]236,
CWTI:JUL/93[42]329, CWTI:NOV/93[24]346,
CWTI:SEP/94[26]400, CWTI:SEP/94[40]403,
CWTI:DEC/95[67]481

ADDITIONAL LISTINGS, GETTY: GETTY:11[19]232, GETTY:9[5]209,
GETTY:9[41]212

ADDITIONAL LISTINGS, MH: MH:APR/92[18]157, MH:JUN/92[50]159,
MH:APR/94[54]176, MH:JUN/94[8]177

BURR, W.J., *Surgeon, 47th New York Infantry;*
GETTY:10[53]225

BURRAGE, CHARLES W., *Lieutenant, 19th Mississippi
Infantry;* GETTY:5[89]162

BURRAGE, HENRY, *Captain, 36th Massachusetts Infantry;*
CWTI:JAN/95[34]427

BURRELL, ISAAC X., *Colonel, 42nd Massachusetts Infantry;*
ACW:JAN/93[51]398

BURROUGH, JEHU A., *Lieutenant, USMC;*
CWTI:APR/92[14]254

BURROUGHS, CHARLES, *Sergeant, 14th Connecticut
Infantry;* B&G:APR/93[12]518

BURT, AUGUSTUS W. JR., *Lieutenant, 7th South Carolina
Infantry;* GETTY:12[111]250

BURT, MASON W., *Major, USA;* GETTY:8[53]203

BURT-STARK HOUSE; ARTICLE: "IN THE LITTLE-KNOWN
BURT-STARK HOUSE, THE DECISION WAS MADE TO
END THE CONFEDERACY," ACW:MAY/92[62]364

BURTON, AMELIA, ACW:SEP/91[46]324

BURTON, ANTHONY B., *Lieutenant, Ohio Light Artillery;*
B&G:AUG/95[8]604

BURTON, ARNOLD, *Lieutenant, 5th Ohio Artillery;*
B&G:AUG/95[8]604

BURTON, DANIEL B., *Private, 22nd Virginia Infantry
Battalion;* CWR:VOL1#3[52]122

BURTON, J.H., *Lieutenant Colonel, CSA;* ACW:JAN/94[18]449

BURTON, JAMES, *civilian;* ACW:JAN/91[8]282

BURTON, JOHN W., *Captain, 6th Alabama Infantry;*
GETTY:12[111]250

BURTON, ROBERT T., *Colonel, Nauvoo Legion;*
ACW:JAN/95[8]502

BUSCHBECK, ADOLPHUS, *Colonel, 27th Pennsylvania
Infantry;* GETTY:8[17]200

BUSH, LOUIS, *Colonel, CSA;* CWR:VOL3#1[1]149,
CWR:VOL4#2[118]169

BUSH, MILTON, *Private, 154th New York Infantry;* ARTICLE:
"RELUCTANT AND UNLUCKY SOLDIER,"
B&G:OCT/93[36]540

BUSH, W.P., *Surgeon, 61st New York Infantry;*
GETTY:10[53]225

BUSHMAN, GEORGE, *civilian;* GETTY:4[65]148

BUSHNELL, CHARLES, *Major, 13th Illinois Infantry;*
CWTI:SEP/94[40]403

BUSHWACKING & BUSHWHACKERS:

ARTICLES: "BITTER BUSHWHACKERS AND JAYHAWKERS,"
ACW:JAN/93[26]395, "THE MEANEST BUSHWHACKER,"
B&G:JUN/91[32]454,

BOOK REVIEWS: *APRIL '65: CONFEDERATE COVERT ACTION
IN THE AMERICAN CIVIL WAR * BLACK FLAG:
GUERRILLA WARFARE ON THE WESTERN BORDER,
1861-1865 * BUSHWHACKERS: THE CIVIL WAR IN
NORTH CAROLINA: THE MOUNTAINS * JENNISON'S
JAYHAWKERS: A CIVIL WAR CAVALRY REGIMENT AND
ITS COMMANDER*

ADDITIONAL LISTING: CWM:AUG/95[58]611

BUSSEY, CYRUS, *Colonel, 3rd Iowa Infantry;*
B&G:AUG/95[8]604, CWNEWS:JAN/94[5],
CWTI:AUG/95[34]457

BUSWELL, NICHOLAS, *93rd Ill. Inf.;* CWR:VOL3#3[59]159

C

CABELL, GEORGE C., *Major, 18th Virginia Infantry;*
CWR:VOL3#2[1]153

CABELL, HENRY C., *Colonel, CSA;* ACW:SEP/94[38]487,
B&G:OCT/93[12]537, B&G:APR/95[8]595, GETTY:5[35]159,
GETTY:8[53]203

CABELL, WILLIAM L., *General, CSA;* ACW:JAN/91[30]286,
ACW:SEP/92[66]381, B&G:JUN/91[10]452,
CWR:VOL1#2[44]114, *photo,* B&G:JUN/91[10]452

CABIN CREEK, CHEROKEE NATION, BATTLE OF;
ACW:JAN/91[30]286, B&G:FEB/92[6]473,
CWM:JAN/92[6]398, CWM:SEP/92[38]443

CABLE, GEORGE W., *Pvt., 4th Miss. Cav.;* MH:DEC/94[46]181

CADWALADER, GEORGE, *General, USA;* AHI:NOV/71[32]136

CADWALLADER, SYLVANUS; ACW:MAY/95[38]526,
B&G:APR/91[8]445, B&G:DEC/92[32]506,
CWTI:FEB/90[46]146

CAIN, BENJAMIN D., GEORGE W. and JAMES M., *2nd
Tennessee Cavalry;* CWR:VOL4#1[1]163

CAIN, JEFF, *civilian;* ACW:SEP/91[22]321

CAIN, M., *Private, Pegram's Battery;* B&G:APR/93[24]520

CAIRO, ILLINOIS; CWTI:FEB/90[26]143

CAKE, HENRY L., *Colonel, 96th Pennsylvania Infantry;*
ARTICLE: "OF BATTLEFIELDS AND BITTER FEUDS: THE
96TH PENNSYLVANIA VOLUNTEERS," CWR:VOL3#3[1]157

CALAIS, MAINE; ARTICLE: "THE GREAT REBEL RAID ON
CALAIS, MAINE," CWTI:SEP/92[40]282

CALDER, WILLIAM, *Lieutenant, 2nd North Carolina Infantry;*
B&G:DEC/95[9]615, CWM:JUL/92[16]428

CALDWELL, CHARLES, *Lieutenant, USN;* MH:AUG/93[47]169

CALDWELL, HENRY, *Colonel, USA;* CWTI:SEP/94[12]398

CALDWELL, HORACE, *Captain, 2nd USSS;*
CWR:VOL2#2[169]

CALDWELL, JAMES F. J., *Captain, 1st South Carolina
Infantry:*
BOOK REVIEW: *A HISTORY OF A BRIGADE OF SOUTH
CAROLINIANS*
ADDITIONAL LISTINGS: ACW:MAR/94[16]458,
CWTI:AUG/90[26]166, CWTI:APR/92[49]260,
GETTY:13[22]254

CALDWELL, JOHN C., *General, USA:*
GENERAL LISTINGS: *Gettysburg,* GETTY:5[47]160,
GETTY:7[29]188, GETTY:8[53]203, GETTY:9[53]214,
GETTY:11[80]235, GETTY:12[7]241, GETTY:12[24]242
ADDITIONAL LISTINGS: ACW:MAR/94[16]458, ACW:MAY/94[12]466,
ACW:SEP/94[38]487, ACW:JUL/95[50]538,
ACW:SEP/95[54]548, B&G:APR/91[8]445,
CWM:MAR/91[50]340, CWM:APR/95[50],
CWR:VOL4#4[47]179, CWTI:AUG/95[24]455,
GETTY:5[35]159, GETTY:5[79]161, GETTY:6[59]174,
GETTY:7[51]190, GETTY:13[50]257, GETTY:10[120]229

CALDWELL, LYCURGUS W.:
BOOK REVIEW: *MY HEART IS SO REBELLIOUS: THE
CALDWELL LETTERS, 1861-1865*
ADDITIONAL LISTING: CWM:MAR/92[56]415

CALDWELL, MATTHEW A., *Private, CSA;* GETTY:10[107]227

CALDWELL, S.B., *Lieutenant, USN;* ACW:MAR/94[35]460

CALDWELL, SUSAN, *civilian;* ARTICLE: "I WAS THERE,"
CWM:MAR/92[56]415

CALEF, JOHN H., *Lieutenant, 2nd U.S. Artillery;*
B&G:DEC/91[12]469, B&G:FEB/95[8]590A,
B&G:JUN/95[36]603A, GETTY:6[13]170, GETTY:11[19]232,
photo, B&G:DEC/91[12]469

CALHOUN, JAMES M., *Mayor, Atlanta;* ACW:NOV/95[74]560,
CWM:JAN/91[28]327, CWM:JAN/92[40]405,
CWTI:SUMMER/89[50]124

CALHOUN, JOHN C.:
ARTICLE: "'A CAST-IRON MAN': JOHN C. CALHOUN,"
AHI:FEB/75[4]157
BOOK REVIEW: *JOHN C. CALHOUN AND THE PRICE OF
UNION: A BIOGRAPHY*
ADDITIONAL LISTINGS: ACW:SEP/94[66], ACW:NOV/94[12]494,
ACW:JAN/95[74]510, ACW:MAR/95[8]512, AHI:JUN/73[4]149,
CWNEWS:AUG/91[4], CWNEWS:APR/93[4],
CWNEWS:SEP/95[33], *photo,* AHI:FEB/75[4]157

CALHOUN, MRS. JOHN C.; AHI:FEB/75[4]157

CALHOUN, JOHN R., *Private, 18th Virginia Infantry;*
CWR:VOL1#3[52]122

CALIFORNIA BATTALION; CWTI:SEP/90[34]176

CALIFORNIA BRIGADE; ACW:MAY/92[8]357,
GETTY:7[97]193

CALIFORNIA COLUMN; ACW:JUL/93[27]423,
B&G:JUN/94[8]568, CWTI:SEP/91[18]227

CALIFORNIA HUNDRED; CWTI:APR/90[74]155A,
CWTI:SEP/91[18]227

CALIFORNIA TROOPS:

1st Cavalry; ACW:JUL/93[27]423, B&G:OCT/91[11]466,
CWM:MAY/92[8]418

1st Infantry; (71st Pennsylvania Infantry);
ACW:SEP/95[10]543, CWR:VOL3#1[31]150, GETTY:7[97]193

2nd Cavalry; CWR:VOL4#2[26]166

3rd Infantry; ACW:MAY/92[8]357

4th Infantry; B&G:OCT/91[11]466

5th Infantry; (106th Pennsylvania Infantry) GETTY:7[97]193

8th Infantry; ACW:MAR/92[62]355

Native Cavalry; B&G:OCT/91[11]466

CALIFORNIA, STATE OF:

ARTICLES: "REBEL PIRATES AND CALIFORNIA GOLD,"
CWTI:JUN/95[48]448, "TRACES OF A DISTANT WAR,"
CWTI:JUN/95[51]449
BOOK REVIEWS: *FORTRESS ALCATRAZ: GUARDIAN OF THE
GOLDEN GATE, THE BEAT OF THE DRUM*

CALLAHAM, SHEROD W., *Lieutenant, 7th South Carolina
Infantry;* GETTY:5[35]159

CALLAHAN, CHARLES M., *Captain, 1st Missouri Light
Artillery;* B&G:AUG/95[8]604

CALLAWAY COUNTY, MISSOURI; ARTICLE: "CALLAWAY
COUNTY, MISSOURI," ACW:MAR/91[62]298

CALLAWAY, FELIX R., *Sergeant, Sumter Artillery;*
CWR:VOL3#2[1]153

CALLIHAN, CHARLES S., *Lt. Col., USA;* CWTI:AUG/95[34]457

CALLIS, JOHN B., *Lieutenant Colonel, 7th Wisconsin Infantry;*
ARTICLE: "A GETTYSBURG ENCOUNTER," GETTY:7[114]194
ADDITIONAL LISTINGS: GETTY:4[115]152, GETTY:6[13]170,
GETTY:11[119]238

CALLOWAY, WILLIAM P., *Captain, USA;* ACW:JUL/93[27]423

CALVERT, JOSEPH C., *Private, Mosby's Ranger;*
CWTI:SEP/90[34]176

CALWAY, THOMAS F., *Lieutenant, USA;* CWM:MAR/91[17]335

CARDER, WILLIAM B., *Lieutenant, 4th Virginia Infantry;*
GETTY:12[111]250

CARDY, J. HENRY, *Private, 6th Wisconsin Infantry;*
GETTY:11[57]233

CAREY, JAMES L., *Lt., 4th Indiana Inf.;* B&G:AUG/95[8]604

CARIKER, JACK, *Private, CSA;* CWTI:SEP/92[31]281

CARLETON, JAMES H., *General, USA;* ACW:JUL/93[27]423,
AHI:JAN/69[56], AHI:OCT/79[20]194, B&G:JUN/94[8]568,
CWTI:SEP/91[18]227, *photo,* AHI:OCT/79[20]194

CARLETON, JOSEPH H., *Captain, 32nd Wisconsin Infantry;*
CWR:VOL2#4[313]146

CARLILE, JOHN S., *Senator, Virginia;* CWTI:AUG/95[54]460

CARLIN, J.C., *Captain, CSN;* ACW:MAY/92[23]360,
CWTI:AUG/95[58]461

CARLIN, WILILAM P., *General, USA;* B&G:FEB/91[8]339,
B&G:OCT/91[11]466, B&G:DEC/95[9]615,
CWR:VOL4#3[65]172, CWTI:SEPT/89[30]129, *photo,*
B&G:DEC/95[9]615

CARLISLE, DAVID, *Private, CSA;* ACW:JUL/94[26]477

CARLISLE, PENNSYLVANIA, CWTI:APR/89[38]111,
CWTI:DEC/89[34]136

CARLTON, HENRY H., *Captain, Troup (Georgia) Artillery;*
ACW:JAN/94[8]447, GETTY:8[53]203

CARLTON, P.C., *Captain, 7th North Carolina Infantry;*
GETTY:8[67]204, GETTY:13[75]259

CARLTON, R.E., *Pvt., 7th Kentucky Inf.;* B&G:AUG/94[22]576

CARMAN, EZRA, *General, USA;* B&G:FEB/91[8]439,
B&G:OCT/95[8]611E, CWM:DEC/94[17]547

CARMICHAEL, THOMAS, *Lt., USA;* CWTI:MAY/92[29]263

CARMICHAEL, THOMAS H., *Lt., USN;* MH:FEB/91[8]151

CARNEGIE, ANDREW; CWM:NOV/91[8]394A

CARNEY, PATRICK, *Lt., 69th NY Inf.;* CWTI:DEC/90[58]185

CARNEY, THOMAS, *Governor, Kansas;* ACW:NOV/94[42]497,
B&G:JUN/91[10]452

CARNEY, WILLIAM H., *Sergeant, 54th Massachusetts
Infantry;* ACW:SEP/91[30]322, ACW:MAR/93[58],
CWTI:DEC/89[42]137

CARNIFEX FERRY, WEST VIRGINIA, BATTLE OF;
ACW:SEP/94[31]486, CWTI:JAN/94[46]364

CARNTON MANSION, FRANKLIN, TENNESSEE;
B&G:OCT/91[11]466, B&G:FEB/92[40]479

CAROLINA CAMPAIGN; see listings under "SHERMAN'S
CAROLINA CAMPAIGN"

CARPENTER'S (VIRGINIA) BATTERY;
CWM:MAY/92[20]420

CARPENTER, ALFRED and CHARLES, *1st Minnesota
Infantry;* GETTY:5[79]161

CARPENTER, B.F., *Private, 34th North Carolina Infantry;*
GETTY:8[67]204

CARPENTER, DANIEL, *civilian;* AHI:AUG/77[30]175

CARPENTER, FRANCIS B., *artist;* ARTICLE: "THE PAINTER
AND THE PRESIDENT," CWTI:FEB/92[21]247

CARPENTER, JOHN C., *Captain, Alleghany Artillery;*
CWR:VOL4#4[70]180, GETTY:4[49]147, GETTY:10[29]222

CARPENTER, LOUIS H., *Lieutenant Colonel, USA;*
AHI:DEC/67[58]114, CWTI:JUN/90[32]159

CARPENTIER, STEVEN, *Captain, Carpentier's Alabama
Artillery;* B&G:AUG/95[8]604

CARPENTIER'S (ALABAMA) BATTERY; B&G:AUG/95[8]604

CARPETBAGGERS; BOOK REVIEWS: *CARPETBAGGER FROM
VERMONT: THE AUTOBIOGRAPHY OF MARSHALL
HARVEY TWITCHELL * THE CONFEDERATE*

*CARPETBAGGERS * THE INVISIBLE EMPIRE * THOSE
TERRIBLE CARPETBAGGERS: A REINTERPRETATION*

CARR, C.C., *Sergeant, 1st U.S. Cavalry;* ACW:JUL/93[42]425

CARR, EUGENE A., *General, USA;*
ARTICLE: "CARR'S PUNITIVE EXPEDITION,"
AHI:DEC/67[58]114

ADDITIONAL LISTINGS: ACW:JUL/93[42]425, ACW:JUL/94[51]480,
AHI:FEB/71[4]131, AHI:NOV/79[32]196, B&G:FEB/94[8]550,
CWR:VOL1#1[42]105, CWR:VOL2#1[19]131,
CWR:VOL2#1[69]133, CWR:VOL3#3[59]159,
CWTI:MAY/91[24]208, CWTI:FEB/92[29]248,
MH:DEC/95[58]188, *photo,* AHI:DEC/67[58]114

CARR, FLAVELL, *Corporal, 5th New York Infantry;*
CWR:VOL1#2[7]111, CWTI:MAY/94[31]382

CARR, JOHN D., *Private, CSA;* CWTI:NOV/93[65]351

CARR, JOSEPH B., *General, USA:*
ARTICLE: "TO UNFLINCHINGLY FACE DANGER AND DEATH:
CARR'S BRIGADE DEFENDS EMMITSBURG ROAD,
GETTY:12[7]241

BOOK REVIEW: *THE MUTINY AT BRANDY STATION: THE
LAST BATTLE OF THE HOOKER BRIGADE*

ADDITIONAL LISTINGS: B&G:APR/91[8]445, B&G:FEB/92[22]476,
CWM:MAY/92[20]420, GETTY:5[79]161, GETTY:8[31]201,
photo, GETTY:12[7]241

CARR, ROBERT B., *Lieutenant, 43rd North Carolina Infantry;*
GETTY:12[111]250

CARRAWAY, PLEASANT T., *Private, 2nd South Carolina
Infantry;* GETTY:5[35]159

CARRELL, THOMAS R., *USN;* ACW:MAR/92[40]353

CARRIER, JOSEPH C., *Chaplain, 6th Missouri Infantry;*
CWM:MAR/91[50]340

CARRINGTON, HENRY B., *General, USA;*
AHI:JUN/66[52]102, CWM:SEP/93[18]494,
CWTI:JUL/94[44]394

CARRINGTON, W.H.D., *Captain, CSA;* CWTI:AUG/90[58]169

CARRINGTON, WILLIAM A., *Surgeon, CSA;*
CWTI:MAR/95[60]439

CARROLL COUNTY RIFLES, (11th Mississippi Infantry);
GETTY:9[98]217

CARROLL, ANNA ELLA:
ARTICLE: "WASHINGTON JOURNALIST AND LOBBYIST
ANNA ELLA CARROLL WAS ABRAHAM LINCOLN'S
SECRET STRATEGIC WEAPON," ACW:MAR/95[8]512

BOOK REVIEW: *NEITHER HEROINE NOR FOOL: ANNA ELLA
CARROLL OF MARYLAND*

CARROLL, CHAS, *Col., 15th TN. Inf.;* CWTI:JAN/95[27]425

CARROLL, COLUMBA, *Mother Superior;* B&G:OCT/93[31]539

CARROLL, DEROSEY, *Colonel, 1st Arkansas Cavalry;*
ACW:NOV/93[26]441, CWTI:FEB/92[29]248

CARROLL, EDWARD, *14th Ohio Infantry;*
CWTI:SUMMER/89[20]121

CARROLL, JOHN, *Cpl., 5th NY Inf.;* CWR:VOL1#2[29]112

CARROLL, SAMUEL S., *Colonel, USA;* ACW:NOV/92[42]388,
ACW:SEP/94[38]487, ACW:JUL/95[50]538,
B&G:APR/95[8]595, B&G:JUN/95[8]600,
CWM:MAR/91[17]335, GETTY:4[49]147, GETTY:4[113]153,
GETTY:7[51]190, GETTY:8[95]205, GETTY:9[61]215,
GETTY:11[57]233, GETTY:12[30]243, GETTY:12[85]248,
GETTY:13[7]253, *photo,* CWM:MAR/91[17]335

CARROLL, WILLIAM H., *General, USA;* ACW:SEP/93[38]434,
ACW:JAN/94[18]449, B&G:FEB/93[12]511,
CWR:VOL4#1[1]163, CWTI:MAR/89[44]105

CASSON, JAMES, *Pvt., 2nd SC Inf.;* GETTY:5[35]159

CASSVILLE, GEORGIA, BATTLE OF; ACW:SEP/94[10]484,
CWM:JAN/91[12]326, CWM:JUL/92[40]432,
CWTI:APR/89[50]112, CWTI:SUMMER/89[13]120

CASTLEBERRY, W.A., *Private, 13th Alabama Infantry;*
GETTY:5[4]156

CASTLEMAN, JOHN B., *Captain, CSA;* B&G:OCT/93[38]541

CASTOR, WILLIAM, *Private, 4th U.S. Artillery;*
GETTY:11[57]233

CATER, DOUGLAS J., *Private, 3rd Texas Cavalry;* BOOK
REVIEW: *AS IT WAS: REMINISCENCES OF A SOLDIER OF
THE THIRD TEXAS CAVALRY AND THE NINETEENTH
LOUISIANA INFANTRY*

CATHEY, ALEXANDER A., *Lieutenant, 34th North Carolina
Infantry;* GETTY:12[111]250

CATLETT STATION, VIRGINIA:
ARTICLE: "STUART'S REVENGE," CWTI:JUN/95[38]447
ADDITIONAL LISTINGS: B&G:AUG/92[11]493, B&G:OCT/92[38]500,
CWR:VOL1#3[28]120, CWTI:DEC/89[34]136,
CWTI:NOV/93[55]350, MH:JUN/94[8]177

CATLIN, THEODORE B., *Colonel, 5th Wisconsin Infantry;*
ACW:MAR/92[30]352

CATTERSON, ROBERT F., *Colonel, USA;* B&G:DEC/95[9]615

CATTERSON, W.C., *Captain, 12th Arkansas Sharpshooter
Battalion;* B&G:FEB/94[8]550

CAUDLE, ALEX, *Pvt., Petersburg Arty.;* ACW:MAR/95[12]513

CAUDLE, JOHN H., *Colonel, CSA;* CWR:VOL4#2[118]169

CAUSES OF THE WAR; ARTICLE: "CIVIL WAR IN THE
MAKING," ACW:MAY/94[43]470

CAVADA, ADOLPHUS F., *Captain, 23rd Pennsylvania
Infantry;* GETTY:10[112]228, GETTY:12[7]241

CAVALRY RAIDS; see listings under **"RAIDS"**

CAVALRY TACTICS and WARFARE:
ARTICLES: "BOOTS AND SADDLES: PART I: THE EASTERN
THEATER," CWTI:APR/92[35]257, "BOOTS AND SADDLES:
PART II: THE WESTERN THEATER," CWTI:MAY/92[48]267
BOOK REVIEWS: *CAVALRY TACTICS: OR, REGULATIONS FOR
THE INSTRUCTION, FORMATIONS, AND MOVEMENTS
OF THE CAVALRY * SPURS TO GLORY * THE STORY OF
THE UNITED STATES CAVALRY; THE UNION CAVALRY
IN THE CIVIL WAR*

CAVANAGH, JAMES, *Major, 69th New York Infantry;*
CWTI:DEC/90[58]185

CAVANAUGH, JOHN, *Chaplain;* B&G:OCT/93[31]539

CAVING BANKS, INDIAN TERRITORY, BATTLE OF;
ACW:JAN/91[30]286, CWM:MAY/93[24]476

CAVINS, ADEN, *Captain, USA;* CWNEWS:JUN/90[4]

CAWTHORN, JAMES, *Colonel, CSA;* ACW:NOV/93[26]441,
CWTI:FEB/92[29]248

CEDAR CREEK BATTLEFIELD FOUNDATION; see listings
under **"PRESERVATION"**

CEDAR CREEK, VIRGINIA, BATTLE OF:
ARTICLES: "BILL MAY: CRUSADER FOR CEDAR CREEK,"
CWM:DEC/95[26]626, "DETAILS OF CEDAR CREEK,"
CWM:OCT/94[38]540, "FAMILY VALUES AT CEDAR
CREEK," CWM:OCT/94[23]535, "TRAVEL,"
MH:OCT/93[76]173
BOOK REVIEWS *THE BATTLE OF CEDAR CREEK: SHOWDOWN
IN THE SHENANDOAH, OCTOBER 1-30, 1864 *
SHERIDAN: THE LIFE AND WARS OF GENERAL PHIL
SHERIDAN * THE GUNS OF CEDAR CREEK*
ADDITIONAL LISTINGS: ACW:MAY/93[14]413, ACW:SEP/94[55]489,
AHI:MAY/71[3]133A, B&G:JUN/94[22]569,

CWM:JAN/91[35]328, CWM:JUL/91[64]375,
CWM:SEP/91[64]387, CWM:MAR/93[24]467,
CWM:SEP/93[24]495, CWM:APR/94[24]505,
CWM:OCT/94[4]532, CWNEWS:MAY/95[33],
CWR:VOL2#1[19]131, CWR:VOL2#3[256],
CWR:VOL3#1[1]149, CWTI:APR/92[35]257, CWTI:SEP/92[18],
CWTI:SEP/94[49]404, MH:APR/95[46]183

CEDAR MOUNTAIN, VIRGINIA, BATTLE OF:
BOOK REVIEW: *STONEWALL JACKSON AT CEDAR MOUNTAIN*
ADDITIONAL LISTINGS: ACW:JUL/91[18]312, ACW:MAR/94[16]458,
ACW:MAR/95[42]517, AHI:MAY/71[3]133A,
AHI:NOV/89[50]288, B&G:APR/91[8]445, B&G:JUN/92[8]487,
B&G:AUG/92[11]493, B&G:OCT/95[32]613,
CWM:MAR/91[65]342, CWM:JUL/92[18]429, CWM:OCT/94[8],
CWM:DEC/94[26]548, CWM:DEC/95[41]630,
CWR:VOL1#1[1]102, CWR:VOL1#3[52]122,
CWR:VOL2#4[346], CWR:VOL3#1[31]150, CWR:VOL3#1[80],
CWR:VOL3#2[70]155, CWTI:APR/92[35]257,
CWTI:NOV/93[55]350, CWTI:JUN/95[38]447

CEDAR RUN, VIRGINIA, BATTLE OF; CWTI:JUN/95[18]444

CELLUM, T.J., *Sgt., 3rd Texas Cavalry;* CWTI:JUL/94[50]395

CENTER, C.O., *Pvt., 52nd NC Inf.;* B&G:APR/93[24]520

CENTRAL RAILROAD BRIDGE, VIRGINIA,
ENGAGEMENT AT; ARTICLE: "The 'Blackberry' Raid,"
GETTY:11[6]231

CENTRALIA, MISSOURI, MASSACRE AT:
ARTICLE: "EVEN IN DEATH, GUERRILLA 'BLOODY BILL'
ANDERSON REMAINED FEARSOME AND DEFIANT,"
ACW:JAN/93[6]391
ADDITIONAL LISTINGS: ACW:MAR/94[6]455, ACW:JUL/95[58],
B&G:JUN/91[10]452, B&G:JUN/91[32]454,
B&G:OCT/91[11]466, CWTI:JAN/94[29]360

"THE CENTURY ILLUSTRATED MONTHLY MAGAZINE",
ARTICLE: "THE 'CENTURY' ART: WHAT WAR LOOKED
LIKE," CWTI:SEP/90[28]175

CEVOR, CHARLES, *Captain, CSA;* AHI:JUN/84[24]239,
B&G:DEC/91[6]468

CHACE, H.C., *Seaman, USN;* B&G:JUN/92[40]489

CHADBOURNE, HENRY A., *Lieutenant, 10th Alabama
Infantry;* GETTY:12[111]250

CHAFFEE, ADNA R., *Lieutenant, USA;* ACW:JUL/93[42]425

CHAFFEE, NEWTON A., *Sergeant, USA;* GETTY:8[17]200

CHAFFIN'S BLUFF, VIRGINIA; ACW:JUL/94[42]479,
ACW:SEP/95[30]545

CHAFFIN, H., *Captain, Louisiana Tigers;* CWTI:MAR/94[48]374

CHALKEY, GEORGE B., *Lieutenant, 14th Virginia Infantry;*
GETTY:12[111]250

CHALMERS, JAMES R., *General, CSA;* ACW:SEP/92[23]377,
ACW:JUL/95[70]540, ACW:NOV/95[48]557,
AHI:APR/74[4]154, B&G:OCT/92[32]499,
B&G:JUN/93[12]524, B&G:DEC/93[12]545,
B&G:DEC/93[52]548, CWM:JUL/92[24]430,
CWR:VOL1#4[v]124, CWR:VOL1#4[42]126,
CWR:VOL2#4[313]146, CWR:VOL4#1[44]164,
CWTI:SEP/93[59]341, CWTI:NOV/93[65]351, *photo,*
CWTI:NOV/93[65]351

CHAMBERLAIN, CYRUS N., *Surgeon, USA;* GETTY:10[53]225

CHAMBERLAIN, D.C., *Lieutenant, 21st Massachusetts
Infantry;* B&G:FEB/95[38]593, B&G:JUN/95[36]603A,

CHAMBERLAIN, DANIEL H.:
ARTICLE: "THE GENTLE CARPETBAGGER: DANIEL H.
CHAMBERLAIN," AHI:JAN/73[28]147

CHANCELLORSVILLE," CWM:DEC/94[40]550,
"ORDNANCE," ACW:MAY/91[8]300
BOOK REVIEWS: *THE CAMPAIGN OF CHANCELLORSVILLE **
CHANCELLORSVILLE AND GETTYSBURG *
CHANCELLORSVILLE BATTLEFIELD SITES *
CHANCELLORSVILLE 1863: THE SOULS OF THE BRAVE
* THE CHANCELLORSVILLE CAMPAIGN: MARCH-MAY
1863 * LEATHERBREECHES: HERO OF
CHANCELLORSVILLE * LEE'S TERRIBLE SWIFT SWORD:
FROM ANTIETAM TO CHANCELLORSVILLE, AN
EYEWITNESS HISTORY * THE U.S. ARMY WAR COLLEGE
GUIDE TO THE BATTLES OF CHANCELLORSVILLE AND
FREDERICKSBURG
GENERAL LISTINGS: *general history,* AHI:MAY/71[3]133A, *in book*
review, ACW:NOV/93[58], CWM:DEC/94[7], CWM:AUG/95[8],
CWM:AUG/95[45], CWNEWS:MAY/89[4],
CWNEWS:APR/93[4], CWR:VOL1#4[77], CWR:VOL2#4[346],
CWR:VOL3#2[105], CWR:VOL3#3[92], CWR:VOL4#3[89],
CWR:VOL4#4[129], *Jackson,* B&G:JUN/92[8]487, *Jackson's*
wounding, ACW:MAY/95[10]523, *O.O. Howard,*
GETTY:11[71]234
ADDITIONAL LISTINGS, ACW: ACW:NOV/91[41]334,
ACW:JUL/92[12]367, ACW:MAR/93[26]404,
ACW:JUL/93[16]422, ACW:JUL/94[18]476,
ACW:JAN/95[46]507, ACW:JUL/95[10]533,
ACW:JUL/95[26]535, ACW:SEP/95[54]548
ADDITIONAL LISTINGS, B&G: B&G:AUG/91[36]462,
B&G:APR/95[8]595
ADDITIONAL LISTINGS, CWM: CWM:MAR/91[35]337,
CWM:JUL/91[28]366, CWM:NOV/91[12]390,
CWM:JUL/92[8]427, CWM:JUL/92[16]428,
CWM:JUL/92[18]429, CWM:SEP/93[8]493,
CWM:SEP/93[24]495, CWM:APR/94[14]503,
CWM:JUN/94[26]512, CWM:OCT/94[26]536,
CWM:DEC/94[4]545, CWM:APR/95[16]571,
CWM:AUG/95[4]601, CWM:DEC/95[34]628
ADDITIONAL LISTINGS, CWR: CWR:VOL1#1[1]102,
CWR:VOL1#1[26]103, CWR:VOL1#2[29]112,
CWR:VOL1#3[v]117, CWR:VOL1#3[52]122,
CWR:VOL2#2[141]137, CWR:VOL2#3[236]143,
CWR:VOL2#4[269]145, CWR:VOL3#1[31]150,
CWR:VOL3#3[1]157, CWR:VOL4#4[i]175
ADDITIONAL LISTINGS, CWTI: CWTI:APR/89[38]111,
CWTI:MAY/89[22]116, CWTI:MAY/89[36]118,
CWTI:DEC/89[34]136, CWTI:SEP/91[31]229,
CWTI:APR/92[35]257, CWTI:SEP/92[42]283,
CWTI:MAY/93[26]318, CWTI:JUL/93[42]329,
CWTI:SEP/93[43]338, CWTI:JUL/94[44]394,
CWTI:MAR/95[26]434, CWTI:JUN/95[32]446,
CWTI:DEC/95[67]481
ADDITIONAL LISTINGS, GETTY: GETTY:6[69]176, GETTY:13[108]261
ADDITIONAL LISTINGS, MH: MH:APR/92[18]157, MH:AUG/94[46]178
CHANDLER, ALBERT A.; CWTI:AUG/95[46]459
CHANDLER, CHARLES L., *Lieutenant Colonel, 57th*
Massachusetts Infantry; ACW:SEP/95[70]549,
B&G:APR/93[12]518
CHANDLER, JASPER M., *civilian;* B&G:FEB/91[20]440
CHANDLER, SIMON C., *Private, 6th Massachusetts Infantry;*
ACW:NOV/95[30]555
CHANDLER, ZACHARIAH M., *Lieutenant Colonel, 78th Ohio*
Infantry; ACW:SEP/93[46]435, AHI:MAY/70[4]126,
B&G:FEB/94[8]550, CWTI:MAR/95[40]436,

CWTI:DEC/95[52]480, GETTY:12[1]240, GETTY:12[85]248,
photo, AHI:MAY/70[4]126
CHANEY, JOHN T., *Captain, 1st Illinois Artillery;*
B&G:AUG/95[8]604
CHANEY, R. ELMORE,, *Private, 2nd South Carolina Infantry;*
GETTY:5[35]159
CHANTILLY, VIRGINIA, BATTLE OF:
ARTICLES: "STONEWALL'S SURPRISE AT OX HILL,"
ACW:JAN/95[54]508, "WE CLEARED THEIR WAY...FIRING
CANISTER," CWTI:MAR/93[20]308
ADDITIONAL LISTINGS: ACW:NOV/92[18]385, ACW:MAY/95[18]524,
AHI:MAY/71[3]133A, B&G:JUN/92[8]487,
CWM:APR/94[14]503, CWM:DEC/94[26]548,
CWR:VOL1#1[1]102, CWR:VOL1#3[52]122,
CWR:VOL2#4[346], CWR:VOL3#1[80]
CHAPLAINS; ARTICLE: "THEIR FAITH BRINGS THEM,"
CWM:MAR/91[50]340
CHAPLIN, DANILE, *Colonel, 1st Maine Heavy Artillery;*
CWR:VOL4#1[78]
CHAPMAN'S DIXIE ARTILLERY; GETTY:6[62]175
CHAPMAN, CONRAD WISE:
ARTICLE: "THE ARTIST AND THE CIVIL WAR,"
AHI:NOV/80[28]211, "MEMOIRS IN OILS,"
CWM:NOV/92[31]449
ADDITIONAL LISTING: CWTI:APR/89[BACK]
CHAPMAN, GEORGE, *General, USA;* B&G:AUG/93[36]533
CHAPMAN, GEORGE, *Private, 126th New York Infantry;*
CWR:VOL1#4[7]125
CHAPMAN, GEORGE H., *Colonel, 12th Illinois Cavalry;*
ACW:MAY/94[35]469, B&G:APR/94[10]558,
B&G:APR/95[8]595, CWTI:APR/92[49]260, GETTY:11[19]232
CHAPMAN, HORATIO, *Private, 20th Connecticut Infantry;*
ACW:SEP/92[47]380
CHAPMAN, JOHN, *Lieutenant, 13th Indiana Cavalry;*
CWTI:MAR/91[46]203
CHAPMAN, JOHN S., *Captain, CSA;* B&G:OCT/94[11]580
CHAPMAN, ROBERT T., *Captain, USN;* B&G:DEC/94[10]585
CHAPMAN, ROBERT, *Lieutenant, CSN;* ACW:MAY/93[62]418,
CWTI:AUG/95[40]458
CHAPMAN, WILLIAM, *Colonel, USA;* ACW:NOV/94[50]498,
B&G:AUG/92[11]493
CHAPMAN, WILLIAM H., *Captain, Dixie Artillery:*
ARTICLE: "TIME LAPSE," CWTI:DEC/90[90]186
ADDITIONAL LISTINGS: CWM:AUG/94[48]529,
CWTI:MAR/91[10]197, CWTI:NOV/93[55]350,
GETTY:10[107]227
CHARLES, WILLIAM, *Private, 154th New York Infantry;*
GETTY:8[17]200
CHARLESTON, SOUTH CAROLINA:
ARTICLES: "COMING TO THE CRISIS: 1860," AHI:JUN/73[4]149,
"SWAMP ANGEL'S REIGN OF TERROR,"
CWM:MAR/92[16]411, "TO HONOR THE DEAD: A PROPER
BURIAL IN CHARLESTON," CWTI:MAR/94[59]376
BOOK REVIEWS: *CHARLESTON'S MARITIME HERITAGE,*
1670-1865: AN ILLUSTRATED HISTORY * CONFEDERATE
CHARLESTON: AN ILLUSTRATED HISTORY OF THE
CITY AND THE PEOPLE DURING THE CIVIL WAR * GATE
OF HELL, CAMPAIGN FOR CHARLESTON HARBOR, 1863
* THE SIEGE OF CHARLESTON, 1861-1865
GENERAL LISTINGS: *Battery Wagner;* CWTI:APR/89[22]108, *Fort*
Gregg; CWTI:APR/89[22]108, *Fort Sumter;*
CWTI:APR/89[22]108, *Immortal Six Hundred,*
GETTY:12[111]250, *in book review,* CWR:VOL3#3[92], *map;*

CWTI:APR/89[22]108, painting by Conrad Wise Chapman;
CWTI:APR/89[BACK], *The Swamp Angel;*
CWTI:APR/89[22]108, photos; ACW:SEP/94[46]488,
CWTI:APR/89[22]108
ADDITIONAL LISTINGS: CWTI:APR/89[32]110,
CWTI:DEC/89[42]137, CWTI:AUG/90[42]167,
CWTI:JAN/94[46]364
CHARLOTTESVILLE (VIRGINIA) ARTILLERY;
B&G:DEC/95[25]616, GETTY:7[124]196
CHASE, DUDLEY H., *Captain, 17th U.S. Infantry;*
CWM:AUG/95[27]605
CHASE, GEORGE H., *Private, Berdan's Sharpshooters;*
CWTI:APR/90[48]154
CHASE, KATE; ACW:JUL/92[8]365A, GETTY:9[122]220
CHASE, SALMON P.:
BOOK REVIEWS: *THE SALMON P. CHASE PAPERS, VOLUME 1,
JOURNALS, 1829-1872 * THE SALMON P. CHASE PAPERS,
VOLUME 1, JOURNALS, 1829-1872, VOLUME 2 *
CORRESPONDENCE, 1823-1857 * SALMON P. CHASE: A
BIOGRAPHY*
GENERAL LISTINGS: *election of 1864,* AHI:OCT/68[4]116,
Gettysburg, GETTY:7[23]187, GETTY:12[85]248, *impeachment
of Andrew Johnson,* AHI:DEC/68[28]118, *in book review,*
CWM:DEC/94[7], CWM:AUG/95[45], CWNEWS:AUG/91[4],
James A. Garfield, AHI:MAY/76[24]167, *Kate Sprague,*
AHI:APR/83[27]233, *Lincoln's assassination;*
CWTI:AUG/90[42]167, *Lincoln's humor,* AHI:NOV/70[22]130,
Nelson-Davis feud, AHI:NOV/72[12]142, *Thaddeus Stevens,*
AHI:JAN/82[16]224, *photo,* AHI:APR/83[27]233
ADDITIONAL LISTINGS: ACW:MAR/94[35]460, ACW:NOV/72[10]141,
AHI:DEC/81[18]223, CWM:APR/95[32]575,
CWTI:JUN/90[46]161, CWTI:FEB/92[21]247,
CWTI:SEP/92[22]279, CWTI:DEC/94[82]418,
CWTI:MAR/95[40]436, CWTI:JUN/95[32]446,
GETTY:9[122]220
CHATFIELD, JOHN L., *Colonel, 6th Connecticut Infantry;*
ACW:SEP/91[30]322
**CHATTANOOGA, TENNESSEE, BATTLE, CAMPAIGN
AND SIEGE OF:**
ARTICLES: "THE 24TH WISCONSIN'S GALLANT BOY
COLONEL, ARTHUR MACARTHUR, PLANTED THE
COLORS ON MISSIONARY RIDGE," ACW:MAR/92[14]350,
"A CONVERSATION WITH PETER COZZENS, THE LAST
HURRAH: BRAGG AND CHATTANOOGA,"
CWM:APR/95[16]571, "CHATTANOOGA RELIEVED!"
CWM:DEC/94[46]552, "CHATTANOOGA'S FRONTIERLIKE
APPEARANCE BELIED ITS STRATEGIC MILITARY
IMPORTANCE AS A RAILROAD CENTER,"
ACW:NOV/95[6]551, "DARING REAR-GUARD DEFENSE,"
ACW:NOV/93[34]442, "GUNBOATS ON THE UPPER
TENNESSEE," CWTI:MAY/93[38]321, "MIRACLE OF THE
RAILS," CWTI:SEP/92[22]279, "TO SAVE AN ARMY,"
CWTI:SEP/94[40]403
BOOK REVIEWS: *CHICKAMAUGA & CHATTANOOGA: THE
BATTLES THAT DOOMED THE CONFEDERACY *
MOUNTAIN TOUCHED WITH FIRE: CHATTANOOGA
BESIEGED, 1863 * PATHS TO VICTORY: A HISTORY AND
TOUR GUIDE OF THE STONES RIVER, CHICKAMAUGA,
CHATTANOOGA, KNOXVILLE AND NASHVILLE * THE
SHIPWRECK OF THEIR HOPES: THE BATTLE FOR
CHATTANOOGA*
GENERAL LISTINGS: *general history,* AHI:MAY/71[3]133A, *in book
review,* ACW:NOV/95[62], CWM:AUG/95[45],

CWM:OCT/95[10], CWR:VOL1#2[78], CWR:VOL4#1[78],
photo, CWTI:FEB/90[46]146
ADDITIONAL LISTINGS: ACW:MAY/91[23]303, ACW:JAN/94[55]453,
ACW:JUL/94[66]481, ACW:NOV/95[6]551,
B&G:JUN/91[42]403, B&G:OCT/92[10]496,
CWM:JAN/91[4]323, CWM:JUL/92[18]429,
CWM:MAR/93[8]465, CWM:MAR/94[8]465,
CWM:DEC/94[46]552, CWM:APR/95[6]571,
CWM:APR/95[16]571, CWR:VOL1#1[73]108,
CWR:VOL1#4[64]127, CWR:VOL1#4[64]128,
CWTI:JAN/95[27]425, CWR:VOL3#2[70]155,
CWR:VOL3#3[59]159, CWTI:SUMMER/89[13]120,
CWTI:SEPT/89[30]129, CWTI:FEB/90[46]146,
CWTI:AUG/91[62]221, CWTI:MAR/93[40]312,
CWTI:JAN/94[35]361, CWTI:MAY/94[50]386,
CWTI:MAR/95[26]434, CWTI:JAN/95[34]427,
CWTI:MAR/95[40]436, MH:DEC/93[12]174
CHAVEZ, MANUEL, *Lt. Col., USA;* B&G:JUN/94[8]568
CHEAIRS, NATHANIEL F., *Major, CSA;* ACW:JUL/94[58],
B&G:FEB/92[10]474
**CHEAT MOUNTAIN, WEST VIRGINIA, BATTLE AND
CAMPAIGN:**
ARTICLE: "GRANNY LEE'S INAUSPICIOUS DEBUT,"
ACW:SEP/94[31]486
ADDITIONAL LISTINGS: ACW:NOV/91[41]334, ACW:JAN/92[50]345,
B&G:OCT/92[32]499, B&G:AUG/93[10]529,
CWM:JUL/92[24]430, CWM:DEC/95[10], CWR:VOL1#4[7]125
CHEATHAM, BENJAMIN F., *General, CSA:*
BOOK REVIEW: *TENNESSEE'S FORGOTTEN WARRIORS:
FRANK CHEATHAM AND HIS CONFEDERATE DIVISION*
GENERAL LISTINGS: *Atlanta Campaign,* ACW:JAN/95[30]505,
ACW:NOV/95[74]560, CWTI:SUMMER/89[20]121,
CWTI:SUMMER/89[32]122, CWTI:SUMMER/89[40]123,
CWTI:SUMMER/89[50]124, *Carolina Campaign,*
B&G:DEC/95[9]615, *Franklin,* ACW:MAR/94[42]461, *in book
review,* ACW:MAR/91[54], CWNEWS:JUL/92[4],
CWR:VOL4#4[129], *Nashville,* ACW:NOV/95[48]557, *order of
battle,* B&G:DEC/93[12]545, B&G:DEC/95[9]615, *Shiloh,*
CWTI:SEP/93[59]341, *Tullahoma Campaign,*
B&G:OCT/92[10]496, *photo,* B&G:DEC/93[12]545
ADDITIONAL LISTINGS: ACW:SEP/92[38]379, B&G:DEC/93[12]545,
B&G:DEC/93[49]547A, B&G:DEC/93[52]548,
B&G:OCT/94[11]580, CWM:JAN/91[12]326,
CWM:APR/95[16]571, CWR:VOL1#3[7]118,
CWR:VOL1#4[v]124, CWR:VOL1#4[42]126,
CWR:VOL1#4[64]127, CWR:VOL3#4[24]162,
CWR:VOL4#1[44]164, CWR:VOL4#3[50]171,
CWTI:APR/89[14]107, CWTI:SEPT/89[30]129,
CWTI:SEP/92[28]280, CWTI:NOV/92[41]291,
CWTI:JAN/93[20]298, CWTI:JAN/95[27]425
CHEATHAM, E. FOSTER, *Captain, CSA;* B&G:OCT/94[11]580
CHEAVENS, HENRY, *Private, 6th Missouri Infantry;*
CWTI:AUG/95[58]461
CHEEK, WILLIAM H., *Colonel, CSA;* CWTI:FEB/91[45]194
CHEEK, WILLIAM M., *Pvt., 26th NC Inf.;* GETTY:5[19]158
CHEESBRO, ALMOND M., *Sergeant, 53rd Pennsylvania
Infantry;* GETTY:11[80]235
CHEEVES, JOSHUA; ACW:MAR/93[8]401
CHEMBERLIN, JOHN, *Sergeant, USA;* GETTY:8[31]201
CHENAULT, D.W., *Col., 11th Kent. Cav.;* B&G:OCT/94[11]580
CHENEY, MATTHEW B., *Captain, 154th New York Infantry;*
GETTY:8[17]200

CHENEY, NEWELL, *Adjutant, 9th New York Cavalry;*
GETTY:11[19]232
CHEROKEE (GEORGIA) ARTILLERY; ACW:NOV/91[22]331,
CWTI:NOV/92[41]291
CHEROKEE BRAVES:
ARTICLE: "MUSKETS AND...TOMAHAWKS," CWM:SEP/92[8]437
ADDITIONAL LISTINGS: B&G:OCT/94[38]582, CWM:SEP/92[8]437,
CWM:SEP/92[38]443
CHEROKEE NATION; CWTI:SEP/90[52]179
CHEROKEE NEUTRAL LANDS; CWTI:SEP/90[52]179
CHESAPEAKE (MARYLAND) ARTILLERY;
GETTY:4[49]147, GETTY:10[29]222
CHESNUT, JAMES JR.; ACW:MAY/93[38]416,
ACW:SEP/93[10]430, CWTI:DEC/90[50]183,
CWTI:JUL/92[29]272
CHESNUT, MARY B.:
BOOK REVIEW: *MARY CHESNUT'S CIVIL WAR*
GENERAL LISTINGS: *Beauregard,* CWTI:JUL/92[29]272, *Fall of
Richmond,* AHI:JAN/74[10]153, *Horace Greeley;*
CWTI:DEC/90[50]183, *in book review,* B&G:FEB/92[26],
CWM:JAN/91[47], CWM:APR/95[8], CWR:VOL2#2[169],
miscegenation, AHI:MAY/77[37]174, *Women in the South,*
AHI:DEC/73[10]152, *photos,* AHI:JAN/74[10]153,
AHI:MAY/77[37]174
ADDITIONAL LISTINGS: ACW:MAY/92[39]362, ACW:SEP/92[38]379,
ACW:SEP/93[10]430, ACW:JUL/94[35]478,
ACW:SEP/94[31]486, ACW:SEP/95[38]546,
B&G:DEC/93[12]545, CWM:MAR/93[32]468,
CWM:DEC/94[17]547, CWM:APR/95[32]575,
CWTI:SUMMER/89[50]124, CWTI:MAR/93[24]309,
CWTI:MAY/93[29]319
CHESTER COUNTY, PENNSYLVANIA: BOOK REVIEW: *"IF
THEE MUST FIGHT" A CIVIL WAR HISTORY OF
CHESTER COUNTY, PENNSYLVANIA*
CHESTER, JAMES, *Capt., 3rd U.S. Arty.;* ACW:JUL/93[42]425
CHESTER, JAMES, *Lt., 1st U.S. Artillery;* GETTY:13[89]260
CHESTER, SAMUEL C., *photographer;* B&G:FEB/94[24]551
CHESTER, THOMAS M., *correspondent:*
BOOK REVIEW: *THOMAS MORRIS CHESTER, BLACK CIVIL
WAR CORRESPONDENT: HIS DISPATCHES FROM THE
VIRGINIA FRONT*
ADDITIONAL LISTING: CWM:AUG/94[30]527
CHESTER, WILLIAM M., *Captain, USA;* GETTY:12[7]241
CHEVES, LANGDON, *Captain, CSA;* AHI:JUN/84[24]239,
B&G:DEC/91[6]468, B&G:AUG/91[20]459
CHEW, HENRY F., *Capt., 12th NJ Inf.;* GETTY:5[89]162
CHEW, R. PRESTON, *Major, CSA;* B&G:OCT/93[12]537,
B&G:APR/94[10]558, B&G:APR/95[8]595,
CWR:VOL4#4[70]180, *photo,* B&G:OCT/93[12]537,
CHICAGO MERCANTILE BATTERY; CWR:VOL2#1[36]132,
CWTI:MAY/91[18]207, MH:JUN/93[82]167
CHICAGO, ILLINOIS; BOOK REVIEW: *RALLY ROUND THE
FLAG: CHICAGO AND THE CIVIL WAR*
CHICKAMAUGA AND CHATTANOOGA NATIONAL
MILITARY PARK; AHI:SEP/90[16]289B,
B&G:OCT/91[11]466, CWR:VOL3#2[102]156
CHICKAMAUGA NATIONAL PARK COMMISSION;
CWM:JUL/92[24]430
CHICKAMAUGA, GEORGIA, BATTLE AND CAMPAIGN
OF:
ARTICLES: "A FEW ARE HOLDING OUT UP YONDER,"
CWTI:SEP/92[31]281, "A FORGOTTEN ACCOUNT OF
CHICKAMAUGA," CWTI:SEP/93[53]340,

"CHICKAMAUGA-CHATTANOOGA NATIONAL MILITARY
PARK CENTENNIAL," AHI:SEP/90[16]289B, "FROM SANTA
ROSA ISLAND TO CHICKAMAUGA: THE FIRST
CONFEDERATE REGIMENT," CWR:VOL1#4[42]126, "RAILS
TO THE RIVER OF DEATH: RAILROADS IN THE
CHICKAMAUGA CAMPAIGN," CWM:NOV/91[50]394
BOOK REVIEWS: *A GUIDE TO THE BATTLE OF CHICKAMAUGA
* THE BATTLE OF CHICKAMAUGA * CHICKAMAUGA &
CHATTANOOGA: THE BATTLES THAT DOOMED THE
CONFEDERACY * GUIDE TO THE BATTLE OF
CHICKAMAUGA * PATHS TO VICTORY: A HISTORY AND
TOUR GUIDE OF THE STONES RIVER, CHICKAMAUGA,
CHATTANOOGA, KNOXVILLE AND NASHVILLE * THE
SHIPWRECK OF THEIR HOPES: THE BATTLES FOR
CHATTANOOGA * THIS TERRIBLE SOUND: THE BATTLE
OF CHICKAMAUGA*
GENERAL LISTINGS: *in book review,* ACW:SEP/94[66],
ACW:NOV/94[66], CWM:OCT/94[8], CWM:APR/95[8],
CWM:AUG/95[8], CWM:AUG/95[45], CWNEWS:OCT/89[4],
CWR:VOL1#2[78], CWR:VOL1#4[77], CWR:VOL4#3[89],
CWR:VOL4#4[129], CWTI:NOV/92[10]
ADDITIONAL LISTINGS, ACW: ACW:MAY/91[23]303,
ACW:MAR/92[14]350, ACW:JUL/92[12]367,
ACW:NOV/92[8]383, ACW:MAR/93[26]404,
ACW:JUL/93[42]425, ACW:NOV/93[42]443,
ACW:JAN/94[55]453, ACW:MAR/94[42]461,
ACW:MAR/94[42]461, ACW:JUL/94[6]473,
ACW:JUL/94[66]480, ACW:MAR/95[26]515,
ACW:MAY/95[49]527, ACW:JUL/95[10]533,
ACW:NOV/95[6]551
ADDITIONAL LISTINGS: AHI:MAY/71[3]133A, B&G:OCT/91[11]466,
B&G:FEB/93[48]515, B&G:AUG/93[34]532,
CWM:JUL/92[24]430, CWM:JUL/92[40]432,
CWM:MAR/93[8]465, CWM:APR/94[8]502,
CWM:DEC/94[26]548, CWM:APR/95[16]571,
CWM:OCT/95[22]614, CWR:VOL1#1[71]107,
CWR:VOL1#4[64]127, CWR:VOL3#2[70]155,
CWTI:APR/89[14]107, CWTI:SUMMER/89[13]120,
CWTI:FEB/90[46]146, CWTI:DEC/90[56]184,
CWTI:AUG/91[62]221, CWTI:SEP/91[31]229,
CWTI:SEP/92[22]279, CWTI:MAR/93[24]309,
CWTI:MAR/93[40]312, CWTI:JAN/94[35]361,
CWTI:MAY/94[50]386, CWTI:JAN/95[27]425,
MH:DEC/93[12]174, MH:OCT/94[20]180
CHICKASAW BLUFFS, MISSISSIPPI, BATTLE OF;
ACW:NOV/91[22]331, ACW:MAY/92[47]363,
ACW:JUL/93[34]424, ACW:MAR/94[58],
ACW:JUL/94[51]480, AHI:MAY/71[3]133A, CWM:APR/95[8],
CWM:AUG/95[45], CWM:DEC/95[10], CWR:VOL2#1[1]130,
CWR:VOL2#1[36]132, CWR:VOL2#1[78],
CWR:VOL3#3[33]158, CWTI:FEB/90[38]145,
CWTI:MAY/91[16]206, CWTI:MAY/91[24]208
CHICKASAW GUARDS, *11th Mississippi Infantry;*
GETTY:9[98]217
CHICKASAW RANGERS; GETTY:12[68]246
CHILD, WILLIAM, *Surgeon, 5th New Hampshire Infantry;*
BOOK REVIEW: *A HISTORY OF THE FIFTH REGIMENT, NEW
HAMPSHIRE VOLUNTEERS, IN THE AMERICAN CIVIL
WAR, 1861-1865*
CHILDERS, SAMUEL P., *Private, 1st Georgia Regulars;*
CWR:VOL2#2[95]135
CHILDERS, WILLIAM W., *Private, Sumter Artillery;*
CWR:VOL3#2[1]153

CHILDREN; ARTICLE: "ARMED ONLY WITH THEIR DRUMS, UNION AND CONFEDERATE DRUMMER BOYS SERVED THEIR CAUSES WITH DISTINCTION," ACW:NOV/92[8]383

CHILDRESS, R., *Pvt., 22nd Virginia Inf.;* CWR:VOL1#3[52]122

CHILDS, HENRY L., *Private, 6th Wisconsin Infantry;* GETTY:11[57]233

CHILDS, J.M., *Lieutenant, CSA;* B&G:OCT/91[11]466

CHILDS, JAMES H., *Colonel, 4th Pennsylvania Cavalry;* B&G:OCT/95[8]611F

CHILTON, GEORGE W., *Major, CSA;* ACW:NOV/93[26]441, CWTI:FEB/92[29]248

CHILTON, J.E., *Sergeant, 1st Kentucky (USA) Cavalry;* B&G:FEB/93[12]511

CHILTON, ROBERT H., *Major, CSA:*
ARTICLE: "CONDUCT UNBECOMING," CWTI:MAR/95[60]439
ADDITIONAL LISTINGS: ACW:SEP/92[30]378, ACW:JAN/94[6]446, CWM:MAR/91[12]333, CWR:VOL1#4[77], *photo,* CWTI:MAR/95[60]439

CHINN, SAM, *Private, CSA;* ACW:MAY/92[30]361

CHISELTINE, PHILIP, *Private, 3rd Maryland Infantry;* B&G:APR/95[24]596

CHISHOLM, DANIEL, *Private, 116th Pennsylvania Infantry:*
BOOK REVIEW: *THE CIVIL WAR NOTEBOOK OF DANIEL CHISHOLM: A CHRONICLE OF DAILY LIFE IN THE UNION ARMY 1864-1865*
ADDITIONAL LISTING: ACW:MAY/94[12]466

CHISOLM, JOHN J., *Surgeon,* BOOK REVIEW: *A MANUAL OF MILITARY SURGERY, FOR THE USE OF SURGEONS IN THE CONFEDERATE ARMY WITH AN APPENDIX OF THE RULES AND REGULATIONS OF THE MEDICAL DEPARTMENT OF THE CONFEDERATE ARMY*

CHISHOLM, JOHN N., *Captain, 9th Alabama Infantry;* GETTY:12[111]250

CHITTY, JOHN E., *Private, 1st Florida Special Battalion;* CWR:VOL3#1[65]151

CHIVINGTON, JOHN M., *Colonel, 1st Colorado Infantry;*
GENERAL LISTINGS: *Indian wars,* AHI:OCT/79[20]194, *letters to the editor,* B&G:AUG/94[6]573, B&G:OCT/94[6]579, CWTI:MAR/91[10]197, *photo,* B&G:JUN/94[8]568
ADDITIONAL LISTINGS: ACW:NOV/91[10]329, ACW:MAY/93[6]410, ACW:JUL/93[27]423, B&G:JUN/94[8]568, CWM:MAY/93[16]475, CWR:VOL2#2[161]139, CWTI:MAR/94[58]375

CHRIST, BENJAMIN C., *Colonel, 50th Pennsylvania Infantry;* ACW:JAN/95[54]508, B&G:APR/94[10]558, B&G:APR/95[8]595, B&G:AUG/95[8]604

CHRIST, JOHN M., *Private, 53rd Pennsylvania Infantry;* GETTY:11[80]235

CHRISTIAN COMMISSION; see listings under **"UNITED STATES CHRISTIAN COMMISSION"**

CHRISTIAN, JONES, *Lieutenant, CSA;* ACW:JUL/95[34]536

CHRISTIAN, WILLIAM E., *Sergeant, 8th Michigan Infantry;*
ARTICLE: "WOUNDED AT THE CRATER," CWTI:MAY/91[74]212

CHRISTIAN, WILLIAM S., *Colonel, 55th Virginia Infantry;* GETTY:8[67]204, GETTY:13[64]258

CHRISTIANCY, HENRY C., *Lieutenant, USA;* GETTY:12[7]241

CHRISTIANCY, JAMES, *Lt., USA;* ACW:NOV/92[26]386

CHRISTIE, DANIEL H., *Colonel, 23rd North Carolina Infantry;* ACW:MAR/95[50]518, B&G:FEB/95[8]590B, CWM:DEC/94[40]550, CWTI:MAY/93[26]318, GETTY:5[13]157

CHRISTMAN, ENOS L., *Captain, 4th Pennsylvania Reserves;* CWR:VOL4#4[1]177

CHRISTY, RICHARD C., *Chaplain, 78th Pennsylvania Infantry;* CWM:MAR/91[50]340

CHURCH, ALBERT E.; B&G:DEC/91[12]469

CHURCH, BENJAMIN B., *Captain, 8th Michigan Infantry;* CWTI:JAN/94[46]364

CHURCH, FRANK L., *Lieutenant, USMC;* CWR:VOL2#3[212]142

CHURCH, LAWRENCE S., *Colonel, 95th Illinois Infantry;* ACW:JAN/91[16]284

CHURCH, MORRIS H., *Captain, USA;* B&G:APR/93[24]520, CWTI:JAN/95[48]429

CHURCHER, J.H., *Sergeant, 2nd Iowa Infantry;* B&G:FEB/92[48]475

CHURCHILL, THOMAS J., *General, CSA;* CWR:VOL2#3[212]142, CWR:VOL4#2[68]167, CWTI:MAY/91[16]206

CHUSTENAHLAH, INDIAN TERRITORY, BATTLE OF; CWM:MAY/93[24]476

CISCO, JOHNNIE, *civilian;* MH:FEB/93[42]164

CITADEL; BOOK REVIEW: *CADETS IN GRAY: THE STORY OF THE CADETS OF THE SOUTH CAROLINA MILITARY ACADEMY AND THE CADET RANGERS IN THE CIVIL WAR*

CITRONELLE, ALABAMA; CWTI:AUG/90[50]168

CITY POINT, VIRGINIA; ACW:JUL/94[42]479, ACW:SEP/95[74]550, CWM:SEP/92[19]440, CWNEWS:NOV/90[4], CWTI:FEB/91[28]192, CWTI:MAR/95[33]435, GETTY:8[121]207, MH:JUN/94[8]177

CIVIL WAR ART; ARTICLE: "THE 'CENTURY' ART: WHAT WAR LOOKED LIKE," CWTI:SEP/90[28]175

CIVIL WAR BATTLEFIELD COMMEMORATIVE COIN ACT; see listings under **"PRESERVATION"**

CIVIL WAR FOUNDATION; see listings under **"PRESERVATION"**

CIVIL WAR ROUND TABLE ASSOCIATES; see listings under **"PRESERVATION"**

CIVIL WAR SITES ADVISORY COMMISSION; see listings under **"PRESERVATION"**

CIVIL WAR SOLDIERS SYSTEM; CWM:JUL/93[35]487

THE CIVIL WAR TRUST; see listings under **"PRESERVATION"**

CIVILIANS:
ARTICLES: "THE CITY OF BROTHERLY HOSPITALITY," CWTI:MAY/94[24]381, "FOR BETTER OR FOR WORSE," CWTI:MAY/92[32]264, "IN HARM'S WAY," CWTI:MAR/93[26]310
BOOK REVIEWS: *A BLOCKADED FAMILY: LIFE IN SOUTHERN ALABAMA DURING THE CIVIL WAR * DAYS OF "UNCERTAINTY AND DREAD": THE ORDEAL ENDURED BY THE CITIZENS AT GETTYSBURG * DEFEND THE VALLEY: A SHENANDOAH FAMILY IN THE CIVIL WAR * DIARY OF A SOUTHERN REFUGEE *LETTER FROM FORREST PLACE: A PLANTATION FAMILY'S CORRESPONDENCE, 1846-1881 * LUCY BRECKINRIDGE OF GROVE HILL: THE JOURNAL OF A VIRGINIA GIRL, 1862-1864 * TRUE TALES OF THE SOUTH AT WAR, HOW SOLDIERS FOUGHT AND FAMILIES LIVED, 1861-1865 * WAR OF ANOTHER KIND: A SOUTHERN COMMUNITY IN THE GREAT REBELLION*

CLAASSEN, PETER J., *Colonel, 132nd New York Infantry;* CWM:SEP/92[16]438

CLACK, FRANKLIN H., *Colonel, 12th Louisiana Infantry Battalion;* CWR:VOL3#1[1]149, CWR:VOL4#2[1]165, CWR:VOL4#2[68]167, CWR:VOL4#2[118]169

CLAGHORN, MRS. JAMES L., *civilian;* GETTY:10[53]225

CLAIBORNE, JOHN H., *Surgeon, 12th Virginia Infantry;* CWR:VOL2#3[236]143

CLAIBORNE, THOMAS, *Captain, CSA;* CWTI:SEP/92[31]281

CLAIBORNE, WILLIAM C., *Captain, Consolidated Crescent Regiment;* CWR:VOL4#2[1]165

CLAIRVILE, WILLIAM H., *Sergeant, USA;* GETTY:5[35]159

CLANHARTY, C.H., *Major, 141st New York Infantry;* CWR:VOL3#2[70]155

CLANTON, JAMES H., *Colonel, 1st Alabama Cavalry;* CWM:JAN/91[40]330, CWR:VOL4#1[44]164

CLANTON, NAT, *Captain, CSA;* ACW:MAR/91[38]296

CLAPP, ALFRED R., *Lieutenant, 126th New York Infantry;* CWR:VOL1#4[7]125

CLARA BARTON NATIONAL HISTORIC SITE; ARTICLE: "CLARA BARTON NATIONAL HISTORIC SITE," AHI:NOV/89[65]289

CLARE, WILLIAM, *Major, CSA;* B&G:DEC/93[12]545

CLARK'S (MISSOURI) ARTILLERY; CWTI:JUL/94[50]395

CLARK'S MILL, MISSOURI, SKIRMISH AT; ACW:JUL/94[8]474

CLARK'S MOUNTAIN, VIRGINIA; B&G:APR/91[8]445

CLARK, A.D., *Sgt., 7th South Carolina Inf.;* GETTY:5[35]159

CLARK, A. JUDSON, *Captain, 2nd New Jersey Artillery;* ACW:MAY/95[30]525, GETTY:5[35]159, GETTY:5[47]160, GETTY:6[59]174

CLARK, A.K., *Private, 5th Georgia Infantry;* ACW:NOV/92[8]383

CLARK, ACHILLES V., *Sergeant, CSA;* AHI:APR/74[4]154, CWTI:JAN/94[35]361

CLARK, AUGUSTUS M., *Surgeon;* B&G:OCT/94[11]580

CLARK, CHARLES, *General, CSA;* ACW:SEP/92[38]379

CLARK, CHARLES, *Private, 8th Louisiana Infantry;* CWTI:FEB/91[12]189

CLARK, EDWARD, *Governor, Texas;* AHI:JUN/70[30]127

CLARK, EDWARD L., *Chaplain, 12th Massachusetts Infantry;* B&G:OCT/95[20]612

CLARK, ERASTUS, *Cpt., 12th Mass. Inf.;* B&G:FEB/95[8]590B

CLARK, GEORGE, *Cpt., 11th Alabama Inf.;* GETTY:12[7]241

CLARK, GEORGE T., *Private, 22nd Virginia Infantry;* CWR:VOL1#3[52]122

CLARK, H.F., *Colonel, USA;* GETTY:11[19]232

CLARK, HARRISON, *Private, 125th New York Infantry;* B&G:FEB/93[40]514, GETTY:7[51]190

CLARK, HENRY T., *Governor, North Carolina;* ACW:JAN/94[18]449

CLARK, HIRAM, *Lieutenant, 185th New York Infantry;* CWR:VOL1#1[35]104

CLARK, HIRAM D., *Private, 125th New York Infantry;* GETTY:10[53]225

CLARK, JAMES F., *Chaplain;* ACW:MAR/94[10]457

CLARK, JOHN, *Colonel, USA;* ACW:JUL/92[41]370, CWR:VOL1#1[42]105

CLARK, JOHN A., *Lieutenant, USA;* ACW:NOV/95[54]558

CLARK, JOHN B., *General, CSA;* ACW:NOV/93[26]441, AHI:JUN/70[30]127, B&G:JUN/91[10]452

CLARK, JOHN M., *Lieutenant, 83rd Pennsylvania Infantry;* GETTY:7[41]189

CLARK, JOHN S., *Lieutenant, 1st Massachusetts Infantry;* GETTY:12[7]241

CLARK, JOSEPH C. JR., *Captain, 4th U.S. Artillery;* CWTI:FEB/92[36]249

CLARK, M.R., *Major, CSA;* B&G:JUN/93[12]524

CLARK, MACAJAH; CWTI:MAR/93[32]311

CLARK, REUBEN G., *Captain, 59th Tennessee Mounted Infantry;* BOOK REVIEWS: *VALLEYS OF THE SHADOW: THE MEMOIR OF CONFEDERATE CAPTAIN REUBEN G. CLARK, COMPANY I, 59TH TENNESSEE MOUNTED INFANTRY*

CLARK, SMITH H., *Captain, 71st Ohio Infantry;* CWTI:JUL/92[42]274

CLARK, TERRENCE, *Major, USA;* ACW:JAN/94[55]453

CLARK, THOMAS M., *Private, 2nd Wisconsin Infantry,* GETTY:11[57]233

CLARK, WALTER, *Major, CSA;* ACW:NOV/93[12]440

CLARK, WILLIAM, *Lieutenant Colonel, USA;* CWTI:MAR/95[40]436

CLARK, WILLIAM, *Private, 13th Pennsylvania Reserves;* CWR:VOL1#3[20]119

CLARK, WILLIAM, *Sergeant, 154th New York Infantry;* GETTY:8[17]200

CLARK, WILLIAM M., *Sergeant, 147th Pennsylvania Infantry;* GETTY:9[81]216

CLARK, WILLIAM S., *Colonel, 21st Massachusetts Infantry;* CWTI:FEB/92[36]249

CLARK, WILLIAM T., *General, USA;* B&G:DEC/95[9]615, CWTI:SUMMER/89[40]123,

CLARKE, GEORGE J., *Lieutenant, USA;* GETTY:4[101]150, GETTY:10[42]224, *photo;* GETTY:10[42]224

CLARKE, HENRY F., *Colonel, USA;* GETTY:10[53]225

CLARKE, MARCELLUS J.; ARTICLE: "WAS ROME CLARKE REALLY 'SUE MUNDY'—OR MERELY THE VICTIM OF AN EDITOR'S DEADLY PRANK?" ACW:JAN/94[10]448

CLARKE, MRS. AMY; AHI:DEC/73[10]152

CLARKE, PIUS J., *Private, 114th Ohio Infantry;* CWTI:AUG/90[64]170

CLARKE, SMITH H., *Captain, 71st Ohio Infantry;* CWTI:JUL/92[42]274

CLARKE, THOMAS W., *Captain, 29th Massachusetts Infantry;* CWTI:APR/90[24]152

CLARKE, WILLIAM F., *Private, 1st Connecticut Cavalry;* ACW:JAN/92[16]340

CLARKSON, BENJAMIN F., *Private, USA;* CWTI:SEP/93[43]338

CLARKSON, J.J., *Colonel, CSA;* CWM:SEP/92[38]443

CLARKSON, JOHN, *civilian;* B&G:AUG/91[11]458

CLARY, ALBERT G., *Commander, USN;* ACW:NOV/92[51]389

CLAY, CASSIUS M.:
ARTICLE: "THE LION OF WHITE HALL," AHI:MAY/69[12]121
BOOK REVIEW: *FAMOUS KENTUCKY DUELS*
ADDITIONAL LISTINGS: CWTI:JUN/90[46]161, *photo;* AHI:MAY/69[12]121

CLAY, CLEMENT, *Senator, Alabama;* ACW:JAN/95[46]507, ACW:JUL/95[44]537, AHI:JUN/70[30]127, AHI:JAN/76[14]164, CWTI:NOV/92[54]293, CWTI:JAN/93[44]302

CLAY, HENRY B., *Captain, CSA;* B&G:FEB/94[62]556

CLAY, HENRY:
BOOK REVIEW: *HENRY CLAY: STATESMAN FOR THE UNION*
ADDITIONAL LISTINGS: AHI:MAY/69[12]121, AHI:JUN/74[12]155, AHI:FEB/75[4]157, CWNEWS:AUG/91[4], CWTI:SEP/92[46]284

CLAY, JAMES, *Pvt., 69th Pennsylvania Inf.;* GETTY:4[89]150

CLAY, JAMES W., *Private, 18th Virginia Infantry;*
GETTY:5[107]164
CLAYPOOL, JOHN, GETTY:7[119]195
CLAYTON, HENRY D., *General, CSA;* ACW:NOV/95[48]557,
B&G:DEC/93[12]545, B&G:DEC/95[9]615,
CWR:VOL1#4[64]127, CWTI:SUMMER/89[20]121,
CWTI:SUMMER/89[40]123, CWTI:SUMMER/89[50]124
CLAYTON, POWELL, *Colonel, USA:*
BOOK REVIEW: *THE HONORABLE POWELL CLAYTON*
ADDITIONAL LISTINGS: AHI:JAN/80[8]197, CWNEWS:APR/90[4],
CWR:VOL1#2[44]114
CLEARY, WILLIAM W., *Major, CSA;* CWTI:NOV/92[54]293
CLEAVELAND, STEPHEN B., *Captain, CSA;*
B&G:JUN/93[12]524
CLEBURNE, PATRICK R., *General, CSA:*
ARTICLES: "CHATTANOOGA RELIEVED!" CWM:DEC/94[46]552,
"CLEBURNE," MH:OCT/94[20]180, "DARING REAR-GUARD
DEFENSE," ACW:NOV/93[34]442, "PAT CLEBURNE'S
MODEST PROPOSAL SENT SHOCKWAVES THROUGH
THE CONFEDERATE ARMY AND THE GOVERNMENT,"
ACW:NOV/93[6]437, "PATRICK RONAYNE CLEBURNE:
SOUTHERN CITIZEN-SOLDIER," CWM:MAR/91[28]336, "TO
SAVE AN ARMY," CWTI:SEP/94[40]403
BOOK REVIEW: *NINE MEN IN GRAY*
GENERAL LISTINGS: *Atlanta Campaign,* ACW:JAN/95[30]505,
CWTI:SUMMER/89[20]121, CWTI:SUMMER/89[32]122,
CWTI:SUMMER/89[40]123, CWTI:SEP/92[28]280, *Black
Confederates,* ACW:NOV/93[6]437, ACW:NOV/95[8]552,
GETTY:6[93]179, *common soldiers,* AHI:APR/68[4]115,
Franklin, ACW:MAR/94[42]461, B&G:OCT/91[11]466,
B&G:DEC/93[12]545, *in book review,* ACW:MAR/95[58],
B&G:DEC/95[30], CWM:MAR/91[74], CWM:APR/95[50],
CWM:AUG/95[45], CWNEWS:APR/92[4],
CWNEWS:MAY/93[4], CWR:VOL1#2[78], CWR:VOL1#4[77],
CWR:VOL4#4[129], CWTI:FEB/91[10], CWTI:APR/92[30],
CWTI:JUL/93[12]
GENERAL LISTINGS, continued: *letters to the editor,*
B&G:FEB/94[6]549, CWM:JAN/91[6]324, CWM:JUL/91[6]355,
CWM:DEC/94[5]546, CWTI:JAN/95[16]421, *Missionary Ridge,*
CWTI:MAR/93[24]309, *Perryville,* CWR:VOL4#3[50]171,
proposal to arm slaves, CWTI:AUG/91[68]222, *Resaca,*
CWTI:NOV/92[41]291, *Tullahoma Campaign,*
B&G:OCT/92[10]496, *Slavery;* CWTI:DEC/89[62]139, *photos;*
ACW:NOV/93[6]437, ACW:NOV/93[34]442,
AHI:APR/68[4]115, AHI:NOV/73[18]151, B&G:OCT/91[11]466,
CWM:MAR/91[28]336, CWM:DEC/94[46]552,
CWR:VOL3#3[59]159, CWTI:SEP/94[40]403
ADDITIONAL LISTINGS: ACW:MAR/91[30]295, ACW:JAN/94[55]453,
ACW:JUL/94[66]481, B&G:AUG/92[40]495,
B&G:DEC/93[52]548, CWM:JAN/91[12]326,
CWM:JAN/91[72]331, CWM:MAR/92[27]412,
CWM:AUG/94[27]526, CWM:OCT/94[48]542,
CWR:VOL1#1[73]108, CWR:VOL1#3[82]123,
CWR:VOL1#4[42]126, CWR:VOL1#4[64]127,
CWR:VOL3#3[59]159, CWTI:AUG/91[62]221,
MH:OCT/93[6]170, MH:OCT/93[20]172
CLEM, JOHN L., *Colonel, USA:*
ARTICLE: "ARMED ONLY WITH THEIR DRUMS, UNION AND
CONFEDERATE DRUMMER BOYS SERVED THEIR
CAUSES WITH DISTINCTION," ACW:NOV/92[8]383
ADDITIONAL LISTINGS: AHI:APR/68[4]115, AHI:JUL/93[40]312,
photo; ACW:NOV/92[8]383

CLEMENCY, ALEX, *Sergeant, 1st Georgia Regulars;*
CWR:VOL2#2[95]135
CLEMENS, SAMUEL L.:
ARTICLE: "EDITORIAL," ACW:MAY/91[6]299
ADDITIONAL LISTINGS: ACW:MAY/91[10]301, CWTI:FEB/90[60]148,
CWTI:MAR/91[34]201, *photos;* ACW:MAY/91[6]299,
AHI:DEC/72[4]144
CLEMENT, ARCHIE; ACW:JAN/93[6]391,
ACW:JAN/93[26]395, B&G:JUN/91[32]454,
CWTI:JAN/94[29]360
CLEMENT, HERMAN, *Private, 9th New Hampshire Infantry;*
CWR:VOL2#2[118]136
CLEMENT, MOSES, *Private, 14th Connecticut Infantry;*
GETTY:9[61]215
CLEMSON, FLORIDE, *Private, CSA;* BOOK REVIEWS: *A REBEL
CAME HOME: THE DIARY AND LETTERS OF FLORIDE
CLEMSON, 1863-1866*
CLENDENIN, DAVID R., *Lieutenant Colonel, 8th Illinois
Cavalry;* ACW:NOV/93[50]444, B&G:DEC/92[8]503,
CWTI:JAN/93[40]301
CLENDENNON, JOSEPH, *civilian;* B&G:FEB/91[20]440
CLEVELAND, AUGUSTUS S., *Private, Sumter Artillery;*
CWR:VOL3#2[1]153, CWR:VOL3#2[61]154
CLEVELAND, GROVER; ARTICLE: "GROVER CLEVELAND
AND THE REBEL BANNERS," CWTI:SEP/93[22]335
CLIFFE, DANIEL B., *Doctor;* B&G:FEB/93[12]511
CLINCH'S LIGHT BATTERY; CWTI:DEC/94[62]415
CLINCH, J.M.H., *Colonel, CSA;* B&G:FEB/91[8]439
CLINCH, NICHOLAS B., *Captain, CSA;* B&G:FEB/91[8]439,
CWTI:DEC/94[62]415
CLINGMAN, THOMAS L., *General, CSA;* B&G:APR/94[10]558,
CWR:VOL4#2[136]
CLINTON, MISSISSIPPI, BATTLE OF: B&G:AUG/95[8]604,
CWR:VOL2#1[36]132
CLITZ, HENRY B., *Lieutenant Colonel, USA;*
ACW:NOV/94[50]498, B&G:DEC/91[12]469, *photo;*
B&G:DEC/91[12]469
CLIVE, MAURICE, *Private, 2nd Michigan Infantry;*
CWTI:JUL/93[14]324
CLOPTON, WILLIAM I., *Lieutenant, CSA;* GETTY:13[64]258
CLOTHING; BOOK REVIEW: *THE LADIES' HAND BOOK OF
FANCY AND ORNAMENTAL WORK: CIVIL WAR ERA*
CLOUD, A.S., *Capt., 16th North Carolina Inf.;* GETTY:8[67]204
CLOUD, MOUNTJOY, *Scout, CSA;* ARTICLE: "THE PLAN TO
KIDNAP LINCOLN THAT FAILED BY ONE DAY,"
AHI:NOV/80[6]208
CLOUD, WILLIAM F., *Colonel, 2nd Kansas Cavalry (Union);*
CWTI:SEP/90[52]179
CLOWER, GUS, *Pvt., 1st GA Regulars;* CWR:VOL2#2[95]135
CLOYD'S MOUNTAIN, WEST VIRGINIA, BATTLE OF:
ARTICLE: "VICIOUS MOUNTAIN ENCOUNTER,"
ACW:MAR/94[27]459
ADDITIONAL LISTINGS: CWNEWS:DEC/93[5],
CWNEWS:JUL/94[25], CWTI:SEP/94[49]404
CLUKE, LEROY S., *Colonel, 8th Kentucky Infantry;*
ACW:SEP/95[22]544, B&G:OCT/94[11]580
CLUTTER'S BATTERY; CWR:VOL1#1[35]104
CLUTTER, V.J., *Lieutenant, Johnson's Artillery;*
CWR:VOL4#4[70]180
COADY, WILLIAM J., *Private, 19th Indiana Infantry,*
GETTY:11[57]233
COAHOMA INVINCIBLES, (11th Mississippi Infantry);
GETTY:9[98]217

COALTER, HENRY T., *Lieutenant, 53rd Virginia Infantry;* GETTY:12[111]250

COATES, B.F., *Lieutenant, 91st Ohio Infantry;* ACW:JUL/94[26]477

COATES, HENRY C., *Captain, 1st Minnesota Infantry;* GETTY:5[79]161,

COATS, ANDREW, *Private, 5th New York Infantry;* CWR:VOL1#2[29]112

COBB'S (GEORGIA) LEGION:
ARTICLE: "THE CAVALRY CLASH AT QUEBEC SCHOOLHOUSE," B&G:FEB/93[24]512
ADDITIONAL LISTINGS: ACW:JUL/92[41]370, ACW:JAN/94[8]447, B&G:OCT/93[12]537, CWM:MAR/93[32]468, CWR:VOL1#4[7]125, CWR:VOL4#4[28]178, CWTI:JUN/90[32]159, GETTY:4[75]149, GETTY:12[68]246

COBB, HOWELL:
ARTICLES: *black soldiers*, ACW:NOV/95[8]552, *Harpers Ferry*, MH:AUG/95[30]185, *James Buchanan*, AHI:MAY/66[12]101, *Peninsula Campaign*, CWM:JUN/95[29]583, *women in the South*, AHI:DEC/73[10]152
ADDITIONAL LISTINGS: ACW:MAR/91[38]296, ACW:JUL/92[22]368, ACW:MAR/93[18]403, ACW:NOV/93[42]443, ACW:JAN/94[8]447, ACW:JAN/94[39]451, AHI:JUN/72[18]139, B&G:FEB/93[40]514, B&G:FEB/95[8]590B, CWR:VOL1#4[7]125, CWR:VOL3#3[1]157, CWR:VOL4#4[28]178, CWTI:AUG/91[68]222, CWTI:SEP/91[23]228, *photo;* ACW:MAR/93[18]403

COBB, JAMES E., *Lieutenant, 5th Texas Infantry;* GETTY:12[1]240, GETTY:12[111]250

COBB, JOHN A., *Sergeant Major, 16th Georgia Infantry;* AHI:APR/68[4]115

COBB, MARY ANN; AHI:DEC/73[10]152

COBB, PHAROAH A., *Major, 2nd Tennesses Cavalry;* CWR:VOL4#1[1]163

COBB, ROBERT, *Captain, Cobb's (Kentucky) Artillery;* B&G:AUG/95[8]604

COBB, THOMAS R.R., *General, CSA:*
ARTICLE: "'THE GLORIOUS LIGHT WENT OUT FOREVER': THE DEATH OF BRIG. GEN. THOMAS R.R. COBB," CWR:VOL4#4[28]178
ADDITIONAL LISTINGS: ACW:SEP/95[54]548, CWM:MAR/93[32]468, CWM:AUG/95[45], CWR:VOL4#4[i]175, CWR:VOL4#4[v]176, CWR:VOL4#4[47]179, CWR:VOL4#4[127]182, CWTI:SEP/94[26]400, *photo;* CWR:VOL4#4[28]178

COBB, WILLIAMSON R.W.:
ARTICLE: "ALABAMA'S WILLIAMSON R.W. COBB MADE A DRAMATIC FINAL APPEARANCE BEFORE THE HOUSE OF REPRESENTATIVES," ACW:MAY/94[8]465

COBB'S (KENTUCKY) ARTILLERY; B&G:AUG/95[8]604

COBHAM, GEORGE A., JR, *Colonel, 111th Pennsylvania Infantry;* CWR:VOL3#2[70]155, GETTY:10[120]229, CWTI:SEPT/89[30]129, CWTI:SEP/94[40]403, *photo;* GETTY:10[120]229

COBURN, JAMES H., *Major, 27th Connecticut Infantry;* GETTY:12[24]242

COBURN, JOHN, *Colonel, 33rd Indiana Infantry;* CWM:JAN/91[28]327, CWTI:SUMMER/89[32]122, CWTI:NOV/92[41]291

COCKE, JOHN K., *Captain, 18th Texas Infantry;* ACW:MAR/93[68]409

COCKE, PHILIP ST. GEORGE, *General, USA;* B&G:JUN/93[32]525, CWTI:MAR/94[48]374, CWTI:JUL/94[44]394

COCKERILL, JOSEPH R., *Colonel, USA;* B&G:AUG/95[8]604

COCKRELL, FRANCIS M., *General, CSA:*
BOOK REVIEW: *IN DEADLY EARNEST: HISTORY OF THE FIRST MISSOURI BRIGADE, CSA*
ADDITIONAL LISTINGS: ACW:NOV/91[22]331, ACW:JUL/94[51]480, ACW:MAR/95[8]512, B&G:AUG/93[24], B&G:FEB/94[8]550, B&G:FEB/94[57]555, CWR:VOL2#1[1]130, CWR:VOL2#1[36]132, CWTI:MAY/91[24]208, MH:JUN/93[82]167, *photos;* B&G:FEB/94[8]550, CWR:VOL2#1[36]132

COCKRELL, MONROE W., *General, CSA;* MH:APR/94[54]176

CODE BREAKING:
ARTICLE: "CODE-CRACKERS," CWTI:AUG/95[46]459
ADDITIONAL LISTING: CWTI:DEC/95[8]474

CODER, DANIEL R., *Lieutenant, 11th Pennsylvania Reserves;* CWR:VOL4#1[1]177

CODORI, NICHOLAS, *civilian;* GETTY:5[107]164

CODY, WILLIAM F.; ACW:JUL/95[58], CWTI:MAY/94[40]383

COEHORN MORTARS; ACW:SEP/93[16]431

COFFEE, J.T., *Colonel, CSA;* ACW:MAR/95[26]515

COFFEEVILLE, MISSISSIPPI, BATTLE OF; CWTI:NOV/92[54]293

COFFEY, ROBERT J., *Sergeant, 4th Vermont Infantry;* CWM:SEP/93[18]494

COFFIN, BENJAMIN F., *Captain, 9th New York Cavalry;* GETTY:11[19]232

COFFIN, CHARLES C., *reporter;* GETTY:7[23]187

COFFIN, W.P., *Captain, 13th Indiana Cavalry;* CWTI:MAR/91[46]203

COFFIN, WILLIAM G., *civilian;* ACW:JAN/91[30]286

COGGESHALL, WILLIAM T., BOOK REVIEW: *COLONEL COGGESHALL-THE MAN WHO SAVED LINCOLN*

COGGIN, JEREMIAH, *Lieutenant, 23rd North Carolina Infantry;* GETTY:12[1]240, GETTY:12[111]250, *photo;* GETTY:12[111]250

COGGSWELL, ZELOTES P., *Captain, USA;* CWTI:MAY/93[35]320

COGHILL, JOHN F., *Captain, 23rd North Carolina Infantry;* B&G:FEB/95[8]590A

COGLEY, J, *Sergeant, USMC;* CWR:VOL2#3[194]141

COGSWELL, JOSEPH H., *Captain, 150th New York Infantry;* GETTY:12[42]244

COGSWELL, MILTON, *Colonel, 42nd New York Infantry;* AHI:FEB/82[36]225, CWTI:MAY/89[14]114

COGSWELL, WILLIAM, *General, USA;* B&G:AUG/95[8]604, B&G:DEC/95[9]615, GETTY:6[69]176

COHEN, A.J., *Major, USA;* CWM:SEP/93[8]493

COHN, ABRAHAM, *Sergeant Major, USA;* CWM:SEP/93[8]493

COID, ARTHUR C., *seaman, CSN;* ACW:SEP/94[46]488

COINER, MARION K., *Private, 52nd Virginia Infantry;* CWTI:MAR/94[29]371

COINS:
ARTICLE: "U.S. MINT TO RELEASE CIVIL WAR COINS," CWTI:JUN/95[10]442
ADDITIONAL LISTINGS: B&G:APR/95[38]598, CWM:JUL/92[27]431, CWM:NOV/92[35]450

COIT, JAMES, *Captain, 14th Connecticut Infantry;* GETTY:9[61]215

COKER HOUSE, (CHAMPION HILL,) MISSISSIPPPI;
ARTICLE: "A MISSISSIPPI HOME STANDS, A SILENT
WITNESS TO A BATTLE," CWTI:MAY/91[18]207
COKER, FRANCIS M., *Lieutenant, Sumter Artillery;*
CWR:VOL3#2[1]153
COLANI, GIOVANNI M., *Lieutenant, 39th New York Infantry;*
ACW:MAY/95[54]528
COLBERT, WALLACE B., *Colonel, 40th Mississippi Infantry;*
CWTI:JUL/94[50]395
COLBURN, ROBERT S., *83rd New York Infantry;*
GETTY:10[7]221
COLBY, SEYMOUR W., *Private, 6th Wisconsin Infantry;*
GETTY:11[57]233
COLBY, WALTER, *Private, 5th New York Infantry;*
CWR:VOL1#2[7]111, CWTI:MAY/94[31]382
COLCLAISAIR, JAMES H.; CWTI:AUG/95[58]461
COLCOCK, BILL, *Lieutenant, 1st South Carolina Artillery;*
B&G:DEC/95[9]615
COLCOCK, CHARLES J., *Colonel, 3rd South Carolina
Cavalry;* CWR:VOL2#3[194]141
COLD HARBOR BATTLEFIELD PARK; ACW:SEP/93[62]436
COLD HARBOR, VIRGINIA, BATTLE OF:
ARTICLES: "THE BLUNT COLLECTION OF COLD HARBOR
PHOTOGRAPHS," B&G:APR/94[47]562A, "GRANT AND
LEE, 1864: FROM THE NORTH ANNA TO THE CROSSING
OF THE JAMES," B&G:APR/94[10]558, "JOSEPH
FINEGAN'S FLORIDA BRIGADE AT COLD HARBOR,"
CWR:VOL3#4[1]161, "NORTH ANNA TO THE CROSSING
OF THE JAMES," B&G:APR/94[59]565, "THE REGIMENT
HAS COVERED ITSELF WITH GLORY': THE 8TH NEW
YORK HEAVIES AT COLD HARBOR," B&G:APR/94[55]564,
"VISITORS TO THE DREADFUL BATTLEGROUND AT
COLD HARBOR CAN ALMOST HEAR THE GUN
HAMMERS CLICKING," ACW:SEP/93[62]436, "WAR COMES
TO HANOVER COUNTY," B&G:APR/94[51]563
BOOK REVIEWS: *BLOODY ROADS SOUTH: THE WILDERNESS
TO COLD HARBOR, MAY-JUNE 1864 * MARCHING TO
COLD HARBOR: VICTORY AND FAILURE, 1864*
GENERAL LISTINGS: *general history,* AHI:MAY/71[3]133A, *in book
review,* CWM:AUG/95[8], CWR:VOL2#1[78],
CWR:VOL2#4[346], CWR:VOL3#3[92], CWR:VOL4#2[136],
CWTI:FEB/90[10], *letters to the editor,* B&G:DEC/94[6]584
ADDITIONAL LISTINGS: ACW:NOV/92[74]390, ACW:MAY/93[14]413,
ACW:SEP/93[8]429, ACW:NOV/93[50]444,
ACW:JUL/94[26]477, ACW:JAN/95[46]507,
ACW:SEP/95[54]548, ACW:SEP/95[74]550,
AHI:OCT/67[26]112, B&G:APR/94[47]562A,
CWM:JUL/91[45]372, CWM:JUL/92[8]427,
CWM:JAN/93[40]461, CWM:OCT/94[17]534,
CWM:OCT/94[34]538, CWM:DEC/94[26]548,
CWM:OCT/95[40]619
ADDITIONAL LISTINGS, continued: CWR:VOL1#1[1]102,
CWR:VOL1#3[52]122, CWR:VOL2#2[141]137,
CWR:VOL2#4[269]145, CWR:VOL3#1[65]151,
CWR:VOL3#2[1]153, CWR:VOL3#3[1]157,
CWR:VOL3#4[1]161, CWTI:MAY/89[36]118,
CWTI:FEB/90[46]146, CWTI:SEP/91[31]229,
CWTI:APR/92[49]260, CWTI:MAY/93[26]318,
CWTI:JAN/95[34]427, CWTI:MAR/95[46]437,
MH:FEB/93[42]164
COLDWATER RIVER, TENNESSEE, BATTLE OF;
ACW:JUL/95[6]531
COLE'S (MARYLAND) CAVALRY; B&G:AUG/94[19]575

COLE, CHARLES H., *Captain, CSA;* ACW:JUL/95[44]537,
B&G:JUN/95[36]603A
COLE, ELEAZER, *Private, 9th Massachusetts Artillery;*
GETTY:5[47]160
COLE, FRANK A., *Private, 126th New York Infantry;*
CWR:VOL1#4[7]125
COLE, HENRY G.; ACW:NOV/93[42]443
COLE, JOHN B., *Lieutenant, CSA;* B&G:OCT/94[11]580
COLEMAN, ANN; AHI:MAY/66[12]101
COLEMAN, CHARLES, *Captain, USA;* B&G:JUN/92[28]
COLEMAN, CICERO, *Lieutenant Colonel, CSA;*
B&G:OCT/94[11]580
COLEMAN, DAVID, *Colonel, CSA;* B&G:DEC/93[12]545,
CWTI:SEP/92[31]281
COLEMAN, G.M., *Captain, CSA;* B&G:OCT/94[11]580
COLEMAN, HENRY E., *Colonel, 12th North Carolina Infantry;*
CWM:MAY/92[34]422
COLEMAN, J.D., *Private, CSA;* CWTI:SEP/91[23]228
COLEMAN, LEWIS M., *Lieutenant Colonel, CSA;*
CWR:VOL1#1[1]102, CWR:VOL4#4[70]180
COLEMAN, W.O., *Colonel, 4th Missouri Cavalry;*
CWTI:FEB/92[42]250
COLES, ROBERT, *Adjutant, 4th Alabama Infantry;*
ACW:NOV/94[18]495
COLFAX, SCHUYLER; AHI:FEB/86[12]257,
CWTI:DEC/95[76]482
COLGROVE, SILAS, *Colonel, 27th Indiana Infantry;*
B&G:FEB/95[8]590C, CWR:VOL1#4[7]125, GETTY:6[7]169,
GETTY:6[69]176, GETTY:7[83]192
COLLAMORE, GEORGE W., *Mayor, Lawrence, Kansas;*
CWM:JAN/92[12]400
COLLECTIBLES:
ARTICLES: "A $2,500 SET OF CIVIL WAR TRADING CARDS?"
CWTI:DEC/91[18]236, "THE ALURE OF THE CIIVL WAR'S
HEFTIEST RELICS," CWTI:DEC/90[20]181,
"COMMEMORATIVE STAMPS: HISTORY MOVES THE
MAIL," CWTI:JUN/90[12]157, "THE RELIABLE
REMINGTON," CWTI:SEP/90[18]172
BOOK REVIEW: *CIVIL WAR AUTOGRAPHS & MANUSCRIPTS:
PRICES CURRENT, 1992*
COLLEY, CHARLES H., *Sergeant, 10th Maine Infantry;*
ARTICLE: "THE STRANGE CASE OF LIEUTENANT COLLEY,
10TH MAINE INFANTRY," B&G:OCT/95[32]613
COLLEY, T.W., *Private, CSA;* ACW:SEP/95[38]546
COLLIER, EDWARD T., *Private, 3rd Massachusetts Infantry;*
ARTICLE: "RUSHED TO THE FRONT," CWTI:JAN/95[82]430
COLLIER, FREDERICK H., *Colonel, 139th Pennsylvania
Infantry;* GETTY:11[91]236
COLLINS, ALPHONZO D.L., *Private, 7th Wisconsin Infantry;*
GETTY:11[57]233
COLLINS, CORDELLO, *Private, 13th Pennsylvania Reserves;*
CWR:VOL1#3[28]120, CWR:VOL1#3[46]121
COLLINS, DICK, *Captain, CSA;* B&G:JUN/91[10]452
COLLINS, GEORGE K., *Captain, 149th New York Infantry:*
BOOK REVIEW: *MEMOIRS OF THE 149TH REGIMENT*
ADDITIONAL LISTINGS: CWR:VOL3#2[70]155,
CWTI:SEPT/89[30]129, GETTY:10[36]223
COLLINS, JEREMIAH, *Private, 150th New York Infantry;*
GETTY:12[42]244
COLLINS, JOHN, *Master, USN;* CWM:JUL/93[24]485
COLLINS, JOHN L., *Private, 8th Pennsylvania Cavalry;*
ACW:JAN/92[10]339

COLLINS, JOSEPH, *Lieutenant Colonel, 18th Louisiana Consolidated Infantry;* CWR:VOL4#2[1]165

COLLINS, JOSEPH, *Private, 1st Virginia Battalion;* CWM:MAR/91[65]342

COLLINS, JOSEPH B., *Captain, USA;* ACW:NOV/94[50]498

COLLINS, NAPOLEON, *Captain, USN;* AHI:JAN/83[10]232

COLLINS, R.M., *Lieutenant, 15th Texas Cavalry;* BOOK REVIEW: *CHAPTERS FROM THE UNWRITTEN HISTORY OF THE WAR BETWEEN THE STATES*

COLLINS, WILLIAM, *Private, 88th Pennsylvania Infantry:*
ARTICLE: "THREE ROADS TO ANDERSONVILLE," B&G:DEC/92[32]506
ADDITIONAL LISTINGS: CWM:JAN/92[16]401, CWTI:SEP/92[40]282, CWTI:JAN/93[10]297

COLLIS, CHARLES H.T., *Colonel, 114th Pennsylvania Infantry;* B&G:APR/93[12]518

COLORADO TROOPS:
ARTICLE: "COLORADO'S FORGOTTEN CONFEDERATES DID THEIR BEST TO SUPPORT THE SOUTHERN CAUSE, BUT TO NO AVAIL," ACW:NOV/91[10]329
BOOK REVIEWS: *THE BIRTH OF COLORADO: A CIVIL WAR PERSPECTIVE*
1st Infantry; ACW:NOV/91[10]329, B&G:JUN/94[8]568, B&G:AUG/94[6]573, CWNEWS:NOV/90[4], CWR:VOL2#2[161]139, CWTI:MAR/94[58]375, CWTI:JUL/94[10]389
2nd Cavalry; ACW:NOV/91[10]329

COLQUITT, ALFRED E., *General, CSA;* ACW:JUL/92[30]369, ACW:SEP/93[31]433, ACW:MAY/95[30]525, B&G:APR/94[10]558, B&G:FEB/95[8]590B, CWR:VOL2#2[156]138, CWR:VOL3#1[65]151, CWR:VOL3#2[1]153, CWR:VOL3#4[1]161, CWTI:DEC/94[32]410, GETTY:11[6]231, MH:JUN/92[50]159, *photo;* ACW:MAY/95[30]525

COLSTON, FRED, *Captain, CSA;* CWTI:AUG/90[26]166

COLSTON, FREDERICK M., *Captain, CSA;* CWTI:SEP/92[42]283

COLSTON, RALEIGH E., *General, CSA:*
ARTICLE: "CONVERSATION IN CONFIDENCE," CWTI:JAN/95[20]422
ADDITIONAL LISTINGS: ACW:SEP/93[31]433, ACW:JAN/95[46]507, ACW:MAR/95[12]513, ACW:MAY/95[30]525, AHI:JUN/70[30]127, B&G:JUN/92[8]487, GETTY:13[108]261, MH:JUN/92[50]159, *photo;* CWTI:JAN/95[20]422

COLT, HENRY V., *Major, USA;* ACW:MAR/91[25]294, CWTI:DEC/91[26]238

COLT, SAMUEL; ACW:JAN/91[8]282, CWTI:SEP/90[18]172

COLTART, JOHN G., *Colonel, CSA;* B&G:DEC/95[9]615

COLUMBIA, SOUTH CAROLINA; BOOK REVIEW: *SHERMAN AND THE BURNING OF COLUMBIA*

COLUMBUS (GEORGIA) ARSENAL; ACW:MAR/91[38]296

COLUMBUS IRON WORKS; ACW:MAR/91[38]296

COLUMBUS, GEORGIA, BATTLE OF:
ARTICLES: "A MOST VOLUNTARY GATHERING," B&G:AUG/94[22]576, "BATTLE FOR THE BRIDGES," ACW:MAR/91[38]296
ADDITIONAL LISTINGS: CWTI:SUMMER/89[20]121, CWTI:AUG/90[42]167, CWTI:AUG/90[50]168, CWTI:NOV/93[74]353, CWTI:JAN/95[27]425

COLUMBUS, KENTUCKY; CWTI:FEB/90[26]143, CWTI:FEB/90[38]145

COLVILLE, WILLIAM, III, *Colonel, 1st Minnesota Infantry:*
ARTICLE: "THE FIRST MINNESOTA AT GETTYSBURG," GETTY:5[79]161
BOOK REVIEWS: *THE LAST FULL MEASURE: THE LIFE AND DEATH OF THE FIRST MINNESOTA VOLUNTEERS*
ADDITIONAL LISTINGS: ACW:JAN/94[62], ACW:NOV/94[76]500, GETTY:10[53]225

COLY, W.H., *Colonel, USA;* ACW:JAN/94[10]448

COMBS, D.S., *Private, Terry's Texas Rangers;* CWM:JUL/92[40]432

COMES, CHARLES L., *Private, 8th Louisiana Infantry;* CWTI:FEB/91[12]189

COMEY, HENRY N., *Lieutenant, 2nd Massachusetts Infantry;* GETTY:6[69]176

COMLY, JAMES M., *Major, 23rd Ohio Infantry;* ACW:MAR/94[27]459, CWTI:OCT/95[48]470

COMMAND AND LEADERSHIP; BOOK REVIEWS: *LEADERSHIP AND COMMAND IN THE AMERICAN CIVIL WAR: PARTNERS IN COMMAND: THE RELATIONSHIPS BETWEEN LEADERS IN THE CIVIL WAR*

COMMANDS:
A series of articles devoted to specific military commands, as published in "America's Civil War" as a separate department.
1st Connecticut Cavalry; ACW:JAN/92[16]340
1st Maryland Infantry (Confederate and Union); ACW:JUL/94[10]475
1st South Carolina Infantry; ACW:NOV/92[10]384
2nd Florida Infantry; ACW:SEP/93[8]429
3rd Minnesota Infantry; ACW:MAY/91[12]302
4th Alabama Infantry; ACW:NOV/94[18]495
4th Wisconsin Cavalry; ACW:MAY/93[12]412
6th New Hampshire Infantry; ACW:MAY/95[18]524
10th Georgia Infantry; ACW:JUL/95[10]533
12th Georgia Infantry; ACW:MAR/94[16]458
14th Kentucky (Union) Cavalry; ACW:SEP/95[22]544
22nd Virginia Battalion; CWTI:APR/90[46]153
56th Virginia Infantry; ACW:MAR/93[10]402
72nd Pennsylvania Infantry; ACW:MAY/92[8]357
96th Ohio Infantry; ACW:SEP/92[16]376
black Confederate soldiers; ACW:NOV/95[8]552
Colorado Confederates; ACW:NOV/91[10]329
III Corps; ACW:JUL/93[16]422
Irish Brigade; ACW:MAY/94[12]466
Nauvoo Legion; ACW:JAN/95[8]502
North Carolina Junior Reserves; ACW:NOV/93[12]440
Petersburg Artillery; ACW:MAR/95[12]513
Vermont Brigade; ACW:JAN/94[8]447
Veteran Reserve Corps; ACW:SEP/94[8]483
Washington Horse Artillery; ACW:JUL/92[12]367

COMMERCE; BOOK REVIEW: *GRAY RAIDERS OF THE SEA: HOW EIGHT CONFEDERATE WARSHIPS DESTROYED THE UNION'S HIGH SEAS COMMERCE*

COMMISSARY; BOOK REVIEW: *A COMMISSARY SERGEANT'S COOKBOOK*

COMMITTEE ON GOVERNMENT CONTRACTS; CWTI:JUN/90[46]161

COMMITTEE ON THE CONDUCT OF THE WAR; see listings under "JOINT CONGRESSIONAL COMMITTEE ON THE CONDUCT OF THE WAR"

COMMITTEE TO SAVE FORT FISHER; B&G:FEB/92[40]479

COMMON SOLDIERS:
ARTICLES: "A GREAT POET'S LETTERS ABOUT WARTIME SUFFERING," AHI:AUG/68[4]115B, "A MATTER OF INJUSTICE: THE SUMMERS-KOONTZ INCIDENT," B&G:FEB/92[32]477, "A POETIC PLEA FROM PRISON," CWTI:MAR/91[28]200, "A WEDDING IN CAMP," B&G:FEB/92[22]476, "COALFIELDS' PERFECT HELL," ACW:MAR/92[22]351, "COLORADO'S FORGOTTEN CONFEDERATES DID THEIR BEST TO SUPPORT THE SOUTHERN CAUSE, BUT TO NO AVAIL," ACW:NOV/91[10]329, "EDITORIAL," ACW:MAY/92[6]356, "THE GENERAL'S TOUR: SEASON OF CHANGE, THE WINTER ENCAMPMENT OF THE ARMY OF THE POTOMAC, DECEMBER 1, 1863-MAY 4, 1864," B&G:APR/91[8]445, "HOW MEN FEEL IN BATTLE," AHI:APR/87[10]261
ARTICLES, continued: "JOURNEY OF THE DEAD," ACW:SEP/94[62]490, "LIMBS MADE AND UNMADE BY WAR," ACW:SEP/95[38]546, "ORDNANCE," ACW:MAR/91[12]292, "PERSONALITY," ACW:SEP/91[8]318, "REMEMBERING A DAY," CWM:OCT/95[55]622, "SERGEANT EDWIN B. BIGELOW'S EXCITING ADVENTURES," B&G:AUG/91[36]462, "THEIR FAITH BRINGS THEM,'" CWM:MAR/91[50]340, "THE TOLL OF WAR," B&G:AUG/92[53]495A, "TWENTY-SEVEN KINDS OF DRUNK: A SAMPLING OF DRUNKEN TALES FROM UNION COURT MARTIAL RECORDS," B&G:APR/95[24]596, "TWO CORPORALS: A TALE OF NATHAN BEDFORD FORREST'S ATTACK AT SULPHUR BRANCH TRESTLE, ALABAMA," B&G:JUN/92[32]488,
BOOK REVIEWS: *THE BLUE AND THE GRAY * THE BOYS' WAR * THE BROTHERS' WAR: CIVIL WAR LETTERS TO THEIR LOVED ONES FROM THE BLUE AND GRAY * THE CONFEDERACY IS ON HER WAY UP THE SPOUT: LETTERS TO SOUTH CAROLINA, 1861-1864 * THE CONFEDEDATE REGULAR ARMY * DEAR WIFE: LETTERS OF A CIVIL WAR SOLDIER * DETAILED MINUTIAE OF SOLDIER LIFE IN THE ARMY OF NORTHERN VIRGINIA 1861-1865 * EMBATTLED COURAGE, THE EXPERIENCE OF COMBAT IN THE AMERICAN CIVIL WAR * GEORGIA IN THE WAR, 1861-1865: A COMPENDIUM OF GEORGIA PARTICIPANTS * GONE FOR A SOLDIER: THE CIVIL WAR MEMOIRS OF PRIVATE ALFRED BELLARD*
BOOK REVIEWS, continued: *HARD MARCHING EVERY DAY: THE CIVIL WAR LETTERS OF PRIVATE WILBUR FISK 1861-1865 * HARDTACK & COFFEE: THE UNWRITTEN STORY OF ARMY LIFE * THE ILLUSTRATED CONFEDERATE READER * THE LIFE OF JOHNNY REB: THE COMMON SOLDIER OF THE CONFEDERACY * NO MIDDLE GROUND: THOMAS WARD OSBORN'S LETTERS FROM THE FIELD: 1862-1864 * "SEEING THE ELEPHANT," RAW RECRUITS AT THE BATTLE OF SHILOH * SOLDIERING IN THE ARMY OF TENNESSEE: A PORTRAIT OF LIFE IN A CONFEDERATE ARMY * SOLDIERS BLUE AND GRAY * THE STORY THE SOLDIERS WOULDN'T TELL: SEX IN THE CIVIL WAR,*
BOOK REVIEWS, continued: *THE TRAINING OF AN ARMY: CAMP CURTIN AND THE NORTH'S CIVIL WAR * TRUE TALES OF THE SOUTH AT WAR, HOW SOLDIERS FOUGHT AND FAMILIES LIVED, 1861-1865 * UPON TENTED FIELD: AN HISTORICAL ACCOUNT OF THE CIVIL WAR AS TOLD BY THE MEN WHO FOUGHT AND GAVE THEIR LIVES * THE*

*VACANT CHAIR: THE NORTHERN SOLDIER LEAVES HOME * VOICES OF THE CIVIL WAR * WEEP NOT FOR ME, DEAR MOTHER * WHAT THEY FOUGHT FOR: 1861-1865 * WHERE THEY LIE*
COMMON, CHARLES, *Private, 52nd Ohio Infantry;* ACW:NOV/92[8]383
COMPANY OF SANTA FE GAMBLERS; B&G:JUN/94[8]568
COMPROMISE OF 1850; ACW:MAR/93[6]400, ACW:MAY/93[47]417, ACW:MAY/94[43]470, AHI:JUN/73[4]149, CWNEWS:AUG/91[4], CWR:VOL3#1[31]150, CWTI:DEC/90[50]183
COMPTON, ALEX, *Sergeant, Virginia Infantry;* GETTY:5[117]165
COMPTON, JAMES, *Captain, 52nd Illinois Infantry;* CWTI:SUMMER/89[40]123
COMPTON, JOHN, *Private, 2nd Wisconsin Infantry,* GETTY:11[57]233
COMPUSERVE; CWTI:OCT/95[40]469
COMPUTERS; ARTICLE: "CIVIL WAR IN CYBERSPACE," CWTI:OCT/95[40]469
COMSTOCK, CYRUS, *Lieutenant Colonel, USA;* ACW:NOV/95[22]554, B&G:APR/94[10]558, B&G:DEC/94[10]585, CWM:SEP/92[19]440, CWTI:APR/92[49]260
CONANT, HORACE, *Major, USA;* ACW:NOV/93[26]441
CONDON, PATRICK, *Captain, 63rd New York Infantry;* CWTI:DEC/90[58]185
CONE, AURELIUS F., *Sergeant, CSA;* CWM:JUL/93[4]482

CONFEDERATE TROOPS:
Military units formed as "Confederate" units
1st & 3rd Confederate Cavalry; B&G:FEB/95[8]590A, CWNEWS:AUG/92[4], CWR:VOL4#1[1]163
1st Confederate Georgia Infantry; ARTICLES: "A LONG ROAD TO BENTONVILLE: THE FIRST CONFEDERATE REGIMENT," CWR:VOL1#4[64]127, "FROM SANTA ROSA ISLAND TO CHICKAMAUGA: THE FIRST CONFEDERATE REGIMENT," CWR:VOL1#4[42]126
1st Confederate Infantry; CWR:VOL1#4[v]124, CWR:VOL2#4[269]145
3rd Confederate Cavalry; ACW:SEP/92[23]377, B&G:AUG/91[11]458
3rd Confederate Infantry; CWTI:SEP/94[40]403
5th Confederate Cavalry; CWTI:SEP/94[40]403
6th Confederate Cavalry; B&G:AUG/91[11]458
7th Confederate Cavalry; ACW:MAR/95[12]513
8th Confederate Cavalry; B&G:AUG/91[11]458, CWTI:DEC/90[56]184
10th Confederate Cavalry; B&G:AUG/91[11]458
Confederate Guards Response Battalion; CWR:VOL3#1[1]149
CONFEDERACY, HISTORY OF; BOOK REVIEW: *THEIR TATTERED FLAGS, THE EPIC OF THE CONFEDERACY*
CONFEDERATE (MISSISSIPPI) RIFLES, (48th Mississippi Infantry); GETTY:4[7]142
CONFEDERATE COMMAND; ARTICLE: "A FAILURE OF COMMAND: THE CONFEDERATE LOSS OF VICKSBURG," CWR:VOL2#1[36]132
CONFEDERATE EXILES, ARTICLE: "CONFEDERATE EXILES," AHI:JUN/70[30]127

CONFEDERATE GENERALS FROM THE NORTH, ARTICLE: "YANKEES IN GRAY," ACW:SEP/92[38]379
CONFEDERATE GENERALS:
ARTICLE: "YOU HAD DONE ME A GREAT INJUSTICE," CWTI:MAR/93[40]312
BOOK REVIEWS: *THE CONFEDERATE GENERAL * MEDICAL HISTORIES OF CONFEDERATE GENERALS*
GENERAL LISTING: *The Great Seal of the Confederacy;* ACW:MAY/92[62]364
CONFEDERATE HIGH COMMAND; BOOK REVIEWS: *THE CONFEDERATE HIGH COMMAND AND RELATED TOPICS * JEFFERSON DAVIS AND HIS GENERALS: THE FAILURE OF CONFEDERATE COMMAND IN THE WEST*
CONFEDERATE NAVAL RAIDERS; BOOK REVIEW: *GRAY RAIDERS OF THE SEA: HOW EIGHT CONFEDERATE WARSHIPS DESTROYED THE UNION'S HIGH SEA COMMERCE*
CONFEDERATE RAILROAD BUREAU; ACW:SEP/95[48]547
CONFEDERATE STATES GOVERNMENT:
ARTICLES: "BERMUDA IS AN UNLIKELY STARTING POINT FOR THOSE TRACING THE MYSTERY OF THE GREAT SEAL OF THE CONFEDERACY," ACW:MAY/93[62]418, "COLONEL GEORGE WASHINGTON RAINS WORKED WONDERS WITH THE CONFEDERACY'S NASCENT NITRE BUREAU," ACW:MAY/94[20]467, "THE VICE PRESIDENT RESIDES IN GEORGIA," CWTI:FEB/91[36]193, "WOLF AT THE DOOR," ACW:NOV/93[42]443
BOOK REVIEWS: *A GOVERNMENT OF OUR OWN: THE MAKING OF THE CONFEDERACY * COMPENDIUM OF THE CONFEDERACY, AN ANNOTATED BIBLIOGRAPHY, 2 VOL. * THE CONFEDERATE REPUBLIC: A REVOLUTION AGAINST POLITICS * DIVIDED WE FALL—ESSAYS ON CONFEDERATE NATION BUILDING * ENCYCLOPEDIA OF THE CONFEDERACY * FINANCIAL FAILURE AND CONFEDERATE DEFEAT * INSIDE THE CONFEDERATE GOVERNMENT: THE DIARY OF ROBERT GARLICK HILL KEAN * JEFFERSON DAVIS AND HIS GENERALS: THE FAILURE OF CONFEDERATE COMMAND IN THE WEST * THE RISE AND FALL OF THE CONFEDERATE GOVERNMENT * WHY THE CONFEDERACY LOST*
CONFEDERATE STATES MARINE CORPS:
ARTICLE: "THE CONFEDERATE STATES MARINES," ACW:MAR/91[14]293
BOOK REVIEWS: *THE CONFEDERATE MARINE CORPS * THE CONFEDERATE STATES MARINE CORPS: THE REBEL LEATHERNECKS*
ADDITIONAL LISTINGS: CWM:JAN/91[47], CWR:VOL2#3[183]140
CONFEDERATE STATES NAVAL ACADEMY; ARTICLE: "THE MIDSHIPMEN OF THE CONFEDERATE NAVAL ACADEMY PUT THEIR OFFICERS' TRAINING TO A LAND-BASED USE," ACW:JUL/92[10]366
CONFEDERATES IN BRAZIL, ARTICLE: "OS CONFEDERADOS," CWTI:JAN/93[26]299
CONFISCATION ACTS; CWM:FEB/95[7], CWTI:DEC/90[50]183
CONGDON, AMOS, *Private, 17th Pennsylvania Infantry;* B&G:APR/91[8]445
CONGER, E.J., *Colonel, USA;* CWTI:MAY/91[48]211
CONGER, GEORGE, *Captain, USA;* AHI:JAN/76[14]164
CONGER, SEYMOUR B., *Major, 3rd West Virginia Cavalry;* B&G:AUG/94[10]574, GETTY:11[19]232
CONGRESS, FEDERAL, BOOK REVIEWS: *THE CONGRESSMAN'S CIVIL WAR*

CONGRESSIONAL JOINT COMMITTEE ON RECONSTRUCTION; CWM:APR/94[32]506
CONINE, JAMES, *Colonel, 5th U.S. Colored Infantry;* B&G:OCT/94[42]583
CONKLING, ROSCOE, *Senator, New York;* ACW:MAR/95[8]512, AHI:MAY/76[24]167, AHI:FEB/82[36]225, AHI:APR/83[27]233, CWTI:MAY/89[21]115, *photos;* AHI:MAY/76[24]167, AHI:APR/83[27]233

CONNECTICUT TROOPS:
BOOK REVIEW: *CONNECTICUT YANKEES AT GETTYSBURG*
1st Artillery; ACW:SEP/93[16]431, ACW:JUL/94[42]479, ACW:SEP/95[30]545
1st Cavalry:
ARTICLE: "FROM WEST VIRGINIA TO APPOMATTOX COURT HOUSE, THE 1ST CONNECTICUT VOLUNTEER CAVALRY FOUGHT WITH HONOR," ACW:JAN/92[16]340
ADDITIONAL LISTINGS: B&G:APR/92[8]481, CWM:APR/94[24]505, CWTI:MAR/95[90]440,
2nd Artillery (Heavy); B&G:APR/94[10]558, B&G:APR/94[55]564, CWM:APR/95[50], CWNEWS:JUN/94[5], CWR:VOL3#3[92], CWTI:SEP/91[61]233, CWTI:MAY/94[24]381, GETTY:12[24]242
5th Infantry; CWM:APR/95[50], CWNEWS:JUN/94[5], CWR:VOL3#3[92], GETTY:7[83]192, GETTY:9[61]215
6th Infantry; ACW:SEP/91[30]322
7th Infantry; ACW:NOV/93[10]439, CWR:VOL3#1[65]151, CWTI:JAN/94[46]364
8th Infantry; B&G:OCT/95[8]611A, GETTY:9[61]215
9th Infantry; CWM:MAR/91[50]340
10th Infantry; ACW:MAY/92[30]361, ACW:JUL/94[42]479, CWTI:MAR/94[38]372, GETTY:9[61]215
11th Infantry; B&G:OCT/95[8]611A
12th Infantry; ACW:MAY/91[38]305, CWR:VOL3#1[1]149
13th Infantry; ACW:MAY/91[38]305, CWR:VOL3#1[1]149, GETTY:9[61]215
14th Infantry:
GENERAL LISTINGS: *Gettysburg,* GETTY:5[89]162, GETTY:6[7]169, GETTY:7[97]193, GETTY:8[95]205, GETTY:8[111]206, GETTY:9[61]215, GETTY:10[53]225, GETTY:12[61]245, *in book review,* B&G:APR/95[30], CWM:APR/95[50], CWNEWS:JUN/94[5], CWR:VOL3#3[92], CWR:VOL4#3[89], CWTI:JUL/93[34]327, *list of monuments,* B&G:OCT/95[8]611A, *photos* ACW:SEP/94[38]487, GETTY:9[61]215
ADDITIONAL LISTINGS: ACW:SEP/94[38]487, ACW:JUL/95[50]538, B&G:APR/91[8]445, B&G:APR/93[12]518, GETTY:13[7]253, GETTY:13[75]259
15th Infantry; ACW:SEP/92[8]374, GETTY:8[95]205
16th Infantry; ACW:JAN/94[55]453, B&G:AUG/93[18]530, B&G:OCT/95[8]611A
17th Infantry; ACW:NOV/92[42]388, ACW:NOV/95[38]556, CWM:APR/95[50], CWNEWS:JUN/94[5], CWR:VOL3#3[92], GETTY:4[49]147, GETTY:4[115]152, GETTY:9[33]211, GETTY:13[7]253
18th Infantry; GETTY:12[42]244
19th Infantry; CWTI:SEP/91[61]233
20th Infantry; ACW:SEP/92[47]380, AHI:OCT/67[26]112, B&G:DEC/95[9]615, CWM:APR/95[50], CWNEWS:JUN/94[5], CWR:VOL3#3[92], CWTI:SUMMER/89[32]122, CWTI:SEP/90[26]174, CWTI:NOV/92[41]291, GETTY:5[117]165, GETTY:6[7]169

21st Infantry; ACW:SEP/93[62]436
27th Infantry:
ARTICLE: "THE 10TH GEORGIA AND 27TH CONNECTICUT IN THE WHEATFIELD; TWO CAPTURED SWORDS AGAINST THEIR FORMER OWNERS," GETTY:12[24]242
GENERAL LISTINGS: *Gettysburg*, GETTY:8[53]203, GETTY:11[80]235, GETTY:12[1]240, *in book review*, CWM:APR/95[50], CWNEWS:JUN/94[5], CWR:VOL3#3[92]
ADDITIONAL LISTING: ACW:JUL/95[10]533
Connecticut Light Battery; CWTI:JAN/94[46]364

CONNALLY, JOHN K., *Colonel, 55th North Carolina Infantry;* GETTY:5[4]156, GETTY:9[98]217
CONNAWAY, CHARLES J.M., *Private, Cobb's Legion;* CWR:VOL4#4[28]178
CONNELL, J., *Lt. Col., 28th Iowa Infantry;* B&G:FEB/94[8]550
CONNELL, JOHN M., *Colonel, 17th Ohio Infantry;* B&G:FEB/93[12]511
CONNELLY, HENRY, *Governor, New Mexico;* B&G:JUN/94[8]568
CONNELLY, JAMES, *Captain, 1st Indiana Heavy Artillery;* ACW:JAN/94[30]450
CONNER, DANIEL E., *civilian;* ACW:NOV/91[10]329
CONNER, JAMES, *General, CSA;* CWTI:FEB/91[45]194
CONNER, PATRICK E., *General, USA;* CWNEWS:DEC/92[4]
CONNER, WILLIAM G., *Major, Jeff Davis Legion;* GETTY:12[68]246
CONNINGTON, THOMAS, *Lieutenant, 1st USSS;* CWTI:JUL/93[42]329
CONNOLLY, JAMES A., *Major, 98th Illinois Infantry;* B&G:OCT/92[32]499, CWTI:SUMMER/89[50]124
CONNOLLY, JAMES S., *Major, 123rd Illinois Infantry;* B&G:OCT/92[10]496
CONNOR, H.C., *Private, Palmetto Sharpshooters;* CWR:VOL3#2[70]155
CONNOR, P.E., *Colonel, USA;* ACW:JAN/95[8]502
CONNORS, RICHARD, *Private, 24th Michigan Infantry;* GETTY:5[19]158
CONOLLY, THOMAS; BOOK REVIEW: *AN IRISHMAN IN DIXIE: THOMAS CONOLLY'S DIARY OF THE FALL OF THE CONFEDERACY*
CONOVER, ISAAC, *Corporal, 37th Illinois Infantry;* CWR:VOL1#1[42]105
CONRAD, JOSEPH, *Colonel, USA;* B&G:DEC/93[12]545
CONRAD, THOMAS N., *Captain, 3rd Virginia Cavalry;* ARTICLES: "THE PLAN TO KIDNAP LINCOLN THAT FAILED BY ONE DAY," AHI:NOV/80[6]208, CWTI:DEC/91[28]239
CONSCRIPTION; see listings under various subjects under "DRAFT"
THE CONSERVATION FUND; see listings under "PRESERVATION"
CONTRABAND RELIEF SOCIETY; ACW:JUL/92[8]365A
CONVERSE, NELSON, *Colonel, 6th New Hampshire Infantry;* ACW:MAY/95[18]524
CONVERSE, ROLLIN, *Captain, USA;* GETTY:4[24]145
CONWAY, P.V.D., *Private, Fredericksburg Artillery;* CWR:VOL1#1[1]102
CONWAY, RACHEL; B&G:OCT/93[31]539
CONY, SAMUEL, *Governor, Maine;* CWTI:SEP/92[40]282
CONYNGHAM, DAVID P., *Captain, USA;* CWM:MAR/91[50]340
COOK, AARON, *Private, 4th Kansas Inf.;* ACW:NOV/94[42]497

COOK, ASA M., *Captain, 8th Massachusetts Artillery;* CWTI:FEB/92[36]249
COOK, E.T., *Sergeant, 5th Ohio Cavalry;* CWR:VOL4#1[44]164
COOK, FERDINAND W.C.; ACW:JAN/94[18]449
COOK, FRANK; ACW:JAN/94[18]449
COOK, GEORGE, *photographer;* B&G:FEB/94[24]551
COOK, HENRY A., *Captain, 72nd Pennsylvania Infantry;* GETTY:5[89]162
COOK, HENRY P., *Sergeant Major, 126th New York Infantry;* CWR:VOL1#4[7]125
COOK, IVEY, *Ensign, 27th Texas Infantry;* CWTI:JUL/94[50]395
COOK, JOHN, *General, USA;* AHI:DEC/71[30]138, B&G:FEB/92[10]474
COOK, JOHN, *Private, 4th U.S. Artillery;* GETTY:11[57]233
COOK, JOHN H., *Private, 6th Wisconsin Infantry,* GETTY:11[57]233
COOK JOSEPH, *Colonel, 1st Texas Heavy Artillery;* ACW:JAN/93[51]398, CWTI:DEC/90[29]182
COOK, MRS. ENOCH H.; AHI:DEC/73[10]152
COOK, MINERVA JANE, *civilian;* B&G:AUG/91[52]464
COOK, PHILIP, *General, CSA;* ACW:MAY/91[38]305
COOK, ROBERT T., *Lieutenant Colonel, Phillips Legion;* CWR:VOL4#4[28]178
COOK, SAMUEL H., *Captain, 1st Colorado Infantry;* ACW:NOV/91[10]329, B&G:JUN/94[8]568
COOK, THOMAS M., *reporter;* ACW:MAY/92[30]361, ACW:JUL/94[42]479, CWM:JUL/92[18]429
COOKE, CHARLES M., *Adjutant, 55th North Carolina Infantry;* GETTY:4[22]144
COOKE, CHAUNCEY, *Private, 25th Wisconsin Infantry;* AHI:APR/68[4]115
COOKE, GILES B., *Adjutant, CSA;* ARTICLE: "THE SWORD AND THE CROSS OF GILES B. COOKE: A CHRISTIAN SOLDIER WITH LEE AND JACKSON," B&G:JUN/93[32]525
COOKE, JAY:
ARTICLE: "INTERVIEW WITH LINCOLN," AHI:NOV/72[10]141
ADDITIONAL LISTINGS: AHI:APR/83[27]233
COOKE, JOHN ESTEN, *Lieutenant, CSA;* ACW:JUL/94[26]477, ACW:JAN/95[10]503, ACW:JUL/95[34]536, CWNEWS:MAY/95[33], CWR:VOL4#4[70]180, CWTI:DEC/89[34]136, CWTI:APR/92[41]258, CWTI:JUL/92[12]270, CWTI:JUN/95[18]444, GETTY:4[65]148, GETTY:8[67]204
COOKE, JOHN R., *General, CSA;* ACW:SEP/93[31]433, B&G:APR/92[8]481, B&G:APR/94[10]558, B&G:APR/95[8]595, CWR:VOL1#3[52]122, CWR:VOL2#4[269]145, CWR:VOL4#4[28]178, CWTI:AUG/90[26]166, CWTI:FEB/91[45]194, CWTI:DEC/94[32]410, GETTY:11[6]231, MH:AUG/95[30]185, *photo;* CWTI:FEB/91[45]194
COOKE, PHILIP ST. GEORGE, *General, USA:*
BOOK REVIEW: *CAVALRY TACTICS: OR, REGULATIONS FOR THE INSTRUCTION, FORMATIONS, AND MOVEMENTS OF THE CAVALRY*
GENERAL LISTINGS: *Gaines' Mill*, CWM:JUN/95[61]593, *Mexican War*, MH:APR/93[39]166, *Mormon confrontation*, AHI:DEC/72[10]145, *pre-war*, AHI:SEP/83[42]235, *sketch;* AHI:DEC/72[10]145
ADDITIONAL LISTINGS: ACW:JUL/93[42]425, ACW:SEP/94[55]489, ACW:NOV/94[50]498, B&G:AUG/91[11]458, CWM:JUN/95[50]589, CWR:VOL2#4[269]145, CWR:VOL4#2[104]168, CWTI:DEC/89[34]136, CWTI:APR/92[35]257

COOLEY, DENNIS N., *civilian;* ACW:JAN/91[30]286
COOLIDGE, R.H., *Major, USA;* ACW:JAN/93[66]399
COOMBS, T.M., *Captain, CSA;* B&G:OCT/94[11]580
COON, DATUS E., *Colonel, USA;* ACW:NOV/95[48]557,
   B&G:DEC/93[12]545
COON, DAVID A., *Lieutenant, 11th North Carolina Infantry;*
   GETTY:12[111]250
COONEY, PETER PAUL, *Chaplain, 35th Indiana Infantry;*
   CWM:MAR/91[50]340
COONLEY, J.F., *photographer;* B&G:FEB/94[24]551
COONS, JOHN, *Colonel, 14th Indiana Infantry;*
   GETTY:12[30]243
COOPER SHOP VOLUNTEER REFRESHMENT SALOON;
   CWTI:MAY/94[24]381
COOPER UNION ADDRESS; ACW:NOV/94[8]493,
   CWTI:DEC/95[40]479
COOPER'S (PENNSYLVANIA) BATTERY;
   AHI:MAY/67[22]107
COOPER, DOUGLAS H., *General, CSA;* ACW:JAN/91[30]286,
   ACW:NOV/91[10]329, CWM:SEP/92[38]443,
   CWM:MAY/93[24]476, B&G:OCT/93[38]541
COOPER, FRED, *Major, 7th New Jersey Infantry;*
   B&G:FEB/92[22]476
COOPER, JAMES H., *Captain, 1st Pennsylvania Artillery;*
   GETTY:11[57]233, GETTY:12[30]243, GETTY:13[22]254
COOPER, JOHN A., *Surgeon, CSA;* CWTI:DEC/94[79]417
COOPER, JOHN B., *Captain, 9th New Hampshire Infantry;*
   CWR:VOL2#2[118]136
COOPER, JOSEPH A., *General, USA;* B&G:DEC/93[12]545
COOPER, PETER, *inventor;* ACW:JUL/93[8]420
COOPER, SAMUEL, *General, CSA:*
GENERAL LISTINGS: *Black Confederates,* GETTY:6[94]180, *in book
   review,* CWM:JAN/91[47], CWM:APR/95[50],
   CWNEWS:JUN/93[5], CWR:VOL1#4[77], *photo;*
   ACW:SEP/92[38]379
ADDITIONAL LISTINGS: ACW:SEP/92[38]379, ACW:MAY/93[38]416,
   ACW:MAR/94[16]458, ACW:JUL/94[35]478,
   ACW:SEP/94[10]484, B&G:FEB/91[20]440,
   B&G:AUG/93[30]531, B&G:FEB/95[8]590B,
   CWR:VOL4#1[1]163, CWTI:MAR/89[28]103,
   CWTI:APR/89[14]107, CWTI:APR/90[46]153,
   CWTI:AUG/91[46]218, CWTI:MAR/93[24]309,
   CWTI:MAR/93[40]312, CWTI:MAR/94[29]371,
   CWTI:JUL/94[44]394, CWTI:MAR/95[60]439,
   GETTY:9[109]218
COOPER, MRS. SAMUEL; B&G:JUN/94[22]569
COOPER, SIMEON, *Private, 126th New York Infantry;*
   CWR:VOL1#4[7]125
COOPER, SIMON W., *Captain, USN;* MH:OCT/91[50]154
COOPER, THOMAS V., *Private, 26th Pennsylvania Infantry;*
   GETTY:12[7]241
COPELAND, JOSEPH, *General, USA;* GETTY:11[19]232
COPPEN'S LOUISIANA BATTALION; see listings under
   "LOUISIANA TROOPS, LOUISIANA TIGERS"
COPPENS, ALFRED, *Major, 1st Louisiana Zouave Battalion;*
   ACW:SEP/95[8]542, CWTI:MAR/89[28]103
COPPENS, GASTON, *Colonel, 1st Louisiana Zouave Battalion;*
   CWTI:MAR/89[28]103
COPPENS, GEORGE A.G., CWM:SEP/93[24]495
"COPPERHEADS:"
ARTICLE: "CLEMENT VALLANDIGHAM," ACW:MAR/91[8]291,
   "PETER GRAY MEEK: STRIDENT COPPERHEAD EDITOR,"
   CWM:APR/95[63]578

GENERAL LISTINGS: *Dr. Richard J. Gatling,* AHI:JUN/66[52]102,
   election of 1864, AHI:OCT/68[4]116, *in book review,*
   ACW:NOV/94[66], CWM:APR/95[50], *Thaddeus Stevens,*
   AHI:JAN/82[16]224
ADDITIONAL LISTINGS: ACW:SEP/93[22]432, ACW:JAN/94[47]452,
   ACW:JUL/95[44]537, B&G:OCT/94[28]581,
   CWM:AUG/95[58]611, CWTI:NOV/92[54]293,
   CWTI:OCT/95[48]470, MH:JUN/91[20]152, MH:FEB/94[8]175
CORBETT, BOSTON, *Sergeant, USA:*
ARTICLE: "WHATEVER BECAME OF BOSTON CORBETT?"
   CWTI:MAY/91[48]211
ADDITIONAL LISTINGS: ACW:MAR/93[35]405,
   CWTI:AUG/90[42]167, CWTI:DEC/91[14]235,
   CWTI:MAY/93[12]316, *photo;* ACW:MAR/93[35]405
CORBY, WILLIAM, *Chaplain, 88th New York Infantry;*
BOOK REVIEW: *MEMORIES OF CHAPLAIN LIFE: THREE
   YEARS WITH THE IRISH BRIGADE IN THE ARMY OF
   THE POTOMAC*
GENERAL LISTINGS: *Gettysburg,* GETTY:10[53]225, *in book review,*
   B&G:AUG/93[24], CWM:FEB/95[7], *letters to the editor,*
   CWM:MAY/91[6]345, *photo;* CWM:MAR/91[50]340
ADDITIONAL LISTINGS: ACW:MAY/94[12]466,
   CWM:MAR/91[17]335, CWM:MAR/91[28]336,
   CWM:MAR/91[50]340
CORCORAN, EDWARD P., *Chaplain, 61st Ohio Infantry;*
   CWM:MAR/91[50]340
CORCORAN, MICHAEL, *General, USA;* ACW:SEP/94[46]488,
   ACW:SEP/95[54]548, B&G:AUG/93[36]533,
   B&G:JUN/94[22]569, CWM:MAR/91[50]340,
   CWM:OCT/95[40]619, CWTI:SEPT/89[46]132,
   CWTI:DEC/90[58]185, GETTY:13[43]256
CORCORAN, MICHAEL, *Lieutenant, 150th New York Infantry;*
   GETTY:12[42]244
CORDREY, FRANCIS, *Private, 126th Ohio Infantry;*
   B&G:JUN/95[8]600
CORINTH, MISSISSIPPI, BATTLE OF:
ARTICLE: "ATTACK WRITTEN DEEP AND CRIMSON,"
   ACW:SEP/91[46]324
BOOK REVIEW: *FROM FORT HENRY TO CORINTH*
ADDITIONAL LISTINGS: ACW:JUL/91[35]314, ACW:SEP/92[8]374,
   AHI:OCT/67[26]112, AHI:MAY/71[3]133A,
   AHI:APR/87[10]261, CWM:MAR/93[8]465,
   CWM:AUG/94[52]530, CWR:VOL1#2[44]114,
   CWR:VOL2#1[36]132, CWR:VOL2#4[269]145,
   CWR:VOL2#4[313]146, CWR:VOL3#3[59]159,
   CWR:VOL4#3[50]171, CWTI:MAR/89[28]103,
   CWTI:FEB/90[32]144, CWTI:JUL/92[29]272,
   CWTI:NOV/92[18]289, CWTI:JAN/93[82]304,
   CWTI:SEP/93[59]341, CWTI:DEC/94[82]418,
   CWTI:JAN/95[27]425
CORKERAN, DENNIS, *Private, Louisiana Tigers;*
   CWTI:MAR/94[48]374
CORKERY, W., *Lieutenant, Guibor's Missouri Battery;*
   B&G:FEB/94[8]550
CORLISS, AUGUSTUS W., *Major, USA;* CWR:VOL1#4[7]125
CORLISS, STEPHEN P., *Private, 4th New York Heavy
   Artillery;* B&G:FEB/93[40]514
CORMIER, NICHOLAS, *Captain, 10th Louisiana Infantry
   Battalion;* CWR:VOL3#1[1]149
CORN EXCHANGE REGIMENT; GETTY:13[7]253
CORNAY, FLORIAN, *Captain, USA;* CWR:VOL4#2[26]166,
   CWR:VOL4#2[118]169

CORNELL, WILLIAM H., *Private, 11th Veteran Reserve Corps;*
B&G:APR/93[24]520

CORNISH, SAMUEL E., *founder of Freedom's Journal;*
AHI:JUN/74[12]155

CORNISH, THEODORE O., *Surgeon, 15th Massachusetts
Infantry;* GETTY:10[53]225

CORPS D' AFRIQUE; CWR:VOL4#2[26]166

CORPS OF ENGINEERS; "THE DELICATE AND
DANGEROUS WORK OF PLACING PONTOON BRIDGES
FELL TO THE CORPS OF ENGINEERS," ACW:MAY/93[8]411

CORPS, ARMY, (FEDERAL):

*The following ARMY CORPS are specific listings. These listings
are incomplete since many articles do not specifically refer to a
particular ARMY CORPS. An example might be an article on
the Battle of Antietam, where the numerical designation of an
ARMY CORPS might not be used, however it is assumed that a
particular CORPS fought there. Consequently, refer to
individual battles for additional information. Also, CORPS in
the Confederate Army are not included in this index because of
conflicts between CORPS numbering (1st, 2nd, etc.) and the
fact that most CORPS were referred to by the name of the
commander, which tended to change as the commanders
changed. Federal CORPS are not listed by commanders names
nor is any attempt to segregate CORPS designation when two
or more of them were merged into an existing or a new CORPS.*

CORPS, I: GENERAL LISTINGS: *Gettysburg;* AHI:MAY/67[22]107,
GETTY:9[5]209, GETTY:9[17]210, GETTY:9[33]211,
GETTY:9[81]216, GETTY:10[7]221, GETTY:10[36]223,
GETTY:10[42]224, GETTY:10[53]225, GETTY:11[19]232,
GETTY:11[71]234, GETTY:12[30]243, GETTY:12[85]248, *in
book review,* CWR:VOL1#2[78], CWR:VOL1#2[78],
CWR:VOL3#4[68], *letters to the editor,* CWTI:FEB/92[8]245
ADDITIONAL LISTINGS, ACW: ACW:JUL/91[18]312,
ACW:MAR/92[30]352, ACW:JUL/92[30]369,
ACW:NOV/92[42]388, ACW:JUL/93[50]426,
ACW:SEP/93[31]433, ACW:MAR/94[50]462,
ACW:SEP/94[38]487, ACW:NOV/94[50]498,
ACW:JAN/95[46]507, ACW:MAR/95[42]517,
ACW:JUL/95[50]538
ADDITIONAL LISTINGS, B&G: B&G:OCT/91[11]466,
B&G:FEB/95[8]590A, B&G:FEB/95[8]590B,
B&G:FEB/95[8]590C, B&G:OCT/95[8]611A
ADDITIONAL LISTINGS, CWM: CWM:MAR/91[17]335,
CWM:MAY/92[15]419, CWM:JUL/92[18]429,
CWM:SEP/93[8]493, CWM:APR/95[42]577,
CWM:AUG/94[60]531, CWM:DEC/95[54]632
ADDITIONAL LISTINGS, CWR: CWR:VOL1#3[28]120,
CWR:VOL2#4[269]145, CWR:VOL3#1[31]150,
CWR:VOL3#3[1]157, CWR:VOL4#4[1]177
ADDITIONAL LISTINGS, CWTI: CWTI:FEB/92[36]249,
CWTI:JAN/93[35]300, CWTI:SEP/93[43]338,
CWTI:NOV/93[24]346
ADDITIONAL LISTINGS, GETTY: GETTY:13[1]252, GETTY:13[7]253,
GETTY:13[33]255, GETTY:13[119]262

CORPS, II:
ARTICLE: "THE UNION SECOND CORPS HOSPITAL AT
GETTYSBURG, JULY 2 TO AUGUST 8, 1863,"
GETTY:10[53]225
GENERAL LISTINGS: Cold Harbor, B&G:APR/94[10]558, Five Forks,
B&G:APR/92[8]481, Gettysburg,, AHI:MAY/67[22]107,
AHI:SUM/88[12]273, GETTY:9[61]215, GETTY:10[112]228,

GETTY:11[57]233, GETTY:11[80]235, GETTY:11[80]235,
GETTY:11[126]239, GETTY:12[7]241, GETTY:12[30]243,
GETTY:12[42]244, GETTY:12[68]246, GETTY:12[85]248,
MH:DEC/91[54]155, *in book review,* ACW:JAN/94[62],
CWNEWS:MAY/89[4], CWNEWS:JAN/91[4],
CWR:VOL1#4[77], CWR:VOL2#1[78], CWR:VOL4#3[89],
CWR:VOL4#4[129], *in order of battle,* B&G:APR/94[10]558,
letters to the editor, CWTI:FEB/92[8]245, *Overland Campaign,*
B&G:APR/94[10]558, *Peninsula Campaign,*
CWM:JUN/95[34]584, *Petersburg, MH:APR/95[46]183,*
Wilderness B&G:APR/95[8]595, *photo, ambulance train at
Gettysburg,* GETTY:10[53]225
ADDITIONAL LISTINGS, ACW: ACW:JUL/91[18]312,
ACW:JAN/92[22]341, ACW:MAR/92[30]352,
ACW:JUL/92[41]370, ACW:SEP/92[30]378,
ACW:JAN/93[43]397, ACW:MAR/93[26]404,
ACW:MAY/93[31]415, ACW:JUL/93[16]422,
ACW:JUL/93[50]426, ACW:MAR/94[50]462,
ACW:MAY/94[12]466, ACW:SEP/94[38]487,
ACW:NOV/94[50]498, ACW:MAY/95[30]525,
ACW:SEP/95[54]548
ADDITIONAL LISTINGS, B&G: B&G:APR/93[12]518,
B&G:APR/94[59]565, B&G:DEC/94[34]587,
B&G:APR/95[8]595, B&G:JUN/95[8]600,
B&G:OCT/95[8]611A, B&G:OCT/95[8]611C,
B&G:OCT/95[32]613
ADDITIONAL LISTINGS, CWM: CWM:MAR/91[17]335,
CWM:MAR/91[17]335, CWM:MAY/92[30]420,
CWM:JUL/92[18]429, CWM:JAN/93[8]456,
CWM:MAR/93[24]467, CWM:OCT/94[17]534,
CWM:FEB/95[30]561, CWM:JUN/95[47]588,
CWM:JUN/95[65]595, CWM:OCT/95[40]619,
CWM:DEC/95[54]632
ADDITIONAL LISTINGS, CWR: CWR:VOL1#3[28]120,
CWR:VOL1#3[52]122, CWR:VOL2#2[141]137,
CWR:VOL2#3[236]143, CWR:VOL2#4[269]145,
CWR:VOL3#1[31]150, CWR:VOL3#1[65]151,
CWR:VOL3#2[1]153, CWR:VOL3#4[1]161,
CWR:VOL4#4[47]179, CWR:VOL4#4[101]181
ADDITIONAL LISTINGS, CWTI: CWTI:AUG/90[26]166,
CWTI:FEB/91[45]194, CWTI:APR/92[49]260,
CWTI:JUL/93[29]326, CWTI:SEP/93[43]338,
CWTI:SEP/94[34]402, CWTI:JAN/95[34]427,
CWTI:AUG/95[24]455
ADDITIONAL LISTINGS, GETTY: GETTY:13[1]252, GETTY:13[43]256,
GETTY:13[50]257, GETTY:13[119]262

CORPS, III:
ARTICLE: "THE ARMY OF THE POTOMAC'S PROUD III CORPS
FELL VICTIM TO INTRA-ARMY POLITICS,"
ACW:JUL/93[16]422
GENERAL LISTINGS: *Falling Waters,* GETTY:9[109]218, *Cold
Harbor,* B&G:APR/94[10]558, *Gettysburg,* GETTY:9[5]209,
GETTY:9[48]213, GETTY:9[53]214, GETTY:10[42]224,
GETTY:10[53]225, GETTY:10[112]228, GETTY:10[120]229,
GETTY:11[19]232, GETTY:11[71]234, GETTY:11[80]235,
GETTY:12[7]241, GETTY:12[85]248, GETTY:12[123]251, *in
book review,* ACW:JAN/94[62], CWR:VOL1#4[77],
CWR:VOL2#2[169], CWR:VOL4#4[129]
ADDITIONAL LISTINGS, ACW: ACW:MAR/91[47]297,
ACW:JUL/91[18]312, ACW:JAN/92[38]343,
ACW:MAR/92[30]352, ACW:NOV/92[18]385,
ACW:MAR/93[26]404, ACW:JUL/93[50]426,
ACW:MAY/94[12]466, ACW:SEP/94[38]487,

ACW:MAY/95[18]524, ACW:MAY/95[30]525,
ACW:JUL/95[50]538
ADDITIONAL LISTINGS, B&G: B&G:AUG/91[32]461,
B&G:FEB/92[22]476, B&G:DEC/94[34]587,
B&G:FEB/95[8]590A, B&G:FEB/95[8]590C,
B&G:OCT/95[20]612
ADDITIONAL LISTINGS, CWM: CWM:MAR/91[17]335,
CWM:MAY/92[20]420, CWM:JUL/92[8]427,
CWM:JAN/93[8]456, CWM:DEC/94[40]550,
CWM:JUN/95[29]583, CWM:JUN/95[34]584,
CWM:JUN/95[47]588, CWM:JUN/95[65]595,
CWM:DEC/95[54]632
ADDITIONAL LISTINGS, CWR: CWR:VOL2#4[269]145,
CWR:VOL3#1[31]150, CWR:VOL3#2[1]153,
CWR:VOL3#3[1]157, CWR:VOL4#2[68]167,
CWR:VOL4#4[1]177
ADDITIONAL LISTINGS, CWTI: CWTI:JUN/90[28]158,
CWTI:SEP/91[31]229, CWTI:NOV/92[49]292,
CWTI:JUL/93[14]324, CWTI:JUL/93[42]329,
CWTI:NOV/93[55]350
ADDITIONAL LISTINGS, GETTY: GETTY:13[1]252, GETTY:13[7]253,
GETTY:13[43]256, GETTY:13[50]257
CORPS, IV: ADDITIONAL LISTINGS: ACW:MAR/92[14]350,
ACW:NOV/93[34]442, ACW:JAN/94[8]447,
ACW:JUL/94[66]481, ACW:NOV/95[48]557,
B&G:DEC/93[12]545, CWM:JUN/95[29]583,
CWM:JUN/95[34]584, CWM:JUN/95[47]588,
CWM:JUN/95[55]591, CWR:VOL2#4[269]145,
CWR:VOL3#1[31]150, CWR:VOL3#2[1]153,
CWR:VOL3#2[70]155, CWR:VOL3#3[1]157,
CWTI:SUMMER/89[13]120, CWTI:SUMMER/89[20]121,
CWTI:SUMMER/89[32]122, CWTI:SUMMER/89[50]124,
CWTI:AUG/90[26]166, CWTI:NOV/92[41]291,
CWTI:MAR/95[40]436, MH:DEC/95[58]188
CORPS, V:
BOOK REVIEW: *REMINISCENCES OF THE FIFTH ARMY CORPS*
GENERAL LISTINGS: *Aldie*, GETTY:11[19]232, *Cold Harbor*,
B&G:APR/94[10]558, *Five Forks*, B&G:APR/92[8]481,
Gettysburg, GETTY:9[41]212, GETTY:9[53]214,
GETTY:10[42]224, GETTY:10[53]225, GETTY:10[112]228,
GETTY:10[120]229, GETTY:11[71]234, GETTY:11[91]236,
GETTY:12[24]242, GETTY:12[85]248, *in book review*,
CWM:DEC/94[7], CWR:VOL1#2[78], CWR:VOL1#3[94],
CWR:VOL2#2[169], CWR:VOL2#3[256], *in order of battle*,
B&G:APR/92[8]481, B&G:APR/94[10]558,
CWM:APR/95[5]570, CWM:DEC/95[5]625, *Manassas, Second*,
AHI:DEC/66[30]105, *Overland Campaign*,
B&G:APR/94[10]558, *Petersburg*, MH:APR/95[46]183,
Wilderness, B&G:APR/95[8]595
ADDITIONAL LISTINGS, ACW: ACW:JUL/91[18]312,
ACW:JAN/92[22]341, ACW:JAN/92[38]343,
ACW:MAR/92[30]352, ACW:NOV/92[10]384,
ACW:MAR/93[26]404, ACW:MAY/93[31]415,
ACW:JUL/93[16]422, ACW:JUL/93[42]425,
ACW:JUL/93[50]426, ACW:SEP/93[31]433,
ACW:MAR/94[50]462, ACW:NOV/94[50]498,
ACW:JAN/95[46]507, ACW:MAY/95[30]525,
ACW:MAY/95[38]526, ACW:JUL/95[34]536
ADDITIONAL LISTINGS, B&G: B&G:APR/91[8]445,
B&G:APR/93[12]518, B&G:AUG/93[30]531,
B&G:OCT/93[12]537, B&G:APR/94[59]565,
B&G:JUN/95[8]600, B&G:JUN/95[36]603A,

B&G:OCT/95[8]611A, B&G:OCT/95[8]611B,
B&G:DEC/95[25]616
ADDITIONAL LISTINGS, CWM: CWM:MAR/91[35]337,
CWM:JUL/92[8]427, CWM:JUL/92[18]429,
CWM:JAN/93[8]456, CWM:MAR/93[24]467,
CWM:AUG/94[48]529, CWM:FEB/95[30]561,
CWM:JUN/95[47]588, CWM:JUN/95[57]592,
CWM:AUG/95[27]605, CWM:DEC/95[54]632
ADDITIONAL LISTINGS, CWR: CWR:VOL1#2[7]111,
CWR:VOL1#2[29]112, CWR:VOL1#3[28]120,
CWR:VOL1#3[52]122, CWR:VOL2#2[141]137,
CWR:VOL2#3[236]143, CWR:VOL2#4[269]145,
CWR:VOL3#3[1]157
ADDITIONAL LISTINGS, CWTI: CWTI:AUG/90[26]166,
CWTI:FEB/91[24]191, CWTI:FEB/91[45]194,
CWTI:SEP/91[31]229, CWTI:APR/92[49]260,
CWTI:JUL/93[42]329, CWTI:NOV/93[55]350,
CWTI:MAY/94[31]382, CWTI:JUL/94[44]394,
CWTI:JUN/95[32]446
ADDITIONAL LISTINGS, GETTY: GETTY:13[7]253, MH:JUN/94[8]177
CORPS, VI:
ARTICLE: "THE THIRD BRIGADE, THIRD DIVISION, SIXTH
CORPS AT GETTYSBURG," GETTY:11[91]236
GENERAL LISTINGS: *Crampton's Gap*, MH:AUG/95[30]185, *Falling
Waters*, GETTY:9[109]218, *Five Forks*, B&G:APR/92[8]481,
Gettysburg, GETTY:10[42]224, GETTY:12[24]242,
GETTY:12[123]251, *in book review*, CWNEWS:OCT/89[4],
CWNEWS:NOV/91[4], CWR:VOL4#3[89], *in order of battle*,
B&G:APR/92[8]481, *letters to the editor*, CWTI:FEB/92[8]245,
Monocacy, B&G:DEC/92[8]503, *Overland Campaign*,
B&G:APR/94[10]558, *Wilderness*, B&G:APR/95[8]595
ADDITIONAL LISTINGS, ACW: ACW:MAY/91[38]305,
ACW:JAN/92[22]341, ACW:MAR/92[30]352,
ACW:JUL/92[30]369, ACW:SEP/92[30]378,
ACW:NOV/92[26]386, ACW:MAR/93[26]404,
ACW:MAY/93[31]415, ACW:JUL/93[16]422,
ACW:JUL/93[50]426, ACW:NOV/93[50]444,
ACW:SEP/94[8]483, ACW:SEP/94[55]489,
ACW:NOV/94[50]498, ACW:MAR/95[42]517,
ACW:MAR/95[70]520
ADDITIONAL LISTINGS, B&G: B&G:APR/91[8]445,
B&G:FEB/93[40]514, B&G:APR/93[12]518,
B&G:APR/94[51]563, B&G:APR/94[59]565,
B&G:JUN/94[22]569, B&G:AUG/94[10]574,
B&G:AUG/94[19]575, B&G:JUN/95[8]600,
B&G:OCT/95[8]611B
ADDITIONAL LISTINGS, CWM: CWM:MAY/92[20]420,
CWM:JAN/93[8]456, CWM:MAR/93[24]467,
CWM:SEP/93[24]495, CWM:JUN/95[47]588
ADDITIONAL LISTINGS, CWR: CWR:VOL1#3[52]122,
CWR:VOL1#4[7]125, CWR:VOL2#3[236]143,
CWR:VOL2#4[269]145, CWR:VOL3#1[31]150,
CWR:VOL3#2[1]153, CWR:VOL3#3[1]157,
CWR:VOL3#4[1]161, CWR:VOL4#4[1]177
ADDITIONAL LISTINGS, CWTI: CWTI:APR/92[49]260,
CWTI:NOV/92[49]292, CWTI:JAN/93[40]301,
CWTI:SEP/93[43]338, CWTI:NOV/93[55]350,
CWTI:JUN/95[32]446
ADDITIONAL LISTINGS, GETTY: GETTY:13[7]253, GETTY:13[119]262
CORPS, VII; MH:OCT/93[76]173
CORPS, VIII; ACW:NOV/93[50]444, B&G:DEC/92[8]503,
CWM:JUL/91[64]375, CWTI:JAN/93[40]301,
MH:OCT/93[76]173

CWTI:MAR/94[24]370, CWTI:AUG/95[24]455,
GETTY:13[119]262
COUCH, WILLIAM, *Private, 1st Wisconsin Artillery;*
B&G:FEB/94[8]550
COUK, A.R., *Lieutenant, 2nd Tennessee Cavalry;*
CWR:VOL4#1[1]163
COULTER, RICHARD, *Colonel, 11th Pennsylvania Infantry;*
ACW:JUL/92[30]369, B&G:APR/92[8]481,
CWTI:APR/92[42]259, GETTY:4[33]146, GETTY:10[7]221,
GETTY:13[33]255, *photo;* GETTY:10[7]221
COULTER, WILLIAM B., *Captain, 53rd Pennsylvania
Infantry;* GETTY:11[80]235
COUNNEL, A.B., *Private, 30th Ohio Infantry;*
CWM:MAY/92[44]423
COUNTERFEITING MONEY; ARTICLE: "SAM UPHAM:
STOREKEEPER AND 'YANKEE SCOUNDREL,'"
CWM:MAR/92[32]413
COURT OF IMPEACHEMENT; AHI:DEC/68[28]118
COURTNEY (VIRGINIA) ARTILLERY; B&G:FEB/95[8]590C
COURTNEY, A.R., *Captain, CSA;* GETTY:10[29]222
COURTS MARTIALS, ARTICLE: "TWENTY-SEVEN KINDS OF
DRUNK: A SAMPLING OF DRUNKEN TALES," FROM
UNION COURT MARTIAL RECORDS," B&G:APR/95[24]596
COVELL, GEORGE W., *Captain, 3rd Missouri Infantry;*
B&G:FEB/94[8]550
COVERT, GEORGE K., *Private, 7th Indiana Infantry;*
CWTI:NOV/93[24]346
COVEY, EDWARD, *Major, USA;* B&G:JUN/94[38]571
COVODE, JOHN, *Congressman, Pennsylvania;*
ACW:JUL/95[16]534, CWTI:DEC/95[24]477
COWAN, ANDREW, *Captain, 1st New York Independent
Battery;* CWTI:SEP/93[43]338, GETTY:4[89]150,
GETTY:7[97]193
COWAN, J., *Lieutenant Colonel, 19th Kentucky Infantry,*
B&G:FEB/94[8]550
COWARD, ASBURY, *Colonel, 5th South Carolina Cavalry;*
ACW:MAY/92[30]361, CWM:JUN/94[26]512,
CWR:VOL3#2[70]155, CWTI:MAR/95[60]439
COWARD, CHARLES A., *10th New Jersey Infantry;*
ACW:MAR/92[22]351
COWPER, JOHN C.C., *Lieutenant, 33rd North Carolina
Infantry;* GETTY:12[111]250
COX, CLAYTON, *Captain, 1st Indiana Heavy Artillery;*
ACW:JAN/94[30]450
COX, EDWARD, *Private, New York Cavalry;* AHI:JUL/93[40]312
COX, FLEET WILLIAM, *Colonel, 40th Virginia Infantry;*
GETTY:13[108]261
COX, JACOB D., *General, USA:*
BOOK REVIEW: *ATLANTA*
GENERAL LISTINGS: *Antietam,* B&G:OCT/95[8]611D, *Gettysburg,*
GETTY:9[81]216, *Manassas, Second,* B&G:AUG/92[11]493,
order of battle, B&G:DEC/93[12]545, *Wilmington/Fort Fisher,*
B&G:DEC/94[10]585, *photo;* CWM:AUG/95[36]608
ADDITIONAL LISTINGS: ACW:JUL/94[66]481, ACW:SEP/94[31]486,
ACW:NOV/95[22]554, B&G:AUG/93[10]529,
B&G:FEB/95[30]591, CWM:JAN/91[12]326,
CWM:AUG/95[36]608, CWR:VOL3#3[59]159,
CWTI:FEB/90[46]146, CWTI:FEB/92[36]249,
CWTI:NOV/92[41]291, CWTI:JAN/95[34]427
COX, JOHN, *Private, 84th New York Infantry;* GETTY:7[83]192
COX, JOHN H., *Sergeant, USA;* CWTI:AUG/95[34]457
COX, SAMUEL, *Scout, USA;* B&G:JUN/91[32]454
COX, WALTER S., *Justice,* AHI:FEB/69[12]119

COX, WILLIAM R., *Colonel, CSA;* ACW:MAY/91[38]305,
ACW:MAR/92[30]352, B&G:APR/94[10]558
COXE, JOHN, *Private, 2nd South Carolina Infantry;*
GETTY:5[35]159
COYLE, JAMES, *Private, 69th Pennsylvania Infantry;*
GETTY:4[89]150
"CRACKER LINE"; CWTI:FEB/90[32]144,
CWTI:FEB/90[46]146, CWTI:MAY/93[38]321
CRAFT, DAVID, *Chaplain, 141st Pennsylvania Infantry;* BOOK
REVIEW: *HISTORY OF THE ONE HUNDRED FORTY-FIRST
REGIMENT PENNSYLVANIA VOLUNTEERS 1862-1865*
CRAIG, JAMES, *General, USA;* B&G:JUN/91[32]454
CRAIG, JOHN, *Major, 147th Pennsylvania Infantry;*
GETTY:9[81]216, GETTY:10[120]229
CRAIGHILL, E.A., *Doctor;* CWM:MAY/91[40]351
CRAM, GEORGE C., *Captain, 6th U.S. Cavalry;*
GETTY:11[19]232
CRAM, THOMAS J., *Colonel, USA:*
BOOK REVIEW: *TO THE GATES OF RICHMOND: THE
PENINSULA CAMPAIGN*
ADDITIONAL LISTINGS: CWR:VOL1#4[7]125
CRAMPTON'S GAP, MARYLAND, BATTLE OF:
ARTICLES: "FIRING THE GAP," ACW:JAN/94[39]451,
"PRESERVATION: 96TH PENNSYLVANIA VOLUNTEERS,"
CWR:VOL3#3[88]160
ADDITIONAL LISTINGS: ACW:JUL/92[30]369, ACW:JUL/93[58],
B&G:FEB/93[40]514, B&G:OCT/95[8]611B,
CWR:VOL2#2[95]135, CWR:VOL2#3[236]143,
CWR:VOL3#3[1]157, CWTI:MAY/89[36]118,
CWTI:SEP/92[42]283, MH:AUG/95[30]185
CRANDALL, WILFORD W., *Private, USA;*
B&G:AUG/93[18]530
CRANDALL, WILLIAM, *Private, 8th Michigan Cavalry;*
B&G:JUN/95[36]603A
CRANDELL, LEVIN, *Lieutenant Colonel, 125th New York
Infantry;* GETTY:7[51]190
CRANE, ALEXANDER B., *Lieutenant Colonel, 85th Indiana
Infantry;* CWTI:SUMMER/89[32]122
CRANE, GEORGE W., *Private, USA;* AHI:APR/68[4]115
CRANE, O.J., *Lieutenant Colonel, 7th Ohio Infantry;*
GETTY:9[81]216
CRANE, STEPHEN; ACW:JUL/94[6]473, CWM:NOV/92[10]447
CRAPSEY, EDWARD, *reporter;* CWTI:SEP/91[31]229
CRATER, (PETERSBURG, VIRGINIA) BATTLE OF:
ARTICLES: "AND FIRE SHALL DEVOUR THEM: THE 9TH NEW
HAMPSHIRE IN THE CRATER," CWR:VOL2#2[118]136,
"BURY THEM IF THEY WON'T MOVE (EXCERPT FROM
*MOTHER, MAY YOU NEVER SEE THE SIGHTS I HAVE
SEEN),* CWTI:APR/90[24]152, "CRATER AT PETERSBURG,"
CWTI:APR/90[24]152, "WOUNDED AT THE CRATER,"
CWTI:MAY/91[74]212
BOOK REVIEWS: *FIELDS OF FURY: FROM THE WILDERNESS
TO THE CRATER: AN EYEWITNESS HISTORY * GLORY
ENOUGH FOR ALL * THE LAST CITADEL: PETERSBURG,
VIRGINIA, JUNE 1864-APRIL 1865 * ON FIELDS OF FURY:
FROM THE WILDERNESS TO THE CRATER, AN
EYEWITNESS HISTORY * THE PETERSBURG
CAMPAIGN: THE BATTLE OF THE CRATER: 'THE
HORRID PIT', JUNE 25 - AUGUST 6, 1864*
GENERAL LISTINGS: *general history,* AHI:MAY/71[3]133A, *in book
review,* CWNEWS:MAY/89[4], CWNEWS:NOV/90[4],
CWNEWS:JAN/91[4], CWNEWS:APR/95[33],
CWR:VOL1#3[94], CWR:VOL2#2[169], CWR:VOL3#4[68],

letters to the editor, CWTI:JUN/95[14]443, *Petersburg,* MH:APR/95[46]183

ADDITIONAL LISTINGS: ACW:NOV/92[74]390, ACW:SEP/93[16]431, ACW:MAY/95[18]524, B&G:AUG/91[32]461, B&G:AUG/92[36], CWM:SEP/92[24]441, CWM:SEP/93[24]495, CWR:VOL2#2[141]137, CWR:VOL2#3[236]143, CWTI:SEP/91[31]229, CWTI:MAY/92[38]265, CWTI:JAN/95[34]427

CRAVEN, JOHN J., *Surgeon, USA;* ACW:MAY/91[62]307, CWTI:MAR/94[38]372

CRAVEN, T.A.M., *Captain, USN;* CWM:JUL/93[24]485

CRAVEN, THOMAS T., *Commodore, USN:*
ARTICLE: "THE DILEMMA OF COMMODORE CRAVEN," CWTI:DEC/94[34]411

ADDITIONAL LISTINGS: ACW:NOV/92[51]389, CWTI:MAR/95[18]432, *photo;* CWTI:DEC/94[34]411

CRAVENS, J.E., *Colonel, 21st Arkansas Infantry;* B&G:FEB/94[8]550

CRAWFORD, CHARLES P., *Captain, Sumter Artillery;* CWR:VOL3#2[1]153

CRAWFORD, JAMES W., *Private, 6th Virginia Cavalry;* CWTI:DEC/91[26]238

CRAWFORD, JOHN B., *Private, 16th Mississippi Infantry;* GETTY:4[7]142,

CRAWFORD, RICHARD T., *Adjutant, 9th Louisiana Infantry;* CWTI:FEB/91[12]189

CRAWFORD, SAMUEL W., *General, USA:*
GENERAL LISTINGS: *Antietam,* B&G:OCT/95[8]611A, *Five Forks,* B&G:APR/92[8]481, *Gettysburg,* GETTY:6[7]169, GETTY:9[53]214, GETTY:11[91]236, *in book review,* ACW:JUL/91[50], ACW:NOV/94[66], B&G:AUG/91[26], B&G:FEB/95[26], *in order of battle,* B&G:APR/92[8]481, B&G:APR/94[10]558, B&G:APR/95[8]595, *Overland Campaign,* B&G:APR/94[10]558, *Wilderness,* B&G:APR/95[8]595, B&G:JUN/95[8]600, *photos;* B&G:APR/92[8]481, B&G:APR/95[8]595, B&G:OCT/95[8]611A

ADDITIONAL LISTINGS: ACW:JUL/92[30]369, ACW:MAR/94[50]462, B&G:APR/93[12]518, B&G:OCT/95[32]613, CWM:MAR/91[65]342, CWR:VOL2#3[236]143, CWTI:FEB/91[45]194, CWTI:APR/92[49]260, CWTI:MAY/92[45]266, CWTI:JUN/95[38]447

CRAWFORD, W.L., *Major, 19th Texas Infantry;* ACW:MAR/93[68]409

CRAWFORD, WILLIAM, *Lieutenant, 13th Alabama Infantry;* GETTY:6[13]170

CRAWFORD, WILLIAM A., *Colonel, 1st Arkansas Cavalry:*
ARTICLES: "RACKENSACKER RAIDERS: CRAWFORD'S FIRST ARKANSAS CAVALRY," CWR:VOL1#2[44]114, "...OUR NOBLEST AND BEST SPIRITS HAVE LAIN DOWN THEIR LIVES..." CWR:VOL1#2[70]115

ADDITIONAL LISTINGS: CWR:VOL1#2[v]110, CWR:VOL1#3[94], *photo;* CWR:VOL1#2[44]114

CRAWFORD, WILLIAM H., *Private, Sumter Artillery;* CWR:VOL3#2[1]153

CRAWFORD, WILLIAM M., *Corporal, 1st Georgia Regulars;* CWR:VOL2#2[95]135

CRAWLEY, ROBERT R., *Private, 22nd Battalion Virginia Infantry;* CWR:VOL1#3[52]122

CREEKMORE, SAMUEL A.J., *Sergeant, Jeff Davis Legion;* GETTY:12[68]246

CREEL, GEORGE, ACW:MAR/95[26]515

CREIGHTON, WILLIAM R., *Colonel, 7th Ohio Infantry;* ACW:NOV/93[34]442, CWM:APR/95[29]574, CWTI:SEP/94[40]403, GETTY:9[81]216

CRENNELL, WILLIAM H., *Lieutenant, USA;* GETTY:9[48]213

CRENSHAW'S (VIRGINIA) ARTILLERY; ARTICLE: "NEVER HEARD BEFORE ON THE AMERICAN CONTINENT," GETTY:10[107]227

CRENSHAW, W.N., *Private, 22nd Battalion Virginia Infantry;* CWR:VOL1#3[52]122

CRENSHAW, WILLIAM G., *Captain, CSA;* CWR:VOL1#1[1]102, CWR:VOL3#4[68], GETTY:10[107]227

CRIBBEN, HENRY, *Lieutenant, USA;* B&G:APR/95[8]595

CRIPPEN, EDWARD, *Corporal, 27th Illinois Infantry;* CWR:VOL3#4[24]162

CRIPPS, HIRAM, *seaman, USN;* B&G:JUN/92[40]489

CRIST, HENRY H., *Private, USA, 33rd Indiana Infantry;* CWTI:SUMMER/89[32]122

CRITTENDEN COMPROMISE; ACW:MAR/93[51]407, CWM:JAN/93[6]455

CRITTENDEN, GEORGE B., *General, CSA:*
ARTICLE: "NORTH'S FIRST VICTORY," ACW:SEP/93[38]434

ADDITIONAL LISTINGS: ACW:JAN/91[22]285, ACW:JUL/93[27]423, ACW:MAR/93[55]408, B&G:FEB/92[10]474, B&G:OCT/92[10]496, B&G:FEB/93[12]511, B&G:JUN/94[8]568, CWR:VOL4#1[1]163, *photos;* ACW:MAR/93[55]408, ACW:SEP/93[38]434, B&G:FEB/93[12]511

CRITTENDEN, JOHN J., *Senator, Kentucky;* ACW:JUL/92[22]368, ACW:MAR/93[51]407, ACW:MAR/93[55]408, AHI:NOV/72[12]142, B&G:FEB/93[12]511

CRITTENDEN, THOMAS L, *General, USA;* ACW:JUL/92[22]368, ACW:MAR/93[51]407, ACW:MAR/93[55]408, ACW:SEP/95[70]549, B&G:OCT/92[10]496, B&G:APR/93[12]518, B&G:APR/94[10]558, CWR:VOL2#4[269]145, CWR:VOL4#1[1]163, *photo;* ACW:MAR/93[55]408

CRITTENDEN, THOMAS T., *General, USA;* ACW:MAY/91[12]302, ACW:JAN/92[47]344, AHI:NOV/72[12]142, B&G:AUG/93[10]529 CWM:JUL/92[24]430, CWM:JUL/92[40]432, CWM:OCT/94[48]542, CWR:VOL4#3[50]171

CROCKER, FREDERICK, *Lieutenant, USN;* CWM:OCT/95[47]620, CWTI:DEC/90[29]182

CROCKER, JULES O.B., *Captain, 9th Virginia Infantry;* GETTY:12[111]250

CROCKER, MARCELLUS M., *General, CSA;* ACW:NOV/91[22]331, CWR:VOL3#3[59]159, CWTI:MAY/91[24]208, MH:JUN/93[82]167

CROCKER, WILLIAM H., *Lieutenant Colonel, 6th New York Cavalry;* GETTY:11[19]232

CROCKETT, LEROY, *Major, 72nd Ohio Infantry;* CWR:VOL4#1[44]164

CROFFUT, WILLIAM, *Private, 1st Minnesota Infantry;* ACW:JAN/94[62]

CROFT, EDWARD, *Georgia Light Artillery;* B&G:AUG/95[8]604

CROFT, EDWARD, *Major, 14th South Carolina Infantry;* GETTY:8[9]199, GETTY:13[22]254

CROFT, SAM, *Private, USA;* AHI:APR/68[4]115

CROMWELL, JAMES, *Major, 124th New York Infantry;* ACW:JUL/95[66]539, CWM:DEC/94[40]550

CROOK, GEORGE, *General, USA:*
ARTICLES: "CONFEDERATES' BRILLIANT EXPLOIT,"
ACW:SEP/91[41]323, "GENERAL CROOK AND THE
PAIUTES," AHI:JUL/73[38]150, "HOW STANDING BEAR
BECAME A PERSON," AHI:APR/71[48]133, "UNION
FORCES ROUTED AGAIN," CWM:AUG/95[35]607,
"VICIOUS MOUNTAIN ENCOUNTER," ACW:MAR/94[27]459
GENERAL LISTINGS: *Cedar Creek,* MH:OCT/93[76]173, *Custer,*
AHI:FEB/71[4]131, *Five Forks,* B&G:APR/92[8]481, *in book
review,* CWNEWS:JUL/90[4], CWNEWS:SEP/90[4], *in order of
battle,* B&G:APR/92[8]481, *Indian Wars,* AHI:JUL/80[36]204,
Kernstown, 1864, B&G:AUG/94[10]574, *letters to the editor,*
B&G:APR/95[5]594, CWTI:JAN/95[16]421, *Little Big Horn,*
AHI:DEC/84[18]243, *post war,* AHI:OCT/79[20]194,
AHI:NOV/79[32]196, MH:FEB/95[18]182, *Third Winchester,*
ACW:MAY/91[38]305, AHI:NOV/80[8]209, *photos;*
ACW:SEP/91[41]323, ACW:SEP/94[55]489,
AHI:AUG/72[24]140, AHI:JUL/73[38]150,
AHI:NOV/79[32]196, AHI:NOV/80[8]209,
CWM:AUG/95[35]607, CWTI:SEP/94[49]404
ADDITIONAL LISTINGS: ACW:JAN/92[22]341, ACW:JAN/93[43]397,
ACW:JUL/94[26]477, ACW:MAY/95[49]527,
AHI:AUG/72[24]140, AHI:FEB/85[10]247,
B&G:AUG/91[11]458, B&G:APR/93[12]518,
CWM:NOV/91[58]394A, CWM:MAY/92[8]418,
CWM:APR/94[24]505, CWTI:APR/92[35]257,
CWTI:SEP/94[49]404, MH:APR/95[46]183
CROOK, WILLIAM, *Sergeant, USA;* CWTI:FEB/91[28]192
CROOKS, SAMUEL J., *Colonel, 8th New York Cavalry;*
CWM:MAY/92[8]418
CROSBY, ALANSON, *Adjutant, 154th New York Infantry;*
GETTY:8[17]200
CROSBY, FRANKLIN B., *Lieutenant, 4th U.S. Artillery;*
ACW:MAY/91[8]300
CROSBY, JOHN K., *Master, USN;* AHI:OCT/95[16]325
CROSBY, JOHN S., *Colonel, USA;* AHI:FEB/85[10]247
CROSMAN, A.F., *Lieutenant Commander, USN;*
CWR:VOL2#3[194]141
CROSS KEYS, VIRGINIA, BATTLE OF:
ARTICLE: "LIVING ON A CIVIL WAR BATTLEFIELD,"
CWTI:JAN/95[22]423
BOOK REVIEWS: *BATTLEFIELD: FARMING A CIVIL WAR
BATTLEGROUND*
ADDITIONAL LISTINGS: ACW:JAN/93[35]396, ACW:MAY/95[54]528,
AHI:MAY/71[3]133A, B&G:JUN/92[8]487,
CWM:JUL/92[16]428, CWM:DEC/95[34]628,
CWR:VOL1#3[28]120, CWR:VOL1#4[7]125,
CWTI:JUN/95[18]444
CROSS, CHARLES, *Lieutenant, 50th New York Infantry;*
ACW:MAY/93[8]411, B&G:DEC/91[12]469,
CWR:VOL4#4[101]181
CROSS, D.W., *Private, 15th Massachusetts Infantry;*
CWTI:SEP/90[26]174
CROSS, EDWARD E., *Colonel, 5th New Hampshire Infantry:*
ARTICLE: "COMPLETELY OUTGENERALLED,"
CWTI:AUG/95[24]455
ADDITIONAL LISTINGS: CWR:VOL3#3[92], CWTI:FEB/90[74]149,
GETTY:8[53]203, GETTY:10[53]225, GETTY:11[80]235,
GETTY:12[24]242, *photos;* CWTI:AUG/95[24]455,
GETTY:10[53]225
CROSS, JAMES E., *Private, 12th New York Infantry;*
B&G:FEB/93[40]514
CROSS, NELSON, *Colonel, USA;* B&G:APR/94[10]558

CROSS, RICHARD, *Berdan's Sharpshooters;*
CWTI:MAR/89[34]104
CROSSDALE, ALBERT, *Private, 109th Pennsylvania Infantry;*
CWTI:SUMMER/89[32]122
CROSSLAND, EDWARD, *Colonel, CSA;* ACW:SEP/92[23]377,
B&G:DEC/93[12]545
CROTCHETT, GEORGE M., *Private, 1st South Carolina
Infantry;* ACW:NOV/92[10]384
CROTTY, DANIEL, *Private, USA;* B&G:APR/95[8]595
CROUNSE, L.L., *Reporter;* GETTY:6[99]181, GETTY:7[23]187
CROWDER, ZERALD, *Private, CSA;* B&G:JUN/95[22]601
CROWE, ROBERT R., *Private, 32nd Wisconsin Infantry;*
CWR:VOL2#4[313]146
CROWELL, JAMES M., *Lieutenant, 28th North Carolina
Infantry;* GETTY:9[109]218
CROWN, WILLIAM, *Private, 22nd Battalion Virginia Infantry;*
CWR:VOL1#3[52]122
CROWNINSHIELD, BENJAMIN, *1st Massachusetts Cavalry;*
B&G:OCT/93[21]538
CROWNINSHIELD, CASPAR, *Captain, USA;*
AHI:FEB/82[36]225
CROWTHER, JAMES, *Colonel, 118th Pennsylvania Infantry;*
B&G:APR/95[8]595
CROXTON, J.H., *Lieutenant, CSA;* B&G:OCT/94[11]580
CROXTON, JOHN T., *General, USA;* ACW:NOV/95[48]557,
B&G:DEC/93[12]545, CWM:OCT/95[36]616
CRUFT, CHARLES, *General, USA;* ACW:NOV/93[34]442,
B&G:DEC/93[12]545, CWTI:SEP/94[40]403
CRUMLEY, W.M., *Private, CSA;* CWR:VOL4#4[28]178
CRUMP, BILLY, *orderly, 23rd Ohio Infantry;*
CWTI:SEP/94[49]404
CRUMP, PLEASANT, *Private, 10th Alabama Infantry;*
B&G:FEB/91[32]441
CRUTCHFIELD, SAMUEL, *Colonel, CSA;*
ACW:MAY/95[30]525
CRUTCHFIELD, STAPLETON, *Colonel, CSA:*
ARTICLE: "VMI'S STAPLETON CRUTCHFIELD LOYALLY
FOLLOWED STONEWALL JACKSON FROM THE CAMPUS
TO THE BATTLEFIELD," ACW:MAY/95[10]523
ADDITIONAL LISTINGS: ACW:JAN/92[22]341, CWR:VOL1#1[1]102,
CWR:VOL4#4[70]180, MH:JUN/92[50]159, *portrait;*
ACW:MAY/95[10]523
CRUTE, WILLIAM T., *Sergeant, 14th Virginia Infantry;*
CWR:VOL1#3[52]122
CRYSTAL SPRINGS (MISSISSIPPI) SOUTHERN RIGHTS,
(16th Mississippi Infantry); GETTY:4[7]142, GETTY:5[89]162,
GETTY:8[111]206
CULBERTSON, JOHN S., B&G:AUG/95[36]607
CULLEN, J.S.D., *Major, CSA;* CWTI:MAR/93[40]312,
GETTY:5[4]156
CULLEN, JOHN, *Private, 6th South Carolina Cavalry;*
CWTI:SEP/90[26]174
CULLIN, LEWIS F., *Private, 10th Virginia Cavalry;*
B&G:DEC/91[38]471
CULLUM, GEORGE W., *General, USA;* ACW:MAY/93[8]411,
B&G:DEC/91[12]469, B&G:APR/92[6]480,
B&G:AUG/93[36]533, CWTI:DEC/94[82]418,
GETTY:11[19]232
CULP, PETER, *scout, USA;* GETTY:11[19]232
CULPEPER ARTILLERY; B&G:DEC/91[34]470
CULPEPER COURT HOUSE, VIRGINIA;
B&G:APR/91[8]445, CWTI:DEC/89[34]136,
CWTI:JUN/90[32]159

CULPEPER, D.J., *Private, Sumter Artillery;*
CWR:VOL3#2[1]153
CULPEPPER (SOUTH CAROLINA) ARTILLERY;
B&G:AUG/95[8]604
CULPEPPER, JAMES F., *Captain, Culpepper's South Carolina Artillery;* B&G:AUG/95[8]604
CUMBERLAND CHURCH, VIRGINIA, BATTLE OF;
CWR:VOL2#3[236]143
CUMBERLAND GAP, KENTUCKY, CAMPAIGNS OF:
ARTICLE: "CONTESTING CUMBERLAND GAP,"
ACW:JUL/91[26]313
ADDITIONAL LISTING: CWTI:FEB/90[26]143
CUMMING, ALFRED, *General, CSA;* ACW:JUL/95[10]533,
CWR:VOL1#4[42]126, CWR:VOL2#1[36]132,
CWR:VOL3#3[59]159
CUMMING, JOSEPH B., *Major, CSA;*
CWTI:SUMMER/89[40]123
CUMMINGS, A. BOYD, *Lieutenant Commander, USN;*
ACW:MAR/92[40]353
CUMMINGS, ALEXANDER; CWTI:JUN/90[46]161
CUMMINGS, ALFRED, *General, CSA;* ACW:NOV/91[22]331,
CWTI:MAY/91[24]208, CWTI:SEPT/89[30]129,
CWTI:DEC/94[49]413
CUMMINGS, DAVID H., *Colonel, CSA;* B&G:FEB/93[12]511
CUMMINGS, HENRY and JAMES, *Sumter Artillery;*
CWR:VOL3#2[1]153
CUMMINGS, J.B., *Colonel, 20th Georgia Infantry;*
CWM:JUN/95[63]594
CUMMINGS, KATE, CWM:MAY/91[26]349, CWR:VOL4#1[78]
CUMMINGS, SIMEON W., *engineer, CSA;* CWTI:MAY/91[8]205
CUMMINS, ROBERT, *Colonel, 142nd Pennsylvania Infantry;*
CWR:VOL4#4[1]177
CUNARD, HENRY E., *Captain, USA;* B&G:AUG/93[10]529
CUNNINGHAM, EDWARD, *Lieutenant Colonel, CSA;*
CWTI:NOV/92[41]291
CUNNINGHAM, GEORGE H., *Private, 15th Massachusetts Infantry;* GETTY:13[43]256
CUNNINGHAM, JAMES, *Lieutenant Colonel, 2nd Alabama Cavalry;* B&G:JUN/93[12]524, CWR:VOL4#1[1]163
CUNNINGHAM, S.A., *Private, CSA;* B&G:FEB/92[10]474,
B&G:OCT/92[10]496
CUNNINGHAM, W. R., *Captain, 14th Kentucky Cavalry;*
B&G:OCT/94[11]580
CURLEY, EDMUND W., *Lieutenant, 16th Mississippi Infantry;*
GETTY:8[111]206
CURRAN, HUGH; CWM:MAR/91[56]341
CURRIDEN, DAVID D., *Private, USA;* B&G:APR/95[8]595
CURRIER & IVES:
PRINTS: "Death of Stonewall Jackson", CWM:NOV/92[24]448,
"Johnston surrendering to Sherman", CWM:NOV/92[24]448
ADDITIONAL LISTING: B&G:FEB/94[24]551
CURRY, WILMOT W., *Sergeant, CSA;* CWTI:SEPT/89[24]128
CURTIN, ANDREW, *Governor, Pennsylvania:*
GENERAL LISTINGS: *Gettysburg,* GETTY:9[53]214,
GETTY:12[97]249, *in book review,* B&G:JUN/93[28], *Lincoln's Gettysburg Address,* GETTY:9[122]220, *photo;*
GETTY:12[97]249
ADDITIONAL LISTINGS: ACW:JAN/92[30]342, ACW:MAR/92[22]351,
ACW:SEP/93[22]432, AHI:JAN/94[50]319,
AHI:NOV/88[37]278, B&G:AUG/95[8]604,
CWM:MAR/91[56]341, CWM:APR/95[63]578,
CWM:OCT/95[55]622, CWM:DEC/95[54]632,
CWR:VOL1#3[20]119, CWR:VOL3#3[1]157,

CWTI:FEB/92[21]247, CWTI:SEP/93[43]338,
CWTI:DEC/95[24]477
CURTIN, JOHN I., *General, USA;* B&G:APR/94[10]558,
B&G:AUG/95[8]604, CWR:VOL3#2[1]153
CURTIN, SAMUEL; CWM:SEP/92[38]443
CURTIS, BENJAMIN R.; AHI:DEC/68[28]118
CURTIS, CHARLES, *Private, USA;* CWM:JAN/92[16]401
CURTIS, FREDERICK, *seaman, USN;* AHI:OCT/75[30]162
CURTIS, HENRY, *Captain, 37th Illinois Infantry;*
CWR:VOL1#1[42]105, CWR:VOL1#4[7]125
CURTIS, JAMES F., *Colonel, USA;* B&G:OCT/91[11]466,
CWTI:SEP/91[18]227, *photo;* B&G:OCT/91[11]466
CURTIS, JOSEPH M, *Private, 30th Maine Infantry;*
ACW:SEP/91[16]320
CURTIS, NEWTON M., *General, USA;* AHI:SEP/83[12]234,
B&G:DEC/94[10]585
CURTIS, ORSON B., *Private, 24th Michigan Infantry;*
GETTY:11[57]233
CURTIS, PLATT, *Private, 150th New York Infantry;*
GETTY:12[42]244
CURTIS, SAMUEL R., *General, USA;* ACW:MAR/94[8]456,
ACW:NOV/94[42]497, AHI:MAY/71[3]133A,
AHI:NOV/72[12]142, B&G:JUN/91[10]452,
CWNEWS:DEC/94[33], CWR:VOL1#1[42]105,
CWR:VOL1#2[44]114, CWR:VOL2#3[212]142,
CWR:VOL3#1[80], CWTI:APR/92[27]256,
CWTI:MAY/92[48]267, MH:DEC/95[58]188, *photo;*
ACW:NOV/94[42]497
CURTIS, SYLVANUS, *Major, 7th Michigan Infantry;*
ACW:JUL/95[50]538
CURTIS, T.A., *Captain, CSA;* CWR:VOL1#1[1]102
CUSHING, ALONZO H., *Captain, USA:*
BOOK REVIEWS: *CUSHING OF GETTYSBURG: THE STORY OF A UNION ARTILLERY COMMANDER*
GENERAL LISTINGS: *Gettysburg,* GETTY:4[89]150,
GETTY:4[113]153, GETTY:5[79]161, GETTY:5[107]164,
GETTY:7[97]193, GETTY:11[71]234, GETTY:12[61]245,
MH:DEC/91[54]155, *letters to the editor,*
CWTI:NOV/93[12]345, MH:AUG/92[8]160, *photo;*
B&G:DEC/91[12]469
ADDITIONAL LISTINGS: ACW:MAY/92[8]357, ACW:MAR/93[10]402,
ACW:JUL/95[50]538, AHI:SUM/88[12]273,
B&G:DEC/91[12]469, CWR:VOL3#2[1]153,
CWTI:JUL/93[29]326, GETTY:13[43]256, GETTY:13[50]257,
GETTY:13[64]258
CUSHING, GEORGE; AHI:AUG/71[22]135
CUSHING, LEAVITT W., *Private, 53rd Pennsylvania Infantry;*
GETTY:11[80]235
CUSHING, SAMUEL T., *Captain, USA;* GETTY:10[42]224
CUSHING, WILLIAM B., *Lieutenant Commander, USN;*
ACW:NOV/91[8]328, B&G:DEC/94[10]585,
B&G:DEC/94[36]588, B&G:JUN/95[36]603A,
CWNEWS:MAY/91[4], *photo;* B&G:DEC/94[10]585
CUSHMAN, PAULINE, *female spy:*
ARTICLE: "PAULINE CUSHMAN: ACTRESS IN THE THEATER OF WAR," AHI:JAN/85[20]245
ADDITIONAL LISTINGS: AHI:DEC/73[10]152, B&G:OCT/92[10]496,
CWTI:JUN/95[51]449, *photos;* AHI:DEC/73[10]152,
AHI:JAN/85[20]245, B&G:OCT/92[10]496
CUSHMAN, W.H., *engineer, USN;* AHI:JAN/83[10]232
CUSICK, CORNELIUS C., *Lieutenant, 132 New York Infantry:*
ARTICLE: "WAREAGLE OF THE TUSCARORAS: LIEUTENANT CORNELIUS C. CUSICK," CWM:SEP/92[16]438

ADDITIONAL LISTINGS: CWNEWS:JAN/94[5], *photo;* CWM:SEP/92[16]438
CUSSON, JOHN, *Captain, CSA:* GETTY:13[64]258
CUSTER, ELIZABETH B.:
BOOK REVIEW: *THE CIVIL WAR MEMORIES OF ELIZABETH BACON CUSTER*
ADDITIONAL LISTINGS: ACW:SEP/95[38]546, *photos;* AHI:FEB/71[4]131, AHI:JUN/76[4]169
CUSTER, GEORGE A., *General, USA:*
ARTICLES: "A FACE IN HISTORY," AHI:OCT/85[38]253, "AMERICAN HISTORY TODAY," AHI:OCT/84[6]241, "THE APPOMATTOX SURRENDER TABLE," CWTI:NOV/93[50]349, "CUSTER'S LAST BATTLE, PART ?" AHI:DEC/84[18]243, "CUSTER'S LAST BATTLE, PART II," AHI:JAN/85[30]246, "CUSTER'S LONG SUMMER," CWTI:MAY/93[35]320, "CUSTER: HERO OR BUTCHER?" AHI:FEB/71[4]131
ARTICLES, continued: "ECHOES FROM THE CUSTER BATTLEFIELD," AHI:DEC/84[10]242, "THE ENDURING CUSTER LEGEND," AHI:JUN/76[4]169, "FORGOTTEN FIELD: THE CAVALRY BATTLE EAST OF GETTYSBURG ON JULY 3, 1963," GETTY:4[75]149, "LOST IN CUSTER'S SHADOW," ACW:SEP/94[55]489, "MELEE IN THE UNDERBRUSH," ACW:NOV/92[26]386, "NEITHER 'HANCOCK THE SUPERB' NOR 'HARD BACKSIDES' CUSTER WON MUCH GLORY IN THE HANCOCK'S WAR FIASCO," ACW:MAY/93[6]410, "SWELTERING SUMMER COLLISION," MH:FEB/93[42]164
BOOK REVIEWS: *A COMPLETE LIFE OF GENERAL GEORGE ARMSTRONG CUSTER * ARCHAEOLOGY, HISTORY, AND CUSTER'S LAST BATTLE: THE LITTLE BIG HORN REEXAMINED * ARCHEOLOGICAL PERSPECTIVES ON THE BATTLE OF LITTLE BIGHORN * BATTLE OF THE ROSEBUD: PRELUDE TO THE LITTLE BIG HORN * CENTENNIAL CAMPAIGN: THE SIOUX WAR OF 1876 * THE CIVIL WAR MEMORIES OF ELIZABETH BACON CUSTER * CUSTER AND HIS TIMES: BOOK III * CUSTER ENGAGES THE HOSTILES * THE CUSTER READER * THE CUSTER TRAGEDY: EVENTS LEADING UP TO AND FOLLOWING THE LITTLE BIG HORN CAMPAIGN OF 1876 * CUSTER VICTORIOUS: THE CIVIL WAR BATTLES OF GENERAL GEORGE ARMSTRONG CUSTER * CUSTER'S LAST, OR THE BATTLE OF LITTLE BIG HORN * CUSTER'S SEVENTH CAVALRY COMES TO DAKOTA*
GENERAL LISTINGS: *Appomattox,* CWTI:MAR/95[20]433, *Beecher's Island, Battle of (Indian Wars),* AHI:DEC/67[4]113, *Brandy Station,* CWTI:JUN/90[32]159, *Buckland,* ACW:JUL/92[41]370, *Cedar Creek,* MH:OCT/93[76]173, *election of 1864,* AHI:OCT/68[4]116, *Falling Waters,* GETTY:9[109]218, *Five Forks,* ACW:MAY/95[38]526, B&G:APR/92[8]481, *Gettysburg,* CWTI:APR/92[35]257, GETTY:4[65]148, GETTY:11[19]232, GETTY:12[68]246, *in book review,* ACW:SEP/95[62], CWM:APR/95[50], CWNEWS:SEP/90[4], CWNEWS:JUL/94[25], CWR:VOL4#2[136], CWR:VOL4#3[89], MH:DEC/92[74]
GENERAL LISTINGS, continued: *in order of battle,* B&G:APR/92[8]481, B&G:APR/94[10]558, *letters to the editor,* B&G:JUN/95[5]599, CWTI:JUL/93[10]323, *Little Big Horn,* MH:AUG/95[82]186, *order of battle,* B&G:APR/95[8]595, *Overland Campaign,* B&G:APR/94[10]558, *post war,* AHI:NOV/79[32]196, *Waynesboro,* CWM:APR/94[24]505, *West Point,* B&G:DEC/91[12]469, *Williamsburg,* ACW:MAR/91[47]297,

Winchester, Third ACW:MAY/91[38]305, ACW:JAN/92[16]340, *Yellow Tavern,* ACW:MAY/94[35]469
PHOTOS: *photo, as cadet;* AHI:FEB/71[4]131, *photo, with dog;* CWTI:MAR/95[46]437, *photos;* ACW:JAN/92[22]341, ACW:JUL/92[41]370, ACW:SEP/94[55]489, AHI:FEB/71[4]131, AHI:JUN/76[4]169, AHI:DEC/84[18]243, AHI:OCT/85[38]253, B&G:OCT/91[11]466, B&G:DEC/91[12]469, B&G:APR/92[8]481, B&G:OCT/93[12]537, GETTY:9[109]218, GETTY:13[89]260, *portrait;* CWM:APR/94[24]505, *sketch;* ACW:SEP/94[55]489
ADDITIONAL LISTINGS, ACW: ACW:JUL/93[50]426, ACW:SEP/94[6]482
ADDITIONAL LISTINGS, AHI: AHI:FEB/85[10]247, AHI:SEP/87[40]263
ADDITIONAL LISTINGS, B&G: B&G:APR/91[8]445, B&G:AUG/91[36]462, B&G:OCT/91[40]467, B&G:JUN/92[46]490, B&G:FEB/93[24]512, B&G:APR/94[51]563, B&G:AUG/94[10]574
ADDITIONAL LISTINGS, CWM: CWM:JAN/93[40]461, CWM:AUG/94[26]525
ADDITIONAL LISTINGS, CWR: CWR:VOL1#1[35]104, CWR:VOL3#2[1]153
ADDITIONAL LISTINGS, CWTI: CWTI:SEP/90[52]179, CWTI:MAY/92[32]264, CWTI:MAY/93[26]318
ADDITIONAL LISTINGS, GETTY: GETTY:13[1]252, GETTY:13[89]260, GETTY:13[108]261, GETTY:13[119]262
ADDITIONAL LISTINGS, MH: MH:OCT/93[12]171, MH:DEC/95[58]188
CUSTER, THOMAS, *Lieutenant, USA;* AHI:JUN/76[4]169, B&G:APR/91[6]444
CUTHBERT, JAMES, *Capt., 2nd SC Inf.;* MH:AUG/95[30]185
CUTLER, LYSANDER, *General, USA:*
BOOK REVIEWS: *CUTLER'S BRIGADE AT GETTYSBURG*
GENERAL LISTINGS: *Gettysburg,* GETTY:4[16]143, GETTY:4[24]145, GETTY:4[33]146, GETTY:4[113]153, GETTY:5[4]156, GETTY:5[13]157, GETTY:5[19]158, GETTY:6[13]170, GETTY:6[29]171, GETTY:7[23]187, GETTY:10[7]221, GETTY:11[71]234, *in book review,* CWR:VOL1#2[78], *Manassas, Second,* B&G:AUG/92[11]493, *Wilderness,* B&G:APR/95[8]595, B&G:JUN/95[8]600
ADDITIONAL LISTINGS: B&G:APR/93[12]518, B&G:APR/94[10]558, B&G:FEB/95[8]590A, B&G:APR/95[8]595, B&G:FEB/95[8]590B, B&G:FEB/95[8]590C, CWR:VOL2#4[269]145, GETTY:13[22]254, GETTY:13[33]255
CUTSHAW, W.E., *Major, CSA;* ACW:MAY/91[38]305, B&G:APR/95[8]595
CUTTER, CHARLES, *Private, 1st Massachusetts Heavy Artillery,* AHI:AUG/68[4]115B
CUTTER, VALENTINE, *Captain, CSA;* CWR:VOL1#1[1]102
CUTTS, ALLEN S., *Colonel, CSA;* B&G:APR/95[8]595, CWR:VOL3#2[1]153, CWR:VOL3#2[61]154
CUTTS, JAMES M., *Captain, USA;* AHI:NOV/70[22]130, B&G:OCT/94[11]580
CUYLER, JOHN M., *Surgeon;* CWM:DEC/95[54]632, GETTY:10[53]225
CYTHIANA, KENTUCKY, ENGAGEMENT AT; MH:JUN/91[20]152

D

D'AQUIN, LOUIS E., *Captain, CSA;* CWR:VOL4#4[70]180
D'ARTOIS, GASTON, *Captain, USA;* ACW:MAR/92[62]355
D'EPINEUIL, LIONEL R., *Colonel, 53rd New York Infantry;*
MH:APR/94[54]176
D'UTASSY, FREDERICK G., *Colonel, 39th New York Infantry:*
ARTICLE: "FLAMBOYANT GARIBALDI GUARDS,"
ACW:MAY/95[54]528
ADDITIONAL LISTINGS: B&G:OCT/95[36]614, CWR:VOL1#4[7]125,
GETTY:7[51]190, MH:OCT/93[20]172, *photo,*
ACW:MAY/95[54]528
DA SARACENA, LEO RIZZO, *Chaplain, 9th Connecticut
Infantry;* CWM:MAR/91[50]340
DABBS HOUSE MEETING; ARTICLE: "THE PENINSULA
CAMPAIGN OF 1862: THE DABBS HOUSE MEETING,"
CWM:JUN/95[53]590
DABNEY, CHISWELL, *Lieutenant, CSA;* B&G:AUG/92[11]493,
CWM:JUL/92[64]434, CWTI:JUN/95[38]447, GETTY:4[65]148
DABNEY, ROBERT L.; B&G:JUN/92[8]487,
CWM:JUN/94[43]517
DADISMAN, WILLIAM M., *Private, 62nd Virginia Infantry;*
B&G:DEC/92[40]508
DAFFAN, L.A., *Private, 5th New York Infantry;*
CWR:VOL1#2[29]112
DAGENFELD, CHARLES, *Captain, 12th Ohio Cavalry;*
B&G:AUG/91[11]458
DAGUERREOTYPE; see listings under **"PHOTOGRAPHY"**
DAHLGREN'S MARINE BATTALION; ARTICLE: "TO THE
SHORES OF CAROLINA: DAHLGREN'S MARINE
BATTALION," CWR:VOL2#3[194]141
DAHLGREN, JOHN A., *Admiral, USN:*
GENERAL LISTINGS: *general history,* AHI:MAY/71[3]133A, *in book
review,* B&G:JUN/95[30], *Savannah,* B&G:FEB/91[8]439,
photo, AHI:MAY/71[3]133A
ADDITIONAL LISTINGS: ACW:JUL/91[8]309, ACW:SEP/91[30]322,
ACW:SEP/92[47]380, ACW:JUL/93[8]420,
CWR:VOL2#3[183]140, CWR:VOL2#3[194]141,
CWTI:DEC/89[42]137, CWTI:SEP/90[34]176,
CWTI:JAN/93[49]303, CWTI:MAR/94[38]372,
CWTI:DEC/94[34]411, CWTI:DEC/94[62]415,
CWTI:OCT/95[32]468
DAHLGREN, ULRIC, *Colonel, USA;* ACW:JUL/91[8]309,
AHI:NOV/85[38]254, B&G:APR/91[8]445,
CWNEWS:MAY/90[4], CWNEWS:NOV/95[29],
CWTI:JUN/90[32]159, CWTI:DEC/91[28]239,
CWTI:DEC/95[76]482, MH:JUN/94[8]177
DAILEY, JAMES, *Private, 11th Mississippi Infantry;*
ACW:MAR/92[10]349
DAINGERFIELD, FAUNTLEROY, *Captain, CSA;*
ACW:JAN/92[47]344, B&G:AUG/93[10]529
DALE, H.W., *Captain, USN;* CWTI:JAN/95[42]428
DALE, JIM, *Private, 3rd Georgia Infantry;* CWTI:SEP/94[26]400
DALE, NICHOLAS H., *Lieutenant Colonel, 2nd Wisconsin
Cavalry;* CWTI:MAY/93[35]320
DALGLISH, W.M., *Lieutenant, 149th Pennsylvania Infantry;*
GETTY:4[24]145
DALLAS, GEORGIA, BATTLE OF; CWM:JAN/91[12]326,
CWTI:JUL/92[10]
DALTON, GEORGIA, BATTLE OF; ACW:NOV/93[34]442,
ACW:JUL/94[66]481, AHI:MAY/71[3]133A,

CWM:JAN/91[12]326, CWM:JAN/91[28]327,
CWTI:SUMMER/89[13]120, CWTI:FEB/90[46]146
DAM NUMBER 1, VIRGINIA, ENGAGEMENT AT;
CWM:JUN/95[29]583
DAMERON, ROBERT B., *Private, 56th Virginia Infantry;*
ACW:MAR/93[10]402
DANA, AMASA, *Captain, 8th Illinois Cavalry;*
B&G:FEB/95[8]590A
DANA, CHARLES A.; AHI:JAN/94[50]319,
B&G:APR/93[12]518, CWM:JUL/92[24]430,
CWM:SEP/92[19]440, CWM:MAR/93[8]465,
CWTI:APR/92[49]260, CWTI:JAN/95[34]427,
CWTI:AUG/95[46]459
DANA, EDMUND L., *Colonel, 143rd Pennsylvania Infantry;*
ACW:JUL/92[41]370, GETTY:12[30]243, GETTY:13[22]254
DANA, GUSTAVUS, *Lieutenant, USA;* GETTY:10[42]224
DANA, NAPOLEON J.T., *General, USA;* ACW:JUL/92[46]371,
ACW:JAN/94[62], ACW:MAR/94[50]462, B&G:OCT/95[8]611A,
CWM:MAY/93[32]477, CWR:VOL3#1[31]150, GETTY:5[79]161
DANA, W.H., *Lieutenant Commander, USN;*
CWTI:DEC/90[29]182
DANCE'S POWHATAN BATTERY; CWR:VOL1#1[35]104
DANCE, HENRY E., *Private, 22nd Virginia Infantry;*
CWR:VOL1#3[52]122
DANCE, WILLIS S., *Captain, Powhatan Artillery;*
CWR:VOL4#4[70]180, GETTY:4[49]147, GETTY:12[30]243
DANDRIDGE, STEVEN, *Private, Rockbridge Artillery;*
CWR:VOL4#4[70]180
DANE, DAN, *Corporal, 29th Pennsylvania Infantry;*
CWR:VOL3#2[70]155
DANE, HENRY, *Lieutenant, USN;* CWTI:DEC/90[29]182
DANIEL, JAMES, *Lieutenant, 7th South Carolina Infantry;*
GETTY:5[35]159
DANIEL, JOHN, *Major, CSA;* B&G:JUN/95[8]600,
GETTY:9[17]210
DANIEL, JUNIUS, *General, CSA;* ACW:JAN/95[46]507,
B&G:FEB/95[8]590B, B&G:APR/95[8]595,
CWR:VOL3#2[1]153, GETTY:4[49]147, GETTY:5[13]157,
GETTY:5[117]165, GETTY:5[128]167, GETTY:6[69]176,
GETTY:7[83]192, GETTY:7[114]194, GETTY:9[17]210,
GETTY:9[81]216, GETTY:10[7]221, GETTY:11[6]231,
GETTY:13[33]255
DANIEL, ROBERT, *Private, 2nd Kentucky Cavalry;*
CWM:MAR/93[16]466
DANIEL, T.M, *Private, 11th Mississippi Infantry;*
CWR:VOL2#4[269]145
DANIEL, WILLIAM, *Surgeon, 7th South Carolina Infantry;*
GETTY:5[35]159
DANIEL, WILLIAM E., *Corporal, Petersburg Artillery;*
ACW:MAR/95[12]513
DANIEL, WILLIAM L., *Lieutenant, CSA;* GETTY:5[35]159
DANIELS, CHARLES P., *Colonel, 5th Georgia Infantry;*
CWR:VOL1#4[42]126
DANIELS, J.M., *Captain, CSA;* CWR:VOL3#3[33]158
DANIELS, MILTON, *Lieutenant, 17th Connecticut Infantry;*
CWNEWS:JUN/94[5]
DANIELS, NATHUM, *Captain, USA;* GETTY:4[101]151
DANTZLER, OMA, *Colonel, CSA;* B&G:DEC/92[40]508
DANVILLE ARTILLERY; GETTY:13[7]253
DANVILLE, KENTUCKY, ENGAGEMENT AT;
CWR:VOL4#1[1]163
DAPLIN (NORTH CAROLINA) RIFLES; GETTY:7[114]194

DARBY, JOHN T., *Surgeon, CSA;* ACW:SEP/95[38]546, B&G:DEC/95[9]615

DARBYTOWN ROAD, VIRGINIA, ENGAGEMENT AT; ARTICLES: "COSTLY UNION RECONNAISSANCE," ACW:JUL/94[42]479, "DARBYTOWN ROAD DEBACLE," ACW:MAY/92[30]361

DARE, GEORGE, *Lieutenant Colonel, 5th Pennsylvania Reserves;* CWR:VOL4#4[1]177

DARIEN, GEORGIA, DESTRUCTION OF; CWR:VOL3#1[80], CWTI:DEC/89[42]137, CWTI:DEC/89[53]138

DARLING, DWIGHT, *Corporal, 9th New Hampshire Infantry;* CWR:VOL2#2[118]136

DARLING, MARCELLUS W., *Private, 154th New York Infantry;* B&G:OCT/93[36]540

DARLINGTON, SOUTH CAROLINA; ARTICLE: "ARTICLE BRINGS NOTICE TO A UNIQUE REBEL," CWTI:JUN/90[57]163

DARRAGH, GILLET, *Private, 19th Indiana Infantry;* CWTI:NOV/93[78]354

DARROW, JOHN, *Private, 82nd New York Infantry;* GETTY:5[79]161

DAUGHTERS OF CHARITY; B&G:OCT/93[31]539

DAVEGA, ISAAC, *Attorney;* ACW:SEP/94[46]488

DAVENPORT, ALFRED, *Private, 5th New York Infantry;* BOOK REVIEW: *CAMP AND FIELD LIFE OF THE FIFTH NEW YORK* ADDITIONAL LISTINGS: ACW:JUL/91[18]312, B&G:AUG/92[11]493, CWR:VOL1#2[7]111, CWR:VOL1#2[29]112, CWTI:MAY/94[31]382

DAVENPORT, DAVID, *Captain, 6th Vermont Infantry;* ACW:JAN/94[8]447, ACW:MAR/94[35]460

DAVENPORT, DUDLEY, *Lieutenant, USN;* AHI:DEC/82[38]231

DAVES, GRAHAM, *Adjutant, CSA;* CWTI:APR/92[49]260

DAVIDSON, GREENLEE, *Captain, Letcher Artillery;* ACW:MAR/95[42]517, CWR:VOL1#1[1]102, CWR:VOL4#4[70]180

DAVIDSON, HENRY, *General, CSA;* CWR:VOL4#1[1]163

DAVIDSON, HUNTER, *Lieutenant, CSN;* ACW:NOV/91[8]328, AHI:NOV/75[38]163, B&G:AUG/91[20]459

DAVIDSON, J.O., *painting "The Battle of New Orleans";* CWM:NOV/92[24]448

DAVIDSON, JAMES, *Lieutenant, 4th U.S. Artillery;* GETTY:9[33]211, GETTY:11[57]233

DAVIDSON, JAMES K., *Private, 4th Iowa Infantry;* B&G:AUG/93[18]530

DAVIDSON, JOHN W., *General, USA;* ACW:MAY/93[12]412, ACW:JAN/94[8]447, CWTI:JUL/93[42]329, CWTI:JUN/95[32]446

DAVIDSON, PETER, *Captain, 2nd Illinois Artillery;* CWR:VOL1#1[42]105

DAVIDSON, WILLIAM, *Private, 5th New York Infantry;* CWR:VOL1#2[7]111

DAVIES, HENRY E., *General, USA;* ACW:JUL/92[41]370, ACW:SEP/94[55]489, B&G:APR/92[8]481, B&G:APR/94[10]558, B&G:APR/95[8]595, CWR:VOL1#2[7]111, MH:FEB/93[42]164

DAVIES, J. MANSFIELD, *Major, 5th New York Infantry;* CWR:VOL1#2[7]111

DAVIES, THOMAS, *General, USA;* ACW:SEP/91[46]324

DAVIS (JEFF) LEGION: ARTICLE: "THE JEFF DAVIS LEGION AT GETTYSBURG," GETTY:12[68]246

ADDITIONAL LISTINGS: B&G:OCT/93[12]537, CWTI:JUN/90[32]159, GETTY:12[1]240,

DAVIS MEMORIAL HOME; CWTI:AUG/91[22]215

DAVIS GUARDS; CWTI:DEC/90[29]182

DAVIS, ARTHUR N., *Captain, USA;* ACW:MAR/93[51]407

DAVIS, BENJAMIN F., *Colonel, USA:* ARTICLE: "ESCAPE FROM HARPERS FERRY," CWM:MAY/92[8]418 BOOK REVIEW: *THE HISTORY OF THE HARPERS FERRY CAVALRY EXPEDITION, SEPTEMBER 14 & 15, 1862* ADDITIONAL LISTINGS: ACW:SEP/94[55]489, CWR:VOL1#4[7]125, CWTI:JUN/90[32]159, CWTI:JUN/90[43]160, GETTY:6[69]176, GETTY:11[19]232, MH:AUG/95[30]185, *photo,* CWM:MAY/92[8]418

DAVIS, BILLY, *Private, 7th Indiana Infantry;* BOOK REVIEWS: *THE CIVIL WAR JOURNAL OF BILLY DAVIS: FROM HOPEWELL, INDIANA TO PORT REPUBLIC, VIRGINIA*

DAVIS, BRYAN, *Lieutenant, 71st Pennsylvania Infantry;* GETTY:7[83]192

DAVIS, CHARLES, *Lieutenant, 1st Massachusetts Cavalry;* B&G:OCT/93[12]537

DAVIS, CHARLES B., *Private, 30th Maine Infantry;* ACW:SEP/91[16]320

DAVIS, CHARLES E., *Private, 13th Massachusetts Infantry;* CWTI:APR/92[49]260

DAVIS, CHARLES H., *Admiral, USN;* ACW:JUL/93[34]424, ACW:MAR/95[18]514, CWNEWS:JAN/91[4], CWTI:DEC/94[34]411

DAVIS, CHRISTOPHER C., *Private, 2nd Mississippi Infantry;* GETTY:4[126]154, GETTY:6[77]177

DAVIS, DAVID, *civilian;* CWTI:JAN/93[10]297

DAVIS, E.J., *Colonel, 1st Texas (Union) Cavalry;* ACW:JUL/92[46]371

DAVIS, EDWIN A., *Corporal, 150th New York Infantry;* GETTY:12[42]244

DAVIS, ELIAS, *Private, 10th Alabama Infantry;* CWM:JUL/92[16]428

DAVIS, GARRETT, *Senator, Kentucky;* AHI:NOV/72[12]142

DAVIS, GEORGE E., *Lieutenant, 10th Vermont Infantry;* ACW:NOV/93[50]444, B&G:DEC/92[8]503

DAVIS, GEORGE H., *Sergeant, 157th New York Infantry;* GETTY:7[83]192

DAVIS, HARRISON, *Lieutenant, 1st Florida Special Battalion;* CWR:VOL3#1[65]151

DAVIS, HASBROUCK, *Lieutenant Colonel, 12th Illinois Cavalry;* CWM:MAY/92[8]418, CWM:APR/95[32]575

DAVIS, J. LUCIUS, *Colonel, 10th Virginia Cavalry;* GETTY:9[109]218, GETTY:13[89]260

DAVIS, JAMES, *Chaplain;* B&G:DEC/92[20]504

DAVIS, JAMES, *Captain, 12th Alabama Infantry;* GETTY:5[117]165

DAVIS, JAMES C., *Captain, 16th Mississippi Infantry;* GETTY:8[111]206

DAVIS, JEFFERSON: ARTICLES: "A REASON TO LOATHE DAVIS," CWTI:AUG/91[68]222, "AN ARMY OF HIS OWN," CWTI:DEC/94[49]413, "BEAUVOIR, WHERE THE LEADER OF A LOST REVOLUTION AND SOME OF HIS TROOPS WAITED OUT THEIR DAYS," CWTI:AUG/91[22]215, "CAMEL CORPS, USA," AHI:DEC/81[8]222, "CHEERS FOR JEFFERSON DAVIS," AHI:MAY/81[8]217, "COMPASSION IS ALWAYS DUE TO AN ENRAGED IMBECILE,"

AHI:FEB/76[14]165, "CONFEDERATE CLOAK AND DAGGER," ACW:JUL/95[44]537

ARTICLES, continued: "DAVIS' LAST RIDE TO RICHMOND," CWTI:MAR/93[32]311, "THE FIRST AND ONLY CONFEDERATE PRESIDENT," CWTI:AUG/91[36]217, "THE GREAT PHILOSOPHICAL COLLISION," CWTI:AUG/91[52]219, "HIS NATION'S COMMANDER IN CHIEF," CWTI:AUG/91[46]218, "JEFF DAVIS' LIVING TOMB," CWTI:MAY/93[20]317, "KIDNAP CAREFULLY PLOTTED," MH:APR/94[54]176, "KING JEFF THE FIRST," CWTI:AUG/91[58]220, "MR. DAVIS BIDS ADIEU," CWM:FEB/95[19]558, "PERSPECTIVES ON THE PAST," AHI:JUL/78[40]182, "PIRATES OR PATRIOTS?" ACW:SEP/94[46]488, "U.S. GRANT AND SIMON BUCKNER: FRIENDS," AHI:MAR/82[8]227, "THE VICE PRESIDENT RESIDES IN GEORGIA," CWTI:FEB/91[36]193, "VICKSBURG: DAVIS, VAN DORN, PEMBERTON—A TRIANGULATION OF SHORTCOMINGS," CWM:AUG/94[52]530, "THE WILL TO WIN AND DENYING REALITY," CWTI:AUG/91[62]221, "'WE WILL VINDICATE THE RIGHT': AN ACCOUNT OF THE LIFE OF JEFFERSON DAVIS," CWTI:AUG/91[29]216

BOOK REVIEWS: *JEFFERSON DAVIS AND HIS GENERALS: THE FAILURE OF CONFEDERATE COMMAND IN THE WEST * JEFFERSON DAVIS'S MEXICAN WAR REGIMENT * JEFFERSON DAVIS, THE MAN AND HIS HOUR * LEE'S DISPATCHES: UNPUBLISHED LETTERS OF GENERAL ROBERT E. LEE, C.S.A. TO JEFFERSON DAVIS AND THE WAR DEPARTMENT OF THE CONFEDERATE STATES OF AMERICA, 1862-65 * THE PAPERS OF JEFFERSON DAVIS: JANUARY 6, 1856-DECEMBER 28, 1860, VOLUME 6 * THE PAPERS OF JEFFERSON, DAVIS, VOLUME 7, 1861 * THE PAPERS OF JEFFERSON DAVIS, VOLUME 8, 1862 * THE RISE AND FALL OF THE CONFEDERATE GOVERNMENT * VARINA: FORGOTTEN FIRST LADY*

GENERAL LISTINGS: *A.S. Johnston,* ACW:SEP/93[6]428, *Atlanta Campaign,* ACW:JAN/95[30]505, CWTI:SEP/92[28]280, *Beauregard,* CWTI:JUL/92[29]272, *Beaver Dam Creek,* CWM:JUN/95[57]592, *black soldiers,* ACW:NOV/93[6]437, ACW:NOV/95[8]552, *Bragg,* CWTI:MAR/93[40]312, *California,* CWTI:JUN/95[48]448, *capture of,* CWTI:AUG/90[50]168, MH:APR/94[54]176, *common soldiers,* AHI:APR/68[4]115, *Confederate attempt to surrender,* CWTI:FEB/91[36]193, *conscription, CWTI:SEP/ 91[23]228, Cumberland Gap,* ACW:JUL/91[26]313

GENERAL LISTINGS, continued: *editorial,* ACW:JAN/91[6]281, *election of 1864,* AHI:OCT/68[4]116, *evacuating Richmond,* CWTI:FEB/91[28]192, *Fall of Richmond,* AHI:JAN/74[10]153, CWR:VOL4#1[78], CWTI:AUG/90[26]166, *Forrest,* CWTI:SEP/93[59]341, *Forts Henry and Donelson,* B&G:FEB/92[10]474, *Francis A. Shoup,* ACW:SEP/94[10]484, *Garnot Wolseley,* CWTI:DEC/94[73]416, *general history,* AHI:MAY/71[3]133A

GENERAL LISTINGS, continued: *Gettysburg,* GETTY:4[7]142, GETTY:4[22]144, GETTY:4[33]146, GETTY:4[113]153, GETTY:5[4]156, GETTY:5[13]157, GETTY:5[19]158, GETTY:5[103]163, GETTY:6[13]170, GETTY:6[29]171, GETTY:7[77]191, GETTY:8[67]204, GETTY:8[95]205, GETTY:8[111]206, GETTY:11[6]231, *Grant,* AHI:DEC/72[4]144, *impeachment of Andrew Johnson,* AHI:DEC/68[28]118, *imprisonment,* CWTI:AUG/90[70]171, GENERAL LISTINGS, continued: *in book review,* ACW:JAN/92[54], ACW:MAY/93[54], ACW:NOV/93[58], ACW:SEP/94[66],

ACW:NOV/94[66], ACW:MAR/95[58], ACW:NOV/95[62], AHI:MAY/82[8], B&G:AUG/91[26], B&G:OCT/93[24], CWM:MAR/91[74], CWM:MAR/92[49], CWM:MAY/93[51], CWM:JUL/93[51], CWM:SEP/93[51], CWM:JUN/94[6], CWM:APR/95[50], CWM:AUG/95[8], CWM:AUG/95[45], CWM:OCT/95[10], CWNEWS:MAY/89[4], CWNEWS:SEP/89[8], CWNEWS:OCT/89[4], CWNEWS:JAN/90[4], CWNEWS:APR/90[4], CWNEWS:NOV/90[4], CWNEWS:JUL/91[4], CWNEWS:NOV/92[4], CWNEWS:APR/93[4], CWNEWS:JUN/93[5], CWNEWS:OCT/93[5], CWNEWS:DEC/93[5], CWNEWS:JAN/94[5], CWNEWS:SEP/95[33], CWR:VOL1#2[78], CWR:VOL2#1[78], CWR:VOL2#2[169], CWR:VOL2#4[346], CWR:VOL3#1[80], CWR:VOL3#3[92], CWR:VOL3#4[68], CWR:VOL4#1[78], CWR:VOL4#2[136], CWR:VOL4#3[37], CWR:VOL4#3[89], CWR:VOL4#4[129], CWTI:AUG/91[18], CWTI:APR/92[30], CWTI:SEP/92[18], CWTI:JUL/93[12], CWTI:JUL/94[18], CWTI:JUN/95[24], CWTI:OCT/95[18], MH:DEC/94[70]

GENERAL LISTINGS, continued: *Jackson's funeral,* CWTI:MAY/89[22]116, *Jackson,* B&G:JUN/92[8]487, *Jake Thompson,* CWTI:NOV/92[54]293, *James B. Gordon,* ACW:JAN/95[10]503, *Johnston's Surrender;* CWTI:APR/90[20]151, *Joseph E. Johnston,* ACW:MAR/94[42]461, CWTI:FEB/90[54]147, CWTI:JAN/95[20]422, *Joe Brown,* CWTI:DEC/94[49]413

GENERAL LISTINGS, continued: *letters to the editor,* CWM:MAY/91[6]345, CWM:DEC/94[5]546, CWM:OCT/95[5]613, CWTI:SEP/91[8]224, CWTI:APR/92[8]252, CWTI:MAY/92[8]261, CWTI:MAY/93[8]315, CWTI:AUG/95[14]454, CWTI:NOV/93[12]345, *Lincoln's assassination,* CWTI:AUG/90[42]167, *Longstreet,* CWTI:NOV/93[55]350, *McClellan,* ACW:NOV/94[50]498, *Mexican War,* AHI:OCT/82[28]230, MH:APR/93[39]166, *Mosby,* CWTI:SEP/90[34]176, *New Mexico Campaign,* B&G:JUN/94[8]568, *Peninsula Campaign,* CWM:JUN/95[24]582, CWM:JUN/95[53]590

GENERAL LISTINGS, continued: *Quantrill,* ACW:MAR/95[26]515, *Robert Anderson,* CWTI:MAY/92[45]266, *Rodes,* Davis, Jefferson, continued: ACW:JAN/95[46]507, *Sabine Pass,* CWM:OCT/95[47]620, *Savannah,* CWTI:DEC/94[62]415, *Seven Pines,* CWM:JUN/95[47]588, *Southern education,* AHI:FEB/80[14]199, *Sterling Price,* ACW:NOV/94[42]497, *Toombs,* CWM:MAR/93[32]468, *Tullahoma Campaign,* B&G:OCT/92[10]496, *Vicksburg Campaign,* B&G:AUG/95[8]604, CWTI:SEPT/89[18]126, CWTI:MAY/91[24]208, *W.H.T. Walker,* CWTI:MAR/93[24]309, *West Virginia Campaign,* ACW:SEP/94[31]486, B&G:AUG/93[10]529, *William T. Sherman,* AHI:JAN/67[4]106, *Winfield Scott,* AHI:JUL/81[20]221,

PAINTINGS, PHOTOS, ETC.: *painting, late years;* CWTI:MAR/93[32]311, *photo of coffin;* CWTI:MAR/93[32]311, *photo of entourage after capture;* CWTI:AUG/90[50]168, *photos;* ACW:JAN/91[10]283, ACW:MAR/93[58], ACW:MAY/93[38]416, AHI:JUN/73[4]149, AHI:JAN/74[10]153, AHI:FEB/76[14]165, B&G:DEC/95[44]617, CWM:JAN/91[28]327, CWM:AUG/94[52]530, CWM:FEB/95[19]558, CWTI:AUG/91[29]216, CWTI:AUG/91[36]217, MH:APR/94[54]176, *portraits,* ACW:JUL/95[44]537,

DAVIS, T.O., *Master, CSN;* CWM:DEC/95[30]627
DAVIS, THEODORE R., *artist;* ACW:JAN/92[10]339,
   CWM:NOV/92[10]447
DAVIS, THOMAS, *General, USA;* ACW:JAN/92[22]341,
   CWNEWS:MAY/89[4]
DAVIS, TIMOTHEUS, *Private, 2nd Tennessee Cavalry;*
   CWR:VOL4#1[1]163
DAVIS, U.Q., *Surgeon, 148th Pennsylvania Infantry;*
   GETTY:10[53]225
DAVIS, VARINA H.:
ARTICLES: "BEAUVOIR, WHERE THE LEADER OF A LOST
   REVOLUTION AND SOME OF HIS TROOPS WAITED OUT
   THEIR DAYS," CWTI:AUG/91[22]215, "FIRST LADIES AT
   WAR," ACW:JAN/94[47]452
BOOK REVIEWS: *JEFFERSON DAVIS * VARINA: FORGOTTEN
   FIRST LADY*
GENERAL LISTINGS: *in book review,* ACW:SEP/95[62], *SIO,*
   B&G:APR/94[34]561, B&G:JUN/94[38]571, *photos;*
   ACW:JAN/94[47]452, AHI:DEC/73[10]152,
   CWTI:AUG/91[29]216, CWTI:AUG/91[36]217
ADDITIONAL LISTINGS: ACW:MAY/92[39]362, ACW:MAY/92[62]364,
   ACW:JUL/92[8]365A, ACW:JAN/93[18]394,
   ACW:MAY/95[38]526, CWTI:AUG/90[50]168,
   CWTI:AUG/91[29]216, CWTI:AUG/91[46]218,
   CWTI:AUG/91[58]220, CWTI:AUG/91[68]222,
   CWTI:MAY/93[20]317, CWTI:MAR/93[32]311,
   CWTI:AUG/95[28]456
DAVIS, W.S., *Lieutenant Colonel, 12th North Carolina Infantry;*
   B&G:FEB/95[8]590B
DAVIS, WALTER, *Lieutenant, 22nd Massachusetts Infantry;*
   GETTY:8[53]203
DAVIS, WILLIAM G.M., *General, CSA;* B&G:FEB/91[20]440
DAVIS, WILLIAM, *Captain, 69th Pennsylvania Infantry;*
   GETTY:4[89]150
DAVIS, WILLIAM, *Captain, CSA;* CWM:MAR/93[16]466
DAVIS, WILLIAM, *Private, 7th Indiana Infantry;* ARTICLE:
   "WHILE FATHER WAS WITH US," CWTI:NOV/93[24]346
DAVIS, WILLIAM P., *Lieutenant Colonel, 23rd Indiana
   Infantry;* B&G:FEB/94[8]550
DAVIS, WILLIAM S., *Lieutenant Colonel, 12th North Carolina
   Infantry;* GETTY:5[13]157
DAVIS, WINIFRED; CWTI:AUG/91[68]222
DAVIS, ZIMMERMAN, *Colonel, CSA;* B&G:DEC/92[20]504
DAVISDON, HUNTER; B&G:OCT/91[6]465
DAVISON, JAMES, *Lieutenant, 4th U.S. Artillery;*
   GETTY:11[57]233
DAWES, RUFUS R., *Colonel, USA:*
GENERAL LISTINGS: *Brawner's Farm,* B&G:AUG/92[11]493,
   Gettysburg, AHI:MAY/67[22]107, GETTY:4[16]143,
   GETTY:4[24]145, GETTY:4[126]154, GETTY:5[4]156,
   GETTY:6[29]171, GETTY:6[77]177, GETTY:7[7]185,
   GETTY:7[83]192, GETTY:9[33]211, GETTY:10[36]223,
   GETTY:11[57]233, *in book review,* CWR:VOL1#2[78],
   CWR:VOL4#4[129]
ADDITIONAL LISTINGS: ACW:JAN/91[38]287, ACW:JUL/92[30]369,
   CWTI:APR/92[42]259, GETTY:13[22]254
DAWKINS, J.B.; ACW:NOV/95[38]556
DAWSON, CHARLES, *civilian;* CWTI:JUN/95[26]445,
DAWSON, D.H., *Private, Sumter Artillery;* CWR:VOL3#2[1]153
DAWSON, E.S., *Captain, CSA;* B&G:OCT/94[11]580
DAWSON, FRANCIS W., *Major CSA;* BOOK REVIEW:
   REMINISCENCES OF CONFEDERATE SERVICE, 1861-1865

DAWSON, GEORGE W., *Private, 25th Virginia Infantry;*
   ARTICLE: "ONE MAN'S STRUGGLE AT RICH MOUNTAIN,"
   B&G:AUG/93[52]534
DAWSON, JOHN, *Mayor, Wilmington;* B&G:DEC/94[10]585
DAWSON, L.L., *Captain, USN;* B&G:DEC/94[10]585
DAWSON, LUCIEN L., *Captain, USMC;*
   CWR:VOL2#3[183]140, CWR:VOL2#3[252]144
DAWSON, NATHANIEL, *Captain, 4th Alabama Infantry;*
   ACW:NOV/94[18]495
DAY, EBENEZER, *Surgeon, 39th New York Infantry;*
   GETTY:10[53]225
DAY, HANNIBAL, *Colonel, 91st Illinois Infantry;*
   ACW:JUL/92[46]371, GETTY:8[53]203, GETTY:9[53]214
DAY, HENRY, *17th Virginia Infantry;* B&G:AUG/92[40]495
DAY, SELDEN A., *Corporal, 7th Ohio Infantry;*
   CWM:APR/95[29]574
DAY, THOMAS G., *Private, 3rd Indiana Cavalry;*
   GETTY:4[115]152
DAY, WILLIAM, *Private, 54th North Carolina Infantry;* ARTICLE:
   "A LOYAL FAMILY MAN," CWTI:DEC/91[82]243
DAYMOND, WILLIAM; CWTI:JAN/93[10]297
DAYTON, L.M., *Colonel, USA;* B&G:FEB/91[8]439,
   CWTI:APR/90[20]151
DAYTON, LEWIS M., *Captain, USA;* AHI:JAN/67[4]106
de BAUN, JAMES, *Major, 9th Louisiana Partisan Rangers;*
   B&G:JUN/93[12]524
de BONGE, GUSTAVE, *Sergeant, 6th Connecticut Infantry;*
   ACW:SEP/91[30]322
de BORDENAVE, FULGENCE, *Captain, 1st Louisiana Zouave
   Battalion;* CWTI:MAR/89[28]103
de CESNOLA, LUIGI P., *Colonel, USA;* ARTICLE: "THE ONLY
   MEDAL OF HONOR EARNED IN THE LOUDOUN VALLEY
   FIGHTING," B&G:OCT/93[21]538
de CHENAL, FRANCOIS; CWTI:DEC/94[73]416
de CHOISEUL, CHARLES, *Lieutenant Colonel, 7th Louisiana
   Infantry;* CWM:SEP/93[24]495, CWTI:MAR/94[48]374
de FOREST, JOHN W., *Captain, USVRC:*
BOOK REVIEW: *A VOLUNTEER'S ADVENTURES: A UNION
   CAPTAIN'S RECORD OF THE CIVIL WAR*
ADDITIONAL LISTINGS: ACW:MAY/91[38]305, ACW:SEP/94[8]483
de FOREST, OTHNEIL, *Colonel, USA;* GETTY:9[109]218,
   MH:OCT/92[51]162
de GOLYER, SAMUEL, *Captain, 8th Michigan Artillery;*
   B&G:FEB/94[8]550
de GOURNAY, PAUL F., *Lieutenant Colonel, CSA;* ARTICLE:
   "WELL-BORN LIEUTENANT COLONEL PAUL FRANCOIS
   DE GOURNAY WAS THE SOUTH'S ADOPTED 'MARQUIS
   IN GRAY.' ACW:SEP/95[8]542
de GROAT, CHARLES H., *Captain, 32nd Wisconsin Infantry;*
   CWR:VOL2#4[313]146, CWR:VOL2#4[343]147
de JANON, PATRICE; B&G:DEC/91[12]469
de LAGNEL, JULIUS A., *General, CSA;* ACW:JAN/92[47]344,
   ACW:JAN/92[50]345, ACW:SEP/92[38]379,
   B&G:AUG/93[10]529, *photo,* B&G:AUG/93[10]529
de MONTIE, SENIAGO; *civilian;* B&G:OCT/94[11]580
de MORSE, CHARLES, *Colonel, CSA;* CWR:VOL1#2[44]114
de NOYELLES (NEW YORK) GUARD; GETTY:6[29]171
**de ORLEANS, FRANCOIS FERDINAND, PRINCE de
   JOINVILLE;** ACW:JAN/94[8]447, CWTI:SEP/91[54]232,
   CWTI:DEC/94[73]416
**de ORLEANS, LOUIS PHILIPPE ALBERT, COMTE de
   PARIS;** ACW:JAN/94[8]447, CWTI:MAY/89[14]114,
   CWTI:SEP/91[54]232, GETTY:4[113]153

de PEYSTER, JOHN W., *General, USA;* ACW:JUL/93[16]422

de POLIGNAC, CAMILLE ARMAND, *General, CSA;*
CWM:MAR/91[74], CWM:APR/95[50], CWR:VOL2#3[212]142,
CWR:VOL4#2[1]165, CWR:VOL4#2[26]166,
CWR:VOL4#2[68]167, MH:APR/94[54]176

de SAUSSURE, WILLIAM D., *Colonel, 15th South Carolina
Infantry;* ACW:JUL/93[58], GETTY:5[35]159, GETTY:8[53]203

de TROBRIAND, PHILIPPE REGIS D. de K., *General, USA;*
ACW:JAN/93[43]397, ACW:JUL/93[16]422,
B&G:FEB/92[22]476, CWM:MAR/91[74],
CWR:VOL2#3[236]143, GETTY:5[35]159, GETTY:7[29]188,
GETTY:8[43]202, GETTY:8[53]203, GETTY:10[120]229,
GETTY:12[85]248, MH:APR/95[46]183

de VECCHI, ARCHILLE, *Captain, 9th Massachusetts Artillery;*
GETTY:5[47]160

DEAL, JOHN, *Private, CSA;* CWM:JUN/95[37]585

DEAN, BENJAMIN, *Colonel, USA;* CWR:VOL3#3[59]159

DEAN, HARRY, *Lieutenant, 7th Ohio Infantry;* GETTY:9[81]216

DEAR, CHARLES, *Mosby's Rangers;* CWM:JAN/93[24]458

DEARING, GEORGE; CWTI:JUL/94[44]394

DEARING, JAMES, *General, CSA;* ACW:JAN/93[43]397,
ACW:MAR/93[10]402, ACW:MAR/95[12]513,
B&G:APR/92[8]481, B&G:APR/92[48]484,
CWM:SEP/92[16]438, CWR:VOL3#2[1]153,
CWTI:SEPT/89[46]132, CWTI:DEC/94[122]419,
GETTY:12[111]250, GETTY:13[64]258

DEAS, GEORGE; CWTI:MAR/95[60]439

DEAS, ZACHARIAH C., *General, CSA;* B&G:DEC/93[12]545,
B&G:DEC/93[30]546, CWTI:DEC/90[56]184,
CWTI:SEP/92[31]281

DEATH; ARTICLE: "ATTITUDES OF DEATH,"
CWTI:JUL/92[36]273

DEATHRAGE, HENRY C., *Private, 2nd Tennessee Cavalry;*
CWR:VOL4#1[1]163

DEAVER, A.E., *Lieutenant, CSA;* B&G:FEB/91[20]440

DEBLANC, ALCIBIADES, *Lieutenant Colonel, 8th Louisiana
Infantry;* CWTI:FEB/91[12]189

DEBLANC, LOUIS, *Captain, 10th Louisiana Infantry;*
CWR:VOL3#1[1]149

DEBOND, J.M., *Captain, 53rd Georgia Infantry;*
CWTI:SEP/90[26]174

DEBOW, JAMES D.B.; CWNEWS:FEB/94[5]

DEBRAY, XAVIER B., *Colonel, 26th Texas Cavalry;*
CWR:VOL2#3[212]142, CWR:VOL4#2[68]167,
CWR:VOL4#2[118]169

DECATUR, ALABAMA; ARTICLE: "A MEMORIAL DIRGE FOR
LINCOLN," B&G:JUN/95[35]602

DECATUR, GEORGIA; CWM:JAN/91[40]330,
CWTI:SUMMER/89[20]121, CWTI:SUMMER/89[50]124

DECKER, ISAAC, *Sergeant, 124th New York Infantry;*
CWM:DEC/94[40]550

DECKER, S.H., *Private, 4th U.S. Artillery;* ACW:SEP/95[38]546

DECOURCEY, JOHN, *Captain, 14th Kentucky Cavalry;*
ACW:SEP/95[22]544

DECOURCY, JOHN F., *Colonel, USA;* ACW:JUL/91[26]313,
CWR:VOL3#3[33]158

DEELY, SIMON, *Private, 5th New York Infantry;*
CWR:VOL1#2[7]111, CWTI:MAY/94[31]382

DEERING, GEORGE A., *Lieutenant, 16th Maine Infantry;*
GETTY:13[33]255

DEES, JOSEPH, *Private, 3rd Georgia Infantry;*
CWTI:SEP/94[26]400

DEETZ, WILLIAM, *Private, 53rd Pennsylvania Infantry;*
GETTY:11[80]235

DEFENDERS AND GREYS (VIRGINIA);
ACW:MAR/93[10]402

DEFREEST, DANIEL and JOHN, *125th New York Infantry;*
CWR:VOL1#4[7]125

DEGNER, CHARLES, *Private, 7th Indiana Infantry;*
B&G:AUG/93[10]529

DEGOLYER, SAMUEL, *Captain, 8th Michigan Battery;*
ACW:NOV/91[22]331

DEGOURNAY, PAUL F., *Lieutenant Colonel, 1st Louisiana
Zouave Battalion;* ACW:JAN/94[30]450, CWTI:MAR/89[28]103

DEGRESS, FRANCIS, *Captain, 1st Illinois Artillery;*
ARTICLES: "CAPTAIN DEGRESS AND THE BEST GUNS IN THE
WORLD," B&G:AUG/95[55]609, "REPORT OF THE BATTLE
OF ATLANTA," B&G:APR/94[28]559
ADDITIONAL LISTINGS: B&G:DEC/94[36]588, B&G:JUN/95[36]603A,
CWTI:SUMMER/89[40]123,   CWTI:SEP/92[28]280,
photos, B&G:APR/94[28]559, B&G:AUG/95[55]609

DEHART, E.P.; B&G:JUN/91[32]454

DEHART, HENRY, *Captain, USA;* ACW:NOV/94[50]498

DEHASS, WILLS, *Colonel, USA;* CWR:VOL4#1[44]164

DEHN, JOHN, *Corporal, 1st Minnesota Infantry;*
GETTY:5[79]161

DEHON, ARTHUR, *Lieutenant, 12th Massachusetts Infantry;*
B&G:OCT/95[20]612, CWR:VOL4#4[1]177

DEITZLER, GEORGE W., *General, USA;* ACW:NOV/93[26]441,
ACW:NOV/94[42]497, B&G:JUN/91[10]452,
CWTI:FEB/92[29]248

DEJEAN, ALBERT, *Captain, 8th Louisiana Infantry;*
CWTI:FEB/91[12]189

DELAWARE TROOPS
1st Cavalry; GETTY:12[42]244,
1st Infantry:
GENERAL LISTINGS: *Gettysburg,* GETTY:5[89]162,
GETTY:7[29]188, GETTY:8[95]205, GETTY:9[61]215,
GETTY:10[53]225, GETTY:12[61]245, *in list,*
CWTI:JUL/93[34]327, *in order of battle,* B&G:APR/92[8]481,
list of monuments, B&G:OCT/95[8]611A, *SIO,*
B&G:JUN/94[38]571
ADDITIONAL LISTINGS: B&G:APR/91[8]445, CWTI:APR/92[49]260
2nd Infantry: ACW:MAY/95[30]525, GETTY:8[53]203,
GETTY:11[80]235, GETTY:12[24]242

DELACY, PATRICK, *Sergeant, 143rd Pennsylvania Infantry;*
B&G:JUN/95[8]600

DELAFIELD, RICHARD, *General, USA;* B&G:DEC/94[10]585,
CWTI:SEPT/89[10]125

DELAND, C.V., *Colonel, 1st Michigan Infantry;*
CWM:SEP/92[24]441

DELANEY, MARTIN, *Private, Letcher Artillery;*
CWR:VOL4#4[70]180

DELANEY, MARTIN R., *Major, USA;* CWTI:DEC/95[52]480

DELANEY, PATRICK, *Private, USA;* CWM:JAN/92[16]401

DELEON, THOMAS C., *Private, USA;* CWTI:AUG/90[26]166,
CWTI:MAY/92[38]265

DELHANEY, JOHN, *Private, CSA;* ACW:MAR/92[54]

DELLZELLE, WILLIAM, *Private, 8th Louisiana Infantry;*
CWTI:FEB/91[12]189

DEMENT, WILLIAM F., *Captain, 1st Maryland (Confederate)
Artillery;* GETTY:4[49]147, GETTY:10[29]222

DEMING, ANDREW J., *Sergeant, 12th Pennsylvania Reserves;*
CWR:VOL1#3[28]120
DEMOBILIZATION OF THE UNION ARMY;
CWTI:AUG/90[70]171
DEMOCRATIC PARTY:
BOOK REVIEW: *LINCOLN AND THE WAR DEMOCRATS: THE
GRAND EROSION OF CONSERVATIVE TRADITION*
ADDITIONAL LISTINGS: AHI:OCT/68[4]116, AHI:DEC/68[28]118,
AHI:JUN/73[4]149
DENICKE, ERNST, *Captain, USA;* GETTY:4[101]151
DENICKE, M., *Lieutenant, USA;* GETTY:4[101]151
DENIG, A.M., *civilian;* B&G:OCT/94[11]580
DENIKE, ABRAM, *Captain, 5th New York Infantry;*
CWR:VOL1#2[7]111
DENISON, ANDREW W., *Colonel, USA;* B&G:APR/92[8]481,
B&G:APR/95[8]595
DENISON, CHARLES W., *Chaplain;* GETTY:6[87]178
DENNIS, ELIAS S., *General, USA;* B&G:APR/93[34]521,
B&G:FEB/94[8]550, CWR:VOL3#3[33]158, *photo,*
B&G:APR/93[34]521
DENNIS, WILLIAM, *Private, Georgia and Mississippi
Regiment;* CWR:VOL1#4[42]126
DENNISON, WILLIAM, *Governor, Ohio;* ACW:JUL/92[22]368,
B&G:OCT/92[10]496, B&G:AUG/93[10]529,
CWTI:AUG/95[46]459
DENOON, CHARLES E., *Lieutenant, 41st Virginia Infantry;*
BOOK REVIEW: *CHARLIE'S LETTERS, THE CIVIL WAR
CORRESPONDENCE*
DENT, S.H., *Captain, CSA;* CWTI:SEP/92[31]281
DENTON, ANDREW R., CWTI:MAR/89[44]105
DENTON, JACOB, *Lieutenant, 124th New York Infantry;*
CWM:DEC/94[40]550
DEPARTMENTS AND DIVISIONS, MILITARY; see listings
under **"MILITARY DEPARTMENTS AND DIVISIONS"**
DERBY, CHARLES A., *Colonel, 44th Alabama Infantry;*
CWTI:SEP/93[53]340
DERBY, N.R., *Surgeon, USA;* CWM:MAY/91[10]347
DERN, GEORGE F., *Captain, 3rd New York Cavalry;*
ACW:MAY/92[30]361
DERRICK, CLARENCE, *Lieutenant Colonel, 23rd Virginia
Battalion;* B&G:DEC/95[5]614A
DERUSSY, RENE E., *Colonel, USA;* ACW:MAR/92[62]355
DESELLEM, J.N., *civilian;* B&G:OCT/94[11]580
DESHLER, JAMES, *General, CSA;* CWR:VOL1#2[78]
DETTLOFF, FERDINAND, *Private, 2nd Wisconsin Infantry,*
GETTY:11[57]233
DEVANE, WILLIAM S., *Lieutenant Colonel, 61st North
Carolina Infantry;* B&G:FEB/95[8]590B, B&G:DEC/95[9]615
DEVENS, CHARLES P., *General, USA;* AHI:MAY/67[22]107,
AHI:FEB/82[36]225, B&G:APR/94[10]558,
CWR:VOL3#1[31]150, CWTI:MAY/89[14]114,
CWTI:MAY/89[50]119, CWTI:JUL/94[20]390
DEVER, N.H., *Private, 51st North Carolina Infantry;*
B&G:APR/93[24]520
DEVEREAUX, ARTHUR, *Colonel, 19th Massachusetts
Infantry;* GETTY:5[79]161, GETTY:7[97]193
DEVIN, THOMAS C., *General, USA:*
GENERAL LISTINGS: *Aldie,* GETTY:11[19]232, *Brandy Station,*
GETTY:11[19]232, *Five Forks,* B&G:APR/92[8]481, *Gettysburg,*
GETTY:4[33]146, GETTY:4[49]147, GETTY:4[75]149,
GETTY:4[101]151, GETTY:11[19]232, GETTY:12[123]251, *in
order of battle,* B&G:APR/92[8]481, B&G:APR/95[8]595, *letters*

to the editor, B&G:JUN/95[5]599, *photos;* B&G:FEB/95[8]590A,
CWM:MAR/91[17]335
ADDITIONAL LISTINGS: ACW:MAY/91[38]305, ACW:MAY/94[35]469,
ACW:SEP/94[55]489, B&G:OCT/93[12]537,
B&G:APR/94[10]558, B&G:FEB/95[8]590A,
B&G:FEB/95[8]590B, CWM:MAR/91[17]335,
CWM:APR/94[24]505, CWR:VOL1#1[35]104,
CWTI:JUN/90[32]159, CWTI:APR/92[35]257,
CWTI:OCT/95[48]470
DEW, R.J., *Private, CSA;* ACW:JAN/92[10]339
DEWEES, JOSHUA, *Private, 92nd Illinois Infantry;*
B&G:APR/93[6]517
DEWEY, GEORGE, *Captain, USN;* ACW:MAR/92[40]353
Di CESNOLA, LOUIS, *Colonel, USA;* B&G:OCT/93[12]537,
B&G:APR/94[6]557

DIARIES, JOURNALS AND LETTERS:
ARTICLES: "ATTACK AND COUNTERATTACK,"
GETTY:4[126]154, GETTY:5[128]167, "DEAR MOTHER,
SINCE LAST I WROTE TO YOU WE HAVE MADE THE FUR
FLY...," CWR:VOL1#3[46]121, "THE FIRST GEORGIA
REGULARS AT SHARPSBURG: RECOLLECTIONS OF THE
MARYLAND CAMPAIGN, 1862," CWR:VOL2#2[95]135,
"GOING BACK INTO THE UNION AT LAST,"
CWTI:FEB/91[12]189, "I SHALL BE A PRISONER,"
CWTI:SEP/91[42]231, "IF THIS CONTINUES THE ARMY OF
THE POTOMAC WILL BE ANNIHILLATED,"
CWM:OCT/95[40]619
ARTICLES, continued: "LETTERS TO THE EDITOR,"
CWTI:JUL/92[8]269, CWTI:SEP/92[10]278, "NEVER HEARD
BEFORE ON THE AMERICAN CONTINENT,"
GETTY:10[107]227, "ON THE RAPPAHANNOCK,
CHRISTMAS DAY, 1862," AHI:DEC/68[25]117, "PRAYING
FOR SOUTHERN VICTORY," CWTI:MAR/91[12]198, "TIRED
SOLDIERS DON'T GO VERY FAST," CWTI:FEB/92[36]249,
"WRITING HOME TO TALLADEGA," CWTI:DEC/90[56]184
BOOK REVIEWS: *THE BROTHERS' WAR: CIVIL WAR LETTERS
TO THEIR LOVED ONES FROM THE BLUE AND GRAY *
CIVIL WAR MEMOIRS OF TWO REBEL SISTERS * THE
CONFEDERACY IS ON HER WAY UP THE SPOUT:
LETTERS TO SOUTH CAROLINA, 1861-1864 * THE
CORMANY DIARIES: A NORTHERN FAMILY IN THE
CIVIL WAR * "DEAR FRIEND ANNA": THE CIVIL WAR
LETTERS OF A COMMON SOLDIER FROM MAINE *
"DEAR MOTHER: DON'T GRIEVE ABOUT ME. IF I GET
KILLED, I'LL ONLY BE DEAD." LETTERS FROM GEORGIA
SOLDIERS IN THE CIVIL WAR * FIELDS OF FURY: FROM
THE WILDERNESS TO THE CRATER: AN EYEWITNESS
HISTORY * FOURTEEN HUNDRED AND 91 DAYS IN THE
CONFEDERATE ARMY * THE LYON CAMPAIGN IN
MISSOURI: BEING A HISTORY OF THE FIRST IOWA
INFANTRY*
Abbott, Henry L.; BOOK REVIEW: *FALLEN LEAVES: THE CIVIL
WAR LETTERS OF MAJOR HENRY LIVERMORE ABBOTT*
Alexander, Edward P.; BOOK REVIEW: *MILITARY MEMOIRS
OF A CONFEDERATE: A CRITICAL NARRATIVE*
Alexander, Bates; ARTICLE: "THROUGH 'MURDEROUS FIRE
AT FREDERICKSBURG,'" CWM:DEC/94[74]555
Andrews, W.H., *Sergeant, 1st Georgia Regulars;* BOOK REVIEW:
*FOOTPRINTS OF A REGIMENT: A RECOLLECTION OF
THE FIRST GEORGIA REGULARS, 1861-1865*
Aschmann, Rudolf; BOOK REVIEW: *MEMOIRS OF A SWISS
OFFICER IN THE AMERICAN CIVIL WAR*

Barber, Charles; BOOK REVIEW: *THE CIVIL WAR LETTERS OF CHARLES BARBER, PRIVATE, 104TH NEW YORK VOLUNTEER INFANTRY*

Barber, Flavel C.; BOOK REVIEW: *HOLDING THE LINE: THE THIRD TENNESSEE INFANTRY, 1861-1864*

Barclay, Ted; BOOK REVIEW: *TED BARCLAY, LIBERTY HALL VOLUNTEERS: LETTERS FROM THE STONEWALL BRIGADE*

Bartlett, Harold J.; BOOK REVIEW: *TO THE SOUND OF MUSKETRY AND TAP OF THE DRUM: A HISTORY OF MICHIGAN'S BATTERY D THROUGH THE LETTERS OF ARTIFICER HAROLD J. BARTLETT, 1861-1864*

Beatty, John; BOOK REVIEW: *THE CITIZEN SOLDIER; OR MEMOIRS OF A VOLUNTEER*

Bellard, Alfred; BOOK REVIEW: *GONE FOR A SOLDIER: THE CIVIL WAR MEMOIRS OF PRIVATE ALFRED BELLARD,* CWNEWS:SEP/92[4]

Benson, Barry W., *Sergeant, CSA;* BOOK REVIEW: *BERRY BENSON'S CIVIL WAR BOOK: MEMOIRS OF A CONFEDERATE SCOUT AND SHARPSHOOTER*

Bevens, William E., *Private, 1st Arkansas Infantry;* BOOK REVIEW: *REMINISCENCES OF A PRIVATE: WILLIAM E. BEVENS OF THE FIRST ARKANSAS INFANTRY, C.S.A.*

Bigelow, Edwin B., ARTICLE: "SERGEANT EDWIN B. BIGELOW'S EXCITING ADVENTURES," B&G:AUG/91[36]462

Bird, Edgeworth & Sallie; BOOK REVIEW: *THE GRANITE FARM LETTERS: THE CIVIL WAR CORRESPONDENCE OF EDGEWORTH AND SALLIE BIRD*

Birmingham, Theodore, *Private, 23rd Michigan Infantry;* BOOK REVIEW: *YOURS IN LOVE: THE BIRMINGHAM CIVIL WAR LETTERS*

Breckinridge, Lucy; BOOK REVIEW: *LUCY BRECKINRIDGE OF GROVE HILL: THE JOURNAL OF A VIRGINIA GIRL, 1862-1864*

Brewster, Charles H.; BOOK REVIEW: *WHEN THIS CRUEL WAR IS OVER: THE CIVIL WAR LETTERS OF CHARLES HARVEY BREWSTER*

Broadhead, Sarah M.; BOOK REVIEW: *THE DIARY OF A LADY OF GETTYSBURG, PENNSYLVANIA*

Browder, George W.; BOOK REVIEW: *THE HEAVENS ARE WEEPING: THE DIARIES OF GEORGE RICHARD BROWDER 1852-1886*

Bull, Rice C.; BOOK REVIEW: *SOLDIERING: THE CIVIL WAR DIARY OF RICE C. BULL*

Burgwyn, William H.S., *Captain, 35th North Carolina Infantry;* BOOK REVIEW: *A CAPTAIN'S WAR: THE LETTERS AND DIARIES OF WILLIAM H.S. BURGWYN, 1861-1865*

Caldwell, Lycurgus; BOOK REVIEW: *MY HEART IS SO REBELLIOUS: THE CALDWELL LETTERS, 1861-1865*

Caldwell, Susan; ARTICLE: "I WAS THERE," CWM:MAR/92[56]415

Carter, Isabel B.; ARTICLE: "PRAYING FOR SOUTHERN VICTORY," CWTI:MAR/91[12]198

Cater, Douglas J.; BOOK REVIEW: *AS IT WAS: REMINISCENCES OF A SOLDIER OF THE THIRD TEXAS CAVALRY AND THE NINETEENTH LOUISIANA INFANTRY*

Chamberlayne, Ham; BOOK REVIEW: *HAM CHAMBERLAYNE—VIRGINIAN: LETTERS AND PAPERS OF AN ARTILLERY OFFICER IN THE WAR FOR SOUTHERN INDEPENDENCE 1861-1865*

Chambers, William Pitt, *Sergeant, 46th Mississippi Infantry;* BOOK REVIEW: *BLOOD & SACRIFICE: THE CIVIL WAR JOURNAL OF A CONFEDERATE SOLDIER*

Chase, Salmon P.; BOOK REVIEW: *THE SALMON P. CHASE PAPERS, VOLUME 1, JOURNALS, 1829-1872, VOLUME 2, CORRESPONDENCE, 1823-1857*

Chisholm, Daniel, *Private, 116th Pennsylvania Infantry;* BOOK REVIEW: *THE CIVIL WAR NOTEBOOK OF DANIEL CHISHOLM: A CHRONICLE OF DAILY LIFE IN THE UNION ARMY 1864-1865*

Clark, Reuben G., *Captain, 59th Tennessee Mounted Infantry;* BOOK REVIEW: *VALLEYS OF THE SHADOW: THE MEMOIR OF CONFEDERATE CAPTAIN REUBEN G. CLARK, COMPANY I, 59TH TENNESSEE MOUNTED INFANTRY*

Clemson, Floride; BOOK REVIEW: *A REBEL CAME HOME: THE DIARY AND LETTERS OF FLORIDE CLEMSON, 1863-1866*

Conolly, Thomas; BOOK REVIEW: *AN IRISHMAN IN DIXIE: THOMAS CONOLLY'S DIARY OF THE FALL OF THE CONFEDERACY*

Crawford, William A.; ARTICLE: "...OUR NOBLEST AND BEST SPIRITS HAVE LAIN DOWN THEIR LIVES..." CWR:VOL1#2[70]115

Curry, Wilmot W.; ARTICLE: "TO THE POTOMAC WITH SERGEANT CURRY," CWTI:SEPT/89[24]128

Davis, Billy; BOOK REVIEW: *THE CIVIL WAR JOURNAL OF BILLY DAVIS*

Denoon, Charles E.; BOOK REVIEW: *CHARLIE'S LETTERS, THE CIVIL WAR CORRESPONDENCE*

Ewell, Richard S., *General, CSA;* BOOK REVIEW: *"OLD BALD HEAD" (GENERAL RICHARD S. EWELL): THE PORTRAIT OF A SOLDIER AND THE MAKING OF A SOLDIER: LETTERS OF GENERAL R.S. EWELL*

Farris, John K.; ARTICLE: "A CONFEDERATE SURGEON'S VIEW OF FORT DONELSON: THE DIARY OF JOHN KENNERLY FARRIS, CWR:VOL1#3[7]118

Favill, John M.; BOOK REVIEW: *THE DIARY OF A YOUNG OFFICER*

Fisk, Wilbur; BOOK REVIEW: *HARD MARCHING EVERY DAY: THE CIVIL WAR, LETTERS OF PRIVATE WILBUR FISK, 1861-1865*

Fox, Gustavus V.; BOOK REVIEW: *CONFIDENTIAL CORRESPONDENCE OF GUSTAVUS VASA FOX*

Fox, Tryphena B.H.; BOOK REVIEW: *A NORTHERN WOMAN IN THE PLANTATION SOUTH: LETTERS OF TRYPHENA BLANCHE HOLDER FOX, 1856-1876*

Fuller, Charles; BOOK REVIEW: *PERSONAL RECOLLECTIONS OF THE WAR OF 1861*

Gantz, Jacob; BOOK REVIEW: *SUCH ARE THE TRIALS: THE CIVIL WAR DIARIES OF JACOB GANTZ*

Garnett, Theodore S.; BOOK REVIEW: *RIDING WITH STUART: REMINISCENCES OF AN AIDE-DE-CAMP*

Gates, Theodore B., *Colonel, 20th New York Militia;* BOOK REVIEW: *THE CIVIL WAR DIARIES OF COL. THEODORE B. GATES, 20TH NEW YORK STATE MILITIA*

Gordon, John B., *General, CSA;*
ARTICLE: "LEST WE FORGET," CWM:JUL/93[56]490,
BOOK REVIEW: *REMINISCENCES OF THE CIVIL WAR*

Greene, William B., *Private, 2nd USSS;* BOOK REVIEW: *LETTERS FROM A SHARPSHOOTER: THE CIVIL WAR LETTERS OF PRIVATE WILLIAM B. GREENE CO. G, 2ND UNITED STATES SHARPSHOOTERS (BERDAN'S), ARMY OF THE POTOMAC*

Grismore, Silas T.; BOOK REVIEW: *THE CIVIL WAR REMINISCENCES OF MAJOR SILAS T. GRISMORE*

Hammond, James Henry; BOOK REVIEW: *SECRET AND SACRED: THE DIARIES OF JAMES HENRY HAMMOND, A SOUTHERN SLAVEHOLDER*

Harris, David G.; BOOK REVIEW: *PIEDMONT FARMER: THE JOURNALS OF DAVID GOLIGHTLY HARRIS, 1855-1870*

Haydon, Charles B., *2nd Michigan Infantry;* BOOK REVIEW: *FOR COUNTRY, CAUSE & LEADER: THE CIVIL WAR JOURNAL OF CHARLES B. HAYDON*

Hazen, William B., *General, USA;* BOOK REVIEW: *A NARRATIVE OF MILITARY SERVICE*

Heyward, Pauline DeCaradeuc; BOOK REVIEW: *A CONFEDERATE LADY COMES OF AGE: THE JOURNAL OF PAULINE DECARADEUC HEYWARD, 1863-1888*

Hodgkins, Joseph E., *Lieutenant, 19th Massachusetts Infantry;* BOOK REVIEW: *THE CIVIL WAR DIARY OF LT. J.E. HODGKINS*

Holmes, Emma; BOOK REVIEW: *THE DIARY OF MISS EMMA HOLMES, 1861-1866*

Holt, Daniel M., *Surgeon, 121st New York Infantry;* BOOK REVIEW: *A SURGEON'S CIVIL WAR: THE LETTERS AND DIARY OF DANIEL M. HOLT, M.D.*

Hood, John B., *General, CSA;* BOOK REVIEW: *ADVANCE AND RETREAT*

Hopkins, Charles; BOOK REVIEW: *THE ANDERSONVILLE DIARY & MEMOIRS OF CHARLES HOPKINS*

Horner, Franklin, *Private, 12th Pennsylvania Infantry;* BOOK REVIEW: *35 DAYS TO GETTYSBURG: THE CAMPAIGN DIARIES OF TWO AMERICAN ENEMIES*

Hudson, Henry, *Private, 202nd Pennsylvania Infantry;* BOOK REVIEW: *CIVIL WAR SKETCHBOOK & DIARY*

Jackman, John S.; BOOK REVIEW: *DIARY OF A CONFEDERATE SOLDIER: JOHN S. JACKMAN OF THE ORPHAN BRIGADE*

Jones, J.B.:
ARTICLE: "HUMBLE BUT OBSERVANT WAR DEPARTMENT CLERK J.B. JONES LEFT BEHIND AN INVALUABLE ACCOUNT OF WARTIME RICHMOND," ACW:JAN/93[18]394
BOOK REVIEW: *A REBEL WAR CLERK'S DIARY*

Kean, Robert G.H.; BOOK REVIEWS: *INSIDE THE CONFEDERATE GOVERNMENT: THE DIARY OF ROBERT GARLICK HILL KEAN*

Keesy, William A.; BOOK REVIEW: *WAR AS VIEWED FROM THE RANKS*

Kennedy, Charles W.; ARTICLE: "THE RED RIVER CAMPAIGN LETTERS OF LT. CHARLES W. KENNEDY, 156TH NEW YORK VOLUNTEER INFANTRY, CWR:VOL4#2[104]168

Kent, William; ARTICLE: "A WILDERNESS MEMORY: ONE MORNING, 30 YEARS AFTER THE BATTLE IT ALL CAME BACK TO HIM," CWTI:MAR/89[34]104

Ladley, Oscar D.; BOOK REVIEW: *HEARTH AND KNAPSACK: THE LADLEY LETTERS, 1857-1880*

Lauderdale, John V., M.D.; BOOK REVIEW: *THE WOUNDED RIVER: THE CIVIL WAR LETTERS OF JOHN VANCE LAUDERDALE, M.D.*

Lee, Elizabeth Blair; BOOK REVIEW: *WARTIME WASHINGTON: THE CIVIL WAR LETTERS OF ELIZABETH BLAIR LEE*

Lee, Robert E.; BOOK REVIEW: *LEE'S DISPATCHES: UNPUBLISHED LETTERS OF GENERAL ROBERT E. LEE, C.S.A. TO JEFFERSON DAVIS AND THE WAR DEPARTMENT OF THE CONFEDERATE STATES OF AMERICA, 1862-65; RECOLLECTIONS AND LETTERS OF GENERAL, ROBERT E. LEE BY HIS SON*

Maher, Thomas F., *Corporal, 5th New York Infantry;* ARTICLE: "I HARDLY HAVE THE HEART TO WRITE THESE FEW LINES...," CWR:VOL1#2[42]113

Markham, Philo A., *Corporal, 154th New York Infantry;* ARTICLE: "PHILO MARKHAM'S LONG WALK," CWTI:MAR/95[26]434

Matrau, Henry, *Private, 6th Wisconsin Infantry;* BOOK REVIEW: *LETTERS HOME: HENRY MATRAU OF THE IRON BRIGADE*

Matteson, Elisha C., ARTICLE: "DEAR SISTER—THEY FIGHT TO WHIP," CWTI:MAY/91[16]206

Mattocks, Charles; BOOK REVIEW: *UNSPOILED HEART: THE JOURNAL OF CHARLES MATTOCKS OF THE 17TH MAINE*

McCaskey, James, *Private, 100th Pennsylvania Infantry,* ARTICLE: "A SCRATCH WITH THE REBELS," CWTI:JAN/94[49]365

McDonald, Cornelia P.; BOOK REVIEW: *A WOMAN'S CIVIL WAR: A DIARY, WITH REMINISCENCES OF THE WAR, FROM MARCH 1862*

McIlvaine, Samuel; BOOK REVIEW: *BY THE DIM AND FLARING LAMPS: THE CIVIL WAR DIARY OF SAMUEL MCILVAINE, FEBRUARY THROUGH JUNE 1862*

McMahon, John T., *Private, 136th New York Infantry;* BOOK REVIEW: *JOHN T. MCMAHON'S: DIARY OF THE 136TH NEW YORK 1861-1865*

Meade, George G., *General, USA;* BOOK REVIEW: *THE LIFE AND LETTERS OF GENERAL GEORGE G. MEADE*

Merrick, Morgan J.; BOOK REVIEW: *FROM DESERT TO BAYOU: THE CIVIL WAR JOURNAL AND SKETCHES OF MORGAN WOLFE MERRICK*

Morgan, Sarah; BOOK REVIEW: *THE CIVIL WAR DIARY OF SARAH MORGAN*

Mosby, John S.; BOOK REVIEW: *THE MEMOIRS OF JOHN S. MOSBY*

Mumford, William T.; ARTICLE: "DIARY OF THE VICKSBURG SIEGE," AHI:DEC/77[46]177

Nelson, George W., *Captain, CSA;* ARTICLE: "LETTERS FROM THE HEART," CWTI:OCT/95[28]467

Omenhausser, John J.; BOOK REVIEW: *SKETCHES FROM PRISON: A CONFEDERATE ARTIST'S RECORD OF LIFE AT POINT LOOKOUT PRISONER OF WAR CAMP, 1863-1865*

Osborn, Thomas W., *Lieutenant Colonel, USA;* BOOK REVIEW: *NO MIDDLE GROUND: THOMAS WARD OSBORN'S LETTERS FROM THE FIELD: 1862-1864*

Pender, William D., *General, CSA;* BOOK REVIEW: *THE GENERAL TO HIS LADY: THE CIVIL WAR LETTERS OF WILLIAM DORSEY PENDER TO FANNY PENDER*

Pettit, Frederick; BOOK REVIEW: *INFANTRYMAN PETTIT: THE CIVIL WAR LETTERS OF CORPORAL FREDERICK PETTIT*

Petty, Elijah P., *Captain, CSA;* BOOK REVIEW: *JOURNEY TO PLEASANT HILL: THE CIVIL WAR LETTERS OF CAPTAIN ELIJAH P. PETTY, WALKER'S TEXAS DIVISION C.S.A.*

Preston, Madge; BOOK REVIEW: *A PRIVATE WAR, LETTERS AND DIARIES OF MADGE PRESTON 1862-1867*

Rorty, James M.; ARTICLE: "I WAS THERE," CWM:MAR/91[14]334

Ross, Lawrence S., *General CSA;* BOOK REVIEW: *PERSONAL CIVIL WAR LETTERS OF GENERAL LAWRENCE SULLIVAN ROSS*

Ruffin, Edmund; BOOK REVIEW: *THE DIARY OF EDMUND RUFFIN, VOLUME III, A DREAM SHATTERED, JUNE, 1863-JUNE 1865*

Russell, William H.; BOOK REVIEW: *WILLIAM HOWARD RUSSELL'S CIVIL WAR: PRIVATE DIARY AND LETTERS 1861-1862*

Seabury, Caroline; BOOK REVIEW: *THE DIARY OF CAROLINE SEABURY, 1854-1863*

Seymour, William J., *Captain, CSA;* BOOK REVIEW: *THE CIVIL WAR MEMOIRS OF CAPTAIN WILLIAM J. SEYMOUR: REMINISCENCES OF A LOUISIANA TIGER*

Shanklin, James M., *Lieutenant Colonel, 42nd Indiana Infantry;* BOOK REVIEW: *DEAREST LIZZIE: THE CIVIL WAR LETTERS OF LT. COL. JAMES MAYNARD SHANKLIN*

Shaw, Robert G.; *Colonel, 54th Massachusetts Infantry;* BOOK REVIEW: *BLUE-EYED CHILD OF FORTUNE: THE CIVIL WAR LETTERS OF COLONEL ROBERT GOULD SHAW*

Stewart, William H.; BOOK REVIEW: *A PAIR OF BLANKETS: WAR-TIME HISTORY IN LETTERS TO THE YOUNG PEOPLE OF THE SOUTH*

Stockton, Joseph; BOOK REVIEW: *WAR DIARY OF BREVET BRIGADIER GENERAL JOSEPH STOCKTON, FIRST LIEUTENANT, CAPTAIN, MAJOR AND LIEUTENANT COLONEL, 72ND REGIMENT ILLLIONIS INFANTRY VOLUTEEERS*

Stokes, William, *General, CSA;* BOOK REVIEW: *SADDLE SOLDIERS: THE CIVIL WAR CORRESPONDENCE OF GENERAL WILLIAM STOKES OF THE 4TH SOUTH CAROLINA CAVALRY*

Stuckenberg, John H.W., *Chaplain, 145th Pennsylvania Infantry;* BOOK REVIEW: *I'M SURROUNDED BY METHODISTS...: DIARY OF JOHN H.W. STUCKENBERG, CHAPLAIN OF THE 145TH PENNSYLVANIA VOLUNTEER INFANTRY*

Sullivan, James P., *Sergeant, 6th Wisconsin Infantry;* BOOK REVIEW: *AN IRISHMAN IN THE IRON BRIGADE: THE CIVIL WAR MEMOIRS OF JAMES P. SULLIVAN, SERGEANT, 6TH WISCONSIN VOLUNTEERS*

Thomas, Ella Gertrude Clanton; BOOK REVIEW: *THE SECRET EYE: THE JOURNAL OF ELLA GERTRUDE CLANTON THOMAS, 1848-1889*

Thomas, Horace H.; ARTICLE: "I WAS AN OGRE," CWM:OCT/94[60]544

Thompson, M. Jeff, *General, CSA;* BOOK REVIEW: *THE CIVIL WAR REMINISCENCES OF GENERAL M. JEFF THOMPSON*

Traweek, Washington B., ARTICLE: "BREAK OUT!" CWTI:DEC/91[26]238

Trimble, Isaac R., *General, CSA;* ARTICLE: "GETTYSBURG: FIGHT ENOUGH IN OLD MAN TRIMBLE TO SATISFY A HERD OF TIGERS, CWM:AUG/94[60]531

Wainwright, Charles S., *Colonel, CSA;* BOOK REVIEW: *A DIARY OF BATTLE: THE PERSONAL JOURNALS OF COLONEL CHARLES S. WAINWRIGHT, 1861-1865*

Wakeman, Sarah; BOOK REVIEW: *AN UNCOMMON SOLDIER: THE CIVIL WAR LETTERS OF SARAH ROSETTA WAKEMAN, ALIAS PVT. LYONS WAKEMAN, 153RD REGIMENT, NEW YORK STATE VOLUNTEERS, 1862-1864*

Ward, W.W., *Colonel, 9th Tennessee Cavalry;* BOOK REVIEW: 'FOR THE SAKE OF MY COUNTRY:' THE DIARY OF COL. W.W. WARD, 9TH TENNESSEE CAVALRY, MORGAN'S BRIGADE, C.S.A.*

Ware, Thomas L., *Private, 15th Georgia Infantry;* BOOK REVIEW: *35 DAYS TO GETTYSBURG: THE CAMPAIGN DIARIES OF TWO AMERICAN ENEMIES*

Weld, Stephen M.; BOOK REVIEW: *WAR LETTERS AND DIARIES OF STEPHEN MINOT WELD, 1861-1865*

White, Daniel, *Private, 144th New York Infantry;* BOOK REVIEW: *DEAR WIFE, LETTERS OF A CIVIL WAR SOLDIER*

White, George R., *Private, 19th Massachusetts Infantry;* BOOK REVIEW: *THE CIVIL WAR: LETTERS HOME FROM GEO. R. WHITE*

White, Wyman, *Sergeant, 2nd USSS;* BOOK REVIEW: *THE CIVIL WAR DIARY OF WYMAN WHITE, FIRST SERGEANT OF COMPANY F, 2ND UNITED STATES SHARPSHOOTER REGIMENT, 1861-1865*

Williams, Alpheus S., *General, USA;* BOOK REVIEW: *FROM THE CANNON'S MOUTH: THE CIVIL WAR LETTERS OF GENERAL ALPHEUS S. WILLIAMS*

Williams, Hiram S.; BOOK REVIEW: *THIS WAR SO HORRIBLE: THE CIVIL WAR DIARY OF HIRAM SMITH WILLIAMS*

Willison, Charles A.; BOOK REVIEW: *A BOY'S SERVICE WITH THE 76TH OHIO*

Wren, James; BOOK REVIEW: *FROM NEW BERN TO FREDERICKSBURG: CAPTAIN JAMES WREN'S DIARY*

Zachry, Alfred, *Private, 3rd Georgia Infantry;* ARTICLE: "FIGHTING WITH THE 3D GEORGIA," CWTI:SEP/94[26]400, "FOUR SHOTS FOR THE CAUSE," CWTI:DEC/94[32]410

DIBBLE, OLIVER, *Private, 8th New York Infantry;* B&G:FEB/95[8]590A

DIBRELL, GEORGE G., *General, CSA;* B&G:AUG/91[11]458, B&G:DEC/95[9]615, CWM:DEC/95[48]631

DICEY, EDWARD, *reporter;* BOOK REVIEW: *SPECTATOR OF AMERICA*

DICK, F.A., *Lieutenant Colonel, USA;* CWTI:AUG/95[58]461

DICKENS, J.L.N., *Captain, CSA;* B&G:OCT/94[11]580

DICKENSON, CRISPEN, *Captain, CSA;* ACW:MAR/94[27]459

DICKENSON, J.D., *Colonel, 7th New Jersey Infantry;* B&G:FEB/92[22]476

DICKERT, D. AUGUSTUS, *Lieutenant, 3rd South Carolina Infantry;* ACW:MAY/92[54], CWR:VOL3#4[1]161, GETTY:5[35]159

DICKEY, CYRUS E., *Captain, USA;* CWR:VOL4#2[68]167

DICKEY, GILBERT, *Lieutenant, 24th Michigan Infantry;* GETTY:5[19]158

DICKEY, WILLIAM H., *Colonel, USA;* CWR:VOL4#2[26]166

DICKINSON, ORMAN, *Private, 126th New York Infantry;* CWR:VOL1#4[7]125

DICKINSON, WILLIAM, *Private, 19th Indiana Infantry;* GETTY:11[57]233

DICKISON, JOHN J., *Lieutenant, CSA;* ARTICLE: "THE GRAY FOX OF DIXIE," NOV/95[38]556

"DICTATOR" MORTAR; ACW:SEP/93[16]431

DIKE, JOHN H., *Captain, 7th Massachusetts Infantry;* ACW:NOV/95[30]555

DILGER, HUBERT, *Captain, 1st Ohio Light Artillery;* ARTICLE: "DIGLER'S BATTERY AT GETTYSBURG," GETTY:4[49]147

BOOK REVIEW: *LEATHERBREECHES: HERO OF CHANCELLORSVILLE*

ADDITIONAL LISTINGS: B&G:AUG/93[36]533, GETTY:4[33]146, GETTY:10[7]221, *photo,* GETTY:4[49]147

DILL, BENJAMIN F., *Colonel, CSA;* ACW:NOV/92[35]387

DILLEN, JOHN, *Private, 53rd Pennsylvania Infantry;*
GETTY:11[80]235
DILLION, RICHARD S., *Captain, 24th Michigan Infantry;*
GETTY:5[19]158
DILLMAN, JOHN, *Private, 89th Ohio Infantry;*
CWTI:SEP/92[31]281
DILLON, EDWARD, *Major, CSA;* ACW:SEP/91[46]324
DILLON, JAMES M., *Chaplain, 182nd New York Infantry;*
CWM:MAR/91[50]340
DILLON, PETER, *civilian;* ACW:MAR/92[22]351
DILTS, GEORGE S., *Surgeon, 5th New York Infantry;*
B&G:APR/95[24]596
DILWORTH, WILLIAM S., *Colonel, 1st Florida Special
Battalion;* CWR:VOL3#1[65]151
DIMAN, THEODORE, *civilian;* GETTY:12[97]249
DIMICK, H.E., *gunsmith;* CWTI:APR/90[48]154
DIMICK, JUSTIN E., *Lieutenant, USA;* B&G:DEC/91[12]469
DIMM, HENRY S., *Captain, 53rd Pennsylvania Infantry;*
GETTY:11[80]235
DIMMICK, MILO M., *civilian;* ACW:SEP/93[22]432
DIMMICK, RICHARD C., *Private, 126th New York Infantry;*
CWR:VOL1#4[7]125
DIMMOCK, CHARLES, *Captain, CSA;* ACW:SEP/94[62]490,
CWTI:APR/89[38]111, GETTY:5[107]164
DIMON, THEODORE, *Surgeon, 2nd Maryland Infantry;*
B&G:DEC/94[28], GETTY:10[53]225, GETTY:12[97]249
DIMOND, JAMES F., *Private, USA;* GETTY:12[7]241
DINSMOOR, SAMUEL P., *Private, 116th Ohio Infantry;*
CWM:OCT/94[23]535
DINSMORE, RICHARD, *Captain, USA;* GETTY:4[101]151
DINWIDDIE COURT HOUSE, VIRGINIA, BATTLE OF;
B&G:APR/92[8]481, B&G:FEB/94[38]553,
CWM:OCT/94[17]534, CWTI:AUG/90[26]166
DIPLOMACY:
BOOK REVIEWS: *DESPERATE DIPLOMACY: WILLIAM H.
SEWARD'S FOREIGN POLICY, 1861 * DIPLOMATIC
HISTORY OF THE SOUTHERN CONFEDERACY * GREAT
BRITAIN AND THE AMERICAN CIVIL WAR * GREAT
BRITAIN AND THE CONFEDERATE NAVY, 1861-1865 *
KING COTTON DIPLOMACY * THE NORTH, THE SOUTH,
AND THE POWERS: 1861-1865 * SQUALL ACROSS THE
ATLANTIC: AMERICAN CIVIL WAR PRIZE CASES AND
DIPLOMACY * THE UNITED STATES AND FRANCE:
CIVIL WAR DIPLOMACY*
DISEASE IN THE CIVIL WAR; ARTICLE: "'THE ARMY
DISEASE,'" AHI:DEC/71[10]137
DISNEY CO., WALT; see listings under **"PRESERVATION"**
DISTRICT OF COLUMBIA:
BOOK REVIEW: *A GUIDE TO CIVIL WAR WASHINGTON*
ADDITIONAL LISTINGS: CWTI:MAY/89[28]117, *photo of "Great
Cavalry Depot";* CWTI:JUN/90[46]161

DISTRICT OF COLUMBIA TROOPS:
1st Cavalry; B&G:APR/92[8]481, B&G:JUN/95[36]603A
2nd Infantry; ACW:NOV/91[16]330
2nd Infantry, Colored; AHI:AUG/68[4]115B

DIVIDSON, CHARLES A., *Lieutenant, 1st Virginia Battalion;*
CWM:MAR/91[65]342
DIX, AUSTIN, *Private, 18th Virginia Infantry;* GETTY:6[94]180
DIX, DOROTHEA:
ARTICLE: "DOROTHEA DIX: FORGOTTEN CRUSADER,"
AHI:JUL/78[11]181

ADDITIONAL LISTINGS: ACW:JAN/92[30]342, B&G:OCT/93[31]539,
CWM:JAN/91[47], CWM:MAY/91[18]348, CWM:APR/94[8]502,
GETTY:8[121]207, GETTY:10[53]225, *painting;*
AHI:JUL/78[11]181, *photos;* ACW:JAN/92[30]342,
AHI:JUL/78[11]181, GETTY:10[53]225
DIX, JOHN A., *General, USA:*
ARTICLE: "THE 'BLACKBERRY RAID,'" GETTY:11[6]231
ADDITIONAL LISTINGS: ACW:JAN/94[47]452, ACW:MAR/94[35]460,
ACW:JAN/95[74]510, AHI:APR/80[21]200,
CWR:VOL1#4[7]125, CWTI:APR/89[14]107,
CWTI:NOV/92[49]292, MH:JUN/91[20]152, *photos;*
AHI:APR/80[21]200, GETTY:11[6]231
DIX-HILL CARTEL; CWR:VOL1#4[7]125,
CWTI:APR/89[14]107, GETTY:12[111]250, GETTY:13[108]261
DIXIE ARTILLERY:
ARTICLE: "TIME LAPSE," CWTI:DEC/90[90]186
ADDITIONAL LISTINGS: CWM:AUG/94[48]529, CWTI:NOV/93[55]350
DIXON, GEORGE E., *Lieutenant, 21st Alabama Infantry;*
AHI:MAY/71[3]133A, AHI:OCT/95[16]325,
B&G:JUN/95[36]603A, CWR:VOL4#3[77]174,
CWTI:SEPT/89[20]127
DIXON, GOODMAN, *Private, Sumter Artillery;*
CWR:VOL3#2[1]153
DIXON, JOHN A., *Captain, CSA;* B&G:DEC/95[9]615
DIXON, WILLIAM T., *Private, 22nd Virginia Infantry;*
CWR:VOL1#3[52]122
DOAN, ISAAC, *Private, 40th Ohio Infantry;*
CWTI:SEP/92[31]281
DOAN, THOMAS, *Lieutenant Colonel, USA;* B&G:DEC/95[9]615
DOANE, GEORGE H., *New Jersey Militia;*
CWM:MAR/91[50]340
DOBBIN, ARCHIBALD S., *Colonel, CSA;* B&G:JUN/91[10]452
DOBBS, JESSE L., *Sergeant, 7th Georgia Infantry;*
B&G:APR/91[32]447
DOBKE, ADOLPHUS, *Lieutenant Colonel, 45th New York
Infantry;* GETTY:10[7]221
DOBY, ALFRED E., *Captain, CSA;* CWM:JUN/94[26]512
DOCKERY, THOMAS, *Colonel, 19th Arkansas Infantry;*
CWR:VOL1#2[44]114, CWR:VOL2#1[36]132
DODD, THEODORE, *Captain, USA;* B&G:JUN/94[8]568
DODD, THOMAS, *Captain, USA;* CWTI:OCT/95[56]471
DODDS, EDWARD E., *Sergeant, 21st New York Cavalry;*
CWM:SEP/93[18]494
DODGE, GRENVILLE M., *General, USA:*
ARTICLE: "SHERMAN'S FEUDING GENERALS,"
CWTI:MAR/95[40]436
BOOK REVIEW: *GRENVILLE M. DODGE: SOLDIER,
POLITICIAN RAILROAD PIONEER*
GENERAL LISTINGS: *Atlanta Campaign,*
CWTI:SUMMER/89[13]120, *in book review,*
CWNEWS:JUL/92[4], *Indian Wars,* AHI:OCT/79[20]194,
Tullahoma Campaign, B&G:OCT/92[10]496, *photos;*
AHI:JUN/71[10]134, CWTI:SUMMER/89[13]120,
CWTI:MAR/95[40]436
ADDITIONAL LISTINGS: ACW:JAN/95[30]505, ACW:NOV/95[74]560,
CWM:JUL/92[18]429, CWM:AUG/94[27]526,
CWM:DEC/95[48]631, CWTI:SUMMER/89[20]121,
CWTI:SUMMER/89[32]122, CWTI:SUMMER/89[40]123,
CWTI:SUMMER/89[50]124, CWTI:NOV/92[41]291,
CWTI:JAN/93[20]298, CWTI:MAR/95[40]436,
CWTI:AUG/95[34]457, MH:DEC/95[58]188
DODGE, HENRY, AHI:MAY/67[34]108
DODGE, THEODORE, *Adjutant, USA;* GETTY:5[117]165

BOOK REVIEWS: *THE AMERICAN CONSCIENCE: THE DRAMA OF THE LINCOLN-DOUGLAS DEBATES * THE FRONTIER, THE UNION AND STEPHEN A. DOUGLAS * LINCOLN VS DOUGLAS: THE GREAT DEBATES CAMPAIGN * THE LINCOLN-DOUGLAS DEBATES: THE FIRST COMPLETE UNEXPURGATED TEXT * LINCOLN, DOUGLAS AND SLAVERY*

GENERAL LISTINGS: *Dred Scott*, AHI:MAY/81[35]218, *in book review*, ACW:SEP/91[54], CWNEWS:JUN/92[4], CWNEWS:SEP/92[4], CWNEWS:JUN/95[33], *Lincoln's humor*, AHI:NOV/70[22]130, *Mormon confrontation*, AHI:DEC/72[10]145, *photos;* AHI:OCT/70[23]129, AHI:NOV/72[37]143, AHI:JUN/73[4]149, AHI:JUL/75[4]160, AHI:NOV/90[44]293, ACW:MAY/93[47]417, ACW:NOV/94[8]493, ACW:MAY/94[43]470

ADDITIONAL LISTINGS: ACW:MAR/91[30]295, ACW:JUL/92[22]368, ACW:NOV/92[35]387, ACW:MAR/93[6]400, ACW:MAR/93[18]403, ACW:MAY/94[43]470, ACW:NOV/94[8]493, AHI:FEB/69[35]120, AHI:JUN/73[4]149, AHI:NOV/84[18]241A, AHI:NOV/88[37]278, AHI:NOV/90[44]293, CWR:VOL3#3[59]159, CWTI:FEB/90[26]143, CWTI:FEB/91[36]193, CWTI:AUG/91[36]217, CWTI:MAY/93[29]319, CWTI:MAY/94[46]385, CWTI:MAR/95[54]438, CWTI:AUG/95[34]457, CWTI:DEC/95[14]475, CWTI:DEC/95[22]476, CWTI:DEC/95[40]479

DOUGLAS, MRS. STEPHEN A.; AHI:OCT/70[23]129

DOUGLASS, FREDERICK:

BOOK REVIEWS: *FREDERICK DOUGLASS * FREDERICK DOUGLASS: AUTOBIOGRAPHIES * FREDERICK DOUGLASS' CIVIL WAR: KEEPING FAITH IN JUBILEE*

GENERAL LISTINGS: *Harpers Ferry Raid, 1859*, AHI:MAR/84[10]236, *in book review*, B&G:JUN/95[30], CWM:AUG/94[9], CWNEWS:JUN/92[4], *letters to the editor*, B&G:APR/95[5]594, *Underground Railroad*, AHI:JAN/78[34]178, *photos;* AHI:JUN/74[12]155, CWTI:DEC/95[52]480

ADDITIONAL LISTINGS: ACW:JUL/91[43]315, ACW:NOV/94[42]497, ACW:NOV/95[54]558, AHI:JUN/74[12]155, CWTI:DEC/89[42]137, CWTI:DEC/89[53]138, CWTI:AUG/90[50]168, CWTI:JUL/92[20]271, CWTI:MAR/94[38]372, CWTI:MAY/94[46]385, CWTI:DEC/95[52]480

DOUGLASS, LEWIS, *Sergeant Major, 54th Massachusetts Infantry;* ACW:SEP/91[30]322, CWTI:DEC/89[42]137

DOUGLASS, WALTER, *Private, 8th New York Cavalry;* CWM:MAY/92[8]418

DOUGLASS, WILLIAM J., *Private, 2nd Tennessee Cavalry;* CWR:VOL4#1[1]163

DOUTH, CALVIN S.; B&G:OCT/93[12]537

DOUTHAT, WILLIAM, *Lieutenant, CSA;* B&G:FEB/94[8]550

DOUTY, CALVIN, *Colonel, 1st Maine Cavalry;* B&G:OCT/93[12]537

DOUTY, JACOB, *Lieutenant, 48th Pennsylvania Infantry;* CWTI:APR/90[24]152, MH:APR/95[46]183

DOW, EDWIN B., *Captain, 6th Maine Light Artillery;* B&G:JUN/95[8]600, GETTY:5[47]160, GETTY:12[42]244

DOW, NEAL, *General, USA;* AHI:NOV/85[38]254, B&G:OCT/94[11]580

DOWD, COLONEL E.F., *Colonel, 24th Mississippi;* CWTI:SEPT/89[30]129

DOWLING, LAWRENCE, *Private, 7th Wisconsin Infantry;* GETTY:11[57]233

DOWLING, RICHARD, *Lieutenant, CSA:*

ARTICLES: "THE MOST EXTRAORDINARY FEAT OF THE WAR," CWM:OCT/95[47]620, "SIX GUNS AGAINST THE FLEET," CWTI:DEC/90[29]182

ADDITIONAL LISTINGS: CWM:APR/95[8], CWTI:MAY/91[8]205, *photo;* CWTI:DEC/90[29]182

DOWNEY, STEPHEN, *Lieutenant Colonel, Potomac Home Brigade;* CWR:VOL1#4[7]125

DOWNIE, MARK, *Major, 1st Minnesota Infantry;* GETTY:5[79]161

DOWNING, CHARLES; CWM:SEP/92[8]437

DOWNING, JACOB, *Captain, USA;* B&G:JUN/94[8]568

DOWNINGTOWN GUARDS (PENNSYLVANIA) GUARDS, (53rd Pennsylvania Infantry); GETTY:11[80]235

DOYLE, EDWARD, *Private, USA;* B&G:APR/95[24]596

DOYLE, JIMMY, *Private, 10th Tennessee Infantry;* CWR:VOL4#3[89]

DOYLE, RICHARD N., *Captain, 8th Michigan Infantry;* CWTI:JAN/94[46]364

DOYLE, WILLIAM E., *Adjutant, 17th Indiana Infantry;* ACW:MAY/95[49]527

DRAFT RIOTS:

ARTICLES: "A TIME OF TERROR," AHI:MAY/76[35]168, "ASHES AND BLOOD: THE NEW YORK CITY DRAFT RIOTS," AHI:AUG/77[30]175, "HOLIDAY IN NEW YORK," CWTI:NOV/92[49]292, "ROWDIES, RIOTS, AND REBELLIONS," AHI:JUN/72[18]139

BOOK REVIEWS: *THE ARMIES OF THE STREETS: THE NEW YORK CITY DRAFT RIOTS OF 1863 * THE NEW YORK CITY DRAFT RIOTS: THEIR SIGNIFICANCE FOR AMERICAN SOCIETY AND POLITICS IN THE AGE OF THE CIVIL WAR*

ADDITIONAL LISTINGS: ACW:SEP/95[54]548, CWM:MAY/92[6]417, CWM:NOV/92[43]452, CWNEWS:APR/92[4], CWTI:DEC/90[50]183, CWTI:MAY/91[34]209, CWTI:JAN/93[49]303, CWTI:AUG/95[90]462, GETTY:5[79]161

DRAFT, CONFEDERATE; ACW:MAY/92[14]358, ACW:SEP/92[54], ACW:MAR/94[16]458, CWR:VOL3#1[1]149, CWR:VOL3#1[65]151, CWTI:FEB/91[36]193, CWTI:AUG/91[52]219, CWTI:AUG/91[58]220, CWTI:SEP/91[23]228, CWTI:DEC/94[49]413, CWTI:MAR/95[18]432

DRAFT, FEDERAL:

ARTICLES: "COALFIELDS' PERFECT HELL," ACW:MAR/92[22]351, "HOLIDAY IN NEW YORK," CWTI:NOV/92[49]292, "JOHN SUMMERFIELD STAPLES BORE THE PRESIDENT'S MUSKET IN THE CIVIL WAR," ACW:NOV/91[16]330, "TIL THE PAPER WORK IS DONE," CWTI:NOV/93[78]354, "WHO ARE EXEMPT," CWTI:SEP/93[50]339

BOOK REVIEWS: *THE NEW YORK CITY DRAFT RIOTS: THEIR SIGNIFICANCE FOR AMERICAN SOCIETY AND POLITICS IN THE AGE OF THE CIVIL WAR * TO RAISE AN ARMY: THE DRAFT COMES TO MODERN AMERICA * WE NEED MEN: THE UNION DRAFT IN THE CIVIL WAR*

ADDITIONAL LISTINGS: CWM:MAY/92[6]417, CWM:NOV/92[43]452, CWM:SEP/93[18]494, CWR:VOL3#4[68], CWTI:FEB/91[36]193, CWTI:AUG/91[58]220, CWTI:SEP/93[22]335, MH:OCT/93[12]171

DRAKE, FRANCES, *Colonel, USA;* CWR:VOL1#2[44]114

DRAKE, JAMES, *Colonel, CSA;* MH:OCT/92[51]162

DRAKE, JEREMIAH C., *Colonel, USA;* B&G:APR/94[10]558

DRAKE, JOHN H., *Lieutenant, 111th New York Infantry;* GETTY:8[95]205

DRANESVILLE, VIRGINIA, BATTLE OF;
ACW:JAN/95[10]503, CWR:VOL1#3[20]119,
CWR:VOL3#2[1]153, CWTI:MAY/89[14]114, GETTY:12[30]243

DRAPER, ALONZO G., *Colonel, USA;* B&G:JUN/95[5]599,
CWM:AUG/94[30]527

DRAPER, JOHN W.; AHI:JAN/77[46]173

DRAYTON, PERCIVAL, *Captain, USN;* ACW:NOV/91[8]328,
CWTI:JAN/94[46]364, CWTI:MAR/94[20]369,
MH:FEB/92[8]156

DRAYTON, THOMAS F., *General, CSA;* B&G:AUG/91[20]459,
CWM:MAY/92[44]423, CWR:VOL2#2[95]135

DRED SCOTT DECISION:
ARTICLE: "A HEAP O' TROUBLE," AHI:MAY/81[35]218,
ACW:SEP/91[54], ACW:MAY/93[47]417, ACW:MAY/94[43]470,
ACW:NOV/94[8]493, AHI:MAY/81[12]101, AHI:JUN/73[4]149,
AHI:MAY/81[35]218, CWM:MAY/91[6]345,
CWNEWS:JUN/92[4], CWR:VOL3#2[105],
CWTI:DEC/95[40]479

DREHER, FERDINAND, *Captain, 20th Massachusetts
Infantry;* AHI:FEB/82[36]225, CWR:VOL3#1[31]150

DRESSER, EDSON, *Captain, 57th Massachusetts Infantry;*
CWTI:APR/90[24]152

DREUX, CHARLES D., *Colonel, 1st Louisiana Infantry;*
CWR:VOL4#2[68]167

DREW, JOHN, *Colonel, 1st Cherokee Mounted Rifles:*
BOOK REVIEWS: *THE CONFEDERATE CHEROKEES: JOHN
DREW'S REGIMENT OF MOUNTED RIFLES*
ADDITIONAL LISTINGS: ACW:JAN/91[30]286, CWM:SEP/92[38]443

DREWRY'S BLUFF, 1862 BATTLE OF:
ARTICLE: "THE PENINSULA CAMPAIGN OF 1862: THE
BATTLE OF DREWRY'S BLUFF," CWM:JUN/95[39]586
ADDITIONAL LISTINGS: ACW:MAR/91[14]293, ACW:JUL/92[10]366,
ACW:JUL/92[12]367, ACW:MAR/94[35]460,
ACW:JUL/94[35]478, ACW:SEP/95[30]545,
AHI:MAY/71[3]133A, CWM:JUL/93[15]484

DREWRY'S BLUFF, 1864 BATTLE OF; ACW:MAY/92[14]358,
ACW:MAR/93[10]402, B&G:APR/94[10]558,
CWR:VOL1#1[35]104, CWTI:DEC/95[76]482

DRIESBACH, TATE R., *Private, 7th Alabama Cavalry;*
B&G:AUG/92[40]495

DRIGGS, JOB S., *Private, 6th Wisconsin Infantry;*
GETTY:11[57]233

DROOP MOUNTAIN, W. VIRGINIA, BATTLE OF: ARTICLE:
"A BATTLE AT DROOP MOUNTAIN: THE
CONFEDERATES' LAST STAND IN WEST VIRGINIA,"
CWTI:MAR/89[16]101

DRUGS; ARTICLE: "WAR'S 'WONDER' DRUGS,"
ACW:MAY/94[51]471

DRUM BARRACKS, WILMINGTON, CALIFORNIA:
ARTICLE: "LOS ANGELES' DRUM BARRACKS,"
CWTI:SEP/91[18]227
BOOK REVIEW: *THE BEAT OF THE DRUM*
ADDITIONAL LISTINGS: B&G:OCT/91[11]466, CWTI:FEB/92[8]245

DRUMMER BOYS; ARTICLE: "ARMED ONLY WITH THEIR
DRUMS, UNION AND CONFEDERATE DRUMMER BOYS
SERVED THEIR CAUSES WITH DISTINCTION,"
ACW:NOV/92[8]383

DRUMMOND, JOHN A., *Sergeant, CSA;* CWTI:DEC/90[29]182

DRYDEN, R.H., *Surgeon;* ACW:JAN/91[10]283

DUANE, JAMES C., *Captain, USA:*

BOOK REVIEW: *MANUAL FOR ENGINEER TROOPS*
ADDITIONAL LISTINGS: ACW:MAY/93[8]411, B&G:APR/95[8]595,
CWTI:APR/92[49]260

DUBBERLY, LEWIS A., *Private, 4th Alabama Infantry;*
CWTI:JUL/92[8]269

DUBOIS, JOHN V., *Lieutenant, USA;* ACW:NOV/93[26]441,
CWTI:FEB/92[29]248

DUBOSE, DUDLEY M., *Colonel, 15th Georgia Infantry;*
B&G:APR/94[10]558, GETTY:13[7]253

DUCAT, ARTHUR, *Colonel, USA;* CWM:MAR/93[8]465

DUCHAMP, ARTHUR, *Private, 8th Louisiana Infantry;*
CWTI:FEB/91[12]189

DUCKETT, T.B., *Private, CSA;* CWTI:FEB/92[42]250

DUDLEY, FREDERICK A., *Surgeon, 14th Connecticut
Infantry;* GETTY:10[53]225

DUDLEY, NATHAN A.M., *Colonel, USA;* CWR:VOL4#2[1]165,
CWR:VOL4#2[68]167

DUDLEY, WILLIAM, *Private, 19th Indiana Infantry;*
GETTY:6[13]170

DUELS; ARTICLE: "YOU HAD DONE ME A GREAT
INJUSTICE," CWTI:MAR/93[40]312

DUFF, JAMES, *Captain, CSA;* ACW:JUL/91[58]316

DUFF, JAMES B., *Private, USA;* GETTY:10[42]224

DUFFEL, MARTIN V.B., *Private, 8th Louisiana Infantry;*
CWTI:FEB/91[12]189

DUFFIE, ALEXANDER; MH:OCT/93[6]170

DUFFIE, ALFRED N., *General, USA:*
GENERAL LISTINGS: *1863 Cavalry Battles,* MH:OCT/92[51]162,
Aldie, GETTY:11[19]232, *Brandy Station,*
CWTI:JUN/90[32]159, GETTY:11[19]232, *in book review,*
CWM:MAR/91[74], *Kernstown, 1864,* B&G:AUG/94[10]574,
photo; CWTI:MAR/89[16]101
ADDITIONAL LISTINGS: ACW:NOV/91[30]332, ACW:SEP/94[55]489,
B&G:OCT/93[12]537, B&G:OCT/93[21]538,
B&G:AUG/94[10]574, B&G:AUG/94[19]575,
CWTI:MAR/89[16]101, CWTI:MAY/92[48]267

DUFFIELD, WILLIAM W., *Colonel, USA;* ACW:MAY/91[12]302

DUFFY, JAMES, *Major, 69th Pennsylvania Infantry;*
GETTY:4[89]150

DUFFY, MICHAEL, *Captain, USA;* GETTY:7[97]193

DUG GAP, GEORGIA, BATTLE OF; CWTI:MAR/95[26]434

DUGAN, CHARLES, *civilian;* ACW:MAR/92[22]351

DUGAN, JIM, *Private, USA;* ACW:NOV/92[8]383

DUGANNE, AUGUSTINE J.H.; B&G:FEB/93[36]

DUKE, BASIL W., *General, CSA;* ACW:JUL/92[10]366,
ACW:JUL/95[44]537, ACW:SEP/95[10]543,
ACW:SEP/95[22]544, ACW:AUG/91[11]458,
B&G:FEB/94[38]553, B&G:OCT/94[6]579,
B&G:OCT/94[11]580, B&G:DEC/94[6]584,
CWM:JAN/93[29]459, CWM:MAR/93[16]466,
CWR:VOL3#1[80], GETTY:11[19]232, MH:JUN/91[20]152,
photo; B&G:OCT/94[11]580

DUKE, R.T.W., *Captain, CSA;* CWTI:APR/89[38]111

DUKES, JOSEPH H., *attorney;* ACW:SEP/94[46]488

DULA, S.A., *Sergeant, 26th North Carolina Infantry;*
GETTY:5[19]158

DULANY, D.H., *Colonel, USA;* CWTI:SEP/90[34]176

DULANY, RICHARD H., *Lieutenant Colonel, 7th Virginia
Cavalry;* B&G:OCT/93[12]537

DULEY, EDMUNG G., *Lieutenant, 1st Maryland (Confederate)
Cavalry;* GETTY:12[111]250

DULL, JOHN, *Captain, USA;* CWTI:AUG/95[34]457

DUMOND, DAVID B., *Private, 19th Indiana Infantry;*
GETTY:11[57]233

DUMONT, EBENEZER, *Colonel, 7th Indiana Infantry;*
ACW:JAN/92[47]344, B&G:AUG/93[10]529

DUMONT, ROBERT S., *Captain, 5th New York Infantry;*
CWR:VOL1#2[7]111

DUNAWAY, WAYLAND F., *Captain, 47th Virginia Infantry;*
CWR:VOL1#3[52]122, GETTY:8[67]204

DUNBAR, AARON, *Private, 93rd Illinois Infantry;*
CWR:VOL3#3[59]159

DUNBAR, CHARLES, *gunner, CSN;* AHI:OCT/75[30]162

DUNCAN, JOHN P., *Lieutenant, Sumter Artillery;*
CWR:VOL3#2[1]153

DUNCAN, JOHNSON K., *General, CSA;* ACW:SEP/92[38]379,
B&G:FEB/92[26], CWNEWS:JAN/92[4], CWR:VOL1#4[77],
MH:AUG/93[47]169

DUNCAN, SAMUEL A., *Colonel, USA;* CWM:AUG/94[30]527

DUNCAN, THOMAS, *Corporal, CSA;* ARTICLE: "TWO
CORPORALS: A TALE OF NATHAN BEDFORD FORREST'S
ATTACK AT SULPHUR BRANCH TRESTLE, ALABAMA,"
B&G:JUN/92[32]488

DUNCAN, THOMAS, *Major, USA;* B&G:JUN/94[8]568,
CWTI:OCT/95[56]471

DUNCAN, WILLIAM, *Captain, 15th Illinois Cavalry;*
B&G:FEB/91[8]439

DUNHAM'S (FLORIDA) LIGHT ARTILLERY;
ACW:NOV/91[64]336

DUNHAM, CYRUS L., *Colonel, USA;* CWM:DEC/95[48]631

DUNHAM, SAMUEL, *Private, 63rd Pennsylvania Infantry;*
B&G:APR/95[8]595, B&G:JUN/95[8]600

DUNLAP, CHARLES W., *Colonel, 21st Iowa Infantry;*
B&G:FEB/94[8]550, B&G:JUN/94[5]567, CWR:VOL2#1[19]131

DUNLAP, EBEN B., *Private, 7th Wisconsin Infantry;*
GETTY:11[57]233

DUNLAP, GEORGE W., *Congressman, Kentucky;*
AHI:NOV/72[12]142

DUNLAP, J.R., *Private, Jeff Davis Legion;* GETTY:12[68]246

DUNLAP, W.W., *Major, CSA;* CW:JUL/94[8]474

DUNLOP, WILLIAM, *Sergeant, 139th Pennsylvania Infantry;*
B&G:APR/91[8]445

DUNN, ANDREW, *Major, CSA;* B&G:JUN/95[8]600

DUNN, JAMES, *Captain, CSA;* ACW:JUL/92[46]371

DUNN, JAMES L., *Surgeon;* AHI:NOV/89[50]288

DUNN, WILLIAM H., *Private, 5th Michigan Cavalry;*
GETTY:13[89]260

DUNN, WILLIAM M., *Captain, USA;* AHI:SEP/87[48]264

DUNNING, WILLIAM B., *Captain, 11th New Hampshire
Infantry;* GETTY:12[7]241

DuPONT, FRANCIS; CWTI:MAR/94[38]372

DuPONT, HENRY A., *Captain, USA;* ACW:MAY/91[38]305,
B&G:DEC/91[12]469, CWM:JAN/93[40]461

DuPONT, SAMUEL F., *Admiral, USN;* ACW:NOV/91[46]335,
AHI:MAY/71[3]133A, B&G:FEB/91[8]439,
CWR:VOL2#3[183]140, CWR:VOL2#3[194]141,
CWR:VOL3#4[24]162, MH:DEC/94[46]181, photo;
ACW:JUL/94[35]478

DuPREE, COLQUITT, *Private, Sumter Artillery;*
CWR:VOL3#2[1]153

DuPREE, T.J., *Private, 7th Tennessee Cavalry;*
B&G:APR/93[34]521

DURAN, GEORGE E.H., *Private, 17th Maine Infantry;*
GETTY:8[43]202

DURANT, T.C., *civilian;* CWTI:MAR/95[54]438

DURDEN, THOMAS J., *Private, 1st Florida Special Battalion;*
CWR:VOL3#1[65]151

DURGIN, GEORGE, *Private, 19th Maine Infantry;*
GETTY:13[50]257

DURHAM, NORTH CAROLINA; ARTICLE: "BENNETT PLACE:
HUMBLE SHRINE TO PEACE," CWTI:APR/90[20]151

DURHAM, OLIVER P., *Private, 2nd Tennessee Cavalry;*
CWR:VOL4#1[1]163

DURRELL, GEORGE W., *Captain, Pennsylvania Artillery;*
B&G:AUG/95[8]604

DURRIVE, EDWARD, JR., *Captain, Durrive's Louisiana
Artillery;* B&G:AUG/95[8]604

DURYEA, HIRAM, *Captain, 5th New York Infantry;*
CWR:VOL1#2[7]111, CWR:VOL1#2[76]116,
CWTI:MAY/94[31]382, *photos;* CWR:VOL1#2[29]112,
CWTI:MAY/94[31]382

DURYEE, ABRAM, *General, USA:*
ARTICLES: "'BOYS, WON'T I MAKE A FINE LOOKING CORPSE?'
DURYEE'S ZOUAVES AT SECOND BULL RUN,"
CWR:VOL1#2[29]112, "DURYEE'S ZOUAVES: THE 5TH
NEW YORK VOLUNTEER INFANTRY," CWR:VOL1#2[7]111
ADDITIONAL LISTINGS: ACW:JUL/92[30]369, ACW:MAR/93[42]406

DUSHANE, NATHAN T., *Colonel, USA;* B&G:APR/94[10]558,
CWR:VOL2#4[269]145

DUSSEAULT, JOHN H., *Private, 39th Massachusetts Infantry;*
CWTI:APR/92[49]260

DUSTIN, DANIEL, *Colonel, USA;* B&G:DEC/95[9]615

DUSTIN, E.F., *Union Veteran;* GETTY:5[123]166

DUTTON'S HILL, KENTUCKY, BATTLE OF;
CWR:VOL4#1[1]163

DUTTON, ARTHUR H., *Captain, USA;* B&G:DEC/91[12]469

DUTTON, NEWELL T., *Sergeant Major, 9th New Hampshire
Infantry;* CWR:VOL2#2[118]136

DUVAL, ISAAC, *Colonel, USA;* ACW:MAY/91[38]305

DUVALL, ELI, *Lieutenant, CSA;* GETTY:4[110]152

DUVALL, ISAAC H., *Colonel, 9th West Virginia Infantry;*
ACW:MAR/94[27]459

DWIGHT, WALTON,, *Lieutenant Colonel, 149th Pennsylvania
Infantry;* GETTY:4[33]146

DWIGHT, WILDER,, *Lieutenant Colonel, 2nd Massachusetts
Infantry;* GETTY:6[69]176

DWIGHT, WILLIAM, *General, USA;* ACW:MAY/91[38]305,
B&G:APR/95[24]596

DWINELL, JUSTIN, *civilian doctor;* GETTY:10[53]225

DWYER, JOHN, *Major, 63rd New York Infantry;*
CWR:VOL4#4[47]179

DWYER, WILLIAM, *Private, CSA;* ACW:JUL/93[27]423

DYE, ISAAC, *Private, USA;* CWTI:DEC/94[62]415

DYE, WILLIAM M., *General, USA;* ACW:MAY/94[26]468,
AHI:JUN/70[30]127, CWR:VOL1#1[42]105

DYER, ALEXANDER B., *General, USA;* CWM:SEP/91[19]380,
AHI:JUN/66[52]102, CWM:SEP/91[19]380

DYER, ALLEN, *sutler, 3rd Georgia Infantry;*
CWTI:SEP/94[26]400

DYER, FRANKLIN J., *Surgeon, 19th Massachusetts Infantry;*
GETTY:10[53]225

DYER, S.M., *Private, 5th Wisconsin Infantry;*
CWM:MAY/91[26]349

DYESS, RUBEN, *Private, Sumter Artillery;* CWR:VOL3#2[1]153

DYOTT, JOHN; AHI:FEB/86[20]258

DYSON, JOHN C., *Sergeant, Sumter Artillery;*
CWR:VOL3#2[1]153

E

EACHO'S FARM, VIRGINIA, ENGAGEMENT AT; ARTICLE: "FROM EACHO'S FARM TO APPOMATTOX: THE FREDERICKSBURG ARTILLERY," CWR:VOL1#1[1]102
EADS, JAMES B.; ACW:MAY/91[54], ACW:SEP/94[74]491, CWTI:MAY/94[16]380
EAKIN, CHANDLER P., *Lt., 1st U.S. Arty;* GETTY:12[30]243
EARHEARD, HYRCANUS, *Sergeant, 8th Louisiana Infantry;* CWTI:FEB/91[12]189
EARL, WILLIAM J., *Pvt., 7th Wisconsin Inf.;* GETTY:11[57]233
EARLE, DAVID, *Adjutant, 15th Mass. Inf.;* GETTY:13[43]256
EARLE, L.W., *Chaplain, 21st Michigan Inf.;* B&G:DEC/95[9]615
EARLY'S WASHINGTON D.C. (1864) RAID; see listings under **"SHENANDOAH VALLEY CAMPAIGN, 1864"**
EARLY, JUBAL A., *General, CSA:*
ARTICLES: "THE FORGOTTEN BATTLE FOR THE CAPITAL," CWTI:JAN/93[40]301, "JUBAL EARLY AT WAYNESBORO: THE LAST HURRAH," CWM:APR/94[24]505, "MONOCACY: THE BATTLE THAT SAVED WASHINGTON," B&G:DEC/92[8]503, "'OLD JUBE' FOOLS THE YANKEES," B&G:AUG/94[19]575, "ROADBLOCK EN ROUTE TO WASHINGTON," ACW:NOV/93[50]444, "SHERIDAN IN THE SHENANDOAH," AHI:NOV/80[8]209, "TRAVEL," MH:OCT/93[76]173, "WHIRLING THROUGH WINCHESTER," ACW:MAY/91[38]305
BOOK REVIEWS: *JUBAL EARLY'S MEMOIRS: AUTOBIOGRAPHICAL SKETCH AND NARRATIVE OF THE WAR BETWEEN THE STATES * JUBAL'S RAID * JUBAL: THE LIFE AND TIMES OF GENERAL JUBAL A. EARLY, CSA * LIEUTENANT GENERAL JUBAL A. EARLY, C.S.A.: AUTOBIOGRAPHICAL SKETCH AND NARRATIVE OF THE WAR BETWEEN THE STATES * SEASON OF FIRE: THE CONFEDERATE STRIKE ON WASHINGTON*
GENERAL LISTINGS: *Antietam,* ACW:JUL/92[30]369, *Cedar Creek,* ACW:SEP/94[55]489, *Cedar Creek,* CWM:OCT/94[38]540, *Chancellorsville,* ACW:JUL/94[18]476, *Confederate exiles,* AHI:JUN/70[30]127, *Davis' funeral,* CWTI:MAR/93[32]311, *Fisher's Hill,* CWTI:AUG/91[12]214, *Fort Stevens,* CWTI:FEB/91[28]192, *Fredericksburg, 1863 battle of,* ACW:SEP/92[30]378, *general history,* AHI:MAY/71[3]133A
GENERAL LISTINGS, continued: *Gettysburg,* ACW:NOV/92[42]388, ACW:MAY/93[14]413, ACW:JAN/95[46]507, B&G:OCT/91[11]466, CWM:NOV/91[12]390, CWM:JAN/93[8]456, CWTI:SEPT/89[46]132, CWTI:MAR/94[24]370, CWTI:SEP/94[34]402, GETTY:4[33]146, GETTY:4[49]147, GETTY:4[65]148, GETTY:4[113]153, GETTY:5[4]156, GETTY:5[103]163, GETTY:6[7]169, GETTY:6[43]173, GETTY:6[69]176, GETTY:6[113]183, GETTY:7[13]186, GETTY:8[17]200, GETTY:9[17]210, GETTY:11[19]232, GETTY:11[71]234, GETTY:11[119]238, GETTY:12[30]243, GETTY:12[123]251
GENERAL LISTINGS, continued: *in book review,* ACW:MAY/91[54], CWM:JAN/91[47], CWM:APR/95[8], CWM:APR/95[50], CWM:AUG/95[45], CWM:OCT/95[10], CWM:DEC/95[10], CWNEWS:APR/91[4], CWNEWS:JUL/91[4], CWNEWS:JAN/92[4], CWNEWS:JUL/94[25], CWR:VOL1#4[77], CWR:VOL3#2[105], CWR:VOL3#4[68], CWR:VOL4#1[78], CWR:VOL4#3[1], CWR:VOL4#4[129], *in order of battle,* B&G:APR/94[10]558, *letters to the editor,* CWM:MAY/92[6]417, CWM:APR/95[5]570,

CWM:AUG/95[5]602, CWM:OCT/95[5]613, CWTI:NOV/92[8]288, CWTI:MAY/93[8]315
GENERAL LISTINGS, continued: *Malvern Hill,* CWTI:JUL/93[29]326, *Manassas, First,* CWTI:MAR/94[48]374, *Manassas, Second,* B&G:AUG/92[11]493, CWTI:JUN/95[18]444, *Mine Run,* ACW:MAR/93[26]404, *order of battle,* B&G:APR/95[8]595, *Overland Campaign,* B&G:APR/94[10]558, *Peninsula Campaign,* CWM:JUN/95[34]584, *Petersburg,* MH:APR/95[46]183, *post-war,* ACW:JUL/95[26]535, *Ramseur,* CWM:JAN/93[40]461, *Rappahannock Station,* ACW:MAR/92[30]352, *Shenandoah Valley Campaign, 1864,* ACW:SEP/94[8]483, ACW:SEP/94[55]489, ACW:MAY/95[38]526, B&G:AUG/94[10]574, CWTI:SEP/91[31]229, CWTI:SEP/91[61]233, CWTI:JUL/92[29]272, CWTI:JAN/95[48]429, CWTI:OCT/95[48]470, *Wilderness,* B&G:APR/95[8]595, B&G:JUN/95[8]600, *Williamsburg,* ACW:MAR/91[47]297, *Winchester,* ACW:JAN/92[16]340, CWM:OCT/95[37]617
PHOTOS: ACW:MAY/91[38]305, ACW:NOV/93[50]444, ACW:JUL/95[26]535, AHI:JUN/70[30]127, AHI:MAY/71[3]133A, AHI:NOV/80[8]209, B&G:DEC/92[8]503, B&G:APR/94[10]558, B&G:AUG/94[19]575, B&G:FEB/95[8]590C, CWTI:JAN/93[40]301
ADDITIONAL LISTINGS, ACW: ACW:SEP/91[41]323, ACW:MAY/93[38]416, ACW:SEP/93[31]433, ACW:MAR/94[16]458, ACW:MAR/94[50]462, ACW:JUL/94[26]477
ADDITIONAL LISTINGS, AHI: AHI:MAR/84[42]238, AHI:OCT/95[24]326
ADDITIONAL LISTINGS, B&G: B&G:JUN/92[53]491, B&G:APR/94[34]561, B&G:FEB/95[8]590A, B&G:FEB/95[8]590B, B&G:FEB/95[8]590C, B&G:DEC/95[25]616
ADDITIONAL LISTINGS, CWM: CWM:SEP/91[64]387, CWM:JAN/92[27]403, CWM:MAY/92[20]420, CWM:JAN/93[35]460, CWM:MAR/93[24]467, CWM:MAY/93[4]472, CWM:SEP/93[24]495, CWM:AUG/94[8]522, CWM:OCT/94[4]532, CWM:OCT/94[26]536, CWM:AUG/95[35]607
ADDITIONAL LISTINGS, CWR: CWR:VOL1#2[44]114, CWR:VOL1#3[52]122, CWR:VOL2#3[183]140, CWR:VOL2#4[269]145, CWR:VOL3#1[31]150, CWR:VOL3#2[1]153, CWR:VOL3#3[1]157, CWR:VOL3#4[1]161, CWR:VOL4#4[70]180
ADDITIONAL LISTINGS, CWTI: CWTI:APR/89[14]107, CWTI:DEC/89[34]136, CWTI:FEB/90[54]147, CWTI:APR/90[56]155, CWTI:SEP/90[26]174, CWTI:FEB/91[12]189, CWTI:FEB/91[45]194, CWTI:APR/92[35]257, CWTI:APR/92[49]260, CWTI:MAY/92[45]266, CWTI:JUL/92[29]272, CWTI:MAR/93[24]309, CWTI:NOV/93[55]350, CWTI:MAR/94[48]374, CWTI:SEP/94[26]400, CWTI:SEP/94[49]404, CWTI:DEC/94[32]410, CWTI:DEC/95[76]482
ADDITIONAL LISTINGS, GETTY: GETTY:13[7]253, GETTY:13[64]258, GETTY:13[108]261
ADDITIONAL LISTINGS, MH: MH:OCT/92[51]162, MH:APR/95[46]183, MH:OCT/95[8]187
EARLY, ROBERT, *CSA Staff officer;* GETTY:9[17]210
EARLY, WILLIAM, *Lt., Alleghany Artillery;* B&G:APR/92[8]481
EARNEST, AUGUST, *Pvt., 24th Michigan Inf.;* GETTY:5[19]158

EAST GULF BLOCKADING SQUADRON:
BOOK REVIEW: *BLOCKADERS, REFUGEES, & CONTRABANDS: CIVIL WAR ON FLORIDA'S GULF COAST*
ADDITIONAL LISTINGS: ACW:NOV/94[58]499, B&G:JUN/92[40]489, CWR:VOL4#2[136]
EASTIN, THOMAS E., *Captain, CSA;* B&G:DEC/94[6]584
EASTMAN, AUSTIN, *Private., Louisiana Tigers;* CWTI:MAR/94[48]374
EASTMAN, FREDERICK, *Lt. Col., USA;* ACW:MAR/91[25]294
EASTMAN, ROBERT L., *Major, USA;* B&G:OCT/93[31]539
EASTON, HEZEKIAH, *Captain, USA;* CWR:VOL3#2[1]153
EASTON, T.E., *Captain, CSA;* B&G:OCT/94[11]580
EATON, JOHN, *Chaplain, 27th Ohio Inf.;* B&G:APR/95[24]596
EBENEZER (VIRGINIA) GREYS; ACW:MAR/93[10]402
EBERT, FREDERICK, *Pvt., 126th NY Inf.;* CWR:VOL1#4[7]125
EBERTS, ANTHONY, *Private, 24th Michigan Infantry,* GETTY:11[57]233, GETTY:9[33]211
EBY, A.M., *Pvt., 147th Pennsylvania Infantry;* GETTY:9[81]216
ECHOLS, JOHN, *General, CSA;* ACW:NOV/93[50]444, B&G:AUG/91[11]458, B&G:DEC/92[8]503, CWR:VOL3#4[1]161, CWTI:MAR/89[16]101, *photos;* B&G:AUG/91[11]458, CWTI:MAR/89[16]101
ECKELS, IRVIN, *Capt., 32nd Wisc. Inf.;* CWR:VOL2#4[313]146
ECKERT, THOMAS T., *Major, USA;* B&G:DEC/93[12]545, CWTI:SEP/92[22]279, CWTI:MAR/94[24]370
ECONOMICS, NORTHERN:
ARTICLE: "THE GREAT CIVIL WAR GOLD HOAX," AHI:APR/80[21]200
BOOK REVIEW: *RED RIVER CAMPAIGN: POLITICS AND COTTON IN THE CIVIL WAR*
ECONOMICS, SOUTHERN:
"SOUTHERN ECONOMY," ACW:JUL/91[14]311
BOOK REVIEW: *NEW MASTERS: NORTHERN PLANTERS DURING THE CIVIL WAR AND RECONSTRUCTION*
ECTOR, MATHEW D., *General, CSA;* B&G:DEC/93[12]545, B&G:AUG/95[8]604, CWR:VOL2#1[36]132, CWTI:MAR/93[24]309
EDDY, HENRY G., *Lt., Illinois Light Arty;* B&G:AUG/95[8]604
EDES, EDWARD L., *Private, USA;* ACW:SEP/93[46]435
EDGAR, GEORGE M., *Colonel, 26th Virginia Battalion;* CWM:OCT/95[37]617, CWR:VOL3#3[33]158, CWTI:MAR/89[16]101
EDGE, JAMES, *Corporal, Sumter Artillery;* CWR:VOL3#2[1]153
EDGELL, FREDERICK M., *Captain, 1st New Hampshire Artillery;* ACW:MAR/94[50], 462GETTY:12[30]243
EDINBOROUGH, CHARLES, *Private, 67th New York Infantry;* B&G:JUN/95[8]600
EDMONDS, S.D., *Pvt., 22nd VA Inf.;* CWTI:MAR/89[16]101
EDMONDS, SARAH, *2nd Michigan Inf.;* CWR:VOL3#2[105]
EDMONDSON, BELLE; BOOK REVIEW: *A LOST HEROINE OF THE CONFEDERACY: THE DIARIES AND LETTERS OF BELLE EDMONDSON*
EDMONDSON, SARAH, *Private, 2nd Michigan Infantry;* CWM:SEP/93[18]494
EDMONDSTON, CATHERINE A.; AHI:DEC/73[10]152, CWM:JAN/91[47]
EDMONDSTON, GABRIEL W., *Sergeant, 41st Virginia Infantry;* B&G:OCT/95[8]611C
EDMUNDSON, THOMAS, *Sergeant, 78th Illinois Infantry;* CWTI:SEP/92[31]281
EDRINGTON, JESSE, *Lieutenant, CSA;* ACW:JAN/94[30]450
EDUCATION; ARTICLE: "THE SPURNED SCHOOLTEACHERS FROM YANKEEDOM," AHI:FEB/80[14]199

EDWARDS, ABIAL H., *Private, 10th and 29th Maine Infantry;*
BOOK REVIEW: *"DEAR FRIEND ANNA": THE CIVIL WAR LETTERS OF A COMMON SOLDIER FROM MAINE*
EDWARDS, ALBERT M., *Captain, 24th Michigan Infantry;* GETTY:5[19]158
EDWARDS, J.D., ARTICLE: "FOCUS: CIVIL WAR PHOTOGRAPHY," AHI:OCT/79[18]193
EDWARDS, J.T., *Pvt., 5th NC Cav.;* ACW:MAR/95[50]518
EDWARDS, JOHN, *Captain, 1st U.S. Artillery;* ACW:NOV/94[50]498, B&G:APR/95[8]595, B&G:AUG/95[8]604
EDWARDS, JOHN F., *Major, CSA;* CWTI:MAR/93[40]312
EDWARDS, JOHN N., *Major, CSA:*
ARTICLE: "JO SHELBY AND HIS SHADOW," ACW:MAR/95[26]515
ADDITIONAL LISTINGS: ACW:JAN/93[26]395, ACW:MAR/95[26]515, B&G:JUN/91[10]452, CWM:MAY/92[6]417, *photos;* ACW:MAR/95[26]515, B&G:JUN/91[10]452
EDWARDS, M.S., *Captain, CSA;* B&G:OCT/94[11]580
EDWARDS, NATHAN M., *Lt., USA;* CWTI:APR/89[22]108
EDWARDS, OLIVER, *Col., 37th Mass. Inf.;* GETTY:13[7]253
EDWARDS, OTIS, *Colonel, USA;* B&G:APR/94[10]558
EDWARDS, WILLIAM, *Private, USA;* ACW:JUL/93[27]423
EFFINGHAM (GEORGIA) HUSSARS; GETTY:12[68]246
EGAN, CONSTANTINE L., *Chaplain, 9th Massachusetts Infantry;* CWM:MAR/91[50]340
EGAN, THOMAS W., *Colonel, 40th New York Infantry;* ACW:JUL/93[16]422, B&G:APR/94[10]558, GETTY:8[53]203, *photo,* CWM:MAR/91[17]335
EGE, JAMES, *Cpl., 93rd Illinois Infantry;* CWR:VOL3#3[59]159
EGGLESTON, BEROTH, *Colonel, 1st Ohio Cavalry;* ACW:MAR/91[38]296
EGGLESTON, JOHN R., *Lieutenant, CSN;* AHI:OCT/75[30]162, AHI:NOV/75[38]163
EGGLESTON, LEWIS, *Pvt., 6th Wisc. Inf.;* GETTY:4[16]143
EGLESTON, ROUSE S., *Captain, 97th New York Infantry;* GETTY:13[33]255
EICHOLTZ, G.C.M., *Capt., 53rd Penna. Inf.;* GETTY:11[80]235
EINHORN, DAVID, *Rabbi;* CWTI:MAY/92[38]265
EINSTEIN, MAX, *Colonel, 27th New York Infantry;* CWNEWS:NOV/92[4]
ELAM, ROBERT S., *Captain, 22nd Virginia Infantry;* GETTY:12[111]250
ELBERT, LEROY S., *Cadet;* B&G:DEC/91[12]469
ELDER, JOHN A., *artist;* ARTICLE: "THE ARTIST AND THE CIVIL WAR," AHI:NOV/80[28]211
ELDER, SAMUEL S., *Captain, 4th U.S. Artillery;* ACW:JUL/92[41]370, B&G:APR/94[10]558
ELDRED, JOHN A., *Captain, 1st Pennsylvania Rifles;* CWR:VOL1#3[20]119
ELDREDGE, WILLIAM J., *Ensign, USN;* B&G:JUN/92[40]489
ELDRIDGE, C.M., *Private, 3rd Tennessee Cavalry (Union);* CWTI:AUG/90[50]168
ELDRIDGE, CHARLES, *Union veteran;* GETTY:7[119]195
ELDRIDGE, E.J., *Surgeon, CSA;* CWR:VOL4#4[28]178
ELDRIEGE, DANIEL, *Lieutenant, 3rd New Hampshire Infantry;* BOOK REVIEW: *THE THIRD NEW HAMPSHIRE AND ALL ABOUT IT*
ELECTION OF 1860; ARTICLE: "COMING TO THE CRISIS: 1860," AHI:JUN/73[4]149
ELECTION OF 1864; ARTICLE: "THE WAR ELECTION OF 1864," AHI:OCT/68[4]116
ELKHORN TAVERN, ARKANSAS, BATTLE OF; see listings under **"PEA RIDGE, ARKANSAS, BATTLE OF"**

ELLET'S MARINE BRIGADE; CWR:VOL2#3[212]142,
  CWR:VOL4#2[26]166
ELLET, ALFRED W., *General, USA;* ACW:JUL/93[34]424,
  CWR:VOL2#3[212]142, CWR:VOL3#3[88]160,
  CWR:VOL4#2[26]166
ELLET, CHARLES R. JR., *Colonel, USA:*
BOOK REVIEW: *CHARLES ELLET, JR: THE ENGINEER AS*
  INDIVIDUALIST
ADDITIONAL LISTINGS: ACW:JUL/93[34]424, ACW:MAR/95[18]514,
  photo; ACW:JUL/93[34]424
ELLETT, JAMES, *Lt., Purcell Artillery;* CWR:VOL4#4[70]180
ELLETT, ROBERT, *Sgt., Purcell Arty.;* CWR:VOL4#4[70]180
ELLETT, THOMAS R., *Captain, Crenshaw's Artillery;*
  B&G:APR/92[8]481, GETTY:10[107]227
ELLIOT, GIL., *Maj., 102nd NY Inf.;* CWTI:SEPT/89[30]129
ELLIOT, ROBERT, *Major, 16th New York Infantry;*
  GETTY:6[33]172
ELLIOT, W.P., *Captain, CSA;* B&G:OCT/94[11]580
ELLIOTT, BENJAMIN, *Colonel, CSA;* ACW:MAR/95[26]515
ELLIOTT, FERGUS, *Sergeant, 109th Pennsylvania Infantry;*
  CWTI:SUMMER/89[32]122
ELLIOTT, GEORGE H., *Captain, USA;* ACW:MAR/92[62]355
ELLIOTT, GEORGE W., *Private, 2nd Tennessee Cavalry;*
  CWR:VOL4#1[1]163
ELLIOTT, GILBERT; BOOK REVIEW: *IRONCLAD OF THE*
  ROANOKE: GILBERT ELLIOTT'S ALBEMARLE
ELLIOTT, J. WALTER, *Private, 44th USCT;*
  B&G:AUG/95[24]605
ELLIOTT, JOSEPH T., *Lieutenant, 124th Indiana Infantry,*
  B&G:AUG/95[24]605, CWTI:AUG/90[50]168, *photo;*
  B&G:AUG/95[24]605
ELLIOTT, STEPHEN, JR., *General, CSA;* B&G:DEC/95[9]615,
  CWR:VOL2#2[118]136
ELLIOTT, W.P., *Major, CSA;* B&G:OCT/94[11]580
ELLIOTT, WASHINGTON L., *General, USA;*
  B&G:DEC/93[12]545
ELLIOTT, WYATT M., *Lieutenant Colonel, 25th Virginia*
  Infantry Battalion; CWM:AUG/94[30]527
ELLIS, AUGUSTUS VAN HORNE, *Colonel, 124th New York*
  Infantry:
ARTICLE: "'FORWARD, MY TULIPS!': THE DAREDEVIL
  ORANGE BLOSSOMS AT CHANCELLORSVILLE,"
  CWM:DEC/94[40]550
BOOK REVIEW: *HISTORY OF THE ONE HUNDRED AND*
  TWENTY-FOURTH REGIMENT, N.Y.S.V.
ADDITIONAL LISTINGS: ACW:JUL/95[66]539, CWM:DEC/94[4]545,
  GETTY:9[5]209, *photo;* CWM:DEC/94[40]550
ELLIS, DANIEL, *Captain, USA:*
ARTICLE: "YANKEE CAPTAIN DANIEL ELLIS: THE OLD RED
  FOX OF EAST TENNESSEE," B&G:APR/92[28]482
ADDITIONAL LISTINGS: ACW:NOV/91[10]329, *photo;*
  B&G:APR/92[28]482
ELLIS, EZEKIEL J., *Captain, CSA;* CWM:FEB/95[28]560
ELLIS, H.C., *Captain, CSA;* B&G:OCT/94[11]580
ELLIS, HORACE, *Private, 7th Wisconsin Infantry,*
  GETTY:9[33]211, GETTY:11[57]233
ELLIS, JOHN, *3rd New Jersey Infantry;* CWTI:MAY/89[36]118
ELLIS, JOHN H., *Cpt., 1st FL Special Bn.;* CWR:VOL3#1[65]151
ELLIS, JOHN W., *Governor of North Carolina;*
  CWTI:APR/89[14]107
ELLIS, THEODORE G., *Major, 14th Connecticut Infantry;*
  ACW:JUL/95[50]538, GETTY:5[89]162, GETTY:9[61]215,
  GETTY:12[61]245

ELLISON, ISAAC B., *Private, 35th Texas Cavalry;*
  B&G:OCT/95[36]614
ELLISON, JAMES H., *Captain, 15th Alabama Infantry;*
  ACW:JAN/92[38]343
ELLMAKER, PETER C., *Colonel, USA;* ACW:MAR/92[30]352
ELLRICH, ERNEST, *Lieutenant, 96th Pennsylvania Infantry;*
  CWR:VOL3#3[1]157
ELLSWORTH, ELMER E., *Colonel, USA:*
ARTICLE: "THE GREATEST LITTLE MAN I EVER MET,"
  AHI:DEC/71[30]138
ADDITIONAL LISTINGS: ACW:JAN/92[38]343, ACW:JUL/92[22]368,
  AHI:DEC/71[30]138, AHI:NOV/90[44]293,
  AHI:JAN/93[61]309, B&G:AUG/93[10]529,
  CWM:NOV/92[24]448, CWM:SEP/93[18]494,
  CWNEWS:AUG/90[4], CWNEWS:AUG/92[4],
  CWR:VOL1#2[7]111,
  CWTI:SEPT/89[44]131, CWTI:MAY/92[32]264,
  CWTI:DEC/95[24]477, GETTY:6[33]172, *photos;*
  AHI:DEC/71[30]138, AHI:NOV/90[44]293
ELLSWORTH, GEORGE A., CWM:NOV/91[58]394A,
  CWM:MAR/93[16]466
ELLSWORTH, STILES B., *civilian;* B&G:OCT/93[36]540
ELMS, GEORGE O., *Lt., 28th LA Inf.;* CWM:SEP/93[18]494
ELTHAM'S LANDING, VIRGINIA, ENGAGEMENT AT:
ARTICLE: "THE PENINSULA CAMPAIGN OF 1862: THE
  ENGAGEMENT AT ELTHAM'S LANDING,"
  CWM:JUN/95[37]585
ELWELL, JOHN J., *Lieutenant Colonel, USA;* CWM:APR/95[8],
  CWTI:MAR/94[38]372, *photo;* CWTI:MAR/94[38]372
ELY, JOHN J., *Major, USA;* B&G:DEC/93[12]545
ELY, RALPH, *Colonel, USA;* CWTI:JAN/95[34]427
ELY, ROBERT B., *Lieutenant, USN,* CWTI:AUG/90[42]167,
  CWTI:JUL/94[30]392
ELZEY, ARNOLD, *General, CSA;* ACW:NOV/94[18]495,
  AHI:APR/85[18]250, B&G:DEC/91[34]470,
  CWM:APR/95[32]575, CWM:AUG/95[30]606,
  CWTI:MAY/89[22]116, CWTI:MAR/93[24]309,
  CWTI:MAR/94[48]374, GETTY:11[6]231, *photo;*
  GETTY:11[6]231
EMACK, JAMES W., *Lieutenant, 7th North Carolina Infantry;*
  ARTICLE: "TIME LAPSE," CWTI:SEP/92[82]286
EMANCIPATION PROCLAMATION:
ARTICLES: "'THE SACRED FIRE OF LIBERTY': THE CREATION
  OF THE AMERICAN BILL OF RIGHTS," AHI:SEP/91[8]297,
  "WAS LINCOLN THE GREAT EMANCIPATOR?"
  CWTI:MAY/94[46]385
BOOK REVIEWS: *BLACK SCARE: THE RACIST RESPONSE TO*
  *EMANCIPATION AND RECONSTRUCTION * LINCOLN*
  AND BLACK FREEDOM
GENERAL LISTINGS: *general history,* AHI:MAY/71[3]133A, *in book*
  review, ACW:NOV/94[66], B&G:OCT/93[24], CWM:FEB/95[7],
  CWNEWS:APR/90[4], CWNEWS:OCT/90[4],
  CWNEWS:APR/91[4], CWNEWS:JUN/92[4],
  CWNEWS:AUG/93[5], *letters to the editor,*
  CWM:MAY/92[6]417, CWM:JAN/93[6]455,
  CWTI:SEP/94[12]398, *Lincoln's humor,* AHI:NOV/70[22]130,
  Thaddeus Stevens, AHI:JAN/82[16]224
ADDITIONAL LISTINGS: ACW:NOV/92[35]387, ACW:JAN/94[47]452,
  ACW:NOV/94[58]499, ACW:NOV/95[8]552,
  AHI:APR/89[13]281, AHI:OCT/95[24]326,
  B&G:APR/92[28]482, CWM:SEP/93[18]494,
  CWM:APR/94[32]506, CWR:VOL3#1[31]150,
  CWTI:DEC/89[42]137, CWTI:FEB/90[38]145,

CWTI:JUN/90[46]161, CWTI:DEC/90[50]183,
CWTI:AUG/91[52]219, CWTI:AUG/91[58]220,
CWTI:FEB/92[21]247, CWTI:MAY/93[20]317,
CWTI:JUN/95[56]450, CWTI:DEC/95[52]480,
CWTI:DEC/95[67]481, MH:JUN/94[8]177

EMERALD GUARDS; MH:DEC/92[74]

EMERSON, FRANK, *Colonel, USA;* CWR:VOL4#2[1]165

EMERSON, JOHN, *Lieutenant, 26th North Carolina Infantry;*
ACW:NOV/94[34]496, GETTY:5[19]158

EMERSON, RALPH WALDO; ACW:MAR/94[10]457,
CWTI:AUG/90[42]167, *photos;* AHI:JUL/78[11]181,
CWTI:AUG/90[42]167

EMERY, GEORGE, *Lt., 9th NH Inf.;* CWR:VOL2#2[118]136

EMIGRANT AID SOCIETY; AHI:JUL/75[4]160,
CWNEWS:JUN/93[5]

EMILIO, LUIS F.; *Captain, 54th Massachusetts Infantry:*
BOOK REVIEWS: *A BRAVE BLACK REGIMENT: HISTORY OF
THE FIFTY-FOURTH REGIMENT OF MASSACHUSETTS
VOLUNTEER INFANTRY*
ADDITIONAL LISTING: ACW:SEP/91[30]322

EMMETT, DAN; B&G:FEB/94[38]553

EMORY, WILLIAM H., *General, USA;* ACW:MAY/91[38]305,
AHI:MAY/67[34]108, AHI:NOV/80[8]209, AHI:SEP/83[42]235,
CWR:VOL3#1[1]149, CWR:VOL4#2[1]165,
CWR:VOL4#2[26]166, CWTI:DEC/90[29]182, *photo;*
CWTI:DEC/90[29]182

ENGELBRECHT, JACOB; *civilian;* ACW:JAN/91[38]287

ENGINEERS:
ARTICLE: "THE 50TH NEW YORK ENGINEERS WERE
INVALUABLE BRIDGE BUILDERS DURING THE
VARIOUS CAMPAIGNS AGAINST LEE,"
ACW:NOV/95[10]553
BOOK REVIEW: *MANUAL FOR ENGINEER TROOPS*

ENGLAND, EDMUND E., *Lieutenant, 21st Virginia Infantry;*
GETTY:13[108]261

ENGLE, JAMES E., *Sergeant, USA;* B&G:DEC/92[40]508

ENGLEHARD, JOSEPH A., *Major, CSA;* GETTY:8[67]204,
GETTY:13[22]254

ENSIGN, NATHAN R., *Sergeant, Georgia Artillery;*
CWR:VOL3#2[1]153

ENTWHISTLE, THOMAS, *Corporal, 3rd New Hampshire
Infantry;* CWR:VOL4#3[1]170

ERICKSON, CHRISTOPHER, *Lieutenant, 9th Massachusetts
Artillery;* GETTY:5[47]160

ERICSSON, JOHN; ACW:MAY/91[54], ACW:MAY/91[62]307,
AHI:JUL/66[32]103, AHI:AUG/69[5]123, AHI:MAY/71[3]133A,
AHI:NOV/75[38]163, AHI:AUG/69[5]123, AHI:NOV/75[38]163,
CWM:JUL/93[15]484, CWM:APR/94[4]501,
MH:AUG/92[26]161, MH:OCT/93[12]171, MH:OCT/93[20]172

ERNST, OSWALD H., *Cadet;* B&G:DEC/91[12]469

ERWIN, EUGENE, *Colonel, 6th Missouri (Confederate)
Infantry;* ACW:JUL/94[51]480, B&G:FEB/94[8]550

ERWIN, LAWSON, *Maj., 16th NC Inf.;* CWR:VOL3#2[105]

ERWIN, WILLIAM P., *Sergeant, 93rd Illinois Infantry;*
CWR:VOL3#3[59]159

ESHLEMAN, BENJAMIN F., *Major, CSA;*
ACW:JUL/92[12]367, B&G:OCT/95[54]614A, GETTY:13[7]253

ESPIONAGE:
ARTICLES: "CONFEDERATE CLOAK AND DAGGER,"
ACW:JUL/95[44]537, "ESPIONAGE," MH:FEB/94[8]175,
MH:JUN/94[8]177, MH:OCT/95[8]187, "NO LADY WAS SHE,"
MH:FEB/91[8]151, "THE SECRETIVE STONEWALL,"
B&G:JUN/92[53]491

ADDITIONAL LISTING: MH:DEC/94[70]

ESSEX (VIRGINIA) LIGHT BRIGADE; ACW:JUL/95[34]536

ESTE, GEORGE P., *Colonel, USA;* B&G:DEC/95[9]615

ESTES, LLEWELLYN G., *Lieutenant, USA;*
B&G:OCT/93[21]538

ETOWAH IRON WORKS; ACW:SEP/91[22]321,
ACW:SEP/94[10]484

EUROPE:
BOOK REVIEWS: *THE SECRET SERVICE OF THE
CONFEDERATE STATES IN EUROPE * WHEN THE GUNS
ROARED*

EUSTIS, GEORGE, *civilian;* ACW:NOV/91[46]335

EUSTIS, HENRY L., *General, USA;* B&G:APR/94[10]558,
B&G:APR/95[8]595, GETTY:5[117]165, GETTY:8[53]203,
GETTY:13[7]253

EVANS, BEVERLY D., *Colonel, CSA;* CWTI:DEC/94[49]413

EVANS, BILL, *Ensign, CSN;* CWTI:AUG/95[40]458

EVANS, BYRON, *Capt., 4th Ohio Infantry;* B&G:DEC/91[38]471

EVANS, CLEMENT A., *General, CSA:*
BOOK REVIEW: *INTREPID WARRIOR: CLEMENT ANSELM
EVANS, CONFEDERATE GENERAL FROM GEORGIA*
ADDITIONAL LISTINGS: CW:NOV/93[50]444, ACW:NOV/95[38]556,
B&G:APR/94[10]558, CWM:SEP/93[24]495,
CWTI:JAN/93[40]301, CWTI:MAR/93[32]311,
CWTI:JUL/93[38]328, CWTI:MAR/95[33]435, GETTY:7[13]186

EVANS, FRANK, *Private, USA;* B&G:APR/93[24]520,
CWTI:JAN/95[48]429

EVANS, HENRY, *Sergeant, 11th Pennsylvania Infantry;*
GETTY:10[7]221

EVANS, HUGH, *Private, 7th Wisconsin Infantry,*
GETTY:9[33]211, GETTY:11[57]233,

EVANS, JAMES, *Lieutenant, CSN;* ACW:SEP/94[46]488

EVANS, JOHN B., *Lieutenant, 10th Georgia Infantry;*
ACW:JUL/95[10]533

EVANS, JOSH, *Captain, 3rd Georgia Infantry;*
CWTI:DEC/94[32]410

EVANS, LEMUEL D., ACW:MAR/95[8]512

EVANS, NATHAN G., *General, CSA:* ACW:NOV/94[18]495,
AHI:FEB/82[36]225, B&G:AUG/92[11]493,
B&G:APR/92[58]485, B&G:AUG/95[8]604,
CWR:VOL2#4[269]145, CWR:VOL3#1[31]150,
CWR:VOL3#1[78]152, CWTI:MAY/89[14]114,
CWTI:SEPT/89[24]128, CWTI:MAR/91[12]198,
CWTI:DEC/91[36]240, CWTI:NOV/93[55]350,
CWTI:JAN/94[46]364, CWTI:MAR/94[48]374,
CWTI:JUL/94[20]390, CWTI:DEC/94[49]413, *photos;*
CWTI:MAY/89[14]114, AHI:FEB/82[36]225

EVANS, PETER, *Colonel, 5th North Carolina Cavalry;*
B&G:OCT/93[12]537

EVANS, TALIAFERRO S., *Major, 11th Mississippi Infantry;*
CWR:VOL2#4[269]145, GETTY:9[98]217

EVANS, THOMAS W.; ARTICLE: "ESPIONAGE,"
MH:OCT/95[8]187

EVANS, WILLIAM, *Sergeant, 6th Wisconsin Infantry;*
GETTY:4[126]154

EVANS, WILLIAM E., *Lieutenant, CSN;* AHI:DEC/82[38]231

EVE, JOSEPH E., *Captain, CSA;* CWTI:SEP/91[23]228

EVEREST, JAMES G., *Captain, 13th Illinois Infantry;*
CWR:VOL2#1[75]134

EVERETT, EDWARD; AHI:NOV/88[37]278,
AHI:NOV/88[43]279, B&G:DEC/95[30], GETTY:9[122]220,
photo; GETTY:9[122]220

EVERETT, JOHN A., *Private, CSA;* ACW:MAY/92[30]361

F

FAGAHY, W.H., *Captain, USA;* CWR:VOL4#1[44]164
FAGAN, JAMES, *General, CSA;* ACW:MAY/93[22]414,
    ACW:MAR/95[34]516, B&G:JUN/91[10]452,
    CWR:VOL1#1[42]105, CWR:VOL1#2[44]114,
    CWR:VOL1#2[70]115, *photo,* B&G:JUN/91[10]452
FAIR OAKS, VIRGINIA, BATTLE OF; see listings under
    "SEVEN PINES, VIRGINIA, BATTLE OF"
FAIRCHILD, CASSIUS, *Colonel, USA;* B&G:DEC/95[9]615
FAIRCHILD, HARRISON S., *Colonel, USA;*
    CWTI:FEB/92[36]249
FAIRCHILD, LUCIUS, *Colonel, 2nd Wisconsin Infantry;*
    AHI:MAY/67[22]107, CWTI:SEP/93[22]335, GETTY:4[24]145,
    GETTY:6[13]170
FAIRFAX, D.M., *Lieutenant, USN;* ACW:NOV/91[46]335
FAIRFAX, JOHN W., *Major, CSA;* CWM:JAN/93[8]456,
    GETTY:4[110]152
FAIRFAX, RANDOLPH, *Private, Rockbridge Artillery;*
    CWR:VOL4#4[70]180
FAIRFIELD, GEORGE, *Sergeant, 6th Wisconsin Infantry;*
    GETTY:4[24]145
FALKNER, WILLIAM C., *Colonel, 2nd Mississippi Infantry;*
ARTICLE: "IN HIS NAMESAKE'S TALENTED HANDS, W.C.
    FALKNER'S CONTENTIOUS LIFE BECAME THE STUFF
    OF LEGEND," ACW:JUL/95[6]531
ADDITIONAL LISTINGS: CWR:VOL2#4[269]145, GETTY:6[77]177
FALLING WATERS, VIRGINIA, BATTLE OF:
ARTICLE: "GETTYSBURG FINALE," ACW:JUL/93[50]426, "THE
    RETREAT FROM GETTYSBURG," CWM:AUG/94[26]525,
    "THE SIXTH MICHIGAN CAVALRY AT FALLING WATERS:
    THE END OF THE GETTYSBURG CAMPAIGN,"
    GETTY:9[109]218
ADDITIONAL LISTINGS: CWR:VOL1#3[52]122, GETTY:4[101]151,
    GETTY:5[19]158, GETTY:8[111]206, GETTY:9[109]218
FANNIN, JAMES H., *Colonel, 1st Georgia Reserves;*
    B&G:AUG/94[22]576
FANNING, WILLIAM F., *Private, 5th Ohio Cavalry;*
    CWR:VOL4#1[44]164
FARIES, THOMAS A., *Captain, CSA;* CWR:VOL4#2[68]167,
    CWR:VOL4#2[118]169
FARINHOLD, BENJAMIN L., *Captain, 53rd Virginia Infantry;*
    CWM:MAY/92[34]422, GETTY:13[1]252, GETTY:13[64]258,
    photos, CWM:MAY/92[34]422, GETTY:13[64]258
FARLEY, PORTER, *Captain, USA;* CWM:MAR/91[35]337,
    GETTY:8[31]201
FARLEY, WILLIAM, *Captain, CSA;* ACW:JUL/95[34]536,
    CWR:VOL1#2[78]
FARMINGTON, TENNESSEE, ENGAGEMENT OF;
    ACW:MAY/95[49]527
FARMVILLE, VIRGINIA, ENGAGEMENT AT;
    CWR:VOL1#1[35]104
FARNHAM, AUGUSTUS B., *Major, 16th Maine Infantry;*
    GETTY:13[33]255
FARNHAM, LEANDER B., *Private, 1st Vermont Heavy
    Artillery;* B&G:AUG/93[18]530
FARNSWORTH, ELON, *General, USA:*
ARTICLE: "ELON FARNSWORTH, THE NORTH'S THIRD 'BOY
    GENERAL,' HAD LITTLE TIME TO ENJOY HIS FAME,"
    ACW:SEP/94[6]482

ADDITIONAL LISTINGS: ACW:JUL/92[41]370, ACW:SEP/94[55]489,
    GETTY:4[65]148, GETTY:4[75]149, GETTY:4[113]153,
    GETTY:11[19]232, GETTY:13[89]260, GETTY:13[108]261
FARNSWORTH, JOHN, *Colonel, 8th Illinois Cavalry;*
    B&G:FEB/93[24]512
FARNSWORTH, JOHN F., *Congressman;* ACW:SEP/94[6]482,
    GETTY:4[75]149
FARNUM, ASA, *Lieutenant, 95th Illinois Infantry;*
    CWM:JAN/91[11]325, CWTI:JAN/93[20]298
FARNUM, J. EGBERT, *Colonel, 70th New York Infantry;*
    B&G:FEB/92[22]476
FARR, WALDO, *Lieutenant, 1st Minnesota Infantry;*
    GETTY:5[79]161
FARRAGUT, LOYALL, *Lieutenant, USN;* ACW:MAR/92[40]353
FARRAGUT, DAVID G., *Admiral, USN:*
ARTICLES: "BRILLIANT VICTORY OVER THE YANKEE FLEET
    ON THE MISSISSIPPI," CWM:APR/95[28]573, "DAMN THE
    TORPEDOES!": THE BATTLE OF MOBILE BAY,"
    CWM:JUL/93[24]485, "DECKS COVERED WITH BLOOD,"
    ACW:MAR/92[40]353, "FULL SPEED AHEAD!,"
    MH:FEB/92[8]156, "GUARDIANS OF MOBILE BAY,"
    CWTI:MAR/94[20]369, "STUNG BY MOSQUITOES,"
    MH:DEC/94[46]181
GENERAL LISTINGS: *Fort Jackson,* ACW:JAN/92[62]346, *general
    history,* AHI:MAY/71[3]133A, *in book review,*
    ACW:MAY/91[54], ACW:MAR/92[54], ACW:JUL/94[58],
    B&G:JUN/94[34], CWNEWS:JAN/91[4], CWNEWS:JUN/92[4],
    CWTI:APR/90[10], *letters to the editor,* MH:FEB/93[10]163,
    Mobile, CWTI:DEC/94[24]409, *New Orleans,*
    ACW:MAY/92[16]359, ACW:MAY/93[12]412,
    ACW:JUL/93[34]424, ACW:JAN/94[70]454,
    CWTI:SEPT/89[20]127, CWTI:MAY/92[38]265,
    CWTI:MAY/93[29]319, CWTI:DEC/94[34]411,
    MH:AUG/93[47]169, *Port Hudson,* ACW:SEP/95[8]542,
    MH:AUG/94[82]179, *Star of the West,* ACW:NOV/93[8]438,
    Vicksburg, AHI:DEC/77[46]177, CWTI:SEPT/89[18]126,
    painting; CWM:JUL/93[24]485, *photos,* ACW:MAR/92[40]353,
    AHI:MAY/71[3]133A, CWTI:DEC/94[34]411,
    MH:FEB/92[8]156, MH:AUG/93[47]169
ADDITIONAL LISTINGS: ACW:JAN/91[47]288, ACW:NOV/91[8]328,
    ACW:NOV/92[51]389, ACW:JAN/93[51]398,
    ACW:JAN/94[30]450, ACW:JUL/94[35]478,
    ACW:SEP/95[30]545, AHI:OCT/95[24]326,
    B&G:DEC/93[52]548, B&G:DEC/94[10]585,
    CWM:SEP/93[18]494, CWM:OCT/95[47]620,
    CWR:VOL2#3[183]140, CWR:VOL3#3[33]158,
    CWR:VOL4#2[26]166, CWTI:AUG/91[52]219,
    CWTI:DEC/95[67]481, CWTI:DEC/95[76]482,
    MH:AUG/92[26]161, MH:OCT/91[50]154, MH:DEC/95[58]188
FARRAND, CHARLES E., *Lieutenant, USA;*
    CWTI:FEB/92[29]248
FARRAND, EBENEEZER, *Captain, CSMC;*
    ACW:MAR/91[14]293, CWM:JUN/95[39]586
FARRAR, ABSALOM H., *Lieutenant, 13th Mississippi Infantry;*
    GETTY:12[111]250
FARRAR, BERNARD G., *Colonel, USA;* B&G:AUG/95[8]604
FARRIS, JOHN K., *Surgeon, 41st Tennessee Infantry:*
ARTICLE: "A CONFEDERATE SURGEON'S VIEW OF FORT
    DONELSON: THE DIARY OF JOHN KENNERLY FARRIS,"
    CWR:VOL1#3[7]118
ADDITIONAL LISTINGS: CWR:VOL1#3[v]117, *photo;*
    CWR:VOL1#3[7]118
FASSITT, JOHN B., *Captain, USA;* GETTY:7[51]190

FAULKNER, WILLIAM; ARTICLE: "OXFORD, MISSISSIPPI, THE HOME OF WILLIAM FAULKNER, PROVIDES A COURSE IN THE SWEEP OF SOUTHERN HISTORY," ACW:JUL/95[70]540

FAUNCE, JOHN, *Captain, USN;* ACW:MAR/94[35]460

FAUST, DANIEL, *Private, 96th Pennsylvania Infantry;* CWR:VOL3#3[1]157

FAVILL, JOHN M., *Lieutenant, 57th New York Infantry:* BOOK REVIEW: *THE DIARY OF A YOUNG OFFICER* ADDITIONAL LISTING: CWM:JUN/95[76]598

FAVORS, WILLIAM W., *Corporal, Sumter Artillery;* CWR:VOL3#2[61]154

FAY, JOHN, *Corporal, 5th New York Infantry;* CWR:VOL1#2[7]111, CWTI:MAY/94[31]382

FAY, JOHN, *Sergeant, CSA;* ACW:SEP/91[41]323

FAY, MICHAEL, *Private, 69th Pennsylvania Infantry;* GETTY:4[89]150

FAYETTE (VIRGINIA) ARTILLERY; CWTI:MAY/89[22]116

FEARING, BENJAMIN D., *General, USA;* B&G:DEC/95[9]615, CWR:VOL4#3[65]172

FEATHER, STEPHEN, *Private, 83rd Pennsylvania Infantry;* ARTICLE: "TIME LAPSE," CWTI:FEB/92[58]251

FEATHERSTON, DANIEL A., *Lieutenant, 11th Mississippi Infantry;* CWR:VOL2#4[269]145

FEATHERSTON, WINFIELD S., *General, CSA;* ACW:NOV/91[22]331, B&G:AUG/91[30]460, B&G:JUN/93[12]524, B&G:DEC/93[12]545, B&G:AUG/95[8]604, CWM:DEC/95[34]628, CWR:VOL2#1[36]132, CWTI:SUMMER/89[32]122, CWTI:FEB/92[10]246

FEATHERSTONE, DANIEL, *Lieutenant, 11th Mississippi Infantry;* GETTY:9[98]217

FEENEY, WILLIAM, *Major, 42nd Mississippi Infantry;* GETTY:4[22]144

FELTON, HERSCHEL, *Corporal, 37th Illinois Infantry;* CWR:VOL1#1[42]105

FENDALL, JAMES R.Y., *Lieutenant, CSMC;* ACW:MAR/91[14]293

FENN, HENRY, *Private, 9th Massachusetts Artillery;* GETTY:5[47]160

FENNER, CHARLES E., *Captain, Fenner's Louisiana Light Artillery;* B&G:AUG/95[8]604, CWR:VOL4#2[68]167

FENTON, F.B., *Lieutenant, 2nd Illinois Artillery;* B&G:FEB/94[8]550

FENTON, WILLIAM M., *Colonel, 8th Michigan Infantry;* CWTI:JAN/94[46]364

FENTRESS, DAVID W., *Surgeon, CSA;* CWR:VOL2#3[212]142

FENWICK, JAMES, *quartermaster, USN;* CWM:JUL/93[15]484

FERGUSON, AUGUSTUS, *Lieutenant, 12th Virginia Infantry;* CWR:VOL2#3[236]143

FERGUSON, CHAMP: BOOK REVIEW: *CHAMP FERGUSON, CONFEDERATE GUERILLA* ADDITIONAL LISTINGS: B&G:AUG/91[52]464, B&G:DEC/91[6]468, CWTI:MAY/94[40]383, *photo;* B&G:AUG/91[52]464

FERGUSON, HARRISON B., *Sergeant, 126th New York Infantry;* GETTY:7[51]190

FERGUSON, JOHN V., *Chaplain, 97th New York Infantry;* GETTY:10[7]221

FERGUSON, MILTON J., *Colonel, CSA;* GETTY:11[19]232, GETTY:12[68]246, GETTY:13[89]260

FERGUSON, O.H.P., *Captain, 111th Pennsylvania Infantry;* CWR:VOL3#2[70]155

FERGUSON, SAMUEL W., *General, CSA;* B&G:AUG/95[8]604, *photo;* AHI:AUG/71[22]135

FERGUSON, SYD, *Mosby's Rangers;* ACW:JUL/94[26]477

FERGUSON, THOMAS B., *Captain, Ferguson's South Carolina Artillery;* B&G:AUG/95[8]604

FERNAL, WILLIAM, *Lieutenant, 12th New Hampshire Infantry;* GETTY:12[7]241

FERNALD, ALBERT, *Private, 20th Maine Infantry;* ACW:MAR/95[12]513

FERRERO, EDWARD, *General, USA;* ACW:MAY/91[23]303, B&G:APR/94[10]558, B&G:APR/94[59]565, B&G:APR/95[8]595, B&G:AUG/95[8]604, CWM:MAY/92[44]423, CWR:VOL2#2[118]136, CWTI:APR/90[24]152, CWTI:FEB/92[36]249, CWTI:MAY/94[50]386, CWTI:JAN/95[34]427, MH:APR/95[46]183, *photo;* CWTI:FEB/92[36]249

FERRIS, ALBERT G., *seaman, CSN;* ACW:SEP/94[46]488

FERRY, MADISON S., *Governor, Florida;* ACW:SEP/94[10]484

FERRY, NOAH, *Major, 5th Michigan Cavalry;* B&G:AUG/91[36]462, GETTY:13[89]260

FESSENDEN, FRANCIS, *Colonel, 30th Maine Infantry;* ACW:SEP/91[16]320

FESSENDEN, WILLIAM P., *Senator, Maine;* AHI:DEC/68[28]118, AHI:JAN/82[16]224, CWTI:AUG/95[54]460, *photo;* CWTI:AUG/95[54]460

FICKEN, MARTIN, *Private, 6th New York Cavalry;* CWM:MAY/92[44]423

FICKLEN, BENJAMIN, *Major, CSA;* ACW:MAY/94[51]471

FICKLIN, JOHN, *Corporal, Sumter Artillery;* CWR:VOL3#2[61]154

FIELD, CHARLES W., *General, CSA:* GENERAL LISTINGS: *Beaver Dam Creek,* CWM:JUN/95[57]592, *Confederate exiles,* AHI:JUN/70[30]127, *Glendale,* CWM:JUN/95[69]596, *in order of battle,* B&G:APR/94[10]558, B&G:APR/95[8]595, *Overland Campaign,* B&G:APR/94[10]558, *Wilderness,* B&G:JUN/95[8]600 ADDITIONAL LISTINGS: ACW:MAY/92[30]361, ACW:JAN/93[43]397, ACW:JUL/94[42]479, ACW:MAY/95[38]526, AHI:SEP/87[40]263, B&G:APR/92[58]485, CWM:JUN/94[26]512, CWM:OCT/94[34]538, CWR:VOL1#3[52]122, CWTI:MAR/93[40]312, CWTI:MAR/95[60]439, GETTY:13[75]259, *photo;* CWR:VOL1#3[52]122

FIELD, HUME R., *Colonel, CSA;* B&G:DEC/93[12]545, B&G:DEC/95[9]615

FIELD, JOSIAH H.V., *Lieutenant, USA;* B&G:DEC/91[12]469

FIELD, SETH R., *Captain, Consolidated Crescent Regiment;* CWR:VOL4#2[1]165

FIELDS, ROBERT S., *Captain, Consolidated Crescent Regiment;* CWR:VOL4#2[68]167

FIFE, WILLIAM E., *Major, CSA;* ACW:MAR/94[27]459

FILBERT, PETER A., *Captain, 96th Pennsylvania Infantry;* CWR:VOL3#3[1]157

FILLMORE, JOHN H., *Private, 6th Wisconsin Infantry,* GETTY:11[57]233

FINANCE; BOOK REVIEWS: *FINANCIAL FAILURE AND CONFEDERATE DEFEAT*

FINECY, WILLIAM, *Sergeant, 72nd Pennsylvania Infantry;* GETTY:7[97]193

FINEGAN, JOSEPH, *General, CSA:* ARTICLE: "JOSEPH FINEGAN'S FLORIDA BRIGADE AT COLD HARBOR," CWR:VOL3#4[1]161

ADDITIONAL LISTINGS: ACW:SEP/93[8]429, ACW:NOV/95[38]556, CWM:MAR/91[74], CWR:VOL1#1[1]102, CWR:VOL2#3[236]143, CWR:VOL2#4[346], CWR:VOL3#1[65]151, CWTI:DEC/94[32]410, *photo;* CWR:VOL3#4[1]161

FINLEY, CLEMENT, *Surgeon General, USA;* CWM:MAY/91[18]348

FINLEY, GEORGE H., *Captain, 2nd Tennessee Cavalry;* CWR:VOL4#1[1]163

FINLEY, GEORGE W., *Captain, 56th Virginia Infantry;* ACW:MAR/93[10]402, GETTY:5[107]164, GETTY:7[97]193, GETTY:12[1]240, GETTY:12[111]250

FINLEY, JAMES B., *Colonel, CSA;* B&G:DEC/93[12]545

FINLEY, JOHN, *Private, 6th Wisconsin Infantry,* GETTY:11[57]233

FINNICUM, MARK, *Lieutenant Colonel, 7th Wisconsin Infantry;* GETTY:4[24]145

FISER, JOHN C., *Colonel, CSA;* ACW:JAN/94[39]451, B&G:DEC/95[9]615, CWR:VOL1#4[7]125, MH:AUG/95[30]185

FISH, GEORGE A., *Sergeant, 1st Connecticut Cavalry;* ACW:JAN/92[16]340

FISH, THOMAS, *Sergeant, 5th New York Infantry;* CWR:VOL1#2[29]112

FISHBACK, WILLIAM, *General, USA;* B&G:JUN/91[10]452

FISHER'S HILL, VIRGINIA, BATTLE OF; AHI:MAY/71[3]133A, CWM:SEP/91[64]387, CWM:JAN/93[40]461, CWM:MAR/93[24]467, CWM:SEP/93[24]495, CWM:APR/94[24]505, CWM:OCT/94[8], CWM:OCT/94[38]540, CWR:VOL2#1[19]131, CWTI:AUG/91[12]214, CWTI:APR/92[35]257, CWTI:SEP/94[49]404, MH:OCT/93[76]173

FISHER, B.F., *Captain, USA;* GETTY:4[110]152, GETTY:10[42]224

FISHER, CHARLES F., *Colonel, 6th North Carolina Infantry;* B&G:DEC/94[10]585

FISHER, GEORGE A., *Lieutenant, USA;* B&G:FEB/91[8]439, GETTY:4[101]151

FISHER, GLIAS, *Private, 77th Illinois Infantry;* B&G:APR/94[34]561

FISHER, JOSEPH W., *Colonel, Pennsylvania Reserve Brigade;* B&G:APR/94[10]558, B&G:APR/95[8]595, CWR:VOL2#4[346], GETTY:11[91]236

FISHER, OLIVER, *Sergeant, 53rd Pennsylvania Infantry;* GETTY:11[80]235

FISHER, ROMANZO, *Sergeant, 92nd Illinois Infantry;* B&G:DEC/92[40]508

FISHER, THOMAS, *Private, 9th Massachusetts Artillery;* GETTY:5[47]160

FISHER, WARREN, *Union veteran;* GETTY:7[119]195

FISK, CLINTON, *General, USA;* B&G:JUN/91[10]452

FISK, D.M., *Corporal, USA;* ACW:MAY/92[30]361

FISK, JOHN, *Colonel, 2nd New York Infantry;* CWM:SEP/92[16]438

FISK, WILBUR, *Private, 2nd Vermont Infantry;* BOOK REVIEWS: *HARD MARCHING EVERY DAY: THE CIVIL WAR LETTERS OF PRIVATE WILBUR FISK 1861-1865* ADDITIONAL LISTINGS: CWM:JUN/95[29]583, CWTI:NOV/92[49]292, CWTI:MAY/94[24]381

FISKE, R. EMMETT, *Captain, 132nd New York Infantry;* CWM:SEP/92[16]438

FISKE, SAM, *Colonel, 14th Connecticut Infantry;* ACW:SEP/94[38]487, GETTY:9[61]215

FISLAR, J.C., *Lieutenant, USA;* AHI:DEC/85[40]255

FISTER, THOMAS D., *Lieutenant, USN;* ACW:MAR/94[35]460

FITCH, MICHAEL H., *Lieutenant Colonel, USA;* B&G:DEC/95[9]615

FITE, JOHN A., *Colonel, 7th Tennessee Infantry;* GETTY:6[13]170, GETTY:12[61]245

FITHIAN, WILLIAM, *Surgeon;* CWR:VOL1#1[42]105

FITZGERALD, JOHN, *Major, 23rd Virginia Infantry;* CWM:MAY/92[20]420

FITZGERALD, MORRIS, *Private, 37th Illinois Infantry;* CWR:VOL1#1[42]105

FITZHUGH'S WOODS, MINNESOTA, SKIRMISH OF; ACW:MAY/91[12]302

FITZHUGH, CHARLES L., *Colonel, USA;* B&G:APR/92[8]481, CWM:APR/94[24]505

FITZHUGH, GEORGE; ARTICLE: "GEORGE FITZHUGH: POLEMICIST FOR THE PECULIAR INSTITUTION," CWM:FEB/95[68]567

FITZHUGH, NORMAN, *Major, CSA;* CWTI:NOV/93[55]350, CWTI:JUN/95[38]447

FITZHUGH, ROBERT H., *Major, USA;* B&G:APR/95[8]595, CWTI:APR/92[49]260

FITZPATRICK, THOMAS, *seaman, USN;* CWM:SEP/93[18]494

FITZSIMMONS, GEORGE H., *Major, USA;* AHI:NOV/85[38]254

FIVE FORKS, VIRGINIA, BATTLE OF: ARTICLE: "THE BATTLE OF FIVE FORKS: FINAL PUSH FOR THE SOUTH SIDE," B&G:APR/92[8]481, "CONFRONTATION AT FIVE FORKS: GENERAL SHERIDAN VS. GENERAL WARREN," CWM:MAR/93[24]467, "WHAT ARE SHAD? (AND HOW DID THEY AFFECT CONFEDERATE FORTUNES AT FIVE FORKS)," B&G:APR/92[48]484 GENERAL LISTINGS: *general history,* AHI:MAY/71[3]133A, *in book review,* CWM:AUG/95[8], *letters to the editor,* B&G:JUN/92[6]486, B&G:DEC/92[6]502, B&G:FEB/93[6]510, *order of battle;* B&G:APR/92[8]481 ADDITIONAL LISTINGS: ACW:JAN/92[16]340, ACW:NOV/92[74]390, ACW:MAY/94[12]466, ACW:MAR/95[12]513, ACW:MAY/95[38]526, ACW:JUL/95[26]535, AHI:SEP/87[40]263, B&G:OCT/91[40]467, B&G:FEB/93[40]514, CWM:JUL/92[8]427, CWM:MAR/93[4]463, CWR:VOL2#3[236]143, CWR:VOL2#4[269]145, CWR:VOL3#1[65]151, CWR:VOL3#2[1]153, CWTI:FEB/90[54]147, CWTI:JUL/94[44]394, *photo;* CWTI:AUG/90[26]166

FLAGLER, DANIEL W., *Lieutenant, USA;* GETTY:9[41]212

FLAGS:

ARTICLES: "EMBATTLED EMBLEM: THE ARMY OF NORTHERN VIRGINIA BATTLE FLAG FROM 1861 TO THE PRESENT," AHI:JAN/94[12]317, "GROVER CLEVELAND AND THE REBEL BANNERS," CWTI:SEP/93[22]335 BOOK REVIEWS: *ADVANCE THE COLORS!: PENNSYLVANIA CIVIL WAR BATTLE FLAGS, VOL. II* **2nd Mississippi Infantry;** GETTY:4[16]143, GETTY:6[77]177 **5th Ohio Cavalry;** CWR:VOL4#1[44]164 **6th Mississippi Infantry;** CWTI:AUG/91[52]219 **8th New York Cavalry;** CWM:MAY/92[8]418 **8th Virginia Infantry;** CWTI:AUG/91[52]219 **11th Mississippi Infantry;** CWR:VOL2#4[269]145 **15th Virginia Infantry;** CWTI:JUL/94[44]394 **16th Maine Infantry;** CWM:MAY/92[15]419, GETTY:13[33]255 **19th Virginia Infantry;** CWTI:JUL/94[44]394

24th Michigan Infantry; GETTY:5[19]158
28th Massachusetts Infantry; CWM:MAR/91[17]335,
  CWTI:DEC/90[58]185
28th Virginia Infantry; B&G:AUG/94[6]573
39th Indiana Infantry; B&G:OCT/95[36]614
81st New York Infantry; B&G:OCT/95[36]614
83d Pennsylvania Infantry; B&G:AUG/94[38]578
145th Pennsylvania Infantry; B&G:AUG/94[38]578
Cherokee Braves; CWM:SEP/92[8]437, CWM:SEP/92[38]443
Choctaw Brigade Flag; CWM:SEP/92[8]437
Museum of the Confederacy; B&G:APR/95[38]598
Restoration; B&G:FEB/91[34]442, B&G:OCT/95[36]614

FLANAGAN, JOHN, *Private, 10th West Virginia Infantry;*
  B&G:OCT/94[28]581
FLANDREAU, STEPHEN B., *Private, 8th Louisiana Infantry;*
  CWTI:FEB/91[12]189
FLANIGAN, HARRIS, *Governor of Arkansas;*
  ACW:SEP/92[66]381, B&G:JUN/91[10]452
FLANIGAN, MARK, *Lieutenant Colonel, 24th Michigan
  Infantry;* CWM:MAR/91[17]335, GETTY:5[19]158
FLANNER, HENRY, *Colonel, CSA;* CWR:VOL2#2[118]136
FLAZER, LEWIS, *Private, 53rd Pennsylvania Infantry;*
  GETTY:11[80]235
FLECK, ANDREW G., *Private, 53rd Pennsylvania Infantry;*
  GETTY:11[80]235
FLEET, CHARLES B., *Sergeant, Fredericksburg Artillery:*
ARTICLE: "THE FREDERICKSBURG ARTILLERY AT
  APPOMATTOX," CWR:VOL1#1[35]104
ADDITIONAL LISTINGS: CWR:VOL1#1[1]102
FLEETWOOD, CHRISTIAN, *Private, USCT;*
  ACW:NOV/95[8]552
FLEMING, C.S., *Captain, 2nd Florida Infantry;*
  ACW:SEP/93[8]429
FLEMING, SETON, *Captain, 2nd Florida Battalion;*
  CWR:VOL3#4[1]161
FLEMING, VIVIAN, *Private, 2nd Richmond Howitzers;*
  CWR:VOL4#4[70]180
FLETCHER, JAMES, *Corporal, 3rd Vermont Infantry;*
  ACW:JAN/94[8]447
FLETCHER, THOMAS, *Colonel, USA;* B&G:JUN/91[10]452
FLING, B.M., *Captain, Maine State Guard;*
  CWTI:SEP/92[40]282
FLIPPIN, J.B., *Sergeant, 3rd Virginia Cavalry;*
  B&G:APR/92[48]484
FLOOD, JOEL, *Major, 2nd Virginia Cavalry;*
  CWR:VOL1#1[35]104
FLORENCE, ALABAMA, ENGAGEMENT AT; ARTICLE:
  "YANKEE INVADERS CAUGHT UNPREPARED,"
  CWM:OCT/95[36]616

FLORIDA TROOPS:
1st Infantry; B&G:AUG/94[22]576, B&G:AUG/95[8]604,
  CWR:VOL3#4[1]161, GETTY:13[50]257
1st Reserves; ACW:NOV/91[64]336
1st Special Battalion:
ARTICLE: "FROM OLUSTEE TO APPOMATTOX: THE 1ST
  FLORIDA SPECIAL BATTALION," CWR:VOL3#1[65]151
BOOK REVIEW: *HEAVY ARTILLERY AND LIGHT INFANTRY: A
  HISTORY OF THE 1ST FLORIDA SPECIAL BATTALION
  AND 10TH INFANTRY REGIMENT, C.S.A.*
ADDITIONAL LISTING: CWR:VOL3#4[1]161

2nd Cavalry:
ARTICLE: "THE GRAY FOX OF DIXIE," ACW:NOV/95[38]556
ADDITIONAL LISTINGS: ACW:NOV/91[64]336, CWR:VOL3#1[65]151
2nd Cavalry, (USCT); ACW:NOV/91[64]336, CWM:APR/95[50],
  CWR:VOL4#2[136]
2nd Infantry:
ARTICLE: "THE 2ND FLORIDA MADE A LONG JOURNEY
  FROM ITS SANDY HOME STATE TO THE KILLING
  FIELDS OF VIRGINIA," ACW:SEP/93[8]429
ADDITIONAL LISTINGS: ACW:SEP/93[8]429, CWR:VOL3#1[65]151,
  CWR:VOL3#4[1]161, CWR:VOL4#2[136], GETTY:8[111]206,
  GETTY:12[7]241, GETTY:12[111]250, GETTY:13[50]257
3rd Infantry; B&G:AUG/95[8]604
4th Infantry; B&G:AUG/95[8]604, CWR:VOL3#4[1]161
5th Cavalry; ACW:NOV/91[64]336
5th Infantry; ACW:SEP/93[8]429, CWR:VOL3#1[65]151,
  CWR:VOL3#4[1]161, GETTY:12[7]241, GETTY:12[111]250
6th Infantry; CWR:VOL3#1[65]151, CWR:VOL3#4[1]161
8th Infantry; ACW:SEP/93[8]429, CWR:VOL3#1[65]151,
  CWR:VOL3#4[1]161, CWR:VOL4#4[101]181,
  CWTI:MAR/89[28]103, GETTY:13[50]257
9th Infantry; CWR:VOL3#1[65]151, CWR:VOL3#4[1]161
10th Infantry:
ARTICLE: "FROM OLUSTEE TO APPOMATTOX: THE 1ST
  FLORIDA SPECIAL BATTALION," CWR:VOL3#1[65]151
BOOK REVIEW: *HEAVY ARTILLERY AND LIGHT INFANTRY: A
  HISTORY OF THE 1ST FLORIDA SPECIAL BATTALION
  AND 10TH INFANTRY REGIMENT, C.S.A.*
ADDITIONAL LISTING: CWR:VOL3#1[65]151
11th Infantry; CWR:VOL3#4[1]161
18th Infantry; B&G:FEB/91[34]442
Dunham's Light Artillery; ACW:NOV/91[64]336
Florida Brigade:
ARTICLE: "JOSEPH FINEGAN'S FLORIDA BRIGADE AT COLD
  HARBOR," CWR:VOL3#4[1]161
ADDITIONAL LISTINGS: ACW:SEP/93[8]429, CWR:VOL3#1[65]151,
  CWR:VOL3#2[1]153, CWR:VOL3#2[61]154, GETTY:5[89]162,
  GETTY:7[51]190
Florida Light Artillery; CWR:VOL3#1[65]151
Gamble's Battery; ACW:NOV/91[64]336
Marion Light Artillery; CWR:VOL3#4[1]161

FLORIDA, STATE OF:
ARTICLE: "THE NORTH'S SOUTHERNMOST OUTPOST,"
  ACW:NOV/94[58]499
BOOK REVIEWS: *BLOCKADERS, REFUGEES &
  CONTRABANDS—CIVIL WAR ON FLORIDA'S GULF
  COAST 1861-65 * CONFEDERATE FLORIDA: THE ROAD
  TO OLUSTEE * FLORIDA DURING THE CIVIL WAR*
FLORY, AARON M., *Lieutenant Colonel, USA;*
  CWR:VOL4#2[1]165
FLOURNOY, GEORGE, *Colonel, 16th Texas Infantry;*
  AHI:JUN/70[30]127, CWR:VOL3#3[33]158
FLOYD, ELDRIDGE G., *Colonel, USA;* AHI:SEP/83[12]234
FLOYD, FREDERICK C., *Sergeant, 40th New York Infantry;*
  ACW:JUL/93[16]422
FLOYD, JAMES; AHI:MAY/66[12]101
FLOYD, JOHN B, *General, CSA:*
ARTICLE: "FORMULA FOR DISASTER," CWM:JAN/92[34]404
GENERAL LISTINGS: *Forts Henry and Donelson,*
  B&G:FEB/92[10]474, *John Brown,* AHI:AUG/76[34]171, *in
  book review,* B&G:APR/91[28], CWM:APR/95[50],
  CWNEWS:APR/92[4], CWNEWS:OCT/92[4], *letters to the*

editor, B&G:APR/92[6]480, *West Virginia campaign,* B&G:AUG/93[10]529, *photos,* ACW:SEP/94[31]486, B&G:FEB/92[10]474, CWM:JAN/92[34]404, CWTI:APR/90[56]155
ADDITIONAL LISTINGS: ACW:JUL/91[43]315, ACW:JUL/92[22]368, ACW:SEP/92[38]379, ACW:MAR/93[10]402, ACW:MAR/93[18]403, ACW:JUL/94[35]478, ACW:SEP/94[31]486, AHI:FEB/76[14]165, B&G:AUG/91[11]458, CWM:JAN/92[4]397, CWR:VOL1#3[7]118, CWR:VOL4#3[50]171, CWTI:DEC/89[34]136, CWTI:FEB/90[26]143, CWTI:APR/90[56]155, CWTI:MAY/92[45]266, CWTI:JUL/92[29]272, CWTI:JUL/93[29]326, CWTI:SEP/93[59]341, CWTI:JUL/94[44]394, CWTI:DEC/94[49]413, CWTI:JAN/95[24]424
FLOYD-JONES, DELANCEY, *Major, 11th U.S. Infantry;* ACW:NOV/94[50]498
FLUKER, OSCAR E., *Corporal, Sumter Artillery;* CWR:VOL3#2[61]154
FLYE, WILLIAM, *Lieutenant, USN;* AHI:NOV/75[38]163, CWM:JUL/93[15]484
FLYNN, CHRISTOPHER, *Corporal, 14th Connecticut Infantry;* GETTY:9[61]215
FLYNN, JOHN H., *engineer;* CWTI:FEB/92[10]246
FOARD, A.J., *Surgeon, CSA;* CWM:MAY/91[10]347
FOERING, JOHN O., *Captain, 28th Ohio Infantry;* GETTY:9[81]216
FOGG, H.M.R., *Major, CSA;* B&G:FEB/93[12]511
FOLEY, JAMES, *Captain, USA;* ACW:MAR/92[46]354
FOLEY, SHADRACK, *Major, 14th Pennsylvania Cavalry;* B&G:JUN/92[46]490, GETTY:11[19]232
FOLEY, THOMAS, *Sergeant, 124th New York Infantry;* CWM:DEC/94[40]550
FOLGER, WILLIAM H., *Captain, 19th Maine Infantry;* GETTY:13[50]257
FOLK, ——, *Colonel, 6th North Carolina Cavalry;* CWM:SEP/92[16]438
FOLLENSBEE, CHARLES, *Captain, 7th Massachusetts Infantry;* ACW:NOV/95[30]555
FOLLETT, CHARLES D., *Captain, 8th New York Cavalry;* B&G:FEB/95[8]590A
FOLLETT, JOSEPH L., *1st Missouri Light Artillery;* B&G:FEB/93[40]514
FOLTZ, CHRISTIAN, *Lieutenant, 116th Pennsylvania Infantry;* CWR:VOL4#4[47]179
FONDA, J.G., *Colonel, 118th Illinois Infantry;* B&G:FEB/94[8]550
FONDA, TEN EYCK H., *telegrapher;* ARTICLE: "A MIDNIGHT RIDE," CWTI:MAR/94[24]370
FONTAINE, JOHN B., *Surgeon, CSA;* ACW:MAY/94[35]469
FONTAINE, LAMAR, *Major, CSA:*
ARTICLE: "A LIFE STORY LARGER THAN LIFE," CWTI:JUN/90[74]164
ADDITIONAL LISTINGS: AHI:JUL/68[31]115A, AHI:DEC/77[46]177
FONTAINE, S.J., *Captain, CSA;* ACW:JAN/93[51]398
FOOSHE, JOHN, *Private, 2nd South Carolina Infantry;* GETTY:5[35]159
FOOT, ALFRED, *Lieutenant, USA;* CWR:VOL1#4[7]125
FOOTE, ANDREW H., *Captain, USN;* B&G:FEB/92[10]474, CWM:FEB/95[32]562, CWR:VOL1#3[7]118, CWR:VOL2#1[36]132, CWTI:FEB/90[26]143, CWTI:FEB/90[32]144, CWTI:MAY/94[16]380, *photo;* B&G:FEB/92[10]474

FOOTE, FRANK, *Private, 48th Mississippi Infantry;* GETTY:4[7]142, GETTY:5[89]162
FOOTE, SHELBY; ARTICLES: "THE CIVIL WAR", CWTI:SEP/90[48]178, "IT WAS JUST MADNESS: INTERVIEW WITH SHELBY FOOTE," ACW:MAR/91[30]295
FORAKER, JOE, *Lieutenant, USA;* B&G:DEC/95[9]615
FORBES, EDWIN, *artist:*
ARTICLE: "THE ARTIST AND THE CIVIL WAR," AHI:NOV/80[28]211
BOOK REVIEW: *THIRTY YEARS AFTER: AN ARTIST'S MEMOIR OF THE CIVIL WAR*
ADDITIONAL LISTINGS: ACW:MAY/94[58], B&G:FEB/94[36], B&G:JUN/94[5]567, CWM:NOV/92[10]447, CWTI:FEB/92[18]
FORBES, EUGENE, *Private, USA;* CWM:JAN/92[16]401
FORBES, HENRY C., *Captain, 7th Illinois Cavalry;* ACW:MAY/92[47]363, B&G:JUN/93[12]524
FORBES, JOHN M.; CWNEWS:JUN/93[5]
FORBES, STEPHEN A., *Sergeant, USA;* B&G:JUN/93[12]524
FORCE, MANNING F., *General, USA:*
BOOK REVIEW: *FROM FORT HENRY TO CORINTH*
ADDITIONAL LISTINGS: ACW:JAN/95[30]505, B&G:AUG/95[8]604, B&G:DEC/95[9]615, CWTI:SUMMER/89[40]123, CWTI:JAN/93[20]298
FORD'S THEATER, WASHINGTON D.C.:
ARTICLES: "EYEWITNESSES REMEMBER THE 'FEARFUL NIGHT,'" CWTI:MAR/93[12]307, "FORD'S THEATRE ON STAGE," AHI:FEB/86[20]258, "FORD'S THEATRE," AHI:FEB/86[12]257, "HERITAGE OR HOAX?" CWTI:SEP/94[24]399, "THE LIVELY PAGEANTRY OF DEATH," CWTI:DEC/95[90]483, "OUR 'OUR AMERICAN COUSIN': A SYNOPSIS," AHI:FEB/86[24]259, "VISITING THE SITE OF ABRAHAM LINCOLN'S ASSASSINATION GIVES HISTORY BUFFS AN EERIE SENSE OF STEPPING BACK IN TIME," ACW:MAY/95[68]529, "WHAT REALLY HAPPENED TO THE ASSASSIN?" CWTI:JUL/92[50]275
ADDITIONAL LISTINGS: ACW:MAR/93[35]405, ACW:SEP/95[62], AHI:APR/86[4], AHI:MAY/86[4], AHI:JUN/86[4], AHI:APR/89[43]284, B&G:DEC/95[44]617, CWTI:DEC/91[28]239, *photos,* AHI:FEB/86[12]257
FORD, A.P., *Corporal, CSA;* B&G:DEC/95[9]615
FORD, ANTONIA, *female spy;* AHI:DEC/73[10]152
FORD, CHARLES, *Captain, 6th Wisconsin Infantry;* GETTY:4[24]145
FORD, CHARLES W., *Private, 126th New York Infantry;* CWR:VOL1#4[7]125
FORD, CHRISTOPHER A., *Private, 2nd Tennessee Cavalry;* CWR:VOL4#1[1]163
FORD, DANIEL, *Private, 9th Massachusetts Infantry;* CWTI:JUN/90[28]158
FORD, GEORGE W., *Major, USA;* CWTI:APR/92[49]260
FORD, JAMES H., *Colonel, USA;* B&G:JUN/91[10]452
FORD, JOHN "RIP", *Colonel, CSA;* ACW:JUL/92[46]371
FORD, JOHN S., *Colonel, CSA;* CWTI:AUG/90[58]169
FORD, T.J., *Sergeant, 24th Wisconsin Infantry;* ACW:MAR/92[14]350
FORD, THOMAS H., *Colonel, USA;* CWR:VOL1#4[7]125, GETTY:7[51]190, MH:AUG/95[30]185
FOREIGN AFFAIRS; ARTICLES: "MONTREAL'S POSH REBEL RENDEVOUS," CWTI:JAN/93[44]302, "THE PRISONER AND THE PRIME MINISTER," CWTI:JUL/93[38]328, "THEY CAME TO WATCH," CWTI:DEC/94[73]416

ADDITIONAL LISTINGS, CWM: CWM:JAN/91[40]330, CWM:MAR/91[39]338, CWM:JUL/92[24]430, CWM:JUL/92[40]432, CWM:JUL/92[4]425, CWM:NOV/92[10]447, CWM:JUN/94[58]519, CWM:OCT/94[48]542, CWM:DEC/94[49]553, CWM:FEB/95[32]562, CWM:FEB/95[36]563

ADDITIONAL LISTINGS, CWR: CWR:VOL1#4[42]126, CWR:VOL1#4[64]127, CWR:VOL2#1[36]132, CWR:VOL2#3[212]142, CWR:VOL2#4[313]146, CWR:VOL3#3[33]158, CWR:VOL4#1[1]163

ADDITIONAL LISTINGS, CWTI: CWTI:FEB/90[38]145, CWTI:FEB/92[42]250, CWTI:MAY/92[74]268, CWTI:JUL/92[42]274, CWTI:MAY/93[38]321, CWTI:SEP/93[14]333, CWTI:JAN/94[18]357, CWTI:MAY/94[44]384

ADDITIONAL LISTINGS: GETTY:11[19]232, MH:DEC/95[58]188

FORREST, WILLIAM M., *Captain, CSA;* CWTI:SEP/93[59]341

FORSHEY, C.G., *Colonel, CSA;* ACW:JAN/93[51]398

FORSYTH, CHARLES, *Lieutenant Colonel, 3rd Alabama Infantry;* B&G:FEB/95[8]590B

FORSYTH, GEORGE A., *Colonel, USA:*

BOOK REVIEW: *HERO OF BEECHER ISLAND: THE LIFE AND MILITARY CAREER OF GEORGE A. FORSYTH*

GENERAL LISTINGS: *Beecher's Island,* AHI:DEC/67[4]113, *Five Forks,* B&G:APR/92[8]481, *photo;* AHI:DEC/67[4]113

FORSYTH, JAMES W.; ACW:JUL/93[42]425, CW:SEP/94[55]489

FORT ANDERSON, NORTH CAROLINA; B&G:DEC/94[10]585, CWM:SEP/92[16]438

FORT BARRANCAS, FLORIDA; CWR:VOL1#4[42]126

FORT BARTOW, NORTH CAROLINA; CWM:FEB/95[49]565

FORT BELKNAP, TEXAS; ACW:NOV/91[10]329

FORT BISLAND, LOUISIANA, BATTLE OF; ACW:MAY/93[54], CWR:VOL3#1[1]149, CWR:VOL4#2[104]168, CWR:VOL4#2[68]167

FORT BLAKELY, ALABAMA:

ARTICLE: "FROZEN IN TIME," CWTI:DEC/94[24]409

ADDITIONAL LISTINGS: ACW:SEP/92[16]376, CWR:VOL1#1[42]105, CWTI:AUG/95[14]454, CWTI:MAR/95[18]432, MH:APR/94[54]176, MH:DEC/95[58]188, *photo;* CWTI:DEC/94[24]409

FORT BLANCHARD, NORTH CAROLINA; CWM:FEB/95[49]565

FORT BLISS, TEXAS; B&G:JUN/94[8]568

FORT BRADY, VIRGINIA; ACW:SEP/95[30]545

FORT BRANCH, NORTH CAROLINA; ACW:MAR/95[12]513

FORT CALHOUN, VIRGINIA; ACW:JAN/95[74]510

FORT CANBY, WASHINGTON; ARTICLE: "FORTS STEVENS AND CANBY STOOD A LONG VIGIL PROTECTING THE PACIFIC COAST FROM ATTACK," ACW:MAR/92[62]355

FORT CASWELL, NORTH CAROLINA; B&G:DEC/94[10]585, CWM:JUN/94[50]518

FORT CLARK, NORTH CAROLINA; ACW:MAR/94[35]460

FORT COBUN, MISSISSIPPI; CWR:VOL3#3[33]158

FORT CRAIG, NEW MEXICO; ACW:JAN/91[10]283, B&G:JUN/94[8]568, CWM:MAY/93[16]475, CWR:VOL2#2[161]139, CWTI:OCT/95[56]471, *photo;* CWTI:OCT/95[56]471

FORT CRATER, VIRGINIA, BATTLE OF; ARTICLE: "FORT CRATER REVISITED: CORRESPONDENCE FROM OUR READERS," CWR:VOL2#4[361]148, "GLORY ENOUGH: THE 148TH PENNSYLVANIA VOLUNTEERS AT FORT CRATER," CWR:VOL2#2[141]137

FORT DARLING, VIRGINIA; CWM:JUL/93[15]484, CWM:JUN/95[39]586

FORT DE RUSSY, LOUISIANA; ACW:JAN/91[16]284, ACW:MAR/95[18]514, CWR:VOL4#2[26]166, CWR:VOL4#2[68]167, CWR:VOL4#2[118]169, MH:DEC/95[58]188

FORT DELAWARE STATE PARK, DELAWARE; ACW:NOV/93[66]445

FORT DELAWARE, DELAWARE:

ARTICLE: "FORT DELAWARE ON THE WATER: A MONUMENT TO RUGGED REBELS," CWTI:JUL/93[20]325, "INFAMOUS FOR DELAWARE WON AN UNWELCOME REPUTATION AS THE 'NORTHERN ANDERSONVILLE,'" ACW:NOV/93[66]445

FORT DICKERSON, KENTUCKY; CWTI:MAY/94[50]386

FORT DONELSON NATIONAL BATTLEFIELD; B&G:FEB/92[10]474, B&G:FEB/92[48]475

FORT DONELSON, TENNESSEE, BATTLE OF:

ARTICLES: "A CONFEDERATE SURGEON'S VIEW OF FORT DONELSON: THE DIARY OF JOHN KENNERLY FARRIS," CWR:VOL1#3[7]118, "FORMULA FOR DISASTER," CWM:JAN/92[34]404, "FORTS HENRY & DONELSON: UNION VICTORY ON THE TWIN RIVERS," B&G:FEB/92[10]474, "FORTS HENRY AND DONELSON FALL TO 'UNCONDITIONAL SURRENDER' GRANT!" CWM:FEB/95[32]562

BOOK REVIEWS: *FORTS HENRY AND DONELSON: THE KEY TO THE HEARTLAND * THE LIFE AND WARS OF GIDEON J. PILLOW * PIERCING THE HEARTLAND: A HISTORY AND TOUR GUIDE OF THE FORT DONELSON, SHILOH, AND PERRYVILLE CAMPAIGNS*

GENERAL LISTINGS: *general history,* AHI:MAY/71[3]133A, *in book review,* ACW:SEP/95[62], B&G:FEB/95[26], CWM:AUG/94[9], CWM:APR/95[50], CWM:JUN/95[6], CWM:AUG/95[45], CWR:VOL4#3[1]170, CWR:VOL4#3[89], CWTI:MAR/94[12], *letters to the editor,* B&G:APR/92[6]480, CWM:JUL/91[6]355, *sketch of fighting,* CWTI:FEB/90[26]143

ADDITIONAL LISTINGS: ACW:JAN/91[22]285, ACW:JUL/92[22]368, ACW:MAR/93[10]402, ACW:SEP/93[6]428, ACW:JAN/94[10]448, ACW:MAR/95[8]512, ACW:SEP/95[38]546, B&G:FEB/92[48]475, CWM:JAN/92[4]397, CWM:MAR/93[8]465, CWM:OCT/95[22]614, CWM:DEC/95[48]631, CWR:VOL1#3[v]117, CWR:VOL2#1[i]129, CWR:VOL2#1[36]132, CWR:VOL3#3[59]159, CWR:VOL3#4[24]162, CWR:VOL4#3[50]171, CWTI:FEB/90[26]143, CWTI:FEB/90[32]144, CWTI:APR/90[56]155, CWTI:AUG/91[62]221, CWTI:JUL/93[14]324, CWTI:SEP/93[18]334, CWTI:SEP/93[59]341, CWTI:DEC/94[57]414, CWTI:DEC/94[79]417, CWTI:DEC/95[67]481

FORT FILLMORE, NEW MEXICO; ACW:JAN/91[10]283, ACW:JUL/93[27]423, B&G:JUN/94[8]568, CWM:MAY/93[16]475, CWR:VOL2#2[161]139, CWTI:OCT/95[56]471

FORT FISHER NATIONAL HISTORIC LANDMARK; CWR:VOL2#3[252]144

FORT FISHER STATE HISTORIC SITE; CWM:JUL/91[35]369, CWM:MAR/91[39]338, CWM:NOV/91[35]392

FORT FISHER, NORTH CAROLINA, BATTLE OF:

ARTICLES: "BEN BUTLER'S POWDER BOAT SCHEME," ACW:JAN/95[38]506, "CAMPAIGN TO SAVE FORT

FISHER," AHI:MAY/91[12]294, "FORT FISHER RECEIVES STATE FUNDS," AHI:MAR/92[8]300, "THE LAST RAYS OF DEPARTING HOPE: THE FALL OF WILMINGTON," B&G:DEC/94[10]585, "SERGEANT EDWARD KING WIGHTMAN: LETTERS HOME DURING THE FORT FISHER CAMPAIGN," AHI:SEP/83[12]234

BOOK REVIEWS: *CONFEDERATE GOLIATH: THE BATTLE OF FORT FISHER*

ADDITIONAL LISTINGS: ACW:JAN/91[47]288, ACW:MAY/92[14]358, ACW:NOV/93[12]440, ACW:SEP/95[30]545, AHI:MAY/71[3]133A, B&G:DEC/91[38]471, B&G:FEB/95[5]589, B&G:DEC/95[9]615, CWM:MAR/91[17]335, CWM:MAR/91[39]338, CWM:JUL/91[35]369, CWM:JUN/94[50]518, CWM:APR/95[50], CWNEWS:DEC/95[29], CWR:VOL2#3[183]140, CWR:VOL2#3[194]141, CWTI:DEC/91[44]241, CWTI:MAY/93[29]319, CWTI:OCT/95[32]468, *photos,* B&G:DEC/94[10]585

FORT GAINES, ALABAMA:

ARTICLE: "GUARDIANS OF MOBILE BAY," CWTI:MAR/94[20]369

ADDITIONAL LISTINGS: CWM:JUL/93[24]485, CWM:AUG/94[25]524, CWR:VOL1#4[v]124, CWR:VOL1#4[64]127, CWTI:DEC/94[24]409, CWTI:JUL/94[10]389, *photo;* CWTI:MAR/94[20]369

FORT GARLAND, COLORADO; ACW:NOV/91[10]329

FORT GIBSON, INDIAN TERRITORY; ACW:JAN/91[30]286

FORT GILMER, VIRGINIA; CWR:VOL1#1[71]107

FORT GREGG, VIRGINIA; ACW:NOV/92[74]390, B&G:AUG/91[30]460, B&G:DEC/91[38]471, CWR:VOL2#3[236]143, CWR:VOL3#2[1]153, CWR:VOL3#2[61]154, CWTI:AUG/90[26]166

FORT GREGG, SOUTH CAROLINA; GETTY:12[111]250

FORT GRIFFIN, TEXAS; CWM:OCT/95[47]620, CWTI:MAY/91[8]205

FORT GRIGSBY, TEXAS; CWTI:DEC/90[29]182

FORT HAMILTON, NEW YORK; CWTI:NOV/92[49]292

FORT HARDEMAN, GEORGIA; B&G:FEB/91[8]439

FORT HARRISON, VIRGINIA, BATTLE OF:

ARTICLE: "COSTLY UNION RECONNAISSANCE," ACW:JUL/94[42]479

ADDITIONAL LISTINGS: ACW:MAY/92[30]361, ACW:SEP/95[74]550, CWM:AUG/94[30]527, CWR:VOL1#1[1]102, CWR:VOL1#1[71]107, CWR:VOL4#2[136], MH:APR/95[46]183, *photo;* ACW:MAY/92[30]361

FORT HASKELL; ACW:NOV/92[74]390

FORT HATTERAS, NORTH CAROLINA; ACW:MAR/94[35]460

FORT HEIMAN, TENNESSEE; B&G:FEB/92[10]474

FORT HENRY, TENNESSEE, BATTLE OF:

ARTICLES: "FORTS HENRY & DONELSON: UNION VICTORY ON THE TWIN RIVERS," B&G:FEB/92[10]474, "FORTS HENRY AND DONELSON FALL TO 'UNCONDITIONAL SURRENDER' GRANT!" CWM:FEB/95[32]562,

BOOK REVIEWS: *FORTS HENRY AND DONELSON: THE KEY TO THE CONFEDERATE HEARTLAND * FROM FORT HENRY TO CORINTH*

GENERAL LISTINGS: *general history,* AHI:MAY/71[3]133A, *in book review,* ACW:SEP/95[62], *in book review,* CWM:JUN/95[6], *letters to the editor,* B&G:APR/92[6]480, *photo (1937);* B&G:FEB/92[10]474

ADDITIONAL LISTINGS: ACW:JAN/91[22]285, ACW:JUL/92[22]368, ACW:MAR/93[8]401, ACW:SEP/93[6]428, ACW:MAR/95[8]512,

CWM:JAN/92[34]404, CWM:MAR/93[8]465, CWR:VOL1#3[7]118, CWR:VOL2#1[36]132, CWTI:FEB/90[26]143, CWTI:FEB/90[32]144, CWTI:DEC/94[57]414

FORT HINDMAN, ARKANSAS, BATTLE OF:
AHI:MAY/71[3]133A, CWR:VOL1#4[77], CWR:VOL2#1[69]133, CWR:VOL3#3[92], CWTI:FEB/90[38]145, CWTI:MAY/94[16]380

FORT HOLMES, NORTH CAROLINA; B&G:DEC/94[10]585

FORT HUGER, NORTH CAROLINA; CWM:FEB/95[49]565

FORT JACKSON, GEORGIA; B&G:FEB/91[8]339

FORT JACKSON, LOUISIANA:

ARTICLE: "FORT JACKSON, GUARDIAN OF NEW ORLEANS AND THE LOWER MISSISSIPPI, WAS LONG THOUGHT TO BE IMPREGNABLE," ACW:JAN/92[62]346

ADDITIONAL LISTINGS: ACW:MAY/92[16]359, ACW:JAN/94[70]454, ACW:SEP/95[8]542, CWR:VOL1#4[77], CWTI:SEPT/91[20]127, CWTI:MAY/93[29]319, CWTI:DEC/94[34]411, MH:FEB/92[8]156, MH:AUG/93[47]169

FORT JEFFERSON, FLORIDA; B&G:APR/92[36]483, CWTI:APR/90[12]150

FORT JOHNSON, SOUTH CAROLINA; CWTI:JAN/94[46]364

FORT LAMAR, SOUTH CAROLINA; CWM:MAY/92[27]421

FORT LEAVENWORTH, KANSAS; ACW:MAR/94[8]456, CWM:SEP/92[8]437, CWTI:SEP/90[52]179, CWTI:MAR/91[34]201

FORT LOUDON, KNOXVILLE, KENTUCKY; CWTI:MAY/94[50]386

FORT MAGRUDER; ACW:MAR/91[47]297, ACW:SEP/93[8]429, CWM:JUN/95[34]584

FORT MAHONE; CWR:VOL3#2[1]153, CWR:VOL3#2[61]154

FORT MASON, TEXAS; ARTICLE: "LEE'S LAST U.S. ARMY POST," B&G:APR/92[58]485

FORT McALLISTER HISTORIC PARK, GEORGIA; B&G:FEB/91[8]339, CWTI:DEC/94[62]415

FORT McALLISTER, GEORGIA:

ARTICLE: "GATEWAY TO THE ATLANTIC," CWTI:DEC/94[62]415

ADDITIONAL LISTINGS: ACW:SEP/92[47]380, B&G:FEB/91[8]439, CWTI:MAR/95[18]432, *photos,* B&G:FEB/91[8]339, CWTI:DEC/94[62]415

FORT McCULLOCH, INDIAN TERRITORY; ACW:JAN/91[30]286

FORT McHENRY, MARYLAND; CWTI:OCT/95[24]466, MH:FEB/91[8]151

FORT McREE; CWR:VOL1#4[42]126

FORT MONROE, VIRGINIA;

ARTICLES: "JEFF DAVIS' LIVING TOMB," CWTI:MAY/93[20]317, "FORT MONROE," ACW:MAY/91[62]307

BOOK REVIEW: *DEFENDER OF THE CHESAPEAKE: THE STORY OF FORT MONROE*

ADDITIONAL LISTINGS: ACW:MAR/91[47]297, ACW:MAR/93[42]406, ACW:JAN/95[74]510, CWM:MAR/91[35]337, CWM:JUN/95[24]582, CWM:JUN/95[76]598, CWR:VOL2#4[269]145, CWR:VOL4#2[68]167, CWTI:JUN/90[28]158, CWTI:AUG/90[70]171, CWTI:AUG/91[68]222, CWTI:MAY/93[29]319, CWTI:MAY/94[40]383, *photos;* AHI:MAY/71[3]133A, ACW:MAY/91[62]307, ACW:MAR/93[42]406

FORT MORGAN, ALABAMA:

ARTICLES: "DETAILS OF THE SIEGE OF FORT MORGAN, ALABAMA," CWM:AUG/94[25]524, "GUARDIANS OF MOBILE BAY," CWTI:MAR/94[20]369

ADDITIONAL LISTINGS: CWM:JUL/93[24]485, CWTI:DEC/94[24]409, MH:FEB/92[8]156

FORT MORTON, VIRGINIA; CWR:VOL2#2[141]137

FORT MOULTRIE, SOUTH CAROLINA;
AHI:MAY/66[12]101, B&G:FEB/91[8]439,
CWR:VOL2#3[194]141, CWTI:MAR/94[38]372,
GETTY:12[111]250

FORT PEMBERTON, MISSISSIPPI; CWR:VOL3#3[59]159

FORT PICKENS, FLORIDA; CWR:VOL1#4[42]126,
CWR:VOL2#4[269]145, CWTI:MAR/93[24]309,
CWTI:MAR/95[8]431

FORT PILLOW, TENNESSEE, BATTLE OF:
ARTICLES: "A LEGACY OF CONTROVERSY: FOR PILLOW STILL STANDS," CWTI:SEP/93[18]334, "BETWIXT WIND AND WATER," CWTI:NOV/93[65]351, "FORT PILLOW: VICTORY OR MASSACRE?" AHI:APR/74[4]154, "WE WILL ALWAYS STAND BY YOU," CWTI:NOV/93[71]352
BOOK REVIEWS: *THE FORT PILLOW MASSACRE: THE REASON WHY * UNERRING FIRE: THE MASSACRE AT FORT PILLOW*
GENERAL LISTINGS: *general history,* AHI:MAY/71[3]133A, *in book review,* CWR:VOL1#3[94], CWTI:MAR/89[10], *letters to the editor,* CWM:NOV/92[6]446, CWM:JUL/93[4]482, CWTI:JAN/94[8]356, CWTI:MAR/94[16]368, CWTI:MAY/94[12]37
ADDITIONAL LISTINGS: ACW:MAR/91[30]295, ACW:MAR/95[18]514, AHI:APR/74[4]154, B&G:DEC/91[38]471, CWM:NOV/92[10]447, CWR:VOL2#4[313]146, CWTI:JAN/94[18]357, CWTI:JAN/94[35]361

FORT PILLOW STATE HISTORIC AREA; ARTICLE: "A LEGACY OF CONTROVERSY: FORT PILLOW STILL STANDS," CWTI:SEP/93[18]334

FORT POINT, CALIFORNIA:
ARTICLE: "TRACES OF A DISTANT WAR," CWTI:JUN/95[51]449
ADDITIONAL LISTING: CWTI:JUN/95[48]448

FORT POWELL; CWM:JUL/93[24]485, CWM:AUG/94[25]524

FORT PULASKI NATIONAL MONUMENT;
B&G:FEB/91[8]339

FORT PULASKI, GEORGIA; ACW:SEP/93[10]430,
ACW:NOV/93[42]443, B&G:FEB/91[8]439,
B&G:OCT/91[11]466, B&G:DEC/94[6]584,
CWM:MAR/91[35]337, CWM:JUN/94[50]518,
CWTI:MAR/93[24]309, CWTI:DEC/94[49]413,
CWTI:OCT/95[28]467, GETTY:12[111]250, *photos,*
B&G:FEB/91[8]439, B&G:OCT/91[11]466

FORT QUITMAN, TEXAS; CWM:MAY/93[16]475

FORT SANDERS, TENNESSEE:
ARTICLE: "ICY ASSAULT ROUTED," ACW:MAY/91[23]303
ADDITIONAL LISTINGS: CWTI:MAR/93[40]312, CWTI:JAN/95[34]427

FORT SCOTT, KANSAS; ACW:JAN/93[26]395,
CWTI:SEP/90[52]179

FORT SEDGWICK, VIRGINIA; CWR:VOL3#2[1]153,
CWTI:AUG/90[26]166

FORT SMITH, ARKANSAS; CWM:SEP/92[38]443

FORT SNELLING, MINNESOTA; ACW:MAY/91[12]302,
ACW:JAN/94[62], GETTY:5[79]161

FORT ST. PHILIP, LOUISIANA; ACW:MAY/92[16]359,
ACW:MAY/93[12]412, ACW:JAN/94[70]454,
ACW:SEP/95[8]542, CWTI:SEPT/89[20]127,
CWTI:MAY/93[29]319, CWTI:DEC/94[34]411,
MH:FEB/92[8]156, MH:AUG/93[47]169

FORT STANTON, NEW MEXICO; ACW:JAN/91[10]283,
CWM:MAY/93[16]475

FORT STEDMAN, VIRGINIA, BATTLE OF:
ARTICLE: "BATTLE IN DESPERATION," CWTI:MAR/95[33]435
ADDITIONAL LISTINGS: ACW:NOV/92[74]390, ACW:MAY/95[38]526,
ACW:SEP/95[74]550, AHI:MAY/71[3]133A,
AHI:SEP/87[40]263, B&G:APR/92[8]481, B&G:APR/92[24],
CWM:SEP/93[24]495, CWR:VOL1#3[94],
CWR:VOL2#3[236]143, CWR:VOL2#4[269]145,
CWTI:FEB/91[28]192, CWTI:FEB/92[18],
CWTI:JAN/95[34]427, MH:APR/95[46]183, *photo;*
CWTI:MAR/95[33]435

FORT STEVENS, OREGON:
ARTICLE: "FORTS STEVENS AND CANBY STOOD A LONG VIGIL PROTECTING THE PACIFIC COAST FROM ATTACK," ACW:MAR/92[62]355, "RECONSTRUCTION OF CIVIL WAR BATTERY UNDER WAY AT OREGON'S FORT STEVENS," AHI:MAR/91[8]293A,
ADDITIONAL LISTING: CWM:JUL/91[35]369

FORT STEVENS, WASHINGTON, D.C.;
ACW:NOV/93[50]444, B&G:DEC/92[8]503, *photo;*
CWTI:JAN/93[40]301

FORT SUMTER, SOUTH CAROLINA:
ARTICLES: "CIVIL WAR IN THE MAKING," ACW:MAY/94[43]470,
"FOCUS: CIVIL WAR PHOTOGRAPHY," AHI:OCT/79[18]193,
"GUSTAVE," CWTI:JUL/92[29]272, "ROBERT ANDERSON: RELUCTANT HERO," CWTI:MAY/92[45]266
BOOK REVIEWS: *FORT SUMTER * SUMTER: THE FIRST DAY OF THE CIVIL WAR*
GENERAL LISTINGS: *general history,* AHI:MAY/71[3]133A, *in book review,* CWR:VOL3#2[105], *James Buchanan,*
AHI:MAY/66[12]101, *letters to the editor,* CWM:MAY/91[6]345,
West Point, B&G:DEC/91[12]469
ADDITIONAL LISTINGS: ACW:MAY/91[31]304, ACW:MAR/93[18]403,
ACW:MAY/93[38]416, ACW:MAR/94[35]460,
ACW:SEP/94[46]488, ACW:NOV/94[58]499,
B&G:FEB/91[8]439, CWM:MAR/92[16]411,
CWM:MAR/93[32]468, CWM:SEP/93[8]493,
CWM:OCT/95[22]614, CWR:VOL1#2[7]111,
CWR:VOL2#3[183]140, CWR:VOL2#3[194]141,
CWR:VOL2#4[269]145, CWTI:APR/89[22]108,
CWTI:AUG/90[42]167, CWTI:AUG/91[36]217,
CWTI:SEP/92[46]284, CWTI:NOV/92[54]293,
CWTI:JAN/94[46]364, CWTI:MAR/94[38]372,
CWTI:DEC/95[52]480, CWTI:DEC/95[67]481

FORT TAYLOR, FLORIDA; ACW:NOV/94[58]499

FORT TOWSON, OKLAHOMA; ARTICLE: "FORT TOWSON: INDIAN TERRITORY POST THAT PLAYED A PART IN THE PEACE," B&G:OCT/94[38]582

FORT UNION, NEW MEXICO; ACW:NOV/91[10]329,
ACW:JUL/93[27]423, B&G:JUN/94[8]568,
CWR:VOL2#2[161]139, CWTI:OCT/95[56]471

FORT WADE, MISSISSIPPI; CWR:VOL3#3[33]158

FORT WAGNER, SOUTH CAROLINA, BATTLE OF; see listings under "BATTERY WAGNER"

FORT WARREN, MASSACHUSETTS; GETTY:10[7]221

FORT WOOL, VIRGINIA; ARTICLE: "VIRGINIA'S FORT WOOL SAW ACTIVE SERVICE FROM THE CIVIL WAR THROUGH WORLD WAR II," ACW:JAN/95[74]510

FORT YUMA, ARIZONA TERRITORY; ACW:JUL/93[27]423

FORT, DEWITT C., *Captain, CSA;* AHI:APR/74[4]154

FORT, ISAAC and SYLVESTER, *6th Wisconsin Infantry,*
GETTY:11[57]233

FORTESCUE, LOUIS, *Captain, USA;* CWR:VOL1#4[7]125,
GETTY:4[101]151

FORTS; BOOK REVIEWS: *THE ARMY CALLED IT HOME: MILITARY INTERIORS OF THE 19TH CENTURY * MR. LINCOLN'S FORTS: A GUIDE TO THE CIVIL WAR DEFENSES OF WASHINGTON*

FOSTER, ADRIAN H., *Private, 126th New York Infantry;* CWR:VOL1#4[7]125

FOSTER, HENRY B., *Private, 2nd Wisconsin Infantry,* GETTY:11[57]233

FOSTER, J.A., *Colonel, CSA;* CWTI:FEB/92[29]248

FOSTER, JAMES P., *Lieutenant Commander, USN;* CWTI:JUL/94[30]392

FOSTER, JAMES W., *Captain, 1st New York Cavalry;* CWTI:SEP/90[34]176

FOSTER, JOHN G., *General, USA;* ACW:SEP/92[47]380, B&G:FEB/91[8]439, CWR:VOL2#3[194]141, GETTY:12[111]250, MH:APR/93[39]166

FOSTER, ROBERT H., *Major, 148th Pennsylvania Infantry;* GETTY:10[53]225

FOSTER, ROBERT S., *General, USA;* ACW:JUL/94[42]479, CWM:AUG/94[30]527, GETTY:11[6]231

FOSTER, SAMUEL T., *Captain, 24-25th Texas Cavalry (dismounted);* CWTI:SUMMER/89[20]121

FOSTERS, FRANKLIN, *Sergeant Major, 9th New Hampshire Infantry;* CWR:VOL2#2[118]136

FOUKE, PHILIP B., *Colonel, 30th Illinois Infantry;* CWR:VOL3#4[24]162

FOURNET, GABIREL, LOUIS and VALSIN A., *10th Louisiana Infantry Battalion;* CWR:VOL3#1[1]149

FOURTEENTH AMENDMENT; AHI:JAN/82[16]224

FOWLER, EDWARD B., *Colonel, 84th New York Infantry;* B&G:AUG/93[36]533, CWR:VOL1#2[78], CWR:VOL4#4[129], GETTY:6[13]170, GETTY:7[83]192

FOWLER, FREDERICK, *Private, 5th New York Infantry;* CWR:VOL1#2[29]112, CWTI:MAY/94[31]382

FOWLER, HENRY, *Private, 12th Alabama Infantry;* ACW:SEP/93[31]433

FOWLER, JOSEPH S., *Senator, Tennessee;* AHI:DEC/68[28]118

FOX'S GAP, MARYLAND, BATTLE OF:
ARTICLE: "THE DEATH OF JESSE RENO," CWM:MAY/92[44]423
ADDITIONAL LISTING: ACW:JUL/93[58]

FOX, CHARLES B., *Colonel, 55th Massachusetts Infantry;* BOOK REVIEW: *RECORD OF THE SERVICE OF THE FIFTY-FIFTH REGIMENT OF MASSACHUSETTS VOLUNTEER INFANTRY*

FOX, GUSTAVUS V.:
BOOK REVIEW: *CONFIDENTIAL CORRESPONDENCE OF GUSTAVUS VASA FOX*
ADDITIONAL LISTINGS: ACW:JAN/92[62]346, ACW:JAN/93[51]398, ACW:JUL/93[34]424, ACW:JAN/95[38]506, ACW:SEP/95[30]545, AHI:MAY/71[3]133A, B&G:DEC/94[10]585, CWTI:JAN/93[10]297, CWTI:OCT/95[32]468, MH:AUG/92[26]161

FOX, HIRAM, *Private, 14th Connecticut Infantry;* GETTY:6[7]169

FOX, JAMES, *engineer, USN;* CWTI:DEC/90[29]182

FOX, THOMAS B., *Captain, 2nd Massachusetts Infantry;* GETTY:6[69]176, GETTY:7[83]192

FOX, TRYPHENA B.H., BOOK REVIEW: *A NORTHERN WOMAN IN THE PLANTATION SOUTH: LETTERS OF TRYPHENA BLANCHE HOLDER FOX, 1856-1876*

FOX, WILLIAM F., *Lieutenant Colonel, USA;* GETTY:12[123]251

FRACHTLING, JULIUS, *Private, 8th Louisiana Infantry;* CWTI:FEB/91[12]189

FRALEY, JAMES M., *Lieutenant, 2nd Tennessee Cavalry;* CWR:VOL4#1[1]163

FRANCE:
BOOK REVIEW: *THE UNITED STATES AND FRANCE: CIVIL WAR DIPLOMACY,* AHI:JAN/75[50]
Mercier, Ambassador Henri; CWTI:MAY/89[28]117
Napoleon III; CWTI:MAY/89[28]117

FRANCINE, LOUIS R., *Colonel, 7th New Jersey Infantry;* B&G:FEB/92[22]476

FRANK, PAUL, *Colonel, 52nd New York Infantry;* ACW:MAY/93[31]415, B&G:APR/95[8]595, CWR:VOL2#4[269]145

FRANKE, WILLIAM, *Private, 24th Michigan Infantry,* GETTY:11[57]233

FRANKENTHAL, MAX; CWTI:MAY/92[38]265

FRANKLIN, A.B., *Lieutenant, 8th Vermont Infantry;* CWR:VOL3#1[1]149

FRANKLIN, CHARLES B., *Private, 16th Massachusetts Infantry;* GETTY:12[7]241

FRANKLIN, EMLEN, *colonel, USA;* CWM:DEC/94[40]550, GETTY:9[5]209

FRANKLIN, TENNESSEE, BATTLE OF:
ARTICLES: "THE GALLANT HOOD OF TEXAS," ACW:MAR/94[42]461, "THE TRIALS AND TRIBULATIONS OF FOUNTAIN BRANCH CARTER AND HIS FRANKLIN, TENNESSEE HOME," B&G:FEB/95[30]591
BOOK REVIEWS: *EMBRACE AN ANGRY WIND * HOOD'S CAMPAIGN FOR TENNESSEE * THE MARCH TO THE SEA, FRANKLIN AND NASHVILLE * SHROUDS OF GLORY*
GENERAL LISTINGS: *in book review,* CWM:JAN/91[47], CWM:OCT/94[8], CWM:APR/95[8], CWM:DEC/95[10], CWR:VOL2#2[169], CWR:VOL4#3[1]170
ADDITIONAL LISTINGS: ACW:MAR/91[30]295, ACW:MAR/92[14]350, B&G:JUN/91[26]453, B&G:OCT/91[11]466, B&G:DEC/91[34]470, B&G:DEC/93[12]545, B&G:JUN/94[32]570, CWM:MAR/91[28]336, CWM:MAR/92[27]412, CWM:DEC/94[49]553, CWR:VOL1#4[64]127, CWTI:FEB/90[54]147, MH:OCT/94[20]180

FRANKLIN, WILLIAM B., *General, USA:*
ARTICLES: "FIRING THE GAP," ACW:JAN/94[39]451, "THE MOST EXTRAORDINARY FEAT OF THE WAR," CWM:OCT/95[47]620
GENERAL LISTINGS: *Chantilly,* ACW:JAN/95[54]508, *Crampton's Gap,* B&G:OCT/95[8]611B, MH:AUG/95[30]185, *Fredericksburg,* AHI:JUN/78[4]180, CWR:VOL4#4[1]177, CWR:VOL4#4[101]181, CWR:VOL4#4[70]180, *general history,* AHI:MAY/71[3]133A, *Glendale,* CWM:JUN/95[69]596, *in book review,* CWM:OCT/94[8], CWM:FEB/95[7], CWNEWS:JAN/91[4], *Kelly's Ford,* ACW:NOV/91[30]332, *letters to the editor,* CWM:DEC/95[5]625, *Peninsula Campaign,* CWM:JUN/95[37]585, *Sabine Pass,* CWTI:DEC/90[29]182, *Savage's Station,* CWM:JUN/95[65]595, *photos;* ACW:JAN/94[39]451, CWM:OCT/95[47]620, CWTI:DEC/90[29]182
ADDITIONAL LISTINGS: ACW:JUL/91[35]314, ACW:MAR/95[42]517, B&G:FEB/93[40]514, CWM:APR/95[39]576, CWR:VOL1#4[7]125, CWR:VOL3#2[1]153, CWR:VOL3#3[1]157, CWR:VOL4#2[1]165,

CWR:VOL4#2[26]166, CWR:VOL4#2[104]168,
CWR:VOL4#4[i]175, CWR:VOL4#4[v]176,
CWR:VOL4#4[1]177, CWTI:DEC/89[62]139,
CWTI:SEP/93[43]338, CWTI:SEP/94[49]404,
MH:DEC/95[58]188

FRASER, J.C., *Captain, Pulaski (Georgia) Artillery;*
GETTY:8[53]203

FRASER, ROBERT, *Private, Rockbridge Artillery;*
CWR:VOL4#4[70]180

FRAYSER'S FARM, VIRGINIA, BATTLE OF; see listings
under **"WHITE OAK SWAMP, VIRGINIA, BATTLE OF"**

FRAYSER, RICHARD E., *Captain, CSA;* ACW:JUL/95[34]536,
GETTY:4[110]152

FRAZEE, HIRAM W., *Sergeant, 2nd New York Artillery;*
AHI:AUG/68[4]115B

FRAZER, CHARLES, *Private, 125th Pennsylvania Infantry;*
B&G:OCT/95[8]611A

FRAZER, JOHN W., *General, CSA;* ACW:JUL/91[26]313,
ACW:JUL/95[44]537, GETTY:13[108]261

FRAZER, PHILIP, *Pvt., 7th Wisc. Inf.,* GETTY:11[57]233

FRAZIER, GEORGE and JOHN C., *2nd Tennessee Cavalry;*
CWR:VOL4#1[1]163

FRAZIER, JULIUS, *Colonel, USA;* ACW:MAR/92[46]354

FRAZIER, ROBERT, *Pvt., 2nd Tenn. Cav.;* CWR:VOL4#1[1]163

FREDERICK, MARYLAND; ARTICLE: "WAR COMES TO
FREDERICK," ACW:JAN/91[38]287

**FREDERICKSBURG & SPOTSYLVANIA NATIONAL
MILITARY PARK;** B&G:FEB/91[34]442,
B&G:DEC/91[38]471, B&G:JUN/94[38]571

FREDERICKSBURG (VIRGINIA) ARTILLERY:
ARTICLES: "THE FIRST GUN AT GETTYSBURG: 'WITH THE
CONFEDERATE ADVANCE GUARD,'" CWR:VOL1#1[26]103,
"THE FREDERICKSBURG ARTILLERY AT APPOMATTOX,"
CWR:VOL1#1[35]104, "FROM EACHO'S FARM TO
APPOMATTOX: THE FREDERICKSBURG ARTILLERY"
CWR:VOL1#1[1]102

ADDITIONAL LISTINGS: B&G:FEB/95[8]590A, CWR:VOL1#1[69]106,
GETTY:10[107]227

**FREDERICKSBURG RAILROAD BRIDGE, VIRGINIA,
ENGAGEMENT OF;** GETTY:11[6]231

FREDERICKSBURG, VIRGINIA; B&G:OCT/91[11]466

**FREDERICKSBURG, VIRGINIA, BATTLE AND
CAMPAIGN OF:**
ARTICLES: "THE 20TH MASSACHUSETTS INFANTRY AND
THE STREET FIGHT FOR FREDERICKSBURG,"
CWR:VOL4#4[101]181, "THE BATTLE OF
FREDERICKSBURG," AHI:JUN/78[4]180, "THE BATTLE OF
FREDERICKSBURG REVISITED," CWR:VOL4#4[i]175,
"'THE BREATH OF HELL'S DOOR': PRIVATE WILLIAM
MCCARTER AND THE IRISH BRIGADE AT
FREDERICKSBURG," CWR:VOL4#4[47]179, "BRIEF
BREACH AT FREDERICKSBURG," ACW:MAR/95[42]517,
"'BUSTED UP AND GONE TO HELL': THE ASSAULT OF
THE PENNSYLVANIA RESERVES AT
FREDERICKSBURG," CWR:VOL4#4[1]177, "DESPERATE
COURAGE," CWTI:DEC/90[58]185, "THE GLORIOUS LIGHT
WENT OUT FOREVER: THE DEATH OF BRIG. GENERAL
THOMAS R.R. COBB," CWR:VOL4#4[28]178,
"INTRODUCTION," CWR:VOL4#4[v]176, "RETURN TO
FREDERICKSBURG," ACW:SEP/92[30]378, "STONEWALL
JACKSON'S ARTILLERISTS AND THE DEFENSE OF THE
CONFEDERATE RIGHT," CWR:VOL4#4[70]180, "THROUGH
'MURDEROUS FIRE AT FREDERICKSBURG,'"

CWM:DEC/94[74]555, "THE YANKEES OF THE
HARD-FIGHTING IRISH BRIGADE WERE SO BRAVE
THAT THE CONFEDERATES HATED HAVING TO SHOOT
THEM," ACW:MAY/94[12]466

BOOK REVIEWS: *ACROSS THE RAPPAHANNOCK: FROM
FREDERICKSBURG TO THE MUD MARCH * THE
ANTIETAM AND FREDERICKSBURG * THE
FREDERICKSBURG CAMPAIGN: DECISION ON THE
RAPPAHANNOCK * LEE'S TERRIBLE SWIFT SWORD *
"STONEWALL" JACKSON AT FREDERICKSBURG: THE
BATTLE OF PROSPECT HILL: DECEMBER 13, 1862 * THE
U.S. ARMY WAR COLLEGE GUIDE TO THE BATTLES OF
CHANCELLORSVILLE AND FREDERICKSBURG*

GENERAL LISTINGS: *general history,* AHI:MAY/71[3]133A, *in book
review,* ACW:MAR/93[58], ACW:SEP/94[66],
ACW:MAY/95[62], CWM:DEC/94[7], CWNEWS:MAY/89[4],
CWNEWS:JAN/91[4], CWNEWS:JAN/93[4],
CWNEWS:APR/93[4], CWR:VOL1#3[94], CWR:VOL1#4[77],
CWR:VOL2#2[169], CWR:VOL2#4[346], CWR:VOL3#1[80],
CWR:VOL3#2[105], CWR:VOL3#3[92], CWR:VOL4#2[136],
letters to the editor, CWTI:JUL/93[10]323

ADDITIONAL LISTINGS: ACW:NOV/91[35]333, ACW:MAY/92[8]357,
ACW:JUL/92[12]367, ACW:NOV/92[8]383,
ACW:MAY/93[8]411, ACW:MAR/94[16]458,
ACW:JAN/95[20]504, ACW:JAN/95[46]507,
ACW:MAY/95[18]524, ACW:SEP/95[54]548,
B&G:JUN/92[8]487, CWM:MAR/91[35]337,
CWM:MAR/91[65]342, CWM:NOV/91[12]390,
CWM:MAY/92[15]419, CWM:JUL/92[8]427,
CWM:SEP/93[24]495, CWM:OCT/95[22]614,
CWM:DEC/95[34]628, CWM:DEC/95[41]630

ADDITIONAL LISTINGS, continued: CWR:VOL1#1[1]102,
CWR:VOL1#1[71]107, CWR:VOL1#2[29]112,
CWR:VOL1#2[42]113, CWR:VOL1#3[28]120,
CWR:VOL1#3[52]122, CWR:VOL2#2[141]137,
CWR:VOL3#1[31]150, CWR:VOL3#2[1]153,
CWR:VOL3#3[1]157, CWTI:APR/89[14]107,
CWTI:APR/89[38]111, CWTI:DEC/89[34]136,
CWTI:SEP/91[31]229, CWTI:DEC/91[82]243,
CWTI:SEP/92[42]283, CWTI:MAY/93[26]318,
CWTI:JUL/93[29]326, CWTI:JUL/93[42]329,
CWTI:MAR/94[38]372, CWTI:JUL/94[44]394,
CWTI:SEP/94[26]400, CWTI:JAN/95[34]427,
CWTI:MAR/95[26]434, CWTI:JUN/95[18]444,
CWTI:JUN/95[90]451, CWTI:DEC/95[67]481,
GETTY:13[108]261, MH:JUN/94[8]177, MH:AUG/94[46]178

FREDERICKSBURG, VIRGINIA, SECOND BATTLE OF;
CWR:VOL3#2[1]153

FREDERICKSON, GEORGE, *Lieutenant, USN;*
AHI:NOV/75[38]163, CWM:JUL/93[15]484

FREE-SOIL PARTY; AHI:OCT/68[4]116

FREEDMEN'S BUREAU:
BOOK REVIEW: *THE FREEDMEN'S BUREAU IN LOUISIANA*
ADDITIONAL LISTINGS: AHI:APR/73[12]148, AHI:JAN/82[16]224,
CWM:FEB/95[68]567, GETTY:11[71]234

FREEDOM; BOOK REVIEWS: *FREEDOM'S LAWMAKERS: A
DIRECTORY OF BLACK OFFICEHOLDERS DURING
RECONSTRUCTION * FREEDOM: A DOCUMENTARY
HISTORY OF EMANCIPATION, 1861-1867 * THE
WARTIME GENESIS OF FREE LABOR: THE UPPER
SOUTH*

FREEMAN, CHRISTOPHER C., *Private, Sumter Artillery;*
CWR:VOL3#2[1]153

FREEMAN, DANIEL B., *Private, 10th Vermont Infantry;* CWR:VOL4#3[89], CWTI:JAN/93[40]301

FREEMAN, GEORGE D., *Private, 53rd Pennsylvania Infantry;* GETTY:11[80]235

FREEMAN, J.R., *Colonel, 2nd Missouri Cavalry;* ACW:MAR/92[46]354

FREEMAN, MAITLAND J., *Private, 7th Wisconsin Infantry,* GETTY:11[57]233

FREEMAN, S.L., *Captain, CSA;* CWM:DEC/95[48]631

FREEMAN, SIMEON N., *Master, USN;* B&G:JUN/92[40]489

FREEMAN, THOMAS J., *Colonel, 22nd Tennessee Infantry;* B&G:JUN/91[10]452, CWR:VOL3#4[24]162

FREEMEN, JAMES, *Private, 2nd Tennessee Cavalry;* CWR:VOL4#1[1]163

FREEPORT DOCTRINE; ACW:MAY/93[47]417

FREMANTLE, ARTHUR J.L.:
BOOK REVIEWS: *THREE MONTHS IN THE SOUTHERN STATES, APRIL-JUNE 1863*
GENERAL LISTINGS: *Bragg,* B&G:OCT/92[10]496, *Gettysburg,* GETTY:4[110]152, GETTY:5[4]156, GETTY:6[94]180, GETTY:6[113]183, GETTY:7[13]186, *in book review,* ACW:MAY/92[54], CWM:MAR/91[74], CWM:DEC/95[10], CWNEWS:OCT/92[4], *letters to the editor,* CWTI:MAR/95[18]432
ADDITIONAL LISTINGS: ACW:JUL/95[10]533, ACW:NOV/95[8]552, CWTI:SEPT/89[46]132, CWTI:DEC/94[73]416, GETTY:13[75]259

FREMONT (ILLINOIS) RIFLES; ARTICLE: "THE FREMONT RIFLES: THE 37TH ILLINOIS AT PEA RIDGE AND PRAIRIE GROVE," CWR:VOL1#1[42]105

FREMONT'S BODYGUARD; ARTICLE: "TAKING OFF THE KID GLOVES," ACW:MAR/92[46]354

FREMONT, JESSIE BENTON:
ARTICLE: "JESSIE BENTON FREMONT," AHI:SEP/87[21]262
BOOK REVIEW: *THE LETTERS OF JESSIE BENTON FREMONT*
ADDITIONAL LISTINGS: AHI:SEP/87[21]262, AHI:MAY/70[4]126

FREMONT, JOHN C., *General, USA:*
ARTICLE: "A SINGLE STEP," CWTI:MAR/94[29]371, "BLACK BEAVER," AHI:MAY/67[34]108, "FREMONT AND HIS FRIEND," AHI:AUG/66[32]104, "JOHN C. FREMONT," AHI:MAY/70[4]126, "TAKING OFF THE KID GLOVES," ACW:MAR/92[46]354
BOOK REVIEW: *FREMONT, PATHMAKER OF THE WEST * THE LETTERS OF JESSIE BENTON FREMONT*
GENERAL LISTINGS: *abolition,* ACW:NOV/95[8]552, *election of 1864,* AHI:OCT/68[4]116, *general history,* AHI:MAY/71[3]133A, *Henry Halleck,* AHI:MAY/78[10]179, *in book review,* ACW:JUL/92[54], CWM:DEC/95[10], *Jackson,* B&G:JUN/92[8]487, *Presidential contender,* ACW:NOV/94[42]497, *Shenandoah Valley,* ACW:JAN/93[35]396, CWTI:JUN/95[18]444, *Thaddeus Stevens,* AHI:JAN/82[16]224, *photos;* ACW:NOV/94[34]496, AHI:AUG/66[32]104, AHI:MAY/70[4]126, AHI:MAY/71[3]133A, AHI:SEP/87[21]262, CWM:MAY/93[8]474, CWTI:FEB/90[26]143, CWTI:SEP/90[22]173, CWTI:MAR/94[29]371
ADDITIONAL LISTINGS: ACW:JUL/91[35]314, ACW:JAN/92[8]338, ACW:MAR/92[6]347, ACW:JUL/92[22]368, ACW:MAR/93[8]401, ACW:MAR/93[18]403, ACW:JUL/93[8]420, ACW:NOV/93[26]441, ACW:NOV/94[34]496, AHI:SEP/87[21]262, AHI:SEP/89[20]286, B&G:FEB/92[10]474, B&G:AUG/92[26]494, B&G:FEB/93[12]511

ADDITIONAL LISTINGS, continued: CWM:MAR/91[39]338, CWM:MAY/93[8]474, CWR:VOL1#1[42]105, CWR:VOL3#4[24]162, CWTI:FEB/90[26]143, CWTI:APR/90[48]154, CWTI:FEB/92[29]248, CWTI:MAR/94[48]374, CWTI:MAY/94[46]385, CWTI:JAN/95[22]423, CWTI:JUN/95[32]446, CWTI:AUG/95[34]457, CWTI:AUG/95[58]461, CWTI:DEC/95[67]481

FRENCH, BASSETT, *Colonel, CSA;* CWM:SEP/91[40]385

FRENCH, BENJAMIN B.; BOOK REVIEW: *WITNESS TO THE YOUNG REPUBLIC: A YANKEE'S JOURNAL, 1828-1870*

FRENCH, DAVID A., *Captain, CSA;* B&G:FEB/92[10]474, B&G:APR/92[6]480

FRENCH, EDWIN W., *Captain, 1st Connecticut Cavalry;* ACW:JAN/92[16]340

FRENCH, HENRY, *Private, 11th Veteran Reserve Corps;* B&G:APR/93[24]520

FRENCH, HENRY, *Commander, CSN;* MH:DEC/94[46]181

FRENCH, HENRY A.L., *Lieutenant, 12th New Hampshire Infantry;* GETTY:12[7]241

FRENCH, JOHN W., *civilian;* B&G:DEC/91[12]469

FRENCH, NAPOLEON B.; B&G:APR/92[6]480

FRENCH, SAMUEL G., *General, CSA;* ACW:SEP/92[38]379, ACW:SEP/94[10]484, ACW:SEP/95[54]548, B&G:DEC/93[12]545, B&G:AUG/95[8]604, CWM:JAN/91[12]326, CWM:DEC/94[49]553, CWNEWS:MAY/90[4], CWR:VOL1#1[1]102, CWR:VOL1#1[73]108, CWR:VOL2#4[269]145, CWR:VOL3#2[1]153, CWR:VOL3#3[59]159, CWTI:SUMMER/89[20]121, CWTI:MAR/93[24]309, MH:APR/94[54]176

FRENCH, WILLIAM H., *General, USA:*
ARTICLE: "'THE MUSKET BALLS FLEW VERY THICK': HOLDING THE LINE AT PAYNE'S FARM," CWM:MAY/92[20]420
GENERAL LISTINGS: *Antietam,* ACW:MAR/94[50]462, B&G:OCT/95[8]611A, *Falling Waters,* GETTY:9[109]218, *Fredericksburg,* CWR:VOL4#4[28]178, *in book review,* CWNEWS:MAY/90[4], CWR:VOL4#2[136], CWR:VOL4#3[1]170, *Jackson,* B&G:JUN/92[8]487, *photo;* ACW:MAR/93[26]404, CWM:MAY/92[20]420
ADDITIONAL LISTINGS: ACW:MAR/92[30]352, ACW:MAR/93[26]404, ACW:JUL/93[50]426, ACW:MAY/94[12]466, ACW:NOV/94[50]498, ACW:NOV/94[58]499, AHI:JUN/78[4]180, B&G:APR/91[8]445, B&G:AUG/91[32]461, CWM:MAR/93[24]467, CWM:VOL3#1[31]150, CWR:VOL3#2[1]153, CWR:VOL4#4[28]178, CWR:VOL4#4[47]179, CWTI:AUG/95[24]455

FREUNTHAL, MAX, *Private, 16th Mississippi Infantry;* CWM:SEP/93[8]493

FRICK, JACOB G., *Lieutenant Colonel, 96th Pennsylvania Infantry;* CWR:VOL3#3[1]157

FRIEND, CHARLES, *Union veteran;* GETTY:7[119]195

FRIEND, THOMAS, *Captain, CSA;* CWTI:JUL/94[44]394

FRIENDS OF SOUTHERN FREEDOM; ACW:NOV/92[35]387

FRITCHIE, BARBARA; ACW:JAN/91[38]287

FRITZ, LEVI J., *Private, 53rd Pennsylvania Infantry;* GETTY:11[80]235

FROBEL, BUSHROD W., *Lieutenant Colonel, CSA;* B&G:FEB/91[8]439, CWNEWS:SEP/94[33]

FRONT ROYAL, VIRGINIA, 1862, BATTLE OF; ACW:JAN/92[8]338, ACW:MAY/92[14]358,

ACW:JUL/94[10]475, ACW:MAY/95[10]523,
CWM:SEP/93[24]495
FROST, DANIEL M, *General, CSA;* ACW:MAY/91[31]304,
ACW:SEP/92[38]379, ACW:MAY/94[26]468,
ACW:SEP/94[10]484, B&G:AUG/93[24], B&G:FEB/94[8]550,
CWM:MAY/93[8]474, CWR:VOL1#1[42]105,
CWTI:MAR/91[34]201, *photo;* CWM:MAY/93[8]474
FROST, FRANK, *Captain, CSA;* B&G:AUG/94[22]576
FROST, GRIFFIN, *Captain, USA;* CWTI:AUG/95[58]461,
CWTI:DEC/95[8]474
FROST, GRIFFIN, *Private, CSA;* BOOK REVIEW: *CAMP AND
PRISON JOURNAL: EMBRACING SCENES IN CAMP ON
THE MARCH AND IN PRISONS*
FRY, BIRKETT A., *General, CSA;* GETTY:13[75]259,
GETTY:6[13]170, GETTY:6[94]180, GETTY:8[67]204,
B&G:APR/94[10]558, B&G:FEB/95[8]590A,
CWR:VOL1#3[52]122, CWTI:JUL/93[34]327,
GETTY:12[61]245, GETTY:13[50]257, ACW:JAN/95[62],
CWTI:SEPT/89[46]132, GETTY:9[61]215
FRY, C.W., *Captain, Orange Artillery;* GETTY:4[33]146,
GETTY:4[49]147, GETTY:5[4]156, GETTY:9[17]210
FRY, DAVENPORT B., *General, CSA;* CWM:OCT/94[8]
FRY, JAMES B., *General, USA;* ACW:NOV/91[16]330,
ACW:SEP/94[8]483, AHI:NOV/72[12]142,
AHI:NOV/88[37]278, B&G:DEC/91[30], B&G:DEC/94[34]587,
CWNEWS:JUL/92[4]
FRY, SPEED S., *General, USA;* ACW:SEP/93[38]434,
B&G:FEB/93[12]511
FRYER, H.C., *Captain, CSA;* CWTI:DEC/94[49]413
FUGER, FREDERICK, *Sergeant, 4th U.S. Artillery;*
CWTI:JUL/93[29]326, MH:DEC/91[54]155
FUGITIVE SLAVE ACT; ACW:MAY/94[43]470,
ACW:NOV/94[42]497, AHI:MAY/66[12]101,
AHI:OCT/70[23]129, AHI:JUN/73[4]149, CWM:JAN/92[57],
CWNEWS:APR/92[4], CWNEWS:NOV/92[4],
CWR:VOL3#1[31]150, CWTI:MAY/93[20]317
FULKERSON, SAMUEL, *Colonel, CSA;* ACW:JAN/93[35]396,
CWTI:JUN/95[18]444
FULLER, BYAM, *Private, 24th Georgia Infantry;*
B&G:APR/93[24]520
FULLER, CHARLES A., *Lieutenant, 61st New York Infantry:*
BOOK REVIEW: *PERSONAL RECOLLECTIONS OF THE WAR OF
1861*
ADDITIONAL LISTINGS: GETTY:4[89]150, GETTY:12[97]249
FULLER, DENNIS M., *Private, 6th Wisconsin Infantry;*
GETTY:11[57]233
FULLER, EMILIUS W., *Captain, 6th New York Infantry;*
CWTI:JAN/95[42]428
FULLER, GUY W., *Captain, 16th Michigan Infantry;*
B&G:OCT/93[12]537, GETTY:6[33]172
FULLER, JOHN W., *General, USA;* B&G:DEC/95[9]615,
CWM:DEC/95[48]631, CWTI:JUL/94[50]395
FULLER, JOSEPH, *Private, CSA;* CWTI:APR/92[49]260
FULLER, WILLIAM A., ACW:SEP/91[22]321,
CWTI:FEB/92[10]246
FULLER, WILLIAM D., *Captain, 11th Louisiana Battalion;*
CWR:VOL4#2[151]170
FULLER, WILLIAM M., *Captain, Consolidated Crescent
Regiment;* CWR:VOL4#2[1]165
FULLERTON, HUGH, *Colonel, USA;* B&G:AUG/95[8]604
FULSHER, WALLACE, *Corporal, USA;* ACW:JUL/94[42]479
FULTON, CHARLES S., *Private, 7th Wisconsin Infantry;*
GETTY:11[57]233

FULTON, JOHN S., *Colonel, CSA;* CWTI:SEP/92[31]281
FULTON, WILLIAM F., *Colonel, 5th Alabama Infantry;*
GETTY:6[13]170, GETTY:7[13]186
FUNK, J.H.S., *Colonel, 5th Virginia Infantry;* CWR:VOL4#3[89],
GETTY:12[42]244
FUNKE, WILLIAM, *Private, 24th Michigan Infantry;*
GETTY:9[33]211
FUNSTEN, OLIVER R., *Colonel, CSA;* ACW:JAN/92[8]338,
CWTI:APR/89[38]111
FURST, LUTHER C., *Sergeant, USA:*
ARTICLE: "A SIGNAL SERGEANT AT GETTYSBURG: THE
DIARY OF LUTHER C. FURST," GETTY:10[42]224
ADDITIONAL LISTINGS: CWR:VOL4#4[1]177, GETTY:4[101]151,
GETTY:8[31]201, GETTY:10[42]224
FUSSEDER, FRANCIS, *Chaplain, 17th Wisconsin Infantry;*
CWM:MAR/91[50]340

G

GACHE, PERE LOUIS-HIPPOLYTE, *Chaplain, Louisiana Infantry;* B&G:AUG/93[24], CWM:SEP/93[24]495
GADBERRY, J.M., *civilian;* ACW:NOV/92[10]384
GADSDEN, JOHN, *attorney;* CWTI:MAY/92[38]265
GAGE'S (HUTCHINSON'S) BATTERY; B&G:AUG/92[40]495
GAGE, JEREMIAH, *Sergeant, 11th Mississippi Infantry;* ACW:MAR/92[10]349, CWR:VOL2#4[269]145
GAGER, EDWIN V., *Lieutenant, USN;* AHI:NOV/75[38]163, CWM:JUL/93[15]484
GAILLARD, FRANKLIN, *Lieutenant Colonel, 2nd South Carolina Infantry;* GETTY:5[35]159
GAILLARD, P.C., *Lieutenant Colonel, 9th South Carolina Infantry;* ACW:SEP/91[30]322, CWTI:JAN/94[46]364
GAINES' MILL, VIRGINIA, BATTLE OF:
ARTICLES: "CHARGE BAYONETS," CWTI:MAY/94[31]382, "DESTINY AT GAINES' MILL: ONE FAMILY'S ORDEAL," CWM:MAR/92[9]410, "DURYEE'S ZOUAVES: THE 5TH NEW YORK VOLUNTEER INFANTRY," CWR:VOL1#2[7]111, "INSPIRED BY ITS GALLANT COLOR-BEARERS, THE 1ST SOUTH CAROLINA MADE A BRAVE CHARGE AT GAINES' MILL," ACW:NOV/92[10]384, "THE PENINSULA CAMPAIGN OF 1862: THE BATTLE OF GAINES' MILL," CWM:JUN/95[61]593, "REGULARS TO THE RESCUE AT GAINES' MILL," ACW:NOV/94[50]498
BOOK REVIEW: *GAINES' MILL TO APPOMATTOX—WACO & MCCLENNAN COUNTY IN HOOD'S TEXAS BRIGADE*
GENERAL LISTINGS: *balloons,* B&G:AUG/91[20]459, *in book review,* CWM:JUN/95[6], CWR:VOL2#3[256], CWR:VOL3#2[105], *Jackson,* B&G:JUN/92[8]487, *letters to the editor,* B&G:DEC/91[6]468, CWM:OCT/94[5]533
ADDITIONAL LISTINGS: ACW:JUL/93[42]425, ACW:MAR/94[42]461, ACW:MAY/94[12]466, ACW:JAN/95[46]507, ACW:SEP/95[54]548, B&G:FEB/95[8]590B, CWM:MAR/92[4]408, CWM:MAR/93[32]468, CWM:SEP/93[24]495, CWM:AUG/95[30]606, CWR:VOL1#1[1]102, CWR:VOL1#2[7]111, CWR:VOL1#2[42]113, CWR:VOL1#3[28]120, CWR:VOL1#3[46]121, CWR:VOL2#4[269]145, CWR:VOL3#2[1]153, CWR:VOL3#3[1]157, CWTI:MAR/89[28]103, CWTI:APR/89[14]107, CWTI:MAY/89[36]118, CWTI:DEC/89[26]135, CWTI:DEC/89[34]136, CWTI:JUN/90[28]158, CWTI:DEC/91[36]240, CWTI:JUL/93[14]324, CWTI:JUL/93[42]329, CWTI:JUL/94[44]394, CWTI:JUN/95[32]446, CWTI:NOV/93[55]350
GAINES, SAM, *Captain, CSA;* B&G:AUG/93[10]529
GAINESVILLE, ALABAMA; CWTI:AUG/90[50]168
GAINESVILLE, FLORIDA; ACW:NOV/95[38]556
GAINESVILLE, TEXAS; CWM:APR/95[8]
GALBRAITH, WILLIAM, *Lieutenant, USA;* GETTY:4[101]151
GALE, GEORGE A., *Capt., 33rd NY Inf.;* CWM:SEP/93[18]494
GALENA, ILLINOIS;
ARTICLE: "GRANT'S EARLY WAR DAYS," ACW:NOV/94[34]496
ADDITIONAL LISTINGS: CWTI:FEB/90[12]141, CWTI:FEB/90[20]142, CWTI:FEB/90[26]143, CWTI:FEB/90[46]146, *photo,* ACW:NOV/94[34]496
GALLAGHER, CHARLIE, *Private, 69th New York Infantry;* CWM:MAR/91[17]335

GALLAGHER, JEREMIAH, *Sergeant, 69th Pennsylvania Infantry;* GETTY:4[89]150
GALLAGHER, THOMAS, *Colonel, USA;* ACW:JUL/92[30]369
GALLAHER, ALBERT H. and THOMAS J., *2nd Tennessee Cavalry;* CWR:VOL4#1[1]163
GALLAHER, JOHN F., *Lieutenant, CSA;* CWR:VOL4#1[1]163
GALLIE, JOHN, *Major, CSA;* B&G:FEB/91[8]339
GALLOWAY, A.H., *Capt., 45th NC Inf.;* B&G:FEB/95[8]590B
GALLOWAY, HENRY, *Sergeant, 92nd Ohio Infantry;* B&G:OCT/94[42]583
GALLOWAY, W.L., *Private, CSA;* CWTI:FEB/92[42]250
GALT, EDWARD, *Captain, CSA;* CWTI:DEC/94[49]413
GALT, F.L., *Lieutenant, CSN;* AHI:OCT/88[38]275
GALVANIZED YANKEES; ARTICLE: "A SOLDIER FOR TWO COUNTRIES," CWTI:MAR/95[90]440
GALVESTON, TEXAS, BATTLE OF; ACW:JAN/93[51]398, CWM:APR/95[8]
GALWAY, THOMAS F., *Private, 8th Ohio Infantry;* ACW:SEP/95[54]548, B&G:JUN/95[8]600, CWTI:NOV/92[49]292, GETTY:6[7]169
GAMBLE PLANTATION, FLORIDA; ARTICLE: "WILY JUDAH BENJAMIN ELUDED A FRENZIED NORTHERN MANHUNT AT FLORIDA'S LUXURIOUS GAMBLE PLANTATION," ACW:JUL/93[66]427
GAMBLE'S (FLORIDA) BATTERY; ACW:NOV/91[64]336
GAMBLE, WILLIAM, *Colonel, USA;* B&G:OCT/93[12]537, B&G:FEB/95[8]590A, CWM:MAR/91[17]335, GETTY:4[101]151, GETTY:4[75]149, GETTY:5[4]156, GETTY:5[103]163, GETTY:6[13]170, GETTY:11[19]232, GETTY:12[123]251, GETTY:13[22]254, *photos;* B&G:FEB/95[8]590A, GETTY:11[19]232
GAMBRILL, JAMES, *civilian;* B&G:DEC/92[8]503
GANAHL, JOSEPH, *Major, CSA;* CWTI:MAR/93[40]312
GANIER, ELIE and F.M., *18th Louisiana Infantry;* CWR:VOL4#2[1]165
GANN, DAVID, *Private, 1st Georgia Regulars;* CWR:VOL2#2[95]135
GANO, RICHARD M., *General, CSA;* CWM:SEP/92[38]443, CWR:VOL1#2[44]114
GANSEVOORT, HENRY S., *Colonel, 13th New York Infantry;* CWR:VOL4#1[78]
GANTT, THOMAS, *Colonel, USA;* CWTI:AUG/95[58]461
GANTZ, JACOB, *Private, 4th Iowa Cavalry;* BOOK REVIEW: *SUCH ARE THE TRIALS: THE CIVIL WAR DIARIES OF JACOB GANTZ*
GARDEN, HUGH, *Captain, Palmetto Light Artillery;* BOOK REVIEW: *SOUTHERN BRONZE: CAPT. GARDEN'S (S.C.) ARTILLERY COMPANY DURING THE WAR BETWEEN THE STATES*
GARDENER, THOMAS, *Corporal, 14th Connecticut Infantry;* GETTY:9[61]215
GARDINER, CHARLES, *Private, 1st Colorado Infantry;* B&G:AUG/94[6]573
GARDINER, HARRISON W., *Private, USA;* GETTY:10[42]224
GARDINER, JAMES, *Private, 36th USCT;* CWM:AUG/94[30]527
GARDINER, JOHN W.T., *Major, USA;* GETTY:8[43]202
GARDNER, ALEXANDER:
ARTICLE: "EDITORIAL," ACW:JAN/92[6]337
BOOK REVIEWS: *WITNESS TO AN ERA: THE LIFE AND PHOTOGRAPHS OF ALEXANDER GARDNER*
GENERAL LISTINGS: *in book review,* CWM:JAN/91[47], CWNEWS:MAY/92[4], *photo of Lincoln, Nicolay and Hay;*

CWTI:APR/89[28]109, *photos;* ACW:JAN/92[54],
ACW:NOV/95[54]558

ADDITIONAL LISTINGS: ACW:JUL/92[30]369, ACW:NOV/95[54]558,
AHI:FEB/86[12]257, AHI:NOV/88[37]278, AHI:SEP/89[20]286,
B&G:OCT/92[38]500, B&G:FEB/94[24]551,
CWTI:DEC/89[26]135, CWTI:MAR/91[22]199,
CWTI:MAY/91[34]209

GARDNER, FRANKLIN, *General, CSA;* ACW:MAR/92[40]353,
ACW:SEP/92[38]379, ACW:JAN/94[30]450,
ACW:SEP/95[8]542, B&G:JUN/93[12]524,
B&G:AUG/95[8]604, CWM:APR/95[28]573,
CWR:VOL2#1[36]132, MH:AUG/94[82]179

GARDNER, HENRY C., *Captain, Louisiana Tigers;*
CWTI:MAR/94[48]374

GARDNER, ISSAC W., *Private, 1st Ohio Light Artillery;*
GETTY:4[49]147

GARDNER, JAMES; B&G:FEB/94[24]551

GARDNER, WASHINGTON W., *Sergeant, 13th U.S. Regulars;*
CWR:VOL2#1[1]130

GARDNER, WILLIAM C., *Private, 6th Wisconsin Infantry:*
GETTY:11[57]233

GARDNER, WILLIAM M., *General, CSA;* B&G:APR/91[32]447,
CWR:VOL3#1[65]151

GARDNER, WILLIAM, *Surgeon, USA;* B&G:AUG/91[52]464,
B&G:DEC/91[6]468

GAREY, BARTLEY, *Corporal, 6th Tennessee Cavalry (Union);*
B&G:DEC/91[38]471, B&G:DEC/92[40]508

GARFIELD, JAMES A., *General, USA:*
ARTICLES: "A PRESIDENTIAL GALLERY," AHI:APR/89[20]282,
"THE ASSASSINATION OF GARFIELD AND THE TRIAL
OF HIS KILLER," AHI:FEB/69[12]119, "BEHIND THE
LINES," CWTI:AUG/90[8]165, "FROM LOG CABIN TO
OBLIVION," AHI:MAY/76[24]167, "THE HEARTBEAT IN
THE WHITE HOUSE," AHI:APR/70[38]125, "'TRUE
AMERICAN MADNESS': INAUGURAL BALLS,"
AHI:NOV/72[37]143

GENERAL LISTINGS: *election of 1864,* AHI:OCT/68[4]116, *Garfield
Monument;* AHI:APR/89[43]284, *Gettysburg,*
GETTY:7[23]187, *in book review,* CWM:DEC/94[7],
CWNEWS:NOV/92[4], CWNEWS:FEB/94[5], *Lawn Field;*
AHI:APR/89[43]284, *Mary Todd Lincoln,* AHI:MAY/75[4]159,
Nelson-Davis feud, AHI:NOV/72[12]142, *Tullahoma
Campaign,* B&G:OCT/92[10]496, *photos;* AHI:FEB/69[12]119,
AHI:APR/70[38]125, AHI:MAY/76[24]167,
AHI:APR/89[20]282, B&G:OCT/92[10]496

ADDITIONAL LISTINGS: ACW:JUL/91[35]314, ACW:JUL/92[62]372,
ACW:SEP/95[6]541, AHI:NOV/89[50]288,
AHI:NOV/90[44]293, B&G:FEB/94[38]553,
CWM:MAR/93[8]465, CWTI:FEB/90[60]148,
CWTI:SEP/90[22]173, CWTI:FEB/92[21]247,
MH:DEC/93[12]174

GARGER, ASHER W., *Lieutenant, Stanton Artillery;*
CWR:VOL4#4[70]180

GARIBALDI GUARDS, (39th New York Infantry):
ARTICLE: "FLAMBOYANT GARIBALDI GUARDS,"
ACW:MAY/95[54]528

ADDITIONAL LISTINGS: GETTY:7[51]190, GETTY:8[95]205,
MH:OCT/93[20]172

GARLAND, AUGUSTUS, *Senator from Arkansas;*
B&G:JUN/91[10]452

GARLAND, SAMUEL, *General, CSA;* ACW:JUL/93[58],
ACW:SEP/93[8]429, ACW:SEP/93[31]433,

B&G:FEB/95[8]590B, CWM:MAY/92[44]423,
CWR:VOL3#2[1]153

GARLAND, WILLIAM H., *Major, CSA;* B&G:JUN/93[12]524

GARNER, DANIEL N., *Sgt., 53rd Penna. Inf.;* GETTY:11[80]235

GARNETT'S FARM, VIRGINIA, BATTLE OF; ARTICLE: "THE
PENINSULA CAMPAIGN OF 1862: THE BATTLE OF
GARNETT'S FARM," CWM:JUN/95[63]594

GARNETT, ALEXANDER Y.P., *Surgeon, CSA;*
CWM:MAY/91[38]

GARNETT, JOHN J., *Major, CSA;* B&G:DEC/91[12]469,
CWR:VOL3#2[1]153

GARNETT, JOSEPH W., *Captain, 69th Pennsylvania Infantry;*
GETTY:7[97]193

GARNETT, RICHARD B., *General, CSA:*
ARTICLE: "THE DEATH AND BURIALS OF GENERAL
RICHARD BROOKE GARNETT," GETTY:5[107]164

GENERAL LISTINGS: *Gettysburg,* CWTI:JUL/93[29]326,
GETTY:4[89]150, GETTY:5[79]161, GETTY:5[103]163,
GETTY:6[33]172, GETTY:7[97]193, GETTY:8[67]204,
GETTY:9[61]215, GETTY:10[112]228, GETTY:12[61]245,
GETTY:12[111]250, MH:DEC/91[54]155, *Jackson,*
B&G:JUN/92[8]487, *in book review,* B&G:APR/95[30],
CWR:VOL4#3[89], *in list,* CWTI:JUL/93[34]327, *letters to the
editor,* CWTI:NOV/93[12]345

ADDITIONAL LISTINGS: ACW:JAN/93[35]396, ACW:SEP/94[62]490,
B&G:OCT/91[40]467, B&G:APR/94[34]561,
CWM:MAR/91[65]342, CWR:VOL3#2[1]153,
CWTI:MAY/89[22]116, CWTI:SEPT/89[46]132,
CWTI:SEP/93[43]338, CWTI:MAR/94[29]371,
CWTI:JUL/94[44]394, GETTY:5[107]164, GETTY:13[50]257,
GETTY:13[64]258, GETTY:13[75]259

GARNETT, ROBERT S., *General, CSA:*
BOOK REVIEW: *BATTLE AT CORRICKS FORD: CONFEDERATE
DISASTER AND LOSS OF A LEADER*
GENERAL LISTINGS: *in book review,* CWNEWS:FEB/94[5], *West
Virginia campaign,* B&G:AUG/93[10]529, *photo;*
B&G:AUG/93[10]529

ADDITIONAL LISTINGS: ACW:NOV/91[41]334, ACW:JAN/92[47]344,
ACW:JAN/92[50]345, ACW:SEP/92[38]379,
B&G:AUG/93[36]533, B&G:DEC/93[30]546,
CWTI:JAN/94[46]364

GARNETT, THEODORE S., *Colonel, 48th Virginia Infantry:*
BOOK REVIEWS: *RIDING WITH STUART: REMINISCENCES OF
AN AIDE-DE-CAMP*
ADDITIONAL LISTINGS: CWM:MAR/91[65]342, GETTY:13[108]261

GARNETT, THOMAS, *Colonel, CSA;* ACW:JUL/91[50]

GARRARD, ISRAEL, *Colonel, 7th Ohio Cavalry;*
CWR:VOL4#1[1]163

GARRARD, KENNER, *General, USA:*
GENERAL LISTINGS: *Atlanta Campaign,*
CWTI:SUMMER/89[13]120, CWTI:SUMMER/89[50]124, *order
of battle,* B&G:DEC/93[12]545, *West Point,*
B&G:DEC/91[12]469, *photos;* B&G:DEC/91[12]469,
B&G:DEC/94[22]586

ADDITIONAL LISTINGS: ACW:MAR/92[30]352, B&G:APR/92[58]485,
B&G:DEC/94[22]586, CWR:VOL1#3[82]123,
CWTI:SUMMER/89[20]121, CWTI:SUMMER/89[40]123,
CWTI:MAY/92[48]267, CWTI:NOV/92[41]291,
GETTY:9[48]213, MH:DEC/95[58]188

GARRARD, THEOPHILUS T., *General, USA;*
ACW:JUL/94[51]480, B&G:FEB/94[8]550

GARRETT, JOHN W., *President of Baltimore & Ohio Railroad;*
ACW:NOV/93[50]444, B&G:DEC/92[8]503,

B&G:AUG/94[10]574, CWM:NOV/91[40]393,
CWTI:APR/89[38]111, CWTI:MAR/91[22]199,
CWTI:SEP/92[22]279, CWTI:JAN/93[40]301
GARRETT, RICHARD; CWTI:MAY/91[48]211
GARRETT, WILLIAM M., *Major, CSA;* B&G:FEB/91[20]440
GARRISON, WILLIAM LLOYD:
GENERAL LISTINGS: *Cassius M. Clay,* AHI:MAY/69[12]121, *in book
review,* CWM:JAN/91[47], CWNEWS:NOV/91[4], *Underground
Railroad,* AHI:JAN/78[34]178, *photos;* ACW:NOV/95[54]558,
CWTI:AUG/90[50]168
ADDITIONAL LISTINGS: ACW:NOV/95[54]558, AHI:JAN/73[28]147,
AHI:JAN/93[61]309, CWTI:DEC/89[42]137,
CWTI:AUG/90[50]168, CWTI:DEC/95[52]480
GARROTT, ISHAM W., *Colonel, 20th Alabama Infantry;*
ACW:JUL/94[51]480, B&G:FEB/94[8]550,
B&G:FEB/94[57]555, CWR:VOL2#1[36]132
GARY, M.M., *Private, 22nd Virginia Infantry;*
CWR:VOL1#3[52]122
GARY, MARTIN W., *General, CSA;* ACW:MAY/92[30]361,
ACW:JUL/94[42]479, AHI:JAN/73[28]147,
CWM:AUG/94[30]527, CWR:VOL3#2[70]155,
CWTI:APR/92[49]260
GARY, SAMUEL W., *Lt., 3rd Virginia Inf.;* GETTY:12[111]250
GASNELL, W.T., *Lieutenant, CSN;* ACW:NOV/91[8]328
GASTON (NORTH CAROLINA) GUARDS; GETTY:5[13]157
GASTON, CHARLES; CWTI:AUG/95[46]459
GASTON, JAMES H., *Capt., 42nd Miss. Inf.;* GETTY:4[22]144
GASTON, STEPHEN M., *Private, 9th Indiana Cavalry;*
B&G:AUG/95[24]605
GATES, THEODORE B.; *Colonel, 20th New York Infantry;*
BOOK REVIEW: *THE CIVIL WAR DIARIES OF COLONEL
THEODORE B. GATES, 20TH NEW YORK STATE MILITIA*
ADDITIONAL LISTINGS: B&G:DEC/93[6]544, B&G:FEB/95[8]590A,
CWNEWS:JUN/92[4], GETTY:4[89]150, GETTY:13[22]254
GATLIN, A.D., *Lieutenant, 11th Mississippi Infantry;*
GETTY:9[98]217
GATLING, DR. RICHARD J.:
ARTICLE: "DR. GATLING AND HIS AMAZING GUN,"
AHI:JUN/66[52]102, "THE SEARCH FOR THE ULTIMATE
WEAPON," CWTI:JAN/93[49]303, "WEAPONRY,"
MH:OCT/93[12]171
ADDITIONAL LISTINGS: ACW:JUL/93[8]420, CWTI:JAN/93[49]303,
photo; AHI:JUN/66[52]102
GATTON, W.F., *Private, 35th Virginia Cavalry;*
B&G:APR/93[24]520
GAULEY BRIDGE, WEST VIRGINIA, BATTLE OF;
ACW:SEP/94[31]486
GAUS, JACOB, *Corporal, CSA;* CWTI:NOV/93[65]351
GAUSE, ISSAC, *Corporal, CSA;* CWM:SEP/93[8]493
GAUSE, W.R., *Colonel, 3rd Missouri (Confederate) Infantry;*
B&G:FEB/94[8]550, CWR:VOL2#1[1]130
GAVIN, JAMES, *Colonel, USA;* CWTI:NOV/93[24]346
GAY, WEED, *guerrilla;* ACW:SEP/95[22]544
GAYLORD, AUGUSTUS, *Adjutant, 4th Wisconsin Infantry;*
ACW:MAY/93[12]412
GEARHART, EDWIN R., *Private, 142nd Pennsylvania
Infantry;* CWR:VOL4#4[1]177
GEARY, EDWARD R., *Lieutenant, Pennsylvania Light
Artillery;* CWNEWS:APR/94[5], CWR:VOL3#2[70]155
GEARY, JOHN W., *General, USA:*
ARTICLES: "MIDNIGHT ENGAGEMENT: GEARY'S WHITE
STAR DIVISION AT WAUHATCHIE, TENNESSEE,
OCTOBER 28-29, 1863," CWR:VOL3#2[70]155

BOOK REVIEW: *A POLITICIAN GOES TO WAR: THE CIVIL WAR
LETTERS OF JOHN WHITE GEARY*
GENERAL LISTINGS: *Gettysburg,* ACW:JAN/92[38]343,
GETTY:4[89]150, GETTY:6[7]169, GETTY:6[69]176,
GETTY:7[29]188, GETTY:7[83]192, GETTY:7[97]193,
GETTY:8[31]201, GETTY:9[53]214, GETTY:9[81]216,
GETTY:10[36]223, GETTY:10[120]229, GETTY:11[80]235,
GETTY:12[42]244, *order of battle,* B&G:DEC/95[9]615,
Savannah, B&G:FEB/91[8]339, *photos;* ACW:JAN/92[38]343,
AHI:JUL/75[4]160, CWR:VOL3#2[70]155,
CWTI:SEP/94[40]403
ADDITIONAL LISTINGS: ACW:JAN/92[10]339, ACW:SEP/92[47]380,
ACW:NOV/92[42]388, ACW:JUL/93[8]420,
ACW:NOV/93[34]442, ACW:MAY/95[30]525,
AHI:JUL/75[4]160, CWM:JAN/91[12]326,
CWM:MAR/91[17]335, CWM:JUL/92[18]429,
CWR:VOL3#2[102]156, CWTI:SUMMER/89[32]122,
CWTI:SEPT/89[30]129, CWTI:MAR/91[12]198,
CWTI:JAN/93[49]303, CWTI:SEP/94[40]403,
CWTI:MAR/95[40]436, CWTI:AUG/95[24]455
GEDDES, JAMES, *Colonel, 8th Iowa Infantry;*
B&G:AUG/95[8]604
GEE, A.L., *sutler;* CWR:VOL3#3[1]157
GEE, GEORGE, *Private, 32nd Wisconsin Infantry;*
CWR:VOL2#4[313]146
GEE, THADDEUS, *Private, 32nd Wisconsin Infantry;*
CWR:VOL2#4[313]146
GEER, DAVID L., *Pvt., 5th Florida Inf.;* CWR:VOL3#4[1]161
GEER, EUGENE P., *Private, 5th New York Infantry;*
CWR:VOL1#2[29]112
GEIGER, HARVEY S., *Private, 53rd Pennsylvania Infantry;*
GETTY:11[80]235
GEISREITER, JACOB, *Private, 1st Minnesota Infantry;*
GETTY:5[79]161
GELEICH, VINCENT, *Surgeon, USA;* B&G:OCT/91[11]466
GENEALOGY; BOOK REVIEW: *GENEALOGY ONLINE:
RESEARCHING YOUR ROOTS*

GENERAL ORDERS:
General Orders #9; CWM:AUG/94[8]522, CWM:JUL/91[8]356,
CWM:AUG/95[17]603
General Orders #11; AHI:JUN/80[49]203,
B&G:JUN/91[10]452, B&G:JUN/91[32]454,
CWM:JAN/92[8]399
General Orders #61; CWTI:MAY/89[22]116
General Orders #62; GETTY:9[5]209
General Orders #72:
ARTICLE: "GENERAL ORDERS NO. 72: 'BY COMMAND OF
GEN. R.E. LEE'," GETTY:7[13]186
ADDITIONAL LISTINGS: GETTY:4[7]142, GETTY:8[127]208
General Orders #100; ARTICLE: "FRANCIS LEIBER'S SEARCH
FOR A MORE HUMANE SHADE OF WAR,"
CWM:AUG/95[58]611
General Orders #100; GETTY:7[29]188

GENERAL'S TOUR:
Title articles from BLUE & GRAY Magazine
Antietam; "FORGOTTEN VALOR: OFF THE BEATEN PATH
AT ANTIETAM: ATTACK OF THE TURNVEREIN,"
B&G:OCT/95[8]611B; DEBACLE IN THE WEST WOODS,"
B&G:OCT/95[8]611A; GUNNERS OF THE 6TH VA. INFY.,"
B&G:OCT/95[8]611C; OLD SIMON," B&G:OCT/95[8]611E;

WHOEVER HEARD OF A DEAD CAVALRYMAN?"
B&G:OCT/95[8]611F; ARTILLERY HELL AND HOT
COFFEE," B&G:OCT/95[8]611D

Bentonville; "THE BATTLE OF BENTONVILLE, MARCH
19-21, 1865: LAST STAND IN THE CAROLINAS,"
B&G:DEC/95[9]615

Five Forks; "THE BATTLE OF FIVE FORKS: FINAL PUSH
FOR THE SOUTH SIDE," B&G:APR/92[8]481

Fort Henry and Donelson; "FORTS HENRY & DONELSON:
UNION VICTORY ON THE TWIN RIVERS,"
B&G:FEB/92[10]474

Gettysburg; "GETTYSBURG VIGNETTES: FIGHT LIKE THE
DEVIL TO HOLD YOUR OWN. GENERAL JOHN BUFORD'S
CAVALRY AT GETTYSBURG;" B&G:FEB/95[8]590A, THAT
ONE ERROR FILLS HIM WITH FAULTS. GEN. ALFRED
IVERSON AND HIS BRIGADE AT GETTYSBURG;"
B&G:FEB/95[8]590B, AT THE TIME IMPRACTICABLE.
DICK EWELL'S DECISION ON THE FIRST DAY AT
GETTYSBURG" B&G:FEB/95[8]590C

Grierson's Raid; "GRIERSON'S RAID: A CAVALRY RAID AT
ITS BEST," B&G:JUN/93[12]524

Haunted Places; "13 HAUNTED PLACES OF THE CIVIL
WAR II," B&G:OCT/91[11]466

Jackson, Mississippi; "RETURN TO JACKSON, JULY 5-25,
1863," B&G:AUG/95[8]604,

Loudoun Valley Cavalary Battles; "THE FIGHT FOR
LOUDOUN VALLEY: ALDIE, MIDDLEBURG AND
UPPERVILLE, VA.," B&G:OCT/93[12]537

Manassas, Second Battle of; "THE SECOND BATTLE OF
MANASSAS: LEE SUPPRESSES THE "MISCREANT"
POPE," B&G:AUG/92[11]493

McCausland's Chambersburg Raid; "MCCAUSLAND'S RAID
AND THE BURNING OF CHAMBERSBURG,"
B&G:AUG/94[10]574

Mill Springs; "THE CAMPAIGN AND BATTLE OF MILL
SPRINGS," B&G:FEB/93[12]511

Monocacy; "MONOCACY: THE BATTLE THAT SAVED
WASHINGTON," B&G:DEC/92[8]503

Morgan's Escape; "JOHN HUNT MORGAN'S ESCAPE FROM
THE OHIO PENITENTIARY," B&G:OCT/94[11]580

Nashville; "THE BATTLE OF NASHVILLE,"
B&G:DEC/93[12]545

New Mexico Campaign; "THE CONFEDERATE INVASION
OF NEW MEXICO," B&G:JUN/94[8]568

Overland Campaign; "GRANT AND LEE, 1864: FROM THE
NORTH ANNA TO THE CROSSING OF THE JAMES,"
B&G:APR/94[10]558, "STRIKE THEM A BLOW: LEE AND
GRANT AT THE NORTH ANNA RIVER," B&G:APR/93[12]518

Port Gibson; "GRANT'S BEACHHEAD FOR THE
VICKSBURG CAMPAIGN: THE BATTLE, OF PORT
GIBSON, MAY 1, 1863," B&G:FEB/94[8]550

Price's 1864 Missouri Campaign; MISSOURI! ONE LAST
TIME—STERLING PRICE'S 1864 MISSOURI
EXPEDITION," B&G:JUN/91[10]452

Saltville; "THE BATTLE OF SALTVILLE—MASSACRE OR
MYTH," B&G:AUG/91[11]458

Savannah; "SAVANNAH: MR. LINCOLN'S CHRISTMAS
PRESENT," B&G:FEB/91[8]439

Thomas J. "Stonewall" Jackson; "STONEWALL JACKSON,"
B&G:JUN/92[8]487

Tullahoma Campaign; "THE DECEPTION OF BRAXTON
BRAGG: THE TULLAHOMA CAMPAIGN, JUNE 23-JULY
4,1863," B&G:OCT/92[10]496

West Point; "MUCH TO SADDEN—AND LITTLE TO CHEER:
THE CIVIL WAR YEARS AT WEST POINT,"
B&G:DEC/91[12]469

West Virginia Campaign; "THE NORTHWESTERN
VIRGINIA CAMPAIGN OF 1861," B&G:AUG/93[10]529

Wilderness "NO TURNING BACK: THE BATTLE OF THE
WILDERNESS, PART I," B&G:APR/95[8]595, "NO TURNING
BACK: THE BATTLE OF THE WILDERNESS, PART II,"
B&G:JUN/95[8]600

Wilmington Campaign; "THE LAST RAYS OF DEPARTING
HOPE: THE FALL OF WILMINGTON," B&G:DEC/94[10]585

Winter Encampment; "SEASON OF CHANGE, THE WINTER
ENCAMPMENT OF THE ARMY OF THE POTOMAC,"
B&G:APR/91[8]445

GENERALS, CONFEDERATE:
ARTICLE: "YOU HAD DONE ME A GREAT INJUSTICE,"
CWTI:MAR/93[40]312
BOOK REVIEWS: *THE CONFEDERATE GENERAL ***
CONFEDERATE GENERALS OF GEORGIA AND THEIR
*BURIAL SITES * MEDICAL HISTORIES OF*
*CONFEDERATE GENERALS * THEY SLEEP BENEATH*
THE MOCKINGBIRD: MISSISSIPPI BURIAL SITES AND
BIOGRAPHIES OF CONFEDERATE GENERALS

GENERALS, FEDERAL; BOOK REVIEW: *LINCOLN'S*
GENERALS

GENTRY, JOSHUA K., *Private, 2nd Tennessee Cavalry;*
CWR:VOL4#1[1]163

GEORGE, DAVID E.; CWTI:OCT/95[14]465

GEORGE, NEWT J., *Lieutenant Colonel, 1st Tennessee*
Infantry; GETTY:6[13]170, GETTY:12[61]245

GEORGIA MILITARY INSTITUTE; ARTICLE: "TRAINING IN
TREASON,'" CWTI:SEP/91[23]228

GEORGIA STATE GOVERNMENT; ARTICLE: "WOLF AT THE
DOOR," ACW:NOV/93[42]443

GEORGIA TROOPS:
1st Cavalry; CWR:VOL4#1[1]163

1st Confederate Georgia Infantry; ARTICLES: "A LONG ROAD
TO BENTONVILLE: THE FIRST CONFEDERATE
REGIMENT (PART II)," CWR:VOL1#4[64]127, "FROM
SANTA ROSA ISLAND TO CHICKAMAUGA: THE FIRST
CONFEDERATE REGIMENT," CWR:VOL1#4[42]126

1st Infantry:
BOOK REVIEWS: *FOOTPRINTS OF A REGIMENT: A*
RECOLLECTION OF THE 1ST GEORGIA REGULARS
ADDITIONAL LISTINGS: ACW:MAY/91[12]302, AHI:MAR/84[42]238,
B&G:AUG/93[10]529, B&G:AUG/95[38],
CWM:MAR/93[32]468, CWTI:MAR/89[28]103,
CWTI:SEP/92[28]280, CWTI:DEC/94[49]413,
CWTI:MAR/95[18]432

1st Local Defense Troops; CWM:SEP/91[10]379

1st Regulars:
ARTICLE: "THE FIRST GEORGIA REGULARS AT
SHARPSBURG: RECOLLECTIONS OF THE MARYLAND
CAMPAIGN, 1862," CWR:VOL2#2[95]135
ADDITIONAL LISTINGS: B&G:FEB/91[8]439, CWM:AUG/95[38]609,
CWR:VOL2#2[156]138, CWR:VOL3#1[65]151

1st Reserves; B&G:AUG/94[22]576, CWR:VOL2#3[194]141,
CWTI:DEC/94[62]415

1st Sharpshooter Battalion; CWR:VOL1#4[64]127

2nd Cavalry; B&G:APR/93[24]520, CWR:VOL4#1[1]163,
CWTI:SEP/93[59]341, CWTI:NOV/93[33]347

2nd Infantry; ACW:MAY/91[12]302, ACW:JUL/95[50]538, AHI:OCT/75[30]162, CWM:MAR/93[32]468, CWM:AUG/95[38]609, CWM:JUN/95[63]594, CWTI:DEC/94[32]410, GETTY:8[53]203

2nd Sharpshooter Battalion; CWR:VOL1#4[42]12 WTI:MAR/95[18]432

3rd Cavalry; B&G:AUG/91[11]458, CWR:VOL4#1[1]163

3rd Infantry; ACW:MAY/95[18]524, ACW:JUL/95[50]538, B&G:AUG/91[30]460, CWR:VOL1#4[7]125, CWTI:DEC/94[32]410

3rd Reserves; B&G:FEB/91[8]439, CWR:VOL2#3[194]141

4th Infantry; B&G:DEC/95[25]616, CWM:JUN/95[55]591, CWR:VOL3#2[1]153, CWTI:APR/90[48]154, CWTI:FEB/92[42]250, CWTI:MAY/94[44]384, CWTI:MAR/95[33]435, GETTY:4[33]146, GETTY:5[107]164

5th Cavalry; B&G:AUG/91[11]458

5th Infantry; ACW:NOV/92[8]383, CWR:VOL1#4[42]126, CWR:VOL2#3[194]141, GETTY:9[53]214

5th Reserves; B&G:FEB/91[8]439

6th Infantry; ACW:SEP/92[47]380, B&G:OCT/95[8]611A, CWR:VOL3#1[65]151

7th Cavalry; B&G:AUG/93[36]533

7th Infantry; ACW:JAN/94[8]447, B&G:APR/91[32]447, CWM:AUG/95[38]609, CWM:JUN/95[29]583, CWM:JUN/95[63]594, GETTY:8[53]203

8th Cavalry; ACW:MAR/95[12]513, B&G:AUG/91[11]458

8th Infantry; ACW:JAN/94[8]447, B&G:APR/91[32]447, CWM:JUN/94[50]518, CWM:JUN/95[29]583, CWM:AUG/95[38]609, CWTI:DEC/89[62]139, GETTY:8[43]202, GETTY:8[53]203, GETTY:12[1]240, GETTY:12[111]250

9th Infantry; B&G:APR/91[32]447, B&G:AUG/92[11]493, CWM:AUG/95[38]609, CWR:VOL2#2[95]135, CWR:VOL3#2[1]153, GETTY:8[43]202, GETTY:8[53]203

9th State Troops; CWTI:MAR/93[24]309

10th Cavalry; B&G:AUG/91[11]458

10th Infantry:
ARTICLES: "THE 10TH GEORGIA AND 27TH CONNECTICUT IN THE WHEATFIELD; TWO CAPTURED SWORDS AGAINST THEIR FORMER OWNERS," GETTY:12[24]242, "THE THOMSON GUARDS FROM GEORGIA'S MCDUFFIE COUNTY SERVED THE CONFEDERACY TO THE BITTER END," ACW:JUL/95[10]533

ADDITIONAL LISTINGS: ACW:JAN/94[39]451, CWR:VOL1#4[7]125, GETTY:5[47]160, GETTY:8[53]203, GETTY:12[1]240 ,

11th Artillery: ARTICLES: "THE SUMTER ARTILLERY: THE STORY OF THE 11TH BATTALION, GEORGIA LIGHT ARTILLERY DURING THE WAR BETWEEN THE STATES," CWR:VOL3#2[1]153, "WILDERNESS TO PETERSBURG: UNPUBLISHED REPORTS OF THE 11TH BATTALION, GEORGIA LIGHT ARTILLERY," CWR:VOL3#2[61]154

11th Infantry: ACW:JAN/94[8]447, AHI:APR/85[18]250, CWM:AUG/95[38]609, GETTY:8[43]202, GETTY:8[53]203

12th Infantry:
ARTICLE: "FOR THE VETERAN 12TH GEORGIA REGIMENT, ROUNDING UP DESERTERS WAS "QUITE A HOLIDAY." ACW:MAR/94[16]458

BOOK REVIEW: *A POST OF HONOR: THE PRYOR LETTERS, 1861-63 * LETTERS FROM CAPT. S. G. PRYOR, TWELFTH GEORGIA REGIMENT AND HIS WIFE, PENELOPE TYSON PRYOR*

ADDITIONAL LISTINGS: ACW:JAN/93[35]396, B&G:AUG/93[10]529, CWTI:MAR/94[29]371, GETTY:4[33]146, GETTY:5[117]165, GETTY:13[108]261

13th Infantry; B&G:APR/95[8]595, CWNEWS:SEP/89[8]

14th Infantry; ACW:MAY/95[30]525, GETTY:13[7]253

15th Infantry:
BOOK REVIEW: *35 DAYS TO GETTYSBURG: THE CAMPAIGN DIARIES OF TWO AMERICAN ENEMIES*

ADDITIONAL LISTINGS: ACW:MAR/93[58], B&G:AUG/92[11]493, B&G:APR/93[40]522, B&G:OCT/93[24], CWM:MAR/93[32]468, CWM:JUN/95[63]594, CWM:AUG/95[38]609, CWNEWS:JUL/93[5], CWR:VOL2#2[95]135, GETTY:8[53]203, GETTY:11[91]236, GETTY:13[7]253

16th Infantry; ACW:MAY/91[23]303, ACW:JAN/94[8]447, AHI:APR/68[4]115, B&G:DEC/92[26], B&G:APR/93[24]520, CWM:JUL/92[16]428, CWR:VOL1#4[7]125, CWR:VOL3#3[1]157, CWTI:MAY/94[50]386, GETTY:8[53]203

17th Infantry; ACW:NOV/95[54]558, CWM:MAR/93[32]468, CWM:FEB/95[7], CWM:AUG/95[38]609, CWTI:DEC/91[36]240, GETTY:8[53]203

18th Infantry; ACW:JUL/92[30]369, B&G:AUG/91[20]459, CWR:VOL1#2[29]112, CWR:VOL1#4[77], CWR:VOL2#3[256], CWR:VOL2#4[269]145, CWR:VOL4#4[28]178, CWTI:DEC/91[36]240, CWTI:SEP/94[12]398, CWTI:SEP/94[26]400, GETTY:8[53]203

19th Cavalry; B&G:JUN/94[38]571

19th Infantry; CWR:VOL1#1[1]102, CWR:VOL3#1[65]151, CWR:VOL4#4[1]177, CWTI:DEC/94[32]410, GETTY:6[13]170

20th Infantry; CWM:JUN/95[63]594, CWM:AUG/95[38]609, GETTY:8[53]203

21st Infantry; ACW:JUL/92[30]369, ACW:MAR/94[50]462, B&G:AUG/92[11]493, CWR:VOL1#3[28]120, CWTI:MAR/94[48]374, GETTY:4[33]146, GETTY:10[120]229

22nd Infantry; ACW:JUL/95[50]538, CWM:JUN/95[55]591, CWR:VOL1#4[7]125, CWTI:SEP/90[26]174, CWTI:DEC/94[32]410, GETTY:12[111]250

23rd Infantry; ACW:MAY/95[30]525, CWR:VOL3#1[65]151, CWTI:JUL/93[42]329

24th Infantry; B&G:APR/93[24]520, CWR:VOL1#4[7]125, CWR:VOL1#4[64]127, CWR:VOL4#4[28]178, GETTY:8[53]203

26th Infantry:
BOOK REVIEW: *SOUTH GEORGIA REBELS: THE 26TH GEORGIA VOLUNTEER INFANTRY*

ADDITIONAL LISTINGS: B&G:AUG/92[11]493, B&G:APR/95[8]595, CWNEWS:SEP/89[8]

27th Infantry; ACW:JUL/92[30]369, CWR:VOL3#1[65]151, CWTI:DEC/94[32]410

28th Artillery; CWR:VOL3#1[65]151

28th Infantry; CWR:VOL3#1[65]151

29th Cavalry; CWTI:JUL/93[74]331

29th Infantry; CWR:VOL1#4[64]127

30th Infantry; CWR:VOL1#4[64]127

31st Infantry; B&G:APR/95[8]595, CWNEWS:SEP/89[8]

32nd Infantry; ACW:SEP/91[30]322, CWR:VOL2#3[194]141, CWR:VOL3#1[65]151

34th Infantry; CWR:VOL2#1[36]132, CWTI:MAY/91[24]208

35th Infantry; B&G:APR/93[12]518, CWM:JUN/95[57]592, CWR:VOL1#1[1]102

36th Infantry; CWR:VOL1#4[v]124, CWR:VOL1#4[42]126, CWR:VOL2#1[36]132

37th Reserves; B&G:AUG/94[22]576

38th Infantry; B&G:APR/95[8]595, B&G:JUN/95[8]600

39th Infantry; CWR:VOL2#1[36]132, CWTI:MAY/91[24]208

40th Infantry; CWTI:SEP/92[28]280
41st Infantry; CWTI:SEP/92[28]280
42nd Infantry; B&G:DEC/95[9]615, CWR:VOL1#1[42]105, CWTI:SEP/92[28]280, CWTI:DEC/94[49]413
43rd Infantry; CWTI:SEP/92[28]280
44th Infantry; ACW:SEP/94[38]487, CWM:JUN/95[57]592, GETTY:4[33]146
45th Infantry; B&G:AUG/92[11]493, B&G:APR/93[12]518, GETTY:10[53]225
47th Infantry; B&G:AUG/95[8]604, CWR:VOL2#3[194]141, CWR:VOL2#3[252]144
48th Infantry; ACW:JAN/92[38]343, ACW:JUL/95[50]538, CWR:VOL1#4[7]125, CWTI:DEC/94[32]410, GETTY:12[111]250
49th Infantry; GETTY:8[43]202, GETTY:12[111]250
50th Infantry; CWM:MAR/93[32]468, GETTY:5[35]159, GETTY:5[47]160, GETTY:8[53]203
51st Infantry; AHI:MAR/84[42]238, GETTY:5[47]160, GETTY:8[53]203
52nd Infantry; CWTI:SEP/92[28]280, CWTI:NOV/92[41]291, CWTI:MAY/93[8]315, CWTI:MAR/94[16]368
53rd Infantry; ACW:JUL/95[10]533, B&G:APR/93[24]520, CWR:VOL1#4[7]125, CWTI:SEP/90[26]174, GETTY:5[47]160, GETTY:8[53]203
55th Infantry; B&G:FEB/91[8]439
56th Infantry; CWR:VOL2#1[36]132
57th Infantry; B&G:AUG/93[36]533, CWR:VOL2#1[36]132
59th Infantry; B&G:JUN/94[38]571, GETTY:8[53]203, GETTY:12[111]250
60th Infantry; B&G:APR/95[8]595, CWNEWS:SEP/89[8]
61st Infantry; B&G:APR/95[8]595, B&G:JUN/95[8]600, CWNEWS:SEP/89[8], CWTI:JAN/93[40]301, GETTY:12[111]250
64th Infantry; B&G:APR/95[5]594, CWR:VOL3#1[65]151
66th Infantry; CWR:VOL1#4[64]127, CWTI:SUMMER/89[40]123
Athens Battalion; B&G:FEB/91[8]439
Augusta Battalion; B&G:FEB/91[8]439
Bonaud's Battalion; CWR:VOL3#1[65]151
Cherokee Artillery; ACW:NOV/91[22]331
Cobb's Legion; ACW:JUL/92[41]370, ACW:JAN/94[8]447, CWM:MAR/93[32]468, CWTI:JUN/90[32]159, GETTY:8[53]203
Columbus Light Artillery; B&G:AUG/95[8]604
Ferrell's Battery; B&G:AUG/94[22]576
Georgia and Mississippi Regiment; CWR:VOL1#4[42]126
Georgia Brigade:
BOOK REVIEW: *THE GEORGIA BRIGADE*
ADDITIONAL LISTINGS: GETTY:11[102]237, GETTY:12[7]241
Georgia Legion; B&G:APR/93[24]520
Georgia State Line; ACW:MAR/91[38]296, CWTI:DEC/94[49]413
Home Guard; ACW:SEP/92[47]380
Independent Battalion Georgia Volunteers; CWR:VOL1#4[42]126
LaGrange Light Guards; B&G:DEC/95[25]616
Lane's Battery; CWR:VOL3#2[1]153
Martin's Light Artillery; B&G:AUG/95[8]604
Nelson's Independent Cavalry; B&G:FEB/91[20]440, B&G:AUG/95[8]604
Oglethorpe Light Artillery; B&G:FEB/91[8]339, GETTY:12[111]250
Phillip's Legion; ACW:JUL/92[41]370, CWTI:APR/89[50]112, GETTY:8[53]203

Pulaski Artillery; GETTY:8[53]203
Russell County Reserves; ACW:MAR/91[38]296
Savannah Guards; ACW:MAR/91[14]293
Sumter Artillery; see listings above under "GEORGIA TROOPS, 11TH ARTILLERY"
Troup Artillery; GETTY:8[53]203
Washington Artillery; CWR:VOL1#4[42]126

GEORGIA, STATE OF; BOOK REVIEWS: *THE CHILDREN OF PRIDE: A TRUE STORY OF GEORGIA AND THE CIVIL WAR * GEORGIA IN THE WAR, 1861-1865: A COMPENDIUM OF GEORGIA PARTICIPANTS * PATRIOTISM FOR PROFIT: GEORGIA'S URBAN ENTERPRENEURS AND THE CONFEDERATE WAR EFFORT*
GERALD, GEORGE B., *Major, 18th Mississippi Infantry;* GETTY:12[7]241
GERHARDT, JOSEPH, *Colonel, USA;* B&G:AUG/95[8]604
GERHART, FREDERICK W., *Private, 125th Pennsylvania Infantry;* B&G:OCT/95[8]611A
GERMANNA'S FORD, VIRGINIA; B&G:APR/91[8]445
GERRETT, WILLIAM, *Private, 95th Illinois Infantry;* ACW:JAN/91[16]284
GERRISH, THEODORE, *Private, 20th Maine Infantry;* ACW:JAN/92[38]343, MH:JUN/92[6]158
GESNER, BROWN, *Surgeon, 10th New York Infantry;* CWM:SEP/93[18]494
GETTY, GEORGE W., *General, USA;* ACW:MAY/91[38]305, ACW:MAY/93[31]415, ACW:SEP/94[55]489, B&G:APR/95[8]595, B&G:JUN/95[8]600, CWR:VOL1#3[52]122, GETTY:11[6]231, *photo;* GETTY:11[6]231
GETTYSBURG ADDRESS:
ARTICLES: "'A FEW APPROPRIATE REMARKS,'" AHI:NOV/88[37]278, "THE FOUNDING FATHERS' 'REPUBLICAN IDEAL,'" NOURISHED ABRAHAM LINCOLN'S BELIEF IN FREEDOM FOR ALL," ACW:NOV/94[8]493, "GETTYSBURG REMEMBERS PRESIDENT LINCOLN," GETTY:9[122]220, "TURNING THE PAGES OF HISTORY: A NEW DRAFT OF THE, GETTYSBURG ADDRESS LOCATED," GETTY:6[107]182, "WHAT DID LINCOLN ACTUALLY SAY?" AHI:NOV/88[43]279
BOOK REVIEWS: *ABRAHAM LINCOLN THE ORATOR: PENETRATING THE LINCOLN LEGEND * THE GETTYSBURG SOLDIERS' CEMETERY AND LINCOLN'S ADDRESS*
ADDITIONAL LISTINGS: ACW:SEP/94[62]490, B&G:JUN/92[46]490, B&G:APR/92[36]483, B&G:APR/93[40]522, CWM:OCT/95[22]614, CWM:DEC/95[10], CWTI:DEC/95[22]476, CWTI:DEC/95[40]479, CWTI:DEC/95[67]481, GETTY:12[97]249, *photo;* GETTY:9[122]220
GETTYSBURG BATTLEFIELD MEMORIAL ASSOCIATION; ACW:MAY/92[8]357, GETTY:11[91]236, GETTY:13[33]255,
GETTYSBURG BATTLEFIELD PRESERVATION ASSOCIATION; see listings under "PRESERVATION"

GETTYSBURG BOOKS:
*A listing of some of the available titles about the battle.
All are reviewed in* Gettysburg Magazine, *Issue 6, page
113.*
*A CASPIAN SEA OF INK: THE MEADE-SICKLES
CONTROVERSY * A VAST SEA OF MISERY * AT
GETTYSBURG: WHAT A GIRL SAW AND HEARD OF THE
BATTLE * THE ATTACK AND DEFENSE OF LITTLE
ROUND TOP * THE BATTLE OF GETTYSBURG *
BATTLES AND LEADERS OF THE CIVIL WAR * THE
CAVALRY AT GETTYSBURG * THE CONFEDERATE
VETERAN * CRISIS AT THE CROSSROADS * FIGHTING
FOR THE CONFEDERACY * THE GETTYSBURG
CAMPAIGN * THE GETTYSBURG CAMPAIGN, JUNE
3-AUGUST 1, 1863 * THE GETTYSBURG DEATH ROSTER
* THE CONFEDERATE HIGH TIDE * GETTYSBURG,
THEN AND NOW * GETTYSBURG: A JOURNEY IN TIME *
GETTYSBURG: THE LONG ENCAMPMENT *
GETTYSBURG: THE SECOND DAY * HANCOCK THE
SUPERB * HERE COME THE REBELS * HIGH TIDE AT
GETTYSBURG * THE IMAGE OF WAR: 1861-1865 * THE
KILLER ANGELS * LEE'S LIEUTENANTS * MEADE OF
GETTYSBURG * MILITARY MEMOIRS OF A
CONFEDERATE * NOTHING BUT GLORY * THE
PHOTOGRAPHIC HISTORY OF THE CIVIL WAR *
PICKETT'S CHARGE * R.E. LEE * REBEL INVASION OF
MARYLAND & PENNSYLVANIA AND THE BATTLE OF
GETTYSBURG * THE RED BADGE OF COURAGE *
REGIMENTAL STRENGTHS AND LOSSES AT
GETTYSBURG * ROADS TO GETTYSBURG * SICKLES
THE INCREDIBLE * THE SOUTHERN HISTORICAL
SOCIETY PAPERS * THE WAR OF THE REBELLION
OFFICIAL RECORDS OF THE UNION AND
CONFEDERATE ARMIES * WASTED VALOR*

GETTYSBURG NATIONAL CEMETERY;
B&G:JUN/93[40]527, CWM:NOV/91[80]396

GETTYSBURG NATIONAL MILITARY PARK: *Note: for
articles related to preservation issues, see listings under*
"PRESERVATION"
ADDITIONAL LISTINGS: B&G:APR/91[36]448, B&G:JUN/91[26]453,
B&G:JUN/92[46]490, B&G:DEC/92[40]508,
B&G:FEB/95[8]590A, B&G:JUN/95[36]603A,
CWM:NOV/91[35]392, CWM:JAN/92[44]406,
CWM:MAR/92[27]412, CWM:MAY/92[6]417,
CWTI:MAY/89[8]113, CWTI:SEP/91[16]226,
CWTI:JUL/92[8]269, CWTI:NOV/92[8]288,
CWTI:JAN/93[35]300, CWTI:SEP/93[38]337,
CWTI:SEP/94[28]401, CWTI:SEP/94[34]402

GETTYSBURG, PENNSYLVANIA, BATTLE OF:
ARTICLES: "THE 10TH GEORGIA AND 27TH CONNECTICUT IN
THE WHEATFIELD; TWO CAPTURED SWORDS AGAINST
THEIR FORMER OWNERS," GETTY:12[24]242, "THE 16TH
MAINE VOLUNTEER INFANTRY AT GETTYSBURG,"
GETTY:13[33]255, "16TH MAINE AT GETTYSBURG,"
CWM:MAY/92[15]419, "THE 72ND PENNSYLVANIA
FOUGHT TWO BATTLES AT GETTYSBURG—A QUARTER
CENTURY APART," ACW:MAY/92[8]357, "A CALL OF
LEADERSHIP: LIEUTENANT COLONEL CHARLES
REDINGTON MUDGE, U.S.V. AND THE SECOND
MASSACHUSETTS INFANTRY AT GETTYSBURG,"
GETTY:6[69]176, "A PERFECT ROAR OF MUSKETRY:
CANDY'S BRIGADE IN THE FIGHT FOR CULP'S HILL,"
GETTY:9[81]216, "A FEDERAL ARTILLERYMAN AT

GETTYSBURG: AN EYEWITNESS, ACCOUNT,"
AHI:MAY/67[22]107, "A GETTYSBURG ENCOUNTER,"
GETTY:7[114]194, "A METEOROLOGICAL AND
ASTRONOMICAL CHRONOLOGY OF THE GETTYSBURG
CAMPAIGN," GETTY:13[7]253, "A MISSISSIPPIAN IN THE
RAILROAD CUT," GETTY:4[22]144, "A REFUGEE FROM
GETTYSBURG," CWTI:DEC/89[16]134, "A SHADOW
PASSING: THE TRAGIC STORY OF NORVAL WELCH AND
THE SIXTEENTH MICHIGAN AT GETTYSBURG AND
BEYOND," GETTY:6[33]172
ARTICLES, continued: "A SIGNAL SERGEANT AT GETTYSBURG:
THE DIARY OF LUTHER C. FURST," GETTY:10[42]224, "A
SURGEON'S HANDIWORK," GETTY:12[83]247, "A TOURIST
AT GETTYSBURG," CWTI:SEP/90[26]174, "A UNION
OFFICER AT GETTYSBURG," AHI:SUM/88[12]273, "A.P.
HILL'S ADVANCE TO GETTYSBURG," GETTY:5[4]156,
"THE AFTERMATH AND RECOVERY OF GETTYSBURG,
PART I," GETTY:11[102]237, "THE AFTERMATH AND
RECOVERY OF GETTYSBURG, PART II," GETTY:12[97]249,
"'AGATE': WHITELAW REID REPORTS FROM
GETTYSBURG," GETTY:7[23]187, "AN ENCOUNTER WITH
BATTERY HELL," GETTY:12[30]243, "AN IRON BRIGADE
CAPTAIN'S REVOLVER IN THE FIGHT ON MCPHERSON'S
RIDGE," GETTY:7[7]185, "ARNOLD'S BATTERY AND THE
26TH NORTH CAROLINA," GETTY:12[61]245, "BAPTISM
OF FIRE: THE NINTH MASSACHUSETTS BATTERY AT
GETTYSBURG, JULY 2, 1863," GETTY:5[47]160, "BATTLE
ON THE BRICKYARD WALL," CWTI:SEP/94[34]402,
"BLACK CONFEDERATES AT GETTYSBURG—1863,"
GETTY:6[94]180, "THE 'BLACKBERRY RAID,'"
GETTY:11[6]231, "BRIG. GENERAL HENRY BAXTER'S
BRIGADE AT GETTYSBURG, JULY 1," GETTY:10[7]221
ARTICLES, continued: "CAPT. JAMES GLENN'S SWORD AND
Private, J. MARSHALL HILL'S, ENFIELD IN THE FIGHT
FOR THE LUTHERAN SEMINARY," GETTY:8[9]199, "CAPT.
MCKEE'S REVOLVER AND CAPT. SELLERS' SWORD
WITH WEED'S BRIGADE ON LITTLE ROUNDTOP,"
GETTY:9[48]213, "CASHTOWN INN," B&G:APR/91[39]449,
"THE COLORS ARE SHROUDED IN MYSTERY,"
GETTY:6[77]177, "THE CONFEDERATE SIGNAL CORPS AT
GETTYSBURG," GETTY:4[110]152, "THE CONGRESSIONAL
RESOLUTION OF THANKS FOR THE FEDERAL VICTORY
AT GETTYSBURG," GETTY:12[85]248, "COURAGE
AGAINST THE TRENCHES: THE ATTACK AND REPULSE
OF STEUART'S BRIGADE ON CULP'S HILL,"
GETTY:7[83]192, "THE DEADLY EMBRACE: THE
MEETING OF THE TWENTY-FOURTH REGIMENT,
MICHIGAN INFANTRY AND THE TWENTY-SIXTH
REGIMENT OF NORTH CAROLINA TROOPS AT
MCPHERSON'S WOODS, GETTYSBURG,
PENNSYLVANIA, JULY 1, 1863," GETTY:5[19]158, "THE
DEATH AND BURIALS OF GENERAL RICHARD BROOKE
GARNETT," GETTY:5[107]164
ARTICLES, continued: "DEFENDING THE CODORI HOUSE AND
CEMETERY RIDGE: TWO SWORDS WITH HARROW'S
BRIGADE IN THE GETTYSBURG CAMPAIGN,"
GETTY:13[43]256, "DEFENDING WATSON'S BATTERY,"
GETTY:9[41]212, "DIGLER'S BATTERY AT GETTYSBURG,"
GETTY:4[49]147, "DON'T LET ME BLEED TO DEATH': THE
WOUNDING OF MAJOR GENERAL WINFIELD SCOTT
HANCOCK," GETTY:6[87]178, "THE DUTCHESS COUNTY
REGIMENT," GETTY:12[42]244, "THE EFFECTS OF
ARTILLERY FIRE ON INFANTRY AT GETTYSBURG,"

GETTY:5[117]165, "ELMINA KEELER SPENCER: MATRON, 147TH NEW YORK," GETTY:8[121]207, "END OF AN ERA: THE 75TH REUNION AT GETTYSBURG," GETTY:7[119]195, "FAILURE ON THE HEIGHTS," ACW:NOV/92[42]388, "FIFTY-THIRD! THE 53RD PENNSYLVANIA VOLUNTEER INFANTRY IN THE GETTYSBURG CAMPAIGN," GETTY:11[80]235, "THE FIGHT FOR LOUDOUN VALLEY: ALDIE, MIDDLEBURG AND UPPERVILLE, VA," B&G:OCT/93[12]537, "THE FIGHTING PROFESSOR: JOSHUA LAWRENCE CHAMBERLAIN," CWM:JUL/92[8]427, "THE FIRST GUN AT GETTYSBURG: 'WITH THE CONFEDERATE ADVANCE GUARD,'" CWR:VOL1#1[26]103, "THE FIRST MINNESOTA AT GETTYSBURG," GETTY:5[79]161

ARTICLES, continued: "FORGOTTEN FIELD: THE CAVALRY BATTLE EAST OF GETTYSBURG ON JULY 3, 1963," GETTY:4[75]149, "FORGOTTEN HERO OF GETTYSBURG," AHI:NOV/93[48]316, "FRANCIS ASBURY WALLER: A MEDAL OF HONOR AT GETTYSBURG," GETTY:4[16]143, "FULL MILITARY HONORS FOR CIVIL WAR DEAD," AHI:NOV/91[16]298, "FURY AT BLISS FARM," ACW:JUL/95[50]538, "GENERAL ORDERS NO. 72: 'BY COMMAND OFGENERAL R.E. LEE,'" GETTY:7[13]186, "GENERALS AT ODDS," MH:AUG/94[46]178, "GEORGE J. GROSS ON HALLOWED GROUND," GETTY:10[112]228, "GEORGE PICKETT: ANOTHER LOOK," CWTI:JUL/94[44]394, "GETTYSBURG AND THE IMMORTAL SIX HUNDRED," GETTY:12[111]250, "GETTYSBURG AND THE SEVENTEENTH MAINE," GETTY:8[43]202, "GETTYSBURG ANNIVERSARY COMMEMORATION," AHI:APR/88[8]268, "GETTYSBURG CONTROVERSIES," GETTY:4[113]153, "THE GETTYSBURG EXPERIENCE OF JAMES J. KIRKPATRICK," GETTY:8[111]206, "GETTYSBURG FINALE," ACW:JUL/93[50]426, "GETTYSBURG REMEMBERS PRESIDENT LINCOLN," GETTY:9[122]220,

ARTICLES, continued: "THE GETTYSBURG DIARY OF LIEUTENANT WILLIAM PEEL," GETTY:9[98]217, "GETTYSBURG REVISITED," GETTY:13[1]252, "GETTYSBURG VIGNETTES #1: FIGHT LIKE THE DEVIL TO HOLD YOUR OWN. GENERAL JOHN BUFORD'S CAVALRY AT GETTYSBURG," B&G:FEB/95[8]590A, "GETTYSBURG VIGNETTES #2: THAT ONE ERROR FILLS HIM WITH FAULTS. GENERAL ALFRED IVERSON AND HIS BRIGADE AT GETTYSBURG," B&G:FEB/95[8]590B, "GETTYSBURG VIGNETTES #3: AT THE TIME IMPRACTICABLE. DICK EWELL'S DECISION ON THE FIRST DAY AT GETTYSBURG," B&G:FEB/95[8]590C, "GETTYSBURG'S ABANDONED WOUNDED," CWM:DEC/95[54]632, "GETTYSBURG: FIGHT ENOUGH IN OLD MAN TRIMBLE TO SATISFY A HERD OF TIGERS," CWM:AUG/94[60]531, "GLORY ENOUGH FOR ALL: LIEUTENANT WILLIAM BROOKE-RAWLE AND THE 3RD PENNSYLVANIA CAVALRY AT GETTYSBURG," GETTY:13[89]260, "GOING BACK INTO THE UNION AT LAST," CWTI:FEB/91[12]189, "THE GORDON-BARLOW STORY, WITH SEQUEL," GETTY:8[5]198, "THE GRANITE GLORY: THE 19TH MAINE AT GETTYSBURG," GETTY:13[50]257

ARTICLES, continued: "THE HARDTACK REGIMENT IN THE BRICKYARD FIGHT," GETTY:8[17]200, "THE HARD-FIGHTING 56TH VIRGINIA'S FINEST HOUR CAME AS THE 'DEADLY DRESS PARADE' OF PICKETT'S CHARGE," ACW:MAR/93[10]402, "HIS LEFT WAS WORTH A GLANCE' MEADE AND THE UNION LEFT ON JULY 2, 1863," GETTY:7[29]188, "HOT SHOT, COLD STEEL," MH:DEC/91[54]155, "HUMBUGGING THE HISTORIAN: A REAPPRAISAL OF LONGSTREET AT GETTYSBURG," GETTY:6[62]175, "HUMPHREYS' DIVISION'S FLANK MARCH TO LITTLE ROUND TOP," GETTY:6[59]174, "I HAVE A GREAT CONTEMPT FOR HISTORY,'" CWTI:SEP/91[31]229, "THE IRON BRIGADE BATTERY AT GETTYSBURG," GETTY:11[57]233, "IT STRUCK HORROR TO US ALL," GETTY:4[89]150, "THE JEFF DAVIS LEGION AT GETTYSBURG," GETTY:12[68]246, "JOHN BUFORD AND THE GETTYSBURG CAMPAIGN," GETTY:11[19]232, "JOHN GIBBON: THE MAN AND THE MONUMENT," GETTY:13[119]262, "JOSEPH W. LATIMER, THE 'BOY MAJOR' AT GETTYSBURG," GETTY:10[29]222, "JOURNEY OF THE DEAD," ACW:SEP/94[62]490

ARTICLES, continued: "KERSHAW'S BRIGADE AT GETTYSBURG," GETTY:5[35]159, "LEE AT GETTYSBURG: THE MAN, THE MYTH, THE RECRIMINATIONS," CWM:JAN/93[8]456, "THE LIEUTENANT WHO ARRESTED A GENERAL," GETTY:4[24]145, "THE LOST HOURS OF 'JEB' STUART," GETTY:4[65]148, "MAJOR JOSEPH H. SAUNDERS, 33RD NORTH CAROLINA, C.S.A.," GETTY:10[102]226, "MANTLED IN FIRE AND SMOKE," ACW:JAN/92[38]343, "MARCH OF THE 124TH NEW YORK TO GETTYSBURG," GETTY:9[5]209, "THE MYSTERIOUS DISAPPEARANCE OF BRIG. General, JOHN R. JONES," GETTY:13[108]261, "NEVER HEARD BEFORE ON THE AMERICAN CONTINENT," GETTY:10[107]227, "NORTH CAROLINA IN THE PICKETT-PETTIGREW-TRIMBLE CHARGE AT GETTYSBURG," GETTY:8[67]204, "NOTHING BUT COWARDS RUN,'" CWM:APR/95[42]577, "O.O. HOWARD'S COMMENCEMENT ADDRESS TO SYRACUSE UNIVERSITY," GETTY:11[71]234, "OVER THE WALL," GETTY:13[64]258

ARTICLES, continued: "THE PHILADELPHIA BRIGADE AT GETTYSBURG," GETTY:7[97]193, "PICKETT'S CHARGE BY THE NUMBERS," CWTI:JUL/93[34]327, "PICKETT'S CHARGE: THE REASON WHY," GETTY:5[103]163, "POSEY'S BRIGADE AT GETTYSBURG, PART I," GETTY:4[7]142, "POSEY'S BRIGADE AT GETTYSBURG, PART II," GETTY:5[89]162, "PURSUING THE ELUSIVE 'CANNONEER'," GETTY:9[33]211, "PRIVATE ROBERT G. CARTER AND THE 22D MASSACHUSETTS AT GETTYSBURG," GETTY:8[53]203, "PYE'S SWORD AT THE RAILROAD CUT," GETTY:6[29]171, "R.S. EWELL'S COMMAND, JUNE 29-JULY 1, 1863," GETTY:9[17]210, "REBELS AT THEIR DOORSTEP," ACW:SEP/93[22]432, "REFLECTIONS ON GETTYSBURG: OR, RETHINKING THE BIG ONE," B&G:FEB/93[48]515, "REMEMBER HARPER'S FERRY!: THE DEGRADATION, HUMILIATION AND REDEMPTION OF Colonel, GEORGE L. WILLARD'S BRIGADE, PART I," GETTY:7[51]190, "REMEMBER HARPER'S FERRY!' THE DEGRADATION, HUMILIATION, AND REDEMPTION OF Colonel, GEORGE L. WILLARD'S BRIGADE, PART II," GETTY:8[95]205

ARTICLES, continued: "REMEMBERING THE 14TH CONNECTICUT VOLUNTEERS," GETTY:9[61]215, "THE RETREAT FROM GETTYSBURG," CWM:AUG/94[26]525, "RETURN TO GETTYSBURG," AHI:JUL/93[40]312, "REUNION AT GETTYSBURG: A REMINISCENCE OF THE FIFTIETH ANNIVERSARY OF THE BATTLE OF

GETTYSBURG JULY 1-5, 1913," GETTY:5[123]166, "RODES ON OAK HILL: A STUDY OF RODES' DIVISION ON THE FIRST DAY OF GETTYSBURG," GETTY:4[33]146, "THE SAVIORS OF LITTLE ROUND TOP," GETTY:8[31]201, "SCENES FROM THE MAKING OF *GETTYSBURG*," B&G:DEC/93[59]549, "SEMINARY RIDGE TO REMAIN UNRESTORED," CWTI:SEP/93[38]337, "THE SIGNAL CORPS AT GETTYSBURG PART II: SUPPORT OF MEADE'S PURSUIT," GETTY:4[101]151, "THE SIXTH MICHIGAN CAVALRY AT FALLING WATERS: THE END OF THE GETTYSBURG CAMPAIGN," GETTY:9[109]218, "SKIRMISHERS," GETTY:6[7]169, "SLAUGHTER AT HOUCK'S RIDGE," CWM:AUG/95[27]605

ARTICLES, continued: "THANKS TO A CHERISHED PHOTOGRAPH, 'THE UNKNOWN SOLDIER OF GETTYSBURG' DID NOT REMAIN UNKNOWN FOR LONG'" ACW:JUL/94[18]476, "THE THIRD BRIGADE, THIRD DIVISION, SIXTH CORPS AT GETTYSBURG," GETTY:11[91]236, "THREE HEROINES OF GETTYSBURG," GETTY:11[119]238, "THROUGH BLOOD AND FIRE AT GETTYSBURG," GETTY:6[43]173, "TO ASSUAGE THE GRIEF: THE GETTYSBURG SAGA OF ISAAC AND MARY STAMPS," GETTY:7[77]191, "TO UNFLINCHINGLY FACE DANGER AND DEATH: CARR'S BRIGADE DEFENDS EMMITSBURG ROAD," GETTY:12[7]241, "TWO NEW YORK SWORDS IN THE FIGHT FOR CULP'S HILL: Colonel, JAMES C. LANE'S AND CAPT. NICHOLAS GRUMBACH'S," GETTY:10[36]223, "TWO ROADS TO GETTYSBURG: THOMAS LEIPER KANE AND THE 13TH PENNSYLVANIA RESERVES," GETTY:9[53]214

ARTICLES, continued: "THE UNION SECOND CORPS HOSPITAL AT GETTYSBURG, JULY 2 TO AUGUST 8, 1863," GETTY:10[53]225, "THE UNMERITED CENSURE OF TWO MARYLAND STAFF OFFICERS, Major, OSMUN LATROBE AND FIRST Lieutenant, W. STUART SYMINGTON," GETTY:13[75]259, "VALLEY OF THE SHADOW OF DEATH: Colonel, STRONG VINCENT AND THE EIGHTY-THIRD PENNSYLVANIA INFANTRY AT LITTLE ROUND TOP," GETTY:7[41]189, "WAR COMES TO PROFESSOR MICHAEL JACOBS," GETTY:6[99]181, "'WHAT A DEADLY TRAP WE WERE IN': ARCHER'S BRIGADE ON JULY 1, 1863," GETTY:6[13]170, "WHO LOST SEMINARY RIDGE?," CWTI:JAN/93[35]300, "WHO WILL FOLLOW ME?," CWTI:JUL/93[29]326, "WILLIAM C. OATES: ON LITTLE ROUND TOP, UNSUNG; IN POSTWAR POLITICS, UNRECONSTRUCTED," CWM:DEC/94[26]548

BOOK REVIEWS: *35 DAYS TO GETTYSBURG * A CASPIAN SEA OF INK: THE MEADE-SICKLES CONTROVERSY * A COLONEL AT GETTYSBURG AND SPOTSYLVANIA: THE LIFE OF COLONEL JOSEPH NEWTON BROWN AND THE BATTLE OF GETTYSBURG * A VAST SEA OF MISERY: A HISTORY AND GUIDE TO THE UNION AND CONFEDERATE FIELD HOSPITALS AT GETTYSBURG JULY 1-NOVEMBER 20, 1863 * THE ATTACK AND DEFENSE OF LITTLE ROUND TOP * THE BACHELDER PAPERS: GETTYSBURG IN THEIR OWN WORDS * THE BATTLE OF GETTYSBURG * THE CAVALRY AT GETTYSBURG: A TACTICAL STUDY OF MOUNTED OPERATIONS DURING THE CIVIL WAR'S PIVOTAL CAMPAIGN * CHANCELLORSVILLE AND GETTYSBURG * CONNECTICUT YANKEES AT GETTYSBURG * CUSHING OF GETTYSBURG * CUTLER'S BRIGADE AT GETTYSBURG * DAYS OF "UNCERTAINTY AND DREAD":*

*THE ORDEAL ENDURED BY THE CITIZENS AT GETTYSBURG * DEATH OF A NATION: THE STORY OF LEE AND HIS MEN AT GETTYSBURG * "THE DEVIL'S TO PAY": GENERAL JOHN BUFORD * THE DIARY OF A LADY OF GETTYSBURG, PENNSYLVANIA*

BOOK REVIEWS, continued: *THE ELEVENTH CORPS ARTILLERY AT GETTYSBURG: THE PAPERS OF MAJOR THOMAS WARD OSBORNE * FIELDS OF GLORY, THE FACTS BOOK OF THE BATTLE OF GETTYSBURG * THE FIRST DAY AT GETTYSBURG: ESSAYS ON UNION AND CONFEDERATE LEADERSHIP * THE FIRST MINNESOTA REGIMENT AT GETTYSBURG * FROM BALL'S BLUFF TO GETTYSBURG...AND BEYOND * FROM MANASSAS TO APPOMATTOX * GENERAL JAMES LONGSTREET: THE, CONFEDERACY'S MOST CONTROVERSIAL SOLDIER * THE GETTYSBURG CAMPAIGN: A STUDY IN COMMAND * THE GETTYSBURG SOLDIERS' CEMETERY AND LINCOLN'S ADDRESS * GETTYSBURG—A BATTLEFIELD ATLAS * GETTYSBURG—CULP'S HILL AND CEMETERY HILL * GETTYSBURG—THE SECOND DAY * GETTYSBURG BATTLEFIELD: THE FIRST DAY'S BATTLEFIELD * GETTYSBURG BATTLEFIELD: THE SECOND AND THIRD DAYS' BATTLEFIELD * GETTYSBURG HOUR-BY-HOUR * GETTYSBURG JULY 1 * GETTYSBURG SOURCES, VOLUME 3*

BOOK REVIEWS, continued: *GETTYSBURG: A BATTLEFIELD ATLAS * GETTYSBURG: A JOURNEY IN TIME * GETTYSBURG: A MEDITATION ON WAR & VALUES * GETTYSBURG: CRISIS OF COMMAND * GETTYSBURG: HISTORICAL ARTICLES OF LASTING INTEREST * GETTYSBURG: THE PAINTINGS OF MORT KUNSTLER * GHOSTS OF GETTYSBURG * HANDS ACROSS THE WALL: THE 50TH AND 75TH REUNIONS OF THE GETTYSBURG BATTLE * HASKELL OF GETTYSBURG, HIS LIFE AND CIVIL WAR PAPERS * HIGH TIDE AT GETTYSBURG * HOLDING THE LEFT AT GETTYSBURG: THE 20TH NEW YORK STATE MILITIA ON JULY 1, 1863 * IN THE BLOODY RAILROAD CUT AT GETTYSBURG * INSCRIPTION AT GETTYSBURG * KILLED IN ACTION: EYEWITNESS ACCOUNTS OF THE LAST MOMENTS OF 100 UNION SOLDIERS WHO DIED AT GETTYSBURG * THE KILLER ANGELS; THE LAST FULL MEASURE * BURIALS IN THE SOLDIER'S NATIONAL CEMETERY AT GETTYSBURG * THE LAST FULL MEASURE: THE LIFE AND DEATH OF THE FIRST MINNESOTA VOLUNTEERS * LEE AND LONGSTREET AT HIGH TIDE * LINCOLN AT GETTYSBURG: THE WORDS THAT REMADE AMERICA * LINCOLN THE WAR PRESIDENT * THE GETTYSBURG LECTURES * THE LONG ROAD TO GETTYSBURG * MEADE OF GETTYSBURG * MORNING AT WILLOUGHBY RUN, JULY 1, 1863*

BOOK REVIEWS, continued: *"OVER A WIDE, HOT...CRIMSON PLAIN": THE STRUGGLE FOR THE BLISS FARM AT GETTYSBURG * PICKETT'S CHARGE: EYEWITNESS ACCOUNTS * SABER AND SCAPEGOAT: J.E.B. STUART AND THE GETTYSBURG CONTROVERSY * THE SECOND DAY AT GETTYSBURG: , ESSAYS ON CONFEDERATE AND UNION LEADERSHIP * THE THIRD DAY AT GETTYSBURG & BEYOND * THREE MONTHS IN THE SOUTHERN STATES, APRIL-JUNE 1863 * TO GETTYSBURG AND BEYOND: THE PARALLEL LIVES OF JOSHUA LAWRENCE CHAMBERLAIN AND EDWARD PORTER ALEXANDER * TO GETTYSBURG AND BEYOND:*

*NEW JERSEY VOLUNTEER INFANTRY * TWO LADIES OF GETTYSBURG * THE U.S. ARMY WAR COLLEGE GUIDE TO THE BATTLE OF GETTYSBURG * WASTED VALOR: THE CONFEDERATE DEAD AT GETTYSBURG * WITH A FLASH OF HIS SWORD: THE WRITINGS OF MAJOR HOLMAN S. MELCHER, 20TH MAINE INFANTRY * WOMEN AT GETTYSBURG, 1863*

GENERAL LISTINGS: *Cashtown Inn,* B&G:OCT/91[11]466, *general history,* AHI:MAY/71[3]133A, *ghosts,* B&G:OCT/91[11]466, *in book review,* ACW:JUL/93[58], ACW:NOV/94[66], CWM:MAY/93[51], CWM:AUG/94[9], CWM:OCT/94[8], CWM:DEC/94[7], CWM:FEB/95[7], CWM:APR/95[50], CWM:AUG/95[8], CWM:AUG/95[45], CWM:OCT/95[10], CWNEWS:MAY/89[4], CWNEWS:JUL/90[4], CWNEWS:SEP/90[4], CWNEWS:MAY/92[4], CWNEWS:JUN/92[4], CWNEWS:OCT/92[4], CWNEWS:NOV/92[4], CWNEWS:SEP/93[5], CWNEWS:JAN/94[5], CWNEWS:APR/94[5], CWR:VOL1#2[78], CWR:VOL1#3[94], CWR:VOL1#4[77], CWR:VOL2#2[169], CWR:VOL2#3[256], CWR:VOL2#4[346], CWR:VOL3#1[80], CWR:VOL3#2[105], CWR:VOL3#3[92], CWR:VOL3#4[68], CWR:VOL4#1[78], CWR:VOL4#3[1]170, CWR:VOL4#4[129], CWTI:NOV/92[10], CWTI:JAN/93[12], CWTI:NOV/93[14]

GENERAL LISTINGS, continued: *Letterman Hospital,* GETTY:12[111]250, *letters to the editor,* B&G:JUN/93[6]523, B&G:APR/94[6]557, CWM:MAY/91[6]345, CWM:JUL/92[6]426, CWM:OCT/95[5]613, CWM:DEC/95[5]625, CWTI:FEB/92[8]245, CWTI:SEP/92[10]278, CWTI:MAY/93[8]315, CWTI:JAN/94[8]356, *Railroad Cut; Gettysburg,* GETTY:9[33]211, *Seminary Ridge; Gettysburg,* GETTY:9[33]211, *Sickles,* CWTI:FEB/92[6]244, *Temperature,* GETTY:10[120]229,

TABLE: Results of individual artillery shots at Gettysburg; causing two or more casualties, GETTY:5[117]165

MOVIES: *Gettysburg:* B&G:OCT/92[26]498, B&G:DEC/92[30]505, B&G:FEB/93[6]510, B&G:FEB/93[40]514, B&G:FEB/94[6]549, B&G:FEB/94[38]553, B&G:APR/94[6]557, CWM:JUL/93[40]488, CWTI:SEP/92[54]285

PHOTOS: *battlefield;* CWTI:SEPT/89[46]132, *Bliss barn site,* GETTY:9[61]215, *Candy's position on Culp's Hill,* GETTY:9[81]216, *Cemetery gatehouse;* GETTY:11[119]238, *dead horses at the Trostle house;* GETTY:11[102]237, *first shot marker;* GETTY:4[113]153, *General Hospital;* GETTY:10[53]225, *Latimer's Grave in Harrisonburg, VA;* GETTY:10[29]222, *Leister house;* GETTY:11[102]237, *Luthern Seminary, modern;* GETTY:8[9]199, *Modern house on location of Ewell's Headquarters,* GETTY:9[17]210, *Monument, 124th New York Infantry Gettysburg,* GETTY:9[5]209, *O'Sullivan, dead on the Rose Farm;* GETTY:11[102]237, *removing dead;* ACW:JUL/93[50]426, *Spring House of Josiah Benner,* GETTY:9[17]210, *Unfinished railroad cut,* GETTY:10[7]221, *Union dead;* GETTY:11[102]237, *Valley of the Shadow of Death, Little Round Top;* GETTY:11[102]237, *View fromBenner's Hill,* GETTY:10[29]222, *William P. Carter's Battery's position on Oak Hill,* GETTY:9[17]210

VIDEOS: *THE BATTLE OF GETTYSBURG IN MINIATURE,* AHI:JAN/90[15], *GETTYSBURG: THE LAST REUNION OF THE BLUE & GRAY,* AHI:JAN/94[28], *THE LAST FULL MEASURE: THE BATTLE OF GETTYSBURG,* AHI:JAN/88[9], *VOICES OF GETTYSBURG: THE THIRD DAY—PICKETT'S CHARGE,* AHI:JUL/91[20]

ADDITIONAL LISTINGS, ACW: ACW:MAR/91[30]295, ACW:MAY/91[8]300, ACW:MAR/92[10]349, ACW:JUL/92[12]367, ACW:MAR/93[26]404, ACW:MAY/93[14]413, ACW:MAY/93[22]414, ACW:MAY/93[31]415, ACW:JUL/93[16]422, ACW:NOV/93[66]445, ACW:JAN/94[47]452, ACW:JUL/94[10]475, ACW:SEP/94[6]482, ACW:SEP/94[38]487, ACW:SEP/94[55]489, ACW:JAN/95[46]507, ACW:JUL/95[10]533, ACW:JUL/95[16]534, ACW:SEP/95[54]548, ACW:NOV/95[54]558

ADDITIONAL LISTINGS, AHI: AHI:JUL/70[12]128, AHI:MAR/84[42]238, AHI:JUL/93[40]312

ADDITIONAL LISTINGS, B&G: B&G:FEB/91[34]442, B&G:AUG/91[36]462, B&G:OCT/91[11]466, B&G:FEB/93[40]514, B&G:OCT/93[38]541, B&G:DEC/93[30]546, B&G:FEB/94[24]551, B&G:AUG/95[32]606

ADDITIONAL LISTINGS, CWM: CWM:MAR/91[14]334, CWM:MAR/91[17]335, CWM:MAR/91[35]337, CWM:MAR/91[50]340, CWM:JUL/91[10]357, CWM:JUL/91[29]367, CWM:NOV/91[12]390, CWM:JUL/92[4]425, CWM:JUL/92[18]429, CWM:JUL/92[64]434, CWM:NOV/92[10]447, CWM:MAR/93[4]463, CWM:MAR/93[24]467, CWM:SEP/93[24]495, CWM:JUN/94[43]517, CWM:OCT/94[17]534, CWM:OCT/94[26]536, CWM:OCT/94[48]542, CWM:DEC/94[26]548, CWM:DEC/94[46]552, CWM:AUG/95[17]603, CWM:AUG/95[56]610, CWM:DEC/95[41]630

ADDITIONAL LISTINGS, CWR: CWR:VOL1#1[1]102, CWR:VOL1#1[71]107, CWR:VOL1#3[28]120, CWR:VOL1#3[52]122, CWR:VOL2#2[141]137, CWR:VOL2#3[236]143, CWR:VOL2#4[269]145, CWR:VOL3#1[31]150, CWR:VOL3#2[1]153, CWR:VOL3#2[70]155, CWR:VOL4#4[i]175, CWR:VOL3#4[1]161

ADDITIONAL LISTINGS, CWTI CWTI:APR/89[38]111, CWTI:MAY/89[36]118, CWTI:SEPT/89[46]132, CWTI:DEC/89[34]136, CWTI:SEP/90[34]176, CWTI:AUG/91[62]221, CWTI:AUG/91[82]223, CWTI:APR/92[35]257, CWTI:NOV/92[49]292, CWTI:JAN/93[35]300, CWTI:MAY/93[26]318, CWTI:MAY/93[74]322, CWTI:JUL/93[20]325, CWTI:JUL/93[64]330, CWTI:SEP/93[53]340, CWTI:MAR/94[24]370, CWTI:SEP/94[26]400, CWTI:DEC/94[42]412, CWTI:DEC/94[73]416, CWTI:MAR/95[26]434, CWTI:JUN/95[8]441, CWTI:AUG/95[24]455, CWTI:OCT/95[28]467, CWTI:DEC/95[22]476

ADDITIONAL LISTINGS, MH: MH:APR/92[18]157

GHOLSON, SAMUEL J., *General, CSA;* B&G:JUN/93[12]524

GIBBES, WADE H., *Major, CSA;* AHI:SEP/87[40]263, B&G:DEC/91[12]469

GIBBON'S INDEPENDENT CAVALRY BATTALION; CWTI:MAR/89[16]101

GIBBON, JOHN, *General, USA:*

ARTICLES: "BATTLE FOUGHT ON PAPER," ACW:MAY/93[31]415, "BRIEF BREACH AT FREDERICKSBURG," ACW:MAR/95[42]517, "JOHN GIBBON: THE MAN AND THE MONUMENT," GETTY:13[119]262

BOOK REVIEW: *IRON BRIGADE GENERAL: JOHN GIBBON, A REBEL IN BLUE*
GENERAL LISTINGS: *Chancellorsville*, CWTI:AUG/95[24]455, *Cold Harbor*, B&G:APR/94[10]558, *Fredericksburg*, AHI:JUN/78[4]180, CWR:VOL4#4[1]177, CWR:VOL4#4[70]180, *Gettysburg*, ACW:JUL/95[50]538, GETTY:4[89]150, GETTY:4[113]153, GETTY:5[79]161, GETTY:5[89]162, GETTY:7[7]185, GETTY:7[29]188, GETTY:7[51]190, GETTY:7[97]193, GETTY:8[5]198, GETTY:9[17]210, GETTY:9[33]211, GETTY:9[61]215, GETTY:10[53]225, GETTY:11[57]233, GETTY:11[80]235, GETTY:12[24]242, GETTY:12[30]243, GETTY:12[42]244, GETTY:12[85]248, MH:DEC/91[54]155
GENERAL LISTINGS, continued: *in book review*, CWM:OCT/94[8], CWM:FEB/95[7], CWNEWS:AUG/90[4], CWNEWS:JUN/92[4], CWNEWS:SEP/94[33], CWNEWS:MAY/95[33], CWR:VOL4#2[136], *in list*, CWTI:JUL/93[34]327, *in order of battle*, B&G:APR/94[10]558, *Little Big Horn*, AHI:DEC/84[18]243, AHI:JAN/85[30]246, *Manassas, Second*, ACW:JUL/91[18]312, B&G:AUG/92[11]493, *Mexican War*, MH:APR/93[39]166, *order of battle*, B&G:APR/95[8]595, *Overland Campaign*, CWTI:SEP/91[31]229, *post war*, AHI:NOV/79[32]196, *Wilderness*, B&G:APR/95[8]595, *photos*, ACW:MAR/95[42]517, AHI:MAY/71[3]133A, B&G:AUG/92[11]493, B&G:APR/94[10]558, GETTY:10[53]225, GETTY:13[119]262
ADDITIONAL LISTINGS: ACW:SEP/92[30]378, ACW:MAY/92[8]357, ACW:JUL/92[30]369, ACW:MAY/93[31]415, AHI:SUM/88[12]273, B&G:APR/93[12]518, B&G:APR/94[55]564, B&G:APR/94[59]565, CWM:JAN/93[16]457, CWR:VOL1#3[52]122, CWR:VOL3#1[31]150, CWR:VOL3#2[1]153, CWTI:APR/89[14]107, CWTI:FEB/91[45]194, GETTY:13[33]255, GETTY:13[43]256, GETTY:13[50]257
GIBBON, NICHOLAS and ROBERT, *28th North Carolina Infantry*; GETTY:13[119]262
GIBBON, THOMAS; CWTI:MAR/89[16]101
GIBBONS, J.R., *Private, CSA*; CWTI:FEB/92[42]250
GIBBS, ALFRED, *Colonel, USA*; ACW:MAY/94[35]469, B&G:APR/91[8]445, B&G:APR/92[8]481
GIBBS, DAVID M., *Sgt., 53rd Penna. Inf.*; GETTY:11[80]235
GIBBS, FRANK C., *Capt., 1st Ohio Arty.*; GETTY:11[91]236
GIBBS, WILLIAM, *Pvt., 95th Illinois Inf.*; CWTI:JAN/93[20]298
GIBSON, AUGUSTUS A., *Captain, 3rd U.S. Artillery*; CWTI:JUL/93[20]325
GIBSON, BRUCE, *Capt., 6th VA Cav.*; CWTI:JUN/90[32]159
GIBSON, DRURY P., *Private, Louisiana Tigers*; CWTI:MAR/94[48]374
GIBSON, HART, *Captain, CSA*; B&G:OCT/94[11]580
GIBSON, JAMES F., ACW:NOV/95[54]558, B&G:FEB/94[24]551
GIBSON, JOHN, *Colonel, 55th Virginia Infantry*; CWTI:JUL/92[20]271
GIBSON, RANDALL L., *General, CSA*; ACW:NOV/95[48]557, B&G:DEC/93[12]545, B&G:JUN/94[34], B&G:FEB/95[35]592, CWM:OCT/95[36]616, CWR:VOL1#2[44]114, CWTI:SUMMER/89[50]124
GIBSON, SAMUEL, *Lieutenant, CSA*; CWTI:JUN/95[38]447
GIBSON, THOMAS W., *attorney*; AHI:NOV/72[12]142
GIBSON, WILLIAM, *Colonel, CSA*; B&G:APR/94[10]558, CWTI:DEC/94[32]410
GIDDINGS, DEWITT C., *Lieutenant Colonel, CSA*; CWR:VOL2#3[212]142
GIDDINGS, GEORGE, *Major, CSA*; ACW:JUL/92[46]371

GIDDINGS, JOSHUA; CWTI:DEC/94[73]416
GIESECKE, JULIUS, *Captain, CSA*; CWTI:JAN/95[42]428
GIFFORD, MARTIN V., *Lieutenant, 83rd Pennsylvania Infantry*; GETTY:7[41]189
GILBERT, CHARLES, *General, USA*; CWR:VOL4#3[50]171, CWTI:NOV/92[18]289
GILBERT, JACOB H., *Captain, 57th North Carolina Infantry*; GETTY:12[111]250
GILBERT, JAMES I., *Colonel, USA*; B&G:DEC/93[12]545
GILBERT, S.C., *Lieutenant, Brooks (South Carolina) Artillery*; GETTY:5[47]160
GILDERSLEEVE, *Captain, 150th New York Infantry*; GETTY:12[42]244
GILES, LEONIDAS B., *Private, Terry's Texas Rangers*; CWM:JUL/92[40]432
GILES, VAL C., *Private, 4th Texas Infantry*; CWTI:MAR/95[46]437, GETTY:6[7]169
GILHAM, WILLIAM, *Colonel, 21st Virginia Infantry*:
BOOK REVIEW: *GILHAM'S MANUAL FOR VOLUNTEERS AND MILITIA*
ADDITIONAL LISTINGS: B&G:AUG/93[10]529, CWM:MAR/91[65]342
GILKERSON, THOMAS E., *Private, CSA*; ACW:MAR/91[25]294
GILL, C.R., *Colonel, 29th Wisconsin Infantry*; B&G:FEB/94[8]550
GILL, ROBERT, *Private, CSA*; ACW:MAY/92[6]356
GILL, SAMUEL W., *Private, 53rd Pennsylvania Infantry*; GETTY:11[80]235
GILLELAND, DANIEL, *Private, CSA*; ACW:JUL/93[27]423
GILLEM, ALVAN C., *General, USA*; AHI:AUG/78[18]183, B&G:AUG/91[11]458, B&G:APR/92[28]482, B&G:FEB/94[62]556
GILLEN, JAMES, *Private, 11th Pennsylvania Infantry*; GETTY:10[7]221
GILLEN, PAUL E., *Chaplain, 170th New York Infantry*; CWM:MAR/91[50]340
GILLESPIE, ANGELA, *Mother Superior*; B&G:OCT/93[31]539
GILLESPIE, H.C., *Lieutenant Colonel, 2nd Tennessee Cavalry*; CWR:VOL4#1[1]163
GILLESPIE, GEORGE L., *Lieutenant, USA*; B&G:DEC/91[12]469
GILLIAM, GEORGE, *Captain, 52nd North Carolina Infantry*; GETTY:12[61]245
GILLIGAN, EDWARD, *Sergeant, 88th Pennsylvania Infantry*; B&G:FEB/95[8]590B, GETTY:10[7]221
GILLIGAN, LUKE, *Private, 5th New York Infantry*; CWR:VOL1#2[7]111, CWTI:MAY/94[31]382
GILLMORE, QUINCY A., *General, USA*:
BOOK REVIEW: *THE BERMUDA HUNDRED CAMPAIGN*
GENERAL LISTINGS: *in book review*, B&G:JUN/95[30], CWM:JAN/91[47], CWNEWS:SEP/90[4], CWNEWS:APR/95[33], *Savannah*, B&G:FEB/91[8]439, *West Point*, B&G:DEC/91[12]469, *painting*; CWM:MAR/92[16]411, *photos*; B&G:FEB/91[8]439, CWTI:APR/89[22]108
ADDITIONAL LISTINGS: ACW:JUL/91[35]314, ACW:SEP/91[30]322, ACW:MAR/95[12]513, ACW:SEP/95[22]544, CWM:MAR/92[4]408, CWM:MAR/92[16]411, CWR:VOL2#3[194]141, CWR:VOL4#1[1]163, CWTI:MAR/89[10], CWTI:APR/89[22]108, CWTI:DEC/89[42]137, CWTI:MAY/93[29]319, CWTI:MAR/94[38]372
GILLOCK, JAMES W., *Lieutenant, 27th Virginia Infantry*; GETTY:12[111]250

GILMAN, LEMUEL, *Captain, 15th Illinois Infantry;*
  CWM:JAN/91[11]325, CWTI:JAN/93[20]298
GILMER, JEREMY F., *General, CSA:*
BOOK REVIEW: *CONFEDERATE ENGINEERS' MAPS*
ADDITIONAL LISTINGS: ACW:JUL/94[42]479, AHI:SEP/83[42]235,
  B&G:FEB/91[8]439, B&G:FEB/92[10]474, B&G:AUG/92[6]492,
  CWR:VOL1#3[7]118, *photo;* B&G:FEB/92[10]474
GILMOR, HARRY, *Major, CSA;* ACW:SEP/91[41]323,
  ACW:NOV/91[30]332, ACW:NOV/91[35]333,
  ACW:JAN/92[16]340, ACW:SEP/92[8]374,
  B&G:AUG/94[10]574, CWNEWS:MAY/94[5],
  GETTY:11[119]238, *photo;* B&G:AUG/94[10]574
GILMORE, JOHN T., *Surgeon, CSA;* CWR:VOL4#4[28]178
GILMORE, PATRICK S.; CWM:MAY/92[27]421,
  CWM:SEP/92[6]436
GILPIN, WILLIAM, *Governor, Colorado;* B&G:AUG/91[11]458,
  ACW:NOV/91[10]329, B&G:JUN/94[8]568,
  CWNEWS:NOV/90[4]
GILSTRAP, L.J., *Private, 6th South Carolina Cavalry;*
  ACW:MAR/95[50]518
GILTNER, HENRY L., *Colonel, CSA;* B&G:AUG/91[11]458,
  B&G:AUG/91[52]464
GIMBALL, HORACE I., *Lieutenant, USN;* ACW:MAR/94[35]460
GIMBEL, FREDERICK L., *Captain, 109th Pennsylvania
  Infantry;* CWR:VOL3#2[70]155
GIRARDEY, ISADORE P., *Captain, CSA;*
  CWR:VOL1#4[42]126
GIRARDEY, VICTOR, *Cpt., 3rd GA Inf.;* CWTI:DEC/94[32]410
GIST, GABRIEL G., *Pvt., 15th SC Inf.;* GETTY:5[35]159
GIST, RICHARD A., *Pvt., 2nd Tenn. Cav.;* CWR:VOL4#1[1]163
GIST, STATES RIGHTS, *General, CSA:*
BOOK REVIEWS: *STATES RIGHTS GIST: A SOUTH CAROLINA
  GENERAL OF THE CIVIL WAR*
ADDITIONAL LISTINGS: B&G:DEC/91[38]471, B&G:AUG/95[8]604,
  B&G:AUG/95[42]608, CWR:VOL2#1[36]132,
  CWTI:SUMMER/89[40]123, CWTI:MAR/93[24]309,
  CWTI:SEP/94[40]403, CWTI:DEC/95[8]474, *photo;*
  B&G:AUG/95[42]608
GIST, WILLIAM M., *Major, CSA;* GETTY:5[35]159
GIVEN, JOHN M., *Pvt., 1st Penna. Arty;* GETTY:12[30]243
GIVINS, WILLIAM, *Private, 53rd Pennsylvania Infantry;*
  GETTY:11[80]235
GLADDEN, ADLEY H., *General, CSA:*
ARTICLE: "A FORGOTTEN REBEL GENERAL,"
  CWTI:MAR/93[50]313
ADDITIONAL LISTINGS: CWR:VOL1#4[42]126, CWTI:JUL/93[10]323,
  photo; CWTI:MAR/93[50]313
GLASGOW, SAMUEL L., *Lieutenant Colonel, 23rd Iowa
  Infantry;* B&G:FEB/94[8]550
GLAZIER, WILLIARD W., *Captain, USA;* B&G:DEC/92[40]508
GLEASON, MICHAEL, *Captain, USN;* B&G:JUN/92[40]489
GLENDALE, VIRGINIA, BATTLE OF, see listings under
  "WHITE OAK SWAMP, VIRGINIA, BATTLE OF"
GLENN, J.M., *Lieutenant, 34th Mississippi Infantry;*
  CWTI:SEPT/89[30]129
GLENN, JAMES, *Major, 149th Pennsylvania Infantry:*
ARTICLE: "CAPT. JAMES GLENN'S SWORD AND PRIVATE J.
  MARSHALL HILL'S ENFIELD IN THE FIGHT FOR THE
  LUTHERAN SEMINARY," GETTY:8[9]199
ADDITIONAL LISTINGS: GETTY:4[24]145, GETTY:8[9]199,
  GETTY:13[22]254
GLOBE TAVERN, VIRGINIA, BATTLE OF: see listings
  under **"WELDON RAILROAD, VIRGINIA, BATTLE OF"**

GLORIETA BATTLEFIELD PRESERVATION SOCIETY;
  see listings under **"PRESERVATION"**
GLORIETA PASS, NEW MEXICO, BATTLE OF:
ARTICLES: "CIVIL WAR ON THE SANTA FE TRAIL:
  PRESERVING THE BATTLEFIELD AT GLORIETA PASS,"
  CWR:VOL2#2[161]139, "THE CONFEDERATE INVASION
  OF NEW MEXICO AND ARIZONA," CWM:MAY/93[16]475,
  "THE CONFEDERATE INVASION OF NEW MEXICO,"
  B&G:JUN/94[8]568, "TO HONOR THE DEAD: LAST TAPS
  AT LA GLORIETA PASS," CWTI:MAR/94[58]375
BOOK REVIEWS: *BLOOD AND TREASURE: CONFEDERATE
  EMPIRE IN THE SOUTHWEST * GLORY, GLORY,
  GLORIETA: THE GETTYSBURG OF THE WEST*
GENERAL LISTINGS: *in book review,* CWM:SEP/92[57],
  CWNEWS:NOV/90[4], CWNEWS:JUN/92[4],
  CWNEWS:AUG/94[33], CWR:VOL4#4[129], *letters to the
  editor,* B&G:DEC/93[6]544, B&G:OCT/94[6]579,
  CWTI:JUL/94[10]389
ADDITIONAL LISTINGS: ACW:JAN/91[10]283, ACW:JUL/93[27]423,
  B&G:FEB/91[34]442, B&G:JUN/93[40]527,
  B&G:JUN/94[8]568, CWM:JUL/93[35]487,
  CWTI:SEP/91[18]227
GLOSKOSKE, JOSEPH, *Captain, USA;* GETTY:4[101]151
GOBIN, J.P.S., *Col., 47th Penna. Inf.;* CWM:NOV/91[80]396
GODDARD, ABLE, *Col., 60th NY Inf.;* CWR:VOL3#2[70]155
GODDARD, CHARLES E., *Private, 1st Minnesota Infantry;*
  ACW:JAN/94[62], GETTY:5[79]161
GODELL, WILLIAM; ACW:NOV/94[42]497
GODLEY, LEONIDAS, *Sergeant, 22nd Iowa Infantry;*
  CWR:VOL2#1[19]131
GODWIN, ARCHIBALD, *Colonel, 57th North Carolina
  Infantry;* ACW:MAR/92[30]352, GETTY:12[30]243
GOEB, JOHN A., *4th U.S. Artillery;* GETTY:11[57]233
GOFF, DAVID, *Colonel, CSA;* B&G:AUG/93[10]529,
  B&G:OCT/94[28]581
GOHIR, EDWARD, *Private, 24th Michigan Infantry,*
  GETTY:9[33]211, GETTY:11[57]233
GOLD HOAX; ARTICLE: "THE GREAT CIVIL WAR GOLD
  HOAX," AHI:APR/80[21]200
GOLDEN GATE NATIONAL RECREATION AREA; ARTICLE:
  "TRACES OF A DISTANT WAR," CWTI:JUN/95[51]449
GOLDSBORO, NORTH CAROLINA; CWTI:SEPT/89[24]128
GOLDSBOROUGH, LOUIS M., *Admiral, USN;* CWM:JUN/95[39]586
GOLDSBOROUGH, WILLIAM W., *Major, 1st Maryland
  (Confederate) Infantry;* CWM:FEB/95[49]565,
  GETTY:7[83]192, GETTY:9[17]210, GETTY:12[1]240,
  GETTY:12[111]250, *photo,* GETTY:12[111]250
GOLDSBY, THOMAS, *Captain, 4th Alabama Infantry;*
  ACW:NOV/94[18]495
GOLDSMITH, WASHINGTON, *Major, CSA;*
  AHI:JUN/70[30]127
GOLDTHWAITE, RICHARD W., *Lieutenant, CSA;*
  ACW:NOV/93[34]442, CWTI:SEP/94[40]403
GOMBITELLI, JAMES, *Chaplain, 13th Pennsylvania Infantry;*
  CWM:MAR/91[50]340
GONCE, JOHN A., *Sgt., 9th Michigan Inf.;* B&G:OCT/94[11]580
GONZALES, CELESTINO, *Captain, 1st Florida Infantry;*
  B&G:AUG/94[22]576, CWTI:JAN/95[27]425
GOOD, WILLIAM H., *Private, 72nd Pennsylvania Infantry;*
  ACW:MAY/92[8]357, CWTI:DEC/90[29]182, GETTY:7[97]193
GOODBRAKE, C., *Surgeon, USA;* CWM:MAY/91[10]347
GOODE, SAMUEL W., *Private, CSA;* CWTI:SEP/91[23]228

GOODELL, WILLIAM, *Corporal, 14th Connecticut Infantry;*
 GETTY:9[61]215
GOODING, JAMES H., *Private, 54th Massachusetts Infantry;*
 AHI:JAN/94[50]319
GOODING, MICHAEL, *Colonel, USA;* ACW:SEP/95[62],
 CWR:VOL4#3[50]171
GOODING, OLIVER P., *Colonel, USA;* CWR:VOL3#1[1]149,
 CWR:VOL4#2[26]166
GOODLOE, HARPER, *Adjutant, USA;* CWR:VOL2#3[212]142
GOODMAN, SAMUEL, *Adjutant, 28th Pennsylvania Infantry;*
 GETTY:9[81]216
GOODMAN, THOMAS M., *Sergeant, Missouri Engineers;*
 B&G:JUN/91[32]454, CWTI:JAN/94[29]360
GOODRICH, CASPAR F., *USN;* ACW:JAN/91[62]289
GOODRICH, WILLIAM B., *Colonel, USA;* ACW:MAR/94[50]462
GOODSPEED, WILBUR F., *Major, USA;* B&G:DEC/93[12]545
GOODWIN, EDWARD, *Colonel, CSA;* B&G:JUN/93[12]524
GOODWIN, STEPHEN H., *Private, 9th Massachusetts
 Artillery;* GETTY:5[47]160
GOODWYN, WILLIAM E., *Private, 22nd Virginia Infantry;*
 CWR:VOL1#3[52]122
GOODYEAR, ROBERT B., *Sergeant, 27th Connecticut
 Infantry;* GETTY:12[24]242
GOOLRICK, JOHN T., *Private, Fredericksburg Artillery;*
 CWR:VOL1#1[1]102
GORDON, FRANK B., *Colonel, CSA;* B&G:JUN/91[10]452
GORDON, GEORGE C., *Captain, 24th Michigan Infantry;*
 GETTY:5[19]158
GORDON, GEORGE H., *General, USA;* ACW:JUL/92[30]369,
 ACW:JAN/95[62], GETTY:6[69]176
GORDON, GEORGE W., *General, CSA;* CWTI:FEB/92[42]250
GORDON, JAMES B., *General, CSA:*
ARTICLE: "JAMES B. GORDON OF NORTH CAROLINA
 BECAME KNOWN AS THE 'MURAT OF THE ARMY OF
 NORTHERN VIRGINIA'," ACW:JAN/95[10]503
ADDITIONAL LISTINGS: ACW:JUL/92[41]370, ACW:MAY/93[14]413,
 ACW:MAY/94[35]469, B&G:APR/95[8]595, *photo;*
 ACW:JAN/95[10]503
GORDON, JAMES, *Captain, Jeff Davis Legion;*
 GETTY:12[68]246
GORDON, JAMES C., *Major, 1st Confederate Georgia Infantry;*
 CWR:VOL1#4[42]126, CWR:VOL1#4[64]127
GORDON, JOHN B., *General, CSA:*
ARTICLES: "BATTLE IN DESPERATION," CWTI:MAR/95[33]435,
 "FOR TWO FORMER CIVIL WAR FOES, THE NEWS OF
 THEIR DEATHS WAS—LIKE MARK TWAIN'S—GREATLY
 EXAGGERATED," ACW:MAY/93[14]413, "THE
 GORDON-BARLOW STORY, WITH SEQUEL,"
 GETTY:8[5]198, "LEST WE FORGET," CWM:JUL/93[56]490
BOOK REVIEWS: *JOHN BROWN GORDON: SOLDIER,
 SOUTHERNER, AMERICAN * REMINISCENCES OF THE
 CIVIL WAR*
GENERAL LISTINGS: *Cedar Creek,* MH:OCT/93[76]173, *Davis'
 funeral,* CWTI:MAR/93[32]311, *Fort Stedman,*
 ACW:MAY/95[38]526, CWTI:FEB/91[28]192, *Gettysburg,*
 GETTY:4[33]146, GETTY:4[113]153, GETTY:6[113]183,
 GETTY:7[13]186, GETTY:9[17]210, GETTY:10[120]229, *in
 book review,* ACW:NOV/94[66], B&G:APR/92[24],
 CWM:NOV/92[55], CWM:APR/95[50], CWNEWS:SEP/90[4],
 CWNEWS:JAN/91[4], CWNEWS:OCT/94[33],
 CWR:VOL1#3[94], CWTI:FEB/90[10], *in order of battle,*
 B&G:APR/94[10]558, *Jackson,* B&G:JUN/92[8]487

GENERAL LISTINGS, continued: *Jefferson Davis,* AHI:MAY/81[8]217,
 Monocacy, ACW:NOV/93[50]444, B&G:DEC/92[8]503,
 CWTI:JAN/93[40]301, *order of battle,* B&G:APR/95[8]595,
 Overland Campaign, B&G:APR/94[10]558, *Petersburg,*
 MH:APR/95[46]183, *post-war,* ACW:JUL/95[26]535, *Sayler's
 Creek,* ACW:JAN/92[22]341, ACW:JAN/93[43]397, *Wilderness;*
 B&G:APR/95[8]595, B&G:JUN/95[8]600, *Winchester, Third,*
 ACW:MAY/91[38]305, ACW:JAN/95[46]507,
 AHI:NOV/80[8]209
PHOTOS: ACW:NOV/93[50]444, ACW:MAY/94[35]469,
 AHI:NOV/80[8]209, AHI:MAY/81[8]217, B&G:DEC/92[8]503,
 B&G:JUN/95[8]600, CWTI:MAR/95[33]435, GETTY:8[5]198
ADDITIONAL LISTINGS: ACW:NOV/92[42]388, ACW:SEP/93[31]433,
 ACW:JAN/95[10]503, ACW:JAN/95[46]507,
 AHI:SEP/87[40]263, B&G:APR/92[48]484,
 B&G:FEB/95[8]590B, B&G:FEB/95[8]590C,
 CWM:JUL/91[46]373, CWM:SEP/93[24]495,
 CWM:JAN/93[40]461, CWM:OCT/94[38]540,
 CWR:VOL1#1[35]104, CWR:VOL2#4[269]145,
 CWR:VOL3#2[1]153, CWTI:AUG/90[26]166,
 CWTI:JUL/93[38]328, CWTI:DEC/94[32]410, GETTY:13[7]253
GORDON-BARLOW INCIDENT; ARTICLE: "THE
 GORDON-BARLOW STORY, WITH SEQUEL,"
 GETTY:8[5]198
GORE, LESLIE, *Corporal, 1st Minnesota Infantry;*
 GETTY:5[79]161
GORE, SILAS, *Private, 141st Pennsylvania Infantry;*
 B&G:JUN/95[36]603A
GORGAS, JOSIAH, *General, CSA:*
BOOK REVIEWS: *PLOUGHSHARES INTO SWORDS: JOSIAH
 GORGAS AND CONFEDERATE ORDNANCE*
ADDITIONAL LISTINGS: ACW:JAN/91[8]282, ACW:MAR/91[38]296,
 ACW:NOV/91[8]328, ACW:SEP/92[38]379,
 ACW:JAN/93[51]398, ACW:JAN/94[18]449,
 ACW:MAY/94[20]467, ACW:MAY/95[38]526,
 CWM:SEP/91[10]379, *photos;* CWM:SEP/91[10]379,
 CWTI:JAN/93[49]303
GORMAN, JOHN, *U.S. Sheriff;* B&G:APR/91[24]446
GORMAN, WILLIS A., *Colonel, 34th New York Infantry;*
 ACW:JAN/94[62], ACW:MAR/94[50]462, B&G:OCT/95[8]611A,
 CWTI:APR/90[48]154, CWR:VOL3#1[78]152, GETTY:5[79]161
GORY, JOHN W., *Colonel, 28th Pennsylvania Infantry;*
 GETTY:10[120]229
GOSDEN, W.W., *Mosby's Ranger;* CWTI:SEP/90[34]176
GOSPORT NAVAL YARD, VIRGINIA; ACW:JAN/91[62]289,
 ACW:MAR/94[35]460, CWR:VOL2#3[183]140,
 CWTI:SEP/94[26]400
GOSS, MARK W., *Lieutenant, USA;* B&G:OCT/94[11]580
GOSS, WARREN L., *Private, 2nd Massachusetts Heavy
 Artillery;* B&G:DEC/92[32]506, CWM:JAN/92[16]401,
 GETTY:9[5]209
GOULD, ANDREW W., *Lieutenant, CSA;* CWTI:JAN/93[12],
 CWTI:JAN/94[35]361
GOULD, J.P., *Colonel, USA;* CWTI:APR/90[24]152
GOULD, N.C., *Captain, CSA;* ACW:MAR/93[51]407
GOULD, ORRIN, *Private, 9th Texas Infantry;*
 ACW:SEP/91[46]324
GOULD, SEWARD F., *Major, 4th New York Heavy Artillery;*
 CWTI:AUG/90[26]166
GOULDEN, W., *Private, 22nd Virginia Infantry;*
 CWR:VOL1#3[52]122
GOURLAY, JEANNE; AHI:FEB/86[20]258

GOURLAY, THOMAS C.; AHI:FEB/86[20]258

GOVAN, DANIEL C., *General, CSA;* ACW:NOV/93[34]442, B&G:DEC/93[12]545, CWTI:SUMMER/89[50]124, CWTI:SEP/94[40]403

GOVERNEMENT, CONFEDERATE; BOOK REVIEWS: *A GOVERNMENT OF OUR OWN: THE MAKING OF THE CONFEDERACY * COMPENDIUM OF THE CONFEDERACY, AN ANNOTATED BIBLIOGRAPHY, 2 VOL. * THE CONFEDERATE REPUBLIC: A REVOLUTION AGAINST POLITICS * DIVIDED WE FALL—ESSAYS ON CONFEDERATE NATION BUILDING * ENCYCLOPEDIA OF THE CONFEDERACY * FINANCIAL FAILURE AND CONFEDERATE DEFEAT * INSIDE THE CONFEDERATE GOVERNMENT: THE DIARY OF ROBERT GARLICK HILL KEAN * JEFFERSON DAVIS AND HIS GENERALS: THE FAILURE OF CONFEDERATE COMMAND IN THE WEST * THE RISE AND FALL OF THE CONFEDERATE GOVERNMENT*

GOVERNMENT, FEDERAL:

ARTICLE: "THE CONGRESSIONAL RESOLUTION OF THANKS FOR THE FEDERAL VICTORY AT GETTYSBURG," GETTY:12[85]248

BOOK REVIEW: *BLUEPRINT FOR MODERN AMERICA: NONMILITARY LEGISLATION OF THE FIRST CIVIL WAR CONGRESS*

GOWAN, GEORGE W., *Colonel, 48th Pennsylvania Infantry;* CWM:JUL/93[46]489, CWM:OCT/94[55]543

GOZELACHOWSKI, ALEXANDER, *Chaplain, 2nd New Mexico Cavalry;* CWM:MAR/91[50]340

GRABER, HENRY W., *Private, Terry's Texas Rangers;* CWM:JUL/92[40]432

GRACE, CHARLES D., *Sergeant, 4th Georgia Infantry;* ARTICLE: "THE MAN WHO SHOT JOHN SEDGWICK: THE TALE OF CHARLES D. GRACE-A SHARPSHOOTER IN THE DOLES-COOK BRIGADE, CSA, B&G:DEC/95[25]616

GRACE, NEWELL, *Lieutenant, 24th Michigan Infantry;* GETTY:5[19]158

GRACIE, ARCHIBALD, *General, CSA;* ACW:MAY/91[23]303, ACW:SEP/92[38]379, AHI:AUG/71[22]135, B&G:DEC/93[30]546, CWTI:MAY/94[50]386, MH:APR/95[46]183

GRAFTON, WEST VIRGINIA, ENGAGEMENT AT; B&G:AUG/93[10]529

GRAHAM HARVEY, *Lieutenant Colonel, USA;* CWR:VOL2#1[19]131

GRAHAM, ARCHIBALD, *Lieutenant, Rockbridge Artillery;* CWR:VOL4#4[70]180

GRAHAM, CHARLES K., *General, USA;* CWM:APR/95[42]577, GETTY:5[35]159, GETTY:5[47]160, GETTY:6[59]174, GETTY:8[31]201, GETTY:8[53]203, GETTY:10[112]228, GETTY:12[7]241

GRAHAM, E.R., *Pvt., 56th Pennsylvania Inf.;* GETTY:9[33]211

GRAHAM, EDWARD, *Captain, Petersburg Artillery;* ACW:MAR/95[12]513, B&G:OCT/94[42]583

GRAHAM, HARVEY, *Colonel, 22nd Iowa Infantry;* CWR:VOL2#1[19]131

GRAHAM, JAMES A., *Captain, 27th North Carolina Infantry;* CWTI:FEB/91[45]194

GRAHAM, JOHN H., *Captain, 5th New York Heavy Artillery;* CWR:VOL1#4[7]125

GRAHAM, JOHN M., *Major, 7th Illinois Cavalry;* B&G:JUN/93[12]524

GRAHAM, NEIL T., *Surgeon, 10th Ohio Infantry;* CWM:SEP/93[18]494

GRAHAM, ROBERT G., *Colonel, 21st South Carolina Infantry;* CWM:JUL/92[16]428

GRAHAM, SMITH, *Private, 140th Pennsylvania Infantry;* B&G:APR/91[8]445

GRAHAM, THOMAS A., *Private, Sumter Artillery;* CWR:VOL3#2[1]153

GRAHAM, THOMAS, *Major, USA;* CWM:JAN/91[40]330

GRAHAM, WILLIAM M., *Captain, 1st U.S. Artillery;* B&G:OCT/93[12]537, GETTY:11[19]232

GRAHAM, ZIBA, *Lieutenant, 16th Michigan Infantry;* GETTY:6[33]172

GRAMMER, WILLIAM B., *Private, 48th Mississippi Infantry;* GETTY:4[7]142

GRANBURY, HIRAM, *General, CSA;* ACW:NOV/93[34]442, B&G:OCT/91[11]466, B&G:DEC/93[12]545, CWR:VOL1#2[78], CWR:VOL3#3[59]159, CWTI:SEP/94[40]403

GRAND ARMY OF THE REPUBLIC CIVIL WAR MUSEUM AND LIBRARY; ARTICLE: "G.A.R. MUSEUM IS A TREASURY OF WAR RELICS," CWTI:SEP/90[22]173

GRAND ARMY OF THE REPUBLIC:

BOOK REVIEWS: *COLLECTING GRAND ARMY OF THE REPUBLIC MEMORABILIA * GLORIOUS CONTENTMENT: THE GRAND ARMY OF THE REPUBLIC 1865-1900*

ADDITIONAL LISTINGS: ACW:SEP/91[8]318, ACW:MAR/95[70]520, AHI:JUL/93[40]312, CWTI:MAY/91[8]205, CWTI:MAY/91[48]211, CWTI:FEB/92[42]250, CWTI:SEP/93[22]335, GETTY:4[24]145, GETTY:5[123]166, GETTY:7[119]195

GRAND COTEAU, LOUISIANA; ACW:SEP/92[16]376

GRAND GULF MILITARY PARK; B&G:FEB/94[57]555

GRAND GULF, MISSISSIPPI, BATTLE OF; ACW:NOV/91[22]331, ACW:MAY/92[47]363, ACW:JUL/94[51]480, B&G:FEB/94[8]550, CWR:VOL2#1[1]130, CWR:VOL2#1[19]131, CWR:VOL2#1[36]132, CWR:VOL3#3[33]158, CWR:VOL4#2[26]166

GRAND JUNCTION, TENNESSEE; CWTI:FEB/90[38]145

GRAND REVIEW, WASHINGTON, D.C.:

BOOK REVIEW: *THE FINAL BIVOUAC: THE SURRENDER PARADE AT APPOMATTOX AND THE DISBANDING OF THE ARMIES*

ADDITIONAL LISTINGS: CWNEWS:MAY/91[4], CWTI:JAN/95[34]427

GRANGER, AMOS P.; ACW:NOV/94[42]497

GRANGER, ERASTUS M., *Lieutenant, 111th New York Infantry;* GETTY:8[95]205

GRANGER, GORDON, *General, USA;* ACW:SEP/92[16]376, ACW:NOV/93[26]441, B&G:OCT/92[10]496, B&G:JUN/94[34], B&G:FEB/95[30]591, CWM:JUL/93[24]485, CWM:OCT/94[48]542, CWM:DEC/94[7], CWNEWS:NOV/91[4], CWNEWS:SEP/92[4], CWR:VOL4#1[1]163, CWTI:SEP/92[31]281, CWTI:MAR/94[20]369, CWTI:DEC/94[24]409, MH:DEC/95[58]188, *photo;* CWTI:SEP/92[31]281

GRANGER, HENRY H., *Captain, 10th Massachusetts Artillery;* CWR:VOL2#1[78]

GRANGER, HENRY W., *Major, 7th Michigan Cavalry;* ACW:MAY/94[35]469

GRANGER, ROBERT S., *General, USA;* CWTI:MAR/91[46]203

GRANNIS, HENRY J., *Sergeant, 12th Iowa Infantry;* B&G:FEB/92[10]474, CWNEWS:NOV/94[33]

GRANT MEMORIAL ASSOCIATION; CWM:JUL/93[4]482

GRANT'S TOMB; B&G:APR/92[36]483

GRANT, GEORGE W., *Lieutenant, 88th Pennsylvania Infantry;*
B&G:AUG/95[36]607, GETTY:10[7]221

GRANT, JULIA DENT:

ARTICLES: "AMERICA'S FIRST LADIES," AHI:MAY/89[26]285,
"FIRST LADIES AT WAR," ACW:JAN/94[47]452, "MRS.
GRANT REMEMBERS JAPAN," AHI:JUN/81[38]220

BOOK REVIEW: *THE PERSONAL MEMOIRS OF JULIA DENT
GRANT*

ADDITIONAL LISTINGS: B&G:FEB/93[61]516, CWTI:FEB/90[20]142,
CWTI:FEB/90[46]146, CWTI:APR/90[56]155,
CWTI:FEB/91[28]192, *photo;* ACW:JAN/94[47]452

GRANT, LEWIS A., *General, USA;* B&G:APR/94[10]558,
B&G:APR/95[8]595, CWM:JUL/91[64]375,
CWM:JAN/91[35]328, GETTY:12[123]251

GRANT, M.S., *General, Kansas Militia;* ACW:NOV/94[42]497,
B&G:JUN/91[10]452

GRANT, NATHANIEL, *civilian;* CWTI:MAR/91[34]201

GRANT, THOMAS, *Pvt., 13th Alabama Inf.;* GETTY:6[13]170

GRANT, ULYSSES S., *General, USA:*

ARTICLES: "A CONVERSATION WITH THE PAST,"
CWTI:APR/90[56]155, "A HILL OF DEATH,"
CWTI:MAY/91[24]208, "A PRESIDENTIAL GALLERY,"
AHI:APR/89[20]282, "A UNION HERO'S FORGOTTEN
RESTING PLACE," CWTI:FEB/90[12]141, "'ALL GOES ON
LIKE A MIRACLE,'" CWTI:APR/92[49]260, "BATTLE IN
DESPERATION," CWTI:MAR/95[33]435, "THE BELKNAP
SCANDAL," AHI:MAY/69[32]122, "BLACK THURSDAY FOR
REBELS," ACW:JAN/92[22]341, "BURNING DOWN THE
SOUTH," CWTI:OCT/95[48]470, "CIVIL WAR'S LONGEST
SIEGE," MH:APR/95[46]183, "CONDITIONAL SURRENDER:
THE DEATH OF U.S. GRANT, AND THE COTTAGE ON
MOUNT MCGREGOR," B&G:FEB/93[61]516, "CROSSED
WIRES," CWTI:DEC/94[57]414, "DEVIL'S OWN DAY,"
ACW:JAN/91[22]285, "THE FALL OF RICHMOND,"
ACW:MAY/95[38]526, "FORTS HENRY AND DONELSON
FALL TO 'UNCONDITIONAL SURRENDER' GRANT!"
CWM:FEB/95[32]562, "FORTS HENRY AND DONELSON:
UNION VICTORY ON THE TWIN RIVERS," B&G:FEB/92[10]474, "GENERAL GRANT IS NEARLY
KILLED AT THE BRADY STUDIO," B&G:FEB/94[32]552

ARTICLES, continued: "THE GRACIOUS VICTOR,"
CWTI:FEB/90[54]147, "GRANT AND LEE, 1864: FROM THE
NORTH ANNA TO THE CROSSING OF THE JAMES,"
B&G:APR/94[10]558, "GRANT'S BEACHHEAD FOR THE
VICKSBURG CAMPAIGN: THE BATTLE OF PORT GIBSON,
MAY 1, 1863," B&G:FEB/94[8]550, "GRANT'S EARLY WAR
DAYS," ACW:NOV/94[34]496, "GRANT'S MISSISSIPPI
GAMBLE," ACW:JUL/94[51]480, "HISTORY COMES HOME,"
CWTI:MAR/95[20]433, "HOMETOWN FRIEND JOHN A.
RAWLINS WAS U. S. GRANT'S 'NEAREST
INDISPENSABLE' OFFICER," ACW:NOV/95[22]554, "IF
THIS CONTINUES THE ARMY OF THE POTOMAC WILL
BE ANNIHILLATED," CWM:OCT/95[40]619, "THE LAST
DAYS OF 'SAM' GRANT," AHI:DEC/72[4]144, "LITERAL
HILL OF DEATH," ACW:NOV/91[22]331, "MEETING AT
THE MCLEAN HOUSE," AHI:SEP/87[48]264, "MIRACLE OF
THE RAILS," CWTI:SEP/92[22]279, "MR. GRANT GOES TO
WASHINGTON," B&G:APR/95[33]597, "NO TURNING
BACK: THE BATTLE OF THE WILDERNESS, PART I,"
B&G:APR/95[8]595

ARTICLES, continued: "NO TURNING BACK: THE BATTLE OF THE
WILDERNESS, PART II - THE FIGHTING ON MAY 6, 1864,"

B&G:JUN/95[8]600, "ONE BRIDGE TOO MANY,"
ACW:JAN/93[43]397, "PERSONALITY: ELIZABETH VAN
LEW," ACW:JUL/91[8]309, "PERSPECTIVES IN THE PAST,"
AHI:AUG/78[31]185, "SHOWDOWN IN THE WEST: GRANT
VS ROSECRANS," CWM:MAR/93[8]465, "STRIKE THEM A
BLOW: LEE AND GRANT AT THE NORTH ANNA RIVER,"
B&G:APR/93[12]518, "TO SAVE AN ARMY,"
CWTI:SEP/94[40]403, "'TRUE AMERICAN MADNESS':
INAUGURAL BALLS," AHI:NOV/72[37]143, "U.S. GRANT
AND SIMON BUCKNER: FRIENDS," AHI:MAR/82[8]227,
"ULYSSES S. GRANT: A KIND OF NORTHERN HERO,"
CWTI:FEB/90[32]144, "ULYSSES S. GRANT: AN UNHAPPY
CIVILIAN," CWTI:FEB/90[26]143, "ULYSSES S. GRANT:
COMMANDER OF ALL UNION ARMIES,"
CWTI:FEB/90[46]146, "ULYSSES S. GRANT: DIFFICULT
LAST DAYS," CWTI:FEB/90[60]148, "ULYSSES S. GRANT:
HIS LIFE AND HARD TIMES," CWTI:FEB/90[20]142,
"ULYSSES S. GRANT: LEADING THE JUGGERNAUT,"
CWTI:FEB/90[38]145, "WHEN ULYSSES S. GRANT
CROSSED THE RAPIDAN, HE COMMENCED THE FINAL
CAMPAIGN OF THE CIVIL WAR," ACW:SEP/95[74]550

BOOK REVIEWS: *THE BATTLE OF BELMONT: GRANT STRIKES
SOUTH * BATTLE IN THE WILDERNESS: GRANT MEETS
LEE * CAMPAIGNING WITH GRANT * CAPTAIN SAM
GRANT * THE GENERALSHIP OF ULYSSES S. GRANT *
GRANT & LEE: A STUDY IN PERSONALITY AND
GENERALSHIP * GRANT MOVES SOUTH * GRANT
TAKES COMMAND * GRANT: A BIOGRAPHY * IF IT
TAKES ALL SUMMER: THE BATTLE OF SPOTSYLVANIA
* LET US HAVE PEACE: ULYSSES S. GRANT AND THE
POLITICS OF WAR AND RECONSTRUCTION, 1861-1868*

BOOK REVIEWS, continued: *LINCOLN FINDS A GENERAL. A
MILITARY HISTORY OF THE CIVIL WAR * THE PAPERS
OF ULYSSES S. GRANT. VOLUME 1: 1837-1861 *
PERSONAL MEMOIRS OF U.S.GRANT * PERSONAL /
SELECTED LETTERS OF ULYSSES S. GRANT * ULYSSES:
A BIOGRAPHICAL NOVEL OF U.S. GRANT * WITH GRANT
AND MEADE: FROM THE WILDERNESS TO
APPOMATTOX*

VIDEO REVIEW: ULYSSES S. GRANT, AHI:JAN/90[22]

GENERAL LISTINGS: *Appomattox Campaign,* CWTI:AUG/90[26]166,
CWTI:SEP/92[42]283, CWTI:NOV/93[50]349,
CWTI:MAR/95[20]433, *assassination of Garfield,*
AHI:FEB/69[12]119, *Belmont,* ACW:NOV/94[34]496,
CWR:VOL3#4[24]162, *birthplace;* AHI:APR/89[43]284, *Cassius
M. Clay,* AHI:MAY/69[12]121, *Champion Hill,*
CWTI:MAY/91[18]207, MH:JUN/93[82]167, *Cold Harbor,*
ACW:SEP/93[62]436, CWR:VOL3#4[1]161, *common soldiers,*
AHI:APR/68[4]115, *Confederate attempt to surrender,*
CWTI:FEB/91[36]193, *Cordelia Harvey,*
CWTI:MAR/89[20]102, *Custer,* AHI:FEB/71[4]131,
AHI:JUN/76[4]169, *demobilization,* CWTI:AUG/90[70]171

GENERAL LISTINGS, continued: *election of 1864,* AHI:OCT/68[4]116,
election of 1876, AHI:NOV/88[28]277, *Eli Parker,*
AHI:NOV/69[13]124, *Fall of Richmond,* AHI:JAN/74[10]153,
Five Forks, B&G:APR/92[8]481, *Fort Donelson,*
CWM:JAN/92[34]404, CWTI:SEP/93[59]341, *Fort Fisher,*
ACW:JAN/95[38]506, *Fort Fisher,* AHI:SEP/83[12]234, *Fort
Pillow,* CWTI:NOV/93[65]351, *Fort Steadman,*
CWTI:MAR/95[33]435, *General Grant National Memorial;*
AHI:APR/89[43]284, *general history,* AHI:MAY/71[3]133A,
Grand Review, ACW:SEP/94[55]489, CWTI:AUG/90[64]170,
Grant Cottage State Historic Site; AHI:APR/89[43]284, *Grant's*

Grant, Ulysses S.

Headquarters Cabin; AHI:APR/89[43]284, *Grierson's Raid,*
B&G:JUN/93[12]524, MH:FEB/95[18]182, *Henry Halleck,*
AHI:MAY/78[10]179, *His funeral;* CWTI:FEB/90[12]141
GENERAL LISTINGS, continued: *in book review,* ACW:NOV/91[54],
ACW:MAR/92[54], ACW:MAY/92[54], ACW:MAY/93[54],
ACW:JUL/93[58], ACW:SEP/93[54], ACW:NOV/93[58],
ACW:MAR/94[58], ACW:MAY/94[58], ACW:JUL/94[58],
ACW:SEP/94[66], ACW:NOV/94[66], ACW:NOV/95[62]
AHI:JAN/84[8], B&G:JUN/95[30], B&G:DEC/95[30],
CWM:JAN/91[47], CWM:SEP/91[58], CWM:JUN/94[6],
CWM:AUG/94[9], CWM:DEC/94[7], CWM:APR/95[8],
CWM:AUG/95[8], CWM:AUG/95[45], CWM:OCT/95[10],
CWM:DEC/95[10], CWNEWS:OCT/89[4],
CWNEWS:AUG/90[4], CWNEWS:SEP/90[4],
CWNEWS:NOV/90[4], CWNEWS:JAN/91[4],
CWNEWS:JUN/91[4], CWNEWS:AUG/92[4],
CWNEWS:SEP/92[4], CWNEWS:NOV/92[4],
CWNEWS:MAY/93[4], CWNEWS:JUN/93[5],
CWNEWS:JAN/94[5], CWNEWS:JUL/94[25],
CWNEWS:APR/95[33], CWNEWS:AUG/95[33],
CWNEWS:SEP/95[33]
GENERAL LISTINGS, continued: *in book review, continued,*
CWR:VOL1#2[78], CWR:VOL1#3[94], CWR:VOL2#1[78],
CWR:VOL2#2[169], CWR:VOL2#3[256], CWR:VOL3#1[80],
CWR:VOL3#3[92], CWR:VOL4#1[78], CWR:VOL4#3[1]170,
CWR:VOL4#3[89], CWR:VOL4#4[129], CWTI:MAR/89[10],
CWTI:FEB/90[10], CWTI:DEC/90[10], CWTI:AUG/91[18],
CWTI:FEB/92[18], CWTI:APR/92[30], CWTI:SEP/92[18],
CWTI:JAN/93[12], CWTI:JUL/94[18], MH:AUG/92[76],
MH:DEC/94[70]
GENERAL LISTINGS, continued: *in order of battle,* B&G:APR/94[10]558,
Indian Wars, AHI:AUG/78[18]183, *Isaac Lynde,*
B&G:JUN/94[8]568, *James A. Garfield,* AHI:MAY/76[24]167,
Jericho Mill, B&G:APR/93[12]518, *John C. Fremont,*
AHI:MAY/70[4]126, *Johnston's surrender;*
CWTI:APR/90[20]151, CWTI:AUG/90[42]167, *Julia Grant,*
ACW:JAN/94[47]452, *Kate Sprague,* AHI:APR/83[27]233,
leadership, CWR:VOL4#1[78], *letters to the editor,*
B&G:APR/93[6]517, B&G:AUG/95[36]607,
CWM:MAR/91[12]333, CWM:JUL/93[4]482,
CWM:SEP/93[4]492, CWM:DEC/94[5]546,
CWTI:FEB/92[8]245, CWTI:NOV/92[8]288,
CWTI:NOV/93[12]345, CWTI:JUN/95[14]443, *Lincoln's
assassination,* ACW:SEP/95[62], *Lincoln's humor,*
AHI:NOV/70[22]130, *Lincoln, at City Point,*
CWTI:FEB/91[28]192, *Lookout Mountain,*
CWTI:SEPT/89[30]129
GENERAL LISTINGS, continued: *Mark Twain,* AHI:AUG/67[50]111,
Mary Ann Bickerdyke, AHI:APR/79[4]186, *Meade,*
CWTI:SEP/91[31]229, *Mexican War,* AHI:MAY/88[38]270,
MH:APR/93[39]166, *Mexico,* MH:AUG/91[45]153, *Monocacy,*
ACW:NOV/93[50]444, *Nelson-Davis feud,* AHI:NOV/72[12]142,
order of battle, B&G:FEB/94[8]550, B&G:APR/95[8]595,
Overland Campaign, ACW:SEP/95[70]549,
CWTI:JAN/93[40]301, *Petersburg,* ACW:NOV/92[74]390,
ACW:JUL/94[42]479, MH:JUN/92[6]158, *prisoner exchange,*
CWM:OCT/95[10], CWM:OCT/95[10], CWTI:JAN/95[48]429,
Sherman on the Presidency, AHI:JAN/77[46]173, *Shiloh,*
CWR:VOL4#1[44]164, *SIO,* B&G:FEB/95[38]593, *slavery,*
ACW:NOV/95[8]552, *soldier's life,* AHI:AUG/72[24]140, *St.
Louis,* ACW:MAY/91[31]304
GENERAL LISTINGS, continued: *Thomas,* ACW:NOV/95[48]557,
Vicksburg, ACW:MAY/92[47]363, ACW:NOV/93[8]438,

AHI:DEC/77[13]176, AHI:DEC/77[46]177,
B&G:AUG/95[8]604, CWM:AUG/94[52]530,
CWR:VOL3#3[33]158, CWTI:SEPT/89[18]126, *West Point,*
AHI:AUG/71[22]135, B&G:DEC/91[12]469, *Wilderness,*
ACW:MAY/93[31]415, ACW:MAY/94[35]469,
CWTI:FEB/90[46]146, *William T. Sherman,*
AHI:JAN/67[4]106, *Winfield Scott,* AHI:JUL/81[20]221
PHOTOS AND PAINTINGS: ACW:JUL/92[54], ACW:NOV/94[34]496,
AHI:JAN/67[4]106, AHI:MAY/69[32]122, AHI:NOV/69[13]124,
AHI:MAY/71[3]133A, AHI:AUG/72[24]140, AHI:DEC/72[4]144,
AHI:NOV/73[18]151, AHI:JUN/76[4]169, AHI:JAN/77[46]173,
AHI:APR/89[20]282, AHI:SEP/89[20]286, AHI:NOV/90[44]293,
B&G:APR/91[8]445, B&G:FEB/92[10]474,
B&G:APR/93[12]518, B&G:JUN/93[12]524,
B&G:FEB/94[8]550, B&G:APR/94[10]558,
B&G:APR/94[34]561, B&G:AUG/94[38]578,
B&G:DEC/94[36]588, B&G:APR/95[8]595,
B&G:APR/95[33]597, B&G:JUN/95[8]600,
CWTI:FEB/90[20]142, CWTI:FEB/90[26]143,
CWTI:FEB/90[32]144, CWTI:FEB/90[38]145,
CWTI:FEB/90[46]146, CWTI:FEB/90[54]147,
CWTI:FEB/90[60]148, CWTI:APR/90[56]155,
CWTI:MAY/91[24]208, CWTI:DEC/94[57]414,
CWTI:DEC/95[67]481, MH:FEB/93[42]164
ADDITIONAL LISTINGS, ACW: ACW:JAN/91[16]284,
ACW:MAR/91[30]295, ACW:MAR/91[38]296,
ACW:MAY/91[10]301, ACW:MAY/91[38]305,
ACW:MAY/91[62]307, ACW:JUL/91[14]311,
ACW:JUL/91[35]314, ACW:SEP/91[41]323,
ACW:SEP/91[46]324, ACW:NOV/91[6]327,
ACW:MAR/92[14]350, ACW:MAY/92[14]358,
ACW:JUL/92[6]365, ACW:JUL/92[22]368,
ACW:JUL/92[62]372, ACW:SEP/92[23]377,
ACW:SEP/92[47]380, ACW:NOV/92[8]383,
ACW:NOV/92[26]386, ACW:NOV/92[35]387,
ACW:MAR/93[8]401, ACW:MAR/93[26]404,
ACW:MAY/93[12]412, ACW:MAY/93[14]413,
ACW:MAY/93[22]414, ACW:MAY/93[38]416,
ACW:JUL/93[6]419, ACW:JUL/93[34]424, ACW:SEP/93[6]428,
ACW:SEP/93[16]431, ACW:NOV/93[34]442,
ACW:JAN/94[18]449, ACW:JAN/94[30]450,
ACW:MAR/94[27]459, ACW:MAY/94[12]466,
ACW:JUL/94[26]477, ACW:JUL/94[66]481,
ACW:SEP/94[10]484, ACW:SEP/94[74]491,
ACW:NOV/94[12]494, ACW:NOV/94[42]497,
ACW:NOV/94[76]500, ACW:JAN/95[10]503,
ACW:JAN/95[46]507, ACW:MAR/95[8]512,
ACW:MAR/95[34]516, ACW:MAR/95[70]520,
ACW:JUL/95[10]533, ACW:JUL/95[26]535,
ACW:SEP/95[6]541, ACW:SEP/95[30]545,
ACW:SEP/95[48]547, ACW:SEP/95[54]548,
ACW:NOV/95[6]551, ACW:NOV/95[8]552,
ACW:NOV/95[10]553
ADDITIONAL LISTINGS, AHI: AHI:NOV/73[18]151,
AHI:NOV/80[8]209, AHI:NOV/84[18]241A,
AHI:JAN/85[10]244, AHI:APR/85[16]249, AHI:APR/85[18]250,
AHI:FEB/86[12]257, AHI:APR/87[10]261, AHI:SEP/87[40]263,
AHI:APR/89[13]281, AHI:NOV/90[44]293,
AHI:NOV/93[48]316, AHI:OCT/95[24]326
ADDITIONAL LISTINGS, B&G: B&G:FEB/91[8]439,
B&G:FEB/91[34]442, B&G:APR/91[8]445,
B&G:JUN/91[10]452, B&G:JUN/91[32]454,
B&G:AUG/91[11]458, B&G:OCT/91[11]466,

B&G:OCT/92[10]496, B&G:DEC/92[8]503,
B&G:AUG/93[36]533, B&G:OCT/93[31]539,
B&G:APR/94[34]561, B&G:JUN/94[38]571,
B&G:AUG/94[10]574, B&G:AUG/94[38]578,
B&G:DEC/94[10]585, B&G:APR/95[24]596,
B&G:DEC/95[9]615, B&G:DEC/95[25]616
ADDITIONAL LISTINGS, CWM: CWM:JAN/91[38]329,
CWM:JAN/91[40]330, CWM:MAR/91[56]341,
CWM:MAY/91[10]347, CWM:MAY/91[31]350,
CWM:MAY/91[40]351, CWM:JUL/91[8]356,
CWM:JUL/91[45]372, CWM:JUL/91[46]373,
CWM:NOV/91[58]394A, CWM:JAN/92[21]402,
CWM:JAN/92[40]405, CWM:MAY/92[34]422,
CWM:JUL/92[24]430, CWM:JUL/92[40]432,
CWM:JUL/92[4]425, CWM:JUL/92[8]427, CWM:SEP/92[8]437,
CWM:SEP/92[16]438, CWM:SEP/92[19]440,
CWM:NOV/92[10]447, CWM:NOV/92[41]451,
CWM:JAN/93[40]461, CWM:MAR/93[4]463,
CWM:MAR/93[24]467, CWM:MAY/93[4]472,
CWM:SEP/93[8]493, CWM:APR/94[24]505,
CWM:JUN/94[26]512, CWM:JUN/94[30]515,
CWM:AUG/94[30]527, CWM:OCT/94[17]534,
CWM:OCT/94[33]538, CWM:DEC/94[46]552,
CWM:FEB/95[30]561, CWM:FEB/95[36]563,
CWM:APR/95[16]571, CWM:APR/95[66]579,
CWM:JUN/95[17]581, CWM:OCT/95[22]614,
CWM:OCT/95[47]620, CWM:DEC/95[35]629,
CWM:DEC/95[48]631
ADDITIONAL LISTINGS, CWR: CWR:VOL1#1[42]105,
CWR:VOL1#2[44]114, CWR:VOL1#3[7]118,
CWR:VOL1#3[52]122, CWR:VOL1#4[42]126,
CWR:VOL1#4[64]127, CWR:VOL2#1[1]130,
CWR:VOL2#1[19]131, CWR:VOL2#1[36]132,
CWR:VOL2#1[75]134, CWR:VOL2#2[118]136,
CWR:VOL2#2[141]137, CWR:VOL2#3[212]142,
CWR:VOL2#3[236]143, CWR:VOL2#4[269]145,
CWR:VOL2#4[313]146, CWR:VOL3#1[65]151,
CWR:VOL3#2[1]153, CWR:VOL3#2[70]155,
CWR:VOL3#3[1]157, CWR:VOL3#3[59]159,
CWR:VOL3#4[1]161, CWR:VOL4#2[26]166
ADDITIONAL LISTINGS, CWTI: CWTI:SUMMER/89[13]120,
CWTI:SUMMER/89[20]121, CWTI:SUMMER/89[34]122,
CWTI:SUMMER/89[40]123, CWTI:DEC/89[34]136,
CWTI:FEB/90[60]148, CWTI:APR/90[24]152,
CWTI:SEP/90[22]173, CWTI:SEP/90[28]175,
CWTI:FEB/91[24]191, CWTI:FEB/91[45]194,
CWTI:MAR/91[28]200, CWTI:MAY/91[24]208,
CWTI:AUG/91[52]219, CWTI:AUG/91[62]221,
CWTI:SEP/91[23]228, CWTI:SEP/91[61]233,
CWTI:DEC/91[28]239, CWTI:APR/92[35]257,
CWTI:MAY/92[20]262, CWTI:MAY/92[38]265,
CWTI:MAY/92[48]267, CWTI:JUL/92[29]272,
CWTI:JUL/92[42]274, CWTI:MAR/93[24]309,
CWTI:MAR/93[40]312, CWTI:MAY/93[26]318,
CWTI:MAY/93[29]319, CWTI:JUL/93[20]325,
CWTI:SEP/93[14]333, CWTI:SEP/93[62]342,
CWTI:NOV/93[33]347, CWTI:NOV/93[78]354,
CWTI:JAN/94[35]361, CWTI:MAY/94[46]385,
CWTI:MAY/94[50]386, CWTI:JUL/94[44]394,
CWTI:JUL/94[50]395, CWTI:SEP/94[40]403,
CWTI:DEC/94[32]410, CWTI:DEC/94[79]417,
CWTI:DEC/94[82]418, CWTI:JAN/95[27]425,
CWTI:JAN/95[34]427, CWTI:JAN/95[48]429,

CWTI:MAR/95[40]436, CWTI:JUN/95[26]445,
CWTI:JUN/95[51]449, CWTI:AUG/95[46]459,
CWTI:OCT/95[32]468, CWTI:DEC/95[14]475,
CWTI:DEC/95[67]481, CWTI:DEC/95[76]482
ADDITIONAL LISTINGS, continued: GETTY:13[89]260,
MH:FEB/92[8]156, MH:FEB/93[42]164, MH:DEC/93[12]174,
MH:JUN/94[8]177, MH:AUG/94[46]178, MH:OCT/94[20]180,
MH:OCT/95[8]187, MH:DEC/95[58]188
GRANVILLE (NORTH CAROLINA) RIFLES;
ACW:MAR/95[50]518, CWTI:MAY/93[26]318, MH:DEC/92[74]
GRATIOT, JOHN, *Colonel, 3rd Arkansas Infantry;*
ACW:NOV/93[26]441, CWTI:FEB/92[29]248
GRATZ, CARY, *Capt., 1st Missouri Inf.;* CWM:SEP/93[8]493
GRATZ, JOSEPH, *Captain, 1st Missouri Cavalry (Confederate);*
CWM:SEP/93[8]493
GRAVATH, GEORGE W., *Sergeant, 22nd Virginia Infantry;*
CWR:VOL1#3[52]122
GRAVELLY RUN, VIRGINIA, ENGAGEMENT OF;
B&G:APR/92[8]481
GRAVERAET, GARRETT A., *Lieutenant, 1st Michigan*
Infantry; CWM:SEP/92[24]441
GRAVERAET, HENRY, *Sergeant, 1st Michigan Infantry;*
CWM:SEP/92[24]441
GRAVES' CUMBERLAND KENTUCKY BATTERY;
B&G:FEB/92[10]474
GRAVES, FRANK, *Lt. Col., USA;* CWTI:JAN/94[46]364
GRAVES, G.A., *Capt., 22nd NC Inf.;* GETTY:12[61]245
GRAVES, HENRY L., *Lieutenant, CSMC;*
ACW:MAR/91[14]293, ACW:MAR/92[54]
GRAVES, J.A., *Col., 47th North Carolina Inf.;* GETTY:8[67]204
GRAVES, RICE E., *Major CSA;* B&G:FEB/92[10]474,
B&G:AUG/95[8]604
GRAY, GEORGE, *Col., 6th Michigan Cav.;* GETTY:9[109]218
GRAY, HENRY, *Colonel, 28th Louisiana Infantry:*
ARTICLE: "HENRY GRAY'S LOUISIANA BRIGADE AT THE
BATTLE OF MANSFIELD APRIL 8, 1864,"
CWR:VOL4#2[1]165
ADDITIONAL LISTINGS: CWM:OCT/94[33]537, CWR:VOL4#2[68]167,
CWR:VOL4#2[118]169, *photo;* CWR:VOL4#2[1]165
GRAY, ISAAC N., *Private, 2nd Mississippi Infantry;*
GETTY:6[77]177
GRAY, JOHN, *Captain, USA;* GETTY:12[111]250
GRAY, M.M., *Captain, CSA;* CWR:VOL4#3[77]174
GRAY, R.S., *Lt., 1st Illinois Artillery;* B&G:APR/94[28]559
GRAYDON, JAMES, *Captain, USA;* B&G:JUN/94[8]568,
CWTI:OCT/95[56]471
GRAYSON, G.W.; BOOK REVIEWS: *A CREEK WARRIOR FOR*
THE CONFEDERACY, THE AUTOBIOGRAPHY OF CHIEF
G.W. GRAYSON
"GREAT CAVALRY DEPOT", WASHINGTON;
CWTI:JUN/90[46]161
GREAT BRITAIN; BOOK REVIEWS: *GREAT BRITAIN AND THE*
AMERICAN CIVIL WAR; GREAT BRITAIN AND THE
CONFEDERATE NAVY 1861-1865
"GREAT LOCOMOTIVE CHASE;" see listings under
"ANDREWS, JAMES J."
GREAT SEAL OF THE CONFEDERACY; ARTICLE:
"BERMUDA IS AN UNLIKELY STARTING POINT FOR
THOSE TRACING THE MYSTERY OF THE GREAT SEAL
OF THE CONFEDERACY," ACW:MAY/93[62]418
ADDITIONAL LISTING; ACW:MAY/92[62]364
GREATHOUSE, RIDGLY, *civilian;* CWTI:JUN/95[48]448
GREAVES, JOHN, *Private, USA;* CWM:JUL/92[27]431

GREBLE, JOHN T., *Lieutenant, 5th New York Infantry;*
ACW:MAR/93[42]406, B&G:DEC/91[12]469,
CWR:VOL1#2[7]111
GREELEY, HORACE:
ARTICLE: "WHERE DO YOU STAND HORACE GREELEY?"
CWTI:DEC/90[50]183
GENERAL LISTINGS: *Davis' release,* CWTI:AUG/90[70]171, *Dred
Scott,* AHI:MAY/81[35]218, *election of 1864,*
AHI:OCT/68[4]116, *Elmer Ellsworth,* AHI:DEC/71[30]138,
Gettysburg, GETTY:7[23]187, *in book review,*
CWNEWS:APR/91[4], CWTI:SEP/90[12], *letters to the editor,*
B&G:AUG/93[6]528, *Stephen A. Douglas,* AHI:OCT/70[23]129,
West Point, B&G:DEC/91[12]469, *photos;*
ACW:NOV/95[54]558, AHI:NOV/72[37]143,
CWTI:DEC/90[50]183
ADDITIONAL LISTINGS: ACW:NOV/94[42]497, ACW:NOV/95[54]558,
CWM:MAR/93[8]465, CWR:VOL3#4[24]162,
CWTI:DEC/91[28]239, CWTI:JAN/93[49]303,
CWTI:MAY/93[20]317, CWTI:MAY/94[46]385
GREEN, BENJAMIN, *Private, 2nd Arkansas Infantry;*
CWTI:FEB/92[42]250
GREEN, C.A., *Captain, Louisiana Guard Artillery;*
GETTY:4[65]148
GREEN, FRANCIS M., *Colonel, 11th Mississippi Infantry;*
ACW:MAR/92[10]349, CWR:VOL2#4[269]145, GETTY:9[98]217
GREEN, HANSON, *Lieutenant, 1st Maryland Cavalry;*
CWM:MAY/92[8]418
GREEN, HENRY, *Sgt., 9th Virginia Inf.;* B&G:APR/93[24]520
GREEN, ISRAEL, *Major CSMC;* ACW:MAR/91[14]293,
AHI:AUG/76[34]171, AHI:MAR/84[10]236,
CWTI:JAN/95[24]424
GREEN, J. EVARTS, *Captain, 15th Massachusetts Infantry;*
GETTY:13[43]256
GREEN, JACOB L., *Captain, USA;* CWTI:MAY/93[35]320
GREEN, JAMES S., *Senator, Missouri;* CWTI:AUG/95[34]457
GREEN, JAMES, *Lieutenant Colonel, 48th New York Infantry;*
ACW:SEP/91[30]322
GREEN, JAMES, *Private, CSA;* ACW:JUL/93[27]423
GREEN, JOHN, *Capt., 150th New York Inf.;* GETTY:12[42]244
GREEN, JOHNNY, *Private, 9th Kentucky (Confederate)
Infantry;* AHI:OCT/67[26]112, CWM:JAN/93[29]459,
CWTI:SUMMER/89[40]123
GREEN, JOSEPH F., *Captain, USN;* CWR:VOL2#3[194]141
GREEN, MARTIN E., *General, CSA;* ACW:SEP/91[46]324,
ACW:NOV/91[22]331, ACW:JUL/94[51]480,
B&G:FEB/94[8]550, B&G:FEB/94[57]555,
CWR:VOL2#1[36]132, CWTI:MAY/91[24]208,
CWTI:AUG/95[34]457, CWTI:DEC/95[8]474, *photo;*
CWTI:AUG/95[34]457
GREEN, PETER V., *Colonel, CSA;* B&G:DEC/95[9]615
GREEN, THOMAS B., *Captain, 6th North Carolina Infantry;*
CWM:SEP/92[16]438
GREEN, THOMAS B., *Captain, 132nd New York Infantry;*
CWM:SEP/92[16]438
GREEN, THOMAS L., *General, CSA:*
ARTICLE: ARTICLE: "BRILLIANT RAID BY GENERAL GREEN,"
CWM:OCT/94[33]537
ADDITIONAL LISTINGS: ACW:SEP/92[16]376, ACW:SEP/92[66]381,
ACW:JAN/93[51]398, B&G:DEC/93[6]544,
B&G:JUN/94[8]568, B&G:AUG/94[6]573,
CWM:MAY/93[16]475, CWM:OCT/94[4]532,
CWM:APR/95[39]576, CWR:VOL2#3[212]142,
CWR:VOL3#1[1]149, CWR:VOL4#2[1]165,

CWR:VOL4#2[26]166, CWR:VOL4#2[68]167,
CWR:VOL4#2[118]169, CWTI:MAY/92[48]267,
CWTI:OCT/95[56]471, *photos,* B&G:JUN/94[8]568,
CWTI:OCT/95[56]471
GREEN, THOMAS S., *Sergeant, Sumter Artillery;*
CWR:VOL3#2[1]153
GREEN, WHARTON, *Lieutenant, CSA;* CWTI:MAY/93[26]318
GREEN, WILLIAM, *Lieutenant, 10th Georgia Infantry;*
ACW:JUL/95[10]533
GREEN, WILLIAM, *Pvt., 4th U.S. Arty;* GETTY:11[57]233
GREENE, ALBERT R., *Lieutenant, 78th New York Infantry;*
CWR:VOL3#2[70]155, CWTI:SEPT/89[30]129
GREENE, GEORGE S., *General, USA:*
GENERAL LISTINGS: *Gettysburg,* GETTY:4[89]150,
GETTY:6[69]176, GETTY:7[83]192, GETTY:7[97]193,
GETTY:9[53]214, GETTY:9[81]216, GETTY:10[36]223,
GETTY:10[120]229, GETTY:11[71]234, GETTY:12[42]244, *in
book review,* B&G:OCT/94[40], CWM:AUG/94[9]
ADDITIONAL LISTINGS: ACW:JUL/92[30]369, ACW:NOV/92[42]388,
ACW:MAR/94[50]462, CWR:VOL3#2[70]155,
CWR:VOL3#2[102]156, CWTI:SEP/93[43]338,
GETTY:13[7]253, GETTY:13[89]260
GREENE, OLIVER D., *Adjutant, USA;* CWR:VOL3#3[1]157
GREENE, S. DANA, *Lieutenant, USN;* AHI:NOV/75[38]163,
CWM:JUL/93[15]484, *photos,* AHI:NOV/75[38]163,
CWM:JUL/93[15]484
GREENE, THEODORE P., *Captain, USN;* B&G:JUN/92[40]489
GREENE, WILLIAM B., *Private, 2nd USSS:*
ARTICLE: "PRIVATE WILLIE GREEN—YANKEE REBEL AND
ANTI-HERO," CWM:DEC/95[59]633
BOOK REVIEWS: *LETTERS FROM A SHARPSHOOTER: THE
CIVIL WAR LETTERS OF PRIVATE WILLIAM B. GREENE
CO. G, 2ND UNITED STATES SHARPSHOOTERS
(BERDAN'S)*
GREENHOW, ROSE O'NEAL; AHI:MAY/71[3]133A,
AHI:DEC/73[10]152, B&G:DEC/94[10]585,
CWTI:MAY/92[38]265, *photo;* AHI:DEC/73[10]152
GREENLAND, W.W., *Sergeant, 125th Pennsylvania Infantry;*
B&G:OCT/95[8]611A
GREENSBORO, NORTH CAROLINA; CWTI:AUG/90[26]166
GREENWALT, ABRAHAM, *Private, USA;* CWM:SEP/93[8]493
GREENWOOD, CHARLES, *Captain, 38th Ohio Infantry;*
B&G:FEB/93[12]511
GREENWOOD, HARRY, *Private, 5th New York Infantry;*
CWR:VOL1#2[29]112
GREER, ELKANAH, *Colonel, 3rd Texas Cavalry:*
BOOK REVIEW: *THE THIRD TEXAS CAVALRY*
ADDITIONAL LISTINGS: ACW:NOV/93[26]441, ACW:MAY/94[58],
CWTI:FEB/92[29]248
GREER, JAMES L., *Private, 2nd Tennessee Cavalry;*
CWR:VOL4#1[1]163
GREGG, DAVID McM., *General, USA:*
ARTICLE: "MELEE IN THE UNDERBRUSH,"
ACW:NOV/92[26]386
GENERAL LISTINGS: *1863 Cavalry Battles,* MH:OCT/92[51]162,
Aldie, B&G:OCT/93[12]537, GETTY:10[42]224,
GETTY:11[19]232, *Brandy Station,* CWTI:JUN/90[32]159,
GETTY:11[19]232, *Falling Waters,* GETTY:9[109]218,
Gettysburg, GETTY:4[65]148, GETTY:4[75]149,
GETTY:7[29]188, GETTY:12[68]246, *in order of battle,*
B&G:APR/94[10]558, B&G:APR/95[8]595, *Overland
Campaign,* B&G:APR/94[10]558, *Trevilian Station,*

MH:FEB/93[42]164, *Wilderness*, B&G:APR/95[8]595, *photos*,
B&G:OCT/93[12]537, GETTY:11[19]232
ADDITIONAL LISTINGS: ACW:JUL/92[41]370, ACW:MAY/94[35]469,
ACW:SEP/94[55]489, B&G:APR/91[8]445,
B&G:DEC/91[34]470, B&G:OCT/93[12]537,
B&G:APR/94[59]565, CWM:JUL/92[64]434,
CWM:APR/95[32]575, CWTI:FEB/91[45]194,
CWTI:APR/92[35]257, GETTY:13[1]252, GETTY:13[89]260
GREGG, EDWARD P., *Lieutenant Colonel, 16th Texas Cavalry;*
CWR:VOL3#3[33]158
GREGG, J. IRVIN, *General, USA;* ACW:NOV/92[26]386,
ACW:JAN/93[43]397, AHI:SEP/87[40]263, B&G:APR/92[8]481,
B&G:OCT/93[12]537,
B&G:APR/94[10]558, B&G:APR/95[8]595, GETTY:4[75]149,
GETTY:12[68]246, GETTY:13[1]252, GETTY:13[89]260,
MH:OCT/92[51]162
GREGG, JOHN, *General, CSA;* ACW:MAY/92[30]361,
ACW:JUL/94[42]479, B&G:APR/94[10]558,
B&G:APR/95[8]595, B&G:JUN/95[8]600, B&G:AUG/95[8]604,
CWM:JUN/94[58]519, CWM:AUG/94[30]527,
CWR:VOL1#1[71]107, CWR:VOL1#3[7]118,
CWR:VOL2#1[36]132, CWR:VOL2#3[256],
CWR:VOL3#3[33]158, CWR:VOL4#3[89],
CWTI:MAR/93[24]309, CWTI:MAR/93[40]312
GREGG, MAXCY, *General, CSA;* ACW:JUL/91[18]312,
ACW:NOV/92[10]384, ACW:MAR/95[42]517,
B&G:AUG/92[11]493, CWM:OCT/94[26]536,
CWM:JUN/95[61]593, CWR:VOL1#1[1]102,
CWR:VOL1#2[7]111, CWR:VOL4#4[1]177,
CWTI:MAY/94[31]382, MH:APR/93[39]166
GREGG, THOMAS, *Sergeant, 3rd Pennsylvania Cavalry;*
GETTY:13[89]260
GREGG, WILLIAM, *guerrilla;* ACW:MAR/95[26]515
GREGORY, EDGAR M., *General, USA;* B&G:APR/92[8]481
GREGORY, JOHN M., JR, *Lieutenant, CSA;* GETTY:7[13]186
GRENAD, BENJAMIN O., *Captain, 1st Florida Special
Battalion;* CWR:VOL3#1[65]151
GRENADA, MISSISSIPPI; CWTI:FEB/90[38]145
GRENFELL, GEORGE ST. LEGER:
ARTICLE: "VISITING CAVALRYMAN'S ORDEAL,"
MH:JUN/91[20]152
ADDITIONAL LISTINGS: CWM:MAR/91[74], CWM:OCT/94[8],
CWNEWS:MAY/94[5]
GRESHAM, THOMAS R., *Lieutenant Colonel, CSA;*
CWR:VOL1#3[52]122, CWTI:JAN/93[20]298
GREUSEL, NICHOLAS, *Colonel, USA;* ACW:MAR/92[14]350,
CWR:VOL1#1[42]105
GRIDLEY, ASAHEL, *General, USA;* AHI:FEB/69[35]120
GRIDLEY, HENRY, *Lieutenant, 150th New York Infantry;*
GETTY:12[42]244
GRIER, D.P., *Colonel, 77th Illinois Infantry;* B&G:FEB/94[8]550
GRIERSON, BENJAMIN F., *General, USA:*
ARTICLES: "BRILLIANT CAVALRY EXPLOIT,"
ACW:MAY/92[47]363, "GRIERSON'S RAID: A CAVALRY
RAID AT ITS BEST," B&G:JUN/93[12]524, "PERSONALITY -
GRIERSON," MH:FEB/95[18]182
GENERAL LISTINGS: *general gistory,* AHI:MAY/71[3]133A, *in book
review,* CWM:DEC/94[7], CWNEWS:JAN/94[5],
CWNEWS:NOV/95[29], *order of battle,* B&G:FEB/94[8]550,
post war, AHI:NOV/79[32]196, *photos;* ACW:MAY/92[47]363,
AHI:NOV/79[10]195, B&G:JUN/93[12]524
ADDITIONAL LISTINGS: ACW:SEP/92[23]377, ACW:MAY/93[12]412,
ACW:SEP/95[48]547, ACW:NOV/95[48]557,

CWM:MAR/93[16]466, CWR:VOL2#1[36]132,
CWR:VOL2#4[313]146, CWTI:MAY/92[48]267,
MH:JUN/93[82]167, MH:DEC/95[58]188
GRIERSON'S RAID:
ARTICLES: "BRILLIANT CAVALRY EXPLOIT,"
ACW:MAY/92[47]363, "GRIERSON'S RAID: A CAVALRY
RAID AT ITS BEST," B&G:JUN/93[12]524, "PERSONALITY -
GRIERSON," MH:FEB/95[18]182, "THE HORSE SOLDIERS
(AUDIO/VIDEO)," B&G:JUN/93[36]526
GENERAL LISTINGS: *in book review,* CWM:DEC/94[7], *in book
review,* CWR:VOL2#1[78], *letters to the editor,*
B&G:AUG/93[6]528, *letters to the editor,* B&G:OCT/93[6]536,
SIO, B&G:DEC/93[30]546, B&G:FEB/94[38]553,
B&G:APR/94[34]561
ADDITIONAL LISTINGS: ACW:JUL/94[8]474, ACW:JUL/94[51]480,
ACW:SEP/95[48]547, B&G:FEB/94[8]550,
CWTI:MAY/92[48]267
GRIFFEN, Z.T., *Private, 122nd New York Infantry;*
B&G:JUN/95[8]600
GRIFFIN, CHARLES, *General, USA:*
GENERAL LISTINGS: *Five Forks,* B&G:APR/92[8]481, *Gettysburg,*
GETTY:6[33]172, *in order of battle,* B&G:APR/92[8]481,
B&G:APR/94[10]558, *in book review,* CWNEWS:JUL/94[25],
letters to the editor, CWM:DEC/95[5]625, *Sayler's Creek,*
ACW:JAN/92[22]341, *West Point,* B&G:DEC/91[12]469,
Wilderness, B&G:APR/95[8]595
ADDITIONAL LISTINGS: ACW:JAN/94[47]452, ACW:MAR/95[12]513,
B&G:APR/93[12]518, B&G:JUN/94[22]569,
CWR:VOL2#2[95]135, CWR:VOL2#3[183]140,
CWTI:APR/92[14]254, CWTI:DEC/95[24]477
GRIFFIN, CHARLES H., *Private, 29th U.S. Colored Troops;*
B&G:AUG/94[38]578
GRIFFIN, E.H., *Private, 5th Alabama Infantry;* GETTY:6[13]170
GRIFFIN, FELIX T., *Lieutenant, Sumter Artillery;*
CWR:VOL3#2[1]153, CWR:VOL3#2[61]154
GRIFFIN, JOEL R., *Captain, CSA;* CWTI:JAN/95[42]428
GRIFFIN, MICAJAH, *Captain, CSA;* B&G:OCT/94[11]580
GRIFFIN, S.H., *Lieutenant Colonel, 31st Louisiana Infantry;*
B&G:FEB/94[8]550
GRIFFIN, SIMON G., *Colonel, 6th New Hampshire Infantry;*
ACW:MAY/95[18]524, B&G:APR/94[10]558,
B&G:APR/95[8]595, B&G:AUG/95[8]604,
CWR:VOL2#2[118]136
GRIFFIN, THOMAS M., *Colonel, 18th Mississippi Infantry;*
ACW:SEP/92[30]378, AHI:FEB/82[36]225
GRIFFIN, TRUMBULL, *Lieutenant, USA;*
CWTI:JAN/93[82]304
GRIFFIN, WILLIAM, *Captain, 2nd Baltimore Battery;*
ACW:MAY/94[35]469, GETTY:13[89]260
GRIFFIN, WILLIAM H., *Captain, 2nd Maryland Battery;*
GETTY:4[75]149, GETTY:12[68]246
GRIFFITH, ANTHONY and FIELDER, *2nd Tennessee
Cavalry;* CWR:VOL4#1[1]163
GRIFFITH, JOSEPH C.; CWTI:MAR/91[22]199
GRIFFITH, JOSEPH E., *Sergeant, 22nd Iowa Infantry;*
B&G:DEC/91[12]469, CWR:VOL2#1[i]129,
CWR:VOL2#1[19]131, CWR:VOL2#1[69]133
GRIFFITH, RICHARD, *General, CSA;* ACW:SEP/92[38]379
GRIFFITHS, HENRY H., *Captain, Iowa Light Artillery;*
B&G:FEB/94[8]550, B&G:AUG/95[8]604
GRIGG, WILLIAM, *Private, Petersburg Artillery;*
ACW:MAR/95[12]513

GRIGGS, CHAUNCY W., *Lieutenant Colonel, USA;*
ACW:MAY/91[12]302
GRIGSBY, A.J., *Colonel, CSA;* ACW:JUL/92[30]369,
ACW:MAR/94[50]462
GRIMBALL, JOHN, *Lieutenant, CSN;* AHI:OCT/88[38]275
GRIMES, ABSALOM, *Captain, CSA:*
ARTICLE: "AB GRIMES," ACW:MAY/91[10]301
ADDITIONAL LISTINGS: ACW:MAY/91[10]301,
CWTI:MAR/91[34]201, CWTI:AUG/95[58]461
GRIMES, BRYAN, *General, CSA;* ACW:MAY/91[38]305,
ACW:JAN/92[22]341, ACW:JAN/93[43]397,
ACW:SEP/93[31]433, B&G:APR/94[10]558,
CWM:JAN/93[40]461, CWTI:MAR/95[33]435,
CWTI:MAR/95[46]437
GRIMES, CARY, *Captain, CSA;* CWM:JUN/95[55]591
GRIMES, JAMES W., *Senator, Iowa;* ACW:JAN/91[62]289,
AHI:DEC/68[28]118, GETTY:12[85]248
GRIMES, JOHN H., *Lieutenant, USMC;* CWTI:APR/92[14]254
GRIMES, STEPHEN, *Captain, 48th Illinois Infantry;*
B&G:FEB/91[8]439, CWTI:DEC/94[62]415
GRIMLER, JOSEPH, *Lieutenant, 83rd Pennsylvania Infantry;*
GETTY:7[41]189
GRIMMETT, JASPER, *Private, 1st Arkansas Cavalry;*
CWR:VOL1#2[70]115
GRIMSLEY, JAMES, *Captain, 1st Indiana Heavy Artillery;*
ACW:JAN/94[30]450
GRINDLAY, JAMES, *Colonel, USA;* B&G:APR/92[8]481
GRINE, PHILIP, *Private, 83rd Pennsylvania Infantry;*
GETTY:7[41]189
GRISAMORE, SILAS T., *Major, 18th Louisiana Infantry:*
BOOK REVIEWS: *THE CIVIL WAR REMINISCENCES OF MAJOR
SILAS T. GRISMORE, C.S.A.*
ADDITIONAL LISTING: CWR:VOL4#2[1]165
GRISWOLDSVILLE, GEORGIA, BATTLE OF;
CWR:VOL1#1[73]108, CWTI:SEP/91[23]228
GRIVOT, M., *General, USA;* CWR:VOL3#1[1]149
GROGAN, CHARLES, *Lieutenant, Mosby's Rangers;*
CWM:JAN/93[24]458
GROGAN, CHARLIE, *ADC, CSA;* GETTY:10[102]226
GROSE, WILLIAM, *General, USA;* B&G:DEC/93[12]545,
CWTI:SEPT/89[30]129
GROSS, GEORGE J., *author;* ARTICLE: "GEORGE J. GROSS ON
HALLOWED GROUND," GETTY:10[112]228
GROSS, SAMUEL D., *Surgeon, USA:*
BOOK REVIEW: *A MANUAL OF MILITARY SURGERY: OR
HINTS ON THE EMERGENCIES OF FIELD, CAMP, AND
HOSPITAL PRACTICE*
ADDITIONAL LISTINGS: ACW:SEP/95[38]546
GROSVENOR, CHARLES H., *Colonel, USA;*
B&G:DEC/93[12]545
GROUT, WILLIE, *Lieutenant, 15th Massachusetts Infantry;*
CWTI:MAY/89[50]119
GROVE, GEORGE A., *Captain, CSA;* B&G:DEC/91[34]470
GROVER, CUVIER, *General, USA;* ACW:MAY/91[38]305,
ACW:JUL/91[18]312, ACW:JAN/94[30]450,
B&G:AUG/92[11]493, CWM:JUN/95[55]591,
CWR:VOL3#1[1]149, CWR:VOL4#2[104]168, *photo;*
B&G:AUG/92[11]493
GROVER, IRA G., *Colonel, 7th Indiana Infantry;*
B&G:FEB/95[8]590C, CWTI:NOV/93[24]346
GROVER, THEODORE, *Private, 24th Michigan Infantry,*
GETTY:9[33]211, GETTY:11[57]233

GROVETON, VIRGINIA, BATTLE OF; CWR:VOL1#1[1]102,
CWR:VOL1#3[28]120, CWR:VOL2#4[269]145
GROWER, WILLIAM, *Major, 17th New York Infantry;*
B&G:AUG/92[11]493
GROWLER, GRIF, *Private, CSA;* ACW:JAN/92[10]339
GRUMBACH, NICHOLAS, *Captain, 149th New York Infantry;*
ARTICLE: "TWO NEW YORK SWORDS IN THE FIGHT FOR
CULP'S HILL: COLONEL JAMES C. LANE'S AND CAPT.
NICHOLAS GRUMBACH'S, GETTY:10[36]223
GRUMMOND, GEORGE W., *Lieutenant Colonel, USA;*
B&G:DEC/95[9]615
GUERILLA WARFARE:
ARTICLES: "A FIGHT FOR MISSOURI," CWTI:AUG/95[34]457,
"THE JAMES BOYS GO TO WAR," CWTI:JAN/94[29]360,
"WILLIAM CLARKE QUANTRILL: TERROR OF THE
BORDER," CWM:JAN/92[8]399
BOOK REVIEWS: *APRIL '65: CONFEDERATE COVERT ACTION
IN THE AMERICAN CIVIL WAR * CHAMP FERGUSON,
CONFEDERATE GUERILLA * INSIDE WAR: THE
GUERRILLA CONFLICT IN MISSOURI DURING THE
AMERICAN CIVIL WAR*
ADDITIONAL LISTINGS: CWM:MAY/92[6]417, CWM:AUG/95[58]611
GUERNSEY, FRANCIS M., *Lieutenant, 32nd Wisconsin
Infantry;* CWR:VOL2#4[313]146
GUERRANT, EDWARD O., *Captain, CSA;*
B&G:AUG/91[11]458, B&G:AUG/91[52]464
GUERRANT, H.L., *Captain, 13th North Carolina Infantry;*
GETTY:8[67]204
GUERRY, THOMAS L., *Private, Sumter Artillery;*
CWR:VOL3#2[1]153
GUIBOR, HENRY, *Captain, CSA;* ACW:NOV/93[26]441,
B&G:FEB/94[8]550, CWR:VOL3#3[33]158
GUIDRY, ALEX, *Lieutenant, CSA;* CWR:VOL4#2[118]169
GUINAN, DENNIS, *Private, 5th New York Infantry;*
CWR:VOL1#2[29]112
GUINEA STATION, VIRGINIA, ENGAGEMENT AT;
B&G:APR/93[12]518, CWTI:MAY/89[22]116
GUITAR, ODON, *Colonel, CSA;* CWR:VOL2#2[169]
GUITEAU, CHARLES J.; AHI:FEB/69[12]119
GUMBART, GEORGE C., *Captain, USA;* B&G:AUG/95[8]604
GUNDERMAN, CONRAD, *Private, 126th New York Infantry;*
CWR:VOL1#4[7]125
GUNN, ORLANDO, *Private, 7th Ohio Infantry;* GETTY:9[81]216
GUNNELL, WILLIAM P., *Surgeon;* CWTI:DEC/91[22]237
GUNSOLLE, JAMES, *Private, 24th Michigan Infantry,*
GETTY:9[33]211, GETTY:11[57]233
GUPPEY, J.J., *Colonel, 23rd Wisconsin Infantry;*
B&G:FEB/94[8]550
GURNEY, WILLIAM, *Corporal, 150th New York Infantry;*
GETTY:12[42]244
GUTHEIM, JAMES, *Rabbi;* CWTI:MAY/92[38]265
GUY, JOHN H., *Captain, CSA;* B&G:FEB/92[10]474
GWIN, WILLIAM M., *Senator, California;* AHI:JUN/70[30]127
GWYN, JAMES, *Colonel, 118th Pennsylvania Infantry;*
B&G:APR/92[8]481, GETTY:8[53]203

H

HAAS, JACOB W., *Captain, 96th Pennsylvania Infantry;*
CWR:VOL3#3[1]157
HABEAS CORPUS ACT OF 1863; AHI:APR/80[21]200
HACKETT, STEPHEN H., *Private, 1st Louisiana Infantry;*
CWR:VOL4#2[68]167
HADDEN, JESSE, *Lieutenant, 1st Indiana Heavy Artillery;*
ACW:JAN/94[30]450
HADILL, H.J., *Colonel, 141st Penn. Inf.;* CWR:VOL1#4[77]
HADLEY, J.V., *Lieutenant, USA;* B&G:APR/95[8]595
HAECKER, WILLIAM J., *Private, 2nd Tennessee Cavalry;*
CWR:VOL4#1[1]163
HAFFY, BERNARD, *Private, 6th Connecticut Infantry;*
ACW:SEP/91[30]322
HAGAN, HENRY, *Corporal, CSA;* ACW:JUL/95[34]536
HAGER, GEORGE, *Captain, 5th New York Infantry;*
CWR:VOL1#2[29]112
HAGNER, P.V., *Major, USA;* ACW:JAN/91[8]282
HAGOOD, JOHNSON, *General, CSA:*
BOOK REVIEW: *MEMOIRS OF THE WAR OF SECESSION*
GENERAL LISTINGS: *Cold Harbor,* B&G:APR/94[10]558, *in order of*
battle, B&G:APR/94[10]558, *letters to the editor,*
CWTI:JUN/95[14]443, *order of battle,* B&G:DEC/95[9]615,
Wilmington/Fort Fisher, B&G:DEC/94[10]585, *photos,*
B&G:DEC/94[10]585, B&G:DEC/95[9]615
ADDITIONAL LISTINGS: ACW:SEP/91[30]322, AHI:JAN/73[28]147,
CWM:MAR/92[16]411, CWM:SEP/92[19]440,
CWR:VOL2#2[156]138, CWTI:JAN/94[46]364
HAHN, MICHAEL, *Governor, Louisiana;* CWR:VOL4#2[26]166
HAIGHT, FLETCHER M., *Judge;* CWTI:MAY/92[20]262
HAINES, WILLIAM P., *Private, 12th New Jersey Infantry;*
GETTY:5[89]162
HAINES, WILLIAM, *General, USA;* CWTI:SEP/92[31]281
HAKES, W.H., *Lt., 125th New York Inf.;* CWR:VOL1#4[7]125
HALDERMAN, HORACE, *Captain, CSA;* CWR:VOL3#3[33]158
HALDERMAN, JOHN A., *Major, CSA;* CWTI:FEB/92[29]248
HALE, JOHN P., *Senator, New Hampshire;*
CWTI:AUG/95[24]455, CWTI:AUG/95[54]460
HALE, THOMAS, *seaman, USN;* B&G:JUN/92[40]489
HALE, WILLIAM H., *Lieutenant, USMC;* CWTI:APR/92[14]254
HALEY, JOHN W., *Private, 17th Maine Infantry:*
BOOK REVIEW: *REBEL YELL AND YANKEE HURRAH: THE*
CIVIL WAR JOURNAL OF A MAINE VOLUNTEER
ADDITIONAL LISTINGS: ACW:SEP/94[38]487, B&G:APR/91[8]445,
B&G:APR/95[8]595, CWR:VOL4#3[1]170,
CWTI:MAY/94[24]381, GETTY:9[5]209, GETTY:10[53]225
HALL, ALBERT E., *Pvt., 154th New York Inf.;* GETTY:8[17]200
HALL, CHARLES, *Private, Mosby's Rangers;*
CWTI:SEP/90[34]176
HALL, CYRUS M., *Sergeant, 17th Maine Infantry;*
B&G:AUG/95[8]604, GETTY:8[43]202
HALL, DANIEL, *Captain, USA;* GETTY:11[71]234
HALL, DELOS, *Capt., 97th New York Inf.;* GETTY:10[7]221
HALL, GEORGE, *Pvt, 53rd Penn. Inf.;* GETTY:11[80]235
HALL, HARMON, *Major, 5th New York Infantry;*
CWTI:MAY/94[31]382
HALL, HARRY, *Capt., 114th Penn. Inf.;* GETTY:5[123]166
HALL, HARVEY, *Lieutenant, 1st Indiana Heavy Artillery;*
ACW:JAN/94[30]450

HALL, ISAAC, *Captain, 97th New York Infantry;*
B&G:FEB/95[8]590B, GETTY:5[117]165, GETTY:10[7]221
HALL, J.M.C., *Colonel, 5th Alabama Infantry;*
CWM:DEC/94[40]550, GETTY:10[7]221
HALL, JAMES A., *Captain, 2nd Maine Battery;*
ACW:JAN/95[20]504, ACW:MAR/95[42]517, GETTY:4[16]143,
GETTY:5[4]156, GETTY:6[13]170, GETTY:6[29]171,
GETTY:8[31]201, GETTY:11[71]234
HALL, JAMES I., *Capt., 9th Tenn. Inf.;* CWTI:NOV/92[41]291
HALL, JAMES S., *Captain, USA;* GETTY:4[101]151,
GETTY:10[42]224
HALL, JOHN C., *Surgeon, 6th Wisc. Inf.;* GETTY:4[24]145
HALL, JOSEPHUS M., *Colonel, 5th Alabama Infantry;*
GETTY:4[33]146
HALL, LOUIS, *Private, Consolidated Crescent Regiment;*
CWR:VOL4#2[68]167
HALL, NORMAN J., *Colonel, USA;* ACW:SEP/92[30]378,
CWR:VOL3#1[31]150, CWR:VOL4#4[101]181,
GETTY:4[89]150, GETTY:5[79]161, GETTY:5[107]164,
GETTY:7[97]193, GETTY:13[1]252, GETTY:13[43]256,
GETTY:13[50]257
HALL, ROBERT R., *Captain, 13th Pennsylvania Reserves;*
B&G:JUN/94[8]568, CWR:VOL1#3[28]120,
CWR:VOL1#3[46]121, CWTI:OCT/95[56]471
HALL, WILLIAM, *Colonel, USA;* ACW:JAN/93[10]393
HALL, WINCHESTER, *Colonel, CSA;* ACW:SEP/94[10]484
HALLAR, CEPHAS, *Private, CSA;* ACW:SEP/91[41]323
HALLECK, HENRY W., *General, USA:*
ARTICLE: "'OLD BRAINS' IN THE NEW WEST,"
AHI:MAY/78[10]179
GENERAL LISTINGS: *Bermuda Hundred,* CWTI:MAY/93[29]319,
Chattanooga, CWTI:SEP/92[22]279, *conscription,*
CWTI:NOV/92[49]292, *Corinth,* CWTI:FEB/90[38]145, *Forts*
Henry and Donelson, B&G:FEB/92[10]474, *general history,*
AHI:MAY/71[3]133A, *Gettysburg Campaign,* GETTY:5[19]158,
GETTY:7[23]187, GETTY:7[29]188, GETTY:9[109]218,
GETTY:11[6]231, *Grant,* CWTI:FEB/90[32]144,
CWTI:FEB/90[46]146, CWTI:DEC/94[57]414, *Harrison's*
Landing, CWM:JUN/95[76]598, *in book review,*
AHI:JAN/84[8], B&G:AUG/95[38], CWM:JAN/91[47],
CWM:APR/95[50], CWNEWS:JUN/90[4],
CWNEWS:JAN/91[4], CWNEWS:AUG/91[4],
CWNEWS:DEC/94[33], CWR:VOL3#3[92], CWTI:DEC/90[10],
Johnston's surrender, CWTI:AUG/90[42]167, *letters to the*
editor, B&G:APR/92[6]480, CWTI:JAN/93[10]297, *Manassas,*
Second, B&G:AUG/92[11]493, *Morgan,* CWM:JAN/93[29]459,
Nelson-Davis feud, AHI:NOV/72[12]142, *Overland Campaign,*
B&G:APR/94[10]558, *Pope,* ACW:JAN/95[54]508, *Price's 1864*
Missouri Campaign, B&G:JUN/91[10]452
GENERAL LISTINGS, continued: *Sherman on the Presidency,*
AHI:JAN/77[46]173, *Sherman,* AHI:JAN/67[4]106, *Tullahoma*
Campaign, B&G:OCT/92[10]496, *Vicksburg,*
ACW:NOV/91[22]331, *West Point,* B&G:DEC/91[12]469, *photo,*
AHI:JAN/67[4]106, AHI:MAY/78[10]179, B&G:FEB/92[10]474,
CWM:AUG/95[58]611, CWTI:DEC/95[67]481
ADDITIONAL LISTINGS: ACW, ACW:JAN/91[22]285,
ACW:MAY/91[12]302, ACW:MAY/91[38]305,
ACW:JUL/91[18]312, ACW:JUL/91[35]314,
ACW:MAR/92[6]347, ACW:MAR/92[46]354,
ACW:SEP/92[16]376, ACW:MAR/93[8]401,
ACW:JUL/93[34]424, ACW:JUL/93[50]426,
ACW:NOV/93[42]443, ACW:NOV/93[50]444,
ACW:MAR/94[27]459, ACW:SEP/94[38]487,

ACW:JAN/95[54]508, ACW:MAR/95[8]512,
ACW:SEP/95[48]547
ADDITIONAL LISTINGS, AHI; AHI:JUL/73[38]150
ADDITIONAL LISTINGS, B&G; B&G:APR/91[8]445,
B&G:AUG/91[11]458, B&G:FEB/92[48]475,
B&G:JUN/93[12]524, B&G:AUG/93[36]533,
B&G:OCT/93[12]537, B&G:DEC/93[12]545,
B&G:AUG/94[10]574, B&G:AUG/94[19]575,
B&G:OCT/94[11]580, B&G:DEC/94[22]586,
B&G:APR/95[33]597, B&G:AUG/95[8]604, B&G:OCT/95[32]613
ADDITIONAL LISTINGS, CWM; CWM:MAR/91[56]341,
CWM:MAY/92[8]418, CWM:MAR/93[8]465,
CWM:MAY/93[4]472, CWM:OCT/94[48]542,
CWM:AUG/95[58]611
ADDITIONAL LISTINGS, CWR; CWR:VOL2#1[1]130,
CWR:VOL2#3[212]142, CWR:VOL2#4[313]146,
CWR:VOL3#1[31]150, CWR:VOL3#3[33]158,
CWR:VOL4#1[44]164, CWR:VOL4#2[26]166
ADDITIONAL LISTINGS, CWTI; CWTI:MAR/89[16]101,
CWTI:DEC/89[62]139, CWTI:FEB/90[26]143,
CWTI:SEP/91[31]229, CWTI:APR/92[49]260,
CWTI:JUL/92[29]272, CWTI:JUL/92[42]274,
CWTI:NOV/92[18]289, CWTI:NOV/93[33]347,
CWTI:JAN/94[46]364, CWTI:DEC/94[57]414,
CWTI:DEC/94[82]418, CWTI:MAR/95[40]436,
CWTI:AUG/95[58]461, CWTI:DEC/95[67]481
ADDITIONAL LISTINGS, continued; GETTY:12[85]248,
MH:AUG/95[30]185, MH:DEC/95[58]188
HALLIBURTON, W.H., *Colonel, CSA;* CWTI:FEB/92[42]250
HALLOWELL, EDWARD N., *Colonel, 54th Massachusetts
Infantry;* ACW:SEP/91[30]322, GETTY:12[111]250
HALLOWELL, NORWOOD P., *Captain, 20th Massachusetts
Infantry;* CWR:VOL3#1[31]150
HALPINE, CHARLES G., *Captain, USA;* CWTI:MAR/94[38]372
HALSEY, D.P., *Adjutant, CSA;* GETTY:5[13]157
HALSTEAD, E.P., *Major, USA;* B&G:APR/95[5]594
HALSTEAD, MARAT; AHI:JUN/73[4]149
HAM, WILLIAM B., *Private, 8th North Carolina Infantry;*
B&G:APR/93[24]520
HAMBLIN, JOSEPH E., *Adjutant, 5th New York Infantry;*
CWR:VOL1#2[7]111
HAMBLIN, JOSEPH, *Lieutenant Colonel, 65th New York
Infantry;* ACW:SEP/92[30]378
HAMBY, J.H., *Captain, CSA;* B&G:OCT/94[11]580
HAMILL, H.M., *Private, 5th Florida Inf.;* CWR:VOL3#4[1]161
HAMILTON, ALFRED, *Surgeon, 148th Pennsylvania Infantry;*
GETTY:10[53]225
HAMILTON, ANDREW G., *Major, 12th Kentucky Cavalry;*
AHI:DEC/85[40]255, AHI:NOV/85[38]254
HAMILTON, CHARLES S., *General, USA;*
ACW:SEP/91[46]324, CWR:VOL4#2[68]167,
CWTI:JUL/94[50]395, CWTI:DEC/94[82]418
HAMILTON, D.H., *Colonel, 1st South Carolina Infantry;*
ACW:NOV/92[10]384
HAMILTON, EVERARD J., *Lieutenant, 8th Louisiana
Infantry;* CWTI:FEB/91[12]189
HAMILTON, FRANK H., *Surgeon, 31st New York Infantry;*
BOOK REVIEW: *A PRACTICAL TREATISE ON MILITARY
SURGERY*
ADDITIONAL LISTING: CWTI:SEP/91[42]231
HAMILTON, JAMES C., *Private, 110th Pennsylvania Infantry;*
B&G:APR/95[8]595

HAMILTON, THEODORE B., *Lieutenant Colonel, 62nd New
York Infantry;* GETTY:11[91]236
HAMILTON, THOMAS A., *Private, CSA;* CWTI:SEP/91[23]228
HAMILTON, WILLIAM D., *Colonel, USA;* CWM:JAN/91[40]330
HAMLIN, CHARLES, *Major, USA;* GETTY:13[50]257
HAMLIN, HANNIBAL; AHI:MAY/69[12]121,
AHI:JAN/85[10]244, AHI:JAN/93[61]309, B&G:APR/91[8]445,
CWTI:SEP/92[46]284, CWTI:AUG/95[54]460,
GETTY:8[53]203, GETTY:12[85]248, *photo;*
AHI:JAN/85[10]244
HAMM, JOHN, *Capt., 37th Ohio Infantry;* CWM:DEC/95[35]629
HAMMAND, JAMES, *Private, Mosby's Rangers;*
CWTI:SEP/90[34]176
HAMMER, ADAM, *Lieutenant Colonel, German Home Guards;*
ACW:MAR/91[62]298
HAMMOND, JAMES H., *civilian;* BOOK REVIEW: *SECRET AND
SACRED: THE DIARIES OF JAMES HENRY HAMMOND, A
SOUTHERN SLAVEHOLDER*
ADDITIONAL LISTING: CWM:AUG/95[45]
HAMMOND, JOHN H., *General, USA;* ACW:NOV/95[48]557,
B&G:APR/93[12]518, B&G:DEC/93[12]545, B&G:APR/95[8]595
HAMMOND, W.M., *Captain, CSA;* GETTY:4[33]146,
GETTY:13[33]255
HAMMOND, WILLIAM A., *Surgeon General, USA;*
ACW:MAY/94[51]471, ACW:MAY/95[8]522,
AHI:APR/85[16]249, CWM:MAY/91[18]348,
CWM:DEC/95[54]632, CWNEWS:NOV/90[4]
HAMPDEN (VIRGINIA) ARTILLERY; GETTY:10[29]222
HAMPTON ROADS, VIRGINIA, BATTLE OF:
BOOK REVIEW: *THUNDER AT HAMPTON ROADS*
ADDITIONAL LISTINGS: ACW:MAR/91[14]293, ACW:JAN/95[74]510,
CWM:JUL/93[15]484, CWM:FEB/95[49]565,
CWM:JUN/95[24]582, CWR:VOL3#3[92],
CWTI:MAR/91[42]202, CWTI:MAY/93[20]317
HAMPTON, FRANK, *Lieutenant Colonel, CSA;*
CWTI:JUN/90[32]159
HAMPTON, WADE, *General, CSA:*
ARTICLE: "SWELTERING SUMMER COLLISION,"
MH:FEB/93[42]164
GENERAL LISTINGS: *1863 Cavalry Battles,* MH:OCT/92[51]162,
Aldie, GETTY:11[19]232, *Bentonville,* CWR:VOL4#3[65]172,
Brandy Station, CWTI:JUN/90[32]159, GETTY:11[19]232,
Buckland, ACW:JUL/92[41]370, *Gettysburg,*
GETTY:12[68]246, GETTY:4[65]148, GETTY:4[75]149,
GETTY:5[107]164, *Haw's Shop,* ACW:SEP/95[74]550, *in book
review,* CWNEWS:AUG/92[4], CWNEWS:OCT/92[4],
CWNEWS:APR/95[33], CWNEWS:OCT/95[33],
CWR:VOL1#2[78], CWR:VOL3#2[105], CWTI:JUL/93[12]
GENERAL LISTINGS, continued: *in order of battle,* B&G:APR/94[10]558,
B&G:APR/95[8]595, B&G:DEC/95[9]615, *Kelly's Ford,*
ACW:NOV/91[30]332, *letters to the editor,* B&G:DEC/93[6]544,
CWTI:MAY/94[12]379, *Overland Campaign,*
B&G:APR/94[10]558, *Peninsula Campaign,*
CWM:JUN/95[37]585, *Petersburg,* MH:APR/95[46]183, *photos;*
AHI:APR/70[11]124, B&G:OCT/93[12]537,
B&G:APR/94[10]558, B&G:DEC/95[9]615,
CWTI:JUN/90[32]159, CWTI:AUG/95[46]459,
GETTY:12[68]246, MH:FEB/93[42]164
ADDITIONAL LISTINGS: ACW:JAN/91[38]287, ACW:JAN/92[16]340,
ACW:NOV/92[26]386, ACW:MAY/94[35]469,
ACW:JUL/94[35]478, ACW:SEP/94[8]483,
ACW:SEP/94[55]489, ACW:JAN/95[10]503,
AHI:JAN/73[28]147, B&G:APR/91[8]445, B&G:FEB/93[24]512,

B&G:APR/93[12]518, B&G:OCT/93[12]537,
B&G:APR/94[59]565, CWTI:SEPT/89[24]128,
CWTI:DEC/91[18]236, CWTI:APR/92[35]257,
CWTI:APR/92[49]260, CWTI:MAY/92[48]267,
CWTI:AUG/95[46]459, CWTI:DEC/95[76]482,
GETTY:13[1]252, GETTY:13[89]260, MH:JUN/94[8]177

HAMPTON'S LEGION:
BOOK REVIEW: *STEPHEN ELLIOTT WELCH OF THE HAMPTON LEGION*
ADDITIONAL LISTINGS: ACW:JUL/92[30]369, ACW:JUL/94[42]479,
ACW:NOV/94[18]495, B&G:DEC/92[20]504,
CWR:VOL1#2[29]112, CWR:VOL1#2[78], CWR:VOL1#4[77],
CWR:VOL2#3[256], CWR:VOL2#4[269]145,
CWR:VOL3#2[70]155, CWR:VOL3#2[102]156,
CWTI:SEPT/89[24]128, CWTI:DEC/91[36]240

HAMRICK, JAMES, *Cpt., 1st Ind.Hvy Art.;* ACW:JAN/94[30]450

HANAN, JOHN, *Private, 5th New York Infantry;*
CWR:VOL1#2[7]111, CWTI:MAY/94[31]382

HANCOCK, CORNELIA, *civilian;* ACW:JUL/93[50]426,
CWM:DEC/95[54]632, GETTY:10[53]225, GETTY:12[97]249

HANCOCK, LITTLETON B., *Private, Sumter Artillery;*
CWR:VOL3#2[1]153

HANCOCK, WINFIELD S., *General, USA:*
ARTICLES: "BATTLE FOUGHT ON PAPER,"
ACW:MAY/93[31]415, "'DON'T LET ME BLEED TO DEATH':
THE WOUNDING OF MAJ. GEN. WINFIELD SCOTT
HANCOCK," GETTY:6[87]178, "NEITHER 'HANCOCK THE
SUPERB' NOR 'HARD BACKSIDES' CUSTER WON MUCH
GLORY IN THE HANCOCK'S WAR FIASCO,"
ACW:MAY/93[54]410 "SUPERB WAS THE DAY,"
ACW:MAR/91[47]297, "TO BE HELD AT ALL HAZARDS,"
CWTI:SEP/93[43]338
BOOK REVIEW: *WINFIELD SCOTT HANCOCK: A SOLDIER'S LIFE*
GENERAL LISTINGS: *Chancellorsville,* ACW:MAY/95[30]525, *Cold
Harbor,* ACW:SEP/93[62]436, B&G:APR/94[10]558, *Custer,*
AHI:FEB/71[4]131, *Fredericksburg,* ACW:MAY/94[12]466,
ACW:SEP/95[54]548, CWR:VOL4#4[28]178,
CWTI:DEC/90[58]185, *general history,* AHI:MAY/71[3]133A
GENERAL LISTINGS, continued: *Gettysburg,* ACW:MAY/92[8]357,
ACW:JUL/93[50]426, ACW:JUL/95[50]538,
AHI:MAY/67[22]107, AHI:SUM/88[12]273,
CWTI:SEPT/89[46]132, CWTI:JUL/93[29]326,
GETTY:4[113]153, GETTY:5[19]158, GETTY:5[79]161,
GETTY:5[89]162, GETTY:5[117]165, GETTY:6[7]169,
GETTY:6[43]173, GETTY:6[87]178, GETTY:7[29]188,
GETTY:7[51]190, GETTY:7[97]193, GETTY:8[43]202,
GETTY:8[95]205, GETTY:9[5]209, GETTY:9[17]210,
GETTY:9[33]211, GETTY:9[61]215, GETTY:9[81]216,
GETTY:10[53]225, GETTY:10[112]228, GETTY:11[19]232,
GETTY:11[71]234, GETTY:11[80]235, GETTY:12[1]240,
GETTY:12[7]241, GETTY:12[24]242, GETTY:12[30]243,
GETTY:12[68]246, GETTY:12[85]248, MH:DEC/91[54]155
GENERAL LISTINGS, continued: *Grand Review,* CWTI:AUG/90[64]170,
in book review, ACW:JAN/94[62], B&G:JUN/94[34],
CWNEWS:SEP/93[5], CWNEWS:MAY/95[33],
CWR:VOL4#3[89], *in order of battle,* B&G:APR/94[10]558,
B&G:APR/95[8]595, *James A. Garfield,* AHI:MAY/76[24]167,
Jericho Mill, B&G:APR/93[12]518, *letters to the editor,*
B&G:JUN/95[5]599, CWM:FEB/95[5]557,
CWTI:FEB/92[8]245, *Los Angeles,* CWTI:SEP/91[18]227,
Morton's Ford, ACW:SEP/94[38]487, *Mosby,*
CWTI:AUG/90[42]167, *Overland Campaign,*

B&G:APR/94[10]558, CWTI:APR/92[49]260, *Peninsula
Campaign,* CWM:JUN/95[34]584, CWM:JUN/95[63]594,
Petersburg, CWTI:APR/90[24]152, CWTI:FEB/91[45]194,
MH:APR/95[46]183, *Spotsylvania,* ACW:MAY/95[18]524,
Wilderness, ACW:MAY/93[31]415, B&G:APR/95[8]595,
B&G:JUN/95[8]600, CWTI:MAR/89[34]104, *photos;*
ACW:MAR/91[47]297, ACW:JAN/94[8]447,
AHI:MAY/71[3]133A, B&G:APR/94[10]558,
B&G:JUN/95[8]600, B&G:DEC/95[44]617,
CWTI:SEP/93[43]338, GETTY:6[87]178, GETTY:8[5]198,
GETTY:10[53]225
ADDITIONAL LISTINGS: ACW:JUL/91[35]314, ACW:SEP/91[41]323,
ACW:NOV/92[8]383, ACW:NOV/92[42]388,
ACW:JUL/93[16]422, ACW:SEP/93[62]436,
ACW:JAN/94[8]447, ACW:JUL/94[26]477,
ACW:NOV/94[76]500, AHI:APR/85[18]250,
B&G:APR/91[8]445, B&G:FEB/93[61]516,
B&G:APR/93[12]518, B&G:JUN/93[40]527,
B&G:AUG/94[10]574, B&G:AUG/94[38]578,
B&G:APR/94[59]565, B&G:DEC/95[44]617
ADDITIONAL LISTINGS, continued: CWM:MAR/91[14]334,
CWM:MAR/91[17]335, CWM:AUG/94[30]527,
CWM:OCT/95[22]614, CWM:OCT/95[40]619,
CWR:VOL1#3[52]122, CWR:VOL2#2[141]137,
CWR:VOL2#4[269]145, CWR:VOL3#1[31]150,
CWR:VOL3#2[1]153, CWR:VOL3#3[1]157,
CWR:VOL3#4[1]161, CWR:VOL4#4[47]179,
CWTI:SEP/91[31]229, CWTI:SEP/91[54]232,
CWTI:JUL/93[34]327, CWTI:DEC/94[32]410,
CWTI:AUG/95[24]455, GETTY:13[1]252, GETTY:13[7]253,
GETTY:13[43]256, GETTY:13[50]257, GETTY:13[64]258,
GETTY:13[119]262, MH:APR/92[18]157, MH:APR/94[54]176

HAND, W.H., *Pvt., 12th South Carolina Infantry;* GETTY:6[7]169
HANDERSON, HENRY E., *Private, 9th Louisiana Infantry;*
GETTY:6[7]169
HANDS, ROBINSON W., *Lieutenant, USN;*
AHI:NOV/75[38]163, CWM:JUL/93[15]484 ,
HANDY, ISAAC W.K., *Chaplain;* CWTI:JUL/93[20]325
HANDY, LEWIS H., *photographer;* B&G:FEB/94[24]551
HANDY, ROBERT, *Commander, USN;* B&G:JUN/92[40]489
HANDY, THOMAS H., *Lieutenant, CSN;* ACW:JUL/93[34]424
HANEY, MILTON L., *Chaplain, 55th Illinois Infantry:*
ARTICLE: "IN THE PULPIT AND IN THE TRENCHES,"
CWTI:SEP/92[28]280
ADDITIONAL LISTINGS: B&G:APR/93[40]522, *photo;*
CWTI:SEP/92[28]280
HANFORD, J. HARVEY, *Private, 124th New York Infantry;*
GETTY:9[5]209
HANGER, JAMES E., *Private, CSA;* ACW:JAN/92[47]344,
B&G:AUG/93[10]529
HANIFEN, MICHAEL, *Private, 1st New Jersey Artillery;* BOOK
REVIEW: *HISTORY OF BATTERY B, FIRST NEW JERSEY
ARTILLERY*
HANKINS, THOMAS J., *Corporal, 2nd Tennessee Cavalry;*
CWR:VOL4#1[1]163
HANKS, JACK, *Private, 14th Kentucky Infantry;*
ACW:SEP/95[22]544
HANNA, EBENEZER, *Private, CSA;* B&G:JUN/94[8]568,
CWM:JUL/93[35]487, CWTI:MAR/94[58]375,
CWTI:JUL/94[10]389
HANNAH, BOB, *Private, 95th Illinois Infantry;*
CWM:JAN/91[11]325
HANNUM, J.A., *seaman, CSN;* ACW:JAN/93[51]398

HANOVER COUNTY, VIRGINIA; ARTICLE: "WAR COMES TO HANOVER COUNTY," B&G:APR/94[51]563

HANOVER COURT HOUSE, VIRGINIA, BATTLE OF; see listings under **"SLASH CHURCH, VIRGINIA, BATTLE OF"**

HANSELL, GEORGE, *Pvt., 72nd Penn. Inf.;* GETTY:7[97]193

HANSON, CHARLES, *Colonel, 20th Kentucky Infantry;* B&G:AUG/91[11]458, CWM:MAR/93[16]466

HANSON, ROGER, *General, CSA;* ACW:JUL/91[12]310, ACW:JUL/92[22]368, B&G:FEB/92[10]474, CWM:MAR/93[16]466, CWM:FEB/95[28]560

HAPPEE, JOHN, *Private, 24th Michigan Infantry;* GETTY:9[33]211, GETTY:11[57]233

HARD ROPE; ARTICLE: "HARD ROPE'S CIVIL WAR," CWTI:SEP/90[52]179

HARD, ABNER, *Private, 8th Illinois Cavalry;* GETTY:11[19]232

HARDAWAY (HURT'S ALABAMA) ARTILLERY; B&G:FEB/95[38]593, B&G:JUN/95[36]603A, GETTY:5[117]165

HARDAWAY, ROBERT A., *Colonel, CSA;* B&G:APR/95[8]595, CWR:VOL1#1[1]102, CWR:VOL1#1[35]104, CWR:VOL4#4[70]180

HARDEE, WILLIE, *Private, CSA;* B&G:DEC/95[9]615

HARDEE, WILLIAM J., *General, CSA:*
GENERAL LISTINGS: *Atlanta Campaign,* ACW:JAN/95[30]505, ACW:NOV/95[74]560, CWM:JAN/91[12]326, CWM:JAN/91[28]327, CWM:MAR/93[32]468, CWTI:SUMMER/89[32]122, CWTI:SUMMER/89[50]124, CWTI:SEP/92[28]280, CWTI:NOV/92[41]291, CWTI:MAR/93[24]309, *black soldiers,* ACW:NOV/93[6]437, *Carolina Campaign,* B&G:DEC/95[9]615, *Davis,* CWTI:AUG/91[36]217, *in book review,* ACW:JUL/94[58], ACW:MAR/95[58], B&G:FEB/95[26], CWNEWS:NOV/89[4], CWR:VOL2#1[78], CWR:VOL4#3[1]170, *Lookout Mountain,* CWTI:SEPT/89[30]129, *Mexican War,* MH:APR/93[39]166, *Missionary Ridge,* CWTI:SEP/94[40]403, *North Carolina Campaign,* ACW:NOV/93[12]440
GENERAL LISTINGS, continued: *order of battle,* B&G:DEC/95[9]615, *Ringgold Gap,* ACW:NOV/93[34]442, *Savannah,* B&G:FEB/91[8]439, CWTI:DEC/94[62]415, *Shiloh,* ACW:JAN/91[22]285, CWTI:SEP/93[59]341, *Tullahoma Campaign,* B&G:OCT/92[10]496, *West Point,* B&G:DEC/91[12]469, *Wilmington/Fort Fisher,* B&G:DEC/94[10]585, *photos,* B&G:FEB/91[8]439, B&G:DEC/91[12]469, B&G:OCT/92[10]496, B&G:DEC/95[9]615, CWTI:DEC/94[62]415
ADDITIONAL LISTINGS: ACW:SEP/92[47]380, ACW:MAR/94[42]461, ACW:SEP/94[10]484, ACW:NOV/94[34]496, AHI:AUG/72[24]140, AHI:OCT/95[24]326, B&G:FEB/92[10]474, B&G:APR/92[58]485, B&G:DEC/92[20]504, B&G:FEB/93[12]511, B&G:OCT/94[11]580, CWM:MAR/91[28]336, CWM:JUL/92[40]432, CWM:MAY/93[8]474, CWM:AUG/94[27]526, CWM:OCT/94[48]542, CWM:APR/95[16]571, CWR:VOL1#2[7]111, CWR:VOL1#3[7]118, CWR:VOL1#4[64]127, CWR:VOL2#3[194]141, CWR:VOL4#1[1]163, CWR:VOL4#1[44]164, CWR:VOL4#3[50]171, CWR:VOL4#3[65]172, CWTI:SUMMER/89[13]120, CWTI:SUMMER/89[20]121, CWTI:SUMMER/89[40]123

HARDEMAN, WILLIAM P., *General, CSA;* AHI:JUN/70[30]127, CWR:VOL2#3[212]142, CWR:VOL4#2[118]169, *photo;* AHI:JUN/70[30]127

HARDEN, HOPKINS, *Lt., 19th Va Inf.;* GETTY:12[111]250

HARDIE, JAMES A., *Colonel, USA;* GETTY:7[29]188

HARDIN, DAVID, *Pvt., Sumter Artillery;* CWR:VOL3#2[1]153

HARDIN, JOHN J.; CWTI:DEC/95[24]477

HARDIN, JOHN WESLEY; ARTICLE: "THE CIVIL WAR WAS A DEADLY CLASSROOM FOR HICKOK, HARDIN, THE JAMESES AND A NUMBER OF OTHER 'STUDENTS,'" ACW:MAR/94[6]455

HARDIN, MARTIN D., *Colonel, USA;* B&G:AUG/92[11]493, B&G:APR/93[12]518, B&G:APR/94[10]558

HARDIN, THOMAS J., *Maj., 19th Miss. Inf.;* GETTY:5[89]162

HARDING, CHESTER, *General, USA;* ACW:MAR/91[62]298, B&G:JUN/91[10]452

HARDISON, J.J., *Pvt., 51st NC Inf.;* B&G:APR/93[24]520

HARDMAN, ASA S., *Pvt., 3rd Indiana Cav.;* GETTY:11[119]238

HARDMAN, LYMAN, *Sgt., 30th Ohio Inf.;* CWTI:DEC/94[62]415

"HARDTACK" REGIMENT; (154th NY Inf.); GETTY:8[17]200

HARDWICKE, WILLIAM W., *Lt., CSA;* GETTY:10[29]222

HARDY, L.T., *Captain, CSA;* CWR:VOL4#1[1]163

HARDY, ROBERT, *Captain, USN;* MH:DEC/94[46]181

HARDY, WASHINGTON M., *Colonel, CSA;* B&G:DEC/95[9]615

HARGRODER, WILLIAM I., *Captain, 7th Louisiana Infantry;* CWR:VOL4#2[118]169

HARISON, RANDOLPH, *Colonel, CSA;* CWR:VOL2#4[361]148

HARKER, CHARLES G., *General, USA;* B&G:DEC/93[52]548, CWM:JAN/91[12]326, CWR:VOL3#4[24]162, CWTI:SEP/92[31]281

HARKER, WILLIAM S., *Private, 12th New Jersey Infantry;* GETTY:5[89]162

HARLAN, EDWARD, *Private, 124th Pennsylvania Infantry;* CWTI:SEP/93[43]338

HARLAN, JAMES, *Senator, Iowa;* CWTI:DEC/95[76]482

HARLAN, JOHN, *Col, 10th Kentucky Inf.;* B&G:FEB/93[12]511

HARLE, WILLIAM, *Captain, USA;* CWTI:AUG/95[34]457

HARLESTON, JOHN; ACW:SEP/94[46]488

HARLING, THOMAS, *Corp., 7th SC Inf.;* GETTY:5[35]159

HARLOW, FRANKLIN P., *Lieutenant Colonel, 7th Massachusetts Infantry;* ACW:SEP/92[30]378

HARLOW, ISAAC, *Lt., 9th NH Inf.;* CWR:VOL2#2[118]136

HARMAN, E.P., *Pvt., 13th Mississippi Inf.;* GETTY:12[7]241

HARMAN, EDWIN H., *Lieutenant Colonel, 45th Virginia Infantry;* ACW:MAR/94[27]459

HARMAN, JOHN A., *Major, CSA;* ACW:JUL/93[50]426, B&G:JUN/92[8]487, CWTI:APR/89[38]111, CWTI:MAR/94[29]371

HARMAN, WILLIAM H., *General, USA;* CWTI:APR/89[38]111

HARMON, A.W., *Col., 12th Virginia Cavalry;* GETTY:11[19]232

HARMON, JOHN A., *Major, CSA;* AHI:JUN/67[31]110

HARMON, WILLIAM, *Lt., 1st Minn. Infantry;* GETTY:5[79]161

HARNEY, FRANK M., *Lieutenant, 14th North Carolina Infantry;* GETTY:4[33]146

HARNEY, THOMAS F.; CWTI:OCT/95[18], CWTI:DEC/95[76]482

HARNEY, WILLIAM S., *General, USA;* ACW:MAR/91[62]298, ACW:MAY/91[31]304, AHI:MAY/67[34]108, CWM:MAY/93[8]474

HARPER, ELLA; AHI:DEC/73[10]152

HARPER, GEORGE, *Private, Sumter Artillery;* CWR:VOL3#2[1]153

HARPER, JOSEPH, *Capt., 9th Ill. Cav.;* CWTI:JAN/93[20]298

HARPER, JOSEPH F., *Pvt., 26th Ind. Inf.;* B&G:APR/93[40]522

HARPER, KENTON, *Col., 5th VA Inf.;* CWM:NOV/91[40]393

HARPER, ROBERT G.; GETTY:9[122]220

HARPER, WILLIAM, *Private, 154th New York Infantry;* CWTI:SEP/92[22]279, GETTY:8[17]200

HARPER, WILLIAM, *Lieutenant, 1st Indiana Heavy Artillery;*
ACW:JAN/94[30]450
HARPERS FERRY ARSENAL:
ARTICLE: "SCHEMES AND TREACHERY: THE 1861 PLOT TO
SEIZE THE ARSENAL AT HARPERS FERRY,"
CWTI:APR/89[38]111
ADDITIONAL LISTING: ACW:JAN/91[8]282
HARPERS FERRY NATIONAL HISTORIC PARK, WEST
VIRGINIA:
ARTICLES: "A LANDSCAPE THAT GAVE SHAPE TO HISTORY,"
CWTI:JAN/95[24]424, "A VISIT TO JOHN BROWN
COUNTRY," CWTI:JUL/92[20]271
ADDITIONAL LISTINGS: B&G:AUG/91[40]463, B&G:OCT/91[11]466,
CWM:MAR/92[27]412, CWR:VOL1#4[74]128
HARPERS FERRY, WEST VIRGINIA:
GENERAL LISTINGS: *general history,* AHI:MAY/71[3]133A, *ghosts of,*
B&G:OCT/91[11]466, *in book review,* CWM:DEC/95[10], *photo*
of B&O Railroad; CWTI:APR/89[38]111, *photos,*
AHI:MAR/84[10]236
ADDITIONAL LISTINGS: ACW:MAR/91[14]293, ACW:MAY/93[38]416,
ACW:JUL/93[8]420, ACW:JUL/93[58], ACW:MAY/94[43]470,
ACW:SEP/94[10]484, ACW:JAN/95[20]504,
B&G:AUG/91[40]463, B&G:OCT/91[40]467,
CWM:NOV/91[40]393, CWR:VOL1#1[1]102,
CWR:VOL2#4[269]145, CWTI:DEC/89[34]136,
CWTI:DEC/95[40]479,
HARPERS FERRY, WEST VIRGINIA, RAID (1859):
ARTICLES: "A VISIT TO JOHN BROWN COUNTRY,"
CWTI:JUL/92[20]271, "GOD'S ANGRY MAN,"
AHI:JAN/86[10]256, "JOHN BROWN'S RAID,"
AHI:AUG/76[34]171, "METEOR OF THE WAR,"
ACW:JUL/91[43]315, "RAID ON HARPERS FERRY,"
AHI:MAR/84[10]236
BOOK REVIEW: *THE OLD MAN: JOHN BROWN AT HARPERS*
FERRY
ADDITIONAL LISTINGS: AHI:JUN/73[4]149, CWM:JUL/91[35]369,
CWM:SEP/92[8]437, CWTI:SEPT/89[40]130,
CWTI:DEC/89[34]136, *photo circa 1859;* CWTI:APR/89[38]111
HARPERS FERRY, WEST VIRGINIA, 1862, BATTLE AND
SIEGE OF:
ARTICLES: "THE 126TH NEW YORK INFANTRY AT HARPERS
FERRY," CWR:VOL1#4[7]125, "ESCAPE FROM HARPERS
FERRY," CWM:MAY/92[8]418, "FIRING THE GAP,"
ACW:JAN/94[39]451, "'REMEMBER HARPER'S FERRY':
THE DEGRADATION, HUMILIATION AND REDEMPTION
OF COL. GEORGE L. WILLARD'S BRIGADE,"
GETTY:7[51]190, "STONEWALL'S FORGOTTEN
MASTERPIECE," MH:AUG/95[30]185
BOOK REVIEW: *THE HISTORY OF THE HARPERS FERRY*
CAVALRY EXPEDITION, SEPTEMBER 14 & 15, 1862
ADDITIONAL LISTINGS: ACW:JUL/92[30]369, ACW:MAY/95[54]528,
B&G:JUN/92[8]487, CWM:OCT/94[26]536,
CWR:VOL1#3[52]122, CWR:VOL1#4[v]124,
CWR:VOL2#2[95]135, CWR:VOL3#1[31]150,
CWTI:JAN/95[24]424
HARPERS FERRY, WEST VIRGINIA, 1863 SURRENDER
OF; CWM:SEP/91[40]385
HARPERS FERRY, WEST VIRGINIA, 1864;
ACW:NOV/93[50]444
HARPERS, H.H., *Capt., 14th SC Inf.;* GETTY:8[9]199
HARRELL, JAMES A., *Pvt., 17th NC Inf.;* ACW:MAR/95[12]513
HARRIGAN, TOM, *Private, 9th Massachusetts Infantry;*
CWTI:JUN/90[28]158

HARRINGTON, DANIEL, *Sergeant, 53rd Pennsylvania*
Infantry; GETTY:11[80]235
HARRINGTON, EBENEZER B., *Lieutenant, 97th New York*
Infantry; GETTY:10[7]221
HARRINGTON, FAZIO, *Lieutenant Colonel, USA;*
CWR:VOL3#4[24]162
HARRINGTON, JOHN M., *Master, USN;* AHI:OCT/75[30]162
HARRINGTON, WILLIAM D., *Private, 3rd North Carolina*
Cavalry; BOOK REVIEWS: *THE DESERTER'S DAUGHTER ***
THE CAPTAIN'S BRIDE, A TALE OF THE WAR
HARRIS, ANDREW L., *Colonel, 75th Ohio Infantry;*
ACW:NOV/92[42]388, GETTY:6[7]169, GETTY:12[30]243
HARRIS, CHARLES, *Private, 7th Wisconsin Infantry,*
GETTY:11[57]233
HARRIS, CHARLES L., *Colonel, 11th Wisconsin Infantry;*
CWR:VOL2#1[19]131, CWR:VOL2#1[69]133
HARRIS, CLARA:
BOOK REVIEW: *HENRY AND CLARA*
ADDITIONAL LISTINGS: ACW:MAY/95[68]529, AHI:FEB/86[12]257,
CWTI:MAR/93[12]307, CWTI:DEC/95[76]482, *photo;*
CWTI:MAR/93[12]307
HARRIS, DAVID G., *Private, CSA;* BOOK REVIEW: *PIEDMONT*
FARMER: THE JOURNALS OF DAVID GOLIGHTLY
HARRIS, 1855-1870
HARRIS, EDWARD P., *Lieutenant, Colonel, 1st Delaware*
Infantry; GETTY:5[89]162, GETTY:9[61]215
HARRIS, IRA, *Senator;* B&G:OCT/93[21]538,
AHI:FEB/86[12]257
HARRIS, ISHAM G, *Governor, Tennessee,* ACW:JAN/91[22]285,
ACW:JUL/92[22]368, ACW:NOV/92[35]387,
ACW:SEP/93[6]428, ACW:JAN/94[18]449,
ACW:MAR/95[26]515, AHI:JUN/70[30]127,
B&G:FEB/92[10]474, B&G:FEB/93[12]511,
B&G:FEB/95[35]592, CWTI:AUG/91[36]217,
CWTI:SEP/93[59]341, *photo; AHI:JUN/70[30]127*
HARRIS, JAMES G., *Major, 7th North Carolina Infantry;*
GETTY:8[67]204, GETTY:13[75]259
HARRIS, JAMES H., *Sgt., 38th USCT;* CWM:AUG/94[30]527
HARRIS, JIMMY, *Private, 5th Texas Infantry;*
CWTI:DEC/91[36]240
HARRIS, JOEL C., ARTICLE: "A VISIT WITH UNCLE REMUS,"
B&G:FEB/93[32]513
HARRIS, JOHN, *Colonel, USMC;* CWR:VOL2#3[183]140,
CWR:VOL2#3[194]141, CWTI:APR/92[14]254, *photo;*
CWR:VOL2#3[183]140
HARRIS, LEONARD, *Colonel, USA;* CWR:VOL4#3[50]171
HARRIS, M.B., *Col., 12th Miss. Inf.;* B&G:APR/93[12]518
HARRIS, NATHAN, *General, CSA:*
ARTICLE: "GENERAL NAT HARRIS' DIARY,"
B&G:AUG/91[30]460
GENERAL LISTINGS: *Gettysburg,* GETTY:4[7]142, *in order of battle,*
B&G:APR/94[10]558, B&G:APR/95[8]595, *letters to the editor,*
B&G:OCT/91[6]465, *photo;* B&G:AUG/91[30]460
ADDITIONAL LISTINGS: ACW:SEP/95[70]549, B&G:AUG/93[36]533,
B&G:DEC/93[30]546, CWR:VOL2#3[236]143, GETTY:5[89]162
HARRIS, ROBERT A., *Captain, Louisiana Tigers;*
CWTI:MAR/94[48]374
HARRIS, ROBERT A., *Lieutenant, Sumter Artillery;*
CWR:VOL3#2[61]154
HARRIS, SAMUEL, *Lt., 5th Michigan Cav.;* GETTY:13[89]260
HARRIS, TOM, *Confederate guerrilla leader;*
ACW:NOV/94[34]496
HARRIS, THOMAS H., *General, CSA;* AHI:AUG/67[50]111

HARRIS, WILLIAM, *Private, 1st Arkansas Cavalry;*
CWR:VOL1#2[70]115
HARRISBURG, PENNSYLVANIA; GETTY:4[7]142,
GETTY:5[4]156
HARRISON'S (VIRGINIA) GUARDS; ACW:MAR/93[10]402
HARRISON'S LANDING, VIRGINIA, BATTLE OF:
ARTICLE: "THE PENINSULA CAMPAIGN OF 1862:
DENOUEMENT AT HARRISON'S LANDING,"
CWM:JUN/95[76]598
ADDITIONAL LISTINGS: ACW:MAR/95[12]513, CWTI:NOV/93[55]350
HARRISON, BENJAMIN, *Colonel, 70th Indiana Infantry:*
ARTICLE: "'TRUE AMERICAN MADNESS': INAUGURAL
BALLS," AHI:NOV/72[37]143
ADDITIONAL LISTINGS: ACW:JAN/94[47]452, AHI:MAY/69[32]122,
AHI:APR/89[43]284, AHI:NOV/90[44]293,
B&G:DEC/93[12]545, CWTI:SUMMER/89[32]122,
CWTI:NOV/92[41]291, CWTI:SEP/93[22]335
HARRISON, BURTON S.; ACW:SEP/91[62]326,
ACW:MAY/95[38]526, CWNEWS:OCT/89[4],
CWTI:JUL/93[20]325, CWTI:MAR/93[32]311
HARRISON, CHARLES, *Colonel, CSA;* CWTI:SEP/90[52]179,
CWTI:MAR/91[10]197
HARRISON, DABNEY C., *Captain, 56th Virginia Infantry;*
ACW:MAR/93[10]402
HARRISON, EDWARD B., *Sergeant, 24th Michigan Infantry;*
GETTY:5[19]158
HARRISON, GEORGE F., *Captain, 4th Virginia Cavalry;*
CWR:VOL1#1[1]102
HARRISON, GEORGE P., *Colonel, 1st Georgia Infantry:*
ARTICLE: "BEHIND THE LINES," CWTI:JUL/92[62]276
ADDITIONAL LISTINGS: B&G:DEC/95[9]615, CWR:VOL2#4[346],
CWR:VOL3#1[65]151, CWTI:DEC/94[49]413,
CWTI:MAR/95[18]432
HARRISON, H.K., *Capt., 7th GA Cav.;* B&G:AUG/93[36]533
HARRISON, ISAAC F., *Lieutenant Colonel, 15th Louisiana
Cavalry;* CWR:VOL2#1[36]132, CWR:VOL3#3[33]158,
CWR:VOL4#2[118]169
HARRISON, JAMES C., *Adjutant, 5th Ohio Cavalry;*
CWR:VOL4#1[44]164
HARRISON, JAMES E., *Colonel, CSA;* CWR:VOL2#3[212]142
HARRISON, RANDOLPH, *Colonel, 46th Virginia Infantry;*
CWR:VOL2#2[141]137
HARRISON, ROBERT B., *Private, 11th Mississippi Infantry;*
CWR:VOL2#4[269]145
HARRISON, ROBERT D., *Captain, 9th Florida Infantry;*
CWR:VOL3#4[1]161
HARRISON, THOMAS J., *Colonel, 4th Tennessee Cavalry
(Union);* ACW:NOV/95[48]557, B&G:DEC/93[12]545,
CWM:JAN/91[40]330, CWM:JUL/92[40]432
HARRISON, WALTER, *Major, CSA;* GETTY:5[107]164,
GETTY:13[64]258
HARRISON, WILLIAM A., *Private, 13th Virginia Cavalry;*
GETTY:13[89]260
HARRISON, WILLIAM, *Sergeant, 53rd Pennsylvania Infantry;*
GETTY:11[80]235
HARROW'S BRIGADE; ARTICLE: "DEFENDING THE CODORI
HOUSE AND CEMETERY RIDGE: TWO SWORDS WITH
HARROW'S BRIGADE IN THE GETTYSBURG CAMPAIGN,"
GETTY:13[43]256
HARROW, WILLIAM, *General, USA:*
ARTICLE: "DEFENDING THE CODORI HOUSE AND
CEMETERY RIDGE: TWO SWORDS WITH HARROW'S

BRIGADE IN THE GETTYSBURG CAMPAIGN,"
GETTY:13[43]256
GENERAL LISTINGS: *Gettysburg,* AHI:SUM/88[12]273,
GETTY:4[89]150, GETTY:5[79]161, GETTY:7[29]188,
GETTY:7[97]193, GETTY:8[95]205, *photo;*
CWM:APR/95[42]577
ADDITIONAL LISTINGS: CWM:APR/95[42]577, CWTI:SEP/94[34]402,
CWTI:SUMMER/89[40]123, GETTY:13[1]252,
GETTY:13[50]257, GETTY:13[119]262
HARROWER, BENJAMIN, *Lieutenant, 1st Indiana Heavy
Artillery;* ACW:JAN/94[30]450
HART, DANIEL, *Captain, 7th New Jersey Infantry;* ARTICLE: "A
WEDDING IN CAMP," B&G:FEB/92[22]476
HART, DAVID, *Private, USA;* B&G:AUG/93[10]529
HART, J.F., *Captain, Hart's Battery;* CWR:VOL4#4[70]180
HART, J.H., *Major, 71st Ohio Infantry;* CWTI:JUL/92[42]274
HART, JAMES F., *Major, Washington (South Carolina)
Artillery;* B&G:OCT/93[12]537, CWTI:JUN/90[32]159,
GETTY:7[124]196, GETTY:11[19]232
HART, JAMES H., *Capt., 1st New Jersey Cav.;* GETTY:4[75]149
HART, JOHN A., *Private, 11th Veteran Reserve Corps;*
B&G:APR/93[24]520
HART, LEVI W., *Captain, 1st Illinois Light Artillery;*
B&G:AUG/95[8]604, B&G:AUG/95[55]609,
CWR:VOL2#1[1]130
HART, NANCY; AHI:DEC/73[10]152, CWTI:SEP/94[12]398,
photo; AHI:DEC/73[10]152
HART, PATRICK, *Captain; 15th New York Light Artillery;*
GETTY:5[47]160, GETTY:8[53]203, GETTY:9[41]212
HART, PATRICK, *Lieutenant, 19th Indiana Infantry;*
B&G:APR/95[24]596
HART, THEODORE, *Corporal, 5th New York Infantry;*
CWR:VOL1#2[7]111, CWR:VOL1#2[29]112,
CWTI:MAY/94[31]382
HART, WILLIAM M., *Captain, 27th Illinois Infantry;*
CWR:VOL3#4[24]162
HARTLEY, HENRY, *Lieutenant, 1st Massachusetts Infantry;*
GETTY:12[7]241
HARTLEY, JOSEPH H., *Sergeant, USMC;*
CWTI:JUN/95[26]445
HARTRANFT, JOHN F., *General, USA:*
BOOK REVIEW: *MAJOR GENERAL JOHN FREDERICK
HARTRANFT, CITIZEN SOLDIER AND PENNSYLVANIA
STATESMAN*
ADDITIONAL LISTINGS: ACW:MAY/91[23]303, B&G:APR/94[10]558,
B&G:APR/95[8]595, CWR:VOL3#2[1]153,
CWR:VOL2#2[118]136, CWTI:FEB/92[36]249,
CWTI:JAN/95[34]427, CWTI:MAR/95[33]435, *photo,*
CWTI:DEC/89[26]135
HARTSHORNE, W. ROSS, *Lieutenant, 13th Pennsylvania
Reserves;* CWR:VOL1#3[28]120
HARTSUFF, GEORGE L., *General, USA:*
ARTICLE: "A STUDY IN VALOR: GEORGE L. HARTSUFF,
MAJOR GENERAL, U.S.A.," B&G:DEC/94[34]587
ADDITIONAL LISTINGS: ACW:JAN/91[38]287, CWTI:JUN/95[38]447,
CWTI:DEC/95[22]476, *photo;* B&G:DEC/94[34]587
HARTSVILLE RAID; ARTICLE: "A BRILLIANT EXPLOIT:
JOHN HUNT MORGAN'S HARTSVILLE RAID,"
CWM:JAN/93[29]459
HARVEY, CORDELIA; ARTICLE: "AN ANGEL FROM
WISCONSIN: A YANKEE GOVERNOR'S WIDOW,"
DEDICATES HERSELF TO COMFORTING THE
WOUNDED," CWTI:MAR/89[20]102

ADDITIONAL LISTINGS: ACW:JAN/92[30]342, AHI:NOV/70[22]130, AHI:NOV/88[37]278, AHI:NOV/90[44]293, AHI:JAN/94[50]319, CWM:JUL/92[8]427, CWTI:MAY/89[14]114, CWTI:DEC/91[28]239, CWTI:SEP/92[22]279, CWTI:SEP/92[46]284, CWTI:JAN/93[44]302, CWTI:OCT/95[32]468, CWTI:DEC/95[22]476, CWTI:DEC/95[52]480, CWTI:DEC/95[76]482

HAYDEN, CHARLES B., *Lieutenant, 2nd Michigan Infantry;* ARTICLE: "FLIGHT TO THE JAMES," CWTI:JUL/93[14]324

HAYDEN, JULIUS, *Lt. Col., 1st Mass. Inf.;* GETTY:12[7]241

HAYDON, CHARLES B., *Lieutenant Colonel, 2nd Michigan Infantry;* BOOK REVIEWS: *FOR COUNTRY, CAUSE & LEADER: THE CIVIL WAR JOURNAL OF CHARLES B. HAYDON*

HAYES, CHARLES S., *Major, 5th Ohio Cavalry;* CWR:VOL4#1[44]164

HAYES, EDWARD, *Capt., 29th Ohio Infantry;* GETTY:9[81]216

HAYES, JOSEPH, *General, USA;* B&G:APR/92[8]481, CWR:VOL2#4[269]145

HAYES, RUTHERFORD B., *General, USA:*
ARTICLES: "A PRESIDENTIAL GALLERY," AHI:APR/89[20]282, "FOCUS: CIVIL WAR PHOTOGRAPHY," AHI:AUG/79[32]191, "THE GLORY YEARS," CWTI:SEP/94[49]404, "MASTER FRAUD OF THE CENTURY': THE DISPUTED ELECTION OF 1876," AHI:NOV/88[28]277, "'RUTHERFRAUD' B. HAYES SURVIVED THE CIVIL WAR TO WIN A HOTLY DISPUTED PRESIDENTIAL ELECTION," ACW:JUL/93[6]419, "'TRUE AMERICAN MADNESS': INAUGURAL BALLS," AHI:NOV/72[37]143

BOOK REVIEWS: *HAYES OF THE TWENTY-THIRD: THE CIVIL WAR VOLUNTEER OFFICER * RUTHERFORD B. HAYES: WARRIOR & PRESIDENT*

GENERAL LISTINGS: *in book review,* ACW:JUL/94[58], ACW:SEP/95[62], *Cedar Creek,* MH:OCT/93[76]173, *Grant,* AHI:DEC/72[4]144, *in book review,* ACW:JUL/93[58], CWNEWS:NOV/92[4], CWR:VOL4#1[78], *John C. Fremont,* AHI:MAY/70[4]126, *letters to the editor,* CWTI:JAN/95[16]421, *Rutherford B. Hayes Presidential Center;* AHI:APR/89[43]284, *photos,* ACW:JUL/93[6]419, AHI:NOV/88[28]277, AHI:APR/89[20]282, B&G:APR/95[38]598, B&G:OCT/95[8]611D, CWTI:SEP/94[49]404

ADDITIONAL LISTINGS: ACW:JUL/91[8]309, ACW:MAR/94[27]459, AHI:APR/89[13]281, AHI:JAN/85[10]244, AHI:NOV/89[50]288, B&G:AUG/91[40]463, B&G:OCT/92[32]499, B&G:FEB/94[38]553, B&G:JUN/94[38]571, B&G:OCT/94[11]580, B&G:APR/95[38]598, B&G:OCT/95[8]611D, CWM:MAR/93[24]467, CWTI:FEB/90[12]141, CWTI:MAY/93[29]319, CWTI:JUL/94[50]395

HAYES, W.A., *Captain, 13th Indiana Cavalry;* CWTI:MAR/91[46]203

HAYES, WILLIAM, *Private, 69th Pennsylvania Infantry;* GETTY:4[89]150

HAYKES, A.S., *Captain, 10th Louisiana Infantry;* CWR:VOL3#1[1]149

HAYMAN, SAMUEL B., *Colonel, USA;* ACW:MAY/95[30]525, GETTY:8[43]202

HAYNE, EDMUND S., *Private, 1st South Carolina Infantry;* ACW:NOV/92[10]384

HAYNE, PAUL H, *poet;* ACW:SEP/92[10]375

HAYNES, A.S., *Major, 11th North Carolina Infantry;* GETTY:8[67]204

HAYNES, MARTIN, *Private, 2nd New Hampshire Infantry;* B&G:AUG/92[11]493, GETTY:9[41]212

HAYNES, MILTON, *Lieutenant Colonel, CSA;* B&G:FEB/92[10]474

HAYNES, R.P., *Sergeant, 26th Virginia Infantry;* B&G:APR/93[24]520

HAYNIE, ISHAM N., *Colonel, USA;* B&G:FEB/92[10]474

HAYS, ALEXANDER, *General, USA:*
ARTICLE: "REBELS ACROSS THE RIVER," ACW:SEP/94[38]487

GENERAL LISTINGS: *Gettysburg,* ACW:JUL/95[50]538, GETTY:4[113]153, GETTY:5[79]161, GETTY:5[89]162, GETTY:7[29]188, GETTY:7[51]190, GETTY:7[97]193, GETTY:8[95]205, GETTY:9[61]215, GETTY:10[53]225, GETTY:12[61]245, GETTY:12[97]249, *in list,* CWTI:JUL/93[34]327, *letters to the editor,* B&G:JUN/95[5]599, *order of battle,* B&G:APR/95[8]595, *Wilderness,* B&G:APR/95[8]595, *photo as young officer;* CWTI:FEB/90[20]142, *photos;* ACW:SEP/94[38]487, ACW:MAY/95[54]528, B&G:APR/91[8]445, B&G:APR/95[8]595

ADDITIONAL LISTINGS: ACW:MAY/95[54]528, B&G:APR/91[8]445, CWR:VOL2#4[269]145, CWTI:MAR/89[34]104, CWTI:JUL/93[42]329, GETTY:8[95]205

HAYS, ALFRED, *Corporal, 53rd Pennsylvania Infantry;* GETTY:11[80]235

HAYS, HARRY T., *General, CSA:*
GENERAL LISTINGS: *Gettysburg,* GETTY:4[49]147, GETTY:5[89]162, GETTY:5[103]163, GETTY:6[7]169, GETTY:6[94]180, GETTY:8[17]200, GETTY:9[17]210, GETTY:10[7]221, GETTY:11[57]233, GETTY:12[30]243, *in book review,* B&G:FEB/92[26], *in book review,* CWNEWS:JAN/92[4], CWR:VOL1#4[77], *order of battle,* B&G:APR/95[8]595, *Wilderness,* B&G:JUN/95[8]600, *photo;* CWM:SEP/93[24]495

ADDITIONAL LISTINGS: ACW:MAR/92[30]352, ACW:JUL/92[30]369, ACW:SEP/92[30]378, B&G:FEB/95[8]590C, B&G:FEB/95[35]592, CWM:MAR/91[17]335, CWM:SEP/93[24]495, CWTI:FEB/91[12]189, CWTI:SEP/94[34]402, CWTI:MAR/95[46]437, GETTY:11[126]239

HAYSLETT, A.J., *Surgeon, CSA;* CWR:VOL4#4[70]180

HAYWARD, GEORGE L., *Lieutenant, 29th Ohio Infantry;* GETTY:7[83]192

HAYWARD, GEORGE, *Lieutenant, 137th New York Infantry;* GETTY:9[81]216

HAYWARD, NATHAN, *Surgeon, 20th Massachusetts Infantry;* GETTY:10[53]225

HAZARD, JOHN, *Captain, USA;* GETTY:9[61]215

HAZEL, EDWIN, *Capt., 12th Mass. Inf.;* GETTY:10[7]221

HAZELTINE, CHARLES, *Private, 22nd Massachusetts Infantry;* GETTY:8[53]203

HAZEN, WILLIAM B., *Corporal., 124th New York Infantry.;* CWM:DEC/94[40]550

HAZEN, WILLIAM B., *General, USA:*
BOOK REVIEW: *A NARRATIVE OF MILITARY SERVICE*

GENERAL LISTINGS: *in book review,* B&G:AUG/93[24], *in book review,* CWM:AUG/95[45], *order of battle,* B&G:DEC/95[9]615, *Nelson-Davis feud,* AHI:NOV/72[12]142, *Savannah,* B&G:FEB/91[8]439, *photos,* B&G:FEB/91[8]439, CWTI:DEC/94[62]415

ADDITIONAL LISTINGS: ACW:SEP/92[47]380, ACW:JUL/94[6]473, CWM:JUL/92[18]429, CWR:VOL3#2[70]155, CWTI:NOV/92[41]291, CWTI:DEC/94[62]415

HAZLETT, CHARLES E, *Lieutenant, 5th U.S. Artillery;*
B&G:DEC/91[12]469, B&G:AUG/92[11]493,
CWR:VOL1#2[29]112, CWR:VOL1#2[42]113, GETTY:6[7]169,
GETTY:6[43]173, GETTY:7[41]189, GETTY:8[31]201,
GETTY:9[48]213, GETTY:11[91]236, *West Point photo;*
B&G:DEC/91[12]469
HEAD, EDWARD, *Pvt., 69th Pennsylvania Inf.;* GETTY:4[89]150
HEAD, THOMAS, *Private, 2nd USSS;* CWTI:JUL/93[42]329
HEAD, TRUMAN; CWTI:JUL/93[42]329
HEAGY, GEORGE W., *Sergeant, 3rd Pennsylvania Cavalry;*
GETTY:13[89]260
HEALY, W.H., *Capt., 8th New York Cav.;* CWM:MAY/92[8]418
HEART, A.Y., *Sergeant, 21st Illinois Inf.;* ACW:NOV/94[34]496
HEARTSILL, W.W.; BOOK REVIEW: *FOURTEEN HUNDRED
AND 91 DAYS IN THE CONFEDERATE ARMY*
HEATH, A.M., *Adj., 12th New Hampshire Inf.;* GETTY:12[7]241
HEATH, FRANCIS E., *Colonel, 19th Maine Infantry;*
GETTY:5[79]161, GETTY:7[97]193, GETTY:13[50]257
HEATH, THOMAS T., *Lieutenant Colonel, 5th Ohio Cavalry;*
CWR:VOL4#1[44]164
HEBERLING, WILLIAM F., *Private, 148th Pennsylvania
Infantry;* CWR:VOL2#2[141]137
HEBERT, JOSEPH, *Captain, 10th Louisiana Infantry
Battalion;* CWR:VOL3#1[1]149
HEBERT, LOUIS, *General, CSA;* ACW:SEP/91[46]324,
ACW:NOV/93[26]441, AHI:DEC/77[46]177,
CWR:VOL1#1[42]105, CWR:VOL2#1[1]130,
CWR:VOL2#1[36]132, CWR:VOL4#3[1]170,
CWTI:FEB/92[29]248, CWTI:JUL/94[50]395
HEBERT, PAUL O., *General, CSA;* ACW:JUL/91[58]316,
ACW:JAN/93[51]398, CWR:VOL3#1[1]149,
CWR:VOL3#3[33]158
HECK, JONATHAN, *Lieutenant Colonel, CSA;*
B&G:AUG/93[10]529, CWNEWS:FEB/94[5]
HEENAN, DENNIS, *Colonel, 116th Pennsylvania Infantry;*
CWR:VOL4#4[47]179, CWTI:DEC/90[58]185
HEFFELFINGER, CHRIS, *Lieutenant, 1st Minnesota Infantry;*
GETTY:5[79]161
HEFFINER JOHN, *Colonel, CSA;* ACW:NOV/91[10]329
HEFLIN, WILLIAM P., *Private, 11th Mississippi Infantry;*
CWR:VOL2#4[269]145, GETTY:9[98]217
HEG, HANS C., *Colonel, 15th Wisconsin Infantry:*
ARTICLE: "COLONEL HEG MEMORIAL PARK,"
B&G:AUG/93[34]532
ADDITIONAL LISTING: AHI:DEC/73[10]152
HEIM, GEORGE, *Pvt., 8th Illinois Cav.;* B&G:FEB/95[8]590A
HEIM, ISAAC, *Corp., 53rd Pennsylvania Inf.;* GETTY:11[80]235
HEIMAN, ADOLPHUS, *Colonel, 10th Tennessee Infantry;*
B&G:DEC/93[52]548, CWR:VOL4#3[89]
HEIMER, FRANK, *Lt., 144th NY Inf.* ACW:MAY/94[51]471
HEINTZELMAN, SAMUEL P., *General, USA:*
ARTICLE: "THE PENINSULA CAMPAIGN OF 1862: THE
BATTLE OF SEVEN PINES," CWM:JUN/95[47]588
GENERAL LISTINGS: *Manassas, Second,* B&G:AUG/92[11]493,
B&G:OCT/95[20]612, *Mexican War,* MH:APR/93[39]166,
Peninsula Campaign, CWM:JUN/95[29]583, *Savage's Station,*
CWM:JUN/95[65]595, *Seven Pines,* CWM:JUN/95[47]588,
Williamsburg, ACW:MAR/91[47]297
ADDITIONAL LISTINGS: ACW:JUL/91[18]312, ACW:NOV/91[30]332,
ACW:NOV/92[18]385, ACW:NOV/94[18]495,
ACW:JAN/95[54]508, ACW:MAY/95[54]528,
CWR:VOL3#2[1]153, CWTI:SEP/91[42]231,

CWTI:MAR/93[20]308, CWTI:JUL/93[14]324, GETTY:9[5]209,
GETTY:13[33]255
HELENA, ARKANSAS, BATTLE OF:
ARTICLE: "DEATH TAKES NO HOLIDAY," ACW:MAY/93[22]414
ADDITIONAL LISTING: ACW:MAR/95[26]515
HELLEDAY, GUSTAVE B., *Major, 99th New York Infantry;*
ACW:JAN/95[74]510
HELLER, GUS, *Private, 49th Pennsylvania Infantry;*
CWTI:SEP/93[43]338
HELLER, HENRY, *Sergeant, USA;* CWM:SEP/93[8]493
HELM, BENJAMIN H., *General, CSA;* ACW:JUL/91[12]310,
ACW:JAN/91[22]285, ACW:MAR/93[55]408,
AHI:NOV/90[44]293, B&G:AUG/95[8]604,
B&G:AUG/95[42]608, CWTI:DEC/95[8]474, *photo;*
B&G:AUG/95[42]608
HEMPSTEAD, CARL, *Private, 1st Arkansas Cavalry;*
CWR:VOL1#2[70]115
HENAGAN, JOHN W., *Colonel, 2nd South Carolina Infantry;*
B&G:APR/93[12]518, B&G:APR/95[8]595, GETTY:5[35]159
HENDERSHOT, ROBERT H., *Private, 8th Michigan Infantry;*
ACW:NOV/92[8]383, CWR:VOL2#1[19]131
HENDERSON, CHARLES L., *Surgeon, 2nd Michigan Cavalry;*
CWNEWS:SEP/92[4]
HENDERSON, D., *seaman, USN,* ACW:SEP/95[38]546
HENDERSON, H.A.M., *Captain, CSA;* CWNEWS:JAN/91[4]
HENDERSON, HENRY E., *Private, 9th Louisiana Infantry;*
GETTY:7[13]186
HENDERSON, JOHN B., *Senator, Missouri;*
AHI:DEC/68[28]118
HENDERSON, JOHN C., *Private, 7th Indiana Infantry;*
CWTI:NOV/93[24]346
HENDERSON, L.B., *Capt., 13th NC Inf.;* GETTY:8[67]204
HENDERSON, LINDSEY L., *Private, 3rd North Carolina
Cavalry;* ACW:MAR/95[50]518
HENDERSON, OCTAVIUS C., *Lieutenant, 1st Virginia
Battalion;* CWM:MAR/91[65]342
HENDERSON, RICHARD H., *Lieutenant, CSMC;*
ACW:MAR/91[14]293
HENDERSON, ROBERT J., *Colonel, CSA;* B&G:DEC/95[9]615
HENDERSON, THOMAS, *Captain, USA;* CWNEWS:JUL/92[4]
HENDERSON, THOMAS J., *Colonel, USA;*
B&G:DEC/94[10]585
HENDRICKSON, T., *Captain, USA;* ACW:NOV/94[50]498
HENDRIX, JOHN, *Private, 13th Alabama Infantry;*
GETTY:6[13]170
HENDRY, GEORGE N., *Captain, 1st Georgia Reserves;*
CWTI:DEC/94[62]415
HENEGAN, JOHN W., *Colonel, CSA;* CWR:VOL3#2[1]153
HENION, HUDSON D., *Private, 126th New York Infantry;*
CWR:VOL1#4[7]125
HENRY, E.E., *Private, 23rd Ohio Infantry;* CWTI:SEP/94[49]404
HENRY, G.A., *Senator, Tennessee;* CWTI:MAY/89[22]116
HENRY, GEORGE E., *Capt., 1st Mass. Inf.;* GETTY:12[7]241
HENRY, GUY V., *Colonel, USA;* B&G:APR/94[10]558,
CWR:VOL3#1[65]151
HENRY, JOHN, *Private, USA;* GETTY:9[81]216
HENRY, MATHIS W., *Major, CSA;* CWR:VOL4#4[70]180,
GETTY:5[117]165
HENRY, WILLIAM D., *Colonel, 10th Vermont Cavalry;*
ACW:NOV/93[50]444, B&G:DEC/92[8]503
HENRY, WILLIAM W., *Captain, CSA;* CWM:APR/94[32]506
HENSON, WILLIAM W., *Sergeant, 2nd Tennessee Cavalry;*
CWR:VOL4#1[1]163

HERBERT, HILARY A., *Lieutenant Colonel, 8th Alabama Infantry;* GETTY:12[7]241

HERBERT, JAMES R., *Lieutenant Colonel, 1st Maryland (Confederate) Battalion;* CWR:VOL1#3[52]122, GETTY:7[83]192

HERBERT, PHILEOMAN, *Colonel, CSA;* ACW:JAN/91[10]283

HERBERT, W.H., *Lieutenant, 70th Ohio Infantry;* CWR:VOL4#1[44]164

HERBURT, THOMAS, *Private, 84th Illinois Infantry;* B&G:DEC/92[32]506

HERDER, JOHN N., *Lieutenant Colonel, USA;* ACW:JUL/94[8]474

HERENDEEN, ORIN J., *Captain, 126th New York Infantry;* CWR:VOL1#4[7]125, GETTY:8[95]205

"HERITAGEPAC"; see listings under **"PRESERVATION"**

HERNDON, JOHN G., *Private, Charlottesville Artillery;* ARTICLE: "A SCHOOLBOY CAVALRYMAN," CWTI:MAR/91[74]204

HERNDON, THOMAS, *Lieutenant, 14th Tennessee Infantry;* ARTICLE: "A TENNESSEE VOLUNTEER," CWTI:AUG/91[82]223

HERNDON, WILLIAM H.:
BOOK REVIEW: *LINCOLN'S HERNDON: A BIOGRAPHY*
GENERAL LISTINGS: *in book review,* CWM:APR/95[50], *Lincoln's humor,* AHI:NOV/70[22]130, *Mary Todd Lincoln,* AHI:MAY/75[4]159, *sketch;* AHI:NOV/70[22]130, AHI:APR/76[32]166
ADDITIONAL LISTINGS: ACW:JUL/92[62]372, ACW:NOV/94[8]493, AHI:APR/76[32]166, CWTI:DEC/95[22]476, CWTI:DEC/95[24]477

HERO, ANDREW, *Captain, CSA;* ACW:JUL/92[12]367

HEROD, ANDREW, *Captain, 1st Mississippi Artillery;* ACW:JAN/94[30]450

HEROLD, DAVID E., AHI:FEB/86[12]257, CWTI:MAY/92[8]261, CWTI:MAY/93[12]316, CWTI:JUN/95[26]445, CWTI:DEC/95[76]482

HERRICK, ANDREW J., *Private, 6th Massachusetts Militia;* ACW:JAN/91[8]282

HERRINGTON, EPHRAIM, *Private, Sumter Artillery;* CWR:VOL3#2[1]153, CWR:VOL3#2[61]154

HERRON, FRANCIS J., *General, USA;* ACW:JUL/92[46]371, ACW:MAY/94[26]468, ACW:SEP/94[10]484, CWR:VOL1#1[42]105

HERRON, FRANK, *Private, 3rd Tennessee Infantry;* ARTICLE: "I LOVE THE WORK 'RAYMOND'," CWM:JUN/94[58]519

HERRON, JAMES H., *Private, 2nd Tennessee Cavalry;* CWR:VOL4#1[1]163

HERZOG, CHARLES, *Lieutenant, USA;* GETTY:4[101]151

HESS, FRANK W., *Captain, 3rd Pennsylvania Cavalry;* GETTY:4[75]149, GETTY:13[89]260

HESSER, THEODORE, *Lieutenant Colonel, 72nd Pennsylvania Infantry;* GETTY:7[97]193

HESSIAN, WILLIAM, *Sergeant, 3rd U.S. Infantry;* ACW:NOV/94[50]498

HESSIE, AUGUSTUS, *Private, 9th Massachusetts Artillery;* GETTY:5[47]160

HETH, HENRY, *General, CSA:*
ARTICLE: "THE SHELTON LAUREL MASSACRE," B&G:FEB/91[20]440
GENERAL LISTINGS: *Chancellorsville,* MH:JUN/92[50]159, *Cold Harbor,* B&G:APR/94[10]558, *Davis' funeral,* CWTI:MAR/93[32]311, *Falling Waters,* GETTY:9[109]218, *Five Forks,* B&G:APR/92[8]481, *Gettysburg,* ACW:MAY/93[14]413,

AHI:MAY/67[22]107, B&G:APR/91[39]449, GETTY:4[7]142, GETTY:4[22]144, GETTY:4[33]146, GETTY:4[49]147, GETTY:4[101]151, GETTY:4[110]152, GETTY:4[113]153, GETTY:5[4]156, GETTY:5[19]158, GETTY:5[103]163, GETTY:5[107]164, GETTY:6[13]170, GETTY:7[124]196, GETTY:8[67]204, GETTY:8[67]204, GETTY:8[95]205, GETTY:8[111]206, GETTY:9[17]210, GETTY:9[98]217, GETTY:10[107]227, GETTY:11[6]231, GETTY:11[19]232, GETTY:11[57]233, GETTY:11[71]234, GETTY:12[61]245, MH:DEC/91[54]155, *in book review,* CWNEWS:OCT/93[5], CWR:VOL3#4[68], *in order of battle,* B&G:APR/94[10]558, B&G:APR/95[8]595, *Mormon confrontation,* AHI:DEC/72[10]145, *Overland Campaign,* B&G:APR/94[10]558, *Wilderness,* B&G:APR/95[8]595, B&G:JUN/95[8]600, *photos;* B&G:FEB/91[20]440, B&G:FEB/95[8]590A, CWTI:APR/90[46]153, GETTY:13[75]259
ADDITIONAL LISTINGS: ACW:SEP/91[62]326, ACW:MAR/92[10]349, ACW:JUL/93[50]426, ACW:SEP/94[38]487, ACW:JAN/95[46]507, AHI:MAR/84[42]238, B&G:FEB/95[8]590A, B&G:FEB/95[8]590B, CWM:JAN/93[8]456, CWM:AUG/94[26]525, CWM:DEC/95[41]630, CWR:VOL1#1[1]102, CWR:VOL1#1[26]103, CWR:VOL1#3[52]122, CWR:VOL2#2[156]138, CWR:VOL2#3[236]143, CWR:VOL2#4[269]145, CWR:VOL3#2[1]153, CWR:VOL4#1[1]163, CWTI:MAR/89[44]105, CWTI:SEPT/89[46]132, CWTI:AUG/90[26]166, CWTI:APR/90[46]153, CWTI:FEB/91[45]194, CWTI:SEP/94[26]400, GETTY:13[22]254, GETTY:13[64]258, GETTY:13[75]259, GETTY:13[108]261, GETTY:13[119]262

HETH, JOHN; CWM:MAR/91[65]342

HEWETT, NORMAN F., *Lieutenant Colonel, USA;* ACW:NOV/94[42]497

HEWIT, HENRY S., *Medical Director;* CWM:MAY/91[10]347

HEWITT, ABRAM S.; CWTI:OCT/95[32]468

HEWITT, SYLVESTER M., *Major, USA;* CWR:VOL1#4[7]125

HEYER, JACOB, *Captain, 23rd Pennsylvania Infantry;* ARTICLE: "A FIGHTING ZOUAVE," CWTI:JUN/95[90]451

HEYWARD, PAULINE D., BOOK REVIEW: *A CONFEDERATE LADY COMES OF AGE: THE JOURNAL OF PAULINE DECARADEUC HEYWARD, 1863-1888*

HIBBARD, ELISHA C., *Major, 24th Wisconsin Infantry;* ACW:MAR/92[14]350

HIBBETT, JEFFERSON J., *Captain, USA;* CWR:VOL1#4[7]125

HIBBS, J.W., *Captain, 13th Virginia Infantry;* CWTI:JUL/93[20]325

HIBBS, WILLIAM, *Private, 6th Michigan Cavalry;* CWTI:SEP/90[34]176

HIBSON, JOSEPH, *Private, 48th New York Infantry;* ACW:SEP/91[30]322

HICK, DAVID, *Private, 37th Illinois Infantry;* CWR:VOL1#1[42]105

HICKENLOOPER, ANDREW, *Captain, 5th Ohio Light Artillery;* ACW:JAN/91[22]285, B&G:OCT/92[26]498

HICKEY, MYRON, *Lieutenant, 5th Michigan Cavalry;* B&G:AUG/91[36]462

HICKMAN, JOHN, *seaman, USN;* ACW:MAR/92[40]353

HICKOK, JAMES B. "WILD BILL"; ARTICLES: "THE CIVIL WAR—AND CREDULOUS LISTENERS—TURNED JIM HICKOK INTO THE FAMOUS 'WILD BILL,'" ACW:MAR/94[8]456, "THE CIVIL WAR WAS A DEADLY

CWTI:APR/92[49]260, CWTI:MAR/93[40]312,
CWTI:NOV/93[55]350, CWTI:JUL/94[44]394,
CWTI:DEC/94[32]410, CWTI:JAN/95[24]424,
CWTI:JAN/95[34]427
ADDITIONAL LISTINGS, GETTY: GETTY:13[22]254, GETTY:13[43]256,
GETTY:13[64]258, GETTY:13[108]261
HILL, BENJAMIN H., *Confederate Congressman;*
AHI:MAY/81[8]217, CWTI:MAY/94[44]384,
CWTI:SUMMER/89[13]120, CWTI:SUMMER/89[20]121
HILL, BENNETT, *Lieutenant Colonel, USA;*
ACW:JUL/95[44]537
HILL, CHARLES, *Colonel, USA;* ACW:JAN/93[66]399
HILL, CHARLES W., *Militia General;* B&G:AUG/93[10]529
HILL, DANIEL H., *General, CSA:*
ARTICLES: "I AM SO UNLIKE OTHER FOLKS: THE SOLDIER
WHO COULD NOT BE UNDERSTOOD,"
CWTI:APR/89[14]107, "THE "BLACKBERRY RAID","
GETTY:11[6]231, "THE PENINSULA CAMPAIGN OF 1862:
THE BATTLE OF SEVEN PINES," CWM:JUN/95[47]588,
"THE PENINSULA CAMPAIGN OF 1862: THE DABBS
HOUSE MEETING," CWM:JUN/95[53]590
BOOK REVIEW: *LEE'S MAVERICK GENERAL, DANIEL HARVEY
HILL*
GENERAL LISTINGS: *Antietam,* ACW:JUL/92[30]369,
B&G:OCT/95[8]611A, CWTI:MAR/93[26]310,
CWTI:SEP/93[43]338, *Bentonville,* CWR:VOL4#3[65]172,
Carolina Campaign, B&G:DEC/95[9]615, *Chattanooga,*
ACW:MAY/91[23]303, *Chickamauga,* CWTI:MAR/93[24]309,
CWTI:JAN/94[35]361, *Gaines' Mill,* ACW:NOV/94[50]498,
CWM:JUN/95[61]593, *Harpers Ferry,* MH:AUG/95[30]185, *in
book review,* ACW:JUL/93[58], CWM:JUN/95[6],
CWNEWS:MAY/92[4], CWNEWS:FEB/94[5],
CWR:VOL3#2[105], *Jackson,* AHI:JUN/67[31]110,
B&G:JUN/92[8]487, *Lee's lost order 191,* ACW:JAN/94[6]446,
letters to the editor, CWM:MAR/91[12]333,
CWM:OCT/95[5]613, *Malvern Hill,* CWM:JUN/95[73]597,
CWTI:JUL/93[38]328, *Mexican War,* MH:APR/93[39]166, *order
of battle,* B&G:DEC/95[9]615, *Peninsula Campaign,*
ACW:MAR/91[47]297, CWM:JUN/95[34]584, *post-war,*
ACW:JUL/95[26]535, *Seven Days,* CWTI:JUL/93[29]326, *Seven
Pines,* CWM:JUN/95[47]588, *South Mountain,*
CWTI:JAN/95[34]427, *Williamsburg,* ACW:MAR/91[47]297,
photos, AHI:JUN/67[31]110, ACW:MAR/93[42]406,
CWTI:APR/89[14]107, GETTY:11[6]231
ADDITIONAL LISTINGS: ACW:JUL/92[12]367, ACW:MAR/93[42]406,
ACW:SEP/93[8]429, ACW:SEP/93[31]433,
ACW:JAN/95[46]507, ACW:SEP/95[54]548,
AHI:APR/85[18]250, B&G:FEB/93[24]512,
B&G:OCT/94[28]581, B&G:FEB/95[8]590B,
B&G:OCT/95[8]611C, CWM:MAR/93[32]468,
CWM:APR/94[8]502, CWM:JUN/94[43]517,
CWR:VOL1#2[7]111, CWR:VOL1#4[7]125,
CWR:VOL1#4[42]126, CWR:VOL2#2[95]135,
CWR:VOL3#1[31]150, CWR:VOL3#2[1]153,
CWR:VOL3#3[1]157, CWR:VOL4#4[70]180,
CWTI:APR/90[56]155, CWTI:FEB/91[12]189,
CWTI:MAR/93[40]312, CWTI:MAY/93[26]318,
CWTI:NOV/93[55]350, CWTI:JUL/94[44]394,
CWTI:DEC/94[57]414, MH:JUN/94[8]177
HILL, DAVID J., *Private, 2nd Mississippi Infantry;*
GETTY:4[126]154, GETTY:6[77]177
HILL, EDWARD, *Lieutenant Colonel, 16th Michigan Infantry;*
GETTY:6[33]172

HILL, G. POWELL, *Paymaster, CSA;* ACW:MAY/95[38]526
HILL, GABRIEL H., *Lieutenant Colonel, CSA;* BOOK REVIEW:
*THE STORY OF THE CONFEDERATE STATES
ORDNANCE WORKS AT TYLER, TEXAS, 1861-1865*
HILL, J. MARSHALL, *Private, 14th South Carolina Infantry;*
ARTICLE: "CAPT. JAMES GLENN'S SWORD AND PVT. J.
MARSHALL HILL'S ENFIELD IN THE FIGHT FOR THE
LUTHERAN SEMINARY," GETTY:8[9]199
HILL, JASPER; CWTI:AUG/95[58]461
HILL, JOHN T., *Major, 12th New Jersey Infantry;*
GETTY:5[89]162
HILL, JOHN, *Private, CSA;* ACW:JUL/93[27]423
HILL, JOSEPH, *photographer;* AHI:FEB/69[35]120
HILL, JOSHUA; ACW:NOV/93[42]443
HILL, ROSWELL S., *Captain, 2nd Indiana Cavalry;*
B&G:AUG/94[22]576
HILL, SYLVESTER G., *Colonel, USA;* B&G:DEC/93[12]545,
CWR:VOL2#3[212]142
HILL, TUCK; B&G:JUN/91[32]454
HILL, W.T., *Captain, 5th Texas Infantry;* CWR:VOL1#2[29]112
HILL, WALLACE, *Captain, 1st West Virginia Artillery;*
GETTY:12[30]243
HILL, WILLIAM A., *Captain, 19th Massachusetts Infantry;*
GETTY:4[89]150, GETTY:7[97]193
HILL, WILLIAM, *Captain, USA;* GETTY:4[101]151
HILL, WILLIAM H., *Private, 13th Misssissippi Infantry;*
GETTY:12[7]241
HILL-JACKSON FEUD; ARTICLE: "THE CORPORAL, THE
HOTHEAD AND THE CRAZY OLD PRESBYTERIAN FOOL,"
CWM:OCT/94[26]536
HILLARD, ABRAHAM, *Private, 6th Pennsylvania Heavy
Artillery;* B&G:FEB/95[38]593
HILLE, F.T., *Captain, CSA;* GETTY:8[67]204
HILLEBRANDT, HUGO, *Major, 39th New York Infantry;*
ACW:MAY/95[54]528, CWR:VOL1#4[7]125, GETTY:7[51]190,
GETTY:8[95]205, *photo,* GETTY:7[51]190
HILLIARD, ABRAHAM, *Private, 6th Pennsylvania Heavy
Artillery;* B&G:JUN/95[36]603A
HILLYEN, WILLIAM R., *Captain, 7th New Jersey Infantry;*
B&G:FEB/92[22]476
HILLYER, EDGAR W., *Major, USA;* B&G:OCT/91[11]466
HILLYER, LORRIE, *Lieutenant, 3rd Georgia Infantry;*
CWTI:DEC/94[32]410
HINCH, THOMAS H., *Lieutenant, 2nd Tennessee Cavalry;*
CWR:VOL4#1[1]163
HINCHBERGER, CHRISTIAN, *Private, 78th Pennsylvania
Infantry;* CWM:DEC/95[26]626
HINCKS, WILLIAM B., *Sergeant Major, 14th Connecticut
Infantry;* GETTY:12[61]245
HINDMAN, THOMAS C., *General, CSA:*
BOOK REVIEWS: *THE LION OF THE SOUTH: GENERAL
THOMAS C. HINDMAN*
ADDITIONAL LISTINGS: ACW:SEP/92[38]379, ACW:MAY/93[22]414,
ACW:NOV/93[6]437, ACW:MAY/94[26]468,
ACW:SEP/94[10]484, AHI:JUN/70[30]127,
B&G:JUN/92[46]490, B&G:FEB/93[36], CWM:JUL/92[24]430,
CWM:SEP/92[38]443, CWM:JAN/93[6]455, CWM:APR/95[50],
CWR:VOL1#1[42]105, CWTI:APR/89[14]107,
CWTI:SEP/92[31]281, CWTI:NOV/92[41]291,
CWTI:MAY/94[16]380, *photos,* ACW:MAY/94[26]468,
AHI:JUN/70[30]127
HINDSALE, JOHN W., *Private, CSA;* ACW:NOV/93[12]440

HINES, T. HENRY, *Captain, CSA;* AHI:JUN/70[30]127, B&G:OCT/94[11]580, CWM:MAR/93[16]466, CWTI:NOV/92[54]293, MH:JUN/91[20]152, *photo;* B&G:OCT/94[11]580

HINKLEY, JULIAN, *Captain, 3rd Wisconsin Infantry;* CWTI:NOV/92[41]291

HINKS, EDWARD, *General, USA;* ACW:MAR/95[12]513

HINMAN, WILLIAM G., *Private, 7th Wisconsin Infantry,* GETTY:11[57]233, GETTY:9[33]211

HINRICHS, OSCAR, *Lieutenant, CSA;* GETTY:13[108]261

HINRICKS, CHARLES, *Captain, USA;* ACW:MAR/91[38]296

HINSON, WILLIAM, *Private, CSA;* ACW:MAY/92[30]361

HINTON, RICHARD, *Major, 1st New York Cavalry;* ACW:JUL/95[8]532

HIPP, CHARLES, *Major, 37th Ohio Infantry;* CWM:DEC/95[35]629

HIRST, BEN,, JOHN and JOSEPH, *14th Connecticut Infantry;* B&G:APR/95[30], CWR:VOL4#3[89], GETTY:9[61]215

HISTORIC AIR TOURS; ARTICLE: "A LIVING MAP OF THE WAR," CWM:JUN/95[79]599

HISTORIC BLAKELEY (ALABAMA) STATE PARK; CWTI:DEC/94[24]409, CWTI:MAR/95[18]432

HISTORIC SAVANNAH (GEORGIA) FOUNDATION; B&G:JUN/91[6]451

HISTORICAL RESEARCH; BOOK REVIEW: *THE NEW HISTORY AND THE OLD: CRITICAL ESSAYS AND REAPPRAISALS*

HISTORY; ARTICLE: "IF HISTORY IS WRITTEN ONLY BY THE WINNERS, THEN WHO REALLY WON THE CIVIL WAR?" ACW:NOV/94[6]492

HITCH, WILLIAM S., *Senator, Delaware;* CWTI:JUL/93[20]325

HITCHCOCK, CHARLES, *Sergeant, 111th New York Infantry;* ACW:JUL/95[50]538, GETTY:8[95]205, GETTY:9[61]215

HITCHCOCK, ETHAN A., *General, USA;* ACW:MAY/95[54]528, MH:APR/93[39]166

HITCHCOCK, HENRY, *Major, USA;* AHI:JAN/67[4]106, CWTI:DEC/94[62]415, CWTI:DEC/94[82]418

HITCHCOCK, ROBERT, *Lieutenant, USMC;* ARTICLE: "ONE MARINE'S BRIEF BATTLE," CWTI:APR/92[14]254

HITE, MAXFIELD, *Sergeant, 31st Ohio Infantry;* ARTICLE: "34-YEAR-OLD FATHER OF SEVEN," CWTI:SEP/93[90]343

HOADLEY, F.W., *Major, CSA;* AHI:DEC/77[46]177

HOBART, HARRISON C., *General, USA;* ACW:JAN/94[55]453, AHI:DEC/85[40]255, B&G:DEC/95[9]615, *photo;* ACW:JAN/94[55]453

HOBBS, CHARLES A., *Sergeant, 99th Illinois Infantry;* B&G:FEB/94[8]550

HOBBS, WILLIAM, *Doctor;* AHI:FEB/69[35]120

HOBSON, EDWARD H., *General, USA;* B&G:AUG/91[11]458, CWM:MAR/93[16]466, *photo;* B&G:AUG/91[52]458

HOCKERSMITH, LORENZO D., *Captain, CSA;* B&G:OCT/94[11]580

HODGDON, JOHN G., *Private, 6th Wisconsin Infantry,* GETTY:11[57]233

HODGE, GEORGE B., *Colonel, CSA;* ACW:MAY/95[49]527

HODGEMAN, RUFUS, *Private, 7th Wisconsin Infantry;* GETTY:9[33]211, GETTY:11[57]233

HODGES, ALPHONSE, *Corporal, 9th New York Cavalry;* B&G:FEB/95[8]590A, GETTY:4[113]153

HODGES, JAMES G., *Colonel, 14th Virginia Infantry;* CWTI:JUL/93[29]326

HODGKINS, JOSEPH E., *Private, 19th Massachusetts Infantry;* BOOK REVIEW: *THE CIVIL WAR DIARY OF LIEUTENANT J.E. HODGKINS*

HODSDON, JOHN L., *Adjutant General, State of Maine;* CWTI:SEP/92[40]282, GETTY:8[43]202

HOFFMAN, JOHN S., *Colonel, 31st Virginia Infantry;* B&G:JUN/95[8]600

HOFFMAN, JOHN W., *Colonel, USA;* B&G:APR/93[12]518

HOFFMAN, LEWIS, *Captain, 4th Ohio Light Artillery;* B&G:AUG/95[8]604

HOFFMAN, WILLIAM, *Colonel, USA;* ACW:MAR/91[25]294, ACW:JAN/93[66]399, B&G:OCT/94[11]580, CWTI:JUL/93[20]325, GETTY:10[102]226

HOFMANN, J. WILLIAM, *Colonel, USA;* B&G:APR/94[10]558, CWTI:NOV/93[24]346, GETTY:4[113]153

HOGE, A.W., *Lieutenant, CSA;* ACW:MAR/94[27]459

HOITT, SAMUEL, *civilian;* B&G:APR/93[24]520, CWTI:JAN/95[48]429

HOKE, JACOB, *civilian;* B&G:AUG/94[10]574, B&G:AUG/94[19]575, GETTY:7[13]186

HOKE, ROBERT F., *General, CSA:*

GENERAL LISTINGS: *Carolina Campaign,* B&G:DEC/95[9]615, *Cold Harbor,* B&G:APR/94[10]558, *Fort Fisher,* ACW:JAN/95[38]506, AHI:SEP/83[12]234, *Gettysburg,* GETTY:12[30]243, *in order of battle,* B&G:APR/94[10]558, B&G:DEC/95[9]615, *Overland Campaign,* B&G:APR/94[10]558, *Petersburg,* MH:APR/95[46]183, *Wilmington/Fort Fisher,* B&G:DEC/94[10]585, *photos;* ACW:MAY/92[30]361, B&G:DEC/94[10]585, B&G:DEC/95[9]615

ADDITIONAL LISTINGS: ACW:MAY/92[30]361, ACW:NOV/92[42]388, ACW:SEP/93[62]436, ACW:NOV/93[12]440, ACW:JUL/94[42]479, ACW:MAR/95[50]518, CWM:JUL/92[16]428, CWM:SEP/92[16]438, CWM:SEP/93[24]495, CWR:VOL1#1[1]102, CWR:VOL3#2[1]153, CWR:VOL3#4[1]161, CWR:VOL4#3[65]172, CWTI:FEB/91[12]189, CWTI:APR/92[49]260, CWTI:JUL/94[44]394

HOLCOMB, PYTHAGORAS, *Captain, 2nd Vermont Artillery;* ACW:JAN/94[30]450

HOLCOMBE, GEORGE P., *Private, 2nd Mississippi Infantry;* GETTY:6[77]177

HOLCOMBE, JAMES P., *civilian;* ACW:NOV/92[51]389, ACW:JUL/95[44]537

HOLD, WILLIAM, *Lieutenant Colonel, 10th Georgia Infantry;* ACW:JUL/95[10]533

HOLDEN, WILLIAM, *Governor, North Carolina;* AHI:APR/73[12]148, AHI:JAN/80[8]197

HOLDER, ROBERT, *Private, 1st Maryland Battalion;* GETTY:9[81]216

HOLDER, WILLIAM D., *Colonel, 17th Mississippi Infantry;* ACW:SEP/92[30]378

HOLLADAY, WALLER, *Private, Charlottesville Artillery;* B&G:DEC/95[25]616

HOLLAND, DANILE P., *Lieutenant Colonel, 1st Florida Special Battalion;* CWR:VOL3#1[65]151

HOLLAND, J.E., *Lieutenant, USA;* B&G:APR/94[10]558

HOLLAND, JOHN C., *Captain, 75th USCT;* CWM:NOV/92[6]446

HOLLAND, JOHN, *Lieutenant, 18th Virginia Infantry;* B&G:APR/92[8]481

HOLLAND, JOHN, *Private, 2nd Wisconsin Infantry,* GETTY:11[57]233

HOLLAND, PHILIP, *Captain, 1st Pennsylvania Rifles;*
CWR:VOL1#3[20]119

HOLLINS, GEORGE N., *Captain, CSN;* ACW:MAY/92[16]359,
CWTI:MAY/92[29]263, MH:FEB/91[8]151,
MH:DEC/94[46]181, *photos;* CWTI:MAY/92[29]263,
MH:DEC/94[46]181

HOLLIS, EDWARD G., *Private, CSA;* GETTY:10[107]227

HOLLIS, MATHEW H., *Private, Sumter Artillery;*
CWR:VOL3#2[1]153

HOLLISTER, OVANDO, *Private, 1st Colorado Infantry;*
ACW:NOV/91[10]329

HOLLOWAY, EDMONDS B., *Colonel, CSA;*
CWTI:MAR/91[34]201

HOLLOWAY, JAMES M., *Surgeon, 18th Mississippi Infantry;*
CWM:JUN/95[29]583

HOLLOWAY, S.D., *Captain, CSA;* B&G:OCT/94[11]580

HOLLOWAY, WILLIAM P., *Lieutenant, 148th Pennsylvania
Infantry;* CWR:VOL2#2[141]137

HOLLOWELL, NORWELL, *Captain, USA;* AHI:FEB/82[36]225

HOLLY SPRINGS, MISSISSIPPI, RAID ON:

BOOK REVIEW: *MOUNTED RAIDS OF THE CIVIL WAR*

GENERAL LISTINGS: *general history,* AHI:MAY/71[3]133A, *in book
review,* CWM:DEC/94[7], CWR:VOL2#1[78], CWTI:DEC/94[18]

ADDITIONAL LISTINGS: ACW:MAY/93[22]414, CWM:AUG/94[52]530,
CWM:DEC/95[48]631, CWR:VOL2#1[36]132,
CWR:VOL2#4[313]146, CWR:VOL3#3[33]158,
CWTI:MAY/92[48]267, CWTI:NOV/93[33]347,
MH:APR/94[54]176

HOLLY, TURNER W., *Private, 2nd South Carolina Cavalry;*
GETTY:12[68]246

HOLLYWOOD MEMORIAL ASSOCIATION;
ACW:SEP/94[62]490

HOLMAN, JOHN B., *Major, CSA;* B&G:FEB/93[40]514

HOLMAN, JOHN H., *Colonel, 26th Missouri Infantry (Union);*
B&G:JUN/95[5]599, CWM:AUG/94[30]527,
CWTI:JUL/94[50]395

HOLMES, EMMA; BOOK REVIEW: *THE DIARY OF MISS EMMA
HOLMES 1861-1866*

HOLMES, EUGENE, *Captain, CSA;* CWTI:JAN/95[42]428

HOLMES, FREDERICK, *Corporal, USA;* GETTY:10[120]229

HOLMES, GEORGE, *Captain, CSMC;* ACW:MAR/91[14]293

HOLMES, HENRY, *Sergeant, CSA;* ACW:JUL/93[27]423

HOLMES, JAMES T., *Major, 52nd Ohio Infantry;*
B&G:DEC/95[9]615, CWTI:MAY/94[40]383

HOLMES, JOHN B., *Major, CSA;* B&G:DEC/91[38]471

HOLMES, OLIVER W. JR, *Captain, 20th Mass. Infantry:*

GENERAL LISTINGS: *Ball's Bluff,* AHI:FEB/82[36]225, *in book
review,* CWNEWS:NOV/92[4], CWNEWS:MAY/93[4], *Lincoln,*
MH:APR/95[46]183, *photos,* AHI:FEB/82[36]225,
CWR:VOL3#1[31]150

ADDITIONAL LISTINGS: ACW:JAN/92[6]337, ACW:NOV/93[50]444,
ACW:MAR/94[50]462, ACW:SEP/95[38]546,
ACW:NOV/95[54]558, AHI:SEP/89[20]286,
B&G:OCT/93[38]541, CWR:VOL3#1[31]150,
CWR:VOL4#4[101]181, CWTI:SEP/91[42]231,
CWTI:JAN/93[40]301

HOLMES, OLIVER W., SR, CWTI:AUG/90[42]167

HOLMES, PHILIP G., *Private, 1st South Carolina Infantry;*
ACW:NOV/92[10]384

HOLMES, SAMUEL A., *Colonel, 56th Illinois Infantry;*
ACW:SEP/91[46]324, ACW:NOV/91[22]331,
CWR:VOL2#1[19]131, CWR:VOL3#3[59]159

HOLMES, THEOPHILIUS H., *General, CSA:*

ARTICLE: "DEATH TAKES NO HOLIDAY," ACW:MAY/93[22]414

GENERAL LISTINGS: *Glendale,* CWM:JUN/95[69]596, *in book review,*
CWM:JUN/95[6], *letters to the editor,* CWTI:JUL/93[10]323,
Mexican War, MH:APR/93[39]166, *Peninsula Campaign,*
CWM:JUN/95[24]582, *photo;* CWTI:SEP/90[52]179

ADDITIONAL LISTINGS: ACW:MAY/93[38]416, ACW:NOV/93[12]440,
ACW:MAY/94[26]468, ACW:MAR/95[12]513,
AHI:NOV/73[18]151, B&G:JUN/95[8]600,
CWM:SEP/92[38]443, CWM:AUG/94[52]530,
CWR:VOL1#1[1]102, CWR:VOL1#1[42]105,
CWR:VOL1#2[44]114, CWR:VOL2#1[36]132,
CWR:VOL3#2[1]153, CWR:VOL3#3[33]158,
CWTI:SEP/90[52]179, CWTI:JUL/94[44]394,
CWTI:JUL/94[82]396, MH:FEB/91[8]151

HOLMES, WILLIAM R., *Lieutenant Colonel, CSA;*
CWM:JUN/95[63]594

HOLROYD, JOSEPH, *Private, CSA;* MH:JUN/91[20]152

HOLSINGER, FRANK, *Captain, 19th U.S. Colored Infantry;*
AHI:OCT/67[26]112

HOLT, BOLLING H., *Colonel, 35th Georgia Infantry;*
B&G:APR/93[12]518

HOLT, DANIEL M., *Surgeon, 121st New York Infantry;* BOOK
REVIEW: *A SURGEON'S CIVIL WAR: THE LETTERS AND
DIARY OF DANIEL M. HOLT, M.D.*

HOLT, JOSEPH, *Surgeon, 2nd Mississippi Infantry;*
GETTY:6[77]177

HOLT, JOSEPH, *Judge Advocate General, USA;*
ACW:JAN/91[8]282, ACW:JUL/92[22]368,
ACW:MAR/93[18]403, CWTI:JUL/92[50]275,
CWTI:JAN/94[46]364, CWTI:JUN/95[26]445, *photo;*
ACW:JUL/92[22]368

HOLT, SAMUEL, *General, USA;* CWTI:JUN/95[32]446

HOLT, WILLIAM, *Captain, CSA;* ACW:JUL/95[10]533

HOLT, WILLIS, *Major, 10th Georgia Infantry;*
ACW:JAN/94[39]451

HOLTON, EDWARD A., *Sergeant, 6th Vermont Infantry;*
ACW:JAN/94[8]447

HOLTZCLAW, JAMES, *General, CSA;* B&G:DEC/93[12]545

HOMEFRONT; ARTICLE: "THE CITY OF BROTHERLY
HOSPITALITY," CWTI:MAY/94[24]381

HOMER, WINSLOW:

ARTICLES: "THE ARTIST AND THE CIVIL WAR,"
AHI:NOV/80[28]211, "EYEWITNESS NEWS,"
CWM:NOV/92[10]447, "MEMOIRS IN OILS,"
CWM:NOV/92[31]449

BOOK REVIEW: *WINSLOW HOMER: PAINTINGS OF THE CIVIL
WAR*

ADDITIONAL LISTINGS: ACW:MAY/94[58], CWTI:AUG/90[70]171,
CWTI:SEP/91[54]232

HOMESTEAD ACT; CWM:FEB/95[7]

HONES, JOHN T., *Major, 26th North Carolina Infantry;*
GETTY:5[19]158

HONEY HILL, SOUTH CAROLINA, BATTLE OF;
CWR:VOL2#3[194]141

HONEY SPRINGS, CHEROKEE NATION, BATTLE OF;
ACW:JAN/91[30]286, B&G:FEB/92[6]473,
CWM:SEP/92[38]443,

HONEY SPRINGS, OKLAHOMA, BATTLEFIELD PARK;
B&G:OCT/93[38]541

HONEYCUT, FRANK, *Private, 26th North Carolina Infantry;*
GETTY:5[19]158

HOOD, JOHN B., *General, CSA:*

ARTICLES: "AS THE SHELLS EXPLODED OVER ATLANTA IN 1864, THE OPPOSING GENERALS OPENED A WAR OF WORDS," ACW:JAN/95[6]501, "THE ATLANTA CAMPAIGN: CHAPTER 3: FIGHTING JOHN HOOD," CWTI:SUMMER/89[32]122, "THE ATLANTA CAMPAIGN," CWM:JAN/91[12]326, "BATTLE MOST DESPERATE AND BLOODY," ACW:JAN/95[30]505, "THE BATTLE OF NASHVILLE," B&G:DEC/93[12]545, "FIGHTING WITH FORREST IN THE TENNESSEE WINTER," ACW:NOV/95[48]557, "THE GALLANT HOOD OF TEXAS," ACW:MAR/94[42]461, "HOW TO LOSE A CITY," CWM:JAN/91[28]327

BOOK REVIEWS: *ADVANCE AND RETREAT: PERSONAL EXPERIENCES IN THE UNITED AND CONFEDERATE STATES ARMIES * THE DEATH OF AN ARMY: THE BATTLE OF NASHVILLE AND HOOD'S RETREAT * DECISION IN THE WEST: THE ATLANTA CAMPAIGN OF 1864 * EMBRACE AN ANGRY WIND; HOOD'S CAMPAIGN FOR TENNESSEE * HOOD'S TEXAS BRIGADE SKETCHBOOK * HOOD'S TEXAS BRIGADE: LEE'S GRENADIER GUARD * JEFFERSON DAVIS AND HIS GENERALS: THE FAILURE OF CONFEDERATE COMMAND IN THE WEST * JOHN BELL HOOD AND THE WAR FOR SOUTHERN INDEPENDENCE * THE MARCH TO THE SEA*

GENERAL LISTINGS: *Allatoona,* ACW:JAN/95[20]504, *Atlanta Campaign,* ACW:MAY/93[12]412, ACW:SEP/94[10]484, ACW:JAN/95[30]505, ACW:NOV/95[22]554, CWM:JAN/91[4]323, CWM:JAN/92[40]405, CWM:AUG/94[27]526, CWM:AUG/95[36]608, CWTI:SUMMER/89[13]120, CWTI:SUMMER/89[20]121, CWTI:SUMMER/89[32]122, CWTI:SUMMER/89[40]123, CWTI:SUMMER/89[50]124, CWTI:FEB/90[54]147, CWTI:SEP/91[23]228, CWTI:FEB/92[10]246, CWTI:MAY/92[48]267, CWTI:JUL/92[29]272, CWTI:SEP/92[28]280, CWTI:NOV/92[41]291, CWTI:MAR/93[24]309, *Antietam,* ACW:JUL/92[30]369, ACW:MAR/94[50]462, B&G:OCT/95[8]611A, GETTY:6[69]176

GENERAL LISTINGS, continued: *black soldiers,* ACW:NOV/95[8]552, *Brandy Station,* CWTI:JUN/90[32]159, GETTY:11[19]232, *Chancellorsville,* ACW:SEP/93[31]433, *Chickamauga,* CWTI:SEP/93[53]340, *Confederate exiles,* AHI:JUN/70[30]127, *Fredericksburg,* CWR:VOL4#4[70]180, *Gaines' Mill,* CWM:JUN/95[61]593, CWTI:MAY/94[31]382, *general history,* AHI:MAY/71[3]133A, *Gettysburg,* ACW:JAN/92[38]343, ACW:SEP/94[55]489, ACW:JUL/95[10]533, CWM:MAR/91[17]335, CWTI:SEPT/89[46]132, GETTY:4[7]142, GETTY:4[101]151, GETTY:4[110]152, GETTY:5[4]156, GETTY:5[35]159, GETTY:5[47]160, GETTY:5[103]163, GETTY:5[107]164, GETTY:5[117]165, GETTY:6[7]169, GETTY:6[33]172, GETTY:6[43]173, GETTY:6[62]175, GETTY:7[41]189, GETTY:7[51]190, GETTY:7[77]191, GETTY:7[124]196, GETTY:8[31]201, GETTY:8[43]202, GETTY:8[53]203, GETTY:9[5]209, GETTY:9[48]213, GETTY:11[71]234, GETTY:12[111]250, MH:AUG/94[46]178

GENERAL LISTINGS, continued: *in book review,* ACW:NOV/93[58], ACW:MAY/94[58], ACW:JUL/94[58], ACW:JAN/95[62], B&G:FEB/92[26], B&G:APR/95[30], CWM:MAY/91[38], CWM:JUL/93[51], CWM:JUN/94[6], CWM:FEB/95[7], CWM:APR/95[8], CWM:APR/95[50], CWM:AUG/95[8], CWM:AUG/95[45], CWNEWS:OCT/89[4],

CWNEWS:NOV/89[4], CWNEWS:MAY/90[4], CWNEWS:NOV/90[4], CWNEWS:MAY/91[4], CWNEWS:APR/92[4], CWNEWS:MAY/93[4], CWR:VOL1#2[78], CWR:VOL2#2[169], CWR:VOL2#3[256], CWR:VOL4#3[1]170, CWR:VOL4#3[89], CWTI:APR/92[30], CWTI:JUL/92[10], CWTI:AUG/95[18], MH:AUG/92[76], *Indian wars,* AHI:OCT/79[20]194, *Johnston,* CWTI:JAN/95[20]422, *letters to the editor,* B&G:APR/94[6]557, CWM:OCT/95[5]613, *loss of leg,* ACW:SEP/95[38]546, *Manassas, Second,* B&G:AUG/92[11]493, *Missionary Ridge,* CWTI:MAR/93[24]309, *Nashville,* ACW:NOV/95[48]557, CWTI:MAY/93[38]321, *Peninsula Campaign,* CWM:JUN/95[37]585, *post-war,* ACW:JUL/95[26]535, *Sherman,* AHI:JAN/67[4]106, *South Mountain,* CWM:MAY/92[44]423

PHOTOS: ACW:NOV/93[42]443, ACW:MAR/94[42]461, ACW:JAN/95[30]505, ACW:NOV/95[48]557, AHI:MAY/71[3]133A, AHI:NOV/73[18]151, B&G:AUG/92[11]493, B&G:DEC/93[12]545, CWM:JAN/91[28]327, CWTI:SUMMER/89[32]122, CWTI:DEC/91[36]240

ADDITIONAL LISTINGS, ACW: ACW:MAR/91[12]292, ACW:MAR/91[30]295, ACW:JUL/91[18]312, ACW:MAR/92[10]349, ACW:MAR/92[14]350, ACW:JUL/92[30]369, ACW:JAN/93[10]393, ACW:MAR/93[10]402, ACW:MAR/93[68]409, ACW:NOV/93[42]443, ACW:MAR/94[27]459, ACW:JUL/94[35]478, ACW:JUL/94[66]481, ACW:NOV/94[76]500, ACW:NOV/95[74]560

ADDITIONAL LISTINGS, AHI: AHI:NOV/73[18]151, AHI:APR/85[18]250, AHI:OCT/95[24]326

ADDITIONAL LISTINGS, B&G: B&G:JUN/91[10]452, B&G:OCT/91[11]466, B&G:DEC/91[34]470, B&G:APR/92[58]485, B&G:FEB/93[12]511, B&G:FEB/95[8]590A, B&G:FEB/95[30]591, B&G:FEB/95[35]592, B&G:OCT/95[8]611F

ADDITIONAL LISTINGS, CWM: CWM:JAN/91[72]331, CWM:MAR/91[28]336, CWM:JUL/92[16]428, CWM:JUL/92[40]432, CWM:MAR/92[9]410, CWM:DEC/94[26]548, CWM:OCT/95[36]616

ADDITIONAL LISTINGS, CWR: CWR:VOL1#1[1]102, CWR:VOL1#1[71]107, CWR:VOL1#1[73]108, CWR:VOL1#2[7]111, CWR:VOL1#3[82]123, CWR:VOL1#4[64]127, CWR:VOL2#1[36]132, CWR:VOL2#2[95]135, CWR:VOL2#4[269]145, CWR:VOL3#2[1]153, CWR:VOL3#3[59]159, CWR:VOL4#3[65]172, CWR:VOL4#4[70]180

ADDITIONAL LISTINGS, CWTI: CWTI:SUMMER/89[13]120, CWTI:SUMMER/89[32]122, CWTI:AUG/91[62]221, CWTI:AUG/91[68]222, CWTI:DEC/91[36]240, CWTI:MAR/93[40]312, CWTI:NOV/93[55]350, CWTI:JAN/94[35]361, CWTI:JUL/94[28]391, CWTI:JUL/94[44]394, CWTI:DEC/94[49]413, CWTI:MAR/95[40]436

ADDITIONAL LISTINGS, GETTY: GETTY:13[1]252, GETTY:13[75]259

ADDITIONAL LISTINGS, MH: MH:APR/94[54]176, MH:OCT/94[20]180, MH:FEB/95[18]182, MH:DEC/95[58]188

HOOKER, GEORGE W., *Lieutenant, USA;* GETTY:6[87]178

HOOKER, JOSEPH E., *General, USA:*

ARTICLES: "COMPLETELY OUTGENERALLED," CWTI:AUG/95[24]455, "FLANK ATTACK," ACW:SEP/93[31]433, "MIRACLE OF THE RAILS,"

CWTI:SEP/92[22]279, "SHERMAN'S FEUDING GENERALS," CWTI:MAR/95[40]436

BOOK REVIEWS: *CHANCELLORSVILLE 1863: THE SOULS OF THE BRAVE*

GENERAL LISTINGS: *1863 Cavalry Battles,* MH:OCT/92[51]162, *Antietam,* ACW:JUL/92[30]369, ACW:MAR/94[50]462, B&G:OCT/95[8]611A, CWTI:SEP/93[43]338, *Atlanta Campaign,* ACW:NOV/95[74]560, CWTI:SUMMER/89[13]120, CWTI:SUMMER/89[20]121, CWTI:SUMMER/89[32]122, CWTI:SUMMER/89[50]124, CWTI:NOV/92[41]291, *Brandy Station,* GETTY:11[19]232, *Chancellorsville,* ACW:MAR/95[70]520, ACW:MAY/95[30]525, ACW:SEP/95[54]548, B&G:JUN/92[8]487, B&G:APR/95[8]595, CWM:DEC/94[40]550, CWTI:APR/92[35]257, CWTI:JUL/94[44]394, GETTY:8[43]202, GETTY:9[53]214, GETTY:9[61]215, MH:JUN/92[50]159, *Chantilly,* ACW:JAN/95[54]508, *Chattanooga,* ACW:MAY/91[23]303, *Fredericksburg,* ACW:MAY/94[12]466, AHI:JUN/78[4]180, CWR:VOL4#4[101]181, CWTI:SEP/94[26]400, *general history,* AHI:MAY/71[3]133A

GENERAL LISTINGS, continued: *in book review,* ACW:JAN/93[58]399, ACW:NOV/95[62], AHI:MAY/69[49], CWM:MAY/91[38], CWM:AUG/94[9], CWM:DEC/94[7], CWM:AUG/95[45], CWNEWS:NOV/91[4], CWNEWS:SEP/92[4], CWNEWS:OCT/92[4], CWNEWS:DEC/92[4], CWNEWS:JUN/93[5], CWNEWS:AUG/93[5], CWNEWS:FEB/95[33], CWNEWS:JUN/95[33], CWNEWS:AUG/95[33], CWR:VOL1#4[77], *letters to the editor,* CWM:DEC/95[5]625, CWTI:FEB/92[8]245, *Lincoln,* ACW:JAN/94[47]452, *Lookout Mountain,* CWTI:SEPT/89[30]129, CWTI:MAR/95[26]434, *Manassas, Second,* ACW:JUL/91[18]312, ACW:JAN/95[54]508, AHI:DEC/66[30]105, B&G:AUG/92[11]493, *Mexican War,* MH:APR/93[39]166, *Missionary Ridge,* CWTI:SEP/94[40]403, *Oak Grove,* CWM:JUN/95[55]591, *Peninsula Campaign,* CWM:JUN/95[34]584, CWM:JUN/95[76]598, *Ringgold Gap,* ACW:NOV/93[34]442, *Williamsburg,* ACW:MAR/91[47]297, *photos,* ACW:NOV/93[34]442, AHI:MAY/71[3]133A, B&G:OCT/93[12]537, CWTI:SEP/92[22]279, CWTI:SEP/94[40]403, CWTI:MAR/95[40]436, GETTY:12[85]248, MH:JUN/92[50]159

ADDITIONAL LISTINGS, ACW: ACW:MAY/91[8]300, ACW:JUL/91[35]314, ACW:NOV/91[30]332, ACW:JAN/92[10]339, ACW:SEP/92[30]378, ACW:NOV/92[18]385, ACW:MAR/93[26]404, ACW:JUL/93[16]422, ACW:JUL/94[66]481, ACW:SEP/94[55]489, ACW:NOV/94[12]494

ADDITIONAL LISTINGS, B&G: B&G:DEC/91[34]470, B&G:FEB/92[22]476, B&G:OCT/93[12]537, B&G:OCT/95[54]614A, B&G:DEC/95[25]616

ADDITIONAL LISTINGS, CWM: CWM:JAN/91[72]331, CWM:JUL/91[43]371, CWM:NOV/91[12]390, CWM:JUL/92[16]428, CWM:JUL/92[18]429, CWM:JAN/93[8]456, CWM:SEP/93[24]495, CWM:JUN/94[26]512, CWM:OCT/94[26]536, CWM:DEC/94[46]552, CWM:APR/95[16]571, CWM:APR/95[32]575, CWM:DEC/95[35]629

ADDITIONAL LISTINGS, CWR: CWR:VOL1#1[1]102, CWR:VOL1#1[26]103, CWR:VOL1#3[28]120, CWR:VOL1#4[64]127, CWR:VOL2#4[269]145, CWR:VOL3#1[31]150, CWR:VOL3#2[1]153, CWR:VOL3#2[70]155, CWR:VOL3#3[1]157, CWR:VOL3#3[59]159

ADDITIONAL LISTINGS, CWTI: CWTI:MAR/89[16]101, CWTI:DEC/89[34]136, CWTI:JUN/90[32]159, CWTI:SEP/90[34]176, CWTI:FEB/91[24]191, CWTI:SEP/91[31]229, CWTI:DEC/91[28]239, CWTI:FEB/92[42]250, CWTI:MAY/92[45]266, CWTI:JUL/92[29]272, CWTI:MAR/93[24]309, CWTI:MAY/93[26]318, CWTI:JUL/93[14]324, CWTI:DEC/94[49]413, CWTI:JAN/95[42]428, CWTI:JUN/95[32]446, CWTI:DEC/95[67]481

ADDITIONAL LISTINGS, GETTY: GETTY:6[69]176, GETTY:8[111]206, GETTY:9[5]209, GETTY:9[41]212, GETTY:9[81]216, GETTY:10[42]224, GETTY:10[53]225, GETTY:11[6]231, GETTY:11[19]232, GETTY:12[85]248, GETTY:13[33]255, GETTY:13[64]258

ADDITIONAL LISTINGS, MH: MH:APR/92[18]157, MH:AUG/94[46]178

HOOKER'S BRIGADE; BOOK REVIEW: *THE MUTINY AT BRANDY STATION: THE LAST BATTLE OF THE HOOKER BRIGADE*

HOOLE, AXALLA J., *Lieutenant Colonel, 8th South Carolina Infantry;* CWR:VOL1#4[7]125

HOOPER, I. HARRIS, *Major, 15th Massachusetts Infantry;* CWM:APR/95[42]577

HOPE, TOM, *Private, 22nd Virginia Infantry;* CWR:VOL1#3[52]122

HOPKINS, ANDREW, *seaman, USN;* ARTICLE: "PRISONER OF CIRCUMSTANCES," CWTI:NOV/92[28]290

HOPKINS, C., *Sergeant, 87th Indiana Infantry;* B&G:APR/94[34]561

HOPKINS, CHARLES, *Private, 1st New Jersey Infantry:*

HOPKINS, CHARLES F., *Lieutenant Colonel, CSA;* CWR:VOL3#1[65]151, CWR:VOL3#4[1]161

BOOK REVIEW: *THE ANDERSONVILLE DIARY & MEMOIRS OF CHARLES HOPKINS*

ADDITIONAL LISTING: B&G:JUN/95[8]600

HOPKINS, EDWARD R.; B&G:DEC/91[12]469

HOPKINS, GEORGE, *Surgeon, USA;* ACW:MAR/93[8]401

HOPKINS, JAMES A., *Captain, 45th North Carolina Infantry;* CWM:MAY/92[15]419, GETTY:13[33]255

HOPKINS, LUTHER W., *Private, 6th Virginia Cavalry;* CWM:NOV/92[64]453

HOPKINS, MRS. ARTHUR F.; AHI:DEC/73[10]152

HOPKINSON, HENRY E., *Ensign, USN;* B&G:JUN/92[40]489

HOPPER, FREDERICK, *Private, 150th New York Infantry;* GETTY:12[42]244

HORCRAFT, T.C., *Private, 34th New York Infantry;* CWTI:SEP/90[26]174

HOREN, THOMAS, *Sergeant, 72nd New York Infantry;* GETTY:13[50]257

HORGAN, WILLIAM, *Major, 28th Massachusetts Infantry;* ACW:MAY/94[12]466

HORNE, ASHLEY, *Colonel, CSA;* ACW:JAN/92[10]339

HORNE, HOSEA, *Private, 36th North Carolina Infantry;* B&G:DEC/94[10]585

HORNER, FRANKLIN, *Private, 12th Pennsylvania Infantry:*

BOOK REVIEWS: *35 DAYS TO GETTYSBURG: THE CAMPAIGN DIARIES OF TWO AMERICAN ENEMIES*

ADDITIONAL LISTING: CWNEWS:JUL/93[5]

HORNER, ROBERT, *Doctor;* GETTY:10[53]225

HORR, JOSEPH L., *Lieutenant, 13th U.S. Regulars;* CWR:VOL2#1[1]130

HORSES AND MULES:

ARTICLES: "THE HARDY MULE GAVE ITS FLOP-EARED ALL—SOMETIMES LITERALLY—FOR THE UNION AND

ACW:JUL/94[18]476, ACW:MAY/95[30]525,
CWTI:AUG/95[24]455, MH:JUN/92[50]159, *Custer,*
AHI:FEB/71[4]131, *Fredericksburg,* CWR:VOL4#4[47]179,
Gatling Gun, AHI:JUN/66[52]102, *Gettysburg,*
ACW:JAN/95[46]507, ACW:JUL/94[18]476,
ACW:MAY/93[14]413, AHI:MAY/67[22]107, GETTY:4[33]146,
GETTY:4[49]147, GETTY:4[75]149, GETTY:4[101]151,
GETTY:4[113]153, GETTY:5[19]158, GETTY:5[117]165,
GETTY:6[7]169, GETTY:6[69]176, GETTY:6[99]181,
GETTY:7[23]187, GETTY:7[29]188, GETTY:7[83]192,
GETTY:8[43]202, GETTY:9[17]210, GETTY:9[81]216,
GETTY:10[7]221, GETTY:11[19]232, GETTY:11[119]238,
GETTY:12[7]241, GETTY:12[30]243, GETTY:12[68]246,
GETTY:12[85]248
GENERAL LISTINGS, continued: *in book review,* ACW:JAN/93[58]399,
CWM:AUG/94[9], CWM:AUG/95[8], CWNEWS:MAY/89[4],
CWNEWS:NOV/91[4], CWNEWS:OCT/93[5],
CWR:VOL3#3[92], CWR:VOL3#4[68], *Indian wars,*
AHI:JUL/80[36]204, *letters to the editor,* B&G:APR/95[5]594,
loss of arm, ACW:SEP/95[38]546, *Missionary Ridge,*
CWTI:SEP/94[40]403, *Nashville,* B&G:DEC/93[12]545, *order of
battle,* B&G:DEC/95[9]615, *Resaca,* CWTI:NOV/92[41]291,
Savannah, ACW:SEP/92[47]380, B&G:FEB/91[8]439,
CWTI:DEC/94[62]415, *West Point,* B&G:DEC/91[12]469,
photos; ACW:JUL/91[35]314, AHI:NOV/73[18]151,
B&G:DEC/95[9]615, CWTI:MAR/95[40]436, GETTY:11[71]234,
GETTY:12[85]248
ADDITIONAL LISTINGS: ACW:JUL/91[35]314, ACW:NOV/92[42]388,
ACW:JUL/93[50]426, ACW:SEP/93[31]433,
ACW:MAR/94[50]462, AHI:NOV/73[18]151,
B&G:OCT/91[11]466, B&G:DEC/92[20]504,
B&G:FEB/95[8]590A, CWM:JAN/91[12]326,
CWM:JAN/92[40]405, CWM:JUL/92[18]429,
CWM:AUG/95[36]608, CWR:VOL1#3[52]122,
CWR:VOL3#1[31]150, CWR:VOL3#2[70]155,
CWR:VOL3#3[59]159, CWR:VOL4#3[65]172,
CWR:VOL4#4[101]181, CWTI:SUMMER/89[20]121,
CWTI:SEP/91[23]228, CWTI:SEP/92[22]279,
GETTY:13[22]254, GETTY:13[89]260
HOWARD, W.P., *General, CSA;* CWM:JAN/92[40]405
HOWARD, WILLIAM H., *Correspondent;* BOOK REVIEW:
*WILLIAM HOWARD RUSSELL'S CIVIL WAR: PRIVATE
DIARY AND LETTERS 1861-1862*
HOWE, ALBION P., *General, USA;* ACW:MAR/92[30]352,
ACW:SEP/92[30]378, B&G:DEC/92[8]503, GETTY:4[113]153,
GETTY:12[123]251
HOWE, CHURCH, *Private, 6th Massachusetts Infantry;*
ACW:NOV/95[30]555
HOWE, ELIAS, *civilian;* AHI:DEC/71[30]138,
B&G:OCT/92[22]497
HOWE, FREDERICK, *Private, 23rd Ohio Cavalry;*
CWM:SEP/93[18]494
HOWE, GEORGE, *Captain, 57th Massachusetts Infantry;*
CWTI:APR/90[24]152
HOWE, JAMES H., *Colonel, 32nd Wisconsin Infantry;*
CWR:VOL2#4[313]146
HOWE, JULIA WARD:
ARTICLES: "'THE BATTLE HYMN OF THE REPUBLIC' ARMED
THE NORTH WITH MORAL CERTITUDE,"
ACW:MAR/94[10]457, "THE MESSAGE OF JULIA WARD
HOWE," CWTI:SEPT/89[40]130, "MINE EYES HAVE SEEN
THE GLORY," AHI:JAN/93[61]309

ADDITIONAL LISTINGS: AHI:OCT/79[10]192, CWM:SEP/92[6]436,
CWM:NOV/92[41]451, *painting;* CWTI:SEPT/89[40]130
HOWE, ORION P., *Private, 55th Illinois Infantry;*
ACW:NOV/92[8]383
HOWE, SAMUEL G.; ACW:JUL/91[43]315
HOWE, TIMOTHY O., *Senator, Michigan;* CWTI:AUG/95[54]460
HOWE, WILLIAM J., *Sergeant, 12th New Hampshire Infantry;*
GETTY:12[7]241
HOWELL, ALBERT, *Lt. Colonel, CSA;* CWTI:DEC/94[49]413
HOWELL, B.K., *Lieutenant, CSMC;* AHI:OCT/88[38]275
HOWELL, EVAN P., *Lieutenant, Martin's Georgia Light
Artillery;* B&G:AUG/95[8]604
HOWELL, HENRY M., *Private, 124th New York Infantry;*
CWM:DEC/94[40]550, GETTY:9[5]209
HOWELL, HORATIO S., *Chaplain, 90th Pennsylvania
Infantry;* GETTY:10[7]221
HOWELL, WILLIAM R., *Private, CSA;* BOOK REVIEW:
*WESTWARD THE TEXANS: THE CIVIL WAR JOURNAL
OF PRIVATE WILLIAM RANDOLPH HOWELL*
HOWELL, WILLIAM, *Corporal, 124th New York Infantry;*
CWM:DEC/94[40]550
HOWGATE, CHARLES, *Private, 150th New York Infantry;*
GETTY:12[42]244
HOWISON, EDWARD, *Corporal, Fredericksburg Artillery;*
CWR:VOL1#1[1]102
HOYT, GEORGE H.; ACW:JUL/91[43]315
HOYT, JAMES A., *Captain, 1st Palmetto Sharpthooters;*
CWM:MAY/92[34]422
HUBBARD, C.C., *Sergeant, 9th New York Infantry;*
B&G:APR/95[24]596
HUBBARD, GEORGE H., *Surgeon, USA;* CWM:MAY/91[10]347
HUBBARD, JAMES M., *Major, USA;* CWR:VOL3#3[33]158
HUBBARD, LUCIUS F., *Colonel, USA;* ACW:NOV/94[76]500,
B&G:DEC/93[12]545
HUBBELL, W.S., *Captain, 21st Connecticut Infantry;*
ACW:SEP/93[62]436
HUBER, LEVI, *Capt., 96th Penn. Inf.;* CWR:VOL3#3[1]157
HUBNER, CHARLES W., *Major, CSA;*
CWTI:SUMMER/89[20]121
HUCKABY, LEANDER, *Private, 11th Mississippi Infantry;*
CWR:VOL2#4[269]145
HUDGINS, FRANCIS, *Sergeant, 38th Georgia Infantry;*
B&G:APR/95[8]595, B&G:JUN/95[8]600
HUDSON, D.L., *Captain, 37th North Carolina Infantry;*
B&G:FEB/95[8]590A
HUDSON, HENRY, *Private, 202nd Pennsylvania Infantry;* BOOK
REVIEW: *CIVIL WAR SKETCHBOOK & DIARY*
HUDSON, JAMES, *Private, 4th Alabama Infantry;*
ACW:NOV/94[18]495
HUDSON, JOHN W., *Lieutenant, 35th Massachusetts Infantry;*
ARTICLE: "'TIRED SOLDIERS DON'T GO VERY FAST',"
CWTI:FEB/92[36]249
HUDSON, WARREN, *Sergeant, 4th Alabama Infantry;*
ACW:NOV/94[18]495
HUEY, PENNOCK, *General, USA;* GETTY:4[75]149
HUFF, ALEXANDER H., *Surgeon,* ACW:MAR/93[8]401
HUFF, JOHN A., *Private, 5th Michigan Cavalry;*
ACW:MAY/94[35]469, MH:FEB/93[42]164
HUFF, JOHN, *Private, USA;* B&G:APR/94[10]558,
B&G:JUN/94[5]567, CWM:SEP/93[18]494
HUFF, JOHN T., *Doctor;* ACW:JAN/92[47]344,
B&G:AUG/93[10]529
HUFFMAN, ISAAC, *civilian;* B&G:OCT/94[11]580

CWNEWS:OCT/94[33], CWNEWS:OCT/95[33],
CWR:VOL2#3[256], CWR:VOL4#3[89], *Shenandoah Valley,*
1864, ACW:JUL/94[26]477, ACW:SEP/94[55]489,
CWM:JAN/92[21]402, *Thaddeus Stevens,* AHI:JAN/82[16]224,
photos, B&G:AUG/94[10]574, CWTI:DEC/91[28]239,
CWTI:OCT/95[48]470

ADDITIONAL LISTINGS: ACW:MAY/91[38]305, ACW:SEP/91[30]322,
ACW:MAR/92[46]354, ACW:MAY/92[14]358,
ACW:JUL/93[10]421, ACW:SEP/93[31]433,
ACW:NOV/93[50]444, B&G:OCT/91[11]466,
B&G:DEC/92[8]503, B&G:AUG/94[10]574,
B&G:AUG/94[19]575, CWM:JUL/91[48]374,
CWM:MAR/92[16]411, CWM:APR/94[24]505,
CWR:VOL1#1[76]109, CWTI:SEP/91[8]224,
CWTI:JAN/93[40]301, CWTI:JAN/94[46]364,
CWTI:MAR/94[38]372, CWTI:MAY/94[46]385,
CWTI:DEC/95[67]481, MH:FEB/93[42]164

HUNTER, J.B., *Captain, CSA;* B&G:OCT/94[11]580
HUNTER, JAMES, *Private, 125th Pennsylvania Infantry;*
B&G:OCT/95[8]611A
HUNTER, MORTON C., *Colonel, USA;* B&G:DEC/95[9]615
HUNTER, ROBERT M.T.; AHI:NOV/70[22]130,
CWTI:FEB/91[36]193
HUNTER, ROBERT W., *Major, CSA;* B&G:APR/92[48]484
HUNTER, SHEROD, *Captain, 2nd Texas Mounted Rifles;*
ACW:JUL/93[27]423, B&G:JUN/94[8]568
HUNTER, THOMAS T., *Commander, CSN;*
CWM:AUG/95[5]602
HUNTER, W.W., *Commodore, CSN;* B&G:FEB/91[8]439
HUNTER, WILLIAM, *Mosby's raider;* CWTI:DEC/91[22]237
HUNTERSON, HARRY, *Private, 88th Pennsylvania Infantry;*
GETTY:10[7]221
HUNTERSON, JOHN C., *Private, 3rd Pennsylvania Cavalry;*
GETTY:13[89]260
HUNTINGTON, JAMES F., *Captain, USA;* GETTY:12[30]243
HUNTINGTON, ROBERT W., *Lieutenant, USMC;*
CWTI:APR/92[14]254
HUNTLEY, JUDSON J., *Lieutenant, 37th Illinois Infantry;*
CWR:VOL1#1[42]105
HUNTON, EPPA, *Colonel, 8th Virginia Infantry:*

GENERAL LISTINGS: *Ball's Bluff,* AHI:FEB/82[36]225, *Five Forks,*
B&G:APR/92[8]481, *Gettysburg,* GETTY:5[107]164, *in order of*
battle, B&G:APR/92[8]481, B&G:APR/94[10]558, *Manassas,*
Second, B&G:AUG/92[11]493, *Overland Campaign,*
B&G:APR/94[10]558

ADDITIONAL LISTINGS: ACW:MAY/93[62]418,
CWTI:MAY/89[14]114, CWTI:APR/92[49]260,
CWTI:NOV/93[55]350, CWTI:JUL/94[20]390,
CWTI:JUL/94[44]394

HUNTON, K.A., *Lieutenant Colonel, Michigan Engineers &*
Mechanics; B&G:FEB/93[12]511
HURLBUT, FREDERICK J., *Colonel, USA;* B&G:DEC/95[9]615
HURLBUT, STEPHEN A., *General, USA:*

GENERAL LISTINGS: *Grierson's Raid,* B&G:JUN/93[12]524, *Jackson,*
Battle of, B&G:AUG/95[8]604, *Shiloh,* ACW:JAN/91[22]285,
Tullahoma Campaign, B&G:OCT/92[10]496, *photos,*
B&G:JUN/93[12]524, CWTI:NOV/93[65]351

ADDITIONAL LISTINGS: ACW:JAN/91[16]284, ACW:SEP/95[48]547,
CWR:VOL2#4[313]146, CWR:VOL4#1[44]164,
CWTI:NOV/93[65]351, CWTI:DEC/94[82]418,
MH:DEC/95[58]188

HURLEY, THOMAS, *Private, 8th Tennessee Cavalry;*
ACW:SEP/95[38]546

HURST, LEVI, *Lieutenant, 13th Indiana Cavalry;*
CWTI:MAR/91[46]203
HURT, W.B., *Captain, Hardaway (Alabama) Artillery;*
CWM:MAY/92[34]422, GETTY:5[117]165
HUSE, CALEB, *Major, USA;* ACW:MAY/92[23]360,
CWTI:JAN/93[49]303, *photo;* ACW:MAY/92[23]360
HUSSEY, CYRUS, *Lieutenant Colonel, 192nd Ohio Infantry;*
B&G:FEB/92[32]477
HUSSEY, GEORGE, *Private, 83rd New York Infantry;*
GETTY:10[7]221
HUSSEY, WILLIAM H.H., *Lieutenant, 2nd Massachusetts*
Cavalry; ARTICLE: "TIME LAPSE," CWTI:APR/90[56]155
HUSTED, NATHANIAL, *Captain, USA;* ACW:JAN/92[38]343
HUSTON, DAN, *Colonel, USA;* CWR:VOL1#1[42]105
HUSTON, JAMES, *Lieutenant Colonel, 82nd New York*
Infantry; GETTY:13[1]252, GETTY:13[43]256
HUTCHERSON, WILLIAM A., *Private, 22nd Virginia Infantry;*
CWR:VOL1#3[52]122
HUTCHINS, A.J., *Private, 25th Ohio Infantry;*
CWM:MAY/91[26]349
HUTCHINS, BENJAMIN T., *Lieutenant, 6th U.S. Cavalry;*
B&G:OCT/93[12]537
HUTCHINSON, CURG, *Mosby's Rangers;* CWM:JAN/93[24]458
HUTCHINSON, R.R., *Major, CSA;* CWM:JAN/93[40]461,
MH:OCT/93[76]173
HUTCHINSON, SAMUEL P., *Adjutant, 71st Pennsylvania*
Infantry; GETTY:7[83]192
HUTCHINSON, WILLIAM, *Lieutenant, CSA;*
AHI:JAN/76[14]164
HUTCHISON, BENJAMIN H., *Lieutenant, 8th Virginia*
Infantry; GETTY:12[111]250
HUTCHISON, WILLIAM F., *Lieutenant, 2nd Tennessee*
Cavalry; CWR:VOL4#1[1]163
HUTTON, CHARLES, *Lieutenant, 24th Michigan Infantry;*
GETTY:5[19]158
HUWALD, G.A., *Lieutenant, CSA;* CWR:VOL4#1[1]163
HUXHAM, SAMUEL, *Corporal, 14th Connecticut Infantry;*
GETTY:6[7]169, GETTY:9[61]215
HUYETTE, ULYSSES L., *Captain, USA;* ACW:MAR/94[50]462
HYAMS, ISSAC, *Lieutenant, CSA;* CWM:SEP/93[8]493
HYATT, ARTHUR W., *Captain, 18th Louisiana Infantry;*
CWM:OCT/94[33]537, CWR:VOL3#1[1]149,
CWR:VOL4#2[1]165
HYDE, BREED N., *Col., 3rd Vermont Inf.;* ACW:JAN/94[8]447
HYDE, JAMES S., *Cpl., 137th NY Inf.;* CWR:VOL3#2[70]155
HYDE, JOHN MCE., *Major, 39th New York Infantry;*
CWTI:AUG/90[26]166
HYDE, JOSEPH E., *Private, 30th Maine Infantry;*
ACW:SEP/91[16]320
HYDE, THOMAS W., *Colonel, 7th Maine Infantry;*
B&G:APR/91[8]445, B&G:JUN/95[8]600, B&G:DEC/95[25]616,
CWM:OCT/94[37]539, CWTI:JUN/95[32]446, *Photo;*
B&G:APR/91[8]445
HYLESTED, WALDEMAR, *Major, 1st Louisiana Zouave*
Battalion; CWTI:MAR/89[28]103
HYMAN, HENRY F., *Capt., 1st Ohio Art.;* GETTY:4[49]147
HYMAN, JOSEPH H., *Colonel, CSA;* B&G:APR/92[8]481,
CWTI:AUG/90[26]166

I

IDAHO TERRITORY OF; ARTICLE: "IDAHO SHOOT-OUT,"
B&G:APR/91[24]446
IDE, JOHN, *Private, 1st USSS;* CWTI:JUL/93[42]329
IDE, WILLIAM, *civilian;* B&G:OCT/94[11]580
IF THE SOUTH HAD WON; ARTICLE: "WHAT MIGHT HAVE
BEEN," CWTI:SEP/94[56]405
IGLEHART, JAMES, *Private, 1st Maryland Battalion;*
GETTY:7[83]192

ILLINOIS TROOPS:

1st Artillery; B&G:OCT/91[11]466, B&G:JUN/95[36]603A
1st Artillery, Battery A; B&G:FEB/92[10]474,
B&G:AUG/95[8]604, CWR:VOL2#1[1]130
1st Artillery, Battery B; B&G:AUG/95[8]604,
CWR:VOL2#1[1]130
1st Artillery, Battery C; B&G:DEC/95[9]615
1st Artillery, Battery E; B&G:AUG/95[8]604
1st Artillery, Battery F; B&G:AUG/95[8]604
1st Artillery, Battery H:
ARTICLE: "CAPTAIN DEGRESS AND THE BEST GUNS IN THE
WORLD," B&G:AUG/95[55]609, "REPORT OF THE BATTLE
OF ATLANTA," B&G:APR/94[28]559
ADDITIONAL LISTINGS: B&G:DEC/94[36]588, B&G:AUG/95[8]604,
CWR:VOL2#1[1]130
1st Artillery, Battery I; B&G:AUG/95[8]604
1st Artillery, Battery K; ACW:JUL/94[8]474,
B&G:JUN/93[12]524
1st Artillery, Battery M; CWTI:SEP/92[31]281
2nd Artillery; ACW:JAN/91[16]284, CWR:VOL1#4[7]125
2nd Artillery, Battery A; B&G:FEB/94[8]550,
B&G:FEB/94[8]550, B&G:AUG/95[8]604,
CWR:VOL1#1[42]105, CWR:VOL2#1[19]131
2nd Artillery, Battery E; B&G:AUG/95[8]604
2nd Artillery, Battery F; ACW:JAN/93[10]393
2nd Artillery, Battery G; B&G:FEB/94[8]550
2nd Artillery, Battery K; B&G:AUG/95[8]604,
MH:FEB/95[18]182
2nd Cavalry; B&G:FEB/94[8]550, B&G:AUG/95[8]604,
CWR:VOL4#1[44]164, CWR:VOL4#2[1]165
3rd Cavalry; B&G:AUG/95[8]604
3rd Infantry; CWTI:MAR/95[46]437
4th Cavalry; CWR:VOL4#1[44]164
4th Infantry; ACW:MAR/93[8]401, CWTI:MAY/93[35]320
5th Cavalry; ACW:SEP/95[48]547, B&G:AUG/95[8]604
5th Infantry; CWR:VOL2#4[343]147
6th Cavalry; ACW:MAY/92[47]363, ACW:JUL/94[8]474,
B&G:JUN/93[12]524, MH:FEB/95[18]182
6th Infantry; ACW:MAY/92[47]363
7th Cavalry; ACW:MAY/92[47]363, B&G:JUN/93[12]524,
MH:FEB/95[18]182
7th Infantry; CWTI:MAR/95[46]437
8th Cavalry:
ARTICLE: "THE CAVALRY CLASH AT QUEBEC
SCHOOLHOUSE," B&G:FEB/93[24]512
GENERAL LISTINGS: *Aldie,* GETTY:11[19]232, *Brandy Station,*
GETTY:11[19]232, *Gettysburg,* GETTY:4[113]153,
GETTY:5[4]156, GETTY:5[123]166, GETTY:6[13]170,
GETTY:11[19]232, *in book review,* CWNEWS:NOV/95[29],
Monocacy, B&G:DEC/92[8]503

ADDITIONAL LISTINGS: ACW:NOV/93[50]444, ACW:SEP/94[6]482,
B&G:OCT/93[12]537, B&G:FEB/95[8]590A,
CWTI:JUN/90[32]159, CWTI:JAN/93[40]301
8th Infantry; B&G:FEB/94[8]550, CWR:VOL3#3[33]158
9th Cavalry; CWTI:JAN/93[20]298
9th Infantry; B&G:FEB/92[10]474, B&G:OCT/93[31]539,
CWR:VOL3#4[24]162
9th Mounted Infantry; CWR:VOL4#1[1]163,
CWTI:SEP/91[23]228
10th Cavalry; ACW:JUL/94[8]474, CWR:VOL3#3[33]158
10th Infantry; B&G:JUN/93[12]524, CWR:VOL2#4[313]146,
CWR:VOL4#3[1]170
11th Cavalry; ACW:SEP/95[48]547, CWR:VOL4#1[44]164
11th Infantry; BOOK REVIEW: *HARD DYING MEN: THE STORY
OF GENERAL W.H.L. WALLACE, GENERAL T.E.G.
RANSOM, AND THEIR "OLD ELEVENTH" ILLINOIS
INFANTRY IN THE AMERICAN CIVIL WAR*
12th Cavalry:
GENERAL LISTINGS: *Gettysburg,* GETTY:4[115]152,
GETTY:6[13]170, GETTY:11[19]232, *Harpers Ferry,*
MH:AUG/95[30]185, *The "Blackberry" Raid,* GETTY:11[6]231
ADDITIONAL LISTINGS: B&G:OCT/93[12]537, B&G:FEB/95[8]590A,
CWM:MAY/92[8]418, CWM:APR/95[32]575,
CWR:VOL1#4[7]125, GETTY:13[22]254
12th Infantry; B&G:FEB/92[10]474
13th Infantry; CWR:VOL2#1[75]134, CWTI:SEP/94[40]403
14th Cavalry; B&G:DEC/94[22]586
15th Cavalry; B&G:FEB/91[8]439, B&G:DEC/92[20]504,
B&G:AUG/95[8]604
15th Infantry; CWM:JAN/91[11]325, CWTI:JAN/93[20]298
16th Infantry; B&G:DEC/95[9]615
17th Cavalry; ACW:JAN/93[26]395, B&G:DEC/93[30]546
17th Infantry; ACW:NOV/94[34]496, CWM:MAR/91[50]340,
GETTY:10[120]229
18th Infantry; CWM:MAR/91[50]340, CWR:VOL2#1[19]131,
CWR:VOL3#4[24]162
19th Infantry; CWM:SEP/93[18]494, MH:DEC/93[12]174
20th Infantry; B&G:APR/93[34]521, B&G:FEB/94[8]550,
CWTI:JAN/93[20]298
21st Infantry; ACW:NOV/94[34]496, CWTI:FEB/90[26]143,
MH:DEC/93[12]174
22nd Infantry; B&G:FEB/94[38]553, CWR:VOL3#4[24]162
23rd Infantry; ACW:MAR/92[46]354, B&G:JUN/95[36]603A,
CWM:MAR/91[50]340, CWM:AUG/95[35]607,
CWR:VOL1#4[7]125
24th Infantry; ACW:NOV/94[34]496
25th Infantry; ACW:NOV/94[34]496
26th Infantry; ACW:JAN/93[8]392, CWR:VOL1#1[73]108
27th Infantry:
ARTICLE: "THE BATTLE OF BELMONT AND THE CITIZEN
SOLDIERS OF THE 27TH ILLINOIS VOLUNTEER
INFANTRY," CWR:VOL3#4[24]162
ADDITIONAL LISTINGS: CWTI:DEC/94[82]418, GETTY:11[19]232
28th Infantry; B&G:AUG/95[8]604, CWR:VOL4#1[44]164
29th Infantry; B&G:FEB/91[34]442, CWR:VOL3#4[24]162
30th Infantry; B&G:APR/93[34]521, B&G:FEB/94[8]550,
CWR:VOL3#4[24]162
31st Infantry:
BOOK REVIEW: *HISTORY 31ST REGIMENT ILLINOIS
VOLUNTEERS ORGANIZED BY JOHN A. LOGAN*
ADDITIONAL LISTINGS: ACW:JAN/93[8]392, B&G:FEB/91[8]439,
B&G:FEB/94[8]550, CWR:VOL3#4[24]162
33rd Infantry; B&G:FEB/94[8]550

34th Infantry; B&G:DEC/95[9]615, CWTI:NOV/92[41]291
36th Infantry; ACW:MAR/94[8]456, CWNEWS:DEC/93[5],
  CWR:VOL1#1[42]105
37th Infantry;
ARTICLE: "THE FREMONT RIFLES: THE 37TH ILLINOIS AT
  PEA RIDGE AND PRAIRIE GROVE," CWR:VOL1#1[42]105
BOOK REVIEW: *THE FREMONT RIFLES: A HISTORY OF THE
  37TH ILLINOIS VENTERAN VOLUNTEER INFANTRY*
ADDITIONAL LISTINGS: ACW:MAY/94[26]468, CWR:VOL1#1[1]102
38th Infantry; CWTI:DEC/94[12]408
39th Infantry; ACW:JUL/94[42]479
40th Infantry; CWM:FEB/95[36]563
41st Infantry; B&G:FEB/92[10]474, B&G:AUG/95[8]604,
  CWR:VOL4#1[44]164, CWTI:APR/89[32]110
42nd Infantry; CWR:VOL3#4[24]162
45th Infantry; ACW:NOV/94[76]500, B&G:FEB/94[8]550
46th Infantry; CWTI:AUG/90[64]170
48th Infantry; B&G:FEB/91[8]439, CWTI:DEC/94[62]415
50th Infantry; CWM:SEP/93[8]493
52nd Infantry; ACW:SEP/91[46]324, B&G:APR/95[24]596,
  CWTI:SUMMER/89[40]123
53rd Infantry; B&G:AUG/95[8]604
55th Infantry; ACW:NOV/92[8]383, ACW:MAR/93[8]401,
  B&G:APR/93[40]522, B&G:OCT/95[5]610,
  CWM:APR/95[66]579, CWR:VOL2#1[1]130,
  CWR:VOL3#4[24]162
56th Infantry; ACW:SEP/91[46]324
57th Infantry; CWR:VOL4#1[1]163
58th Infantry;
ARTICLE: "IN THE PULPIT AND IN THE TRENCHES,"
  CWTI:SEP/92[28]280
ADDITIONAL LISTINGS: CWM:MAR/91[50]340,
  CWTI:SUMMER/89[13]120
59th Infantry; CWR:VOL1#1[42]105, CWTI:SEPT/89[30]129
62nd Infantry; MH:OCT/93[20]172
65th Infantry; ACW:MAR/94[42]461, ACW:MAY/95[54]528,
  B&G:FEB/92[40]479, CWR:VOL1#4[7]125
66th Infantry; CWTI:SUMMER/89[50]124,
  CWTI:APR/90[48]154, CWTI:NOV/92[41]291
72nd Infantry;
BOOK REVIEW: *WAR DIARY OF BREVET BRIGADIER GENERAL
  JOSEPH STOCKTON, FIRST LIEUTENANT, CAPTAIN,
  MAJOR AND LIEUTENANT COLONEL 72ND REGIMENT
  ILLINOIS INFANTRY VOLUNTEEERS (FIRST BOARD OF
  TRADE REGIMENT)*
ADDITIONAL LISTINGS: CWR:VOL2#4[313]146, CWR:VOL4#3[1]170,
  GETTY:10[120]229
73rd Infantry;
BOOK REVIEW: *A HISTORY OF THE 73RD ILLINOIS*
ADDITIONAL LISTINGS: B&G:DEC/92[40]508,
  CWTI:SUMMER/89[32]122
75th Infantry; CWTI:SEPT/89[30]129
77th Infantry; B&G:FEB/94[8]550, B&G:APR/94[34]561,
  CWR:VOL2#1[19]131, CWR:VOL4#2[1]165
78th Infantry; CWTI:SUMMER/89[50]124,
  CWTI:SEP/92[31]281
81st Infantry; B&G:FEB/94[8]550, CWTI:JAN/93[20]298
82nd Infantry; ACW:NOV/92[42]388, CWM:SEP/93[8]493,
  CWTI:MAY/92[38]265, GETTY:4[49]147, GETTY:7[83]192
84th Infantry; B&G:DEC/92[32]506, CWTI:SEPT/89[30]129
85th Infantry; CWR:VOL3#4[24]162
86th Infantry; CWTI:MAY/94[40]383

90th Infantry; CWM:MAR/91[50]340, CWR:VOL1#1[73]108,
  CWTI:DEC/94[62]415
91st Infantry; ACW:JUL/92[46]371
92nd Infantry; B&G:DEC/92[40]508, B&G:APR/93[6]517
93rd Infantry;
ARTICLE: "COLONEL HOLDEN PUTNAM AND THE 93D
  ILLINOIS VOLUNTEER INFANTRY," CWR:VOL3#3[59]159
ADDITIONAL LISTINGS: CWR:VOL2#4[313]146
94th Infantry; CWR:VOL1#1[42]105
ARTICLE: "95TH ILLINOIS," ACW:JAN/91[16]284, "YOUR
  CHARLIE," CWTI:JAN/93[20]298
ADDITIONAL LISTINGS: CWM:JAN/91[11]325, CWTI:JAN/93[20]298
95th Infantry; CWTI:SEPT/89[30]129, CWTI:SEP/92[31]281
97th Infantry;
BOOK REVIEW: *A FRENCHMAN FIGHTS FOR THE UNION:
  VICTOR VIFQUAIN AND THE 97TH ILLINOIS*
ADDITIONAL LISTINGS: B&G:FEB/94[8]550, CWR:VOL2#1[19]131
98th Infantry; ACW:MAY/95[49]527, B&G:OCT/92[10]496,
  GETTY:10[120]229
99th Infantry; B&G:FEB/94[8]550, CWR:VOL3#4[24]162
104th Infantry; CWTI:SUMMER/89[32]122
105th Infantry; CWTI:NOV/92[41]291
107th Infantry; B&G:APR/94[34]561
108th Infantry; B&G:AUG/92[40]495, B&G:FEB/94[8]550
111th Infantry; B&G:FEB/91[8]439, CWTI:DEC/94[62]415
112th Infantry; B&G:AUG/93[18]530, CWR:VOL4#1[1]163,
  CWTI:MAY/94[50]386
113th Infantry; CWR:VOL2#1[1]130
114th Infantry; CWR:VOL2#4[313]146
116th Infantry; B&G:FEB/91[8]439, CWR:VOL2#1[1]130,
  CWTI:DEC/94[62]415, CWTI:JUN/95[14]443
118th Infantry; B&G:FEB/94[8]550, B&G:AUG/95[8]604
119th Infantry; CWM:DEC/95[48]631, CWR:VOL2#3[212]142
120th Infantry; CWR:VOL2#4[313]146
123rd Infantry; ACW:MAY/95[49]527, B&G:OCT/92[10]496,
  B&G:OCT/92[32]499, GETTY:10[120]229
124th Infantry; B&G:FEB/94[8]550
125th Infantry; CWTI:JAN/93[20]298
127th Infantry; CWR:VOL2#1[1]130
129th Infantry; CWTI:SUMMER/89[32]122
130th Infantry; B&G:FEB/94[8]550, CWR:VOL2#1[19]131,
  CWR:VOL4#2[1]165
146th Infantry; CWTI:AUG/90[50]168
149th Infantry; B&G:FEB/94[38]553
150th Infantry; CWTI:SEP/92[31]281
155th Infantry; B&G:FEB/94[38]553
Charmichael's Cavalry Battalion; CWR:VOL4#1[44]164
Chicago Board of Trade Battery; ACW:MAY/95[49]527
Chicago Fire Zouaves; AHI:DEC/71[30]138
Chicago Light Battery; CWR:VOL3#4[24]162
Chicago Mercantile Battery; B&G:AUG/95[8]604,
  CWM:APR/95[39]576, CWR:VOL2#1[36]132,
  CWR:VOL4#2[1]165, CWTI:MAY/91[18]207
Cogswell's Battery; B&G:AUG/95[8]604
Kane County Cavalry; B&G:AUG/95[8]604
Thielemann's (Illinois) Cavalry; B&G:AUG/95[8]604

ILLINOIS, STATE OF; BOOK REVIEWS: *ILLINOIS IN THE
  CIVIL WAR * RALLY ROUND THE FLAG: CHICAGO AND
  THE CIVIL WAR*
IMBODEN, JOHN D., *General, CSA:*
GENERAL LISTINGS: *Falling Waters*, GETTY:9[109]218, *Gettysburg*,
  B&G:APR/91[39]449, GETTY:5[4]156, GETTY:5[103]163,

2nd Infantry; B&G:AUG/94[22]576

3rd Artillery; CWR:VOL2#3[212]142

3rd Cavalry:

GENERAL LISTINGS: *Aldie,* GETTY:11[19]232, *Gettysburg,*
GETTY:4[115]152, GETTY:6[13]170, GETTY:11[19]232,
GETTY:11[119]238, *SIO,* B&G:AUG/93[36]533

ADDITIONAL LISTINGS: B&G:FEB/93[24]512, B&G:OCT/93[12]537,
B&G:FEB/95[8]590A, CWTI:JUN/90[32]159,
CWTI:APR/92[49]260, GETTY:13[22]254

3rd Infantry; B&G:OCT/95[8]611A, CWTI:APR/92[49]260

4th Cavalry; B&G:AUG/94[22]576, B&G:AUG/95[8]604

5th Artillery; CWTI:NOV/92[41]291

5th Cavalry; B&G:OCT/92[38]500

6th Infantry; ACW:JAN/92[47]344, B&G:AUG/93[10]529

7th Infantry:

BOOK REVIEW: *THE CIVIL WAR JOURNAL OF BILLY DAVIS:
FROM HOPEWELL, INDIANA TO PORT REPUBLIC*

ADDITIONAL LISTINGS: ACW:JAN/92[47]344, ACW:JUL/92[30]369,
B&G:AUG/93[10]529, B&G:OCT/95[8]611A,
B&G:DEC/95[5]614A, CWNEWS:NOV/90[4],
CWTI:NOV/93[24]346, *photo,* CWTI:NOV/93[24]346

8th Cavalry; CWM:JAN/91[40]330

9th Infantry; B&G:AUG/93[10]529, B&G:FEB/94[8]550

9th Cavalry:

ARTICLE: "TWO CORPORALS: A TALE OF NATHAN BEDFORD
FORREST'S ATTACK AT SULPHUR BRANCH TRESTLE,
ALABAMA," B&G:JUN/92[32]488

ADDITIONAL LISTINGS: ACW:MAY/91[38]305, B&G:AUG/95[24]605

9th Infantry; ACW:JAN/92[47]344, B&G:AUG/93[10]529,
CWTI:SEPT/89[30]129

9th Cavalry; ACW:NOV/95[48]557

10th Infantry; ACW:SEP/93[38]434, B&G:FEB/93[12]511,
B&G:AUG/93[10]529, B&G:JUN/95[36]603A,
CWNEWS:JUL/92[4]

11th Artillery; AHI:JAN/67[4]106

11th Cavalry; CWTI:MAR/91[46]203

11th Infantry; ACW:MAY/91[38]305, ACW:NOV/93[50]444,
ACW:JUL/94[51]480, B&G:DEC/92[8]503, B&G:FEB/94[8]550,
CWNEWS:AUG/92[4], CWTI:MAR/91[28]200,
CWTI:JAN/93[40]301

12th Cavalry; GETTY:11[19]232

12th Infantry; B&G:AUG/93[10]529, CWR:VOL1#1[73]108

13th Cavalry; CWTI:MAR/91[46]203

13th Infantry; CWTI:SEP/90[52]179

14th Infantry:

GENERAL LISTINGS: *Gettysburg,* GETTY:4[115]152,
GETTY:9[33]211, GETTY:12[30]243, *list of monuments,*
B&G:OCT/95[8]611A

ADDITIONAL LISTINGS: ACW:JAN/92[50]345, ACW:NOV/92[42]388,
ACW:SEP/94[31]486, B&G:AUG/93[10]529,
B&G:APR/95[8]595, B&G:JUN/95[8]600,
CWM:MAR/91[17]335, CWTI:NOV/92[49]292

15th Artillery; CWR:VOL1#4[7]125

15th Infantry; B&G:AUG/93[10]529

16th Infantry; B&G:FEB/94[8]550

16th Mounted Infantry; CWR:VOL4#2[1]165

17th Infantry:

GENERAL LISTINGS: *Lightning Brigade,* B&G:OCT/92[32]499,
Tullahoma Campaign, B&G:OCT/92[10]496

ADDITIONAL LISTINGS: ACW:MAY/95[49]527, B&G:OCT/92[32]499,
CWM:JUL/92[24]430

18th Artillery; ACW:SEP/95[10]543, B&G:AUG/94[22]576,
B&G:OCT/92[32]499

18th Infantry: B&G:FEB/94[8]550, CWR:VOL1#1[42]105

19th Artillery; B&G:DEC/95[9]615

19th Infantry:

GENERAL LISTINGS: *Gettysburg,* GETTY:5[4]156, GETTY:5[19]158,
GETTY:6[13]170, GETTY:7[7]185, GETTY:11[57]233, *list of
monuments,* B&G:OCT/95[8]611A, *Manassas, Second,*
B&G:AUG/92[11]493, *SIO,* B&G:JUN/95[36]603A, *photo;*
B&G:OCT/94[42]583

ADDITIONAL LISTINGS: ACW:JUL/92[30]369, AHI:JAN/94[50]319,
B&G:AUG/93[10]529, B&G:FEB/95[8]590A,
B&G:APR/95[8]595, B&G:APR/95[24]596,
CWM:MAR/91[17]335, CWM:JAN/93[16]457,
CWTI:NOV/93[78]354, GETTY:13[22]254, GETTY:13[119]262

20th Infantry:

GENERAL LISTINGS; *Gettysburg,* GETTY:8[43]202,
GETTY:8[53]203, GETTY:9[5]209

ADDITIONAL LISTINGS: ACW:MAY/95[30]525, AHI:OCT/75[30]162,
B&G:APR/93[12]518, CWM:JUN/95[55]591,
CWTI:NOV/92[49]292

21st Infantry; CWR:VOL3#1[1]149

22nd Infantry; ACW:SEP/95[62], AHI:NOV/72[12]142

23rd Infantry; B&G:FEB/94[8]550

24th Infantry; B&G:FEB/94[8]550, B&G:FEB/94[57]555

25th Infantry; B&G:FEB/92[10]474, B&G:APR/92[36]483,
B&G:APR/93[40]522, CWR:VOL2#4[313]146,
CWTI:AUG/95[58]461

26th Infantry; ACW:MAY/94[26]468, CWM:OCT/94[33]537,
CWR:VOL1#1[42]105

27th Infantry:

GENERAL LISTINGS: *Gettysburg,* GETTY:4[113]153,
GETTY:6[7]169, GETTY:6[69]176, GETTY:7[83]192,
GETTY:12[42]244, *Harpers Ferry,* MH:AUG/95[30]185

ADDITIONAL LISTINGS: ACW:JAN/91[38]287, ACW:MAY/91[8]300,
ACW:JUL/92[30]369, ACW:JUL/93[58], ACW:JAN/94[6]446,
ACW:JAN/94[39]451, B&G:FEB/95[8]590C,
CWR:VOL1#4[7]125, CWR:VOL3#2[70]155,
CWTI:SEP/92[22]279, CWTI:NOV/92[49]292,
MH:JUN/94[8]177

28th Infantry; B&G:OCT/95[8]611A

32nd Infantry; B&G:JUN/95[5]599, CWM:JUL/92[40]432,
CWM:SEP/93[8]493

33rd Infantry; CWM:JAN/91[28]327,
CWTI:SUMMER/89[32]122

34th Infantry; ACW:JUL/92[46]371, B&G:FEB/94[8]550,
B&G:OCT/94[42]583, CWTI:AUG/90[58]169

35th Infantry; CWM:MAR/91[50]340, CWTI:SEPT/89[30]129

36th Infantry; CWM:APR/95[66]579, CWTI:SEPT/89[30]129

38th Infantry; CWTI:SEPT/89[30]129

39th Infantry; *Tullahoma Campaign,* B&G:OCT/92[10]496,
photo of flag, B&G:OCT/95[36]614

40th Infantry; CWTI:JUN/95[14]443

42nd Infantry:

BOOK REVIEW: *DEAREST LIZZIE: THE CIVIL WAR LETTERS
OF LT. COL. JAMES MAYNARD SHANKLIN*

ADDITIONAL LISTINGS: B&G:AUG/95[24]605, CWTI:SEPT/89[30]129

43rd Infantry; ACW:MAY/93[22]414, CWR:VOL1#2[44]114

46th Infantry; AHI:DEC/71[10]137, B&G:FEB/94[8]550,
B&G:FEB/94[57]555, CWR:VOL4#2[1]165

47th Infantry; ACW:JUL/94[51]480, B&G:FEB/94[8]550,
CWTI:MAY/91[24]208

48th Infantry; CWTI:JUL/94[50]395

49th Infantry; B&G:FEB/94[8]550, CWR:VOL2#1[19]131

54th Infantry; B&G:FEB/94[8]550, B&G:AUG/95[8]604

12th Infantry:
BOOK REVIEW: *UNIVERSITY RECRUITS, BATTERY C, 12TH IOWA INFANTRY REGIMENT 1861-1865*
GENERAL LISTINGS: ACW:JAN/91[22]285, ACW:SEP/92[23]377, B&G:FEB/92[10]474

13th Infantry; ACW:JAN/93[10]393

14th Infantry; ACW:JAN/91[22]285, B&G:FEB/92[10]474, CWTI:AUG/90[50]168

15th Infantry; ACW:JAN/93[10]393, CWTI:SUMMER/89[50]124

16th Infantry; ACW:JAN/93[10]393, CWTI:SUMMER/89[40]123

17th Infantry; ACW:SEP/91[46]324

18th Infantry; CWR:VOL1#2[44]114, CWR:VOL2#1[19]131

19th Infantry; ACW:MAY/94[26]468, CWM:OCT/94[33]537, CWR:VOL1#1[42]105

20th Infantry; ACW:MAY/94[26]468, CWM:OCT/94[33]537, CWR:VOL1#1[42]105

21st Infantry; B&G:FEB/94[8]550, B&G:JUN/94[5]567, CWR:VOL2#1[19]131

22nd Infantry:
ARTICLE: "INTO THE BREACH: THE 22ND IOWA INFANTRY AT THE RAILROAD REDOUBT," CWR:VOL2#1[19]131
BOOK REVIEW: *REMINISCENCES OF THE 22ND IOWA INFANTRY*
GENERAL LISTINGS: *order of battle*, B&G:FEB/94[8]550, *SIO*, B&G:JUN/94[38]571, B&G:JUN/95[36]603A
ADDITIONAL LISTINGS: ACW:MAY/91[38]305, B&G:FEB/94[8]550, CWR:VOL2#1[i]129, CWR:VOL2#1[69]133

23rd Infantry; B&G:FEB/94[8]550, CWR:VOL2#1[19]131, CWR:VOL3#3[33]158, CWTI:JAN/94[8]356

24th Infantry; B&G:FEB/94[8]550, CWR:VOL2#1[i]129, CWR:VOL4#2[1]165

25th Infantry; CWM:MAY/91[10]347, CWTI:SEP/94[40]403

26th Infantry; ACW:SEP/95[38]546, CWTI:SEP/94[40]403

27th Infantry; B&G:AUG/92[40]495

28th Infantry; B&G:FEB/94[8]550, CWR:VOL2#1[i]129, CWR:VOL4#2[1]165

29th Infantry; ACW:MAY/93[22]414

30th Infantry; CWTI:SEP/94[40]403

33rd Infantry; ACW:MAY/93[22]414, CWR:VOL1#2[44]114

35th Infantry; CWR:VOL2#3[212]142

36th Infantry; ACW:MAY/93[22]414, B&G:DEC/93[30]546, CWR:VOL1#2[44]114

37th Infantry; AHI:APR/68[4]115, B&G:OCT/94[42]583, B&G:DEC/94[36]588, CWTI:DEC/95[8]474

39th Infantry; CWR:VOL3#3[59]159

57th Infantry; B&G:AUG/92[40]495

Dubuque Battery; CWTI:MAY/91[16]206

Iowa Brigade; ARTICLE: "AT THE BATTLE OF ATLANTA, THE IOWA BRIGADE SACRIFICED ITSELF TO BUY TIME FOR ITS COMRADES," ACW:JAN/93[10]393

Iowa Light Artillery, 1st Battery; B&G:FEB/94[8]550, B&G:AUG/95[8]604

Light Artillery, 2nd Battery; B&G:AUG/95[8]604

IOWA, STATE OF; BOOK REVIEW: *IOWA VALOR*

IREDELL, CADWALLADER J., *Captain, 1st North Carolina Cavalry;* CWM:JUL/92[16]428

IRELAND, DAVID, *Colonel, 137th New York Infantry;* CWR:VOL3#2[70]155, CWTI:SEPT/89[30]129, CWTI:NOV/92[41]291, CWTI:SEP/94[40]403, GETTY:7[83]192

IRELAND, JOHN, *Chaplain, 5th Minnesota Infantry;* ACW:NOV/94[76]500, CWM:MAR/91[50]340

IRISH (MISSOURI) DRAGOONS; ACW:MAR/92[46]354

IRISH BEND, LOUISIANA, BATTLE OF;
CWR:VOL3#1[1]149, CWR:VOL3#1[78]152

IRISH BRIGADE:
ARTICLE:S "'THE BREATH OF HELL'S DOOR': PRIVATE WILLIAM MCCARTER AND THE IRISH BRIGADE AT FREDERICKSBURG," CWR:VOL4#4[47]179, "DESPERATE COURAGE," CWTI:DEC/90[58]185, "THE FIGHTING IRISH," CWM:MAR/91[17]335, "MEAGHER OF THE SWORD," ACW:SEP/95[54]548, "THE YANKEES OF THE HARD-FIGHTING IRISH BRIGADE WERE SO BRAVE THAT THE CONFEDERATES HATED HAVING TO SHOOT THEM," ACW:MAY/94[12]466
BOOK REVIEWS: *THE IRISH BRIGADE * MEMORIES OF CHAPLAIN LIFE: THREE YEARS WITH THE IRISH BRIGADE IN THE ARMY OF THE POTOMAC * THE STORY OF THE 116TH REGIMENT PENNSYLVANIA INFANTRY*
GENERAL LISTINGS: *common soldiers*, AHI:APR/68[4]115, *Gettysburg*, GETTY:4[89]150, GETTY:5[35]159, GETTY:6[59]174, GETTY:8[53]203, *in book review*, CWNEWS:MAY/91[4], *letters to the editor*, CWM:MAY/91[6]345, CWM:SEP/92[6]436
ADDITIONAL LISTINGS: ACW:NOV/94[50]498, ACW:SEP/95[70]549, B&G:APR/91[8]445, B&G:OCT/95[8]611B, B&G:OCT/95[36]614, CWM:MAR/91[14]334, CWM:MAR/91[50]340, CWM:SEP/93[18]494, CWM:SEP/93[24]495, CWR:VOL4#4[v]176, CWR:VOL4#4[127]182, CWTI:AUG/95[24]455, CWTI:SEP/91[42]231, MH:OCT/93[20]172

IRISH SOLDIERS:
ARTICLES: "'THEIR FAITH BRINGS THEM'," CWM:MAR/91[50]340, "VIRGINIA'S FIGHTING IRISH," CWM:MAR/91[65]342
BOOK REVIEW: *REBEL SONS OF ERIN, A CIVIL WAR HISTORY OF THE TENTH TENNESSEE INFANTRY (IRISH), CONFEDERATE STATES VOLUNTEERS*
ADDITIONAL LISTING: CWM:MAY/91[6]345

IRON BRIGADE:
ARTICLES: "THE FORGING OF THE IRON BRIGADE," CWM:JAN/93[16]457, "THE IRON BRIGADE BATTERY AT GETTYSBURG," GETTY:11[57]233
BOOK REVIEWS: *AN IRISHMAN IN THE IRON BRIGADE: THE CIVIL WAR MEMOIRS OF JAMES P. SULLIVAN, SERGEANT, 6TH WISCONSIN VOLUNTEERS * THE IRON BRIGADE * IRON BRIGADE GENERAL: JOHN GIBBON, A REBEL IN BLUE * LETTERS HOME: HENRY MATRAU OF THE IRON BRIGADE*
GENERAL LISTINGS: *Antietam;* CWTI:MAR/89[28]103, *Brawner's Farm*, B&G:AUG/92[11]493, *Gettysburg*, GETTY:4[16]143, GETTY:4[24]145, GETTY:4[33]146, GETTY:4[113]153, GETTY:4[126]154, GETTY:5[4]156, GETTY:5[19]158, GETTY:5[117]165, GETTY:6[7]169, GETTY:6[13]170, GETTY:6[29]171, GETTY:7[7]185, GETTY:7[23]187, GETTY:7[114]194, GETTY:8[9]199, GETTY:9[33]211, GETTY:11[19]232, GETTY:11[57]233, GETTY:11[71]234, *in book review*, CWM:APR/95[50], CWNEWS:OCT/93[5], CWR:VOL1#2[78], *Wilderness*, B&G:APR/95[8]595, B&G:JUN/95[8]600, *photo*, B&G:OCT/94[42]583
ADDITIONAL LISTINGS: ACW:MAY/92[8]357, ACW:JUL/92[30]369, ACW:MAY/93[31]415, ACW:JAN/95[46]507, ACW:MAR/95[42]517, B&G:APR/93[12]518, B&G:FEB/95[8]590A, CWM:MAR/91[17]335, CWM:SEP/92[8]437, CWM:JAN/93[16]457, CWM:SEP/93[24]495, CWM:FEB/95[30]561,

J

JACKLIN, RUFUS, W., *Private, 16th Michigan Infantry;*
GETTY:6[33]172
JACKMAN, JOHN S., *Private, CSA;* BOOK REVIEWS: *DIARY OF A
CONFEDERATE SOLDIER: JOHN S. JACKMAN OF THE
ORPHAN BRIGADE*
JACKMAN, SIDNEY D., *Colonel, CSA;* ACW:NOV/94[42]497,
B&G:JUN/91[10]452
JACKSON, A.J., *Private, CSA;* CWTI:DEC/94[49]413
JACKSON, ALFRED E., *General, CSA;* B&G:FEB/91[6]438,
&G:APR/91[6]444, B&G:AUG/91[11]458, *photo;*
B&G:AUG/91[52]458
JACKSON, ANNA M.; ACW:SEP/93[31]433,
CWTI:MAY/89[22]116, *photo,* AHI:JUN/67[31]110
JACKSON, CALIB, *Governor, Tennessee;* AHI:AUG/67[50]111
JACKSON, CLAIBORNE F., *Governor, Missouri;*
ACW:MAR/91[62]298, ACW:MAY/91[31]304,
ACW:MAR/92[46]354, ACW:NOV/93[26]441,
CWM:MAY/93[8]474, CWNEWS:MAY/92[4],
CWTI:MAR/91[34]201, CWTI:FEB/92[29]248,
CWTI:JUL/94[50]395, CWTI:AUG/95[34]457
JACKSON, CONRAD F., *General, USA;* B&G:AUG/93[36]533,
CWR:VOL4#4[1]177, CWTI:JUL/93[10]323, *photo;*
CWR:VOL4#4[1]177
JACKSON, GILMER G., *Private, Jeff Davis Artillery;*
CWTI:DEC/91[26]238
JACKSON, H.E., *Private, Cobb's Legion;* GETTY:12[68]246
JACKSON, HENRY, *Private, USA;* CWM:SEP/93[18]494
JACKSON, HENRY R., *General, CSA:*
GENERAL LISTINGS: *Nashville,* B&G:DEC/93[12]545, *West Virginia
campaign,* B&G:AUG/93[10]529
ADDITIONAL LISTINGS: ACW:JAN/92[50]345, ACW:SEP/94[31]486,
B&G:DEC/93[12]545, CWR:VOL1#4[64]127,
CWTI:DEC/94[49]413, CWTI:MAR/95[18]432,
CWTI:JUN/95[18]444
JACKSON, ISAAC, *Private, 11th Veteran Reserve Corps;*
B&G:APR/93[24]520
JACKSON, J. THOMPSON, *Lieutenant, USA;* GETTY:13[7]253
JACKSON, J. WARREN, *Lieutenant, 8th Louisiana Infantry;*
ARTICLE: "GOING BACK INTO THE UNION AT LAST,"
CWTI:FEB/91[12]189
JACKSON, JAMES S., *General, USA;* ACW:MAR/93[51]407,
AHI:NOV/72[12]142, B&G:DEC/95[9]615,
CWR:VOL4#3[50]171
JACKSON, JAMES T., *civilian;* ACW:JUL/92[22]368
JACKSON, JOHN, *Colonel, 3rd New Hampshire Infantry;*
ACW:SEP/91[30]322
JACKSON, JOHN K., *General, CSA;* CWR:VOL1#4[v]124,
CWR:VOL1#4[42]126, CWR:VOL1#4[64]127,
CWTI:SEPT/89[30]129, *photo;* CWR:VOL1#4[42]126
JACKSON, JOSEPH W., *Lieutenant, CSA;* CWM:SEP/93[24]495
JACKSON, MARY ANNA, B&G:JUN/92[8]487
JACKSON, MISSISSIPPI, BATTLE OF:
ARTICLES: "FIGHTING ERUPTS AT JACKSON, MISSISSIPPI,"
CWM:AUG/95[26]604, "RETURN TO JACKSON, JULY 5-25,
1863," B&G:AUG/95[8]604
ADDITIONAL LISTINGS: CWR:VOL2#1[19]131, CWR:VOL2#1[78],
CWTI:FEB/90[38]145
JACKSON, NATHANIEL J., *General, USA;* B&G:DEC/95[9]615

JACKSON, OSCAR, *Colonel, 63rd Ohio Infantry;*
ACW:SEP/91[46]324, CWTI:DEC/94[62]415
JACKSON, R.A., *Lieutenant, 22nd Virginia Infantry;*
CWR:VOL1#3[52]122
JACKSON, R. STARK, *Lieutenant, 8th Louisiana Infantry;*
CWTI:FEB/91[12]189
JACKSON, THOMAS E., *Captain, Charlottesville (Virginia)
Artillery;* GETTY:7[124]196
JACKSON, THOMAS J., *General, CSA:*
ARTICLES: "A SINGLE STEP," CWTI:MAR/94[29]371, "ARNOLD
VS. ARNOLD: THE STRANGE AND HITHERTO UNTOLD
STORY OF THE DIVORCE OF STONEWALL JACKSON'S
SISTER," B&G:OCT/94[28]581, "COMMAND SHIFT
DICTATED," MH:JUN/92[50]159, "THE CORPORAL, THE
HOTHEAD AND THE CRAZY OLD PRESBYTERIAN FOOL,"
CWM:OCT/94[26]536, "DIMINUTIVE BUT FEISTY,
CHARLES CARTER RANDOLPH WAS STONEWALL
JACKSON'S PET CADET'" ACW:JUL/93[10]421, "FIRE AND
FURY AT CATHERINE'S FURNACE," ACW:MAY/95[30]525,
"FLANK ATTACK," ACW:SEP/93[31]433
ARTICLES, continued: "THE GREAT TRAIN ROBBERY,"
CWM:NOV/91[40]393, "HENRY KYD DOUGLAS
CHALLENGED BY HIS PEERS," CWM:SEP/91[40]385,
"LEE'S LIEUTENANTS: STONEWALL JACKSON,"
CWM:JUL/92[16]428, "MEMORIES OF STONEWALL,"
CWM:APR/94[14]503, "THE PENINSULA CAMPAIGN OF
1862: THE DABBS HOUSE MEETING,"
CWM:JUN/95[53]590, "PERSONAL REMINISCENCES OF
'STONEWALL' JACKSON," CWTI:JUN/95[18]444, "RETURN
TO THE KILLING GROUND," ACW:JUL/91[18]312,
"SECOND MANASSAS: ENFILADING THUNDER,"
CWM:AUG/94[48]529, "THE SECRETIVE STONEWALL,"
B&G:JUN/92[53]491, "STARS IN THEIR COURSES,"
ACW:NOV/91[41]334
ARTICLES, continued: "'STONEWALL' JACKSON'S LAST MARCH: A
LAVISH STATE FUNERAL FOR A SOUTHERN HERO,"
CWTI:MAY/89[22]116, "STONEWALL IN THE VALLEY,"
ACW:JAN/93[35]396, "STONEWALL JACKSON,"
B&G:JUN/92[8]487, "'STONEWALL' JACKSON—A
MEMOIR," AHI:JUN/67[31]110, "STONEWALL JACKSON'S
ARTILLERISTS AND THE DEFENSE OF THE
CONFEDERATE RIGHT," CWR:VOL4#4[70]180,
"STONEWALL'S FORGOTTEN MASTERPIECE,"
MH:AUG/95[30]185, "STONEWALL'S SURPRISE AT OX
HILL," ACW:JAN/95[54]508, "STREET NAMED FOR
'LITTLE SORREL,'" CWTI:APR/92[41]258, "VALOR OF
OHIOANS AT THE BATTLE OF KERNSTOWN,"
CWM:APR/95[29]574, "VMI'S STAPLETON CRUTCHFIELD
LOYALLY FOLLOWED STONEWALL JACKSON FROM
THE CAMPUS TO THE BATTLEFIELD,"
ACW:MAY/95[10]523, "WHO'S UP AND WHO'S DOWN IN
CIVIL WAR HISTORY: ONE'S REPUTATION
INCREASINGLY DEPENDS ON WHO'S TELLING THE
TALE," ACW:MAR/95[6]511
BOOK REVIEWS: *A BULLET FOR STONEWALL *
CHANCELLORSVILLE 1863: THE SOULS OF THE BRAVE
* THE CLASS OF 1846: FROM WEST, POINT TO
APPOMATTOX: STONEWALL JACKSON, GEORGE
MCCLELLAN, AND THEIR BROTHERS * THE
DESTRUCTIVE WAR—WILLIAM TECUMSEH SHERMAN,
STONEWALL JACKSON, AND THE AMERICANS * THE
HISTORY OF THE HARPERS FERRY CAVALRY
EXPEDITION, SEPTEMBER 14 & 15, 1862*

CWM:NOV/92[41]451, CWM:MAR/93[32]468,
CWM:MAY/93[4]472, CWM:SEP/93[8]493,
CWM:SEP/93[24]495, CWM:JUN/94[23]510,
CWM:JUN/94[26]512, CWM:JUN/94[27]513,
CWM:JUN/94[43]517, CWM:OCT/94[4]532,
CWM:OCT/94[55]543, CWM:DEC/94[4]545,
CWM:DEC/94[17]547, CWM:DEC/94[26]548,
CWM:DEC/94[34]549, CWM:DEC/94[40]550,
CWM:APR/95[32]575, CWM:JUN/95[82]600,
CWM:AUG/95[4]601, CWM:AUG/95[17]603,
CWM:AUG/95[30]606, CWM:AUG/95[38]609,
CWM:OCT/95[22]614, CWM:OCT/95[38]618,
CWM:DEC/95[41]630

ADDITIONAL LISTINGS, CWR: CWR:VOL1#1[1]102,
CWR:VOL1#1[26]103, CWR:VOL1#2[29]112,
CWR:VOL1#3[28]120, CWR:VOL1#3[52]122,
CWR:VOL1#4[v]124, CWR:VOL1#4[7]125,
CWR:VOL1#4[74]128, CWR:VOL2#1[36]132,
CWR:VOL2#2[95]135, CWR:VOL2#4[269]145,
CWR:VOL3#1[1]149, CWR:VOL3#1[31]150,
CWR:VOL3#2[1]153, CWR:VOL3#3[33]158,
CWR:VOL4#2[26]166, CWR:VOL4#2[68]167,
CWR:VOL4#4[i]175

ADDITIONAL LISTINGS, CWTI: CWTI:APR/89[14]107,
CWTI:APR/89[38]111, CWTI:DEC/89[34]136,
CWTI:MAR/91[12]198, CWTI:MAR/91[74]204,
CWTI:AUG/91[46]218, CWTI:SEP/91[42]231,
CWTI:DEC/91[36]240, CWTI:APR/92[35]257,
CWTI:MAY/92[20]262, CWTI:SEP/92[42]283,
CWTI:JAN/93[40]301, CWTI:MAY/93[26]318,
CWTI:MAR/93[40]312, CWTI:JUL/93[42]329,
CWTI:NOV/93[55]350, CWTI:MAR/94[48]374,
CWTI:JUL/94[44]394, CWTI:DEC/94[73]416,
CWTI:JAN/95[24]424, CWTI:JAN/95[34]427,
CWTI:MAR/95[46]437, CWTI:OCT/95[90]472,
CWTI:DEC/95[14]475, CWTI:DEC/95[67]481

ADDITIONAL LISTINGS, GETTY: GETTY:6[33]172, GETTY:6[69]176,
GETTY:6[94]180, GETTY:9[17]210, GETTY:10[29]222,
GETTY:13[108]261

ADDITIONAL LISTINGS, MH: MH:FEB/92[8]156, MH:APR/92[18]157

JACKSON, WILLIAM, *Corporal, 124th New York Infantry;*
CWM:DEC/94[40]550

JACKSON, WILLIAM H. "RED", *General, CSA:*
GENERAL LISTINGS: *Jackson, Battle of,* B&G:AUG/95[8]604, *order of
battle,* B&G:DEC/93[12]545, B&G:AUG/95[8]604, *Tullahoma
Campaign,* B&G:OCT/92[10]496, *photo;* B&G:AUG/95[8]604
ADDITIONAL LISTINGS: B&G:APR/93[34]521, B&G:DEC/93[52]548,
CWM:JAN/91[12]326, CWTI:SUMMER/89[50]124

JACKSON, WILLIAM H., *Sergeant, 53rd Pennsylvania
Infantry;* GETTY:7[119]195, GETTY:11[80]235

JACKSON, WILLIAM L. "MUDWALL", *General, CSA:*
GENERAL LISTINGS: *Monocacy,* B&G:DEC/92[8]503, *West Virginia
campaign,* B&G:AUG/93[10]529
ADDITIONAL LISTINGS: ACW:MAY/91[38]305, B&G:FEB/91[6]438,
B&G:AUG/94[19]575, CWTI:MAR/89[16]101

JACKSON, WILLIAM M., *Private, 53rd Georgia Infantry;*
B&G:APR/93[24]520

JACKSON-HILL FEUD:
ARTICLE: "THE CORPORAL, THE HOTHEAD AND THE CRAZY
OLD PRESBYTERIAN FOOL," CWM:OCT/94[26]536
ADDITIONAL LISTING: CWR:VOL1#1[1]102

JACKSONVILLE, FLORIDA: ARTICLE: "THE *MAPLE LEAF*
ESCAPE,"

ADDITIONAL LISTING: CWTI:AUG/95[10]453

JACOBS, HENRY E., *civilian;* GETTY:7[13]186,
GETTY:9[122]220

JACOBS, MICHAEL, *civilian:*
ARTICLE: "WAR COMES TO PROFESSOR MICHAEL JACOBS,"
GETTY:6[99]181
ADDITIONAL LISTINGS: GETTY:7[13]186, GETTY:7[97]193,
GETTY:11[102]237, GETTY:13[7]253, *photo;* GETTY:6[99]181

JACOBS, VALENTINE, *Corporal, 19th Indiana Infantry;*
CWTI:NOV/93[78]354

JAMES CREEK GUARDS (PENNSYLVANIA) GUARDS,
(53rd Pennsylvania Infantry); GETTY:11[80]235

JAMES RIVER SQUADRON; ACW:MAR/91[14]293,
ACW:SEP/95[30]545, CWM:DEC/95[10]

JAMES, BUSHROD W., *Doctor, USA;* GETTY:10[53]225,
GETTY:11[102]237

JAMES, CYRUS W., *Private, 9th New York Cavalry;*
GETTY:11[19]232

JAMES, FRANK:
ARTICLE: "THE JAMES BOYS GO TO WAR,"
CWTI:JAN/94[29]360
ADDITIONAL LISTINGS: ACW:MAR/94[6]455, ACW:MAR/95[26]515,
ACW:JUL/95[58], B&G:JUN/91[32]454, B&G:OCT/91[11]466,
CWM:JAN/92[8]399, *photos,* ACW:JAN/93[26]395,
B&G:OCT/91[11]466, CWTI:JAN/94[29]360

JAMES, GARTH W., *Lieutenant, 54th Massachusetts Infantry;*
ACW:SEP/91[30]322, CWTI:DEC/89[42]137

JAMES, JESSE:
ARTICLES: "THE CIVIL WAR WAS A DEADLY CLASSROOM
FOR HICKOK, HARDIN, THE JAMESES AND A NUMBER
OF OTHER 'STUDENTS,'" ACW:MAR/94[6]455, "THE
JAMES BOYS GO TO WAR," CWTI:JAN/94[29]360
GENERAL LISTINGS: *in book review,* ACW:JUL/95[58],
CWTI:MAY/89[44], *letters to the editor,* B&G:OCT/91[6]465,
B&G:DEC/92[6]502, CWTI:MAY/94[12]379, *photo of farm;*
B&G:OCT/91[11]466, *photos;* ACW:JAN/93[26]395,
ACW:MAR/94[6]455, B&G:OCT/91[11]466,
CWTI:JAN/94[29]360
ADDITIONAL LISTINGS: ACW:JAN/93[26]395, ACW:MAR/95[26]515,
B&G:JUN/91[32]454, B&G:OCT/91[11]466,
B&G:OCT/95[36]614, CWM:JAN/92[8]399

JAMES, MILES, *Corporal, 36th USCT;* CWM:AUG/94[30]527

JAMES, ROBERT, *Lieutenant, 4th U.S. Artillery;*
GETTY:12[7]241, GETTY:12[42]244

JAMESON, CHARLES D., *Colonel, 2nd Maine Infantry;*
CWR:VOL4#1[78]

JAMIESON, SAMUEL, *Private, CSA;* B&G:OCT/95[36]614

JAMISON, JOSHUA, *Corporal, 22nd South Carolina Infantry;*
CWTI:JAN/94[46]364

JANES, HENRY, *Surgeon;* CWM:DEC/95[54]632,
GETTY:10[53]225

JANSEN, THEODORE, *Private, 27th Illinois Infantry;*
CWR:VOL3#4[24]162

JAPAN; ARTICLE: "SHOGUNATE DEFIED," MH:OCT/91[50]154

JAQUES, CHARLES B., *Surgeon, 7th New Jersey Infantry;*
B&G:FEB/92[22]476

JARED, ARCHIBALD S., *Private, 28th Tennessee Infantry;*
B&G:APR/91[36]448

JARVIS, WILLIAM, *Private, Georgia and Mississippi Regiment;*
CWR:VOL1#4[42]126

JASPER (MISSISSIPPI) GRAYS, *16th Mississippi Infantry;*
GETTY:4[7]142

JOHNSON, ——, *Sergeant, 12th New Hampshire Infantry;*
GETTY:12[7]241

JOHNSON, A.V.E., *Major, 39th Missouri Infantry;*
B&G:JUN/91[32]454, B&G:OCT/91[11]466,
CWTI:JAN/94[29]360

JOHNSON, ADAM R., *General, CSA:*
ARTICLE: "FIELDS WITHOUT HONOR: TWO AFFAIRS IN
TENNESSEE," CWTI:JUL/92[42]274
ADDITIONAL LISTINGS: ACW:MAR/93[51]407, ACW:MAR/93[55]408,
CWM:MAR/93[16]466

JOHNSON, AMOS, *Lieutenant, USN;* CWTI:DEC/90[29]182

JOHNSON, ANDREW:
ARTICLES: "A PRESIDENTIAL GALLERY," AHI:APR/89[20]282,
"'THE MOST HEROIC ACT IN AMERICAN HISTORY,'"
AHI:DEC/68[28]118
BOOK REVIEWS: *THE IMPEACHMENT AND TRIAL OF ANDREW
JOHNSON * IMPEACHMENT OF A PRESIDENT:
ANDREW JOHNSON, THE BLACKS AND
RECONSTRUCTION * THE PAPERS OF ANDREW
JOHNSON*
GENERAL LISTINGS: *election of 1864,* AHI:OCT/68[4]116, *in book
review,* ACW:MAY/93[54], ACW:SEP/93[54], ACW:SEP/94[66],
B&G:JUN/92[28], CWTI:SEP/92[18], CWTI:OCT/95[18], *Isaac
Lynde,* B&G:JUN/94[8]568, *Ku Klux Klan,* AHI:JAN/80[8]197,
letters to the editor, CWTI:APR/92[8]252, CWTI:MAY/92[8]261,
CWTI:MAY/94[12]379, MH:FEB/93[10]163, *Thaddeus Stevens,*
AHI:JAN/82[16]224, *Andrew Johnson Birthplace;*
AHI:APR/89[43]284, *Andrew Johnson National Historic Site;*
AHI:APR/89[43]284, *Johnston's Surrender;*
CWTI:APR/90[20]151, *Lincoln's assassination;*
CWTI:AUG/90[42]167, *photos,* AHI:DEC/68[28]118,
AHI:APR/89[20]282
ADDITIONAL LISTINGS: ACW:JAN/91[30]286, ACW:MAY/91[12]302,
ACW:JUL/91[26]313, ACW:JUL/92[6]365,
ACW:NOV/92[35]387, ACW:SEP/94[55]489,
ACW:JUL/95[26]535, ACW:SEP/95[54]548,
AHI:JAN/73[28]147, AHI:JUL/76[19]170, AHI:JAN/85[10]244,
AHI:APR/89[13]281, AHI:MAY/89[26]285,
B&G:FEB/93[12]511, B&G:DEC/93[52]548,
B&G:FEB/94[38]553, B&G:DEC/95[44]617,
CWM:MAR/93[8]465, CWM:APR/94[8]502,
CWTI:FEB/90[60]148, CWTI:APR/90[12]150,
CWTI:AUG/90[64]170, CWTI:AUG/90[70]171,
CWTI:DEC/91[28]239, CWTI:JUL/92[42]274,
CWTI:NOV/92[54]293, CWTI:MAR/93[12]307,
CWTI:MAY/93[29]319, CWTI:MAY/93[35]320,
CWTI:JAN/94[35]361, CWTI:MAY/94[40]383,
CWTI:DEC/94[79]417, CWTI:DEC/95[76]482,
MH:FEB/94[8]175

JOHNSON, AXEL, *Private, 1st Illinois Artillery;*
B&G:APR/94[28]559

JOHNSON, B.T., *Colonel, CSA;* ACW:JUL/92[30]369

JOHNSON, BENJAMIN W., *Colonel, 15th Arkansas Infantry;*
CWM:JUN/94[25]511

JOHNSON, BRADLEY T., *General, CSA:*
GENERAL LISTINGS: *letters to the editor,* B&G:DEC/93[6]544,
Manassas, 2nd, B&G:AUG/92[11]493, *Monocacy,*
B&G:DEC/92[8]503, *photo;* B&G:AUG/94[10]574
ADDITIONAL LISTINGS: ACW:JAN/91[38]287, ACW:MAY/91[38]305,
ACW:NOV/93[50]444, ACW:JUL/94[10]475,
ACW:JUL/94[66]481, B&G:APR/94[59]565,
B&G:AUG/94[10]574, CWM:JUL/92[16]428,

CWTI:DEC/91[28]239, CWTI:JAN/95[27]425,
CWTI:DEC/95[76]482

JOHNSON, BUSHROD R., *General, CSA:*
GENERAL LISTINGS: *Chickamauga,* CWTI:SEP/92[31]281,
CWTI:SEP/93[53]340, *Five Forks,* B&G:APR/92[8]481,
FortsHenry and Donelson, B&G:FEB/92[10]474, *in order of
battle,* B&G:APR/92[8]481, *Knoxville,* ACW:MAY/91[23]303,
CWTI:MAR/93[40]312, CWTI:MAY/94[50]386, *letters to the
editor,* B&G:APR/92[6]480, *Sayler's Creek,*
ACW:JAN/92[22]341, *Tullahoma Campaign,*
B&G:OCT/92[10]496, *photos,* ACW:SEP/92[38]379,
B&G:FEB/92[10]474, B&G:APR/92[8]481,
CWTI:SEP/92[31]281
ADDITIONAL LISTINGS: ACW:SEP/92[38]379, ACW:JAN/93[43]397,
B&G:DEC/93[52]548, CWM:SEP/91[35]384,
CWM:JUL/92[24]430, CWR:VOL1#3[7]118,
CWR:VOL2#2[141]137, CWR:VOL2#3[236]143,
CWR:VOL4#3[50]171, CWTI:FEB/90[26]143,
CWTI:AUG/90[26]166, CWTI:JUL/94[44]394,
CWTI:JAN/95[27]425, CWTI:MAR/95[33]435

JOHNSON, C.J., *Sergeant, 1st Illinois Artillery;*
B&G:APR/94[28]559

JOHNSON, CHARLES, *seaman, USN;* ACW:NOV/92[51]389

JOHNSON, CHARLES, *Private, 150th New York Infantry;*
ACW:JAN/95[74]510, GETTY:12[42]244

JOHNSON, CHARLES B., *Private, 130th Illinois Infantry;*
B&G:FEB/94[8]550

JOHNSON, CHARLES F., *Colonel, USVRC;* ACW:SEP/94[8]483

JOHNSON, CHARLES R., *Corporal, 16th Massachusetts
Infantry;* GETTY:12[7]241

JOHNSON, CURTIS, *Private, 15th Kansas Cavalry;*
B&G:JUN/91[10]452

JOHNSON, EASTMAN:
ARTICLE: "THE ARTIST AND THE CIVIL WAR,"
AHI:NOV/80[28]211
ADDITIONAL LISTING: ACW:MAY/94[58]

JOHNSON, EDWARD, *General, CSA:*
ARTICLES: "LEE FOILS MEADE AT MINE RUN,"
CWM:DEC/94[44]551, "'THE MUSKET BALLS FLEW VERY
THICK': HOLDING THE LINE AT PAYNE'S FARM,"
CWM:MAY/92[20]420
GENERAL LISTINGS: *Gettysburg,* GETTY:4[49]147,
GETTY:4[65]148, GETTY:5[4]156, GETTY:5[35]159,
GETTY:5[103]163, GETTY:5[117]165, GETTY:6[7]169,
GETTY:6[69]176, GETTY:7[77]191, GETTY:7[83]192,
GETTY:9[17]210, GETTY:9[81]216, GETTY:10[29]222,
GETTY:10[36]223, GETTY:12[30]243, GETTY:12[42]244
GENERAL LISTINGS, continued: *in book review,* CWR:VOL2#4[346],
CWR:VOL3#3[92], *Jackson,* B&G:JUN/92[8]487, *Nashville,*
B&G:DEC/93[12]545, *order of battle,* B&G:APR/95[8]595, *West
Virginia campaign,* B&G:AUG/93[10]529, *Wilderness,*
B&G:APR/95[8]595, *photo;* B&G:AUG/93[10]529,
CWM:MAY/92[20]420, CWM:DEC/94[44]551,
CWTI:MAR/94[29]371, GETTY:9[17]210
ADDITIONAL LISTINGS: ACW:MAR/92[30]352, ACW:NOV/92[42]388,
ACW:MAR/94[16]458, ACW:SEP/94[38]487,
AHI:APR/85[18]250, B&G:FEB/95[8]590C,
CWM:MAY/92[4]416, CWM:JAN/93[8]456,
CWM:SEP/93[24]495, CWM:AUG/94[60]531,
CWM:OCT/95[36]616, CWTI:SEP/90[26]174,
CWTI:FEB/91[12]189, CWTI:MAR/94[29]371,
CWTI:DEC/94[32]410, GETTY:13[89]260, GETTY:13[108]261

JOHNSON, GEORGE, *Private, USA;* ACW:JUL/93[27]423

JOHNSON, GEORGE E., *Captain, 29th Pennsylvania Infantry;* GETTY:7[83]192

JOHNSON, GEORGE H., *Private, 1st Florida Special Battalion;* CWR:VOL3#1[65]151

JOHNSON, GEORGE W., *Governor, Kentucky;* ACW:JUL/91[12]310

JOHNSON, GILBERT D., *Corporal, 12th Michigan Infantry;* ACW:JAN/91[22]285

JOHNSON, GILBERT M.L., *Colonel, 13th Indiana Cavalry;* B&G:DEC/93[12]545, CWTI:MAR/91[46]203

JOHNSON, GILES N., *Private, 154th New York Infantry;* CWTI:MAR/95[26]434

JOHNSON, HERSCHEL V., *Congressman from Georgia;* ACW:NOV/93[6]437, ACW:NOV/93[42]443

JOHNSON, HIRAM, *Sergeant, 26th North Carolina Infantry;* GETTY:5[19]158

JOHNSON, HOMER B., *Private, 1st Ohio Light Artillery;* GETTY:4[49]147

JOHNSON, I.N., *Corporal, 6th Kentucky Infantry;* AHI:DEC/85[40]255

JOHNSON, J.J., *Private, 22nd Virginia Infantry;* CWR:VOL1#3[52]122

JOHNSON, JAMES, *seaman, USN;* ACW:NOV/92[51]389

JOHNSON, JAMES B., *Adjutant, 5th Florida Infantry;* GETTY:12[7]241

JOHNSON, JAMES C., *Lieutenant Colonel, 22nd Virginia Infantry;* CWR:VOL1#3[52]122

JOHNSON, JOHN, *Private, 7th Wisconsin Infantry;* GETTY:9[33]211, GETTY:11[57]233

JOHNSON, JOHN and MICHAEL, *51st North Carolina Infantry;* CWTI:JAN/95[48]429

JOHNSON, JOHN O., *Private, 6th Wisconsin Infantry;* GETTY:4[16]143

JOHNSON, JOHN O. and MICHAEL, *31st North Carolina Infantry;* B&G:JUN/93[6]523

JOHNSON, JOHN O., *Sergeant, USA;* B&G:APR/93[12]518

JOHNSON, JOHN R., *Corporal, CSA;* GETTY:10[107]227

JOHNSON, MARMADUKE, *Lieutenant Colonel, CSA;* CWR:VOL1#1[1]102, CWR:VOL1#1[35]104

JOHNSON, MISCAL, *Colonel, 3rd Missouri Cavalry;* ACW:MAR/92[46]354

JOHNSON, OSCAR, *Private, 30th Maine Infantry;* ACW:SEP/91[16]320

JOHNSON, PRESTON, *Private, 2nd Wisconsin Infantry;* GETTY:11[57]233

JOHNSON, R.J., *Private, 10th Georgia Infantry;* ACW:JUL/95[10]533

JOHNSON, R.M., *Major, USA;* CWR:VOL1#1[73]108

JOHNSON, REVERDY; ACW:JAN/91[62]289, CWTI:OCT/95[48]470

JOHNSON, RICHARD W., *General, USA:*
GENERAL LISTINGS: *letters to the editor,* CWTI:AUG/95[14]454, *Nashville,* B&G:DEC/93[12]545
ADDITIONAL LISTINGS: ACW:NOV/95[48]557, B&G:APR/92[58]485, B&G:DEC/93[12]545, CWR:VOL1#4[42]126

JOHNSON, ROBERT D., *Colonel, 23rd North Carolina Infantry;* GETTY:4[33]146

JOHNSON, THOMAS, *Corporal, 11th New Jersey Infantry;* GETTY:12[7]241

JOHNSON, W.H., *Private, 12th New Jersey Infantry;* GETTY:5[89]162

JOHNSON, WILLIAM, *Corporal, CSA;* ACW:JAN/93[43]397

JOHNSON, WILLIAM A., *Lieutenant, 2nd South Carolina Infantry;* GETTY:5[35]159

JOHNSON, WILLIAM K., *Corporal, 8th Louisiana Infantry;* CWTI:FEB/91[12]189

JOHNSON, WILLIAM L., *Private, 6th Wisconsin Infantry;* GETTY:11[57]233

JOHNSON, WILLIAM T., *Captain, 18th Virginia Infantry;* GETTY:12[111]250

JOHNSON-CRITTENDEN RESOLUTIONS; AHI:JAN/82[16]224

JOHNSONVILLE, TENNESSEE, RAID; CWTI:NOV/93[74]353, CWTI:JAN/94[35]361

JOHNSTON, ALBERT SIDNEY, *General, CSA:*
ARTICLES: "DEVIL'S OWN DAY," ACW:JAN/91[22]285, "THE FINAL RESTING PLACE OF GENERAL ALBERT SIDNEY JOHNSTON," B&G:FEB/95[35]592, "FORTS HENRY & DONELSON: UNION VICTORY ON THE TWIN RIVERS," B&G:FEB/92[10]474, "NO ONE COULD HAVE LIVED UP TO ALBERT SIDNEY JOHNSTON'S REPUTATION—NOT EVEN JOHNSTON," ACW:SEP/93[6]428
BOOK REVIEWS: *ALBERT SIDNEY JOHNSTON: SOLDIER OF THREE REPUBLICS * FAMOUS KENTUCKY DUELS * JEFFERSON DAVIS AND HIS GENERALS: THE FAILURE OF CONFEDERATE COMMAND IN THE WEST*
GENERAL LISTINGS: *Davis,* CWTI:AUG/91[29]216, CWTI:AUG/91[62]221, *general history,* AHI:MAY/71[3]133A, *in book review,* B&G:OCT/93[24], CWM:MAY/91[38], CWM:FEB/95[7], CWM:APR/95[50], CWNEWS:JUN/93[5], CWR:VOL2#1[78], CWR:VOL2#2[169], CWR:VOL4#3[1], *letters to the editor,* B&G:JUN/92[6]486, *Morman Campaign,* ACW:JAN/95[8]502, AHI:DEC/72[10]145, *trading cards,* CWTI:DEC/91[18]236, *photos,* ACW:SEP/93[6]428, AHI:MAY/71[3]133A, AHI:NOV/73[18]151, B&G:FEB/92[10]474, B&G:FEB/93[12]511, B&G:FEB/95[35]592, CWTI:AUG/91[46]218, *sketch;* AHI:DEC/72[10]145
ADDITIONAL LISTINGS: ACW:JUL/91[12]310, ACW:JUL/92[22]368, ACW:NOV/92[35]387, ACW:SEP/93[38]434, ACW:MAR/94[42]461, AHI:NOV/73[18]151, AHI:OCT/95[24]326, B&G:APR/92[58]485, B&G:FEB/93[12]511, CWM:MAY/91[10]347, CWM:JAN/92[34]404, CWM:JUL/92[40]432, CWM:MAY/93[4]472, CWM:MAY/93[16]475, CWM:FEB/95[32]562, CWR:VOL1#2[44]114, CWR:VOL1#3[7]118, CWR:VOL2#1[36]132, CWR:VOL3#3[33]158, CWR:VOL3#4[24]162, CWR:VOL4#1[44]164, CWR:VOL4#3[50]171
ADDITIONAL LISTINGS, continued: CWTI:FEB/90[26]143, CWTI:FEB/90[32]144, CWTI:AUG/91[46]218, CWTI:AUG/91[52]219, CWTI:MAY/92[45]266, CWTI:MAY/92[48]267, CWTI:JUL/92[29]272, CWTI:MAR/93[50]313, CWTI:SEP/93[22]335, CWTI:SEP/93[43]338, CWTI:AUG/95[46]459, CWTI:JUN/95[48]448, MH:OCT/94[20]180

JOHNSTON, ANDREW B., *Lieutenant, Crenshaw's Artillery;* GETTY:10[107]227,

JOHNSTON, EDWARD; ACW:JAN/93[35]396

JOHNSTON, G.K., *Surgeon, USA;* GETTY:10[53]225

JOHNSTON, GEORGE D., *General, CSA;* B&G:DEC/93[12]545, B&G:DEC/95[9]615

JOHNSTON, J. STODDARD; CWR:VOL4#3[50]171

JOHNSTON, JAMES D., *Captain, CSN;* CWM:JUL/93[24]485

JOHNSTON, JAMES S., *Private, 11th Mississippi Infantry;* ACW:JUL/93[58]

JOHNSTON, JOHN W., *Major, Botetourt Artillery;* B&G:DEC/93[12]545, B&G:FEB/94[8]550

JOHNSTON, JOSEPH E., *General, CSA:*

ARTICLES: "THE ATLANTA CAMPAIGN," CWM:JAN/91[12]326, "THE BATTLE OF BENTONVILLE, MARCH 19-21, 1865: LAST STAND IN THE CAROLINAS," B&G:DEC/95[9]615, "THE BATTLE THAT SHOULD NOT HAVE BEEN," CWTI:NOV/92[41]291, "CONVERSATION IN CONFIDENCE," CWTI:JAN/95[20]422, "EDITORIAL," ACW:JAN/91[6]281, "HOW TO LOSE A CITY," CWM:JAN/91[28]327, "LAST STAND IN THE CAROLINAS: THE BATTLE OF BENTONVILLE. AN INTERVIEW WITH AUTHOR MARK L. BRADLEY," CWR:VOL4#3[65]172

ARTICLES, continued: "THE PENINSULA CAMPAIGN OF 1862: THE ENGAGEMENT AT ELTHAM'S LANDING," CWM:JUN/95[37]585, "THE PENINSULA CAMPAIGN OF 1862: THE BATTLE OF DREWRY'S BLUFF," CWM:JUN/95[39]586, "THE PENINSULA CAMPAIGN OF 1862: THE BATTLE OF SEVEN PINES," CWM:JUN/95[47]588, "THE PENINSULA CAMPAIGN OF 1862: THE BATTLE OF SLASH CHURCH," CWM:JUN/95[43]587, "THE PENINSULA CAMPAIGN OF 1862: THE BATTLE OF WILLIAMSBURG," CWM:JUN/95[34]584, "THE PENINSULA CAMPAIGN OF 1862; PRELUDE: THE LEGIONS GATHER," CWM:JUN/95[24]582, "THE PENINSULA CAMPAIGN OF 1862: THE SIEGE OF YORKTOWN AND ENGAGEMENTS ALONG THE WARWICK RIVER," CWM:JUN/95[29]583

BOOK REVIEWS: *DECISION IN THE WEST: THE ATLANTA CAMPAIGN OF 1864 * DESTROYER OF THE IRON HORSE: GENERAL JOSEPH E. JOHNSTON AND CONFEDERATE RAIL TRANSPORT, 1861-1865 * JEFFERSON DAVIS AND HIS GENERALS: THE FAILURE OF CONFEDERATE COMMAND IN THE WEST * JOSEPH E. JOHNSTON: A CIVIL WAR BIOGRAPHY * THE MARCH TO THE SEA * NARRATIVE OF MILITARY OPERATIONS, DIRECTED DURING THE LATE WAR BETWEEN THE STATES, TO THE GATES OF RICHMOND: THE PENINSULA CAMPAIGN*

GENERAL LISTINGS: *Alexander Stephens,* CWTI:FEB/91[36]193, *Atlanta Campaign,* ACW:JUL/94[66]481, ACW:JAN/95[30]505, ACW:NOV/95[74]560, CWM:JAN/91[4]323, CWM:JAN/91[40]330, CWR:VOL1#3[82]123, CWTI:SUMMER/89[13]120, CWTI:SUMMER/89[20]121, CWTI:SUMMER/89[32]122, CWTI:SUMMER/89[40]123, CWTI:SUMMER/89[50]124, CWTI:FEB/90[54]147, CWTI:SEP/91[23]228, *Davis,* CWTI:AUG/91[29]216, CWTI:AUG/91[52]219, CWTI:AUG/91[62]221, *Fair Oaks,* ACW:SEP/95[54]548, *general history,* AHI:MAY/71[3]133A, *Grierson's Raid,* B&G:JUN/93[12]524

GENERAL LISTINGS, continued: *in book review,* ACW:MAR/94[58], ACW:SEP/94[66], ACW:NOV/94[66], ACW:JAN/95[62], ACW:MAR/95[58], B&G:APR/91[28], B&G:APR/95[30], CWM:JAN/91[47], CWM:MAR/92[49], CWM:JUL/93[51], CWM:JUN/94[6], CWM:OCT/94[8], CWM:APR/95[8], CWM:JUN/95[6], CWM:OCT/95[10], CWNEWS:OCT/89[4], CWNEWS:NOV/90[4], CWNEWS:MAY/91[4], CWNEWS:AUG/92[4], CWNEWS:MAY/92[4], CWNEWS:NOV/92[4], CWNEWS:MAY/93[4],

CWNEWS:MAY/94[5], CWR:VOL2#1[78], CWR:VOL2#2[169], CWR:VOL1#2[78], CWR:VOL1#3[94], CWR:VOL2#3[256], CWR:VOL3#2[105], CWR:VOL4#1[78], CWR:VOL4#4[129], CWTI:APR/92[30], CWTI:JUL/94[18], CWTI:AUG/95[18]

GENERAL LISTINGS, continued: *Jackson,* B&G:JUN/92[8]487, B&G:AUG/95[8]604, *Johnston's surrender,* CWTI:AUG/90[26]166, CWTI:AUG/90[42]167, *letters to the editor,* CWTI:MAR/93[8]306, *Manassas,* ACW:JAN/95[46]507, CWTI:MAR/91[12]198, CWTI:AUG/91[46]218, CWTI:APR/92[35]257, *Mexican War,* MH:APR/93[34]165, MH:APR/93[39]166, *North Carolina Campaign,* ACW:NOV/93[12]440, *order of battle,* B&G:AUG/95[8]604, B&G:DEC/95[9]615, *Peninsula Campaign,* ACW:JAN/94[8]447, ACW:JUL/95[34]536, CWM:JUN/95[76]598, *post-war,* ACW:JUL/95[26]535, *Shenandoah Valley,* ACW:NOV/94[18]495, *surrender of;* CWTI:APR/90[20]151, *Thomas J. Jackson,* AHI:JUN/67[31]110, *Vicksburg,* ACW:NOV/91[22]331, AHI:DEC/77[13]176, CWTI:FEB/90[38]145, CWTI:MAY/91[24]208, *William T. Sherman,* AHI:JAN/67[4]106, *Wilmington/Fort Fisher,* B&G:DEC/94[10]585, *Winfield Scott,* AHI:FEB/76[14]165, AHI:JUL/81[20]221

PHOTOS: *photo of headquarters flag;* CWTI:SUMMER/89[20]121, *photos;* AHI:MAY/71[3]133A, AHI:NOV/73[18]151, B&G:AUG/95[8]604, B&G:DEC/95[9]615, CWM:JAN/91[28]327, CWM:JUN/95[24]582, CWR:VOL2#1[36]132, CWTI:SUMMER/89[13]120, CWTI:AUG/91[46]218, CWTI:JUL/92[29]272, CWTI:NOV/92[41]291, CWTI:JAN/95[20]422

ADDITIONAL LISTINGS, ACW: ACW:MAR/91[30]295, ACW:MAR/91[47]297, ACW:MAY/91[23]303, ACW:SEP/91[46]324, ACW:NOV/91[6]327, ACW:NOV/91[8]328, ACW:NOV/91[41]334, ACW:JAN/92[22]341, ACW:MAR/92[10]349, ACW:MAY/92[39]362, ACW:SEP/92[38]379, ACW:SEP/92[47]380, ACW:NOV/92[10]384, ACW:JAN/93[18]394, ACW:JAN/93[43]397, ACW:MAY/93[38]416, ACW:JUL/93[66]427, ACW:NOV/93[6]437, ACW:NOV/93[42]443, ACW:MAR/94[42]461, ACW:JUL/94[66]481, ACW:SEP/94[6]482, ACW:SEP/94[10]484, ACW:NOV/94[50]498, ACW:JAN/95[20]504, ACW:MAR/95[12]513, ACW:MAR/95[50]518, ACW:SEP/95[38]546, ACW:SEP/95[48]547, ACW:SEP/95[74]550, ACW:NOV/95[10]553

ADDITIONAL LISTINGS, AHI: AHI:NOV/73[18]151, AHI:OCT/95[24]326

ADDITIONAL LISTINGS, B&G: B&G:FEB/91[8]439, B&G:DEC/92[20]504, B&G:FEB/93[48]515, B&G:DEC/93[12]545, B&G:JUN/94[22]569, B&G:FEB/95[8]590B, B&G:FEB/95[8]590C

ADDITIONAL LISTINGS, CWM: CWM:MAR/91[28]336, CWM:MAY/91[26]349, CWM:JUL/92[16]428, CWM:JUL/92[40]432, CWM:JAN/93[29]459, CWM:MAR/93[32]468, CWM:APR/94[8]502, CWM:JUN/94[23]510, CWM:JUN/94[43]517, CWM:AUG/94[27]526, CWM:AUG/94[52]530, CWM:OCT/94[26]536, CWM:OCT/94[48]542, CWM:APR/95[16]571, CWM:AUG/95[26]604, CWM:AUG/95[30]606, CWM:AUG/95[38]609, CWM:OCT/95[22]614, CWM:OCT/95[40]619

JOHNSTON, MRS. JOSEPH E., B&G:JUN/94[22]569

JOHNSTON, ROBERT A., *Private, 19th Massachusetts
Infantry;* B&G:AUG/93[18]530

JOHNSTON, ROBERT D., *General, CSA;*
ACW:MAY/91[38]305, B&G:APR/95[8]595, B&G:JUN/95[8]600

JOHNSTON, SAMUEL R., *Captain, CSA;* GETTY:5[4]156,
GETTY:6[62]175, MH:AUG/94[46]178

JOHNSTON, WILLIAM, *Captain, 10th Georgia Infantry;*
ACW:JUL/95[10]533

JOHNSTON, WILLIAM, *Private, 3rd Vermont Infantry;*
ACW:NOV/92[8]383

JOHNSTON, WILLIAM H., *Captain, 23rd North Carolina
Infantry;* GETTY:5[13]157

JOHNSTON, WILLIAM P., *Colonel, CSA;*
ACW:MAY/92[14]358, CWTI:AUG/90[50]168,
CWTI:JUL/93[20]325

JOHNSTONE, ROBERT, *Colonel, 5th New York Infantry;*
CWTI:DEC/91[22]237

JOINER, A., *Sergeant, 13th Virginia Infantry;*
B&G:APR/93[24]520

JOINT COMMITTEE ON RECONSTRUCTION;
AHI:JAN/82[16]224

**JOINT CONGRESSIONAL COMMITTEE ON THE
CONDUCT OF THE WAR:**
GENERAL LISTINGS: *Fort Pillow,* AHI:APR/74[4]154, *heneral
history,* AHI:MAY/71[3]133A, *Gettysburg,* GETTY:10[112]228,
GETTY:12[85]248, *in book review,* ACW:NOV/91[54],
CWM:DEC/94[7], CWNEWS:JAN/91[4]
ADDITIONAL LISTINGS: ACW:JUL/91[35]314, ACW:JUL/93[16]422,
ACW:MAR/95[8]512, B&G:APR/91[8]445,
CWM:JUL/91[27]365, CWM:APR/94[32]506,
CWM:APR/95[32]575, CWM:JUN/95[17]581,
CWR:VOL3#1[31]150, CWR:VOL3#1[78]152,
CWR:VOL4#2[26]166, CWTI:MAY/89[14]114,
CWTI:MAY/89[21]115, CWTI:SEP/91[31]229,
CWTI:SEP/93[18]334, CWTI:NOV/93[65]351,
CWTI:OCT/95[32]468, GETTY:6[59]174

JONAS, CHARLES H., *Corporal, 12th Arkansas Infantry;*
CWM:SEP/93[8]493

JONAS, EDWARD, *Lieutenant Colonel, 50th Illinois Infantry;*
CWM:SEP/93[8]493

JONES RIFLES (PENNSYLVANIA) GUARDS, 53rd
Pennsylvania Infantry; GETTY:11[80]235

JONES, A.J., *Private, 24th Wisconsin Infantry;*
ACW:MAR/92[14]350

JONES, A. STOKES, *Surgeon, 72nd Pennsylvania Infantry;*
GETTY:10[53]225

JONES, ARCHER F., *Corporal, 53rd Pennsylvania Infantry;*
GETTY:11[80]235

JONES, BRYAN, *Private, 5th North Carolina Infantry;*
B&G:DEC/94[36]588

JONES, BUSHROD, *Colonel, CSA;* CWTI:SUMMER/89[40]123

JONES, CADWALLADER, *Captain, 12th South Carolina
Infantry;* GETTY:6[7]169, GETTY:13[7]253

JONES, CATESBY ap R., *Lieutenant, CSN;*
ACW:JUL/94[35]478, AHI:OCT/75[30]162,
AHI:NOV/75[38]163, CWTI:MAR/91[42]202

JONES, CHARLES C., *Reverend:*
BOOK REVIEW: *THE CHILDREN OF PRIDE: A TRUE STORY OF
GEORGIA AND THE CIVIL WAR*
ADDITIONAL LISTING: CWNEWS:NOV/92[4]

JONES, CLARRISA F., *civilian;* GETTY:10[53]225

JONES, DAVID. R., *General, CSA:*
ARTICLE: "THE BATTLE AT THOROUGHFARE GAP,"
CWM:AUG/95[38]609
GENERAL LISTINGS: *in book review,* ACW:JAN/95[62],
CWNEWS:SEP/94[33], CWR:VOL4#2[136], *Manassas, Second,*
B&G:AUG/92[11]493, *Mexican War,* MH:APR/93[39]166,
Peninsula Campaign, CWM:JUN/95[63]594
ADDITIONAL LISTINGS: ACW:JUL/91[18]312, CWR:VOL2#2[95]135,
CWR:VOL3#2[1]153, CWTI:NOV/93[55]350,
CWTI:MAR/95[60]439, GETTY:13[75]259

JONES, E.P., *Colonel, CSA;* CWTI:JUL/93[20]325

JONES, EDWARD F., *Colonel, 6th Massachusetts Infantry;*
ACW:NOV/95[30]555

JONES, EDWARD S., *Lieutenant Colonel, 3rd Pennsylvania
Cavalry;* GETTY:13[89]260

JONES, EGBERT J., *Colonel, 4th Alabama Infantry;*
ACW:NOV/94[18]495

JONES, ELISHA, *Corporal, 29th Pennsylvania Infantry;*
CWR:VOL3#2[70]155

JONES, FLORA M.; AHI:DEC/73[10]152

JONES, FRANCES, *Doctor;* B&G:AUG/92[40]495,
CWTI:JAN/93[10]297

JONES, FRANK, *Major, 2nd Virginia Cavalry;* CWM:APR/95[8]

JONES, HILARY P., *Lieutenant Colonel, CSA:*
GENERAL LISTINGS: *Five Forks,* B&G:APR/92[8]481, *Gettysburg,*
GETTY:4[49]147, GETTY:4[65]148, GETTY:9[17]210, *in order
of battle,* B&G:APR/92[8]481
ADDITIONAL LISTING: B&G:FEB/95[8]590C

JONES, J.L., *Colonel, CSA;* B&G:OCT/94[11]580

JONES, J.P., *Colonel, CSA;* CWM:NOV/91[50]394

JONES, J. WILLIAM, *Chaplain, CSA;* BOOK REVIEW:
*PERSONAL REMINISCENCES OF GENERAL ROBERT E.
LEE,* CWNEWS:NOV/91[4]

JONES, JAMES H., *Corporal, USMC;* CWTI:APR/92[14]254

JONES, JEFFERSON F., *Colonel, USA;* ACW:MAR/91[62]298

JONES, JOHN, *Colonel, CSA;* GETTY:13[75]259

JONES, JOHN B.,
ARTICLE: "HUMBLE BUT OBSERVANT WAR DEPARTMENT
   CLERK J.B. JONES LEFT BEHIND AN INVALUABLE
   ACCOUNT OF WARTIME RICHMOND," ACW:JAN/93[18]394
BOOK REVIEW: *A REBEL WAR CLERK'S DIARY*
ADDITIONAL LISTINGS: ACW:JAN/91[10]283, ACW:SEP/92[38]379,
   ACW:NOV/93[42]443, CWM:SEP/93[8]493,
   CWTI:AUG/91[58]220, CWTI:JUL/92[29]272
JONES, JOHN F., *Corporal, 3rd Georgia Infantry;*
   CWTI:SEP/94[26]400
JONES, JOHN J., *Major, 26th North Carolina Infantry;*
   GETTY:5[19]158, GETTY:8[67]204, GETTY:12[61]245
JONES, JOHN M., *General, CSA:*
GENERAL LISTINGS: *Gettysburg,* GETTY:5[103]163,
   GETTY:5[107]164, GETTY:7[83]192, GETTY:9[17]210,
   GETTY:9[81]216, GETTY:10[29]222, GETTY:12[42]244, *order
   of battle,* B&G:APR/95[8]595, *photo;* B&G:APR/95[8]595
ADDITIONAL LISTINGS: ACW:NOV/92[42]388, B&G:APR/95[8]595,
   CWM:MAY/92[20]420, GETTY:13[108]261
JONES, JOHN R., *General, CSA:*
ARTICLE: "THE MYSTERIOUS DISAPPEARANCE OF BRIG.
   GENERAL JOHN R. JONES," GETTY:13[108]261
GENERAL LISTINGS: *Chancellorsville,* MH:JUN/92[50]159, *photo;*
   GETTY:13[108]261
ADDITIONAL LISTINGS: ACW:JUL/92[30]369, ACW:JUL/95[44]537,
   GETTY:13[1]252
JONES, JOHN S., *Captain, CSA;* GETTY:5[107]164
JONES, JOHN T., *Major, CSA;* GETTY:8[67]204
JONES, JOHN W.; CWM:MAY/92[6]417
JONES, JOSEPH, *Major, CSA;* ACW:MAY/95[8]522
JONES, MARCELLUS E., *Lieutenant, 8th Illinois Cavalry;*
   B&G:FEB/95[8]590A, CWNEWS:NOV/95[29],
   GETTY:4[113]153, GETTY:6[13]170, GETTY:11[19]232
JONES, MILTON R., *Lieutenant, 16th Mississippi Infantry;*
   GETTY:8[111]206
JONES, NATHAN L., *Sergeant, 1st Florida Special Battalion;*
   CWR:VOL3#1[65]151
JONES, O.G., *Corporal, CSA;* CWTI:AUG/90[58]169
JONES, PATRICK H., *Colonel, 154th New York Infantry;*
   B&G:OCT/93[36]540
JONES, RICHARD W., *Major, CSA;* CWR:VOL2#3[236]143
JONES, ROBERT B., *Colonel, USA;* CWTI:AUG/90[58]169
JONES, ROBERT T., *Sergeant, 53rd Virginia Infantry;*
   GETTY:13[64]258
JONES, ROGER, *Lieutenant, USA;* ACW:JAN/91[8]282
JONES, S.W., *Captain, 150th Pennsylvania Infantry;*
   GETTY:4[24]145
JONES, SAMUEL, *General, CSA;* ACW:NOV/91[64]336,
   B&G:APR/91[32]447, B&G:AUG/91[11]458,
   B&G:JUN/93[32]525, CWNEWS:JAN/91[4],
   CWR:VOL1#4[42]126, CWR:VOL2#3[194]141,
   CWR:VOL3#1[65]151, CWR:VOL3#4[1]161,
   CWTI:MAR/89[16]101, GETTY:12[111]250
JONES, SAMUEL C., *Lieutenant, 22nd Iowa Infantry;*
   B&G:FEB/94[8]550, CWR:VOL2#1[19]131
JONES, THEODORE, *Colonel, 30th Ohio Infantry;*
   B&G:APR/94[28]559, B&G:DEC/95[9]615,
   CWTI:DEC/94[62]415
JONES, THOMAS G., *Private, CSA;* CWTI:MAR/95[33]435
JONES, THOMAS M., *Colonel, CSA;* CWR:VOL4#3[50]171
JONES, TOM M., *Private, 51st Ohio Infantry;*
   B&G:JUN/95[36]603A

JONES, W.H., *Private, 3rd Georgia Infantry;*
   CWTI:SEP/94[26]400
JONES, WALTER, *Private, 26th North Carolina Infantry;*
   GETTY:5[19]158
JONES, WELLS S., *Colonel, USA;* B&G:DEC/95[9]615,
   CWTI:DEC/94[62]415
JONES, WILLIAM, *Lieutenant Colonel, 40th Ohio Infantry;*
   CWTI:SEP/92[31]281
JONES, WILLIAM, *Private, 19th Maine Infantry;*
   B&G:AUG/93[18]530
JONES, WILLIAM E., *General, CSA:*
ARTICLE: "DETAILS OF THE BATTLE AT PIEDMONT,"
   CWM:JUN/94[27]513
BOOK REVIEW: *GRUMBLE: THE W.E. JONES BRIGADE 1863-64*
GENERAL LISTINGS: *Brandy Station,* GETTY:11[19]232, *general
   history,* AHI:MAY/71[3]133A, *Gettysburg,* GETTY:5[103]163,
   GETTY:9[5N]209, *in book review,* CWM:FEB/95[7],
   CWNEWS:NOV/95[29], *letters to the editor,*
   B&G:OCT/94[6]579, *Saltville,* B&G:AUG/91[11]458
ADDITIONAL LISTINGS: ACW:NOV/91[30]332, ACW:JAN/92[47]344,
   ACW:JUL/92[41]370, B&G:OCT/93[12]537,
   B&G:AUG/94[10]574, CWTI:JUN/90[32]159,
   CWTI:MAY/92[48]267
JONES, WILLIS F., *Major, CSA;* ACW:JUL/94[42]479
JONESBORO, GEORGIA, BATTLE OF; ACW:JUL/91[12]310,
   ACW:NOV/95[74]560, AHI:MAY/71[3]133A,
   CWM:JAN/91[12]326, CWR:VOL1#1[73]108,
   CWR:VOL1#4[64]127, CWTI:SUMMER/89[50]124
JORDAN, THOMAS, *General, CSA;* B&G:JUN/92[32]488,
   CWM:MAR/92[16]411, CWTI:JUL/92[29]272
JORDAN, THOMAS J., *Colonel, 9th Pennsylvania Cavalry;*
   B&G:DEC/95[9]615, MH:JUN/91[20]152
JORDAY, WILLIAM H., *Corporal, 9th U.S. Infantry;*
   ACW:MAR/92[62]355
JOSKINS, JOE, *Private, 5th New York Infantry;*
   CWR:VOL1#2[29]112
JOSLIN, GEORGE C., *Lieutenant Colonel, 15th Massachusetts
   Infantry;* CWM:APR/95[42]577
JOUETT, JAMES E., *Commander, USN;* MH:FEB/92[8]156
JUDAH, HENRY M., *General, USA;* CWM:MAR/93[16]466,
   CWTI:NOV/92[41]291, CWTI:MAR/95[40]436
JUDD, WILLARD B., *Corporal, 97th New York Infantry;*
   GETTY:8[95]205, GETTY:10[7]221, GETTY:13[33]255
JUDGE, FRANK, *Sergeant, 79th New York Infantry;*
   ACW:MAY/91[23]303
JUDKINS, WILLIAM A., *Lieutenant, USA;* B&G:OCT/94[11]580
JUDSON, AMOS M., *Captain, 83rd Pennsylvania Infantry;*
   GETTY:7[41]189
JUDSON, SHELDON, *Private, 2nd Wisconsin Infantry;*
   B&G:AUG/92[11]493
JUMP, ABRAHAM L., *17th Illinois Cavalry;*
   B&G:DEC/93[30]546
JUNKIN, GEORGE, *Lieutenant, CSA;* CWM:APR/95[29]574

K

KABLETOWN, VIRGINIA, SKIRMISH AT;
ACW:JUL/94[26]477
KAMMERLING, GUSTAVE, *Lieutenant Colonel, 9th Ohio Infantry;* B&G:FEB/93[12]511
KANAWAH VALLEY CAMPAIGN; BOOK REVIEW: *WAR DIARIES: THE 1861 KANAWHA VALLEY CAMPAIGN*
KANE, GEORGE P., *Baltimore Police Chief;*
CWTI:OCT/95[24]466, ACW:JAN/92[30]342,
ACW:NOV/95[30]555
KANE, THOMAS L., *General, USA;* GETTY:7[83]192,
GETTY:9[53]214, GETTY:9[81]216, GETTY:10[120]229,
photos; ACW:NOV/92[42]388, CWR:VOL1#3[20]119,
CWR:VOL1#3[28]120, GETTY:9[53]214

KANSAS TROOPS:

1st Cavalry; ACW:NOV/94[42]497
1st Infantry; ACW:NOV/93[26]441
1st Infantry, (Colored); ACW:JAN/91[30]286,
B&G:FEB/92[6]473, B&G:FEB/94[38]553,
CWM:JAN/92[6]398, CWR:VOL1#2[44]114
2nd Cavalry; ACW:NOV/93[26]441, ACW:NOV/94[42]497,
CWR:VOL1#2[44]114, CWTI:SEP/90[52]179
2nd Infantry; CWTI:FEB/92[29]248, CWTI:JAN/94[29]360
2nd Militia; B&G:JUN/91[10]452
3rd Indian Home Guard Regiment; BOOK REVIEW: *THE CONFEDERATE CHEROKEES: JOHN DREW'S REGIMENT OF MOUNTED RIFLES*
4th Infantry; ARTICLE: "KANSAS MINUTEMEN: MISSOURI'S SAVIORS," ACW:NOV/94[42]497
4th Militia; ACW:NOV/94[42]497
5th Cavalry; ACW:MAY/93[22]414, ACW:MAR/95[34]516,
CWR:VOL1#2[44]114
6th Cavalry; CWM:SEP/92[38]443, CWR:VOL1#2[44]114
7th Cavalry:
BOOK REVIEW: *JENNISON'S JAYHAWKERS: A CIVIL WAR CAVLRY REGIMENT AND ITS COMMANDER*
ADDITIONAL LISTINGS: ACW:SEP/92[23]377, ACW:JAN/93[26]395,
ACW:NOV/94[42]497, ACW:SEP/95[48]547
8th Infantry: B&G:AUG/92[40]495
9th Cavalry: CWM:SEP/92[38]443, CWTI:SEP/90[52]179
10th Infantry: B&G:OCT/95[36]614, CWTI:JAN/93[20]298
14th Cavalry: CWR:VOL1#2[44]114
15th Cavalry: B&G:JUN/91[10]452
Fort Leavenworth; CWTI:SEP/90[52]179
Fort Scott; CWTI:SEP/90[52]179
Kansas Brigade; ACW:MAY/94[26]468
South Kansas-Texas Mounted Regiment;
CWTI:FEB/92[29]248

KANSAS, STATE OF:

ARTICLES: "BLEEDING KANSAS," AHI:JUL/75[4]160, "THE MEANEST BUSHWHACKER," B&G:JUN/91[32]454
BOOK REVIEWS:
A FRONTIER STATE AT WAR: KANSAS 1861-1865
KANSAS-MISSOURI CIVIL WAR; ARTICLE: "BITTER BUSHWHACKERS AND JAYHAWKERS,"
ACW:JAN/93[26]395

KANSAS-NEBRASKA ACT:
ARTICLE: "BLEEDING KANSAS," AHI:JUL/75[4]160
GENERAL LISTINGS: *impeachment of Andrew Johnson,*
AHI:DEC/68[28]118, *in book review,* ACW:SEP/91[54],
ACW:JUL/95[58], CWNEWS:AUG/91[4], CWNEWS:SEP/92[4],
CWNEWS:JUN/95[33], *James Buchanan,*
AHI:MAY/66[12]101, *Stephen A. Douglas,* AHI:OCT/70[23]129
ADDITIONAL LISTINGS: ACW:JUL/91[43]315, ACW:JAN/93[26]395,
ACW:MAR/93[6]400, ACW:MAR/93[18]403,
ACW:MAY/93[47]417, ACW:MAY/94[43]470,
ACW:NOV/94[8]493, ACW:NOV/94[42]497,
AHI:JUN/73[4]149, AHI:MAY/81[35]218, AHI:DEC/81[18]223,
CWTI:SEPT/89[40]130, CWTI:DEC/90[50]183,
CWTI:FEB/91[36]193, CWTI:AUG/91[36]217,
CWTI:JAN/94[29]360, CWTI:DEC/95[40]479
KAPP, FRIEDRICH, *editor;* CWTI:JUN/95[32]446
KAPPESSER, PETER, *Private, 149th New York Infantry;*
CWTI:SEPT/89[30]129
KARNS, MARK, *Captain, USA;* B&G:AUG/92[11]493
KARNS, N.H., *Sergeant, 18th Ohio Infantry;*
CWTI:AUG/90[50]168
KARPELES, LEOPOLD, *Lieutenant, Colonel, 57th Massachusetts Infantry;* ACW:SEP/95[70]549,
B&G:APR/93[12]518, CWM:SEP/93[8]493
KAUFFMAN, SCOTT W., *Private, USA;* GETTY:10[42]224
KAUFMAN, SAMUEL A., *Private, 53rd Pennsylvania Infantry;*
GETTY:11[80]235
KAUFMANN, SIGISMUND, *editor;* CWTI:JUN/95[32]446
KAUTZ, AUGUST V., *General, USA;* ACW:JAN/92[16]340,
ACW:MAY/92[30]361, ACW:JUL/94[42]479,
ACW:MAR/95[12]513, CWM:MAR/91[74],
CWM:MAY/92[34]422
KAVANAUGH, F.E., *Major, CSA;* ACW:JUL/92[46]371
KEAN, ROBERT G.H., *Chief, Confederate Bureau of War:*
BOOK REVIEWS: *INSIDE THE CONFEDERATE GOVERNMENT: THE DIARY OF ROBERT GARLICK HILL KEAN*
ADDITIONAL LISTINGS: CWTI:APR/89[14]107, GETTY:11[6]231
KEARNS, J.V., *Private, 13th U.S. Regulars;* CWR:VOL2#1[1]130
KEARNY, PHILIP, *Major, USA;* GETTY:12[7]241
KEARNY, PHILIP J., *General, USA:*
ARTICLES: "HOTHEADED, FLAMBOYANT 'FIGHTING PHIL' KEARNY WAS ONE OF THE UNION'S MOST CELEBRATED DAREDEVILS," ACW:NOV/92[18]385,
"STONEWALL'S SURPRISE AT OX HILL,"
ACW:JAN/95[54]508
GENERAL LISTINGS: *in book review,* CWNEWS:SEP/93[5],
CWNEWS:JUN/94[5], CWR:VOL1#4[77], CWR:VOL3#4[68],
general history, AHI:MAY/71[3]133A, *Manassas, Second,*
AHI:DEC/66[30]105, B&G:AUG/92[11]493, *Mexican War,*
MH:APR/93[39]166, *Oak Grove,* CWM:JUN/95[55]591,
Peninsula Campaign, CWM:JUN/95[34]584, *Williamsburg,*
ACW:MAR/91[47]297, *sketch;* ACW:JAN/95[54]508
ADDITIONAL LISTINGS: ACW:JUL/91[18]312, ACW:JUL/93[16]422,
ACW:JAN/95[54]508, ACW:SEP/95[38]546,
AHI:APR/85[18]250, CWR:VOL1#3[52]122,
CWTI:MAY/89[36]118, CWTI:MAY/92[38]265,
CWTI:JUL/93[14]324, CWTI:NOV/93[55]350
KEARNY, STEPHEN WATTS; AHI:AUG/66[32]104,
AHI:SEP/87[21]262
KEATING, MARY DE CHANTAL; B&G:OCT/93[31]539

KECKLEY, ELIZABETH:
ARTICLE: "ELIZABETH KECKLEY MADE THE LONG
JOURNEY FROM SLAVERY TO THE WHITE HOUSE, AS
MARY LINCOLN'S DRESSMAKER," ACW:JUL/92[8]365A
ADDITIONAL LISTING: ACW:JAN/94[47]452
KEEFE, PAT; *civilian;* CWM:JAN/92[12]400
KEEFER, BERNADINE; B&G:OCT/93[31]539
KEELE, JOSEPH, *Sergeant Major, USA;* B&G:APR/93[12]518
KEELER, ——, *Lieutenant, 95th Illinois Infantry;*
CWM:JAN/91[11]325
KEELER, WILLIAM F., *Lieutenant, USN;* AHI:NOV/75[38]163,
CWM:JUN/95[39]586, *photos,* AHI:NOV/75[38]163,
CWM:JUL/93[15]484
KEENE, HENRY T., *Master, USN;* CWTI:JUL/94[30]392
KEENE, LAURA:
ARTICLE: "LAURA KEENE, A BIOGRAPHY,"
AHI:MAY/91[18]293C
ADDITIONAL LISTINGS: AHI:FEB/86[12]257, AHI:FEB/86[20]258,
photo; AHI:FEB/86[20]258
KEENEN, JAMES, *Private, 2nd Georgia Infantry;*
AHI:OCT/75[30]162
KEENEY, JOHN, *Corporal, 5th New York Infantry;*
CWR:VOL1#2[7]111, CWTI:MAY/94[31]382
KEESY, WILLIAM A., *Private, 55th Ohio Infantry:* BOOK REVIEW:
WAR AS VIEWED FROM THE RANKS
KEHOE, JACK, *civilian;* ACW:MAR/92[22]351
KEIFER, J. WARREN, *Colonel, 3rd Ohio Infantry;*
ACW:MAR/91[14]293, ACW:MAY/91[38]305,
B&G:AUG/93[10]529
KEIGWIN, JAMES, *Colonel, 49th Indiana Infantry;*
B&G:FEB/94[8]550, B&G:AUG/95[8]604
KEIL, F.W., *Private, 35th Ohio Infantry;* B&G:APR/94[6]557
KEILEY, ANTHONY, *Private, CSA;* ACW:MAR/91[25]294
KEISER, HENRY, *Private, 96th Pennsylvania Infantry;*
CWR:VOL3#3[1]157
KEITH, JAMES A., *Lieutenant Colonel, 64th North Carolina
Infantry;* B&G:FEB/91[20]440
KEITH, JOHN A., *Colonel, 1st Indiana Heavy Artillery;*
ACW:JAN/94[30]450
KEITT, LAWRENCE M., *Colonel, 20th South Carolina
Infantry;* ACW:SEP/92[10]375, ACW:MAR/93[18]403,
B&G:APR/94[10]558, CWM:AUG/95[45],
CWNEWS:FEB/94[5], CWR:VOL3#4[1]161
KELL, JOHN M., *Lieutenant, CSN:*
ARTICLE: "CRUISE AND COMBATS OF THE *ALABAMA*,"
AHI:OCT/88[38]275
GENERAL LISTINGS: *in book review,* CWNEWS:AUG/92[4], *letters to
the editor,* CWTI:MAY/91[8]205, *photos;* AHI:DEC/82[38]231,
AHI:JAN/83[10]232, AHI:OCT/88[38]275
ADDITIONAL LISTINGS: ACW:SEP/95[30]545, AHI:DEC/82[38]231,
AHI:JAN/83[10]232
KELLAR, ANDREW J., *Colonel CSA;* B&G:DEC/93[12]545
KELLEHER, JOHN, *Captain, 8th New Hampshire Infantry;*
CWR:VOL3#1[1]149
KELLER, ANDREW J., *Colonel, CSA;* B&G:DEC/93[12]545
KELLERMAN, WILLIAM H., *Private, 148th Pennsylvania
Infantry;* CWR:VOL2#2[141]137
KELLEY, ABBY; BOOK REVIEW: *AHEAD OF HER TIME: ABBY
KELLEY AND THE POLITICS OF ANTISLAVERY*
KELLEY, BANJAMIN F., *General, USA:*
ARTICLE: "CONFEDERATES' BRILLIANT EXPLOIT,"
ACW:SEP/91[41]323

GENERAL LISTINGS: *West Virginia campaign,* B&G:AUG/93[10]529,
photos, ACW:SEP/91[41]323, B&G:AUG/93[10]529,
B&G:AUG/94[10]574, B&G:OCT/94[28]581
ADDITIONAL LISTINGS: ACW:JAN/92[8]338, ACW:JAN/92[47]344,
B&G:AUG/94[10]574, B&G:OCT/94[28]581,
CWM:APR/94[24]505, CWTI:MAR/89[16]101,
CWTI:FEB/91[12]189, CWTI:DEC/94[73]416
KELLEY, DAVID C., *Lieutenant, Colonel, CSA;*
ACW:MAR/93[51]407, B&G:DEC/93[12]545,
B&G:DEC/93[52]548, CWTI:SEP/93[59]341
KELLEY, TAPPAN W., *Lieutenant, USA;* B&G:AUG/94[10]574
KELLEY, WILLIAM, *Private, 24th Michigan Infantry;*
GETTY:5[19]158
KELLOG, FRANK, *Private, 24th Michigan Infantry,*
GETTY:9[33]211, GETTY:11[57]233
KELLOGG, ELISHA S., *Colonel, 2nd Connecticut Heavy
Artillery;* B&G:APR/94[10]558
KELLOGG, HENRY C., *General, CSA;* B&G:DEC/95[9]615
KELLOGG, JOHN A., *Colonel, USA;* B&G:APR/92[8]481
KELLOGG, JOSIAH H., *Colonel, 17th Pennsylvania Cavalry;*
GETTY:11[19]232
KELLOGG, ROBERT, *Sergeant, 16th Connecticut Infantry;*
B&G:AUG/93[18]530
KELLY'S FORD, VIRGINIA, BATTLE OF:
ARTICLES: "BEAUTY, SALLIE AND FATE," ACW:NOV/91[35]333,
"MELEE ON SAINT PATRICK'S DAY," ACW:NOV/91[30]332
ADDITIONAL LISTINGS: CWTI:APR/92[35]257, CWTI:JAN/94[42]363
KELLY, ALEXANDER, *Sergeant, 5th USCT;*
CWM:AUG/94[4]520, CWM:AUG/94[30]527
KELLY, D.C., *Colonel, CSA;* B&G:JUN/92[32]488
KELLY, DANIEL S., *Civilian;* GETTY:11[71]234
KELLY, GEORGE W., *Private, 26th North Carolina Infantry;*
GETTY:5[19]158
KELLY, HENRY B., *Colonel, 8th Louisiana Infantry;*
CWTI:MAR/94[48]374
KELLY, I.F., *Captain, 6th Wisconsin Infantry;* GETTY:4[24]145
KELLY, J.H., *Lieutenant Colonel, 114th Ohio Infantry;*
B&G:FEB/94[8]550
KELLY, JAMES E., *Private, 56th Pennsylvania Infantry;*
ACW:SEP/95[38]546
KELLY, JOHN, *Private, USA;* MH:FEB/93[42]164
KELLY, JOHN, *Private, 9th Massachusetts Artillery;*
GETTY:5[47]160
KELLY, JOHN H., *General, CSA;* CWTI:DEC/90[56]184
KELLY, LAWRENCE, *Private, 1st Massachusetts Infantry;*
GETTY:6[7]169
KELLY, PATICK, *Colonel, 88th New York Infantry:*
GENERAL LISTINGS: *Gettysburg,* GETTY:5[35]159,
GETTY:6[59]174, GETTY:8[53]203, GETTY:11[80]235
ADDITIONAL LISTINGS: ACW:MAY/94[12]466, ACW:SEP/95[54]548,
CWM:MAR/91[17]335, CWR:VOL4#4[47]179,
CWTI:DEC/90[58]185
KELLY, PETER, *Private, USA;* CWM:MAR/91[14]334
KELLY, ROBERT P., *civilian;* ARTICLE: "PERSONALITY,"
ACW:JAN/91[10]283
KELLY, SAMUEL C., *Captain, 30th Alabama Infantry;*
B&G:FEB/94[8]550
KELLY, THOMAS F., *Chaplain, 90th Illinois Infantry;*
CWM:MAR/91[50]340
KELLY, THOMAS J., *Chaplain, 9th Illinois Infantry;*
B&G:OCT/93[31]539

KELLY, TIMOTHY W., *Captain, 164th New York Infantry;*
ARTICLE: "'IF THIS CONTINUES THE ARMY OF THE
POTOMAC WILL BE ANNIHILLATED',"
CWM:OCT/95[40]619
ADDITIONAL LISTINGS: CWM:OCT/95[4]612, CWM:OCT/95[40]619
KELLY, WILLIAM, *Private, 4th U.S. Artillery;*
GETTY:11[57]233
KELSEY, CHARLES T., *Surgeon, USA;* GETTY:10[53]225
KELSEY, ROBERT, *Corporal, 13th Pennsylvania Reserves;*
CWR:VOL1#3[46]121
KELSO, JOHN R., *scout;* ACW:MAR/94[8]456
KELZLE, HENRY, *Private, 37th Illinois Infantry;*
CWR:VOL1#1[42]105
KEMP, DANIEL F., *seaman, USN,* ARTICLE: "NAVY LIFE ON
THE MISSISSIPPI RIVER," CWTI:MAY/94[16]380
KEMP, WILLIAM H., *Lieutenant, 2nd Maryland Cavalry
(Confederate);* B&G:AUG/94[10]574
KEMPER, JOHN H., *Major, 10th New York Cavalry;*
GETTY:4[65]148
KEMPER, JAMES L., *General, CSA:*
BOOK REVIEWS: *THE CONFEDERACY'S FORGOTTEN SON:
MAJOR GENERAL JAMES LAWSON KEMPER C.S.A.*
GENERAL LISTINGS: *Gettysburg,* GETTY:4[89]150,
GETTY:5[79]161, GETTY:5[103]163, GETTY:5[107]164,
GETTY:8[67]204, GETTY:10[112]228, GETTY:12[61]245,
MH:DEC/91[54]155, *in book review,* CWNEWS:SEP/95[33], *in
list,* CWTI:JUL/93[34]327, *Manassas, Second,*
B&G:AUG/92[11]493
ADDITIONAL LISTINGS: ACW:JUL/91[18]312, B&G:APR/93[12]518,
B&G:APR/94[34]561, CWM:AUG/94[60]531,
CWR:VOL2#4[269]145, CWTI:MAY/89[22]116,
CWTI:SEPT/89[46]132, CWTI:MAR/93[40]312,
CWTI:NOV/93[55]350, CWTI:JUL/94[44]394,
GETTY:13[75]259
KEMPTON, GEORGE, *Lieutenant, 9th Massachusetts Artillery;*
GETTY:5[47]160
KENAN, DANIEL L., *Colonel, CSA;* B&G:DEC/95[9]615
KENAN, JAMES, *Captain, 43rd North Carolina Infantry;*
GETTY:7[114]194
KENAN, LEWIS H., *Captain, 1st Georgia Regulars;*
CWR:VOL2#2[95]135
KENAN, THOMAS S., *Colonel, 43rd North Carolina Infantry:*
ARTICLE: "A GETTYSBURG ENCOUNTER," GETTY:7[114]194
ADDITIONAL LISTINGS: GETTY:7[83]192, GETTY:9[81]216
KENDALL, CHARLES, *Captain, USA;* GETTY:4[101]151
KENDALL, WARREN L., *Private, 20th Maine Infantry;*
GETTY:6[43]173
KENDRICK, HENRY L., B&G:DEC/91[12]469
KENDRUM, PETER, *Private, Terry's Texas Rangers;*
CWM:JUL/92[40]432
KENLY, JOHN R., *Colonel, 1st Maryland Infantry (Union);*
ACW:JUL/92[41]370, ACW:JAN/93[35]396,
ACW:JUL/94[10]475, CWR:VOL1#2[78]
KENNEDY, CHARLES W., *Lieutenant, 156th New York
Infantry;* ARTICLE: "THE RED RIVER CAMPAIGN LETTERS
OF LIEUTENANT CHARLES W. KENNEDY, 156TH NEW
YORK VOLUNTEER INFANTRY," CWR:VOL4#2[104]168
KENNEDY, FELIX, *Private, Terry's Texas Rangers;*
CWM:JUL/92[40]432
KENNEDY, JOHN, *Sergeant, 95th Illinois Infantry;*
CWTI:JAN/93[20]298
KENNEDY, JOHN A., *civilian;* ACW:JAN/92[30]342,
AHI:AUG/77[30]175

KENNEDY, JOHN D., *General, CSA;* B&G:DEC/95[9]615,
GETTY:5[35]159
KENNEDY, JOHN W., *Private, 19th Indiana Infantry,*
GETTY:11[57]233
KENNEDY, ROBERT, *Major, USA;* ACW:SEP/91[41]323
KENNEDY, WILLIAM B., *Private, 1st North Carolina Cavalry;*
ACW:MAR/95[50]518
**KENNESAW MOUNTAIN NATIONAL BATTLEFIELD
PARK:**
ARTICLE: "KENNESAW MOUNTAIN BATTLEFIELD PARK AND
THE ATLANTA CYCLORAMA GIVE VISITORS A GOOD
TASTE OF THE ATLANTA CAMPAIGN,"
ACW:NOV/95[74]560
ADDITIONAL LISTINGS: B&G:DEC/92[40]508, CWM:JAN/91[72]331
KENNESAW MOUNTAIN, GEORGIA, BATTLE OF:
ARTICLE: "KENNESAW MOUNTAIN BATTLEFIELD PARK AND
THE ATLANTA CYCLORAMA GIVE VISITORS A GOOD
TASTE OF THE ATLANTA CAMPAIGN,"
ACW:NOV/95[74]560
BOOK REVIEW: *KENNESAW MOUNTAIN AND THE ATLANTA
CAMPAIGN: A TOUR GUIDE*
GENERAL LISTINGS: *general history,* AHI:MAY/71[3]133A, *in book
review,* ACW:MAR/94[58], CWM:MAR/92[49],
CWR:VOL4#3[1]170, CWTI:MAY/92[18], *letters to the editor,*
CWTI:JUL/93[10]323
ADDITIONAL LISTINGS: ACW:JUL/94[6]473, ACW:SEP/94[10]484,
CWM:JAN/91[12]326, CWM:JAN/91[72]331,
CWM:JUL/92[18]429, CWR:VOL1#3[82]123,
CWR:VOL1#4[64]127, CWR:VOL3#4[24]162,
CWTI:SUMMER/89[13]120, CWTI:FEB/92[10]246,
CWTI:MAR/93[24]309, CWTI:DEC/94[49]413,
CWTI:MAR/95[40]436
KENNICOTT, RANSOM, *Captain, USA;* CWR:VOL1#1[42]105
KENNISON, WILLIAM, *Master, USN;* AHI:OCT/75[30]162
KENNON, BEVERLY, *Captain, CSN;* ACW:MAY/92[16]359,
ACW:SEP/94[74]491, MH:AUG/93[47]169
KENNY, DENNIS, *Captain, 1st Ohio Artillery;*
B&G:FEB/93[12]511
KENT, DOUGLAS, *civilian;* CWTI:JAN/95[48]429
KENT, DUFF, *civilian;* B&G:APR/93[24]520
KENT, J. FORD, *Lieutenant, USA;* B&G:APR/91[8]445
KENT, JACOB; B&G:DEC/91[12]469
KENT, JOSEPH, *civilian;* B&G:AUG/91[11]458
KENT, THOMAS N., *Captain, 48th Georgia Infantry;*
GETTY:12[111]250
KENT, WILLIAM B., *Private, 1st U.S. Sharpshooters;*
B&G:APR/95[8]595

KENTUCKY TROOPS:

1st Brigade; BOOK REVIEW: *HISTORY OF THE FIRST
KENTUCKY BRIGADE*
1st Cavalry, (Confederate); ACW:MAR/93[51]407,
ACW:JAN/94[10]448, B&G:AUG/91[11]458,
B&G:OCT/91[11]466, B&G:OCT/92[10]496,
CWM:OCT/94[48]542, CWR:VOL3#2[1]153
1st Cavalry, (Union); B&G:FEB/93[12]511,
B&G:OCT/94[42]583, B&G:DEC/94[22]586,
CWR:VOL4#1[1]163
1st Infantry, (Confederate); ACW:JUL/92[22]368,
B&G:APR/91[32]447, CWTI:MAR/94[48]374
1st Infantry, (Union); CWM:APR/95[66]579
1st/3rd Mounted Rifles, (Confederate); B&G:AUG/92[40]495

2nd Cavalry, (Confederate); ACW:SEP/95[10]543,
B&G:OCT/94[11]580, CWR:VOL3#3[33]158,
CWTI:DEC/94[79]417, MH:JUN/91[20]152
2nd Cavalry, (Union); CWM:JAN/91[40]330,
CWM:MAR/93[16]466
2nd Infantry, (Confederate); ACW:JUL/91[12]310,
ACW:JUL/92[22]368, B&G:FEB/92[10]474,
B&G:OCT/94[11]580, CWM:JAN/93[29]459,
CWTI:DEC/94[79]417, CWTI:MAR/95[46]437
2nd Infantry, (Union); CWM:APR/95[66]579
2nd Mounted Infantry, (Confederate); B&G:FEB/91[8]439
3rd Cavalry, (Confederate); ACW:SEP/92[23]377
3rd Cavalry, (Union); ACW:MAR/93[51]407
3rd Infantry (Confederate); AHI:MAY/71[3]133A,
CWR:VOL2#1[36]132, CWTI:JUL/94[50]395
3rd Mounted Rifles; ACW:SEP/95[22]544
4th Cavalry, (Confederate); B&G:AUG/91[11]458
4th Infantry, (Confederate); ACW:JUL/91[12]310,
ACW:MAR/93[55]408, ACW:JAN/94[10]448
4th Infantry, (Union); ACW:MAR/93[55]408,
ACW:SEP/93[38]434, B&G:FEB/93[12]511
4th Mounted Infantry, (Confederate); B&G:FEB/91[8]439,
CWTI:SEP/91[23]228
5th Cavalry, (Union); ACW:MAR/94[27]459,
ACW:SEP/95[22]544, B&G:OCT/94[11]580
6th Cavalry, (Confederate); CWTI:MAY/93[38]321
6th Infantry, (Confederate); ACW:JUL/91[12]310
6th Infantry, (Union); AHI:NOV/72[12]142,
AHI:DEC/85[40]255
7th Cavalry, (Confederate); CWR:VOL4#1[1]163
7th Cavalry, (Union); B&G:AUG/94[22]576
7th Infantry, (Union); B&G:FEB/94[8]550
8th Cavalry, (Confederate); MH:JUN/93[82]167
8th Infantry, (Confederate); CWR:VOL2#1[36]132
8th Infantry, (Union); CWR:VOL2#1[36]132,
CWTI:SEPT/89[30]129
9th Cavalry, (Confederate); B&G:AUG/91[11]458,
CWTI:SEP/94[40]403
9th Cavalry, (Union); CWR:VOL4#1[1]163
9th Infantry, (Confederate); AHI:OCT/67[26]112,
CWM:JAN/93[29]459, CWTI:SUMMER/89[20]121,
CWTI:SUMMER/89[50]124
9th Mounted Infantry, (Confederate); B&G:FEB/91[8]439
10th Cavalry, (Confederate); ACW:MAR/93[51]407,
B&G:AUG/91[11]458, CWM:MAR/93[16]466
10th Cavalry, (Union); ACW:SEP/95[22]544,
CWR:VOL4#1[1]163
10th Infantry, (Union); B&G:FEB/93[12]511
10th Mounted Rifles, (Confederate); B&G:AUG/91[11]458
10th Partisan Rangers; ACW:MAR/93[51]407,
B&G:OCT/94[11]580
11th Cavalry, (Confederate); B&G:OCT/94[11]580
11th Cavalry, (Union); B&G:AUG/91[11]458
11th Infantry, (Confederate); B&G:OCT/94[11]580
11th Infantry, (Union); CWTI:MAY/94[50]386
12th Cavalry, (Confederate); CWTI:MAY/92[74]268,
12th Cavalry, (Union); AHI:NOV/85[38]254
12th Infantry, (Union); ACW:SEP/93[38]434,
B&G:FEB/93[12]511, CWTI:MAY/94[50]386
13th Cavalry, (Confederate); B&G:AUG/91[11]458
14th Cavalry, (Confederate); B&G:OCT/94[11]580

14th Cavalry, (Union):
ARTICLE: "THE 14TH KENTUCKY CAVALRY'S 'ORPHAN
BATTALION' FOUGHT TO KEEP THE BLUEGRASS STATE
IN UNION HANDS," ACW:SEP/95[22]544
ADDITIONAL LISTINGS: ACW:SEP/95[22]544, CWM:MAR/93[16]466,
CWR:VOL4#1[1]163
15th Infantry, (Union); CWTI:MAY/93[38]321
17th Infantry, (Union); ACW:MAR/93[55]408
19th Infantry, (Union); B&G:FEB/94[8]550,
CWR:VOL4#2[1]165
20th Infantry, (Union); CWM:MAR/93[16]466
22th Infantry, (Union); B&G:FEB/94[8]550
22th Mounted Infantry, (Union); B&G:AUG/91[11]458
30th Mounted Infantry, (Union); B&G:AUG/91[11]458
35th Mounted Infantry, (Union); B&G:AUG/91[11]458
37th Mounted Infantry, (Union); B&G:AUG/91[11]458
39th Mounted Infantry, (Union); B&G:AUG/91[11]458
40th Mounted Infantry, (Union); B&G:AUG/91[11]458
45th Mounted Infantry, (Union); B&G:AUG/91[11]458,
CWTI:NOV/93[78]354
52nd Infantry, (Union); CWTI:JUL/92[42]274
Cobb's Artillery; B&G:AUG/95[8]604
Graves Cumberland Battery; B&G:FEB/92[10]474
Kentucky Home Guard; B&G:FEB/93[12]511
Kentucky State Guard; ACW:JUL/91[12]310,
ACW:JUL/92[22]368, CWTI:APR/90[56]155,
Orphan Brigade:
ARTICLE: "ORPHAN BRIGADE," ACW:JUL/91[12]310
BOOK REVIEWS: *DIARY OF A CONFEDERATE SOLDIER: JOHN
S. JACKMAN OF THE ORPHAN BRIGADE * THE ORPHAN
BRIGADE*
ADDITIONAL LISTINGS: ACW:MAR/91[54], ACW:JAN/94[10]448,
CWM:FEB/95[28]560, CWTI:SUMMER/89[50]124
KENTUCKY, STATE OF:
ARTICLE: "KENTUCKY NEUTRALITY THREATENED,"
ACW:JUL/92[22]368
BOOK REVIEWS: *WAR IN KENTUCKY: FROM SHILOH TO
PERRYVILLE*
KEOGH, MYLES, *Lieutenant Colonel, USA:*
BOOK REVIEW: *MYLES KEOGH, THE LIFE AND LEGEND OF
AN, 'IRISH DRAGOON' IN THE SEVENTH CAVALRY*
GENERAL LISTINGS: *Gettysburg,* GETTY:11[19]232, *Little Big Horn,*
AHI:JAN/85[30]246
KEPHARDT, JAMES, *Private, 13th U.S. Regulars;*
CWR:VOL2#1[1]130
KERNSTOWN, VIRGINIA, FIRST BATTLE OF:
ARTICLE: "VALOR OF OHIOANS AT THE BATTLE OF
KERNSTOWN," CWM:APR/95[29]574
ADDITIONAL LISTINGS: ACW:NOV/91[41]334, ACW:MAY/92[14]358,
AHI:MAY/71[3]133A, CWTI:MAR/94[29]371
KERNSTOWN, VIRGINIA, SECOND BATTLE OF:
CWM:JAN/93[40]461, CWM:AUG/95[35]607,
MH:OCT/93[76]173, MH:APR/95[46]183
KERR, JAMES, *Lieutenant Colonel, USA;* B&G:OCT/95[8]611F
KERR, JOHN H., *Sergeant, USA;* GETTY:9[48]213
KERR, T.R., *Captain, 14th Pennsylvania Cavalry;*
B&G:AUG/94[10]574
KERR, WILLIAM, *Captain, 72nd Pennsylvania Infantry;*
GETTY:7[97]193
KERSHAW'S BRIGADE; BOOK REVIEW: *HISTORY OF
KERSHAW'S BRIGADE*

KERSHAW, JOSEPH B., *General, CSA:*
ARTICLES: "DETAILS OF CEDAR CREEK," CWM:OCT/94[38]540,
"KERSHAW'S BRIGADE AT GETTYSBURG,"
GETTY:5[35]159
GENERAL LISTINGS: *Cedar Creek,* MH:OCT/93[76]173, *Crampton's Gap,* ACW:JAN/94[39]451, *Fall of Richmond,*
AHI:JAN/74[10]153, *Gettysburg,* GETTY:5[47]160,
GETTY:5[103]163, GETTY:5[117]165, GETTY:8[53]203,
GETTY:9[41]212, GETTY:9[53]214, GETTY:10[120]229,
GETTY:11[80]235, GETTY:11[91]236, *Harpers Ferry,*
GETTY:7[51]190, MH:AUG/95[30]185, *in book review,*
CWM:APR/95[8], CWNEWS:SEP/92[4], CWNEWS:SEP/94[33],
in order of battle, B&G:APR/94[10]558, *Jericho Mill,*
B&G:APR/93[12]518, *order of battle,* B&G:APR/95[8]595,
Overland Campaign, B&G:APR/94[10]558, *Peninsula Campaign,* ACW:MAR/91[47]297, *Savage's Station,*
CWM:JUN/95[65]595, *Wilderness,* B&G:JUN/95[8]600, *photos,*
B&G:APR/94[10]558, CWM:OCT/94[38]540, *sketch;*
CWTI:MAY/94[50]386
ADDITIONAL LISTINGS: ACW:MAY/91[38]305, ACW:JAN/92[22]341,
ACW:JAN/93[43]397, ACW:SEP/93[62]436,
ACW:MAR/94[50]462, ACW:MAY/94[12]466,
ACW:MAY/95[38]526, AHI:JAN/73[28]147,
AHI:SEP/87[40]263, CWM:JAN/93[40]461,
CWM:JUN/94[26]512, CWM:OCT/94[4]532,
CWR:VOL1#4[7]125, CWR:VOL1#4[74]128,
CWR:VOL2#2[95]135, CWR:VOL3#4[1]161,
CWR:VOL4#4[28]178, CWTI:AUG/90[26]166,
CWTI:SEP/92[31]281, CWTI:MAR/93[40]312,
CWTI:MAY/94[50]386
KERSHNER, JONATHAN, *Lieutenant, 3rd Illinois Cavalry;*
B&G:AUG/95[8]604
KERWOOD, ASBURY L., *Private, 57th Indiana Infantry;*
ACW:SEP/93[46]435
KESTER, JOHN W., *Colonel, 1st New Jersey Cavalry;*
ACW:NOV/92[26]386
KESTERSON, WILLIAM, *Private, 52nd Virginia Infantry;*
CWTI:MAR/94[29]371
KETCHAM, EDWARD H., *Private, 120th New York Infantry;*
B&G:FEB/93[36]
KETCHAM, HIRAM, *Corporal, 124th New York Infantry;*
CWM:DEC/94[40]550
KETCHAM, J.L., *70th Indiana Infantry;*
CWTI:SUMMER/89[32]122
KETCHAM, JOHN H., *Colonel, 150th New York Infantry;*
GETTY:12[42]244
KETCHAM, JOHN T., *Private, 4th New York Cavalry;*
B&G:FEB/93[36]
KETZLE, HENRY, *Sergeant, 37th Illinois Infantry;*
CWR:VOL1#1[42]105
KEY WEST NAVAL STATION; ACW:NOV/94[58]499
KEY WEST, FLORIDA; ARTICLE: "THE NORTH'S
SOUTHERNMOST OUTPOST," ACW:NOV/94[58]499
KEY, JOHN F., *Union Veteran;* GETTY:5[123]166
KEY, PHILIP BARTON; AHI:SEP/82[40]229
KEYES, ERASMUS D., *General, USA:*
GENERAL LISTINGS: *The "Blackberry" Raid,* GETTY:11[6]231,
Peninsula Campaign, CWM:JUN/95[29]583, *Seven Pines,*
CWM:JUN/95[47]588, *photo;* GETTY:11[6]231
ADDITIONAL LISTINGS: ACW:JAN/94[8]447, CWR:VOL3#1[31]150,
CWR:VOL3#2[1]153
KEYSTONE BATTERY OF PHILADELPHIA;
GETTY:5[47]160

KIDD, EDWIN C., *Lieutenant, 28th Louisiana Infantry;*
CWR:VOL4#2[1]165
KIDD, J.H., *Major, USA;* MH:FEB/93[42]164
KIDD, JAMES H., *Major, 6th Michigan Cavalry;*
GENERAL LISTINGS: *Falling Waters,* GETTY:9[109]218, *Gettysburg,*
GETTY:10[120]229, *photo;* GETTY:9[109]218
ADDITIONAL LISTINGS: ACW:JUL/92[41]370, ACW:NOV/92[26]386,
GETTY:13[89]260
KIDD, WILLIAM, *Private, 11th Mississippi Infantry;*
CWR:VOL2#4[269]145
KIDDER, ROSCOE, *Private, 9th New Hampshire Infantry;*
CWR:VOL2#2[118]136
KIEFFER, HARRY, *Private, 150th Pennsylvania Infantry;*
GETTY:5[117]165
KIGGINS, JOHN, *Private, 149th New York Infantry;*
CWTI:SEPT/89[30]129
KILE, JOSEPH, *Private, 53rd Pennsylvania Infantry;*
GETTY:11[80]235
KILGORE, BENJAMIN, *Doctor;* B&G:JUN/93[12]524
KILGORE, DAWSON, *Lieutenant Colonel, USA;*
CWR:VOL1#2[44]114
KILIAN, D.W., *Captain, 5th Tennessee Mounted Infantry;*
CWTI:MAY/93[8]315
KILPATRICK, FRANKLIN W., *Colonel, 1st South Carolina Infantry;* CWR:VOL3#2[70]155
KILPATRICK, ROBERT, *Lieutenant Colonel, 5th Ohio Infantry;* CWTI:NOV/92[41]291
KILPATRICK, HUGH JUDSON, *General, USA:*
ARTICLE: "PELL-MELL CAVALRY CHASE," ACW:JUL/92[41]370
GENERAL LISTINGS: *1863 cavalry battles,* MH:OCT/92[51]162,
Aldie, B&G:OCT/93[12]537, *Atlanta Campaign,*
ACW:NOV/95[74]560, CWTI:JAN/93[20]298, *Big Bethel,*
ACW:MAR/93[42]406, *Buckland,* ACW:JAN/95[10]503,
Carolina Campaign, B&G:DEC/95[9]615, *common soldiers,*
AHI:AUG/68[4]115B, *Falling Waters,* GETTY:9[109]218,
Gettysburg, ACW:SEP/94[6]482, GETTY:4[65]148,
GETTY:4[75]149, GETTY:7[29]188, GETTY:9[116]219,
GETTY:11[19]232, *in book review,* CWM:DEC/94[7],
CWNEWS:NOV/95[29], *Millen,* CWTI:SEP/91[23]228, *North
Carolina Campaign,* ACW:NOV/93[12]440, *order of battle,*
B&G:DEC/95[9]615, *relics,* B&G:JUN/91[38]455, *Savannah,*
B&G:FEB/91[8]439, CWTI:DEC/94[62]415, *West Point,*
B&G:DEC/91[12]469, *photos,* B&G:APR/91[8]445,
B&G:OCT/93[12]537, CWTI:MAY/92[48]267, *photo, West
Point;* B&G:DEC/91[12]469
ADDITIONAL LISTINGS: ACW:SEP/92[47]380, ACW:JUL/93[50]426,
ACW:SEP/94[38]487, ACW:SEP/94[55]489,
AHI:NOV/85[38]254, B&G:APR/91[8]445,
B&G:OCT/93[21]538, CWM:DEC/94[17]547,
CWM:APR/95[32]575, CWR:VOL1#2[7]111,
CWR:VOL1#2[29]112, CWR:VOL2#4[269]145,
CWTI:SUMMER/89[50]124, CWTI:JUN/90[32]159,
CWTI:DEC/91[28]239, CWTI:MAY/92[48]267,
CWTI:NOV/92[41]291, CWTI:DEC/94[32]410,
CWTI:DEC/95[76]482, GETTY:13[64]258, GETTY:13[89]260,
GETTY:13[108]261
KILPATRICK-DAHLGREN RAID; MH:JUN/94[8]177
KIMBALL, CHARLES B., *Lieutenant, Wisconsin Light
Artillery;* B&G:FEB/94[8]550
KIMBALL, EDGAR A., *Lieutenant Colonel, 9th New York
Infantry;* B&G:AUG/93[36]533, CWM:FEB/95[7],
CWTI:SEPT/89[74]133

KIMBALL, JOHN W., *Lieutenant Colonel, 15th Massachusetts Infantry;* ACW:MAR/94[50]462

KIMBALL, NATHAN B., *General, USA:*
ARTICLE: "VALOR OF OHIOANS AT THE BATTLE OF KERNSTOWN," CWM:APR/95[29]574
ADDITIONAL LISTINGS: ACW:JAN/92[50]345, ACW:JAN/93[35]396, ACW:SEP/94[31]486, B&G:AUG/93[10]529, B&G:DEC/93[12]545, B&G:AUG/95[8]604, CWR:VOL4#4[28]178, CWTI:JAN/94[20]358

KIMBROUGH, A.L., *Sergeant, 11th Mississippi Infantry;* CWR:VOL2#4[269]145

KIMBROUGH, JOHN, *Captain, USA;* CWTI:AUG/95[34]457

KIMMEL, JOSEPH, *Private, 51st Ohio Infantry;* CWTI:NOV/92[41]291

KINCAID, GEORGE W., *Colonel, USA;* CWTI:DEC/95[8]474

KINCAID, J.M., *Captain, 52nd North Carolina Infantry;* GETTY:12[61]245

KING WILLIAM (VIRGINIA) ARTILLERY; GETTY:4[33]146, GETTY:4[49]147, GETTY:9[17]210

KING, ALBERT W., *Private, 100th Ohio Infantry;* B&G:AUG/95[24]605

KING, CHARLES, *Private, 49th Pennsylvania Infantry;* B&G:DEC/92[38]507, CWTI:SEP/93[43]338

KING, CURTIS, *Private, 47th Iowa Infantry;* AHI:APR/68[4]115

KING, ELLISON, *civilian;* B&G:FEB/91[20]440

KING, FLOYD, *Lieutenant Colonel, CSA;* ACW:NOV/93[50]444, B&G:DEC/92[8]503

KING, HENRY, *Captain, USA;* B&G:OCT/95[8]611F

KING, HENRY, *Sergeant, 3rd Arkansas Infantry;* GETTY:5[117]165

KING, HOUSTON, *Captain, Clark's Missouri Artillery;* B&G:AUG/95[8]604

KING, JOHN, *Private, 25th Virginia Infantry;* CWM:NOV/92[64]453

KING, JOHN H., *General, USA;* CWTI:SEP/92[31]281

KING, LEANDER G., *Captain, 16th Massachusetts Infantry;* GETTY:12[7]241

KING, PORTER, *Captain, 4th Alabama Infantry;* ACW:NOV/94[18]495

KING, ROBERT H., *Lieutenant, USA;* ACW:MAR/93[51]407

KING, RUFUS, *General, USA;* ACW:JUL/91[18]312, AHI:DEC/66[30]105, B&G:DEC/91[12]469, B&G:AUG/92[11]493, CWM:JAN/93[16]457

KING, THOMAS, *Private, 2nd District Colored Infantry;* AHI:AUG/68[4]115B

KING, WILLIAM, *civilian;* ACW:NOV/93[42]443, B&G:FEB/91[8]439

KINGFIELD, DANIEL, *Private, 19th Indiana Infantry,* GETTY:11[57]233

KINGSBURY, HENRY W., *Captain, USA;* ACW:NOV/94[50]498, B&G:DEC/91[12]469

KINKEAD, WILLIAM H., *Private, 53rd Pennsylvania Infantry;* GETTY:11[80]235

KINNEAR, ROBERT, *Private, 13th Pennsylvania Reserves;* CWR:VOL1#3[46]121

KINNEY, DANIEL F., *Lieutenant, 7th North Carolina Infantry;* GETTY:8[67]204

KINNEY, THOMAS J., *Colonel, 119th Illinois Infantry;* CWR:VOL2#3[212]142

KINSMAN, THOMAS J., *Colonel, 23rd Iowa Infantry;* CWR:VOL2#1[19]131

KINZIE, DAVID H., *Lieutenant, 5th U.S. Artillery;* GETTY:12[1]240, GETTY:12[42]244, GETTY:12[83]247

KIRBY, EDMUND, *Lieutenant, 1st U.S. Artillery;* B&G:DEC/91[12]469, B&G:APR/92[36]483

KIRBY, GEORGE, *Major, CSA;* CWTI:MAY/93[35]320

KIRBY, ISAAC M., *Colonel, USA;* B&G:DEC/93[12]545

KIRK, JAMES, *Colonel, 3rd North Carolina Mounted Infantry (Union);* ACW:NOV/93[12]440

KIRK, JOHN L., *Private, 1st Tennessee (Union) Cavalry;* B&G:FEB/91[20]440

KIRK, JONATHAN C., *Sergeant, 20th Indiana Infantry;* B&G:APR/93[12]518

KIRKLAND, RICHARD R., *Sergeant, 2nd South Carolina Infantry;* ACW:MAR/93[58], CWM:OCT/95[22]614

KIRKLAND, WILLIAM W., *General, CSA:*
GENERAL LISTINGS: *in order of battle,* B&G:APR/94[10]558, B&G:APR/95[8]595, B&G:DEC/95[9]615, *Wilmington/Fort Fisher,* B&G:DEC/94[10]585, B&G:APR/95[8]595
ADDITIONAL LISTINGS: B&G:DEC/94[10]585, CWR:VOL1#3[52]122, CWR:VOL2#4[269]145

KIRKLEY, J.W., *Private, 1st Maryland Infantry;* BOOK REVIEW: *HISTORICAL RECORD OF THE FIRST REGIMENT MARYLAND INFANTRY*

KIRKPATRICK, JAMES J., *Sergeant, 16th Mississippi Infantry:*
ARTICLE: "THE GETTYSBURG EXPERIENCE OF JAMES J. KIRKPATRICK," GETTY:8[111]206
ADDITIONAL LISTINGS: GETTY:4[7]142, GETTY:5[89]162, GETTY:8[111]206

KIRKPATRICK, SAMUEL C., *Colonel, 72nd Indiana Infantry;* B&G:OCT/92[32]499

KIRKPATRICK, T.J., *Captain, Amherst (Virginia) Artillery;* GETTY:7[124]196

KIRKWOOD, SAMUEL J., *Governor, Iowa;* CWR:VOL2#1[19]131, CWTI:AUG/95[34]457

KISE, WILLIAM C., *Lieutenant Colonel, 10th Indiana Infantry;* B&G:FEB/93[12]511

KISER, WALLACE, *Private, 126th New York Infantry;* CWR:VOL1#4[7]125

KISER, WILLIAM, *Lieutenant Colonel, 10th Indiana Infantry;* ACW:SEP/93[38]434

KISTLER, DANIEL, *Captain, 11th Pennsylvania Infantry;* MH:OCT/92[51]162

KITCHING, J. HOWARD, *Colonel, USA;* B&G:APR/91[8]445, B&G:APR/94[10]558, B&G:APR/95[8]595

KITE, ANDREW J., *Sergeant, 7th Virginia Cavalry;* B&G:FEB/92[32]477, B&G:JUN/92[6]486

KITE, JOSHUA, *Private, 7th Virginia (Union) Infantry;* GETTY:12[1]240

KITTINGER, MARTIN S., *Surgeon, 100th New York Infantry;* CWTI:MAR/94[38]372

KITTOE, EDWARD D., *Colonel, USA;* AHI:JAN/67[4]106

KITTRELL SPRINGS, NORTH CAROLINA; ARTICLE: "RESORT OF THE DEAD," ACW:MAR/95[50]518

KLAUSS, MARTIN, *Captain, Indiana Light Artillery;* B&G:FEB/94[8]550

KLECKNER, JACOB H., *Private, 53rd Pennsylvania Infantry;* GETTY:11[80]235

KLINEFELTER, HENRY G., *Private, 7th Wisconsin Infantry,* GETTY:9[33]211, GETTY:11[57]233

KNAP'S INDEPENDENT BATTERY; GETTY:9[81]216

KNAP, JOSEPH M., *Captain, Knap's Independent Battery;* B&G:FEB/95[8]590C, CWTI:AUG/95[24]455, GETTY:9[81]216

KNAPP, EDWIN, *Private, 126th New York Infantry;* CWR:VOL1#4[7]125

KNAPP, HENRY J., *Private, 137th New York Infantry;*
GETTY:9[81]216
KNAPP, JOHN, *Lieutenant Colonel, 1st Missouri Infantry;*
ACW:MAY/91[31]304
KNAUSS, WILLIAM H., *Private, USA;* B&G:AUG/95[42]608
KNEFFLER, FREDERICK, *General, USA;*
B&G:DEC/93[12]545, CWTI:SEP/92[10]278
KNEISLEY, J.W., *Captain, CSA;* MH:APR/95[74]184
KNIGHT, CHARLES O., *Private, Fredericksburg Artillery;*
CWR:VOL1#1[1]102
KNIGHT, CHARLES, *Corporal, 9th New Hampshire Infantry;*
CWR:VOL2#2[118]136
KNIGHT, DANIEL W.S., *Private, CSA;* B&G:AUG/93[10]529
KNIGHT, JOHN W., *Private, 19th Indiana Infantry,*
GETTY:11[57]233
KNIGHT, LEROY, *Private, 2nd Tennessee Cavalry;*
CWR:VOL4#1[1]163
KNIGHT, NAPOLEON, *Major, 1st Delaware Cavalry;*
GETTY:12[42]244
KNIGHT, WILLIAM J., *Corporal, USA;* ACW:SEP/91[22]321
KNIGHTS OF THE GOLDEN CIRCLE; AHI:NOV/88[28]277,
B&G:OCT/92[30], CWR:VOL4#4[129], CWTI:MAY/92[8]261,
CWTI:NOV/92[54]293, CWTI:JAN/95[27]425,
MH:JUN/91[20]152
KNIGHTS, J.S., *Corporal, 7th Massachusetts Infantry;*
ACW:NOV/95[30]555
KNIPE, JOSEPH F., *General, USA;* ACW:NOV/95[48]557,
B&G:DEC/93[12]545
KNOW-NOTHING PARTY; BOOK REVIEW: *NATIVISM AND
SLAVERY, THE NORTHERN KNOW NOTHINGS & THE
POLITICS OF THE 1850'S*
KNOWLES, CEDAR C., *Captain, 1st Alabama Infantry;*
GETTY:10[102]226, GETTY:13[108]261
KNOWLES, JACK, *Sergeant, 3rd New York Infantry;*
AHI:SEP/83[12]234
KNOWLTON, JULIUS, *Sergeant, 14th Connecticut Infantry;*
GETTY:9[61]215
KNOX, DAVID, *photographer;* B&G:FEB/94[24]551
KNOX, JAMES S., CWTI:MAR/93[12]307
KNOX, THOMAS, *Correspondent;* ACW:NOV/92[6]382,
ACW:NOV/95[54]558, GETTY:12[97]249
KNOXVILLE, TENNESSEE CAMPAIGN:
ARTICLES: "ICY ASSAULT ROUTED," ACW:MAY/91[23]303,
"REMNANTS OF CIVIL WAR KNOXVILLE,"
CWTI:MAY/94[50]386
BOOK REVIEW: *PATHS TO VICTORY: A HISTORY AND TOUR
GUIDE OF THE STONES RIVER, CHICKAMAUGA,
CHATTANOOGA, KNOXVILLE AND NASHVILLE
CAMPAIGNS*
GENERAL LISTINGS: *in book review,* ACW:SEP/94[66],
CWM:DEC/94[7], CWM:AUG/95[45], CWR:VOL2#2[169],
letters to the editor, CWTI:SEP/94[12]398
ADDITIONAL LISTINGS: ACW:SEP/92[38]379, ACW:JUL/95[10]533,
CWM:NOV/91[50]394, CWM:JUL/92[40]432,
CWM:OCT/94[60]544, CWR:VOL1#1[71]107,
CWTI:MAR/89[16]101, CWTI:SEPT/89[30]129,
CWTI:MAR/93[40]312, CWTI:JAN/95[34]427,
CWTI:MAR/95[26]434
KOCHER, CONRAD, *Private, 24th Michigan Infantry,*
GETTY:11[57]233, GETTY:9[33]211
KOCHERSPERGER, CHARLES, *Lieutenant Colonel, 69th
Pennsylvania Infantry;* GETTY:7[97]193

KOENIG, EMIL, *Captain, 58th New York Infantry;*
GETTY:4[49]147
KOFFMAN, C.C., *Lieutenant, 1st Iowa Cavalry;*
CWTI:MAY/93[35]320
KOHLER, JOHN B., *Major, 21st Pennsylvania Infantry;*
GETTY:10[42]224, GETTY:11[91]236
KOLB'S FARM, VIRGINIA, BATTLE OF;
ACW:MAY/91[8]300, ACW:NOV/95[74]560
KOLBE, GUSTAVE, *Private, 12th Missouri Infantry;*
B&G:APR/95[24]596
KOONTZ, ISAAC N., and JACOB D., *7th Virginia Cavalry:*
ARTICLE: "A MATTER OF INJUSTICE: THE
SUMMERS—KOONTZ INCIDENT," B&G:FEB/92[32]477
ADDITIONAL LISTING: B&G:JUN/92[6]486
KORCHERSPERGER, WILLIAM, *Sergeant, USA;*
B&G:AUG/94[10]574
KOUNTZ, JOHN, *Private, 37th Ohio Infantry;*
CWM:DEC/95[35]629
KRESS, J.A., *Colonel, USA;* GETTY:6[13]170
KRUPP, MORGAN, *Private, 167th Pennsylvania Infantry;*
GETTY:11[6]231
KRZYZANOWSKI, WLADIMIR, *General, USA;*
ACW:NOV/92[42]388, B&G:AUG/92[11]493,
B&G:FEB/95[8]590C, GETTY:9[17]210, GETTY:12[30]243,
GETTY:13[7]253
KU KLUX KLAN:
ARTICLES: "LEADER OF THE KLAN: THE LIFE OF NATHAN
BEDFORD FORREST PART III," CWTI:JAN/94[35]361,
"RULE BY TERROR, PART I," AHI:JAN/80[8]197
GENERAL LISTINGS: *in book review,* ACW:SEP/93[54],
CWTI:SEPT/89[28], CWNEWS:OCT/90[4],
CWNEWS:JAN/91[4], *letters to the editor,* B&G:APR/94[6]557,
CWM:MAY/92[6]417, CWM:MAY/93[6]473,
CWTI:SEP/93[8]332, CWTI:MAY/94[12]379
ADDITIONAL LISTINGS: ACW:MAR/91[30]295, ACW:MAY/93[14]413,
AHI:APR/73[12]148, CWM:NOV/92[43]452,
CWM:MAR/93[36]469, CWM:JUL/92[24]430,
CWTI:SEPT/89[18]126, CWTI:DEC/89[62]139,
CWTI:MAY/91[48]211, CWTI:MAR/93[32]311,
CWTI:SEP/93[14]333, CWTI:SEP/93[62]342,
CWTI:JAN/94[18]357
KUHLMAN, HENRY, *Private, 47th Ohio Infantry;*
ACW:SEP/95[38]546
KUHN, JOHN, *civilian;* GETTY:8[17]200
KUHN, JOHN H., *Lieutenant Colonel, CSA;* CWR:VOL4#1[1]163
KUHN, JOHN H., *Major, 9th Illinois Mounted Infantry;*
CWR:VOL4#1[1]163
KURZ & ALLISON; *painting "Fort Pillow";*
CWM:NOV/92[24]448, *print "Lincoln and his Generals";*
CWM:NOV/92[24]448, *print "Siege of Vicksburg";*
CWM:NOV/92[24]448
KYDD, WILLIAM, *Sergeant Major, 16th Michigan Infantry;*
GETTY:6[33]172
KYLE, DAVID J., *Private, CSA;* CWR:VOL1#3[52]122
KYLE, FERGUSON, *Captain, Terry's Texas Rangers;*
CWM:JUL/92[40]432
KYLE, OSCEOLA, *Lieutenant Colonel, CSA;*
B&G:DEC/95[9]615, CWR:VOL1#4[64]127
KYLE, W.E., *Lieutenant, CSA;* B&G:APR/95[5]594

L

LA GRANGE, TENNESSEE; AHI:MAY/71[3]133A,
B&G:JUN/93[12]524, CWTI:FEB/90[38]145
LABADIEVILLE, LOUISIANA, BATTLE OF;
CWR:VOL3#1[1]149
LACEY, WILLIAM A., *Lieutenant, 3rd Louisiana Infantry;*
CWTI:FEB/92[29]248
LACHLISON, J.E., *Private, Oglethorpe Light Infantry;*
B&G:APR/91[32]447
LACY, BEVERLY T.; B&G:JUN/92[8]487, B&G:JUN/95[8]600,
CWM:JUL/92[16]428, CWR:VOL2#4[346],
CWTI:MAY/89[22]116
LADD, LUTHER, *Private, 7th Massachusetts Infantry;*
ACW:NOV/95[30]555
LADIES AID SOCIETY; GETTY:8[121]207
LADIES RELIEF HOSPITAL; CWM:MAY/91[40]351
LADLEY, OSCAR D., *Private, 16th Ohio Infantry;* BOOK
REVIEWS: *HEARTH AND KNAPSACK: THE LADLEY
LETTERS 1857-1880*
LADY, DANIEL, *civilian;* GETTY:4[65]148
LAFAYETTE, TENNESSEE, ENGAGEMENT AT;
CWR:VOL2#4[313]146
LAGRANGE, OSCAR H., *Colonel, USA;* B&G:AUG/94[22]576,
CWTI:MAY/94[44]384, CWTI:JAN/95[27]425
LAIBOLDT, BERNARD, *Colonel, USA;* CWTI:SEP/92[31]281
LAIRD, JOHN B., *Surgeon, 4th Ohio Infantry;*
GETTY:10[53]225
LAKE, GREGG, *Private, 1st Maryland Battalion;*
GETTY:9[81]216
LAMAR (MISSISSIPPI) RIFLES; ACW:MAR/92[10]349,
GETTY:9[98]217
LAMAR, BASIL, *Colonel, CSA;* B&G:FEB/93[40]514
LAMAR, JEFFERSON, *Colonel, CSA;* B&G:FEB/93[40]514
LAMAR, JOHN H., *Colonel, 61st Georgia Infantry;*
CWTI:JAN/93[40]301
LAMAR, LUCIUS Q.C., *Colonel, CSA:*
BOOK REVIEW: *L.Q.C. LAMAR: PRAGMATIC PATRIOT*
ADDITIONAL LISTINGS: B&G:AUG/91[30]460, CWM:MAY/92[6]417
LAMAR, THOMAS G., *Colonel, 1st South Carolina Artillery;*
CWTI:JAN/94[46]364
LAMASON, B.P., *civilian;* CWTI:MAR/95[54]438
LAMB, HUGH L. and JAMES H., *2nd Tennessee Cavalry;*
CWR:VOL4#1[1]163
LAMB, MILES, *Private, Sumter Artillery;* CWR:VOL3#2[1]153
LAMB, SAMUEL, *Captain, USA;* CWTI:MAR/94[38]372
LAMB, WILLIAM, *Colonel, CSA:*
GENERAL LISTINGS: *in book review,* B&G:OCT/91[34],
Wilmington/Fort Fisher, AHI:SEP/83[12]234,
B&G:DEC/94[10]585, *photo,* B&G:DEC/94[10]585
ADDITIONAL LISTINGS: ACW:MAY/92[14]358, ACW:NOV/93[12]440,
ACW:JAN/95[38]506
LAMB, WILLIAM, *Sergeant, 3rd South Carolina Infantry;*
GETTY:5[35]159par
LAMBERT, LOUIS A., *Chaplain, 18th Illinois Cavalry;*
CWM:MAR/91[50]340
LAMBERT, R.A., *Private, 42nd Alabama Infantry;*
B&G:DEC/95[9]615
LAMBERTH, BILL, *Private, 3rd Georgia Infantry;*
CWTI:SEP/94[26]400

LAMBERTSON, G.W., *Sergeant, 7th Tennessee Infantry;*
GETTY:6[13]170
LAMKIN, JAMES N., *Captain, CSA;* AHI:SEP/87[40]263
LAMON, WARD HILL:
GENERAL LISTINGS: *election of 1864,* AHI:OCT/68[4]116, *Lincoln's
Gettysburg Address,* GETTY:9[122]220, *Lincoln's humor,*
AHI:NOV/70[22]130, *photos,* ACW:JAN/92[30]342,
AHI:NOV/70[22]130, AHI:NOV/90[44]293
ADDITIONAL LISTINGS: ACW:JAN/92[30]342, AHI:NOV/88[37]278,
AHI:NOV/90[44]293, CWTI:MAR/91[22]199,
CWTI:MAR/95[54]438, CWTI:DEC/95[24]477
LAMOUNTAIN, JOHN:
BOOK REVIEW: *AERONAUTICS IN THE UNION AND
CONFEDERATE ARMIES*
ADDITIONAL LISTINGS: AHI:JUN/84[24]239, B&G:DEC/91[6]468
LAMPHERE, CHARLES H., *Captain, USA;* B&G:AUG/95[8]604
LAMPLEY, WILLIAM, *Colonel, 45th Alabama Infantry;*
CWTI:SUMMER/89[50]124
LAMSON, CHARLES, *Master, USN;* CWTI:DEC/90[29]182
LAMSON, HORACE P., *Lieutenant Colonel, 4th Indiana
Cavalry;* B&G:AUG/94[22]576
LAMSON, MYRON H., *Sergeant, USA;* CWTI:MAR/95[54]438
LANABEE, OSCAR G, *Private, 1st Pennsylvania Artillery;*
GETTY:12[30]243
LANCASTER, JAMES M., *Lieutenant, USA;*
B&G:DEC/91[12]469
LANCASTER, LEONARD, *Lieutenant, USA;*
CWTI:MAY/93[35]320
LAND, EBEN, *Private, 16th Massachusetts Infantry;*
GETTY:12[7]241
LAND, LEWIS J., *Lieutenant, 111th Illinois Infantry;*
CWTI:DEC/94[62]415
LANDER, FREDERICK W., *General, USA;*
ACW:JAN/92[47]344, AHI:APR/68[4]115, B&G:AUG/93[10]529
LANDERS, ELI P., *Sergeant, 16th Georgia Infantry;* BOOK
REVIEW: *WEEP NOT FOR ME, DEAR MOTHER*
LANDGRAEBER, CLEMENS, *Captain, USA;*
B&G:AUG/95[8]604
LANDIS, JOHN D., *Captain, Landis' Missouri Battery;*
B&G:FEB/94[8]550
LANDON, WILLIAM D.F., *Lieutenant, 14th Indiana Infantry;*
B&G:JUN/95[8]600
LANDRAM, WILLIAM J., *Colonel, USA;* B&G:FEB/94[8]550,
B&G:AUG/95[8]604, CWR:VOL2#1[19]131,
CWR:VOL4#2[1]165, CWR:VOL4#2[68]167
LANDREGAN, JAMES, *Private, 13th Pennsylvania Reserves;*
GETTY:9[53]214, GETTY:10[120]229
LANE, BENJAMIN, *Lieutenant, 9th Florida Infantry;*
CWR:VOL3#4[1]161
LANE, FREDERICK A.; CWTI:FEB/92[21]247
LANE, HARRIET; AHI:MAY/66[12]101
LANE, JAMES C., *Colonel, 102nd New York Infantry;* ARTICLE:
"TWO NEW YORK SWORDS IN THE FIGHT FOR CULP'S
HILL: COLONEL JAMES C. LANE'S AND CAPT.
NICHOLAS GRUMBACH'S," GETTY:10[36]223
LANE, JAMES H., *General, CSA:*
GENERAL LISTINGS: *Chancellorsville,* MH:JUN/92[50]159, *Falling
Waters,* GETTY:9[109]218, *Gettysburg,* GETTY:4[115]152,
GETTY:8[9]199, GETTY:8[67]204, GETTY:8[95]205,
GETTY:10[102]226, GETTY:11[57]233, GETTY:12[61]245, *in
list,* CWTI:JUL/93[34]327, *in order of battle,*
B&G:APR/94[10]558, B&G:APR/95[8]595, *letters to the editor,*
B&G:AUG/91[6]457, B&G:APR/95[5]594, *Peninsula*

Campaign, CWM:JUN/95[43]587, *Wilderness,*
B&G:APR/95[8]595, *photos,* B&G:FEB/95[8]590A,
CWTI:FEB/91[45]194, GETTY:8[67]204
ADDITIONAL LISTINGS: ACW:NOV/92[42]388, ACW:MAR/95[42]517,
ACW:MAY/95[18]524, B&G:APR/93[12]518,
B&G:FEB/95[8]590A, CWR:VOL1#1[26]103,
CWR:VOL1#3[52]122, CWR:VOL2#4[269]145,
CWR:VOL3#2[1]153, CWR:VOL4#4[70]180,
CWTI:FEB/91[45]194, CWTI:APR/92[49]260,
CWTI:SEP/92[82]286, CWTI:SEP/94[26]400, GETTY:13[1]252,
GETTY:13[22]254, GETTY:13[75]259, GETTY:13[119]262
LANE, JAMES H., *Senator, Kansas;*
GENERAL LISTINGS: *Bloody Kansas,* AHI:JUL/75[4]160,
impeachment of Andrew Johnson, AHI:DEC/68[28]118, *in book
review,* B&G:FEB/93[36], CWNEWS:OCT/93[5], *letters to the
editor,* CWM:MAY/92[6]417, *Price's 1864 Missouri Campaign,*
B&G:JUN/91[10]452, *photo;* AHI:JUL/75[4]160, *portrait;*
CWTI:JUN/90[54]162
ADDITIONAL LISTINGS: ACW:JAN/91[30]286, ACW:JAN/93[26]395,
ACW:MAR/94[8]456, ACW:MAY/94[26]468,
B&G:DEC/91[12]469, CWTI:JUN/90[54]162
LANE, JOHN, *Lieutenant Colonel, Sumter Artillery;*
B&G:DEC/91[12]469, CWR:VOL3#2[1]153, GETTY:4[49]147,
GETTY:5[89]162, *photo,* CWR:VOL3#2[1]153
LANE, JOHN Q., *Colonel, USA;* B&G:DEC/93[12]545
LANE, JOHN R., *Lieutenant Colonel, 26th North Carolina
Infantry;* GETTY:5[19]158
LANE, JOSEPH, *Senator,* B&G:DEC/91[12]469
LANE, MISS HARRIET; AHI:DEC/71[30]138
LANE, WALTER P., *Colonel, CSA;* CWR:VOL4#2[68]167,
CWR:VOL4#2[118]169
LANFORD, FRANCIS M., *Sergeant, 7th South Carolina
Infantry;* GETTY:5[35]159
LANG, DAVID, *Colonel:*
GENERAL LISTINGS: *Gettysburg,* GETTY:5[79]161,
GETTY:5[89]162, GETTY:7[51]190, GETTY:12[7]241, *in list,*
CWTI:JUL/93[34]327
ADDITIONAL LISTINGS: CWR:VOL2#3[236]143, CWR:VOL3#4[1]161,
GETTY:13[1]252, GETTY:13[50]257
LANG, WILLIS, *Captain, CSA;* ACW:NOV/95[62],
CWTI:OCT/95[56]471
LANGDON, F.W., *civilian;* ACW:MAR/92[22]351
LANGFORD, J.R., *Private, 10th Georgia Infantry;*
ACW:JUL/95[10]533
LANGLEY, I.W., *Colonel, 125th Illinois Infantry;*
CWTI:JAN/93[20]298
LANGLEY, JAMES W., *Lieutenant Colonel, USA;*
B&G:DEC/95[9]615
LANGLEY, JOHN F., *Captain, 12th New Hampshire Infantry;*
GETTY:12[7]241
LANGSTON, DAVID, *Lieutenant Colonel, 3rd South Carolina
Infantry;* GETTY:5[35]159
LANGSTON, DAVID M.H., *Captain, 8th South Carolina
Infantry;* GETTY:5[35]159
LANIER, SIDNEY; ARTICLE: "GEORGIA POET SIDNEY
LANIER QUICKLY WENT FROM LIGHTHEARTED
VOLUNTEER TO DISILLUSIONED VETERAN,"
ACW:SEP/92[6]373
LANPHERE, CHARLES H., *Captain, 1st Michigan Artillery;*
B&G:FEB/94[8]550, B&G:AUG/95[8]604
LANSING, WILLIAM N., *Lieutenant, 1st Illinois Artillery;*
B&G:AUG/95[8]604

LAPHAM, C.N., *Corporal, 1st Vermont Cavalry;*
ACW:SEP/95[38]546
LARDNER, JAMES L., *Flag Officer, USN;* B&G:JUN/92[40]489
LAREY, PETER H., *Major, Independent Battalion Georgia
Volunteers;* CWR:VOL1#4[42]126
LARIMORE, C.P., and GEORGE K., *2nd Tennessee Cavalry;*
CWR:VOL4#1[1]163
LARNER, NOBEL D., *civilian;* ACW:NOV/91[16]330
LAROCQUE, JEREMIAH; ACW:SEP/94[46]488
LARRABEE, LUCIUS S., *Captain, 44th New York Infantry;*
ACW:JAN/92[38]343
LARY, WASHINGTON T., *Lieutenant Colonel, CSA;*
CWM:JAN/91[40]330
LASH, JACOB A., *Major, CSA;* B&G:DEC/93[12]545
LASSITER, W.H., *Private, Sumter Artillery;* CWR:VOL3#2[1]153
LAST DAYS OF THE CIVIL WAR:
ARTICLES: "LAST DAYS OF THE CIVIL WAR: AMERICA LOOKS
TO THE FUTURE," CWTI:AUG/90[70]171, "LAST DAYS OF
THE CIVIL WAR: 'GOD'S WILL BE DONE,'"
CWTI:AUG/90[50]168, "LAST DAYS OF THE CIVIL WAR: 'IT
WAS A TERRIBLE CALAMITY BEYOND DESCRIPTION,'"
CWTI:AUG/90[64]170, "LAST DAYS OF THE CIVIL WAR:
'THE LAST GUN HAD BEEN FIRED,'" CWTI:AUG/90[58]169,
"LAST DAYS OF THE CIVIL WAR: 'SUCCESS WAS
EMINENTLY A HAPPY, A GLORIOUS ONE,'"
CWTI:AUG/90[26]166, "LAST DAYS OF THE CIVIL WAR:
'THE WHOLE COUNTRY SEEMED TO BE ALIVE WITH
DEMONS,'" CWTI:AUG/90[42]167
LATANE, WILLIAM, *Captain, CSA;* ACW:JUL/95[34]536,
CWM:JUN/95[50]589, CWTI:DEC/89[34]136
LATCH, EDWARD, *Ensign, USN;* ACW:MAR/92[40]353
LATHAM, A.C., *Captain, Branch (North Carolina) Artillery;*
GETTY:5[47]160
LATHAM, GEORGE R., *Captain, 2nd West Virginia Infantry;*
B&G:AUG/93[10]529, CWTI:MAR/94[29]371
LATHE, JAMES, *Sergeant, 9th New Hampshire Infantry;*
CWR:VOL2#2[118]136
LATHROP, JOHN, *Captain, 35th Massachusetts Infantry;*
CWTI:FEB/92[36]249
LATIMER, JOSEPH W., *Major, CSA:*
ARTICLE: "JOSEPH W. LATIMER, THE 'BOY MAJOR' AT
GETTYSBURG," GETTY:10[29]222
GENERAL LISTINGS: *Gettysburg,* GETTY:4[49]147,
GETTY:5[117]165, GETTY:7[83]192, GETTY:9[81]216,
GETTY:10[29]222, GETTY:12[30]243, *photo,* GETTY:10[29]222
ADDITIONAL LISTINGS: ACW:NOV/92[42]388, CWR:VOL1#1[1]102,
CWR:VOL4#4[70]180, CWR:VOL4#4[127]182
LATIMER, THOMAS, *civilian;* GETTY:10[29]222
LATROBE LIGHT GUARDS (PENNSYLVANIA) GUARDS,
(53rd Pennsylvania Infantry); GETTY:11[80]235
LATROBE, FREDERICK, *civilian;* GETTY:7[77]191
LATROBE, OSMUN, *Colonel, CSA:*
ARTICLE: "THE UNMERITED CENSURE OF TWO MARYLAND
STAFF OFFICERS, MAJOR OSMUN LATROBE AND FIRST
LIEUTENANT, W. STUART SYMINGTON," GETTY:13[75]259
ADDITIONAL LISTINGS: AHI:SEP/87[40]263, GETTY:13[1]252, *photo,*
GETTY:13[75]259
LATROBE, STUART, *Private, 1st Maryland Cavalry;*
B&G:AUG/94[10]574
LATROP, WILLIAM H., *Colonel, USA;* B&G:JUN/92[32]488
LAUDERDALE, JOHN V., *Surgeon, USA;* BOOK REVIEW: *THE
WOUNDED RIVER: THE CIVIL WAR LETTERS OF JOHN
VANCE LAUDERDALE, M.D.*

LAUMAN, JACOB G., *General, USA:*
GENERAL LISTINGS: *Fort Donelson,* B&G:FEB/92[10]474, *Jackson, Battle of,* B&G:AUG/95[8]604, *order of battle,* B&G:AUG/95[8]604, *photo,* B&G:AUG/95[8]604
ADDITIONAL LISTINGS: B&G:AUG/95[8]604, CWR:VOL3#4[24]162, CWR:VOL4#1[44]164
LAUREL BRIGADE; ACW:JUL/92[41]370, B&G:FEB/92[32]477, MH:FEB/93[42]164
LAUVE, N., *Captain, 1st Louisiana Zouave Battalion;* CWTI:MAR/89[28]103
LAVERY, JOHN T., *Captain, 18th Louisiana Infantry;* CWR:VOL4#2[1]165
LAW, EVANDER M., *General, CSA:*
BOOK REVIEW: *THE POWER THAT GOVERNS: THE EVOLUTION OF JUDICIAL ACTIVISM IN A MIDWESTERN STATE, 1840-1890*
GENERAL LISTINGS: *Carolina Campaign,* B&G:DEC/95[9]615, *Chickamauga,* CWTI:SEP/92[31]281, *Cold Harbor,* B&G:APR/94[10]558, *Gettysburg,* GETTY:5[103]163, GETTY:6[7]169, GETTY:6[62]175, GETTY:8[31]201, GETTY:8[53]203, GETTY:11[19]232, GETTY:12[111]250, *in book review,* CWR:VOL2#4[346], *in order of battle,* B&G:APR/94[10]558, B&G:DEC/95[9]615, *Manassas, Second,* B&G:AUG/92[11]493, *Wilderness,* B&G:JUN/95[8]600
ADDITIONAL LISTINGS: ACW:MAY/91[23]303, ACW:JAN/92[38]343, ACW:JUL/92[30]369, ACW:JUL/93[50]426, ACW:SEP/93[62]436, ACW:JUL/94[42]479, ACW:SEP/94[6]482, ACW:NOV/94[18]495, ACW:SEP/95[74]550, B&G:APR/93[12]518, CWM:JAN/93[8]456, CWM:JUN/94[26]512, CWM:DEC/94[26]548, CWM:AUG/95[38]609, CWR:VOL2#4[269]145, CWR:VOL3#2[1]153, CWR:VOL3#2[70]155, CWR:VOL3#2[102]156, CWR:VOL3#4[1]161, CWR:VOL4#4[70]180, CWTI:DEC/91[36]240, CWTI:MAR/93[40]312, CWTI:SEP/93[53]340, CWTI:NOV/93[55]350, CWTI:JUL/94[44]394, GETTY:13[64]258
LAW, P.L., *Captain, USN;* ACW:JAN/93[51]398
LAWLER, MICHAEL K., *General, USA;* B&G:APR/93[34]521, B&G:AUG/95[8]604, CWR:VOL1#1[42]105, CWR:VOL2#1[1]130, CWR:VOL2#1[19]131, CWR:VOL2#1[36]132, CWR:VOL2#1[69]133
LAWLEY, FRANCIS C., *reporter;* ACW:MAY/95[38]526, CWM:DEC/95[10], CWTI:DEC/91[44]241
LAWRENCE, AMOS A.; AHI:JUL/75[4]160, CWNEWS:JUN/93[5]
LAWRENCE, KANSAS, MASSACRE:
ARTICLES: "BITTER BUSHWHACKERS AND JAYHAWKERS," ACW:JAN/93[26]395, "BLOODY KANSAS...WITNESSES TO QUANTRILL'S RAID IN LAWRENCE AND THEIR STORIES," CWM:JAN/92[12]400
BOOK REVIEWS: *BLOODY DAWN: THE STORY OF THE LAWRENCE MASSACRE*
ADDITIONAL LISTINGS: ACW:JAN/93[6]391, ACW:MAR/94[6]455, ACW:NOV/94[42]497, B&G:OCT/91[11]466, B&G:JUN/91[10]452, B&G:JUN/91[32]454, CWM:JAN/92[8]399, CWM:MAY/92[6]417, CWTI:JAN/94[29]360
LAWRENCE, ROBERT J., *Lieutenant Colonel, CSA;* B&G:DEC/95[9]615
LAWRENCE, SAMUEL B., *Captain, USA;* CWTI:JAN/93[40]301
LAWRENCE, SAMUEL C., *Colonel, USA;* CWTI:MAY/91[34]209

LAWSON, JOHN H., *Private, USA;* B&G:DEC/92[40]508
LAWSON, JUNIOUS, *Private, 22nd Iowa Infantry;* CWR:VOL2#1[19]131
LAWSON, ORRIS A., *Captain, 3rd Ohio Infantry;* B&G:AUG/93[10]529
LAWSON, THOMAS, *Surgeon General, USA:*
BOOK REVIEW: *REGULATIONS FOR THE MEDICAL DEPARTMENT OF THE ARMY*
ADDITIONAL LISTING: CWM:MAY/91[18]348
LAWSON'S (PENNSYLVANIA) GUARDS; 53rd Pennsylvania Infantry, GETTY:11[80]235
LAWTON, ALEXANDER R., *General, CSA:*
GENERAL LISTINGS: *Manassas, Second,* B&G:AUG/92[11]493, B&G:AUG/92[11]493, *Savannah,* B&G:FEB/91[8]439, *photos,* B&G:FEB/91[8]439, CWM:JUL/91[48]374
ADDITIONAL LISTINGS: ACW:JUL/91[18]312, ACW:JUL/92[30]369, ACW:JAN/95[54]508, AHI:JUN/70[30]127, B&G:FEB/91[8]439, CWM:NOV/91[50]394, CWM:JUL/92[16]428, CWM:JAN/93[16]457, CWTI:JUL/93[29]326, CWTI:JUN/95[18]444
LAWTON, AMBROSE R., *General, CSA;* B&G:AUG/91[20]459
LAWTON, J.K., *Colonel, 2nd Georgia Cavalry;* CWTI:NOV/93[33]347
LEA, EDWARD, *Lieutenant Commander, USN;* ACW:JAN/93[51]398
LEA, J.M., *civilian;* B&G:DEC/93[12]545
LEA, JOHN W., *Captain, CSA;* ARTICLE: "THE MURDER OF A SCALAWAG," AHI:APR/73[12]148
LEACE, OLIVER, *Private, 53rd Pennsylvania Infantry;* GETTY:11[80]235
LEACH, J.A., *Private, 1st South Carolina Infantry;* GETTY:13[22]254
LEACH, LEBBEUS, *Captain, 29th Massachusetts Infantry;* ACW:JAN/95[74]510
LEADBETTER, DANVILLE, *General, CSA;* ACW:MAY/91[23]303, ACW:SEP/92[38]379, AHI:JUN/70[30]127, B&G:APR/92[28]482, CWTI:MAR/93[40]312, CWTI:MAY/94[50]386
LEADERSHIP; BOOK REVIEWS: *DOUGLAS SOUTHALL FREEMAN ON LEADERSHIP * LEADERSHIP DURING THE CIVIL WAR * THE SECOND DAY AT GETTYSBURG: ESSAYS ON CONFEDERATE AND UNION LEADERSHIP*
LEAKE, JOSEPH B., *Lieutenant Colonel, 20th Iowa Infantry;* CWM:OCT/94[33]537, CWR:VOL1#1[42]105
LEALE, CHARLES A., *Surgeon, USA;* ACW:MAY/95[68]529
LEAMING, MACK J., *Lieutenant, 13th Tennessee Cavalry (Union);* AHI:APR/74[4]154, CWTI:NOV/93[65]351
LEARY, JACOB, *Private, 100th Pennsylvania Infantry;* CWTI:JAN/94[49]365
LEARY, LEWIS; CWM:SEP/92[8]437
LEASURE, DANIEL, *Colonel, USA;* B&G:AUG/92[11]493, B&G:APR/95[8]595, B&G:JUN/95[8]600, B&G:AUG/95[8]604, CWTI:JAN/94[46]364
LEAVITT, ARCHIBALD D., *Major, 16th Maine Infantry;* GETTY:13[33]255
LEAVITT, AUBREY, *Lieutenant, 16th Maine Infantry;* CWM:MAY/92[15]419
LEBANON, KENTUCKY, SKIRMISH AT; B&G:OCT/94[11]580
LEBARNES, JOHN W., *Lieutenant, 20th Massachusetts Infantry;* ACW:JUL/91[43]315, CWR:VOL3#1[31]150
LEDLIE, JAMES H., *General, USA;* ACW:SEP/95[70]549, B&G:APR/93[12]518, B&G:APR/93[23]519,

B&G:APR/94[10]558, CWR:VOL1#3[94],
CWR:VOL2#2[118]136, CWTI:APR/90[24]152,
CWTI:JAN/95[34]427, MH:APR/95[46]183, *photos*,
B&G:APR/93[12]518

LEDUC, WILLIAM G., *General, USA;* CWTI:NOV/92[8]288

LEDWELL, WILLIAM, *Private, 5th Ohio Cavalry;*
CWR:VOL4#1[44]164

LEDYARD, WILLIAM, *Lieutenant, 33rd North Carolina
Infantry;* GETTY:12[111]250

LEDYARD, WILLIAM N., *Lieutenant, 3rd Alabama Infantry;*
GETTY:12[111]250

LEE (VIRGINIA) ARTILLERY; GETTY:4[49]147

LEE'S MILL, VIRGINIA, BATTLE OF; ACW:JAN/94[8]447

LEE, AGNES; B&G:JUN/95[22]601

LEE, ALBERT L., *General USA;* CWM:APR/95[39]576,
CWR:VOL1#1[42]105, CWR:VOL4#2[1]165,
CWR:VOL4#2[26]166, MH:DEC/95[58]188

LEE, ALFRED, *Private, 82nd Ohio Infantry;*
B&G:FEB/95[8]590C

LEE, ANNE CARTER; ARTICLE: "GENTLE ANNIE GOES
HOME: ROBERT E. LEE'S DAUGHTER RETURNS TO
VIRGINIA AFTER 132 YEARS," B&G:JUN/95[22]601

LEE, AUGUSTUS H., *Major, 3rd Georgia Infantry;*
CWTI:SEP/94[26]400,

LEE, BENJAMIN, *Captain, 126th New York Infantry;*
GETTY:7[51]190

LEE, EDWIN G., *General CSA;* ARTICLE: "CONFEDERATE
GENERAL EDWIN LEE WAS A CREDIT TO HIS FAMOUS
NAME," ACW:MAY/92[14]358

LEE, ELEANOR AGNES; CWM:JUL/91[16]358

LEE, ELIZABETH BLAIR, *General;* BOOK REVIEWS: *WARTIME
WASHINGTON: THE CIVIL WAR LETTERS OF
ELIZABETH BLAIR LEE*

LEE, FITZHUGH, *General, CSA:*
ARTICLE: "MELEE ON SAINT PATRICK'S DAY,"
ACW:NOV/91[30]332
BOOK REVIEWS: *THE FITZHUGH LEE SAMPLER * GENERAL
FITZHUGH LEE * GENERAL LEE*
GENERAL LISTINGS: *1863 cavalry battles,* MH:OCT/92[51]162,
Antietam, ACW:JUL/92[30]369, *Appomattox Campaign,*
CWTI:AUG/90[26]166, *Brandy Station,* CWTI:JUN/90[32]159,
Buckland, ACW:JUL/92[41]370, *Chancellorsville,*
MH:JUN/92[50]159, *Five Forks,* ACW:MAY/95[38]526,
B&G:APR/92[8]481, *Gettysburg,* GETTY:4[65]148,
GETTY:4[75]149, GETTY:4[113]153, GETTY:5[103]163,
GETTY:6[62]175, GETTY:10[42]224, GETTY:12[68]246, *Haw's
Shop,* ACW:SEP/95[74]550, *in book review,* ACW:MAY/91[54],
CWM:FEB/95[7], CWNEWS:NOV/89[4], CWNEWS:JAN/91[4],
CWNEWS:OCT/92[4], *Indian wars,* AHI:OCT/79[20]194, *in
order of battle,* B&G:APR/92[8]481, B&G:APR/94[10]558,
B&G:APR/95[8]595, *Manassas, 2nd,* B&G:AUG/92[11]493,
Overland Campaign, B&G:APR/94[10]558, *Peninsula
Campaign,* CWM:JUN/95[50]589, *post-war,*
ACW:JUL/95[26]535, *Sayler's Creek,* ACW:JAN/92[22]341,
Trevilian Station, MH:FEB/93[42]164, *West Point,*
B&G:DEC/91[12]469, *Yellow Tavern,* ACW:MAY/94[35]469,
photos, ACW:NOV/91[30]332, B&G:APR/92[8]481
ADDITIONAL LISTINGS: ACW:JAN/91[38]287, ACW:MAY/91[38]305,
ACW:SEP/91[41]323, ACW:NOV/91[35]333,
ACW:NOV/92[26]386, ACW:JAN/93[43]397,
ACW:JUL/93[50]426, ACW:SEP/93[31]433,
ACW:SEP/93[62]436, ACW:JUL/94[35]478,
ACW:JAN/95[10]503, ACW:MAR/95[12]513,

ACW:JUL/95[34]536, B&G:APR/92[48]484,
B&G:OCT/92[38]500, B&G:OCT/93[12]537,
CWM:MAY/92[34]422, CWM:APR/94[32]506,
CWM:JUN/94[43]517, CWM:OCT/94[17]534,
CWM:OCT/95[37]617, CWR:VOL2#2[156]138,
CWR:VOL3#2[1]153, CWR:VOL3#4[1]161,
CWR:VOL4#4[28]178, CWTI:DEC/89[34]136,
CWTI:DEC/91[22]237, CWTI:APR/92[35]257,
CWTI:NOV/93[50]349, CWTI:JUL/94[44]394,
CWTI:JUN/95[38]447, CWTI:OCT/95[90]472,
GETTY:13[89]260, MH:APR/94[54]176

LEE, FRANCIS, *Corporal, 124th New York Infantry;*
CWM:DEC/94[40]550

LEE, GEORGE W., *Captain, CSA;* CWR:VOL1#4[42]126

LEE, GEORGE W.C., *General, CSA;* ACW:JAN/92[22]341,
AHI:SEP/87[40]263, B&G:FEB/94[24]551,
B&G:JUN/95[22]601, CWM:JUL/91[48]374,
CWTI:DEC/89[34]136, *photos,* CWM:JUL/91[16]358,
CWTI:AUG/90[42]167

LEE, HENRY, *Captain, CSA;* GETTY:4[65]148,
GETTY:12[68]246

LEE, JAMES, *Private, 37th Illinois Infantry;*
CWR:VOL1#1[42]105

LEE, JOHN J., *Private, 7th Wisconsin Infantry;*
GETTY:11[57]233

LEE, MARY CUSTIS, B&G:JUN/95[22]601, *photos,*
B&G:JUN/95[22]601, CWM:JUL/91[16]358

LEE, MILDRED CHILDE; CWM:JUL/91[16]358

LEE, ORLANDO H., *Lieutenant, USA;* B&G:OCT/91[11]466

LEE, ROBERT E., *General, CSA:*
ARTICLES: "A CONTEMPORARY HERO," CWM:JUL/91[26]364,
"A FAMILY TREE ROOTED IN HISTORY: A LEE FAMILY
ALBUM," CWM:JUL/91[16]358, "A MATTER OF PRINCIPLE:
ROBERT E. LEE AND THE CONSTITUTION OF THE
UNITED STATES," CWM:APR/94[32]506, "ALL GOES ON
LIKE A MIRACLE," CWTI:APR/92[49]260, "AUDACITY TO
WHAT PURPOSE?" CWM:JUL/91[28]366, "THE BATTLE OF
FREDERICKSBURG," AHI:JUN/78[4]180, "BATTLE IN
DESPERATION," CWTI:MAR/95[33]435, "BLACK
THURSDAY FOR REBELS," ACW:JAN/92[22]341, "BLOOD
POURED LIKE WATER," ACW:MAR/94[50]462,
"BRILLIANCE TO NO ADVANTAGE," CWM:JUL/91[24]361,
"CIVIL WAR'S LONGEST SIEGE," MH:APR/95[46]183,
"COMMAND SHIFT DICTATED," MH:JUN/92[50]159
ARTICLES, continued: "DOUBLY MISSED OPPORTUNITY,"
ACW:MAR/93[26]404, "THE ESSENTIAL LEE: A
20TH-CENTURY SCRAPBOOK," CWM:JUL/91[22]359,
"FAILURE ON THE HEIGHTS," ACW:NOV/92[42]388, "THE
FALL OF RICHMOND," ACW:MAY/95[38]526, "THE FIELD
GLASSES OF ROBERT E. LEE," B&G:AUG/95[32]606,
"FLANK ATTACK," ACW:SEP/93[31]433, "GENERAL
ORDERS NO. 72: 'BY COMMAND OF GEN. R. E. LEE,'"
GETTY:7[13]186, "GENERALS AT ODDS,"
MH:AUG/94[46]178, "GENTLE ANNIE GOES HOME:
ROBERT E. LEE'S DAUGHTER RETURNS TO VIRGINIA
AFTER 132 YEARS," B&G:JUN/95[22]601, "GETTYSBURG
FINALE," ACW:JUL/93[50]426, "GRANNY LEE'S
INAUSPICIOUS DEBUT," ACW:SEP/94[31]486, "GRANT
AND LEE, 1864: FROM THE NORTH ANNA TO THE
CROSSING OF THE JAMES," B&G:APR/94[10]558
ARTICLES, continued: "HISTORY COMES HOME,"
CWTI:MAR/95[20]433, "I WAS THERE," CWM:JUL/91[8]356,
"I WILL TAKE ALL THE RESPONSIBILITY,"

CWM:JUL/91[46]373, "JEB STUART'S DARING RECONNAISSANCE," ACW:JUL/95[34]536, "LEADERSHIP THROUGH DIPLOMACY," CWM:JUL/91[31]368, "LEE AT GETTYSBURG: THE MAN, THE MYTH, THE RECRIMINATIONS," CWM:JAN/93[8]456, "LEE FOILS MEADE AT MINE RUN," CWM:DEC/94[44]551, "LEE'S LAST U.S. ARMY POST," B&G:APR/92[58]485, "LEE'S LIEUTENANTS," CWM:JUL/92[16]428, "LEGEND VS. HISTORY," CWM:JUL/91[27]365, "LEXINGTON: LEE'S LAST RETREAT," CWM:JUL/91[48]374, "LIFE AFTER SURRENDER FOR REBEL WARRIORS," ACW:JUL/95[26]535

ARTICLES, continued: "MASTER OF THE BOLD FRON," CWM:JUL/91[29]367, "MEETING AT THE MCLEAN HOUSE," AHI:SEP/87[48]264, "MR. LEE OF VIRGINIA: A CONVERSATION WITH EMORY M. THOMAS," CWM:AUG/95[17]603, "NEAR KILLING ME," CWM:JUL/91[40]370, "NHS MEMBER NEWS," AHI:AUG/75[48]161, "NO TURNING BACK: THE BATTLE OF THE WILDERNESS, PART I," B&G:APR/95[8]595, "NO TURNING BACK: THE BATTLE OF THE WILDERNESS, PART II—THE FIGHTING ON MAY 6, 1864," B&G:JUN/95[8]600, "THE NORTHWESTERN VIRGINIA CAMPAIGN OF 1861," B&G:AUG/93[10]529, "ONE BRIDGE TOO MANY," ACW:JAN/93[43]397, "THE ONLY PROPER COURSE," CWM:JUL/91[24]360

ARTICLES, continued: (all of the following listings are sub-titles for the article titled "The Peninsula Campaign of 1862): "THE PENINSULA CAMPAIGN OF 1862: STUART'S RIDE AROUND MCCLELLAN," CWM:JUN/95[50]589; "THE BATTLE OF BEAVER DAM CREEK," CWM:JUN/95[57]592; "THE BATTLE OF DREWRY'S BLUFF," CWM:JUN/95[39]586; "THE BATTLE OF GAINES' MILL," CWM:JUN/95[61]593; "THE BATTLE OF GLENDALE," CWM:JUN/95[69]596; "THE BATTLE OF MALVERN HILL," CWM:JUN/95[73]597; "THE BATTLE OF OAK GROVE," CWM:JUN/95[55]591; "THE BATTLE OF SAVAGE'S STATION," CWM:JUN/95[65]595; "THE BATTLE OF SEVEN PINES," CWM:JUN/95[47]588; "THE BATTLE OF SLASH CHURCH," CWM:JUN/95[43]587; "THE BATTLE OF WILLIAMSBURG," CWM:JUN/95[34]584; "THE DABBS HOUSE MEETING," CWM:JUN/95[53]590; "THE SIEGE OF YORKTOWN AND ENGAGEMENTS ALONG THE WARWICK RIVER," CWM:JUN/95[29]583; "THE ENGAGEMENT AT ELTHAM'S LANDING," CWM:JUN/95[37]585; "PRELUDE: THE, LEGIONS GATHER," CWM:JUN/95[24]582

ARTICLES, continued: "PERSPECTIVES ON THE PAST," AHI:NOV/76[29]172, "THE REALIST," CWM:JUL/91[25]362, "REGULARS TO THE RESCUE AT GAINES' MILL," ACW:NOV/94[50]498, "RETURN TO THE KILLING GROUND," ACW:JUL/91[18]312, "THE SECOND BATTLE OF MANASSAS: LEE SUPPRESSES THE 'MISCREANT' POPE," B&G:AUG/92[11]493, "SECOND MANASSAS: ENFILADING THUNDER," CWM:AUG/94[48]529, "SNIFFING THE WIND," CWM:JUL/91[43]371, "THE SOUL OF THE ARMY," CWM:JUL/91[45]372, "STARS IN THEIR COURSES," ACW:NOV/91[41]334, "STRIKE THE PHRASE 'STRIKE THE TENT,'" CWTI:SEP/90[47]177, "STRIKE THEM A BLOW: LEE AND GRANT AT THE NORTH ANNA RIVER," B&G:APR/93[12]518, "'THOSE PEOPLE,'" CWM:JUL/91[10]357, "TO BE HELD AT ALL HAZARDS," CWTI:SEP/93[43]338, "WHO'S UP AND WHO'S DOWN IN CIVIL WAR HISTORY: ONE'S REPUTATION INCREASINGLY DEPENDS ON WHO'S TELLING THE

TALE," ACW:MAR/95[6]511, "WHOEVER LOST ROBERT E. LEE'S 'LOST ORDER,' A DELIGHTED GEORGE MCCLELLAN FOUND IT," ACW:JAN/94[6]446, "WITH LEE AT APPOMATTOX," AHI:SEP/87[40]263, "'YOU ARE THE ARMY,'" CWM:JUL/91[25]363

BOOK REVIEWS: *ABANDONED BY LINCOLN: A MILITARY BIOGRAPHY OF GENERAL JOHN POPE * THE ARMY OF NORTHERN VIRGINIA * THE ARMY OF ROBERT E. LEE * BATTLE IN THE WILDERNESS: GRANT MEETS LEE * CHANCELLORSVILLE 1863: THE SOULS OF THE BRAVE * THE COURT MARTIAL OF ROBERT E. LEE: A HISTORICAL NOVEL * DEATH OF A NATION: THE STORY OF LEE AND HIS MEN AT GETTYSBURG * GENERAL LEE * GENERAL LEE: HIS CAMPAIGNS IN VIRGINIA 1861-1865 WITH PERSONAL REMINISCENCES * GETTYSBURG: CRISIS OF COMMAND * GRANT & LEE: A STUDY IN PERSONALITY AND GENERALSHIP * IF IT TAKES ALL SUMMER: THE BATTLE OF SPOTSYLVANIA * THE LEE GIRLS*

BOOK REVIEWS, continued: *LEE AND JACKSON: CONFEDERATE CHIEFTONS * LEE AND LONGSTREET AT HIGH TIDE: GETTYSBURG IN LIGHT OF THE OFFICIAL RECORDS * LEE CONSIDERED: GENERAL ROBERT E. LEE AND CIVIL WAR HISTORY * LEE'S ADJUTANT: THE WARTIME LETTERS OF COLONEL WALTER HERRON TAYLOR, 1862-1865 * LEE'S COLONELS: A BIOGRAPHICAL REGISTER OF THE FIELD OFFICERS OF THE ARMY OF NORTHERN VIRGINIA * LEE'S DISPATCHES: UNPUBLISHED LETTERS OF GENERAL ROBERT E. LEE, C.S.A. TO JEFFERSON DAVIS AND THE WAR DEPARTMENT OF THE CONFEDERATE STATES OF AMERICA, 1862-65 * LEE'S LAST CAMPAIGN * LEE'S LIEUTENANTS: A STUDY IN COMMAND * LEE'S MAVERICK GENERAL: DANIEL HARVEY HILL * LEE'S TARNISHED LIEUTENANT: JAMES LONGSTREET AND HIS PLACE IN SOUTHERN HISTORY * LEE'S TERRIBLE SWIFT SWORD: FROM ANTIETAM TO CHANCELLORSVILLE, AN EYEWITNESS TO HISTORY*

BOOK REVIEWS, continued: *LEE: THE LAST YEARS * THE LEE'S OF VIRGINIA * THE LONG ARM OF LEE, OR THE HISTORY OF THE ARTILLERY OF THE ARMY OF NORTHERN VIRGINIA WITH A BRIEF ACCOUNT OF THE CONFEDERATE BUREAU OF ORDNANCE, * THE LONG ARM OF LEE * THE MARBLE MAN: ROBERT E. LEE AND HIS IMAGE IN AMERICAN SOCIETY * PERSONAL REMINISCENCES OF GENERAL ROBERT E. LEE * R.E. LEE: A BIOGRAPHY * RECOLLECTIONS AND LETTERS OF GENERAL ROBERT E. LEE BY HIS SON * RETURN TO BULL RUN: THE CAMPAIGN AND BATTLE OF SECOND MANASSAS * ROBERT E. LEE AT SEWELL MOUNTAIN: THE WEST VIRGINIA CAMPAIGN * ROBERT E. LEE: A PORTRAIT 1807-1861 * THE SEVEN DAYS: THE EMERGENCE OF LEE * TO THE GATES OF RICHMOND: THE PENINSULA CAMPAIGN * THE WARTIME PAPERS OF R.E. LEE,*

GENERAL LISTINGS: *1863 cavalry battles,* MH:OCT/92[51]162, *22nd Virginia Battalion,* CWTI:APR/90[46]153, *Alexander Stephens,* CWTI:FEB/91[36]193, *Antietam,* ACW:JUL/92[30]369, B&G:OCT/95[8]611A, CWM:JAN/92[44]406, CWTI:MAR/93[26]310, *Appomattox,* CWTI:AUG/90[26]166, CWTI:SEP/92[42]283, CWTI:NOV/93[50]349, CWTI:MAR/95[20]433, *Battle of Falling Waters,* GETTY:9[109]218, *Beauregard,* CWTI:JUL/92[29]272,

B&G:APR/95[8]595, B&G:JUN/95[8]600, B&G:JUN/95[22]601, B&G:AUG/95[32]606, CWM:JUL/91[10]357, CWM:JUL/91[16]358, CWM:JUL/92[16]428, CWM:APR/94[32]506, CWM:JUN/95[50]589, CWM:AUG/95[17]603, CWTI:AUG/90[42]167, *portrait by C.C. Beale;* CWTI:APR/89[14]107, *portrait;* AHI:JUL/81[20]221, *post war photo,* B&G:APR/92[58]485, *sketch of meeting with Grant at Appomattox;* CWTI:FEB/90[54]147, *sketch;* CWM:SEP/93[8]493

VIDEO: "ROBERT E. LEE," AHI:JAN/90[22]

ADDITIONAL LISTINGS, ACW: ACW:JAN/91[8]282, ACW:JAN/91[38]287, ACW:MAR/91[30]295, ACW:MAY/91[23]303, ACW:MAY/91[38]305, ACW:MAY/91[62]307, ACW:JUL/91[35]314, ACW:SEP/91[41]323, ACW:SEP/91[62]326, ACW:NOV/91[6]327, ACW:NOV/91[8]328, ACW:NOV/91[30]332, ACW:NOV/91[35]333, ACW:NOV/91[64]336, ACW:JAN/92[47]344, ACW:JAN/92[50]345, ACW:JAN/92[62]346, ACW:MAR/92[30]352, ACW:MAY/92[14]358, ACW:MAY/92[30]361, ACW:JUL/92[41]370, ACW:NOV/92[10]384, ACW:NOV/92[18]385, ACW:NOV/92[26]386, ACW:JAN/93[18]394, ACW:JAN/93[35]396, ACW:MAY/93[14]413, ACW:MAY/93[22]414, ACW:MAY/93[38]416, ACW:MAY/93[62]418, ACW:JUL/93[66]427, ACW:SEP/93[22]432, ACW:NOV/93[12]440, ACW:NOV/93[50]444, ACW:NOV/93[66]445, ACW:MAR/94[27]459, ACW:MAR/94[42]461, ACW:MAY/94[12]466, ACW:JUL/94[18]476, ACW:JUL/94[26]477, ACW:JUL/94[35]478, ACW:JUL/94[42]479, ACW:SEP/94[10]484, ACW:SEP/94[38]487, ACW:SEP/94[55]489, ACW:SEP/94[62]490, ACW:JAN/95[20]504, ACW:JAN/95[30]505, ACW:JAN/95[46]507, ACW:MAR/95[70]520, ACW:MAY/95[10]523, ACW:JUL/95[10]533, ACW:JUL/95[50]538, ACW:SEP/95[30]545, ACW:SEP/95[38]546, ACW:SEP/95[48]547, ACW:NOV/95[54]558, ACW:NOV/95[74]560

ADDITIONAL LISTINGS, AHI: AHI:DEC/74[12]156, AHI:NOV/80[8]209, AHI:MAR/84[42]238, AHI:APR/85[18]250, AHI:OCT/95[24]326

ADDITIONAL LISTINGS, B&G: B&G:FEB/91[8]439, B&G:APR/91[8]445, B&G:OCT/91[11]466, B&G:DEC/91[34]470, B&G:AUG/92[40]495, B&G:OCT/92[32]499, B&G:OCT/92[38]500, B&G:DEC/92[8]503, B&G:FEB/93[24]512, B&G:FEB/93[40]514, B&G:JUN/93[32]525, B&G:OCT/93[12]537, B&G:FEB/94[24]551, B&G:APR/94[34]561, B&G:AUG/94[10]574, B&G:DEC/94[10]585, B&G:DEC/94[36]588, B&G:FEB/95[8]590B, B&G:FEB/95[8]590C, B&G:APR/95[33]597, B&G:AUG/95[8]604, B&G:DEC/95[9]615

ADDITIONAL LISTINGS, CWM: CWM:JAN/91[12]326, CWM:JAN/91[28]327, CWM:MAR/91[17]335, CWM:JUL/91[4]354, CWM:SEP/91[10]379, CWM:SEP/91[40]385, CWM:NOV/91[12]390, CWM:NOV/91[58]394A, CWM:JAN/92[27]403, CWM:JAN/92[34]404, CWM:MAR/92[9]410, CWM:MAY/92[8]418, CWM:MAY/92[15]419, CWM:MAY/92[20]420, CWM:MAY/92[34]422, CWM:MAY/92[44]423, CWM:JUL/92[8]427,

CWM:JUL/92[16]428, CWM:JUL/92[40]432, CWM:JUL/92[64]434, CWM:SEP/92[16]438, CWM:SEP/92[19]440, CWM:NOV/92[41]451, CWM:JAN/93[40]461, CWM:MAR/93[8]465, CWM:MAR/93[32]468, CWM:MAY/93[4]472, CWM:SEP/93[24]495, CWM:SEP/93[35]497, CWM:APR/94[24]505, CWM:JUN/94[14]509, CWM:JUN/94[27]513, CWM:JUN/94[43]517, CWM:AUG/94[8]522, CWM:AUG/94[26]525, CWM:AUG/94[30]527, CWM:AUG/94[60]531, CWM:OCT/94[4]532, CWM:OCT/94[17]534, CWM:OCT/94[34]538, CWM:OCT/94[38]540, CWM:OCT/94[48]542, CWM:DEC/94[26]548, CWM:DEC/94[34]549, CWM:FEB/95[30]561, CWM:APR/95[32]575, CWM:JUN/95[17]581, CWM:AUG/95[4]601, CWM:AUG/95[30]606, CWM:AUG/95[38]609, CWM:OCT/95[22]614, CWM:OCT/95[38]618, CWM:OCT/95[40]619

ADDITIONAL LISTINGS, CWR: CWR:VOL1#1[1]102, CWR:VOL1#1[26]103, CWR:VOL1#1[35]104, CWR:VOL1#1[71]107, CWR:VOL1#2[29]112, CWR:VOL1#2[44]114, CWR:VOL1#3[28]120, CWR:VOL1#3[52]122, CWR:VOL1#4[v]124, CWR:VOL1#4[7]125, CWR:VOL1#4[74]128, CWR:VOL2#1[1]130, CWR:VOL2#1[36]132, CWR:VOL2#2[95]135, CWR:VOL2#2[141]137, CWR:VOL2#2[156]138, CWR:VOL2#3[183]140, CWR:VOL2#3[212]142, CWR:VOL2#3[236]143, CWR:VOL2#3[252]144, CWR:VOL2#4[269]145, CWR:VOL3#1[31]150, CWR:VOL3#2[1]153, CWR:VOL3#2[70]155, CWR:VOL3#3[1]157, CWR:VOL3#3[33]158, CWR:VOL3#4[1]161, CWR:VOL4#2[68]167, CWR:VOL4#3[65]172

ADDITIONAL LISTINGS, CWTI: CWTI:MAR/89[28]103, CWTI:SUMMER/89[13]120, CWTI:SUMMER/89[40]123, CWTI:FEB/90[46]146, CWTI:APR/90[24]152, CWTI:JUN/90[32]159, CWTI:FEB/91[12]189, CWTI:FEB/91[24]191, CWTI:FEB/91[28]192, CWTI:AUG/91[46]218, CWTI:AUG/91[52]219, CWTI:AUG/91[68]222, CWTI:SEP/91[31]229, CWTI:SEP/91[42]231, CWTI:DEC/91[18]236, CWTI:DEC/91[28]239, CWTI:DEC/91[44]241, CWTI:APR/92[35]257, CWTI:SEP/92[22]279, CWTI:SEP/92[31]281, CWTI:SEP/92[42]283, CWTI:NOV/92[18]289, CWTI:NOV/92[49]292, CWTI:MAR/93[40]312, CWTI:MAY/93[26]318, CWTI:MAY/93[29]319, CWTI:JUL/93[14]324, CWTI:SEP/93[14]333, CWTI:NOV/93[55]350, CWTI:JAN/94[18]357, CWTI:MAR/94[29]371, CWTI:JUL/94[44]394, CWTI:SEP/94[8]397, CWTI:SEP/94[49]404, CWTI:DEC/94[32]410, CWTI:DEC/94[73]416, CWTI:JAN/95[27]425, CWTI:JAN/95[34]427, CWTI:JAN/95[42]428, CWTI:JAN/95[48]429, CWTI:MAR/95[60]439, CWTI:AUG/95[28]456, CWTI:AUG/95[46]459, CWTI:DEC/95[14]475, CWTI:DEC/95[67]481, CWTI:DEC/95[76]482

ADDITIONAL LISTINGS, GETTY: GETTY:13[22]254, GETTY:13[64]258, GETTY:13[75]259, GETTY:13[108]261

ADDITIONAL LISTINGS, MH: MH:FEB/91[8]151, MH:JUN/91[20]152, MH:FEB/92[8]156, MH:APR/92[18]157, MH:FEB/93[42]164, MH:APR/94[54]176, MH:AUG/95[30]185

LEE, ROBERT E., JR, *Private, CSA:*
BOOK REVIEW: *RECOLLECTIONS AND LETTERS OF GENERAL ROBERT E. LEE BY HIS SON*
ADDITIONAL LISTING: CWTI:APR/89[38]111
LEE, S.W., *Private, 8th North Carolina Infantry;*
B&G:APR/93[24]520
LEE, SAMUEL P., *Admiral, USN;* ACW:MAY/92[14]358,
ACW:JUL/94[35]478, B&G:DEC/94[10]585,
CWM:JUN/94[50]518, CWR:VOL2#3[183]140
LEE, STEPHEN D., *General, CSA:*
ARTICLE: "SECOND MANASSAS: ENFILADING THUNDER,"
CWM:AUG/94[48]529
GENERAL LISTINGS: *Antietam,* B&G:OCT/95[8]611D, *Atlanta Campaign,* ACW:NOV/95[74]560, CWTI:SUMMER/89[50]124,
Champion's Hill, ACW:NOV/91[22]331, *in book review,*
B&G:FEB/92[26], CWM:APR/95[8], CWM:APR/95[50],
CWNEWS:OCT/89[4], CWNEWS:DEC/95[29],
CWR:VOL3#2[105], *in order of battle,* B&G:DEC/93[12]545,
letters to the editor, B&G:AUG/95[36]607, *Manassas, Second,*
B&G:AUG/92[11]493, GETTY:6[62]175, *Nashville,*
ACW:NOV/95[48]557, *Peninsula Campaign,*
CWM:JUN/95[63]594, *Vicksburg,* AHI:DEC/77[13]176,
AHI:DEC/77[46]177, CWTI:SEPT/89[18]126,
CWTI:MAY/91[24]208, *West Point,* B&G:DEC/91[12]469,
photos, ACW:SEP/92[23]377, B&G:AUG/92[11]493
ADDITIONAL LISTINGS: ACW:JUL/91[18]312, ACW:JUL/92[12]367,
ACW:JUL/92[30]369, ACW:SEP/92[23]377,
ACW:SEP/92[38]379, ACW:MAR/94[42]461,
ACW:SEP/95[48]547, AHI:NOV/73[18]151,
B&G:DEC/91[34]470, B&G:DEC/93[12]545,
B&G:DEC/93[52]548, CWM:JAN/91[12]326,
CWM:JAN/91[40]330, CWM:OCT/95[36]616,
CWM:DEC/95[41]630, CWR:VOL1#1[73]108,
CWR:VOL1#4[64]127, CWR:VOL1#4[74]128,
CWR:VOL2#1[19]131, CWR:VOL2#1[36]132,
CWR:VOL2#1[75]134, CWR:VOL3#2[1]153,
CWTI:MAR/93[32]311, CWTI:NOV/93[55]350,
CWTI:JAN/94[35]361, CWTI:DEC/94[34]411,
GETTY:11[71]234, MH:DEC/95[58]188
LEE, SYDNEY S., *Admiral, CSA;* ARTICLE: "HANDSOMEST MAN IN THE CONFEDERACY," ACW:JUL/94[35]478
LEE, THOMAS, *Lieutenant, 148th Pennsylvania Infantry;*
CWR:VOL2#2[141]137
LEE, WILLIAM H.F., *General, CSA:*
GENERAL LISTINGS: *1863 cavalry battles,* MH:OCT/92[51]162, *The "Blackberry" Raid,* GETTY:11[6]231, *Brandy Station,*
GETTY:11[19]232, *Buckland,* ACW:JUL/92[41]370, *Five Forks,* B&G:APR/92[8]481, *Gettysburg,* GETTY:12[68]246, *in book review,* CWM:OCT/94[8], CWM:AUG/95[45], *in order of battle,* B&G:APR/92[8]481, B&G:APR/94[10]558, *order of battle,* B&G:APR/95[8]595, *Overland Campaign,*
B&G:APR/94[10]558, *Peninsula Campaign,*
CWM:JUN/95[50]589, *West Virginia campaign,*
B&G:AUG/93[10]529, *photo;* ACW:JAN/93[43]397,
CWM:JUL/91[16]358, CWTI:DEC/89[34]136,
CWTI:JUN/90[32]159
ADDITIONAL LISTINGS: ACW:NOV/91[30]332, ACW:JAN/92[16]340,
ACW:JAN/92[22]341, ACW:JAN/92[50]345,
ACW:JAN/93[43]397, ACW:SEP/94[31]486,
ACW:SEP/94[55]489, ACW:MAY/95[10]523,
ACW:MAY/95[38]526, ACW:JUL/95[34]536,
B&G:APR/93[12]518, B&G:OCT/93[12]537,
B&G:JUN/95[22]601, CWM:JUL/91[10]357,

CWM:APR/95[32]575, CWR:VOL1#3[52]122,
CWR:VOL4#4[28]178, CWTI:DEC/89[34]136,
CWTI:JUN/90[32]159, CWTI:JUN/90[43]160,
CWTI:FEB/91[45]194, CWTI:APR/92[35]257,
CWTI:JUN/95[38]447
LEE, WESLEY, *Private, 102nd Ohio Infantry;*
B&G:AUG/95[24]605
LEE, WILLIAM M., *servant to General Lee;* B&G:APR/91[40]450
LEE, WILLIAM O., *Sergeant, 7th Michigan Cavalry;* BOOK
REVIEW: *PERSONAL AND HISTORICAL SKETCHES AND FACIAL HISTORY OF AND BY MEMBERS OF THE SEVENTH REGIMENT MICHIGAN VOLUNTEER CAVALRY 1862-1865*
LEE, WILLIAM R., *Colonel, 20th Massachusetts Infantry;*
AHI:FEB/82[36]225, CWR:VOL3#1[31]150,
CWR:VOL4#4[101]181, CWTI:MAY/89[14]114
LEE, WILLS, *Private, 2nd Richmond Howitzers;*
CWR:VOL4#4[70]180
LEE-LONGSTREET CONTROVERSY; GETTY:4[113]153
LEECH, MARGARET; AHI:OCT/79[10]192
LEEFELDT, HENRY, *Captain, 16th Iowa Infantry;*
ACW:JAN/93[10]393
LEES, I.W.; CWTI:JUN/95[48]448
LEGAL TENDER ACT; CWM:FEB/95[7]
LEGGETT, MORTIMER D., *General, USA;*
ACW:JAN/95[30]505, ACW:NOV/95[74]560,
CWTI:SUMMER/89[40]123, CWTI:SUMMER/89[50]124,
CWTI:JAN/93[20]298
LEGION OF HONOR; ACW:JUL/94[26]477
LEHMAN, ALBERT, *Private, USA;* CWM:MAY/93[8]474
LEHMAN, ED, *Private, USA;* CWTI:FEB/92[29]248
LEHMANN, EDWARD, *Private, 1st U.S. Cavalry;*
ACW:NOV/93[26]441
LEIB, HERMANN, *Colonel, USA;* CWR:VOL3#3[33]158
LEIER, JACOB, *Private, 20th New York Infantry;*
B&G:OCT/95[8]611B
LEIGH, BENJAMIN W., *Major, 7th Ohio Infantry;*
GETTY:9[81]216
LEIGH, WATKINS, *Major, CSA;* GETTY:10[120]229
LEINBACH, JULIUS A., *Private, 26th North Carolina Infantry;*
GETTY:5[19]158
LEISENRING, GEORGE, *Private, USA;* CWM:JUL/92[27]431
LEISTER, LYDIA, *civilian;* GETTY:6[77]177,
GETTY:11[102]237
LEITH, DALLAS, *Private, 6th Virginia Cavalry;*
CWM:NOV/92[64]453
LEITNER, WILLIAM Z., *Captain, 2nd South Carolina Infantry;*
GETTY:5[35]159
LEMAGIC, CHARLES L., *Chaplain, 2nd Louisiana Cavalry (Union);* CWM:MAR/91[50]340
LEMON, CHARLES, *Major, USA;* B&G:FEB/95[8]590A
LENERIUEX, FRANCIS M., *Sergeant, 15th South Carolina Infantry;* GETTY:5[35]159
LEON, PIERRE, *seaman, USN;* CWTI:DEC/94[12]408
LEONARD, JOHN, *Lieutenant Colonel, 72nd New York Infantry;* CWM:MAY/92[20]420
LEONARD, SAMUEL H., *Colonel, 13th Massachusetts Infantry;*
B&G:APR/95[8]595, GETTY:13[33]255
LEONARD, WILLIAM, *Private, USA;* ACW:JUL/93[27]423
LEPPIEN, GEORGE F., *Captain, 5th Maine Light Artillery;*
B&G:AUG/92[11]493, B&G:OCT/95[20]612
LESLEY, JOHN, *Major, CSA;* ACW:JUL/93[66]427
LESLEY, JAMES, JR; MH:OCT/95[8]187

LESLIE, FRANK; ARTICLE: "THE FRANK LESLIES,"
AHI:JUL/70[12]128

LESTER, ANDREW, *Pvt., 22nd VA Inf.,* CWR:VOL1#3[52]122

LESTER, HENRY C., *Colonel, 3rd Minnesota Infantry;*
ACW:MAY/91[12]302

LESUEUR, CHARLES M., *Captain, CSA;* ACW:JUL/93[27]423

LETCHER (VIRGINIA) ARTILLERY; GETTY:4[33]146

LETCHER, JOHN, *Governor, Virginia:*
BOOK REVIEW: *JOHN LETCHER OF VIRGINIA: THE STORY OF VIRGINIA'S CIVIL WAR GOVERNOR*
ADDITIONAL LISTINGS: ACW:MAY/92[14]358, ACW:JAN/92[47]344,
ACW:JUL/95[34]536, B&G:AUG/91[11]458,
B&G:FEB/92[32]477, B&G:AUG/93[10]529,
B&G:FEB/94[8]550, B&G:AUG/94[10]574,
CWM:MAR/91[65]342, CWM:JUL/91[48]374,
CWM:JAN/92[21]402, CWTI:MAY/89[22]116,
CWTI:DEC/89[34]136, CWTI:MAY/92[29]263,
CWTI:MAR/94[29]371, CWTI:JUN/95[18]444,
CWTI:JUN/95[38]447, CWTI:OCT/95[48]470,
GETTY:11[6]231, MH:FEB/91[8]151, *photo,*
CWTI:APR/89[38]111

LETCHER, MARGARET; ARTICLE: "I WAS THERE,"
CWM:JAN/92[21]402

LETCHER, SAM HOUSTON, *Lieutenant, CSA;*
CWM:JUL/91[48]374

LETTERMAN, JOHATHAN, *Surgeon, USA;* B&G:DEC/94[28],
CWM:MAY/91[26]349, CWM:DEC/95[54]632,
GETTY:10[53]225, GETTY:11[102]237

LETTERS & DIARIES:

Also, see listing under **"DIARIES, JOURNALS & LETTERS"**
ARTICLES: "ATTACK AND COUNTERATTACK,"
GETTY:4[126]154, GETTY:5[128]167, "DIARY OF THE
VICKSBURG SIEGE," AHI:DEC/77[46]177, "GOING BACK
INTO THE UNION AT LAST," CWTI:FEB/91[12]189,
"I WAS THERE," CWM:MAR/91[14]334,
CWM:MAR/92[56]415, "LETTERS TO THE EDITOR,"
CWTI:JUL/92[8]269, CWTI:SEP/92[10]278, "NEVER HEARD
BEFORE ON THE AMERICAN CONTINENT,"
GETTY:10[107]227, "ON THE RAPPAHANNOCK,
CHRISTMAS DAY, 1862," AHI:DEC/68[25]117, "TO THE
POTOMAC WITH SERGEANT CURRY,"
CWTI:SEPT/89[24]128, "WRITING HOME TO TALLADEGA,"
CWTI:DEC/90[56]184
BOOK REVIEWS: *AS IT WAS: REMINISCENCES OF A SOLDIER
OF THE THIRD TEXAS CAVALRY AND THE
NINETEENTH LOUISIANA INFANTRY * THE BROTHERS'
WAR: CIVIL WAR LETTERS TO THEIR LOVED ONES
FROM THE BLUE AND GRAY * THE CITIZEN SOLDIER;
OR MEMOIRS OF A VOLUNTEER * CIVIL WAR MEMOIRS
OF TWO REBEL SISTERS * THE CONFEDERACY IS ON
HER WAY UP THE SPOUT: LETTERS TO SOUTH
CAROLINA, 1861-1864 * "DEAR FRIEND ANNA": THE
CIVIL WAR LETTERS OF A COMMON SOLDIER FROM
MAINE * "DEAR MOTHER: DON'T GRIEVE ABOUT ME. IF
I GET KILLED, I'LL ONLY BE DEAD." LETTERS FROM
GEORGIA SOLDIERS IN THE CIVIL WAR * FIELDS OF
FURY: FROM THE WILDERNESS TO, THE CRATER: AN
EYEWITNESS HISTORY * MEMOIRS OF A SWISS
OFFICER IN THE AMERICAN CIVIL WAR * PERSONAL
RECOLLECTIONS OF THE WAR OF 1861*
Abbott, Henry L.; BOOK REVIEW: *FALLEN LEAVES: THE CIVIL
WAR LETTERS OF MAJOR HENRY LIVERMORE ABBOTT*

Andrews, W.H.; BOOK REVIEW: *FOOTPRINTS OF A REGIMENT:
A RECOLLECTION OF THE FIRST GEORGIA REGULARS
1861-1865*

Barber, Charles; BOOK REVIEW: *THE CIVIL WAR LETTERS OF
CHARLES BARBER, PRIVATE, 104TH NEW YORK
VOLUNTEER INFANTRY*

Bartlett, Harold J.; BOOK REVIEW: *TO THE SOUND OF
MUSKETRY AND TAP OF THE DRUM: A HISTORY OF
MICHIGAN'S BATTERY D THROUGH THE LETTERS OF
ARTIFICER HAROLD J. BARTLETT, 1861-1864*

Bellard, Alfred; BOOK REVIEW: *GONE FOR A SOLDIER: THE
CIVIL WAR MEMOIRS OF PRIVATE ALFRED BELLARD,*

Bevens, William E.; BOOK REVIEW: *REMINISCENCES OF A
PRIVATE: WILLIAM E. BEVENS OF THE FIRST
ARKANSAS INFANTRY, C.S.A.*

Bird, Edgeworth and Sallie; BOOK REVIEWS: *THE GRANITE
FARM LETTERS: THE CIVIL WAR CORRESPONDENCE
OF EDGEWORTH & SALLIE BIRD*

Birmingham, Theodore; BOOK REVIEW: *YOURS IN LOVE: THE
BIRMINGHAM CIVIL WAR LETTERS*

Breckinridge, Lucy; BOOK REVIEW: *LUCY BRECKINRIDGE OF
GROVE HILL: THE JOURNAL OF A VIRGINIA GIRL,
1862-1864*

Brewster, Charles H.; BOOK REVIEWS: *WHEN THIS CRUEL
WAR IS OVER: THE CIVIL WAR LETTERS OF CHARLES
HARVEY BREWSTER*

Browder, George R.; BOOK REVIEW: *THE HEAVENS ARE
WEEPING: THE DIARIES OF GEORGE RICHARD
BROWDER 1852-1886*

Burgwyn, William H.; BOOK REVIEWS: *A CAPTAIN'S WAR: THE
LETTERS AND DIARIES OF WILLIAM H.S. BURGWYN,
1861-1865*

Caldwell, Lycurgus; BOOK REVIEW: *MY HEART IS SO
REBELLIOUS: THE CALDWELL LETTERS, 1861-1865*

Chamberlayne, John H.; BOOK REVIEW: *HAM
CHAMBERLAYNE—VIRGINIAN: LETTERS AND PAPERS
OF AN ARTILLERY OFFICER IN THE WAR FOR
SOUTHERN INDEPENDENCE 1861-1865*

Chisholm, Daniel; BOOK REVIEW: *THE CIVIL WAR NOTEBOOK
OF DANIEL CHISHOLM: A CHRONICLE OF DAILY LIFE
IN THE UNION ARMY 1864-1865*

Clemson, Floride; BOOK REVIEW: *A REBEL CAME HOME: THE
DIARY AND LETTERS OF FLORIDE CLEMSON, 1863-1866*

Conolly, Thomas; BOOK REVIEW: *AN IRISHMAN IN DIXIE:
THOMAS CONOLLY'S DIARY OF THE FALL OF THE
CONFEDERACY*

Cormany, —; BOOK REVIEW: *THE CORMANY DIARIES: A
NORTHERN FAMILY IN THE CIVIL WAR*

Davis, Billy; BOOK REVIEW: *THE CIVIL WAR JOURNAL OF
BILLY DAVIS*

Denoon, Charles E.; BOOK REVIEW: *CHARLIE'S LETTERS, THE
CIVIL WAR CORRESPONDENCE*

Ewell, Richard S.; BOOK REVIEW: *"OLD BALD HEAD" THE
PORTRAIT OF A SOLDIER AND THE MAKING OF A
SOLDIER: LETTERS OF GENERAL R.S. EWELL*

Favill, John M.; BOOK REVIEW: *THE DIARY OF A YOUNG
OFFICER*

Fisk, Wilbur; BOOK REVIEWS: *HARD MARCHING EVERY DAY:
THE CIVIL WAR LETTERS OF PRIVATE WILBUR FISK,
1861-1865*

Fox, Gustavus V.; BOOK REVIEW: *CONFIDENTIAL
CORRESPONDENCE OF GUSTAVUS VASA FOX*

STUCKENBERG, CHAPLAIN OF THE 145TH
PENNSYLVANIA VOLUNTEER INFANTRY

Sullivan, James P.; BOOK REVIEW: *AN IRISHMAN IN THE
IRON BRIGADE: THE CIVIL WAR MEMOIRS OF JAMES P.
SULLIVAN, SERGEANT, 6TH WISCONSIN VOLUNTEERS*

Thomas, Ella; BOOK REVIEW: *THE SECRET EYE: THE
JOURNAL OF ELLA GERTRUDE CLANTON THOMAS*

Thompson, M. Jeff; BOOK REVIEW: *THE CIVIL WAR
REMINISCENCES OF GENERAL M. JEFF THOMPSON*

Wakeman, Sarah; BOOK REVIEW: *AN UNCOMMON SOLDIER:
THE CIVIL WAR LETTERS OF SARAH ROSETTA
WAKEMAN, ALIAS PVT. LYONS WAKEMAN, 153RD
REGIMENT, NEW YORK STATE VOLUNTEERS, 1862-1864*

Ward, W.W.; BOOK REVIEW: *'FOR THE SAKE OF MY COUNTRY:'
THE DIARY OF COL. W.W. WARD, 9TH TENNESSEE
CAVALRY, MORGAN'S BRIGADE, C.S.A.*

Weld, Stephen M.; BOOK REVIEW: *WAR LETTERS AND
DIARIES OF STEPHEN MINOT WELD, 1861-1865*

White, Daniel; BOOK REVIEW: *DEAR WIFE, LETTERS OF A
CIVIL WAR SOLDIER*

White, George R., BOOK REVIEW: *THE CIVIL WAR: LETTERS
HOME FROM GEO. R. WHITE*

Williams, Alpheus S.; BOOK REVIEW: *FROM THE CANNON'S
MOUTH: THE CIVIL WAR LETTERS OF GENERAL
ALPHEUS S. WILLIAMS*

Wren, James; BOOK REVIEWS: *FROM NEW BERN TO
FREDERICKSBURG: CAPTAIN JAMES WREN'S DIARY*

Zachry, Alfred; ARTICLE: "FIGHTING WITH THE 3D
GEORGIA," CWTI:SEP/94[26]400

LEVANS, ELDRIDGE, *Lieutenant, 88th Pennsylvania Infantry;*
GETTY:10[7]221

LEVENSALLER, HENRY C., *Surgeon, 19th Maine Infantry;*
GETTY:10[53]225

LEVY, BENJAMIN, *Private, 40th New York Infantry;*
CWM:SEP/93[8]493

LEVY, JOHN, *Private, 3rd Georgia Infantry;*
CWTI:SEP/94[26]400

LEWIS' FARM, VIRGINIA, BATTLE OF; B&G:APR/92[8]481

LEWIS, ASA, *Corporal, 6th Kentucky Infantry;*
ACW:JUL/91[12]310

LEWIS, CHARLES L., *Private, 2nd Tennessee Cavalry;*
CWR:VOL4#1[1]163

LEWIS, CHARLES, *Colonel, CSA;* ACW:JUL/93[42]425

LEWIS, DAVID, *Private, Pennsylvania Light Artillery;*
ACW:MAY/95[62]

LEWIS, EDWARD, *Corporal, 5th New York Infantry;*
CWR:VOL1#2[42]113

LEWIS, FREDERICK, *Lieutenant, 5th New York Infantry;*
CWR:VOL1#2[29]112, CWR:VOL1#2[42]113

LEWIS, GEORGE; GETTY:9[41]212

LEWIS, JAMES, *Governor of Wisconsin;* CWTI:MAR/89[20]102

LEWIS, HENRY, *Lieutenant, CSN;* ARTICLE: "NO LADY WAS
SHE," CWTI:MAY/92[29]263, MH:FEB/91[8]151

LEWIS, JAMES, *Captain, USMC;* CWR:VOL2#3[183]140

LEWIS, JAMES H., *Lieutenant Colonel, CSA;*
B&G:DEC/95[9]615

LEWIS, JAMES H., *Private, 2nd Wisconsin Infantry,*
GETTY:11[57]233

LEWIS, JIM, *black servant to Stonewall Jackson;*
GETTY:6[94]180

LEWIS, JOHN L., *General, CSA;* CWR:VOL3#1[1]149,
CWR:VOL4#2[1]165, CWR:VOL4#2[118]169

LEWIS, RICHARD, *Lieutenant, Palmetto Sharpshooters;*
CWR:VOL3#2[70]155

LEWIS, THOMAS, *Private, Sumter Artillery;*
CWR:VOL3#2[1]153

LEWIS, TREVANION D., *Colonel, 8th Louisiana Infantry;*
CWTI:FEB/91[12]189

LEWIS, W. GASTON, *General, CSA;* B&G:APR/94[10]558,
CWTI:APR/92[42]259, GETTY:9[81]216

LEWIS, WARNER, *Colonel, CSA;* CWTI:SEP/90[52]179

LEWIS, WILBUR F., *Captain, 5th New York Infantry;*
CWR:VOL1#2[29]112, CWR:VOL1#2[42]113

LEWIS, WILLIAM G., *Lieutenant Colonel, 43rd North Carolina
Infantry;* GETTY:13[33]255

LEXINGTON, MISSOURI, BATTLE OF;
ACW:MAY/91[10]301, CWTI:JAN/94[29]360

LEXINGTON, TENNESSEE, ENGAGEMENT AT;
CWM:DEC/95[48]631

LEXINGTON, VIRGINIA; ARTICLE: "LEXINGTON: LEE'S
LAST RETREAT," CWM:JUL/91[48]374

LEYARD, WILLIAM N., *Lieutenant, 3rd Alabama Infantry;*
GETTY:12[1]240

LIBERTY HALL (VIRGINIA) VOLUNTEERS; BOOK REVIEWS:
*TED BARCLAY, LIBERTY HALL VOLUNTEERS: LETTERS
FROM THE STONEWALL BRIGADE*

LIDDELL, PHILIP F., *Lieutenant Colonel, 11th Mississippi
Infantry;* CWR:VOL2#4[269]145, GETTY:9[98]217

LIDDELL, ST. JOHN R., *General, CSA;* B&G:OCT/92[32]499,
B&G:JUN/94[34], CWR:VOL4#2[26]166,
CWR:VOL4#2[118]169, CWR:VOL4#3[50]171

LIDDICK, DANIEL, *Private, 133rd Pennsylvania Infantry;*
B&G:OCT/94[42]583

LIEBER, FRANCIS, *Doctor:*
ARTICLE: "FRANCIS LIEBER'S SEARCH FOR A MORE
HUMANE SHADE OF WAR," CWM:AUG/95[58]611
ADDITIONAL LISTING: B&G:DEC/92[38]507

LIEPS, DAVID, *Private, 1st Wisconsin Artillery;*
B&G:FEB/94[8]550

LIGAL, JOHN, *Private, 9th Massachusetts Artillery;*
GETTY:5[47]160

LIGHTBURN, JOSEPH A.J., *General, USA;*
B&G:AUG/95[8]604, CWTI:SUMMER/89[40]123,
CWTI:SEP/92[28]280, CWTI:JAN/93[20]298

LIGHTFOOT, J., *Private, 22nd Virginia Infantry;*
CWR:VOL1#3[52]122

LIGHTFOOT, J.N., *Lieutenant Colonel, 6th Alabama Infantry;*
ACW:JAN/95[46]507

LIGHTNER, DANIEL, *Private, 53rd Pennsylvania Infantry;*
GETTY:11[80]235

LIGHTNING BRIGADE:
ARTICLES: "LIGHTING BRIGADE STRIKES FIGHTING JOE,"
ACW:MAY/95[49]527, "MOST SPLENDID PIECE OF
STRATEGY," CWM:OCT/94[48]542, "THE STEADIEST BODY
OF MEN I EVER SAW: JOHN T. WILDER AND THE
LIGHTNING BRIGADE," B&G:OCT/92[32]499
ADDITIONAL LISTINGS: B&G:OCT/92[10]496, B&G:APR/93[6]517,
CWM:JUL/92[24]430, CWM:OCT/94[4]532,
CWTI:MAY/92[48]267

LIKENS, JAMES B., *Colonel, CSA;* CWR:VOL4#2[118]169

LILLEY, ROBERT D., *Colonel, 25th Virginia Infantry;*
B&G:AUG/93[10]529, B&G:APR/94[10]558

LILLY, ELI, *Major, USA;* ACW:SEP/95[10]543,
B&G:JUN/92[32]488, B&G:OCT/92[10]496,

B&G:OCT/92[32]499, CWM:JUL/92[24]430, *photo;*
B&G:OCT/92[32]499
LILLY, HENRY C., *Colonel, 14th Kentucky Cavalry;*
ACW:SEP/95[22]544
LILLY, WILLIAM, *Sergeant, 149th New York Infantry;*
CWR:VOL4#3[1]170
LINCOLN, ABRAHAM:
ARTICLES: "A FEW APPROPRIATE REMARKS,"
AHI:NOV/88[37]278, "A MAN OF SORROWS,"
CWTI:DEC/95[24]477, "A MEMORIAL DIRGE FOR
LINCOLN," B&G:JUN/95[35]602, "A PAPER LINK TO A
CONSPIRACY," CWTI:SEP/91[15]225, "A PRESIDENTIAL
GALLERY," AHI:APR/89[20]282, "A ROLLING MEMENTO,"
CWTI:MAR/95[54]438, "A SHRINE IN THE GOLDEN
STATE," CWTI:MAY/92[20]262, "ABRAHAM LINCOLN,
INVENTOR," AHI:JAN/81[4]213, "AFTER LIFE'S FITFUL
FEVER," AHI:MAR/93[50]310, "THE ART OF REA REDIFER:
INTERPRETATIONS OF LINCOLN," B&G:OCT/92[55]501,
"AT NEW SALEM, LINCOLN MADE A STARTLING
TRANSFORMATION FROM COUNTRY BUMPKIN TO
POLISHED LAWYER," ACW:MAR/94[66]463, "BOOTH
DERRINGER AUCTIONED," AHI:OCT/94[8]321, "CLOAK &
DAGGER FIASCO," ACW:JAN/92[30]342, "COLLECTING
LINCOLN," CWTI:DEC/95[30]478, "DEAR MR. LINCOLN,"
AHI:JAN/94[50]319
ARTICLES, continued: "EYEWITNESSES REMEMBER THE
'FEARFUL NIGHT'," CWTI:MAR/93[12]307, "THE FALL OF
RICHMOND," ACW:MAY/95[38]526, "FIFTEEN
PRESIDENTIAL DECISIONS THAT SHAPED AMERICA,"
AHI:APR/89[36]283, "FIRST BLOOD IN BALTIMORE,"
ACW:NOV/95[30]555, "THE FOUNDING FATHERS'
'REPUBLICAN IDEAL' NOURISHED ABRAHAM
LINCOLN'S BELIEF IN FREEDOM FOR ALL,"
ACW:NOV/94[8]493, "GETTYSBURG FINALE,"
ACW:JUL/93[50]426, "GETTYSBURG REMEMBERS
PRESIDENT LINCOLN," GETTY:9[122]220, "THE GREAT
DEBATE," ACW:MAY/93[47]417, "THE HAPPIEST DAY OF
HIS LIFE," CWTI:DEC/95[76]482, "THE HEARTBEAT IN
THE WHITE HOUSE," AHI:APR/70[38]125, "I MYSELF WAS
AT THE FRONT," CWTI:FEB/91[28]192, "I SHOULD NOT
SAY ANY FOOLISH THINGS," CWTI:DEC/95[22]476,
"INTERVIEW WITH LINCOLN," AHI:NOV/72[10]141, "JOHN
SUMMERFIELD STAPLES BORE THE PRESIDENT'S
MUSKET IN THE CIVIL WAR," ACW:NOV/91[16]330, "THE
LAST BEST HOPE OF EARTH: ABRAHAM LINCOLN AND
THE PROMISE OF AMERICA," AHI:NOV/93[16]314
ARTICLES, continued: "LINCOLN AND THE IRONCLADS COME TO
TELEVISION," CWTI:MAR/91[42]202, "THE LINCOLN
FAMILY ALBUM," AHI:NOV/90[44]293, "LINCOLN HOME
REOPENS," AHI:MAY/88[5]269, "LINCOLN HOME TO BE
RESTORED," AHI:JUN/85[53]252, "LINCOLN MORE THAN
COUNTRY LAWYER," AHI:SEP/92[11]303, "LINCOLN
MUSEUM TO RELOCATE," AHI:JUL/93[14]311,
"LINCOLN'S DICTATORSHIP," AHI:NOV/71[32]136,
"LINCOLN'S FIRST LOVE," CWTI:DEC/95[40]479,
"LINCOLN'S GRATITUDE REGAINED,"
B&G:DEC/92[38]507, "LINCOLN'S HUMOR,"
AHI:NOV/70[22]130, "LINCOLN'S 'LOST' TELEGRAM,"
CWTI:MAR/91[22]199, "LINCOLN'S MURDER: THE SIMPLE
CONSPIRACY THEORY," CWTI:DEC/91[28]239,
"LINCOLN'S SECRET ARMS RACE," CWTI:OCT/95[32]468,
"LINCOLNIANA UNCOVERED," AHI:NOV/88[6]276

ARTICLES, continued: "THE LITTLE GIANT," AHI:OCT/70[23]129,
"THE LIVELY PAGEANTRY OF DEATH,"
CWTI:DEC/95[90]483, "THE LONG TRIP HOME,"
AHI:JUL/95[30]324, "THE LOST LINCOLN
PHOTOGRAPHS," AHI:FEB/69[35]120, "THE MAN AT THE
WHITE HOUSE WINDOW," CWTI:DEC/95[52]480, "MINE
EYES HAVE SEEN THE GLORY," CWTI:SEP/93[30]336,
"MR. LINCOLN'S SPRINGFIELD," AHI:MAR/89[26]280, "OH,
DEM BONES, DEM DRY BONES," CWTI:SEP/91[41]230,
"ON HISTORY'S SLIGHTER SIDE," AHI:JUN/79[19]188,
"THE PAINTER AND THE PRESIDENT,"
CWTI:FEB/92[21]247, "THE PLAIN TRUTH WAS TOO
PLAIN FOR HORACE LURTON," CWTI:DEC/94[79]417,
"THE PLAN TO KIDNAP LINCOLN THAT FAILED BY ONE
DAY," AHI:NOV/80[6]208, "THE PLOT TO ROB LINCOLN'S
TOMB," AHI:JAN/71[12]131, "THE PRESIDENT AT PLAY,"
CWTI:DEC/95[14]475
ARTICLES, continued: "RE-CREATING THE GREAT DEBATE,"
AHI:DEC/94[68]322, "SOME THOUGHTS FOR THE
PRESIDENT'S CONSIDERATION," CWTI:SEP/92[46]284,
"TESTS ON LINCOLN'S TISSUE POSTPONED,"
AHI:SEP/92[11]304, "TRAGEDIAN'S GREATEST ROLE,"
ACW:MAR/93[35]405, "TRIED BY WAR,"
CWTI:DEC/95[67]481, "TRUE AMERICAN MADNESS:
INAUGURAL BALLS," AHI:NOV/72[37]143, "TURNING THE
PAGES OF HISTORY: A NEW DRAFT OF THE,
GETTYSBURG ADDRESS LOCATED," GETTY:6[107]182,
"THE UNDISTINGUISHED WOODRUFF GUN HAD ONLY
ONE TRUE SUPPORTER, ABRAHAM LINCOLN—BUT ONE
WAS ENOUGH," ACW:JUL/94[8]474, "VISITING THE SITE
OF ABRAHAM LINCOLN'S ASSASSINATION GIVES
HISTORY BUFFS AN EERIE SENSE OF STEPPING BACK
IN TIME," ACW:MAY/95[68]529, "THE WAR ELECTION OF
1864," AHI:OCT/68[4]116, "WAS LINCOLN THE GREAT
EMANCIPATOR?" CWTI:MAY/94[46]385, "WASHINGTON
JOURNALIST AND LOBBYIST ANNA ELLA CARROLL
WAS ABRAHAM LINCOLN'S SECRET STRATEGIC
WEAPON," ACW:MAR/95[8]512, "WHAT DID LINCOLN
ACTUALLY SAY?" AHI:NOV/88[43]279, "WHAT REALLY
HAPPENED TO THE ASSASSIN?" CWTI:JUL/92[50]275,
"WHATEVER BECAME OF BOSTON CORBETT?"
CWTI:MAY/91[48]211, "WHO'S UP AND WHO'S DOWN IN
CIVIL WAR HISTORY: ONE'S REPUTATION
INCREASINGLY DEPENDS ON WHO'S TELLING THE
TALE, ACW:MAR/95[6]511, "WHY SHOULD THE SPIRIT OF
MORTAL BE PROUD?" AHI:APR/76[32]166
BOOK REVIEWS: *A RISING THUNDER: FROM LINCOLN'S
ELECTION TO THE BATTLE OF BULL RUN, AN
EYEWITNESS HISTORY * A. LINCOLN: HIS LAST 24
HOURS * ABANDONED BY LINCOLN: A MILITARY
BIOGRAPHY OF GENERAL JOHN POPE * ABRAHAM
LINCOLN AND THE SECOND AMERICAN REVOLUTION *
ABRAHAM LINCOLN AT CITY POINT * ABRAHAM
LINCOLN THE ORATOR: PENETRATING THE LINCOLN
LEGEND * ABRAHAM LINCOLN'S FLAG * ABRAHAM
LINCOLN, 1809-1858 * ABRAHAM LINCOLN, A
BIOGRAPHY * ABRAHAM LINCOLN * ABRAHAM
LINCOLN: A HISTORY * ABRAHAM LINCOLN: A PRESS
PORTRAIT * ABRAHAM LINCOLN: HIS STORY IN HIS
OWN WORDS *ABRAHAM LINCOLN: SOURCES AND
STYLE OF LEADERSHIP *ABRAHAM LINCOLN: THE
MAN BEHIND THE MYTHS*

BOOK REVIEWS, continued: *THE AMERICAN CONSCIENCE: THE DRAMA OF THE LINCOLN-DOUGLAS DEBATES * THE ASSASSINATION OF LINCOLN: HISTORY AND MYTH * BLACK EASTER: THE ASSASSINATION OF ABRAHAM LINCOLN * BUILDING THE MYTH: SELECTED SPEECHES MEMORIALIZING ABRAHAM LINCOLN * CIVIL WAR JUSTICE: UNION ARMY EXECUTIONS UNDER LINCOLN * THE COLLECTED WORKS OF ABRAHAM LINCOLN, 1848-1865 (VOLUME II) SECOND SUPPLEMENT * THE COLLECTED WORKS OF ABRAHAM LINCOLN: SUPPLEMENT 1832-1865, NUMBER 7 * COLLECTED WORKS OF ABRAHAM LINCOLN * COLONEL COGGESHALL—THE MAN WHO SAVED LINCOLN * COME RETRIBUTION: THE CONFEDERATE SECRET SERVICE AND THE ASSASSINATION OF LINCOLN*

BOOK REVIEWS, continued: *DEAR MR. LINCOLN: LETTERS TO THE PRESIDENT * THE FACE OF LINCOLN * THE FATE OF LIBERTY: ABRAHAM LINCOLN AND CIVIL LIBERTIES * THE GETTYSBURG SOLDIERS' CEMETERY AND LINCOLN'S ADDRESS * THE GREAT AMERICAN MYTH: THE TRUE STORY OF LINCOLN'S MURDER * HERNDON'S LINCOLN: THE TRUE STORY OF A GREAT LIFE * THE HISTORIAN'S LINCOLN: PSEUDOHISTORY, PSYCHOHISTORY, AND HISTORY * THE HISTORIAN'S LINCOLN: REBUTTALS: WHAT THE UNIVERSITY PRESS WOULD NOT PRINT * THE INNER WORLD OF ABRAHAM LINCOLN * IT DIDN'T HAPPEN THE WAY YOU THINK. THE LINCOLN ASSASSINATION: WHAT THE EXPERTS MISSED * THE JEWEL OF LIBERTY: ABRAHAM LINCOLN'S RE-ELECTION AND THE END OF SLAVERY * THE LAST BEST HOPE OF EARTH: ABRAHAM LINCOLN AND THE PROMISE OF AMERICA*

BOOK REVIEWS, continued: *THE LINCOLN FAMILY * THE LINCOLN IMAGE * THE LINCOLN MURDER CONSPIRACIES * THE LINCOLN NO ONE KNOWS * THE LINCOLN PERSUASION: REMAKING AMERICAN LIBERALISM * THE LINCOLN-DOUGLAS DEBATES: THE FIRST COMPLETE, UNEXPURGATED TEXT * LINCOLN AND BLACK FREEDOM * LINCOLN AND HIS GENERALS * LINCOLN AND THE ECONOMICS OF THE AMERICAN DREAM * LINCOLN AND THE MUSIC OF THE CIVIL WAR * LINCOLN AND THE TOOLS OF WAR * LINCOLN AND THE WAR DEMOCRATS: THE GRAND EROSION OF CONSERVATIVE TRADITION * LINCOLN AT GETTYSBURG: THE WORDS THAT REMADE AMERICA * LINCOLN COLLECTOR * LINCOLN DAY BY DAY*

BOOK REVIEWS, continued: *LINCOLN FINDS A GENERAL: A MILITARY STUDY OF THE CIVIL WAR * LINCOLN IN AMERICAN MEMORY * LINCOLN IN PHOTOGRAPHS * LINCOLN MEMORIAL * LINCOLN ON DEMOCRACY * LINCOLN THE PRESIDENT * LINCOLN THE WAR PRESIDENT, THE GETTYSBURG LECTURES * LINCOLN VS DOUGLAS: THE GREAT DEBATES CAMAPIGN, * LINCOLN'S GENERALS * LINCOLN'S LOST SPEECH * LINCOLN'S LOYALISTS: UNION SOLDIERS FROM THE CONFEDERACY * LINCOLN'S PREPARATION FOR GREATNESS * LINCOLN, DOUGLAS AND SLAVERY * LINCOLN, LAND, AND LABOR, 1809-60 * LINCOLN, THE SOUTH, AND SLAVERY: THE POLITICAL DIMENSION * LINCOLN, THE WAR PRESIDENT: THE GETTYSBURG LECTURES * LINCOLN * LINCOLN: SPEECHES AND WRITINGS*

BOOK REVIEWS, continued: *"NO SORROW LIKE OUR SORROW": NORTHERN PROTESTANT MINISTERS AND THE ASSASSINATION OF LINCOLN * POLITICAL PARTIES AND AMERICAN POLITICAL DEVELOPMENT FROM THE AGE OF JACKSON TO THE AGE OF LINCOLN * PRELUDE TO GREATNESS: LINCOLN IN THE 1850'S * THE PRESIDENCY OF ABRAHAM LINCOLN * PRESIDENT LINCOLN'S THIRD LARGEST CITY, BROOKLYN AND THE CIVIL WAR * THE PRESIDENT'S WIFE: MARY TODD LINCOLN * THE SHADOWS RISE: ABRAHAM LINCOLN AND THE ANN RUTLEDGE LEGEND * WASHINGTON D.C., IN LINCOLN'S TIME * WILLIAM HENRY SEWARD: LINCOLN'S RIGHT HAND * WITH MALICE TOWARD NONE: THE LIFE OF ABRAHAM LINCOLN * WITNESS TO AN ERA: THE LIFE AND PHOTOGRAPHY OF ALEXANDER GARDNER; THE CIVIL WAR, LINCOLN, AND THE WEST*

COMPILATIONS: *The Abraham Lincoln Encyclopedia,* CWTI:DEC/95[67]481, *Abraham LIncoln: His Speeches and Writings,* CWTI:DEC/95[40]479, *Abraham Lincoln: Speeches and Writings,* CWTI:DEC/95[40]479, *Lincoln in American Memory,* CWTI:DEC/95[67]481, *Lincoln on Democracy,* CWTI:DEC/95[40]479, *Political Thought of Abraham Lincoln,* CWTI:DEC/95[40]479, *Portable Abraham Lincoln,* CWTI:DEC/95[40]479, *Selected Writings and Speeches of Lincoln,* CWTI:DEC/95[40]479, *Uncollected Letters of Abraham Lincoln,* CWTI:DEC/95[40]479

GENERAL LISTINGS: *1864 election,* CWTI:FEB/90[54]147, *abolition,* ACW:NOV/95[8]552, *Abraham Lincoln Birthplace National Historic Site;* AHI:APR/89[43]284, *Ambrose E. Burnside,* CWTI:JAN/95[34]427, *Antietam,* CWM:NOV/91[35]392, CWM:JAN/92[44]406, *Atlanta Campaign,* ACW:NOV/95[22]554, CWTI:SUMMER/89[50]124, *Ball's Bluff,* CWTI:MAY/89[14]114, *balloons,* AHI:JUN/84[24]239, *"The Battle Hymn of the Republic";* ACW:MAR/94[10]457, CWTI:SEPT/89[40]130, *Benjamin H. Helm,* ACW:MAR/93[55]408, *blockade,* ACW:JAN/91[47]288, *Bloody Kansas,* AHI:JUL/75[4]160, *call for volunteers,* ACW:JUL/94[10]475, CWTI:MAY/94[24]381, *Cassius M. Clay,* AHI:MAY/69[12]121, *Chancellorsville,* MH:JUN/92[50]159, *Chantilly,* ACW:JAN/95[54]508, *Charles P. Stone,* CWTI:MAY/89[21]115, *Chattanooga,* CWTI:SEP/92[22]279, *colored troops,* CWTI:DEC/89[42]137, *Common Soldiers,* AHI:APR/68[4]115, *conscription,* ACW:MAR/92[22]351, CWTI:NOV/92[49]292, *Cooper Union Address,* ACW:NOV/94[8]493, B&G:FEB/94[24]551, *Cordelia Harvey;* CWTI:MAR/89[20]102, *Cumberland Gap,* ACW:JUL/91[26]313

GENERAL LISTINGS, continued: *David G. Farragut,* ACW:SEP/95[30]545, *David Hunter,* CWTI:JAN/94[46]364, CWTI:MAR/94[38]372, *Don C. Buell,* CWTI:NOV/92[18]289, *editorial,* ACW:JAN/91[6]281, ACW:MAR/91[6]290, *election,* CWTI:MAR/95[8]431, *Eli Parker,* AHI:NOV/69[13]124, *Elmer Ellsworth,* AHI:DEC/71[30]138, *espionage,* MH:FEB/94[8]175, *Ford's Theatre;* AHI:APR/89[43]284, *Fort Calhoun,* ACW:JAN/95[74]510, *Fort Fisher,* ACW:JAN/95[38]506, *Fort Pillow,* CWTI:NOV/93[65]351, *Fort Sumter,* CWTI:MAY/92[45]266, *Fredericksburg,* AHI:JUN/78[4]180, *General History,* AHI:MAY/71[3]133A, *George B. McClellan,* ACW:SEP/95[54]548, *George E. Pickett,* CWTI:JUL/94[44]394, *George H. Thomas,* ACW:NOV/95[48]557, *Gettysburg Address,* ACW:SEP/94[8]483, ACW:SEP/94[62]490, CWTI:DEC/95[40]479, *Gettysburg,* B&G:FEB/93[48]515, GETTY:6[99]181, GETTY:7[7]185, GETTY:7[51]190,

GETTY:8[43]202, GETTY:9[5]209, GETTY:9[109]218,
GETTY:12[85]248, GETTY:12[97]249
GENERAL LISTINGS, continued: *gold hoax,* AHI:APR/80[21]200, *Grant,*
ACW:MAR/94[27]459, ACW:NOV/94[34]496,
ACW:MAR/95[70]520, CWTI:FEB/90[32]144,
CWTI:FEB/90[46]146, *Harpers Ferry Raid, 1859,*
AHI:MAR/84[10]236, *Harrison's Landing,*
CWM:JUN/95[76]598, *Henry Halleck,* AHI:MAY/78[10]179,
Hermann Haupt, ACW:JUL/95[16]534, *Hiram Berdan,*
CWTI:JUL/93[42]329, *Horace Greeley,* CWTI:DEC/90[50]183,
impeachment of Andrew Johnson, AHI:DEC/68[28]118
GENERAL LISTINGS, continued: *in book review,* ACW:MAY/91[54],
ACW:JAN/92[54], ACW:MAY/92[54], ACW:JUL/92[54],
ACW:NOV/92[58], ACW:JAN/93[58], ACW:MAY/94[58],
ACW:SEP/95[62], ACW:NOV/95[62], AHI:JAN/84[8],
B&G:APR/91[28], B&G:FEB/95[26], CWM:JAN/91[47],
CWM:JUL/93[51], CWM:MAR/91[74], CWM:JUN/94[6],
CWM:AUG/94[9], CWM:DEC/94[7], CWM:FEB/95[7],
CWM:APR/95[50], CWM:AUG/95[45], CWNEWS:JAN/90[4],
CWNEWS:APR/90[4], CWNEWS:JUN/90[4],
CWNEWS:SEP/90[4], CWNEWS:OCT/90[4],
CWNEWS:JAN/91[4], CWNEWS:JUN/91[4],
CWNEWS:JUL/91[4], CWNEWS:NOV/91[4],
CWNEWS:JAN/92[4], CWNEWS:JUN/92[4],
CWNEWS:DEC/92[4], CWNEWS:JAN/93[4],
CWNEWS:AUG/93[5], CWNEWS:NOV/93[5],
CWNEWS:JAN/95[25], CWR:VOL2#3[256],
CWR:VOL2#4[346], CWR:VOL3#1[80], CWR:VOL3#3[92],
CWR:VOL3#4[68], CWR:VOL4#1[78], CWR:VOL4#3[89],
CWR:VOL4#4[129], CWTI:DEC/91[12], CWTI:MAY/92[18],
CWTI:NOV/93[14], CWTI:JUL/94[18], MH:DEC/93[90],
MH:DEC/94[70]
GENERAL LISTINGS, continued: *indians,* CWM:MAY/93[24]476, *James
Buchanan,* AHI:MAY/66[12]101, *Johnathan Walker,*
CWTI:DEC/91[48]242, *John Basil Turchin,*
ACW:SEP/95[6]541, *John C. Calhoun,* AHI:FEB/75[4]157,
John C. Fremont, CWTI:MAR/94[29]371, *John H. Morgan,*
CWM:JAN/93[29]459, *Julia Ward Howe,*
CWTI:SEPT/89[40]130, *Kaplan photo,* B&G:FEB/95[5]589,
leadership, CWR:VOL4#1[78], *Lee's lost order 191,*
ACW:JAN/94[6]446, *letters to editor,* AHI:MAY/86[4],
AHI:JUN/86[4], B&G:FEB/92[6]473, B&G:FEB/94[6]549,
B&G:DEC/94[6]584, CWM:MAY/91[6]345,
CWM:JAN/92[6]398, CWM:MAY/92[6]417,
CWM:JUL/93[4]482, CWM:SEP/93[4]492,
CWM:AUG/94[6]521, CWM:DEC/94[5]546,
CWM:FEB/95[5]557, CWM:OCT/95[5]613,
CWM:DEC/95[5]625, CWTI:DEC/91[14]235,
CWTI:MAY/92[8]261, CWTI:JAN/93[10]297,
CWTI:JAN/94[8]356, CWTI:SEP/94[12]398,
CWTI:OCT/95[14]465, MH:FEB/93[10]163, *Lincoln Boyhood
National Memorial;* AHI:APR/89[43]284, *Lincoln's Tomb;*
AHI:APR/89[43]284
GENERAL LISTINGS, continued: *Marfan's disease,*
CWTI:SEP/91[41]230, *Mary Todd Lincoln,*
ACW:JAN/94[47]452, AHI:MAY/75[4]159, *Mary Walker,*
CWTI:MAY/94[40]383, *medical,* CWM:SEP/91[35]384, *Mobile,*
CWM:JUL/93[24]485, *Monocacy,* ACW:NOV/93[50]444,
Mormon confrontation, AHI:DEC/72[10]145, *mutiny,*
CWTI:JUN/95[32]446, *New Mexico Campaign,*
B&G:JUN/94[8]568, *Peninsula Campaign,*
ACW:JAN/94[8]447, ACW:NOV/94[50]498,
CWM:JUN/95[24]582, CWM:JUN/95[53]590,

CWTI:JAN/94[20]358, GETTY:9[61]215, *prisoners,*
CWTI:APR/92[23]255, *railroads,* CWM:NOV/91[12]390,
rapid-fire weapons, ACW:JUL/93[8]420, *Red River Campaign,*
ACW:MAR/95[34]516, CWR:VOL4#2[26]166, *Russian Navy,*
AHI:JAN/81[18]214, *Rutherford B. Hayes,*
CWTI:SEP/94[49]404
GENERAL LISTINGS, continued: *Savannah,* B&G:FEB/91[8]439,
sculpture by Sarah Ames; CWTI:APR/89[28]109, *Simon
Cameron,* CWTI:JUN/90[46]161, *Slavery,*
CWTI:DEC/89[62]139, *Solomon P. Chase,* CWM:DEC/95[10],
Thaddeus Stevens, AHI:JAN/82[16]224, *The <u>Princeton</u>
Explosion,* AHI:AUG/69[5]123, *trans-continental railroad,*
AHI:JUN/71[10]134, *Tullahoma Campaign,*
CWM:OCT/94[48]542, *Vicksburg,* ACW:JUL/94[51]480, *visits
Richmond,* CWR:VOL4#1[78], *volunteers,*
CWTI:NOV/93[78]354, *weapons,* CWTI:JAN/93[49]303, *West
Point,* B&G:DEC/91[12]469, *West Virginia campaign,*
B&G:AUG/93[10]529, *Wilderness,* B&G:JUN/95[8]600,
Willard's Hotel, AHI:OCT/79[10]192, *William Harney,*
CWM:MAY/93[8]474, *William T. Sherman,* AHI:JAN/67[4]106,
Williamson R.W. Cobb, ACW:MAY/94[8]465
PHOTOS: ACW:JAN/92[30]342, ACW:NOV/94[8]493,
ACW:MAR/95[6]511, AHI:OCT/68[4]116, AHI:FEB/69[35]120,
AHI:MAY/71[3]133A, AHI:JUN/73[4]149, AHI:SEP/89[20]286,
AHI:NOV/90[44]293, B&G:FEB/94[24]551,
B&G:OCT/94[42]583, CWTI:APR/89[28]109,
CWTI:FEB/92[21]247, CWTI:DEC/95[22]476,
CWTI:DEC/95[40]479, CWTI:DEC/95[52]480
PHOTOS, PORTRAITS, ETC.: *early photo;* AHI:APR/76[32]166,
CWTI:SEP/92[46]284, *painting;* CWTI:FEB/90[46]146, *portrait
by Healy;* ACW:MAY/93[47]417, *portrait;* AHI:APR/89[20]282,
photo at home in Springfield; ACW:MAY/93[47]417, *photo of
"portrait" with his head on Fremont's body;*
CWTI:SEP/90[22]173, *photo with Nicolay and Hay by
Alexander Gardner;* CWTI:APR/89[28]109, *photo with
Pinkerton and McClernand;* CWTI:MAR/91[22]199, *photo,
Gettysburg Address,* GETTY:9[122]220
ADDITIONAL LISTINGS, ACW: ACW:JAN/91[10]283,
ACW:JAN/91[16]284, ACW:JAN/91[38]287,
ACW:MAR/91[8]291, ACW:MAR/91[30]295,
ACW:MAR/91[38]296, ACW:MAR/91[47]297,
ACW:MAY/91[10]301, ACW:MAY/91[31]304,
ACW:MAY/91[38]305, ACW:MAY/91[62]307,
ACW:JUL/91[6]308, ACW:JUL/91[18]312,
ACW:JUL/91[35]314, ACW:SEP/91[62]326,
ACW:NOV/91[10]329, ACW:NOV/91[30]332,
ACW:NOV/91[46]335, ACW:JAN/92[22]341,
ACW:JAN/92[62]346, ACW:MAR/92[14]350,
ACW:MAR/92[46]354, ACW:MAY/92[14]358,
ACW:MAY/92[23]360, ACW:MAY/92[47]363,
ACW:JUL/92[22]368, ACW:JUL/92[62]372,
ACW:SEP/92[16]376, ACW:SEP/92[30]378,
ACW:SEP/92[47]380, ACW:SEP/92[66]381,
ACW:NOV/92[8]383, ACW:NOV/92[10]384,
ACW:NOV/92[18]385, ACW:NOV/92[35]387,
ACW:JAN/93[35]396, ACW:JAN/93[51]398,
ACW:MAR/93[6]400, ACW:MAR/93[8]403,
ACW:MAY/93[12]412, ACW:JUL/93[6]419,
ACW:JUL/93[10]421, ACW:JUL/93[27]423,
ACW:JUL/93[66]427, ACW:SEP/93[8]429,
ACW:SEP/93[22]432, ACW:SEP/93[31]433,
ACW:SEP/93[46]435, ACW:NOV/93[26]441,
ACW:NOV/93[42]443, ACW:JAN/94[10]448,

ACW:JAN/94[70]454, ACW:MAR/94[35]460,
ACW:MAY/94[43]470, ACW:SEP/94[46]488,
ACW:NOV/94[58]499, ACW:JAN/95[8]502,
ACW:MAR/95[26]515, ACW:NOV/95[74]560

ADDITIONAL LISTINGS, AHI: AHI:JUN/73[4]149, AHI:DEC/74[12]156,
AHI:NOV/80[8]209, AHI:DEC/81[18]223, AHI:MAR/84[42]238,
AHI:NOV/84[18]241A, AHI:JAN/85[10]244,
AHI:OCT/85[38]253, AHI:FEB/86[12]257, AHI:FEB/86[20]258,
AHI:SEP/87[21]262, AHI:SEP/87[40]263, AHI:NOV/88[28]277,
AHI:APR/89[13]281, AHI:SEP/89[20]286, AHI:NOV/89[50]288,
AHI:MAR/92[52]301, AHI:JAN/93[61]309,
AHI:NOV/93[48]316, AHI:OCT/95[24]326

ADDITIONAL LISTINGS, B&G: B&G:APR/91[8]445,
B&G:APR/91[24]446, B&G:JUN/91[26]453,
B&G:AUG/91[40]463, B&G:OCT/91[11]466,
B&G:OCT/91[40]467, B&G:FEB/92[22]476,
B&G:FEB/92[40]479, B&G:APR/92[36]483,
B&G:JUN/92[46]490, B&G:OCT/92[10]496,
B&G:DEC/92[8]503, B&G:DEC/92[40]508,
B&G:FEB/93[12]511, B&G:JUN/93[12]524,
B&G:AUG/93[36]533, B&G:OCT/93[12]537,
B&G:OCT/93[21]538, B&G:OCT/93[31]539,
B&G:DEC/93[12]545, B&G:FEB/94[8]550,
B&G:FEB/94[24]551, B&G:AUG/94[10]574,
B&G:OCT/94[11]580, B&G:OCT/94[42]583,
B&G:DEC/94[10]585, B&G:APR/95[8]595,
B&G:APR/95[24]596, B&G:APR/95[33]597,
B&G:JUN/95[36]603A, B&G:OCT/95[8]611A,
B&G:DEC/95[44]617

ADDITIONAL LISTINGS, CWM: CWM:MAR/91[56]341,
CWM:MAY/91[18]348, CWM:JAN/92[27]403,
CWM:JAN/92[40]405, CWM:JUL/92[4]425,
CWM:JUL/92[18]429, CWM:SEP/92[16]438,
CWM:NOV/92[43]452, CWM:JAN/93[40]461,
CWM:MAR/93[4]463, CWM:MAY/93[16]475,
CWM:JUL/93[2]481, CWM:JUL/93[35]487,
CWM:SEP/93[2]491, CWM:SEP/93[8]493,
CWM:SEP/93[18]494, CWM:APR/94[8]502,
CWM:APR/94[32]506, CWM:JUN/94[14]509,
CWM:DEC/94[17]547, CWM:DEC/94[40]550,
CWM:DEC/94[46]552, CWM:FEB/95[19]558,
CWM:FEB/95[68]567, CWM:APR/95[32]575,
CWM:JUN/95[17]581, CWM:AUG/95[38]609,
CWM:OCT/95[22]614, CWM:OCT/95[47]620,
CWM:OCT/95[55]622

ADDITIONAL LISTINGS, CWR: CWR:VOL1#1[73]108,
CWR:VOL2#1[1]130, CWR:VOL2#2[118]136,
CWR:VOL2#3[194]141, CWR:VOL2#4[313]146,
CWR:VOL3#1[31]150, CWR:VOL3#3[1]157,
CWR:VOL3#3[33]158, CWR:VOL3#3[59]159,
CWR:VOL3#4[24]162

ADDITIONAL LISTINGS, CWTI: CWTI:MAR/89[16]101,
CWTI:MAY/89[14]114, CWTI:MAY/89[36]118,
CWTI:FEB/90[38]145, CWTI:APR/90[56]155,
CWTI:SEP/90[22]173, CWTI:SEP/90[52]179,
CWTI:FEB/91[36]193, CWTI:AUG/91[36]217,
CWTI:AUG/91[46]218, CWTI:AUG/91[52]219,
CWTI:AUG/91[68]222, CWTI:SEP/91[31]229,
CWTI:FEB/92[42]250, CWTI:APR/92[35]257,
CWTI:JAN/93[8]296, CWTI:JAN/93[40]301,
CWTI:MAY/93[12]316, CWTI:MAY/93[20]317,
CWTI:MAY/93[29]319, CWTI:MAY/93[35]320,
CWTI:JUL/93[20]325, CWTI:JUL/93[29]326,

CWTI:SEP/93[14]333, CWTI:SEP/93[22]335,
CWTI:NOV/93[71]352, CWTI:JAN/94[29]360,
CWTI:MAR/94[48]374, CWTI:MAY/94[50]386,
CWTI:JUL/94[30]392, CWTI:JUL/94[44]394,
CWTI:SEP/94[24]399, CWTI:DEC/94[73]416,
CWTI:DEC/94[82]418, CWTI:JAN/95[48]429,
CWTI:MAR/95[33]435, CWTI:MAR/95[40]436,
CWTI:MAR/95[46]437, CWTI:JUN/95[51]449,
CWTI:JUN/95[56]450, CWTI:AUG/95[34]457,
CWTI:OCT/95[8]463, CWTI:OCT/95[24]466,
CWTI:DEC/95[6]473

ADDITIONAL LISTINGS, GETTY: GETTY:10[42]224

ADDITIONAL LISTINGS, MH: MH:JUN/91[20]152, MH:FEB/92[8]156,
MH:APR/92[18]157, MH:OCT/92[51]162, MH:FEB/93[42]164,
MH:AUG/93[47]169, MH:OCT/93[6]170, MH:OCT/93[20]172,
MH:OCT/93[76]173, MH:DEC/93[12]174, MH:JUN/94[8]177,
MH:AUG/94[82]179, MH:DEC/94[46]181, MH:APR/95[46]183,
MH:AUG/95[30]185, MH:OCT/95[8]187

VIDEO: "ABRAHAM LINCOLN," AHI:SEP/89[25],
CWTI:SEP/90[12], "OUT OF THE WILDERNESS: THE LIFE
OF ABRAHAM LINCOLN," AHI:AUG/94[22]

LINCOLN'S ASSASSINATION:

ARTICLES: "A PAPER LINK TO A CONSPIRACY,"
CWTI:SEP/91[15]225, "BEHIND THE LINES,"
CWTI:AUG/90[8]165, "BOOTH DERRINGER AUCTIONED,"
AHI:OCT/94[8]321, "EYEWITNESSES REMEMBER THE
'FEARFUL NIGHT,'" CWTI:MAR/93[12]307, "FORD'S
THEATRE ON STAGE," AHI:FEB/86[20]258, "FORD'S
THEATRE," AHI:FEB/86[12]257, "HERITAGE OR HOAX?"
CWTI:SEP/94[24]399, "HISTORIANS OPPOSE OPENING OF
BOOTH GRAVE," CWTI:JUN/95[26]445, "LINCOLN'S
MURDER: THE SIMPLE CONSPIRACY THEORY,"
CWTI:DEC/91[28]239, "THE LONG TRIP HOME,"
AHI:JUL/95[30]324, "MORAL VICTORY IN THE CRUSADE
TO CLEAR MUDD," CWTI:MAY/93[12]316, "TRAGEDIAN'S
GREATEST ROLE," ACW:MAR/93[35]405, "VISITING THE
SITE OF ABRAHAM LINCOLN'S ASSASSINATION GIVES,
HISTORY BUFFS AN EERIE SENSE OF STEPPING BACK
IN TIME," ACW:MAY/95[68]529, "WHAT REALLY
HAPPENED TO THE ASSASSIN?" CWTI:JUL/92[50]275,
"WHATEVER BECAME OF BOSTON CORBETT?"
CWTI:MAY/91[48]211

BOOK REVIEWS: *A BULLET FOR LINCOLN * A. LINCOLN: HIS
LAST 24 HOURS, * APRIL '65: CONFEDERATE COVERT
ACTION IN THE AMERICAN CIVIL WAR * THE
ASSASSINATION OF LINCOLN: HISTORY AND MYTH *
BLACK EASTER: THE ASSASSINATION OF ABRAHAM
LINCOLN * COME RETRIBUTION: THE CONFEDERATE
SECRET SERVICE AND THE ASSASSINATION OF
LINCOLN * THE GREAT AMERICAN MYTH: THE TRUE
STORY OF LINCOLN'S MURDER * IT DIDN'T HAPPEN
THE WAY YOU THINK. THE LINCOLN ASSASSINATION:
WHAT THE EXPERTS MISSED * "NO SORROW LIKE OUR
SORROW": NORTHERN PROTESTANT MINISTERS AND
THE ASSASSINATION OF LINCOLN * OUT OF THE
STORM: THE END OF THE CIVIL WAR (APRIL-JUNE 1865)*

GENERAL LISTINGS: *Ford's Theatre;* AHI:APR/89[43]284, *in book
review,* ACW:SEP/95[62], *letters to editor,* AHI:APR/86[4],
AHI:MAY/86[4], AHI:JUN/86[4], CWTI:MAY/92[8]261,
CWTI:MAY/93[8]315, CWTI:JAN/95[16]421, *photo of weapon
used to assassinate Lincoln,* CWTI:AUG/90[42]167, *photo, in
casket;* CWTI:AUG/90[42]167

ADDITIONAL LISTINGS: ACW:SEP/93[8]429, ACW:JAN/94[47]452, ACW:JUL/94[26]477, AHI:OCT/86[22]260, B&G:JUN/95[36]603A, CWM:JUL/91[4]354, CWM:MAY/93[32]477, CWTI:FEB/90[60]148, CWTI:APR/90[12]150, CWTI:AUG/90[42]167, CWTI:AUG/90[50]168, CWTI:FEB/91[28]192, CWTI:AUG/91[68]222, CWTI:DEC/91[8]234, CWTI:JAN/93[8]296, CWTI:JAN/93[44]302, CWTI:JUL/93[20]325, CWTI:AUG/95[46]459

LINCOLN'S GETTYSBURG ADDRESS: see listings under "GETTYSBURG ADDRESS"

LINCOLN, BENJAMIN, *Major, 2nd USCT;* ACW:NOV/91[64]336

LINCOLN, JACOB B., *Private, 33rd Virginia Infantry;* CWM:JUL/91[48]374

LINCOLN, MARY TODD:

ARTICLES: "AMERICA'S FIRST LADIES," AHI:MAY/89[26]285, "FIRST LADIES AT WAR," ACW:JAN/94[47]452, "MARY TODD LINCOLN," AHI:MAY/75[4]159

BOOK REVIEWS: *MARY TODD LINCOLN: A BIOGRAPHY,* AHI:FEB/88[8], *THE PRESIDENT'S WIFE: MARY TODD LINCOLN*

GENERAL LISTINGS: *in book review,* B&G:DEC/95[30], CWNEWS:NOV/90[4], *Richmond,* CWTI:AUG/90[26]166, *photos,* ACW:JAN/94[47]452, AHI:NOV/72[37]143, AHI:MAY/75[4]159, AHI:NOV/90[44]293, CWTI:FEB/91[28]192, CWTI:DEC/95[24]477, CWTI:DEC/95[40]479

ADDITIONAL LISTINGS: ACW:JUL/91[8]309, ACW:JUL/92[8]365A, ACW:JUL/92[62]372, AHI:FEB/69[35]120, AHI:FEB/85[36]248, AHI:FEB/86[12]257, AHI:MAR/89[26]280, AHI:NOV/90[44]293, AHI:MAR/93[50]310, B&G:DEC/91[12]469, B&G:APR/95[33]597, B&G:AUG/95[8]604, CWTI:MAY/89[14]114, CWTI:FEB/91[28]192, CWTI:MAR/95[54]438, CWTI:AUG/95[54]460, CWTI:DEC/95[24]477, CWTI:DEC/95[40]479, CWTI:DEC/95[90]483, GETTY:9[122]220

LINCOLN, ROBERT T.:

ARTICLES: "'HILDENE' WAS THE RESIDENCE AND REFUGE OF ABRAHAM LINCOLN'S LAST SURVIVING SON, ROBERT TODD LINCOLN," ACW:JUL/92[62]372, "THE SECOND TRAGIC LINCOLN," AHI:FEB/85[36]248,

GENERAL LISTINGS: *assassination of Garfield,* AHI:FEB/69[12]119, *Mary Todd Lincoln,* AHI:MAY/75[4]159, *Lincoln's humor,* AHI:NOV/70[22]130, *photos,* AHI:JAN/71[12]131, AHI:MAY/75[4]159, AHI:FEB/85[36]248, AHI:NOV/90[44]293, CWTI:FEB/91[28]192, CWTI:DEC/95[24]477

ADDITIONAL LISTINGS: ACW:MAR/93[35]405, ACW:JAN/94[47]452, AHI:FEB/69[35]120, AHI:JAN/71[12]131, AHI:SEP/87[48]264, AHI:MAR/89[26]280, AHI:NOV/90[44]293, B&G:FEB/93[12]511, CWTI:FEB/91[28]192, CWTI:DEC/95[76]482

LINCOLN, THOMAS "TAD": AHI:MAY/75[4]159, CWTI:FEB/92[21]247, *photos,* AHI:MAY/75[4]159, CWTI:FEB/91[28]192, CWTI:DEC/95[24]477

LINCOLN-DOUGLAS DEBATES:

ARTICLE: "RE-CREATING THE GREAT DEBATE," AHI:DEC/94[68]322

BOOK REVIEWS: *THE AMERICAN CONSCIENCE: THE DRAMA OF THE LINCOLN-DOUGLAS DEBATES * THE LINCOLN-DOUGLAS DEBATES: THE FIRST COMPLETE*

*UNEXPURGATED TEXT * LINCOLN, DOUGLAS AND SLAVERY*

VIDEO: *THE LINCOLN-DOUGLAS DEBATES OF 1858,* AHI:OCT/94[28]

ADDITIONAL LISTINGS: ACW:NOV/94[8]493, AHI:FEB/69[35]120, CWR:VOL3#3[59]159

LINDLEY, JONATHAN F., *Private, 7th Georgia Infantry;* B&G:APR/91[32]447

LINDSAY, ROBERT H., *Colonel, CSA;* CWM:OCT/95[36]616

LINDSEY, DANIEL W., *Colonel, USA;* B&G:AUG/95[8]604

LINEBAUGH, JOHN H., *correspondent;* ACW:NOV/92[35]387

LINGO, CAWSAY and HENRY, *22nd Iowa Infantry;* CWR:VOL2#1[19]131

LINGO, JOSEPH, *Private, 11th Veteran Reserve Corps;* B&G:APR/93[24]520

LINGO, MILTON, *Private, 22nd Iowa Infantry;* CWR:VOL2#1[19]131

LINING, CHARLES, *Surgeon, CSN;* ACW:MAY/91[46]306

LINN, JOHN B., *civilian;* GETTY:12[97]249

LINN, JOHN B., *Lieutenant, 51st Pennsylvania Infantry;* CWTI:SEP/90[26]174

LINSCOTT, ARAD H., *Private, 20th Maine Infantry;* GETTY:6[43]173

LINTHICUM, CHARLES F., *Captain, USA;* GETTY:5[107]164

LIPMAN, ADOLPH, *Private, 9th Massachusetts Artillery;* GETTY:5[47]160

LIPPINCOTT, CHARLES E., *Colonel, 33rd Illinois Infantry;* B&G:FEB/94[8]550

LIPSCOMB, WILLIAM H., *Lieutenant, CSA;* ACW:MAR/94[27]459

LISSAVSKI, ADMIRAL, *Commander of the Russian Baltic Fleet;* CWTI:MAY/89[28]117

LIST, SAMUEL V., *Private, 7th Indiana Infantry;* CWTI:NOV/93[24]346

LITTLE BIG HORN, BATTLE OF; ARTICLES: "CUSTER'S LAST BATTLE, PART I," AHI:DEC/84[18]243, "CUSTER'S LAST BATTLE, PART II," AHI:JAN/85[30]246, "ECHOES FROM THE CUSTER BATTLEFIELD," AHI:DEC/84[10]242

LITTLE ROCK, ARKANSAS, REUNION, ARTICLE: "THE GRAY REUNION," CWTI:FEB/92[42]250

LITTLE ROCK, ARKANSAS; ACW:MAY/94[26]468, CWR:VOL1#2[44]114

LITTLE, BENJAMIN F., *Captain, 52nd North Carolina Infantry;* GETTY:8[67]204, GETTY:13[75]259

LITTLE, LEWIS H., *General, CSA;* B&G:AUG/93[24], CWTI:MAR/91[34]201, CWTI:JUL/94[50]395

LITTLE, WILLIAM, *Private, 88th Pennsylvania Infantry;* GETTY:10[7]221

LITTLE, WILLIAM M., *Private, 8th Louisiana Infantry;* CWTI:FEB/91[12]189

LITTLEFIELD, D.W., *Lieutenant, 7th Michigan Cavalry;* B&G:OCT/93[12]537

LITTLEJOHN, JOSEPH B., *Sergeant Major, 8th Louisiana Infantry;* CWTI:FEB/91[12]189

LITTLEJOHN, THOMAS M., *Private, 13th South Carolina Infantry;* GETTY:13[22]254

LITTLEPAGE, HARDIN B., *Lieutenant, CSN;* AHI:OCT/75[30]162, AHI:NOV/75[38]163

LIVENS, CHARLES, *Private, 7th Wisconsin Infantry,* GETTY:11[57]233

LIVERMORE, MARY A., *civilian;* AHI:APR/79[4]186

LIVERMORE, THOMAS L., *Captain, USA;* GETTY:10[53]225

LIVINGSTON, JOHN, *Sergeant, 3rd Georgia Infantry;*
   CWTI:DEC/94[32]410
LIVINGSTONE, THOMAS R., *Major, USA;*
   CWTI:SEP/90[52]179
LLEWELLYN, DAVID H., *Surgeon, CSN;* ACW:MAY/95[8]522,
   AHI:OCT/88[38]275
LLEWELLYN, SAMUEL, *Private, USA;* ACW:SEP/91[22]321
LLOYD, JOHN M.; CWTI:MAY/92[8]261
LLOYD, W.D.C., *Major, CSA;* CWR:VOL1#4[42]126
LLOYD, WILLIAM H., *Captain, 11th New Jersey Infantry;*
   GETTY:12[7]241
LLOYDS, W.P., *Captain, CSA;* CWR:VOL3#2[1]153
LOCHREN, WILLIAM, *Lieutenant, 1st Minnesota Infantry;*
   ACW:NOV/94[76]500, GETTY:5[79]161
LOCHRY, JOHN, *Captain, 98th Ohio Infantry;*
   CWTI:SEP/92[31]281
LOCKE, FREDERICK T., *Colonel, USA;* B&G:DEC/95[25]616
LOCKE, ROBERT W., *Captain, 42nd Mississippi Infantry;*
   GETTY:4[22]144
LOCKE, VERNON G., *Captain, CSN;* ACW:NOV/92[51]389
LOCKE, WILLIAM H., *Private, 11th Pennsylvania Infantry;*
   GETTY:10[7]221
LOCKETT, SAMUEL, *Major, CSA;* CWR:VOL2#1[36]132
LOCKHART, W.G., *Private, 3rd Arkansas Infantry;*
   B&G:JUN/95[8]600
LOCKREN, WILLIAM, *Private, 1st Minnesota Infantry;*
   ACW:JAN/94[62]
LOCKRIDGE, S.A., *Major, CSA;* CWM:MAY/93[16]475
LOCKWOOD, HENRY H., *General, USA:*
   GENERAL LISTINGS: *Gettysburg,* GETTY:7[29]188,
      GETTY:7[51]190, GETTY:7[83]192, GETTY:12[42]244, *in
      order of battle,* B&G:APR/94[10]558
   ADDITIONAL LISTINGS: ACW:NOV/92[42]388, ACW:MAY/93[12]412
LOCKWOOD, ROBERT, *Captain, CSN;* ACW:JAN/91[47]288
LOCKWOOD, THOMAS J., *Captain, CSN;*
   ACW:JAN/91[47]288, ACW:MAY/92[23]360
LOCOMOTIVE CHASE; see listings under **"ANDREWS,
   JAMES J."**

LOCOMOTIVES:
General; ACW:SEP/91[22]321, CWTI:FEB/92[10]246, *photo,*
   ACW:SEP/91[22]321
Missouri; CWTI:FEB/92[10]246
Texas; ACW:SEP/91[22]321, CWTI:FEB/92[10]246
William R. Smith; ACW:SEP/91[22]321
Yonah; ACW:SEP/91[22]321

LOEHR, CHARLES T., *Sergeant, 1st Virginia Infantry;*
   B&G:APR/93[12]518
LOFTIN, FRANK S., *Private, CSA;* CWTI:SEP/91[23]228
LOGAN'S CROSS ROADS, KENTUCKY, BATTLE OF; see
   listings under **"MILL SPRINGS, KENTUCKY, BATTLE
   OF"**
LOGAN, DORASTER B., *Captain, 11th New Jersey Infantry;*
   GETTY:12[7]241
LOGAN, JOHN A., *General, USA:*
   ARTICLE: "SHERMAN'S FEUDING GENERALS,"
      CWTI:MAR/95[40]436
   BOOK REVIEW: *HISTORY 31ST REGIMENT ILLINOIS
      VOLUNTEERS ORGANIZED BY JOHN A. LOGAN*
   GENERAL LISTINGS: *Atlanta Campaign,*
      CWTI:SUMMER/89[13]120, CWTI:SUMMER/89[20]121,
      CWTI:SUMMER/89[32]122, CWTI:SUMMER/89[40]123,

CWTI:SUMMER/89[50]124, *Forts Henry and Donelson,*
   B&G:FEB/92[10]474, *Mary Ann Bickerdyke,*
   AHI:APR/79[4]186, *order of battle,* B&G:FEB/94[8]550,
   B&G:DEC/95[9]615, *photo of statue;* MH:JUN/93[82]167,
   photos, ACW:JUL/91[35]314, AHI:DEC/68[28]118,
   AHI:APR/79[4]186, CWR:VOL3#4[24]162,
   CWTI:SUMMER/89[50]124, CWTI:MAR/95[40]436
ADDITIONAL LISTINGS: ACW:JUL/91[35]314, ACW:NOV/91[22]331,
   ACW:NOV/92[8]383, ACW:NOV/94[34]496,
   ACW:JAN/95[30]505, ACW:NOV/95[74]560,
   B&G:DEC/93[12]545, B&G:FEB/94[8]550,
   CWM:JAN/91[12]326, CWM:AUG/94[27]526,
   CWR:VOL1#1[73]108, CWR:VOL2#1[36]132,
   CWR:VOL2#4[313]146, CWR:VOL3#3[59]159,
   CWR:VOL3#4[24]162, CWTI:SUMMER/89[40]123,
   CWTI:FEB/91[18]190, CWTI:MAY/91[24]208,
   CWTI:SEP/92[28]280, CWTI:NOV/92[41]291,
   CWTI:DEC/94[49]413, CWTI:MAR/95[40]436
LOGAN, JOHN T., *civilian;* ACW:MAR/91[8]291
LOGAN, JOSHUA, *General, USA;* AHI:JAN/82[16]224
LOGAN, MATTHEW D., *Captain, CSA;* B&G:DEC/94[6]584
LOGAN, ROBERT D., *Captain, CSA;* B&G:OCT/94[11]580,
   B&G:DEC/94[6]584
LOGAN, SAMUEL M., *Captain, 1st Colorado Infantry;*
   ACW:NOV/91[10]329
LOGAN, T.M., *Colonel, USA;* GETTY:11[6]231
LOGUE, DANIEL C., *Doctor, USN;* AHI:NOV/75[38]163,
   CWM:JUL/93[15]484
LOHMANN, WILLIAM; CWTI:AUG/95[58]461
LOMAX, LUNSFORD L., *General, CSA;* ACW:MAY/91[38]305,
   ACW:JUL/92[41]370, ACW:MAY/94[35]469,
   ACW:SEP/94[55]489, B&G:OCT/93[12]537,
   B&G:APR/94[10]558, B&G:APR/95[8]595,
   CWM:JAN/93[40]461, CWM:APR/94[24]505, CWM:FEB/95[7],
   CWTI:APR/92[35]257
LOMAX, WILLIAM G., *Private, 2nd South Carolina Infantry;*
   GETTY:5[35]159
LONDON, H.A., *Private, 2nd North Carolina;* GETTY:5[117]165
LONG, ARMISTEAD L., *General, CSA:*
   GENERAL LISTINGS: *Gettysburg,* GETTY:4[65]148,
      GETTY:4[113]153, GETTY:5[4]156, GETTY:7[13]186, *in order
      of battle,* B&G:APR/94[10]558, B&G:APR/95[8]595, *Monocacy,*
      B&G:DEC/92[8]503
   ADDITIONAL LISTINGS: ACW:JAN/93[43]397, B&G:APR/93[12]518,
      B&G:APR/95[8]595, CWM:JAN/93[8]456,
      CWR:VOL1#1[35]104, CWR:VOL4#4[70]180
LONG, BENJAMIN, *Private, 3rd Texas Cavalry;*
   ACW:MAY/94[58]
LONG, CORNELIUS, *Corporal, 1st Florida Special Battalion;*
   CWR:VOL3#1[65]151
LONG, ELI, *General, USA;* ACW:NOV/91[10]329,
   ACW:MAY/95[49]527
LONG, GREEN B., *Lieutenant, 11th Virginia Infantry;*
   GETTY:12[111]250
LONG, HENRY W., *Lieutenant, 9th Florida Infantry;*
   CWR:VOL3#4[1]161
LONG, JOSEPH M. JR, *Private, 2nd South Carolina Artillery;*
   B&G:FEB/95[38]593, B&G:JUN/95[36]603A
LONG, REUBEN M., *Lieutenant, 9th Pennsylvania Reserves;*
   CWR:VOL4#4[1]177
LONG, WILLIAM A., *Private, 8th New York Cavalry;*
   CWM:MAY/92[8]418

ADDITIONAL LISTINGS, B&G: B&G:APR/91[8]445,
  B&G:OCT/91[11]466, B&G:FEB/92[40]479,
  B&G:APR/92[28]482, B&G:APR/92[48]484,
  B&G:OCT/92[32]499, B&G:DEC/92[8]503,
  B&G:FEB/93[40]514, B&G:APR/93[12]518,
  B&G:OCT/93[12]537, B&G:OCT/93[38]541,
  B&G:APR/94[10]558, B&G:JUN/94[8]568,
  B&G:AUG/94[10]574, B&G:FEB/95[35]592,
  B&G:OCT/95[54]614A, B&G:DEC/95[44]617
ADDITIONAL LISTINGS, CWM: CWM:JUL/91[24]360,
  CWM:JUL/91[40]370, CWM:NOV/91[50]394,
  CWM:MAY/92[8]418, CWM:JUL/92[24]430,
  CWM:JUL/92[40]432, CWM:MAR/93[8]465,
  CWM:MAR/93[32]468, CWM:JUN/94[43]517,
  CWM:AUG/94[26]525, CWM:AUG/94[60]531,
  CWM:OCT/94[26]536, CWM:OCT/94[34]538,
  CWM:DEC/94[26]548, CWM:APR/95[16]571,
  CWM:APR/95[32]575, CWM:JUN/95[17]581,
  CWM:AUG/95[17]603, CWM:AUG/95[38]609,
  CWM:OCT/95[22]614
ADDITIONAL LISTINGS, CWR: CWR:VOL1#1[1]102,
  CWR:VOL1#1[26]103, CWR:VOL1#1[35]104,
  CWR:VOL1#1[71]107, CWR:VOL1#2[29]112,
  CWR:VOL1#3[52]122, CWR:VOL1#4[7]125,
  CWR:VOL2#1[36]132, CWR:VOL2#2[156]138,
  CWR:VOL2#2[95]135, CWR:VOL2#3[236]143,
  CWR:VOL2#4[269]145, CWR:VOL3#1[31]150,
  CWR:VOL3#2[1]153, CWR:VOL3#2[70]155,
  CWR:VOL4#4[28]178
ADDITIONAL LISTINGS, CWTI: CWTI:MAR/89[28]103,
  CWTI:APR/89[14]107, CWTI:JUN/90[32]159,
  CWTI:SEP/90[34]176, CWTI:FEB/91[12]189,
  CWTI:AUG/91[62]221, CWTI:SEP/91[31]229,
  CWTI:MAR/93[40]312, CWTI:JUL/94[44]394,
  CWTI:SEP/94[40]403, CWTI:JAN/95[34]427,
  CWTI:JUN/95[18]444, CWTI:DEC/95[67]481
ADDITIONAL LISTINGS, GETTY: GETTY:13[1]252, GETTY:13[43]256,
  GETTY:13[64]258, GETTY:13[75]259
ADDITIONAL LISTINGS, MH: MH:JUN/92[50]159, MH:JUN/94[8]177,
  MH:AUG/95[30]185
LONGUST, HUGH, *railroad engineer;* CWM:NOV/91[40]393
LOOKOUT MOUNTAIN, TENNESSEE, BATTLE OF:
ARTICLE: "A BATTLE ABOVE THE CLOUDS,"
  CWTI:SEPT/89[30]129
BOOK REVIEW: *THE SHIPWRECK OF THEIR HOPES: THE
  BATTLES FOR CHATTANOOGA*
ADDITIONAL LISTINGS: ACW:JAN/92[10]339, ACW:NOV/95[6]551,
  ACW:NOV/95[62], CWM:JUL/92[24]430,
  CWM:DEC/94[46]552, CWR:VOL1#4[64]127,
  CWR:VOL1#4[74]128, CWR:VOL2#1[36]132,
  CWR:VOL3#2[70]155, CWR:VOL3#3[59]159,
  CWTI:SEPT/89[30]129, CWTI:FEB/90[46]146
LOOMIS, CYRUS, *Captain, USA;* B&G:OCT/91[11]466
LOOMIS, DAVID, *Private, 14th Michigan Infantry;*
  B&G:JUN/94[38]571
LOOMIS, JOHN M., *Colonel, USA;* B&G:AUG/95[8]604,
  CWR:VOL1#1[73]108, CWR:VOL3#3[59]159
LOOMIS, REUBEN, *Colonel, 6th Illinois Cavalry;*
  ACW:MAY/92[47]363, B&G:JUN/93[12]524
LOONEY, WILLIAM, *Private, 1st Virginia Battalion;*
  CWM:MAR/91[65]342

LOOP, CHARLES B., *Major, 95th Illinois Infantry;* ARTICLES: "I
  WAS THERE," CWM:JAN/91[11]325, "YOUR CHARLIE,"
  CWTI:JAN/93[20]298
LOPER, BENJAMIN, *Private, 98th Ohio Infantry;*
  B&G:OCT/94[42]583
LORD, DANIEL, *attorney;* ACW:SEP/94[46]488
LORD, NATHAN, *Colonel, 6th Vermont Infantry;*
  ACW:JAN/94[8]447, CWM:JUN/95[29]583
LORD, RICHARD S.C., *Captain, 1st U.S. Cavalry;*
  GETTY:11[19]232
LORD, STEPHEN D., *Private, Consolidated Crescent Regiment;*
  CWR:VOL4#2[1]165
LORD, THOMAS J., *Captain, Lincoln Cavalry;*
  B&G:APR/95[24]596
LORENDO, VICTOR, *Private, 7th Massachusetts Infantry;*
  ACW:NOV/95[30]555
LORING, WILLIAM C., *Colonel, USA;* CWTI:OCT/95[56]471
LORING, WILLIAM W., *General, CSA:*
GENERAL LISTINGS: *Carolina Campaign,* B&G:DEC/95[9]615,
  Champion Hill, ACW:NOV/91[22]331, CWTI:MAY/91[24]208,
  MH:JUN/93[82]167, *Confederate exiles,* AHI:JUN/70[30]127,
  Grierson's Raid, B&G:JUN/93[12]524, *in book review,*
  CWM:APR/95[50], CWNEWS:AUG/92[4],
  CWNEWS:FEB/94[5], *Jackson, Battle of,* B&G:AUG/95[8]604,
  Lee, CWM:AUG/95[17]603, *Nashville,* B&G:DEC/93[12]545,
  order of battle, B&G:DEC/93[12]545, B&G:AUG/95[8]604,
  B&G:DEC/95[9]615, *Thomas J. Jackson,* B&G:JUN/92[8]487,
  West Virginia campaign, B&G:AUG/93[10]529, *photos,*
  ACW:SEP/94[31]486, B&G:JUN/93[12]524,
  B&G:AUG/95[8]604, CWR:VOL2#1[36]132
ADDITIONAL LISTINGS: ACW:JAN/92[50]345, ACW:JUL/93[27]423,
  ACW:NOV/93[8]438, ACW:JUL/94[51]480,
  ACW:SEP/94[31]486, ACW:NOV/95[74]560,
  B&G:FEB/94[8]550, B&G:JUN/94[8]568,
  CWM:JAN/91[12]326, CWM:MAR/91[65]342,
  CWR:VOL1#1[73]108, CWR:VOL2#1[i]129,
  CWR:VOL2#1[1]130, CWR:VOL2#1[36]132,
  CWR:VOL3#3[33]158, CWR:VOL4#3[65]172,
  CWTI:SUMMER/89[20]121, CWTI:SUMMER/89[50]124,
  CWTI:NOV/92[41]291, CWTI:JUN/95[18]444
THE LOST CAUSE:
ARTICLE: "HOW WAS THE LOST CAUSE LOST?"
  CWM:AUG/94[8]522, "IF HISTORY IS WRITTEN ONLY BY
  THE WINNERS, THEN WHO REALLY WON THE CIVIL
  WAR?" ACW:NOV/94[6]492
BOOK REVIEW: *JUBAL: THE LIFE AND TIMES OF JUBAL A.
  EARLY, CSA, DEFENDER OF THE LOST CAUSE*
GENERAL LISTINGS: *in book review,* ACW:SEP/94[66],
  CWM:JAN/92[57], CWM:AUG/95[45], CWM:OCT/95[10],
  CWM:DEC/95[50], CWNEWS:OCT/89[4],
  CWNEWS:AUG/91[4], CWNEWS:NOV/91[4],
  CWR:VOL2#1[78], CWR:VOL4#3[1]170, CWR:VOL4#3[89],
  letters to the editor, CWM:MAY/92[6]417, CWM:APR/95[5]570
ADDITIONAL LISTINGS: CWM:JUL/91[22]359, CWM:JUN/94[43]517,
  CWTI:MAR/93[32]311
LOTT, JACOB, *civilian;* GETTY:4[65]148
LOTT, JONNY, *Private, USA;* ACW:SEP/95[38]546
LOUCK, ABRAHAM, *Private, 8th New York Cavalry;*
  CWM:MAY/92[8]418
LOUGHBOROUGH, JAMES M., *Major, CSA;*
  AHI:DEC/77[13]176

LOUGHBOROUGH, MARY ANN W., *civilian;*
BOOK REVIEW: *MY CAVE LIFE IN VICKSBURG,*
   CWNEWS:NOV/90[4]
ADDITIONAL LISTINGS: AHI:DEC/77[13]176, CWTI:SEPT/89[18]126

LOUISIANA TROOPS:
BOOK REVIEWS *GUIDE TO LOUISIANA CONFEDERATE*
   MILITARY UNITS 1861-1865
1st Artillery; ARTICLE: "DIARY OF THE VICKSBURG SIEGE,"
   AHI:DEC/77[46]177
1st Artillery, (Heavy); B&G:FEB/94[8]550,
   CWR:VOL3#3[33]158
1st Artillery, (Heavy), African Descent; B&G:FEB/92[6]473,
   CWM:JAN/92[6]398
1st Brigade; CWM:SEP/93[24]495
1st Cavalry; ACW:SEP/95[22]544, CWR:VOL4#1[1]163
1st Infantry; ACW:SEP/92[38]379, ACW:NOV/92[42]388,
   CWM:MAR/91[17]335, CWM:JUN/95[55]591,
   CWR:VOL4#2[68]167, CWTI:MAR/89[28]103,
   CWTI:FEB/91[12]189, CWTI:MAR/93[50]313,
   GETTY:9[81]216, GETTY:12[111]250
1st Special Battalion, (Louisiana Tigers):
ARTICLES: "JEFF DAVIS' PET WOLVES: THE 1ST LOUISIANA
   ZOUAVE BATTALION DID NOT DESERVE ITS MEAN
   REPUTATION...," CWTI:MAR/89[28]103, "WHEAT'S
   TIGERS," CWTI:MAR/94[48]374
ADDITIONAL LISTING: CWM:SEP/93[24]495
2nd Brigade; CWM:SEP/93[24]495, CWTI:JUL/93[38]328
2nd Cavalry; CWR:VOL3#1[1]149, CWR:VOL4#2[118]169,
   MH:DEC/95[58]188
2nd Cavalry, (Union); CWM:MAR/91[50]340
2nd Infantry; ACW:NOV/92[42]388, ACW:JAN/94[8]447,
   CWM:MAR/91[17]335, CWM:JUN/95[29]583,
   CWTI:SEP/90[26]174
2nd Infantry, (Colored); AHI:MAY/71[3]133A
2nd Mounted Infantry, (Union); CWR:VOL4#2[1]165
3rd Battalion; CWTI:MAR/89[28]103
3rd Infantry:
BOOK REVIEW: *A SOUTHERN RECORD: THE HISTORY OF*
   THE THIRD REGIMENT LOUISIANA INFANTRY
ADDITIONAL LISTINGS: ACW:NOV/93[26]441, CWR:VOL1#1[42]105,
   CWTI:FEB/92[29]248, CWTI:JUL/94[50]395,
   CWTI:MAR/95[46]437
4th Cavalry; CWR:VOL3#1[1]149
4th Infantry; B&G:DEC/92[32]506, B&G:JUN/93[12]524,
   CWR:VOL1#2[44]114, CWTI:JAN/94[46]364
5th Infantry; ACW:MAR/92[30]352, B&G:DEC/93[30]546,
   CWM:MAR/91[17]335, GETTY:8[17]200
6th Brigade; MH:OCT/93[20]172
6th Infantry; ACW:MAR/92[30]352, ACW:JUL/92[30]369,
   ACW:SEP/92[30]378, B&G:OCT/95[8]611A,
   CWM:MAR/91[17]335, CWM:SEP/93[18]494,
   CWR:VOL1#4[77], CWTI:FEB/91[12]189,
   CWTI:MAR/94[48]374, GETTY:8[17]200
7th Cavalry; CWR:VOL3#1[1]149, CWR:VOL4#2[118]169
7th Infantry; ACW:MAR/92[30]352, CWM:SEP/93[24]495,
   CWTI:MAR/94[48]374, GETTY:8[17]200
8th Infantry:
ARTICLE: "GOING BACK INTO THE UNION AT LAST,"
   CWTI:FEB/91[12]189
ADDITIONAL LISTINGS: ACW:MAR/92[30]352, CWNEWS:OCT/89[4],
   CWTI:FEB/91[12]189, CWTI:MAR/94[48]374,
   GETTY:6[94]180, GETTY:8[17]200

9th Infantry; ACW:MAR/92[30]352, ACW:MAY/93[54],
   CWM:SEP/93[24]495, CWR:VOL4#2[26]166,
   CWTI:FEB/91[12]189, CWTI:MAR/94[48]374, GETTY:6[7]169,
   GETTY:7[13]186, GETTY:8[17]200, GETTY:13[7]253
9th Infantry, (African Descent); CWR:VOL3#3[33]158
9th Partisan Rangers; B&G:JUN/93[12]524
10th Infantry Battalion:
ARTICLE: "THE YELLOW JACKETS: THE 10TH LOUISIANA
   INFANTRY BATTALION," CWR:VOL3#1[1]149
ADDITIONAL LISTINGS: CWR:VOL3#1[78]152, CWR:VOL4#2[1]165,
   CWR:VOL4#2[68]167
10th Infantry; ACW:NOV/92[42]388, B&G:AUG/93[24],
   CWM:MAR/91[17]335, CWM:SEP/93[18]494,
   CWM:SEP/93[24]495, CWM:JUN/95[29]583,
   CWTI:JUL/93[38]328, GETTY:12[111]250
11th Infantry Battalion; CWR:VOL4#2[68]167,
   CWR:VOL4#2[151]170
11th Infantry; CWR:VOL3#4[24]162, CWR:VOL4#2[68]167
11th Infantry, (African Descent); CWR:VOL3#3[33]158
12th Artillery; ACW:JAN/94[30]450
12th Artillery, (Heavy); ACW:SEP/95[8]542,
   CWM:APR/95[28]573
12th Infantry; ACW:NOV/91[22]331, CWR:VOL2#1[36]132,
   CWR:VOL3#1[1]149, CWR:VOL4#2[68]167,
   CWR:VOL4#2[151]170
13th & 20th Consolidated Infantry; CWM:FEB/95[28]560
13th Cavalry; CWR:VOL3#3[33]158
13th Infantry; B&G:AUG/95[8]604, CWR:VOL1#2[44]114
13th Infantry, (African Descent); CWR:VOL3#3[33]158
13th Partisan Rangers; CWR:VOL4#2[68]167
14th Infantry; ACW:SEP/92[38]379, ACW:NOV/92[42]388,
   B&G:AUG/93[24], CWM:MAR/91[17]335,
   CWM:SEP/93[24]495, CWTI:JUN/90[28]158
14th Sharpshooter Battalion; CWM:FEB/95[28]560
15th Cavalry; CWR:VOL2#1[36]132, CWR:VOL3#3[33]158
15th Infantry; ACW:NOV/92[42]388, CWM:MAR/91[17]335,
   CWTI:MAR/89[28]103, CWTI:MAR/94[48]374
16th & 25th Consolidated Infantry; CWM:FEB/95[28]560
17th Infantry; B&G:FEB/94[8]550
18th Consolidated Infantry:
BOOK REVIEW: *THE CIVIL WAR REMINISCENCES OF MAJOR*
   SILAS T. GRISAMORE, C.S.A.
ADDITIONAL LISTINGS: CWM:APR/95[50], CWNEWS:APR/90[4],
   CWR:VOL3#1[1]149, CWR:VOL4#2[1]165,
   CWR:VOL4#2[68]167, CWR:VOL4#2[118]169
19th Infantry; CWM:AUG/95[26]604, CWNEWS:JUL/92[4],
   CWR:VOL1#2[44]114
20th Infantry; B&G:AUG/95[8]604, MH:OCT/93[20]172
21st Infantry; ACW:SEP/92[38]379, AHI:MAR/84[42]238,
   CWR:VOL2#1[36]132
22nd Infantry; AHI:MAR/84[42]238
24th Infantry; CWR:VOL4#2[1]165, CWR:VOL4#2[68]167,
   CWR:VOL4#2[151]170
26th Infantry; ACW:SEP/94[10]484
27th Infantry; ACW:SEP/94[10]484, CWR:VOL2#1[1]130
28th Infantry; ACW:SEP/94[10]484, CWM:SEP/93[18]494,
   CWR:VOL3#1[1]149, CWR:VOL4#2[1]165,
   CWR:VOL4#2[68]167, CWR:VOL4#2[118]169
31st Infantry; B&G:FEB/94[8]550, CWR:VOL4#2[68]167
33rd Infantry; CWR:VOL3#1[1]149
Confederate Guards Response Battalion;
   CWM:OCT/94[33]537, CWR:VOL4#2[1]165

Consolidated Crescent Regiment:
ARTICLE: "A DEATH AT MANSFIELD: COL. JAMES HAMILTON BEARD AND THE CONSOLIDATED CRESCENT REGIMENT," CWR:VOL4#2[68]167
ADDITIONAL LISTING: CWM:APR/95[28]573, CWR:VOL3#1[1]149, CWR:VOL4#2[1]165
Coppen's Zouaves:
ARTICLE: "FOCUS: CIVIL WAR PHOTOGRAPHY," AHI:JAN/81[27]215
ADDITIONAL LISTING: CWM:SEP/93[24]495
D'Aquin's Battery; ACW:MAR/94[50]462
Donaldsonville Artillery; GETTY:5[4]156, GETTY:13[7]253
Durrive's Light Artillery; B&G:AUG/95[8]604
Fenner's Light Artillery; B&G:JUN/93[12]524, B&G:AUG/95[8]604
Gray's Brigade; ARTICLE: "HENRY GRAY'S LOUISIANA BRIGADE AT THE BATTLE OF MANSFIELD, APRIL 8, 1864," CWR:VOL4#2[1]165
Lafourche Militia Regiment; CWR:VOL3#1[1]149
Louisiana Brigade; ACW:MAY/93[54], B&G:FEB/92[26], CWM:MAY/92[20]420, CWR:VOL1#1[42]105, CWTI:MAR/94[48]374, CWTI:MAR/95[33]435
Louisiana Guard Artillery; ACW:MAR/92[30]352, B&G:FEB/95[8]590C, CWM:JAN/92[44]406, GETTY:4[65]148
Louisiana Native Guards; AHI:MAY/71[3]133A, CWM:JAN/92[44]406, GETTY:6[94]180, MH:AUG/94[82]179
Louisiana Tigers:
ARTICLES: "JEFF DAVIS' PET WOLVES: THE 1ST LOUISIANA ZOUAVE BATTALION DID NOT DESERVE ITS MEAN REPUTATION...," CWTI:MAR/89[28]103, "GOING BACK INTO THE UNION AT LAST," CWTI:FEB/91[12]189, "THE LOUISIANA TIGERS," CWM:SEP/93[24]495, "WHEAT'S TIGERS," CWTI:MAR/94[48]374
BOOK REVIEWS: *THE CIVIL WAR MEMOIRS OF CAPTAIN WILLIAM J. SEYMOUR: REMINISCENCES OF A LOUISIANA TIGER*
GENERAL LISTINGS: *Gettysburg,* GETTY:11[91]236, *Gettysburg,* GETTY:12[30]243, *in book review,* B&G:FEB/92[26], *letters to the editor,* B&G:DEC/95[5]614A, CWTI:MAY/91[8]205
ADDITIONAL LISTINGS: ACW:MAR/92[30]352, ACW:MAY/93[54], ACW:NOV/94[18]495, B&G:FEB/95[8]590C, B&G:DEC/95[5]614A, CWM:MAR/91[17]335, CWM:MAR/91[65]342, CWR:VOL1#4[77], CWTI:MAY/91[8]205, GETTY:5[123]166, MH:OCT/93[20]172
Madison Infantry; B&G:DEC/92[32]506
Orleans Independent Artillery; ACW:SEP/95[8]542
Pointe Coupee Artillery; B&G:AUG/94[22]576, CWR:VOL2#1[36]132
Terrebonne Militia Regiment; CWR:VOL3#1[1]149
Washington Artillery:
BOOK REVIEW: *IN CAMP AND BATTLE WITH THE WASHINGTON ARTILLERY*
ADDITIONAL LISTINGS: ACW:JAN/93[43]397, B&G:OCT/92[38]500, B&G:DEC/93[30]546, B&G:AUG/95[8]604, CWM:FEB/95[28]560, CWM:AUG/95[26]604, CWR:VOL4#3[50]171, CWR:VOL4#4[28]178, CWTI:SEPT/89[46]132, CWTI:NOV/93[55]350
Washington Horse Artillery:
ARTICLE: "ALREADY OWNING A PROUD PEDIGREE, THE WASHINGTON HORSE ARTILLERY ADDED LUSTER TO THE CONFEDERATE CAUSE," ACW:JUL/92[12]367
ADDITIONAL LISTINGS: ACW:SEP/92[30]378, ACW:NOV/92[74]390
Watson's Battery; CWR:VOL3#4[24]162

LOUISIANA, STATE OF: BOOK REVIEWS: *THE CIVIL WAR IN LOUISIANA * THE CONDUCT OF THE FEDERAL TROOPS IN LOUISIANA DURING THE INVASIONS OF 1863 AND 1864 * CRUCIBLE OF RECONSTRUCTION: WAR, RADICALISM, AND RACE IN LOUISIANA, 1862-1877 * THE FREEDMEN'S BUREAU IN LOUISIANA * LOUISIANA NECKTIES: LOUISIANA RAILROADS IN THE CIVIL WAR * PORTRAITS OF CONFLICT: A PHOTOGRAPHIC HISTORY OF LOUISIANA IN THE CIVIL WAR*
LOVE, ANDREW P., *Captain, CSA;* GETTY:12[68]246
LOVE, D.C., *Private, 11th Mississippi Infantry;* CWR:VOL2#4[269]145
LOVE, HIRAM, *Major, 2nd Iowa Cavalry;* ACW:JUL/94[8]474, B&G:JUN/93[12]524
LOVE, JAMES D., *Sergeant, 11th Mississippi Infantry;* CWR:VOL2#4[269]145, GETTY:9[98]217
LOVEJOY'S STATION, GEORGIA, BATTLE OF; ACW:JUL/91[12]310, CWTI:SUMMER/89[50]124
LOVEJOY, ELIJAH P., *Chaplain;* ACW:NOV/95[54]558
LOVEJOY, OWEN; CWTI:FEB/92[21]247
LOVELL, C.S., *Major, USA;* ACW:NOV/94[50]498
LOVELL, CHARLES S.; ACW:NOV/94[50]498
LOVELL, DON G., *Captain, USA;* ACW:JUL/92[41]370
LOVELL, MANSFIELD, *General, CSA:*
GENERAL LISTINGS: *in book review,* CWM:APR/95[50], CWNEWS:SEP/95[33], *Yellow Fever,* AHI:MAY/67[42]109
ADDITIONAL LISTINGS: ACW:SEP/91[46]324, B&G:DEC/93[30]546, CWR:VOL2#1[36]132, CWR:VOL3#1[1]149, CWTI:MAR/93[24]309, CWTI:MAY/93[29]319
LOVIE, HENRY, *artist;* CWM:NOV/92[10]447
LOVILL, E.F., *Captain, 28th North Carolina Infantry;* GETTY:8[67]204
LOVING, STARLING, *civilian;* B&G:OCT/94[11]580
LOW, JOHN, *Lieutenant, CSN;* CWTI:DEC/91[44]241
LOWE, AARON B., *Lieutenant, 16th Mississippi Infantry;* GETTY:8[111]206
LOWE, BUD, *Private, 34th Mississippi Infantry;* CWTI:SEPT/89[30]129
LOWE, ISAAC, JAMES and JOHN, *92nd Ohio Infantry;* B&G:JUN/95[36]603A
LOWE, J.A., *Lieutenant, 26th North Carolina Infantry;* GETTY:5[19]158
LOWE, J.G., *Captain, USA;* CWM:JAN/92[12]400
LOWE, JOHN, *Lieutenant, CSN;* AHI:OCT/88[38]275
LOWE, S.D., *Colonel, 28th North Carolina Infantry;* GETTY:8[67]204
LOWE, THADDEUS S.C.:
ARTICLES: "BALLOONS: AMERICA'S FIRST AIR FORCE," AHI:JUN/84[24]239, "FOCUS: CIVIL WAR PHOTOGRAPHY," AHI:JAN/80[29]198
BOOK REVIEW: *AERONAUTICS IN THE UNION AND CONFEDERATE ARMIES*
GENERAL LISTINGS: *balloons,* B&G:AUG/91[20]459, *Ball's Bluff,* AHI:FEB/82[36]225, *general history,* AHI:MAY/71[3]133A, *letters to the editor,* B&G:DEC/91[6]468
LOWE, WILLIAM W., *Colonel, USA;* CWTI:JUL/92[42]274
LOWELL, CHARLES R.; *Colonel, 2nd Massachusetts Cavalry;* CWNEWS:SEP/90[4], CWR:VOL4#1[78], CWTI:SEP/90[34]176
LOWELL, JAMES R., AHI:JUL/78[11]181, CWTI:AUG/90[42]167
LOWELL, NELSON, *Private, 9th Massachusetts Artillery;* GETTY:5[47]160

LOWRANCE, WILLIAM L., *General, CSA;*
ACW:JUL/95[50]538, GETTY:6[7]169, GETTY:8[67]204,
GETTY:11[57]233, GETTY:13[1]252
LOWREY, MARK P., *General, CSA;* ACW:NOV/93[34]442,
B&G:DEC/93[12]545, CWTI:SUMMER/89[50]124,
CWTI:SEP/94[40]403
LOWRY, ROBERT, *Colonel, 6th Mississippi Infantry;*
B&G:DEC/93[12]545, B&G:FEB/94[8]550,
CWR:VOL2#1[36]132
LOWRY, WILLIAM B., *Lieutenant Colonel, 11th Mississippi
Infantry;* CWR:VOL2#4[269]145
LOWTHER, ALEXANDER A., *Major, 15th Alabama Infantry;*
ACW:JAN/92[38]343
LOYALL, B.P., *Captain, CSN;* ACW:JUL/92[10]366
LUBBOCK, FRANCIS, *Governor, Texas;* ACW:JAN/93[51]398,
ACW:MAY/95[38]526, CWR:VOL1#4[77],
CWTI:MAR/93[32]311, CWTI:JUL/93[20]325
LUBBOCK, THOMAS S., *Colonel, Terry's Texas Rangers;*
CWM:JUL/92[40]432, CWR:VOL2#3[212]142
LUCAS, JESSE, *Captain, USA;* ACW:JAN/93[10]393
LUCAS, THOMAS J., *Colonel, 16th Indiana Infantry;*
B&G:FEB/94[8]550, CWR:VOL4#2[1]165,
CWR:VOL4#2[68]167
LUCE, STEPHEN B., *Lieutenant, USN;* ACW:JAN/91[62]289
LUCKENBILL, LEWIS, *Private, 96th Pennsylvania Infantry;*
CWR:VOL3#3[1]157
LUCKIE, A.T., *Private, CSA;* CWTI:SEP/91[23]228
LUCKIE, L.P., *Captain, 3rd Georgia Infantry;*
CWTI:DEC/94[32]410
LUDLOW, BENJAMIN C., *Major, USA;* GETTY:6[59]174,
GETTY:8[31]201
LUKER, AUGUSTUS, *Sergeant, 118th Pennsylvania Infantry;*
GETTY:8[53]203
LUMPKIN, JOSEPH H., *Private, CSA;* CWR:VOL4#4[28]178
LUMSDEN'S ALABAMA BATTERY; B&G:DEC/93[52]548
LUMSDEN, CHARLES L., *Captain, CSA;* B&G:DEC/93[12]545,
GETTY:10[107]227
LUND, HERMAN, *Captain, 16th Illinois Infantry;*
B&G:DEC/95[9]615
LUNDY, WILLIAM, *Private, CSA;* B&G:FEB/91[32]441
LUNT, WILLIAM, *Colonel, USA;* CWTI:MAY/94[50]386
LURTON, HORACE:
ARTICLE: "THE PLAIN TRUTH WAS TOO PLAIN FOR HORACE
LURTON," CWTI:DEC/94[79]417
ADDITIONAL LISTING: CWM:OCT/95[53]621
LUSE, HENRY W., *Lieutenant Colonel, 77th New York Infantry;*
ACW:SEP/92[30]378
LUSK, LYCURGUS D., *Captain, 22nd New York Cavalry;*
B&G:FEB/92[32]477
LUTRY, WARREN S., *Captain, CSA;* CWTI:MAR/89[16]101
LUTZ, CHARLES F., *8th Louisiana Infantry;* GETTY:6[94]180
LYDECKER, GARRETT J., *cadet;* B&G:DEC/91[12]469
LYLE, JOSEPH B., *Captain, CSA;* ARTICLE: "STUNNING
SOUTHERN HEROISM," CWM:OCT/94[34]538
LYLE, PETER, *Colonel, USA;* ACW:MAR/95[42]517,
B&G:APR/94[10]558
LYLES, WILLIAM D., *Surgeon, CSA;* CWM:MAY/91[10]347
LYMAN, CHAUNCY A., *Major, 7th Pennsylvania Reserves;*
CWM:DEC/94[74]555
LYMAN, JONAS, *Lieutenant Colonel, 203rd Pennsylvania
Infantry;* B&G:DEC/94[10]585
LYMAN, THEODORE, *Colonel, USA:*

BOOK REVIEWS: *WITH GRANT AND MEADE: FROM THE
WILDERNESS TO APPOMATTOX,* CWNEWS:DEC/95[29],
CWR:VOL4#2[136]
ADDITIONAL LISTINGS: ACW:MAY/93[31]415, B&G:APR/95[8]595,
B&G:APR/95[33]597, B&G:JUN/95[8]600,
CWM:MAR/93[24]467, CWTI:AUG/90[26]166,
CWTI:FEB/91[24]191, CWTI:SEP/91[31]229,
CWTI:MAY/93[29]319, GETTY:11[19]232, MH:JUN/92[6]158,
photo; CWTI:FEB/91[24]191
LYNCH, BILLY, *Private, Terry's Texas Rangers;*
CWM:JUL/92[40]432
LYNCH, JAMES C., *Captain, 106th Pennsylvania Infantry;*
GETTY:5[89]162, GETTY:6[7]169, GETTY:7[97]193
LYNCH, WILLIAM F., *Captain, CSN;* B&G:AUG/95[38],
CWM:FEB/95[49]565, CWR:VOL2#3[212]142
LYNCHBURG, VIRGINIA; ARTICLE: "A HEALING PLACE,"
CWM:MAY/91[40]351
LYNCHBURG, VIRGINIA, BATTLE OF;
ACW:JUL/94[26]477, B&G:AUG/94[10]574,
CWTI:MAY/93[26]318
LYNDE, ISAAC, *Major, USA;* ACW:JAN/91[10]283,
ACW:JUL/93[27]423, B&G:JUN/94[8]568, CWR:VOL4#4[129],
CWTI:OCT/95[56]471
LYNN, JOHN R., *Private, 29th Ohio Infantry;*
ACW:SEP/91[41]323, GETTY:9[81]216
LYON, ARTHUR P., *Sergeant, 15th Pennsylvania Cavalry;*
CWTI:MAY/93[38]321
LYON, HYLAN B., *General, CSA;* CWTI:MAY/93[38]321,
MH:JUN/93[82]167
LYON, ISAAC, *Captain, USA;* GETTY:4[101]150,
GETTY:4[101]151
LYON, NATHANIEL, *General, USA:*
ARTICLES: "A MIGHTY MEAN-FOWT FIGHT,"
ACW:NOV/93[26]441, CWTI:FEB/92[29]248, "DEATH
STRUGGLE FOR MISSOURI," CWM:MAY/93[8]474,
"UNPROVOKED TRAGICOMEDY IN ST. LOUIS,"
ACW:MAY/91[31]304
BOOK REVIEWS: *DAMNED YANKEE: THE LIFE OF GENERAL
NATHANIEL LYON * THE LYON CAMPAIGN IN
MISSOURI: BEING A HISTORY OF THE FIRST IOWA
INFANTRY*
ADDITIONAL LISTINGS: AHI:MAY/71[3]133A, ACW:MAR/91[62]298,
ACW:MAY/91[10]301, ACW:MAR/92[46]354,
ACW:JUL/92[8]365A, ACW:SEP/92[38]379,
ACW:JAN/93[26]395, ACW:MAR/94[8]456, ACW:MAY/94[58],
CWM:SEP/92[38]443, CWM:SEP/93[8]493,
CWTI:FEB/90[26]143, CWTI:MAR/91[34]201,
CWTI:JAN/94[29]360, MH:APR/95[74]184, *photo,*
CWM:MAY/93[8]474, *sketch;* CWTI:FEB/92[29]248
LYON, R.W., *Lieutenant, 102nd Pennsylvania Infantry;*
GETTY:11[91]236
LYONS, BENJAMIN R., *Lieutenant, USA;*
CWTI:JAN/94[46]364
LYTLE, ROBERT, *Lieutenant, 27th Illinois Infantry;*
CWR:VOL3#4[24]162
LYTLE, WILLIAM H., *General, USA;* B&G:OCT/92[32]499,
CWR:VOL4#3[50]171, CWTI:DEC/90[56]184

M

MABRY, HINCHIE, *Colonel, 3rd Confederate Cavalry Brigade;*
ACW:SEP/92[23]377, ACW:MAR/93[68]409
MABRY, JOSEPH A.; CWTI:MAY/94[50]386
MACARTHUR, ARTHUR, JR., *Colonel, USA:*
ARTICLE: "THE 24TH WISCONSIN'S GALLANT BOY COLONEL,
ARTHUR MACARTHUR, PLANTED THE COLORS ON
MISSIONARY RIDGE," ACW:MAR/92[14]350
ADDITIONAL LISTING: B&G:FEB/93[40]514
MACAULAY, DAN, *Colonel, 11th Indiana Infantry;*
B&G:FEB/94[8]550, CWTI:MAR/91[28]200
MACBETH, CHARLES, *Mayor, Charleston;*
CWM:MAR/92[16]411
MACCONNELL, CHARLES C., *Lieutenant, 5th U.S. Artillery;*
GETTY:9[41]212
MACDONALD, CHRISTINE; CWTI:JUL/93[38]328
MACDONALD, SANDFIELD, *Canadian Prime Minister;*
CWTI:JUL/93[38]328
MACDOUGALL, CLINTON D., *Colonel, 111th New York
Infantry;* B&G:APR/94[10]558, CWTI:AUG/90[26]166,
GETTY:7[51]190, GETTY:8[95]205, *photo,* GETTY:7[51]190
MACFARLAND, JAMES E., *civilian;* ACW:NOV/91[46]335
MACINTOSH, DAVID G., *General, CSA;* CWM:DEC/95[41]630
MACK, ALBERT G., *Captain, 18th New York Artillery;*
ACW:JAN/94[30]450, CWTI:JAN/93[49]303
MACK, SAMUEL A., *Lieutenant, 13th Pennsylvania Reserves;*
CWR:VOL1#3[28]120, CWR:VOL1#3[46]121
MACKALL, WILLIAM W., *Colonel, CSA;* ACW:MAR/95[58],
B&G:OCT/92[10]496, CWTI:JUL/93[10]323
MACKENZIE, RANALD S., *General, USA:*
BOOK REVIEWS: *BAD HAND: A BIOGRAPHY OF GENERAL
RANALD S. MACKENZIE * THE MOST PROMISING
YOUNG OFFICER: A LIFE OF RANALD SLIDELL
MACKENZIE*
GENERAL LISTINGS: *Custer,* AHI:FEB/71[4]131, *Five Forks,*
B&G:APR/92[8]481, *Gettysburg,* GETTY:6[59]174,
GETTY:8[31]201, *in book review,* CWM:APR/95[50],
CWR:VOL4#3[89], *in order of battle,* B&G:APR/92[8]481, *post
war,* AHI:NOV/79[32]196, *West Point,* B&G:DEC/91[12]469,
photo, B&G:DEC/91[12]469
MACKEY, EDWIN I., *Pvt., 7th Wisconsin Inf.;* GETTY:11[57]233
MACKEY, T.J., *Captain, CSA;* B&G:JUN/91[10]452
MACLAUCHLAN, JACK, *Corporal, 29th Pennsylvania
Infantry;* CWR:VOL3#2[70]155
MACON (GEORGIA) CENTRAL ORDNANCE
LABORATORY; AHI:NOV/73[18]151
MACON, GEORGIA; B&G:APR/93[40]522,
CWTI:SUMMER/89[20]121, CWTI:SUMMER/89[50]124
MACON, MILES C., *Captain, CSA;* GETTY:13[64]258
MACRAE, WILLIAM, *General, CSA;* CWTI:AUG/90[26]166,
CWTI:FEB/91[45]194
MACVEAGH, WAYNE; GETTY:9[122]220
MACWILLIE, M.H.; ACW:JAN/91[10]283
MACY, GEORGE N., *General, USA;* B&G:JUN/95[8]600,
CWNEWS:MAY/95[33], CWR:VOL3#1[31]150,
CWR:VOL4#4[101]181, MH:AUG/95[70], *photo,*
CWR:VOL4#4[101]181
MADDEN, WILLIAM, *Pvt., 44th Ohio Inf.;* B&G:AUG/95[24]605
MADDUX, CAB, *Mosby's Rangers;* ACW:JUL/94[26]477,
CWM:JAN/93[24]458

MADILL, HENRY J., *General, USA;* CWTI:AUG/90[26]166
MADISON (LOUISIANA) LIGHT ARTILLERY;
GETTY:5[47]160
MADISON (PENNSYLVANIA) GUARDS, (53rd Pennsylvania
Infantry); GETTY:11[80]235
MADISON INFANTRY; B&G:DEC/92[32]506
MADISON, GEORGE T., *Captain, CSA;* ACW:NOV/91[10]329,
CWTI:MAR/91[10]197
MAFFETT, ROBERT C., *Major, 3rd South Carolina Infantry;*
GETTY:5[35]159
MAFFIT, E.A., *Midshipman, CSN;* AHI:OCT/88[38]275
MAFFITT, JOHN N., *Captain, CSN:*
ARTICLE: "A SON OF OLD NEPTUNE," CWTI:DEC/91[44]241
BOOK REVIEWS: *HIGH SEAS CONFEDERATE: THE LIFE AND
TIMES OF JOHN NEWLAND MAFFITT*
GENERAL LISTINGS: *general history,* AHI:MAY/71[3]133A, *in book
review,* B&G:AUG/92[36], B&G:AUG/95[38], *photos,*
AHI:DEC/82[38]231, CWTI:DEC/91[44]241
ADDITIONAL LISTINGS: ACW:JAN/91[47]288, AHI:DEC/82[38]231,
B&G:DEC/94[10]585, CWTI:DEC/89[10]133,
CWTI:AUG/95[40]458

MAGAZINES:
ARTICLE: *"CENTURY MAGAZINE";* CWTI:APR/89[14]107
BOOK REVIEW: *LESLIE'S ILLUSTRATED CIVIL WAR,*
CWNEWS:JUL/93[5]
Army and Navy Journal; GETTY:12[85]248
Atlantic Monthly; ACW:MAR/94[10]457, GETTY:12[85]248

MAGEE, B.F., *Sergeant, 72nd Indiana Infantry;*
ACW:MAY/95[49]527
MAGEE, GUSTAVUS S., *Captain, 11th Kentucky Infantry;*
B&G:OCT/94[11]580
MAGILL, JACOB, *Private, 53rd Pennsylvania Infantry;*
GETTY:11[80]235
MAGILL, ROBERT J., *Lieutenant, 1st Georgia Regulars;*
CWR:VOL2#2[95]135
MAGILL, ROBERT M., *Private, 39th Georgia Infantry;*
CWTI:MAY/91[24]208
MAGILTON, ALBERT L., *Colonel, 7th Pennsylvania Reserves;*
ACW:JUL/92[30]369, CWM:DEC/94[74]555,
CWR:VOL4#4[1]177
MAGILTON, WILLIAM, *Colonel, USA;* CWR:VOL4#4[1]177
MAGOFFIN, BERIAH, *Governor, Kentucky;*
ACW:JUL/91[26]313, ACW:JUL/92[22]368,
ACW:JAN/94[10]448, B&G:FEB/93[12]511,
CWR:VOL4#3[50]171
MAGOFFIN, EBENEZER, *Colonel, CSA;* CWTI:AUG/95[58]461
MAGOFFIN, JAMES; AHI:SEP/83[42]235
MAGRUDER, A.B., *Major, CSA;* CWTI:MAR/95[60]439
MAGRUDER, GEORGE, *Lieutenant, USA;* B&G:OCT/95[36]614
MAGRUDER, JOHN B., *General, CSA:*
ARTICLES: "MOST DISGRACEFUL AFFAIR,"
ACW:JAN/93[51]398, "THE PENINSULA CAMPAIGN OF
1862: THE SIEGE OF YORKTOWN AND ENGAGEMENTS
ALONG THE WARWICK RIVER," CWM:JUN/9 "SUPERB
WAS THE DAY," ACW:MAR/91[47]297
GENERAL LISTINGS: *Big Bethel,* ACW:MAR/93[42]406, *Galveston,*
ACW:MAR/94[35]460, *in book review,* B&G:AUG/93[24],
CWM:JUN/95[6], *letters to the editor,* CWM:JAN/93[6]455,
Malvern Hill, CWM:JUN/95[73]597, *Mexican War,*
B&G:JUN/92[8]487, MH:APR/93[39]166, *Monitor* vs. *Virginia,*
AHI:OCT/75[30]162, *Peninsula Campaign,*

15th Infantry; CWM:SEP/92[8]437
16th Infantry:
ARTICLES: "16TH MAINE AT GETTYSBURG,"
CWM:MAY/92[15]419, "THE 16TH MAINE VOLUNTEER
INFANTRY AT GETTYSBURG," GETTY:13[33]255
GENERAL LISTINGS: *Chancellorsville*, GETTY:13[33]255,
Fredericksburg, GETTY:13[33]255, *Gettysburg*,
GETTY:4[33]146, GETTY:4[115]152, GETTY:5[117]165,
GETTY:6[7]169, GETTY:10[7]221, *in book review*,
CWNEWS:AUG/90[4], *in order of battle*, B&G:APR/92[8]481,
photo of officers, CWM:MAY/92[15]419, *photo of flag*,
CWM:MAY/92[15]419, GETTY:13[33]255
ADDITIONAL LISTINGS: ACW:MAR/95[42]517, AHI:DEC/73[10]152,
CWM:MAY/92[4]416, CWTI:JAN/93[35]300, GETTY:13[1]252,
GETTY:13[7]253
17th Infantry:
ARTICLE: "GETTYSBURG AND THE SEVENTEENTH MAINE,"
GETTY:8[43]202
BOOK REVIEWS: *REBEL YELL AND YANKEE HURRAH: THE
CIVIL WAR JOURNAL OF A MAINE VOLUNTEER *
"UNSPOILED HEART"; THE JOURNAL OF CHARLES
MATTOCKS OF THE 17TH MAINE*
GENERAL LISTINGS: *Gettysburg*, GETTY:4[113]153,
GETTY:8[43]202, GETTY:8[53]203, GETTY:9[5]209,
GETTY:10[53]225
ADDITIONAL LISTINGS: ACW:SEP/94[38]487, B&G:APR/91[8]445,
B&G:APR/95[8]595, CWM:SEP/92[8]437, CWM:AUG/95[45],
CWTI:MAR/89[34]104, CWTI:MAY/94[24]381,
GETTY:8[43]202
18th Infantry; GETTY:8[43]202
19th Infantry:
ARTICLE: "THE GRANITE GLORY: THE 19TH MAINE AT
GETTYSBURG," GETTY:13[50]257
GENERAL LISTINGS: *Gettysburg*, GETTY:4[89]150,
GETTY:5[79]161, GETTY:6[7]169, GETTY:8[43]202,
GETTY:9[17N]210, GETTY:10[53]225, *in list*,
CWTI:JUL/93[34]327, *photo of officers*, GETTY:13[50]257
ADDITIONAL LISTINGS: ACW:JAN/93[43]397, B&G:AUG/93[18]530,
CWM:APR/95[42]577, GETTY:13[1]252, GETTY:13[7]253
20th Infantry:
ARTICLES: "THE FIGHTING PROFESSOR: JOSHUA
LAWRENCE CHAMBERLAIN," CWM:JUL/92[8]427,
"THROUGH BLOOD AND FIRE AT GETTYSBURG,"
GETTY:6[43]173
BOOK REVIEWS: *IN THE HANDS OF PROVIDENCE: JOSHUA L.
CHAMBERLAIN & THE AMERICAN CIVIL WAR * THE
TWENTIETH MAINE * WITH A FLASH OF HIS SWORD:
THE WRITINGS OF MAJOR HOLMAN S. MELCHER, 20TH
MAINE INFANTRY*
GENERAL LISTINGS: *Five Forks*, B&G:APR/92[8]481, *Gettysburg*,
GETTY:5[103]163, GETTY:6[33]172, GETTY:6[113]183,
GETTY:7[41]189, GETTY:8[31]201, GETTY:8[43]202,
GETTY:9[41]212, GETTY:10[112]228, GETTY:12[97]249, *in
book review*, CWNEWS:SEP/89[8], CWNEWS:JUL/90[4],
CWNEWS:JUL/93[5], CWR:VOL2#2[169], CWR:VOL2#3[256],
CWR:VOL2#4[346], CWR:VOL4#1[78], CWTI:NOV/92[10],
CWTI:MAY/93[18], CWTI:JUN/95[24], *in order of battle*,
B&G:APR/92[8]481, *photo of monument*, GETTY:7[41]189
ADDITIONAL LISTINGS: ACW:JAN/92[38]343, ACW:MAR/95[12]513,
ACW:MAY/95[62], AHI:JUL/93[40]312, AHI:NOV/93[48]316,
B&G:APR/91[8]445, B&G:OCT/93[12]537,
B&G:OCT/94[42]583, CWM:DEC/94[26]548,

CWTI:JUL/93[42]329, CWTI:MAY/94[40]383,
GETTY:13[1]252, GETTY:13[7]253
27th Infantry:
BOOK REVIEW: *A SHOWER OF STARS; THE MEDAL OF HONOR
AND THE 27TH MAINE*
ADDITIONAL LISTINGS: CWM:SEP/92[8]437, CWTI:SEP/94[12]398
29th Infantry; CWM:OCT/94[8], CWTI:FEB/91[66]196
30th Infantry; ARTICLE: "30TH MAINE," ACW:SEP/91[16]320
31st Infantry; ACW:MAY/95[18]524, CWR:VOL2#2[118]136,
CWR:VOL4#1[78]
32nd Infantry; ACW:MAY/95[18]524, CWR:VOL2#2[118]136
Bangor Light Infantry; CWR:VOL4#1[78]

MAITLAND, WILLIAM; *civilian;* CWR:VOL4#2[26]166
MAJOR, JAMES P., *General, CSA;* CWM:OCT/94[33]537,
CWR:VOL2#3[212]142, CWR:VOL4#2[1]165,
CWR:VOL4#2[26]166, CWR:VOL4#2[68]167,
CWR:VOL4#2[118]169
MAJOR, ROBERT, *Sergeant Major, 5th Ohio Cavalry;*
CWR:VOL4#1[44]164
MAKEPEACE, A.J., *Captain, 19th Indiana Infantry;*
AHI:JAN/94[50]319
MALLORY, BUDDY, *Midshipman, CSN;* ACW:JUL/92[10]366
MALLORY, ROBERT H., *Private, Crenshaw's Artillery;*
GETTY:10[107]227
MALLORY, STEPHEN R.:
GENERAL LISTINGS: *Virginia vs U.S. fleet*, AHI:OCT/75[30]162,
evacuation of Richmond, ACW:SEP/95[30]545, *fall of
Richmond*, ACW:MAY/95[38]526, *general history*,
AHI:MAY/71[3]133A, *in book review*, ACW:MAR/92[54],
ACW:JUL/95[58], CWM:OCT/94[8], CWNEWS:JUN/92[4],
CWNEWS:JUL/92[4], CWNEWS:AUG/92[4],
CWNEWS:MAY/95[33], CWR:VOL3#3[92], *Ironclads*,
MH:AUG/92[26]161, *photos*, AHI:MAY/71[3]133A,
CWTI:DEC/91[44]241, CWTI:AUG/95[40]458
ADDITIONAL LISTINGS: ACW:NOV/91[8]328, ACW:MAY/92[14]358,
ACW:JUL/92[10]366, ACW:JAN/93[58]399,
ACW:JUL/94[35]478, ACW:NOV/94[58]499,
AHI:DEC/82[38]231, AHI:JAN/83[10]232, CWM:JUL/93[2]481,
CWM:JUL/93[15]484, CWM:JUL/93[30]486,
CWTI:AUG/90[42]167, CWTI:AUG/91[36]217,
CWTI:DEC/91[44]241, CWTI:MAY/92[29]263,
CWTI:JUL/94[30]392, CWTI:AUG/95[40]458,
MH:FEB/91[8]151
MALLORY, W.B., *Captain, CSA;* CWTI:APR/89[38]111
MALLOY, THOMAS P., *Lieutenant, 7th North Carolina
Infantry;* GETTY:13[75]259
MALONEY, PATRICK, *Private, 2nd Wisconsin Infantry;*
CWM:MAR/91[17]335
MALONEY, WILLIAM H., *Private, McNeill's Rangers;*
B&G:AUG/94[10]574
MALTBY, JASPER A., *Colonel, 45th Illinois Infantry;*
B&G:FEB/94[8]550
MALVERN HILL, VIRGINIA, BATTLE OF:
ARTICLE: "THE PENINSULA CAMPAIGN OF 1862: THE
BATTLE OF MALVERN HILL," CWM:JUN/95[73]597
ADDITIONAL LISTINGS: ACW:MAR/94[42]461, ACW:MAY/94[12]466,
ACW:MAR/95[12]513, ACW:MAR/95[70]520,
ACW:JUL/95[10]533, ACW:SEP/95[54]548,
AHI:MAY/71[3]133A, B&G:APR/92[36]483,
CWM:JUL/91[28]366, CWM:JAN/92[68]407,
CWM:MAR/93[32]468, CWM:APR/94[14]503,
CWM:DEC/94[34]549, CWM:APR/95[50], CWR:VOL1#1[1]102,

CWR:VOL1#2[7]111, CWR:VOL1#3[28]120,
CWR:VOL2#4[269]145, CWR:VOL2#4[346],
CWR:VOL3#1[31]150, CWR:VOL3#3[1]157,
CWTI:APR/89[14]107, CWTI:JUN/90[28]158,
CWTI:JUL/93[14]324, CWTI:JUL/93[29]326,
CWTI:JUL/93[38]328, CWTI:JUL/93[42]329,
CWTI:NOV/93[55]350, CWTI:JAN/94[20]358,
CWTI:MAR/95[18]432, CWTI:MAR/95[60]439

MANEY, FRANK, *Captain, CSA;* B&G:FEB/92[10]474

MANEY, GEORGE E., *General, CSA;* ACW:JAN/95[30]505,
B&G:OCT/91[11]466, B&G:DEC/93[52]548,
CWR:VOL1#4[42]126, CWR:VOL4#3[50]171,
CWTI:SUMMER/89[20]121, CWTI:SUMMER/89[32]122

MANGES, HENRY F., *Lieutenant, 53rd Pennsylvania Infantry;*
GETTY:11[80]235

MANGUM, ADOLPHUS W., *Chaplain, 6th North Carolina
Infantry;* ARTICLE: "PRISON CHAPLAIN AND HISTORIAN,"
CWTI:NOV/93[114]355

MANGUM, WILLIAM P., *Lieutenant, 6th North Carolina
Infantry;* CWTI:NOV/93[114]355

MANIGAULT, ARTHUR M., *General, CSA:*
BOOK REVIEW: *A CAROLINIAN GOES TO WAR: THE CIVIL
WAR NARRATIVE OF ARTHUR MIDDLETON
MANIGAULT, BRIGADIER GENERAL, C.S.A.*
ADDITIONAL LISTINGS: B&G:OCT/91[11]466, B&G:OCT/92[32]499,
B&G:APR/94[28]559, B&G:JUN/94[34], CWM:JUL/92[24]430,
CWTI:SUMMER/89[40]123, CWTI:SUMMER/89[50]124,
CWTI:SEP/92[31]281, CWTI:SEP/92[28]280

MANLEY, BASIL, *Captain, CSA;* ACW:JAN/94[39]451

MANLY, B.C., *Captain, 1st North Carolina Artillery;*
GETTY:8[53]203

MANN, A. DUDLEY; AHI:JUN/70[30]127

MANN, ARTHUR B., *Lieutenant, 53rd Pennsylvania Infantry;*
GETTY:11[80]235

MANN, CHARLES, *Captain, 1st Missouri Artillery;*
B&G:AUG/95[8]604

MANN, HORACE; CWM:JAN/91[47]

MANN, ISAAC, *Lieutenant, 71st Ohio Infantry;*
CWTI:JUL/92[42]274

MANN, NEHEMIAH, *Captain, USA;* B&G:OCT/93[12]537

MANN, WILLIAM D., *Colonel, 7th Michigan Cavalry;*
GETTY:13[89]260

MANN, WILLIAM E., *General, CSA;* CWTI:SEP/94[26]400

MANASSAS NATIONAL BATTLEFIELD PARK;
B&G:JUN/91[26]453, B&G:AUG/94[34]577A,
CWM:JUL/91[35]369, CWM:SEP/91[35]384,
CWM:NOV/91[35]392, CWM:OCT/95[27]615

MANASSAS, VIRGINIA, FIRST BATTLE OF:
ARTICLES: "THE 4TH ALABAMA INFANTRY UNWITTINGLY
HELPED CREATE A CIVIL WAR LEGEND AT MANASSAS,"
ACW:NOV/94[18]495, "THE CIVIL WAR'S FIRST
MONUMENT: BARTOW'S MARKER AT MANASSAS,"
B&G:APR/91[32]447
BOOK REVIEWS: *A RISING THUNDER: FROM LINCOLN'S
ELECTION TO THE BATTLE OF BULL RUN, AN
EYEWITNESS HISTORY * THE FIRST BATTLE OF
MANASSAS*
GENERAL LISTINGS: *general history,* AHI:MAY/71[3]133A, *in book
review,* ACW:JAN/94[62], ACW:JUL/94[58], CWM:AUG/95[45],
CWNEWS:OCT/90[4], CWR:VOL1#2[78], CWR:VOL1#3[94],
CWR:VOL2#2[169], CWR:VOL3#2[105], CWR:VOL4#3[89],
Monuments, B&G:APR/91[32]447

ADDITIONAL LISTINGS: ACW:NOV/91[8]328, ACW:NOV/91[41]334,
ACW:MAR/92[10]349, ACW:MAY/92[14]358,
ACW:JUL/92[12]367, ACW:MAY/93[38]416,
ACW:SEP/94[31]486, ACW:JAN/95[20]504,
ACW:JAN/95[46]507, ACW:MAY/95[54]528,
ACW:SEP/95[54]548, ACW:NOV/95[8]552,
B&G:DEC/91[34]470, B&G:JUN/94[22]569,
CWM:MAR/91[35]337, CWM:JAN/92[27]403,
CWM:JUL/92[16]428, CWM:JUN/94[50]518,
CWM:DEC/94[49]553, CWM:JUN/95[24]582,
CWM:AUG/95[38]609, CWM:OCT/95[22]614,
CWR:VOL1#3[20]119, CWR:VOL2#3[183]140,
CWR:VOL2#4[269]145, CWR:VOL3#1[31]150,
CWR:VOL3#2[1]153, CWTI:MAY/89[36]118,
CWTI:SEPT/89[24]128, CWTI:DEC/89[34]136,
CWTI:AUG/91[46]218, CWTI:APR/92[14]254,
CWTI:APR/92[35]257, CWTI:JAN/93[40]301

MANASSAS, VIRGINIA, SECOND BATTLE OF:
ARTICLES: "AN EYEWITNESS ACCOUNT OF SECOND BULL
RUN," AHI:DEC/66[30]105, "THE BLOODY FIFTH,"
CWTI:DEC/91[36]240, "'BOYS, WON'T I MAKE A FINE
LOOKING CORPSE?' DURYEE'S ZOUAVES AT SECOND
BULL RUN," CWR:VOL1#2[29]112, "COL. FLETCHER
WEBSTER'S LAST LETTER: I SHALL NOT SPARE
MYSELF," B&G:OCT/95[20]612, "THE FORGING OF THE
IRON BRIGADE," CWM:JAN/93[16]457, "'NEAR KILLING
ME,'" CWM:JUL/91[40]370, "RETURN TO THE KILLING
GROUND," ACW:JUL/91[18]312, "THE SECOND BATTLE
OF MANASSAS: LEE SUPPRESSES THE 'MISCREANT'
POPE," B&G:AUG/92[11]493, "SECOND MANASSAS:
ENFILADING THUNDER," CWM:AUG/94[48]529,
"STANDOFF AT BRAWNER'S FARM," CWM:AUG/95[30]606,
"WE CLEARED THEIR WAY...FIRING CANISTER,"
CWTI:MAR/93[20]308
BOOK REVIEWS: *ABANDONED BY LINCOLN: A MILITARY
BIOGRAPHY OF GENERAL JOHN POPE * RETURN TO
BULL RUN: THE CAMPAIGN AND BATTLE OF SECOND
MANASSAS * SECOND MANASSAS BATTLEFIELD MAP
STUDY—ACCOMPANIED BY 16 SEPARATE COLORED
MAPS*
GENERAL LISTINGS: *general history,* AHI:MAY/71[3]133A, *in book
review,* ACW:SEP/94[66], CWM:OCT/94[8], CWM:AUG/95[8],
CWNEWS:OCT/90[4], CWR:VOL1#2[78], CWR:VOL1#3[94],
CWR:VOL2#4[346], CWR:VOL3#2[105], CWR:VOL3#3[92],
CWR:VOL3#4[68], CWR:VOL4#1[78], *Jackson,*
B&G:JUN/92[8]487, *letters to the editor,* B&G:OCT/92[22]497,
West Point, B&G:DEC/91[12]469, *Maps;* AHI:DEC/66[30]105
ADDITIONAL LISTINGS: ACW:JUL/92[12]367, ACW:JUL/93[10]421,
ACW:JUL/93[58], ACW:SEP/93[8]429, ACW:JAN/95[54]508,
ACW:MAR/95[42]517, AHI:MAR/84[42]238,
B&G:AUG/91[32]461, B&G:DEC/91[34]470,
B&G:AUG/92[53]496A, B&G:FEB/95[8]590C,
CWM:MAY/91[8]346, CWM:MAY/91[26]349,
CWM:JUL/91[28]366, CWM:NOV/91[12]390,
CWM:JUL/92[18]429, CWM:MAR/93[32]468,
CWM:SEP/93[24]495, CWM:OCT/94[26]536,
CWM:DEC/94[26]548, CWM:AUG/95[38]609,
CWM:DEC/95[34]628, CWM:DEC/95[41]630,
CWM:DEC/95[59]633, CWR:VOL1#1[1]102,
CWR:VOL1#2[v]110, CWR:VOL1#3[28]120,
CWR:VOL1#3[52]122, CWR:VOL2#1[36]132,
CWR:VOL2#4[269]145, CWR:VOL3#1[31]150,
CWR:VOL3#3[1]157, CWTI:MAR/89[28]103,

CWTI:APR/89[14]107, CWTI:AUG/91[82]223,
CWTI:FEB/92[58]251, CWTI:APR/92[35]257,
CWTI:JUL/93[29]326, CWTI:JAN/95[34]427,
CWTI:JUN/95[38]447, CWTI:NOV/93[55]350,
GETTY:13[119]262, MH:APR/92[18]157, MH:JUN/94[8]177,
MH:AUG/94[46]178, MH:AUG/95[30]185
MANNES, FREDERICK, *Sergeant, 72nd Pennsylvania
Infantry;* GETTY:7[97]193
MANNING, BENJAMIN, *Sergeant, 37th Illinois Infantry;*
CWR:VOL1#1[42]105
MANNING, JACOB H., *Captain, CSA;* GETTY:4[110]152
MANNING, JOHN, *Private, 19th Indiana Infantry;*
B&G:APR/95[24]596
MANNING, PEYTON T., *Captain, CSA;* CWTI:NOV/93[55]350,
GETTY:4[110]152
MANNING, VAN H., *Colonel, CSA;* ACW:MAR/94[50]462,
CWR:VOL3#2[1]153
MANNING, WALLACE, *Private, 31st North Carolina Infantry;*
B&G:APR/93[24]520
MANSFIELD, F., *Colonel, 54th Indiana Infantry;*
B&G:FEB/94[8]550
MANSFIELD, J.B., *Private, 26th North Carolina Infantry;*
GETTY:5[19]158
MANSFIELD, JOHN, *Major, 2nd Wisconsin Infantry;*
GETTY:6[13]170
MANSFIELD, JOHN, *Major, 6th Michigan Infantry;*
GETTY:5[19]158
MANSFIELD, JOSEPH F.K., *General, USA;*
ACW:JUL/92[30]369, ACW:JUL/93[8]420,
ACW:MAR/94[50]462, ACW:JAN/95[74]510,
ACW:MAY/95[54]528, AHI:DEC/71[30]138,
AHI:OCT/75[30]162, B&G:OCT/95[8]611A,
CWM:JUL/92[18]429, CWTI:MAY/92[38]265
MANSFIELD, LOUISIANA, BATTLE OF:
ARTICLES: "A DEATH AT MANSFIELD: COLONEL JAMES
HAMILTON BEARD AND THE CONSOLIDATED
CRESCENT REGIMENT," CWR:VOL4#2[68]167, "HENRY
GRAY'S LOUISIANA BRIGADE AT THE BATTLE OF
MANSFIELD, APRIL 8, 1864," CWR:VOL4#2[1]165, "RED
RIVER BLUES," CWM:APR/95[39]576
ADDITIONAL LISTINGS: ACW:SEP/91[16]320, ACW:JUL/92[46]371,
ACW:MAR/93[68]409, ACW:MAY/93[54],
ACW:MAR/95[34]516, AHI:MAY/71[3]133A,
CWNEWS:SEP/92[4], CWR:VOL2#3[212]142,
CWR:VOL2#3[252]144, CWR:VOL3#1[1]149,
CWR:VOL4#2[26]166, CWR:VOL4#2[104]168,
CWR:VOL4#2[118]169, CWR:VOL4#2[151]170,
MH:DEC/95[58]188
MANSHIP, CHARLES H., *civilian;* B&G:AUG/95[8]604
MANSON, MAHLON D., *Colonel, USA;* AHI:NOV/72[12]142,
B&G:FEB/93[12]511
MAPS: *A listing of articles and books only relating to maps and
map sets.*
ARTICLES: "A LIVING MAP OF THE WAR," CWM:JUN/95[79]599,
"MAPPING THE CIVIL WAR," CWTI:NOV/92[60]294
BOOK REVIEWS: *AMERICAN HERITAGE BATTLE MAPS OF THE
CIVIL WAR * THE ATLAS FOR THE AMERICAN CIVIL
WAR * THE ATLAS OF THE CIVIL WAR * CIVIL WAR
NEWSPAPER MAPS: A HISTORICAL ATLAS * CIVIL WAR
NEWSPAPER MAPS: A CARTOBIBLIOGRAPHY OF THE
NORTHERN DAILY PRESS * CONFEDERATE
ENGINEERS' MAPS * GETTYSBURG BATTLEFIELD: THE
FIRST DAY'S BATTLEFIELD * GETTYSBURG*

*BATTLEFIELD: THE SECOND AND THIRD DAYS'
BATTLEFIELD * GETTYSBURG: A BATTLEFIELD ATLAS,
* MAPPING FOR STONEWALL: THE CIVIL WAR SERVICE
OF JED HOTCHKISS * MAPPING THE CIVIL WAR:
FEATURING RARE MAPS FROM THE LIBRARY OF
CONGRESS * SECOND MANASSAS BATTLEFIELD MAP
STUDY*
MARABLE, JOSEPH G., *Lieutenant, 11th Mississippi Infantry;*
CWR:VOL2#4[269]145
MARBAKER, THOMAS D., *Private, 11th New Jersey Infantry:*
BOOK REVIEW: *HISTORY OF THE ELEVENTH NEW JERSEY
VOLUNTEERS*
ADDITIONAL LISTING: GETTY:11[102]237
MARBLE, FRANK, *Captain, USA;* CWTI:JUL/93[42]329
MARCH TO THE SEA; see listings under **"SHERMAN'S
SAVANNAH CAMPAIGN"**
MARCHAND, JOHN B., *Captain, USN;* ACW:NOV/91[46]335
MARCHANT, JOHN J., *Private, Sumter Artillery;*
CWR:VOL3#2[1]153
MARCHBANKS, GEORGE, *Lieutenant, CSA;*
CWTI:SEP/92[31]281
MARCHBANKS, WILLIAM, *Captain, CSA;*
ACW:JAN/93[26]395
MARCY, GEORGE O., *Major, 1st Connecticut Cavalry;*
ACW:JAN/92[16]340
MARCY, RANDOLPH B., *Captain, USA;* AHI:MAY/67[34]108,
AHI:DEC/72[10]145, AHI:OCT/79[20]194
MARCY, WILLIAM L.; AHI:SEP/83[42]235
MARGEDANT, WILLIAM C., *Captain, USA;*
CWTI:NOV/92[60]294
MARIETTA, GEORGIA; CWTI:SUMMER/89[13]120,
CWTI:SUMMER/89[20]121, CWTI:SUMMER/89[50]124
MARIGNY, MANDEVILLE, *Colonel, 10th Louisiana Infantry;*
CWTI:JUL/93[38]328
MARINE BRIGADE; ACW:JUL/93[34]424,
CWR:VOL2#3[212]142, CWR:VOL4#2[26]166
MARINE CORPS; see listings under **"CONFEDERATE
STATES MARINE CORPS"** and **"UNITED STATES
MARINE CORPS"**
MARION, WILLIAM P., *Private, 11th Mississippi Infantry;*
CWR:VOL2#4[269]145
MARITIME LAW; ARTICLE: "PIRATES OR PATRIOTS?,"
ACW:SEP/94[46]488
MARKEL, WILLIAM L., *Colonel, USA;* GETTY:11[19]232
MARKELL, CATHERINE, *civilian;* ACW:JAN/91[38]287
MARKELL, WILLIAM L., *Lieutenant Colonel, 8th New York
Cavalry;* B&G:FEB/95[8]590A
MARKEY, LAWRENCE, *Private, 5th New York Artillery;*
B&G:APR/95[24]596
MARKHAM, HENRY C., *Lieutenant, USA;* CWTI:DEC/95[8]474
MARKHAM, PHILO A., *Corporal, 154th New York Infantry;*
ARTICLE: "PHILO MARKHAM'S LONG WALK,"
CWTI:MAR/95[26]434
MARKHAM, SYLVANUS, *Private, 44th New York Infantry;*
CWTI:MAR/95[26]434
MARKLAND, A. H., *Colonel, USA;* ACW:SEP/92[47]380,
B&G:FEB/91[8]439, CWTI:DEC/94[62]415
MARKS' MILL, ARKANSAS, BATTLE OF;
CWR:VOL1#2[44]114
MARKS, ALBERT S., *Colonel, 17th Tennessee Infantry;*
CWR:VOL4#3[50]171
MARKS, SAMUEL, *Colonel, 11th Louisiana Infantry;*
CWR:VOL3#4[24]162

MARKS, SAMUEL B., *Lieutenant Colonel, USA;*
CWR:VOL1#2[44]114
MARLIN, JAMES L., *Private, 2nd Delaware Infantry;*
B&G:JUN/94[38]571
MARLOTT, WILLIAM, *Private, 37th Illinois Infantry;*
CWR:VOL1#1[42]105
MARMADUKE, HENRY H., *Lieutenant, CSN;*
AHI:OCT/75[30]162
MARMADUKE, JOHN S., *General, CSA:*
GENERAL LISTINGS: *in book review,* CWR:VOL2#2[169], *letters to the editor,* CWM:JAN/93[6]455, *Price's 1864 Missouri Campaign,* B&G:JUN/91[10]452, *photo,* B&G:JUN/91[10]452
ADDITIONAL LISTINGS: ACW:JAN/93[26]395, ACW:MAY/93[22]414, ACW:MAY/94[26]468, ACW:SEP/94[10]484, CWM:OCT/95[53]621, CWR:VOL1#1[42]105, CWR:VOL1#2[44]114, CWR:VOL2#3[212]142
MARR, JOHN Q., *Captain, CSA;* B&G:OCT/93[6]536, CWTI:DEC/91[14]235
MARROW, ISAAC H., *Colonel, USA;* B&G:AUG/93[10]529
MARSH, C.H., *Private, CSA;* CWTI:SEP/91[23]228
MARSH, CALEB P.; AHI:MAY/69[32]122
MARSH, FRED H., *Captain, 46th Illinois Infantry;*
CWTI:AUG/90[64]170
MARSH, JOHN G., *Lieutenant, 29th Ohio Infntry;*
GETTY:9[81]216
MARSH, SIMEON, *Private, 11th Mississippi Infantry;*
ACW:MAR/92[10]349
MARSHALL, CHARLES, *Colonel, CSA:*
ARTICLE: "I WAS THERE," CWM:JUL/91[8]356
GENERAL LISTINGS: *Gettysburg,* GETTY:4[65]148, GETTY:4[113]153, GETTY:5[4]156, GETTY:6[62]175, GETTY:9[17]210, *letters to editor,* AHI:MAR/88[4]
ADDITIONAL LISTINGS: AHI:SEP/87[48]264, B&G:JUN/93[32]525, CWM:SEP/92[19]440, CWM:JAN/93[8]456, CWM:AUG/95[17]603, CWTI:AUG/90[26]166, CWTI:SEP/92[42]283, CWTI:JUL/94[44]394, CWTI:MAR/95[20]433
MARSHALL, CHARLES H., *New York Defense Committee;*
ACW:SEP/94[46]488
MARSHALL, ELISHA G., *Colonel, USA;* B&G:APR/94[10]558, B&G:APR/95[8]595, CWTI:APR/90[24]152
MARSHALL, HUMPHREY, *General, CSA:*
ARTICLE: "TIME LAPSE," CWTI:MAR/89[44]105
BOOK REVIEW: *FAMOUS KENTUCKY DUELS*
ADDITIONAL LISTINGS: ACW:SEP/95[22]544, AHI:MAY/76[24]167, B&G:AUG/91[11]458
MARSHALL, J.K., *Colonel, 52nd North Carolina Infantry;*
CWTI:JUL/93[34]327, GETTY:8[67]204, GETTY:12[61]245, GETTY:13[1]252, GETTY:13[75]259
MARSHALL, JAMES, *Captain, USN;* AHI:APR/74[4]154, CWTI:NOV/93[65]351,
MARSHALL, JOHN, *Colonel, 4th Texas Infantry;* ARTICLE: "DESTINY AT GAINES'S MILL: ONE FAMILY'S ORDEAL," CWM:MAR/92[9]410
MARSHALL, JOHN E., *Captain, USA;* AHI:JAN/67[4]106
MARSHALL, LUCIUS E., *Private, 7th Wisconsin Infantry,*
GETTY:9[33]211, GETTY:11[57]233
MARSHALL, MATTHIAS M., *Chaplain;* ARTICLE: "RESORT OF THE DEAD," ACW:MAR/95[50]518
MARSHALL, THOMAS, *Colonel, CSA;* CWM:APR/95[8]
MARSHALL, WILLIAM, *Colonel, CSA; 7th Virginia Cavalry;*
B&G:JUN/95[36]603A

MARSHALL, WILLIAM, *Private, 95th Illinois Infantry;*
CWM:JAN/91[11]325, CWTI:JAN/93[20]298
MARSHALL, W.R., *Captain, CSA;* CWR:VOL4#1[1]163
MARSHALL, WILLIAM R., *Colonel, 7th Minnesota Infantry;*
ACW:NOV/94[76]500, ACW:SEP/92[23]377, CWTI:AUG/90[70]171
MARSHALL, WALTER, *Colonel, CSA;* CWM:JUL/91[40]370, CWM:JUL/92[64]434, CWTI:MAR/95[20]433
MARSTON, DANIEL, *Captain, 16th Maine Infantry;*
GETTY:13[33]255
MARSTON, GILMAN, *General, USA;* B&G:APR/94[10]558
MARSTON, JOHN, *Captain, CSN;* AHI:OCT/75[30]162
MARSTON, WARD, *Major, USMC;* CWR:VOL2#3[183]140
MARTIN, ALONZO, *civilian;* ACW:SEP/91[22]321
MARTIN, ARTHUR H., *Lieutenant, CSA;* CWR:VOL4#2[1]165, CWR:VOL4#2[118]169
MARTIN, AUGUSTUS P., *Colonel, USA;* GETTY:8[31]201, GETTY:9[41]212, GETTY:11[91]236
MARTIN, HOMER D., *artist;* CWTI:SEP/91[54]232
MARTIN, J.W., *Lieutenant, 6th Independent New York Battery;*
ACW:MAY/95[30]525
MARTIN, JAMES G., *General, CSA;* B&G:APR/94[10]558, CWR:VOL3#4[1]161, CWTI:SEP/92[28]280
MARTIN, JOHN, *civilian;* B&G:APR/93[24]520, CWTI:JAN/95[48]429
MARTIN, JOHN D., *Colonel, CSA;* CWTI:JUL/94[50]395
MARTIN, JOHN M., *Lieutenant Colonel, 6th Florida Battalion;*
CWR:VOL3#4[1]161
MARTIN, JOHN S., *Private, 11th Veteran Reserve Corps;*
B&G:APR/93[24]520
MARTIN, JOSEPH, *Captain, 6th New York Artillery;*
CWTI:JUN/90[32]159
MARTIN, KNOTT, *Captain, 8th Massachusetts Infantry;*
ACW:NOV/95[30]555
MARTIN, LUTHER, *Captain, 11th New Jersey Infantry;*
GETTY:12[7]241
MARTIN, MICHAEL F., *Chaplain, 69th Pennsylvania Infantry;*
CWM:MAR/91[50]340
MARTIN, R.M., *Lieutenant, CSA;* CWTI:JUL/92[42]274
MARTIN, RAWLEY W., *Colonel, 53rd Virginia Infantry;*
CWTI:JUL/93[29]326, GETTY:13[64]258
MARTIN, ROBERT M., *Colonel, CSA;* ACW:MAR/93[51]407, ACW:JUL/95[44]537, CWTI:NOV/92[54]293
MARTIN, SAMUEL, *Major, USA;* ACW:JAN/94[10]448
MARTIN, SYLVESTER, *Lieutenant, 88th Pennsylvania Infantry;* GETTY:10[7]221
MARTIN, W.G., *Private, 13th Alabama Infantry;*
GETTY:6[13]170
MARTIN, WILLIAM, *Private, 4th Alabama Infantry;*
B&G:FEB/91[34]442
MARTIN, WILLIAM T., *General, CSA:* ACW:JUL/95[34]536, B&G:OCT/92[10]496, CWR:VOL4#1[1]163, CWTI:SUMMER/89[50]124, CWTI:DEC/90[56]184, CWTI:NOV/92[41]291, CWTI:MAR/93[40]312, GETTY:12[1]240, GETTY:12[68]246
MARTINDALE, JAMES H., *General, USA;* B&G:APR/94[10]558
MARTINDALE, JOHN H., *Colonel, USA;* B&G:APR/94[10]558, CWM:JUN/95[43]587, CWR:VOL2#4[269]145
MARVIN, A.S., *Captain, USA;* GETTY:8[31]201
MARVIN, MATTHEW, *Private, 1st Minnesota Infantry;*
GETTY:5[79]161, GETTY:10[53]225
MARYE, ALFRED J., *Private, Fredericksburg Artillery;*
CWR:VOL1#1[1]102

MARYE, EDWARD A., *Captain, Fredericksburg Artillery:*
ARTICLE: "THE FIRST GUN AT GETTYSBURG: 'WITH THE
  CONFEDERATE ADVANCE GUARD,'" CWR:VOL1#1[26]103
ADDITIONAL LISTINGS: B&G:FEB/95[8]590A, CWR:VOL1#1[1]102,
  CWR:VOL1#1[26]103, CWR:VOL4#4[70]180, GETTY:5[4]156,
  GETTY:10[107]227, *photo,* CWR:VOL1#1[1]102
MARYE, LAWRENCE S., *Captain, CSA;* GETTY:10[29]222

MARYLAND TROOPS:
1st Artillery (Confederate):
BOOK REVIEW: *THE PERSONAL MEMOIRS OF JONATHAN
  THOMAS SCHARF OF THE FIRST MARYLAND
  ARTILLERY*
ADDITIONAL LISTINGS: B&G:OCT/95[8]611A, GETTY:4[49]147,
  GETTY:10[29]222
1st Artillery, (Union); ACW:JAN/94[39]451
1st Artillery, Battery A; B&G:OCT/95[8]611A
1st Artillery, Battery D; B&G:OCT/95[8]611A
1st Cavalry, (Confederate); ACW:JUL/92[41]370,
  B&G:JUN/91[6]451, B&G:AUG/94[10]574,
  CWR:VOL1#4[7]125, CWTI:JUL/93[20]325, GETTY:4[75]149,
  GETTY:9[17]210, GETTY:12[111]250, GETTY:13[7]253
1st Cavalry, (Union); B&G:APR/92[8]481,
  CWM:MAY/92[8]418, CWTI:JUN/90[32]159, GETTY:13[89]260
1st Infantry, (Confederate):
ARTICLE: "ACCOMPANIED BY CRIES OF 'GO IT, BOYS!
  MARYLAND WHIP MARYLAND!' TWO 1ST MARYLAND
  INFANTRIES CLASHED," ACW:JUL/94[10]475
ADDITIONAL LISTINGS: ACW:NOV/92[42]388, CWNEWS:AUG/92[4],
  CWR:VOL1#3[28]120, CWTI:MAR/94[48]374,
  GETTY:7[83]192, GETTY:9[53]214, GETTY:9[81]216,
  GETTY:12[1]240, GETTY:12[42]244, GETTY:12[111]250
1st Infantry, (Union):
ARTICLE: "ACCOMPANIED BY CRIES OF 'GO IT, BOYS!
  MARYLAND WHIP MARYLAND!' TWO 1ST MARYLAND
  INFANTRIES CLASHED," ACW:JUL/94[10]475
BOOK REVIEW: *HISTORICAL RECORD OF THE FIRST
  REGIMENT, MARYLAND INFANTRY*
ADDITIONAL LISTINGS: ACW:JAN/93[35]396, B&G:APR/92[8]481
1st Eastern Shore Regiment; GETTY:7[83]192
1st Potomac Home Brigade; ACW:NOV/93[50]444,
  B&G:DEC/92[8]503, CWM:MAY/92[8]418,
  CWR:VOL1#4[7]125, GETTY:7[83]192, GETTY:12[42]244
2nd Artillery; GETTY:4[75]149, GETTY:13[89]260
2nd Infantry (Confederate); ACW:JUL/94[10]475,
  AHI:AUG/68[4]115B, B&G:DEC/94[28], B&G:OCT/95[8]611A,
  CWR:VOL1#2[7]111, CWR:VOL1#3[52]122,
  CWR:VOL3#4[1]161, GETTY:7[83]192
2nd Infantry, (Union); ACW:MAY/95[18]524,
  CWR:VOL2#2[118]136
2nd Potomac Home Brigade; B&G:AUG/94[10]574
3rd Infantry, (Confederate); CWTI:APR/90[24]152
3rd Infantry, (Union); B&G:DEC/92[8]503,
  B&G:APR/95[24]596, B&G:JUN/95[8]600,
  B&G:OCT/95[8]611A
3rd Potomac Home Brigade; ACW:NOV/93[50]444
4th Artillery (Confederate); CWR:VOL4#4[70]180,
  GETTY:4[49]147, GETTY:10[29]222
4th Infantry, (Union); B&G:APR/92[8]481
5th Infantry, (Union); ACW:JUL/94[10]475,
  B&G:OCT/95[8]611A
6th Infantry, (Union); ACW:JUL/94[10]475,
  AHI:AUG/68[4]115B, CWM:NOV/92[64]453

7th Infantry, (Union); B&G:APR/92[8]481
8th Infantry, (Union); B&G:APR/92[8]481
11th Infantry, (Union); ACW:NOV/93[50]444,
  B&G:AUG/91[40]463
Baltimore Light Artillery; ACW:NOV/93[50]444,
  ACW:MAY/94[35]469, B&G:AUG/94[10]574
Brockenbrough's Battery; ACW:MAR/94[50]462
Chesapeake Artillery; CWR:VOL4#4[70]180, GETTY:4[49]147,
  GETTY:10[29]222
Cole's Cavalry; B&G:AUG/94[10]57, B&G:AUG/94[19]575
Dement's Battery; CWR:VOL4#4[70]180
Griffin's Battery; ACW:JUL/92[41]370
Maryland Light Artillery; GETTY:9[81]216
Patapsco Guards; B&G:AUG/94[10]574
Purnell Cavalry Troop; GETTY:4[75]149, GETTY:13[89]260

MARYLAND, STATE OF; BOOK REVIEWS: *EVENTS OF THE
  CIVIL WAR IN WASHINGTON COUNTY, MARYLAND, *
  *ROSTER OF CIVIL WAR SOLDIERS FROM WASHINGTON
  COUNTY, MARYLAND*
MASKEW, JOHN, *Lieutenant, 1st Louisiana Infantry;*
  GETTY:12[111]250
MASON, A.P., *Private, 1st Massachusetts Infantry;*
  GETTY:12[7]241
MASON, ALEXANDER M., *Lieutenant, CSA;*
  AHI:JUN/70[30]127
MASON, CHARLES; CWTI:NOV/93[55]350
MASON, EDWARD C., *Colonel, USA;* B&G:DEC/93[12]545
MASON, ELIHU, *Sergeant, USA;* ACW:SEP/91[22]321
MASON, GEORGE J., *Corporal, 154th New York Infantry;*
  GETTY:8[17]200
MASON, HERBERT, *Lieutenant, 20th Massachusetts Infantry;*
  CWR:VOL3#1[31]150
MASON, J. CASS; *civilian;* B&G:AUG/95[24]605,
  CWM:MAY/93[32]477, CWNEWS:NOV/92[4],
  CWTI:AUG/90[42]167, CWTI:AUG/90[50]168
MASON, JAMES M.:
ARTICLE: "HIGH SEAS BROUHAHA," ACW:NOV/91[46]335
ADDITIONAL LISTINGS: ACW:MAY/92[23]360, ACW:MAY/93[62]418,
  AHI:JUN/70[30]127, AHI:FEB/75[4]157,
  CWTI:DEC/89[10]133, CWTI:JAN/93[44]302, *photos,*
  ACW:NOV/91[46]335, CWTI:MAY/89[28]117
MASON, JOHN S., *General, USA;* B&G:OCT/94[11]580
MASON, JULIUS W., *Captain, 5th U.S. Cavalry;*
  GETTY:11[19]232
MASON, LABERT, *Lieutenant, CSA;* CWR:VOL4#2[104]168
MASON, RODNEY, *Colonel, 71st Ohio Infantry;*
  CWTI:JUL/92[42]274
MASSACHUSETTS HISTORICAL SOCIETY;
  B&G:JUN/91[26]453

MASSACHUSETTS TROOPS:
1st Artillery; GETTY:5[117]165
1st Artillery, Battery M; AHI:AUG/68[4]115B
1st Cavalry:
GENERAL LISTINGS: *1863 cavalry battles,* MH:OCT/92[51]162,
  Aldie, GETTY:11[19]232, *Gettysburg,* GETTY:4[75]149,
  GETTY:12[85]248, *in book review,* MH:DEC/92[74]
ADDITIONAL LISTINGS: ACW:NOV/91[30]332, ACW:NOV/92[26]386,
  B&G:OCT/93[12]537, B&G:OCT/93[21]538,
  CWTI:JUN/90[32]159, CWTI:AUG/90[64]170

1st Infantry:
GENERAL LISTINGS: *Gettysburg,* GETTY:6[7]169, GETTY:12[7]241, *in book review,* CWM:APR/95[50], CWNEWS:JUN/95[33], *Manassas, Second,* B&G:AUG/92[11]493
ADDITIONAL LISTINGS: ACW:NOV/95[30]555, B&G:APR/91[8]445, B&G:FEB/93[40]514, CWM:JUN/95[55]591, CWTI:JUL/93[42]329, GETTY:13[7]253
1st Sharpshooters; GETTY:13[75]259
2nd Artillery; CWR:VOL4#2[1]165, CWTI:MAY/93[74]322
2nd Artillery, (Heavy); B&G:DEC/92[32]506
2nd Cavalry; B&G:APR/92[8]481, B&G:OCT/94[42]583, CWR:VOL4#1[78], CWTI:APR/90[74]155A, CWTI:JUN/90[32]159, CWTI:SEP/90[34]176, GETTY:11[6]231
2nd Infantry:
ARTICLE: "A CALL OF LEADERSHIP: LT. COL. CHARLES REDINGTON MUDGE, U.S.V. AND THE SECOND MASSACHUSETTS INFANTRY AT GETTYSBURG," GETTY:6[69]176
GENERAL LISTINGS: *Antietam,* GETTY:6[69]176, *Gettysburg,* GETTY:4[113]153, GETTY:7[83]192, GETTY:11[91]236, GETTY:12[42]244, *in book review,* B&G:OCT/93[24], CWR:VOL3#1[80], *SIO,* CWM:NOV/92[6]446, *photo of Lt. Col. Wilder Dwight,* CWTI:MAY/89[BC], *photo of monument on Culp's Hill,* GETTY:6[69]176
ADDITIONAL LISTINGS: ACW:JUL/92[30]369, ACW:MAR/94[50]462, B&G:FEB/95[8]590C, CWM:JAN/92[40]405, CWTI:DEC/89[42]137, CWTI:NOV/92[49]292, CWTI:JUL/93[42]329, GETTY:6[69]176
3rd Artillery; CWTI:MAY/93[74]322, GETTY:9[41]212, GETTY:11[91]236
3rd Artillery, Battery C; GETTY:9[41]212, GETTY:11[91]236
3rd Cavalry; B&G:FEB/94[38]553, CWR:VOL4#2[1]165
3rd Infantry; ACW:NOV/95[30]555, CWTI:JAN/95[82]430
4th Cavalry; ACW:MAY/95[38]526, AHI:JAN/74[10]153, CWNEWS:JUN/95[33]
4th Infantry; ACW:JAN/93[18]394, ACW:MAR/93[42]406, ACW:JAN/94[30]450, ACW:NOV/95[30]555, CWTI:SEPT/89[44]131, CWTI:AUG/90[42]167
5th Artillery; GETTY:5[47]160, GETTY:8[53]203, GETTY:9[41]212
5th Cavalry; AHI:JAN/73[28]147
6th Infantry:
ARTICLE: "FIRST BLOOD IN BALTIMORE," ACW:NOV/95[30]555
ADDITIONAL LISTINGS: ACW:JAN/91[8]282, ACW:JAN/92[30]342, B&G:AUG/95[38], B&G:DEC/95[44]617, CWR:VOL3#1[1]149, CWTI:OCT/95[24]466
7th Artillery; GETTY:11[6]231
7th Infantry; GETTY:8[53]203, GETTY:11[6]231
8th Artillery; CWTI:FEB/92[36]249
8th Infantry; ACW:NOV/95[30]555
9th Artillery:
ARTICLE: "BAPTISM OF FIRE: THE NINTH MASSACHUSETTS BATTERY AT GETTYSBURG, JULY 2, 1863," GETTY:5[47]160
ADDITIONAL LISTINGS: AHI:APR/68[4]115, B&G:APR/91[8]445, GETTY:5[35]159, GETTY:5[47]160, GETTY:7[51]190, GETTY:8[53]203, GETTY:10[120]229, GETTY:12[42]244
9th Infantry:
ARTICLE: "ON TO PRISON," CWTI:JUN/90[28]158
ADDITIONAL LISTINGS: ACW:NOV/92[10]384, B&G:APR/93[12]518, CWM:MAR/91[50]340, CWTI:JUN/90[28]158, GETTY:4[113]153

10th Artillery; BOOK REVIEWS: *THE HISTORY OF THE TENTH MASSACHUSETTS BATTERY OF LIGHT ARTILLERY*
10th Infantry:
BOOK REVIEWS: *WHEN THIS CRUEL WAR IS OVER: THE CIVIL WAR LETTERS OF CHARLES HARVEY BREWSTER*
ADDITIONAL LISTING: GETTY:8[53]203
11th Infantry:
BOOK REVIEW: *THE MUTINY AT BRANDY STATION: THE LAST BATTLE OF THE HOOKER BRIGADE*
ADDITIONAL LISTINGS: ACW:MAY/95[30]525, B&G:AUG/92[11]493, CWM:AUG/95[38]609, CWM:JUN/95[55]591, CWNEWS:JUN/95[33], GETTY:12[7]241
12th Infantry:
ARTICLE: "COL. FLETCHER WEBSTER'S LAST LETTER: I SHALL NOT SPARE MYSELF," B&G:OCT/95[20]612
ADDITIONAL LISTINGS: ACW:JUL/92[30]369, ACW:MAR/95[42]517, AHI:JAN/93[61]309, B&G:AUG/92[11]493, B&G:DEC/94[34]587, B&G:FEB/95[8]590B, CWM:AUG/95[38]609, CWR:VOL2#4[269]145, CWTI:SEPT/89[44]131, GETTY:4[33]146, GETTY:5[128]167, GETTY:10[7]221, GETTY:13[33]255
13th Infantry; B&G:APR/91[8]445, B&G:AUG/92[11]493, B&G:OCT/95[20]612, CWM:SEP/93[32]496, CWM:AUG/95[38]609, CWTI:APR/92[49]260, GETTY:4[33]146, GETTY:4[115]152, GETTY:10[7]221, GETTY:13[7]253, GETTY:13[33]255
15th Artillery; CWTI:DEC/94[24]409
15th Infantry:
ARTICLES: "FORGOTTEN VALOR: OFF THE BEATEN PATH AT ANTIETAM: DEBACLE IN THE WEST WOODS," B&G:OCT/95[8]611A, "NOTHING BUT COWARDS RUN," CWM:APR/95[42]577
BOOK REVIEW: *FROM BALL'S BLUFF TO GETTYSBURG...AND BEYOND*
GENERAL LISTINGS: *Gettysburg,* GETTY:5[79]161, GETTY:5[89]162, GETTY:7[29]188, GETTY:10[53]225, MH:DEC/91[54]155, *in book review,* CWR:VOL2#2[169], *in list,* CWTI:JUL/93[34]327
ADDITIONAL LISTINGS: ACW:MAR/94[50]462, ACW:JUL/95[50]538, AHI:FEB/82[36]225, B&G:OCT/95[8]611A, CWR:VOL3#1[31]150, CWTI:MAY/89[14]114, CWTI:MAY/89[50]119, CWTI:SEP/90[26]174, CWTI:JUL/94[20]390, GETTY:13[1]252, GETTY:13[43]256, GETTY:13[50]257
16th Infantry; CWNEWS:JUN/95[33], CWTI:JUN/90[28]158, GETTY:12[7]241
18th Infantry; B&G:APR/95[8]595
19th Infantry:
BOOK REVIEWS: *THE CIVIL WAR DIARY OF LT. J.E. HODGKINS * THE CIVIL WAR: LETTERS HOME, FROM GEO. R. WHITE * HISTORY OF THE NINETEENTH REGIMENT, MASSACHUSETTS VOLUNTEER INFANTRY, 1861-1965*
GENERAL LISTINGS: *Gettysburg,* GETTY:4[89]150, GETTY:5[79]161, GETTY:5[107]164, GETTY:7[97]193, GETTY:10[53]225, GETTY:12[7]241, GETTY:13[7]253, GETTY:13[43]256, MH:OCT/93[20]172, *letters to the editor,* CWTI:NOV/93[12]345
ADDITIONAL LISTINGS: ACW:MAY/92[8]357, ACW:MAR/94[50]462, AHI:FEB/82[36]225, B&G:AUG/93[18]530, CWM:MAR/91[17]335, CWR:VOL3#1[31]150, CWR:VOL4#4[101]181

20th Infantry:
ARTICLES: "THE 20TH MASSACHUSETTS INFANTRY AND THE STREET FIGHT FOR FREDERICKSBURG," CWR:VOL4#4[101]181, "THE COPPERHEAD REGIMENT: THE 20TH MASSACHUSETTS INFANTRY," CWR:VOL3#1[31]150

BOOK REVIEWS: *THE CIVIL WAR: THE NANTUCKET EXPERIENCE * THE TWENTIETH REGIMENT OF MASSACHUSETTS VOLUNTEER INFANTRY 1861-1865*

GENERAL LISTINGS: *Gettysburg*, GETTY:5[117]165, GETTY:10[53]225, *in book review*, B&G:APR/92[24], CWNEWS:JUL/90[4], CWNEWS:JAN/91[4], CWNEWS:JAN/93[4], MH:AUG/95[70], *letters to the editor*, CWTI:NOV/93[12]345

ADDITIONAL LISTINGS: ACW:MAR/94[50]462, AHI:FEB/82[36]225, B&G:APR/91[8]445, B&G:JUN/95[8]600, CWR:VOL3#1[31]150, CWR:VOL3#1[78]152, CWR:VOL4#4[i]175, CWR:VOL4#4[v]176, CWR:VOL4#4[101]181, CWR:VOL4#4[127]182, CWTI:MAY/89[14]114, CWTI:MAY/89[21]115, CWTI:MAY/89[BACK], GETTY:13[43]256

21st Infantry; ACW:SEP/92[8]374, ACW:JAN/95[54]508, B&G:FEB/95[38]593, B&G:OCT/95[8]611A, CWM:MAY/92[44]423, CWR:VOL2#2[118]136, CWTI:APR/90[24]152, CWTI:FEB/91[24]191, CWTI:FEB/92[36]249, CWTI:MAY/94[24]381

22nd Infantry:
ARTICLE: "PVT. ROBERT G. CARTER AND THE 22D MASSACHUSETTS AT GETTYSBURG," GETTY:8[53]203

ADDITIONAL LISTINGS: B&G:APR/93[12]518, CWM:NOV/91[35]392, GETTY:10[120]229

23rd Infantry; CWNEWS:JUL/93[5], CWTI:MAR/95[46]437

27th Infantry; BOOK REVIEW: *THE LONG ROAD FOR HOME: THE CIVIL WAR EXPERIENCES OF FOUR FARMBOY SOLDIERS OF THE TWENTY-SEVENTH MASSACHUSETTS REGIMENT OF VOLUNTEER INFANTRY AS TOLD BY THEIR PERSONAL CORRESPONDENCE, 1861-1864*

28th Infantry:
BOOK REVIEW: *FROM CAVEN TO COLD HARBOR: THE LIFE OF COLONEL RICHARD BYRNES*

ADDITIONAL LISTINGS: ACW:MAY/94[12]466, ACW:JAN/95[54]508, ACW:SEP/95[54]548, CWM:MAR/91[17]335, CWM:MAR/91[50]340, CWR:VOL4#4[47]179, CWTI:DEC/90[58]185, CWTI:JAN/94[46]364, GETTY:8[53]203, GETTY:10[53]225, GETTY:13[7]253, *photo of flag*, CWTI:DEC/90[58]185

29th Infantry; ACW:MAY/91[23]303, ACW:MAY/94[12]466, ACW:JAN/95[74]510, ACW:SEP/95[54]548, CWTI:APR/90[24]152, CWTI:MAY/94[50]386

31st Infantry; ACW:JAN/94[30]450, CWR:VOL4#2[1]165

32nd Infantry; B&G:APR/92[8]481, GETTY:6[7]169, GETTY:8[53]203

33rd Infantry; GETTY:4[115]152

34th Infantry; B&G:FEB/92[26]

35th Infantry:
ARTICLE: "TIRED SOLDIERS DON'T GO VERY FAST," CWTI:FEB/92[36]249

ADDITIONAL LISTINGS: B&G:APR/93[12]518, B&G:AUG/95[8]604, B&G:OCT/95[8]611A, CWM:MAY/92[44]423, CWTI:APR/90[24]152

36th Infantry; CWTI:JAN/95[34]427

37th Infantry; ACW:MAR/91[14]293, ACW:MAY/91[38]305, CWTI:NOV/92[49]292, CWTI:MAR/93[8]306, GETTY:5[117]165, GETTY:8[53]203, GETTY:13[7]253

38th Infantry; ACW:JAN/94[30]450, CWR:VOL3#1[1]149, CWR:VOL4#2[104]168

39th Infantry; B&G:APR/91[8]445, B&G:APR/92[8]481, CWTI:APR/92[49]260

42nd Infantry; ACW:JAN/93[51]398, GETTY:10[53]225

43rd Infantry; CWM:DEC/94[5]546

44th Infantry; ACW:MAY/94[51]471

45th Infantry; ACW:MAY/94[51]471, B&G:OCT/93[31]539

52nd Infantry; AHI:OCT/80[45]207

53rd Infantry; ACW:JAN/94[30]450, CWR:VOL3#1[1]149

54th Infantry:
ARTICLES: "CARNIVAL OF DEATH," ACW:SEP/91[30]322, "I WANT YOU TO PROVE YOURSELVES MEN," CWTI:DEC/89[42]137

BOOK REVIEWS: *A BRAVE BLACK REGIMENT: HISTORY OF THE 54TH REGIMENT OF MASSACHUSETTS VOLUNTEER INFANTRY,1863-1865 * BLUE-EYED CHILD OF FORTUNE: THE CIVIL WAR LETTERS OF COLONEL ROBERT GOULD SHAW * GATE OF HELL: CAMPAIGN FOR CHARLESTON HARBOR, 1863*

GENERAL LISTINGS: *Immortal Six Hundred*, GETTY:12[111]250, *in book review*, ACW:MAR/93[58], B&G:OCT/93[24], B&G:JUN/95[30], CWM:JUL/91[58], CWM:APR/95[8], CWNEWS:OCT/90[4], CWNEWS:NOV/91[4], CWNEWS:NOV/92[4], CWNEWS:APR/95[33], CWTI:JUL/93[12], *in the movie* GLORY, CWTI:DEC/89[53]138, *letters to the editor*, B&G:FEB/92[6]473, CWM:JAN/91[6]324, CWM:JAN/92[6]398, *SIO*, B&G:FEB/91[34]442, CWM:NOV/92[6]446, *sketch of attack at Fort Wagner*, CWTI:DEC/89[42]137

ADDITIONAL LISTINGS: ACW:SEP/91[6]317, AHI:JAN/94[50]319, B&G:AUG/91[32]461, B&G:OCT/91[11]466, B&G:FEB/94[38]553, B&G:APR/95[38]598, CWM:JAN/91[35]328, CWM:MAR/91[39]338, CWM:MAR/92[4]408, CWM:NOV/92[24]448, CWM:AUG/94[30]527, CWR:VOL3#1[31]150, CWR:VOL3#1[65]151, CWTI:DEC/89[42]137, CWTI:DEC/89[62]139, CWTI:AUG/90[42]167, CWTI:MAR/94[38]372, MH:AUG/94[82]179

55th Infantry:
BOOK REVIEW: *RECORD OF THE SERVICE OF THE FIFTY-FIFTH REGIMENT OF MASSACHUSETTS VOLUNTEER INFANTRY*

ADDITIONAL LISTING: CWR:VOL2#3[194]141

56th Infantry; B&G:APR/93[12]518, CWR:VOL2#2[118]136, CWTI:APR/90[24]152

57th Infantry:
ARTICLE: "BURY THEM IF THEY WON'T MOVE, (EXCERPT FROM *MOTHER, MAY YOU NEVER SEE THE SIGHTS I HAVE SEEN*)," CWTI:APR/90[24]152

BOOK REVIEWS: *MOTHER MAY YOU NEVER SEE THE SIGHTS I'VE SEEN: THE FIFTY-SEVENTH MASSACHUSETTS VOLUNTEERS IN THE ARMY OF THE POTOMAC 1864-1865*

ADDITIONAL LISTINGS: ACW:SEP/95[70]549, B&G:APR/93[12]518, B&G:APR/94[47]562A, CWTI:MAY/92[38]265, CWTI:JAN/95[34]427

58th Infantry; CWR:VOL2#2[118]136

59th Infantry; B&G:APR/94[47]562A

Andrews' Sharpshooters; GETTY:8[95]205

Boston Light Infantry; CWTI:SEPT/89[44]131

MASSACHUSETTS, STATE OF; BOOK REVIEW: *THE CIVIL WAR: THE NANTUCKET EXPERIENCE*

MASSACRES:
ARTICLE: "CONTROVERSY: WHAT MAKES A MASSACRE?" B&G:AUG/91[52]464

BOOK REVIEW: *BLOODY DAWN: THE STORY OF THE LAWRENCE MASSACRE*

Centralia; see listings under CENTRALIA, MISSOURI, MASSACRE AT"

Fort Pillow; see listings under "FORT PILLOW, TENNESSEE, BATTLE OF"

Lawrence, Kansas: see listings under "LAWRENCE, KANSAS, MASSACRE AT"

Saltville; see listings under "SALTVILLE, VIRGINIA, BATTLE OF"

Sand Creek; see listings under "SAND CREEK MASSACRE"

MASSIE, THOMAS, *Lieutenant Colonel, 12th Virginia Cavalry;* B&G:OCT/93[12]537

MASTEN, CHARLES H. and JAMES H., *13th Pennsylvania Reserves;* CWR:VOL1#3[46]121

MASTERSON, W.J.; CWTI:AUG/95[58]461

MATHER, SAMUEL W., *Lieutenant, USN;* ACW:SEP/94[46]488

MATRAU, HENRY, *Lieutenant, 6th Wisconsin Infantry;* BOOK REVIEWS: *LETTERS HOME: HENRY MATRAU OF THE IRON BRIGADE*

MATTESON, DANIEL M., *Private, USA;* CWTI:MAY/91[16]206

MATTESON, ELISHA C., *Private, 9th Iowa Infantry;* ARTICLE: "DEAR SISTER—THEY FIGHT TO WHIP," CWTI:MAY/91[16]206

MATTHEIS, CHARLES L., *Colonel, USA;* CWM:DEC/94[46]552

MATTHEWS, EZRA W., *Captain, 1st Pennsylvania Artillery;* GETTY:12[30]243

MATTHEWS, STANLEY, *General, USA;* AHI:NOV/72[12]142

MATTHIES, CHARLES L., *General, USA;* B&G:AUG/95[8]604, CWR:VOL3#3[59]159

MATTIES, CHARLES L., *Colonel, 5th Iowa Infantry;* AHI:APR/87[10]261, CWR:VOL3#3[59]159

MATTOCKS, CHARLES, *Private, 17th Maine Infantry;* BOOK REVIEW: *"UNSPOILED HEART"; THE JOURNAL OF CHARLES MATTOCKS OF THE 17TH MAINE*

MATVIN, AZOR, *Lieutenant, 5th New York Infantry;* CWTI:MAY/94[31]382

MAUCH CHUNK, PENNSYLVANIA; ARTICLE: "REBELS AT THEIR DOORSTEP," ACW:SEP/93[22]432

MAUK, JOHN W., *Corporal, 138th Pennsylvania Infantry;* CWM:OCT/94[26]536, CWTI:SEP/92[42]283

MAULL, JOHN F., *Sergeant, Jeff Davis Artillery;* CWTI:DEC/91[26]238

MAULSBY, WILLIAM B., *Colonel, 1st Maryland Potomac Home Brigade;* CWR:VOL1#4[7]125, GETTY:7[83]192, GETTY:12[42]244

MAURICE, THOMAS D., *Major, USA;* B&G:APR/94[28]559

MAURIN, VICTOR, *Captain, Donaldsonville Artillery;* GETTY:13[75]259

MAURY, DABNEY H., *General, CSA:*
GENERAL LISTINGS: *Davis' funeral,* CWTI:MAR/93[32]311, *in book review,* ACW:MAY/93[54], ACW:JAN/95[62], B&G:JUN/94[34], CWR:VOL4#2[136], CWR:VOL4#3[1]170

ADDITIONAL LISTINGS: ACW:SEP/91[46]324, ACW:SEP/92[23]377, ACW:SEP/92[38]379, ACW:SEP/94[10]484,

ACW:SEP/95[48]547, CWM:JAN/91[40]330, CWR:VOL2#1[36]132, CWR:VOL4#3[77]174, CWTI:SEPT/89[20]127, CWTI:DEC/94[24]409, CWTI:JUL/94[50]395

MAURY, MATTHEW F.:
ARTICLE: "THE FIRST ATLANTIC CABLE," AHI:JAN/73[4]146, "MATTHEW FONTAINE MAURY: UNRECOGNIZED CONFEDERATE NAVY HERO," CWM:JUL/93[30]486

GENERAL LISTINGS: *in book review,* B&G:AUG/92[36], *letters to the editor,* B&G:OCT/91[6]465, CWM:APR/94[4]501, *post war Mexico,* ACW:MAR/95[26]515, *photos,* AHI:JAN/73[4]146, CWM:JUL/93[30]486, CWTI:AUG/95[40]458

ADDITIONAL LISTINGS: ACW:NOV/91[8]328, AHI:DEC/82[38]231, AHI:OCT/88[38]275, MH:FEB/91[8]151, CWTI:AUG/95[40]458

MAURY, WILLIAM L., *Captain, CSN;* ARTICLE: "RELUCTANT RAIDER," CWTI:AUG/95[40]458

MAXEY, SAMUEL B., *General, CSA:*
ARTICLE: "FORT TOWSON: INDIAN TERRITORY POST THAT PLAYED A PART IN THE PEACE," B&G:OCT/94[38]582

ADDITIONAL LISTINGS: B&G:AUG/95[8]604, CWR:VOL1#2[44]114, *photo,* B&G:OCT/94[38]582

MAXIMILIAN, EMPEROR:
ARTICLE: "FRENCH MEDDLING IN MEXICO ALMOST LED TO A POST-CIVIL WAR CONFRONTATION WITH THE UNITED STATES," ACW:JUL/92[6]365,

ADDITIONAL LISTINGS: ACW:JUL/92[46]371, ACW:MAR/95[26]515, CWTI:DEC/90[29]182, *photo,* ACW:JUL/92[6]365

MAXON, DANIEL B., *Lieutenant, 4th Wisconsin Infantry;* ACW:MAY/93[12]412

MAXWELL, D.E., *Private, 2nd Florida Infantry;* ACW:SEP/93[8]429

MAXWELL, R.A., *Colonel, USA;* AHI:JUN/66[52]102

MAY, HENRY C., *Surgeon, 5th New York Infantry;* CWR:VOL1#2[7]111

MAY, JAMES, *Captain, 15th Massachusetts Infantry;* GETTY:13[1]252, GETTY:13[43]256

MAY, JOHN F., *Surgeon;* CWTI:JUL/92[50]275

MAY, MARCELLUS, *Corporal, 53rd Pennsylvania Infantry;* GETTY:11[80]235

MAY, SAMUEL, *Private, 3rd Georgia Infantry;* CWTI:SEP/94[26]400

MAY, SAMUEL H., *Lieutenant, 10th Louisiana Infantry;* GETTY:12[111]250

MAY, W.H., *Captain, 3rd Alabama Infantry;* GETTY:5[128]167

MAYER, MAURICE, *attorney;* ACW:SEP/94[46]488

MAYES, JOEL B., *Captain, Cherokee Braves;* CWM:SEP/92[8]437

MAYNARD, EDWARD, *Surgeon;* B&G:DEC/94[28]

MAYNARD, HORACE, *Congressman, Tennessee;* ACW:JUL/91[26]313, B&G:FEB/93[12]511

MAYO, JAMES M., *Captain, 4th North Carolina Cavalry;* GETTY:13[108]261

MAYO, JOHN A., *Private, Crenshaw's Artillery;* GETTY:10[107]227

MAYO, JOSEPH C., *Colonel, 3rd Virginia Infantry:*
GENERAL LISTINGS: *The "Blackberry" Raid,* GETTY:11[6]231, *fall of Richmond,* AHI:JAN/74[10]153, *Five Forks,* B&G:APR/92[8]481, *Gettysburg,* GETTY:5[107]164, *in book review,* CWR:VOL4#1[78], *in order of battle,* B&G:APR/92[8]481

ADDITIONAL LISTINGS: ACW:SEP/91[62]326, ACW:JAN/93[18]394, CWR:VOL1#3[52]122, CWTI:MAY/89[22]116, CWTI:JUL/94[44]394, GETTY:13[50]257, GETTY:13[75]259

MAYO, PETER H., *Private, CSA;* ACW:MAY/95[38]526

MAYO, ROBERT M., *Colonel, 47th Virginia Infantry;*
CWR:VOL1#3[52]122, GETTY:8[67]204

MAYUADIER, WILLIAM, *civilian;* CWTI:APR/89[38]111

McABEE, HARRY M., *Surgeon, 4th Ohio Infantry;*
GETTY:10[53]225

McADAMS, DANIEL, *Private, 20th Massachusetts Infantry;*
CWR:VOL4#4[101]181

McALLISTER, DAVID, *Sergeant, 48th Pennsylvania Infantry;*
CWM:MAR/91[56]341

McALLISTER, JOHN, *Private, Petersburg Artillery;*
ACW:MAR/95[12]513

McALLISTER, JOSEPH L., *Lieutenant Colonel, CSA;*
B&G:FEB/91[8]439

McALLISTER, RICHARD, *Lieutenant, USN;*
CWTI:MAY/93[38]321

McALLISTER, ROBERT, *Colonel, 11th New Jersey Infantry;*
ACW:JUL/93[16]422, B&G:JUN/95[8]600, B&G:APR/95[8]595,
CWM:MAY/92[20]420, CWNEWS:JUN/95[33],
CWTI:FEB/91[45]194, GETTY:12[7]241, GETTY:13[7]253,
photo, GETTY:12[7]241

McARTHUR, HENRY, *Sergeant, 75th New York
Infantry;*CWTI:DEC/90[29]182

McARTHUR, JOHN, *General, USA;* ACW:JAN/91[16]284,
ACW:SEP/91[46]324, ACW:NOV/94[76]500,
B&G:FEB/92[10]474, B&G:DEC/93[12]545,
B&G:AUG/95[8]604, MH:DEC/95[58]188, *photo,*
B&G:DEC/93[12]545

McATEE, FRANCIS, *Chaplain, 31st New York Infantry;*
CWM:MAR/91[50]340

McBETH, JAMES, *Private, 5th New York Infantry;*
CWTI:MAY/94[31]382

McBRIDE, ANDREW, *Sergeant, 4th U.S. Artillery;*
GETTY:11[57]233

McBRIDE, JAMES D., *General, USA;* ACW:MAR/92[46]354,
ACW:NOV/93[26]441, CWTI:FEB/92[29]248

McBRIDE, ROBERT, *Captain, 72nd Pennsylvania Infantry;*
ACW:MAR/92[8]357, CWR:VOL[7[97]193

McCABE, CHARLES C., *Chaplain, USA;* ACW:MAR/94[10]457

McCABE, W. GORDON, *Adjutant, CSA;* B&G:APR/92[8]481,
CWR:VOL1#1[1]102, CWR:VOL3#4[68], CWTI:APR/89[38]111

McCAFFREY, EDWARD, *Sergeant, 155th New York Infantry;*
CWM:MAR/91[50]340

McCAIN, W.D., *Colonel, 4th Kansas Infantry;*
ACW:NOV/94[42]497

McCALL, GEORGE A., *General, USA;* ACW:NOV/94[50]498,
ACW:MAR/95[70]520, AHI:FEB/82[36]225, CWM:APR/95[50],
CWM:JUN/95[6], CWM:JUN/95[57]592, CWM:JUN/95[61]593,
CWM:JUN/95[69]596, CWR:VOL1#3[28]120,
CWR:VOL3#1[80], CWTI:MAY/89[14]114,
CWTI:JUN/90[28]158, CWTI:MAR/91[12]198,
CWTI:MAY/94[31]382, GETTY:9[53]214

McCALL, MICHAEL, *Private, 53rd Pennsylvania Infantry;*
GETTY:11[80]235

McCALL, WILLIAM, *Lieutenant, USA;* AHI:DEC/67[4]113

McCALLA (SOUTH CAROLINA) RIFLES; GETTY:8[9]199

McCALLUM, DANIEL C., *Colonel, USA;* CWM:NOV/91[12]390,
CWTI:SEP/92[22]279

McCANDLESS, WILLIAM, *Colonel, USA;* B&G:APR/95[8]595,
CWR:VOL1#3[28]120, CWR:VOL4#4[1]177,
GETTY:11[91]236, GETTY:9[53]214, *photo,*
CWR:VOL4#4[1]177

McCANN RIFLES (PENNSYLVANIA) GUARDS, (53rd
Pennsylvania Infantry); GETTY:11[80]235

McCARDELL, WILLIAM H., *Private, 2nd Florida Cavalry;*
ACW:NOV/95[38]556

McCARREN, JOSEPH, *Private, 7th Ohio Infantry;*
GETTY:9[81]216

McCARTER, WILLIAM, *Private, 116th Pennsylvania Infantry;*
ARTICLE: "'THE BREATH OF HELL'S DOOR': PRIVATE
WILLIAM MCCARTER AND THE IRISH BRIGADE AT
FREDERICKSBURG," CWR:VOL4#4[47]179
ADDITIONAL LISTINGS: CWR:VOL4#4[127]182,
CWTI:DEC/90[58]185, *photo,* CWR:VOL4#4[47]179

McCARTHY, CARLTON, *Private, Cutshaw's Richmond
Howitzers;* ACW:MAR/91[12]292

McCARTHY, E.S., *Captain, 1st Richmond Howitzers;*
GETTY:8[53]203

McCARTHY, JAMES, *Private, 5th New York Infantry;*
CWR:VOL1#2[42]113

McCARTY, THOMAS L., *Private, 4th Texas Infantry;*
CWM:AUG/94[30]527

McCASKEY, JAMES, *Private, 100th Pennsylvania Infantry;*
ARTICLE: "A SCRATCH WITH THE REBELS,"
CWTI:JAN/94[49]365

McCAULEY, CHARLES S., *Captain, USN;*
ACW:MAR/94[35]460

McCAULEY, JAMES, *Sergeant, 7th Pennsylvania Reserves;*
CWM:DEC/94[74]555, CWR:VOL4#4[1]177

McCAULEY, LEVI G., *Major, 7th Pennsylvania Reserves;*
CWM:DEC/94[74]555

McCAUSLAND'S CHAMBERSBURG RAID: ARTICLES:
"MCCAUSLAND'S RAID AND THE BURNING OF
CHAMBERSBURG," B&G:AUG/94[10]574, "'OLD JUBE'
FOOLS THE YANKEES," B&G:AUG/94[19]575

McCAUSLAND, JOHN, *General, CSA:*
ARTICLES: "MCCAUSLAND'S RAID AND THE BURNING OF
CHAMBERSBURG," B&G:AUG/94[10]574, "'OLD JUBE'
FOOLS THE YANKEES," B&G:AUG/94[19]575
BOOK REVIEWS: *SOUTHERN REVENGE! CIVIL WAR HISTORY
OF CHAMBERSBURG, PENNSYLVANIA * TIGER JOHN:
THE REBEL WHO BURNED CHAMBERSBURG *
UNRECONSTRUCTED REBEL: THE LIFE OF GENERAL
JOHN MCCAUSLAND, C.S.A.*
GENERAL LISTINGS: *Custer,* AHI:JUN/76[4]169, *in book review,*
CWM:APR/95[50], *letters to the editor,* B&G:OCT/94[6]579,
Monocacy, B&G:DEC/92[8]503, *photos,* B&G:DEC/92[8]503,
B&G:AUG/94[10]574
ADDITIONAL LISTINGS: ACW:MAY/91[38]305, ACW:NOV/93[50]444,
ACW:MAR/94[27]459, B&G:JUN/95[36]603A,
CWTI:JAN/93[40]301

McCAW, JAMES B.; ACW:MAY/95[8]522

McCAWLEY, CHARLES G., *Captain, USMC;*
CWR:VOL2#3[194]141

McCLAIN, DOUGLAS, *Sergeant, 28th Pennsylvania Infantry;*
GETTY:9[81]216

McCLANAHAN, JOHN R., *Colonel, CSA;* ACW:NOV/92[35]387

McCLANAHAN, WILLIAM, *Captain, CSA;*
CWTI:MAR/91[34]201

McCLEAVE, WILLIAM, *Captain, 1st California Dragoons;*
ACW:JUL/93[27]423

McCLELAND, WILLIAM, *Private, 88th New York Infantry;*
CWR:VOL4#4[47]179

McCLELLAN, ARTHUR, *Lieutenant, USA;* B&G:APR/91[8]445

ADDITIONAL LISTINGS, B&G: B&G:AUG/92[11]493,
B&G:OCT/92[26]498, B&G:FEB/93[24]512,
B&G:FEB/93[40]514, B&G:AUG/93[55]535,
B&G:FEB/94[8]550, B&G:FEB/95[8]590B,
B&G:APR/95[24]596, B&G:JUN/95[22]601,
B&G:JUN/95[36]603A, B&G:OCT/95[8]611D,
B&G:OCT/95[8]611F, B&G:OCT/95[32]613

ADDITIONAL LISTINGS, CWM: CWM:MAR/91[56]341,
CWM:MAY/91[18]348, CWM:JUL/91[10]357,
CWM:JUL/91[24]361, CWM:NOV/91[12]390,
CWM:NOV/91[58]394A, CWM:JAN/92[27]403,
CWM:MAR/92[9]410, CWM:MAR/92[32]413,
CWM:MAY/92[34]422, CWM:JUL/92[16]428,
CWM:NOV/92[10]447, CWM:NOV/92[24]448,
CWM:JAN/93[16]457, CWM:MAR/93[4]463,
CWM:MAR/93[8]465, CWM:MAR/93[32]468,
CWM:MAY/93[4]472, CWM:JUL/93[35]487,
CWM:SEP/93[24]495, CWM:APR/94[14]503,
CWM:DEC/94[74]555, CWM:FEB/95[49]565,
CWM:JUN/95[17]581, CWM:JUN/95[55]591,
CWM:OCT/95[22]614, CWM:OCT/95[55]622,
CWM:DEC/95[54]632

ADDITIONAL LISTINGS, CWR CWR:VOL1#1[1]102,
CWR:VOL1#1[71]107, CWR:VOL1#2[7]111,
CWR:VOL1#2[29]112, CWR:VOL1#3[28]120,
CWR:VOL1#4[7]125, CWR:VOL2#2[95]135,
CWR:VOL2#2[156]138, CWR:VOL2#4[269]145,
CWR:VOL2#4[313]146, CWR:VOL3#1[31]150,
CWR:VOL3#2[1]153, CWR:VOL3#3[1]157,
CWR:VOL4#1[1]163, CWR:VOL4#2[68]167,
CWR:VOL4#4[1]177, CWR:VOL4#4[47]179

ADDITIONAL LISTINGS, CWTI: CWTI:APR/89[14]107,
CWTI:MAY/89[14]114, CWTI:MAY/89[36]118,
CWTI:DEC/89[34]136, CWTI:FEB/90[26]143,
CWTI:FEB/90[32]144, CWTI:AUG/91[46]218,
CWTI:SEP/91[31]229, CWTI:SEP/91[42]231,
CWTI:SEP/91[54]232, CWTI:APR/92[35]257,
CWTI:MAY/92[29]263, CWTI:NOV/92[18]289,
CWTI:NOV/92[60]294, CWTI:MAY/93[29]319,
CWTI:MAY/93[35]320, CWTI:JUL/93[14]324,
CWTI:JUL/93[29]326, CWTI:NOV/93[24]346,
CWTI:JAN/94[46]364, CWTI:MAR/94[29]371,
CWTI:MAR/94[48]374, CWTI:MAY/94[31]382,
CWTI:JUL/94[20]390, CWTI:JUL/94[44]394,
CWTI:SEP/94[49]404, CWTI:JUN/95[38]447,
CWTI:JUN/95[51]449, CWTI:AUG/95[46]459,
CWTI:OCT/95[48]470, CWTI:DEC/95[52]480,
CWTI:DEC/95[67]481

ADDITIONAL LISTINGS, GETTY: GETTY:6[43]173, GETTY:7[41]189,
GETTY:9[41]212, GETTY:10[42]224, GETTY:10[53]225,
GETTY:11[19]232

ADDITIONAL LISTINGS, MH: MH:APR/92[18]157, MH:OCT/93[20]172,
MH:DEC/93[12]174, MH:JUN/94[8]177, MH:APR/95[46]183,
MH:AUG/95[30]185

McCLELLAN, GEORGE R., *Lieutenant Colonel, 5th Tennessee*
Cavalry, B&G:FEB/93[12]511, CWR:VOL4#1[1]163

McCLELLAN, HENRY B., *Major, CSA:*
BOOK REVIEW: *I RODE WITH JEB STUART: THE LIFE AND*
CAMPAIGNS OF MAJOR GENERAL J.E.B. STUART
GENERAL LISTINGS: *Brandy Station,* GETTY:11[19]232, *Gettysburg,*
GETTY:4[65]148, GETTY:4[75]149, GETTY:4[115]152
ADDITIONAL LISTINGS: ACW:NOV/91[30]332, ACW:MAR/94[58],
ACW:MAY/94[35]469, CWNEWS:MAY/95[33],

CWR:VOL1#2[78], CWTI:JUN/90[32]159,
CWTI:APR/92[35]257, MH:OCT/92[51]162

McCLELLAN, J.F., *Lieutenant Colonel, 4th Florida Battalion;*
CWR:VOL3#4[1]161

McCLELLAN, WILLIAM C., *Private, 9th Alabama Infantry;*
CWM:JUL/92[16]428

McCLELLAND, MATTHEW, *seaman, USN;*
ACW:MAR/92[40]353

McCLELLAND, W.H., *Captain, Jeff Davis Legion;*
GETTY:12[68]246

McCLENDON, WILLIAM, *Private, 15th Alabama Infantry;*
ACW:JUL/94[42]479

McCLENNAN, MATTHEW R., *Colonel, USA;*
ACW:NOV/93[50]444, CWTI:JAN/93[40]301

McCLERNAND, JOHN A. *General, USA:*
GENERAL LISTINGS: *Champion's Hill,* MH:JUN/93[82]167, *Forts*
Henry and Donelson, B&G:FEB/92[10]474, *general history,*
AHI:MAY/71[3]133A, *in book review,* CWR:VOL2#1[78], *order*
of battle, &G:FEB/94[8]550, *Port Gibson,*
ACW:JUL/94[51]480, *Shiloh,* ACW:JAN/91[22]285, *Vicksburg,*
ACW:NOV/91[22]331, B&G:AUG/95[8]604,
CWTI:FEB/90[46]146, CWTI:MAY/91[24]208, *photos,*
ACW:JUL/91[35]314, B&G:FEB/92[10]474,
B&G:FEB/94[8]550, CWTI:MAR/91[22]199
ADDITIONAL LISTINGS: ACW:JUL/91[35]314, ACW:SEP/92[16]376,
ACW:NOV/94[34]496, ACW:NOV/94[76]500,
B&G:FEB/94[8]550, B&G:FEB/94[57]555,
CWM:FEB/95[32]562, CWR:VOL2#1[i]129,
CWR:VOL2#1[1]130, CWR:VOL2#1[19]131,
CWR:VOL2#1[36]132, CWR:VOL2#1[69]133,
CWR:VOL3#3[33]158, CWR:VOL3#3[59]159,
CWR:VOL3#4[24]162, CWR:VOL4#1[44]164,
CWR:VOL4#2[26]166, CWTI:FEB/90[38]145,
CWTI:MAR/91[22]199, CWTI:MAY/91[16]206,
CWTI:MAY/94[16]380, CWTI:DEC/94[82]418,
MH:APR/94[54]176

McCLESKEY, JAMES R., *Lieutenant, CSA;*
CWTI:SEP/91[23]228

McCLINTOCK, JAMES, *Captain, USA;* B&G:FEB/91[8]439

McCLINTOCK, JAMES R., *civilian;* AHI:OCT/95[16]325,
CWTI:SEPT/89[20]127

McCLOSKEY, JAMES, *Captain, CSN;* CW:JUL/93[34]424,
ACW:MAR/95[18]514

McCLOSKEY, JAMES, *seaman, USN* B&G:JUN/92[40]489

McCLUNG, HUGH L.W., *Captain, Tennessee Artillery;*
B&G:AUG/91[11]458, B&G:FEB/93[12]511,

McCLUNG, RICHARD L., *Captain, CSA;* CWM:JUN/94[25]511

McCLURE, A.K., *Colonel, USA;* GETTY:13[64]258

McCLURE, ALEXANDER K.; *civilian;* ACW:MAR/92[22]351,
CWM:MAR/91[56]341, CWTI:JUN/90[46]161, *photo,*
CWM:MAR/91[56]341

McCLURE, J.R., *Private, 14th Indiana Infantry;*
GETTY:9[33]211

McCLURE, W.P., *postmaster;* ACW:NOV/91[10]329

McCLURE, WILLIAM S., *Major, 8th Illinois Cavalry;*
GETTY:11[19]232

McCLURG, ALEXANDER C., *Colonel, USA;*
AHI:NOV/72[12]142, CWR:VOL4#3[65]172

McCOLLUM, BERNARD, *Chaplain, 116th Pennsylvania*
Infantry; CWM:MAR/91[50]340

McCOMAS, BENJAMIN, *Lieutenant, CSA;* B&G:APR/92[6]480

McCOMAS, WILLIAM, *Captain, CSA;* B&G:APR/92[6]480

McCOMB, WILLIAM, *General, CSA;* ACW:SEP/92[38]379,
CWR:VOL1#3[52]122
McCONAUGHY, DAVID, *civilian;* GETTY:11[19]232,
GETTY:11[119]238, GETTY:12[97]249
McCONNELL, CHARLES H., *Sergeant, 24th Michigan
Infantry;* GETTY:5[19]158
McCONNELL, HENRY K., *Captain, 71st Ohio Infantry;*
CWTI:JUL/92[42]27
McCONNELL, ROBERT, *Captain, 150th New York Infantry;*
GETTY:12[42]244
McCONNELL, WILLIAM, *civilian;* B&G:APR/91[24]446
McCOOK, ALEXANDER M., *General, USA:*
GENERAL LISTINGS: *in book review,* ACW:SEP/95[62],
CWNEWS:FEB/94[5], CWR:VOL4#3[1]170, *letters to the
editor,* CWTI:MAR/93[8]306, *Nelson-Davis feud,*
AHI:NOV/72[12]142, *Tullahoma Campaign,*
B&G:OCT/92[10]496, *West Point,* B&G:DEC/91[12]469
ADDITIONAL LISTINGS: B&G:OCT/91[11]466, CWM:JUL/92[24]430,
CWM:OCT/94[48]542, CWR:VOL4#3[50]171,
CWTI:NOV/92[18]289
McCOOK, DANIEL; ACW:NOV/95[74]560,
CWM:JAN/91[12]326, CWM:APR/94[8]502,
CWTI:MAY/94[40]383
McCOOK, EDWARD M., *General, USA;* ACW:MAY/95[49]527,
B&G:DEC/93[12]545, CWTI:SUMMER/89[50]124,
CWTI:MAY/92[48]267
McCOOK, EDWIN S., *Colonel, 31st Illinois Infantry;*
B&G:FEB/94[8]550
McCOOK, ROBERT L., *General, USA;* ACW:SEP/93[38]434,
B&G:JUN/92[6]490, B&G:FEB/93[12]511,
B&G:AUG/93[10]529
McCORKLE, BAXTER, *Lieutenant, CSA;* CWR:VOL4#4[70]180
McCORKLE, JOHN:
BOOK REVIEW: *THREE YEARS WITH QUANTRILL, A TRUE
STORY TOLD BY HIS SCOUT JOHN MCCORKLE*
ADDITIONAL LISTING: ACW:JAN/93[26]395
McCORMICK, BERNARD, *Private, 5th New York Infantry;*
CWR:VOL1#2[42]113
McCORMICK, DICK, *photographer;* B&G:FEB/94[24]551
McCORMICK, FRANK, *Private, 97th New York Infantry;*
GETTY:9[33]211
McCORMICK, GEORGE, *Captain, 7th Michigan Cavalry;*
CWNEWS:JAN/92[4]
McCORMICK, MATTHIAS, *Private, 1st Florida Special
Battalion;* CWR:VOL3#1[65]151
McCORMICK, OSCAR F., *Private, 8th Louisiana Infantry;*
CWTI:FEB/91[12]189
McCORQUADALE, M., *Private, 51st North Carolina Infantry;*
B&G:APR/93[24]520
McCOSKER, JOHN, *Chaplain, 55th Pennsylvania Infantry;*
CWM:MAR/91[50]340
McCOUBREY, JAMES, *Private, 111th New York Infantry;*
GETTY:8[95]205
McCOWN, JAMES L., *Private, 5th Virginia Infantry;*
CWTI:JUL/93[20]325
McCOWN, JAMES, *Colonel, CSA;* CWR:VOL2#1[1]130
McCOWN, JOHN P., *General, CSA;* B&G:OCT/92[10]496,
CWTI:AUG/91[36]217
McCOY, JAMES C., *Major, USA;* AHI:JAN/67[4]106
McCOY, PETER, *civilian;* B&G:FEB/91[20]440
McCOY, T., *Sergeant, 3rd New Jersey Infantry;*
CWTI:MAY/89[36]118

McCRACKEN, GEORGE W., *Private, 10th Pennsylvania
Reserves;* CWR:VOL4#4[1]177
McCRACKEN, PATRICK, *civilian;* B&G:JUN/95[8]600
McCRADY, EDWARD, *Colonel, 1st South Carolina Infantry;*
B&G:AUG/92[11]493
McCRAY, THOMAS H., *Colonel, CSA;* B&G:JUN/91[10]452
McCREA, TULLY, *cadet;* B&G:DEC/91[12]469
McCREARY, COMILLUS W., *Major, CSA;* GETTY:13[22]254
McCREARY, JAMES B., *Lieutenant, Colonel, 11th Kentucky
Cavalry;* B&G:OCT/94[11]580, B&G:DEC/94[6]584
McCREARY, JOHN, *civilian;* GETTY:6[7]169
McCREARY, KATE; GETTY:9[122]220
McCREARY, WILLIAM, *Captain, USA;* GETTY:4[101]151
McCREEDY, W.W., *Captain, CSA;* GETTY:5[19]158
McCREERY, WILLIAM, *Colonel, 21st Michigan Infantry;*
ACW:JAN/94[55]453
McCRORY, LEWIS W., *Lieutenant, 100th Ohio Infantry;*
B&G:AUG/95[24]605
McCROSSIN, BERNARD, *Chaplain, 69th New York Militia;*
CWM:MAR/91[50]340
McCULLEY, WILLIAM H., *Private, 2nd Tennessee Cavalry;*
CWR:VOL4#1[1]163
McCULLOCH, BEN, *General, CSA:*
ARTICLES: "A MIGHTY MEAN-FOWT FIGHT,"
ACW:NOV/93[26]441, CWTI:FEB/92[29]248
BOOK REVIEWS: *BEN MCCULLOCH AND THE FRONTIER
MILITARY TRADITION*
GENERAL LISTINGS: *in book review,* CWR:VOL4#3[1]170, *Mexican
War,* AHI:OCT/82[28]230, *Mormon confrontation,*
AHI:DEC/72[10]145, *Wilson's Creek,* ACW:MAR/94[8]456,
photos, ACW:NOV/93[26]441, CWM:MAY/93[16]475
ADDITIONAL LISTINGS: ACW:MAR/92[46]354, ACW:SEP/92[38]379,
B&G:APR/93[34]521, CWM:SEP/92[8]437,
CWM:SEP/92[38]443, CWM:MAY/93[8]474,
CWM:SEP/93[8]493, CWR:VOL1#1[42]105,
CWR:VOL2#3[212]142, CWR:VOL3#3[33]158
McCULLOCH, HENRY E., *General, CSA;* CWR:VOL3#3[33]158
McCULLOCH, ROBERT, *Colonel, CSA;* ACW:SEP/92[23]377,
CWTI:NOV/93[65]351, *photo,* CWTI:NOV/93[65]351
McCULLOCH, R.E., *Private, 14th Tennessee Infantry;*
GETTY:6[13]170
McCULLOUGH, J.W., *Surgeon, 1st Delaware Infantry;*
GETTY:10[53]225
McCURVEY, T.W., *Private, 16th Georgia Infantry;*
B&G:APR/93[24]520
McCUTCHEON, JAMES, *Captain, 15th South Carolina
Infantry;* GETTY:5[35]159
McDANIEL, JAMES, *Private, 2nd Tennessee Cavalry;*
CWR:VOL4#1[1]163
McDANIEL, REASON, *Private, 19th Indiana Infantry;*
GETTY:11[57]233
McDANIEL, ZEDEKIAH, *Lieutenant, CSN;*
ACW:NOV/91[8]328, ACW:SEP/94[74]491,
CWM:DEC/95[30]627
McDANIEL, ZERE, *Lieutenant, CSA;* BOOK REVIEW: *THE
SINKING OF THE USS CAIRO;* CWM:APR/95[50],
CWNEWS:FEB/94[5]
McDAVID, PETER A., *Lieutenant, Palmetto Sharpshooters;*
CWR:VOL3#2[70]155
McDERMOTT, ANTHONY W., *Private, 69th Pennsylvania
Infantry;* GETTY:4[89]150, GETTY:7[97]193
McDERMOTT, JOHN, *Private, 24th Michigan Infantry;*
GETTY:11[57]233, GETTY:9[33]211

McDERMOTT, JOHN P., *Private, 2nd Wisconsin Infantry;*
GETTY:11[57]233

McDIVITT, JOHN, *Private, 46th Pennsylvania Infantry;*
CWM:AUG/95[5]602

McDONALD, ANGUS, *Colonel, CSA;* ACW:JAN/92[8]338

McDONALD, B.B., *Major, 101st Ohio Infantry;*
AHI:DEC/85[40]255

McDONALD, CORNELIA PEAKE; BOOK REVIEWS: *A WOMAN'S CIVIL WAR: A DIARY, WITH REMINISCENCES OF THE WAR, FROM MARCH 1862*

McDONALD, GEORGE M., *Sergeant, 2nd Tennessee Cavalry;*
CWR:VOL4#1[1]163

McDONALD, HUGH, *Captain, 13th Pennsylvania Reserves;*
CWR:VOL1#3[20]119, CWR:VOL1#3[28]120,
CWR:VOL4#4[1]177

McDONALD, JAMES H., *Captain, 50th New York Engineers;*
ACW:NOV/95[10]553

McDONALD, JOHN, *Private, 4th New York Infantry;*
B&G:APR/95[24]596

McDONOUGH, CHARLES, *Private, Mosby's Ranger;*
ACW:JUL/94[26]477, CWTI:SEP/90[34]176

McDONOUGH, JAMES S., *Private, 2nd Tennessee Cavalry;*
CWR:VOL4#1[1]163

McDOUGAL, DAVID S., *Commander, USN;* MH:OCT/91[50]154

McDOUGALL, ARCHIBALD L., *Colonel, USA;*
B&G:FEB/95[8]590C, GETTY:6[7]169, GETTY:7[83]192

McDOUGALL, CHARLES; ACW:MAR/93[8]401

McDOUGALL, HENRY G., *Private, 6th Wisconsin Infantry,*
GETTY:11[57]233

McDOUGALL, JAMES A., *Senator, California;*
CWTI:AUG/95[54]460

McDOUGALL, THOMAS M., *Captain, USA;*
MH:AUG/95[82]186

McDOUGLE, W.T., *Private, 126th Ohio Infantry;*
CWTI:JAN/93[40]301

McDOW, J.T., *Sergeant, 4th South Carolina Cavalry;*
ACW:MAR/95[50]518

McDOWALL, GEORGE M., *Captain, 2nd South Carolina Infantry;* GETTY:5[35]159

McDOWELL, JESSE, *Private, 2nd Tennessee Cavalry;*
CWR:VOL4#1[1]163

McDOWELL, JOSEPH N., *Doctor;* CWTI:AUG/95[58]461

McDOWELL, R.A., *Lieutenant, 11th Mississippi Infantry;*
GETTY:9[98]217

McDOWELL, VIRGINIA, BATTLE OF:
ARTICLE: "A SINGLE STEP," CWTI:MAR/94[29]371
BOOK REVIEW: *JACKSON'S VALLEY CAMPAIGN: THE BATTLE OF MCDOWELL, MARCH 11-MAY 18, 1862*
ADDITIONAL LISTINGS: ACW:JAN/92[16]340, AHI:MAY/71[3]133A,
AHI:MAR/84[42]238, CWTI:JUN/95[18]444

McDOWELL, WILLIAM, *Sergeant, 5th New York Infantry;*
CWR:VOL1#2[29]112

McDOWELL, IRVIN; *General, USA:*
ARTICLE: "GENERAL IRVIN MCDOWELL: GENEROUS TO A FAULT," CWM:JUN/95[82]600
GENERAL LISTINGS: *Chantilly,* ACW:JAN/95[54]508, *general history,* AHI:MAY/71[3]133A, *in book review,*
ACW:NOV/94[66], B&G:JUN/94[34], CWM:DEC/95[10],
CWNEWS:JUN/91[4], CWR:VOL3#1[80], *Jackson,*
B&G:JUN/92[8]487, *Manassas, First,* ACW:JUL/95[16]534,
CWTI:APR/92[35]257, CWTI:MAR/94[48]374, *Manassas, Second,* ACW:NOV/94[18]495, ACW:JAN/95[54]508,
AHI:DEC/66[30]105, B&G:AUG/92[11]493,

B&G:OCT/95[20]612, GETTY:11[19]232, *Mexican War,*
MH:APR/93[39]166, *Shenandoah Valley Campaign,*
ACW:JAN/92[8]338, *Signal Corps,* ACW:JAN/95[20]504,
William T. Sherman, AHI:JAN/67[4]106, *photos,*
AHI:MAY/71[3]133A, B&G:AUG/92[11]493,
CWM:JUN/95[82]600
ADDITIONAL LISTINGS: ACW:MAR/91[30]295, ACW:JUL/91[18]312,
ACW:MAY/92[14]358, ACW:MAY/93[38]416,
ACW:SEP/94[31]486, ACW:NOV/94[50]498,
AHI:JUL/73[38]150, B&G:DEC/94[34]587,
B&G:OCT/95[32]613, CWM:NOV/91[12]390,
CWR:VOL2#4[269]145, CWTI:AUG/91[46]218,
CWTI:APR/92[14]254, CWTI:MAY/92[45]266,
CWTI:JUL/92[29]272, CWTI:NOV/93[55]350,
CWTI:MAR/94[29]371, CWTI:JUN/95[51]449,
CWTI:DEC/95[67]481, MH:APR/92[18]157, MH:APR/94[54]176

McELHANY, WILLIAM; CWTI:AUG/95[58]461

McELRATH, THOMPSON P., *Lieutenant, 5th U.S. Artillery;*
GETTY:9[41]212

McELROY, JOHN, *Private, USA;* CWM:JAN/92[16]401,
CWM:OCT/95[10]

McELROY, JOHN S., *Colonel, 16th North Carolina Infantry;*
CWR:VOL4#4[70]180

McELWAIN, ANDREW J., *civilian;* B&G:AUG/94[10]574

McELWEE, GEORGE, *Corporal, Baltimore Light Artillery;*
B&G:AUG/94[10]574

McENERY, JOHN, *Lieutenant Colonel, CSA;*
CWTI:JAN/94[46]364

McFARLAND, EDWIN D., *Sergeant, 57th Massachusetts Infantry;* ACW:SEP/95[70]549

McFARLAND, GEORGE, *Colonel, 151st Pennsylvania Infantry;*
GETTY:8[9]199, GETTY:13[22]254

McFARLAND, LOUIS B., *Lieutenant, 9th Tennessee Infantry;*
B&G:AUG/94[22]576

McFARLAND, SAMUEL, *Lieutenant Colonel, 19th Iowa Infantry;* CWR:VOL1#1[42]105

McFARLAND, WILLIAM H., *Private, 5th Wisconsin Infantry;*
CWM:MAY/91[26]349

McFARLAND, WILLIAM, *Private, 42nd Indiana Infantry;*
B&G:AUG/95[24]605

McGAILLIARD, W.N., *Lieutenant, 8th Louisiana Infantry;*
CWTI:FEB/91[12]189

McGANN, FRANCIS, *Private, 4th U.S. Artillery;*
GETTY:11[57]233

McGARR, OWEN, *Private, 1st U.S. Artillery;*
ACW:JUL/93[42]425

McGARRAH, JOHN L., *Corporal, 11th Georgia Artillery;*
CWR:VOL3#2[1]153

McGAVOCK, RANDAL W., *Colonel, 10th Tennessee Infantry;*
CWNEWS:JUN/95[33]

McGAVOCK, RANDALL W., *Lieutenant Colonel, 10th Tennessee Infantry;* BOOK REVIEW: *REBEL SONS OF ERIN, A CIVIL WAR HISTORY OF THE TENTH TENNESSEE INFANTRY (IRISH), CONFEDERATE STATES VOLUNTEERS*

McGEE, BENJAMIN F., *Sergeant, 72nd Indiana Infantry;*
B&G:DEC/94[22]586

McGEE, DENNIS, *Captain, 1st Pennsylvania Rifles;*
CWR:VOL1#3[20]119

McGEE, ISAAC, *Private, 7th Indiana Infantry;*
CWTI:NOV/93[24]346

McGEE, JAMES, *Captain, 69th New York Infantry;*
ACW:MAY/94[12]466

McGEHEE, CHARLEY, *Private, Terry's Texas Rangers;*
CWM:JUL[92[40]432

McGEHEE, E., *Lieutenant, 22nd Virginia Infantry;*
CWR:VOL1#3[52]122

McGEORGE, JOHN, *Sergeant, 1st Illinois Artillery;*
B&G:APR/94[28]559

McGHEE, JAMES, *Colonel, CSA;* B&G:JUN/91[10]452

McGHEE, JOSEPH, *Private, 150th New York Infantry;*
GETTY:12[42]244

McGIFFEN, BENJAMIN F., *Corporal, 148th Pennsylvania
Infantry;* CWR:VOL2#2[141]137

McGILL, JOHN, *Sergeant, 150th New York Infantry;*
GETTY:12[42]244

McGILL, W.J., *Colonel, 1st Georgia Regulars;*
CWR:VOL2#2[95]135

McGILVERY, FREEMAN, *Colonel, USA;* GETTY:5[47]160,
GETTY:7[51]190, GETTY:9[41]212, GETTY:9[61]215,
GETTY:11[71]234, GETTY:12[30]243, GETTY:12[42]244,
photo, GETTY:5[47]160

McGIMSEY, WILLIAM C., *Lieutenant, 8th Louisiana Infantry;*
CWTI:FEB/91[12]189

McGINNIS, GEORGE F., *General, USA;* ACW:NOV/91[22]331,
B&G:FEB/94[8]550, CWR:VOL2#1[36]132,
CWTI:MAY/91[24]208

McGINNIS, WILLIAM A., *Lieutenant, 19th Massachusetts
Infantry;* CWM:MAR/91[17]335

McGOWAN, JOHN, *Captain, USN;* ACW:NOV/93[8]438

McGOWAN, SAMUEL, *General, CSA:*
GENERAL LISTINGS: *Chancellorsville,* MH:JUN/92[50]159, *Five
Forks,* B&G:APR/92[8]481, *Gettysburg,* GETTY:8[67]204,
Manassas, Second, B&G:AUG/92[11]493, *order of battle,*
B&G:APR/95[8]595, *Wilderness,* B&G:JUN/95[8]600
ADDITIONAL LISTINGS: B&G:FEB/93[40]514, CWR:VOL1#1[26]103,
CWR:VOL3#2[1]153, CWR:VOL3#2[61]154,
CWTI:AUG/90[26]166, CWTI:FEB/91[45]194,
CWTI:APR/92[49]260

McGOWEN, NED; CWTI:JAN/95[42]428

McGOWN, THOMAS S., *Captain, Patapsco (Maryland) Guards;*
B&G:AUG/94[10]574

McGRATH, EUGENE, *Captain, USA;* CWR:VOL1#4[7]125

McGRATH, JAMES, *civilian;* B&G:JUN/93[12]524

McGRATH, MICHAEL H., *Lieutenant, 15th New York
Engineers;* CWR:VOL4#4[101]181

McGRAW'S (VIRGINIA) BATTERY; ACW:MAY/95[30]525

McGRAW, JOSEPH, *Captain, Purcell Artillery;*
CWM:MAR/91[17]335

McGREGOR, WILLIAM M, *Captain, CSA;* B&G:APR/92[8]481

McGUFFAGE, WILLIAM, *Private, 5th New York Infantry;*
CWR:VOL1#2[29]112

McGUIRE, HUNTER H., *Surgeon, CSA:*
ARTICLE: "MEMORIES OF STONEWALL," CWM:APR/94[14]503
BOOK REVIEW: *STONEWALL JACKSON'S SURGEON, HUNTER
HOLMES MCGUIRE; A BIOGRAPHY]*
GENERAL LISTINGS: *Gettysburg,* GETTY:11[126]239, *Jackson,*
B&G:JUN/92[8]487, *letters to the editor, CWM:JUL/91[6]355,
photos,* CWM:SEP/91[40]385, CWM:APR/94[14]503
ADDITIONAL LISTINGS: ACW:JUL/91[18]312, ACW:MAY/95[8]522,
CWM:MAY/91[40]351, CWM:SEP/91[40]385,
CWM:JUL/92[16]428, CWM:OCT/94[26]536,
CWTI:MAY/89[22]116

McGUIRE, JUDITH W.; BOOK REVIEW: *DIARY OF A
SOUTHERN REFUGEE*

McGUIRE, ROBERT, *Lieutenant, 116th Pennsylvania Infantry;*
CWTI:DEC/90[58]185

McGUIRE, ROBERT, *Private, 53rd Pennsylvania Infantry;*
GETTY:11[80]235

McGUIRK, JOHN, *Colonel, CSA;* CWTI:NOV/93[65]351

McHORNEY, B.F., *civilian;* CWTI:JAN/95[42]428

McILHATTAN, DAVID, *Private, 148th Pennsylvania Infantry;*
GETTY:10[53]225

McILHENNY, WILLIAM A., *civilian,* GETTY:9[122]220

McILVAINE, H.B., *Major, 5th New York Artillery;*
CWR:VOL1#4[7]125

McILVAINE, SAMUEL, *Private, 10th Indiana Infantry;* BOOK
REVIEW: *BY THE DIM AND FLARING LAMPS: THE CIVIL
WAR DIARY OF SAMUEL MCILVAINE, FEBRUARY
THROUGH JUNE 1862*

McILWAIN, JAMES I., *Private, 11th Pennsylvania Infantry;*
CWM:MAR/93[56]471

McINTIRE, DANIEL M., *Private, CSA;* ACW:MAR/91[62]298

McINTOSH, DANIEL N., *Colonel, Creek and Seminole
Mounted Rifles;* ACW:JAN/91[30]286

McINTOSH, DAVID G., *Colonel, Pee Dee Artillery;*
B&G:APR/94[10]558, B&G:APR/95[8]595,
B&G:APR/94[10]558, CWR:VOL1#1[1]102,
CWR:VOL4#4[70]180, GETTY:5[4]156, GETTY:13[7]253,
photo, CWR:VOL4#4[70]180

McINTOSH, JAMES, *General, CSA;* ACW:NOV/93[26]441,
B&G:APR/93[34]521, CWM:SEP/92[38]443,
CWM:MAY/93[24]476, CWTI:FEB/92[29]248,
CWTI:MAY/92[48]267

McINTOSH, JOHN B., *General, USA;* ACW:MAY/91[38]305,
ACW:NOV/91[30]332, ACW:JAN/92[16]340,
B&G:APR/94[10]558, B&G:APR/95[8]595, GETTY:4[75]149,
GETTY:13[89]260, *photo,* GETTY:13[89]260

McINTOSH, LUCAS, *Lieutenant, Fredericksburg Artillery;*
CWR:VOL1#1[35]104

McINTOSH, WILLIAM M., *Colonel, 15th Georgia Infantry;*
CWM:JUN/95[63]594

McINTRYE, BENJAMIN, *Sergeant, 19th Iowa Infantry;*
CWR:VOL1#1[42]105

McINTYRE, D.M., *Lieutenant, 38th North Carolina Infantry;*
GETTY:8[67]204

McIVER, JOHN K., *Captain, 8th South Carolina Infantry;*
GETTY:5[35]159

McIVOR, JAMES P., *Colonel, USA;* B&G:APR/93[12]518

McKAMEY, MARSHALL, *Private, CSA;* B&G:FEB/91[20]440

McKAY, CHARLES W., *Private, 154th New York Infantry;*
GETTY:8[17]200

McKAY, DAVID, *Surgeon, USA;* B&G:APR/95[24]596

McKEAGE, JOHN, *Captain, USA;* ACW:MAR/94[50]462

McKEAN, THOMAS, *General, USA;* ACW:SEP/91[46]324

McKEE, ABRAM W., *Captain, CSA;* B&G:OCT/94[6]579

McKEE, EDWARD, *Chaplain, 116th Pennsylvania Infantry;*
CWM:MAR/91[50]340, GETTY:10[53]225

McKEE, JAMES C., *Surgeon, USA;* ACW:JUL/93[27]423

McKEE, JOEL, *Captain, CSA;* CWTI:MAR/91[10]197

McKEE, SAMUEL, *Captain, 14th Kentucky Cavalry;*
ACW:SEP/95[22]544

McKEE, SAMUEL A., *Captain, 155th Pennsylvania Infantry;*
GETTY:9[48]213

McKEEN, HENRY B., *Colonel, USA;* B&G:APR/94[10]558

McKEEN, JAMES, *Private, 17th Maine Infantry;*
GETTY:8[43]202

McKEEVER, JOSEPH, *Private, 69th Pennsylvania Infantry;* GETTY:4[89]150, GETTY:7[97]193

McKELL, WILLIAM, *Sergeant, 89th Ohio Infantry;* CWTI:SEP/92[31]281

McKELVAINE, R.P., *Lieutenant Colonel, 34th Mississippi Infantry;* CWTI:SEPT/89[30]129

McKENDREE, GEORGE, *Lieutenant, CSA;* CWR:VOL4#4[70]180

McKENNA, JAMES, *civilian;* ACW:SEP/93[22]432

McKENNEY, WILLIAM, *Private, 27th/47th Iowa Infantry;* B&G:AUG/92[40]495

McKENZIE, GEORGE, *Private, 2nd South Carolina Infantry;* GETTY:5[35]159

McKENZIE, HENRY, *seaman, USN;* B&G:JUN/92[40]489

McKERNAN, MICHAEL, *Private, CSA;* CWTI:DEC/90[29]182

McKIE, THOMAS F., *Private, 11th Mississippi Infantry;* ACW:MAR/92[10]349

McKIM, RANDOLPH H., *Lieutenant, 1st North Carolina Infantry;* ACW:JUL/94[10]475, GETTY:5[4]156, GETTY:7[83]192, GETTY:9[17N]210

McKINLEY, WILLIAM, *Major, USA:*
ARTICLES: "BEHIND THE LINES," CWTI:AUG/90[8]165, "THE HEARTBEAT IN THE WHITE HOUSE," AHI:APR/70[38]125, "TRUE AMERICAN MADNESS: INAUGURAL BALLS," AHI:NOV/72[37]143
GENERAL LISTINGS: *in book review,* CWNEWS:NOV/92[4], *Trevilian Station,* MH:FEB/93[42]164, *list of monuments,* B&G:OCT/95[8]611A, *McKinley National Memorial;* AHI:APR/89[43]284, *photos,* AHI:NOV/72[37]143, CWTI:SEP/94[49]404
ADDITIONAL LISTINGS: ACW:MAY/91[38]305, ACW:MAY/95[6]521, B&G:FEB/94[38]553, B&G:OCT/95[8]611D, CWTI:JUL/94[50]395, CWTI:SEP/94[49]404, GETTY:13[89]260

McKINNEY, A.J., *Chaplain, 71st Ohio Infantry;* CWTI:JUL/92[42]274

McKINNEY, CHRISTOPHER C., *Lieutenant Colonel, CSA;* B&G:DEC/95[9]615

McKINNEY, ROBERT M., *Colonel, 15th North Carolina Infantry;* ACW:JAN/94[8]447

McKINNEY, WILLIAM, *Lieutenant Colonel, 15th North Carolina Infantry;* CWM:JUN/95[29]583

McKINSTRY, ALEXANDER, *Colonel, CSA;* B&G:OCT/92[10]496

McKINSTRY, JUSTUS, *General, USA:*
ARTICLE: "UNION QUARTERMASTER JUSTUS MCKINSTRY, A HANDY MAN WITH A LEDGER BOOK, PRACTICED UNIQUE BOOKKEEPING," ACW:MAR/92[6]347
ADDITIONAL LISTINGS: ACW:MAR/92[46]354, ACW:NOV/94[34]496

McKNIGHT, CHARLES, *Captain, 88th Pennsylvania Infantry;* B&G:OCT/95[36]614

McKNIGHT, WILLIAM, *seaman, USN;* MH:AUG/93[47]169

McKOIN, JOHN; ACW:MAR/94[8]456

McLAFLIN, EDWARD, *Captain, 1st Indiana Heavy Artillery;* ACW:JAN/94[30]450

McLAIN, WILLIAM, *civilian;* B&G:APR/92[28]482

McLANE, JOHN W., *Colonel, 83rd Pennsylvania Infantry;* CWTI:FEB/92[58]251, GETTY:7[41]189

McLAUGHLEN, NAPOLEON B.; CWTI:MAR/95[33]435

McLAUGHLIN, AUGUSTUS, *Lieutenant, CSN;* CWNEWS:JAN/90[4]

McLAUGHLIN, J.A., *Lieutenant Colonel, 47th Indiana Infantry;* B&G:FEB/94[8]550

McLAUGHLIN, JOHN, *Private, 6th Wisconsin Infantry,* GETTY:11[57]233

McLAUGHLIN, WILLIAM, *Major, CSA;* CWTI:MAR/89[16]101

McLAWS, LAFAYETTE, *General, CSA:*
ARTICLE: "FIRING THE GAP," ACW:JAN/94[39]451
GENERAL LISTINGS: *Antietam,* B&G:OCT/95[8]611A, *Carolina Campaign,* B&G:DEC/95[9]615, *Chancellorsville,* ACW:MAY/95[30]525, MH:JUN/92[50]159, *Davis' funeral,* CWTI:MAR/93[32]311, *Gettysburg,* GETTY:4[113]153, GETTY:5[4]156, GETTY:5[35]159, GETTY:5[79]161, GETTY:5[103]163, GETTY:6[62]175, GETTY:7[51]190, GETTY:7[77]191, GETTY:7[124]196, GETTY:8[53]203, GETTY:10[42]224, GETTY:10[120]229, GETTY:11[71]234, GETTY:11[91]236, GETTY:12[7]241, GETTY:12[42]244, MH:AUG/94[46]178, *Harpers Ferry,* GETTY:7[51]190, MH:AUG/95[30]185, *in book review,* ACW:JUL/93[58], ACW:SEP/94[66], CWNEWS:APR/92[4], *Knoxville,* ACW:MAY/91[23]303, *letters to the editor,* CWM:OCT/95[5]613, *Longstreet,* CWTI:JUL/92[29]272, CWTI:MAR/93[40]312, *Malvern Hill,* CWM:JUN/95[73]597, *Mexican War,* MH:APR/93[39]166, *order of battle,* B&G:DEC/95[9]615, *Savannah,* B&G:FEB/91[8]439, *Seven Pines,* CWM:JUN/95[47]588, *Upperville,* B&G:OCT/93[12]537, *Williamsburg,* ACW:MAR/91[47]297, *photos,* ACW:JAN/94[39]451, B&G:FEB/91[8]439, CWTI:MAR/93[40]312, MH:AUG/95[30]185
ADDITIONAL LISTINGS: ACW:MAR/91[12]292, ACW:JUL/92[30]369, ACW:SEP/92[30]378, ACW:SEP/92[47]380, ACW:JUL/93[50]426, ACW:SEP/93[31]433, ACW:JAN/94[8]447, ACW:MAR/94[50]462, ACW:JUL/95[10]533, CWM:MAY/92[8]418, CWM:JUL/92[16]428, CWM:JUL/92[40]432, CWM:JAN/93[8]456, CWM:JUN/94[43]517, CWM:DEC/95[54]632, CWR:VOL1#4[7]125, CWR:VOL3#2[1]153, CWR:VOL3#3[1]157, CWR:VOL4#2[68]167, CWR:VOL4#3[65]172, CWR:VOL4#4[28]178, CWR:VOL4#4[101]181, CWTI:APR/89[14]107, CWTI:SEPT/89[46]132, CWTI:SEP/91[23]228, CWTI:NOV/93[55]350, CWTI:MAY/94[50]386, CWTI:SEP/94[26]400, CWTI:JAN/95[24]424, GETTY:13[7]253, GETTY:13[75]259

McLAWS, W.R.; CWTI:MAR/93[40]312

McLEAN, E.W., *Captain, CSA;* B&G:OCT/94[11]580

McLEAN, HANCOCK T., *Lieutenant, 6th U.S. Cavalry;* B&G:AUG/94[10]574

McLEAN, JOSEPH A., *Adjutant, 14th Pennslyvania Infantry;* ARTICLE: "THE TOLL OF WAR," B&G:AUG/92[53]495A

McLEAN, NATHAN C., *Colonel, 75th Ohio Infantry;* ACW:JAN/93[35]396

McLEAN, NATHANIEL C., *Colonel, USA;* B&G:AUG/91[11]458, B&G:AUG/92[11]493, B&G:OCT/95[20]612, CWTI:MAR/94[29]371

McLEAN, WILBER, *civilian;* CWM:JUL/91[8]356, CWM:JUL/92[8]427, CWTI:FEB/90[54]147, CWTI:AUG/90[26]166, CWTI:SEP/92[42]283, CWTI:NOV/93[50]349, CWTI:MAR/95[20]433

McLEAN, WILLIAM, *Colonel, USA;* ACW:MAY/93[22]414

McLEMORE, WILLIAM S., *Colonel, 8th Tennessee Cavalry;* ACW:MAR/93[51]407, B&G:DEC/95[9]615

McLENDON, WILLIAM, *Private, 15th Alabama Infantry;* B&G:AUG/92[11]493

McLEOD, ALEXANDER, *Chaplain, 84th Pennsylvania Infantry;* CWM:SEP/93[18]494

McLIN, J.B., *Colonel, CSA;* CWR:VOL4#1[1]163
McLURE, JOHN, *Private, 14th Indiana Infantry;*
B&G:APR/95[8]595
McLURE, PARK, *Captain;* CWTI:SEP/90[52]179
McMAHAN, ARNOLD, *Major, USA;* CWTI:SEP/92[31]281
McMAHAN, M.V., *Colonel, CSA;* CWR:VOL2#3[212]142,
CWR:VOL4#2[118]169
McMAHON, BERNARD J., *Captain, 71st Pennsylvania
Infantry;* GETTY:7[97]193
McMAHON, JAMES P., *Colonel, USA;* CWM:OCT/95[40]619
McMAHON, JOHN T., *Sergeant, (136th New York Infantry);*
BOOK REVIEWS: *JOHN T. MCMAHON'S DIARY OF THE 136TH
NEW YORK 1861-1865*
McMAHON, LAURENCE S., *Chaplain, 28th Massachusetts
Infantry;* CWM:MAR/91[50]340
McMAHON, MARTIN T., *General, USA;* ACW:SEP/93[62]436,
ACW:MAR/95[70]520, B&G:DEC/95[25]616,
CWM:MAR/91[50]340, GETTY:10[42]224, GETTY:12[123]251
McMANUS, ANDREW, *Captain, 69th Pennsylvania Infantry;*
GETTY:7[97]193
McMATH, JOSEPH, *Corporal, Sumter Artillery;*
CWR:VOL3#2[1]153
McMICHAEL, RICHARDS, *Lieutenant Colonel, 53rd
Pennsylvania Infantry;* GETTY:11[80]235
McMILLAN, JAMES W., *Colonel, USA;* CWR:VOL3#1[1]149
McMILLAN, ROBERT, *Colonel, CSA;* CWTI:DEC/90[58]185
McMULLEN, J.P., *Chaplain,* CWTI:NOV/92[41]291
McMULLEN, JORDAN J., *Private, 1st Georgia Regulars;*
CWR:VOL2#2[95]135
McMILLEN, WILLIAM J., *Colonel, USA;* B&G:DEC/93[12]545,
B&G:AUG/95[8]604
McMULLIN, JAMES R., *Captain, 1st Ohio Artillery;* ARTICLE:
"FORGOTTEN VALOR: OFF THE BEATEN PATH AT
ANTIETAM: ARTILLERY HELL AND HOT COFFEE,"
B&G:OCT/95[8]611D
McMURRAY, JOHN, *Captain, 6th USCT;* CWM:AUG/94[30]527
McMURRAY, WILLIAM, *Lieutenant, 20th Tennessee Infantry;*
CWTI:SUMMER/89[20]121, CWTI:NOV/92[41]291
McMURTREY, E.L., *Major, CSA;* CWR:VOL1#2[44]114
McNAIR, EVANDER, *General, CSA;* ACW:SEP/92[66]381,
B&G:AUG/95[8]604, CWR:VOL1#1[42]105,
CWR:VOL2#1[36]132, CWTI:MAR/93[24]309
McNALLY, C.H., *Lieutenant, USA;* ACW:JUL/93[27]423
McNARY, GEORGE H., *Lieutenant, USA;* GETTY:10[42]224
McNEIL, ALEXANDER, *Lieutenant, 2nd South Carolina
Infantry;* GETTY:5[35]159
McNEIL, CHARLES, *Sergeant, CSA;* B&G:AUG/94[22]576
McNEIL, HUGH, *Colonel, USA;* CWR:VOL1#3[20]119,
CWR:VOL1#3[28]120, GETTY:9[53]214, GETTY:10[120]229,
photo, CWR:VOL1#3[20]119
McNEIL, JOHN, *General, USA;* ACW:MAR/91[62]298,
B&G:JUN/91[10]452
McNEIL, JOHN R., *Private, Sumter Artillery;*
CWR:VOL3#2[1]153
McNEILL, ARCHIBALD, *Captain, CSA;* ACW:JUL/93[66]427
McNEILL, JESSE, *Captain, CSA:*
ARTICLE: "CONFEDERATES' BRILLIANT EXPLOIT,"
ACW:SEP/91[41]323
ADDITIONAL LISTING: CWM:APR/94[24]505
McNEILL, JOHN, *General, USA;* B&G:JUN/91[10]452,
CWR:VOL1#2[44]114
McNEILL, JOHN H. "HANSE", *Captain, CSA;*
ACW:SEP/91[41]323, B&G:AUG/94[10]574

McNEILY, JOHN S., *Lieutenant, Hurricane (Mississippi) Rifles;*
GETTY:7[77]191
McNEILY, W.P., *Lieutenant, 9th Massachusetts Artillery;*
GETTY:5[47]160
McNULTY, JOHN, *Lieutenant, Baltimore Light Artillery;*
B&G:AUG/94[10]574
McPHAIL, JAMES L., CWTI:DEC/95[76]482
McPHAIL, JOHN B., *Major, 56th Virginia Infantry;*
ACW:MAR/93[10]402
McPHERSON, JAMES B., *General, USA:*
ARTICLES: "FIGHTING AT ATLANTA," CWM:AUG/94[27]526,
"SHERMAN'S FEUDING GENERALS," CWTI:MAR/95[40]43
GENERAL LISTINGS: *Atlanta Campaign,* ACW:JUL/94[66]481,
ACW:JAN/95[30]505, CWM:JAN/91[12]326,
CWM:AUG/95[36]608, CWTI:SUMMER/89[13]120,
CWTI:SUMMER/89[20]121, CWTI:SUMMER/89[40]123,
CWTI:SEP/91[23]228, CWTI:SEP/92[28]280, *Champion's Hill,*
MH:JUN/93[82]167, *in book review,* CWM:MAY/91[38],
CWNEWS:APR/93[4], CWR:VOL4#3[89], *Jackson,*
B&G:AUG/95[8]604, *letters to the editor,* CWTI:MAR/93[8]306,
CWTI:JUL/93[10]323, *order of battle,* B&G:FEB/94[8]550,
Port Gibson, ACW:JUL/94[51]480, *Resaca,*
CWTI:NOV/92[41]291, *Vicksburg,* ACW:NOV/95[22]554,
CWTI:MAY/91[24]208, *photo, where we was killed;*
CWTI:SUMMER/89[40]123, *photos,* B&G:FEB/94[8]550,
CWM:AUG/94[27]526, CWTI:SUMMER/89[13]120,
CWTI:MAR/95[40]436
ADDITIONAL LISTINGS: ACW:JUL/91[35]314, ACW:NOV/91[22]331,
ACW:JAN/93[10]393, ACW:SEP/95[48]547,
ACW:NOV/95[74]560, AHI:NOV/73[18]151,
B&G:DEC/93[12]545, B&G:FEB/94[8]550,
B&G:FEB/94[57]555, CWM:JAN/91[11]325,
CWM:JAN/91[72]331, CWM:JUN/94[58]519,
CWR:VOL1#3[82]123, CWR:VOL2#1[19]131,
CWR:VOL2#1[36]132, CWR:VOL2#4[313]146,
CWR:VOL3#3[33]158, CWR:VOL3#3[59]159,
CWTI:NOV/92[60]294, CWTI:JAN/93[20]298,
CWTI:MAR/93[24]309, MH:DEC/95[58]188
McPHERSON, W.D., *Captain, USA;* CWM:DEC/95[59]633
McQUADE, ——, *USA;* *Colonel, 14th New York Infantry;*
CWTI:JUN/90[28]158
McQUAQUE, A., *Private, 31st North Carolina Infantry;*
B&G:APR/93[24]520
McQUEEN, A.G., *Lieutenant Colonel, 1st Iowa Cavalry;*
CWTI:MAY/93[35]320
McQUEEN, JOHN A., *Lieutenant, 15th Illinois Infantry;*
ARTICLE: "MY FRIEND, THE ENEMY," B&G:DEC/92[20]504
McQUESTEN, JAMES F., *Captain, USA;* B&G:DEC/91[12]469
McRAE, ALEXANDER, *Captain, USA;* CWM:MAY/93[16]475,
CWTI:OCT/95[56]471, B&G:JUN/94[8]568
McRAE, C.D., *Lieutenant, 2nd Texas Mounted Rifles;*
ACW:JUL/91[58]316
McRAE, COLIN J., *General, CSA;* AHI:JUN/70[30]127
McRAE, D., *Private, 13th Mississippi Infantry;* GETTY:10[53]225
McRAE, D.K., *Colonel, 5th North Carolina Infantry;*
ACW:MAR/91[47]297, ACW:JUL/92[30]369,
B&G:FEB/95[8]590B
McRAE, DANDRIDGE, *General, CSA;* ACW:MAY/91[12]302,
ACW:MAY/93[22]414
McRAE, JOHN, *Governor, Mississippi;* AHI:JUN/70[30]127
McRAE, WILLIAM, *civilian;* AHI:DEC/77[13]176
McRAE, WILLIAM, *Colonel, CSA;* B&G:APR/92[8]481

McRAVEN (VICKSBURG, MISSISSIPPI) PLANTATION; B&G:OCT/91[11]466

McVAY, FRANCIS, JAMES and MICHAEL, *14th Connecticut Infantry;* GETTY:9[61]215

McWHORTER, JAMES, *Lieutenant, 3rd Georgia Infantry;* CWTI:DEC/94[32]410

MEAD, CHRISTOPHER, *Corporal, 12th New Jersey Infantry;* GETTY:5[89]162

MEADE, GEORGE G., *General, USA:*

ARTICLES: "THE ARMY OF THE POTOMAC'S PROUD III CORPS FELL VICTIM TO INTRA-ARMY POLITICS," ACW:JUL/93[16]422, "BLACK THURSDAY FOR REBELS," ACW:JAN/92[22]341, "DOUBLY MISSED OPPORTUNITY," ACW:MAR/93[26]404, "THE FALL OF RICHMOND," ACW:MAY/95[38]526, "GETTYSBURG FINALE," ACW:JUL/93[50]426, "HIS LEFT WAS WORTH A GLANCE: MEADE AND THE UNION LEFT ON JULY 2, 1863," GETTY:7[29]188, "I HAVE A GREAT CONTEMPT FOR HISTORY,'" CWTI:SEP/91[31]229, "LEE FOILS MEADE AT MINE RUN," CWM:DEC/94[44]551

BOOK REVIEWS: *A CASPIAN SEA OF INK: THE MEADE-SICKLES CONTROVERSY * THE BATTLE OF GETTYSBURG * THE LIFE AND LETTERS OF GEORGE GORDON MEADE, MAJOR-GENERAL UNITED STATES ARMY * MEADE OF GETTYSBURG * MEADE'S HEADQUARTERS, 1863-1865: LETTERS OF COLONEL THEODORE LYMAN FROM THE WILDERNESS TO APPOMATTOX * WITH GRANT AND MEADE: FROM THE WILDERNESS TO APPOMATTOX*

GENERAL LISTINGS: *Antietam,* ACW:JUL/92[30]369, *Appomattox Campaign,* CWTI:AUG/90[26]166, *Ball's Bluff,* AHI:FEB/82[36]225, *Beaver Dam Creek,* CWM:JUN/95[57]592, *Benjamin F. Butler,* CWTI:MAY/93[29]319, *The "Crater",* CWTI:APR/90[24]152, *Chancellorsville,* ACW:MAY/95[30]525, *Cold Harbor,* ACW:SEP/93[62]436, B&G:APR/94[10]558, CWR:VOL3#4[1]161, *Falling Waters,* GETTY:9[109]218, *Five Forks,* B&G:APR/92[8]481, *Fredericksburg,* ACW:MAR/95[42]517, AHI:JUN/78[4]180, CWR:VOL4#4[1]177, CWR:VOL4#4[70]180, *Gaines' Mill,* CWM:JUN/95[61]593, *general history,* AHI:MAY/71[3]133A

GENERAL LISTINGS, continued: *Gettysburg,* ACW:JAN/92[38]343, ACW:NOV/92[42]388, AHI:SUM/88[12]273, CWM:JUL/92[8]427, CWM:JAN/93[8]456, CWM:DEC/95[54]632, CWTI:SEPT/89[46]132, CWTI:AUG/91[62]221, CWTI:MAR/94[24]370, GETTY:4[7]142, GETTY:4[49]147, GETTY:4[101]151, GETTY:4[110]152, GETTY:4[113]153, GETTY:5[19]158, GETTY:5[47]160, GETTY:5[79]161, GETTY:5[103]163, GETTY:6[7]169, GETTY:6[33]172, GETTY:6[43]173, GETTY:6[59]174, GETTY:6[77]177, GETTY:6[87]178, GETTY:7[23]187, GETTY:7[51]190, GETTY:7[97]193, GETTY:8[31]201, GETTY:8[43]202, GETTY:8[53]203, GETTY:8[67]204, GETTY:8[111]206, GETTY:8[127]208, GETTY:9[5]209, GETTY:9[53]214, GETTY:9[61]215, GETTY:9[81]216, GETTY:10[7]221, GETTY:10[36]223, GETTY:10[42]224, GETTY:10[53]225, GETTY:10[107]227, GETTY:10[112]228, GETTY:11[19]232, GETTY:11[71]234, GETTY:11[80]235, GETTY:11[91]236, GETTY:11[102]237, GETTY:12[7]241, GETTY:12[30]243, GETTY:12[42]244, GETTY:12[68]246, GETTY:12[85]248, GETTY:12[97]249, MH:DEC/91[54]155, MH:AUG/94[46]178

GENERAL LISTINGS, continued: *Grand Review,* ACW:SEP/94[55]489, CWTI:AUG/90[64]170, *Grant,* ACW:NOV/94[34]496, *in book review,* ACW:MAY/94[58], ACW:SEP/94[66], CWM:DEC/94[7], CWM:FEB/95[7], CWM:AUG/95[45], CWNEWS:MAY/90[4], CWNEWS:AUG/90[4], CWNEWS:SEP/90[4], CWNEWS:JAN/91[4], CWNEWS:JUN/91[4], CWNEWS:JUL/91[4], CWNEWS:APR/92[4], CWNEWS:AUG/92[4], CWNEWS:MAY/93[4], CWNEWS:JUN/93[5], CWNEWS:AUG/95[33], CWNEWS:SEP/95[33], CWNEWS:NOV/95[29], CWNEWS:DEC/95[29], CWR:VOL2#2[169], CWR:VOL4#3[89], CWTI:MAR/94[12], MH:AUG/92[76], *in order of battle,* B&G:APR/94[10]558, *Jericho Mill,* B&G:APR/93[12]518, *Kelly's Ford,* ACW:NOV/91[30]332, *letters to the editor,* B&G:JUN/93[6]523, CWTI:FEB/92[8]245, CWTI:APR/92[8]252

GENERAL LISTINGS, continued: *Mexican War,* AHI:MAY/88[38]270, MH:APR/93[34]165, MH:APR/93[39]166, *order of battle,* B&G:APR/95[8]595, *Overland Campaign,* B&G:APR/94[10]558, *Petersburg,* CWTI:FEB/91[28]192, CWTI:FEB/91[45]194, MH:APR/95[46]183, *Post War,* AHI:AUG/78[33]184, *Rappahannock Station,* ACW:MAR/92[30]352, *West Point,* B&G:DEC/91[12]469, *Wilderness,* ACW:MAY/93[31]415, B&G:APR/95[8]595, B&G:JUN/95[8]600, *Winfield Scott,* AHI:JUL/81[20]221

PHOTOS: ACW:MAR/93[26]404, AHI:MAY/71[3]133A, B&G:APR/91[8]445, B&G:APR/93[12]518, B&G:APR/94[10]558, B&G:APR/95[8]595, CWM:DEC/94[44]551, CWR:VOL4#4[1]177, CWTI:APR/90[24]152, CWTI:FEB/91[24]191, CWTI:SEP/91[31]229, GETTY:12[85]248

ADDITIONAL LISTINGS, ACW: ACW:MAR/91[30]295, ACW:JUL/91[35]314, ACW:NOV/91[41]334, ACW:JUL/92[41]370, ACW:NOV/92[8]383, ACW:NOV/92[26]386, ACW:MAY/93[14]413, ACW:NOV/93[50]444, ACW:MAR/94[27]459, ACW:MAY/94[35]469, ACW:SEP/94[38]487, ACW:SEP/94[55]489, ACW:JAN/95[20]504, ACW:MAR/95[42]517, ACW:MAR/95[70]520, ACW:JUL/95[26]535, ACW:JUL/95[50]538, ACW:SEP/95[74]550

ADDITIONAL LISTINGS, AHI: AHI:APR/85[18]250, AHI:NOV/88[37]278

ADDITIONAL LISTINGS, B&G: B&G:APR/91[8]445, B&G:APR/91[36]448, B&G:AUG/91[32]461, B&G:DEC/91[34]470, B&G:OCT/92[10]496, B&G:DEC/92[8]503, B&G:APR/93[12]518, B&G:OCT/93[12]537, B&G:FEB/94[8]550, B&G:FEB/95[8]590A, B&G:APR/95[33]597

ADDITIONAL LISTINGS, CWM: CWM:NOV/91[12]390, CWM:MAY/92[8]418, CWM:MAY/92[15]419, CWM:MAY/92[20]420, CWM:JUL/92[16]428, CWM:JUL/92[18]429, CWM:SEP/92[19]440, CWM:MAR/93[24]467, CWM:AUG/94[60]531, CWM:FEB/95[30]561, CWM:JUN/95[17]581, CWM:AUG/95[27]605

ADDITIONAL LISTINGS, CWR: CWR:VOL1#3[28]120, CWR:VOL1#3[46]121, CWR:VOL1#3[52]122, CWR:VOL2#2[118]136, CWR:VOL2#2[141]137, CWR:VOL2#3[212]142, CWR:VOL2#4[269]145, CWR:VOL3#2[70]155, CWR:VOL3#3[1]157, CWR:VOL3#4[1]161

ADDITIONAL LISTINGS, CWTI: CWTI:MAY/89[28]117, CWTI:MAY/89[36]118, CWTI:DEC/89[34]136, CWTI:FEB/90[46]146, CWTI:SEP/90[22]173, CWTI:SEP/90[34]176, CWTI:FEB/91[24]191, CWTI:APR/92[35]257, CWTI:MAY/92[45]266,

CWTI:SEP/92[28]280, CWTI:NOV/92[49]292,
CWTI:JAN/95[34]427, CWTI:MAR/95[33]435,
CWTI:DEC/95[67]481, CWTI:DEC/95[76]482
ADDITIONAL LISTINGS, GETTY: GETTY:13[7]253, GETTY:13[50]257,
GETTY:13[89]260, GETTY:13[119]262
ADDITIONAL LISTINGS, MH: MH:APR/92[18]157, MH:FEB/93[42]164,
MH:JUN/94[8]177
VIDEO: "MEADE OF GETTYSBURG," CWTI:NOV/93[14]
MEADE, GEORGE G. JR., *Major, USA;* B&G:DEC/91[12]469,
GETTY:10[53]225, GETTY:11[102]237
MEADE, JOHN S.; CWTI:SEP/91[31]229
MEADE-SICKLES CONTROVERSY: GETTY:4[115]152,
GETTY:6[113]183
MEADOR, W.J., *Private, 22nd Virginia Infantry;*
CWR:VOL1#3[52]122
MEAGHER, JOSEPHINE; B&G:OCT/93[31]539
MEAGHER, THOMAS F., *General, USA:*
ARTICLES: "THE FIGHTING IRISH," CWM:MAR/91[17]335,
"MEAGHER OF THE SWORD," ACW:SEP/95[54]548
GENERAL LISTINGS: *in book review,* CWM:MAR/91[74],
CWM:FEB/95[7], CWNEWS:AUG/93[5], *Sickles murder trial,*
ACW:SEP/95[54]548, *photos,* ACW:SEP/95[54]548,
CWM:MAR/91[28]336, CWTI:DEC/90[58]185
ADDITIONAL LISTINGS: ACW:MAY/94[12]466, ACW:SEP/95[70]549,
B&G:OCT/95[36]614, CWM:MAR/91[14]334,
CWM:MAR/91[28]336, CWM:MAR/91[50]340,
CWM:MAR/92[27]412, CWR:VOL4#4[47]179,
CWTI:DEC/90[58]185, CWTI:SEP/91[42]231,
CWTI:MAY/94[31]382, CWTI:SEP/94[26]400,
CWTI:AUG/95[24]455
MEBANE, JOHN, *Captain, Johnston's Tennessee Artillery;*
B&G:AUG/95[8]604
MECHANICSVILLE, VIRGINIA, BATTLE OF; see listings
under "**BEAVER DAM CREEK, VIRGINIA, BATTLE OF**"

MEDAL OF HONOR:
ARTICLE: "A SHOWER OF STARS AT NEW MARKET
HEIGHTS," CWM:AUG/94[30]527
BOOK REVIEWS: *A SHOWER OF STARS; THE MEDAL OF
HONOR AND THE 27TH MAINE * ABOVE AND BEYOND:
A HISTORY OF THE MEDAL OF HONOR FROM THE CIVIL
WAR TO VIETNAM * THE GREAT LOCOMOTIVE CHASE:
MORE ON THE ANDREWS RAID AND THE FIRST MEDAL
OF HONOR*
Anderson, Peter, *Private, 1st Wisconsin Infantry;*
B&G:DEC/95[9]615
Andrews' Raiders; see listings under "**ANDREWS, JAMES J.**"
Bacon, Elijah, *Private, 14th Connecticut Infantry;*
GETTY:9[61]215
Barnum, Henry, *Colonel, 149th New York Infantry;*
CWTI:SEPT/89[30]129
Black, John Charles, *Lieutenant Colonel, 37th Illinois Infantry;*
CWR:VOL1#1[42]105
Blickensderfer, Milton A., *Sergeant, 126th Ohio Infantry:*
ARTICLE: "MEDAL OF HONOR RECIPIENT,"
CWTI:AUG/95[90]462
ADDITIONAL LISTING: CWTI:DEC/95[8]474
Brown, Jerry Z., *Captain, 148th Pennsylvania Infantry;*
CWR:VOL2#2[141]137
Brown, Morris, *Captain, 126th New York Infantry;*
CWR:VOL1#4[7]125, GETTY:8[95]205
Buckles, Abram J.; *Sergeant, B&G:APR/95[8]595*

Burke, Thomas, *Private, 97th New York Infantry;*
B&G:FEB/91[34]442
Butterfield, Daniel; CWTI:JUN/95[32]446
Carney, William H.; *Sergeant, 54th Massachusetts Infantry;*
ACW:SEP/91[30]322, ACW:MAR/93[58], CWTI:DEC/89[42]137
Cart, Jacob, *Private, 7th Pennsylvania Reserves;*
CWR:VOL4#4[1]177
Chamberlain, Joshua L.; *General;* ACW:JAN/92[38]343,
CWR:VOL2#3[256]
Clark, Harrison, *Private, 125th New York Infantry;*
B&G:FEB/93[40]514, GETTY:7[51]190
Cohn, Abraham, *Captain, 68th New York Infantry;*
CWM:SEP/93[8]493, CWTI:MAY/92[38]265
Corliss, Stephen P., *4th New York Artillery;*
B&G:FEB/93[40]514
Cross, James E., *12th New York Infantry;* B&G:FEB/93[40]514
Custer, Thomas, *Lieutenant;* B&G:APR/91[6]444
Cutts, James M., *Captain;* AHI:NOV/70[22]130
Davis, George E., *10th Vermont Infantry;* ACW:NOV/93[50]444,
B&G:DEC/92[8]503
DeLacy, Patrick, *Sergeant, 143rd Pennsylvania Infantry;*
B&G:JUN/95[8]600
di Cesnola, Luigi P., *Colonel;* ARTICLE: "THE ONLY MEDAL OF
HONOR EARNED IN THE LOUDOUN VALLEY FIGHTING,"
B&G:OCT/93[21]38, B&G:APR/94[6]557
Dodds, Edward E., *Sergeant, 21st New York Cavalry;*
CWM:SEP/93[18]494
Donohue, Timothy, *Private;* CWTI:DEC/90[58]185
Dore, George H., *Sergeant;* GETTY:8[95]205
DuPont, Henry; B&G:DEC/91[12]469
Fitzpatrick, Thomas, *USN;* CWM:SEP/93[18]494
Flynn, Christopher; *Corporal, 14th Connecticut Infantry;*
GETTY:9[61]215
Follett, Joseph L., *1st Missouri Artillery;* B&G:FEB/93[40]514
Force, Manning F.; ACW:JAN/95[30]505
Gause, Issac, *Corporal;* CWM:SEP/93[8]493
Godley, Leonidas, *Sergeant, 22nd Iowa Infantry;*
CWR:VOL2#1[19]131
Greenwalt, Abraham, *Private, 104th Ohio Infantry;*
CWM:SEP/93[8]493, CWTI:MAY/92[38]265
Haney, Milton L., *55th Illinois Infantry;* B&G:APR/93[40]522,
CWTI:SEP/92[28]280
Heller, Henry, *Private, 66th Ohio Infantry;* CWM:SEP/93[8]493,
CWTI:MAY/92[38]265
Hibson, Joseph, *Private, 48th New York Infantry;*
ACW:SEP/91[30]322
Hickman, John; ACW:MAR/92[40]353
Hill, Edward; *Captain;* GETTY:6[33]172
Howard, Oliver O.; GETTY:11[71]234
Howe, Orion P., *55th Illinois Infantry;* ACW:NOV/92[8]383
Johnson, R.M., *Major, 100th Indiana Infantry;*
CWR:VOL1#1[73]108
Kappesser, Peter, *Private, 149th New York Infantry;*
CWTI:SEPT/89[30]129
Karpeles, Leopold, *57th Massachusetts Infantry;*
ACW:SEP/95[70]549, CWM:SEP/93[8]493,
CWTI:MAY/92[38]265,
Keele, Joseph, *170th New York Infantry;* B&G:APR/93[12]518
Kelly, Alexander, *Sergeant, USCT;* CWM:AUG/94[4]520,
CWM:AUG/94[30]527
Kephardt, James, *Private, 13th U.S. Regulars;*
CWR:VOL2#1[1]130
King, Robert H.; B&G:FEB/93[40]514

Kirk, Jonathan C., *20th Indiana Infantry;* B&G:APR/93[12]518

Knight, Charles, *Corporal, 9th New Hampshire Infantry;* CWR:VOL2#2[118]136

Lawson, John H., *Private;* B&G:DEC/92[40]508

Leon, Pierre, CWTI:DEC/94[12]408

Levy, Benjamin B., *1st New York Infantry;* CWM:SEP/93[8]493, CWTI:MAY/92[38]265

MacArthur, Arthur; ACW:MAR/92[14]350

Mattocks, Charles, *Major, 17th Maine Infantry;* CWR:VOL4#3[37], CWR:VOL4#4[129]

McClelland, Matthew; ACW:MAR/92[40]353

Miles, Nelson A.; ACW:MAY/95[30]525

Miller, William E.; GETTY:13[89]260

Murphy, Michael C., B&G:APR/93[12]518

Nibbe, John H., B&G:FEB/91[34]442

Norton, Oliver W.; B&G:AUG/93[30]531

O'Brien, Henry D., *Corporal, 1st Minnesota Infantry;* ACW:JAN/94[62]

O'Connor, T., *1st U.S. Cavalry;* ACW:JUL/93[42]425

O'Neil, S., *Corporal, 7th U.S. Infantry;* ACW:JUL/93[42]425

Orbanski, David, *Private, 58th Ohio Infantry;* CWM:SEP/93[8]493, CWTI:MAY/92[38]265

Patterson, John H., *11th U.S. Infantry;* B&G:FEB/93[40]514

Pelham, William, *USN;* CWM:SEP/93[18]494

Pitman, George A., *Sergeant, 1st New York Cavalry;* CWR:VOL3#2[1]153

Post, Philip S., *General;* B&G:APR/91[36]448

Postles, James P., *Captain;* GETTY:5[89]162

Potter, Norman; *Sergeant, 149th New York Infantry;* CWTI:SEPT/89[30]129

Purcell, Hiram; *Sergeant;* CWM:JUN/95[47]588

Quinlan, James, *Major, 88th New York Infantry;* ACW:MAY/94[12]466

Rafferty, Peter, *Private, 69th New York Infantry;* ACW:MAY/94[12]466

Reed, Charles, *Private, 9th Massachusetts Artillery;* GETTY:5[47]160

Roberts, Otis O.; ACW:MAR/92[30]352

Rush, John; ACW:MAR/92[40]353

Schorn, Charles, *1st West Virginia Cavalry;* CWR:VOL3#2[1]153

Scott, Alexander; *B&G:DEC/92[8]503*

Scott, Julian; CWTI:SEP/91[54]232

Shafter, William O.; BOOK REVIEW: *"PECOS BILL": A MILITARY BIOGRAPHY OF WILLIAM R. SHAFTER*

Sherman, Marshall, *Private, 1st Minnesota Infantry;* GETTY:5[79]161

Shivers, John, *Private, USMC;* CWM:SEP/93[18]494

Simons, Charles, *Sergeant, 9th New Hampshire Infantry;* CWR:VOL2#2[118]136

Stahel, Julius; MH:OCT/93[6]170

Stephens, William G.; CWTI:SEP/91[18]227

Thomas, Stephen, *General;* CWR:VOL3#1[1]149

Tobie, Edward P.; CWTI:FEB/91[66]196

Tozier, Andrew J., *Sergeant, 2nd Maine Infantry;* CWTI:NOV/92[10]

Twombly, Voltaire P., *Private, 2nd Iowa Infantry:*

ARTICLE: "VOLTAIRE P. TWOMBLY, 2ND IOWA INFANTRY, MEDAL OF HONOR," B&G:FEB/92[48]475

ADDITIONAL LISTING: B&G:FEB/92[10]474

Valentine, Joseph E.; ACW:MAR/92[40]353

Vifquain, Victor, *General;* CWNEWS:SEP/94[33], MH:APR/94[54]176

von Vegesack, Ernst; B&G:OCT/95[8]611B

Walker, Mary;

ARTICLE: "MARY WALKER: SAMARITAN OR CHARLATAN," CWTI:MAY/94[40]383

ADDITIONAL LISTINGS: CWM:APR/94[8]502, CWTI:SEP/94[12]398

Wall, Jerry, *Private, 126th New York Infantry;* CWR:VOL1#4[7]125, GETTY:8[95]205

Waller, Francis A.; ARTICLE: "FRANCIS ASBURY WALLER: A MEDAL OF HONOR AT GETTYSBURG," GETTY:4[16]143

Ward, Nelson W., *Sergeant, 11th Pennsylvania Cavalry;* CWM:MAY/92[34]422

Whitman, Frank M., *Corporal, 35th Massachusetts Infantry;* CWTI:FEB/92[36]249

Wilkins, Leander, *Private, 9th New Hampshire Infantry;* CWR:VOL2#2[118]136

William Johnston, *3rd Vermont Infantry;* ACW:NOV/92[8]383

Wllliams, Leroy, *Sergeant, 8th New York Heavy Artillery;* B&G:APR/94[55]564

Wisner, Lewis; CWM:DEC/94[40]550

Wood, Daniel A., *Private, 1st Virginia Cavalry;* B&G:FEB/91[34]442

MEDALS:

Davis Guards Medal; CWTI:DEC/90[29]182

Medal of Honor: see various listings under **"MEDAL OF HONOR"**

MEDFORD HISTORICAL SOCIETY MUSEUM; ARTICLE: "TREASURE IN THE ATTIC," CWTI:MAY/91[34]209

MEDICAL BUREAU OF THE UNITED STATES ARMY; GETTY:12[97]249

MEDICAL PURVEYOR'S DEPARTMENT; GETTY:8[121]207

MEDICAL SCIENCE; ARTICLE: "ATTITUDES OF DEATH," CWTI:JUL/92[36]273

MEDICAL: also see various listings under **"HOSPITALS, CONFEDERATE, FEDERAL AND GENERAL INFORMATION"**

ARTICLES: "A CONFEDERATE SURGEON'S VIEW OF FORT DONELSON: THE DIARY OF JOHN KENNERLY FARRIS," CWR:VOL1#3[7]118, "A HEALING PLACE," CWM:MAY/91[40]351, "A SURGEON'S HANDIWORK," GETTY:12[83]247, "THE ARMY DISEASE," AHI:DEC/71[10]137, "THE *CONFEDERATE STATES MEDICAL & SURGICAL JOURNAL* WAS AN INVALUABLE CONDUIT TO SOUTHERN DOCTORS IN THE FIELD," ACW:MAY/95[8]522, "CONFIDENT PLANS, GRIM REALITY," CWM:MAY/91[18]348, "GETTYSBURG'S ABANDONED WOUNDED," CWM:DEC/95[54]632, "HOW IT FELT TO BE SHOT AT," AHI:OCT/67[26]112, "I SHALL BE A PRISONER," CWTI:SEP/91[42]231, "INVISIBLE ENEMIES," CWM:MAY/91[26]349, "THE LADY'S CARRYING A SCALPEL?," CWM:APR/94[8]502, "LIMBS MADE AND UNMADE BY WAR," ACW:SEP/95[38]546

ARTICLES, continued: "ORDNANCE," ACW:SEP/91[10]319, "THE UNION SECOND CORPS HOSPITAL AT GETTYSBURG, JULY 2 TO AUGUST 8, 1863," GETTY:10[53]225, "TWENTY-SEVEN KINDS OF DRUNK: A SAMPLING OF DRUNKEN TALES FROM UNION COURT MARTIAL RECORDS," B&G:APR/95[24]596, "WAR'S 'WONDER' DRUGS," ACW:MAY/94[51]471, "WITH A CONFEDERATE SURGEON AT VICKSBURG," AHI:JUL/68[31]115A, "THE WOUNDED OF SHILOH," CWM:MAY/91[10]347

BOOK REVIEWS: *A CONFEDERATE NURSE: THE DIARY OF ADA W. BACOT, 1860-1863 * A MANUAL OF MILITARY SURGERY, FOR THE USE OF SURGEONS IN THE CONFEDERATE ARMY; WITH AN APPENDIX OF THE RULES AND REGULATIONS OF THE MEDICAL DEPARTMENT OF THE CONFEDERATE ARMY * A MANUAL OF MILITARY SURGERY: OR HINTS ON THE EMERGENCIES OF FIELD, CAMP, AND HOSPITAL PRACTICE * A MANUAL OF MINOR SURGERY * A PRACTICAL TREATISE ON MILITARY SURGERY * A SURGEON'S CIVIL WAR: THE LETTERS AND DIARY OF DANIEL M. HOLT, M.D. * A VAST SEA OF MISERY: A HISTORY AND GUIDE TO THE UNION AND CONFEDERATE FIELD HOSPITALS AT GETTYSBURG JULY 1-NOVEMBER 20, 1863 * A WOMAN OF VALOR: CLARA BARTON AND THE CIVIL WAR * AN ALPHABETICAL LIST OF THE BATTLES OF THE WAR OF THE REBELLION, WITH DATES, FROM FT. SUMTER, SC, APRIL AND 13, 1861, TO KIRBY SMITH'S SURRENDER, MAY 26, 1865 * AN EPITOME OF PRACTICAL SURGERY FOR FIELD AND HOSPITAL * CIVIL WAR MEDICINE: CARE AND COMFORT OF THE WOUNDED, * CONFEDERATE HOSPITALS ON THE MOVE: SAMUEL H. STOUT AND THE ARMY OF TENNESSEE * DOCTORS IN GRAY: THE CONFEDERATE MEDICAL SERVICE * DOCTORS IN BLUE: THE MEDICAL HISTORY OF THE UNION ARMY IN THE CIVIL WAR, * FARMCARTS TO FORDS: A HISTORY OF THE MILITARY AMBULANCE, 1790-1925 * GUNSHOT WOUNDS AND OTHER INJURIES OF NERVES*

BOOK REVIEWS, continued: *HAND-BOOK FOR THE MILITARY SURGEON: BEING A COMPENDIUM OF THE DUTIES OF THE MEDICAL OFFICER IN THE FIELD, THE SANITARY NAGEMENT OF THE CAMP, THE PREPARATION OF FOOD, ETC.... * HAND-BOOK OF SURGICAL OPERATIONS * IN HOSPITAL AND CAMP: THE CIVIL WAR THROUGH THE EYES OF ITS DOCTORS AND NURSES * KILLED IN ACTION: EYEWITNESS ACCOUNTS OF THE LAST MOMENTS OF 100 UNION SOLDIERS WHO DIED AT GETTYSBURG * MANUAL OF MILITARY SURGERY, PREPARED FOR THE USE OF THE CONFEDERATE STATES ARMY BY ORDER OF THE SURGEON-GENERAL * THE MEDICAL AND SURGICAL HISTORY OF THE WAR OF THE REBELLION. (1861-1865) * MEDICAL HISTORIES OF CONFEDERATE GENERALS * MEDICAL-MILITARY PORTRAITS OF UNION AND CONFEDERATE GENERALS*

BOOK REVIEWS, continued: *MICROBES AND MINIE BALLS: AN ANNOTATED BIBLIOGRAPHY OF CIVIL WAR MEDICINE * REGULATIONS FOR THE MEDICAL DEPARTMENT OF THE ARMY * THE STORY THE SOLDIERS WOULDN'T TELL: SEX IN THE CIVIL WAR * TREATISE ON GUN-SHOT WOUNDS: WRITTEN FOR AND DEDICATED TO SURGEONS OF THE CONFEDERATE STATES ARMY * THE WOUNDED RIVER: THE CIVIL WAR LETTERS OF JOHN VANCE LAUDERDALE, M.D.*

Yellow Fever: "A LONG WAR AND A SICKLY SEASON," B&G:JUN/92[40]489, "YELLOW FEVER," AHI:MAY/67[42]109

MEDILL, WILLIAM H., *Major, 8th Illinois Cavalry;* B&G:FEB/93[24]512, GETTY:11[19]232

MEEK, PETER G., ARTICLE: "PETER GRAY MEEK: STRIDENT COPPERHEAD EDITOR," CWM:APR/95[63]578

MEGLONE, WHITNEY W., *Private, 2nd Kentucky Cavalry;* CWM:MAR/93[16]466

MEHRINGER, JOHN, *Colonel, USA;* B&G:DEC/93[12]545

MEIGS, JOHN R., *Major, USA;* B&G:DEC/91[12]469, CWTI:OCT/95[48]470, *photo,* B&G:DEC/91[12]469

MEIGS, MONTGOMERY C.:
ARTICLES: "A PEEK INTO THE PAST," CWTI:AUG/95[10]453, "METICULOUS MR. MEIGS," AHI:NOV/80[34]212

BOOK REVIEWS: *QUARTERMASTER GENERAL OF THE UNION ARMY: A BIOGRAPHY OF M.C. MEIGS*

ADDITIONAL LISTINGS: GETTY:12[97]249, B&G:DEC/91[12]469, CWM:NOV/91[58]394A, CWTI:DEC/95[67]481, CWTI:MAR/95[8]431, B&G:APR/91[40]450, AHI:JAN/84[8], *photo,* AHI:NOV/80[34]212

MEITTENGER, GUSTAVUS, *Chaplain, 2nd New York Infantry;* CWM:MAR/91[50]340

MELCHER, HOLMAN S., *Major, 20th Maine Infantry:*
BOOK REVIEWS: *WITH A FLASH OF HIS SWORD: THE WRITINGS OF MAJOR HOLMAN S. MELCHER, 20TH MAINE INFANTRY*

ADDITIONAL LISTINGS: ACW:JAN/92[38]343, GETTY:6[43]173

MELCHER, SAMUEL H., *Surgeon, USA;* ACW:NOV/93[26]441

RICHARD KING MELLON FOUNDATION; B&G:JUN/92[6]486

MELOY, GEORGE, *Private, 5th New York Infantry;* CWR:VOL1#2[7]111

MELTON, ISAAC W., *Colonel, 28th Louisiana Infantry;* CWR:VOL4#2[118]169

MELVILLE, HERMAN:
BOOK REVIEWS: *THE CIVIL WAR WORLD OF HERMAN MELVILLE*

POEM: "BALL'S BLUFF"; CWTI:MAY/89[14]114

MELVIN, JOHN; BOOK REVIEW: *NORTH INTO FREEDOM: THE AUTOBIOGRAPHY OF JOHN MALVIN, FREE NEGRO, 1795-1880*

MELVIN, THAYER, *Major, USA;* ACW:SEP/91[41]323

MEMMINGER, CHRISTOPHER G.:
BOOK REVIEW: *FINANCIAL FAILURE AND CONFEDERATE DEFEAT*

ADDITIONAL LISTINGS: ACW:JUL/91[8]309, ACW:JUL/91[14]311, B&G:FEB/92[26], CWM:MAR/91[74], CWM:MAR/92[32]413, CWM:MAR/92[49], CWTI:AUG/91[36]217, CWTI:AUG/95[46]459

MEMPHIS, TENNESSEE, BATTLE OF; ACW:NOV/92[35]387, ACW:MAR/95[18]514, CWTI:FEB/90[38]145, MH:DEC/95[58]188

MENDENHALL, GEORGE, *surgeon;* B&G:OCT/94[28]581

MENGES, JACOB, *Private, 11th Pennsylvania Infantry;* GETTY:10[7]221

MENNET, OVERTON, *Union veteran;* GETTY:7[119]195

MERCER, HUGH W., *General, CSA;* AHI:MAR/84[42]238, CWTI:SEP/92[28]280

MERCER, JOHN T., *Colonel, 21st Georgia Infantry;* GETTY:4[33]146

MERCER, O.E., *Lieutenant, 20th North Carolina Infantry;* B&G:FEB/95[8]590B

MERCIER, HENRI, *French ambassador;* CWTI:MAY/89[28]117, CWTI:DEC/90[50]183

MEREDITH, SOLOMON, *General, USA:*
GENERAL LISTINGS: *Gettysburg,* AHI:MAY/67[22]107, GETTY:4[33]146, GETTY:5[4]156, GETTY:5[19]158, GETTY:6[13]170, GETTY:6[29]171, GETTY:7[23]187, GETTY:11[57]233, GETTY:11[71]234, *in book review,* CWR:VOL1#2[78], *Manassas, Second,* B&G:AUG/92[11]493

ADDITIONAL LISTINGS: CWM:JAN/93[16]457, CWR:VOL1#3[52]122, CWR:VOL2#4[269]145, GETTY:13[22]254

MEREDITH, SULLIVAN A., *General, USA;* GETTY:7[77]191, GETTY:10[102]226

MERICLE, ALBERT, *Captain, 154th New York Infantry;* GETTY:8[17]200

MERIDIAN CAMPAIGN: ACW:SEP/95[48]547, CWR:VOL2#4[313]146, CWR:VOL2#4[343]147, CWR:VOL4#2[26]166

MERION, NATHANIEL, *Civilian;* B&G:OCT/94[11]580

MERKLE, CHARLES, *Lieutenant, USA;* B&G:FEB/95[8]590C

MERRELL, JOSEPH W., *Captain, 27th Illinois Infantry;* CWR:VOL3#4[24]162

MERRIAM, WALDO, *Lieutenant Colonel, 16th Massachusetts Infantry;* GETTY:12[7]241

MERRICK, MORGAN W., *Private, 2nd Texas Mounted Rifles;* BOOK REVIEWS: *FROM DESERT TO BAYOU: THE CIVIL WAR JOURNAL AND SKETCHES OF MORGAN WOLFE MERRICK*

MERRILL, CHARLES B., *Lieutenant Colonel, 17th Maine Infantry;* GETTY:8[43]202

MERRILL, JAMES, *Lieutenant, 7th Rhode Island Infantry;* CWTI:AUG/90[64]170

MERRILL, LEWIS, *Colonel, USA;* CWR:VOL1#2[44]114

MERRILL, RANSOM P., *civilian;* B&G:FEB/91[20]440

MERRILL, SAMUEL, *Colonel, 21st Iowa Infantry;* B&G:FEB/94[8]550

MERRILL, WILLIAM E., *Colonel, USA;* CWTI:NOV/92[60]294

MERRIMON, AUGUSTUS S., *civilian;* B&G:FEB/91[20]440

MERRITT, WESLEY, *General, USA:*
GENERAL LISTINGS: "LOST IN CUSTER'S SHADOW," ACW:SEP/94[55]489
GENERAL LISTINGS: *3rd Winchester,* ACW:MAY/91[38]305, *Aldie,* GETTY:11[19]232, *Brandy Station,* GETTY:11[19]232, *Cedar Creek,* MH:OCT/93[76]173, *Five Forks,* B&G:APR/92[8]481, *Gettysburg,* GETTY:4[101]151, GETTY:4[75]149, GETTY:11[19]232, *in order of battle,* B&G:APR/92[8]481, B&G:APR/94[10]558, B&G:APR/95[8]595, *Overland Campaign,* B&G:APR/94[10]558, *Sayler's Creek,* ACW:JAN/92[22]341, *Trevilian Station,* MH:FEB/93[42]164, *Yellow Tavern,* ACW:MAY/94[35]469, *photos,* ACW:JAN/93[43]397, ACW:SEP/94[55]489, GETTY:11[19]232
ADDITIONAL LISTINGS: ACW:JUL/92[41]370, ACW:SEP/94[6]482, ACW:SEP/94[38]487, B&G:APR/91[8]445, B&G:AUG/94[10]574, CWM:JAN/93[40]461, CWTI:JUN/90[32]159, CWTI:APR/92[35]257, CWTI:MAY/92[32]264, GETTY:13[89]260

MERRITT, WILLIAM H., *Lieutenant Colonel, 1st Iowa Infantry;* CWTI:FEB/92[29]248

MERRIWETHER, CLAYTON, *Captain, CSA;* CWM:MAR/93[16]466

MERRIWETHER, NED, *Captain, 1st Kentucky Cavalry* ACW:MAR/93[51]407

MERRYMAN, JAMES H., *Lieutenant, USN;* ACW:MAR/94[35]460, AHI:DEC/82[38]231

MERRYMAN, JOHN, *Lieutenant, USA;* AHI:NOV/71[32]136

MERSY, AUGUST, *Colonel, USA;* B&G:APR/94[28]559, CWTI:SUMMER/89[50]124, CWTI:SEP/92[28]280

MERWIN, HENRY C., *Lieutenant Colonel, 27th Connecticut Infantry:*
ARTICLE: "THE 10TH GEORGIA AND 27TH CONNECTICUT IN THE WHEATFIELD; TWO CAPTURED SWORDS AGAINST THEIR FORMER OWNERS," GETTY:12[24]242

ADDITIONAL LISTINGS: GETTY:11[80]235, GETTY:12[1]240, GETTY:12[24]242

MERWIN, S.E. JR., *Captain, USA;* GETTY:12[24]242

MESSENGER, N.C.; CWR:VOL2#1[69]133

MESSENGER, NICHOLAS G., *Sergeant, 22nd Iowa Infantry;* CWR:VOL2#1[i]129, CWR:VOL2#1[19]131

MESSICK, NATHAN, *Captain, 1st Minnesota Infantry;* GETTY:5[79]161

METCALF, F.M., *Private, 65th New York Infantry;* B&G:JUN/95[8]600

METCALF, JAMES, *civilian;* B&G:FEB/91[20]440

METCALF, THOMAS S., *Captain, 3rd Georgia Infantry;* CWTI:SEP/94[26]400

METZGER, JACOB, *Private, 4th Kansas Infantry;* ACW:NOV/94[42]497

MEW MARKET BATTLEFIELD HISTORICAL PARK; B&G:APR/91[36]448

MEWS, JESSE W., *72nd Pennsylvania Infantry;* GETTY:7[97]193

MEXICAN WAR:
ARTICLES: "IMPOSSIBLE CAMPAIGN ATTEMPTED," MH:APR/93[34]165, "NAKED SWORD IN HAND," MH:AUG/91[45]153, "THE PROVING GROUND," AHI:MAY/88[38]270, "TESTING FOR A FUTURE WAR," MH:APR/93[39]166
BOOK REVIEW: *JEFFERSON DAVIS' MEXICAN WAR REGIMENT*
ADDITIONAL LISTINGS: ACW:NOV/94[12]494, CWNEWS:NOV/93[5]

MEXICO, 1865; ARTICLE: "FRENCH MEDDLING IN MEXICO ALMOST LED TO A POST-CIVIL WAR CONFRONTATION WITH THE UNITED STATES," ACW:JUL/92[6]365

MEYER, HENRY C., *Captain, 24th New York Cavalry;* B&G:OCT/93[12]537

MEYER, THOMAS, *Sergeant, 148th Pennsylvania Infantry;* GETTY:11[102]237

MEYERS, ABRAHAM C., *Quartermaster General, CSA;* CWNEWS:NOV/92[4]

MEYSENBURG, THEODORE A., *Colonel, USA;* GETTY:11[71]234

MICHELBACHER, M.J., *Rabbi;* CWM:SEP/93[8]493

MICHIE, HENRY C.; *Captain, 56th Virginia Infantry;* ACW:MAR/93[10]402

MICHIE, PETER S., *Lieutenant, Corps of Engineers;* B&G:DEC/91[12]469, CWTI:APR/89[22]108

MICHIGAN TROOPS:
1st Artillery; CWM:JAN/91[40]330, CWNEWS:APR/92[4]
1st Artillery, Battery G; B&G:AUG/95[8]604
1st Cavalry; ACW:JUL/92[41]370, ACW:NOV/92[26]386, ACW:MAY/94[35]469, ACW:SEP/94[55]489, B&G:AUG/91[36]462, B&G:APR/92[8]481, GETTY:4[75]149, GETTY:9[109]218, GETTY:13[1]252, GETTY:13[89]260
1st Engineers; CWTI:MAY/93[38]321
1st Infantry:
ARTICLE: "THE CHIPPEWA SHARPSHOOTERS OF COMPANY K," CWM:SEP/92[24]441
GENERAL LISTINGS: *Five Forks,* B&G:APR/92[8]481, *in order of battle,* B&G:APR/92[8]481, *order of battle,* B&G:DEC/95[9]615, *Wilderness,* B&G:APR/95[8]595
ADDITIONAL LISTINGS: CWM:SEP/92[24]441, CWR:VOL2#4[269]145

Cavalry Brigade; ACW:JUL/92[41]370, ACW:MAY/94[35]469, GETTY:4[75]149, GETTY:9[109]218, GETTY:10[120]229, GETTY:13[89]260, *photo of monument*, GETTY:4[75]149
Coldwater Battery; B&G:AUG/93[10]529
Engineeers & Mechanics; B&G:FEB/93[12]511, B&G:DEC/95[9]615
Michigan Brigade; ACW:JUL/92[41]370, ACW:MAY/94[35]469, GETTY:10[120]229

MICHLER, NATHANIEL, *Major, USA;* CWTI:APR/92[49]260
MICKLE, WILLIAM N., *Lieutenant, 37th North Carolina Infantry;* GETTY:8[67]204
MICKLER, THOMAS, *Captain, 1st Florida Special Battalion;* CWR:VOL3#1[65]151
MIDDLEBURG, VIRGINIA, BATTLE OF:
ARTICLE: "THE FIGHT FOR LOUDOUN VALLEY: ALDIE, MIDDLEBURG AND UPPERVILLE, VA," B&G:OCT/93[12]537
ADDITIONAL LISTINGS: ACW:JUL/93[8]420, B&G:OCT/93[12]537, CWTI:DEC/89[34]136, CWTI:SEP/90[34]176, GETTY:4[7]142, MH:OCT/92[51]162
MIDDLETON, SAMUEL, *Private, 3rd New Jersey Infantry;* CWTI:MAY/89[36]118
MIGNAULT, NAPOLEON, *Chaplain, 17th Wisconsin Infantry;* CWM:MAR/91[50]340
MILES, BENJAMIN B., *Surgeon, USA;* CWR:VOL1#4[7]125
MILES, DAVID, *Lieutenant Colonel, USA;* B&G:DEC/95[9]615
MILES, DIXON S., *Colonel, USA;* ACW:MAY/95[54]528, CWM:MAY/92[8]418, CWR:VOL1#4[7]125, CWR:VOL1#4[7]125, MH:AUG/95[30]185, GETTY:7[51]190, *photo*, MH:AUG/95[30]185
MILES, JOHN W., *Private, 2nd Wisconsin Infantry,* GETTY:11[57]233
MILES, WILLIAM P.; CWNEWS:FEB/94[5]
MILES, WILLIAM R., *Colonel, CSA;* B&G:JUN/93[12]524
MILES, NELSON A., *General, USA:*
ARTICLE: "THE GREAT PULLMAN STRIKE!" AHI:APR/71[37]132
BOOK REVIEWS: *THE MOST FAMOUS SOLDIER IN AMERICA: A BIOGRAPHY OF NELSON A. MILES * PERSONAL RECOLLECTIONS & OBSERVATIONS OF GENERAL NELSON A. MILES * THE SEARCH FOR GENERAL MILES*
GENERAL LISTINGS: *Cold Harbor,* B&G:APR/94[10]558, *Custer,* AHI:FEB/71[4]131, *Five Forks,* B&G:APR/92[8]481, *in book review,* CWR:VOL4#1[78], *in order of battle,* B&G:APR/94[10]558, B&G:APR/95[8]595, *Indian Wars,* AHI:JUL/80[36]204, *post war,* AHI:NOV/79[32]196, *photos,* AHI:APR/71[37]132, AHI:JUN/76[4]169, AHI:JUL/80[36]204
ADDITIONAL LISTINGS: ACW:JAN/93[43]397, ACW:MAY/95[30]525, CWR:VOL2#2[141]137, CWR:VOL2#3[236]143, CWTI:AUG/90[26]166, CWTI:FEB/91[45]194, CWTI:AUG/91[68]222
MILFORD STATION, VIRGINIA, ENGAGEMENT AT; B&G:APR/93[12]518
MILHOLLIN, JOHN F., *Captain, CSA; Phillip's (Georgia) Legion;* ARTICLE: "TIME LAPSE," CWTI:APR/89[50]112

MILITARY DEPARTMENTS, DISTRICTS AND DIVISIONS, CONFEDERATE:
Department of Alabama and West Florida; CWR:VOL1#4[42]126

Department of Alabama, Mississippi and East Lousiana; ACW:SEP/95[48]547, CWR:VOL1#3[94], CWTI:NOV/93[65]351, CWTI:JAN/94[35]361
Department of Arizona; CWM:MAY/93[16]475
Department of East Tennessee; B&G:FEB/91[20]440, CWR:VOL4#1[1]163
Department of Mississippi and East Louisiana; B&G:AUG/95[8]604, CWM:APR/95[28]573, CWR:VOL2#1[36]132, CWR:VOL2#1[78], CWTI:MAY/91[24]208, CWTI:SEP/92[18], CWTI:NOV/92[54]293
Department of North Carolina and Southern Virginia; CWTI:APR/89[14]107
Department of North Carolina; CWM:JUN/95[24]582
Department of Northern Virginia; CWM:JUN/95[24]582, CWTI:APR/89[14]107
Department of Richmond; CWTI:MAY/89[22]116
Department of South; ACW:SEP/92[47]380
Department of South Carolina and Georgia; CWTI:JAN/94[46]364
Department of South Carolina, Georgia and Florida; B&G:DEC/95[9]615, CWR:VOL2#1[36]132
Department of Southwest Virginia; B&G:AUG/91[11]458
Department of Tennessee; CWTI:SUMMER/89[20]121
Department of Texas; ACW:JUL/91[58]316
Department of the Trans-Mississippi:
BOOK REVIEWS: *KIRBY SMITH'S CONFEDERACY: THE TRANS-MISSISSIPPI SOUTH, 1863-1865*
ADDITIONAL LISTINGS: ACW:MAR/93[68]409, ACW:MAY/93[22]414, AHI:NOV/73[18]151, B&G:JUN/91[10]452, CWR:VOL4#2[26]166, CWTI:MAR/89[10]
Department of Western Virginia & East Tennessee; CWTI:MAR/89[16]101
District of Arkansas; B&G:JUN/91[10]452
District of Georgia; CWTI:APR/89[14]107
District of South Carolina, Georgia and Florida; CWR:VOL3#4[1]161
District of Western Louisiana; CWR:VOL4#2[26]166, CWR:VOL4#2[1]165, CWR:VOL4#2[68]167
District of the Gulf; CWM:JAN/91[40]330
District of the Pamlico (North Carolina); CWTI:APR/89[14]107
District of the Rio Grande; ACW:JUL/91[58]316
Division of Florida; ACW:NOV/91[64]336
Division of the West; B&G:DEC/95[9]615

MILITARY DEPARTMENTS, DISTRICTS AND DIVISIONS, FEDERAL:
Department of Mississippi and Eastern Louisiana; ACW:SEP/94[10]484
Department of Missouri; CWTI:FEB/90[26]143, MH:DEC/95[58]188
Department of Oregon; ACW:MAR/92[62]355
Department of Susquehanna; B&G:AUG/94[10]574
Department of Virginia and North Carolina; B&G:DEC/94[10]585, CWTI:MAY/93[29]319
Department of West Tennessee; ACW:SEP/92[23]377
Department of West Virginia; B&G:AUG/94[10]574, B&G:AUG/94[19]575, CWTI:MAR/89[16]101
Department of the Cumberland; ACW:NOV/92[6]382, AHI:JAN/67[4]106, MH:DEC/95[58]188

Department of the Gulf; ACW:SEP/94[10]484,
CWR:VOL2#3[212]142, CWR:VOL4#2[26]166,
CWTI:MAY/93[29]319
Department of the Ohio; ACW:SEP/91[22]321,
ACW:SEP/95[22]544, B&G:FEB/93[12]511,
B&G:AUG/93[10]529, B&G:OCT/94[11]580,
CWTI:FEB/90[26]143, CWTI:MAR/95[40]436
Department of the South; ACW:SEP/91[30]322,
CWM:MAR/92[16]411, CWTI:DEC/89[42]137,
CWTI:JAN/94[46]364
Department of the Susquehanna; ACW:MAR/92[22]351,
B&G:AUG/94[10]574
Department of the West; ACW:MAR/92[46]354,
ACW:NOV/93[26]441, CWTI:APR/90[48]154
District of Kansas and the Indian Territory;
ACW:NOV/94[42]497
District of North Alabama; CWTI:MAR/91[46]203
District of North Missouri; B&G:JUN/91[10]452
District of West Tennessee; MH:DEC/95[58]188
District of the Border; B&G:JUN/91[10]452,
CWM:JAN/92[8]399
District of the Frontier; CWM:JAN/92[8]399
Middle Department; B&G:AUG/94[10]574
Middle Department of Maryland; ACW:NOV/93[50]444
Military District of Cairo; AHI:NOV/73[18]151
Military District of Southeastern Missouri;
CWTI:FEB/90[26]143
Military Division of the Gulf; CWTI:MAY/93[35]320
Military Division of the Mississippi; AHI:NOV/73[18]151,
B&G:AUG/94[22]576, CWTI:MAR/95[40]436
Military Division of West Mississippi; CWR:VOL1#1[42]105

MILITARY ORGANIZATION; BOOK REVIEW: *THE UNION
ARMY, 1861-1865: ORGANIZATION AND OPERATIONS.
VOLUME I: THE EASTERN THEATRE * THE UNION
ARMY, 1861-1865: ORGANIZATION AND OPERATIONS,
VOLUME II: THE WESTERN THEATRE*
MILL SPRINGS BATTLEFIELD ASSOCIATION;
B&G:OCT/92[26]498, B&G:FEB/93[40]514
MILL SPRINGS, KENTUCKY, BATTLE OF:
ARTICLES: "THE CAMPAIGN AND BATTLE OF MILL
SPRINGS," B&G:FEB/93[12]511, "NORTH'S FIRST
VICTORY," ACW:SEP/93[38]434
GENERAL LISTINGS: *general history*, AHI:MAY/71[3]133A,
in book review, CWNEWS:OCT/93[5], *letters to the editor*,
B&G:JUN/93[6]523, B&G:AUG/93[6]528, B&G:APR/94[6]557,
B&G:AUG/93[36]607
ADDITIONAL LISTINGS: ACW:JAN/91[22]285, ACW:JUL/91[26]313,
B&G:FEB/92[40]479, B&G:JUN/92[46]490,
B&G:FEB/93[12]511, CWM:JAN/93[35]460,
CWR:VOL4#1[1]163, CWTI:SEP/93[59]341,
CWTI:SEP/93[90]343
MILLA, J.G.; CWTI:JAN/93[49]303
MILLAR, J. CLYDE, *Lieutenant, 153rd Pennsylvania Infantry;*
GETTY:12[30]243
MILLEDGE, GEORGE, *Corporal, 66th Ohio Infantry;*
GETTY:9[81]216
MILLER, ABRAM S., *Colonel, 72nd Indiana Infantry;*
ACW:MAY/95[49]527, B&G:OCT/92[32]499,
B&G:DEC/94[22]586
MILLER, ANDREW J., *civilian;* B&G:AUG/94[10]574
MILLER, BURTON, *Private, 6th Wisconsin Infantry,*
GETTY:11[57]233

MILLER, CLELL; B&G:OCT/91[11]466
MILLER, DAVID R., *civilian;* ACW:JUL/92[30]369
MILLER, DORA, *civilian in Vicksburg;* CWTI:SEPT/89[18]126
MILLER, FRANCIS, *Lieutenant Colonel, 147th New York
Infantry;* GETTY:5[4]156
MILLER, FRANK, *Lieutenant, 9th Georgia State Troops;*
CWTI:MAR/93[24]309
MILLER, HUGH R., *Colonel, 52nd Mississippi Infantry;*
GETTY:9[98]217
MILLER, J.L., *Colonel, 12th South Carolina Infantry;*
GETTY:6[7]169
MILLER, JAMES T., *Private, 111th Pennsylvania Infantry;*
CWR:VOL3#2[70]155
MILLER, JOHN F., *General, USA;* ACW:NOV/95[66]559,
B&G:DEC/93[12]545
MILLER, JOHN K., *Colonel, USA;* B&G:APR/92[28]482
MILLER, JOHN M., *Captain, USA;* CWTI:AUG/95[34]457
MILLER, JONATHAN, *Lieutenant, 1st Kentucky Cavalry;*
B&G:FEB/93[12]511
MILLER, MARK S., *Captain, CSA;* CWR:VOL1#2[44]114
MILLER, MATHEW A., *Captain, CSA;* B&G:JUN/94[38]571
MILLER, MERRIT B., *Captain, CSA;* ACW:JUL/92[12]367
MILLER, OBED P., *Captain, Louisiana Tigers;*
CWTI:MAR/94[48]374
MILLER, OSCAR, *Private, CSA;* B&G:AUG/91[11]458
MILLER, S.C., *Private, 76th Pennsylvania Infantry;*
ACW:SEP/91[30]322
MILLER, SAMUEL H., *Private, 14th Kentucky Cavalry;*
CWM:MAR/93[16]466
MILLER, T.C.H., *Colonel, 17th Tennessee Infantry;*
B&G:FEB/93[12]511
MILLER, THOMAS W., *Lieutenant, 55th Ohio Infantry;*
GETTY:4[24]145
MILLER, WILLIAM E., *Captain, 3rd Pennsylvania Cavalry;*
GETTY:4[75]149, GETTY:12[68]246, GETTY:13[89]260, *photo,*
GETTY:13[89]260
MILLER, WILLIAM, *General, CSA;* ACW:NOV/91[64]336
MILLICAN, WILLIAM T., *Lieutenant Colonel, 15th Georgia
Infantry;* CWM:JUN/95[63]594
MILLIKEN'S BEND, LOUISIANA, BATTLE OF;
AHI:MAY/71[3]133A, B&G:FEB/92[6]473, B&G:FEB/94[8]550,
CWM:JAN/92[6]398, CWR:VOL3#3[33]158,
CWR:VOL3#3[88]160
MILLISON, JESSE, *Captain, 29th Pennsylvania Infantry;*
CWTI:SEPT/89[30]129
MILLS, CHARLES, *Surgeon, 125th Illinois Infantry;*
CWTI:JAN/93[20]298
MILLS, GEORGE H., *Private, 16th North Carolina Infantry:*
BOOK REVIEW: *THE HISTORY OF THE 16TH NORTH
CAROLINA REGIMENT IN THE CIVIL WAR*
ADDITIONAL LISTING: CWR:VOL4#4[70]180
MILLS, J.D., *inventor;* ACW:JUL/93[8]420
MILLS, LUTHER R., *Private, 26th Virginia Infantry;*
CWR:VOL3#4[1]161
MILLS, ROGER Q., *Private, CSA;* CWTI:FEB/92[29]248
MILLS, THOMAS, *Private, 11th Battalion, Georgia Light
Artillery;* CWR:VOL3#2[1]153
MILLSPAUGH, THEODORE, *Captain, 5th West Virginia
Cavalry;* B&G:OCT/94[28]581
MILNE, JOSEPH S., *Lieutenant, 1st Rhode Island Artillery;*
CWTI:SEP/90[26]174

MILROY, ROBERT H., *General, USA:*
GENERAL LISTINGS: *general history,* AHI:MAY/71[3]133A,
Gettysburg, GETTY:5[4]156, GETTY:11[6]231, *in book review,*
CWM:JAN/91[47], CWR:VOL3#3[92], *Manassas, Second,*
B&G:AUG/92[11]493, *Nashville,* B&G:DEC/93[12]545, *West
Virginia Campaign,* B&G:AUG/93[10]529, *Winchester, Second,*
CWNEWS:APR/92[4], *photo,* CWTI:MAR/94[29]371
ADDITIONAL LISTINGS: ACW:JAN/92[47]344, ACW:JAN/93[35]396,
B&G:OCT/93[12]537, B&G:OCT/93[21]538,
CWM:JUL/91[10]357, CWM:JUL/92[18]429,
CWTI:FEB/91[12]189, CWTI:MAR/94[29]371,
CWTI:JUN/95[18]444
MILTON, BILLY, *Captain, 20th Massachusetts Infantry;*
CWR:VOL3#1[31]150
MILTON, JOHN, *Governor, Florida;* ACW:SEP/93[8]429,
CWR:VOL3#4[1]161
MILTON, RICHARD S., *Lieutenant, 9th Massachusetts
Artillery;* GETTY:5[47]160
MIMMS, HENRY, *Private, 32nd Texas Cavalry;*
ACW:MAR/93[68]409
MIMS, ROBERT L., *Sergeant, 7th South Carolina Infantry;*
GETTY:5[35]159
MINA, LUCY, *civilian;* CWM:MAY/91[40]351
MINDIL, GEORGE, *Colonel, USA;* B&G:DEC/95[9]615
MINE CREEK, KANSAS, BATTLE OF; CWM:DEC/95[10]
MINE RUN, VIRGINIA, CAMPAIGN OF:
ARTICLES: "DOUBLY MISSED OPPORTUNITY,"
ACW:MAR/93[26]404, "LEE FOILS MEADE AT MINE RUN,"
CWM:DEC/94[44]551
BOOK REVIEW: *MINE RUN: A CAMPAIGN OF LOST
OPPORTUNITIES, OCTOBER 21, 1863-MAY 1, 1864*
GENERAL LISTINGS: *general history,* AHI:MAY/71[3]133A, *in book
review,* CWM:OCT/94[8], CWNEWS:MAY/89[4],
CWR:VOL1#4[77], CWR:VOL2#4[346]
ADDITIONAL LISTINGS: ACW:SEP/94[38]487, ACW:JAN/95[10]503,
B&G:APR/91[8]445, B&G:DEC/91[34]470, B&G:APR/95[8]595,
B&G:DEC/95[25]616, CWM:MAY/92[4]416,
CWM:MAY/92[20]420, CWM:JUL/92[8]427,
CWM:SEP/93[24]495, CWR:VOL1#1[1]102,
CWR:VOL1#3[52]122, CWR:VOL3#2[1]153,
CWR:VOL3#3[1]157, CWTI:MAY/89[36]118,
CWTI:APR/90[46]153, CWTI:SEP/91[31]229
MINIE', CLAUDE E., *inventor of the minie ball;*
CWTI:SEPT/89[10]125
MINIGERODE, CHARLES, *Reverend;* ACW:MAY/94[35]469
MINNEGERODE, CHARLES, *Lieutenant, CSA;*
ACW:NOV/91[30]332, CWR:VOL4#1[78]
MINNESOTA SIOUX INDIAN UPRISING:
BOOK REVIEW: *THROUGH DAKOTA EYES: NARRATIVE
ACCOUNTS OF THE MINNESOTA INDIAN WAR OF 1862*
ADDITIONAL LISTING: ACW:MAY/91[12]302

MINNESOTA TROOPS:
ARTICLE: "SIX PAINTINGS IN MINNESOTA'S CAPITOL
BUILDING VIVIDLY RE-CREATE THE YOUNG STATE'S
CIVIL WAR SERVICE," ACW:NOV/94[76]500
1st Artillery; CWR:VOL4#1[44]164, B&G:JUN/95[36]603A,
CWTI:MAR/95[18]432
1st Artillery, (Heavy); B&G:FEB/91[32]441,
CWTI:JUL/92[8]269
1st Cavalry; CWM:MAR/91[50]340

1st Infantry:
BOOK REVIEWS: *THE FIRST MINNESOTA REGIMENT AT
GETTYSBURG * THE LAST FULL MEASURE: THE LIFE
AND DEATH OF THE FIRST MINNESOTA VOLUNTEERS*
GENERAL LISTINGS: *Gettysburg,* GETTY:4[89]150,
GETTY:5[79]161, GETTY:10[53]225, *in book review,*
CWR:VOL3#2[105], *in list,* CWTI:JUL/93[34]327, *letters to the
editor,* B&G:OCT/95[5]610
ADDITIONAL LISTINGS: GETTY:13[1]252, GETTY:13[43]256,
GETTY:13[50]257
ADDITIONAL LISTINGS: ACW:MAR/94[50]462, ACW:NOV/94[76]500,
AHI:JUL/93[40]312, B&G:APR/91[8]445,
CWM:APR/95[42]577, CWR:VOL2#2[95]135,
CWTI:NOV/92[49]292, CWTI:SEP/94[34]402
2nd Infantry; ACW:SEP/93[38]434, ACW:NOV/94[76]500,
B&G:OCT/92[32]499, B&G:FEB/93[12]511,
B&G:APR/94[6]557, CWTI:SEP/92[31]281
3rd Infantry:
ARTICLE: "COMMANDS (THE 3RD MINNESOTA),"
ACW:MAY/91[12]302
ADDITIONAL LISTING: CWTI:NOV/93[33]347
4th Infantry; ACW:NOV/94[76]500, AHI:MAY/71[3]133A,
CWTI:JUL/94[50]395
5th Infantry; ACW:NOV/94[76]500, CWM:MAR/91[50]340
7th Infantry; ACW:SEP/92[23]377, ACW:NOV/94[76]500,
CWTI:AUG/90[70]171
8th Infantry; ACW:NOV/94[76]500
9th Infantry; ACW:NOV/94[76]500, CWM:SEP/92[8]437
10th Infantry; ACW:NOV/94[76]500
MINNICH, J.W., *Lieutenant, CSA;* ACW:SEP/95[8]542
MINOR, CARTER N.B., *Private, Rockbridge Artillery;*
CWR:VOL4#4[70]180
MINOR, PHINEAS R., *Captain, 5th Ohio Cavalry;*
CWR:VOL4#1[44]164
MINOR, ROBERT, *Lieutenant, CSN;* AHI:OCT/75[30]162
MINORITIES; ARTICLE: "THE FIGHTING MINORITY,"
CWTI:MAY/92[38]265
MINTON, THOMAS, *Private, 26th North Carolina Infantry;*
CWTI:FEB/91[45]194
MINTY, ROBERT H., *Colonel, USA;* ACW:MAY/95[49]527,
B&G:OCT/92[10]496, CWM:JUL/92[24]430,
CWR:VOL4#1[1]163, CWTI:MAY/92[48]267
MINTZER, WILLIAM M., *Captain, 53rd Pennsylvania Infantry;*
GETTY:11[80]235
MINUTE, FRANZ, *Private, 1st Louisiana Zouave Battalion;*
CWTI:MAR/89[28]103
MISCEGENATION; ARTICLE: "THIS 'ONE GREAT EVIL',"
AHI:MAY/77[37]174
MISENHEIMER, MARION A., *Private, 3rd Tennessee Infantry;*
ACW:SEP/95[38]546,
MISSIONARY RIDGE, TENNESSEE, BATTLE OF; see
listings under "**CHATTANOOGA, TENNESSEE, BATTLE
OF**"
MISSISSIPPI MARINE BRIGADE; CWR:VOL2#3[183]140,
CWR:VOL3#3[33]158
MISSISSIPPI SQUADRON; ACW:JUL/93[8]420,
CWR:VOL4#2[26]166

MISSISSIPPI TROOPS:
1st Artillery; ACW:NOV/91[22]331, CWR:VOL2#1[36]132,
CWTI:MAY/91[24]208
1st Artillery, Battery B; ACW:JAN/94[30]450,
B&G:FEB/94[8]550, CWM:JUN/94[25]511

ADDITIONAL LISTINGS: B&G:AUG/92[40]495,
  CWR:VOL2#4[269]145, CWTI:JUL/93[34]327, GETTY:4[7]142,
  GETTY:5[4]156, GETTY:7[13]186, GETTY:10[53]225
43rd Infantry; CWR:VOL2#4[269]145, CWTI:MAR/95[46]437,
  GETTY:9[98]217
44th Infantry; ACW:MAR/91[12]292
46th Infantry:
BOOK REVIEW: *BLOOD & SACRIFICE: THE CIVIL WAR
  JOURNAL OF A CONFEDERATE SOLDIER*
ADDITIONAL LISTINGS: ACW:SEP/92[38]379, ACW:JUL/94[51]480,
  B&G:FEB/94[8]550, CWM:DEC/94[49]553
48th Infantry:
GENERAL LISTINGS: *Gettysburg,* GETTY:4[7]142, GETTY:5[89]162,
  GETTY:8[111]206, GETTY:9[61]215
ADDITIONAL LISTINGS: ACW:MAY/95[30]525, ACW:JUL/95[50]538,
  CWR:VOL3#2[1]153
52nd Infantry; GETTY:9[98]217
Crystal Springs Southern Rights; GETTY:5[89]162,
  GETTY:8[111]206
Culbertson's Artillery; CWR:VOL2#1[36]132
Georgia and Mississippi Regiment; CWR:VOL1#4[42]126
Jeff Davis Legion; CWTI:JUN/90[32]159
Jefferson Davis Legion; ACW:JUL/92[41]370
Lamar Rifles; ACW:MAR/92[10]349
Mississippi Brigade; GETTY:7[51]190
Noxubee Rifles; ACW:MAR/92[10]349
O'Connor Rifles; GETTY:6[77]177
Pettus Flying Artillery; CWR:VOL2#1[36]132
Swett's Battery; CWR:VOL3#3[59]159
University Greys:
ARTICLE: "OLE MISS' SPIRITED UNIVERSITY GREYS LEFT
  THEIR QUIET UNIVERSITY CAMPUS FOR THE WAR'S
  WORST BATTLEFIELDS," ACW:MAR/92[10]349
ADDITIONAL LISTING: ACW:MAR/92[10]349
Ward's Battery; CWR:VOL3#2[1]153

MISSISSIPPI, STATE OF; BOOK REVIEWS: *PORTRAITS OF
  CONFLICT: A PHOTOGRAPHIC HISTORY OF
  MISSISSIPPI IN THE CIVIL WAR*
MISSOURI COMPROMISE; ACW:SEP/91[54],
  ACW:MAY/93[47]417, ACW:MAY/94[43]470,
  AHI:MAY/66[12]101, AHI:OCT/70[23]129, AHI:JUN/73[4]149,
  AHI:JUL/75[4]160, AHI:DEC/81[18]223,
  CWNEWS:AUG/91[4], CWNEWS:JUN/95[33]

MISSOURI TROOPS:
1st Artillery, (Union); ACW:MAY/93[22]414,
  B&G:FEB/93[40]514, CWR:VOL4#2[26]166
1st Artillery, Battery A, (Union); B&G:FEB/94[8]550,
  B&G:AUG/95[8]604
1st Artillery, Battery C, (Union); B&G:AUG/95[8]604
1st Artillery, Battery D, (Union); CWR:VOL1#1[42]105
1st Artillery, Battery E, (Union); CWM:OCT/94[33]537
1st Brigade:
BOOK REVIEWS: *THE CONFEDERACY'S FIGHTING CHAPLAIN:
  FATHER JOHN B. BANNON * IN DEADLY EARNEST:
  HISTORY OF THE FIRST MISSOURI BRIGADE, CSA *
  THE SOUTH'S FINEST: THE FIRST MISSOURI
  CONFEDERATE BRIGADE FROM PEA RIDGE TO
  VICKSBURG*
ADDITIONAL LISTINGS: B&G:AUG/93[24], CWM:OCT/95[10],
  CWNEWS:JUN/93[5]

1st Cavalry, (Confederate); ACW:MAR/92[46]354,
  AHI:DEC/77[46]177, CWM:SEP/93[8]493,
  CWR:VOL2#1[36]132
1st Infantry; ACW:MAY/91[31]304, B&G:DEC/95[9]615
1st Infantry, (Confederate); B&G:FEB/94[8]550,
  CWR:VOL2#1[1]130, CWR:VOL2#1[36]132
1st Infantry, (Union); ACW:NOV/93[26]441,
  CWM:SEP/93[8]493, CWR:VOL1#2[44]114,
  CWTI:FEB/92[29]248
1st Militia; B&G:JUN/91[10]452
1st Northeast Home Guards; CWTI:AUG/95[34]457,
  CWTI:DEC/95[8]474, MH:APR/95[74]184
1st-4th Infantry; CWR:VOL3#3[59]159
2nd Artillery, Battery E; CWR:VOL1#2[44]114
2nd Artillery, Battery F; B&G:AUG/95[8]604
2nd Cavalry, (State Militia); ACW:MAR/92[46]354
2nd Cavalry, (Union); ACW:MAR/92[46]354,
  CWR:VOL1#2[44]114
2nd Infantry; ACW:MAY/91[31]304, B&G:FEB/94[8]550
2nd Infantry, (Confederate); ACW:NOV/91[22]331,
  AHI:MAR/84[42]238, B&G:FEB/94[8]550,
  CWR:VOL2#1[36]132
2nd Infantry, (Union); ACW:MAR/92[46]354,
  ACW:NOV/93[26]441, CWTI:FEB/92[29]248
3rd Cavalry; ACW:MAR/92[46]354, CWR:VOL2#1[36]132
3rd Infantry; ACW:MAY/91[31]304, ACW:NOV/91[22]331,
  ACW:MAR/92[46]354, ACW:NOV/93[26]441,
  ACW:JUL/94[51]480, B&G:FEB/94[8]550,
  CWR:VOL2#1[1]130, CWR:VOL2#1[36]132,
  CWTI:FEB/92[29]248, CWTI:SEP/94[40]403
3rd Militia; B&G:OCT/91[40]467
4th Cavalry; ACW:MAR/95[26]515, CWR:VOL3#1[80],
  CWTI:FEB/92[42]250
4th Infantry, (Confederate); CWR:VOL2#1[36]132
5th Cavalry; B&G:JUN/91[10]452
5th Infantry; ACW:MAY/91[31]304, B&G:FEB/94[8]550
5th Infantry, (Confederate):
BOOK REVIEW: *WESTERNERS IN GRAY: THE MEN AND
  MISSIONS OF THE ELITE FIFTH MISSOURI INFANTRY
  REGIMENT*
ADDITIONAL LISTINGS: ACW:NOV/91[22]331, ACW:JUL/94[51]480,
  B&G:FEB/94[8]550, CWR:VOL2#1[36]132
5th Infantry, (Union); ACW:NOV/93[26]441,
  CWTI:FEB/92[29]248
6th Artillery; CWR:VOL4#2[1]165
6th Cavalry, (Union); B&G:AUG/95[8]604, CWR:VOL4#2[1]165
6th Infantry; B&G:FEB/94[8]550, CWM:MAR/91[50]340,
  CWTI:DEC/94[62]415, CWTI:AUG/95[58]461
6th Infantry, (Confederate); ACW:NOV/91[22]331,
  ACW:JUL/94[51]480, B&G:FEB/94[8]550,
  CWR:VOL2#1[36]132
6th Infantry, (Union); B&G:FEB/91[8]439, CWR:VOL2#1[1]130
7th Cavalry; CWR:VOL1#2[44]114
7th Infantry, (Union); ACW:MAY/94[26]468,
  B&G:FEB/94[8]550
8th Infantry, (Union); ACW:MAY/91[12]302,
  CWR:VOL2#1[1]130
9th Cavalry, (Union); CWR:VOL2#2[169]
9th Infantry; CWR:VOL1#1[42]105
9th Infantry, (Confederate); ACW:MAY/93[22]414,
  CWR:VOL2#2[169]
10th Cavalry; ACW:MAR/91[38]296, B&G:JUN/91[10]452
10th Cavalry, (Union); B&G:AUG/95[8]604

10th Infantry; CWTI:AUG/90[42]167
10th Infantry, (Confederate); ACW:MAY/93[22]414
10th Infantry, (Union); ACW:MAR/91[38]296
11th Cavalry; B&G:JUN/91[10]452
11th Infantry, (Union); ACW:SEP/91[46]324
12th Infantry, (Union); B&G:APR/95[24]596,
   CWR:VOL1#1[42]105, CWTI:MAY/91[16]206,
   CWTI:SEP/94[40]403
15th Cavalry, (Confederate); B&G:FEB/93[40]514
15th Cavalry, (Union); B&G:OCT/91[40]467
15th Infantry, (Union); MH:OCT/93[20]172
17th Infantry, (Union); CWTI:SEP/94[40]403,
   MH:OCT/93[20]172
18th Infantry, (Union); B&G:DEC/95[9]615
21st Infantry, (Union); ACW:JAN/91[22]285,
   ACW:SEP/94[10]484, CWTI:DEC/95[8]474
25th Infantry, (Union); ACW:JAN/91[22]285,
   ACW:SEP/94[10]484
26th Infantry, (Union); CWR:VOL3#3[59]159,
   CWTI:JUL/94[50]395
29th Infantry, (Union); ACW:NOV/93[34]442,
   CWTI:SEP/94[40]403
31st Infantry, (Union); CWTI:SEP/94[40]403
33rd Enrolled Militia; B&G:JUN/91[32]454
33rd Infantry, (Union); ACW:MAY/93[22]414,
   CWR:VOL2#3[212]142
35th Infantry; (Union); ACW:MAY/93[22]414,
   CWTI:DEC/94[82]418
39th Infantry; (Union); B&G:JUN/91[32]454,
   CWTI:JAN/94[29]360
44th Infantry; (Union); CWR:VOL4#3[1]170
55th Provisional Enrolled Militia; B&G:JUN/91[32]454
Bledsoe's Light Artillery; B&G:AUG/95[8]604
Clark's Artillery; B&G:AUG/95[8]604, CWTI:JUL/94[50]395
German Home Guard; ACW:MAR/91[62]298
Guibor's Battery; B&G:FEB/94[8]550, CWR:VOL2#1[36]132
Irish Dragoons; ACW:MAR/92[46]354
Iron Brigade; B&G:JUN/91[10]452
Landis' Battery; B&G:FEB/94[8]550, CWR:VOL2#1[36]132
Mann's Artillery; CWR:VOL4#1[44]164
Missouri Brigade; CWR:VOL2#1[36]132, CWTI:MAY/91[24]208
Missouri Home Guard:
ARTICLE: "TAKING OFF THE KID GLOVES,"
   ACW:MAR/92[46]354
ADDITIONAL LISTINGS: ACW:MAY/91[31]304, ACW:SEP/91[50]325,
   ACW:MAR/92[46]354, ACW:JUL/92[22]368,
   ACW:NOV/93[26]441, B&G:FEB/93[36], B&G:FEB/94[8]550,
   CWR:VOL1#1[42]105, CWTI:MAR/91[34]201,
   CWTI:FEB/92[29]248, CWTI:JUL/94[50]395,
   CWTI:AUG/95[34]457, CWTI:AUG/95[58]461
Wade's Battery; CWR:VOL2#1[36]132

MISSOURI, STATE OF:
ARTICLES: "A FIGHT FOR MISSOURI," CWTI:AUG/95[34]457,
   "DEATH STRUGGLE FOR MISSOURI," CWM:MAY/93[8]474,
   "THE GENERAL'S TOUR: MISSOURI! ONE LAST
   TIME—STERLING PRICE'S 1864 MISSOURI
   EXPEDITION," B&G:JU N/91[10]452, "THE MEANEST
   BUSHWHACKER," B&G:JUN/91[32]454, "TRAVEL
   (CALLAWAY COUNTY, MISSOURI)," ACW:MAR/91[62]298
BOOK REVIEWS: *CIVIL WAR IN THE OZARKS * WITH PORTER
   IN NORTH MISSOURI: A CHAPTER IN THE HISTORY OF
   THE WAR BETWEEN THE STATES*

MISSOURI-KANSAS CIVIL WAR; ARTICLE: "BITTER
   BUSHWHACKERS AND JAYHAWKERS,"
   ACW:JAN/93[26]395
MITCHEL, ORMSBY M., *General, USA;* ACW:MAY/91[12]302,
   ACW:SEP/91[22]321, B&G:DEC/91[38]471,
   B&G:JUN/95[36]603A, CWTI:MAY/93[38]321,
   MH:DEC/93[12]174, *photo,* CWTI:MAY/93[38]321
MITCHEL, WILLIE, *Private, 1st Virginia Infantry;*
   CWM:MAR/91[17]335
MITCHELL, ACKBER O., *Major, 44th Ohio Mounted Infantry;*
   CWR:VOL4#1[1]163
MITCHELL, BARTON W., *Corporal, 27th Indiana Infantry;*
   ACW:JAN/94[6]446, ACW:JAN/94[39]451,
   CWM:MAR/91[12]333, MH:AUG/95[30]185
MITCHELL, GEORGE, *Sergeant, 5th New York Infantry;*
   CWR:VOL1#2[7]111, CWR:VOL1#2[29]112,
   CWTI:MAY/94[31]382
MITCHELL, ISAAC, *Corporal, USA;* ACW:MAR/93[51]407
MITCHELL, JAMES, *Captain, CSA;* B&G:OCT/94[11]580,
   GETTY:5[35]159
MITCHELL, JAMES A., *Captain, Ohio Light Artillery;*
   B&G:FEB/94[8]550
MITCHELL, JOHN, *Lieutenant, 154th New York Infantry;*
   GETTY:8[17]200
MITCHELL, JOHN, *Private, 66th Ohio Infantry;*
   GETTY:9[81]216
MITCHELL, JOHN, *Sergeant, 4th U.S. Artillery;*
   CWM:MAR/91[17]335, GETTY:11[57]233
MITCHELL, JOHN G., *General, USA;* B&G:DEC/95[9]615,
   B&G:DEC/93[12]545, CWTI:SEP/92[31]281, *photo,*
   AHI:NOV/79[10]195
MITCHELL, JOHN K., *Commander, CSN;*
   ACW:MAY/92[16]359, ACW:SEP/95[30]545, B&G:AUG/95[38],
   MH:AUG/93[47]169
MITCHELL, JOSEPH, *Sergeant, 42nd Virginia Cavalry;*
   B&G:APR/93[24]520
MITCHELL, ONGE, *Private, 7th Ohio Infantry;*
   CWTI:SEP/92[22]279
MITCHELL, ROBERT, *Captain, CSA;* B&G:APR/93[12]518
MITCHELL, ROBERT B., *General, USA;* AHI:NOV/72[12]142,
   B&G:OCT/92[10]496, CWR:VOL4#3[50]171,
   CWTI:FEB/92[29]248, CWTI:MAY/92[48]267
MITCHELL, S.W., *Sergeant, Essex Light Brigade;*
   ACW:JUL/95[34]536
MITCHELL, W.G., *Major, USA;* ACW:MAY/93[31]415,
   CWTI:APR/92[49]260, GETTY:6[87]178
MITTS, JOHN P., *Private, 2nd Tennessee Cavalry;*
   CWR:VOL4#1[1]163
MIX, JAMES, *Lieutenant, 137th New York Infantry;*
   CWR:VOL3#2[70]155
MIXSON, FRANK M., *Private, 1st South Carolina Infantry;*
   CWR:VOL3#2[70]155
MIZNER, JOHN K., *Colonel, USA;* CWTI:JUL/94[50]395
MOBBERLY, JOHN W.; BOOK REVIEW: *ROUGH-RIDING
   SCOUT: THE STORY OF JOHN W. MOBBERLY,
   LOUDOUN'S OWN CIVIL WAR GUERRILLA HERO*
MOBILE BAY, ALABAMA, BATTLE and SIEGE OF:
ARTICLES: A.J. SMITH'S ROVING 'GORILLAS,'"
   MH:DEC/95[58]188, "'DAMN THE TORPEDOES!': THE
   BATTLE OF MOBILE BAY," CWM:JUL/93[24]485, "'FULL
   SPEED AHEAD!,'" MH:FEB/92[8]156, "GUARDIANS OF
   MOBILE BAY," CWTI:MAR/94[20]369

BOOK REVIEWS: *MOBILE BAY AND THE MOBILE CAMPAIGN: THE LAST GREAT BATTLES OF THE CIVIL WAR*
ADDITIONAL LISTINGS: ACW:JUL/92[12]367, ACW:SEP/95[48]547, CWM:SEP/93[18]494, CWR:VOL1#1[42]105, CWR:VOL1#4[42]126, CWR:VOL2#1[36]132, CWR:VOL2#3[183]140, CWTI:APR/90[10], CWTI:JUL/94[10]389, CWTI:DEC/94[24]409, MH:APR/94[54]176

MOBILE, ALABAMA:
BOOK REVIEW: *CONFEDERATE MOBILE*
GENERAL LISTING: *ordnance explosion*, CWTI:AUG/90[64]170
ADDITIONAL LISTINGS: ACW:JAN/93[51]398, CWTI:SEPT/89[20]127, CWTI:AUG/90[26]166

MOBLEY, J.M., *Lieutenant, CSA*; CWTI:JAN/95[42]428
MOCKBEE, R.T., *Private, 14th Tennessee Infantry*; GETTY:6[13]170
MODERN WARFARE; BOOK REVIEW: *THE AMERICAN CIVIL WAR AND THE ORIGINS OF MODERN WARFARE*
MOHAN, MICHAEL, *Private, 109th Pennsylvania Infantry*; CWTI:SUMMER/89[32]122
MOIR, JAMES, *Captain, Royal Navy*; ACW:NOV/91[46]335
MOLINEUX, EDWARD, *Colonel, USA*; ACW:MAY/91[38]305
MOLLOY, THOMAS P., *Lieutenant, 7th North Carolina Infantry*; GETTY:8[67]204
MILITARY ORDER OF THE LOYAL LEGION OF THE UNITED STATES (M.O.LL.U.S.); ACW:NOV/94[34]496, CWTI:MAY/91[34]209, GETTY:7[97]193, GETTY:9[33]211, GETTY:11[57]233, GETTY:13[89]260, GETTY:13[119]262
MOLLY MAGUIRES:
ARTICLE: "'IT WAS OPEN, DEFIANT REBELLION'," CWM:MAR/91[56]341
ADDITIONAL LISTINGS: ACW:SEP/93[22]432, CWM:MAR/91[4]332, CWM:JUL/91[6]355, CWNEWS:NOV/95[29]
MONAGHAN, WILLIAM, *Colonel, CSA*; B&G:APR/94[10]558, CWM:MAR/91[17]335, CWM:SEP/93[24]495
MONCK, SIR CHARLES S.; *Governor General of Canada*; ACW:NOV/91[46]335
USS MONITOR vs *CSS VIRGINIA*; see listings under "NAVAL WARFARE" and "SHIPS, BOATS, VESSELS, ETC."
MONNAHAN, HENRY, *Private, 24th Michigan Infantry*; GETTY:9[33]211
MONOCACY NATIONAL BATTLEFIELD PARK:
ARTICLE: "BATTLE OF MONOCACY PRESERVATION MESSAGE," B&G:DEC/92[53]509
ADDITIONAL LISTINGS: B&G:DEC/92[8]503, B&G:DEC/93[6]544
MONOCACY, MARYLAND, BATTLE OF:
ARTICLES: "THE FORGOTTEN BATTLE FOR THE CAPITAL," CWTI:JAN/93[40]301, "MONOCACY: THE BATTLE THAT SAVED WASHINGTON," B&G:DEC/92[8]503, "ROADBLOCK EN ROUTE TO WASHINGTON," ACW:NOV/93[50]444
BOOK REVIEWS: *JUBAL EARLY'S RAID ON WASHINGTON: 1864 * SEASON OF FIRE: THE CONFEDERATE STRIKE ON WASHINGTON*
ADDITIONAL LISTINGS: ACW:MAY/93[14]413, ACW:JUL/94[26]477, AHI:MAY/71[3]133A, B&G:APR/93[6]517, B&G:AUG/94[10]574, CWM:SEP/93[24]495, CWTI:DEC/90[10], CWTI:MAY/93[26]318
MONROE, CHARLES, *Corporal, 1st Ohio Artillery*; GETTY:4[49]147
MONROE, J. ALBERT, *Captain, 1st Rhode Island Artillery*; ACW:MAR/94[50]462

MONROE, JAMES, *Colonel, 123rd Illinois Infantry*; ACW:MAY/95[49]527
MONTAGUE, GEORGE L., *Colonel, 37th Massachusetts Infantry*; GETTY:13[7]253
MONTEIRO, ARISTIDES, *Doctor, CSA*; CWM:JUL/93[4]482
MONTGOMERY, ALABAMA; CWTI:MAR/89[28]103
MONTGOMERY, CHARLES, *Lieutenant, 5th New York Infantry*; CWTI:MAY/94[31]382
MONTGOMERY, J.T., *Captain, Jeff Davis Artillery*;CWTI:DEC/91[26]238
MONGTOMERY, JAMES, *Colonel, 2nd South Carolina Infantry (Colored)*; AHI:JUL/75[4]160, CWR:VOL1#1[76]109, CWTI:DEC/89[42]137, CWTI:MAR/94[38]372
MONTGOMERY, JAMES G., *Captain, 1st Georgia Regulars*; CWR:VOL2#2[95]135
MONTGOMERY, MILTON, *Colonel, USA*; B&G:DEC/95[9]615
MONTGOMERY, WALTER A., *Captain, 12th North Carolina Infantry*; B&G:FEB/95[8]590B, GETTY:5[13]157
MONTGOMERY, WILLIAM, *Private, Phillips Legion*; CWR:VOL4#4[28]178
MONTJOY, RICHARD, *Mosby's Ranger*; CWTI:SEP/90[34]176
MONUMENTS, ETC; ARTICLES: "THE CIVIL WAR'S FIRST MONUMENT: BARTOW'S MARKER AT MANASSAS," B&G:APR/91[32]447, "FORGOTTEN VALOR: OFF THE BEATEN PATH AT ANTIETAM: DEBACLE IN THE WEST WOODS," B&G:OCT/95[8]611A, "FORGOTTEN VALOR: OFF THE BEATEN PATH AT ANTIETAM: WHOEVER HEARD OF A DEAD CAVALRYMAN?" B&G:OCT/95[8]611F, "FORGOTTEN VALOR: OFF THE BEATEN PATH AT ANTIETAM: ATTACK OF THE TURNVEREIN," B&G:OCT/95[8]611B, "FORGOTTEN VALOR: OFF THE BEATEN PATH AT ANTIETAM: OLD SIMON," B&G:OCT/95[8]611E
MOODY, DANIEL N., *Colonel, CSA*; CWM:OCT/94[38]540
MOODY, GEORGE V., *Captain, Madison (Louisiana) Artillery*; GETTY:5[47]160
MOODY, GIDEON C., *Colonel, 19th Indiana Infantry*; B&G:AUG/93[10]529
MOODY, GRANVILLE, *Colonel, USA*; B&G:FEB/94[38]553
MOODY, JEREMIAH, *Private, Petersburg Artillery*; ACW:MAR/95[12]513
MOODY, WILLIAM H., *Lieutenant Colonel, 139th Pennsylvania Infantry*; GETTY:11[91]236
MOODY, YOUNG M., *General, CSA*; B&G:APR/92[8]481
MOON, JESSE W., *Sergeant, 88th Ohio Infantry*; B&G:OCT/94[11]580
MOON, W.H., *Surgeon, 13th Alabama Infantry*; CWTI:JUL/93[20]325, GETTY:6[13]170
MOON, WILLIAM P., *Lieutenant, 7th Georgia Infantry*; B&G:APR/91[32]447
MOONEY, ROBERT, *Major, Cole's Maryland Cavalry*; B&G:AUG/94[19]575
MOONEY, THOMAS F., *Chaplain, 69th New York Militia*; CWM:MAR/91[50]340
MOONLIGHT, THOMAS, *Colonel, USA*; B&G:JUN/91[10]452
MOOR, AUGUSTUS, *Colonel, 28th Ohio Infantry*; ACW:JAN/91[38]287, B&G:OCT/94[28]581, CWTI:MAR/89[16]101
MOORE'S MILL, MISSOURI, BATTLE OF; CWNEWS:DEC/92[4], CWR:VOL2#2[169]
MOORE, A.H., *Lieutenant, 7th Tennessee Infantry*; GETTY:6[13]170
MOORE, ABSALOM B., *Colonel, USA*; CWM:JAN/93[29]459

MOORE, CALEB, *Captain, 8th New York Cavalry;*
CWM:MAY/92[8]418

MOORE, CHARLES D., *Captain, Consolidated Crescent Regiment;* CWR:VOL4#2[1]165

MOORE, DAVID, *Colonel, USA;* B&G:DEC/93[12]545, CWTI:AUG/95[34]457, CWTI:DEC/95[8]474, MH:APR/95[74]184, MH:DEC/95[58]188, *photo,* CWTI:AUG/95[34]457

MOORE, F.M., *Colonel, 83rd Ohio Infantry;* B&G:FEB/94[8]550

MOORE, FRANK A., *Lieutenant, McNally's Arkansas Artillery;* B&G:AUG/95[8]604

MOORE, GEORGE H., *Private, 111th Pennsylvania Infantry;* CWR:VOL3#2[70]155

MOORE, H.C., *Lieutenant, 38th North Carolina Infantry;* GETTY:8[67]204

MOORE, HENRY, *Sergeant, 4th U.S. Artillery;* GETTY:9[33]211, GETTY:11[57]233

MOORE, HENRY W., *civilian;* B&G:FEB/91[20]440

MOORE, J.C., *Private, 25th Arkansas Infantry;* CWTI:SEP/92[31]281

MOORE, J. SCOTT, *Private, 14th Virginia Cavalry;* B&G:AUG/94[10]574

MOORE, JAMES W., *Private, 7th Wisconsin Infantry,* GETTY:11[57]233

MOORE, JANE B., *civilian;* GETTY:10[53]225

MOORE, JESSE, *Colonel, 89th Ohio Infantry;* CWTI:SEP/92[31]281

MOORE, JOHN B., *Private, 24th Michigan Infantry;* GETTY:9[33]211, GETTY:11[57]233

MOORE, JOHN C., *General, CSA;* ACW:SEP/91[46]324, CWR:VOL1#4[64]127, CWR:VOL2#1[36]132, CWTI:SEPT/89[30]129

MOORE, JOHN V., *Private, 11th Mississippi Infantry;* ACW:MAR/92[10]349, CWR:VOL2#4[269]145

MOORE, JOHN W., *Colonel, 203rd Pennsylvania Infantry;* B&G:DEC/94[10]585,

MOORE, JONATHAN B., *Colonel, USA;* B&G:DEC/93[12]545, MH:DEC/95[58]188

MOORE, JOSEPH A., *Captain, 147th Pennsylvania Infantry;* GETTY:9[81]216

MOORE, JULIUS H.; *civilian;* B&G:FEB/91[20]440

MOORE, L.C., *Captain, 1st Pennsylvania Artillery;* GETTY:12[30]243

MOORE, N.B., *Private, 12th Illinois Cavalry;* GETTY:4[115]152

MOORE, ORLANDO H., *Colonel, CSA;* B&G:DEC/93[12]545, B&G:DEC/94[10]585, CWM:MAR/93[16]466, CWR:VOL1#4[64]127

MOORE, ROBERT, *Corporal, 4th U.S. Artillery;* GETTY:11[57]233

MOORE, ROBERT A., *Private, 17th Mississippi Infantry;* GETTY:13[7]253

MOORE, SAMUEL, *Captain, 12th New Jersey Infantry;* ACW:JUL/95[50]538

MOORE, SAMUEL A., *Lieutenant Colonel, 14th Connecticut Infantry;* ACW:SEP/94[38]487, GETTY:5[89]162, GETTY:9[61]215, *photo,* ACW:SEP/94[38]487

MOORE, SAMUEL P., *Surgeon General, CSA:*
ARTICLE: "THE *CONFEDERATE STATES MEDICAL & SURGICAL JOURNAL* WAS AN INVALUABLE CONDUIT TO SOUTHERN DOCTORS IN THE FIELD," ACW:MAY/95[8]522
ADDITIONAL LISTINGS: ACW:MAY/94[51]471, CWNEWS:NOV/90[4]

MOORE, SILAS R., *Private, 10th West Virginia Infantry;* B&G:OCT/94[28]581

MOORE, THOMAS O., *Governor, Louisiana;* ACW:JAN/92[62]346, AHI:MAY/67[42]109, CWR:VOL3#1[1]149

MOORE, W.R., *Colonel, 2nd Florida Infantry;* ACW:SEP/93[8]429

MOORE, W.T., *Private, CSA;* ACW:NOV/91[22]331

MOORE, WILBER, *Private, 154th New York Infantry;* GETTY:8[17]200

MOORE, WILLIAM, *Captain, 27th Illinois Infantry;* CWR:VOL3#4[24]162

MOORE, WILLIAM E., *Captain, Consolidated Crescent Regiment;* CWR:VOL4#2[68]167

MOORE, WILLIAM H., *Colonel, 11th Mississippi Infantry;* CWR:VOL2#4[269]145, GETTY:9[98]217

MOORE, WILLIAM H., *Lieutenant, 25th Alabama Infantry;* ARTICLE: "WRITING HOME TO TALLADEGA," CWTI:DEC/90[56]184

MOORE, WILLIAM M., *Colonel, 43rd Mississippi Infantry;* CWTI:MAR/95[46]437

MOORMAN, M.N., *Captain, CSA;* B&G:OCT/93[12]537, CWR:VOL4#4[70]180

MORAN, BENJAMIN; ACW:MAY/91[46]306

MORAN, FRANK E., *Colonel, 73rd New York Infantry:*
ARTICLE: "ESCAPE FROM LIBBY PRISON, PART I," AHI:NOV/85[38]254, "ESCAPE FROM LIBBY PRISON, PART II" AHI:DEC/85[40]255
ADDITIONAL LISTING: GETTY:5[47]160

MORAN, THOMAS, *Private, USA;* ARTICLE: "A POETIC PLEA FROM PRISON," CWTI:MAR/91[28]200

MORDECAI, ALFRED, *Major, USA;* ACW:JAN/91[8]282

MOREHEAD, CHARLES S., *Governor, Kentucky;* AHI:JUN/70[30]127

MOREHEAD, JAMES T., *Colonel, 53rd North Carolina Infantry;* GETTY:5[128]167

MOREHEAD, TURNER G., *Colonel, 106th Pennsylvania Infantry;* ACW:MAR/94[50]462, GETTY:7[97]193

MORELAND, THOMAS A., *Lieutenant, CSA;* B&G:OCT/94[11]580

MORELL, GEORGE W., *General, USA:*
GENERAL LISTINGS: *Gaines' Mill,* CWM:JUN/95[61]593, *Gettysburg,* GETTY:12[85]248, *Peninsula Campaign,* CWM:JUN/95[43]587, *Second Manassas,* AHI:DEC/66[30]105
ADDITIONAL LISTINGS: ACW:NOV/94[50]498, CWR:VOL2#4[269]145, CWTI:JUN/90[28]158, CWTI:JUL/93[42]329

MOREY, SIDNEY S., *Lieutenant, 13th Vermont Infantry;* GETTY:6[87]178

MORGAN'S 2ND KENTUCKY RAID: B&G:OCT/93[38]541

MORGAN'S INDIANA AND OHIO RAID;
BOOK REVIEW: *MOUNTED RAIDS OF THE CIVIL WAR*
ADDITIONAL LISTINGS: B&G:DEC/93[30]546, B&G:APR/94[34]561, B&G:OCT/94[11]580

MORGAN, CALVIN C., *Captain, CSA;* B&G:OCT/94[11]580

MORGAN, CHARLES H., *Lieutenant, 21st Wisconsin Infantry;* AHI:NOV/85[38]254, AHI:DEC/85[40]255, GETTY:13[50]257

MORGAN, CHARLES L., *Colonel, CSA;* CWR:VOL1#4[77], CWR:VOL2#3[212]142

MORGAN, CHARLTON H., *Captain, CSA;* B&G:OCT/94[11]580

MORGAN, EDMUND, *Governor, New York;* CWR:VOL1#4[7]125, CWTI:JUN/95[32]446, GETTY:9[5]209, GETTY:12[42]244

MORGAN, GEORGE N., *Colonel, USA;* GETTY:5[79]161
MORGAN, GEORGE W., *General, USA;* ACW:JUL/91[26]313,
CWR:VOL4#1[1]163, *photo,* AHI:NOV/79[10]195
MORGAN, JAMES D., *General, USA;* CWR:VOL4#3[65]172,
B&G:DEC/95[9]615, B&G:DEC/95[9]615, *photo,*
B&G:DEC/95[9]615
MORGAN, JAMES M., *Midshipman, CSN;*
ACW:MAY/92[16]359, AHI:DEC/82[38]231,
MH:DEC/94[46]181
MORGAN, JOHN H., *General, CSA:*
ARTICLES: "A BRILLIANT EXPLOIT: JOHN HUNT MORGAN'S
HARTSVILLE RAID," CWM:JAN/93[29]459, "CROSSING
THE LINE: BRAGG VS MORGAN," CWM:MAR/93[16]466,
"JOHN HUNT MORGAN'S ESCAPE FROM THE OHIO
PENITENTIARY," B&G:OCT/94[11]580, "MORGAN'S
BLOODY SHIRT," B&G:FEB/94[62]556
BOOK REVIEW: *CORYDON: THE FORGOTTEN BATTLE OF THE
CIVIL WAR * FOR THE SAKE OF MY COUNTRY: THE
DIARY OF COLONEL W.W. WARD, 9TH TENNESSEE
CAVALRY, MORGAN'S BRIGADE, C.S.A. * REBEL
RAIDER: THE LIFE OF GENERAL JOHN HUNT MORGAN*
GENERAL LISTINGS: *1862 Kentucky Raid,* CWTI:MAY/92[48]267,
Atlanta Campaign, CWTI:SUMMER/89[13]120, *death of,*
CWM:OCT/94[60]544, *general history,* AHI:MAY/71[3]133A, *in
book review,* ACW:SEP/95[62], CWM:MAR/91[74],
CWM:DEC/94[7], CWNEWS:JAN/94[5],
CWNEWS:NOV/95[29], CWR:VOL2#2[169],
CWR:VOL4#2[136], *in list,* B&G:OCT/94[11]580, *letters to the
editor,* B&G:DEC/94[6]584, B&G:AUG/95[36]607,
B&G:FEB/95[5]589, CWM:MAY/92[6]417, *Tullahoma
Campaign,* B&G:OCT/92[10]496, *photos,* AHI:MAY/71[3]133A,
B&G:OCT/94[11]580, CWM:MAR/93[16]466
ADDITIONAL LISTINGS, ACW: ACW:MAY/91[12]302,
ACW:JUL/92[22]368, ACW:MAR/93[51]407,
ACW:JAN/94[10]448, ACW:MAR/94[27]459,
ACW:JUL/94[26]477, ACW:MAR/95[26]515,
ACW:SEP/95[10]543, ACW:SEP/95[22]544,
ACW:NOV/95[66]559
ADDITIONAL LISTINGS, AHI: AHI:NOV/73[18]151,
AHI:JAN/76[14]164, AHI:JAN/85[20]245
ADDITIONAL LISTINGS, B&G: B&G:FEB/91[20]440,
B&G:AUG/91[11]458, B&G:FEB/92[40]479,
B&G:APR/92[28]482, B&G:OCT/92[32]499,
B&G:FEB/93[12]511, B&G:FEB/93[48]515,
B&G:APR/93[34]521, B&G:OCT/93[38]541,
B&G:AUG/94[10]574, B&G:OCT/94[42]583
ADDITIONAL LISTINGS, CWM: CWM:NOV/91[58]394A,
CWM:MAY/92[34]422, CWM:JUL/92[24]430,
CWM:MAR/93[4]463, CWM:OCT/94[48]542,
CWR:VOL4#1[1]163
ADDITIONAL LISTINGS, CWTI: CWTI:SUMMER/89[20]121,
CWTI:NOV/92[54]293, CWTI:NOV/93[33]347,
CWTI:SEP/94[49]404, CWTI:DEC/94[82]418
ADDITIONAL LISTINGS, OTHER: GETTY:13[108]261,
MH:JUN/91[20]152
MORGAN, JOHN W., *Private, CSA;* AHI:AUG/68[4]115B
MORGAN, MARTHA "MATTIE"; B&G:OCT/94[11]580
MORGAN, MICHAEL R., *General, USA;* AHI:SEP/87[48]264,
B&G:DEC/93[30]546
MORGAN, NANCY, *Nancy Harts Women's Militia Company;*
ARTICLE: "GEORGIA'S NANCY HARTS," CWTI:MAY/94[44]384
MORGAN, Q.B., *Private, 13th Virginia Artillery;*
CWR:VOL1#3[52]122

MORGAN, RICHARD C., *Captain, CSA;* B&G:OCT/94[11]580
MORGAN, ROBERT W., *Private, CSA;* CWNEWS:APR/90[4],
GETTY:6[94]180
MORGAN, SARAH:
BOOK REVIEW: *THE CIVIL WAR DIARY OF SARAH MORGAN*
ADDITIONAL LISTING: AHI:DEC/73[10]152
MORGAN, THOMAS J., *Colonel, 14th U.S. Colored Infantry;*
B&G:DEC/93[12]545
MORGAN, THOMAS S., *Captain, CSA;* B&G:OCT/94[11]580,
CWM:MAR/93[16]466
MORGAN, WILLIAM, *Colonel, 1st Virginia Cavalry;*
ACW:NOV/91[30]332, CWR:VOL2#4[313]146,
GETTY:4[65]148, GETTY:12[68]246, GETTY:13[89]260
MORGAN, WILLIAM C., *Captain, 3rd Maine Infantry;*
GETTY:12[24]242
MORGAN, WILLIAM H., *Private, CSA;* B&G:APR/93[12]518
MORGAN, WILLIAM H., *Colonel, USA;* CWR:VOL2#4[313]146
MORGANZIA BEND, LOUISIANA, SKIRMISH AT;
MH:APR/94[54]176
MORHOUS, HENRY, *Sergeant, 123rd New York Infantry;*
ACW:MAY/91[8]300
MORIARTY, JOHN D., *Major, Excelsior Brigade;*
B&G:APR/95[24]596
MORILL, WALTER, *Captain, 20th Maine Infantry;*
ACW:JAN/92[38]343
MORLEY, THOMAS, *Captain, 12th Pennsylvania Cavalry;*
B&G:OCT/93[21]538
MORMON CONFRONTATION; ARTICLE: "'TO MEET A
REBELLION'," AHI:DEC/72[10]145
MORRILL, HENRY L., *Adjutant, 1st Iowa Cavalry;*
CWTI:MAY/93[35]320
MORRILL, WALTER G., *Captain, 20th Maine Infantry;*
GETTY:6[43]173, GETTY:8[31]201
MORRIS (VIRGINIA) ARTILLERY; GETTY:4[33]146,
GETTY:4[49]147, GETTY:6[7]169
MORRIS, C.O., *Private, 10th Georgia Infantry;*
ACW:JUL/95[10]533
MORRIS, CHARLES M., *Lieutenant, CSN;* AHI:JAN/83[10]232
MORRIS, DWIGHT W., *Colonel, 14th Connecticut Infantry;*
GETTY:9[61]215
MORRIS, GEORGE N., *Lieutenant, USN;* AHI:OCT/75[30]162
MORRIS, J.L., *Surgeon, 150th Pennsylvania Infantry;*
GETTY:10[53]225
MORRIS, ROBERT, *Major, 6th Pennsylvania Cavalry;*
CWTI:JUN/90[32]159
MORRIS, ROBERT, *Private, 24th Michigan Infantry,*
GETTY:9[33]211, GETTY:11[57]233
MORRIS, ROBERT, JR., *Colonel, USA;* GETTY:7[77]191,
GETTY:11[19]232
MORRIS, THOMAS A., *General, USA;* ACW:JAN/92[47]344,
B&G:AUG/93[10]529
MORRIS, W.G., *Colonel, 37th North Carolina Infantry;*
GETTY:8[67]204
MORRIS, WILLIAM H., *General, USA;* B&G:APR/95[8]595,
B&G:JUN/95[8]600, B&G:DEC/95[25]616
MORRIS, WILLIAM S.; CWM:NOV/91[58]394A
MORRISON, DAVID, *Lieutenant Colonel, USA;*
CWTI:JAN/94[46]364
MORRISON, EMMETT, *Lieutenant Colonel, 15th Virginia
Infantry;* CWTI:AUG/90[26]166
MORRISON, FRANCIS W., *Surgeon, 4th Ohio Infantry;*
GETTY:10[53]225

MORRISON, J.J., *Colonel, 1st Georgia Cavalry;*
CWR:VOL4#1[1]163
MORRISON, JAMES, *Captain, CSA;* CWTI:MAY/89[22]116
MORRISON, JAMES J., *Captain, USN;* ACW:MAR/94[35]460
MORRISON, JAMES J., *Colonel, CSA;* CWR:VOL4#1[1]163
MORRISON, JOHN, *Private, 22nd Massachusetts Infantry;*
GETTY:8[53]203
MORRISON, JOSEPH, *Captain, CSA;* ACW:MAY/95[10]523,
CWM:APR/94[14]503
MORRISON, PETER, *Corporal, 9th New Hampshire Infantry;*
CWNEWS:MAY/89[4]
MORRISON, ROBERT G., *Lieutenant Colonel, 34th Indiana
Infantry;* CWTI:AUG/90[58]169
MORRISON, W.W., *Major, CSA;* CWTI:MAY/89[22]116
MORRISON, WILLIAM R., *Colonel, USA;* B&G:FEB/92[10]474
MORROW, BEN; B&G:JUN/91[32]454
MORROW, HENRY, *Colonel, 24th Michigan Infantry;*
CWM:JAN/93[16]457, GETTY:5[19]158, GETTY:7[7]185
MORROW, KEITH G., *Major, 5th Indiana Infantry;*
CWM:MAR/94[1]205
MORSE, A.P., *Lieutenant, 6th New York Infantry;*
CWTI:JAN/95[42]428
MORSE, CHARLES F., *Colonel, 2nd Massachusetts Infantry;*
B&G:FEB/95[8]590C, GETTY:7[83]192
MORSE, CHARLES M., *civilian;* CWTI:MAR/89[28]103
MORSE, CHARLES P., *Major, 2nd Massachusetts Infantry;*
GETTY:6[69]176
MORSE, GEORGE W., *arms inventor;* ACW:JAN/94[18]449
MORSE, SAMUEL F.B.; B&G:FEB/94[24]551
MORTIMORE, WILLIAM, *Captain, USA;* CWTI:OCT/95[56]471
MORTON'S FORD, VIRGINIA, BATTLE OF:
ARTICLE: "REBELS ACROSS THE RIVER," ACW:SEP/94[38]487
ADDITIONAL LISTING: B&G:APR/91[8]445
MORTON, GEORGE P., *Private, 31st Virginia Infantry;*
B&G:AUG/93[10]529
MORTON, JEREMIAH; B&G:DEC/91[34]470
MORTON, JOHN W., *Captain, 1st Tennessee Infantry:*
BOOK REVIEW: *THE ARTILLERY OF NATHAN BEDFORD
FORREST'S CAVALRY*
ADDITIONAL LISTINGS: B&G:JUN/92[32]488, B&G:DEC/93[12]545
MORTON, OLIVER P., *Governor, Indiana;* ACW:JUL/91[6]308,
ACW:JUL/92[22]368, AHI:JUN/66[52]102,
AHI:NOV/72[12]142, B&G:OCT/95[36]614,
CWTI:JAN/93[49]303
MORTON, PHILO S., *Lieutenant, 100th Pennsylvania Infantry;*
CWTI:JAN/94[49]365
MORTON, SIDNEY G., *Private, 17th Maine Infantry;*
GETTY:8[43]202
MORTON, ST. CLAIR, *Major, USA;* CWTI:APR/90[24]152
MOSBY, JOHN S., *Colonel, CSA:*
ARTICLES: A MATCH FOR MOSBY?" ACW:JUL/94[26]477, "THE
GRAY GHOST STORY," B&G:APR/94[31]560, "HOW TO
STEAL A GENERAL," CWTI:DEC/91[22]237, "INSIDE
MOSBY'S CONFEDERACY," CWTI:SEP/90[34]176, "JOHN
SINGLETON MOSBY AND THE 'GREENBACK RAID,'"
CWM:JAN/93[24]458
BOOK REVIEWS: *43RD BATTALION VIRGINIA CAVALRY
MOSBY'S COMMAND * THE MEMOIRS OF JOHN S.
MOSBY * MOSBY'S CONFEDERACY: A GUIDE TO THE
ROADS AND SITES OF COLONEL JOHN SINGLETON
MOSBY * MOSBY'S RANGERS*
GENERAL LISTINGS: *1863 cavalry battles,* MH:OCT/92[51]162,
Aldie, GETTY:11[19]232, *general history,*

AHI:MAY/71[3]133A, *Gettysburg,* GETTY:4[65]148,
GETTY:4[113]153, GETTY:7[124]196, GETTY:12[111]250, *in
book review,* ACW:MAY/95[62], CWM:AUG/95[8],
CWNEWS:MAY/90[4], CWNEWS:JUN/91[4],
CWR:VOL4#1[78], CWTI:OCT/95[18], *letters to the editor,*
CWM:MAR/91[12]333, CWM:MAY/92[6]417,
CWM:JAN/93[6]455, CWM:JUL/93[4]482,
CWM:AUG/94[6]521, CWTI:MAR/91[10]197,
CWTI:FEB/91[8]188, CWTI:JUL/93[10]323, *Peninsula
Campaign,* CWM:JUN/95[50]589, *television,*
B&G:FEB/91[38]443, *photos,* ACW:JUL/94[26]477,
ACW:JUL/95[34]536, AHI:MAY/71[3]133A,
B&G:APR/91[8]445, B&G:APR/94[31]560,
CWTI:SEP/90[34]176, CWTI:DEC/95[76]482
ADDITIONAL LISTINGS: ACW:MAR/91[30]295, ACW:SEP/91[41]323,
ACW:SEP/93[22]432, ACW:SEP/94[55]489,
ACW:MAR/95[26]515, ACW:MAY/95[54]528,
ACW:JUL/95[34]536, ACW:SEP/95[10]543,
AHI:MAR/84[42]238, B&G:APR/91[8]445,
B&G:FEB/93[48]515, B&G:OCT/93[12]537,
B&G:AUG/94[10]574, B&G:AUG/94[19]575,
B&G:AUG/95[22]608, CWM:MAR/92[56]415,
CWM:JUN/94[14]509, CWM:JUN/94[23]510,
CWR:VOL1#3[28]120, CWTI:DEC/89[34]136,
CWTI:AUG/90[42]167, CWTI:SEP/90[18]172,
CWTI:DEC/90[58]185, CWTI:MAY/91[48]211,
CWTI:JUL/92[12]270, CWTI:JUL/94[44]394,
CWTI:JUN/95[38]447, CWTI:OCT/95[48]470,
CWTI:DEC/95[76]482, GETTY:10[42]224, GETTY:10[102]226
MOSBY, PAULINE, CWTI:SEP/90[34]176
MOSEBUCK, AUGUSTUS, *Private, 8th Louisiana Infantry;*
CWTI:FEB/91[12]189
MOSELEY, WILLIAM G.; CWR:VOL4#2[118]169
MOSES, FRANK J., *Governor, South Carolina;*
AHI:JAN/73[28]147
MOSES, WEBSTER, *Private, 7th Kansas Cavalry;*
ACW:JAN/93[26]395
MOSGROVE, GEORGE E., *Private, CSA;*
B&G:AUG/91[11]458, B&G:AUG/91[52]464
MOSHER, CHARLIE, *Private, 85th New York Infantry;* BOOK
REVIEW: *CHARLIE MOSHER'S CIVIL WAR*
MOSMAN, CHESLEY A., *Lieutenant, 59th Illinois Infantry;*
CWTI:SUMMER/89[20]121
MOTT, GERSHOM, *General, USA;* ACW:NOV/91[30]332,
ACW:JUL/93[16]422, ACW:MAY/93[31]415,
B&G:FEB/92[22]476, B&G:APR/94[10]558,
B&G:APR/95[8]595, B&G:JUN/95[8]600, CWR:VOL1#3[52]122
MOTT, RANDOLPH L., *Colonel, USA;* ACW:MAR/91[38]296
MOTT, SAMUEL, *Lieutenant Colonel, 57th Ohio Infantry;*
CWTI:SUMMER/89[50]124
MOTT, THADDEUS P., *Captain, 3rd New York Artillery;*
ACW:JAN/94[8]447, CWM:JUN/95[29]583
MOUAT, DAVID, *Private, 29th Pennsylvania Infantry;*
CWR:VOL3#2[70]155
MOULDING, JOHN, *Private, USA;* B&G:JUN/93[12]524
MOULTON, ANDREW, *Private, 9th New Hampshire Infantry;*
CWR:VOL2#2[118]136
MOULTON, CHARLES H., *Private, 34th Massachusetts
Infantry;* BOOK REVIEW: *FORT LYON TO HARPERS FERRY:
ON THE BORDER OF NORTH AND SOUTH WITH
"RAMBLING JOUR"*
MOUNT McGREGOR MEMORIAL ASSOCIATION;
B&G:FEB/93[61]516

MOUNT McGREGOR, NEW YORK; B&G:APR/93[6]517,
B&G:JUN/93[6]523
MOUNTJOY, RICHARD, *Captain, CSA;* ACW:JUL/94[26]477
MOUTON, ALFRED, *General, CSA:*
BOOK REVIEW: *ACADIAN GENERAL: ALFRED MOUTON AND
THE CIVIL WAR*
ADDITIONAL LISTINGS: CWM:OCT/94[33]537, CWM:APR/95[39]576,
CWM:APR/95[50], CWNEWS:DEC/93[5], CWR:VOL3#1[1]149,
CWR:VOL4#2[1]165, CWR:VOL4#2[26]166,
CWR:VOL4#2[118]169, CWR:VOL4#2[68]167
MOUTON, WILLIAM, *Major, 18th Louisiana Consolidated
Infantry;* CWR:VOL4#2[1]165

MOVIES, TELEVISION AND VIDEO:
ARTICLES: "A LEG UP ON JOHN BELL HOOD,"
B&G:JUN/91[42]456, "THE CIVIL WAR IS ON A ROLL,"
B&G:APR/91[40]450, "CIVIL WAR JOURNAL"
CWTI:MAR/94[44]373, CWTI:JUL/94[10]389, "CIVIL WAR
SERIES AIRS ON PBS," AHI:SEP/90[16]289A, "EDITORIAL,"
ACW:SEP/91[6]317, "GRAY GHOST; B&G:FEB/91[38]443,
"THE GRAY GHOST STORY," B&G:APR/94[31]560,
"JEFFERSON DAVIS' GREATEST MISTAKE,"
B&G:FEB/91[38]443, "LINCOLN AND THE IRONCLADS
COME TO TELEVISION," CWTI:MAR/91[42]202, "THE
MONITOR VS. THE *MERRIMACK:* A LOVE STORY?"
CWM:MAR/91[43]339, "STRANGE BEDFELLOWS,"
B&G:FEB/92[36]478
A Perfect Tribute; CWTI:MAR/91[42]202
A Defense of General Joseph E. Johnston;
B&G:FEB/91[38]443
A Fair Rebel (1914); B&G:FEB/91[38]443
Abraham Lincoln, AHI:SEP/89[25], CWTI:SEP/90[10]
An Occurrence at Owl Creek Bridge; ACW:SEP/91[6]317
Andersonville; B&G:FEB/95[38]593
Atlanta: Yankees Invate the Deep South, AHI:NOV/89[27]
The Battle of Gettysburg in Miniature, AHI:JAN/90[15],
CWTI:SEPT/89[28]
The Battle of Shiloh, AHI:APR/88[13]
Birth of a Nation; ACW:SEP/91[6]317, B&G:FEB/91[38]443,
CWTI:DEC/89[62]139
Black Easter: The Assassination of Abraham Lincoln,
CWTI:NOV/92[10]
Bloody Shenandoah: The Valley Campaign In All Its Fury,
ACW:MAY/92[54], CWM:MAR/92[49], CWTI:FEB/92[18]
USS Cairo; B&G:APR/91[40]450
Civil War Cinema; B&G:FEB/91[38]443, CWTI:SEP/91[10]
The Civil War (Ken Burns):
ARTICLE: "THE CIVIL WAR," CWTI:SEP/90[48]178
GENERAL LISTINGS: *editorial,* ACW:JAN/91[6]281, *in book review,*
CWM:JUN/94[6], CWNEWS:JUN/91[4], CWTI:AUG/91[18],
letters to the editor, CWM:JAN/91[6]324,
CWM:MAR/91[12]333, CWM:MAY/91[6]345,
CWM:NOV/91[6]389, CWTI:FEB/91[8]188,
CWTI:MAR/91[10]197, CWTI:APR/92[8]252,
CWTI:JUL/93[10]323
ADDITIONAL LISTINGS: ACW:MAR/91[30]295, ACW:MAR/95[6]511,
B&G:FEB/91[6]438, B&G:JUN/91[26]453,
B&G:JUN/91[42]456, B&G:AUG/91[40]463,
CWM:MAY/91[31]350, CWM:NOV/91[6]389,
CWM:NOV/91[35]392
The Divided House: The Second American Revolution,
CWTI:JUN/90[20]

**The Divided Union: The Story of the Great American War,
1961-1865,** AHI:SUM/88[8], B&G:APR/91[40]450
Echoes of Glory, CWM:SEP/92[57]
Echoes of the Blue & Gray, CWTI:FEB/90[10],
CWTI:DEC/90[10]
Federal Enlisted Uniforms of the Civil War,
B&G:APR/91[40]450, CWTI:MAR/91[18]
The Fugitive (1910); B&G:FEB/91[38]443
Gettysburg:
ARTICLES: "CAMP TALK EXTRA: **GETTYSBURG,** A LESSON
IN FOREIGN," POLICY B&G:FEB/94[39]554, "FILM
ADAPTATION OF *KILLER ANGELS* REACHES SCREEN,"
AHI:NOV/93[28]315, **"GETTYSBURG:** HOW A PRIZE
WINNING NOVEL BECAME A MOTION PICTURE,"
CWTI:NOV/93[40]348, "THE *KILLER ANGELS /
GETTYSBURG,"* CWM:JUL/93[40]488, "SCENES FROM
THE MAKING OF **GETTYSBURG,"** B&G:DEC/93[59]549
GENERAL LISTINGS: *letters to the editor,* B&G:APR/94[6]557,
B&G:FEB/93[6]510, B&G:FEB/94[6]549, CWTI:JAN/94[8]356,
CWTI:MAR/94[16]368
ADDITIONAL LISTINGS: ACW:MAR/95[6]511, AHI:AUG/94[22],
B&G:OCT/92[26]498, B&G:DEC/93[30]546,
B&G:DEC/93[59]549, B&G:FEB/94[38]553,
CWM:DEC/94[26]548, CWR:VOL4#4[v]176,
CWTI:MAR/94[44]373
Gettysburg: The Last Reunion of the Blue & Gray,
AHI:JAN/94[28],
Glory:
ARTICLE: "THE MAKING OF **GLORY,** CWTI:DEC/89[53]138
GENERAL LISTINGS: *in book review,* B&G:OCT/93[24],
CWM:JUL/91[58], CWNEWS:JUL/93[5], CWTI:JUL/93[12],
letters to the editor, CWM:JAN/91[6]324
ADDITIONAL LISTINGS: ACW:MAR/91[30]295, CWM:JAN/91[35]328,
CWM:MAR/91[39]338, CWM:MAR/91[43]339,
B&G:FEB/94[38]553, CWM:JUL/93[40]488
Gone With the Wind:
ARTICLE: "THE FILM THAT MADE ME: 50 YEARS AFTER
GWTW IS RELEASED AN HISTORIAN GETS AROUND TO
SAYING THANK YOU," CWTI:SUMMER/89[6]119A
ADDITIONAL LISTINGS: ACW:SEP/91[6]317, B&G:APR/94[34]561,
CWTI:DEC/89[62]139
The Great Locomotive Chase; ACW:SEP/91[6]317
Guns of the Civil War, AHI:AUG/94[22], CWTI:JUL/94[18]
"Helmira" 1864-1865, CWM:OCT/95[10]
The Horse Soldiers:
ARTICLE: "THE HORSE SOLDIERS," B&G:JUN/93[36]526
ADDITIONAL LISTINGS: B&G:JUN/93[12]524, MH:FEB/95[18]182
House With Closed Shutters (1910); B&G:FEB/91[38]443
The Ironclads; B&G:APR/91[40]450, B&G:JUN/91[42]456,
CWTI:MAR/91[42]202
The Last Full Measure: The Battle of Gettysburg,
AHI:JAN/88[9]
The Lincoln-Douglas Debates OF 1858, ACW:OCT/94[28]
The Little Shephard of Kingdom Come; ACW:SEP/91[6]317
Meade of Gettysburg, CWTI:NOV/93[14]
Out of the Wilderness: The Life of Abraham Lincoln,
AHI:AUG/94[22], CWTI:MAR/94[12]
Petersburg; B&G:JUN/91[42]456
Quest for the *Monitor,* AHI:MAY/91[22]
The Red Badge of Courage; ACW:SEP/91[6]317
Robert E. Lee, AHI:JAN/90[22]
Shenandoah; ACW:SEP/91[6]317

Smithsonian's Great Battles of the Civil War,
ACW:JUL/93[58], CWTI:JUL/93[12]
Son of the Morning Star; B&G:JUN/91[42]456
Spotsylvania; B&G:JUN/91[42]456
Stonewall Jackson; Robert E. Lee; Ulysses S. Grant. Civil War Generals, CWTI:DEC/89[20]
Thomas J. Jackson, AHI:JAN/90[22]
Touring Civil War Battlefields, AHI:NOV/88[8]
The True Story of *GLORY* Continues, CWM:JUL/91[58]
Twilight of the Blue And Gray; B&G:APR/91[40]45
Ulysses S. Grant, AHI:JAN/90[22]
Voices of Gettysburg: The Third Day—Pickett's Charge,
AHI:JUL/91[20], B&G:FEB/91[38]443
Witness to the Storm: Part 1, The Civil War Photographers, AHI:NOV/87[8]

MOWER, JAMES A.; CWR:VOL2#4[313]146
MOWER, JOSEPH A., *General, USA;* B&G:JUN/91[10]452,
B&G:AUG/95[8]604, B&G:DEC/95[9]615,
CWM:JUL/92[18]429, CWR:VOL2#3[212]142,
CWR:VOL3#3[88]160, CWR:VOL4#2[26]166,
CWR:VOL4#3[65]172, CWTI:JUL/94[50]395,
MH:DEC/95[58]188, *photo,* AHI:NOV/79[10]195
MOWER, WILBUR F., *Sergeant, 16th Maine Infantry;*
CWM:MAY/92[15]419, GETTY:13[33]255
MOWRY, SYLVESTER; ACW:JUL/93[27]423
MOYLAN, MYLES, *Captain, USA;* MH:AUG/95[82]186
MOYNAHAN, HENRY, *Private, 24th Michigan Infantry,*
GETTY:11[57]233
MUD MARCH; B&G:FEB/92[22]476
MUDD, JOSEPH A., *Private, CSA;*
BOOK REVIEWS: *WITH PORTER IN NORTH MISSOURI: A CHAPTER IN THE HISTORY OF THE WAR BETWEEN THE STATES*
MUDD, SAMUEL A., *Surgeon;*
ARTICLES: "MORAL VICTORY IN THE CRUSADE TO CLEAR MUDD," CWTI:MAY/93[12]316, "MUDD MUSEUM," AHI:FEB/88[12]267, "RULING IN MUDD CASE OVERTURNED," AHI:JAN/93[8]307, "WHAT REALLY HAPPENED TO THE ASSASSIN?" CWTI:JUL/92[50]275
ADDITIONAL LISTINGS: AHI:FEB/86[12]257, B&G:JUN/91[26]453,
B&G:OCT/91[40]467, B&G:APR/92[36]483,
B&G:DEC/92[40]508, CWTI:AUG/90[8]165,
CWTI:MAR/91[28]200, CWTI:MAY/92[8]261,
CWTI:SEP/93[8]332, MH:JUN/91[20]152, *photo,*
CWTI:MAR/91[28]200
MUDGE, CHARLES R., *Lieutenant Colonel, 2nd Massachusetts Infantry;*
ARTICLE: "A CALL OF LEADERSHIP: LIEUTENANT COLONEL CHARLES REDINGTON MUDGE, U.S.V. AND THE SECOND MASSACHUSETTS INFANTRY AT GETTYSBURG," GETTY:6[69]176
ADDITIONAL LISTINGS: GETTY:7[83]192, GETTY:12[7]241
MUDGET, LEWIS P., *Major, 86th USCT;* CWR:VOL4#1[78]
MUELLER, J. MAX, *Captain, USA;* GETTY:4[115]152
MUELLER, MICHAEL, *Captain, Indiana Light Artillery;*
B&G:AUG/95[8]604
MUFFLY, J.W., *Adjutant, 148th Pennsylvania Infantry;* BOOK
REVIEW: *THE STORY OF OUR REGIMENT,*
CWR:VOL4#3[1]170
MUHLENBERG, CHARLES P., *Lieutenant, 5th U.S. Artillery;*
CWTI:FEB/92[36]249

MUHLENBERG, EDWARD D., *Lieutenant, 4th U.S. Artillery;*
ACW:MAY/91[8]300, B&G:FEB/95[8]590C, GETTY:7[83]192,
GETTY:9[81]216
MUHLENGERG, FRANK, *Captain, 13th U.S. Regulars;*
CWR:VOL2#1[1]130
MULHOLLAND, ST. CLAIR A., *Major, 116th Pennsylvania Infantry;*
BOOK REVIEW: *THE STORY OF THE 116TH REGIMENT PENNSYLVANIA INFANTRY*
ADDITIONAL LISTINGS: ACW:MAY/94[12]466,
CWM:MAR/91[17]335, CWM:MAR/91[50]340,
CWNEWS:JAN/93[4], CWR:VOL2#2[141]137,
CWR:VOL4#4[47]179, CWTI:DEC/90[58]185, GETTY:5[35]159
MULLEN, DANIEL, *Chaplain, 9th Connecticut Infantry;*
CWM:MAR/91[50]340
MULLER, CHARLES and LOUIS, *1st Minnesota Infantry;*
GETTY:5[79]161, GETTY:10[53]225
MULLIGAN, JAMES A., *Colonel, 23rd Illinois Infantry;*
ACW:MAR/92[46]354, B&G:JUN/95[36]603A,
CWM:AUG/95[35]607
MULLINS, GORDON C., *Captain, CSA;* B&G:OCT/94[11]580
MULLINS, MARTIN, *Private, 52nd Illinois Infantry;*
B&G:APR/95[24]596
MULLIS, JOSEPH M, *Private, 19th Georgia Cavalry;*
B&G:JUN/94[38]571
MUMFORD, WILLIAM B., *civilian;* CWTI:MAY/93[29]319
MUMFORD, WILLIAM T., *Lieutenant, 1st Louisiana Artillery;*
ARTICLE: "DIARY OF THE VICKSBURG SIEGE,"
AHI:DEC/77[46]177
MUNCH, EMIL, *Captain, 1st Minnesota Battery;*
B&G:JUN/95[36]603A, CWR:VOL4#1[44]164
MUNFORD, JOHN D.; CWM:MAR/91[65]342
MUNFORD, THOMAS T., *General, CSA:*
GENERAL LISTINGS: *1863 cavalry battles,* MH:OCT/92[51]162,
Aldie, GETTY:10[42]224, GETTY:11[19]232, *Brandy Station,*
GETTY:11[19]232, *Five Forks,* B&G:APR/92[8]481, *Gettysburg,*
GETTY:4[65]148, *in order of battle,* B&G:APR/92[8]481,
Manassas, Second, B&G:AUG/92[11]493
ADDITIONAL LISTINGS: ACW:JAN/93[43]397, ACW:SEP/93[31]433,
ACW:JAN/94[39]451, B&G:APR/92[48]484,
B&G:FEB/93[24]512, B&G:OCT/93[12]537,
CWR:VOL3#3[1]157, CWTI:JUN/90[32]159,
CWTI:APR/92[35]257
MUNFORDVILLE, KENTUCKY, SKIRMISH AT;
B&G:OCT/92[32]499
MUNGER, BENNETT, *Captain, USA;* CWTI:DEC/91[26]238
MUNNERLYN, CHARLES J., *Colonel, CSA;*
ACW:NOV/95[38]556
MUNNIE, ROBERT, *Private, 5th New York Infantry;*
CWR:VOL1#2[29]112
MUNROE, CHARLES, *Private, 1st Ohio Light Artillery;*
GETTY:4[49]147
MUNROE, DUNCAN, *Private, 51st North Carolina Infantry;*
B&G:APR/93[24]520
MUNROE, FRANK, *Lieutenant, USMC;* CWTI:APR/92[14]254
MUNSELL, GEORGE N., *Surgeon, 35th Massachusetts Infantry;* CWTI:FEB/92[36]249
MUNSON, FRED, *Sergeant, 97th New York Infantry;*
GETTY:10[7]221
MUNSON, JOHN, *Mosby's Ranger;* ACW:SEP/95[10]543
MURFREE, JAMES, *Surgeon, CSA;* B&G:AUG/91[11]458
MURFREESBORO, TENNESSEE, BATTLE OF; see listings under **"STONES RIVER, TENNESSEE, BATTLE OF"**

MURFREESBORO, TENNESSEE, FORREST'S RAID ON;
B&G:OCT/92[10]496, B&G:DEC/93[12]545,
B&G:OCT/95[5]610, CWTI:NOV/93[33]347
MURPHEY, JOSIAH F., *Private, 20th Massachusetts Infantry:*
BOOK REVIEW: *THE CIVIL WAR: THE NANTUCKET
EXPERIENCE*
ADDITIONAL LISTING: CWR:VOL4#4[101]181
MURPHY, ANTHONY, *civilian;* ACW:SEP/91[22]321
MURPHY, ISAAC, *Governor, Arkansas;* ACW:MAY/91[12]302
MURPHY, JAMES C., *Captain, 7th Louisiana Infantry;*
CWR:VOL4#2[118]169
MURPHY, JEDIDIAH, *Private, 150th New York Infantry;*
GETTY:12[42]244
MURPHY, JEREMIAH, *Private, 6th Wisconsin Infantry;*
GETTY:11[57]233
MURPHY, JOHN R., *Lieutenant, 8th Louisiana Infantry;*
CWTI:FEB/91[12]189
MURPHY, MICHAEL C., *Colonel, USA;* B&G:APR/93[12]51,
CWM:OCT/95[40]619
MURPHY, PATRICK J.R., *Chaplain, 58th Illinois Cavalry;*
CWM:MAR/91[50]340
MURPHY, THOMAS, *Private, 8th Louisiana Infantry;*
CWTI:FEB/91[12]189
MURPHY, THOMAS H., *Lieutenant, CSA;* ACW:NOV/91[64]336
MURPHY, WILLIAM B., *Sergeant, 2nd Mississippi Infantry;*
CWM:MAR/91[17]335, GETTY:4[16]143, GETTY:4[126]154,
GETTY:6[77]177, GETTY:9[98]217
MURPHY, WILLIAM B., *Sergeant, 6th Wisconsin Infantry;*
GETTY:6[77]177
MURRAH, PENDLETON, *Governor of Texas;*
AHI:JUN/70[30]127, CWTI:AUG/90[70]171
MURRAY, ALBERT M., *Lieutenant, USA;* B&G:DEC/91[12]469
MURRAY, CHARLES H., *Lieutenant, 5th Ohio Cavalry;*
CWR:VOL4#1[44]164
MURRAY, EIL H., *Major, 3rd Kentucky Cavalry;*
ACW:MAR/93[51]407
MURRAY, J. OGDEN; CWTI:FEB/92[42]250
MURRAY, JAMES, *Sergeant Major, Petersburg Artillery;*
ACW:MAR/95[12]513
MURRAY, JOHN P., *Colonel, 28th Tennessee Infantry;*
B&G:FEB/93[12]511
MURRAY, ROBERT, *Surgeon, USA;* CWM:MAY/91[10]347
MURRAY, THOMAS, *Private, 5th Ohio Cavalry;*
CWR:VOL4#1[44]164
MURRAY, WILLIAM, *Sergeant, 52nd Georgia Infantry;*
CWTI:NOV/92[41]291
MURRAY, WILLIAM H., *Captain, 1st Maryland (Confederate)
Battalion;* GETTY:7[83]192
MURREY, MICHAEL, *Private, 70th Ohio Infantry;*
CWTI:DEC/94[62]415

MUSEUMS:
A.K. Smiley Library; ARTICLE: "A SHRINE IN THE GOLDEN
STATE," CWTI:MAY/92[20]262
Abraham Lincoln Museum; B&G:FEB/91[34]442
Andersonville:
ARTICLE: "POW MUSEUM AT ANDERSONVILLE,"
AHI:NOV/92[16]305
ADDITIONAL LISTING: CWM:JUL/92[27]431
Army Quartermaster Musuem, Fort Lee, Virginia;
ACW:NOV/92[74]390
Atlanta Cyclorama; ACW:NOV/95[74]560,
CWTI:FEB/92[10]246

Atlanta History Museum; ARTICLE: "ATLANTA HISTORY
MUSEUM ESTABLISHED," AHI:NOV/93[12]313
ADDITIONAL LISTING: B&G:OCT/94[42]583
Baltimore & Ohio Railroad Museum; CWTI:OCT/95[24]466
Branson Civil War Museum; B&G:FEB/94[38]553
Carter House, Franklin, Tennessee; B&G:OCT/93[38]541
Civil War Library and Museum in Philadelphia;
B&G:DEC/92[40]508, CWM:NOV/92[6]446
Confederate Memorial Hall; B&G:FEB/92[40]479
Confederate Museum at St. George, Bermuda;
ACW:MAY/93[62]418, CWTI:DEC/89[10]133
Confederate Naval Museum, Columbus, Georgia; ARTICLE:
"GEORGIA'S ENDANGERED REBEL GUNBOATS,"
CWTI:NOV/93[74]353
Cumberland Science Museum; B&G:DEC/93[52]548
Drum Barracks Civil War Muesum; ARTICLE: "LOS
ANGELES' DRUM BARRACKS," CWTI:SEP/91[18]227
Fort Gaines, Alabama; CWTI:MAR/94[20]369
"G.A.R. MUSEUM IS A TREASURY OF WAR RELICS,"
CWTI:SEP/90[22]173
**The Grand Army of the Republic Civil War Museum and
Library of Philadelphia,** B&G:APR/92[36]483
Hoover Museum; B&G:OCT/94[42]583
Kennedy Farm (John Brown's house); CWTI:JUL/92[20]271
Kennesaw, Georgia; CWTI:FEB/92[10]246
Lincoln Memorial Shrine; ARTICLE: "A SHRINE IN THE
GOLDEN STATE," CWTI:MAY/92[20]262
Lincoln Museum of Fort Wayne; AHI:JUL/93[14]311,
B&G:APR/92[36]483, CWM:MAR/93[36]469
**Louisiana Historical Association's Memorial Hall
Confederate Museum;** ARTICLE: "NEW ORLEANS' HAVEN
FOR HISTORY," CWTI:AUG/95[28]456
Louisiana State Museum in New Orleans;
CWTI:SEPT/89[20]127
Manassas Museum; ARTICLE: "STONEWALL JACKSON
RETURNS TO MANASSAS," AHI:JAN/93[8]308
ADDITIONAL LISTING: B&G:APR/93[40]522
Medford Historical Society Museum:
ARTICLE: "TREASURE IN THE ATTIC," CWTI:MAY/91[34]209
ADDITIONAL LISTING: CWTI:OCT/95[18]
Mudd Museum; ARTICLE: "MUDD MUSEUM,"
AHI:FEB/88[12]267
Museum of American Financial History;
B&G:DEC/94[36]588
Museum of New Mexico; CWTI:MAR/94[58]375
Museum of the Confederacy:
ARTICLES: "CONFEDERATE WHITE HOUSE OPENS,"
AHI:SUM/88[10]272 "EMBATTLED EMBLEM: THE ARMY
OF NORTHERN VIRGINIA BATTLE FLAG FROM 1861 TO
THE PRESENT," AHI:JAN/94[12]317, "TRAVEL, MUSEUM
OF THE CONFEDERACY," ACW:SEP/91[62]326
ADDITIONAL LISTINGS: ACW:MAY/93[62]418, B&G:DEC/92[40]508,
B&G:AUG/93[36]533, B&G:APR/94[34]561,
B&G:JUN/94[38]571, B&G:AUG/94[6]573,
B&G:OCT/94[6]579, B&G:DEC/94[36]588,
B&G:APR/95[38]598, CWTI:JUL/94[8]388, MH:DEC/92[74]
National Building Museum; ARTICLE: "A PEEK INTO THE
PAST," CWTI:AUG/95[10]453
National Civil War Museum, Gettysburg;
B&G:AUG/95[42]608
ARTICLE: "NATIONAL MUSEUM OF CIVIL WAR MEDICINE,"
AHI:JAN/94[17]318

ADDITIONAL LISTINGS: B&G:AUG/93[36]533, B&G:APR/92[36]483, B&G:DEC/93[30]546, CWM:JUL/93[35]487

National Museum of Health, National Archives; B&G:AUG/95[42]608

National Museum of the U.S. Army; ARTICLE: "NEW ARMY MUSEUM PLANNED," CWTI:OCT/95[10]464

New Market Battlefield; B&G:OCT/92[26]498

New York State Military Heritage Museum; CWM:JAN/92[27]403

Siege Museum, Petersburg, Virginia; ACW:NOV/92[74]390

St. Albans Historical Museum; B&G:OCT/94[42]583

Surratt Museum; ARTICLE: "SURRATT MUSEUM," AHI:SUM/88[10]272

Tennessee State Museum; B&G:DEC/93[52]548

United States Civil War Center; ARTICLE: "A SUPERHIGHWAY FOR CIVIL WAR INFORMATION," CWTI:JAN/95[30]426

Valentine Museum:
ARTICLES: "RICHMOND MUSEUM CELEBRATES FIRST YEAR," CWTI:JUN/95[10]442, "VALENTINE MUSEUM EXPANDS TO TREDEGAR IRON WORKS," AHI:JUL/91[14]296, "WORKING PEOPLE IN RICHMOND: LIFE AND LABOR IN AN INDUSTRIAL CITY, 1865-1920," AHI:SEP/91[8]298
ADDITIONAL LISTING: CWM:SEP/91[27]382

White House of the Confederacy; BOOK REVIEW: *WHITE HOUSE OF THE CONFEDERACY*

MUSIC:

"Battle Hymn of the Republic":
ARTICLES: "'THE BATTLE HYMN OF THE REPUBLIC' ARMED THE NORTH WITH MORAL CERTITUDE," ACW:MAR/94[10]457, "WORDS ABOUT THE MUSIC," CWTI:SEPT/89[44]131

"Homespun Songs of the Civil War"; CWTI:APR/90[10]

Miscellaneous:
ARTICLES: "THE CIVIL WAR IS ON A ROLL (AUDIO/VIDEO)," B&G:APR/91[40]450, "STRANGE BEDFELLOWS (AUDIO/VIDEO)," B&G:FEB/92[36]478, "THE TRUE STORY OF TAPS," B&G:AUG/93[30]531
BOOK REVIEW: *BALLADS OF THE BLUE AND GRAY*

Dan Emmett; B&G:FEB/94[38]553

The Civil War (Ken Burns); B&G:APR/91[40]450

The Civil War - Music and Sounds; B&G:APR/91[40]450

MUSSELWHITE, WORLEY, *civilian;* B&G:AUG/91[11]458

MUTINIES:
ARTICLE: "MUTINY AT THE FRONT," CWTI:JUN/95[32]446
BOOK REVIEW: *THE MUTINY AT BRANDY STATION: THE LAST BATTLE OF THE HOOKER BRIGADE,* CWNEWS:JUN/95[33]

MY WAR:

A series of brief articles in *Civil War Times Illustrated* featuring one individual.

Addison-Darneille, Henrietta S. ARTICLE: "FOR BETTER OR FOR WORSE," CWTI:MAY/92[32]264

Benjamin, Samuel N., *Lieutenant, Battery E, 2nd U.S. Artillery;* ARTICLE: "WE CLEARED THEIR WAY...FIRING CANISTER," CWTI:MAR/93[20]308

Blacknall, Charles, *Colonel, 23rd North Carolina Infantry;* ARTICLE: "I'LL LIVE YET TO DANCE ON THAT FOOT," CWTI:MAY/93[26]318

Cross, Edward E., *Colonel, 5th New Hampshire Infantry;* ARTICLE: "COMPLETELY OUTGENERALLED," CWTI:AUG/95[24]455

Davis, William, *Private, 7th Indiana Infantry;* ARTICLE: "WHILE FATHER WAS WITH US," CWTI:NOV/93[24]346

Fonda, Ten Eyck Hilton, *telegrapher;* ARTICLE: "A MIDNIGHT RIDE," CWTI:MAR/94[24]370

Hitchcock, Robert E., *Lieutenant, USMC;* ARTICLE: "ONE MARINE'S BRIEF BATTLE," CWTI:APR/92[14]254

Hopkins, Andrew, *seaman, USN;* ARTICLE: "PRISONER OF CIRCUMSTANCES," CWTI:NOV/92[28]290

Hudson, John W. *Lieutenant, USA;* ARTICLE: "TIRED SOLDIERS DON'T GO VERY FAST," CWTI:FEB/92[36]249

Johnston, Joseph E., *General, CSA;* ARTICLE: "CONVERSATION IN CONFIDENCE," CWTI:JAN/95[20]422

Kemp, Daniel F., *seaman, USN;* ARTICLE: "NAVY LIFE ON THE MISSISSIPPI RIVER," CWTI:MAY/94[16]380

Loop, Charles B., *Major, 95th Illinois Infantry;* ARTICLE: "YOUR CHARLIE," CWTI:JAN/93[20]298

Markham, Philo A., *154th New York Infantry;* ARTICLE: "PHILO MARKHAM'S LONG WALK," CWTI:MAR/95[26]434

Matteson, Elisha, *Private, 9th Iowa Infantry;* ARTICLE: "DEAR SISTER—THEY FIGHT TO WHIP," CWTI:MAY/91[16]206

Nelson, George W., *Captain, CSA;* ARTICLE: "LETTERS FROM THE HEART," CWTI:OCT/95[28]467

Perry, William F., *General, CSA;* ARTICLE: "A FORGOTTEN ACCOUNT OF CHICKAMAUGA," CWTI:SEP/93[53]340

Ratcliffe, Laura; ARTICLE: "LETTERS TO LAURA," CWTI:JUL/92[12]270

Sherman, William T.; ARTICLE: "SHERMAN REVEALS SOMETHING ABOUT HIS STRATEGY," CWTI:JUL/94[28]391

Stuart, James E.B.; ARTICLE: "LETTERS TO LAURA," CWTI:JUL/92[12]270

Taliaferro, William B., *General, CSA;* ARTICLE: "PERSONAL REMINISCENCES OF 'STONEWALL' JACKSON," CWTI:JUN/95[18]444

Traweek, Washington B.; ARTICLE: "BREAK OUT!" CWTI:DEC/91[26]238

Wipperman, Henry; ARTICLE: "IN A NUTSHELL," CWTI:JAN/94[24]359

Zachry, Alfred, *Private, 3rd Georgia Infantry;* ARTICLES: "FIGHTING WITH THE 3D GEORGIA, PART I," CWTI:SEP/94[26]400, "FOUR SHOTS FOR THE CAUSE, PART II," CWTI:DEC/94[32]410

MYER, ALBERT J., *Colonel, USA;* ACW:JAN/95[20]504, CWTI:AUG/95[46]459, CWTI:DEC/95[8]474, GETTY:4[101]151, GETTY:4[110]152, GETTY:10[42]224, *photos,* CWTI:AUG/95[46]459, GETTY:10[42]224

MYER, THIES N., *Captain, USN;* ACW:SEP/94[46]488

MYERS, FRANK, *Lieutenant, 1st Georgia Regulars;* CWR:VOL2#2[95]135

MYERS, FRANK, *Sergeant, 6th Virginia Infantry;* ACW:JAN/91[38]287

MYERS, VICTOR, *civilian;* CWTI:JUN/95[56]450

MYERS, WHITTAKER, *Captain, CSA;* CWTI:JAN/95[42]428

MYRICK, W.E., *Private, CSA;* CWTI:SEP/91[23]228

MYTON, THOMAS W., *Private, 148th Pennsylvania Infantry;* CWR:VOL2#2[141]137

N

NADENBOUSCH, JOHN Q.A., *Colonel, 2nd Virginia Cavalry;*
GETTY:4[65]148, GETTY:13[89]260
NAFF, JAMES T., *Lieutenant, 2nd Tennessee Cavalry;*
CWR:VOL4#1[1]163
NAGLE, JAMES, *Colonel, USA;* ACW:MAY/95[18]524,
B&G:AUG/92[11]493, CWTI:FEB/92[36]249, *photo,*
CWTI:MAR/95[46]437
NAGLE, WILLIAM J., *Captain, 88th New York Infantry;*
CWTI:DEC/90[58]185
NAGLEY, JAMES, *General, USA;* B&G:DEC/93[52]548
NAIL, JAMES B., *Private, 2nd Tennessee Cavalry;*
CWR:VOL4#1[1]163
NAMOZINE CHURCH, VIRGINIA, BATTLE OF;
B&G:APR/91[6]444
NANCE, DAVID C., *Private, Parson's Texas Cavalry;* BOOK
REVIEW: *THE RAGGED REBEL: A COMMON SOLDIER IN
W.H. PARSON'S TEXAS CAVALRY, 1861-1865*
NANCE, JAMES D., *Colonel, 3rd South Carolina Infantry;*
B&G:JUN/95[8]600, GETTY:5[35]159, GETTY:10[107]227,
photo, B&G:JUN/95[8]600
NANCY HARTS, (Women's Militia Company); ARTICLE:
"GEORGIA'S NANCY HARTS," CWTI:MAY/94[44]384
NANTUCKET; BOOK REVIEW: *THE CIVIL WAR: THE
NANTUCKET EXPERIENCE*
NAPIER, T.A., *Colonel, CSA;* CWM:DEC/95[48]631
NAPOLEON III; ACW:JUL/92[46]371, CWTI:MAY/89[28]117,
CWTI:DEC/90[50]183
NASH, CHARLES E., *Captain, 19th Maine Infantry;*
GETTY:13[50]257
NASH, EUGENE, *Private, 44th New York Infantry;*
GETTY:6[33]172
NASH, MICHAEL, *Chaplain, 6th New York Infantry;*
CWM:MAR/91[50]340
NASHVILLE CAMPAIGN; BOOK REVIEW: *PATHS TO VICTORY:
A HISTORY AND TOUR GUIDE OF THE STONES RIVER,
CHICKAMAUGA, CHATTANOOGA, KNOXVILLE AND
NASHVILLE CAMPAIGNS*
NASHVILLE, TENNESSEE, BATTLE AND CAMAPIGN OF:
ARTICLES: "THE BATTLE OF NASHVILLE,"
B&G:DEC/93[12]545, "CIVIL WAR SITES IN NASHVILLE,"
B&G:DEC/93[52]548, "FIGHTING WITH FORREST IN THE
TENNESSEE WINTER," ACW:NOV/95[48]557, "THE
GALLANT HOOD OF TEXAS," ACW:MAR/94[42]461, "SEARS
OBLIVIOUS TO LOSS OF LEG," CWM:DEC/94[49]553
BOOK REVIEWS: *THE DEATH OF AN ARMY: THE BATTLE OF
NASHVILLE AND HOOD'S RETREAT * EMBRACE AN
ANGRY WIND—THE CONFEDERACY'S LAST HURRAH:
SPRING HILL, FRANKLIN, AND NASHVILLE * HOOD'S
CAMPAIGN FOR TENNESSEE * THE MARCH TO THE
SEA, FRANKLIN AND NASHVILLE * SHROUDS OF
GLORY: FROM ATLANTA TO NASHVILLE*
GENERAL LISTINGS: *general history,* AHI:MAY/71[3]133A, *in book
review,* ACW:NOV/94[66], CWM:JAN/91[47], CWM:OCT/94[8],
CWM:APR/95[8], CWNEWS:AUG/92[4], CWR:VOL4#3[89],
letters to the editor, B&G:APR/94[6]557, CWTI:AUG/95[14]454,
photo, ACW:NOV/95[48]557
ADDITIONAL LISTINGS: ACW:NOV/94[76]500, B&G:JUN/94[32]570,
CWM:MAR/91[28]336, CWR:VOL1#4[64]127,

CWTI:FEB/90[46]146, CWTI:FEB/90[54]147,
CWTI:JAN/94[35]361, MH:APR/94[54]176, MH:FEB/95[18]182
NASSAU, BERMUDA; ACW:NOV/92[51]389
NAST, THOMAS; CWM:NOV/92[10]447
NATIONAL BANKING ACT; CWM:FEB/95[7]
NATIONAL COMMISSION ON HISTORIC SITES;
B&G:FEB/92[40]479
NATIONAL PARKS & CONSERVATION ASSOCIATION;
CWTI:JUN/90[6]156
NATIONAL REGISTER OF HISTORIC PLACES;
B&G:APR/94[61]566
NATIONAL SUBCRIPTION ACT; ACW:MAR/92[22]351
**NATURAL BRIDGE, (FLORIDA) BATTLEFIELDS STATE
HISTORIC SITE;** ACW:NOV/91[64]336
NATURAL BRIDGE, (FLORIDA), BATTLE OF; ARTICLE: "AT
NATURAL BRIDGE, CONFEDERATE FORCES WON THEIR
LAST BATTLE OF THE WAR," ACW:NOV/91[64]336
NAUVOO LEGION; ARTICLE: "UTAH'S EXPERIENCED
NAUVOO LEGION SERVED BOTH THE UNITED STATES
AND THE MORMON CHURCH," ACW:JAN/95[8]502
NAVAL ORDNANCE WORKS, MOBILE, ALABAMA;
CWTI:JAN/93[49]303
NAVAL SHIPS, BOATS, ETC.; see all listings under **"SHIPS,
BOATS, VESSELS, ETC."**
NAVAL WARFARE:
ARTICLES: "A SON OF OLD NEPTUNE," CWTI:DEC/91[44]241,
"BRAVING THE YANKEE BLOCKADE,"
ACW:JAN/91[47]288, "CONFEDERATE MIKE USINA: 'BOY'
SEA FOX," CWM:JUN/94[50]518, "CRUISERS FOR THE
CONFEDERACY, PART I," AHI:DEC/82[38]231, "CRUISERS
FOR THE CONFEDERACY, PART II," AHI:JAN/83[10]232,
"THE *CSS H.L. HUNLEY:* SOLVING A 131-YEAR-OLD
MYSTERY," CWR:VOL4#3[77]174, *CSS MANASSAS,*
GUARDIAN OF NEW ORLEANS, WAS THE FIRST
CONFEDERATE IRONCLAD TO MENACE THE UNION
FLEET," ACW:MAY/92[16]359, "DESPERATE IRONCLAD
ASSAULT AT TRENT'S REACH," ACW:SEP/95[30]545, "THE
DILEMMA OF COMMODORE CRAVEN,"
CWTI:DEC/94[34]411, "GREAT GUNBOAT CHASE,"
CWTI:JUL/94[30]392, "GUARDIANS OF THE COAST,"
ACW:MAR/94[35]460, "GUNBOATS ON THE UPPER
TENNESSEE," CWTI:MAY/93[38]321
ARTICLES, continued: "HIGH SEAS HIJACK," ACW:NOV/92[51]389,
"IT WAS A GREAT VICTORY," AHI:OCT/75[30]162, "THE
MIDSHIPMEN OF THE CONFEDERATE NAVAL
ACADEMY PUT THEIR OFFICERS' TRAINING TO A
LAND-BASED USE," ACW:JUL/92[10]366, "ON THE
MUDDY YAZOO RIVER, ONE MORNING, THE UNION
GUNBOAT *CAIRO* MADE UNWANTED NAVAL HISTORY,"
ACW:SEP/94[74]491, "RAIDER OF THE ARCTIC SEAS,"
ACW:MAY/91[46]306, "RELUCTANT RAIDER,"
CWTI:AUG/95[40]458, "TORPEDOES, THE
CONFEDERACY'S DREADED 'INFERNAL MACHINES',"
MADE MANY A UNION SEA CAPTAIN UNEASY,"
ACW:NOV/91[8]328, "THE UNION NAVAL EXPEDITION ON
THE RED RIVER MARCH 12-MAY 22, 1864,"
CWR:VOL4#2[26]166
BOOK REVIEWS: *A GUNBOAT NAMED DIANA * THE ATLANTIC
COAST * THE BLOCKADE RUNNERS: TRUE TALES OF
RUNNING THE YANKEE BLOCKADE OF THE
CONFEDERATE COAST * BLOCKADERS, REFUGEES, &
CONTRABANDS: CIVIL WAR ON FLORIDA'S GULF
COAST * THE CIVIL WAR AT SEA * COMBINED*

*OPERATIONS IN THE CIVIL WAR * THE CONFEDERATE PRIVATEERS * CONFEDERATE STATES NAVY RESEARCH GUIDE * DAMN THE TORPEDOES! NAVAL INCIDENTS OF THE CIVIL WAR * FROM CAPE CHARLES TO CAPE FEAR: THE NORTH ALTANTIC BLOCKADING SQUADRON DURING THE CIVIL WAR*
BOOK REVIEWS, continued: *GRAY RAIDERS OF THE SEA: HOW EIGHT CONFEDERATE WARSHIPS DESTROYED THE UNION'S HIGH SEA COMMERCE, * GREAT BRITAIN AND THE CONFEDERATE NAVY, 1861-1865 * GUNS ON THE WESTERN WATERS: THE STORY OF RIVER GUNBOATS IN THE CIVIL WAR * HIGH SEAS CONFEDERATE: THE LIFE AND TIMES OF JOHN NEWLAND MAFFITT * HISTORY OF THE CONFEDERATES STATES NAVY * LIFELINE OF THE CONFEDERACY: BLOCKADE RUNNING DURING THE CIVIL WAR * MEMOIRS OF SERVICE AFLOAT * NAVY GRAY: A STORY OF THE CONFEDERATE NAVY ON THE CHATTAHOOCHEE AND APALACHICOLA RIVERS * RISE OF THE IRONCLADS * SHIPS VERSUS SHORE: CIVIL WAR ENGAGEMENTS ALONG SOUTHERN SHORES AND RIVERS * THE SINKING OF THE USS CAIRO * THUNDER AT HAMPTON ROADS * UNDER TWO FLAGS: THE AMERICAN NAVY IN THE CIVIL WAR * WARSHIPS OF THE CIVIL WAR NAVIES*
ADDITIONAL LISTINGS: ACW:JUL/92[10]366, CWNEWS:NOV/95[29]

NEAFIE, ALFRED, *Lieutenant Colonel, 156th New York Infantry;* CWR:VOL4#2[104]168

NEAL, SAMUEL, *Lieutenant, 10th Georgia Infantry;* ACW:JUL/95[10]533

NEAR, CHARLES R., *Lieutenant, 20th New York Infantry;* B&G:APR/95[24]596

NEBINGER, ANDREW, *surgeon;* CWTI:MAY/94[24]381

NEBRASKA TROOPS:
1st Infantry; ACW:NOV/94[34]496
NEBRASKA, STATE OF; CWNEWS:JUN/95[33]
NEEDHAM, SUMNER H., *Corporal, 7th Massachusetts Infantry;* ACW:NOV/95[30]555
NEELY, J.J., *Colonel, CSA;* CWTI:NOV/93[65]351
NEFF, D.C., *civilian;* B&G:OCT/94[11]580
NEFF, JOHN, *Colonel, 33rd Virginia Infantry;* B&G:AUG/92[11]493
NEILL, THOMAS H., *General, USA;* ACW:SEP/92[30]378, B&G:APR/94[10]558, B&G:APR/95[8]595, B&G:JUN/95[8]600, GETTY:7[83]192, GETTY:10[42]224
NELLIS, JOSEPH G., *Private, 83rd Pennsylvania Infantry;* GETTY:7[41]189
NELMS, W.G., *Captain, 11th Mississippi Infantry;* CWR:VOL2#4[269]145
NELMS, W.G., *Captain, 55th North Carolina Infantry;* CWR:VOL2#4[269]145
NELSON'S INDEPENDENT COMPANY OF PARTISAN RANGERS; B&G:FEB/91[20]440
NELSON, GEORGE W., *Captain, CSA;* ARTICLE: "LETTERS FROM THE HEART," CWTI:OCT/95[28]467
NELSON, J.A., *Private, 22nd Virginia Infantry;* CWR:VOL1#3[52]122
NELSON, JOE, *Mosby's raider;* CWTI:DEC/91[22]237
NELSON, JOSEPH, *Lieutenant, CSA;* ACW:JUL/94[26]477
NELSON, PETER, *Major, 66th New York Infantry;* GETTY:6[59]174

NELSON, ROBERT M., *Sergeant, 13th U.S. Regulars;* CWR:VOL2#1[1]130
NELSON, THOMAS, *Captain, Nelson's Independent Georgia Cavalry;* B&G:FEB/91[20]440, B&G:AUG/95[8]604
NELSON, WILLIAM, *General, USA:*
ARTICLES: "BRAWLING YANKEE BRASS," ACW:JUL/91[35]314, "'BULL' AND THE 'DAMNED PUPPY': A CIVIL WAR TRAGEDY," AHI:NOV/72[12]142, "EDITORIAL, WILLIAM 'BULL' NELSON," ACW:JUL/91[6]308
ADDITIONAL LISTINGS: ACW:JAN/91[22]285, ACW:JUL/91[26]313, ACW:JUL/92[22]368, B&G:DEC/91[38]471, B&G:OCT/92[32]499, B&G:APR/95[8]595, B&G:DEC/95[9]615, CWM:MAY/91[6]345, CWM:APR/95[66]579, CWTI:SEP/92[18], *photos,* AHI:NOV/72[12]142, CWM:APR/95[66]579
NESBITT, OTHO, *civilian;* B&G:AUG/94[10]574
NESHOBA RIFLES, (11th Mississippi Infantry); GETTY:9[98]217
NESMITH, JAMES W.; CWTI:AUG/95[54]460
NETHERCUTT, JOHN H., *Colonel, CSA;* B&G:DEC/95[9]615
NETTLES, T.D., *Captain, Valverde Artillery;* CWR:VOL4#2[68]167, CWR:VOL4#2[118]169
NEVIN, DAVID J., *Colonel, USA:*
ARTICLE: "THE THIRD BRIGADE, THIRD DIVISION, SIXTH CORPS AT," GETTYSBURG. GETTY:11[91]236,
ADDITIONAL LISTINGS: GETTY:10[42]224, *photo,* GETTY:11[91]236
NEVIN, JOHN I., *Major, 93rd Pennsylvania Infantry;* GETTY:11[91]236
NEW BERNE, NORTH CAROLINA, BATTLE OF:
GENERAL LISTINGS: *in book review,* ACW:JUL/94[58], CWR:VOL2#2[169], *letters to the editor,* B&G:OCT/95[5]610, CWM:MAR/91[12]333
ADDITIONAL LISTINGS: B&G:DEC/94[10]585, CWM:SEP/92[16]438, CWR:VOL3#2[1]153, CWTI:JUL/94[44]394, CWTI:JAN/95[34]427
NEW ENGLAND EMIGRANT AID COMPANY; ACW:NOV/94[42]497

NEW HAMPSHIRE TROOPS:
1st Artillery; ACW:MAR/94[50]462, GETTY:9[33]211, GETTY:12[30]243
1st Cavalry; CWM:APR/94[24]505
1st Infantry; CWTI:APR/92[49]260
2nd Infantry:
GENERAL LISTINGS: *Gettysburg,* GETTY:8[53]203, GETTY:9[41]212, *Manassas, Second,* B&G:AUG/92[11]493
ADDITIONAL LISTING: GETTY:13[7]253
3rd Infantry:
BOOK REVIEW: *THE THIRD NEW HAMPSHIRE AND ALL ABOUT IT*
ADDITIONAL LISTINGS: ACW:SEP/91[30]322, ACW:JUL/94[42]479, CWTI:APR/89[22]108
5th Infantry:
ARTICLE: "COMPLETELY OUTGENERALLED," CWTI:AUG/95[24]455
BOOK REVIEW: *A HISTORY OF THE FIFTH REGIMENT, NEW HAMPSHIRE VOLUNTEERS, IN THE AMERICAN CIVIL WAR, 1861-1865*
GENERAL LISTINGS: *Gettysburg,* GETTY:6[7]169, GETTY:8[53]203, GETTY:11[80]235, *photo, building bridge,* ACW:JUL/95[34]536
ADDITIONAL LISTINGS: ACW:MAR/91[12]292, CWM:DEC/95[59]633, CWR:VOL2#3[236]143, CWTI:FEB/90[74]149, CWTI:SEP/91[42]231

6th Infantry:
ARTICLE: "THE 'BULLY 6TH NEW HAMPSHIRE' FOUGHT REBELS FROM THE COAST OF NORTH CAROLINA TO THE TRENCHES OF VICKSBURG," ACW:MAY/95[18]524
ADDITIONAL LISTINGS: ACW:MAY/95[18]524, B&G:AUG/92[11]493, B&G:JUN/95[8]600, CWM:MAY/92[44]423, CWTI:JAN/95[34]427
7th Infantry; ACW:SEP/91[6]317, ACW:SEP/91[30]322, CWM:JAN/92[16]401, CWR:VOL3#1[65]151
8th Infantry; ACW:JAN/94[30]450, CWR:VOL3#1[1]149
8th Infantry, (Mounted); CWR:VOL4#2[1]165, CWR:VOL4#2[68]167
9th Infantry:
ARTICLE: "AND FIRE SALL DEVOUR THEM: THE 9TH NEW HAMPSHIRE IN THE CRATER," CWR:VOL2#2[118]136
BOOK REVIEW: *RACE OF THE SOIL: THE NINTH NEW HAMPSHIRE REGIMENT IN THE CIVIL WAR*
ADDITIONAL LISTINGS: ACW:MAY/95[18]524, CWM:MAY/92[44]423, CWNEWS:DEC/93[5], CWTI:JAN/95[34]427
11th Infantry; ACW:MAY/95[18]524, CWR:VOL2#2[118]136
12th Infantry:
BOOK REVIEW: *HISTORY OF THE TWELFTH REGIMENT, NEW HAMPSHIRE VOLUNTEERS, IN THE WAR OF THE REBELLION*
ADDITIONAL LISTINGS: ACW:SEP/93[62]436, ACW:SEP/95[74]550, B&G:APR/94[10]558, GETTY:12[7]241, GETTY:13[7]253
13th Infantry; ACW:MAY/94[51]471, B&G:FEB/92[40]479, B&G:OCT/95[8]611A, GETTY:11[6]231
14th Infantry; ACW:MAY/91[38]305, AHI:FEB/75[35]158
15th Infantry; GETTY:9[41]212

NEW HAVEN GRAYS MILITIA; GETTY:12[24]242
NEW HOPE CHURCH, GEORGIA, BATTLE OF;
ACW:JUL/94[66]481, B&G:DEC/91[34]470, CWM:JAN/91[72]331, CWM:JUL/92[18]429, CWM:JUL/92[40]432, CWTI:SUMMER/89[13]120, CWTI:MAR/95[40]436

NEW JERSEY TROOPS:

1st Artillery; B&G:JUN/95[36]603A, CWM:MAR/91[17]335, GETTY:5[47]160
1st Artillery, Battery B:
BOOK REVIEW: *HISTORY OF BATTERY B, FIRST NEW JERSEY ARTILLERY*
ADDITIONAL LISTINGS: CWM:JUN/95[55]591, CWTI:AUG/90[26]166, GETTY:13[7]253
1st Brigade, ACW:NOV/92[18]385, B&G:OCT/95[8]611A, CWTI:MAY/89[36]118, GETTY:6[7]169
1st Cavalry:
BOOK REVIEW: *JERSEY CAVALIERS: A HISTORY OF THE FIRST NEW JERSEY VOLUNTEER CAVALRY, 1861-1865*
ADDITIONAL LISTINGS: ACW:NOV/92[26]386, B&G:DEC/91[34]470, B&G:APR/92[8]481, CWM:APR/95[32]575, CWM:AUG/95[38]609, CWTI:DEC/91[22]237, GETTY:4[75]149
1st Infantry; B&G:JUN/95[8]600, B&G:OCT/95[8]611A, CWNEWS:MAY/90[4], CWTI:MAY/89[36]118
2nd Artillery, Battery B; GETTY:5[35]159, GETTY:6[59]174
2nd Infantry; CWM:JUN/95[63]594, CWTI:MAY/89[36]118
3rd Cavalry; B&G:APR/92[8]481, MH:OCT/93[20]172

3rd Infantry:
ARTICLE: "GIVE MY LOVE TO ALL: A LIEUTENANT'S LETTERS TOLD THE STORY OF THE 3RD NEW JERSEY INFANTRY," CWTI:MAY/89[36]118
ADDITIONAL LISTING: CWM:APR/94[24]505
4th Cavalry; CWR:VOL1#3[28]120
4th Infantry; ACW:MAY/91[38]305, CWTI:MAY/89[36]118
5th Infantry; AHI:FEB/75[35]158, CWNEWS:SEP/92[4], CWTI:DEC/91[12], CWTI:JUL/92[74]277, GETTY:8[53]203
6th Infantry; CWTI:JAN/93[10]297, GETTY:8[53]203
7th Infantry:
ARTICLE: "A WEDDING IN CAMP," B&G:FEB/92[22]476
ADDITIONAL LISTINGS: B&G:FEB/92[22]476, GETTY:8[53]203
8th Infantry; B&G:FEB/92[22]476, GETTY:4[113]153, GETTY:8[43]202, GETTY:8[53]203
10th Cavalry; MH:FEB/93[42]164
10th Infantry; ACW:MAY/91[38]305, ACW:MAR/92[22]351, CWTI:MAY/89[36]118
11th Infantry:
BOOK REVIEW: *HISTORY OF THE ELEVENTH NEW JERSEY VOLUNTEERS*
GENERAL LISTINGS: *Gettysburg,* GETTY:11[102]237, GETTY:12[7]241, *in book review,* CWNEWS:JUN/95[33]
ADDITIONAL LISTINGS: ACW:JUL/93[16]422, B&G:APR/91[8]445, CWM:MAY/92[20]420
12th Infantry:
BOOK REVIEW: *TO GETTYSBURG AND BEYOND: THE TWELFTH NEW JERSEY VOLUNTEER INFANTRY, II CORPS, ARMY OF THE POTOMAC, 1862-1865*
GENERAL LISTINGS: *Gettysburg,* GETTY:5[89]162, GETTY:7[29]188, GETTY:7[97]193, GETTY:8[95]205, GETTY:9[61]215, GETTY:10[53]225, GETTY:11[102]237, GETTY:12[61]245, GETTY:12[97]249, *in list,* CWTI:JUL/93[34]327, *photos of monument,* GETTY:4[7]142, GETTY:5[89]162
ADDITIONAL LISTINGS: ACW:SEP/94[38]487, B&G:JUN/95[8]600, CWR:VOL2#4[269]145, GETTY:13[75]259
13th Infantry:
BOOK REVIEW: *REMINISCENCES OF THE THIRTEENTH REGIMENT NEW JERSEY VOLUNTEERS*
GENERAL LISTINGS: *Antietam,* GETTY:6[69]176, *Gettysburg,* GETTY:6[7]169, GETTY:12[42]244, *list of monuments,* B&G:OCT/95[8]611A
ADDITIONAL LISTINGS: ACW:MAR/94[50]462, B&G:OCT/95[8]611E, GETTY:13[7]253
14th Infantry:
BOOK REVIEW: *UPON THE TENTED FIELD*
ADDITIONAL LISTINGS: ACW:NOV/93[50]444, B&G:DEC/92[8]503, CWM:NOV/92[6]446, CWTI:JAN/93[40]301
15th Infantry:
BOOK REVIEW: *THREE ROUSING CHEERS: A HISTORY OF THE FIFTEENTH NEW JERSEY FROM FLEMINGTON TO APPOMATTOX*
ADDITIONAL LISTINGS: ACW:MAY/91[38]305, B&G:APR/91[8]445, B&G:FEB/92[22]476, CWR:VOL3#3[1]157, CWR:VOL3#3[88]160, CWTI:MAY/89[36]118, CWTI:SEP/90[22]173, GETTY:13[7]253
23rd Infantry; ACW:MAR/92[22]351, CWR:VOL3#3[88]160, CWTI:MAY/89[36]118
28th Infantry; B&G:FEB/95[38]593, B&G:JUN/95[36]603A
29th Infantry; CWNEWS:NOV/91[4]
33rd Infantry; CWNEWS:AUG/92[4], CWTI:SUMMER/89[32]122, CWTI:NOV/92[41]291

39th Infantry; CWR:VOL3#2[1]153
Hexamer's Battery; B&G:OCT/95[8]611A

NEW JERSEY, STATE OF; BOOK REVIEWS: *CUMBERLAND COUNTY AND SOUTH JERSEY DURING THE CIVIL WAR * JERSEY BLUE: CIVIL WAR POLITICS IN NEW JERSEY, 1854-1865*
NEW MADRID, MISSOURI; AHI:MAY/71[3]133A, ACW:JAN/91[54]
NEW MANCHESTER, GEORGIA; ARTICLE: "TOTAL WAR COMES TO NEW MANCHESTER," B&G:DEC/94[22]586
NEW MARKET CROSSROADS, VIRGINIA, BATTLE OF; see listings under **"WHITE OAK SWAMP, VIRGINIA, BATTLE OF"**
NEW MARKET HEIGHTS, VIRGINIA, BATTLE OF; ARTICLE: "A SHOWER OF STARS AT NEW MARKET HEIGHTS," CWM:AUG/94[30]527
NEW MARKET, VIRGINIA, 1862 BATTLE OF:
BOOK REVIEW: *THE NEW MARKET CAMPAIGN*
GENERAL LISTINGS: *general history*, AHI:MAY/71[3]133A, *in book review*, CWR:VOL4#3[89], *letters to the editor*, CWM:JAN/91[6]324
ADDITIONAL LISTINGS: CWM:JAN/92[21]402, CWM:JUN/94[27]513, CWTI:OCT/95[48]470
NEW MARKET, VIRGINIA, 1864 BATTLE OF:
ARTICLE: "DIMINUTIVE BUT FEISTY, CHARLES CARTER RANDOLPH WAS STONEWALL JACKSON'S PET CADET," ACW:JUL/93[10]421
BOOK REVIEW: *THE BATTLE OF NEW MARKET*
ADDITIONAL LISTINGS: ACW:NOV/93[50]444, AHI:MAR/84[42]238, B&G:DEC/95[5]614A, CWM:NOV/92[41]451, CWTI:FEB/90[46]146, MH:OCT/93[6]170
NEW MEXICO CAMPAIGN:
ARTICLES: "BATTLE FOR THE RIO GRANDE," CWTI:OCT/95[56]471, "THE CONFEDERATE INVASION OF NEW MEXICO AND ARIZONA," CWM:MAY/93[16]475, "THE CONFEDERATE INVASION OF NEW MEXICO," B&G:JUN/94[8]568, "PERSONALITY, COLONEL JOHN R. BAYLOR," ACW:JAN/91[10]283
BOOK REVIEWS: *BLOOD AND TREASURE: CONFEDERATE EMPIRE IN THE SOUTHWEST * REBELS ON THE RIO GRANDE: THE CIVIL WAR JOURNAL OF A.B. PETICOLAS * WESTWARD THE TEXANS: THE CIVIL WAR JOURNAL OF PRIVATE WILLIAM R. HOWELL*
GENERAL LISTINGS: *in book review*, CWM:MAR/92[49], *letters to the editor*, B&G:AUG/94[6]573, B&G:OCT/94[6]579
ADDITIONAL LISTINGS: ACW:JAN/91[10]283, ACW:NOV/91[10]329, ACW:JUL/93[27]423
NEW MEXICO TERRITORY; ACW:JUL/93[27]423, B&G:JUN/94[8]568

NEW MEXICO TROOPS:
1st Infantry; B&G:JUN/94[8]568, CWM:MAR/91[50]340, CWTI:OCT/95[56]471
2nd Cavalry; CWM:MAR/91[50]340
2nd Infantry; CWM:MAR/91[50]340, CWTI:OCT/95[56]471
5th Infantry; B&G:JUN/94[8]568
Company of Santa Fe Gamblers; B&G:JUN/94[8]568

NEW ORLEANS, LOUISIANA, BATTLE OF:
ARTICLES: "EDITORIAL," MH:AUG/93[6]168, "FORT JACKSON, GUARDIAN OF NEW ORLEANS AND THE LOWER MISSISSIPPI, WAS LONG THOUGHT TO BE IMPREGNABLE," ACW:JAN/92[62]346, *"CSS MANASSAS,* GUARDIAN OF NEW ORLEANS, WAS THE FIRST CONFEDERATE IRONCLAD TO MENACE THE UNION FLEET," ACW:MAY/92[16]359, "STEADY BOYS, STEADY!" MH:AUG/93[47]169, "STUNG BY MOSQUITOES," MH:DEC/94[46]181
BOOK REVIEW: *THE NIGHT THE WAR WAS LOST*
NEW ORLEANS, OCCUPATION OF; ARTICLE: "THE BEAST OF NEW ORLEANS," CWTI:MAY/93[29]319
NEW SALEM, ILLINOIS; ARTICLE: "AT NEW SALEM, LINCOLN MADE A STARTLING TRANSFORMATION FROM COUNTRY BUMPKIN TO POLISHED LAWYER," ACW:MAR/94[66]463
NEW YORK CITY DRAFT RIOTS: also, see other listings under **"DRAFT RIOTS"**
ARTICLES: "A TIME OF TERROR," AHI:MAY/76[35]168, "'ASHES AND BLOOD': THE NEW YORK CITY DRAFT RIOTS," AHI:AUG/77[30]175
BOOK REVIEWS: *THE ARMIES OF THE STREETS: THE NEW YORK CITY DRAFT RIOTS OF 1863 * THE CIVIL WAR AND NEW YORK CITY * THE MAN WHO TRIED TO BURN NEW YORK * THE NEW YORK CITY DRAFT RIOTS: THEIR SIGNIFICANCE FOR AMERICAN SOCIETY AND POLIICS IN THE AGE OF THE CIVIL WAR*
ADDITIONAL LISTINGS: CWTI:DEC/90[50]183, MH:OCT/93[12]171, *photo of Printing House Square;* CWTI:DEC/90[50]183
NEW YORK STOCK EXCHANGE; AHI:APR/80[21]200

NEW YORK TROOPS:
1st Artillery:
GENERAL LISTINGS: *Gettysburg*, GETTY:5[123]166, GETTY:9[41]212, GETTY:10[29]222, GETTY:11[119]238, *photos*, ACW:SEP/93[8]429, CWM:JUN/95[65]595
ADDITIONAL LISTINGS: ACW:MAR/91[47]297, CWTI:SUMMER/89[32]122, GETTY:13[7]253
1st Artillery, Battery A; ACW:SEP/93[8]429, B&G:AUG/94[10]574
1st Artillery, Battery B; B&G:APR/92[8]481, CWM:MAR/91[14]334, CWM:MAR/91[17]335, GETTY:5[47]160
1st Artillery, Battery C; GETTY:11[91]236
1st Artillery, Battery D:
GENERAL LISTINGS: *Gettysburg*, GETTY:8[53]203, *in order of battle*, B&G:APR/92[8]481, *Overland Campaign*, B&G:APR/94[10]558
ADDITIONAL LISTING: B&G:APR/95[8]595
1st Artillery, Battery E; ACW:JAN/94[8]447
1st Artillery, Battery E & L; GETTY:12[30]243
1st Artillery, Battery G; GETTY:5[35]159, GETTY:8[53]203, GETTY:9[41]212
1st Artillery, Battery H; B&G:APR/92[8]481, B&G:APR/95[8]595
1st Artillery, Battery I; ACW:NOV/92[42]388, GETTY:4[49]147, GETTY:6[7]169, GETTY:8[17]200, GETTY:8[43]202, GETTY:9[33]211, GETTY:10[29]222, GETTY:11[19]232, GETTY:12[30]243
1st Artillery, Battery L; B&G:APR/95[8]595, GETTY:5[117]165, GETTY:10[29]222, GETTY:13[22]254
1st Artillery, Battery M; B&G:FEB/95[8]590C
1st Artillery, Independent; GETTY:4[89]150, GETTY:7[97]193
1st Cavalry; ACW:JUL/95[8]532, AHI:DEC/85[40]255, B&G:APR/92[8]481, B&G:OCT/93[12]537, B&G:AUG/94[10]574, CWM:APR/94[24]505, CWR:VOL1#1[35]104, CWR:VOL3#2[1]153,

CWTI:JUN/90[32]159, CWTI:SEP/90[34]176,
GETTY:13[89]260

1st Dragoons; ACW:MAY/91[38]305

1st Engineers; CWM:MAR/92[16]411

1st Fire Zouaves; ACW:JAN/92[38]343

1st Infantry; ACW:MAR/93[42]406, ACW:JAN/95[54]508,
ACW:MAY/95[30]525, CWTI:MAY/92[38]265,
CWTI:JUL/93[14]324, CWTI:DEC/95[24]477,
GETTY:5[117]165

1st Infantry, (Mounted); B&G:FEB/95[38]593,
B&G:JUN/95[36]603A

1st Sharpshooters; B&G:APR/92[8]481

2nd Artillery; AHI:AUG/68[4]115B, B&G:AUG/95[8]604

2nd Artillery, (Heavy); B&G:AUG/92[11]493,
B&G:APR/94[47]562A, CWM:SEP/92[8]437,
CWR:VOL2#3[236]143, *photo*, ACW:NOV/94[12]494

2nd Cavalry:
GENERAL LISTINGS: *1863 cavalry battles*, MH:OCT/92[51]162, *in
order of battle*, B&G:APR/92[8]481
ADDITIONAL LISTINGS: ACW:MAY/91[38]305, ACW:JUL/92[41]370,
AHI:JUL/93[40]312, B&G:OCT/93[12]537,
CWM:APR/95[32]575, CWTI:JUN/90[32]159

2nd Infantry; ACW:MAR/93[42]406, CWM:MAR/91[50]340,
CWM:SEP/92[16]438, CWR:VOL4#1[78], GETTY:12[7]241

2nd Infantry, (Mounted); B&G:APR/92[8]481

2nd Militia; GETTY:13[43]256

3rd Artillery; ACW:JAN/94[8]447, CWM:JUN/95[29]583,
CWTI:AUG/90[42]167

3rd Cavalry; ACW:MAY/92[30]361, ACW:MAR/95[12]513

3rd Infantry; ACW:MAR/93[42]406, AHI:SEP/83[12]234,
CWR:VOL1#2[7]111

4th Artillery; B&G:JUN/95[36]603A, GETTY:8[31]201,
GETTY:8[53]203, GETTY:9[5]209

4th Artillery, (Heavy); B&G:FEB/93[40]514,
CWTI:AUG/90[26]166

4th Cavalry; ACW:NOV/91[30]332, B&G:FEB/93[36],
B&G:OCT/93[12]537, B&G:OCT/93[21]538, MH:OCT/92[51]162

4th Infantry; B&G:APR/95[24]596, B&G:OCT/95[8]611A

5th Artillery; AHI:NOV/88[37]278, B&G:APR/95[24]596,
GETTY:5[47]160

5th Artillery, (Heavy); B&G:JUN/95[36]603A,
CWR:VOL1#4[7]125

5th Cavalry; ACW:MAY/91[38]305, ACW:JUL/92[41]370,
B&G:APR/93[12]518, B&G:APR/95[8]595, B&G:JUN/95[8]600,
CWM:APR/94[24]505, CWTI:DEC/91[22]237

5th Infantry:
ARTICLES: "'BOYS, WON'T I MAKE A FINE LOOKING CORPSE?'
DURYE'S ZOUAVES AT SECOND BULL RUN,"
CWR:VOL1#2[29]112, "CHARGE BAYONETS,"
CWTI:MAY/94[31]382, "DURYE'S ZOUAVES: THE 5TH NEW
YORK VOLUNTEER INFANTRY," CWR:VOL1#2[7]111, "I
HARDLY HAVE THE HEART TO WRITE THESE FEW
LINES..." CWR:VOL1#2[42]113
BOOK REVIEW: *CAMP AND FIELD LIFE OF THE FIFTH NEW
YORK*
GENERAL LISTINGS: *Five Forks*, B&G:APR/92[8]481, *in book review*,
CWNEWS:NOV/91[4], CWNEWS:AUG/92[4],
CWR:VOL3#2[105], *in order of battle*, B&G:APR/92[8]481,
Manassas, Second, AHI:DEC/66[30]105, B&G:AUG/92[11]493
ADDITIONAL LISTINGS: ACW:JUL/91[18]312, ACW:MAR/93[42]406,
CWM:MAR/93[24]467, CWR:VOL1#2[v]110,
CWR:VOL1#2[7]111, CWR:VOL1#2[29]112,

CWR:VOL1#2[76]116, CWTI:DEC/89[26]135,
CWTI:DEC/91[36]240, GETTY:12[42]244

6th Artillery; ACW:NOV/91[30]332, ACW:MAY/95[30]525,
CWTI:JUN/90[32]159

6th Cavalry:
GENERAL LISTINGS: *Gettysburg*, GETTY:4[113]153,
GETTY:6[87]178, GETTY:11[19]232, *in order of battle*,
B&G:APR/92[8]481
ADDITIONAL LISTINGS: ACW:MAY/94[35]469, ACW:MAY/95[30]525,
B&G:FEB/95[8]590A, CWM:MAY/92[44]423,
CWTI:JUN/90[32]159, CWTI:MAY/93[35]320

6th Infantry; ACW:MAR/91[14]293, CWM:MAR/91[50]340,
CWR:VOL1#4[42]126, CWTI:JAN/95[42]428

7th Artillery, (Heavy); B&G:APR/94[10]558,
B&G:APR/94[55]564

7th Infantry; ACW:MAR/93[42]406, AHI:MAY/71[3]133A,
B&G:JUN/95[36]603A, CWR:VOL1#2[7]111

7th Militia; B&G:OCT/93[24], CWTI:DEC/89[42]137

8th Artillery, (Heavy):
ARTICLE: "'THE REGIMENT HAS COVERED ITSELF WITH
GLORY': THE 8TH NEW YORK HEAVIES AT COLD
HARBOR," B&G:APR/94[55]564
ADDITIONAL LISTINGS: ACW:JUL/93[16]422, B&G:APR/94[59]565

8th Cavalry:
ARTICLE: "ESCAPE FROM HARPERS FERRY,"
CWM:MAY/92[8]418
GENERAL LISTINGS: *Brandy Station*, GETTY:11[19]232, *Falling
Waters*, GETTY:9[109]218, *flag*, CWM:MAY/92[8]418,
Gettysburg, GETTY:4[115]152, GETTY:6[13]170,
GETTY:11[19]232, *Harpers Ferry*, MH:AUG/95[30]185, *in
order of battle*, B&G:APR/92[8]481
ADDITIONAL LISTINGS: ACW:SEP/94[55]489, B&G:APR/91[8]445,
B&G:FEB/95[8]590A, CWM:MAY/92[4]416,
CWM:SEP/92[8]437, CWM:APR/94[24]505,
CWTI:JUN/90[32]159, CWTI:APR/92[49]260,
GETTY:13[22]254

8th Infantry; ACW:SEP/93[8]429, ACW:NOV/94[18]495,
B&G:JUN/95[36]603A, CWR:VOL1#4[7]125,
CWR:VOL3#4[1]161, CWTI:MAY/92[38]265,
CWTI:JAN/95[22]423

9th Artillery, (Heavy); ACW:NOV/93[50]444,
B&G:DEC/92[8]503, CWTI:JAN/93[40]301

9th Cavalry:
GENERAL LISTINGS: *common soldiers*, AHI:AUG/68[4]115B,
Gettysburg, GETTY:4[33]146, GETTY:4[113]153,
GETTY:11[19]232, *in order of battle*, B&G:APR/92[8]481
9th Cavalry; AHI:JUL/93[40]312, B&G:FEB/95[8]590A,
B&G:FEB/95[8]590B, CWTI:JUN/90[32]159

9th Infantry; B&G:APR/95[24]596, B&G:OCT/95[8]611A,
CWM:FEB/95[7], CWNEWS:AUG/92[4],
CWTI:SEPT/89[46]132, GETTY:10[7]221

10th Cavalry; ACW:NOV/92[26]386, B&G:APR/92[8]481,
B&G:OCT/93[12]537, CWTI:JUN/90[32]159, GETTY:4[65]148,
GETTY:4[75]149, GETTY:13[89]260

10th Infantry; ACW:JUL/91[18]312, ACW:SEP/94[38]487,
CWM:SEP/93[18]494, CWM:APR/95[32]575,
CWNEWS:NOV/89[4], CWR:VOL1#2[7]111,
CWR:VOL1#2[29]112, CWR:VOL1#2[76]116,
CWTI:MAY/93[20]317, CWTI:MAY/94[31]382, GETTY:9[61]215

11th Cavalry; B&G:OCT/93[21]538

11th Infantry; ACW:JAN/92[38]343, AHI:DEC/71[30]138,
AHI:AUG/77[30]175, B&G:AUG/93[10]529,
CWTI:APR/92[14]254

GETTY:10[7]221, *letters to the editor,* B&G:OCT/95[5]610, *SIO,* B&G:APR/92[36]483
ADDITIONAL LISTINGS: ACW:NOV/92[42]388, B&G:FEB/95[8]590A, B&G:APR/95[24]596
46th Infantry; ACW:JAN/95[54]508, B&G:AUG/95[8]604, CWM:MAY/92[44]423, CWR:VOL1#1[42]105, CWTI:JAN/94[46]364
47th Infantry; CWR:VOL3#1[65]151, GETTY:10[53]225
48th Infantry; ACW:SEP/91[30]322, CWR:VOL3#1[65]151
49th Infantry; B&G:JUN/95[8]600, CWTI:JUN/95[32]446
50th Engineers:
ARTICLE: "THE 50TH NEW YORK ENGINEERS WERE INVALUABLE BRIDGE BUILDERS DURING THE VARIOUS CAMPAIGNS AGAINST LEE," ACW:NOV/95[10]553
ADDITIONAL LISTINGS: B&G:APR/91[8]445, CWR:VOL4#4[101]181
50th Infantry; ACW:MAY/93[8]411
51st Infantry; ACW:MAY/94[6]464, B&G:OCT/94[42]583, B&G:DEC/94[36]588, B&G:OCT/95[8]611A, CWM:MAY/92[44]423, CWTI:FEB/92[36]249
52nd Infantry; ACW:MAY/95[30]525, CWR:VOL2#4[269]145, GETTY:8[53]203
53rd Infantry; CWNEWS:SEP/94[33], MH:APR/94[54]176
54th Infantry; GETTY:6[7]169
55th Infantry; ACW:JUL/93[16]422, GETTY:8[43]202, MH:OCT/93[20]172
56th Infantry; CWTI:JAN/93[49]303, CWTI:MAR/94[38]372, CWTI:JAN/95[34]427
57th Infantry; ACW:MAY/95[30]525, CWM:JUN/95[76]598, CWR:VOL4#3[1]170, GETTY:8[53]203, GETTY:10[53]225, GETTY:13[7]253
58th Infantry:
GENERAL LISTINGS: *Gettysburg,* GETTY:12[30]243, GETTY:4[49]147, GETTY:5[117]165, *SIO,* B&G:JUN/95[36]603A
ADDITIONAL LISTING: CWTI:SEP/92[22]279
59th Infantry:
GENERAL LISTINGS: *Gettysburg,* GETTY:4[89]150, *letters to the editor,* CWTI:NOV/93[12]345, *list of monuments,* B&G:OCT/95[8]611A
ADDITIONAL LISTINGS: ACW:MAR/94[50]462, B&G:OCT/95[8]611A, CWR:VOL4#4[101]181
60th Infantry; ACW:MAR/94[50]462, CWR:VOL3#2[70]155, CWTI:SUMMER/89[32]122, CWTI:SEPT/89[30]129, GETTY:9[81]216, GETTY:10[36]223, GETTY:13[7]253
61st Infantry:
BOOK REVIEWS: *PERSONAL RECOLLECTIONS OF THE WAR OF 1861*
GENERAL LISTINGS: *Gettysburg,* GETTY:4[89]150, GETTY:8[53]203, GETTY:10[53]225, GETTY:12[97]249, *in book review,* CWNEWS:JUL/91[4]
ADDITIONAL LISTINGS: B&G:APR/91[8]445, CWR:VOL2#3[236]143
62nd Infantry; ACW:SEP/92[30]378, CWM:MAY/91[26]349, GETTY:11[91]236
63rd Infantry:
GENERAL LISTINGS: *Gettysburg,* GETTY:8[53]203, GETTY:10[53]225, *photo,* CWM:MAR/91[17]335
ADDITIONAL LISTINGS: ACW:MAY/94[12]466, ACW:SEP/95[54]548, B&G:APR/91[8]445, CWM:MAR/91[50]340, CWR:VOL4#4[47]179, CWTI:DEC/90[58]185
64th Infantry; GETTY:8[53]203, GETTY:10[53]225, GETTY:11[80]235, GETTY:12[24]242, *photo, building bridge,* ACW:JUL/95[34]536

65th Infantry; AHI:AUG/77[30]175, ACW:SEP/92[30]378, B&G:JUN/95[8]600, CWR:VOL1#2[7]111
66th Infantry; GETTY:6[59]174, GETTY:8[53]203, GETTY:10[53]225
67th Infantry; B&G:JUN/95[8]600, *photo, on parade,* CWTI:DEC/90[58]185
68th Infantry; B&G:APR/93[12]518, CWM:DEC/94[17]547, CWTI:MAY/92[38]265, GETTY:12[30]243, GETTY:13[7]253
69th Infantry:
GENERAL LISTINGS: *Gettysburg,* GETTY:8[53]203, GETTY:10[53]225, GETTY:11[126]239, *in book review,* CWNEWS:JUL/90[4], CWR:VOL3#2[105], CWR:VOL3#4[68], *letters to the editor,* CWM:SEP/92[6]436
ADDITIONAL LISTINGS: ACW:MAY/94[12]466, ACW:SEP/94[46]488, ACW:SEP/95[54]548, ACW:SEP/95[70]549, B&G:OCT/95[36]614, CWM:MAR/91[14]334, CWM:MAR/91[17]335, CWM:MAR/91[50]340, CWM:SEP/93[18]494, CWR:VOL4#4[47]179, CWTI:MAY/89[36]118, CWTI:DEC/90[58]185, CWTI:APR/92[14]254
70th Infantry; CWM:MAY/92[20]420, B&G:FEB/92[22]476, CWTI:JAN/95[16]421
71st Infantry; GETTY:6[59]174, GETTY:9[5]209, GETTY:12[7]241
72nd Infantry; CWM:MAY/92[20]420, GETTY:6[59]174, GETTY:12[7]241, GETTY:13[50]257
73rd Infantry; AHI:DEC/85[40]255, CWM:MAR/91[50]340, GETTY:5[47]160
75th Infantry; B&G:JUN/95[36]603A, CWR:VOL3#1[1]149, CWTI:DEC/90[29]182
76th Infantry:
GENERAL LISTINGS: *Gettysburg,* GETTY:4[115]152, GETTY:5[4]156, GETTY:6[13]170, GETTY:10[36]223, *Manassas, Second,* B&G:AUG/92[11]493
ADDITIONAL LISTINGS: B&G:JUN/95[8]600, CWM:JAN/92[16]401, CWM:JAN/93[16]457, GETTY:13[7]253
77th Infantry: ACW:SEP/92[30]378, CWR:VOL3#3[1]157, CWTI:MAY/94[24]381, CWTI:JUN/95[32]446
78th Infantry; ACW:MAR/94[50]462, CWM:NOV/91[35]392, CWR:VOL3#2[70]155, CWTI:SEPT/89[30]129, GETTY:7[83]192, GETTY:12[42]244
79th Infantry; ACW:MAY/91[23]303, ACW:JAN/95[54]508, CWTI:JAN/94[46]364, CWTI:MAY/94[12]379, CWTI:MAY/94[50]386
80th Infantry:
BOOK REVIEW: *HOLDING THE LEFT AT GETTYSBURG: THE 20TH NEW YORK STATE MILITIA ON JULY 1, 1863*
GENERAL LISTINGS: *Gettysburg,* GETTY:5[79]161, *in book review,* B&G:AUG/93[24], CWNEWS:JUL/95[61], *in list,* CWTI:JUL/93[34]327, *letters to the editor,* B&G:DEC/93[6]544
ADDITIONAL LISTINGS: B&G:FEB/95[8]590A, GETTY:13[22]254
81st Infantry; B&G:OCT/95[36]614
82nd Infantry:
GENERAL LISTINGS: *Gettysburg,* GETTY:5[79]161, GETTY:7[29]188, *in list,* CWTI:JUL/93[34]327, *SIO,* B&G:JUN/95[36]603A
ADDITIONAL LISTINGS: ACW:MAR/94[50]462, ACW:JUL/95[50]538, CWM:APR/95[42]577, GETTY:13[1]252, GETTY:13[43]256, GETTY:13[50]257
83rd Infantry: ACW:MAR/95[42]517, B&G:FEB/95[8]590B, CWM:AUG/95[38]609, GETTY:4[33]146, GETTY:5[13]157, GETTY:10[7]221, GETTY:13[33]255

84th Infantry:
GENERAL LISTINGS: *Gettysburg*, GETTY:4[16]143, GETTY:5[4]156, GETTY:5[123]166, GETTY:6[13]170, GETTY:6[29]171, GETTY:7[83]192, GETTY:8[121]207, GETTY:10[36]223, *in book review*, CWNEWS:JUL/95[61], CWR:VOL1#2[78], CWR:VOL4#4[129], *letters to the editor*, B&G:FEB/94[6]549, *list of monuments*, B&G:OCT/95[8]611A
ADDITIONAL LISTINGS: ACW:NOV/92[42]388, B&G:APR/91[32]447, B&G:FEB/95[8]590A, CWM:AUG/95[38]609

85th Infantry:
BOOK REVIEWS: *CHARLIE MOSHER'S CIVIL WAR * THE PLYMOUTH PILGRIMS: A HISTORY OF THE EIGHTY-FIFTH NEW YORK INFANTRY IN THE CIVIL WAR*
ADDITIONAL LISTING: CWM:JAN/92[16]401

86th Infantry:
GENERAL LISTINGS: *Chancellorsville*, GETTY:9[5]209, *Gettysburg*, GETTY:5[103]163, GETTY:8[53]203, GETTY:9[5]209
ADDITIONAL LISTINGS: CWM:SEP/92[8]437, CWM:DEC/94[40]550, CWTI:JUN/90[32]159, GETTY:9[5]209

87th Infantry; CWM:JUN/95[55]591

88th Infantry; ACW:MAY/94[12]466, ACW:SEP/95[54]548, CWM:MAR/91[28]336, CWM:MAR/91[50]340, CWR:VOL4#4[47]179, CWTI:DEC/90[58]185, CWTI:AUG/95[24]455, GETTY:8[53]203, GETTY:10[53]225

89th Infantry; CWR:VOL3#1[31]150, CWR:VOL4#4[101]181

91st Infantry; B&G:APR/92[8]481

93rd Infantry; B&G:APR/91[8]445, B&G:JUN/95[36]603A, GETTY:13[7]253

94th Infantry:
GENERAL LISTINGS: *Gettysburg*, GETTY:4[33]146, GETTY:4[115]152, GETTY:6[7]169, GETTY:10[7]221, *in order of battle*, B&G:APR/92[8]481
ADDITIONAL LISTINGS: ACW:MAR/95[42]517, GETTY:13[33]255

95th Infantry:
GENERAL LISTINGS: *Gettysburg*, GETTY:5[4]156, GETTY:6[13]170, GETTY:6[29]171, *in order of battle*, B&G:APR/92[8]481, *SIO*, B&G:FEB/92[40]479
ADDITIONAL LISTINGS: B&G:FEB/95[8]590A, CWM:JAN/93[16]457

96th Infantry; CWTI:JAN/94[8]356

97th Infantry:
GENERAL LISTINGS: *Gettysburg*, GETTY:4[33]146, GETTY:5[13]157, GETTY:5[117]165, GETTY:5[128]167, GETTY:9[33]211, GETTY:10[7]221, GETTY:11[57]233, GETTY:11[119]238, *in order of battle*, B&G:APR/92[8]481, *ISO*, B&G:FEB/91[34]442, *letters to the editor*, B&G:AUG/95[36]607, *Manassas, Second*, GETTY:10[7]221
ADDITIONAL LISTINGS: ACW:MAR/95[42]517, B&G:FEB/95[8]590B, CWTI:JAN/93[35]300, GETTY:13[33]255

98th Infantry; CWM:SEP/92[8]437

99th Infantry; ACW:JAN/95[74]510, CWR:VOL2#4[269]145, GETTY:11[6]231

100th Infantry; ACW:SEP/91[30]322, ACW:MAY/92[30]361, CWTI:MAR/94[38]372, CWTI:MAY/94[16]380

101st Infantry; ACW:JAN/95[54]508, CWM:MAY/91[8]346, CWM:SEP/92[8]437

102nd Infantry:
ARTICLE: "TWO NEW YORK SWORDS IN THE FIGHT FOR CULP'S HILL: COL. JAMES C. LANE'S AND CAPT. NICHOLAS GRUMBACH'S," GETTY:10[36]223
ADDITIONAL LISTINGS: CWM:NOV/91[35]392, CWR:VOL3#2[70]155, CWTI:SEPT/89[30]129, GETTY:12[42]244

103rd Infantry; GETTY:11[6]231

104th Infantry:
BOOK REVIEW: *CIVIL WAR LETTERS OF CHARLES BARBER, PRIVATE, 104TH NEW YORK VOLUNTEER INFANTRY*
GENERAL LISTINGS: *Gettysburg*, GETTY:4[33]146, GETTY:10[7]221, *in order of battle*, B&G:APR/92[8]481, *list of monuments*, B&G:OCT/95[8]611A
ADDITIONAL LISTINGS: ACW:MAR/95[42]517, CWM:SEP/93[32]496, CWTI:MAY/92[32]264, GETTY:13[7]253, GETTY:13[22]254, GETTY:13[33]255

106th Infantry; ACW:NOV/93[50]444, B&G:DEC/92[8]503, CWTI:JAN/93[40]301

107th Infantry; GETTY:12[42]244

108th Infantry:
GENERAL LISTINGS: *Gettysburg*, GETTY:6[7]169, GETTY:8[67]204, GETTY:8[95]205, GETTY:9[61]215, GETTY:10[53]225, GETTY:11[126]239, *in list*, CWTI:JUL/93[34]327
ADDITIONAL LISTINGS: ACW:SEP/94[38]487, CWM:SEP/93[18]494, CWTI:APR/92[49]260

110th Infantry: CWR:VOL3#1[1]149, CWTI:DEC/90[29]182, CWNEWS:JUL/95[61]

111th Infantry:
GENERAL LISTINGS: *Gettysburg*, GETTY:5[79]161, GETTY:7[51]190, GETTY:8[95]205, GETTY:9[61]215, GETTY:10[53]225, GETTY:11[102]237, *in list*, CWTI:JUL/93[34]327, *photo of monument*, GETTY:8[95]205
ADDITIONAL LISTINGS: ACW:SEP/94[38]487, ACW:MAY/95[54]528, ACW:JUL/95[50]538, CWR:VOL1#4[7]125, CWR:VOL2#4[269]145

114th Infantry; ACW:MAY/91[38]305

115th Infantry; ACW:MAY/95[54]528, CWR:VOL1#4[7]125, CWR:VOL3#1[65]151

116th Infantry; ACW:MAY/91[38]305

117th Infantry; B&G:DEC/94[10]585, GETTY:11[6]231

118th Infantry; B&G:APR/94[10]558, B&G:OCT/95[36]614, GETTY:11[6]231

119th Infantry; CWTI:SUMMER/89[32]122, GETTY:12[30]243, GETTY:13[7]253

120th Infantry; CWM:FEB/95[30]561

121st Infantry:
BOOK REVIEWS: *A SURGEON'S CIVIL WAR: THE LETTERS AND DIARY OF DANIEL M. HOLT, M.D.*
GENERAL LISTINGS: *Gettysburg*, GETTY:10[53]225, GETTY:11[71]234, *in order of battle*, B&G:APR/92[8]481
ADDITIONAL LISTINGS: ACW:MAR/92[30]352, ACW:JAN/95[62], CWR:VOL3#3[1]157

122nd Infantry; B&G:JUN/95[8]600, CWR:VOL4#3[1]170

123rd Infantry; ACW:MAY/91[8]300, ACW:SEP/93[62]436, CWTI/8907SUMMER/89[32]122, GETTY:5[117]165, GETTY:6[7]169, GETTY:7[83]192

124th Infantry:
ARTICLE: "'FORWARD, MY TULIPS!': THE DAREDEVIL ORANGE BLOSSOMS AT CHANCELLORSVILLE," CWM:DEC/94[40]550
BOOK REVIEWS: *HISTORY OF THE ONE HUNDRED AND TWENTY-FOURTH REGIMENT, N.Y.S.V. * THAT REGIMENT OF HEROES*
GENERAL LISTINGS: *Gettysburg*, GETTY:8[53]203, GETTY:9[5]209, GETTY:9[5N]209, GETTY:12[1]240
ADDITIONAL LISTINGS: ACW:JUL/92[30]369, ACW:JUL/95[66]539, B&G:JUN/95[8]600, CWM:DEC/94[4]545, CWTI:JUN/90[32]159, CWTI:MAY/94[24]381, GETTY:13[7]253

125th Infantry:
GENERAL LISTINGS: *Gettysburg,* GETTY:7[51]190, GETTY:8[95]205, GETTY:9[61]215, GETTY:10[53]225, *in list,* CWTI:JUL/93[34]327
ADDITIONAL LISTINGS: ACW:JUL/95[50]538, B&G:FEB/93[40]514, CWR:VOL1#4[7]125, CWTI:AUG/90[26]166

126th Infantry:
ARTICLE: "THE 126TH NEW YORK INFANTRY AT HARPERS FERRY," CWR:VOL1#4[7]125
GENERAL LISTINGS: *Gettysburg,* GETTY:7[51]190, GETTY:8[67]204, GETTY:8[95]205, GETTY:9[61]215, GETTY:10[53]225, GETTY:12[97]249, MH:DEC/91[54]155, *Harpers Ferry,* MH:AUG/95[30]185, *in list,* CWTI:JUL/93[34]327, *photo of monument,* GETTY:8[95]205
ADDITIONAL LISTINGS: ACW:SEP/94[38]487, B&G:APR/91[8]445, CWR:VOL1#4[v]124, CWR:VOL1#4[74]128, CWR:VOL2#4[269]145, GETTY:13[7]253, GETTY:13[75]259

127th Infantry; GETTY:11[6]231, MH:APR/94[54]176
128th Infantry; CWR:VOL4#2[104]168, MH:OCT/93[76]173
129th Infantry; AHI:OCT/67[26]112, B&G:APR/94[55]564

132nd Infantry:
ARTICLE: "WAREAGLE OF THE TUSCARORAS: LIEUTENANT CORNELIUS C. CUSICK," CWM:SEP/92[16]438
ADDITIONAL LISTINGS: B&G:OCT/95[5]610, CWM:SEP/92[8]437, CWNEWS:JAN/94[5], CWR:VOL3#2[105]

134th Infantry; ACW:JUL/94[18]476, CWTI:SEP/94[34]402, GETTY:8[17]200

136th Infantry:
BOOK REVIEW: *JOHN T. MCMAHON'S DIARY OF THE 136TH NEW YORK 1861-1865*
ADDITIONAL LISTING: GETTY:6[7]169

137th Infantry:
GENERAL LISTINGS: *Gettysburg,* GETTY:7[83]192, GETTY:7[97]193, GETTY:9[81]216, GETTY:10[36]223
ADDITIONAL LISTINGS: CWR:VOL3#2[102]156, CWR:VOL3#2[70]155, CWTI:SEPT/89[30]129

140th Infantry:
BOOK REVIEW: *SONS OF OLD MONROE: A REGIMENTAL HISTORY OF PATRICK O'RORKE'S 140TH NEW YORK VOLUNTEER INFANTRY*
GENERAL LISTINGS: *Gettysburg,* GETTY:5[103]163, GETTY:6[33]172, GETTY:6[43]173, GETTY:7[41]189, GETTY:8[31]201, GETTY:9[48]213, *in book review,* CWNEWS:AUG/92[4], *in order of battle,* B&G:APR/92[8]481
ADDITIONAL LISTINGS: ACW:JAN/92[38]343, B&G:APR/95[8]595, B&G:JUN/95[8]600, CWM:MAR/91[17]335, CWM:MAR/91[35]337, CWM:JAN/92[16]401, GETTY:13[7]253

141st Infantry; CWM:NOV/91[28]391, CWR:VOL3#2[70]155, CWR:VOL3#2[102]156
142nd Infantry; B&G:DEC/94[10]585

144th Infantry:
BOOK REVIEW: *DEAR WIFE, LETTERS OF A CIVIL WAR SOLDIER*
ADDITIONAL LISTINGS: ACW:MAY/94[51]471, AHI:NOV/92[16], CWR:VOL2#3[194]141

145th Infantry; B&G:APR/93[12]518, GETTY:9[48]213
146th Infantry; B&G:DEC/91[12]469, B&G:APR/92[8]481, B&G:APR/95[8]595, CWM:NOV/92[64]453, GETTY:8[31]201, GETTY:13[7]253

147th Infantry:
ARTICLE: "ELMINA KEELER SPENCER: MATRON, 147TH NEW YORK," GETTY:8[121]207

GENERAL LISTINGS: *Gettysburg,* GETTY:5[4]156, GETTY:6[13]170, GETTY:6[29]171, GETTY:12[1]240, *in book review,* CWM:APR/95[50], CWNEWS:JUL/95[61], CWNEWS:NOV/95[29], *in order of battle,* B&G:APR/92[8]481
ADDITIONAL LISTING: B&G:APR/95[8]595

148th Infantry; CWR:VOL3#2[70]155

149th Infantry:
ARTICLE: "TWO NEW YORK SWORDS IN THE FIGHT FOR CULP'S HILL: COL. JAMES C. LANE'S AND CAPT. NICHOLAS GRUMBACH'S," GETTY:10[36]223
BOOK REVIEW: *MEMOIRS OF THE 149TH REGIMENT*
ADDITIONAL LISTINGS: CWR:VOL3#2[70]155, CWTI:SEPT/89[30]129, CWTI:JAN/94[8]356, GETTY:4[89]150, GETTY:7[83]192, GETTY:13[7]253

150th Infantry:
ARTICLE: "THE DUTCHESS COUNTY REGIMENT," GETTY:12[42]244
GENERAL LISTINGS: *Gettysburg,* GETTY:7[83]192, GETTY:12[1]240, *Savannah,* B&G:FEB/91[8]439, *photo of monument,* GETTY:12[42]244
ADDITIONAL LISTING: B&G:JUN/92[46]490

151st Infantry; ACW:NOV/93[50]444, B&G:DEC/92[8]503, CWTI:JUN/95[26]445
152nd Infantry; ACW:SEP/94[38]487, B&G:JUN/95[8]600

153rd Infantry:
BOOK REVIEWS: *AN UNCOMMON SOLDIER: THE CIVIL WAR LETTERS OF SARAH ROSETTA WAKEMAN, ALIAS PVT. LYONS WAKEMAN, 153RD REGIMENT, NEW YORK STATE VOLUNTEERS*
ADDITIONAL LISTINGS: ACW:MAY/91[38]305, AHI:FEB/75[35]158

154th Infantry:
ARTICLES: "THE HARDTACK REGIMENT IN THE BRICKYARD FIGHT," GETTY:8[17]200, "PHILO MARKHAM'S LONG WALK," CWTI:MAR/95[26]434, "THANKS TO A CHERISHED PHOTOGRAPH, THE UNKNOWN SOLDIER OF GETTYSBURG' DID NOT REMAIN UNKNOWN FOR LONG," ACW:JUL/94[18]476
ADDITIONAL LISTINGS: B&G:OCT/93[36]540, B&G:OCT/93[38]541, CWTI:SEP/92[22]279, CWTI:SEP/94[34]402, *Gettysburg,* GETTY:5[123]166

155th Infantry; CWM:MAR/91[50]340, CWM:OCT/95[40]619

156th Infantry:
ARTICLE: "THE RED RIVER CAMPAIGN LETTERS OF LT. CHARLES W. KENNEDY, 156TH NEW YORK VOLUNTEER INFANTRY," CWR:VOL4#2[104]168
ADDITIONAL LISTING: ACW:MAY/91[38]305

157th Infantry: ACW:MAY/91[38]305, ACW:NOV/92[42]388, GETTY:4[49]147, GETTY:7[83]192, GETTY:12[111]250
161st Infantry: CWTI:DEC/90[29]182
162nd Infantry: CWTI:DEC/90[29]182

164th Infantry:
ARTICLE: "IF THIS CONTINUES THE ARMY OF THE POTOMAC WILL BE ANNIHILLATED," CWM:OCT/95[40]619
ADDITIONAL LISTINGS: ACW:JUL/91[50], ACW:JUL/93[16]422

165th Infantry; ACW:SEP/91[16]320
169th Infantry; B&G:FEB/95[38]593, B&G:JUN/95[36]603A, B&G:OCT/95[36]614, GETTY:11[6]231
170th Infantry; B&G:APR/93[12]518, CWM:MAR/91[50]340
175th Infantry; CWR:VOL4#2[104]168
176th Infantry; CWTI:AUG/90[42]167
179th Infantry; CWTI:APR/90[24]152
182nd Infantry; B&G:APR/93[12]518, CWM:MAR/91[50]340

184th Infantry; CWNEWS:JUL/95[61]
185th Infantry; B&G:APR/92[8]481, CWR:VOL1#1[35]104
187th Infantry; B&G:APR/92[8]481
188th Infantry; B&G:APR/92[8]481
189th Infantry; B&G:APR/92[8]481
192nd Infantry; B&G:FEB/92[32]477
DeNoyelles Guard (95th New York Infantry);
GETTY:6[29]171
Excelsior Brigade; AHI:APR/85[16]249, CWM:JUN/95[34]584
Fire Zouaves; CWTI:MAY/89[36]118, CWTI:DEC/89[34]136
Independent Battery; ACW:MAY/91[38]305
National Zouaves; ACW:SEP/94[38]487

NEW YORK, STATE OF; BOOK REVIEW: *BUGLES ECHO ACROSS THE VALLEY: NORTHERN OSWEGO COUNTY, NEW YORK AND THE CIVIL WAR*
NEWBERRY, JOHN S., *civilian;* CWM:MAY/91[10]347
NEWBY, WILLIAM, *Private, 40th Illinois Infantry;* ARTICLE: "THE RETURN OF WILLIAM NEWBY: A CIVIL WAR MYSTERY," CWM:FEB/95[36]563
NEWCOMB, GEORGE, *Private, 154th New York Infantry;* GETTY:8[17]200
NEWCOMBE, JOHN M., *Captain, USA;* CWNEWS:MAY/91[4]
NEWCOMER, C.A., *Private, Cole's Maryland Cavalry;* B&G:AUG/94[10]574
NEWHALL, WALTER S., *Captain, 3rd Pennsylvania Cavalry;* GETTY:4[75]149, GETTY:13[89]260
NEWMAN, APLHEUS G., *Private, Crenshaw's Artillery;* GETTY:10[107]227
NEWMAN, L.H., *Lieutenant, USN;* CWM:JUL/93[15]484
NEWSOME, ELLEN K., AHI:DEC/73[10]152

NEWSPAPERS AND MAGAZINES:
ARTICLES: "BESIDES FIGHTING CONFEDERATES, WILLIAM SHERMAN ALSO FOUGHT WITH NORTHERN WAR CORRESPONDENTS," ACW:NOV/92[6]382, "HOW THE WAR CHANGED AMERICA'S NEWSPAPERS," ACW:NOV/95[54]558
BOOK REVIEWS: *CIVIL WAR NEWSPAPER MAPS: A HISTORICAL ATLAS * CIVIL WAR NEWSPAPER MAPS: A CARTOBIBLIOGRAPHY OF THE NORTHERN DAILY PRESS * THE IMAGE OF WAR, THE PICTORIAL REPORTING OF THE AMERICAN CIVIL WAR*
Alton "Observer"; ACW:NOV/95[54]558
Atlanta "Intelligencer"; CWM:JAN/92[40]405
"Atlantic Monthly"; ACW:NOV/95[54]558, CWTI:SEPT/89[40]130, CWTI:SEPT/89[44]131
Augusta "Constitutionalist"; CWTI:AUG/90[50]168,
Baltimore "Union"; ACW:JAN/92[30]342, ACW:MAY/94[8]465
Bellefonte "Democrat Watchman"; CWM:APR/95[63]578
Boston "Journal"; AHI:NOV/88[37]278, CWTI:AUG/90[26]166, CWTI:FEB/91[28]192, GETTY:7[23]187
Boston "Post"; AHI:FEB/82[36]225
Boston "Transcript"; CWTI:AUG/90[50]168
Brooklyn "Eagle"; AHI:APR/80[21]200
Brooklyn "Standard"; ACW:MAY/94[6]464
Century Magazine; GETTY:4[113]153, GETTY:4[24]145
Charleston "Courier"; CWM:JAN/93[29]459
Charleston "Mercury"; ACW:SEP/92[10]375, ACW:SEP/94[46]488, CWM:JUN/94[6], CWNEWS:APR/91[4], CWTI:DEC/95[22]476

Chattanooga "Daily Rebel"; ACW:NOV/92[6]382, ACW:NOV/92[35]387, B&G:OCT/92[32]499, B&G:FEB/95[30]591
Chicago "Evening Journal"; CWM:MAR/91[50]340, CWTI:SEP/92[22]279
Chicago "Press & Tribune"; ARTICLE: "RE-CREATING THE GREAT DEBATE," AHI:DEC/94[68]322
Chicago "Times":
ARTICLE: "RE-CREATING THE GREAT DEBATE," AHI:DEC/94[68]322
ADDITIONAL LISTING: AHI:NOV/88[43]279
Chicago "Tribune"; AHI:JAN/93[61]309, CWR:VOL3#4[24]162, CWTI:FEB/91[28]192, GETTY:9[122]220
Cincinnati "Daily Commercial"; AHI:JAN/67[4]106, AHI:NOV/88[37]278, B&G:DEC/91[12]469, CWM:APR/95[66]579, CWTI:SUMMER/89[32]122
Cincinnati "Daily Gazette":
ARTICLE: "'AGATE': WHITELAW REID REPORTS FROM GETTYSBURG," GETTY:7[23]187
ADDITIONAL LISTINGS: B&G:AUG/93[10]529, CWR:VOL4#1[44]164, GETTY:4[49]14
Cincinnati "Times"; AHI:NOV/72[12]142
Columbus "Daily South Carolinian"; CWTI:AUG/90[50]168
Columbus "Enquirer"; ACW:MAR/91[38]296
Columbus "Sun"; ACW:MAR/91[38]296
Columbus "Times"; ACW:MAR/91[38]296
Dayton "Journal"; ACW:MAR/91[8]291
Detroit "Advertiser and Tribune"; CWM:SEP/92[24]441
Detroit "Daily Tribune"; CWM:SEP/92[8]437
Detroit "Free Press"; CWM:SEP/93[18]494, GETTY:7[7]185
Frank Leslie's Illustrated Newspaper:
ARTICLE: "THE FRANK LESLIES," AHI:JUL/70[12]128
BOOK REVIEW: *LESLIE'S ILLUSTRATED CIVIL WAR*
ADDITIONAL LISTINGS: ACW:SEP/92[8]374, B&G:FEB/94[24]551
Frederick "Examiner"; ACW:JAN/91[38]287
Fredericksburg "News"; CWR:VOL1#1[1]102
Freedom's Journal; AHI:JUN/74[12]155
Harper's Illustrated News; AHI:JUL/70[12]128
Harper's Weekly; ACW:JAN/92[10]339, ACW:JAN/92[54], ACW:SEP/92[8]374, ACW:NOV/95[54]558, AHI:NOV/88[37]278, CWM:NOV/92[10]447, CWTI:APR/89[22]108, CWTI:SEPT/89[20]127
Harrisburg, "The Patriot and Union"; GETTY:9[122]220
Harrisburg, "Telegraph"; CWTI:JUN/90[46]161
Houston "Telegraph"; CWTI:DEC/89[26]135
Jacksonville, "Free Trader"; CWTI:AUG/90[50]168
Knoxville "Daily Register"; ACW:NOV/92[35]387, B&G:JUN/93[32]525
Leavenworth "Daily Times"; CWTI:AUG/90[26]166
London "TImes":
ARTICLE: "*LONDON TIMES* CORRESPONDENT WILLIAM HOWARD RUSSELL TOURED A VICTORY-MADDENED SOUTH IN MID-1861," ACW:SEP/93[10]430
ADDITIONAL LISTING: ACW:MAY/95[38]526
Louisville "Daily Journal"; ACW:JAN/94[10]448, CWM:JUN/94[6], CWM:JAN/93[29]459
Macon "Daily Telegraph"; CWM:JAN/92[40]405,CWR:VOL1#4[42]126
Memphis "Appeal":
ARTICLE: "DEFIANT REBEL NEWSPAPER," ACW:NOV/92[35]387
ADDITIONAL LISTING: ACW:NOV/92[6]382
Mesilla "Times"; ACW:JAN/91[10]283

Milwaukee "Sunday Telegraph"; GETTY:4[24]145
Mississippi "Whig"; MH:FEB/95[18]182
Missouri "Republican"; ACW:MAY/91[31]304
Missouri "Democrat"; ACW:MAR/92[46]354,
  ACW:NOV/94[42]497
Natchez "Courier"; GETTY:12[68]246
National Tribune; GETTY:9[33]211
New Orleans "Daily Picayune"; CWTI:MAR/89[28]103,
  CWTI:SEPT/89[20]127, MH:DEC/94[46]181
New Orleans "Crescent"; ACW:NOV/95[54]558,
  CWM:JUN/94[6]
New York "Daily News"; AHI:APR/80[21]200
New York "Evening News"; ACW:JUL/93[8]420,
  AHI:JAN/81[18]214, CWTI:SEP/92[22]279
New York "Journal of Commerce"; AHI:APR/80[21]200
New York "Herald"; ACW:JUL/91[35]314,
  ACW:NOV/91[16]330, ACW:MAY/92[30]361,
  ACW:NOV/92[6]382, ACW:JAN/94[47]452,
  ACW:JUL/94[42]479, ACW:SEP/94[46]488,
  AHI:OCT/68[4]116, AHI:JAN/81[18]214, AHI:NOV/88[37]278,
  AHI:JAN/93[61]309, B&G:DEC/91[12]469,
  B&G:DEC/92[32]506, B&G:FEB/94[24]551,
  B&G:DEC/95[9]615, CWM:JUL/92[18]429,
  CWR:VOL1#2[7]111, CWTI:JUN/90[46]161,
  CWTI:AUG/90[58]169, CWTI:SEP/91[31]229,
  CWTI:SEP/92[42]283, CWTI:JUN/95[38]447,
  GETTY:12[85]248, GETTY:12[97]249, MH:JUN/94[8]177
New York "Leader"; ACW:MAY/94[6]464
New York "Post"; CWTI:SEP/91[54]232, CWTI:JAN/93[49]303
New York "Times"; ACW:NOV/91[16]330,
  ACW:NOV/91[22]331, ACW:NOV/91[46]335, ACW:JAN/92[54],
  ACW:JAN/92[6]337, ACW:JAN/92[30]342,
  ACW:MAR/92[22]351, ACW:MAY/92[30]361,
  ACW:JAN/93[26]395, ACW:JAN/93[58]399,
  ACW:SEP/94[55]489, ACW:JAN/95[54]508,
  AHI:OCT/68[4]116, AHI:DEC/68[28]118, AHI:APR/80[21]200,
  B&G:FEB/91[20]440, B&G:DEC/92[38]507,
  B&G:JUN/93[12]524, CWM:JUL/92[18]429,
  CWM:MAY/93[32]477, CWTI:MAY/89[14]114,
  CWTI:AUG/90[26]166, CWTI:AUG/90[42]167,
  CWTI:AUG/90[58]169, CWTI:AUG/90[64]170,
  CWTI:FEB/91[28]192, CWTI:DEC/91[28]239,
  CWTI:APR/92[35]257, CWTI:OCT/95[48]470,
  GETTY:6[99]181, GETTY:7[23]187, GETTY:13[108]261,
  MH:OCT/93[12]171
New York "Tribune"; ACW:JAN/92[30]342,
  ACW:NOV/92[6]382, ACW:NOV/93[50]444,
  ACW:MAR/94[35]460, ACW:MAY/95[54]528,
  ACW:NOV/95[54]558, AHI:OCT/68[4]116,
  AHI:DEC/68[28]118, AHI:NOV/71[32]136,
  AHI:DEC/71[30]138, AHI:AUG/77[30]175,
  AHI:MAY/81[35]218, AHI:JAN/93[61]309,
  B&G:DEC/91[12]469, B&G:APR/92[28]482,
  B&G:APR/95[8]595, CWNEWS:APR/91[4],
  CWTI:SEPT/89[44]131, CWTI:AUG/90[50]168,
  CWTI:AUG/90[70]171, CWTI:SEP/90[12],
  CWTI:DEC/90[50]183, CWTI:AUG/91[46]218,
  CWTI:DEC/91[28]239, CWTI:SEP/91[42]231,
  CWTI:SEP/91[54]232, CWTI:JAN/93[49]303,
  CWTI:MAY/93[20]317, CWTI:DEC/95[22]476,
  MH:JUN/94[8]177, GETTY:7[23]187
New York "World"; ACW:MAY/95[38]526, AHI:APR/80[21]200,
  AHI:JAN/82[16]224

"North Carolina Standard"; CWM:JUN/94[6]
Petersburg "Express"; CWTI:AUG/90[50]168
Philadelphia "Daily Age"; AHI:NOV/88[37]278
Philadelphia "Daily Evening Bulletin"; GETTY:12[85]248
Philadelphia "Evening Journal"; CWM:SEP/92[8]437
Philadelphia "Inquirer"; ACW:NOV/95[54]558,
  AHI:DEC/68[28]118, AHI:NOV/88[43]279,
  CWM:MAR/92[32]413, CWM:JUL/92[18]429
Philadelphia "Weekly Press":
  ARTICLE: "GEORGE J. GROSS ON HALLOWED GROUND,"
  GETTY:10[112]228
  ADDITIONAL LISTINGS: CWNEWS:SEP/90[4], GETTY:4[113]153,
  GETTY:11[126]239
Philadelphia "Weekly Times"; MH:JUN/94[8]177
Raleigh "Daily Confederate"; ACW:MAR/95[50]518
Raleigh "Observer"; GETTY:8[67]204
Richmond "Daily Dispatch"; ACW:JAN/93[18]394,
  ACW:MAR/93[42]406, CWTI:AUG/91[68]222,
  CWTI:MAY/94[40]383
Richmond "Daily Inquirer":
  ARTICLE: "NEVER HEARD BEFORE ON THE AMERICAN
  CONTINENT," GETTY:10[107]227
  ADDITIONAL LISTINGS: ACW:NOV/95[8]552, ACW:SEP/92[38]379,
  ACW:NOV/95[54]558, CWTI:MAY/89[22]116,
  GETTY:4[113]153, GETTY:8[67]204
Richmond "Examiner"; ACW:SEP/92[38]379,
  ACW:MAY/93[38]416, ACW:JUL/93[34]424,
  ACW:NOV/93[42]443, B&G:APR/91[8]445,
  CWTI:AUG/91[58]220, CWTI:MAY/94[40]383
Richmond "Sentinel"; ACW:NOV/95[8]552
Richmond "Times-Dispatch"; GETTY:5[19]158
Richmond "Whig"; ACW:MAR/92[22]351, ACW:JAN/93[18]394,
  ACW:SEP/93[22]432, CWNEWS:APR/91[4]
"Rocky Mountain News"; ACW:NOV/91[10]329
Savannah "Republican"; CWR:VOL3#1[65]151
Shreveport "News"; CWR:VOL4#2[68]167,
  CWR:VOL4#2[118]169
Southern Illustrated News; CWM:NOV/92[10]447
Southern Magazine; GETTY:4[113]153
St. Louis "Democrat"; GETTY:7[23]187
Tallahassee "Floridian and Journal"; CWR:VOL3#1[65]151
"Telegraph and Confederate"; CWM:JAN/92[40]405
Vicksburg "Daily Citizen"; AHI:DEC/77[13]176,
  B&G:AUG/95[8]604, CWTI:SEPT/89[18]126
Vicksburg "Daily Herald"; B&G:OCT/91[11]466
Washington "Telegraph"; ACW:SEP/92[66]381
Washington "Chronicle"; GETTY:10[112]228,
  GETTY:12[85]248
Wilmington "Daily North Carolinian"; B&G:DEC/94[10]585

NEWPORT, RHODE ISLAND; ARTICLE: "U.S. NAVAL
  ACADEMY," ACW:JAN/91[62]289
NEWTON STATION, MISSISSIPPI; ACW:MAY/92[47]363,
  B&G:JUN/93[12]524, B&G:AUG/93[6]528, MH:FEB/95[18]182
NEWTON, GEORGE A., *Private, 129th Illinois Infantry;*
  CWTI:SUMMER/89[32]122
NEWTON, ISAAC, *Lieutenant, USN;* AHI:NOV/75[38]163,
  CWTI:DEC/95[24]477, *photo,* AHI:NOV/75[38]163
NEWTON, J., *Lieutenant, USN;* CWM:JUL/93[15]484
NEWTON, JAMES M., *Lieutenant Colonel, 6th Georgia
  Infantry;* B&G:OCT/95[8]611A

ADDITIONAL LISTINGS: B&G:DEC/94[10]585, ACW:JUL/93[34]424, ACW:JAN/95[38]506, CWTI:DEC/94[34]411, CWTI:DEC/95[76]482

NORTH CAROLINA TROOPS:

ARTICLE: "NORTH CAROLINA IN THE PICKETT-PETTIGREW-TRIMBLE CHARGE AT GETTYSBURG," GETTY:8[67]204

BOOK REVIEWS: *A TARHEEL CONFEDERATE AND HIS FAMILY * BUSHWHACKERS: THE CIVIL WAR IN NORTH CAROLINA: THE MOUNTAINS * THE CIVIL WAR IN NORTH CAROLINA * NORTH CAROLINA AND THE COMING OF THE CIVIL WAR * NORTH CAROLINA TROOPS, 1861-1865: A ROSTER, VOLUME XII, 49TH-52ND REGIMENTS * NORTH CAROLINA TROOPS, 1861-1865: A ROSTER, VOL. XIII INFANTRY * SILK FLAGS AND COLD STEEL: THE CIVIL WAR IN NORTH CAROLINA. VOL. 1: THE PEIDMONT*

1st Artillery; B&G:DEC/94[10]585

1st Artillery, Battery A; GETTY:8[53]203

1st Cavalry:
GENERAL LISTINGS: *Gettysburg,* GETTY:4[75]149, GETTY:12[68]246, *in order of battle,* B&G:APR/92[8]481
ADDITIONAL LISTINGS: ACW:JUL/92[41]370, ACW:JAN/95[10]503, ACW:MAR/95[50]518, B&G:DEC/91[34]470, B&G:APR/93[24]520, B&G:OCT/93[12]537, B&G:JUN/95[8]600, CWM:JUL/92[16]428, CWTI:JUN/90[32]159, CWTI:FEB/91[45]194, GETTY:13[89]260

1st Infantry; ACW:JUL/92[30]369, ACW:MAR/93[42]406, ACW:JAN/95[10]503, CWM:MAY/92[20]420, CWM:JUN/95[57]592, CWR:VOL1#2[7]111, CWTI:APR/89[14]107, GETTY:7[83]192, GETTY:9[17]210

1st Infantry, (Union); CWR:VOL3#1[65]151

1st Junior Reserves; ACW:NOV/93[12]440, ACW:MAR/95[50]518

2nd Artillery; B&G:DEC/94[10]585

2nd Cavalry:
GENERAL LISTINGS: *Brandy Station,* GETTY:11[19]232, *in order of battle,* B&G:APR/92[8]481, *letters to the editor,* B&G:APR/91[6]444
ADDITIONAL LISTINGS: ACW:JUL/92[41]370, ACW:JAN/95[10]503, B&G:OCT/93[12]537, CWM:SEP/93[18]494, CWTI:JUN/90[32]159, CWTI:FEB/91[45]194

2nd Infantry; ACW:MAR/92[30]352, CWM:JUL/92[16]428, GETTY:4[33]146, GETTY:5[117]165, GETTY:13[33]255

2nd Infantry, (Mounted); B&G:OCT/94[42]583, CWM:SEP/92[8]437

2nd Infantry, (Union); ACW:SEP/93[54]54, B&G:APR/92[28]482

2nd Junior Reserves; ACW:NOV/93[12]440, ACW:MAR/95[50]518

3rd Cavalry; B&G:APR/92[8]481, CWTI:FEB/91[45]194

3rd Infantry; ACW:JUL/92[30]369, B&G:APR/95[8]595, CWM:MAY/92[20]420, GETTY:7[83]192

3rd Infantry, (Mounted, Union); ACW:NOV/93[12]440

4th Cavalry; ACW:JUL/92[41]370, ACW:JAN/95[10]503, B&G:APR/92[8]481, GETTY:13[108]261

4th Infantry; CWM:JUL/92[16]428, GETTY:4[33]146, GETTY:12[111]250, GETTY:13[33]255

4th Junior Reserves; ACW:NOV/93[12]440

5th Cavalry; ACW:JUL/92[41]370, ACW:JAN/95[10]503, ACW:MAR/95[50]518, B&G:APR/92[36]483,

B&G:OCT/93[12]537, CWR:VOL4#1[1]163, CWTI:FEB/91[45]194

5th Infantry; ACW:MAR/91[47]297, AHI:APR/68[4]115, B&G:DEC/94[36]588, B&G:FEB/95[8]590B, B&G:JUN/95[36]603A, CWTI:SEP/93[43]338, GETTY:5[13]157, GETTY:10[7]221, GETTY:12[111]250

5th Junior Reserves; ACW:NOV/93[12]440

6th Cavalry; CWM:SEP/92[16]438

6th Infantry; ACW:MAR/92[30]352, ACW:JUL/92[30]369, ACW:NOV/92[42]388, ACW:MAR/94[50]462, ACW:NOV/94[18]495, B&G:AUG/93[10]529, B&G:DEC/94[10]585, CWR:VOL2#4[269]145, CWR:VOL3#2[105], CWNEWS:OCT/89[4], CWTI:NOV/93[114]355, GETTY:8[17]200

6th Junior Reserves; ACW:NOV/93[12]440

7th Infantry:
GENERAL LISTINGS: *Gettysburg,* GETTY:8[67]204, *in book review,* CWNEWS:OCT/89[4], *in list,* CWTI:JUL/93[34]327, *Manassas, Second,* B&G:AUG/92[11]493
ADDITIONAL LISTINGS: ACW:MAR/95[42]517, CWTI:SEP/92[82]286, GETTY:13[22]254, GETTY:13[75]259

7th Junior Reserves; ACW:NOV/93[12]440, CWR:VOL2#3[194]141

8th Infantry; B&G:APR/93[24]520, B&G:APR/94[10]558, CWM:FEB/95[49]565

8th Junior Reserves; ACW:NOV/93[12]440

9th Junior Reserves; ACW:NOV/93[12]440

10th Infantry; B&G:DEC/94[10]585

11th Infantry:
GENERAL LISTINGS: *Gettysburg,* GETTY:5[19]158, GETTY:8[67]204, *Immortal Six Hundred (in list),* GETTY:12[111]250, *in list,* CWTI:JUL/93[34]327
ADDITIONAL LISTINGS: B&G:JUN/95[8]600, GETTY:13[75]259

12th Infantry:
GENERAL LISTINGS: *Gettysburg,* GETTY:4[33]146, GETTY:5[13]157, GETTY:7[114]194, GETTY:10[7]221, GETTY:12[111]250, GETTY:13[33]255
ADDITIONAL LISTINGS: B&G:FEB/95[8]590B, CWM:MAY/92[34]422

13th Infantry; CWTI:AUG/90[26]166, CWTI:MAY/93[26]318, CWTI:JUL/93[34]327, CWTI:SEP/94[26]400, GETTY:8[67]204, GETTY:11[57]233

14th Infantry; CWTI:MAR/95[46]437, GETTY:4[33]146, GETTY:6[7]169, GETTY:13[7]253, GETTY:13[33]255

15th Infantry; ACW:JAN/94[8]447, CWM:JUN/95[29]583, CWR:VOL1#4[7]125, CWR:VOL3#3[1]157

16th Cavalry; B&G:APR/92[8]481

16th Infantry:
BOOK REVIEWS: *THE HISTORY OF THE 16TH NORTH CAROLINA REGIMENT IN THE CIVIL WAR*
GENERAL LISTINGS: *Gettysburg,* GETTY:8[67]204, GETTY:11[57]233, GETTY:12[61]245, *in list,* CWTI:JUL/93[34]327
ADDITIONAL LISTINGS: B&G:APR/93[12]518, CWR:VOL4#4[70]180

17th Infantry; ACW:MAR/95[12]513

18th Infantry:
GENERAL LISTINGS: *Chancellorsville,* MH:JUN/92[50]159, *Falling Waters,* GETTY:9[109]218, *Gettysburg,* GETTY:8[67]204, *in list,* CWTI:JUL/93[34]327
ADDITIONAL LISTING: CWR:VOL1#3[52]122

19th Infantry:
GENERAL LISTINGS: *Gettysburg,* GETTY:4[33]146, GETTY:5[13]157, GETTY:8[67]204, GETTY:10[7]221,

GETTY:12[1]240, GETTY:12[111]250, *Immortal Six Hundred,*
GETTY:12[111]250, *in book review,* CWNEWS:SEP/95[33]
ADDITIONAL LISTINGS: B&G:FEB/95[8]590B, GETTY:13[33]255
20th Infantry; AHI:APR/85[18]250, B&G:AUG/92[11]493,
GETTY:8[17]200, GETTY:10[53]225
21st Infantry:
GENERAL LISTINGS: *Gettysburg,* GETTY:8[67]204,
GETTY:11[57]233, GETTY:12[61]245, *Immortal Six Hundred,*
GETTY:12[111]250, *in list,* CWTI:JUL/93[34]327
ADDITIONAL LISTINGS: B&G:APR/93[24]520, CWR:VOL1#1[1]102,
CWTI:FEB/91[45]194, CWTI:APR/92[49]260
23rd Infantry:
GENERAL LISTINGS: *Gettysburg,* GETTY:4[33]146,
GETTY:5[13]157, GETTY:10[7]221, GETTY:12[1]240,
GETTY:12[111]250, *Immortal Six Hundred,*
GETTY:12[111]250, ACW:MAR/91[47]297, ACW:MAY/91[38]305,
ACW:MAR/95[50]518, B&G:FEB/95[8]590A,
B&G:FEB/95[8]590B, CWTI:MAY/93[26]318
24th Infantry; B&G:APR/92[8]481, GETTY:11[6]231
25th Infantry; B&G:APR/92[8]481
26th Infantry:
ARTICLES: "ARNOLD'S BATTERY AND THE 26TH NORTH
CAROLINA," GETTY:12[61]245, "THE DEADLY EMBRACE:
THE MEETING OF THE TWENTY-FOURTH REGIMENT,
MICHIGAN INFANTRY AND THE TWENTY-SIXTH
REGIMENT OF NORTH CAROLINA TROOPS AT
McPHERSON'S WOODS, GETTYSBURG, PENNSYLVANIA,
JULY 1, 1863," GETTY:5[19]158
GENERAL LISTINGS: *Gettysburg,* GETTY:4[113]153,
GETTY:7[7]185, GETTY:8[67]204, GETTY:12[1]240,
GETTY:12[61]245, GETTY:12[111]250, *Immortal Six Hundred
(in list),* GETTY:12[111]250, *in book review,* CWM:APR/95[50],
CWR:VOL4#2[136], *in list,* CWTI:JUL/93[34]327, *SIO,*
B&G:DEC/93[30]546
ADDITIONAL LISTINGS: B&G:FEB/95[8]590A, B&G:JUN/95[8]600,
CWM:AUG/94[26]525, CWTI:FEB/91[45]194, GETTY:13[1]252
27th Infantry; CWM:NOV/92[64]453, CWR:VOL4#4[28]178,
CWTI:AUG/90[26]166, CWTI:FEB/91[45]194,
MH:AUG/95[30]185
28th Infantry; CWM:JUN/95[43]587, CWR:VOL1#4[7]125,
CWTI:FEB/91[45]194, CWTI:JUL/93[34]327, GETTY:8[67]204,
GETTY:9[109]218, GETTY:13[119]262
30th Infantry; GETTY:4[33]146, GETTY:13[33]255
31st Infantry; ACW:SEP/91[30]322, B&G:APR/93[24]520,
B&G:JUN/93[6]523
32nd Cavalry; ACW:MAR/95[50]518
32nd Infantry; CWTI:DEC/89[42]137, GETTY:4[33]146,
GETTY:9[81]216, GETTY:13[33]255
33rd Infantry:
ARTICLE: "MAJ. JOSEPH H. SAUNDERS, 33RD NORTH
CAROLINA, C.S.A.," GETTY:10[102]226
GENERAL LISTINGS: *Falling Waters,* GETTY:9[109]218, *Gettysburg,*
GETTY:8[67]204, GETTY:12[111]250, *Immortal Six Hundred,*
GETTY:12[111]250, *in list,* CWTI:JUL/93[34]327
ADDITIONAL LISTINGS: ACW:MAY/95[18]524, AHI:JUN/70[30]127,
CWTI:FEB/91[45]194, GETTY:13[75]259
34th Infantry:
GENERAL LISTINGS: *Falling Waters,* GETTY:9[109]218, *Gettysburg,*
GETTY:11[57]233, *Gettysburg,* GETTY:8[67]204, *Immortal Six
Hundred,* GETTY:12[111]250, *in list,* CWTI:JUL/93[34]327
ADDITIONAL LISTING: GETTY:13[75]259

35th Infantry:
BOOK REVIEW: *A CAPTAIN'S WAR: THE LETTERS AND
DIARIES OF WILLIAM H.S. BURGWYN, 1861-1865*
ADDITIONAL LISTINGS: B&G:APR/92[8]481, CWR:VOL4#2[136]
36th Infantry: B&G:DEC/94[10]585
37th Infantry; ACW:MAR/95[42]517, B&G:APR/93[12]518,
CWM:JUN/95[43]587, CWTI:JUL/93[34]327, GETTY:8[67]204,
GETTY:12[111]250
38th Infantry; CWM:JUN/95[57]592, CWTI:JUL/93[34]327,
GETTY:6[7]169, GETTY:8[67]204, GETTY:11[57]233
40th Infantry; B&G:DEC/95[9]615
42nd Infantry; B&G:DEC/94[10]585
43rd Infantry;
GENERAL LISTINGS: *Gettysburg,* GETTY:4[33]146,
GETTY:7[114]194, GETTY:9[81]216, *Immortal Six Hundred,*
GETTY:12[111]250
ADDITIONAL LISTINGS: B&G:APR/93[12]518, CWTI:APR/92[42]259,
GETTY:13[7]253, GETTY:13[33]255
44th Infantry; B&G:APR/93[24]520, CWTI:MAY/89[22]116,
CWTI:AUG/90[26]166, CWTI:FEB/91[45]194,
GETTY:5[19]158, GETTY:11[6]231
45th Infantry; B&G:FEB/95[8]590B, CWM:MAY/92[15]419,
GETTY:10[102]226, GETTY:11[6]231, GETTY:13[33]255
46th Infantry; CWR:VOL4#4[28]178, GETTY:10[102]226,
GETTY:11[6]231
47th Infantry:
GENERAL LISTINGS: *Gettysburg,* GETTY:5[19]158,
GETTY:8[67]204, GETTY:12[61]245, *in list,*
CWTI:JUL/93[34]327, *letters to the editor,*
B&G:AUG/95[36]607, *SIO,* B&G:OCT/95[36]614
ADDITIONAL LISTINGS: B&G:APR/93[24]520, B&G:FEB/95[8]590A,
CWTI:FEB/91[45]194, GETTY:13[75]259
48th Infantry; CWM:JUN/95[55]591
49th Infantry; B&G:APR/92[8]481
51st Infantry; ACW:SEP/91[30]322, B&G:APR/93[24]520,
B&G:APR/94[10]558, CWTI:DEC/89[42]137,
CWTI:JAN/95[48]429
52nd Infantry:
GENERAL LISTINGS: *Gettysburg,* GETTY:5[19]158,
GETTY:8[67]204, GETTY:9[61]215, GETTY:12[61]245,
GETTY:13[75]259, *in list,* CWTI:JUL/93[34]327, *letters to the
editor,* B&G:APR/95[5]594, B&G:AUG/95[36]607
ADDITIONAL LISTINGS: B&G:APR/93[24]520, B&G:FEB/95[8]590A,
CWTI:AUG/90[26]166
53rd Infantry; B&G:FEB/95[8]590B, GETTY:4[33]146,
GETTY:4[33]146, GETTY:5[128]167, GETTY:13[33]255
54th Infantry; ACW:MAR/92[30]352, ACW:JAN/93[43]397,
CWNEWS:OCT/89[4], CWTI:DEC/91[82]243
55th Infantry:
GENERAL LISTINGS: *Gettysburg,* GETTY:4[22]144, GETTY:5[4]156,
GETTY:6[29]171, GETTY:8[67]204, *in list,*
CWTI:JUL/93[34]327
ADDITIONAL LISTINGS: CWR:VOL2#4[269]145, GETTY:9[98]217,
GETTY:13[75]259
56th Infantry; B&G:APR/92[8]481
57th Infantry; ACW:MAR/92[30]352, ACW:NOV/94[66],
GETTY:8[17]200, GETTY:12[30]243, GETTY:12[111]250
59th Infantry; ACW:JAN/95[10]503
61st Infantry; B&G:FEB/95[8]590B
63rd Infantry; ACW:JAN/95[10]503
64th Infantry; B&G:FEB/91[20]440
65th Infantry; B&G:APR/92[36]483

67th Infantry; CWM:SEP/92[16]438
68th Infantry;
BOOK REVIEW: *A TARHEEL CONFEDERATE AND HIS FAMILY*
ADDITIONAL LISTING: CWTI:JAN/95[42]428
69th Infantry; CWM:JUN/94[27]513
70th Infantry; ACW:MAR/95[50]518
70th Junior Reserves; ACW:NOV/93[12]440
70th Infantry; ACW:MAR/95[50]518
71st Junior Reserves; ACW:NOV/93[12]440
72nd Junior Reserves; ACW:NOV/93[12]440
Army of Northern Virginia Brigades; ARTICLE: "CHARGE OF
   THE TARHEEL BRIGADES," CWTI:FEB/91[45]194
Duplin Rifles; GETTY:7[114]194
Gaston Guards; GETTY:5[13]157
Granville Rifles; ACW:MAR/95[50]518, CWTI:MAY/93[26]318
Junior Reserves; ARTICLE: "THE NORTH CAROLINA JUNIOR
   RESERVES FOUGHT WITH A FIERCENESS THAT BELIED
   THEIR YOUTH," ACW:NOV/93[12]440
Latham's Battery; CWR:VOL4#4[70]180
**Lloyd's Battery;,D CWR:VOL3#2[1]153
North Carolina Reserves Brigade; B&G:DEC/95[9]615
Southerland's Battery; B&G:DEC/94[10]585
Thomas Legion; CWM:SEP/92[8]437
Wilmington Horse Artillery; B&G:DEC/94[10]585

NORTH CAROLINA, STATE OF:
BOOK REVIEWS: *A TARHEEL CONFEDERATE AND HIS FAMILY
   * THE CIVIL WAR IN NORTH CAROLINA * NORTH
   CAROLINA AND THE COMING OF THE CIVIL WAR * SILK
   FLAGS AND COLD STEEL: THE CIVIL WAR IN NORTH
   CAROLINA. VOL. 1: THE PIEDMONT*
NORTH, CHARLES, *Private, 1st Minnesota Infantry;*
   GETTY:5[79]161
NORTHON, JOHN, *Private, 5th Michigan Cavalry;*
   B&G:AUG/91[36]462
NORTHROP, BIRDSEY G.; B&G:DEC/91[12]469
NORTHROP, LUCIUS B., *Colonel, CSA:*
BOOK REVIEW: *NINE MEN IN GRAY,* CWNEWS:NOV/94[33]
ADDITIONAL LISTING: CWM:APR/95[50]
NORTHROP, RUFUS, *Private, 90th Pennsylvania Infantry;*
   GETTY:10[7]221
NORTHRUP, CHARLES, *Major, 97th New York Infantry;*
   GETTY:10[7]221
NORTHWEST CONSPIRACY; B&G:OCT/93[38]541,
   CWTI:JAN/93[44]302, MH:JUN/91[20]152
NORTON, CHARLES E.; CWTI:AUG/90[42]167
NORTON, GEORGE F., *Major, 1st Virginia Infantry;*
   B&G:APR/93[12]518
NORTON, GEORGE W., *Lieutenant, 1st Ohio Artillery;*
   GETTY:12[30]243
NORTON, HENRY, *Private, 8th New York Cavalry;*
   CWM:MAY/92[8]418
NORTON, JOHN, *Captain, 6th Massachusetts Infantry;*
   ACW:NOV/95[30]555
NORTON, JOHN, *civilian;* B&G:FEB/91[20]440
NORTON, JOSEPH, *Private, 5th Michigan Cavalry;*
   B&G:AUG/95[24]605
NORTON, LEMUEL B., *Captain, USA;* B&G:APR/91[8]445,
   GETTY:4[101]151, GETTY:7[29]188, GETTY:8[31]201,
   GETTY:10[42]224, MH:JUN/94[8]177, *photo,*
   B&G:APR/91[8]445
NORTON, OLIVER W., *Sergeant, 83rd Pennsylvania Infantry:*
ARTICLE: "THE TRUE STORY OF TAPS," B&G:AUG/93[30]531

BOOK REVIEW: *THE ATTACK AND DEFENSE OF LITTLE
   ROUND TOP*
GENERAL LISTINGS: *Gettysburg,* GETTY:6[33]172,
   GETTY:7[41]189, GETTY:7[97]193, GETTY:8[31]201,
   GETTY:10[112]228, *letters to the editor,* B&G:DEC/92[6]502
ADDITIONAL LISTINGS: B&G:AUG/93[30]531, CWTI:JAN/94[20]358
NORTON, WALTER B., *Private, 8th New York Cavalry;*
   GETTY:4[115]152
NORWOOD, JOHN K., *Private, 9th Massachusetts Artillery;*
   GETTY:5[47]160
NORWOOD, THOMAS L., *Lieutenant, 37th North Carolina
   Infantry;* GETTY:8[67]204
NOWLEN, GARRETT, *Lieutenant 116th Pennsylvania
   Infantry;* CWTI:DEC/90[58]185
NOXUBEE (MISSISSIPPI) RIFLES; ACW:MAR/92[10]349,
   GETTY:9[98]217
NOYES, E.M., *Lieutenant, USA;* ACW:JAN/94[8]447,
   CWM:JUN/95[29]583
NUECES, TEXAS, BATTLE OF; ARTICLE: "TRAVEL,
   COMFORT, TEXAS," ACW:JUL/91[58]316
NUGENT, EDWARD, *inventor;* ACW:JUL/93[8]420
NUGENT, JAMES H., *Lieutenant, USA;* CWM:AUG/95[35]607
NUGENT, ROBERT, *Colonel, 69th New York Infantry;*
   ACW:MAY/94[12]466, ACW:SEP/95[54]548,
   AHI:AUG/77[30]175, CWR:VOL4#4[47]179,
   CWTI:AUG/90[26]166, CWTI:DEC/90[58]185, *photos,*
   CWM:MAR/91[17]335, CWTI:DEC/90[58]185
NUGENT, WILLIAM L., *Lieutenant, 28th Mississippi Infantry;*
   CWTI:NOV/92[106]295
NULL, THEODORE, *Lieutenant, 12th New Jersey Infantry;*
   ACW:SEP/94[38]487
NUNEZ, FELIX E., *Lieutenant, 18th Louisiana Infantry;*
   CWR:VOL4#2[1]165

NURSES:
ARTICLE: "SISTERS AND NUNS WHO WERE NURSES DURING
   THE CIVIL WAR," B&G:OCT/93[31]539
Harvey, Cordelia; ARTICLE: "AN ANGEL FORM WISCONSIN:
   A YANKEE GOVERNOR'S WIDOW DEDICATES HERSELF
   TO COMFORTING THE WOUNDED," CWTI:MAR/89[20]102

NUTTING, OSCAR F., *Lieutenant, Wisconsin Light Artillery;*
   B&G:AUG/95[8]604

O

O'BEIRNE, JAMES R., *Captain, 37th New York Infantry;* CWM:MAR/91[50]340

O'BRIEN, BILLY, *Pvt., 11th Miss. Inf.;* CWR:VOL2#4[269]145

O'BRIEN, EDWARD, *Chaplain, 17th Illinois Cavalry;* CWM:MAR/91[50]340

O'BRIEN, HENRY, *Col., 11th NY Inf.;* AHI:AUG/77[30]175

O'BRIEN, HENRY D., *Corporal, 1st Minnesota Infantry;* ACW:JAN/94[62], GETTY:5[79]161

O'BRIEN, MICHAEL, *Private, Louisiana Tigers;* CWTI:MAR/94[48]374

O'BRIEN, NICHOLAS, *Chaplain, 28th Massachusetts Infantry;* CWM:MAR/91[50]340

O'CALLAGHAN, JOSEPH, *Chaplain, 69th New York Militia;* CWM:MAR/91[50]340

O'CONNELL, JOHN D., *Captain, USA;* ACW:NOV/94[50]498

O'CONNELL, MALACHI, *Captain, 24th Michigan Infantry;* GETTY:5[19]158

O'CONNER, LAWRENCE L., *Lieutenant, USA;* CWTI:DEC/91[22]237

O'CONNOR (MISSISSIPPI) RIFLES, (2nd Mississippi Infantry); GETTY:6[77]177

O'CONNOR, EDGAR, *Col., 2nd Wisc. Inf.;* B&G:AUG/92[11]493

O'CONNOR, PAT, *Sergeant, 15th Alabama Infantry;* ACW:JAN/92[38]343, CWM:DEC/94[26]548

O'CONNOR, T., *Private, 1st U.S. Cavalry;* ACW:JUL/93[42]425

O'CONNOR, WILLIAM, *Sergeant, USMC;* CWTI:JAN/94[46]364

O'DANIEL, W.J., *Pvt., 5th North Carolina Inf.;* GETTY:5[13]157

O'DONNELL, MALACHI, *Captain, 24th Michigan Infantry;* CWM:MAR/91[17]335

O'DONOHUE, WILLIAM, *Private, USA;* CWM:MAR/91[14]334

O'HAGAN, JOSEPH B., *Chaplain, 73rd New York Infantry;* CWM:MAR/91[50]340

O'HARA, TIMOTHY, *Col., 12th Ala. Inf.;* B&G:DEC/92[8]503

O'HERN, J.D., *Lt., 2nd Florida Battalion;* CWR:VOL3#4[1]161

O'HIGGINS, WILLIAM T., *Chaplain, 10th Ohio Infantry;* CWM:MAR/91[50]340

O'KANE, DENNIS, *Colonel, 69th Pennsylvania Infantry;* CWM:MAR/91[17]335, GETTY:4[89]150

O'MEAGHER, WILLIAM, *Surgeon, 69th New York Infantry;* GETTY:10[53]225

O'NEAL, A.M., *1st Confederate Battalion;* B&G:FEB/95[8]590A,

O'NEAL, CHARLES, *seaman, USN;* AHI:OCT/75[30]162

O'NEAL, EDWARD A., *Colonel, CSA:*
GENERAL LISTINGS: *Gettysburg,* GETTY:4[33]146, GETTY:4[49]147, GETTY:5[13]157, GETTY:5[128]167, GETTY:6[69]176, GETTY:7[83]192, GETTY:9[17]210, GETTY:9[81]216, GETTY:10[7]221, GETTY:12[111]250, *in book review,* CWNEWS:OCT/93[5], *letters to the editor,* B&G:AUG/95[36]607
ADDITIONAL LISTINGS: ACW:SEP/93[31]433, ACW:JAN/95[46]507, B&G:FEB/95[8]590B, CWM:MAR/91[17]335, CWM:DEC/94[40]550, CWTI:SUMMER/89[32]122, GETTY:13[33]255

O'NEAL, JOHN, *Pvt., 19th Indiana Infantry,* GETTY:11[57]233

O'NEAL, JOHN W.C., *civilian;* GETTY:5[107]164, GETTY:7[114]194, GETTY:12[97]249

O'NEIL, S., *Corporal, 7th U.S. Infantry;* ACW:JUL/93[42]425

O'NEILL, JOHN, *Colonel, 116th Pennsylvania Infantry:*

ARTICLE: "FENIAN RAIDS AGAINST CANADA," AHI:AUG/78[33]184
ADDITIONAL LISTINGS: AHI:AUG/78[33]184, CWTI:DEC/90[58]185

O'NEILL, JOSEPH, *Major, 63rd New York Infantry;* CWR:VOL4#4[47]179, CWTI:DEC/90[58]185

O'REILLY, BERNARD, *Chaplain, 69th New York Infantry;* CWM:MAR/91[50]340

O'REILLY, THOMAS, *Chaplain, USA;* ARTICLE: "FATHER THOMAS O'REILLY: A SAVIOR OF ATLANTA," CWM:JAN/92[40]405

O'RORKE, PADDY, *Colonel, 140th New York Infantry:*
ARTICLE: "THE IDEAL OF A SOLDIER AND A GENTLEMAN," CWM:MAR/91[35]337
BOOK REVIEW: *SONS OF OLD MONROE: A REGIMENTAL HISTORY OF PATRICK O'RORKE'S 140TH NEW YORK VOLUNTEER INFANTRY*
GENERAL LISTINGS: *Gettysburg,* GETTY:6[33]172, GETTY:6[43]173, GETTY:7[41]189, GETTY:8[31]201, GETTY:9[48]213, GETTY:10[112]228, *West Point,* B&G:DEC/91[12]469, *photos,* B&G:DEC/91[12]469, CWM:MAR/91[35]337, *photo of monument,* GETTY:6[43]173
ADDITIONAL LISTINGS: ACW:JAN/92[38]343, CWM:MAR/91[17]335, CWM:MAR/91[35]337

O'SULLIVAN, TIMOTHY, *photographer;* ACW:NOV/95[54]558, AHI:SEP/89[20]286, B&G:OCT/92[38]500, B&G:FEB/94[24]551, CWTI:MAY/91[34]209, *photo,* B&G:FEB/94[24]551

O'TOOLE, JERRY, *Sgt., 2nd Florida Cav.;* ACW:NOV/95[38]556

OAK GROVE, VIRGINIA, BATTLE OF:
ARTICLE: "THE PENINSULA CAMPAIGN OF 1862: THE BATTLE OF OAK GROVE," CWM:JUN/95[55]591
ADDITIONAL LISTING: CWTI:JUL/93[14]324

OAKLEY, GEORGE, *Private, 24th Michigan Infantry,* GETTY:9[33]211, GETTY:11[57]233

OATES, JAMES, *Lieutenant, 9th Illinois Mounted Infantry;* CWTI:SEP/91[23]228

OATES, JOHN A., *Lieutenant, 15th Alabama Infantry;* ACW:JAN/92[38]343, CWM:DEC/94[26]548

OATES, WILLIAM C., *Colonel, 15th Alabama Infantry:*
ARTICLE: "WILLIAM C. OATES: ON LITTLE ROUND TOP, UNSUNG; IN POSTWAR POLITICS, UNRECONSTRUCTED," CWM:DEC/94[26]548
BOOK REVIEW: *THE WAR BETWEEN THE UNION AND THE CONFEDERACY AND ITS LOST OPPORTUNITIES WITH A HISTORY OF THE 15TH ALABAMA REGIMENT AND THE FORTY-EIGHT BATTLES IN WHICH IT WAS ENGAGED*
GENERAL LISTINGS: *Gettysburg,* GETTY:7[41]189, GETTY:7[13]186, *Wilderness,* B&G:JUN/95[8]600
ADDITIONAL LISTINGS: ACW:JAN/92[38]343, ACW:SEP/93[62]436, CWM:JUL/92[8]427, CWM:DEC/94[4]545, CWTI:JUL/93[42]329, CWTI:SEP/93[53]340, CWTI:MAR/94[48]374, GETTY:13[7]253, MH:APR/92[18]157

OATIS, MARTIN A., *Major, CSA;* B&G:DEC/95[9]615

OBENCHAIN, FRANCIS G., *Sergeant, CSA;* ACW:JUL/94[51]480, B&G:FEB/94[8]550, B&G:FEB/94[57]555

OBERLIN, OHIO:
ARTICLE: "THE TOWN THAT STARTED THE CIVIL WAR," AHI:SEP/90[20]290
BOOK REVIEWS: *THE TOWN THAT STARTED THE CIVIL WAR*

OBLATE SISTERS OF PROVIDENCE; B&G:OCT/93[31]539

OCEAN POND, FLORIDA, BATTLE OF; see listings under "OLUSTEE, FLORIDA, BATTLE OF"

OCHILTREE, W.B., *Col., 18th Texas Inf.;* ACW:MAR/93[68]409

ODEN, H.P., *Capt., 30th Alabama Inf.;* CWR:VOL2#1[19]131

ODEN, JOHN, *Lt., 10th Alabama Inf.;* CWTI:FEB/90[74]149

ODLUM, F.A., *Captain, CSA;* CWM:OCT/95[47]620,
CWTI:DEC/90[29]182

OFFICERS, (IN GENERAL); ARTICLE: "HOW TO PICK OUT
BAD OFFICERS," CWTI:MAR/91[46]203

OGDEN, F.N., *Major, CSA;* AHI:DEC/77[46]177

OGLESBY, RICHARD, *Colonel, USA;* ACW:JUL/92[22]368,
CWTI:DEC/95[24]477

OGLETHORPE (GEORGIA) LIGHT ARTILLERY;
B&G:APR/91[32]447, GETTY:12[111]250

OGLETHORPE (GEORGIA) LIGHT INFANTRY,
B&G:FEB/91[8]339, CWTI:SEPT/89[24]128

OHAVER, JOHN, *7th Indiana Infantry;* B&G:FEB/92[40]479

OHIO TROOPS:

1st Artillery; B&G:AUG/93[10]529, B&G:OCT/95[8]611D,
GETTY:9[5]209, GETTY:9[41]212

1st Artillery, Battery B; B&G:FEB/93[12]511

1st Artillery, Battery C; B&G:FEB/93[12]511

1st Artillery, Battery D; GETTY:9[41]212

1st Artillery, Battery H; GETTY:12[30]243

1st Artillery, Battery I:
ARTICLE: "DIGLER'S BATTERY AT GETTYSBURG,"
GETTY:4[49]147

ADDITIONAL LISTINGS: CWNEWS:OCT/90[4], GETTY:4[33]146,
GETTY:10[7]221, *photo, modern,* GETTY:4[49]14

1st Artillery, Battery L:
GENERAL LISTINGS: *Gettysburg,* GETTY:8[31]201,
GETTY:11[91]236, *letters to the editor,* CWM:DEC/95[5]625

1st Artillery, (Heavy); GETTY:12[1]240

1st Artillery, Independent Battery:
ARTICLE: "FORGOTTEN VALOR: OFF THE BEATEN PATH AT
ANTIETAM: ARTILLERY HELL AND HOT COFFEE,"
B&G:OCT/95[8]611D

ADDITIONAL LISTING: B&G:OCT/95[8]611A

1st Cavalry; B&G:AUG/93[10]529

1st Infantry; ACW:MAR/91[38]296, B&G:JUN/95[36]603A,
B&G:OCT/95[36]614

2nd Artillery; B&G:FEB/94[8]550, B&G:AUG/95[8]604

2nd Cavalry; B&G:APR/92[8]481, CWM:MAY/92[34]422,
CWM:APR/94[24]505, CWR:VOL4#1[1]163,
CWTI:OCT/95[48]470

2nd Infantry; ACW:SEP/91[22]321, B&G:AUG/95[24]605,
CWTI:SEPT/89[30]129

3rd Infantry; ACW:NOV/92[8]383, B&G:AUG/93[10]529,
CWR:VOL4#3[1]170, MH:DEC/93[12]174

4th Artillery; B&G:AUG/95[8]604

4th Artillery, Independent Battery; B&G:AUG/95[8]604

4th Cavalry; CWM:JUL/92[40]432

4th Infantry;
GENERAL LISTINGS: *Gettysburg,* GETTY:4[115]152,
GETTY:10[53]225, *West Virginia campaign,*
B&G:AUG/93[10]529

ADDITIONAL LISTINGS: ACW:NOV/92[42]388, B&G:DEC/91[38]471,
B&G:APR/93[12]518, B&G:OCT/94[11]580, GETTY:13[7]253

5th Artillery; ACW:JAN/91[22]285, B&G:OCT/92[26]498,
B&G:AUG/95[8]604

5th Cavalry:
ARTICLE: "SCOUTING FOR ULYSSES S. GRANT: THE 5TH
OHIO CAVALRY IN THE SHILOH CAMPAIGN,"
CWR:VOL4#1[44]164

GENERAL LISTINGS: *Gettysburg,* GETTY:6[77]177, *Savannah,*
B&G:FEB/91[8]439, *photo of flag,* CWR:VOL4#1[44]164

5th Infantry:
GENERAL LISTINGS: *Gettysburg,* GETTY:7[83]192, *Gettysburg,*
GETTY:9[81]216, *list of monuments,* B&G:OCT/95[8]611A,
photo of monument, GETTY:7[83]192

ADDITIONAL LISTINGS: ACW:JUL/92[30]369, ACW:MAR/94[50]462,
CWTI:SEPT/89[30]129, CWTI:FEB/90[32]144,
CWTI:NOV/92[41]291

6th Cavalry; ACW:NOV/91[30]332, ACW:NOV/92[26]386,
B&G:APR/92[8]481, B&G:OCT/93[12]537,
CWTI:JUN/90[32]159, MH:OCT/92[51]162

6th Infantry:
ARTICLE: "SHILOH, WHERE DEATH KNOWS NO
DISTINCTION," CWM:APR/95[66]579

ADDITIONAL LISTING: CWM:MAY/91[10]347

7th Artillery; B&G:AUG/95[8]604

7th Cavalry; B&G:FEB/94[38]553, CWR:VOL4#1[1]163,
CWTI:JAN/93[49]303

7th Infantry;
ARTICLE: "VALOR OF OHIOANS AT THE BATTLE OF
KERNSTOWN," CWM:APR/95[29]574

ADDITIONAL LISTINGS: ACW:JUL/92[30]369, ACW:MAR/94[50]462,
ACW:MAY/95[30]525, B&G:OCT/95[8]611A,
CWTI:SEPT/89[30]129, CWTI:DEC/89[26]135,
CWTI:SEP/92[22]279, CWTI:AUG/95[24]455, GETTY:9[81]216

8th Artillery; B&G:OCT/94[28]581, B&G:AUG/95[8]604

8th Infantry:
GENERAL LISTINGS: *Gettysburg,* GETTY:6[7]169, GETTY:8[95]205,
GETTY:9[61]215, GETTY:10[53]225, *in list,*
CWTI:JUL/93[34]327, *list of monuments,*
B&G:OCT/95[8]611A, *Wilderness,* B&G:JUN/95[8]600

ADDITIONAL LISTINGS: ACW:NOV/92[42]388, ACW:SEP/94[38]487,
B&G:JUN/95[8]600, CWM:MAR/91[17]335,
CWR:VOL1#3[52]122, CWR:VOL2#4[269]145,
CWR:VOL4#4[47]179, CWTI:NOV/92[49]292,
GETTY:13[75]259

9th Artillery; B&G:FEB/93[12]511

9th Cavalry; B&G:DEC/92[40]508, CWM:JAN/91[40]330

9th Infantry:
GENERAL LISTINGS: *in order of battle,* B&G:FEB/93[12]511, *letters
to the editor,* B&G:APR/94[6]557, B&G:AUG/95[36]607, *West
Virginia campaign,* B&G:AUG/93[10]529

ADDITIONAL LISTING: ACW:SEP/93[38]434, B&G:FEB/93[12]511

10th Infantry; CWM:MAR/91[50]340, CWM:SEP/93[18]494,
CWTI:MAY/93[38]321

11th Artillery; CWTI:JUL/94[50]395

11th Infantry; B&G:OCT/95[8]611A, B&G:OCT/95[8]611D,
CWTI:JUL/94[50]395

12th Cavalry; B&G:AUG/91[11]458, B&G:AUG/91[52]464

12th Infantry; ACW:MAR/94[27]459, B&G:OCT/95[8]611A,
B&G:OCT/95[8]611D, CWTI:MAR/89[16]101

13th Artillery; ACW:JAN/91[22]285, CWR:VOL4#1[44]164

13th Cavalry; B&G:APR/92[8]481

14th Artillery; ACW:NOV/95[48]557

14th Infantry:
ARTICLE: "THERE WILL BE HOME MADE THUNDER HERE,"
CWTI:SUMMER/89[20]121

ADDITIONAL LISTINGS: ACW:JAN/92[47]344, B&G:FEB/93[12]511,
B&G:AUG/93[10]529, B&G:AUG/93[24]

15th Artillery; B&G:AUG/95[8]604

15th Infantry; B&G:OCT/94[11]580, B&G:AUG/93[10]529

16th Artillery; B&G:FEB/94[8]550, B&G:AUG/95[8]604, CWTI:MAY/91[24]208

16th Artillery, Independent Battery; B&G:AUG/95[8]604

16th Infantry;
GENERAL LISTINGS: *in book review,* B&G:APR/91[28], *in book review,* CWNEWS:AUG/91[4], *order of battle,* B&G:FEB/94[8]550
ADDITIONAL LISTINGS: ACW:JAN/92[47]344, B&G:AUG/93[10]529

17th Artillery; ACW:SEP/92[16]376, B&G:FEB/94[8]550, B&G:AUG/95[8]604

17th Artillery, Independent Battery; B&G:AUG/95[8]604

17th Infantry; B&G:FEB/93[12]511

18th Infantry; ACW:JAN/92[47]344, B&G:AUG/93[10]529, CWTI:AUG/90[50]168, MH:DEC/93[12]174

19th Infantry; B&G:AUG/93[10]529

20th Artillery; CWM:SEP/93[18]494

20th Infantry; AHI:DEC/77[13]176, CWNEWS:SEP/91[4], CWTI:SEPT/89[18]126

21st Infantry; ACW:SEP/91[22]321, B&G:AUG/91[40]463, B&G:APR/93[40]522, CWTI:SEP/92[31]281, *photo,* CWTI:SEP/92[31]281

22nd Infantry; B&G:DEC/91[12]469

23rd Cavalry; CWM:SEP/93[18]494

23rd Infantry:
ARTICLE: "FOCUS: CIVIL WAR PHOTOGRAPHY," AHI:AUG/79[32]191
BOOK REVIEW: *HAYES OF THE TWENTY-THIRD: THE CIVIL WAR VOLUNTEER OFFICER*
ADDITIONAL LISTINGS: ACW:JUL/93[6]419, ACW:JUL/93[58], ACW:JUL/94[26]477, B&G:OCT/91[40]467, B&G:OCT/95[8]611A, B&G:OCT/95[8]611D, CWTI:MAY/92[38]265, CWTI:JUL/94[50]395, CWTI:SEP/94[49]404, CWTI:OCT/95[48]470, *photo,* ACW:MAR/94[27]459

24th Infantry; B&G:AUG/93[10]529, CWM:APR/95[66]579, CWTI:SEPT/89[30]129

25th Infantry; ACW:NOV/92[42]388, B&G:DEC/92[40]508, B&G:AUG/93[10]529, CWM:MAY/91[26]349, CWTI:MAR/94[29]371, GETTY:6[7]169, GETTY:12[30]243, GETTY:13[7]253

27th Infantry; ACW:SEP/91[46]324, B&G:APR/95[24]596, CWTI:SUMMER/89[40]123

28th Infantry; B&G:OCT/94[28]581, B&G:OCT/95[8]611A, B&G:OCT/95[8]611D, CWTI:MAR/89[16]101

29th Infantry:
GENERAL LISTINGS: *Gettysburg,* GETTY:7[83]192, GETTY:9[81]216, *letters to the editor,* B&G:DEC/95[5]614A
ADDITIONAL LISTINGS: CWTI:SUMMER/89[32]122, GETTY:13[7]253

30th Infantry:
GENERAL LISTINGS: *list of monuments,* B&G:OCT/95[8]611A, *Savannah,* B&G:FEB/91[8]439, *SIO,* CWTI:JUN/95[14]443
ADDITIONAL LISTINGS: B&G:APR/94[28]559, B&G:OCT/95[8]611D, CWM:MAY/92[44]423, CWTI:DEC/94[62]415

31st Infantry; B&G:FEB/93[12]511, B&G:FEB/94[38]553, CWTI:SEPT/89[30]129, CWTI:SEP/93[90]343

32nd Infantry; ACW:JAN/93[35]396, B&G:FEB/94[8]550, B&G:APR/95[24]596, CWR:VOL1#4[7]125, CWTI:MAR/94[29]371

33rd Infantry; ACW:SEP/91[22]321, CWTI:SEPT/89[30]129

34th Infantry; CWTI:MAR/89[16]101

35th Infantry; B&G:APR/94[6]557

36th Infantry; ACW:MAR/94[27]459, B&G:OCT/95[8]611A, B&G:OCT/95[8]611D, CWM:AUG/95[35]607, CWTI:SEP/94[49]404

37th Infantry; CWM:DEC/95[35]629

38th Infantry; B&G:FEB/93[12]511

39th Infantry; ACW:SEP/91[46]324, CWTI:SUMMER/89[40]123

40th Infantry; CWTI:SEPT/89[30]129, CWTI:SEP/92[31]281

41st Infantry; B&G:DEC/93[12]545, CWR:VOL3#2[105]

42nd Infantry; ACW:SEP/92[16]376, AHI:MAY/76[24]167

43rd Infantry; B&G:FEB/94[8]550

44th Infantry; B&G:AUG/95[24]605

44th Infantry, (Mounted); CWR:VOL4#1[1]163

45th Infantry; CWTI:MAY/94[50]386

45th Infantry, (Mounted); CWR:VOL4#1[1]163

46th Infantry; B&G:AUG/92[40]495, B&G:DEC/93[30]546

47th Infantry; ACW:SEP/95[38]546, B&G:FEB/91[8]439, CWTI:DEC/94[62]415

48th Infantry; B&G:FEB/94[8]550, CWM:APR/95[66]579, CWR:VOL2#1[19]131, CWR:VOL4#2[1]165

51st Infantry; B&G:JUN/95[36]603A, CWTI:SEPT/89[30]129, CWTI:NOV/92[41]291

52nd Infantry:
BOOK REVIEW: *THE FIFTY-SECOND OHIO VOLUNTEER INFANTRY: THEN AND NOW, VOLUME I*
ADDITIONAL LISTINGS: ACW:NOV/92[8]383, B&G:DEC/95[9]615, CWM:APR/94[8]502, CWTI:NOV/92[41]291, CWTI:MAY/94[40]383

53rd Infantry; ACW:JAN/91[22]285, AHI:OCT/67[26]112, B&G:APR/94[28]559, MH:OCT/94[20]180

54th Infantry; B&G:FEB/91[8]439, B&G:AUG/92[40]495, CWR:VOL2#1[1]130, CWR:VOL4#1[44]164, CWTI:DEC/94[62]415

55th Infantry:
GENERAL LISTINGS: *Gettysburg,* GETTY:4[24]145, GETTY:4[115]152, GETTY:5[117]165, *in book review,* CWNEWS:OCT/92[4], *Manassas, Second,* B&G:AUG/92[11]493
ADDITIONAL LISTING: GETTY:13[7]253

56th Infantry; ACW:JUL/94[51]480, B&G:FEB/94[8]550, CWR:VOL4#2[1]165

57th Infantry; CWR:VOL2#1[1]130, CWR:VOL4#1[44]164, CWTI:SUMMER/89[50]124, CWTI:SEP/92[28]280

58th Infantry; CWTI:MAY/92[38]265

59th Infantry; CWR:VOL4#1[1]163

60th Infantry; CWR:VOL1#4[7]125

61st Infantry:
GENERAL LISTINGS: *Gettysburg,* GETTY:4[49]147, GETTY:7[83]192
ADDITIONAL LISTINGS: ACW:NOV/92[42]388, B&G:FEB/95[8]590A, CWM:MAR/91[50]340

62nd Infantry; ACW:SEP/91[30]322, ACW:JUL/94[42]479

63rd Infantry; ACW:SEP/91[46]324, CWTI:JAN/93[82]304, CWTI:DEC/94[62]415

64th Infantry; B&G:JUN/94[38]571, CWNEWS:OCT/92[4]

66th Infantry:
GENERAL LISTINGS: *Gettysburg,* GETTY:9[81]216, GETTY:12[42]244, *list of monuments,* B&G:OCT/95[8]611A
ADDITIONAL LISTINGS: ACW:JUL/92[30]369, ACW:MAR/94[50]462, CWTI:SEPT/89[30]129, CWTI:MAY/92[38]265

66th Infantry; ACW:SEP/91[30]322, ACW:JUL/94[42]479, CWTI:MAY/92[38]265

68th Infantry; B&G:FEB/94[8]550

70th Infantry; B&G:FEB/91[8]439, CWR:VOL4#1[44]164, CWTI:SUMMER/89[50]124, CWTI:DEC/94[62]415

71st Infantry; ARTICLE: "FIELDS WITHOUT HONOR: TWO AFFAIRS IN TENNESSEE," CWTI:JUL/92[42]274

72nd Infantry; CWR:VOL2#4[313]146, CWR:VOL4#1[44]164

73rd Infantry:
GENERAL LISTINGS: *Manassas, Second,* B&G:AUG/92[11]493, *SIO,* B&G:DEC/93[30]546, B&G:OCT/94[42]583
ADDITIONAL LISTINGS: B&G:AUG/92[53]495A

75th Infantry: ACW:NOV/92[42]388, ACW:JAN/93[35]396, ACW:NOV/95[38]556, B&G:APR/91[28], CWTI:MAR/94[29]371, GETTY:6[7]169, GETTY:12[30]243

76th Infantry:
BOOK REVIEW: *A BOY'S SERVICE WITH THE 76TH OHIO*
ADDITIONAL LISTINGS: ACW:NOV/93[34]442, AHI:JAN/67[4]106, CWTI:MAY/91[16]206, CWTI:SEP/94[40]403

77th Infantry; CWR:VOL1#2[44]114, CWR:VOL4#1[44]164

78th Infantry; B&G:FEB/94[8]550, B&G:AUG/95[8]604

81st Infantry; B&G:APR/94[28]559, CWM:APR/95[66]579, CWTI:NOV/92[41]291

82nd Infantry; ACW:JAN/93[35]396, B&G:AUG/92[11]493, B&G:FEB/95[8]590C, CWTI:MAY/94[12]379, CWTI:MAR/94[29]371

83rd Infantry; B&G:AUG/92[40]495, B&G:FEB/94[8]550, CWR:VOL4#2[1]165

87th Infantry; CWR:VOL1#4[7]125

88th Infantry; B&G:OCT/94[11]580, CWTI:SEPT/89[30]129

89th Infantry; CWTI:SEP/92[31]281, CWTI:SEP/93[90]343

91st Infantry; ACW:MAR/94[27]459, ACW:JUL/94[26]477, CWTI:MAR/89[16]101

92nd Infantry; B&G:OCT/94[42]583, B&G:JUN/95[36]603A, CWTI:JUN/95[14]443

94th Infantry; B&G:APR/94[34]561

96th Infantry:
ARTICLE: "THE FARM BOYS IN THE 96TH OHIO REGIMENT FOUND THEMSELVES KNEE-DEEP IN ALLIGATORS IN LOUISIANA," ACW:SEP/92[16]376
ADDITIONAL LISTINGS: CWR:VOL4#2[1]165, CWR:VOL4#2[68]167

98th Infantry; B&G:OCT/94[42]583, B&G:DEC/95[9]615, CWTI:SEP/92[31]281

99th Infantry; B&G:AUG/93[36]533

100th Infantry; B&G:AUG/95[24]605

101st Infantry; AHI:DEC/85[40]255

102nd Infantry:
ARTICLE: "A MEMORIAL DIRGE FOR LINCOLN," B&G:JUN/95[35]602
ADDITIONAL LISTING: B&G:AUG/95[24]605

104th Infantry; B&G:DEC/94[10]585, CWTI:MAY/92[38]265

107th Infantry; GETTY:12[30]243

108th Infantry; B&G:DEC/95[9]615

110th Infantry; ACW:NOV/93[50]444, CWM:NOV/92[64]453, CWTI:JAN/93[40]301

111th Infantry; CWTI:DEC/94[62]415

114th Infantry; B&G:FEB/94[8]550, B&G:OCT/95[36]614, CWTI:AUG/90[64]170

115th Infantry; B&G:AUG/95[24]605

116th Infantry; CWM:OCT/94[23]535

120th Infantry; ACW:JUL/94[51]480, B&G:FEB/94[8]550, CWNEWS:NOV/92[4], CWR:VOL4#2[26]166, CWR:VOL4#2[118]169, CWTI:MAY/92[38]265

121st Infantry; B&G:DEC/95[9]615, CWTI:SEP/92[31]281

122nd Infantry; ACW:NOV/93[50]444, ACW:MAR/94[10]457, B&G:JUN/95[8]600, CWTI:SEPT/89[40]130, CWTI:JAN/93[40]301

125th Infantry:

BOOK REVIEWS: *YANKEE TIGERS: THROUGH THE CIVIL WAR WITH THE 125TH OHIO*
GENERAL LISTINGS: B&G:AUG/93[24], CWNEWS:JAN/94[5], CWTI:NOV/92[10]
ADDITIONAL LISTING: B&G:OCT/91[11]466

126th Infantry; ACW:NOV/93[50]444, B&G:JUN/95[8]600, CWTI:JAN/93[40]301, CWTI:AUG/95[90]462

128th Infantry; ACW:JAN/93[66]399

144th Infantry; ACW:NOV/93[50]444, B&G:DEC/92[8]503

148th Infantry; CWTI:DEC/95[52]480

149th Infantry; ACW:NOV/93[50]444, B&G:DEC/92[8]503

152nd National Guard; B&G:AUG/94[10]574

155th National Guard; B&G:OCT/95[36]614

156th National Guard; B&G:AUG/94[10]574

159th Infantry, (Mounted); B&G:DEC/92[8]503

163rd Infantry; B&G:DEC/92[40]508

165th National Guard; B&G:AUG/94[10]574

170th Infantry; B&G:AUG/92[40]495

173rd Infantry; B&G:FEB/94[38]553

192nd Infantry; B&G:FEB/92[32]477

OHLMAN, MICHAEL; ACW:MAR/93[8]401

OKEY, CORNELIUS, *Private, 6th Wisconsin Infantry;* GETTY:4[16]143

OKOLONA, MISSISSIPPI, BATTLE OF; CWM:JUL/92[48]433, CWR:VOL2#4[313]146

OLDEN, CHARLES, *Governor of New Jersey;* CWTI:MAY/89[36]118

OLDHAM, WILLIAMSON S., *Captain, Terry's Texas Rangers;* CWM:MAR/92[9]410

OLDROYD, OSBORN, *Sergeant, 20th Ohio Infantry;* AHI:DEC/77[13]176, CWTI:SEPT/89[18]126

OLDS, FRED A., *correspondent;* GETTY:5[19]158

OLIPHANT, DAVID, *Capt., 5th Mich. Cav.;* GETTY:4[101]151

OLIVER, JOHN M., *Colonel, USA;* ACW:SEP/91[46]324, B&G:DEC/95[9]615, CWTI:DEC/94[62]415

OLIVER, LEON, *Corporal, 5th New York Infantry;* CWR:VOL1#2[7]111, CWTI:MAY/94[31]382

OLMSTEAD, CHARLES H., *Colonel, CSA;* B&G:FEB/91[8]439, B&G:OCT/91[11]466

OLMSTEAD, FREDERICK LAW, *U.S. Sanitary Commission:*
BOOK REVIEW: *FLO: A BIOGRAPHY OF FREDERICK LAW OLMSTEAD*
GENERAL LISTINGS: *Gettysburg,* GETTY:9[116]219, *in book review,* B&G:AUG/94[30], *slavery,* AHI:APR/70[11]124, *photo,* GETTY:9[116]219
ADDITIONAL LISTINGS: CWM:MAY/91[18]348, CWM:JUN/94[28]514

OLNEY, AMOS M.C., *Sergeant, 1st Rhode Island Artillery;* GETTY:12[61]245

OLSON, G., *Sergeant, 1st Illinois Artillery;* B&G:APR/94[28]559

OLUSTEE, FLORIDA, BATTLE OF:
ARTICLE: "FROM OLUSTEE TO APPOMATTOX: THE 1ST FLORIDA SPECIAL BATTALION," CWR:VOL3#1[65]151
BOOK REVIEWS: *THE BATTLE OF OLUSTEE: THE CIVIL WAR IN FLORIDA * CONFEDERATE FLORIDA: THE ROAD TO OLUSTEE*
ADDITIONAL LISTINGS: ACW:NOV/91[64]336, ACW:NOV/93[10]439, ACW:NOV/95[38]556, AHI:MAY/71[3]133A, B&G:APR/95[5]594, CWM:JAN/92[16]401, CWM:NOV/92[24]448, CWR:VOL2#4[346], CWR:VOL3#4[1]161, CWR:VOL4#3[1]170

OMENHAUSSER, JOHN J., *Private, 46th Virginia Infantry;* BOOK REVIEW: *SKETCHES FROM PRISON: A CONFEDERATE ARTIST'S RECORD OF LIFE AT POINT LOOKOUT PRISONER OF WAR CAMP, 1863-1865*
ONONDAGA COUNTY ANTI-SLAVERY SOCIETY; ACW:NOV/94[42]497
ONSTOTT, WILLIAM H., *Private, 27th Illinois Infantry;* CWR:VOL3#4[24]162
OPDYCKE, EMERSON, *Colonel, USA;* ACW:MAR/92[14]350, B&G:OCT/91[11]466, B&G:AUG/93[24], B&G:DEC/93[12]545, CWR:VOL4#3[1]170, CWTI:NOV/92[10]
OPDYKE, GEORGE, *Mayor, New York City;* AHI:AUG/77[30]175
OPIE, J.N., *Private, 6th Virginia Cavalry;* GETTY:11[19]232
ORANGE (VIRGINIA) ARTILLERY; *Gettysburg,* GETTY:4[33]146, *Gettysburg,* GETTY:4[49]147
ORBANSKY, DAVID, *Private, USA;* CWM:SEP/93[8]493
ORD, EDWIN O.C., *General, USA:*
BOOK REVIEW: *APPOMATTOX COMMANDER: THE STORY OF GENERAL E.O.C. ORD*
GENERAL LISTINGS: *Five Forks,* B&G:APR/92[8]481, *Henry Halleck,* AHI:MAY/78[10]179, *Indian wars,* AHI:OCT/79[20]194, *ISO,* B&G:FEB/91[34]442, *Jackson, Battle of,* B&G:AUG/95[8]604, *Lincoln,* CWTI:FEB/91[28]192, *Mary Todd Lincoln,* AHI:MAY/75[4]159, *order of battle,* B&G:AUG/95[8]604, *Petersburg,* MH:APR/95[46]183, *Sayler's Creek,* ACW:JAN/92[22]341, *photos,* AHI:MAY/75[4]159, AHI:MAY/78[10]179, B&G:AUG/95[8]604
ADDITIONAL LISTINGS: ACW:JAN/93[43]397, ACW:NOV/93[50]444, ACW:JAN/94[47]452, AHI:SEP/87[48]264, CWM:MAR/93[8]465, CWM:AUG/94[30]527, CWR:VOL2#2[118]136, CWR:VOL2#3[236]143, CWR:VOL3#2[1]153, CWTI:NOV/93[50]349, CWTI:JUL/94[50]395, CWTI:DEC/95[24]477, GETTY:13[119]262
ORD, WILLIAM, *Captain, 19th Indiana Infantry;* AHI:JAN/94[50]319,

ORDNANCE:

Specific articles from the Department in ACW: also, see section under **"WEAPONS"** for additional specific weapons.
50th New York Engineers; ARTICLE: "THE 50TH NEW YORK ENGINEERS WERE INVALUABLE," BRIDGE BUILDERS DURING THE VARIOUS CAMPAIGNS AGAINST LEE," ACW:NOV/95[10]553
Body armor; ARTICLE: "KNIGHTLY ARMOR, THOUGH APPEALING TO ROMANTICS, FOUND," LITTLE FAVOR WITH CIVIL WAR VETERANS," ACW:SEP/92[8]374
British rifles; ARTICLE: "THE READY AVAILABILITY OF BRITISH RIFLES ENABLED," BOTH NORTH AND SOUTH TO ARM THEMSELVES QUICKLY," ACW:JAN/93[8]392
Confederate Naval Academy; ARTICLE: "THE MIDSHIPMENT OF THE CONFEDERATE NAVAL," ACADEMY PUT THEIR OFFICERS' TRAINING TO A LAND-BASED USE," ACW:JUL/92[10]366
Drummer Boys; ARTICLE: "ARMED ONLY WITH THEIR DURMS, UNION AND CONFEDERATE DRUMMER," BOYS SERVED THEIR CAUSES WITH DISTINCTION," ACW:NOV/92[8]383
Explosion at Mobile; CWTI:AUG/90[64]170
Field Artillery; ARTICLE: "CIVIL WAR FIELD ARTILLERY BRIDGED THE GAP BETWEEN NAPOLEON AND WORLD WAR I," ACW:NOV/94[12]494

Handguns; ARTICLE: "NORTHERN MANUFACTURERS, SURPRISED BY THE WAR, SCRAMBLED TO," PRODUCE RELIABLE HANDGUNS FOR UNION FORCES," ACW:MAR/92[8]348
Hospital ships; ARTICLE: "*D.A. JANUARY* AND HER SISTER HOSPITAL," STEAMERS SAVED COUNTLESS LIVES DURING THE CIVIL WAR," ACW:MAR/93[8]401
Mortars; ARTICLE: "WHEN BIG GUNS COULD NOT PENETRATE FORTIFIED SOUTHERN," WALLS, FEDERAL MORTARS LOBBED SHELLS OVER THEM," ACW:SEP/93[16]431
Mountain Howitzer; ARTICLE: "CONFEDERATE GUNNERS AFFECTIONATELY CALLED THEIR," HARD-WORKING LITTLE MOUNTAIN HOWITZERS 'BULL PUPS'," ACW:SEP/95[10]543
Mules; ARTICLE: "THE HARDY MULE GAVE ITS FLOP-EARED ALL_-SOMETIMES LITERALLY—FOR THE UNION AND CONFEDERACY," ACW:JAN/92[10]339
Music; ARTICLE: "'THE BATTLE HYMN OF THE REPUBLIC' ARMED THE NORTH WITH MORAL CERTITUDE," ACW:MAR/94[10]457
Pontoon Bridges; ARTICLE: "THE DELICATE AND DANGEROUS WORK OF PLACING," PONTOON BRIDGES FELL TO THE CORPS OF ENGINEERS," ACW:MAY/93[8]411
Rains, George W.; ARTICLE: "COLONEL GEORGE WASHINGTON RAINS WORKED WONDERS WITH THE CONFEDERACY'S NASCENT NITRE BUREAU," ACW:MAY/94[20]467
Rapid-fire weapons; ARTICLE: "MALFUNCTIONS AND A SHORTSIGHTED ORDNANCE DEPARTMENT," DELAYED THE DEVELOPMENT OF RAPID-FIRE WEAPONS," ACW:JUL/93[8]420
Star of the West; ARTICLE: "ELEGANT, LUXURIOUS *STAR OF THE WEST* MET A DECIDEDLY UNROMANTIC FATE IN THE MISSISSIPPI DELTA," ACW:NOV/93[8]438
Starr revolvers and carbines; ARTICLE: "CONNECTICUT YANKEE EBEN T. STARR'S PISTOLS AND CARBINES HELPED BOLSTER THE UNION'S WAR EFFORT," ACW:SEP/94[24]485
Queen of the West; ARTICLE: "THE SIDE-WHEEL STEAMER *QUEEN OF THE WEST* WAS ALSO VARIOUSLY THE QUEEN OF BOTH THE NORTH AND THE SOUTH," ACW:MAR/95[18]514
United States Military Railroad; ARTICLE: "WHEN SECRETARY OF WAR EDWIN STANTON NEEDED A GOOD MAN TO," RUN HIS VITAL RAILROADS, HE SENT FOR HERMAN HAUPT," ACW:JUL/95[16]534
Weapons, procurement of; ARTICLE: "THE ARMS-STARVED CONFEDERACY EXPLORED ALL AVENUES," TO ACQUIRE THE WEAPONS ITS SOLDIERS DESPERATELY NEEDED," ACW:JAN/94[18]449
Woodruff Gun; ARTICLE: "THE UNDISTINGUISHED WOODRUFF GUN HAD ONLY ONE," TRUE SUPPORTER, ABRAHAM LINCOLN—BUT ONE WAS ENOUGH," ACW:JUL/94[8]474
OREGON, STATE OF:
ARTICLE: "FORTS STEVENS AND CANBY STOOD A LONG VIGIL PROTECTING THE PACIFIC COAST FROM ATTACK," ACW:MAR/92[62]355
ADDITIONAL LISTING: CWM:JUL/91[35]369
ORLEANS INDEPENDENT ARTILLERY; ACW:SEP/95[8]542
ORME, WILLIAM W., *General, USA;* B&G:OCT/94[11]580, CWR:VOL1#1[42]105

ORPHAN BRIGADE:
ARTICLE: "ORPHAN BRIGADE," ACW:JUL/91[12]310
BOOK REVIEWS: *DIARY OF A CONFEDERATE SOLDIER: JOHN S. JACKMAN OF THE ORPHAN BRIGADE * THE ORPHAN BRIGADE*
ADDITIONAL LISTINGS: ACW:MAR/91[54], ACW:JUL/94[10]448, CWM:FEB/95[28]560, CWTI:SUMMER/89[50]124
ORR, HENRY, *Private, CSA;* CWR:VOL2#3[212]142
ORR, JAMES, *Private, CSA;* MH:JUN/91[20]152
ORR, JEHU A., *Colonel, CSA;* B&G:AUG/95[8]604
ORTEJAS, PREDENCIO, *Captain, CSA;* CWR:VOL3#1[65]151
ORTH, JOHN, *Private, 24th Michigan Infantry;* GETTY:9[33]211, GETTY:11[57]233
ORWIN, ROBERT D.; ACW:JAN/91[8]282
OSBORN, T.W., *Major, USA;* GETTY:8[95]205
OSBORN, THOMAS W. *Lieutenant Colonel, USA:*
BOOK REVIEWS: *THE ELEVENTH CORPS ARTILLERY AT GETTYSBURG: THE PAPERS OF MAJOR THOMAS WARD OSBORNE * NO MIDDLE GROUND:THOMAS WARD OSBORN'S LETTERS FROM THE FIELD (1862-1864)*
ADDITIONAL LISTINGS: GETTY:4[33]146, GETTY:4[49]147 GETTY:9[61]215, GETTY:11[71]234
OSBOURN, ROBERT, *seaman, CSN;* ACW:NOV/92[51]389
OSTERHAUS, PETER J., *General, USA:*
GENERAL LISTINGS: *Common Soldiers,* AHI:APR/68[4]115, *in book review,* CWM:MAR/91[74], *Jackson, Battle of,* B&G:AUG/95[8]604, *order of battle,* B&G:FEB/94[8]550, B&G:AUG/95[8]604, *Savannah,* B&G:FEB/91[8]439, *photos,* AHI:APR/68[4]115, CWTI:SEPT/89[30]129
ADDITIONAL LISTINGS: ACW:NOV/91[22]331, ACW:SEP/92[47]380, ACW:NOV/93[26]441, ACW:NOV/93[34]442, ACW:JUL/94[51]480, B&G:FEB/94[8]550, CWM:JUL/92[18]429, CWM:SEP/92[38]443, CWR:VOL1#1[42]105, CWR:VOL2#1[19]131, CWR:VOL3#3[59]159, CWTI:SEPT/89[30]129, CWTI:MAY/91[24]208, CWTI:FEB/92[29]248, CWTI:SEP/94[40]403, CWTI:MAR/95[40]436, CWTI:OCT/95[48]470
OSTRANDER, DANIEL, *Corporal, 150th New York Infantry;* GETTY:12[42]244
OTEY, LUCY W., *civilian;* CWM:MAY/91[40]351
OTIS, ELMER, *Captain, 4th U.S. Cavalry;* ACW:NOV/91[10]329, CWR:VOL4#1[1]163
OTTO, JOHN H., *Lieutenant, USA;* B&G:FEB/91[8]439
OUELLET, THOMAS, *Chp., 69th NY Inf.;* CWM:MAR/91[50]340
OULD, ROBERT, *Commissioner of Prisoner Exchange;* B&G:DEC/92[32]506, GETTY:7[77]191, GETTY:10[102]226
"OUR AMERICAN COUSIN":
ARTICLE: "'OUR AMERICAN COUSIN': A SYNOPSIS," AHI:FEB/86[24]259
ADDITIONAL LISTING: AHI:JUN/86[4]
OURY, GRANVILLE, *civilian;* ACW:JAN/91[10]283, ACW:JUL/93[27]423
OUTLAW, EDWARD R., *Lieutenant, 11th North Carolina Infantry;* GETTY:13[75]259
OVERLAND CAMPAIGN, VIRGINIA, 1864:
ARTICLES: "ALL GOES ON LIKE A MIRACLE," CWTI:APR/92[49]260, "GRANT AND LEE, 1864: FROM THE NORTH ANNA TO THE CROSSING OF THE JAMES," B&G:APR/94[10]558, "IF THIS CONTINUES THE ARMY OF THE POTOMAC WILL BE ANNIHILLATED," CWM:OCT/95[40]619, "NO TURNING BACK: THE BATTLE OF THE WILDERNESS, PART I," B&G:APR/95[8]595, "NO

TURNING BACK: THE BATTLE OF THE WILDERNESS, PART II—THE FIGHTING ON MAY 6, 1864," B&G:JUN/95[8]600, "NORTH ANNA TO THE CROSSING OF THE JAMES," THE TOUR B&G:APR/94[59]565, "WHEN ULYSSES S. GRANT CROSSED THE RAPIDAN, HE COMMENCED THE FINAL CAMPAIGN OF THE CIVIL WAR," ACW:SEP/95[74]550
BOOK REVIEWS: *THE BATTLE OF THE WILDERNESS MAY 5-6, 1864 * BLOODY ROADS SOUTH: THE WILDERNESS TO COLD HARBOR, MAY-JUNE, 1864 * MARCHING TO COLD HARBOR: VICTORY AND FAILURE, 1864 *NO TURNING BACK: THE BEGINNING OF THE END OF THE CIVIL WAR, MARCH-JUNE, 1864 * ON FIELDS OF FURY: FROM THE WILDERNESS TO THE CRATER, AN EYEWITNESS HISTORY * THE VIRGINIA CAMPAIGN OF 1864 AND 1865 * WITH GRANT & MEADE: FROM THE WILDERNESS TO APPOMATTOX*
GENERAL LISTINGS: *in book review,* CWM:OCT/95[10], CWM:DEC/95[10], CWNEWS:MAY/89[4], CWNEWS:NOV/90[4], CWR:VOL1#2[78], CWR:VOL1#3[94], CWR:VOL2#1[78], CWR:VOL2#4[346], CWR:VOL4#4[129]
ADDITIONAL LISTINGS: ACW:MAY/93[31]415, ACW:SEP/94[38]487, ACW:JAN/95[10]503, ACW:JAN/95[46]507, ACW:SEP/95[70]549, ACW:NOV/95[10]553, CWM:MAR/93[24]467, CWM:SEP/93[24]495, CWM:OCT/94[17]534, CWM:OCT/94[26]536, CWM:OCT/95[4]612, CWR:VOL1#1[1]102, CWR:VOL3#2[1]153, CWR:VOL3#4[1]161, CWTI:SEP/91[31]229, CWTI:SEP/91[61]233, CWTI:NOV/93[78]354
OVERMAN, G.A., *Pvt., 13th Mississippi Inf.;* GETTY:10[53]225
OWEN, — *Captain, 5th Ohio Cavalry;* GETTY:6[77]177
OWEN, HENRY T., *Capt., 18th Virginia Inf.;* GETTY:5[107]164
OWEN, JOSHUA T., *General, USA;* ACW:SEP/94[38]487, B&G:APR/94[10]558, B&G:APR/95[8]595, B&G:JUN/95[8]600, GETTY:7[97]193
OWEN, RICHARD, *Colonel, USA;* B&G:AUG/95[8]604
OWEN, THOMAS H., *Colonel, 3rd Virginia Cavalry;* ACW:NOV/91[30]332, ACW:JUL/92[41]370, B&G:OCT/93[12]537
OWEN, U.G., *Surgeon;* CWTI:MAY/94[40]383
OWEN, W.G., *Captain, CSA;* B&G:OCT/94[11]580
OWEN, WILLIAM, *Lieutenant Colonel, CSA;* ACW:JAN/91[38]287, ACW:SEP/95[38]546, CWTI:SEP/92[31]281
OWEN, WILLIAM M., *Captain, Washington Artillery;* ACW:JUL/92[12]367, GETTY:13[75]259, MH:JUN/92[6]158
OWENS, RICHARD, *Colonel, USA;* B&G:AUG/95[8]604
OWENS, TOM, *Lieutenant Colonel, CSA;* MH:OCT/92[51]162
OX FORD, VIRGINIA, BATTLEFIELD PARK; B&G:APR/94[59]565
OX FORD, VIRGINIA, BATTLE OF; ACW:SEP/95[70]549, B&G:APR/93[12]518
OXFORD, MISSISSIPPI, BATTLE OF; ACW:JUL/95[70]540
OXFORD, MISSISSIPPI; ARTICLE: "OXFORD, MISSISSIPPI, THE HOME OF WILLIAM FAULKNER PROVIDES A COURSE IN THE SWEEP OF SOUTHERN HISTORY," ACW:JUL/95[70]540

P-Q

PACE, THOMAS N., *Lt. Col., 1st IN Cav.;* ACW:MAY/93[22]414
PACIFIC RAILROAD ACT; CWM:FEB/95[7]
PACKARD, ELBRIDGE E., *Private, 2nd Wisconsin Infantry,* GETTY:11[57]233
PACKARD, JOHN H., *Surgeon, USA;* BOOK REVIEW: *A MANUAL OF MINOR SURGERY,* CWNEWS:SEP/91[4]
PACKER, ASA; ACW:SEP/93[22]432
PADUCAH, KENTUCKY; CWTI:FEB/90[26]143
PAGE, CHARLES, *reporter;* B&G:APR/95[8]595
PAGE, CHARLES D., *Pvt., 14th Conn. Inf.;* GETTY:5[89]162
PAGE, G.S., *Sergeant, 2nd Iowa Infantry;* B&G:FEB/92[48]475
PAGE, R.C.M., *Major, Morris Artillery;* B&G:APR/95[8]595, GETTY:4[33]146, GETTY:4[49]147, GETTY:10[7]221
PAGE, RICHARD L., *General, CSA;* B&G:JUN/94[34], CWM:AUG/94[25]524, CWTI:MAR/94[20]369, *photo,* CWM:AUG/94[25]524
PAGE, THOMAS, *Captain, CSN;* ARTICLE: "THE DILEMMA OF COMMODORE CRAVEN," CWTI:DEC/94[34]411
PAGE, THOMAS J., *Major, CSA;* CWR:VOL3#2[1]153
PAGE, WILLIAM, *artist;* CWTI:SEP/91[54]232
PAGE, WILLIAM H., *Surgeon, USA;* ARTICLE: "I SHALL BE A PRISONER," CWTI:SEP/91[42]231
PAINE, CHARLES J., *General, USA;* B&G:DEC/94[10]585, CWM:AUG/94[30]527
PAINE, HALBERT E., *Colonel, 4th Wisconsin Infantry;* ACW:MAY/93[12]412, CWR:VOL3#1[1]149
PAINE, LEWIS; ACW:MAR/92[8]348, ACW:SEP/93[8]429, AHI:FEB/86[12]257, CWTI:DEC/91[28]239, CWNEWS:OCT/94[33], *photo,* CWTI:DEC/91[28]239
PAINE, SUMNER, *Lt., 20th Mass. Inf.;* CWR:VOL3#1[31]150
PAINE, WILLIAM H., *Captain, USA;* GETTY:7[29]188
PALFREY, FRANCIS W., *Lieutenant, 20th Massachusetts Infantry;* CWNEWS:JAN/91[4], CWR:VOL3#1[31]150
PALMER, DAVID, *Cpl.,, 8th Iowa In.;* CWM:MAY/91[10]347
PALMER, F.B., *Lt., 1st Georgia Regulars;* CWR:VOL2#2[95]135
PALMER, INNIS, *General, USA;* B&G:APR/92[58]485, CWM:JUN/95[55]591
PALMER, J.G., *Major, 66th Ohio Infantry;* GETTY:9[81]216
PALMER, JOHN B., *Colonel, CSA;* B&G:FEB/91[20]440,
PALMER, JOHN M., *General, USA:*
ARTICLE: "SHERMAN'S FEUDING GENERALS," CWTI:MAR/95[40]436
ADDITIONAL LISTINGS: ACW:NOV/93[34]442, CWM:AUG/95[36]608, CWTI:SUMMER/89[13]120, CWTI:SUMMER/89[20]121, CWTI:SUMMER/89[32]122, CWTI:SUMMER/89[40]123, CWTI:SUMMER/89[50]124, CWTI:NOV/92[41]291, CWTI:MAR/95[40]436, CWTI:AUG/95[14]454, CWTI:DEC/95[40]479, *photos,* CWTI:SUMMER/89[13]120, CWTI:MAR/95[40]436
PALMER, JOSEPH B., *General, CSA:*
BOOK REVIEW: *TENNESSEE'S BATTERED BRIGADIER: THE LIFE OF GENERAL JOSEPH B. PALMER*
ADDITIONAL LISTINGS: B&G:DEC/95[9]615, CWR:VOL1#3[7]118
PALMER, OLIVER H., *Colonel, USA;* CWR:VOL4#4[28]178
PALMER, RICHARD, *seaman, CSN;* ACW:SEP/94[46]488
PALMER, URIAH, *Pvt., 6th Wisconsin Inf.;* GETTY:11[57]233
PALMER, W.R., *Mosby's Ranger;* CWTI:SEP/90[34]176
PALMER, WILLIAM, *inventor;* ACW:JUL/93[8]420
PALMER, WILLIAM, *Lieutenant, CSA;* B&G:JUN/95[8]600

PALMER, WILLIAM H., *Colonel, CSA;* B&G:JUN/95[8]600, CWTI:SEP/92[42]283
PALMER, WILLIAM J., *General, USA;* CWTI:APR/92[8]252
PALMETTO (SOUTH CAROLINA) BATTERY; AHI:APR/68[4]115, B&G:DEC/91[38]471
PALMETTO (SOUTH CAROLINA) SHARPSHOOTERS; GETTY:6[33]172
PALMITO RANCH, TEXAS, BATTLE OF:
ARTICLE: "WAR'S LAST BATTLE," ACW:JUL/92[46]371
BOOK REVIEW: *OUT OF THE STORM: THE END OF THE CIVIL WAR (APRIL-JUNE 1865)*
ADDITIONAL LISTINGS: AHI:MAR/84[42]238, CWTI:AUG/90[58]169
PAMPLIN PARK CIVIL WAR SITE; B&G:FEB/93[40]514
PAMUNKEY RIFLES; GETTY:13[64]258
PARDEE, ARIO J., *Lieutenant Colonel, 147th Pennsylvania Infantry;* B&G:DEC/95[9]615, CWTI:SUMMER/89[32]122, GETTY:7[83]192, GETTY:10[120]229, *photo,* GETTY:9[81]216
PARDEE, D.A., *Lt. Col., 42nd Ohio Inf.;* B&G:FEB/94[8]550
PARHAM, R.T.B., *Lt., 1st Florida Inf.;* B&G:AUG/94[22]576
PARHAM, WILLIAM A., *Colonel, CSA;* ACW:JAN/94[39]451, CWR:VOL3#3[1]157
PARKE, JOHN G., *General, USA;* B&G:APR/92[8]481, B&G:AUG/95[8]604, CWR:VOL3#2[1]153, CWTI:JAN/95[34]427, CWTI:MAR/95[33]435, *photo,* B&G:AUG/95[8]604
PARKE, LEMUEL, *Capt., 27th Ill. Inf.;* CWR:VOL3#4[24]162
PARKER'S (VIRGINIA) BATTERY;
BOOK REVIEW: *PARKER'S VIRGINIA BATTERY, C.S.A.*
ADDITIONAL LISTINGS: ACW:MAY/92[62]364, CWNEWS:APR/91[4], CWR:VOL1#1[35]104, CWTI:MAY/94[50]386
PARKER'S CROSS ROADS, TENNESSEE, BATTLE OF;
ARTICLE: "AGAINST ALL ODDS: FORREST'S GREAT WEST TENNESSEE RAID," CWM:DEC/95[48]631
ADDITIONAL LISTING: CWTI:NOV/93[33]347
PARKER, ELI S., *Colonel, USA:*
ARTICLES: "AN IROQUOIS AT APPOMATTOX," CWM:SEP/92[19]440, "HASANOANDA OF THE TONAWANDA SENECAS," CWM:SEP/92[18]439, "'ONE REAL AMERICAN'," AHI:NOV/69[13]124
BOOK REVIEWS: *THE IROQUOIS IN THE CIVIL WAR: FROM BATTLEFIELD TO RESERVATION*
ADDITIONAL LISTINGS: AHI:SEP/87[48]264, CWM:JUL/91[8]356, CWM:SEP/92[8]437, CWM:SEP/92[16]438, CWM:SEP/92[38]443, CWNEWS:JAN/94[5], CWR:VOL3#2[105], *photos,* AHI:NOV/69[13]124, CWM:SEP/92[19]440, CWTI:FEB/90[54]147
PARKER, FOXHALL A., *Commander, USN;* ACW:JUL/92[10]366, CWR:VOL2#3[194]141
PARKER, FRANCIS H., *Cadet;* B&G:DEC/91[12]469
PARKER, J.R., *Lieutenant Colonel, 48th Ohio Infantry;* B&G:FEB/94[8]550, CWM:APR/95[39]576
PARKER, JOHN F., ACW:JAN/94[47]452, AHI:FEB/86[12]257
PARKER, JOHN H., *Captain, USA;* AHI:JUN/66[52]102
PARKER, JOSEPH, *Surgeon* ACW:MAR/93[8]401
PARKER, LUTHER H., *Sergeant, 12th New Hampshire Infantry;* GETTY:12[7]241
PARKER, SIMON, *Sergeant, 5th New York Infantry;* CWR:VOL1#2[7]111, CWTI:MAY/94[31]382
PARKER, THEODORE; ACW:JUL/91[43]315
PARKER, THOMAS H., *Captain, 51st Pennsylvania Infantry;* BOOK REVIEW: *HISTORY OF THE 51ST REGIMENT OF P.V. AND V.V.*

PARKER, W. W., *Major, Virginia Battery;* AHI:SEP/87[40]263, CWM:AUG/94[48]529, GETTY:5[47]160
PARKER, WILLIAM, *Colonel, CSA;* CWR:VOL1#4[7]125
PARKER, WILLIAM, *Private, Petersburg Artillery;* ACW:MAR/95[12]513
PARKER, WILLIAM, *Captain, CSA;* CWTI:MAY/94[50]386
PARKER, WILLIAM A., *Cmdr., USN;* ACW:SEP/95[30]545
PARKER, WILLIAM H., *Lieutenant, CSN;* ACW:JUL/92[10]366, AHI:OCT/75[30]162
PARKER, WILLIAM W., *Major, Parker's Virginia Battery;* ACW:MAY/92[62]364, CWNEWS:APR/91[4], CWR:VOL1#1[35]104, CWTI:MAY/94[50]386
PARKHILL, GEORGE W., *Captain, 2nd Florida Infantry;* ACW:SEP/93[8]429
PARKHURST, JOHN C., *Lieutenant Colonel, 9th Michigan Infantry;* B&G:OCT/95[5]610, CWTI:NOV/93[33]347
PARKMAN, FRANCIS; CWTI:AUG/90[42]167
PARKMAN, THEODORE; CWNEWS:MAY/93[4]
PARKS, CHARLES S., *Pvt., 118th NY Inf.;* B&G:OCT/95[36]614
PARKS, J.C., *Pvt., 22nd Virginia Inf.;* B&G:APR/93[24]520
PARKS, MARCUS A., *Lieutenant Colonel, 52nd North Carolina Infantry;* GETTY:8[67]204, GETTY:12[61]245
PARKS, R.E., *Captain, CSA;* CWTI:JUL/93[20]325
PARMATER, N.L., *Private, 29th Ohio Infantry;* GETTY:9[81]216
PARR, ALVIN, *Pvt., 1st Georgia Regulars;* CWR:VOL2#2[95]135
PARROTT, ENOCH G., *Captain, USN;* ACW:SEP/94[46]488
PARROTT, JACOB, *Private, USA;* ACW:SEP/91[22]321
PARROTT, ROBERT P.; B&G:DEC/91[12]469, CWTI:OCT/95[32]468
PARSLEY, RICHARD, *28th Tenn. Inf.;* B&G:DEC/91[38]471
PARSLEY, WILLIAM M., *Major, 3rd North Carolina Infantry;* GETTY:7[83]192
PARSONS, CHARLES C., *Lt., USA;* B&G:DEC/91[12]469
PARSONS, EDWARD, *Sergeant, 9th New Hampshire Infantry;* CWR:VOL2#2[118]136
PARSONS, EDWIN B., *Captain, 24th Wisconsin. Infantry;* ACW:MAR/92[14]350
PARSONS, MONROE M., *General, CSA;* AHI:JUN/70[30]127, CWR:VOL2#3[212]142
PARSONS, MOSBY M., *General, CSA;* ACW:MAY/93[22]414, ACW:NOV/93[26]441, CWR:VOL1#4[77], CWR:VOL4#2[68]167
PARSONS, THOMAS W., *Private, 14th Kentucky Cavalry;* ACW:SEP/95[22]544
PARSONS, WILLIAM H., *Colonel, CSA;*
ARTICLE: "CHASING BANKS OUT OF LOUISIANA: PARSON'S TEXAS CAVALRY IN THE RED RIVER CAMPAIGN," CWR:VOL2#3[212]142
BOOK REVIEWS: *BETWEEN THE ENEMY AND TEXAS: PARSON'S TEXAS CAVALRY IN THE CIVIL WAR* *THE RAGGED REBEL: A COMMON SOLDIER IN W.H. PARSON'S TEXAS CAVALRY, 1861-1865*
ADDITIONAL LISTINGS: CWR:VOL2#3[252]144, CWR:VOL4#2[26]166, CWR:VOL4#2[118]169, *photo,* CWR:VOL2#3[212]142
PART, ROBERT E., *Captain, CSA;* GETTY:12[111]250
PARTIRDGE, BENJAMIN F., *Lieutenant, 16th Michigan Infantry;* GETTY:6[33]172
PARTISAN RANGER LAW; CWTI:SEP/90[34]176
PARTRIDGE, CHARLES, *Private, 96th Illinois Infantry;* CWTI:SEPT/89[30]129
PARTRIDGE, FREDERICK, *Lieutenant Colonel, 13th Illinois Infantry;* CWTI:SEP/94[40]403

PARTRIDGE, WILLIAM T., *Captain, 5th New York Infantry;* CWR:VOL1#2[7]111, CWTI:MAY/94[31]382
PASSALAIGUE, CHARLES S., *Lieutenant, CSN;* ACW:SEP/94[46]488
PATAPSCO (MARYLAND) GUARDS; B&G:AUG/94[10]574
PATE, HENRY C., *Colonel, 5th Virginia Cavalry;* ACW:NOV/91[30]332, ACW:NOV/91[35]333, ACW:MAY/94[35]469
PATON, CHARLES, *Pvt., 24th Michigan Inf.,* GETTY:11[57]233
PATRICK, ALBERT, *Pvt., 1st Ind. Cav.;* ACW:MAR/95[34]516
PATRICK, J.N., *Pvt., 26th Virginia Inf.;* B&G:APR/93[24]520
PATRICK, JOHN H., *Col., 5th Ohio Infantry;* GETTY:9[81]216
PATRICK, MARSENA R., *General, USA;*
GENERAL LISTINGS: *Gettysburg,* GETTY:9[98]217, *in book review,* CWNEWS:AUG/93[5], *letters to the editor,* B&G:DEC/94[6]584, *Manassas, 2nd,* B&G:AUG/92[11]493, *order of battle,* B&G:APR/95[8]595, *Veteran Reserve Corps,* AHI:FEB/75[35]158, *Wilderness,* B&G:APR/95[8]595, *photos,* AHI:FEB/75[35]158, B&G:APR/91[8]445
ADDITIONAL LISTINGS: ACW:MAR/92[30]352, ACW:JUL/92[30]369, B&G:APR/91[8]445, B&G:AUG/91[40]463, B&G:APR/93[12]518, CWM:JAN/93[16]457, CWM:AUG/94[60]531, CWR:VOL3#2[1]153, CWTI:MAR/94[38]372, CWTI:JUN/95[32]446, GETTY:12[85]248
PATRICK, RICHARD F., *Lieutenant, 55th Ohio Infantry;* CWNEWS:OCT/92[4]
PATRICK, SIDNEY V., *Private, 5th Texas Infantry;* CWR:VOL1#2[29]112
PATTEE, JOHN A., *Pvt., 24th Michigan Inf.;* GETTY:11[57]233
PATTEN, CHARLES, *Pvt., 24th Michigan Inf.;* GETTY:9[33]211
PATTEN, GEORGE W., *Captain, 73rd Illinois Infantry;* CWR:VOL4#3[1]170
PATTEN, JOHN A., *Pvt., 24th Michigan Inf.;* GETTY:9[33]211
PATTERSON, EDMUND D., *Captain, 9th Alabama Infantry;* CWM:JUN/95[29]583, GETTY:7[13]186
PATTERSON, EDMUND K., *Captain, 88th Pennsylvania Infantry;* GETTY:10[7]221
PATTERSON, EMANUAL, *Private, 6th USCT;* CWM:AUG/94[30]527
PATTERSON, FERDINAND; B&G:APR/91[24]446
PATTERSON, GEORGE M., *Captain, Sumter Artillery;* CWR:VOL3#2[1]153
PATTERSON, JAMES, *Pvt., 5th NY Inf.;* CWR:VOL1#2[29]112
PATTERSON, JOHN H., *11th U.S. Infantry;* B&G:FEB/93[40]514
PATTERSON, JOHN W., *Colonel, 102nd Pennsylvania Infantry;* GETTY:11[91]236
PATTERSON, REUBEN, *former slave;* CWTI:FEB/92[42]250
PATTERSON, ROBERT, *General, USA;* AHI:JUL/81[20]221, MH:APR/93[34]165
PATTERSON, W.W., *Captain, CSA;* ACW:MAR/94[50]462
PATTERSON, WILLIAM T., *Sergeant, USA;* CWTI:OCT/95[48]470
PATTISON, THOMAS, *Colonel, USA;* CWR:VOL1#1[42]105
PATTON, ARCHIBALD, *Lieutenant Colonel, 1st Arkansas Infantry;* AHI:MAR/84[42]238
PATTON, GEORGE S., *Colonel, 22nd Virginia Infantry;*
ARTICLE: "ANCESTRAL GRAY CLOUD OVER PATTON," AHI:MAR/84[42]238, "CONFEDERATES ROUTED AT WINCHESTER!" CWM:OCT/95[37]617
GENERAL LISTINGS: *in order of battle,* B&G:APR/94[10]558, *letters to the editor,* B&G:DEC/95[5]614A, *photo,* AHI:MAR/84[42]238

ADDITIONAL LISTINGS: AHI:MAR/84[42]238, CWR:VOL3#4[1]161, CWTI:MAR/89[16]101

PATTON, ISAAC WILLIAMS, *Colonel, CSA*; AHI:MAR/84[42]238

PATTON, JAMES F.; AHI:MAR/84[42]238

PATTON, JOHN, *Colonel, Missouri Militia*; AHI:MAR/84[42]238

PATTON, JOHN M., *Colonel, CSA*; AHI:MAR/84[42]238, CWM:AUG/95[38]609

PATTON, JOHN R., *Cadet, VMI*; AHI:MAR/84[42]238

PATTON, THOMAS, *Colonel, 2nd Missouri Infantry*; AHI:MAR/84[42]238

PATTON, THOMAS, *Private, 14th Kentucky Infantry*; ACW:SEP/95[22]544

PATTON, WALLER T., *Colonel, CSA*; ARTICLE: "ANCESTRAL GRAY CLOUD OVER PATTON," AHI:MAR/84[42]238

PATTON, WILLIAM M., *cadet, VMI*; AHI:MAR/84[42]238

PAUL, E.A., *reporter*; ACW:SEP/94[55]489

PAUL, GABIREL R., *General, USA*;
GENERAL LISTINGS: *Gettysburg*, GETTY:4[33]146, GETTY:10[7]221, *New Mexico Campaign*, B&G:JUN/94[8]568, *photo*, B&G:JUN/94[8]568
ADDITIONAL LISTINGS: B&G:FEB/95[8]590B, CWM:MAY/92[15]419, GETTY:13[1]252, GETTY:13[33]255

PAUL, JAMES, *Confederate veteran*; GETTY:7[119]195

PAULDING, HIRAM; ACW:NOV/92[51]389

PAULETTE, SAM, *Pvt., 18th Virginia Inf.*; B&G:APR/92[8]481

PAULLIN, WILLIAM, *aeronaut*; B&G:DEC/91[6]468

PAXTON, ELISHA F., *General, CSA*; CWM:JUL/91[48]374, CWTI:MAY/89[22]116, MH:JUN/92[50]159

PAXTON, FRANK; ACW:MAY/92[14]358

PAXTON, JOHN R., *Private, 140th Pennsylvania Infantry*; ARTICLE: "ON THE RAPPAHANNOCK, CHRISTMAS DAY, 1862," AHI:DEC/68[25]117

PAYNE'S FARM, VIRGINIA, BATTLE OF:
ARTICLE: "'THE MUSKET BALLS FLEW VERY THICK': HOLDING THE LINE AT PAYNE'S FARM," CWM:MAY/92[20]420
ADDITIONAL LISTINGS: CWM:MAY/92[4]416, CWM:SEP/93[24]495, CWM:DEC/94[44]551, CWR:VOL1#4[77]

PAYNE, ALEXANDER, *Lieutenant, CSA*; B&G:OCT/93[12]537

PAYNE, DANIEL, *Corporal, 13th U.S. Infantry*; CWM:JUN/94[30]515, CWR:VOL2#1[1]130

PAYNE, DOLPHUS S., *U.S. Marshall*; B&G:APR/91[24]446

PAYNE, EUGENE B., *Capt., 37th Ill. Inf.*; CWR:VOL1#1[42]105

PAYNE, JAMES E., *civilian*; CWTI:MAR/91[34]201

PAYNE, JOHN, *Lt., CSN*; AHI:OCT/95[16]325, CWR:VOL4#3[77]174

PAYNE, JOHN, *Pvt., Crenshaw Artillery*; CWR:VOL4#4[70]180

PAYNE, OLIVER B., *Captain, USA*; CWTI:AUG/95[34]457

PAYNE, TOM, *Corp., 37th Illinois Inf.*; CWR:VOL1#1[42]105

PAYNE, WILLIAM H.F., *General, CSA*; ACW:MAY/91[38]305, B&G:APR/92[8]481, GETTY:4[65]148, MH:OCT/93[76]173

PAYTON, GREEN, *Major, CSA*; ACW:SEP/93[31]433

PEA RIDGE NATIONAL MILITARY PARK; CWR:VOL1#1[42]105

PEA RIDGE, ARKANSAS, BATTLE OF:
ARTICLE: "THE FREMONT RIFLES: THE 37TH ILLINOIS AT PEA RIDGE AND PRAIRIE GROVE," CWR:VOL1#1[42]105
BOOK REVIEWS: *PEA RIDGE: CIVIL WAR CAMPAIGN IN THE WEST * THE SOUTH'S FINEST: THE FIRST MISSOURI CONFEDERATE BRIGADE FROM PEA RIDGE TO VICKSBURG*

GENERAL LISTINGS: *general history*, AHI:MAY/71[3]133A, *in book review*, ACW:MAY/94[58], B&G:APR/94[24], CWM:APR/95[50], CWM:OCT/95[10], CWNEWS:DEC/93[5], CWR:VOL3#4[68]
ADDITIONAL LISTINGS: ACW:MAY/91[10]301, ACW:MAR/94[8]456, ACW:MAY/94[26]468, B&G:AUG/92[26]494, CWM:SEP/92[38]443, CWR:VOL1#2[44]114, CWR:VOL2#1[36]132, CWTI:MAY/91[16]206, CWTI:MAY/92[48]267, CWTI:JUL/94[82]396

PEABODY, EVERETT, *Colonel, USA*; ACW:JAN/91[22]285

PEABODY, WILLIAM, *Private, 57th Massachusetts Infantry*; CWR:VOL1#3[94]

PEACHTREE CREEK, GEORGIA, BATTLE OF;
ACW:MAR/92[14]350, ACW:NOV/92[35]387, ACW:NOV/95[74]560, AHI:MAY/71[3]133A, CWM:JAN/91[12]326, CWM:JAN/92[40]405, CWR:VOL1#2[78], CWR:VOL1#4[64]127, CWTI:SUMMER/89[32]122, CWTI:SUMMER/89[40]123

PEACOCK, WILLIAM, *Private, 9th Indiana Cavalry*; B&G:AUG/95[24]605,

PEARCE, JOHN, *Master, USN*; CWTI:MAY/94[16]380

PEARCE, JOHN B., *Lt., 32nd Ohio Inf.*; CWR:VOL1#4[7]125

PEARCE, N. BARTLETT, *General, CSA*; ACW:NOV/93[26]441, CWTI:FEB/92[29]248

PEARCE, WALTER, *Ensign, USN*; MH:OCT/91[50]154

PEARSALL, URI B., *Lt. Col., 99th USCT*; ACW:NOV/91[64]336

PEARSON, ALFRED L., *Colonel, USA*; B&G:APR/92[8]481

PEARSON, HENRY, *Lieutenant Colonel, 6th New Hampshire Infantry*; ACW:MAY/95[18]524, B&G:AUG/92[11]493, CWTI:JAN/95[34]427

PEARSON, J.M., *Lieutenant, CSA*; CWR:VOL2#1[19]131

PEARSON, WILLIAM, *Private, 148th Pennsylvania Infantry*; CWR:VOL2#2[141]137

PECK, A.W., *Lt., 17th Connecticut Infantry*; GETTY:9[33]211

PECK, ABEL, *Sgt., 24th Michigan Infantry*; GETTY:5[19]158

PECK, CASSIUS, *Private, Berdan's Sharpshooters*; CWTI:MAR/89[34]104

PECK, FRANK H., *Lieutenant Colonel, 12th Connecticut Infantry*; ACW:MAY/91[38]305

PECK, HERBERT, *Sgt., 5th NY Inf.*; CWR:VOL1#2[29]112

PECK, JOHN J., *General, USA*; ACW:JUL/93[16]422

PECK, WILLIAM R., *General, CSA*; CWM:SEP/93[24]495, CWTI:MAR/94[48]374

PEDDICORD, J.M., *Sergeant, USMC*; CWTI:JUN/95[26]445

PEE DEE (SOUTH CAROLINA) ARTILLERY, CWR:VOL1#1[1]102, GETTY:10[107]227

PEEBLES' FARM, VIRGINIA, BATTLE OF; ACW:MAR/95[12]513, CWNEWS:MAY/89[4]

PEEK, JOHN, *Capt., 64th NC Inf.*; B&G:FEB/91[20]440

PEEL, WILLIAM, *Lieutenant, 11th Mississippi Infantry*; GETTY:12[1]240, GETTY:7[13]186, GETTY:9[98]217

PEEPLES, SAMUEL, *Lieutenant, 5th U.S. Artillery*; GETTY:7[51]190, GETTY:9[41]212

PEETS, GEORGE, *Surgeon, 21st Mississippi Infantry*; GETTY:7[77]191

PEGRAM, JOHN, *General, CSA*:
GENERAL LISTINGS: *3rd Winchester*, ACW:MAY/91[38]305, *in book review*, CWNEWS:FEB/94[5], *order of battle*, B&G:APR/95[8]595, *West Virginia campaign*, B&G:AUG/93[10]529, *photo*, B&G:AUG/93[10]529
ADDITIONAL LISTINGS: ACW:JAN/92[47]344, ACW:JAN/92[50]345, B&G:APR/92[8]481, B&G:OCT/92[26]498, B&G:APR/95[8]595,

CWM:JAN/92[27]403, CWM:NOV/92[64]453, CWM:DEC/95[41]630, CWR:VOL4#1[1]163

PEGRAM, WILLIAM: *the following listings might be for William J. or William J.R. Pegram*
GENERAL LISTINGS: *Beaver Dam Creek,* CWM:JUN/95[57]592, *Cold Harbor,* B&G:APR/94[10]558, *Gettysburg,* GETTY:5[4]156, GETTY:9[61]215, GETTY:11[71]234, *in book review,* CWM:APR/95[50]
ADDITIONAL LISTINGS: ACW:MAY/95[30]525, AHI:SEP/87[40]263, CWM:JAN/93[40]461, CWR:VOL1#1[1]102, CWR:VOL1#3[52]122, CWR:VOL3#2[1]153

PEGRAM, WILLIAM J., *Lieutenant Colonel, CSA:*
GENERAL LISTINGS: *Five Forks,* B&G:APR/92[8]481, *Gettysburg,* GETTY:5[89]162, GETTY:6[13]170, *Harpers Ferry,* MH:AUG/95[30]185, *in order of battle,* B&G:APR/92[8]481, *order of battle,* B&G:APR/95[8]595, *Wilderness,* B&G:JUN/95[8]600, *photo,* CWR:VOL4#4[70]180
ADDITIONAL LISTINGS: ACW:JUL/95[50]538, B&G:APR/93[12]518, CWM:MAR/91[17]335, CWR:VOL1#1[26]103, CWR:VOL1#1[35]104, CWR:VOL3#2[1]153, CWR:VOL4#4[70]180, CWTI:FEB/91[45]194

PEGRAM, WILLIAM R.J., *Major, CSA:*
ARTICLE: "THE LORD'S YOUNG ARTILLERIST: A CONVERSATION WITH PETER S. CARMICHAEL," CWM:DEC/95[41]630
BOOK REVIEW: *NINE MEN IN GRAY*
ADDITIONAL LISTINGS: GETTY:10[107]227, *photo,* CWM:DEC/95[41]630

PEIKS, J.D., *Pvt., 47th Virginia Infantry;* B&G:APR/93[24]520
PEIRSON, CHARLES, *Lieutenant, USA;* AHI:FEB/82[36]225
PELHAM HISTORICAL ASSOCIATION; B&G:DEC/92[40]508
PELHAM, JOHN, *Major, CSA:*
ARTICLE: "BEAUTY, SALLIE AND FATE," ACW:NOV/91[35]333, "STONEWALL JACKSON'S ARTILLERISTS AND THE DEFENSE OF THE CONFEDERATE RIGHT," CWR:VOL4#4[70]180
GENERAL LISTINGS: *Brawner's Farm,* B&G:AUG/92[11]493, *Fredericksburg,* CWR:VOL4#4[1]177, *in book review,* ACW:MAR/94[58], CWNEWS:MAY/94[5], CWR:VOL4#3[89], *Kelly's Ford,* ACW:NOV/91[30]332, *letters to the editor,* B&G:FEB/91[6]438, B&G:DEC/93[6]544, *Peninsula Campaign,* CWM:JUN/95[76]598, *West Point,* B&G:DEC/91[12]469, *photos,* ACW:NOV/91[35]333, ACW:MAR/94[58], B&G:DEC/91[12]469, CWR:VOL4#4[70]180
ADDITIONAL LISTINGS: ACW:JUL/92[30]369, ACW:MAR/94[50]462, B&G:APR/91[8]445, B&G:DEC/91[34]470, B&G:OCT/92[38]500, B&G:DEC/92[40]508, B&G:OCT/93[49]543, B&G:FEB/94[38]553, CWM:DEC/94[74]555, CWR:VOL1#1[1]102, CWR:VOL4#4[i]175, CWR:VOL4#4[127]182, CWTI:APR/92[35]257, CWTI:NOV/93[24]346

PELHAM, WILLIAM, *seaman, USN;* CWM:SEP/93[18]494
PELICAN, PETER, *Private, 36th Illinois Infantry;* ACW:MAR/94[8]456, CWNEWS:DEC/93[5]
PELLEY, JOHN, *Pvt., 5th Ohio Cavalry;* CWR:VOL4#1[44]164
PELTIER, PIERRE D., *Surgeon, 126th New York Infantry;* GETTY:10[53]225
PEMBER, PHEOBE YATES:
BOOK REVIEW: *A SOUTHERN WOMAN'S STORY*
GENERAL LISTINGS: *in book review,* CWR:VOL4#1[78], *Women in the South,* AHI:DEC/73[10]152, *photo,* AHI:DEC/73[10]152
ADDITIONAL LISTINGS: ACW:MAY/92[39]362, ACW:MAY/95[38]526, CWTI:AUG/90[26]166, CWTI:MAY/92[38]265

PEMBERTON, JOHN C. *General, CSA:*
ARTICLES: "A HILL OF DEATH," CWTI:MAY/91[24]208, "EDITORIAL," ACW:NOV/91[6]327, "LITERAL HILL OF DEATH," ACW:NOV/91[22]331, "VICKSBURG: DAVIS, VAN DORN, PEMBERTON—A TRIANGULATION OF SHORTCOMINGS," CWM:AUG/94[52]530
BOOK REVIEWS: *PEMBERTON, A BIOGRAPHY*
GENERAL LISTINGS: *Champion's Hill,* MH:JUN/93[82]167, *general history,* AHI:MAY/71[3]133A, *Grierson's Raid,* B&G:JUN/93[12]524, *in book review,* ACW:NOV/93[58], B&G:FEB/92[26], CWR:VOL2#1[78], CWR:VOL2#2[169], CWR:VOL4#3[89], *Jefferson Davis,* CWTI:AUG/91[62]221, *Mexican War,* MH:APR/93[39]166, *Port Gibson,* B&G:FEB/94[8]550, *Secessionville,* CWTI:JAN/94[46]364, *Vicksburg,* ACW:JAN/91[16]284, AHI:DEC/77[46]177, B&G:AUG/95[8]604, *photos,* ACW:NOV/91[6]327, AHI:DEC/77[13]176, AHI:MAY/71[3]133A, B&G:FEB/94[8]550, B&G:JUN/93[12]524, CWM:AUG/94[52]530, CWR:VOL2#1[36]132, CWTI:MAY/91[24]208
ADDITIONAL LISTINGS: ACW:MAY/91[10]301, ACW:MAY/92[47]363, ACW:SEP/92[38]379, ACW:JUL/94[51]480, ACW:SEP/94[10]484, ACW:NOV/94[76]500, AHI:NOV/73[18]151, AHI:DEC/77[13]176, AHI:OCT/95[24]326, B&G:DEC/95[25]616, CWM:MAY/91[31]350, CWM:MAR/93[16]466, CWM:APR/95[28]573, CWM:DEC/95[48]631, CWR:VOL1#1[42]105, CWR:VOL2#1[i]129, CWR:VOL2#1[1]130, CWR:VOL2#1[19]131, CWR:VOL2#1[36]132, CWR:VOL3#3[33]158, CWR:VOL3#3[59]159, CWTI:SEPT/89[18]126, CWTI:FEB/90[46]146, CWTI:MAY/91[18]207, CWTI:AUG/91[62]221, CWTI:NOV/92[54]293, CWTI:MAR/93[24]309, CWTI:NOV/93[33]347, CWTI:JUL/94[44]394, CWTI:AUG/95[46]459, CWTI:DEC/95[67]481

PENAIR, GEORGE, *Pvt., 88th Penna. Inf.;* GETTY:10[7]221
PENDER, WILLIAM D., *General, CSA:*
BOOK REVIEWS: *THE GENERAL TO HIS LADY: THE CIVIL WAR LETTERS OF WILLIAM DORSEY PENDER TO FANNY PENDER*
GENERAL LISTINGS: *Beaver Dam Creek,* CWM:JUN/95[57]592, *Chancellorsville,* CWM:APR/94[14]503, *Gettysburg,* GETTY:4[7]142, GETTY:5[4]156, GETTY:5[19]158, GETTY:5[89]162, GETTY:5[103]163, GETTY:5[107]164, GETTY:7[13]186, GETTY:8[9]199, GETTY:8[67]204, GETTY:8[111]206, GETTY:9[17]210, GETTY:9[98]217, GETTY:10[7]221, GETTY:10[102]226, GETTY:10[107]227, GETTY:11[57]233, GETTY:11[71]234, MH:DEC/91[54]155, *Harpers Ferry,* MH:AUG/95[30]185, *in book review,* ACW:JUL/91[50], CWM:AUG/95[8], CWR:VOL3#2[105], CWR:VOL4#3[1]170, *letters to the editor,* B&G:APR/95[5]594, *Manassas, Second,* B&G:AUG/92[11]493, *Seven Pines,* CWM:JUN/95[47]588, *photo,* GETTY:13[22]254
ADDITIONAL LISTINGS: ACW:NOV/92[42]388, ACW:SEP/93[31]433, ACW:JUL/95[50]538, AHI:APR/85[18]250, B&G:FEB/95[8]590A, CWM:MAY/92[15]419, CWM:JAN/93[8]456, CWM:AUG/94[26]525, CWM:AUG/94[60]531, CWR:VOL1#1[1]102, CWR:VOL1#1[26]103, CWR:VOL1#3[52]122, CWR:VOL1#4[7]125, CWR:VOL2#4[269]145, CWR:VOL4#4[70]180, CWTI:FEB/91[12]189,

CWTI:NOV/93[55]350, GETTY:13[1]252, GETTY:13[22]254, GETTY:13[33]255, GETTY:13[75]259, GETTY:13[108]261

PENDERGRASS, R.W., *Private, 2nd Tennessee Cavalry;*
CWR:VOL4#1[1]163

PENDERGRAST, GARRETT J., *Flag Officer, USN;*
ACW:SEP/94[46]488

PENDLETON, ALEXANDER S. "SANDIE", *Lieutenant Colonel, CSA:*
GENERAL LISTINGS: *Gettysburg,* GETTY:5[107]164, GETTY:6[94]180, GETTY:7[13]186, GETTY:9[17]210, *Jackson,* B&G:JUN/92[8]487

ADDITIONAL LISTING: CWTI:MAY/89[22]116

PENDLETON, GEORGE, *election of 1864;* AHI:OCT/68[4]116

PENDLETON, WILLIAM N., *General, CSA:*
ARTICLE: "NEAR DISASTER ON THE POTOMAC," CWM:OCT/95[38]618

GENERAL LISTINGS: *Gettysburg,* GETTY:4[113]153, GETTY:5[4]156, GETTY:5[107]164, GETTY:7[13]186, *in book review,* CWNEWS:JAN/91[4], CWR:VOL3#4[68], *letters to the editor,* CWTI:NOV/92[8]288, *post-war,* ACW:JUL/95[26]535

ADDITIONAL LISTINGS: ACW:MAY/92[14]358, ACW:JUL/92[12]367, ACW:SEP/92[30]378, ACW:MAR/93[26]404, ACW:MAR/94[50]462, ACW:SEP/94[10]484, ACW:MAY/95[10]523, B&G:DEC/91[34]470, B&G:APR/93[12]518, B&G:FEB/95[8]590C, CWM:JUL/91[46]373, CWM:JUL/91[48]374, CWM:JAN/93[8]456, CWM:JUN/94[43]517, CWR:VOL1#1[1]102, CWR:VOL2#2[95]135, CWR:VOL3#2[1]153, CWR:VOL4#4[28]178, CWTI:SEPT/89[46]132, GETTY:13[75]259

PENGEL, CHARLES, *Sergeant, USA;* B&G:FEB/95[8]590A

PENINSULA CAMPAIGN, VIRGINIA, 1862:
ARTICLE: "DETAILS FROM WHITE HOUSE ON THE PENINSULA," CWM:JUN/94[28]514, "JEB STUART'S DARING RECONNAISSANCE," ACW:JUL/95[34]536, "THE PENINSULA CAMPAIGN OF 1862: DENOUEMENT AT HARRISON'S LANDING," CWM:JUN/95[76]598, "THE PENINSULA CAMPAIGN OF 1862: STUART'S RIDE AROUND MCCLELLAN," CWM:JUN/95[50]589, "THE PENINSULA CAMPAIGN OF 1862: THE BATTLE OF BEAVER DAM CREEK," CWM:JUN/95[57]592, "THE PENINSULA CAMPAIGN OF 1862: THE BATTLE OF DREWRY'S BLUFF," CWM:JUN/95[39]586, "THE PENINSULA CAMPAIGN OF 1862: THE BATTLE OF GAINES'S MILL," CWM:JUN/95[61]593, "THE PENINSULA CAMPAIGN OF 1862: THE BATTLE OF GARNETT'S FARM," CWM:JUN/95[63]594, "THE PENINSULA CAMPAIGN OF 1862: THE BATTLE OF GLENDALE," CWM:JUN/95[69]596, "THE PENINSULA CAMPAIGN OF 1862: THE BATTLE OF MALVERN HILL," CWM:JUN/95[73]597, "THE PENINSULA CAMPAIGN OF 1862: THE BATTLE OF OAK GROVE," CWM:JUN/95[55]591

ARTICLES, continued: "THE PENINSULA CAMPAIGN OF 1862: THE BATTLE OF SAVAGE'S STATION," CWM:JUN/95[65]595, "THE PENINSULA CAMPAIGN OF 1862: THE BATTLE OF SEVEN PINES," CWM:JUN/95[47]588, "THE PENINSULA CAMPAIGN OF 1862: THE BATTLE OF SLASH CHURCH," CWM:JUN/95[43]587, "THE PENINSULA CAMPAIGN OF 1862: THE BATTLE OF WILLIAMSBURG," CWM:JUN/95[34]584, "THE PENINSULA CAMPAIGN OF 1862: THE DABBS HOUSE MEETING," CWM:JUN/95[53]590, "THE PENINSULA CAMPAIGN OF

1862: THE SIEGE OF YORKTOWN AND ENGAGEMENTS ALONG THE WARWICK RIVER," CWM:JUN/95[29]583, "THE PENINSULA CAMPAIGN OF 1862: THE ENGAGEMENT AT ELTHAM'S LANDING," CWM:JUN/95[37]585, "THE PENINSULA CAMPAIGN OF 1862; PRELUDE: THE LEGIONS GATHER," CWM:JUN/95[24]582

BOOK REVIEWS: *THE BATTLE OF SEVEN PINES * HISTORY OF THE PENNSYLVANIA RESERVE CORPS * THE PENINSULA CAMPAIGN OF 1862: YORKTOWN TO THE SEVEN DAYS * THE PENINSULA: MCCLELLAN'S CAMPAIGN OF 1862 * THE RISE AND FALL OF THE CONFEDERATE GOVERNMENT * THE OTHER SIDE OF THE WAR; WITH THE ARMY OF THE POTOMAC: LETTERS FROM THE HEADQUARTERS OF THE U.S. SANITARY COMMISSION DURING THE PENINSULA CAMPAIGN * TO THE GATES OF RICHMOND: THE PENINSULA CAMPAIGN*

GENERAL LISTINGS: *general history,* AHI:MAY/71[3]133A, *in book review,* CWM:APR/95[50], CWM:JUN/95[6], CWNEWS:OCT/89[4], CWNEWS:JUN/90[4], CWR:VOL1#3[94], MH:DEC/94[70], *letters to the editor,* CWM:OCT/94[5]533, *torpedoes,* ACW:NOV/91[8]328, *photo,* ACW:JUL/95[34]536

ADDITIONAL LISTINGS, ACW: ACW:NOV/91[41]334, ACW:NOV/92[10]384, ACW:MAY/93[38]416, ACW:JUL/93[8]420, ACW:MAR/94[35]460, ACW:MAY/94[12]466, ACW:JUL/94[35]478, ACW:SEP/94[55]489, ACW:JAN/95[10]503, ACW:JAN/95[46]507, ACW:MAR/95[12]513, ACW:MAR/95[70]520, ACW:SEP/95[8]542, ACW:NOV/95[10]553

ADDITIONAL LISTINGS, CWM: CWM:MAR/91[50]340, CWM:MAR/91[56]341, CWM:MAY/91[18]348, CWM:JUL/91[10]357, CWM:SEP/91[24]381, CWM:SEP/92[8]437, CWM:SEP/93[24]495, CWM:DEC/94[34]549, CWM:JUN/95[17]581, CWM:JUN/95[82]600, CWM:OCT/95[22]614

ADDITIONAL LISTINGS, CWR: CWR:VOL1#1[1]102, CWR:VOL1#2[29]112, CWR:VOL1#4[7]125, CWR:VOL2#3[236]143, CWR:VOL2#4[269]145, CWR:VOL3#2[1]153, CWR:VOL3#3[1]157, CWR:VOL4#4[47]179

ADDITIONAL LISTINGS, CWTI: CWTI:MAR/89[28]103, CWTI:APR/89[14]107, CWTI:DEC/89[34]136, CWTI:AUG/91[58]220, CWTI:SEP/91[31]229, CWTI:SEP/91[42]231, CWTI:SEP/91[54]232, CWTI:NOV/92[60]294, CWTI:MAY/93[20]317, CWTI:JUL/93[14]324, CWTI:NOV/93[55]350, CWTI:JAN/94[20]358, CWTI:MAR/94[48]374, CWTI:MAY/94[31]382, CWTI:JUL/94[44]394

PENN, DAVIDSON B., *Colonel, CSA;* ACW:MAR/92[30]352, GETTY:13[108]261

PENN, ELIJAH G., *Lt., 5th Ohio Cavalry;* CWR:VOL4#1[44]164

PENNINGTON, ALEXANDER C.M., *Colonel, 2nd U.S.:*
GENERAL LISTINGS: *Five Forks,* B&G:APR/92[8]481, *Gettysburg,* GETTY:4[75]149, GETTY:12[68]246, *in order of battle,* B&G:APR/92[8]481

ADDITIONAL LISTINGS: ACW:JUL/92[41]370, CWM:APR/94[24]505, GETTY:13[89]260, MH:FEB/93[42]164

PENNINGTON, EDWARD, *civilian;* GETTY:10[112]228

PENNOCK, ALEX M., *Captain, USN;* ACW:JUL/93[34]424

PENNSYLVANIA COAL MINERS; ARTICLE: "IT WAS OPEN, DEFIANT REBELLION'," CWM:MAR/91[56]341

PENNSYLVANIA TROOPS:

1st Artillery; B&G:FEB/94[24]551, CWTI:SUMMER/89[32]122, GETTY:13[22]254

1st Artillery, Battery A; CWR:VOL1#3[20]119

1st Artillery, Battery B; B&G:APR/95[8]595, GETTY:10[29]222, GETTY:11[57]233

1st Artillery, Battery F; ACW:JUL/92[30]369

1st Artillery, Battery F & G:
ARTICLE: "AN ENCOUNTER WITH BATTERY HELL," GETTY:12[30]243
GENERAL LISTINGS: *Gettysburg*, GETTY:4[49]147, GETTY:9[33]211, GETTY:12[1]240
ADDITIONAL LISTING: ACW:NOV/92[42]388

1st Artillery, Battery G; CWTI:DEC/91[36]240

1st Cavalry; ACW:NOV/92[26]386, B&G:APR/92[8]481, CWTI:JUN/90[32]159

1st Reserves; B&G:APR/93[12]518, CWR:VOL1#2[7]111, CWTI:MAY/94[31]382, GETTY:10[42]224, GETTY:11[91]236

1st Rifles; see listings under **"13th RESERVES"** and **"BUCKTAILS"**

2nd Artillery (Heavy); CWTI:APR/90[24]152

2nd Cavalry; CWTI:SEP/90[26]174, GETTY:11[102]237, GETTY:12[97]249

2nd Reserves; B&G:APR/95[8]595, CWR:VOL4#4[1]177, GETTY:6[7]169, GETTY:11[91]236, GETTY:13[7]253

3rd Artillery, (Heavy); CWTI:JAN/95[42]428, GETTY:4[65]148, GETTY:13[89]260

3rd Cavalry;
ARTICLES: "FORGOTTEN VALOR: OFF THE BEATEN PATH AT ANTIETAM: WHOEVER HEARD OF A DEAD CAVALRYMAN?" B&G:OCT/95[8]611F, "GLORY ENOUGH FOR ALL': LT. WILLIAM BROOKE-RAWLE AND THE 3RD PENNSYLVANIA CAVALRY AT GETTYSBURG," GETTY:13[89]260
ADDITIONAL LISTINGS: ACW:NOV/91[30]332, ACW:JAN/95[10]503, B&G:APR/93[12]518, GETTY:4[75]149, GETTY:12[68]246, GETTY:13[1]252

3rd Infantry; B&G:OCT/95[8]611A, CWR:VOL4#4[1]177

4th Cavalry; ACW:NOV/91[30]332, ACW:NOV/92[26]386, B&G:APR/92[8]481, B&G:OCT/95[8]611F, B&G:OCT/93[12]537, GETTY:7[29]188

4th Reserves; ACW:MAR/94[27]459, B&G:OCT/95[8]611A, CWR:VOL4#4[1]177

5th Cavalry; B&G:APR/92[8]481, B&G:OCT/95[8]611F, CWM:MAY/92[34]422, *photo*, CWTI:JUN/90[46]161

5th Reserves:
BOOK REVIEW: *THE LIFE AND ANCESTRY OF JOHN THISTLEWAITE BAYNES (1833-1891)*
GENERAL LISTINGS: *Gettysburg*, GETTY:9[53]214, GETTY:10[53]225, *in book review*, CWR:VOL2#4[346]
ADDITIONAL LISTINGS: CWR:VOL1#3[20]119, CWR:VOL1#3[28]120, CWR:VOL4#4[1]177

6th Artillery (Heavy); B&G:FEB/95[38]593, B&G:JUN/95[36]603A

6th Cavalry; ACW:SEP/94[55]489, B&G:DEC/91[12]469, B&G:APR/92[8]481, CWTI:JUN/90[32]159, CWTI:JUN/90[43]160, GETTY:11[19]232

6th Reserves; B&G:APR/95[8]595, CWM:NOV/91[66]395, CWR:VOL3#2[1]153, CWR:VOL1#3[20]119, CWR:VOL4#4[1]177, GETTY:11[91]236

7th Cavalry; B&G:OCT/92[10]496, B&G:APR/92[8]481, B&G:DEC/93[30]546, CWTI:NOV/93[33]347

7th Reserves; B&G:APR/95[8]595, B&G:OCT/95[8]611A, CWM:DEC/94[74]555, CWR:VOL4#4[1]177

8th Cavalry; ACW:JAN/92[10]339, ACW:MAY/95[30]525, CWR:VOL1#1[1]102, CWR:VOL1#3[52]122, CWTI:SEP/94[18], GETTY:4[75]149

8th Reserves; ACW:JUL/92[30]369, B&G:OCT/95[8]611A, CWR:VOL4#4[1]177

9th Cavalry; B&G:OCT/92[10]496, MH:JUN/91[20]152

9th Reserves; ACW:JUL/92[30]369, ACW:JAN/93[8]392, CWR:VOL1#3[20]119, CWR:VOL4#4[1]177, GETTY:9[53]214

10th Reserves; B&G:APR/93[12]518, CWR:VOL1#3[20]119, CWR:VOL3#2[1]153, CWR:VOL4#4[1]177, GETTY:9[53]214

11th Cavalry; B&G:APR/92[8]481, CWM:MAY/92[34]422, GETTY:11[6]231

11th Infantry;
GENERAL LISTINGS: *1863 cavalry battles*, MH:OCT/92[51]162, *Five Forks*, B&G:APR/92[8]481, *Gettysburg*, GETTY:4[33]146, GETTY:9[33]211, GETTY:9[81]216, GETTY:10[7]221, GETTY:11[57]233, *in order of battle*, B&G:APR/92[8]481, *letters to the editor*, B&G:JUN/95[5]599, CWTI:JUL/92[8]269, *Manassas, First*, GETTY:10[7]221, *Manassas, Second*, B&G:AUG/92[11]493, *SIO*, B&G:OCT/95[36]614, CWTI:JUN/95[14]443
ADDITIONAL LISTINGS: ACW:JUL/92[30]369, ACW:MAR/95[42]517, B&G:FEB/95[8]590B, B&G:OCT/95[20]612, CWM:MAR/93[56]471, CWM:AUG/95[38]609, CWTI:APR/92[42]259, GETTY:13[33]255

11th Reserves; B&G:APR/93[12]518, B&G:APR/95[8]595, CWR:VOL4#4[1]177, GETTY:9[53]214, GETTY:11[91]236

12th Cavalry:
ARTICLE: "FORGOTTEN VALOR: OFF THE BEATEN PATH AT ANTIETAM: WHOEVER HEARD OF A DEAD CAVALRYMAN?" B&G:OCT/95[8]611F
ADDITIONAL LISTINGS: B&G:OCT/93[21]538, B&G:AUG/94[10]574, B&G:OCT/95[8]611F

12th Infantry:
BOOK REVIEW: *35 DAYS TO GETTYSBURG: THE CAMPAIGN DIARIES OF TWO AMERICAN ENEMIES*
ADDITIONAL LISTINGS: ACW:JUL/92[30]369, ACW:MAR/94[50]462, B&G:OCT/95[8]611A, CWNEWS:SEP/92[4], CWR:VOL3#2[1]153

12th Reserves:
GENERAL LISTINGS: *Gettysburg*, GETTY:9[53]214, *in book review*, CWNEWS:JUL/93[5], CWR:VOL2#4[346], *SIO*, B&G:AUG/93[36]533
ADDITIONAL LISTINGS: ACW:MAR/93[58], B&G:OCT/93[24], CWM:JUN/95[57]592, CWR:VOL1#3[20]119, CWR:VOL4#4[1]177

13th Reserves: also, see listings under **"42nd INTANTRY and BUCKTAIL REGIMENTS"** in the Pennsylvania Troops Section
ARTICLES: "THE BLOODY ROAD TO SPOTSYLVANIA: PENNSYLVANIA BUCKTAILS, PART TWO, CWR:VOL1#3[28]120, "LIFE ON THE SKIRMISH LINE: THROUGH THE WAR WITH THE PENNSYLVANIA BUCKTAILS, CWR:VOL1#3[20]119
GENERAL LISTINGS: *Chancellorsville*, GETTY:9[53]214, *Fredericksburg*, GETTY:9[53]214, *Gettysburg*, GETTY:6[7]169, GETTY:8[9]199, GETTY:9[53]214, GETTY:10[120]229, GETTY:11[91]236, GETTY:11[126]239, *Harrisburg, VA, Battle*

of, GETTY:9[53]214, *in book review,* CWNEWS:APR/95[33], *photo,* GETTY:9[53]214

ADDITIONAL LISTINGS: B&G:DEC/92[26], B&G:APR/93[12]518, B&G:APR/95[8]595, CWM:MAR/91[50]340, CWR:VOL1#3[v]117, CWR:VOL3#2[1]153, CWR:VOL4#4[1]177, CWTI:JUL/93[42]329, GETTY:9[53]214, GETTY:11[91]236

14th Cavalry; B&G:JUN/92[46]490, B&G:AUG/94[10]574, CWTI:MAR/89[16]101, GETTY:11[19]232

14th Infantry; B&G:AUG/92[53]495A

15th Cavalry; CWTI:APR/92[8]252, CWTI:MAY/93[38]321

16th Cavalry; ACW:NOV/91[30]332, B&G:OCT/93[12]537, CWTI:JUL/94[10]389

16th Cavalry; ACW:MAY/94[35]469, ACW:MAY/95[30]525, B&G:FEB/95[8]590A, CWM:NOV/91[35]392, CWTI:JUN/90[32]159, GETTY:4[113]153, GETTY:11[19]232

17th Infantry; ACW:MAY/94[35]469, B&G:APR/91[8]445

18th Cavalry; ACW:MAY/91[38]305, ACW:JUL/92[41]370, GETTY:9[109]218

19th Cavalry; ACW:NOV/95[48]557

19th Infantry:

BOOK REVIEW: *'THIS WAR IS AN AWFUL THING...': CIVIL WAR LETTERS OF THE NATIONAL GUARDS, THE 19TH AND 90TH PENNSYLVANIA VOLUNTEERS*

ADDITIONAL LISTING: GETTY:5[13]157

20th Cavalry; B&G:APR/92[8]481

21st Infantry; GETTY:11[91]236

22nd Cavalry; B&G:AUG/94[10]574

23rd Infantry:

GENERAL LISTINGS: *Gettysburg,* GETTY:10[112]228, *in book review,* CWNEWS:AUG/92[4]

ADDITIONAL LISTINGS: CWTI:MAY/89[36]118, CWTI:JUN/95[90]451

25th Infantry; CWR:VOL3#3[1]157

26th Emergency Militia; CWM:NOV/91[35]392, GETTY:5[4]156

26th Infantry:

GENERAL LISTINGS: *Gettysburg,* GETTY:12[7]241, *in book review,* CWNEWS:JUN/95[33]

ADDITIONAL LISTING: CWM:MAY/92[20]420

27th Infantry; ACW:JUL/94[18]476, CWR:VOL1#3[28]120, CWR:VOL3#3[59]159, CWTI:SEP/94[34]402, GETTY:8[17]200

28th Infantry:

GENERAL LISTINGS: *Gettysburg,* GETTY:6[7]169, GETTY:9[81]216, GETTY:10[120]229, *in book review,* CWNEWS:APR/94[5]

ADDITIONAL LISTINGS: ACW:JUL/93[8]420, ACW:MAR/94[50]462, ACW:MAY/95[30]525, CWR:VOL3#2[70]155, CWTI:SEPT/89[30]129, CWTI:JAN/93[49]303, CWTI:AUG/95[24]455

29th Infantry:

GENERAL LISTINGS: *Gettysburg,* GETTY:7[83]192, GETTY:9[53]214, GETTY:10[120]229

ADDITIONAL LISTINGS: CWR:VOL3#2[102]156, CWR:VOL3#2[70]155, CWTI:SEPT/89[30]129

30th Reserves; B&G:DEC/92[26]

34th Militia; ACW:SEP/93[22]432

42nd Infantry: also, see listings under **"13th RESERVES and BUCKTAIL REGIMENTS"** in the Pennsylvania Troops Section

ARTICLE: "LIFE ON THE SKIRMISH LINE: THROUGH THE WAR WITH THE PENNSYLVANIA BUCKTAILS," CWR:VOL1#3[20]119,

GENERAL LISTINGS: *Gettysburg,* GETTY:8[9]199, GETTY:9[53]214, *in book review,* B&G:DEC/92[26]

ADDITIONAL LISTING: CWR:VOL1#3[v]117

45th Infantry; B&G:AUG/95[8]604, B&G:OCT/95[8]611A, B&G:OCT/95[36]614, CWM:MAY/92[44]423, CWR:VOL2#2[141]137

46th Infantry; ACW:JUL/92[30]369, CWM:AUG/95[5]602 GETTY:7[83]192

47th Infantry; CWM:NOV/91[80]396

48th Infantry:

ARTICLE: "BURY THEM IF THEY WON'T MOVE (EXCERPT FROM *MOTHER, MAY YOU NEVER SEE THE SIGHTS I HAVE SEEN,*) CWTI:APR/90[24]152

GENERAL LISTINGS: *general history,* AHI:MAY/71[3]133A, *in book review,* CWNEWS:SEP/91[4], CWNEWS:NOV/92[4], *list of monuments,* B&G:OCT/95[8]611A, *Petersburg,* MH:APR/95[46]183

ADDITIONAL LISTINGS: ACW:NOV/92[74]390, ACW:MAY/95[18]524, CWM:MAR/91[56]341, CWM:MAY/92[44]423, CWM:JUL/93[46]489, CWM:OCT/94[55]543, CWTI:JAN/95[34]427

49th Infantry; ACW:MAR/91[14]293, ACW:MAR/91[47]297, ACW:MAR/92[30]352, ACW:SEP/92[30]378, CWM:NOV/91[35]392, CWM:OCT/94[37]539, CWM:JUN/95[63]594, CWR:VOL3#3[1]157, CWTI:SEP/93[43]338

50th Infantry; ACW:JAN/95[54]508, ACW:MAY/95[18]524, B&G:OCT/95[8]611A, CWTI:JAN/94[46]364

51st Infantry:

BOOK REVIEW: *HISTORY OF THE 51ST REGIMENT OF P.V. AND V.V.*

ADDITIONAL LISTINGS: ACW:JAN/95[54]508, B&G:OCT/95[8]611A, CWM:MAY/92[44]423, CWNEWS:NOV/95[29], CWTI:SEP/90[26]174, CWTI:FEB/92[36]249

53rd Infantry:

ARTICLE: "FIFTY-THIRD! THE 53RD PENNSYLVANIA VOLUNTEER INFANTRY IN THE GETTYSBURG CAMPAIGN," GETTY:11[80]235

ADDITIONAL LISTINGS: GETTY:8[53]203, GETTY:12[24]242

54th Infantry; CWTI:JAN/94[8]356

55th Infantry; B&G:OCT/94[42]583, CWM:MAR/91[50]340, CWTI:FEB/92[58]251, GETTY:8[31]201

56th Infantry:

GENERAL LISTINGS: *Gettysburg,* GETTY:4[115]152, GETTY:5[4]156, GETTY:6[13]170, GETTY:9[33]211, *in order of battle,* B&G:APR/92[8]481, *Manassas, Second,* B&G:AUG/92[11]493

ADDITIONAL LISTINGS: ACW:SEP/95[38]546, B&G:JUN/95[8]600, CWM:JAN/93[16]457

56th Infantry; CWM:MAR/91[17]335

61st Infantry; ACW:SEP/92[30]378

62nd Infantry; CWTI:JUN/90[28]158, GETTY:8[53]203, GETTY:11[91]236

63rd Infantry; ACW:JUL/93[16]422, ACW:MAY/95[54]528, B&G:JUN/95[8]600, CWM:JUN/95[55]591, CWM:JUN/95[76]598, CWNEWS:APR/94[5], CWR:VOL3#4[1]161, CWTI:JUL/93[14]324, GETTY:7[51]190

67th Infantry; B&G:OCT/95[36]614, CWTI:MAY/93[8]315

69th Infantry:

ARTICLE: "IT STRUCK HORROR TO US ALL," GETTY:4[89]150

GENERAL LISTINGS: *Gettysburg,* GETTY:5[107]164, GETTY:7[97]193, GETTY:10[53]225, MH:DEC/91[54]155, *in list,* CWTI:JUL/93[34]327

ADDITIONAL LISTINGS: ACW:MAY/92[8]357, AHI:FEB/75[35]158, CWM:MAR/91[50]340, CWTI:JUL/93[29]326, GETTY:13[7]253, GETTY:13[43]256, GETTY:13[50]257

71st Infantry:

GENERAL LISTINGS: *Gettysburg*, GETTY:4[89]150, GETTY:5[107]164, GETTY:7[97]193, GETTY:9[61]215, GETTY:10[36]223, *in list*, CWTI:JUL/93[34]327

ADDITIONAL LISTINGS: ACW:MAY/92[8]357, ACW:NOV/92[42]388, ACW:MAR/93[10]402, ACW:JUL/95[50]538, AHI:FEB/82[36]225, CWR:VOL3#1[31]150, CWTI:MAY/89[14]114, CWTI:JUL/93[29]326, CWTI:JUL/94[20]390, GETTY:13[7]253, GETTY:13[50]257

72nd Infantry:

ARTICLE: "THE 72ND PENNSYLVANIA FOUGHT TWO BATTLES AT GETTYSBURG—A QUARTER CENTURY APART," ACW:MAY/92[8]357

GENERAL LISTINGS: *Gettysburg*, GETTY:4[89]150, GETTY:4[113]153, GETTY:5[89]162, GETTY:5[107]164, GETTY:7[97]193, GETTY:10[53]225, *in list*, CWTI:JUL/93[34]327, *photo of monument*, GETTY:7[97]193

ADDITIONAL LISTINGS: CWTI:JUL/93[29]326, GETTY:13[7]253

73rd Infantry; ACW:JUL/94[18]476, CWR:VOL3#3[59]159, CWTI:SEP/94[34]402, GETTY:8[17]200

74th Infantry; B&G:FEB/95[8]590A, GETTY:4[49]147, MH:OCT/93[20]172

75th Infantry; GETTY:10[53]225

76th Infantry; ACW:SEP/91[30]322, CWTI:MAR/94[38]372

77th Infantry; AHI:NOV/85[38]254, B&G:OCT/94[42]583, CWR:VOL1#4[42]126

78th Infantry; ACW:NOV/95[66]559, CWM:MAR/91[50]340, CWM:DEC/95[26]626

81st Infantry; ACW:SEP/93[22]432, CWR:VOL2#3[236]143, CWTI:JUL/93[29]326, CWTI:AUG/95[24]455, GETTY:8[53]203

82nd Infantry; CWTI:MAY/89[36]118

83rd Infantry:

ARTICLE: "VALLEY OF THE SHADOW OF DEATH: COL. STRONG VINCENT AND THE EIGHTY-THIRD PENNSYLVANIA INFANTRY AT LITTLE ROUND TOP," GETTY:7[41]189

GENERAL LISTINGS: *Gettysburg*, GETTY:6[33]172, GETTY:6[43]173, GETTY:8[31]201, *in book review*, AHI:AUG/78[49], CWR:VOL2#2[169], CWR:VOL2#3[256], *in order of battle*, B&G:APR/92[8]481, *letters to the editor*, B&G:JUN/95[5]599, *Manassas, Second*, B&G:AUG/92[11]493

ADDITIONAL LISTINGS: ACW:JAN/92[38]343, B&G:APR/91[8]445, B&G:APR/93[12]518, B&G:OCT/93[12]537, B&G:APR/95[8]595, CWM:DEC/94[26]548, CWTI:FEB/92[58]251, GETTY:13[7]253

84th Infantry; CWM:SEP/93[18]494, CWNEWS:JUN/95[33], GETTY:12[7]241

85th Infantry; ACW:JUL/94[42]479

87th Infantry; ACW:NOV/93[50]444, B&G:DEC/92[8]503, CWTI:JAN/93[40]301, GETTY:9[122]220

88th Infantry:

GENERAL LISTINGS: *Andersonville*, B&G:DEC/92[32]506, *Gettysburg*, GETTY:4[33]146, GETTY:5[13]157, GETTY:5[128]167, GETTY:10[7]221, GETTY:11[126]239, GETTY:12[111]250, GETTY:12[123]251, *in order of battle*, B&G:APR/92[8]481, *letters to the editor*, B&G:AUG/95[36]607, *Manassas, Second*, B&G:AUG/92[11]493, GETTY:10[7]221, *SIO*, B&G:OCT/95[36]614

ADDITIONAL LISTINGS: ACW:MAR/95[42]517, B&G:AUG/92[53]496A, B&G:DEC/92[32]506, B&G:FEB/95[8]590B, CWM:JAN/92[16]401, GETTY:13[33]255

90th Infantry:

BOOK REVIEW: *"THIS WAR IS AN AWFUL THING...": CIVIL WAR LETTERS OF THE NATIONAL GUARDS, THE 19TH AND 90TH PENNSYLVANIA VOLUNTEERS*

GENERAL LISTINGS: *Gettysburg*, GETTY:4[33]146, GETTY:5[117]165, GETTY:10[7]221, GETTY:12[123]251, *list of monuments*, B&G:OCT/95[8]611A, B&G:OCT/95[8]611F

ADDITIONAL LISTINGS: ACW:MAR/95[42]517, B&G:FEB/95[8]590B, B&G:OCT/95[8]611F, CWTI:MAR/95[18]432, GETTY:13[33]255

91st Infantry:

GENERAL LISTINGS: *Chancellorsville*, GETTY:9[48]213, *Fredericksburg*, GETTY:9[48]213, *Gettysburg*, GETTY:8[31]201, GETTY:9[48]213, *in order of battle*, B&G:APR/92[8]481

ADDITIONAL LISTING: B&G:APR/95[8]595

93rd Infantry; B&G:APR/91[8]445, GETTY:11[91]236

95th Infantry; ACW:SEP/92[30]378, CWM:JUN/95[37]585

96th Infantry:

ARTICLES: "96TH PENNSYLVANIA VOLUNTEERS," CWR:VOL3#3[88]160, "OF BATTLEFIELDS AND BITTER FEUDS: THE 96TH PENNSYLVANIA VOLUNTEERS," CWR:VOL3#3[1]157

ADDITIONAL LISTINGS: ACW:JAN/94[39]451, B&G:APR/91[8]445, CWR:VOL3#3[1]157

97th Infantry; B&G:JUN/93[28], B&G:DEC/94[10]585, B&G:FEB/95[38]593, B&G:JUN/95[36]603A, GETTY:10[7]221

98th Infantry; GETTY:10[42]224, GETTY:11[91]236

99th Infantry; CWM:MAR/91[17]335, GETTY:8[53]203, GETTY:9[5]209

100th Infantry:

BOOK REVIEW: *CAMPAIGNING WITH THE ROUNDHEADS: THE HISTORY OF THE 100TH PENNSYLVANIA VOLUNTEER INFANTRY REGIMENT, 1861-1865 * INFANTRYMAN PETTIT: THE CIVIL WAR LETTERS OF CORPORAL FREDERICK PETTIT*

ADDITIONAL LISTINGS: ACW:JAN/95[54]508, B&G:OCT/95[8]611A, CWM:MAY/92[44]423, CWTI:APR/90[24]152, CWTI:JAN/94[46]364, CWTI:JAN/94[49]365

102nd Infantry; ACW:SEP/92[30]378, GETTY:4[24]145, GETTY:11[91]236

104th Infantry; CWM:JUN/95[47]588, CWTI:MAR/95[46]437

105th Infantry:

BOOK REVIEW: *HISTORY OF THE ONE HUNDRED AND FIFTH REGIMENT OF PENNSYLVANIA VOLUNTEERS*

ADDITIONAL LISTING: GETTY:9[5]209

106th Infantry:

GENERAL LISTINGS: *Gettysburg*, GETTY:5[89]162, GETTY:5[123]166, GETTY:6[7]169, GETTY:7[97]193, GETTY:9[61]215, GETTY:10[53]225, *in list*, CWTI:JUL/93[34]327

ADDITIONAL LISTINGS: ACW:MAY/92[8]357, ACW:MAR/94[50]462, ACW:JUL/95[50]538, GETTY:13[7]253

107th Infantry:

GENERAL LISTINGS: *Gettysburg*, GETTY:4[33]146, GETTY:9[33]211, GETTY:10[7]221, *in order of battle*, B&G:APR/92[8]481

ADDITIONAL LISTINGS: ACW:MAR/95[42]517, GETTY:13[33]255

109th Infantry; CWR:VOL3#2[70]155, CWTI:SUMMER/89[32]122, GETTY:9[53]214

110th Infantry; B&G:APR/95[8]595, GETTY:8[43]202, CWTI:MAY/93[8]315

111th Infantry:
GENERAL LISTINGS: *Gettysburg,* GETTY:7[83]192, GETTY:9[53]214, GETTY:10[120]229
ADDITIONAL LISTINGS: CWR:VOL3#2[70]155, CWR:VOL3#2[102]156, CWTI:SEPT/89[30]129

112th Infantry; B&G:AUG/92[40]495, B&G:APR/95[24]596

114th Infantry; B&G:APR/91[8]445, B&G:APR/93[12]518, CWTI:DEC/89[26]135, GETTY:5[123]166, GETTY:12[7]241

115th Infantry; B&G:OCT/94[42]583, GETTY:4[113]153, GETTY:6[59]174, GETTY:8[53]203

116th Infantry:
ARTICLE: "'THE BREATH OF HELL'S DOOR': PRIVATE WILLIAM MCCARTER AND THE IRISH BRIGADE AT FREDERICKSBURG," CWR:VOL4#4[47]179
BOOK REVIEWS: *THE CIVIL WAR NOTEBOOK OF DANIEL CHISHOLM: A CHRONICLE OF DAILY LIFE IN THE UNION ARMY 1864-1865 * THE STORY OF THE 116TH REGIMENT PENNSYLVANIA INFANTRY*
ADDITIONAL LISTINGS: ACW:MAY/94[12]466, ACW:SEP/95[54]548, CWM:MAR/91[17]335, CWM:MAR/91[50]340, CWNEWS:JAN/93[4], CWR:VOL2#2[141]137, CWTI:DEC/90[58]185, GETTY:4[113]153, GETTY:8[53]203

118th Infantry:
GENERAL LISTINGS: *Five Forks,* B&G:APR/92[8]481, *Gettysburg,* GETTY:5[47]160, GETTY:6[43]173, *in order of battle,* B&G:APR/92[8]481
ADDITIONAL LISTINGS: ACW:MAR/92[30]352, CWM:NOV/92[64]453, CWTI:JUL/93[42]329, GETTY:13[7]253

119th Infantry; ACW:MAR/92[30]352, ACW:SEP/92[30]378, CWR:VOL3#3[1]157

121st Infantry; B&G:FEB/95[8]590A, B&G:APR/92[8]481, B&G:APR/95[8]595, B&G:AUG/95[36]607, CWR:VOL4#4[1]177, GETTY:13[22]254

122nd Infantry; CWM:DEC/94[40]550, GETTY:9[5]209

124th Infantry; B&G:OCT/95[8]611A, CWTI:SEP/93[43]338

125th Infantry:
ARTICLE: "FORGOTTEN VALOR: OFF THE BEATEN PATH AT ANTIETAM: DEBACLE IN THE WEST WOODS," B&G:OCT/95[8]611A
ADDITIONAL LISTINGS: ACW:MAR/94[50]462, B&G:DEC/93[30]546, B&G:OCT/95[8]611A, B&G:OCT/95[8]611F

127th Infantry; CWR:VOL4#4[101]181

128th Infantry; ACW:JUL/92[30]369, B&G:OCT/95[8]611A, CWTI:SEP/92[82]286

129th Infantry; CWR:VOL3#3[1]157

130th Infantry; B&G:OCT/95[8]611A, GETTY:9[61]215

132nd Infantry; ACW:SEP/93[22]432, B&G:OCT/95[8]611A, B&G:OCT/95[8]611F

133rd Infantry; B&G:OCT/94[42]583

136th Infantry; ACW:MAR/95[42]517

137th Infantry; B&G:OCT/95[8]611A

138th Infantry; ACW:NOV/93[50]444, CWM:OCT/94[26]536, CWTI:SEP/92[42]283, CWTI:JAN/93[40]301, GETTY:11[119]238

139th Infantry; B&G:APR/91[8]445, GETTY:11[91]236

140th Infantry:
ARTICLE: "ON THE RAPPAHANNOCK, CHRISTMAS DAY, 1862," AHI:DEC/68[25]117
BOOK REVIEW: *INSCRIPTION AT GETTYSBURG*
GENERAL LISTINGS: *Gettysburg,* GETTY:4[113]153, GETTY:5[35]159, GETTY:8[53]203, GETTY:10[53]225

ADDITIONAL LISTINGS: B&G:APR/91[8]445, CWR:VOL2#3[236]143, CWTI:AUG/90[26]166

141st Infantry:
BOOK REVIEW: *HISTORY OF THE ONE HUNDRED FORTY-FIRST REGIMENT PENNSYLVANIA VOLUNTEERS 1862-1865*
ADDITIONAL LISTINGS: B&G:APR/93[12]518, B&G:JUN/95[36]603A

142nd Infantry; B&G:APR/92[8]481, CWR:VOL4#4[1]177, GETTY:4[24]145, GETTY:13[22]254

143rd Infantry:
GENERAL LISTINGS: *Gettysburg,* GETTY:4[24]145, GETTY:4[33]146, GETTY:12[30]243
ADDITIONAL LISTINGS: ACW:JUL/92[41]370, B&G:APR/95[8]595, B&G:JUN/95[8]600

145th Infantry:
BOOK REVIEW: *I'M SURROUNDED BY METHODISTS...: DIARY OF JOHN H.W. STUCKENBERG, CHAPLAIN OF THE 145TH PENNSYLVANIA VOLUNTEER INFANTRY*
ADDITIONAL LISTINGS: CWM:NOV/91[35]392, GETTY:8[53]203, GETTY:11[80]235, GETTY:11[102]237, GETTY:12[24]242

146th Infantry; MH:DEC/95[58]188

147th Infantry; CWTI:SUMMER/89[32]122, CWTI:SEPT/89[30]129, GETTY:9[81]216, GETTY:10[120]22

148th Infantry:
ARTICLES: "FORT CRATER REVISITED: CORRESPONDENCE FROM OUR READERS," CWR:VOL2#4[361]148, "GLORY ENOUGH: THE 148TH PENNSYLVANIA VOLUNTEERS AT FORT CRATER," CWR:VOL2#2[141]137, "REMEMBERING A DAY," CWM:OCT/95[55]622
BOOK REVIEWS: *THE STORY OF OUR REGIMENT: A HISTORY OF THE 148TH PENNSYLVANIA VOLUNTEERS*
GENERAL LISTINGS: *Gettysburg,* GETTY:6[7]169, GETTY:8[53]203, GETTY:10[53]225, GETTY:11[80]235, GETTY:11[102]237, GETTY:12[97]249
ADDITIONAL LISTINGS: ACW:MAY/95[30]525, B&G:APR/91[8]445, CWM:NOV/91[80]396, CWR:VOL2#4[361]148

149th Infantry:
ARTICLE: "CAPT. JAMES GLENN'S SWORD AND PVT. J. MARSHALL HILL'S ENFIELD IN THE FIGHT FOR THE LUTHERAN SEMINARY," GETTY:8[9]199
BOOK REVIEWS: *THE 149TH PENNSYLVANIA VOLUNTEER INFANTRY UNIT IN THE CIVIL WAR*
GENERAL LISTINGS: *Gettysburg,* GETTY:4[7]142, GETTY:4[24]145, GETTY:4[33]146, GETTY:8[9]199, GETTY:9[53]214, GETTY:9[98]217
ADDITIONAL LISTINGS: B&G:APR/95[8]595, GETTY:13[22]254

150th Infantry:
GENERAL LISTINGS: *Gettysburg,* GETTY:10[53]225, GETTY:4[24]145, GETTY:4[33]146, GETTY:4[113]153, GETTY:5[117]165, GETTY:5[123]166, GETTY:6[59]174, GETTY:8[9]199, GETTY:9[53]214, *in book review,* CWR:VOL3#2[105]
ADDITIONAL LISTINGS: B&G:APR/91[8]445, CWR:VOL1#3[52]122, CWTI:SEP/90[26]174, GETTY:13[7]253, GETTY:13[22]254

151st Infantry; CWTI:SEP/90[26]174, CWTI:JUL/93[34]327, GETTY:5[79]161, GETTY:13[22]254

153rd Infantry; GETTY:12[30]243, GETTY:13[7]253

155th Infantry:
GENERAL LISTINGS: *Five Forks,* B&G:APR/92[8]481, *Gettysburg,* GETTY:9[48]213, *in order of battle,* B&G:APR/92[8]481
ADDITIONAL LISTINGS: B&G:APR/95[8]595, GETTY:13[7]253

157th Infantry; AHI:FEB/75[35]158, B&G:APR/92[8]481

167th Infantry; GETTY:11[6]231

176th Infantry; ACW:NOV/91[16]330
178th Infantry; ACW:NOV/91[16]330
190th Infantry; B&G:APR/92[8]481, CWR:VOL1#3[28]120
191st Infantry; B&G:APR/92[8]481
198th Infantry; ACW:MAR/93[10]402, B&G:APR/92[8]481,
  CWM:JUL/92[8]427, CWR:VOL1#1[35]104
200th Infantry; ACW:NOV/92[74]390
202nd Infantry:
BOOK REVIEW: *CIVIL WAR SKETCHBOOK & DIARY*
ADDITIONAL LISTING: ACW:SEP/93[22]432
203rd Infantry; B&G:DEC/94[10]585
209th Infantry; CWTI:AUG/90[64]170
210th Infantry; B&G:APR/92[8]481
212th Infantry; B&G:AUG/93[36]533
Artillery, Miscellaneous Listings:
Independent Battery; ACW:JUL/92[30]369, ACW:MAY/95[30]525,
  CWR:VOL3#2[70]155, GETTY:9[33]211
Pennsylvania Light Artillery; ACW:MAY/95[30]525,
  ACW:MAY/95[62], B&G:FEB/95[8]590C, B&G:AUG/95[8]604,
  GETTY:5[47]160, GETTY:8[53]203, GETTY:9[41]212
Bucktail Regiments: listings not related to the 13th Reserves
  or the 42nd Infantry
ARTICLES: "THE BLOODY ROAD TO SPOTSYLVANIA:
  PENNSYLVANIA BUCKTAILS, PART TWO,"
  CWR:VOL1#3[28]120, "'DEAR MOTHER, SINCE LAST I
  WROTE TO YOU WE HAVE MADE THE FUR FLY...',"
  CWR:VOL1#3[46]121, "LIFE ON THE SKIRMISH LINE:
  THROUGH THE WAR WITH THE PENNSYLVANIA
  BUCKTAILS," CWR:VOL1#3[20]119
GENERAL LISTINGS: *Gettysburg,* GETTY:4[24]145,
  GETTY:4[33]146, GETTY:8[9]199, GETTY:9[53]214, *in book
  review,* CWM:OCT/95[10], CWNEWS:APR/95[33], *Manassas,
  Second,* AHI:DEC/66[30]105
ADDITIONAL LISTINGS: ACW:JAN/92[8]338, ACW:MAR/94[27]459,
  B&G:APR/95[8]595, CWM:FEB/95[30]561,
  CWR:VOL1#3[v]117, CWR:VOL3#2[1]153,
  CWR:VOL4#4[1]177, CWTI:JUL/93[42]329, GETTY:13[22]254
Cooper's Battery; AHI:MAY/67[22]107
Keystone Battery of Philadelphia; GETTY:5[47]160
Knap's Pennsylvania Artillery:
BOOK REVIEW: *HURRAH FOR THE ARTILLERY! KNAP'S
  INDEPENDENT BATTERY "E", PENNSYLVANIA LIGHT
  ARTILLERY*
ADDITIONAL LISTINGS: CWR:VOL3#2[70]155, CWR:VOL3#2[102]156
Pennsylvania Reserve Corps, Miscellaneous Listings:
ARTICLE: "'BUSTED UP AND GONE TO HELL': THE ASSAULT
  OF THE PENNSYLVANIA RESERVES AT
  FREDERICKSBURG," CWR:VOL4#4[1]177
BOOK REVIEWS: *HISTORY OF THE PENNSYLVANIA RESERVE
  CORPS: A COMPLETE RECORD OF THE ORGANIZATION;
  AND OF ITS DIFFERENT COMPANIES*
GENERAL LISTINGS: *Gettysburg,* GETTY:11[91]236,
  GETTY:12[85]248, *in book review,* CWR:VOL3#1[80],
  Manassas, Second, AHI:DEC/66[30]105, B&G:AUG/92[11]493
ADDITIONAL LISTINGS: ACW:MAR/95[42]517, AHI:DEC/66[30]105,
  B&G:APR/93[12]518, B&G:APR/94[10]558,
  CWTI:SEP/91[31]229, GETTY:11[91]236
Philadelphia Brigade:
ARTICLE: "THE PHILADELPHIA BRIGADE AT GETTYSBURG,"
  GETTY:7[97]193
ADDITIONAL LISTINGS: ACW:MAY/92[8]357, ACW:MAR/94[50]462,
  AHI:JUL/93[40]312, B&G:JUN/95[8]600,
  B&G:OCT/95[8]611A, CWM:JUN/95[65]595,

GETTY:4[113]153, GETTY:5[117]165, GETTY:10[7]221,
  GETTY:10[112]228, GETTY:12[1]240, GETTY:13[7]253,
  GETTY:13[43]256, GETTY:13[50]257
Zouaves d'Afrique; ACW:JUL/92[30]369

PENNSYLVANIA, STATE OF:
BOOK REVIEWS: *ADVANCE THE COLORS: PENNSYLVANIA
  CIVIL WAR BATTLE FLAGS, VOLUME II * ANOTHER
  CIVIL WAR; LABOR, CAPITAL, AND THE STATE IN THE
  ANTHRACITE REGIONS OF PENNSYLVANIA, 1840-68 *
  LEHIGH COUNTY PENNSYLVANIA IN THE CIVIL WAR,
  AN ACCOUNT*
PENNYPACKER, GALUSHA, *Gen., USA;* B&G:DEC/94[10]585
PENROSE, CHARLES B., *Captain, USA;*
  CWTI:FEB/91[28]192, CWTI:DEC/95[76]482
PENROSE, WILLIAM H., *Colonel, USA;* B&G:APR/94[10]558
PENSACOLA, FLORIDA; CWTI:MAR/89[28]103
PERCELL ARTILLERY; GETTY:10[107]227
PERIAM, JOSEPH, *Capt., 1st Minnesota Inf.;* GETTY:5[79]161
PERKINS' LANDING, LOUISIANA, SKIRMISH AT;
  CWR:VOL3#3[33]158
PERKINS, AUGUSTUS, *Captain, 50th New York Engineers;*
  ACW:NOV/95[10]553
PERKINS, CHARLES C., *Private, 1st Massachusetts Infantry;*
  B&G:APR/91[8]445, GETTY:12[7]241
PERKINS, E.P., *Sgt., 1st Minnesota Infantry;* GETTY:5[79]161
PERKINS, JOHN, *post war Mexico;* ACW:MAR/95[26]515
PERKINS, LYNVILLE J., *Major, 50th Virginia Infantry;*
  GETTY:13[108]261
PERKINS, M.B., *Captain, CSA;* B&G:OCT/94[11]580
PERKINS, SANFORD H., *Lieutenant Colonel, 14th Connecticut
  Infantry;* GETTY:9[61]215
PERRIGO, ABLE, *Pvt., 53rd Penna. Inf.;* GETTY:11[80]235
PERRIN'S BRIGADE; ARTICLE: "PERRIN'S BRIGADE ON
  JULY 1, 1863," GETTY:13[22]254
PERRIN, ABNER, *General, CSA:*
ARTICLE: "PERRIN'S BRIGADE ON JULY 1, 1863,"
  GETTY:13[22]254
GENERAL LISTINGS: *Falling Waters,* GETTY:9[109]218, *Gettysburg,*
  GETTY:5[19]158, GETTY:5[117]165, GETTY:6[7]169,
  GETTY:8[9]199, GETTY:8[67]204, GETTY:10[7]221,
  GETTY:11[57]233, *order of battle,* B&G:APR/95[8]595,
  GETTY:13[1]252, GETTY:13[33]255, *photo,* GETTY:13[22]254
PERRIN, ROBERT O., *Captain, Jeff Davis Legion;*
  GETTY:12[68]246
PERRIN, W.S., *Lt., 1st Rhode Island Artillery;* GETTY:4[89]150
PERRINE, THOMAS A., *Private, USA;* ACW:SEP/95[38]546
PERRY, E. WOOD, *artist;* CWTI:SEP/91[54]232
PERRY, EDWARD A., *General, CSA;* ACW:SEP/93[8]429,
  B&G:APR/93[12]518, B&G:APR/95[8]595, CWR:VOL2#4[346],
  CWR:VOL3#1[65]151, CWR:VOL3#2[1]153,
  CWR:VOL3#2[61]154, CWR:VOL3#4[1]161, GETTY:13[50]257
PERRY, GEORGE, *Lieutenant, 20th Massachusetts Infantry;*
  CWR:VOL3#1[31]150
PERRY, HORATIO, *civilian;* CWTI:DEC/94[34]411
PERRY, JOSEPH A., *Lt., 17th Maine Inf.;* GETTY:8[43]202
PERRY, L.J., *Lt., 1st South Carolina Inf.;* CWR:VOL3#2[70]155
PERRY, MADISON S., *Governor, Florida;* CWR:VOL3#1[65]151
PERRY, WILLIAM F., *Colonel, CSA:*
ARTICLE: "A FORGOTTEN ACCOUNT OF CHICKAMAUGA,"
  CWTI:SEP/93[53]340
ADDITIONAL LISTINGS: ACW:MAY/92[30]361, ACW:JUL/94[42]479,
  B&G:APR/95[8]595, B&G:JUN/95[8]600, CWM:DEC/94[26]548

PERRY, WILLIAM H., *Colonel, 44th Alabama Infantry;*
GETTY:13[7]253
PERRYVILLE BATTLEFIELD STATE HISTORIC SITE;
CWTI:NOV/92[18]289
PERRYVILLE, KENTUCKY, BATTLE OF:
ARTICLES: "A WADE IN THE HIGH TIDE AT PERRYVILLE,"
CWTI:NOV/92[18]289, "AT PERRYVILLE, DON CAROLS
BUELL WON A BATTLEFIELD VICTORY BUT LOST A
POLITICAL WAR," ACW:SEP/95[6]541, "MAJOR GENERAL
SIMON B. BUCKNER'S UNPUBLISHED AFTER-ACTION
REPORT ON THE BATTLE OF PERRYVILLE,"
CWR:VOL4#3[50]171
BOOK REVIEWS: *PIERCING THE HEARTLAND: A HISTORY
AND TOUR GUIDE OF THE FORT DONELSON, SHILOH,
AND PERRYVILLE CAMPAIGNS * WAR IN KENTUCKY:
FROM SHILOH TO PERRYVILLE*
GENERAL LISTINGS: *general history,* AHI:MAY/71[3]133A, *ghosts of,*
B&G:OCT/91[11]466, *in book review,* ACW:SEP/95[62],
CWR:VOL4#2[136], *letters to the editor,* CWTI:MAR/93[8]306,
ISO, B&G:FEB/91[34]442
ADDITIONAL LISTINGS: ACW:MAY/91[23]303, ACW:JUL/91[26]313,
ACW:MAR/92[14]350, ACW:NOV/94[6]492,
CWM:JUL/92[40]432, CWM:OCT/94[48]542,
CWM:APR/95[16]571, CWR:VOL2#1[36]132,
CWR:VOL2#4[313]146, CWR:VOL4#1[1]163,
CWTI:MAY/92[48]267, CWTI:NOV/93[33]347

PERSONALITY:
As listed in the Department in *America's Civil War.*
Barlow, Francis C.; ARTICLE: "FOR TWO FORMER CIVIL WAR
FOES, THE NEWS OF THEIR DEATHS WAS—LIKE MARK
TWAIN'S—GREATLY EXAGGERATED,"
ACW:MAY/93[14]413
Buchanan, James; ARTICLE: "WEAK, EAGER-TO-PLEASE
JAMES BUCHANAN WATCHED IN HORROR AS THE
AMERICAN NATION SPLIT INTO WARRING HALVES,"
ACW:MAR/93[18]403
Carroll, Anna Ella; ARTICLE: "WASHINGTON JOURNALIST
AND LOBBYIST ANNA ELLA CARROLL WAS ABRAHAM
LINCOLN'S SECRET STRATEGIC WEAPON,"
ACW:MAR/95[8]512
Clarke, Marcellus J. "Rome"; ARTICLE: "WAS ROME CLARKE
REALLY "SUE MUNDY"—OR MERELY THE VICTIM OF
AN EDITOR'S DEADLY PRANK?" ACW:JAN/94[10]448
Cobb, Williamson R.W.; ARTICLE: "ALABAMA'S WILLIAMSON
R.W. CODD MADE A DRAMATIC FINAL APPEARANCE
BEFORE THE HOUSE OF REPRESENTATIVES,"
ACW:MAY/94[8]465
Crutchfield, Stapleton; ARTICLE: "VMI'S STAPLETON
CRUTCHFIELD LOYALLY FOLLOWED STONEWALL
JACKSON FROM THE CAMPUS TO THE BATTLEFIELD,"
ACW:MAY/95[10]523
de Gournay, Paul Francois; ARTICLE: "WELL-BORN
LIEUTENANT COLONEL PAUL FRANCOIS DE GOURNAY
WAS THE SOUTH'S ADOPTED 'MARQUIS IN GRAY,'"
ACW:SEP/95[8]542
Gordon, James B.; ARTICLE: "JAMES B. GORDON OF NORTH
CAROLINA BECAME KNOWN AS THE 'MURAT OF THE
ARMY OF NORTHERN VIRGINIA,'" ACW:JAN/95[10]503
Gordon, John B.; ARTICLE: "FOR TWO FORMER CIVIL WAR
FOES, THE NEWS OF THEIR DEATHS WAS—LIKE MARK
TWAIN'S—GREATLY EXAGGERATED,"
ACW:MAY/93[14]413

Grimes, Ab; ARTICLE: "IRREPRESSIBLE AB GRIMES RISKED
EVERYTHING TO CARRY THE MAIL TO LONELY
CONFEDERATES," ACW:MAY/91[10]301
Hawley, Harriet; ARTICLE: "INDEFATIGABLE HARRIET
HAWLEY SACRIFICED HEALTH AND HOME FOR THE
SOLDIERS SHE CALLED 'HER BOYS'," ACW:NOV/93[10]439
Henry Timrod; ARTICLE: "SOUTH CAROLINA'S HENRY
TIMROD WAS THE POET LAUREATE OF THE
CONFEDERACY'S BEGINNING AND END,"
ACW:SEP/92[10]375
Hickok, James Butler "Wild Bill"; ARTICLE: "THE CIVIL
WAR—AND CREDULOUS LISTENERS—TURNED JIM
HICKOK INTO THE FAMOUS 'WILD BILL,'"
ACW:MAR/94[8]456
Humiston, Amos, 154th New York Infantry; ARTICLE:
"THANKS TO A CHERISHED PHOTOGRAPH, 'THE
UNKNOWN SOLDIER OF GETTYSBURG' DID NOT
REMAIN UNKNOWN FOR LONG," ACW:JUL/94[18]476
Jones, John B.; ARTICLE: "HUMBLE BUT OBSERVANT WAR
DEPARTMENT CLERK J.B. JONES LEFT BEHIND AN
INVALUABLE ACCOUNT OF WARTIME RICHMOND,"
ACW:JAN/93[18]394
Lee, Edwin G., CSA; ARTICLE: "CONFEDERATE GENERAL
EDWIN LEE WAS A CREDIT TO HIS FAMOUS NAME,"
ACW:MAY/92[14]358
Lincoln, Abraham; ARTICLE: "THE FOUNDING FATHERS'
'REPUBLICAN IDEAL' NOURISHED ABRAHAM
LINCOLN'S BELIEF IN FREEDOM FOR ALL,"
ACW:NOV/94[8]493
MacArthur, Arthur; ARTICLE: "THE 24TH WISCONSIN'S
GALLANT BOY COLONEL, ARTHUR MACARTHUR,
PLANTED THE COLORS ON MISSIONARY RIDGE,"
ACW:MAR/92[14]350
Philip Kearny; ARTICLE: "HOTHEADED, FLAMBOYANT
'FIGHTING PHIL' KEARNY WAS ONE OF THE UNION'S
MOST CELEBRATED DAREDEVILS," ACW:NOV/92[18]385
Pulitzer, Joseph; ARTICLE: "HUNGARIAN IMMIGRANT
TURNED UNION SOLDIER, JOSEPH PULITZER WOULD
ONE DAY BECOME A JOURNALISTIC TITAN,"
ACW:JUL/95[8]532
Rawlins, John A.; ARTICLE: "HOMETOWN FRIEND JOHN A.
RAWLINS WAS U.S. GRANT'S 'NEAREST
INDISPENSABLE' OFFICER," ACW:NOV/95[22]554
Russell, William H.; ARTICLE: 'LONDON TIMES'
CORRESPONDENT WILLIAM HOWARD RUSSELL
TOURED A VICTORY-MADDENED SOUTH IN MID-1861,"
ACW:SEP/93[10]430
Shoup, Francis A.; ARTICLE: "INDIANA-BORN FRANCIS
ASBURY SHOUP SPENT HIS ENTIRE ADULT LIFE
DEFENDING THE SOUTH HE LOVED SO WELL,"
ACW:SEP/94[10]484

PETELER, FRANCIS, *Lieutenant Colonel, 2nd USSS;*
CWTI:JUL/93[42]329
PETER, WALTER G., *Lieutenant, CSA;* B&G:OCT/92[10]496
PETERKIN, JOSHUA; ACW:MAY/94[35]469
PETERS, GEORGE, *Doctor;* B&G:OCT/92[10]496
PETERS, PHILLIP, *Lieutenant, USA;* B&G:FEB/94[8]550
PETERS, RICHARD, *civilian;* CWM:JUN/94[50]518
PETERS, WILLIAM, *Col., 21st VA Cav.;* B&G:AUG/94[10]574
PETERS, WILLIAM H.; ACW:MAR/94[35]460
PETERSBURG ARTILLERY; ARTICLE: "THE MEN OF THE
STALWART PETERSBURG ARTILLERY SERVED FROM

THE BEGINNING OF THE WAR TO THE END,"
ACW:MAR/95[12]513

PETERSBURG NATIONAL BATTLEFIELD PARK;
ACW:NOV/92[74]390, B&G:APR/92[8]481,
CWM:JUL/91[35]369, CWR:VOL2#2[156]138,
CWTI:DEC/90[18]180, MH:JUN/92[6]158

PETERSBURG, VIRGINIA, BATTLE, CAMPAIGN AND SIEGE OF:
ARTICLES: "ACTION SOUTH OF PETERSBURG,"
CWM:FEB/95[30]561, "AND FIRE SHALL DEVOUR THEM:
THE 9TH NEW HAMPSHIRE IN THE CRATER,"
CWR:VOL2#2[118]136, "BATTLE IN DESPERATION,"
CWTI:MAR/95[33]435, "BURY THEM IF THEY WON'T
MOVE (EXCERPT FROM *MOTHER, MAY YOU NEVER SEE
THE SIGHTS I HAVE SEEN*,) CWTI:APR/90[24]152, "CIVIL
WAR'S LONGEST SIEGE," MH:APR/95[46]183, "GLORY
ENOUGH: THE 148TH PENNSYLVANIA VOLUNTEERS AT
FORT CRATER," CWR:VOL2#2[141]137, "LIKE
VICKSBURG, STRATEGIC PETERSBURG ENDURED AN
INTENSE UNION SIEGE, ONLY TO FALL IN THE END,"
ACW:NOV/92[74]390, "SIEGE CITY, USA,"
MH:JUN/92[6]158, "WILDERNESS TO PETERSBURG:
UNPUBLISHED REPORTS OF THE 11TH BATTALION,
GEORGIA LIGHT ARTILLERY," CWR:VOL3#2[61]154

BOOK REVIEWS: *THE BATTLE OF OLD MEN AND YOUNG
BOYS, JUNE 9, 1864: THE PETERSBURG CAMPAIGN *
DARK AND CRUEL WAR: THE DECISIVE MONTHS OF
THE CIVIL WAR, SEPTEMBER-DECEMBER 1864 * THE
LAST CITADEL: PETERSBURG VIRGINIA, JUNE
1864—APRIL 1865 * THE PETERSBURG CAMPAIGN JUNE
1864-APRIL 1865 * THE PETERSBURG CAMPAIGN: THE
BATTLE OF OLD MEN AND YOUNG BOYS, JUNE 9, 1864 *
THE PETERSBURG CAMPAIGN: THE BATTLE OF THE
CRATER: 'THE HORRID PIT', JUNE 25 - AUGUST 6, 1864 *
THE PETERSBURG CAMPAIGN: THE DESTRUCTION OF
THE WELDON RAILROAD (DEEP BOTTOM, GLOBE
TAVERN, AND REAMS STATION, AUGUST 14-25, 1864 *
RICHMOND REDEEMED: THE SIEGE AT PETERSBURG*

GENERAL LISTINGS: *Fort Gregg;* CWTI:AUG/90[26]166, *Fort
Sedgwick;* CWTI:AUG/90[26]166, *general history,*
AHI:MAY/71[3]133A, *in book review,* CWR:VOL1#2[78],
CWR:VOL2#2[169], CWR:VOL2#4[346]

ADDITIONAL LISTINGS, ACW: ACW:JAN/92[16]340,
ACW:MAY/93[14]413, ACW:MAR/95[50]518,
ACW:MAY/95[18]524, ACW:SEP/95[30]545,
ACW:SEP/95[74]550

ADDITIONAL LISTINGS, AHI: AHI:SEP/87[40]263

ADDITIONAL LISTINGS, B&G: B&G:APR/92[8]481,
B&G:FEB/93[40]514

ADDITIONAL LISTINGS, CWM: CWM:MAY/92[34]422,
CWM:MAR/93[24]467, CWM:SEP/93[24]495,
CWM:AUG/94[30]527, CWM:OCT/94[17]534,
CWM:OCT/94[26]536, CWM:OCT/94[34]538,
CWM:OCT/95[40]619

ADDITIONAL LISTINGS, CWR: CWR:VOL1#1[35]104,
CWR:VOL1#3[52]122, CWR:VOL2#4[269]145,
CWR:VOL3#1[65]151, CWR:VOL3#3[1]157,
CWR:VOL3#4[1]161

ADDITIONAL LISTINGS, CWTI: CWTI:SEPT/89[24]128,
CWTI:FEB/90[46]146, CWTI:FEB/90[54]147,
CWTI:AUG/90[26]166, CWTI:FEB/91[36]193,
CWTI:FEB/91[45]194, CWTI:FEB/92[42]250,

CWTI:SEP/92[42]283, CWTI:JAN/95[34]427,
CWTI:JAN/95[48]429, CWTI:DEC/95[76]482

PETICOLAS, A.B., *Private, CSA;*
BOOK REVIEW: *REBELS ON THE RIO GRANDE: THE CIVIL
WAR JOURNAL OF A.B. PETICOLAS*
ADDITIONAL LISTING: B&G:JUN/94[8]568

PETRIE, PETER B., *Captain, 2nd Maryland Potomac Home
Brigade;* B&G:AUG/94[10]574

PETTES, WILLIAM H., *Lieutenant Colonel, 50th New York
Engineers;* ACW:NOV/95[10]553

PETTIGREW, JAMES J., *General, CSA:*
ARTICLE: "THE RETREAT FROM GETTYSBURG,"
CWM:AUG/94[26]525

BOOK REVIEWS: *CAROLINA CAVALIER: THE LIFE AND MIND
OF JAMES JOHNSTON PETTIGREW*

GENERAL LISTINGS: *Falling Waters,* GETTY:9[109]218, *Gettysburg,*
GETTY:4[49]147, GETTY:5[4]156, GETTY:5[19]158,
GETTY:5[79]161, GETTY:5[103]163, GETTY:5[107]164,
GETTY:6[13]170, GETTY:7[97]193, GETTY:7[124]196,
GETTY:8[67]204, GETTY:8[95]205, GETTY:9[61]215,
GETTY:9[98]217, GETTY:10[42]224, GETTY:10[102]226,
GETTY:11[6]231, GETTY:11[19]232, GETTY:12[61]245,
MH:DEC/91[54]155, *in list,* CWTI:JUL/93[34]327, *letters to the
editor,* CWTI:DEC/94[12]408, *photos,* CWM:AUG/94[26]525,
GETTY:11[19]232, GETTY:13[75]259

ADDITIONAL LISTINGS: ACW:MAR/92[10]349, ACW:JUL/93[50]426,
B&G:FEB/95[8]590A, CWM:JAN/93[8]456,
CWR:VOL1#1[26]103, CWR:VOL1#3[52]122,
CWR:VOL2#4[269]145, CWTI:SEPT/89[46]132,
CWTI:JUL/93[29]326, CWTI:JUL/94[44]394,
CWTI:SEP/94[26]400, GETTY:13[7]253, GETTY:13[64]258,
GETTY:13[75]259

PETTINGILL, C.S., ACW:MAR/92[8]348

PETTIS, GEORGE, *Lieutenant, 1st California Cavalry;*
ACW:SEP/95[10]543

PETTIT, FRED, *Private, USA;* CWTI:JAN/95[34]427

PETTIT, FREDERICK, *Corporal, 100th Pennsylvania Infantry;*
BOOK REVIEW: *INFANTRYMAN PETTIT: THE CIVIL WAR
LETTERS OF CORPORAL FREDERICK PETTIT,*
CWNEWS:MAY/92[4]

PETTIT, IRA, *Pvt., 11th U.S. Infantry;* CWTI:NOV/92[49]292

PETTIT, MARVIN D., *Lieutenant, 111th Pennsylvania
Infantry;* CWR:VOL3#2[70]155

PETTIT, RUFUS D., *Captain, USA;* CWTI:AUG/95[24]455

PETTUS FLYING ARTILLERY; B&G:FEB/94[8]550,
B&G:FEB/94[57]555

PETTUS, ALFRED, *Colonel, CSA;* CWTI:SEPT/89[30]129

PETTUS, EDMUND W., *General, CSA;* B&G:DEC/93[12]545,
B&G:FEB/94[8]550, B&G:DEC/95[9]615,
CWR:VOL1#4[64]127, CWR:VOL2#1[19]131,
CWTI:SEPT/89[30]129

PETTUS, JOHN J., *Governor, Mississippi;*
B&G:JUN/93[12]524, GETTY:7[77]191, GETTY:9[98]217,
GETTY:12[68]246

PETTY, ELIJAH P., *Captain, 17th Texas Infantry:*
BOOK REVIEW: *JOURNEY TO PLEASANT HILL: THE CIVIL
WAR LETTERS OF CAPTAIN ELIJAH P. PETTY,
WALKER'S TEXAS DIVISION C.S.A.*
ADDITIONAL LISTING: CWR:VOL2#3[212]142

PEYTON, BALIE, *Lt., 20th Tennessee Inf.;* B&G:FEB/93[12]511

PEYTON, CHARLES S., *Major, 19th Virginia Infantry;*
CWTI:JUL/94[44]394, GETTY:5[107]164, GETTY:5[117]165

PFIEFF, LOUIS, *Lt., 3rd Illinois Inf.;* CWTI:MAR/95[46]437

PHELAN, JOHN A., *Private, 13th U.S. Regulars;*
  CWR:VOL2#1[1]130
PHELPS, DEWARD, *Surgeon, USA;* CWM:APR/94[8]502
PHELPS, J.W., *civilian;* GETTY:8[17]200
PHELPS, JOHN, *Congressman, Missouri;* ACW:NOV/93[26]441
PHELPS, SETH L., *Commander, USN;* B&G:FEB/92[10]474,
  CWR:VOL4#2[26]166
PHELPS, WALTER, *Colonel, USA;* ACW:JUL/92[30]369
PHILADELPHIA BRIGADE; see listing under
  "PENNSYLVANIA TROOPS"
PHILADELPHIA NAVAL YARD, CWTI:MAY/94[24]381
PHILADELPHIA, PENNSYLVANIA:
ARTICLES: "THE CITY OF BROTHERLY HOSPITALITY,"
  CWTI:MAY/94[24]381, "G.A.R. MUSEUM IS A TREASURY
  OF WAR RELICS," CWTI:SEP/90[22]173
PHILBROOK, ALVAH, *Major, 24th Wisconsin Infantry;*
  ACW:MAR/92[14]350
PHILIP, J.V.N., *Lieutenant, USN;* B&G:JUN/92[40]489
PHILIPPI, WEST VIRGINIA, BATTLE OF:
ARTICLES: "CONFUSED FIRST FIGHT," ACW:JAN/92[47]344,
  "FORGOTTEN FEDERAL SUCCESS," ACW:JAN/92[50]345
ADDITIONAL LISTINGS: AHI:MAY/71[3]133A, B&G:AUG/93[10]529,
  B&G:AUG/93[55]535
PHILIPS, MARTIN, *Pvt., 19th Indiana Inf.,* GETTY:11[57]233
PHILLIP'S (GEORGIA) LEGION; ACW:JUL/92[41]370,
  CWTI:APR/89[50]112
PHILLIP'S (SOUTH CAROLINA) LEGION; GETTY:12[68]246
PHILLIPS, ALEX, *Captain, CSA;* CWTI:SEP/94[26]400
PHILLIPS, CHARLES, *Private, 22nd Massachusetts Infantry;*
  GETTY:8[53]203
PHILLIPS, CHARLES A., *Major, 5th Massachusetts Artillery;*
  CWR:VOL3#2[1]153, GETTY:5[47]160, GETTY:8[53]203
PHILLIPS, DINWIDDIE B., *Surgeon, CSN;*
  AHI:OCT/75[30]162, AHI:NOV/75[38]163
PHILLIPS, EDWIN D.; B&G:DEC/91[12]469
PHILLIPS, GEORGE, *Captain, USN;* CWTI:AUG/95[40]458
PHILLIPS, HENRY; *Col., 70th OH Inf.;* CWTI:DEC/94[62]415
PHILLIPS, JAMES, *Lieutenant, CSA;* CWR:VOL2#3[236]143
PHILLIPS, JAMES, *Pvt., 8th LA Inf.* CWTI:FEB/91[12]189
PHILLIPS, JAMES E., *Sergeant, 12th Virginia Infantry;*
  ARTICLE: "FINAL MARCH TO APPOMATTOX: THE 12TH
  VIRGINIA INFANTRY APRIL 2-12, AN EYEWITNESS
  ACCOUNT," CWR:VOL2#3[236]143
PHILLIPS, JOHN F., *Colonel, USA;* B&G:JUN/91[10]452
PHILLIPS, PHILIP, *attorney;* CWTI:MAY/92[38]265
PHILLIPS, PHILO, *Captain, 126th New York Infantry;*
  CWR:VOL1#4[7]125
PHILLIPS, RODNEY E., *Private, 8th Louisiana Infantry;*
  CWTI:FEB/91[12]189
PHILLIPS, WENDELL; AHI:OCT/68[4]116,
  CWNEWS:JUN/93[5], CWTI:DEC/89[42]137,
  CWTI:AUG/90[50]168, CWTI:MAY/94[46]385
PHILLIPS, WILLIAM, *Colonel, Georgia Militia;*
  CWTI:SEP/91[23]228, CWTI:JAN/93[10]297,
  CWTI:DEC/94[49]413
PHILLIPS, WILLIAM A., *Colonel, First Indian Home Guard;*
  ACW:JAN/91[30]286, CWM:SEP/92[38]443

PHOTOGRAPHERS:

Barnard, George N.; BOOK REVIEW: GEORGE N. BARNARD:
  PHOTOGRAPHER OF SHERMAN'S CAMPAIGNS,
  B&G:APR/91[28]

Brady, Mathew; BOOK REVIEW: *MATHEW BRADY: HIS LIFE
  AND PHOTOGRAPHS*
Gardner, Alexander; BOOK REVIEW: *WITNESS TO AN
  ERA:THE LIFE AND PHOTOGRAPHS OF ALEXANDER
  GARDNER*
Tyson, Charles J.; CWTI:DEC/89[16]134

PHOTOGRAPHS: BOOK REVIEWS: *THE BLUE AND THE GRAY
  * CATALOGUE OF CIVIL WAR PHOTOGRAPHERS *
  HOOD'S TEXAS BRIGADE SKETCHBOOK * MY
  BROTHER'S FACE: PORTRAITS OF THE CIVIL WAR IN
  PHOTOGRAPHS, DIARIES, AND LETTERS * STILL MORE
  CONFEDERATE FACES*
PHOTOGRAPHY:
ARTICLES: "THE BLUNT COLLECTION OF COLD HARBOR
  PHOTOGRAPHS," B&G:APR/94[47]562A, "CATALOGUE OF
  CIVIL WAR PHOTOGRAPHERS"; CWTI:DEC/89[26]135,
  "ENDURING IMAGES OF A NATION DIVIDED: THE
  GREAT PRINTMAKERS OF THE CIVIL WAR,"
  CWM:NOV/92[24]448, "FOCUS: CIVIL WAR
  PHOTOGRAPHY," AHI:MAY/79[35]187, AHI:JUN/79[22]189,
  AHI:JUL/79[50]190, AHI:AUG/79[32]191, AHI:OCT/79[18]193,
  AHI:NOV/79[10]195, AHI:JAN/80[29]198, AHI:APR/80[39]201,
  AHI:MAY/80[29]202,
  AHI:JUN/80[49]203, AHI:JUL/80[29]203A,
  AHI:AUG/80[26]206, AHI:OCT/80[45]207,
  AHI:NOV/80[17]210, AHI:JAN/81[27]215, AHI:FEB/81[21]216
  "LITTLE WINDOWS ON HISTORY," CWTI:DEC/89[26]135,
  "MATHEW B. BRADY: A MAN WITH A VISION,"
  B&G:FEB/94[24]551, "PHOTOGRAPHY: MIRROR OF THE
  PAST," AHI:SEP/89[20]286, "TREASURE IN THE ATTIC,"
  CWTI:MAY/91[34]209
BOOK REVIEWS: *THE AMERICAN DAGUERREOTYPE, * THE
  CIVIL WAR—AN AERIAL PORTRAIT * CONFEDERATE
  FACES * DISTANT THUNDER: A PHOTOGRAPHIC ESSAY
  ON THE AMERICAN CIVIL WAR * GEORGE N. BARNARD:
  PHOTOGRAPHER OF SHERMAN'S CAMPAIGNS * THE
  IMAGE OF WAR, THE PICTORIAL REPORTING OF THE
  AMERICAN CIVIL WAR * IMAGES OF THE CIVIL WAR *
  INTRODUCTION TO CIVIL WAR PHOTOGRAPHY *
  LANDSCAPES OF THE CIVIL WAR: NEWLY DISCOVERED
  PHOTOGRAPHS FROM THE MEDFORD HISTORICAL
  SOCIETY * LESLIE'S ILLUSTRATED CIVIL WAR*
BOOK REVIEWS, continued: *MATHEW BRADY: HIS LIFE AND
  PHOTOGRAPHS * MINE EYES HAVE SEEN THE GLORY:
  THE CIVIL WAR IN ART * MORE CONFEDERATE FACES *
  MY BROTHER'S FACE: PORTRAITS OF THE CIVIL WAR
  IN PHOTOGRAPHS, DIARIES AND LETTERS *
  PORTRAITS OF CONFLICT: A PHOTOGRAPHIC HISTORY
  OF LOUISIANA IN THE CIVIL WAR *TOUCHED BY FIRE:
  A PHOTOGRAPHIC PORTRAIT OF THE CIVIL WAR,
  VOLUME I * TRACES OF WAR: PHOTOGRAPHY, AND
  THE CRISIS OF THE UNION * WITNESS TO AN ERA:
  THE LIFE AND PHOTOGRAPHY OF ALEXANDER
  GARDNER; THE CIVIL WAR, LINCOLN, AND THE WEST*
Ambrotype; CWTI:DEC/89[26]135
Cartes de visite:
ARTICLE: "PHOTOGRAPHY: MIRROR OF THE PAST,"
  AHI:SEP/89[20]286
ADDITIONAL LISTINGS: B&G:FEB/93[24]551, CWTI:DEC/89[26]135
Daguerrotype:
ARTICLE: "PHOTOGRAPHY: MIRROR OF THE PAST,"
  AHI:SEP/89[20]286

ADDITIONAL LISTING: B&G:FEB/94[24]551, CWTI:DEC/89[26]135
Michigan Photographic Historical Society;
  B&G:JUN/91[26]453
Tintype:
ARTICLE: "PHOTOGRAPHY: MIRROR OF THE PAST,"
  AHI:SEP/89[20]286

PIATT, ABRAM S.; GETTY:9[5]209
PICACHO PASS, ARIZONA, SKIRMISH AT:
ARTICLE: "WAR'S WESTERNMOST BATTLE,"
  ACW:JUL/93[27]423
ADDITIONAL LISTING: B&G:JUN/94[8]568
PICKENS, FRANCIS W., ACW:NOV/92[10]384,
  ACW:NOV/93[8]438, CWTI:MAY/92[45]266,
  CWTI:JAN/94[46]364
PICKENS, S.B., *Col., 12th Alabama Infantry;* GETTY:10[7]221
PICKERILL, WILLIAM N., *Corporal, 3rd Indiana Cavalry;*
  B&G:FEB/93[24]512
PICKERING, W.A., *Private, CSA;* CWR:VOL1#4[42]126
PICKETT'S CHARGE: (Pickett-Pettigrew-Trimble Charge)
ARTICLES: "THE DEATH AND BURIALS OF GENERAL
  RICHARD BROOKE GARNETT," GETTY:5[107]164, "'DON'T
  LET ME BLEED TO DEATH': THE WOUNDING OF MAJ.
  GEN. WINFIELD SCOTT HANCOCK," GETTY:6[87]178,
  "GENERALS AT ODDS," MH:AUG/94[46]178, "GEORGE
  PICKETT: ANOTHER LOOK," CWTI:JUL/94[44]394, "THE
  HARD-FIGHTING 56TH VIRGINIA'S FINEST HOUR CAME
  AS THE 'DEADLY DRESS PARADE' OF PICKETT'S
  CHARGE," ACW:MAR/93[10]402, "HOT SHOT, COLD
  STEEL," MH:DEC/91[54]155, "IT STRUCK HORROR TO US
  ALL," GETTY:4[89]150, "NORTH CAROLINA IN THE
  PICKETT-PETTIGREW-TRIMBLE CHARGE AT
  GETTYSBURG," GETTY:8[67]204, "OVER THE WALL,"
  GETTY:13[64]258, "PICKETT'S CHARGE BY THE
  NUMBERS," CWTI:JUL/93[34]327, "PICKETT'S CHARGE:
  THE REASON WHY," GETTY:5[103]163, "THE UNMERITED
  CENSURE OF TWO MARYLAND STAFF OFFICERS, MAJ.
  OSMUN LATROBE AND FIRST LT. W. STUART
  SYMINGTON," GETTY:13[75]259
BOOK REVIEWS: *DEATH OF A NATION * GETTYSBURG: THE
  FINAL FURY * HIGH TIDE AT GETTYSBURG * LEE AND
  LONGSTREET AT GETTYSBURG * LEE'S LIEUTENANTS
  * NOTHING BUT GLORY * PICKETT'S CHARGE *
  PICKETT'S CHARGE: EYEWITNESS ACCOUNTS * R.E.
  LEE * THEY MET AT GETTYSBURG * THE THIRD DAY AT
  GETTYSBURG & BEYOND*
GENERAL LISTINGS: *in book review,* ACW:SEP/94[66],
  ACW:MAY/95[62], CWM:MAR/92[49], CWM:AUG/94[9],
  CWM:OCT/94[8], CWM:APR/95[50], CWNEWS:NOV/91[4],
  CWNEWS:OCT/92[4], CWNEWS:SEP/95[33],
  CWR:VOL2#2[169], CWR:VOL3#2[105], CWR:VOL4#1[78],
  CWR:VOL4#3[89], CWR:VOL4#4[129], CWTI:MAR/95[14]
  letters to the editor, B&G:AUG/94[6]573, CWTI:FEB/92[8]245,
  CWTI:NOV/93[12]345, CWTI:DEC/94[12]408
ADDITIONAL LISTINGS, ACW: ACW:MAR/91[30]295,
  ACW:MAY/92[8]357, ACW:JUL/92[12]367,
  ACW:JUL/93[50]426, ACW:SEP/93[8]429, ACW:JAN/94[62],
  ACW:SEP/94[6]482, ACW:SEP/94[62]490,
  ACW:JAN/95[46]507, ACW:MAR/95[6]511,
  ACW:SEP/95[54]548
ADDITIONAL LISTINGS, AHI: AHI:MAR/84[42]238,
  AHI:SUM/88[12]273

ADDITIONAL LISTINGS, B&G: B&G:AUG/91[36]462,
  B&G:OCT/91[40]467, B&G:FEB/93[40]514,
  B&G:FEB/93[48]515, B&G:APR/94[34]561
ADDITIONAL LISTINGS, CWM: CWM:MAR/91[14]334,
  CWM:JUL/92[8]427, CWM:JAN/93[8]456,
  CWM:SEP/93[24]495, CWM:OCT/94[17]534,
  CWM:OCT/95[22]614
ADDITIONAL LISTINGS, CWR: CWR:VOL1#1[26]103,
  CWR:VOL1#3[v]117, CWR:VOL3#1[31]150
ADDITIONAL LISTINGS, CWTI: CWTI:SEP/91[31]229
ADDITIONAL LISTINGS, GETTY: GETTY:4[75]149, GETTY:4[101]151,
  GETTY:4[126]154, GETTY:5[19]158, GETTY:5[89]162,
  GETTY:5[117]165, GETTY:5[123]166, GETTY:6[7]169,
  GETTY:6[94]180, GETTY:6[99]181, GETTY:7[23]187,
  GETTY:7[97]193, GETTY:8[9]199, GETTY:8[43]202,
  GETTY:8[95]205, GETTY:8[111]206, GETTY:8[127]208,
  GETTY:9[81]216, GETTY:11[57]233, GETTY:11[102]237,
  GETTY:11[119]238, GETTY:12[61]245, GETTY:12[85]248,
  GETTY:12[97]249, GETTY:12[111]250, GETTY:13[50]257
PICKETT'S MILL, GEORGIA, BATTLE OF;
  ACW:SEP/95[38]546, ACW:NOV/95[74]560,
  CWM:JAN/91[12]326, CWM:JAN/91[72]331,
  CWTI:JUL/92[10], CWTI:MAR/95[40]436
PICKETT, CHARLES, *Major, CSA;* CWTI:JUL/94[44]394
PICKETT, EDWARD, *Colonel, 21st Tennessee Infantry;*
  CWR:VOL3#4[24]162
PICKETT, GEORGE E., *General, CSA:*
ARTICLES: "GEORGE PICKETT: ANOTHER LOOK,"
  CWTI:JUL/94[44]394, "PICKETT'S CHARGE: THE REASON
  WHY," GETTY:5[103]163
GENERAL LISTINGS: *Five Forks,* ACW:MAY/95[38]526,
  B&G:APR/92[8]481, CWTI:AUG/90[26]166, *Fredericksburg,*
  ACW:MAY/94[12]466, *general history,* AHI:MAY/71[3]133A,
  Gettysburg, AHI:SUM/88[12]273, CWM:JAN/93[8]456,
  CWTI:SEPT/89[46]132, CWTI:JUL/93[29]326,
  CWTI:SEP/94[26]400, GETTY:4[7]142, GETTY:4[113]153,
  GETTY:5[4]156, GETTY:5[35]159, GETTY:5[79]161,
  GETTY:5[107]164, GETTY:5[117]165, GETTY:6[7]169,
  GETTY:7[13]186, GETTY:7[97]193, GETTY:7[124]196,
  GETTY:8[67]204, GETTY:9[61]215, GETTY:10[102]226,
  GETTY:10[112]228, GETTY:11[71]234, GETTY:12[61]245,
  GETTY:12[111]250, MH:AUG/94[46]178
GENERAL LISTINGS, continued: *in book review,* ACW:SEP/93[54],
  ACW:JAN/95[62], CWNEWS:MAY/90[4],
  CWNEWS:APR/95[33], CWR:VOL4#1[78], CWR:VOL4#2[136],
  CWTI:MAR/95[14], *in list,* CWTI:JUL/93[34]327, *in order of
  battle,* B&G:APR/92[8]481, B&G:APR/94[10]558, *letters to the
  editor,* B&G:APR/94[6]557, CWM:MAR/91[12]333,
  CWTI:JAN/94[8]356, CWTI:DEC/94[12]408, *Mexican War,*
  MH:APR/93[39]166, *Overland Campaign,*
  B&G:APR/94[10]558, CWTI:APR/92[49]260, *Peninsula
  Campaign,* CWM:JUN/95[34]584, *Petersburg,*
  CWTI:JUL/92[29]272, MH:APR/95[46]183, *post-war,*
  ACW:JUL/95[26]535, *Sayler's Creek,* ACW:JAN/92[22]341,
  Seven Pines, CWM:JAN/93[49]303, *SIO,* B&G:APR/93[40]522,
  B&G:AUG/93[36]533, *West Point,* B&G:DEC/91[12]469,
  photos, ACW:SEP/94[62]490, B&G:APR/92[8]481,
  CWM:JAN/93[8]456, CWTI:JUL/94[44]394
ADDITIONAL LISTINGS, ACW: ACW:NOV/91[41]334,
  ACW:MAR/92[10]349, ACW:JUL/93[50]426,
  ACW:SEP/93[8]429, ACW:SEP/93[62]436,
  ACW:SEP/94[62]490, ACW:SEP/95[54]548
ADDITIONAL LISTINGS, AHI: AHI:APR/85[18]250, AHI:SEP/87[40]263

PLEASANTON, ALFRED, *General, USA:*
GENERAL LISTINGS: *1863 cavalry battles,* MH:OCT/92[51]162,
  Aldie, Virginia, B&G:OCT/93[12]537, GETTY:10[42]224,
  GETTY:11[19]232, *Brandy Station,* CWM:JAN/92[44]406,
  CWTI:JUN/90[32]159, *Falling Waters,* GETTY:9[109]218,
  general history, AHI:MAY/71[3]133A, *Gettysburg,*
  AHI:SUM/88[12]273, GETTY:4[75]149, GETTY:4[113]153,
  GETTY:6[69]176, GETTY:7[29]188, GETTY:7[41]189,
  GETTY:11[19]232, GETTY:11[71]234, GETTY:12[68]246,
  Kelly's Ford, ACW:NOV/91[30]332, *Missouri,*
  MH:DEC/95[58]188, *Price's 1864 Missouri Campaign,*
  B&G:JUN/91[10]452, *Red River,* CWTI:MAY/92[48]267,
  photos, ACW:JUL/92[41]370, B&G:JUN/91[10]452,
  B&G:OCT/93[12]537, CWTI:JUN/90[32]159,
  CWTI:SEP/90[34]176
ADDITIONAL LISTINGS: ACW:JUL/92[41]370, ACW:JUL/93[50]426,
  ACW:MAY/94[35]469, ACW:SEP/94[6]482,
  ACW:SEP/94[55]489, ACW:NOV/94[42]497,
  ACW:MAR/95[26]515, ACW:MAY/95[30]525,
  B&G:APR/91[8]445, B&G:FEB/93[24]512,
  B&G:OCT/93[21]538, B&G:FEB/95[8]590A,
  B&G:APR/95[8]595, B&G:OCT/95[8]611F,
  CWM:APR/95[32]575, CWR:VOL1#2[44]114,
  CWR:VOL3#1[31]150, CWTI:DEC/89[34]136,
  CWTI:SEP/90[34]176, CWTI:APR/92[35]257,
  CWTI:NOV/93[24]346, CWTI:MAR/94[67]377,
  GETTY:13[89]260, MH:JUN/94[8]177
PLEASANTS, HENRY, *Colonel, 48th Pennsylvania Infantry;*
  CWTI:APR/90[24]152, CWTI:JAN/95[34]427,
  MH:APR/95[46]183
PLEASANTS, REUBEN B., *Sergeant, 2nd Richmond
  Howitzers;* CWR:VOL4#4[70]180
PLUM RUN BEND, BATTLE OF; CWTI:SEP/93[18]334
PLUM, WILLIAM R., *Captain, USA;* CWTI:AUG/95[46]459,
  CWTI:DEC/95[8]474
PLUMB, ISAAC, *Capt., 61st New York Inf.;* B&G:APR/91[8]445
PLUMMER, JOSEPH B., *Captain, 1st U.S. Infantry;*
  ACW:NOV/93[26]441, CWTI:FEB/92[29]248
PLYMELL, CALVEN, *Private, Sumter Artillery;*
  CWR:VOL3#2[1]153
PLYMOUTH, NORTH CAROLINA, BATTLE OF;
  B&G:AUG/95[38]
PLYMPTON, PETER, *Captain, USA;* CWTI:OCT/95[56]471
POAGUE, WILLIAM T., *Captain, CSA;* ACW:JAN/92[8]338,
  ACW:JAN/92[10]339, ACW:MAR/94[50]462,
  B&G:APR/95[8]595, B&G:JUN/95[8]600, CWR:VOL3#2[1]153,
  CWR:VOL3#4[68], CWR:VOL4#4[70]180, GETTY:8[67]204,
  photo, CWR:VOL4#4[70]180
POCHE, FELIX, *Private, CSA;* CWR:VOL4#2[68]167
POCHE, S. ALEXANDER, *Captain, 18th Louisiana Infantry;*
  CWR:VOL4#2[1]165
POE'S CAVALRY BATTALION; BOOK REVIEW: *RANKS OF
  HONOR: A REGIMENTAL HISTORY OF THE ELEVENTH
  ARKANSAS INFANTRY REGIMENT & POE'S CAVALRY
  BATTALION C.S.A. 1861-1865*
POE, JAMES T., *Major, CSA;* CWR:VOL1#2[44]114
POE, ORLANDO M., *General, USA:*
GENERAL LISTINGS: *in book review,* CWR:VOL3#4[68], *Savannah,*
  B&G:FEB/91[8]439, *West Virginia campaign,*
  B&G:AUG/93[10]529, *photo,* AHI:JAN/67[4]106
ADDITIONAL LISTINGS: ACW:MAY/91[23]303, ACW:SEP/92[47]380,
  CWTI:SEP/91[23]228, CWTI:MAY/94[50]386

POETRY:
BOOK REVIEWS: *THE COLUMBIA BOOK OF CIVIL WAR
  POETRY: FROM WHITMAN TO WALCOTT * THE POETRY
  OF THE AMERICAN CIVIL WAR*
POEM: *"BALL'S BLUFF";* CWTI:MAY/89[14]114
POINT COUPEE (LOUISIANA) ARTILLERY;
  B&G:AUG/94[22]576
POISON SPRINGS, ARKANSAS, BATTLE OF;
  CWR:VOL1#2[44]114
POLAND, JOHN S., *Captain, USA;* ACW:NOV/94[50]498,
  GETTY:6[59]174, GETTY:9[41]212
POLIGNAC, CAMILLE A.J.M., *General, CSA;*
  ACW:MAR/93[68]409, CWR:VOL4#2[118]169
POLITICAL CARTOONS; AHI:OCT/68[4]116
POLITICS:
ARTICLES: "THE EVOLVING PRESIDENCY,"
  AHI:APR/89[13]281, "POLITICAL BUTTONS,"
  AHI:NOV/84[18]241A, "SPEAKING OF THE
  VICE-PRESIDENCY...," AHI:JAN/85[10]244, "THE WAR
  ELECTION OF 1864," AHI:OCT/68[4]116
BOOK REVIEWS: *A CRISIS OF REPUBLICANISM: AMERICAN
  POLITICS DURING THE CIVIL WAR * THE
  CONFEDERATE REPUBLIC: A REVOLUTION AGAINST
  POLITICS * COTTON & CAPITOL: BOSTON
  BUSINESSMEN AND ANTISLAVERY REFORM, 1854-1868
  * THE FIRE-EATERS * THE LINCOLN PERSUASION:
  REMAKING AMERICAN LIBERALISM * LINCOLN, THE
  SOUTH, AND SLAVERY: THE POLITICAL DIMENSION *
  NATIVISM AND SLAVERY, THE NORTHERN KNOW
  NOTHINGS & THE POLITICS OF THE 1850'S * THE
  NATURAL SUPERIORITY OF SOUTHERN POLITICANS *
  POLITICAL PARTIES AND AMERICAN POLITICAL
  DEVELOPMENT FROM THE AGE OF JACKSON TO THE
  AGE OF LINCOLN * THE POLITICS OF UNION:
  NORTHERN POLITICS DURING THE CIVIL WAR * WHY
  THE SOUTH LOST THE CIVIL WAR*
ADDITIONAL LISTINGS: CWNEWS:JUL/91[4], CWTI:JUN/90[46]161
POLK, LEONIDAS, *General, CSA:*
BOOK REVIEWS: *THE BATTLE OF BELMONT: GRANT STRIKES
  SOUTH * GENERAL LEONIDAS POLK, C.S.A., THE
  FIGHTING BISHOP*
GENERAL LISTINGS: *Atlanta Campaign,* ACW:NOV/95[74]560,
  CWM:JAN/91[12]326, CWTI:SUMMER/89[13]120, *Belmont,*
  CWR:VOL3#4[24]162, *Chattanooga,* ACW:MAY/91[23]303,
  CWTI:MAR/93[24]309, *Chickamauga,* CWTI:SEP/92[31]281,
  common soldiers, AHI:APR/68[4]115, *Davis,*
  CWTI:AUG/91[62]221, *Forts Henry and Donelson,*
  B&G:FEB/92[10]474, *in book review,* B&G:APR/91[28],
  B&G:FEB/92[26], B&G:FEB/95[26], CWM:MAR/92[49],
  CWM:APR/95[50], CWNEWS:JAN/93[4], CWR:VOL2#1[78],
  CWR:VOL2#2[169], CWTI:FEB/91[10], *letter about Bragg,*
  CWTI:APR/89[14]107, *Resaca,* CWTI:NOV/92[41]291, *Shiloh,*
  ACW:JAN/91[22]285, *Tullahoma Campaign,*
  B&G:OCT/92[10]496, *West Point,* B&G:DEC/91[12]469, *photo,*
  CWTI:APR/89[14]107
ADDITIONAL LISTINGS: ACW:JUL/92[22]368, ACW:SEP/92[38]379,
  ACW:NOV/92[35]387, ACW:MAR/93[58], ACW:JUL/94[58],
  ACW:JUL/94[66]481, ACW:SEP/95[48]547,
  AHI:NOV/73[18]151, AHI:OCT/95[24]326,
  B&G:DEC/91[34]470, B&G:FEB/93[12]511,
  B&G:OCT/94[11]580, CWM:JAN/91[72]331,
  CWM:MAY/91[10]347, CWM:APR/95[16]571,
  CWR:VOL1#3[7]118, CWR:VOL1#4[42]126,

ACW:JAN/94[30]450, "TRAVEL—PORT HUDSON,"
MH:AUG/94[82]179
GENERAL LISTINGS: *general history,* AHI:MAY/71[3]133A,
Grierson's Raid, B&G:JUN/93[12]524, *in book review,*
CWNEWS:APR/91[4], CWR:VOL1#3[94], CWR:VOL4#3[89],
letters to the editor, B&G:FEB/92[6]473, CWM:JAN/92[6]398
GENERAL LISTINGS: ACW:MAR/91[30]295, ACW:MAY/92[47]363,
ACW:SEP/92[38]379, ACW:JAN/93[51]398,
ACW:MAY/93[12]412, ACW:JUL/93[34]424,
ACW:SEP/95[8]542, CWM:SEP/93[8]493,
CWTI:FEB/90[38]145, CWTI:FEB/90[38]145,
CWTI:JAN/93[49]303, CWR:VOL1#3[7]118,
CWR:VOL2#1[36]132, CWR:VOL3#1[1]149,
CWR:VOL3#1[31]150, CWR:VOL4#2[26]166,
CWR:VOL4#2[104]168
PORT JERVIS, NEW YORK; CWTI:JAN/95[48]429
PORT REPUBLIC, VIRGINIA, BATTLE OF;
ACW:JAN/92[10]339, ACW:MAY/95[10]523,
AHI:MAY/71[3]133A, B&G:JUN/92[8]487,
CWM:JUL/92[16]428, CWM:SEP/93[24]495,
CWM:JUN/94[27]513, CWR:VOL1#4[7]125,
CWTI:JAN/95[22]423, CWTI:JUN/95[18]444
PORT ROYAL, SOUTH CAROLINA; AHI:MAY/71[3]133A,
ACW:MAR/91[14]293
PORTER, ANDREW, *General, USA;* B&G:APR/95[24]596,
CWR:VOL2#3[183]140
PORTER, ANTHONY T., *Chaplain;* ARTICLE: "MY FRIEND,
THE ENEMY," B&G:DEC/92[20]504
PORTER, DAVID D., *Admiral, USN:*
ARTICLE: "GRANT'S MISSISSIPPI GAMBLE,"
ACW:JUL/94[51]480, "THE UNION NAVAL EXPEDITION
ON THE RED RIVER, MARCH 12-MAY 22, 1864,"
CWR:VOL4#2[26]166
GENERAL LISTINGS: *Cold Harbor,* B&G:APR/94[10]558, *Fall of
Richmond,* CWTI:AUG/90[26]166, *Fort Fisher,*
ACW:NOV/93[12]440, ACW:JAN/95[38]506,
AHI:SEP/83[12]234, *Fort Jackson,* ACW:JAN/92[62]346,
general history, AHI:MAY/71[3]133A, *Grierson's Raid,*
B&G:JUN/93[12]524, *in book review,* ACW:MAR/92[54],
B&G:OCT/91[34], CWNEWS:NOV/90[4],
CWNEWS:MAY/91[4], CWNEWS:JUL/95[61],
CWR:VOL2#1[78], CWTI:AUG/91[18], CWTI:JUL/94[18],
letters to the editor, B&G:FEB/95[5]589, *New Orleans,*
CWTI:MAY/93[29]319, MH:AUG/93[47]169, *Red River,*
ACW:MAR/95[34]516, *Vicksburg,* AHI:DEC/77[46]177,
CWTI:SEPT/89[18]126, CWTI:FEB/90[38]145,
Wilmington/Fort Fisher, B&G:DEC/94[10]585 *photo, with
Meade;* CWTI:SEP/91[31]229, *photos,* ACW:JUL/94[35]478,
AHI:MAY/71[3]133A, B&G:FEB/94[8]550,
B&G:DEC/94[10]585, CWR:VOL4#2[26]166
ADDITIONAL LISTINGS: ACW:JAN/91[47]288, ACW:JUL/91[35]314,
ACW:MAY/92[16]359, ACW:MAY/93[12]412,
ACW:MAY/93[22]414, ACW:JUL/93[8]420,
ACW:JUL/93[34]424, ACW:SEP/93[10]430,
ACW:MAR/94[35]460, ACW:JUL/94[35]478,
ACW:SEP/94[74]491, ACW:SEP/95[30]545 AHI:DEC/81[8]222,
B&G:FEB/94[8]550, CWM:JUL/93[24]485,
CWM:APR/95[39]576, CWR:VOL2#1[1]130,
CWR:VOL2#1[36]132, CWR:VOL2#3[183]140,
CWR:VOL2#3[212]142, CWR:VOL3#3[33]158,
CWR:VOL4#2[1]165, CWR:VOL4#2[68]167,
CWR:VOL4#2[104]168, CWR:VOL4#2[118]169,
CWTI:FEB/91[28]192, CWTI:MAR/95[33]435,

CWTI:AUG/95[40]458, CWTI:OCT/95[32]468,
CWTI:DEC/95[67]481, CWTI:DEC/95[76]482,
MH:FEB/92[8]156, MH:JUN/93[82]167, MH:APR/94[54]176,
MH:DEC/95[58]188
PORTER, FITZ JOHN, *General, USA:*
ARTICLES: "THE PENINSULA CAMPAIGN OF 1862: THE
BATTLE OF SLASH CHURCH," CWM:JUN/95[43]587, "THE
PENINSULA CAMPAIGN OF 1862: THE BATTLE OF
GAINES' MILL," CWM:JUN/95[61]593
GENERAL LISTINGS: *Beaver Dam Creek,* CWM:JUN/95[57]592,
court-martial, B&G:JUN/94[22]569, *Gaines' Mill,*
ACW:NOV/94[50]498, *in book review,* ACW:JAN/91[54],
B&G:AUG/93[24], CWNEWS:OCT/90[4],
CWNEWS:JAN/91[4], CWNEWS:APR/92[4],
CWR:VOL3#1[80], *letters to the editor,* CWM:OCT/94[5]533,
CWM:DEC/95[5]625, CWTI:JUN/95[14]443, *Malvern Hill,*
CWM:JUN/95[73]597, *Manassas, Second,*
ACW:JUL/91[18]312, B&G:AUG/92[11]493,
B&G:OCT/95[20]612, GETTY:6[62]175, *Mormon confrontation,*
AHI:DEC/72[10]145, *Peninsula Campaign,*
ACW:JUL/94[34]536, *photos,* ACW:NOV/94[50]498,
B&G:AUG/92[11]493
ADDITIONAL LISTINGS: ACW:JUL/91[35]314, ACW:NOV/92[10]384,
ACW:JUL/93[42]425, ACW:SEP/94[55]489,
ACW:JAN/95[54]508, B&G:AUG/91[32]461,
B&G:JUN/94[8]568, B&G:JUN/95[36]603A,
CWM:JUL/91[10]357, CWM:JUL/91[40]370,
CWM:AUG/94[48]529, CWR:VOL1#2[7]111,
CWR:VOL1#2[29]112, CWR:VOL1#3[28]120,
CWR:VOL1#3[52]122, CWR:VOL2#4[269]145,
CWR:VOL3#1[31]150, CWR:VOL3#2[1]153,
CWR:VOL3#3[1]157, CWTI:MAR/91[18],
CWTI:JUL/93[42]329, CWTI:SEP/93[43]338,
CWTI:NOV/93[55]350, CWTI:JAN/94[46]364,
CWTI:MAR/94[48]374, CWTI:MAY/94[31]382,
CWTI:JUL/94[44]394, CWTI:DEC/94[82]418,
GETTY:7[41]189, GETTY:9[41]212
PORTER, HENRY O., *Lieutenant, USN;* ACW:MAR/94[35]460
PORTER, HORACE, *Colonel, USA:*
BOOK REVIEW: *CAMPAIGNING WITH GRANT*
ADDITIONAL LISTINGS: ACW:SEP/93[62]436, ACW:JAN/94[47]452,
AHI:SEP/87[48]264, B&G:APR/95[8]595, B&G:APR/95[33]597,
B&G:JUN/95[8]600, CWM:JUL/91[8]356,
CWM:SEP/92[19]440, CWTI:FEB/90[12]141,
CWTI:APR/90[56]155, CWTI:AUG/90[26]166,
CWTI:APR/92[49]260, CWTI:MAR/94[16]368
PORTER, JOHN N., *Corporal, 154th New York Infantry;*
ACW:SEP/91[22]321, GETTY:8[17]200
PORTER, JOSEPH C., *Colonel, CSA:*
BOOK REVIEW: *WITH PORTER IN NORTH MISSOURI: A
CHAPTER IN THE HISTORY OF THE WAR BETWEEN THE
STATES*
ADDITIONAL LISTING: B&G:JUN/91[32]454
PORTER, PETER, *Col., 8th NY Arty.;* B&G:APR/94[55]564
PORTER, PETER A., *Colonel, 129th New York Infantry;*
AHI:OCT/67[26]112
PORTER, PLEASANT, *Creek Mounted Volunteers;*
CWM:SEP/92[8]437
PORTER, R.K., *Chaplain, CSA;* CWR:VOL4#4[28]178
PORTER, THOMAS K., *Lieutenant, CSN;* AHI:JAN/83[10]232
PORTER, WASH, *Pvt., 95th Illinois Inf.;* ACW:JAN/91[16]284
PORTER, WILLIAM D., *Commander, USN;*
ACW:JUL/93[34]424, ACW:SEP/95[8]542

PORTER, WILLIAM S.; B&G:AUG/95[36]607
PORTERFIELD, GEORGE A., *Colonel, CSA:*
ARTICLE: "CONFUSED FIRST FIGHT," ACW:JAN/92[47]344
ADDITIONAL LISTINGS: ACW:JAN/92[50]345, B&G:AUG/93[10]529
PORTLAND, MAINE; CWM:SEP/93[4]492
PORTSMOUTH, VIRGINIA, *U.S. Navy Yard;*
CWTI:APR/89[38]111
POSEY, CARNOT, *General, CSA:*
ARTICLE: "DEATH OF ANOTHER GENERAL,"
CWM:DEC/95[34]628, "POSEY'S BRIGADE AT
GETTYSBURG, PART I," GETTY:4[7]142, "POSEY'S
BRIGADE AT GETTYSBURG, PART II," GETTY:5[89]162
GENERAL LISTINGS: *Gettysburg,* GETTY:4[7]142, GETTY:5[79]161,
GETTY:7[77]191, GETTY:8[111]206, GETTY:9[61]215,
GETTY:9[98]217, GETTY:12[1]240, GETTY:12[7]241
ADDITIONAL LISTINGS: ACW:MAY/95[30]525, ACW:JUL/95[50]538,
CWR:VOL3#2[1]153, GETTY:4[7]142
POST, J.P., *Colonel, Illinois Infantry;* B&G:FEB/94[8]550
POST, PHILIP S., *General, USA;* B&G:APR/91[36]448,
B&G:DEC/93[12]545
POSTAL SERVICE, CONFEDERATE; ACW:MAY/92[6]356
POSTLES, J. PARKE, *Captain, 1st Delaware Infantry;*
GETTY:5[89]162, GETTY:9[61]215
POSTLETHWAITE, SAMUEL, *Private, 21st Mississippi
Infantry;* ARTICLE: "LOST SOUL: A YANKEE'S FIGHT FOR A
REBEL'S DIGNITY," CWM:DEC/94[34]549
ADDITIONAL LISTING: CWM:APR/95[5]570
POTTER, EDWARD E., *General, USA;* ACW:MAR/95[12]513
POTTER, NORMAN, *Sergeant, 149th New York Infantry;*
CWTI:SEPT/89[30]129
POTTER, ROBERT B., *General, USA;* ACW:MAY/95[18]524,
B&G:APR/94[10]558, B&G:APR/95[8]595, B&G:JUN/95[8]600,
B&G:AUG/95[8]604, CWR:VOL2#2[118]136,
CWR:VOL2#3[194]141, CWTI:APR/90[24]152,
CWTI:FEB/92[36]249, CWTI:MAY/94[50]386,
MH:APR/95[46]183
POTTER, WILLIAM, *Lt., 12th New Jersey Inf.;* GETTY:5[89]162
POTTER, WILLIAM, *Surgeon, 57th New York Infantry;*
GETTY:10[53]225
POTTS, BENJAMIN F., *Captain, First Independent Indiana
Battery;* CWR:VOL1#4[7]125
POTTS, BENJAMIN F., *General, USA;* B&G:FEB/94[8]550,
B&G:DEC/95[9]615
POTTS, J.R., *Lt., Latham's Battery;* CWR:VOL4#4[70]180
POUNDS, MERRIMAN, *Private, 3rd Georgia Infantry;*
CWTI:DEC/94[32]410
POWE, THOMAS E., *Captain, 8th South Carolina Infantry;*
GETTY:5[35]159
POWELL, BENJAMIN M., *Private, 1st South Carolina
Infantry;* B&G:DEC/95[25]616
POWELL, EUGENE, *Colonel, 66th Ohio Infantry;*
GETTY:9[81]216, GETTY:12[42]244
POWELL, FRANK M., *Lieutenant, 142nd Pennsylvania
Infantry;* GETTY:4[24]145
POWELL, FRANK M., *Colonel, CSA;* CWR:VOL2#3[256]
POWELL, LEWIS P., *Private, 2nd Florida
Infantry;*ACW:SEP/93[8]429
POWELL, LEWIS T.; ACW:JUL/94[26]477,
B&G:JUN/95[36]603A, CWNEWS:OCT/94[33],
CWTI:MAY/92[8]261, CWTI:DEC/95[76]482
POWELL, R.M., *Colonel, 5th Texas Infantry;* GETTY:6[43]173
POWELL, RICHARD, *Surgeon, 88th New York Infantry;*
GETTY:10[53]225

POWELL, ROBERT M., *Colonel, 5th Texas Infantry;*
GETTY:7[41]189
POWELL, SAMUEL, *Colonel, 29th Tennessee Infantry; in order
of battle,* B&G:FEB/93[12]511,
POWELL, SAMUEL, *Colonel, CSA;* CWR:VOL4#3[50]171,
POWELL, THOMAS N., *Major, 10th Louisiana Infantry;*
CWM:MAR/91[17]335,
POWELL, WILLIAM, *Colonel, USA;* ACW:MAY/91[38]305
POWER, JAMES, *Sgt., 57th Mass. Inf.;* CWR:VOL1#3[94]
POWER, THOMAS B., *Captain, CSN;* ACW:NOV/92[51]389
POWERS, CHARLES J., *Colonel, 108th New York Infantry;*
ACW:SEP/94[38]487, B&G:APR/91[8]445
POWERS, GEORGE L., *Private, 2nd Wisconsin Infantry,*
GETTY:11[57]233
POWERS, O.R., *Lieutenant, 37th Illinois Infantry;*
CWR:VOL1#1[42]105
PRAIRIE GROVE BATTLEFIELD STATE PARK;
B&G:JUN/92[46]490
PRAIRIE GROVE, ARKANSAS, BATTLE OF:
ARTICLES: "THE FREMONT RIFLES: THE 37TH ILLINOIS AT
PEA RIDGE AND PRAIRIE GROVE," CWR:VOL1#1[42]105,
"SLUGFEST IN THE OZARKS," ACW:MAY/94[26]468
ADDITIONAL LISTINGS: ACW:SEP/94[10]484, B&G:OCT/95[36]614,
CWM:SEP/92[38]443, CWTI:JAN/94[29]360
PRAIRIE RIFLES, 11th Mississippi Infantry; GETTY:9[98]217
PRANG & COMPANY; CWM:NOV/92[24]448
PRATHER, JOHN S., *Lieutenant Colonel, 8th Confederate
Cavalry;* B&G:AUG/91[11]458
PRATT'S (TEXAS) BATTERY; CWR:VOL2#3[212]142
PRATT, GEORGE W., *Colonel, USA;* CWNEWS:AUG/93[5]
PRATT, JOHN G., *General, CSA;* CWR:VOL3#1[1]149
PRATT, JOSEPH L., *Private, 1st Pennsylvania Infantry;*
CWR:VOL4#4[1]177
PREBLE, GEORGE H., *Captain, USN;* AHI:DEC/82[38]231,
CWR:VOL2#3[194]141
PRENTICE, GEORGE D., *newspaper editor;*
ACW:JAN/94[10]448
PRENTISS, BENJAMIN M., *General, USA:*
ARTICLE: "DEATH TAKES NO HOLIDAY," ACW:MAY/93[22]414
ADDITIONAL LISTINGS: ACW:JAN/91[22]285, ACW:SEP/92[38]379,
ACW:SEP/94[10]484, ACW:NOV/94[34]496,
B&G:JUN/93[12]524, CWM:MAY/93[8]474,
CWR:VOL4#1[44]164, CWTI:FEB/90[32]144,
CWTI:MAR/93[50]313, *photo,* ACW:MAY/93[22]414
PRENTISS, CLIFTON K., *Colonel, 6th Maryland Infantry;*
AHI:AUG/68[4]115B
PRENTISS, PHILO, *civilian;* B&G:APR/93[24]520,
CWTI:JAN/95[48]429
PRESCOTT, ALBERT, *Colonel, 57th Massachusetts Infantry;*
ACW:SEP/95[70]549, CWTI:APR/90[24]152
PRESCOTT, GEORGE L., *Colonel, 32nd Massachusetts
Infantry;* GETTY:6[7]169, GETTY:8[53]203

PRESERVATION:
ARTICLES: "CAMP TALK," B&G:JUN/91[26]453, "CIVIL WAR
MAGAZINE'S FIRST ANNUAL ENDANGERED
BATTLEFIELDS LIST," CWM:JAN/92[44]406, "CIVIL WAR
ON THE SANTA FE TRAIL: PRESERVING THE
BATTLEFIELD AT GLORIETA PASS,"
CWR:VOL2#2[161]139, "DESTROYING HISTORY HURTS
TOO MUCH," CWM:JUL/92[64]434A, "DISCOVERY TRAIL
LINKS CIVIL WAR SITES," AHI:JUL/95[9]323, "DISNEY'S
AMERICA THEME PARK PLANNED," AHI:MAR/94[6]320,

"HISTORIC DESIGNATION COSTS TOO MUCH," CWM:JUL/92[64]434, "HOW TO SAVE A BATTLEFIELD: DOCUMENT THE ACTION," CWM:NOV/91[66]395, "HOW TO SAVE A BATTLEFIELD," CWM:MAY/91[50]352, "INSIDE PRESERVATION, INSIDE CIVIL WAR ROUNDTABLE ASSOCIATES," CWM:SEP/93[40]498, "INSIDE PRESERVATION, INSIDE THE ASSOCIATION FOR THE PRESERVATION OF CIVIL WAR SITES," CWM:MAY/93[40]479

ARTICLES, continued: "INSIDE PRESERVATION, INSIDE THE CIVIL WAR TRUST," CWM:MAR/93[40]470, "INSIDE PRESERVATION, INSIDE...THE FEDERAL GOVERNMENT," CWM:APR/94[40]507, "LIVING ON A CIVIL WAR BATTLEFIELD," CWTI:JAN/95[22]423, "LOST SOUL: YANKEE'S FIGHT FOR A REBEL'S DIGNITY," CWM:DEC/94[34]549, "MORE TROUBLE AT BRANDY STATION," B&G:DEC/93[31]547, "THE PRESERVATION REPORT," CWR:VOL1#1[69]106, CWR:VOL1#2[76]116, CWR:VOL2#1[69]133, CWR:VOL2#3[252]144, CWR:VOL2#4[343]147, CWR:VOL3#1[78]152, CWR:VOL3#2[102]156, CWR:VOL3#3[88]160, CWR:VOL4#4[127]182, "WAR AND PAINT," CWM:OCT/94[55]543

BOOK REVIEWS: *BATTLEFIELD: FARMING A CIVIL WAR BATTLEGROUND * THE CIVIL WAR ROUND TABLE: FIFTY YEARS OF SCHOLARSHIP AND FELLOWSHIP * LOOK TO THE EARTH: HISTORICAL ARCHAEOLOGY AND THE AMERICAN CIVIL WAR * PAVING OVER THE PAST: A HISTORY AND GUIDE TO CIVIL WAR BATTLEFIELD PRESERVATION*

CSS Alabama; B&G:DEC/93[30]546, CWM:SEP/91[35]384

Aldie, Virginia; B&G:AUG/94[38]578, CWM:JUN/94[14]509

American Battlefield Protection Foundation; CWM:JUL/91[35]369, CWM:MAR/92[27]412, CWM:MAY/92[27]421

American Battlefield Protection Plan; CWR:VOL1#4[74]128

American Battlefield Protection Program; B&G:JUN'92[46]490, CWM:MAR/92[27]412, CWM:APR/94[40]507

Antietam National Battlefield Park, Maryland:

ARTICLES: "ANTIETAM 'CORNFIELD' DONATED," AHI:NOV/89[11]292, "MASTER PLAN APPROVED FOR PRESERVING ANTIETAM NATIONAL BATTLEFIELD," AHI:JAN/93[8]306

ADDITIONAL LISTINGS: B&G:APR/91[36]448, B&G:JUN/95[36]603A, B&G:OCT/95[36]614, CWM:MAY/91[31]350, CWM:JAN/92[27]403, CWM:JAN/92[44]406, CWM:MAY/93[35]478, CWM:JUL/93[35]487, CWM:JUL/93[46]489, CWR:VOL1#1[69]106, CWR:VOL3#3[88]160, CWTI:OCT/95[10]464

Appomattox Court House, Virginia:

ARTICLE: "HISTORY COMES HOME," CWTI:MAR/95[20]433

ADDITIONAL LISTING: CWR:VOL2#3[252]144

archaeology; BOOK REVIEW: *LOOK TO THE EARTH: HISTORICAL ARCHAEOLOGY AND THE AMERICAN CIVIL WAR*

Arkansas Post National Memorial; CWR:VOL2#1[69]133

Arlington House, Arlington, Virginia; B&G:AUG/95[42]608

Association for the Preservation of Civil War Sites:

ARTICLES: "BATTLEFIELD PRESERVATION IN CENTRAL VIRGINIA," B&G:APR/94[61]566, "DISNEY'S AMERICA: THE MOUSE IN THE SOUTH?" B&G:JUN/94[62]572,

"INSIDE PRESERVATION, INSIDE THE ASSOCIATION FOR THE PRESERVATION OF CIVIL WAR SITES,"

ADDITIONAL LISTINGS, B&G: B&G:FEB/93[40]514, B&G:APR/93[23]519, B&G:AUG/93[10]529, B&G:AUG/93[36]533, B&G:APR/94[6]557, B&G:APR/94[34]561, B&G:AUG/94[34]577A, B&G:AUG/94[38]578, B&G:DEC/94[36]588, B&G:FEB/95[38]593, B&G:JUN/95[36]603A, B&G:AUG/95[42]608, B&G:OCT/95[36]614

ADDITIONAL LISTINGS, CWM: CWM:MAR/91[39]338, CWM:MAY/91[31]350, CWM:SEP/91[35]384, CWM:JAN/92[27]403, CWM:JAN/92[44]406, CWM:MAR/92[27]412, CWM:JUL/92[64]434, CWM:SEP/92[33]442, CWM:NOV/92[35]450, CWM:MAR/93[36]469, CWM:MAR/93[40]470, CWM:MAY/93[40]479 CWM:JUL/93[46]489, CWM:SEP/93[35]497, CWM:APR/94[4]501, CWM:APR/94[40]507, CWM:JUN/94[14]509, CWM:AUG/95[5]602

ADDITIONAL LISTINGS, CWR: CWR:VOL1#1[69]106, CWR:VOL1#2[v]110, CWR:VOL1#2[7]111, CWR:VOL1#4[v]124, CWR:VOL2#4[343]147

ADDITIONAL LISTINGS, CWTI: CWTI:JUN/90[6]156, CWTI:JUN/90[43]160, CWTI:AUG/91[12]214, CWTI:JAN/94[42]363, CWTI:OCT/95[10]464

Association for the Preservation of Historic Antiquities; B&G:APR/94[61]566

Atlanta Cyclorama; ARTICLE: "ATLANTA'S RESTORED CYCLORAMA," CWTI:FEB/91[18]190

Atlanta Historical Society; B&G:JUN/93[40]527, B&G:OCT/94[42]583, CWR:VOL1#4[74]128

Ball's Bluff; B&G:OCT/95[36]614, CWR:VOL3#1[78]152

Battlefield Preservation Advisory Coalition; CWM:NOV/92[35]450, CWM:JUL/93[35]487, CWM:SEP/93[40]498

Belle Isle Prison; CWM:MAY/93[35]478

Bentonville Battleground Historical Association;

ARTICLE: "THE BENTONVILLE BATTLEFIELD TODAY," CWR:VOL4#3[75]173

ADDITIONAL LISTINGS: B&G:DEC/95[9]615, B&G:DEC/95[44]617, CWR:VOL1#4[74]128, CWR:VOL4#3[75]173, CWM:JUL/92[27]431, CWM:JUL/93[46]489

Big Bethel, Virginia; CWR:VOL1#2[76]116

Big Blue River; B&G:JUN/91[26]453

Black River Bridge; CWR:VOL2#1[69]133

Brandy Station, Virginia:

ARTICLES: "A NEW BATTLE FLARES AT BRANDY STATION," CWTI:JUN/90[43]160, "BEHIND THE LINES," CWTI:NOV/93[8]344, "DISASTER AT BRANDY STATION," B&G:APR/94[35]562, "FLANK ATTACK," CWTI:JUL/94[38]393, "IRRECONCILABLE DIFFERENCES," CWTI:JAN/94[42]363, "MORE TROUBLE AT BRANDY STATION," B&G:DEC/93[31]547

ADDITIONAL LISTINGS: B&G:APR/91[36]448, B&G:JUN/92[46]490, B&G:DEC/93[30]546, B&G:FEB/94[38]553, B&G:APR/94[34]561, B&G:JUN/94[38]571, B&G:AUG/94[38]578, B&G:FEB/95[38]593, CWM:MAR/91[80]343, CWM:SEP/91[35]384, CWM:NOV/91[66]395, CWM:JAN/92[44]406, CWM:MAR/92[27]412, CWM:MAY/92[27]421, CWM:JUL/92[27]431, CWM:JUL/92[64]434, CWM:NOV/92[35]450, CWM:JAN/93[35]460, CWM:MAR/93[6]464,

CWM:MAR/93[36]469, CWM:SEP/93[35]497,
CWM:SEP/93[40]498, CWM:APR/94[19]504,
CWM:APR/94[40]507 CWTI:DEC/94[12]408

Brandy Station Foundation:
ARTICLES: "BEHIND THE LINES," CWTI:FEB/91[6]187,
"IRRECONCILABLE DIFFERENCES,: CWTI:JAN/94[42]363
ADDITIONAL LISTINGS: B&G:FEB/91[34]442, B&G:APR/91[6]438,
B&G:APR/91[36]448, B&G:JUN/91[6]451, B&G:OCT/91[6]465,
B&G:APR/94[34]561, B&G:APR/94[35]562,
CWM:JAN'91[38]329, CWM:NOV/91[35]392,
CWM:JAN/92[44]406, CWM:MAY/92[64]424,
CWM:JUL/92[27]431, CWM:JUL/92[64]434,
CWM:NOV/92[35]450, CWM:JAN/93[35]460,
CWM:SEP/93[35]497, CWM:SEP/93[40]498,
CWM:APR/94[19]504, CWM:APR/94[40]507,
CWTI:FEB/91[6]187

Brice's Cross Roads; B&G:AUG/94[38]578
Bristoe Station; CWM:MAY/91[50]352, CWM:SEP/91[35]384
Byram's Ford, Missouri; CWM:JAN/92[44]406
Camp Chase Memorial Association; B&G:FEB/94[38]553,
B&G:OCT/94[6]579, B&G:AUG/95[42]608

Cedar Creek, Virginia:
ARTICLES: "BILL MAY: CRUSADER FOR CEDAR CREEK,"
CWM:DEC/95[26]626, "FAMILY VALUES AT CEDAR
CREEK," CWM:OCT/94[23]535,
ADDITIONAL LISTINGS:CWM:JAN/92[27]403, CWM:JAN/92[44]406,
CWM:JAN/93[35]460, CWM:FEB/95[5]557,
CWM:AUG/95[5]602

Cedar Creek Battlefield Foundation:
ARTICLE: "BILL MAY: CRUSADER FOR CEDAR CREEK,"
CWM:DEC/95[26]626
ADDITIONAL LISTINGS: CWM:JAN/92[27]403,
CWM:MAR/92[27]412, CWM:OCT/94[23]535,
CWM:AUG/95[5]602, MH:OCT/93[76]173

Cedar Mountain; B&G:APR/94[34]561, CWR:VOL1#1[69]106
Central Virginia; ARTICLE: "BATTLEFIELD PRESERVATION
IN CENTRAL VIRGINIA," B&G:APR/94[61]566
Chamberlain, Joshua L.; B&G:OCT/94[42]583
Champion Hill, Mississippi; CWM:MAY/91[31]350,
CWR:VOL2#1[69]133
Chancellorsville, Virginia; B&G:AUG/93[36]533,
CWM:JUL/93[46]489, CWR:VOL1#1[69]106
Chantilly, Virginia; CWM:MAY/91[50]352,
CWM:MAY/93[40]479, B&G:APR/94[6]557, B&G:AUG/94[6]573
Charleston, South Carolina; ARTICLE: "TO HONOR THE
DEAD: A PROPER BURIAL IN CHARLESTON,"
CWTI:MAR/94[59]376
Chickamauga and Chattanooga National Military Park;
B&G:FEB/95[38]593, CWR:VOL1#4[74]128,
CWR:VOL3#2[102]156
Chickasaw Bayou, Mississippi; CWR:VOL2#1[69]133
City Point, Virginia; CWM:JUL/93[46]489
Civil War Battlefield Commemorative Coin Act of 1992;
B&G:FEB/93[40]514, B&G:APR/95[38]598,
CWM:JUL/92[27]431, CWM:NOV/92[35]450
Civil War Foundation; CWM:JAN/91[38]329
Civil War Round Table Associates:
ARTICLE: "INSIDE PRESERVATION, INSIDE CIVIL WAR
ROUNDTABLE ASSOCIATES," CWM:SEP/93[40]498
ADDITIONAL LISTINGS: CWM:NOV/92[35]450,
CWM:MAR/93[40]470, CWM:MAY/93[40]479,
CWM:JUL/93[35]487, CWM:JUL/93[46]489,
CWM:APR/94[4]501, CWM:APR/94[19]504,

CWM:JUN/94[14]509, CWR:VOL1#1[69]106,
CWR:VOL1#2[v]110, CWTI:APR/89[8]106,
CWTI:JUN/90[6]156, CWTI:JAN/94[42]363

Civil War Sites Advisory Commission; B&G:DEC/91[38]471,
CWM:MAR/93[40]470, CWM:SEP/93[35]497,
CWM:SEP/93[56]499, CWM:APR/94[40]507,
CWM:JUN/94[14]509
Civil War Soldiers System; CWM:JUL/93[35]487
Civil War Trust; B&G:APR/94[35]562,
ARTICLE: "INSIDE PRESERVATION, INSIDE THE CIVIL WAR
TRUST," CWM:MAR/93[40]470
ADDITIONAL LISTINGS: B&G:FEB/93[40]514, B&G:JUN/93[40]527,
B&G:APR/94[35]562, CWM:NOV/92[35]450,
CWM:MAY/93[40]479, CWM:JUL/93[35]487,
CWM:SEP/93[35]497, CWM:SEP/93[40]498,
CWM:APR/94[19]504, CWM:APR/94[40]507
Coker House Preservation Committee; CWTI:MAY/91[18]207
Conservation Fund:
ARTICLE: "INSIDE PRESERVATION, INSIDE THE
CONSERVATION FUND," CWM:JUL/93[46]489
ADDITIONAL LISTINGS: B&G:AUG/91[40]463, B&G:FEB/92[40]479,
B&G:APR/92[8]481, B&G:JUN/92[46]490,
B&G:OCT/92[26]498, B&G:DEC/92[40]508,
B&G:AUG/93[36]533, B&G:AUG/94[38]578,
CWM:JUL/91[35]369, CWM:JAN/92[44]406,
CWM:NOV/92[35]450, CWM:MAY/93[40]479,
CWM:JUL/93[35]487, CWM:SEP/92[33]442,
CWM:SEP/93[35]497, CWM:APR/94[4]501,
CWM:APR/94[40]507, CWTI:JUN/90[6]156
Crampton's Gap, Maryland; ARTICLE: "96TH PENNSYLVANIA
VOLUNTEERS," CWR:VOL3#3[88]160
The Crater, Petersburg, Virginia:
ARTICLE: "THE PRESERVATION REPORT: A HISTORY OF THE
CRATER BATTLEFIELD, 1865-1992," CWR:VOL2#2[156]138
ADDITIONAL LISTING: CWR:VOL2#4[343]147
Cross Keys, VIrginia; ARTICLES: "LIVING ON A CIVIL WAR
BATTLEFIELD," CWTI:JAN/95[22]423, "PRESERVATION
NEWS," CWTI:AUG/95[10]453
Disney's America:
ARTICLES: "THE DISNEY PARK LOOMS," CWM:JUN/94[14]509,
"DISNEY'S AMERICA: GUEST EDITORIAL,"
B&G:AUG/94[34]577A, "DISNEY'S AMERICA: THE MOUSE
IN THE SOUTH?" B&G:JUN/94[62]572, "DISNEY'S
AMERICA THEME PARK PLANNED," AHI:MAR/94[6]320,
"THE THEME PARK—ADIEU AND ACCELERANDO?"
CWM:JUN/94[23]510
GENERAL LISTINGS: *letters to the editor,* B&G:JUN/94[5]567,
B&G:AUG/94[6]573, B&G:OCT/94[6]579, CWM:AUG/94[6]521,
CWM:FEB/95[5]557, CWM:APR/95[5]570
ADDITIONAL LISTINGS: B&G:JUN/94[38]571, B&G:DEC/94[36]588,
CWM:OCT/95[27]615, CWM:DEC/95[4]624
Fisher's Hill, Virginia; CWM:MAY/91[31]350,
CWM:MAY/93[40]479, CWM:JUL/93[46]489,
CWR:VOL1#4[v]124
Five Forks, Virginia; B&G:FEB/93[40]514,
CWM:JUL/91[35]369, CWM:JUL/93[46]489,
CWR:VOL2#4[343]147
Flags; B&G:AUG/94[38]578, B&G:OCT/95[36]614
Fort Blakely; CWTI:MAR/95[18]432
Fort Delaware; CWM:MAR/91[39]338
Fort DeRussy, Louisiana; CWR:VOL2#3[252]144,
CWTI:OCT/95[10]464

Fort Fisher National Historic Landmark:
ARTICLE: "FORT FISHER RECEIVES STATE FUNDS,"
AHI:MAR/92[8]300
ADDITIONAL LISTINGS: B&G:DEC/94[10]585, B&G:DEC/94[36]588,
CWM:MAR/91[39]338, CWM:JUL/91[35]369,
CWM:NOV/91[35]392, CWR:VOL2#3[252]144
Fort Mahone, Petersburg; CWR:VOL2#4[343]147
Fort Pickens, FLorida; CWR:VOL1#4[74]128
Fort Sedgwick, Petersburg, Virginia; CWR:VOL2#4[343]147
Fort Stedman, Petersburg, Virginia; CWR:VOL2#4[343]147
Fort Stevens, Oregon; CWM:JUL/91[35]369
Fox's Gap, Maryland; CWM:SEP/93[35]497
Franklin Memorial Association; B&G:APR/95[38]598
Franklin, Tennessee; B&G:JUN/94[38]571,
CWR:VOL1#4[74]128
Fredericksburg & Spotsylvania National Military Park;
B&G:JUN/94[38]571, B&G:FEB/95[38]593,
CWM:JUL/93[46]489, CWM:JAN/93[64]462,
CWM:SEP/93[35]497, CWM:FEB/95[7], CWR:VOL1#1[69]106,
CWR:VOL3#3[88]160, CWR:VOL4#4[127]182,
CWTI:OCT/95[10]464
Friends of Shiloh Battlefield; CWM:JUL/93[35]487
Friends of Harpers Ferry National Park;
B&G:AUG/91[40]463
Friends of the National Parks at Gettysburg;
B&G:APR/91[36]448, B&G:OCT/94[42]583,
B&G:AUG/95[42]608, B&G:OCT/95[36]614
Gaines' Mill, Virginia; CWR:VOL1#2[76]116
Garnett, Richard B.; CWR:VOL1#2[v]110
General James Longstreet Memorial Committee;
B&G:JUN/94[38]571, CWM:SEP/92[33]442
Gettysburg Battlefield Preservation Association:
ARTICLE: "CONGRESS QUESTIONS GETTYSBURG LAND
DEAL," CWTI:SEP/94[28]401
ADDITIONAL LISTINGS: B&G:OCT/91[40]467, B&G:FEB/92[40]479,
B&G:DEC/92[40]508, CWM:SEP/91[35]384,
CWM:JAN/92[44]406, CWM:SEP/92[33]442,
CWTI:JUN/90[6]156, CWTI:SEP/91[16]226,
CWTI:APR/92[42]259, CWTI:MAY/92[8]261,
CWTI:JUL/92[8]269, CWTI:JAN/93[8]296,
CWTI:JAN/93[35]300, CWTI:MAY/93[8]315
Gettysburg National Military Park:
ARTICLES: "BATTLE ON THE BRICKYARD WALL,"
CWTI:SEP/94[34]402, "BEHIND THE LINES,"
CWTI:SEP/91[16]226, "CAMP TALK EXTRA: GETTYSBURG,
A LESSON IN FOREIGN POLICY," B&G:FEB/94[39]554,
"CONGRESS QUESTIONS GETTYSBURG LAND DEAL,"
CWTI:SEP/94[28]401, "SEMINARY RIDGE TO REMAIN
UNRESTORED," CWTI:SEP/93[38]337, "WHERE DID
SEMINARY RIDGE GO?" CWTI:APR/92[42]259, "WHO LOST
SEMINARY RIDGE?," CWTI:JAN/93[35]300
ADDITIONAL LISTINGS: B&G:APR/91[36]448, B&G:APR/93[40]522,
B&G:JUN/93[40]527, B&G:DEC/93[30]546,
B&G:JUN/95[36]603A, CWM:MAY/91[31]350,
CWM:SEP/91[35]384, CWM:NOV/91[35]392,
CWM:JAN/92[44]406, CWM:MAR/92[27]412,
CWM:SEP/92[33]442, CWM:JAN/93[35]460,
CWM:JUL/93[46]489, CWM:APR/94[40]507,
CWTI:MAY/89[8]113, CWTI:JUL/92[8]269,
CWTI:SEP/92[54]285, CWTI:NOV/92[8]288,
CWTI:JAN/93[8]296, CWTI:MAY/93[8]315
Glendale, Virginia; B&G:DEC/94[36]588, CWM:JUN/94[14]509

Glorieta Pass, New Mexico:
ARTICLE: "CIVIL WAR ON THE SANTA FE TRAIL:
PRESERVING THE BATTLEFIELD AT GLORIETA PASS,"
CWR:VOL2#2[161]139, "TO HONOR THE DEAD: LAST TAPS
AT LA GLORIETA PASS," CWTI:MAR/94[58]375
ADDITIONAL LISTINGS: B&G:JUN/93[40]527, B&G:AUG/93[36]533,
CWM:JUL/93[35]487, CWM:JUL/93[46]489
Glorieta Battlefield Preservation Society;
B&G:FEB/91[34]442, B&G:JUN/94[8]568,
CWR:VOL2#2[161]139
Grand Gulf Military Monument Park; CWR:VOL2#1[69]133,
CWTI:OCT/95[10]464
Grant's Canal; CWM:JUL/93[46]489
Grant's Tomb National Monument:
ARTICLE: "FRIENDS OF GRANT'S TOMB FORMED,"
AHI:MAR/94[10]320
ADDITIONAL LISTINGS: B&G:FEB/93[61]516, B&G:AUG/93[36]533,
B&G:AUG/94[38]578, B&G:DEC/94[36]588,
B&G:DEC/95[44]617, CWM:JUL/93[4]482, CWM:OCT/94[5]533
Greenawalt House, Chambersburg, Pennsylvania;
B&G:JUN/95[36]603A
Griswoldville; CWTI:OCT/95[10]464
Grove Farm, Antietam; B&G:JUN/95[36]603A
Hancock's Tomb; B&G:DEC/95[44]617
Harpers Ferry National Historical Park:
ARTICLE: "THE PRESERVATION REPORT,"
CWR:VOL1#4[74]128
ADDITIONAL LISTINGS: CWM:JUL/91[35]369, CWM:MAR/92[27]412,
B&G:JUN/93[40]527, CWM:JUL/93[46]489,
B&G:AUG/93[36]533, B&G:FEB/95[38]593
Hatcher's Run; CWM:JAN/92[27]403, CWR:VOL2#4[343]147
HeritagePac:
ARTICLE: "BEHIND THE LINES," CWTI:JUN/90[6]156
ADDITIONAL LISTINGS: CWM:NOV/92[35]450, CWTI:APR/89[8]106
Historic Air Tours; ARTICLE: "A LIVING MAP OF THE WAR,"
CWM:JUN/95[79]599
Historic Fredericksburg Foundation; CWM:JUL/92[64]434
Historic Savannah Foundation; B&G:JUN/91[6]451
History Camp; ARTICLE: "CIVIL WAR HISTORY CAMP:
PASSING THE TORCH TO OUR KIDS," CWM:FEB/95[26]559
Honey Springs Battlefield Park; B&G:OCT/93[38]541,
CWR:VOL2#3[252]144
CSS Hunley; B&G:JUN/95[36]603A
Iowa monuments; BOOK REVIEW: *HANDBOOK FOR IOWA
SOLDIERS' AND SAILORS'*
Irish Brigade Association; B&G:OCT/95[36]614,
CWM:MAR/92[27]412
J.E.B. Stuart Birthplace Preservation Trust;
B&G:JUN/94[38]571, CWM:JAN/91[35]328,
CWM:NOV/91[35]392
Thomas J. Jackson; B&G:AUG/95[42]608
Jenkins' Ferry; CWR:VOL1#2[76]116
John Pelham Historical Association; B&G:FEB/94[38]553
Johnson's Island Preservation Society:
ARTICLE: "JOHNSON'S ISLAND PRESERVATION SOCIETY,"
CWM:OCT/95[53]621
ADDITIONAL LISTINGS: CWM:JUL/91[35]369, CWM:OCT/95[53]621
Johnson, Andrew; B&G:DEC/95[44]617
Kennesaw National Battlefield Park; B&G:FEB/95[38]593,
B&G:AUG/95[42]608, CWM:SEP/91[35]384,
CWR:VOL1#4[74]128
Libby Prison; CWM:OCT/94[55]543

CWTI:MAR/89[10], *Iuka,* CWTI:JUL/94[50]395, *letters to the editor,* B&G:OCT/91[6]465, CWM:JAN/93[6]455, CWTI:DEC/95[8]474, *pre-war,* AHI:SEP/83[42]235, *Wilson's Creek,* ACW:MAR/94[8]456, CWTI:FEB/92[29]248, *photos,* ACW:NOV/93[26]441, AHI:JUN/70[30]127, B&G:JUN/91[10]452, CWTI:FEB/92[29]248, CWTI:JUL/94[50]395

ADDITIONAL LISTINGS, ACW: ACW:JAN/91[30]286, ACW:MAR/91[62]298, ACW:MAY/91[10]301, ACW:SEP/91[46]324, ACW:SEP/91[50]325, ACW:NOV/91[10]329, ACW:MAR/92[46]354, ACW:JAN/93[26]395, ACW:MAR/93[68]409, ACW:MAR/94[8]456, ACW:NOV/94[76]500, ACW:MAR/95[26]515

ADDITIONAL LISTINGS, AHI: AHI:JUN/70[30]127, AHI:APR/87[10]261

ADDITIONAL LISTINGS, B&G: B&G:JUN/91[10]452, B&G:APR/92[36]483, B&G:APR/93[34]521, B&G:FEB/94[8]550

ADDITIONAL LISTINGS, CWM: CWM:JAN/92[8]399, CWM:SEP/92[38]443, CWM:MAR/93[8]465, CWM:MAY/93[8]474, CWM:AUG/94[52]530

ADDITIONAL LISTINGS, CWR: CWR:VOL1#1[42]105, CWR:VOL1#2[44]114, CWR:VOL1#2[76]116, CWR:VOL2#1[36]132, CWR:VOL2#4[313]146, CWR:VOL3#4[24]162, CWR:VOL4#3[50]171

ADDITIONAL LISTINGS, CWTI: CWTI:AUG/90[70]171, CWTI:SEP/90[52]179, CWTI:MAR/91[34]201, CWTI:MAY/91[16]206, CWTI:MAY/92[48]267, CWTI:JAN/93[44]302, CWTI:JAN/94[29]360, CWTI:AUG/95[58]461

ADDITIONAL LISTINGS, MH: MH:DEC/95[58]188

PRICELA, MISSOURI, DESTRUCTION OF; CWM:MAY/92[6]417

PRIEST, ALONZA, *Private, 6th Wisconsin Infantry,* GETTY:11[57]233

PRIME, RALPH, *Lieutenant, 5th New York Infantry;* CWR:VOL1#2[7]111, CWTI:MAY/94[31]382

PRINCE, EDWARD, *Colonel, 7th Illinois Cavalry;* ACW:MAY/92[47]363, ACW:JUL/94[8]474, B&G:JUN/93[12]524

PRINCE, HENRY, *General, USA;* CWM:MAY/92[20]420, CWNEWS:MAY/90[4]

PRINCE, J.R., *Captain, 11th Mississippi Infantry;* CWR:VOL2#4[269]145

PRINCE, ROBERT H., *Private, 22nd Battalion Virginia Infantry;* CWR:VOL1#3[52]122

PRINCE, WILLIAM E., *Major, USA;* CWTI:MAR/91[34]201

PRINZ, GEORGE, *civilian;* B&G:AUG/93[10]529

PRISONER EXCHANGES; B&G:APR/93[24]520

PRISONS:
BOOK REVIEWS: *CAMP AND PRISON JOURNAL: EMBRACING SCENES IN CAMP ON THE MARCH AND IN PRISONS * CIVIL WAR PRISONS & ESCAPES, A DAY-BY-DAY CHRONICLE*

PRISONS, CONFEDERATE:
Andersonville National Cemetery; CWM:APR/95[8]
Andersonville:
ARTICLES: "THE ANDERSONVILLE ARTIST," B&G:AUG/93[18]530, "ANDERSONVILLE PRISON REVAMPED," AHI:DEC/87[8]266, "THE COST OF CAPTURE," CWTI:APR/92[23]255, "'THE MOST HORRIBLE BARBARISM,'" CWM:JAN/92[16]401, "NORTHERN HELL ON EARTH," ACW:MAR/91[25]294, "POW MUSEUM AT

ANDERSONVILLE," AHI:NOV/92[16]305, "THREE ROADS TO ANDERSONVILLE," B&G:DEC/92[32]506
BOOK REVIEWS: *THE ANDERSONVILLE DIARY & MEMOIRS OF CHARLES HOPKINS * ANDERSONVILLE: THE LAST DEPOT*
GENERAL LISTINGS: *Andersonville; election of 1864,* AHI:OCT/68[4]116, *in book review,* ACW:NOV/92[58], B&G:APR/93[30], B&G:JUN/91[22], CWM:MAY/91[34], CWNEWS:AUG/91[4], *in book review,* CWNEWS:JAN/91[4], CWR:VOL4#3[1]170, *letters to the editor,* B&G:DEC/92[6]502, B&G:OCT/93[6]536, B&G:APR/94[6]557, CWTI:JUL/92[8]269, CWTI:DEC/94[12]408, *photo,* CWTI:APR/92[23]255
ADDITIONAL LISTINGS: ACW:MAY/91[8]300, ACW:JAN/93[10]393, ACW:NOV/93[66]445, ACW:NOV/93[10]439, ACW:MAY/95[8]522, AHI:NOV/89[50]288, B&G:AUG/91[36]462, B&G:AUG/95[24]605, B&G:OCT/95[36]614, CWM:JAN/92[4]397, CWM:JUL/92[27]431, CWM:SEP/92[24]441, CWM:OCT/94[17]534, CWM:DEC/94[17]547, CWM:FEB/95[36]563, CWM:APR/95[42]577, CWR:VOL1#4[7]125, CWTI:SUMMER/89[50]124, CWTI:AUG/90[42]167, CWTI:MAY/91[48]211, CWTI:FEB/92[42]250, CWTI:JUL/93[20]325, CWTI:NOV/93[78]354, CWTI:DEC/94[32]410, CWTI:OCT/95[28]467, GETTY:12[111]250
VIDEO: *THE ANDERSONVILLE TRIAL,* AHI:MAY/91[22]
Belle Isle:
ARTICLE: "ON TO PRISON," CWTI:JUN/90[28]158
ADDITIONAL LISTINGS: AHI:NOV/85[38]254, B&G:AUG/91[36]462, B&G:DEC/92[32]506, CWM:JAN/92[16]401, CWM:MAY/93[35]478, CWM:APR/95[42]577, CWTI:MAR/95[26]434, GETTY:12[24]242, *photo of prisoner,* ACW:MAR/95[50]518, AHI:MAY/71[3]133A
Cahaba:
BOOK REVIEWS: *CAHABA PRISON AND THE SULTANA DISASTER*
ADDITIONAL LISTINGS: ACW:NOV/92[58], B&G:JUN/92[32]488, B&G:APR/93[30], B&G:AUG/95[24]605, CWTI:AUG/90[42]167, *map,* B&G:JUN/92[32]488
Camp Ford, Texas; ARTICLE: "GREAT ESCAPE FROM REBEL PRISON," ACW:MAR/95[34]516
Castle Thunder; ACW:SEP/91[22]321, AHI:DEC/85[40]255, CWM:APR/94[8]502, CWTI:MAY/94[40]383, CWTI:DEC/95[76]482, *photo,* CWTI:JUN/90[28]158
Danville; CWM:OCT/95[40]619
Libby:
ARTICLES: "ESCAPE FROM LIBBY," ACW:JAN/94[55]453, "ESCAPE FROM LIBBY PRISON, PART I," AHI:NOV/85[38]254, "ESCAPE FROM LIBBY PRISON, PART II," AHI:DEC/85[40]255, "ON TO PRISON," CWTI:JUN/90[28]158
BOOK REVIEW: *LIBBY LIFE: EXPERIENCES OF A PRISONER OF WAR IN RICHMOND, VA 1863-1864*
GENERAL LISTINGS: *Confederate exiles,* AHI:JUN/70[30]127, *Fall of Richmond,* AHI:JAN/74[10]153, *Gettysburg,* GETTY:10[7]221, GETTY:10[53]225, GETTY:12[24]242, *in book review,* B&G:FEB/93[36], CWNEWS:OCT/89[4], *letters to the editor,* B&G:FEB/95[5]589, *sketch,* CWTI:NOV/92[28]290, *photos,* ACW:JAN/94[55]453, AHI:NOV/85[38]254, AHI:DEC/85[40]255
ADDITIONAL LISTINGS: ACW:MAY/91[12]302, ACW:JUL/91[8]309, ACW:NOV/92[18]385, ACW:MAR/94[10]457,

ACW:JUL/94[26]477, ACW:MAY/95[18]524,
ACW:SEP/95[22]544, AHI:FEB/82[36]225,
AHI:APR/85[18]250, AHI:NOV/88[28]277,
B&G:AUG/91[36]462, B&G:OCT/93[21]538,
B&G:DEC/93[30]546, B&G:JUN/94[22]569,
B&G:OCT/95[8]611A, B&G:OCT/95[36]614,
CWM:OCT/94[55]543, CWM:OCT/95[40]619,
CWR:VOL1#3[46]121, CWTI:SEPT/89[40]130,
CWTI:JUN/90[32]159, CWTI:DEC/91[22]237,
CWTI:NOV/92[28]290, CWTI:NOV/93[78]354,
CWTI:MAR/95[26]434, CWTI:DEC/95[76]482,
GETTY:10[42]224, GETTY:13[33]255, MH:APR/94[54]176

Salisbury:
BOOK REVIEW: *THE SALISBURY PRISON: CASE STUDY OF
CONFEDERATE MILITARY PRISONS, 1861-1865*
ADDITIONAL LISTINGS: B&G:APR/92[28]482, CWM:OCT/95[40]619,
CWTI:NOV/93[114]355

PRISONS, FEDERAL:
Alton; CWTI:JUL/94[82]396
Camp Butler; CWR:VOL1#4[77]
Camp Chase; ACW:SEP/95[22]544, B&G:AUG/91[40]463,
B&G:OCT/94[11]580, B&G:OCT/94[28]581,
CWTI:DEC/94[79]417, CWNEWS:JAN/92[4],
CWR:VOL1#2[78], *photo,* B&G:OCT/91[11]466
Camp Dennison; ACW:SEP/95[22]544
Camp Douglas; B&G:FEB/92[10]474, B&G:DEC/92[6]502,
B&G:OCT/93[38]541, B&G:AUG/94[38]578
Camp Morton; B&G:FEB/91[34]442, CWTI:APR/90[56]155
Camp Stanton; B&G:FEB/94[38]553
Elmira;
ARTICLES: "BREAK OUT!" CWTI:DEC/91[26]238, "NORTHERN
HELL ON EARTH," ACW:MAR/91[25]294, "THE TRACK IS
CLEAR TO SHOHOLA: DISASTER ON THE ROAD TO
ELMIRA," B&G:APR/93[24]520
ADDITIONAL LISTINGS: B&G:JUN/93[6]523, CWM:APR/95[50],
CWM:OCT/95[10], CWR:VOL3#2[105], CWTI:JAN/95[48]429,
photo, ACW:MAR/91[25]294
Forest Hall Military Prison; AHI:FEB/75[35]158,
CWM:APR/94[8]502
Fort Columbus; CWM:SEP/92[8]437, CWTI:JUL/93[38]328
Fort Delaware: .
ARTICLE: "FORT DELAWARE ON THE WATER: A MONUMENT
TO RUGGED REBELS," CWTI:JUL/93[20]325, "INFAMOUS
FOR DELAWARE WON AN UNWELCOME REPUTATION
AS THE 'NORTHERN ANDERSONVILLE',"
ACW:NOV/93[66]445
GENERAL LISTINGS: *Gettysburg,* GETTY:6[77]177, *in book review,*
CWNEWS:JAN/94[5], CWR:VOL1#2[78], CWR:VOL3#1[80],
CWR:VOL4#2[136], *letters to the editor,* CWTI:NOV/93[12]345,
SIO, B&G:DEC/91[38]471, *photo,* CWTI:JUL/93[20]325
ADDITIONAL LISTINGS: ACW:SEP/95[8]542, B&G:DEC/92[26],
CWM:MAR/91[39]338, CWR:VOL2#3[236]143,
CWR:VOL2#4[269]145, CWTI:MAY/92[29]263,
CWTI:JUL/93[74]331, CWTI:JAN/95[42]428,
CWTI:OCT/95[28]467, GETTY:12[1]240, GETTY:12[68]246,
GETTY:12[111]250, GETTY:13[1]252, GETTY:13[108]261
Fort Jefferson:
ARTICLE: "A POETIC PLEA FROM PRISON,"
CWTI:MAR/91[28]20,
ADDITIONAL LISTINGS: CWTI:MAY/93[12]316, MH:JUN/91[20]152,
photo, CWTI:MAR/91[28]200

Fort Lafayette; ACW:JAN/93[66]399, ACW:SEP/94[46]488,
ACW:JUL/95[44]537, CWR:VOL3#1[31]150,
CWTI:MAY/89[14]114, CWTI:MAY/89[21]115, GETTY:11[6]231
Fort McHenry; ACW:SEP/91[41]323, ACW:JUL/95[44]537,
CWTI:MAY/93[26]318, GETTY:6[77]177, GETTY:12[111]250,
GETTY:13[1]252, GETTY:13[108]261, MH:APR/94[54]176
Fort Warren; ACW:SEP/91[41]323, ACW:NOV/91[46]335,
ACW:MAR/94[35]460, ACW:SEP/94[46]488,
B&G:FEB/94[8]550, CWR:VOL4#3[50]171, CWR:VOL4#3[89],
CWTI:FEB/91[36]193, CWTI:MAY/91[34]209,
CWTI:JUL/93[38]328, *photo,* CWTI:JUL/93[38]328
Fort Wool, Virginia; ACW:JAN/95[74]510
Gratiot Street (St. Louis):
ARTICLE: "A HELL ON EARTH," CWTI:AUG/95[58]461
ADDITIONAL LISTINGS: ACW:MAY/91[10]301, CWR:VOL4#3[37],
CWTI:DEC/95[8]474
Johnson's Island:
ARTICLE: "A LONE STATUE AND AN EMPTY CONFEDERATE
GRAVEYARD ARE THE ONLY REMINDERS OF THE
JOHNSON'S ISLAND PRISON," ACW:JAN/93[66]399
ADDITIONAL LISTINGS: ACW:JUL/95[44]537, B&G:FEB/91[34]442,
B&G:AUG/91[40]463, B&G:OCT/94[11]580,
CWM:OCT/95[53]621, CWR:VOL2#4[269]145,
CWR:VOL3#4[68], CWTI:FEB/91[36]193,
CWTI:AUG/91[82]223, CWTI:NOV/92[54]293,
CWTI:MAY/93[26]318, CWTI:DEC/94[79]417,
CWTI:JAN/95[42]428, CWTI:JUN/95[90]451,
CWTI:OCT/95[28]467, GETTY:7[114]194, GETTY:9[98]217,
GETTY:10[53]225, GETTY:12[1]240, GETTY:13[108]261,
photo, GETTY:13[108]261
Ohio Penitentiary:
ARTICLE: "JOHN HUNT MORGAN'S ESCAPE FROM THE OHIO
PENITENTIARY," B&G:OCT/94[11]580
ADDITIONAL LISTINGS: B&G:FEB/95[5]589, CWM:MAR/93[16]466,
photos, B&G:OCT/94[11]580
Old Capital; *in book review,* CWM:APR/95[50],
ACW:JUL/93[10]421, CWR:VOL4#2[136],
CWTI:DEC/91[22]237, CWTI:APR/92[23]255,
CWTI:SEP/92[42]283, CWTI:MAY/93[26]318,
CWTI:DEC/95[76]482, GETTY:12[111]250, *photo,*
AHI:FEB/75[35]158
Point Lookout:
BOOK REVIEW: *SKETCHES FROM PRISON: A CONFEDERATE
ARTIST'S RECORD OF LIFE AT POINT LOOKOUT
PRISONER OF WAR CAMP, 1863-1865*
GENERAL LISTINGS: *Gettysburg,* GETTY:6[77]177, *in book review,*
CWM:FEB/95[7], CWM:APR/95[50], CWR:VOL3#4[68],
CWR:VOL4#1[78]
ADDITIONAL LISTINGS: ACW:MAR/91[25]294, ACW:SEP/92[6]373,
B&G:APR/93[24]520, CWM:OCT/95[10],
CWR:VOL2#4[269]145, CWTI:DEC/91[26]238,
CWTI:MAY/93[26]318, CWTI:JAN/95[48]429,
CWTI:OCT/95[28]467, GETTY:10[102]226
Prince Street Prison; ACW:NOV/91[16]330
Rock Island; B&G:DEC/92[6]502, MH:JUN/91[20]152

PRITCHETT, JAMES M., *Lieutenant Commander, USN;*
ACW:MAY/93[22]414
PRIVATEERS; BOOK REVIEW: *THE CONFEDERATE
PRIVATEERS,* CWM:JAN/91[47]
PROCTOR, AUSTIN, *Private, Crenshaw's Artillery;*
GETTY:10[107]227

PROCTOR, JAMES S., *Private, Georgia Light Artillery;*
  CWR:VOL3#2[1]153
PRODIGY; CWTI:OCT/95[40]469
PROSKAUER, ADOLPH, *Major, 12th Alabama Infantry;*
  CWM:SEP/93[8]493
PROVOST GUARD; BOOK REVIEW: *REBEL WATCHDOG: THE
  CONFEDERATE STATES ARMY PROVOST GUARD*
PRUYN, ROBERT, *Captain, CSA;* MH:AUG/94[82]179
PRUYN, ROBERT H., *civilian;* MH:OCT/91[50]154
PRYCE, SAMUEL D., *Captain, USA;* CWR:VOL2#1[19]131
PRYOR, ROGER A., *General, CSA;* ACW:MAR/91[47]297,
  ACW:SEP/93[8]429, B&G:AUG/91[26], CWM:SEP/92[19]440,
  CWTI:MAR/89[28]103, CWTI:JUL/92[29]272,
  CWTI:MAR/95[60]439
PRYOR, SHEPHERD G., *Captain, CSA;* BOOK REVIEW: *A POST
  OF HONOR: THE PRYOR LETTERS 1861-63; LETTERS
  FROM CAPT. S.G. PRYOR, TWELFTH GEORGIA
  REGIMENT AND HIS WIFE, PENELOPE TYSON PRYOR*
PUGH, GEORGE E., *Senator, OHIO;* AHI:JUN/73[4]149
PUGH, ISAAC C., *Colonel, USA;* B&G:AUG/95[8]604
PULASKI (GEORGIA) ARTILLERY; CWTI:FEB/92[29]248,
  GETTY:8[53]203
PULITZER, JOSEPH, *Private, 1st New York Cavalry;* ARTICLE:
  "HUNGARIAN IMMIGRANT TURNED UNION SOLDIER,
  JOSEPH PULITZER WOULD ONE DAY BECOME A
  JOURNALISTIC TITAN," ACW:JUL/95[8]532
PULLER, JOHN, *Lt., 5th Virginia Arty.;* ACW:NOV/91[30]332
PULLIAM, ROBERT C., *Capt., 2nd SC Inf.;* GETTY:5[35]159
PURCELL (VIRGINIA) ARTILLERY; CWM:MAR/91[17]335,
  CWM:JUN/95[57]592, CWM:DEC/95[41]630,
  CWR:VOL1#2[44]114, GETTY:9[61]215
PURCELL, HIRAM, *Sgt., 104th PA Inf.;* CWM:JUN/95[47]588
PURDEN, WILLIAM H., *Captain, CSA;* CWTI:SEP/91[23]228
PURDY, JOHN, *Pvt., 2nd Kentucky Cav.;* CWM:MAR/93[16]466
PURNELL (MARYLAND) CAVALRY; GETTY:4[75]149,
  GETTY:13[89]260
PURSEL, THOMAS C., *Captain, 11th Indiana Infantry;*
  CWTI:MAR/91[28]200
PURSLEY, LAFAYETTE, *Pvt., 19th IN Inf.,* GETTY:11[57]233
PURVIANCE, H.Y., *Captain, USN;* AHI:OCT/75[30]162
PURYEAR, JOHN, *Private, CSA;* ACW:JUL/94[26]477
PUTEGNAT, JOHN P., *Sergeant, Jeff Davis Artillery;*
  CWTI:DEC/91[26]238
PUTHAM, HOLDEN, CWR:VOL3#3[59]159
PUTHAM, JOHN, *Captain, USA;* AHI:FEB/82[36]225
PUTNAM, GEORGE H., *Captain, 176th New York Infantry;*
  CWTI:AUG/90[42]167
PUTNAM, HALDIMAND S., *Colonel, USA;*
  ACW:SEP/91[30]322, CWTI:DEC/89[42]137
PUTNAM, HOLDEN, *Colonel, 93rd Illinois Volunteer Infantry;*
  ARTICLE: "COLONEL HOLDEN PUTNAM AND THE 934D
  ILLINOIS VOLUNTEER INFANTRY," CWR:VOL3#3[59]159
PUTNAM, JAMES F., *Captain, Ohio Light Artillery;*
  B&G:AUG/95[8]604
PUTNAM, JOHN C., *Cpt., 20th Mass. Inf.;* CWR:VOL3#1[31]150
PUTNAM, SALLIE A.B., ACW:JAN/93[18]394
PUTNAM, WILLIAM L., *Lieutenant, 20th Massachusetts
  Infantry;* CWR:VOL3#1[31]150
PYE, EDWARD, *Colonel, 95th New York Infantry;* ARTICLE:
  "PYE'S SWORD AT THE RAILROAD CUT," GETTY:6[29]171
PYLE, HOWARD; CWTI:SEPT/89[24]128
PYRON, CHARLES L., *Major, 2nd Texas Mounted Rifles;*
  B&G:JUN/94[8]568, CWM:MAY/93[16]475,

CWR:VOL2#2[161]139, CWTI:MAR/94[58]375,
  CWTI:OCT/95[56]471
PYWELL, WILLIAM R., *photographer;* B&G:FEB/94[24]551

Q

QUADT, CHARLES, *Private 24th Michigan Infantry,*
  GETTY:9[33]211, GETTY:11[57]233
QUAKERS; BOOK REVIEW: *INDIANA QUAKERS CONFRONT
  THE CIVIL WAR*
QUANTRILL, WILLIAM S.;
ARTICLES: "BLOODY KANSAS...WITNESSES TO QUANTRILL'S
  RAID IN LAWRENCE AND THEIR STORIES,"
  CWM:JAN/92[12]400, "WILLIAM CLARKE QUANTRILL:
  TERROR OF THE BORDER," CWM:JAN/92[8]399
BOOK REVIEWS: *BLOODY DAWN: THE STORY OF THE
  LAWRENCE MASSACRE * DARK FRIDAY: THE STORY OF
  QUANTRILL'S LAWRENCE RAID * THREE YEARS WITH
  QUANTRILL, A TRUE STORY TOLD BY HIS SCOUT JOHN
  MCCORKLE*
GENERAL LISTINGS: *Bloody Kansas,* AHI:JUL/75[4]160, *death of,*
  CWTI:AUG/90[64]170, *in book review,* ACW:JUL/95[58],
  B&G:FEB/93[36], B&G:AUG/93[24], CWTI:MAY/89[44], *letters
  to the editor,* B&G:OCT/91[6]465, B&G:APR/93[6]517,
  CWM:SEP/91[6]377, CWM:MAY/92[6]417,
  CWM:SEP/92[6]436, CWM:JAN/93[6]455,
  CWTI:MAY/94[12]379, *Price's 1864 Missouri Campaign,*
  B&G:JUN/91[10]452, *photos,* CWM:JAN/92[8]399,
  CWTI:JAN/94[29]360
ADDITIONAL LISTINGS: ACW:NOV/91[10]329, ACW:JAN/93[26]395,
  ACW:JAN/94[10]448, ACW:MAR/94[6]455,
  ACW:NOV/94[42]497, CW:MAR/95[26]515,
  B&G:JUN/91[32]454, B&G:OCT/91[11]466,
  CWM:JAN/92[4]397, CWM:SEP/92[38]443,
  CWM:MAY/93[35]478, CWTI:MAY/91[48]211,
  CWTI:FEB/92[42]250, CWTI:JAN/94[29]360
QUARLES, T.P., *Sergeant, 7th South Carolina Infantry;*
  GETTY:5[35]159
QUARLES, WILLIAM A., *General, CSA;* B&G:DEC/93[12]545
QUEBEC SCHOOLHOUSE, MARYLAND, ENGAGEMENT
  AT:
ARTICLE: "THE CAVALRY CLASH AT QUEBEC
  SCHOOLHOUSE," B&G:FEB/93[24]512
ADDITIONAL LISTING: B&G:DEC/93[6]544
QUERRY, MATTHIAS, *Pvt., 53rd PA. Inf.;* GETTY:11[80]235
QUILLIAM, JAMES D., *Private, 154th New York Infantry;*
  GETTY:8[17]200
QUINBY, ISAAC F., *General, USA;* CWR:VOL2#1[19]131,
  CWR:VOL3#3[59]159
QUINLAN, JAMES, *Maj., 88th NY Inf.;* ACW:MAY/94[12]466
QUINN, GEORGE W., *Private, 31st Illinois Infantry;*
  B&G:FEB/91[8]439, GETTY:11[71]234
QUINN, THOMAS, *Chaplain, 1st Rhode Island Artillery;*
  CWM:MAR/91[50]340
QUINT, LOUIS; GETTY:7[119]195,
QUINT, MONROE, *Pvt., 17th Maine Infantry;* GETTY:8[43]202
QUITMAN, JOHN A.; CWNEWS:FEB/94[5]

R

RABB, JAMES D., *cadet;* B&G:DEC/91[12]469
RACE, CHARLES N., *Captain, USA;* CWTI:JUL/93[42]329
RACE, LESTER, *Corp., 53rd Penna. Inf.;* GETTY:11[80]235
RADCLIFFE, LAURA; AHI:DEC/73[10]152
RADFORD, WILLIAM, *Commodore, USN;* ACW:SEP/95[30]545
RADICAL REPUBLICANS; ACW:MAR/92[46]354,
    AHI:OCT/68[4]116, AHI:DEC/68[28]118, AHI:APR/73[12]148,
    AHI:JUL/76[19]170, GETTY:12[85]248
RAE, THOMAS W., *Engineer, USN;* ARTICLE: "'THE LITTLE
    MONITOR SAVED OUR LIVES,'" AHI:JUL/66[32]103
RAFFERTY, PETER, *Private, 69th New York Infantry;*
    ACW:MAY/94[12]466
RAFFERTY, THOMAS, *Colonel, USA;* GETTY:10[112]228
RAGLAND, JOHN M, *Sergeant, 1st-4th Missouri Infantry;*
    CWR:VOL3#3[59]159
RAGNET, HENRY W., *Major, CSA;* B&G:JUN/94[8]568,
    CWTI:MAR/94[58]375, CWTI:JUL/94[10]389,
    CWTI:OCT/95[56]471

RAIDS:

Andrew's Raid: see listings under **"ANDREWS, JAMES J."**
Calais Maine; ARTICLE: "THE GREAT REBEL RAID ON
    CALAIS, MAINE," CWTI:SEP/92[40]282
Camden, South Carolina, 1864; CWTI:AUG/90[42]167,
Grierson's Raid: see listings under **GRIERSON'S RAID"**
Holly Springs, Mississippi, Raid:
BOOK REVIEW: *MOUNTED RAIDS OF THE CIVIL WAR*
GENERAL LISTINGS: *general history,* AHI:MAY/71[3]133A, *in book
    review,* CWM:DEC/94[7], CWR:VOL2#1[78], CWTI:DEC/94[18]
ADDITIONAL LISTINGS: ACW:MAY/93[22]414, AHI:MAY/71[3]133A,
    CWM:AUG/94[52]530, CWM:DEC/95[48]631,
    CWR:VOL2#1[36]132, CWR:VOL2#1[78],
    CWR:VOL2#4[313]146, CWR:VOL3#3[33]158,
    CWTI:MAY/92[48]267, CWTI:NOV/93[33]347,
    CWTI:DEC/94[18], MH:APR/94[54]176
Selma (Alabama) Raid: see listings under **"SELMA, ALABAMA,
    BATTLE OF"**
Stoneman's Chancellorsville Raid; ARTICLE: "FAILURE OR
    HARBINGER," CWM:APR/95[32]575
Streight's Raid; see listings under **"STREIGHT'S RAID"**
ADDITIONAL LISTINGS: CWM:OCT/94[48]542,
    CWTI:MAY/92[48]267, CWTI:JAN/94[35]361
Wilson-Kautz Raid, ACW:JAN/92[16]340

RAILEY, MARTIN, *civilian;* ACW:NOV/91[10]329
RAILROAD CONSTRUCTION CORPS;
    CWM:NOV/91[28]391, CWNEWS:JUN/91[4]

RAILROADS:

ARTICLES: "A ROLLING MEMENTO," CWTI:MAR/95[54]438,
    "THE GREAT LOCOMOTIVE WRECK,"
    CWTI:JAN/95[48]429, "THE GREAT TRAIN ROBBERY,"
    CWM:NOV/91[40]393, "HAUPT'S INNOVATIONS...KEPT
    THE NORTHERN TRAINS ON TRACK,"
    CWM:NOV/91[28]391, "HERMAN HAUPT'S RAILROADS:
    BEANPOLES AND CORNSTALKS," CWM:NOV/91[12]390,
    "MIRACLE OF THE RAILS," CWTI:SEP/92[22]279, "RAILS
    TO THE RIVER OF DEATH: RAILROADS IN THE

CHICKAMAUGA CAMPAIGN," CWM:NOV/91[50]394,
    "WRECKING ON THE RAILROAD," ACW:SEP/95[48]547
BOOK REVIEWS: *THE CONFEDERACY AS A REVOLUTIONARY
    EXPERIENCE * DESTROYER OF THE IRON HORSE:
    GENERAL JOSEPH E. JOHNSTON AND CONFEDERATE
    RAIL TRANSPORT, 1861-1865 * THE GREAT
    LOCOMOTIVE CHASE: MORE ON THE ANDREWS RAID
    AND THE FIRST MEDAL OF HONOR * LOUISIANA
    NECKTIES: LOUISIANA RAILROADS IN THE CIVIL WAR
    * THE RAILROADS OF THE CONFEDERACY * SOUTHERN
    RAILROAD MAN: CONDUCTOR N.J. BELL'S
    RECOLLECTIONS OF THE CIVIL WAR ERA *
    SOUTHWEST VIRGINIA'S RAILROAD: MODERNIZATION
    AND THE SECTIONAL CRISIS * VICTORY RODE THE
    RAILS: THE STRATEGIC, PLACE OF THE RAILROADS IN
    THE CIVIL WAR * VIRGINIA RAILROADS IN THE CIVIL
    WAR*
GENERAL LISTINGS: *letters to the editor,* CWTI:NOV/92[8]288,
    CWTI:JUN/95[14]443, CWTI:AUG/95[14]454, *photo of the
    Chattahoochee River bridge;* CWTI:SUMMER/89[20]121,
    photo, destruction of; ACW:SEP/95[48]547, *photos,*
    CWM:NOV/91[12]390, CWM:NOV/91[28]391
Alabama & Mississipi River; ACW:SEP/95[48]547
Alabama & Tennessee; AHI:NOV/73[18]151
Aquia & Richmond; CWM:APR/95[32]575
Atlanta & West Point; ACW:JUL/94[66]481,
    CWTI:SUMMER/89[50]124
Atlantic & Gulf; ACW:SEP/92[47]380, B&G:FEB/91[8]439,
    CWTI:DEC/94[62]415
Atlantic & North Carolina; B&G:DEC/95[9]615
Atlantic & West; ACW:JUL/94[66]481
Augusta; CWM:JAN/91[12]326
Baltimore & Ohio:
ARTICLE: "THE GREAT TRAIN ROBBERY," CWM:NOV/91[40]393
GENERAL LISTINGS: *Gettysburg,* GETTY:10[42]224, *in book review,*
    CWM:NOV/91[73], CWR:VOL4#3[89], *photo,*
    CWTI:APR/89[38]111
ADDITIONAL LISTINGS: ACW:SEP/91[41]323, ACW:JAN/92[47]344,
    ACW:NOV/93[50]444, ACW:SEP/94[31]486,
    AHI:AUG/76[34]171, AHI:NOV/80[8]209, AHI:JUL/95[30]324,
    B&G:JUN/92[8]487, B&G:DEC/92[8]503,
    B&G:AUG/93[10]529, B&G:AUG/94[10]574,
    B&G:AUG/94[19]575, CWM:NOV/91[12]390,
    CWM:JAN/93[24]458, CWM:APR/94[24]505,
    CWR:VOL2#2[95]135, CWR:VOL3#2[70]155,
    CWTI:MAR/89[16]101, CWTI:APR/89[38]111,
    CWTI:AUG/90[42]167, CWTI:MAR/91[22]199,
    CWTI:MAY/92[48]267, CWTI:SEP/92[22]279,
    CWTI:JAN/93[40]301, CWTI:JAN/95[24]424,
    GETTY:11[80]235, GETTY:12[42]244, GETTY:12[68]246,
    GETTY:13[75]259
Central of Georgia; ACW:SEP/92[47]380, B&G:FEB/91[8]339
Charleston & Savannah; ACW:SEP/92[47]380,
    CWR:VOL2#3[194]141
Charleston; ACW:SEP/92[47]380, B&G:FEB/91[8]439
Chattanooga & Memphis; CWTI:SEPT/89[30]129
Chesapeake & Ohio; GETTY:9[109]218
City Point; ACW:MAY/95[38]526, MH:APR/95[46]183
Columbus; CWM:JAN/91[40]330
Cumberland Valley; B&G:AUG/94[10]574,
    CWM:NOV/91[12]390
Danville; ACW:MAY/95[38]526

Richmond & York River; ACW:JUL/95[34]536,
B&G:AUG/91[20]459, CWM:JUN/94[28]514,
CWM:JUN/95[39]586, CWM:JUN/95[50]589,
CWM:JUN/95[57]592, CWM:JUN/95[63]594,
CWR:VOL3#1[31]150, CWTI:JUL/93[29]326, GETTY:11[6]231
Savannah & Charleston; B&G:FEB/91[8]439
Savannah and Gulf; B&G:FEB/91[8]439,
Seaboard & Roanoke; CWTI:JAN/95[42]428
Selma & Jackson; CWR:VOL2#4[313]146
South Side; B&G:APR/92[8]481, CWM:JUL/91[46]373,
CWR:VOL2#3[236]143, CWTI:AUG/90[26]166
Southern Mississippi; ACW:SEP/95[48]547
Southern; ACW:NOV/91[22]331, ACW:JAN/92[16]340,
ACW:MAY/92[47]363, ACW:NOV/92[74]390,
ACW:JAN/93[43]397, ACW:MAY/95[38]526,
B&G:AUG/95[8]604, CWM:MAY/91[40]351,
CWM:MAY/92[34]422, CWM:MAR/93[24]467,
CWR:VOL1#2[44]114, CWR:VOL2#1[19]131,
CWR:VOL2#2[141]137, CWR:VOL3#2[70]155,
MH:APR/95[46]183
State of Georgia; CWTI:FEB/92[10]246
Tennessee & Alabama; B&G:FEB/95[30]591,
CWR:VOL2#4[313]146, CWTI:JAN/94[35]361
Texas & New Orleans; CWM:OCT/95[47]620
United States Military Railroad:
ARTICLE: "HERMAN HAUPT'S RAILROADS: BEANPOLES TO
CORNSTALKS," CWM:NOV/91[12]390, "WHEN SECRETARY
OF WAR EDWIN STANTON NEEDED A GOOD MAN TO
RUN HIS VITAL RAILROADS, HE SENT FOR HERMAN
HAUPT," ACW:JUL/95[16]534
ADDITIONAL LISTINGS: AHI:JUL/95[30]324, B&G:AUG/91[32]461,
CWM:NOV/91[4]388, CWM:NOV/91[12]390,
CWTI:FEB/91[24]191, CWTI:FEB/92[10]246,
CWTI:MAR/95[54]438
Vicksburg & Jackson; B&G:AUG/95[8]604, CWR:VOL2#1[78]
Vicksburg; B&G:JUN/93[12]524
Virginia & Tennessee; ACW:MAR/94[27]459,
B&G:AUG/91[11]458, B&G:JUN/93[32]525,
CWM:MAY/91[40]351, CWTI:MAR/89[16]101,
CWTI:SEP/94[49]404
Virginia Central; ACW:JUL/91[18]312, ACW:NOV/92[26]386,
ACW:MAY/94[35]469, B&G:APR/91[8]445,
B&G:APR/93[12]518, B&G:APR/94[10]558,
B&G:AUG/94[10]574, CWM:MAR/91[65]342,
CWM:MAY/91[40]351, CWM:NOV/91[73],
CWM:APR/94[24]505, CWM:JUN/95[43]587,
CWTI:APR/89[38]111, CWTI:MAY/89[22]116,
CWTI:DEC/91[36]240, CWTI:NOV/93[55]350,
GETTY:11[6]231, MH:FEB/93[42]164
Virginia; CWM:MAY/91[40]351
Weldon & Petersburg; MH:APR/95[46]183
Weldon; ACW:NOV/92[74]390, ACW:JUL/93[16]422,
ACW:SEP/93[8]429, B&G:APR/92[8]481, CWM:JUL/92[8]427,
CWM:OCT/95[40]619, CWNEWS:JAN/92[4],
CWR:VOL1#3[52]122, CWR:VOL2#2[141]137,
CWR:VOL2#4[269]145, CWR:VOL3#3[1]157,
CWTI:FEB/91[45]194, CWTI:DEC/94[32]410,
CWTI:JAN/95[34]427
Western & Atlantic:
ARTICLE: "AT HOME WITH THE GENERAL,"
CWTI:FEB/92[10]246
ADDITIONAL LISTINGS: ACW:SEP/91[22]321, ACW:NOV/93[42]443,
ACW:MAR/94[42]461, ACW:JUL/94[66]481,

AHI:NOV/73[18]151, B&G:JUN/93[12]524, B&G:APR/95[30],
CWM:JAN/91[12]326, CWM:JAN/91[40]330,
CWM:NOV/91[50]394, CWM:JUL/92[24]430,
CWNEWS:MAY/93[4], CWR:VOL1#3[82]123,
CWR:VOL3#3[59]159, CWR:VOL4#1[1]163,
CWTI:SUMMER/89[13]120, CWTI:SUMMER/89[50]124,
CWTI:FEB/91[18]190, CWTI:SEP/91[23]228,
CWTI:NOV/93[33]347, CWTI:SEP/94[40]403,
CWTI:DEC/94[49]413, CWTI:MAR/95[40]436
Western Maryland; CWM:NOV/91[12]390
Wilmington & Weldon; B&G:DEC/94[10]585,
B&G:DEC/95[9]615
Winchester & Harpers Ferry; CWR:VOL1#4[7]125
Winchester & Potomac; CWM:NOV/91[40]393
York River; CWM:NOV/91[4]388

RAILWAYS AND TELEGRAPH ACT; CWM:NOV/91[12]390
RAINE, C.I., *Captain, Lee Artillery;* GETTY:4[49]147
RAINE, CHARLES J., *Captain, CSA;* CWR:VOL4#4[70]180,
GETTY:10[29]222
RAINES, WILLIAM A., *Lieutenant, 11th Mississippi Infantry;*
ACW:MAR/92[10]349
RAINEY, THEOPHILUS, *Private, Petersburg Artillery;*
ACW:MAR/95[12]513
RAINS, GABRIEL J., *General, CSA;* ACW:NOV/91[8]328,
ACW:MAY/92[62]364, ACW:JAN/95[46]507,
CWTI:SEP/90[34]176, CWTI:DEC/95[76]482
RAINS, GEORGE W., *Colonel, CSA:*
ARTICLES: "BULWARK OF THE BELEAGUERED
CONFEDERACY," CWM:SEP/91[10]379, "COLONEL
GEORGE WASHINGTON RAINS WORKED WONDERS
WITH THE CONFEDERACY'S NASCENT NITRE BUREAU,"
ACW:MAY/94[20]467
ADDITIONAL LISTINGS: CWM:SEP/91[4]376, CWR:VOL3#4[68],
photo, CWM:SEP/91[10]379
RAINS, JAMES S., *General, CSA;* ACW:NOV/93[26]441,
B&G:DEC/93[52]548, CWTI:FEB/92[29]248
RALSTON, GEORGE, *Captain, CSA;* CWR:VOL3#1[1]149
RALSTON, R., *Musician, 26th Iowa Infantry;*
ACW:SEP/95[38]546
RAMMEL, JOEL B., *Sgt., 3rd Penna. Cav.;* GETTY:13[89]260
RAMSAY, GEORGE D., *General, USA;* CWTI:JAN/93[49]303
RAMSAY, H. ASHTON, *Engineer, CSN;* AHI:OCT/75[30]162,
AHI:NOV/75[38]163
RAMSAY, JAMES G.; AHI:DEC/73[10]152
RAMSDELL, HENRY, *Adjutant, 124th New York Infantry;*
ACW:JUL/95[66]539
RAMSEUR, STEPHEN D. *General, CSA:*
ARTICLE: "STEPHEN DODSON RAMSEUR,"
CWM:JAN/93[40]461
GENERAL LISTINGS: *Cedar Creek,* ACW:SEP/94[55]489,
MH:OCT/93[76]173, *Chancellorsville,* MH:JUN/92[50]159,
Gettysburg, GETTY:4[33]146, GETTY:4[49]147,
GETTY:5[13]157, GETTY:5[117]165, GETTY:6[7]169,
GETTY:9[17]210, GETTY:10[7]221, *in book review,*
CWNEWS:SEP/90[4], CWNEWS:OCT/94[33], *in order of
battle,* B&G:APR/94[10]558, B&G:APR/95[8]595, *Monocacy,*
ACW:NOV/93[50]444, B&G:DEC/92[8]503, *Overland
Campaign,* B&G:APR/94[10]558, *Stephenson's Depot,*
B&G:AUG/94[10]574, *Third Winchester,* ACW:MAY/91[38]305,
AHI:NOV/80[8]209, *West Point,* B&G:DEC/91[12]469,
Wilderness, B&G:APR/95[8]595, B&G:JUN/95[8]600, *photo,*
CWM:JAN/93[40]461

ADDITIONAL LISTINGS: ACW:NOV/92[42]388, ACW:SEP/93[31]433, ACW:SEP/94[38]487, ACW:JAN/95[46]507, AHI:APR/85[18]250, B&G:FEB/95[8]590B, CWM:SEP/91[64]387, CWM:JUL/92[16]428, CWM:OCT/94[38]540, CWTI:JAN/93[40]301, CWTI:MAY/93[26]318, GETTY:13[33]255, GETTY:13[108]261

RAMSEY, ALAN, *Lieutenant, USMC;* CWTI:APR/92[14]254

RAMSEY, ALEXANDER, *Governor, Minnesota;* ACW:MAY/91[12]302, ACW:NOV/94[76]500, GETTY:5[79]161

RAMSEY, GEORGE D., *General, USA;* CWTI:DEC/90[18]180

RAMSEY, JOHN, *General, USA;* CWTI:AUG/90[26]166

RAMSEY, MRS. J.G.; AHI:DEC/73[10]152

RAMSOUR, O.A., *Lt., 11th North Carolina Inf.;* GETTY:8[67]204

RANDAL, HORACE, *Colonel, CSA;* CWR:VOL3#3[33]158, CWR:VOL4#2[68]167

RANDALL, CHARLES B., *Lieutenant Colonel, 149th New York Infantry;* CWR:VOL3#2[70]155, GETTY:10[36]223

RANDALL, HORACE D., *Lieutenant, Sumter Artillery;* CWR:VOL3#2[1]153

RANDALL, WILLIAM, *Lt., 1st Mich. Inf.;* CWM:SEP/92[24]441

RANDLETT, JAMES F., *Major, USA;* ACW:MAY/92[30]361

RANDOL, ALANSON M., *Captain, 1st U.S. Artillery:*
GENERAL LISTINGS: *Gettysburg,* GETTY:4[75]149, GETTY:11[19]232, *Manassas, Second,* AHI:DEC/66[30]105
ADDITIONAL LISTINGS: B&G:OCT/93[12]537, CWM:JUN/95[69]596, GETTY:13[89]260

RANDOLPH, AUGUSTE, *Lieutenant, 9th Louisiana Infantry;* CWTI:FEB/91[12]189

RANDOLPH, CHARLES C., *cadet, VMI;* ARTICLE: "DIMINUTIVE BUT FEISTY, CHARLES CARTER RANDOLPH WAS," STONEWALL JACKSON'S PET CADET," ACW:JUL/93[10]421

RANDOLPH, GEORGE, *Major, CSA;* ACW:MAR/93[42]406, CWR:VOL1#2[7]111

RANDOLPH, GEORGE E., *Captain, USA;* GETTY:9[41]212

RANDOLPH, GEORGE W., *General, CSA:*
BOOK REVIEW: *GEORGE WYTHE RANDOLPH AND THE CONFEDERATE ELITE*
GENERAL LISTINGS: *in book review,* CWM:APR/95[50], *torpedoes,* ACW:NOV/91[8]328, *photo,* B&G:OCT/92[38]500
ADDITIONAL LISTINGS: ACW:SEP/93[8]429, ACW:NOV/93[42]443, B&G:OCT/92[38]500, CWM:APR/94[32]506, CWM:JUN/95[29]583, CWR:VOL2#1[36]132, CWTI:APR/89[14]107, CWTI:DEC/94[73]416, CWTI:DEC/95[76]482

RANDOLPH, JOHN; CWNEWS:SEP/95[33]

RANDOLPH, MERIWETHER L., *Captain, CSA;* GETTY:4[110]152

RANK IN THE MILITARY; ARTICLE: "A PROBLEM OF RANK," CWTI:FEB/91[52]195

RANK, WILLIAM D., *Captain, 3rd Pennsylvania Heavy Artillery;* GETTY:4[65]148, GETTY:13[89]260

RANKIN, ARTHUR, *Colonel, USA;* CWM:SEP/93[18]494

RANKIN, JAMES and REUBEN, *2nd Tennessee Cavalry;* CWR:VOL4#1[1]163

RANKIN, ROBERT, *Lieutenant, CSA;* B&G:DEC/94[10]585

RANKIN, WILLIAM A., *Lieutenant Colonel, 9th Mississippi Infantry;* ACW:JAN/91[22]285

RANSOM, DUNBAR R., *Captain, 3rd U.S. Artillery;* B&G:APR/94[10]558, GETTY:12[7]241

RANSOM, JOHN, *Private, USA;* CWM:JAN/92[16]401, CWM:AUG/95[45], CWM:OCT/95[10], CWTI:APR/92[23]255

RANSOM, MATTHEW W., *General, CSA;* B&G:APR/92[8]481, B&G:APR/92[48]484, CWR:VOL4#2[136], CWTI:JUL/94[44]394

RANSOM, ROBERT, *General, CSA;* ACW:NOV/93[50]444, ACW:MAR/94[50]462, ACW:JAN/95[10]503, AHI:JUN/78[4]180, B&G:DEC/92[8]503, CWM:JUN/95[73]597, CWR:VOL4#4[28]178, GETTY:11[6]231

RANSOM, THOMAS E.G., *General, USA:*
BOOK REVIEW: *HARD DYING MEN: THE STORY OF GENERAL W.H.L. WALLACE, GENERAL T.E.G. RANSOM, AND THEIR "OLD ELEVENTH" ILLINOIS INFANTRY*
ADDITIONAL LISTINGS: CWM:JAN/91[11]325, CWR:VOL4#2[26]166, CWR:VOL4#2[1]165, CWTI:SUMMER/89[50]124, CWTI:JAN/93[20]298

RAPHALL, MORRIS J., *Rabbi;* CWTI:MAY/92[38]265

RAPPAHANNOCK STATION, VIRGINIA, BATTLE OF:
ARTICLE: "DARING NIGHT ASSAULT," ACW:MAR/92[30]352
ADDITIONAL LISTINGS: B&G:APR/91[8]445, CWM:JUL/92[8]427, CWNEWS:OCT/89[4], CWTI:JAN/94[42]363

RATCHFORD, JAMES W., *Lieutenant, CSA;* CWM:JUN/95[61]593

RATCLIFFE, LAURA:
ARTICLE: "LETTERS TO LAURA," CWTI:JUL/92[12]270
ADDITIONAL LISTING: CWTI:NOV/92[8]288

RATCLIFFE, W.D., *Capt., 14th Kent. Inf.;* ACW:SEP/95[22]544

RATCLIFFE, WALTER J., *Private, Crenshaw's Artillery;* GETTY:10[107]227

RATHBONE, HENRY R., *Major, USA:*
BOOK REVIEW: *HENRY AND CLARA,* ACW:SEP/95[62]
ADDITIONAL LISTINGS: ACW:MAY/95[68]529, AHI:FEB/86[12]257, CWTI:MAR/93[12]307, CWTI:SEP/94[24]399, CWTI:DEC/95[76]482, CWTI:DEC/95[90]483, *photo,* CWTI:MAR/93[12]307

RATLIFF, ROBERT W., *General, USA;* B&G:AUG/91[11]458, B&G:AUG/91[52]464, *photo,* B&G:AUG/91[52]458

RAUCH, —, *Lt., 14th South Carolina Inf.;* GETTY:9[116]219

RAUCH, WILLIAM, *Sergeant, 13th Pennsylvania Reserve;* CWR:VOL1#3[28]120

RAUGH, JAMES J., *Private, 53rd Pennsylvania Infantry;* GETTY:11[80]235

RAUM, GREEN, *Colonel, USA;* CWR:VOL3#3[59]159

RAWLES, JACOB, *Capt., 5th U.S. Arty.;* ACW:JAN/94[30]450

RAWLEY, CHARLES W., *General, CSA;* CWR:VOL3#1[1]149

RAWLINGS, BENJAMIN C., *Private, Crenshaw's Artillery;* GETTY:10[107]227

RAWLINS, JOHN A., *General, USA:*
ARTICLE: "HOMETOWN FRIEND JOHN A. RAWLINS WAS U.S. GRANT'S 'NEAREST INDISPENSABLE' OFFICER," ACW:NOV/95[22]554
ADDITIONAL LISTINGS: AHI:MAY/69[32]122, AHI:SEP/87[48]264, B&G:APR/95[8]595, B&G:APR/95[33]597, CWM:SEP/92[19]440, CWM:AUG/95[8], CWR:VOL3#4[24]162, CWTI:FEB/90[46]146, CWTI:MAY/91[24]208, CWTI:DEC/94[82]418, *photo,* CWTI:FEB/90[46]146

RAWSON, CHARLES H., *Surgeon, 5th Iowa Infantry;* AHI:DEC/71[10]137

RAY, POLLY; AHI:DEC/73[10]152

RAY, R., *Private, 1st Illinois Artillery;* B&G:APR/94[28]559

RAYMOND (MISSISSIPPI) FENCIBLES, (12th Mississippi Infantry); GETTY:4[7]142

RAYMOND, MISSISSIPPI, BATTLE OF:
ARTICLE: "I LOVE THE WORK 'RAYMOND'," CWM:JUN/94[58]519
ADDITIONAL LISTINGS: B&G:AUG/95[8]604, CWR:VOL2#1[19]131, CWR:VOL2#1[36]132, CWR:VOL2#1[78], CWR:VOL3#3[33]158, CWR:VOL4#3[89]
RAYNER, KENNETH; BOOK REVIEW: *KENNETH AND JOHN B. RAYNER AND THE LIMITS OF SOUTHERN DISSENT*
RAYNOR, W.H., *Colonel, 56th Ohio Infantry;* B&G:FEB/94[8]550, CWR:VOL4#2[1]165
READ, CHARLES W., *Lieutenant, CSN:*
ARTICLE: "THE GREAT GUNBOAT CHASE," CWTI:JUL/94[30]392
BOOK REVIEW: *NINE MEN IN GRAY*
GENERAL LISTINGS: *in book review,* ACW:JAN/93[58]399, CWM:APR/95[50], CWNEWS:MAY/91[4], *letters to the editor,* CWM:SEP/93[4]492, *photos,* AHI:DEC/82[38]231, CWTI:JUL/94[30]392
ADDITIONAL LISTINGS: ACW:MAR/94[35]460, ACW:SEP/95[30]545, AHI:DEC/82[38]231, CWTI:AUG/90[42]167
READ, SPENCER A., *Pvt., 2nd Tenn. Cav.;* CWR:VOL4#1[1]163
READ, THEODORE, *General, USA;* ACW:JAN/92[22]341, ACW:JAN/93[43]397
READ, THOMAS, *Pvt., 72nd Penna. Inf.;* ACW:MAY/92[8]357
READY, MARTHA "MATTIE"; B&G:OCT/94[11]580
REAGAN, JAMES S.; ACW:JUL/93[27]423
REAGAN, JOHN H.; ACW:MAY/92[62]364, ACW:MAY/95[38]526, CWR:VOL2#3[212]142, CWTI:AUG/90[50]168, CWTI:AUG/91[36]217
REAL, MICHAEL, *Pvt., 1st Indiana Cav.;* ACW:MAR/95[34]516
REAM'S STATION, VIRGINIA, BATTLE OF:
ARTICLE: "CHARGE OF THE TARHEEL BRIGADES," CWTI:FEB/91[45]194
BOOK REVIEW: *THE PETERSBURG CAMPAIGN: THE DESTRUCTION OF THE WELDON RAILROAD (DEEP BOTTOM, GLOBE TAVERN, AND REAMS STATION, AUGUST 14-25, 1864*
ADDITIONAL LISTINGS: ACW:JAN/92[16]340, ACW:JUL/93[16]422, ACW:SEP/93[8]429, ACW:SEP/95[74]550, CWM:MAY/92[8]418, CWM:OCT/95[40]619, CWM:DEC/95[41]630, CWR:VOL1#1[1]102, CWR:VOL2#1[78], CWR:VOL2#2[141]137, CWR:VOL2#3[236]143, CWR:VOL3#1[65]151, CWR:VOL3#3[1]157, CWTI:FEB/91[45]194
REARDON, JOHN, *Private, 3rd Georgia Infantry;* CWTI:DEC/94[32]410
REASER, PHILIP, *Pvt., 26th VA Battalion;* B&G:APR/93[24]520
REBERSBURG, PENNSYLVANIA; ARTICLE: "REMEMBERING A DAY," CWM:OCT/95[55]622
RECONSTRUCTION ACTS; CWTI:FEB/90[60]148
RECONSTRUCTION:
ARTICLES: "THE GENTLE CARPETBAGGER: DANIEL H. CHAMBERLAIN," AHI:JAN/73[28]147, "THE MURDER OF A SCALAWAG," AHI:APR/73[12]148, "WILLIAM C. OATES: ON LITTLE ROUND TOP, UNSUNG; IN POSTWAR POLITICS, UNRECONSTRUCTED," CWM:DEC/94[26]548
BOOK REVIEWS: *A COMPROMISE OF PRINCIPLE: CONGRESSIONAL REPUBLICANS AND RECONSTRUCTION, 1863-1869 * THE ABOLITIONIST LEGACY: FROM RECONSTRUCTION TO THE NAACP * AN OLD CREED FOR THE NEW SOUTH PRO-SLAVERY IDEOLOGY AND HISTORIOGRAPHY, 1865-1918 * BLACK SCARE: THE RACIST RESPONSE TO EMANCIPATION*

AND RECONSTRUCTION * THE CRISIS OF THE AMERICAN REPUBLIC: A HISTORY OF THE CIVIL WAR AND RECONSTRUCTION ERA * CRUCIBLE OF RECONSTRUCTION: WAR, RADICALISM, AND RACE IN LOUISIANA, 1862-1877 * FREEDOM'S LAWMAKERS: A DIRECTORY OF BLACK OFFICEHOLDERS DURING RECONSTRUCTION * THE IMPACT OF THE CIVIL WAR AND RECONSTRUCTION ON ARKANSAS*
BOOK REVIEWS, continued: *IMPEACHMENT OF A PRESIDENT: ANDREW JOHNSON, THE BLACKS AND RECONSTRUCTION * LEE CONSIDERED: GENERAL ROBERT E. LEE AND CIVIL WAR HISTORY * LET US HAVE PEACE: ULYSSES S. GRANT AND THE POLITICS OF WAR AND RECONSTRUCTION, 1861-1868 * NEW MASTERS: NORTHERN PLANTERS DURING THE CIVIL WAR AND RECONSTRUCTION * ORDEAL BY FIRE: THE CIVIL WAR AND RECONSTRUCTION * RETREAT FROM RECONSTRUCTION * THE ROMANCE OF REUNION: NORTHERNERS AND THE SOUTH, 1865-1900 * THE TROUBLE THEY SEEN: BLACK PEOPLE TELL THE STORY OF RECONSTRUCTION*
GENERAL LISTINGS: *in book review,* AHI:OCT/73[49], CWM:AUG/95[45], MH:AUG/92[76], *Thaddeus Stevens,* AHI:JAN/82[16]224
ADDITIONAL LISTINGS: CWM:APR/94[32]506, CWM:DEC/94[17]547, CWTI:DEC/89[62]139, CWTI:FEB/90[60]148, CWTI:AUG/90[64]170, CWTI:SEP/90[28]175, CWTI:SEP/93[14]333, CWTI:JAN/94[35]361
RECRUITING; ARTICLE: "TIL THE PAPER WORK IS DONE," CWTI:NOV/93[78]354
RED RIVER CAMPAIGN:
ARTICLES: "A DEATH AT MANSFIELD: COLONEL JAMES HAMILTON BEARD AND THE CONSOLIDATED CRESCENT REGIMENT," CWR:VOL4#2[68]167, "A.J. SMITH'S ROVING 'GORILLAS'," MH:DEC/95[58]188, "CHASING BANKS OUT OF LOUISIANA: PARSON'S TEXAS CAVALRY IN THE RED RIVER CAMPAIGN," CWR:VOL2#3[212]142, "COMMANDS, 95TH ILLINOIS," ACW:JAN/91[16]284, "THE FARM BOYS IN THE 96TH OHIO REGIMENT FOUND THEMSELVES KNEE-DEEP IN ALLIGATORS IN LOUISIANA," ACW:SEP/92[16]376, "HENRY GRAY'S LOUISIANA BRIGADE AT THE BATTLE OF MANSFIELD APRIL 8, 1864," CWR:VOL4#2[1]165, "THE RED RIVER CAMPAIGN LETTERS OF LIEUTENANT CHARLES W. KENNEDY, 156TH NEW YORK VOLUNTEER INFANTRY," CWR:VOL4#2[104]168, "RED RIVER BLUES," CWM:APR/95[39]576, "THE UNION NAVAL EXPEDITION ON THE RED RIVER, MARCH 12-MAY 22, 1864," CWR:VOL4#2[26]166, "UNPUBLISHED AFTER-ACTION REPORTS FROM THE RED RIVER CAMPAIGN," CWR:VOL4#2[118]169
BOOK REVIEWS: *THE RED RIVER CAMPAIGN: ESSAYS ON UNION AND CONFEDERATE LEADERSHIP * RED RIVER CAMPAIGN: POLITICS AND COTTON IN THE CIVIL WAR*
GENERAL LISTINGS: *general history,* AHI:MAY/71[3]133A, *in book review,* ACW:MAY/93[54], CWNEWS:OCT/89[4], CWNEWS:APR/90[4], CWR:VOL2#4[346], CWR:VOL4#3[1]170
ADDITIONAL LISTINGS: ACW:SEP/91[16]320, ACW:SEP/92[23]377, ACW:MAY/93[12]412, ACW:JUL/93[34]424, ACW:MAR/95[18]514, ACW:MAR/95[34]516, B&G:OCT/94[38]582, CWM:OCT/95[47]620, CWM:OCT/95[63]623, CWR:VOL1#2[44]114, CWR:VOL2#1[19]131, CWR:VOL2#3[252]144,

REBELLION: A COMPILATION OF THE OFFICIAL
RECORDS OF THE UNION AND CONFEDERATE ARMIES

REFORD, WILLIAM, *Captain, 24th Michigan Infantry;*
GETTY:5[19]158

REID, EDWARD F., *Private, 3rd Indiana Cavalry;*
GETTY:11[19]232

REID, J.S., *Captain, CSA;* ACW:NOV/93[26]441

REID, JAMES S., *Lt. Col., 3rd GA Inf.;* CWTI:SEP/94[26]400

REID, JOHN C., *Captain, USA;* AHI:NOV/88[28]277

REID, RAYMOND J., *Adjutant, 2nd Florida Infantry;*
GETTY:12[7]241

REID, SAMUEL J., *Captain, CSA;* CWTI:JAN/94[46]364

REID, WHITELAW;
ARTICLE: "'AGATE': WHITELAW REID REPORTS FROM
GETTYSBURG," GETTY:7[23]187
ADDITIONAL LISTINGS: ACW:JUL/91[35]314, B&G:AUG/93[10]529

REILLY'S BATTERY; CWM:MAR/91[17]335

REILLY, JAMES, *Major, Rowan (North Carolina) Artillery;*
B&G:DEC/94[10]585, CWM:MAR/91[17]335, GETTY:5[47]160

REILLY, JAMES W., *General, USA;* CWM:AUG/95[36]608,
CWTI:SUMMER/89[50]124

REILLY, MICHAEL; B&G:FEB/94[38]553

REILLY, O.T., ARTICLE: "O.T. REILLY, BATTLEFIELD GUIDE,"
B&G:OCT/95[54]614A

REILY, JAMES, *Colonel, CSA;* ACW:JUL/93[27]423

REINHARDT, JOHN H., *Private, 16th Georgia Infantry;*
CWM:JUL/92[16]428

RELIC HUNTING, ARTICLE: "HUNTING HISTORY,"
CWM:SEP/91[48]386

RELICS; ARTICLES: "THE B.H. TEAGUE COLLECTION OF
CONFEDERATE RELICS AND CURIOS,"
B&G:JUN/91[38]455, "THE WAR'S MOST DANGEROUS
RELICS," CWTI:DEC/94[42]412

RELIGION:
BOOK REVIEWS: *THE CONFEDERACY'S FIGHTING CHAPLAIN:
FATHER JOHN B. BANNON * THE FOURTH CAREER OF
JOHN B. BANNON: ST LOUIS PASTOR, SOUTHERN
CHAPLAIN, CONFEDERATE AGENT, IRISH JESUIT
ORATOR * GOD ORDAINED THIS WAR: SERMONS ON
THE SECTIONAL CRISIS, 1830-1865 * 'NO SORROW LIKE
OUR SORROW': NORTHERN PROTESTANT MINISTERS
AND THE ASSASSINATION OF LINCOLN * WHERE THEY
LIE, THE STORY OF JEWISH SOLDIERS OF THE NORTH
AND SOUTH WHOSE DEATHS OCCURRED DURING THE
CIVIL WAR, 1861-1865*
ADDITIONAL LISTING: *photo,* CWTI:JUN/90[28]158

REMINGTON, FREDERIC, CWTI:SUMMER/89[20]121

REMINGTON, WILLIAM N., *Lieutenant, 6th Wisconsin
Infantry;* GETTY:4[16]143

RENO, JESSE L., *General, USA:*
ARTICLE: "THE DEATH OF JESSE RENO," CWM:MAY/92[44]423
GENERAL LISTINGS: *in book review,* ACW:JUL/93[58],
ACW:JAN/95[62], CWR:VOL4#2[136], *Manassas, Second,*
AHI:DEC/66[30]105, B&G:AUG/92[11]493,
B&G:OCT/95[20]612, *photo,* CWM:MAY/92[44]423
ADDITIONAL LISTINGS: ACW:JUL/91[18]312, ACW:JAN/95[54]508,
ACW:MAY/95[18]524, CWM:SEP/93[35]497,
CWTI:MAR/93[20]308, CWTI:SEP/94[26]400,
CWTI:SEP/94[49]404, CWTI:JAN/95[34]427

RENO, MARCUS A., *Major, USA:*
BOOK REVIEW: *FAINT THE TRUMPET SOUNDS; THE LIFE
AND TRIAL OF MAJOR RENO*

GENERAL LISTINGS: *Custer,* AHI:JUN/76[4]169, *Little Big Horn,*
AHI:DEC/84[10]242, AHI:DEC/84[18]243,
AHI:JAN/85[30]246, MH:AUG/95[82]186, *photo,*
AHI:JUN/76[4]169

RENSHAW, WILLIAM B., *Commodore, USN;*
ACW:JAN/93[51]398

REPETTI, ALEXANDER, *Lieutenant Colonel, 39th New York
Infantry;* ACW:MAY/95[54]528, B&G:OCT/95[36]614

REPUBLICAN PARTY:
BOOK REVIEW: *A COMPROMISE OF PRINCIPLE:
CONGRESSIONAL REPUBLICANS AND
RECONSTRUCTION, 1863-1869*
ADDITIONAL LISTINGS: AHI:OCT/68[4]116, AHI:DEC/68[28]118,
AHI:JUN/73[4]149

REQUA, JOSEPHUS; B&G:DEC/94[28], CWTI:JAN/93[49]303

RESACA, GEORGIA, BATTLE OF:
ARTICLE: "THE BATTLE THAT SHOULD NOT HAVE BEEN,"
CWTI:NOV/92[41]291
GENERAL LISTINGS: *general history,* AHI:MAY/71[3]133A, *in book
review,* CWM:AUG/95[45], *letters to the editor,*
CWTI:MAR/93[8]306
ADDITIONAL LISTINGS: ACW:MAR/92[14]350, ACW:JUL/94[66]481,
CWM:JAN/91[12]326, CWM:NOV/91[50]394,
CWM:JUL/92[40]432, CWR:VOL1#1[73]108,
CWTI:SUMMER/89[13]120, CWTI:SUMMER/89[20]121,
CWTI:MAR/95[40]436

RESEARCH:
ARTICLE: "FINDING CIVIL WAR ANCESTORS MADE EASIER,"
AHI:JAN/94[18]319
BOOK REVIEW: *THE SUPPLEMENT TO THE OFFICIAL
RECORDS, VOLS. 1-3*

REULS, J.W., *Pvt., 31st NC Inf.;* B&G:APR/93[24]520

REUNIONS:
ARTICLES: "THE GRAY REUNION," CWTI:FEB/92[42]250,
"PERSONALITY," ACW:SEP/91[8]318
BOOK REVIEW: *HANDS ACROSS THE WALL: THE 50TH AND
75TH REUNIONS OF THE GETTYSBURG BATTLE*
Gettysburg, 50th:
ARTICLES: "REUNION AT GETTYSBURG: A REMINISCENCE
OF THE FIFTIETH ANNIVERSARY OF THE BATTLE OF
GETTYSBURG JULY 1-5, 1913," GETTY:5[123]166,
"RETURN TO GETTYSBURG," AHI:JUL/93[40]312
ADDITIONAL LISTING: GETTY:7[119]195
Gettysburg, 75th:
ARTICLE: "END OF AN ERA: THE 75TH REUNION AT
GETTYSBURG," GETTY:7[119]195
BOOK REVIEW: *GETTYSBURG: THE LAST REUNION OF THE
BLUE & GRAY*
ADDITIONAL LISTINGS: AHI:JUL/93[40]312, CWM:AUG/95[56]610,
GETTY:8[127]208

REVENUE CUTTER SERVICE; ARTICLE: "GUARDIANS OF
THE COAST," ACW:MAR/94[35]460

REVERE, JOSEPH W., *General, USA;* B&G:FEB/92[22]476

REVERE, PAUL J., *Major, 20th Massachusetts Infantry;*
ACW:JUL/91[8]309, AHI:FEB/82[36]225,
CWR:VOL3#1[31]150, *photo,* CWR:VOL3#1[31]150

REX, GEORGE, *Surgeon;* CWTI:AUG/95[58]461

REYNOLDS, A.E., *Colonel, CSA;* ACW:NOV/91[22]331

REYNOLDS, ALEXANDER W., *General, CSA;*
AHI:JUN/70[30]127, CWR:VOL2#1[36]132,
CWTI:MAR/89[44]105

REYNOLDS, C.E., *Union Veteran;* GETTY:5[123]166
REYNOLDS, DANIEL H, *General, CSA;* ACW:SEP/92[38]379,
  B&G:DEC/93[12]545, B&G:DEC/95[9]615,
  CWTI:SUMMER/89[32]122, *photo,* B&G:DEC/95[9]615
REYNOLDS, E. MCDONALD, *Captain, USMC;*
  CWR:VOL2#3[194]141
REYNOLDS, FRANCIS, *Surgeon, 88th New York Infantry;*
  GETTY:10[53]225
REYNOLDS, GILBERT H., *Captain, 1st New York Light
  Artillery;* GETTY:5[117]165, GETTY:12[30]243
REYNOLDS, J.E., *Pvt., 30th Miss. Inf.;* CWTI:SEPT/89[30]129
REYNOLDS, JACK, *Lieutenant, USN;* CWTI:DEC/90[29]182
REYNOLDS, JAMES, *Private, CSA;* ACW:NOV/91[10]329
REYNOLDS, JOHN A., *Major, USA;* B&G:DEC/95[9]615,
  CWR:VOL3#2[70]155, CWTI:SUMMER/89[32]122
REYNOLDS, JOHN F., *General, USA:*
GENERAL LISTINGS: *Beaver Dam Creek,* CWM:JUN/95[57]592,
  Chancellorsville, CWTI:AUG/95[24]455, *Fredericksburg,*
  ACW:MAR/95[42]517, CWR:VOL4#4[1]177,
  CWR:VOL4#4[70]180, *Gaines' Mill,* CWM:JUN/95[61]593,
  Gettysburg, AHI:MAY/67[22]107, B&G:OCT/91[11]466,
  GETTY:4[7]142, GETTY:4[24]145, GETTY:4[49]147,
  GETTY:4[113]153, GETTY:5[4]156, GETTY:5[13]157,
  GETTY:5[19]158, GETTY:5[47]160, GETTY:6[7]169,
  GETTY:6[13]170, GETTY:6[43]173, GETTY:6[69]176,
  GETTY:7[7]185, GETTY:7[23]187, GETTY:7[124]196,
  GETTY:8[111]206, GETTY:8[121]207, GETTY:9[17]210,
  GETTY:9[53]214, GETTY:9[61]215, GETTY:10[7]221,
  GETTY:10[42]224, GETTY:11[19]232, GETTY:11[57]233,
  GETTY:11[71]234, GETTY:11[119]238, GETTY:12[85]248
GENERAL LISTINGS, continued: *in book review,* CWM:FEB/95[7],
  CWR:VOL1#2[78], CWR:VOL3#4[68], CWR:VOL4#4[129],
  Indian wars, AHI:OCT/79[20]194, *Mexican War,*
  MH:APR/93[39]166, *Manassas, Second,* AHI:DEC/66[30]105,
  B&G:AUG/92[11]493, B&G:OCT/95[20]612,
  CWTI:NOV/93[55]350, *SIO,* B&G:OCT/94[42]583, *West Point,*
  AHI:AUG/71[22]135, B&G:DEC/91[12]469, *photos,*
  AHI:DEC/66[30]105, B&G:DEC/91[12]469,
  B&G:AUG/92[11]493, B&G:FEB/95[8]590A,
  CWM:MAR/91[17]335, CWM:DEC/94[74]555,
  CWTI:SEP/91[31]229, GETTY:11[19]232
ADDITIONAL LISTINGS: ACW:JUL/91[18]312, ACW:JUL/91[35]314,
  ACW:JUL/93[50]426, B&G:OCT/93[12]537,
  B&G:FEB/94[24]551, B&G:APR/94[34]561,
  B&G:FEB/95[8]590A, CWM:MAR/91[17]335,
  CWM:MAY/92[15]419, CWM:JAN/93[8]456,
  CWM:AUG/94[48]529, CWM:AUG/94[60]531,
  CWM:DEC/94[74]555, CWR:VOL1#1[26]103,
  CWR:VOL1#2[29]112, CWR:VOL1#3[28]120,
  CWR:VOL2#4[269]145, CWR:VOL3#1[31]150,
  CWR:VOL3#3[1]157, CWTI:FEB/91[12]189,
  CWTI:SEP/91[31]229, CWTI:JUL/93[42]329,
  CWTI:NOV/93[24]346, GETTY:13[33]255, GETTY:13[119]262
REYNOLDS, JOHN G., *Lieutenant Colonel, USMC;*
  CWR:VOL2#3[183]140, CWR:VOL2#3[194]141,
  CWTI:APR/92[14]254
REYNOLDS, JOSEPH J., *General, USA;* ACW:JAN/92[50]345,
  ACW:SEP/94[31]486, B&G:OCT/92[10]496,
  B&G:AUG/93[10]529
REYNOLDS, ORIN, *Pvt., 9th Mass. Arty.;* GETTY:5[47]160
REYNOLDS, REUBEN O., *Major, 11th Mississippi Infantry;*
  CWR:VOL2#4[269]145, GETTY:9[98]217
REYNOLDS, S.H., *Captain, CSA;* B&G:FEB/91[20]440

REYNOLDS, THOMAS C., *Confederate Governor of Missouri;*
  ACW:NOV/94[42]497, B&G:JUN/91[10]452,
  B&G:OCT/91[6]465, CWM:JAN/92[8]399
REYNOLDS, W.W., *Lieutenant Colonel, 15th Arkansas Infantry;*
  B&G:FEB/94[8]550
RHEA, MATT, *Capt., 13th Tennessee Inf.;* CWR:VOL3#4[24]162
RHETT, A. BURNETT, *Major, CSA;* B&G:DEC/95[9]615
RHETT, ROBERT B.; AHI:JUN/73[4]149, AHI:FEB/75[4]157,
  CWM:JUN/94[6], CWM:AUG/95[45], CWNEWS:FEB/94[5],
  CWR:VOL2#1[78], *photo,* AHI:JUN/73[4]149
RHETT, THOMAS, *Colonel, CSA;* CWTI:MAR/95[60]439
RHIENHARDT, CHARLES, *Private, 1st Ohio Artillery;*
  GETTY:4[49]147
RHIND, ALEXANDER C., *Commander, USN;*
  ACW:JAN/95[38]506, B&G:DEC/94[10]585
RHINEHART, ALFRED, *Captain, 148th Pennsylvania
  Infantry;* CWR:VOL2#2[141]137

RHODE ISLAND TROOPS:

1st Artillery; ACW:MAY/95[30]525, CWM:MAR/91[50]340,
  CWM:MAY/92[20]420, CWR:VOL4#4[101]181,
  CWTI:SEP/90[26]174, GETTY:9[41]212, GETTY:9[61]215
1st Artillery, Battery A:
ARTICLE: "ARNOLD'S BATTERY AND THE 26TH NORTH
  CAROLINA," GETTY:12[61]245
ADDITIONAL LISTINGS: ACW:MAR/94[50]462, CWR:VOL4#4[28]178,
  GETTY:4[89]150, GETTY:5[89]162, GETTY:7[51]190,
  GETTY:7[97]193, GETTY:8[95]205
1st Artillery, Battery B; ACW:JUL/95[50]538,
  CWM:MAR/91[17]335, GETTY:4[89]150, GETTY:5[79]161,
  GETTY:5[89]162, GETTY:7[97]193, GETTY:12[61]245,
  GETTY:13[43]256
1st Artillery, Battery D; ACW:MAR/94[50]462
1st Artillery, Battery E; GETTY:13[7]253
1st Cavalry; ACW:NOV/91[30]332, ACW:JAN/95[54]508,
  B&G:OCT/93[12]537, CWTI:JUN/90[32]159,
  MH:OCT/92[51]162
1st Infantry; ARTICLE: "IN BOOK REVIEW," ACW:JUL/94[58]
2nd Infantry; ACW:MAR/91[14]293, CWTI:MAR/94[48]374,
  GETTY:13[7]253
4th Artillery, Battery B; ACW:MAY/92[8]357
4th Infantry; GETTY:11[6]231
5th Infantry; ACW:JUL/94[58]
7th Cavalry; CWM:MAY/92[8]418
7th Infantry; B&G:APR/94[34]561, B&G:AUG/95[8]604,
  CWTI:AUG/90[26]166, CWTI:AUG/90[64]170,
  CWTI:APR/92[49]260
9th Infantry; GETTY:8[43]202

RHODES, A.C., *Lieutenant, Loudoun Virginia Rangers;*
  CWTI:NOV/92[28]290
RHODES, CHARLES D., *Captain, USA;* ACW:SEP/92[8]374
RHODES, JABEZ R., *Captain, Georgia and Mississippi
  Regiment;* CWR:VOL1#4[42]126
RHODES, ROBERT, *Master, USN;* CWTI:DEC/90[29]182
RHODES, THOMAS C., *Captain, CSA;* B&G:JUN/93[12]524
RICE, ADDISON G., *Col., 154th NY Inf.;* B&G:OCT/93[36]540
RICE, CHARLES S., *Capt., Ohio Arty.;* B&G:AUG/95[8]604
RICE, EDMUND, *Major, 19th Massachusetts Infantry;*
  GETTY:5[79]161, GETTY:7[97]193
RICE, ELLIOTT W., *General, USA;* B&G:DEC/95[9]615
RICE, HORACE, *Major, 29th Tennessee Infantry;*
  B&G:FEB/93[12]511

RICE, JAMES C., *General, USA;* ACW:JAN/92[38]343,
ACW:JAN/95[46]507, B&G:APR/91[8]445, B&G:APR/95[8]595,
B&G:APR/95[8]595, B&G:JUN/95[8]600, GETTY:6[33]172,
GETTY:6[43]173, GETTY:7[41]189, GETTY:8[31]201

RICE, JOE, *Private, 3rd Georgia Infantry;*
CWTI:SEP/94[26]400, CWTI:DEC/94[32]410

RICE, R.S., *Captain, Danville Artillery;* GETTY:13[7]253

RICE, RALSA C., *Private, 125th Ohio Infantry;* BOOK REVIEWS:
*YANKEE TIGERS: THROUGH THE CIVIL WAR WITH THE
125T OHIO*

RICE, SAMUEL, *Colonel, USA;* ACW:MAY/93[22]414

RICE, WILLIAM G., *Lt. Col., 3rd SC Battalion;* GETTY:5[35]159

RICH MOUNTAIN BATTLEFIELD FOUNDATION;
B&G:AUG/93[10]529

RICH MOUNTAIN, WEST VIRGINIA, BATTLE OF:
ARTICLES: "THE NORTHWESTERN VIRGINIA CAMPAIGN OF
1861," B&G:AUG/93[10]529, "ONE MAN'S STRUGGLE AT
RICH MOUNTAIN," B&G:AUG/93[52]534, "PRESERVING
BEVERLY AND THE RICH MOUNTAIN BATTLEFIELD,"
B&G:AUG/93[55]535
ADDITIONAL LISTINGS: AHI:MAY/71[3]133A, B&G:OCT/92[26]498,
B&G:AUG/93[10]529

RICH, EDWIN, *Pvt., 1st Maryland Cav.;* CWTI:JUL/93[20]325

RICH, JABEZ C., *Lieutenant, CSMC;* ACW:MAR/91[14]293

RICHARD, JOHN C., *Captain, 1st Florida Special Battalion;*
CWR:VOL3#1[65]151

RICHARD, JOSEPH H., *Private, 88th Pennsylvania Infantry;*
GETTY:10[7]221

RICHARD, M.E., *Captain, USA;* B&G:APR/91[8]445

RICHARDS, ADOLPHUS, *Captain, CSA;* ACW:JUL/94[26]477

RICHARDS, EVAN, *Lt. Col., 20th Ill. Inf.;* B&G:FEB/94[8]550

RICHARDS, JOSEPH H., *Captain, 88th Pennsylvania
Infantry;* B&G:FEB/95[8]590B, GETTY:10[7]221

RICHARDS, MATTHEW, *Lieutenant Colonel, 96th
Pennsylvania Infantry;* CWR:VOL3#3[1]157

RICHARDS, SAMUEL, *civilian;* ACW:SEP/95[38]546

RICHARDSON, ALBERT C.; BOOK REVIEW: *LOST LOVE: A
TRUE STORY OF PASSION MURDER, AND JUSTICE IN
OLD NEW YORK*

RICHARDSON, ALBERT D., *reporter;* B&G:APR/92[28]482,
CWTI:SEP/91[42]231

RICHARDSON, BUFORD, *Private, 7th Indiana Infantry;*
CWTI:NOV/93[24]346

RICHARDSON, C.A., *Captain, 14th Connecticut Infantry;*
GETTY:8[95]205, GETTY:9[61]215

RICHARDSON, CHARLES, *Lieutenant Colonel, CSA;*
CWR:VOL3#2[1]153, B&G:APR/95[8]595

RICHARDSON, CHARLES A., *Captain, 126th New York
Infantry;* CWR:VOL1#4[7]125

RICHARDSON, D.S., *Pvt., 1st Mass. Inf.;* GETTY:12[7]241

RICHARDSON, HENRY B., *Captain, CSA;* GETTY:9[17]210

RICHARDSON, HOLLON, *Captain, 7th Wisconsin Infantry;*
GETTY:7[23]187

RICHARDSON, ISRAEL B., *General, USA:*
GENERAL LISTINGS: *Antietam,* B&G:OCT/95[8]611C, *in book review,*
CWNEWS:JAN/91[4], CWR:VOL3#4[68], *list of monuments,*
B&G:OCT/95[8]611A
ADDITIONAL LISTINGS: ACW:MAR/94[50]462, ACW:MAY/94[12]466,
ACW:SEP/95[54]548, B&G:OCT/95[8]611A,
CWR:VOL1#4[7]125, CWR:VOL3#1[31]150,
CWTI:JUL/93[14]324, CWTI:SEP/93[43]338, GETTY:11[80]235

RICHARDSON, JOHN B., *Captain, CSA;* ACW:JUL/92[12]367

RICHARDSON, JOHN, *Lieutenant, 11th Mississippi Infantry;*
GETTY:9[98]217

RICHARDSON, JOHN Q., *Major, 52nd North Carolina
Infantry;* GETTY:8[67]204, GETTY:12[61]245

RICHARDSON, MAL, *Private, 3rd Georgia Infantry;*
CWTI:SEP/94[26]400

RICHARDSON, R., *Col., 17th LA Inf.;* B&G:FEB/94[8]550

RICHARDSON, ROBERT V., *Colonel, USA;*
AHI:JUN/70[30]127, B&G:JUN/93[12]524

RICHARDSON, SAMUEL, *Surgeon, 13th New Hampshire
Infantry;* B&G:FEB/92[40]479

RICHARDSON, TOBIAS G., *Surgeon, CSA;* CWM:MAY/91[38]

RICHARDSON, WESLEY, *Private, 7th Wisconsin Infantry,*
GETTY:11[57]233

RICHARDSON, WILLIAM, *Captain, CSA;*
CWTI:NOV/93[33]347

RICHMOND (VIRGINIA) HOWITZERS; ACW:SEP/94[62]490,
AHI:JAN/74[10]153, CWR:VOL1#1[35]104, GETTY:8[53]203

RICHMOND ARMORY; ACW:MAY/95[38]526

RICHMOND NATIONAL BATTLEFIELD PARK;
B&G:APR/92[36]483, CWM:MAY/92[27]421,
B&G:APR/94[47]562A, B&G:APR/94[59]565

RICHMOND, CALVIN D., *Lieutenant, 32nd Wisconsin
Infantry;* CWR:VOL2#4[313]146

RICHMOND, KENTUCKY, BATTLE OF; ACW:JUL/91[6]308,
CWR:VOL4#2[68]167, MH:OCT/94[20]180

RICHMOND, NATHANIEL P., *Colonel, USA;*
GETTY:9[109]218, GETTY:11[19]232

RICHMOND, VIRGINIA, BATTLES AND SIEGE OF:
ARTICLES: "THE 'BLACKBERRY RAID'," GETTY:11[6]231,
"DESPERATE IRONCLAD ASSAULT AT TRENT'S REACH,"
ACW:SEP/95[30]545, "THE FALL OF RICHMOND,"
ACW:MAY/95[38]526, "HUMBLE BUT OBSERVANT WAR
DEPARTMENT CLERK J.B. JONES LEFT BEHIND AN
INVALUABLE ACCOUNT OF WARTIME RICHMOND,"
ACW:JAN/93[18]394, "RICHMOND FALLS!"
AHI:JAN/74[10]153, "WORKING PEOPLE IN RICHMOND:
LIFE AND LABOR IN AN INDUSTRIAL CITY, 1865-1920,"
AHI:SEP/91[8]298
BOOK REVIEWS: *AN IRISHMAN IN DIXIE: THOMAS
CONOLLY'S DIARY OF THE FALL OF THE
CONFEDERACY * CITY UNDER SIEGE: RICHMOND IN
THE CIVIL WAR * FOUR DAYS IN 1865: THE FALL OF
RICHMOND * RICHMOND REDEEMED: THE SIEGE AT
PETERSBURG * RICHMOND: THE STORY OF A CITY *
TO THE GATES OF RICHMOND: THE PENINSULA
CAMPAIGN*
ADDITIONAL LISTINGS: CWTI:APR/89[38]111,
CWTI:DEC/89[34]136, CWTI:JUN/90[28]158,
CWTI:AUG/90[26]166, *photos of destruction;*
ACW:MAY/95[38]526, AHI:JAN/74[10]153

RICKARDS, WILLIAM, *Colonel, 29th Pennsylvania Infantry;*
CWR:VOL3#2[70]155, GETTY:10[120]229

RICKER, ELBRIDGE G., *Major, 5th Ohio Cavalry;*
CWR:VOL4#1[44]164

RICKETTS, FRANCIS; ARTICLE: "A WIFE'S DEVOTION: THE
STORY OF JAMES AND FANNY RICKETTS,"
B&G:JUN/94[22]569

RICKETTS, JAMES B., *General, USA:*
ARTICLES: "A WIFE'S DEVOTION: THE STORY OF JAMES AND
FANNY RICKETTS," B&G:JUN/94[22]569, "THE BATTLE AT
THOROUGHFARE GAP," CWM:AUG/95[38]609

GENERAL LISTINGS: *Gettysburg,* GETTY:11[57]233, *in book review,* CWR:VOL4#3[89], *in order of battle,* B&G:APR/94[10]558, *Manassas, Second,* B&G:APR/91[32]447, B&G:AUG/92[11]493, *Monocacy,* B&G:DEC/92[8]503, *order of battle,* B&G:APR/95[8]595, *Overland Campaign,* B&G:APR/94[10]558, *photos,* B&G:DEC/92[8]503, B&G:JUN/94[22]569, CWTI:JAN/93[40]301
ADDITIONAL LISTINGS: ACW:MAY/91[38]305, ACW:JUL/91[18]312, ACW:JUL/92[30]369, ACW:NOV/93[50]444, B&G:OCT/95[20]612, CWM:AUG/94[48]529, CWTI:JAN/93[40]301, CWTI:NOV/93[55]350
RICKETTS, R. BRUCE, *Captain, 1st Pennsylvania Artillery:*
ARTICLE: "AN ENCOUNTER WITH BATTERY HELL," GETTY:12[30]243
ADDITIONAL LISTINGS: ACW:NOV/92[42]388, GETTY:4[49]147, GETTY:9[33]211, GETTY:12[1]240, *photo,* GETTY:12[30]243
RICKEY, L.D., *Sergeant, 42nd Alabama Infantry;* CWTI:NOV/92[41]291
RIDDLE, A.J., B&G:OCT/93[6]536
RIDDLE, ALBERT G., *Representative from Ohio;* CWTI:JUN/90[46]161
RIDDLE, ANDREW J., *artist;* ARTICLE: "THE ANDERSONVILLE ARTIST," B&G:AUG/93[18]530
RIDDLE, HUGH, *civilian;* CWTI:JAN/95[48]429
RIDDLE, THOMAS, *Pvt., 12th Tenn. Inf.;* ACW:SEP/91[8]318
RIDDLE, WILLIAM, *Major, USA;* CWM:MAR/91[17]335, GETTY:5[19]158
RIDER, JOHN D., *Pvt., 24th Michigan Inf.;* GETTY:5[19]158
RIDGEWAY, JAMES, *attorney;* ACW:SEP/94[46]488
RIDGEWAY, THOMAS J., *civilian;* B&G:APR/93[24]520, CWTI:JAN/95[48]429
RIDGWAY, JOHN, *Pvt., 11th Alabama Inf.;* GETTY:12[7]241
RIDLEY, SAMUEL J., *Captain, 1st Mississippi Artillery;* ACW:NOV/91[22]331, CWTI:MAY/91[24]208
RIFLE, JOSEPH, *Sergeant, USA;* B&G:OCT/94[11]580
RIGBY, SILAS P., *Captain, USA;* CWR:VOL1#4[7]125
RIGBY, WILLIAM T., *Capt., 24th IA Inf.;* CWR:VOL2#1[75]134
RIGGIN, JOHN, *Colonel, USA;* CWR:VOL3#3[33]158
RIGGINS, JAMES H., *Pvt., 1st Penna. Arty.;* GETTY:12[30]243
RIGGS, KATE; CWM:JAN/92[12]400
RIGGS, SAMUEL A., *judge;* CWM:JAN/92[12]400
RIGHTOR, NICHOLAS, *Lieutenant Colonel, Consolidated Crescent Regiment;* CWR:VOL4#2[68]167
RIHL, WILLIAM, *Corporal, USA;* B&G:AUG/94[10]574
RILEY, A.C., *Colonel, 1st Missouri Infantry;* B&G:FEB/94[8]550, CWR:VOL2#1[1]130
RILEY, CHARLES H., *Lieutenant, 143rd Pennsylvania Infantry;* GETTY:4[24]145
RILEY, EDWIN, *Private, USA;* B&G:APR/95[24]596
RILEY, F.A., *ships pilot;* B&G:AUG/92[40]495
RILEY, FRANKLIN L., *Private, 16th Mississippi Infantry;* GETTY:4[7]142, GETTY:5[89]162, GETTY:7[13]186
RILEY, SYLVESTER, *Sergeant, 97th New York Infantry;* B&G:FEB/95[8]590B, GETTY:10[7]221
RINEHART, LEVI, *civilian;* GETTY:4[65]148
RING, C.P., *Captain, CSA;* CWM:SEP/93[24]495
RINGGOLD GAP, GEORGIA, BATTLE OF; ARTICLE: "DARING REAR-GUARD DEFENSE," ACW:NOV/93[34]442
RION, JAMES H., *Colonel, 6th South Carolina Infantry;* B&G:DEC/92[40]508, CWTI:MAY/94[12]379
RIOTS; see listings under **"DRAFT RIOTS"** and **"NEW YORK CITY"**

RIPLEY, EDWARD H., *Colonel, 9th Vermont Infantry;* CWTI:OCT/95[18], CWTI:DEC/95[76]482
RIPLEY, HORACE, *Pvt., 7th Wisconsin Inf.,* GETTY:11[57]233
RIPLEY, JAMES W., *General, USA:*
ARTICLE: "MALFUNCTIONS AND A SHORTSIGHTED ORDNANCE DEPARTMENT DELAYED THE DEVELOPMENT OF RAPID-FIRE WEAPONS," ACW:JUL/93[8]420
ADDITIONAL LISTINGS: ACW:JAN/91[8]282, AHI:JUN/66[52]102, CWNEWS:APR/91[4], CWTI:JUL/93[42]329
RIPLEY, ROSWELL S., *General, CSA;* ACW:JUL/92[30]369, ACW:SEP/92[38]379, ACW:JUL/94[8]474, AHI:JUN/70[30]127, B&G:DEC/95[9]615, CWM:JUN/95[57]592
RIPLEY, WILLIAM W.Y., *Lieutenant Colonel, 1st USSS;* CWTI:JUL/93[42]329
RISON, HENRY, *Pvt., 7th Tennessee Inf.;* GETTY:6[13]170
RITCHIE, ALEXANDER H.; CWTI:FEB/92[21]247
RITTENHOUSE, BENJAMIN F., *Lieutenant, 5th United States Artillery;* GETTY:8[31]201, GETTY:9[48]213
RITTNER, SIMON, *Private, USA;* CWTI:MAR/94[58]375, CWTI:JUL/94[10]389
RIVER DEFENSE FLEET; ACW:MAY/92[16]359, ACW:MAR/95[18]514
RIVES' FARM, VIRGINIA, BATTLE OF; ACW:MAR/95[12]513
RIZER, MARTIN, *Surgeon, 72nd Pennsylvania Infantry;* GETTY:10[53]225
ROACH, WILLIAM A., *Private, 3rd North Carolina Cavalry;* ACW:MAR/95[50]518
ROANOKE ISLAND, VIRGINIA, BATTLE OF:
ARTICLE: "DISASTER AT ROANOKE ISLAND," CWM:FEB/95[49]565
ADDITIONAL LISTINGS: CWM:AUG/95[5]602, CWR:VOL2#3[183]140, CWTI:SEP/94[26]400
ROBB, MATTHEW, *Lt., 22nd Iowa Inf.;* CWR:VOL2#1[19]131
ROBBINS, JAMES L., *Lt., 7th Mich. Inf.;* ACW:NOV/95[10]553
ROBERSON, ADAM, JOHN and SAMUEL, *2nd Tennessee Cavalry;* CWR:VOL4#1[1]163
ROBERTS, B.E., *Captain, CSA;* B&G:OCT/94[11]580
ROBERTS, BENJAMIN S., *General, USA:*
GENERAL LISTINGS: *Confederate exiles,* AHI:JUN/70[30]127, *New Mexico Campaign,* B&G:JUN/94[8]568, *photo,* CWTI:OCT/95[56]471
ADDITIONAL LISTINGS: CWM:MAY/93[16]475, CWTI:OCT/95[56]471
ROBERTS, CHARLES, *Colonel, USA;* B&G:AUG/92[11]493
ROBERTS, CHRISTIAN, *Captain, CSA;* B&G:AUG/93[10]529, B&G:OCT/93[6]536
ROBERTS, M.P., *Lieutenant, CSA;* B&G:FEB/91[20]440
ROBERTS, OTIS O., *Sergeant, USA;* ACW:MAR/92[30]352
ROBERTS, PETER, *Private, USA;* CWM:JUL/92[27]431
ROBERTS, SAMUEL B., *Major, 72nd Pennsylvania Infantry;* ACW:MAY/92[8]357, GETTY:7[97]193
ROBERTS, THOMAS A., *Colonel, 17th Maine Infantry;* GETTY:8[43]202
ROBERTS, WILLIAM L, *Lieutenant, 17th Maine Infantry;* GETTY:8[43]202
ROBERTS, WILLIAM P., *Colonel, 2nd North Carolina Cavalry;* B&G:APR/92[8]481, CWTI:FEB/91[45]194
ROBERTSON, A.C., *Lt., 9th NY Cav.;* B&G:FEB/95[8]590B
ROBERTSON, BEVERLY H., *General, CSA: 1863 cavalry battles,* MH:OCT/92[51]162, *Brandy Station,* GETTY:11[19]232, *Gettysburg,* GETTY:6[94]180, GETTY:7[124]196, *Manassas, Second,* B&G:AUG/92[11]493, *photo,* B&G:OCT/93[12]537

ADDITIONAL LISTINGS: B&G:JUN/92[53]491, B&G:OCT/92[38]500, B&G:OCT/93[12]537, CWTI:APR/89[14]107, CWTI:JUN/90[32]159, CWTI:NOV/93[55]350

ROBERTSON, FELIX H., *General, CSA:*

GENERAL LISTINGS: *Gettysburg,* GETTY:5[123]166, *in list,* B&G:AUG/91[11]458, *Saltville, Battle of,* B&G:AUG/91[11]458, B&G:AUG/91[52]464, *West Point,* B&G:DEC/91[12]469, *photo,* B&G:AUG/91[11]458

ADDITIONAL LISTINGS: B&G:AUG/91[11]458, CWTI:MAR/93[50]313

ROBERTSON, GEORGE, *Private, Petersburg Artillery;* ACW:MAR/95[12]513,

ROBERTSON, J.N., *Lt., 52nd NC Inf.;* GETTY:12[61]245

ROBERTSON, JAMES M., *Captain, 22nd Iowa Infantry;* ACW:NOV/94[50]498, B&G:APR/94[10]558, B&G:APR/95[8]595, CWR:VOL2#1[19]131

ROBERTSON, JEROME B., *General, CSA:*

GENERAL LISTINGS: *Gettysburg,* GETTY:5[107]164, GETTY:8[43]202, GETTY:8[53]203, GETTY:9[5]209, *in book review,* CWR:VOL2#3[256], *Saltville,* B&G:AUG/91[11]458, *photo,* CWTI:DEC/91[36]240

ADDITIONAL LISTINGS: ACW:MAY/91[23]303, ACW:JAN/92[38]343, CWM:JUN/94[26]512, CWR:VOL1#2[29]112, CWR:VOL3#2[70]155, CWTI:DEC/91[36]240, CWTI:MAR/93[40]312, CWTI:SEP/93[53]340

ROBERTSON, JOSEPH E., *Private, 22nd Battalion Virginia Infantry;* CWR:VOL1#3[52]122

ROBERTSON, PETER, *Private, 106th New York Infantry;* CWTI:JAN/93[40]301

ROBERTSON, ROBERT, *Lieutenant, 93rd New York Infantry;* B&G:APR/91[8]445

ROBERTSON, SAMUEL, *Private, USA;* ACW:SEP/91[22]321

ROBESON, THOMAS, *Captain, 2nd Massachusetts Infantry;* GETTY:6[69]176

ROBINS, J.B., *Pvt., 8th SC Inf.;* CWTI:SEP/90[26]174

ROBINSON, A.D., *Major, USA;* CWTI:MAY/91[48]211

ROBINSON, A.H., *Private, 24th Michigan Infantry;* GETTY:9[33]211, GETTY:11[57]233

ROBINSON, ALBERT, *Private, USA;* B&G:OCT/95[8]611A

ROBINSON, BENJAMIN, *Captain, CSA;* B&G:FEB/95[8]590A, B&G:FEB/95[8]590B, B&G:AUG/95[36]607

ROBINSON, CHARLES, *Governor, Missouri;* ACW:JAN/93[26]395, AHI:JUL/75[4]160

ROBINSON, GILBERT P., *Lieutenant Colonel 179th New York Infantry;* CWTI:APR/90[24]152

ROBINSON, HARAI, *Colonel, USA;* CWR:VOL4#2[1]165

ROBINSON, J.W., *Cpl., 2nd Iowa Infantry;* B&G:FEB/92[48]475

ROBINSON, JAMES S., *General, USA;* B&G:DEC/95[9]615, CWTI:NOV/92[41]291, CWTI:NOV/92[54]293

ROBINSON, JOHN C., *General, USA:*

GENERAL LISTINGS: *Gettysburg,* AHI:MAY/67[22]107, GETTY:4[33]146, GETTY:4[49]147, GETTY:7[29]188, GETTY:9[17]210, GETTY:11[19]232, GETTY:11[57]233, GETTY:11[71]234, GETTY:11[126]239, GETTY:12[30]243, *letters to the editor,* B&G:APR/95[5]594, *Manassas, Second,* B&G:AUG/92[11]493, *Oak Grove,* CWM:JUN/95[55]591, *order of battle,* B&G:APR/95[8]595, *Wilderness,* B&G:APR/95[8]595

ADDITIONAL LISTINGS: ACW:MAY/91[38]590B, CWM:MAR/91[17]335, CWM:MAY/92[15]419, GETTY:10[7]221, GETTY:13[33]255

ROBINSON, N.T., *Captain, CSA;* CWR:VOL4#1[1]163

ROBINSON, OSCAR D., *Lieutenant, 9th New Hampshire Infantry;* CWR:VOL2#2[118]136

ROBINSON, PALATINE, *Colonel, CSA;* ACW:JUL/93[27]423

ROBINSON, W.W., *Col., 7th Wisconsin Inf.;* GETTY:13[22]254

ROBINSON, WILLIAM B., *Captain, 13th North Carolina Infantry;* GETTY:8[67]204

ROBINSON, WILLIAM G., *Colonel, 2nd North Carolina Cavalry;* CWM:SEP/93[18]494

ROBINSON, WILLIAM P., *Lieutenant, Ringgold's Battery;* ACW:MAR/94[27]459

ROBINSON, WILLIAM W., *Colonel, 7th Wisconsin Infantry;* B&G:APR/94[10]558, B&G:JUN/94[38]571, GETTY:4[24]145, GETTY:6[13]170

ROBISON, JAMES D., *Surgeon, 16th Ohio Infantry;* B&G:AUG/93[10]529

ROCHE, T.C., *photographer;* B&G:FEB/94[24]551

ROCHELLE, JAMES H., *Lieutenant, CSN;* AHI:NOV/75[38]163

ROCHESTER, E.T., *Captain, CSA;* B&G:OCT/94[11]580

ROCK CREEK, MISSOURI, BATTLE OF; ARTICLE: "THE BATTLE OF ROCK CREEK," CWTI:MAR/91[34]201

ROCKBRIDGE (VIRGINIA) ARTILLERY; ACW:JAN/92[8]338, ACW:MAR/92[30]352, ACW:MAR/94[50]462, AHI:JUN/67[31]110, AHI:SEP/87[40]263, B&G:JUN/92[8]487, B&G:DEC/95[5]614A, CWM:AUG/94[30]527, GETTY:13[75]259

ROCKWELL, J.L., *106th Pennsylvania Inf.;* GETTY:5[123]166

ROCKWOOD, GEORGE C., *photographer;* B&G:FEB/94[24]551

ROCKWOOD, W.A., *Major, USA;* B&G:OCT/92[32]499

RODDEY, PHILLIP D., *General, CSA;* CWR:VOL2#4[313]146, CWTI:JAN/94[39]362

RODENBOUGH, THEOPHILUS F., *General, USA;* ACW:JAN/92[10]339, ACW:MAY/94[35]469, GETTY:11[19]232

RODER, JOHN W., *Lieutenant, USA;* CWM:MAY/92[20]420, CWR:VOL3#2[1]153

RODERMEL, DEWITT, *Corporal, 118th Pennsylvania Infantry;* GETTY:8[53]203

RODES, ROBERT E., *General, CSA:*

ARTICLES: "FLANK ATTACK," ACW:SEP/93[31]433, "ROBERT RODES, WARRIOR IN GRAY," ACW:JAN/95[46]507, "RODES ON OAK HILL: A STUDY OF RODES' DIVISION ON THE FIRST DAY OF GETTYSBURG," GETTY:4[33]146

GENERAL LISTINGS: *Brandy Station,* GETTY:11[19]232, *Chancellorsville,* ACW:MAY/95[30]525, GETTY:9[17]210, MH:JUN/92[50]159, *Gettysburg,* GETTY:4[49]147, GETTY:4[65]148, GETTY:5[4]156, GETTY:5[13]157, GETTY:5[103]163, GETTY:5[117]165, GETTY:5[128]167, GETTY:6[7]169, GETTY:6[69]176, GETTY:6[99]181, GETTY:7[83]192, GETTY:7[114]194, GETTY:8[67]204, GETTY:9[17]210, GETTY:9[81]216, GETTY:11[19]232, GETTY:11[57]233, GETTY:11[71]234, GETTY:12[111]250, GETTY:12[30]243, *in book review,* CWM:AUG/94[9], CWNEWS:OCT/93[5], CWR:VOL4#3[1]170, *in order of battle,* B&G:APR/95[8]595, B&G:APR/94[10]558, *letters to the editor,* B&G:AUG/95[36]607, *Monocacy,* ACW:NOV/93[50]444, B&G:DEC/92[8]503, *Overland Campaign,* B&G:APR/94[10]558, *Third Winchester,* ACW:MAY/91[38]305, AHI:NOV/80[8]209, *Wilderness,* B&G:APR/95[8]595, *photos,* ACW:SEP/93[31]433, ACW:JAN/95[46]507, AHI:NOV/80[8]209, B&G:FEB/95[8]590B, CWM:MAR/91[17]335, GETTY:9[17]210

ADDITIONAL LISTINGS: ACW:MAR/92[30]352, ACW:NOV/92[42]388, ACW:MAR/93[26]404, ACW:JUL/93[50]426, ACW:SEP/93[31]433, B&G:AUG/91[32]461, B&G:FEB/95[8]590A, B&G:FEB/95[8]590B, B&G:FEB/95[8]590C, B&G:DEC/95[25]616, CWM:MAR/91[17]335, CWM:MAY/92[15]419, CWM:JAN/93[8]456, CWM:JAN/93[40]461,

CWM:SEP/93[8]493, CWR:VOL3#3[1]157,
CWTI:SEPT/89[46]132, CWTI:JAN/93[40]301,
GETTY:13[1]252, GETTY:13[7]253, GETTY:13[33]255,
GETTY:13[75]259, GETTY:13[108]261
RODGERS, BENJAMIN F., *Captain, 2nd Illinois Artillery;*
B&G:AUG/95[8]604
RODGERS, CHRISTOPHER R.P., *Lieutenant, USN;*
ACW:JAN/91[62]289
RODGERS, CLAYTON E., *Lieutenant, USA;* GETTY:13[22]254
RODGERS, HIRAM C., *Colonel, USA;* GETTY:9[81]216
RODGERS, JOHN I., *Cadet;* B&G:DEC/91[12]469
RODGERS, JOHN, *Commodore, USN;* ACW:MAR/94[35]460,
B&G:FEB/92[10]474, CWM:JUN/95[39]586,
CWTI:MAY/94[16]380
RODMAN, ISSAC P., *General, USA;* B&G:OCT/95[8]611A
ROE, G.H., *Private, 45th Georgia Infantry;* GETTY:10[53]225
ROE, HENRY, *Lieutenant, USA;* CWM:APR/95[39]576
ROEBLING, WASHINGTON A., *Lieutenant, USA;*
GETTY:8[31]201
ROEMER, JACOB, *Captain, 2nd New York Artillery;*
B&G:AUG/95[8]604
ROGER, WILLIAM W., *Captain, 3rd Pennsylvania Cavalry;*
GETTY:13[89]260
ROGERS, CLAYTON E., *Lieutenant, 6th Wisconsin Infantry;*
ARTICLE: "THE LIEUTENANT WHO ARRESTED A
GENERAL," GETTY:4[24]145
ROGERS, EARL M., *Captain, 6th Wisconsin Infantry;*
B&G:JUN/95[8]600, GETTY:4[16]143, GETTY:4[24]145
ROGERS, ELIZA B., *civilian;* CWTI:JUL/92[50]275
ROGERS, GEORGE W., *Sergeant, 2nd Tennessee Cavalry;*
CWR:VOL4#1[1]163
ROGERS, JAMES M., *Private, 11th Tennessee Infantry;*
ACW:SEP/95[38]546
ROGERS, JIM, *Private, 7th Wisconsin Infantry;*
GETTY:9[33]211
ROGERS, JOAB B., *Captain, 1st Connecticut Cavalry;*
ACW:JAN/92[16]340
ROGERS, JOHN, *Private, 1st Arkansas Cavalry;*
CWR:VOL1#2[70]115
ROGERS, JOSEPHINE, *civilian;* B&G:FEB/93[40]514
ROGERS, WILLIAM F., *Captain, USN;* ACW:MAR/94[35]460
ROGERS, WILLIAM P., *Colonel, 2nd Texas Infantry;*
ACW:SEP/91[46]324, ACW:SEP/92[8]374
ROGERS, WILLIAM P., *Colonel, USA;* AHI:APR/87[10]261
ROGERS, WILLIAM W., *Captain, 3rd Pennsylvania Cavalry;*
GETTY:4[75]149
ROHLFING, CHRISTIAN, *Private, 69th Pennsylvania
Infantry;* GETTY:4[89]150
ROLLINS, A.S., *Private, 95th Illinois Infantry;*
ACW:JAN/91[16]284
ROLLINS, JAMES H., *Cadet;* B&G:DEC/91[12]469
ROLLINS, JAMES S.; B&G:JUN/91[32]454
ROMAN, ALFRED, *Captain, CSA;* CWTI:JUL/92[29]272
ROME, GEORGIA; ACW:SEP/94[10]484
ROMNEY, VIRGINIA, CAMPAIGN; ACW:JAN/92[8]338,
CWM:APR/95[8], CWTI:JUN/95[18]444
RONALD, CHARLES A., *Colonel, CSA;* ACW:JUL/91[50]
RONCKENDORF, WILLIAM, *Commander, USN;*
B&G:JUN/92[40]489
ROOKE (PENNSYLVANIA) GUARDS, (53rd Pennsylvania
Infantry) GETTY:11[80]235
ROOKIE, J., *photographer;* B&G:FEB/94[24]551

ROOKS, ALONZO, *Private, 1st Ohio Artillery;*
B&G:OCT/95[8]611D
ROONEY, BLANCHE; B&G:OCT/93[31]539
ROOT, ADRIAN R., *Colonel, 94th New York Infantry;*
ACW:MAR/95[42]517, GETTY:13[33]255
ROOT, FRANK, *Private,* GETTY:9[33]211
ROOT, JOHN H., *Lieutenant, 53rd Pennsylvania Infantry;*
GETTY:11[80]235
ROPES, HENRY, *Lieutenant, 20th Massachusetts Infantry;*
CWR:VOL3#1[31]150, CWR:VOL4#4[101]181
ROPES, JOHN C., *Captain, USA;* GETTY:12[111]250
RORSCH, DAVID W., *Captain, 16th Massachusetts Infantry;*
GETTY:12[7]241
RORTY, JAMES M., *Captain, 1st New York Light Artillery;*
ARTICLE: "I WAS THERE," CWM:MAR/91[14]334
ADDITIONAL LISTINGS: CWM:MAR/91[14]334,
CWM:MAR/91[17]335, CWR:VOL4#3[89], GETTY:5[47]160
ROSA, ARTHUR S., *Surgeon, 52nd Ohio Infantry;*
CWTI:MAY/94[40]383
ROSE, JULIUS D., *Chaplain, 7th New Jersey Infantry;*
B&G:FEB/92[22]476
ROSE, THOMAS E., *Colonel, 77th Pennsylvania Infantry;*
ACW:JUL/91[8]309, ACW:JAN/94[55]453,
AHI:NOV/85[38]254, AHI:DEC/85[40]255
ROSECRANS, WILLIAM S., *General, USA;*
ARTICLES: "A FIERCE LITTLE FIGHT IN MISSISSIPPI,"
CWTI:JUL/94[50]395, "THE DECEPTION OF BRAXTON
BRAGG: THE TULLAHOMA CAMPAIGN, JUNE 23-JULY 4,
1863," B&G:OCT/92[10]496, "MOST SPLENDID PIECE OF
STRATEGY," CWM:OCT/94[48]542, "SHOWDOWN IN THE
WEST: GRANT VS ROSECRANS," CWM:MAR/93[8]465
BOOK REVIEWS: *MOUNTAINS TOUCHED BY FIRE:
CHATTANOOGA BESIEGED, 1863 * THIS TERRIBLE
SOUND: THE BATTLE OF CHICKAMAUGA*
GENERAL LISTINGS: *Chattanooga,* CWTI:SEP/92[22]279,
Chickamauga, ACW:MAR/95[26]515, CWM:NOV/91[50]394,
CWTI:SEP/93[53]340, CWTI:NOV/93[33]347, *election of 1864,*
AHI:OCT/68[4]116, *general history,* AHI:MAY/71[3]133A, *in
book review,* ACW:MAR/91[54], ACW:SEP/95[62],
CWM:SEP/91[58], CWM:MAY/93[51], CWM:DEC/94[7],
CWNEWS:APR/90[4], CWNEWS:JUN/91[4],
CWNEWS:FEB/94[5], CWR:VOL4#4[129], CWTI:SEP/92[18],
*Iuka, CWM:MAR/93[8]465, CWTI:JUL/94[50]395, James A.
Garfield,* AHI:MAY/76[24]167, *letters to the editor,*
B&G:JUN/93[6]523, *Lightning Brigade,* B&G:OCT/92[32]499,
Lookout Mountain, CWTI:SEPT/89[30]129, *Pilot Knob,*
B&G:JUN/91[10]452, *Price's 1864 Missouri Campaign,*
B&G:JUN/91[10]452, *rapid-fire weapons,* ACW:JUL/93[8]420,
West Point, B&G:DEC/91[12]469, *West Virginia Campaign,*
ACW:SEP/94[31]486, B&G:AUG/93[10]529, *photos,*
AHI:MAY/71[3]133A, AHI:NOV/73[18]151,
B&G:JUN/91[10]452, B&G:OCT/92[10]496,
B&G:AUG/93[10]529, CWM:OCT/94[48]542,
CWTI:JUL/94[50]395
ADDITIONAL LISTINGS, ACW: ACW:MAR/91[30]295,
ACW:MAY/91[23]303, ACW:JUL/91[12]310,
ACW:JUL/91[35]314, ACW:SEP/91[46]324,
ACW:JAN/92[8]338, ACW:JAN/92[50]345,
ACW:NOV/92[8]383, ACW:JUL/93[34]424,
ACW:JAN/94[47]452, ACW:NOV/95[6]551,
ACW:NOV/95[66]559
ADDITIONAL LISTINGS, AHI: AHI:APR/87[10]261, AHI:NOV/73[18]151

ADDITIONAL LISTINGS, B&G: B&G:OCT/91[11]466,
B&G:OCT/92[26]498, B&G:AUG/93[34]532,
B&G:OCT/93[31]539, B&G:FEB/94[38]553,
B&G:DEC/94[34]587
ADDITIONAL LISTINGS, CWM: CWM:JUL/92[18]429,
CWM:JUL/92[24]430, CWM:JAN/93[29]459,
CWM:MAR/93[4]463, CWM:MAR/93[16]466,
CWM:OCT/94[4]532, CWM:DEC/94[46]552,
CWM:APR/95[16]571, CWM:OCT/95[47]620
ADDITIONAL LISTINGS, CWR: CWR:VOL1#4[42]126,
CWR:VOL1#4[64]127, CWR:VOL2#1[36]132,
CWR:VOL2#4[313]146, CWR:VOL3#2[70]155,
CWR:VOL4#1[1]163
ADDITIONAL LISTINGS, CWTI: CWTI:APR/89[14]107,
CWTI:SUMMER/89[13]120, CWTI:FEB/90[46]146,
CWTI:AUG/91[62]221, CWTI:SEP/91[31]229,
CWTI:MAY/92[48]267, CWTI:SEP/92[28]280,
CWTI:JAN/93[20]298, CWTI:MAR/93[40]312,
CWTI:MAY/93[38]321, CWTI:JAN/94[35]361,
CWTI:JAN/94[46]364, CWTI:DEC/94[82]418,
CWTI:DEC/95[67]481
ADDITIONAL LISTINGS, OTHER: GETTY:10[120]229,
MH:DEC/95[58]188
ROSENGARTEN, JOSEPH G., *Major, USA;* GETTY:4[113]153
ROSS, ANTHONY, *Pvt., 73rd Ohio Inf.;* B&G:OCT/94[42]583
ROSS, DANIEL, *Private, 4th U.S. Artillery;* ARTICLE:
"INFANTRY VOLUNTEERS, UNION ARTILLERY
BATTERIES," ACW:MAY/91[8]300
ROSS, EDMUND G., *Senator, Kansas:*
ARTICLE: "THE MOST HEROIC ACT IN AMERICAN HISTORY,"
AHI:DEC/68[28]118
BOOK REVIEW: *THE IMPEACHMENT AND TRIAL OF ANDREW
JOHNSON*
ROSS, EDWARD T.F., CWTI:MAR/95[18]432
ROSS, HUGH M., *Captain, Sumter Artillery;*
CWR:VOL3#2[1]153, CWR:VOL3#2[61]154
ROSS, JOHN, *Cherokee Chief;* ACW:JAN/91[30]286,
B&G:OCT/94[38]582, CWM:SEP/92[38]443, *photo,*
ACW:JAN/91[30]286
ROSS, LAWRENCE S., *General, CSA:*
BOOK REVIEW: *PERSONAL CIVIL WAR LETTERS OF GENERAL
LAWRENCE SULLIVAN ROSS*
ADDITIONAL LISTINGS: ACW:JAN/92[10]339, B&G:DEC/93[12]545
ROSS, LEVI, *Sgt., 86th Illinois Infantry;* CWTI:MAY/94[40]383
ROSS, MARION, *Sergeant Major, USA;* ACW:SEP/91[22]321
ROSS, REUBEN, *Captain, CSA;* B&G:FEB/92[10]474
ROSS, WILLIAM H., *Lt. Col., USA;* B&G:DEC/95[9]615
ROSSELL, NATHAN B., *Major, 3rd U.S. Infantry;*
ACW:NOV/94[50]498
ROSSER, THOMAS L., *General, CSA:*
ARTICLE: "JEB STUART AND HIS RELUCTANT
CAVALRYMAN," B&G:OCT/92[38]500
GENERAL LISTINGS: *1863 cavalry battles,* MH:OCT/92[51]162,
Aldie, GETTY:11[19]232, *Buckland,* ACW:JUL/92[41]370,
Custer, AHI:FEB/71[4]131, AHI:JUN/76[4]169, *Five Forks,*
ACW:MAY/95[38]526, B&G:APR/92[8]481, *in book review,*
B&G:FEB/91[28], CWNEWS:SEP/90[4], *in order of battle,*
B&G:APR/92[8]481, B&G:APR/94[10]558, B&G:APR/95[8]595,
letters to the editor, B&G:FEB/93[6]510, *post-war,*
ACW:JUL/95[26]535, *Trevilian Station,* MH:FEB/93[42]164,
West Point, B&G:DEC/91[12]469, *Wilderness,*
B&G:APR/95[8]595, *photos,* AHI:JUN/76[4]169,
B&G:APR/92[8]481, B&G:OCT/92[38]500

ADDITIONAL LISTINGS: ACW:SEP/91[41]323, ACW:NOV/91[30]332,
ACW:JAN/92[16]340, ACW:JAN/92[22]341,
ACW:JUL/92[12]367, ACW:NOV/92[26]386,
ACW:JAN/93[49]397, ACW:MAY/94[35]469,
ACW:SEP/94[55]489, B&G:FEB/92[32]477,
B&G:APR/92[48]484, B&G:AUG/93[55]535,
B&G:OCT/93[12]537, B&G:OCT/94[28]581,
CWM:APR/94[24]505, CWR:VOL4#4[70]180,
CWTI:JUN/90[32]159, CWTI:APR/92[35]257,
CWTI:JUL/92[12]270, CWTI:JAN/94[29]360,
CWTI:JUL/94[44]394, CWTI:JUN/95[38]447
ROSSMAN, ALEXANDER C., *Lieutenant, 5th Ohio Cavalry;*
CWR:VOL4#1[44]164
ROSSVILLE GAP, GEORGIA; ACW:NOV/93[34]442
ROSWELL, GEORGIA:
ARTICLE: "TOTAL WAR COMES TO NEW MANCHESTER,"
B&G:DEC/94[22]586
BOOK REVIEW: *CHARGED WITH TREASON: ORDEAL OF 400
MILL WORKERS DURING MILITARY OPERATIONS IN
ROSWELL GEORGIA, 1864-1865*
ADDITIONAL LISTING: CWTI:SUMMER/89[20]121
ROSZELL, WILLIAM T., *Private, 7th Indiana Infantry;*
CWTI:NOV/93[24]346
ROTTAKEN, HERBERT, *Captain, USA;* CWR:VOL4#2[1]165
ROUND MOUNTAIN, INDIAN TERRITORY, BATTLE OF;
CWM:MAY/93[24]476
ROUNTREE, LEONIDES C., *Major, 13th Texas Infantry;*
CWM:OCT/94[33]537
ROUSE, MILTON, *Lt., 12th Virginia Cav.;* CWR:VOL1#4[7]125
ROUSSEAU, LOVELL H., *General, USA:*
ARTICLE: "JADED MULES, TWISTED RAILS, AND RAZED
DEPOTS," CWM:JAN/91[40]330
ADDITIONAL LISTINGS: ACW:JUL/92[22]368, B&G:OCT/91[11]466,
B&G:JUN/92[32]488, CWR:VOL4#3[50]171,
CWTI:SUMMER/89[50]124, CWTI:OCT/95[48]470, *photo,*
CWM:JAN/91[40]330
ROUTT, HENRY L., *attorney;* CWTI:MAR/91[34]201
ROWAN (NORTH CAROLINA) ARTILLERY;
GETTY:5[47]160
ROWE, PERRY, *Private, 19th Indiana Infantry,*
GETTY:11[57]233
ROWLAND, ALBERT B., *Lieutenant, USA;*
CWM:JUL/92[27]431
ROWLAND, THOMAS, *Cadet;* B&G:DEC/91[12]469
ROWLETT'S STATION, KENTUCKY, ENGAGEMENT AT;
B&G:APR/94[34]561, CWM:SEP/93[8]493
ROWLEY, THOMAS A., *General, USA:*
ARTICLE: "THE LIEUTENANT WHO ARRESTED A GENERAL,"
GETTY:4[24]145
ADDITIONAL LISTINGS: AHI:MAY/67[22]107, GETTY:9[17]210,
GETTY:11[91]236, GETTY:11[19]232, GETTY:11[71]234,
GETTY:13[22]254
ROWLEY, W.R., *Capt., 9th Ohio Cavalry;* CWR:VOL4#1[44]164
ROY, THOMAS B., *Lt. Col., CSA;* B&G:DEC/95[9]615
ROY, WILLIAM, *Capt., 1st Indiana Art.;* ACW:JAN/94[30]450
ROYAL, THOMAS, *Private, Sumter Artillery;*
CWR:VOL3#2[1]153
ROYALL, WILLIAM, *Colonel, USA;* ACW:JUL/95[34]536,
AHI:DEC/67[58]114, CWM:FEB/95[7], CWM:JUN/95[50]589,
ROYER, HENRY, *Capt., 96th Penna. Inf.;* CWR:VOL3#3[1]157
ROYSTER, JAMES M., *Lieutenant, 37th North Carolina
Infantry;* GETTY:8[67]204
ROYSTON, S.M., *civilian;* B&G:AUG/94[10]574

ROYSTON, W.B., *Sergeant, 5th Texas Infantry;*
CWTI:DEC/91[36]240

RUBERY, ALFRED, *civilian;* CWTI:JUN/95[48]448

RUCKER, EDMUMD W., *Colonel, CSA;* ACW:NOV/95[48]557,
B&G:DEC/93[12]545, CWTI:JAN/94[39]362

RUDGE, FRANK R., *Corporal, 4th U.S. Artillery;*
GETTY:11[57]233

RUE, GEORGE W., *Major, CSA;* CWM:MAR/93[16]466

RUEHLE, JOHN V., *Lieutenant Colonel, 16th Michigan
Infantry;* GETTY:6[33]172

RUFF, SOLON Z., *Colonel, 18th Georgia Infantry;*
CWTI:MAR/93[40]312, CWTI:SEP/94[12]398

RUFFIN, EDMUND:
BOOK REVIEW: *THE DIARY OF EDMUND RUFFIN, VOLUME III,
A DREAM SHATTERED, JUNE, 1863-JUNE 1865*
GENERAL LISTINGS: *death of,* CWTI:AUG/90[64]170, *in book review,*
B&G:AUG/91[26], CWNEWS:FEB/94[5],
CWNEWS:SEP/94[33], CWNEWS:DEC/94[33],
CWNEWS:SEP/95[33], *letters to the editor,*
CWM:SEP/91[6]377, *portrait,* CWTI:AUG/90[64]170
ADDITIONAL LISTING: CWTI:FEB/91[36]193

RUGER, EDWARD, *Captain, USA;* CWM:JAN/91[40]330,
CWNEWS:APR/90[4]

RUGER, THOMAS H., *General, USA:*
GENERAL LISTINGS: *Gettysburg,* GETTY:6[69]176,
GETTY:7[29]188, GETTY:7[83]192, GETTY:9[81]216,
GETTY:10[36]223, GETTY:12[42]244
ADDITIONAL LISTINGS: ACW:NOV/92[42]388, B&G:FEB/95[8]590C,
CWR:VOL1#4[64]127

RUGGLES, DANIEL, *General, CSA:*
GENERAL LISTINGS: *Grierson's Raid,* B&G:JUN/93[12]524, *Port
Hudson,* MH:AUG/94[82]179, *photo,* B&G:JUN/93[12]524
ADDITIONAL LISTINGS: ACW:JAN/91[22]285, ACW:SEP/92[38]379,
B&G:JUN/95[8]600, CWR:VOL1#1[1]102,
CWR:VOL1#2[44]114

RUGGLES, G.D., *Colonel, USA;* GETTY:11[19]232

RUMSEY, ISRAEL P., *Lieutenant, 1st Illinois Artillery;*
B&G:AUG/95[8]604

RUNKLE, BENJAMIN P., *Colonel, 45th Ohio Mounted
Infantry;* CWR:VOL4#1[1]163

"RUSH'S LANCERS", see listings under **"PENNSYLVANIA
TROOPS, 6TH CAVALRY"**

RUSH, JOHN, *seaman, USN;* ACW:MAR/92[40]353

RUSH, LEVI, *Private, 150th New York Infantry;*
GETTY:12[42]244

RUSH, RICHARD, *Colonel, 6th Pennsylvania Cavalry;*
GETTY:11[19]232

RUSHBY, THOMAS, *Lieutenant, USA;* GETTY:4[101]151

RUSS, EDWARD L., *Sergeant, 125th Pennsylvania Infantry;*
B&G:OCT/95[8]611A

RUSS, SUL; ACW:SEP/92[38]379

RUSSEL, JAMES, *Private, 2nd Wisconsin Infantry,*
GETTY:11[57]233

RUSSELL, A.A., *Colonel, 4th Alabama Cavalry;*
CWM:DEC/95[48]631

RUSSELL, A.J., *Captain, 141st New York Infantry:*
ARTICLE: "FOCUS: CIVIL WAR PHOTOGRAPHY,"
AHI:JUL/79[50]190
ADDITIONAL LISTINGS: CWM:NOV/91[28]391, CWTI:MAY/91[34]209

RUSSELL, CHARLES H., *Captain, 1st Maryland Cavalry;*
CWR:VOL1#4[7]125

RUSSELL, DAVID A., *General, USA:*
GENERAL LISTINGS: *Brandy Station,* GETTY:11[19]232, *in order of
battle,* B&G:APR/94[10]558, *Overland Campaign,*
B&G:APR/94[10]558
ADDITIONAL LISTINGS: ACW:MAY/91[38]305, ACW:MAR/92[30]352,
ACW:SEP/92[30]378, B&G:APR/95[8]595,
CWTI:JUN/90[32]159, CWTI:JUN/95[32]446

RUSSELL, HENRY, *Private, 72nd Pennsylvania Infantry;*
GETTY:7[97]193

RUSSELL, IRA, *Private, 11th Mississippi Infantry;*
CWR:VOL2#4[269]145

RUSSELL, JERRY; see listings under **"PRESERVATION:
CIVIL WAR ROUND TABLE ASSOCIATES,
HERITAGEPAC and RUSSELL, JERRY"**

RUSSELL, JOHN H., *Lieutenant, USMC;* CWR:VOL1#4[42]126

RUSSELL, LORD JOHN, *British foreign secretary;*
CWTI:MAY/89[28]117

RUSSELL, RICHARD B., *Corporal, 2nd Florida Cavalry;*
ACW:NOV/95[38]556

RUSSELL, ROBERT M, *Colonel, 12th Tennessee Infantry;*
CWR:VOL3#4[24]162

RUSSELL, WILLIAM H., *correspondent:*
ARTICLE: *"LONDON TIMES* CORRESPONDENT WILLIAM
HOWARD RUSSELL TOURED A VICTORY-MADDENED
SOUTH IN MID-1861," ACW:SEP/93[10]430
ADDITIONAL LISTINGS: CWM:MAR/91[74], CWTI:JAN/93[44]302

RUSSIA; CWTI:MAY/89[28]117

RUSSIAN NAVY; ARTICLE: "OUR GOOD FRIENDS, THE
RUSSIANS," AHI:JAN/81[18]214

RUST, ALBERT, *Colonel, CSA;* ACW:SEP/91[46]324,
ACW:JAN/92[50]345, ACW:SEP/94[31]486,
B&G:AUG/93[10]529

RUST, HENRY A., *Adjutant, USA;* CWR:VOL3#4[24]162

RUST, LEVI, *Private, 150th New York Infantry;*
GETTY:12[42]244

RUTHERFORD, FRIEND S., *Colonel, 97th Illinois Infantry;*
B&G:FEB/94[8]550

RUTHERFORD, GUS, *Lieutenant, 1st Georgia
Regulars;* CWR:VOL2#2[95]135

RUTHERFORD, JOHN C., *Adjutant, CSA;*
CWR:VOL4#4[28]178

RUTLEDGE, A.M., *Captain, Tennessee Artillery;*
B&G:FEB/93[12]511

RUTLEDGE, ANN; BOOK REVIEW: *THE SHADOWS RISE:
ABRAHAM LINCOLN AND THE ANN RUTLEDGE LEGEND*

RUTTER, SAMUEL H., *Sergeant Major, 53rd Pennsylvania
Infantry;* GETTY:11[80]235

RYAN, GEORGE, *Colonel, 140th New York Infantry;*
B&G:APR/95[8]595, CWM:MAR/91[17]335,
CWM:MAR/91[35]337, CWNEWS:APR/94[5]

RYAN, WHITE G., *Captain, CSA;* ACW:MAR/94[27]459

RYAN, WILLIAM A., *Major, CSA;* B&G:DEC/95[9]615

RYDER, OSCAR, *Sergeant, 7th New York State Militia;*
AHI:MAY/71[3]133A

RYERSON, HENRY O., *Colonel, USA;* ACW:MAR/92[22]351

RYLAND, THOMAS M., *Private, Fredericksburg Artillery;*
CWR:VOL1#1[1]102

S

SABINE CROSS ROADS, LOUISIANA, BATTLE OF; see
listings under "MANSFIELD, LOUISIANA, BATTLE OF"
SABINE PASS BATTLE GROUND STATE HISTORICAL
PARK; CWM:OCT/95[47]620
SABINE PASS, TEXAS, BATTLE OF:
ARTICLES "THE MOST EXTRAORDINARY FEAT OF THE WAR,"
CWM:OCT/95[47]620, "SIX GUNS AGAINST THE FLEET,"
CWTI:DEC/90[29]182
GENERAL LISTINGS: *in book review,* CWM:APR/95[8], *letter to the
editor,* CWTI:MAY/91[8]205
ADDITIONAL LISTINGS: ACW:JAN/93[51]398, CWR:VOL3#1[1]149,
CWTI:DEC/90[29]182
SABRE, G.W., *Private, USA;* CWM:JAN/92[16]401
SACHS, MAX, *Lt., 32nd Indiana Infantry;* CWM:SEP/93[8]493
SACKET, D.B., *Colonel, USA;* GETTY:11[19]232
SACKETT, DARIUS, *Pvt., 126th NY Inf.;* CWR:VOL1#4[7]125
SACKETT, JOSEPH, *Corporal, 13th Illinois Infantry;*
CWTI:SEP/94[40]403
SACKETT, WILLIAM, *Colonel, 9th New York Cavalry;*
GETTY:11[19]232
SACRAMENTO, KENTUCKY, SKIRMISH AT:
ARTICLE: "FORREST'S FIRST FIGHT," ACW:MAR/93[51]407
ADDITIONAL LISTING: CWTI:SEP/93[59]341
SAFFORD, WINFIELD, *Lieutenant, 24th Michigan Infantry;*
GETTY:5[19]158
SAHM, NICHOLAS, *Lt., 1st New York Arty.;* GETTY:6[7]169
SAINT GAUDENS, AUGUSTUS:
ARTICLE: "AUGUSTUS SAINT GAUDENS AND THE SHERMAN
MEMORIAL," CWM:NOV/92[43]452
ADDITIONAL LISTING: CWTI:DEC/89[53]138
SALE, HENRY, *Lieutenant, CSA;* B&G:FEB/91[20]440
SALEM CHURCH, VIRGINIA, BATTLE OF;
CWR:VOL3#3[1]157, CWR:VOL3#3[88]160
SALLING, JOHN, *Private, USA;* ACW:SEP/91[8]318,
B&G:FEB/91[32]441, CWTI:MAY/92[8]261,
CWTI:JUL/92[8]269
SALMOND, THOMAS W., *Surgeon;* GETTY:5[35]159
SALOMON, CHARLES E., *Colonel, 5th Missouri Infantry;*
CWTI:FEB/92[29]248
SALOMON, EDWARD, *Governor, Wisconsin;*
ACW:MAY/93[12]412
SALOMON, FREDERICK, *General, USA;* ACW:MAY/93[22]414
SALT LAKE CITY, UTAH; ACW:JAN/95[8]502
SALTVILLE, VIRGINIA, BATTLE OF:
ARTICLES "THE BATTLE OF SALTVILLE—MASSACRE OR
MYTH," B&G:AUG/91[11]458, "CONTROVERSY: WHAT
MAKES A MASSACRE?," B&G:AUG/91[52]464
BOOK REVIEW: *SOUTHWEST VIRGINIA IN THE CIVIL WAR:
THE BATTLE FOR SALTVILLE*
GENERAL LISTINGS: *in book review,* CWNEWS:FEB/94[5],
CWR:VOL3#1[80], *letters to the editor,* B&G:OCT/91[6]465,
B&G:DEC/91[6]468, B&G:APR/92[6]480, *modern photo's;*
B&G:AUG/91[52]458
ADDITIONAL LISTING: ACW:MAR/94[27]459
SALYER, LOGAN H.N., *Lieutenant Colonel, 50th Virginia
Infantry;* GETTY:10[29]222
SAMKINS, T.C., *Pvt., 2nd Georgia Cavalry;* B&G:APR/93[24]520
SAMPLE, HUGH, *Captain, USA;* CWTI:AUG/95[34]457

SAMPLE, JEREMIAH, *Captain, 139th Pennsylvania Infantry;*
GETTY:11[91]236
SAMPSON, JOHN C., *Lieutenant, 9th New Hampshire
Infantry;* CWR:VOL2#2[118]136
SAN FRANCISCO, CALIFORNIA:
ARTICLE: "TRACES OF A DISTANT WAR," CWTI:JUN/95[51]449
ADDITIONAL LISTING: CWTI:OCT/95[14]465
SANBORN, FRANKLIN B.; ACW:JUL/91[43]315
SANBORN, JOHN B., *General, USA:* ACW:NOV/91[22]331,
ACW:NOV/94[76]500, B&G:JUN/91[10]452,
CWR:VOL2#1[19]131, CWR:VOL3#3[59]159,
CWTI:JUL/94[50]395, *photo,* B&G:JUN/91[10]452
SANBORN, JOHN B., *Pvt., 6th Wisc. Inf.,* GETTY:11[57]233
SAND CREEK MASSACRE:
BOOK REVIEW: *WOLVES FOR THE BLUE SOLDIERS: INDIAN
SCOUTS AND AUXILIARIES WITH THE UNITED STATES
ARMY, 1860-90]*
GENERAL LISTINGS: *in book review,* CWM:JAN/91[47],
CWM:APR/95[50], *letters to the editor,* CWTI:MAR/91[10]197,
CWTI:DEC/91[14]235
ADDITIONAL LISTINGS: ACW:MAY/93[6]410, B&G:JUN/94[8]568,
CWM:SEP/92[57], CWR:VOL2#2[161]139
SANDER, WILLIAM, *Colonel, 5th Kentucky Cavalry;*
ACW:SEP/95[22]544
SANDERLIN, NOAH, *Private, Georgia and Mississippi
Regiment;* CWR:VOL1#4[42]126
SANDERLIN, WILLIS B., *Captain, 68th North Carolina
Infantry;* CWTI:JAN/95[42]428
SANDERS, ADDISON, *Lt. Col., USA;* ACW:JAN/93[10]393
SANDERS, GEORGE N.:
ARTICLE: "ST. ALBANS HAS BEEN SURPRISED,"
AHI:JAN/76[14]164
ADDITIONAL LISTINGS: AHI:JUN/70[30]127, CWTI:JAN/93[44]302
SANDERS, J.C.C., *General, CSA;* B&G:APR/94[10]558,
CWTI:APR/90[24]152, CWTI:DEC/94[32]410
SANDERS, JAMES, *Private, CSA;* B&G:AUG/91[11]458
SANDERS, JOHN W., *Corporal, Sumter Artillery;*
CWR:VOL3#2[61]154
SANDERS, T.C., *Captain, CSA;* B&G:FEB/93[12]511
SANDERS, WILLIAM, *Sergeant, 95th Illinois Infantry;*
CWM:JAN/91[11]325, CWTI:JAN/93[20]298
SANDERS, WILLIAM P., *General, USA;* ACW:MAY/91[23]303,
CWR:VOL4#1[1]163, CWTI:MAR/93[40]312,
CWTI:MAY/94[50]386
SANDERSON, HENRY, *Private, 96th Ohio Infantry;*
ACW:SEP/92[16]376
SANDS, GEORGE N.; CWTI:OCT/95[18]
SANDS, HENRY, *seaman, USN* B&G:DEC/94[10]585
SANDS, JAMES G.; CWM:JAN/92[12]400
SANFORD, GEORGE, *Captain, USA;* ACW:SEP/94[55]489
SANFORD, J.F., *Pvt., 44th NC Inf.;* B&G:APR/93[24]520
SANFORD, JOSEPH, *Private, Fredericksburg Artillery;*
CWR:VOL1#1[1]102
SANFORD, WILLIAM P., *Colonel, USA;* B&G:AUG/95[8]604
SANGER, EUGENE L., *Surgeon;* ACW:MAR/91[25]294,
CWM:OCT/95[10]
SANGER, WILLIAM D., *Major, 5th Ohio Cavalry;*
CWR:VOL4#1[44]164
SANGFORD, W.B., *Pvt., 16th Georgia Inf.;* B&G:APR/93[24]520
SANITARY FAIRS; BOOK REVIEW: *SANITARY FAIRS: A
PHILATELIC AND HISTORICAL STUDY OF CIVIL WAR
BENEVOLENCES*
SANSOM, EMMA; AHI:DEC/73[10]152

SCHOFIELD, JOHN M., *General, USA:*
ARTICLE: "SHERMAN'S FEUDING GENERALS,"
CWTI:MAR/95[40]436
GENERAL LISTINGS: *Atlanta Campaign,* ACW:JUL/94[66]481,
ACW:JAN/95[30]505, ACW:NOV/95[74]560,
CWM:JAN/91[12]326, CWM:AUG/94[27]526,
CWTI:SUMMER/89[13]120, CWTI:SUMMER/89[20]121,
CWTI:SUMMER/89[32]122, CWTI:SUMMER/89[50]124,
CWTI:SEP/92[28]280, CWTI:NOV/92[41]291, *Camp Jackson,*
ACW:MAY/91[31]304, *Franklin,* ACW:MAR/94[42]461, *in book
review,* B&G:AUG/92[36], CWM:SEP/92[57],
CWR:VOL2#1[78], CWTI:APR/92[30], *Indian Wars,*
AHI:AUG/78[18]183, *Jackson, Battle of,* B&G:AUG/95[8]604,
John C. Fremont, AHI:MAY/70[4]126, *Nashville,*
ACW:NOV/95[48]557, B&G:DEC/93[12]545, *order of battle,*
B&G:DEC/93[12]545, *Sherman's Carolina Campaign,*
B&G:DEC/95[9]615, *Wilmington/Fort Fisher,*
B&G:DEC/94[10]585, *Wilson's Creek,* CWTI:FEB/92[29]248,
photos, ACW:MAR/94[42]461, B&G:DEC/91[12]469,
B&G:DEC/94[10]585, CWTI:SUMMER/89[13]120,
CWTI:MAR/95[40]436
ADDITIONAL LISTINGS: ACW:NOV/93[26]441, ACW:MAY/94[26]468,
AHI:JUL/73[38]150, AHI:NOV/73[18]151, AHI:SEP/87[40]263,
B&G:AUG/91[11]458, B&G:OCT/91[11]466,
B&G:DEC/94[22]586, B&G:FEB/95[30]591,
CWM:JAN/91[40]330, CWM:MAR/91[28]336,
CWM:SEP/92[38]443, CWM:MAY/93[8]474,
CWM:AUG/95[36]608, CWR:VOL1#1[42]105,
CWR:VOL1#3[82]123, CWR:VOL1#4[64]127,
CWR:VOL4#3[65]172, CWTI:SEP/90[52]179,
CWTI:DEC/94[82]418, CWTI:MAR/95[33]435,
MH:OCT/94[20]180, MH:DEC/95[58]188
SCHOONMAKER, JAMES, *Colonel, USA;* ACW:MAY/91[38]305
SCHOONMAKER, JOHN N., *Colonel, 14th Pennsylvania
Cavalry;* CWTI:MAR/89[16]101
SCHOONOVER, JOHN, *Lieutenant, 11th New Jersey Infantry;*
GETTY:12[7]241
SCHOONOVER, RANDOLPH, *Private, 23rd Iowa Infantry;*
CWTI:JAN/94[8]356
SCHORN, CHARLES, *Private, 1st West Virginia Cavalry;*
CWR:VOL3#2[1]153
SCHRAUM, LOUIS, *Lieutenant, USA;* CWTI:JUL/94[50]395
SCHREYER, PHILIP R., *Captain, 53rd Pennsylvania Infantry;*
GETTY:11[80]235
SCHROYER, M.S., *Sgt.., 147th Penna. Inf.;* GETTY:10[120]229
SCHUETZENBACH, EDWARD, *Lt, USA;* CWTI:FEB/92[29]248
SCHUPPERT, M., *Surgeon, CSA;* BOOK REVIEW: *TREATISE ON
GUN-SHOT WOUNDS: WRITTEN FOR AND DEDICATED
TO SURGEON OF THE CONFEDERATE STATES ARMY*
SCHURZ, CARL, *General, USA:*
ARTICLE: "HOW STANDING BEAR BECAME A PERSON,"
AHI:APR/71[48]133
BOOK REVIEW: *CARL SCHURZ: A BIOGRAPHY*
GENERAL LISTINGS: *Gettysburg,* GETTY:4[33]146,
GETTY:4[49]147, GETTY:6[7]169, GETTY:7[29]188,
GETTY:9[17]210, GETTY:10[7]221, GETTY:11[71]234,
GETTY:12[30]243, *in book review,* CWM:MAR/91[74],
CWTI:MAR/94[12], *Kate Sprague,* AHI:APR/83[27]233,
Manassas, Second, B&G:AUG/92[11]493, *photo,*
ACW:NOV/92[42]388
ADDITIONAL LISTINGS: ACW:NOV/92[42]388, CWM:JUL/92[18]429,
CWR:VOL3#2[70]155, CWTI:MAY/92[38]265,
MH:OCT/93[6]170

SCOGIN, JOHN, *Capt., Georgia Battery;* CWR:VOL1#4[42]126
SCOTT, ADDISON L., *Private, 154th New York Infantry;*
GETTY:8[17]200
SCOTT, ALEXANDER, *Corporal, 10th Vermont Infantry;*
B&G:DEC/92[8]503
SCOTT, CHARLES, *Major, 4th Alabama Infantry;*
ACW:NOV/94[18]495, ACW:MAR/95[8]512,
CWTI:MAY/92[32]264
SCOTT, COCKRELL, *Private, 7th Wisconsin Infantry,*
GETTY:9[33]211, GETTY:11[57]233
SCOTT, DRED; see listings under "DRED SCOTT DECISION"
SCOTT, G.W., *Private, 22nd Battalion Virginia Infantry;*
CWR:VOL1#3[52]122
SCOTT, GEORGE W., *Lieutenant Colonel, 5th Florida Cavalry;*
ACW:NOV/91[64]336, AHI:JAN/76[14]164,
CWR:VOL2#3[236]143
SCOTT, HENRY, *Private, Sumter Artillery;* CWR:VOL3#2[1]153
SCOTT, HENRY M., *Captain, 70th Ohio Infantry;*
CWTI:SUMMER/89[50]
SCOTT, HENRY P., *Lieutenant, 5th Massachusetts Artillery;*
GETTY:9[41]212
SCOTT, ISAAC, *Surgeon, 7th West Virginia Infantry;*
GETTY:10[53]225
SCOTT, J.M., *Pvt., Fredericksburg Artillery;* CWR:VOL1#1[1]102
SCOTT, JACK, *Pvt., 42nd Mississippi Inf.;* GETTY:4[22]144
SCOTT, JOHN, *Major, CSA;* ACW:JUL/94[26]477
SCOTT, JOHN, *Sergeant, USA;* ACW:SEP/91[22]321
SCOTT, JOHN K., *civilian;* CWTI:SEPT/89[20]127
SCOTT, JOHN S., *Colonel, 1st Louisiana Cavalry;*
ACW:MAY/95[49]527, ACW:SEP/95[22]544,
CWR:VOL4#1[1]163
SCOTT, JOSEPH R., *Colonel, 19th Illinois Infantry;*
CWM:SEP/93[18]494
SCOTT, JULIAN, *artist;* ARTICLES: "A SOLDIER'S
SKETCHBOOK," CWTI:SEP/91[54]232, "MEMOIRS IN
OILS," CWM:NOV/92[31]449
SCOTT, JULIAN, *Pvt., 3rd Vermont Inf.;* ACW:JAN/94[8]447
SCOTT, LEMUEL, *Capt., 84th Ill. Inf.;* CWTI:SEPT/89[30]129
SCOTT, MILO, *civilian;* B&G:OCT/94[11]580
SCOTT, MITCHELL, *Private, 42nd Mississippi Infantry;*
GETTY:4[22]144
SCOTT, ROBERT K., *General, USA;* B&G:FEB/94[8]550,
CWM:AUG/94[27]526, CWTI:JAN/93[20]298
SCOTT, ROBERT N., *Major, USA;* ACW:SEP/95[54]548
SCOTT, THADDEUS, *Colonel, 12th Georgia Infantry;*
ACW:MAR/94[16]458
SCOTT, THOMAS, *Asst. Secretary of War;* ACW:JAN/94[47]452,
CWTI:SEP/92[22]279
SCOTT, THOMAS A.; ACW:MAR/95[8]512
SCOTT, THOMAS M., *General, CSA;*
CWTI:SUMMER/89[32]122, CWTI:DEC/94[82]418
SCOTT, WILLIAM, *Pvt., 3rd Vermont Inf.;* CWTI:SEP/91[54]232
SCOTT, WILLIAM C., *Colonel, 44th Virginia Infantry;*
B&G:AUG/93[10]529, CWTI:MAR/94[29]371
SCOTT, WILLIAM F., *Captain, 4th Iowa Cavalry:*
BOOK REVIEW: *THE STORY OF A CAVALRY, REGIMENT: THE
CAREER OF THE FOURTH IOWA VETERAN
VOLUNTEERS, FROM KANSAS TO GEORGIA, 1861-1865*
ADDITIONAL LISTING: ACW:JUL/94[8]474
SCOTT, WILLIAM W., *Captain, 1st Florida Special Battalion;*
CWR:VOL3#1[65]151
SCOTT, WINFIELD, *Captain, 126th New York Infantry;*
CWR:VOL1#4[7]125, GETTY:13[75]259

SCOTT, WINFIELD, *General, USA:*
ARTICLES: "COMPASSION IS ALWAYS DUE TO AN ENRAGED
IMBECILE," AHI:FEB/76[14]165, "IMPOSSIBLE CAMPAIGN
ATTEMPTED," MH:APR/93[34]165, "WINFIELD SCOTT,
PART I, THE SOLDIER," AHI:JUN/81[10]219, "WINFIELD
SCOTT, PART II: THE COMMANDER," AHI:JUL/81[20]221
GENERAL LISTINGS: *Beauregard,* CWTI:JUL/92[29]272, *Cassius M.
Clay,* AHI:MAY/69[12]121, *Fort Sumter,*
CWTI:MAY/92[45]266, *Henry Halleck,* AHI:MAY/78[10]179, *in
book review,* ACW:MAR/92[54], ACW:JUL/94[58],
ACW:JUL/95[58], CWM:AUG/94[9], CWNEWS:MAY/91[4],
CWR:VOL3#3[92], CWR:VOL4#3[89], CWTI:MAY/92[18],
MH:DEC/94[70], MH:AUG/95[70], *Jackson,*
B&G:JUN/92[8]487, *James Buchanan,* AHI:MAY/66[12]101,
letters to the editor, B&G:APR/92[6]480, B&G:DEC/93[6]544,
CWM:DEC/94[5]546, *Lincoln's dictatorship,*
AHI:NOV/71[32]136, *Mexican War,* AHI:OCT/82[28]230,
AHI:MAY/88[38]270, MH:AUG/91[45]153, *Mormon
confrontation,* AHI:DEC/72[10]145, *Peninsula Campaign,*
CWM:JUN/95[24]582, *West Point,* B&G:DEC/91[12]469,
photos, AHI:FEB/76[14]165, AHI:JUN/81[10]219,
B&G:DEC/91[12]469, CWM:DEC/94[5]546,
CWTI:DEC/95[67]481
ADDITIONAL LISTINGS, ACW: ACW:JAN/91[8]282,
ACW:NOV/91[41]334, ACW:JAN/92[30]342,
ACW:MAY/92[39]362, ACW:NOV/92[18]385,
ACW:MAR/93[6]400, ACW:MAR/93[18]403,
ACW:JUL/93[42]425, ACW:SEP/93[38]434,
ACW:JAN/94[47]452, ACW:MAR/94[27]459,
ACW:JUL/94[8]471, ACW:SEP/94[31]486, ACW:SEP/94[46]488
ADDITIONAL LISTINGS, AHI: AHI:DEC/71[30]138,
AHI:NOV/72[10]141, AHI:JUN/78[4]180, AHI:DEC/81[18]223
ADDITIONAL LISTINGS, B&G: B&G:FEB/93[12]511,
B&G:FEB/93[48]515, B&G:JUN/94[22]569
ADDITIONAL LISTINGS, CWM: CWM:JAN/92[34]404,
CWM:MAR/93[32]468, CWM:MAY/93[4]472,
CWM:MAY/93[8]474, CWM:FEB/95[49]565,
CWM:AUG/95[17]603
ADDITIONAL LISTING, CWR: CWR:VOL4#2[26]166
ADDITIONAL LISTINGS, CWTI: CWTI:APR/89[14]107,
CWTI:MAY/89[14]114, CWTI:FEB/92[29]248,
CWTI:APR/92[35]257, CWTI:MAY/92[38]265,
CWTI:JUL/94[44]394, CWTI:MAR/94[48]374,
CWTI:DEC/95[22]476, CWTI:DEC/95[40]479,
CWTI:DEC/95[67]481
SCRANTON, SAM, *Sgt., 14th Connecticut Inf.;* GETTY:9[61]215
SCRIPTURE, CLARK, *Lieutenant, 1st Ohio Light Artillery;*
GETTY:4[49]147
SCRUGGS, LAWRENCE H., *Lieutenant Colonel, 4th Alabama
Infantry;* GETTY:7[41]189
SCULLY, THOMAS, *Chaplain, 9th Massachusetts Infantry;*
CWM:MAR/91[50]340
SCURRY, WILLIAM R., *Lieutenant Colonel, 4th Texas Mounted
Volunteers:*
GENERAL LISTINGS: *in book review,* CWR:VOL4#3[1]170, *letters to
the editor,* B&G:OCT/94[6]579, *photo,* B&G:JUN/94[8]568
ADDITIONAL LISTINGS: ACW:JAN/93[51]398, B&G:JUN/94[8]568
CWM:MAY/93[16]475, CWR:VOL2#2[161]139,
CWR:VOL4#2[26]166, CWR:VOL4#2[68]167,
CWTI:MAR/94[58]375, CWTI:OCT/95[56]471
SEABURY, CAROLINE; BOOK REVIEW: *THE DIARY OF
CAROLINE SEABURY 1854-1863*
SEABURY, ROBERT, *Captain, USA;* ACW:SEP/94[38]487

SEAGRAVES, MICHAEL, *Private, 19th Indiana Infantry,*
GETTY:11[57]233
SEAL, ——, *Lieutenant, 42nd Mississippi Infantry;*
GETTY:10[53]225
SEALS, BOWMAN, *free man of color;* AHI:JUN/74[12]155
SEAMANS, ISAAC A., *Lieutenant, 126th New York Infantry;*
CWR:VOL1#4[7]125
SEARLE, CHARLES P., *Captain, 6th Iowa Infantry;*
AHI:OCT/67[26]112
SEARS, CLAUDIUS W., *General, CSA:*
ARTICLE: "SEARS OBLIVIOUS TO LOSS OF LEG,"
CWM:DEC/94[49]553
GENERAL LISTINGS: *Nashville,* B&G:DEC/93[12]545, *order of battle,*
B&G:DEC/93[12]545, B&G:FEB/94[8]550
ADDITIONAL LISTINGS: ACW:SEP/92[38]379, B&G:FEB/94[8]550
SEARS, CYRUS, *Lt., 11th Ohio Battery;* CWTI:JUL/94[50]395
SEARS, HENRY W., *Lieutenant, 2nd Michigan Cavalry;*
B&G:APR/95[24]596
SEATON, JOHN, *Captain, USA;* CWR:VOL3#4[24]162
SEAY, MILTON, *Private, CSA;* B&G:APR/93[12]518
SECESSION:
BOOK REVIEWS: *THE ROAD TO DISUNION: SECESSIONISTS
AT BAY 1776-1854*
SECESSIONVILLE, SOUTH CAROLINA, BATTLE OF:
ARTICLES: "A BLOODY HALF-HOUR," CWTI:JAN/94[46]364, "A
SCRATCH WITH THE REBELS," CWTI:JAN/94[49]365
ADDITIONAL LISTING: CWM:MAY/92[27]421
SECOND CONFISCATION ACT; AHI:JAN/82[16]224
SECORD, SOLOMON, *Surgeon, USA;* CWM:SEP/93[18]494
SECRET SERVICE, CONFEDERATE: also, see additional
listings under **"SPIES"**
BOOK REVIEWS: *APRIL '65: CONFEDERATE COVERT ACTION
IN THE AMERICAN CIVIL WAR * THE SECRET SERVICE
OF THE CONFEDERATE STATES IN EUROPE*
SEDBERRY, T.D., *Captain, 19th Texas Infantry;*
ACW:MAR/93[68]409
SEDDON, JAMES A.,
GENERAL LISTINGS: *Gettysburg,* GETTY:11[6]231, *in book review,*
CWNEWS:MAY/90[4], *letters to the editor,*
CWTI:MAR/91[10]197, *Mosby,* CWTI:SEP/90[34]176, *Price's
1864 Missouri Campaign,* B&G:JUN/91[10]452, *W.H.T.
Walker,* CWTI:MAR/93[24]309
ADDITIONAL LISTINGS: ACW:MAY/91[23]303, ACW:MAY/92[14]358,
ACW:NOV/93[42]443, B&G:FEB/91[20]440,
B&G:APR/91[8]445, B&G:OCT/94[11]580,
B&G:FEB/95[8]590B, B&G:AUG/95[8]604,
CWM:MAR/91[65]342, CWM:JUL/91[10]357,
CWM:AUG/95[58]611, CWR:VOL1#1[1]102,
CWR:VOL2#4[269]145, CWR:VOL4#4[70]180,
CWTI:AUG/91[58]220, CWTI:AUG/91[62]221,
CWTI:APR/92[49]260, CWTI:NOV/92[54]293,
CWTI:MAR/93[40]312, CWTI:JUL/94[44]394,
GETTY:13[75]259, MH:AUG/94[46]178
SEDGWICK, JOHN, *General, USA:*
ARTICLES: "GENERAL JOHN SEDGWICK BUILT A
LUXURIOUS RETIREMENT HOME IN CORNWALL
HOLLOW, BUT HE DID NOT LIVE TO USE IT,"
ACW:MAR/95[70]520, "THE MAN WHO SHOT JOHN
SEDGWICK: THE TALE OF CHARLES D. GRACE—A
SHARPSHOOTER IN THE DOLES-COOK BRIGADE, CSA,"
B&G:DEC/95[25]616, "THE PENINSULA CAMPAIGN OF
1862: THE BATTLE OF SEVEN PINES,"
CWM:JUN/95[47]588

GENERAL LISTINGS: *Antietam,* ACW:MAR/94[50]462,
ACW:MAR/95[70]520, B&G:OCT/95[8]611A,
CWTI:SEP/93[43]338, GETTY:6[69]176, *Falling Waters,*
GETTY:9[109]218, *Chancellorsville,* ACW:MAR/95[70]520,
MH:JUN/92[50]159, *general history,* AHI:MAY/71[3]133A,
Gettysburg, GETTY:4[101]151, GETTY:6[7]169,
GETTY:8[53]203, GETTY:10[42]224, GETTY:11[19]232,
GETTY:11[71]234, GETTY:11[91]236, GETTY:12[123]251, *in
book review,* CWM:AUG/94[9], CWM:DEC/94[7],
CWM:FEB/95[7], CWR:VOL4#3[1]170, *letters to the editor,*
B&G:DEC/95[5]614A, *Malvern Hill,* ACW:MAR/95[70]520,
Mexican War, MH:APR/93[39]166, *order of battle,*
B&G:APR/95[8]595, *Overland Campaign,* B&G:APR/94[10]558
GENERAL LISTINGS, continued: *Peninsula Campaign,*
ACW:MAR/95[70]520, *Rappahannock Station,*
ACW:MAR/92[30]352, *Seven Pines,* CWM:JUN/95[47]588,
Spotsylvania, ACW:MAR/95[70]520, *Wilderness,*
B&G:APR/95[8]595, B&G:JUN/95[8]600, *painting of death of;*
CWTI:APR/90[48]154, *photos,* ACW:MAR/92[30]352,
ACW:MAR/93[26]404, B&G:APR/91[8]445,
B&G:JUN/95[8]600, B&G:OCT/95[8]611A,
B&G:DEC/95[5]614A, B&G:DEC/95[25]616
ADDITIONAL LISTINGS: ACW:SEP/92[30]378, ACW:SEP/93[31]433,
ACW:SEP/94[38]487, B&G:APR/91[8]445,
B&G:AUG/91[32]461, B&G:FEB/95[8]590B,
CWM:MAY/92[20]420, CWR:VOL2#4[269]145,
CWR:VOL3#1[31]150, CWR:VOL3#2[1]153,
CWR:VOL3#3[1]157, CWTI:MAY/89[36]118,
CWTI:APR/90[48]154, CWTI:MAR/93[24]309,
CWTI:SEP/94[26]400, CWTI:AUG/95[24]455
SEDGWICK, WILLIAM D., *Major, USA;* AHI:OCT/67[26]112
SEDINGER, JAMES, *Lt., 8th VA Cav.;* B&G:AUG/94[10]574
SEELEY, AARON P., *Captain, 126th New York Infantry;*
GETTY:7[51]190, GETTY:8[95]205
SEELEY, FRANCIS W., *Lieutenant, 4th U.S. Artillery;*
CWR:VOL3#2[1]153, GETTY:5[79]161, GETTY:12[7]241
SEFTON, JEFFERSON, *Union veteran;* GETTY:5[123]166
SEGOINE, JESSE, *Colonel, 111th New York Infantry;*
CWR:VOL1#4[7]125, GETTY:7[51]190
SEIBERT, JOHN, *Pvt., 53rd Penna. Inf.;* GETTY:11[80]235
SEIBERT, JUSTUS, *Colonel, USA;* GETTY:11[19]232
SEILER, GEROGE A.C., *Colonel, USA;* GETTY:12[30]243
SELDON, HENRY R., *Captain, USA;* B&G:JUN/94[8]568,
CWTI:OCT/95[56]471
SELFFRICH, WILLIAM, *Chaplain;* GETTY:11[102]237
SELFRIDGE, ALEXANDER W., *Captain, 46th Pennsylvania
Infantry;* GETTY:7[83]192
SELFRIDGE, JAMES L., *Colonel, USA;* B&G:DEC/95[9]615
SELFRIDGE, THOMAS O., *Lieutenant, USN;*
ACW:MAY/93[62]418, ACW:SEP/94[74]491,
AHI:OCT/75[30]162, CWR:VOL2#3[212]142,
CWR:VOL4#2[26]166
SELLARS, ALFRED J., *Lieutenant Colonel, 19th Pennsylvania
Infantry;* GETTY:5[13]157, GETTY:10[7]221
SELLERS, ELI G., *Capt., 91st Penna. Inf.;* GETTY:9[48]213
SELLMER, CHARLES, *Lieutenant, 11th Maine Infantry;*
CWM:MAR/92[16]411, CWTI:APR/89[22]108
SELLS, ORANGE, *Captain, 12th Ohio Cavalry;*
B&G:AUG/91[52]464
SELMA, ALABAMA, BATTLE OF; ACW:MAR/91[38]296,
ACW:SEP/95[48]547, CWTI:AUG/90[26]166,
CWTI:MAY/92[48]267, CWTI:MAY/94[44]384
SEMMES, BENEDICT J., *Captain, CSA;* CWM:APR/94[8]502

SEMMES, OLIVER J., *Major, CSA;* CWM:OCT/94[33]537,
CWR:VOL3#1[1]149, CWR:VOL4#2[118]169,
CWTI:JAN/95[42]428
SEMMES, PAUL J., *General, CSA:*
GENERAL LISTINGS: *Gettysburg,* GETTY:5[35]159,
GETTY:5[103]163, GETTY:5[107]164, GETTY:8[53]203,
GETTY:9[53]214, GETTY:11[80]235, GETTY:11[91]236,
GETTY:11[102]237, GETTY:12[24]242, *Peninsula Campaign,*
ACW:MAR/91[47]297, *Harpers Ferry,* MH:AUG/95[30]185,
Savage's Station, CWM:JUN/95[65]595
ADDITIONAL LISTINGS: ACW:JAN/94[39]451, ACW:MAR/94[50]462,
ACW:JUL/95[10]533, CWR:VOL1#4[7]125,
CWTI:SEPT/89[46]132, CWTI:SEP/94[26]400
SEMMES, RAPAHEL, *Admiral, CSN:*
ARTICLES: "CRUISE AND COMBATS OF THE *ALABAMA*,"
AHI:OCT/88[38]275, "I TOLD HIM I SHOULD BURN HIS
SHIP," CWM:FEB/95[73]568
BOOK REVIEWS: *CONFEDERATE RAIDER: RAPHAEL SEMMES
OF THE ALABAMA," * MEMOIRS OF SERVICE AFLOAT*
GENERAL LISTINGS: *evacuation of Richmond,* ACW:MAY/95[38]526,
ACW:SEP/95[30]545, *general history,* AHI:MAY/71[3]133A, *in
book review,* ACW:JAN/93[58]399, B&G:AUG/92[36],
CWNEWS:SEP/89[8], CWNEWS:MAY/91[4],
CWNEWS:AUG/92[4], *letters to the editor,*
CWM:MAR/92[6]409, *photos,* AHI:MAY/71[3]133A,
AHI:JAN/83[10]232, CWM:FEB/95[73]568,
CWTI:AUG/95[40]458
ADDITIONAL LISTINGS: ACW:SEP/91[62]326, ACW:JUL/92[10]366,
ACW:SEP/94[46]488, AHI:DEC/82[38]231,
AHI:JAN/83[10]232, AHI:OCT/88[32]274,
B&G:AUG/91[40]463, CWTI:DEC/94[73]416,
CWTI:JAN/95[42]428
SEMMES, THOMAS J., *civilian;* B&G:APR/91[32]447,
SEMMILROGGE, WILLIAM, *Private, USA;*
ACW:JUL/93[27]423
SEMPLE'S ALABAMA BATTERY; ACW:NOV/93[34]442,
SEMPLE, HENRY C., *Captain, CSA;* CWR:VOL4#3[50]171
SENATE COMMITTEE ON MILITARY AFFAIRS;
GETTY:12[1]240
SENATE COMMITTEE ON TERRITORIES;
CWTI:JUN/90[54]162
SENATOBIA (MISSISSIPPI) INVINCIBLES, (42nd
Mississippi Infantry); GETTY:4[22]144
SENECA MILLS, MARYLAND; CWTI:SEP/90[34]176
SERRELL, EDWARD W., *Colonel, 1st New York Engineers;*
CWM:MAR/92[16]411
SESSIONS, N., *Private, 1st USSS;* B&G:JUN/95[8]600
SEVEN DAY'S (VIRGINIA) CAMPAIGN: also, see listings for
other actions under **"PENINSULA CAMPAIGN"**
ARTICLES: "THE PENINSULA CAMPAIGN OF 1862:
DENOUEMENT AT HARRISON'S LANDING,"
CWM:JUN/95[76]598, "THE PENINSULA CAMPAIGN OF
1862: THE BATTLE OF BEAVER DAM CREEK,"
CWM:JUN/95[57]592, "THE PENINSULA CAMPAIGN OF
1862: THE BATTLE OF GAINES'S MILL,"
CWM:JUN/95[61]593, "THE PENINSULA CAMPAIGN OF
1862: THE BATTLE OF GARNETT'S FARM,"
CWM:JUN/95[63]594, "THE PENINSULA CAMPAIGN OF
1862: THE BATTLE OF GLENDALE," CWM:JUN/95[69]596,
"THE PENINSULA CAMPAIGN OF 1862: THE BATTLE OF
MALVERN HILL," CWM:JUN/95[73]597, "THE PENINSULA
CAMPAIGN OF 1862: THE BATTLE OF SAVAGE'S
STATION," CWM:JUN/95[65]595

BOOK REVIEWS: *THE PENINSULA CAMPAIGN OF 1862: YORKTOWN TO THE SEVEN DAYS * THE SEVEN DAYS: THE EMERGENCE OF LEE * TO THE GATES OF RICHMOND: THE PENINSULA CAMPAIGN*

GENERAL LISTINGS: *general history*, AHI:MAY/71[3]133A, *in book review*, ACW:SEP/94[66], CWM:OCT/94[8], CWM:APR/95[50], CWNEWS:MAY/91[4], CWNEWS:JUN/94[5], CWR:VOL2#4[346], CWR:VOL3#2[105], CWR:VOL4#3[89], *Jackson*, B&G:JUN/92[8]487, *letters to the editor*, CWM:OCT/94[5]533, CWM:OCT/95[5]613

ADDITIONAL LISTINGS: ACW:NOV/91[41]334, CWM:SEP/93[24]495, CWM:OCT/94[26]536, CWM:DEC/94[26]548, CWM:AUG/95[17]603, CWM:AUG/95[30]606, CWM:DEC/95[41]630, CWR:VOL1#1[1]102, CWR:VOL1#1[71]107, CWR:VOL1#3[v]117, CWR:VOL1#3[52]122, CWR:VOL2#1[36]132, CWR:VOL2#4[269]145, CWR:VOL3#1[31]150, CWR:VOL3#2[1]153, CWR:VOL3#3[1]157, CWTI:DEC/89[34]136, CWTI:AUG/91[58]220, CWTI:DEC/91[36]240, CWTI:JUL/93[14]324, CWTI:JUL/93[42]329, CWTI:NOV/93[55]350, CWTI:JAN/94[20]358, CWTI:MAY/94[31]382, CWTI:MAR/95[60]439, CWTI:DEC/95[67]481

SEVEN PINES, VIRGINIA, BATTLE OF:

ARTICLES: "THE PENINSULA CAMPAIGN OF 1862: THE BATTLE OF SEVEN PINES," CWM:JUN/95[47]588, "STUNNING SOUTHERN HEROISM," CWM:OCT/94[34]538

BOOK REVIEW: *THE BATTLE OF SEVEN PINES*

GENERAL LISTINGS: *balloons*, AHI:JUN/84[24]239, *in book review*, CWR:VOL3#2[105], *Peninsula Campaign*, CWM:JUN/95[76]598

ADDITIONAL LISTINGS: ACW:MAR/92[10]349, ACW:NOV/92[18]385, ACW:JUL/93[8]420, ACW:SEP/93[8]429, ACW:MAY/94[12]466, ACW:NOV/94[50]498, ACW:JAN/95[46]507, ACW:MAR/95[50]518, ACW:MAR/95[70]520, ACW:JUL/95[34]536, ACW:SEP/95[54]548, B&G:DEC/91[34]470, CWM:SEP/93[24]495, CWM:JUN/94[26]512, CWM:JUN/94[28]514, CWR:VOL1#1[1]102, CWR:VOL1#3[52]122, CWR:VOL2#4[269]145, CWR:VOL3#1[31]150, CWR:VOL3#2[1]153, CWTI:MAR/89[44]105, CWTI:APR/89[14]107, CWTI:DEC/89[34]136, CWTI:AUG/91[52]219, CWTI:SEP/91[42]231, CWTI:JAN/93[49]303, CWTI:MAY/93[26]318, CWTI:JUL/93[29]326, CWTI:JUL/94[44]394

SEWARD, SAMUEL, *Lt., 14th Connecticut Inf.;* GETTY:9[61]215

SEWARD, WILLIAM H.:

ARTICLE: "SOME THOUGHTS FOR THE PRESIDENT'S CONSIDERATION," CWTI:SEP/92[46]284

BOOK REVIEWS: *DESPERATE DIPLOMACY: WILLIAM H. SEWARD'S FOREIGN POLICY, 1861 * WILLIAM HENRY SEWARD * WILLIAM HENRY SEWARD: LINCOLN'S RIGHT HAND*

GENERAL LISTINGS: *attempted assassination*, CWTI:DEC/91[28]239, *Ball's Bluff*, AHI:FEB/82[36]225, *Bloody Kansas*, AHI:JUL/75[4]160, *Cassius M. Clay*, AHI:MAY/69[12]121, *Eli Parker*, AHI:NOV/69[13]124, *Gettysburg*, GETTY:8[43]202, GETTY:9[61]215, *gold hoax*, AHI:APR/80[21]200, *Grant*, CWTI:FEB/90[46]146, *in book review*, ACW:MAY/93[54], CWM:DEC/95[10], CWNEWS:OCT/94[33], CWTI:SEP/94[18], CWTI:OCT/95[18], *John Brown*, AHI:JAN/86[10]256, *letters to the editor*,

CWTI:JAN/93[10]297, *Lincoln's Gettysburg Address*, GETTY:9[122]220, *Nelson-Davis feud*, AHI:NOV/72[12]142, *Southern education*, AHI:FEB/80[14]199, *Willard's Hotel*, AHI:OCT/79[10]192, *photo*, CWTI:SEP/92[46]284

ADDITIONAL LISTINGS: ACW:JUL/91[43]315, ACW:NOV/91[46]335, ACW:JAN/92[30]342, ACW:MAR/92[8]348, ACW:JUL/92[6]365, ACW:SEP/93[8]429, ACW:SEP/93[46]435, ACW:MAY/95[38]526, AHI:JAN/73[4]146, AHI:JUN/73[4]149, AHI:JAN/81[18]214, AHI:NOV/88[37]278, AHI:APR/89[13]281, B&G:DEC/92[38]507, B&G:APR/95[33]597, CWM:SEP/92[8]437, CWM:SEP/92[19]440, CWM:OCT/95[47]620, CWR:VOL4#2[26]166, CWTI:MAY/89[14]114, CWTI:MAY/89[28]117, CWTI:AUG/90[26]166, CWTI:DEC/90[50]183, CWTI:AUG/91[52]219, CWTI:FEB/92[21]247, CWTI:SEP/92[22]279, CWTI:JUL/93[14]324, CWTI:JUL/93[38]328, CWTI:DEC/94[34]411, CWTI:DEC/94[73]416, CWTI:MAR/95[8]431, CWTI:JUN/95[56]450, CWTI:AUG/95[54]460, CWTI:DEC/95[40]479, CWTI:DEC/95[67]481, CWTI:DEC/95[76]482, MH:OCT/95[8]187

SEWARD, WILLIAM H. JR., *Colonel, 9th New York Heavy Artillery;* ACW:NOV/93[50]444, B&G:DEC/92[8]503

SEWELL MOUNTAIN, WEST VIRGINIA, BATTLE OF: BOOK REVIEW: *ROBERT E. LEE AT SEWELL MOUNTAIN: THE WEST VIRGINIA CAMPAIGN*

SEX IN THE CIVIL WAR: BOOK REVIEWS: *DIVIDED HOUSES: GENDER AND THE CIVIL WAR * THE STORY THE SOLDIERS WOULDN'T TELL: SEX IN THE CIVIL WAR*

SEYMOUR, FREDERICK J., *Lieutenant, 14th Connecticut Infantry;* ACW:JUL/95[50]538, GETTY:9[61]215

SEYMOUR, HORATIO, *Governor, New York:*

GENERAL LISTINGS: *Gettysburg*, GETTY:9[61]215, *gold hoax*, AHI:APR/80[21]200, *Kate Sprague*, AHI:APR/83[27]233

ADDITIONAL LISTINGS: ACW:MAR/91[8]291, AHI:AUG/77[30]175, CWTI:FEB/90[60]148

SEYMOUR, ISAAC G., *Colonel, 6th Louisiana Infantry;* CWR:VOL1#4[77], CWTI:MAR/94[48]374

SEYMOUR, TRUMAN, *General, USA:*

GENERAL LISTINGS: *Beaver Dam Creek*, CWM:JUN/95[57]592, *in book review*, ACW:JAN/95[62], *order of battle*, B&G:APR/95[8]595, *Sayler's Creek*, ACW:JAN/92[22]341, *West Point*, B&G:DEC/91[12]469, *Wilderness*, B&G:JUN/95[8]600

ADDITIONAL LISTINGS: ACW:SEP/91[30]322, ACW:NOV/95[38]556, B&G:AUG/93[30]531, CWR:VOL1#2[7]111, CWR:VOL3#1[65]151, CWR:VOL3#4[1]161, CWTI:DEC/89[42]137

SEYMOUR, WILLIAM, *Captain, 1st Pennsylvania Artillery;* GETTY:12[30]243

SEYMOUR, WILLIAM J., *Captain, Louisiana Tigers:*

BOOK REVIEWS: *THE CIVIL WAR MEMOIRS OF CAPTAIN WILLIAM J. SEYMOUR: REMINISCENCES OF A LOUISIANA TIGER*

ADDITIONAL LISTINGS: CWM:SEP/93[24]495, GETTY:7[13]186, GETTY:9[17N]210

SHACKELFORD, BESSIE, *civilian;* ACW:NOV/91[30]332, ACW:NOV/91[35]333

SHACKELFORD, JAMES M., *General, USA;* ACW:JUL/91[26]313

SHACKLETT, BENJAMIN W., *Major, CSA;* CWTI:AUG/95[34]457, MH:APR/95[74]184

SHACKLETT, KITTY, *civilian;* MH:OCT/92[51]162

SHADEL, HENRY, *Corp., 28th Penna. Inf.;* GETTY:9[81]216

SHADRACH, PHILIP, *Private, USA;* ACW:SEP/91[22]321

SHAFER, EMANUEL, *Private, Georgia and Mississippi Regiment;* CWR:VOL1#4[42]126

SHAFER, JEROME, *Pvt., 154th New York Inf.;* GETTY:8[17]200

SHAFER, LEVI S., *Sergeant, 8th Illinois Cavalry;* B&G:FEB/95[8]590A, GETTY:11[19]232

SHAFTER, WILLIAM R., *Colonel, 17th U.S. Colored Infantry:*
BOOK REVIEW: *"PECOS BILL": A MILITARY BIOGRAPHY OF WILLIAM R. SHAFTER*
ADDITIONAL LISTING: B&G:DEC/93[12]545

SHALER, ALEXANDER, *General, USA;* ACW:SEP/92[30]378, B&G:APR/95[8]595, B&G:JUN/95[8]600, GETTY:6[69]176, GETTY:7[83]192

SHANE, JOHN, *Col., 13th Iowa Infantry;* ACW:JAN/93[10]393

SHANE, WASHINGTON C., *Adjutant, CSA;* B&G:OCT/94[11]580

SHANGHAI STEAM NAVIGATION COMPANY; MH:OCT/91[50]154

SHANKLIN, JAMES M., *Lieutenant Colonel, 42nd Indiana Infantry;* BOOK REVIEW: *DEAREST LIZZIE: THE CIVIL WAR LETTERS OF LIEUTENANT COLONEL JAMES MAYNARD SHANKLIN*

SHANKS, DAVID, *Colonel, CSA;* B&G:JUN/91[10]452, CWR:VOL1#2[44]114

SHANKS, JAMES, *Private, CSA;* MH:JUN/91[20]152

SHANKS, THOMAS H., *Captain, Petersburg Artillery;* ACW:MAR/95[12]513, B&G:OCT/94[11]580

SHANKS, WILLIAM F.G., *correspondent;* ACW:JUL/91[35]314

SHANNON'S SCOUTS, TERRY'S TEXAS RANGERS; CWM:JUL/92[40]432

SHANNON, ALEXANDER M., *Captain, Terry's Texas Rangers;* CWM:JUL/92[40]432

SHANNON, ALICE, *civilian;* CWTI:SEPT/89[18]126

SHANNON, GEORGE, *Captain, 11th Mississippi Infantry;* CWR:VOL2#4[269]145

SHANNON, MARSHALL H., *Sergeant, 154th New York Infantry;* GETTY:8[17]200

SHANNON, SAMUEL D., *Lieutenant, CSA;* GETTY:5[89]162

SHARP, JACOB H., *General, CSA;* B&G:DEC/93[12]545, CWTI:SUMMER/89[40]123

SHARP, REDFORD, *Surgeon, 15th New Jersey Infantry;* B&G:FEB/92[22]476

SHARP, THOMAS, *Private, 2nd West Virginia Infantry;* CWTI:AUG/90[50]168

SHARP, THOMAS R., *Captain, CSA;* CWM:NOV/91[40]393

SHARP, W.W., *Surgeon, 140th Pennsylvania Infantry;* GETTY:10[53]225

SHARPE, C.W., *Private, Sumter Artillery;* CWR:VOL3#2[1]153

SHARPE, GEORGE H., *General, USA;* ACW:JUL/91[8]309, AHI:SEP/87[48]264, CWTI:AUG/95[46]459, GETTY:11[19]232

SHARPE, JACOB, *Colonel, 156th New York Infantry;* ACW:MAY/91[38]305, CWR:VOL4#2[104]168

SHARPE, RICHARD, *civilian;* ACW:SEP/93[22]432

SHARPSBURG, MARYLAND, BATTLE OF; see listings under "ANTIETAM, MARYLAND, BATTLE OF"

SHARPSHOOTERS: see listings under "UNITED STATES SHARPSHOOTERS"

SHATTUCK, LUCIUS L., *Lieutenant, 24th Michigan Infantry;* GETTY:5[19]158

SHAUGHTER, PHILIP, *Colonel, CSA;* AHI:MAR/84[42]238

SHAW, A.O., *Surgeon, 20th Maine Infantry;* CWM:JUL/92[8]427

SHAW, EDWARD, *Master, USN;* ACW:JUL/93[34]424

SHAW, HENRY M., *Colonel, 8th North Carolina Infantry;* CWM:FEB/95[49]565

SHAW, ROBERT G., *Colonel, 54th Massachusetts Infantry:*
ARTICLE: "CARNIVAL OF DEATH," ACW:SEP/91[30]322
BOOK REVIEWS: *BLUE-EYED CHILD OF FORTUNE: THE CIVIL WAR LETTERS OF COLONEL ROBERT GOULD SHAW * GATE OF HELL: CAMPAIGN FOR CHARLESTON HARBOR, 1863*
GENERAL LISTINGS: *in book review,* B&G:JUN/95[30], CWM:AUG/94[9], CWNEWS:NOV/92[4], *in the movie "GLORY";* CWTI:DEC/89[53]138, *Winchester,* GETTY:6[69]176, *photos,* ACW:SEP/91[30]322, CWTI:DEC/89[42]137
ADDITIONAL LISTINGS: ACW:MAY/93[14]413, B&G:FEB/94[38]553, B&G:APR/95[38]598, CWR:VOL1#1[76]109, CWR:VOL3#1[31]150, CWTI:DEC/89[42]137, CWTI:DEC/89[62]139, CWTI:MAR/94[38]372

SHAW, WILLIAM T., *Colonel, USA;* CWR:VOL2#3[212]142

SHEADS, CARRIE S., *civilian:*
ARTICLE: "THREE HEROINES OF GETTYSBURG," GETTY:11[119]238
ADDITIONAL LISTING: GETTY:10[7]221

SHEAFFER, DANIEL, *civilian;* GETTY:11[119]238

SHEARS, THEODORE, *Private, 126th New York Infantry;* CWR:VOL1#4[7]125

SHEDD, W., *Lt. Col., 30th Illinois Infantry;* B&G:FEB/94[8]550

SHEERAN, JAMES B., *Chaplain, 14th Louisiana Infantry;* B&G:AUG/93[24], CWM:MAR/91[17]335

SHEETZ, H.A., *Lieutenant, USA;* CWR:VOL3#3[59]159

SHEFFIELD, JAMES L., *Colonel, CSA;* CWTI:SEP/93[53]340

SHEHHAN, JOHN, *Pvt., 4th U.S. Artillery;* GETTY:11[57]233

SHELBY, JOSEPH O., *General, CSA:*
ARTICLE: "JO SHELBY AND HIS SHADOW," ACW:MAR/95[26]515
GENERAL LISTINGS: *Confederate exiles,* AHI:JUN/70[30]127, *in book review,* CWNEWS:JAN/94[5], CWTI:MAR/89[10], *letters to the editor,* CWM:MAY/92[6]417, CWM:JAN/93[6]455, *sketch;* ACW:MAR/95[26]515, *photo,* B&G:JUN/91[10]452
ADDITIONAL LISTINGS: ACW:SEP/92[66]381, ACW:JAN/93[26]395, ACW:JAN/94[18]449, ACW:MAR/94[8]456, ACW:MAY/94[26]468, ACW:SEP/94[10]484, ACW:NOV/94[42]497, B&G:JUN/91[10]452, B&G:FEB/93[40]514, B&G:FEB/94[38]553, CWM:JAN/92[8]399, CWM:SEP/92[38]443, CWM:SEP/93[8]493, CWR:VOL1#1[42]105, CWR:VOL1#2[44]114, CWTI:AUG/90[70]171, CWTI:JAN/94[29]360, CWTI:DEC/94[82]418, CWTI:MAR/95[46]437

SHELDEN, EDGAR, *Pvt., 150th NY Inf.;* GETTY:12[42]244

SHELDON, GEORGE W., *Corporal, 126th New York Infantry;* CWR:VOL1#4[7]125, CWR:VOL1#4[7]125

SHELDON, LIONEL A., *Colonel, USA;* ACW:JUL/94[51]480, B&G:FEB/94[8]550

SHELDON, RALPH, *Capt., 2nd Kent. Inf.;* B&G:OCT/94[11]580

SHELLEY, CHARLES M., *Colonel, 30th Alabama Infantry;* B&G:DEC/93[12]545, B&G:FEB/94[8]550, CWR:VOL2#1[19]131

SHELLEY, JACOB D., *Lieutenant Colonel, 11th Louisiana Infantry;* CWR:VOL4#2[68]167

SHELMIRE, JOHN, *Major, USA;* B&G:DEC/91[34]470

SHELTON LAUREL MASSACRE: "THE SHELTON LAUREL MASSACRE," B&G:FEB/91[20]440

order of battle, B&G:APR/95[8]595, *Overland Campaign,* B&G:APR/94[10]558, *Perryville,* CWR:VOL4#3[50]171, CWTI:NOV/92[18]289

GENERAL LISTINGS, continued: *post war,* AHI:OCT/79[20]194, AHI:NOV/79[32]196, *Sayler's Creek,* ACW:JAN/93[43]397, *Shenandoah Valley Campaign, 1864,* ACW:MAY/95[38]526, CWM:MAR/93[24]467, CWTI:FEB/90[54]147, CWTI:MAY/93[26]318, CWTI:JUL/93[38]328, *Stones River,* B&G:OCT/91[11]466, *West Point,* B&G:DEC/91[12]469, *Wilderness,* B&G:APR/95[8]595, *Winchester,* ACW:JAN/95[46]507, CWM:OCT/95[37]617, *Yellow Tavern,* ACW:JAN/95[10]503, *painting on horse;* CWTI:FEB/90[54]147, *photo, (pre-war);* AHI:AUG/72[24]140, *photos,* ACW:JAN/92[22]341, ACW:SEP/94[55]489, AHI:NOV/70[22]130, AHI:MAY/71[3]133A, AHI:NOV/80[8]209, AHI:FEB/85[10]247, B&G:OCT/91[11]466, B&G:APR/92[8]481, CWM:MAR/93[24]467, CWTI:DEC/89[34]136, CWTI:SEP/92[18], CWTI:OCT/95[48]470

ADDITIONAL LISTINGS, ACW: ACW:JAN/91[22]285, ACW:MAR/91[30]295, ACW:JUL/91[35]314, ACW:SEP/91[41]323, ACW:JAN/92[10]339, ACW:JAN/92[16]340, ACW:MAR/92[14]350, ACW:JUL/92[6]365, ACW:NOV/92[26]386, ACW:NOV/92[74]390, ACW:MAY/93[14]413, ACW:SEP/93[31]433, ACW:SEP/93[62]436, ACW:MAY/94[12]466, ACW:SEP/94[55]489

ADDITIONAL LISTINGS, AHI: AHI:DEC/74[12]156, AHI:MAR/84[42]238, AHI:SEP/87[48]264, AHI:OCT/95[24]326

ADDITIONAL LISTINGS, B&G: B&G:APR/91[8]445, B&G:OCT/92[38]500, B&G:FEB/93[40]514, B&G:APR/93[12]518, B&G:APR/94[59]565, B&G:AUG/94[10]574, B&G:FEB/95[35]592, B&G:DEC/95[9]615

ADDITIONAL LISTINGS, CWM: CWM:JAN/91[35]328, CWM:JUL/91[35]369, CWM:SEP/91[64]387, CWM:JAN/92[27]403, CWM:MAR/92[4]408, CWM:MAY/92[34]422, CWM:JUL/92[8]427, CWM:JUL/92[24]430, CWM:NOV/92[10]447, CWM:JAN/93[24]458, CWM:JAN/93[40]461, CWM:MAR/93[4]463, CWM:MAY/93[4]472, CWM:SEP/93[24]495, CWM:APR/94[24]505, CWM:OCT/94[17]534, CWM:DEC/95[26]626

ADDITIONAL LISTINGS, CWR: CWR:VOL1#1[35]104, CWR:VOL2#1[i]129, CWR:VOL2#1[19]131, CWR:VOL2#3[236]143, CWR:VOL3#2[1]153, CWR:VOL3#4[24]162

ADDITIONAL LISTINGS, CWTI: CWTI:DEC/89[34]136, CWTI:AUG/91[62]221, CWTI:SEP/91[8]224, CWTI:SEP/91[54]232, CWTI:DEC/91[18]236, CWTI:APR/92[35]257, CWTI:APR/92[49]260, CWTI:MAY/92[32]264, CWTI:JAN/93[40]301, CWTI:SEP/94[49]404, CWTI:DEC/95[52]480, CWTI:DEC/95[67]481

ADDITIONAL LISTINGS, OTHER: GETTY:13[89]260, MH:FEB/93[42]164, MH:OCT/93[6]170, MH:APR/95[46]183

SHERMAN MILITARY TELEGRAPH SYSTEM; ACW:JAN/95[20]504

SHERMAN, JOHN, *Senator:*
GENERAL LISTINGS: *election of 1864,* AHI:OCT/68[4]116, *in book review,* CWM:FEB/95[7], *James A. Garfield,* AHI:MAY/76[24]167, *William T. Sherman,* AHI:JAN/67[4]106, *photo,* AHI:JAN/67[4]106

ADDITIONAL LISTINGS: ACW:MAR/92[22]351, B&G:APR/93[12]518, AHI:APR/89[13]281

SHERMAN, MARSHALL, *Private, 1st Minnesota Infantry;* ACW:JAN/94[62], GETTY:5[79]161

SHERMAN, MATTHEW, *Captain, USA;* B&G:OCT/91[11]466

SHERMAN, THOMAS W., *General, USA;* ACW:JAN/94[30]450, CWM:MAR/91[35]337, CWTI:MAY/91[74]212

SHERMAN, WILLIAM T., *General, USA:*
ARTICLES: "A DRIVING TOUR OF NORTH GEORGIA TRACES WILLIAM T. SHERMAN'S CAUTIOUS ADVANCE TO ATLANTA," ACW:JUL/94[66]481, "AS THE SHELLS EXPLODED OVER ATLANTA IN 1864, THE OPPOSING GENERALS OPENED A WAR OF WORDS," ACW:JAN/95[6]501, "THE ATLANTA CAMPAIGN," CWM:JAN/91[12]326, "AUGUSTUS SAINT GAUDENS AND THE SHERMAN MEMORIAL," CWM:NOV/92[43]452, "BATTLE MOST DESPERATE AND BLOODY," ACW:JAN/95[30]505, "THE BATTLE OF BENTONVILLE, MARCH 19-21, 1865: LAST STAND IN THE CAROLINAS," B&G:DEC/95[9]615, "THE BATTLE THAT SHOULD NOT HAVE BEEN," CWTI:NOV/92[41]291, "BESIDES FIGHTING CONFEDERATES, WILLIAM SHERMAN ALSO FOUGHT WITH NORTHERN WAR CORRESPONDENTS," ACW:NOV/92[6]382, "BURNING DOWN THE SOUTH," CWTI:OCT/95[48]470, "CHATTANOOGA RELIEVED!" CWM:DEC/94[46]552, "CITY FOR THE TAKING," ACW:SEP/92[47]380, "DEVIL'S OWN DAY," ACW:JAN/91[22]285, "FATHER THOMAS O'REILLY: A SAVIOR OF ATLANTA," CWM:JAN/92[40]405, "GATEWAY TO THE ATLANTIC," CWTI:DEC/94[62]415

ARTICLES, continued: "HEROISM OF SHERMAN'S SOLDIERS AT TUNNEL HILL," CWM:DEC/95[35]629, "I HEREBY TENDER YOU MY SERVICES," CWTI:SEP/93[62]342, "LAST STAND IN THE CAROLINAS: THE BATTLE OF BENTONVILLE. AN INTERVIEW WITH AUTHOR MARK L. BRADLEY," CWR:VOL4#3[65]172, "RETURN TO JACKSON, JULY 5-25, 1863," B&G:AUG/95[8]604, "SHERMAN MOVES ON ATLANTA," CWM:AUG/95[36]608, "SHERMAN REVEALS SOMETHING ABOUT HIS STRATEGY," CWTI:JUL/94[28]391, "SHERMAN'S FEUDING GENERALS," CWTI:MAR/95[40]436, "THIS THANKLESS OFFICE," AHI:JAN/77[46]173, "TOTAL WAR COMES TO NEW MANCHESTER," B&G:DEC/94[22]586, "WILLIAM T. SHERMAN," AHI:JAN/67[4]106, "WOLF AT THE DOOR," ACW:NOV/93[42]443, "WRECKING ON THE RAILROAD," ACW:SEP/95[48]547

BOOK REVIEWS: *THE CAMPAIGN FOR ATLANTA & SHERMAN'S MARCH TO THE SEA * CHARGED WITH TREASON: ORDEAL OF 400 MILL WORKERS DURING MILITARY OPERATIONS IN ROSWELL GEORGIA, 1864-1865 * CITIZEN SHERMAN * DECISION IN THE WEST: THE ATLANTA CAMPAIGN OF 1864 * THE DESTRUCTIVE WAR—WILLIAM TECUMSEH SHERMAN, STONEWALL JACKSON, AND THE AMERICANS * THE MARCH TO THE SEA AND BEYOND: SHERMAN'S TROOPS IN THE SAVANNAH AND CAROLINAS CAMPAIGNS * THE MARCH TO THE SEA * MARCHING THROUGH GEORGIA: THE STORY OF SOLDIERS AND CIVILIANS DURING SHERMAN'S CAMPAIGN * MEMOIRS OF GENERAL W.T. SHERMAN * SHERMAN AND THE BURNING OF COLUMBIA * SHERMAN AT WAR * SHERMAN: A SOLDIER'S PASSION FOR ORDER * SHERMAN: FIGHTING PROPHET * MERCHANT OF TERROR,*

CWTI:JAN/94[35]361, CWTI:JAN/94[46]364,
CWTI:MAY/94[50]386, CWTI:DEC/94[49]413,
CWTI:JAN/95[30]426, CWTI:JAN/95[34]427,
CWTI:JAN/95[42]428, CWTI:MAR/95[26]434,
CWTI:MAR/95[33]435, CWTI:JUN/95[51]449,
CWTI:DEC/95[52]480, CWTI:DEC/95[67]481,
CWTI:DEC/95[76]482
ADDITIONAL LISTINGS, MH: MH:DEC/93[12]174, MH:APR/94[54]176,
MH:APR/95[46]183, MH:DEC/95[58]188
SHERMAN'S CAROLINA CAMPAIGN:
ARTICLES: "THE BATTLE OF BENTONVILLE, MARCH 19-21,
1865: LAST STAND IN THE CAROLINAS,"
B&G:DEC/95[9]615, "LAST STAND IN THE CAROLINAS:
THE BATTLE OF BENTONVILLE. AN INTERVIEW WITH
AUTHOR MARK L. BRADLEY," CWR:VOL4#3[65]172
BOOK REVIEWS: *THE MARCH TO THE SEA AND BEYOND:
SHERMAN'S TROOPS IN THE SAVANNAH AND
CAROLINAS CAMPAIGNS * THE MARCH TO THE SEA *
THE MARCH TO THE SEA, FRANKLIN AND NASHVILLE *
SHERMAN AND THE BURNING OF COLUMBIA*
ADDITIONAL LISTINGS: ACW:NOV/93[58], AHI:MAY/71[3]133A,
CWTI:APR/89[32]110
SHERMAN'S MERIDIAN CAMPAIGN;
CWR:VOL2#4[313]146, CWR:VOL2#4[343]147
**SHERMAN'S SAVANNAH CAMPAIGN (MARCH TO THE
SEA):**
ARTICLES: "A DRIVING TOUR OF NORTH GEORGIA TRACES
WILLIAM T. SHERMAN'S CAUTIOUS ADVANCE TO
ATLANTA," ACW:JUL/94[66]481, "AS THE SHELLS
EXPLODED OVER ATLANTA IN 1864, THE OPPOSING
GENERALS OPENED A WAR OF WORDS,"
ACW:JAN/95[6]501, "THE ATLANTA CAMPAIGN,"
CWM:JAN/91[12]326, "BURNING DOWN THE SOUTH,"
CWTI:OCT/95[48]470, "CITY FOR THE TAKING,"
ACW:SEP/92[47]380, "GATEWAY TO THE ATLANTIC,"
CWTI:DEC/94[62]415, "SAVANNAH: MR. LINCOLN'S
CHRISTMAS PRESENT," B&G:FEB/91[8]439, "SHERMAN
MOVES ON ATLANTA," CWM:AUG/95[36]608, "TOTAL WAR
COMES TO NEW MANCHESTER," B&G:DEC/94[22]586,
"WRECKING ON THE RAILROAD," ACW:SEP/95[48]547
BOOK REVIEWS: *THE CAMPAIGN FOR ATLANTA & SHERMAN'S
MARCH TO THE SEA * DECISION IN THE WEST: THE
ATLANTA CAMPAIGN OF 1864 * THE MARCH TO THE
SEA * THE MARCH TO THE SEA, FRANKLIN AND
NASHVILLE * THE MARCH TO THE SEA AND BEYOND:
SHERMAN'S TROOPS IN THE SAVANNAH AND
CAROLINAS CAMPAIGNS * MARCHING THROUGH
GEORGIA: THE STORY OF SOLDIERS AND CIVILIANS
DURING SHERMAN'S CAMPAIGN * TO THE SEA, A
HISTORY AND TOUR GUIDE OF SHERMAN'S MARCH*
GENERAL LISTINGS: *editorial*, ACW:JAN/91[6]281, *in book review*,
ACW:MAR/94[58], CWM:AUG/95[8], CWTI:MAY/92[18]
ADDITIONAL LISTINGS: ACW:NOV/93[42]443, ACW:JAN/95[30]505,
B&G:FEB/91[8]439, B&G:OCT/91[11]466, B&G:DEC/95[9]615,
CWM:JAN/92[40]405, CWM:JUL/92[18]429,
CWR:VOL2#4[313]146, CWR:VOL4#3[65]172,
CWTI:APR/89[32]110, CWTI:OCT/95[48]470,
MH:DEC/95[58]188
SHERRELL, EDWARD W., *Colonel, USA;* CWTI:APR/89[22]108
SHERRILL, ELIAKIM E., *Colonel, 126th New York Infantry;*
CWR:VOL1#4[7]125, GETTY:7[51]190, GETTY:9[61]215,
MH:AUG/95[30]185, *photos*, CWR:VOL1#4[7]125,
GETTY:7[51]190

SHERRILL, SAMUEL S., *Private, 2nd Tennessee Cavalry;*
CWR:VOL4#1[1]163
SHERWIN, THOMAS, *Lieutenant Colonel, 22nd Massachusetts
Infantry;* GETTY:8[53]203
SHERWOOD, JULIUS, *Captain, 6th Pennsylvania Infantry;*
CWR:VOL1#3[20]119
SHIELDS, DAVID, *Captain, USA;* ACW:MAY/95[54]528,
GETTY:8[95]205
SHIELDS, JAMES, *Pvt., 48th PA. Inf.;* CWM:MAR/91[56]341,
SHIELDS, JAMES, *General, USA:*
GENERAL LISTINGS: *general history*, AHI:MAY/71[3]133A, *in book
review*, CWM:MAR/91[74], CWNEWS:JAN/93[4], *Jackson*,
B&G:JUN/92[8]487, *Winfield Scott*, AHI:JUL/81[20]221
ADDITIONAL LISTINGS: ACW:JAN/92[8]338, ACW:JAN/93[35]396,
CWM:APR/95[29]574, CWTI:MAR/94[48]374,
CWTI:JAN/95[22]423, CWTI:JUN/95[18]444
SHIELDS, JEFFERSON; CWTI:FEB/92[42]250
SHIELDS, JOHN, *Capt., 53rd Penna. Inf.;* GETTY:11[80]235
SHIELDS, THOMAS, *Private, 62nd New York Infantry;*
CWM:MAY/91[26]349
SHILOH NATIONAL MILITARY BATTLEFIELD PARK;
B&G:JUN/91[26]453, B&G:APR/92[36]483,
B&G:APR/93[40]522, B&G:JUN/93[40]527,
CWM:JAN/91[38]329
SHILOH, TENNESSEE, BATTLE OF:
ARTICLES: "DEVIL'S OWN DAY," ACW:JAN/91[22]285,
"SCOUTING FOR ULYSSES S. GRANT: THE 5TH OHIO
CAVALRY IN THE SHILOH CAMPAIGN,"
CWR:VOL4#1[44]164, "SHILOH, WHERE DEATH KNOWS
NO DISTINCTION," CWM:APR/95[66]579, "THE WOUNDED
OF SHILOH," CWM:MAY/91[10]347
BOOK REVIEWS: *PIERCING THE HEARTLAND: A HISTORY
AND TOUR GUIDE OF THE FORT DONELSON, SHILOH,
AND PERRYVILLE CAMPAIGNS * "SEEING THE
ELEPHANT" RAW RECRUITS AT THE BATTLE OF
SHILOH * WAR IN KENTUCKY: FROM SHILOH TO
PERRYVILLE*
VIDEO REVIEW: *THE BATTLE OF SHILOH*, AHI:APR/88[13]
GENERAL LISTINGS: *Cleburne*, MH:OCT/94[20]180, *general history*,
AHI:MAY/71[3]133A, *in book review*, ACW:MAR/94[58],
CWM:AUG/95[45], *painting*; CWTI:FEB/90[32]144
ADDITIONAL LISTINGS, ACW: ACW:MAY/91[12]302,
ACW:JUL/91[12]310, ACW:JUL/92[12]367,
ACW:NOV/92[8]383, ACW:NOV/92[35]387,
ACW:MAY/93[22]414, ACW:JUL/93[34]424,
ACW:SEP/93[6]428, ACW:SEP/93[38]434,
ACW:NOV/93[50]444, ACW:JUL/94[6]473,
ACW:SEP/94[10]484, ACW:NOV/94[76]500,
ACW:JAN/95[30]505, ACW:SEP/95[6]541
ADDITIONAL LISTINGS, CWM: CWM:MAR/91[28]336,
CWM:JUL/92[40]432, CWM:MAR/93[8]465,
CWM:SEP/93[8]493, CWM:OCT/95[22]614,
CWM:DEC/95[48]631
ADDITIONAL LISTINGS, CWR: CWR:VOL1#2[44]114,
CWR:VOL1#2[70]115, CWR:VOL2#1[19]131,
CWR:VOL2#1[36]132, CWR:VOL4#2[1]165
ADDITIONAL LISTINGS, CWTI: CWTI:FEB/90[32]144,
CWTI:FEB/90[38]145, CWTI:MAR/91[28]200,
CWTI:AUG/91[52]219, CWTI:JUL/92[29]272,
CWTI:JUL/92[42]274, CWTI:JAN/93[40]301,
CWTI:MAR/93[50]313, CWTI:SEP/93[59]341,
CWTI:JAN/95[27]425, CWTI:DEC/95[67]481
SHIMEALL, DAVID, *Pvt., 2nd Wisc. Inf.,* GETTY:11[57]233

General Quitman; ACW:MAY/92[16]359

Georgia:

ARTICLE: ARTICLE: "RELUCTANT RAIDER," CWTI:AUG/95[40]458

GENERAL LISTINGS: *in book review,* B&G:AUG/92[36],
CWNEWS:AUG/92[4], *sketch,* CWTI:AUG/95[40]458

ADDITIONAL LISTINGS: ACW:JAN/93[58]399, AHI:DEC/82[38]231,
AHI:JAN/83[10]232, B&G:FEB/91[8]439, CWM:JUL/93[30]486

Giraffe; ACW:JAN/91[47]288

Gladiator; ARTICLE: "VERY JAWS OF CAPTURE,"
ACW:MAY/92[23]360

Gordon; ACW:NOV/91[46]335

Governor Moore; ACW:MAY/92[16]359, MH:AUG/93[47]169

Grand Era; ACW:JUL/93[34]424

Hunley:

ARTICLES: "THE *CSS H.L. HUNLEY:* SOLVING A
131-YEAR-OLD MYSTERY," CWR:VOL4#3[77]174, "*CSS
HUNLEY* FOUND,"AHI:OCT/95[16]325, "DIVERS FIND
WRECK OF CONFEDERATE SECRET WEAPON,"
CWTI:OCT/95[10]464, "SEARCH ENDS FOR
CONFEDERATE SUB," B&G:JUN/95[36]603A

BOOK REVIEW: *DANGER BENEATH THE WAVES*

GENERAL LISTINGS: *general history,* AHI:MAY/71[3]133A, *in book
review,* CWR:VOL3#3[92], CWTI:APR/90[10]

ADDITIONAL LISTINGS: ACW:JAN/93[58]399, AHI:MAY/71[3]133A,
CWTI:SEPT/89[20]127

Huntress; ACW:MAR/91[14]293

Isaac Wells; B&G:DEC/94[10]585

Isabel; ACW:MAY/92[23]360

Isondiga; B&G:FEB/91[8]439

Ivy; ACW:MAY/92[16]359, MH:DEC/94[46]181

J.B. White; AHI:NOV/75[38]163

Jackson:

ARTICLE: "GEORGIA'S ENDANGERED REBEL GUNBOATS,"
CWTI:NOV/93[74]353

ADDITIONAL LISTINGS: ACW:MAY/92[16]359, MH:AUG/93[47]169,
MH:DEC/94[46]181

Jamestown; ACW:MAR/91[14]293, AHI:OCT/75[30]162,
AHI:NOV/75[38]163

Jeff Davis; ACW:SEP/94[46]488

Jessie; ACW:JAN/91[47]288, CWM:JUN/94[50]518

John F. Carr; ACW:JAN/93[51]398

Josiah H. Bell; CWTI:DEC/90[29]182

Judah; ACW:MAR/91[14]293, CWR:VOL1#4[42]126

Kate; ACW:MAY/92[23]360

LaCrosse; CWR:VOL4#2[118]169

Lafourche; CWR:VOL4#2[118]169

Leopard; CWM:JUN/94[50]518

Lillian; CWTI:DEC/91[44]241

Little Flora; CWM:JUN/94[50]518

Little Hattie; B&G:DEC/94[10]585

Louis d'Or; CWR:VOL4#2[68]167

Louisiana; ACW:JAN/92[62]346, ACW:MAY/92[16]359,
MH:AUG/93[47]169

Lucy Gwin; ACW:JAN/93[51]398

Lynchburg; ACW:SEP/94[46]488

Macon; ACW:SEP/92[47]380, B&G:FEB/91[8]439

Manassas:

ARTICLES: "*CSS MANASSAS,* GUARDIAN OF NEW ORLEANS,
WAS THE FIRST CONFEDERATE IRONCLAD TO MENACE
THE UNION FLEET," ACW:MAY/92[16]359, "STUNG BY
MOSQUITOES," MH:DEC/94[46]181

ADDITIONAL LISTINGS: ACW:MAY/92[16]359, CWNEWS:AUG/91[4],
MH:AUG/93[47]169

Maple Leaf; B&G:DEC/93[30]546

Margaret; ACW:JAN/91[47]288, CWM:JUN/94[50]518

Mary Celeste; CWM:JUN/94[50]518

May Duke; B&G:FEB/92[10]474

McRae; ACW:MAR/91[14]293, ACW:MAY/92[16]359,
CWTI:JUL/94[30]392, MH:AUG/93[47]169, MH:DEC/94[46]181

Merrimack, see listings under *Virginia;* AHI:OCT/75[30]162

Milledgeville; B&G:FEB/91[8]439

Mississippi; ACW:JAN/92[62]346, ACW:MAY/92[16]359

Modern Greece; B&G:DEC/94[36]588

Morgan; CWM:JUL/93[24]485

Moro; ACW:JUL/93[34]424

Mosher; ACW:JAN/92[62]346

Nashville:

GENERAL LISTINGS: *in book review,* B&G:AUG/92[36],
CWNEWS:AUG/92[4]

ADDITIONAL LISTINGS: ACW:NOV/91[46]335, ACW:JAN/93[58]399,
B&G:FEB/91[8]439

Nassau; CWTI:DEC/91[44]241

Neaffie; CWR:VOL1#4[42]126

Neptune; ACW:JAN/93[51]398

New Falls City; CWR:VOL4#2[26]166

North Carolina; ACW:SEP/94[46]488, CWTI:AUG/95[40]458

Oreto; B&G:FEB/95[26]

Owl; ACW:JAN/91[47]288, CWTI:DEC/91[44]241

Paint Rock; B&G:OCT/92[32]499

Palmetto State; CWR:VOL2#2[95]135, CWR:VOL4#3[77]174,
MH:AUG/92[26]161

Patrick Henry; ACW:MAR/91[14]293, ACW:JUL/92[10]366,
ACW:MAY/95[38]526, AHI:OCT/75[30]162,
AHI:NOV/75[38]163, CWM:JUN/95[39]586,
CWM:AUG/95[5]602, *photo,* ACW:JUL/92[10]366

Paul Jones; CWR:VOL2#1[69]133

Petrel; ACW:SEP/94[46]488

Pioneer; ACW:SEP/94[46]488, CWNEWS:AUG/91[4],
CWR:VOL4#3[77]174, CWTI:SEPT/89[20]127

Planter; BOOK REVIEW: *GULLAH STATESMAN, ROBERT
SMALLS FROM SLAVERY TO CONGRESS, 1839-1915*

Queen of the West:

ARTICLE: "THE SIDE-WHEEL STEAMER *QUEEN OF THE
WEST* WAS ALSO VARIOUSLY THE QUEEN OF BOTH
THE NORTH AND THE SOUTH," ACW:MAR/95[18]514

ADDITIONAL LISTING: CWTI:JAN/95[42]428

R.E. Lee; ACW:JAN/91[47]288, ACW:MAY/92[23]360

Raleigh; AHI:NOV/75[38]163

Rappahannock; AHI:DEC/82[38]231, AHI:JAN/83[10]232,
CWTI:MAY/92[29]263, CWTI:AUG/95[40]458

Rattlesnake; CWM:JUN/94[50]518

Rebecca Hertz; B&G:FEB/91[8]439

Resolute; ACW:MAR/91[14]293, B&G:FEB/91[8]439

Retribution; ACW:NOV/92[51]389

Richmond; ACW:JAN/91[47]288, ACW:MAY/92[16]359,
ACW:SEP/95[30]545

Roebuck; CWTI:DEC/90[29]182

Runion; CWR:VOL1#3[7]118

Sallie Magee; ACW:SEP/94[46]488

Sampson; ACW:MAR/91[14]293, ACW:SEP/92[47]380,
B&G:FEB/91[8]439

Savannah:

ARTICLE: "PIRATES OR PATRIOTS?" ACW:SEP/94[46]488

ADDITIONAL LISTINGS: ACW:MAR/91[14]293, ACW:SEP/92[47]380,
B&G:FEB/91[8]439, CWM:SEP/93[4]492, CWTI:DEC/91[44]241

Scorpion; ACW:SEP/95[30]545
Seabird; CWTI:MAY/92[38]265, CWTI:SEP/94[26]400
Selma; CWM:JUL/93[24]485
Shenandoah:
ARTICLES: "THE FANTASTIC VOYAGE OF THE *CSS SHENANDOAH,* CWM:JUL/93[8]483, "RAIDER OF THE ARCTIC SEAS," ACW:MAY/91[46]306
GENERAL LISTINGS: *in book review,* B&G:AUG/92[36], CWNEWS:OCT/90[4], CWNEWS:MAY/91[4], CWNEWS:APR/92[4], CWNEWS:AUG/92[4], CWTI:APR/90[10], CWTI:JUN/90[20], CWTI:AUG/90[64]170, *letters to the editor,* CWM:SEP/93[4]492, *photos,* ACW:MAY/91[46]306, AHI:JAN/83[10]232
ADDITIONAL LISTINGS: ACW:MAY/91[54], ACW:MAR/92[62]355, AHI:JAN/83[10]232, CWTI:AUG/90[64]170, CWTI:JUN/95[51]449
St. Philip; ACW:NOV/93[8]438
Star of the West:
ARTICLES: "ELEGANT, LUXURIOUS *STAR OF THE WEST* MET A DECIDEDLY UNROMANTIC FATE IN THE MISSISSIPPI DELTA," ACW:NOV/93[8]438
ADDITIONAL LISTING: ACW:NOV/93[8]438
Stonewall:
ARTICLE: "THE DILEMMA OF COMMODORE CRAVEN," CWTI:DEC/94[34]411
ADDITIONAL LISTINGS: B&G:OCT/91[6]465, CWTI:MAR/95[18]432
Stormy Petrel; B&G:DEC/94[36]588
Sumter:
ARTICLE: "'I TOLD HIM I SHOULD BURN HIS SHIP'," CWM:FEB/95[73]568
GENERAL LISTINGS: *in book review,* B&G:AUG/92[36], CWNEWS:AUG/92[4], CWTI:JUN/90[20], *letters to the editor,* CWTI:MAY/91[8]205
ADDITIONAL LISTINGS: ACW:MAR/91[14]293, ACW:JAN/93[58]399, ACW:JUL/95[58], AHI:DEC/82[38]231, AHI:JAN/83[10]232, AHI:OCT/88[38]275
Swan; ACW:SEP/92[47]380, B&G:FEB/91[8]439
Tacony; ACW:MAR/94[35]460, ACW:SEP/94[46]488
Tallahassee:
GENERAL LISTINGS: *general history,* AHI:MAY/71[3]133A, *in book review,* B&G:AUG/92[36], CWNEWS:AUG/92[4], CWTI:JUN/90[20], *letters to the editor,* CWM:MAY/91[6]345
ADDITIONAL LISTINGS: ACW:JAN/93[58]399, AHI:JAN/83[10]232, B&G:DEC/94[10]585, CWM:JUN/94[50]518
Teaser:
GENERAL LISTINGS: *balloons,* B&G:AUG/91[20]459, *letters to the editor,* B&G:OCT/91[6]465, B&G:DEC/91[6]468
ADDITIONAL LISTINGS: AHI:OCT/75[30]162, AHI:NOV/75[38]163, AHI:JUN/84[24]239, B&G:DEC/93[30]546
Tennessee:
BOOK REVIEW: *MOBILE BAY AND THE MOBILE CAMPAIGN: THE LAST GREAT BATTLES OF THE CIVIL WAR*
ADDITIONAL LISTINGS: CWM:JUL/93[24]485, CWTI:MAR/94[20]369, MH:AUG/92[26]161
Theodora; ACW:NOV/91[46]335, ACW:MAY/92[23]360
Torpedo; CWTI:FEB/91[36]193
Tuscaloosa; AHI:OCT/88[38]275
Tuscarora; ACW:MAY/92[16]359, MH:DEC/94[46]181
Uncle Ben; CWTI:DEC/90[29]182
Underwriter; ACW:JUL/92[10]366
Virginia:
ARTICLES: "FIRST CLASH OF THE IRONCLADS," AHI:NOV/75[38]163, "IT WAS A GREAT VICTORY,"

AHI:OCT/75[30]162, "LINCOLN AND THE IRONCLADS COME TO TELEVISION," CWTI:MAR/91[42]202, "'THE LITTLE *MONITOR* SAVED OUR LIVES,'" AHI:JUL/66[32]103
GENERAL LISTINGS: *audio/visual,* B&G:JUN/91[42]456, *general history,* AHI:MAY/71[3]133A, *in book review,* ACW:MAY/91[54], CWM:DEC/95[10], CWNEWS:JAN/90[4], CWNEWS:MAY/91[4], CWNEWS:AUG/92[4], CWNEWS:NOV/92[4], CWNEWS:APR/94[5], CWR:VOL3#3[92], *letters to the editor,* CWM:OCT/95[5]613
ADDITIONAL LISTINGS: ACW:MAR/91[14]293, ACW:MAY/91[62]307, ACW:JUL/92[10]366, ACW:JAN/93[58]399, ACW:MAR/94[35]460, ACW:JUL/94[35]478, ACW:JAN/95[74]510, AHI:NOV/75[38]163, AHI:JAN/83[10]232, B&G:FEB/91[8]439, B&G:AUG/92[40]495, CWM:MAR/91[43]339, CWM:SEP/91[24]381, CWM:JUL/93[15]484, CWM:JUL/93[24]485, CWM:FEB/95[49]565, CWM:JUN/95[24]582, CWM:JUN/95[29]583, CWM:JUN/95[37]585, CWM:JUN/95[39]586, CWTI:AUG/91[58]220, CWTI:MAY/93[20]317, MH:AUG/92[26]161, MH:APR/94[54]176
Virginia II; ACW:MAY/95[38]526, ACW:SEP/95[30]545
Webb; ACW:JAN/91[47]288, ACW:JUL/93[34]424
Whisper; CWM:JUN/94[50]518
William H. Webb; ACW:MAR/95[18]514, CWTI:AUG/90[42]167
Wilmington; B&G:DEC/94[10]585
Winifred; ACW:SEP/94[46]488
Winslow; CWTI:SEP/94[26]400

SHIPS, BOATS, VESSELS, ETC., — FEDERAL:

An alphabetical listing of all ships, boats, vessels, etc. that served the Union.
ARTICLE: "GUN PLATFORMS AT SEA," MH:AUG/92[26]161
Abigail; ACW:MAY/91[46]306
Acacia; ACW:NOV/92[51]389
Addison F. Andrews; AHI:JAN/81[18]214
Adelaide; ACW:MAY/91[46]306, CWR:VOL1#2[7]111
Adriatic; AHI:JAN/83[10]232
Agawam; ACW:NOV/92[51]389, ACW:JAN/95[38]506, B&G:DEC/93[30]546, B&G:FEB/94[38]553, B&G:APR/94[34]561
Alabama; CWR:VOL1#2[7]111
Alabatross; ACW:JUL/93[34]424, B&G:DEC/93[30]546, B&G:FEB/94[38]553, B&G:APR/94[34]561, CWM:APR/95[28]573
Alice Dean; CWM:MAR/93[16]466
Alice Vivian; CWR:VOL4#2[26]166
Alina; ACW:MAY/91[46]306
Allegheny; B&G:JUN/95[36]603A
Alligator; ACW:SEP/94[74]491
Althea; ACW:NOV/91[8]328
America; ACW:JAN/91[62]289
Anacostia; ACW:JAN/95[74]510
Anashe; CWTI:JUN/95[48]448
Aquila; CWTI:JUN/95[48]448
Arago; CWR:VOL2#3[194]141, CWTI:MAR/94[38]372
Archer; ACW:MAR/94[35]460, AHI:DEC/82[38]231
Ariel; CWR:VOL2#3[194]141
Arizona; ACW:MAR/95[18]514, B&G:DEC/93[30]546, B&G:FEB/94[38]553, B&G:APR/94[34]561, CWM:OCT/95[47]620, CWTI:DEC/90[29]182
Aroostook; ACW:MAR/94[35]460, CWM:JUN/95[39]586, CWM:JUN/95[69]596

Ashuelot; ACW:MAR/94[35]460
Aster; B&G:DEC/94[36]588
Atlanta; ACW:SEP/95[30]545
Atlantic; CWTI:MAR/95[8]431
Avenger; CWR:VOL4#2[26]166
Baltic; ACW:JAN/91[62]289, ACW:MAR/94[35]460,
   CWTI:MAY/92[45]266
Baron de Kalb; CWTI:MAY/94[16]380
Bat; CWTI:FEB/91[28]192, CWTI:DEC/95[76]482
Benefit; CWR:VOL4#2[26]166
Benton; ACW:JUL/93[34]424, ACW:JUL/94[51]480,
   B&G:FEB/94[8]550, CWR:VOL3#3[33]158,
   CWR:VOL4#2[26]166
Berkshire; ACW:SEP/94[46]488
Black Hawk; CWR:VOL2#3[212]142, CWR:VOL4#2[26]166,
   CWTI:MAY/94[16]380
Bold Hunter; CWTI:AUG/95[40]458
Bostona No. 2; CWR:VOL4#1[44]164
Bronx; ACW:MAR/94[35]460
Brooklyn; ACW:NOV/91[8]328, ACW:MAY/92[16]359,
   ACW:MAR/93[18]403, AHI:MAY/66[12]101,
   AHI:SEP/83[12]234, CWM:JUL/93[24]485,
   CWM:FEB/95[73]568, CWTI:MAR/94[20]369,
   CWTI:DEC/94[34]411, MH:FEB/92[8]156, MH:AUG/93[47]169
Brother Johathan; CWTI:JUN/95[48]448
Brunswick; ACW:MAY/91[46]306, AHI:JAN/83[10]232
C.P. Williams; CWR:VOL2#3[194]141
Cahawba; CWR:VOL1#2[29]112, CWTI:JAN/95[42]428
Cairo:
ARTICLES: "ON THE MUDDY YAZOO RIVER ONE MORNING,
   THE UNION GUNBOAT *CAIRO* MADE UNWANTED
   NAVAL HISTORY," ACW:SEP/94[74]491, "TORPEDOES
   SINK YANKEE GUNBOAT!" CWM:DEC/95[30]627
BOOK REVIEWS: *THE SINKING OF THE USS CAIRO*
ADDITIONAL LISTINGS: ACW:NOV/91[8]328, CWM:APR/94[4]501,
   CWR:VOL4#1[44]164
Caleb Cushing; ACW:NOV/92[51]389, ACW:JAN/93[58]399,
   ACW:MAR/94[35]460, CWTI:JUL/94[30]392
Calhoun; ACW:MAR/95[18]514
Camanche; MH:AUG/92[26]161
Canonicus; CWTI:MAR/94[38]372, MH:AUG/92[26]161
Carondelet; ACW:NOV/91[8]328, B&G:FEB/92[10]474,
   B&G:FEB/94[8]550, CWR:VOL1#3[7]118,
   CWR:VOL3#3[33]158, CWR:VOL4#2[26]166,
   CWTI:MAY/94[16]380
Casco; ACW:MAR/94[35]460, AHI:DEC/82[38]231
Catskill; CWR:VOL3#1[31]150
Catskill; MH:FEB/93[10]163
Cayuga; ACW:MAY/92[16]359, B&G:DEC/93[30]546,
   B&G:FEB/94[38]553, B&G:APR/94[34]561,
   CWTI:DEC/90[29]182, MH:AUG/93[47]169
Chamberlin; B&G:DEC/94[10]585
Champion; CWTI:JUL/94[30]392
Champion #3; CWR:VOL4#2[26]166, CWR:VOL4#2[118]169
Champion #5; CWR:VOL4#2[26]166
Chancellor; CWR:VOL3#4[24]162
Chapman; CWTI:JUN/95[48]448
Charles McDougall; ACW:MAR/93[8]401
Charter Oak; ACW:MAY/91[46]306
Chattanooga; CWTI:MAY/93[38]321
Chesapeake:
ARTICLE: "HIGH SEAS HIJACK," ACW:NOV/92[51]389
ADDITIONAL LISTINGS: ACW:MAR/94[35]460, AHI:DEC/82[38]231

Chickasaw; CWM:JUL/93[24]485, MH:AUG/92[26]161
Chillicothe; ACW:NOV/93[8]438, CWR:VOL4#2[26]166
Choctaw; CWR:VOL3#3[33]158, CWR:VOL4#2[26]166,
   CWTI:JUL/94[30]392
Chotank; ACW:SEP/94[46]488
Cimarron; CWR:VOL2#3[194]141
Cincinnati:
ARTICLE: "NAVY LIFE ON THE MISSISSIPPI RIVER,"
   CWTI:MAY/94[16]380
ADDITIONAL LISTINGS: AHI:JUL/68[31]115A,
   B&G:FEB/92[10]474,*photo,* CWTI:MAY/94[16]380
City Belle; CWR:VOL4#2[26]166, CWR:VOL4#2[118]169
City of Alton; ACW:MAR/93[8]401
City of Bath; CWTI:AUG/95[40]458
City of Louisiana; ACW:MAR/93[8]401
City of Madison; CWTI:JUN/95[56]450
City of Memphis; ACW:MAR/93[8]401, AHI:APR/79[4]186,
   CWM:MAY/91[10]347
Clara Bell; CWR:VOL4#2[26]166
Clara Dolsen; CWTI:MAY/94[16]380
Clarence; ACW:JAN/93[58]399, ACW:MAR/94[35]460,
   AHI:DEC/82[38]231
Clifton; ACW:JAN/93[51]398, CWM:OCT/95[47]620,
   CWTI:DEC/90[29]182
Colorado; ACW:MAR/91[14]293, B&G:DEC/94[10]585,
   CWR:VOL1#4[42]126
Columbia; ACW:MAR/94[35]460, CWTI:MAY/92[29]263
Columbine; ACW:NOV/95[38]556
Columbus; ACW:MAR/94[35]460, CWTI:DEC/95[76]482
Comanche; CWTI:JUN/95[48]448
Commodore Jones; ACW:NOV/91[8]328
Commodore Perry; CWM:MAY/91[10]347
Conestoga; B&G:FEB/92[10]474
Congress:
GENERAL LISTINGS: *audio/visual,* B&G:JUN/91[42]456, *in book
   review,* ACW:MAY/91[54], CWNEWS:APR/94[5]
ADDITIONAL LISTINGS: ACW:JUL/94[35]478, AHI:JUL/66[32]103,
   AHI:OCT/75[30]162, AHI:NOV/75[38]163,
   CWM:JUL/93[15]484
Connecticut; CWTI:DEC/89[10]133
Constitution; ACW:JAN/91[62]289, ACW:NOV/95[30]555,
   CWTI:AUG/95[40]458
Corypheus; ACW:JAN/93[51]398
Covington; CWR:VOL4#2[26]166, CWR:VOL4#2[104]168
Covington #25; CWR:VOL4#2[118]169
Crescent City; CWM:MAY/91[10]347, GETTY:12[1]240,
   GETTY:12[111]250
Crescent; B&G:APR/93[24]520, CWTI:JAN/95[48]429
Cricket; CWR:VOL4#2[26]166,
Cumberland:
GENERAL LISTINGS: *audio/visual,* B&G:JUN/91[42]456, *in book
   review,* ACW:MAY/91[54], CWM:DEC/95[10],
   CWNEWS:APR/94[5], *SIO,* B&G:JUN/95[36]603A
ADDITIONAL LISTINGS: ACW:MAR/94[35]460, ACW:JUL/94[35]478,
   AHI:JUL/66[32]103, AHI:OCT/75[30]162, AHI:NOV/75[38]163,
   CWM:JUL/93[15]484
Cushing; AHI:DEC/82[38]231
Cuyahoga; ACW:MAR/94[35]460
Cyane; CWTI:JUN/95[48]448
D.A. January:
ARTICLE: "*D.A. JANUARY* AND HER SISTER HOSPITAL
   STEAMERS SAVED COUNTLESS LIVES DURING THE
   CIVIL WAR," ACW:MAR/93[8]401

J.B. Goody Friends; CWR:VOL4#1[44]164
J.C. Swan; ACW:MAY/91[31]304, ACW:MAR/93[8]401
J.R. Williams; ACW:JAN/91[30]286, CWM:SEP/92[38]443
J.S. Pringle; ACW:MAR/93[8]401
J.W. Seaver; CWTI:AUG/95[40]458
Jacob Bell; CWTI:DEC/91[44]241
James Adger; ACW:NOV/91[46]335, ACW:MAY/92[23]360
James Funk; AHI:JAN/83[10]232
James Maury; ACW:MAY/91[46]306, AHI:JAN/83[10]232
James S. Chambers; ARTICLE: "A LONG WAR AND A SICKLY
  SEASON," B&G:JUN/92[40]489
Jesse K. Bell; CWR:VOL3#3[59]159
Jireh Swift; ACW:MAY/91[46]306
John Adams; ACW:JAN/91[62]289
John B. McCombs; CWM:MAR/93[16]466
John J. Roe; CWM:MAY/91[10]347
John S. Shriver; CWTI:JUL/93[20]325
John Warner; CWR:VOL4#2[26]166, CWR:VOL4#2[104]168
John Watts; CWTI:AUG/95[40]458
Joseph; ACW:SEP/94[46]488
Joseph H. Toone; MH:DEC/94[46]181
Juliet; CWR:VOL4#2[26]166, CWR:VOL4#2[118]169
Kankakee; ACW:MAR/94[35]460
Kate Prince; ACW:MAY/91[46]306
Kearsarge:
GENERAL LISTINGS: *general history*, AHI:MAY/71[3]133A, *in book
  review*, CWNEWS:JAN/90[4]
ADDITIONAL LISTINGS: ACW:MAY/91[46]306, ACW:SEP/94[46]488,
  AHI:JAN/83[10]232, AHI:OCT/88[38]275,
  B&G:APR/91[36]448, B&G:AUG/92[40]495,
  CWM:SEP/91[35]384, CWM:SEP/92[33]442,
  CWTI:DEC/94[34]411, CWTI:AUG/95[40]458,
  MH:OCT/91[50]154
Kennebec; MH:AUG/93[47]169
Keokuk; ACW:JAN/95[38]506, CWR:VOL2#3[194]141
Kewanee; ACW:MAR/94[35]460
Key West; CWTI:NOV/93[74]353
Keystone State; ACW:JAN/91[47]288, AHI:JUN/73[4]149
Kineo; ACW:MAY/92[16]359, CWM:APR/95[28]573
Lackawanna; CWM:JUL/93[24]485, CWTI:JUL/94[30]392
Lafayette; ACW:JUL/94[51]480, CWR:VOL4#2[26]166,
  CWTI:AUG/90[42]167, CWTI:JUL/94[30]392
Lancaster; ACW:JUL/93[34]424
Lehigh; MH:FEB/93[10]163
Lewis Cass; ACW:MAR/94[35]460
Lexington; ACW:JAN/91[22]285, ACW:JUL/92[22]368,
  B&G:FEB/92[10]474, CWR:VOL3#3[33]158,
  CWR:VOL4#1[44]164, CWR:VOL4#2[26]166,
  CWTI:MAY/94[16]380, CWTI:JUL/94[30]392
Liberty; CWTI:NOV/93[65]351
Little Eastern; GETTY:13[108]261
Lizzie M. Stacey; ACW:MAY/91[46]306
Louisiana:
GENERAL LISTINGS: *in book review*, ACW:MAY/91[54], *letters to the
  editor*, B&G:FEB/95[5]589
ADDITIONAL LISTINGS: ACW:SEP/92[16]376, ACW:JAN/95[38]506,
  B&G:FEB/94[8]550, B&G:DEC/94[10]585,
  B&G:DEC/94[36]588, CWR:VOL4#2[26]166,
  CWTI:MAY/94[16]380
Luminary; B&G:AUG/95[24]605
M. Small; ACW:JAN/95[38]506
Macedonian; ACW:JAN/91[62]289
Magnolia; ACW:JUL/94[51]480

Mahoning; ACW:MAR/94[35]460
Malvern; B&G:DEC/94[10]585, CWTI:FEB/91[28]192,
  CWTI:OCT/95[18], CWTI:DEC/95[76]482
Manhattan; CWM:JUL/93[24]485, CWTI:AUG/90[42]167,
  CWTI:JUL/94[30]392, MH:AUG/92[26]161
Maple Leaf:
ARTICLES: "CIVIL WAR STEAMSHIP YIELDS
  ARCHAEOLOGICAL TROVE," AHI:NOV/89[8]291, "THE
  MAPLE LEAF ESCAPE," CWTI:JAN/95[42]428, *"MAPLE
  LEAF* RELICS," CWTI:AUG/95[10]453
ADDITIONAL LISTINGS: CWTI:JAN/95[42]428, CWTI:JUN/95[14]443
Maratanza; AHI:JUN/84[24]239
Marblehead; ACW:JAN/91[62]289, CWR:VOL2#3[194]141
Margaret; MH:FEB/91[8]151
Maria Denning; ACW:JAN/91[16]284
Marigold; B&G:JUN/92[40]489
Marion; ACW:JAN/91[62]289
Marmora; ACW:SEP/94[74]491, CWM:DEC/95[30]627
Mary Alvina; ACW:MAR/94[35]460
Mary Pierce; MH:FEB/91[8]151
Mary Washington; CWTI:MAY/92[29]263
Massachusetts; ACW:MAR/91[14]293, ACW:JAN/94[70]454
Massasoit; ACW:SEP/95[30]545
Matilda; CWM:AUG/94[30]527
Mendola; ACW:MAY/92[23]360
Merrimack; ACW:MAR/93[42]406, ACW:MAR/94[35]460,
  ACW:JUL/94[35]478, CWM:OCT/95[5]613
Metacomet; MH:FEB/92[8]156
Miami; ACW:MAR/94[35]460, CWTI:MAR/95[46]437
Miantonomoh; MH:AUG/92[26]161
Michigan; ACW:JUL/95[44]537, CWTI:NOV/92[54]293,
  CWTI:MAY/94[16]380, CWTI:JUN/95[56]450,
  MH:FEB/94[8]175, *photos*, ACW:JUL/95[44]537,
  CWTI:JUN/95[56]450
Milo; ACW:MAY/91[46]306
Minnehaha; CWM:MAY/91[10]347
Minnesota:
ARTICLE: "'THE LITTLE *MONITOR* SAVED OUR LIVES',"
  AHI:JUL/66[32]103
GENERAL LISTINGS: *Fort Fisher*, B&G:DEC/94[10]585, *letters to the
  editor*, B&G:OCT/91[6]465
ADDITIONAL LISTINGS: ACW:NOV/91[8]328, ACW:JUL/94[35]478,
  ACW:SEP/94[46]488, ACW:JAN/95[74]510,
  AHI:OCT/75[30]162, AHI:NOV/75[38]163,
  CWM:JUL/93[15]484, CWTI:MAY/93[20]317
Mississippi; ACW:MAY/91[54], ACW:MAR/92[40]353,
  ACW:MAY/92[16]359, ACW:JUL/93[34]424,
  CWM:APR/95[28]573, MH:OCT/91[50]154, MH:AUG/93[47]169
Moderator; B&G:FEB/94[8]550
Monadnock; MH:AUG/92[26]161
Monarch; ACW:MAR/95[18]514
Monitor:
ARTICLES: "COOPERATIVE EFFORT PLANNED FOR
  RECOVERY OF THE *MONITOR*, AHI:MAY/85[6]251, "FIRST
  CLASH OF THE IRONCLADS," AHI:NOV/75[38]163,
  "LINCOLN AND THE IRONCLADS COME TO
  TELEVISION," CWTI:MAR/91[42]202, "RAISE THE
  MONITOR: CAN WE? ... SHOULD WE?" CWM:JUL/93[15]484
VIDEO: *QUEST FOR THE MONITOR*, AHI:MAY/91[22]
GENERAL LISTINGS: *audio/visual*, B&G:JUN/91[42]456, *general
  history*, AHI:MAY/71[3]133A, *in book review*,
  ACW:MAY/91[54], ACW:MAR/92[54], CWNEWS:JAN/90[4],
  CWNEWS:MAY/91[4], CWNEWS:NOV/92[4],

Samson; CWTI:JUL/94[30]392

Samuel Orr; ACW:JUL/92[22]368

San Jacinto; ACW:NOV/91[46]335, ACW:NOV/92[51]389, B&G:JUN/92[40]489, CWTI:JAN/93[44]302, CWTI:DEC/94[73]416, *sketch,* B&G:JUN/92[40]489

Santee; ACW:JAN/91[62]289, MH:DEC/94[46]181

Saranac; CWM:JUL/93[8]483

Sassacuss; ACW:JAN/95[38]506

Sciota; MH:AUG/93[47]169

Sebago; ACW:NOV/92[51]389

Seminole; CWM:MAR/91[14]334

Shubrick; CWTI:JUN/95[48]448

Signal; ACW:SEP/94[74]491, CWM:DEC/95[30]627, CWR:VOL4#2[26]166, CWR:VOL4#2[104]168

Signal #8; CWR:VOL4#2[118]169

Smith Briggs; CWTI:NOV/92[28]290

Sonoma; CWR:VOL2#3[194]141, *photo,* ACW:MAY/92[23]360

Sophia Thornton; ACW:MAY/91[46]306

South Carolina; ACW:JAN/93[51]398, CWR:VOL2#3[194]141, MH:DEC/94[46]181

Spalding; CWR:VOL1#2[7]111

Springfield; B&G:DEC/91[38]471

Spuyten Duyvil; ACW:SEP/95[30]545

St. Lawrence; ACW:SEP/94[46]488, AHI:OCT/75[30]162

St. Louis:
ARTICLE: "FOCUS: CIVIL WAR PHOTOGRAPHY," AHI:JUN/79[22]189, ADDITIONAL LISTING: B&G:FEB/92[10]474

St. Nicholas; CWTI:MAY/92[29]263, MH:FEB/91[8]151, MH:DEC/94[46]181

Star of the West:
ARTICLE: "ELEGANT, LUXURIOUS *STAR OF THE WEST* MET A DECIDEDLY UNROMANTIC FATE IN THE MISSISSIPPI DELTA," ACW:NOV/93[8]438
GENERAL LISTINGS: *James Buchanan,* AHI:MAY/66[12]101, *in book review,* CWNEWS:APR/92[4], *sketch of,* ACW:NOV/93[8]438
ADDITIONAL LISTINGS: ACW:MAR/93[18]403, CWTI:MAY/92[45]266, CWTI:NOV/92[54]293

Stephen Decatur; ACW:MAR/93[8]401

Suffolk; CWTI:DEC/90[29]182

Suliote; AHI:JAN/83[10]232

Sultana:
ARTICLES: "THE CRIPPLING OF THE *SULTANA:* THE REAL PICTURE," B&G:AUG/95[24]605, "DISASTER ON THE MISSISSIPPI! THE *SULTANA* GOES DOWN," CWM:MAY/93[32]477, "STEAMER *SULTANA* MEMORIALIZED," AHI:NOV/89[20]287
BOOK REVIEWS: *CAHABA PRISON AND THE SULTANA DISASTER * THE SULTANA TRAGEDY: AMERICA'S GREATEST MARITIME DISASTER*
GENERAL LISTINGS: *in book review,* CWNEWS:MAY/91[4], CWTI:APR/90[10], *letters to the editor,* B&G:OCT/95[5]610, *SIO,* B&G:DEC/92[40]508, *photos,* ACW:NOV/92[58], B&G:AUG/95[24]605, CWM:MAY/93[32]477, CWTI:AUG/90[50]168
ADDITIONAL LISTINGS: B&G:JUN/92[32]488, CWTI:AUG/90[42]167, CWTI:AUG/90[50]168

Sumter; ACW:MAY/92[23]360

Susan Abigail; ACW:MAY/91[46]306, AHI:JAN/83[10]232

Susan; ACW:MAY/91[46]306

Susquehanna; B&G:DEC/94[10]585

Suwanee; ACW:MAY/91[46]306, CWM:JUL/93[8]483

Switzerland; ACW:JUL/93[34]424

Tacony; ACW:JAN/93[58]399, AHI:DEC/82[38]231, B&G:DEC/94[10]585

Tawah; CWTI:NOV/93[74]353

Tecumseh (transport); CWR:VOL4#1[44]164

Tecumseh:
BOOK REVIEW: *MOBILE BAY AND THE MOBILE CAMPAIGN: THE LAST GREAT BATTLES OF THE CIVIL WAR*
ADDITIONAL LISTINGS: ACW:NOV/91[8]328, CWM:JUL/93[24]485, CWTI:MAR/94[20]369, MH:FEB/92[8]156, MH:AUG/92[26]161

Tennessee; CWTI:AUG/90[42]167, CWTI:MAY/93[38]321

Thomas; CWTI:DEC/90[29]182

Ticonderoga; ACW:NOV/92[51]389

Tigress; ACW:JAN/91[22]285, CWTI:MAY/91[16]206

Tioga; B&G:JUN/92[40]489

Tuscumbia; ACW:JUL/94[51]480, B&G:FEB/94[8]550

Tyler; ACW:JAN/91[22]285, ACW:MAY/93[22]414, B&G:FEB/92[10]474, CWR:VOL4#1[44]164

Uncle Sam; B&G:FEB/92[10]474

Undine; B&G:APR/91[36]448, B&G:OCT/91[40]467, CWM:MAR/91[39]338, CWTI:MAR/94[16]368

United States; ACW:MAR/94[35]460

Vanderbilt; CWTI:AUG/95[40]458

Varuna; ACW:MAY/92[16]359

Velocity; ACW:JAN/93[51]398

Vermont; CWR:VOL2#3[194]141

Vicksburg; ACW:NOV/92[51]389

Vincennes; ACW:MAY/92[16]359, MH:DEC/94[46]181

Vindicator; CWTI:JUL/94[30]392

Von Phul; ACW:MAR/93[8]401

W.B. Terry; ACW:JUL/92[22]368

W.W. Coit; B&G:FEB/91[8]439

Wabash; B&G:DEC/94[10]585, CWR:VOL2#3[194]141, CWTI:MAR/94[38]372

Wachusett; ACW:MAY/91[46]306, AHI:MAY/71[3]133A, AHI:JAN/83[10]232, CWM:JUL/93[8]483

War Eagle; CWM:MAY/91[10]347

Warner; CWR:VOL4#2[26]166, CWR:VOL4#2[118]169

Washington; ACW:MAR/94[35]460

Water Witch; ACW:MAY/92[16]359, MH:DEC/94[46]181

Wayanda; ACW:MAR/94[35]460

Webb; CWTI:JUL/94[30]392

Weehawken; MH:AUG/92[26]161

Westfield; ACW:JAN/93[51]398

Whistling Wind; ACW:MAR/94[35]460

White Cloud; ACW:MAR/93[8]401

Whitehall; AHI:JUL/66[32]103

Wilderness; ACW:JAN/95[38]506

William Aiken; ACW:MAR/94[35]460

William Allen; ACW:JAN/95[38]506

William Bell; AHI:JAN/83[10]232

William Thompson; ACW:MAY/91[46]306, CWM:JUL/93[8]483

Winnebago; CWM:JUL/93[24]485, MH:AUG/92[26]161

Winona; MH:AUG/93[47]169

Woodford; ACW:MAR/93[8]401, CWR:VOL4#2[26]166, CWR:VOL4#2[118]169

Wyalusing; ACW:NOV/91[8]328

Wyoming:
ARTICLE: "SHOGUNATE DEFIED," MH:OCT/91[50]154
ADDITIONAL LISTINGS: CWTI:JUN/95[48]448, *sketch,* MH:OCT/91[50]154

CWM:MAR/91[17]335, CWM:JUL/92[18]429,
CWM:JAN/93[8]456, CWM:DEC/94[40]550,
CWR:VOL3#1[31]150, CWTI:SEP/90[26]174,
CWTI:SEP/91[31]229, CWTI:JUL/93[42]329,
GETTY:13[43]256, GETTY:13[50]257
SICKLES, TERESA; ARTICLE: "THE SAD, SHATTERED LIFE
OF TERESA SICKLES," AHI:SEP/82[40]229
SIGEL, FRANZ, *General, USA:*
ARTICLE: "A MIGHTY MEAN-FOWT FIGHT,"
ACW:NOV/93[26]441, "I'M GOING TO FIGHTS MIT SIGEL,"
B&G:AUG/92[26]494
BOOK REVIEWS: *YANKEE DUTCHMAN: THE LIFE OF FRANZ
SIGEL*
GENERAL LISTINGS: *Camp Jackson*, ACW:MAY/91[31]304, *general
history*, AHI:MAY/71[3]133A, *in book review*,
ACW:MAY/94[58], CWM:MAR/91[74], CWM:APR/95[50],
CWR:VOL4#3[89], *letters to the editor*, CWM:JAN/91[6]324,
Manassas, Second, AHI:DEC/66[30]105, B&G:AUG/92[11]493,
Monocacy, B&G:DEC/92[8]503, *Wilson's Creek*,
CWTI:FEB/92[29]248, *photos*, ACW:NOV/93[26]441,
CWTI:FEB/92[29]248
ADDITIONAL LISTINGS: ACW:JUL/91[18]312, ACW:SEP/91[41]323,
ACW:JAN/92[16]340, ACW:JUL/93[10]421,
ACW:SEP/93[22]432, ACW:NOV/93[50]444,
ACW:MAR/94[27]459, AHI:MAY/76[35]168,
B&G:AUG/91[11]458, B&G:APR/93[12]518,
B&G:OCT/95[32]613, CWM:NOV/92[41]451,
CWM:MAY/93[8]474, CWM:APR/94[24]505,
CWR:VOL1#1[42]105, CWTI:FEB/90[46]146,
CWTI:SEP/90[26]174, CWTI:MAR/91[34]201,
CWTI:MAR/93[20]308, CWTI:MAY/93[29]319,
CWTI:MAR/95[26]434, CWTI:JUN/95[32]446,
CWTI:DEC/95[67]481,
SIGFRIED, JOSHUA K., *Colonel, USA;* B&G:APR/94[10]558,
B&G:APR/95[8]595
SIGNAL CORPS, CONFEDERATE:
ARTICLE: "THE CONFEDERATE SIGNAL CORPS AT
GETTYSBURG," GETTY:4[110]152
ADDITIONAL LISTING: ACW:JAN/95[20]504
SIGNAL CORPS, FEDERAL:
ARTICLES: "MEMBERS OF THE U.S. SIGNAL CORPS EARNED
THE PROUD NICKNAME 'KNIGHTS WITHOUR ARMOR,'"
ACW:JAN/95[20]504, "THE SIGNAL CORPS AT
GETTYSBURG PART II: SUPPORT OF MEADE'S
PURSUIT," GETTY:4[101]151
ADDITIONAL LISTING: GETTY:7[29]188
SIGSBEE, CHARLES, *USN;* ACW:JAN/91[62]289
SILL, JOSHUA W., *General, USA;* CWR:VOL4#1[1]163
SILVERS, GOLDEN, *Captain, 4th Kansas Infantry;*
ACW:NOV/94[42]497
SIM, THOMAS, *Doctor, USA;* GETTY:10[112]228
SIMMOND, SETH J., *Captain, Kentucky Artillery;*
CWTI:MAR/89[16]101
SIMMONS, H.H., *Captain, 2nd Florida Cavalry;*
ACW:NOV/91[64]336
SIMMONS, SENECA, *Colonel, USA;* CWR:VOL1#3[28]120
SIMMONS, MRS. WILLIAM A., ACW:MAY/95[38]526
SIMMS, CHARLES C., *Lieutenant, CSN;* AHI:OCT/75[30]162
SIMMS, JAMES P., *Colonel, CSA;* ACW:JUL/95[10]533,
CWM:OCT/94[38]540
SIMMS, JOHN D., *Lieutenant, CSMC;* ACW:MAR/91[14]293
SIMMS, R.M., *Major, CSA;* AHI:SEP/87[40]263
SIMMS, ROBERT, *Lt., New Jersey Arty.;* ACW:MAY/95[30]525

SIMMS, WILLIAM G., *poet;* ACW:SEP/92[10]375
SIMON, ARTHUR F., *Major, 10th Louisiana Infantry;*
CWR:VOL3#1[1]149
SIMON, CHARLES, *Sergeant, 9th New Hampshire Infantry;*
CWR:VOL2#2[118]136
SIMOND, HENRY L, *seaman, USN;* B&G:JUN/92[40]489
SIMONS, EZRA, *Chaplain, 125th New York Infantry;*
CWTI:AUG/90[26]166, GETTY:7[51]190, GETTY:8[95]205
SIMONSON, PETER, *Captain, 5th Indiana Artillery;*
CWTI:NOV/92[41]291
SIMONTON, CHARLES, *Colonel, CSA;* B&G:DEC/94[10]585
SIMPSON, B.C., *Corp., 5th Texas Inf.;* CWTI:DEC/91[36]240
SIMPSON, DICK, *Private, 3rd South Carolina Infantry;*
BOOK REVIEWS: *FAR, FAR FROM HOME: THE WARTIME
LETTERS OF DICK AND TALLY SIMPSON, 3RD SOUTH
CAROLINA VOLUNTEERS*
SIMPSON, GEORGE, *Sergeant, 125th Pennsylvania Infantry;*
B&G:OCT/95[8]611A, B&G:OCT/95[8]611F
SIMPSON, JOHN R., *Sergeant, 125th Pennsylvania Infantry;*
B&G:OCT/95[8]611A
SIMPSON, LUCY FAUCETT; AHI:DEC/73[10]152
SIMPSON, MATTHEW, *Methodist Bishop;* AHI:DEC/68[28]118
SIMPSON, NICHOLAS and ROBERT, *1st Ohio Heavy
Artillery;* GETTY:12[1]240
SIMPSON, TALIAFERRO, *Private, 3rd South Carolina
Infantry;* CWR:VOL4#4[129]
SIMPSON, WILLIAM T., *Private, 28th Pennsylvania Infantry;*
GETTY:9[81]216, GETTY:10[7]221
SIMS, FREDERICK W., *Major, CSA;* CWM:NOV/91[50]394
SIMS, WILLIAM, *Private, CSA;* B&G:AUG/93[10]529
SINCLAIR, ARTHUR, *Lieutenant, CSN:*
BOOK REVIEW: *TWO YEARS ON THE ALABAMA.*
ADDITIONAL LISTING: AHI:OCT/88[38]275
SINCLAIR, CHARLES H., *Ensign, USN;* CWTI:JUL/94[30]392
SINCLAIR, GEORGE, *Sgt., 5th NY Inf.;* CWR:VOL1#2[29]112
SINCLAIR, GEORGE T., *Midshipman, CSN;*
AHI:OCT/88[38]275
SINCLAIR, WILLIAM, *Colonel, USA;* CWR:VOL4#4[1]177
SIPLE, GEORGE W., *Lieutenant, CSA;* CWTI:MAR/89[16]101
SISTERS OF CHARITY OF MOTHER SETON;
B&G:FEB/94[6]549
SISTERS OF CHARITY OF NAZARETH;
B&G:OCT/93[31]539, B&G:FEB/94[6]549
SISTERS OF CHARITY OF ST. VINCENT DE PAUL;
B&G:FEB/94[6]549
SISTERS OF MERCY; B&G:OCT/93[31]539,
B&G:FEB/94[6]549
SISTERS OF OUR LADY MT. CARMEL;
B&G:OCT/93[31]539, B&G:FEB/94[6]549
SISTERS OF OUR LADY OF MERCY; B&G:FEB/94[6]549
SISTERS OF PROVIDENCE; B&G:OCT/93[31]539,
B&G:FEB/94[6]549
SISTERS OF ST. DOMINIC; B&G:FEB/94[6]549
SISTERS OF ST. FRANCIS; B&G:OCT/93[31]539
SISTERS OF ST. JOSEPH, B&G:OCT/93[31]539,
B&G:FEB/94[6]549
SISTERS OF THE HOLY CROSS; B&G:OCT/93[31]539,
B&G:FEB/94[6]549
SISTERS OF THE POOR OF ST. FRANCIS;
B&G:FEB/94[6]549
SKELLY, DANIEL, *civilian;* GETTY:5[107]164,
GETTY:9[122]220, GETTY:10[53]225

SKELLY, JOHNSTON H., *Corporal, 87th Pennsylvania Infantry;* GETTY:9[122]220, GETTY:11[119]238
SKERETT, J.S., *Lt. Commander, USN;* CWTI:JAN/93[49]303
SKINNER, FREDERICK, *Colonel, 1st Virginia Infantry;* B&G:AUG/92[11]493
SKIRMISHERS; ARTICLE: "SKIRMISHERS," GETTY:6[7]169
SLACK, JAMES R., *General, USA;* ACW:NOV/91[22]331, B&G:FEB/94[8]550, B&G:AUG/95[8]604, CWR:VOL2#1[36]132, CWTI:MAY/91[24]208
SLACK, WILLIAM B., *Major, USMC;* CWTI:APR/92[14]254
SLACK, WILLIAM Y., *General, CSA;* ACW:NOV/93[26]441, CWTI:FEB/92[29]248
SLAGLE, J.F., *Maj., 149th Pennsylvania Inf.;* GETTY:13[22]254
SLASH CHURCH, VIRGINIA, BATTLE OF; ARTICLE: "THE PENINSULA CAMPAIGN OF 1862: THE BATTLE OF SLASH CHURCH," CWM:JUN/95[43]587
SLATON, HENRY T., *Sgt., Sumter Arty.;* CWR:VOL3#2[61]154
SLATTER, W.J., *civilian;* B&G:AUG/94[22]576
SLATTERLY, D.P., *Master, USN;* CWTI:JUL/94[30]392
SLAUGHTER, JAMES E., *General, CSA;* ACW:JUL/92[46]371, AHI:JUN/70[30]127, AHI:MAR/84[42]238, CWTI:AUG/90[58]169
SLAUGHTER, JOHN, *Maj., 34th Ala. Inf.;* CWTI:SEP/92[31]281
SLAUGHTER, MERCER, *cadet;* AHI:MAR/84[42]238
SLAUGHTER, PHILIP P., *Lieutenant Colonel, 56th Virginia Infantry;* ACW:MAR/93[10]402
SLAUGHTER, WILLIAM B., *Corporal, 22nd Virginia Infantry;* AHI:MAR/84[42]238, CWR:VOL1#3[52]122
SLAVENS, SAMUEL, *Private, USA;* ACW:SEP/91[22]321
SLAVERY AND SLAVES:
ARTICLES: "AN UNPLEASANT RELIC," CWTI:DEC/91[48]242, "BEFORE FREEDOM CAME: AFRICAN-AMERICAN LIFE IN THE ANTEBELLUM SOUTH, 1790-1865," AHI:JUL/91[10]295, "CIVIL WAR IN THE MAKING," ACW:MAY/94[43]470, "ELIZABETH KECKLEY MADE THE LONG JOURNEY FROM SLAVERY TO THE WHITE HOUSE, AS MARY LINCOLN'S DRESSMAKER," ACW:JUL/92[8]365A, "ESCAPED SLAVES ON THE UNDERGROUND RAILROAD FOUND WELCOME HAVENS IN OHIO'S OBERLIN AND WELLINGTON," ACW:MAY/94[66]472, "GEORGE FITZHUGH: POLEMICIST FOR THE PECULIAR INSTITUTION," CWM:FEB/95[68]567, "GIVE THE BLACKS TEXAS," CWTI:JUN/90[54]162, "MINE EYES HAVE SEEN THE GLORY," CWTI:SEP/93[30]336, "THE MYTH OF THE UNDERGROUND RAILROAD," AHI:JAN/78[34]178, "NOT QUITE FREE: THE FREE NEGRO BEFORE THE CIVIL WAR," AHI:JUN/74[12]155, "ONTARIO LAUNCHES TOUR OF UNDERGROUND RAILROAD SITES," AHI:JUL/92[10]302, "SLAVERY," AHI:APR/70[11]124, "THIS 'ONE GREAT EVIL,'" AHI:MAY/77[37]174, "WAS LINCOLN THE GREAT EMANCIPATOR?" CWTI:MAY/94[46]385
BOOK REVIEWS: *AHEAD OF HER TIME: ABBY KELLEY AND THE POLITICS OF ANTISLAVERY * ALLIES FOR FREEDOM: BLACKS AND JOHN BROWN * THE AMERICAN INDIAN AS SLAVEHOLDER AND SECESSIONIST * AMERICAN NEGRO SLAVERY: A DOCUMENTARY HISTORY * AN OLD CREED FOR THE NEW SOUTH, PRO-SLAVERY IDEOLOGY AND HISTORIOGRAPHY, 1865-1918 * BLOCKADERS, REFUGEES & CONTRABANDS—CIVIL WAR ON FLORIDA'S GULF COAST 1861-65 * CELIA, A SLAVE * CONSTITUTIONS AND CONSTITUTIONALISM IN THE*

*SLAVEHOLDING SOUTH * COTTON & CAPITOL: BOSTON BUSINESSMEN AND ANTISLAVERY REFORM, 1854-1868*
BOOK REVIEWS, continued: *DRIFT TOWARD DISSOLUTION: THE VIRGINIA SLAVERY DEBATE OF 1831-1832 * FREDERICK DOUGLASS * FREEDOM: A DOCUMENTARY HISTORY OF EMANCIPATION, 1861-1867 * FREEDOM: A DOCUMENTARY HISTORY OF EMANCIPATION, 1861-1867, SERIES I, VOLUME III: THE WARTIME GENESIS OF FREE LABOR: LOWER SOUTH * GULLAH STATESMAN, ROBERT SMALLS FROM SLAVERY TO CONGRESS, 1839-1915 * INDUSTRIAL SLAVERY IN THE OLD SOUTH * THE JEWEL OF LIBERTY: ABRAHAM LINCOLN'S RE-ELECTION AND THE END OF SLAVERY * KENNETH AND JOHN B. RAYNER AND THE LIMITS OF SOUTHERN DISSENT * LINCOLN, DOUGLAS AND SLAVERY*
BOOK REVIEWS, continued: *LINCOLN, THE SOUTH, AND SLAVERY: THE POLITICAL DIMENSION * MARKETS AND PRODUCTION, VOLUME ONE. CONDITIONS OF SLAVE LIFE AND THE TRANSITION TO FREEDOM, VOLUME TWO * MEN AND BROTHERS, ANGLO-AMERICAN ANTISLAVERY COOPERATION * NATIVISM AND SLAVERY, THE NORTHERN KNOW NOTHINGS & THE POLITICS OF THE 1850'S * NORTH INTO FREEDOM: THE AUTOBIOGRAPHY OF JOHN MALVIN, FREE NEGRO, 1795-1880 * THE OVERSEER: PLANTATION MANAGEMENT IN THE OLD SOUTH * ROLL, JORDAN, ROLL: THE WORLD THE SLAVES MADE * THE SLAVE COMMUNITY: PLANTATION LIFE IN THE ANTEBELLUM SOUTH * SLAVERY ATTACKED—SOUTHERN SLAVES AND THEIR ALLIES * SOUTHERN NEGROES, 1861-1865*
BOOK REVIEWS, continued: *STRAINED SISTERHOOD: GENDER AND CLASS IN THE BOSTON FEMALE ANTI-SLAVERY SOCIETY * THIS SPECIES OF PROPERTY: SLAVE LIFE AND CULTURE IN THE OLD SOUTH * THE TROUBLE THEY SEEN: BLACK PEOPLE TELL THE STORY OF RECONSTRUCTION * TUMULT AND SILENCE AT SECOND CREEK: AN INQUIRY INTO A CIVIL WAR SLAVE CONSPIRACY * THE WARTIME GENESIS OF FREE LABOR: THE UPPER SOUTH * WITHOUT CONSENT OF CONTRACT: THE RISE AND FALL OF AMERICAN SLAVERY—EVIDENCE AND METHODS*
GENERAL LISTINGS: *general history,* AHI:MAY/71[3]133A, *in book review,* CWM:JUN/94[6], CWNEWS:MAY/91[4], CWNEWS:JUL/95[61], *letters to the editor,* CWM:SEP/91[6]377, CWM:NOV/91[6]389, CWM:MAY/92[6]417, CWM:JUL/92[6]426, CWTI:SEP/94[12]398, CWTI:JAN/95[16]421, *Sherman on the Presidency,* AHI:JAN/77[46]173, *Thaddeus Stevens,* AHI:JAN/82[16]224, *photo of a black camp follower;* CWTI:APR/89[32]110, *sketch of camp scene;* CWTI:APR/89[32]110, *sketch of slaves following troops;* CWTI:APR/89[32]109, *photo of trader's cells;* CWTI:SEP/93[59]341
ADDITIONAL LISTINGS: ACW:NOV/94[8]493, ACW:NOV/94[42]497, AHI:MAY/76[48], CWM:JUL/91[27]365, CWM:APR/95[63]578, CWM:DEC/95[41]630, CWR:VOL3#1[31]150, CWTI:AUG/91[62]221, CWTI:SEP/93[59]341, CWTI:MAR/94[38]372
SLAY, ELIJAH, *Capt., 16th Mississippi Inf.;* GETTY:8[111]206
SLAYBACK, ALONZO, *Lt. Col., USA;* B&G:JUN/91[10]452
SLAYMAN, REUBEN, *Pvt., 53rd Penna. Inf.;* GETTY:11[80]235

SLEEPER, J. HENRY, *Captain, 10th Massachusetts Artillery;* CWR:VOL2#1[78]

SLEMMER, ADAM, *Lieutenant, USA;* CWR:VOL1#4[42]126

SLEMMONS, WILLIAM, *Colonel, CSA;* B&G:JUN/91[10]452

SLEMONS, W.F., *Col., 2nd Arkansas Cav.;* CWR:VOL1#2[44]114

SLIDELL, JOHN:
ARTICLE: "HIGH SEAS BROUHAHA," ACW:NOV/91[46]335
GENERAL LISTINGS: *Bloody Kansas,* AHI:JUL/75[4]160, *Fort Donelson,* B&G:FEB/92[10]474, *Mexican War,* MH:APR/93[34]165, *photo,* CWTI:MAY/89[28]117
ADDITIONAL LISTINGS: ACW:MAY/92[23]360, AHI:JUN/70[30]127, AHI:JUN/73[4]149, CWTI:MAY/89[28]117, CWTI:JUL/92[29]272, CWTI:NOV/92[54]293, CWTI:JAN/93[44]302, MH:OCT/95[8]187

SLIGER, J.E., *Lt., 28th Louisiana Infantry;* CWR:VOL4#2[1]165

SLINGLUFF, FIELDER, *Private, 1st Maryland Cavalry (Confederate);* B&G:AUG/94[10]574

SLISBY, ALONZO, *Private, 1st Ohio Artillery;* GETTY:4[49]147

SLOAN, JOHN A., *Pvt., 27th NC Inf.;* CWM:NOV/92[64]453

SLOAN, THOMAS F., *civilian;* B&G:AUG/94[10]574

SLOAN, THOMAS J., *Col., 124th Ill. Inf.;* B&G:FEB/94[8]550

SLOANE, J.B.E., *Col., 4th SC Inf.;* CWTI:MAR/91[12]198

SLOCOMB, CUTHBERT H., *Captain, Washington Artillery;* ACW:JUL/92[12]367, B&G:AUG/95[8]604,CWM:AUG/95[26]604

SLOCUM, HENRY W., *General, USA:*
GENERAL LISTINGS: *Bentonville,* ACW:NOV/93[12]440, CWR:VOL4#3[65]172, *Carolina Campaign,* B&G:DEC/95[9]615, *Chancellorsville,* ACW:MAY/95[30]525, *Crampton's Gap,* ACW:JAN/94[39]451, *Gaines's Mill,* CWM:JUN/95[61]593, *Gettysburg,* GETTY:4[101]151, GETTY:4[49]147, GETTY:6[7]169, GETTY:6[69]176, GETTY:7[23]187, GETTY:7[29]188, GETTY:7[83]192, GETTY:8[31]201, GETTY:9[81]216, GETTY:10[36]223, GETTY:11[71]234, GETTY:11[119]238, GETTY:12[30]243, GETTY:12[42]244, GETTY:12[85]248, *in book review,* CWM:DEC/94[7], CWM:APR/95[50], CWNEWS:SEP/93[5], CWR:VOL3#3[92], *order of battle,* B&G:DEC/95[9]615, *Savannah,* ACW:SEP/92[47]380, B&G:FEB/91[8]439, *photos,* ACW:MAY/91[8]300, B&G:FEB/91[8]439, B&G:DEC/95[9]615
ADDITIONAL LISTINGS: ACW:MAY/91[8]300, ACW:NOV/92[42]388, ACW:NOV/94[50]498, B&G:OCT/91[11]466, B&G:FEB/95[8]590C, CWM:JAN/91[12]326, CWM:JAN/92[40]405, CWM:JUL/92[18]429, CWR:VOL3#3[1]157, CWTI:SUMMER/89[50]124, CWTI:SEP/91[23]228, CWTI:AUG/95[24]455, GETTY:13[119]262

SLOUGH, JOHN P., *Colonel, 1st Colorado Infantry;* ACW:NOV/91[10]329, B&G:JUN/94[8]568, B&G:OCT/94[6]579, CWM:MAY/93[16]475, CWR:VOL2#2[161]139, CWTI:SEP/91[18]227, CWTI:MAR/94[58]375, CWTI:JUL/94[10]389

SLOUGH, NELSON, *Lt. Col., 20th NC Inf.;* B&G:FEB/95[8]590B

SLOUGH, R.H., *Mayor, Mobile;* CWTI:DEC/94[24]409

SMALL, ABNER R., *Major, 16th Maine Infantry;* AHI:DEC/73[10]152, CWM:MAY/92[15]419, GETTY:5[117]165, GETTY:13[7]253, GETTY:13[33]255, *photo,* CWM:MAY/92[15]419

SMALL, ELLSBERRY T., *Captain, USA;* CWTI:AUG/95[34]457

SMALL, JOHN, *Pvt., 7th Wisconsin Infantry,* GETTY:11[57]233

SMALL, WILLIAM F., *General, USA;* CWM:JUL/92[27]431

SMALLEY, HENRY A., *Colonel, 5th Vermont Infantry;* ACW:JAN/94[8]447

SMALLS, ROBERT, *ex-slave;* BOOK REVIEW: *GULLAH STATESMAN, ROBERT SMALLS FROM SLAVERY TO CONGRESS, 1839-1915*

SMART, BENJAMIN, *Corporal, 2nd Maine Infantry;* CWR:VOL4#1[78]

SMART, CHARLES, *Surgeon, 63rd New York Infantry;* GETTY:10[53]225

SMART, CHARLES H., *Private, 13th U.S. Regulars;* CWR:VOL2#1[1]130

SMART, FREDERICK G., *Private, 5th New York Infantry;* CWTI:MAY/94[31]382

SMATLEY, G.C., *Private, Georgia Legion;* B&G:APR/93[24]520

SMEAD, ——, *Captain, 5th U.S. Artillery;* AHI:DEC/66[30]105

SMEAD, ABNER, *Pvt., 12th Georgia Inf.;* GETTY:13[108]261

SMEAD, ABNER, *Colonel, CSA;* GETTY:9[17N]210

SMEDLEY, ABEL B., *Major, 32nd Wisconsin Infantry;* CWR:VOL2#4[313]146

SMEDLEY, CHARLES, *Corporal, 90th Pennsylvania Infantry;* CWTI:MAR/95[18]432

SMITH, A.D., *Lt. Col., 1st SC Inf.;* CWTI:JAN/94[46]364

SMITH, A.J., *Pvt., 33rd Alabama Infantry;* AHI:JUL/93[40]312

SMITH, ABNER C., *Corporal, 20th Connecticut Infantry;* B&G:DEC/95[9]615

SMITH, ALBERT G., *Private, 51st North Carolina Infantry;* CWTI:JAN/95[48]429

SMITH, ALFRED, *Maj., 150th New York Inf.;* GETTY:12[42]244

SMITH, ALFRED B., *civilian;* GETTY:12[42]244

SMITH, ALFRED C., *Sergeant, 2nd Mississippi Infantry;* ARTICLE: "'SWAMP RANGER' AND CAVALRYMAN," CWTI:NOV/92[106]295

SMITH, ANDREW, *Pvt., 49th Penna. Inf.;* CWTI:SEP/93[43]338

SMITH, ANDREW J., *General, USA:*
ARTICLES: "A.J. SMITH'S ROVING 'GORILLAS,'" MH:DEC/95[58]188, "FEDERALS' RISKY PURSUIT," ACW:SEP/92[23]377
GENERAL LISTINGS: *Jackson, Battle of,* B&G:AUG/95[8]604, *Nashville,* B&G:DEC/93[12]545, *order of battle,* B&G:DEC/93[12]545, B&G:FEB/94[8]550, B&G:AUG/95[8]604, *Price's 1864 Missouri Campaign,* B&G:JUN/91[10]452, *photos,* ACW:SEP/92[23]377, MH:DEC/95[58]188
ADDITIONAL LISTINGS: ACW:SEP/91[16]320, ACW:NOV/91[22]331, B&G:FEB/94[8]550, CWM:JAN/91[40]330, CWM:MAY/91[31]350, CWM:APR/95[39]576, CWR:VOL1#2[44]114, CWR:VOL2#1[36]132, CWR:VOL2#3[212]142, CWR:VOL4#2[1]165, CWR:VOL4#2[26]166, CWR:VOL4#2[104]168, CWTI:MAY/91[24]208, CWTI:MAY/92[48]267, CWTI:JAN/93[20]298, CWTI:JAN/94[35]361, CWTI:DEC/94[24]409

SMITH, AUGUST, *Pvt., 1st Minnesota Inf.;* GETTY:5[79]161

SMITH, B.H., *Lt. Col., 2nd Michigan Cav.;* CWTI:MAR/91[46]203

SMITH, BAXTER, *Colonel, CSA;* B&G:DEC/95[9]615

SMITH, BENJAMIN B., *Sergeant, 1st Georgia Regulars;* CWR:VOL2#2[95]135

SMITH, BENJAMIN F., *Colonel, USA;* B&G:APR/94[10]558

SMITH, C. SHALER, *engineer;* CWM:SEP/91[10]379

SMITH, CALEB B.; CWTI:DEC/95[24]477

SMITH, CHARLES, *Lt. Col., 1st ME Cav.;* B&G:OCT/93[12]537

SMITH, CHARLES C., *Captain, 13th U.S. Regulars;* CWR:VOL2#1[1]130

SMITH, CHARLES F., *General, USA;* ACW:JUL/91[35]314, B&G:FEB/92[10]474, B&G:FEB/92[48]475,

SMITH, JASON B., *Captain, 1st Illinois Artillery;*
ACW:JUL/94[8]474, B&G:JUN/93[12]524
SMITH, JEFF, *Lieutenant, CSA;* B&G:AUG/94[10]574
SMITH, JOE, *Lt., 4th Texas Infantry;* CWTI:JUL/93[42]329
SMITH, JOHN, *Private, Botetourt Artillery;* B&G:FEB/94[8]550
SMITH, JOHN, *Private, USMC;* CWR:VOL1#4[42]126
SMITH, JOHN D., *Corporal, 19th Maine Infantry;*
GETTY:9[17N]210, GETTY:13[50]257
SMITH, JOHN E., *General, USA;* AHI:NOV/69[13]124,
B&G:FEB/94[8]550, B&G:DEC/95[9]615,
CWM:SEP/92[19]440, CWR:VOL2#4[313]146,
CWR:VOL3#3[59]159, CWTI:JAN/93[20]298,
CWTI:MAY/93[35]320
SMITH, JOHN F., *Lieutenant Colonel, CSA;* B&G:DEC/95[9]615
SMITH, JOHN L., *Cpl., 118th Penna. Inf.;* ACW:MAR/92[30]352
SMITH, JOHN S., *Adj. 20th Alabama Inf.;* B&G:FEB/94[8]550
SMITH, JOSEPH, *Pvt., 11th Miss. Inf.;* CWR:VOL2#4[269]145
SMITH, JOSEPH B., *Lieutenant, USN;* AHI:OCT/75[30]162
SMITH, JOSEPH R., *46th Ohio Infantry;* B&G:DEC/93[30]546
SMITH, JOSHUA K., *Pvt., 2nd Tenn. Cav.;* CWR:VOL4#1[1]163
SMITH, LEE, *Private, CSA;* B&G:AUG/91[52]464
SMITH, LEON, *Major, CSA;* ACW:JAN/93[51]398,
CWTI:DEC/90[29]182
SMITH, LEWIS, *Sgt. 125th New York Inf.;* GETTY:7[51]190
SMITH, LOT, *Captain, Nauvoo Legion;* ACW:JAN/95[8]502
SMITH, LUCIAS H., *Captain, CSA;* B&G:FEB/91[20]440
SMITH, MELANCTHON, *Colonel, CSA;* B&G:DEC/93[12]545
SMITH, MARSHALL J., *Lieutenant Colonel, CSA;* ARTICLE:
"BRILLIANT VICTORY OVER THE YANKEE FLEET ON
THE MISSISSIPPI," CWM:APR/95[28]573
SMITH, MARTIN L., *General, CSA:*
GENERAL LISTINGS: *Atlanta,* B&G:APR/94[28]559, *Champion's Hill,*
MH:JUN/93[82]167, *Vicksburg,* AHI:DEC/77[46]177,
Wilderness, B&G:JUN/95[8]600, *photo,* CWR:VOL2#1[36]132
ADDITIONAL LISTINGS: ACW:SEP/92[38]379, ACW:SEP/94[10]484,
B&G:APR/93[12]518, CWR:VOL2#1[19]131,
CWR:VOL2#1[36]132
SMITH, MELANCHTON, *Captain, USN;* ACW:MAR/92[40]353
SMITH, MILO, *Colonel, USA;* B&G:AUG/95[8]604,
CWTI:JAN/93[20]298
SMITH, MORGAN L., *General, USA;* CWR:VOL2#1[69]133,
CWR:VOL3#3[59]159, CWR:VOL4#1[44]164,
CWTI:SEP/92[28]280
SMITH, MOSES, *Col., 11th Missouri Cav.;* B&G:JUN/91[10]452
SMITH, MYRON, *Sgt., 111th Penna. Inf.;* CWR:VOL3#2[70]155
SMITH, N.H., *Lieutenant, CSA;* CWM:OCT/95[47]620
SMITH, NAT S., *Capt., 13th NC Inf.;* GETTY:8[67]204
SMITH, NORMENT, *Private, Mosby's Ranger;*
CWTI:SEP/90[34]176
SMITH, ORLANDO, *Colonel, USA;* CWR:VOL3#2[70]155,
GETTY:11[19]232
SMITH, PETER, *Pvt., 6th Wisconsin Infantry,* GETTY:11[57]233
SMITH, PRESTON, *Colonel, CSA;* CWR:VOL1#4[42]126,
CWR:VOL4#3[50]171
SMITH, RICHARD P., *Colonel, 71st Pennsylvania Infantry;*
CWTI:JUL/94[20]390, GETTY:7[83]192, GETTY:7[97]193,
photo, GETTY:7[97]193
SMITH, ROBERT, *Lieutenant Colonel, 13th Virginia Reserve
Battalion;* B&G:AUG/91[11]458
SMITH, ROBERT F., *Col., 16th Ill. Inf.;* ACW:NOV/94[34]496
SMITH, ROGER, *Private, 2nd Texas Infantry;* CWM:APR/95[8]
SMITH, STEPHEN, *Pvt., 7th NH Inf.;* ACW:SEP/91[30]322

SMITH, STEPHEN, *Surgeon, CSA;* BOOK REVIEW: *HAND-BOOK
OF SURGICAL OPERATIONS*
SMITH, THOMAS, *Adjutant, 22nd Battalion Virginia Infantry;*
CWR:VOL1#3[52]122
SMITH, THOMAS, *Lieutenant Colonel, CSA;*
ACW:MAY/91[38]305, ACW:MAR/94[27]459
SMITH, THOMAS B., *General, CSA;* B&G:DEC/93[12]545,
B&G:DEC/93[49]547A, B&G:DEC/93[52]548,
CWNEWS:JUL/93[5]
SMITH, THOMAS KILBY, *General, USA;*
B&G:AUG/91[30]460, B&G:AUG/92[40]495,
CWR:VOL2#1[1]130, CWR:VOL3#3[33]158,
CWR:VOL4#2[26]166, MH:DEC/95[58]188
SMITH, W.E., *Private, CSA;* CWTI:FEB/92[42]250
SMITH, W.H., *Pvt., 18th Virginia Infantry;* CWR:VOL1#3[52]122
SMITH, W.H., *Private, 8th New York Cavalry;* GETTY:4[115]152
SMITH, W.P., *civilian;* CWTI:SEP/92[22]279
SMITH, W. WILLARD, *Captain, USA;* GETTY:12[97]249
SMITH, WALTER, *privateer;* B&G:JUN/94[22]569
SMITH, WILLARD, *Pvt., 24th Michigan Inf.,* GETTY:11[57]233
SMITH, WILLIAM, *Captain, USA;* GETTY:12[97]249
SMITH, WILLIAM, *Colonel, CSA;* GETTY:6[69]176
SMITH, WILLIAM "EXTRA BILLY", *General, CSA;*
ACW:NOV/92[42]388, AHI:APR/85[18]250,
B&G:APR/91[8]445, B&G:DEC/91[34]470,
B&G:FEB/95[8]590C, CWR:VOL2#4[269]145,
CWTI:NOV/93[24]346, GETTY:9[17]210, GETTY:9[81]216
SMITH, WILLIAM, *Pvt., 3rd Vermont Inf.;* ACW:JAN/94[8]447
SMITH, WILLIAM A., *Sergeant, 2nd Tennessee Cavalry;*
CWR:VOL4#1[1]163
SMITH, WILLIAM F. "BALDY", *General, USA:*
BOOK REVIEW: *THE BERMUDA HUNDRED CAMPAIGN*
GENERAL LISTINGS: *Crampton's Gap,* B&G:OCT/95[8]611B,
Gettysburg, GETTY:4[65]148, *in book review,*
CWTI:MAR/89[10], *in order of battle,* B&G:APR/94[10]558,
Overland Campaign, B&G:APR/94[10]558, *Peninsula
Campaign,* CWM:JUN/95[29]583, CWM:JUN/95[34]584,
CWM:JUN/95[63]594, *Petersburg,* MH:APR/95[46]183,
Williamsburg, ACW:MAR/91[47]297
ADDITIONAL LISTINGS: ACW:JUL/91[35]314, ACW:SEP/93[62]436,
ACW:JAN/94[8]447, ACW:JAN/94[39]451,
ACW:SEP/95[74]550, B&G:FEB/91[34]442,
B&G:APR/94[51]563, CWM:OCT/94[37]539,
CWR:VOL3#2[70]155, CWR:VOL3#3[1]157,
CWR:VOL3#3[59]159, CWR:VOL3#4[1]161,
CWTI:SEP/91[31]229, CWTI:SEP/91[54]232,
CWTI:APR/92[49]260, CWTI:MAY/93[29]319,
CWTI:JAN/94[20]358, GETTY:5[103]163
SMITH, WILLIAM HENRY; CWTI:SEP/94[49]404
SMITH, WILLIAM K., *civilian;* CWM:NOV/91[58]394A
SMITH, WILLIAM M., *Captain, CSA;* CWR:VOL4#1[1]163
SMITH, WILLIAM SOOY, *General, USA:*
GENERAL LISTINGS: *Grierson's Raid,* B&G:JUN/93[12]524,
MH:FEB/95[18]182, *Jackson, Battle of,* B&G:AUG/95[8]604,
order of battle, B&G:AUG/95[8]604, *photo,* B&G:JUN/93[12]524
ADDITIONAL LISTINGS: ACW:MAR/95[42]517, ACW:SEP/95[48]547,
CWR:VOL2#4[313]146, CWTI:JAN/94[35]361
SMITH, WILLIAM ST. CLAIR, *Captain, 6th Louisiana
Infantry;* CWM:SEP/93[18]494
SMITH, WYATT, *Pvt., 3rd Georgia Inf.;* CWTI:SEP/94[26]400
SMITH, XANTHUS R., *artist;* ARTICLE: "MEMOIRS IN OILS,"
CWM:NOV/92[31]449

2nd Infantry, Colored; CWTI:MAR/94[38]372
2nd Infantry, Union; CWTI:DEC/89[42]137
2nd Rifles, CWR:VOL3#2[70]155
3rd Cavalry; CWR:VOL2#3[194]141, CWR:VOL2#3[252]144
3rd Infantry:
BOOK REVIEWS: *FAR, FAR FROM HOME: THE WARTIME LETTERS OF DICK AND TALLY SIMPSON, 3RD SOUTH CAROLINA VOLUNTEERS*
GENERAL LISTINGS: *Gettysburg,* GETTY:5[35]159, GETTY:5[47]160, GETTY:8[53]203, *in book review,* CWNEWS:APR/92[4], CWNEWS:OCT/95[33], CWR:VOL4#4[129]
ADDITIONAL LISTINGS: ACW:MAY/92[54], ACW:JUL/93[58], ACW:MAR/94[50]462, B&G:APR/93[12]518, B&G:JUN/95[8]600, CWR:VOL1#4[7]125, CWTI:MAY/94[50]386
4th Cavalry:
BOOK REVIEWS: *SADDLE SOLDIERS: THE CIVIL WAR CORRESPONDENCE OF GENERAL WILLIAM STOKES OF THE 4TH SOUTH CAROLINA CAVALRY*
GENERAL LISTINGS: *in book review,* CWNEWS:JAN/92[4], CWNEWS:OCT/92[4], CWR:VOL1#2[78], *Overland Campaign,* B&G:APR/94[10]558
ADDITIONAL LISTINGS: ACW:NOV/92[26]386, ACW:MAR/95[50]518, B&G:DEC/92[20]504
4th Infantry; CWR:VOL2#4[269]145, CWTI:MAR/91[12]198, CWTI:MAR/94[48]374
5th Cavalry:
GENERAL LISTINGS: *in book review,* CWNEWS:JAN/92[4], CWR:VOL1#2[78], *Overland Campaign,* B&G:APR/94[10]558
ADDITIONAL LISTINGS: ACW:JUL/91[50], ACW:MAY/92[30]361, ACW:NOV/92[26]386, ACW:MAR/95[50]518, B&G:DEC/92[20]504
5th Infantry; CWM:JUN/94[26]512, CWM:OCT/94[34]538, CWR:VOL3#2[70]155
6th Cavalry:
GENERAL LISTINGS: *in book review,* B&G:FEB/91[28], CWNEWS:JAN/92[4], CWR:VOL1#2[78]
ADDITIONAL LISTINGS: ACW:MAR/95[50]518, B&G:DEC/92[20]504, CWR:VOL3#2[1]153, CWTI:SEP/90[26]174
6th Infantry; CWM:JUN/94[26]512, CWR:VOL3#2[70]155, CWTI:MAY/94[12]379
7th Cavalry; ACW:MAY/92[30]361, CWM:JUL/92[16]428
7th Infantry:
GENERAL LISTINGS: *Gettysburg,* GETTY:5[35]159, GETTY:5[47]160, GETTY:5[117]165, GETTY:8[53]203, *Immortal Six Hundred,* GETTY:12[111]250, *in book review,* CWNEWS:APR/92[4], *letters to the editor,* CWTI:MAY/94[12]379
ADDITIONAL LISTINGS: ACW:MAY/94[12]466, ACW:MAR/94[50]462, B&G:APR/93[12]518, CWR:VOL1#4[7]125
8th Infantry:
GENERAL LISTINGS: *Gettysburg,* GETTY:5[35]159, GETTY:5[47]160, GETTY:8[53]203, *in book review,* CWNEWS:APR/92[4]
ADDITIONAL LISTINGS: ACW:JAN/92[16]340, ACW:MAR/94[50]462, CWR:VOL1#4[7]125, CWTI:SEP/90[26]174
9th Infantry; CWTI:JAN/94[46]364
10th Infantry; CWTI:SUMMER/89[50]124
12th Cavalry; B&G:FEB/91[8]439
12th Infantry;
GENERAL LISTINGS: *Gettysburg,* GETTY:6[7]169, *in book review,* CWNEWS:MAY/89[4], *Manassas, 2nd,* B&G:AUG/92[11]493

ADDITIONAL LISTINGS: ACW:NOV/92[10]384, CWM:SEP/92[8]437, CWTI:SEP/90[26]174, GETTY:13[1]252, GETTY:13[7]253, GETTY:13[22]254
13th Infantry:
GENERAL LISTINGS: *Gettysburg,* GETTY:6[94]180, *in book review,* CWNEWS:MAY/89[4], *Manassas, Second,* B&G:AUG/92[11]493
ADDITIONAL LISTINGS: ACW:NOV/92[10]384, CWTI:SEP/90[26]174, GETTY:13[1]252, GETTY:13[22]254
14th Infantry:
ARTICLE: "CAPT. JAMES GLENN'S SWORD AND PRIVATE J. MARSHALL HILL'S ENFIELD IN THE FIGHT FOR THE LUTHERAN SEMINARY," GETTY:8[9]199
BOOK REVIEW: *A COLONEL AT GETTYSBURG AND SPOTSYLVANIA: THE LIFE OF COLONEL JOSEPH NEWTON BROWN AND THE BATTLE OF GETTYSBURG AND SPOTSYLVANIA*
GENERAL LISTINGS: B&G:APR/93[12]518, GETTY:9[109]218, GETTY:9[116]219, GETTY:13[1]252, GETTY:13[22]254
15th Infantry:
GENERAL LISTINGS: *Gettysburg,* GETTY:5[35]159, GETTY:5[47]160, GETTY:8[53]203, *in book review,* CWNEWS:APR/92[4]
ADDITIONAL LISTING: B&G:DEC/95[25]616
17th Infantry; B&G:APR/92[8]481
18th Infantry; B&G:APR/92[8]481
20th Infantry; B&G:APR/94[10]558, CWNEWS:APR/92[4], CWR:VOL3#4[1]161
21st Infantry; CWM:JUL/92[16]428
22nd Infantry; B&G:APR/92[8]481, CWM:JUL/92[16]428, CWTI:JAN/94[46]364
23rd Infantry; B&G:APR/92[8]481
25th Infantry; B&G:DEC/92[40]508, B&G:DEC/94[10]585, CWTI:JAN/93[49]303
26th Infantry; B&G:APR/92[8]481, CWR:VOL2#2[141]137
27th Infantry; B&G:DEC/94[10]585
30th Infantry; ACW:SEP/92[10]375
Bachman's Battery; CWR:VOL2#3[194]141
Brunson's Battery; ACW:MAY/95[30]525
Charleston Light Infantry; CWTI:JAN/94[46]364
Cobb Legion; B&G:OCT/93[12]537
Culpepper's Artillery; B&G:AUG/95[8]604
Eutaw Battalion; CWTI:JAN/94[46]364
Ferguson's Light Artillery; B&G:AUG/95[8]604
Hampton's Legion; ACW:JUL/94[42]479, ACW:NOV/94[18]495, CWR:VOL3#2[70]155 <dd more of these?>>
Hart's Battery; ACW:JUL/92[41]370, CWR:VOL4#4[70]180
Jeff Davis Legion; B&G:OCT/93[12]537
Kershaw's Brigade; BOOK REVIEW: *HISTORY OF KERSHAW'S BRIGADE*
MacBeth Light Artillery; B&G:AUG/95[8]604
McCalla Rifles; GETTY:8[9]199
Oglethorpe Rifles; CWM:JUN/94[50]518
Palmetto Light Artillery, Battery B:
BOOK REVIEW: *SOUTHERN BRONZE: CAPT. GARDEN'S (S.C.) ARTILLERY COMPANY DURING THE WAR BETWEEN THE STATES*
ADDITIONAL LISTINGS: B&G:AUG/95[8]604, *photo,* AHI:APR/68[4]115
Palmetto Sharpshooters; CWM:JUN/95[34]584, CWR:VOL3#2[70]155, GETTY:6[33]172
Pee Dee Artillery; CWR:VOL4#4[70]180, CWTI:JAN/94[46]364, GETTY:10[107]227
South Carolina Sharpshooter Battalion; GETTY:6[7]169
Waite's Battery; B&G:AUG/94[22]576

Washington (South Carolina) Artillery; GETTY:11[19]232

SOUTH CAROLINA, STATE OF:
BOOK REVIEW: *CADETS IN GRAY: THE STORY OF THE
    CADETS OF THE SOUTH CAROLINA MILITARY
    ACADEMY AND THE CADET RANGERS IN THE CIVIL
    WAR * PRELUDE TO CIVIL WAR: THE NULLIFICATION
    CONTROVERSY IN SOUTH CAROLINA, 1816-1836*
SOUTH MOUNTAIN, MARYLAND, BATTLE OF:
ARTICLE: "THE DEATH OF JESSE RENO," CWM:MAY/92[44]423
BOOK REVIEW: *BEFORE ANTIETAM: THE BATTLE FOR
    SOUTH MOUNTAIN * THE BIVOUACS OF THE DEAD:
    THE STORY OF THOSE WHO DIED AT ANTIETAM AND
    SOUTH MOUNTAIN*
GENERAL LISTINGS: ACW:JAN/91[38]287, ACW:JUL/92[30]369,
    ACW:MAR/93[10]402, ACW:JAN/95[46]507,
    ACW:MAY/95[18]524, B&G:FEB/95[8]590B,
    CWM:SEP/91[40]385, CWM:MAY/92[8]418,
    CWR:VOL1#3[28]120, CWR:VOL2#4[269]145,
    CWR:VOL3#3[1]157, CWTI:APR/89[14]107,
    CWTI:MAY/89[36]118, CWTI:SEP/91[31]229,
    CWTI:FEB/92[36]249, CWTI:SEP/94[49]404
SOUTHERLAND (NORTH CAROLINA) BATTERY;
    B&G:DEC/94[10]585
SOUTHERN (MISSISSIPPI) GUARDS; GETTY:12[68]246
SOUTHERN CLAIMS COMMISSION; BOOK REVIEWS:
    *SOUTHERN LOYALISTS IN THE CIVIL WAR: THE
    SOUTHERN CLAIMS COMMISSION*
SOUTHERN ECONOMY; ARTICLE: "ORDNANCE, SOUTHERN
    ECONOMY," ACW:JUL/91[14]311
SOUTHERN FAMILY; BOOK REVIEW: *DEFEND THE VALLEY:
    A SHENANDOAH FAMILY IN THE CIVIL WAR*
SOUTHERN GUARDS; GETTY:12[68]246
SOUTHERN HISTORICAL SOCIETY; GETTY:4[113]153
SOUTHERN HISTORY AND SOUTHERN NATIONALISM:
ARTICLE: "THE SPURNED SCHOOLTEACHERS FROM
    YANKEEDOM," AHI:FEB/80[14]199
BOOK REVIEWS: *THE BURDEN OF SOUTHERN HISTORY *
    CIVIL WARS: WOMEN AND THE CRISIS OF SOUTHERN
    NATIONALISM * IN THE CAGE: EYEWITNESS
    ACCOUNTS OF THE FREED NEGRO IN SOUTHERN
    SOCIETY, 1877-1929 * INDUSTRIAL SLAVERY IN THE
    OLD SOUTH * THE SLAVE COMMUNITY: PLANTATION
    LIFE IN THE ANTEBELLUM SOUTH*
SOUTHERN TELEGRAPH COMPANY;
    CWM:NOV/91[58]394A
SOUTHWICK, THOMAS, *Private, 5th New York Infantry;*
    CWR:VOL1#2[7]111, CWTI:MAY/94[31]382
SOVEREIGN, FREDERICK, *Adjutant, 5th New York Infantry;*
    CWR:VOL1#2[29]112
SOVEREIGN, T., *Chaplain, 5th New Jersey Infantry;*
    B&G:FEB/92[22]476
SOWERINE, ISAAC, *Pvt., 19th Indiana Inf.,* GETTY:11[57]233
SOWERS, RICHARD, *Private, CSA;* ACW:JUL/94[26]477
SPALDING, GEORGE, *Colonel, 12th Tennessee (Union)
    Cavalry;* ACW:NOV/95[48]557
SPANGLER, DANIEL, *civilian;* GETTY:4[65]148
SPANGLER, EDMAN; ACW:MAY/95[68]529,
    AHI:FEB/86[12]257, CWTI:MAY/92[8]261
SPANGLER, EDWARD; CWTI:APR/90[12]150
SPANISH FORT, MOBILE, ALABAMA; ACW:SEP/92[16]376,
    CWTI:DEC/94[24]409, MH:DEC/95[58]188
SPARKMAN, JAMES, *Captain, CSA;* ACW:JAN/94[30]450

SPARKS, HENRY, *Sgt., 3rd Indiana Cav.;* B&G:FEB/95[8]590A
SPARTANS AND GUARDS (VIRGINIA);
    ACW:MAR/93[10]402
SPAULDING, IRA, *Lieutenant Colonel, 50th New York
    Engineers;* ACW:MAY/93[8]411, ACW:NOV/95[10]553,
    CWR:VOL4#4[101]181, CWTI:APR/92[49]260
SPAULDING, JOSEPH W., *Captain, 19th Maine Infantry;*
    GETTY:13[50]257
SPAULDING, LYMAN, *Colonel, 23rd Michigan Infantry;*
    CWTI:NOV/92[41]291
SPAULDING, WILLIAM, *Pvt., 24th Mich. Inf.;* GETTY:5[19]158
SPAULDING, ZEPHARIAH, *Major, 27th Ohio Infantry;*
    ACW:SEP/91[46]324
SPAYBERRY, HARVEY, *Captain, Georgia and Mississippi
    Regiment;* CWR:VOL1#4[42]126
SPEAR, ELLIS, *Captain, 20th Maine Infantry;* GETTY:6[43]173
SPEAR, GEORGE C., *Colonel, USA;* ACW:SEP/92[30]378
SPEAR, EDWARD, *Captain, Ohio Light Artillery;*
    B&G:AUG/95[8]604
SPEAR, SAMUEL P, *Colonel, 11th Pennsylvania Cavalry;*
GENERAL LISTINGS: *The "Blackberry" Raid,* GETTY:11[6]231, *Five
    Forks,* B&G:APR/92[8]481, *in order of battle,*
    B&G:APR/92[8]481, *photo,* GETTY:11[6]231
ADDITIONAL LISTINGS: ACW:MAY/92[30]361, CWTI:FEB/91[45]194
SPEARS, JAMES G., *General, USA;* ACW:JUL/91[26]313
SPECHT, MICHAEL, *Sergeant, 72nd Pennsylvania Infantry;*
    GETTY:5[107]164

SPECIAL ORDERS:
Special Order Number 19; GETTY:6[13]170
Special Order Number 191:
ARTICLES: "ESPIONAGE," MH:JUN/94[8]177, "WHOEVER LOST
    ROBERT E. LEE'S 'LOST ORDER,' A DELIGHTED GEORGE
    MCCLELLAN FOUND IT," ACW:JAN/94[6]446
GENERAL LISTINGS: *Harpers Ferry,* MH:AUG/95[30]185, *in book
    review,* CWNEWS:JAN/91[4], *letters to the editor,*
    CWM:MAR/91[12]333
ADDITIONAL LISTINGS: ACW:JAN/91[38]287, ACW:JUL/93[58],
    ACW:JAN/94[39]451, ACW:JAN/95[46]507,
    B&G:FEB/93[24]512, B&G:JUL/91[24]361,
    CWM:SEP/91[40]385, CWM:MAY/92[8]418,
    CWR:VOL1#4[7]125, CWTI:APR/89[14]107
Special Order Number 286; MH:APR/92[18]157

SPEED, FREDERIC, *Captain, 5th Maine Infantry;*
    B&G:AUG/95[24]605, CWNEWS:NOV/92[4], GETTY:7[7]185
SPEED, JAMES, *Attorney;* ACW:JUL/91[6]308,
    ACW:MAR/93[55]408, AHI:NOV/72[12]142,
    AHI:NOV/88[37]278, B&G:FEB/93[12]511
SPEED, JOSHUA; CWM:DEC/94[17]547
SPEED, WILLIAM J., *Captain, 24th Michigan Infantry:*
ARTICLE: "AN IRON BRIGADE CAPTAIN'S REVOLVER IN THE
    FIGHT ON MCPHERSON'S RIDGE," GETTY:7[7]185
ADDITIONAL LISTING: GETTY:7[7]185
SPEER, JOHN, *editor;* CWM:JAN/92[12]400
SPEESE, A.J., *Pvt., 3rd Pennsylvania Cav.;* GETTY:13[89]260
SPEICE, HENRY, *Sgt., 53rd Penna. Inf.;* GETTY:11[80]235
SPEIGHT, JOSEPH W., *Colonel, CSA;* CWM:OCT/94[33]537
SPELLMAN, DOMINICK, *Private, 1st South Carolina Infantry;*
    ACW:NOV/92[10]384
SPELLMAN, HENRY P., *Captain, USA;* CWTI:AUG/95[34]457

SPELMAN, FRANCIS, *Sergeant, 5th New York Infantry;*
  CWR:VOL1#2[v]110, CWR:VOL1#2[29]112,
  CWTI:MAY/94[31]382
SPENCE, BELDIN, *Lt., 1st Pennsylvania Inf.;* GETTY:12[30]243
SPENCER, CHRISTOPHER, *inventor;* B&G:OCT/92[32]499,
  CWM:JUL/92[24]430
SPENCER, ELMINA KEELER, *Matron, 147th New York
  Infantry:*
  ARTICLE: "ELMINA KEELER SPENCER: MATRON, 147TH NEW
  YORK," GETTY:8[121]207
  ADDITIONAL LISTINGS: GETTY:12[1]240, *photo,* GETTY:8[121]207
SPENCER, GEORGE E., *Colonel, USA;* B&G:DEC/95[9]615,
  CWNEWS:APR/90[4]
SPENCER, J.G., *Private, CSA;* CWTI:MAY/91[18]207
SPENCER, JOHN S., *Lt., 12th VA Inf.;* CWR:VOL2#3[236]143
SPENCER, T. RUSH, *Surgeon, USA;* B&G:OCT/95[32]613
SPERRY, JOHN J., *Capt., 106th Penna. Inf.;* GETTY:5[89]162
SPICELY, WILLIAM T., *Colonel, USA;* B&G:AUG/95[8]604
SPICER, DANIEL, *Private, 11th Veteran Reserve Corps;*
  B&G:APR/93[24]520
SPICLY, WILLIAM T., *Col., 24th Ind. Inf.;* B&G:FEB/94[8]550
SPIEGEL, MARCUS M., *Colonel, 120th Ohio Infantry;*
  ACW:JUL/94[51]480, B&G:FEB/94[8]550,
  CWNEWS:NOV/92[4], *photo,* CWTI:MAY/92[38]265

SPIES:
  ARTICLES: "CODE-CRACKERS," CWTI:AUG/95[46]459,
  "CONFEDERATE CLOAK AND DAGGER,"
  ACW:JUL/95[44]537
  BOOK REVIEWS: *APRIL '65: CONFEDERATE COVERT ACTION
  IN THE AMERICAN CIVIL WAR * BLUE AND GRAY ROSES
  OF INTRIGUE * COME RETRIBUTION: THE
  CONFEDERATE SECRET SERVICE AND THE
  ASSASSINATION OF LINCOLN * THE SECRET SERVICE
  OF THE CONFEDERATE STATES IN EUROPE * SPIES &
  SPYMASTERS OF THE CIVIL WAR*
  ADDITIONAL LISTINGS: CWM:SEP/93[18]494, CWTI:DEC/95[8]474,
  MH:DEC/94[70]
  Boyd, Belle; B&G:DEC/92[40]508, B&G:APR/93[40]522,
  CWM:SEP/93[18]494, CWM:SEP/93[24]495
  Pinkerton, Allen; see listings under **"PINKERTON, ALLEN"**
  Van Lew, Elizabeth; see listings under **"VAN LEW,
  ELIZABETH"**
  Zarvona, Richard Thomas; ARTICLE: "THE FRENCH LADY,"
  CWTI:MAY/92[29]263

SPINNER, FRANCIS E., *U.S. Treasurer;* ACW:NOV/92[8]383
SPIVEY, LITTLETON E., *Lieutenant, Sumter Artillery;*
  CWR:VOL3#2[1]153
SPOFFORD, JOHN P., *Lieutenant Colonel, 97th New York
  Infantry;* GETTY:10[7]221, GETTY:13[33]255
SPOONER, LYSANDER; CWM:DEC/94[5]546
SPOOR, NELSON T., *Captain, USA;* B&G:AUG/95[8]604
SPOTSYLVANIA NATIONAL MILITARY PARK;
  ACW:SEP/95[74]550, B&G:APR/93[12]518
SPOTSYLVANIA, VIRGINIA, BATTLE OF:
  ARTICLES: "THE BLOODY ROAD TO SPOTSYLVANIA:
  PENNSYLVANIA BUCKTAILS, PART TWO,"
  CWR:VOL1#3[28]120, "THE MAN WHO SHOT JOHN
  SEDGWICK: THE TALE OF CHARLES D. GRACE—A
  SHARPSHOOTER IN THE DOLES-COOK BRIGADE, CSA,"
  B&G:DEC/95[25]616

  BOOK REVIEWS: *A COLONEL AT GETTYSBURG AND
  SPOTSYLVANIA: THE LIFE OF COLONEL JOSEPH
  NEWTON BROWN AND THE BATTLE OF GETTYSBURG
  AND SPOTSYLVANIA * BLOODY ROADS SOUTH: THE
  WILDERNESS TO COLD HARBOR, MAY-JUNE 1864 * IF IT
  TAKES ALL SUMMER: THE BATTLE OF SPOTSYLVANIA*
  GENERAL LISTINGS: *general history,* AHI:MAY/71[3]133A, *in book
  review,* CWNEWS:MAY/89[4], CWR:VOL1#4[77],
  CWR:VOL2#1[78], CWTI:FEB/90[10]
  ADDITIONAL LISTINGS: ACW:JAN/92[16]340, ACW:MAY/93[14]413,
  ACW:SEP/93[62]436, ACW:JUL/94[26]477,
  ACW:JAN/95[46]507, ACW:MAR/95[70]520,
  ACW:MAY/95[18]524, ACW:SEP/95[74]550,
  B&G:JUN/94[38]571, CWM:JUL/92[8]427,
  CWM:SEP/93[8]493, CWM:SEP/93[24]495,
  CWM:OCT/94[17]534, CWM:OCT/95[40]619,
  CWR:VOL1#1[1]102, CWR:VOL1#3[52]122,
  CWR:VOL2#2[118]136, CWR:VOL2#2[141]137,
  CWR:VOL3#2[1]153, CWR:VOL3#3[1]157,
  CWR:VOL3#2[61]154, CWR:VOL3#4[1]161,
  CWTI:FEB/90[46]146, CWTI:SEP/91[61]233,
  CWTI:DEC/91[26]238, CWTI:DEC/94[32]410,
  CWTI:JAN/95[34]427
SPRAGUE, ASA W., *Lt., 24th Michigan Inf.;* GETTY:5[19]158
SPRAGUE, CHARLES, *Pvt. 6th Wisc. Inf.,* GETTY:11[57]233
SPRAGUE, JOHN W., *Colonel, 63rd Ohio Infantry;*
  ACW:SEP/91[46]324, CWTI:JAN/93[82]304
SPRAGUE, KATE CHASE:
  ARTICLE: "THE LIFE OF KATE CHASE SPRAGUE,"
  AHI:APR/83[27]233
  GENERAL LISTINGS: *Mary Todd Lincoln,* AHI:MAY/75[4]159,
  Willard's Hotel, AHI:OCT/79[10]192, *photos,*
  AHI:OCT/79[10]192, AHI:APR/83[27]233
SPRAGUE, MAHLON, *Corporal, 5th New Jersey Infantry;*
  ARTICLE: "PATRIOTIC SON OF A SEAMAN,"
  CWTI:JUL/92[74]277
SPRANKLE, PETER D., *Lieutenant, 148th Pennsylvania
  Infantry;* CWR:VOL2#2[141]137
SPRENGER, GEORGE F., *Sergeant, 124th New York Infantry;*
  CWM:DEC/94[40]550
SPRING HILL, TENNESSEE, BATTLE OF:
  BOOK REVIEWS: *EMBRACE AN ANGRY WIND—THE
  CONFEDERACY'S LAST HURRAH: SPRING HILL,
  FRANKLIN, AND NASHVILLE*
  ADDITIONAL LISTINGS: ACW:MAR/94[42]461, B&G:FEB/95[30]591,
  CWM:JAN/91[47], CWM:MAR/91[28]336, CWM:OCT/94[8],
  CWR:VOL1#4[64]127
SPRINGFIELD ARSENAL; ACW:JAN/91[8]282
SPRINGFIELD, ILLINOIS; ARTICLE: "MR. LINCOLN'S
  SPRINGFIELD," AHI:MAR/89[26]280
SPRINGFIELD, MISSOURI, BATTLE OF; ARTICLE: "TAKING
  OFF THE KID GLOVES," ACW:MAR/92[46]354
SPURLORK, ALTEN, *Doctor;* B&G:JUN/93[12]524
SPURR, THOMAS, *Lt., 125th Penna. Inf.;* B&G:OCT/95[8]611A
SQUIRES, MILES T., *Captain, CSA;* MH:AUG/93[47]169
ST. ALBAN'S, VERMONT, RAID ON:
  ARTICLE: "ST. ALBANS HAS BEEN SURPRISED,"
  AHI:JAN/76[14]164
  GENERAL LISTINGS: *letters to the editor,* B&G:FEB/91[6]438,
  B&G:APR/91[6]444, *St. Albans Historical Museum;*
  B&G:OCT/94[42]583
  ADDITIONAL LISTINGS: CWTI:SEP/92[40]282, CWTI:JAN/93[44]302,
  MH:FEB/94[8]175

ST. AUGUSTINE (FLORIDA) RIFLES; ACW:SEP/93[8]429
ST. JOHN, ISAAC M., ARTICLE: "'THEY ALSO SERVE, WHO...':
   JONATHAN HARALSON AND THE SELMA NITRIARY,"
   CWM:SEP/91[34]383,
ST. LAWRENCE HALL, MONTREAL, CANADA; ARTICLE:
   "MONTREAL'S POSH REBEL RENDEVOUS,"
   CWTI:JAN/93[44]302
ST. LOUIS, MISSOURI; ARTICLE: "UNPROVOKED
   TRAGICOMEDY IN ST. LOUIS," ACW:MAY/91[31]304
ST. MARKS, FLORIDA; ACW:NOV/91[64]336
ST. MARTIN, VICTOR, *Cpt., 9th LA Inf.;* CWTI:FEB/91[12]189
STACEY, ALBERT H., *Pvt, 126th NY Inf.;.* CWR:VOL1#4[7]125
STACKPOLE, THOMAS, *Captain, USA;* ACW:JAN/94[47]452,
   CWTI:DEC/95[24]477
STACY, BRAZILLIAH, *Lieutenant Colonel, USA;*
   B&G:AUG/91[11]458
STAFFORD, LEROY A., *General, CSA:*
GENERAL LISTINGS: *Manassas, Second,* B&G:AUG/92[11]493, *order
   of battle,* B&G:APR/95[8]595, *Wilderness,* B&G:JUN/95[8]600
ADDITIONAL LISTINGS: B&G:APR/95[8]595, CWM:MAY/92[20]420,
   CWM:SEP/93[24]495, CWM:DEC/94[44]551,
   CWR:VOL1#3[52]122, CWTI:MAR/95[46]437
STAGG, PETER, *Colonel, 1st Michigan Cavalry;*
   ACW:NOV/92[26]386, B&G:APR/92[8]481
STAHEL, JULIUS, *General, USA:*
GENERAL LISTINGS: *1863 cavalry battles,* MH:OCT/92[51]162,
   Gettysburg, GETTY:11[19]232, *letters to the editor,*
   B&G:DEC/95[5]614A
ADDITIONAL LISTINGS: ACW:MAY/95[54]528, AHI:JUN/81[38]220,
   B&G:OCT/93[12]537, CWTI:OCT/95[48]470, MH:OCT/93[6]170
STAINROOK, HENRY J., *Colonel, USA;* ACW:MAR/94[50]462
STAINS, SAMUEL F., *Private, 53rd Pennsylvania Infantry;*
   GETTY:11[80]235
STAMP COLLECTING AND STAMPS:
ARTICLES: "COMMEMORATIVE STAMPS: HISTORY MOVES
   THE MAIL," CWTI:JUN/90[12]157 "CIVIL WAR STAMPS,"
   AHI:JUL/95[9]323, "CIVIL WAR STAMPS,"
   CWTI:JUN/95[10]442
BOOK REVIEW: *SANITARY FAIRS: A PHILATELIC AND
   HISTORICAL STUDY OF CIVIL WAR BENEVOLENCES*
ADDITIONAL LISTING: B&G:FEB/95[38]593, B&G:DEC/95[44]617,
   CWTI:FEB/91[8]188
STAMPER, JOHN, *Pvt., 26th NC Inf.;* GETTY:5[19]158
STAMPS, ISAAC, *Captain, 21st Mississippi Infantry:*
ARTICLE: "TO ASSUAGE THE GRIEF: THE GETTYSBURG
   SAGA OF ISAAC AND MARY STAMPS," GETTY:7[77]191
ADDITIONAL LISTING: GETTY:12[1]240
STANBURY, HENRY, *civilian;* AHI:DEC/68[28]118
STANDART, WILLIAM E., *Captain, 1st Ohio Light Artillery;*
   B&G:FEB/93[12]511
STANDIFER, LUKE L., *Corporal, 2nd Tennessee Cavalry;*
   CWR:VOL4#1[1]163
STANFIELD, CHARLES, *Private, 96th Ohio Infantry;*
   ACW:SEP/92[16]376
STANLEY, DAVID S., *General, USA:*
GENERAL LISTINGS: *Custer,* AHI:FEB/71[4]131, *in book review,*
   CWM:FEB/95[7], *Tullahoma Campaign,* B&G:OCT/92[10]496
ADDITIONAL LISTINGS: ACW:SEP/91[46]324, ACW:MAR/92[14]350,
   ACW:NOV/93[26]441, ACW:MAR/94[42]461,
   CWM:OCT/94[48]542, CWTI:SUMMER/89[50]124,
   CWTI:MAY/92[48]267, CWTI:JUL/94[50]395,
   CWTI:MAR/95[40]436
STANLEY, ISHAM, *civilian;* B&G:AUG/94[22]576

STANLEY, J.R., *seaman, USN;* CWR:VOL2#3[194]141
STANLEY, T.R., *Col., 18th Ohio Infantry;* B&G:AUG/93[10]529
STANNARD, GEORGE J., *General, USA:*
GENERAL LISTINGS: *Gettysburg,* AHI:SUM/88[12]273,
   GETTY:5[79]161, GETTY:5[117]165, GETTY:6[87]178,
   GETTY:10[7]221, GETTY:10[112]228, *in order of battle,*
   B&G:APR/94[10]558, *letters to the editor,* B&G:JUN/95[5]599
ADDITIONAL LISTINGS: ACW:SEP/93[8]429, CWR:VOL1#4[7]125,
   CWR:VOL3#1[31]150, CWTI:SEPT/89[46]132,
   GETTY:13[50]257
STANSBURY, SMITH, *Major, CSA;* CWTI:DEC/89[10]133
STANTON, DAVID L., *Colonel, USA;* B&G:APR/92[8]481
STANTON, EDWIN M.:
ARTICLE: "WHEN SECRETARY OF WAR EDWIN STANTON
   NEEDED A GOOD MAN TO RUN HIS VITAL RAILROADS,
   HE SENT FOR HERMAN HAUPT," ACW:JUL/95[16]534
GENERAL LISTINGS: *Andrew Johnson,* CWTI:FEB/90[60]148,
   Appomattox, CWTI:FEB/90[54]147, *Cedar Creek,*
   MH:OCT/93[76]173, *Charles Ellet,* ACW:MAR/95[18]514,
   Charles P. Stone, CWTI:MAY/89[21]115, *Confederate attempt
   to surrender,* CWTI:FEB/91[36]193, *Cordelia Harvey,*
   CWTI:MAR/89[20]102, *Daniel E. Sickles,* CWTI:FEB/92[6]244,
   editorial, ACW:JAN/91[6]281, *Fort Pillow,*
   CWTI:NOV/93[65]351, *Fort Wool,* ACW:JAN/95[74]510, *George
   H. Thomas,* ACW:NOV/95[48]557, *Gettysburg,*
   CWTI:MAR/94[24]370, GETTY:4[24]145, GETTY:4[101]151,
   GETTY:7[23]187, *gold hoax,* AHI:APR/80[21]200, *Grand
   Review,* CWTI:AUG/90[64]170, *Horace H. Lurton,*
   CWTI:DEC/94[79]417, *impeachment of Andrew Johnson,*
   AHI:DEC/68[28]118
GENERAL LISTINGS, continued: *in book review,* ACW:NOV/95[62],
   AHI:JAN/84[8], B&G:JUN/95[30], CWM:DEC/94[7],
   CWM:FEB/95[7], CWM:JUN/95[6], CWM:DEC/95[10],
   CWNEWS:AUG/91[4], CWR:VOL4#4[129], *John A.
   Rawlins, ACW:NOV/95[22]554, John W. Booth,*
   CWTI:JUN/95[26]445, *letter to editor,* AHI:MAY/86[4], *letters
   to the editor,* CWTI:JAN/93[10]297, *Lincoln as lawyer,*
   AHI:APR/76[32]166, *Lincoln's assassination,*
   ACW:MAY/95[68]529, *Lincoln's humor,* AHI:NOV/70[22]130,
   Monocacy, ACW:NOV/93[50]444, *Nelson-Davis feud,*
   AHI:NOV/72[12]142, *Peninsula Campaign,*
   CWM:JUN/95[24]582, *railroads,* CWM:NOV/91[12]390, *Sickles
   murder trial,* ACW:SEP/95[54]548, *Thaddeus Stevens,*
   AHI:JAN/82[16]224, *Ulysses S. Grant,* CWTI:FEB/90[46]146,
   CSS *Virginia,* ACW:JUL/94[35]478, *West Point,*
   B&G:DEC/91[12]469, *painting;* CWTI:FEB/90[32]144, *photos,*
   AHI:DEC/68[28]118, AHI:APR/80[21]200, AHI:NOV/90[44]293
ADDITIONAL LISTINGS, ACW: ACW:JAN/91[8]282,
   ACW:MAR/91[25]294, ACW:MAY/91[38]305,
   ACW:JUL/91[18]312, ACW:JUL/91[35]314,
   ACW:NOV/91[22]331, ACW:NOV/91[30]332,
   ACW:MAR/92[22]351, ACW:SEP/92[8]374,
   ACW:NOV/92[8]383, ACW:JAN/93[51]398,
   ACW:MAR/93[18]403, ACW:SEP/93[38]434,
   ACW:MAR/94[35]460, ACW:SEP/94[55]489,
   ACW:JAN/95[20]504, ACW:MAR/95[8]512,
   ACW:MAY/95[38]526, ACW:MAY/95[54]528
ADDITIONAL LISTINGS, AHI: AHI:FEB/69[35]120,
   AHI:FEB/82[36]225, AHI:FEB/86[12]257, AHI:NOV/88[37]278,
   AHI:NOV/90[44]293
ADDITIONAL LISTINGS, B&G: B&G:FEB/91[8]439,
   B&G:APR/91[8]445, B&G:OCT/92[10]496, B&G:DEC/92[8]503,
   B&G:FEB/93[12]511, B&G:DEC/93[12]545,

B&G:FEB/94[32]552, B&G:JUN/94[22]569,
B&G:OCT/94[11]580, B&G:DEC/94[22]586,
B&G:FEB/95[8]590A, B&G:APR/95[33]597,
B&G:OCT/95[32]613, B&G:DEC/95[44]617
ADDITIONAL LISTINGS, CWM: CWM:MAR/91[56]341,
CWM:MAY/91[18]348, CWM:NOV/91[58]394A,
CWM:MAR/92[32]413, CWM:MAR/93[8]465,
CWM:MAY/93[32]477, CWM:SEP/93[18]494,
CWM:APR/94[8]502, CWM:OCT/94[48]542,
CWM:APR/95[32]575, CWM:JUN/95[17]581
ADDITIONAL LISTINGS, CWR: CWR:VOL4#2[26]166
ADDITIONAL LISTINGS, CWTI: CWTI:FEB/91[28]192,
CWTI:AUG/91[46]218, CWTI:SEP/91[31]229,
CWTI:DEC/91[28]239, CWTI:APR/92[49]260,
CWTI:SEP/92[22]279, CWTI:SEP/92[40]282,
CWTI:NOV/92[54]293, CWTI:MAY/93[29]319,
CWTI:JUL/93[20]325, CWTI:JAN/94[46]364,
CWTI:DEC/94[57]414, CWTI:DEC/94[82]418,
CWTI:JAN/95[34]427, CWTI:MAR/95[40]436,
CWTI:MAR/95[54]438, CWTI:JUN/95[32]446,
CWTI:DEC/95[76]482, CWTI:DEC/95[90]483
ADDITIONAL LISTINGS, GETTY: GETTY:10[102]226,
GETTY:12[85]248, GETTY:12[111]250
ADDITIONAL LISTINGS, MH: MH:JUN/91[20]152, MH:APR/92[18]157,
MH:DEC/93[12]174, MH:APR/94[54]176
STANTON, ELIZABETH C.; CWTI:DEC/90[50]183
STANTON, S.S., *Col., 25th Tennessee Inf.;* B&G:FEB/93[12]511
STAPLES, JOHN S., *Private, 2nd District of Columbia Infantry;*
ARTICLE: "JOHN SUMMERFIELD STAPLES BORE THE
PRESIDENT'S MUSKET IN THE CIVIL WAR,"
ACW:NOV/91[16]330
STARBIRD, ISAAC W., *Captain, 19th Maine Infantry;*
GETTY:13[50]257
STARK, BENJAMIN, *Senator, Oregon;* ARTICLE: "A TRAITOR
IN THE SENATE," CWTI:AUG/95[54]460
STARKE, PETER B., *General, CSA;* B&G:AUG/94[38]578,
B&G:AUG/95[8]604, CWR:VOL2#4[343]147
STARKE, WILLIAM E., *General, CSA;* ACW:JUL/91[18]312,
ACW:JUL/92[30]369, ACW:JAN/95[54]508,
ACW:MAY/95[18]524, B&G:AUG/92[11]493,
B&G:OCT/95[8]611A, CWM:JAN/93[16]457,
CWM:SEP/93[24]495, CWTI:MAR/89[28]103
STARKWEATHER, JOHN, *Colonel, USA;*
CWR:VOL4#3[50]171, CWTI:NOV/92[18]289
STARLING, SAMUEL M.; ACW:MAR/93[55]408
STARNES, JAMES W., *Colonel, 3rd Tennessee Cavalry;*
ACW:MAR/93[51]407, CWM:DEC/95[48]631,
CWR:VOL4#1[1]163
STARR EBENEZER T.; ARTICLE: "CONNECTICUT YANKEE
EBEN T. STARR'S PISTOLS AND CARBINES HELPED
BOLSTER THE UNION'S WAR EFFORT,"
ACW:SEP/94[24]485
STARR, JOSEPH B., *Lieutenant Colonel, North Carolina
Junior Reserves Brigade;* B&G:DEC/95[9]615
STARR, MATHEW, *Major, USA;* ACW:JUL/94[8]474
STARR, SAMUEL H., *Major, 6th United States Cavalry;*
B&G:OCT/93[12]537, GETTY:11[19]232
STATHAM, CHARLES W., *Lieutenant, Lee Artillery;*
B&G:AUG/93[10]529, CWR:VOL4#4[70]180
STAUFFER, N.B., *Pvt., 42nd NC Inf.;* B&G:APR/93[24]520
STAUGHTON, HOMER, *Major,* ACW:JAN/92[38]343
STAUNTON (VIRGINIA) ARTILLERY; B&G:FEB/95[8]590C,
CWM:JAN/92[68]407

**STAUNTON RIVER BRIDGE, VIRGINIA, ENGAGEMENT
AT;** ARTICLE: "OLD MEN AND YOUNG BOYS,"
CWM:MAY/92[34]422
STEADMAN, ARTHUR, *Private, 19th Indiana Infantry,*
GETTY:11[57]233
STEADMAN, GEORGE, *Private, USA;* B&G:JUN/93[12]524
STEARNS, AUSTIN, *Pvt., 13th Mass. Inf.;* ACW:MAR/95[42]517
STEARNS, GEORGE L.; CWNEWS:JUN/93[5]
STEBBINS, JOHN W., *Private, 9th New York Cavalry;*
AHI:JUL/93[40]312
STEBBINS, JOSEPH, *Quartermaster, USN;*
B&G:JUN/92[40]489
STEBBINS, SAMUEL, *Pvt., 1st Minn. Inf.;* CWTI:NOV/93[14]
STEDMAN, CHARLES M., *Major, 44th North Carolina
Infantry;* CWTI:FEB/91[45]194
STEDMAN, GRIFFIN A., *General, USA;* B&G:APR/94[10]558
STEEDMAN, JAMES B., *General, USA;* ACW:JAN/92[47]344,
B&G:FEB/93[12]511, B&G:AUG/93[10]529
B&G:DEC/93[12]545, CWR:VOL4#1[1]163,
CWR:VOL4#3[50]171, CWTI:SEP/92[31]281
STEELE'S BAYOU EXPEDITION; CWR:VOL2#1[78]
STEELE'S CAMDEN EXPEDITION; ACW:MAR/95[34]516,
CWR:VOL1#2[44]114
STEELE'S GREENVILLE EXPEDITION; CWR:VOL2#1[78]
STEELE, CHARLES W., *Sergeant, 20th Maine Infantry;*
GETTY:6[43]173
STEELE, FREDERICK, *General, USA:*
GENERAL LISTINGS: *in book review,* B&G:JUN/94[34], *Jackson,
Battle of,* B&G:AUG/95[8]604, *order of battle,*
B&G:AUG/95[8]604, *Price's 1864 Missouri Campaign,*
B&G:JUN/91[10]452, *photo,* B&G:AUG/95[8]604
ADDITIONAL LISTINGS: ACW:SEP/92[66]381, ACW:MAR/93[68]409,
ACW:MAY/93[22]414, ACW:NOV/93[26]441,
ACW:MAR/95[34]516, CWR:VOL1#1[42]105,
CWR:VOL1#2[44]114, CWR:VOL2#1[78],
CWR:VOL2#3[212]142, CWR:VOL3#3[59]159,
CWR:VOL4#2[26]166, CWTI:FEB/92[29]248,
CWTI:APR/92[27]256, CWTI:DEC/94[24]409,
MH:APR/94[54]176, MH:DEC/95[58]188
STEELE, OLIVER, *Major, CSA;* CWR:VOL2#1[19]131
STEELE, THEOPHILUS, *Major, CSA;* CWR:VOL4#1[1]163
STEELE, WILLIAM, *General, CSA;* ACW:SEP/92[38]379,
CWR:VOL1#2[44]114, CWR:VOL2#3[212]142,
CWR:VOL4#2[1]165, CWR:VOL4#2[118]169
STEEN, ALEXANDER E., *General, USA;* ACW:NOV/93[26]441,
CWTI:FEB/92[29]248
STEFFEN, EDWARD W., *Private, 121st Pennsylvania Infantry;*
CWR:VOL4#4[1]177
STEFFY, JOHN, *Pvt., 55th Penna. Inf.;* B&G:OCT/94[42]583
STEGMAN, LEWIS R., *Lieutenant Colonel, 102nd New York
Infantry; Gettysburg,* GETTY:10[36]223, GETTY:12[42]244
STEINER, JOHN A., *Major, USA;* CWR:VOL1#4[7]125
STEINER, LEWIS, *surgeon;* ACW:JAN/91[38]287,
GETTY:6[94]180
STENSEL, MARTIN L., *Colonel, CSA;* B&G:APR/92[8]481
STEPHENS, ALEXANDER:
ARTICLE: "THE VICE PRESIDENT RESIDES IN GEORGIA,"
CWTI:FEB/91[36]192
GENERAL LISTINGS: *Confederate attempt to surrender,*
CWTI:FEB/91[36]193, *in book review,* ACW:MAR/95[58],
CWM:JUN/94[6], CWM:AUG/95[45], CWNEWS:OCT/92[4],
Jefferson Davis, CWTI:AUG/91[36]217, *letters to the editor,*

CWM:AUG/94[6]521, *women in the South,*
AHI:DEC/73[10]152, *sketch;* AHI:NOV/70[22]130
ADDITIONAL LISTINGS: ACW:SEP/91[54], ACW:SEP/91[62]326,
ACW:MAY/92[62]364, ACW:NOV/93[42]443,
ACW:MAY/95[38]526, B&G:APR/91[32]447,
CWM:JAN/91[28]327, CWM:MAR/93[32]468,
CWM:AUG/94[8]522, CWR:VOL4#4[28]178,
CWTI:MAY/89[22]116, CWTI:AUG/91[52]219,
CWTI:AUG/91[58]220, CWTI:DEC/91[28]239,
CWTI:FEB/92[21]247, CWTI:MAY/94[46]385,
CWTI:DEC/94[79]417, CWTI:DEC/95[22]476,
CWTI:DEC/95[76]482
STEPHENS, ALFRED H., *Surgeon, 6th Ohio Infantry;*
CWM:MAY/91[10]347
STEPHENS, EDMUND, *Sergeant, 9th Louisiana Infantry;*
CWM:SEP/93[24]495
STEPHENS, JOHN A., *Lieutenant, CSA;* CWTI:FEB/91[36]193
STEPHENS, JOHN W., *Senator, North Carolina;* ARTICLE: "THE
MURDER OF A SCALAWAG," AHI:APR/73[12]148
STEPHENS, LINTON; ACW:NOV/93[42]443,
CWTI:AUG/91[52]219
STEPHENS, THOMAS A., *Colonel, USA;* CWTI:MAY/93[35]320
STEPHENS, WILLIAM G., *Private, USA;* CWTI:SEP/91[18]227
STEPHENS, WINSTON, *Captain, 1st Florida Special
Battalion;* CWR:VOL3#1[65]151
STEPHENSON'D DEPOT, VIRGINIA, BATTLE OF;
CWM:JAN/93[40]461, CWM:AUG/95[35]607,
CWM:OCT/95[37]617
STEPHENSON, P.D., *Pvt., 13th Ark. Inf.;* ACW:JAN/92[10]339
STEPHEST, HERMANN, *Private, 24th Michigan Infantry,*
GETTY:11[57]233
STERL, OSCAR W., *Colonel, USA;* B&G:DEC/94[10]585
STETSON, JOHN L., *Lieutenant Colonel, 59th New York
Infantry;* B&G:OCT/95[8]611A
STEUART'S BRIGADE; ARTICLE: AGAINST THE TRENCHES:
THE ATTACK AND REPULSE OF STEUART'S BRIGADE
ON CULP'S HILL," GETTY:7[83]192
ADDITIONAL LISTING: GETTY:9[81]216
STEUART, GEORGE H., *General, CSA:*
ARTICLE: "COURAGE AGAINST THE TRENCHES: THE
ATTACK AND REPULSE OF STEUART'S BRIGADE ON
CULP'S HILL," GETTY:GETTY:9[81]216,
GENERAL LISTINGS: *Five Forks,* B&G:APR/92[8]481, *Gettysburg,*
CWR:VOL2#2[141]137, GETTY:5[103]163, GETTY:5[107]164,
GETTY:6[69]176, GETTY:9[17]210, GETTY:10[36]223,
GETTY:12[42]244, *in order of battle,* B&G:APR/92[8]481,
order of battle, B&G:APR/95[8]595, *Wilderness,*
B&G:APR/95[8]595, *photos,* B&G:APR/95[8]595,
CWM:MAY/92[20]420
ADDITIONAL LISTINGS: ACW:NOV/92[42]388, ACW:SEP/94[38]487,
AHI:APR/85[18]250, CWM:MAY/92[20]420,
CWTI:MAY/89[22]116, GETTY:5[4]156
STEVENS, A.H., *Major, 4th Massachusetts Infantry;*
ACW:JAN/93[18]394
STEVENS, CHARLES, *Private, 29th Georgia Cavalry;* ARTICLE:
"A RELUCTANT REBEL SOLDIER," CWTI:JUL/93[74]331
STEVENS, CLEMENT H., *General, CSA;* ACW:SEP/92[38]379,
CWR:VOL1#4[64]127
STEVENS, EDMUND L., *Lieutenant, 54th Massachusetts
Infantry;* CWTI:AUG/90[42]167
STEVENS, EDWARD, *civilian;* CWTI:MAY/89[36]118
STEVENS, EDWARD, *Pvt., 1st Minn. Inf.;* CWTI:NOV/93[14]

STEVENS, GEORGE, *Surgeon, USA;* CWTI:APR/92[49]260,
CWTI:MAY/94[24]381,
STEVENS, GEORGE H., *Lieutenant Colonel, 2nd Wisconsin
Infantry;* GETTY:6[13]170
STEVENS, GREENLEAF T., *Captain, 5th Maine Artillery;*
GETTY:4[33]146, GETTY:8[9]199, GETTY:11[57]233,
GETTY:12[30]243, GETTY:13[22]254
STEVENS, HAZARD, *Captain, USA;* ACW:JAN/95[54]508,
B&G:APR/95[8]595
STEVENS, HENRY S., *Chaplain, 12th New Jersey Infantry;*
ACW:JUL/95[50]538,
STEVENS, HENRY S., *Chaplain, 14th Connecticut Infantry;*
GETTY:9[61]215, GETTY:12[61]245, GETTY:13[75]259
STEVENS, ISAAC I., *General, CSA:*
ARTICLE: "STONEWALL'S SURPRISE AT OX HILL,"
ACW:JAN/95[54]508
GENERAL LISTINGS: *Indian Wars,* AHI:OCT/79[20]194, *Manassas,
Second,* B&G:AUG/92[11]493, *Mexican War,*
MH:APR/93[39]166, *sketch;* CWTI:JAN/94[46]364,
ACW:JAN/95[54]508
ADDITIONAL LISTINGS: ACW:MAR/92[62]355, CWR:VOL1#3[52]122,
CWTI:MAR/93[20]308, CWTI:JAN/94[46]364,
CWTI:JAN/95[34]427
STEVENS, L.H., *Lieutenant, USA;* GETTY:7[51]190
STEVENS, THADDEUS:
ARTICLES: "OLD THAD STEVENS," AHI:DEC/81[18]223, "OLD
THAD STEVENS," AHI:JAN/82[16]224
GENERAL LISTINGS: *Gettysburg,* GETTY:7[13]186, *in book review,*
ACW:NOV/91[54], ACW:MAY/93[54], *photos,*
AHI:DEC/68[28]118, AHI:DEC/81[18]223, AHI:JAN/82[16]224
ADDITIONAL LISTINGS: ACW:MAR/91[30]295,
CWTI:JUN/90[46]161, CWTI:DEC/91[28]239,
CWTI:SEP/94[26]400, CWTI:DEC/95[52]480,
GETTY:13[64]258, GETTY:13[7]253
STEVENS, THOMAS H., *Cmdr., USMC;* CWR:VOL2#3[194]141
STEVENS, W.R., *Private, Sumter Artillery;* CWR:VOL3#2[1]153
STEVENS, WALTER H., *General, CSA;* ACW:SEP/92[38]379
STEVENS, WILBUR F., *Captain, 29th Ohio Infantry;*
GETTY:9[81]216
STEVENS, WILLIAM H., *Captain, 148th Pennsylvania
Infantry;* CWR:VOL2#2[141]137
STEVENSON, CARTER L., *General, CSA:*
GENERAL LISTINGS: *Champion's Hill,* CWTI:MAY/91[24]208,
MH:JUN/93[82]167, *Grierson's Raid,* B&G:JUN/93[12]524, *in
book review,* CWNEWS:AUG/92[4], CWR:VOL3#1[80], *order of
battle,* B&G:DEC/93[12]545, B&G:DEC/95[9]615, *Vicksburg,*
AHI:DEC/77[46]177, CWTI:MAR/89[44]105, *photos,*
CWR:VOL2#1[36]132, CWTI:SEPT/89[30]129
ADDITIONAL LISTINGS: ACW:NOV/91[22]331, ACW:NOV/95[48]557,
CWR:VOL2#1[i]129, CWR:VOL2#1[36]132,
CWR:VOL3#3[59]159, CWTI:SUMMER/89[20]121,
CWTI:SUMMER/89[40]123, CWTI:SEPT/89[30]129,
CWTI:NOV/92[41]291, CWTI:DEC/94[49]413
STEVENSON, JAMES, *Captain, 1st New York Cavalry;*
B&G:AUG/94[10]574
STEVENSON, JOHN A., *civilian;* ACW:MAY/92[16]359,
MH:DEC/94[46]181
STEVENSON, JOHN D., *General, USA;* ACW:NOV/91[22]331,
B&G:FEB/94[8]550, CWTI:MAY/91[24]208
STEVENSON, THOMAS G., *General, USA;*
ACW:SEP/91[30]322, B&G:APR/95[8]595,
CWTI:DEC/89[42]137

STEVENSON, WILLIAM H., *Lieutenant, USA; 118th New York Infantry;* GETTY:11[6]231

STEWART, ALEXANDER P., *General, CSA;*
GENERAL LISTINGS: *Atlanta Campaign,* CWTI:SEP/92[28]280, *Carolina Campaign,* B&G:DEC/95[9]615, *Ezra Church,* CWTI:SUMMER/89[50]124, *Franklin,* B&G:OCT/91[11]466, *Nashville,* ACW:NOV/95[48]557, B&G:DEC/93[12]545, *order of battle,* B&G:DEC/93[12]545, B&G:DEC/95[9]615, *photo,* B&G:DEC/93[12]545
ADDITIONAL LISTINGS: ACW:SEP/92[38]379, ACW:MAR/94[42]461, ACW:JAN/95[30]505, B&G:OCT/91[11]466, B&G:OCT/92[32]499, B&G:DEC/93[12]545, B&G:DEC/93[52]548, CWM:JAN/91[12]326, CWM:MAR/91[28]336, CWM:JUL/92[24]430, CWM:OCT/94[48]542, CWR:VOL1#4[42]126, CWR:VOL4#3[50]171, CWR:VOL4#3[65]172, CWTI:SUMMER/89[20]121, CWTI:SUMMER/89[32]122, CWTI:SUMMER/89[40]123, CWTI:NOV/92[41]291, CWTI:MAR/93[24]309, CWTI:DEC/94[49]413

STEWART, HENRY W., *Private, 6th Michigan Cavalry;* GETTY:9[109]218

STEWART, JAMES, *Captain, 4th U.S. Artillery:*
ARTICLE: "A FEDERAL ARTILLERYMAN AT GETTYSBURG: AN EYEWITNESS ACCOUNT," AHI:MAY/67[22]107
GENERAL LISTINGS: *Gettysburg,* GETTY:4[24]145, GETTY:4[33]146, GETTY:5[117]165, GETTY:9[33]211, GETTY:10[7]221, GETTY:11[57]233, GETTY:12[30]243, GETTY:13[22]254, GETTY:13[33]255, *photo of grave;* GETTY:11[57]233, *photo,* GETTY:11[57]233

STEWART, JAMES, *Corporal, Pennsylvania Light Artillery;* CWNEWS:APR/94[5]

STEWART, JAMES, *seaman, USN;* CWTI:MAY/94[16]380

STEWART, LORENZO C., *Private, 14th New York Artillery;* AHI:DEC/71[10]137

STEWART, NIXON B., *Chaplain, 52nd Ohio Infantry;* CWTI:NOV/92[41]291, CWTI:MAY/94[40]383

STEWART, ROBERT R., *Colonel, 11th Indiana Cavalry;* B&G:DEC/93[12]545, CWTI:MAR/91[46]203

STEWART, TOM, *Captain, 1st Maryland Battalion;* GETTY:9[81]216

STEWART, WILLIAM H., *Major, 61st Virginia Infantry:*
BOOK REVIEW: *A PAIR OF BLANKETS: WAR-TIME HISTORY IN LETTERS TO THE YOUNG PEOPLE OF THE SOUTH*
ADDITIONAL LISTING: GETTY:5[117]165

STEWART, WILLIAM, *Captain, 11th Pennsylvania Reserves;* CWR:VOL2#4[269]145, CWR:VOL4#4[1]177

STEWART, WILLIAM S., *Surgeon, 83rd Pennsylvania Infantry;* B&G:JUN/95[5]599

STILES, ISRAEL N., *Colonel, USA;* B&G:DEC/93[12]545

STILES, JAMES, *Lieutenant, 97th New York Infantry;* GETTY:10[7]221

STILES, JOHN, *Colonel, USA;* B&G:OCT/95[20]612

STILES, RICHARD C., *Surgeon;* GETTY:10[53]225

STILES, ROBERT, *Major, USA;* ACW:JAN/92[22]341, ACW:SEP/95[62], B&G:AUG/92[11]493, CWTI:APR/92[49]260, GETTY:11[102]237

STILES, THOMAS T., *Private, 53rd Pennsylvania Infantry;* GETTY:11[80]235

STILLMAN, BENJAMIN H., *Private, 7th Wisconsin Infantry,* GETTY:11[57]233

STILLMAN, GEORGE L., *Lieutenant, Michigan Light Artillery;* B&G:AUG/95[8]604

STIMERS, ALBAN, *Lieutenant, USN;* AHI:NOV/75[38]163

STIVERS, JOSEPH, *Major, 14th Kentucky Infantry;* ACW:SEP/95[22]544

STOCK, CHRISTIAN, *Lieutenant, 1st New York Light Artillery;* GETTY:6[7]169

STOCKING, JOHN, *Master, USN;* CWM:JUL/93[15]484

STOCKTON, JOSEPH, *General, USA;* BOOK REVIEW: *WAR DIARY OF BREVET BRIGADIER GENERAL JOSEPH STOCKTON, FIRST LIEUTENANT, CAPTAIN, MAJOR AND LIEUTENANT COLONEL 72ND REGIMENT ILLINOIS INFANTRY VOLUNTEERS*

STOCKTON, ROBERT F., *Captain, USN;* ARTICLE: "THE *PRINCETON* EXPLOSION," AHI:AUG/69[5]123

STOCKTON, THOMAS B.W., *Colonel, 16th Michigan Infantry;* B&G:FEB/92[22]476, GETTY:6[33]172

STOCKTON, WILLIAM S., *Lieutenant, 71st Pennsylvania Infantry;* GETTY:7[97]193

STOCKWELL, ELISHA, *Private, 14th Wisconsin Infantry;* ACW:MAR/92[54], AHI:OCT/67[26]112, CWTI:DEC/89[26]135

STODDARD, AZRO, *Lieutenant, CSA;* ACW:NOV/93[8]438

STODDARD, E.M., *Master, USN* AHI:JAN/83[10]232

STODDARD, GEORGE G., *Lieutenant, USN;* CWR:VOL2#3[194]141

STODDARD, WILLIAM O.; CWTI:DEC/95[52]480

STODDER, L.N., *Master, USN;* CWM:JUL/93[15]484

STODDER, LOUIS N., *Lieutenant, USN;* AHI:NOV/75[38]163

STOECKL, EDOUARD DE, *Russian Minister to Washington;* CWTI:MAY/89[28]117

STOKE, FRANK, *Private, USA;* GETTY:11[102]237

STOKER, WILLIAM E., *Private, CSA;* ARTICLE: "EDITORIAL," ACW:MAY/92[6]356

STOKES, JAMES H., *Captain, Chicago Board of Trade Battery;* ACW:MAY/95[49]527

STOKES, WILLIAM, *Lieutenant Colonel, 4th South Carolian Cavalry;* BOOK REVIEW: *SADDLE SOLDIERS: THE CIVIL WAR CORRESPONDENCE OF GENERAL WILLIAM STOKES OF THE 4TH SOUTH CAROLINA CAVALRY*

STONE MOUNTAIN, GEORGIA; CWTI:SUMMER/89[20]121, CWTI:SUMMER/89[40]123

STONE, C.F., *Captain, USA;* GETTY:4[101]151

STONE, CHARLES P., *General, USA:*
ARTICLE: "GENERAL STONE'S SHAME," CWTI:MAY/89[21]115
GENERAL LISTINGS: AHI:JUN/70[30]127, AHI:FEB/82[36]225, CWR:VOL3#1[31]150, CWR:VOL4#2[26]166, CWTI:MAY/89[14]114, CWTI:JUL/94[20]390, GETTY:7[97]193, *photo,* CWTI:MAY/89[21]115

STONE, EDWARD; CWR:VOL3#1[78]152

STONE, GEORGE A., *Colonel, USA;* B&G:DEC/95[9]615

STONE, HENRY L., *Captain, USA;* B&G:DEC/93[49]547A, CWM:JAN/93[29]459

STONE, J.M., *Colonel, CSA;* CWR:VOL2#4[269]145

STONE, J., *Major, USA;* MH:JUN/91[20]152

STONE, JOHN M., *Lieutenant, 2nd Maryland Infantry;* GETTY:7[83]192

STONE, JOHN M., *Colonel, 2nd Mississippi Infantry:*
GENERAL LISTINGS: *Gettysburg,* GETTY:4[22]144, GETTY:5[4]156, GETTY:6[77]177, *order of battle,* B&G:APR/95[8]595
ADDITIONAL LISTINGS: B&G:JUN/95[8]600, CWR:VOL2#4[269]145, GETTY:4[126]154, GETTY:9[98]217

STONE, KATE; AHI:DEC/73[10]152

STONE, MARTIN, *Captain, 2nd Pennsylvania Cavalry;* GETTY:11[102]237

STONE, ORRIN B., *Private, 13th Pennsylvania Infantry;* CWR:VOL1#3[28]120

STONE, ROBERT, *Colonel, CSA;* CWR:VOL2#3[212]142, CWR:VOL4#2[118]169

STONE, ROY, *Colonel, 42nd Pennsylvania Infantry:*
GENERAL LISTINGS: *Gettysburg,* GETTY:4[33]146, GETTY:5[117]165, GETTY:8[9]199, GETTY:9[17]210, GETTY:9[53]214, GETTY:11[19]232, *in book review,* CWM:OCT/95[10], CWNEWS:APR/95[33], *order of battle,* B&G:APR/95[8]595, *Wilderness,* B&G:APR/95[8]595
ADDITIONAL LISTINGS: ACW:JAN/95[46]507, CWR:VOL1#3[20]119, CWR:VOL1#3[28]120, GETTY:13[33]255

STONE, SPENCER C., *Private, 2nd Tennessee Cavalry;* CWR:VOL4#1[1]163

STONE, WILLIAM F., *Private, 53rd Pennsylvania Infantry;* GETTY:11[80]235

STONE, WILLIAM H., *Colonel, USA;* B&G:AUG/95[8]604

STONE, WILLIAM M., *Captain, CSA;* GETTY:12[68]246

STONE, WILLIAM M., *General, USA;* ACW:JUL/94[51]480, B&G:FEB/94[8]550, CWR:VOL2#1[19]131

STONE, ZEKE, *scout;* ACW:MAR/94[8]456

STONEMAN'S CHANCELLORSVILLE RAID; ARTICLE: "FAILURE OR HARBINGER," CWM:APR/95[32]575

STONEMAN, GEORGE, *General, USA:*
ARTICLE: "FAILURE OR HARBINGER," CWM:APR/95[32]575
GENERAL LISTINGS: *Atlanta Campaign,* CWTI:NOV/92[41]291, *Gaines' Mill,* ACW:NOV/94[50]498, *general history,* AHI:MAY/71[3]133A, *in book review,* ACW:JAN/95[62], CWM:DEC/94[7], CWNEWS:NOV/89[4], CWNEWS:NOV/95[29], CWR:VOL4#2[136], *Kelly's Ford,* ACW:NOV/91[30]332, *letters to the editor,* B&G:APR/95[5]594, *photos,* CWM:DEC/94[7], CWM:APR/95[32]575, CWTI:MAR/95[46]437
ADDITIONAL LISTINGS: ACW:JAN/92[16]340, ACW:SEP/94[55]489, B&G:AUG/91[11]458, B&G:APR/92[28]482, B&G:APR/92[58]485, B&G:OCT/93[12]537, B&G:DEC/94[22]586, B&G:FEB/95[8]590B, CWM:JAN/91[12]326, CWM:MAY/92[8]418, CWR:VOL1#3[82]123, CWR:VOL2#2[156]138, CWTI:SUMMER/89[50]124, CWTI:DEC/90[18]180, CWTI:SEP/91[18]227, CWTI:SEP/91[23]228, CWTI:APR/92[35]257, CWTI:MAY/92[48]267, CWTI:JAN/93[49]303, GETTY:11[19]232

STONES RIVER NATIONAL BATTLEFIELD; B&G:OCT/92[10]496, CWM:JUL/91[35]369

STONES RIVER, TENNESSEE, BATTLE OF:
ARTICLES: "COMMANDS, THE 3RD MINNESOTA," ACW:MAY/91[12]302, "TENACITY OF SOLDIERS OF THE DEEP SOUTH AT MURFREESBORO," CWM:FEB/95[28]560
BOOK REVIEWS: *NO BETTER PLACE TO DIE: THE BATTLE OF STONES RIVER * PATHS TO VICTORY: A HISTORY AND TOUR GUIDE OF THE STONES RIVER, CHICKAMAUGA, CHATTANOOGA, KNOXVILLE AND NASHVILLE CAMPAIGNS * STONES RIVER: BLOODY WINTER IN TENNESSEE*
ADDITIONAL LISTINGS: ACW:MAR/91[54], ACW:JUL/91[12]310, ACW:JUL/94[58], ACW:NOV/94[76]500, ACW:NOV/95[66]559, AHI:MAY/71[3]133A, AHI:NOV/73[18]151, B&G:OCT/91[11]466, B&G:OCT/92[10]496, CWM:JAN/92[34]404, CWM:OCT/94[48]542, CWM:APR/95[16]571, CWM:OCT/95[22]614, CWR:VOL1#4[42]126, CWR:VOL4#1[1]163, CWR:VOL4#1[78], CWTI:JAN/95[27]425

STONEWALL BRIGADE:
BOOK REVIEWS: *FOUR YEARS IN THE STONEWALL BRIGADE * TED BARCLAY, LIBERTY HALL VOLUNTEERS: LETTERS FROM THE STONEWALL BRIGADE (1861-1864)*
GENERAL LISTINGS: *Gettysburg,* GETTY:4[65]148, GETTY:4[75]149, GETTY:6[7]169, GETTY:6[69]176, GETTY:7[83]192, GETTY:9[81]216, GETTY:12[42]244, *in book review,* CWNEWS:JUL/92[4], CWR:VOL2#4[346], *Jackson's funeral,* CWTI:MAY/89[22]116, *Jackson,* B&G:JUN/92[8]487, *Manassas, Second,* B&G:AUG/92[11]493, *Monocacy,* B&G:DEC/92[8]503, *Wilderness,* B&G:JUN/95[8]600
ADDITIONAL LISTINGS: ACW:JUL/91[18]312, ACW:NOV/91[41]334, ACW:MAY/92[14]358, ACW:JUL/92[30]369, ACW:NOV/92[42]388, ACW:JAN/93[35]396, ACW:JAN/95[46]507, ACW:JAN/95[54]508, B&G:JUN/92[8]487, CWM:JUL/91[48]374, CWM:MAY/92[20]420, CWM:JAN/93[16]457, CWM:SEP/93[24]495, CWTI:MAR/94[29]371, GETTY:4[65]148, GETTY:13[89]260

STOREY, J.H.R., *Sergeant, 109th Pennsylvania Infantry;* CWR:VOL3#2[70]155

STOREY, MOORFIELD; BOOK REVIEW: *MOORFIELD STOREY AND THE ABOLITIONIST TRADITION,* AHI:DEC/72[49]

STOREY, RICHARD L., *Colonel, CSA;* CWTI:DEC/94[49]413

STORICK, ADAM, *civilian;* GETTY:4[65]148

STORKE, CHARLES A., *Colonel, 36th Wisconsin Infantry;* B&G:APR/94[59]565

STOTLER, PETER P., *31st Ohio Infantry;* B&G:FEB/94[38]553

STOUGH, ISRAEL, *Colonel, 153rd Ohio National Guard;* B&G:AUG/94[10]574

STOUGHTON, EDWIN H., *General, USA:*
ARTICLE: "HOW TO STEAL A GENERAL," CWTI:DEC/91[22]237
GENERAL LISTINGS: *general history,* AHI:MAY/71[3]133A, *in book review,* ACW:MAY/91[54], B&G:FEB/92[26]
ADDITIONAL LISTINGS: ACW:JAN/94[8]447, CWR:VOL1#3[28]120, CWTI:SEP/90[34]176, CWTI:JUL/92[12]270, MH:OCT/92[51]162

STOUGHTON, HOMER; CWTI:JUL/93[42]329

STOUT, SAMUEL H., *Surgeon, CSA;* BOOK REVIEWS: *CONFEDERATE HOSPITALS ON THE MOVE: SAMUEL H. STOUT AND THE ARMY OF TENNESSEE*

STOUT, WILLIAM L., *Lieutenant, 27th Illinois Infantry;* CWR:VOL3#4[24]162

STOVALL, MARCELLUS A., *General, CSA;* B&G:DEC/93[12]545, B&G:AUG/95[8]604, CWTI:SEP/92[28]280, CWTI:NOV/92[41]291, CWTI:DEC/94[49]413

STOWE, HARRIET BEECHER:
GENERAL LISTINGS: *Bloody Kansas,* AHI:JUL/75[4]160, *in book review,* CWM:AUG/94[9]
ADDITIONAL LISTINGS: AHI:JUN/73[4]149, CWM:MAY/92[15]419, CWM:SEP/93[18]494

STOWE, JOHN, *Private, 9th Massachusetts Light Artillery;* GETTY:5[47]160

STOWE, JONATHAN P., *Sergeant, 125th Pennsylvania Infantry;* B&G:OCT/95[8]611A

STOWE, W.A., *Colonel, 16th North Carolina Infantry;* B&G:APR/93[12]518

STOWERS, GEORGE E., *Surgeon;* ACW:MAR/93[51]407

STRACHAN, ROBERT, *Private, 5th New York Infantry;* CWR:VOL1#2[7]111, CWR:VOL1#2[29]112, CWTI:MAY/94[31]382

STRAHL, OTHO, *General, CSA;* ACW:SEP/92[38]379, B&G:OCT/91[11]466, CWR:VOL1#3[7]118, CWR:VOL1#4[42]126

STRANGE, JOHN B., *Lieutenant Colonel, CSA;* CWTI:JUL/94[44]394, GETTY:13[75]259

STRATEGY, CONFEDERATE; BOOK REVIEW: *CIVIL WAR COMMAND AND STRATEGY: THE PROCESS OF VICTORY AND DEFEAT * THE CONFEDERATE HIGH COMMAND AND RELATED TOPICS*

STRATFORD, RICHARD, *Sergeant, 1st Pennsylvania Artillery;* GETTY:12[30]243

STRATTON, AZARIAH, *Corporal, 12th New Jersey Infantry;* GETTY:5[89]162

STRATTON, ISAAC, *Sergeant, 7th Ohio Infantry;* GETTY:9[81]216

STRATTON, W.H.H., *Private, 12th New Jersey Infantry;* GETTY:5[89]162

STRECHABOCK, JOHN, *Sergeant, 116th Pennsylvania Infantry;* CWR:VOL4#4[47]179

STREETER, EDWIN, *Corporal, 20th Wisconsin Infantry;* CWR:VOL1#1[42]105

STREIGHT'S RAID:
BOOK REVIEW: *MOUNTED RAIDS OF THE CIVIL WAR*
ADDITIONAL LISTINGS: CWM:OCT/94[48]542, CWTI:MAY/92[48]267, CWTI:JAN/94[35]361

STREIGHT, ABEL D., *General, USA:*
BOOK REVIEW: *MOUNTED RAIDS OF THE CIVIL WAR*
GENERAL LISTINGS: *Female spy,* AHI:DEC/73[10]152, *in book review,* CWM:DEC/94[7], CWNEWS:NOV/95[29], *order of battle,* B&G:DEC/93[12]545, *photos,* CWTI:NOV/93[33]347
ADDITIONAL LISTINGS: ACW:JUL/91[8]309, B&G:JUN/93[12]524, B&G:OCT/94[11]580, CWM:OCT/94[48]542, CWTI:SEP/91[23]228, CWTI:MAY/92[48]267, CWTI:NOV/93[33]347, CWTI:JAN/94[35]361

STRIBLING, JOHN M., *Lieutenant, CSN;* AHI:DEC/82[38]231

STRICKLAND, FRANCIS, *Sergeant, 154th New York Infantry;* GETTY:8[17]200

STRICKLAND, T.J., *Private, 51st North Carolina Infantry;* B&G:APR/93[24]520

STRICKLAND, WILLIAM, *Private, 53rd Pennsylvania Infantry;* GETTY:11[80]235

STRICKLER, W.R., *Private, 125th Pennsylvania Infantry;* B&G:OCT/95[8]611A

STRINE, ROBERT P., *Corporal, 53rd Pennsylvania Infantry;* GETTY:11[80]235

STRINGFELLOW, FRANK, *Scout, CSA;* B&G:APR/91[8]445

STRINGHAM, SILAS H.; ACW: MAR/94[35]460, ACW:SEP/94[46]488

STRONG, DANIEL G., *Chaplain, 4th Ohio Infantry;* GETTY:10[53]225

STRONG, GEORGE C., *General, USA;* ACW:SEP/91[30]322, B&G:DEC/91[12]469, B&G:AUG/93[36]533, CWTI:DEC/89[42]137, CWTI:MAR/94[38]372

STRONG, GEORGE TEMPLETON:
GENERAL LISTINGS: *editorial,* ACW:MAR/91[6]290, *in book review,* B&G:JUN/95[30], *photo,* CWTI:SEP/90[48]178
ADDITIONAL LISTINGS: ACW:MAY/93[38]416, CWTI:AUG/90[26]166

STRONG, HENRY B., *Colonel, 6th Louisiana Infantry;* ACW:JUL/92[30]369, B&G:OCT/95[8]611A, CWM:SEP/93[24]495

STRONG, JAMES, *Lieutenant, USA;* GETTY:9[48]213

STRONG, LORENZO, *Private, 9th New York Cavalry;* AHI:AUG/68[4]115B

STRONG, ROBERT, *Private, 105th Illinois Infantry;* CWTI:NOV/92[41]291

STRONG, WILLIAM E., *Lieutenant Colonel, USA;* CWTI:SUMMER/89[40]123

STROTHER, DAVID H., *Colonel, USA:*
ARTICLE: "EYEWITNESS NEWS," CWM:NOV/92[10]447
ADDITIONAL LISTINGS: ACW:JAN/91[38]287, B&G:AUG/92[11]493, CWM:NOV/92[10]447, CWR:VOL4#3[89]

STROTHER, JOSEPHUS E., *Private, Sumter Artillery;* CWR:VOL3#2[1]153

STROUSE, THOMAS, *Private, 8th New York Cavalry;* CWM:MAY/92[8]418

STRUTHERS, JEANNIE G.; CWTI:MAR/93[12]307

STUART BIRTHPLACE PRESERVATION TRUST; B&G:APR/92[36]483, CWM:JAN/91[35]328, CWM:NOV/91[35]392

STUART HORSE ARTILLERY:
ARTICLE: "ROBERT F. BECKHAM: THE MAN WHO COMMANDED STUART'S HORSE ARTILLERY AFTER PELHAM FELL," B&G:DEC/91[34]470
ADDITIONAL LISTINGS: ACW:NOV/91[30]332, ACW:NOV/91[35]333, CWM:NOV/91[66]395, ACW:MAR/94[50]462, CWM:NOV/91[66]395, CWR:VOL4#4[70]180, CWTI:NOV/93[24]346

STUART'S CHAMBERSBURG RAID; CWM:DEC/94[7]

STUART'S FIRST RIDE AROUND MCCLELLAN; ARTICLE: "THE PENINSULA CAMPAIGN OF 1862: STUART'S RIDE AROUND MCCLELLAN," CWM:JUN/95[50]589

STUART, CHARLES, *Captain, 5th Tennessee Mounted Infantry;* CWTI:MAY/93[8]315

STUART, CHARLES B., *Colonel, 50th New York Engineers;* ACW:NOV/95[10]553

STUART, DAVID, *Colonel, USA;* CWR:VOL2#1[69]133, CWTI:JUL/92[42]274

STUART, FLORA; ACW:MAY/94[35]469

STUART, JAMES, *Captain, 4th U.S. Artillery;* GETTY:11[57]233

STUART, JAMES E.B., *General, CSA:*
ARTICLES: "THE BATTLE OF BRANDY STATION," CWTI:JUN/90[32]159, "BEAUTY, SALLIE AND FATE," ACW:NOV/91[35]333, "COMMAND SHIFT DICTATED," MH:JUN/92[50]159, "FORGOTTEN FIELD: THE CAVALRY BATTLE EAST OF GETTYSBURG ON JULY 3, 1963," GETTY:4[75]149, "JEB STUART AND HIS RELUCTANT CAVALRYMAN," B&G:OCT/92[38]500, "JEB STUART'S DARING RECONNAISSANCE," ACW:JUL/95[34]536, "JEB STUART'S LAST RIDE," ACW:MAY/94[35]469, "LEE'S LIEUTENANT: J.E.B. STUART," CWM:JUL/92[16]428, "LETTERS TO LAURA," CWTI:JUL/92[12]270, "MELEE ON SAINT PATRICK'S DAY," ACW:NOV/91[30]332, "PELL-MELL CAVALRY CHASE," ACW:JUL/92[41]370, "THE PENINSULA CAMPAIGN OF 1862: STUART'S RIDE AROUND MCCLELLAN," CWM:JUN/95[50]589, "THE REAL J.E.B. STUART," CWTI:DEC/89[34]136, "SHELLS AND SABER POINTS," MH:OCT/92[51]162, "STUART'S REVENGE," CWTI:JUN/95[38]447, "THE LOST HOURS OF "JEB" STUART," GETTY:4[65]148, "TIME LAPSE," CWTI:APR/89[50]112
BOOK REVIEWS: *BOLD DRAGOON: THE LIFE OF J.E.B. STUART * I ROAD WITH JEB STUART: THE LIFE AND CAMPAIGNS OF MAJOR GENERAL J.E.B. STUART * JEB STUART * THE LETTERS OF MAJOR GENERAL JAMES E.B. STUART * RIDING WITH STUART: REMINISCENCES*

OF AN AIDE-DE-CAMP * SABER AND SCAPEGOAT: J.E.B.
STUART AND THE GETTYSBURG CONTROVERSY *
THEY FOLLOWED THE PLUME: THE STORY OF J.E.B.
STUART AND HIS STAFF * WAR YEARS WITH JEB
STUART * STUART

GENERAL LISTINGS: *Aldie,* B&G:OCT/93[12]537, GETTY:11[19]232,
Antietam, ACW:JUL/92[30]369, ACW:JUL/93[10]421, *Brandy
Station,* CWM:JAN/92[44]406, GETTY:8[111]206,
GETTY:11[19]232, *Chancellorsville,* ACW:SEP/93[31]433,
ACW:JAN/95[46]507, CWTI:AUG/95[24]455, *Crampton's Gap,*
ACW:JAN/94[39]451, *first ride around McClellan,*
ACW:JUL/95[34]536, *Falling Waters,* GETTY:9[109]218,
Fredericksburg, CWR:VOL4#4[70]180, *general history,*
AHI:MAY/71[3]133A

GENERAL LISTINGS, continued: *Gettysburg,* ACW:MAY/93[14]413,
B&G:APR/91[39]449, B&G:OCT/91[11]466,
CWM:JAN/93[8]456, GETTY:4[101]151, GETTY:4[110]152,
GETTY:4[113]153, GETTY:5[4]156, GETTY:5[35]159,
GETTY:5[103]163, GETTY:6[113]183, GETTY:7[124]196,
GETTY:9[17]210, GETTY:9[53]214, GETTY:9[61]215,
GETTY:10[42]224, GETTY:11[19]232, GETTY:11[71]234,
GETTY:11[80]235, GETTY:12[42]244, GETTY:12[111]250,
MH:AUG/94[46]178, *Harpers Ferry Raid, 1859,*
AHI:MAR/84[10]236, CWTI:JAN/95[24]424, *in book review,*
ACW:MAY/91[54], ACW:MAY/94[58], ACW:SEP/94[66],
CWM:MAR/91[74], CWM:DEC/94[7], CWM:APR/95[8],
CWM:APR/95[50], CWM:AUG/95[8],
CWM:AUG/95[45],CWM:FEB/95[7], CWNEWS:JAN/91[4],
CWNEWS:APR/91[4], CWNEWS:NOV/91[4],
CWNEWS:JUN/93[5], CWNEWS:OCT/93[5],
CWNEWS:NOV/95[29], CWR:VOL1#3[94],
CWR:VOL4#3[1]170, CWTI:SEP/92[18], MH:DEC/94[70]

GENERAL LISTINGS, continued: *Indian wars,* AHI:OCT/79[20]194,
J.E.B. Stuart Birthplace Preservation Trust, Inc.;
CWM:JAN/91[35]328, CWM:NOV/91[35]392, *John Brown,*
AHI:AUG/76[34]171, AHI:JAN/86[10]256,
CWTI:JUL/92[20]271, *letters to the editor,*
CWM:JAN/91[6]324, CWM:NOV/92[6]446,
CWM:OCT/95[5]613, CWTI:MAY/91[8]205, *Manassas, First,*
CWTI:APR/92[35]257, *Manassas, Second,*
ACW:JUL/91[18]312, B&G:AUG/92[11]493, *order of battle,*
B&G:APR/95[8]595, *Overland Campaign,*
B&G:APR/94[10]558, *Peninsula Campaign,*
ACW:MAR/91[47]297, CWM:JUN/95[50]589,
CWM:JUN/95[53]590, CWTI:JAN/94[20]358, *Thomas J.
Jackson,* AHI:JUN/67[31]110, *West Point,*
B&G:DEC/91[12]469, *Wilderness,* B&G:APR/95[8]595,
B&G:JUN/95[8]600, *in painting;* ACW:JAN/91[38]287,
CWM:JUL/92[16]428, *painting at Battle Abbey;*
CWTI:DEC/89[34]136, *photos,* AHI:MAY/71[3]133A,
AHI:AUG/76[34]171, B&G:AUG/91[11]458,
B&G:DEC/91[34]470, B&G:AUG/92[11]493,
B&G:OCT/92[38]500, B&G:OCT/93[12]537,
CWM:JAN/91[35]328, CWTI:DEC/89[34]136,
CWTI:JUN/90[32]159, CWTI:JUN/95[38]447,
MH:JUN/92[50]159

ADDITIONAL LISTINGS, ACW: ACW:JAN/91[38]287,
ACW:MAR/91[30]295, ACW:SEP/91[62]326,
ACW:NOV/91[41]334, ACW:NOV/92[26]386,
ACW:MAR/93[10]402, ACW:MAR/93[26]404,
ACW:MAY/93[62]418, ACW:JAN/94[6]446,
ACW:MAR/94[27]459, ACW:MAR/94[50]462,
ACW:JUL/94[26]477, ACW:JUL/94[35]478,

ACW:SEP/94[55]489, ACW:NOV/94[50]498,
ACW:JAN/95[10]503, ACW:JAN/95[54]508,
ACW:MAR/95[26]515, ACW:SEP/95[10]543

ADDITIONAL LISTINGS, AHI: AHI:APR/85[18]250

ADDITIONAL LISTINGS, B&G: B&G:APR/91[8]445,
B&G:AUG/91[36]462, B&G:DEC/91[34]470,
B&G:APR/92[36]483, B&G:FEB/93[24]512,
B&G:JUN/93[40]527, B&G:OCT/93[49]543,
B&G:JUN/94[22]569, B&G:FEB/95[8]590B,
B&G:AUG/95[32]606, B&G:DEC/95[25]616

ADDITIONAL LISTINGS, CWM: CWM:JAN/91[35]328,
CWM:JUL/91[43]369, CWM:NOV/91[58]394A,
CWM:MAY/92[8]418, CWM:JUL/92[18]429,
CWM:JUL/92[64]434, CWM:MAR/93[24]467,
CWM:MAR/93[32]468, CWM:SEP/93[18]494,
CWM:JUN/94[14]509, CWM:OCT/94[17]534,
CWM:DEC/94[26]548, CWM:AUG/95[17]603,
CWM:AUG/95[30]606, CWM:DEC/95[41]630

ADDITIONAL LISTINGS, CWR: CWR:VOL1#3[20]119,
CWR:VOL1#3[28]120, CWR:VOL1#3[v]117,
CWR:VOL1#3[52]122, CWR:VOL1#4[7]125,
CWR:VOL3#2[1]153, CWR:VOL4#4[28]178

ADDITIONAL LISTINGS, CWTI: CWTI:APR/89[14]107,
CWTI:JUN/90[28]158, CWTI:SEP/90[34]176,
CWTI:MAR/91[12]198, CWTI:DEC/91[18]236,
CWTI:DEC/91[22]237, CWTI:JUL/93[29]326,
CWTI:NOV/93[24]346, CWTI:NOV/93[55]350,
CWTI:MAR/94[67]377, CWTI:DEC/94[73]416,
CWTI:JUN/95[18]444

ADDITIONAL LISTINGS, GETTY: GETTY:13[1]252, GETTY:13[7]253,
GETTY:13[89]260, GETTY:13[108]261

ADDITIONAL LISTINGS, MH: MH:FEB/91[8]151, MH:FEB/92[8]156,
MH:FEB/93[42]164, MH:JUN/94[8]177

STUART, JOHN T.; AHI:JAN/71[12]131

STUART, SAMUEL, *Private, 46th Indiana Infantry;*
AHI:DEC/71[10]137

STUART, WILLIAM D., *Colonel, 56th Virginia Infantry;*
ACW:MAR/93[10]402, GETTY:5[107]164

STUCKENBERG, JOHN H.W., *Chaplain, 145th Pennsylvania
Infantry:*

BOOK REVIEW: *I'M SURROUNDED BY METHODISTS...: DIARY
OF JOHN H.W. STUCKENBERG, CHAPLAIN OF THE
145TH PENNSYLVANIA VOLUNTEER INFANTRY*

ADDITIONAL LISTING: GETTY:11[102]237

STUDENT UNREST; ARTICLE: "ROWDIES, RIOTS, AND
REBELLIONS," AHI:JUN/72[18]139

STURDEVANT, JAMES K., *8th Iowa Infantry;*
B&G:DEC/93[30]546

STURGES, OSCAR, *Private, 5th New York Infantry;*
CWR:VOL1#2[29]112

STURGESS, R.H., *Colonel, 8th Illinois Infantry;*
B&G:FEB/94[8]550

STURGIS, SAMUEL, *General, USA: Antietam,*
CWTI:FEB/92[36]249, *Brice's Cross Roads,*
B&G:AUG/94[38]578, *Custer,* AHI:JUN/76[4]169, *General
History,* AHI:MAY/71[3]133A, *in book review,*
ACW:JAN/95[62], CWM:OCT/94[8], CWM:FEB/95[7],
CWNEWS:JAN/94[5], CWNEWS:SEP/94[33],
CWR:VOL4#2[136], *post war,* AHI:NOV/79[32]196, *Wilson's
Creek,* CWTI:FEB/92[29]248, *photos,* CWM:MAY/93[8]474,
CWTI:FEB/92[29]248, CWTI:JAN/94[35]361

ADDITIONAL LISTINGS: ACW:JAN/91[16]284, ACW:JUL/91[18]312,
ACW:MAR/92[46]354, ACW:SEP/92[23]377,

ACW:NOV/93[26]441, ACW:MAY/95[18]524,
CWM:MAY/93[8]474, CWTI:MAY/92[48]267,
CWTI:JAN/94[35]361, MH:APR/92[18]157,
MH:FEB/95[18]182, MH:DEC/95[58]188
STUYVESANT, MOSES, *Gunner, USN;* AHI:OCT/75[30]162
STYLES, GEORGE, *Sergeant, USA;* GETTY:11[91]236
STYLES, WILLIAM, *Lieutenant, 7th Illinois Cavalry;*
B&G:JUN/93[12]524
SUDDATH, JAMES B., *Sergeant, 7th South Carolina Infantry;*
GETTY:5[35]159
SUDSBURG, JOSEPH M., *Colonel, 3rd Maryland Infantry;*
B&G:APR/94[10]558, B&G:JUN/95[8]600
"SUE MUNDY", ARTICLE: "WAS ROME CLARKE REALLY 'SUE
MUNDY'—OR MERELY THE VICTIM OF AN EDITOR'S
DEADLY PRANK?" ACW:JAN/94[10]448
SUFFOLK, VIRGINIA, CAMPAIGN:
BOOK REVIEWS: *THE SIEGE OF SUFFOLK: THE FORGOTTEN
CAMPAIGN, APRIL 11-MAY 4, 1863*
ADDITIONAL LISTINGS: CWR:VOL3#2[1]153,
CWTI:SEPT/89[74]132A
SUGGETT, THOMAS, *Captain, 24th Michigan Infantry;*
GETTY:5[19]158
SUGGS, CYRUS A., *Colonel, CSA;* CWTI:SEP/92[31]281
SULAKOWSKI, VALERY, *Colonel, 14th Louisiana Infantry;*
CWM:SEP/93[24]495, GETTY:13[64]258
SULLIVAN, ALGERNON S., *Attorney;* ACW:SEP/94[46]488
SULLIVAN, CARY, *Private, 76th New York Infantry;*
CWM:JAN/92[16]401
SULLIVAN, JAMES P., *Sergeant, 6th Wisconsin Infantry:*
BOOK REVIEWS: *AN IRISHMAN IN THE IRON BRIGADE: THE
CIVIL WAR MEMOIRS OF JAMES P. SULLIVAN,
SERGEANT, 6TH WISCONSIN VOLUNTEERS*
ADDITIONAL LISTINGS: *Gettysburg,* GETTY:4[24]145, *in book review,*
CWR:VOL1#2[78]
SULLIVAN, JEREMIAH C., *General, USA;*
ACW:SEP/91[46]324, CWM:DEC/95[48]631,
CWTI:NOV/93[33]347, CWTI:JUL/94[50]395
SULLIVAN, TIMOTHY, *Colonel, USA;* B&G:AUG/92[11]493
SULLY, ALFRED, *Colonel, USA:*
GENERAL LISTINGS: *Gettysburg,* GETTY:5[79]161, *Indian Wars,*
AHI:OCT/79[20]194, *in book review,* CWM:OCT/95[10]
**SULPHUR BRANCH TRESTLE, ALABAMA, SKIRMISH
AT;** ARTICLE: "TWO CORPORALS: A TALE OF NATHAN
BEDFORD FORREST'S ATTACK AT SULPHUR BRANCH
TRESTLE, ALABAMA," B&G:JUN/92[32]488
SULTANA **DISASTER:**
ARTICLES: "THE CRIPPLING OF THE *SULTANA:* THE REAL
PICTURE," B&G:AUG/95[24]605, "DISASTER ON THE
MISSISSIPPI! THE *SULTANA* GOES DOWN,"
CWM:MAY/93[32]477, "STEAMER *SULTANA*
MEMORIALIZED," AHI:NOV/89[20]287
BOOK REVIEWS: *CAHABA PRISON AND THE SULTANA
DISASTER * THE SULTANA TRAGEDY: AMERICA'S
GREATEST MARITIME DISASTER*
GENERAL LISTINGS: *in book review,* CWNEWS:MAY/91[4],
CWTI:APR/90[10], *letters to the editor,* B&G:OCT/95[5]610,
photos, B&G:AUG/95[24]605, CWTI:AUG/90[50]168
ADDITIONAL LISTINGS: B&G:JUN/92[32]488, CWTI:AUG/90[42]167,
CWTI:AUG/90[50]168
SUMMERHAYES, JOHN, *Major, 20th Massachusetts Infantry;*
CWR:VOL4#4[101]181

SUMMERS-KOONTZ INCIDENT; ARTICLE: "A MATTER OF
INJUSTICE: THE SUMMERS-KOONTZ INCIDENT,"
B&G:FEB/92[32]477
SUMMERS, GEORGE W., *Captain, 7th Virginia Cavalry:*
ARTICLE: "A MATTER OF INJUSTICE: THE
SUMMERS-KOONTZ INCIDENT," B&G:FEB/92[32]477
ADDITIONAL LISTING: B&G:JUN/92[6]486
SUMMERS, SAMUEL W., *Colonel, 7th Iowa Cavalry:*
ARTICLE: "SOUTHERN-BORN UNION COLONEL,"
CWTI:MAY/94[82]387
ADDITIONAL LISTING: CWTI:SEP/94[12]398
SUMNER, CHARLES:
BOOK REVIEW: *THE SELECTED LETTERS OF CHARLES
SUMNER*
GENERAL LISTINGS: *in book review,* ACW:MAY/93[54], *Mary Todd
Lincoln,* AHI:MAY/75[4]159, *Thaddeus Stevens,*
AHI:JAN/82[16]224, *photo,* CWTI:AUG/95[54]460
ADDITIONAL LISTINGS: ACW:MAR/91[30]295, AHI:JAN/73[28]147,
AHI:JAN/83[10]232, CWM:FEB/95[68]567,
CWR:VOL3#1[31]150, CWTI:MAY/89[21]115,
CWTI:SEP/92[46]284, CWTI:JUL/93[38]328,
CWTI:AUG/95[54]460, CWTI:DEC/95[52]480,
CWTI:DEC/95[76]482
SUMNER, EDWIN V., *General, USA:*
ARTICLE: "BLOOD POURED LIKE WATER,"
ACW:MAR/94[50]462
GENERAL LISTINGS: *Antietam,* B&G:OCT/95[8]611A,
CWTI:SEP/93[43]338, GETTY:11[71]234, *Chantilly,*
ACW:JAN/95[54]508, *Fredericksburg,* AHI:JUN/78[4]180,
CWR:VOL4#4[70]180, *in book review,* CWM:FEB/95[7],
CWR:VOL4#3[89] *Indian wars,* AHI:OCT/79[20]194,
Peninsula Campaign, CWM:JUN/95[34]584, *Savage's Station,*
CWM:JUN/95[65]595, *Seven Pines,* CWM:JUN/95[47]588,
Simon Cameron, CWTI:JUN/90[46]161, *Williamsburg,*
ACW:MAR/91[47]297, *photo,* B&G:OCT/95[8]611A
ADDITIONAL LISTINGS: ACW:MAR/94[50]462, ACW:MAR/95[70]520,
ACW:SEP/95[54]548, AHI:AUG/72[24]140,
B&G:FEB/95[8]590B, CWM:JUL/92[18]429,
CWR:VOL2#4[269]145, CWR:VOL3#1[31]150,
CWR:VOL3#2[1]153, CWR:VOL4#4[i]175,
CWR:VOL4#4[v]176, CWR:VOL4#4[101]181,
CWTI:JAN/95[34]427
SUMTER ARTILLERY BATTALION, GETTY:4[49]147,
GETTY:5[89]162
SUMTER-PICKENS PLAN; CWTI:JAN/93[10]297
SUNDLEY, DAVID R., *Colonel, 31st Alabama Infantry;*
B&G:FEB/94[8]550
SUNSHINE CHURCH, GEORGIA, BATTLE OF;
B&G:FEB/95[8]590B, CWTI:SUMMER/89[50]124
SUNSTROM, MARK, *Lieutenant, USN;* AHI:NOV/75[38]163,
CWM:JUL/93[15]484
SUPLEE, ANDREW C., *Captain, 72nd Pennsylvania Infantry;*
GETTY:5[89]162
SUPPLIES; BOOK REVIEW: *THE HISTORICAL SUPPLY
CATALOG*
SURBY, RICHARD W., *Sergeant, 7th Illinois Cavalry;*
ACW:MAY/92[47]363, B&G:JUN/93[12]524
SURGET, EUSTACE, *Major, CSA;* CWR:VOL4#2[118]169
SURRATT, JOHN H.; ACW:MAY/92[14]358,
AHI:FEB/86[12]257, CWTI:DEC/91[28]239,
CWTI:JUN/95[26]445, CWTI:DEC/95[76]482
SURRATT, MARY E.:
ARTICLE: "SURRATT MUSEUM," AHI:SUM/88[10]272

ADDITIONAL LISTINGS: B&G:DEC/92[40]508, B&G:JUN/93[40]527, CWTI:APR/90[12]150, CWTI:AUG/90[8]165, CWTI:DEC/91[28]239, CWTI:MAY/92[8]261, CWTI:JAN/93[8]296, CWTI:SEP/94[24]399, CWTI:DEC/95[90]483, *photo*, CWTI:DEC/91[28]239

SUTHERLAND'S STATION, VIRGINIA, BATTLE OF; CWTI:AUG/90[26]166

SUTHERLAND, SAMUEL, *civilian;* ACW:JAN/94[18]449

SUTTON, JAMES S., *Lieutenant Colonel, CSA;* CWTI:OCT/95[56]471

SUTTON, JOHN S., *Lieutenant Colonel, 7th Texas Mounted Volunteers;* B&G:JUN/94[8]568

SUTTON, JOSEPH J., *Private, 91st Ohio Infantry;* CWTI:MAR/89[16]101

SWAFFORD, THOMAS A., *Private, 2nd Tennessee Cavalry;* CWR:VOL4#1[1]163

SWAIN, JULIUS, *Lieutenant, USA;* GETTY:4[101]151

SWAIN, LUCIEN, *Corporal, 5th New York Infantry;* CWR:VOL1#2[29]112

SWAIN, M.S., *Colonel, CSA;* AHI:JUN/70[30]127

SWAIN, WILMON W., *Lieutenant, 8th Ohio Cavalry;* B&G:OCT/94[28]581

"SWAMP ANGEL":
ARTICLE: "SWAMP ANGEL'S REIGN OF TERROR," CWM:MAR/92[16]411

ADDITIONAL LISTINGS: CWM:JAN/93[35]460, CWTI:APR/89[22]108

SWAN, HENRY R., *Lieutenant, 8th New York Heavy Artillery;* B&G:APR/94[55]564, CWR:VOL3#4[1]161

SWAN, WILLIAM, *Lieutenant Colonel, USA;* B&G:APR/95[8]595

SWANSON, WILLIAM G., *Colonel, 61st Alabama Infantry;* B&G:APR/95[8]595

SWAP, ANDREW, *Corporal, 37th Illinois Infantry;* CWR:VOL1#1[42]105

SWARTWOUT, HENRY A., *Captain, 5th New York Infantry;* CWR:VOL1#2[7]111

SWAYER, FRANKLIN, *Lieutenant Colonel, 8th Ohio Infantry;* GETTY:8[95]205

SWEANEY, JOHN R., *Lieutenant, Pettus Flying Artillery;* B&G:FEB/94[8]550

SWEENY, THOMAS W., *General, USA:*
GENERAL LISTINGS: *in book review*, CWNEWS:JUL/92[4], *post war,* AHI:AUG/78[33]184, *photo*, AHI:AUG/78[33]184

ADDITIONAL LISTINGS: ACW:SEP/91[46]324, ACW:NOV/93[26]441, ACW:JUL/94[66]481, B&G:AUG/93[36]533, CWM:MAY/93[8]474, CWTI:SUMMER/89[40]123, CWTI:FEB/92[29]248, CWTI:NOV/92[41]291, CWTI:MAR/95[40]436

SWEET, H.W.S., *Captain, 146th New York Infantry;* B&G:APR/95[8]595

SWEETAPPLE, J., *Private, 95th Illinois Infantry;* ACW:JAN/91[16]284

SWEITZER, JACOB B., *Colonel, USA:*
GENERAL LISTINGS: *Gettysburg,* GETTY:6[7]169, GETTY:8[53]203, GETTY:9[41]212, GETTY:9[53]214, GETTY:10[120]229, GETTY:11[91]236, *in order of battle,* B&G:APR/94[10]558, B&G:APR/95[8]595

ADDITIONAL LISTING: B&G:APR/93[12]518

SWETT, LEONARD, *civilian;* CWTI:JAN/93[10]297

SWILLING, JACK, *Lieutenant, CSA;* ACW:JUL/92[46]371, ACW:JUL/93[27]423

SWINTON, WILLIAM, *reporter;* ACW:JAN/93[58]399, ACW:MAY/93[31]415, CWTI:OCT/95[48]470, GETTY:4[113]153

SWITZER, JACOB, *Private, 22nd Iowa Infantry;* CWR:VOL2#1[19]131

SYKES, W.L., *Lieutenant Colonel, 5th Mississippi Infantry;* CWR:VOL1#4[42]126

SYKES, GEORGE, *General, USA:*
ARTICLES: "GEORGE J. GROSS ON HALLOWED GROUND," GETTY:10[112]228, "REGULARS TO THE RESCUE AT GAINES' MILL," ACW:NOV/94[50]498

BOOK REVIEWS: *SYKES' REGULAR INFANTRY DIVISION 1861-1864: A HISTORY OF REGULAR UNITED STATES INFANTRY OPERATIONS IN THE CIVIL WAR'S EASTERN THEATRE*

GENERAL LISTINGS: *Antietam,* B&G:OCT/95[8]611F, *Gaines' Mill,* CWM:JUN/95[61]593, *Gettysburg,* ACW:JAN/92[38]343, GETTY:4[101]151, GETTY:6[33]172, GETTY:6[43]173, GETTY:6[59]174, GETTY:7[29]188, GETTY:7[41]189, GETTY:8[31]201, GETTY:8[53]203, GETTY:9[17]210, GETTY:9[41]212, GETTY:9[48]213, GETTY:9[53]214, GETTY:11[71]234, GETTY:11[80]235, GETTY:12[7]241, *Manassas, 2nd,* B&G:AUG/92[11]493, *Mexican War,* MH:APR/93[39]166, *photos,* CWM:AUG/95[27]605, GETTY:10[112]228

ADDITIONAL LISTINGS: ACW:JUL/93[50]426, B&G:APR/91[8]445, CWM:MAR/93[24]467, CWM:AUG/95[27]605, CWR:VOL1#2[7]111, CWR:VOL2#2[95]135, CWR:VOL3#3[1]157, CWTI:APR/89[14]107, CWTI:APR/92[14]254, CWTI:MAY/94[31]382

SYMINGTON, W. STUART, *Lieutenant, CSA:*
ARTICLE: "THE UNMERITED CENSURE OF TWO MARYLAND STAFF OFFICERS, MAJOR OSMUN LATROBE AND FIRST LIEUTENANT W. STUART SYMINGTON," GETTY:13[75]259

ADDITIONAL LISTINGS: GETTY:13[1]252, GETTY:13[75]259, *photo,* GETTY:13[75]259

SYRACUSE (KANSAS) COMPANY; ACW:NOV/94[42]497

SYRACUSE UNION ANTI-SLAVERY SOCIETY; ACW:NOV/94[42]497

SZINK, JACOB, *Lieutenant Colonel, 125th Pennsylvania Infantry;* B&G:OCT/95[8]611A

T

TACTICS; BOOK REVIEWS: *BATTLE TACTICS OF THE CIVIL WAR * UNITED STATES INFANTRY AND RIFLE TACTICS*
TAFT, CHARLES S., *Surgeon, USA*; ACW:MAY/95[68]529, B&G:DEC/95[44]617
TAFT, EDWARD P., *Major, USA*; B&G:DEC/92[8]503
TAFT, ELIJAH D., *Captain, 5th New York Artillery*; GETTY:5[47]160
TAGGERT, ROBERT, *Lieutenant, 9th Pennsylvania Reserves*; CWR:VOL4#4[1]177
TAIT, ROBERT, *Sergeant, 53rd Pennsylvania Infantry*; GETTY:11[80]235
TAKATS, FRANCIS, *Captain, 39th New York Infantry*; ACW:MAY/95[54]528
TALADRID, DAMASIO, *Chaplain, 1st New Mexico Cavalry*; CWM:MAR/91[50]340
TALBOTT, EDWARD, *Captain, 123rd Illinois Infantry*; ACW:MAY/95[49]527
TALCOTT, T.M.R., *Colonel, CSA*; ACW:JAN/93[43]397
TALIAFERRO, A.G., *Colonel, CSA*; CWM:JAN/93[16]457
TALIAFERRO, WILLIAM B., *General, CSA*:
ARTICLE: "PERSONAL REMINISCENCES OF 'STONEWALL' JACKSON," CWTI:JUN/95[18]444
GENERAL LISTINGS: *Carolina Campaign*, B&G:DEC/95[9]615, *Manassas, 2nd*, B&G:AUG/92[11]493, *order of battle*, B&G:DEC/95[9]615, *West Point*, B&G:DEC/91[12]469, *photos*, B&G:DEC/95[9]615, CWTI:JUN/95[18]444
ADDITIONAL LISTINGS: ACW:JUL/91[18]312, ACW:SEP/91[30]322, ACW:JAN/92[47]344, B&G:AUG/93[10]529, CWM:JAN/93[16]457, CWM:AUG/95[30]606, CWR:VOL1#3[52]122, CWR:VOL4#4[70]180, CWTI:DEC/89[42]137, CWTI:NOV/93[55]350, CWTI:MAR/94[29]371
TALLADEGA, ALABAMA; CWTI:DEC/90[56]184
TALLAHASSEE, FLORIDA; ACW:NOV/91[64]336
TALLMAN, WILLIAM H.H., *Sergeant, 66th Ohio Infantry*; GETTY:9[81]216
TALTY, HUGH, *Private, 6th Wisconsin Infantry*; GETTY:4[24]145
TAMMANY REGIMENT; (42nd New York Infantry); CWTI:MAY/89[14]114
TANEY, ROGER B.; ACW:MAR/91[6]290, AHI:NOV/71[32]136, CWTI:DEC/95[52]480
TANNATT, THOMAS R., *Colonel, USA*; B&G:APR/94[10]558
TANNER, LINN, *Private, CSA*; ACW:JAN/92[10]339
TANNER, W.A., *Lieutenant, Courtney Artillery*; CWR:VOL4#4[70]180
TANNER, W.R., *Private, 13th South Carolina Infantry*; GETTY:13[22]254
TANSILL, ROBERT, *Colonel, CSA*; CWR:VOL1#3[52]122
TAPPAN, JAMES C., *General, CSA*; CWR:VOL3#3[33]158, CWR:VOL3#4[24]162, CWR:VOL4#2[68]167, *photo*, CWR:VOL3#4[24]162
TAPPAN, LEWIS; ACW:NOV/94[42]497
TAPPAN, SAMUEL F., *Lieutenant Colonel, 1st Colorado Infantry*; CWTI:MAR/94[58]375, CWTI:JUL/94[10]389

TARGET:
an occasional department in CWTI
Bennett Place State Historic Site, ARTICLE: "BENNETT PLACE: HUMBLE SHRINE TO PEACE," CWTI:APR/90[20]151
A.K. Smiley Library; ARTICLE: "A SHRINE IN THE GOLDEN STATE," CWTI:MAY/92[20]262
Andersonville Prison; ARTICLE: "THE COST OF CAPTURE," CWTI:APR/92[23]255
Atlanta Cyclorama; ARTICLE: "ATLANTA'S RESTORED CYCLORAMA," CWTI:FEB/91[18]190
Brown, John; ARTICLE: "A VISIT TO JOHN BROWN COUNTRY," CWTI:JUL/92[20]271
Coker House, Champion Hill; ARTICLE: "A MISSISSIPPI HOME STANDS, A SILENT WITNESS TO A BATTLE," CWTI:MAY/91[18]207
Drum Barracks; ARTICLE: "LOS ANGELES' DRUM BARRACKS," CWTI:SEP/91[18]227
Harpers Ferry National Historical Park; ARTICLE: "A VISIT TO JOHN BROWN COUNTRY," CWTI:JUL/92[20]271

TARRANT, EASTHAM, *Private, CSA*; B&G:FEB/93[12]511
TASSILLIER, LOUIS, *Captain, 39th New York Infantry*; ACW:MAY/95[54]528
TATE, JOSEPH W., *Private, 2nd Tennessee Cavalry*; CWR:VOL4#1[1]163,
TATE, THEODORE H., *Surgeon, 3rd Pennsylvania Cavalry*; GETTY:13[89]260
TATTNALL, JOSIAH, *Captain, CSN*; ACW:MAR/91[14]293, ACW:JUL/94[35]478, ACW:JUL/95[26]535, CWM:JUN/94[50]518, CWTI:DEC/91[44]241, *sketch*; CWTI:DEC/91[44]241
TAYLOE, EDWARD P., *Lieutenant Colonel, 22nd Virginia Infantry*; CWR:VOL1#3[52]122, CWTI:APR/90[46]153
TAYLOE, GEORGE E., *Colonel, CSA*; CWR:VOL2#3[236]143, CWTI:DEC/94[32]410
TAYLOR, ALFRED W., *Colonel, 4th New York Infantry*; B&G:APR/95[24]596
TAYLOR, BENJAMIN F., *correspondent*; CWM:MAR/91[50]340
TAYLOR, CHARLES, *Colonel, USA*; GETTY:9[53]214
TAYLOR, CHARLES A., *Private, 7th Massachusetts Infantry*; ACW:NOV/95[30]555
TAYLOR, CHARLES F., *Colonel, 13th Pennsylvania Reserves*; CWR:VOL1#3[20]119, CWR:VOL1#3[28]120, CWR:VOL4#4[1]177, GETTY:9[53]214, *photo*, CWR:VOL1#3[20]119
TAYLOR, CHARLES H.; CWR:VOL1#3[46]121
TAYLOR, DANIEL, *Private, USA*; AHI:APR/74[4]154
TAYLOR, EZRA, *Captain, USA*; CWR:VOL3#4[24]162
TAYLOR, FLETCHER; CWTI:JAN/94[29]360
TAYLOR, GEORGE W., *Private, 2nd Tennessee Cavalry*; CWR:VOL4#1[1]163
TAYLOR, GEORGE W., *General, USA*; B&G:AUG/92[11]493, CWTI:MAY/89[36]118, *photo*, CWTI:MAY/89[36]118
TAYLOR, ISAAC, *Private, 1st Minnesota Infantry*; GETTY:5[79]161
TAYLOR, JAMES; B&G:FEB/94[36]
TAYLOR, JAMES E. *artist*:
BOOK REVIEW: *THE JAMES E. TAYLOR SKETCHBOOK: WITH SHERIDAN UP THE SHENANDOAH VALLEY IN 1864: LEAVES FROM A SPECIAL ARTISTS SKETCHBOOK AND DIARY*

ADDITIONAL LISTINGS: ACW:SEP/94[55]489, CWM:NOV/92[10]447, CWTI:SUMMER/89[40]123

TAYLOR, JAMES H., *Private, 1st South Carolina Infantry;* ACW:NOV/92[10]384

TAYLOR, JAMES N., *Captain, CSA; in list,* B&G:OCT/94[11]580,

TAYLOR, JOHN; CWNEWS:SEP/95[33]

TAYLOR, JOHN D., *Lieutenant Colonel, CSA;* B&G:DEC/95[9]615

TAYLOR, JOHN P., *Colonel, 1st Pennsylvania Cavalry;* ACW:NOV/92[26]386

TAYLOR, JOHN R., *Surgeon;* B&G:OCT/91[11]466

TAYLOR, JOHN T., *Colonel, CSA;* ACW:JUL/93[66]427

TAYLOR, JOHN T., *Lieutenant, 5th Ohio Cavalry;* CWR:VOL4#1[44]164

TAYLOR, KINCHEN, *Private, 17th North Carolina Infantry;* ACW:MAR/95[12]513

TAYLOR, MURRAY F., *Lieutenant, CSA;* B&G:OCT/91[11]466

TAYLOR, NELSON, *General, USA;* ACW:MAR/95[42]517, B&G:AUG/92[11]493

TAYLOR, O.B., *Captain, Virginia Battery;* AHI:SEP/87[40]263, GETTY:5[47]160

TAYLOR, OLIVER, *Private, 37th Virginia Infantry;* GETTY:9[81]216

TAYLOR, PATRICK, *Private, 1st Minnesota Infantry;* GETTY:5[79]161

TAYLOR, PETER A., *Captain, USA;* GETTY:4[101]151, GETTY:8[31]201, GETTY:10[42]224

TAYLOR, RICHARD H., *General, CSA:*
ARTICLES: "RED RIVER BLUES," CWM:APR/95[39]576, "UNPUBLISHED AFTER-ACTION REPORTS FROM THE RED RIVER CAMPAIGN," CWR:VOL4#2[118]169
BOOK REVIEWS: *DESTRUCTION AND RECONSTRUCTION: PERSONAL EXPERIENCES IN THE LATE WAR * NINE MEN IN GRAY * RICHARD TAYLOR: SOLDIER PRINCE OF DIXIE*
GENERAL LISTINGS: *general history,* AHI:MAY/71[3]133A, *in book review,* CWM:APR/95[50], CWM:JUL/93[51], CWNEWS:SEP/92[4], CWNEWS:JAN/94[5], CWR:VOL4#3[1]170, *Jackson,* B&G:JUN/92[8]487, *letters to the editor,* CWTI:MAY/94[12]379, *Shenandoah Valley,* ACW:MAY/95[10]523, *surrender,* CWTI:AUG/90[50]168, *photos,* CWM:SEP/93[24]495, CWM:OCT/94[33]537
ADDITIONAL LISTINGS: ACW:SEP/91[16]320, ACW:SEP/92[23]377, ACW:SEP/92[38]379, ACW:SEP/92[47]380, ACW:JAN/93[35]396, AHI:NOV/73[18]151, B&G:JUN/91[10]452, B&G:JUN/94[8]568, B&G:FEB/95[35]592, CWM:SEP/93[24]495, CWM:OCT/94[33]537, CWR:VOL1#2[44]114, CWR:VOL2#3[212]142, CWR:VOL3#1[1]149, CWR:VOL3#3[33]158, CWR:VOL4#2[1]165, CWR:VOL4#2[26]166, CWR:VOL4#2[68]167, CWR:VOL4#2[104]168, CWTI:JUL/92[29]272, CWTI:NOV/92[60]294, CWTI:MAR/93[24]309, CWTI:JAN/94[35]361, CWTI:MAR/94[48]374, CWTI:JUN/95[18]444, MH:OCT/93[20]172, MH:DEC/95[58]188

TAYLOR, SAMUEL B., *Captain, 10th Kentucky Infantry;* B&G:OCT/94[11]580, CWM:MAR/93[16]466

TAYLOR, T.T., *Colonel, USA;* ACW:MAR/92[46]354

TAYLOR, THOMAS H., *Colonel, CSA;* ACW:SEP/94[10]484, ACW:SEP/94[46]488, AHI:DEC/77[46]177, CWR:VOL2#1[36]132

TAYLOR, W.H., *Colonel, 12th Mississippi Infantry;* ACW:JUL/95[50]538

TAYLOR, WALTER H., *Lieutenant Colonel, CSA:*
BOOK REVIEWS: *LEE'S ADJUTANT: THE WARTIME LETTERS OF COLONEL WALTER HERRON TAYLOR, 1862-1865 * GENERAL LEE: HIS CAMPAIGNS IN VIRGINIA 1861-1865, WITH PERSONAL REMINISCENCES*
GENERAL LISTINGS: *Gettysburg,* GETTY:4[65]148, GETTY:4[113]153, GETTY:5[4]156, GETTY:6[62]175, GETTY:7[13]186, GETTY:8[67]204, GETTY:9[17]210, GETTY:10[29]222, *Wilderness,* B&G:APR/95[8]595, *photos,* ACW:JAN/93[43]397, CWTI:AUG/90[42]167
ADDITIONAL LISTINGS: ACW:MAR/93[26]404, B&G:JUN/93[32]525, B&G:FEB/94[24]551, CWM:JAN/93[8]456, CWM:JUN/94[43]517, CWTI:APR/90[46]153, CWTI:SEP/92[42]283, CWTI:SEP/94[40]403, CWTI:JUL/94[44]394, GETTY:13[108]261

TAYLOR, WILLIAM H., *Colonel, 12th Mississippi Infantry;* GETTY:4[7]142, GETTY:5[89]162

TAYLOR, WILLIAM H.H., *Colonel, 5th Ohio Cavalry;* CWR:VOL4#1[44]164

TAYLOR, WILLIAM T., JR., *Corporal, Petersburg Artillery;* ACW:MAR/95[12]513

TEA, RICHARD, *Private, 4th U.S. Artillery;* GETTY:11[57]233

TEAGUE, B.H., ARTICLE: "THE B.H. TEAGUE COLLECTION OF CONFEDERATE RELICS AND CURIOS," B&G:JUN/91[38]455

TEARS, DAVID O., *Lieutenant, USA;* GETTY:11[6]231

TEAVIS, TURNER; AHI:JAN/76[14]164

TEEL, TREVANION T., *Captain, CSA;* B&G:JUN/94[8]568

TEGENER, FRITZ, *civilian;* ACW:JUL/91[58]316

TELEGRAPH; also, see listings under **"UNITED STATES TELEGRAPH SERVICE"**
ARTICLE: "THE TELEGRAPH GOES TO WAR," CWM:NOV/91[58]394A
ADDITIONAL LISTINGS: ACW:JAN/95[20]504, GETTY:4[101]150, GETTY:4[101]151

TELEVISION: see listings under **"MOVIES"**

TEMPLIN, WILLIAM H., *Private, Jeff Davis Artillery;* CWTI:DEC/91[26]238

TENNESSEE TROOPS:

1st Artillery; ACW:JAN/94[30]450

1st Artillery, (East Tennessee); B&G:FEB/94[62]556,

1st Cavalry; CWR:VOL4#1[1]163

1st Cavalry, East Tennessee); CWR:VOL4#1[1]163

1st Cavalry, (Union); B&G:FEB/91[20]440, B&G:APR/92[28]482

1st Infantry:
GENERAL LISTINGS: *Gettysburg,* GETTY:6[13]170, GETTY:9[61]215, GETTY:12[61]245, GETTY:12[123]251, *in book review,* CWNEWS:JAN/90[4], *in list,* CWTI:JUL/93[34]327
ADDITIONAL LISTINGS: ACW:SEP/95[38]546, B&G:FEB/95[8]590A, CWR:VOL1#1[1]102, CWR:VOL1#3[52]122, CWR:VOL2#1[36]132, CWR:VOL2#4[269]145, CWTI:SUMMER/89[20]121, CWTI:AUG/90[42]167, CWTI:SEP/92[28]280, CWTI:DEC/94[49]413

1st Infantry, (Union); B&G:FEB/93[12]511

1st/27th Infantry (Consolidated); B&G:AUG/95[36]607

2nd Cavalry:
ARTICLE: "DEFENDING THE CONFEDERATE HEARTLAND: COMPANY F OF HENRY ASHBY'S 2ND TENNESSEE CAVALRY," CWR:VOL4#1[1]163

ADDITIONAL LISTINGS: ACW:MAY/92[47]363, B&G:JUN/93[12]524, CWR:VOL1#2[44]114, CWTI:NOV/93[65]351

2nd Cavalry, (Union); BOOK REVIEW: *LOYAL MOUNTAIN TROOPERS: THE SECOND AND THIRD TENNESSEE CAVALRY IN THE CIVIL WAR, REMINISCENCES OF LIEUTENANT JOHN W. ANDES AND MAJOR WILL A. MCTEER*

2nd Infantry; CWR:VOL1#1[1]102, CWR:VOL3#4[24]162, CWTI:SEP/94[40]403, MH:FEB/91[8]151

2nd Infantry, (Union); B&G:FEB/93[12]511

2nd Mounted Rifles (Union); B&G:OCT/94[42]583

3rd Cavalry; CWR:VOL4#1[1]163,

3rd Cavalry, (Union):

BOOK REVIEW: *LOYAL MOUNTAIN TROOPERS: THE SECOND AND THIRD TENNESSEE CAVALRY IN THE CIVIL WAR, REMINISCENCES OF LIEUTENANT JOHN W. ANDES AND MAJOR WILL A. MCTEER*

ADDITIONAL LISTINGS: B&G:JUN/92[32]488, CWTI:AUG/90[50]168

3rd Infantry:

ARTICLE: "I LOVE THE WORK 'RAYMOND,'" CWM:JUN/94[58]519

BOOK REVIEW: *HOLDING THE LINE: THE HISTORY OF THE THIRD TENNESSEE INFANTRY, 1861-1864*

ADDITIONAL LISTINGS: ACW:SEP/95[38]546, B&G:FEB/92[10]474, CWR:VOL2#1[36]132, CWR:VOL4#1[78]

4th Cavalry; ACW:MAR/93[51]407, B&G:AUG/91[11]458, B&G:DEC/95[9]615, CWM:DEC/95[48]631, CWR:VOL4#1[1]163

4th Cavalry, (Union); CWM:JAN/91[40]330

4th Infantry; ACW:SEP/92[38]379, B&G:FEB/91[8]439

4th Infantry, (Union); B&G:APR/92[28]482

5th Cavalry; CWR:VOL4#1[1]163

5th Infantry; CWR:VOL4#2[68]167, CWTI:MAY/92[74]268, CWTI:DEC/94[79]417

5th Mounted Infantry; CWTI:MAY/93[8]315

6th Cavalry; B&G:DEC/92[40]508, CWR:VOL4#1[1]163

6th Cavalry, (Union); B&G:DEC/91[38]471

7th Cavalry; B&G:APR/93[34]521,CWTI:JAN/93[12]

7th Infantry:

GENERAL LISTINGS: *Falling Waters,* GETTY:9[109]218, *Gettysburg,* GETTY:6[13]170, GETTY:9[61]215, GETTY:12[61]245, GETTY:12[123]251, *in list,* CWTI:JUL/93[34]327

ADDITIONAL LISTINGS: ACW:SEP/92[38]379, ACW:MAY/95[30]525, B&G:FEB/95[8]590A, CWR:VOL1#1[1]102, CWR:VOL1#3[52]122

8th Cavalry; ACW:MAR/93[51]407, B&G:AUG/91[11]458, CWM:DEC/95[48]631

8th Cavalry, (Union); ACW:SEP/95[38]546

8th Infantry, (Union); CWM:OCT/94[60]544

9th Cavalry:

BOOK REVIEWS: *'FOR THE SAKE OF MY COUNTRY:' THE DIARY OF COLONEL W.W. WARD, 9TH TENNESSEE CAVALRY, MORGAN'S BRIGADE, C.S.A.*

ADDITIONAL LISTINGS: ACW:MAY/92[47]363, B&G:JUN/93[12]524, B&G:FEB/94[62]556, CWM:DEC/95[48]631, CWR:VOL4#1[1]163

9th Infantry; B&G:AUG/94[22]576, CWTI:NOV/92[41]291

10th Cavalry; B&G:OCT/94[42]583

10th Infantry:

BOOK REVIEW: *REBEL SONS OF ERIN: A CIVIL WAR HISTORY OF THE TENTH TENNESSEE INFANTRY (IRISH), CONFEDERATE STATES VOLUNTEERS*

GENERAL LISTINGS: *Fort Donelson,* B&G:FEB/92[10]474, *letters to the editor,* CWM:JUL/91[6]355

ADDITIONAL LISTING: B&G:DEC/93[52]548

10th/30th Infantry (Consolidated); CWR:VOL2#1[36]132

11th Infantry; ACW:SEP/95[38]546

12th Cavalry; ACW:NOV/95[48]557,

12th Cavalry, (Union); ACW:NOV/95[48]557

12th Infantry; ACW:SEP/91[8]318, CWR:VOL3#4[24]162

13th Cavalry, (Union); B&G:AUG/91[11]458, B&G:APR/92[28]482, CWTI:SEP/93[18]334, CWTI:NOV/93[65]351

13th Infantry; CWR:VOL3#4[24]162

13th Infantry, (Union); CWTI:JAN/94[35]361

14th Infantry:

GENERAL LISTINGS: *Falling Waters,* GETTY:9[109]218, *Gettysburg,* GETTY:6[13]170, GETTY:6[94]180, GETTY:9[61]215, GETTY:12[61]245, GETTY:12[123]251, *in list,* CWTI:JUL/93[34]327, *SIO,* CWTI:MAR/95[18]432

ADDITIONAL LISTINGS: ACW:SEP/92[38]379, ACW:MAY/95[30]525, B&G:FEB/95[8]590A, CWR:VOL1#1[1]102, CWR:VOL1#3[52]122, CWTI:AUG/91[82]223

15th Infantry; B&G:AUG/94[22]576, CWR:VOL3#4[24]162, CWTI:JAN/95[27]425

15th/27th Infantry (Consolidated); CWTI:JAN/95[27]425

16th Cavalry; CWR:VOL4#1[1]163

17th Infantry; ACW:SEP/93[38]434, B&G:FEB/93[12]511, CWR:VOL4#3[50]171

19th Infantry; ACW:SEP/93[38]434, B&G:FEB/93[12]511

20th Infantry; ACW:SEP/93[38]434, B&G:OCT/92[10]496, B&G:FEB/93[12]511, B&G:DEC/93[12]545, B&G:DEC/93[52]548, B&G:JUN/94[32]570, B&G:FEB/95[30]591, B&G:APR/95[38]598, CWTI:SUMMER/89[20]121, CWTI:NOV/92[41]291

21st Infantry; CWR:VOL3#4[24]162

22nd Infantry; CWR:VOL3#4[24]162

23rd Infantry; MH:OCT/94[20]180

25th Infantry; ACW:SEP/93[38]434, B&G:FEB/93[12]511

26th Infantry; ACW:NOV/95[66]559

28th Infantry; ACW:SEP/93[38]434, B&G:APR/91[36]448, B&G:DEC/91[38]471, B&G:FEB/93[12]511

29th Infantry; ACW:SEP/93[38]434, B&G:FEB/93[12]511

30th Infantry; B&G:FEB/92[10]474, B&G:FEB/92[48]475, B&G:OCT/94[42]583, B&G:DEC/94[36]588

37th Infantry; CWTI:JAN/95[27]425

38th Infantry; CWR:VOL4#4[129]

41st Infantry:

ARTICLE: "A CONFEDERATE SURGEON'S VIEW OF FORT DONELSON: THE DIARY OF JOHN KENNERLY FARRIS," CWR:VOL1#3[7]118

ADDITIONAL LISTINGS: B&G:FEB/92[10]474, B&G:OCT/92[10]496, CWR:VOL1#3[v]117, CWR:VOL2#1[36]132

43rd Infantry; CWTI:MAR/89[44]105

50th Infantry; CWR:VOL2#1[36]132

55th Infantry; B&G:JUN/93[12]524

59th Infantry, (Mounted);

BOOK REVIEWS: *VALLEYS OF THE SHADOW: THE MEMOIR OF CONFEDERATE CAPTAIN REUBEN G. CLARK, COMPANY I, 59TH TENNESSEE MOUNTED INFANTRY*

60th Infantry; CWR:VOL2#1[36]132

61st Infantry; CWR:VOL2#1[36]132

62nd Infantry; CWR:VOL2#1[36]132

4th Cavalry; CWR:VOL2#3[212]142, CWR:VOL4#4[129]
4th Infantry:
BOOK REVIEW: *GAINES' MILL TO APPOMATTOX—WACO &*
MCCLENNAN COUNTY IN HOOD'S TEXAS BRIGADE
GENERAL LISTINGS: *Gettysburg,* GETTY:5[103]163,
GETTY:5[117]165, GETTY:6[7]169, GETTY:6[33]172,
GETTY:6[43]173, GETTY:7[13]186, GETTY:7[41]189,
GETTY:8[53]203, GETTY:10[53]225, *in book review,*
CWR:VOL1#4[77], CWR:VOL2#3[256]
ADDITIONAL LISTINGS: ACW:MAR/91[12]292, ACW:JUL/92[30]369,
ACW:MAR/94[42]461, CWM:MAR/92[9]410,
CWM:JUL/92[40]432, CWM:AUG/94[30]527,
CWM:JUN/95[37]585, CWR:VOL1#1[71]107,
CWR:VOL1#2[29]112, CWR:VOL2#4[269]145,
CWTI:DEC/89[26]135,
CWTI:DEC/91[36]240, CWTI:JUL/93[42]329,
CWTI:MAR/95[46]43
4th Infantry, (Mounted); B&G:JUN/94[8]568,
B&G:OCT/94[6]579, CWM:MAY/93[16]475,
CWTI:OCT/95[56]471
4th Mounted Rifles; CWR:VOL2#2[161]139,
CWTI:MAR/94[58]375
5th Cavalry; ACW:SEP/91[8]318, CWR:VOL2#3[212]142,
CWR:VOL4#4[129]
5th Infantry:
ARTICLE: "THE BLOODY FIFTH," CWTI:DEC/91[36]240
GENERAL LISTINGS: *Gettysburg,* GETTY:5[103]163,
GETTY:6[13]170, GETTY:6[33]172, GETTY:6[43]173,
GETTY:7[41]189, GETTY:8[53]203, GETTY:12[1]240,
GETTY:12[111]250, *Immortal Six Hundred,*
GETTY:12[111]250, *in book review,* CWR:VOL1#4[77],
CWR:VOL2#3[256]
ADDITIONAL LISTINGS: ACW:MAR/91[12]292, ACW:JUL/92[30]369,
ACW:MAR/94[50]462, B&G:JUN/95[8]600,
CWM:JUL/92[40]432, CWR:VOL1#1[71]107,
CWR:VOL1#2[29]112, CWR:VOL2#4[269]145,
CWTI:NOV/93[55]350
5th Infantry, (Mounted); B&G:JUN/94[8]568,
CWR:VOL3#1[1]149, CWTI:OCT/95[56]471
5th Mounted Rifles; CWR:VOL2#2[161]139,
CWTI:MAR/94[58]375
6th Cavalry; B&G:AUG/95[8]604, CWNEWS:JUL/95[61]
6th Cavalry, (Dismounted); CWR:VOL3#3[33]158
6th Infantry; CWR:VOL1#2[78], CWTI:SUMMER/89[20]121,
CWTI:SEP/94[40]403
7th Cavalry; ACW:JAN/93[51]398, CWR:VOL2#3[212]142,
CWR:VOL3#1[1]149, CWR:VOL4#4[129]
7th Infantry; AHI:JUL/93[40]312, B&G:OCT/95[36]614,
CWR:VOL2#1[36]132, CWTI:SEP/94[40]403
7th Infantry, (Mounted); B&G:JUN/94[8]568,
CWTI:OCT/95[56]471
7th Mounted Rifles; CWTI:MAR/94[58]375
8th Cavalry; ACW:MAY/91[12]302, B&G:AUG/91[11]458,
B&G:JUN/95[5]599, B&G:OCT/95[5]610, B&G:DEC/95[9]615,
CWM:JUL/92[40]432, CWR:VOL3#3[33]158,
CWR:VOL4#1[1]163
9th Infantry; ACW:SEP/91[46]324, B&G:OCT/94[38]582
10th Infantry; CWR:VOL1#2[78], CWTI:SEP/94[40]403
11th Cavalry; B&G:AUG/91[11]458
11th Infantry; CWR:VOL3#3[33]158
12th Cavalry; CWR:VOL2#3[212]142
12th Infantry; CWR:VOL3#3[33]158,

13th Cavalry; CWM:OCT/94[33]537, CWR:VOL2#3[212]142,
CWR:VOL3#1[1]149
13th Cavalry, (Dismounted); CWR:VOL3#3[33]158
13th Infantry; CWM:OCT/94[33]537
14th Infantry; CWR:VOL3#3[33]158
15th Cavalry; BOOK REVIEW: *CHAPTERS FROM THE*
UNWRITTEN HISTORY OF THE WAR BETWEEN THE
STATES
15th Infantry; CWM:OCT/94[33]537, CWR:VOL2#3[212]142,
CWTI:SEP/94[40]403
16th Cavalry, (Dismounted); CWR:VOL3#3[33]158
16th Infantry; CWNEWS:OCT/95[33], CWR:VOL2#3[212]142,
CWR:VOL3#3[33]158, CWR:VOL4#3[1]170
17th Cavalry; B&G:APR/94[34]561
17th Cavalry, (Dismounted); CWTI:SEP/94[40]403
17th Infantry; CWR:VOL2#3[212]142, CWR:VOL3#3[33]158
18th Cavalry, (Dismounted); CWTI:SUMMER/89[40]123,
CWTI:SEP/94[40]403
18th Infantry; ACW:MAR/93[68]409, CWR:VOL3#3[33]158,
CWR:VOL3#3[88]160
19th Cavalry; CWR:VOL2#3[212]142
19th Infantry; ACW:MAR/93[68]409, CWR:VOL3#3[33]158
21st Infantry; CWR:VOL2#3[212]142
22nd Cavalry, (Dismounted); CWR:VOL2#3[212]142
22nd Infantry; CWR:VOL3#3[33]158
23rd Cavalry; CWR:VOL2#3[212]142, CWR:VOL4#2[26]166
24th Cavalry, (Dismounded); CWTI:SEP/94[40]403
24th/25th Cavalry, (Dismounted);
CWTI:SUMMER/89[20]121, CWTI:SUMMER/89[40]123
25th Cavalry (Dismounted); CWTI:SEP/94[40]403
26th Cavalry; CWR:VOL2#3[212]142, CWR:VOL4#2[68]167
27th Cavalry; CWR:VOL3#3[33]158, CWTI:JUL/94[50]395
29th Infantry; ACW:JAN/91[30]286
31st Cavalry, (Dismounted); CWR:VOL2#3[212]142
32nd Cavalry; ACW:MAR/93[68]409
33rd Cavalry; ACW:MAR/93[68]409
34th Cavalry, (Dismounted); CWR:VOL2#3[212]142
35th Cavalry; B&G:OCT/95[36]614, CWR:VOL2#3[212]142
36th Cavalry; CWR:VOL2#3[212]142, CWR:VOL4#2[26]166
Cypress Rangers; BOOK REVIEW: *THE CYPRESS RANGERS IN*
THE CIVIL WAR
Granbury's Texas Brigade; CWR:VOL1#2[78]
Hood's Texas Brigade:
BOOK REVIEWS: *CONFEDERATE CAPITAL AND HOOD'S TEXAS*
*BRIGADE * GAINES' MILL TO APPOMATTOX—WACO &*
*MCCLENNAN COUNTY IN HOOD'S TEXAS BRIGADE ***
HOOD'S TEXAS BRIGADE SKETCHBOOK OF GENERAL
*R.S. EWELL * HOOD'S TEXAS BRIGADE: LEE'S*
*GRENADIER GUARD * A TEXAN IN SEARCH OF A FIGHT.*
BEING THE DIARY AND LETTERS OF A PRIVATE
SOLDIER IN HOOD'S TEXAS BRIGADE
ADDITIONAL LISTINGS: ACW:JUL/92[30]369, ACW:MAY/92[30]361,
ACW:MAR/94[42]461, ACW:JUL/94[42]479,
ACW:JAN/95[30]505, B&G:JUN/95[8]600,
B&G:OCT/95[8]611A, CWM:MAR/92[9]410,
CWM:JUL/92[40]432, CWM:SEP/92[8]437,
CWM:AUG/94[30]527, CWM:OCT/94[34]538,
CWM:DEC/94[26]548, CWR:VOL1#1[71]107,
CWR:VOL1#2[7]111, CWR:VOL1#2[29]112,
CWR:VOL1#3[28]120, CWR:VOL2#1[36]132,
CWR:VOL2#4[269]145, CWTI:SEP/93[53]340,
CWTI:NOV/93[55]350, CWTI:MAY/94[31]382,
CWTI:SEP/94[40]403, CWTI:DEC/94[32]410

CWTI:FEB/90[54]147, *order of battle,* B&G:DEC/93[12]545,
Tullahoma Campaign, B&G:OCT/92[10]496
PHOTOS: AHI:MAY/71[3]133A, AHI:NOV/73[18]151,
B&G:JUN/92[46]490, B&G:OCT/92[10]496,
B&G:FEB/93[12]511, B&G:DEC/93[12]545,
CWM:DEC/94[46]552, CWTI:SUMMER/89[13]120,
CWTI:MAR/95[40]436
ADDITIONAL LISTINGS, ACW: ACW:JAN/91[22]285,
ACW:JUL/91[12]310, ACW:JUL/91[26]313,
ACW:JUL/91[35]314, ACW:NOV/92[8]383,
ACW:JAN/93[10]393, ACW:SEP/93[38]434,
ACW:MAR/94[42]461, ACW:JUL/94[66]481
ADDITIONAL LISTINGS, AHI: AHI:JUL/73[38]150,
AHI:NOV/73[18]151, AHI:JUN/80[49]203, AHI:OCT/95[24]326
ADDITIONAL LISTINGS, B&G: B&G:JUN/91[10]452,
B&G:AUG/91[11]458, B&G:OCT/91[11]466,
B&G:APR/92[58]485, B&G:JUN/92[46]490,
B&G:OCT/92[26]498, B&G:DEC/93[49]547A,
B&G:DEC/93[52]548, B&G:JUN/94[32]570,
B&G:DEC/94[22]586, B&G:FEB/95[30]591, B&G:DEC/95[9]615
ADDITIONAL LISTINGS, CWM: CWM:SEP/91[35]384,
CWM:JUL/92[18]429, CWM:JUL/92[24]430,
CWM:MAR/93[8]465, CWM:APR/94[8]502,
CWM:OCT/94[48]542, CWM:DEC/94[46]552
ADDITIONAL LISTINGS, CWR: CWR:VOL1#3[82]123,
CWR:VOL1#4[64]127, CWR:VOL2#4[313]146,
CWR:VOL3#2[70]155, CWR:VOL3#3[59]159
ADDITIONAL LISTINGS, CWTI: CWTI:SEP/91[23]228,
CWTI:MAY/94[40]383, CWTI:JUL/94[28]391,
CWTI:MAR/95[26]434, CWTI:DEC/95[67]481
ADDITIONAL LISTINGS, MH: MH:DEC/93[12]174, MH:APR/94[54]176,
MH:DEC/95[58]188
THOMAS, HAMPTON S., *Captain, 1st New Jersey Cavalry;*
GETTY:13[89]260
THOMAS, HENRY G., *Colonel, USA;* B&G:APR/94[10]558,
B&G:APR/95[8]595
THOMAS, HORACE H., *Lieutenant, USA;* ARTICLE: "I WAS AN
OGRE," CWM:OCT/94[60]544
THOMAS, ISAAC N., *Private, 2nd Tennessee Cavalry;*
CWR:VOL4#1[1]163
THOMAS, JOHN A., *Corporal, 3rd South Carolina Infantry;*
GETTY:5[35]159
THOMAS, JOHN F., *Captain, 117th New York Infantry;*
B&G:DEC/94[10]585
THOMAS, KEEFER, *civilian;* B&G:DEC/92[8]503
THOMAS, L.P., *Major, 42nd Georgia Infantry;*
B&G:DEC/95[9]615
THOMAS, LARKIN, *Private, 26th North Carolina Infantry;*
GETTY:5[19]158
THOMAS, LEWIS P., *Private, 3rd South Carolina Infantry;*
GETTY:5[35]159
THOMAS, LORENZO, *General, USA;* ACW:MAY/95[54]528,
AHI:DEC/68[28]118, AHI:MAY/71[3]133A,
B&G:FEB/93[12]511, CWTI:APR/92[35]257,
CWTI:JUL/93[38]328, CWTI:DEC/94[57]414
THOMAS, RICHARD; MH:FEB/91[8]151
THOMAS, SAMPSON A., *Sergeant, 16th Maine Infantry;*
CWM:MAY/92[15]419, GETTY:13[33]255
THOMAS, STEPHEN, *General, USA;* CWR:VOL3#1[1]149,
THOMAS, THOMAS S., *Private, 3rd South Carolina Infantry;*
GETTY:5[35]159
BOOK REVIEW: *CONFEDERATE COLONEL AND CHEROKEE
CHIEF: THE LIFE OF WILLIAM HOLLAND THOMAS*

ADDITIONAL LISTING: CWM:SEP/92[8]437
THOMAS, WILLIAM R., *Lieutenant, 3rd South Carolina
Infantry;* GETTY:5[35]159
THOMASON, IRA G., *Private, 8th Louisiana Infantry;*
CWTI:FEB/91[12]189
THOMPKINS, HAVILAND, *Major, 14th Illinois Cavalry;*
B&G:DEC/94[22]586
THOMPSON, A.J., *Captain, USA;* CWM:AUG/94[27]526
THOMPSON, BENJAMIN W., *Captain, 111th New York
Infantry;* GETTY:7[51]190, GETTY:8[95]205,
GETTY:10[53]225, GETTY:11[102]237
THOMPSON, BILL, *Private, 7th Indiana Infantry;*
CWTI:NOV/93[24]346
THOMPSON, CHARLES R., *Colonel, USA;*
B&G:DEC/93[12]545
THOMPSON, E.W., *Captain, USA;* CWR:VOL3#1[1]149
THOMPSON, ED PORTER; BOOK REVIEW: *HISTORY OF THE
FIRST KENTUCKY BRIGADE*
THOMPSON, EDWARD W., *Private, USA;* CWM:SEP/93[18]494
THOMPSON, ELBERT, *Private, 11th Mississippi Infantry;*
CWR:VOL2#4[269]145
THOMPSON, FLEMING W., *Sergeant, 11th Alabama Infantry;*
GETTY:12[7]241
**THOMPSON, FRANKLIN, (aka SARAH EMMA
EDMONDS);** *2nd Michigan Infantry;* CWR:VOL3#2[105]
THOMPSON, GEORGE, *Captain, 69th Pennsylvania Infantry;*
GETTY:4[89]150
THOMPSON, GEORGE W., *Private, 53rd Pennsylvania
Infantry;* GETTY:11[80]235
THOMPSON, HENRY E., *Lieutenant Colonel, 7th Michigan
Cavalry;* ACW:JUL/92[41]370
THOMPSON, JACOB, *Major, USA:*
ARTICLES: "CONFEDERATE CLOAK AND DAGGER,"
ACW:JUL/95[44]537, "ESPIONAGE," MH:FEB/94[8]175,
"THE GREATEST SCOUNDREL," CWTI:NOV/92[54]293
ADDITIONAL LISTINGS: ACW:NOV/91[22]331, ACW:NOV/93[8]438,
AHI:JUN/70[30]127, CWTI:JAN/93[44]302,
CWTI:MAY/93[8]315, *photos,* CWTI:NOV/92[54]293,
MH:FEB/94[8]175
THOMPSON, JAMES, *Captain, Pennsylvania Light Artillery;*
GETTY:5[47]160, GETTY:8[53]203, GETTY:9[41]212
THOMPSON, JOHN K., *Captain, USA;* CWTI:MAR/89[16]101
THOMPSON, JOHN L., *Colonel, 1st New Hampshire Cavalry;*
CWM:APR/94[24]505
THOMPSON, M. JEFF, *General, CSA:*
BOOK REVIEW: *THE CIVIL WAR REMINISCENCES OF
GENERAL M. JEFF THOMPSON*
GENERAL LISTINGS: *letters to the editor,* CWM:JAN/93[6]455, *Price's
1864 Missouri Campaign,* B&G:JUN/91[10]452, *photo,*
B&G:JUN/91[10]452
ADDITIONAL LISTINGS: ACW:JUL/92[22]368, ACW:JAN/93[26]395,
ACW:NOV/94[34]496, ACW:JUL/95[44]537,
CWM:MAY/93[8]474, CWM:OCT/95[53]621,
CWR:VOL3#4[24]162, GETTY:13[108]261
THOMPSON, ORVILLE, *Lieutenant, 7th Indiana Infantry;*
CWTI:NOV/93[24]346
THOMPSON, R.H., *Private, 22nd Virginia Infantry;*
CWR:VOL1#3[52]122
THOMPSON, RICHARD S., *Captain, 12th New Jersey
Infantry;* ACW:JUL/95[50]538, GETTY:5[89]162
THOMPSON, S. MILLET, *Lieutenant, 13th New Hampshire
Infantry;* ACW:MAY/94[51]471

THOMPSON, WILLIAM C., *Captain, 6th Mississippi Infantry;* ACW:JUL/94[51]480, B&G:FEB/94[8]550

THOMPSON, WILLIAM P., *Colonel, 19th Virginia Cavalry;* CWTI:MAR/89[16]101

THOMSON (GEORGIA) GUARDS; ARTICLE: "THE THOMSON GUARDS FROM GEORGIA'S MCDUFFIE COUNTY SERVED THE CONFEDERACY TO THE BITTER END," ACW:JUL/95[10]533

THOMSON, CLIFFORD, *Lieutenant, 1st New York Cavalry;* B&G:OCT/93[12]537

THOMSON, J.W., *Major, CSA;* ACW:JAN/93[43]397

THOMSON, JIM, *Lieutenant, CSA;* ACW:JAN/92[8]338

THOMSON, RUFFIN, *Lieutenant, CSMC;* ACW:MAR/91[14]293

THOMSON, THOMAS, *Colonel, 2nd South Carolina Rifles;* CWR:VOL3#2[70]155

THOMSON, WILLIAM, *surgeon;* CWTI:JUL/92[36]273

THORN, ELIZABETH C., *Civilian;* ARTICLE: "THREE HEROINES OF GETTYSBURG," GETTY:11[119]238

THORN, PETER, *Private, 138th Pennsylvania Infantry;* GETTY:11[119]238

THORNBURG, W.L., *Captain, 38th North Carolina Infantry;* GETTY:8[67]204

THORNE, PLATT M, *Captain, 150th New York Infantry;* GETTY:12[42]244

THORNSBURY, SAM, *Private, 8th Louisiana Infantry;* CWTI:FEB/91[12]189

THORNTON, WILLIAM A., *General, USA;* CWTI:JUL/92[8]269

THORNTON, WILLIAM E., *Private, 24th Michigan Infantry,* GETTY:9[33]211, GETTY:11[57]233

THOROUGHFARE GAP, VIRGINIA, BATTLE OF; ARTICLE: "THE BATTLE AT THOROUGHFARE GAP," CWM:AUG/95[38]609

THORP, JOHN, *Captain, 47th New York Infantry;* CWTI:FEB/91[45]194

THORPE, EDGAR A., *Private, 2nd Wisconsin Infantry,* GETTY:9[33]211, GETTY:11[57]233

THORPE, P.H., *Colonel, CSA;* B&G:OCT/94[11]580

THRAILKILL, JOHN; ACW:JAN/93[26]395

THRASHER, GEORGE, *Sergeant, 1st Kentucky (USA) Cavalry;* B&G:FEB/93[12]511

THRESHER, A.M., *Lieutenant, 3rd Georgia Infantry;* CWTI:DEC/94[32]410

THROOP, GEORGE, *Lieutenant, Chicago Mercantile Battery;* CWR:VOL4#2[1]165

THRUSTON, SEPTHEN, *Colonel, CSA;* CWM:MAY/92[20]420

THURMAN, JOHN, *Private, Petersburg Artillery;* ACW:MAR/95[12]513

THURSTON, AHAZ R., *Private, 7th Wisconsin Infantry,* GETTY:9[33]211, GETTY:11[57]233

THURSTON, WILLIAM, *Corporal, 1st Pennsylvania Artillery;* GETTY:12[30]243

TIBBATTS, J.W., *Lieutenant, USA;* ACW:JAN/91[16]284

TIBBITS, HOWARD, *Master, USN;* CWTI:DEC/90[29]182

TIBBLES, CHARLES E., and GEORGE W., *4th Iowa Infantry;* B&G:AUG/93[18]530

TICKFAW BRIDGE, BATTLE OF; B&G:JUN/93[12]524

TIDBALL'S HORSE ARTILLERY; GETTY:11[19]232

TIDBALL, JOHN C., *Captain, USA:*
GENERAL LISTINGS: *Gettysburg,* GETTY:11[19]232, *in order of battle,* B&G:APR/94[10]558, *order of battle,* B&G:APR/95[8]595, *Overland Campaign,* B&G:APR/94[10]558, *West Point,* B&G:DEC/91[12]469, *photo,* GETTY:11[19]232

ADDITIONAL LISTINGS: ACW:NOV/94[50]498, B&G:JUN/95[36]603A

TIDBALL, WILLIAM, *Colonel, USA;* ACW:MAR/94[50]462

TIEBOUT, SAMUEL, *Sergeant, 5th New York Infantry;* CWTI:MAY/94[31]382

TIER, ED, *Private, 12th New Jersey Infantry;* GETTY:5[89]162

TILDEN, CHARLES W., *Colonel, 16th Maine Infantry;* ACW:MAR/95[42]517, CWM:MAY/92[15]419, GETTY:13[1]252, GETTY:13[33]255, *photo,* CWM:MAY/92[15]419

TILDEN, SAMUEL J.; AHI:NOV/88[28]277

TILGHMAN, LLOYD, *General, CSA:*
GENERAL LISTINGS: *Champion's Hill,* MH:JUN/93[82]167, *Grierson's Raid,* B&G:JUN/93[12]524, *photos,* ACW:NOV/91[22]331, B&G:FEB/92[10]474

ADDITIONAL LISTINGS: ACW:SEP/91[50]325, ACW:NOV/91[22]331, ACW:JUL/92[22]368, B&G:FEB/92[10]474, B&G:DEC/93[30]546, B&G:FEB/94[57]555, CWM:MAY/91[31]350, CWM:FEB/95[32]562, CWR:VOL1#3[7]118, CWR:VOL2#1[36]132, CWR:VOL2#1[69]133, CWTI:MAY/91[18]207, CWTI:MAY/91[24]208, MH:APR/94[54]176

TILLERY, GAYNAM T., *Private, 2nd Tennessee Cavalry;* CWR:VOL4#1[1]163

TILLMAN, JAMES D., *Colonel, CSA;* B&G:DEC/95[9]615

TILLSON, DAVIS, *General, USA;* B&G:APR/92[28]482

TILLSON, JOHN Q., *Colonel, USA;* CWR:VOL2#4[313]146

TILLSON, JOHN, *Colonel, USA;* B&G:DEC/95[9]615

TILTON, WILLIAM S., *Colonel, USA;* GETTY:5[47]160, GETTY:8[53]203, GETTY:9[41]212, GETTY:10[120]229

TIMBERLAKE, JOHN C., *Colonel, CSA;* GETTY:13[64]258

TIME LAPSE:

a department that appears in CWTI

Baldwin, James, *Sergeant, 3rd Arkansas Infantry (Union);* ARTICLE: "A FREEDMAN IN THE UNION ARMY," CWTI:JAN/94[82]366

Blakely, Edward, *Corporal, 63rd Ohio Infantry;* ARTICLE: "OVERCOME BY THE SCARS OF WAR," CWTI:JAN/93[82]304

Blickensderfer, Milton A., *Sergeant, 126th Ohio Infantry;* ARTICLE: "MEDAL OF HONOR RECIPIENT," CWTI:AUG/95[90]462

Cashner, John, Jr.,; *Private, 3th Indiana Infantry;* CWTI:SEP/90[52]179

Chapman, William H., CWTI:DEC/90[90]186

Christian, William E., *Sergeant;* ARTICLE: "WOUNDED AT THE CRATER," CWTI:MAY/91[74]212

Collier, Edward T., *Private, 3rd Massachusetts Infantry;* ARTICLE: "RUSHED TO THE FRONT," CWTI:JAN/95[82]430

Day, William, *Private;* ARTICLE: "A LOYAL FAMILY MAN," CWTI:DEC/91[82]243

Emack, James H., *Lieutenant, 7th North Carolina Infantry;* CWTI:SEP/92[82]286

Fontaine, Lamar, *Major;* ARTICLE: "A LIFE STORY LARGER THAN LIFE," CWTI:JUN/90[74]164

Gladden, Adley H., *General, CSA;* ARTICLE: "A FORGOTTEN REBEL GENERAL," CWTI:MAR/93[50]313

Grout, Willie; CWTI:MAY/89[50]119

Herndon, Thomas, *Lieutenant;* ARTICLE: "A TENNESSEE VOLUNTEER," CWTI:AUG/91[82]223

Herndon, John G., *Private;* ARTICLE: "A SCHOOLBOY CAVALRYMAN," CWTI:MAR/91[74]204

Heyer, Jacob, *Captain, 23rd Pennsylvania Infantry;* ARTICLE: "A FIGHTING ZOUAVE," CWTI:JUN/95[90]451

Hite, Maxfield, *Sergeant, 31st Ohio Infantry;* ARTICLE: "34-YEAR-OLD FATHER OF SEVEN," CWTI:SEP/93[90]343

Hussey, W.H.H., *Lieutenant;* CWTI:APR/90[74]155A

Kimball, Edgar A., *Major, 9th New York Infantry;* CWTI:SEPT/89[74]133

Mangum, Adolphus W., *Chaplain, 6th North Carolina Infantry;* ARTICLE: "PRISON CHAPLAIN AND HISTORIAN," CWTI:NOV/93[114]355

Milhollin, John F. *Captain;* CWTI:APR/89[50]112

Oden, John; CWTI:FEB/90[74]149

Pierce, Joseph, *Corporal, 14th Connecticut Infantry;* ARTICLE: "AN ORIENTAL YANKEE SOLDIER," CWTI:SEP/94[90]406

Price, Thomas J., *Private, 12th Mississippi Infantry;* ARTICLE: "A SOLDIER FOR TWO COUNTRIES," CWTI:MAR/95[90]440

Price, William C., *Major, CSA;* ARTICLE: "U.S. TREASURER, REBEL SOLDIER," CWTI:JUL/94[82]396

Shirkey, Samuel B., *Private, 1st Virginia Cavalry;* ARTICLE: "A VIRGINIA CAVALRYMAN," CWTI:OCT/95[90]472

Smith, Alfred C., *Sergeant, 2nd Mississippi Infantry;* ARTICLE: "'SWAMP RANGER' AND CAVALRYMAN," CWTI:NOV/92[106]295

Sprague, Mahlon, *Corporal, 5th New Jersey Infantry;* ARTICLE: "PATRIOTIC SON OF A SEAMAN," CWTI:JUL/92[74]277

Stephen Feather, *Private, 83rd Pennsylvania Infantry;* CWTI:FEB/92[58]251

Stevens, Charles, *Private, 29th Georgia Cavalry;* ARTICLE: "A RELUCTANT REBEL SOLDIER," CWTI:JUL/93[74]331

Summers, Samuel W., *Colonel, 7th Iowa Cavalry;* ARTICLE: "SOUTHERN-BORN UNION COLONEL," CWTI:MAY/94[82]387

Tobie, Edward and Leroy; ARTICLE: "THE TOBIE BROTHERS' WAR," CWTI:FEB/91[66]196

Tyler, Henry A., *5th Tennessee Infantry;* ARTICLE: "A COLLEAGUE OF GENERAL FORREST," CWTI:MAY/92[74]268

Usina, Michael; *8th Georgia Regiment;* CWTI:DEC/89[82]140

Walcott, Aaron F., *Lieutenant, 2nd Massachusetts Artillery;* ARTICLE: "A VETERAN OF 33 BATTLES," CWTI:MAY/93[74]322

Warner, Irwin E.; ARTICLE: "LIES, DISGRACE, REDEMPTION," CWTI:SEP/91[61]233

White, Elijah, *Lieutenant Colonel, CSA;* ARTICLE: "A CAVALRYMAN WITHOUT FANFARE," CWTI:DEC/94[122]419

Williams, George H., *Private, 10th Virginia Infantry;* ARTICLE: "KILLED AT BRANDY STATION," CWTI:MAR/94[67]377

Williams, Thomas J., *Captain, 1st Arkansas Infantry (Union);* CWTI:APR/92[27]256

TIME, KEEPING TRACK OF; ARTICLE: "DID ANYBODY REALLY KNOW WHAT TIME IT WAS," B&G:AUG/91[32]461

TIMM, AUGUST, *Lieutenant, 16th Iowa Infantry;* ACW:JAN/93[10]393

TIMROD, HENRY:
ARTICLE: "SOUTH CAROLINA'S HENRY TIMROD WAS THE POET LAUREATE OF THE CONFEDERACY'S BEGINNING AND END," ACW:SEP/92[10]375
ADDITIONAL LISTINGS: ACW:SEP/92[6]373, *photo,* ACW:SEP/92[10]375

TINES, PATRICK S., *Captain, 69th Pennsylvania Infantry;* GETTY:4[89]150

TINKER, CHARLES A.; CWTI:AUG/95[46]459

TINKHAM, HENRY, *Lieutenant, USA;* CWTI:MAY/93[35]320

TISDALE, WILLIAM D., *Lieutenant, 12th Arkansas Sharpshooters;* B&G:FEB/94[8]550

TISDEL, JAMES, *Captain, USA;* CWTI:JAN/93[20]298

TISSOT, PETER, *Chaplain, 37th New York Infantry;* CWM:MAR/91[50]340

TITUS, RICHARD, *Lieutenant, 150th New York Infantry;* GETTY:12[42]244

TOBIAS, JOHN B., *Private, 8th Pennsylvania Reserves;* CWR:VOL4#4[1]177

TOBIE, EDWARD and LEROY; ARTICLE: "THE TOBIE BROTHERS' WAR," CWTI:FEB/91[66]196

TOD, DAVID, *Governor, Ohio;* B&G:OCT/94[11]580

TODD'S TAVERN, VIRGINIA, BATTLE OF;
ACW:SEP/94[55]489, CWM:NOV/92[64]453, CWM:MAR/93[24]467, CWTI:APR/92[35]257

TODD, DAVID H., *Lieutenant, CSA;* ACW:JUL/91[8]309

TODD, GEORGE, *Surgeon, CSA;* ACW:JAN/93[26]395, B&G:JUN/91[32]454, CWM:JAN/92[8]399, CWNEWS:OCT/93[5], CWR:VOL4#4[28]178, CWTI:JAN/94[29]360

TODD, GEORGE F., *Captain, 4th Georgia Infantry;* B&G:DEC/95[25]616

TODD, J. SCOTT, *Sergeant, CSA;* CWTI:SEP/91[23]228

TODD, WILLIAM, *Private, 79th New York Infantry;* ACW:MAY/91[23]303

TOFFEY, D., *Seaman, USN;* AHI:NOV/75[38]163

TOFFEY, JOHN J.; CWTI:AUG/90[42]167

TOLEN, JOHN, *Captain, 6th Louisiana Infantry;* CWM:SEP/93[18]494

TOLLETT, HENRY G., *Private, 2nd Tennessee Cavalry;* CWR:VOL4#1[1]163

TOLLISON, E.T., *Private, CSA;* CWR:VOL3#2[70]155

TOLMAN, ALVIN, *Union veteran;* GETTY:7[119]195

TOM'S BROOK, VIRGINIA, BATTLE OF;
ACW:SEP/94[55]489, CWM:JAN/93[40]461

TOMB, JAMES, *Engineer, CSN;* MH:AUG/93[47]169

TOMLINSON, A.A., *Private, 10th Louisiana Infantry;* CWR:VOL3#1[1]141

TOMLINSON, B.B., *Private, 11th Mississippi Infantry;* CWR:VOL2#4[269]145

TOMMY, JOHN, *Private, 70th New York Infantry;* CWTI:JAN/95[16]421

TOMPKINS, CHARLES H., *Colonel, 1st Rhode Island Artillery;* B&G:APR/94[10]558, B&G:APR/95[8]595, B&G:DEC/95[25]616, CWR:VOL4#4[101]181

TOMPKINS, JOHN A., *Major, USA; 1st Rhode Island Artillery;* ACW:MAR/94[50]462, B&G:APR/95[8]595

TOMPKINS, SALLY L.; ACW:MAY/92[39]362, AHI:DEC/73[10]152, *photos,* ACW:MAY/92[39]362, AHI:DEC/73[10]152

TONGUE, LEVI, *Private, 6th Wisconsin Infantry;* GETTY:4[24]145

TOOF, S.C., *editor;* ACW:NOV/92[35]387

TOOMBS, ROBERT A., *General, CSA:*
ARTICLE: "THE CONTENTIOUS ROBERT TOOMBS," CWM:MAR/93[32]468
GENERAL LISTINGS: *Jefferson, Davis,* CWTI:AUG/91[36]217, *letters to the editor,* CWM:DEC/94[5]546, *Manassas, Second,* B&G:APR/91[32]447, B&G:AUG/92[11]493, *Peninsula Campaign,* CWM:JUN/95[63]594, *photos,* AHI:JUN/72[18]139, CWM:MAR/93[32]468

ADDITIONAL LISTINGS: ACW:SEP/93[46]435, ACW:NOV/93[42]443, AHI:JUN/70[30]127, AHI:JUN/72[18]139, CWM:SEP/92[8]437, CWM:MAR/93[4]463, CWM:AUG/94[8]522, CWR:VOL2#2[95]135, CWTI:SUMMER/89[20]121, CWTI:FEB/91[36]193, CWTI:SEP/93[43]338, CWTI:NOV/93[55]350

TOOMBS, SAMUEL, *Private, 13th New Jersey Infantry;* BOOK REVIEW: *REMINISCENCES OF THE THIRTEENTH REGIMENT NEW JERSEY VOLUNTEERS*

TOON, THOMAS F., *Colonel, 20th North Carolina Infantry;* B&G:APR/94[10]558, GETTY:4[33]146

TORBERT, ALFRED T.A., *General, USA:*

GENERAL LISTINGS: *Gettysburg,* GETTY:6[7]169, *in order of battle,* B&G:APR/94[10]558, B&G:APR/95[8]595, *Overland Campaign,* B&G:APR/94[10]558, *Trevilian Station,* MH:FEB/93[42]164, *Winchester, Third,* ACW:MAY/91[38]305, AHI:NOV/80[8]209, *Wilderness,* B&G:APR/95[8]595

ADDITIONAL LISTINGS: ACW:JAN/92[16]340, ACW:NOV/92[26]386, ACW:JAN/94[39]451, ACW:SEP/94[55]489, B&G:APR/91[8]445, B&G:FEB/92[32]477, B&G:APR/93[12]518

TORGERSON, WILLIAM, *painting of St. George, Bermuda;* CWTI:DEC/89[10]133

TORPEDO BUREAU:

ARTICLE: "TORPEDOES, THE CONFEDERACY'S DREADED 'INFERNAL MACHINES' MADE MANY A UNION SEA CAPTAIN UNEASY," ACW:NOV/91[8]328

ADDITIONAL LISTING: CWTI:DEC/95[76]482

TORSCH, JOHN W., *Captain, 1st Maryland Battalion;* GETTY:7[83]192, GETTY:9[81]216

TOTTEN, JAMES, *Captain, 2nd U.S. Artillery;* ACW:NOV/93[26]441, CWR:VOL1#1[42]105, CWTI:FEB/92[29]248

TOTTEN, JOSEPH G., *General, USA:*

GENERAL LISTINGS: *Mexican War,* MH:APR/93[39]166, *Savannah,* B&G:FEB/91[8]439, *West Point,* B&G:DEC/91[12]469

ADDITIONAL LISTINGS: ACW:MAR/92[62]355, ACW:JAN/95[74]510

TOTTY, JOHN H., *Private, 1st Georgia Regulars;* CWR:VOL2#2[95]135

TOUCEY, ISAAC, *Secretary of the Navy;* ACW:MAY/91[54]

TOULMIN, HARRY T., *Colonel, CSA;* B&G:DEC/95[9]615

TOURGEE, ALBION W.; AHI:APR/73[12]148, CWNEWS:APR/90[4]

TOURISON, ASHTON S. and WILLIAM L., *147th Pennsylvania Infantry;* GETTY:9[81]216

TOURS; ARTICLE: "HOW TO TOUR A BATTLEFIELD," CWM:MAR/92[40]414

TOURTELLOTTE, JOHN E., *Colonel, 4th Minnesota Infantry;* ACW:NOV/94[76]500

TOWER, CHARLEMAGNE, *Captain, USA;* ACW:MAR/92[22]351

TOWER, ZEALOUS B., *General, USA:*

GENERAL LISTINGS: *Manassas, Second,* B&G:AUG/92[11]493, B&G:OCT/95[20]612, *Mexican War,* MH:APR/93[39]166, *West Point,* B&G:DEC/91[12]469, *photo,* B&G:OCT/95[20]612

TOWN, CHARLES H., *Colonel, 1st Michigan Cavalry;* ACW:JUL/92[41]370, GETTY:4[75]149, GETTY:13[89]260

TOWNSEND, B.R., *Colonel, 2nd U.S. Colored Infantry;* ACW:NOV/91[64]336

TOWNSEND, COPELAND, *civilian;* ACW:NOV/91[10]329, CWTI:MAR/91[10]197

TOWNSEND, EDWARD D., *General, USA;* ACW:MAR/91[25]294, B&G:DEC/94[34]587,

CWM:MAR/91[56]341, GETTY:13[33]255, *photo, with Lincoln's casket;* CWTI:AUG/90[42]167

TOWNSEND, FREDERICK, *Colonel, 3rd New York Infantry;* ACW:MAR/93[42]406

TOWNSEND, GEORGE A., *reporter;* ACW:MAY/95[38]526, B&G:FEB/94[24]551, CWTI:DEC/91[28]239

TOWNSEND, HURLBERT G., *cadet;* B&G:DEC/91[12]469

TOZIER, ANDREW J., *Sergeant, 20th Maine Infantry;* CWM:JUL/92[8]427, CWR:VOL4#1[78], CWTI:NOV/92[10], GETTY:6[43]173

TRABUE, ROBERT, *Colonel, 4th Kentucky Infantry;* ACW:JUL/91[12]310

TRACEY, E.B., *Captain, CSA;* ACW:NOV/91[64]336

TRACY, BENJAMIN F., *Colonel, USA;* CWM:OCT/95[10]

TRACY, BUFORD A., *Captain, CSA;* B&G:OCT/94[11]580

TRACY, CHESTER, *Private, 93rd Illinois Infantry;* CWR:VOL3#3[59]159

TRACY, EDWARD D., *General, CSA;* ACW:JUL/94[51]480, ACW:NOV/94[18]495, B&G:FEB/94[8]550, B&G:FEB/94[57]555, CWR:VOL2#1[36]132, *photo,* B&G:FEB/94[8]550

TRACY, GEORGE T., *Private, 10th Kansas Infantry;* B&G:AUG/93[36]533

TRADING CARDS; ARTICLE: "A $2,500 SET OF CIVIL WAR TRADING CARDS?" CWTI:DEC/91[18]236

TRAFTON, GEORGE W., *Captain, USA;* B&G:JUN/93[12]524

TRAFTON, L.W., *Captain, CSA;* B&G:OCT/94[11]580

TRAINOR, JOSEPH, *Private, 88th Pennsylvania Infantry;* GETTY:10[7]221

TRAVEL:

ARTICLE: "HOW TO TOUR A BATTLEFIELD," CWM:MAR/92[40]414

BOOK REVIEWS: *A GUIDE TO CIVIL WAR WASHINGTON * CIVIL WAR BATTLEFIELDS: A TOURING GUIDE * THE INSIDERS' GUIDE TO THE CIVIL WAR: THE EASTERN THEATER * TOURING THE MIDDLE TENNESSEE BACKROADS*

Beauvoir, Biloxi, Mississippi; CWTI:AUG/91[22]215

Bermuda; ARTICLE: "BERMUDA IS AN UNLIKELY STARTING POINT FOR THOSE TRACING THE MYSTERY OF THE GREAT SEAL OF THE CONFEDERACY," ACW:MAY/93[62]418

Burt-Stark House; ARTICLE: "IN THE LITTLE-KNOWN BURT-STARK HOUSE, THE DECISION WAS MADE TO END THE CONFEDERACY," ACW:MAY/92[62]364

USS Cairo; ARTICLE: "ON THE MUDDY YAZOO RIVER ONE MORNING, THE UNION GUNBOAT *CAIRO* MADE UNWANTED NAVAL HISTORY," ACW:SEP/94[74]491

Cold Harbor; ARTICLE: "VISITORS TO THE DREADFUL BATTLEGROUND AT COLD HARBOR CAN ALMOST HEAR THE GUN HAMMERS CLICKING," ACW:SEP/93[62]436,

Ford's Theatre; ARTICLE: "VISITING THE SITE OF ABRAHAM LINCOLN'S ASSASSINATION GIVES HISTORY BUFFS AN EERIE SENSE OF STEPPING BACK IN TIME," ACW:MAY/95[68]529

Fort Delaware; ARTICLE: "INFAMOUS FOR DELAWARE WON AN UNWELCOME REPUTATION AS THE 'NORTHERN ANDERSONVILLE,'" ACW:NOV/93[66]445

Fort Jackson, Louisiana; ARTICLE: "FORT JACKSON, GUARDIAN OF NEW ORLEANS AND THE LOWER MISSISSIPPI, WAS LONG THOUGHT TO BE IMPREGNABLE," ACW:JAN/92[62]346

Fort Wool, Virginia; ARTICLE: "VIRGINIA'S FORT WOOL SAW ACTIVE SERVICE FROM THE CIVIL WAR THROUGH WORLD WAR II," ACW:JAN/95[74]510

Gamble Plantation, Ellenton, Florida; ARTICLE: "WILY JUDAH BENJAMIN ELUDED A FRENZIED NORTHERN MANHUNT AT FLORIDA'S LUXURIOUS GAMBLE PLANTATION," ACW:JUL/93[66]427

Grant's Overland Campaign; ARTICLE: "WHEN ULYSSES S. GRANT CROSSED THE RAPIDAN, HE COMMENCED THE FINAL CAMPAIGN OF THE CIVIL WAR," ACW:SEP/95[74]550

Jefferson, Texas; ARTICLE: "SHADOWED BY ITS CHARACTERISTIC CYPRESS TREES, JEFFERSON PLAYED A SIGNIFICANT ROLE IN CIVIL WAR-ERA TEXAS," ACW:MAR/93[68]409

Johnson's Island; ARTICLE: "A LONE STATUE AND AN EMPTY CONFEDERATE GRAVEYARD ARE THE ONLY REMINDERS OF THE JOHNSON'S ISLAND PRISON," ACW:JAN/93[66]399

Kennesaw Mountain Battlefield Park; ARTICLE: "KENNESAW MOUNTAIN BATTLEFIELD PARK AND THE ATLANTA CYCLORAMA GIVE VISITORS A GOOD TASTE OF THE ATLANTA," ACW:NOV/95[74]560

Minnesota; ARTICLE: "SIX PAINTINGS IN MINNESOTA'S CAPITOL BUILDING VIVIDLY RE-CREATE THE YOUNG STATE'S CIVIL WAR SERVICE," ACW:NOV/94[76]500

Natural Bridge, Virginia; ARTICLE: "AT NATURAL BRIDGE, CONFEDERATE FORCES WON THEIR LAST BATTLE OF THE WAR," ACW:NOV/91[64]336

New Salem, Illinois; ARTICLE: "AT NEW SALEM, LINCOLN MADE A STARTLING TRANSFORMATION FROM COUNTRY BUMPKIN TO POLISHED LAWYER," ACW:MAR/94[66]463

Newport, Rhode Island; ARTICLE: "U.S. NAVAL ACADEMY," ACW:JAN/91[62]289

North Georgia; ARTICLE: "A DRIVING TOUR OF NORTH GEORGIA TRACES WILLIAM T. SHERMAN'S CAUTIOUS ADVANCE TO ATLANTA," ACW:JUL/94[66]481

Oberlin, Ohio; ACW:MAY/94[66]472

Oxford, Mississippi; ARTICLE: "OXFORD, MISSISSIPPI, THE HOME OF WILLIAM FAULKNER PROVIDES A COURSE IN THE SWEEP OF SOUTHERN HISTORY," ACW:JUL/95[70]540

Petersburg; ARTICLE: "LIKE VICKSBURG, STRATEGIC PETERSBURG ENDURED AN INTENSE UNION SIEGE, ONLY TO FALL IN THE END," ACW:NOV/92[74]390

Sedgwick House, Cornwall Hollow, Connecticut; ARTICLE: "GENERAL JOHN SEDGWICK BUILT A LUXURIOUS RETIREMENT HOME IN CORNWALL HOLLOW, BUT HE DID NOT LIVE TO USE IT," ACW:MAR/95[70]520

Ship Island, Mississippi; ACW:JAN/94[70]454

Tudor Hall; ARTICLE: "CHILDHOOD HOME OF AN AMERICAN ARCH-VILLAIN," CWTI:APR/90[12]150

Vicksburg National Military Park; ARTICLE: "ON THE MUDDY YAZOO RIVER ONE MORNING, THE UNION GUNBOAT *CAIRO* MADE UNWANTED NAVAL HISTORY," ACW:SEP/94[74]491

Washington, Arkansas; ARTICLE: "THE APTLY NAMED TOWN OF WASHINGTON WAS, FOR A TIME, THE CAPITAL OF CONFEDEREATE ARKANSAS," ACW:SEP/92[66]381

TRAVERS, G.W., *Lieutenant Colonel, 46th New York Infantry;* B&G:AUG/95[8]604

TRAWEEK, WASHINGTON B., *Private, Jeff Davis Artillery;* ARTICLE: "BREAK OUT!" CWTI:DEC/91[26]238

TRAYLOR, ALBERT T., *Lieutenant, 7th South Carolina Infantry;* GETTY:5[35]159

TREASON; ARTICLE: "TRAINING IN TREASON," CWTI:SEP/91[23]228

TREATY OF KANAZAWA; MH:OCT/91[50]154

TREDEGAR IRON WORKS:
ARTICLES: "TREDEGAR IRON WORKS: ARSENAL OF THE SOUTH," CWM:SEP/91[24]381, "TREDEGAR," CWM:SEP/91[27]382, "VALENTINE MUSEUM EXPANDS TO TREDEGAR IRON WORKS," AHI:JUL/91[14]296
BOOK REVIEW: *IRONMAKER TO THE CONFEDERACY: JOSEPH R. ANDERSON AND THE TREDEGAR IRON WORKS*
ADDITIONAL LISTINGS: ACW:MAY/94[20]467, ACW:MAY/95[38]526, AHI:NOV/73[18]151, AHI:JAN/74[10]153, CWM:SEP/91[4]376, CWM:JUN/95[43]587, CWR:VOL1#1[1]102, CWTI:JUN/90[28]158, CWTI:JAN/93[49]303, *photos,* CWM:SEP/91[24]381, CWM:JUN/95[24]582

TREICHEL, CHARLES, *Captain, 3rd Pennsylvania Cavalry;* GETTY:4[75]149, GETTY:13[89]260

TREMAIN, HENRY; GETTY:4[113]153

TRENHOLM, GEORGE A.; ACW:MAY/95[38]526

***"TRENT* AFFAIR":**
ARTICLE: "HIGH SEAS BROUHAHA," ACW:NOV/91[46]335
GENERAL LISTINGS: ACW:NOV/91[46]335, ACW:NOV/92[51]389, AHI:JUN/80[6], CWNEWS:OCT/90[4], CWTI:SEP/92[46]284, CWTI:JAN/93[44]302, CWTI:DEC/94[73]416

TRENT'S REACH, VIRGINIA, BATTLE OF; ARTICLE: "DESPERATE IRONCLAD ASSAULT AT TRENT'S REACH," ACW:SEP/95[30]545

TREPP, CASPAR, *Lieutenant Colonel, Berdan's Sharpshooters;* CWTI:JUL/93[42]329

TREVILIAN STATION, VIRGINIA, BATTLE OF:
ARTICLE: "SWELTERING SUMMER COLLISION," MH:FEB/93[42]164
BOOK REVIEWS: *BATTLE OF TREVILIAN STATION WITH EYEWITNESS MEMOIRS * EYEWITNESS TO WAR 1861-1865: MEMOIRS OF MEN WHO FOUGHT IN THE BATTLE OF TREVILIAN STATION 11-12 JUNE 1864, VOL. I*
ADDITIONAL LISTINGS: ACW:SEP/94[55]489, CWM:OCT/94[17]534, CWR:VOL1#2[78], CWTI:APR/92[35]257

TREZEVANT, E.B., *Lieutenant, CSA;* CWTI:JUL/94[50]395

TRIGG, ROBERT, *Colonel, CSA;* B&G:AUG/91[11]458

TRIMBLE, A.M., *Private, 93rd Illinois Infantry;* CWR:VOL3#3[59]159

TRIMBLE, EDWIN, *Colonel, CSA;* B&G:AUG/91[11]458

TRIMBLE, ISAAC R., *General, CSA:*
ARTICLE: "GETTYSBURG: FIGHT ENOUGH IN OLD MAN TRIMBLE TO SATISFY A HERD OF TIGERS," CWM:AUG/94[60]531
GENERAL LISTINGS: *Gettysburg,* GETTY:5[107]164, GETTY:8[67]204, GETTY:8[95]205, GETTY:9[17]210, GETTY:9[61]215, GETTY:10[29]222, GETTY:10[102]226, GETTY:12[1]240, GETTY:12[61]245, MH:DEC/91[54]155, *in book review,* CWTI:MAR/94[12], *in list,* CWTI:JUL/93[34]327, *letters to the editor,* CWTI:DEC/94[12]408, *Manassas, Second,* ACW:JUL/91[18]312, B&G:AUG/92[11]493, *photo,* GETTY:13[75]259

ADDITIONAL LISTINGS: ACW:JUL/92[30]369, ACW:JAN/93[35]396, ACW:JUL/95[44]537, CWM:JAN/93[8]456, CWM:JAN/93[16]457, CWM:DEC/94[26]548, CWM:OCT/95[53]621, CWM:DEC/95[34]628, CWR:VOL2#4[269]145, CWTI:SEPT/89[46]132, CWTI:JUL/93[29]326, CWTI:NOV/93[55]350, CWTI:JUL/94[44]394, CWTI:DEC/94[79]417, CWTI:JAN/95[22]423, GETTY:13[64]258, GETTY:13[75]259, GETTY:13[108]261

TRIPLER, CHARLES S., *Major, USA:*
BOOK REVIEW: *HAND-BOOK FOR THE MILITARY SURGEON: BEING A COMPENDIUM OF THE DUTIES OF THE MEDICAL OFFICER IN THE FIELD, THE SANITARY MANAGEMENT OF THE CAMP, THE PREPARATION OF FOOD, ETC....*
ADDITIONAL LISTINGS: B&G:AUG/91[40]463, CWM:MAY/91[18]348 *photo,* CWM:MAY/91[18]348

TRIMBLE, JOHN J., *Lieutenant, 12th New Jersey Infantry;* GETTY:5[89]162

TRIMBLE, WILLIAM F., *Colonel, 60th Ohio Infantry;* CWR:VOL1#4[7]125, GETTY:7[51]190

TRIPLER, WILLIAM, *Surgeon, USA;* ARTICLE: "DETAILS FROM WHITE HOUSE ON THE PENINSULA," CWM:JUN/94[28]514

TRIPP, BRADFORD H., *7th Wisconsin Infantry;* GETTY:4[115]152

TROSLE, ABRAHAM, *civilian;* GETTY:5[47]160, GETTY:11[102]237

TROTH'S LANDING, ENGAGEMENT AT; ACW:SEP/95[8]542

TROUP (GEORGIA) ARTILLERY; GETTY:8[53]203

TROUPE ARTILLERY; CWTI:MAR/95[46]437

TROUT, BEN G., *Private, 7th Indiana Infantry;* CWTI:NOV/93[24]346

TROUT, BILLIE, *Private, CSA;* CWM:JUL/93[24]485

TROW, HARRISON; B&G:JUN/91[32]454

TROWBRIDGE, LUTHER S., *Major, 5th Michigan Cavalry;* GETTY:13[89]260

TRUE, CLINTON, *Colonel, 11th Kentucky Cavalry;* B&G:AUG/91[11]458

TRUES, WILLIAM S., *Colonel, USA;* B&G:APR/94[10]558

TRUESDAIL, WILLIAM, *General, USA;* AHI:JAN/85[20]245

TRUEX, WILLIAM S., *Colonel, USA;* ACW:NOV/93[50]444, B&G:APR/94[10]558, CWTI:JAN/93[40]301

TRUMAN, BENAJMIN C., *reporter;* CWTI:AUG/90[26]166

TRUMAN, JAMES, *Private, 5th New York Infantry;* CWTI:MAY/94[31]382

TRUMAN, LUCIUS, *Lieutenant, 13th Pennsylvania Reserves;* CWR:VOL1#3[46]121

TRUMBELL, H. CLAY, *Chaplain, 10th Connecticut Infantry;* ACW:JUL/94[42]479

TRUMBULL, LYMAN, *Senator, Illinois:*
GENERAL LISTINGS: *election of 1864,* AHI:OCT/68[4]116, *impeachment of Andrew Johnson,* AHI:DEC/68[28]118, *West Point,* B&G:DEC/91[12]469, *photo,* CWTI:AUG/95[54]460
ADDITIONAL LISTINGS: CWTI:JUN/90[46]161, CWTI:MAY/94[46]385, CWTI:AUG/95[54]460

TRUSTON, WENTWORTH, *Private, USA;* ACW:JUL/93[27]423

TSCHUDY, MARTIN, *Lieutenant Colonel, 9th Pennsylvania Infantry;* GETTY:4[89]150

TSHUDY, MARTIN, *Lieutenant Colonel, 69th New York Infantry;* CWM:MAR/91[17]335

TUBMAN, HARRIET; CWTI:MAR/94[38]372

TUCKER, A.W., *Private, 124th New York Infantry;* GETTY:9[5]209

TUCKER, BEVERLY; CWM:SEP/91[6]377, CWTI:JAN/93[44]302

TUCKER, FRANCIS M., *Seaman, CSN;* CWM:DEC/95[30]627

TUCKER, GEORGE, *Private, 1st Indiana Cavalry;* ACW:MAR/95[34]516, CWNEWS:SEP/95[33]

TUCKER, GEORGE W., *Sergeant, CSA:*
ARTICLE: "HILL'S FAVORITE COURIER," CWTI:SEP/92[42]283
ADDITIONAL LISTINGS: AHI:SEP/87[48]264, CWTI:SEP/92[42]283, CWTI:NOV/92[8]288

TUCKER, JAMES, *Captain, 9th Florida Infantry;* CWR:VOL3#4[1]161

TUCKER, JOHN R., *Commander, CSN;* ACW:JAN/92[22]341, AHI:OCT/75[30]162, CWM:FEB/95[49]565, CWM:AUG/95[5]602, *photo,* CWM:FEB/95[49]565

TUCKER, JOSEPH T., *Colonel, CSA;* B&G:OCT/94[11]580

TUCKER, MARTIN and MICHAEL, *1st Indiana Cavalry;* ACW:MAR/95[34]516

TUCKER, NATHANIEL B.; CWNEWS:FEB/94[5]

TUCKERMAN, S. CARY, *Lieutenant, USA;* GETTY:4[101]151

TUCSON, ARIZONA; ACW:JUL/93[27]423

TUITS, JAMES, *Private, 5th New York Infantry;* CWR:VOL1#2[7]111, CWTI:MAY/94[31]382

TULLAHOMA CAMPAIGN:
ARTICLES: "THE DECEPTION OF BRAXTON BRAGG: THE TULLAHOMA CAMPAIGN, JUNE 23-JULY 4, 1863," B&G:OCT/92[12]496, "MOST SPLENDID PIECE OF STRATEGY," CWM:OCT/94[48]542
ADDITIONAL LISTINGS: ACW:MAR/91[30]295, B&G:JUN/93[6]523, CWM:NOV/91[50]394, CWM:JUL/92[18]429, CWM:JUL/92[24]430, CWM:MAR/93[8]465, CWM:MAR/93[24]467, CWM:OCT/94[4]532

TULLIFINNY CROSSROADS, SOUTH CAROLINA, ENGAGEMENT AT; CWR:VOL2#3[194]141

TULLOS (TENNESSEE) RANGERS; CWR:VOL4#1[1]163

TUNNARD, W. *Private, 3rd Louisiana Infantry;* BOOK REVIEW: *A SOUTHERN RECORD: THE HISTORY OF THE THIRD REGIMENT LOUISIANA INFANTRY*

TUNNEL HILL, GEORGIA, BATTLE OF:
ARTICLES: "CHATTANOOGA RELIEVED!" CWM:DEC/94[46]552, "HEROISM OF SHERMAN'S SOLDIERS AT TUNNEL HILL," CWM:DEC/95[35]629
ADDITIONAL LISTINGS: ACW:JUL/94[66]481, CWM:APR/95[16]571, CWR:VOL1#1[73]108, CWR:VOL1#4[64]127, CWR:VOL3#3[59]159

TUPELO, MISSISSIPPI, BATTLE OF:
ARTICLE: "FEDERALS' RISKY PURSUIT," ACW:SEP/92[23]377
ADDITIONAL LISTINGS: ACW:SEP/92[23]377, CWTI:JAN/94[35]361

TURBERVILLE, GEORGE, *Private, Mosby's Ranger;* CWTI:SEP/90[34]176

TURCHIN, (TURCHININOFF), JOHN B., *Colonel, USA:*
ARTICLE: "A UNION COLONEL WAS THE RUSSIAN CONNECTION IN THE AMERICAN CIVIL WAR," MH:DEC/93[12]174
ADDITIONAL LISTINGS: ACW:SEP/95[6]541, AHI:JAN/81[18]214, CWM:MAR/91[74], CWM:SEP/93[18]494, CWR:VOL3#2[70]155, MH:OCT/93[6]170

TURNBULL, JOHN G., *Lieutenant, 3rd U.S. Artillery;* ACW:MAY/95[30]525, CWR:VOL3#2[1]153, GETTY:5[79]161, GETTY:7[51]190, GETTY:12[7]241

TURNER MOVEMENT:
ARTICLE: "MUTINY AT THE FRONT," CWTI:JUN/95[32]446
ADDITIONAL LISTING: B&G:OCT/95[8]611B
TURNER'S GAP, MARYLAND, BATTLE OF;
ACW:JUL/93[58], ACW:JAN/94[39]451, B&G:FEB/95[8]590B,
CWR:VOL1#3[28]120, CWR:VOL3#2[1]153
TURNER, C., *Lieutenant Colonel, 108th Illinois Infantry;*
B&G:FEB/94[8]550
TURNER, GEORGE W.; CWTI:JAN/95[24]424
TURNER, HENRY M., *Chaplain, 1st U.S. Colored Infantry;*
CWTI:APR/89[32]110
TURNER, IKE, *Captain, 5th Texas Infantry;*
ACW:JUL/92[30]369, CWTI:DEC/91[36]240
TURNER, IRA, *Private, 2nd South Carolina Infantry;*
GETTY:5[35]159
TURNER, J. MCLEOD, *Lieutenant Colonel, 7th North Carolina
Infantry;* GETTY:8[67]204, GETTY:13[75]259
TURNER, JOSEPH, *Sergeant, 118th Pennsylvania Infantry;*
GETTY:8[53]203
TURNER, NAT; AHI:JUN/74[12]155
TURNER, PETER, *Private, Georgia and Mississippi Regiment;*
CWR:VOL1#4[42]126
TURNER, T.T., *Captain, CSA;* B&G:FEB/95[8]590C,
GETTY:9[17]210
TURNER, THOMAS P., *Major, USA;* AHI:JUN/70[30]127,
AHI:DEC/85[40]255
TURNER, VINES E., *Captain, 23rd North Carolina Infantry;*
B&G:FEB/95[8]590B, GETTY:5[13]157
TURNER, W.S., *civilian;* ACW:NOV/95[8]552
TURNER, WILLIAM T., *Lieutenant, CSA;* CWTI:SEP/90[34]176
"TURNERS"; ARTICLE: "MUTINY AT THE FRONT,"
CWTI:JUN/95[32]446
TURNEY, J.B., *Captain, 13th Alabama Infantry;*
GETTY:5[4]156, GETTY:6[13]170
TURPIN, WILLIAM H., *53rd Virginia Infantry;*
GETTY:5[123]166
TUTTLE, DANIEL, *civilian;* B&G:APR/93[24]520
TUTTLE, J.W., *Colonel, USA;* CWTI:AUG/95[58]461
TUTTLE, JAMES, *Colonel, 2nd Iowa Infantry;*
B&G:FEB/92[48]475
TUTTLE, JAMES M., *General, USA;* B&G:AUG/95[8]604
TUTTLE, JOHN R., *Private, 126th New York Infantry;*
CWR:VOL1#4[7]125
TWAIN, MARK; ARTICLE: "THE PRIVATE HISTORY OF A
CAMPAIGN THAT FAILED," AHI:AUG/67[50]111
TWIGGS, DAVID E., *General, CSA:*
GENERAL LISTINGS: *Indian wars,* AHI:OCT/79[20]194, *Mexican
War,* AHI:MAY/88[38]270, MH:AUG/91[45]153,
MH:APR/93[34]165, *Winfield Scott,* AHI:JUL/81[20]221, *photo,*
CWM:MAY/93[16]475
ADDITIONAL LISTINGS: ACW:MAR/93[58], ACW:JAN/94[70]454,
CWTI:MAY/93[29]319
TWILLEY, BEN, *Private, 1st Maryland Battalion;*
GETTY:9[81]216
TWIST, RUSSELL P., *Lieutenant, Ohio Light Artillery;*
B&G:AUG/95[8]604
TWITCHELL, MARSHALL H.; BOOK REVIEWS:
*CARPETBAGGER FROM VERMONT: THE
AUTOBIOGRAPHY OF MARSHALL HARVEY TWITCHELL,*
CWM:JAN/91[35], CWNEWS:JAN/90[4]
TWOMBLY, VOLTAIRE P., *Corporal, 2nd Iowa Infantry:*
ARTICLE: "VOLTAIRE P. TWOMBLY, 2ND IOWA INFANTRY,
MEDAL OF HONOR," B&G:FEB/92[48]475

ADDITIONAL LISTINGS: B&G:FEB/92[10]474, *photo,*
B&G:FEB/92[48]475
TYLER, CHARLES, *Colonel, CSA;* B&G:JUN/91[10]452
TYLER, DANIEL; CWM:MAR/91[35]337
TYLER, ELNATHAN, *Corporal, 14th Connecticut Infantry;*
GETTY:9[61]215
TYLER, ERASMUS B., *General, USA;* ACW:JAN/93[35]396,
B&G:DEC/92[8]503, CWM:APR/95[29]574,
CWTI:NOV/93[55]350, *photo,* B&G:DEC/92[8]503
TYLER, HENRY A., *Captain, 5th Tennessee Infantry;* ARTICLE:
"A COLLEAGUE OF GENERAL FORREST,"
CWTI:MAY/92[74]268
TYLER, JAMES R., *Lieutenant, 1st Virginia Battalion;*
CWM:MAR/91[65]342
TYLER, NAT, *Major, CSA;* B&G:AUG/93[10]529
TYLER, ROBERT, *Union veteran;* GETTY:7[119]195
TYLER, ROBERT C., *General, CSA:*
ARTICLES: "A MOST VOLUNTARY GATHERING,"
B&G:AUG/94[22]576, "OUT OF THE SHADOWS,"
CWTI:JAN/95[27]425
ADDITIONAL LISTINGS: CWTI:MAY/94[44]384, *photos,*
B&G:AUG/94[22]576, CWTI:JAN/95[27]425
TYLER, ROBERT C., *Lieutenant Colonel, 15th Tennessee
Infantry;* CWR:VOL3#4[24]162
TYLER, ROBERT O., *General, USA;* B&G:APR/93[12]518,
B&G:APR/94[10]558, B&G:APR/94[55]564,
CWM:OCT/95[40]619, GETTY:5[47]160, GETTY:12[30]243
TYNDALE, HECTOR, *Colonel, USA;* ACW:MAR/94[50]462,
CWR:VOL3#2[70]155
TYRRELL, WILLIAM, *Sergeant, 116th Pennsylvania Infantry;*
CWTI:DEC/90[58]185
TYSON, CHARLES J.; CWTI:DEC/89[16]134

U

ULRICH, GEORGE, *civilian;* ACW:MAR/92[22]351
UNDERGROUND RAILROAD:
ARTICLES: "ESCAPED SLAVES ON THE UNDERGROUND
RAILROAD FOUND WELCOME HAVENS IN OHIO'S
OBERLIN AND WELLINGTON," ACW:MAY/94[66]472, "THE
MYTH OF THE UNDERGROUND RAILROAD,"
AHI:JAN/78[34]178
ADDITIONAL LISTINGS: ACW:JUL/91[8]309, ACW:JAN/94[47]452,
ACW:NOV/94[42]497, CWM:SEP/93[18]494,
CWTI:FEB/91[66]196, CWTI:MAR/94[38]372,
CWTI:JUN/95[56]450
UNDERHILL, CHARLES, *Private, 9th New Hampshire
Infantry;* CWR:VOL2#2[118]136
UNDERWOOD, GEORGE C., *Surgeon, 26th North Carolina
Infantry;* GETTY:5[19]158
UNDERWOOD, JOHN, *Lieutenant, USN;* ACW:MAR/94[35]460
UNIFORMS:
ARTICLE: "THE FIELD GLASSES OF ROBERT E. LEE,"
B&G:AUG/95[32]606
BOOK REVIEWS: *AMERICAN MILITARY, SOURCEBOOK AND
DIRECTORY THE WHO'S WHO IN MILITARIA * CIVIL
WAR CANTEENS * COLLECTING GRAND ARMY OF THE
REPUBLIC MEMORABILIA * CONFEDERATE BELT
BUCKLES & PLATES * THE LADIES' HAND BOOK OF
FANCY AND ORNAMENTAL WORK: CIVIL WAR ERA *
NOTES ON MILITARY ETIQUETTE * UNIFORMS OF THE
CIVIL WAR IN COLOR * ZOUAVES: THE FIRST AND THE
BRAVEST*
UNION ARMY; BOOK REVIEW: *THE UNION ARMY, 1861-1865:
ORGANIZATION AND OPERATIONS, VOLUME I: THE
EASTERN THEATER*
UNION DEFENSE COMMITTEE; ACW:MAY/95[54]528
UNION (PENNSYLVANIA) GUARDS; (53rd Pennsylvania
Infantry); GETTY:11[80]235
UNION LEAGUE;, ACW:JUL/91[58]316, AHI:OCT/68[4]116,
AHI:APR/73[12]148
UNION VOLUNTEER REFRESHMENT SALOON;
CWTI:MAY/94[24]381
UNITED CONFEDERATE VETERANS;
ACW:MAY/93[14]413, AHI:JUL/93[40]312,
CWTI:FEB/92[42]250, GETTY:5[123]166, GETTY:7[119]195
UNITED DAUGHTERS OF THE CONFEDERACY:
ARTICLE: "SEN. CAROL MOSELEY-BRAUN AND THE
POLITICS OF SYMBOLISM: UDC LOSES LOGO BATTLE,"
B&G:OCT/93[39]542
GENERAL LISTINGS: *letters to the editor,* B&G:OCT/92[22]497,
B&G:FEB/94[6]549, B&G:JUN/94[5]567
ADDITIONAL LISTINGS: ACW:NOV/92[10]384, AHI:DEC/74[12]156,
B&G:AUG/93[55]535, B&G:FEB/94[57]555,
B&G:JUN/94[38]571, B&G:FEB/95[35]592,
B&G:FEB/95[38]593, CWM:JUL/93[35]487,
CWTI:MAR/94[59]376
**UNITED STATES ARMY MILITARY HISTORY
INSTITUTE;** B&G:JUN/92[46]490
UNITED STATES CHRISTIAN COMMISSION:
GENERAL LISTINGS: *Gettysburg,* GETTY:6[43]173,
GETTY:8[17]200, GETTY:10[53]225, GETTY:12[97]249, *photo,*
GETTY:10[53]225

ADDITIONAL LISTINGS: B&G:APR/91[8]445, CWM:DEC/95[54]632,
CWTI:SEPT/89[44]131, CWTI:DEC/95[24]477
UNITED STATES CIVIL WAR CENTER; ARTICLE: "A
SUPERHIGHWAY FOR CIVIL WAR INFORMATION,"
CWTI:JAN/95[30]426

UNITED STATES COLORED TROOPS:
also, see individual state listings
1st Artillery, (Heavy); B&G:AUG/91[36]462
1st Infantry; CWTI:APR/89[32]110, CWTI:MAY/93[20]317
2nd Cavalry; CWM:AUG/94[30]527, CWR:VOL4#2[136]
2nd Infantry; ACW:NOV/91[64]336, ACW:NOV/95[38]556,
CWM:APR/95[50], CWR:VOL4#2[136], CWTI:DEC/89[42]137,
CWTI:MAY/93[20]317
3rd Infantry; CWM:AUG/94[30]527
4th Artillery; CWTI:SEP/93[18]334, CWTI:JAN/94[35]361,
4th Infantry; B&G:JUN/95[36]603A, CWM:AUG/94[30]527
5th Cavalry; GENERAL LISTINGS: *Saltville,* B&G:AUG/91[11]458,
B&G:AUG/91[52]464, *in list,* B&G:AUG/91[11]458
5th Infantry; B&G:OCT/94[42]583
6th Artillery, (Heavy); CWTI:NOV/93[65]351
6th Cavalry; GENERAL LISTINGS: *Battle of Saltville,*
B&G:AUG/91[11]458, B&G:AUG/91[52]464, *in list,*
B&G:AUG/91[11]458
6th Infantry; CWM:AUG/94[30]527
8th Infantry; ACW:JUL/94[42]479, CWM:NOV/92[24]448,
CWR:VOL3#1[65]151, CWR:VOL3#4[1]161
10th Artillery, (Heavy); B&G:FEB/92[6]473,
CWM:JAN/92[6]398
10th Infantry; AHI:AUG/68[4]115B
11th Infantry; CWTI:SEP/93[18]334, CWTI:NOV/93[65]351,
CWTI:JAN/94[35]361
13th Infantry; B&G:DEC/93[12]545
14th Infantry; &G:DEC/93[12]545
17th Infantry; B&G:DEC/93[12]545
19th Infantry; AHI:OCT/67[26]112
22nd Infantry; CWM:AUG/94[30]527
27th Infantry; B&G:DEC/94[10]585
29th Infantry; B&G:AUG/94[38]578
31st Infantry; ACW:SEP/95[38]546
32nd Infantry; CWTI:AUG/90[42]167
33rd Infantry; B&G:FEB/92[6]473, CWM:JAN/92[6]398
36th Infantry; CWM:AUG/94[30]527
37th Infantry; B&G:JUN/95[5]599
38th Infantry; CWM:AUG/94[30]527
44th Infantry; B&G:AUG/95[24]605
56th Infantry; CWTI:JAN/94[82]366
62nd Infantry; ACW:JUL/92[46]371, CWTI:AUG/90[58]169
73rd Infantry; CWM:NOV/92[6]446, CWTI:DEC/94[24]409
79th Infantry; B&G:FEB/92[6]473, CWM:JAN/92[6]398
86th Infantry; CWR:VOL4#1[78]
99th Infantry; ACW:NOV/91[64]336
102nd Infantry; CWTI:APR/89[32]110, CWTI:AUG/90[42]167
107th Infantry; AHI:APR/68[4]115
108th Infantry; CWTI:APR/89[32]110
109th Infantry; CWM:JAN/91[35], CWNEWS:JAN/90[4]
111th Infantry; B&G:JUN/92[32]488
119th Infantry; GETTY:12[42]244

UNITED STATES CONGRESS; BOOK REVIEW: *BLUEPRINT
FOR MODERN AMERICA: NONMILITARY LEGISLATION
OF THE FIRST CIVIL WAR CONGRESS*

UNITED STATES MILITARY RAILROAD:
ARTICLES: "HERMAN HAUPT'S RAILROADS: BEANPOLES
AND CORNSTALKS," CWM:NOV/91[12]390, "WHEN
SECRETARY OF WAR EDWIN STANTON NEEDED A
GOOD MAN TO RUN HIS VITAL RAILROADS, HE SENT
FOR HERMAN HAUPT," ACW:JUL/95[16]534
ADDITIONAL LISTINGS: AHI:JUL/95[30]324, B&G:AUG/91[32]461,
CWM:NOV/91[4]388, CWM:NOV/91[12]390,
CWTI:FEB/91[24]191, CWTI:FEB/92[10]246,
CWTI:MAR/95[54]438
UNITED STATES MILITARY TELEGRAPH CORPS:
ARTICLE: "THE TELEGRAPH GOES TO WAR,"
CWM:NOV/91[58]394A
GENERAL LISTINGS: *Beardslee*, ACW:JAN/95[20]504, *Gettysburg*,
GETTY:4[101]151, *letters to the editor*, CWTI:DEC/95[8]474,
photo, CWTI:DEC/94[57]414
ADDITIONAL LISTINGS: CWTI:SEP/92[22]279,
CWTI:DEC/94[57]414, CWTI:AUG/95[46]459
UNITED STATES NAVAL ACADEMY; ARTICLE: "TRAVEL,
U.S. NAVAL ACADEMY," ACW:JAN/91[62]289
UNITED STATES SANITARY COMMISSION:
ARTICLE: "DETAILS FROM WHITE HOUSE ON THE
PENINSULA," CWM:JUN/94[28]514
BOOK REVIEWS: *THE RISE AND FALL OF THE CONFEDERATE
GOVERNMENT SANITARY COMMISSION DURING THE
PENINSULA CAMPAIGN * SANITARY FAIRS: A
PHILATELIC AND HISTORICAL STUDY OF CIVIL WAR
BENEVOLENCES*
GENERAL LISTINGS: *Gettysburg*, GETTY:6[99]181,
GETTY:8[121]207, GETTY:9[116]219, GETTY:10[53]225,
GETTY:12[97]249, *Mary Ann Bickerdyke*, AHI:APR/79[4]186
ADDITIONAL LISTINGS: ACW:JAN/91[38]287, ACW:NOV/92[8]383,
ACW:JUL/93[50]426, ACW:SEP/95[38]546,
AHI:JAN/93[61]309, B&G:APR/91[8]445,
CWM:MAY/91[10]347, CWM:MAY/91[18]348,
CWTI:MAR/89[20]102, CWTI:SEPT/89[40]130,
CWTI:MAR/93[26]310,
CWTI:MAR/94[38]372, CWTI:AUG/95[58]461

UNITED STATES SHARPSHOOTERS:
1st Regiment:
ARTICLE: "THE MOST DANGEROUS SET OF MEN,"
CWTI:JUL/93[42]329
BOOK REVIEW: *CIVIL WAR CHIEF OF SHARPSHOOTERS
HIRAM BERDAN: MILITARY COMMANDER AND
FIREARMS INVENTOR*
GENERAL LISTINGS: *Gettysburg*, GETTY:7[29]188,
GETTY:8[53]203, GETTY:9[5]209, *in book review*,
CWM:AUG/95[45], CWNEWS:JAN/91[4], CWR:VOL4#4[129]
ADDITIONAL LISTINGS: ACW:MAR/92[30]352, ACW:NOV/92[10]384,
ACW:MAY/95[30]525, B&G:FEB/95[8]590A,
B&G:APR/95[8]595, B&G:JUN/95[8]600,
CWM:JUN/95[63]594, CWTI:MAR/89[34]104
2nd Regiment:
ARTICLE: "THE MOST DANGEROUS SET OF MEN,"
CWTI:JUL/93[42]329
BOOK REVIEWS: *CIVIL WAR CHIEF OF SHARPSHOOTERS
HIRAM BERDAN: MILITARY COMMANDER AND
FIREARMS INVENTOR * THE CIVIL WAR DIARY OF
WYMAN WHITE, FIRST SERGEANT OF COMPANY F,
UNITED STATES SHARPSHOOTER REGIMENT, 1861-1865
* LETTERS FROM A SHARPSHOOTER: THE CIVIL WAR*

*LETTERS OF PRIVATE WILLIAM B. GREENE, COLONEL,
2ND UNITED STATES SHARPSHOOTERS (BERDAN'S)*
GENERAL LISTINGS: *Gettysburg*, GETTY:8[53]203, GETTY:9[5]209,
GETTY:9[33]211, GETTY:9[48]213, *in Book Review*,
MH:DEC/92[74], *Manassas, Second*, B&G:AUG/92[11]493
ADDITIONAL LISTINGS: ACW:JAN/92[38]343, ACW:MAY/95[30]525,
CWM:DEC/94[26]548, CWTI:JUL/93[42]329

UNITED STATES SIGNAL CORPS; ARTICLE: "MEMBERS OF
THE U.S. SIGNAL CORPS EARNED THE PROUD
NICKNAME 'KNIGHTS WITHOUT ARMOR,'"
ACW:JAN/95[20]504

UNITED STATES TROOPS:
ARTICLES: "A SIGNAL SERGEANT AT GETTYSBURG: THE
DIARY OF LUTHER C. FURST," GETTY:10[42]224,
"MEMBERS OF THE U.S. SIGNAL CORPS EARNED THE
PROUD NICKNAME 'KNIGHTS WITHOUR ARMOR,'"
ACW:JAN/95[20]504, "NORTH'S UNSUNG REGULARS,"
ACW:JUL/93[42]425, "REGULARS TO THE RESCUE AT
GAINES' MILL," ACW:NOV/94[50]498
BOOK REVIEWS: *FRONTIER REGULARS, THE UNITED STATES
ARMY AND THE INDIAN, 1866-1891 * THE REGULAR
ARMY ON THE EVE OF THE CIVIL WAR * SYKES'
REGULAR INFANTRY DIVISION, 1861-1864: A HISTORY
OF REGULAR UNITED STATES INFANTRY OPERATIONS
IN THE CIVIL WAR'S EASTERN THEATER * THE UNITED
STATES INFANTRY: AN ILLUSTRATED HISTORY
1775-1918*
1st Artillery; AHI:DEC/66[30]105, CWR:VOL1#4[42]126,
CWR:VOL2#3[194]141
1st Artillery, Battery A; ACW:JAN/94[30]450,
ACW:MAR/94[50]462
1st Artillery, Battery B; ACW:MAY/92[30]361
1st Artillery, Battery E & G; ACW:JUL/93[42]425,
B&G:OCT/93[12]537, GETTY:9[41]212, GETTY:11[19]232,
GETTY:13[89]260
1st Artillery, Battery H; GETTY:12[30]243
1st Artillery, Battery I; B&G:APR/92[36]483, GETTY:4[89]150,
GETTY:5[89]162, GETTY:7[51]190, GETTY:8[95]205,
GETTY:9[61]215
1st Artillery, Battery H & I; B&G:APR/92[8]481
1st Artillery, Battery K; GETTY:11[19]23
1st Cavalry; *Aldie*, GETTY:11[19]232, *Gettysburg*,
GETTY:11[19]232, *in order of battle*, B&G:APR/92[8]481,
photo, ACW:JUL/93[42]425
ADDITIONAL LISTINGS: ACW:JUL/93[42]425, ACW:NOV/94[50]498,
B&G:OCT/93[12]537, B&G:JUN/94[8]568,
CWTI:JUN/90[32]159, CWTI:FEB/92[29]248
1st Engineers; CWTI:DEC/90[29]182
1st Infantry; ACW:SEP/91[46]324, ACW:NOV/93[26]441,
CWR:VOL2#1[19]131
1st Sharpshooters; GETTY:12[7]241
2nd Artillery; ACW:MAY/91[23]303, ACW:NOV/93[26]441,
B&G:JUN/95[36]603A, CWR:VOL1#2[7]111,
CWTI:MAY/89[36]118, CWTI:MAY/94[50]386,
GETTY:7[29]188, GETTY:13[89]260
2nd Artillery, Battery A:
GENERAL LISTINGS: *Five Forks*, B&G:APR/92[8]481, *Gettysburg*,
GETTY:6[13]170
ADDITIONAL LISTINGS: B&G:FEB/95[8]590A, GETTY:11[19]232
2nd Artillery, Battery B & L; GETTY:11[19]232

2nd Artillery, Battery E; B&G:AUG/95[8]604,
CWTI:MAR/93[20]308
2nd Artillery, Battery M; GETTY:12[68]246
2nd Cavalry:
BOOK REVIEWS: *CRY COMANCHE: THE 2ND U.S. CAVALRY IN TEXAS, 1855-1861 * FROM EVERGLADE TO CANON WITH THE SECOND DRAGOONS * WITHOUT QUARTER: THE WICHITA EXPEDITION AND THE FIGHT ON CROOKED CREEK*
ADDITIONAL LISTINGS: ACW:JUL/93[42]425, ACW:SEP/94[55]489,
ACW:NOV/94[50]498, ACW:JUL/95[34]536,
B&G:JUN/94[8]568, CWR:VOL4#1[44]164,
CWTI:MAY/89[36]118, CWTI:JUN/90[32]159,
CWTI:FEB/92[29]248, GETTY:11[19]232, MH:FEB/93[42]164
2nd Infantry; CWM:MAY/93[8]474, CWR:VOL1#4[7]125,
CWTI:FEB/92[29]248
3rd Artillery; ACW:JUL/93[42]425, CWTI:JUL/93[20]325,
CWTI:MAY/94[31]382, CWTI:JUN/95[51]449
3rd Artillery, Battery E; ACW:MAY/92[30]361
3rd Artillery, Batteries F & K; ACW:MAY/95[30]525
GETTY:7[51]190, GETTY:12[7]241
3rd Artillery, Battery L; CWTI:JAN/94[8]356
3rd Artillery, Battery L & M; CWTI:MAR/95[18]432
3rd Cavalry; B&G:JUN/94[8]568
3rd Infantry; ACW:NOV/94[50]498, B&G:APR/95[24]596,
CWR:VOL3#3[1]157, GETTY:11[91]236
4th Artillery; ACW:MAR/93[10]402, ACW:SEP/95[38]546,
CWTI:JUL/93[29]326, MH:DEC/91[54]155, *photo,*
ACW:JUL/93[42]425
4th Artillery, Battery A:
GENERAL LISTINGS: *Gettysburg,* GETTY:4[89]150,
GETTY:5[107]164, GETTY:7[97]193, GETTY:12[61]245,
MH:DEC/91[54]155, *in book review,* CWM:APR/95[50],
CWR:VOL4#3[89]
ADDITIONAL LISTINGS: ACW:MAY/92[8]357, CWM:MAR/91[17]335
4th Artillery, Battery B:
ARTICLES: "A FEDERAL ARTILLERYMAN AT GETTYSBURG: AN EYEWITNESS ACCOUNT," AHI:MAY/67[22]107, "THE IRON BRIGADE BATTERY AT GETTYSBURG," GETTY:11[57]233
GENERAL LISTINGS: *Five Forks,* B&G:APR/92[8]481, *Gettysburg,*
GETTY:4[33]146, GETTY:4[113]153, GETTY:5[117]165,
GETTY:8[9]199, GETTY:9[33]211, GETTY:10[7]221,
GETTY:10[29]222, GETTY:12[30]243, *in book review,*
CWM:APR/95[50], CWNEWS:JUN/92[4], *in order of battle,*
B&G:APR/92[8]481
ADDITIONAL LISTINGS: CWM:MAR/91[17]335,
CWM:JAN/93[16]457, CWTI:JAN/93[35]300,
GETTY:13[22]254, GETTY:13[33]255
4th Artillery, Battery C; CWM:DEC/94[40]550,
GETTY:5[79]161
4th Artillery, Battery C & F; B&G:APR/92[8]481
4th Artillery, Battery E; ACW:JUL/92[41]370,
CWTI:FEB/92[36]249
4th Artillery, Battery F; ARTICLE: "ORDNANCE, INFANTRY VOLUNTEERS, UNION ARTILLERY BATTERIES," ACW:MAY/91[8]300
4th Artillery, Battery G; B&G:FEB/95[8]590C,
GETTY:4[49]147
4th Artillery, Battery K; GETTY:5[79]161, GETTY:12[7]241,
GETTY:12[42]244
4th Cavalry; ACW:JUL/93[42]425, ACW:NOV/95[48]557,
CWR:VOL4#1[1]163, CWR:VOL4#1[44]164

4th Infantry; B&G:APR/95[24]596
5th Artillery:
GENERAL LISTINGS: *Gettysburg,* GETTY:9[33]211,
GETTY:9[41]212, GETTY:12[42]244, *Manassas, Second,*
AHI:DEC/66[30]105, *West Point,* B&G:DEC/91[12]469
ADDITIONAL LISTINGS: ACW:MAY/91[8]300, ACW:JUL/93[42]425,
CWR:VOL4#2[1]165
5th Artillery, Battery A; CWTI:FEB/92[36]249
5th Artillery, Battery C; CWR:VOL3#3[1]157, GETTY:5[79]161
5th Artillery, Battery D:
GENERAL LISTINGS: *Gettysburg,* GETTY:6[43]173,
GETTY:7[41]189, GETTY:8[31]201, GETTY:8[53]203,
GETTY:9[48]213
ADDITIONAL LISTINGS: CWR:VOL1#2[29]112, CWR:VOL1#2[42]113,
CWTI:JUN/90[28]158, CWTI:APR/92[14]254
5th Artillery, Battery D & G; B&G:APR/92[8]481
5th Artillery, Battery F; ACW:JAN/94[8]447
5th Artillery, Battery G; ACW:JAN/94[30]450
5th Artillery, Battery I; GETTY:5[47]160, GETTY:6[7]169,
GETTY:7[51]190, GETTY:11[91]236
5th Artillery, Battery K; AHI:JAN/67[4]106, GETTY:7[83]192,
GETTY:9[81]216, GETTY:12[1]240, GETTY:12[42]244,
GETTY:12[83]247
5th Cavalry:
GENERAL LISTINGS: *Gettysburg,* GETTY:11[19]232, *in order of battle,* B&G:APR/92[8]481
ADDITIONAL LISTINGS: ACW:NOV/91[30]332, ACW:JUL/93[42]425,
ACW:NOV/94[50]498, ACW:JUL/95[34]536,
B&G:OCT/93[12]537, CWM:JUN/95[50]589,
CWTI:JUN/90[32]159, MH:APR/94[54]176
5th Infantry; B&G:JUN/94[8]568
6th Cavalry:
BOOK REVIEW: *FROM YORKTOWN TO SANTIAGO WITH THE SIXTH U.S. CAVALRY*
GENERAL LISTINGS: *Aldie,* GETTY:11[19]232, *Gettysburg,*
GETTY:11[19]232, *in order of battle,* B&G:APR/92[8]481
ADDITIONAL LISTINGS: ACW:JUL/93[42]425, B&G:OCT/93[12]537,
B&G:AUG/94[10]574, CWM:JUN/95[50]589,
CWTI:JUN/90[32]159
6th Infantry; ACW:NOV/94[50]498, AHI:DEC/66[30]105,
CWR:VOL1#2[29]112
7th Infantry; ACW:JUL/93[42]425, B&G:JUN/94[8]568
8th Infantry; ACW:MAR/92[62]355, B&G:JUN/94[8]568,
B&G:APR/95[24]596
9th Infantry; ACW:MAR/92[62]355
10th Infantry; ACW:NOV/94[50]498
11th Infantry; ACW:JUL/93[42]425, ACW:NOV/94[50]498,
AHI:DEC/66[30]105, B&G:APR/91[8]445,
B&G:APR/93[12]518, CWTI:NOV/92[49]292
12th Infantry; ACW:JUL/93[42]425, ACW:NOV/94[50]498,
B&G:FEB/93[40]514, B&G:APR/93[12]518,
B&G:AUG/93[18]530, CWR:VOL1#2[7]111,
CWTI:MAY/94[31]382
13th Infantry:
GENERAL LISTINGS: "THE ASSAULT ON VICKSBURG,"
CWM:JUN/94[30]515, "THE FIRST HONOR AT VICKSBURG: THE 1ST BATTALION, 13TH U.S. INFANTRY," CWR:VOL2#1[1]130
ADDITIONAL LISTINGS: ACW:JUL/93[42]425, CWR:VOL2#1[i]129,
CWR:VOL2#1[69]133
14th Infantry; ACW:JUL/93[42]425, ACW:NOV/94[50]498,
CWR:VOL1#3[94], CWTI:APR/92[14]254, GETTY:10[42]224
15th Infantry; ACW:JUL/93[42]425, B&G:JUN/95[36]603A

16th Infantry; ACW:JUL/93[42]425, B&G:JUN/95[36]603A
17th Infantry; ACW:JUL/93[42]425, ACW:NOV/94[50]498, CWM:AUG/95[27]605, GETTY:13[7]253
18th Infantry:
GENERAL LISTINGS: *Gettysburg,* GETTY:11[57]233, *letters to the editor,* B&G:APR/94[6]557, *SIO,* B&G:JUN/95[36]603A
ADDITIONAL LISTINGS: ACW:JUL/93[42]425, AHI:NOV/85[38]254
19th Infantry; ACW:JUL/93[42]425, B&G:JUN/95[36]603A, GETTY:7[51]190
23rd Infantry; CWTI:APR/92[14]254

UNITED STATES VETERAN RESERVE CORPS:
ARTICLES: "ALTHOUGH CRIPPLED IN BODY, THE SOLDIERS IN THE VETERAN RESERVE CORPS WERE WHOLE AND STRONG IN SPIRIT," ACW:SEP/94[8]483, "CONDEMNED YANKS," AHI:FEB/75[35]158
ADDITIONAL LISTINGS: AHI:JUL/95[30]324
1st Regiment, AHI:FEB/75[35]158
3rd Regiment; ACW:SEP/94[8]483
7th Regiment; CWTI:JUN/95[90]451
8th Regiment; ACW:SEP/94[8]483
11th Regiment; B&G:APR/93[24]520, CWTI:JAN/95[48]429
16th Regiment; ACW:SEP/94[8]483
18th Regiment; ACW:SEP/94[8]483
20th Regiment; B&G:APR/93[24]520, CWTI:JAN/95[48]429
23rd Regiment; CWTI:AUG/90[50]168

UNIVERSITY (MISSISSIPPI) GREYS:
ARTICLE: "OLE MISS' SPIRITED UNIVERSITY GREYS LEFT THEIR QUIET UNIVERSITY CAMPUS FOR THE WAR'S WORST BATTLEFIELDS," ACW:MAR/92[10]349
ADDITIONAL LISTING: GETTY:9[98]217
UPHAM, SAM, ARTICLE: "SAM UPHAM: STOREKEEPER AND 'YANKEE SCOUNDREL,'" CWM:MAR/92[32]413
UPJOHN, CHARLES, *Private, 7th Pennsylvania Reserves;* CWR:VOL4#4[1]177
UPPERMAN, JAMES H.; CWTI:DEC/95[24]477
UPPERVILLE, VIRGINIA, BATTLE OF:
ARTICLE: "THE FIGHT FOR LOUDOUN VALLEY: ALDIE, MIDDLEBURG AND UPPERVILLE, VA," B&G:OCT/93[12]537
ADDITIONAL LISTINGS: B&G:OCT/93[12]537, CWTI:DEC/89[34]136, GETTY:9[5]209
UPSON, THEODORE F., *Private, USA;* ACW:JAN/92[10]339
UPTON, EMORY, *General, USA:*
BOOK REVIEW: *UPTON AND THE ARMY*
GENERAL LISTINGS: *in book review,* B&G:FEB/91[28], CWM:DEC/95[10], CWNEWS:JAN/94[5], *in order of battle,* B&G:APR/94[10]558, B&G:APR/95[8]595, *Overland Campaign,* B&G:APR/94[10]558, *West Point,* B&G:DEC/91[12]469, *photo,* B&G:DEC/91[12]469
ADDITIONAL LISTINGS: ACW:MAR/91[38]296, ACW:MAR/92[30]352, ACW:JAN/95[46]507, B&G:FEB/92[22]476, B&G:AUG/93[30]531, B&G:JUN/94[38]571, CWR:VOL2#2[156]138, CWR:VOL3#3[1]157
UPTON, JOHN C., *Colonel, 5th Texas Infantry;* CWTI:DEC/91[36]240
URBAN, JOHN, *Private, Pennsylvania Reserves;* ACW:MAY/94[35]469
URQUART, DAVID, *Lieutenant Colonel, CSA;* B&G:FEB/91[20]440
URQUHART, CHARLES, *Surgeon;* B&G:APR/95[8]595

URQUHART, MOSES, *Captain, 98th Ohio Infantry;* CWTI:SEP/92[31]281
URSLINE NUNS; B&G:FEB/94[6]549
USHER, FRED, *Private, 8th Illinois Cavalry;* GETTY:11[19]232
USHER, JOHN P., *Secretary of the Interior;* GETTY:9[122]220
USINA, MICHAEL, *Private, 8th Georgia Infantry;* CWTI:DEC/89[82]140
USINA, MICHAEL P., *Lieutenant, CSN;* ARTICLE: "CONFEDERATE MIKE USINA: "BOY" SEA FOX," CWM:JUN/94[50]518
UNITED STATE MILITARY ACADEMY: see listings under **"WEST POINT"**
UNITED STATES MARINE CORPS:
ARTICLES: "SOME NOTES ON THE CIVIL WAR-ERA MARINE CORPS," CWR:VOL2#3[183]140, "TO THE SHORES OF CAROLINA: DAHLGREN'S MARINE BATTALIONS," CWR:VOL2#3[194]141
ADDITIONAL LISTINGS: CWR:VOL2#3[252]144, CWTI:APR/92[14]254
UTAH TERRITORY:
ARTICLE: "UTAH'S EXPERIENCED NAUVOO LEGION SERVED BOTH THE UNITED STATES AND THE MORMON CHURCH," ACW:JAN/95[8]502
ADDITIONAL LISTING: B&G:JUN/94[8]568
UTOY CREEK, GEORGIA, BATTLE OF; ACW:NOV/95[74]560, CWM:AUG/95[36]608, CWR:VOL1#4[64]127, CWTI:SUMMER/89[50]124
UTZ, JAMES S., *Lieutenant, 3rd Richmond Howitzers;* CWR:VOL4#4[70]180

V

VAIL, JOSEPH, *Sergeant, 5th New York Infantry;*
CWR:VOL1#2[7]111, CWTI:MAY/94[31]382
VALENTINE, JACOB, *Lieutenant, CSA;* CWM:SEP/93[8]493
VALENTINE, JOSEPH E., *Seaman, USN;*
ACW:MAR/92[40]353
VALLANDIGHAM, CLEMENT L.:
ARTICLES: "EDITORIAL," ACW:MAR/91[6]290, "PERSONALITY,
CLEMENT VALLANDIGHAM," ACW:MAR/91[8]291
GENERAL LISTINGS: *in book review,* CWM:DEC/95[10], *photo,*
ACW:MAR/91[8]291
ADDITIONAL LISTINGS: ACW:JUL/95[44]537, B&G:OCT/94[28]581,
CWM:AUG/95[58]611, CWR:VOL3#1[31]150,
CWTI:DEC/90[50]183, CWTI:NOV/92[54]293
VALLEAU, JOHN M., *Corporal, 109th Pennsylvania Infantry;*
CWTI:SUMMER/89[32]122
VALVERDE, NEW MEXICO, BATTLE OF:
ARTICLES: "BATTLE FOR THE RIO GRANDE,"
CWTI:OCT/95[56]471, "THE CONFEDERATE INVASION OF
NEW MEXICO AND ARIZONA," B&G:JUN/94[8]568,
CWM:MAY/93[16]475
GENERAL LISTINGS: *in book review,* CWM:MAR/92[49],
CWNEWS:AUG/94[33], *letters to the editor,* B&G:DEC/93[6]544
ADDITIONAL LISTINGS: ACW:JAN/91[10]283, ACW:JUL/93[27]423,
ACW:NOV/95[62], B&G:JUN/94[8]568, CWR:VOL2#2[161]139
VAN AERNAM, HENRY, *Surgeon, 154th New York Infantry;*
CWTI:MAR/95[26]434, GETTY:8[17]200
VAN ALEN, JAMES H., *General, USA;* ACW:MAY/95[30]525,
CWTI:MAY/89[21]115
VAN ALSTYNE, JOHN, *Corporal, 150th New York Infantry;*
GETTY:12[42]244
VAN BRUNT, G.J., *Captain, USN;* AHI:JUL/66[32]103
VAN CLEVE, HORATIO P., *Colonel, 2nd Minnesota Infantry;*
B&G:FEB/93[12]511
VAN CLEVE, PETER, *Colonel, 2nd Massachusetts Infantry;*
CWM:NOV/92[6]446
VAN DE GRAAF, A.S., *Major, 5th Alabama Battalion;*
B&G:FEB/95[8]590A, GETTY:6[13]170
VAN DEN CORPUT, MAX, *Captain, USA;*
CWTI:NOV/92[41]291
VAN DORN RESERVES, (11th Mississippi Infantry);
GETTY:9[98]217
VAN DORN, EARL, *General, CSA:*
ARTICLE: "ATTACK WRITTEN DEEP AND CRIMSON,"
ACW:SEP/91[46]324, "COURT-MARTIAL OF VAN DORN,"
ACW:SEP/91[50]325, "VICKSBURG: DAVIS, VAN DORN,
PEMBERTON—A TRIANGULATION OF SHORTCOMINGS,"
CWM:AUG/94[52]530
BOOK REVIEW: *VAN DORN: THE LIFE AND TIMES OF A
CONFEDERATE GENERAL*
GENERAL LISTINGS: *captures* Star of the West, ACW:NOV/93[8]438,
Corinth, CWM:MAR/93[8]465, *general history,*
AHI:MAY/71[3]133A, *Holly Springs Raid,*
CWM:DEC/95[48]631, CWTI:FEB/90[38]145, *in book review,*
ACW:MAY/94[58], B&G:FEB/92[26], CWM:DEC/94[7],
CWM:FEB/95[7], CWNEWS:NOV/89[4],
CWNEWS:DEC/94[33], CWNEWS:SEP/95[33],
CWNEWS:NOV/95[29], CWR:VOL2#1[78], CWR:VOL3#1[80],
CWR:VOL3#4[68], CWR:VOL4#3[1]170, *Indian wars,*
AHI:OCT/79[20]194, *Iuka,* CWM:MAR/93[8]465, *Julia Grant,*

ACW:JAN/94[47]452, *Mexican War,* MH:APR/93[39]166,
Price's 1864 Missouri B&G:JUN/91[10]452, *Tullahoma*
B&G:OCT/92[10]496, *Vicksburg,* CWTI:SEPT/89[18]126,
photos, CWM:AUG/94[52]530, CWM:MAR/93[8]465
ADDITIONAL LISTINGS, ACW: ACW:JAN/91[16]284,
ACW:JUL/91[12]310, ACW:JAN/93[51]398,
ACW:MAY/93[22]414, ACW:SEP/93[31]433,
ACW:MAR/94[42]461, ACW:MAY/94[26]468,
ACW:JUL/94[51]480, ACW:NOV/94[76]500
ADDITIONAL LISTINGS, AHI: AHI:NOV/73[18]151
ADDITIONAL LISTINGS, B&G: B&G:APR/92[58]485,
B&G:AUG/92[26]494, B&G:FEB/94[57]555,
B&G:JUN/94[8]568
ADDITIONAL LISTINGS, CWM: CWM:SEP/92[38]443,
CWM:MAR/93[8]465, CWM:OCT/94[48]542
ADDITIONAL LISTINGS, CWR: CWR:VOL1#1[42]105,
CWR:VOL1#1[73]108, CWR:VOL1#2[44]114,
CWR:VOL1#4[42]126, CWR:VOL2#1[i]129,
CWR:VOL2#1[36]132, CWR:VOL2#4[313]146,
CWR:VOL3#3[33]158, CWR:VOL4#3[50]171
ADDITIONAL LISTINGS, CWTI: CWTI:FEB/91[36]193,
CWTI:MAY/92[48]267, CWTI:NOV/92[18]289,
CWTI:NOV/93[33]347, CWTI:MAR/94[48]374,
CWTI:JUL/94[50]395, CWTI:DEC/94[82]418
ADDITIONAL LISTINGS, MH: MH:JUN/93[82]167
VAN DUZER, JOHN C., *Colonel, USA;* B&G:DEC/93[12]545,
CWTI:DEC/94[57]414
VAN HORN, BURT, *Congressman, New York;*
CWM:SEP/92[16]438
VAN HORN, ROBERT T., *Mayor, Kansas City;*
CWTI:MAR/91[34]201
VAN HORN, THOMAS B., *Colonel, USA;* CWTI:NOV/92[60]294
VAN LEW, ELIZABETH L.:
ARTICLE: "PERSONALITY, ELIZABETH VAN LEW,"
ACW:JUL/91[8]309
GENERAL LISTINGS: *in book review,* MH:DEC/93[90],
MH:DEC/94[70], *letters to the editor,* CWTI:DEC/94[12]408,
photo, ACW:JUL/91[8]309
ADDITIONAL LISTINGS: ACW:SEP/94[62]490, AHI:DEC/73[10]152
VAN METER, DAVID, *civilian;* ACW:SEP/91[41]323
VAN RENSSELAER, WALTER, *Major, USA;* GETTY:13[7]253
VAN TOOTH, JAMES, *Private, 19th Indiana Infantry;*
CWTI:NOV/93[78]354
VAN VALKENBURG, JAMES D., *Lieutenant Colonel, 61st
Georgia Infantry;* B&G:APR/95[8]595, CWTI:JAN/93[40]301
VAN WINKLE, PETER G., *Senator, West Virginia;*
AHI:DEC/68[28]118
VAN WYCK, CHARLES H., *Colonel, 56th New York Infantry;*
CWTI:MAR/94[38]372
VAN ZANDT, KLEBER M., *Major, 7th Texas Infantry;*
B&G:OCT/95[36]614
VANALSTINE, HART W., *Private, 11th Veteran Reserve Corps;*
B&G:APR/93[24]520
VANCE, JOSEPH W., *Colonel, USA;* CWR:VOL4#2[1]165,
CWR:VOL4#2[68]167
VANCE, ZEBULON B., *Governor, North Carolina;*
GENERAL LISTINGS: *Wilmington/Fort Fisher,* B&G:DEC/94[10]585,
women in the South, AHI:DEC/73[10]152, *photos,*
AHI:DEC/73[10]152, B&G:FEB/91[20]440
ADDITIONAL LISTINGS: ACW:NOV/92[42]388, ACW:NOV/93[12]440,
AHI:JAN/83[10]232, B&G:FEB/91[20]440,
B&G:JUN/95[22]601, CWM:AUG/94[8]522,
CWTI:APR/89[14]107, CWTI:DEC/90[18]180,

CWTI:FEB/91[45]194, CWTI:AUG/91[58]220,
GETTY:8[67]204,GETTY:11[6]231
VANDECAR, ISAAC L., *Private, 24th Michigan Infantry,*
GETTY:9[33]211, GETTY:11[57]233
VANDENBURGH VOLLEY GUN; CWTI:DEC/90[18]180
VANDENBURGH, ORIGEN; CWTI:JAN/93[49]303
VANDEVENTER, ALEXANDER S., *Colonel, 50th Virginia
Infantry;* GETTY:13[108]261
VANDEVER, WILLIAM, *General, USA;* B&G:DEC/95[9]615,
CWR:VOL1#1[42]105
VANDIVER, JOE, *Sergeant, CSA;* ACW:SEP/91[41]323
VANDLING, GEORGE, *Private, 53rd Pennsylvania Infantry;*
GETTY:11[80]235
VANHEE, CHARLES, *Private, 3rd U.S. Infantry;*
B&G:APR/95[24]596
VANHOOSE, WILLIAM, *Private, 45th Kentucky Infantry;*
CWTI:NOV/93[78]354
VANMETER, JONATHAN, *Private, 27th Illinois Infantry;*
CWR:VOL3#4[24]162
VANNORMAN, OZRO, *Private, 11th Veteran Reserve Corps;*
B&G:APR/93[24]520
VARIAN, AUGUSTUS L., *Sergeant, 2nd Mississippi Infantry;*
GETTY:6[77]177
VASSAR, THOMAS, *Chaplain, 150th New York Infantry;*
GETTY:12[42]244
VAUGHAN, ALFRED J., *Colonel, CSA;* CWR:VOL3#4[24]162
VAUGHAN, GEORGE W., *Corporal, Petersburg Artillery;*
ACW:MAR/95[12]513
VAUGHAN, HENRY, *Private, 47th Virginia Infantry;*
B&G:APR/93[24]520
VAUGHAN, ALFRED J.; CWR:VOL3#4[24]162
VAUGHAN, JOHN C., *General, CSA;* ACW:NOV/91[22]331,
B&G:AUG/91[11]458, B&G:AUG/94[10]574,
CWM:JAN/93[40]461, CWR:VOL2#1[36]132,
CWR:VOL4#4[129], CWTI:NOV/92[41]291
VAUTIER, JOHN D., *Private, 88th Pennsylvania Infantry;*
B&G:AUG/92[11]493, GETTY:5[13]157, GETTY:10[7]221,
GETTY:12[123]251
VAY, JAMES S., *Lieutenant, 8th Louisiana Infantry;*
CWTI:FEB/91[12]189
VEALE, GEORGE, *Colonel, USA;* B&G:JUN/91[10]452
VEATCH, JAMES, *General, USA;* CWR:VOL2#4[313]146
VEAZEY, WHEELOCK, *Colonel, 16th Vermont Infantry;*
GETTY:6[87]178
VEIL, CHARLES H., *Private, 9th Pennsylvania Reserves;*
CWR:VOL4#4[1]177, GETTY:4[113]153
VELAZQUEZ, LORETA JANETA; CWR:VOL3#2[105]
VELIE, ABRAM, *Private, 24th Michigan Infantry,*
GETTY:9[33]211, GETTY:11[57]233
VENABLE, ANDREW R., *Major, CSA;* ACW:MAR/94[58],
GETTY:4[65]148, GETTY:12[68]246
VENABLE, CHARLES S., *Colonel, CSA;* ACW:MAY/92[30]361,
ACW:MAY/94[35]469, B&G:APR/93[12]518,
B&G:APR/94[10]558, B&G:APR/95[8]595,
B&G:OCT/93[49]543, CWM:JUL/91[40]370,
CWM:JAN/93[8]456, CWM:JUN/94[43]517,
CWTI:NOV/93[55]350, CWTI:DEC/94[32]410,
GETTY:4[113]153, GETTY:5[4]156, GETTY:9[17]210,
GETTY:9[17N]210
VERDIERSVILLE, VIRGINIA, RAID ON:
ARTICLE: "STUART'S REVENGE," CWTI:JUN/95[38]447
ADDITIONAL LISTINGS: B&G:AUG/92[11]493, CWTI:NOV/93[55]350

VERDIGRIS RIVER, BATTLE OF; ARTICLE: "HARD ROPE'S
CIVIL WAR," CWTI:SEP/90[52]179
VERMONT BRIGADE:
ARTICLE: "THE VERMONT BRIGADE HAD THE DUBIOUS
HONOR OF LOSING MORE MEN THAN ANY OTHER
BRIGADE IN THE CIVIL WAR," ACW:JAN/94[8]447
BOOK REVIEW: *FULL DUTY: VERMONTERS IN THE CIVIL WAR*
GENERAL LISTINGS: *Gettysburg,* GETTY:10[112]228, *letters to the
editor,* B&G:JUN/95[5]599, *list of monuments,*
B&G:OCT/95[8]611A
ADDITIONAL LISTINGS: B&G:APR/95[8]595, CWM:JUL/91[64]375,
CWR:VOL3#1[31]150, CWTI:NOV/92[49]292,
GETTY:12[123]251, GETTY:10[7]221, GETTY:10[112]228
VERMONT HISTORICAL SOCIETY; B&G:FEB/91[34]442

VERMONT TROOPS:
BOOK REVIEW: *FULL DUTY: VERMONTERS IN THE CIVIL WAR*
1st Artillery, (Heavy); B&G:AUG/93[18]530
1st Cavalry; ACW:JUL/92[41]370, ACW:MAY/94[35]469,
ACW:SEP/94[6]482, ACW:SEP/95[38]546, B&G:APR/91[8]445,
B&G:APR/92[8]481, GETTY:4[115]152, GETTY:9[109]218
1st Infantry; ACW:MAR/93[42]406, CWR:VOL1#2[7]111,
CWTI:APR/92[49]260
2nd Artillery; ACW:JAN/94[30]450
2nd Infantry:
BOOK REVIEWS: *HARD MARCHING EVERY DAY: THE CIVIL
WAR LETTERS OF PRIVATE WILBUR FISK, 1861-1865*
ADDITIONAL LISTINGS: ACW:JAN/94[8]447, AHI:MAR/93[20],
B&G:AUG/95[38], B&G:OCT/95[8]611A, CWR:VOL3#3[1]157,
CWTI:APR/92[14]254, CWTI:NOV/92[49]292,
CWTI:MAY/94[24]381
3rd Infantry:
BOOK REVIEW: *BUCK'S BOOK: A VIEW OF THE 3RD VERMONT
INFANTRY REGIMENT*
ADDITIONAL LISTINGS: ACW:NOV/92[8]383, ACW:JAN/94[8]447,
CWM:JUN/95[29]583, CWTI:SEP/91[54]232,
CWTI:NOV/92[49]292
4th Infantry; ACW:JAN/94[8]447, B&G:JUN/91[6]451,
CWM:JAN/91[35], CWM:SEP/93[18]494,
CWM:JUN/95[63]594, CWTI:DEC/91[22]237,
CWTI:NOV/92[49]292
5th Infantry; ACW:JAN/94[8]447, CWR:VOL3#3[1]157,
CWTI:NOV/92[49]292
6th Infantry; ACW:JAN/94[8]447, B&G:DEC/95[25]616,
CWM:JUN/95[29]583, CWR:VOL3#3[1]157,
CWTI:NOV/92[49]292
8th Infantry; ACW:MAY/91[38]305, CWR:VOL3#1[1]149
9th Infantry; CWR:VOL1#4[7]125
10th Cavalry; B&G:DEC/92[8]503
10th Infantry; ACW:NOV/93[50]444, B&G:DEC/92[8]503,
CWR:VOL4#3[89], CWTI:JAN/93[40]301
12th Infantry; B&G:APR/91[32]447, B&G:OCT/95[36]614,
CWR:VOL3#1[31]150, CWTI:DEC/91[22]237,
GETTY:5[107]164
13th Infantry:
GENERAL LISTINGS: *Gettysburg,* GETTY:4[89]150,
GETTY:5[79]161, GETTY:6[87]178, *in list,*
CWTI:JUL/93[34]327
ADDITIONAL LISTINGS: ACW:JUL/95[50]538, CWR:VOL3#1[31]150,
CWTI:DEC/91[22]237, GETTY:6[7]169, GETTY:13[7]253
15th Infantry; CWR:VOL3#1[31]150, CWTI:DEC/91[22]237,
CWTI:JUL/93[34]327, GETTY:5[117]165, GETTY:9[5]209

16th Infantry; CWR:VOL3#1[31]150, CWTI:DEC/91[22]237, CWTI:JUL/93[34]327, GETTY:6[87]178
17th Infantry; ACW:MAY/95[18]524, CWR:VOL2#2[118]136

VESSELS, CHARLES B., *Private, 72nd Pennsylvania Infantry;* ACW:MAY/92[8]357, GETTY:7[97]193
VETERANS: ARTICLES: "THE GREAT IMPOSTORS," B&G:FEB/91[32]441, "PERSONALITY, VETERANS," ACW:SEP/91[8]318
VICK, J.W., *Captain, 7th North Carolina Infantry;* GETTY:8[67]204
VICK, THOMAS E., *Colonel, CSA;* CWR:VOL3#1[1]149
VICKSBURG COMMUNITY OF OUR LADY OF MERCY; B&G:OCT/93[31]539
VICKSBURG (MISSISSIPPI) VOLUNTEERS, (48th Mississippi Infantry); GETTY:4[7]142
VICKSBURG NATIONAL BATTLEFIELD PARK; B&G:FEB/94[57]555, B&G:AUG/95[8]604, CWR:VOL2#1[i]129, CWR:VOL2#1[69]133, CWR:VOL2#1[75]134, CWTI:MAY/91[18]207, MH:JUN/93[82]167
VICKSBURG NATIONAL MILITARY PARK COMMISSION; CWR:VOL2#1[75]134
VICKSBURG, MISSISSIPPI, BATTLE, CAMPAIGN AND SIEGE OF:
ARTICLES: "A FAILURE OF COMMAND: THE CONFEDERATE LOSS OF VICKSBURG," CWR:VOL2#1[36]132, "A HILL OF DEATH," CWTI:MAY/91[24]208, "A SUPERIOR SOUTHERN MUSEUM: VICKSBURG, MISSISSIPPI," CWTI:SEPT/89[18]126, "THE ARCHIVAL HOLDINGS OF VICKSBURG NATIONAL MILITARY PARK," CWR:VOL2#1[75]134, "THE ASSAULT ON VICKSBURG," CWM:JUN/94[30]515, "BATTLE OF PORT GIBSON, MISSISSIPPI," B&G:FEB/94[57]555, "CIVILIAN LIFE DURING THE SIEGE OF VICKSBURG," AHI:DEC/77[13]176, "DIARY OF THE VICKSBURG SIEGE," AHI:DEC/77[46]177, "FIGHTING ERUPTS AT JACKSON, MISSISSIPPI," CWM:AUG/95[26]604, "THE FIRST HONOR AT VICKSBURG: THE 1ST BATTALION 13TH U.S. INFANTRY," CWR:VOL2#1[1]130, "FOCUS: CIVIL WAR PHOTOGRAPHY," AHI:AUG/80[26]206, "GRANT'S BEACHHEAD FOR THE VICKSBURG CAMPAIGN: THE BATTLE OF PORT GIBSON, MAY 1, 1863," B&G:FEB/94[8]550, "GRANT'S MISSISSIPPI GAMBLE," ACW:JUL/94[51]480
ARTICLES, continued: "INTO THE BREACH: THE 22ND IOWA INFANTRY AT THE RAILROAD REDOUBT," CWR:VOL2#1[19]131, "JOHN WALKER'S TEXAS DIVISION AND ITS EXPEDITION TO RELIEVE FORTRESS VICKSBURG," CWR:VOL3#3[33]158, "LITERAL HILL OF DEATH," ACW:NOV/91[22]331, "MISSISSIPPI'S CHAMPION'S HILL IS AN IMPORTANT, IF FORGOTTEN, BATTLEFIELD," MH:JUN/93[82]167, "RETURN TO JACKSON, JULY 5-25, 1863," B&G:AUG/95[8]604, "VICKSBURG REVISITED," CWR:VOL2#1[i]129, "VICKSBURG: DAVIS, VAN DORN, PEMBERTON—A TRIANGULATION OF SHORTCOMINGS," CWM:AUG/94[52]530, "WITH A CONFEDERATE SURGEON AT VICKSBURG," AHI:JUL/68[31]115A
BOOK REVIEWS: *THE CAMPAIGN FOR VICKSBURG * MY CAVE LIFE IN VICKSBURG * PEMBERTON: A BIOGRAPHY, * REBEL VICTORY AT VICKSBURG * SEVEN STORY MOUNTAIN: THE UNION AT VICKSBURG, * THE*

*SOUTH'S FINEST: THE FIRST MISSOURI CONFEDERATE BRIGADE FROM PEA RIDGE TO VICKSBURG * REMINISCENCES OF THE 22ND IOWA INFANTRY * THE VICKSBURG*
GENERAL LISTINGS: *general history,* AHI:MAY/71[3]133A, *Grierson's Raid,* B&G:JUN/93[12]524, *in book review,* ACW:MAY/92[54], ACW:NOV/93[58], CWM:AUG/95[45], CWNEWS:OCT/90[4], CWNEWS:JAN/91[4], CWR:VOL2#1[78], CWR:VOL2#2[169], CWR:VOL3#1[80], CWR:VOL3#4[68], CWTI:SEP/92[18], *photo of captured artillery;* CWTI:FEB/90[38]145, *photo of Old Court House;* CWTI:SEPT/89[28]126, *photo of Union "tinclad" gunboats at Vicksburg;* CWTI:FEB/90[38]145, *photo of waterfront;* ACW:MAY/93[22]414
ADDITIONAL LISTINGS, ACW: ACW:JAN/91[16]284, ACW:MAY/91[10]301, ACW:JUL/91[12]310, ACW:NOV/91[6]327, ACW:NOV/91[8]328, ACW:MAY/92[47]363, ACW:SEP/92[16]376, ACW:MAR/93[8]401, ACW:MAY/93[14]413, ACW:MAY/93[22]414, ACW:JUL/93[34]424, ACW:JAN/94[30]450, ACW:SEP/94[10]484, ACW:SEP/94[74]491, ACW:MAR/95[8]512, ACW:MAR/95[18]514, ACW:MAR/95[34]516, ACW:MAY/95[18]524, ACW:SEP/95[8]542
ADDITIONAL LISTINGS, AHI: AHI:JUL/76[19]170, AHI:APR/87[10]261
ADDITIONAL LISTINGS, B&G: B&G:FEB/94[8]550
ADDITIONAL LISTINGS, CWM: CWM:JAN/91[4]323, CWM:MAY/92[34]422, CWM:MAR/93[16]466, CWM:OCT/94[48]542, CWM:DEC/94[34]549, CWM:DEC/95[30]627, CWM:DEC/95[48]631
ADDITIONAL LISTINGS, CWR: CWR:VOL1#1[42]105, CWR:VOL1#1[73]108, CWR:VOL1#4[42]126, CWR:VOL1#4[64]127, CWR:VOL2#1[69]133, CWR:VOL2#1[75]134, CWR:VOL2#4[269]145, CWR:VOL2#4[313]146, CWR:VOL3#3[88]160, CWR:VOL4#2[26]166
ADDITIONAL LISTINGS, CWTI: CWTI:MAR/89[44]105, CWTI:FEB/90[38]145, CWTI:FEB/90[46]146, CWTI:FEB/90[54]147, CWTI:MAR/91[28]200, CWTI:MAY/91[16]206, CWTI:AUG/91[62]221, CWTI:MAR/93[24]309, CWTI:JUL/93[64]330, CWTI:NOV/93[33]347, CWTI:JAN/95[34]427, CWTI:DEC/95[67]481
ADDITIONAL LISTINGS, MH: MH:FEB/92[8]156, MH:DEC/95[58]188
VIDEO: see listings under **MOVIES, TELEVISION & VIDEO"**
VIELE, EGBERT L., *General, USA;* ACW:MAR/94[35]460
VIFQUAIN, VICTOR, *General, USA:*
ARTICLE: "KIDNAP CAREFULLY PLOTTED," MH:APR/94[54]176
BOOK REVIEW: *A FRENCHMAN FIGHTS FOR THE UNION: VICTOR VIFQUAIN AND THE 97TH ILLINOIS*
VIGILINI, JOHN P., *Captain, CSA;* ACW:NOV/93[26]441
VILLARD, HENRY, *reporter;* AHI:APR/80[21]200
VILLEPIGUE, JOHN B., *General, CSA;* CWR:VOL1#4[42]126, CWTI:NOV/92[54]293
VINCENT, ALBERT O., *Lieutenant, 2nd U.S. Artillery;* GETTY:11[19]232
VINCENT, BOYD, *Captain, USA;* GETTY:7[41]189
VINCENT, CEVIN, *Private, CSA;* CWR:VOL4#2[118]169
VINCENT, FERRELL; AHI:JUN/70[30]127
VINCENT, STRONG, *Colonel, USA:*
ARTICLE: "VALLEY OF THE SHADOW OF DEATH: COLONEL STRONG VINCENT AND THE EIGHTY-THIRD

PENNSYLVANIA INFANTRY AT LITTLE ROUND TOP," GETTY:7[41]189

GENERAL LISTINGS: *Aldie*, GETTY:11[19]232, *Gettysburg*, GETTY:5[103]163, GETTY:6[33]172, GETTY:6[43]173, GETTY:6[59]174, GETTY:8[31]201, GETTY:8[53]203, GETTY:9[41]212, GETTY:9[53]214, *in book review*, CWR:VOL2#3[256], *Upperville*, B&G:OCT/93[12]537, *photos*, B&G:OCT/93[12]537, GETTY:8[31]201

ADDITIONAL LISTINGS: ACW:JAN/92[38]343, CWM:JUL/92[8]427, CWM:DEC/94[26]548, MH:OCT/92[51]162

VINCENT, THOMAS M., *General, USA*; CWTI:AUG/90[70]171

VINCENT, WILLIAM G., *Colonel, 2nd Louisiana Cavalry*; CWR:VOL3#1[1]149, CWR:VOL4#2[26]166, CWR:VOL4#2[68]167, CWR:VOL4#2[118]169

VINING'S STATION, GEORGIA; CWTI:SUMMER/89[20]121

VINSON, JOHN, *Private, 26th North Carolina Infantry*; GETTY:5[19]158

VIRGINIA MILITARY INSTITUTE:

ARTICLE: "DIMINUTIVE BUT FEISTY, CHARLES CARTER RANDOLPH WAS STONEWALL JACKSON'S PET CADET," ACW:JUL/93[10]421

GENERAL LISTINGS: *Gettysburg*, GETTY:4[33]146, GETTY:10[29]222, GETTY:12[111]250, *in book review*, CWNEWS:MAY/92[4], *letters to the editor*, CWM:JAN/91[6]324, B&G:AUG/92[6]492

ADDITIONAL LISTINGS: ACW:NOV/91[41]334, B&G:APR/91[36]448, B&G:DEC/92[8]503, B&G:AUG/94[10]574, CWM:JUL/91[48]374, CWM:JAN/92[21]402, CWM:MAY/92[34]422, CWTI:MAY/89[22]116, CWTI:MAR/94[29]371, CWTI:OCT/95[48]470

VIRGINIA TROOPS:

1st Artillery; GETTY:12[30]243

1st Cavalry:

GENERAL LISTINGS: *1863 cavalry battles*, MH:OCT/92[51]162, *Gettysburg*, GETTY:4[65]148, GETTY:12[68]246, *in book review*, ACW:MAY/91[54], CWM:FEB/95[7], *in order of battle*, B&G:APR/92[8]481, *Thomas J. Jackson*, AHI:JUN/67[31]110

ADDITIONAL LISTINGS: ACW:NOV/91[30]332, ACW:NOV/91[35]333, ACW:JUL/92[41]370, ACW:MAY/94[35]469, ACW:JUL/95[34]536, B&G:OCT/93[12]537, CWM:JUN/95[37]585, CWM:JUN/95[50]589, CWTI:DEC/89[34]136, CWTI:MAR/91[12]198, CWTI:APR/92[35]257, CWTI:OCT/95[90]472, GETTY:13[89]260

1st Cavalry, (Union); B&G:FEB/91[34]442

1st Infantry:

GENERAL LISTINGS: *Gettysburg*, GETTY:5[103]163, GETTY:10[53]225, GETTY:12[97]249, *in list*, CWTI:JUL/93[34]327, *in order of battle*, B&G:APR/92[8]481, *letters to the editor*, B&G:APR/94[6]557, CWM:JUL/91[6]355, *Manassas, Second*, B&G:AUG/92[11]493

ADDITIONAL LISTINGS: ACW:SEP/94[62]490, B&G:APR/93[12]518, B&G:OCT/95[20]612, B&G:OCT/95[32]613, CWM:MAR/91[17]335, CWM:MAR/91[65]342

1st Infantry, (Union); ACW:JAN/92[47]344

2nd Artillery; CWR:VOL1#3[52]122, CWTI:APR/90[46]153

GENERAL LISTINGS: *1863 cavalry battles*, MH:OCT/92[51]162, *Five Forks*, B&G:APR/92[8]481, *Gettysburg*, GETTY:4[65]148, *in book review*, CWM:APR/95[8], *in order of battle*, B&G:APR/92[8]481, *letters to the editor*, B&G:DEC/95[5]614A, *Manassas, 2nd*, B&G:AUG/92[11]493

ADDITIONAL LISTINGS: ACW:NOV/91[30]332, ACW:JUL/92[41]370, ACW:SEP/93[31]433, B&G:OCT/93[12]537, B&G:OCT/93[21]538, CWR:VOL1#1[35]104, GETTY:13[75]259

2nd Infantry

GENERAL LISTINGS: *Brawner's Farm*, B&G:AUG/92[11]493, *Gettysburg*, GETTY:4[75]149, GETTY:6[7]169, GETTY:7[83]192, *Jackson*, B&G:JUN/92[8]487, *Manassas, Second*, B&G:AUG/92[11]493

ADDITIONAL LISTINGS: ACW:MAY/92[14]358, ACW:MAY/95[10]523, CWM:MAY/91[40]351, CWM:AUG/95[30]606, CWR:VOL1#1[1]102, CWR:VOL3#3[1]157, CWR:VOL3#3[33]158, GETTY:13[89]260

3rd Cavalry; ACW:NOV/91[30]332, ACW:JUL/92[41]370, ACW:MAY/95[30]525, AHI:NOV/80[6]208, B&G:APR/92[8]481, B&G:APR/92[48]484, B&G:OCT/93[12]537, CWR:VOL1#1[1]102

3rd Infantry:

GENERAL LISTINGS: *1863 cavalry battles*, MH:OCT/92[51]162, *Five Forks*, B&G:APR/92[8]481, *Gettysburg*, GETTY:5[107]164, *Immortal Six Hundred (in list)*, GETTY:12[111]250, *in list*, CWTI:JUL/93[34]327, *in order of battle*, B&G:APR/92[8]481, *letters to the editor*, B&G:APR/94[6]557

ADDITIONAL LISTINGS: ACW:MAR/93[42]406, ACW:MAR/95[50]518, CWTI:JUL/94[44]394, GETTY:13[7]253, GETTY:13[50]257, GETTY:13[75]259

4th Artillery; GETTY:10[29]222

4th Cavalry:

GENERAL LISTINGS: *1863 cavalry battles*, MH:OCT/92[51]162, *Gettysburg*, GETTY:4[65]148, GETTY:4[75]149, *in order of battle*, B&G:APR/92[8]481, *Manassas, 2nd*, B&G:AUG/92[11]493

ADDITIONAL LISTINGS: ACW:NOV/91[30]332, ACW:JUL/92[41]370, ACW:JUL/95[34]536, B&G:OCT/92[38]500, B&G:OCT/93[12]537, B&G:APR/94[59]565, CWM:JUL/91[40]370, CWM:JUN/95[50]589, CWR:VOL1#1[1]102, CWTI:JUN/90[32]159, CWTI:JUN/95[38]447

4th Infantry:

BOOK REVIEW: *TED BARCLAY, LIBERTY HALL VOLUNTEERS: LETTERS FROM THE STONEWALL BRIGADE*

GENERAL LISTINGS: *Gettysburg*, GETTY:9[81]216, GETTY:12[42]244, GETTY:12[61]245, *Immortal Six Hundred*, GETTY:12[111]250, *in book review*, CWM:MAY/93[51], *Jackson*, B&G:JUN/92[8]487

ADDITIONAL LISTINGS: CWM:JUN/95[29]583, CWTI:MAY/89[22]116, CWTI:JUL/93[20]325

4th Reserves; B&G:AUG/91[11]458

5th Cavalry:

GENERAL LISTINGS: *1863 cavalry battles*, MH:OCT/92[51]162, *Aldie*, GETTY:11[19]232, *in order of battle*, B&G:APR/92[8]481

ADDITIONAL LISTINGS: ACW:NOV/91[30]332, ACW:JUL/92[41]370, ACW:MAY/94[35]469, B&G:OCT/92[38]500, B&G:OCT/93[12]537, MH:OCT/92[51]162

5th Infantry:

GENERAL LISTINGS: *Gettysburg*, GETTY:7[83]192, GETTY:12[42]244, *Jackson*, B&G:JUN/92[8]487, *letters to the editor*, CWTI:JAN/95[16]421

ADDITIONAL LISTINGS: ACW:JAN/93[35]396, B&G:DEC/95[5]614A, CWM:NOV/91[40]393, CWTI:MAY/89[36]118, CWTI:JUL/93[20]325

6th Cavalry;

GENERAL LISTINGS: ACW:JUL/92[41]370, ACW:JUL/93[10]421, B&G:APR/92[8]481, B&G:OCT/93[12]537,

CWM:NOV/92[64]453, CWTI:JUN/90[32]159,
CWTI:DEC/91[26]238, GETTY:11[19]232

6th Infantry:
ARTICLE: "FORGOTTEN VALOR: OFF THE BEATEN PATH AT
ANTIETAM: GUNNERS OF THE 6TH VA. INFY,"
B&G:OCT/95[8]611C

ADDITIONAL LISTINGS: ACW:JAN/91[38]287, ACW:JAN/94[39]451,
CWM:JUN/95[39]586, CWR:VOL1#4[7]125,
CWR:VOL2#3[236]143

7th Cavalry:
GENERAL LISTINGS: *Gettysburg*, GETTY:11[19]232, *in order of
battle*, B&G:APR/92[8]481, *letters to the editor*,
B&G:JUN/92[6]486, *SIO*, B&G:JUN/95[36]603A

ADDITIONAL LISTINGS: ACW:SEP/91[41]323, ACW:JUL/92[41]370,
B&G:FEB/92[32]477, B&G:JUN/92[53]491,
B&G:OCT/93[12]537, CWTI:JUN/90[32]159,
CWTI:MAR/91[74]204, CWTI:DEC/94[122]419

7th Infantry:
GENERAL LISTINGS: *Immortal Six Hundred (in list)*,
GETTY:12[111]250, *in book review*, CWM:APR/95[8],
CWNEWS:APR/94[5], *in list*, CWTI:JUL/93[34]327, *in order of
battle*, B&G:APR/92[8]481, *letters to the editor*,
B&G:APR/94[6]557

ADDITIONAL LISTINGS: AHI:MAR/84[42]238, B&G:OCT/95[20]612,
CWM:MAR/91[17]335

7th Infantry, (Union); GETTY:12[1]240

8th Cavalry; B&G:APR/92[8]481, B&G:APR/93[40]522,
B&G:AUG/94[10]574, CWTI:OCT/95[90]472

8th Infantry:
GENERAL LISTINGS: *Gettysburg*, GETTY:5[107]164,
GETTY:5[117]165, GETTY:12[111]250, *Immortal Six
Hundred*, GETTY:12[111]250, *in order of battle*,
B&G:APR/92[8]481

ADDITIONAL LISTINGS: ACW:MAR/93[10]402, AHI:FEB/82[36]225,
CWM:MAR/91[17]335, CWM:JAN/93[8]456,
CWR:VOL3#1[31]150, CWR:VOL3#1[78]152,
CWTI:MAY/89[14]114, CWTI:MAR/91[12]198,
CWTI:AUG/91[52]219, CWTI:NOV/93[55]350,
CWTI:JUL/94[20]390

9th Cavalry:
BOOK REVIEW: *A LIEUTENANT OF CAVALRY IN LEE'S ARMY*

ADDITIONAL LISTINGS: ACW:JUL/92[41]370, ACW:JUL/95[34]536,
B&G:APR/92[8]481, B&G:APR/93[12]518, B&G:APR/95[8]595,
CWM:JUN/95[50]589, CWTI:DEC/89[34]136,
CWTI:FEB/91[45]194, CWTI:JUN/95[38]447,
GETTY:4[65]148, GETTY:13[89]260

9th Infantry:
GENERAL LISTINGS: *Five Forks*, B&G:APR/92[8]481, *Immortal Six
Hundred*, GETTY:12[111]250, *in list*, CWTI:JUL/93[34]327, *in
order of battle*, B&G:APR/92[8]481, *letters to the editor*,
B&G:APR/94[6]557

ADDITIONAL LISTINGS: ACW:MAR/94[27]459, B&G:APR/93[24]520,
B&G:AUG/93[10]529, CWM:MAR/91[17]335,
CWTI:APR/89[14]107, CWTI:JUL/93[29]326, GETTY:13[7]253

10th Cavalry:
GENERAL LISTINGS: *Battle of Falling Waters*, GETTY:9[109]218,
Brandy Station, GETTY:11[19]232, *in order of battle*,
B&G:APR/92[8]481, *SIO*, B&G:DEC/91[38]471

ADDITIONAL LISTINGS: ACW:JUL/92[41]370, CWTI:FEB/91[45]194,
CWTI:MAR/91[12]198, CWTI:OCT/95[90]472,
GETTY:13[89]260

10th Infantry; ACW:MAR/91[25]294, ACW:NOV/92[42]388,
B&G:APR/95[8]595, CWM:MAY/92[20]420,

CWR:VOL4#1[1]163, CWTI:MAR/94[29]371,
CWTI:MAR/94[67]377, GETTY:7[83]192

10th Mounted Rifles; B&G:AUG/91[11]458

11th Cavalry:
GENERAL LISTINGS: *Aldie*, GETTY:11[19]232, *Brandy Station*,
GETTY:11[19]232, *Gettysburg*, GETTY:11[19]232, *in order of
battle*, B&G:APR/92[8]481

ADDITIONAL LISTINGS: ACW:SEP/91[41]323, B&G:AUG/93[10]529,
B&G:OCT/93[12]537, CWR:VOL3#2[1]153,
CWTI:JUN/90[32]159

11th Infantry:
GENERAL LISTINGS: *Immortal Six Hundred (in list)*,
GETTY:12[111]250, *in book review*, CWNEWS:NOV/91[4], *in
list*, CWTI:JUL/93[34]327, *in order of battle*,
B&G:APR/92[8]481

ADDITIONAL LISTINGS: ACW:JUL/92[41]370, B&G:APR/93[12]518,
B&G:APR/93[40]522, B&G:AUG/93[36]533,
B&G:OCT/95[20]612

12th Cavalry:
GENERAL LISTINGS: *Aldie*, GETTY:11[19]232, *Brandy Station*,
GETTY:11[19]232, *in order of battle*, B&G:APR/92[8]481,
letters to the editor, CWTI:NOV/92[8]288

ADDITIONAL LISTINGS: ACW:NOV/91[30]332, ACW:JUL/92[41]370,
B&G:OCT/93[12]537, CWTI:JUN/90[32]159,
CWTI:SEP/92[42]283, CWTI:MAR/94[67]377

12th Infantry:
ARTICLE: "FINAL MARCH TO APPOMATTOX: THE 12TH
VIRGINIA INFANTRY APRIL 2-12, AN EYEWITNESS
ACCOUNT," CWR:VOL2#3[236]143

ADDITIONAL LISTINGS: ACW:JAN/94[39]451, B&G:AUG/92[11]493,
B&G:JUN/95[8]600, B&G:OCT/95[36]614,
CWM:NOV/92[64]453, CWR:VOL1#4[7]125,
CWR:VOL2#3[236]143, CWR:VOL2#3[252]144,
CWTI:DEC/94[32]410

13th Artillery Battalion; CWR:VOL1#3[52]122

13th Cavalry; ACW:JUL/92[41]370, B&G:APR/92[8]481,
B&G:OCT/93[12]537, GETTY:11[19]232, GETTY:13[89]260

13th Infantry:
GENERAL LISTINGS: *in book review*, CWNEWS:JUL/92[4],
CWNEWS:OCT/92[4], *letters to the editor*,
CWTI:JAN/95[16]421, *SIO*, B&G:JUN/95[36]603A

ADDITIONAL LISTINGS: ACW:MAR/94[50]462, B&G:APR/93[24]520,
B&G:DEC/95[25]616, CWR:VOL1#3[28]120,
CWTI:JUL/93[20]325

13th Reserves; B&G:AUG/91[11]458

14th Cavalry; B&G:APR/92[8]481, B&G:AUG/93[10]529,
B&G:AUG/94[10]574, CWTI:MAR/89[16]101,
GETTY:13[89]260

14th Infantry:
GENERAL LISTINGS: *Gettysburg*, GETTY:7[124]196,
GETTY:9[61]215, GETTY:9[81]216, *Immortal Six Hundred*,
GETTY:12[111]250, *in list*, CWTI:JUL/93[34]327, *in order of
battle*, B&G:APR/92[8]481

ADDITIONAL LISTINGS: B&G:AUG/93[10]529, CWR:VOL1#3[52]122,
CWTI:JUL/93[29]326

15th Cavalry; ACW:JUL/92[41]370, ACW:MAY/94[35]469,
GETTY:11[6]231

15th Infantry; B&G:APR/92[8]481, CWR:VOL1#4[7]125,
CWR:VOL4#2[68]167, CWTI:AUG/90[26]166

16th Cavalry; B&G:APR/92[8]481, CWTI:MAR/89[16]101,
GETTY:13[89]260

16th Infantry; ACW:JAN/94[39]451, ACW:MAY/95[30]525,
CWR:VOL1#4[7]125, GETTY:7[124]196

Liberty Hall Volunteers; BOOK REVIEW: *TED BARCLAY,
LIBERTY HALL VOLUNTEERS: LETTERS FROM THE
STONEWALL BRIGADE*
Lynchburg Battery; ACW:MAR/94[50]462
Marion Heavy Artillery; B&G:JUN/95[36]603A
McGraw's Battery; ACW:MAY/95[30]525
McGregor's Battery; ACW:JUL/92[41]370,
CWTI:FEB/91[45]194
Moorman's Battery; ACW:JUL/92[41]370,
CWR:VOL4#4[70]180
Morris Artillery; GETTY:4[33]146, GETTY:4[49]147,
GETTY:6[7]169
Neblett Heavy Artillery; B&G:JUN/95[36]603A
Orange Artillery; GETTY:4[33]146, GETTY:4[49]147,
GETTY:10[7]221
Pamunkey Heavy Artillery; B&G:JUN/95[36]603A
Pamunkey Rifles; GETTY:13[64]258
Parker's Battery:
BOOK REVIEW: *PARKER'S VIRGINIA BATTERY, C.S.A.*
ADDITIONAL LISTINGS: ACW:SEP/92[30]378, CWR:VOL1#1[35]104,
B&G:APR/93[12]518, CWTI:MAY/94[50]386
Partisan Rangers; GETTY:9[109]218
Pegram's Battery; B&G:APR/93[24]520
Petersburg Artillery; ARTICLE: "THE MEN OF THE
STALWART PETERSBURG ARTILLERY SERVED FROM
THE BEGINNING OF THE WAR TO THE END,"
ACW:MAR/95[12]513
Poague's Artillery; B&G:JUN/95[8]600
Powhatan Artillery; CWR:VOL4#4[70]180
Purcell Artillery; CWM:MAR/91[17]335, CWM:JUN/95[57]592,
CWM:DEC/95[41]630 CWR:VOL1#2[44]114,
CWR:VOL4#4[70]180, GETTY:9[61]215
Richmond Heavy Artillery; ACW:JAN/92[22]341
Richmond Howitzers; ACW:SEP/94[38]487,
ACW:SEP/94[62]490, CWR:VOL1#1[35]104,
CWR:VOL3#2[1]153, CWR:VOL4#4[70]180, GETTY:8[53]203
Ringgold's Battery; ACW:MAR/94[27]459
Rockbridge Artillery; ACW:JAN/92[8]338,
ACW:MAR/92[30]352, ACW:NOV/92[42]388,
ACW:MAR/94[50]462, AHI:JUN/67[31]110,
AHI:SEP/87[40]263, B&G:JUN/92[8]487,
B&G:DEC/95[5]614A, CWM:AUG/94[30]527,
CWR:VOL4#4[70]180, GETTY:13[75]259
Southside Heavy Artillery; B&G:JUN/95[36]603A
Stanton Artillery; CWR:VOL4#4[70]180
Star Artillery; B&G:AUG/93[10]529
Staunton Artillery; B&G:FEB/95[8]590C, CWM:JAN/92[68]407
Virginia Artillery; GETTY:5[47]160, GETTY:10[29]222
Washington Artillery; GETTY:13[7]253

VIRGINIA, STATE OF:
BOOK REVIEWS: *BACK DOOR TO RICHMOND: THE BERMUDA
HUNDRED CAMPAIGN, APRIL-JUNE 1864 * CIVIL WAR
VIRGINIA: BATTLEGROUND FOR A NATION *
LEXINGTON AND ROCKBRIDGE COUNTY IN THE CIVIL
WAR * VIRGINIA RAILROADS IN THE CIVIL WAR * THE
WAR AND LOUISA COUNTY 1861-1865*
VIZETELLY, FRANK; CWM:NOV/92[10]447
VLIET, JOHN, *Lieutenant, 20th New York State Militia;*
B&G:FEB/94[6]549
VODGES, I., *Major, USA;* CWR:VOL1#4[42]126
VOELKER, LOUIS, *Captain, USA;* CWTI:NOV/92[41]291

VOELKNER, LEWIS, *Lieutenant, 2nd Missouri Light Artillery;*
B&G:AUG/95[8]604
VOGELSANG, PETER, *Lieutenant, 54th Massachusetts
Infantry;* CWM:NOV/92[6]446
VOGT, JOHN, *civilian;* CWTI:JAN/95[48]429
VOLCK, ADALBERT, *cartoonist;* ACW:JAN/92[30]342
VOLCK, FREDERICK, *artist;* CWTI:MAY/89[22]116
VOLLUM, EDWARD P., *Surgeon;* GETTY:10[53]225
VOLZ, GOTLIEB, *Private, 11th Veteran Reserve Corps;*
B&G:APR/93[24]520
von AMSBERG, GEORGE, *Colonel, USA;*
B&G:FEB/95[8]590A, GETTY:4[33]146, GETTY:4[49]147,
GETTY:7[83]192, GETTY:10[7]221
von BORCKE, HEROS, *Major, CSA:*
ARTICLE: "PRUSSIAN GIANT IN GRAY: MAJOR JOHANN
HEINRICH HEROS VON BORCKE," B&G:OCT/93[49]543
GENERAL LISTINGS: *Brandy Station,* GETTY:11[19]232, *in book
review,* ACW:MAR/94[58], CWM:MAR/91[74],
CWNEWS:MAY/94[5], CWNEWS:MAY/95[33], *letters to the
editor,* B&G:DEC/93[6]544, B&G:FEB/94[6]549, *Manassas,
Second,* B&G:AUG/92[11]493, *photos,* B&G:OCT/93[49]543,
B&G:DEC/93[6]544
ADDITIONAL LISTINGS: ACW:JUL/94[35]478, ACW:JUL/95[34]536,
B&G:FEB/91[38]443, B&G:OCT/93[12]537,
CWR:VOL4#4[70]180, CWTI:DEC/89[34]136,
CWTI:DEC/94[73]416, GETTY:13[75]259, MH:OCT/93[6]170
von GILSA, LEOPOLD, *Colonel, USA;* ACW:NOV/92[42]388,
GETTY:4[33]146, GETTY:9[17]210, GETTY:12[30]243
von HAMMERSTEIN, HERBERT, *Lieutenant Colonel, 78th
New York Infantry;* CWR:VOL3#2[70]155, GETTY:12[42]244
von KOERBER, V.E., *Captain, USA;* B&G:OCT/93[12]537
von SCHRADER, ALEXANDER, *Colonel, USA;*
AHI:NOV/85[38]254
von STEINWEHR, ADOLPH, *General, USA:*
GENERAL LISTINGS: *Gettysburg,* GETTY:4[49]147,
GETTY:5[19]158, GETTY:6[7]169, GETTY:7[29]188,
GETTY:11[19]232
ADDITIONAL LISTINGS: B&G:AUG/94[38]578, CWR:VOL3#2[70]155,
CWTI:AUG/91[52]219
von VEGESACK, ERNST, *Colonel, 20th New York Infantry;*
B&G:OCT/95[8]611B, CWTI:JUN/95[32]446
von ZEPPELIN, FERDINAND; AHI:JUN/84[24]239
von ZINKEN, LEON, *Colonel, 13th and 20th Louisiana
Infantry;* ACW:MAR/91[38]296, B&G:AUG/95[8]604
VOSBURG, SHELDON, *Lieutenant, 1st Wisconsin Cavalry;*
B&G:AUG/94[22]576
VOSBURGH, EMORY K., *Private, 154th New York Infantry;*
CWTI:MAR/95[26]434
VOSS, ARNO, *Colonel, 12th Illinois Cavalry;*
CWM:MAY/92[8]418
VOSS, W.H., *Private, 21st North Carolina Infantry;*
GETTY:10[53]225
VOTAW, MAHLON, *Sergeant, 123rd Illinois Infantry;*
ACW:MAY/95[49]527
VREDENBURGH, PETER, *Major, 14th New Jersey Infantry:*
BOOK REVIEW: *UPON THE TENTED FIELD*
ADDITIONAL LISTING: CWM:NOV/92[6]446, CWTI:JAN/93[40]301

W-Y-Z

WADDELL, JAMES, *Captain, Alabama Battery;*
ACW:MAR/91[38]296, ACW:NOV/91[22]331,
CWTI:JUN/95[51]449

WADDELL, JAMES I., *Lieutenant, CSN:*
ARTICLE: "THE FANTASTIC VOYAGE OF THE *CSS
SHENANDOAH,* CWM:JUL/93[8]483, "RAIDER OF THE
ARCTIC SEAS," ACW:MAY/91[46]306
GENERAL LISTINGS: *general history,* AHI:MAY/71[3]133A, *in book
review,* CWNEWS:MAY/91[4], CWTI:APR/90[10], *letters to the
editor,* CWM:SEP/93[4]492, *photos,* ACW:MAY/91[46]306,
AHI:JAN/83[10]232, CWM:JUL/93[8]483,
ADDITIONAL LISTING: AHI:JAN/83[10]232

WADE, BANJAMIN, *Senator from Ohio:*
GENERAL LISTINGS: *election of 1864,* AHI:OCT/68[4]116,
Gettysburg, GETTY:7[23]187, GETTY:11[19]232,
GETTY:12[85]248, *impeachment of Andrew Johnson,*
AHI:DEC/68[28]118, *Lincoln's assassination,*
CWTI:AUG/90[42]167, *Lincoln's humor,* AHI:NOV/70[22]130,
West Point, B&G:DEC/91[12]469, *photo,* GETTY:12[85]248
ADDITIONAL LISTINGS: ACW:MAR/95[8]512, CWR:VOL3#1[31]150,
CWTI:MAY/89[21]115, CWTI:MAY/93[29]319,
CWTI:DEC/95[52]480

WADE, E.H., *Sergeant, CSA;* B&G:APR/93[12]518

WADE, JAMES F., *Lieutenant, 6th U.S. Cavalry, photo;*
B&G:AUG/91[11]458, B&G:OCT/93[12]537, GETTY:11[19]232

WADE, JENNIE, *civilian;* GETTY:6[7]169, GETTY:9[122]220,
GETTY:10[7]221, GETTY:11[119]238

WADE, THOMAS M, *Private, Rockbridge Artillery;*
CWR:VOL4#4[70]180

WADE, WILLIAM, *Colonel, CSA;* B&G:FEB/94[8]550,
CWR:VOL3#3[33]158

WADE-DAVIS BILL; AHI:OCT/68[4]116, AHI:JAN/82[16]224

WADLIA, ANDREW, *Captain, 3rd New Hampshire Infantry;*
CWTI:APR/89[22]108

WADSWORTH, CRAIG W., *Captain, USA;* GETTY:4[24]145,
GETTY:6[13]170

WADSWORTH, JAMES S., *General, USA:*
GENERAL LISTINGS: *Gettysburg,* AHI:MAY/67[22]107,
GETTY:4[16]143, GETTY:4[24]145, GETTY:4[113]153,
GETTY:5[4]156, GETTY:5[19]158, GETTY:5[117]165,
GETTY:6[13]170, GETTY:6[69]176, GETTY:7[23]187,
GETTY:7[29]188, GETTY:7[83]192, GETTY:9[81]216,
GETTY:10[7]221, GETTY:10[36]223, GETTY:11[19]232,
GETTY:11[57]233, GETTY:11[71]234, GETTY:11[126]239,
GETTY:12[30]243, *in book review,* CWR:VOL1#2[78],
CWR:VOL4#4[129], *order of battle,* B&G:APR/95[8]595,
Wilderness, B&G:JUN/95[8]600, *photo,* B&G:JUN/95[8]600
ADDITIONAL LISTINGS: ACW:NOV/92[42]388, ACW:MAY/93[31]415,
ACW:JUL/93[50]426, ACW:JAN/95[46]507,
B&G:FEB/95[8]590A, B&G:JUN/95[8]600,
CWR:VOL2#4[269]145, CWTI:NOV/93[24]346,
CWTI:DEC/94[32]410, GETTY:13[22]254, GETTY:13[33]255

WADSWORTH, WILLIAM H.; ACW:SEP/95[22]544

WAFER, FRANCIS M., *Surgeon, 108th New York Infantry;*
GETTY:10[53]225, GETTY:11[126]239

WAGGAMAN, EUGENE, *Colonel, 10th Louisiana Infantry:*
ARTICLE: "THE PRISONER AND THE PRIME MINISTER,"
CWTI:JUL/93[38]328

ADDITIONAL LISTINGS: CWM:SEP/93[18]494, CWM:SEP/93[24]495,
CWTI:MAR/95[33]435, *photo,* CWTI:JUL/93[38]328

WAGNER, ANDREW, *Captain, 24th Michigan Infantry;*
GETTY:5[19]158

WAGNER, ORLANDO, *Lieutenant, USA;* ACW:MAR/91[47]297

WAGNER, SAMUEL C., *Captain, USA;* GETTY:13[89]260,

WAGNER, THOMAS M., *Lieutenant Colonel, CSA;*
ACW:SEP/91[30]322, CWTI:JAN/94[46]364

WAINWRIGHT, CHARLES F., *General, USA:*
BOOK REVIEW: *A DIARY OF BATTLE: THE PERSONAL
JOURNALS OF COLONEL CHARLES S. WAINWRIGHT,
1861-1865*
GENERAL LISTINGS: *Five Forks,* B&G:APR/92[8]481, *Gettysburg,*
GETTY:5[117]165, GETTY:9[33]211, GETTY:10[29]222,
GETTY:11[19]232, GETTY:11[57]233, GETTY:11[71]234,
GETTY:12[30]243, *in book review,* CWR:VOL3#1[80],
CWR:VOL4#4[129], *in order of battle,* B&G:APR/92[8]481,
B&G:APR/94[10]558, B&G:APR/95[8]595, *photo,*
GETTY:12[30]243
ADDITIONAL LISTINGS: B&G:APR/91[8]445, B&G:APR/93[12]518,
B&G:APR/95[8]595, CWTI:APR/92[49]260,
CWTI:MAR/95[33]435, GETTY:4[49]147, GETTY:13[22]254

WAINWRIGHT, JOHATHAN, *Commander, USN;*
ACW:JAN/93[51]398, ACW:MAR/94[35]460

WAINWRIGHT, WILLIAM, *Colonel, 76th New York Infantry;*
B&G:AUG/92[11]493

WAKEFIELD, E., *Major, 7th Missouri (Union) Infantry;*
B&G:FEB/94[8]550

WAKEFIELD, GEORGE, *Corporal, 9th New Hampshire
Infantry;* CWR:VOL2#2[118]136

WAKEMAN, LYONS, *Private, 153rd New York Infantry:*
ARTICLE: "THE PRIVATE LYONS WAKEMAN—A SOLDIER
WITH A SECRET," CWM:OCT/95[63]623
BOOK REVIEWS: *AN UNCOMMON SOLDIER: THE CIVIL WAR
LETTERS OF SARAH ROSETTA WAKEMAN, ALIAS
PRIVATE LYONS WAKEMAN, 153RD REGIMENT, NEW
YORK STATE VOLUNTEERS, 1862-1864*

WALCOTT, AARON F., *Captain, 3rd Massachusetts Artillery:*
ARTICLE: "A VETERAN OF 33 BATTLES," CWTI:MAY/93[74]322
ADDITIONAL LISTINGS: GETTY:9[41]212, GETTY:11[91]236

WALCOTT, ALFRED F., *Lieutenant, 21st Massachusetts
Infantry;* CWTI:FEB/92[36]249

WALCOTT, CHARLES C., *General, USA;* B&G:OCT/94[11]580,
CWR:VOL1#1[73]108, CWR:VOL3#3[59]159,
CWTI:SUMMER/89[40]123

WALCOTT, CHARLES F., *Captain, 21st Massachusetts
Infantry;* CWTI:MAY/94[24]381

WALDRON, WILLIAM H., *Captain, 16th Maine Infantry;*
CWM:MAY/92[15]419, GETTY:13[33]255

WALDROP, RICHARD W., *Private, 21st Virginia Infantry;*
CWM:JUL/92[16]428

WALES, NATHANIEL, *Adjutant, 35th Massachusetts Infantry;*
CWTI:FEB/92[36]249

WALES, NATHANIEL, *General, USA;* ACW:SEP/92[8]374

WALKE, HENRY, *Captain, USN;* ACW:NOV/91[8]328,
ACW:JUL/93[34]424, ACW:SEP/94[74]491,
B&G:FEB/92[10]474, CWTI:DEC/94[34]411

WALKER'S TEXAS DIVISION:
ARTICLE: "JOHN WALKER'S TEXAS DIVISION AND ITS
EXPEDITION TO RELIEVE FORTRESS VICKSBURG,"
CWR:VOL3#3[33]158
BOOK REVIEW: *THE CAMPAIGNS OF WALKER'S TEXAS
DIVISION*

ADDITIONAL LISTINGS: CWR:VOL3#3[88]160, CWR:VOL4#2[1]165,
  CWR:VOL4#2[26]166, CWR:VOL4#2[68]167
WALKER, ALDACE F.; CWTI:SEP/91[54]232
WALKER, C.J., *Colonel, 14th Kentucky Infantry;*
  ACW:SEP/95[22]544
WALKER, CALVIN H., *Colonel, 3rd Tennessee Infantry;*
  CWM:JUN/94[58]519
WALKER, E.J., *Surgeon, 121st New York Infantry;*
  GETTY:10[53]225
WALKER, ELIJAH, *Colonel, 4th Maine Infantry;*
  GETTY:9[5]209
WALKER, FRANCIS, *Colonel, USA;* GETTY:4[89]150
WALKER, FRANCIS A., *Colonel;* ACW:JAN/93[58]399,
  ACW:MAY/93[31]415, ACW:SEP/94[38]487,
  B&G:APR/91[8]445, GETTY:4[115]152, GETTY:6[87]178
WALKER, FRANCIS M., *Lieutenant Colonel, 19th Tennessee
  Infantry;* B&G:FEB/93[12]511
WALKER, GARDNER, *Major, USA;* GETTY:12[7]241
WALKER, GEORGE E., *Private, 24th Michigan Infantry,*
  GETTY:9[33]211, GETTY:11[57]233
WALKER, GEORGE W., *Sergeant, 2nd Tennessee Cavalry;*
  CWR:VOL4#1[1]163
WALKER, HENRY H., *General, CSA;* B&G:APR/95[8]595,
  CWR:VOL1#3[52]122, CWR:VOL2#4[269]145,
  CWTI:APR/90[46]153, *photo,* CWR:VOL1#3[52]122
WALKER, ISAAC E., *Private, 2nd Tennessee Cavalry;*
  CWR:VOL4#1[1]163
WALKER, ISHAM, *Private, 9th Mississippi Infantry;*
  AHI:JUN/84[24]239, B&G:AUG/91[20]459
WALKER, J. KNOX, *Colonel, Walker's Legion;*
  CWR:VOL3#4[24]162
WALKER, JAMES, *artist;* ARTICLE: "THE ARTIST AND THE
  CIVIL WAR," AHI:NOV/80[28]211
WALKER, JAMES A., *General, CSA:*
BOOK REVIEW: *STONEWALL JIM: A BIOGRAPHY OF GENERAL
  JAMES A. WALKER, C.S.A*
ADDITIONAL LISTINGS: *Gettysburg,* GETTY:4[65]148,
  GETTY:5[103]163, GETTY:6[7]169, GETTY:6[69]176,
  GETTY:7[83]192, GETTY:9[81]216, GETTY:12[42]244, *order
  of battle,* B&G:APR/95[8]595, *Wilderness,* B&G:JUN/95[8]600
ADDITIONAL LISTINGS: ACW:JUL/92[30]369, ACW:NOV/92[42]388,
  B&G:APR/95[8]595, CWTI:MAR/95[33]435, GETTY:13[89]260
WALKER, JAMES E., *Surgeon, USA;* GETTY:10[53]225
WALKER, JAMES H.; CWM:MAY/92[20]420
WALKER, JAMES W., *Lieutenant, 2nd Tennessee Cavalry;*
  CWR:VOL4#1[1]163
WALKER, JOHATHAN, *Captain, USA;* ARTICLE: "AN
  UNPLEASANT RELIC," CWTI:DEC/91[48]242
WALKER, JOHN G., *General, CSA:*
ARTICLE: "JOHN WALKER'S TEXAS DIVISION AND ITS
  EXPEDITION TO RELIEVE FORTRESS VICKSBURG,"
  CWR:VOL3#3[33]158
BOOK REVIEW: *THE CAMPAIGNS OF WALKER'S TEXAS
  DIVISION*
GENERAL LISTINGS: *Antietam,* B&G:OCT/95[8]611A, *Harpers Ferry,*
  MH:AUG/95[30]185, *in book review,* CWNEWS:OCT/95[33],
  photo, MH:AUG/95[30]185
ADDITIONAL LISTINGS: ACW:JUL/92[30]369, ACW:JUL/93[58],
  ACW:MAR/94[50]462, CWM:APR/95[39]576,
  CWR:VOL1#4[7]125, CWR:VOL2#3[212]142,
  CWR:VOL3#1[1]149, CWR:VOL3#3[33]158,
  CWR:VOL3#3[88]160, CWR:VOL4#2[1]165,

CWR:VOL4#2[26]166, CWR:VOL4#2[68]167,
  CWTI:AUG/90[58]169, CWTI:JAN/95[24]424
WALKER, JOSEPH, *Colonel, Palmetto Sharpshooters;*
  CWR:VOL3#2[70]155
WALKER, LEICESTER, *Lieutenant, 5th U.S. Cavalry;*
  B&G:OCT/93[12]537
WALKER, LEROY P., *General, CSA;* ACW:JUL/92[22]368,
  AHI:JUN/84[24]239, CWTI:FEB/91[36]193,
  CWTI:AUG/91[36]217, CWTI:AUG/91[46]218,
  CWTI:DEC/91[44]241, CWTI:FEB/92[29]248,
  CWTI:MAR/93[24]309, MH:FEB/91[8]151
WALKER, LUCIUS M., *General, CSA;* ACW:SEP/92[38]379,
  ACW:MAY/93[22]414
WALKER, MARY *Doctor:*
ARTICLE: "MARY WALKER: SAMARITAN OR CHARLATAN,"
  CWTI:MAY/94[40]383
ADDITIONAL LISTINGS: CWM:APR/94[8]502, CWTI:SEP/94[12]398,
  photo, CWTI:MAY/94[40]383
WALKER, MOSES B., *Colonel, 31st Ohio Infantry;*
  B&G:FEB/93[12]511
WALKER, NORMAN S., *Major, CSA;* ACW:MAY/93[62]418,
  CWTI:DEC/89[10]133
WALKER, R. LINDSAY, *Colonel, CSA:*
GENERAL LISTINGS: *in book review,* CWR:VOL3#4[68], *in order of
  battle,* B&G:APR/94[10]558, *order of battle,*
  B&G:APR/95[8]595, *photo,* CWR:VOL4#4[70]180
ADDITIONAL LISTINGS: CWR:VOL1#1[1]102, CWR:VOL1#1[26]103,
  CWR:VOL1#2[44]114, CWR:VOL3#2[1]153,
  CWR:VOL4#4[70]180, CWTI:SEPT/89[46]132,
  GETTY:13[75]259
WALKER, ROBERT, *Private, CSA;* ACW:JUL/94[26]477
WALKER, ROBERT J., *Governor, Kansas;* ACW:SEP/91[54]
WALKER, TANDY, CWM:JAN/93[6]455, CWR:VOL1#2[44]114
WALKER, THADDEUS J., *Private, CSA;* ACW:MAR/94[16]458
WALKER, THOMAS, *Lieutenant Colonel, 111th Pennsylvania
  Infantry;* B&G:FEB/94[38]553, B&G:APR/94[34]561,
  CWR:VOL3#2[70]155, GETTY:10[120]229
WALKER, THOMAS, *Private, Crenshaw's Artillery;*
  GETTY:10[107]227
WALKER, THOMAS M., *Lieutenant Colonel, 111th
  Pennsylvania Infantry;* GETTY:7[83]192
WALKER, WILLIAM, *Lieutenant Colonel, 28th Louisiana
  Infantry;* CWR:VOL4#2[1]165, CWR:VOL4#2[118]169
WALKER, WILLIAM, *Private, 5th New York Infantry;*
  CWR:VOL1#2[29]112
WALKER, WILLIAM H.T., *General, CSA:*
ARTICLE: "I SHALL MAKE HIM REMEMBER THIS INSULT,"
  CWTI:MAR/93[24]309
BOOK REVIEW: *TO THE MANNER BORN: THE LIFE OF
  GENERAL WILLIAM H.T. WALKER*
GENERAL LISTINGS: *black soldiers,* ACW:NOV/93[6]437, *Jackson,
  Battle of,* B&G:AUG/95[8]604, *letters to the editor,*
  CWM:DEC/94[5]546, CWTI:JUL/93[10]323,
  CWTI:MAR/95[18]432, *order of battle,* B&G:AUG/95[8]604,
  Vicksburg, B&G:AUG/95[8]604, *photos,* ACW:MAR/95[58],
  CWTI:MAR/93[24]309
ADDITIONAL LISTINGS: ACW:JAN/95[30]505, CWM:JUL/92[24]430,
  CWR:VOL1#3[82]123, CWR:VOL1#4[42]126,
  CWR:VOL1#4[64]127, CWR:VOL2#1[36]132,
  CWTI:SUMMER/89[20]121, CWTI:SUMMER/89[32]122,
  CWTI:SEPT/89[30]129, CWTI:SEP/91[23]228,
  CWTI:SEP/92[28]280, CWTI:NOV/92[41]291,
  CWTI:MAR/94[48]374, CWTI:DEC/94[49]413

WALL, JERRY, *Private, 126th New York Infantry;*
CWR:VOL1#4[7]125, GETTY:8[95]205
WALLACE, ALEXANDER, *Private, Fredericksburg Artillery;*
CWR:VOL1#1[1]102
WALLACE, E.P., *Private, 22nd Battalion Virginia Infantry;*
CWR:VOL1#3[52]122
WALLACE, GEORGE, *Private, 3rd Georgia Infantry;*
CWTI:SEP/94[26]400
WALLACE, JAMES, *Colonel, 1st Maryland Eastern Shore
Regiment;* GETTY:12[42]244
WALLACE, JONATHAN, *Private, CSA;* AHI:AUG/68[4]115B
WALLACE, LEW, *General, USA:*
ARTICLES: "MONOCACY: THE BATTLE THAT SAVED
WASHINGTON," B&G:DEC/92[8]503, "ROADBLOCK EN
ROUTE TO WASHINGTON," ACW:NOV/93[50]44
BOOK REVIEWS: *LEW WALLACE: MILITANT ROMANTIC ∗
SEASON OF FIRE: THE CONFEDERATE STRIKE ON
WASHINGTON*
GENERAL LISTINGS: *election of 1876,* AHI:NOV/88[28]277, *Forts
Henry and Donelson,* B&G:FEB/92[10]474, *in book review,*
CWNEWS:APR/91[4], CWNEWS:OCT/94[33], *letters to the
editor,* CWTI:MAY/93[8]315, *Monocacy,* CWTI:JAN/93[40]301,
MH:APR/95[46]183, *Shenandoah Valley Campaign, 1864,*
B&G:AUG/94[10]574, *Shiloh,* ACW:JAN/91[22]285, *photos,*
B&G:FEB/92[10]474, B&G:DEC/92[8]503,
CWM:JUL/91[48]374, CWTI:FEB/90[32]144,
CWTI:DEC/91[28]239
ADDITIONAL LISTINGS: ACW:JUL/92[46]371, ACW:JUL/93[34]424,
ACW:JUL/94[26]477, B&G:DEC/92[53]509,
B&G:JUN/94[8]568, B&G:OCT/95[36]614,
CWM:JAN/93[38]329, CWM:JAN/93[40]461,
CWM:SEP/93[24]495, CWM:FEB/95[32]562,
CWR:VOL4#1[44]164, CWTI:AUG/90[58]169,
CWTI:MAR/91[28]200, CWTI:MAY/91[47]210
WALLACE, MATTHEW H., *Sergeant, 4th Illinois Cavalry;*
ACW:MAR/93[8]401
WALLACE, PATRICK, *Private, 4th U.S.;* GETTY:9[33]211,
GETTY:11[57]233
WALLACE, WILLIAM H.L., *General, USA:*
BOOK REVIEW: *HARD DYING MEN: THE STORY OF GENERAL
W.H.L. WALLACE, GENERAL T.E.G. RANSOM, AND THEIR
"OLD ELEVENTH" ILLINOIS INFANTRY*
ADDITIONAL LISTINGS: ACW:JAN/91[22]285, B&G:FEB/92[10]474,
CWR:VOL4#1[44]164
WALLACE, WALTER, *Lieutenant, 24th Michigan Infantry;*
GETTY:5[19]158
WALLACE, WARD G., *Private, 7th Texas Infantry;*
AHI:JUL/93[40]312
WALLACE, WILLIAM, *Colonel, 2nd South Carolina Infantry;*
GETTY:5[35]159
WALLACE, WILLIAM, *Colonel, 15th Ohio Infantry;*
B&G:OCT/94[11]580
WALLACE, WILLIAM, *Paymaster, USA;* ACW:JAN/94[47]452
WALLACE, WILLIAM H., *General, CSA;* B&G:APR/92[8]481
WALLACE, WILLIAM W., *Private, 125th Pennsylvania
Infantry;* B&G:OCT/95[8]611A
WALLER, EDWARD, *Major, 13th Texas Cavalry;*
CWR:VOL3#1[1]149
WALLER, EDWIN, *Major, CSA;* ACW:JAN/91[10]283
WALLER, FRANCIS A., *Major, 6th Wisconsin Infantry:*
ARTICLE: "FRANCIS ASBURY WALLER: A MEDAL OF HONOR
AT GETTYSBURG," GETTY:4[16]143
ADDITIONAL LISTING: GETTY:4[126]154

WALLER, THOMAS, *Private, 6th Wisconsin Infantry;*
GETTY:4[16]143
WALLING, WILLIAM W., *Lieutenant, 142nd New York
Infantry;* AHI:SEP/83[12]234, B&G:DEC/94[10]585
WALLIS, WILLIAM, *Lieutenant, 30th Alabama Infantry;*
CWR:VOL2#1[19]131
WALSH, JAMES W., *Captain, 3rd Pennsylvania Cavalry;*
GETTY:4[75]149, GETTY:13[89]260
WALT, A.J., *AAG, CSA;* CWR:VOL4#2[118]169
WALTER, GEORGE, *Captain, CSA;* CWR:VOL1#2[78]
WALTER, T. FRANK, *Captain, USA;* ACW:SEP/93[22]432
WALTERS, JOHN L., *Lieutenant, USA;* ACW:MAR/93[51]407
WALTHALL, EDWARD C., *General, CSA:*
GENERAL LISTINGS: *in book review,* CWNEWS:JUL/92[4],
CWR:VOL3#1[80], *in order of battle,* B&G:FEB/93[12]511,
B&G:DEC/93[12]545, B&G:DEC/95[9]615, *Nashville,*
B&G:DEC/93[12]545
ADDITIONAL LISTINGS: ACW:NOV/95[48]557, CWR:VOL1#4[64]127,
CWR:VOL4#3[65]172, CWTI:SUMMER/89[20]121,
CWTI:SUMMER/89[50]124, CWTI:SEPT/89[30]129
WALTHALL, WILLIAM T.; CWM:JAN/91[40]330
WALTMAN, DAVID P., *Private, 53rd Pennsylvania Infantry;*
GETTY:11[80]235
WALTON, J.B., *Colonel, CSA;* ACW:JUL/92[12]367,
ACW:SEP/92[30]378, CWTI:SEPT/89[46]132,
GETTY:4[115]152
WALTON, SIMEON, *Lieutenant Colonel, 23rd Virginia
Infantry;* CWM:MAY/92[20]420
WALTON, WILLIAM, *Lieutenant, 2nd Virginia Cavalry;*
B&G:OCT/93[12]537
WALTON, WILLIAM, *Lieutenant, 21st Texas Infantry;*
CWR:VOL2#3[212]142
WALWORTH, WILLIAM, *Lieutenant, USA;* GETTY:11[91]236
WANGELIN, HUGO, *Colonel, USA;* CWTI:SUMMER/89[40]123
WAR CONTRACTS; ARTICLE: "HE WOULD STEAL?"
CWTI:JUN/90[46]161
WAR IN THE WEST; "THE OTHER CIVIL WAR,"
AHI:NOV/73[18]151
WARD, GEORGE H., *Colonel, 15th Massachusetts Infantry;*
CWM:APR/95[42]577, GETTY:13[43]256
WARD, GEORGE T., *Colonel, 2nd Florida Infantry;*
ACW:SEP/93[8]429, CWR:VOL3#2[1]153
WARD, JAMES H., *Lieutenant, USN;* CWTI:MAY/92[29]263,
MH:FEB/91[8]151
WARD, JOHN H.H., *General, USA:*
GENERAL LISTINGS: *Gettysburg,* GETTY:8[43]202,
GETTY:8[53]203, GETTY:9[5]209, GETTY:10[112]228, *order
of battle,* B&G:APR/95[8]595, *SIO,* B&G:DEC/92[40]508
ADDITIONAL LISTINGS: B&G:FEB/92[22]476
WARD, LYMAN M., *Colonel, USA;* B&G:DEC/93[12]545,
CWR:VOL4#2[26]166
WARE, EUGENE F., *Private, 1st Iowa Infantry:*
BOOK REVIEW: *THE LYON CAMPAIGN IN MISSOURI: BEING A
HISTORY OF THE FIRST IOWA INFANTRY*
ADDITIONAL LISTING: CWM:MAY/92[34]422
WARD, ROBERT F., *Lieutenant, 42nd Mississippi Infantry;*
GETTY:4[22]144
WARD, W.N., *Major, CSA;* CWTI:JUL/94[44]394
WARD, WILLIAM G., *Colonel, 12th New York Militia;*
CWR:VOL1#4[7]125
WARD, WILLIAM T., *General, USA;* B&G:DEC/95[9]615,
CWTI:SUMMER/89[32]122, CWTI:NOV/92[41]291

WARD, WILLIAM W., *Colonel, 9th Tennessee Cavalry:*
BOOK REVIEWS: *FOR THE SAKE OF MY COUNTRY: THE DIARY OF COLONEL W.W. WARD, 9TH TENNESSEE CAVALRY, MORGAN'S BRIGADE, C.S.A*
ADDITIONAL LISTING: B&G:OCT/94[11]580
WARDER, E.D., *Captain, CSA;* B&G:OCT/94[11]580
WARDROP, DAVID, *Colonel, USA;* GETTY:11[6]231
WARE, EUGENE F., *Private, 1st Iowa Infantry;*
ACW:NOV/93[26]441
WARE, THOMAS L., *Sergeant, 15th Georgia Infantry;*
BOOK REVIEWS: *35 DAYS TO GETTYSBURG: THE CAMPAIGN DIARIES OF TWO AMERICAN ENEMIES*
WARGAMMING; BOOK REVIEW: *WARGAMMING IN HISTORY: THE AMERICAN CIVIL WAR*
WARING, GEORGE E., *Major, Colonel, 39th New York Infantry;* ACW:MAY/95[54]528, MH:FEB/95[18]182
WARING, JOSEPH F., *Captain, CSA;* GETTY:12[68]246
WARING, WILLIAM, *Chaplain, 102nd U.S. Colored Infantry;*
CWTI:APR/89[32]110
WARLEY, ALEXANDER F., *Lieutenant, CSN;*
ACW:MAY/92[16]359, MH:AUG/93[47]169, MH:DEC/94[46]181
WARMOUTH, HENRY C., *Lieutenant, Colonel, USA;*
B&G:FEB/94[8]550, CWNEWS:APR/90[4]
WARNER, GEORGE, *Private, 20th Connecticut Infantry;*
GETTY:5[117]165
WARNER, IRWIN E., *Private, 2nd Connecticut Heavy Artillery;*
ARTICLE: "LIES, DISGRACE, REDEMPTION,"
CWTI:SEP/91[61]233
WARNER, LEWIS D., *Major, 154th New York Infantry;*
GETTY:8[17]200
WARNER, WILLARD, *Lieutenant Colonel, 76th Ohio Infantry;*
AHI:JAN/67[4]106, CWNEWS:APR/90[4],
CWTI:SUMMER/89[50]124, CWTI:SEP/94[40]403
WARNER, SOLOMON, *civilian;* ACW:JUL/93[27]423
WARREN (MISSISSIPPI) LIGHT ARTILLERY;
GETTY:4[7]142
WARREN (MISSISSIPPI) RIFLES, (19th Mississippi Infantry); GETTY:4[7]142
WARREN, EDGAR, *Captain, USA;* GETTY:8[31]201
WARREN, EDWARD T.H., *Colonel, 10th Virginia Infantry;*
GETTY:7[83]192
WARREN, EDWARD, *Surgeon, CSA;* BOOK REVIEW: *AN EPITOME OF PRACTICAL SURGERY FOR FIELD AND HOSPITAL*
WARREN, GEORGE, *Captain, 3rd New York Infantry;*
AHI:SEP/83[12]234
WARREN, GOUVERNEUR K., *General, USA:*
ARTICLE: "CONFRONTATION AT FIVE FORKS: GENERAL SHERIDAN VS. GENERAL WARREN," CWM:MAR/93[24]467
GENERAL LISTINGS: *Cold Harbor,* B&G:APR/94[10]558, *Five Forks,* ACW:MAY/95[38]526, B&G:APR/92[8]481, *Gaines' Mill,* CWM:JUN/95[61]593, *Gettysburg,* ACW:JAN/92[38]343, CWM:JUL/92[8]427, GETTY:6[33]172, GETTY:6[43]173, GETTY:6[59]174, GETTY:7[29]188, GETTY:7[41]189, GETTY:8[31]201, GETTY:9[48]213, GETTY:10[42]224, GETTY:10[112]228, GETTY:11[71]234, GETTY:12[30]243, GETTY:12[85]248, *in book review,* CWNEWS:APR/92[4], CWNEWS:MAY/90[4], CWNEWS:JUL/94[25], CWR:VOL1#2[78], MH:AUG/92[76], *in order of battle,* B&G:APR/92[8]481, B&G:APR/94[10]558, *letters to the editor,* CWM:APR/95[5]570, *Manassas, Second,* ACW:JUL/91[18]312, AHI:DEC/66[30]105, B&G:AUG/92[11]493, *Mine Run,* ACW:MAR/93[26]404, *order of battle,* B&G:APR/95[8]595

GENERAL LISTINGS, continued: *Overland Campaign,* B&G:APR/94[10]558, *Peninsula Campaign,* CWM:JUN/95[43]587, *Petersburg,* MH:APR/95[46]183, *Wilderness,* B&G:APR/95[8]595, B&G:JUN/95[8]600, *photo,* AHI:DEC/66[30]105, B&G:APR/92[8]481, B&G:APR/93[12]518, B&G:APR/95[8]595, CWM:MAR/93[24]467, GETTY:6[43]173, GETTY:8[31]201
ADDITIONAL LISTINGS: ACW:JUL/91[18]312, ACW:JUL/91[35]314, ACW:JUL/92[41]370, ACW:SEP/92[30]378, ACW:NOV/92[26]386, ACW:MAR/93[26]404, ACW:SEP/93[62]436, ACW:SEP/94[38]487, ACW:NOV/94[50]498, B&G:APR/91[8]445, B&G:APR/93[12]518, B&G:APR/94[59]565, B&G:DEC/95[25]616, CWM:MAR/91[35]337, CWM:SEP/91[35]384, CWM:MAY/92[20]420, CWM:MAR/93[4]463, CWM:OCT/94[17]534, CWM:FEB/95[30]561, CWR:VOL1#2[7]111, CWR:VOL1#2[29]112, CWR:VOL1#3[52]122, CWR:VOL2#4[269]145, CWR:VOL3#1[31]150, CWR:VOL3#4[1]161, CWTI:AUG/90[26]166, CWTI:SEP/91[31]229, CWTI:MAY/94[31]382, CWTI:DEC/94[32]410, GETTY:13[119]262
WARREN, H.N., *Major, 142nd Pennsylvania Infantry;*
GETTY:4[24]145
WARREN, J.C., *Lieutenant, 52nd North Carolina Infantry;*
GETTY:12[61]245
WARREN, JOHN, *Captain, 8th New Hampshire Infantry;*
CWR:VOL3#1[1]149
WARREN, LEANDER, *civilian;* GETTY:11[19]232
WARREN, NATHANIEL, *Private, 30th Maine Infantry;*
ACW:SEP/91[16]320
WARREN, T.J., *Captain, 13th South Carolina Infantry;*
CWTI:SEP/90[26]174
WARRINGTON NAVY YARD, PENSACOLA, FLORIDA;
ACW:MAR/91[14]293
WARWICK RIVER LINE; CWM:JUN/95[29]583
WARWICK, NOBLE, *Corporal, 13th U.S. Infantry;*
CWM:JUN/94[30]515, CWR:VOL2#1[1]130
WASDEN, J., *Colonel, 22nd Georgia Infantry;*
CWTI:SEP/90[26]174
WASH, W.A., *Captain, CSA;* ACW:JAN/93[66]399
WASHBURN, CADWALLADER C., *General, USA;*
ACW:SEP/92[16]376, ACW:SEP/92[23]377, CWTI:MAY/93[35]320, CWTI:NOV/93[71]352, CWTI:JAN/94[35]361, CWTI:DEC/94[82]418, MH:DEC/95[58]188
WASHBURN, ELISHA, *Lieutenant Colonel, CSA;*
B&G:DEC/95[9]615
WASHBURN, FRANCIS, *Colonel, USA;* ACW:JAN/92[22]341, ACW:JAN/93[43]397
WASHBURN, GEORGE, *Private, 108th New York Infantry;*
GETTY:6[7]169
WASHBURN, H.D., *Colonel, 18th Indiana Infantry;*
B&G:FEB/94[8]550
WASHBURN, HENRY S., *Private, 1st Massachusetts Infantry;*
GETTY:12[7]241
WASHBURN, I.B., *Surgeon, USA;* AHI:DEC/71[10]137
WASHBURN, ISRAEL, JR., *Governor, Maine;*
ACW:MAY/95[62], GETTY:8[43]202, GETTY:10[53]225
WASHBURNE, ELIHU B., *Congressman;* ACW:JAN/92[30]342, ACW:NOV/94[34]496, CWTI:FEB/90[32]144, CWTI:DEC/94[82]418, GETTY:12[85]248

WASHINGTON ARTILLERY: B&G:AUG/92[11]493,
B&G:OCT/92[38]500, B&G:DEC/93[30]546,
B&G:AUG/95[8]604, CWTI:SEPT/89[46]132, GETTY:6[62]175,
GETTY:13[7]253, GETTY:13[75]259
WASHINGTON (GEORGIA) ARTILLERY;
CWR:VOL1#4[42]126
WASHINGTON (SOUTH CAROLINA) ARTILLERY;
GETTY:7[124]196
WASHINGTON D.C.:
ARTICLE: "CAPITAL FOLLY," ACW:MAY/93[38]416
BOOK REVIEWS: *A GUIDE TO CIVIL WAR WASHINGTON, **
JUBAL'S RAID * MR. LINCOLN'S FORTS: A GUIDE TO
THE CIVIL WAR DEFENSES OF WASHINGTON * SEASON
OF FIRE: THE CONFEDERATE STRIKE ON
WASHINGTON * WARTIME WASHINGTON: THE CIVIL
WAR LETTERS OF ELIZABETH BLAIR LEE *
WASHINGTON D.C., IN LINCOLN'S TIME
ADDITIONAL LISTINGS: CWNEWS:DEC/92[4]
CWTI:SEPT/89[40]130, CWTI:DEC/89[34]136
WASHINGTON HORSE ARTILLERY:
ARTICLE: "ALREADY OWNING A PROUD PEDIGREE, THE
WASHINGTON HORSE ARTILLERY ADDED LUSTER TO
THE CONFEDERATE CAUSE," ACW:JUL/92[12]367
ADDITIONAL LISTINGS: ACW:SEP/92[30]378, ACW:NOV/92[74]390
WASHINGTON LIGHT ARTILLERY; ACW:JAN/93[43]397
WASHINGTON LIGHT INFANTRY; CWTI:DEC/89[42]137
WASHINGTON NAVY YARD; CWTI:APR/92[14]254
WASHINGTON'S ARTILLERY OF CHARLESTON;
CWTI:SEPT/89[24]128
WASHINGTON, (STATE OF); ARTICLE: "FORTS STEVENS
AND CANBY STOOD A LONG VIGIL PROTECTING THE
PACIFIC COAST FROM ATTACK," ACW:MAR/92[62]355
WASHINGTON, ARKANSAS; ARTICLE: "THE APTLY NAMED
TOWN OF WASHINGTON WAS, FOR A TIME, THE
CAPITAL OF CONFEDEREATE ARKANSAS,"
ACW:SEP/92[66]381
WASHINGTON, EDWARD C., *Captain, 13th U.S. Infantry;*
CWM:JUN/94[30]515, CWR:VOL2#1[1]130,
CWR:VOL2#1[69]133
WASHINGTON, JAMES B., *cadet;* B&G:DEC/91[12]469
WASHINGTON, JOHN A., *Colonel, CSA;* ACW:JAN/92[50]345,
ACW:SEP/94[31]486, B&G:OCT/92[32]499,
B&G:AUG/93[10]529
WASHINGTON, LEWIS T.; ACW:JUL/91[43]315
WATERHOUSE, ALLEN C., *Captain, 1st Illinois Artillery;*
B&G:AUG/95[8]604, B&G:DEC/95[9]615
WATERHOUSE, RICHARD, *Colonel, 19th Texas Infantry;*
ACW:MAR/93[68]409, CWR:VOL3#3[33]158
WATERMAN, CHARLES D., *Lieutenant, USA;*
B&G:DEC/91[12]469
WATERS, JOHN, *Private, 2nd Tennessee Cavalry;*
CWR:VOL4#1[1]163,
WATIE, SALADIN R., *Captain, Cherokee Braves;*
CWM:SEP/92[38]443
WATIE, STAND, *General, CSA:*
ARTICLES: "FORT TOWSON: INDIAN TERRITORY POST THAT
PLAYED A PART IN THE PEACE." B&G:OCT/94[38]582,
"FROM TAHLEQUAH TO BOGGY DEPOT: STAND WATIE'S
CIVIL WAR," CWM:SEP/92[38]443, "INDIANS BLUE AND
GRAY," ACW:JAN/91[30]286
GENERAL LISTINGS: *common soldiers,* AHI:APR/68[4]115, *letters to*
the editor, CWM:JAN/93[6]455, *Price's 1864 Missouri*
Campaign, B&G:JUN/91[10]452, *Surrender of;*

CWTI:APR/90[20]151, *photos,* ACW:JAN/91[30]286,
B&G:OCT/94[38]582, CWM:SEP/92[38]443
ADDITIONAL LISTINGS: CWM:SEP/92[8]437, CWM:MAY/93[24]476,
CWTI:AUG/90[64]170
WATIES, JOHN, *Captain, Palmetto Light Artillery;*
B&G:AUG/95[8]604
WATKINS, ELIHU P., *Colonel, CSA;* B&G:DEC/93[12]545
WATKINS, SAM R., *Private, 1st Tennessee Infantry;*
ACW:NOV/93[42]443, ACW:NOV/94[6]492,
ACW:SEP/95[38]546, CWTI:SUMMER/89[20]121,
CWTI:AUG/90[42]167, CWTI:SEP/92[28]280,
CWTI:DEC/94[49]413
WATKINS, THOMAS, *Lieutenant, CSA;* B&G:AUG/93[10]529
WATKINS, WILLIAM M., *Colonel, CSA;* B&G:DEC/93[12]545
WATROUS, JEROME A., *Adjutant, 6th Wisconsin Infantry;*
CWR:VOL1#2[78], GETTY:4[16]143, GETTY:4[24]145
WATSON, ALONZO, *Private, 15th Alabama Infantry;*
B&G:AUG/92[11]493
WATSON, BAXTER, *civilian;* CWTI:SEPT/89[20]127
WATSON, CLEMENT S., *Lieutenant, CSA;*
CWM:FEB/95[28]560
WATSON, DAVID, *Captain, 2nd Richmond Howitzers;*
CWR:VOL4#4[70]180
WATSON, J. CRITTENDEN, *Lieutenant, USN;*
ACW:NOV/91[8]328
WATSON, JESSE E., *civilian;* B&G:OCT/94[11]580
WATSON, MALBONE F., *Lieutenant, 5th U.S. Artillery;*
GETTY:5[47]160, GETTY:7[51]190, GETTY:9[41]212
WATSON, PETER H., *Assistant Secretary of War;*
CWM:NOV/91[12]390
WATSON, S.D., *Sergeant, 51st North Carolina Infantry;*
B&G:APR/93[24]520
WATSON, THOMAS E., *Private, 10th Georgia Infantry;*
ACW:JUL/95[10]533
WATSON, WILLIAM, *surgeon;* CWM:DEC/95[54]632
WATSON, WILLIAM A., *Lieutenant, USN;* B&G:JUN/92[40]489
WATSON, WILLIAM L., *Lieutenant, 21st Wisconsin Infantry;*
AHI:NOV/85[38]254, AHI:DEC/85[40]255
WATT, JOHN; CWTI:DEC/95[24]477
WATTERS, ZACHARIAH L., *Colonel, CSA;*
B&G:DEC/93[12]545
WATTERSON, HENRY, *editor;* B&G:OCT/92[32]499
WATTS, A.T., *Colonel, CSA;* CWTI:MAY/92[38]265
WATTS, JACK, *Private, Petersburg Artillery;*
ACW:MAR/95[12]513
WATTS, JAMES, *Colonel, 2nd Virginia Cavalry;*
B&G:OCT/93[12]537, B&G:OCT/93[21]538
WATTS, JAMES, *Master, USN;* AHI:JAN/83[10]232
WATTS, JOHN W., *Sergeant, 3rd South Carolina Infantry;*
GETTY:5[35]159
WATTS, JOSIAH, *Doctor;* B&G:JUN/93[12]524
WATTS, N.G., *Major, CSA;* AHI:DEC/77[46]177
WAUD, ALFRED R., *artist:*
ARTICLE: "THE ARTIST AND THE CIVIL WAR,"
AHI:NOV/80[28]211
BOOK REVIEW: *OUR SPECIAL ARTIST*
ADDITIONAL LISTINGS: B&G:FEB/92[22]476, B&G:FEB/94[24]551,
B&G:FEB/94[36], B&G:JUN/94[5]567, CWM:NOV/92[10]447
WAUD, WILLIAM; B&G:FEB/94[36], CWM:NOV/92[10]447
WAUGH, JAMES L., *Captain, 5th New York Infantry;*
CWR:VOL1#2[7]111,
WAUHATCHIE JUNCTION, TENNESSEE, ENGAGEMENT
AT; CWR:VOL3#2[70]155, CWR:VOL3#2[102]156

WAUL, THOMAS, *Colonel, CSA;* CWR:VOL2#1[19]131,
  CWR:VOL4#2[68]167
WAY, WILLIAM B., *Lieutenant Colonel, USA;*
  B&G:DEC/95[9]615
WAY, WILLIAM C., *Chaplain, 24th Michigan Infantry;*
  GETTY:5[19]158, GETTY:10[53]225
WAYNE, HENRY C., *Adjutant General, State of Georgia;*
  CWTI:SEP/91[23]228
WAYNE, RICHARD A., *Colonel, 1st Georgia Regulars;*
  CWR:VOL2#2[95]135
WAYNESBORO, VIRGINIA, BATTLE OF:
ARTICLE: "JUBAL EARLY AT WAYNESBORO: THE LAST
  HURRAH," CWM:APR/94[24]505
ADDITIONAL LISTING: ACW:JAN/92[16]340
WEAKLEY, JAMES G., *Corporal, 3rd Pennsylvania Cavalry;*
  GETTY:13[89]260

WEAPONS:

ARTICLE: "LINCOLN'S SECRET ARMS RACE,"
  CWTI:OCT/95[32]468
BOOK REVIEWS: *AN INTRODUCTION OT CIVIL WAR SMALL
  ARMS * ARMING THE SUCKERS, 1861-1865 *
  CONFEDERATE ARMS * LINCOLN AND THE TOOLS OF
  WAR * THE STORY OF THE CONFEDERATE STATES
  ORDNANCE WORKS AT TYLER, TEXAS, 1861-1865*
VIDEO REVIEW: *GUNS OF THE CIVIL WAR,* AHI:AUG/94[22]
Ambulance; BOOK REVIEW: *FARMCARTS TO FORDS: A
  HISTORY OF THE MILITARY AMBULANCE, 1790-1925*
Ammunition; *Maynard tape primer;* CWTI:SEPT/89[10]125
Animals; CWTI:MAR/95[46]437,
Arms and Equipment; BOOK REVIEW: *ARMS AND EQUIPMENT
  OF THE CONFEDERACY * ARMS AND EQUIPMENT OF
  THE UNION*

(ARTILLERY):
ARTICLES: "THE ALLURE OF THE CIVIL WAR'S HEFTIEST
  RELICS," CWTI:DEC/90[20]181, "CIVIL WAR FIELD
  ARTILLERY BRIDGED THE GAP BETWEEN NAPOLEON
  AND WORLD WAR I," ACW:NOV/94[12]494, "THE EFFECTS
  OF ARTILLERY FIRE ON INFANTRY AT GETTYSBURG,"
  GETTY:5[117]165, "THE WAR'S MOST DANGEROUS
  RELICS," CWTI:DEC/94[42]412
BOOK REVIEWS: *INTRODUCTION TO FIELD ARTILLERY
  ORDNANCE 1861-1865: A PICTORIAL STUDY OF CIVIL
  WAR ARTILLERY PROJECTILES * ARTILLERY HELL:
  THE EMPLOYMENT OF ARTILLERY AT ANTIETAM, *
  CUSHING OF GETTYSBURG: THE STORY OF A UNION
  ARTILLERY COMMANDER * THE LONG ARM OF LEE, OR
  THE HISTORY OF THE ARTILLERY OF THE ARMY OF
  NORTHERN VIRGINIA A BRIEF ACCOUNT OF THE
  CONFEDERATE BUREAU OF ORDNANCE * ARTILLERY
  HELL: THE EMPLOYMENT OF ARTILLERY AT
  ANTIETAM * THE LONG ARM OF LEE OR THE HISTORY
  OF THE ARTILLERY OF THE ARMY OF NORTHERN
  VIRGINIA*
TABLE: Results of individual artillery shots at Gettysburg causing
  two or more casualties, GETTY:5[117]165
Armstrong rifle; ACW:NOV/94[12]494
Blakely rifle; ACW:NOV/94[12]494
Delafield Rifle, 20 Pound; CWTI:DEC/90[20]181
James Rifle, 24 Pound; ACW:NOV/94[12]494,
  CWTI:DEC/90[20]181
Model 1841 6-Pounder; CWTI:DEC/90[20]181

Model 1857 12-Pounder Napoleon; CWTI:DEC/90[20]181
Model 1861 Ordnance Rifle; ACW:NOV/94[12]494,
  CWTI:DEC/90[20]181
Mountain Howitzer; ARTICLE: "CONFEDERATE GUNNERS
  AFFECTIONATELY CALLED THEIR HARD-WORKING
  LITTLE MOUNTAIN HOWITZERS 'BULL PUPS,'"
  ACW:SEP/95[10]543
Parrott rifle; ACW:NOV/94[12]494, *photos,*
  CWTI:OCT/95[32]468
Parrott rifle, 10 Pound; CWTI:DEC/90[20]181
Swamp Angel; ARTICLE: "THE SWAMP ANGEL: LOVED IN
  TRENTON AND HATED IN CHARLESTON,"
  CWTI:APR/89[22]108
Whitworth cannon; ACW:NOV/94[12]494, GETTY:5[117]165
Wiard, 12-Pound; CWTI:DEC/90[20]181
Woodruff Gun; ARTICLE: "THE UNDISTINGUISHED
  WOODRUFF GUN HAD ONLY ONE," TRUE SUPPORTER,
  ABRAHAM LINCOLN—BUT ONE WAS ENOUGH,"
  ACW:JUL/94[8]474

Balloons; ARTICLE: "THE CONFEDERATE BALLOON CORPS,"
  B&G:AUG/91[20]459
Canteens; BOOK REVIEW: *CIVIL WAR CANTEENS,*
  CWNEWS:MAY/91[4]
Carbines; ARTICLE: "CONNECTICUT YANKEE EBEN T.
  STARR'S PISTOLS AND CARBINES," HELPED BOLSTER
  THE UNION'S WAR EFFORT," ACW:SEP/94[24]485
Dogs; "FAITHFUL FRIENDS," CWTI:MAR/95[46]437
Earthworks:
ARTICLE: "THE 'SHOUPADE' REDOUBTS: JOSEPH E.
  JOHNSTON'S CHATTAHOOCHEE RIVER LINE,"
  CWR:VOL1#3[82]123,
ADDITIONAL LISTINGS: CWR:VOL1#3[v]117, CWR:VOL2#3[256]
Edged, Bowie Knife:
BOOK REVIEW: *CONFEDERATE EDGED WEAPONS*
ADDITIONAL LISTING: CWTI:SUMMER/89[40]123
Gatling Gun:
ARTICLE: "DR. GATLING AND HIS AMAZING GUN,"
  AHI:JUN/66[52]102, "WEAPONRY," MH:OCT/93[12]171
ADDITIONAL LISTINGS: AHI:SUMMER/88[6], *photos,*
  AHI:JUN/66[52]102
Greek Fire; CWTI:APR/89[22]108
Machine Gun; ARTICLE: "THE SEARCH FOR THE ULTIMATE
  WEAPON," CWTI:JAN/93[49]303
Horses and Mules: ARTICLE: "THE HARDY MULE GAVE ITS
  FLOP-EARED ALL—SOMETIMES LITERALLY—FOR THE
  UNION AND CONFEDERACY," ACW:JAN/92[10]339,
  "STREET NAMED FOR 'LITTLE SORREL,'"
  CWTI:APR/92[41]258
Mortars; ARTICLE: "WHEN BIG GUNS COULD NOT
  PENETRATE FORTIFIED SOUTHERN WALLS, FEDERAL
  MORTARS LOBBED SHELLS OVER THEM,"
  ACW:SEP/93[16]431

(PISTOLS and REVOLVERS):
ARTICLE: "CONNECTICUT YANKEE EBEN T. STARR'S
  PISTOLS AND CARBINES HELPED BOLSTER THE
  UNION'S WAR EFFORT," ACW:SEP/94[24]485
BOOK REVIEWS: *THE CONFEDERATE BRASS-FRAMED COLT &
  WHITNEY * CONFEDERATE HANDGUNS * THE
  ORIGINAL CONFEDERATE COLT*
Colt Model 1849; GETTY:9[48]213
Colt Model 1860; ACW:MAR/92[8]348

LeFaucheux revolver; ACW:MAR/92[8]348
LeMat; CWTI:SEPT/89[10]125
Minie' Pistol Carbine; CWTI:SEPT/89[10]125
Navy Revolver, .36 Caliber, Manhattan Series III; ARTICLE:
"AN IRON BRIGADE CAPTAIN'S REVOLVER IN THE
FIGHT ON MCPHERSON'S RIDGE," GETTY:7[7]185
Perrin; ACW:MAR/92[8]348
Pettingill revolver; ACW:MAR/92[8]348
Remington .44 Cal:
ARTICLE: "THE RELIABLE REMINGTON," CWTI:SEP/90[18]172
ADDITIONAL LISTING: ACW:MAR/92[8]348
Smith & Wesson revolver; ACW:MAR/92[8]348
Springfield pistol-carbine; ACW:MAR/92[8]348
Starr Revolver:
ARTICLE: "CONNECTICUT YANKEE EBEN T. STARR'S
PISTOLS AND CARBINES HELPED BOLSTER THE
UNION'S WAR EFFORT," ACW:/SEP/94[24]485
ADDITIONAL LISTING: ACW:MAR/92[8]348

Procurement of; ARTICLE: "THE ARMS-STARVED
CONFEDERACY EXPLORED ALL AVENUES," TO
ACQUIRE THE WEAPONS ITS SOLDIERS DESPERATELY
NEEDED," ACW:JAN/94[18]449

(RAPID FIRE):
ARTICLE: "MALFUNCTIONS AND A SHORTSIGHTED
ORDNANCE DEPARTMENT DELAYED THE
DEVELOPMENT OF RAPID-FIRE WEAPONS,"
ACW:JUL/93[8]420
Ager "Coffee Mill" gun; ACW:JUL/93[8]420,
CWTI:JAN/93[49]303
Gatling gun; see listings under GATLING, DR. RICHARD J."
Requa gun; ACW:JUL/93[8]420, CWTI:JAN/93[49]303
Vandenburgh gun:
ARTICLE: "THE PETERSBURG 'FOLLY GUN,'"
CWTI:DEC/90[18]180
ADDITIONAL LISTINGS: CWTI:DEC/90[18]180, CWTI:JAN/93[49]30

(RIFLES):
ARTICLE: "THE RIFLE MUSKET," ACW:JAN/91[8]282
Springfield Model 1855 Rifle Musket; CWTI:SEPT/89[10]125
Springfield Model 1861 Rifle Musket:
ARTICLE: "THE UNION'S MOST READY RIFLE: THE MODEL
1861 SPRINGFIELD RIFLE MUSKET,"
CWTI:SEPT/89[10]125
ADDITIONAL LISTING: CWTI:SEPT/89[10]125
British Sharpshooter; CWTI:APR/90[48]154
Enfield Rifle Musket:
ARTICLE: "CAPT. JAMES GLENN'S SWORD AND PRIVATE J.
MARSHALL HILL'S ENFIELD IN THE FIGHT FOR THE
LUTHERAN SEMINARY," GETTY:8[9]199, "THE READY
AVAILABILITY OF BRITISH RIFLES ENABLED BOTH
NORTH AND SOUTH TO ARM THEMSELVES QUICKLY,"
ACW:JAN/93[8]392
ADDITIONAL LISTINGS: CWTI:SEPT/89[10]125,
CWTI:APR/90[48]154
Henry; CWTI:APR/90[48]154
Kerr; CWTI:APR/90[48]154
Minie' Rifle; CWTI:SEPT/89[10]125
Sharps; CWTI:APR/90[48]154
Whitworth:
BOOK REVIEW: *THE CONFEDERATE WHITWORTH
SHARPSHOOTERS*

ADDITIONAL LISTING: CWTI:APR/90[48]154
Sniper; CWTI:APR/90[48]154

(SWORDS):
BOOK REVIEWS: *A PHOTOGRAPHIC SUPPLEMENT OF
CONFEDERATE SWORDS * AMERICAN SWORDS AND
SWORD MAKERS * HANDBOOK OF CONFEDERATE
SWORDS*
Collins & Co. Model 1850 Field and Staff Officer's Sword;
GETTY:12[24]242
U.S. Model 1850 Field and Staff Officer's Sword; ARTICLE:
"PYE'S SWORD AT THE RAILROAD CUT," GETTY:6[29]171

Telescopic Sights; ARTICLE: "DEATH AT A DISTANCE,"
CWTI:APR/90[48]154

Torpedoes:
ARTICLES: "ON THE MUDDY YAZOO RIVER ONE MORNING,
THE UNION GUNBOAT *CAIRO* MADE UNWANTED
NAVAL HISTORY," ACW:SEP/94[74]491, "TORPEDOES
SINK YANKEE GUNBOAT!" CWM:DEC/95[30]627,
"TORPEDOES, THE CONFEDERACY'S DREADED
'INFERNAL MACHINES' MADE MANY A UNION SEA
CAPTAIN UNEASY," ACW:NOV/91[8]328
BOOK REVIEW: *DAMN THE TORPEDOES! NAVAL INCIDENTS
OF THE CIVIL WAR*

WEAVER, FRANCIS A., *Private, 53rd Pennsylvania Infantry;*
GETTY:11[80]235
WEAVER, H.E., *Corporal, 2nd Iowa Infantry;*
B&G:FEB/92[48]475
WEAVER, OMAR, *Lieutenant, Woodreuffs Arkansas Battery;*
CWM:MAY/93[8]474
WEAVER, RUFUS, *civilian;* ACW:SEP/94[62]490,
GETTY:12[97]249
WEAVER, SAMUEL B., *Private, 92nd Ohio Infantry;*
B&G:JUN/95[36]603A
WEAVER, SAMUEL, *civilian;* ACW:SEP/94[62]490,
GETTY:5[107]164, GETTY:12[97]249
WEBB, ALEXANDER S., *General, USA:*
BOOK REVIEW: *THE PENINSULA: MCCLELLAN'S CAMPAIGN
OF 1862*
GENERAL LISTINGS: MH:DEC/91[54]155, AHI:SUM/88[12]273,
Gettysburg, GETTY:4[89]150, GETTY:4[113]153,
GETTY:5[79]161, GETTY:5[107]164, GETTY:5[123]166,
GETTY:6[7]169, GETTY:6[87]178, GETTY:7[29]188,
GETTY:7[97]193, GETTY:8[95]205, GETTY:10[7]221,
GETTY:10[36]223, GETTY:10[53]225, GETTY:10[112]228,
GETTY:11[71]234, *in book review,* CWR:VOL3#1[80], *order of
battle,* B&G:APR/95[8]595, *Wilderness,* B&G:JUN/95[8]600
ADDITIONAL LISTINGS: ACW:MAY/92[8]357, ACW:SEP/94[38]487,
CWTI:JUL/93[29]326, GETTY:13[43]256, GETTY:13[50]257
WEBB, JAMES, *Private, 5th New York Infantry;*
CWR:VOL1#2[29]112
WEBB, JOSEPH, *Doctor, USA;* CWTI:SEP/94[49]404
WEBB, NATHAN, *Captain, 1st Maine Cavalry;*
B&G:OCT/93[21]538
WEBB, THOMAS J., *Private, 1st Maryland Battalion;*
GETTY:9[81]216
WEBBER, THOMAS B., *Major, 2nd Kentucky Cavalry;*
B&G:OCT/94[11]580
WEBER, MAX, *Colonel, 20th New York Infantry;*
B&G:OCT/95[8]611B, CWTI:JUN/95[32]446

WEBER, PETER, *Corporal, 53rd Pennsylvania Infantry;*
GETTY:11[80]235

WEBER, PETER A., *Major, 6th Michigan Cavalry;*
GETTY:9[109]218, GETTY:13[89]260

WEBRE, J. SEPTIME, *Lieutenant, 18th Louisiana Infantry;*
CWR:VOL4#2[1]165

WEBSTER, FLETCHER, *Colonel, 12th Massachusetts Infantry:*
ARTICLE: "COLONEL FLETCHER WEBSTER'S LAST LETTER:
I SHALL NOT SPARE MYSELF, B&G:OCT/95[20]612
ADDITIONAL LISTINGS: AHI:JAN/93[61]309, B&G:AUG/92[11]493,
GETTY:10[7]221, *photo,* B&G:OCT/95[20]612

WEBSTER, GEORGE, *Colonel, USA;* CWR:VOL4#3[50]171

WEBSTER, JOSEPH D., *General, USA;* B&G:DEC/94[22]586

WEED, MINOT S., *Private, 24th Michigan Infantry,*
GETTY:9[33]211, GETTY:11[57]233

WEED, STEPHEN H., *General, USA:*
GENERAL LISTINGS: *Gettysburg,* GETTY:6[33]172,
GETTY:6[43]173, GETTY:8[31]201, GETTY:8[53]203,
GETTY:9[48]213, GETTY:9[53]214, GETTY:10[42]224,
GETTY:10[112]228, GETTY:11[71]234
ADDITIONAL LISTINGS: ACW:NOV/94[50]498, GETTY:6[7]169,
GETTY:9[41]212, GETTY:13[119]262

WEED, THURLOW; CWTI:DEC/95[24]477,
CWTI:DEC/95[40]479

WEEKS, B.S., *Master, USN;* CWTI:DEC/90[29]182

WEEKS, E.C., *Major, USA;* ACW:NOV/91[64]336

WEEKS, HENRY A., *Colonel, USA;* B&G:AUG/92[11]493

WEEMS, J.B., *Colonel, 10th Georgia Infantry;*
ACW:JUL/95[10]533

WEER, NORMAN, *Captain, 123rd New York Infantry;*
GETTY:6[7]169

WEER, WILLIAM, *Colonel, USA;* ACW:JAN/91[30]286,
CWM:SEP/92[38]443

WEIDRICH, MICHAEL, *Captain, USA;* GETTY:11[119]238

WEIGHTMAN, RICHARD H., *Colonel, CSA;*
ACW:NOV/93[26]441, CWTI:FEB/92[29]248

WEIKERT, GEORGE, *civilian;* GETTY:5[47]160,
GETTY:7[29]188, GETTY:8[31]201

WEINERT, RICHARD P., *Private, 1st Confederate Cavalry;*
BOOK REVIEW: *THE CONFEDERATE REGULAR ARMY*

WEIR, GULIAN V., *Lieutenant, 5th U.S. Artillery;*
GETTY:5[79]161

WEIR, JAMES, *Private, 5th New York Infantry;*
CWR:VOL1#2[7]111

WEIR, ROBERT W.; B&G:DEC/91[12]469

WEIR, THOMAS B., *Captain, USA;* MH:AUG/95[82]186

WEISAGER, DANIEL A., *General, CSA;* CWR:VOL1#3[52]122,
CWTI:APR/90[24]152, CWTI:FEB/91[45]194,
CWTI:DEC/94[32]410

WEISIGER, DAVID A., *Colonel, CSA;* B&G:APR/94[10]558,
CWR:VOL2#3[236]143

WEISS, FRANCIS, *Lieutenant Colonel, 20th New York Infantry;*
CWTI:JUN/95[32]446

WEITZEL, GODFREY, *General, USA:*
GENERAL LISTINGS: *fall of Richmond,* ACW:MAY/95[38]526, *Fort
Fisher,* ACW:JAN/95[38]506, AHI:SEP/83[12]234, *in book
review,* CWR:VOL4#1[78], *letters to the editor,*
B&G:JUN/95[5]599, *Sabine Pass,* CWTI:DEC/90[29]182,
photos, B&G:DEC/94[10]585, CWTI:DEC/90[29]182
ADDITIONAL LISTINGS: ACW:JUL/91[8]309, ACW:SEP/91[62]326,
ACW:JAN/94[30]450, ACW:JUL/94[42]479,
B&G:DEC/94[10]585, CWR:VOL3#1[1]149,
CWTI:DEC/95[76]482

WELCH, D.W., *Private, 126th Ohio Infantry;* B&G:JUN/95[8]600

WELCH, NORVAL E., *Lieutenant Colonel, 16th Michigan
Infantry:*
ARTICLE: "A SHADOW PASSING: THE TRAGIC STORY OF
NORVAL WELCH AND THE SIXTEENTH MICHIGAN AT
GETTYSBURG AND BEYOND," GETTY:6[33]172
ADDITIONAL LISTING: GETTY:8[31]201

WELCH, SPENCER, *Surgeon, 13th South Carolina Infantry;*
GETTY:6[94]180, GETTY:13[22]254

WELD, STEPHEN M., *Lieutenant Colonel, 56th Massachusetts
Infantry:*
BOOK REVIEW: *WAR LETTERS AND DIARIES OF STEPHEN
MINOT WELD, 1861-1865*
ADDITIONAL LISTINGS: B&G:APR/93[12]518, CWTI:APR/90[24]152,
GETTY:11[19]232

WELDON RAILROAD, VIRGINIA, BATTLE OF:
BOOK REVIEW: *THE PETERSBURG CAMPAIGN: THE
DESTRUCTION OF THE WELDON RAILROAD (DEEP
BOTTOM, GLOBE TAVERN, AND REAMS STATION,
AUGUST 14-25, 1864*
GENERAL LISTINGS: *in book review,* CWM:AUG/95[8],
CWNEWS:SEP/91[4], CWR:VOL1#2[78], CWR:VOL1#3[94]
ADDITIONAL LISTINGS: ACW:SEP/95[74]550,
CWR:VOL2#3[236]143, CWTI:FEB/91[45]194

WELDON, J.W., *Private, 53rd Georgia Infantry;*
CWTI:SEP/90[26]174

WELLER, F.J., *Captain, CSA;* ACW:JAN/94[30]450

WELLES, GIDEON:
GENERAL LISTINGS: *de Pont,* CWTI:MAR/94[38]372, *Fort Fisher,*
ACW:JAN/95[38]506, *Gettysburg,* GETTY:12[85]248, *general
history,* AHI:MAY/71[3]133A, *impeachment of Andrew
Johnson,* AHI:DEC/68[28]118, *in book review,*
ACW:MAY/91[54], B&G:JUN/95[30], CWNEWS:JAN/91[4],
CWNEWS:JUN/92[4], CWNEWS:FEB/95[33],
CWR:VOL3#3[92], *Ironclads,* MH:AUG/92[26]161, *letters to
the editor,* B&G:DEC/91[6]468, CWTI:JAN/93[10]297, *Mary
Todd Lincoln,* ACW:JAN/94[47]452, *Nelson-Davis feud,*
AHI:NOV/72[12]142, *The Princeton Explosion,*
AHI:AUG/69[5]123, *Wilmington/Fort Fisher,*
B&G:DEC/94[10]585, *photos,* ACW:NOV/92[51]389,
AHI:MAY/71[3]133A, B&G:DEC/94[10]585,
CWTI:DEC/94[34]411
ADDITIONAL LISTINGS: ACW:JAN/91[62]289, ACW:JUL/91[35]314,
ACW:NOV/91[46]335, ACW:NOV/92[8]383,
ACW:NOV/92[51]389, ACW:JAN/93[51]398,
ACW:JAN/94[47]452, ACW:MAR/94[35]460,
ACW:JUL/94[35]478, ACW:SEP/94[46]488,
ACW:SEP/95[30]545, AHI:JAN/81[18]214,
AHI:DEC/82[38]231, AHI:JAN/83[10]232, AHI:FEB/86[12]257,
B&G:FEB/92[10]474, B&G:APR/95[33]597,
CWM:JUL/93[2]481, CWM:JUL/93[24]485,
CWR:VOL2#3[183]140, CWR:VOL2#3[194]141,
CWTI:MAY/89[28]117, CWTI:FEB/91[28]192,
CWTI:FEB/92[21]247, CWTI:APR/92[14]254,
CWTI:DEC/94[34]411, CWTI:OCT/95[32]468,
MH:FEB/92[8]156, MH:AUG/93[47]169

WELLMAN, JOHN F., *Sergeant, 154th New York Infantry;*
GETTY:8[17]200

WELLS, EDWARD, *Private, 4th South Carolina Cavalry;*
CWNEWS:OCT/92[4]

WELLS, ELIAS, *Private, USA;* AHI:APR/74[4]154

WELLS, J., *Private, 1st Kentucky Cavalry;* B&G:OCT/91[11]466

WELLS, JAMES, *Private, 6th New York Cavalry;*
GETTY:6[87]178
WELLS, JAMES F., *Captain, 137th New York Infantry;*
CWR:VOL3#2[70]155
WELLS, JAMES M., *Captain, 111th Pennsylvania Infantry;*
GETTY:10[120]229
WELLS, JOHN H., *Captain, 5th New York Infantry;*
CWR:VOL1#2[7]111
WELLS, WILLIAM, *Colonel, USA;* B&G:APR/92[8]481,
CWM:APR/94[24]505
WELSH, PETER, *Sergeant, 28th Massachusetts Infantry;*
ACW:MAY/94[12]466
WELSH, STEPHEN E., *Captain, Hampton's Legion;* BOOK
REVIEW: *STEPHEN ELLIOTT WELCH OF THE HAMPTON
LEGION*
WELSH, THOMAS, *General, USA;* B&G:AUG/95[8]604,
WELTON, EVERAD, *Sergeant, 24th Michigan Infantry;*
GETTY:5[19]158
WELTON, ISAAC, *Lieutenant, CSA;* ACW:SEP/91[41]323
WEMYSS, JAMES, *Captain, 36th Alabama Infantry;*
CWTI:NOV/92[41]291
WERT, H. HOWARD, *civilian;* GETTY:10[53]225,
GETTY:11[102]237
WERT, J. HOWARD, *Lieutenant, 209th Pennsylvania Infantry;*
CWTI:AUG/90[64]170, CWTI:DEC/94[42]412
WERTZ, O. SIMEON, *Private, 13th South Carolina Infantry;*
GETTY:13[22]254
WESCOTT, J.B., *Private, 20th Maine Infantry;*
GETTY:12[97]249
WESSELLS, HENRY, *General, USA;* CWNEWS:AUG/90[4]
WESSELS, —, *Captain, USA;* AHI:SUM/88[12]273
WESSON, EDWIN, *gunsmith;* CWTI:APR/90[48]154
WEST GULF BLOCKADING SQUADRON;
CWM:OCT/95[47]620, CWNEWS:JAN/91[4],
CWR:VOL3#3[33]158, MH:AUG/93[47]169
WEST POINT FOUNDRY (NEW YORK);
CWTI:APR/89[22]108
WEST POINT, GEORGIA, BATTLE OF:
ARTICLE: "A MOST VOLUNTARY GATHERING,"
B&G:AUG/94[22]576
ADDITIONAL LISTING: B&G:OCT/94[6]579
WEST POINT, NEW YORK, (United States Military Academy):
ARTICLES: "MUCH TO SADDEN—AND LITTLE TO CHEER:
THE CIVIL WAR YEARS AT WEST POINT,"
B&G:DEC/91[12]469, "REBELS FROM WEST POINT,"
AHI:APR/85[18]250, "'THIS MONOTONOUS LIFE,'"
AHI:AUG/71[22]135
BOOK REVIEWS: *THE CLASS OF 1846: FROM WEST POINT TO
APPOMATTOX: STONEWALL JACKSON, GEORGE
MCCLELLAN, AND THEIR BROTHERS * DUTY, HONOR,
COUNTRY. A HISTORY OF WEST POINT * REBELS FROM
WEST POINT*
GENERAL LISTINGS: *Roster of Graduates, classes of 1861-1865;*
B&G:DEC/91[12]469, *photos;* B&G:DEC/91[12]469
ADDITIONAL LISTINGS: CWTI:SUMMER/89[13]120,
CWTI:FEB/90[12]141, CWTI:APR/90[46]153,
CWTI:APR/90[56]155, GETTY:11[71]234
WEST VIRGINIA CAMPAIGN, 1861:
ARTICLES: "GRANNY LEE'S INAUSPICIOUS DEBUT,"
ACW:SEP/94[31]486, "THE NORTHWESTERN VIRGINIA
CAMPAIGN OF 1861," B&G:AUG/93[10]529
BOOK REVIEWS: *A PICTORIAL GUIDE TO WEST VIRGINIA'S
CIVIL WAR SITES AND RELATED INFORMATION * CIVIL*

*WAR IN CABELL COUNTY, WEST VIRGINIA 1861-1865, *
MILITARY OPERATIONS IN JEFFERSON COUNTY WEST
VIRGINIA 1861-1865*
ADDITIONAL LISTING: CWTI:MAR/89[16]101

WEST VIRGINIA TROOPS:
1st Artillery; CWTI:MAR/89[16]101, GETTY:12[30]243
1st Artillery, Battery C; VOL1#3[28]120
1st Cavalry; ACW:JUL/92[41]370, B&G:APR/92[8]481,
CWM:APR/94[24]505, CWR:VOL3#2[1]153,
CWTI:MAR/94[29]371, GETTY:4[115]152, GETTY:9[109]218
1st Infantry; B&G:AUG/93[10]529
2nd Cavalry; B&G:APR/92[8]481, CWTI:MAR/89[16]101
2nd Infantry; B&G:AUG/93[10]529, CWTI:AUG/90[50]168,
CWTI:MAR/94[29]371
2nd Mounted Infantry; CWTI:MAR/89[16]101
3rd Cavalry; B&G:APR/92[8]481, B&G:AUG/94[10]574,
B&G:FEB/95[8]590A, CWTI:JUN/90[32]159, GETTY:11[19]232
3rd Infantry; ACW:JAN/93[35]396, CWTI:MAR/94[29]371
3rd Mounted Infantry; CWTI:MAR/89[16]101
5th Cavalry; B&G:OCT/94[28]581
5th Infantry; B&G:AUG/92[11]493, CWTI:SEP/94[49]404,
CWTI:JAN/95[16]421
6th Infantry; B&G:AUG/94[10]574
7th Infantry; ACW:NOV/92[42]388, B&G:JUN/94[38]571
GETTY:4[115]152, GETTY:10[53]225
8th Mounted Infantry; CWTI:MAR/89[16]101
9th Infantry; ACW:MAR/94[27]459
10th Infantry; B&G:OCT/94[28]581, CWM:AUG/95[35]607,
CWTI:MAR/89[16]101
11th Infantry; B&G:AUG/94[10]574
12th Infantry; CWTI:MAY/94[12]379
13th Infantry; CWTI:SEP/94[49]404, CWTI:JAN/95[16]421
14th Infantry; ACW:MAR/94[27]459
15th Infantry; ACW:MAR/94[27]459, CWTI:MAR/94[16]368
Bath County Cavalry; B&G:AUG/93[10]529
Grafton Guards; B&G:AUG/93[10]529
Letcher Guards; B&G:AUG/93[10]529

WEST, A.A., *Colonel, CSA;* CWR:VOL4#2[118]169
WEST, ALONZO, *Sergeant, 1st Maryland Cavalry;*
B&G:JUN/91[6]451
WEST, EDWIN, *Captain, 1st Florida Special Battalion;*
CWR:VOL3#1[65]151
WEST, EMMET C., *Private, 2nd Wisconsin Cavalry;*
CWTI:MAY/93[35]320
WEST, FREDERICK L., *Sergeant, 154th New York Infantry;*
GETTY:8[17]200
WEST, GEORGE W., *Major, 17th Maine Infantry;*
GETTY:8[43]202
WEST, J.A.A., *Captain, CSA;* CWR:VOL4#2[26]166
WEST, JAMES S., *Captain, CSA;* AHI:MAY/71[3]133A
WEST, JOHN A., *cadet;* B&G:DEC/91[12]469
WEST, JOHN C., *Private, 4th Texas Infantry:*
BOOK REVIEW: *A TEXAN IN SEARCH OF A FIGHT. BEING THE
DIARY AND LETTERS OF A PRIVATE SOLDIER IN
HOOD'S TEXAS BRIGADE*
ADDITIONAL LISTING: GETTY:6[7]169
WEST, JOHN T., *Lieutenant, 61st Virginia Infantry;*
GETTY:6[7]169
WEST, KIRKPATRICK; ARTICLES: "A NOVEL HISTORY OF
THE CIVIL WAR," CWM:AUG/94[40]528, "A NOVEL
HISTORY OF THE CIVIL WAR: KIRKPATRICK WEST

REPORTS ON THE WILSON'S CREEK,"
CWM:DEC/94[60]554, "THE CIVIL WAR JOURNALS AND
DISPATCHES OF KIRKPATRICK WEST...,
CWM:JUN/94[34]516, "THE WARTIME JOURNALS,
DISPATCHES, & SELECTED CORRESPONDENCE OF
KIRKPATRICK WEST, CWM:OCT/94[41]541
WEST, LEWIS, *Captain, USN;* B&G:FEB/91[8]439
WEST, ROBERT M., *Colonel, 5th Pennsylvania Cavalry;*
ACW:MAY/92[30]361, B&G:APR/92[8]481,
CWM:MAY/92[34]422, GETTY:11[6]231
WEST, SPEIGHT B., *Captain, 5th North Carolina Infantry;*
B&G:FEB/95[8]590B, GETTY:5[13]157
WEST, THEODORE S., *Lieutenant Colonel, 24th Wisconsin
Infantry;* ACW:MAR/92[14]350, ACW:JAN/94[55]453
WEST, WILLIAM, *Private, 1st Illinois Artillery;*
B&G:APR/94[28]559
WESTBROOK ROBERT, *Private, 49th Pennsylvania Infantry;*
CWTI:SEP/93[43]338
WESTCOTT, JOHN, *Major, CSA;* CWR:VOL3#1[65]151
WESTERN FLOTILLA; ACW:JUL/93[34]424
WESTERN GULF BLOCKADING SQUADRON;
MH:FEB/92[8]156
WESTERN SANITARY COMMISSION; CWTI:MAR/89[20]102
WESTFALL, E.D., *civilian;* B&G:DEC/95[9]615
WESTLAKE, OSCAR, *Lieutenant, 3rd New Jersey Infantry;*
CWTI:MAY/89[36]118
WESTON, JAMES A., *Major, 33rd North Carolina Infantry;*
AHI:JUN/70[30]127
WESTPORT, MISSOURI, BATTLE OF:
ARTICLE: "KANSAS MINUTEMEN: MISSOURI'S SAVIORS,"
ACW:NOV/94[42]497
ADDITIONAL LISTINGS: ACW:MAR/94[8]456, B&G:JUN/91[10]452,
CWM:JAN/92[8]399, CWM:JAN/92[44]406,
CWR:VOL1#2[44]114
WESTVILLE (MISSISSIPPI) GUARDS, (16th Mississippi
Infantry); GETTY:4[7]142, GETTY:5[89]162
WETHERBY, LYMAN, *Private, 11th Veteran Reserve Corps;*
B&G:APR/93[24]520
WETMORE, HENRY S., *Captain, 9th Ohio Battery;*
B&G:FEB/93[12]511
WEVER, CLARK R., *Colonel, USA;* B&G:DEC/95[9]615
WEYGANT, CHARLES H., *Lieutenant Colonel, 124th New York
Infantry;*
BOOK REVIEW: *HISTORY OF THE ONE HUNDRED AND
TWENTY-FOURTH REGIMENT, N.Y.S.V.*
ADDITIONAL LISTINGS: B&G:JUN/95[8]600, CWTI:MAY/94[24]381,
GETTY:9[5]209, *photo,* CWM:DEC/94[40]550
WHARTON, GABRIEL C., *General, CSA;*
ACW:MAY/91[38]305, ACW:JAN/92[16]340,
ACW:MAR/93[10]402, B&G:APR/94[10]558,
CWM:JAN/93[40]461, CWM:APR/94[24]505,
CWR:VOL3#2[1]153, CWR:VOL3#2[61]154,
CWR:VOL3#4[1]161, CWTI:AUG/95[46]459
WHARTON, HENRY C., *cadet;* B&G:DEC/91[12]469
WHARTON, JOHN A., *General, CSA;* ACW:MAY/95[49]527,
CWM:JUL/92[40]432, CWR:VOL2#3[212]142,
CWR:VOL4#1[1]163, CWR:VOL4#2[1]165,
CWR:VOL4#2[118]169, CWR:VOL4#3[50]171,
CWTI:MAY/92[48]267, CWTI:NOV/93[33]347
WHARTON, R.W., *Major, 1st North Carolina Infantry;*
GETTY:9[17]210
WHEAT, CHATHAM R., *Major, CSA:*
ARTICLE: "WHEAT'S TIGERS," CWTI:MAR/94[48]374

ADDITIONAL LISTINGS: ACW:MAY/93[54], ACW:JUL/94[35]478,
ACW:NOV/94[18]495, CWM:SEP/93[24]495,
MH:OCT/93[20]172
WHEATON, FRANK, *General, USA;* ACW:JAN/92[22]341,
B&G:APR/94[10]558, B&G:APR/95[8]595, GETTY:11[91]236
WHEELER, CHARLES C., *Captain, 1st New York Artillery;*
ACW:JAN/94[8]447
WHEELER, JAMES T., *Colonel, CSA;* CWR:VOL4#1[1]163
WHEELER, JOHN E., *Sergeant, 3rd Georgia Infantry;*
CWTI:SEP/94[26]400
WHEELER, SAMUEL H, *Lieutenant, 2nd Tennessee Cavalry;*
CWR:VOL4#1[1]163
WHEELER, WILLIAM, *Lieutenant, 13th New York Artillery;*
GETTY:4[33]146, GETTY:4[49]147
WHEELER, JOSEPH, *General, CSA:*
ARTICLES: "FIGHTING JOE WHEELER TRADED HIS
CONFEDERATE GRAY FOR ARMY BLUE IN THE
SPANISH-AMERICAN WAR," ACW:MAY/95[6]521, "HOW
'FIGHTIN' JOE' WHEELER GOT HIS TRENCHES DUG,"
AHI:FEB/82[48]226, "LIGHTING BRIGADE STRIKES
FIGHTING JOE," ACW:MAY/95[49]527
GENERAL LISTINGS: *Atlanta Campaign,* ACW:NOV/95[74]560,
CWM:JAN/91[12]326, CWTI:SUMMER/89[13]120,
CWTI:SUMMER/89[20]121, CWTI:SUMMER/89[32]122,
CWTI:SUMMER/89[40]123, CWTI:SUMMER/89[50]124,
CWTI:NOV/92[41]291, CWTI:JAN/93[20]298, *Carolina
Campaign,* B&G:DEC/95[9]615, *Chickamauga,*
CWTI:SEP/92[31]281, *Gatling Gun,* AHI:JUN/66[52]102, *in
book review,* CWM:DEC/94[7], CWNEWS:NOV/95[29], *order of
battle,* B&G:DEC/95[9]615, *relics,* B&G:JUN/91[38]455,
Savannah, B&G:FEB/91[8]439, *Tullahoma Campaign,*
B&G:OCT/92[10]496, *photo, Spanish-American War;*
ACW:MAY/95[49]527, *photo,* B&G:OCT/92[10]496
ADDITIONAL LISTINGS: ACW:JUL/91[12]310, ACW:SEP/92[38]379,
ACW:SEP/92[47]380, ACW:JUL/93[27]423,
ACW:JAN/95[30]505, AHI:APR/85[18]250,
AHI:OCT/95[24]326, B&G:JUN/94[8]568,
CWM:JUL/91[35]369, CWM:JUL/92[40]432,
CWM:OCT/94[48]542, CWR:VOL1#1[73]108,
CWR:VOL1#3[82]123, CWR:VOL2#3[212]142,
CWR:VOL4#1[1]163, CWR:VOL4#3[50]171,
CWR:VOL4#3[65]172, CWTI:SEP/91[23]228,
CWTI:FEB/92[42]250, CWTI:MAY/92[48]267,
CWTI:SEP/92[28]280, CWTI:JUL/93[20]325,
CWTI:NOV/93[33]347, CWTI:JAN/94[35]361,
CWTI:MAY/94[44]384, CWTI:MAY/94[50]386,
CWTI:SEP/94[40]403
WHEELOCK, CHARLES, *Colonel, 97th New York Infantry;
Gettysburg,* ACW:MAR/95[42]517, GETTY:5[13]157,
GETTY:10[7]221, GETTY:11[119]238, *photo,* GETTY:10[7]221
WHELAN, HENRY C., *Major, 6th Pennsylvania Cavalry;*
GETTY:11[19]232
WHELAN, PETER, *Chaplain;* CWTI:APR/92[23]255
WHELEN, WILLIAM, *Surgeon, USA;* CWTI:APR/92[14]254
WHERRY, WILLIAM M., *Captain, USA;* CWTI:FEB/92[29]248
WHETSTONE, W.D., *Private, 21st Alabama Infantry;*
ACW:SEP/92[8]374
WHIG PARTY; AHI:OCT/68[4]116, AHI:JUN/73[4]149
WHIGHAM, JACK & JOHN, *5th New York Infantry;*
CWR:VOL1#2[7]111, CWR:VOL1#2[29]112
WHILDLY, WILLIAM, *Adjutant, 69th Pennsylvania Infantry;*
GETTY:4[89]150

WHIPPLE, AMIEL, *General, USA;* ACW:MAY/95[30]525,
  CWM:DEC/94[40]550, CWR:VOL4#3[1]170, GETTY:9[5]209
WHIPPLE, HENRY F., *Sergeant, 154th New York Infantry;*
  GETTY:8[17]200
WHISKEY RING; AHI:MAY/69[32]122
WHISTLER, JOSEPH N.G., B&G:DEC/91[12]469
WHITAKER, ALEXANDER H., *Lieutenant, 9th Massachusetts
  Artillery;* GETTY:5[47]160
WHITAKER, EDWARD W., *Lieutenant Colonel, 1st Connecticut
  Cavalry;* ACW:JAN/92[16]340, CWM:APR/94[24]505
WHITAKER, JOHN, *Lieutenant, 53rd Pennsylvania Infantry;*
  GETTY:11[80]235
WHITAKER, WALTER C., *General, USA;* B&G:DEC/93[12]545
WHITAKER, WILLIAM A., *Captain, 7th Louisiana Infantry;*
  CWR:VOL4#2[118]169
WHITE HALL (VIRGINIA) GUARDS; ACW:MAR/93[10]402
WHITE OAK SWAMP, VIRGINIA, BATTLE OF:
ARTICLE: "THE PENINSULA CAMPAIGN OF 1862: THE
  BATTLE OF GLENDALE," CWM:JUN/95[69]596
ADDITIONAL LISTINGS: B&G:APR/92[8]481, CWR:VOL1#3[28]120,
  CWR:VOL1#3[52]122, CWR:VOL3#1[31]150,
  CWR:VOL3#1[80], CWTI:APR/89[14]107,
  CWTI:JUN/95[32]446
WHITE SULPHER SPRINGS, WEST VIRGINIA;
  ACW:SEP/94[31]486, CWTI:MAR/89[16]101
WHITE'S (TENNESSEE) BATTERY; CWR:VOL4#1[1]163
WHITE, ALEXANDER, *Captain, 14th Louisiana Infantry;*
  CWM:SEP/93[24]495
WHITE, AMMI M., *civilian;* ACW:JUL/93[27]423
WHITE, CARR B., *Colonel, USA;* ACW:MAR/94[27]459,
  ACW:JUL/94[26]477
WHITE, D.G., *Colonel, CSA;* B&G:DEC/95[9]615
WHITE, DANIEL B., *Private, 144th New York Infantry;* BOOK
  REVIEWS: *DEAR WIFE: LETTERS OF A CIVIL WAR SOLDIER*
WHITE, EDWARD, *Lieutenant, CSA;* ACW:MAR/92[40]353
WHITE, ELIJAH, *Colonel, 35th Virginia Cavalry:*
ARTICLE: "A CAVALRYMAN WITHOUT FANFARE,"
  CWTI:DEC/94[122]419
ADDITIONAL LISTINGS: ACW:SEP/91[41]323, ACW:MAY/95[62],
  CWTI:JUN/90[32]159, *photo,* CWTI:DEC/94[122]419
WHITE, FRANK, *Major, USA;* ACW:MAR/92[46]354
WHITE, GEORGE R., *Private, 19th Massachusetts Infantry;*
  BOOK REVIEW: *THE CIVIL WAR: LETTERS HOME FROM
  GEO. R. WHITE*
WHITE, HARRY, *Colonel, USA;* AHI:NOV/85[38]254
WHITE, HORACE, AHI:APR/80[21]200, CWTI:DEC/95[22]476
WHITE, JOHN C., *Lieutenant, 20th Massachusetts Infantry;*
  CWR:VOL3#1[31]150
WHITE, JOHN E., *Private, 53rd Pennsylvania Infantry;*
  GETTY:11[80]235
WHITE, JOHN M., *Major, 6th South Carolina Infantry;*
  CWR:VOL3#2[70]155
WHITE, JULIUS, *General, USA;* ACW:MAY/95[54]528,
  CWM:SEP/91[40]385, CWM:MAY/92[8]418,
  CWR:VOL1#1[1]102, CWR:VOL1#1[42]105,
  CWR:VOL1#4[7]125, CWTI:FEB/91[45]194,
  CWTI:JAN/95[24]424, MH:AUG/95[30]185
WHITE, LORENZO D., *civilian;* B&G:OCT/94[28]581
WHITE, LUTHER, *Private, 20th Massachusetts Infantry;*
  GETTY:5[117]165
WHITE, NATHAN, *Private, 88th Pennsylvania Infantry;*
  ACW:MAR/95[42]517

WHITE, OSCAR, *Major, 48th Virginia Infantry;*
  GETTY:13[108]261
WHITE, PATRICK H., *Captain, Chicago Mercantile Battery;*
  B&G:AUG/95[8]604, CWR:VOL4#2[1]165
WHITE, SAMUEL, *Private, 3rd Georgia Infantry;*
  CWTI:DEC/94[32]410
WHITE, THOMAS, *Private, USA;* B&G:AUG/91[11]458
WHITE, THOMAS A., *Captain, CSA;* CWTI:DEC/94[62]415
WHITE, THOMAS S., *Major, CSA;* B&G:FEB/91[8]439
WHITE, WILLIAM J., *Captain, CSA;* B&G:JUN/95[22]601
WHITE, WILLIAM S., *Private, 3rd Richmond Howitzers;*
  CWR:VOL4#4[70]180
WHITE, WILLIAM W., *Colonel, CSA;* GETTY:12[123]251
WHITE, WYMAN, *Sergeant, 2nd USSS;* BOOK REVIEW: *THE
  CIVIL WAR DIARY OF WYMAN WHITE, FIRST SERGEANT
  OF COMPANY F, 2ND UNITED STATES SHARPSHOOTER
  REGIMENT, 1861-1865*
WHITEAKER, JOHN, *Governor, Oregon;* CWTI:AUG/95[54]460
WHITEHEAD, GERRARD I., *Lieutenant, 6th Pennsylvania
  Cavalry;* B&G:OCT/93[12]537
WHITEHORNE, JAMES E., *Sergeant, 12th Virginia Infantry;*
  ARTICLE: "FINAL MARCH TO APPOMATTOX: THE 12TH
  VIRGINIA INFANTRY APRIL 2-12, AN EYEWITNESS
  ACCOUNT," CWR:VOL2#3[236]143
WHITEHOUSE, STEPHEN C., *Captain, 16th Maine Infantry;*
  CWM:MAY/92[15]419, GETTY:13[33]255
WHITELEY, RICHARD H., *Major, 2nd Georgia Battalion
  Sharpshooters;* CWR:VOL1#4[42]126
WHITESCARVER, GEORGE; *Lieutenant, 6th Michigan
  Cavalry;* CWTI:SEP/90[34]176, CWTI:DEC/91[22]237
WHITESIDE, NEWT, *Lieutenant, USA;* B&G:FEB/93[40]514
WHITFIELD, GEORGE, *Major, CSA;* ACW:SEP/95[48]547
WHITFIELD, JOHN W., *General, CSA;* B&G:AUG/95[8]604,
WHITFORD, EDWARD, *Major, 67th North Carolina Infantry;*
  CWM:SEP/92[16]438
WHITFORD, J.N., *Colonel, CSA;* CWM:SEP/92[16]438
WHITFORD, JOHN H., *Colonel, 67th North Carolina Infantry;*
  CWM:SEP/92[16]438
WHITIKER, WALTER, *General, USA;* CWTI:SEPT/89[30]129
WHITING, CHARLES J., *Major, 5th U.S. Cavalry;*
  ACW:NOV/91[10]329, ACW:JUL/93[42]425,
  ACW:NOV/94[50]498, GETTY:11[19]232, GETTY:11[19]232
WHITING, H. REES, *Lieutenant, 24th Michigan Infantry;*
  GETTY:5[19]158
WHITING, J.W., *Colonel, CSA;* CWM:JUL/93[24]485
WHITING, WILLIAM, *Major, CSA;* ACW:SEP/93[10]430
WHITING, WILLIAM H.C., *General, CSA:*
ARTICLE: "THE PENINSULA CAMPAIGN OF 1862: THE
  BATTLE OF SEVEN PINES," CWM:JUN/95[47]588
GENERAL LISTINGS: *Gaines' Mill,* CWM:JUN/95[61]593, *in book
  review,* B&G:OCT/91[34], CWR:VOL1#2[78], *Peninsula
  Campaign,* CWM:JUN/95[37]585, *Wilmington/Fort Fisher,*
  B&G:DEC/94[10]585, *photo,* B&G:DEC/94[10]585
ADDITIONAL LISTINGS: ACW:MAR/95[70]520,
  CWR:VOL2#4[269]145, CWTI:APR/89[14]107,
  CWTI:DEC/91[36]240, GETTY:9[98]217
WHITING, WILLIAM W.; CWM:JAN/92[68]407
WHITMAN, FRANK M., *Corporal, 35th Massachusetts Infantry;*
  CWTI:FEB/92[36]249
WHITMAN, GEORGE, *Private, 51st New York Infantry;*
  ACW:MAY/94[6]464, CWTI:JAN/95[34]427
WHITMAN, ROBERT, *Private, 3rd Georgia Infantry;*
  CWTI:SEP/94[26]400

WHITMAN, WALT:
ARTICLES: "A GREAT POET'S LETTERS ABOUT WARTIME
SUFFERING," AHI:AUG/68[4]115B, "'I WAS THERE,'"
CWM:MAY/91[8]346, "WALT WHITMAN'S CIVIL WAR WAS
ON LONG TOUR OF NORTHERN HOSPITALS AND THEIR
SUFFERERS," ACW:MAY/94[6]464
GENERAL LISTINGS: *in book review,* CWR:VOL3#1[80], *letter to the
editor,* CWTI:DEC/91[14]235, *painting of;*
AHI:AUG/68[4]115B, *photo,* CWTI:AUG/90[42]167
ADDITIONAL LISTINGS: B&G:APR/91[8]445, CWM:MAY/91[18]348,
CWTI:AUG/90[42]167, CWTI:SEP/92[22]279
WHITNEY, ADDISON O., *Private, 7th Massachusetts Infantry;*
ACW:NOV/95[30]555
WHITNEY, JOHN H., *Lieutenant, 5th New York Infantry;*
CWTI:MAY/94[31]382
WHITSITT, WILLIAM J., *Captain, 1st Confederate Georgia
Infantry;* CWR:VOL1#4[64]127
WHITTAKER, FREDERICK, *Captain, 6th New York Cavalry;*
CWTI:MAY/93[35]320
WHITTAKER, *Colonel, 6th Kentucky Infantry;*
AHI:NOV/72[12]142
WHITTELSEY, C.H., *Captain, 1st Pennsylvania Artillery;*
GETTY:12[30]243
WHITTER, CHARLES A., *Major, USA;* B&G:DEC/95[25]616
WHITTICK, ROBERT, *Private, 69th Pennsylvania Infantry;*
GETTY:4[89]150
WHITTIER, CHARLES, *Major, 20th Massachusetts Infantry;*
CWR:VOL3#1[31]150
WHITTIER, JOHN GREENLEAF; ACW:JAN/93[26]395
WHITTING, SAMUEL, *U.S. Consul;* ACW:MAY/92[23]360
WHITTLE, POWHATAN B., *Lieutenant, Colonel, 38th Virginia
Infantry;* ACW:MAR/91[47]297, CWM:JUL/92[16]428
WHITTLE, WILLIAM, *Lieutenant, CSN;* ACW:MAY/91[46]306,
AHI:OCT/88[38]275, AHI:JAN/83[10]232, CWM:JUL/93[8]483
WHYTAL, JAMES, *Private, USA;* CWR:VOL1#2[29]112
WICKES, EDWARD, *Captain, 150th New York Infantry;*
GETTY:12[42]244
WICKHAM, WILLIAMS C., *General, CSA:*
GENERAL LISTINGS: *1863 cavalry battles,* MH:OCT/92[51]162, *in
order of battle,* B&G:APR/94[10]558, B&G:APR/95[8]595,
Manassas, Second, B&G:AUG/92[11]493
ADDITIONAL LISTINGS: ACW:JUL/92[41]370, ACW:NOV/92[26]386,
ACW:MAY/94[35]469, ACW:JUL/95[34]536,
B&G:OCT/93[12]537, CWTI:JUN/95[38]447
WIDENER, JOSEPH, *Private, 3rd Georgia Infantry;*
CWTI:SEP/94[26]400
WIDNEY, LYMAN, *Sergeant, USA;* B&G:DEC/95[9]615
WIEDRICH, MICHAEL, *Captain, 1st New York Light Artillery;*
ACW:NOV/92[42]388, GETTY:4[49]147, GETTY:6[7]169,
GETTY:8[17]200, GETTY:9[33]211, GETTY:11[19]232,
GETTY:11[57]233, GETTY:12[30]243
WIGFALL, LOUIS T., *Senator from Texas:*
GENERAL LISTINGS: *in book review,* ACW:SEP/94[66],
B&G:AUG/91[26], CWM:AUG/95[45], CWNEWS:FEB/94[5],
CWR:VOL1#4[77], CWR:VOL2#3[256], *photo,*
AHI:JUN/70[30]127
ADDITIONAL LISTINGS: ACW:SEP/93[10]430, ACW:NOV/93[58],
AHI:JUN/70[30]127, CWR:VOL1#1[71]107,
CWTI:SUMMER/89[13]120, CWTI:SEPT/89[24]128,
CWTI:AUG/91[62]221, CWTI:DEC/91[36]240
WIGGINS, JOHN C., *Lieutenant, USA;* B&G:APR/91[8]445,
GETTY:4[101]150

WIGHAM, JOHN, *Private, 5th New York Infantry;*
CWTI:MAY/94[31]382
WIGHT, EDWIN B., *Lieutenant Colonel, 24th Michigan
Infantry;* GETTY:5[19]158, GETTY:7[7]185
WIGHTMAN, EDWARD K., *Sergeant Major, 3rd New York
Infantry;* ARTICLE: "SERGEANT EDWARD KING
WIGHTMAN: LETTERS HOME DURING THE FORT
FISHER CAMPAIGN," AHI:SEP/83[12]234
WILBOURN, CHRISTOPHER C., *Lieutenant Colonel, CSA;*
B&G:JUN/93[12]524
WILBOURN, RICHARD E., *Captain, CSA;* GETTY:4[110]152
WILCOX, CADMUS M., *General, CSA:*
GENERAL LISTINGS: *Cold Harbor,* ACW:SEP/93[62]436, *Confederate
exiles,* AHI:JUN/70[30]127, *Five Forks,* B&G:APR/92[8]481,
Gettysburg, GETTY:4[115]152, GETTY:5[79]161,
GETTY:5[89]162, GETTY:5[107]164, GETTY:7[51]190,
GETTY:8[67]204, GETTY:9[5]209, GETTY:11[19]232,
GETTY:12[7]241, MH:DEC/91[54]155, *Glendale,*
CWM:JUN/95[69]596, *in book review,* ACW:JAN/94[62],
ACW:JAN/95[62], CWM:MAR/92[49], CWNEWS:SEP/93[5],
CWR:VOL4#2[136], *in list,* CWTI:JUL/93[34]327, *in order of
battle,* B&G:APR/94[10]558, B&G:APR/95[8]595, *Manassas,
Second,* B&G:AUG/92[11]493, *Peninsula Campaign,*
CWM:JUN/95[34]584, *Wilderness,* B&G:APR/95[8]595,
B&G:JUN/95[8]600, *photo,* AHI:JUN/70[30]127
ADDITIONAL LISTINGS: ACW:JUL/91[18]312, ACW:SEP/92[30]378,
ACW:JUL/93[27]423, ACW:SEP/93[8]429,
ACW:SEP/93[31]433, ACW:JUL/95[10]533,
AHI:APR/85[18]250, B&G:AUG/91[30]460,
B&G:APR/93[12]518, B&G:JUN/94[8]568,
CWR:VOL2#3[236]143, CWR:VOL2#4[269]145,
CWR:VOL3#2[1]153, CWR:VOL3#3[1]157,
CWTI:SEPT/89[46]132, CWTI:AUG/90[26]166,
CWTI:FEB/91[45]194, CWTI:JUL/93[29]326,
CWTI:NOV/93[55]350, CWTI:JUL/94[44]394,
CWTI:MAR/95[33]435, GETTY:13[50]257, GETTY:13[64]258,
GETTY:13[75]259
WILCOX, CHARLES E., *Sergeant, 33rd Illinois Infantry;*
B&G:FEB/94[8]550
WILCOX, GEORGE, *Captain, 26th North Carolina Infantry;*
GETTY:5[19]158, GETTY:8[67]204
WILCOX, HARRY, *Lieutenant, 1st New York Cavalry;*
AHI:DEC/85[40]255
WILCOX, JOHN, *Lieutenant, USA;* B&G:FEB/92[10]474
WILCOXON, ALBERT H., *Colonel, 17th Connecticut Infantry;*
ACW:NOV/95[38]556
WILD, EDWARD A., *General, USA;* ACW:JAN/94[47]452
WILDCAT MOUNTAIN, KENTUCKY, BATTLE OF;
B&G:FEB/93[12]511
WILDER, JOHN T., *Colonel, USA:*
ARTICLES: "LIGHTING BRIGADE STRIKES FIGHTING JOE,"
ACW:MAY/95[49]527, "MOST SPLENDID PIECE OF
STRATEGY," CWM:OCT/94[48]542, "THE STEADIEST BODY
OF MEN I EVER SAW: JOHN T. WILDER AND THE
LIGHTNING BRIGADE," B&G:OCT/92[32]499, "WE'LL TRY
FIGHTING FOR AWHILE'...JOHN T. WILDER,"
CWM:JUL/92[24]430
GENERAL LISTINGS: *letters to the editor,* B&G:APR/93[6]517,
Tullahoma Campaign, B&G:OCT/92[10]496, *photo,*
CWM:JUL/92[24]430, CWM:OCT/94[48]542,
B&G:OCT/92[32]499
ADDITIONAL LISTINGS: ACW:NOV/95[6]551, B&G:OCT/91[11]466,
CWM:OCT/94[4]532, CWTI:MAY/92[48]267

WILDER, THEODORE, *Private, 7th Ohio Infantry;*
GETTY:9[81]216

WILDERNESS, VIRGINIA, BATTLE AND CAMPAIGN OF:

ARTICLES: "BATTLE FOUGHT ON PAPER,"
ACW:MAY/93[31]415, "NO TURNING BACK: THE BATTLE
OF THE WILDERNESS, PART I," B&G:APR/95[8]595, "NO
TURNING BACK: THE BATTLE OF THE WILDERNESS,
PART II—THE FIGHTING ON MAY 6, 1864,"
B&G:JUN/95[8]600, "TRAGEDY IN THE WILDERNESS,"
CWM:JUN/94[26]512, "WILDERNESS TO PETERSBURG:
UNPUBLISHED REPORTS OF THE 11TH BATTALION,
GEORGIA LIGHT ARTILLERY," CWR:VOL3#2[61]154

BOOK REVIEWS: *THE BATTLE OF THE WILDERNESS MAY 5-6,
1864 * BATTLE IN THE WILDERNESS: GRANT MEETS
LEE * BLOODY ROADS SOUTH: THE WILDERNESS TO
COLD HARBOR, MAY-JUNE 1864 * INTO THE
WILDERNESS WITH THE ARMY OF THE POTOMAC * ON
FIELDS OF FURY: FROM THE WILDERNESS TO THE
CRATER: AN EYEWITNESS HISTORY * THE
WILDERNESS CAMPAIGN: MAY 1864 * WITH GRANT
AND MEADE: FROM THE WILDERNESS TO
APPOMATTOX*

GENERAL LISTINGS: *general history,* AHI:MAY/71[3]133A, *in book
review,* ACW:NOV/91[54], CWM:AUG/95[45],
CWNEWS:MAY/89[4], CWNEWS:JAN/91[4],
CWR:VOL1#3[94], CWR:VOL1#4[77], CWR:VOL3#2[105],
CWR:VOL4#4[129], CWTI:FEB/90[10], CWTI:JAN/93[12],
letters to the editor, B&G:JUN/95[5]599

ADDITIONAL LISTINGS, ACW: ACW:SEP/93[62]436,
ACW:NOV/93[50]444, ACW:MAY/94[35]469,
ACW:JUL/94[26]477, ACW:JAN/95[10]503,
ACW:JAN/95[46]507, ACW:MAY/95[18]524,
ACW:SEP/95[54]548, ACW:SEP/95[74]550

ADDITIONAL LISTINGS, CWM: CWM:MAY/91[40]351,
CWM:JUL/91[45]372, CWM:JUL/92[8]427,
CWM:JUL/92[16]428, CWM:SEP/92[24]441,
CWM:NOV/92[64]453, CWM:MAR/93[24]467,
CWM:SEP/93[24]495, CWM:OCT/94[17]534,
CWM:OCT/94[34]538

ADDITIONAL LISTINGS, CWR: CWR:VOL1#1[1]102,
CWR:VOL1#1[71]107, CWR:VOL1#3[52]122,
CWR:VOL2#2[141]137, CWR:VOL3#2[1]153,
CWR:VOL3#3[1]157, CWR:VOL3#4[1]161

ADDITIONAL LISTINGS, CWTI: CWTI:MAR/89[34]104,
CWTI:DEC/89[34]136, CWTI:FEB/90[46]146,
CWTI:SEP/91[31]229, CWTI:MAY/92[38]265,
CWTI:SEP/92[42]283, CWTI:JUL/93[42]329,
CWTI:DEC/94[32]410

WILDES, ASA W., *Colonel, 16th Maine Infantry;*
CWM:MAY/92[15]419, GETTY:13[33]255

WILDES, THOMAS F., *General, USA;* CWTI:OCT/95[48]470

WILES, GREENBURY P., *Colonel, 78th Ohio Infantry;*
B&G:AUG/95[8]604, B&G:DEC/95[9]615

WILKERSON, FRANK, *Private, USA;* ACW:MAY/92[54]

WILKES, CHARLES D., *Admiral, USN:*
ARTICLE: "HIGH SEAS BROUHAHA," ACW:NOV/91[46]335
BOOK REVIEW: *AUTOBIOGRAPHY OF READ ADMIRAL
CHARLES WILKES, U.S. NAVY, 1798-1877*
ADDITIONAL LISTINGS: ACW:NOV/92[51]389, *photo,*
ACW:NOV/91[46]335

WILKES, JOHN, *Captain, USN;* CWTI:JAN/93[44]302

WILKESON, BAYARD, *Lieutenant, 4th U.S. Artillery;*
B&G:FEB/95[8]590C

WILKINS, F.G., *civilian;* ACW:MAR/91[38]296

WILKINS, LEANDER, *Private, 9th New Hampshire Infantry;*
CWR:VOL2#2[118]136

WILKINSON (MISSISSIPPI) RIFLES; GETTY:4[7]142

WILKINSON, ADAM, *Private, 11th Veteran Reserve Corps;*
B&G:APR/93[24]520

WILKINSON, ANDREW J., *Private, 7th Wisconsin Infantry,*
GETTY:9[33]211, GETTY:11[57]233

WILKINSON, JOHN, *Captain, CSN;* ACW:JAN/91[47]288,
ACW:MAY/94[51]471, CWTI:DEC/89[10]133

WILKINSON, JOHN C., *Colonel, 8th Mississippi Infantry;*
CWR:VOL1#4[42]126, CWR:VOL1#4[64]127

WILKINSON, JOSHUA S., *Private, 15th West Virginia
Infantry;* CWTI:MAR/94[16]368

WILKINSON, MORTON W., *Senator, Minnesota;*
GETTY:5[79]161

WILKINSON, W.H., *Major, CSA;* B&G:DEC/95[9]615

WILL, DAVID, *civilian;* GETTY:4[65]148

WILLARD'S BRIGADE: ARTICLES: "REMEMBER HARPER'S
FERRY!' THE DEGRADATION, HUMILIATION AND
REDEMPTION OF COLONEL GEORGE L. WILLARD'S
BRIGADE, PART I," GETTY:7[51]190, "REMEMBER
HARPER'S FERRY!' THE DEGRADATION, HUMILIATION
AND REDEMPTION OF COLONEL GEORGE L. WILLARD'S
BRIGADE, PART II," GETTY:8[95]205

WILLARD'S HOTEL; ARTICLE: "WILLARD'S OF
WASHINGTON," AHI:OCT/79[10]192

WILLARD, GEORGE L., *Colonel, 125th New York Infantry:*
ARTICLES: "REMEMBER HARPER'S FERRY!' THE
DEGRADATION, HUMILIATION AND REDEMPTION OF
COLONEL GEORGE L. WILLARD'S BRIGADE, PART I,"
GETTY:7[51]190, "REMEMBER HARPER'S FERRY!' THE
DEGRADATION, HUMILIATION AND REDEMPTION OF
COLONEL GEORGE L. WILLARD'S BRIGADE, PART II,"
GETTY:8[95]205

GENERAL LISTINGS: *Gettysburg,* GETTY:5[79]161, GETTY:6[7]169,
GETTY:9[61]215, *photo,* GETTY:7[51]190

ADDITIONAL LISTINGS: ACW:JUL/95[50]538, CWR:VOL1#4[7]125

WILLCOX, LYMAN, *Captain, 3rd Michigan Cavalry;*
CWTI:JUL/94[50]395

WILLCOX, ORLANDO B., *General, USA:*
GENERAL LISTINGS: *Gettysburg,* GETTY:7[7]185, *in order of battle,*
B&G:APR/94[10]558, *order of battle,* B&G:APR/95[8]595

ADDITIONAL LISTINGS: B&G:APR/93[12]518, CWM:MAY/92[44]423,
CWR:VOL1#1[1]102, CWR:VOL1#3[52]122,
CWR:VOL2#2[118]136, CWR:VOL2#4[269]145,
CWTI:APR/90[24]152, CWTI:FEB/91[45]194,
CWTI:FEB/92[36]249 CWTI:JAN/95[34]427,
CWTI:MAR/95[33]435

WILLET, THOMAS, *Chaplain, 69th New York Infantry;*
CWM:SEP/93[18]494, GETTY:10[53]225, GETTY:11[126]239

WILLETT, FRANK, *Private, 8th New York Cavalry;*
GETTY:6[13]170

WILLETT, ISAAC, *Captain, USN;* ACW:NOV/92[51]389

WILLETT, THOMAS, *Chaplain, 69th New York Infantry;*
CWTI:DEC/90[58]185

WILLEY, WILLIAM J., *Lieutenant Colonel, 31st Virginia
Infantry;* B&G:AUG/93[10]529

WILLIAMS ALPHEUS S., *General, USA:*
ARTICLE: "ALPHEUS WILLIAMS 'OLD PAP,'"
CWM:JUL/92[18]429

GENERAL LISTINGS: *Antietam,* B&G:OCT/95[8]611A, *Atlanta
Campaign,* CWTI:SUMMER/89[32]122, *Carolina Campaign,*

B&G:DEC/95[9]615, *Gettysburg*, GETTY:5[103]163,
GETTY:6[69]176, GETTY:7[29]188, GETTY:7[83]192,
GETTY:9[17]210, GETTY:9[81]216, GETTY:12[42]244, *order
of battle*, B&G:DEC/95[9]615, *Savannah*, B&G:FEB/91[8]439,
photos, B&G:DEC/95[9]615, CWM:JUL/92[18]429,
CWTI:NOV/92[41]291
ADDITIONAL LISTINGS: ACW:JAN/92[10]339, ACW:JUL/92[30]369,
ACW:SEP/92[47]380, ACW:NOV/92[42]388,
ACW:JAN/94[6]446, AHI:APR/85[18]250,
B&G:FEB/95[8]590C, CWM:JUL/92[4]425,
CWTI:SUMMER/89[50]124, CWTI:NOV/92[60]294,
CWTI:MAR/95[40]436, CWTI:AUG/95[24]455
WILLIAMS, D. RUFUS, *Captain, CSA;* B&G:OCT/94[11]580,
CWTI:JAN/93[49]303
WILLIAMS, FRANK, *Mosby's raider;* CWTI:DEC/91[22]237
WILLIAMS, G.C., *Sergeant, 14th U.S. Infantry;*
ACW:NOV/94[50]498
WILLIAMS, GEORGE F., *reporter;* CWTI:SEP/91[31]229
WILLIAMS, GEORGE H., *Private, 10th Virginia Infantry;*
ARTICLE: "KILLED AT BRANDY STATION,"
CWTI:MAR/94[67]377
WILLIAMS, HENRY, *Private, 95th Illinois Infantry;*
ACW:JAN/91[16]284
WILLIAMS, HENRY L.N., *Major, 9th Louisiana Infantry;*
CWTI:FEB/91[12]189
WILLIAMS, HIRAM S., *Private, 40th Alabama Infantry:*
BOOK REVIEWS: *THIS WAR SO HORRIBLE: THE CIVIL WAR
DIARY OF HIRAM SMITH WILLIAMS*
ADDITIONAL LISTING: B&G:DEC/95[9]615
WILLIAMS, J. BYRD, *Captain, 11th Mississippi Infantry;*
GETTY:9[98]217
WILLIAMS, JAMES M., *Colonel, CSA;* ACW:NOV/92[42]388,
CWR:VOL1#2[44]114, GETTY:9[81]216, MH:DEC/92[74]
WILLIAMS, JAS. H., *Private, 53rd Georgia Infantry;*
B&G:APR/93[24]520
WILLIAMS, JESSE M., *Colonel, CSA;* GETTY:7[83]192,
GETTY:10[36]223
WILLIAMS, JOHN, *Private, 3rd Georgia Infantry;*
CWTI:DEC/94[32]410
WILLIAMS, JOHN B., *Major, CSA;* CWR:VOL2#3[212]142
WILLIAMS, JOHN J., *Private, 34th Indiana Infantry;*
CWTI:AUG/90[58]169
WILLIAMS, JOHN L., *Private, USA;* ACW:MAR/93[51]407
WILLIAMS, JOHN S., *General, CSA;* B&G:AUG/91[11]458
WILLIAMS, JOSEPH P., *Lieutenant, 11th Mississippi Infantry;*
GETTY:9[98]217
WILLIAMS, LAWRENCE A., *Colonel, CSA;*
B&G:OCT/92[10]496, B&G:DEC/92[6]502
WILLIAMS, LEROY, *Sergeant, 8th New York Heavy Artillery;*
B&G:APR/94[55]564
WILLIAMS, LEWIS B., *Colonel, 1st Virginia Infantry;*
GETTY:5[103]163
WILLIAMS, NELSON G.; CWR:VOL4#1[44]164
WILLIAMS, OLIVER, *Lieutenant, 20th North Carolina
Infantry;* B&G:FEB/95[8]590B, GETTY:5[13]157
WILLIAMS, PETER, *Lieutenant, USN;* AHI:NOV/75[38]163
WILLIAMS, ROBERT, *Colonel, 14th Kentucky Infantry;*
ACW:SEP/95[22]544, CWTI:JAN/94[46]364
WILLIAMS, SAM, *editor;* ACW:SEP/92[66]381
WILLIAMS, SAMUEL C., *Lieutenant Colonel, CSA;*
B&G:DEC/93[12]545, GETTY:13[22]254
WILLIAMS, SAMUEL J., *Colonel, 19th Indiana Infantry;*
GETTY:6[13]170

WILLIAMS, SETH, *General, USA:*
GENERAL LISTINGS: *Gettysburg*, GETTY:9[5]209,
GETTY:9[116]219, GETTY:12[85]248
ADDITIONAL LISTINGS: ACW:JAN/93[43]397, AHI:SEP/87[48]264,
AHI:JAN/94[50]319, B&G:AUG/91[32]461,
CWR:VOL3#3[1]157
WILLIAMS, SEWELL, *Private, Mosby's Ranger;*
CWTI:SEP/90[34]176
WILLIAMS, SOLOMON, *Colonel, 2nd North Carolina Cavalry;*
GETTY:11[19]232
WILLIAMS, STEPHEN M., BOOK REVIEW: *FROM THE
CANNON'S MOUTH: THE CIVIL WAR LETTERS OF
GENERAL ALPHEUS S. WILLIAMS*
WILLIAMS, THOMAS, *Corporal, 10th West Virginia Infantry;*
B&G:OCT/94[28]581
WILLIAMS, THOMAS, *General, USA;* ACW:MAY/93[12]412,
CWNEWS:MAY/92[4], *photos*, AHI:DEC/68[28]118,
AHI:JAN/82[16]224
WILLIAMS, THOMAS J., *Captain, 1st Arkansas Infantry
(Union);* ARTICLE: "TIME LAPSE," CWTI:APR/92[27]256
WILLIAMS, TITUS V., *Colonel, 37th Virginia Infantry;*
CWM:MAY/92[20]420
WILLIAMS, WALTER, *Private, CSA;* ACW:SEP/91[8]318,
B&G:FEB/91[32]441, B&G:APR/91[40]450,
B&G:JUN/91[6]451, CWTI:MAY/92[8]261, CWTI:JUL/92[8]269
WILLIAMS, WASHINGTON F., *Private, 11th Battalion,
Georgia Artillery;* CWR:VOL3#2[1]153
WILLIAMS, WINFIELD S., *Private, 7th Wisconsin Infantry,*
GETTY:9[33]211, GETTY:11[57]233
WILLIAMSBURG, VIRGINIA, BATTLE OF:
ARTICLES: "THE PENINSULA CAMPAIGN OF 1862: THE
BATTLE OF WILLIAMSBURG," CWM:JUN/95[34]584,
"SUPERB WAS THE DAY," ACW:MAR/91[47]297
ADDITIONAL LISTINGS: ACW:JUL/93[16]422, ACW:NOV/94[50]498,
B&G:AUG/91[30]460, CWM:MAR/91[50]340,
CWR:VOL3#1[31]150, CWTI:MAR/91[12]198
WILLIAMSON, HENRY F., *Captain, CSA;* CWR:VOL3#1[1]149
WILLIAMSON, JAMES, *Colonel, USA;* CWTI:SEP/94[40]403
WILLIAMSON, JAMES A., *Colonel USA;* ACW:NOV/93[34]442
WILLIAMSON, JAMES J., *Mosby's Rangers:*
BOOK REVIEW: *MOSBY'S RANGERS*
ADDITIONAL LISTINGS: ACW:JUL/94[26]477, CWTI:SEP/90[34]176
WILLIAMSPORT, VIRGINIA; GETTY:9[109]218
WILLICH, AUGUST, *General, USA;* B&G:OCT/92[10]496,
B&G:JUN/95[5]599, CWM:JUL/92[40]432,
CWM:SEP/93[8]493, CWTI:NOV/92[41]291
WILLIS, BARNEYH, *Lieutenant, 3rd Georgia Infantry;*
CWTI:SEP/94[26]400
WILLIS, EDWARD, *Colonel, 12th Georgia Infantry;*
ACW:MAR/94[16]458, ACW:MAY/95[10]523,
B&G:APR/94[10]558, GETTY:5[117]165
WILLIS, EDWARD S., *Cadet;* B&G:DEC/91[12]469
WILLIS, G.T., *Captain, 1st Confederate Georgia Infantry;*
CWR:VOL1#4[42]126
WILLIS, HOLMES, *Private, 8th Louisiana Infantry;*
CWTI:FEB/91[12]189
WILLIS, R.L., *Private, 9th Massachusetts Light Artillery;*
GETTY:5[47]160
WILLIS, REUBEN G., *Private, 13th Virginia Infantry;*
B&G:DEC/95[25]616
WILLIS, TOM, *Private, 13th Sough Carolina Infantry;*
GETTY:13[22]254

WILSON, JOHN P., *Private, 100th Pennsylvania Infantry;* CWTI:JAN/94[49]365

WILSON, JOHN W., *Surgeon, 73rd Pennsylvania Infantry;* B&G:FEB/92[40]479

WILSON, LAWRENCE, *Sergeant, 7th Ohio Infantry;* GETTY:9[81]216

WILSON, LYMAN D., *Private, USA;* GETTY:13[22]254

WILSON, PHIL, *Sergeant, 5th New York Infantry;* CWR:VOL1#2[7]111, CWR:VOL1#2[29]112, CWTI:MAY/94[31]382

WILSON, THOMAS F., *US Consul to Brazil;* AHI:JAN/83[10]232

WILSON, WILLIAM, *Colonel, 6th New York Infantry;* CWR:VOL1#4[42]126

WILSON, WILLIAM A., *Private, 4th Illinois Infantry;* CWTI:MAY/93[35]320

WILSON, WILLIAM C., *Major, 104th New York Infantry;* CWTI:MAY/92[32]264

WILSON, WILLIAM L., *Adjutant, 142nd Pennsylvania Infantry;* GETTY:4[24]145

WILSON, WILLIAM P., *Lieutenant, 53rd Pennsylvania Infantry;* GETTY:11[80]235

WILSON-KAUTZ RAID: ACW:JAN/92[16]340

WILTSHIRE, JIM, *Mosby's Rangers;* CWM:JAN/93[24]458

WIMBERLY, A.M., and JOHN C., *2nd Tennessee Cavalry;* CWR:VOL4#1[1]163

WINCHESTER, VIRGINIA, FIRST BATTLE OF; CWM:MAY/92[8]418, CWR:VOL2#4[346]

WINCHESTER, VIRGINIA, SECOND BATTLE OF:
ARTICLE: "UNION FORCES ROUTED AGAIN," CWM:AUG/95[35]607
BOOK REVIEWS: *THE SECOND BATTLE OF WINCHESTER, JUNE 12-15, 1863*
ADDITIONAL LISTINGS: CWM:JAN/91[47], CWM:SEP/93[24]495, CWR:VOL1#4[77]

WINCHESTER, VIRGINIA, THIRD BATTLE OF:
ARTICLES: "CONFEDERATES ROUTED AT WINCHESTER!" CWM:OCT/95[37]617, "SHERIDAN IN THE SHENANDOAH," AHI:NOV/80[8]209, "WHIRLING THROUGH WINCHESTER," ACW:MAY/91[38]305
GENERAL LISTINGS: *election of 1864,* AHI:OCT/68[4]116, *in book review,* CWM:OCT/94[8], *general history,* AHI:MAY/71[3]133A, *letters to the editor,* B&G:JUN/95[5]599
ADDITIONAL LISTINGS: ACW:JAN/92[16]340, ACW:JAN/95[46]507, ACW:MAR/95[50]518, AHI:MAR/84[42]238, CWM:JAN/93[40]461, CWM:MAR/93[24]467, CWM:SEP/93[24]495, CWM:APR/94[24]505, CWR:VOL2#1[19]131, CWR:VOL3#3[1]157, CWTI:APR/92[35]257, CWTI:MAY/93[26]318, MH:OCT/93[76]173

WINCHESTER, VIRGINIA:
ARTICLE: "FOCUS: CIVIL WAR PHOTOGRAPHY," AHI:NOV/80[17]210
ADDITIONAL LISTINGS: CWTI:DEC/89[34]136

WINCLER, CLINTON M., *Captain, 4th Texas Infantry;* BOOK REVIEW: *CONFEDERATE CAPITAL AND HOOD'S TEXAS BRIGADE*

WINDER, CHARLES S., *General, CSA;* ACW:JAN/92[8]338, B&G:JUN/92[8]487, CWTI:MAR/94[29]371, CWTI:JUN/95[18]444

WINDER, JOHN H., *General, CSA:*
BOOK REVIEWS: *GENERAL JOHN H. WINDER, C.S.A.*

GENERAL LISTINGS: *Andersonville,* B&G:DEC/92[32]506, *in book review,* B&G:JUN/95[30], CWM:OCT/95[10], *Mexican War,* MH:APR/93[39]166, *photo,* B&G:AUG/93[18]530
ADDITIONAL LISTINGS: AHI:DEC/85[40]255, B&G:AUG/93[18]530, CWTI:MAY/89[22]116, CWTI:APR/92[23]255, MH:APR/94[54]176

WINDER, JOSEPH, *Private, 10th U.S. Colored Infantry;* AHI:AUG/68[4]115B

WINDER, RICHARD, *Major, CSA;* CWTI:APR/92[23]255

WINDER, WILLIAM, *Captain, USA;* CWTI:JUN/95[51]449

WINE, JAMES, *Private, 19th Indiana Infantry,* GETTY:11[57]233

WINEGAR, CHARLES, *Captain, 1st New York Artillery;* B&G:FEB/91[8]339, B&G:FEB/91[8]439, B&G:FEB/95[8]590C

WINEGAR, DANIEL G., *Private, 95th Illinois Infantry;* ACW:JAN/91[16]284

WING, HENRY, *reporter;* B&G:APR/95[8]595, B&G:JUN/95[8]600

WING, JOHN P., *Private, 150th New York Infantry;* GETTY:12[42]244

WINGFIELD, GEORGE, *Private, Petersburg Artillery;* ACW:MAR/95[12]513

WINGFIELD, JOHN T., *Captain, Sumter Artillery:*
ARTICLE: "WILDERNESS TO PETERSBURG: UNPUBLISHED REPORTS OF THE 11TH BATTALION, GEORGIA LIGHT ARTILLERY," CWR:VOL3#2[61]154
ADDITIONAL LISTING: CWR:VOL3#2[1]153

WINGO, EDMOND T., *Colonel, CSA;* CWTI:FEB/92[29]248

WINKELMAIER, LOUIS, *Captain, USA;* B&G:APR/95[24]596

WINKLER, CLINTON M., *Colonel, CSA;* CWR:VOL2#3[256]

WINN, DAVID R.E., *Lieutenant Colonel, 4th Georgia Infantry;* GETTY:5[107]164

WINSLOW, CLEVELAND, *Captain, 5th New York Infantry;* CWR:VOL1#2[7]111, CWR:VOL1#2[29]112, CWTI:MAY/94[31]382

WINSLOW, EDWARD F., *Colonel, USA;* ACW:MAR/91[38]296, ACW:SEP/95[48]547, B&G:JUN/91[10]452, B&G:AUG/95[8]604, CWNEWS:JAN/94[5]

WINSLOW, FRANCIS, *Lieutenant, USN;* MH:DEC/94[46]181, B&G:JUN/92[40]489

WINSLOW, GEORGE B., *Captain, 1st New York Light Artillery;* GETTY:8[43]202, GETTY:8[53]203

WINSLOW, GORDON, *Chaplain, 5th New York Infantry;* CWR:VOL1#2[7]111, CWTI:MAY/94[31]382

WINSLOW, JOHN, *Captain, USN;* AHI:OCT/88[38]275

WINSLOW, JOHN A., *Lieutenant, USA;* ACW:JUL/95[58], AHI:JAN/83[10]232, CWTI:DEC/94[34]411

WINSLOW, MIRON, *Private, 5th New York Infantry;* CWR:VOL1#2[7]111, CWTI:MAY/94[31]382

WINSLOW, THOMAS, *Lieutenant, USA;* CWR:VOL1#3[28]120

WINSTON, F.V., *Captain, 13th Virginia Infantry;* ACW:MAR/94[50]462

WINSTON, JOHN R., *Major, 45th North Carolina Infantry;* GETTY:10[102]226

WINTERMEYER, GUSTAVUS, *Lieutenant, 4th Wisconsin Infantry;* ACW:MAY/93[12]412

WINTHROP, FRED, *Captain, 12th U.S. Infantry;* B&G:APR/92[8]481, B&G:APR/93[12]518

WINTHROP, ROBERT C.; CWTI:OCT/95[48]470

WINTHROP, THEODORE, *Major, USA;* ACW:MAR/93[42]406, CWNEWS:MAY/93[4]

WINTRINGER, NATHAN, *civilian;* B&G:AUG/95[24]605, CWM:MAY/93[32]477

36th Infantry:
GENERAL LISTINGS: *Cold Harbor*, B&G:APR/94[10]558, *Gettysburg*, GETTY:7[97]193, GETTY:10[53]225, *SIO*, B&G:JUN/95[36]603A
ADDITIONAL LISTINGS: ACW:JUL/93[16]422, B&G:APR/94[59]565
46th Infantry; CWTI:AUG/90[50]168
50th Infantry; GETTY:4[24]145
Light Artillery; B&G:FEB/94[8]550, B&G:AUG/95[8]604
Sharpshooters Regiment; MH:OCT/93[20]172

WISDOM, D.M., *Colonel, CSA;* AHI:APR/74[4]154
WISE, HENRY A., *General, CSA:*
ARTICLE: "DISASTER AT ROANOKE ISLAND," CWM:FEB/95[49]565
GENERAL LISTINGS: *The "Blackberry" Raid,* GETTY:11[6]231, *Five Forks,* B&G:APR/92[8]481, *in book review,* CWNEWS:OCT/92[4], CWR:VOL4#3[1]170, *in order of battle,* B&G:APR/92[8]481, *John Brown,* ACW:JUL/91[43]315, AHI:AUG/76[34]171, *letters to the editor,* CWM:SEP/91[6]377, *Thomas J. Jackson,* B&G:JUN/92[8]487, *West Virginia campaign,* B&G:AUG/93[10]529, *photos,* ACW:SEP/94[31]486, CWM:JUL/91[48]374, CWM:FEB/95[49]565, CWTI:APR/89[38]111
ADDITIONAL LISTINGS: ACW:JAN/92[22]341, ACW:JAN/93[43]397, ACW:SEP/94[31]486, ACW:MAR/95[12]513, AHI:MAR/84[10]236, CWM:JUL/91[25]363, CWM:JUL/91[46]373, CWR:VOL1#3[7]118, CWR:VOL2#2[141]137, CWTI:APR/89[38]111, CWTI:JUL/94[44]394, CWTI:JAN/95[24]424, CWTI:OCT/95[32]468
WISE, JENNINGS C.:
BOOK REVIEWS: *THE LONG ARM OF LEE OR THE HISTORY OF THE ARTILLERY OF THE ARMY OF NORTHERN VIRGINIA*
ADDITIONAL LISTING: CWR:VOL1#1[1]102
WISE, JOHN, *Governor, Virginia;* ACW:MAR/93[18]403, ACW:JUL/93[10]421, ACW:JUL/94[35]478
WISE, JOHN:
BOOK REVIEW: *AERONAUTICS IN THE UNION AND CONFEDERATE ARMIES*
ADDITIONAL LISTINGS: ACW:JAN/92[22]341, ACW:MAY/92[54]
WISE, MICAJAH, *Union veteran;* GETTY:5[123]166
WISE, O. JENNINGS, *Captain, CSA;* CWM:FEB/95[49]565
WISE, PEYTON, *Lieutenant Colonel, CSA;* CWR:VOL2#4[361]148
WISELY, LUKE, *Private, 9th New York Infantry;* B&G:APR/95[24]596
WISNER, LEWIS, *Private, 124th New York Infantry;* CWM:DEC/94[40]550
WISTER, LANGHORNE, *Colonel, 150th Pennsylvania Infantry;* CWR:VOL1#3[20]119, GETTY:4[33]146
WITCHER, VINCENT, *Captain, 34th Virginia Cavalry Battalion;* B&G:AUG/91[11]458
WITCHER, WILLIAM A., *Captain, 21st Virginia Infantry;* GETTY:13[108]261
WITCHERT, PHILIP, *Private, 11th Veteran Reserve Corps;* B&G:APR/93[24]520
WITHENBURY, WELLINGTON W., *civilian;* CWR:VOL4#2[26]166
WITHER, JOHN; CWR:VOL1#3[7]118
WITHERS, ELIJAH B., *Colonel, 13th North Carolina Infantry;* GETTY:8[67]204

WITHERS, JONES M., *General, USA;* CWM:JAN/91[40]330, CWR:VOL4#1[1]163
WITHERS, WILLIAM; AHI:FEB/86[20]258, CWTI:MAR/93[12]307
WITHERSPOON, W.W., *Colonel, 36th Mississippi Infantry;* CWR:VOL2#1[1]130
WITHERSPOON, WILLIAM, *Private, 7th Tennessee Cavalry;* B&G:APR/93[34]521
WITMOYER, JOHN, *Private, 11th Pennsylvania Infantry;* GETTY:10[7]221
WITT, ALLEN R., *Colonel, 10th Arkansas Infantry;* CWTI:JAN/95[42]428
WOFFORD, WILLIAM T., *General, CSA:*
GENERAL LISTINGS: *Gettysburg,* GETTY:5[35]159, GETTY:5[47]160, GETTY:5[103]163, GETTY:7[51]190, GETTY:8[53]203, GETTY:9[53]214, GETTY:10[42]224, GETTY:10[120]229, GETTY:11[91]236, *in order of battle,* B&G:APR/94[10]558, *letters to the editor,* CWTI:SEP/94[12]398, *order of battle,* B&G:APR/95[8]595, *Overland Campaign,* B&G:APR/94[10]558, *Wilderness,* B&G:JUN/95[8]600, *photo,* CWTI:MAY/94[50]386
ADDITIONAL LISTINGS: ACW:MAY/91[23]303, ACW:JUL/92[30]369, ACW:MAY/95[30]525, CWM:JUN/94[26]512, CWTI:MAR/93[40]312, CWTI:MAY/94[50]386, CWTI:SEP/94[26]400, GETTY:13[7]253
WOLCOTT, DAVID A., *Sergeant, 1st Ohio Cavalry;* B&G:AUG/93[10]529
WOLCOTT, JOHN W., *Captain, 1st Maryland Battery;* ACW:JAN/94[39]451, CWTI:MAR/93[20]308
WOLD, FRED, *Surgeon, 39th New York Infantry;* GETTY:10[53]225
WOLF, ALEXANDER, *Private, 2nd Mississippi Infantry;* GETTY:6[77]177
WOLF, J.B., *Captain, CSA;* CWTI:JAN/95[42]428
WOLFE, EDWARD H., *Colonel, USA;* B&G:DEC/93[12]545
WOLFE, GEORGE, *Lieutenant, USA;* CWTI:JUL/93[20]325
WOLFE, SIMEON K., *editor;* CWM:MAR/93[16]466
WOLFORD, DANIEL, *Private, 138th Pennsylvania Infantry;* CWM:OCT/94[26]536, CWTI:SEP/92[42]283
WOLFORD, FRANK, *Colonel, 1st Kentucky (USA) Cavalry;* B&G:FEB/93[12]511, CWR:VOL4#1[1]163
WOLLAM, JOHN, *Private, USA;* ACW:SEP/91[22]321
WOLSELEY, GARNET, *Lieutenant Colonel, British Army:*
BOOK REVIEW: *THE AMERICAN CIVIL WAR: AN ENGLISH VIEW*
GENERAL LISTINGS: ACW:NOV/91[46]335, CWM:DEC/95[10], CWTI:DEC/94[73]416
WOLVERTON, ALONZO, *Lieutenant, 9th Ohio Cavalry, 20th Ohio Artillery;* B&G:DEC/92[40]508, CWM:SEP/93[18]494
WOMAN'S RIGHTS SOCIETY; CWTI:AUG/90[50]168
WOMEN IN THE SOUTH, ARTICLE: "WOMEN OF THE LOST CAUSE," AHI:DEC/73[10]152
WOMEN SOLDIERS, BOOK REVIEW: *PATRIOTS IN DISGUISE*
WOMEN'S RELIEF ASSOCIATION; CWM:APR/94[8]502

WOMEN'S RIGHTS:
Anthony, Susan B.; CWTI:DEC/90[50]183
Stanton, Elizabeth Cady; CWTI:DEC/90[50]183

WOMEN IN THE CIVIL WAR:
ARTICLES: "ARNOLD VS. ARNOLD: THE STRANGE AND HITHERTO UNTOLD STORY OF THE DIVORCE OF STONEWALL JACKSON'S SISTER," B&G:OCT/94[28]581,

"ELIZABETH KECKLEY MADE THE LONG JOURNEY FROM SLAVERY TO THE WHITE HOUSE, AS MARY LINCOLN'S DRESSMAKER," ACW:JUL/92[8]365A, "ELMINA KEELER SPENCER: MATRON, 147TH NEW YORK," GETTY:8[121]207, "GENTLE ANNIE GOES HOME: ROBERT E. LEE'S DAUGHTER RETURNS TO VIRGINIA AFTER 132 YEARS," B&G:JUN/95[22]601, "GEORGIA'S NANCY HARTS," CWTI:MAY/94[44]384, "THE LADY'S CARRYING A SCALPEL?" CWM:APR/94[8]502, "SISTERS AND NUNS WHO WERE NURSES DURING THE CIVIL WAR," B&G:OCT/93[31]539, "SOUTHERN BELLES AT WAR," ACW:MAY/92[39]362, "TOTAL WAR COMES TO NEW MANCHESTER," B&G:DEC/94[22]586, "WASHINGTON JOURNALIST AND LOBBYIST ANNA ELLA CARROLL WAS ABRAHAM LINCOLN'S SECRET STRATEGIC WEAPON," ACW:MAR/95[8]512

BOOK REVIEWS: *A NORTHERN WOMAN IN THE PLANTATION SOUTH: LETTERS OF TRYPHENA BLANCHE HOLDER FOX, 1856-1876 * AN UNCOMMON SOLDIER: THE CIVIL WAR LETTERS OF SARAH ROSETTA WAKEMAN, ALIAS PRIVATE LYONS WAKEMAN, 153RD REGIMENT, NEW YORK STATE VOLUNTEERS, 1862-1864 * A CONFEDERATE NURSE: THE DIARY OF ADA W. BACOT, 1860-1863 * A LOST HEROINE OF THE CONFEDERACY * A SOUTHERN WOMAN'S STORY * A WOMAN'S CIVIL WAR: A DIARY, WITH REMINISCENCES OF THE WAR, FROM MARCH 1862 * AHEAD OF HER TIME: ABBY KELLEY AND THE POLITICS OF ANTISLAVERY * AN UNCOMMON SOLDIER: THE CIVIL WAR LETTERS OF SARAH ROSETTA WAKEMAN, ALIAS PRIVATE LYONS WAKEMAN, 153RD REGIMENT, NEW YORK STATE VOLUNTEERS, 1862-1864 * BLUE AND GRAY ROSES OF INTRIGUE * CELIA, A SLAVE*

BOOK REVIEWS, continued: *CHARGED WITH TREASON: ORDEAL OF 400 MILL WORKERS DURING MILITARY OPERATIONS IN ROSWELL GEORGIA, 1864-1865 * THE CIVIL WAR DIARY OF MARTHA ABERNATHY, WIFE OF DR. C.C. ABERNATHY OF PULASKI, TENNESSEE * CIVIL WAR HEROINES: THE COGGESHALL LADIES * CIVIL WAR LADIES, FASHIONS AND NEEDLE-ARTS OF THE EARLY 1869'S * THE CIVIL WAR MEMORIES OF ELIZABETH BACON CUSTER * CIVIL WAR MEMOIRS OF TWO REBEL SISTERS * CIVIL WARS: WOMEN AND THE CRISIS OF SOUTHERN NATIONALISM * THE DIARY OF A LADY OF GETTYSBURG, PENNSYLVANIA * DIARY OF A SOUTHERN REFUGEE * EMMA'S WORLD: AN INITMATE LOOK AT LIVES TOUCHED BY THE CIVIL WAR ERA*

BOOK REVIEWS, continued: *HEARTS OF FIRE: SOLDIER WOMEN OF THE CIVIL WAR * IN JOY AND IN SORROW: WOMEN, FAMILY, AND MARRIAGE IN THE VICTORIAN SOUTH, 1830-1900 * THE LADIES' HAND BOOK OF FANCY AND ORNAMENTAL WORK: CIVIL WAR ERA, * THE LEE GIRLS * LUCY BRECKINRIDGE OF GROVE HILL: THE JOURNAL OF A VIRGINIA GIRL, 1862-1864 * MARGARET JUNKIN PRESTON: A BIOGRAPHY * MY CAVE LIFE IN VICKSBURG * PATRIOTS IN DISGUISE: WOMEN WARRIORS OF THE CIVIL WAR * STRAINED SISTERHOOD: GENDER AND CLASS IN THE BOSTON FEMALE ANTI-SLAVERY SOCIETY * TARA REVISITED: WOMEN, WAR, AND THE PLANTATION LEGEND * TRIALS AND TRIUMPHS: WOMEN OF THE AMERICAN CIVIL WAR * TWO LADIES OF GETTYSBURG, * WOMEN AT GETTYSBURG, 1863 * WOMEN IN THE CIVIL WAR*

Harvey, Cordelia; CWTI:MAR/89[20]102

Hawley, Harriet; ARTICLE: "INDEFATIGABLE HARRIET HAWLEY SACRIFICED HEALTH AND HOME FOR THE SOLDIERS SHE CALLED 'HER BOYS,'" ACW:NOV/93[10]439

Heyward, Pauline DeCaradeuc; BOOK REVIEW: *A CONFEDERATE LADY COMES OF AGE: THE JOURNAL OF PAULINE DECARADEUC HEYWARD, 1863-1888*

Lee, Elizabeth Blair; BOOK REVIEW: *WARTIME WASHINGTON: THE CIVIL WAR LETTERS OF ELIZABETH BLAIR LEE*

McDonald, Cornelia P.; BOOK REVIEW: *A WOMAN'S CIVIL WAR: A DIARY, WITH REMINISCENCES OF THE WAR*

Morgan, Sarah; BOOK REVIEW: *THE CIVIL WAR DIARY OF SARAH MORGAN*

Seabury, Caroline; BOOK REVIEW: *THE DIARY OF CAROLINE SEABURY 1854-1863*

WOOD LAKE, MINNESOTA, ENGAGEMENT AT; ACW:MAY/91[12]302

WOOD, ALEXANDER H., *Sergeant, 6th New York Cavalry;* CWM:MAY/92[44]423

WOOD, ALMON A., *Lieutenant, 110th New York Infantry;* CWR:VOL3#1[1]149

WOOD, ARTHUR, *Private, USA;* B&G:JUN/93[12]524

WOOD, C.A., *Lieutenant Colonel, 11th Wisconsin Infantry;* B&G:FEB/94[8]550

WOOD, CHARLES S., *Surgeon, 66th New York Infantry;* GETTY:10[53]225

WOOD, D.H., *Major, CSA;* ACW:MAY/95[38]526

WOOD, EPHRAIM, *Captain, 111th New York Infantry;* CWR:VOL1#4[7]125, GETTY:8[95]205, GETTY:10[53]225

WOOD, FERNANDO, *Mayor, New York:*
GENERAL LISTINGS: *Draft Riots,* AHI:AUG/77[30]175, *in book review,* CWM:JAN/91[35], CWNEWS:APR/92[4]

WOOD, GEORGE, *river pilot;* ACW:JUL/93[34]424, ACW:MAR/95[18]514

WOOD, JOHN, *Governor, Illinois;* ACW:JUL/94[8]474

WOOD, JOHN, *photographer;* B&G:FEB/94[24]551

WOOD, JOHN TAYLOR, *Commander, CSN:*
GENERAL LISTINGS: *letters to the editor,* CWM:MAY/91[6]345, CWM:MAR/91[12]333, *photo,* AHI:OCT/75[30]162
ADDITIONAL LISTINGS: ACW:JAN/95[74]510, ACW:NOV/95[38]556, AHI:OCT/75[30]162, AHI:JAN/83[10]232, B&G:DEC/92[8]503, CWM:JUN/94[50]518, CWTI:MAR/93[32]311, CWTI:JUL/94[44]394

WOOD, JOSEPH, *civilian;* B&G:FEB/91[20]440

WOOD, JULIUS V., *Private, 96th Ohio Infantry;* ACW:SEP/92[16]376

WOOD, MARK, *Sergeant, USA;* ACW:SEP/91[22]321

WOOD, PETER P., *Captain, 1st Illinois Artillery;* B&G:AUG/95[8]604, CWR:VOL2#1[1]130

WOOD, STERLING A., *General, CSA;* CWR:VOL4#3[50]171

WOOD, T. HIRAM, *Lieutenant, 10th Georgia Infantry;* ACW:JUL/95[10]533

WOOD, TALLMADGE, *Private, 150th New York Infantry;* GETTY:12[42]244

WOOD, THOMAS J., *General, USA:*
GENERAL LISTINGS: *Nashville,* B&G:DEC/93[12]545, *order of battle,* B&G:DEC/93[12]545, *William T. Sherman,* AHI:JAN/67[4]106
ADDITIONAL LISTINGS: ACW:JUL/91[35]314, ACW:NOV/95[48]557, B&G:DEC/93[52]548, CWM:JUL/92[24]430, CWTI:SUMMER/89[20]121, CWTI:MAR/95[40]436

WOOD, THOMAS W., *artist:*
ARTICLE: "THE ARTIST AND THE CIVIL WAR,"
AHI:NOV/80[28]211
PAINTING: "The Return of the Flags"; CWTI:AUG/90[58]169

WOOD, W.S., *Private, Terry's Texas Rangers;*
CWM:JUL/92[40]432

WOOD, WALES W., *Adjutant, 95th Illinois Infantry;*
ACW:JAN/91[16]284

WOOD, WILLIAM B., *Colonel, 16th Alabama Infantry;*
B&G:FEB/93[12]511

WOODBURY, D.B., *photographer;* B&G:FEB/94[24]551

WOODBURY, DANIEL P., *General, USA;*
ACW:NOV/95[10]553, CWR:VOL4#4[101]181

WOODBURY, JOHN D., *Captain, 1st New York Light Artillery;*
CWTI:SUMMER/89[32]122

WOODHEAD, JAMES, *Private, 84th New York Infantry;*
GETTY:5[123]166

WOODING, G.W., *Captain, Danville Artillery;*
CWR:VOL4#4[70]180

WOODRING, DANIEL W., *Private, 148th Pennsylvania Infantry;* CWR:VOL2#2[141]137

WOODRUFF, GEORGE A., *Captain, 1st U.S. Artillery:*
Gettysburg, AHI:SUM/88[12]273, GETTY:4[89]150,
GETTY:5[89]162, GETTY:7[51]190, GETTY:8[95]205,
GETTY:9[61]215, *West Point,* B&G:DEC/91[12]469
ADDITIONAL LISTINGS: ACW:MAY/92[8]357, ACW:MAR/94[50]462,
CWR:VOL3#2[1]153

WOODRUFF, JAMES; ARTICLE: "THE UNDISTINGUISHED
WOODRUFF GUN HAD ONLY ONE TRUE SUPPORTER,
ABRAHAM LINCOLN—BUT ONE WAS ENOUGH,"
ACW:JUL/94[8]474

WOODRUFF, JOHN G., *Captain, USA;* AHI:APR/74[4]154

WOODRUFF, WILLIAM E., *Captain, Pulaski Battery;*
ACW:NOV/93[26]441, CWTI:FEB/92[29]248

WOODS, CHARLES R., *General, USA;* ACW:NOV/93[34]442,
B&G:APR/94[28]559, B&G:AUG/95[8]604,
B&G:DEC/95[9]615, CWR:VOL4#1[44]164,
CWTI:SUMMER/89[50]124, CWTI:NOV/92[41]291,
CWTI:SEP/92[28]280, CWTI:JAN/93[20]298,
CWTI:SEP/94[40]403

WOODS, GEORGE H., *Lieutenant, USA;* ACW:JAN/94[62]

WOODS, J.G., *Private, 22nd Virginia Infantry;*
CWR:VOL1#3[52]122

WOODS, J.T., *Surgeon, 96th Ohio Infantry;* ACW:SEP/92[16]376

WOODS, JAMES, *Colonel, USA;* CWTI:SUMMER/89[32]122

WOODS, JOSEPH J., *Colonel, USA;* B&G:AUG/95[8]604

WOODS, MICHAEL., *Colonel, 46th Alabama Infantry;*
ACW:NOV/91[22]331, B&G:FEB/94[8]550,
CWR:VOL2#1[19]131

WOODS, PENVIL, *Private, 5th North Carolina Infantry;*
B&G:FEB/95[8]590B

WOODS, PHILO, *Sergeant, 12th Iowa Infantry;*
CWNEWS:NOV/94[33]

WOODS, W.W., *Captain, USA;* CWTI:JAN/93[20]298

WOODS, WILLIAM B., *General, USA;* B&G:DEC/95[9]615

WOODSON, B.H., *Colonel, CSA;* CWTI:SEP/90[52]179

WOODSON, BLAKE, *Major, CSA;* ACW:SEP/91[41]323

WOODSON, H.M., *Private, 34th Mississippi Infantry;*
CWTI:SEPT/89[30]129

WOODWARD, BENJAMIN, *Civilian, Physician;*
AHI:APR/79[4]186

WOODWARD, EVAN M., *Adjutant, 2nd Pennsylvania Reserves;*
CWR:VOL4#4[1]177

WOODWARD, EVAN M., CWR:VOL4#4[1]177

WOODWARD, ORPHEUS S., *Captain, 83rd Pennsylvania
Infantry;* GETTY:7[41]189, GETTY:8[31]201

WOODWARD, SAMUEL, *Lieutenant, USA;* ACW:JUL/94[8]474,
B&G:JUN/93[12]524

WOODWARD, THOMAS G., *Lieutenant Colonel, CSA;*
CWTI:JUL/92[42]274

WOOL, JOHN E., *General, USA;* ACW:JAN/94[47]452,
AHI:OCT/79[20]194, AHI:OCT/82[28]230,
CWR:VOL1#4[7]125, CWTI:MAY/92[38]265,
MH:APR/93[34]165

WOOLLARD, LEANDER G., *Captain, 2nd Mississippi Infantry:*
ARTICLE: "A MISSISSIPPIAN IN THE RAILROAD CUT,"
GETTY:4[22]144
ADDITIONAL LISTING: GETTY:7[13]186

WOOLSEY, CHARLES, *Captain, USA;* GETTY:9[116]219

WOOLSEY, GEORGE ANNA M., *civilian;* GETTY:9[116]219,
GETTY:10[53]225

WOOLSEY, JANE N., *civilian;* GETTY:10[53]225

WOOLSON, ALBERT, *Private, 1st Minnesota Heavy Artillery;*
ACW:SEP/91[8]318, B&G:FEB/91[32]441,
B&G:APR/91[40]450, GETTY:7[119]195

WOOLWORTH, RICHARD H., *Colonel, 4th Pennsylvania
Reserves;* ACW:MAR/94[27]459, CWR:VOL4#4[1]177

WOOSTER, WILLIAM B., *Colonel, 20th Connecticut Infantry;*
GETTY:5[117]165

WOOTEN, SHADE, *Captain, 27th North Carolina Infantry;*
CWTI:FEB/91[45]194

WORDEN, JOHN L., *Captain, USN;* AHI:JUL/66[32]103,
AHI:NOV/75[38]163, CWM:JUL/93[15]484, *photo,*
AHI:NOV/75[38]163

WORK, GEORGE T., *Major, 22nd Pennsylvania Cavalry;*
B&G:AUG/94[10]574

WORK, PHILLIP A., *Lieutenant Colonel, 1st Texas Infantry;*
ACW:JUL/92[30]369, CWR:VOL1#1[71]107

WORLD WIDE WEB; CWTI:OCT/95[40]469

WORLEY, C.L.F., *Private, 5th Alabama Infantry;*
GETTY:6[13]170

WORSHAM, JOHN H., *Private, 21st Virginia Infantry;*
BOOK REVIEW: *ONE OF JACKSON'S FOOT CAVALRY BY JOHN
H. WORSHAM, F. COMPANY, 21ST VIRGINIA INFANTRY*
ADDITIONAL LISTINGS: B&G:DEC/91[6]468, B&G:DEC/92[8]503,
B&G:APR/95[8]595

WORTH, ALONZO K., *Private, 16th Massachusetts Infantry;*
GETTY:12[7]241

WORTH, BENJAMIN F., *Private, 16th Maine Infantry;*
GETTY:13[33]255

WORTHEN, G.K., *Private, 12th New Hampshire Infantry;*
GETTY:12[7]241

WORTHINGTON, JAMES F., *Sergeant, 2nd Tennessee
Cavalry;* CWR:VOL4#1[1]163,

WORTHINGTON, JOHN T., *civilian;* CWTI:JAN/93[40]301

WORTHINGTON, MARY R.; CWTI:JAN/93[40]301

WORTHINGTON, SAMUEL P., *Private, 2nd Tennessee
Cavalry;* CWR:VOL4#1[1]163

WORTHINGTON, W.J., *Major, 22nd Kentucky Infantry
(Union);* B&G:FEB/94[8]550

WORTHINGTON, WILLIAM J., *Lieutenant, 2nd Tennessee
Cavalry;* CWR:VOL4#1[1]163

WRANGHAM, THOMAS J., *Corporal, 123rd New York
Infantry;* GETTY:6[7]169

WRATH, ROBERT, *Sergeant, 53rd Pennsylvania Infantry;*
GETTY:11[80]235

ADDITIONAL LISTINGS: ACW:JAN/95[10]503, B&G:OCT/92[38]500, B&G:OCT/93[49]543, CWM:SEP/93[18]494, CWTI:DEC/89[34]136, CWTI:APR/92[35]257, MH:FEB/93[42]164

YORK, ZEBULON, *General, CSA;* ACW:MAY/91[38]305, ACW:SEP/92[38]379, ACW:NOV/93[50]444, B&G:DEC/92[8]503, B&G:APR/94[10]558, CWM:SEP/93[24]495, CWTI:JAN/93[40]301

YORKTOWN, VIRGINIA, BATTLE OF:
ARTICLE: "THE PENINSULA CAMPAIGN OF 1862: THE SIEGE OF YORKTOWN AND ENGAGEMENTS ALONG THE WARWICK RIVER," CWM:JUN/95[29]583

BOOK REVIEWS: *THE PENINSULA CAMPAIGN OF 1862: YORKTOWN TO THE SEVEN DAYS*

ADDITIONAL LISTINGS: ACW:MAR/91[47]297, ACW:JUL/93[16]422, ACW:SEP/93[16]431, ACW:NOV/94[50]498, CWM:JUN/95[17]581, CWNEWS:JUN/94[5], CWTI:MAR/89[28]103

YOST, GEORGE, *Lieutenant, 126th New York Infantry;* GETTY:8[95]205

YOUNG, ALBERT, *Private, 6th Wisconsin Infantry;* GETTY:4[24]145

YOUNG, BENNETT H., *Lieutenant, CSA:*
ARTICLE: "ST. ALBANS HAS BEEN SURPRISED," AHI:JAN/76[14]164

ADDITIONAL LISTINGS: ACW:JUL/95[44]537, AHI:JUN/70[30]127, AHI:JUL/93[40]312, B&G:FEB/93[12]511, CWTI:NOV/92[54]293, MH:FEB/94[8]175, *photo;* AHI:JAN/76[14]164

YOUNG, BRIGHAM; ACW:JAN/95[8]502

YOUNG, CHARLES P. and GEORGE S., *Crenshaw's Artillery;* GETTY:10[107]227

YOUNG, CLAUS, *Private, 19th Indiana Infantry,* GETTY:11[57]233

YOUNG, HENRY C., *Major, USA;* ACW:SEP/91[41]323, ACW:MAR/93[55]408, CWTI:JUN/95[26]445

YOUNG, J.J., *Captain, CSA;* GETTY:8[67]204

YOUNG, JESSE B., *Lieutenant, 84th Pennsylvania Infantry;* GETTY:9[5]209, GETTY:12[7]241

YOUNG, JOHN, *Confederate veteran;* GETTY:7[119]195

YOUNG, LOUIS G., *Captain, CSA;* CWTI:FEB/91[45]194, GETTY:5[4]156, GETTY:5[19]158, GETTY:8[67]204

YOUNG, PIERCE M.B., *General, CSA:*
GENERAL LISTINGS: *Gettysburg,* GETTY:12[68]246, *in order of battle,* B&G:APR/94[10]558, B&G:APR/95[8]595, *Savannah,* B&G:FEB/91[8]439, *photos;* B&G:FEB/91[8]439, B&G:FEB/93[24]512

ADDITIONAL LISTINGS: ACW:JUL/92[41]370, B&G:FEB/93[24]512, CWM:JUL/92[16]428

YOUNG, SMITH, *Private, 6th Wisconsin Infantry,* GETTY:11[57]233

YOUNG, THOMAS, *Master, USN;* AHI:JAN/83[10]232

YOUNG, WILLIAM C., *Captain, USA;* ACW:MAR/93[55]408, B&G:AUG/95[8]604

YOUNG, WILLIAM H., *Colonel, USA;* GETTY:13[89]260

YOUNGER, COLEMAN:
GENERAL LISTINGS: *in book review,* ACW:JUL/95[58], *letters to the editor,* B&G:DEC/92[6]502, CWTI:MAY/94[12]379, *photo;* ACW:JAN/93[26]395

ADDITIONAL LISTINGS: ACW:MAR/94[6]455, B&G:JUN/91[32]454, B&G:OCT/91[11]466, CWTI:JAN/94[29]360

YOUNGER, JIM; ACW:MAR/94[6]455, B&G:OCT/91[11]466

YOUNGER, JOHN, *Private, 12th U.S. Infantry;* B&G:AUG/93[18]530

YULEE, DAVID L.; ACW:NOV/95[38]556

Z

ZACHARIAS, DANIEL, *Reverend;* ACW:JAN/91[38]287

ZACHARIAS, DAVID, *Private, 5th South Carolina Cavalry;* ACW:JUL/91[50]

ZACHRY, ALFRED, *Private, 3rd Georgia Infantry;* "FIGHTING WITH THE 3D GEORGIA, PART I," CWTI:SEP/94[26]400, "FOUR SHOTS FOR THE CAUSE, PART II," CWTI:DEC/94[32]410

ZACHRY, CHARLES T., *Colonel, CSA;* ACW:MAR/92[46]354

ZAGONYI, CHARLES, *Colonel, USA;* ACW:MAR/92[46]354, B&G:DEC/95[9]615

ZAIZER, JOHN, *Private, 115th Ohio Infantry;* B&G:AUG/95[24]605

ZARVONA, RICHARD T., *Confederate Spy;* ARTICLE: "THE FRENCH LADY," CWTI:MAY/92[29]263

ZEEK, ELIAS A., *Private, 125th Pennsylvania Infantry;* B&G:OCT/95[8]611A

ZEIDERS, JAMES R., *Sergeant, 53rd Pennsylvania Infantry;* GETTY:11[80]235

ZEILEN, JACOB, *Major, USMC;* CWR:VOL2#3[183]140, CWR:VOL2#3[194]141, CWTI:APR/92[14]254

ZENTMEYER, DAVID, *Adjutant, 5th Pennsylvania Reserves;* CWR:VOL4#4[1]177

ZENTMEYER, FRANK, *Major, 5th Pennsylvania Reserves;* CWR:VOL4#4[1]177

ZIEGLER, WILLIAM T., *civilian;* CWTI:DEC/94[42]412

ZIMMERMAN, WILLIAM W., *Private, 19th Indiana Infantry,* GETTY:11[57]233

ZINN, DANIEL W., *Private, 38th Illinois Infantry;* CWTI:DEC/94[12]408

ZISGEN, JOSEPH, *Private, 16th New York Cavalry;* CWTI:JUN/95[26]445

ZOLLICOFFER, FELIX, *General, CSA:*
ARTICLES: "THE CAMPAIGN AND BATTLE OF MILL SPRINGS," B&G:FEB/93[12]511, "NORTH'S FIRST VICTORY," ACW:SEP/93[38]434

ADDITIONAL LISTINGS: ACW:JUL/91[26]313, ACW:JUL/92[22]368, B&G:FEB/92[40]479, B&G:JUN/92[46]490, B&G:FEB/93[40]514, B&G:DEC/93[52]548, CWM:JAN/93[35]460, CWR:VOL4#1[1]163, *photos;* ACW:SEP/93[38]434, AHI:NOV/73[18]151, B&G:FEB/93[12]511

ZOOK, SAMUEL K., *General, USA:*
GENERAL LISTINGS: *Gettysburg,* GETTY:4[113]153, GETTY:5[35]159, GETTY:6[59]174, GETTY:8[53]203, GETTY:10[53]225, GETTY:11[80]235, GETTY:12[24]242, *in book review,* CWNEWS:SEP/92[4]

ADDITIONAL LISTINGS: ACW:MAY/94[12]466, CWR:VOL4#4[47]179, CWTI:SEP/90[26]174

ZYLA, ANTHONY, *Chaplain, 39th New York Infantry;* ACW:MAY/95[54]528

THE CIVIL WAR TIMES ILLUSTRATED, MINI-INDEX

Listing articles and book reviews from **Civil War Times, Illustrated** *from March, 1989 through December, 1995. Authors of articles will be found in the* CWTI Numerical Listings of Articles *section, while the author of books (book reviews) and the issues where they were published can be found in the* Book Reviews by Title *section.*

A

ADDISON-DARNEILLE, HENRIETTA S.; ARTICLE: "FOR BETTER OR FOR WORSE," CWTI:MAY/92[32]264
AGNEW, SAMUEL A., *Chaplain;* ARTICLE: "CIVILIAN AT BRICE'S CROSS ROADS," CWTI:JAN/94[39]362

ALABAMA TROOPS:
25th Infantry; ARTICLE: "WRITING HOME TO TALLADEGA," CWTI:DEC/90[56]184

ALEXANDER, EDWARD P., *General, CSA:*
ARTICLE: "WHY WE LOST AT GETTYSBURG: EXCERPT FROM *FIGHTING FOR THE CONFEDERACY*," CWTI:SEPT/89[46]132
BOOK REVIEW: *TO GETTYSBURG AND BEYOND: THE PARALLEL LIVES OF JOSHUA LAWRENCE CHAMBERLAIN AND EDWARD PORTER ALEXANDER*
ALTERNATIVE HISTORY; ARTICLE: "WHAT MIGHT HAVE BEEN," CWTI:SEP/94[56]405
AMES, SARAH, *civilian;* ARTICLE: "MRS. AMES AND MR. LINCOLN: HOW A SCULPTOR CAPTURED A GREAT AMERICAN'S SPIRIT IN A STONE AND A PHOTOGRAPH," CWTI:APR/89[28]109
ANALYSIS OF THE WAR; ARTICLE: "THE WAR WE NEVER FINISHED," CWTI:DEC/89[62]139
ANDERSON, ROBERT, *General, USA;* ARTICLE: "ROBERT ANDERSON: RELUCTANT HERO," CWTI:MAY/92[45]266
ANDERSONVILLE NATIONAL MILITARY CEMETERY; ARTICLE: "THE COST OF CAPTURE," CWTI:APR/92[23]255
ANDREWS, JAMES J.; ARTICLE: "AT HOME WITH THE GENERAL," CWTI:FEB/92[10]246
ANDREWS, W.H., *Private, 1st Georgia Infantry;* BOOK REVIEW: *FOOTPRINTS OF A REGIMENT: A RECOLLECTION OF THE 1ST GEORGIA REGULARS*
ANTIETAM, MARYLAND, BATTLE OF:
ARTICLE: "ATTITUDES OF DEATH," CWTI:JUL/92[36]273, "IN HARM'S WAY," CWTI:MAR/93[26]310, "TO BE HELD AT ALL HAZARDS," CWTI:SEP/93[43]338
BOOK REVIEW: *LEE'S TERRIBLE SWIFT SWORD: FROM ANTIETAM TO CHANCELLORSVILLE, AN EYEWITNESS TO HISTORY*

ANTIQUES; ARTICLE: "COLLECTING LINCOLN," CWTI:DEC/95[30]478
APPOMATTOX COURT HOUSE CAMPAIGN, VIRGINIA:
ARTICLES: "THE APPOMATTOX SURRENDER TABLE," CWTI:NOV/93[50]349, "HISTORY COMES HOME," CWTI:MAR/95[20]433, "LAST DAYS OF THE CIVIL WAR: 'SUCCESS WAS EMINENTLY A HAPPY, A GLORIOUS ONE,'" CWTI:AUG/90[26]166
BOOK REVIEW: *OUT OF THE STORM: THE END OF THE CIVIL WAR (APRIL-JUNE 1865)*
APPOMATTOX COURT HOUSE NATIONAL HISTORIC PARK; ARTICLE: "HISTORY COMES HOME," CWTI:MAR/95[20]433
ARKANSAS, STATE OF; BOOK REVIEW: *RAGGED AND SUBLIME: THE CIVIL WAR IN ARKANSAS*
ARMAMENT; ARTICLE: "LINCOLN'S SECRET ARMS RACE," CWTI:OCT/95[32]468
ARMISTEAD, LEWIS A., *General, CSA;* ARTICLE: "WHO WILL FOLLOW ME?," CWTI:JUL/93[29]326
ARMY OF TENNESSEE; BOOK REVIEW: *SOLDIERING IN THE ARMY OF TENNESSEE: A PORTRAIT OF LIFE IN A CONFEDERATE ARMY*

ARTISTS:
ARTICLE: "MINE EYES HAVE SEEN THE GLORY," CWTI:SEP/93[30]336
Carpenter, Francis B.; ARTICLE: "THE PAINTER AND THE PRESIDENT," CWTI:FEB/92[21]247
Kuntsler, Mort; BOOK REVIEW: *IMAGES OF THE CIVIL WAR*
Scott, Julian; ARTICLE: "A SOLDIER'S SKETCHBOOK," CWTI:SEP/91[54]232

ATLANTA, GEORGIA, BATTLE AND CAMPAIGN:
ARTICLE: "THE ATLANTA CAMPAIGN: CHAPTER 1: THE MANEUVERS BEGIN," CWTI:SUMMER/89[13]120, "THE ATLANTA CAMPAIGN: CHAPTER 2: UP AGAINST THE DEFENSES," CWTI:SUMMER/89[20]121, "THE ATLANTA CAMPAIGN: CHAPTER 3: FIGHTING JOHN HOOD," CWTI:SUMMER/89[20]122, "THE ATLANTA CAMPAIGN: CHAPTER 4: THE DEATHS OF FRIENDS AND FOES," CWTI:SUMMER/89[40]123, "THE ATLANTA CAMPAIGN: CHAPTER 5: THE PRIZE I FOUGHT FOR," CWTI:SUMMER/89[50]124, "THE BATTLE THAT SHOULD NOT HAVE BEEN," CWTI:NOV/92[41]291
BOOK REVIEW: *SHROUDS OF GLORY: FROM ATLANTA TO NASHVILLE*
ATLANTA CYCLORAMA; ARTICLE: "ATLANTA'S RESTORED CYCLORAMA," CWTI:FEB/91[18]190

B

BAD OFFICERS; ARTICLE: "HOW TO PICK OUT BAD OFFICERS," CWTI:MAR/91[46]203
BALDWIN, JAMES, *Sergeant, 3rd Arkansas Infantry (Union);* ARTICLE: "A FREEDMAN IN THE UNION ARMY," CWTI:JAN/94[82]366
BALLS BLUFF BATTLEFIELD AND NATIONAL CEMETERY; ARTICLE: "BALL'S BLUFF ABOVE THE POTOMAC," CWTI:JUL/94[20]390

BALL'S BLUFF, VIRGINIA, BATTLE OF; ARTICLE: "BALL'S BLUFF ABOVE THE POTOMAC," CWTI:JUL/94[20]390, "THE DEFINITION OF DISASTER," CWTI:MAY/89[14]114

BALTIMORE, MARYLAND; ARTICLE: "SHADOWS OF CIVIL WAR BALTIMORE," CWTI:OCT/95[24]466

BARTON, CLARA; ARTICLE: "A WOMAN OF VALOR," CWTI:MAR/94[38]372

BATTERY WAGNER, SOUTH CAROLINA, BATTLE OF; BOOK REVIEW: *GATE OF HELL: CAMPAIGN FOR CHARLESTON HARBOR, 1863*

BEAUREGARD, PIERRE G.T., *General, CSA;* ARTICLE: "GUSTAVE," CWTI:JUL/92[29]272

BEAUVOIR, (BILOXI) MISSISSIPPI; ARTICLE: "BEAUVOIR, WHERE THE LEADER OF A LOST REVOLUTION AND SOME OF HIS TROOPS WAITED OUT THEIR DAYS, CWTI:AUG/91[22]215

BELLARD, ALFRED, *Private, 5th New Jersey Infantry;* BOOK REVIEW: *GONE FOR A SOLDIER: THE CIVIL WAR MEMOIRS OF PRIVATE ALFRED BELLARD*

BENJAMIN, SAMUEL N., *Lieutenant, 2nd U.S. Artillery;* ARTICLE: "WE CLEARED THEIR WAY ... FIRING CANISTER," CWTI:MAR/93[20]308

BENNETT PLACE STATE HISTORIC SITE, NORTH CAROLINA; ARTICLE: "BENNETT PLACE: HUMBLE SHRINE TO PEACE," CWTI:APR/90[20]151

BERDAN, HIRAM, *Colonel, USA;* ARTICLES: "DEATH AT A DISTANCE," CWTI:APR/90[48]154, "THE MOST DANGEROUS SET OF MEN," CWTI:JUL/93[42]329

BERDAN'S SHARPSHOOTERS; ARTICLE: "THE MOST DANGEROUS SET OF MEN," CWTI:JUL/93[42]329

BERKELEY PLANTATION; ARTICLE: "McCLELLAN'S PLANTATION," CWTI:JAN/94[20]358

BERMUDA HUNDRED CAMPAIGN; BOOK REVIEW: *BACK DOOR TO RICHMOND: THE BERMUDA HUNDRED CAMPAIGN, APRIL-JUNE 1864*

BERMUDA; ARTICLE: "ISLAND HAVEN FOR A STRUGGLING CONFEDERACY," CWTI:DEC/89[10]133

BLACK CONFEDERATE SOLDIERS; ARTICLE: "ARTICLE BRINGS NOTICE TO A UNIQUE REBEL," CWTI:JUN/90[57]163

BLACK SOLDIERS; ARTICLES: "I WANT YOU TO PROVE YOURSELVES MEN," CWTI:DEC/89[42]137, "THEY ARE INVINCIBLE: TWO BLACK ARMY CHAPLAINS GET A LOOK AT SHERMAN'S ARMY," CWTI:APR/89[32]110

BLACKNALL, CHARLES C., *Colonel 23rd North Carolina Infantry;* ARTICLE: "I'LL LIVE YET TO DANCE ON THAT FOOT," CWTI:MAY/93[26]318

BLAIR, FRANCIS P. JR.; ARTICLE: "SHERMAN'S FEUDING GENERALS," CWTI:MAR/95[40]436

BLAKELY, EDWARD, *Corporal, 63rd Ohio Infantry;* ARTICLE: "OVERCOME BY THE SCARS OF WAR," CWTI:JAN/93[82]304

BLICKENSDERFER, MILTON A., *Sergeant, 126th Ohio Infantry;* ARTICLE: "MEDAL OF HONOR RECIPIENT," CWTI:AUG/95[90]462

BLOCKADE RUNNING; ARTICLE: "THE GREAT GUNBOAT CHASE," CWTI:JUL/94[30]392

BOOK REVIEW: *LIFELINE OF THE CONFEDERACY: BLOCKADE RUNNING DURING THE CIVIL WAR*

BOOTH, JOHN WILKES:
ARTICLES: "A PAPER LINK TO A CONSPIRACY," CWTI:SEP/91[15]225, "CHILDHOOD HOME OF AN AMERICAN ARCH-VILLAIN," CWTI:APR/90[12]150,

"EYEWITNESSES REMEMBER THE "FEARFUL NIGHT" CWTI:MAR/93[12]307, "HERITAGE OR HOAX?," CWTI:SEP/94[24]399, "HISTORIANS OPPOSE OPENING OF BOOTH GRAVE," CWTI:JUN/95[26]445, "LINCOLN'S MURDER: THE SIMPLE CONSPIRACY THEORY," CWTI:DEC/91[28]239, "MORAL VICTORY IN THE CRUSADE TO CLEAR MUDD," CWTI:MAY/93[12]316, "WHAT REALLY HAPPENED TO THE ASSASSIN?," CWTI:JUL/92[50]275, "WHATEVER BECAME OF BOSTON CORBETT?," CWTI:MAY/91[48]211

BOOK REVIEW: *APRIL '65: CONFEDERATE COVERT ACTION IN THE AMERICAN CIVIL WAR*

BRAGG, BRAXTON, *General, CSA:*
ARTICLES: "A FEW ARE HOLDING OUT UP YONDER," CWTI:SEP/92[31]281, "A WADE IN THE HIGH TIDE AT PERRYVILLE," CWTI:NOV/92[18]289, "MIRACLE OF THE RAILS," CWTI:SEP/92[22]279, "TIME LAPSE," CWTI:MAR/89[34]104, "TO SAVE AN ARMY," CWTI:SEP/94[40]403

BOOK REVIEW: *JEFFERSON DAVIS AND HIS GENERALS: THE FAILURE OF CONFEDERATE COMMAND IN THE WEST*

BRANDY STATION, VIRGINIA, BATTLE OF; ARTICLE: "BATTLE OF BRANDY STATION," CWTI:JUN/90[32]159

BRANDY STATION FOUNDATION; ARTICLES: "BEHIND THE LINES," CWTI:FEB/91[6]187, "IRRECONCILABLE DIFFERENCES," CWTI:JAN/94[42]363

BRANDY STATION PRESERVATION; ARTICLE: "A NEW BATTLE FLARES AT BRANDY STATION," CWTI:JUN/90[43]160, "BEHIND THE LINES," CWTI:NOV/93[8]344, "FLANK ATTACK," CWTI:JUL/94[38]393, "IRRECONCILABLE DIFFERENCES," CWTI:JAN/94[42]363

BRAZIL CONFEDERATES; ARTICLE: "OS CONFEDERADOS," CWTI:JAN/93[26]299

BREVET PROMOTION SYSTEM; ARTICLE: "A PROBLEM OF RANK," CWTI:FEB/91[52]195

BRICE'S CROSS ROADS, MISSISSIPPI, BATTLE OF; ARTICLE: "A CIVILIAN AT BRICE'S CROSS ROADS," CWTI:JAN/94[39]362

BROWN, HENRY; *Private, black Confederate soldier;* ARTICLE: "ARTICLE BRINGS NOTICE TO A UNIQUE REBEL," CWTI:JUN/90[57]163

BROWN, JOHN; ARTICLE: "A VISIT TO JOHN BROWN COUNTRY," CWTI:JUL/92[20]271

BROWN, JOSEPH E.; ARTICLE: "AN ARMY OF HIS OWN," CWTI:DEC/94[49]413

BUCKNER, SIMON B., *General, CSA;* ARTICLE: "A CONVERSATION WITH THE PAST," CWTI:APR/90[56]155

BUELL, DON C., *General, USA;* ARTICLE: "A WADE IN THE HIGH TIDE AT PERRYVILLE," CWTI:NOV/92[18]289

BUFORD, NAPOLEON BONAPARTE, *General, USA;* ARTICLE: "NAPOLEON BONAPARTE: THE OTHER BUFORD," CWTI:DEC/94[82]418

BURNSIDE, AMBROSE E. *General, USA;* ARTICLE: "BURNSIDE'S GEOGRAPHY CLASS, by George Skoch, CWTI:JAN/95[34]427, "REMNANTS OF CIVIL WAR KNOXVILLE," CWTI:MAY/94[50]386

BUTLER, BENJAMIN F., *General, USA;* ARTICLE: "THE BEAST OF NEW ORLEANS," CWTI:MAY/93[29]319

BOOK REVIEW: *CONFEDERATE GOLIATH: THE BATTLE OF FORT FISHER*

C

CALAIS, MAINE; ARTICLE: "THE GREAT REBEL RAID ON CALAIS, MAINE," CWTI:SEP/92[40]282

CALIFORNIA, STATE OF; ARTICLE: "A.K. SMILEY LIBRARY: A SHRINE IN THE GOLDEN STATE," CWTI:MAY/92[20]262, "REBEL PIRATES AND CALIFORNIA GOLD," CWTI:JUN/95[48]448, "TRACES OF A DISTANT WAR," CWTI:JUN/95[51]449

CAMERON, SIMON; *Secretary of War;* ARTICLE: "HE WOULD STEAL?," CWTI:JUN/90[46]161

CANADA; ARTICLE: "MONTREAL'S POSH REBEL RENDEVOUS," CWTI:JAN/93[44]302, "STOLEN SOLDIERS, CWTI:JUN/95[56]450

CANBY, EDWARD R.S., *General, USA;* ARTICLE: "BATTLE FOR THE RIO GRANDE," CWTI:OCT/95[56]471

CARPENTER, FRANCIS B., *artist;* ARTICLE: "THE PAINTER AND THE PRESIDENT," CWTI:FEB/92[21]247

CARPETBAGGERS; BOOK REVIEW: *THE INVISIBLE EMPIRE*

CARTER, ISABEL B.; ARTICLE: "PRAYING FOR SOUTHERN VICTORY," CWTI:MAR/91[12]198

CASHNER, JOHN JR., *Private, 13th Indiana Infantry;* ARTICLE: "TIME LAPSE," CWTI:SEP/90[74]180

CATLETT'S STATION, VIRGINIA, RAID ON; ARTICLE: "STUART'S REVENGE," CWTI:JUN/95[38]447

CAVALRY WARFARE; ARTICLE: "BOOTS AND SADDLES: PART I: THE EASTERN THEATER," CWTI:APR/92[35]257, "BOOTS AND SADDLES: PART II: THE WESTERN THEATER," CWTI:MAY/92[48]267

CEDAR MOUNTAIN, VIRGINIA, BATTLE OF; BOOK REVIEW: *STONEWALL JACKSON AT CEDAR MOUNTAIN*

CHAMBERLAIN, JOSHUA L., *General, USA;* BOOK REVIEW: *"BAYONET! FORWARD": MY CIVIL WAR REMINISCENCES * IN THE HANDS OF PROVIDENCE: JOSHUA L. CHAMBERLAIN AND THE AMERICAN CIVIL WAR * TO GETTYSBURG AND BEYOND: THE PARALLEL LIVES OF JOSHUA LAWRENCE CHAMBERLAIN AND EDWARD PORTER ALEXANDER*

CHAMPION HILL, MISSISSIPPI, BATTLE OF; ARTICLE: "A HILL OF DEATH," CWTI:MAY/91[24]208, "A MISSISSIPPI HOME STANDS, A SILENT WITNESS TO A BATTLE," CWTI:MAY/91[18]207

CHANCELLORSVILLE, VIRGINIA, BATTLE OF:
ARTICLE: "COMPLETELY OUTGENERALLED," CWTI:AUG/95[24]455
BOOK REVIEW: *LEE'S TERRIBLE SWIFT SWORD: FROM ANTIETAM TO CHANCELLORSVILLE, AN EYEWITNESS TO HISTORY*

CHANTILLY, VIRGINIA, BATTLE OF; ARTICLE: "WE CLEARED THEIR WAY ... FIRING CANISTER," CWTI:MAR/93[20]308

CHAPMAN, WILLIAM H., *Lieutenant Colonel, Dixie Artillery;* ARTICLE: "TIME LAPSE," CWTI:DEC/90[90]186

CHARLESTON, South Carolina; ARTICLE: "TO HONOR THE DEAD: A PROPER BURIAL IN CHARLESTON," CWTI:MAR/94[59]376

CHATTANOOGA, GEORGIA, BATTLE AND SIEGE OF:
ARTICLE: "GUNBOATS ON THE UPPER TENNESSEE," CWTI:MAY/93[38]321, "MIRACLE OF THE RAILS," CWTI:SEP/92[22]279, "TO SAVE AN ARMY," CWTI:SEP/94[40]403

BOOK REVIEW: *CHICKAMAUGA & CHATTANOOGA: THE BATTLES THAT DOOMED THE CONFEDERACY * THE SHIPWRECK OF THEIR HOPES: THE BATTLES FOR CHATTANOOGA*

CHICKAMAUGA, GEORGIA, BATTLE OF:
ARTICLE: "A FEW ARE HOLDING OUT UP YONDER," CWTI:SEP/92[31]281, "A FORGOTTEN ACCOUNT OF CHICKAMAUGA," CWTI:SEP/93[53]340
BOOK REVIEWS: *CHICKAMAUGA & CHATTANOOGA: THE BATTLES THAT DOOMED THE CONFEDERACY * GUIDE TO THE BATTLE OF CHICKAMAUGA * THE SHIPWRECK OF THEIR HOPES: THE BATTLES FOR CHATTANOOGA*

CHILTON, ROBERT H., *Colonel, CSA;* ARTICLE: "CONDUCT UNBECOMING," CWTI:MAR/95[60]439

CHRISTIAN, WILLIAM E., *Sergeant, 8th Michigan Infantry;* ARTICLE: "WOUNDED AT THE CRATER," CWTI:MAY/91[74]212

CIVIL WAR ART; ARTICLE: "THE 'CENTURY' ART: WHAT WAR LOOKED LIKE," CWTI:SEP/90[28]175

CIVILIANS; ARTICLES: "THE CITY OF BROTHERLY HOSPITALITY," CWTI:MAY/94[24]381, "FOR BETTER OR FOR WORSE," CWTI:MAY/92[32]264, "IN HARM'S WAY," CWTI:MAR/93[26]310

CLEBURNE, PATRICK R. *General, CSA;* ARTICLE: "TO SAVE AN ARMY," CWTI:SEP/94[40]403

CLEVELAND, GROVER; ARTICLE: "GROVER CLEVELAND AND THE REBEL BANNERS," CWTI:SEP/93[22]335

CODE BREAKING; ARTICLE: "CODE-CRACKERS," CWTI:AUG/95[46]459

COINS; ARTICLE: "U.S. MINT TO RELEASE CIVIL WAR COINS," CWTI:JUN/95[10]442

COKER HOUSE, MISSISSIPPI; (CHAMPION HILL BATTLEFIELD), ARTICLE: "A MISSISSIPPI HOME STANDS, A SILENT WITNESS TO A BATTLE," CWTI:MAY/91[18]207

COLD HARBOR, VIRGINIA, BATTLE OF; BOOK REVIEW: *BLOODY ROADS SOUTH: THE WILDERNESS TO COLD HARBOR, MAY-JUNE 1864*

COLLIER, EDWARD T.; *Private, 3rd Massachusetts Infantry;* ARTICLE: "RUSHED TO THE FRONT," CWTI:JAN/95[82]430

COLSTON, RALEIGH E., *General, CSA;* ARTICLE: "CONVERSATION IN CONFIDENCE," CWTI:JAN/95[20]422

COMMAND AND LEADERSHIP; BOOK REVIEW: *LEADERSHIP AND COMMAND IN THE AMERICAN CIVIL WAR * PARTNERS IN COMMAND: THE RELATIONSHIPS BETWEEN LEADERS IN THE CIVIL WAR*

COMMON SOLDIERS:
ARTICLE: "A POETIC PLEA FROM PRISON," CWTI:MAR/91[28]200
BOOK REVIEWS: *GONE FOR A SOLDIER: THE CIVIL WAR MEMOIRS OF PRIVATE ALFRED BELLARD * THE BROTHER'S WAR: CIVIL WAR LETTERS TO THEIR LOVED ONES FROM THE BLUE AND GRAY * HARDTACK & COFFEE: THE UNWRITTEN STORY OF ARMY LIFE * SOLDIERING IN THE ARMY OF TENNESSEE: A PORTRAIT OF LIFE IN A CONFEDERATE ARMY*

COMPUTERS; ARTICLE: "CIVIL WAR N CYBERSPACE," CWTI:OCT/95[40]469

CONFEDERATE GENERALS; ARTICLE: "YOU HAD DONE ME A GREAT INJUSTICE," CWTI:MAR/93[40]312

CONFEDERATE GOVERNMENT:
ARTICLE: "THE VICE PRESIDENT RESIDES IN GEORGIA," CWTI:FEB/91[36]193

BOOK REVIEW: *A GOVERNMENT OF OUR OWN: THE MAKING OF THE CONFEDERACY * FINANCIAL FAILURE AND CONFEDERATE DEFEAT*

CONFEDERATES IN BRAZIL; ARTICLE: "OS CONFEDERADOS," CWTI:JAN/93[26]299

CONGRESS, FEDERAL; BOOK REVIEW: *THE CONGRESSMAN'S CIVIL WAR*

CONSCRIPTION, FEDERAL:
ARTICLES: "WHO ARE EXEMPT," CWTI:SEP/93[50]339, "HOLIDAY IN NEW YORK," CWTI:NOV/92[49]292, "'TIL THE PAPER WORK IS DONE CWTI:NOV/93[78]354
BOOK REVIEW: *WE NEED MEN: THE UNION DRAFT IN THE CIVIL WAR*

CORBETT, BOSTON; ARTICLE: "WHATEVER BECAME OF BOSTON CORBETT?," CWTI:MAY/91[48]211

THE "CRATER", PETERSBURG, VIRGINIA, BATTLE OF:
ARTICLE: "BURY THEM IF THEY WON'T MOVE (EXCERPT FROM *MOTHER, MAY YOU NEVER SEE THE SIGHTS I HAVE SEEN),"* CWTI:APR/90[24]152, "WOUNDED AT THE CRATER" CWTI:MAY/91[74]212
BOOK REVIEW: *GLORY ENOUGH FOR ALL * THE LAST CITADEL: PETERSBURG, VIRGINIA, JUNE 1864-APRIL 1865 * ON FIELDS OF FURY: FROM THE WILDERNESS TO THE CRATER, AN EYEWITNESS HISTORY*

CRAVEN, THOMAS T., *Commodore, USN;* ARTICLE: "THE DILEMMA OF COMMODORE CRAVEN," CWTI:DEC/94[34]411

CROSS KEYS, VIRGINIA, BATTLE OF; ARTICLE: "LIVING ON A CIVIL WAR BATTLEFIELD," CWTI:JAN/95[22]423

CROSS, EDWARD E., *Colonel, 5th New Hampshire Infantry;* ARTICLE: "COMPLETELY OUTGENERALLED," CWTI:AUG/95[24]455

CUSTER, GEORGE A., *General, USA;* ARTICLE: "THE APPOMATTOX SURRENDER TABLE," CWTI:NOV/93[50]349, "CUSTER'S LONG SUMMER," CWTI:MAY/93[35]320

D

DARLINGTON, SOUTH CAROLINA; ARTICLE: "ARTICLE BRINGS NOTICE TO A UNIQUE REBEL

DAVIS, JEFFERSON:
ARTICLES: *A REASON TO LOATHE DAVIS* CWTI:AUG/91[68]222, "AN ARMY OF HIS OWN," CWTI:DEC/94[49]413, "BEAUVOIR, WHERE THE LEADER OF A LOST REVOLUTION AND SOME OF HIS TROOPS WAITED OUT THEIR DAYS," CWTI:AUG/91[22]215, 'DAVIS' LAST RIDE TO RICHMOND," CWTI:MAR/93[32]311, "THE FIRST AND ONLY CONFEDERATE PRESIDENT," CWTI:AUG/91[36]217, "THE GREAT PHILOSOPHICAL COLLISION," CWTI:AUG/91[52]219, "HIS NATION'S COMMANDER IN CHIEF," CWTI:AUG/91[46]218, "JEFF DAVIS' LIVING TOMB" CWTI:MAY/93[20]317, "KING JEFF THE FIRST," CWTI:AUG/91[58]220, "THE VICE PRESIDENT RESIDES IN GEORGIA," CWTI:FEB/91[36]193, "WE WILL VINDICATE THE RIGHT: AN ACCOUNT OF THE LIFE OF JEFFERSON DAVIS," CWTI:AUG/91[29]216, "THE WILL TO WIN AND DENYING REALITY," CWTI:AUG/91[62]221
BOOK REVIEW: *JEFFERSON DAVIS AND HIS GENERALS: THE FAILURE OF CONFEDERATE COMMAND IN THE WEST*

DAVIS, VARINA H.; ARTICLE: "BEAUVOIR, WHERE THE LEADER OF A LOST REVOLUTION AND SOME OF HIS TROOPS WAITED OUT THEIR DAYS," CWTI:AUG/91[22]215

DAVIS, WILLIAM, *Private, 7th Indiana Infantry;* ARTICLE: "WHILE FATHER WAS WITH US," CWTI:NOV/93[24]346

DAY, WILLIAM, *Private, 54th North Carolina Infantry;* ARTICLE: "A LOYAL FAMILY MAN," CWTI:DEC/91[82]243

DEATH; ARTICLE: "ATTITUDES OF DEATH," CWTI:JUL/92[36]273

DIXIE ARTILLERY; ARTICLE: "TIME LAPSE," CWTI:DEC/90[90]186

DODGE, GRENVILLE M. *General, USA;* ARTICLE: "SHERMAN'S FEUDING GENERALS," CWTI:MAR/95[40]436

DOGS; ARTICLE: "FAITHFUL FRIENDS," CWTI:MAR/95[46]437

DOUGLASS, FREDERICK; BOOK REVIEW: *FREDERICK DOUGLASS * FREDERICK DOUGLASS: AUTOBIOGRAPHIES*

DOWLING, RICHARD, *Lieutenant, CSA;* ARTICLE: "SIX GUNS AGAINST THE FLEET,:" CWTI:DEC/90[29]182

DRAFT AND DRAFT RIOTS; see listings under "CONSCRIPTION"

DROOP MOUNTAIN, WEST VIRGINIA, BATTLE OF; ARTICLE: "A BATTLE AT DROOP MOUNTAIN: THE CONFEDERATES' LAST STAND IN WEST VIRGINIA," CWTI:MAR/89[16]101

DRUM BARRACKS; ARTICLE: "LOS ANGELES' DRUM BARRACKS," CWTI:SEP/91[18]227

DUELS; ARTICLE: "YOU HAD DONE ME A GREAT INJUSTICE," CWTI:MAR/93[40]312

DURHAM, NORTH CAROLINA; ARTICLE: "BENNETT PLACE: HUMBLE SHRINE TO PEACE," CWTI:APR/90[20]151

E

EARLY, JUBAL A. *General, CSA:*
ARTICLE: "THE FORGOTTEN BATTLE FOR THE CAPITAL," CWTI:JAN/93[40]301
BOOK REVIEW: *JUBAL: THE LIFE AND TIMES OF GENERAL JUBAL A. EARLY, C.S.A., DEFENDER OF THE LOST CAUSE * JUBAL EARLY'S RAID ON WASHINGTON, 1864*

EMACK, JAMES WILLIAM, *Lieutenant, 7th North Carolina Infantry;* ARTICLE: "TIME LAPSE," CWTI:SEP/92[82]286

EMANCIPATION PROCLAMATION; ARTICLE: "WAS LINCOLN THE GREAT EMANCIPATOR?" CWTI:MAY/94[46]385

F

FARRAGUT, DAVID G., *Admiral, USN;* ARTICLE: "GUARDIANS OF MOBILE BAY," CWTI:MAR/94[20]369

FEATHER, STEPHEN, *Private, 83rd Pennsylvania Infantry;* ARTICLE: "TIME LAPSE," CWTI:FEB/92[58]251

FERGUSON, CHAMP; BOOK REVIEW: *CHAMP FERGUSON, CONFEDERATE GUERILLA*

FINANACE; BOOK REVIEW: *FINANCIAL FAILURE AND CONFEDERATE DEFEAT*

FLAGS; ARTICLE: "GROVER CLEVELAND AND THE REBEL BANNERS," CWTI:SEP/93[22]335

FONDA, TEN EYCK HILTON; *telegrapher;* ARTICLE: "A MIDNIGHT RIDE," CWTI:MAR/94[24]370

FONTAINE, LAMAR, *Major, CSA;* ARTICLE: "A LIFE STORY LARGER THAN LIFE," CWTI:JUN/90[74]164

FORD'S THEATER, WASHINGTON, D.C.; ARTICLES: "EYEWITNESSES REMEMBER THE 'FEARFUL NIGHT,'" CWTI:MAR/93[12]307, "HERITAGE OR HOAX?" CWTI:SEP/94[24]399, "THE LIVELY PAGEANTRY OF DEATH," CWTI:DEC/95[90]483, "WHAT REALLY HAPPENED TO THE ASSASSIN?" CWTI:JUL/92[50]275

FOREIGN AFFAIRS; ARTICLES: "MONTREAL'S POSH REBEL RENDEVOUS," CWTI:JAN/93[44]302, "THE PRISONER AND THE PRIME MINISTER," CWTI:JUL/93[38]328, "RUMORS OF WAR: RUSSIAN BATTLE FLEETS VISIT UNION PORTS IN 1863," CWTI:MAY/89[28]117, "THEY CAME TO WATCH," CWTI:DEC/94[73]416

FORREST, NATHAN B., *General, CSA:*
ARTICLES: "A CIVILIAN AT BRICE'S CROSS ROADS," CWTI:JAN/94[39]362, "A LEGACY OF CONTROVERSY: FORT PILLOW STILL STANDS," CWTI:SEP/93[18]334, "BETWIXT WIND AND WATER," CWTI:NOV/93[65]351, "THE GREAT DECEIVER: THE LIFE OF NATHAN BEDFORD FORREST," CWTI:NOV/93[33]347, "I HEREBY TENDER YOU MY SERVICES," CWTI:SEP/93[62]342, "LEADER OF THE KLAN: THE LIFE OF NATHAN BEDFORD FORREST," CWTI:JAN/94[35]361, "MILLIONAIRE REBEL RAIDER: THE LIFE OF NATHAN BEDFORD FORREST," CWTI:SEP/93[59]341, "WE WILL ALWAYS STAND BY YOU," CWTI:NOV/93[71]352
BOOK REVIEW: *A BATTLE FROM THE START: THE LIFE OF NATHAN BEDFORD FORREST * UNERRING FIRE: THE MASSACRE AT FORT PILLOW*

FORSYTH, GEORGE A., *Captain, USA;* BOOK REVIEW: *HERO OF BEECHER ISLAND: THE LIFE AND MILITARY CAREER OF GEORGE A. FORSYTH*

FORT BLAKELY, ALABAMA; ARTICLE: "FROZEN IN TIME," CWTI:DEC/94[24]409

FORT DELAWARE; ARTICLE: "FORT DELAWARE ON THE WATER: A MONUMENT TO RUGGED REBELS," CWTI:JUL/93[20]325

FORT FISHER, NORTH CAROLINA; BOOK REVIEW: *CONFEDERATE GOLIATH: THE BATTLE OF FORT FISHER*

FORT GAINES, ALABAMA; ARTICLE: "GUARDIANS OF MOBILE BAY," CWTI:MAR/94[20]369

FORT MCALLISTER, GEORGIA; ARTICLE: "GATEWAY TO THE ATLANTIC," CWTI:DEC/94[62]415

FORT MONROE, VIRGINIA; ARTICLE: "JEFF DAVIS' LIVING TOMB," CWTI:MAY/93[20]317

FORT MORGAN, ALABAMA; ARTICLE: "GUARDIANS OF MOBILE BAY," CWTI:MAR/94[20]369

FORT PILLOW MASSACRE:
ARTICLE: "A LEGACY OF CONTROVERSY: FORT PILLOW STILL STANDS," CWTI:SEP/93[18]334, "BETWIXT WIND AND WATER," CWTI:NOV/93[65]351, "WE WILL ALWAYS STAND BY YOU," CWTI:NOV/93[71]352
BOOK REVIEW: *UNERRING FIRE: THE MASSACRE AT FORT PILLOW*

FORT PILLOW STATE HISTORIC AREA; ARTICLE: "A LEGACY OF CONTROVERSY: FORT PILLOW STILL STANDS," CWTI:SEP/93[18]334

FORT POINT, CALIFORNIA; ARTICLE: "TRACES OF A DISTANT WAR," CWTI:JUN/95[51]449

FORT STEDMAN, VIRGINIA, BATTLE OF; ARTICLE: "BATTLE IN DESPERATION," CWTI:MAR/95[33]435

FORT SUMTER, SOUTH CAROLINA, BATTLE OF:
ARTICLE: "GUSTAVE," CWTI:JUL/92[29]272, "ROBERT ANDERSON: RELUCTANT HERO," CWTI:MAY/92[45]266
BOOK REVIEW: *SUMTER: THE FIRST DAY OF THE CIVIL WAR*

FORT WAGNER, SOUTH CAROLINA; see listings under **"BATTERY WAGNER"**

FRANKLIN, TENNESSEE, BATTLE OF; BOOK REVIEW: *EMBRACE AN ANGRY WIND—THE CONFEDERACY'S LAST HURRAH: SPRING HILL, FRANKLIN, AND NASHVILLE * SHROUDS OF GLORY: FROM ATLANTA TO NASHVILLE*

FREDERICKSBURG, VIRGINIA, BATTLE OF:
ARTICLE: "DESPERATE COURAGE", CWTI:DEC/90[58]185
BOOK REVIEW: *LEE'S TERRIBLE SWIFT SWORD: FROM ANTIETAM TO CHANCELLORSVILLE, AN EYEWITNESS TO HISTORY*

FREMONT, JOHN C.; *General, USA;* ARTICLE: "A SINGLE STEP," CWTI:MAR/94[29]371

G

GAINES' MILL, VIRGINIA, BATTLE OF; ARTICLE: "CHARGE BAYONETS," CWTI:MAY/94[31]382

GALVANIZED YANKEES; ARTICLE: "A SOLDIER FOR TWO COUNTRIES," CWTI:MAR/95[90]440

GARFIELD, JAMES A., *General, USA,* ARTICLE: "BEHIND THE LINES," CWTI:AUG/90[8]165

GATLING GUNS; ARTICLE: "THE SEARCH FOR THE ULTIMATE WEAPON," CWTI:JAN/93[49]303

GENEALOGY; BOOK REVIEW: *GENEALOGY ONLINE: RESEARCHING YOUR ROOTS*

GENERALS, CONFEDERATE; ARTICLE: "YOU HAD DONE ME A GREAT INJUSTICE," CWTI:MAR/93[40]312

GENERALS, FEDERAL; BOOK REVIEW: *LINCOLN'S GENERALS*

GEORGIA MILITARY INSTITUTE; ARTICLE: "TRAINING IN TREASON," CWTI:SEP/91[23]228

GEORGIA TROOPS:
1st Infantry, BOOK REVIEW: *FOOTPRINTS OF A REGIMENT: A RECOLLECTION OF THE 1ST GEORGIA REGULARS*

GETTYSBURG NATIONAL MILITARY PARK; ARTICLE: "WHERE DID SEMINARY RIDGE GO?," CWTI:APR/92[42]259

GETTYSBURG PRESERVATION; ARTICLE: "BATTLE ON THE BRICKYARD WALL," CWTI:SEP/94[34]402, "CONGRESS QUESTIONS GETTYSBURG LAND DEAL," CWTI:SEP/94[28]401

GETTYSBURG, PENNSYLVANIA, BATTLE OF:
ARTICLES: "A REFUGEE FROM GETTYSBURG," CWTI:DEC/89[16]134, "A TOURIST AT GETTYSBURG," CWTI:SEP/90[26]174, "BATTLE ON THE BRICKYARD WALL," CWTI:SEP/94[34]402, "GEORGE PICKETT: ANOTHER LOOK," CWTI:JUL/94[44]394, "GOING BACK INTO THE UNION AT LAST," CWTI:FEB/91[12]189, "I HAVE A GREAT CONTEMPT FOR HISTORY," CWTI:SEP/91[31]229, "PICKETT'S CHARGE BY THE NUMBERS,"

CWTI:JUL/93[34]327, "SEMINARY RIDGE TO REMAIN UNRESTORED," CWTI:SEP/93[38]337, "WHO LOST SEMINARY RIDGE?" CWTI:JAN/93[35]300, "WHO WILL FOLLOW ME?," CWTI:JUL/93[29]326

BOOK REVIEW: *THE BATTLE OF GETTYSBURG * GETTYSBURG: A MEDITATION ON WAR AND VALUES * GETTYSBURG: CULP'S HILL AND CEMETERY HILL * THE THIRD DAY AT GETTYSBURG AND BEYOND*

GLADDEN, ADLEY H., *General, CSA;* ARTICLE: "A FORGOTTEN REBEL GENERAL," CWTI:MAR/93[50]313

GLORIETA PASS; ARTICLE: "TO HONOR THE DEAD: LAST TAPS AT LA GLORIETA PASS," CWTI:MAR/94[58]375

GOLDEN GATE NATIONAL RECREATION AREA, CALIFORNIA; ARTICLE: "TRACES OF A DISTANT WAR," CWTI:JUN/95[51]449

GORDON, JOHN B., *General, CSA;* ARTICLE: "BATTLE IN DESPERATION," CWTI:MAR/95[33]435

GOVERNMENT, CONFEDERATE; BOOK REVIEWS: *A GOVERNMENT OF OUR OWN: THE MAKING OF THE CONFEDERACY * FINANCIAL FAILURE AND CONFEDERATE DEFEAT*

GRAND ARMY OF THE REPUBLIC; ARTICLE: "G.A.R. MUSEUM IS A TREASURY OF WAR RELICS," CWTI:SEP/90[22]173

GRANT, ULYSSES S., *General, USA:*
ARTICLES: "A CONVERSATION WITH THE PAST," CWTI:APR/90[56]155, "A HILL OF DEATH," CWTI:MAY/91[24]208, "A UNION HERO'S FORGOTTEN RESTING PLACE," CWTI:FEB/90[12]141, "BATTLE IN DESPERATION" CWTI:MAR/95[33]435, "BURNING DOWN THE SOUTH," CWTI:OCT/95[48]470, "CROSSED WIRES," CWTI:DEC/94[57]414, "THE GRACIOUS VICTOR," CWTI:FEB/90[54]147, "HISTORY COMES HOME," CWTI:MAR/95[20]433, "MIRACLE OF THE RAILS," CWTI:SEP/92[22]279, "TO SAVE AN ARMY," CWTI:SEP/94[40]403, "ULYSSES S. GRANT: A KIND OF NORTHERN HERO," CWTI:FEB/90[32]144, "ULYSSES S. GRANT: AN UNHAPPY CIVILIAN," CWTI:FEB/90[26]143, "ULYSSES S. GRANT: COMMANDER OF ALL UNION ARMIES," CWTI:FEB/90[46]146, "ULYSSES S. GRANT: DIFFICULT LAST DAYS," CWTI:FEB/90[60]148, "ULYSSES S. GRANT: HIS LIFE AND HARD TIMES," CWTI:FEB/90[20]142, "ULYSSES S. GRANT: LEADING THE JUGGERNAUT," CWTI:FEB/90[38]145, "ALL GOES ON LIKE A MIRACLE," CWTI:APR/92[49]260

BOOK REVIEW: *ULYSSES: A BIOGRAPHICAL NOVEL OF U.S. GRANT*

GREELEY, HORACE, ARTICLE: "WHERE DO YOU STAND HORACE GREELEY?" CWTI:DEC/90[50]183

GUERILLA WARFARE:
ARTICLES: "A FIGHT FOR MISSOURI," CWTI:AUG/95[34]457, "THE JAMES BOYS GO TO WAR," CWTI:JAN/94[29]360

BOOK REVIEWS: *APRIL '65: CONFEDERATE COVERT ACTION IN THE AMERICAN CIVIL WAR * CHAMP FERGUSON, CONFEDERATE GUERILLA * INSIDE WAR: THE GUERRILLA CONFLICT IN MISSOURI DURING THE AMERICAN CIVIL WAR*

H

HANCOCK, WINFIELD S., *General, USA;* ARTICLE: "TO BE HELD AT ALL HAZARDS," CWTI:SEP/93[43]338

HANEY, MILTON, *Chaplain, 55th Illinois Infantry;* ARTICLE: "IN THE PULPIT AND IN THE TRENCHES," CWTI:SEP/92[28]280

HARPERS FERRY NATIONAL HISTORICAL PARK; ARTICLE: "A LANDSCAPE THAT GAVE SHAPE TO HISTORY, CWTI:JAN/95[24]424, "A VISIT TO JOHN BROWN COUNTRY," CWTI:JUL/92[20]271

HARPERS FERRY, WEST VIRGINIA, 1859 RAID ON; ARTICLE: "A VISIT TO JOHN BROWN COUNTRY," CWTI:JUL/92[20]271

HARPERS FERRY, WEST VIRGINIA, 1861 RAID ON; ARTICLE: "SCHEMES AND TREACHERY: THE 1861 PLOT TO SEIZE THE ARSENAL AT HARPERS FERRY," CWTI:APR/89[38]111

HARRISON, GEORGE P. Jr., *Colonel, CSA;* ARTICLE: "BEHIND THE LINES," CWTI:JUL/92[62]276

HARVEY, CORDELIA; ARTICLE: "AN ANGEL FROM WISCONSIN: A YANKEE GOVERNOR'S WIDOW DEDICATES HERSELF TO COMFORTING THE WOUNDED," CWTI:MAR/89[20]102

HAYDEN, CHARLES B., *Lieutenant, 2nd Michigan Infantry;* ARTICLE: "FLIGHT TO THE JAMES," CWTI:JUL/93[14]324

HAYES, RUTHERFORD B., *General, USA;* ARTICLE: "THE GLORY YEARS," CWTI:SEP/94[49]404

HERITAGEPAC; ARTICLE: "BEHIND THE LINES," CWTI:JUN/90[6]156

HERNDON, JOHN G., *Private, Charlottesville Artillery;* ARTICLE: "A SCHOOLBOY CAVALRYMAN," CWTI:MAR/91[74]204

HERNDON, THOMAS, *Lieutenant, 14th Tennessee Infantry;* ARTICLE: "A TENNESSEE VOLUNTEER," CWTI:AUG/91[82]223

HERNDON, WILLIAM H.; BOOK REVIEW: *LINCOLN'S HERNDON: A BIOGRAPHY*

HEYER, JACOB, *Captain, 23rd Pennsylvania Infantry;* ARTICLE: "A FIGHTING ZOUAVE," CWTI:JUN/95[90]451

HILL, AMBROSE P., *General, CSA;* ARTICLE: "HILL'S FAVORITE COURIER," CWTI:SEP/92[42]283

HILL, DANIEL H., *General, CSA;* ARTICLE: "I AM SO UNLIKE OTHER FOLKS: THE SOLDIER WHO COULD NOT BE UNDERSTOOD," CWTI:APR/89[14]107

HITCHCOCK, ROBERT E., *Lieutenant, USMC;* ARTICLE: "ONE MARINE'S BRIEF BATTLE," CWTI:APR/92[14]254

HITE, MAXFIELD, *Sergeant, 31st Ohio Infantry;* ARTICLE: "34-YEAR-OLD FATHER OF SEVEN," CWTI:SEP/93[90]343

HOMEFRONT; ARTICLE: "THE CITY OF BROTHERLY HOSPITALITY," CWTI:MAY/94[24]381

HOOD, JOHN B., *General, CSA;* BOOK REVIEW: *JEFFERSON DAVIS AND HIS GENERALS: THE FAILURE OF CONFEDERATE COMMAND IN THE WEST*

HOOKER, JOSEPH E., *General, USA;* ARTICLES: "COMPLETELY OUTGENERALLED," CWTI:AUG/95[24]455, "MIRACLE OF THE RAILS," CWTI:SEP/92[22]279, "SHERMAN'S FEUDING GENERALS," CWTI:MAR/95[40]436

HOPKINS, ANDREW, *Seaman, USN;* ARTICLE: "PRISONER OF CIRCUMSTANCES," CWTI:NOV/92[28]290

HORSES; ARTICLE: "STREET NAMED FOR 'LITTLE SORREL,'" CWTI:APR/92[41]258

HOTCHKISS, JEDEDIAH, *Major, CSA;* ARTICLE: "MAPPING THE CIVIL WAR," CWTI:NOV/92[60]294

HOWARD, OLIVER O., *General, USA;* ARTICLE: "SHERMAN'S FEUDING GENERALS," CWTI:MAR/95[40]436

HOWE, JULIA WARD; ARTICLE: "THE MESSAGE OF JULIA WARD HOWE," CWTI:SEPT/89[40]130

HUDSON, JOHN W., *Lieutenant, 35th Massachusetts Infantry;* ARTICLE: "TIRED SOLDIERS DON'T GO VERY FAST," CWTI:FEB/92[36]249

HUMOR; ARTICLE: "WHO ARE EXEMPT," CWTI:SEP/93[50]339

HUNTER, DAVID, *General, USA;* ARTICLE: "BURNING DOWN THE SOUTH," CWTI:OCT/95[48]470

HUSSEY, WILLIAM H.H., *Lieutenant, 2nd Massachusetts Cavalry;* ARTICLE: "TIME LAPSE," CWTI:APR/90[56]155

I

IF THE SOUTH HAD WON; ARTICLE: "WHAT MIGHT HAVE BEEN," CWTI:SEP/94[56]405

ILLINOIS TROOPS:

58th Infantry; ARTICLE: "IN THE PULPIT AND IN THE TRENCHES," CWTI:SEP/92[28]280

95th Infantry; ARTICLE: "YOUR CHARLIE," CWTI:JAN/93[20]298

INDIANS, (OSAGE); ARTICLE: "HARD ROPE'S CIVIL WAR," CWTI:SEP/90[52]179

IRISH BRIGADE; ARTICLE: "DESPERATE COURAGE," CWTI:DEC/90[58]185

IUKA, MISSISSIPPI, BATTLE OF; ARTICLE: "A FIERCE LITTLE FIGHT IN MISSISSIPPI," CWTI:JUL/94[50]395

J

JACKSON, J. WARREN, *Lieutenant, 8th Louisiana Infantry;* ARTICLE: "GOING BACK INTO THE UNION AT LAST," CWTI:FEB/91[12]189

JACKSON, THOMAS J., *General, CSA:*

ARTICLES: "A SINGLE STEP," CWTI:MAR/94[29]371, "PERSONAL REMINISCENCES OF 'STONEWALL' JACKSON," CWTI:JUN/95[18]444, "STREET NAMED FOR 'LITTLE SORREL'," CWTI:APR/92[41]258, "'STONEWALL' JACKSON'S LAST MARCH: A LAVISH STATE FUNERAL FOR A SOUTHERN HERO," CWTI:MAY/89[22]116

BOOK REVIEW: *THE DESTRUCTIVE WAR: WILLIAM TECUMSEH SHERMAN, STONEWALL JACKSON, AND THE AMERICANS * LOST VICTORIES: THE MILITARY GENIUS OF STONEWALL JACKSON * STONEWALL JACKSON AT CEDAR MOUNTAIN * STONEWALL: A BIOGRAPHY OF GENERAL THOMAS J. JACKSON*

JACKSONVILLE, FLORIDA; ARTICLE: "THE *MAPLE LEAF* ESCAPE," CWTI:JAN/95[42]428

JAMES, FRANK AND JESSE; ARTICLE: "THE JAMES BOYS GO TO WAR," CWTI:JAN/94[29]360

JOHNSON, ADAM R., *General, CSA;* ARTICLE: "FIELDS WITHOUT HONOR: TWO AFFAIRS IN TENNESSEE," CWTI:JUL/92[42]274

JOHNSTON, ALBERT S., *General, CSA;* BOOK REVIEW: *JEFFERSON DAVIS AND HIS GENERALS: THE FAILURE OF CONFEDERATE COMMAND IN THE WEST*

JOHNSTON, JOSEPH E.:

ARTICLES: "THE BATTLE THAT SHOULD NOT HAVE BEEN," CWTI:NOV/92[41]291, "CONVERSATION IN CONFIDENCE," CWTI:JAN/95[20]422

BOOK REVIEW: *JEFFERSON DAVIS AND HIS GENERALS: THE FAILURE OF CONFEDERATE COMMAND IN THE WEST * JOSEPH E. JOHNSTON: A CIVIL WAR BIOGRAPHY*

K

KEMP, DANIEL F., *Seaman, USN;* ARTICLE: "NAVY LIFE ON THE MISSISSIPPI RIVER," CWTI:MAY/94[16]380

KNOXVILLE, TENNESSEE, BATTLE OF; ARTICLE: "REMNANTS OF CIVIL WAR KNOXVILLE," CWTI:MAY/94[50]386

KU KLUX KLAN; ARTICLE: "LEADER OF THE KLAN: THE LIFE OF NATHAN BEDFORD FORREST, PART III," CWTI:JAN/94[35]361

L

LAST DAYS OF THE CIVIL WAR; ARTICLES: "LAST DAYS OF THE CIVIL WAR: 'SUCCESS WAS ANEMINENTLY A HAPPY, A GLORIOUS ONE,'" CWTI:AUG/90[26]166, "LAST DAYS OF THE CIVIL WAR: "THE WHOLE COUNTRY SEEMED TO BE ALIVE WITH DEMONS," CWTI:AUG/90[42]167, "LAST DAYS OF THE CIVIL WAR: 'GOD'S WILL BE DONE,'" CWTI:AUG/90[50]168, "LAST DAYS OF THE CIVIL WAR: 'THE LAST GUN HAD BEEN FIRED,'" CWTI:AUG/90[58]169, "LAST DAYS OF THE CIVIL WAR: 'IT WAS A TERRIBLE CALAMITY BEYOND DESCRIPTION,'" CWTI:AUG/90[64]170, "LAST DAYS OF THE CIVIL WAR: AMERICA LOOKS TO THE FUTURE," CWTI:AUG/90[70]171

LEE, ROBERT E., *General, CSA:*

ARTICLES: "ALL GOES ON LIKE A MIRACLE," CWTI:APR/92[49]260, "BATTLE IN DESPERATION," CWTI:MAR/95[33]435, "HISTORY COMES HOME," CWTI:MAR/95[20]433, "TO BE HELD AT ALL HAZARDS," CWTI:SEP/93[43]338, "STRIKE THE PHRASE 'STRIKE THE TENT,'" CWTI:SEP/90[47]177

BOOK REVIEWS: *ABANDONED BY LINCOLN: A MILITARY BIOGRAPHY OF GENERAL JOHN POPE * THE ARMY OF ROBERT E. LEE * THE COURT MARTIAL OF ROBERT E. LEE: A HISTORICAL NOVEL * LEE CONSIDERED: GENERAL ROBERT E. LEE AND CIVIL WAR HISTORY * LEE'S TERRIBLE SWIFT SWORD: FROM ANTIETAM TO CHANCELLORSVILLE, AN EYEWITNESS TO HISTORY * TO THE GATES OF RICHMOND: THE PENINSULA CAMPAIGN*

LETTERS AND DIARIES:
ARTICLE: "I SHALL BE A PRISONER," CWTI:SEP/91[42]231, "TIRED SOLDIERS DON'T GO VERY FAST," CWTI:FEB/92[36]249
BOOK REVIEW: *GONE FOR A SOLDIER: THE CIVIL WAR MEMOIRS OF PRIVATE ALFRED BELLARD*
Carter, Isabel B., ARTICLE: "PRAYING FOR SOUTHERN VICTORY," CWTI:MAR/91[12]198
Curry, Wilmot W., *Sergeant, USA;* ARTICLE: "TO THE POTOMAC WITH SERGEANT CURRY," CWTI:SEPT/89[24]128
Jackson, J. Warren, ARTICLE: "GOING BACK INTO THE UNION AT LAST," CWTI:FEB/91[12]189
Hayden, Charles B., *Lieutenant, 2nd Michigan Infantry;* ARTICLE: "FLIGHT TO THE JAMES," CWTI:JUL/JUL/93[14]324
Kemp, Daniel F., *Seaman, USN;* ARTICLE: "NAVY LIFE ON THE MISSISSIPPI RIVER," CWTI:MAY/94[16]380
Kent, William; ARTICLE: "A WILDERNESS MEMORY: ONE MORNING, 30 YEARS AFTER THE BATTLE IT ALL CAME BACK TO HIM," CWTI:MAR/89[34]104
Markham, Philo A., *Corporal, 154th New York Infantry;* ARTICLE: "PHILO MARKHAM'S LONG WALK," CWTI:MAR/95[26]434
Matteson, Elisha C., *Private, USA;* ARTICLE: "DEAR SISTER—THEY FIGHT TO WHIP," CWTI:MAY/91[16]206
McCaskey, James, *Private, 100th Pennsylvania Infantry;* ARTICLE: "A SCRATCH WITH THE REBELS," CWTI:JAN/94[49]365
Moore, William H., ARTICLE: "WRITING HOME TO TALLADEGA," CWTI:DEC/90[56]184
Nelson, George W., *Captain, CSA;* ARTICLE: "LETTERS FROM THE HEART," CWTI:OCT/95[28]467
Traweek, Washington B., ARTICLE: "BREAK OUT!," CWTI:DEC/91[26]238
Zachry, Alfred, *Private, 3rd Georgia Infantry;* ARTICLE: "FIGHTING WITH THE 3D GEORGIA, PART I," CWTI:SEP/94[26]400, "FOUR SHOTS FOR THE CAUSE, PART II" CWTI:DEC/94[32]410

LINCOLN, ABRAHAM:
ARTICLES: "A MAN OF SORROWS," CWTI:DEC/95[24]477, "A ROLLING MEMENTO," CWTI:MAR/95[54]438, "A SHRINE IN THE GOLDEN STATE," CWTI:MAY/92[20]262, "COLLECTING LINCOLN," CWTI:DEC/95[30]478, "EYEWITNESSES REMEMBER THE 'FEARFUL NIGHT,'" CWTI:MAR/93[12]307, "THE HAPPIEST DAY OF HIS LIFE," CWTI:DEC/95[76]482, "I MYSELF WAS AT THE FRONT,'" CWTI:FEB/91[28]192, "I SHOULD NOT SAY ANY FOOLISH THINGS,'" CWTI:DEC/95[22]476, "LINCOLN AND THE IRONCLADS COME TO TELEVISION," CWTI:MAR/91[42]202, "LINCOLN'S 'LOST' TELEGRAM," CWTI:MAR/91[22]199, "LINCOLN'S FIRST LOVE," CWTI:DEC/95[40]479, "LINCOLN'S SECRET ARMS RACE," CWTI:OCT/95[32]468, "THE LIVELY PAGEANTRY OF DEATH," CWTI:DEC/95[90]483, "THE MAN AT THE WHITE HOUSE WINDOW," CWTI:DEC/95[52]480, "MINE EYES HAVE SEEN THE GLORY," CWTI:SEP/93[30]336, "OH, DEM BONES, DEM DRY BONES," CWTI:SEP/91[41]230, "THE PAINTER AND THE PRESIDENT," CWTI:FEB/92[21]247, "THE PLAIN TRUTH WAS TOO PLAIN FOR HORACE LURTON," CWTI:DEC/94[79]417, "THE PRESIDENT AT PLAY," CWTI:DEC/95[14]475, "SOME THOUGHTS FOR THE PRESIDENT'S CONSIDERATION," CWTI:SEP/92[46]284, "TRIED BY WAR," CWTI:DEC/95[67]481, "WAS LINCOLN THE GREAT EMANCIPATOR?, CWTI:MAY/94[46]385, "WHAT REALLY HAPPENED TO THE ASSASSIN?," CWTI:JUL/92[50]275, "WHATEVER BECAME OF BOSTON CORBETT?," CWTI:MAY/91[48]211
BOOK REVIEWS: *A RISING THUNDER: FROM LINCOLN'S ELECTION TO THE BATTLE OF BULL RUN, AN EYEWITNESS HISTORY * ABANDONED BY LINCOLN: A MILITARY BIOGRAPHY OF GENERAL JOHN POPE * ABRAHAM LINCOLN AND THE SECOND AMERICAN REVOLUTION * ABRAHAM LINCOLN, 1809-1858 * ABRAHAM LINCOLN, A BIOGRAPHY * ABRAHAM LINCOLN: A HISTORY * BLACK EASTER: THE ASSASSINATION OF ABRAHAM LINCOLN * COLLECTED WORKS OF ABRAHAM LINCOLN * COME RETRIBUTION * THE FACE OF LINCOLN * THE FATE OF LIBERTY: ABRAHAM LINCOLN AND CIVIL LIBERTIES * HERNDON'S LINCOLN: THE TRUE STORY OF A GREAT LIFE * THE HISTORIAN'S LINCOLN: PSEUDOHISTORY, PSYCHOHISTORY AND HISTORY * THE LINCOLN IMAGE * THE LINCOLN MURDER CONSPIRACIES * THE LINCOLN NO ONE KNOWS * LINCOLN * LINCOLN AND HIS GENERALS * LINCOLN AND THE ECONOMICS OF THE AMERICAN DREAM * LINCOLN COLLECTOR * LINCOLN DAY BY DAY * LINCOLN IN PHOTOGRAPHS * LINCOLN THE PRESIDENT * LINCOLN: SPEECHES AND WRITINGS * PRELUDE TO GREATNESS: LINCOLN IN THE 1850'S * THE PRESIDENCY OF ABRAHAM LINCOLN * WILLIAM HENRY SEWARD: LINCOLN'S RIGHT HAND * WITH MALICE TOWARD NONE*

LINCOLN'S ASSASSINATION:
ARTICLES: "A PAPER LINK TO A CONSPIRACY," CWTI:SEP/91[15]225, "BEHIND THE LINES," CWTI:AUG/90[8]165, "EYEWITNESSES REMEMBER THE 'FEARFUL NIGHT,'" CWTI:MAR/93[12]307, "HERITAGE OR HOAX?" CWTI:SEP/94[24]399, "HISTORIANS OPPOSE OPENING OF BOOTH GRAVE," CWTI:JUN/95[26]445, "LINCOLN'S MURDER: THE SIMPLE CONSPIRACY THEORY," CWTI:DEC/91[28]239, "MORAL VICTORY IN THE CRUSADE TO CLEAR MUDD," CWTI:MAY/93[12]316, "WHAT REALLY HAPPENED TO THE ASSASSIN?" CWTI:JUL/92[50]275, "WHATEVER BECAME OF BOSTON CORBETT?," CWTI:MAY/91[48]211
BOOK REVIEWS: *A BULLET FOR LINCOLN * APRIL '65: CONFEDERATE COVERT ACTION IN THE AMERICAN CIVIL WAR * BLACK EASTER: THE ASSASSINATION OF ABRAHAM LINCOLN * OUT OF THE STORM: THE END OF THE CIVIL WAR (APRIL-JUNE 1865)*
LITTLE ROCK, ARKANSAS, REUNION; ARTICLE: "THE GRAY REUNION," CWTI:FEB/92[42]250
LOGAN, JOHN A., *General, USA;* ARTICLE: "SHERMAN'S FEUDING GENERALS CWTI:MAR/95[40]436
LONGSTREET, JAMES, *General, CSA;* ARTICLES: "GENERAL JAMES LONGSTREET," CWTI:NOV/93[55]350, "REMNANTS OF CIVIL WAR KNOXVILLE," CWTI:MAY/94[50]386
LOOKOUT MOUNTAIN, TENNESSEE, BATTLE OF; ARTICLE: "A BATTLE ABOVE THE CLOUDS," CWTI:SEPT/89[30]129
LOOP, CHARLES B., *Major, 95th Illinois Infantry;* ARTICLE: "YOUR CHARLIE," CWTI:JAN/93[20]298

LOUISIANA, STATE OF:
ARTICLE: "GOING BACK INTO THE UNION AT LAST,"
CWTI:FEB/91[12]189
BOOK REVIEW: *GUIDE TO LOUISIANA CONFEDERATE MILITARY UNITS*

LOUISIANA TROOPS:
1st Special Battalion; ARTICLE: "WHEAT'S TIGERS,"
CWTI:MAR/94[48]374
1st Zouave Battalion; ARTICLE: "JEFF DAVIS' PET WOLVES: THE 1ST LOUISIANA ZOUAVE BATTALION DID NOT DESERVE ITS MEAN REPUTATION," CWTI:MAR/89[28]103
8th Infantry; ARTICLE: "GOING BACK INTO THE UNION AT LAST," CWTI:FEB/91[12]189

LURTON, HORACE; ARTICLE: "THE PLAIN TRUTH WAS TOO PLAIN FOR HORACE LURTON," CWTI:DEC/94[79]417
LYON, NATHANIEL, *General, USA;* ARTICLE: "A MIGHTY MEAN-FOWT FIGHT'," CWTI:FEB/92[29]248

M

MACKENZIE, RANALD S., *General, USA;* BOOK REVIEW: *THE MOST PROMISING YOUNG OFFICER: A LIFE OF RANALD SLIDELL MACKENZIE*
MAFFITT, JOHN N., *Captain, CSN;* ARTICLE: "A SON OF OLD NEPTUNE," CWTI:DEC/91[44]241

MAINE TROOPS:
2nd Infantry; BOOK REVIEW: *SECOND TO NONE: THE STORY OF THE 2D MAINE VOLUNTEERS, "THE BANGOR REGIMENT"*
MANASSAS, VIRGINIA, FIRST BATTLE OF; BOOK REVIEW: *A RISING THUNDER: FROM LINCOLN'S ELECTION TO THE BATTLE OF BULL RUN, AN EYEWITNESS HISTORY*
MANASSAS, VIRGINIA, SECOND BATTLE OF:
ARTICLES: "THE BLOODY FIFTH," CWTI:DEC/91[36]240, "WE CLEARED THEIR WAY ... FIRING CANISTER," CWTI:MAR/93[20]
BOOK REVIEW: *ABANDONED BY LINCOLN: A MILITARY BIOGRAPHY OF GENERAL JOHN POPE*
MANGUM, ADOLPHUS W., *Chaplain, 6th North Carolina Infantry;* ARTICLE: "PRISON CHAPLAIN AND HISTORIAN" CWTI:NOV/93[11]
MAPS:
ARTICLE: "MAPPING THE CIVIL WAR," CWTI:NOV/92[60]294
BOOK REVIEWS: *AMERICAN HERITAGE BATTLE MAPS OF THE CIVIL WAR * THE ATLAS OF THE CIVIL WAR * CIVIL WAR NEWSPAPER MAPS: A CARTOBIBLIOGRAPHY OF THE NORTHERN PRESS*
MARCH TO THE SEA; see listings under **"SHERMAN'S MARCH TO THE SEA"**
MARINE CORPS, CONFEDERATE STATES; BOOK REVIEW: *THE CONFEDERATE STATES MARINE CORPS: THE REBEL LEATHERNECKS*
MARKHAM, PHILO A., *Corporal, 154th New York Infantry;* ARTICLE: "PHILO MARKHAM'S LONG WALK," CWTI:MAR/95[26]434

MARSHALL, HUMPHREY; ARTICLE: "TIME LAPSE," CWTI:MAR/89[44]105

MASSACHUSETTS TROOPS:
9th Infantry; ARTICLE: "ON TO PRISON," CWTI:JUN/90[28]158
35th Infantry; ARTICLE: "TIRED SOLDIERS DON'T GO VERY FAST," CWTI:FEB/92[36]249
54th Infantry:
ARTICLE: "I WANT YOU TO PROVE YOURSELVES MEN," CWTI:DEC/89[42]137
BOOK REVIEW: *GATE OF HELL: CAMPAIGN FOR CHARLESTON HARBOR, 1863*
57th Infantry; ARTICLE: "BURY THEM IF THEY WON'T MOVE (EXCERPT FROM *MOTHER, MAY YOU NEVER SEE THE SIGHTS I HAVE SEEN*), CWTI:APR/90[24]152

MATTESON, ELISHA C., *Private, 9th Iowa Infantry;* ARTICLE: "DEAR SISTER—THEY FIGHT TO WHIP," CWTI:MAY/91[16]206
MAURY, WILLIAM L., *Captain, CSN;* ARTICLE: "RELUCTANT RAIDER," CWTI:AUG/95[40]458
McCASKEY, JAMES, *Private, 100th Pennsylvania Infantry;* ARTICLE: "A SCRATCH WITH THE REBELS," CWTI:JAN/94[49]365
McCLELLAN, GEORGE B., *General, USA:*
ARTICLES: "LINCOLN'S 'LOST' TELEGRAM," CWTI:MAR/91[22]199, "MCCLELLAN'S PLANTATION," CWTI:JAN/94[20]358, "TO BE HELD AT ALL HAZARDS," CWTI:SEP/93[43]338
BOOK REVIEW: *TO THE GATES OF RICHMOND: THE PENINSULA CAMPAIGN*
McCULLOCH, BENJAMIN, *General, CSA;* ARTICLE: "A MIGHTY MEAN-FOWT FIGHT," CWTI:FEB/92[29]248
McDONALD, CORNELIA PEAKE; BOOK REVIEW: *A WOMAN'S CIVIL WAR: A DIARY, WITH REMINISCENCES OF THE WAR, FROM MARCH 1862*
McDOWELL, VIRGINIA, BATTLE OF; ARTICLE: "A SINGLE STEP," CWTI:MAR/94[29]371
McKINLEY, WILLIAM; ARTICLE: "BEHIND THE LINES," CWTI:AUG/90[8]165
McPHERSON, JAMES B., *General, USA;* ARTICLE: "SHERMAN'S FEUDING GENERALS," CWTI:MAR/95[40]436
MEADE, GEORGE G. *General, USA;* ARTICLE: "I HAVE A GREAT CONTEMPT FOR HISTORY," CWTI:SEP/91[31]229
MEDAL OF HONOR:
Blickensderfer, Milton A., *Sergeant, 126th Ohio Infantry;* ARTICLE: "MEDAL OF HONOR RECIPIENT," CWTI:AUG/95[90]462
Walker, Mary; ARTICLE: "MARY WALKER: SAMARITAN OR CHARLATAN," CWTI:MAY/94[40]383
MEDFORD HISTORICAL SOCIETY MUSEUM; ARTICLE: "TREASURE IN THE ATTIC," CWTI:MAY/91[34]209
MEDICAL:
ARTICLE: "ATTITUDES OF DEATH," CWTI:JUL/92[36]273, "I SHALL BE A PRISONER," CWTI:SEP/91[42]231
BOOK REVIEW: *CIVIL WAR MEDICINE: CARE AND COMFORT OF THE WOUNDED * SCIENCE AND MEDICINE IN THE OLD SOUTH*
MEIGS, MONTGOMERY C., *General, USA;* ARTICLE: "A PEEK INTO THE PAST," CWTI:AUG/95[10]453
MELVILLE, HERMAN; BOOK REVIEW: *THE CIVIL WAR WORLD OF HERMAN MELVILLE*

MILHOLLIN, JOHN F., *Captain, CSA, Phillip's (Georgia) Legion;* ARTICLE: "TIME LAPSE," CWTI:APR/89[50]112

MILITARY ORGANIZATION; BOOK REVIEW: *THE UNION ARMY, 1861-1865: ORGANIZATION AND OPERATIONS, VOLUME II: THE WESTERN THEATRE*

MINNESOTA TROOPS:
1st Infantry; BOOK REVIEW: *THE LAST FULL MEASURE: THE LIFE AND DEATH OF THE FIRST MINNESOTA VOLUNTEERS*

MINORITIES; ARTICLE: "THE FIGHTING MINORITY," CWTI:MAY/92[38]265
MISSIONARY RIDGE, TENNESSEE, BATTLE OF; ARTICLE: "TO SAVE AN ARMY," CWTI:SEP/94[40]403
BOOK REVIEW: *THE SHIPWRECK OF THEIR HOPES: THE BATTLES FOR CHATTANOOGA*
MISSOURI, STATE OF; ARTICLE: "A FIGHT FOR MISSOURI," CWTI:AUG/95[34]457
MOBILE BAY, ALABAMA, BATTLE OF; BOOK REVIEW: *GUARDIANS OF MOBILE BAY * CONFEDERATE MOBILE*
MONOCACY, MARYLAND, BATTLE OF; ARTICLE: "THE FORGOTTEN BATTLE FOR THE CAPITAL," CWTI:JAN/93[40]301
MOORE, WILLIAM H., *Lieutenant, 25th Alabama Infantry;* ARTICLE: "WRITING HOME TO TALLADEGA," CWTI:DEC/90[56]184
MORAN, THOMAS, *Private, USA;* ARTICLE: "A POETIC PLEA FROM PRISON," CWTI:MAR/91[28]200
MORGAN, NANCY, ARTICLE: "GEORGIA'S NANCY HARTS," CWTI:MAY/94[44]384
MOSBY, JOHN S., ARTICLES: *Colonel, CSA;* "HOW TO STEAL A GENERAL," CWTI:DEC/91[22]237, "INSIDE MOSBY'S CONFEDERACY," CWTI:SEP/90[34]176

MOVIES:
Gettysburg: ARTICLE: "GETTYSBURG: HOW A PRIZE WINNING NOVEL BECAME A MOTION PICTURE," CWTI:NOV/93[40]348
Glory: ARTICLE: "THE MAKING OF *GLORY,*" CWTI:DEC/89[53]138
Gone With the Wind: ARTICLE: "THE FILM THAT MADE ME: 50 YEARS AFTER GWTW IS RELEASED AN HISTORIAN GETS AROUND TO SAYING THANK YOU," CWTI:SUMMER/89[6]

MUDD, SAMUEL; ARTICLE: "MORAL VICTORY IN THE CRUSADE TO CLEAR MUDD," CWTI:MAY/93[12]316, "WHAT REALLY HAPPENED TO THE ASSASSIN? CWTI:JUL/92[50]275

MUSEUMS:
A.K. Smiley Library; ARTICLE: "A SHRINE IN THE GOLDEN STATE," CWTI:MAY/92[20]262
Confederate Naval Museum, Columbus, Georgia; ARTICLE: "GEORGIA'S ENDANGERED REBEL GUNBOATS," CWTI:NOV/93[74]353
Drum Barracks Civil War Muesum; ARTICLE: "LOS ANGELES' DRUM BARRACKS," CWTI:SEP/91[18]227
G.A.R. Museum, ARTICLE: "G.A.R. MUSEUM IS A TREASURY OF WAR RELICS," CWTI:SEP/90[22]173

Lincoln Memorial Shrine; ARTICLE: "A SHRINE IN THE GOLDEN STATE," CWTI:MAY/92[20]262
Louisiana Historical Association's Memorial Hall Confederate Museum; ARTICLE: "NEW ORLEANS' HAVEN FOR HISTORY," CWTI:AUG/95[28]456
Medford Historical Society Museum; ARTICLE: "TREASURE IN THE ATTIC," CWTI:MAY/91[34]209
National Building Museum; ARTICLE: "A PEEK INTO THE PAST," CWTI:AUG/95[10]453
National Museum of the U.S. Army; ARTICLE: "NEW ARMY MUSEUM PLANNED," CWTI:OCT/95[10]464
United States Civil War Center; ARTICLE: "A SUPERHIGHWAY FOR CIVIL WAR INFORMATION," CWTI:JAN/95[30]426
Valentine Riverside Museum; ARTICLE: "RICHMOND MUSEUM CELEBRATES FIRST YEAR," CWTI:JUN/95[10]442

MUTINIES; ARTICLE: "MUTINY AT THE FRONT," CWTI:JUN/95[32]446
MY WAR: see listings in the Consolidated Listings Section on page 227.

N

NANCY HARTS, (WOMEN'S MILITIA COMPANY); ARTICLE: "GEORGIA'S NANCY HARTS," CWTI:MAY/94[44]384
NASHVILLE, TENNESSEE, BATTLE OF; BOOK REVIEWS: *EMBRACE AN ANGRY WIND—THE CONFEDERACY'S LAST HURRAH: SPRING HILL, FRANKLIN, AND NASHVILLE * SHROUDS OF GLORY: FROM ATLANTA TO NASHVILLE*
NAVAL SHIPS, ETC.; see listings under "**SHIPS, BOATS, VESSELS**"
NAVAL WARFARE:
ARTICLES: "A SON OF OLD NEPTUNE," CWTI:DEC/91[44]241, "THE DILEMMA OF COMMODORE CRAVEN," CWTI:DEC/94[34]411, "THE GREAT GUNBOAT CHASE," CWTI:JUL/94[30]392, "GUNBOATS ON THE UPPER TENNESSEE," CWTI:MAY/93[38]321, "RELUCTANT RAIDER," CWTI:AUG/95[40]458
BOOK REVIEWS: *DAMN THE TORPEDOES! NAVAL INCIDENTS OF THE CIVIL WAR * SHIPS VERSUS SHORE: CIVIL WAR ENGAGEMENTS ALONG SOUTHERN SHORES AND RIVERS*
NELSON, GEORGE W., *Captain, CSA;* ARTICLE: "LETTERS FROM THE HEART," CWTI:OCT/95[28]467
NEW MEXICO CAMPAIGN; ARTICLE: "BATTLE FOR THE RIO GRANDE," CWTI:OCT/95[56]471
NEW ORLEANS, LOUISIANA, OCCUPATION OF; ARTICLE: "THE BEAST OF NEW ORLEANS," CWTI:MAY/93[29]319
NEWSPAPERS; BOOK REVIEW: *CIVIL WAR NEWSPAPER MAPS: A CARTOBIBLIOGRAPHY OF THE NORTHERN PRESS*

NEW HAMPSHIRE TROOPS:
5th Infantry; ARTICLE: "COMPLETELY OUTGENERALLED," CWTI:AUG/95[24]455

NEW JERSEY, STATE OF: BOOK REVIEW: *JERSEY BLUE: CIVIL WAR POLITICS IN NEW JERSEY, 1854-1865*

NEW JERSEY TROOPS:
3rd Infantry; ARTICLE: "GIVE MY LOVE TO ALL: A LIEUTENANT'S LETTERS TOLD THE STORY OF THE 3RD NEW JERSEY INFANTRY," CWTI:MAY/89[36]118
14th Infantry; BOOK REVIEW: *UPON THE TENTED FIELD*

NEW YORK TROOPS:
5th Infantry; ARTICLE: "CHARGE BAYONETS," CWTI:MAY/94[31]382
20th Infantry; ARTICLE: "MUTINY AT THE FRONT," CWTI:JUN/95[32]446
154th Infantry; ARTICLE: "PHILO MARKHAM'S LONG WALK," CWTI:MAR/95[26]434

NORTH CAROLINA, STATE OF; ARTICLE: "BENNETT PLACE: HUMBLE SHRINE TO PEACE," CWTI:APR/90[20]151, "CHARGE OF THE TARHEEL BRIGADES," CWTI:FEB/91[45]194
NOVELS; BOOK REVIEW: *THE COURT MARTIAL OF ROBERT E. LEE: A HISTORICAL NOVEL * ULYSSES: A BIOGRAPHICAL NOVEL OF U.S. GRANT*

O

OFFICERS, (IN GENERAL); ARTICLE: "HOW TO PICK OUT BAD OFFICERS," CWTI:MAR/91[46]203

OHIO TROOPS:
14th Infantry; ARTICLE: "THERE WILL BE HOME-MADE THUNDER HERE," CWTI:SUMMER/89[20]
71st Infantry; ARTICLE: "FIELDS WITHOUT HONOR: TWO AFFAIRS IN TENNESSEE," CWTI:JUL/92[42]274
125th Infantry; BOOK REVIEW: *YANKEE TIGERS: THROUGH THE CIVIL WAR WITH THE 125T OHIO*

OVERLAND CAMPAIGN, (VIRGINIA, 1864):
ARTICLE: "ALL GOES ON LIKE A MIRACLE," CWTI:APR/92[49]260
BOOK REVIEW: *NO TURNING BACK: THE BEGINNING OF THE END OF THE CIVIL WAR, MARCH-JUNE, 1864 * ON FIELDS OF FURY: FROM THE WILDERNESS TO THE CRATER, AN EYEWITNESS HISTORY*

P

PAGE, THOMAS, *Captain, CSN;* ARTICLE: "THE DILEMMA OF COMMODORE CRAVEN," CWTI:DEC/94[34]411
PAGE, WILLIAM H., *Surgeon, USA;* ARTICLE: "I SHALL BE A PRISONER," CWTI:SEP/91[42]231
PALMER, JOHN M., *General, USA;* ARTICLE: "SHERMAN'S FEUDING GENERALS," CWTI:MAR/95[40]436
PALMITO RANCH, TEXAS, BATTLE OF; BOOK REVIEW: *OUT OF THE STORM: THE END OF THE CIVIL WAR (APRIL-JUNE 1865)*
PEMBERTON, JOHN C., *General, CSA:*
ARTICLE: "A HILL OF DEATH," CWTI:MAY/91[24]208

BOOK REVIEW: *PEMBERTON, A BIOGRAPHY*
PENINSULA CAMPAIGN; BOOK REVIEW: *TO THE GATES OF RICHMOND: THE PENINSULA CAMPAIGN*

PENNSYLVANIA TROOPS:
148th Infantry; ARTICLE: "BURY THEM IF THEY WON'T MOVE," CWTI:APR/90[24]152

PENNSYLVANIA, STATE OF; ARTICLE: "G.A.R. MUSEUM IS A TREASURY OF WAR RELICS," CWTI:SEP/90[22]173
PERRY, WILLIAM F., *General, CSA;* ARTICLE: "A FORGOTTEN ACCOUNT OF CHICKAMAUGA," CWTI:SEP/93[53]340
PERRYVILLE, KENTUCKY, BATTLE OF; ARTICLE: "A WADE IN THE HIGH TIDE AT PERRYVILLE," CWTI:NOV/92[18]289
PETERSBURG (VIRGINIA) CAMPAIGN AND SIEGE OF:
ARTICLES: "BATTLE IN DESPERATION," CWTI:MAR/95[33]435, "BURY THEM IF THEY WON'T MOVE," CWTI:APR/90[24]152
BOOK REVIEW: *THE LAST CITADEL: PETERSBURG, VIRGINIA, JUNE 1864-APRIL 1865*
PHILADELPHIA, PENNSYLVANIA; ARTICLE: "THE CITY OF BROTHERLY HOSPITALITY," CWTI:MAY/94[24]381, "G.A.R. MUSEUM IS A TREASURY OF WAR RELICS," CWTI:SEP/90[22]173
PHOTOGRAPHY:
ARTICLES: "LITTLE WINDOWS ON HISTORY," CWTI:DEC/89[26]135, "TREASURE IN THE ATTIC," CWTI:MAY/91[34]209
BOOK REVIEWS: *THE BLUE AND THE GRAY * LANDSCAPES OF THE CIVIL WAR: NEWLY DISCOVERED PHOTOGRAPHS FROM THE MEDFORD HISTORICAL SOCIETY*
PICKETT, GEORGE E., *General, CSA;* ARTICLE: "GEORGE PICKETT: ANOTHER LOOK," CWTI:JUL/94[44]394
PIERCE, JOSEPH, *Corporal, 14th Connecticut Infantry;* ARTICLE: "AN ORIENTAL YANKEE SOLDIER," CWTI:SEP/94[90]406
PILLOW, GIDEON J., *General, CSA;* BOOK REVIEW: *THE LIFE AND WARS OF GIDEON PILLOW*
POETRY; BOOK REVIEW: *THE COLUMBIA BOOK OF CIVIL WAR POETRY: FROM WHITMAN TO WALCOTT*
POPE, JOHN, *General, USA;* BOOK REVIEW: *ABANDONED BY LINCOLN: A MILITARY BIOGRAPHY OF GENERAL JOHN POPE*

PRESERVATION, BATTLEFIELD AND OTHER:
Appomattox Court House, Virginia; ARTICLE: "HISTORY COMES HOME," CWTI:MAR/95[20]433
Atlanta Cyclorama; ARTICLE: "ATLANTA'S RESTORED CYCLORAMA," CWTI:FEB/91[18]190
Brandy Station, Virginia; ARTICLES: "A NEW BATTLE FLARES AT BRANDY STATION," CWTI:JUN/90[43]160, "BEHIND THE LINES," CWTI:NOV/93[8]344, "FLANK ATTACK," CWTI:JUL/94[38]393, "IRRECONCILABLE DIFFERENCES," CWTI:JAN/94[42]363
Charleston, South Carolina; ARTICLE: "TO HONOR THE DEAD: A PROPER BURIAL IN CHARLESTON," CWTI:MAR/94[59]376
Cross Keys, Virginia; ARTICLE: "LIVING ON A CIVIL WAR BATTLEFIELD," CWTI:JAN/95[22]423, "PRESERVATION NEWS," CWTI:AUG/95[10]453
Gettysburg, Pennsylvania; ARTICLES: "BEHIND THE LINES," CWTI:SEP/91[16]226, "CONGRESS QUESTIONS GETTYSBURG LAND DEAL," CWTI:SEP/94[28]401, "SEMINARY RIDGE TO REMAIN UNRESTORED,"

CWTI:SEP/93[38]337, "WHERE DID SEMINARY RIDGE GO?" CWTI:APR/92[42]259, "WHO LOST SEMINARY RIDGE?" CWTI:JAN/93[35]300

Glorieta Pass, New Mexico; ARTICLE: "TO HONOR THE DEAD: LAST TAPS AT LA GLORIETA PASS," CWTI:MAR/94[58]375

HERITAGEPAC; ARTICLE: "BEHIND THE LINES," CWTI:JUN/90[6]156

Maple Leaf; ARTICLE: "THE *MAPLE LEAF* ESCAPE," CWTI:JAN/95[42]428

PRESTON, MARGARET JUNKIN; BOOK REVIEW: *MARGARET JUNKIN PRESTON: A BIOGRAPHY*

PRICE, STERLING, *General, CSA;* ARTICLE: "A FIERCE LITTLE FIGHT IN MISSISSIPPI," CWTI:JUL/94[50]395

PRICE, THOMAS J., *Private, 12th Mississippi Infantry;* ARTICLE: "A SOLDIER FOR TWO COUNTRIES," CWTI:MAR/95[90]440

PRICE, WILLIAM C., *Major, CSA;* ARTICLE: "U.S. TREASURER, REBEL SOLDIER," CWTI:JUL/94[82]396

PRISONS, CONFEDERATE:
Andersonville, Georgia; BOOK REVIEW: *ANDERSONVILLE: THE LAST DEPOT*

Belle Isle, Virginia; ARTICLE: "ON TO PRISON," CWTI:JUN/90[28]158

Libby, Virginia; ARTICLE: "ON TO PRISON," CWTI:JUN/90[28]158

PRISONS, FEDERAL:
Gratiot Street (St. Louis); ARTICLE: "A HELL ON EARTH," CWTI:AUG/95[58]461

Fort Jefferson; Florida; ARTICLE: "A POETIC PLEA FROM PRISON," CWTI:MAR/91[28]200

Fort Delaware, Delaware; ARTICLE: "FORT DELAWARE ON THE WATER: A MONUMENT TO RUGGED REBELS," CWTI:JUL/93[20]325

Elmira, New York; ARTICLE: "BREAK OUT!" CWTI:DEC/91[26]238

PRISONS, GENERAL INFORMATION; BOOK REVIEW: *CIVIL WAR PRISONS AND ESCAPES: A DAY-BY-DAY CHRONICLE*

R

RAIDS; ARTICLE: "HOW TO STEAL A GENERAL," CWTI:DEC/91[22]237

RAILROADS:
Western and Atlantic; ARTICLE: "AT HOME WITH THE GENERAL," CWTI:FEB/92[10]246

RAILROADS, GENERAL INFORMATION; ARTICLES: "A ROLLING MEMENTO," CWTI:MAR/95[54]438, "THE GREAT LOCOMOTIVE WRECK," CWTI:JAN/95[48]429, "MIRACLE OF THE RAILS," CWTI:SEP/92[22]279

RANK IN THE MILITARY; ARTICLE: "A PROBLEM OF RANK," CWTI:FEB/91[52]195

RATCLIFFE, LAURA; ARTICLE: "LETTERS TO LAURA," CWTI:JUL/92[12]270

READ, CHARLES W., *Lieutenant, CSA;* ARTICLE: "THE GREAT GUNBOAT CHASE," CWTI:JUL/94[30]392

REAMS STATION, VIRGINIA, SECOND BATTLE OF; ARTICLE: "CHARGE OF THE TARHEEL BRIGADES," CWTI:FEB/91[45]194

RECONSTRUCTION; BOOK REVIEW: *THE CRISIS OF THE AMERICAN REPUBLIC: A HISTORY OF THE CIVIL WAR AND RECONSTRUCTION ERA*

RECRUITING; ARTICLE: "'TIL THE PAPER WORK IS DONE," CWTI:NOV/93[78]354

REENACTING; ARTICLE: "THE ALLURE OF THE CIVIL WAR'S HEFTIEST RELICS," CWTI:DEC/90[20]181

RELICS; ARTICLE: "THE WAR'S MOST DANGEROUS RELICS," CWTI:DEC/94[42]412

RESACA, GEORGIA, BATTLE OF; ARTICLE: "THE BATTLE THAT SHOULD NOT HAVE BEEN," CWTI:NOV/92[41]291

RICE, RALSA C., *Private, 125th Ohio Infantry;* BOOK REVIEW: *YANKEE TIGERS: THROUGH THE CIVIL WAR WITH THE 125T OHIO*

RICHMOND, VIRGINIA, SIEGE OF (1864-1865); BOOK REVIEW: *CITY UNDER SIEGE: RICHMOND IN THE CIVIL WAR*

ROCK CREEK, MISSOURI, BATTLE OF; ARTICLE: "THE BATTLE OF ROCK CREEK," CWTI:MAR/91[34]201

ROSECRANS, WILLIAM S., *General, USA;* ARTICLE: "A FIERCE LITTLE FIGHT IN MISSISSIPPI," CWTI:JUL/94[50]395

S

SABINE PASS, TEXAS, BATTLE OF; ARTICLE: "SIX GUNS AGAINST THE FLEET," CWTI:DEC/90[29]182

SAN FRANCISCO, CALIFORNIA; ARTICLE: "TRACES OF A DISTANT WAR," CWTI:JUN/95[51]449

SAVANNAH, GEORGIA, BATTLE AND SIEGE OF; ARTICLE: "GATEWAY TO THE ATLANTIC," CWTI:DEC/94[62]415

SOUTH CAROLINA, STATE OF; BOOK REVIEW: *ARTICLE BRINGS NOTICE TO A UNIQUE REBEL * SUMTER: THE FIRST DAY OF THE CIVIL WAR*

SCALES, ALFRED M., *General, CSA;* ARTICLE: "CHARGE OF THE TARHEEL BRIGADES," CWTI:FEB/91[45]194

SCHOFIELD, JOHN M., *General, USA;* ARTICLE: "SHERMAN'S FEUDING GENERALS," CWTI:MAR/95[40]436

SCOTT, JULIAN, *artist;* ARTICLE: "A SOLDIER'S SKETCHBOOK," CWTI:SEP/91[54]232

SECESSIONVILLE, SOUTH CAROLINA, BATTLE OF; ARTICLES: "A BLOODY HALF-HOUR," CWTI:JAN/94[46]364, "A SCRATCH WITH THE REBELS," CWTI:JAN/94[49]365

SEMMES, RAPHAEL, *Admiral, CSN;* BOOK REVIEW: *CONFEDERATE RAIDER: RAPHAEL SEMMES OF THE ALABAMA*

SEWARD, WILLIAM H.:
ARTICLE: "SOME THOUGHTS FOR THE PRESIDENT'S CONSIDERATION," CWTI:SEP/92[46]284
BOOK REVIEW: *WILLIAM HENRY SEWARD: LINCOLN'S RIGHT HAND*

SHAW, ROBERT G., *Colonel, USA;* BOOK REVIEW: *BLUE-EYED CHILD OF FORTUNE: THE CIVIL WAR LETTERS OF ROBERT GOULD SHAW*

SHENANDOAH VALLEY CAMPAIGN, 1862; ARTICLE: "A SINGLE STEP," CWTI:MAR/94[29]371

SHENANDOAH VALLEY CAMPAIGN, 1864; BOOK REVIEW: *JUBAL EARLY'S RAID ON WASHINGTON, 1864*

SHERIDAN, PHILIP H. *General, USA:*
ARTICLE: "THE APPOMATTOX SURRENDER TABLE," CWTI:NOV/93[50]349, "BURNING DOWN THE SOUTH," CWTI:OCT/95[48]470

BOOK REVIEWS: *SHERIDAN: THE LIFE AND WARS OF GENERAL PHIL SHERIDAN*

SHERMAN, WILLIAM T., *General, USA:*
ARTICLES: "THE BATTLE THAT SHOULD NOT HAVE BEEN," CWTI:NOV/92[41]291, "BURNING DOWN THE SOUTH," CWTI:OCT/95[48]470, "GATEWAY TO THE ATLANTIC," CWTI:DEC/94[62]415, "I HEREBY TENDER YOU MY SERVICES," CWTI:SEP/93[62]342, "SHERMAN REVEALS SOMETHING ABOUT HIS STRATEGY," CWTI:JUL/94[28]391, "SHERMAN'S FEUDING GENERALS," CWTI:MAR/95[40]436

BOOK REVIEWS: *THE DESTRUCTIVE WAR: WILLIAM TECUMSEH SHERMAN, STONEWALL JACKSON, AND THE AMERICANS * MARCHING THROUGH GEORGIA: THE STORY OF SOLDIERS AND CIVILIANS DURING SHERMAN'S CAMPAIGN * SHERMAN AT WAR * SHERMAN: A SOLDIER'S PASSION FOR ORDER * SHERMAN: MERCHANT OF TERROR, ADVOCATE OF PEACE*

SHERMAN'S MARCH TO THE SEA:
ARTICLE: "GATEWAY TO THE ATLANTIC," CWTI:DEC/94[62]415

BOOK REVIEW: *MARCHING THROUGH GEORGIA: THE STORY OF SOLDIERS AND CIVILIANS DURING SHERMAN'S CAMPAIGN*

SHIPS, BOATS, VESSELS, ETC., CONFEDERATE:

Alabama; BOOK REVIEW: *CONFEDERATE RAIDER: RAPHAEL SEMMES OF THE ALABAMA*

Chattahoochee; ARTICLE: "GEORGIA'S ENDANGERED REBEL GUNBOATS," CWTI:NOV/93[74]353

Georgia; ARTICLE: "RELUCTANT RAIDER," CWTI:AUG/95[40]458

Hunley; ARTICLE: "DIVERS FIND WRECK OF CONFEDERATE SECRET WEAPON," CWTI:OCT/95[10]464

Jackson; ARTICLE: "GEORGIA'S ENDANGERED REBEL GUNBOATS," CWTI:NOV/93[74]353

Stonewall; ARTICLE: "THE DILEMMA OF COMMODORE CRAVEN," CWTI:DEC/94[34]411

submarines; ARTICLE: "THE MYSTERY SUB OF JACKSON SQUARE," CWTI:SEPT/89[20]127

Virginia; ARTICLE: "LINCOLN AND THE IRONCLADS COME TO TELEVISION," CWTI:MAR/91[42]202

SHIPS, BOATS, VESSELS, ETC., FEDERAL:

Cincinnati; ARTICLE: "NAVY LIFE ON THE MISSISSIPPI RIVER," CWTI:MAY/94[16]380

Housatonic; ARTICLE: "DIVERS FIND WRECK OF CONFEDERATE SECRET WEAPON," CWTI:OCT/95[10]464

Monitor; ARTICLE: "LINCOLN AND THE IRONCLADS COME TO TELEVISION," CWTI:MAR/91[42]202

Maple Leaf; ARTICLE: "THE *MAPLE LEAF* ESCAPE," CWTI:JAN/95[42]428, *MAPLE LEAF* RELICS," CWTI:AUG/95[10]453

Sultana; BOOK REVIEW: *THE SULTANA, TRAGEDY: AMERICA'S GREATEST MARITIME DISASTER*

SHIRKEY, SAMUEL B., *Private, 1st Virginia Cavalry;* ARTICLE: "A VIRGINIA CAVALRYMAN," CWTI:OCT/95[90]472

SHOHOLA, PENNSYLVANIA, TRAIN WRECK; ARTICLE: "THE GREAT LOCOMOTIVE WRECK," CWTI:JAN/95[48]429

SIBLEY, HENRY H., *General, CSA;* ARTICLE: "BATTLE FOR THE RIO GRANDE," CWTI:OCT/95[56]471

SICKLES, DANIEL E., *General, USA;* ARTICLE: "BEHIND THE LINES," CWTI:FEB/92[6]244

SLAVERY:
ARTICLES: "AN UNPLEASANT RELIC," CWTI:DEC/91[48]242, "GIVE THE BLACKS TEXAS," CWTI:JUN/90[54]162, "MINE EYES HAVE SEEN THE GLORY," CWTI:SEP/93[30]336, "WAS LINCOLN THE GREAT EMANCIPATOR?," CWTI:MAY/94[46]385

BOOK REVIEW: *FREDERICK DOUGLASS*

SMITH, ALFRED C., *Sergeant, 2nd Mississippi Infantry;* ARTICLE: "SWAMP RANGER' AND CAVALRYMAN," CWTI:NOV/92[106]29

SNIPERS; ARTICLE: "DEATH AT A DISTANCE," CWTI:APR/90[48]154

SOUTHERN NATIONALISM; BOOK REVIEW: *CIVIL WARS: WOMEN AND THE CRISIS OF SOUTHERN NATIONALISM*

SPIES:
ARTICLES: "CODE-CRACKERS," CWTI:AUG/95[46]459, "THE FRENCH LADY," CWTI:MAY/92[29]263

BOOK REVIEW: *SPIES & SPYMASTERS OF THE CIVIL WAR*

SPOTSYLVANIA, VIRGINIA, BATTLE OF; BOOK REVIEWS: *BLOODY ROADS SOUTH: THE WILDERNESS TO COLD HARBOR, MAY-JUNE 1864 * IF IT TAKES ALL SUMMER: THE BATTLE OF SPOTSYLVANIA*

SPRAGUE, MAHLON, *Corporal, 5th New Jersey Infantry;* ARTICLE: "PATRIOTIC SON OF A SEAMAN," CWTI:JUL/92[74]277

SPRING HILL, TENNESSEE, BATTLE OF; BOOK REVIEW: *EMBRACE AND ANGRY WIND — THE CONFEDERACY'S LAST HURRAH: SPRING HILL, FRANKLIN, AND NASHVILLE*

ST. LAWRENCE HALL, MONTREAL, CANADA; ARTICLE: "MONTREAL'S POSH REBEL RENDEVOUS," CWTI:JAN/93[44]302

STAMP COLLECTING; ARTICLES: "CIVIL WAR STAMPS," CWTI:JUN/95[10]442, "COMMEMORATIVE STAMPS: HISTORY MOVES THE MAIL," CWTI:JUN/90[12]157

STARK, BENJAMIN, *Senator, Oregon;* ARTICLE: "A TRAITOR IN THE SENATE," CWTI:AUG/95[54]460

STEPHENS, ALEXANDER; ARTICLE: "THE VICE PRESIDENT RESIDES IN GEORGIA," CWTI:FEB/91[36]193

STEVENS, CHARLES, *Private, 29th Georgia Cavalry;* ARTICLE: "A RELUCTANT REBEL SOLDIER," CWTI:JUL/93[74]331

STONE, CHARLES P., *General, USA;* ARTICLE: "GENERAL STONE'S SHAME," CWTI:MAY/89[21]115

STOUGHTON, EDWIN H., *General, USA;* ARTICLE: "HOW TO STEAL A GENERAL," CWTI:DEC/91[22]237

STRATEGY; BOOK REVIEW: *CIVIL WAR COMMAND AND STRATEGY: THE PROCESS OF VICTORY AND DEFEAT*

STUART, JAMES E.B., ARTICLES: *General, CSA;* "THE BATTLE OF BRANDY STATION," CWTI:JUN/90[32]159, "LETTERS TO LAURA," CWTI:JUL/92[12]270, "THE REAL J.E.B. STUART," CWTI:DEC/89[34]136, "STUART'S REVENGE," CWTI:JUN/95[38]447, "TIME LAPSE," CWTI:APR/89[50]112

SULTANA DISASTER; BOOK REVIEW: *THE SULTANA. TRAGEDY: AMERICA'S GREATEST MARITIME DISASTER*
SUMMERS, SAMUEL W., *Colonel, 7th Iowa Cavalry;* ARTICLE: "SOUTHERN-BORN UNION COLONEL" CWTI:MAY/94[82]387

T

TACTICS; BOOK REVIEW: *BATTLE TACTICS OF THE CIVIL WAR*
TALIAFERRO, WILLIAM B., *General, CSA;* ARTICLE: "PERSONAL REMINISCENCES OF 'STONEWALL' JACKSON," CWTI:JUN/95[18]444
TARGET: see listings in the Consolidated Listings Section on page 328
TAYLOR, RICHARD H., *General, CSA;* BOOK REVIEW: *RICHARD TAYLOR: SOLDIER PRINCE OF DIXIE*
TELEVISION; ARTICLE: "LINCOLN AND THE IRONCLADS COME TO TELEVISION," CWTI:MAR/91[42]202, "REMOTE HISTORY," CWTI:MAR/94[44]373
TEXAS BRIGADE; ARTICLE: "THE BLOODY FIFTH," CWTI:DEC/91[36]240
THOMAS, GEORGE H., *General, USA;* ARTICLES: "A FEW ARE HOLDING OUT UP YONDER," CWTI:SEP/92[31]281, "SHERMAN'S FEUDING GENERALS," CWTI:MAR/95[40]436
THOMPSON, JACOB; ARTICLE: "THE GREATEST SCOUNDREL," CWTI:NOV/92[54]293
THOMPSON, M. JEFF, *General, CSA;* BOOK REVIEW: *THE CIVIL REMINISCENCES OF GENERAL M. JEFF THOMPSON*
TIME LAPSE: see listings in the Consolidated Listings Section on page 335.
TOBIE, EDWARD and LEROY; ARTICLE: "THE TOBIE BROTHERS' WAR," CWTI:FEB/91[66]196
TRADING CARDS; ARTICLE: "A $2,500 SET OF CIVIL WAR TRADING CARDS?" CWTI:DEC/91[18]236
TRAWEEK, WASHINGTON B., *Private, Jeff Davis Artillery;* ARTICLE: "BREAK OUT!" CWTI:DEC/91[26]238
TREASON; ARTICLE: "TRAINING IN TREASON," CWTI:SEP/91[23]228
TUCKER, GEORGE W. Jr., *Sergeant, CSA;* ARTICLE: "HILL'S FAVORITE COURIER," CWTI:SEP/92[42]283
"TURNERS"; ARTICLE: "MUTINY AT THE FRONT," CWTI:JUN/95[32]446

TEXAS TROOPS:
5th Infantry; ARTICLE: "THE BLOODY FIFTH," CWTI:DEC/91[36]240

TEXAS, STATE OF:
ARTICLES: "GIVE THE BLACKS TEXAS," CWTI:JUN/90[54]162, "SIX GUNS AGAINST THE FLEET," CWTI:DEC/90[29]182
BOOK REVIEW: *TEXAS: THE DARK CORNER OF THE CONFEDERACY*
TYLER, HENRY A., *Captain, 5th Tennessee Infantry;* ARTICLE: "A COLLEAGUE OF GENERAL FORREST," CWTI:MAY/92[74]268
TYLER, ROBERT C., *General, CSA;* ARTICLE: "OUT OF THE SHADOWS," CWTI:JAN/95[27]425

U

UNITED STATES CIVIL WAR CENTER; ARTICLE: "A SUPERHIGHWAY FOR CIVIL WAR INFORMATION," CWTI:JAN/95[30]426
UNITED STATES SHARPSHOOTERS; ARTICLE: "THE MOST DANGEROUS SET OF MEN," CWTI:JUL/93[42]329

V

VALVERDE, NEW MEXICO, BATTLE OF; ARTICLE: "BATTLE FOR THE RIO GRANDE," CWTI:OCT/95[56]471
VAN DORN, EARL, *General, CSA;* ARTICLE: "VAN DORN: THE LIFE AND TIMES OF A CONFEDERATE GENERAL," CWTI:DEC/94[18]
VERDIERSVILLE, VIRGINIA, RAID ON; ARTICLE: "STUART'S REVENGE," CWTI:JUN/95[38]447
VERDIGRIS RIVER, KANSAS INDIAN RESERVE, BATTLE OF; ARTICLE: "HARD ROPE'S CIVIL WAR," CWTI:SEP/90[52]179
VICKSBURG, MISSISSIPPI, BATTLE AND CAMPAIGN; ARTICLE: "A HILL OF DEAT," CWTI:MAY/91[24]208, "A SUPERIOR SOUTHERN MUSEUM: VICKSBURG, MISSISSIPPI"
VIDEO REVIEW; *BLACK EASTER: THE ASSASSINATION OF ABRAHAM LINCOLN,* CWTI:NOV/92[10], *BLOODY SHENANDOAH,* CWTI:FEB/92[18], *CIVIL WAR CINEMA, VOL. I,* CWTI:SEP/91[10], *FEDERAL ENLISTED UNIFORMS OF THE CIVIL WAR,* CWTI:MAR/91[18], *GUNS OF THE CIVIL WAR,* CWTI:JUL/94[18], *MEADE OF GETTYSBURG,* CWTI:NOV/93[14], *OUT OF THE WILDERNESS: THE LIFE OF ABRAHAM LINCOLN,* CWTI:MAR/94[12], *SMITHSONIAN'S GREAT BATTLES OF THE CIVIL WAR,* CWTI:JUL/93[12]

VIRGINIA TROOPS:
22nd Infantry Battalion; ARTICLE: "IN A MOST DISGRACEFUL MANNER," CWTI:APR/90[46]153

VIRGINIA, STATE OF:
VRENDENBURGH, PETER, JR., *Major, 14th New Jersey Infantry;* BOOK REVIEW *UPON THE TENTED FIELD*

W

WAGGAMAN, EUGENE, *Lieutenant Colonel, 2nd Louisiana Brigade;* "ARTICLE: "THE PRISONER AND THE PRIME MINISTER," CWTI:JUL/93[38]328
WALCOTT, AARON F., *Lieutenant, 2nd Massachusetts Artillery;* "ARTICLE: *A VETERAN OF 33 BATTLES,*" CWTI:MAY/ 93[74]322
WALKER, JOHNATHAN, *Captain, USA;* ARTICLE: "AN UNPLEASANT RELIC," CWTI:DEC/91[48]242
WALKER, MARY, *Doctor;* ARTICLE: "MARY WALKER: SAMARITAN OR CHARLATAN," CWTI:MAY/94[40]383

WALKER, W.H.T., *General, CSA;* ARTICLE: "I SHALL MAKE HIM REMEMBER THIS INSULT," CWTI:MAR/93[24]309

WAR CONTRACTS; ARTICLE: "HE WOULD STEAL?," CWTI:JUN/90[46]161

WARFARE; BOOK REVIEW: *A COUNTRY MADE BY WAR. FROM THE REVOLUTION TO VIETNAM — THE STORY OF AMERICA'S RISE TO POWER*

WARNER, IRWIN E., *Private, 2nd Connecticut Heavy Artillery;* ARTICLE: "LIES, DISGRACE, REDEMPTION," CWTI:SEP/91[61]233

WASHINGTON, D.C., ARTICLE: "A GUIDE TO CIVIL WAR WASHINGTON," CWTI:OCT/95[18]

WEAPONS:

Artillery; ARTICLES: "THE ALLURE OF THE CIVIL WAR'S HEFTIEST RELICS," CWTI:DEC/90[20]181, "THE SWAMP ANGEL: LOVED IN TRENTON AND HATED IN CHARLESTON," CWTI:APR/89[22]108, "THE WAR'S MOST DANGEROUS RELICS," CWTI:DEC/94[42]412

Dogs; ARTICLE: "FAITHFUL FRIENDS," CWTI:MAR/95[46]437

Machine Gun; ARTICLE: "THE PETERSBURG 'FOLLY GUN'" CWTI:DEC/90[18]180, "THE SEARCH FOR THE ULTIMATE WEAPON," CWTI:JAN/93[49]303

Pistol, Remington, .44 CAL; ARTICLE: "THE RELIABLE REMINGTON," CWTI:SEP/90[18]172

Rifle; ARTICLES: "DEATH AT A DISTANCE," CWTI:APR/90[48]154, "THE UNION'S MOST READY RIFLE: THE MODEL 1861 SPRINGFIELD RIFLE MUSKET," CWTI:SEPT/89[10]125

WEAPONS, GENERAL INFORMATION; ARTICLE: "LINCOLN'S SECRET ARMS RACE," CWTI:OCT/95[32]468

WHEAT, CHATHAM R., *Major, CSA;* ARTICLE: "WHEAT'S TIGERS," CWTI:MAR/94[48]374

WHITE, ELIJAH, *Colonel, CSA;* ARTICLE: "A CAVALRYMAN WITHOUT FANFARE," CWTI:DEC/94[122]419

WILDERNESS, VIRGINIA, BATTLE OF; BOOK REVIEWS: *BLOODY ROADS SOUTH: THE WILDERNESS TO COLD HARBOR, MAY-JUNE 1864 * ON FIELDS OF FURY: FROM THE WILDERNESS TO THE CRATER, AN EYEWITNESS HISTORY*

WILLIAMS, GEORGE H., *Private, 10th Virginia Infantry;* ARTICLE: "KILLED AT BRANDY STATION," CWTI:MAR/94[67]377

WILLIAMS, THOMAS J., *Captain, 1st Arkansas Infantry (Union);* ARTICLE: "TIME LAPSE," CWTI:APR/92[27]256

WILSON'S CREEK, MISSOURI, BATTLE OF; ARTICLE: "A MIGHTY MEAN-FOWT FIGHT," CWTI:FEB/92[29]248

WIPPERMAN, HENRY; ARTICLE: "IN A NUTSHELL," CWTI:JAN/94[24]359

WOMEN:

ARTICLE: "GEORGIA'S NANCY HARTS," CWTI:MAY/94[44]384

BOOK REVIEWS: *A WOMAN'S CIVIL WAR: A DIARY, WITH REMINISCENCES OF THE WAR, FROM MARCH 1862 * CIVIL WARS: WOMEN AND THE CRISIS OF SOUTHERN NATIONALISM * IN JOY AND IN SORROW: WOMEN, FAMILY, AND MARRIAGE IN THE VICTORIAN SOUTH, 1830-1900 * TARA REVISITED: WOMEN, WAR, AND THE PLANTATION LEGEND*

Z

ZACHRY, ALFRED, *Private, 3rd Georgia Infantry;* ARTICLE: "FIGHTING WITH THE 3D GEORGIA," CWTI:SEP/94[26]400, "FOUR SHOTS FOR THE CAUSE," CWTI:DEC/94[32]410

ZARVONA, RICHARD T., ARTICLE: "THE FRENCH LADY," CWTI:MAY/92[29]263

LIST OF ARTICLES, BY AUTHOR

Abel, Ernest L.:
"CLOAK & DAGGER FIASCO," ACW:JAN/92[30]342
"FAITHFUL FRIENDS," CWTI:MAR/95[46]437
Able, James A. Jr.; "THE GRAY FOX OF DIXIE,"
ACW:NOV/95[38]556
Abner, Rhonda; "ROME CLARKE, AKA 'SUE MUNDY,'"
(PERSONALITY)," ACW:JAN/94[10]448
Abolins, Andrea; "OH, DEM BONES, DEM DRY BONES
(LEGACY)," CWTI:SEP/91[41]230
Adams, Cicero; "LEE'S LIEUTENANT: J.E.B. STUART,"
CWM:JUL/92[16]428
Addison-Darneille, Henrietta S. (edited by Richard A.
Wood); "FOR BETTER OR FOR WORSE (MY WAR),"
CWTI:MAY/92[32]264
Adelman, Gary; "THE THIRD BRIGADE, THIRD DIVISION,
SIXTH CORPS AT GETTYSBURG, GETTY:11[91]236
Agnew, Samuel A.; "A CIVILIAN AT BRICE'S CROSS
ROADS," CWTI:JAN/94[39]362
Aikey, Michael; "FLAMBOYANT GARIBALDI GUARDS,"
ACW:MAY/95[54]528
Aimone, Alan and Barbara; "MUCH TO SADDEN—AND
LITTLE TO CHEER: THE CIVIL WAR YEARS AT WEST
POINT (GENERAL'S TOUR)," B&G:DEC/91[12]469
Alberts, Don E.; "CIVIL WAR ON THE SANTA FE TRAIL:
PRESERVING THE BATTLEFIELD AT GLORIETA PASS,"
CWR:VOL2#2[161]139
Albro, Walt; "THE FORGOTTEN BATTLE FOR THE
CAPITAL," CWTI:JAN/93[40]301
Alexander, Bates, (edited by Frank O'Reilly); "THROUGH
MURDEROUS FIRE AT FREDERICKSBURG,"
CWM:DEC/94[74]555
Alexander, E. Porter; (edited by Gary W. Gallagher):
"WHY WE LOST AT GETTYSBURG: EXCERPT FROM
FIGHTING FOR THE CONFEDERACY,"
CWTI:SEPT/89[46]132
"WITH LEE AT APPOMATTOX," AHI:SEP/87[40]263
Alexander, Hudson:
"A MEMORIAL DIRGE FOR LINCOLN," B&G:JUN/95[35]602
"THE TRIALS AND TRIBULATIONS OF FOUNTAIN BRANCH
CARTER AND HIS FRANKLIN, TENNESSEE HOME,"
B&G:FEB/95[30]591
Alexander, Ted:
"THE CHIPPEWA SHARPSHOOTERS OF COMPANY K,"
CWM:SEP/92[24]441
"FORGOTTEN VALOR: OFF THE BEATEN PATH AT
ANTIETAM: ARTILLERY HELL AND HOT COFFEE (THE
GENERAL'S TOUR)," B&G:OCT/95[8]611D
"FORGOTTEN VALOR: OFF THE BEATEN PATH AT
ANTIETAM: ATTACK OF THE TURNVEREIN (THE
GENERAL'S TOUR)," B&G:OCT/95[8]611B
"FORGOTTEN VALOR: OFF THE BEATEN PATH AT
ANTIETAM: DEBACLE IN THE WEST WOODS (THE
GENERAL'S TOUR)," B&G:OCT/95[8]611A
"FORGOTTEN VALOR: OFF THE BEATEN PATH AT
ANTIETAM: GUNNERS OF THE 6TH VA. INFY. (THE
GENERAL'S TOUR)," B&G:OCT/95[8]611C

"FORGOTTEN VALOR: OFF THE BEATEN PATH AT
ANTIETAM: OLD SIMON (THE GENERAL'S TOUR),"
B&G:OCT/95[8]611E
"FORGOTTEN VALOR: OFF THE BEATEN PATH AT
ANTIETAM: WHOEVER HEARD OF A DEAD
CAVALRYMAN? (THE GENERAL'S TOUR),"
B&G:OCT/95[8]611F
"MCCAUSLAND'S RAID AND THE BURNING OF
CHAMBERSBURG (THE GENERAL'S TOUR),
B&G:AUG/94[10]574
"MUSKETS AND . . . TOMAHAWKS," CWM:SEP/92[8]437
"O.T. REILLY, BATTLEFIELD GUIDE," B&G:OCT/95[54]615A
"OLD JUBE' FOOLS THE YANKEES," B&G:AUG/94[19]575
Alison, Dr. Joseph Dill; "WITH A CONFEDERATE SURGEON
AT VICKSBURG," AHI:JUL/68[31]115A
Allardice, Bruce; "OUT OF THE SHADOWS,"
CWTI:JAN/95[27]425
Allen, Christopher J.; "DEVIL'S OWN DAY,"
ACW:JAN/91[22]285
Allen, Randall; "A MOST VOLUNTARY GATHERING,"
B&G:AUG/94[22]576
Ambrose, Stephen E.:
"THIS MONOTONOUS LIFE," AHI:AUG/71[22]135
"WILLIAM T. SHERMAN," AHI:JAN/67[4]106
Anderson, Bill; "SOUTHERN ECONOMY (ORDNANCE),"
ACW:JUL/91[14]311
Anderson, Ella; "ELIZABETH VAN LEW (PERSONALITY),"
ACW:JUL/91[8]309
Anderson, William T.; "MR. LINCOLN'S SPRINGFIELD,"
AHI:MAR/89[26]280
Andrew, Richard:
"THE CORPORAL, THE HOTHEAD AND THE CRAZY OLD
PRESBYTERIAN FOOL," CWM:OCT/94[26]536
"DISASTER AT ROANOKE ISLAND," CWM:FEB/95[49]565
Andrews, Harris; "HAUPT'S INNOVATIONS. . .KEPT THE
NORTHERN TRAINS ON TRACK," CWM:NOV/91[28]391
Andrews, W.H.; "THE FIRST GEORGIA REGULARS AT
SHARPSBURG: RECOLLECTIONS OF THE MARYLAND
CAMPAIGN, 1862," CWR:VOL2#2[95]135
Andrus, Michael J.; "THE PENINSULA CAMPAIGN OF 1862:
THE BATTLE OF BEAVER DAM CREEK,"
CWM:JUN/95[57]592
Anthis, Judith; "THE CONFEDERATE BALLOON CORPS,"
B&G:AUG/91[20]459
Anthony, Carl S.; "FIRST LADIES AT WAR,"
ACW:JAN/94[47]452
Antonucci, Michael; "CODE-CRACKERS,"
CWTI:AUG/95[46]459
Archer, John M.:
"AN ORIENTAL YANKEE SOLDIER (TIME LAPSE),"
CWTI:SEP/94[90]406
"FURY AT BLISS FARM," ACW:JUL/95[50]538
"REMEMBERING THE 14TH CONNECTICUT VOLUNTEERS,"
GETTY:9[61]215
Armstrong, Hugh; "FULL SPEED AHEAD!" MH:FEB/92[8]156
Arnold, Peri E.; "FIFTEEN PRESIDENTIAL DECISIONS
THAT SHAPED AMERICA," AHI:APR/89[36]283
Atwood, Thomas; "THE TOBIE BROTHERS' WAR (TIME
LAPSE)," CWTI:FEB/91[66]196

Bailey, Anne J.; "CHASING BANKS OUT OF LOUISIANA:
PARSON'S TEXAS CAVALRY IN THE RED RIVER
CAMPAIGN," CWR:VOL2#3[212]142

Baker, Pricilla R.; "13 HAUNTED PLACES OF THE CIVIL WAR II," B&G:OCT/91[11]466

Balderston, Thomas; "THE SAD, SHATTERED LIFE OF TERESA SICKLES," AHI:SEPT/82[40]229

Baldwin, Leo T.; "FIRST BLOOD IN BALTIMORE," ACW:NOV/95[30]555

Ballard, Michael B.:
"CHEERS FOR JEFFERSON DAVIS," AHI:MAY/81[8]217
"DAVIS' LAST RIDE TO RICHMOND," CWTI:MAR/93[32]311

Banks, Ron; "DEATH AT A DISTANCE," CWTI:APR/90[48]154

Barns, Leslie; "WASHINGTON, ARKANSAS (TRAVEL)," ACW:SEP/92[66]381

Baxter, Phyllis; "PRESERVING BEVERLY AND THE RICH MOUNTAIN BATTLEFIELD," B&G:AUG/93[55]535

Beames, Barry; "JEFFERSON, TEXAS (TRAVEL)," ACW:MAR/93[68]409

Bearss, Edwin C.; "VICKSBURG REVISITED," CWR:VOL2#1[i]129

Beaudot, William J.K.; "FRANCIS ASBURY WALLER: A MEDAL OF HONOR AT GETTYSBURG," GETTY:4[16]143

Bellard, Alfred; "CONDEMNED YANKS," AHI:FEB/75[35]158

Benjamin, Samuel N.; (edited by Cury Johnson) "WE CLEARED THEIR WAY. . .FIRING CANISTER (MY WAR)," CWTI:MAR/93[20]308

Bennett, Brian A.:
"ESCAPE FROM HARPERS FERRY," CWM:MAY/92[8]418
"THE IDEAL OF A SOLDIER AND A GENTLEMAN," CWM:MAR/91[35]337
"THE MOST HORRIBLE BARBARISM," CWM:JAN/92[16]401

Bennett, Keith W.; "GUN PLATFORMS AT SEA," MH:AUG/92[26]161

Bentley, Jack L.; "FORTS STEVENS AND CANBY (TRAVEL)," ACW:MAR/92[62]355

Berger, Diana S.; "THE TRACK IS CLEAR TO SHOHOLA: DISASTER ON THE ROAD TO ELMIRA," B&G:APR/93[14]520

Bergeron Jr., Arthur W.:
"BRILLIANT RAID BY GENERAL GREEN (DISPATCHES)," CWM:OCT/04[47]537
"BRILLIANT VICTORY OVER THE YANKEE FLEET ON THE MISSISSIPPI (DISPATCHES)," CWM:APR/95[28]573
"DETAILS OF THE SIEGE OF FORT MORGAN, ALABAMA (DISPATCHES)," CWM:AUG/94[25]524
"FIGHTING ERUPTS AT JACKSON, MISSISSIPPI (DISPATCHES)," CWM:AUG/95[26]604
"HENRY GRAY'S LOUISIANA BRIGADE AT THE BATTLE OF MANSFIELD, APRIL 8, 1864," CWR:VOL4#2[1]165
"PARTICULARS OF THE BATTLE AT PORT HUDSON (DISPATCHES)," CWM:JUN/94[25]511
"SEARS OBLIVIOUS TO LOSS OF LEG (DISPATCHES)," CWM:DEC/94[30]627
"TENACITY OF SOLDIERS OF THE DEEP SOUTH AT MURFREESBORO (DISPATCHES)," CWM:FEB/95[28]560
"TORPEDOES SINK YANKEE GUNBOAT! (DISPATCHES)," CWM:DEC/95[30]627
"YANKEE INVADERS CAUGHT UNPREPARED (DISPATCHES)," CWM:OCT/95[36]616
"THE YELLOW JACKETS: THE 10TH LOUISIANA INFANTRY BATTALION, CWR:VOL3#1[1]149

Bergmooser, Mark; "HOW THE WAR CHANGED AMERICA'S NEWSPAPERS," ACW:NOV/95[54]558

Berman, Harvey J.:
"FORT DELAWARE (TRAVEL)," ACW:NOV/93[66]445

"FORT MONROE, VIRGINIA (TRAVEL)," ACW:MAY/91[62]307

Biggs, Greg:
"A LEG UP ON JOHN BELL HOOD (AUDIO/VIDEO)," B&G:JUN/91[42]456
"THE CIVIL WAR IS ON A ROLL (AUDIO/VIDEO)," B&G:APR/91[40]450
"THE GRAY GHOST STORY (AUDIO/VIDEO)," B&G:APR/94[31]560
"THE HORSE SOLDIERS (AUDIO/VIDEO)," B&G:JUN/93[36]526
"JEFFERSON DAVIS' GREATEST MISTAKE (AUDIO/VIDEO)," B&G:FEB/91[38]443
"THE "SHOUPADE" REDOUBTS: JOSEPH E. JOHNSTON'S CHATTAHOOCHEE RIVER LINE," CWR:VOL1#3[82]123
"STRANGE BEDFELLOWS (AUDIO/VIDEO)," B&G:FEB/92[36]478

Bigham, John Mills; "THE B.H. TEAGUE COLLECTION OF CONFEDERATE RELICS AND CURIOS, B&G:JUN/91[38]455

Bilby, Joseph; "GIVE MY LOVE TO ALL: A LIEUTENANT'S LETTERS TOLD THE STORY OF THE 3RD NEW JERSEY INFANTRY," CWTI:MAY/89[36]118

Bird, Roy; "JO SHELBY AND HIS SHADOW," ACW:MAR/95[26]515

Bivin, Ken; "THE FALL OF RICHMOND," ACW:MAY/95[38]526

Black, Linda G.:
"A WIFE'S DEVOTION: THE STORY OF JAMES AND FANNY RICKETTS," B&G:JUN/94[22]569
"CHARLES CARTER RANDOLPH (PERSONALITY)," ACW:JUL/93[10]421
"GETTYSBURG REMEMBERS PRESIDENT LINCOLN," GETTY:9[122]220
"HARRIET HAWLEY (PERSONALITY)," ACW:NOV/93[10]439
"THREE HEROINES OF GETTYSBURG," GETTY:11[119]238

Blacknall, Charles; "I'LL LIVE YET TO DANCE ON THAT FOOT (MY WAR)," CWTI:MAY/93[26]318

Blair, William A.:
"FRANCIS LEIBER'S SEARCH FOR A MORE HUMANE SHADE OF WAR," CWM:AUG/95[58]611
"GENERAL IRVIN MCDOWELL: GENEROUS TO A FAULT," CWM:JUN/95[82]600
"GEORGE FITZHUGH: POLEMICIST FOR THE PECULIAR INSTITUTION," CWM:FEB/95[68]567
"PETER GRAY MEEK: STRIDENT COPPERHEAD EDITOR," CWM:APR/95[63]578
"THE PRIVATE LYONS WAKEMAN—A SOLDIER WITH A SECRET CWM:OCT/95[63]623
"PRIVATE WILLIE GREENE—YANKEE REBEL AND ANTI-HERO," CWM:DEC/95[59]633

Bluford, Robert Jr.; "BATTLEFIELD PRESERVATION IN CENTRAL VIRGINIA," B&G:APR/94[61]566

Blumberg, Arnold; "THE ARMS-STARVED CONFEDERACY... (ORDNANCE)," ACW:JAN/94[18]449

Bogue, Hardy Z. III; "1ST SOUTH CAROLINA (COMMANDS)," ACW:NOV/92[10]384

Bolte', Philip L:
"AGAINST ALL ODDS: FORREST'S GREAT WEST TENNESSEE RAID," CWM:DEC/95[48]631
"COMMAND SHIFT DICTATED," MH:JUN/92[50]159
"RAPID-FIRE WEAPONS (ORDNANCE)," ACW:JUL/93[8]420

Bonney, Usher P.; "LEE'S LIEUTENANTS: JAMES LONGSTREET," CWM:JUL/92[16]428A

Bonomo, Aimee; "U.S. SIGNAL CORPS (ORDNANCE)," ACW:JAN/95[20]504

Boritt, Gabor S.:
"THE ART OF REA REDIFER: INTERPRETATIONS OF
LINCOLN," B&G:OCT/92[55]501
"THE PRESIDENT AT PLAY," CWTI:DEC/95[14]475
Bowen, Thomas E., Jr.; "A FORGOTTEN REBEL GENERAL
(TIME LAPSE)," CWTI:MAR/93[50]313
Bowen, Roland E.; "NOTHING BUT COWARDS RUN,"
CWM:APR/95[42]577
Bradley, Mark L.; "THE BATTLE OF BENTONVILLE,
MARCH 19-21, 1865: LAST STAND IN THE CAROLINAS
(THE GENERAL'S TOUR)," B&G:DEC/95[9]615
Brewer, Captain James D.; "THE BATTLE OF BRITTON'S
LANE: THE CLIMAX OF ARMSTRONG'S RAID,"
B&G:APR/93[34]521
Brightman Jr., Austin C.; "GLORY ENOUGH: THE 148TH
PENNSYLVANIA VOLUNTEERS FORT CRATER,"
CWR:VOL2#2[141]137
Brinsfield, John W.; "IN THE PULPIT AND IN THE
TRENCHES," CWTI:SEP/92[28]280
Brock, Darryl E.; "THE CONFEDERATE STATES MEDICAL
& SURGICAL JOURNAL (ORDNANCE),"
ACW:MAY/95[8]522
Brockway, Michael D.; "COMFORT, TEXAS (TRAVEL),"
ACW:JUL/91[58]316
Brooks, Tom; "MANY A HARD FOUGHT FIELD: THE 22ND
BATTALION VIRGINIA INFANTRY," CWR:VOL1#3[52]122
Brooksher, William R.; "BETWIXT WIND AND WATER,"
CWTI:NOV/93[65]351
Broome, Doyle:
"MOST SPLENDID PIECE OF STRATEGY,"
CWM:OCT/94[48]542
"WE'LL TRY FIGHTING FOR AWHILE. . .JOHN T. WILDER,"
CWM:JUL/92[24]430
Broun, William Le Roy; "I WAS THERE," CWM:SEP/91[8]378
Brown, D. Alexander:
"BEECHER'S ISLAND," AHI:DEC/67[4]113
"THE BELKNAP SCANDAL," AHI:MAY/69[32]1
"BLACK BEAVER," AHI:MAY/67[32]108
"GERONIMO," AHI:JUL/80[36]204
"HOW STANDING BEAR BECAME A PERSON,"
AHI:APR/71[48]133
"THE LAST DAYS OF "SAM" GRANT," AHI:DEC/72[4]144
"ONE REAL AMERICAN," AHI:NOV/69[13]124
Brown, Kent Masterson:
"LEE AT GETTYSBURG: THE MAN, THE MYTH, THE
RECRIMINATIONS," CWM:JAN/93[8]456
"MASTER OF THE BOLD FRONT," CWM:JUL/91[29]367
Brown, William D.; "A FREEDMAN IN THE UNION ARMY
(TIME LAPSE)," CWTI:JAN/94[82]366
Brugioni, Dino A.; "THE MEANEST BUSHWHACKER,"
B&G:JUN/91[32]454
Bryant, Garry; "A LOYAL FAMILY MAN (TIME LAPSE),"
CWTI:DEC/91[82]243
Buckner, Simon B., (edited by Kenneth Hafendorfer); "MAJOR
GENERAL SIMON B. BUCKNER'S UNPUBLISHED
AFTER-ACTION REPORT ON THE BATTLE OF
PERRYVILLE," CWR:VOL4#3[50]171
Bundy, Gloria; "IN A NUTSHELL (MY WAR),"
CWTI:JAN/94[24]359
Burden, Jeffry C.; "INTO THE BREACH: THE 22ND IOWA
INFANTRY AT THE RAILROAD REDOUBT,
CWR:VOL2#1[19]131

Burks, Ned:
"INSIDE PRESERVATION, INSIDE THE ASSOCIATION FOR
THE PRESERVATION OF CIVIL WAR SITES,"
CWM:MAY/93[40]479
"INSIDE PRESERVATION, INSIDE...THE FEDERAL
GOVERNMENT," CWM:APR/94[40]507
Burlingame, Michael; "A MAN OF SORROWS,"
CWTI:DEC/95[24]477
Burns, Ken; "THE REALIST," CWM:JUL/91[25]362
Bush, Garry L.; "THE SIXTH MICHIGAN CAVALRY AT
FALLING WATERS: THE END OF THE GETTYSBURG
CAMPAIGN," GETTY:9[109]218
Buttafuso, Bob; "HUNTING HISTORY," CWM:SEP/91[48]386
Byers, S.H.M.; "HOW MEN FEEL IN BATTLE,"
AHI:APR/87[10]261

Caldwell, Susan; "I WAS THERE," CWM:MAR/92[56]415
Calkins, Chris M.:
"THE BATTLE OF FIVE FORKS: FINAL PUSH FOR THE
SOUTH SIDE (THE GENERAL'S TOUR)," B&G:APR/92[8]481
"FINAL MARCH TO APPOMATTOX: THE 12TH VIRGINIA
INFANTRY APRIL 2-12, AN EYEWITNESS ACCOUNT,"
CWR:VOL2#3[236]143
"I WILL TAKE ALL THE RESPONSIBILITY,"
CWM:JUL/91[46]373
"THE PETERSBURG 'FOLLY GUN' (LEGACY),"
CWTI:DEC/90[18]180
"THE PRESERVATION REPORT: A HISTORY OF THE
CRATER BATTLEFIELD, 1865-1992," CWR:VOL2#2[156]138
Cameron, Alexander W.:
"A SIGNAL SERGEANT AT GETTYSBURG: THE DIARY OF
LUTHER C. FURST," GETTY:10[42]224
"THE SAVIORS OF LITTLE ROUND TOP," GETTY:8[31]201
Cameron, Colonel Bill; "THE SIGNAL CORPS AT
GETTYSBURG PART II: SUPPORT OF MEADE'S PURSUIT,"
GETTY:4[101]151
Campbell, Eric A.:
"THE AFTERMATH AND RECOVERY OF GETTYSBURG,
PART I," GETTY:11[102]237
"THE AFTERMATH AND RECOVERY OF GETTYSBURG,
PART II" GETTY:12[97]249
"REMEMBER HARPER'S FERRY! THE DEGRADATION,
HUMILIATION, AND REDEMPTION OF COL. GEORGE L.
WILLARD'S BRIGADE, PART I," GETTY:7[51]190
"REMEMBER HARPER'S FERRY! THE DEGRADATION,
HUMILIATION, AND REDEMPTION OF COL. GEORGE L.
WILLARD'S BRIGADE, PART II," GETTY:8[95]205
"BAPTISM OF FIRE: THE NINTH MASSACHUSETTS
BATTERY AT GETTYSBURG, JULY 2, 1863," GETTY:5[47]160
Candenquist, Arthur:
"DID ANYBODY REALLY KNOW WHAT TIME IT WAS?"
B&G:AUG/91[32]461
"THE GREAT TRAIN ROBBERY," CWM:NOV/91[40]393
Candido, Jeane H.; "SISTERS AND NUNS WHO WERE
NURSES DURING THE CIVIL WAR," B&G:OCT/93[31]539
Cantrell, Kimberly B.; "BATTLE FOR THE BRIDGES,"
ACW:MAR/91[38]296
Carmichael, Peter S.:
"NEVER HEARD BEFORE ON THE AMERICAN CONTINENT,"
GETTY:10[107]227
"THE PENINSULA CAMPAIGN OF 1862: STUART'S RIDE
AROUND MCCLELLAN," CWM:JUN/95[50]589

"THE PENINSULA CAMPAIGN OF 1862: THE BATTLE OF MALVERN HILL," CWM:JUN/95[73]597

"THE PENINSULA CAMPAIGN OF 1862: THE BATTLE OF SAVAGE'S STATION," CWM:JUN/95[65]595

Caroli, Betty Boyd; "AMERICA'S FIRST LADIES," AHI:MAY/89[26]285

Carr, Major Eugene A.; "CARR'S PUNITIVE EXPEDITION," AHI:DEC/67[58]114

Carroll, Edward; "THERE WILL BE HOME MADE THUNDER HERE (SIDEBAR)," CWTI:SUMMER/89[20]121A

Carroon, Robert G.; "U.S. TREASURER, REBEL SOLDIER," CWTI:JUL/94[82]396

Carter, Caroline; "FAMILY VALUES AT CEDAR CREEK," CWM:OCT/94[23]535

Carter, Chip:
"AT HOME WITH THE GENERAL (TARGET)," CWTI:FEB/92[10]246
"ATLANTA'S RESTORED CYCLORAMA (TARGET)," CWTI:FEB/91[18]190

Carter, Isabel B.; "PRAYING FOR SOUTHERN VICTORY (MY WAR)," CWTI:MAR/91[12]198

Cassidy, Patricia:
"BLOODY KANSAS ... WITNESSES TO QUANTRILL'S RAID IN LAWRENCE AND THEIR STORIES," CWM:JAN/92[12]400
"MEMOIRS IN OILS," CWM:NOV/92[31]449

Castel, Albert:
"ARNOLD VS. ARNOLD: THE STRANGE AND HITHERTO UNTOLD STORY OF THE DIVORCE OF STONEWALL JACKSON'S SISTER," B&G:OCT/94[28]581
"THE BATTLE THAT SHOULD NOT HAVE BEEN," CWTI:NOV/92[41]291
"BLEEDING KANSAS," AHI:JUL/75[4]160
"THE FILM THAT MADE ME: 50 YEARS AFTER GWTW IS RELEASED AN HISTORIAN GETS AROUND TO SAYING THANK YOU," CWTI:SUMMER/1989[6]119A
"FORT PILLOW: VICTORY OR MASSACRE?" AHI:APR/74[4]154
"MARY WALKER: SAMARITAN OR CHARLATAN," CWTI:MAY/94[40]383
"WILLIAM CLARKE QUANTRILL: TERROR OF THE BORDER," CWM:JAN/92[8]399
"WINFIELD SCOTT, PART I, THE SOLDIER," AHI:JUN/81[10]219
"WINFIELD SCOTT, PART II: THE COMMANDER," AHI:JUL/81[20]221

Cates, C. Pat:
"A LONG ROAD TO BENTONVILLE: THE FIRST CONFEDERATE REGIMENT (PART II)," CWR:VOL1#4[64]127
"FROM SANTA ROSA ISLAND TO CHICKAMAUGA: THE FIRST CONFEDERATE REGIMENT, CWR:VOL1#4[42]126

Chalmers, David:
"RULE BY TERROR, PART I," AHI:JAN/80[8]197
"RULE BY TERROR, PART II," AHI:FEB/80[28]199A

Chamberlain, Joshua L.; "THROUGH BLOOD AND FIRE AT GETTYSBURG," GETTY:6[43]173

Cheeks, Robert C.:
"BLOOD POURED LIKE WATER," ACW:MAR/94[50]462
"CARNAGE IN A CORNFIELD," ACW:JUL/92[30]369
"FAILURE ON THE HEIGHTS," ACW:NOV/92[42]388
"FIRE AND FURY AT CATHERINE'S FURNACE," ACW:MAY/95[30]525

Clark, James R.; "THE COST OF CAPTURE (TARGET)," CWTI:APR/92[23]255

Clark, Jim:
"ATLANTA CAMPAIGN (TRAVEL)," ACW:JUL/94[66]481
"KENNESAW MOUNTAIN BATTLEFIELD PARK AND THE ATLANTA CYCLORAMA," ACW:NOV/95[74]560

Cleary, Ben:
"A LIVING MAP OF THE WAR," CWM:JUN/95[79]599
"WAR AND PAINT," CWM:OCT/94[55]543

Cleaveland, R. Chris; "GEORGIA'S NANCY HARTS," CWTI:MAY/94[44]384

Cochran, Darrell:
"CONFEDERATES' BRILLIANT EXPLOIT," ACW:SEP/91[41]323
"GRANNY LEE'S INAUSPICIOUS DEBUT," ACW:SEP/94[31]486

Cochran, Jai S.; "THE CONTENTIOUS ROBERT TOOMBS," CWM:MAR/93[32]468

Cochrane, Alice LeRoy; "BERMUDA (TRAVEL)," ACW:MAY/93[62]418

Comtois, Pierre:
"UTAH'S NAUVOO LEGION (COMMANDS)," ACW:JAN/95[8]502
"WAR'S LAST BATTLE," ACW:JUL/92[46]371

Conklin, E.F.; "ELMINA KEELER SPENCER: MATRON, 147TH NEW YORK," GETTY:8[121]207

Connelly, Thomas L.; "THE OTHER CIVIL WAR," AHI:NOV/73[18]151

Conrad, James L.; "TRAINING IN TREASON," CWTI:SEP/91[23]228

Conrad, Robert J.; "CUSTER'S LONG SUMMER," CWTI:MAY/93[35]320

Cook, Adrian; "ASHES AND BLOOD: THE NEW YORK CITY DRAFT RIOTS," AHI:AUG/77[30]175

Cooke, Jay; "INTERVIEW WITH LINCOLN," AHI:NOV/72[10]141

Cooling, B. Franklin:
"FORTS HENRY & DONELSON: UNION VICTORY ON THE TWIN RIVERS," B&G:FEB/92[10]474
"MONOCACY: THE BATTLE THAT SAVED WASHINGTON (THE GENERAL'S TOUR)," B&G:DEC/92[8]503
"PATRICK RONAYNE CLEBURNE: SOUTHERN CITIZEN-SOLDIER," CWM:MAR/91[28]336

Cooney, Charles F.; "THE GENERAL'S BADGE OF HONOR," AHI:APR/85[16]249

Coski, John M.:
"THE 'BANDBOX REGIMENT': THE 32ND WISCONSIN VOLUNTEER INFANTRY," CWR:VOL2#4[313]146
"THE PENINSULA CAMPAIGN OF 1862: DENOUEMENT AT HARRISON'S LANDING," CWM:JUN/95[76]598

Cotton, Dr. Gordon; "A SUPERIOR SOUTHERN MUSEUM: VICKSBURG, MISSISSIPPI," CWTI:SEPT/89[18]126

Cox, James A.; "FORT DELAWARE ON THE WATER: A MONUMENT TO RUGGED REBELS," CWTI:JUL/93[20]325

Cozzens, Peter:
"A FEW ARE HOLDING OUT UP YONDER," CWTI:SEP/92[31]281
"TO SAVE AN ARMY," CWTI:SEP/94[40]403

Crawford, Frank; "D.A. JANUARY, HOSPITAL SHIP, (ORDNANCE)," ACW:MAR/93[8]401

Crawford, Mark J.; "RESORT OF THE DEAD," ACW:MAR/95[50]518

Crawford, William A.; ". . .OUR NOBLEST AND BEST SPIRITS HAVE LAIN DOWN THEIR LIVES...," CWR:VOL1#2[70]115

Crews, Ed; "PETERSBURG," ACW:NOV/92[74]390

Criswell, Howard Jr.; "A CONVERSATION WITH THE PAST," CWTI:APR/90[56]155
Cross, David F.; "MANTLED IN FIRE AND SMOKE," ACW:JAN/92[38]343
Cross, Edward E.; "COMPLETELY OUTGENERALLED (MY WAR)," CWTI:AUG/95[24]455
Crowe, Elizabeth P.; "CIVIL WAR IN CYBERSPACE," CWTI:OCT/95[40]469
Cubbison, Douglas R.:
"MIDNIGHT ENGAGEMENT: GEARY'S WHITE STAR DIVISION A WAUHATCHIE, TENNESSEE, OCTOBER 28-29, 1863," CWR:VOL3#2[70]155
"THE PRESERVATION REPORT," CWR:VOL3#2[102]156
Cullen, Joseph P.; "RICHMOND FALLS!" AHI:JAN/74[10]153
Cummings, John F. III; "NORTH ANNA RIVER: THE PAST RECLAIMED," B&G:APR/93[23]519
Curry, Wilmot W., (edited by Paula Mitchell Mark); "TO THE POTOMAC WITH SERGEANT CURRY," CWTI:SEPT/89[24]128
CWTI Editors; "STRIKE THE PHRASE 'STRIKE THE TENT'," CWTI:SEP/90[47]177
Czech, Kenneth P.:
"ARMOR (ORDNANCE)," ACW:SEP/92[8]374
"HIGH SEAS BROUHAHA," ACW:NOV/91[46]335
"RAIDER OF THE ARCTIC SEAS," ACW:MAY/91[46]306
"RUMORS OF WAR: RUSSIAN BATTLE FLEETS VISIT UNION PORT IN 1863," CWTI:MAY/89[28]117

Datto, John N.; "GRIERSON (PERSONALITY)," MH:FEB/95[18]182
Dave, Wilkinson; "THE MODOC INDIAN WAR," AHI:AUG/78[18]183
Davis, Danny; "RETURN TO FREDERICKSBURG," ACW:SEP/92[30]378
Davis, Elias; "LEE'S LIEUTENANTS: STONEWALL JACKSON," CWM:JUL/92[16]428
Davis, Stephen R.:
"THE 11TH MISSISSIPPI INFANTRY IN THE ARMY OF NORTHERN VIRGINIA," CWR:VOL2#4[269]145
"THE DEATH AND BURIALS OF GENERAL RICHARD BROOKE GARNETT," GETTY:5[107]164
"DEATH TAKES NO HOLIDAY," ACW:MAY/93[22]414
"UNIVERSITY GREYS (COMMANDS)," ACW:MAR/92[10]349
Davis, Thomas; "SHOGUNATE DEFIED," MH:OCT/91[50]154
Davis, William C.:
"CONFEDERATE EXILES," AHI:JUN/70[30]127
"FIRST CLASH OF THE IRONCLADS," AHI:NOV/75[38]163
"IT WAS A GREAT VICTORY," AHI:OCT/75[30]162
"JOHN C. FREMONT," AHI:MAY/70[4]126
Dawson, Gladys; "CLEMENT VALLANDIGHAM (PERSONALITY)," ACW:MAR/91[8]291
DeForest, Tim; "BRILLIANT CAVALRY EXPLOIT," ACW:MAY/92[47]363
DeGress, Captain Francis; (edited by C. Chris Evans); "REPORT OF THE BATTLE OF ATLANTA, B&G:APR/94[28]559
Delaney, Norman C.:
"CRUISERS FOR THE CONFEDERACY, PART I," AHI:DEC/82[38]231
"CRUISERS FOR THE CONFEDERACY, PART II," AHI:JAN/83[10]232
Denault, Patricia; "THE LITTLE GIANT," AHI:OCT/70[23]129

Denkhaus, Ray; "JOHN PAUL STRAIN (ARTISTS)," ACW:JAN/95[70]509
Dougherty, Captain William E.; "AN EYEWITNESS ACCOUNT OF SECOND BULL RUN," AHI:DEC/66[30]105
Downs, David B.; "HIS LEFT WAS WORTH A GLANCE: MEADE AND THE UNION LEFT ON JULY 2, 1863," GETTY:7[29]188
Driscoll, T. Jeff:
"THE CITY OF BROTHERLY HOSPITALITY," CWTI:MAY/94[24]381
"HOLIDAY IN NEW YORK," CWTI:NOV/92[49]292
"THE VERMONT BRIGADE (COMMANDS)," ACW:JAN/94[8]447
Dugan, Gene; "THE NORTH CAROLINA JUNIOR RESERVES (COMMANDS)," ACW:NOV/93[12]440
Dunkelman, Mark H.:
"THE HARDTACK REGIMENT IN THE BRICKYARD FIGHT," GETTY:8[17]200
"RELUCTANT AND UNLUCKY SOLDIER," B&G:OCT/93[36]540
Durham, Roger S.:
"SAVANNAH: MR. LINCOLN'S CHRISTMAS PRESENT (THE GENERAL'S TOUR)," B&G:FEB/91[8]439
"THE MAN WHO SHOT JOHN SEDGWICK: THE TALE OF CHARLES D. GRACE — A SHARPSHOOTER IN THE DOLES-COOK BRIGADE," B&G:DEC/95[25]616

Earp, Charles A.; "HILL'S FAVORITE COURIER," CWTI:SEP/92[42]283
Ebeling, Andrea E.A.; "BEHIND THE LINES," CWTI:JUL/92[62]276
Ebersole, David S.; "POLITICAL BUTTONS," AHI:NOV/84[18]241A
Ecelbarger, Gary; "SLAUGHTER AT HOUCK'S RIDGE (DISPATCHES)," CWM:AUG/95[27]605
Eckhardt, C.F.; "A PROBLEM OF RANK," CWTI:FEB/91[52]195
Edgerton, C.R.; "MULES (ORDNANCE)," ACW:JAN/92[10]339
Editors Of Blue & Gray Magazine; "THE DEATH OF COL. WILLIAM SHY," B&G:DEC/93[49]547A
Eggert, Gerald G.; "THE GREAT PULLMAN STRIKE!" AHI:APR/71[37]132
Ellertsen, Peter; "THE BATTLE OF BELMONT AND THE CITIZEN SOLDIERS OF THE 27TH ILLINOIS VOLUNTEER INFANTRY," CWR:VOL3#4[24]162
Ellis, Allen; "YANKEE CAPTAIN DANIEL ELLIS: THE OLD RED FOX OF EAST TENNESSEE," B&G:APR/92[28]482
Ellis, Garrison; "EDITOR'S REPORT," CWM:APR/94[2]500
Elmore, Thomas L.:
"A METEOROLOGICAL AND ASTRONOMICAL CHRONOLOGY OF THE GETTYSBURG CAMPAIGN," GETTY:13[7]253
"COURAGE AGAINST THE TRENCHES: THE ATTACK AND REPULSE OF STEUART'S BRIGADE ON CULP'S HILL," GETTY:7[83]192
"THE EFFECTS OF ARTILLERY FIRE ON INFANTRY AT GETTYSBURG," GETTY:5[117]165
"SKIRMISHERS," GETTY:6[7]169
Engle, E. Prescott; "STONEWALL'S FORGOTTEN MASTERPIECE," MH:AUG/95[30]185
Eppinga, Jane; "WAR'S WESTERNMOST BATTLE," ACW:JUL/93[27]423
Ernst, Kathleen:
"AN ANGEL FROM WISCONSIN: A YANKEE GOVERNOR'S WIDOW DEDICATES HERSELF TO COMFORTING THE WOUNDED," CWTI:MAR/89[20]102

"TWO 1ST MARYLAND INFANTRIES (COMMANDS),"
ACW:JUL/94[10]475
"WAR COMES TO FREDERICK," ACW:JAN/91[38]287
Evans, David:
"THE ATLANTA CAMPAIGN: CHAPTER 1: THE
MANEUVERS BEGIN," CWTI:SUMMER/89[13]120
"THE ATLANTA CAMPAIGN: CHAPTER 2: UP AGAINST
THE DEFENSES," CWTI:SUMMER/89[20]121
"THE ATLANTA CAMPAIGN: CHAPTER 3: FIGHTING JOHN
HOOD," CWTI:SUMMER/89[20]122
"THE ATLANTA CAMPAIGN: CHAPTER 4: THE DEATHS OF
FRIENDS AND FOES," CWTI:SUMMER/89[40]123
"THE ATLANTA CAMPAIGN: CHAPTER 5: THE PRIZE I
FOUGHT FOR," CWTI:SUMMER/89[50]124
"CAPTAIN DEGRESS AND THE BEST GUNS IN THE
WORLD," B&G:AUG/95[55]609
"THAT DEVIL—NATHAN BEDFORD FORREST,"
CWM:JUL/92[48]433
Evans, E. Chris; "RETURN TO JACKSON, JULY 5-25, 1863
(THE GENERAL'S TOUR)," B&G:AUG/95[8]604
Evans, Michael W.; "2ND FLORIDA (COMMANDS),"
ACW:SEP/93[8]429
Evans, Thomas J.; "THE STRANGE CASE OF LIEUTENANT
COLLEY, 10TH MAINE INFANTRY," B&G:OCT/95[32]613

Faeder, Gustav S.:
"JEB STUART AND HIS RELUCTANT CAVALRYMAN,"
B&G:OCT/92[38]500
"SUPERB WAS THE DAY," ACW:MAR/91[47]297
Faller, Phillip E.; "POUNDING PORT HUDSON,"
ACW:JAN/94[30]450
Fanton, Ben:
"BATTLE ON THE BRICKYARD WALL," CWTI:SEP/94[34]402
"THE UNKNOWN SOLDIER OF GETTYSBURG
(PERSONALITY)," ACW:JUL/94[18]476
Farris, John K., (edited by Jim Stanbery); "A CONFEDERATE
SURGEON'S VIEW OF FORT DONELSON: DIARY OF
JOHN KENNERLY FARRIS," CWR:VOL1#3[7]118
Feis, William B.; "THE DECEPTION OF BRAXTON BRAGG:
THE TULLAHOMA CAMPAIGN, JUNE 23 - JULY 4, 1863
(THE GENERAL'S TOUR)," B&G:oct/92[10]496
Feldner, Emmitt B.:
"4TH WISCONSIN (COMMANDS)," ACW:MAY/93[12]412
"JEB STUART'S DARING RECONNAISSANCE,"
ACW:JUL/95[34]536
Felton, Silas:
"THE IRON BRIGADE BATTERY AT GETTYSBURG,"
GETTY:11[57]233
"PURSUING THE ELUSIVE 'CANNONEER'," GETTY:9[33]211
Ferling, John E.; "THE EVOLVING PRESIDENCY,"
AHI:APR/89[13]
Feuer, A.B.:
"STEADY BOYS, STEADY!" MH:AUG/93[47]169
"WEAPONRY," MH:OCT/93[12]171
Filzen, Lydia C.; "THE LADY'S CARRYING A SCALPEL?,"
CWM:APR/94[8]502
Filzen, Lydia C.; "MY FRIEND, THE ENEMY,"
B&G:DEC/92[20]504
First, Pasco E.; "ELIZABETH KECKLEY (PERSONALITY),"
ACW:JUL/92[6]365
Fishburne, C.D.; "STONEWALL JACKSON—A MEMOIR,"
AHI:JUN/67[31]110

Fitts, Deborah:
"CIVIL WAR MAGAZINE'S FIRST ANNUAL ENDANGERED
BATTLEFIELDS LIST," CWM:JAN/92[44]406
"THE DISNEY PARK LOOMS," CWM:JUN/94[14]509
Fitzgerald, William S.; "WE WILL ALWAYS STAND BY YOU,"
CWTI:NOV/93[71]352
Fleek, Sherman L.; "LOST IN CUSTER'S SHADOW,"
ACW:SEP/94[55]489
Fleet, Charles B., (edited by Chris Calkins); "THE
FREDERICKSBURG ARTILLERY AT APPOMATTOX,"
CWR:VOL1#1[35]104
Fleming, Candace; "AFTER LIFE'S FITFUL FEVER,"
AHI:MAR/93[50]310
Fleming, Martin K.:
"THE NORTHWESTERN VIRGINIA CAMPAIGN 1861 (THE
GENERAL'S TOUR)," B&G:AUG/93[10]529
"ONE MAN'S STRUGGLE AT RICH MOUNTAIN,"
B&G:AUG/93[52]534
Fleming, Thomas; "THE RACE TO PROMONTORY,"
AHI:JUN/71[10]134
Foley, Edward; "THE GREAT REBEL RAID ON CALAIS,
MAINE," CWTI:SEP/92[40]282
Fonvielle, Chris; "THE LAST RAYS OF DEPARTING HOPE:
THE FALL OF WILMINGTON," B&G:DEC/94[10]585
Fordney, Ben; "FAILURE OR HARBINGER,"
CWM:APR/95[32]575
Fordney, Chris:
"EYEWITNESS NEWS," CWM:NOV/92[10]447
"INSIDE PRESERVATION, INSIDE CIVIL WAR ROUNDTABLE
ASSOCIATES," CWM:SEP/93[40]498
"INSIDE PRESERVATION, INSIDE THE CIVIL WAR TRUST,"
CWM:MAR/93[40]470
"INSIDE PRESERVATION, INSIDE THE CONSERVATION
FUND," CWM:JUL/93[46]489
Forster, Greg:
"ALPHEUS WILLIAMS 'OLD PAP'," CWM:JUL/92[18]429
"SHERMAN'S FEUDING GENERALS," CWTI:MAR/95[40]436
Fox, Dorothy; "CHILDHOOD HOME OF AN AMERICAN
ARCH-VILLAIN," CWTI:APR/90[12]150
Freedman, Roma S.; "PERSPECTIVES," MH:OCT/93[20]172
Frobouck, Jo Ann:
"HISTORIC DESIGNATION COSTS TOO MUCH,"
CWM:JUL/92[64]434
"IN HARM'S WAY," CWTI:MAR/93[26]310
Frye, Dennis E.:
"BRILLIANCE TO NO ADVANTAGE," CWM:JUL/91[24]361
"HENRY KYD DOUGLAS CHALLENGED BY HIS PEERS,"
CWM:SEP/91[40]385
Fryer, Kenneth D.; "MEDAL OF HONOR RECIPIENT (TIME
LAPSE)," CWTI:AUG/95[90]462

Gaddy, David W.; "THE CONFEDERATE SIGNAL CORPS AT
GETTYSBURG," GETTY:4[110]152
Gainer, Lucia A.; "TURNER ASHBY (PERSONALITY),"
ACW:JAN/92[8]338
Gallagher, Gary W.:
"AUDACITY TO WHAT PURPOSE?" CWM:JUL/91[28]366
"HOW WAS THE LOST CAUSE LOST?" CWM:AUG/94[8]522
"STEPHEN DODSON RAMSEUR," CWM:JAN/93[40]461
Gara, Larry; "THE MYTH OF THE UNDERGROUND
RAILROAD," AHI:JAN/78[34]178
Gauss, John; "GIVE THE BLACKS TEXAS,"
CWTI:JUN/90[54]162

Gibney, John M.; "A SHADOW PASSING: THE TRAGIC STORY OF NORVAL WELCH AND THE SIXTEENTH MICHIGAN AT GETTYSBURG AND BEYOND," GETTY:6[33]172

Gibson, John M. Jr.; "BATTLE OF MONOCACY PRESERVATION MESSAGE," B&G:DEC/92[53]509

Gilbert, Thomas D.; "MR. GRANT GOES TO WASHINGTON," B&G:APR/95[33]597

Gillespie, Michael L.:
"THE BATTLE OF ROCK CREEK," CWTI:MAR/91[34]201
"THE GREAT GUNBOAT CHASE," CWTI:JUL/94[30]392
"*QUEEN OF THE WEST),*" ACW:MAR/95[18]514

Glynn, Gary:
"BLACK THURSDAY FOR REBELS," ACW:JAN/92[22]341
"MEAGHER OF THE SWORD," ACW:SEP/95[54]548

Goble, William C.; "BRITISH RIFLES (ORDNANCE)," ACW:JAN/93[8]392

Godfrey, Captain Edward S.:
"CUSTER'S LAST BATTLE, PART I," AHI:DEC/84[18]243
"CUSTER'S LAST BATTLE, PART II," AHI:JAN/85[30]246

Godley, L.N.; "CALLAWAY COUNTY, MISSOURI (TRAVEL)," ACW:MAR/91[62]298

Goldy, James; "THE SWAMP ANGEL: LOVED IN TRENTON AND HATED IN CHARLESTON," CWTI:APR/89[22]108

Goodman, Al W. Jr.:
"GRANT'S MISSISSIPPI GAMBLE," ACW:JUL/94[51]480
"MISSISSIPPI'S CHAMPION'S HILL IS AN IMPORTANT, IF FORGOTTEN, BATTLEFIELD," MH:JUN/93[82]167

Goodwin, Glenn:
"THE CONFEDERATE INVASION OF NEW MEXICO AND ARIZONA," CWM:MAY/93[16]475
"THE MOST EXTRAORDINARY FEAT OF THE WAR," CWM:OCT/95[47]620

Gordon, John B.; "LEST WE FORGET," CWM:JUL/93[56]490

Grab, Ernest O.; "ESPIONAGE," MH:OCT/95[8]187

Gragg, Rod; "A BLOODY HALF-HOUR," CWTI:JAN/94[46]364

Graham, Adele; "AB GRIMES (PERSONALITY)," ACW:MAY/91[10]301

Grant, Julia Dent; "MRS. GRANT REMEMBERS JAPAN," AHI:JUN/81[38]220

Greenberg, Henry J.; "PICKETT'S CHARGE: THE REASON WHY," GETTY:5[103]163

Greene, A. Wilson:
"DISNEY'S AMERICA: GUEST EDITORIAL," B&G:AUG/94[34]577
"LEADERSHIP THROUGH DIPLOMACY," CWM:JUL/91[31]368

Greezicki, Roger J.; "HUMBUGGING THE HISTORIAN: A REAPPRAISAL OF LONGSTREET AT GETTYSBURG," GETTY:6[62]175

Griffin, D. Massy; "RODES ON OAK HILL: A STUDY OF RODES' DIVISION ON THE FIRST DAY OF GETTYSBURG," GETTY:4[33]146

Grimsley, Mark:
"A REASON TO LOATHE DAVIS," CWTI:AUG/91[68]222
"A WADE IN THE HIGH TIDE AT PERRYVILLE," CWTI:NOV/92[18]289
"BURNING DOWN THE SOUTH," CWTI:OCT/95[48]470
"THE DEFINITION OF DISASTER," CWTI:MAY/89[14]114
"THE FIRST AND ONLY CONFEDERATE PRESIDENT: CHAPTER 2," CWTI:AUG/91[36]217
"THE GRACIOUS VICTOR: CHAPTER 6," CWTI:FEB/90[54]147
"THE GREAT DECEIVER: THE LIFE OF NATHAN BEDFORD FORREST, PART II," CWTI:NOV/93[33]347

"THE GREAT PHILOSOPHICAL COLLISION: CHAPTER 4," CWTI:AUG/91[52]219
"HIS NATION'S COMMANDER IN CHIEF: CHAPTER 3," CWTI:AUG/91[46]218
"KING JEFF THE FIRST: CHAPTER 5," CWTI:AUG/91[58]220
"LEADER OF THE KLAN: THE LIFE OF NATHAN BEDFORD FORREST, PART III, CWTI:JAN/94[35]361
"MILLIONAIRE REBEL RAIDER: THE LIFE OF NATHAN BEDFORD FORREST, PART 1, CWTI:SEP/93[59]341
"ULYSSES S. GRANT: A KIND OF NORTHERN HERO: CHAPTER 3," CWTI:FEB/90[32]144
"ULYSSES S. GRANT: AN UNHAPPY CIVILIAN: CHAPTER 2," CWTI:FEB/90[26]143
"ULYSSES S. GRANT: COMMANDER OF ALL UNION ARMIES: CHAPTER 5," CWTI:FEB/90[46]146
"ULYSSES S. GRANT: DIFFICULT LAST DAYS: CHAPTER 7," CWTI:FEB/90[60]148
"ULYSSES S. GRANT: HIS LIFE AND HARD TIMES: CHAPTER 1 (A TOUGH FATHER DECIDES HIS SON HAS LITTLE POTENTIAL)," CWTI:FEB/90[20]142
"ULYSSES S. GRANT: LEADING THE JUGGERNAUT: CHAPTER 4," CWTI:FEB/90[38]145
"WE WILL VINDICATE THE RIGHT': AN ACCOUNT OF THE LIFE OF JEFFERSON DAVIS, CHAPTER 1," CWTI:AUG/91[29]216
"THE WILL TO WIN AND DENYING REALITY: CHAPTER 6," CWTI:AUG/91[62]221

Groome, Doyle D. Jr.; "DARING REAR-GUARD DEFENSE," ACW:NOV/93[34]442

Gustaitis, Joseph:
"A PRESIDENTIAL GALLERY," AHI:APR/89[20]282
"HENRY TIMROD (PERSONALITY)," ACW:SEP/92[10]375

Guttman, Jon:
"DONNA J. NEARY (ARTISTS)," ACW:SEP/95[70]549
"FORGOTTEN FEDERAL SUCCESS," ACW:JAN/92[50]345
"JEB STUART'S LAST RIDE," ACW:MAY/94[35]469
"HEAVY ARTILLERY (ORDNANCE)," ACW:SEP/93[16]431
"*CSS MANASSAS* (ORDNANCE)," ACW:MAY/92[16]359

Hadden, R. Lee:
"THE DEADLY EMBRACE: THE MEETING OF THE TWENTY-FOURTH REGIMENT, MICHIGAN INFANTRY AND THE TWENTY-SIXTH REGIMENT OF NORTH CAROLINA TROOPS AT MCPHERSON'S WOODS, GETTYSBURG, PENNSYLVANIA, JULY 1, 1863," GETTY:5[19]158
"THE GRANITE GLORY: THE 19TH MAINE AT GETTYSBURG," GETTY:13[50]257

Hagerman, George; "THE MIDSHIPMEN OF THE CONFEDERATE NAVAL ACADEMY (ORDNANCE)," ACW:JUL/92[10]366

Haines, Douglas C.; "A.P. HILL'S ADVANCE TO GETTYSBURG," GETTY:5[4]156

Haley, Thomas; "THE PRESERVATION REPORT," CWR:VOL1#1[69]106

Hall, Clark B.:
"THE BATTLE OF BRANDY STATION," CWTI:JUN/90[32]159
"DESTROYING HISTORY HURTS TOO MUCH," CWM:JUL/92[64]434A
"DISASTER AT BRANDY STATION," B&G:APR/94[35]562

"SEASON OF CHANGE, THE WINTER ENCAMPMENT OF THE ARMY OF THE POTOMAC, DECEMBER 1, 1863 — MAY 4, 1864 (THE GENERAL'S TOUR)," B&G:APR/91[8]445

"HOW TO SAVE A BATTLEFIELD: DOCUMENT THE ACTION," CWM:NOV/91[66]395

"KILLED AT BRANDY STATION (TIME LAPSE)," CWTI:MAR/94[67]377

"ROBERT F. BECKHAM: THE MAN WHO COMMANDED STUART'S HORSE ARTILLERY AFTER PELHAM FELL," B&G:DEC/91[34]470

Hall, James O.; "THE SHELTON LAUREL MASSACRE," B&G:FEB/91[20]440

Halsey, Ashley; "ANCESTRAL GRAY CLOUD OVER PATTON," AHI:MAR/84[42]238

Hanchett, William:
"THE HAPPIEST DAY OF HIS LIFE," CWTI:DEC/95[76]482
"LINCOLN'S MURDER: THE SIMPLE CONSPIRACY THEORY," CWTI:DEC/91[28]239

Hanley, Ray; "THE GRAY REUNON," CWTI:FEB/92[42]250

Hanson, Rich; "ATHENS BATTLEFIELD (TRAVEL)," MH:APR/95[74]184

Harris, Brayton:
"A NOVEL HISTORY OF THE CIVIL WAR," CWM:AUG/94[40]528
"CONFIDENT PLANS, GRIM REALITY," CWM:MAY/91[18]348
"INVISIBLE ENEMIES," CWM:MAY/91[26]349

Harris, Shawn C.; "STONEWALL IN THE VALLEY," ACW:JAN/93[35]396

Harrison, Lowell H.:
"A CAST-IRON MAN: JOHN C. CALHOUN," AHI:FEB/75[4]157
"THE LION OF WHITE HALL," AHI:MAY/69[12]121
"NOT QUITE FREE: THE FREE NEGRO BEFORE THE CIVIL WAR," AHI:JUN/74[12]155
"ROWDIES, RIOTS, AND REBELLIONS," AHI:JUN/72[18]139

Harrison, Noel G.; "THE BATTLE AT THOROUGHFARE GAP," CWM:AUG/95[38]609

Hartley, Chris; "GENERAL JAMES B. GORDON (PERSONALITY)," ACW:JAN/95[10]503

Hartwig, D. Scott; "IT STRUCK HORROR TO US ALL," GETTY:4[89]150

Haskell, Frank A.; "A UNION OFFICER AT GETTYSBURG," AHI:SUM/88[12]273

Haskew, Michael E.:
"CIVIL WAR'S LONGEST SIEGE," MH:APR/95[46]183
"ICY ASSAULT ROUTED," ACW:MAY/91[23]303

Hassler, Warren W., Jr.:
"PERSPECTIVES ON THE PAST," AHI:NOV/76[29]172
"PERSPECTIVES ON THE PAST," AHI:JUL/78[40]182
"PERSPECTIVES ON THE PAST," AHI:AUG/78[31]185

Hattaway, Herman; "BALLOONS: AMERICA'S FIRST AIR FORCE," AHI:JUN/84[24]239

Haughton, Phyllis; "PRISONER OF CIRCUMSTANCES (MY WAR)," CWTI:NOV/92[28]290

Hauptman, Laurence M.; "WAREAGLE OF THE TUSCARORAS: LIEUTENANT CORNELIUS C. CUSICK," CWM:SEP/92[16]438

Haydon, Charles, (edited by Stephen W. Sears); "FLIGHT TO THE JAMES," CWTI:JUL/93[14]324

Hemingway, Al:
"1ST CONNECTICUT VOLUNTEER CAVALRY (COMMANDS)," ACW:JAN/92[16]340
"A MIGHTY MEAN-FOWT FIGHT," ACW:NOV/93[26]441
"FORD'S THEATER (TRAVEL)," ACW:MAY/95[68]529

"'HILDENE' (TRAVEL)," ACW:JUL/92[62]372

"GENERAL JOHN SEDGWICK'S HOME IN CORNWALL HOLLOW (TRAVEL)," ACW:MAR/95[70]520

"METEOR OF THE WAR," ACW:JUL/91[43]315

"U.S. NAVAL ACADEMY (TRAVEL)," ACW:JAN/91[62]289

"VISITING CAVALRYMAN'S ORDEAL," MH:JUN/91[20]152

"WHIRLING THROUGH WINCHESTER," ACW:MAY/91[38]305

Henneke, Ben Graf; "LAURA KEENE, A BIOGRAPHY," AHI:MAY/91[18]293

Hennessy, John:
"HOW TO SAVE A BATTLEFIELD," CWM:MAY/91[50]352
"NEAR KILLING ME," CWM:JUL/91[40]370
"THE SECOND BATTLE OF MANASSAS: "LEE SUPPRESSES THE "MISCREANT" POPE (THE GENERAL'S TOUR)," B&G:AUG/92[11]493
"STUART'S REVENGE," CWTI:JUN/95[38]447
"THE TOLL OF WAR," B&G:AUG/92[53]496A

Herdegen, Lance J.; "THE LIEUTENANT WHO ARRESTED A GENERAL," GETTY:4[24]145

Herek, Raymond J.; "WHO ARE EXEMPT," CWTI:SEP/93[50]339

Herndon, Chesley C., Jr.; "A TENNESSEE VOLUNTEER (TIME LAPSE)," CWTI:AUG/91[82]223

Herr, Pamela; "JESSIE BENTON FREMONT," AHI:SEP/87[21]262

Herron, Frank, (edited by William J. Miller); "I LOVE THE WORK 'RAYMOND'," CWM:JUN/94[58]519

Hill, Ed; "A FIGHTING ZOUAVE," CWTI:JUN/95[90]451

Hillhouse, Don; "FROM OLUSTEE TO APPOMATTOX: THE 1ST FLORIDA SPECIAL BATTALION," CWR:VOL3#1[65]151

Hitchcock, Robert E., (edited by David M. Sullivan; "ONE MARINE'S BRIEF BATTLE (MY WAR)," CWTI:APR/92[14]254

Hodge, Alan; "BILL MAY: CRUSADER FOR CEDAR CREEK," CWM:DEC/95[26]626

Hoffert, Sylvia; "THIS 'ONE GREAT EVIL'," AHI:MAY/77[37]174

Holm, Ed; "PHOTOGRAPHY: MIRROR OF THE PAST," AHI:SEP/89[20]286

Holzer, Harold:
"A FEW APPROPRIATE REMARKS," AHI:NOV/88[37]278
"A UNION HERO'S FORGOTTEN RESTING PLACE," CWTI:FEB/90[12]141
"DEAR MR. LINCOLN," AHI:JAN/94[50]319A
"ENDURING IMAGES OF A NATION DIVIDED: THE GREAT PRINTMAKERS OF THE CIVIL WAR," CWM:NOV/92[24]448
"EYEWITNESSES REMEMBER THE 'FEARFUL NIGHT'," CWTI:MAR/93[12]307
"FORD'S THEATRE," AHI:FEB/86[12]257
"FORGOTTEN HERO OF GETTYSBURG," AHI:NOV/93[48]316
"I MYSELF WAS AT THE FRONT," CWTI:FEB/91[28]192
"I SHOULD NOT SAY ANY FOOLISH THINGS," CWTI:DEC/95[22]476
"LINCOLN'S SECRET ARMS RACE," CWTI:OCT/95[32]468
"MINE EYES HAVE SEEN THE GLORY," CWTI:SEP/93[30]336
"MRS. AMES AND MR. LINCOLN: HOW A SCULPTOR CAPTURED A GREAT AMERICAN'S SPIRIT IN A STONE AND A PHOTOGRAPH," CWTI:APR/89[28]109
"RAID ON HARPERS FERRY," AHI:MAR/84[10]236
"RE-CREATING THE GREAT DEBATE," AHI:DEC/94[68]322

Hoover, Robert L; "OS CONFEDERADOS," CWTI:JAN/93[26]299

Hopkins, Alice K.; "SOUTHERN BELLES AT WAR," ACW:MAY/92[39]362

Hopkins, Counce; "PAULINE CUSHMAN: ACTRESS IN THE THEATER OF WAR," AHI:JAN/85[20]245

Horn, John:
"THE ARMY OF THE POTOMAC'S PROUD III CORPS FELL VICTIM TO INTRA-ARMY POLITICS," ACW:JUL/93[16]422
"CHARGE OF THE TARHEEL BRIGADES," CWTI:FEB/91[45]194

Hosler, Joseph:
"A SHRINE IN THE GOLDEN STATE," CWTI:MAY/92[20]262
"LOS ANGELES' DRUM BARRACKS (TARGET)," CWTI:SEP/91[18]227

Houck, Peter W.; "A HEALING PLACE," CWM:MAY/91[40]351

Howard, Oliver O.; "O.O. HOWARD'S COMMENCEMENT ADDRESS TO SYRACUSE UNIVERSITY," GETTY:11[71]234

Howard, Thomas W.; "JOURNEY OF THE DEAD," ACW:SEP/94[62]490

Hudson, John W., (edited by John M. Priest); "TIRED SOLDIERS DON'T GO VERY FAST," CWTI:FEB/92[36]249

Huelskamp, John W.; "COLONEL HOLDEN PUTNAM AND THE 93D ILLINOIS VOLUNTEER INFANTRY," CWR:VOL3#3[59]159

Hughes, Brent; "SAM UPHAM: STOREKEEPER AND YANKEE SCOUNDREL," CWM:MAR/92[32]413

Hughes, Michael; "I'M GOING TO FIGHTS' MIT SIGEL," B&G:AUG/92[26]494

Hutton, Paul A.; "PHIL SHERIDAN'S CRUSADE FOR YELLOWSTONE," AHI:FEB/85[10]247

Imhof, John D.; "TWO ROADS TO GETTYSBURG: THOMAS LEIPER KANE AND THE 13TH PENNSYLVANIA RESERVES," GETTY:9[53]214

Ingram, Roswell S.; "MORGAN'S BLOODY SHIRT," B&G:FEB/94[62]556

Jackson, Jack; "THE GREAT LOCOMOTIVE WRECK," CWTI:JAN/95[48]429

Jackson, William; "THE KILLER ANGELS / GETTYSBURG," CWM:JUL/93[40]488

Jackson, R. Starke, (submitted by Terry L. Jones); "GOING BACK INTO THE UNION AT LAST (MY WAR)," CWTI:FEB/91[12]189

Jaffee, Walter W.; "REBEL PIRATES AND CALIFORNIA GOLD," CWTI:JUN/95[48]448

James, Garry:
"HERITAGE OR HOAX?" CWTI:SEP/94[24]399
"THE RELIABLE REMINGTON (COLLECTIBLE)," CWTI:SEP/90[18]172
"THE SEARCH FOR THE ULTIMATE WEAPON," CWTI:JAN/93[49]303
"THE UNION'S MOST READY RIFLE: THE MODEL 1861 SPRINGFIELD RIFLE MUSKET," CWTI:SEPT/89[10]125

James, Robert F.:
"JOHN A. RAWLINS (PERSONALITY)," ACW:NOV/95[22]554
"PHIL KEARNY (PERSONALITY)," ACW:NOV/92[18]385
"STONEWALL'S SURPRISE AT OX HILL," ACW:JAN/95[54]508

Jensen, Clara C.; "ANNA ELLA CARROLL (PERSONALITY)," ACW:MAR/95[8]512

Jepsen, Thomas C.:
"CROSSED WIRES," CWTI:DEC/94[57]414
"THE TELEGRAPH GOES TO WAR," CWM:NOV/91[58]394A

Johannsen, Robert W.; "COMING TO THE CRISIS: 1860," AHI:JUN/73[4]149

Johnson, Avis E.; "HANDSOMEST MAN IN THE CONFEDERACY," ACW:JUL/94[35]478

Johnson, Charles F.; *"THREE WEEKS AT GETTYSBURG BY GEORGE ANNA M. WOOLSEY,"* GETTY:9[116]219

Johnson, Norman K.:
"COLONEL JOHN R. BAYLOR (PERSONALITY)" ACW:JAN/91[10]283
"FRANCIS ASBURY SHOUP (PERSONALITY)," ACW:SEP/94[10]484
"YANKEES IN GRAY," ACW:SEP/92[38]379

Johnston, Joseph E.; "CONVERSATION IN CONFIDENCE (MY WAR)," CWTI:JAN/95[20]422

Joiner, Gary D.; "THE UNION NAVAL EXPEDITION ON THE RED RIVER, MARCH 12-MAY 22, 1864," CWR:VOL4#2[26]166

Jones, James P. Jr.; "'BULL' AND THE 'DAMNED PUPPY': A CIVIL WAR TRAGEDY," AHI:NOV/72[12]142

Jones, Michael D.:
"JEFF DAVIS' PET WOLVES: THE 1ST LOUISIANA ZOUAVE BATTALION DID NOT DESERVE ITS MEAN REPUTATION," CWTI:MAR/89[28]103
"WILLIAM C. OATES: ON LITTLE ROUND TOP, UNSUNG; IN POSTWAR POLITICS, UNRECONSTRUCTED," CWM:DEC/94[26]548

Jones, Terry L.:
"THE LOUISIANA TIGERS," CWM:SEP/93[24]49
"WHEAT'S TIGERS," CWTI:MAR/94[48]374

Jordan, William B., Jr.; "GETTYSBURG AND THE SEVENTEENTH MAINE," GETTY:JAN/93[43]202

Jorgensen, C. Peter:
"THE ALURE OF THE CIIVL WAR'S HEFTIEST RELICS," CWTI:DEC/90[20]181
"GETTYSBURG: HOW A PRIZE WINNING NOVEL BECAME A MOTION PICTURE," CWTI:NOV/93[40]348
"THE MAKING OF *"GLORY,"* CWTI:DEC/89[53]138
"THE WAR'S MOST DANGEROUS RELICS," CWTI:DEC/94[42]412

Jorgensen, Jay A.:
"JOSEPH W. LATIMER, THE 'BOY MAJOR' AT GETTYSBURG," GETTY:JAN/93[29]222
"SCOUTING FOR ULYSSES S. GRANT: THE 5TH OHIO CAVALRY IN THE SHILOH CAMPAIGN," CWR:VOL4#1[44]164

Joseph, Cullen:
"THE BATTLE OF FREDERICKSBURG," AHI:JUN/78[4]180
"DOROTHEA DIX: FORGOTTEN CRUSADER," AHI:JUL/78[11]181

Joslyn, Mauriel:
"GETTYSBURG AND THE IMMORTAL SIX HUNDRED," GETTY:12[111]250
"LT. COL. PAUL FRANCOIS DE GOURNAY (PERSONALITY)," ACW:SEPT/95[8]542

Karle, Theodore J.; "TIME LAPSE," CWTI:FEB/92[58]251

Katz, D. Mark; "A FACE IN HISTORY," AHI:OCT/85[38]253

Kauffman, Michael W.; "HISTORIANS OPPOSE OPENING OF BOOTH GRAVE," CWTI:JUN/95[26]445

Kaufman, Kara; "MATTHEW FONTAINE MAURY: UNRECOGNIZED CONFEDERATE NAVY HERO," CWM:JUL/93[30]486

Keenan, Jerry:
"FIGHTING WITH FORREST IN THE TENNESSEE WINTER," ACW:NOV/95[48]557
"THE GALLANT HOOD OF TEXAS," ACW:MAR/94[42]463

Kell, John McIntosh; "CRUISE AND COMBATS OF THE *ALABAMA,*" AHI:OCT/88[38]275

Keller, Allan; "JOHN BROWN'S RAID," AHI:AUG/76[34]171

Kellmeyer, Steven; "A UNION COLONEL WAS THE RUSSIAN CONNECTION IN THE AMERICAN CIVIL WAR," MH:DEC/93[12]174

Kelly, C. Brian; "SIEGE CITY, USA," MH:JUN/92[6]158

Kelly, Timothy W., (edited by Elaine Pease); "IF THIS CONTINUES THE ARMY OF THE POTOMAC WILL BE ANNIHILLATED," CWTI:OCT/95[40]619

Kemp, Daniel F., (edited by John D. Milligan); "NAVY LIFE ON THE MISSISSIPPI RIVER (MY LIFE)," CWTI:MAY/94[16]380

Kennedy, Charles W.; "THE RED RIVER CAMPAIGN LETTERS OF LT. CHARLES W. KENNEDY, 156TH NEW YORK VOLUNTEER INFANTRY," CWR:VOL4#2[104]168

Kent, William; "A WILDERNESS MEMORY: ONE MORNING, 30 YEARS AFTER THE BATTLE IT ALL CAME BACK TO HIM," CWTI:MAR/89[34]104

Kepf, Kenneth M.; "DIGLER'S BATTERY AT GETTYSBURG," GETTY:4[49]147

Kerrihard, Bo; "BITTER BUSHWHACKERS AND JAYHAWKERS," ACW:JAN/93[26]395

Kerwood, John R.:
"THE ASSASSINATION OF GARFIELD AND THE TRIAL OF HIS KILLER," AHI:FEB/69[12]119
"THE PLOT TO ROB LINCOLN'S TOMB," AHI:JAN/71[12]131

King, Kendall J.; "BOLD, BUT NOT TOO BOLD," ACW:MAR/93[42]406

Klein, Frederic S.:
"MAN ON A TIGHTROPE," AHI:MAY/66[12]101
"THE WAR ELECTION OF 1864," AHI:OCT/68[4]116

Klement, Frank L.; "SERGEANT EDWIN B. BIGELOW'S EXCITING ADVENTURES," B&G:AUG/91[36]462

Kliger, Paul I.; "THE CONFEDERATE INVASION OF NEW MEXICO (THE GENERAL'S TOUR)," B&G:JUN/94[8]568

Kloeppel, James E.:
"THE MYSTERY SUB OF JACKSON SQUARE," CWTI:SEPT/89[20]127
"SWAMP ANGEL'S REIGN OF TERROR," CWM:MAR/92[16]411

Knudsen, Dean; "SOUTHERN-BORN UNION COLONEL (TIME LAPSE)," CWTI:MAY/94[82]387

Kopp, April; "CAMEL CORPS, USA," AHI:DEC/81[8]222

Koty, Katheryn; "IDAHO SHOOT-OUT," B&G:APR/91[24]446

Kowell, Brian D.; "PELL-MELL CAVALRY CHASE," ACW:JUL/92[41]370

Krehbiel, Randy; "INDIANS BLUE AND GRAY," ACW:JAN/91[30]286

Krick, Robert E.L.:
"THE CIVIL WAR'S FIRST MONUMENT: BARTOW'S MARKER AT MANASSAS," B&G:APR/91[32]447
"DEATH OF ANOTHER GENERAL (DISPATCHES)," CWM:DEC/95[34]628
"LEE FOILS MEADE AT MINE RUN (DISPATCHES)," CWM:DEC/94[44]551
"NEAR DISASTER ON THE POTOMAC," CWM:OCT/95[38]618
"THE PENINSULA CAMPAIGN OF 1862: THE BATTLE OF GAINES' MILL," CWM:JUN/95[61]593
"THE PENINSULA CAMPAIGN OF 1862: THE BATTLE OF SLASH CHURCH," CWM:JUN/95[43]587
"THE PENINSULA CAMPAIGN OF 1862: THE DABBS HOUSE MEETING," CWM:JUN/95[53]590
"THE RETREAT FROM GETTYSBURG (DISPATCHES), CWM:AUG/94[26]525

"STANDOFF AT BRAWNER'S FARM (DISPATCHES)," CWM:AUG/95[30]606
"STUNNING SOUTHERN HEROISM," CWM:OCT/94[34]538
"TRAGEDY IN THE WILDERNESS (DISPATCHES)," CWM:JUN/94[26]512

Krick, Robert K.:
"A CONTEMPORARY HERO," CWM:JUL/91[26]364
"FROM EACHO'S FARM TO APPOMATTOX: THE FREDERICKSBURG ARTILLERY," CWR:VOL1#1[1]102
"GENERAL NAT HARRIS' DIARY," B&G:AUG/91[30]460

Krolick, Marshall D.; "FORGOTTEN FIELD: THE CAVALRY BATTLE EAST OF GETTYSBURG ON JULY 3, 1863," GETTY:4[75]149

Kross, Gary:
"GETTYSBURG VIGNETTES #1: FIGHT LIKE THE DEVIL TO HOLD YOUR OWN. GENERAL JOHN BUFORD'S CAVALRY AT GETTYSBURG (THE GENERAL'S TOUR)," B&G:FEB/95[8]590A
"GETTYSBURG VIGNETTES #2: THAT ONE ERROR FILLS HIM WITH FAULTS. GEN. ALFRED IVERSON AND HIS BRIGADE AT GETTYSBURG (THE GENERAL'S TOUR)," B&G:FEB/95[8]590B
"GETTYSBURG VIGNETTES #3: AT THE TIME IMPRACTICABLE. DICK EWELL'S DECISION ON THE FIRST DAY AT GETTYSBURG (THE GENERAL'S TOUR)," B&G:FEB/95[8]590C

Kurtz, Henry I.; "A SOLDIER'S LIFE," AHI:AUG/72[24]140

Kushlan, Jim:
"A PAPER LINK TO A CONSPIRACY (COLLECTIBLE)," CWTI:SEP/91[15]225
"BENNETT PLACE: HUMBLE SHRINE TO PEACE (TARGET)," CWTI:APR/90[20]151
"THE "CENTURY" ART: WHAT WAR LOOKED LIKE (LEGACY)," CWTI:SEP/90[28]175
"THE LIVELY PAGEANTRY OF DEATH," CWTI:DEC/95[90]483
"TREASURE IN THE ATTIC," CWTI:MAY/91[34]209

Labadie, Paul G.; "96TH OHIO REGIMENT (COMMANDS)," ACW:SEP/92[16]376

Lalire, Gregory; "TRAVEL," MH:OCT/93[76]173

Lambert, C.S.; "THE *CSS ALABAMA* LOST AND FOUND," AHI:OCT/88[32]274

Lang, Dan; "72ND PENNSYLVANIA (COMMANDS)," ACW:MAY/92[8]357

Lang, David; "LAST STAND IN THE CAROLINAS: THE BATTLE OF BENTONVILLE. AN INTERVIEW WITH AUTHOR MARK L. BRADLEY," CWR:VOL4#3[65]172

Largent, F. Brisco; "EBEN T. STARR'S PISTOLS AND CARBINES (ORDNANCE)," ACW:SEP/94[24]485

LaRocca, Charles J.; "FORWARD, MY TULIPS!: THE DAREDEVIL ORANGE BLOSSOMS AT CHANCELLORSVILLE," CWM:DEC/94[40]550

Lash, Gary G.:
"BRIG. GEN. HENRY BAXTER'S BRIGADE AT GETTYSBURG, JULY 1," GETTY:10[7]221
"THE CONGRESSIONAL RESOLUTION OF THANKS FOR THE FEDERAL VICTORY AT GETTYSBURG," GETTY:12[85]248
"MARCH OF THE 124TH NEW YORK TO GETTYSBURG," GETTY:9[5]209
"THE PHILADELPHIA BRIGADE AT GETTYSBURG," GETTY:7[97]193

Lawliss, Chuck; "A VISIT TO JOHN BROWN COUNTRY (TARGET)," CWTI:JUL/92[20]271

Massey, Mary Elizabeth; "MARY TODD LINCOLN," AHI:MAY/75[4]159

Matteson, Elisha C.; "DEAR SISTER — THEY FIGHT TO WHIP (MY WAR)," CWTI:MAY/91[16]206

Maust, Roland R.; "THE UNION SECOND CORPS HOSPITAL AT GETTYSBURG, JULY 2 TO AUGUST 8, 1863," GETTY:10[53]225

Mayers, Adam:
"MONTREAL'S POSH REBEL RENDEVOUS," CWTI:JAN/93[44]302
"THE PRISONER AND THE PRIME MINISTER," CWTI:JUL/93[38]328
"STOLEN SOLDIERS," CWTI:JUN/95[56]450
"THEY CAME TO WATCH," CWTI:DEC/94[73]416

0**McAdams, Benton;** "NAPOLEON BONAPARTE: THE OTHER BUFORD," CWTI:DEC/94[82]418

McBride, Lela J.; "WHATEVER BECAME OF BOSTON CORBETT?" CWTI:MAY/91[48]211

McCarthy, Linda; "LEST WE FORGET," CWM:MAY/91[64]353

McCaskey, James; "A SCRATCH WITH THE REBELS," CWTI:JAN/94[49]365

McCormack, Jack; "THE FIGHTING IRISH," CWM:MAR/91[17]335

McCulloch, Ian; "BILLY AND JOHNNY CANUCK," CWM:SEP/93[18]494

McFall, J. Arthur; "GRANT'S EARLY WAR DAYS," ACW:NOV/94[34]496

McFarland, Bill; "WOUNDED AT THE CRATER (TIME LAPSE)," CWTI:MAY/91[74]212

McFarland, Gerald; "A LEGACY LEFT BEHIND," AHI:MAR/84[20]237

McGinty, Brian:
"A HEAP O'TROUBLE," AHI:MAY/81[35]218
"EDWIN BOOTH: PRINCE OF TRAGEDY," AHI:OCT/86[22]260
"OLD BRAINS' IN THE NEW WEST," AHI:MAY/78[10]179
"ROBERT ANDERSON: RELUCTANT HERO," CWTI:MAY/92[45]266

McIntosh, Suzanne V.; "VETERANS (PERSONALITY)," ACW:SEP/91[8]318

McIver, Stuart; "THE MURDER OF A SCALAWAG," AHI:APR/73[12]148

McKay, John E.; "AN ARMY OF HIS OWN," CWTI:DEC/94[49]413

McKenna, Mark:
"THE FINAL RESTING PLACE OF GENERAL ALBERT SIDNEY JOHNSTON," B&G:FEB/95[35]592
"LEE'S LAST U.S. ARMY POST," B&G:APR/92[58]485

McKenzie, John D.:
"CONFRONTATION AT FIVE FORKS: GENERAL SHERIDAN VS. GENERAL WARREN," CWM:MAR/93[24]467
"SHOWDOWN IN THE WEST: GRANT VS. ROSECRANS," CWM:MAR/93[8]465

McMurry, Richard M.; "THE WAR WE NEVER FINISHED," CWTI:DEC/89[62]139

McPherson, James M.:
"DISNEY'S AMERICA: GUEST EDITORIAL," B&G:AUG/94[34]577A
"TRIED BY WAR," CWTI:DEC/95[67]481

Meier, Neal:
"DISNEY'S AMERICA: THE MOUSE IN THE SOUTH?" B&G:JUN/94[62]572
"MORE TROUBLE AT BRANDY STATION," B&G:DEC/93[31]547

"PRUSSIAN GIANT IN GRAY: MAJ. JOHANN HEINRICH HEROS VON BORCKE," B&G:OCT/93[49]543

Meinhard, Robert W.; "THE FIRST MINNESOTA AT GETTYSBURG," GETTY:5[79]161

Meketa, Jacqueline D.; "A POETIC PLEA FROM PRISON," CWTI:MAR/91[28]200

Melton, Maurice; "THE GENTLE CARPETBAGGER: DANIEL H. CHAMBERLAIN," AHI:JAN/73[28]147

Mertz, Gergory A.:
"NO TURNING BACK: THE BATTLE OF THE WILDERNESS, PART I (THE GENERAL'S TOUR)," B&G:APR/95[8]595
"NO TURNING BACK: THE BATTLE OF THE WILDERNESS, PART II — THE FIGHTING ON MAY 6, 1864 (THE GENERAL'S TOUR)," B&G:JUN/95[8]600
"STONEWALL JACKSON'S ARTILLERISTS AND THE DEFENSE OF THE CONFEDERATE RIGHT," CWR:VOL4#4[70]180

Meyers, Jerry:
"BEAUTY, SALLIE AND FATE," ACW:NOV/91[35]333
"MELEE ON SAINT PATRICK'S DAY," ACW:NOV/91[30]332
"SHELLS AND SABER POINTS," MH:OCT/92[51]162

Milano, Anthony J.:
"A CALL OF LEADERSHIP: LT. COL. CHARLES REDINGTON MUDGE, U.S.V. AND THE SECOND MASSACHUSETTS INFANTRY AT GETTYSBURG," GETTY:6[69]176
"THE COPPERHEAD REGIMENT: THE 20TH MASSACHUSETTS INFANTRY," CWR:VOL3#1[31]150
"PVT. ROBERT G. CARTER AND THE 22D MASSACHUSETTS AT GETTYSBURG," GETTY:8[53]203

Miles, Jim; "THE ATLANTA CAMPAIGN," CWM:JAN/91[12]326

Miller, Edward S.:
"A LONG WAR AND A SICKLY SEASON," B&G:JUN/92[40]489
"THE DILEMMA OF COMMODORE CRAVEN," CWTI:DEC/94[34]411
"HIGH SEAS HIJACK," ACW:NOV/92[51]389

Miller, Ilana D.; "WILLIAM HOWARD RUSSELL (PERSONALITY)," ACW:SEP/93[10]430

Miller, J. Michael:
"PERRIN'S BRIGADE ON JULY 1, 1863," GETTY:13[22]254
"STRIKE THEM A BLOW: LEE AND GRANT AT THE NORTH ANNA RIVER (THE GENERAL'S TOUR)," B&G:APR/93[12]518

Miller, M.C.; "*STAR OF THE WEST* (ORDNANCE)," ACW:NOV/93[8]438

Miller, Richard F.; "THE 20TH MASSACHUSETTS INFANTRY AND THE STREET FIGHT FOR FREDERICKSBURG," CWR:VOL4#4[101]181

Miller, William J.:
"A CONVERSATION WITH JAMES M. MCPHERSON," CWM:AUG/94[17]523
"A CONVERSATION WITH JEFFRY D. WERT," CWM:JUN/94[43]517
"A CONVERSATION WITH KEITH ROCCO," CWM:FEB/95[57]566
"A CONVERSATION WITH NOAH ANDRE TRUDEAU," CWM:OCT/94[17]534
"A CONVERSATION WITH PETER COZZENS, THE LAST HURRAH: BRAGG AND CHATTANOOGA," CWM:APR/95[16]571
"A CONVERSATION WITH THOMAS P. LOWRY," CWM:DEC/94[17]547
"THE BLOODY ROAD TO SPOTSYLVANIA: PENNSYLVANIA BUCKTAILS, PART TWO," CWR:VOL1#3[28]120

"CITIZEN ANNIE: A CONVERSATION WITH PRESERVATIONIST ANNIE SNYDER," CWM:OCT/95[27]615

"DEAR MOTHER, SINCE LAST I WROTE TO YOU WE HAVE MADE THE FUR FLY...", CWR:VOL1#3[46]121

"DETAILS FROM WHITE HOUSE ON THE PENINSULA," CWM:JUN/94[28]514

"GEORGE B. MCCLELLAN — RIGHT-SIDE OUT: A CONVERSATION WITH JOSEPH L. HARSH," CWM:JUN/95[17]581

"'I TOLD HIM I SHOULD BURN HIS SHIP'" CWM:FEB/95[73]568

"LEXINGTON: LEE'S LAST RETREAT," CWM:JUL/91[48]374

"LIFE ON THE SKIRMISH LINE: THROUGH THE WAR WITH THE PENNSYLVANIA BUCKTAILS," CWR:VOL1#3[20]119

"THE LORD'S YOUNG ARTILLERIST": A CONVERSATION WITH PETER S. CARMICHAEL," CWM:DEC/95[41]630

"THE *MONITOR VS. THE MERRIMACK:* A LOVE STORY?" CWM:MAR/91[43]339

"MR. DAVIS BIDS ADIEU," CWM:FEB/95[19]558

"MR. LEE OF VIRGINIA: A CONVERSATION WITH EMORY M. THOMAS," CWM:AUG/95[17]603

"THE PENINSULA CAMPAIGN OF 1862: THE BATTLE OF DREWRY'S BLUFF," CWM:JUN/95[39]586

"THE PENINSULA CAMPAIGN OF 1862: THE BATTLE OF GLENDALE," CWM:JUN/95[69]596

"THE PENINSULA CAMPAIGN OF 1862: THE BATTLE OF OAK GROVE," CWM:JUN/95[55]591

"THE PENINSULA CAMPAIGN OF 1862; PRELUDE: THE LEGIONS GATHER," CWM:JUN/95[24]582

"THE THEME PARK—ADIEU AND ACCELERANDO?" CWM:JUN/94[23]510

"TRAGIC LOSS OF LIFE AT ANTIETAM (DISPATCHES)," CWM:OCT/94[37]539

Millett, Allen; "CAMP TALK EXTRA: GETTYSBURG A LESSON IN FOREIGN POLICY," B&G:FEB/94[39]554

Mitchell, Joseph B.; "YOU ARE THE ARMY," CWM:JUL/91[25]363

Moen, Margaret; "SIX PAINTINGS IN MINNESOTA'S CAPITOL BUILDING (TRAVEL)," ACW:NOV/94[76]500

Mohon, James L.; "DEFENDING THE CONFEDERATE HEARTLAND: COMPANY F OF HENRY ASHBY'S 2ND TENNESSEE CAVALRY," CWR:VOL4#1[1]163

Monson, Nels J.:
"COLONEL HEG MEMORIAL PARK," B&G:AUG/93[34]532
"ARTHUR MACARTHUR (PERSONALITY)," ACW:MAR/92[14]350

Moore, Robert H. II:
"A MATTER OF INJUSTICE: THE SUMMERS—KOONTZ INCIDENT," B&G:FEB/92[32]477
"A SCHOOLBOY CAVALRYMAN (TIME LAPSE)," CWTI:MAR/91[74]204

Moore, William H.; "WRITING HOME TO TALLADEGA (MY WAR)," CWTI:DEC/90[56]184

Moran, Captain Frank E.:
"ESCAPE FROM LIBBY PRISON, PART I," AHI:NOV/85[38]254
"ESCAPE FROM LIBBY PRISON, PART II," AHI:DEC/85[40]255

Morgan, Mark; "THE PRESERVATION REPORT," CWR:VOL2#1[69]133

Morris, Roy Jr.:
"A WAR OF WORDS," ACW:JAN/95[6]501
"ALEXANDER GARDNER," ACW:JAN/92[6]337
"BLOODY BILL ANDERSON," ACW:JAN/93[6]391
"ALBERT SIDNEY JOHNSTON," ACW:SEP/93[6]428

"AMBROSE BIERCE," ACW:JUL/94[6]473
"CHATTANOOGA," ACW:NOV/95[6]551
"CIVIL WAR HISTORY," ACW:MAR/95[6]511
"CLEMENT VALLANDIGHAM," ACW:MAR/91[6]290
"COMMON SOLDIERS," ACW:MAY/92[6]356
"DON CARLOS BUELL," ACW:SEP/95[6]541
"FRANKLIN PIERCE," ACW:MAR/93[6]400
"HICKOK, HARDIN, AND THE JAMESES," ACW:MAR/94[6]455
"IT WAS JUST MADNESS: INTERVIEW WITH SHELBY FOOTE," ACW:MAR/91[30]295
"JOHN C. PEMBERTON," ACW:NOV/91[6]327
"JOSEPH E. JOHNSTON," ACW:JAN/91[6]281
"JOSEPH WHEELER," ACW:MAY/95[6]521
"JUSTUS MCKINSTRY," ACW:MAR/92[6]347
"LEE'S LOST ORDER," ACW:JAN/94[6]446
"MASTER FRAUD OF THE CENTURY": THE DISPUTED ELECTION OF 1876," AHI:NOV/88[28]277
"MATHEW BRADY," ACW:JAN/92[6]337
"MEXICO," ACW:JUL/92[6]365
"MOVIES," ACW:SEP/91[6]317
"PAT CLEBURNE," ACW:NOV/93[6]437
"RUTHERFRAUD' B. HAYES," ACW:JUL/93[6]419
"SAM CLEMENS," ACW:MAY/91[6]299
"SIDNEY LANIER," ACW:SEP/92[6]373
"THE STEADIEST BODY OF MEN I EVER SAW: JOHN T. WILDER AND THE LIGHTNING BRIGADE," B&G:OCT/92[32]499
"SWELTERING SUMMER COLLISION," MH:FEB/93[42]164
"W.C. FALKNER," ACW:JUL/95[6]531
"WALT WHITMAN," ACW:MAY/94[6]464
"WHO REALLY WON THE CIVIL WAR?" ACW:NOV/94[6]492
"WILLIAM SHERMAN AND WAR CORRESPONDENTS," ACW:NOV/92[6]382
"WILLIAM 'BULL' NELSON," ACW:JUL/91[6]308
"WINFIELD S. HANCOCK," ACW:MAY/93[6]410

Mosser, Jeffrey:
"GATEWAY TO THE ATLANTIC," CWTI:DEC/94[62]415
"I SHALL MAKE HIM REMEMBER THIS INSULT," CWTI:MAR/93[24]309

Motts, Warren E.:
"GENERAL GRANT IS NEARLY KILLED AT THE BRADY STUDIO," B&G:FEB/94[32]552
"MATHEW B. BRADY: A MAN WITH A VISION," B&G:FEB/94[24]551

Mullins, Michael A.; "THE FREMONT RIFLES: THE 37TH ILLINOIS AT PEA RIDGE AND PRAIRIE GROVE," CWR:VOL1#1[42]105

Mumford, William T.; "DIARY OF THE VICKSBURG SIEGE," AHI:DEC/77[46]177

Murfin, James V.; "THE SECRETIVE STONEWALL," B&G:JUN/92[53]491

Myers, J. Jay; "WHO WILL FOLLOW ME?" CWTI:JUL/93[29]326

Nash, Howard P. Jr.; "THE PRINCETON EXPLOSION," AHI:AUG/69[5]123

Naversen, Kenneth; "THE RETURN OF WILLIAM NEWBY: A CIVIL WAR MYSTERY," CWM:FEB/95[36]563

Neeley, E.J.; "LOST IMAGE OF A SOUTHERN HERO," B&G:JUN/94[32]570

Neely, Mark E., Jr.:
"THE LINCOLN FAMILY ALBUM," AHI:NOV/90[44]293
"LINCOLN'S FIRST LOVE," CWTI:DEC/95[40]479

Nelson, David K.; "A ROLLING MEMENTO,"
CWTI:MAR/95[54]438

Nelson, Chris, (edited by Chris Fordney); "LETTERS FROM
THE HEART (MY WAR)," CWTI:OCT/95[28]467

"Nemo"; "SHILOH, WHERE DEATH KNOWS NO
DISTINCTION," CWM:APR/95[66]579

Neul, Robert C.:
"BATTLE MOST DESPERATE AND BLOODY,"
ACW:JAN/95[30]505
"DOUBLY MISSED OPPORTUNITY," ACW:MAR/93[26]404
"FEDERALS' RISKY PURSUIT," ACW:SEP/92[23]377
"NORTH'S FIRST VICTORY," ACW:SEP/93[38]434
"SLUGFEST IN THE OZARKS," ACW:MAY/94[26]468

New, M. Christopher; "TRAGEDIAN'S GREATEST ROLE,"
ACW:MAR/93[35]405

Newell, Mark M.; "THE *CSS H.L. HUNLEY*: SOLVING A
131-YEAR-OLD MYSTERY," CWR:VOL4#3[77]174

Newton, Steven H.:
"THE PENINSULA CAMPAIGN OF 1862: THE BATTLE OF
SEVEN PINES," CWM:JUN/95[47]588
"THE PENINSULA CAMPAIGN OF 1862: THE ENGAGEMENT
AT ELTHAM'S LANDING," CWM:JUN/95[37]585

Nichols, William C.; "NATURAL BRIDGE, VIRGINIA
(TRAVEL)," ACW:NOV/91[64]336

Niderost, Eric:
"THE GREAT DEBATE," ACW:MAY/93[47]417
"NEW SALEM, ILLINOIS (TRAVEL)," ACW:MAR/94[66]463
"TRACES OF A DISTANT WAR," CWTI:JUN/95[51]449

Nolan, Alan T.:
"THE FORGING OF THE IRON BRIGADE,"
CWM:JAN/93[16]457
"LEGEND VS. HISTORY," CWM:JUL/91[27]365
"THOSE PEOPLE," CWM:JUL/91[10]357

Norder, Steve; "A MIGHTY MEAN-FOWT FIGHT,"
CWTI:FEB/92[29]248

Norris, David A.:
"MOUNTAIN HOWITZERS (ORDNANCE)," ACW:SEP/95[10]543
"PETERSBURG ARTILLERY (COMMANDS),"
ACW:MAR/95[12]513
"WAR'S 'WONDER' DRUGS," ACW:MAY/94[51]471

Northrop, L.B.; "A HILL OF DEATH," CWTI:MAY/91[24]208

Norville, Charles R.; "TREDEGAR IRON WORKS: ARSENAL
OF THE SOUTH," CWM:SEP/91[24]381

O'Brien, Kevin E.:
"A PERFECT ROAR OF MUSKETRY": CANDY'S BRIGADE IN
THE FIGHT FOR CULP'S HILL," GETTY:9[81]216
"THE BREATH OF HELL'S DOOR: PRIVATE WILLIAM
MCCARTER AND THE IRISH BRIGADE AT
FREDERICKSBURG", CWR:VOL4#4[47]179
"GLORY ENOUGH FOR ALL: LT. WILLIAM BROOKE-RAWLE
AND THE 3RD PENNSYLVANIA CAVALRY AT
GETTYSBURG," GETTY:13[89]260
"IRISH BRIGADE (COMMANDS)," ACW:MAY/94[12]466
"TO UNFLINCHINGLY FACE DANGER AND DEATH: CARR'S
BRIGADE DEFENDS EMMITSBURG ROAD,"
GETTY:12[7]241
"VALLEY OF THE SHADOW OF DEATH: COL. STRONG
VINCENT AND THE EIGHTY-THIRD PENNSYLVANIA
INFANTRY AT LITTLE ROUND TOP," GETTY:7[41]189

O'Brien, Tom; "BATTLE FOR THE RIO GRANDE,"
CWTI:OCT/95[56]471

O'Brien, William M.; "A SAD RETURN TO THE TRAIL OF
TEARS," CWM:MAY/93[24]476

O'Connor, Adrian; "OLD MEN AND YOUNG BOYS,"
CWM:MAY/92[34]422

O'Neill, Robert F. Jr.:
"THE FIGHT FOR LOUDOUN VALLEY: ALDIE,
MIDDLEBURG AND UPPERVILLE, VA. (THE GENERAL'S
TOUR)," B&G:OCT/93[12]537
"THE ONLY MEDAL OF HONOR EARNED IN THE LOUDOUN
VALLEY FIGHTING," B&G:OCT/93[21]538

O'Reilly, Frank A.; "BUSTED UP AND GONE TO HELL: THE
ASSAULT OF THE PENNSYLVANIA RESERVES AT
FREDERICKSBURG," CWR:VOL4#4[1]177

Oates, Stephen B.:
"A WOMAN OF VALOR," CWTI:MAR/94[38]372
"GOD'S ANGRY MAN," AHI:JAN/86[10]256
"THE MAN AT THE WHITE HOUSE WINDOW,"
CWTI:DEC/95[52]480
"WHY SHOULD THE SPIRIT OF MORTAL BE PROUD?"
AHI:APR/76[32]166

Ostendorf, Lloyd:
"LINCOLN'S 'LOST' TELEGRAM (LEGACY),"
CWTI:MAR/91[22]199
"THE LOST LINCOLN PHOTOGRAPHS," AHI:FEB/69[35]120
"TURNING THE PAGES OF HISTORY: A NEW DRAFT OF
THE GETTYSBURG ADDRESS LOCATED," GETTY:6[107]182

Otott, George; "THE RAGGED OLD FIRST: THE FIRST TEXAS
VOLUNTEER INFANTRY," CWR:VOL1#1[71]107

Pagano, John D.; "6TH NEW HAMPSHIRE (COMMANDS),"
ACW:MAY/95[18]524

Page, Dave:
"A FIGHT FOR MISSOURI," CWTI:AUG/95[34]457
"PORT HUDSON (TRAVEL)," MH:AUG/94[82]179

Page, William H.; "I SHALL BE A PRISONER,"
CWTI:SEP/91[42]231

Parachin, Victor M.; "THE BATTLE HYMN OF THE
REPUBLIC (ORDNANCE)," ACW:MAR/94[10]457

Parks, Michael W.; "ECHOES FROM THE CUSTER
BATTLEFIELD," AHI:DEC/84[10]242

Parramore, Tom; "THE *MAPLE LEAF* ESCAPE,"
CWTI:JAN/95[42]428

Partin, Winfred; "CONTESTING CUMBERLAND GAP"
ACW:JUL/91[26]313

Patchan, Scott C.:
"ACTION SOUTH OF PETERSBURG (DISPATCHES),"
CWM:FEB/95[30]561
"CONFEDERATES ROUTED AT WINCHESTER!
(DISPATCHES)," CWM:OCT/95[37]617
"DETAILS OF CEDAR CREEK (DISPATCHES),"
CWM:OCT/94[38]540
"DETAILS OF THE BATTLE AT PIEDMONT (DISPATCHES),"
CWM:JUN/94[27]513
"HEROISM OF SHERMAN'S SOLDIERS AT TUNNEL HILL
(DISPATCHES)," CWM:DEC/95[35]629
"UNION FORCES ROUTED AGAIN (DISPATCHES),"
CWM:AUG/95[35]607
"VALOR OF OHIOANS AT THE BATTLE OF KERNSTOWN
(DISPATCHES)," CWM:APR/95[29]574

Patience, David A.; "LIES, DISGRACE, REDEMPTION (TIME
LAPSE)," CWTI:SEP/91[61]233

Patrick, Kathy; "OBERLIN AND WELLINGTON OHIO
(TRAVEL)," ACW:MAY/94[66]472

"COLORADO CONFEDERATES (COMMANDS),"
ACW:NOV/91[10]329
"NO LADY WAS SHE," MH:FEB/91[8]151
"PIRATES OR PATRIOTS?," ACW:SEP/94[46]488
Rice, Thomas E.; "DESPERATE COURAGE,"
CWTI:DEC/90[58]185
Richey, David; "WILLIAMSON R.W. COBB (PERSONALITY),"
ACW:MAY/94[8]465
Roach, Harry; "LITTLE WINDOWS ON HISTORY,"
CWTI:DEC/89[26]135
Robbins, Peggy:
"A SON OF OLD NEPTUNE," CWTI:DEC/91[44]241
"ABRAHAM LINCOLN, INVENTOR," AHI:JAN/81[4]213
"AUDACIOUS RAILROAD CHASE," ACW:SEP/91[22]321
"CIVILIAN LIFE DURING THE SIEGE OF VICKSBURG,"
AHI:DEC/77[13]176
"DEFIANT REBEL NEWSPAPER," ACW:NOV/92[35]387
"THE FIGHTING MINORITY," CWTI:MAY/92[38]265
"GENERAL GRANT'S 'CALICO COLONEL,'" AHI:APR/79[4]186
"THE GLORY YEARS," CWTI:SEP/94[49]404
"THE GREATEST SCOUNDREL," CWTI:NOV/92[54]293
"HOW 'FIGHTIN' JOE' WHEELER GOT HIS TRENCHES
DUG," AHI:FEB/82[48]226
"JOSEPH PULITZER (PERSONALITY)," ACW:JUL/95[8]532
"THE MESSAGE OF JULIA WARD HOWE,"
CWTI:SEPT/89[40]130
"ON HISTORY'S SLIGHTER SIDE," AHI:JUN/79[19]188
"THE PLAN TO KIDNAP LINCOLN THAT FAILED BY ONE
DAY," AHI:NOV/80[6]208
"TRUE AMERICAN MADNESS: INAUGURAL BALLS,"
AHI:NOV/72[37]143
"U.S. GRANT AND SIMON BUCKNER: FRIENDS,"
AHI:MAR/82[8]227
"WHERE DO YOU STAND HORACE GREELEY?"
CWTI:DEC/90[50]183
Roberson, Elizabeth W.; "GENTLE ANNIE GOES HOME:
ROBERT E. LEE'S DAUGHTER RETURNS TO VIRGINIA
AFTER 132 YEARS," B&G:JUN/95[22]601
Roberts, Russell; "G.A.R. MUSEUM IS A TREASURY OF WAR
RELICS (TARGET)," CWTI:SEP/90[22]173
Robertson, James I. Jr.:
"THE CIVIL WAR," AHI:MAY/71[3]133A
"STONEWALL JACKSON (THE GENERAL'S TOUR),"
B&G:JUN/92[8]487
Robertson, William G.; "RAILS TO THE RIVER OF DEATH:
RAILROADS IN THE CHICKAMAUGA CAMPAIGN,"
CWM:NOV/91[50]394
Rodgers, Thomas G.; "THE 4TH ALABAMA INFANTRY
(COMMANDS)," ACW:NOV/94[18]495

Rogge, Robert E.:
"CROSSING THE LINE: BRAGG VS MORGAN,"
CWM:MAR/93[16]466
"WRECKING ON THE RAILROAD," ACW:SEP/95[48]547
Rollins, Richard:
"THE 100TH INDIANA INFANTRY," CWR:VOL1#1[73]108
"BLACK CONFEDERATES AT GETTYSBURG — 1863,"
GETTY:6[94]180
Rolston, Les; "LOST SOUL: A YANKEE'S FIGHT FOR A
REBEL'S DIGNITY," CWM:DEC/94[34]549
Ronan, James B. II:
"NORTH'S UNSUNG REGULARS," ACW:JUL/93[42]425

"REGULARS TO THE RESCUE AT GAINES' MILL,"
ACW:NOV/94[50]498
Rorty, James McKay, (edited by Brian Pohanka); "I WAS
THERE," CWM:MAR/91[14]334
Ross, D. Reid:
"KANSAS MINUTEMEN: MISSOURI'S SAVIORS,"
ACW:NOV/94[42]497
"INFANTRY VOLUNTEERS, UNION ARTILLERY BATTERIES
(ORDNANCE)," ACW:MAY/91[8]300
Roth, Dave:
"GRIERSON'S RAID: A CAVALRY RAID AT ITS BEST (THE
GENERAL'S TOUR)," B&G:JUN/93[12]524
"JOHN HUNT MORGAN'S ESCAPE FROM THE OHIO
PENITENTIARY (THE GENERAL'S TOUR),"
B&G:OCT/94[11]580
"SCENES FROM THE MAKING OF *GETTYSBURG,*"
B&G:DEC/93[59]549
"SO—WHAT ARE SHAD? (AND HOW DID THEY AFFECT
CONFEDERATE FORTUNES AT FIVE FORKS),"
B&G:APR/92[48]484
Rourke, Norman E.; "*MAPLE LEAF* RELICS (NEWS),"
CWTI:AUG/95[10]453A
Roy, Caesar A.; "WAS LINCOLN THE GREAT
EMANCIPATOR?" CWTI:MAY/94[46]385
Rucker, Mark; "AN ALL-AMERICAN SPORT IN AN
ALL-AMERICAN WAR," CWM:SEP/93[32]496
Ruffner, Kevin C.:
"MADE IN SPRINGFIELD," CWM:SEP/91[19]380
"VIRGINIA'S FIGHTING IRISH," CWM:MAR/91[65]342
Rushing, Anthony C.; "RACKENSACKER RAIDERS:
CRAWFORD'S FIRST ARKANSAS CAVALRY,"
CWR:VOL1#2[44]114
Russell, Jerry L.; "BEHIND THE LINES," CWTI:JUN/90[6]156
Ruston, Guy J.; "ESPIONAGE," MH:FEB/94[8]175
Rutherford, Phillip R.:
"A BATTLE ABOVE THE CLOUDS," CWTI:SEPT/89[30]129
"SIX GUNS AGAINST THE FLEET," CWTI:DEC/90[29]182
Ryan, David D.:
"MEMORIES OF STONEWALL," CWM:APR/94[14]503
"OVERLAND CAMPAIGN (TRAVEL)," ACW:SEP/95[74]550
"RAISE THE MONITOR: CAN WE? ... SHOULD WE?"
CWM:JUL/93[15]484
Ryan, Jeffrey T.:
"SOME NOTES ON THE CIVIL WAR-ERA MARINE CORPS,"
CWR:VOL2#3[183]140
"TO THE SHORES OF CAROLINA: DAHLGREN'S MARINE
BATTALIONS," CWR:VOL2#3[194]141

Sabine, David B.; "DR. GATLING AND HIS AMAZING GUN,"
AHI:JUN/66[52]102
Salecker, Gene; "THE CRIPPLING OF THE *SULTANA*: THE
REAL PICTURE," B&G:AUG/95[24]605
Sallee, Scott E.:
"14TH KENTUCKY CAVALRY (COMMANDS),"
ACW:SEP/95[22]544
"MISSOURI! ONE LAST TIME — STERLING PRICE'S 1864
MISSOURI EXPEDITION (THE GENERAL'S TOUR),"
B&G:JUN/91[10]452
Salta, Remo; "GUARDIANS OF THE COAST,"
ACW:MAR/94[35]460
Samito, Christian G.; "ROBERT RODES, WARRIOR IN GRAY,"
ACW:JAN/95[46]507

Sanders, Evelin; "FORT TOWSON: INDIAN TERRITORY
POST THAT PLAYED A PART IN THE PEACE,"
B&G:OCT/94[38]582

Sasser, Michael; "THE NORTH'S SOUTHERNMOST
OUTPOST," ACW:NOV/94[58]499

Sauers, Richard A.:
"THE 16TH MAINE VOLUNTEER INFANTRY AT
GETTYSBURG," GETTY:13[33]255
"FIFTY-THIRD! THE 53RD PENNSYLVANIA VOLUNTEER
INFANTRY IN THE GETTYSBURG CAMPAIGN,"
GETTY:11[80]235
"GETTYSBURG CONTROVERSIES," GETTY:4[113]153

Savas, Theodore P.:
"A DEATH AT MANSFIELD: COL. JAMES HAMILTON BEARD
AND THE CONSOLIDATED CRESCENT REGIMENT,"
CWR:VOL4#2[68]167
"THE BATTLE OF FREDERICKSBURG REVISITED,"
CWR:VOL4#4[i]175
"BULWARK OF THE BELEAGUERED CONFEDERACY,"
CWM:SEP/91[10]379
"'THE MUSKET BALLS FLEW VERY THICK': HOLDING THE
LINE AT PAYNE'S FARM," CWM:MAY/92[20]420

Sayers, Brian S.; "LIFE AFTER SURRENDER FOR REBEL
WARRIORS," ACW:JUL/95[26]535

Schafer, Elizabeth D.; "JADED MULES, TWISTED RAILS,
AND RAZED DEPOTS," CWM:JAN/91[40]330

Schafer, Louis S.; "COLONEL GEORGE WASHINGTON
RAINS (ORDNANCE)," ACW:MAY/94[20]467

Schell, Ernest; "OUR GOOD FRIENDS, THE RUSSIANS,"
AHI:JAN/81[18]214

Schlegel, Jacob; "A TIME OF TERROR," AHI:MAY/76[35]168

Schmidt, Curt; "OVERCOME BY THE SCARS OF WAR (TIME
LAPSE)," CWTI:JAN/93[82]304

Schuessler, Raymond; "COMMEMORATIVE STAMPS:
HISTORY MOVES THE MAIL," CWTI:JUN/90[12]157

Schultz, Fred L.; "TRAVEL AND ENTERTAINMENT GUIDE,"
AHI:FEB/82[48]228

Schurr, Cathleen; "CLARA BARTON: FOUNDER OF THE
AMERICAN RED CROSS," AHI:NOV/89[50]288

Schurter, Melvin; "PATRIOTIC SON OF A SEAMAN (TIME
LAPSE)," CWTI:JUL/92[74]277

Scott, Carole E.; "TOTAL WAR COMES TO NEW
MANCHESTER," B&G:DEC/94[22]586

Seideman, Tony; "MCCLELLAN'S PLANTATION,"
CWTI:JAN/94[20]358

Selcer, Richard F.:
"BRAWLING YANKEE BRASS," ACW:JUL/91[35]314
"CONDUCT UNBECOMING," CWTI:MAR/95[60]439
"ESPIONAGE," MH:JUN/94[8]177
"GEORGE PICKETT: ANOTHER LOOK," CWTI:JUL/94[44]394

Seldon, W. Lynn Jr.; "MUSEUM OF THE CONFEDERACY
(TRAVEL)," ACW:SEP/91[62]326

Shearer, D. H.; "A TRAITOR IN THE SENATE,"
CWTI:AUG/95[54]460

Sheely, Jo An; "34-YEAR-OLD FATHER OF SEVEN,"
CWTI:SEP/93[90]343

Sherman, William T.:
"SHERMAN REVEALS SOMETHING ABOUT HIS STRATEGY
(MY WAR)," CWTI:JUL/94[28]391
"THIS THANKLESS OFFICE," AHI:JAN/77[46]173

Shevchuk, Paul M.; "THE LOST HOURS OF 'JEB' STUART,"
GETTY:4[65]148

Shingleton, Royce:
"CONFEDERATE MIKE USINA: 'BOY' SEA FOX,"
CWM:JUN/94[50]518
"THE SWORD AND THE CROSS OF GILES B. COOKE": A
CHRISTIAN SOLDIER WITH LEE AND JACKSON,"
B&G:JUN/93[32]525

Shoemaker, Arthur; "HARD ROPE'S CIVIL WAR,"
CWTI:SEP/90[52]179

Shulman, Terry:
"REFLECTIONS ON GETTYSBURG: OR, RETHINKING THE
BIG ONE," B&G:FEB/93[48]515
"TO BE HELD AT ALL HAZARDS," CWTI:SEP/93[43]338
"WHAT REALLY HAPPENED TO THE ASSASSIN?"
CWTI:JUL/92[50]275

Sibert, James; "A BATTLE AT DROOP MOUNTAIN: THE
CONFEDERATES' LAST STAND IN WEST VIRGINIA,"
CWTI:MAR/89[16]101

Sipkoff, Martin:
"CONGRESS QUESTIONS GETTYSBURG LAND DEAL,"
CWTI:SEP/94[28]401
"FLANK ATTACK," CWTI:JUL/94[38]393
"IRRECONCILABLE DIFFERENCES," CWTI:JAN/94[42]363
"SEMINARY RIDGE TO REMAIN UNRESTORED,"
CWTI:SEP/93[38]337
"WHERE DID SEMINARY RIDGE GO?" CWTI:APR/92[42]259
"WHO LOST SEMINARY RIDGE?" CWTI:JAN/93[35]300

Skidmore, Richard S.; "WHILE FATHER WAS WITH US (MY
WAR)," CWTI:NOV/93[24]346

Skoch, George F.:
"THE BLOODY FIFTH," CWTI:DEC/91[36]240
"BURNSIDE'S GEOGRAPHY CLASS," CWTI:JAN/95[34]427
"CASHTOWN INN," B&G:APR/91[39]449
"MIRACLE OF THE RAILS," CWTI:SEP/92[22]279
"STONEWALL JACKSON'S LAST MARCH": A LAVISH STATE
FUNERAL FOR A SOUTHERN HERO," CWTI:MAY/89[22]116

Slosman, Everett L.; "SNOWBALL FIGHTS (ORDNANCE),"
ACW:MAR/91[12]292

Sloss, Frank H.; "FORGOTTEN MEN," AHI:DEC/74[12]156

Smith, Edward C.; "NEW SOUTH: THE MAKING OF A
MEMORIAL," CWM:NOV/92[41]451

Smith, Everard H., (edited by); "LEE'S LIEUTENANTS,"
CWM:JUL/92[16]428

Smith, Gerald J.; "12TH GEORGIA REGIMENT
(COMMANDS)," ACW:MAR/94[16]458

Smith, Jeffrey H.; "KIDNAP CAREFULLY PLOTTED,"
MH:APR/94[54]176

Smith, Robert B.:
"HOT SHOT, COLD STEEL," MH:DEC/91[54]155
"THE JAMES BOYS GO TO WAR," CWTI:JAN/94[29]360

Smith, Robert P., Jr.:
"IMPOSSIBLE CAMPAIGN ATTEMPTED," MH:APR/93[34]165
"TESTING FOR A FUTURE WAR," MH:APR/93[39]166

Snair, Dale S.:
"A COLLEAGUE OF GENERAL FORREST (TIME LAPSE),"
CWTI:MAY/92[74]268
"SWAMP RANGER AND CAVALRYMAN (TIME LAPSE),"
CWTI:NOV/92[106]295

Snow, Constance; "NEW ORLEANS' HAVEN FOR HISTORY,"
CWTI:AUG/95[28]456

Soltysiak, Harry A.; "THE PINKERTON BOMB,"
AHI:MAR/92[52]301

Spach, John T.; "ONE BRIDGE TOO MANY,"
ACW:JAN/93[43]397

Speer, Lonnie R.; "A HELL ON EARTH," CWTI:AUG/95[58]461

Speicher, James L; "THE SUMTER ARTILLERY: THE STORY OF THE 11TH BATTALION, GEORGIA LIGHT ARTILLERY DURING THE WAR BETWEEN THE STATES," CWR:VOL3#2[1]153

Spiegel, Allen D.; "JOHN SUMMERFIELD STAPLES (PERSONALITY)," ACW:NOV/91[16]330

Staff, Richmond National Battlefield Park:
"GRANT AND LEE, 1864: FROM THE NORTH ANNA TO THE CROSSING OF THE JAMES (THE GENERAL'S TOUR)," B&G:APR/94[10]558
"NORTH ANNA TO THE CROSSING OF THE JAMES (THE GENERAL'S TOUR)," B&G:APR/94[59]565

Stanbery, Jim; "A FAILURE OF COMMAND: THE CONFEDERATE LOSS OF VICKSBURG," CWR:VOL2#1[36]132

Stanchak, John E.:
"A BIG WAR ON A SMALL SCREEN," CWTI:SEP/90[48]178
"A LEGACY OF CONTROVERSY: FORT PILLOW STILL STANDS," CWTI:SEP/93[18]334
"A MISSISSIPPI HOME STANDS, A SILENT WITNESS TO A BATTLE (TARGET)," CWTI:MAY/91[18]207
"BALL'S BLUFF ABOVE THE POTOMAC," CWTI:JUL/94[20]390
"BEAUVOIR, WHERE THE LEADER OF A LOST REVOLUTION AND SOME OF HIS TROOPS WAITED OUT THEIR DAYS (TARGET)," CWTI:AUG/91[22]215
"LINCOLN AND THE IRONCLADS COME TO TELEVISION," CWTI:MAR/91[42]202

Stanley, James; "A VISIT WITH UNCLE REMUS," B&G:FEB/93[32]513

Stebbins, Philip E.; "LINCOLN'S DICTATORSHIP," AHI:NOV/71[32]136

Steenburn, Colonel Donald H.:
"GUNBOATS ON THE UPPER TENNESSEE," CWTI:MAY/93[38]321
"TWO CORPORALS: A TALE OF NATHAN BEDFORD FORREST'S ATTACK AT SULPHUR BRANCH TRESTLE, ALABAMA," B&G:JUN/92[32]488

Stefanon, Dyon:
"PICKETT'S CHARGE BY THE NUMBERS," CWTI:JUL/93[34]327
"STREET NAMED FOR 'LITTLE SORREL,'" CWTI:APR/92[41]258

Steger, Jennifer Lee; "IRONIES OF THE CIVIL WAR," CWM:OCT/95[22]614

Steiger, Bill; "TO HONOR THE DEAD: A PROPER BURIAL IN CHARLESTON," CWTI:MAR/94[59]376

Stenson, James B.; "THAT'S OUR FLAG, TOO!" AHI:JUL/76[19]170

Stephenson, Jon:
"DAMN THE TORPEDOES!: THE BATTLE OF MOBILE BAY," CWM:JUL/93[24]485
"LITERAL HILL OF DEATH," ACW:NOV/91[22]331

Stetser, L. Gordon, Jr.; "NORTHERN MANUFACTURERS (ORDNANCE)," ACW:MAR/92[8]348

Stevens, Peter F.; "CLEBURNE (PERSONALITY)," MH:OCT/94[20]180
"THE PROVING GROUND," AHI:MAY/88[38]270

Stevenson, James A.; "ABRAHAM LINCOLN (PERSONALITY)," ACW:NOV/94[8]493

Stevenson, Richard W.; "MAPPING THE CIVIL WAR," CWTI:NOV/92[60]294

Stewart, James; "A FEDERAL ARTILLERYMAN AT GETTYSBURG: AN EYEWITNESS ACCOUNT," AHI:MAY/67[22]107

Stinson, Byron:
"THE ARMY DISEASE," AHI:DEC/71[10]137
"THE FRANK LESLIES," AHI:JUL/70[12]128
"YELLOW FEVER," AHI:MAY/67[42]109

Stokes, G.P.:
"HERMAN HAUPT'S RAILROADS: BEANPOLES AND CORNSTALKS," CWM:NOV/91[12]390
"NAKED SWORD IN HAND," MH:AUG/91[45]153

Storch, Marc & Beth; "WHAT A DEADLY TRAP WE WERE IN: ARCHER'S BRIGADE ON JULY 1, 1863," GETTY:6[13]170

Stratton, Robert E.; "THE APPOMATTOX SURRENDER TABLE," CWTI:NOV/93[50]349

Stuart, James E. B.; "LETTERS TO LAURA (MY WAR)," CWTI:JUL/92[12]270

Stuntz, Margaret L.; "LIGHTING BRIGADE STRIKES FIGHTING JOE," ACW:MAY/95[49]527

Sturm, Jean; "FORD'S THEATRE ON STAGE," AHI:FEB/86[20]258

Suhr, Robert C.:
"ATTACK WRITTEN DEEP AND CRIMSON," ACW:SEP/91[46]324
"COURT-MARTIAL OF VAN DORN," ACW:SEP/91[50]325
"KENTUCKY NEUTRALITY THREATENED," ACW:JUL/92[22]368
"THE RIFLE MUSKET (ORDNANCE)," ACW:JAN/91[8]282
"TORPEDOES," ACW:NOV/91[8]328
"UNION'S HARD-LUCK IRONCLAD," ACW:JUL/93[34]424

Sullivan, David M.; "THE CONFEDERATE STATES MARINES (COMMANDS)," ACW:MAR/91[14]293

Sutherland, Daniel E.; "STARS IN THEIR COURSES," ACW:NOV/91[41]334

Svenson, Peter; "LIVING ON A CIVIL WAR BATTLEFIELD," CWTI:JAN/95[22]423

Swerkstrom, Buz; "WARTIME READING RAGE," ACW:SEP/93[46]435

Swisher, James K.; "FLANK ATTACK," ACW:SEP/93[31]433

Sword, Wiley:
"THE 10TH GEORGIA AND 27TH CONNECTICUT IN THE WHEATFIELD; TWO CAPTURED SWORDS AGAINST THEIR FORMER OWNERS," GETTY:12[24]242
"AN IRON BRIGADE CAPTAIN'S REVOLVER IN THE FIGHT ON MCPHERSON'S RIDGE," GETTY:7[7]185
"THE BATTLE OF NASHVILLE (THE GENERAL'S TOUR)," B&G:DEC/93[12]545
"CAPT. JAMES GLENN'S SWORD AND PVT. J. MARSHALL HILL'S ENFIELD IN THE FIGHT FOR THE LUTHERAN SEMINARY," GETTY:8[9]199
"CAPT. MCKEE'S REVOLVER AND CAPT. SELLERS' SWORD WITH WEED'S BRIGADE ON LITTLE ROUND TOP," GETTY:9[48]213
"COL. FLETCHER WEBSTER'S LAST LETTER: I SHALL NOT SPARE MYSELF," B&G:OCT/95[20]612
"DEFENDING THE CODORI HOUSE AND CEMETERY RIDGE: TWO SWORDS WITH HARROW'S BRIGADE IN THE GETTYSBURG CAMPAIGN," GETTY:13[43]256
"HOW IT FELT TO BE SHOT AT," AHI:OCT/67[26]112
"PYE'S SWORD AT THE RAILROAD CUT," GETTY:6[29]171

"TWO NEW YORK SWORDS IN THE FIGHT FOR CULP'S HILL: COL. JAMES C. LANE'S AND CAPT. NICHOLAS GRUMBACH'S," GETTY:10[36]223

Tackach, James; "OXFORD, MISSISSIPPI (TRAVEL)," ACW:JUL/95[70]540

Taliaferro, William B.; "PERSONAL REMINISCENCES OF "STONEWALL" JACKSON (MY WAR)," CWTI:JUN/95[18]444

Tate, Roger; "THE CAMPAIGN AND BATTLE OF MILL SPRINGS (THE GENERAL'S TOUR)," B&G:FEB/93[12]511

Tate, Thomas K.; "PONTOON BRIDGES (ORDNANCE)," ACW:MAY/93[8]411

Taylor, John M.:
"COMPASSION IS ALWAYS DUE TO AN ENRAGED IMBECILE," AHI:FEB/76[14]165
"FENIAN RAIDS AGAINST CANADA," AHI:AUG/78[33]184
"GROVER CLEVELAND AND THE REBEL BANNERS," CWTI:SEP/93[22]335
"THE PAINTER AND THE PRESIDENT," CWTI:FEB/92[21]247
"RELUCTANT RAIDER," CWTI:AUG/95[40]458
"SOME THOUGHTS FOR THE PRESIDENT'S CONSIDERATION," CWTI:SEP/92[46]284
"WILLARD'S OF WASHINGTON," AHI:OCT/79[10]192

Taylor, Michael W.:
"NORTH CAROLINA IN THE PICKETT-PETTIGREW-TRIMBLE CHARGE AT GETTYSBURG," GETTY:8[67]204
"THE UNMERITED CENSURE OF TWO MARYLAND STAFF OFFICERS, MAJ. OSMUN LATROBE AND FIRST LT. W. STUART SYMINGTON," GETTY:13[75]259

Templeton, James M. Jr.; "A SOLDIER FOR TWO COUNTRIES (TIME LAPSE)," CWTI:MAR/95[90]440

Thomas, Emory M.; "THE REAL J.E.B. STUART," CWTI:DEC/89[34]136

Thomas, Horace H., (edited by William J. Miller); "I WAS AN OGRE," CWM:OCT/94[60]544

Thompson, Ann E.:
"KEITH ROCCO (ARTISTS)," ACW:MAR/95[66]519
"RICK REEVES (ARTISTS)," ACW:NOV/95[66]559

Thompson, Phillip F.; "SECOND MANASSAS: ENFILADING THUNDER," CWM:AUG/94[48]529

Tibbals, Richard K.; "RUSHED TO THE FRONT (TIME LAPSE)," CWTI:JAN/95[82]430

Tidwell, William A.; "TIME LAPSE," CWTI:SEP/92[82]286

Titterton, Robert J.; "A SOLDIER'S SKETCHBOOK," CWTI:SEP/91[54]232

Tobey, Franklin J. Jr.; "THE MYSTERY OF HARVARD'S CIVIL WAR LIZARD (LEGACY)," CWTI:FEB/91[24]191

Tomasak, Pete; "AN ENCOUNTER WITH BATTERY HELL," GETTY:12[30]243

Tooley, Mark; "END OF AN ERA: THE 75TH REUNION AT GETTYSBURG," GETTY:7[119]195

Topps, David; "THE DUTCHESS COUNTY REGIMENT," GETTY:12[42]244

Traweek, Washington B., (submitted by Robert H. Moore II); "BREAK OUT! (MY WAR)," CWTI:DEC/91[26]238

Trefousse, Hans L.:
"OLD THAD STEVENS, PART I," AHI:DEC/81[18]223
"OLD THAD STEVENS, PART II," AHI:JAN/82[16]224

Trenka, John R.; "VICIOUS MOUNTAIN ENCOUNTER," ACW:MAR/94[27]459

Treon, Diane:
"A LANDSCAPE THAT GAVE SHAPE TO HISTORY," CWTI:JAN/95[24]424
"A SUPERHIGHWAY FOR CIVIL WAR INFORMATION," CWTI:JAN/95[30]426
"HISTORY COMES HOME," CWTI:MAR/95[20]433

Trimble, Isaac R.; "GETTYSBURG: FIGHT ENOUGH IN OLD MAN TRIMBLE TO SATISFY A HERD OF TIGERS," CWM:AUG/94[60]531

Trimble, Tony L.:
"'AGATE': WHITELAW REID REPORTS FROM GETTYSBURG," GETTY:7[23]187
"DEATH STRUGGLE FOR MISSOURI," CWM:MAY/93[8]474

Trinque, Bruce A.:
"ARNOLD'S BATTERY AND THE 26TH NORTH CAROLINA," GETTY:12[61]245
"BATTLE FOUGHT ON PAPER," ACW:MAY/93[31]415
"REBELS ACROSS THE RIVER," ACW:SEP/94[38]487

Tripp, John R.; "95TH ILLINOIS (COMMANDS)," ACW:JAN/91[16]284

Trudeau, Noah Andre:
"ALL GOES ON LIKE A MIRACLE," CWTI:APR/92[49]260
"THE 'BLACKBERRY RAID,'" GETTY:11[6]231
"COSTLY UNION RECONNAISSANCE," ACW:JUL/94[42]479
"DARBYTOWN ROAD DEBACLE," ACW:MAY/92[30]361
"FIELDS WITHOUT HONOR: TWO AFFAIRS IN TENNESSEE," CWTI:JUL/92[42]274
"I HAVE A GREAT CONTEMPT FOR HISTORY," CWTI:SEP/91[31]229
"LAST DAYS OF THE CIVIL WAR: CHAPTER 1: 'SUCCESS WAS EMINENTLY A HAPPY, A GLORIOUS ONE,'" CWTI:AUG/90[26]166
"LAST DAYS OF THE CIVIL WAR: CHAPTER 2: 'THE WHOLE COUNTRY SEEMED TO BE ALIVE WITH DEMONS,'" CWTI:AUG/90[42]167
"LAST DAYS OF THE CIVIL WAR: CHAPTER 3: 'GOD'S WILL BE DONE,'" CWTI:AUG/90[50]168
"LAST DAYS OF THE CIVIL WAR: CHAPTER 4: 'THE LAST GUN HAD BEEN FIRED'," CWTI:AUG/90[58]169
"LAST DAYS OF THE CIVIL WAR: CHAPTER 5: 'IT WAS A TERRIBLE CALAMITY BEYOND DESCRIPTION,'" CWTI:AUG/90[64]170
"LAST DAYS OF THE CIVIL WAR: EPILOGUE: AMERICA LOOKS TO THE FUTURE," CWTI:AUG/90[70]171
"WHAT MIGHT HAVE BEEN," CWTI:SEP/94[56]405

Tucker, James B.; "GREAT ESCAPE FROM REBEL PRISON," ACW:MAR/95[34]516

Tullai, Martin D.; "SPEAKING OF THE VICE-PRESIDENCY...," AHI:JAN/85[10]244

Twain, Mark; "THE PRIVATE HISTORY OF A CAMPAIGN THAT FAILED," AHI:AUG/67[50]111

Tyler, Greg; "ARTICLE BRINGS NOTICE TO A UNIQUE REBEL," CWTI:JUN/90[57]163

Tyson, Charles J.; "A REFUGEE FROM GETTYSBURG," CWTI:DEC/89[16]134

Unknown, (submitted by Ken E. Pluskatt); "ON TO PRISON (MY WAR)," CWTI:JUN/90[28]158

Unnerstall, Jay; "UNPROVOKED TRAGICOMEDY IN ST. LOUIS," ACW:MAY/91[31]304

Urner, Martin J.; "A CAVALRYMAN WITHOUT FANFARE (TIME LAPSE)," CWTI:DEC/94[122]419

Urwin, Gregory J.W.:
"I WANT YOU TO PROVE YOURSELVES MEN,"
CWTI:DEC/89[42]137
"TIME LAPSE," CWTI:APR/92[27]256
Utley, Robert M.:
"THE BLUECOATS, PART I," AHI:OCT/79[20]194
"THE BLUECOATS, PART II," AHI:NOV/79[32]196
"CUSTER: HERO OR BUTCHER?," AHI:FEB/71[4]131A
"THE ENDURING CUSTER LEGEND," AHI:JUN/76[4]169
"GENERAL CROOK AND THE PAIUTES," AHI:JUL/73[38]150

Vannoy, Allyn R.; "THE IOWA BRIGADE (COMMANDS),"
ACW:JAN/93[10]393
Venner, Thomas; "'TIL THE PAPER WORK IS DONE,"
CWTI:NOV/93[78]354
Viering, Peter B.; "A MATTER OF PRINCIPLE: ROBERT E.
LEE AND THE CONSTITUTION OF THE UNITED
STATES," CWM:APR/94[32]506
Vogler, James N. Jr.; "THE SOUL OF THE ARMY,"
CWM:JUL/91[45]372

Walcott, William O.; "A VETERAN OF 33 BATTLES (TIME
LAPSE)," CWTI:MAY/93[74]322
Walden, Geoffrey R.; "ORPHAN BRIGADE (COMMANDS),"
ACW:JUL/91[12]310
Walls, Matthew S.; "NORTHERN HELL ON EARTH"
ACW:MAR/91[25]294
Walsh, Michael G.; "AN UNPLEASANT RELIC (LEGACY),"
CWTI:DEC/91[48]242
Ward, Clyde; "VISIONARY FOR THE UNION,"
MH:APR/92[18]157
Ward, David A.; "OF BATTLEFIELDS AND BITTER FEUDS:
THE 96TH PENNSYLVANIA VOLUNTEERS,"
CWR:VOL3#3[1]157
Ward, John K.:
"THE BROTHERS' WAR," ACW:MAR/93[55]408
"FORREST'S FIRST FIGHT," ACW:MAR/93[51]407
Ward, Leo; "IT WAS OPEN, DEFIANT REBELLION,"
CWM:MAR/91[56]341
Warnes, Kathy; "ESCAPE FROM LIBBY," ACW:JAN/94[55]453
Waters, Zack C.; "JOSEPH FINEGAN'S FLORIDA BRIGADE
AT COLD HARBOR," CWR:VOL3#4[1]161
Weber, Barbara; "JAMES BUCHANAN (PERSONALITY),"
ACW:MAR/93[18]403
Webster, Donald B. Jr.; "FREMONT AND HIS FRIEND,"
AHI:AUG/66[32]104
Weddle, Kevin J.; "THE 3RD MINNESOTA (COMMANDS),"
ACW:MAY/91[12]302
Welch, Richard F.; "GETTYSBURG FINALE,"
ACW:JUL/93[50]426
Welsh, Bill; "FIRING THE GAP," ACW:JAN/94[39]451
Wensyel, James W.; "RETURN TO GETTYSBURG,"
AHI:JUL/93[40]312
Wert, Jeffry D.:
"A SINGLE STEP," CWTI:MAR/94[29]371
"GENERAL JAMES LONGSTREET," CWTI:NOV/93[55]350
"GENERALS AT ODDS," MH:AUG/94[46]178
"THE GREAT CIVIL WAR GOLD HOAX," AHI:APR/80[21]200
"I AM SO UNLIKE OTHER FOLKS": THE SOLDIER WHO
COULD NOT BE UNDERSTOOD," CWTI:APR/89[14]107
"INSIDE MOSBY'S CONFEDERACY," CWTI:SEP/90[34]176
"JOHN SINGLETON MOSBY AND THE GREENBACK RAID,"
CWM:JAN/93[24]458

"REMEMBERING A DAY," CWM:OCT/95[55]622
"RETURN TO THE KILLING GROUND," ACW:JUL/91[18]312
"SHERIDAN IN THE SHENANDOAH," AHI:NOV/80[8]209
"YOU HAD DONE ME A GREAT INJUSTICE,"
CWTI:MAR/93[40]312
Wesolowski, Wayne E.; "THE LONG TRIP HOME,"
AHI:JUL/95[30]324
Whitehorne, J.W.A.; "JUBAL EARLY AT WAYNESBORO: THE
LAST HURRAH," CWM:APR/94[24]505
Whitman, Walt:
"A GREAT POET'S LETTERS ABOUT WARTIME SUFFERING,"
AHI:AUG/68[4]115B
"I WAS THERE," CWM:MAY/91[8]346
Whitney, Joseph L.; "THE TRUE STORY OF TAPS,"
B&G:AUG/93[30]531
Wicker, Tom; "THE ONLY PROPER COURSE,"
CWM:JUL/91[24]360
Wiley, Bell I.:
"JOHNNY REB AND BILLY YANK," AHI:APR/68[4]115
"SLAVERY," AHI:APR/70[11]124A
"THE SPURNED SCHOOLTEACHERS FROM YANKEEDOM,"
AHI:FEB/80[14]199
"WOMEN OF THE LOST CAUSE," AHI:DEC/73[10]152
Wilkinson, Warren; "BURY THEM IF THEY WON'T MOVE
(EXCERPT FROM *MOTHER, MAY YOU NEVER SEE THE
SIGHTS I HAVE SEEN),"* CWTI:APR/90[24]152
Williams, Edward B.:
"CITY FOR THE TAKING," ACW:SEP/92[47]380
"JOHN B. GORDON AND FRANCIS BARLOW
(PERSONALITY)," ACW:MAY/93[14]413
Wilson, James H.; "VIRGINIA'S FORT WOOL (TRAVEL),"
ACW:JAN/95[74]510
Wilson, Ronald G.; "MEETING AT THE MCLEAN HOUSE,"
AHI:SEP/87[48]264
Wingfield, John T., (edited by James L. Speicher);
"WILDERNESS TO PETERSBURG: UNPUBLISHED
REPORTS OF THE 11TH BATTALION, GEORGIA LIGHT
ARTILLERY," CWR:VOL3#2[61]154
Winschel, Terrence J.:
"A FIERCE LITTLE FIGHT IN MISSISSIPPI,"
CWTI:JUL/94[50]395
"THE ARCHIVAL HOLDINGS OF VICKSBURG NATIONAL
MILITARY PARK," CWR:VOL2#1[75]134
"BATTLE OF PORT GIBSON, MISSISSIPPI, (THE GENERAL'S
TOUR), B&G:FEB/94[57]555
"THE COLORS ARE SHROUDED IN MYSTERY,"
GETTY:6[77]177
"THE FIRST HONOR AT VICKSBURG: THE 1ST BATTALION,
13TH U.S. INFANTRY," CWR:VOL2#1[1]130
"THE GETTYSBURG EXPERIENCE OF JAMES J.
KIRKPATRICK," GETTY:8[111]206
"THE GETTYSBURG DIARY OF LIEUTENANT WILLIAM
PEEL," GETTY:9[98]217
"GRANT'S BEACHHEAD FOR THE VICKSBURG CAMPAIGN:
THE BATTLE OF PORT GIBSON, MAY 1, 1863 (THE
GENERAL'S TOUR)," B&G:FEB/94[8]550
"THE JEFF DAVIS LEGION AT GETTYSBURG,"
GETTY:12[68]246
"JOHN WALKER'S TEXAS DIVISION AND ITS EXPEDITION
TO RELIEVE FORTRESS VICKSBURG," CWR:VOL3#3[33]158
"POSEY'S BRIGADE AT GETTYSBURG, PART I,"
GETTY:4[7]142

"POSEY'S BRIGADE AT GETTYSBURG, PART II,"
GETTY:5[89]162
"TO ASSUAGE THE GRIEF: THE GETTYSBURG SAGA OF
ISAAC AND MARY STAMPS," GETTY:7[77]191
Wittenberg, Eric J.:
"THE FIGHTING PROFESSOR: JOSHUA LAWRENCE
CHAMBERLAIN," CWM:JUL/92[8]427
"JOHN BUFORD AND THE GETTYSBURG CAMPAIGN,"
GETTY:11[19]232
"ROADBLOCK EN ROUTE TO WASHINGTON,"
ACW:NOV/93[50]444
Wood, Stephanie:
"LONGSTREET AT GETTYSBURG," CWM:AUG/95[56]610
"TOM BROADFOOT—OLD SOURCES TO LIGHT,"
CWM:APR/95[25]572
Woodbury, David A.:
"AN IROQUOIS AT APPOMATTOX," CWM:SEP/92[19]440
"THE ASSAULT ON VICKSBURG," CWM:JUN/94[30]515
"CHATTANOOGA RELIEVED! (DISPATCHES),"
CWM:DEC/94[46]552
"FIGHTING AT ATLANTA (DISPATCHES),"
CWM:AUG/94[27]526
"FORTS HENRY AND DONELSON FALL TO
UNCONDITIONAL' SURRENDER GRANT! (DISPATCHES),"
CWM:FEB/95[32]562
"FROM TAHLEQUAH TO BOGGY DEPOT: STAND WATIE'S
CIVIL WAR," CWM:SEP/92[38]443
"SHERMAN MOVES ON ATLANTA (DISPATCHES),"
CWM:AUG/95[36]608
Woods, James A.:
"DEFENDING WATSON'S BATTERY," GETTY:9[41]212
"HUMPHREYS' DIVISION'S FLANK MARCH TO LITTLE
ROUND TOP," GETTY:6[59]174
Woods, Stephanie; "CIVIL WAR HISTORY CAMP: PASSING
THE TORCH TO OUR KIDS," CWM:FEB/95[26]559
Woodworth, Steven E.:
"CAPITAL FOLLY," ACW:MAY/93[38]416
"FORMULA FOR DISASTER," CWM:JAN/92[34]404
"HOW TO LOSE A CITY," CWM:JAN/91[28]327
"THE PENINSULA CAMPAIGN OF 1862: THE BATTLE OF
WILLIAMSBURG," CWM:JUN/95[34]584
"RED RIVER BLUES," CWM:APR/95[39]576
"VICKSBURG: DAVIS, VAN DORN, PEMBERTON—A
TRIANGULATION OF SHORTCOMINGS,"
CWM:AUG/94[52]530
Wormack, Tom; "CIVIL WAR IN THE MAKING,"
ACW:MAY/94[43]470
Wright, Benjamin F; "GEORGIA'S ENDANGERED REBEL
GUNBOATS," CWTI:NOV/93[74]353
Wright, Mike; "J.B. JONES (PERSONALILTY),"
ACW:JAN/93[18]394
Wright, Steven J.:
"DON'T LET ME BLEED TO DEATH: THE WOUNDING OF
MAJ. GEN. WINFIELD SCOTT HANCOCK," GETTY:6[87]178
"JOHN GIBBON: THE MAN AND THE MONUMENT,"
GETTY:13[119]262
Wukovits, John F.; "DECKS COVERED WITH BLOOD,"
ACW:MAR/92[40]353
Wyckoff, Mac; "KERSHAW'S BRIGADE AT GETTYSBURG,"
GETTY:5[35]159

Yandoh, Judith:
"BRIEF BREACH AT FREDERICKSBURG,"
ACW:MAR/95[42]517
"MUTINY AT THE FRONT," CWTI:JUN/95[32]446
"TAKING OFF THE KID GLOVES," ACW:MAR/92[46]354
Young, William A. Jr.; "56TH VIRGINIA (COMMANDS),"
ACW:MAR/93[10]402
Young, Mel; "SOMEONE SHOULD SAY KADDISH,"
CWM:SEP/93[8]493

Zachry, Alfred:
"FIGHTING WITH THE 3D GEORGIA, PART I (MY WAR),"
CWTI:SEP/94[26]400
"FOUR SHOTS FOR THE CAUSE (MY WAR),"
CWTI:DEC/94[32]410
Zachry, Juanita D.; "GUNBOAT *CAIRO* (TRAVEL),"
ACW:SEP/94[74]491
Zaworski, Robert E., M.D.; "THE FIELD GLASSES OF
ROBERT E. LEE," B&G:AUG/95[32]606
Zbick, Jim:
"COALFIELDS' PERFECT HELL," ACW:MAR/92[22]351
"REBELS AT THEIR DOORSTEP," ACW:SEP/93[22]432
"STAPLETON CRUTCHFIELD (PERSONALITY),"
ACW:MAY/95[10]523
Zebrowski, Carl:
"FROZEN IN TIME," CWTI:DEC/94[24]409
"GUARDIANS OF MOBILE BAY," CWTI:MAR/94[20]369
"JEFF DAVIS' LIVING TOMB (TARGET)," CWTI:MAY/93[20]317
"MORAL VICTORY IN THE CRUSADE TO CLEAR MUDD,"
CWTI:MAY/93[12]316
"REMOTE HISTORY," CWTI:MAR/94[44]373
"WHY THE SOUTH LOST THE CIVIL WAR," AHI:OCT/95[24]326
Zeinert, Karen; "SHIP ISLAND (TRAVEL),"
ACW:JAN/94[70]454
Zentner, Joseph L.:
"FLORIDA'S GAMBLE PLANTATION (TRAVEL),"
ACW:JUL/93[66]427
"FORT JACKSON (TRAVEL)," ACW:JAN/92[62]346
Ziral, James; "ISLAND HAVEN FOR A STRUGGLING
CONFEDERACY," CWTI:DEC/89[10]133
Zwemer, John; "THE THOMSON GUARDS (COMMANDS),"
ACW:JUL/95[10]533

BOOK REVIEWS, BY AUTHOR

—; *A HISTORY OF THE 73RD ILLINOIS*, CWR:VOL4#3[1], *reviewed by* Wiley Sword

—; *AMERICAN HERITAGE BATTLE MAPS OF THE CIVIL WAR*, CWTI:SEP/94[18]

—; *THE ANDERSONVILLE TRIAL*, AHI:MAY/91[22]

—; *ARMY OF THE POTOMAC SERIES*, CWNEWS:DEC/94[33], *reviewed by* Blake A. Magner

—; *BLACK EASTER: THE ASSASSINATION OF ABRAHAM LINCOLN*, CWTI:NOV/92[10]

—; *GENERAL MICAH JENKINS AND THE PALMETTO SHARPSHOOTERS*, CWM:APR/95[8], *reviewed by* Charles R. Norville

—; *HISTORY 31ST REGIMENT ILLINOIS VOLUNTEERS ORGANIZED BY JOHN A. LOGAN*, CWNEWS:OCT/92[4], *reviewed by* Anne J. Bailey

—; *INSTRUCTIONS FOR OFFICERS AND NON-COMMISSION OFFICERS ON OUTPOST AND PATROL DUTY AND TROOPS IN CAMPAIGN*, CWNEWS:APR/92[4], *reviewed by* Frank Piatek

—; *JUDAH P. BENJAMIN: THE JEWISH CONFEDERATE*, AHI:JAN/89[10]

—; *MANUAL OF MILITARY SURGERY, PREPARED FOR THE USE OF THE CONFEDERATE STATES ARMY BY ORDER OF THE SURGEON-GENERAL*, CWNEWS:NOV/90[4], *reviewed by* Dr. Harris D. Riley Jr.

—; *REGULATIONS FOR THE MEDICAL DEPARTMENT OF THE ARMY*, CWNEWS:NOV/90[4], *reviewed by* Harris D. Riley Jr.

—; *WHITE HOUSE OF THE CONFEDERACY*, CWR:VOL3#3[92], *reviewed by* Eugene H. Berwanger

Abbott, Henry L., (edited by Robert G. Scott); *FALLEN LEAVES: THE CIVIL WAR LETTERS OF MAJOR HENRY LIVERMORE ABBOTT*, B&G:APR/92[24], *reviewed by* John M. Priest, CWM:FEB/95[42], *reviewed by* Gary W. Gallagher, CWNEWS:JAN/93[4], *reviewed by* William F. Howard

Abbott, Richard H.; *COTTON & CAPITOL: BOSTON BUSINESSMEN AND ANTISLAVERY REFORM, 1854-1868*, CWNEWS:JUN/93[5], *reviewed by* Gregory J.Y. Urwin

Abel, Annie E.:
THE AMERICAN INDIAN AS SLAVEHOLDER AND SECESSIONIST, CWNEWS:JUL/93[5], *reviewed by* Robert D. Norris Jr.
THE AMERICAN INDIAN IN THE CIVIL WAR, CWNEWS:JUL/93[5], *reviewed by* Robert D. Norris Jr.
THE AMERICAN INDIAN AND THE END OF THE CONFEDERACY: 1863-1866, CWNEWS:FEB/94[5], *reviewed by* Ted Alexander

Abell, Sam; *THE CIVIL WAR — AN AERIAL PORTRAIT*, B&G:FEB/91[28], *reviewed by* William D. Matter, CWNEWS:SEP/90[4], *reviewed by* Michael Hughes, CWTI:SEP/90[12]

Abernathy, Martha, (edited by Elizabeth P. Dargen); *THE CIVIL WAR DIARY OF MARTHA ABERNATHY, WIFE OF DR. C.C. ABERNATHY OF PULASKI, TENNESSEE*, CWNEWS:APR/95[33], *reviewed by* DeAnne Blanton

Adams, Charles S.; *MILITARY OPERATIONS IN JEFFERSON COUNTY, WEST VIRGINIA 1861-1865*, CWNEWS:AUG/95[33], *reviewed by* Ted Alexander

Adams, E.D.; *GREAT BRITAIN AND THE AMERICAN CIVIL WAR*, AHI:JAN/75[50], *reviewed by* Jon M. Nielson

Adams, George W.; *DOCTORS IN BLUE: THE MEDICAL HISTORY OF THE UNION ARMY IN THE CIVIL WAR*, CWM:MAY/91[38], *reviewed by* Gary W. Gallagher

Adams, Michael C.C.; *FIGHTING FOR DEFEAT: UNION MILITARY FAILURE IN THE EAST 1861-1865*, CWNEWS:AUG/93[5], *reviewed by* David F. Riggs

Aimone, Alan C.; *A USER'S GUIDE TO THE OFFICIAL RECORDS OF THE AMERICAN CIVIL WAR*, CWTI:SEP/93[26]

Aimone, Barbara A.; *A USER'S GUIDE TO THE OFFICIAL RECORDS OF THE AMERICAN CIVIL WAR*, CWNEWS:FEB/94[5], *reviewed by* Blake A. Magner

Albaugh III, William A.:
A PHOTOGRAPHIC SUPPLEMENT OF CONFEDERATE SWORDS, CWNEWS:AUG/95[33], *reviewed by* Dale E. Biever
CONFEDERATE ARMS, CWNEWS:AUG/95[33], *reviewed by* Dale E. Biever
THE CONFEDERATE BRASS-FRAMED COLT & WHITNEY, CWNEWS:AUG/95[33], *reviewed by* Dale E. Biever
CONFEDERATE EDGED WEAPONS, CWNEWS:AUG/95[33], *reviewed by* Dale E. Biever
CONFEDERATE FACES, CWNEWS:AUG/95[33], *reviewed by* Michael J. Winey
CONFEDERATE HANDGUNS, CWNEWS:AUG/95[33], *reviewed by* Dale E. Biever
HANDBOOK OF CONFEDERATE SWORDS, CWNEWS:AUG/95[33], *reviewed by* Dale E. Biever
MORE CONFEDERATE FACES, CWNEWS:AUG/95[33], *reviewed by* Michael J. Winey
THE ORIGINAL CONFEDERATE COLT, CWNEWS:AUG/95[33], *reviewed by* Dale E. Biever
THE STORY OF THE CONFEDERATE STATES ORDNANCE WORKS AT TYLER, TEXAS, 1861-1865, CWNEWS:AUG/95[33], *reviewed by* Norman E. Rourke

Albright, Harry; *GETTYSBURG: CRISIS OF COMMAND*, CWNEWS:NOV/92[4], *reviewed by* William Marvel

Alexander, Edward Porter:
FIGHTING FOR THE CONFEDERACY: THE PERSONAL RECOLLECTIONS OF GENERAL EDWARD PORTER ALEXANDER, (edited by Gary W. Gallagher), CWM:FEB/95[42]564, *reviewed by* Gary W. Gallagher, CWM:APR/95[50], *reviewed by* Gary W. Gallagher, CWNEWS:JUL/94[25], *reviewed by* Michael Cavanaugh, CWNEWS:NOV/89[4], *reviewed by* Michael Mullins, CWNEWS:SEP/90[4], *reviewed by* Michael Mullins
MILITARY MEMOIRS OF A CONFEDERATE: A CRITICAL NARRATIVE, CWM:FEB/95[42]564, *reviewed by* Gary W. Gallagher, CWTI:SEP/93[26], *reviewed by* Edward D.C. Campbell

Alexander, Kevin; *LOST VICTORIES: THE MILITARY GENIUS OF STONEWALL JACKSON*, CWM:MAY/93[51], *reviewed by* Brandon Beck

Alexander, Ted; *SOUTHERN REVENGE! CIVIL WAR HISTORY OF CHAMBERSBURG, PENNSYLVANIA*, CWNEWS:APR/91[4], *reviewed by* Steven J. Wright

Allan, William; *THE ARMY OF NORTHERN VIRGINIA*, CWM:JUN/95[6], *reviewed by* Gary W. Gallagher

Allen, Henry W.; *THE CONDUCT OF THE FEDERAL TROOPS IN LOUISIANA, DURING THE INVASIONS OF 1863 AND 1864*, CWNEWS:MAY/90[4], *reviewed by* J. Tracy Power

Allen, Thomas B.; *THE BLUE AND THE GRAY,*
ACW:MAR/93[58], *reviewed by* Jon Guttman,
CWNEWS:APR/93[4], *reviewed by* Frank J. Piatek,
CWTI:JAN/93[12]

Alotta, Robert I.; *CIVIL WAR JUSTICE: UNION ARMY
EXECUTIONS UNDER LINCOLN,* CWNEWS:SEP/90[4],
reviewed by Robert D. Norris Jr.

Amadon, George F.; *RISE OF THE IRONCLADS,*
CWNEWS:NOV/92[4], *reviewed by* David F. Riggs

Ambrose, Stephen E.:
DUTY, HONOR, COUNTRY. A HISTORY OF WEST POINT,
AHI:DEC/66[17], *reviewed by* Wilber S. Nye
UPTON AND THE ARMY, CWM:APR/95[50], *reviewed by* Gary
W. Gallagher

Ambrosius, Lloyd E., (edited by); *A CRISIS OF
REPUBLICANISM: AMERICAN POLITICS DURING THE
CIVIL WAR,* CWNEWS:JAN/92[4], *reviewed by* Michael
Parrish

Amchan, Arthur J.:
*HEROES, MARTYRS AND SURVIVORS OF THE CIVIL WAR:
THE GENERATION THAT FOUGHT THE WAR AND ITS
LEGACY,* CWNEWS:NOV/92[4], *reviewed by* Robert Norris
*THE MOST FAMOUS SOLDIER IN AMERICA: A BIOGRAPHY
OF NELSON A. MILES,* CWNEWS:JUL/91[4], *reviewed by*
Robert D. Norris Jr.

Ammen, Daniel; *THE ATLANTIC COAST,*
CWNEWS:MAY/91[4], *reviewed by* Frank Piatek

Anbinder, Tyler; *NATIVISM AND SLAVERY, THE
NORTHERN KNOW NOTHINGS & THE POLITICS OF THE
1850'S,* CWNEWS:JAN/94[5], *reviewed by* John L. Farber

Anderson, David D.; *ABRAHAM LINCOLN,* AHI:JUL/70[50]

Anderson, Gary C.; *THROUGH DAKOTA EYES: NARRATIVE
ACCOUNTS OF THE MINNESOTA INDIAN WAR OF 1862,*
CWNEWS:JUN/90[4], *reviewed by* Kevin J. Weddle

Andes, John W., (edited by Charles S. McCammon); *LOYAL
MOUNTAIN TROOPERS: THE SECOND AND THIRD
TENNESSEE CAVALRY IN THE CIVIL WAR,
REMINISCENCES OF LIEUTENANT JOHN W. ANDES
AND MAJOR WILL A. MCTEER,* CWNEWS:NOV/93[5],
reviewed by William L. Shea

Andrews, W.H.; (edited by Richard M. McMurry);
*FOOTPRINTS OF A REGIMENT: A RECOLLECTION OF
THE 1ST GEORGIA REGULARS,* B&G:APR/93[30], *reviewed
by* Robert E. L. Krick, CWTI:JAN/93[12],
CWNEWS:OCT/94[33], *reviewed by* Brandon Beck

Angle, Craig; *THE GREAT LOCOMOTIVE CHASE: MORE
ON THE ANDREWS RAID AND THE FIRST MEDAL OF
HONOR,* CWNEWS:NOV/93[5], *reviewed by* Larry G. Gray

Angle, Paul M.:
A PICTORIAL HISTORY OF THE CIVIL WAR YEARS,
AHI:JAN/68[55]
ABRAHAM LINCOLN; A HISTORY, AHI:FEB/67[57], *reviewed
by* Ralph Adams Brown

Arceneaux, William; *ACADIAN GENERAL: ALFRED
MOUTON AND THE CIVIL WAR,* CWNEWS:APR/90[4],
reviewed by Frank Piatek

Archive Society; *ARCHIVE OF THE CIVIL WAR,*
ACW:JUL/92[54], *reviewed by* Jon Guttman

Armstrong, Richard L.; *JACKSON'S VALLEY CAMPAIGN:
THE BATTLE OF MCDOWELL, MARCH 11-MAY 18, 1862,*
CWM:JAN/91[47], *reviewed by* Gary W. Gallagher

Arner, Frederick B.; *THE MUTINY AT BRANDY STATION:
THE LAST BATTLE OF THE HOOKER BRIGADE,*

B&G:OCT/94[40], *reviewed by* John M. Priest,
CWNEWS:JUN/95[33], *reviewed by* Jeffry D. Wert

Aschmann, Rudolf (edited by, Heinz K. Meier); *MEMOIRS OF
A SWISS OFFICER IN THE AMERICAN CIVIL WAR,*
CWNEWS:JAN/91[4], *reviewed by* Michael Mullins

Bacon, Edward; *AMONG THE COTTON THIEVES,*
CWNEWS:MAY/92[4], *reviewed by* Jock Baird

Bacot, Ada W., (edited by Jean V. Berlin); *A CONFEDERATE
NURSE: THE DIARY OF ADA W. BACOT, 1860-1863,*
CWNEWS:FEB/95[33], *reviewed by* Linda G. Black

Baden, Waldo, (edited by); *BUILDING THE MYTH:
SELECTED SPEECHES MEMORIALIZING ABRAHAM
LINCOLN,* CWM:JAN/92[57], *reviewed by* Gary W. Gallagher

Bailey, Anne J.; *BETWEEN THE ENEMY AND TEXAS:
PARSON'S TEXAS CAVALRY IN THE CIVIL WAR,*
CWNEWS:OCT/90[4], *reviewed by* Robert D. Norris

Baker, Gary R.; *CADETS IN GRAY: THE STORY OF THE
CADETS OF THE SOUTH CAROLINA MILITARY ACADEMY
AND THE CADET RANGERS IN THE CIVIL WAR,*
B&G:FEB/91[28], *reviewed by* Richard M. McMurry,
CWNEWS:JAN/92[4], *reviewed by* Brandon Beck

Baker, Jean H.; *MARY TODD LINCOLN: A BIOGRAPHY,*
AHI:FEB/88[8]

Ball, Douglas B.; *FINANCIAL FAILURE AND CONFEDERATE
DEFEAT,* ACW:JAN/92[54], *reviewed by* Bill Anderson,
B&G:FEB/92[26], *reviewed by* James F. Morgan,
CWM:MAR/92[49], *reviewed by* Gary W. Gallagher,
CWNEWS:NOV/91[4], *reviewed by* Theodore P. Savas,
CWTI:DEC/91[12]

Ballard, Michael B.:
LANDSCAPES OF BATTLE: THE CIVIL WAR,
CWNEWS:APR/90[4], *reviewed by* Barry Popchock
PEMBERTON, A BIOGRAPHY, B&G:AUG/92[36], *reviewed by*
Lawrence L. Hewitt, CWM:MAY/92[59], *reviewed by* Charles R.
Norville, CWNEWS:AUG/92[4], *reviewed by* Terrence J.
Winschel, CWR:VOL2#1[78], *reviewed by* Theodore P. Savas,
CWTI:SEP/92[18], *reviewed by* Noah Andre Trudeau

Barber, Charles; *THE CIVIL WAR LETTERS OF CHARLES
BARBER PRIVATE 104TH NEW YORK VOLUNTEER
INFANTRY,* CWNEWS:NOV/92[4], *reviewed by* Steven J.
Wright

Barber, Flavel C., (edited by Robert H. Ferrell); *HOLDING THE
LINE: THE THIRD TENNESSEE INFANTRY, 1861-1864,*
CWM:AUG/95[45], *reviewed by* Gary W. Gallagher,
CWR:VOL4#3[37]

Barclay, Ted, (edited by Charles W. Turner); *TED BARCLAY,
LIBERTY HALL VOLUNTEERS: LETTERS FROM THE
STONEWALL BRIGADE,* B&G:DEC/92[26], *reviewed by* James
I. Robertson, CWNEWS:AUG/93[5], *reviewed by* Frank J. Piatek

Bartlett, Asa W.; *HISTORY OF THE TWELFTH REGIMENT,
NEW HAMPSHIRE VOLUNTEERS, IN THE WAR OF THE
REBELLION,* CWR:VOL4#3[1], *reviewed by* James I. Robertson

Barton, O.S.; *THREE YEARS WITH QUANTRILL, A TRUE
STORY TOLD BY HIS SCOUT JOHN MCCORKLE,*
CWNEWS:SEP/95[33], *reviewed by* Norman E. Rourke

Basler, Roy P.:
*THE COLLECTED WORKS OF ABRAHAM LINCOLN,
1848-1865 (VOLUME II) SECOND SUPPLEMENT,*
CWNEWS:JAN/92[4], *reviewed by* Dr. Allen C. Guelzo
*THE COLLECTED WORKS OF ABRAHAM LINCOLN:
SUPPLEMENT 1832-1865, NUMBER 7,* AHI:MAY/76[48],
reviewed by Robert D. Hoffsommer

COLLECTED WORKS OF ABRAHAM LINCOLN, CWTI:DEC/95[38]

Bates, Colonel Charles F.; *CUSTER ENGAGES THE HOSTILES*, AHI:JUN/74[49]

Baumann, Ken; *ARMING THE SUCKERS, 1861-1865*, CWNEWS:AUG/91[4], *reviewed by* Blake Magner

Baynes, Richard C., (Compiled by); *THE LIFE AND ANCESTRY OF JOHN THISTLEWAITE BAYNES* (1833-1891), CWNEWS:JAN/90[4], *reviewed by* Frank J. Piatek

Beale, G.W.; *A LIEUTENANT OF CAVALRY IN LEE'S ARMY*, CWR:VOL4#3[37]

Bearss, Edwin C.:
THE CAMPAIGN FOR VICKSBURG, CWR:VOL2#1[78], *reviewed by* George Otott Jr.
REBEL VICTORY AT VICKSBURG, CWNEWS:JAN/91[4], *reviewed by* Terrence Winschel
THE VICKSBURG CAMPAIGN, CWM:FEB/95[42]564, *reviewed by* Gary W. Gallagher

Beatty, John; *THE CITIZEN SOLDIER; OR MEMOIRS OF A VOLUNTEER*, CWR:VOL4#3[1], *reviewed by* Peter Cozzens

Beaudot, William J.K.; *AN IRISHMAN IN THE IRON BRIGADE: THE CIVIL WAR MEMOIRS OF JAMES P. SULLIVAN, SERGEANT, 6TH WISCONSIN VOLUNTEERS*, CWM:FEB/95[7], *reviewed by* Ben Maryniak, CWM:APR/95[50], *reviewed by* Gary W. Gallagher, CWNEWS:MAY/94[5], *reviewed by* Kevin E. O'Brien

Beauregard, P.G.T.; *THE MILITARY OPERATIONS OF GENERAL BEAUREGARD IN THE WAR BETWEEN THE STATES 1861-1865*, CWM:FEB/95[42]564, *reviewed by* Gary W. Gallagher

Becker, Carl M., (edited by); *HEARTH AND KNAPSACK: THE LADLEY LETTERS, 1857-1880*, B&G:APR/91[28], *reviewed by* Dave Roth

Bell, Nimrod J., (edited by James A. Ward); *SOUTHERN RAILROAD MAN: CONDUCTOR N.J. BELL'S RECOLLECTIONS OF THE CIVIL WAR ERA*, CWNEWS:OCT/95[33], *reviewed by* Kemp Burpeau, CWR:VOL4#4[129], *reviewed by* Arthur W. Bergeron Jr.

Bellard, Alfred, (edited by David H. Donald); *GONE FOR A SOLDIER: THE CIVIL WAR MEMOIRS OF PRIVATE ALFRED BELLARD*, CWNEWS:SEP/92[4], *reviewed by* Brian C. Pohanka, CWTI:DEC/91[12]

Belohavek, John M., (edited by); *DIVIDED WE FALL — ESSAYS ON CONFEDERATE NATION BUILDING*, CWNEWS:JUL/92[4], *reviewed by* Dale Phillips

Benedict, Michael Les; *A COMPROMISE OF PRINCIPLE: CONGRESSIONAL REPUBLICANS AND RECONSTRUCTION, 1863-1869*, AHI:JUN/75[50], *reviewed by* Maury Klein

Bennett, Brian A.; *SONS OF OLD MONROE: A REGIMENTAL HISTORY OF PATRICK O'RORKE'S 140TH NEW YORK VOLUNTEER INFANTRY*, CWNEWS:APR/94[5], *reviewed by* Brian Pohanka

Bennett, Gerald R.; *DAYS OF "UNCERTAINTY AND DREAD": THE ORDEAL ENDURED BY THE CITIZENS AT GETTYSBURG*, CWNEWS:APR/95[33], *reviewed by* Blake A. Magner

Benson, Berry, (edited by Susan W. Benson); *BERRY BENSON'S CIVIL WAR BOOK: MEMOIRS OF A CONFEDERATE SCOUT AND SHARPSHOOTER*, CWM:APR/95[50], *reviewed by* Gary W. Gallagher, CWNEWS:SEP/94[33], *reviewed by* T. Michael Parrish, CWR:VOL3#2[105], *reviewed by* John McGlone

Bergeron, Arthur W. Jr.:
THE CIVIL WAR REMINISCENCES OF MAJOR SILAS T. GRISAMORE, C.S.A., B&G:JUN/94[34], *reviewed by* Gordon Jones
CONFEDERATE MOBILE, B&G:OCT/92[30], *reviewed by* Florence F. Corley, *CONFEDERATE MOBILE* CWTI:JAN/93[12]
GUIDE TO LOUISIANA CONFEDERATE MILITARY UNITS 1861-1865, CWNEWS:APR/91[4], *reviewed by* Michael Cavanaugh, CWTI:DEC/89[20], *reviewed by* Gary W. Gallagher

Beringer, Richard E.:
THE ELEMENTS OF CONFEDERATE DEFEAT: NATIONALISM, WAR AIMS, AND RELIGION, CWNEWS:OCT/90[4], *reviewed by* Michael Parrish
WHY THE SOUTH LOST THE CIVIL WAR, AHI:JAN/87[49]

Berlin, Ira, (edited by):
FREEDOM: A DOCUMENTARY HISTORY OF EMANCIPATION, 1861-1867, CWM:AUG/95[45], *reviewed by* Gary W. Gallagher
FREEDOM: A DOCUMENTARY HISTORY OF EMANCIPATION, 1861-1867, SERIES I, VOLUME III: THE WARTIME GENESIS OF FREE LABOR: THE LOWER SOUTH, CWNEWS:NOV/91[4], *reviewed by* Gregory J.W. Urwin
THE WARTIME GENESIS OF FREE LABOR: THE UPPER SOUTH, CWM:AUG/95[45], *reviewed by* Gary W. Gallagher

Bernard, Kenneth A.; *LINCOLN AND THE MUSIC OF THE CIVIL WAR* AHI:JUN/68[51], *reviewed by* Robert D. Hoffsommer

Bernath, Stuart L.; *SQUALL ACROSS THE ATLANTIC: AMERICAN CIVIL WAR PRIZE CASES AND DIPLOMACY*, AHI:JAN/75[50], *reviewed by* Jon M. Nielson

Bernstein, Iver; *THE NEW YORK CITY DRAFT RIOTS: THEIR SIGNIFICANCE FOR AMERICAN SOCIETY AND POLIICS IN THE AGE OF THE CIVIL WAR*, CWNEWS:AUG/91[4], *reviewed by* Rob Rago

Berringer, Richard; *WHY THE SOUTH LOST THE CIVIL WAR*, CWNEWS:AUG/92[4], *reviewed by* Michael Russert

Berwanger, Eugene H.; *THE BRITISH FOREIGN SERVICE AND THE AMERICAN CIVIL WAR*, CWR:VOL4#3[37]

Bevens, William E. (edited by Daniel E. Sutherland); *REMINISCENCES OF A PRIVATE: WILLIAM E. BEVENS OF THE FIRST ARKANSAS INFANTRY, C.S.A.*, CWNEWS:JUL/93[5], *reviewed by* Larry J. Daniel

Beveridge, Albert J.; *ABRAHAM LINCOLN, 1809-1858*, CWTI:DEC/95[38]

Bezdek, Richard; *AMERICAN SWORDS AND SWORD MAKERS*, CWNEWS:OCT/94[33], *reviewed by* Ron G. Hickox

Bicknell, Rev. George W.; *HISTORY OF THE FIFTH MAINE REGIMENT*, CWNEWS:OCT/89[4], *reviewed by* Barry Popchock

Bigelow, John Jr.; *THE CAMPAIGN OF CHANCELLORSVILLE*, CWM:FEB/95[42]564, *reviewed by* Gary W. Gallagher

Bilby, Joseph G.; *THREE ROUSING CHEERS: A HISTORY OF THE FIFTEENTH NEW JERSEY FROM FLEMINGTON TO APPOMATTOX*, CWNEWS:JUN/94[5], *reviewed by* Michael Cavanaugh

Billings, John D.:
HARDTACK & COFFEE: THE UNWRITTEN STORY OF ARMY LIFE, CWNEWS:DEC/94[33], *reviewed by* William F. Howard, CWTI:NOV/93[14]

*THE HISTORY OF THE TENTH MASSACHUSETTS
BATTERY OF LIGHT ARTILLERY,* CWR:VOL2#1[78],
reviewed by William Marvel
*THE HISTORY OF THE TENTH MASSACHUSETTS
BATTERY OF LIGHT ARTILLERY,* CWR:VOL4#3[1],
reviewed by William Marvel
Bird, Edgeworth & Sallie, (edited by John Rozier); *THE
GRANITE FARM LETTERS: THE CIVIL WAR
CORRESPONDENCE OF EDGEWORTH & SALLIE BIRD,*
CWNEWS:OCT/89[4], *reviewed by* Steve War,
CWTI:JUN/90[20]
Birmingham, Theodore, (edited by Zoe von Ende Lappin);
*YOURS IN LOVE: THE BIRMINGHAM CIVIL WAR
LETTERS,* CWNEWS:JAN/91[4]
Black, Robert C., III; *THE RAILROADS OF THE
CONFEDERACY,* CWM:NOV/91[73], *reviewed by* Gary W.
Gallagher
Blackerby, Hubert C.; *BLACKS IN THE BLUE AND GRAY:
AFRO-AMERICAN SERVICE IN THE CIVIL WAR,*
CWNEWS:MAY/92[4], *reviewed by* Robert L. Uzzel
Blackford, William W.; *WAR YEARS WITH JEB STUART,*
CWM:AUG/95[45], *reviewed by* Gary W. Gallagher,
CWNEWS:AUG/94[33], *reviewed by* Jerry Holsworth
Blair, William Alan; *A POLITICIAN GOES TO WAR: THE
CIVIL WAR LETTERS OF JOHN WHITE GEARY,*
CWNEWS:SEP/95[33], *reviewed by* Ethan Rafuse
Blakey, Arch F.; *GENERAL JOHN H. WINDER, C.S.A.,*
B&G:DEC/91[30], *reviewed by* R. Frank Saunders,
CWM:MAY/91[34], *reviewed by* William J. Miller,
CWNEWS:AUG/91[4], *reviewed by* John Marszalek
Blassingame, John W.; *THE SLAVE COMMUNITY:
PLANTATION LIFE IN THE ANTEBELLUM SOUTH,*
AHI:JUN/80[6], *reviewed by* Larry Gara
Bleser, Carol, (edited by); *IN JOY AND IN SORROW:
WOMEN, FAMILY, AND MARRIAGE IN THE VICTORIAN
SOUTH, 1830-1900,* CWTI:MAY/91[12], *reviewed by* Andrea
Abolins
Blessington, J.P.; *THE CAMPAIGNS OF WALKER'S TEXAS
DIVISION,* CWNEWS:OCT/95[33], *reviewed by* Richard M.
McMurry, CWR:VOL4#3[1], *reviewed by* T. Michael Parrish
Blight, David W.; *FREDERICK DOUGLASS' CIVIL WAR:
KEEPING FAITH IN JUBILEE,* CWM:JAN/91[47], *reviewed
by* Gary W. Gallagher, CWNEWS:NOV/91[4], *reviewed by*
David G. Martin
Blue, John, (edited by Dan Oates); *HANGING ROCK REBEL:
LT. JOHN BLUE'S WAR IN WEST VIRGINIA THE
SHENANDOAH VALLEY,* CWM:FEB/95[7], *reviewed by* Scott
C. Patchan, CWNEWS:JAN/95[25], *reviewed by* Stephen L.
Ritchie
Boatner, Mark M. III; *THE CIVIL WAR DICTIONARY,*
CWM:NOV/92[55], CWM:FEB/95[42], *reviewed by* Gary W.
Gallagher
Boge, Georgia; *PAVING OVER THE PAST: A HISTORY AND
GUIDE TO CIVIL WAR BATTLEFIELD PRESERVATION,*
CWM:APR/94[51], *reviewed by* Chris Fordney,
CWNEWS:MAY/94[5], *reviewed by* Blake A. Magner
Bogue, Allan G.; *THE CONGRESSMAN'S CIVIL WAR,*
CWNEWS:JUL/91[4], *reviewed by* J. Tracy Power,
CWTI:APR/90[10]
Boney, F.N.; *JOHN LETCHER OF VIRGINIA: THE STORY
OF VIRGINIA'S CIVIL WAR GOVERNOR,* AHI:JUL/67[57],
reviewed by Ralph Adams Brown

Boritt, Gabor S.:
*THE HISTORIAN'S LINCOLN: PSEUDOHISTORY,
PSYCHOHISTORY, AND HISTORY,* CWN:MAY/90[4],
reviewed by Dr. Allen C. Guelzo, CWTI:SEPT/89[29]
*THE HISTORIAN'S LINCOLN: REBUTTALS. WHAT THE
UNIVERSITY PRESS WOULD NOT PRINT,*
CWNEWS:MAY/90[4],*reviewed by* Dr. Allen C. Guelzo
*LINCOLN AND THE ECONOMICS OF THE AMERICAN
DREAM,* CWTI:DEC/95[38]
*LINCOLN THE WAR PRESIDENT, THE GETTYSBURG
LECTURES,* B&G:FEB/94[36], *reviewed by* John F. Marszalek,
CWNEWS:JUL/93[5], *reviewed by* Allen C. Guelzo
LINCOLN'S GENERALS B&G:AUG/95[38], *reviewed by*
Lawrence L. Heewit, CWM:AUG/95[45], *reviewed by* Gary W.
Gallagher, CWNEWS:AUG/95[33], *reviewed by* Willis R.
Kocher, CWTI:JUN/95[24]
WHY THE CONFEDERACY LOST B&G:OCT/92[30], *reviewed by*
Steve Davis, CWNEWS:APR/93[4], *reviewed by* Michael
Russert, CWR:VOL2#3[256], *reviewed by* Archie P. McDonald
Bosse, David, (Compiled by):
*CIVIL WAR NEWSPAPER MAPS: A CARTOBIBLIOGRAPHY
OF THE NORTHERN PRESS,* B&G:AUG/94[30], *reviewed by*
Steve Davis, CWTI:JAN/94[10]
CIVIL WAR NEWSPAPER MAPS: A HISTORICAL ATLAS,
B&G:AUG/94[30], *reviewed by* Steve Davis
Bowen, Roland E., (edited by Gregory A. Coco); *FROM BALL'S
BLUFF TO GETTYSBURG . . . AND BEYOND: THE CIVIL
WAR LETTERS OF PVT ROLAND E. BOWEN, 15TH MASS
INF 1861-1864,* CWM:APR/95[42]577
Bowers, John; *CHICKAMAUGA & CHATTANOOGA: THE
BATTLES THAT DOOMED THE CONFEDERACY,*
B&G:OCT/94[40], *reviewed by* Steve Davis, CWM:DEC/94[7],
reviewed by David A. Woodbury, CWNEWS:NOV/94[33],
reviewed by Larry J. Daniel, CWR:VOL4#3[89], *reviewed by*
David E. Long, CWTI:JAN/95[12]
Braden, Waldo W., (edited by); *BUILDING THE MYTH:
SELECTED SPEECHES MEMORIALIZING ABRAHAM
LINCOLN,* CWNEWS:JUN/92[4], *reviewed by* David F. Riggs
Bradley, Erwin Stanley; *SIMON CAMERON, LINCOLN'S
SECRETARY OF WAR: A POLITICAL BIOGRAPHY,*
AHI:OCT/67[63], *reviewed by* Russell F. Weigley
Brady, James P.; *HURRAH FOR THE ARTILLERY! KNAP'S
INDEPENDENT BATTERY E, PENNSYLVANIA LIGHT
ARTILLERY,* CWNEWS:APR/94[5], *reviewed by* Steven J.
Wright
Brandt, Nat:
THE MAN WHO TRIED TO BURN NEW YORK, AHI:FEB/87[6]
THE TOWN THAT STARTED THE CIVIL WAR,
CWM:JAN/91[35], CWNEWS:APR/92[4], *reviewed by* Gregory
J.W. Irwin
Brandt, Robert; *TOURING THE MIDDLE TENNESSEE
BACKROADS,* CWNEWS:DEC/95[29], *reviewed by* Blake A.
Magner
Breckinridge, Lucy, (edited by Mary D. Robertson); *LUCY
BRECKINRIDGE OF GROVE HILL: THE JOURNAL OF A
VIRGINIA GIRL, 1862-1864,* CWNEWS:AUG/95[33], *reviewed
by* DeAnne Blanton
Brewster, Charles H. (edited by David W. Blight); *WHEN THIS
CRUEL WAR IS OVER: THE CIVIL WAR LETTERS OF
CHARLES HARVEY BREWSTER,* CWNEWS:SEP/94[33],
reviewed by William F. Howard, CWR:VOL3#4[68], *reviewedby*
William A. Taylor

Bridges, Hal; *LEE'S MAVERICK GENERAL: DANIEL HARVEY HILL,* CWM:JAN/92[57], *reviewed by* Gary W. Gallagher, CWNEWS:SEP/93[5], *reviewed by* Kevin J. Weddle

Broadhead, Sarah M.; *THE DIARY OF A LADY OF GETTYSBURG, PENNSYLVANIA,* CWNEWS:JAN/92[4], *reviewed by* Linda Breedlove

Brooks, Noah, (edited by Herbert Mitgang); *WASHINGTON D.C., IN LINCOLN'S TIME,* CWNEWS:AUG/91[4], *reviewed by* Michael Policatti

Brooks, Ulysses R.; *BUTLER AND HIS CAVALRY IN THE WAR OF SECESSION 1861-1865,* CWNEWS:JAN/92[4], *reviewed by* Richard A. Sauers, CWR:VOL1#2[78], *reviewed by* James Harwick, Jr.

Browder, George R, (edited by Richard L. Troutman); *THE HEAVENS ARE WEEPING: THE DIARIES OF GEORGE RICHARD BROWDER 1852-1886,* CWNEWS:JAN/90[4], *reviewed by* Jeffry D. Wert

Brown, Herbert O.; *FIELDS OF GLORY, THE FACTS BOOK OF THE BATTLE OF GETTYSBURG,* CWNEWS:NOV/91[4], *reviewed by* Blake Magner

Brown, Jack I.; *THE SHADE OF THE TREES,* CWNEWS:MAY/90[4], *reviewed by* William Howard

Brown, Kent Masterson; *CUSHING OF GETTYSBURG: THE STORY OF A UNION ARTILLERY COMMANDER,* B&G:DEC/94[28], *reviewed by* William Marvel, CWM:APR/95[50], *reviewed by* Gary W. Gallagher, CWR:VOL4#3[89], *reviewed by* Mike Cantor

Brown, Louis A.; *THE SALISBURY PRISON: A CASE STUDY OF CONFEDERATE MILITARY PRISONS, 1861-1865,* CWNEWS:MAY/93[4], *reviewed by* William Marvel

Brown, Russell K.; *TO THE MANNER BORN: THE LIFE OF GENERAL WILLIAM H.T. WALKER,* ACW:MAR/95[58], *reviewed by* Nat C. Hughes, B&G:APR/95[30], *reviewed by* Christopher Losson, CWM:AUG/95[45], *reviewed by* Gary W. Gallagher, CWR:VOL4#3[37], CWR:VOL4#4[129], *reviewed by* Anne J. Bailey

Brown, Varina D.; *A COLONEL AT GETTYSBURG AND SPOTSYLVANIA: THE LIFE OF COLONEL JOSEPH NEWTON BROWN AND THE BATTLE OF GETTYSBURG AND SPOTSYLVANIA,* CWNEWS:MAY/89[4], *reviewed by* Allen Guelzo

Brown, William L. III; *THE ARMY CALLED IT HOME: MILITARY INTERIORS OF THE 19TH CENTURY,* CWNEWS:OCT/93[5],*reviewed by* Michael Russert

Browning, Robert M. Jr.; *FROM CAPE CHARLES TO CAPE FEAR: THE NORTH ALTANTIC BLOCKADING SQUADRON DURING THE CIVIL WAR,* CWM:APR/95[50], *reviewed by* Gary W. Gallagher, CWNEWS:OCT/95[33], *reviewed by* Richard A. Sauers, CWR:VOL3#3[92], *reviewed by* Mitchell Yockelson

Bruce, George A.; *THE TWENTIETH REGIMENT OF MASSACHUSETTS VOLUNTEER INFANTRY 1861-1865,* CWNEWS:SEP/90[4], *reviewed by* William F. Howard

Bruce, Robert W.; *LINCOLN AND THE TOOLS OF WAR,* CWNEWS:APR/91[4], *reviewed by* Gregory Urwin

Bryan, George S.; *THE GREAT AMERICAN MYTH: THE TRUE STORY OF LINCOLN'S MURDER,* B&G:APR/91[28], *reviewed by* Michael W. Kauffman, CWNEWS:JUN/92[4], *reviewed by* Terrence J. Winschel

Bryant, William O.; *CAHABA PRISON AND THE <u>SULTANA</u> DISASTER,* B&G:JUN/91[22], *reviewed by* Jerry O. Potter, CWNEWS:JAN/91[4], *reviewed by* Theodore P. Savas

Buck, Erastus, (edited by John E. Balzer); *BUCK'S BOOK: A VIEW OF THE 3RD VERMONT INFANTRY REGIMENT,* CWNEWS:JAN/95[25], *reviewed by* Blake A. Magner

Buell, Augustus; *THE CANNONEER,* CWNEWS:JUN/92[4], *reviewed by* Judy Yandoh

Buker, George E.; *BLOCKADERS, REFUGEES & CONTRABANDS — CIVIL WAR ON FLORIDA'S GULF COAST 1861-65,* CWM:APR/95[50], *reviewed by* Gary W. Gallagher, CWNEWS:NOV/94[33], *reviewed by* Clint Johnson, CWR:VOL4#2[136], *reviewed by* Daniel E. Sutherland

Bull, Rice C., (edited by K. Jack Bauer); *SOLDIERING: THE CIVIL WAR DIARY OF RICE C. BULL,* CWM:FEB/95[42]564, *reviewed by* Gary W. Gallagher

Bulloch, James D.; *THE SECRET SERVICE OF THE CONFEDERATE STATES IN EUROPE,* CWNEWS:JUL/90[4],*reviewed by* Gregory Mertz

Burgess, Lauren Cook, (edited by); *AN UNCOMMON SOLDIER: THE CIVIL WAR LETTERS OF SARAH ROSETTA WAKEMAN, ALIAS PVT. LYONS WAKEMAN, 153RD REGIMENT, NEW YORK STATE VOLUNTEERS, 1862-1864,* B&G:FEB/95[26], *reviewed by* Holly A. Robinson

Burgwyn, William H.S., (edited by Herbert M. Schiller); *A CAPTAIN'S WAR: THE LETTERS OF DIARIES OF WILLIAM H.S. BURGWYN, 1861-1865,* B&G:OCT/94[40], *reviewed by* Ben Smith, CWM:APR/95[50], *reviewed by* Gary W. Gallagher, CWNEWS:SEP/95[33], *reviewed by* Michael J. Winey, CWR:VOL4#2[136], *reviewed by* Leonne M. Hudson

Burlingame, Michael; *THE INNER WORLD OF ABRAHAM LINCOLN,* B&G:DEC/95[30], *reviewed by* David E. Long, CWM:DEC/95[10], *reviewed by* J. Jeffrey Cox, CWNEWS:JUN/95[33], *reviewed by* Allen C. Guelzo

Burnside, William H.; *THE HONORABLE POWELL CLAYTON,* CWNEWS:OCT/92[4], *reviewed by* J. Tracy Power

Burton, E. Milby; *THE SIEGE OF CHARLESTON 1861-1865,* CWNEWS:JUN/92[4], *reviewed by* J. Tracy Power

Busey, John; *THE LAST FULL MEASURE: BURIALS IN THE SOLDIER'S NATIONAL CEMETERY AT GETTYSBURG,* CWNEWS:JUL/90[4], *reviewed by* Michael Cavanaugh

Byers, Samuel H.M.; *WITH FIRE AND SWORD* B&G:APR/93[30], *reviewed by* Wiley Sword, CWNEWS:AUG/95[33], *reviewed by* Kevin J. Weddle

Caldwell, J.F.J.; *A HISTORY OF A BRIGADE OF SOUTH CAROLINIANS,* CWR:VOL4#3[1], *reviewed by* Michael P. Musick

Caldwell, Lycurgus W., (edited by J. Michael Welton); *MY HEART IS SO REBELLIOUS: THE CALDWELL LETTERS, 1861-1865,* CWNEWS:JAN/93[4], *reviewed by* Sarah W. Wiggins

Caldwell, Willie W.; *STONEWALL JIM: A BIOGRAPHY OF GENERAL JAMES A. WALKER, C.S.A.,* CWNEWS:JUL/92[4], *reviewed by* Kemp Burpeau

Calkins, Chris; *THE FINAL BIVOUAC: THE SURRENDER PARADE AT APPOMATTOX AND THE DISBANDING OF THE ARMIES, APRIL 10-MAY 20, 1865,* CWNEWS:MAY/89[4], *reviewed by* Michael Parrish

Callahan, James M.; *DIPLOMATIC HISTORY OF THE SOUTHERN CONFEDERACY,* AHI:JAN/75[50], *reviewed by* Jon M. Nielson

Camper, Charles; *HISTORICAL RECORD OF THE FIRST REGIMENT MARYLAND INFANTRY,* CWNEWS:AUG/92[4], *reviewed by* Michael A. Hughes, CWR:VOL1#2[78], *reviewed by* Francis M. Kirby

Cannan, John:
THE ATLANTA CAMPAIGN: MAY-NOVEMBER, 1864,
CWNEWS:NOV/92[4], *reviewed by* Anne J. Bailey
THE WILDERNESS CAMPAIGN: MAY 1864,
CWNEWS:JUN/95[33], *reviewed by* Jock Baird
Cantrell, Gregg; *KENNETH AND JOHN B. RAYNER AND THE LIMITS OF SOUTHERN DISSENT,*
CWNEWS:JUN/94[5], *reviewed by* Spencer Gill
Carey, D.L.; *DISTANT DRUMS,* CWNEWS:SEP/92[4], *reviewed by* Kemp Burpeau
Carlson, Paul; *"PECOS BILL": A MILITARY BIOGRAPHY OF WILLIAM R. SHAFTER,* CWNEWS:APR/91[4], *reviewed by* Robert D. Norris Jr.
Carter, Robert G.; *FOUR BROTHERS N BLUE: OR SUNSHINE AND SHADOWS OF THE WAR OF THE REBELLION: A STORY OF THE GREAT CIVIL WAR FROM BULL RUN TO APPOMATTOX,* CWM:FEB/95[42]564, *reviewed by* Gary W. Gallagher
Carter, W.H.; *FROM YORKTOWN TO SANTIAGO WITH THE SIXTH U.S. CAVALRY,* CWNEWS:SEP/91[4], *reviewed by* David F. Riggs
Casdorph, Paul D.; *LEE AND JACKSON: CONFEDERATE CHIEFTONS,* ACW:JUL/93[58], *reviewed by* Michael D. Hull, CWM:JAN/93[57], *reviewed by* Joseph A. Scotchie, CWNEWS:NOV/93[5], *reviewed by* Jeffry D. Wert
Casler, John O.; *FOUR YEARS IN THE STONEWALL BRIGADE,* CWR:VOL4#3[1], *reviewed by* John M. Coski
Castel, Albert:
A FRONTIER STATE AT WAR: KANSAS, 1861-1865,
B&G:FEB/93[36], *reviewed by* Thomas Goodrich, CWNEWS:OCT/93[5], *reviewed by* Norman E. Rourke
DECISION IN THE WEST: THE ATLANTA CAMPAIGN OF 1864, B&G:APR/93[30], *reviewed by* Larry J. Daniel, CWM:JUL/93[51], *reviewed by* Judge Ben Smith, CWM:FEB/95[42]564, *reviewed by* Gary W. Gallagher, CWNEWS:MAY/94[5], *reviewed by* John Faber, CWR:VOL2#4[346], *reviewed by* Richard M. McMurry
GENERAL STERLING PRICE AND THE CIVIL WAR IN THE WEST, CWM:APR/95[50], *reviewed by* Gary W. Gallagher
Cater, Douglas J.; *AS IT WAS: REMINISCENCES OF A SOLDIER OF THE THIRD TEXAS CAVALRY AND THE NINETEENTH LOUISIANA INFANTRY,*
CWNEWS:JUL/92[4], *reviewed by* Robert D. Norris Jr.
Catton, Bruce:
A STILLNESS AT APPOMATTOX, CWR:VOL4#3[1], *reviewed by* Glenn LaFantasie
THE ARMY OF THE POTOMAC TRILOGY — MR. LINCOLN'S ARMY, GLORY ROAD, AND A STILLNESS AT APPOMATTOX, CWM:FEB/95[42]564, *reviewed by* Gary W. Gallagher
GRANT MOVES SOUTH, CWM:FEB/95[42]564, *reviewed by* Gary W. Gallagher
GRANT TAKES COMMAND AHI:AUG/69[48], *reviewed by* Robert D. Hoffsommer, CWM:FEB/95[42]564, *reviewed by* Gary W. Gallagher
Cavada, F.F.; *LIBBY LIFE: EXPERIENCES OF A PRISONER OF WAR IN RICHMOND, VA 1863-1864,* CWR:VOL4#4[129], *reviewed by* Frank G. Prator
Cavanaugh, Michael; *THE PETERSBURG CAMPAIGN: THE BATTLE OF THE CRATER: "THE HORRID PIT", JUNE 25-AUGUST 6, 1864,* CWNEWS:JUL/90[4], *reviewed by* J. Tracy Power

Chalfant, William Y.:
WITHOUT QUARTER: THE WICHITA EXPEDITION AND THE FIGHT ON CROOKED CREEK, CWM:FEB/95[7], *reviewed by* William J. Miller, CWNEWS:APR/93[4], *reviewed by* Robert D. Norris Jr.
CHEYENNES AND HORSE SOLDIERS, CWM:FEB/95[7], *reviewed by* William J. Miller
Chamberlain, Joshua L.:
"BAYONET! FORWARD": MY CIVIL WAR REMINISCENCES, CWTI:JUN/95[24]
THE PASSING OF THE ARMIES: AN ACCOUNT OF THE FINAL CAMPAIGN OF THE ARMY OF THE POTOMAC, BASED UPON PERSONAL RECOLLECTIONS,
CWM:FEB/95[42]564, *reviewed by* Gary W. Gallagher
Chamberlayne, Ham, (edited by Churchill G. Chamberlayne);
HAM CHAMBERLAYNE — VIRGINIAN: LETTERS AND PAPERS OF AN ARTILLERY OFFICER IN THE WAR FOR SOUTHERN INDEPENDENCE 1861-1865, CWR:VOL3#4[68], *reviewed by* Michael A. Cavanaugh
Chambers, John W. II; *TO RAISE AN ARMY: THE DRAFT COMES TO MODERN AMERICA,* AHI:SUM/88[4]
Chambers, William Pitt; *BLOOD & SACRIFICE: THE CIVIL WAR JOURNAL OF A CONFEDERATE SOLDIER,*
CWM:AUG/95[45], *reviewed by* Gary W. Gallagher
Chance, Josephy E.; *JEFFERSON DAVIS'S MEXICAN WAR REGIMENT,* CWM:JAN/92[57], *reviewed by* Gary W. Gallagher, CWNEWS:NOV/93[5], *reviewed by* Robert D. Norris Jr., CWNEWS:JAN/93[4], *reviewed by* Robert D. Norris Jr.
Chandler, David L.; *THE NATURAL SUPERIORITY OF SOUTHERN POLITICANS,* AHI:OCT/78[26], *reviewed by* David Lindsey
Chase, Lynn M.; *THE UNITED STATES AND FRANCE: CIVIL WAR DIPLOMACY,* AHI:JAN/75[50], *reviewed by* Jon M. Nielson
Chase, Salmon P., (edited by John Niven):
THE SALMON P. CHASE PAPERS, VOLUME 1, JOURNALS, 1829-1872, CWM:AUG/95[45], *reviewed by* Gary W. Gallagher, CWNEWS:DEC/94[33], *reviewed by* Michael Parrish
THE SALMON P. CHASE PAPERS, VOLUME 2, CORRESPONDENCE, 1823-1857, CWM:AUG/95[45], *reviewed by* Gary W. Gallagher
Chesebrough, David B.; *"NO SORROW LIKE OUR SORROW": NORTHERN PROTESTANT MINISTERS AND THE ASSASSINATION OF LINCOLN,* CWNEWS:FEB/95[33], *reviewed by* Larry G. Gray, CWR:VOL4#3[37]
Chesebrough, David B., (edited by); *GOD ORDAINED THIS WAR: SERMONS ON THE SECTIONAL CRISIS, 1830-1865,* CWM:JAN/92[57], *reviewed by* Gary W. Gallagher, CWNEWS:NOV/92[4], *reviewed by* Allen C. Guelzo
Chester, Thomas M., (edited by R.J.M. Blackett); *THOMAS MORRIS CHESTER, BLACK CIVIL WAR CORRESPONDENT: HIS DISPATCHES FROM THE VIRGINIA FRONT,* CWNEWS:SEP/90[4], *reviewed by* Gregory J.W. Irwin
Child, William; *A HISTORY OF THE FIFTH REGIMENT, NEW HAMPSHIRE VOLUNTEERS,* IN THE AMERICAN CIVIL WAR, 1861-1865, CWR:VOL3#3[92], *reviewed by* Patrick S. Brady
Chisholm, Daniel, (edited by W. Springer Menge); *THE CIVIL WAR NOTEBOOK OF DANIEL CHISHOLM: A CHRONICLE OF DAILY LIFE IN THE UNION ARMY 1864-1865,*
CWNEWS:MAY/91[4], *reviewed by* Jeffry D. Wert

Chisolm, J. Julian; *A MANUAL OF MILITARY SURGERY, FOR THE USE OF SURGEONS IN THE CONFEDERATE ARMY; WITH AN APPENDIX OF THE RULES AND REGULATIONS OF THE MEDICAL DEPARTMENT OF THE CONFEDERATE ARMY,* CWNEWS:JUL/91[4], *reviewed by* Harris D. Riley

Christ, Mark K.; *RAGGED AND SUBLIME: THE CIVIL WAR IN ARKANSAS,* CWTI:JUN/95[24]

Cisco, Walter B.; *STATES RIGHTS GIST: A SOUTH CAROLINA GENERAL OF THE CIVIL WAR,* ACW:SEP/92[54], *reviewed by* Jon Guttman, B&G:OCT/92[30], *reviewed by* Christopher Losson, CWR:VOL2#2[169], *reviewed by* George E. Otott, Jr.

Cist, Henry M.; *THE ARMY OF THE CUMBERLAND,* CWNEWS:JUN/91[4], *reviewed by* Jeffry D. Wert

Clark, Charles B.; *UNIVERSITY RECRUITS, COMPANY C, 12TH IOWA INFANTRY REGIMENT 1861-1865,* CWNEWS:NOV/94[33], *reviewed by* Hugh G. Earnhart

Clark, Reuben G., (edited by Willene B. Clark); *VALLEYS OF THE SHADOW: THE MEMOIR OF CONFEDERATE CAPTAIN REUBEN G. CLARK, COMPANY I, 59TH TENNESSEE MOUNTED INFANTRY,* CWM:AUG/95[45], *reviewed by* Gary W. Gallagher, CWR:VOL4#3[37]

Cleaves, Freeman; *MEADE OF GETTYSBURG,* CWM:DEC/94[7], *reviewed by* Gary W. Gallagher, CWNEWS:OCT/92[4], *reviewed by* Frank Piatek

Clemson, Floride, (edited by Ernest M. Lander Jr.); *A REBEL CAME HOME: THE DIARY AND LETTERS OF FLORIDE CLEMSON, 1863-1866,* CWM:JAN/91[47], *reviewed by* Gary W. Gallagher, CWNEWS:MAY/91[4], *reviewed by* Brandon Beck

Clinton, Catherine; *DIVIDED HOUSES: GENDER AND THE CIVIL WAR,* CWNEWS:FEB/94[5], *reviewed by* Allen C. Guelzo

Clinton, Catherine; *TARA REVISITED: WOMEN, WAR, AND THE PLANTATION LEGEND,* CWTI:AUG/95[18]

Coates, Earl J.; *AN INTRODUCTION OT CIVIL WAR SMALL ARMS,* CWNEWS:MAY/92[4], *reviewed by* Russ Pritchard

Coburn, Mark; *TERRIBLE INNOCENCE, GENERAL SHERMAN AT WAR,* CWNEWS:JAN/94[5], *reviewed by* John F. Marszalek

Coco, Gregory A.:

A VAST SEA OF MISERY: A HISTORY AND GUIDE TO THE UNION AND CONFEDERATE FIELD HOSPITALS AT GETTYSBURG JULY 1-NOVEMBER 20, 1863, CWNEWS:NOV/89[4], *reviewed by* William Howard

FROM BALL'S BLUFF TO GETTYSBURG . . . AND BEYOND, CWR:VOL4#4[129], *reviewed by* Mitchell Yockelson

KILLED IN ACTION: EYEWITNESS ACCOUNTS OF THE LAST MOMENTS OF 100 UNION SOLDIERS WHO DIED AT GETTYSBURG, CWNEWS:DEC/93[5], *reviewed by* David F. Riggs

WASTED VALOR: THE CONFEDERATE DEAD AT GETTYSBURG, CWNEWS:APR/92[4], *reviewed by* Dr. David G. Martin

Coddington, Edwin B.; *THE GETTYSBURG CAMPAIGN: A STUDY IN COMMAND,* AHI:DEC/68[50], *reviewed by* E.E. Billings, CWM:FEB/95[42]564, *reviewed by* Gary W. Gallagher

Coffin, Howard; *FULL DUTY: VERMONTERS IN THE CIVIL WAR,* B&G:FEB/95[26], *reviewed by* Albert Castel, CWNEWS:JUN/94[5], *reviewed by* Blake A. Magner

Cohen, Stan B.:

A PICTORIAL GUIDE TO WEST VIRGINIA'S CIVIL WAR SITES AND RELATED INFORMATION, CWNEWS:NOV/91[4], *reviewed by* Frank Piatek

HANDS ACROSS THE WALL: THE 50TH AND 75TH REUNIONS OF THE GETTYSBURG BATTLE, CWNEWS:MAY/95[33], *reviewed by* Allen C. Guelzo

Coker, P.C. III; *CHARLESTON'S MARITIME HERITAGE, 1670-1865: AN ILLUSTRATED HISTORY,* AHI:JAN/89[10]

Coleman, Winston Jr.; *FAMOUS KENTUCKY DUELS,* AHI:JUL/70[50], *reviewed by* William C. Davis

Collins, George K.; *MEMOIRS OF THE 149TH REGIMENT,* CWR:VOL4#3[1], *reviewed by* Harry Pfanz

Collins, R.M.; *CHAPTERS FROM THE UNWRITTEN HISTORY OF THE WAR BETWEE THE STATES,* CWR:VOL1#2[78], *reviewed by* George Otott Jr.

Colt, Margaretta B.; *DEFEND THE VALLEY: A SHENANDOAH FAMILY IN THE CIVIL WAR,* CWM:APR/95[8], *reviewed by* Gary Ecelbarger, CWNEWS:FEB/95[33], *reviewed by* Jeffry D. Wert

Combined Books, (edited by); *THE CIVIL WAR BOOK OF LISTS,* CWNEWS:OCT/94[33], *reviewed by* Robert D. Quigley, CWTI:JAN/94[10]

Conklin, E.F.; *WOMEN AT GETTYSBURG, 1863,D* CWNEWS:JUN / 94[5], *reviewed by* DeAnne Blanton

Connelly, Thomas L.:

ARMY OF THE HEARTLAND: THE ARMY OF TENNESSEE, 1861-1862, CWM:FEB/95[42]564, *reviewed by* Gary W. Gallagher

AUTUMN OF GLORY: THE ARMY OF TENNESSEE, 1862-1865, CWM:FEB/95[42]564, *reviewed by* Gary W. Gallagher

THE MARBLE MAN: ROBERT E. LEE AND HIS IMAGE IN AMERICAN SOCIETY, CWM:JUL/91[58],*reviewed by* Gary W. Gallagher

Conolly, Thomas, (edited by Nelson D. Lankford); *AN IRISHMAN IN DIXIE: THOMAS CONOLLY'S DIARY OF THE FALL OF THE CONFEDERACY,* CWNEWS:SEP/89[8], *reviewed by* Robert D. Norris

Conway, W. Fred; *CORYDON: THE FORGOTTEN BATTLE OF THE CIVIL WAR,* CWNEWS:JUN/92[4], *reviewed by* Steven J. Wright

Conyngham, David P.; *THE IRISH BRIGADE AND ITS CAMPAIGNS,* CWM:FEB/95[7], *reviewed by* William J. Miller

Cook, Adrian; *THE ARMIES OF THE STREETS: THE NEW YORK CITY DRAFT RIOTS OF 1863,* AHI:JAN/76[39], *reviewed by* David Lindsey

Cooke, Philip St. George; *CAVALRY TACTICS: OR, REGULATIONS FOR THE INSTRUCTION, FORMATIONS, AND MOVEMENTS OF THE CAVALRY,* CWNEWS:DEC/95[29], *reviewed by* Dave Hannah

Cooling, Benjamin F. III:

JUBAL EARLY'S RAID ON WASHINGTON: 1864, CWNEWS:MAY/91[4], *reviewed by* Harris D. Riley Jr., CWTI:DEC/90[10], *reviewed by* Jeffry D. Wert

FORTS HENRY AND DONELSON: THE KEY TO THE CONFEDERATE HEARTLAND, CWM:FEB/95[42]564, *reviewed by* Gary W. Gallagher

MR. LINCOLN'S FORTS: A GUIDE TO THE CIVIL WAR DEFENSES OF WASHINGTON, CWNEWS:APR/90[4], *reviewed by* Steve Ward

SYMBOL, SWORD AND SHIELD: DEFENDING WASHINGTON DURING THE CIVIL WAR, CWNEWS:DEC/92[4], *reviewed by* Barry Popchock

Cooper, George; *LOST LOVE: A TRUE STORY OF PASSION, MURDER, AND JUSTICE IN OLD NEW YORK,* CWNEWS:JAN/95[25], *reviewed by* DeAnne Blanton

Corby, William, (edited by Lawrence F. Kohl); *MEMORIES OF CHAPLAIN LIFE: THREE YEARS WITH THE IRISH BRIGADE IN THE ARMY OF THE POTOMAC,* CWNEWS:JAN/94[5], *reviewed by* Gary Augustine

Cormier, Steven A.; *THE SIEGE OF SUFFOLK: THE FORGOTTEN CAMPAIGN, APRIL 11-MAY 4, 1863,* B&G:APR/91[28], *reviewed by* Keith Bohannon, CWNEWS:MAY/90[4], *reviewed by* Theodore P. Savas

Cornwell, Bernard:
COPPERHEAD, CWNEWS:NOV/95[29], *reviewed by* Judy Yandoh
REBEL, CWNEWS:FEB/95[33], *reviewed by* Sarah W. Wiggins

Coryell, Janet L.; *NEITHER HEROINE NOR FOOL: ANNA ELLA CARROLL OF MARYLAND,* CWM:JAN/91[47], *reviewed by* Gary W. Gallagher

Coulling, Mary P.; *THE LEE GIRLS,D* CWNEWS:APR/94[5], *reviewed by* Linda G. Black

Coulling, Mary P.; *MARGARET JUNKIN PRESTON: A BIOGRAPHY,* CWNEWS:SEP/94[33], *reviewed by* Linda G. Black, CWTI:MAR/94[12], *reviewed by* Wendy Hamand Venet

Cox, Jacob D.; *ATLANTA,* CWNEWS:NOV/91[4], *reviewed by* John F. Marszalek

Cox, Jacob D.; *THE MARCH TO THE SEA, FRANKLIN AND NASHVILLE,* CWNEWS:NOV/91[4], *reviewed by* John F. Marszalek

Cox, LaWanda; *LINCOLN AND BLACK FREEDOM,* CWNEWS:JUL/95[61], *reviewed by* Judy Yandoh

Cozzens, Peter:
NO BETTER PLACE TO DIE: THE BATTLE OF STONES RIVER, ACW:MAR/91[54], *reviewed by* Phil Noblitt, CWNEWS:APR/90[4], *reviewed by* John Marszalek
THE SHIPWRECK OF THEIR HOPES: THE BATTLE FOR CHATTANOOGA, B&G:JUN/95[30], *reviewed by* James J. Cooke, CWM:FEB/95[42]564, *reviewed by* Gary W. Gallagher, CWNEWS:MAY/95[33], *reviewed by* Richard M. McMurry, CWR:VOL4#3[37], CWR:VOL4#4[129], *reviewed by* Eugene H. Berwanger, CWTI:JUN/95[24]
THIS TERRIBLE SOUND: THE BATTLE OF CHICKAMAUGA, B&G:AUG/93[24], *reviewed by* Steven E. Woodworth, CWM:MAY/93[51], *reviewed by* John M. Priest, CWM:FEB/95[42]564, *reviewed by* Gary W. Gallagher, CWNEWS:FEB/94[5], *reviewed by* Dr. David Martin

Craft, David; *HISTORY OF THE ONE HUNDRED FORTY-FIRST REGIMENT PENNSYLVANIA VOLUNTEERS 1862-1865,* CWR:VOL1#4[77], *reviewed by* David A. Woodbury

Cresap, Bernarr; *APPOMATTOX COMMANDER: THE STORY OF GENERAL E.O.C. ORD,* AHI:FEB/82[9], *reviewed by* Richard J. Sommers

Crissey, Elwell; *LINCOLN'S LOST SPEECH,* AHI:JUN/68[51], *reviewed by* Robert D. Hoffsommer

Crist, Elwood W.; *"OVER A WIDE, HOT, . . . CRIMSON PLAIN": THE STRUGGLE FOR THE BLISS FARM AG GETTYSBURG, JULY 2ND AND 3RD, 1863,* CWNEWS:JAN/95[25], *reviewed by* Dr. Richard A. Sauers

Crist, Lynda L., (edited by):
THE PAPERS OF JEFFERSON DAVIS: JANUARY 6, 1856-DECEMBER 28, 1860, VOLUME 6, CWNEWS:AUG/90[4], *reviewed by* Theodore P. Savas
THE PAPERS OF JEFFERSON DAVIS, VOLUME 7, 1861, CWNEWS:DEC/92[4], *reviewed by* Theodore P. Savas
THE PAPERS OF JEFFERSON DAVIS. VOL. 8: 1862, B&G:OCT/95[28], *reviewed by* Steve Davis, CWM:JUN/95[6], *reviewed by* Gary W. Gallagher, CWNEWS:DEC/95[29], *reviewed by* Theodore P. Savas

Crofts, Daniel W.; *RELUCTANT CONFEDERATES, UPPER SOUTH UNIONISTS IN THE SECESSION CRISIS,* CWNEWS:JAN/90[4], *reviewed by* David martin

Crook, D. P.; *THE NORTH, THE SOUTH AND THE POWERS 1861-1865,* AHI:DEC/76[50], *reviewed by* Maury Klein, AHI:JAN/75[50], *reviewed by* Jon M. Nielson

Cross, Harold; *THEY SLEEP BENEATH THE MOCKINGBIRD: MISSISSIPPI BURIAL SITES AND BIOGRAPHIES OF CONFEDERATE GENERALS,* CWR:VOL4#3[37]

Crouch, Richard E.; *ROUGH-RIDING SCOUT: THE STORY OF JOHN W. MOBBERLY, LOUDOUN'S OWN CIVIL WAR GUERRILLA HERO,* ACW:MAY/95[62], *reviewed by* Jon Guttman

Crowe, Elizabeth P.; *GENEALOGY ONLINE: RESEARCHING YOUR ROOTS,* CWTI:JUN/95[24]

Culpepper, Marilyn M.; *TRIALS AND TRIUMPHS: WOMEN OF THE AMERICAN CIVIL WAR,* CWNEWS:AUG/93[5], *reviewed by* Sarah W. Wiggins

Cunningham, Horace H.; *DOCTOR'S IN GRAY: THE CONFEDERATE MEDICAL SERVICE,* CWM:MAY/91[38], *reviewed by* Gary W. Gallagher, CWM:APR/95[50], *reviewed by* Gary W. Gallagher

Cuomo, Mario M., (edited by); *LINCOLN ON DEMOCRACY,* B&G:OCT/91[34], *reviewed by* John S. Peterson, CWM:MAR/91[42], *reviewed by* William J. Miller, CWNEWS:JUL/92[4], *reviewed by* Jock Baird

Current, Richard N.:
ENCYCLOPEDIA OF THE CONFEDERACY CWNEWS:MAY/94[5], *reviewed by* Blake A. Magner, CWR:VOL3#4[68], *reviewed by* Theodore P. Savas, CWTI:SEP/94[18]
LINCOLN'S LOYALISTS: UNION SOLDIERS FROM THE CONFEDERACY, ACW:SEP/93[54], *reviewed by* Richard F. Welch, B&G:APR/94[24], *reviewed by* Earl J. Hess
THOSE TERRIBLE CARPETBAGGERS: A REINTERPRETATION, CWNEWS:APR/90[4], *reviewed by* Robert D. Norris

Curry, Leonard P.; *BLUEPRINT FOR MODERN AMERICA: NONMILITARY LEGISLATION OF THE FIRST CIVIL WAR CONGRESS,* CWM:FEB/95[7], *reviewed by* Gary W. Gallagher

Custer, Elizabeth B., (edited by Arlene Reynolds); *THE CIVIL WAR MEMORIES OF ELIZABETH BACON CUSTER,* CWNEWS:APR/95[33], *reviewed by* Jeffry D. Wert

Cutrer, Thomas W.; *BEN MCCULLOCH AND THE FRONTIER MILITARY TRADITION,* B&G:APR/94[24], *reviewed by* Anne J. Bailey, CWM:APR/95[50], *reviewed by* Gary W. Gallagher, CWNEWS:DEC/93[5], *reviewed by* Norman E. Rourke, CWR:VOL3#4[68], *reviewed by* David P. Smith

Dabney, Virginius; *RICHMOND: THE STORY OF A CITY,* AHI:AUG/77[49], *reviewed by*

Daly, Louise H.; *ALEXANDER CHEVES HASKELL: THE PORTRAIT OF A MAN,* CWNEWS:OCT/90[4], *reviewed by* Michael Russert

Daniel, Larry J.; *SOLDIERING IN THE ARMY OF TENNESSEE: A PORTRAIT OF LIFE IN A CONFEDERATE ARMY,* ACW:SEP/92[54], *reviewed by* Richard F. Welch, B&G:AUG/92[36], *reviewed by* Steve Davis, CWNEWS:MAY/93[4], *reviewed by* Michael A. Cavanaugh, CWR:VOL2#1[78], *reviewed by* James Harwick, Jr.

Darling, Roger; *CUSTER'S SEVENTH CAVALRY COMES TO DAKOTA,* CWNEWS:JUL/90[4], *reviewed by* Brian Pohanka

Davenport, Alfred; *CAMP AND FIELD LIFE OF THE FIFTH NEW YORK,* CWR:VOL4#3[1], *reviewed by* Brian C. Pohanka

Davis, Billy, (edited by Richard S. Skidmore); *THE CIVIL WAR JOURNAL OF BILLY DAVIS,* CWNEWS:NOV/90[4], *reviewed by* Frank J. Piatek

Davis, David Brion; *THE PROBLEM OF SLAVERY IN THE AGE OF REVOLUTION, 1770-1823,* AHI:MAY/76[48], *reviewed by* Bell I. Wiley

Davis, James H.; *THE CYPRESS RANGERS IN THE CIVIL WAR,* CWNEWS:MAY/93[4], *reviewed by* Kemp Burpeau

Davis, Jefferson:
THE RISE AND FALL OF THE CONFEDERATE GOVERNMENT, CWM:JAN/91[47], *reviewed by* Gary W. Gallagher, CWM:JUN/95[6], *reviewed by* Gary W. Gallagher
THE PAPERS OF JEFFERSON DAVIS, VOLUME 7, 1861, (edited by Lynda L. Crist), B&G:DEC/93[24]

Davis, Keith F.; *GEORGE N. BARNARD: PHOTOGRAPHER OF SHERMAN'S CAMPAIGNS,* B&G:APR/91[28], *reviewed by* Henry Deeks

Davis, Varina; *JEFFERSON DAVIS,* CWNEWS:MAY/92[4], *reviewed by* Michael Russert

Davis, William C.:
A GOVERNMENT OF OUR OWN: THE MAKING OF THE CONFEDERACY, CWM:AUG/95[45], *reviewed by* Gary W. Gallagher, CWR:VOL4#3[37], CWTI:JUN/95[24], *reviewed by* Steven E. Woodworth
BRECKINRIDGE: STATESMAN, SOLDIER, SYMBOL, CWM:FEB/95[42]564, *reviewed by* Gary W. Gallagher
BROTHER AGAINST BROTHER, AHI:SEP/84[50]
THE CONFEDERATE GENERAL, CWM:FEB/95[42]564, *reviewed by* Gary W. Gallagher, CWNEWS:DEC/93[5], *reviewed by* Blake A. Magner, CWR:VOL3#1[80], *reviewed by* Theodore P. Savas
DEAR WIFE: LETTERS OF A CIVIL WAR SOLDIER, AHI:NOV/92[16]
THE DEEP WATERS OF THE PROUD: VOLUME ONE OF THE IMPERILED UNION, 1861-1865, AHI:MAY/82[8], *reviewed by* James I. Robertson
DIARY OF A CONFEDERATE SOLDIER: JOHN S. JACKMAN OF THE ORPHAN BRIGADE, B&G:OCT/91[34], *reviewed by* Larry J. Daniel
JEFFERSON DAVIS, THE MAN AND HIS HOUR, ACW:MAR/93[58], *reviewed by* Phil Noblitt, B&G:DEC/92[26], *reviewed by* Judith Lee Hallock, CWM:MAR/93[51], CWNEWS:JAN/93[4], *reviewed by* John F. Marszalek, CWR:VOL2#1[78], *reviewed by* Theodore P. Savas
THE ORPHAN BRIGADE AHI:DEC/80[7], *reviewed by* James I. Robertson Jr., CWR:VOL1#1[1], *reviewed by* Craig L. Symonds
TOUCHED BY FIRE: A PHOTOGRAPHIC PORTRAIT OF THE CIVIL WAR, VOLUME I, AHI:JUN/86[8]
TOUCHED BY FIRE: A PHOTOGRAPHIC PORTRAIT OF THE CIVIL WAR, VOLUME II, AHI:MAY/87[9]

Dawson, Francis W.; *REMINISCENCES OF CONFEDERATE SERVICE 1861-1865,* CWNEWS:DEC/95[29], *reviewed by* David E. Long

De Forest, John W., (edited by James H. Croushore); *A VOLUNTEER'S ADVENTURES: A UNION CAPTAIN'S RECORD OF THE CIVIL WAR,* CWM:FEB/95[42]564, *reviewed by* Gary W. Gallagher

de Joinville, Prince; *THE ARMY OF THE POTOMAC: ITS ORGANIZATION, ITS COMMANDER, AND ITS CAMPAIGN,* CWM:JUN/95[6], *reviewed by* William J. Miller

de Paris, Comte; *HISTORY OF THE CIVIL WAR IN AMERICA,* CWM:JUN/95[6], *reviewed by* William J. Miller

DeCredico, Mary A.; *PATRIOTISM FOR PROFIT: GEORGIA'S URBAN ENTERPRENEURS AND THE CONFEDERATE WAR EFFORT,* CWNEWS:JUL/92[4], *reviewed by* Linda G. Black

Dedmondt, Glenn; *SOUTHERN BRONZE: CAPT. GARDEN'S (S.C.) ARTILLERY COMPANY DURING THE WAR BETWEEN THE STATES,* CWNEWS:SEP/94[33], *reviewed by* Theodore P. Savas

Dell, Christopher; *LINCOLN AND THE WAR DEMOCRATS: THE GRAND EROSION OF CONSERVATIVE TRADITION* AHI:JUN/76[50], *reviewed by* Lowell H. Harrison

Denney, Robert E.:
THE CIVIL WAR YEARS: A DAY-BY-DAY CHRONICLE OF THE LIFE OF A NATION, B&G:DEC/93[24], *reviewed by* Lawrence F. Kohl
CIVIL WAR MEDICINE: CARE AND COMFORT OF THE WOUNDED, CWTI:JUN/95[24]
CIVIL WAR PRISONS & ESCAPES, A DAY-BY-DAY CHRONICLE, ACW:SEP/94[66], *reviewed by* Rober L. Vance, CWNEWS:FEB/95[33], *reviewed by* Michael Russert, CWTI:MAY/94[20]
CIVIL WAR YEARS: A DAILY ACCOUNT OF THE LIFE OF A NATION, CWTI:JAN/93[12]
THE CIVIL WAR YEARS — A DAY BY DAY CHRONICLE OF THE LIFE OF A NATION, CWNEWS:AUG/94[33], *reviewed by* Dale K. Phillips

Denoon, Charles E., (edited by Richard T. Couture); *CHARLIE'S LETTERS, THE CIVIL WAR CORRESPONDENCE,* CWNEWS:OCT/90[4], *reviewed by* Ron Rago

Dew, Charles B.; *IRONMAKER TO THE CONFEDERACY: JOSEPH R. ANDERSON AND THE TREDEGAR IRON WORKS,* AHI:DEC/66[17], *reviewed by* Ralph Adams Brown

DeWitt, David Miller; *THE IMPEACHMENT AND TRIAL OF ANDREW JOHNSON,* AHI:JAN/68[55], *reviewed by* Colonel J.E. Raymond

Dicey, Edward, (edited by Herbert Mitgang); *SPECTATOR OF AMERICA,* CWNEWS:MAY/91[4], *reviewed by* Mark Snell

Dickert, D. Augustus; *HISTORY OF KERSHAW'S BRIGADE,* CWNEWS:APR/92[4], *reviewed by* Michael Russert

Dillon, Merton L.; *SLAVERY ATTACKED: SOUTHERN SLAVES AND THEIR ALLIES, 1619-1865,* CWM:JAN/92[57], *reviewed by* Gary W. Gallagher, CWNEWS:JUL/92[4], *reviewed by* Kemp Burpeau

Dimond, E. Gray, (edited by); *LETTER FROM FORREST PLACE: A PLANTATION FAMILY'S CORRESPONDENCE, 1846-1881,* CWNEWS:APR/95[33], *reviewed by* Linda G. Black

Dixon, David; *HERO OF BEECHER ISLAND: THE LIFE AND MILITARY CAREER OF GEORGE A. FORSYTH,* CWTI:AUG/95[18]

Donald, David Herbert:
LINCOLN, CWTI:DEC/95[38]
LINCOLN'S HERNDON: A BIOGRAPHY, CWTI:SEPT/89[28]

Donnelly, Ralph W.; *THE CONFEDERATE STATES MARINE CORPS: THE REBEL LEATHERNECKS,* CWM:JAN/91[47], *reviewed by* Gary W. Gallagher, CWTI:JUN/90[20], *reviewed by* David M. Sullivan

Dornbusch, Charles E.:
MILITARY BIBLIOGRAPHY OF THE CIVIL WAR, AHI:JAN/68[55], CWM:FEB/95[42]564, *reviewed by* Gary W. Gallagher
REGIMENTAL PUBLICATIONS AND PERSONAL NARRATIVES OF THE CIVIL WAR, AHI:JAN/68[55]

Doubleday, Abner; *CHANCELLORSVILLE AND GETTYSBURG,* CWNEWS:NOV/91[4], *reviewed by* Michael Winey

Douglas, Henry Kyd; *I RODE WITH STONEWALL,* CWM:NOV/92[55]

Douglass, Frederick, (edited by Henry Louis Gates Jr.); *FREDERICK DOUGLASS: AUTOBIOGRAPHIES,* CWTI:JUL/94[18]

Dowdey, Clifford:
DEATH OF A NATION: THE STORY OF LEE AND HIS MEN AT GETTYSBURG, CWNEWS:MAY/89[4], *reviewed by* Mike Russert
LEE'S LAST CAMPAIGN, CWNEWS:MAY/94[5], *reviewed by* Kemp Burpeau
THE SEVEN DAYS: THE EMERGENCE OF LEE, CWM:JUN/95[6], *reviewed by* Gary W. Gallagher, CWNEWS:OCT/89[4], *reviewed by* Kevin J. Weddle, CWNEWS:JAN/95[25], *reviewed by* Kemp Burpeau
THE WARTIME PAPERS OF R. E. LEE, CWM:JUL/91[58], *reviewed by* Gary W. GallagherCWM:JUN/95[6], *reviewed by* Gary W. Gallagher

Drickamer, Lee C., (edited by); *FORT LYON TO HARPERS FERRY: ON THE BORDER OF NORTH AND SOUTH WITH "RAMBLING JOUR" B&G:FEB/ 92[26],* *reviewed by* Dave Roth

Driver, Robert J. Jr.; *LEXINGTON AND ROCKBRIDGE COUNTY IN THE CIVIL WAR,* CWNEWS:AUG/91[4], *reviewed by* Barry Popchock

Duane, J.C.; *MANUAL FOR ENGINEER TROOPS,* CWNEWS:NOV/92[4], *reviewed by* William Marvel

Dufour, Charles L.:
THE NIGHT THE WAR WAS LOST, CWNEWS:JUN/92[4], *reviewed by* Dale Phillips, CWNEWS:SEP/95[33], *reviewed by* Terrence J. Winschel
MEN IN GRAY CWM:APR/95[50], *reviewed by* Gary W. Gallagher, CWNEWS:NOV/94[33], *reviewed by* Stephen L. Ritchie

Dunlay, Thomas; *WOLVES FOR THE BLUE SOLDIERS: INDIAN SCOUTS AND AUXILIARIES WITH THE UNITED STATES ARMY, 1860-90,* CWNEWS:SEP/95[33], *reviewed by* Ted Alexander

Dunnigan, James F.; *SHOOTING BLANKS,* MH:AUG/95[70]

Durkin, James, (edited by); *"THIS WAR IS AN AWFUL THING . . .": CIVIL WAR LETTERS OF THE NATIONAL GUARDS, THE 19TH AND 90TH PENNSYLVANIA VOLUNTEERS,* CWNEWS:AUG/95[33], *reviewed by* Dr. Richard Sauers

Durrill, Wayne K.; *WAR OF ANOTHER KIND: A SOUTHERN COMMUNITY IN THE GREAT REBELLION,* CWR:VOL4#4[129], *reviewed by* Nancy Smith

Dustin, Fred; *THE CUSTER TRAGEDY: EVENTS LEADING UP TO AND FOLLOWING THE LITTLE BIG HORN CAMPAIGN OF 1876,* CWNEWS:JUN/91[4], *reviewed by* Michael Mullins

Dyer, Frederick H.; *A COMPENDIUM OF THE WAR OF THE REBELLION,* CWM:FEB/95[42]564, *reviewed by* Gary W. Gallagher

Early, Jubal A., (edited by Craig L. Symonds):
JUBAL EARLY'S MEMOIRS: AUTOBIOGRAPHICAL SKETCH AND NARRATIVE OF THE WAR BETWEEN THE STATES, CWNEWS:APR/91[4], *reviewed by* William G. Robertson
LIEUTENANT GENERAL JUBAL ANDERSON EARLY C.S.A.: AUTOBIOGRAPHICAL SKETCH AND NARRATIVE OF THE WAR BETWEEN THE STATES, CWM:FEB/95[42], *reviewed by* Gary W. Gallagher, CWM:OCT/95[10], *reviewed by* Gary W. Gallagher, CWNEWS:SEP/90[4]

Eckert, Ralph L.; *JOHN BROWN GORDON: SOLDIER, SOUTHERNER, AMERICAN,* CWNEWS:JUN/90[4], *reviewed by* Barry Popchock

Edmondson, Belle, (edited by); *A LOST HEROINE OF THE CONFEDERACY: THE DIARIES AND LETTERS OF BELLE EDMONDSON,* B&G:FEB/92[26], *reviewed by* Anne J. Bailey

Edmonston William E. Jr., (edited by); *UNFURL THE FLAGS: REMEMBRANCES OF THE AMERICAN CIVIL WAR,* CWNEWS:APR/91[4], *reviewed by* Michael Policatti

Edwards, Abial H., (edited by Beverly H. Kallgren); *"DEAR FRIEND ANNA": THE CIVIL WAR LETTERS OF A COMMON SOLDIER FROM MAINE,* CWM:OCT/94[8], *reviewed by* Scott C. Patchan

Eicher, David J.; *CIVIL WAR BATTLEFIELDS: A TOURING GUIDE* CWNEWS:DEC/95[29], *reviewed by* Blake A. Magner

Einhorn, Lois; *ABRAHAM LINCOLN THE ORATOR: PENETRATING THE LINCOLN LEGEND,* B&G:OCT/93[24], *reviewed by* Harold Holzer

Eldridge, Daniel; *THE THIRD NEW HAMPSHIRE AND ALL ABOUT IT,* CWR:VOL4#3[1], *reviewed by* Chris E. Fonvielle

Elliott, Robert G.:
A TARHEEL CONFEDERATE AND HIS FAMILY, CWNEWS:JAN/92[4], *reviewed by* Jeffry D. Wert
IRONCLAD OF THE ROANOKE: GILBERT ELLIOTT'S ALBEMARLE, B&G:AUG/95[38], *reviewed by* Maurice Melton, CWR:VOL4#3[37]

Emilio, Luis F.; *A BRAVE BLACK REGIMENT: HISTORY OF THE 54TH REGIMENT OF MASSACHUSETTS VOLUNTEER INFANTRY, 1863-1865,* CWNEWS:JUL/93[5], *reviewed by* Judith Yandoh, CWR:VOL1#1[76], *reviewed by* Zoyd Luce, CWR:VOL4#3[1], *reviewed by* Leonne M. Hudson, CWR:VOL4#3[1], *reviewed by* Stephen Engle

Engel, Stephen D.; *YANKEE DUTCHMAN: THE LIFE OF FRANZ SIGEL,* CWM:APR/95[50], *reviewed by* Gary W. Gallaghe, CWNEWS:APR/94[5], *reviewed by* Norman E. Rourke

Estaville Jr., Lawrence E.; *LOUISIANA NECKTIES: LOUISIANA RAILROADS IN THE CIVIL WAR,* CWNEWS:APR/92[4], *reviewed by* Terrence J. Winschel

Evans, Eli N.; *JUDAH P. BENJAMIN: THE JEWISH CONFEDERATE,* CWNEWS:MAY/89[4], *reviewed by* J. Tracy Power

Evans, Thomas J.; *MOSBY'S CONFEDERACY: A GUIDE TO THE ROADS AND SITES OF COLONEL JOHN SINGLETON MOSBY,* CWM:MAY/92[59], *reviewed by* WIlliam J. Miller, CWNEWS:NOV/91[4], *reviewed by* Jeffry D. Wert

Everson, Guy R.; *FAR, FAR FROM HOME,* CWNEWS:OCT/95[33], *reviewed by* Kemp Burpeau, CWR:VOL4#4[129], *reviewed by* Leonne M. Hudson

Ewing, Joseph H.; *SHERMAN AT WAR,* CWNEWS:MAY/93[4], *reviewed by* Anne J. Bailey, CWTI:JAN/93[12]

Faherty, William B.; *THE FOURTH CAREER OF JOHN B. BANNON: ST. LOUIS PASTOR, SOUTHERN CHAPLAIN, CONFEDERATE AGENT, IRISH JESUIT ORATOR,* CWNEWS:DEC/95[29], *reviewed by* Ted Alexander

Farwell, Byron; *STONEWALL: A BIOGRAPHY OF GENERAL THOMAS J. JACKSON,* ACW:NOV/93[58], *reviewed by* Michael D. Hull, CWM:JUL/93[51], *reviewed by* John Christian, CWNEWS:OCT/94[33], *reviewed by* Theodore P. Savas, CWTI:MAY/93[18], *reviewed by* George Skoch

Faust, Drew G.:
THE CREATION OF CONFEDERATE NATIONALISM: IDEOLOGY AND IDENTITY IN THE CIVIL WAR SOUTH, CWNEWS:AUG/90[4], *reviewed by* Dr. Allen C. Guelzo
SOUTHERN STORIES, CWNEWS:DEC/95[29], *reviewed by* Judy Yandoh

Faust, Patricia L., (edited by); *HISTORICAL TIMES ILLUSTRATED ENCYCLOPEDIA OF THE CIVIL WAR,* AHI:FEB/87[6], CWM:FEB/95[42]564, *reviewed by* Gary W. Gallagher

Favill, John M.; *THE DIARY OF A YOUNG OFFICER,* CWR:VOL4#3[1], *reviewed by* John M. Coski

Fehrenbacher, Don E.:
CONSTITUTIONS AND CONSTITUTIONALISM IN THE SLAVEHOLDING SOUTH, CWNEWS:APR/91[4], *reviewed by* Kemp Burpeau
LINCOLN: SPEECHES AND WRITINGS, CWTI:APR/90[10], *reviewed by* Harold Holzer
PRELUDE TO GREATNESS: LINCOLN IN THE 1850'S, CWTI:DEC/95[38]

Fellman, Michael; *CITIZEN SHERMAN,* CWNEWS:DEC/95[29], *reviewed by* Norman E. Rourke

Fellman, Michael; *INSIDE WAR: THE GUERRILLA CONFLICT IN MISSOURI DURING THE AMERICAN CIVIL WAR,* CWTI:MAY/89[44], *reviewed by* Albert Castel

Ferrell, Robert H.; *HOLDING THE LINE: THE HISTORY OF THE THIRD TENNESSEE INFANTRY,* CWM:APR/95[8], *reviewed by* Charles R. Norville

Ferris, Norman B.; *DESPERATE DIPLOMACY: WILLIAM H. SEWARD'S FOREIGN POLICY, 1861,* AHI:NOV/77[48], *reviewed by* Albert Castel

Field, Ron; *1ST SOUTH CAROLINA VOLUNTEERS (GREGG'S),* CWNEWS:NOV/92[4], *reviewed by* Michael J. Winey

Finfrock, Bradley; *ACROSS THE RAPPAHONNOCK: FROM FREDERICKSBURG TO THE MUD MARCH,* CWNEWS:SEP/95[33], *reviewed by* David F. Riggs

Fisk, Wilbur, (edited by Emil Rosenblatt); *HARD MARCHING EVERY DAY: THE CIVIL WAR LETTERS OF PRIVATE WILBUR FISK, 1861-1865,* CWM:FEB/95[42]564, *reviewed by* Gary W. Gallagher, CWNEWS:APR/93[4], *reviewed by* Michael Russert

Fladeland, Betty; *MEN AND BROTHERS, ANGLO-AMERICAN ANTISLAVERY COOPERATION,* AHI:JUN/74[49]

Fleischman, Paul; *BULL RUN,* CWNEWS:JUL/95[61], *reviewed by* Dr. David Martin

Flood, Charles Bracelen; *LEE: THE LAST YEARS* AHI:FEB/82[9], *reviewed by* Patricia L. Faust

Fogel, Robert W.:
MARKETS AND PRODUCTION, VOLUME ONE. CONDITIONS OF SLAVE LIFE AND THE TRANSITION TO FREEDOM, VOLUME TWO, CWNEWS:NOV/93[5], *reviewed by* Judy Yandoh

WITHOUT CONSENT OF CONTRACT: THE RISE AND FALL OF AMERICAN SLAVERY — EVIDENCE AND METHODS (VOLUME IV), CWNEWS:NOV/93[5], *reviewed by* Gregory J.W. Urwin

Foner, Eric; *FREEDOM'S LAWMAKERS: A DIRECTORY OF BLACK OFFICEHOLDERS DURING RECONSTRUCTION* CWM:AUG/95[45], *reviewed by* Gary W. Gallagher

Foote, Shelby; *THE CIVIL WAR: A NARRATIVE,* CWR:VOL4#3[1], *reviewed by* Craig L. Symonds

Forbes, Edwin; *THIRTY YEARS AFTER: AN ARTIST'S MEMOIR OF THE CIVIL WAR,* CWM:APR/95[50], *reviewed by* Gary W. Gallagher

Force, Manning F.; *FROM FORT HENRY TO CORINTH,* CWNEWS:SEP/91[4], *reviewed by* William G. Robertson

Forman, Stephen M.; *A GUIDE TO CIVIL WAR WASHINGTON,* B&G:OCT/95[28], *reviewed by* David E. Roth, CWNEWS:DEC/95[29], *reviewed by* Blake A. Magner, CWTI:OCT/95[18]

Fowler, William M. Jr.; *UNDER TWO FLAGS: THE AMERICAN NAVY IN THE CIVIL WAR* ACW:MAY/91[54], *reviewed by* Kenneth P. Czech, ACW:MAR/92[54], *reviewed by* John R. Satterfield, CWNEWS:JUN/92[4], *reviewed by* Barry Popchock

Fowler, Arlen L.; *THE BLACK INFANTRY IN THE WEST, 1869-1891,* AHI:NOV/71[48], *reviewed by* Benjamin Quarles

Fox, Charles B.; *RECORD OF THE SERVICE OF THE FIFTY-FIFTH REGIMENT OF MASSACHUSETTS VOLUNTEER INFANTRY,* CWR:VOL4#3[1], *reviewed by* Noah Andre Trudeau

Fox, Gustavus V., (edited by Robert M. Thompson); *CONFIDENTIAL CORRESPONDENCE OF GUSTAVUS VASA FOX,* CWNEWS:JAN/91[4], *reviewed by* Kevin Weddel

Fox, Richard A. Jr.; *ARCHAEOLOGY, HISTORY, AND CUSTER'S LAST BATTLE: THE LITTLE BIG HORN REEXAMINED,* CWNEWS:AUG/94[33], *reviewed by* Brian C. Pohanka

Fox, Tryphena B.H., (edited by Wilma King); *A NORTHERN WOMAN IN THE PLANTATION SOUTH: LETTERS OF TRYPHENA BLANCHE HOLDER FOX, 1856-1876* CWM:APR/95[50], *reviewed by* Gary W. Gallagher

Frank, Joseph A.; *"SEEING THE ELEPHANT" RAW RECRUITS AT THE BATTLE OF SHILOH,* CWM:JAN/91[47], *reviewed by* Gary W. Gallagher, CWNEWS:MAY/92[4], *reviewed by* John M. Marszalek

Frassanito, William A.; *GETTYSBURG: A JOURNEY IN TIME,* AHI:MAY/76[48], *reviewed by* Robert D. Hoffsommer

Frayss'e, Olivier; *LINCOLN, LAND, AND LABOR, 1809-60,* CWM:DEC/95[10], *reviewed by* J. Jeffrey Cox

Frazier, Donald S.; *BLOOD & TREASURE: CONFEDERATE EMPIRE IN THE SOUTHWEST,* ACW:NOV/95[62], *reviewed by* Maureen Creamer, CWR:VOL4#3[37], CWR:VOL4#4[129], *reviewed by* Melvin C. Johnson

Frederickson, George M.; *THE INNER CIVIL WAR,* CWNEWS:OCT/95[33], *reviewed by* Spencer Gill

Freehling, Alison G.; *DRIFT TOWARD DISSOLUTION: THE VIRGINIA SLAVERY DEBATE OF 1831-1832,* AHI:OCT/83[62], *reviewed by* David J. Bodenhamer

Freehling, William W.:
PRELUDE TO CIVIL WAR: THE NULLIFICATION CONTROVERSY IN SOUTH CAROLINA, 1816-1836, AHI:FEB/67[57], *reviewed by* Ralph Adams Brown

THE ROAD TO DISUNION: SECESSIONISTS AT BAY, 1776-1854, CWM:SEP/91[58], *reviewed by* Edward C. Smith, CWNEWS:AUG/91[4], *reviewed by* Michael Parrish

Freeman, Douglas S.:

DOUGLAS SOUTHALL FREEMAN ON LEADERSHIP, CWR:VOL4#1[78], *reviewed by* Brandon H. Beck

LEE'S DISPATCHES: UNPUBLISHED LETTERS OF GENERAL ROBERT E. LEE, C.S.A. TO JEFFERSON DAVIS AND THE WAR DEPARTMENT OF THE CONFEDERATE STATES OF AMERICA, CWM:JUL/91[58], CWR:VOL4#3[37]

LEE'S LIEUTENANTS: A STUDY IN COMMAND, CWM:FEB/95[42]564, *reviewed by* Gary W. Gallagher, CWM:APR/95[8], *reviewed by* Gary W. Gallagher, CWM:JUN/95[6], *reviewed by* Gary W. Gallagher, CWR:VOL4#3[1], *reviewed by* Gary W. Gallagher, CWR:VOL4#3[1], *reviewed by* Lawrence L. Hewitt, CWR:VOL4#3[1], *reviewed by* Theodore P. Savas

R.E. LEE: A BIOGRAPHY, CWM:FEB/95[42]564, *reviewed by* Gary W. Gallagher, CWM:APR/95[8], *reviewed by* Gary W. Gallagher, CWM:JUN/95[6], *reviewed by* William J. Miller

Freeman, Frank R.; *MICROBES AND MINIE BALLS: AN ANNOTATED BIBLIOGRAPHY OF CIVIL WAR MEDICINE,* B&G:DEC/94[28], *reviewed by* Steve Davis

Freidel, Frank; *UNION PAMPHLETS OF THE CIVIL WAR,* AHI:JUN/68[51], *reviewed by* Robert D. Hoffsommer

Fremantle, Arthur J.L.; *THREE MONTHS IN THE SOUTHERN STATES: APRIL-JUNE 1863,* CWM:OCT/94[8], *reviewed by* Gary W. Gallagher, CWNEWS:OCT/92[4], *reviewed by* Dr. David G. Martin

French, Benjamin B., (edited by Donald P. Cole); *WITNESS TO THE YOUNG REPUBLIC: A YANKEE'S JOURNAL, 1828-1870,* CWM:JAN/91[47], *reviewed by* Gary W. Gallagher

Frost, Griffin; *CAMP AND PRISON JOURNAL: EMBRACING SCENES IN CAMP ON THE MARCH AND IN PRISONS,* CWR:VOL4#3[37], CWR:VOL4#4[129], *reviewed by* Frank G. Prator

Fuchs, Richard L.; *UNERRING FIRE: THE MASSACRE AT FORT PILLOW,* CWTI:AUG/95[18]

Fuller, Charles A.; *PERSONAL RECOLLECTIONS OF THE WAR OF 1861,* B&G:APR/91[28], *reviewed by* Mark Dunkelman, CWR:VOL4#1[78], *reviewed by* Michael Russert

Fuller, J.F.C.:

THE GENERALSHIP OF ULYSSES S. GRANT, CWM:JAN/92[57], *reviewed by* Gary W. Gallagher

GRANT & LEE: A STUDY IN PERSONALITY AND GENERALSHIP CWM:DEC/95[10], *reviewed by* Gary W. Gallagher

Furgurson, Ernest B.; *CHANCELLORSVILLE 1863: THE SOULS OF THE BRAVE,* ACW:MAY/94[58], *reviewed by* Daniel M. Laney, CWM:AUG/94[9], *reviewed by* Brandon Beck, CWNEWS:JUN/93[5], *reviewed by* David F. Riggs, CWR:VOL3#1[80], *reviewed by* Robert E.L. Krick

Gaines, W. Craig; *THE CONFEDERATE CHEROKEES: JOHN DREW'S REGIMENT OF MOUNTED RIFLES,* CWNEWS:AUG/90[4], *reviewed by* Robert D. Norris Jr., CWR:VOL4#3[1], *reviewed by* David Woodbury

Galbraith, Loretta, (edited by); *A LOST HEROINE OF THE CONFEDERACY,* CWNEWS:JUL/92[4], *reviewed by* Judy Yandoh

Gallagher, Gary W.:

ANTIETAM: ESSAYS ON THE 1862 MARYLAND CAMPAIGN, CWNEWS:APR/90[4], *reviewed by* Michael Mullins

THE FIRST DAY AT GETTYSBURG: ESSAYS ON UNION AND CONFEDERATE LEADERSHIP, CWNEWS:OCT/93[5], *reviewed by* Mark Snell

THE FREDERICKSBURG CAMPAIGN: DECISION ON THE RAPPAHANNOCK, B&G:DEC/95[30], *reviewed by* John J. Hennessy, CWNEWS:SEP/95[33], *reviewed by* Jeffry D. Wert, CWR:VOL4#4[129], *reviewed by* David P. Smith

THE SECOND DAY AT GETTYSBURG: ESSAYS ON CONFEDERATE AND UNION LEADERSHIP, CWM:APR/95[50], CWNEWS:APR/94[5], *reviewed by* David F. Riggs

THE THIRD DAY AT GETTYSBURG & BEYOND, B&G:APR/95[30], *reviewed by* Jeffry D. Wert, CWNEWS:FEB/95[33], *reviewed by* Michael Russert, CWR:VOL4#3[89], *reviewed by* Michael A. Cavanaugh, CWTI:MAR/95[14], *reviewed by* Diane Treon

Gallaway, B.P.:

THE RAGGED REBEL: A COMMON SOLDIER IN W.H. PARSON'S TEXAS CAVALRY, 1861-1865, CWNEWS:OCT/89[4], *reviewed by* David F. Riggs

TEXAS, THE DARK CORNER OF THE CONFEDERACY, CWM:APR/95[8], *reviewed by* James A. Ramage, CWTI:JUN/95[24]

Gambone, A.M.; *MAJOR GENERAL JOHN FREDERICK HARTRANFT, CITIZEN SOLDIER AND PENNSYLVANIA STATESMAN,* CWNEWS:NOV/95[29], *reviewed by* Frank J. Piatek

Gantz, Jacob, (edited by Kathleen Davis); *SUCH ARE THE TRIALS: THE CIVIL WAR DIARIES OF JACOB GANTZ,* CWNEWS:SEP/92[4], *reviewed by* Robert D. Norris Jr.

Gara, Larry; *THE PRESIDENCY OF FRANKLIN PIERCE,* CWM:JAN/92[57], *reviewed by* Gary W. Gallagher

Garner, Stanton; *THE CIVIL WAR WORLD OF HERMAN MELVILLE,* CWM:APR/95[50], *reviewed by* Gary W. Gallagher, CWR:VOL4#1[78], *reviewed by* Helen P. Trimpi, CWTI:MAY/94[20], *reviewed by* Richard Pindell

Garnett, Theodore S.; *RIDING WITH STUART: REMINISCENCES OF AN AIDE-DE-CAMP* CWM:OCT/94[8], *reviewed by* Theodore C. Mahr, CWNEWS:MAY/95[33], *reviewed by* Jerry W. Holsworth, CWR:VOL4#3[37]

Garrison, Webb; *THE LINCOLN NO ONE KNOWS,* CWM:SEP/93[51], *reviewed by* Kemp P. Burpeau, CWTI:SEP/94[18], *reviewed by* Lloyd Ostendorf

Gates, Theodore, (edited by Seward R. Osborne); *THE CIVIL WAR DIARIES OF COL. THEODORE B. GATES, 20TH NEW YORK STATE MILITIA,* B&G:AUG/93[24], *reviewed by* Theodore P. Savas

Gavin, William G.; *CAMPAIGNING WITH THE ROUNDHEADS: THE HISTORY OF THE 100TH PENNSYLVANIA VOLUNTEER INFANTRY REGIMENT, 1861-1865,* CWNEWS:MAY/91[4], *reviewed by* Ron Rago

Geary, James W.; *WE NEED MEN: THE UNION DRAFT IN THE CIVIL WAR,* B&G:DEC/91[30], *reviewed by* Frank J. Welcher, CWM:MAR/92[49], *reviewed by* Gary W. Gallagher, CWNEWS:JUL/92[4], *reviewed by* Michael Russert, CWTI:JUL/92[10]

Geier, Clarence R. Jr.; *LOOK TO THE EARTH: HISTORICAL ARCHAEOLOGY AND THE AMERICAN CIVIL WAR,* CWR:VOL4#3[37]

Geiger, Joe, Jr.; *CIVIL WAR IN CABELL COUNTY, WEST VIRGINIA 1861-1865,* CWNEWS:DEC/93[5], *reviewed by* Frank J. Piatek

Genco, James G.; *TO THE SOUND OF MUSKETRY AND TAP OF THE DRUM: A HISTORY OF MICHIGAN'S BATTERY D THROUGH THE LETTERS OF ARTIFICER HAROLD J. BARTLETT, 1861-1864,* CWNEWS:APR/92[4], *reviewed by* Harris D. Riley

Genealogical Publishing; *ROLL OF HONOR: NAMES OF SOLDIERS WHO DIED IN DEFENSE OF THE AMERICAN UNION, INTERRED IN THE NATIONAL CEMETERIES,* CWNEWS:OCT/95[33], *reviewed by* Michael A. Cavanaugh

Genovese, Eugene D.; *ROLL, JORDAN, ROLL: THE WORLD THE SLAVES MADE,* AHI:MAY/76[48], *reviewed by* Bell I. Wiley

Gentile, Gary; *IRONCLAD LEGACY: BATTLE OF THE USS MONITOR,* CWNEWS:NOV/95[29], *reviewed by* Gary Augustine

Gilham, William; *GILHAM'S MANUAL FOR VOLUNTEERS AND MILITIA,* CWNEWS:JUN/94[5], *reviewed by* David Hannah

Gillette, William:
JERSEY BLUE: CIVIL WAR POLITICS IN NEW JERSEY, 1854-1865, CWTI:JUN/95[24]
RETREAT FROM RECONSTRUCTION, AHI:AUG/80[47], *reviewed by* Larry Gara

Gilmer, Jeremy F.; *CONFEDERATE ENGINEERS' MAPS,* CWNEWS:AUG/91[4], *reviewed by* Blake Magner

Gladstone, William A.:
MEN OF COLOR, CWNEWS:NOV/94[33], *reviewed by* Michael J. McAfee
UNITED STATES COLORED TROOPS 1863-1867, CWNEWS:OCT/90[4], *reviewed by* Gregory J.W. Urwin

Glasgow, William M. Jr.; *NORTHERN VIRGINIA'S OWN: THE 17TH VIRGINIA INFANTRY REGIMENT, CONFEDERATE STATES ARMY,* CWNEWS:APR/92[4], *reviewed by* Dr. Allen C. Guelzo

Glatthaar, Joseph T.:
FORGED IN BATTLE: THE CIVIL WAR ALLIANCE OF BLACK SOLDIERS AND WHITE OFFICERS, B&G:JUN/91[22], *reviewed by* Lawrence L. Hewitt, B&G:AUG/91[26], *reviewed by* Lawrence L. Hewitt, CWNEWS:JUL/90[4], *reviewed by* Gregory J.W. Irwin
THE MARCH TO THE SEA AND BEYOND: SHERMAN'S TROOPS IN THE SAVANNAH AND CAROLINAS CAMPAIGNS, CWM:FEB/95[42]564, *reviewed by* Gary W. Gallagher
PARTNERS IN COMMAND: THE RELATIONSHIPS BETWEEN LEADERS IN THE CIVIL WAR CWTI:JUL/94[18], *reviewed by* Stephen D. Engle

Gleason, Michael P.; *THE INSIDERS' GUIDE TO THE CIVIL WAR IN THE EASTERN THEATER,* CWM:FEB/95[7], *reviewed by* William J. Miller, CWNEWS:DEC/95[29], *reviewed by* Blake A. Magner

Gleeson, Ed; *REBEL SONS OF ERIN, A CIVIL WAR HISTORY OF THE TENTH TENNESSEE INFANTRY (IRISH), CONFEDERATE STATES VOLUNTEERS,* CWNEWS:JUN/95[33], *reviewed by* Michael A. Cavanaugh, CWR:VOL4#3[89], *reviewed by* George Otott

Godbold, E. Stanley Jr.; *CONFEDERATE COLONEL AND CHEROKEE CHIEF: THE LIFE OF WILLIAM HOLLAND THOMAS,* CWNEWS:JUN/92[4], *reviewed by* Jeffry Wert

Golay, Michael; *TO GETTYSBURG AND BEYOND: THE PARALLEL LIVES OF JOSHUA LAWRENCE CHAMBERLAIN AND EDWARD PORTER ALEXANDER,*

ACW:MAY/95[62], *reviewed by* Roy Morris Jr., AHI:JUN/95[28], CWTI:JUN/95[24]

Gooding, James H., (edited by); *ON THE ALTAR OF FREEDOM: A BLACK SOLDIER'S CIVIL WAR LETTERS FROM THE FRONT,* CWNEWS:NOV/92[4], *reviewed by* Gregory J.W. Irwin

Goodrich, Thomas:
BLACK FLAG: GUERRILLA WARFARE ON THE WESTERN BORDER, 1861-1865, ACW:JUL/95[58], *reviewed by* Richard Gilbert
BLOODY DAWN: THE STORY OF THE LAWRENCE MASSACRE, B&G:JUN/92[28], *reviewed by* Harris D. Riley Jr., CWNEWS:OCT/93[5], *reviewed by* Mike Cavanaugh

Gordon, John B.; *REMINISCENCES OF THE CIVIL WAR,* CWM:APR/95[50], *reviewed by* Gary W. Gallagher

Gosnell, H. Allen; *GUNS ON THE WESTERN WATERS: THE STORY OF RIVER GUNBOATS IN THE CIVIL WAR,* CWNEWS:JUL/95[61], *reviewed by* Norman E. Rourke

Gottschalk, Phil; *IN DEADLY EARNEST: HISTORY OF THE FIRST MISSOURI BRIGADE CSA,* B&G:APR/93[30], *reviewed by* Jerry Russel, CWNEWS:NOV/92[4], *reviewed by* Kemp Burpeau, CWR:VOL2#2[169], *reviewed by* Theodore P. Savas

Graf, Leroy P., (edited by); *THE PAPERS OF ANDREW JOHNSON,* AHI:MAY/68[48], *reviewed by* Bell I. Wiley, AHI:FEB/72[49]

Gragg, Rod:
CONFEDERATE GOLIATH: THE BATTLE OF FORT FISHER, B&G:OCT/91[34], *reviewed by* Stephen R. Wise, CWM:MAR/91[42], *reviewed by* William J. Miller, CWNEWS:JUN/91[4], *reviewed by* Richard M. McMurry, CWTI:AUG/91[18]
THE ILLUSTRATED CONFEDERATE READER, B&G:FEB/91[28], *reviewed by* Garold L. Cole, CWNEWS:JUN/92[4], *reviewed by* Blake Magner

Graham, Martin F.; *MINE RUN: A CAMPAIGN OF LOST OPPORTUNITIES, OCTOBER 21, 1863-MAY 1, 1864,* CWNEWS:MAY/90[4], *reviewed by* Lawrence F. Kohl

Gramm, Kent; *GETTYSBURG: A MEDITATION ON WAR & VALUES,* B&G:AUG/94[30], *reviewed by* Richard Pindell, CWM:FEB/95[7], *reviewed by* Gordon Shay, CWNEWS:JUN/95[33], *reviewed by* Mark A. Snell, CWR:VOL4#4[129], *reviewed by* David P. Smith, CWTI:MAR/95[14], *reviewed by* Diane Treon

Grant, Julia Dent, (edited by John Y. Simon); *THE PERSONAL MEMOIRS OF JULIA DENT GRANT,* AHI:FEB/76[50], *reviewed by* Bell I. Wiley

Grant, Ulysses S.; *PERSONAL MEMOIRS OF U.S. GRANT,* CWM:FEB/95[42]564, *reviewed by* Gary W. Gallagher, CWM:AUG/95[8], *reviewed by* Gary W. Gallagher

Gray, John S.; *CENTENNIAL CAMPAIGN: THE SIOUX WAR OF 1876,* CWNEWS:JUN/91[4], *reviewed by* Brian Pohanka

Grayson, George W., (edited by David Baird); *A CREEK WARRIOR FOR THE CONFEDERACY, THE AUTOBIOGRAPHY OF CHIEF G. W. GRAYSON,* CWNEWS:APR/90[4], *reviewed by* Ron Rago, CWNEWS:SEP/92[4], *reviewed by* Robert D. Norris Jr.

Greene, Francis V.; *THE MISSISSIPPI;* CWNEWS:APR/91[4], *reviewed by* Jeffry Wert

Greene, William B.; *LETTERS FROM A SHARPSHOOTER: THE CIVIL WAR LETTERS OF PRIVATE WILLIAM B. GREENE CO. G, 2ND UNITED STATES SHARPSHOOTERS (BERDAN'S), ARMY OF THE POTOMAC,* CWR:VOL4#3[37], CWNEWS:JAN/95[25]

Greenstone, J. David; *THE LINCOLN PERSUASION: REMAKING AMERICAN LIBERALISM,* CWNEWS:MAY/95[33], *reviewed by* Allen C Guelzo

Greiner, James M., (edited by); *A SURGEON'S CIVIL WAR: THE LETTERS AND DIARY OF DANIEL M. HOLT., M.D.,* ACW:JAN/95[62]

Grier, Clarence R. Jr., (edited by); *LOOK TO THE EARTH: HISTORICAL ARCHAEOLOGY AND THE AMERICAN CIVIL WAR,* CWM:DEC/95[10], *reviewed by* Charles R. Norville

Griess, Thomas E., (edited by):
THE AMERICAN CIVIL WAR, CWNEWS:JAN/90[4], *reviewed by* Blake Magner
THE ATLAS FOR THE AMERICAN CIVIL WAR, CWNEWS:JAN/90[4], *reviewed by* Blake Magner

Griffith, Paddy; *BATTLE TACTICS OF THE CIVIL WAR,* CWNEWS:JAN/90[4], *reviewed by* A. Wilson Greene, CWTI:SEPT/89[28]

Grisamore, Silas T., (edited by Arthur W Bergeron Jr.); *THE WAR REMINISCENCES OF MAJOR SILAS T. GRISAMORE,* CWM:APR/95[50], *reviewed by* Gary W. Gallagher, CWNEWS:DEC/93[5], *reviewed by* Richard M. McMurry

Groene, Bertram H.; *TRACING YOUR CIVIL WAR ANCESTER,* CWNEWS:DEC/94[33], *reviewed by* Sarah W. Wiggins

Groom, Winston; *SHROUDS OF GLORY: FROM ATLANTA TO NASHVILLE,* CWTI:AUG/95[18], *reviewed by*

Gross, Samuel D.; *A MANUAL OF MILITARY SURGERY: OR HINTS ON THE EMERGENCIES* OF FIELD, CAMP, AND HOSPITAL PRACTICE, CWNEWS:NOV/90[4], *reviewed by* Dr. Harris D. Riley Jr.

Grunder, Charles S.; *THE SECOND BATTLE OF WINCHESTER, JUNE 12-15, 1863,* CWM:JAN/91[47], *reviewed by* Gary W. Gallagher, CWNEWS:APR/92[4], *reviewed by* J. Tracy Power

Guelzo, Allen C.; *THE CRISIS OF THE AMERICAN REPUBLIC: A HISTORY OF THE CIVIL WAR AND RECONSTRUCTION ERA,* CWTI:OCT/95[18]

Gunn, James R.; *UNITED STATES INFANTRY AND RIFLE TACTICS,* CWNEWS:DEC/95[29], *reviewed by* Dave Hannah

Hagerman, Edward; *THE AMERICAN CIVIL WAR AND THE ORIGINS OF MODERN WARFARE,* CWNEWS:MAY/90[4], *reviewed by* Brian C. Pohanka, CWM:DEC/94[7], *reviewed by* General Philip L. Bolt'e

Hagood, Johnson; *MEMOIRS OF THE WAR OF SECESSION,* CWNEWS:SEP/91[4], *reviewed by* William Blake

Hague, Parthenia A., (edited by Elizabeth Fox-Genovese); *A BLOCKADED FAMILY: LIFE IN SOUTHERN ALABAMA DURING THE CIVIL WAR,* B&G:AUG/92[36], *reviewed by* Maxine Turner

Haiber, Robert; *THE FIRST MINNESOTA REGIMENT AT GETTYSBURG,* CWNEWS:MAY/93[4], *reviewed by* Dr. Allen C. Guelzo

Hale, Douglas; *THE THIRD TEXAS CAVALRY IN THE CIVIL WAR,* ACW:MAY/94[58], *reviewed by* Kenneth P. Czech, CWR:VOL4#3[1], *reviewed by* Archie P. McDonald, CWNEWS:NOV/94[33], *reviewed by* Kemp Burpeau

Haley, John; *REBEL YELL AND YANKEE HURRAH: THE CIVIL WAR JOURNAL OF A MAINE VOLUNTEER,* CWR:VOL4#3[1], *reviewed by* John Hennessy

Hall, Richard; *PATRIOTS IN DISGUISE: WOMEN WARRIORS OF THE CIVIL WAR,* ACW:JUL/94[58], *reviewed* by Michael D. Hull, B&G:JUN/94[34], *reviewed by* Lauren Cook Burgess, CWNEWS:OCT/93[5], *reviewed by* Lauren C. Burgess, CWR:VOL3#2[105], *reviewed by* Anne J. Bailey

Haller, John S. Jr.; *FARMCARTS TO FORDS: A HISTORY OF THE MILITARY AMBULANCE,* 1790-1925, CWNEWS:DEC/93[5], *reviewed by* Harris D. Riley Jr.

Halliburton, Lloyd, (edited b); *SADDLE SOLDIERS: THE CIVIL WAR CORRESPONDENCE OF GENERAL WILLIAM STOKES OF THE 4TH SOUTH CAROLINA CAVALRY,* CWNEWS:NOV/94[33], *reviewed by* Gregory J.W. Urwin

Hallock, Judith L.; *BRAXTON BRAGG AND CONFEDERATE DEFEAT, VOL II,* B&G:AUG/92[36], *reviewed by* Richard M. McMurry, CWNEWS:JUL/93[5], *reviewed by* William L. Shea, CWR:VOL2#2[169], *reviewed by* Larry J. Daniel

Hamblen, Charles P.; *CONNECTICUT YANKEES AT GETTYSBURG,* CWM:APR/95[50], *reviewed by* Gary W. Gallagher, CWNEWS:JUN/94[5], *reviewed by* David Ward, CWR:VOL3#3[92], *reviewed by* Kevin E. O'Brien

Hamilton, Charles; *LINCOLN IN PHOTOGRAPHS,* CWTI:DEC/95[38]

Hamilton, Frank H.; *A PRACTICAL TREATISE ON MILITARY SURGERY,* CWNEWS:JUL/91[4], *reviewed by* Harris D. Riley, M.D.

Hamlin, Percy G.; *"OLD BALD HEAD" (GENERAL RICHARD S. EWELL): THE PORTRAIT OF A SOLDIER AND THE MAKING OF A SOLDIER: LETTERS OF GENERAL R.S. EWELL,* CWNEWS:OCT/89[4], *reviewed by* Richard Sauers

Hammond, James Henry, (edited by Carol Bleser); *SECRET AND SACRED: THE DIARIES OF JAMES HANRY HAMMOND, A SOUTHERN SLAVEHOLDER,* CWTI:APR/89[12], *reviewed by* James Street Jr.

Hanchett, William; *THE LINCOLN MURDER CONSPIRACIES,* CWTI:DEC/95[38]

Hanifen, Michael; *HISTORY OF BATTERY B, FIRST NEW JERSEY ARTILLERY,* CWNEWS:NOV/92[4], *reviewed by* Allen C. Guelzo

Hansen, Debra G.; *STRAINED SISTERHOOD: GENDER AND CLASS IN THE BOSTON FEMALE ANTI-SLAVERY SOCIETY,* CWNEWS:SEP/94[33], *reviewed by* DeAnne Blanton

Harper, Douglas R.; *"IF THEE MUST FIGHT" A CIVIL WAR HISTORY OF CHESTER COUNTY, PENNSYLVANIA,* CWNEWS:JUL/92[4], *reviewed by* Michael Cavanaugh

Harris, David G., (edited by Philip N. Racine); *PIEDMONT FARMER: THE JOURNALS OF DAVID GOLIGHTLY HARRIS, 1855-1870,* CWM:MAR/92[49], *reviewed by* Gary W. Gallagher

Harris, William C.; *NORTH CAROLINA AND THE COMING OF THE CIVIL WAR,* CWNEWS:SEP/89[8], *reviewed by* Michael Russert

Harrison, Noel G.; *CHANCELLORSVILLE BATTLEFIELD SITES,* CWM:MAR/92[49], *reviewed by* Gary W. Gallagher

Hart, B. H. Liddell; *SHERMAN: SOLDIER REALIST,* CWNEWS:JAN/94[5], *reviewed by* John F. Marszalek, CWR:VOL4#3[1], *reviewed by* John T. Hubbell

Hartje, Robert G.; *VAN DORN: THE LIFE AND TIMES OF A CONFEDERATE GENERAL,* CWTI:DEC/94[18], *reviewed by* Terrence J. Winschel

Hartley, Florence; *THE LADIES' HAND BOOK OF FANCY AND ORNAMENTAL WORK: CIVIL WAR ERA,* CWNEWS:MAY/93[4], *reviewed by* Linda G. Black

Haskell, Mrs. E.F.; *CIVIL WAR COOKING: THE HOUSEKEEPER'S ENCYCLOPEDIA,* CWNEWS:AUG/93[5], *reviewed by* Linda G. Black

Haskell, Frank A.:
THE BATTLE OF GETTYSBURG, CWNEWS:SEP/95[33],
reviewed by David F. Riggs
*HASKELL OF GETTYSBURG, HIS LIFE AND CIVIL WAR
PAPERS*, CWNEWS:AUG/90[4], reviewed by Michael Winey
Hasselby, Peter; *THE CONFEDERATE MARINE CORPS*,
CWNEWS:JUN/91[4], reviewed by Richard M. McMurry
Hattaway, Herman; *HOW THE NORTH WON: A MILITARY
HISTORY OF THE CIVIL WAR*, AHI:JAN/84[8], reviewed by
Lowell H. Harrison, CWM:FEB/95[42]564, reviewed by Gary
W. Gallagher
Haupt, Herman; *REMINISCENCES OF GENERAL HERMAN
HAUPT*, CWNEWS:JUN/91[4], reviewed by Terrence Winschel
Hauptman, Dr. Laurence M.; *THE IROQUOIS IN THE CIVIL
WAR: FROM BATTLEFIELD TO RESERVATION*,
ACW:SEP/94[66], reviewed by Brian Temple,
CWM:APR/95[50], reviewed by Gary W. Gallagher,
CWNEWS:JAN/94[5], reviewed by Ted Alexander,
CWR:VOL3#2[105], reviewed by Paul N. Beck
Haydon, Charles B., (edited by Stephen W. Sears); *FOR
COUNTRY, CAUSE & LEADER: THE CIVIL WAR
JOURNAL OF CHARLES B. HAYDON*, CWM:APR/94[51],
reviewed by Judge Ben Smith, CWM:FEB/95[42]564, reviewed
by Gary W. Gallagher, CWNEWS:DEC/93[5], reviewed by
Brian Pohanka
Haydon, F. Stansbury; *AERONAUTICS IN THE UNION AND
CONFEDERATE ARMIES*, CWNEWS:SEP/90[4], reviewed by
Steven J. Wright
Haythornthwaite, Philip; *UNIFORMS OF THE CIVIL WAR
IN COLOR*, CWNEWS:APR/92[4], reviewed by William Marvel
Hazen, William B.; *A NARRATIVE OF MILITARY SERVICE*,
CWM:AUG/95[45], reviewed by Gary W. Gallagher
Hearn, Chester G.:
*GRAY RAIDERS OF THE SEA: HOW EIGHT CONFEDERATE
WARSHIPS DESTROYED THE UNION'S HIGH SEA
COMMERCE*, ACW:JAN/93[58]399, reviewed by Jon Guttman,
B&G:AUG/92[36], reviewed by A. Robert Holcombe Jr.,
CWNEWS:AUG/92[4], reviewed by J. Tracy Power
*MOBILE BAY AND THE MOBILE CAMPAIGN: THE LAST
GREAT BATTLES OF THE CIVIL WAR*, B&G:JUN/94[34],
reviewed by Stephen R. Wise, CWNEWS:OCT/94[33], reviewed
by Larry J. Daniel
Heartsill, William H.; *FOURTEEN HUNDRED AND 91 DAYS
IN THE CONFEDERATE ARMY*, CWR:VOL1#4[77], reviewed
by Anne J. Bailey
Heckman, Richard Allen; *LINCOLN VS DOUGLAS: THE
GREAT DEBATES CAMAPIGN*, AHI:OCT/67[64]
Heidler, David S.; *PULLING THE TEMPLE DOWN: THE
FIRE-EATERS AND THE DESTRUCTION OF THE UNION*,
CWM:AUG/95[45], reviewed by Gary W. Gallagher,
CWNEWS:SEP/95[33], reviewed by Stephen D. Engle
Heleniak, Robert J., (edited by):
*THE CONFEDERATE HIGH COMMAND AND RELATED
TOPICS*, B&G:AUG/91[26], reviewed by Steven E. Woodworth,
CWNEWS:OCT/90[4]
*LEADERSHIP DURING THE CIVIL WAR. THE 1989 DEEP
DELTA CIVIL WAR SYMPOSIUM: THEMES IN HONOR OF
T. HARRY WILLIAMS*, CWM:APR/95[50], reviewed by Gary
W. Gallagher, CWNEWS:APR/94[5], reviewed by Michael
Russert, CWR:VOL3#4[68], reviewed by William D. Pederson
Heller, J. Roderick, (edited by); *THE CONFEDERACY IS ON
HER WAY UP THE SPOUT: LETTERS TO SOUTH*

CAROLINA, 1861-1864, CWM:MAR/93[51],
CWNEWS:NOV/94[33], reviewed by J. Tracy Power
Henderson, G.F.R.; *STONEWALL JACKSON AND THE
AMERICAN CIVIL WAR*, CWM:JAN/91[47], reviewed by Gary
W. Gallagher, CWM:FEB/95[42]564, reviewed by Gary W.
Gallagher, CWM:DEC/95[10], reviewed by Gary W. Gallagher
Hendrickson, Robert; *SUMTER: THE FIRST DAY OF THE
CIVIL WAR*, ACW:JAN/91[54], reviewed by Robert I. Alotta,
B&G:AUG/91[26], reviewed by David R. Ruth,
CWNEWS:JUL/91[4], reviewed by William G. Robertson,
CWTI:SEP/90[12], reviewed by Brian McGinty
Hennessy, John J.:
THE FIRST BATTLE OF MANASSAS, CWNEWS:NOV/90[4],
reviewed by Kemp Burpeau
*RETURN TO BULL RUN, THE CAMPAIGN AND BATTLE OF
SECOND MANASSAS*, CWM:NOV/92[55],
CWM:FEB/95[42]564, reviewed by Gary W. Gallagher,
CWNEWS:JUN/93[5], reviewed by Frank Piatek,
CWR:VOL3#1[80], reviewed by Peter S. Carmichael
*SECOND MANASSAS BATTLEFIELD MAP STUDY —
ACCOMPANIED BY 16 SEPARATE COLORED MAPS*,
CWM:MAR/92[49], reviewed by Gary W. Gallagher,
CWNEWS:JUL/92[4], reviewed by Michael Mullins
Herdegen, Lance J.; *IN THE BLOODY RAILROAD CUT AT
GETTYSBURG*, CWR:VOL1#2[78], reviewed by David A.
Woodbury, CWR:VOL4#3[1], reviewed by Craig L. Symonds
Herndon, William H.; *HERNDON'S LINCOLN: THE TRUE
STORY OF A GREAT LIFE*, CWTI:DEC/95[38]
Herr, Pamela, (edited by); *THE LETTERS OF JESSIE
BENTON FREMONT* AHI:JUL/93[19]
Herrington, William D., (edited by W. Keats Sparrow):
THE CAPTAIN'S BRIDE, A TALE OF THE WAR,
CWNEWS:FEB/94[5], reviewed by Linda G. Black
THE DESERTER'S DAUGHTER, CWNEWS:FEB/94[5], reviewed
by Linda G. Black
Hess, Earl J.; *LIBERTY, VIRTUE, AND PROGRESS:
NORTHERNERS AND THEIR WAR FOR UNION*,
CWNEWS:NOV/90[4], reviewed by Mark Snell
Hewett, Janet, (edited by):
*SUPPLEMENT TO THE OFFICIAL RECORDS OF THE UNION
AND CONFEDERATE ARMIES*, CWM:FEB/95[7], reviewed by
Charles R. Norville, CWR:VOL4#3[37]
THE SUPPLEMENT TO THE OFFICIAL RECORDS, VOLS. 1-3,
B&G:FEB/95[26], reviewed by Steve Davis
Heyward, Pauline D., (edited by Mary D. Robertson); *A
CONFEDERATE LADY COMES OF AGE: THE JOURNAL
OF PAULINE DECARADEUC HEYWARD, 1863-1888*,
CWNEWS:APR/93[4], reviewed by Sarah W. Wiggins
Hickens, Victor; *ILLINOIS IN THE CIVIL WAR*,
AHI:FEB/67[57], reviewed by Ralph Adams Brown,
CWNEWS:SEP/92[4], reviewed by Jeffry D. Wert
Hillhouse, Don; *HEAVY ARTILLERY AND LIGHT INFANTRY:
A HISTORY OF THE 1ST FLORIDA SPECIAL BATTALION
AND 10TH INFANTRY REGIMENT, C.S.A.*,
CWR:VOL2#4[346], reviewed by George Otott Jr.
Himmelfarb, Gertrude; *THE NEW HISTORY AND THE OLD:
CRITICAL ESSAYS AND REAPPRAISALS*,
CWTI:MAR/89[10], reviewed by Albert Castel
Hirshson, Stanley P.; *GRENVILLE M. DODGE: SOLDIER,
POLITICIAN, RAILROAD PIONEER*, AHI:AUG/67[59]
Hitt, Michael D.; *CHARGED WITH TREASON: ORDEAL OF
400 MILL WORKERS DURING MILITARY OPERATIONS IN*

ROSWELL GEORGIA, 1864-1865, CWNEWS:NOV/93[5], *reviewed by* Michael Russert

Hixson, William B. Jr; *MOORFIELD STOREY AND THE ABOLITIONIST TRADITION*, AHI:DEC/72[49], *reviewed by* Gossie H. Hudson

Hodgkins, Joseph E., (edited by Kenneth C. Turino); *THE CIVIL WAR DIARY OF LT. J.E. HODGKINS*, CWNEWS:NOV/95[29]

Hoehling, A.A.:
DAMN THE TORPEDOES! NAVAL INCIDENTS OF THE CIVIL WAR, CWNEWS:MAY/91[4], *reviewed by* Allen Guelzo, CWNEWS:OCT/94[33], *reviewed by* Michael Russert, CWTI:APR/90[10]
LAST TRAIN FROM ATLANTA, CWNEWS:SEP/93[5], *reviewed by* Norman E. Rourke
THUNDER AT HAMPTON ROADS, CWNEWS:APR/94[5], *reviewed by* Dale K. Phillips

Hoig, Stan; *TRIBAL WARS OF THE SOUTHERN PLAINS*, CWNEWS:FEB/95[33], *reviewed by* Robert D. Norris Jr.

Holmes, James T.; *FIFTY-SECOND OHIO VOLUNTEER INFANTRY: THEN AND NOW, VOLUME I*, CWR:VOL4#3[1], *reviewed by* Albert Castel

Holmes, Emma, (edited by John F. Marszalek); *THE DIARY OF MISS EMMA HOLMES, 1861-1866*, CWM:APR/95[8], *reviewed by* F. Gordon Shay

Holt, Daniel M., (edited by James M. Greiner); *A SURGEON'S CIVIL WAR: THE LETTERS AND DIARY OF DANIEL M. HOLT, M.D.*, CWM:DEC/95[10], *reviewed by* Kevin Conley Ruffner, CWNEWS:JUL/95[61], *reviewed by* Harris D. Riley Jr.

Holt, Michael F.; *POLITICAL PARTIES AND AMERICAN POLITICAL DEVELOPMENT FROM THE AGE OF JACKSON TO THE AGE OF LINCOLN*, CWNEWS:JUN/93[5], *reviewed by* John L. Farber

Holzer, Harold, (edited by):
DEAR MR. LINCOLN: LETTERS TO THE PRESIDENT, B&G:DEC/94[28], *reviewed by* Michael C. C. Adam, CWNEWS:FEB/95[33], *reviewed by* Allen C. Guelzo
LINCOLN ON DEMOCRACY, AHI:MAR/91[8]293B
THE LINCOLN-DOUGLAS DEBATES: THE FIRST COMPLETE UNEXPURGATED TEXT, B&G:JUN/94[34], *reviewed by* Scott W. Smith, CWNEWS:JUL/94[25], *reviewed by* William F. Howard, CWR:VOL3#2[105], *reviewed by* James Marten
MINE EYES HAVE SEEN THE GLORY: THE CIVIL WAR IN ART, ACW:MAY/94[58], *reviewed by* Lori Anne Dickens, CWNEWS:NOV/95[29], *reviewed by* Douglas Kinnett

Homer, Winslow, (edited by Marc Simpson); *WINSLOW HOMER: PAINTINGS OF THE CIVIL WAR* CWNEWS:JUL/91[4], *reviewed by* Anne J. Bailey

Hood, John B.; *ADVANCE AND RETREAT: PERSONAL EXPERIENCES IN THE UNITED STATES AND CONFEDERATE STATES ARMIES*, ACW:NOV/94[66], *reviewed by* Michael D. Hull, CWM:OCT/94[8], *reviewed by* Jim Percoco, CWM:FEB/95[42], *reviewed by* Gary W. Gallagher, CWM:APR/95[50], *reviewed by* Gary W. Gallagher

Hoogenboom, Ari; *RUTHERFORD B. HAYES: WARRIOR & PRESIDENT* CWNEWS:DEC/95[29], *reviewed by* Michael Russert

Hoover, Dwight W.; *UNDERSTANDING NEGRO HISTORY, EDITED BY*, AHI:JUN/69[46], *reviewed by* Albert Castel

Hopkins, Charles, (edited by William B. Styple); *THE ANDERSONVILLE DIARY & MEMOIRS OF CHARLES HOPKINS*, CWNEWS:MAY/90[4], *reviewed by* Jeffry D. Wert

Horan, James D.; *THE PINKERTONS: THE DETECTIVE DYNASTY THAT MADE HISTORY*, AHI:MAY/69[49], *reviewed by* J. E. Raymond

Horn, John:
THE PETERSBURG CAMPAIGN JUNE 1864-APRIL 1865, CWNEWS:APR/95[33], *reviewed by* Clint Johnson
THE PETERSBURG CAMPAIGN: THE DESTRUCTION OF THE WELDON RAILROAD (DEEP BOTTOM, GLOBE TAVERN, AND REAMS STATION AUGUST 14-25, 1864, CWNEWS:JAN/92[4], *reviewed by* William F. Howard

Horn, Stanley F.; *THE ARMY OF TENNESSEE* CWM:APR/95[8], *reviewed by* Gary W. Gallagher, CWNEWS:MAY/94[5], *reviewed by* Harris D. Riley Jr.

Horner, Dave; *THE BLOCKADE RUNNERS: TRUE TALES OF RUNNING THE YANKEE BLOCKADE OF THE CONFEDERATE COAST*, CWNEWS:OCT/94[33], *reviewed by* Gary Augustine

Hornsby, Alton Jr.; *IN THE CAGE: EYEWITNESS ACCOUNTS OF THE FREED NEGRO IN SOUTHERN SOCIETY, 1877-1929*, AHI:NOV/71[48], *reviewed by* Benjamin Quarles

Hotchkiss, Jedediah; *MAKE ME A MAP OF THE VALLEY: THE CIVIL WAR JOURNAL OF STONEWALL JACKSON'S TOPOGRAPHER*, CWM:FEB/95[42]564, *reviewed by* Gary W. Gallagher

Howard, Martin, (edited by Martin Crawford); *WILLIAM HOWARD RUSSELL'S CIVIL WAR: PRIVATE DIARY AND LETTERS 1861-1862*, CWNEWS:OCT/93[5], *reviewed by* Steven J. Wright

Howell, William R., (edited by Jerry D. Thompson); *WESTWARD THE TEXANS: THE CIVIL WAR JOURNAL OF PRIVATE WILLIAM RANDOLPH HOWELL*, CWM:MAR/92[49], *reviewed by* Gary W. Gallagher, CWNEWS:JUN/92[4], *reviewed by* Anne J. Bailey

Hudson, Henry; *CIVIL WAR SKETCHBOOK & DIARY*, CWNEWS:OCT/89[4], *reviewed by* Barry Popchock

Huffstodt, Jim; *HARD DYING MEN: THE STORY OF GENERAL W.H.L. WALLACE, GENERAL T.E.G. RANSOM, AND THEIR "OLD ELEVENTH" ILLINOIS INFANTRY*, B&G:APR/93[30], *reviewed by* B. Franklin Cooling

Hughes, Nathaniel C.:
THE BATTLE OF BELMONT: GRANT STRIKES SOUTH, ACW:JUL/92[54], *reviewed by* Roy Morris Jr., B&G:APR/92[24], *reviewed by* Michael L. Gillespie, CWM:MAR/92[49], *reviewed by* Gary W. Gallagher, CWNEWS:JAN/93[4], *reviewed by* Dr. Richard A. Sauers, CWR:VOL2#1[78], *reviewed by* David A. Woodbury
THE LIFE AND WARS OF GIDEON J. PILLOW, B&G:FEB/95[26], *reviewed by* Michael L. Gillespie, CWM:AUG/94[9], *reviewed by* Glenn Goodwin, CWM:APR/95[50], *reviewed by* Gary W. Gallagher, CWNEWS:DEC/94[33], *reviewed by* Barry Popchock, CWTI:MAR/94[12]

Hughett, Barbara; *THE CIVIL WAR ROUND TABLE: FIFTY YEARS OF SCHOLARSHIP AND FELLOWSHIP*, B&G:APR/91[28], *reviewed by* Steve Davis, CWNEWS:NOV/90[4], *reviewed by* Jerry Russell

Humphreys, A.A.; *THE VIRGINIA CAMPAIGN OF 1864 AND 1865*, CWNEWS:JAN/91[4], *reviewed by* Michael J. Winey

Hunt, Roger D.; *BREVET BRIGADIER GENERALS IN BLUE*, CWNEWS:SEP/90[4], *reviewed by* Michael Mullins

Hutton, Paul A.:
THE CUSTER READER, B&G:JUN/93[28], *reviewed by* Neil C.
   Mangum, CWM:APR/95[50], *reviewed by* Gary W. Gallagher,
   CWNEWS:JUN/93[5], *reviewed by* Brian Pohanka
PHIL SHERIDAN AND HIS ARMY, AHI:SEP/85[10]

Jackman, John S., (edited by William C. Davis); *DIARY OF A
   CONFEDERATE SOLDIER: JOHN S. JACKMAN OF THE
   ORPHAN BRIGADE,* CWNEWS:JUL/91[4], *reviewed by*
   William G. Robertson
Jamieson, Perry D.; *DEATH IN SEPTEMBER: THE
   ANTIETAM CAMPAIGN,* CWNEWS:DEC/95[29], *reviewed by*
   Ted Alexander
Jimerson, Randall C.; *THE PRIVATE CIVIL WAR: POPULAR
   THOUGHT DURING THE SECTIONAL CONFLICT,*
   CWNEWS:OCT/89[4], *reviewed by* William Howard
Johannsen, Robert W.:
THE FRONTIER, THE UNION, AND STEPHEN A. DOUGLAS,
   CWNEWS:SEP/90[4], *reviewed by* Steven Ward
*LINCOLN, THE SOUTH, AND SLAVERY: THE POLITICAL
   DIMENSION,* CWM:JAN/92[57], *reviewed by* Gary W.
   Gallagher, CWNEWS:JUN/95[33], *reviewed by* John L. Farber
Johns, John E.; *FLORIDA DURING THE CIVIL WAR,*
   CWNEWS:AUG/93[5], *reviewed by* Harris D. Riley Jr.
Johnson, Curt; *ARTILLERY HELL: THE EMPLOYMENT OF
   ARTILLERY AT ANTIETAM, B&G:OCT / 95[28], reviewed by*
   John M. Priest, CWNEWS:DEC/95[29], *reviewed by* Ted
   Alexander
Johnston, Joseph E.; *NARRATIVE OF MILITARY
   OPERATIONS DIRECTED DURING THE LATE WAR
   BETWEEN THE STATES,* CWM:JAN/91[47], *reviewed by*
   Gary W. Gallagher, CWM:FEB/95[42], *reviewed by* Gary W.
   Gallagher, CWM:JUN/95[6], *reviewed by* Gary W. Gallagher
Johnson, Ludwell H.; *RED RIVER CAMPAIGN: POLITICS
   AND COTTON IN THE CIVIL WAR,* CWM:FEB/95[42]564,
   reviewed by Gary W. Gallagher
Johnson, Neil; *THE BATTLE OF GETTYSBURG,*
   CWTI:APR/90[10]
Johnson, Robert U.; *BATTLES AND LEADERS OF THE
   CIVIL WAR,* CWM:FEB/95[42]564, *reviewed by* Gary W.
   Gallagher
Johnston, Angus J.; *VIRGINIA RAILROADS IN THE CIVIL
   WAR,* CWM:NOV/91[73], *reviewed by* Gary W. Gallagher
Jones, Archer; *CIVIL WAR COMMAND AND STRATEGY:
   THE PROCESS OF VICTORY AND DEFEAT,*
   CWTI:NOV/92[10], *reviewed by* James M. McPherson
Jones, Charles E.; *GEORGIA IN THE WAR, 1861-1865: A
   COMPENDIUM OF GEORGIA PARTICIPANTS,*
   B&G:AUG/91[26], *reviewed by* William H. Bragg
Jones, J. William:
*PERSONAL REMINISCENCES OF GENERAL ROBERT E.
   LEE,* CWNEWS:NOV/91[4], *reviewed by* Michael Pollcatti
THE SOUTHERN HISTORICAL SOCIETY PAPERS,
   CWM:FEB/95[42]564, *reviewed by* Gary W. Gallagher
Jones, John B., (edited by Earl Schenck Miers); *A REBEL WAR
   CLERK'S DIARY,* CWM:APR/95[50], *reviewed by* Gary W.
   Gallagher
Jones, S.C., (edited by Jeffry Burden); *REMINISCENCES OF
   THE 22ND IOWA INFANTRY,* CWNEWS:JUN/94[5], *reviewed
   by* Larry J. Daniel
Jones, Terry L.; *THE CIVIL WAR MEMOIRS OF CAPTAIN
   WILLIAM J. SEYMOUR,* B&G:FEB/92[26], *reviewed by*
   Donald Pfanz

Jones, Tom; *HOOD'S TEXAS BRIGADE SKETCHBOOK,*
   CWNEWS:OCT/89[4], *reviewed by* Blake Magner
Jones, Virgil C.; *THE CIVIL WAR AT SEA,*
   CWNEWS:APR/92[4], *reviewed by* Jeffry D. Wert
Jordan, David M.; *WINFIELD SCOTT HANCOCK: A
   SOLDIER'S LIFE,* CWNEWS:MAY/90[4], *reviewed by* Richard
   Sauers
Jordan, Ervin L. Jr.; *BLACK CONFEDERATES AND
   AFRO-YANKEES IN CIVIL WAR VIRGINIA,*
   CWM:AUG/95[45], *reviewed by* Gary W. Gallagher
Jordan, Weymouth T. Jr.:
*NORTH CAROLINA TROOPS 1861-1865, A ROSTER, VOLUME
   XII, 49TH-52ND REGIMENTS,* CWNEWS:APR/92[4], *reviewed
   by* Michael Cavanaugh
*NORTH CAROLINA TROOPS, 1861-1865, A ROSTER, VOLUME
   XIII, INFANTRY,* CWM:APR/95[50], *reviewed by* Gary W.
   Gallagher, CWNEWS:APR/94[5], *reviewed by* Michael
   Cavanaugh
Jordan, Winthrop D.; *TUMULT AND SILENCE AT SECOND
   CREEK: AN INQUIRY INTO A CIVIL WAR SLAVE
   CONSPIRACY ,CWNEWS:APR/95[33], reviewed by* Jeffry D.
   Wert
Josephy, Alvin M.; *THE CIVIL WAR IN THE AMERICAN
   WEST,* CWM:SEP/92[57], *reviewed by* David Woodbury,
   CWNEWS:DEC/92[4], *reviewed by* Robert D. Norris Jr.
Joslyn, Richard S.; *NOTES ON MILITARY ETIQUETTE,*
   CWNEWS:APR/92[4], *reviewed by* Steven J. Wright
Judge, Joseph; *SEASON OF FIRE: THE CONFEDERATE
   STRIKE ON WASHINGTON,* CWNEWS:MAY/95[33], *reviewed
   by* Brandon H. Beck, CWR:VOL4#3[89], *reviewed by* Donna
   Neiger

Kafka, F.L.; *TUNNEL TO GLORY,* CWTI:MAR/93[10], *reviewed
   by* Noah Andre Trudeau
Kantor, Alvin R.; *SANITARY FAIRS: A PHILATELIC AND
   HISTORICAL STUDY OF CIVIL WAR BENEVOLENCES,*
   B&G:DEC/93[24], *reviewed by* Christopher Losson,
   CWNEWS:NOV/93[5], *reviewed by* Cheryl Allen-Munley
Karamanski, Theodore J.; *RALLY ROUND THE FLAG:
   CHICAGO AND THE CIVIL WAR,* CWNEWS:NOV/93[5],
   reviewed by Dale K. Phillips
Katcher, Philip:
THE ARMY OF ROBERT E. LEE, CWNEWS:NOV/95[29],
   reviewed by Stephen L. Ritchi, CWTI:DEC/94[18]
UNION FORCES OF THE AMERICAN CIVIL WAR
   CWNEWS:NOV/91[4], *reviewed by* Brian Paohanka
Katz, D. Mark; *WITNESS TO AN ERA: THE LIFE AND
   PHOTOGRAPHS OF ALEXANDER GARDNER,*
   CWM:MAY/94[34], *reviewed by* William J. Miller,
   CWNEWS:OCT/94[4], *reviewed by* Jeffry D. Wert
Katz, William L.:
EYEWITNESS: THE NEGRO IN AMERICAN HISTORY,
   AHI:JUN/68[51], *reviewed by* Robert D. Hoffsommer
*THE BLACK WEST: A DOCUMENTARY AND PICTORIAL
   HISTORY,* AHI:DEC/72[49], *reviewed by* Gossie H. Hudson
Kean, Robert G.H., (edited by Edward Younger); *INSIDE THE
   CONFEDERATE GOVERNMENT: THE DIARY OF ROBERT
   GARLICK HILL KEAN,* CWM:APR/95[50], *reviewed by* Gary W.
   Gallagher, CWNEWS:DEC/95[29], *reviewed by* David E. Long
Keen, Hugh C.; *43RD BATTALION VIRGINIA CAVALRY,
   MOSBY'S COMMAND,* CWNEWS:MAY/94[5], *reviewed by*
   Jeffry D. Wert

Keesy, William A.; *WAR AS VIEWED FROM THE RANKS,* CWNEWS:OCT/92[4], *reviewed by* Terrence J. Winschel

Kelbough, Ross J.; *INTRODUCTION TO CIVIL WAR PHOTOGRAPHY,* CWNEWS:AUG/92[4]

Keller, S. Roger:
EVENTS OF THE CIVIL WAR IN WASHINGTON COUNTY, MARYLAND, CWNEWS:JUL/95[61], *reviewed by* Ted Alexander
ROSTER OF CIVIL WAR SOLDIERS FROM WASHINGTON COUNTY, MARYLAND, CWNEWS:AUG/94[33], *reviewed by* Ted Alexander

Kelley, Tom; *A COMMISSARY SERGEANT'S COOKBOOK,* CWNEWS:OCT/93[5], *reviewed by* Linda G. Black

Kelly, C. Brian; *BEST LITTLE STORIES FROM THE CIVIL WAR,* ACW:SEP/95[62], *reviewed by* Michael D. Hull, CWNEWS:OCT/95[33], *reviewed by* Frank J. Piatek

Kelly, Dennis; *KENNESAW MOUNTAIN AND THE ATLANTA CAMPAIGN: A TOUR GUIDE,* CWNEWS:NOV/91[4], *reviewed by* Michael Mullins

Kennedy, Frances H.; *THE CIVIL WAR BATTLEFIELD GUIDE,* CWNEWS:NOV/90[4], *reviewed by* David F. Riggs

Kennedy, James R.; *THE SOUTH WAS RIGHT!* CWNEWS:OCT/94[33], *reviewed by* Richard McMurry

Kennett, Lee; *MARCHING THROUGH GEORGIA: THE STORY OF SOLDIERS AND CIVILIANS DURING SHERMAN'S CAMPAIGN,* CWTI:AUG/95[18], *reviewed by* Mark Grimsley

Kerby, Robert L.; *KIRBY SMITH'S CONFEDERACY: THE TRANS-MISSISSIPPI SOUTH, 1863-1865,* B&G:FEB/92[26], *reviewed by* Thomas Goodrich, CWNEWS:SEP/92[4], *reviewed by* Harris D. Riley Jr., CWR:VOL2#2[169], *reviewed by* Anne J. Bailey

Kerlin, Robert H.; *CONFEDERATE GENERALS OF GEORGIA AND THEIR BURIAL SITES,* CWR:VOL4#3[37]

Keyser, Carl A.; *LEATHERBREECHES: HERO OF CHANCELLORSVILLE,* CWNEWS:OCT/90[4], *reviewed by* David G. Martin

King, Benjamin:
A BULLET FOR LINCOLN, CWTI:NOV/93[14]
A BULLET FOR STONEWALL, CWM:SEP/91[58], *reviewed by* William J. Miller

Kinsley, Ardyce; *THE FITZHUGH LEE SAMPLER,* ACW:JAN/93[58]399, *reviewed by* Nan Siegel, CWNEWS:NOV/93[5], *reviewed by* Stephen L. Ritchie

Klein, Frederic S.; *THE DOUGLAS DIARY,* AHI:MAY/74[49], *reviewed by* Lowell H. Harrison

Klement, Frank L.; *THE GETTYSBURG SOLDIERS' CEMETERY AND LINCOLN'S ADDRESS,* B&G:DEC/95[30], *reviewed by* Benedict R. Maryniak, CWM:APR/95[50], *reviewed by* Gary W. Gallagher, CWNEWS:JUL/94[25], *reviewed by* Michael Russert

Kloeppel, James E.; *DANGER BENEATH THE WAVES,* CWNEWS:MAY/89[4], *reviewed by* Barry Popchock

Knauss, William H.; *THE STORY OF CAMP CHASE,* CWNEWS:JAN/92[4], *reviewed by* Frank J. Piatek

Koch, Freda P.:
CIVIL WAR HEROINES: THE COGGESHALL LADIES, CWNEWS:MAY/95[33], *reviewed by* DeAnne Blanton
COLONEL COGGESHALL — THE MAN WHO SAVED LINCOLN, CWNEWS:FEB/95[33], *reviewed by* Frank J. Piatek

Krick, Robert K.:
STONEWALL JACKSON AT CEDAR MOUNTAIN, ACW:JUL/91[50], *reviewed by* Kenneth P. Czech,

CWM:JAN/91[47], *reviewed by* Gary W. Gallagher, CWM:FEB/95[42]564, *reviewed by* Gary W. Gallagher, CWNEWS:SEP/90[4], *reviewed by* Jeffry D. Wert, CWTI:SEP/90[12]
LEE'S COLONELS: A BIOGRAPHICAL REGISTER OF THE FIELD OFFICERS OF THE ARMY OF NORTHERN VIRGINIA, CWM:FEB/95[42]564, *reviewed by* Gary W. Gallagher
PARKER'S VIRGINIA BATTERY, C.S.A., CWNEWS:APR/91[4], *reviewed by* Brandon Beck

Kunstler, Mort; *IMAGES OF THE CIVIL WAR,* CWNEWS:NOV/93[5], *reviewed by* Tom Low, CWTI:JAN/93[12]

Laas, Virginia Jeans,(edited by); *WARTIME WASHINGTON: THE CIVIL WAR LETTERS OF ELIZABETH BLAIR LEE,* AHI:MAR/92[24]

Ladd, David L., (edited by); *THE BACHELDER PAPERS: GETTYSBURG IN THEIR OWN WORDS,* CWNEWS:DEC/95[29], *reviewed by* D. Scott Hartwig, CWR:VOL4#3[37]

Ladley, Oscar D., (edited by Carl M. Becker); *HEARTH AND KNAPSACK: THE LADLEY LETTERS, 1857-1880,* CWNEWS:AUG/91[4], *reviewed by* Michael A. Hughes

Lambert, Dobbie; *THE W.E. JONES BRIGADE 1863-64,* CWNEWS:FEB/94[5], *reviewed by* Kemp Burpeau

Landers, Eli Pinson, (edited by Elizabeth W. Robinson); *WEEP NOT FOR ME, DEAR MOTHER,* B&G:DEC/92[26], *reviewed by* Garold L. Cole

Lane, Mills; *"DEAR MOTHER: DON'T GRIEVE ABOUT ME. IF I GET KILLED, I'LL ONLY BE DEAD." LETTERS FROM GEORGIA SOLDIERS IN THE CIVIL WAR,* CWM:FEB/95[42]564, *reviewed by* Gary W. Gallagher

Langellier, John P.; *MYLES KEOGH, THE LIFE AND LEGEND OF AN "IRISH DRAGOON" IN THE SEVENTH CAVALRY,* CWNEWS:JAN/93[4], *reviewed by* Dr. Richard A. Sauers

LaRocca, Charles; *THAT REGIMENT OF HEROES,* CWNEWS:OCT/93[5], *reviewed by* Michael Russert

Larson, Rebecca D.; *BLUE AND GRAY ROSES OF INTRIGUE,* CWNEWS:FEB/94[5], *reviewed by* DeAnne Blanton

Lash, Jeffrey N.; *DESTROYER OF THE IRON HORSE: GENERAL JOSEPH E. JOHNSTON AND CONFEDERATE RAIL TRANSPORT, 1861-1865,* B&G:FEB/92[26], *reviewed by* Steve Davis, CWM:JAN/92[57], *reviewed by* Gary W. Gallagher, CWNEWS:JUL/91[4], *reviewed by* Mike Mullins

Lauderdale, John V., (edited by, Peter Josyph); *THE WOUNDED RIVER: THE CIVIL WAR LETTERS OF JOHN VANCE LAUDERDALE, M.D.,* CWM:APR/94[51], *reviewed by* Courtney B. WIlson, CWNEWS:FEB/94[5], *reviewed by* Anne J. Bailey

Lavery, Dennis S.; *IRON BRIGADE GENERAL: JOHN GIBBON, A REBEL IN BLUE,* CWM:APR/95[50], *reviewed by* Gary W. Gallagher, B&G:JUN/94[34], *reviewed by* A. WIlson Greene

Leckie, Robert; *NONE DIED IN VAIN: THE SAGA OF THE AMERICAN CIVIL WAR,* B&G:APR/92[24], *reviewed by* J. Tracy Power, CWNEWS:JAN/91[4], *reviewed by* William Marvel

Leckie, William H.; *THE BUFFALO SOLDIERS. A NARRATIVE OF THE NEGRO, CAVALRY IN THE WEST* AHI:AUG/67[59], *reviewed by* Wilber S. Nye

Lee, Elizabeth Blair, (edited by Virginia Jean Laas); *WARTIME WASHINGTON: THE CIVIL WAR LETTERS OF ELIZABETH BLAIR LEE,* CWNEWS:APR/93[4], *reviewed by* Linda Black

Lee, Fitzhugh; *GENERAL LEE*, CWNEWS:JUL/91[4], *reviewed by* Terrence Winschel

Lee, Robert E.:

LEE'S DISPATCHES: UNPUBLISHED LETTERS OF GENERAL ROBERT E. LEE, C.S.A. TO JEFFERSON DAVIS AND THE WAR DEPARTMENT, CWM:FEB/95[42]564, *reviewed by* Gary W. Gallagher

RECOLLECTIONS AND LETTERS OF GENERAL ROBERT E. LEE BY HIS SON, CWNEWS:MAY/89[4], *reviewed by* Michael Parrish

THE WARTIME PAPERS OF ROBERT E. LEE, CWM:JAN/91[47], *reviewed by* Gary W. Gallagher, CWM:FEB/95[42]564, *reviewed by* Gary W. Gallagher

Lee, William O., (compiled by); *PERSONAL AND HISTORICAL SKETCHES AND FACIAL HISTORY OF AND BY MEMBERS OF THE SEVENTH REGIMENT MICHIGAN VOLUNTEER CAVALRY 1862-1865*, CWNEWS:JAN/92[4]

Leslie, Frank; *LESLIE'S ILLUSTRATED CIVIL WAR*, CWR:VOL2#4[346], *reviewed by* Anne J. Bailey

Lesser, W. Hunter; *BATTLE AT CORRICKS FORD: CONFEDERATE DISASTER AND LOSS OF A LEADER*, CWNEWS:NOV/95[29], *reviewed by* Steven J. Wright

Lewis, Gene D.; *CHARLES ELLET, JR.: THE ENGINEER AS INDIVIDUALIST*, AHI:JUN/69[46], *reviewed by* Robert D. Hoffsommer

Lewis, Lloyd:

THE ASSASSINATION OF LINCOLN: HISTORY AND MYTH, ACW:JAN/95[62], CWM:FEB/95[7], *reviewed by* J. Jeffery Cox

CAPTAIN SAM GRANT, CWM:FEB/95[42], *reviewed by* Gary W. Gallagher

SHERMAN: FIGHTING PROPHET, CWM:FEB/95[42], *reviewed by* Gary W. Gallagher, CWM:APR/95[50], *reviewed by* Gary W. Gallagher, CWNEWS:APR/95[33], *reviewed by* Michael Russert, CWR:VOL3#4[68], *reviewed by* Archie P. McDonald

Lewis, Thomas; *THE GUNS OF CEDAR CREEK*, CWNEWS:SEP/90[4], *reviewed by* Richard Sauers

Lienthal, Edward T.; *SACRED GROUND: AMERICANS AND THEIR BATTLEFIELDS*, CWNEWS:AUG/93[5], *reviewed by* Mark Stephens

Lind, Henry C., (edited by); *THE LONG ROAD FOR HOME: THE CIVIL WAR EXPERIENCES OF FOUR FARMBOY SOLDIERS OF THE TWENTY-SEVENTH MASSACHUSETTS REGIMENT OF VOLUNTEER INFANTRY AS TOLD BY THEIR PERSONAL CORRESPONDENCE, 1861-1864*, CWNEWS:JAN/94[5], *reviewed by* Dr. Richard A. Sauers

Linderman, Gerald F.; *EMBATTLED COURAGE, THE EXPERIENCE OF COMBAT IN THE AMERICAN CIVIL WAR*, AHI:NOV/87[8], CWR:VOL4#3[1], *reviewed by* John F. Marszalek

Livingston, E.A.; *PRESIDENT LINCOLN'S THIRD LARGEST CITY, BROOKLYN AND THE CIVIL WAR*, CWNEWS:JUL/95[61], *reviewed by* Frank J. Piatek

Long, David E.; *THE JEWEL OF LIBERTY: ABRAHAM LINCOLN'S RE-ELECTION AND THE END OF SLAVERY*, B&G:JUN/95[30], *reviewed by* Michael W. Kauffman, CWM:DEC/95[10], *reviewed by* J. Jeffrey Cox, CWNEWS:APR/95[33], *reviewed by* Gregory J.W. Urwin, CWR:VOL4#3[37]

Long, E.B.:

THE CIVIL WAR DAY BY DAY: AN ALMANAC 1861-1865, CWM:FEB/95[42], *reviewed by* Gary W. Gallagher

COLLECTING GRAND ARMY OF THE REPUBLIC MEMORABILIA, CWNEWS:JUL/91[4], *reviewed by* Steve Wright

Longacre, Edward G.:

THE CAVALRY AT GETTYSBURG: A TACTICAL STUDY OF MOUNTED OPERATIONS DURING THE CIVIL WAR'S PIVOTAL CAMPAIGN, (JUNE 4-JULY 1863), CWNEWS:APR/95[33], *reviewed by* Dr. Richard A. Sauers

JERSEY CAVALIERS: A HISTORY OF THE FIRST NEW JERSEY VOLUNTEER CAVALRY, 1861-1865, CWNEWS:JAN/95[25], *reviewed by* Michael Russert

MOUNTED RAIDS OF THE CIVIL WAR, CWM:DEC/94[7], *reviewed by* James A. Ramage, CWNEWS:NOV/95[29], *reviewed by* Gregory J.W. Urwin

TO GETTYSBURG AND BEYOND: THE TWELFTH NEW JERSEY VOLUNTEER INFANTRY, II CORPS, ARMY OF THE POTOMAC, 1862-1865, CWNEWS:MAY/89[4], *reviewed by* Mike Mullins

Longford, Lord; *ABRAHAM LINCOLN*, AHI:OCT/76[49], *reviewed by* Robert D. Hoffsommer

Longstreet, Helen D.; *LEE AND LONGSTREET AT HIGH TIDE: GETTYSBURG IN LIGHT OF THE OFFICIAL RECORDS*, CWNEWS:JAN/91[4], *reviewed by* Richard Sauers

Longstreet, James; *FROM MANASSAS TO APPOMATTOX: MEMOIRS OF THE CIVIL WAR IN AMERICA*, CWM:SEP/92[57], *reviewed by* John Michael Priest, CWM:FEB/95[42]564, *reviewed by* Gary W. Gallagher

Lonn, Ella:

FOREIGNERS IN THE CONFEDERACY, CWM:MAR/91[74], *reviewed by* Gary W. Gallagher

FOREIGNERS IN THE UNION ARMY AND NAVY, CWM:MAR/91[74], *reviewed by* Gary W. Gallagher

Loomis, David; *THE HOBBY, A GUIDE TO HAVING 'CIVIL' REENACTMENT, VOLUME 1*, CWNEWS:NOV/93[5], *reviewed by* David Hann

Losson, Christopher; *TENNESSEE'S FORGOTTEN WARRIORS: FRANK CHEATHAM AND HIS CONFEDERATE DIVISION*, CWM:JAN/91[47], *reviewed by* Gary W. Gallagher, CWNEWS:SEP/91[4], *reviewed by* Steve Wright, CWTI:FEB/91[10]

Loughborough, Mary; *MY CAVE LIFE IN VICKSBURG*, CWNEWS:NOV/90[4], *reviewed by* David Riggs

Lowry, Don:

DARK AND CRUEL WAR: THE DECISIVE MONTHS OF THE CIVIL WAR, SEPTEMBER-DECEMBER 1864, ACW:JUL/94[58], *reviewed by* Philip L. Bolte

NO TURNING BACK, THE BEGINNING OF THE END OF THE CIVIL WAR: MARCH-JUNE 1864, ACW:NOV/92[58], *reviewed by* Jon Guttman, B&G:OCT/92[30], *reviewed by* Richard A. Sauers, CWNEWS:MAY/93[4], *reviewed by* Steven J. Wright, CWTI:APR/92[30], CWTI:JAN/93[12]

Lowry, Thomas P.; *THE STORY THE SOLDIERS WOULDN'T TELL — SEX IN THE CIVIL WAR*, ACW:JAN/95[62], B&G:FEB/95[26], *reviewed by* Herbert M. Schiller, M.D, CWM:DEC/94[17]547, CWNEWS:APR/95[33], *reviewed by* Ted Alexander, CWR:VOL4#3[37]

Lucas, Marion B.; *SHERMAN AND THE BURNING OF COLUMBIA*, CWNEWS:JAN/90[4], *reviewed by* David Ward

Luvaas, Dr. Jay:

THE U.S. ARMY WAR COLLEGE GUIDE TO THE BATTLES OF CHANCELLORSVILLE AND FREDERICKSBURG, CWNEWS:NOV/89[4], *reviewed by* David G. Martin

THE U.S. ARMY WAR COLLEGE GUIDE TO THE BATTLE OF GETTYSBURG, AHI:DEC/86[6]
Lyman, Darryl; *CIVIL WAR WORDBOOK,* CWTI:MAY/94[20]
Lyman, Theodore:
WITH GRANT & MEADE: FROM THE WILDERNESS TO APPOMATTOX, CWNEWS:DEC/95[29], *reviewed by* Kevin E. O'Brien, CWR:VOL4#2[136], *reviewed by* M. Jane Johansson
MEADE'S HEADQUARTERS, 1863-1865: LETTERS OF COLONEL THEODORE LYMAN FROM THE WILDERNESS TO APPOMATTOX, CWM:DEC/94[7], *reviewed by* Gary W. Gallagher

Macaluso, Gregory J.; *THE FORT PILLOW MASSACRE: THE REASON WHY,* CWNEWS:APR/91[4], *reviewed by* Michael Policatti
Madden, David; *CLASSICS OF CIVIL WAR FICTION,* CWNEWS:MAY/93[4], *reviewed by* Michael Russert
Mahood, Wayne; *CHARLIE MOSHER'S CIVIL WAR,* (edited by), B&G:AUG/95[38], *reviewed by* Warren Wilkinson
Mahood, Wayne; *THE PLYMOUTH PILGRIMS: A HISTORY OF THE EIGHTY-FIFTH NEW YORK INFANTRY IN THE CIVIL WAR,* B&G:APR/91[28], *reviewed by* E. A. Livingston, CWNEWS:AUG/90[4], *reviewed by* Frank Piatek
Mahr, Theodore C.; *THE BATTLE OF CEDAR CREEK: SHOWDOWN IN THE SEHNANDOAH, OCTOBER 1-30, 1864,* B&G:OCT/93[24], *reviewed by* Jeffry D. Wert
Mallon, Thomas; *HENRY AND CLARA,* ACW:SEP/95[62], *reviewed by* Cowan Brew
Maltz, Earl M; *CIVIL RIGHTS, THE CONSTITUTION, AND CONGRESS, 1863-1869,* CWM:MAR/92[49], *reviewed by* Gary W. Gallagher
Maney, R. Wayne; *MARCHING TO COLD HARBOR: VICTORY & FAILURE, 1864,* B&G:JUN/95[30], *reviewed by* Robert E. L. Krick, CWNEWS:MAY/95[33], *reviewed by* Ethan S. Rafuse, CWR:VOL4#4[129], *reviewed by* Marshall Scott
Mangum, Neil C.; *BATTLE OF THE ROSEBUD: PRELUDE TO THE LITTLE BIG HORN,* CWNEWS:JUL/90[4], *reviewed by* Michael Mullins
Manigault, Arthur M., (edited by R. Lockwood Tower); *A CAROLINIAN GOES TO WAR: THE CIVIL WAR NARRATIVE OF ARTHUR MIDDLETON MANIGAULT, BRIGADIER GENERAL, C.S.A.,* CWM:FEB/95[42], *reviewed by* Gary W. Gallagher
Mann, Jonathan; *LINCOLN COLLECTOR,* CWTI:DEC/95[38]
Marbaker, Thomas D.; *HISTORY OF THE ELEVENTH NEW JERSEY VOLUNTEERS,* CWNEWS:JAN/92[4], *reviewed by* William Marvel
Marcot, Roy M.; *CIVIL WAR CHIEF OF SHARPSHOOTERS HIRAM BERDAN: MILITARY COMMANDER AND FIREARMS INVENTOR,* B&G:FEB/91[28], *reviewed by* Geoff Walden, CWNEWS:OCT/90[4], *reviewed by* Steven J. Wright
Marius, Richard, (edited by); *THE COLUMBIA BOOK OF CIVIL WAR POETRY: FROMD WHITMAN TO WALCOTT,* CWTI:JAN/95[12]
Markle, Donald E.; *SPIES & SPYMASTERS OF THE CIVIL WAR,* CWTI:JAN/95[12], MH:DEC/94[70]
Marszalek, John F.; *SHERMAN: A SOLDIER'S PASSION FOR ORDER,* ACW:MAR/94[58], *reviewed by* Phil Noblitt, B&G:APR/94[24], *reviewed by* Denis Kelly, CWM:JUN/94[6], *reviewed by* Steven E. Woodworth, CWM:FEB/95[42]564, *reviewed by* Gary W. Gallagher, CWTI:SEP/93[26], *reviewed by* David Evans

Marten, James; *TEXAS DIVIDED: LOYALTY AND DISSENT IN THE LONE STAR STATE 1856-1874,* CWM:MAR/92[49], *reviewed by* Gary W. Gallagher, CWNEWS:AUG/91[4], *reviewed by* T. Michael Parrish
Martin, David G.:
THE CHANCELLORSVILLE CAMPAIGN: MARCH-MAY 1863, CWNEWS:DEC/92[4], *reviewed by* Brandon Beck
GETTYSBURG, JULY 1, CWNEWS:NOV/95[29], *reviewed by* Kevin E. O'Brien
Martin, Samuel J.; *THE ROAD TO GLORY, CONFEDERATE GENERAL RICHAR S. EWELL,* CWNEWS:DEC/92[4], *reviewed by* J. Tracy Power, CWR:VOL2#1[78], *reviewed by* James Harwick Jr.
Martini, John A.; *FORTRESS ALCATRAZ: GUARDIAN OF THE GOLDEN GATE,* CWNEWS:APR/93[4], *reviewed by* Michael Russert
Marvel, William:
ANDERSONVILLE: THE LAST DEPOT, B&G:JUN/95[30], *reviewed by* Tom Watson Brow, CWM:AUG/95[45], *reviewed by* Gary W. Gallagher, CWM:OCT/95[10], *reviewed by* Jim Percoco, CWR:VOL4#3[37], CWR:VOL4#3[89], *reviewed by* Anne J. Bailey, CWTI:MAR/95[14]
BURNSIDE, B&G:AUG/92[36], *reviewed by* Lawrence A. Kohl, CWM:FEB/95[42]564, *reviewed by* Gary W. Gallagher, CWNEWS:JUN/93[5], *reviewed by* John Farber, CWR:VOL2#2[169], *reviewed by* David A. Woodbury
RACE OF THE SOIL: THE NINTH NEW HAMPSHIRE REGIMENT IN THE CIVIL WAR, CWNEWS:MAY/89[4], *reviewed by* Harris D. Riley Jr.
SOUTHWEST VIRGINIA IN THE CIVIL WAR: THE BATTLES FOR SALTVILLE, CWNEWS:DEC/93[5], *reviewed by* J. Tracy Power
Massey, Mary E.; *WOMEN IN THE CIVIL WAR,* CWNEWS:NOV/95[29], *reviewed by* DeAnne Blanton
Maser, Louis P., (edited by); "...THE REAL WAR WILL NEVER GET IN THE BOOKS", CWM:AUG/94[9], *reviewed by* Charles Norvill, CWNEWS:NOV/94[33], *reviewed by* Stehen D. Engle, CWR:VOL4#4[129], *reviewed by* Ron Calkins, CWTI:SEP/93[26]
Matrau, Henry, (edited by Marcia Reid-Green); *LETTERS HOME: HENRY MATRAU OF THE IRON BRIGADE* CWM:APR/95[50], *reviewed by* Gary W. Gallagher, CWR:VOL3#3[92], *reviewed by* Donald E. Rynold
Matter, William D.; *IF IT TAKES ALL SUMMER: THE BATTLE OF SPOTSYLVANIA,* CWM:FEB/95[42]564, *reviewed by* Gary W. Gallagher, CWNEWS:NOV/89[4], *reviewed by* Robert Swope
Matthews, Richard E.:
THE 149TH PENNSYLVANIA VOLUNTEER INFANTRY UNIT IN THE CIVIL WAR, CWM:OCT/95[10], *reviewed by* Scott C. Patchan, CWNEWS:APR/95[33], *reviewed by* Frank J. Piatek, CWR:VOL4#3[37]
LEHIGH COUNTY PENNSYLVANIA IN THE CIVIL WAR, AN ACCOUNT, CWNEWS:MAY/92[4], *reviewed by* Michael Cavanaugh
Mattocks, Charles, (edited by Philip N. Racine); *"UNSPOILED HEART"; THE JOURNAL OF CHARLES MATTOCKS OF THE 17TH MAINE,* CWM:AUG/95[45], *reviewed by* Gary W. Gallagher, CWR:VOL4#3[37], CWR:VOL4#4[129], *reviewed by* Ted Alexander
McAfee, Michael J.; *ZOUAVES: THE FIRST AND THE BRAVEST,* CWNEWS:NOV/91[4], *reviewed by* Kathryn Jorgensen, CWNEWS:AUG/92[4], *reviewed by* Dr. Richard A. Sauers

McCarley, J. Britt; *THE ATLANTA CAMPAIGN — A CIVIL WAR DRIVING TOUR*, CWNEWS:NOV/90[4], *reviewed by* Kemp Burpeau

McCarthy, Carlton; *DETAILED MINUTIAE OF SOLDIER LIFE IN THE ARMY OF NORTHERN* VIRGINIA 1861-1865, CWNEWS:DEC/95[29], *reviewed by* Frank J. Piatek

McClellan, General George B., (edited by Stephen W. Sears): *THE CIVIL WAR PAPERS OF GEORGE B. MCCLELLAN: SELECTED CORRESPONDENCE, 1860-1865*, CWM:FEB/95[42]564, *reviewed by* Gary W. Gallagher, CWNEWS:JUN/90[4], *reviewed by* Dr. Allen Guelzo

MCCLELLAN'S OWN STORY, CWM:JUN/95[6], *reviewed by* William J. Miller

McClellan, Henry B.; *I ROAD WITH JEB STUART: THE LIFE AND CAMPAIGNS OF MAJOR GENERAL J.E.B. STUART*, CWM:AUG/95[45], *reviewed by* Gary W. Gallagher

McClure, A. K.; *THE ANNALS OF THE WAR, WRITTEN BY LEADING PARTICIPANTS NORTH AND SOUTH*, CWM:FEB/95[42]564, *reviewed by* Gary W. Gallagher

McConnell, Stuart; *GLORIOUS CONTENTMENT: THE GRAND ARMY OF THE REPUBLIC, 1865-1900*, CWM:JUN/94[6], *reviewed by* William J. Miller, CWNEWS:NOV/94[33], *reviewed by* Allen C. Guelzo

McCutchan, Kenneth P.; *DEAREST LIZZIE: THE CIVIL WAR LETTERS OF LT. COL. JAMES MAYNARD SHANKLIN*, CWNEWS:OCT/89[4], *reviewed by* Frank Piatek

McDonald, Cornelia Peake, (edited by Minrose C. Gwinn);*A WOMAN'S CIVIL WAR: A DIARY, WITH REMINISCENCES OF THE WAR, FROM MARCH 1862*, CWM:APR/95[50], *reviewed by* Gary W. Gallagher, CWTI:JAN/93[12]

McDonald, Archie, (edited by); *A NATION OF SOVERIGN STATES: SECESSION AND WAR IN THE CONFEDERACY*, CWNEWS:AUG/95[33], *reviewed by* Stephen D. Engle

McDonough, James L.: *STONES RIVER: BLOODY WINTER IN TENNESSEE*, ACW:MAR/91[54]

WAR IN KENTUCKY: FROM SHILOH TO PERRYVILLE, ACW:SEP/95[62], *reviewed by* Kenneth P. Czech, B&G:AUG/95[38], *reviewed by* Steven E. Woodworth, CWR:VOL4#2[136], *reviewed by* Theodore P. Savas, CWR:VOL4#3[37]

McDowell, Don; *THE BEAT OF THE DRUM*, CWNEWS:DEC/94[33], *reviewed by* Mark Stephens

McFeely, William S.: *FREDERICK DOUGLASS*, CWNEWS:JUL/92[4], *reviewed by* Gregory J.W. Urwin, CWTI:SEP/91[10], *reviewed by* Sarah W. Wiggins

GRANT: A BIOGRAPHY, AHI:DEC/81[48], *reviewed by* Maury Klein

PERSONAL / SELECTED LETTERS OF ULYSSES S. GRANT, AHI:JAN/91[8]

McGlone, John, (edited by); *JOURNAL OF CONFEDERATE HISTORY*, CWNEWS:NOV/90[4], *reviewed by* David F. Riggs

McGuire, Judith W.; *DIARY OF A SOUTHERN REFUGEE*, CWNEWS:MAY/89[4], *reviewed by* Terrence Winschel

McIlvaine, Samuel, (edited by Clayton E. Cramer); *BY THE DIM AND FLARING LAMPS: THE CIVIL WAR DIARY OF SAMUEL MCILVAINE, FEBRUARY THROUGH JUNE 1862*, CWNEWS:JUL/92[4], *reviewed by* Dr. Allen C. Cuelzo

McKay, Ernest A.; *THE CIVIL WAR AND NEW YORK CITY*, CWM:JAN/91[35], CWNEWS:APR/92[4], *reviewed by* Kemp Burpeau

McKinney, Francis F.; *EDUCATION IN VIOLENCE: THE LIFE OF GEORGE H. THOMAS AND THE HISTORY OF THE ARMY OF THE CUMBERLAND*, CWM:SEP/91[58], *reviewed by* Charles R. Norville, CWNEWS:AUG/92[4], *reviewed by* Richard M. McMurry

McKinney, Tim; *ROBERT E. LEE AT SEWELL MOUNTAIN: THE WEST VIRGINIA CAMPAIGN*, CWNEWS:OCT/92[4], *reviewed by* Michael Policatti

McLaurin, Melton A.; *CELIA, A SLAVE*, CWNEWS:APR/93[4], *reviewed by* John F. Marszalek

McLean, James L.: *CUTLER'S BRIGADE AT GETTYSBURG*, CWNEWS:FEB/95[33], *reviewed by* Michael Russert, CWR:VOL4#3[37]

GETTYSBURG SOURCES, VOLUME 3, CWNEWS:SEP/91[4], *reviewed by* Michael J. Winey

McMahon, John T., (edited by John M. Priest); *JOHN T. MCMAHON'S DIARY OF THE 136TH NEW YORK: 1861-1864*, CWNEWS:JAN/95[25], CWR:VOL3#2[105]

McMurray, Richard M.: *ARMY OF THE HEARTLAND*, CWM:APR/95[8], *reviewed by* Gary W. Gallagher

AUTUMN OF GLORY, CWM:APR/95[8], *reviewed by* Gary W. Gallagher

JOHN BELL HOOD AND THE WAR FOR SOUTHERN INDEPENDENCE, AHI:NOV/83[46], *reviewed by* Emory M. Thomas, CWM:FEB/95[42], *reviewed by* Gary W. Gallagher, CWM:APR/95[8], *reviewed by* Gary W. Gallagher, CWNEWS:AUG/93[5], *reviewed by* Kemp Burpeau

TWO GREAT REBEL ARMIES: AN ESSAY IN CONFEDERATE MILITARY HISTORY, CWM:APR/95[8], *reviewed by* Gary W. Gallagher, CWM:FEB/95[42], *reviewed by* Gary W. Gallagher, CWNEWS:NOV/89[4], *reviewed by* Michael Mullins

McPherson, James M.: *THE ABOLITIONIST LEGACY: FROM RECONSTRUCTION TO THE NAACP*, AHI:JUL/78[42]

ABRAHAM LINCOLN AND THE SECOND AMERICAN REVOLUTION, CWM:MAY/91[34], *reviewed by* Edward C. Smith, CWNEWS:JUN/92[4], *reviewed by* Jeffry D. Wert, CWTI:AUG/91[18], *reviewed by* Harold Holzer

THE ATLAS OF THE CIVIL WAR, AHI:JUN/95[28], CWNEWS:APR/95[33], *reviewed by* Blake A. Magner, CWTI:JUN/95[24]

GETTYSBURG: THE PAINTINGS OF MORT KUNSTLER, CWNEWS:JUN/95[33], *reviewed by* Kevin J. Weddle

IMAGES OF THE CIVIL WAR MH:FEB/93[77]

ORDEAL BY FIRE: THE CIVIL WAR AND RECONSTRUCTION, AHI:NOV/82[9], *reviewed by* Edward G. Longacre

WHAT THEY FOUGHT FOR, 1861-1865, ACW:NOV/94[66], *reviewed by* Ken Bivin, CWNEWS:JUL/95[61], *reviewed by* Allen C. Guelzo, CWR:VOL4#1[78], *reviewed by* Glenn W. LaFantasie, CWR:VOL4#3[37], CWTI:SEP/94[18], *reviewed by* Herman M. Hattaway

McWhiney, Grady: *ATTACK AND DIE: CIVIL WAR MILITARY TACTICS AND THE SOUTHERN HERITAGE*, CWM:FEB/95[42]564, *reviewed by* Gary W. Gallagher

BATTLE IN THE WILDERNESS: GRANT MEETS LEE, CWNEWS:DEC/95[29], *reviewed by* Ted Alexander

LEE'S DISPATCHES: UNPUBLISHED LETTERS OF GENERAL ROBERT E. LEE, C.S.A. TO JEFFERSON DAVIS

AND THE WAR DEPARTMENT OF THE CONFEDERATE STATES OF AMERICA, 1862-65, CWM:AUG/95[45]

Meade, General George G.:
THE BATTLE OF GETTYSBURG, CWNEWS:JAN/90[4], *reviewed by* Richard Sauers
THE LIFE AND LETTERS OF GENERAL GEORGE G. MEADE, CWM:DEC/94[7], *reviewed by* Gary W. Gallagher, CWM:FEB/95[42], *reviewed by* Gary W. Gallagher, CWR:VOL4#3[37]

Meade, Robert Douthat; *JUDAH P. BENJAMIN: CONFEDERATE STATESMAN,* CWNEWS:JUL/91[4], *reviewed by* Thomas E. Schott

Melcher, Holman S., (edited by William B. Styple); *WITH A FLASH OF HIS SWORD, THE WRITINGS OF MAJOR HOLMAN S. MELCHER, 20TH MAINE INFANTRY,* B&G:DEC/94[28], *reviewed by* Richard Rollins, CWNEWS:JUL/94[25], *reviewed by* Blake A. Magner

Mellon, James; *THE FACE OF LINCOLN,* CWTI:DEC/95[38]

Melton, Jack W. Jr.; *INTRODUCTION TO FIELD ARTILLERY ORDNANCE 1861-1865: A PICTORIAL STUDY OF CIVIL WAR ARTILLERY PROJECTILES,* B&G:FEB/95[26], *reviewed by* Dean S. Thomas

Melvin, John, (edited by Allen Peskin); *NORTH INTO FREEDOM: THE AUTOBIOGRAPHY OF JOHN MALVIN, FREE NEGRO, 1795-1880,* CWNEWS:MAY/89[4], *reviewed by* J. Tracy Power

Merideth, Lee W., (compiled by):
CIVIL WAR TIMES AND CIVIL WAR TIMES ILLUSTRATED 30 YEAR COMPREHENSIVE INDEX (APRIL 1859-FEBRUARY 1989), CWNEWS:APR/91[4], *reviewed by* Kathryn Jorgensen
THE GUIDE TO CIVIL WAR PERIODICALS, VOLUME I, 1991, B&G:JUN/92[28], *reviewed by* David Roth, CWM:MAY/92[59], *reviewed by* Thomas A. Lewis, CWNEWS:APR/91[4], *revieded by* Katheryn Jorgenson, CWR:VOL2#2[169], *reviewed by* Col. Milton B. Halsey

Merli, Frank J.; *GREAT BRITAIN AND THE CONFEDERATE NAVY, 1861-1865,* AHI:JAN/75[50], *reviewed by* Jon M. Nielson

Merrick, Morgan W., (edited by Jerry D. Thompson); *FROM DESERT TO BAYOU: THE CIVIL WAR JOURNAL AND SKETCHES OF MORGAN WOLFE MERRICK,* B&G:OCT/92[30], *reviewed by* Nat C. Hughes Jr, CWNEWS:APR/92[4], *reviewed by* Anne J. Bailey

Merrill, James M.; *SPURS TO GLORY; THE STORY OF THE UNITED STATES CAVALRY,* AHI:FEB/67[57], *reviewed by* Ralph Adams Brown

Meyer, Steve; *IOWA VALOR,* CWM:OCT/95[10], *reviewed by* David A. Woodbury

Middleton, Lee; *HEARTS OF FIRE: SOLDIER WOMEN OF THE CIVIL WAR,* CWNEWS:AUG/94[33], *reviewed by* Linda G. Black

Miers, Earl Schenck, (edited by); *LINCOLN DAY BY DAY,* CWTI:DEC/95[38]

Miles, Jim:
FIELDS OF GLORY, A HISTORY AND TOUR GUIDE TO THE ATLANTA CAMPAIGN, CWNEWS:SEP/93[5], *reviewed by* John F. Marszalek
PATHS TO VICTORY: A HISTORY AND TOUR GUIDE OF THE STONES RIVER, CHICKAMAUGA, CHATTANOOGA, KNOXVILLE AND NASHVILLE CAMPAIGNS, CWNEWS:AUG/94[33], *reviewed by* Richard M. McMurry
PIERCING THE HEARTLAND: A HISTORY AND TOUR GUIDE OF THE FORT DONELSON, SHILOH, AND

PERRYVILLE CAMPAIGNS, CWNEWS:AUG/94[33], *reviewed by* Richard M. McMurry
TO THE SEA, A HISTORY AND TOUR GUIDE OF SHERMAN'S MARCH, CWNEWS:SEP/93[5], *reviewed by* John F. Marszalek

Miles, Nelson A.; *PERSONAL RECOLLECTIONS & OBSERVATIONS OF GENERAL NELSON A. MILES,* CWNEWS:DEC/94[33], *reviewed by* Norman E. Rourke

Miller, Edward A. Jr.; *GULLAH STATESMAN, ROBERT SMALLS FROM SLAVERY TO CONGRESS, 1839-1915,* CWNEWS:JUL/95[61], *reviewed by* John F. Marszalek

Miller, Howard; *ABRAHAM LINCOLN'S FLAG,* CWNEWS:NOV/95[29], *reviewed by* Steven J. Wright

Miller, Richard F.; *THE CIVIL WAR: THE NANTUCKET EXPERIENCE,* CWNEWS:MAY/95[33], *reviewed by* Blake A. Magner, MH:AUG/95[70]

Miller, William J.:
MAPPING FOR STONEWALL: THE CIVIL WAR SERVICE OF JED HOTCHKISS, B&G:DEC/94[28], *reviewed by* Archie P. McDonald, CWNEWS:FEB/94[5], *reviewed by* Blake A. Magner
THE PENINSULA CAMPAIGN OF 1862: YORKTOWN TO THE SEVEN DAYS, VOLUME ONE, CWNEWS:JUN/94[5], *reviewed by* Michael Russert
THE PENINSULA CAMPAIGN OF 1862: YORKTOWN TO THE SEVEN DAYS, VOLUME II, CWM:APR/95[50], *reviewed by* Gary W. Gallagher, CWNEWS:AUG/95[33], *reviewed by* Ethan Rafuse
THE TRAINING OF AN ARMY: CAMP CURTIN AND THE NORTH'S CIVIL WAR, B&G:JUN/91[22], *reviewed by* Richard A. Sauers, CWNEWS:NOV/91[4], *reviewed by* Frank J. Piatek, CWM:JAN/91[47], *reviewed by* Gary W. Gallagher

Mills, Gary B.; *SOUTHERN LOYALISTS IN THE CIVIL WAR: THE SOUTHERN CLAIMS COMMISSION,* CWNEWS:MAY/95[33], *reviewed by* Michael A. Cavanaugh, CWR:VOL4#3[37]

Mills, George H.; *THE HISTORY OF THE 16TH NORTH CAROLINA REGIMENT IN THE CIVIL WAR,* CWNEWS:JUN/94[5], *reviewed by* Allen Guelzo, CWR:VOL3#2[105], *reviewed by* Michael Russert

Mills, Robert L.; *IT DIDN'T HAPPEN THE WAY YOU THINK. THE LINCOLN ASSASSINATION: WHAT THE EXPERTS MISSED,* CWNEWS:OCT/94[33], *reviewed by* Seven J. Wright

Mitchell, Reid; *THE VACANT CHAIR: THE NORTHERN SOLDIER LEAVES HOME,* CWM:APR/94[51], *reviewed by* John M. Priest, CWNEWS:MAY/94[5], *reviewed by* Spencer Gill, CWR:VOL4#1[78], *reviewed by* John F. Marszalek

Mitchell, Silas W.; *GUNSHOT WOUNDS AND OTHER INJURIES OF NERVES,* CWNEWS:NOV/90[4], *reviewed by* Dr. Harris D. Riley Jr.

Mitgang, Herbert, (edited by); *ABRAHAM LINCOLN: A PRESS PORTRAIT,* CWNEWS:APR/91[4], *reviewed by* Michael Russert

Moe, Richard; *THE LAST FULL MEASURE: THE LIFE AND DEATH OF THE FIRST MINNESOTA VOLUNTEERS,* ACW:JAN/94[62], *reviewed by* Jon Guttman, B&G:APR/94[24], *reviewed by* Theodore P. Savas, CWM:JAN/93[57], CWNEWS:SEP/93[5], *reviewed by* Kevin E. O'Brien, CWR:VOL4#3[1], *reviewed by* Craig L. Symonds, CWR:VOL4#3[1], *reviewed by* Steven E. Woodworth, CWTI:NOV/93[14], *reviewed by* Frank Jossi

Moebs, Thomas T.; *CONFEDERATE STATES NAVY RESEARCH GUIDE,* CWNEWS:SEP/93[5], *reviewed by* Gary Augustine

Mohr, James C., (edited by); *THE CORMANY DIARIES: A NORTHERN FAMILY IN THE CIVIL WAR,* AHI:MAY/83[48], *reviewed by* Reid Mitchell

Moneyhon, Carl H.; *THE IMPACT OF THE CIVIL WAR AND RECONSTRUCTION ON ARKANSAS,* CWM:AUG/95[45], *reviewed by* Gary W. Gallagher

Morford, T.C.; *FIFTY YEARS AGO: A BRIEF HISTORY OF THE 29TH REGIMENT NEW JERSEY VOLUNTEERS IN THE CIVIL WAR,* CWNEWS:NOV/91[4], *reviewed by* William Marvel

Morga, William James; *AUTOBIOGRAPHY OF READ ADMIRAL CHARLES WILKES, U.S. NAVY, 1798-1877,* AHI:JUN/80[6], *reviewed by* Norman C. Delaney

Morgan, Sarah, (edited by Charles East); *THE CIVIL WAR DIARY OF SARAH MORGAN,* B&G:APR/92[24], *reviewed by* Judy Anthis, CWNEWS:JAN/93[4], *reviewed by* Anne J. Bailey

Morris, Roy Jr.; *SHERIDAN: THE LIFE AND WARS OF GENERAL PHIL SHERIDAN,* CWTI:SEP/92[18], *reviewed by* Edward Longacre

Morrow, John A.; *THE CONFEDERATE WHITWORTH SHARPSHOOTERS,* CWNEWS:APR/92[4], *reviewed by* Gary Augustine

Morsberger, Robert E.; *LEW WALLACE: MILITANT ROMANTIC,* AHI:MAR/82[49], *reviewed by* John S. Patterson

Morton, John Watson; *THE ARTILLERY OF NATHAN BEDFORD FORREST'S CAVALRY,* CWNEWS:JAN/90[4], *reviewed by* Dr. Allen C. Guelzo

Mosby, John S., (edited by Charles W. Russell); *THE MEMOIRS OF JOHN S. MOSBY,* CWR:VOL1#3[94], *reviewed by* Theodore P. Savas

Moskow, Shirley B.; *EMMA'S WORLD: AN INITMATE LOOK AT LIVES TOUCHED BY THE CIVIL WAR ERA,* CWNEWS:MAY/92[4], *reviewed by* Sarah W. Wiggins

Motts, Wayne E.; *"TRUST IN GOD AND FEAR NOTHING": GENERAL LEWIS A ARMISTEAD, C.S.A.,* CWNEWS:MAY/95[33], *reviewed by* Michael Russert

Mudd, Joseph A.; *WITH PORTER IN NORTH MISSOURI: A CHAPTER IN THE HISTORY OF THE WAR BETWEEN THE STATES,* B&G:FEB/93[36], *reviewed by* Donal J. Stanton, CWNEWS:DEC/92[4], *reviewed by* Larry J. Daniel

Muffly, J.W.; *THE STORY OF OUR REGIMENT A HISTORY OF THE 148TH PENNSYLVANIA VOLUNTEERS,* CWR:VOL4#3[1], *reviewed by* Brian C. Pohanka, CWR:VOL4#3[37]

Muir, Doroth T.; *MOUNT VERNON: THE CIVIL WAR YEARS,* CWNEWS:OCT/94[33], *reviewed by* Blake A. Magner

Mulholland, St. Clair A.; *THE STORY OF THE 116TH REGIMENT PENNSYLVANIA INFANTRY,* CWNEWS:JAN/92[4], *reviewed by* Dr. Allen C. Guelzo

Mullinax, Steve E.; *CONFEDERATE BELT BUCKLES & PLATES,* CWNEWS:OCT/92[4], *reviewed by* Michael J. Winey

Mullins, Michael A.:
AMERICAN NEGRO SLAVERY: A DOCUMENTARY HISTORY, AHI:FEB/77[49], *reviewed by* Bell I. Wiley
THE FREMONT RIFLES: A HISTORY OF THE 37TH ILLINOIS VETERAN VOLUNTEER INFANTRY, CWNEWS:JUL/90[4], *reviewed by* James I. Robertson Jr.

Mumma, Wilmer M.:
ANTIETAM, THE AFTERMATH, CWNEWS:APR/94[5], *reviewed by* Blake A. Magner
OUT OF THE PAST, CWNEWS:APR/94[5], *reviewed by* Blake A. Magner

Mundy, James H.; *SECOND TO NONE: THE STORY OF THE 2D MAINE VOLUNTEERS, "THE BANGOR REGIMENT",* CWNEWS:JUL/93[5], *reviewed by* Kevin E. O'brien, CWR:VOL4#1[78], *reviewed by* Andrew MacIsaac, CWTI:NOV/92[10]

Murphy, James B.; *L.Q.C. LAMAR: PRAGMATIC PATRIOT,* AHI:OCT/73[49], *reviewed by* Richard M. McMurry

Murphy, Jim:
THE BOYS' WAR ACW:MAR/92[54], *reviewed by* Kenneth P. Czech
THE LONG ROAD TO GETTYSBURG, CWNEWS:AUG/93[5], *reviewed by* Allen C. Guelzo

Murray, Alton J.; *SOUTH GEORGIA REBELS: THE 26TH GEORGIA VOLUNTEER INFANTRY,* CWNEWS:MAY/92[4], *reviewed by* Dale K. Phillips

Myers, Robert M.; *THE CHILDREN OF PRIDE: A TRUE STORY OF GEORGIA AND THE CIVIL WAR,* AHI:APR/85[7]

Nagel, Paul C.; *THE LEES OF VIRGINIA,* CWNEWS:JUL/92[4], *reviewed by* Linda L. Breedlove

Nash, Eugene; *A HISTORY OF THE FORTY-FOURTH REGIMENT NEW YORK VOLUNTEER INFANTRY,* CWNEWS:AUG/90[4], *reviewed by* William F. Howard

National Geographic Society; *THE CIVIL WAR,* AHI:DEC/87[6]

National Park Service:
APPOMATTOX COURT HOUSE, AHI:OCT/87[10]
FORT SUMTER, AHI:OCT/87[10]
LINCOLN MEMORIAL, AHI:OCT/87[10]

Neal, Diane; *THE LION OF THE SOUTH: GENERAL THOMAS C. HINDMAN,* B&G:JUN/94[34], *reviewed by* Larry J. Daniel, CWM:APR/95[50], *reviewed by* Gary W. Gallagher, CWNEWS:DEC/94[33], *reviewed by* Michael Cavanaugh, CWR:VOL4#1[78], *reviewed by* Stephen D. Engle

Neely, Mark E. Jr., (edited by Herb S. Crumb):
THE FATE OF LIBERTY: ABRAHAM LINCOLN AND CIVIL LIBERTIES, CWTI:DEC/95[38], CWNEWS:OCT/92[4], *reviewed by* Kemp Burpeau, CWNEWS:NOV/92[4], *reviewed by* William Marvel,
THE LAST BEST HOPE OF EARTH: ABRAHAM LINCOLN AND THE PROMISE OF AMERICA, AHI:JAN/94[20]
THE LINCOLN FAMILY, CWNEWS:JUN/92[4], *reviewed by* Kale K. Phillips
THE LINCOLN IMAGE, CWTI:DEC/95[38]
MINE EYES HAVE SEEN THE GLORY: THE CIVIL WAR IN ART, AHI:MAR/94[23], AHI:MAY/94[58], *reviewed by* Lori Anne Dickens, CWN:NOV/95[29], *reviewed by* Douglas Kinnett

Neff, Robert O.; *TENNESSEE'S BATTERED BRIGADIER: THE LIFE OF GENERAL JOSEPH B. PALMER,* B&G:OCT/93[24], *reviewed by* Paul Kallina, CWM:JUL/93[51], *reviewed by* Richard M. McMurry, CWNEWS:APR/91[4], *reviewed by* Matthew Penrod, CWNEWS:OCT/92[4], *reviewed by* Blake Magner, CWNEWS:SEP/93[5], *reviewed by* Blake A. Magner

Nelson, Jacquelyn S.; *INDIANA QUAKERS CONFRONT THE CIVIL WAR,* B&G:FEB/93[36], *reviewed by* Benedict R. Maryniak

Nelson, Truman; *THE OLD MAN: JOHN BROWN AT HARPERS FERRY,* AHI:JAN/75[50], *reviewed by* Allan Keller

Nesbitt, Mark:
35 DAYS TO GETTYSBURG: THE CAMPAIGN DIARIES OF TWO AMERICAN ENEMIES, ACW:MAR/93[58], *reviewed by* Robert I. Alotta, B&G:OCT/93[24], *reviewed by* D. Scott

Hartwig, CWNEWS:JUL/93[5], *reviewed by* Dr. Richard A. Sauers, CWR:VOL2#4[346], *reviewed by* Michael Russert

GHOSTS OF GETTYSBURG, CWNEWS:SEP/93[5], *reviewed by* Blake A. Magner

SABER AND SCAPEGOAT: J.E.B. STUART AND THE GETTYSBURG CONTROVERSY, B&G:JUN/95[30], *reviewed by* Theodore C. Mahr, CWM:AUG/95[8], *reviewed by* John Divine, CWNEWS:MAY/95[33], *reviewed by* Jeffry D. Wert

Ness, George T.; *THE REGULAR ARMY ON THE EVE OF THE CIVIL WAR*, CWNEWS:APR/92[4], *reviewed by* Richard M. McMurry

Nevins, Allen; *FREMONT, PATHMAKER OF THE WEST*, CWNEWS:SEP/93[5], *reviewed by* Norman E. Rourke

Newton, Steven H.; *THE BATTLE OF SEVEN PINES*, CWM:JUN/95[6], *reviewed by* Gary W. Gallagher

Nichols, Isaac T.; *CUMBERLAND COUNTY AND SOUTH JERSEY DURING THE CIVIL WAR*, CWNEWS:JUN/94[5], *reviewed by* Blake A. Magner

Nichols, James L.; *GENERAL FITZHUGH LEE*, CWNEWS:JAN/91[4], *reviewed by* Ron Rago

Nicolay, John G.; *ABRAHAM LINCOLN: A HISTORY*, CWTI:DEC/95[38]

Niven, John; *JOHN C. CALHOUN AND THE PRICE OF UNION: A BIOGRAPHY*, CWNEWS:AUG/90[4], *reviewed by* Michael Parrish

Niven, John; *SALMON P. CHASE: A BIOGRAPHY*, CWM:DEC/95[10], *reviewed by* Carmen Brissett Grayson

Noe, Kenneth W.; *SOUTHWEST VIRGINIA'S RAILROAD: MODERNIZATION AND THE SECTIONAL CRISIS*, CWM:AUG/95[45], *reviewed by* Gary W. Gallagher

Nofi, Albert A.:
A CIVIL WAR TREASURY: BEING A MISCELLANY OF ARMS AND ARTILLERY, FACTS AND FIGURES, LEGENDS AND LORE, MUSES AND MINSTRELS AND PERSONALITIES AND PEOPLE, B&G:JUN/93[28], *reviewed by* Rod Gragg, CWNEWS:AUG/93[5], *reviewed by* Barry Popchock, CWTI:MAY/93[18]

THE CIVIL WAR NOTEBOOK: A COLLECTION OF LITTLE-KNOWN FACTS AND OTHER ODDS-AND-ENDS ABOUT THE CIVIL WAR, CWNEWS:APR/94[5], *reviewed by* Michael Russert, CWTI:JAN/94[10]

THE GETTYSBURG CAMPAIGN: JUNE-JULY 1863 (REVISED EDITION), CWNEWS:APR/94[5], *reviewed by* Kevin E. O'Brien

Nolan, Alan T.:
THE IRON BRIGADE, CWR:VOL4#3[1], *reviewed by* Craig L. Symonds

LEE CONSIDERED: GENERAL ROBERT E. LEE AND CIVIL WAR HISTORY, ACW:NOV/91[54], *reviewed by* Phil Noblitt, B&G:FEB/92[26], *reviewed by* Dennie E. Frye, CWM:JUL/91[58], *reviewed by* Gary W. Gallagher, CWM:JAN/92[57], *reviewed by* Gary W. Gallagher, CWNEWS:SEP/91[4], *reviewed by* Richard M. McMurry, CWTI:DEC/91[12], *reviewed by* Mark Grimsley

Nolan, Dick; *BENJAMIN FRANKLIN BUTLER: THE DAMNEDEST YANKEE*, CWNEWS:SEP/92[4], *reviewed by* William Marvel

Norton, Oliver W.; *THE ATTACK AND DEFENSE OF LITTLE ROUND TOP*, AHI:AUG/78[49], *reviewed by* Edward G. Longacre

Nulty, William H.; *CONFEDERATE FLORIDA: THE ROAD TO OLUSTEE*, B&G:AUG/91[26], *reviewed by* Arch F. Blakey, CWM:JAN/91[47], *reviewed by* Gary W. Gallagher,

CWNEWS:MAY/92[4], *reviewed by* Kemp Burpeau, CWNEWS:JUN/94[5], *reviewed by* Stephen D. Engle

Numbers, Ronald L., (edited by); *SCIENCE AND MEDICINE IN THE OLD SOUTH*, CWTI:DEC/89[20]

O'Reilly, Frank A.; *"STONEWALL" JACKSON AT FREDERICKSBURG: THE BATTLE OF PROSPECT HILL, DECEMBER 13, 1862*, CWM:FEB/95[7], *reviewed by* David A. Woodbury

Oates, Stephen B.:
A WOMAN OF VALOR: CLARA BARTON AND THE CIVIL WAR, AHI:APR/95[26], CWM:APR/95[8], *reviewed by* Jim Percoco, CWTI:MAR/94[38]37

ABRAHAM LINCOLN: THE MAN BEHIND THE MYTHS, AHI:SEP/84[50]

TO PURGE THIS LAND WITH BLOOD, AHI:NOV/70[48], *reviewed by* Robert D. Hoffsommer

WITH MALICE TOWARD NONE: THE LIFE OF ABRAHAM LINCOLN, AHI:AUG/77[49], CWTI:DEC/95[38]

THE WAR BETWEEN THE UNION AND THE CONFEDERACY AND ITS LOST OPPORTUNITIES WITH A HISTORY OF THE 15TH ALABAMA REGIMENT AND THE FORTY-EIGHT BATTLES IN WHICH IT WAS ENGAGED, CWR:VOL2#4[346], *reviewed by* Glenn LaFantasie

Olsen, Bernard A., (editor); *UPON TENTED FIELD: AN HISTORICAL ACCOUNT OF THE CIVIL WAR AS TOLD BY THE MEN WHO FOUGHT AND GAVE THEIR LIVES*, B&G:AUG/94[30], *reviewed by* Chris Calkins, CWNEWS:OCT/94[33], *reviewed by* Stephen D. Engle

Omenhausser, John J., (edited by Ross M. Kimmel); *SKETCHES FROM PRISON: A CONFEDERATE ARTIST'S RECORD OF LIFE AT POINT LOOKOUT PRISONER OF WAR CAMP, 1863-1865*, CWNEWS:JUN/92[4], *reviewed by* Michael Mull

Osborne, Charles C.; *JUBAL: THE LIFE AND TIMES OF JUBAL A. EARLY, CSA, DEFENDER OF THE LOST CAUSE*, B&G:FEB/94[36], *reviewed by* J. Tracy Power, CWM:NOV/92[55], CWNEWS:JUN/93[5], *reviewed by* Kevin J. Weddle, CWTI:JAN/93[12], *reviewed by* Jeffry D. Wert

Osborne, Seward R.; *THE CIVIL WAR DIARIES OF COL. THEODORE B. GATES, 20TH NEW YORK STATE MILITIA*, CWNEWS:JUN/92[4], *reviewed by* Richard A. Sauers, CWNEWS:AUG/93[5], *reviewed by* Brian Pohanka

Osborne, Thomas W., (edited by Herb S. Crumb):
THE ELEVENTH CORPS ARTILLERY AT GETTYSBURG: THE PAPERS OF MAJOR THOMAS WARD OSBORNE, CWNEWS:OCT/92[4], *reviewed by* Michael J. Winey

NO MIDDLE GROUND: THOMAS WARD OSBORN'S LETTERS FROM THE FIELD (1862-1864), B&G:FEB/95[26], *reviewed by* Philip N. Racine, CWNEWS:MAY/95[33], *reviewed by* Michael J. Winey

Owen, William M.; *IN CAMP AND BATTLE WITH THE WASHINGTON ARTILLERY*, CWR:VOL4#3[1], *reviewed by* John M. Coski

Owens, Leslie H.; *THIS SPECIES OF PROPERTY: SLAVE LIFE AND CULTURE IN THE OLD SOUTH*, AHI:FEB/77[49], *reviewed by* Bell I. Wiley

Owsley, Frank; *KING COTTON DIPLOMACY*, AHI:JAN/75[50], *reviewed by* Jon M. Nielson

Packard, John H.; *A MANUAL OF MINOR SURGERY*, CWNEWS:SEP/91[4], *reviewed by* Harris D. Riley

Page, Dave; *SHIPS VERSUS SHORE: CIVIL WAR ENGAGEMENTS ALONG SOUTHERN SHORES AND RIVERS,* CWTI:JUN/95[24]

Palfrey, Francis W.; *THE ANTIETAM AND FREDERICKSBURG,* CWNEWS:JAN/91[4], *reviewed by* Judy Yandoh

Palladino, Grace; *ANOTHER CIVIL WAR; LABOR, CAPITAL, AND THE STATE IN THE ANTHRACITE REGIONS OF PENNSYLVANIA, 1840-68,* CWM:JAN/91[47], *reviewed by* Gary W. Gallagher

Palmer, Beverly W.; *THE SELECTED LETTERS OF CHARLES SUMNER,* CWM:JAN/91[47], *reviewed by* Gary W. Gallagher

Paludan, Philip S.:
"A PEOPLE'S CONTEST:" THE UNION AND CIVIL WAR, 1861-1865, CWNEWS:JUN/90[4], *reviewed by* Mark A. Snell
THE PRESIDENCY OF ABRAHAM LINCOLN, CWTI:MAR/95[14]

Panger, Daniel; *SOLDIER BOYS,* CWNEWS:MAY/89[4], *reviewed by* Dr. Allen Guelzo

Parker, Thomas H.; *HISTORY OF THE 51ST REGIMENT OF P.V. AND V.V.,* CWR:VOL4#3[1], *reviewed by* Richard A. Sauers

Parks, Joseph H.:
GENERAL EDMUND KIRBY SMITH, C.S.A., CWNEWS:MAY/93[4], *reviewed by* Harris D. Riley Jr.
GENERAL LEONIDAS POLK, C.S.A., THE FIGHTING BISHOP, CWNEWS:JUN/93[5], *reviewed by* Norman E. Rourke

Parrish, Michael:
RICHARD TAYLOR: SOLDIER PRINCE OF DIXIE, ACW:MAY/93[54], *reviewed by* Nat C. Hughes, B&G:FEB/93[36], *reviewed by* Richard McMurry, CWM:SEP/93[51], *reviewed by* Keith A. Hardison, CWM:FEB/95[42]564, *reviewed by* Gary W. Gallagher, CWNEWS:OCT/93[5], *reviewed by* Theodore P. Savas, CWR:VOL2#4[346], *reviewed by* Arthur W. Bergeron Jr., CWTI:JUL/93[12], *reviewed by* Gerard Patterson

Parsons, David K.; *BUGLES ECHO ACROSS THE VALLEY: NORTHERN OSWEGO COUNTY, NEW YORK AND THE CIVIL WAR,* CWNEWS:JUL/95[61], *reviewed by* Michael Russert

Patterson, Gerard A.; *REBELS FROM WEST POINT,* AHI:APR/88[14]

Pauley, Michael J.; *UNRECONSTRUCTED REBEL: THE LIFE OF GENERAL JOHN MCCAUSLAND, C.S.A.,* CWNEWS:SEP/94[33], *reviewed by* Jerry Holsworth

Pember, Phoebe Yates; *A SOUTHERN WOMAN'S STORY,* CWR:VOL4#3[1], *reviewed by* Tom Broadfoot

Pender, William D., (edited by William W. Hassler); *THE GENERAL TO HIS LADY: THE CIVIL WAR LETTERS OF WILLIAM DORSEY PENDER TO FANNY PENDER,* CWM:FEB/95[42]564, *reviewed by* Gary W. Gallagher

Perret, Geoffrey; *A COUNTRY MADE BY WAR. FROM THE REVOLUTION TO VIETNAM — THE STORY OF AMERICA'S RISE TO POWER,* CWTI:DEC/89[20], *reviewed by* Richard Pindell

Peterson, Merrill D.; *LINCOLN IN AMERICAN MEMORY,* CWNEWS:JUN/95[33], *reviewed by* Spencer Gill

Peticolas, A.B., (edited by Don E. Alberts); *REBELS ON THE RIO GRANDE: THE CIVIL WAR JOURNAL OF A.B. PETICOLAS,* CWNEWS:AUG/94[33], *reviewed by* Norman E. Rourke

Pettit, Frederick, (edited by William G. Gavin); *INFANTRYMAN PETTIT: THE CIVIL WAR LETTERS OF CORPORAL FREDERICK PETTIT,* CWNEWS:MAY/92[4], *reviewed by* Steven J. Wright

Petty, Elijah P., (edited by Norman D. Brown); *JOURNEY TO PLEASANT HILL: THE CIVIL WAR LETTERS OF CAPTAIN ELIJAH P. PETTY, WALKER'S TEXAS DIVISION C.S.A.,* CWM:FEB/95[42]564, *reviewed by* Gary W. Gallagher

Pfanz, Donald C.:
ABRAHAM LINCOLN AT CITY POINT, CWNEWS:NOV/90[4], *reviewed by* William Blake
GETTYSBURG — CULP'S HILL AND CEMETERY HILL, B&G:OCT/94[40], *reviewed by* Wayne E. Motts, CWM:AUG/94[9], *reviewed by* J. Jeffery Cox, CWM:FEB/95[42], *reviewed by* Gary W. Gallagher, CWNEWS:APR/94[5], *reviewed by* Jeffry D. Wert, CWR:VOL3#4[68], *reviewed by* David P. Smith, CWTI:MAR/94[12], *reviewed by* Terry Shulman
GETTYSBURG — THE SECOND DAY, CWM:FEB/95[42], *reviewed by* Gary W. Gallagher

Phillips, Charles; *MY BROTHER'S FACE: PORTRAITS OF THE CIVIL WAR IN PHOTOGRAPHS, DIARIES AND LETTERS,* CWM:JUL/93[51], *reviewed by* Courtney Wilson, CWNEWS:OCT/93[5], *reviewed by* Michael J. Winey

Phillips, Christopher; *DAMNED YANKEE: THE LIFE OF GENERAL NATHANIEL LYON,* B&G:JUN/91[22], *reviewed by* John S. Peterson, CWM:JAN/91[47], *reviewed by* Gary W. Gallagher, CWNEWS:MAY/92[4], *reviewed by* Robert Norris Jr.

Phillips, David L.; *TIGER JOHN: THE REBEL WHO BURNED CHAMBERSBURG,* CWM:APR/95[50], *reviewed by* Gary W. Gallagher, CWNEWS:AUG/92[4], *reviewed by* Michael Cavanaugh, CWNEWS:JUL/94[25], *reviewed by* Ted Alexander

Phillips, Edward H.; *THE LOWER SHENANDOAH VALLEY IN THE CIVIL WAR: THE IMPACT OF WAR UPON THE CIVILIAN POPULATION AND UPON CIVIL INSTITUTIONS,* CWNEWS:AUG/94[33], *reviewed by* David F. Rigg

Phipps, Michael; *"THE DEVIL'S TO PAY": GENERAL JOHN BUFORD,* CWNEWS:OCT/95[33], *reviewed by* Michael Russert

Phoenix Militaria, Inc.; *AMERICAN MILITARY, SOURCEBOOK AND DIRECTORY THE WHO'S WHO IN MILITARIA,* CWNEWS:APR/90[4], *reviewed by* Russ A. Prichard

Pierce, Michael D.; *THE MOST PROMISING YOUNG OFFICER: A LIFE OF RANALD SLIDELL MACKENZIE,* CWM:APR/95[50], *reviewed by* Gary W. Gallagher, CWNEWS:NOV/94[33], *reviewed by* Robert D. Norris Jr., CWTI:MAY/94[20], *reviewed by* Robert Barr Smith

Pinkerton, Allan; *THE SPY OF THE REBELLION,* CWNEWS:APR/91[4], *reviewed by* Frank Piatek

Piston, William G.; *LEE'S TARNISHED LIEUTENANT: JAMES LONGSTREET AND HIS PLACE IN SOUTHERN HISTORY,* AHI:APR/88[14]

Poe, Clarence, (edited by) *TRUE TALES OF THE SOUTH AT WAR, HOW SOLDIERS FOUGHT AND FAMILIIES LIVED, 1861-1865,* CWNEWS:OCT/95[33], *reviewed by* John F. Marszalek

Pohanka, Brian C.:
DISTANT THUNDER: A PHOTOGRAPHIC ESSAY ON THE AMERICAN CIVIL WAR, AHI:APR/89[10], CWNEWS:OCT/89[4], *reviewed by* Barry Popchock
DON TROIANI'S CIVIL WAR, CWNEWS:DEC/95[29], *reviewed by* Blake A. Magner

Pollard, William C., Jr.; *DARK FRIDAY: THE STORY OF QUANTRILL'S LAWRENCE RAID,* CWNEWS:JUL/92[4], *reviewed by* Harris D. Riley Jr.

Pond, George E.; *THE SHENANDOAH VALLEY IN 1864, THE CAMPAIGN OF SHERIDAN,* CWNEWS:MAY/91[4], *reviewed by* Steven J. Wright

Porter, Horace; *CAMPAIGNING WITH GRANT,* CWM:FEB/95[42]564, *reviewed by* Gary W. Gallagher

Potter, Jerry O.; *THE SULTANA TRAGEDY,* ACW:NOV/92[58], *reviewed by* Mike Haskew, B&G:APR/93[30], *reviewed by* William Marvel, CWNEWS:NOV/92[4], *reviewed by* Terrency J. Winschel, CWTI:JUL/92[10]

Powell, Lawrence N.; *NEW MASTERS: NORTHERN PLANTERS DURING THE CIVIL WAR AND RECONSTRUCTION,* AHI:DEC/80[7], *reviewed by* Larry Gara

Preston, Madge, (edited by Virginia Walcott Beauchamp); *A PRIVATE WAR, LETTERS AND DIARIES OF MADGE PRESTON 1862-1867,* CWNEWS:APR/90[4], *reviewed by* Judy Yandoh

Priest, John M.:
ANTIETAM: THE SOLDIER'S BATTLE, CWNEWS:JUN/90[4], *reviewed by* J. Tracy Power
BEFORE ANTIETAM: THE BATTLE FOR SOUTH MOUNTAIN, ACW:JUL/93[58], *reviewed by* Jon Guttman, CWNEWS:JUN/93[5], *reviewed by* Jeffry Wert, CWR:VOL3#2[105], *reviewed by* Theodore P. Savas
FROM NEW BERN TO FREDERICKSBURG: CAPTAIN JAMES WREN'S DIARY, ACW:NOV/91[54], *reviewed by* Jon Guttman
JOHN T. MCMAHON'S DIARY OF THE 136TH NEW YORK 1861-1865, CWR:VOL3#4[68], *reviewed by* Charles J. Jones

Pryor, Charles R.; *A POST OF HONOR: THE PRYOR LETTERS, 1861-63; LETTERS FROM CAPT. S. G. PRYOR, TWELFTH GEORGIA REGIMENT AND HIS WIFE, PENELOPE TYSON PRYOR,* CWM:FEB/95[42]564, *reviewed by* Gary W. Gallagher

Pullen, John J.:
A SHOWER OF STARS; THE MEDAL OF HONOR AND THE 27TH MAINE, AHI:FEB/67[57], *reviewed by* Ralph Adams Brown
THE TWENTIETH MAINE, AHI:FEB/67[57], *reviewed by* Ralph Adams Brown, CWR:VOL4#3[1], *reviewed by* William Marvel, CWR:VOL4#3[1], *reviewed by* Alan T. Nolan

Quarles, Benjamin; *ALLIES FOR FREEDOM: BLACKS AND JOHN BROWN,* AHI:AUG/75[50], *reviewed by* Allan Keller

Quigley, Robert D.; *CIVIL WAR SPOKEN HERE,* ACW:JAN/95[62], *reviewed by* Al Hemingway, CWR:VOL4#2[136], *reviewed by* Archie P. McDonald, CWTI:MAY/94[20]

Rable, George C.:
CIVIL WARS: WOMEN AND THE CRISIS OF SOUTHERN NATIONALISM, CWNEWS:AUG/90[4], *reviewed by* Judy Yandoh, CWTI:DEC/89[20]
THE CONFEDERATE REPUBLIC: A REVOLUTION AGAINST POLITICS, CWM:AUG/95[45], *reviewed by* Gary W. Gallaghe, CWNEWS:FEB/95[33], *reviewed by* Michael Parrish, CWR:VOL4#3[37]

Radley, Kenneth; *REBEL WATCHDOG: THE CONFEDERATE STATES ARMY PROVOST GUARD,* CWNEWS:JUL/90[4], *reviewed by* Michael Parrish

Ramage, James A.; *REBEL RAIDER: THE LIFE OF GENERAL JOHN HUNT MORGAN,* CWM:FEB/95[42]564, *reviewed by* Gary W. Gallagher

Randall,, James G.; *LINCOLN THE PRESIDENT,* CWTI:DEC/95[38]

Raphael, Morris; *A GUNBOAT NAMED <u>DIANA,</u>* CWNEWS:NOV/94[33], *reviewed by* Dale K. Phillips

Rawley, James A.; *THE POLITICS OF UNION: NORTHERN POLITICS DURING THE CIVIL WAR,* CWNEWS:SEP/91[4], *reviewed by* Kemp Burpeau

Rawls, Walton; *GREAT CIVIL WAR HEROES AND THEIR BATTLES,* AHI:MAY/86[6]

Ray, Frederic E.; *OUR SPECIAL ARTIST,* ACW:MAR/95[58], *reviewed by* Michael D. Hull

Reck, W. Emerson; *A. LINCOLN: HIS LAST 24 HOURS,* AHI:SEP/87[8], CWNEWS:JUN/92[4], *reviewed by* Terrence J. Winschel

Redding, Saunders; *THE NEGRO,* AHI:JUN/68[51], *reviewed by* Robert D. Hoffsommer

Reed, Rowena; *COMBINED OPERATIONS IN THE CIVIL WAR,* CWM:JUN/95[6], *reviewed by* William J. Miller, CWM:APR/95[50], *reviewed by* Gary W. Gallagher, CWNEWS:DEC/95[29], *reviewed by* Frank J. Piatek

Reese, Timothy J.; *SYKES' REGULAR INFANTRY DIVISION, 1861-1864: A HISTORY OF REGULAR UNITED STATES INFANTRY OPERATIONS IN THE CIVIL WAR'S EASTERN THEATER,* CWNEWS:JUL/91[4], *reviewed by* Richard M. McMurry, CWR:VOL1#3[94], *reviewed by* Col. M.B. Halsey

Regimental Studies ; *CIVIL WAR REGIMENTS: A JOURNAL OF THE AMERICAN CIVIL WAR,* CWM:MAR/91[42], *reviewed by* William J. Miller

Reid-Green, Marcia; *LETTERS HOME: HENRY MATRAU OF THE IRON BRIGADE,* CWNEWS:AUG/94[33], *reviewed by* Dr. Richard A. Sauers

Remini, Robert V.; *HENRY CLAY: STATESMAN FOR THE UNION,* CWNEWS:DEC/92[4], *reviewed by* Richard M. McMurry

Rhea, Gordon C.; *THE BATTLE OF THE WILDERNESS MAY 5-6, 1864,* B&G:APR/95[30], *reviewed by* Noah Andre Trudeau, CWM:AUG/95[45], *reviewed by* Gary W. Gallagher, CWNEWS:NOV/95[29], *reviewed by* Theodore P. Savas, CWR:VOL4#3[89], *reviewed by* Robert E. L. Krick

Rice, Ralsa C.; *YANKEE TIGERS: THROUGH THE CIVIL WAR WITH THE 125TH OHIO,* CWNEWS:JAN/94[5], *reviewed by* Barry Popchock

Rinhart, Floyd; *THE AMERICAN DAGUERREOTYPE,* AHI:FEB/82[9], *reviewed by* Frederic Ray

Roach, Harry; *GETTYSBURG HOUR-BY-HOUR,* CWNEWS:NOV/95[29], *reviewed by* Steven J. Wright

Robert's, Bobby; *PORTRAITS OF CONFLICT: A PHOTOGRAPHIC HISTORY OF MISSISSIPPI IN THE CIVIL WAR,* CWM:APR/95[50], *reviewed by* Gary W. Gallagher, CWNEWS:SEP/91[4], *reviewed by* Larry J. Daniel, CWNEWS:JAN/94[5], *reviewed by* Larry J. Daniel

Robertson, James I., Jr.:
CIVIL WAR VIRGINIA, BATTLEGROUND FOR A NATION, CWM:JUL/91[58], *reviewed by* Charles R. Norville, CWNEWS:AUG/92[4], *reviewed by* J. Tracy Power, CWNEWS:DEC/93[5], *reviewed by* Frank J. Piatek, CWTI:SEP/91[10]
CIVIL WAR! AMERICA BECOMES ONE NATION, CWM:NOV/92[55], CWNEWS:JAN/94[5], *reviewed by* Linda G. Black

GENERAL A.P. HILL: THE STORY OF A CONFEDERATE WARRIOR, CWM:FEB/95[42]564, *reviewed by* Gary W. Gallagher

SOLDIERS BLUE AND GRAY, CWNEWS:SEP/89[8], *reviewed by* Ron Rago, CWTI:MAY/89[44], *reviewed by* Terry L. Jones

Robertson, William G.:
BACK DOOR TO RICHMOND: THE BERMUDA HUNDRED CAMPAIGN, APRIL-JUNE 1864, CWTI:MAR/89[10], *reviewed by* Howard C. Westwood

THE BATTLE OF OLD MEN AND YOUNG BOYS, JUNE 9, 1864: THE PETERSBURG CAMPAIGN, CWNEWS:SEP/90[4], *reviewed by* Dave Riggs

THE PETERSBURG CAMPAIGN: THE BATTLE OF OLD MEN AND YOUNG BOYS, JUNE 9, 1864, CWM:JAN/91[47], *reviewed by* Gary W. Gallagher

Robinson, Charles M. III:
BAD HAND: A BIOGRAPHY OF GENERAL RANALD S. MACKENZIE, CWNEWS:JUL/94[25], *reviewed by* Michael Russert

SHARK OF THE CONFEDERACY: THE STORY OF THE CSS ALABAMA, ACW:JUL/95[58], *reviewed by* Jon Guttman

Robinson, Paul Dean; *TWO LADIES OF GETTYSBURG* AHI:JUL/74[50], *reviewed by*

Robinson, William M.; *THE CONFEDERATE PRIVATEERS,* CWM:JAN/91[47], *reviewed by* Gary W. Gallagher, CWNEWS:AUG/91[4], *reviewed by* Anne J. Bailey

Rodenbough, Theodore F.; *FROM EVERGLADE TO CANON WITH THE SECOND DRAGOONS,* CWR:VOL4#3[1], *reviewed by* William J. Miller

Roland, Charles P.:
ALBERT SIDNEY JOHNSTON: SOLDIER OF THREE REPUBLICS, CWM:FEB/95[42]564, *reviewed by* Gary W. Gallagher

THE AMERICAN ILIAD: THE STORY OF THE CIVIL WAR, B&G:FEB/92[26], *reviewed by* Brian C. Pohanka, CWM:JAN/92[57], *reviewed by* Gary W. Gallagher, CWNEWS:SEP/92[4], *reviewed by* Dr. Richard A. Sauers

Rollins, Richard, (edited by); *PICKETT'S CHARGE: EYEWITNESS ACCOUNTS,* CWNEWS:OCT/94[33], *reviewed by* Jeffry D. Wert

Roper, Laura Wood; *FLO: A BIOGRAPHY OF FREDERICK LAW OLMSTEAD,* AHI:MAY/74[49], *reviewed by* Lowell H. Harrison

Roper, Peter W.; *JEDEDIAH HOTCHKISS: REBEL MAPMAKER AND VIRGINIA BUSINESSMAN,* CWNEWS:APR/93[4], *reviewed by* Jeffry D. Wert, CWR:VOL2#3[256], *reviewed by* Robert E. L. Krick

Ropes, John C.; *THE ARMY UNDER POPE,* CWNEWS:JAN/91[4], *reviewed by* Judy Yandoh

Rosen, Robert N.; *CONFEDERATE CHARLESTON: AN ILLUSTRATED HISTORY OF THE CITY AND THE PEOPLE DURING THE CIVIL WAR,* CWNEWS:AUG/95[33], *reviewed by* John G. Secondari

Rosenblatt Emil, (edited by); *HARD MARCHING EVERY DAY: THE CIVIL WAR LETTERS OF PRIVATE WILBUR FISK, 1861-1865 (2ND VERMONT INFANTRY),* AHI:MAR/93[20], B&G:AUG/93[24], *reviewed by* Theodore P. Savas

Ross, Ishbel; *THE PRESIDENT'S WIFE: MARY TODD LINCOLN,* AHI:JAN/75[50], *reviewed by* Robert D. Hoffsommer

Ross, Lawrence S., (compiled by Perry W. Shelton); *PERSONAL CIVIL WAR LETTERS OF GENERAL LAWRENCE SULLIVAN ROSS,* CWNEWS:JUL/95[61], *reviewed by* Jerry W. Holsworth

Rowley, James A.; *TURNING POINTS OF THE CIVIL WAR,* CWNEWS:OCT/90[4], *reviewed by* Kemp Burpeau

Royster, Charles; *THE DESTRUCTIVE WAR — WILLIAM TECUMSEH SHERMAN, STONEWALL JACKSON, AND THE AMERICANS,* ACW:NOV/92[58], *reviewed by* Richard F. Welch, AHI:JAN/91[8], CWM:MAR/92[49], *reviewed by* John M. Priest, CWNEWS:OCT/92[4], *reviewed by* Kemp Burpeau, CWTI:MAY/92[18], *reviewed by* Mark Grimsley

Ruffin, Edmund, (edited by William K. Scarborough); *THE DIARY OF EDMUND RUFFIN, VOLUME III, A DREAM SHATTERED, JUNE, 1863-JUNE 1865,* CWNEWS:AUG/90[4], *reviewed by* Michael Mullins

Rushing, Anthony; *RANKS OF HONOR: A REGIMENTAL HISTORY OF THE ELEVENTH ARKANSAS INFANTRY REGIMENT & POE'S CAVALRY BATTALION C.S.A. 1861,* CWR:VOL1#3[94], *reviewed by* James Harwick Jr.

Russell, Don; *CUSTER'S LAST, OR THE BATTLE OF LITTLE BIG HORN,* AHI:MAY/68[49], *reviewed by* Wilber S. Nye

Ryan, David D.; *FOUR DAYS IN 1865: THE FALL OF RICHMOND,* CWR:VOL4#1[78], *reviewed by* Jon L. Wakelyn, MH:DEC/93[90]

Sacks, Howard L.; *WAY UP NORTH IN DIXIE: A BLACK FAMILY'S CLAIM TO THE CONFEDERATE ANTHEM,* CWTI:JAN/95[12]

Sanders, Steven; *IRONMAIDENS,* CWNEWS:FEB/94[5], *reviewed by* Gary Augustine

Sauers, Richard A.:
A CASPIAN SEA OF INK: THE MEADE-SICKLES CONTROVERSY, CWNEWS:MAY/90[4], *reviewed by* Michael Russert

ADVANCE THE COLORS!: PENNSYLVANIA CIVIL WAR BATTLE FLAGS, VOL. II, B&G:JUN/93[28], *reviewed by* Paul Ellingson, CWNEWS:DEC/92[4], *reviewed by* Michael J. Winey

Savage, Douglas; *THE COURT MARTIAL OF ROBERT E. LEE: A HISTORICAL NOVEL,* CWTI:JAN/94[10]

Savas, Theodore P.:
THE CAMPAIGN FOR ATLANTA & SHERMAN'S MARCH TO THE SEA, VOLUMES I & II, ACW:JAN/95[62], B&G:APR/95[30], *reviewed by* Edwin C. Bearss, CWNEWS:MAY/94[5], *reviewed by* Richard McMurry, CWR:VOL4#3[37]

CIVIL WAR REGIMENTS, CWNEWS:AUG/91[4], *reviewed by* William Marvel

THE RED RIVER CAMPAIGN: ESSAYS ON UNION AND CONFEDERATE LEADERSHIP, CWR:VOL4#3[37]

Scaife, William R.:
THE CAMPAIGN FOR ATLANTA, CWNEWS:MAY/92[4], *reviewed by* William Marvel

THE CHATTAHOOCHEE RIVER LINE, AN AMERICAN MAGINOT, CWNEWS:MAY/93[4], *reviewed by* Anne J. Bailey, CWR:VOL2#3[256], *reviewed by* Theodore P. Savas

THE GEORGIA BRIGADE; CWNEWS:SEP/89[8], *reviewed by* William Howard

HOOD'S CAMPAIGN FOR TENNESSEE, CWM:JAN/91[47], *reviewed by* Gary W. Gallagher

THE MARCH TO THE SEA, CWM:JAN/91[47], *reviewed by* Gary W. Gallagher

Scarborough, William K.; *THE OVERSEER: PLANTATION MANAGEMENT IN THE OLD SOUTH,* AHI:FEB/67[57], *reviewed by* Ralph Adams Brown

Scharf, J. Thomas:
HISTORY OF THE CONFEDERATES STATES NAVY,
CWNEWS:OCT/90[4], *reviewed by* Brandon Beck
*THE PERSONAL MEMOIRS OF JONATHAN THOMAS
SCHARF OF THE FIRST MARYLAND ARTILLERY,*
CWR:VOL3#3[92], (edited by Tom Kelley) *reviewed by*
Brandon Beck
Schiller, Herbert M.:
*A CAPTAIN'S WAR: THE LETTERS AND DIARIES OF
WILLIAM H.S. BURGWYN, 1861-1865,* ACW:NOV/94[66],
reviewed by William J. Shepherd
THE BERMUDA HUNDRED CAMPAIGN,
CWNEWS:NOV/89[4], *reviewed by* Kevin J. Weddle
Schlesinger, Keith R.; *THE POWER THAT GOVERNS: THE
EVOLUTION OF JUDICIAL ACTIVISM IN A MIDWESTERN
STATE, 1840-1890,* CWNEWS:JUN/92[4], *reviewed by* Kemp
Burpeau
Schmidt, Lewis G.; *THE BATTLE OF OLUSTEE: THE CIVIL
WAR IN FLORIDA,* CWNEWS:JUL/91[4], *reviewed by* Michael
Policatti
Schroeder-Lein, Glenna R.; *CONFEDERATE HOSPITALS
ON THE MOVE: SAMUEL H. STOUT AND THE ARMY OF
TENNESSEE,* B&G:AUG/94[30], *reviewed by* Frank R.
Freemon, CWM:APR/95[50], *reviewed by* Gary W. Gallagher,
CWNEWS:APR/95[33], *reviewed by* Frank J. Piatek,
CWR:VOL4#1[78], *reviewed by* Wayman D. Norman, M.D.,
CWR:VOL4#3[37]
Schultz, Duane; *GLORY ENOUGH FOR ALL,*
CWTI:JAN/94[10], *reviewed by* Noah Andre Trudeau
Schuppert, M.; *TREATISE ON GUN-SHOT WOUNDS:
WRITTEN FOR AND DEDICATED TO SURGEON OF THE
CONFEDERATE STATES ARMY,* CWNEWS:AUG/91[4],
reviewed by Harris D. Riley Jr.
Schutz, Wallace J.; *ABANDONED BY LINCOLN: A
MILITARY BIOGRAPHY OF GENERAL JOHN POPE,*
ACW:JAN/91[54], *reviewed by* John Guttman,
CWM:JAN/91[47], *reviewed by* Gary W. Gallagher,
CWNEWS:OCT/90[4], *reviewed by* Anne J. Bailey,
CWTI:MAR/91[18], *reviewed by* John Hennessy
Scott, Douglas D.; *ARCHEOLOGICAL PERSPECTIVES ON
THE BATTLE OF LITTLE BIGHORN,* CWNEWS:JUN/91[4],
reviewed by Brian Pohanka
Scott, Kate M.; *HISTORY OF THE ONE HUNDRED AND
FIFTH REGIMENT OF PENNSYLVANIA VOLUNTEERS,*
CWR:VOL4#1[78], *reviewed by* Kevin E. O'Brien
Scott, Kim A., (compiled by); *MANUSCRIPT RESOURCES
FOR THE CIVIL WAR,* CWNEWS:JAN/92[4], *reviewed by*
Michael Mullins
Scott, Robert G.; *INTO THE WILDERNESS WITH THE
ARMY OF THE POTOMAC,* ACW:JAN/94[62], *reviewed by*
Jerry Keenan
Scott, Robert; *GLORY, GLORY, GLORIETA: THE
GETTYSBURG OF THE WEST,* CWNEWS:FEB/94[5],
reviewed by Kemp Burpeau
Scott, William F.; *THE STORY OF A CAVALRY REGIMENT:
THE CAREER OF THE FOURTH IOWA VETERAN
VOLUNTEERS, FROM KANSAS TO GEORGIA, 1861-1865,*
CWNEWS:JAN/94[5], *reviewed by* Gregory J.W. Urwin,
CWR:VOL3#1[80], *reviewed by* Leonne M. Hudson
Seabury, Caroline, (edited by Suzanne L. Bunkers); *THE
DIARY OF CAROLINE SEABURY, 1854-1863,*
CWNEWS:NOV/92[4]

Seagrave, Ronald R.; *CIVIL WAR AUTOGRAPHS &
MANUSCRIPTS: PRICES CURRENT, 1992,*
CWNEWS:JUL/92[4], *reviewed by* Blake A. Magner
Sears, Stephen W.:
THE CIVIL WAR: A TREASURY OF ART AND LITERATURE,
AHI:SEP/93[24], CWNEWS:FEB/95[33], *reviewed by* Sarah W.
Wiggins
THE CIVIL WAR PAPERS OF GEORGE B. MCCLELLAN,
CWM:JUN/95[6], *reviewed by* William J. Miller
*FOR COUNTRY, CAUSE & LEADER: THE CIVIL WAR
JOURNAL OF CHARLES B. HAYDON,* CWR:VOL3#4[68],
reviewed by Frank l. Byrne
GEORGE B. MCCLELLAN: THE YOUNG NAPOLEON,
AHI:NOV/88[10], CWM:FEB/95[42], *reviewed by* Gary W.
Gallagher
LANDSCAPE TURNED RED: THE BATTLE OF ANTIETAM,
CWM:NOV/92[55], CWM:FEB/95[42]564, *reviewed by* Gary W.
Gallagher
*TO THE GATES OF RICHMOND: THE PENINSULA
CAMPAIGN,* B&G:AUG/93[24], *reviewed by* Judith L. Anthis,
CWM:JUN/95[6], *reviewed by* William J. Miller,
CWNEWS:MAY/93[4], *reviewed by* Blake A. Magner,
CWR:VOL3#1[80], *reviewed by* William J. Miller,
CWTI:MAR/93[10]
Semmes, Raphael; *MEMOIRS OF SERVICE AFLOAT,*
CWR:VOL4#3[1], *reviewed by* Maxine Turner
Sensing, Thurman; *CHAMP FERGUSON, CONFEDERATE
GUERILLA,* CWTI:JUL/94[18]
Serrano, D.A.; *STILL MORE CONFEDERATE FACES,*
B&G:JUN/93[28], *reviewed by* Jai S. Cochran,
CWNEWS:MAY/93[4], *reviewed by* WIlliam F. Howard
Seymour, William J.; (edited by Terry L. Jones), *THE CIVIL
WAR MEMOIRS OF CAPTAIN WILLIAM J. SEYMOUR:
REMINISCENCES OF A LOUISIANA TIGER,*
CWM:MAR/92[49], *reviewed by* Gary W. Gallagher,
CWNEWS:JAN/92[4], *reviewed by* Michael Parrish,
CWR:VOL1#4[77], *reviewed by* Robert K. Krick
Shaara, Michael; *THE KILLER ANGELS,* CWM:NOV/92[55]
Shackelford, George G.; *GEORGE WYTHE RANDOLPH AND
THE CONFEDERATE ELITE,* CWNEWS:JAN/90[4], *reviewed
by* Michael Parrish
Shaw, Maurice F.; *STONEWALL JACKSON'S SURGEON,
HUNTER HOLMES MCGUIRE; A BIOGRAPHY,*
CWNEWS:JUL/94[25], *reviewed by* Michael A. Cavanaugh
Shaw, Robert Gould, (edited by Russell Duncan); *BLUE-EYED
CHILD OF FORTUNE: THE CIVIL WAR LETTERS OF
ROBERT GOULD SHAW,* B&G:OCT/91[24], *reviewed by*
Warren Wilkinson, CWM:FEB/95[42], *reviewed by* Gary W.
Gallagher, CWNEWS:MAY/93[4] *reviewed by* William Marvel,
CWR:VOL2#1[80], *reviewed by* Stephen D. Engle,
CWR:VOL4#3[1], *reviewed by* Stephen Engle, CWTI:JUL/93[12]
Shea, William L.; *PEA RIDGE: CIVIL WAR CAMPAIGN IN
THE WEST,* B&G:AUG/93[24], *reviewed by* Leo E. Huff,
CWM:FEB/95[42]564, *reviewed by* Gary W. Gallagher,
CWR:VOL3#1[80], *reviewed by* Edward A. Hagerty,
CWNEWS:DEC/94[33], *reviewed by* Robert D. Norris Jr.
Shep, R.L.:
CIVIL WAR ERA ETIQUETTE, CWNEWS:JAN/90[4], *reviewed
by* Terry Winschel
*CIVIL WAR LADIES, FASHIONS AND NEEDLE-ARTS OF THE
EARLY 1869'S,* CWNEWS:JUN/90[4], *reviewed by* Kathryn
Jorgensen

Sheridan, Philip H.; *PERSONAL MEMOIRS OF PHILIP HENRY SHERIDAN, GENERAL, UNITED STATES ARMY*, CWM:FEB/95[42]564, *reviewed by* Gary W. Gallagher

Sherman, W. T.; *MEMOIRS OF GENERAL W.T. SHERMAN*, CWM:FEB/95[42], *reviewed by* Gary W. Gallagher, CWM:AUG/95[8], *reviewed by* Gary W. Gallagher

Shingleton, Royce; *HIGH SEAS CONFEDERATE: THE LIFE AND TIMES OF JOHN NEWLAND MAFFITT*, B&G:FEB/95[26], *reviewed by* Arthur W. Bergeron, CWM:AUG/95[45], *reviewed by* Gary W. Gallagher CWNEWS:SEP/95[33], *reviewed by* Gary Augustine

Shue, Richard S.; *MORNING AT WILLOUGHBY RUN, JULY 1, 1863*, CWNEWS:FEB/95[33], *reviewed by* Blake A. Magner, CWR:VOL4#4[129], *reviewed by* Edward J. Hagerty

Siegel, David S.; *THE USED BOOK LOVER'S GUIDE TO THE MID-ATLANTIC STATES*, CWNEWS:FEB/95[33], *reviewed by* Blake A Magner

Sifakis, Steward; *COMPENDIUM OF THE CONFEDERATE ARMIES*, CWM:APR/95[8], *reviewed by* Charles R. Norville, CWNEWS:DEC/92[4], *reviewed by* Jeffry D. Wert, CWR:VOL3#1[80], *reviewed by* Theodore P. Savas

Sigelschiffer, Saul; *THE AMERICAN CONSCIENCE: THE DRAMA OF THE LINCOLN-DOUGLAS DEBATES*, AHI:JUL/75[50], *reviewed by* Gary R. Planck

Silber, Nina; *THE ROMANCE OF REUNION: NORTHERNERS AND THE SOUTH, 1865-1900*, CWNEWS:JUL/95[61], *reviewed by* Larry J. Daniel

Silverstone, Paul H.; *WARSHIPS OF THE CIVIL WAR NAVIES*, CWNEWS:JUL/91[4], *reviewed by* William F. Howard

Simon, John Y.:
THE CONTINUING CIVIL WAR: ESSAYS IN HONOR OF THE CIVIL WAR ROUND TABLE OF CHICAGO, CWNEWS:DEC/92[4], *reviewed by* Blake A. Magner
LINCOLN'S PREPARATION FOR GREATNESS, AHI:JUN/68[51], *reviewed by* Robert D. Hoffsommer
THE PAPERS OF ULYSSES S. GRANT. VOLUME 1: 1837-1861, AHI:NOV/67[57], *reviewed by* WILBER S. NYE
THE SHADOWS RISE: ABRAHAM LINCOLN AND THE ANN RUTLEDGE LEGEND, CWM:APR/95[50], *reviewed by* Gary W. Gallagher

Simpson, Brooks D.; *LET US HAVE PEACE: ULYSSES S. GRANT AND THE POLITICS OF WAR AND DRECONSTRUCTION, 1861-1868*, B&G:JUN/92[28], *reviewed by* Michael C.C. Adams, CWM:JAN/92[57], *reviewed by* Gary W. Gallagher, CWNEWS:JAN/93[4], *reviewed by* David F. Riggs

Simpson, Colonel Harold B.:
BRAWLING BRASS: NORTH AND SOUTH, CWNEWS:APR/92[4], *reviewed by* Theodore P. Savas
CRY COMANCHE: THE 2ND U.S. CAVALRY IN TEXAS, 1855-1861, CWNEWS:NOV/89[4], *reviewed by* Robert Norris
GAINES' MILL TO APPOMATTOX — WACO & McCLENNAN COUNTY IN HOOD'S TEXAS BRIGADE, CWNEWS:SEP/89[8], *reviewed by* Blake Magner
HOOD'S TEXAS BRIGADE: LEE'S GRENADIER GUARD, CWR:VOL2#3[256], *reviewed by* Archie P. McDonald

Simpson, Dick, (edited by Guy R. Everson); *FAR, FAR FROM HOME: THE WARTIME LETTERS OF DICK AND TALLY SIMPSON, 3RD SOUTH CAROLINA VOLUNTEERS*, CWM:APR/95[8], *reviewed by* Charles R. Norville, CWR:VOL4#3[37]

Sinclair, Arthur; *TWO YEARS ON THE ALABAMA*, CWNEWS:JAN/90[4], *reviewed by* Brandon Beck

Skidmore, Richard S., (edited by); *THE CIVIL WAR JOURNAL OF BILLY DAVIS: FROM HOPEWELL, INDIANA TO PORT REPUBLIC, VIRGINIA*, B&G:APR/91[28], *reviewed by* Paul Kallina

Skimin, Robert; *ULYSSES: A BIOGRAPHICAL NOVEL OF U.S. GRANT*, CWTI:JAN/95[12], *reviewed by* Brooks D. Simpson

Smith, David P.; *FRONTIER DEFENSE IN THE CIVIL WAR: TEXAS' RANGERS AND REBELS*, B&G:AUG/93[24], *reviewed by* William L. Shea, CWNEWS:DEC/92[4], *reviewed by* Robert D. Norris Jr., CWNEWS:DEC/94[33], *reviewed by* Norman E. Rourke

Smith, Duane A.; *THE BIRTH OF COLORADO: A CIVIL WAR PERSPECTIVE*, CWM:JAN/91[47], *reviewed by* Gary W. Gallagher, CWNEWS:NOV/90[4], *reviewed by* Theodore P. Savas

Smith, Elbert B.; *FRANCIS PRESTON BLAIR*, AHI:JUL/80[50], *reviewed by* Lowell H. Harrison

Smith, Gene; *AMERICAN GOTHIC: THE STORY OF AMERICA'S LEGENDARY THEATRICAL FAMILY - JUNIUS, EDWIN AND JOHN WILKES BOOTH*, AHI:MAR/93[20]

Smith, Jeffrey H.; *A FRENCHMAN FIGHTS FOR THE UNION: VICTOR VIFQUAIN AND THE 97TH ILLINOIS*, CWNEWS:SEP/94[33], *reviewed by* Blake A. Magner

Smith, John D.; *AN OLD CREED FOR THE NEW SOUTH, PRO-SLAVERY IDEOLOGY AND HISTORIOGRAPHY, 1865-1918*, CWNEWS:APR/93[4], *reviewed by* John F. Marszalek

Smith, Stephen; *HAND-BOOK OF SURGICAL OPERATIONS*, CWNEWS:SEP/91[4], *reviewed by* Harris D. Riley

Smith, Stuart W.; *DOUGLAS SOUTHALL FREEMAN ON LEADERSHIP*, B&G:APR/94[24], *reviewed by* Peter S. Carmichael

Smithsonian Institution; *SMITHSONIAN'S GREAT BATTLES OF THE CIVIL WAR, VOLUME IV*, ACW:JUL/93[58]

Smyer, Ingrid; *VARINA: FORGOTTEN FIRST LADY*, CWNEWS:OCT/95[33], *reviewed by* Frank J. Piatek

Sommers, Richard J.; *RICHMOND REDEEMED: THE SIEGE AT PETERSBURG*, CWM:FEB/95[42]564, *reviewed by* Gary W. Gallagher

Sorrel, Gilbert Moxley; *RECOLLECTIONS OF A CONFEDERATE STAFF OFFICER*, CWM:FEB/95[42]564, *reviewed by* Gary W. Gallagher

Spink, Barry L.; *FROM CAVEN TO COLD HARBOR: THE LIFE OF COLONEL RICHARD BYRNES*, CWNEWS:JUN/95[33], *reviewed by* Blake A. Magner

Spruill, Matt; *GUIDE TO THE BATTLE OF CHICKAMAUGA*, CWM:APR/95[50], *reviewed by* Gary W. Gallagher, CWTI:JAN/94[10], *reviewed by*

Stampp, Kenneth:
AMERICA IN 1857 ACW:SEP/91[54], *reviewed by* Ken Bivin
THE IMPERILED UNION: ESSAYS ON THE BACKGROUND OF THE CIVIL WAR, AHI:JUL/80[50], *reviewed by* Joe Gray Taylor

Stanchak, John E.; *LESLIE'S ILLUSTRATED CIVIL WAR*, AHI:MAR/93[20], B&G:FEB/94[36], *reviewed by* Steve Davis, CWNEWS:JUL/93[5], *reviewed by* Michael Russert

Standley, Gerald, (edited by); *THE BATTLE OF CHICKAMAUGA*, CWNEWS:AUG/90[4], *reviewed by* Jeffry D. Wert

Stanton, Donal J.; *THE CIVIL WAR REMINISCENCES OF GENERAL M. JEFF THOMPSON*, CWTI:MAR/89[10], *reviewed by* Phillip Rutherford

Starobin, Robert S.; *INDUSTRIAL SLAVERY IN THE OLD SOUTH*, AHI:NOV/70[48], *reviewed by* Robert D. Hoffsommer

Starr, Stephen Z.:
JENNISON'S JAYHAWKERS: A CIVIL WAR CAVLRY REGIMENT AND ITS COMMANDER, CWNEWS:JAN/95[25], *reviewed by* Anne J. Bailey
THE UNION CAVALRY IN THE CIVIL WAR, CWM:FEB/95[42]564, *reviewed by* Gary W. Gallagher

Stavis, Barrie; *JOHN BROWN: THE SWORD AND THE WORD*, AHI:NOV/70[48], *reviewed by* Robert D. Hoffsommer

Steele, Phillip W.; *CIVIL WAR IN THE OZARKS*, CWNEWS:DEC/95[29], *reviewed by* John S. Benson

Steiner, Paul E.; *MEDICAL-MILITARY PORTRAITS OF UNION AND CONFEDERATE GENERALS*, CWM:MAY/91[38], *reviewed by* Gary W. Gallagher

Steinmetz, Lee, (edited by); *THE POETRY OF THE AMERICAN CIVIL WAR*, CWNEWS:NOV/93[5], *reviewed by* Linda G. Black

Stephens, Robert G.; *INTREPID WARRIOR: CLEMENT ANSELM EVANS, CONFEDERATE GENERAL FROM GEORGIA — LIFE, LETTERS, AND DIARIES OF THE WAR*, CWM:FEB/95[42]564, *reviewed by* Gary W. Gallagher

Sterling, Dorothy:
AHEAD OF HER TIME: ABBY KELLEY AND THE POLITICS OF ANTISLAVERY, CWNEWS:NOV/92[4], *reviewed by* Linda G. Black
THE TROUBLE THEY SEEN: BLACK PEOPLE TELL THE STORY OF RECONSTRUCTION, AHI:FEB/77[49], *reviewed by* Bell I. Wiley

Stern, Philip Van Doren; *WHEN THE GUNS ROARED*, AHI:JUN/66[59]

Stevens, Joseph E.; *AMERICA'S NATIONAL BATTLEFIELD PARKS: A GUIDE*, B&G:DEC/91[30], *reviewed by* Jerry L. Russell, CWNEWS:MAY/92[4] *reviewed by* Michael Mullins

Stevenson, Paul; *WARGAMMING IN HISTORY: THE AMERICAN CIVIL WAR*, CWNEWS:AUG/92[4], *reviewed by* Dr. Martin G. Martin

Stewart, William H.; *A PAIR OF BLANKETS: WAR-TIME HISTORY IN LETTERS TO THE YOUNG PEOPLE OF THE SOUTH*, CWNEWS:OCT/90[4], *reviewed by* Richard M. McMurry

Stiles, T.J.; *IN THEIR OWN WORDS: CIVIL WAR COMMANDERS*, CWTI:AUG/95[18]

Stockdale, Paul H.; *THE DEATH OF AN ARMY: THE BATTLE OF NASHVILLE AND HOOD'S RETREAT*, CWNEWS:JUL/93[5], *reviewed by* Dale K. Phillips

Stockton, Joseph; *WAR DIARY OF BREVET BRIGADIER GENERAL JOSEPH STOCKTON, FIRST LIEUTENANT, CAPTAIN, MAJOR AND LIEUTENANT COLONEL 72ND REGIMENT ILLINOIS INFANTRY VOLUNTEEERS (FIRST BOARD OF TRADE REGIMENT)*, CWNEWS:AUG/90[4], *reviewed by* Ron Rago

Stokes, William, (edited by Lloyd Halliburton); *SADDLE SOLDIERS: THE CIVIL WAR CORRESPONDENCE OF GENERAL WILLIAM STOKES OF THE 4TH SOUTH CAROLINA CAVALRY*, CWR:VOL3#3[92], *reviewed by* George Otott

Stonesifer, Roy P. Jr.; *THE LIFE AND WARS OF GIDEON J. PILLOW*, ACW:JUL/94[58], *reviewed by* John Wilson

Stotelmyer, Steven R.; *THE BIVOUACS OF THE DEAD: THE STORY OF THOSE WHO DIED AT ANTIETAM AND SOUTH MOUNTAIN*, CWNEWS:SEP/93[5], *reviewed by* Kevin Weddle

Straubling, Harold E.; *IN HOSPITAL AND CAMP: THE CIVIL WAR THROUGH THE EYES OF ITS DOCTORS AND NURSES*, CWNEWS:MAY/94[5], *reviewed by* Harris D. Riley

Strayer, Larry M., (edited by); *ECHOES OF BATTLE: THE ATLANTA CAMPAIGN*, B&G:JUN/92[28], *reviewed by* Stephen Davis, CWNEWS:JUL/92[4], *reviewed by* Gary Augustine

Struill, Matt, (edited by); *A GUIDE TO THE BATTLE OF CHICKAMAUGA*, CWR:VOL4#1[78], *reviewed by* Howard L. Sandefer

Stuart, James E.B., (edited by Adele H. Mitchell); *THE LETTERS OF MAJOR GENERAL JAMES E.B. STUART*, CWM:FEB/95[42]564, *reviewed by* Gary W. Gallagher

Stuckenberg, John H.W., (edited by David T. Hendrick); *I'M SURROUNDED BY METHODISTS...: DIARY OF JOHN H.W. STUCKENBERG, CHAPLAIN OF THE 145TH PENNSYLVANIA VOLUNTEER INFANTRY*, CWNEWS:DEC/95[29], *reviewed by,* Ethan S. Rafuse

Sullivan, Constance, (edited by); *LANDSCAPES OF THE CIVIL WAR: NEWLY DISCOVERED PHOTOGRAPHS FROM THE MEDFORD HISTORICAL SOCIETY*, CWTI:OCT/95[18]

Sullivan, George; *MATHEW BRADY: HIS LIFE AND PHOTOGRAPHS*, CWNEWS:JUN/95[33]

Sutherland, Daniel E.; *THE CONFEDERATE CARPETBAGGERS*, CWNEWS:OCT/89[4], *reviewed by* Brandon Beck

Svenson, Peter; *BATTLEFIELD: FARMING A CIVIL WAR BATTLEGROUND*, AHI:MAY/93[22], CWNEWS:NOV/93[5], *reviewed by* Mark Stephens

Swank, Walbrook D.:
BATTLE OF TREVILIAN STATION WITH EYEWITNESS MEMOIRS, CWNEWS:OCT/95[33], *reviewed by* Frank J. Piatek
EYEWITNESS TO WAR 1861-1865: MEMOIRS OF MEN WHO FOUGHT IN THE BATTLE OF TREVILIAN STATION 11-12 JUNE 1864, VOL. I, CWNEWS:OCT/92[4], *reviewed by* Michael Russert
THE WAR AND LOUISA COUNTY 1861-1865, CWNEWS:OCT/92[4], *reviewed by* Michael Russert

Sweet, Timothy; *TRACES OF WAR: PHOTOGRAPHY, AND THE CRISIS OF THE UNION*, CWNEWS:MAY/92[4], *reviewed by* Jeffry D. Wert

Sword, Wiley; *EMBRACE AN ANGRY WIND — THE CONFEDERACY'S LAST HURRAH: SPRING HILL, FRANKLIN AND NASHVILLE*, B&G:AUG/92[36], *reviewed by* Albert Castel, CWNEWS:OCT/92[4], *reviewed by* Tom Low, CWTI:APR/92[30], *reviewed by* Noah Andre Trudeau

Sword, Wiley; *MOUNTAIN TOUCHED WITH FIRE: CHATTANOOGA BESIEGED, 1863*, ACW:NOV/95[62], *reviewed by* Ken Bivin, B&G:DEC/95[30], *reviewed by* Steven E. Woodworth, CWNEWS:OCT/95[33], *reviewed by* John G. Secondari

Sylvia, Stephen W.; *CIVIL WAR CANTEENS*, CWNEWS:MAY/91[4], *reviewed by* C. Peter Jorgensen

Symonds, Craig L.:
GETTYSBURG—A BATTLEFIELD ATLAS, B&G:JUN/93[28], *reviewed by* William A. Young Jr., CWNEWS:NOV/92[4], *reviewed by* Blake Magner
JOSEPH E. JOHNSTON: A CIVIL WAR BIOGRAPHY, ACW:NOV/93[58], *reviewed by* Richard F. Welch, CWNEWS:JUN/93[5], *reviewed by* T. Michael Parrish, CWTI:JUL/92[10], *reviewed by* Albert Castel

Sypher, J.R.; *HISTORY OF THE PENNSYLVANIA RESERVE CORPS: A COMPLETE RECORD OF THE ORGANIZATION; AND OF ITS DIFFERENT COMPANIES*, B&G:DEC/92[26],

reviewed by Steven J. Wright, CWM:JUN/95[6], *reviewed by* Gary W. Gallagher

Tappert, Annette, (edited by); *THE BROTHER'S WAR: CIVIL WAR LETTERS TO THEIR LOVED ONES FROM THE BLUE AND GRAY,* CWNEWS:JUN/90[4], *reviewed by* Michael A. Hughes, CWTI:SEPT/89[28], *reviewed by* Sarah Woolfork Wiggins

Taylor, James E.; *THE JAMES E. TAYLOR SKETCHBOOK WITH SHERIDAN UP THE SHENANDOAH VALLEY IN 1864: LEAVES FROM A SPECIAL ARTIST'S SKETCHBOOK AND DIARY,* CWNEWS:NOV/89[4], *reviewed by* Brian Pohanka

Taylor, John M.; *CONFEDERATE RAIDER: RAPHAEL SEMMES OF THE <u>ALABAMA</u>* ACW:JUL/95[58], *reviewed by* Jon Guttman, CWTI:MAR/95[14]

Taylor, John M.; *WILLIAM HENRY SEWARD: LINCOLN'S RIGHT HAND,* AHI:MAR/92[20], *reviewed by,* CWNEWS:OCT/92[4], *reviewed by* Gregory J.W. Urwin, CWTI:DEC/91[12], *reviewed by*

Taylor, Richard; *DESTRUCTION AND RECONSTRUCTION: PERSONAL EXPERIENCES IN THE LATE WAR,* CWM:FEB/95[42], *reviewed by* Gary W. Gallagher

Taylor, Walter H.; *GENERAL LEE: HIS CAMPAIGNS IN VIRGINIA 1861-1865, WITH PERSONAL REMINISCENCES,* CWM:AUG/95[45], *reviewed by* Gary W. Gallagher, CWM:FEB/95[42]564, *reviewed by* Gary W. Gallagher

Terrell, John Upton; *FAINT THE TRUMPET SOUNDS; THE LIFE AND TRIAL OF MAJOR RENO,* AHI:FEB/67[57], *reviewed by* Ralph Adams Brown

Thatcher, Marshall P.; *A HUNDRED BATTLES IN THE WEST. ST. LOUIS TO ATLANTA, 1861-1865. THE SECOND MICHIGAN CAVALRY,* CWNEWS:NOV/91[4], *reviewed by* John F. Marszalek, CWNEWS:SEP/92[4], *reviewed by* John F. Marszalek

Thienel, Phillip M.; *SEVEN STORY MOUNTAIN: THE UNION CAMPAIGN AT VICKSBURG* CWNEWS:SEP/95[33], *reviewed by* Terrence J. Winschel

Thomas, Benjamin; *ABRAHAM LINCOLN, A BIOGRAPHY,* CWTI:DEC/95[38]

Thomas, Ella G.C.; *<u>THE SECRET EYE: THE JOURNAL OF ELLA GERTRUDE CLANTON THOMAS, 1848-1889,</u>* CWM:JAN/91[47], *reviewed by* Gary W. Gallagher

Thomas, Emory M.:
BOLD DRAGOON: THE LIFE OF J.E.B. STUART, AHI:OCT/86[8], CWM:FEB/95[42], *reviewed by* Gary W. Gallagher

THE CONFEDERACY AS A REVOLUTIONARY EXPERIENCE, CWM:NOV/91[73], *reviewed by* Gary W. Gallagher, CWNEWS:APR/93[4], *reviewed by* Dale Phillips

ROBERT E. LEE: A BIOGRAPHY CWNEWS:AUG/95[33], *reviewed by* T. Michael Parrish

Thomas, Henry W.; *HISTORY OF THE DOLES-COOK BRIGADE,* CWR:VOL4#3[1], *reviewed by* Robert E.L. Krick

Thompson, Ed Porter; *HISTORY OF THE FIRST KENTUCKY BRIGADE,* CWR:VOL4#3[1], *reviewed by* William C. Davis

Thomason, John W. Jr.; *JEB STUART,* CWM:AUG/95[45], *reviewed by* Gary W. Gallagher, CWNEWS:SEP/95[33], *reviewed by* John G. Secondari, CWR:VOL4#3[89], *reviewed by* Billy B. Hathorn

Thompson, M. Jeff, (edited by Donald J. Stanton); *THE CIVIL WAR REMINISCENCES OF GENERAL M. JEFF THOMPSON,* CWNEWS:JUN/90[4], *reviewed by* Jeffry D. Wert

Thompson, William F.; *THE IMAGE OF WAR, THE PICTORIAL REPORTING OF THE AMERICAN CIVIL WAR,* CWNEWS:DEC/95[29]

Tidwell, William A.:
APRIL '65: CONFEDERATE COVERT ACTION IN THE AMERICAN CIVIL WAR, CWNEWS:AUG/95[33], *reviewed by* Michael P. Musick, CWTI:OCT/95[18], *reviewed by* WIlliam Hanchett

COME RETRIBUTION: THE CONFEDERATE SECRET SERVICE AND THE ASSASSINATION OF LINCOLN, CWNEWS:MAY/90[4], *reviewed by* Brandon Bec, CWTI:DEC/95[38]

Time-Life Books:
ABOVE AND BEYOND: A HISTORY OF THE MEDAL OF HONOR FROM THE CIVIL WAR TO VIETNAM, AHI:JAN/86[9]

ARMS AND EQUIPMENT OF THE CONFEDERACY, MH:DEC/92[74]

ECHOES OF GLORY, MH:DEC/92[74]

Tischler, Allan L.; *THE HISTORY OF THE HARPERS FERRY CAVALRY EXPEDITION, SEPTEMBER 14 & 15, 1862,* CWNEWS:MAY/95[33], *reviewed by* Michael Russert

Tolman, Newton F.; *THE SEARCH FOR GENERAL MILES,* AHI:FEB/69[49], *reviewed by* D. Alexander Brown

Toombs, Samuel; *REMINISCENCES OF THE THIRTEENTH REGIMENT NEW JERSEY VOLUNTEERS,* CWNEWS:JUL/95[61], *reviewed by* Michael Russert

Tourgee, Albion W.; *THE INVISIBLE EMPIRE,* CWTI:SEPT/89[28]

Tower, R. Lockwood, (edited by); *LEE'S ADJUTANT: THE WARTIME LETTERS OF COLONEL WALTER HERRON TAYLOR, 1862-1865,* CWNEWS:DEC/95[29], *reviewed by* John S. Benson

Tredway, G.R.; *THE WAY IT WAS: A NOVEL OF THE CIVIL WAR,* CWNEWS:SEP/95[33], *reviewed by* Blake A. Magner

Trefousse, Hans L.:
CARL SCHURZ: A BIOGRAPHY, AHI:DEC/82[10], *reviewed by* Charles Royster

IMPEACHMENT OF A PRESIDENT: ANDREW JOHNSON, THE BLACKS AND RECONSTRUCTION, AHI:AUG/75[50], *reviewed by* Gerald G. Eggert

IMPEACHMENT OF A PRESIDENT: ANDREW JOHNSON, THE BLACKS AND RECONSTRUCTION, AHI:OCT/78[26], *reviewed by* David Lindsey

Tripler, Charles S.; *HAND-BOOK FOR THE MILITARY SURGEON: BEING A COMPENDIUM OF THE DUTIES OF THE MEDICAL OFFICER IN THE FIELD, THE SANITATION, MANAGEMENT OF THE CAMP, THE PREPARATION OF FOOD,* CWNEWS:AUG/91[4]

Trotter, William R.:
BUSHWHACKERS! THE CIVIL WAR IN NORTH CAROLINA, VOL. 2, THE MOUNTAINS, CWNEWS:JAN/90[4], *reviewed by* Steven J. Wright, CWNEWS:NOV/92[4], *reviewed by* Steven J. Wright

THE CIVIL WAR IN NORTH CAROLINA, CWNEWS:OCT/95[33], *reviewed by* Jerry W. Holsworth

SILK FLAGS AND COLD STEEL: THE CIVIL WAR IN NORTH CAROLINA. VOL. 1: THE PIEDMONT, CWNEWS:OCT/89[4], *reviewed by* J. Tracy Power

Trout, Robert J.; *THEY FOLLOWED THE PLUME: THE STORY OF J.E.B. STUART AND HIS STAFF,* ACW:MAR/94[58], *reviewed by* Jon Guttman, B&G:FEB/94[36], *reviewed by* John Hennessy, CWNEWS:MAY/94[5], *reviewed by* Ted Alexander

Trudeau, Noah Andre:
BLOODY ROADS SOUTH: THE WILDERNESS TO COLD HARBOR, MAY-JUNE 1864, CWNEWS:SEP/90[4], *reviewed by* Mark Snell, CWTI:FEB/90[10], *reviewed by* Gary W. Gallagher
THE LAST CITADEL: PETERSBURG, VIRGINIA, JUNE 1864-APRIL 1865, B&G:APR/92[24], *reviewed by* Neal Meier, CWNEWS:AUG/92[4], *reviewed by* Frank J. Piatek, CWTI:FEB/92[18], *reviewed by* Gary W. Gallagher
OUT OF THE STORM: THE END OF THE CIVIL WAR (APRIL-JUNE 1865), CWTI:DEC/94[18], *reviewed by* John J. Hennessy

Trulock, Alice R.:
IN THE HANDS OF PROVIDENCE: JOSHUA L. CHAMBERLAIN & THE AMERICAN CIVIL WAR, B&G:FEB/93[36], *reviewed by* Eric J. Wittenberg, CWM:FEB/95[42]564, *reviewed by* Gary W. Gallagher, CWNEWS:AUG/92[4], *reviewed by* Brian C. Pohanka, CWR:VOL2#3[256], *reviewed by* Kevin E. O'Brien, CWTI:MAY/93[18]

Tucker, Glenn; *HIGH TIDE AT GETTYSBURG,* AHI:JAN/75[50], *reviewed by* Robert D. Hoffsommer

Tucker, Philip T.:
THE CONFEDERACY'S FIGHTING CHAPLAIN: FATHER JOHN B. BANNON, B&G:AUG/93[24], *reviewed by* Benedict R. Maryniak, CWM:OCT/95[10], *reviewed by* Rev. C. K. Norville, CWNEWS:JUN/93[5], *reviewed by* Larry G. Gray, CWR:VOL4#2[136], *reviewed by* Haskell Monroe
THE SOUTH'S FINEST: THE FIRST MISSOURI CONFEDERATE BRIGADE FROM PEA RIDGE TO VICKSBURG, CWR:VOL4#1[78], *reviewed by* Marius Carriere, CWM:APR/95[50], *reviewed by* Gary W. Gallagher, CWNEWS:DEC/94[33], *reviewed by* Robert D. Norris Jr.
WESTERNERS IN GRAY: THE MEN AND MISSIONS OF THE ELITE FIFTH MISSOURI INFANTRY REGIMENT, B&G:DEC/95[30], *reviewed by* Larry J. Daniel

Tunnard, W.H.; *A SOUTHERN RECORD: THE HISTORY OF THE THIRD REGIMENT LOUISIANA INFANTRY,* CWR:VOL4#3[1], *reviewed by* Arthur W. Bergeron Jr.

Tunnell, Ted; *CRUCIBLE OF RECONSTRUCTION: WAR, RADICALISM, AND RACE IN LOUISIANA, 1862-1877,* CWNEWS:JAN/95[25], *reviewed by* Larry G. Gray

Turner, Charles W.; *TED BARCLAY, LIBERTY HALL VOLUNTEERS: LETTERS FROM THE STONEWALL BRIGADE,* CWM:MAY/93[51], *reviewed by* John M. Priest, CWR:VOL2#4[346], *reviewed by* Brendon H. Beck

Turner, Edward R.; *THE NEW MARKET CAMPAIGN,* CWNEWS:MAY/92[4], *reviewed by* Charles Culbertson

Turner, George E.; *VICTORY RODE THE RAILS: THE STRATEGIC PLACE OF THE RAILROADS IN THE CIVIL WAR,* CWM:NOV/91[73], *reviewed by* Gary W. Gallagher, CWNEWS:MAY/94[5], *reviewed by* Michael J. Winey

Turner, Maxine; *NAVY GRAY: A STORY OF THE CONFEDERATE NAVY ON THE CHATTAHOOCHEE AND APALACHICOLA RIVERS,* CWNEWS:JAN/90[4], *reviewed by* Harris D. Riley Jr.

Twitchell, Marshall H., (edited by Ted Tunnell); *CARPETBAGGER FROM VERMONT: THE*

AUTOBIOGRAPHY OF MARSHALL HARVEY TWITCHELL, CWM:JAN/91[35], CWNEWS:JAN/90[4], *reviewed by* Steven J. Wright

U.S. Surgeon General; *THE MEDICAL AND SURGICAL HISTORY OF THE WAR OF THE REBELLION. (1861-1865),* CWM:MAY/91[38], *reviewed by* Gary W. Gallagher

U.S. War Department; *THE WAR OF THE REBELLION: A COMPILATION OF THE OFFICIAL RECORDS OF THE UNION AND CONFEDERATE ARMIES,* CWM:FEB/95[42]564, *reviewed by* Gary W. Gallagher

Univsity Publishers of America; *CIVIL WAR UNIT HISTORIES: REGIMENTAL HISTORIES AND PERSONAL NARRATIVES,* CWR:VOL4#1[78], *reviewed by* Theodore P. Savas

Urwin, Gregory J.W.:
CUSTER AND HIS TIMES: BOOK III, CWNEWS:JUN/91[4], *reviewed by* Brian Pohanka
CUSTER VICTORIOUS: THE CIVIL WAR BATTLES OF GENERAL GEORGE ARMSTRONG CUSTER, AHI:SEP/83[6], *reviewed by* Albert Castel
THE UNITED STATES INFANTRY: AN ILLUSTRATED HISTORY 1775-1918, CWNEWS:SEP/92[4], *reviewed by* Brian Pohanka

Utley, Robert M.:
FRONTIER REGULARS, THE UNITED STATES ARMY AND THE INDIAN, 1866-1891, AHI:JUN/74[49], *reviewed by* D. Alexander Brown
FRONTIERSMEN IN BLUE; THE UNITED STATES ARMY AND THE INDIAN, 1848-1865, AHI:JAN/69[56], *reviewed by* D. Alexander Brown

van Creveld, Martin; *TECHNOLOGY AND WAR: FROM 2000 B.C. TO THE PRESENT,* CWTI:MAY/89[44], *reviewed by* Richard Pindell

Van Deusen, Glyndon G.; *WILLIAM HENRY SEWARD,* AHI:FEB/68[57], *reviewed by* James I. Robertson Jr.

Van Horne, Thomas B.; *HISTORY OF THE ARMY OF THE CUMBERLAND: ITS ORGANIZATION, CAMPAIGNS, AND BATTLES,* CWNEWS:APR/90[4], *reviewed by* Gregory Mertz

Vandiver, Frank E.:
BLOOD BROTHER: A SHORT HISTORY OF THE CIVIL WAR B&G:OCT/93[24], *reviewed by* James A. Ramage, CWNEWS:OCT/93[5], *reviewed by* Richard M. McMurry, CWR:VOL3#1[80], *reviewed by* Steven J. Wright
MIGHTY STONEWALL, CWM:FEB/95[42], *reviewed by* Gary W. Gallagher
PLOUGHSHARES INTO SWORDS: JOSIAH GORGAS AND CONFEDERATE ORDNANCE, CWM:FEB/95[42], *reviewed by* Gary W. Gallagher, CWR:VOL4#3[37], *reviewed by* CWR:VOL4#4[129], *reviewed by* Archie P. McDonald
THEIR TATTERED FLAGS, THE EPIC OF THE CONFEDERACY, AHI:JUL/70[50]

Vandiver, Frank; *JUBAL'S RAID,* CWNEWS:OCT/94[33], *reviewed by* Jerry Holsworth

Vann Woodward, C.:
THE BURDEN OF SOUTHERN HISTORY, AHI:FEB/69[49]
MARY CHESNUT'S CIVIL WAR, AHI:SEP/82[8], *reviewed by* Joe Gray Taylor

Vetter, Charles E.:

SHERMAN: MERCHANT OF TERROR, ADVOCATE OF
PEACE B&G:DEC/92[26], *reviewed by* Steve Davis,
CWNEWS:DEC/92[4], *reviewed by* William MarveL,
CWR:VOL2#3[256], *reviewed by* Lee Kennett,
CWTI:SEP/92[18]

Vrendenburgh, Peter, Jr.; *UPON THE TENTED FIELD,*
CWTI:SEP/94[18], *reviewed by* edited by Bernard Olsen

Wainwright, Charles A., (edited by Allen Nevins); *A DIARY OF
BATTLE: THE PERSONAL JOURNALS OF COLONEL
CHARLES S. WAINWRIGHT, 1861-1865,*
CWM:FEB/95[42]564, *reviewed by* Gary W. Gallagher

Waite, Ernest L.; *HISTORY OF THE NINETEENTH
REGIMENT, MASSACHUSETTS VOLUNTEER* INFANTRY,
1861-1965, CWNEWS:JUL/90[4], *reviewed by* Dr. Allen C.
Guelzo

Wakeman, Sarah R., (edited by Lauren Cook Burgess); *AN
UNCOMMON SOLDIER: THE CIVIL WAR LETTERS OF
SARAH ROSETTA WAKEMAN, ALIAS PVT. LYONS
WAKEMAN, 153RD REGIMENT, NEW YORK STATE
VOLUNTEERS, 1862-1864,* CWNEWS:APR/95[33]

Wallace, Willard M.; *SOUL OF THE LION: A BIOGRAPHY
OF GENERAL JOSHUA L. CHAMBERLAIN,*
CWNEWS:NOV/92[4], *reviewed by* Mark A. Snell

Walsh, edited by, John E.; *THE SHADOWS RISE:
ABRAHAM LINCOLN AND THE ANN* RUTLEDGE
LEGEND, CWNEWS:SEP/94[33], *reviewed by* Allen C. Guelzo

Walters, Sara G.; *INSCRIPTION AT GETTYSBURG,*
CWNEWS:SEP/92[4], *reviewed by* Dr. Richard A. Sauers

Walther, Eric H.; *THE FIRE-EATERS,* CWNEWS:FEB/94[5],
reviewed by Jock Baird

Ward, Geoffrey C.; *THE CIVIL WAR: AN ILLUSTRATED
HISTORY,* CWNEWS:JUN/91[4], *reviewed by* Gregory J. W.
Irwin, CWTI:DEC/90[10], *reviewed by*

Ward, William W., (edited by R.B. Rosenburg); *'FOR THE
SAKE OF MY COUNTRY:' THE DIARY OF COL. W.W.
WARD, 9TH TENNESSEE CAVALRY, MORGAN'S
BRIGADE, C.S.A.,* CWNEWS:JAN/94[5], *reviewed by* Sarah
W. Wiggins, CWR:VOL3#1[80]

Ware, Eugene F.; *THE LYON CAMPAIGN IN MISSOURI:
BEING A HISTORY OF THE FIRST IOWA INFANTRY,*
CWNEWS:JAN/92[4], *reviewed by* Robert D. Norris Jr.,
CWR:VOL1#4[77], *reviewed by* James Harwick Jr.

Warner, Ezra J.:
*GENERALS IN BLUE: LIVES OF THE UNION
COMMANDERS,* CWM:FEB/95[42], *reviewed by* Gary W.
Gallagher
*GENERALS IN GRAY: LIVES OF THE CONFEDERATE
COMMANDERS,* CWM:FEB/95[42], *reviewed by* Gary W.
Gallagher

Warren, Edward; *AN EPITOME OF PRACTICAL SURGERY
FOR FIELD AND HOSPITAL,* CWNEWS:JUL/91[4], *reviewed
by* Harris D. Riley M.D.

Waugh, John C.; *THE CLASS OF 1846 FROM WEST POINT
TO APPOMATTOX,* ACW:JAN/95[62], *reviewed by* Michael D.
Hull, CWM:OCT/94[8], *reviewed by* Charles R. Norville,
CWNEWS:SEP/94[33], *reviewed by* Thomas Low,
CWR:VOL4#2[136], *reviewed by* Joseph G. Dawson III,
CWR:VOL4#3[37]

Webb, Alexander S.; *THE PENINSULA: MCCLELLAN'S
CAMPAIGN OF 1862,* CWNEWS:MAY/91[4], *reviewed by*
Richard A. Sauers

Weed, Cora C., (compiled by); *HANDBOOK FOR IOWA
SOLDIERS' AND SAILORS' MONUMENT,* CWR:VOL4#3[37]

Weigley, Russell F.; *QUARTERMASTER GENERAL OF THE
UNION ARMY: A BIOGRAPHY OF M.C. MEIGS,*
CWM:FEB/95[42], *reviewed by* Gary W. Gallagher

Weinert, Richard P. Jr.:
THE CONFEDERATE REGULAR ARMY, B&G:OCT/91[34],
reviewed by Robert K. Krick, CWNEWS:AUG/92[4], *reviewed by*
William G. Robertson
*DEFENDER OF THE CHESAPEAKE: THE STORY OF FORT
MONROE,* CWNEWS:JUN/91[4], *reviewed by* Kevin Weddle

Welch, Stephen E., (edited by John M. Priest); *STEPHEN
ELLIOTT WELCH OF THE HAMPTON LEGION,*
CWM:APR/95[8], *reviewed by* Charles R. Norville

Welcher, Frank J.:
*THE UNION ARMY, 1861-1865 ORGANIZATION AND
OPERATIONS, OPERATIONS, VOLUME I: THE EASTERN
THEATER,* B&G:APR/91[28], *reviewed by* William Glenn
Robertson, CWR:VOL1#2[78], *reviewed by* Theodore P. Savas
*THE UNION ARMY, 1861-1865 ORGANIZATION AND
OPERATIONS, VOLUME II: THE WESTERN THEATRE,*
CWM:APR/95[50], *reviewed by* Gary W. Gallagher,
CWNEWS:SEP/94[33], *reviewed by* Anne J. Bailey,
CWR:VOL3#3[92], *reviewed by* Theodore P. Savas,
CWTI:JAN/94[10]

Weld, Stephen M.; *WAR LETTERS AND DIARIES OF
STEPHEN MINOT WELD, 1861-1865,* CWM:FEB/95[42]564,
reviewed by Gary W. Gallagher

Wellikoff, Alan; *THE HISTORICAL SUPPLY CATALOG,*
CWNEWS:NOV/94[33], *reviewed by* Dave Hann

Wells, J.W.:
*AN ALPHABETICAL LIST OF THE BATTLES OF THE WAR OF
THE REBELLION, WITH DATES, FROM FT. SUMTER, SC,
APRIL ++ CWNEWS:SEP/ 91[4], AND 13, 1861, TO KIRBY
SMITH'S SURRENDER, MAY 26, 1865,*
MEDICAL HISTORIES OF CONFEDERATE GENERALS,
CWNEWS:NOV/95[29], *reviewed by* Harris D. Riley M.D.

Wert, Jeffry D.:
*GENERAL JAMES LONGSTREET: THE CONFEDERACY'S
MOST CONTROVERSIAL SOLDIER,* ACW:SEP/94[66],
reviewed by Richard F. Welch, B&G:DEC/94[28], *reviewed by*
Steven W. Woodworth, CWNEWS:JUL/94[25], *reviewed by* Ted
Alexander, MH:AUG/94[70]
MOSBY'S RANGERS, ACW:MAY/91[54], *reviewed by* Nat C.
Hughes, B&G:FEB/92[26], *reviewed by* Maynard Schrock,
CWNEWS:JAN/91[4], *reviewed by* Richard McMurry

West, John C.; *A TEXAN IN SEARCH OF A FIGHT. BEING
THE DIARY AND LETTERS OF A PRIVATE SOLDIER IN
HOOD'S TEXAS BRIGADE,* CWR:VOL4#3[37]

Westwood, Howard C.; *BLACK TROOPS, WHITE
COMMANDERS AND FREEDMEN DURING THE CIVIL
WAR,* B&G:FEB/93[36], *reviewed by* Richard Rollins,
CWR:VOL2#3[256], *reviewed by* Steven E. Woodworth

Weygant, Charles H.; *HISTORY OF THE ONE HUNDRED
AND TWENTY-FOURTH REGIMENT, N.Y.S.V.,*
CWR:VOL4#3[1], *reviewed by* Brian C. Pohanka

Wheeler, Richard:
*A RISING THUNDER: FROM LINCOLN'S ELECTION TO THE
BATTLE OF BULL RUN, AN EYEWITNESS HISTORY,*
ACW:NOV/94[66], *reviewed by* Al Hemingway,
CWNEWS:OCT/95[33], *reviewed by* Ethan S. Rafuse,
CWR:VOL4#3[37], CWTI:MAY/94[20], CWTI:JUN/95[24]

ON FIELDS OF FURY: FROM THE WILDERNESS TO THE CRATER: AN EYEWITNESS HISTORY, ACW:MAY/92[54], *reviewed by* Albert Hemingway, CWNEWS:AUG/92[4], *reviewed by* William Blake, CWTI:AUG/91[18]

LEE'S TERRIBLE SWIFT SWORD: FROM ANTIETAM TO CHANCELLORSVILLE, AN EYEWITNESS HISTORY, ACW:JAN/93[58]399, *reviewed by* Albert Hemingway, CWNEWS:APR/93[4], *reviewed by* Frank J. Piatek, CWTI:SEP/92[18]

VOICES FROM THE CIVIL WAR, ACW:SEP/91[54], *reviewed by* Albert Hemingway, AHI:JUL/77[50], *reviewed by* Bell I. Wiley, CWNEWS:JAN/92[4], *reviewed by* Michael Policatti

WITNESS TO APPOMATTOX, CWNEWS:AUG/90[4], *reviewed by* Thomas E. Schott

Whitaker, Frederick:
A COMPLETE LIFE OF GENERAL GEORGE ARMSTRONG CUSTER, CWR:VOL3#3[92], *reviewed by* Patrick S. Brady
A COMPLETE LIFE OF GENERAL GEORGE ARMSTRONG CUSTER, CWR:VOL3#3[92], *reviewed by* Patrick S. Brady

White, Daniel, (edited by Jack C. Davis); *DEAR WIFE, LETTERS OF A CIVIL WAR SOLDIER*, CWNEWS:APR/94[5], *reviewed by* Michael Russert

White, George R., (edited by Bob Bartosz); *THE CIVIL WAR: LETTERS HOME FROM GEO. R. WHITE*, CWNEWS:JAN/95[25], *reviewed by* Blake A. Magner

White, Howard Ashley; *THE FREEDMEN'S BUREAU IN LOUISIANA*, AHI:AUG/70[50], *reviewed by* E.E. Billings

White, Wyman, (edited by Russell C. White); *THE CIVIL WAR DIARY OF WYMAN WHITE, FIRST SERGEANT OF COMPANY F, 2ND UNITED STATES SHARPSHOOTER REGIMENT*, CWR:VOL2#2[169]

Whitehorne, Joseph W.A.; *THE BATTLE OF NEW MARKET*, CWNEWS:APR/90[4], *reviewed by* Jeffry D. Wert

Wideman, John C.; *THE SINKING OF THE USS CAIRO,* CWM:APR/95[50], *reviewed by* Gary W. Gallagher, CWNEWS:FEB/94[5], *reviewed by* William Shea

Wiley, Bell I.:
THE LIFE OF JOHNNY REB: THE COMMON SOLDIER OF THE CONFEDERACY, CWM:OCT/95[10], *reviewed by* Gary W. Gallagher
THE PLAIN PEOPLE OF THE CONFEDERACY, CWM:OCT/95[10], *reviewed by* Gary W. Gallagher
SOUTHERN NEGROES, 1861-1865, CWM:OCT/95[10], *reviewed by* Gary W. Gallagher

Wilkinson, Warren:
MOTHER MAY YOU NEVER SEE THE SIGHTS I HAVE SEEN: THE FIFTY-SEVENTH MASSACHUSETTS VETERAN VOLUNTEERS IN THE ARMY OF THE POTOMAC 1864-1865, B&G:APR/91[28], *reviewed by* Benedict R. Maryniak, CWNEWS:NOV/90[4], *reviewed by* Michael Cavanaugh, CWR:VOL1#3[94], *reviewed by* Richard Rollins, CWR:VOL4#3[1], *reviewed by* Pat Brennan, CWR:VOL4#3[1], *reviewed by* Lesley J. Gore, CWR:VOL4#3[1], *reviewed by* Emory M. Thomas

Williams, Alpheus S., (edited by Milo M. Quaife); *FROM THE CANNON'S MOUTH: THE CIVIL WAR LETTERS OF GENERAL ALPHEUS S. WILLIAMS*, CWM:FEB/95[42]564, *reviewed by* Gary W. Gallagher

Williams, Frank J., (edited by); *ABRAHAM LINCOLN: SOURCES AND STYLE OF LEADERSHIP*, CWM:DEC/95[10], *reviewed by* J. Jeffrey Cox

Williams, Griffith H.; *BALLADS OF THE BLUE AND GRAY*, CWNEWS:AUG/93[5], *reviewed by* Linda G. Black

Williams, Hiram S., (edited by Lewis N. Wynne); *THIS WAR SO HORRIBLE: THE CIVIL WAR DIARY OF HIRAM SMITH WILLIAMS*, CWM:APR/95[50], *reviewed by* Gary W. Gallagher, CWR:VOL4#1[78], *reviewed by* James Marten

Williams, Kenneth P.; *LINCOLN FINDS A GENERAL. A MILITARY HISTORY OF THE CIVIL WAR*, CWM:FEB/95[42]564, *reviewed by* Gary W. Gallagher

Williams, T. Harry;
HAYES OF THE 23RD, THE CIVIL WAR VOLUNTEER OFFICER, CWM:FEB/95[42]564, *reviewed by* Gary W. Gallagher, CWNEWS:NOV/95[29], *reviewed by* Frank J. Piatek
LINCOLN AND HIS GENERALS, CWTI:DEC/95[38]

Williamson, James J.; *MOSBY'S RANGERS*, CWR:VOL4#3[1], *reviewed by* Jeffry D. Wirt

Wills, Brian Steel; *A BATTLE FROM THE START: THE LIFE OF NATHAN BEDFORD FORREST*, ACW:SEP/93[54], *reviewed by* Michael D. Hull, B&G:FEB/93[36], *reviewed by* James J. Cooke, CWNEWS:APR/93[4], *reviewed by* Michael Russert, CWTI:JAN/93[12], *reviewed by* Edwin C. Bearss

Wills, Garry; *LINCOLN AT GETTYSBURG: THE WORDS THAT REMADE AMERICA*, CWNEWS:JAN/93[4], *reviewed by* Dr. Allen C. Cuelzo

Willson, Charles A.; *A BOY'S SERVICE WITH THE 76TH OHIO*, CWM:DEC/95[10], *reviewed by* Scott C. Patchan

Wilson, Clyde N.; *CAROLINA CAVALIER: THE LIFE AND MIND OF JAMES JOHNSTON PETTIGREW*, B&G:JUN/91[22], *reviewed by* William Garrett Piston, CWM:JAN/91[47], *reviewed by* Gary W. Gallagher, CWNEWS:MAY/92[4], *reviewed by* Judy Yandoh

Wilson, Ephraim A.; *MEMOIRS OF THE WAR*, CWR:VOL4#3[1], *reviewed by* John M. Coski

Winkler, A.V.; *CONFEDERATE CAPITAL AND HOOD'S TEXAS BRIGADE*, CWR:VOL1#4[77], *reviewed by* Theodore P. Savas

Winters, John D.; *THE CIVIL WAR IN LOUISIANA*, CWNEWS:SEP/92[4], *reviewed by* William F. Howard

Wintz, William D., (edited by); *CIVIL WAR MEMOIRS OF TWO REBEL SISTERS*, CWNEWS:MAY/91[4], *reviewed by* Michael Russert

Wise, Jennings C.; *THE LONG ARM OF LEE OR THE HISTORY OF THE ARTILLERY OF THE ARMY OF NORTHERN VIRGINIA*, CWM:FEB/95[42]564, CWNEWS:JUL/90[4], *reviewed by* Michael Russert, CWNEWS:SEP/93[5], *reviewed by* Brandon H. Beck

Wise, Stephen R.:
GATE OF HELL: CAMPAIGN FOR CHARLESTON HARBOR, 1863, B&G:JUN/95[30], *reviewed by* Robert N. Rosen, CWM:AUG/95[45], *reviewed by* Gary W. Gallagher, CWNEWS:APR/95[33], *reviewed by* Dr. Richard A. Sauers, CWR:VOL4#3[37], CWTI:SEP/94[18]
LIFELINE OF THE CONFEDERACY: BLOCKADE RUNNING DURING THE CIVIL WAR, B&G:APR/91[28], *reviewed by* Robert Holcombe, CWNEWS:JUN/90[4], *reviewed by* Terrence J. Winschel, CWTI:JUN/90[20]

Witham, George F.; *CATALOGUE OF CIVIL WAR PHOTOGRAPHERS* CWNEWS:MAY/90[4], *reviewed by* Michael A. Hughes

Wolselsy, Garnet, (edited by James A. Rawley); *THE AMERICAN CIVIL WAR: AN ENGLISH VIEW*, CWM:DEC/95[10], *reviewed by* Gary W. Gallagher

Wood, Forest G.; *BLACK SCARE: THE RACIST RESPONSE TO EMANCIPATION AND RECONSTRUCTION*, AHI:JUN/69[46], *reviewed by* Albert Castel

Woodward, Harold R. Jr. *THE CONFEDERACY'S FORGOTTEN SON: MAJOR GENERAL JAMES LAWSON KEMPER C.S.A.,* CWNEWS:APR/94[5], *reviewed by* Jeffry D. Wert, CWR:VOL4#1[78], *reviewed by* Homer Blass

Woodworth, Stephen E.:
JEFFERSON DAVIS AND HIS GENERALS: THE FAILURE OF CONFEDERATE COMMAND IN THE WEST, ACW:MAY/91[54], *reviewed by* Richard F. Welch, B&G:APR/91[28], *reviewed by* James L. McDonough, CWM:JAN/91[47], *reviewed by* Gary W. Gallagher, CWNEWS:JAN/91[4], *reviewed by* Anne J. Bailey, CWTI:FEB/91[10], *reviewed by* David Evans
LEADERSHIP AND COMMAND IN THE AMERICAN CIVIL WAR, CWTI:AUG/95[18]

Worsham, John H., (edited by James I. Robertson Jr.):
COMPEDIUM OF THE CONFEDERACY, AN ANNOTATED BIBLIOGRAPHY, 2 VOL., CWNEWS:MAY/90[4], *reviewed by* Michael Cavanaugh
ONE OF JACKSON'S FOOT CAVALRY BY JOHN H. WORSHAM, F. COMPANY, 21ST VIRGINIA INFANTRY, CWNEWS:MAY/89[4], *reviewed by* J. Tracy Power

Wren, James, (edited by John M. Priest); *FROM NEW BERN TO FREDERICKSBURG: CAPTAIN JAMES WREN'S DIARY,* CWNEWS:SEP/91[4], *reviewed by* Kevin J. Weddle

Wright, Mike; *CITY UNDER SIEGE: RICHMOND IN THE CIVL WAR,* CWTI:AUG/95[18]

Wright, Stephen J.; *THE IRISH BRIGADE,* CWNEWS:JAN/93[4], *reviewed by* Kevin E. O'Brien

Wyckoff, Mac; *A HISTORY OF THE 2ND SOUTH CAROLINA INFANTRY: 1861-65,* CWM:APR/95[8], *reviewed by* Charles R. Norville

Wyeth, John A.; *THAT DEVIL FORREST: LIFE OF GENERAL NATHAN BEDFORD FORREST,* CWNEWS:JAN/91[4], *reviewed by* Theodore P. Savas

Young, Mel; *WHERE THEY LIE, THE STORY OF JEWISH SOLDIERS OF THE NORTH AND SOUTH WHOSE DEATHS OCCURRED DURING THE CIVIL WAR,* ACW:JUL/91[50], *reviewed by* Nat C. Hughes Jr., CWNEWS:NOV/92[4], *reviewed by* Dr. David Martin

Younger, Robert, (edited by); *GETTYSBURG: HISTORICAL ARTICLES OF LASTING INTEREST,* CWNEWS:NOV/89[4], *reviewed by* Dr. Allen C. Guelzo

Zarefsky, David; *LINCOLN, DOUGLAS AND SLAVERY,* CWNEWS:NOV/94[33], *reviewed by* Judy Yandoh

BOOK REVIEWS, BY BOOK TITLE

1ST SOUTH CAROLINA VOLUNTEERS (GREGG'S),, by Ron Field, CWNEWS:NOV/92[4], *reviewed by,* Michael J. Winey

35 DAYS TO GETTYSBURG: THE CAMPAIGN DIARIES OF TWO AMERICAN ENEMIES, by Mark Nesbitt, ACW:MAR/93[58], *reviewed by,* Robert I. Alotta, CWNEWS:JUL/93[5], *reviewed by,* Dr. Richard A. Sauers, CWR:VOL2#4[346], *reviewed by,* Michael Russert

43RD BATTALION VIRGINIA CAVALRY, MOSBY'S COMMAND, by Hugh C. Keen, CWNEWS:MAY/94[5], *reviewed by,* Jeffry D. Wert

THE 149TH PENNSYLVANIA VOLUNTEER INFANTRY UNIT IN THE CIVIL WAR, by Richard E. Matthews, B&G:OCT/93[24], *reviewed by,* D. Scott Hartwig, CWM:0CT/95[10], *reviewed by,* Scott C. Patchan, CWNEWS:APR/95[33], *reviewed by,* Frank J. Piatek, CWR:VOL4#3[37]

"A PEOPLE'S CONTEST:" THE UNION AND CIVIL WAR 1861-1865, by Philip S. Paludan, CWNEWS:JUN/90[4], *reviewed by* Mark A. Snell

A BATTLE FROM THE START: THE LIFE OF NATHAN BEDFORD FORREST, by Brian Steel Wills, ACW:SEP/93[54], *reviewed by* Michael D. Hull, B&G:FEB/93[36], *reviewed by* James J. Cooke, CWNEWS:APR/93[4], *reviewed by* Michael Russert, CWTI:JAN/93[12], *reviewed by* Edwin C. Bearss

A BLOCKADED FAMILY: LIFE IN SOUTHERN ALABAMA DURING THE CIVIL WAR, by Parthenia A. Hague, (edited by Elizabeth Fox-Genovese), B&G:AUG/92[36], *reviewed by* Maxine Turner

A BOY'S SERVICE WITH THE 76TH OHIO, by Charles A. Willson, CWM:DEC/95[10], *reviewed by* Scott C. Patchan

A BRAVE BLACK REGIMENT: HISTORY OF THE 54TH REGIMENT OF MASSACHUSETTS VOLUNTEER INFANTRY, 1863-1865, Luis F. Emilio, (edited by Gregory J.W. Urwin), CWNEWS:JUL/93[5], *reviewed by* Judith Yandoh, CWR:VOL1#1[76], *reviewed by* Zoyd Luce, CWR:VOL4#3[1], *reviewed by* Stephen Engle, CWR:VOL4#3[1], *reviewed by* Leonne M. Hudson

A BULLET FOR LINCOLN, by Benjamin King, CWTI:NOV/93[14]

A BULLET FOR STONEWALL, by Benjamin King, CWM:SEP/91[58], *reviewed by* William J. Miller

A CAPTAIN'S WAR: THE LETTERS AND DIARIES OF CAPTAIN W.H.S. BURGWYN, by W.H.S. Burgwyn, (edited by Herbert M. Schiller), ACW:NOV/94[66], *reviewed by* William J. Shepher, B&G:OCT/94[40], *reviewed by* Ben Smith, CWNEWS:SEP/95[33], *reviewed by* Michael J. Winey, CWM:APR/95[50], *reviewed by* Gary W. Gallagher, CWR:VOL4#2[136], *reviewed by* Leonne M. Hudson

A CAROLINIAN GOES TO WAR: THE CIVIL WAR NARRATIVE OF ARTHUR MIDDLETON MANIGAULT, BRIGADIER GENERAL, C.S.A., by Arthur M. Manigault, (edited by R. Lockwood Tower), CWM:FEB/95[42]564, *reviewed by* Gary W. Gallagher

A CASPIAN SEA OF INK: THE MEADE-SICKLES CONTROVERSY, by Richard A. Sauers, CWNEWS:MAY/90[4], *reviewed by* Michael Russert

A CIVIL WAR TREASURY: BEING A MISCELLANY OF ARMS AND ARTILLERY, FACTS AND FIGURES, LEGENDS AND LORE, MUSES AND MINSTRELS AND PERSONALITIES AND PEOPLE, by Albert A. Nofi, B&G:JUN/93[28], *reviewed by* Rod Gragg, CWNEWS:AUG/93[5], *reviewed by* Barry Popchock, CWTI:MAY/93[18]

A COLONEL AT GETTYSBURG AND SPOTSYLVANIA: THE LIFE OF COLONEL JOSEPH NEWTON BROWN AND THE BATTLE OF GETTYSBURG AND SPOTSYLVANIA, by Varina D. Brown, CWNEWS:MAY/89[4], *reviewed by* Allen Guelzo

A COMMISSARY SERGEANT'S COOKBOOK, by Tom Kelley, CWNEWS:OCT/93[5], *reviewed by* Linda G. Black

A COMPENDIUM OF THE WAR OF THE REBELLION, by Frederick H. Dyer, CWM:FEB/95[42]564, *reviewed by* Gary W. Gallagher

A COMPLETE LIFE OF GENERAL GEORGE ARMSTRONG CUSTER, by Frederick Whitaker, CWR:VOL3#3[92], *reviewed by* Patrick S. Brady

A COMPROMISE OF PRINCIPLE: CONGRESSIONAL REPUBLICANS AND RECONSTRUCTION, 1863-1869, by Michael Les Benedict, AHI:JUN/75[50], *reviewed by* Maury Klein

A CONFEDERATE LADY COMES OF AGE: THE JOURNAL OF PAULINE DECARADEUC HEYWARD, 1863-1888, by Pauline D. Heyward, (edited by Mary D. Robertson), CWNEWS:APR/93[4], *reviewed by* Sarah W. Wiggins

A CONFEDERATE NURSE: THE DIARY OF ADA W. BACOT, 1860-1863, by Ada W. Bacot, (edited by Jean V. Berlin), CWNEWS:FEB/95[33], *reviewed by* Linda G. Black

A COUNTRY MADE BY WAR — FROM THE REVOLUTION TO VIETNAM, THE STORY OF AMERICA'S RISE TO POWER, by Geoffrey Perret, CWTI:DEC/89[20], *reviewed by* Richard Pindell

A CREEK WARRIOR FOR THE CONFEDERACY, THE AUTOBIOGRAPHY OF CHIEF G.W. GRAYSON, by G.W. Grayson, (edited by David Baird), CWNEWS:APR/90[4], *reviewed by* Ron Rago, CWNEWS:SEP/92[4], *reviewed by* Robert D. Norris Jr.

A CRISIS OF REPUBLICANISM: AMERICAN POLITICS DURING THE CIVIL WAR, (edited by) Lloyd E. Ambrosius, CWNEWS:JAN/92[4], *reviewed by* Michael Parrish

A DIARY OF BATTLE: THE PERSONAL JOURNALS OF COLONEL CHARLES, S. WAINWRIGHT, 1861-1865 by Charles A. Wainwright, (edited by ++, llen Nevins) CWM:FEB/95[42]564, *reviewed by* Gary W. Gallagher

A FRENCHMAN FIGHTS FOR THE UNION: VICTOR VIFQUAIN AND THE 97TH ILLINOIS, by Jeffrey H. Smith, CWNEWS:SEP/94[33], *reviewed by* Blake A. Magner

A FRONTIER STATE AT WAR: KANSAS 1861-1865, by Albert Castel, B&G:FEB/93[36], *reviewed by* Thomas Goodrich, CWNEWS:OCT/93[5], *reviewed by* Norman E. Rourke

A GOVERNMENT OF OUR OWN: THE MAKING OF THE CONFEDERACY, by William C. Davis, CWM:AUG/95[45], *reviewed by* Gary W. Gallagher, CWR:VOL4#3[37], CWTI:JUN/95[24], *reviewed by* Steven E. Woodworht

A GUIDE TO CIVIL WAR WASHINGTON, by Stephen M. Forman, B&G:OCT/95[28], *reviewed by* David E. Roth, CWNEWS:DEC/95[29], *reviewed by* Blake A. Magner, CWTI:OCT/95[18]

A GUIDE TO THE BATTLE OF CHICKAMAUGA, (edited by) Matt Struill, CWR:VOL4#1[78], *reviewed by* Howard L. Sandefer

A GUNBOAT NAMED *DIANA*, by Morris Raphael, CWNEWS:NOV/94[33], *reviewed by* Dale K. Phillips

A HISTORY OF A BRIGADE OF SOUTH CAROLINIANS, by J.F.J. Caldwell, CWR:VOL4#3[1], *reviewed by* Michael P. Musick

A HISTORY OF THE 2ND SOUTH CAROLINA INFANTRY: 1861-65, by Mac Wyckoff, CWM:APR/95[8], *reviewed by* Charles R. Norvill

A HISTORY OF THE 73RD ILLINOIS, CWR:VOL4#3[1], *reviewed by* Wiley Sword

A HISTORY OF THE FIFTH REGIMENT, NEW HAMPSHIRE VOLUNTEERS IN THE AMERICAN CIVIL WAR, 1861-1865, by William Child, CWR:VOL3#3[92], *reviewed by* Patrick S. Brady

A HISTORY OF THE FORTY-FOURTH REGIMENT NEW YORK VOLUNTEER INFANTRY, by Eugene Nash, CWNEWS:AUG/90[4], *reviewed by* William F. Howard

A HUNDRED BATTLES IN THE WEST. ST. LOUIS TO ATLANTA, 1861-1865. THE SECOND MICHIGAN CAVALRY, by Marshall P. Thatcher, CWNEWS:SEP/92[4], *reviewed by* John F. Marszalek

A LIEUTENANT OF CAVALRY IN LEE'S ARMY, by G.W. Beale, CWR:VOL4#3[37]

A LOST HEROINE OF THE CONFEDERACY, by Loretta Galbraith, edited by, CWNEWS:JUL/92[4], *reviewed by* Judy Yandoh

A LOST HEROINE OF THE CONFEDERACY: THE DIARIES AND LETTERS OF BELLE EDMONDSON, (edited by) Belle Edmondson, B&G:FEB/92[26], *reviewed by* Anne J. Bailey

A MANUAL OF MILITARY SURGERY, FOR THE USE OF SURGEONS IN THE CONFEDERATE ARMY; WITH AN APPENDIX OF THE RULES AND REGULATIONS OF THE MEDICAL DEPARTMENT OF THE CONFEDERATE ARMY, by J. Julian Chisolm, CWNEWS:JUL/91[4], *reviewed by* Harris D. Riley, M.D.

A MANUAL OF MILITARY SURGERY: OR HINTS ON THE EMERGENCIES OF FIELD, CAMP, AND HOSPITAL PRACTICE, by Samuel D. Gross, CWNEWS:NOV/90[4], *reviewed by* Dr. Harris D. Riley M.D.

A MANUAL OF MINOR SURGERY, by John H. Packard, CWNEWS:SEP/91[4], *reviewed by* Harris D. Riley M.D.

A NARRATIVE OF MILITARY SERVICE, by William B. Hazen, CWM:AUG/95[45], *reviewed by* Gary W. Gallagher

A NATION OF SOVERIGN STATES: SECESSION AND WAR IN THE CONFEDERACY, (edited by) Archie McDonald, CWNEWS:AUG/95[33], *reviewed by* Stephen D. Engle

A NORTHERN WOMAN IN THE PLANTATION SOUTH: LETTERS OF TRYPHENA BLANCHE HOLDER FOX, 1856-1876, Tryphena B.H. Fox, (edited by) Wilma King), CWM:APR/95[50], *reviewed by* Gary W. Gallagher

A PAIR OF BLANKETS: WAR-TIME HISTORY IN LETTERS TO THE YOUNG PEOPLE OF THE SOUTH, by William H. Stewart, CWNEWS:OCT/90[4], *reviewed by* Richard M. McMurry

A PHOTOGRAPHIC SUPPLEMENT OF CONFEDERATE SWORDS, by William A. Albaugh III, CWNEWS:AUG/95[33], *reviewed by* Dale E. Biever

A PICTORIAL GUIDE TO WEST VIRGINIA'S CIVIL WAR SITES AND RELATED INFORMATION, by Stan B. Cohen, CWNEWS:NOV/91[4], *reviewed by* Frank Piatek

A PICTORIAL HISTORY OF THE CIVIL WAR YEARS, by Paul M. Angle, AHI:JAN/68[55]

A POLITICIAN GOES TO WAR: THE CIVIL WAR LETTERS OF JOHN WHITE GEARY, by William Alan Blair, CWNEWS:SEP/95[33], *reviewed by* Ethan Rafuse

A POST OF HONOR: THE PRYOR LETTERS, 1861-63; LETTERS FROM CAPT. S.G. PRYOR, TWELFTH GEORGIA REGIMENT AND HIS WIFE, PENELOPE TYSON PRYOR, by Charles R. Pryor, CWM:FEB/95[42]564, *reviewed by* Gary W. Gallagher

A PRACTICAL TREATISE ON MILITARY SURGERY, by Frank H. Hamilton, CWNEWS:JUL/91[4], *reviewed by* Harris D. Riley, M.D.

A PRIVATE WAR, LETTERS AND DIARIES OF MADGE PRESTON 1862-1867, by Madge Preston, (edited by Virginia Walcott Beauchamp), CWNEWS:APR/90[4], *reviewed by* Judy Yandoh

A REBEL CAME HOME: THE DIARY AND LETTERS OF FLORIDE CLEMSON, 1863-1866, by Floride Clemson (edited by Ernest M. Lander Jr.), CWM:JAN/91[47], *reviewed by* Gary W. Gallagher, CWNEWS:MAY/91[4], *reviewed by* Brandon Beck

A REBEL WAR CLERK'S DIARY, by John B. Jones, (edited by Earl Schenck Miers), CWM:APR/95[50], *reviewed by* Gary W. Gallagher

A RISING THUNDER: FROM LINCOLN'S ELECTION TO THE BATTLE OF BULL RUN, AN EYEWITNESS HISTORY, by Richard Wheeler, ACW:NOV/94[66], *reviewed by* Al Hemingway, CWNEWS:OCT/95[33], *reviewed by* Ethan S. Rafuse, CWR:VOL4#3[37], CWTI:MAY/94[20], CWTI:JUN/95[24]

A SHOWER OF STARS; THE MEDAL OF HONOR AND THE 27TH MAINE, by John L. Pullen, AHI:FEB/67[57], *reviewed by* Ralph Adams Brown

A SOUTHERN RECORD: THE HISTORY OF THE THIRD REGIMENT LOUISIANA INFANTRY, by W.H. Tunnard, CWR:VOL4#3[1], *reviewed by* Arthur W. Bergeron

A SOUTHERN WOMAN'S STORY, by Phoebe Yates Pember, CWR:VOL4#3[1], *reviewed by* Tom Broadfoot

A STILLNESS AT APPOMATTOX, by Bruce Catton, CWR:VOL4#3[1], *reviewed by* Glenn LaFantasie

A SURGEON'S CIVIL WAR: THE LETTERS AND DIARY OF DANIEL M. HOLT, M.D., by Daniel M. Holt, (edited by James M. Greiner), ACW:JAN/95[62], CWM:DEC/95[10], *reviewed by* Kevin Conley Ruffner, CWNEWS:JUL/95[61], *reviewed by* Harris D. Riley M.D.

A TARHEEL CONFEDERATE AND HIS FAMILY, by Robert G. Elliott, CWNEWS:JAN/92[4], *reviewed by* Jeffry D. Wert

A USER'S GUIDE TO THE OFFICIAL RECORDS OF THE AMERICAN CIVIL WAR, by Barbara A. Aimone, CWNEWS:FEB/94[5], *reviewed by* Blake A. Magner

A USER'S GUIDE TO THE OFFICIAL RECORDS OF THE AMERICAN CIVIL WAR, by Alan C. Aimone, CWTI:SEP/93[26]

A VAST SEA OF MISERY: A HISTORY AND GUIDE TO THE UNION AND CONFEDERATE FIELD HOSPITALS AT GETTYSBURG JULY 1-NOVEMBER 20, 1864, by Gregory A. Coco, CWNEWS:NOV/89[4], *reviewed by* William Howard

A VOLUNTEER'S ADVENTURES: A UNION CAPTAIN'S RECORD OF THE CIVIL WAR, by John W. De Forest, (edited by James H. Croushore), CWM:FEB/95[42]564, *reviewed by* Gary W. Gallagher

A WOMAN OF VALOR: CLARA BARTON AND THE CIVIL WAR, by Stephen B. Oates, AHI:APR/95[26], CWM:APR/95[8], *reviewed by* Jim Percoco, CWTI:MAR/94[38]37, *reviewed by*

A WOMAN'S CIVIL WAR: A DIARY, WITH REMINISCENCES OF THE WAR, FROM MARCH 1862, by Cornelia P. McDonald, (edited by Minrose C. Gwinn), CWM:APR/95[50], *reviewed by* Gary W. Gallagher, CWTI:JAN/93[12], *reviewed by*

A. LINCOLN: HIS LAST 24 HOURS, by W. Emerson Reck, AHI:SEP/87[8], CWNEWS:JUN/92[4], *reviewed by* Terrence J. Winsch

ABANDONED BY LINCOLN: A MILITARY BIOGRAPHY OF GENERAL JOHN POPE, by Wallace J. Schutz, ACW:JAN/91[54], *reviewed by* John Guttman, CWM:JAN/91[47], *reviewed by* Gary W. Gallagher, CWNEWS:OCT/90[4], *reviewed by* Anne J. Bailey, CWTI:MAR/91[18], *reviewed by* John Hennessy

FALLEN LEAVES: THE CIVIL WAR LETTERS OF MAJOR HENRY LIVERMORE ABBOTT, by Henry L. Abbott (edited by Robert G. Scott), CWM:FEB/95[42]564, *reviewed by* Gary W. Gallagher

THE ABOLITIONIST LEGACY: FROM RECONSTRUCTION TO THE NAACP, by James M. McPherson, AHI:JUL/78[42]

ABOVE AND BEYOND: A HISTORY OF THE MEDAL OF HONOR FROM THE CIVIL WAR TO VIETNAM, by Time-Life Books, AHI:JAN/86[9]

ABRAHAM LINCOLN AND THE SECOND AMERICAN REVOLUTION, by James M. McPherson, CWM:MAY/91[34], *reviewed by* Edward C. Smith, CWNEWS:JUN/92[4], *reviewed by* Jeffry D. Wert, CWTI:AUG/91[18], *reviewed by* Harold Holzer

ABRAHAM LINCOLN AT CITY POINT, by Donald C. Pfanz, CWNEWS:NOV/90[4], *reviewed by* William Blake

ABRAHAM LINCOLN THE ORATOR: PENETRATING THE LINCOLN LEGEND, by Lois Einhorn, B&G:OCT/93[24], *reviewed by* Harold Holzer

ABRAHAM LINCOLN'S FLAG, by Howard Miller, CWNEWS:NOV/95[29], *reviewed by* Steven J. Wright

ABRAHAM LINCOLN, 1809-1858, by Albert J. Beveridge, CWTI:DEC/95[38]

ABRAHAM LINCOLN, A BIOGRAPHY, by Benjamin Thomas, CWTI:DEC/95[38]

ABRAHAM LINCOLN, by David D. Anderson, AHI:JUL/70[50]

ABRAHAM LINCOLN, by Lord Longford, AHI:OCT/76[49], *reviewed by* Robert D. Hoffsommer

ABRAHAM LINCOLN: A HISTORY, by John G. Nicolay, CWTI:DEC/95[38]

ABRAHAM LINCOLN: A PRESS PORTRAIT, (edited by) Herbert Mitgan, CWNEWS:APR/91[4], *reviewed by* Michael Russert

ABRAHAM LINCOLN: SOURCES AND STYLE OF LEADERSHIP, (edited by) Frank J. Williams, CWM:DEC/95[10], *reviewed by* J. Jeffrey Cox

ABRAHAM LINCOLN: THE MAN BEHIND THE MYTHS, by Stephen B. Oates, AHI:SEP/84[50]

ABRAHAM LINCOLN; A HISTORY, by Paul M. Angle, AHI:FEB/67[57], *reviewed by* Ralph Adams Brown

ACADIAN GENERAL: ALFRED MOUTON AND THE CIVIL WAR, by William Arceneaux, CWNEWS:APR/90[4], *reviewed by* Frank Piatek

ACROSS THE RAPPAHONNOCK: FROM FREDERICKSBURG TO THE MUD MARCH, by Bradley Finfrock, CWNEWS:SEP/95[33], *reviewed by* David F. Riggs

ADVANCE AND RETREAT: PERSONAL EXPERIENCES IN THE UNITED STATES AND CONFEDERATE STATES ARMIES, by John B. Hood, ACW:NOV/94[66], *reviewed by* Michael D. Hull, CWM:OCT/94[8], *reviewed by* Jim Percoco, CWM:FEB/95[42], *reviewed by* Gary W. Gallagher, CWM:APR/95[50], *reviewed by* Gary W. Gallagher

ADVANCE THE COLORS!: PENNSYLVANIA CIVIL WAR BATTLE FLAGS, II, by Richard A. Sauers, B&G:JUN/93[28], *reviewed by* Paul Ellingson, CWNEWS:DEC/92[4], *reviewed by* Michael J. Winey

AERONAUTICS IN THE UNION AND CONFEDERATE ARMIES, by F. Stansbury Haydon, CWNEWS:SEP/90[4], *reviewed by* Steven J. Wright

AHEAD OF HER TIME: ABBY KELLEY AND THE POLITICS OF ANTISLAVERY, by Dorothy Sterling, CWNEWS:NOV/92[4], *reviewed by* Linda G. Black

ALBERT SIDNEY JOHNSTON: SOLDIER OF THREE REPUBLICS, by Charles P. Roland, CWM:FEB/95[42]564, *reviewed by* Gary W. Gallagher

MILITARY MEMOIRS OF A CONFEDERATE: A CRITICAL NARRATIVE, by E. Porter Alexander, CWM:FEB/95[42], *reviewed by* Gary W. Gallagher

ALEXANDER CHEVES HASKELL: THE PORTRAIT OF A MAN, by Louise H. Daly, CWNEWS:OCT/90[4], *reviewed by* Michael Russert

ALLIES FOR FREEDOM: BLACKS AND JOHN BROWN, by Benjamin Quarles, AHI:AUG/75[50], *reviewed by* Allan Keller

AMERICA IN 1857, by Kenneth Stampp, ACW:SEP/91[54], *reviewed by* Ken Bivin

AMERICA'S NATIONAL BATTLEFIELD PARKS: A GUIDE, by Joseph E. Stevens, B&G:DEC/91[30], *reviewed by* Jerry L. Russell, CWNEWS:MAY/92[4], *reviewed by* Michael Mullins

THE AMERICAN CIVIL WAR AND THE ORIGINS OF MODERN WARFARE, by Edward Hagerman, CWM:DEC/94[7], *reviewed by* General Philip L. Bolte', CWNEWS:MAY/90[4], *reviewed by* Brian C. Pohanka

THE AMERICAN CIVIL WAR, (edited by) Thomas E. Griess, CWNEWS:JAN/90[4], *reviewed by* Blake Magner

THE AMERICAN CIVIL WAR: AN ENGLISH VIEW, by Garnet Wolselsy, (edited by James A. Rawley), CWM:DEC/95[10], *reviewed by* Gary W. Gallagher

THE AMERICAN CONSCIENCE: THE DRAMA OF THE LINCOLN-DOUGLAS DEBATES, by Saul Sigelschiffer, AHI:JUL/75[50], *reviewed by* Gary R. Planck

THE AMERICAN DAGUERREOTYPE, by Floyd Rinhart, AHI:FEB/82[9], *reviewed by* Frederic Ray

THE AMERICAN INDIAN AND THE END OF THE CONFEDERACY: 1863-1866, by Annie H. Abel, CWNEWS:JUL/93[5], *reviewed by* Robert D. Norris Jr., CWNEWS:FEB/94[5], *reviewed by* Ted Alexander

AMERICAN GOTHIC: THE STORY OF AMERICA'S LEGENDARY THEATRICAL FAMILY — JUNIUS, EDWIN AND JOHN WILKES BOOTH, by Gene Smith, AHI:MAR/93[20]

AMERICAN HERITAGE BATTLE MAPS OF THE CIVIL WAR, CWTI:SEP/94[18]

AMERICAN MILITARY, SOURCEBOOK AND DIRECTORY THE WHO'S WHO IN MILITARIA, by Phoenix Militaria, Inc., CWNEWS:APR/90[4], *reviewed by* Russ A. Prichard

AMERICAN NEGRO SLAVERY: A DOCUMENTARY
HISTORY, (edited by) Michael Mullin, AHI:FEB/77[49],
reviewed by Bell I. Wiley

AMERICAN SWORDS AND SWORD MAKERS, by Richard
Bezdek, CWNEWS:OCT/94[33], *reviewed by* Ron G. Hickox

AMONG THE COTTON THIEVES, by Edward Bacon,
CWNEWS:MAY/92[4], *reviewed by* Jock Baird

AN ALPHABETICAL LIST OF THE BATTLES OF THE
WAR OF THE REBELLION, WITH DATES, FROM FT.
SUMTER, SC, APRIL 12 AND 13, 1861, TO KIRBY
SMITH'S SURRENDER, MAY 26, 1865, by J.W. Wells,
CWNEWS:SEP/91[4]

AN AMERICAN ILIAD: THE STORY OF THE CIVIL WAR,
by Charles P. Roland, B&G:FEB/92[26], *reviewed by* Brian C.
Pohanka, CWM:JAN/92[57], *reviewed by* Gary W. Gallagher,
CWNEWS:SEP/92[4], *reviewed by* Dr. Richard A. Sauers

AN EPITOME OF PRACTICAL SURGERY FOR FIELD
AND HOSPITAL, by Edward Warren, CWNEWS:JUL/91[4],
reviewed by Harris D. Riley, M.D.

AN INTRODUCTION OT CIVIL WAR SMALL ARMS, by
Earl J. Coates, CWNEWS:MAY/92[4], *reviewed by* Russ
Pritchard

AN IRISHMAN IN DIXIE: THOMAS CONOLLY'S DIARY
OF THE FALL OF THE CONFEDERACY, by Thomas
Conolly (edited by Nelson D. Lankford), CWNEWS:SEP/89[8],
reviewed by Robert D. Norris

AN IRISHMAN IN THE IRON BRIGADE: THE CIVIL WAR
MEMOIRS OF JAMES P. SULLIVAN, SERGEANT, 6TH
WISCONSIN VOLUNTEERS, by William J.K. Beaudot,
CWM:FEB/95[7], *reviewed by* Ben Maryniak,
CWM:APR/95[50], *reviewed by* Gary W. Gallagher,
CWNEWS:MAY/94[5], *reviewed by* Kevin E. O'Brien

AN OLD CREED FOR THE NEW SOUTH, PRO-SLAVERY
IDEOLOGY AND HISTORIOGRAPHY, 1865-1918, by John
D. Smith, CWNEWS:APR/93[4], *reviewed by* John F. Marszalek

AN UNCOMMON SOLDIER: THE CIVIL WAR LETTERS
OF SARAH ROSETTA WAKEMAN, ALIAS PVT. LYONS
WAKEMAN, 153RD REGIMENT, ORK STATE
VOLUNTEERS, 1862-1864, (edited by) Lauren Cook Burgess,
B&G:FEB/95[26], *reviewed by* Holly A. Robinson,
CWNEWS:APR/95[33]

THE ANDERSONVILLE DIARY & MEMOIRS OF
CHARLES HOPKINS, by Charles Hopkins, (edited by
William B. Styple), CWNEWS:MAY/90[4], *reviewed by* Jeffry
D. Wert

ANDERSONVILLE: THE LAST DEPOT, by William Marvel,
B&G:JUN/95[30], *reviewed by* Tom Watson Brown,
CWM:AUG/95[45], *reviewed by* Gary W. Gallagher,
CWM:OCT/95[10], *reviewed by* Jim Percoco, CWR:VOL4#3[37],
CWR:VOL4#3[89], *reviewed by* Anne J. Bailey,
CWTI:MAR/95[14]

THE ANNALS OF THE WAR, WRITTEN BY LEADING
PARTICIPANTS NORTH AND SOUTH, by A.K. McClure,
CWM:FEB/95[42]564, *reviewed by* Gary W. Gallagher

ANOTHER CIVIL WAR; LABOR, CAPITAL, AND THE
STATE IN THE ANTHRACITE REGIONS OF
PENNSYLVANIA, 1840-68, by Grace Palladino,
CWM:JAN/91[47], *reviewed by* Gary W. Gallagher

THE ANTIETAM AND FREDERICKSBURG, by Francis W.
Palfrey, CWNEWS:JAN/91[4], *reviewed by* Judy Yandoh

ANTIETAM, THE AFTERMATH, by Wilmer M. Mumma,
CWNEWS:APR/94[5], *reviewed by* Blake A. Magner

ANTIETAM: ESSAYS ON THE 1862 MARYLAND
CAMPAIGN, (edited by) Gary W. Gallagher,
CWNEWS:APR/90[4], *reviewed by* Michael Mullins

ANTIETAM: THE SOLDIER'S BATTLE, by John M. Priest,
CWNEWS:JUN/90[4], *reviewed by* J. Tracy Power

APPOMATTOX COMMANDER: THE STORY OF GENERAL
E.O.C. ORD, by Bernarr Cresap, AHI:FEB/82[9], *reviewed by*
Richard J. Sommers

APRIL '65: CONFEDERATE COVERT ACTION IN THE
AMERICAN CIVIL WAR, by William A. Tidwell,
CWNEWS:AUG/95[33], *reviewed by* Michael P. Musick,
CWTI:OCT/95[18], *reviewed by* WIlliam Hanchett

ARCHAEOLOGY, HISTORY, AND CUSTER'S LAST
BATTLE: THE LITTLE BIG HORN REEXAMINED, by
Richard A. Fox Jr., CWNEWS:AUG/94[33], *reviewed by* Brian
C. Pohanka

ARCHEOLOGICAL PERSPECTIVES ON THE BATTLE OF
LITTLE BIGHORN, by Douglas D. Scott,
CWNEWS:JUN/91[4], *reviewed by* Brian Pohanka

ARCHIVE OF THE CIVIL WAR, by Archive Society,
ACW:JUL/92[54], *reviewed by* Jon Guttman

THE ARMIES OF THE STREETS: THE NEW YORK CITY
DRAFT RIOTS OF 1863, by Adrian Cook, AHI:JAN/76[39],
reviewed by David Lindsey

ARMING THE SUCKERS, 1861-1865, by Ken Baumann,
CWNEWS:AUG/91[4], *reviewed by* Blake Magner

ARMS AND EQUIPMENT OF THE CONFEDERACY, by
Time-Life, MH:DEC/92[74]

ARMS AND EQUIPMENT OF THE UNION, by Time-Life,
MH:DEC/92[74]

THE ARMY CALLED IT HOME: MILITARY INTERIORS OF
THE 19TH CENTURY, by William L. Brown III,
CWNEWS:OCT/93[5], *reviewed by* Michael Russert

THE ARMY OF NORTHERN VIRGINIA, by William Allan,
CWM:JUN/95[6], *reviewed by* Gary W. Gallagher

THE ARMY OF ROBERT E. LEE, by Philip Katcher,
CWNEWS:NOV/95[29], *reviewed by* Stephen L. Ritchie,
CWTI:DEC/94[18], *reviewed by*

THE ARMY OF TENNESSEE, by Stanley F. Horn,
CWM:APR/95[8], *reviewed by* Gary W. Gallagher,
CWNEWS:MAY/94[5], *reviewed by* Harris D. Riley M.D.

THE ARMY OF THE CUMBERLAND, by Henry M. Cist,
CWNEWS:JUN/91[4], *reviewed by* Jeffry D. Wert

THE ARMY OF THE POTOMAC TRILOGY — MR
LINCOLN'S ARMY, GLORY ROAD, AND A STILLNESS
AT APPOMATTOX, by Bruce Catton, CWM:FEB/95[42],
reviewed by Gary W. Gallagher

THE ARMY OF THE POTOMAC: ITS ORGANIZATION, ITS
COMMANDER, AND ITS CAMPAIGN, by Prince de
Joinville, CWM:JUN/95[6], *reviewed by* William J. Miller

THE ARMY UNDER POPE, by John C. Ropes,
CWNEWS:JAN/91[4], *reviewed by* Judy Yandoh

ARMY OF THE HEARTLAND, by Richard M. McMurray,
CWM:APR/95[8], *reviewed by* Gary W. Gallagher

ARMY OF THE HEARTLAND: THE ARMY OF
TENNESSEE, 1861-1862, by Thomas L. Connelly,
CWM:FEB/95[42]564

ARMY OF THE POTOMAC SERIES, CWNEWS:DEC/94[33],
reviewed by Blake A. Magner

ARTILLERY HELL: THE EMPLOYMENT OF ARTILLERY
AT ANTIETAM, by Curt Johnson, B&G:OCT/95[28], *reviewed*
by John M. Priest, CWNEWS:DEC/95[29], *reviewed by* Ted
Alexander

THE ARTILLERY OF NATHAN BEDFORD FORREST'S CAVALRY, by John Watson Morton, CWNEWS:JAN/90[4], *reviewed by* Dr. Allen C. Guelzo

AS IT WAS: REMINISCENCES OF A SOLDIER OF THE THIRD TEXAS CAVALRY AND THE NINETEENTH LOUISIANA INFANTRY, by Douglas J. Cater, CWNEWS:JUL/92[4], *reviewed by* Robert D. Norris Jr.

THE ASSASSINATION OF LINCOLN: HISTORY AND MYTH, by Lloyd Lewis, ACW:JAN/95[62], CWM:FEB/95[7], *reviewed by* J. Jeffery Cox

THE ATLANTA CAMPAIGN — A CIVIL WAR DRIVING TOUR, by J. Britt McCarley, CWNEWS:NOV/90[4], *reviewed by* Kemp Burpeau

THE ATLANTA CAMPAIGN: MAY-NOVEMBER, 1864, by John Cannan, CWNEWS:NOV/92[4], *reviewed by* Anne J. Bailey

ATLANTA, by Jacob D. Cox, CWNEWS:NOV/91[4], *reviewed by* John F. Marszalek

THE ATLANTIC COAST, by Daniel Ammen, CWNEWS:MAY/91[4], *reviewed by* Frank Piatek

THE ATLAS FOR THE AMERICAN CIVIL WAR, (edited by) Thomas E. Griess, CWNEWS:JAN/90[4], *reviewed by* Blake Magner

THE ATLAS OF THE CIVIL WAR, (edited by) James M. McPherson, AHI:JUN/95[28], CWNEWS:APR/95[33], *reviewed by* Blake A. Magner, CWTI:JUN/95[24],

THE ATTACK AND DEFENSE OF LITTLE ROUND TOP, by Oliver W. Norton, AHI:AUG/78[49], *reviewed by* Edward G. Longacre

ATTACK AND DIE: CIVIL WAR MILITARY TACTICS AND THE SOUTHERN HERITAGE, by Grady McWhiney, CWM:FEB/95[42]564, *reviewed by* Gary W. Gallagher

AUTOBIOGRAPHY OF READ ADMIRAL CHARLES WILKES, U.S. NAVY 1798-1877, by William James Morgan, AHI:JUN/80[6], *reviewed by* Norman C. Delaney

AUTUMN OF GLORY, by Richard M. McMurray, CWM:APR/95[8], *reviewed by* Gary W. Gallagher

AUTUMN OF GLORY: THE ARMY OF TENNESSEE, 1862-1865, by Thomas L. Connelly, The *Civil War Magazine* 100 Books CWM:FEB/95[42]564, *reviewed by* Gary W. Gallagher

THE BACHELDER PAPERS: GETTYSBURG IN THEIR OWN WORDS, (edited by) David L. Ladd, CWNEWS:DEC/95[29], *reviewed by* D. Scott Hartwig, CWR:VOL4#3[37]

BACK DOOR TO RICHMOND: THE BERMUDA HUNDRED CAMPAIGN, APRIL-JUNE 1864, by William G. Robertson, CWTI:MAR/89[10], *reviewed by* Howard C. Westwood

BAD HAND: A BIOGRAPHY OF GENERAL RANALD S. MACKENZIE, by Charles M. Robinson III, CWNEWS:JUL/94[25], *reviewed by* Michael Russert

BALLADS OF THE BLUE AND GRAY, by Griffith H. Williams, CWNEWS:AUG/93[5], *reviewed by* Linda G. Black

THE BATTLE OF BELMONT: GRANT STRIKES SOUTH, by Nathaniel C. Hughes, ACW:JUL/92[54], *reviewed by* Roy Morris Jr., B&G:APR/92[24], *reviewed by* Michael L. Gillespe, CWM:MAR/92[49], *reviewed by* Gary W. Gallagher, CWNEWS:JAN/93[4], *reviewed by* Dr. Richard A. Sauers, CWR:VOL2#1[78], *reviewed by* David A. Woodbury

THE BATTLE OF CEDAR CREEK: SHOWDOWN IN THE SHENANDOAH, OCTOBER 1-30, 1864, by Theodore C. Mahr, B&G:OCT/93[24], *reviewed by* Jeffry D. Wert

THE BATTLE OF CHICKAMAUGA, (edited by) Gerald Standley, CWNEWS:AUG/90[4], *reviewed by* Jeffry D. Wert

THE BATTLE OF GETTYSBURG, by Frank A. Haskell, CWNEWS:SEP/95[33], *reviewed by* David F. Riggs

THE BATTLE OF GETTYSBURG, by Neil Johnson, CWTI:APR/90[10]

THE BATTLE OF GETTYSBURG, by George G. Meade, CWNEWS:JAN/90[4], *reviewed by* Richard Sauers

THE BATTLE OF NEW MARKET, by Joseph W.A. Whitehorne, CWNEWS:APR/90[4], *reviewed by* Jeffry D. Wert

THE BATTLE OF OLD MEN AND YOUNG BOYS, JUNE 9 1864: THE PETERSBURG CAMPAIGN, by William G. Robertson, CWNEWS:SEP/90[4], *reviewed by* Dave Riggs

THE BATTLE OF OLUSTEE: THE CIVIL WAR IN FLORIDA, by Lewis G. Schmidt, CWNEWS:JUL/91[4], *reviewed by* Michael Policatti

THE BATTLE OF SEVEN PINES, by Steven H. Newton, CWM:JUN/95[6], *reviewed by* Gary W. Gallagher

THE BATTLE OF THE WILDERNESS MAY 5-6, 1864, by Gordon C. Rhea, B&G:APR/95[30], *reviewed by* Noah Andre Trudeau, CWM:AUG/95[45], *reviewed by* Gary W. Gallagher, CWNEWS:NOV/95[29], *reviewed by* Theodore P. Savas, CWR:VOL4#3[89], *reviewed by* Robert E. L. Krick

BATTLE AT CORRICKS FORD: CONFEDERATE DISASTER AND LOSS OF A LEADER, by W. Hunter Lesser, CWNEWS:NOV/95[29], *reviewed by* Steven J. Wright

BATTLE IN THE WILDERNESS: GRANT MEETS LEE, by Grady McWhiney, CWNEWS:DEC/95[29], *reviewed by* Ted Alexander

BATTLE OF THE ROSEBUD: PRELUDE TO THE LITTLE BIG HORN, by Neil C. Mangum, CWNEWS:JUL/90[4], *reviewed by* Michael Mullins

BATTLE OF TREVILIAN STATION WITH EYEWITNESS MEMOIRS, by Walbrook D. Swank, CWNEWS:OCT/95[33], *reviewed by* Frank J. Piatek

BATTLE TACTICS OF THE CIVIL WAR, by Paddy Griffith, CWNEWS:JAN/90[4], *reviewed by* A. Wilson Greene, CWTI:SEPT/89[28]

BATTLEFIELD: FARMING A CIVIL WAR BATTLEGROUND, by Peter Svenson, AHI:MAY/93[22], CWNEWS:NOV/93[5], *reviewed by* Mark Stephens

BATTLES AND LEADERS OF THE CIVIL WAR, by Robert U. Johnson, CWM:FEB/95[42], *reviewed by* Gary W. Gallagher

"BAYONET! FORWARD": MY CIVIL WAR REMINISCENCES, by Joshua L. Chamberlain, CWTI:JUN/95[24]

THE BEAT OF THE DRUM, by Don McDowell, CWNEWS:DEC/94[33], *reviewed by* Mark Stephens

BEFORE ANTIETAM: THE BATTLE FOR SOUTH MOUNTAIN, by John M. Priest, ACW:JUL/93[58], *reviewed by* Jon Guttma, CWNEWS:JUN/93[5], *reviewed by* Jeffry Wert, CWR:VOL3#2[105], *reviewed by* Theodore P. Savas

BEN MCCULLOCH AND THE FRONTIER MILITARY TRADITION, by Thomas W. Cutrer, B&G:APR/94[24], *reviewed by* Anne J. Bailey, CWM:APR/95[50], *reviewed by* Gary W. Gallagher, CWNEWS:DEC/93[5], *reviewed by* Norman E. Rourke, CWR:VOL3#4[68], *reviewed by* David P. Smith

BENJAMIN FRANKLIN BUTLER: THE DAMNEDEST YANKEE, by Dick Nolan, CWNEWS:SEP/92[4], *reviewed by* William Marvel

THE BERMUDA HUNDRED CAMPAIGN, by Herbert M. Schiller, CWNEWS:NOV/89[4], *reviewed by* Kevin J. Weddle

BERRY BENSON'S CIVIL WAR BOOK: MEMOIRS OF A CONFEDERATE SCOUT AND SHARPSHOOTER, by Berry Benson, (edited by Susan W. Benson), CWM:APR/95[50], *reviewed by* Gary W. Gallagher, CWNEWS:SEP/94[33], *reviewed by* T. Michael Parrish, CWR:VOL3#2[105], *reviewed by* John McGlone

BEST LITTLE STORIES FROM THE CIVIL WAR, by C. Brian Kelly, ACW:SEP/95[62], *reviewed by* Michael D. Hull, CWNEWS:OCT/95[33], *reviewed by* Frank J. Piatek

BETWEEN THE ENEMY AND TEXAS: PARSON'S TEXAS CAVALRY IN THE CIVIL WAR, by Anne J. Bailey, CWNEWS:OCT/90[4], *reviewed by* Robert D. Norris

THE BIRTH OF COLORADO: A CIVIL WAR PERSPECTIVE, by Duane A. Smith, CWNEWS:NOV/90[4], *reviewed by* Theodore P. Savas

THE BIRTH OF COLORADO: A CIVL WAR PERSPECTIVE, by Duane A. Smith, CWM:JAN/91[47], *reviewed by* Gary W. Gallagher

THE BIVOUACS OF THE DEAD: THE STORY OF THOSE WHO DIED AT ANTIETAM AND SOUTH MOUNTAIN, by Steven R. Stotelmyer, CWNEWS:SEP/93[5], *reviewed by* Kevin Weddle

THE BLACK INFANTRY IN THE WEST, 1869-1891, by Arlen L. Fowler, AHI:NOV/71[48], *reviewed by* Benjamin Quarles

THE BLACK WEST: A DOCUMENTARY AND PICTORIAL HISTORY by William Loren Katz, AHI:DEC/72[49], *reviewed by* Gossie H. Hudson

BLACK CONFEDERATES AND AFRO-YANKEES IN CIVIL WAR VIRGINIA, by Ervin L. Jordan Jr., CWM:AUG/95[45], *reviewed by* Gary W. Gallagher

BLACK FLAG: GUERRILLA WARFARE ON THE WESTERN BORDER 1861-1865, by Thomas Goodrich, ACW:JUL/95[58], *reviewed by* Richard Gilbert

BLACK SCARE: THE RACIST RESPONSE TO EMANCIPATION AND RECONSTRUCTION, by Forest G. Wood, AHI:JUN/69[46], *reviewed by* Albert Castel

BLACK TROOPS, WHITE COMMANDERS AND FREEDMEN DURING THE CIVIL WAR, by Howard C. Westwood, B&G:FEB/93[36], *reviewed by* Richard Rollin, CWR:VOL2#3[256], *reviewed by* Steven E. Woodworth

BLACKS IN THE BLUE AND GRAY: AFRO-AMERICAN SERVICE IN THE CIVIL WAR, by Hubert C. Blackerby, CWNEWS:MAY/92[4], *reviewed by* Robert L. Uzzel

THE BLOCKADE RUNNERS: TRUE TALES OF RUNNING THE YANKEE BLOCKADE OF THE CONFEDERATE COAST, by Dave Horner, CWNEWS:OCT/94[33], *reviewed by* Gary Augustine

BLOCKADERS, REFUGEES & CONTRABANDS — CIVIL WAR ON FLORIDA'S GULF COAST 1861-65 by George E. Buker, CWM:APR/95[50], *reviewed by* Gary W. Gallagher, CWNEWS:NOV/94[33], *reviewed by* Clint Johnson, CWR:VOL4#2[136], *reviewed by* Daniel E. Sutherland

BLOOD & SACRIFICE: THE CIVIL WAR JOURNAL OF A CONFEDERATE SOLDIER, by William Pitt Chambers (edited by Richard A. Baumgartner), CWM:AUG/95[45], *reviewed by* Gary W. Gallagher

BLOOD AND TREASURE: CONFEDERATE EMPIRE IN THE SOUTHWEST, by Donald S. Frazier, ACW:NOV/95[62], *reviewed by* Maureen Creamer, CWR:VOL4#3[37], CWR:VOL4#4[129], *reviewed by* Melvin C. Johnson

BLOOD BROTHERS: A SHORT HISTORY OF THE CIVIL WAR, by Frank E. Vandiver, B&G:OCT/93[24], *reviewed by* James A. Ramage, CWNEWS:OCT/93[5], *reviewed by* Richard M. McMurry, CWR:VOL3#1[80], *reviewed by* Steven J. Wright

BLOODY DAWN: THE STORY OF THE LAWRENCE MASSACRE, by Thomas Goodrich, B&G:JUN/92[28], *reviewed by* Harris D. Riley, M.D., CWNEWS:OCT/93[5], *reviewed by* Mike Cavanaugh

BLOODY ROADS SOUTH: THE WILDERNESS TO COLD HARBOR, MAY-JUNE 1864, by Noah Andre Trudeau, CWNEWS:SEP/90[4], *reviewed by* Mark Snell, CWTI:FEB/90[10], *reviewed by* Gary W. Gallagher

THE BLUE AND THE GRAY, by Thomas B. Allen, ACW:MAR/93[58], *reviewed by* Jon Guttman, CWNEWS:APR/93[4], *reviewed by* Frank J. Piatek, CWTI:JAN/93[12]

BLUE AND GRAY ROSES OF INTRIGUE, by Rebecca D. Larson, CWNEWS:FEB/94[5], *reviewed by* DeAnne Blanton

BLUE-EYED CHILD OF FORTUNE: THE CIVIL WAR LETTERS OF ROBERT GOULD SHAW, by Robert G. Shaw, (edited by Russell Duncan), B&G:OCT/93[24], *reviewed by* Warren Wilkinson, CWM:FEB/95[42]564, *reviewed by* Gary W. Gallagher, CWNEWS:MAY/93[4], *reviewed by* William Marvel, CWR:VOL3#1[80], *reviewed by* Stephen D. Engle, CWR:VOL4#3[1], *reviewed by* Stephen Engle, CWTI:JUL/93[12]

BLUEPRINT FOR MODERN AMERICA: NONMILITARY LEGISLATION OF THE FIRST CIVIL WAR CONGRESS, by Leonard P. Curry, CWM:FEB/95[7], *reviewed by* Gary W. Gallagher

BOLD DRAGOON: THE LIFE OF J.E.B. STUART, by Emory M. Thomas, AHI:OCT/86[8], CWM:FEB/95[42]564, *reviewed by* Gary W. Gallagher

THE BOYS' WAR, by Jim Murphy, ACW:MAR/92[54], *reviewed by* Kenneth P. Czech

BRAXTON BRAGG AND CONFEDERATE DEFEAT, VOL II, by Judith L. Hallock, CWR:VOL2#2[169], *reviewed by* Larry J. Daniel

BRAWLING BRASS: NORTH AND SOUTH, by Harold B. Simpson, CWNEWS:APR/92[4], *reviewed by* Theodore P. Savas

BRAXTON BRAGG AND CONFEDERATE DEFEAT, VOL II, by Judith L. Hallock, B&G:AUG/92[36], *reviewed by* Richard M. McMurry, CWNEWS:JUL/93[5], *reviewed by* William L. Shea, CWR:VOL2#2[169], *reviewed by* Larry J. Daniel

BRECKINRIDGE: STATESMAN, SOLDIER, SYMBOL, by William C. Davis, CWM:FEB/95[42]564, *reviewed by* Gary W. Gallagher

BREVET BRIGADIER GENERALS IN BLUE, by Roger D. Hunt, CWNEWS:SEP/90[4], *reviewed by* Michael Mullins

THE BRITISH FOREIGN SERVICE AND THE AMERICAN CIVIL WAR, by Eugene H. Berwanger, CWR:VOL4#3[37]

BROTHER AGAINST BROTHER, by William C Davis, AHI:SEP/84[50]

THE BROTHER'S WAR: CIVIL WAR LETTERS TO THEIR LOVED ONES FROM THE BLUE AND GRAY, (edited by) Annette Tappert, CWNEWS:JUN/90[4], *reviewed by* Michael A. Hughes, CWTI:SEPT/89[28], *reviewed by* Sarah Woolfork Wiggins

BUCK'S BOOK: A VIEW OF THE 3RD VERMONT INFANTRY REGIMENT, by Erastus Buck, (edited by John E. Balzer), CWNEWS:JAN/95[25], *reviewed by* Blake A. Magner

THE BUFFALO SOLDIERS. A NARRATIVE OF THE NEGRO CAVALRY IN THE WEST, by William H. Leckie, AHI:AUG/67[59], *reviewed by* Wilber S. Nye

BUGLES ECHO ACROSS THE VALLEY: NORTHERN OSWEGO COUNTY NEW YORK AND THE CIVIL WAR, by David K. Parsons, CWNEWS:JUL/95[61], *reviewed by* Michael Russert

BUILDING THE MYTH: SELECTED SPEECHES MEMORIALIZING ABRAHAM LINCOLN, (edited by Waldo W. Baden), CWM:JAN/92[57], *reviewed by* Gary W. Gallagher, CWNEWS:JUN/92[4], *reviewed by* David F. Riggs

BULL RUN, by Paul Fleischman, CWNEWS:JUL/95[61], *reviewed by* Dr. David Martin

THE BURDEN OF SOUTHERN HISTORY, by C. Vann Woodward, AHI:FEB/69[49]

BURNSIDE, by William Marvel, B&G:AUG/92[36], *reviewed by* Lawrence A. Kohl, CWM:FEB/95[42]564, *reviewed by* Gary W. Gallagher, CWNEWS:JUN/93[5], *reviewed by* John Farber, CWR:VOL2#2[169], *reviewed by* David A. Woodbury

BUSHWHACKERS! THE CIVIL WAR IN NORTH CAROLINA, VOL. 2, THE MOUNTAINS, by William R. Trotter, CWNEWS:JAN/90[4], *reviewed by* Steven J. Wright, CWNEWS:NOV/92[4], *reviewed by* Steven J. Wright

BENJAMIN FRANKLIN BUTLER: THE DAMNEDEST YANKEE, by Dick Nolan, CWNEWS:SEP/92[4], *reviewed by* William Marvel

BUTLER AND HIS CAVALRY IN THE WAR OF SECESSION 1861-1865, by Ulysses R. Brooks, CWNEWS:JAN/92[4], *reviewed by* Richard A. Sauers, CWR:VOL1#2[78], *reviewed by* James Harwick Jr.

BY THE DIM AND FLARING LAMPS: THE CIVIL WAR DIARY OF SAMUEL MCILVAINE, FEBRUARY THROUGH JUNE 1862, by Samuel McIlvaine, (edited by Clayton E. Cramer), CWNEWS:JUL/92[4], *reviewed by* Dr. Allen C. Guelzo

CADETS IN GRAY: THE STORY OF THE CADETS OF THE SOUTH CAROLINA MILITARY ACADEMY AND THE CADET RANGERS IN THE CIVIL WAR, by Gary R. Baker, B&G:FEB/91[28], *reviewed by* Richard M. McMurry, CWNEWS:JAN/92[4], *reviewed by* Brandon Beck

CAHABA PRISON AND THE *SULTANA* DISASTER, by William O. Bryant, B&G:JUN/91[22], *reviewed by* Jerry O. Potter, CWNEWS:JAN/91[4], *reviewed by* Theodore P. Savas

JOHN C. CALHOUN AND THE PRICE OF UNION: A BIOGRAPHY, by John Niven, CWNEWS:AUG/90[4], *reviewed by* Michael Parrish

CAMP AND FIELD LIFE OF THE FIFTH NEW YORK, by Alfred Davenport, CWR:VOL4#3[1], *reviewed by* Brian C. Pohanka

CAMP AND PRISON JOURNAL: EMBRACING SCENES IN CAMP ON THE MARCH AND IN PRISONS, by Griffin Frost, CWR:VOL4#3[37], CWR:VOL4#4[129], *reviewed by* Frank G. Prator

THE CAMPAIGN FOR ATLANTA & SHERMAN'S MARCH TO THE SEA, ESSAYS ON THE 1864 GEORGIA CAMPAIGNS, VOL I & 11, (edited by) Theodore P. Savas, ACW:JAN/95[62], B&G:APR/95[30], *reviewed by* Edwin C. Bearss, CWNEWS:MAY/94[5], *reviewed by* Richard McMurry, CWR:VOL4#3[37]

THE CAMPAIGN FOR ATLANTA, by William R. Scaife, CWNEWS:MAY/92[4], *reviewed by* William Marvel

THE CAMPAIGN FOR VICKSBURG, by Edwin C. Bearss, CWR:VOL2#1[78], *reviewed by* George Otott Jr.

THE CAMPAIGN OF CHANCELLORSVILLE, by John Bigelow Jr., CWM:FEB/95[42]564, *reviewed by* Gary W. Gallagher

CAMPAIGNING WITH GRANT, by Horace Porter, CWM:FEB/95[42]564, *reviewed by* Gary W. Gallagher

CAMPAIGNING WITH THE ROUNDHEADS: THE HISTORY OF THE 100TH PENNSYLVANIA VOLUNTEER INFANTRY REGIMENT, 1861-1865, by William G. Gavin, CWNEWS:MAY/91[4], *reviewed by* Ron Rago

THE CAMPAIGNS OF WALKER'S TEXAS DIVISION, by J.P. Blessington, CWNEWS:OCT/95[33], *reviewed by* Richard M. McMurry, CWR:VOL4#3[1], *reviewed by* T. Michael Parrish

THE CANNONEER, by Augustus Buell, CWNEWS:JUN/92[4], *reviewed by* Judy Yandoh

CAPTAIN SAM GRANT, by Lloyd Lewis, CWM:FEB/95[42]564, *reviewed by* Gary W. Gallagher

THE CAPTAIN'S BRIDE, A TALE OF THE WAR, by William D. Herrington, (edited by W. Keats Sparrow), CWNEWS:FEB/94[5], *reviewed by* Linda G. Black

CARL SCHURZ: A BIOGRAPHY, by Hans L. Trefousse, AHI:DEC/82[10], *reviewed by* Charles Royster

CAROLINA CAVALIER: THE LIFE AND MIND OF JAMES JOHNSTON PETTIGREW, by Clyde N. Wilson, B&G:JUN/91[22], *reviewed by* William Garrett Piston, CWM:JAN/91[47], *reviewed by* Gary W. Gallagher, CWNEWS:MAY/92[4], *reviewed by* Judy Yandoh

CARPETBAGGER FROM VERMONT: THE AUTOBIOGRAPHY OF MARSHALL HARVEY TWITCHELL, by Marshall H. Twitchell, (edited by Ted Tunnell), CWM:JAN/91[35], CWNEWS:JAN/90[4], *reviewed by* Steven J. Wright

CATALOGUE OF CIVIL WAR PHOTOGRAPHERS, by George F. Witham, CWNEWS:MAY/90[4], *reviewed by* Michael A. Hughes

THE CAVALRY AT GETTYSBURG: A TACTICAL STUDY OF MOUNTED OPERATIONS DURING THE CIVIL WAR'S PIVOTAL CAMPAIGN, (JUNE 4 - JULY 1863), by Edward G. Longacre, CWNEWS:APR/95[33]

CAVALRY TACTICS: OR, REGULATIONS FOR THE INSTRUCTION, FORMATIONS, AND MOVEMENTS OF THE CAVALRY, by Philip St. George Cooke, CWNEWS:DEC/95[29], *reviewed by* Dave Hanna

CELIA, A SLAVE, by Melton A. McLaurin, CWNEWS:APR/93[4], *reviewed by* John F. Marszalek

CENTENNIAL CAMPAIGN: THE SIOUX WAR OF 1876, by John S. Gray, CWNEWS:JUN/91[4], *reviewed by* Brian Pohanka

CHAMP FERGUSON, CONFEDERATE GUERILLA, by Thurman Sensing, CWTI:JUL/94[18]

THE CHANCELLORSVILLE CAMPAIGN: MARCH, - MAY 1863, by David G. Martin, CWNEWS:DEC/92[4], *reviewed by* Brandon Beck

CHANCELLORSVILLE 1863: THE SOULS OF THE BRAVE, by Ernest B. Furgurson, ACW:MAY/94[58], *reviewed by* Daniel M. Laney, CWM:AUG/94[9], *reviewed by* Brandon Beck, CWNEWS:JUN/93[5], *reviewed by* David F. Riggs, CWR:VOL3#1[80], *reviewed by* Robert E. L. Krick

CHANCELLORSVILLE AND GETTYSBURG, by Abner Doubleday, CWNEWS:NOV/91[4], *reviewed by* Michael Winey

CHANCELLORSVILLE BATTLEFIELD SITES, by Noel G. Harrison, CWM:MAR/92[49], *reviewed by* Gary W. Gallagher

CHAPTERS FROM THE UNWRITTEN HISTORY OF THE WAR BETWEEN THE STATES, by R.M. Collins, CWR:VOL1#2[78], *reviewed by* George Otott

by) Roy P. Basler, CWNEWS:JAN/92[4], *reviewed by* Dr. Allen C. Guelzo

THE COLLECTED WORKS OF ABRAHAM LINCOLN: SUPPLEMENT 1832-1865, NUMBER 7, (edited by) Roy P. Basler, AHI:MAY/76[48], *reviewed by* Robert D. Hoffsommer

COLLECTED WORKS OF ABRAHAM LINCOLN, by Roy P. Basler, edited by, CWTI:DEC/95[38]

COLLECTING GRAND ARMY OF THE REPUBLIC MEMORABILIA, by R. Brad Long, CWNEWS:JUL/91[4], *reviewed by* Steve Wright

COLONEL COGGESHALL — THE MAN WHO SAVED LINCOLN, by Freda P. Koch, CWNEWS:FEB/95[33], *reviewed by* Frank J. Piatek

THE COLUMBIA BOOK OF CIVIL WAR POETRY: FROM WHITMAN TO WALCOTT, (edited by) Richard Marius, CWTI:JAN/95[12]

COMBINED OPERATIONS IN THE CIVIL WAR, by Rowena Reed, CWM:APR/95[50], *reviewed by* Gary W. Gallagher, CWM:JUN/95[6], *reviewed by* William J. Miller, CWNEWS:DEC/95[29], *reviewed by* Frank J. Piatek

COME RETRIBUTION: THE CONFEDERATE SECRET SERVICE AND THE ASSASSINATION OF LINCOLN, by William A. Tidwell, CWNEWS:MAY/90[4], *reviewed by* Brandon Beck, CWTI:DEC/95[38]

COMPENDIUM OF THE CONFEDERACY, AN ANNOTATED BIBLIOGRAPHY, 2 VOL., (compiled by) John H. Wright, CWNEWS:MAY/90[4], *reviewed by* Michael Cavanaugh

COMPENDIUM OF THE CONFEDERATE ARMIES, by Stewart Sifakis, CWM:APR/95[8], *reviewed by* Charles R. Norville, CWR:VOL3#1[80], *reviewed by* Theodore P. Savas

COMPENDIUM OF THE CONFEDERATE ARMIES: FLORIDA AND ARKANSAS, by Steward Sifakis, CWNEWS:DEC/92[4], *reviewed by* Jeffry D. Wert

THE CONDUCT OF THE FEDERAL TROOPS IN LOUISIANA DURING THE INVASIONS OF 1863 AND 1864, by Henry W. Allen, CWNEWS:MAY/90[4], *reviewed by* J. Tracy Power

THE CONFEDERACY AS A REVOLUTIONARY EXPERIENCE, by Emory M. Thomas, CWM:NOV/91[73], *reviewed by* Gary W. Gallagher, CWNEWS:APR/93[4], *reviewed by* Dale Phillips

THE CONFEDERACY IS ON HER WAY UP THE SPOUT: LETTERS TO SOUTH CAROLINA, 1861-1864, (edited by) Roderick Heller, III, CWM:MAR/93[51], CWNEWS:NOV/94[33], *reviewed by* J. Tracy Power

THE CONFEDERACY'S FIGHTING CHAPLAIN — FATHER JOHN B. BANNON, by Phillip T. Tucker, B&G:AUG/93[24], *reviewed by* Benedict R. Marynick, CWM:OCT/95[10], *reviewed by* Rev. C. K. Norville, CWNEWS:JUN/93[5], *reviewed by* Larry G. Gray, CWR:VOL4#2[136], *reviewed by* Haskell Monroe

THE CONFEDERACY'S FORGOTTEN SON: MAJOR GENERAL JAMES LAWSON KEMPER C.S.A., by Harold R. Woodward Jr., CWR:VOL4#1[78], *reviewed by* Homer Blass

THE CONFEDERATE BRASS-FRAMED COLT & WHITNEY, by William A. Albaugh III, CWNEWS:AUG/95[33], *reviewed by* Dale E. Biever

THE CONFEDERATE CARPETBAGGERS, by Daniel E. Sutherland, CWNEWS:OCT/89[4], *reviewed by* Brandon Beck

THE CONFEDERATE CHEROKEES: JOHN DREW'S REGIMENT OF MOUNTED RIFLES, by W. Craig Gaines, CWNEWS:AUG/90[4], *reviewed by* Robert D. Norris, CWR:VOL4#3[1], *reviewed by* David Woodbury

THE CONFEDERATE GENERAL, (edited by) William C. Davis, CWM:FEB/95[42]564, *reviewed by* Gary W. Gallagher, CWNEWS:DEC/93[5], *reviewed by* Blake A. Magner, CWR:VOL3#1[80], *reviewed by* Theodore P. Savas

THE CONFEDERATE HIGH COMMAND AND RELATED TOPICS, (edited by) Roman J. Heleniak, B&G:AUG/91[26], *reviewed by* Steven E. Woodworth, B&G:JUN/91[22], *reviewed by* Steven E. Woodworth

THE CONFEDERATE MARINE CORPS, by Peter Hasselby, CWNEWS:JUN/91[4], *reviewed by* Richard M. McMurry

THE CONFEDERATE PRIVATEERS, by William M. Robinson Jr., CWM:JAN/91[47], *reviewed by* Gary W. Gallagher, CWNEWS:AUG/91[4], *reviewed by* Anne J. Bailey

THE CONFEDERATE REGULAR ARMY, by Richard P. Weinert Jr., B&G:OCT/91[34], *reviewed by* Robert K. Krick, CWNEWS:AUG/92[4], *reviewed by* William G. Roberts

THE CONFEDERATE REPUBLIC: A REVOLUTION AGAINST POLITICS, by George C. Rable, CWM:AUG/95[45], *reviewed by* Gary W. Gallagher, CWNEWS:FEB/95[33], *reviewed by* Michael Parrish, CWR:VOL4#3[37]

THE CONFEDERATE STATES MARINE CORPS: THE REBEL LEATHERNECKS, by Ralph W. Donnelly, CWM:JAN/91[47], *reviewed by* Gary W. Gallagher, CWTI:JUN/90[20], *reviewed by* David M. Sullivan

THE CONFEDERATE WHITWORTH SHARPSHOOTERS, by John A. Morrow, CWNEWS:APR/92[4], *reviewed by* Gary Augustine

CONFEDERATE ARMS, by William A. Albaugh III, CWNEWS:AUG/95[33], *reviewed by* Dale E. Biever

CONFEDERATE BELT BUCKLES & PLATES, by Steve E. Mullinax, CWNEWS:OCT/92[4], *reviewed by* Michael J. Winey

CONFEDERATE CAPITAL AND HOOD'S TEXAS BRIGADE, by A.V. Winkler, CWR:VOL1#4[77], *reviewed by* Theodore P. Savas

CONFEDERATE CHARLESTON: AN ILLUSTRATED HISTORY OF THE CITY AND THE PEOPLE DURING THE CIVIL WAR ,by Robert N. Rosen, CWNEWS:AUG/95[33], *reviewed by* John G. Secondari

CONFEDERATE COLONEL AND CHEROKEE CHIEF: THE LIFE OF WILLIAM HOLLAND THOMAS, by E. Stanley Godbold Jr., CWNEWS:JUN/92[4], *reviewed by* Jeffry Wert

CONFEDERATE EDGED WEAPONS, by William A. Albaugh III, CWNEWS:AUG/95[33], *reviewed by* Dale E. Biever

CONFEDERATE ENGINEERS' MAPS, by Jeremy F. Gilmer, CWNEWS:AUG/91[4], *reviewed by* Blake Magner

CONFEDERATE FACES, by William A. Albaugh, CWNEWS:AUG/95[33], *reviewed by* Michael J. Winey

CONFEDERATE FLORIDA: THE ROAD TO OLUSTEE, by William H. Nulty, B&G:AUG/91[26], *reviewed by* Arch F. Blakey, CWM:JAN/91[47], *reviewed by* Gary W. Gallagher, CWNEWS:MAY/92[4], *reviewed by* Kemp Burpeau, CWNEWS:JUN/94[5], *reviewed by* Stephen D. Engle

CONFEDERATE GENERALS OF GEORGIA AND THEIR BURIAL SITES, by Robert H. Kerlin, CWR:VOL4#3[37]

CONFEDERATE GOLIATH: THE BATTLE OF FORT FISHER, by Rod Gragg, B&G:OCT/91[34], *reviewed by* Stephen R. Wise, CWM:MAR/91[42], *reviewed by* William J. Miller, CWNEWS:JUN/91[4], *reviewed by* Richard M. McMurry, CWTI:AUG/91[18]

CONFEDERATE HANDGUNS, by William A. Albaugh III, CWNEWS:AUG/95[33], *reviewed by* Dale E. Biever

CONFEDERATE HOSPITALS ON THE MOVE: SAMUEL H. STOUT AND THE ARMY OF TENNESSEE, by Glenna R. Schroeder-Lein, B&G:AUG/94[30], *reviewed by* Frank R. Freemon, CWM:APR/95[50], *reviewed by* Gary W. Gallagher, CWNEWS:APR/95[33], *reviewed by* Frank J. Piatek, CWR:VOL4#1[78], *reviewed by* Wayman D. Norman, CWR:VOL4#3[37], *reviewed by*

CONFEDERATE MOBILE, by Arthur W. Bergeron Jr., B&G:OCT/92[30], *reviewed by* Florence F. Corley, CWTI:JAN/93[12]

CONFEDERATE RAIDER: RAPHAEL SEMMES OF THE *ALABAMA*, by John M. Taylor, ACW:JUL/95[58], *reviewed by* Jon Guttman, CWTI:MAR/95[14]

CONFEDERATE STATES NAVY RESEARCH GUIDE, by Thomas T. Moebs, CWNEWS:SEP/93[5], *reviewed by* Gary Augustine

CONFIDENTIAL CORRESPONDENCE OF GUSTAVUS VASA FOX, by Gustavus V. Fox, (edited by Robert M. Thompson,) CWNEWS:JAN/91[4], *reviewed by* Kevin Weddle

THE CONGRESSMAN'S CIVIL WAR, by Allen G. Bogue, CWNEWS:JUL/91[4], *reviewed by* J. Tracy Power, CWTI:APR/90[10]

CONNECTICUT YANKEES AT GETTYSBURG, by Charles B. Hamblen, CWM:APR/95[50], *reviewed by* Gary W. Gallagher, CWNEWS:JUN/94[5], *reviewed by* David Ward, CWR:VOL3#3[92], *reviewed by* Kevin E. O'Brien

CONSTITUTIONS AND CONSTITUTIONALISM IN THE SLAVEHOLDING SOUTH, by Don E. Fehrenbacher, CWNEWS:APR/91[4], *reviewed by* Kemp Burpeau

THE CONTINUING CIVIL WAR: ESSAYS IN HONOR OF THE CIVIL WAR ROUND TABLE OF CHICAGO, (edited by) John Y. Simon, CWNEWS:DEC/92[4], *reviewed by* Blake A. Magner

COPPERHEAD, by Bernard Cornwell, CWNEWS:NOV/95[29], *reviewed by* Judy Yandoh

THE CORMANY DIARIES: A NORTHERN FAMILY IN THE CIVIL WAR, (edited by) James C. Mohr, AHI:MAY/83[48], *reviewed by* Reid Mitchell

CORYDON: THE FORGOTTEN BATTLE OF THE CIVIL WAR, by W. Fred Conway, CWNEWS:JUN/92[4], *reviewed by* Steven J. Wright

COTTON & CAPITOL: BOSTON BUSINESSMEN AND ANTISLAVERY REFORM, 1854-1868, by Richard H. Abbott, CWNEWS:JUN/93[5], *reviewed by* Gregory J.Y. Urwin

THE COURT MARTIAL OF ROBERT E. LEE: A HISTORICAL NOVEL, by Douglas Savage, CWTI:JAN/94[10]

THE CREATION OF CONFEDERATE NATIONALISM: IDEOLOGY AND IDENTITY IN THE CIVIL WAR SOUTH, by Drew G. Faust, CWNEWS:AUG/90[4], *reviewed by* Dr. Allen C. Guelzo

THE CRISIS OF THE AMERICAN REPUBLIC: A HISTORY OF THE CIVIL WAR AND RECONSTRUCTION ERA, by Allen C. Guelzo, CWTI:OCT/95[18]

CRUCIBLE OF RECONSTRUCTION: WAR, RADICALISM, AND RACE IN LOUISIANA, 1862-1877, by Ted Tunnell, CWNEWS:JAN/95[25], *reviewed by* Larry G. Gray

CRY COMANCHE: THE 2ND U.S. CAVALRY IN TEXAS, 1855-1861, by Colonel Harold B. Simpson, CWNEWS:NOV/89[4], *reviewed by* Robert Norris

CUMBERLAND COUNTY AND SOUTH JERSEY DURING THE CIVIL WAR, by Isaac T. Nichols, CWNEWS:JUN/94[5], *reviewed by* Blake A. Magner

CUSHING OF GETTYSBURG: THE STORY OF A UNION ARTILLERY COMMANDER, B&G:DEC/94[28], *reviewed by* William Marvel, CWM:APR/95[50], *reviewed by* Gary W. Gallagher, CWR:VOL4#3[89], *reviewed by* Mike Cantor

A COMPLETE LIFE OF GENERAL GEORGE ARMSTRONG CUSTER, by Frederick Whitaker, CWR:VOL3#3[92], *reviewed by* Patrick S. Brady

THE CUSTER READER, (edited by) Paul Andrew Hutton, B&G:JUN/93[28], *reviewed by* Neil C. Mangum, CWM:APR/95[50], *reviewed by* Gary W. Gallagher, CWNEWS:JUN/93[5], *reviewed by* Brian Pohanka

THE CUSTER TRAGEDY: EVENTS LEADING UP TO AND FOLLOWING THE LITTLE BIG HORN CAMPAIGN OF 1876, by Fred Dustin, CWNEWS:JUN/91[4], *reviewed by* Michael Mullins

CUSTER AND HIS TIMES: BOOK III, (edited by) Gregory J. Urwin, CWNEWS:JUN/91[4], *reviewed by* Brian Pohanka

CUSTER ENGAGES THE HOSTILES, by Colonel Charles F. Bates, AHI:JUN/74[49]

CUSTER VICTORIOUS: THE CIVIL WAR BATTLES OF GENERAL GEORGE ARMSTRONG CUSTER, by Gregory J.W. Urwin, AHI:SEP/83[6], *reviewed by* Albert Castel

CUSTER'S LAST, OR THE BATTLE OF LITTLE BIG HORN, by Don Russell, AHI:MAY/68[49], *reviewed by* Wilber S. Nye

CUSTER'S SEVENTH CAVALRY COMES TO DAKOTA, by Roger Darling, CWNEWS:JUL/90[4], *reviewed by* Brian Pohanka

CUTLER'S BRIGADE AT GETTYSBURG, by James L. McLean Jr., CWNEWS:FEB/95[33], *reviewed by* Michael Russert, CWR:VOL4#3[37]

THE CYPRESS RANGERS IN THE CIVIL WAR, by James H. Davis, CWNEWS:MAY/93[4], *reviewed by* Kemp Burpeau

DAMN THE TORPEDOES! NAVAL INCIDENTS OF THE CIVIL WAR, by A.A. Hoehling, CWNEWS:MAY/91[4], *reviewed by* Allen Guelzo, CWNEWS:OCT/94[33], *reviewed by* Michael Russert, CWTI:APR/90[10]

DAMNED YANKEE: THE LIFE OF GENERAL NATHANIEL LYON, by Christopher Phillips, B&G:JUN/91[22], *reviewed by* John S. Peterson, CWM:JAN/91[47], *reviewed by* Gary W. Gallagher, CWNEWS:MAY/92[4], *reviewed by* Robert Norris Jr.

DANGER BENEATH THE WAVES, by James E. Kloeppel, CWNEWS:MAY/89[4], *reviewed by* Barry Popchock

DARK AND CRUEL WAR: THE DECISIVE MONTHS OF THE CIVIL WAR SEPTEMBER-DECEMBER 1864, by Don Lowry, ACW:JUL/94[58], *reviewed by* Philip L. Bolte

DARK FRIDAY: THE STORY OF QUANTRILL'S LAWRENCE RAID, by William C. Pollard Jr., CWNEWS:JUL/92[4], *reviewed by* Harris D. Riley Jr.

DAYS OF "UNCERTAINTY AND DREAD": THE ORDEAL ENDURED BY THE CITIZENS AT GETTYSBURG, by Gerald R. Bennett, CWNEWS:APR/95[33], *reviewed by* Blake A. Magner

"DEAR FRIEND ANNA": THE CIVIL WAR LETTERS OF A COMMON SOLDIER FROM MAINE, by Abial H. Edwards, (edited by Beverly H. Kallgren), CWM:OCT/94[8], *reviewed by* Scott C. Patchan

"DEAR MOTHER: DON'T GRIEVE ABOUT ME. IF I GET KILLED, I'LL ONLY BE DEAD." LETTERS FROM GEORGIA SOLDIERS IN THE CIVIL WAR, by Mills Lane, CWM:FEB/95[42]564, *reviewed by* Gary W. Gallagher

BRIGADE, C.S.A., by W.W. Ward, (edited by R.B. Rosenburg), CWNEWS:JAN/94[5], *reviewed by* Sarah W. Wiggins

FOR COUNTRY, CAUSE & LEADER: THE CIVIL WAR JOURNAL OF CHARLES B. HAYDON, by Charles B. Haydon, (edited by Stephen W. Sears), CWM:APR/94[51], *reviewed by* Judge Ben Smith, CWM:FEB/95[42]564, *reviewed by* Gary W. Gallagher, CWNEWS:DEC/93[5], *reviewed by* Brian Pohanka, CWR:VOL3#4[68], *reviewed by* Frank l. Byrne

FOREIGNERS IN THE CONFEDERACY, by Ella Lonn, CWM:MAR/91[74], *reviewed by* Gary W. Gallagher

FOREIGNERS IN THE UNION ARMY AND NAVY, by Ella Lonn, CWM:MAR/91[74], *reviewed by* Gary W. Gallagher

FORGED IN BATTLE: THE CIVIL WAR ALLIANCE OF BLACK SOLDIERS AND WHITE OFFICERS, by Joseph T. Glatthaar, B&G:AUG/91[26], *reviewed by* Lawrence L. Hewitt, CWNEWS:JUL/90[4], *reviewed by* Gregory J.W. Irwin

THE FORT PILLOW MASSACRE: THE REASON WHY, by Gregory J. Macaluso, CWNEWS:APR/91[4], *reviewed by* Michael Policatti

FORT LYON TO HARPERS FERRY: ON THE BORDER OF NORTH AND SOUTH WITH "RAMBLING JOUR", (edited by) Lee C. Drickamer, B&G:FEB/92[26], *reviewed by* Dave Roth

FORTRESS ALCATRAZ: GUARDIAN OF THE GOLDEN GATE, by John A. Martini, CWNEWS:APR/93[4], *reviewed by* Michael Russert

FORTS HENRY AND DONELSON: THE KEY TO THE CONFEDERATE HEARTLAND, by Benjamin F. Cooling, CWM:FEB/95[42], *reviewed by* Gary W. Gallagher

FOUR BROTHERS IN BLUE: OR SUNSHINE AND SHADOWS OF THE WAR OF THE REBELLION: A STORY OF THE GREAT CIVIL WAR FROM BULL RUN TO APPOMATTOX, by Robert G. Carter, CWM:FEB/95[42]564, *reviewed by* Gary W. Gallagher

FOUR DAYS IN 1865: THE FALL OF RICHMOND, by David D. Ryan, CWR:VOL4#1[78], *reviewed by* Jon L. Wakelyn, MH:DEC/93[90]

FOUR YEARS IN THE STONEWALL BRIGADE, by John O. Casler, CWR:VOL4#3[1], *reviewed by* John M. Coski

FOURTEEN HUNDRED AND 91 DAYS IN THE CONFEDERATE ARMY, by William H. Heartsill, CWR:VOL1#4[77], *reviewed by* Anne J. Bailey

THE FOURTH CAREER OF JOHN B. BANNON: ST. LOUIS PASTOR, SOUTHERN CHAPLAIN, CONFEDERATE AGENT, IRISH JESUIT ORATOR, by William B. Faherty, CWNEWS:DEC/95[29], *reviewed by* Ted Alexander

FRANCIS PRESTON BLAIR, by Elbert B. Smith, AHI:JUL/80[50], *reviewed by* Lowell H. Harrison

FREDERICK DOUGLASS' CIVIL WAR: KEEPING FAITH IN JUBILEE, by David W. Blight, CWM:JAN/91[47], *reviewed by* Gary W. Gallagher, CWNEWS:NOV/91[4], *reviewed by* David G. Martin

FREDERICK DOUGLASS, by William S. McFeely, CWNEWS:JUL/92[4], *reviewed by* Gregory J.W. Urwin, CWTI:SEP/91[10], *reviewed by* Sarah W. Wiggins

FREDERICK DOUGLASS: AUTOBIOGRAPHIES, by Frederick Douglass, (edited by enry Louis Gates Jr.), CWTI:JUL/94[18]

THE FREDERICKSBURG CAMPAIGN: DECISION ON THE RAPPAHANNOCK, (edited by) Gary W. Gallagher, B&G:DEC/95[30], *reviewed by* John J. Hennessy,

CWNEWS:SEP/95[33], *reviewed by* Jeffry D. Wert, CWR:VOL4#4[129], *reviewed by* David P. Smith

THE FREEDMEN'S BUREAU IN LOUISIANA, by Howard Ashley White, AHI:AUG/70[50], *reviewed by* E.E. Billings

FREEDOM'S LAWMAKERS: A DIRECTORY OF BLACK OFFICEHOLDERS DURING RECONSTRUCTION, by Eric Foner, CWM:AUG/95[45], *reviewed by* Gary W. Gallagher

FREEDOM: A DOCUMENTARY HISTORY OF EMANCIPATION, 1861-1867, (edited by) Ira Berlin, CWM:AUG/95[45], *reviewed by* Gary W. Gallagher

FREEDOM: A DOCUMENTARY HISTORY OF EMANCIPATION, 1861-1867, SERIES I, VOLUME III: THE WARTIME GENESIS OF FREE LABOR: THE LOWER SOUTH, (edited by) Ira Berlin, CWNEWS:NOV/91[4], *reviewed by* Gregory J.W. Urwin

THE FREMONT RIFLES: A HISTORY OF THE 37TH ILLINOIS VETERAN VOLUNTEER INFANTRY, by Michael A. Mullins, CWNEWS:JUL/90[4], *reviewed by* James I. Robertson

FREMONT, PATHMAKER OF THE WEST, by Allen Nevins, CWNEWS:SEP/93[5], *reviewed by* Norman E. Rourke

FROM BALL'S BLUFF TO GETTYSBURG . . . AND BEYOND: THE CIVIL WAR LETTERS OF PVT ROLAND E. BOWEN, 15TH MASS INF 1861-1864, by Roland E. Bowen, (edited by Gregory A. Coco), CWM:APR/95[42]577, CWR:VOL4#4[129], *reviewed by* Mitchell Yockelson

FROM CAPE CHARLES TO CAPE FEAR: THE NORTH ALTANTIC BLOCKADING SQUADRON DURING THE CIVIL WAR, by Robert M. Browning, CWM:APR/95[50], *reviewed by* Gary W. Gallagher, CWNEWS:OCT/95[33], *reviewed by* Richard A. Sauers, CWR:VOL3#3[92], *reviewed by* Mitchell Yockelson

FROM CAVEN TO COLD HARBOR: THE LIFE OF COLONEL RICHARD BYRNES, by Barry L. Spink, CWNEWS:JUN/95[33], *reviewed by* Blake A. Magner

FROM DESERT TO BAYOU: THE CIVIL WAR JOURNAL AND SKETCHES OF MORGAN WOLFE MERRICK, by Morgan W. Merrick, (edited by Jerry D. Thompson), B&G:OCT/92[30], *reviewed by* Nat C. Hughes Jr., CWNEWS:APR/92[4], *reviewed by* Anne J. Bailey

FROM EVERGLADE TO CANON WITH THE SECOND DRAGOONS, by Theodore F. Rodenbough, CWR:VOL4#3[1], *reviewed by* William J. Miller

FROM FORT HENRY TO CORINTH, by Manning F. Force, CWNEWS:SEP/91[4], *reviewed by* William G. Roberts

FROM MANASSAS TO APPOMATTOX: MEMOIRS OF THE CIVIL WAR IN AMERICA, by James Longstreet, CWM:SEP/92[57], *reviewed by* John Michael Priest, CWM:FEB/95[42], *reviewed by* Gary W. Gallagher

FROM NEW BERN TO FREDERICKSBURG: CAPTAIN JAMES WREN'S DIARY, by James Wren, (edited by John M. Priest), ACW:NOV/91[54], *reviewed by* Jon Guttman, CWNEWS:SEP/91[4], *reviewed by* Kevin J. Weddle

FROM THE CANNON'S MOUTH: THE CIVIL WAR LETTERS OF GENERAL ALPHEUS S. WILLIAMS, by Alpheus S. Williams, (edited by Milo M. Quaife), CWM:FEB/95[42], *reviewed by* Gary W. Gallagher

FROM YORKTOWN TO SANTIAGO WITH THE SIXTH U.S. CAVALRY, by W. H. Carter, CWNEWS:SEP/91[4], *reviewed by* David F. Riggs

THE FRONTIER, THE UNION, AND STEPHEN A. DOUGLAS, by Robert W. Johannsen, CWNEWS:SEP/90[4], *reviewed by* Steven Ward

FRONTIER DEFENSE IN THE CIVIL WAR: TEXAS' RANGERS AND REBELS, by David Smith, B&G:AUG/93[24], *reviewed by* William L. Shea, CWNEWS:DEC/92[4], *reviewed by* Robert D. Norris Jr., CWNEWS:DEC/94[33], *reviewed by* Norman E. Rourke

FRONTIER REGULARS, THE UNITED STATES ARMY AND THE INDIAN, 1866-1891, by Robert M. Utley, AHI:JUN/74[49], *reviewed by* D. Alexander Brown

FRONTIERSMEN IN BLUE: THE UNITED STATES ARMY AND THE INDIAN, 1848-1865, by Robert M. Utley, AHI:JAN/69[56], *reviewed by* D. Alexander Brown

FULL DUTY: VERMONTERS IN THE CIVIL WAR, by Howard Coffin, B&G:FEB/95[26], *reviewed by* Albert Castel, CWNEWS:JUN/94[5], *reviewed by* Blake A. Magner

GAINES' MILL TO APPOMATTOX — WACO & MCCLENNAN COUNTY IN, HOOD'S TEXAS BRIGADE, by Harold B. Simpson, CWNEWS:SEP/89[8], *reviewed by* Blake Magner

GATE OF HELL: CAMPAIGN FOR CHARLESTON HARBOR, 1863, by Stephen R. Wise, B&G:JUN/95[30], *reviewed by* Robert N. Rosen, CWM:AUG/95[45], *reviewed by* Gary W. Gallagher, CWNEWS:APR/95[33], *reviewed by* Dr. Richard A. Sauers, CWR:VOL4#3[37], CWTI:SEP/94[18]

GENEALOGY ONLINE: RESEARCHING YOUR ROOTS, by Elizabeth P. Crowe, CWTI:JUN/95[24]

THE GENERAL TO HIS LADY: THE CIVIL WAR LETTERS OF WILLIAM DORSEY PENDER TO FANNY PENDER, by William D. Pender, (edited by William W. Hassler), CWM:FEB/95[42]564, *reviewed by* Gary W. Gallagher

GENERAL A.P. HILL: THE STORY OF A CONFEDERATE WARRIOR, by James I. Robertson Jr., CWM:FEB/95[42], *reviewed by* Gary W. Gallagher

GENERAL EDMUND KIRBY SMITH, CSA, by Joseph H. Parks, CWNEWS:MAY/93[4], *reviewed by* Harris D. Riley M.D.

GENERAL FITZHUGH LEE, by James L. Nichols, CWNEWS:JAN/91[4], *reviewed by* Ron Rago

GENERAL JAMES LONGSTREET: THE SOUTH'S MOST CONTROVERSIAL SOLDIER, A BIOGRAPHY, by Jeffry D. Wert, ACW:SEP/94[66], *reviewed by* Richard F. Welch, B&G:DEC/94[28], *reviewed by* Steven W. Woodworth, CWNEWS:JUL/94[25], *reviewed by* Ted Alexander, MH:AUG/94[70], *reviewed by*

GENERAL JOHN H. WINDER, C.S.A., by Arch F. Blakey, B&G:DEC/91[30], *reviewed by* R. Frank Saunders, CWM:MAY/91[34], *reviewed by* William J. Miller, CWNEWS:AUG/91[4], *reviewed by* John Marszalek

GENERAL LEE, by Fitzhugh Lee, CWNEWS:JUL/91[4], *reviewed by* Terrence Winschel

GENERAL LEE: HIS CAMPAIGNS IN VIRGINIA 1861-1865, WITH PERSONAL REMINISCENCES, by Walter H. Taylor, CWM:FEB/95[42], *reviewed by* Gary W. Gallagher, CWM:AUG/95[45], *reviewed by* Gary W. Gallagher

GENERAL LEONIDAS POLK, C.S.A., THE FIGHTING BISHOP, by Joseph H. Parks, CWNEWS:JUN/93[5], *reviewed by* Norman E. Rourke

GENERAL MICAH JENKINS AND THE PALMETTO SHARPSHOOTERS, CWM:APR/95[8], *reviewed by* Charles R. Norville

GENERAL STERLING PRICE AND THE CIVIL WAR IN THE WEST, by Albert Castel, CWM:APR/95[50], *reviewed by* Gary W. Gallagher

GENERALS IN BLUE: LIVES OF THE UNION COMMANDERS, by Ezra J. Warner, CWM:FEB/95[42], *reviewed by* Gary W. Gallagher

GENERALS IN GRAY: LIVES OF THE CONFEDERATE COMMANDERS, by Ezra J. Warner, CWM:FEB/95[42]564, *reviewed by* Gary W. Gallagher

THE GENERALSHIP OF ULYSSES S. GRANT, by J.F.C. Fuller, CWM:JAN/92[57], *reviewed by* Gary W. Gallagher

GEORGE B. MCCLELLAN: THE YOUNG NAPOLEON, by Stephen W. Sears, AHI:NOV/88[10], CWM:FEB/95[42], *reviewed by* Gary W. Gallagher

GEORGE N. BARNARD: PHOTOGRAPHER OF SHERMAN'S CAMPAIGNS, by Keith F. Davis, B&G:APR/91[28], *reviewed by* Henry Deeks

GEORGE WYTHE RANDOLPH AND THE CONFEDERATE ELITE, by George G. Shackelford, CWNEWS:JAN/90[4], *reviewed by* Michael Parrish

THE GEORGIA BRIGADE, by William R. Scaife, CWNEWS:SEP/89[8], *reviewed by* William Howard

GEORGIA IN THE WAR, 1861-1865: A COMPENDIUM OF GEORGIA PARTICIPANTS, by Charles E. Jones, B&G:AUG/91[26], *reviewed by* William H. Bragg

THE GETTYSBURG CAMPAIGN: A STUDY IN COMMAND, by Edwin B. Coddington, AHI:DEC/68[50], *reviewed by* E.E. Billings, CWM:FEB/95[42]564, *reviewed by* Gary W. Gallagher

THE GETTYSBURG CAMPAIGN: JUNE-JULY 1863, (REVISED EDITION), by Albert A. Nofi, CWNEWS:APR/94[5], *reviewed by* Kevin E. O'Brien

THE GETTYSBURG SOLDIERS' CEMETERY AND LINCOLN'S ADDRESS, (edited by) Frank L. Klement, B&G:DEC/95[30], *reviewed by* Benedict R. Maryniak, CWM:APR/95[50], *reviewed by* Gary W. Gallagher, CWNEWS:JUL/94[25], *reviewed by* Michael Russert

GETTYSBURG — A BATTLEFIELD ATLAS, by Craig L. Symonds, B&G:JUN/93[28], *reviewed by* William A. Young, CWNEWS:NOV/92[4], *reviewed by* Blake Magner

GETTYSBURG — CULP'S HILL AND CEMETERY HILL, by Harry W. Pfanz, B&G:OCT/94[40], *reviewed by* Wayne E. Motts, CWM:FEB/95[42]564, *reviewed by* Gary W. Gallagh

GETTYSBURG — THE SECOND DAY, by Harry W. Pfanz, ks CWM:FEB/95[42], *reviewed by* Gary W. Gallagher

GETTYSBURG BATTLEFIELD: THE FIRST DAY'S BATTLEFIELD, CWM:AUG/95[45], *reviewed by* Gary W. Gallagher

GETTYSBURG BATTLEFIELD: THE SECOND AND THIRD DAYS' BATTLEFIELD, CWM:AUG/95[45], *reviewed by* Gary W. Gallagher

GETTYSBURG HOUR-BY-HOUR, by Harry Roach, CWNEWS:NOV/95[29], *reviewed by* Steven J. Wright

GETTYSBURG JULY 1, by David G. Martin, CWNEWS:NOV/95[29], *reviewed by* Kevin E. O'Brien

GETTYSBURG SOURCES, VOLUME 3, (compiled by) James L. McLean Jr., CWNEWS:SEP/91[4], *reviewed by* Michael J. Winey

GETTYSBURG: A JOURNEY IN TIME, by William A. Frassanito, AHI:MAY/76[48], *reviewed by* Robert D. Hoffsommer

GETTYSBURG: A MEDITATION ON WAR & VALUES, by Kent Gramm, B&G:AUG/94[30], *reviewed by* Richard Pindell, CWM:FEB/95[7], *reviewed by* Gordon Shay, CWNEWS:JUN/95[33], *reviewed by* Mark A. Snell, CWR:VOL4#4[129], *reviewed by* David P. Smith, CWTI:MAR/95[14], *reviewed by* Diane Treon

by Ernest L. Waite, CWNEWS:JUL/90[4], *reviewed by* Dr. Allen C. Guelzo

HISTORY OF THE ONE HUNDRED AND FIFTH REGIMENT OF PENNSYLVANIA VOLUNTEERS by Kate M. Scott, CWR:VOL4#1[78], *reviewed by* Kevin E. O'Brien

HISTORY OF THE ONE HUNDRED AND TWENTY-FOURTH REGIMENT, N.Y.S.V., by Charles H. Weygant, CWR:VOL4#3[1], *reviewed by* Brian C. Pohanka

HISTORY OF THE ONE HUNDRED FORTY-FIRST REGIMENT, PENNSYLVANIA VOLUNTEERS 1862-1865, by David Craft, CWR:VOL1#4[77], *reviewed by* David A. Woodbury

HISTORY OF THE PENNSYLVANIA RESERVE CORPS: A COMPLETE RECORD OF THE ORGANIZATION; AND OF ITS DIFFERENT COMPANIES, by Joshah R. Sypher, B&G:DEC/92[26], *reviewed by* Steven J. Wright, CWM:JUN/95[6], *reviewed by* Gary W. Gallagher

THE HISTORY OF THE TENTH MASSACHUSETTS BATTERY OF LIGHT ARTILLERY, by John D. Billings, CWR:VOL2#1[78], *reviewed by* William Marvel

HISTORY OF THE TWELFTH REGIMENT, NEW HAMPSHIRE VOLUNTEERS, IN THE WAR OF THE REBELLION, by Asa W. Bartlett, CWR:VOL4#3[1], *reviewed by* James I. Robertson

THE HOBBY, A GUIDE TO HAVING 'CIVIL' REENACTMENTS, VOLUME 1, by David Loomis, CWNEWS:NOV/93[5], *reviewed by* David Hannah

HOLDING THE LEFT AT GETTYSBURG: THE 20TH NEW YORK STATE MILITIA ON JULY 1, 1863, by Seward R. Osborne, CWNEWS:JUN/92[4], *reviewed by* Richard A. Sauers

HOLDING THE LINE: THE HISTORY OF THE THIRD TENNESSEE INFANTRY, by Blavel C. Barber, (edited by Robert H. Ferrell), CWM:APR/95[8], *reviewed by* Charles R. Norville, CWM:AUG/95[45], *reviewed by* Gary W. Gallagher, CWR:VOL4#3[37]

WINSLOW HOMER: PAINTINGS OF THE CIVIL WAR, by Winslow Homer (edited by Marc Simpson), CWNEWS:JUL/91[4], *reviewed by* Anne J. Bailey

THE HONORABLE POWELL CLAYTON, by William H. Burnside, CWNEWS:OCT/92[4], *reviewed by* J. Tracy Power

HOOD'S CAMPAIGN FOR TENNESSEE, by William R. Scaife, CWM:JAN/91[47], *reviewed by* Gary W. Gallagher

HOOD'S TEXAS BRIGADE SKETCHBOOK, by Tom Jones, CWNEWS:OCT/89[4], *reviewed by* Blake Magner

HOOD'S TEXAS BRIGADE: LEE'S GRENADIER GUARD, by Harold B. Simpson, CWR:VOL2#3[256], *reviewed by* Archie P. McDonald

HOW THE NORTH WON: A MILITARY HISTORY OF THE CIVIL WAR, by Herman Hattaway, AHI:JAN/84[8], *reviewed by* Lowell H. Harrison, CWM:FEB/95[42], *reviewed by* Gary W. Gallagher

HURRAH FOR THE ARTILLERY! KNAP'S INDEPENDENT BATTERY "E", PENNSYLVANIA LIGHT ARTILLERY, by James P. Brady, CWNEWS:APR/94[5], *reviewed by* Steven J. Wright

I RODE WITH JEB STUART: THE LIFE AND CAMPAIGNS OF MAJOR GENERAL J.E.B. STUART, by Henry B. McClellan, CWM:AUG/95[45], *reviewed by* Gary W. Gallagher

I RODE WITH STONEWALL, by Henry Kyd Douglas, CWM:NOV/92[55], *reviewed by*

I'M SURROUNDED BY METHODISTS . . .: DIARY OF JOHN H.W. STUCKENBERG, CHAPLAIN OF THE 145TH PENNSYLVANIA VOLUNTEER INFANTRY, by John H.W. Stuckenberg, (edited by David T. Hendrick), CWNEWS:DEC/95[29],

"IF THEE MUST FIGHT" A CIVIL WAR HISTORY OF CHESTER COUNTY, PENNSYLVANIA, by Douglas R. Harper, CWNEWS:JUL/92[4], *reviewed by* Michael Cavanaugh

IF IT TAKES ALL SUMMER: THE BATTLE OF SPOTSYLVANIA, by William D. Matter, CWM:FEB/95[42], *reviewed by* Gary W. Gallagher, CWNEWS:NOV/89[4], *reviewed by* Robert Swope

ILLINOIS IN THE CIVIL WAR, by Victor Hickens, AHI:FEB/67[57], *reviewed by* Ralph Adams Brown, CWNEWS:SEP/92[4], *reviewed by* Jeffry D. Wert

THE ILLUSTRATED CONFEDERATE READER, (edited by Rod Gragg), B&G:FEB/91[28], *reviewed by* Garold L. Cole, CWNEWS:JUN/92[4], *reviewed by* Blake Magner

THE IMAGE OF WAR, THE PICTORIAL REPORTING OF THE AMERICAN CIVIL WAR, by William F. Thompson, CWNEWS:DEC/95[29], *reviewed by* Frank J. Piatek

IMAGES OF THE CIVIL WAR, by Mort Kunstler, CWNEWS:NOV/93[5], *reviewed by* Tom Low, CWTI:JAN/93[12], MH:FEB/93[77]

THE IMPACT OF THE CIVIL WAR AND RECONSTRUCTION ON ARKANSAS, by Carl H. Moneyhon, CWM:AUG/95[45], *reviewed by* Gary W. Gallagher

THE IMPEACHMENT AND TRIAL OF ANDREW JOHNSON, by David Miller DeWitt, AHI:JAN/68[55], *reviewed by* Col. J. E. Raymond

IMPEACHMENT OF A PRESIDENT: ANDREW JOHNSON, THE BLACKS AND RECONSTRUCTION, by Hans L. Trefousse, AHI:AUG/75[50], *reviewed by* Gerald G. Eggert, AHI:OCT/78[26], *reviewed by* David Lindsey

THE IMPERILED UNION: ESSAYS ON THE BACKGROUND OF THE CIVIL WAR, by Kenneth M. Stampp, AHI:JUL/80[50], *reviewed by* Joe Gray Taylor

IN CAMP AND BATTLE WITH THE WASHINGTON ARTILLERY, by William M. Owen, CWR:VOL4#3[1], *reviewed by* John M. Coski

IN DEADLY EARNEST: HISTORY OF THE FIRST MISSOURI BRIGADE, C.S.A., by Phil Gottschalk, B&G:APR/93[30], *reviewed by* Jerry Russell, CWNEWS:NOV/92[4], *reviewed by* Kemp Burpeau, CWR:VOL2#2[169], *reviewed by* Theodore P. Savas

IN HOSPITAL AND CAMP: THE CIVIL WAR THROUGH THE EYES OF ITS DOCTORS AND NURSES, by Harold E. Straubling, CWNEWS:MAY/94[5], *reviewed by* Harris D. Riley M.D.

IN JOY AND IN SORROW: WOMEN, FAMILY, AND MARRIAGE IN THE VICTORIAN SOUTH, 1830-1900, (edited by) Carol Bleser, CWTI:MAY/91[12], *reviewed by* Andrea Abolins

IN THE BLOODY RAILROAD CUT AT GETTYSBURG, by Lance J. Herdegen, CWR:VOL1#2[78], *reviewed by* David A. Woodbury, CWR:VOL4#3[1], *reviewed by* Craig L. Symonds

IN THE CAGE: EYEWITNESS ACCOUNTS OF THE FREED NEGRO IN SOUTHERN SOCIETY, 1877-1929, by Alton Hornsby Jr., AHI:NOV/71[48], *reviewed by* Benjamin Quarles

IN THE HANDS OF PROVIDENCE: JOSHUA L. CHAMBERLAIN & THE AMERICAN CIVIL WAR, by Alice R. Trulock, B&G:FEB/93[36], *reviewed by* Eric J. Wittenberg, CWM:FEB/95[42], *reviewed by* Gary W. Gallagher,

CWNEWS:AUG/92[4], *reviewed by* Brian C. Pohanka,
CWR:VOL2#3[256], *reviewed by* Kevin E. O'Brien,
CWTI:MAY/93[18], *reviewed by*

IN THEIR OWN WORDS: CIVIL WAR COMMANDERS, by
T.J. Stiles, CWTI:AUG/95[18]

INDIANA QUAKERS CONFRONT THE CIVIL WAR, by
Jacquelyn S. Nelson, B&G:FEB/93[36], *reviewed by* Benedict
R. Maryni

INDUSTRIAL SLAVERY IN THE OLD SOUTH, by Robert S.
Starobin, AHI:NOV/70[48], *reviewed by* Robert D. Hoffsommer

**INFANTRYMAN PETTIT: THE CIVIL WAR LETTERS OF
CORPORAL FREDERICK PETTIT,** by Frederick Pettit,
(edited by William G. Gavin), CWNEWS:MAY/92[4], *reviewed
by* Steven J. Wright

THE INNER CIVIL WAR, by George M. Frederickson,
CWNEWS:OCT/95[33], *reviewed by* Spencer Gill

THE INNER WORLD OF ABRAHAM LINCOLN, by Michael
Burlingame, B&G:DEC/95[30], *reviewed by* David E. Long,
CWM:DEC/95[10], *reviewed by* J. Jeffrey Cox,
CWNEWS:JUN/95[33], *reviewed by* Allen C. Guelzo

INSCRIPTION AT GETTYSBURG, by Sara G. Walters,
CWNEWS:SEP/92[4], *reviewed by* Dr. Richard A. Sauers

**INSIDE THE CONFEDERATE GOVERNMENT: THE
DIARY OF ROBERT GARLICK HILL KEAN,** by Robert
G.H. Kean, (edited by Edward Younger), CWM:APR/95[50],
reviewed by Gary W. Gallagher, CWNEWS:DEC/95[29],
reviewed by David E. Long

**INSIDE WAR: THE GUERRILLA CONFLICT IN
MISSOURI DURING THE AMERICAN CIVIL WAR,** by
Michael Fellman, CWTI:MAY/89[44], *reviewed by* Albert Castel

**THE INSIDERS' GUIDE TO THE CIVIL WAR IN THE
EASTERN THEATER,** by Michael P. Gleason,
CWM:FEB/95[7], *reviewed by* William J. Miller,
CWNEWS:DEC/95[29], *reviewed by* Blake A. Magner

**INSTRUCTIONS FOR OFFICERS AND
NON-COMMISSION OFFICERS ON OUTPOST AND
PATROL DUTY AND TROOPS IN CAMPAIGN,**
CWNEWS:APR/92[4], *reviewed by* Frank Piatek

**INTO THE WILDERNESS WITH THE ARMY OF THE
POTOMAC,** by Robert G. Scott, ACW:JAN/94[62], *reviewed by*
Jerry Keenan

**INTREPID WARRIOR: CLEMENT ANSELM EVANS,
CONFEDERATE GENERAL FROM GEORGIA — LIFE,
LETTERS, AND DIARIES OF THE WAR,** by Robert G.
Stephens, CWM:FEB/95[42], *reviewed by* Gary W. Gallagher

INTRODUCTION TO CIVIL WAR PHOTOGRAPHY, by Ross
J. Kelbough, CWNEWS:AUG/92[4]

**INTRODUCTION TO FIELD ARTILLERY ORDNANCE
1861-1865: A PICTORIAL STUDY OF CIVIL WAR
ARTILLERY PROJECTILES,** by Jack W. Melton Jr.,
B&G:FEB/95[26], *reviewed by* Dean S. Thomas

THE INVISIBLE EMPIRE, by Albion W. Tourgee,
CWTI:SEPT/89[28]

IOWA VALOR, by Steve Meyer, CWM:OCT/95[10], *reviewed by*
David A. Woodbury

THE IRISH BRIGADE AND ITS CAMPAIGNS, by David P.
Conyngham, CWM:FEB/95[7], *reviewed by* William J. Miller

THE IRISH BRIGADE, by Stephen J. Wright,
CWNEWS:JAN/93[4], *reviewed by* Kevin E. O'Brien

THE IRON BRIGADE, by Alan Nolan, CWR:VOL4#3[1],
reviewed by Craig L. Symonds

**IRON BRIGADE GENERAL: JOHN GIBBON, A REBEL IN
BLUE,** by Dennis S. Lavery, B&G:JUN/94[34], *reviewed by* A.

WIlson Green, CWM:APR/95[50], *reviewed by* Gary W.
Gallagher

IRONCLAD LEGACY: BATTLE OF THE *USS MONITOR*, by
Gary Gentile, CWNEWS:NOV/95[29], *reviewed by* Gary
Augustine

**IRONCLAD OF THE ROANOKE: GILBERT ELLIOTT'S
ALBEMARLE,** by Robert G. Elliott, B&G:AUG/95[38], *reviewed
by* Maurice Melton, CWR:VOL4#3[37]

IRONMAIDENS, by Steven Sanders, CWNEWS:FEB/94[5],
reviewed by Gary Augustine

**IRONMAKER TO THE CONFEDERACY: JOSEPH R.
ANDERSON AND THE TREDEGAR IRON WORKS,** by
Charles B. Dew, AHI:DEC/66[17], *reviewed by* Ralph Adams
Brown

**THE IROQUOIS IN THE CIVIL WAR: FROM
BATTLEFIELD TO RESERVATION,** by Lawrence M.
Hauptman, ACW:SEP/94[66], *reviewed by* Brian Temple,
CWM:APR/95[50], *reviewed by* Gary W. Gallagher,
CWNEWS:JAN/94[5], *reviewed by* Ted Alexander,
CWR:VOL3#2[105], *reviewed by* Paul N. Beck

**IT DIDN'T HAPPEN THE WAY YOU THINK. THE
LINCOLN ASSASSINATION: WHAT THE EXPERTS
MISSED,** by Robert L. Mills, CWNEWS:OCT/94[33], *reviewed
by* Steven J. Wright

**JACKSON'S VALLEY CAMPAIGN: THE BATTLE OF
MCDOWELL, MARCH 11-MAY 18, 1862,** by Richard L.
Armstrong, CWM:JAN/91[47], *reviewed by* Gary W. Gallagher

**THE JAMES E. TAYLOR SKETCHBOOK: WITH
SHERIDAN UP THE SHENANDOAH VALLEY IN 1864:
LEAVES FROM A SPECIAL ARTI by** James E. Taylor,
SKETCHBOOK AND DIARY, CWNEWS:NOV/89[4],
reviewed by Brian Pohanka

JEB STUART, by John W. Thomason Jr., CWM:AUG/95[45],
reviewed by Gary W. Gallagher, CWNEWS:SEP/95[33],
reviewed by John G. Secondari, CWR:VOL4#3[89], *reviewed by*
Billy B. Hathorn

**JEDEDIAH HOTCHKISS: REBEL MAPMAKER AND
VIRGINIA BUSINESSMAN,** by Peter W. Roper,
CWNEWS:APR/93[4], *reviewed by* Jeffry D. Wert,
CWR:VOL2#3[256], *reviewed by* Robert E. L. Krick

**JEFFERSON DAVIS AND HIS GENERALS: THE FAILURE
OF CONFEDERATE COMMAND IN THE WEST,** by
Stephen E. Woodworth, ACW:MAY/91[54], *reviewed by* Richard
F. Welch, B&G:APR/91[28], *reviewed by* James L. McDonough,
CWM:JAN/91[47], *reviewed by* Gary W. Gallagher,
CWNEWS:JAN/91[4], *reviewed by* Anne J. Bailey,
CWTI:FEB/91[10], *reviewed by* David Evans

JEFFERSON DAVIS' MEXICAN WAR REGIMENT, by
Joseph E. Chance, WM:JAN/92[57], *reviewed by* Gary W.
Gallagher, CWNEWS:JAN/93[4], *reviewed by* Robert D. Norris
Jr., CWNEWS:NOV/93[5], *reviewed by* Robert D. Norris Jr.

JEFFERSON DAVIS, THE MAN AND HIS HOUR, by William
C. Davis, ACW:MAR/93[58], *reviewed by* Phil Noblitt,
B&G:DEC/92[26], *reviewed by* Judith Lee Hallock,
CWM:MAR/93[51], CWNEWS:JAN/93[4], *reviewed by* John F.
Marszalek, CWR:VOL2#1[78], *reviewed by* Theodore P. Savas

JEFFERSON DAVIS, by Varina Davis, CWNEWS:MAY/92[4],
reviewed by Michael Russert

**JENNISON'S JAYHAWKERS: A CIVIL WAR CAVLRY
REGIMENT AND ITS COMMANDER,** by Stephen Z. Starr,
CWNEWS:JAN/95[25], *reviewed by* Anne J. Bailey

THE LIFE AND WARS OF GIDEON J. PILLOW, by
Nathaniel C. Hughes Jr., ACW:JUL/94[58], *reviewed by* John
Wilso, B&G:FEB/95[26], *reviewed by* Michael L. Gillespie,
CWM:AUG/94[9], *reviewed by* Glenn Goodwin,
CWM:APR/95[50], *reviewed by* Gary W. Gallagher,
CWNEWS:DEC/94[33], *reviewed by* Barry Popchock,
CWTI:MAR/94[12]

THE LIFE AND WARS OF GENERAL PHIL SHERIDAN, by
Roy Morris, MH:AUG/92[76]

**THE LIFE OF JOHNNY REB: THE COMMON SOLDIER
OF THE CONFEDERACY,** by Bell I. Wiley,
CWM:OCT/95[10], *reviewed by* Gary W. Gallagher

**LIFELINE OF THE CONFEDERACY: BLOCKADE
RUNNING DURING THE CIVIL WAR,** by Stephen R. Wise,
B&G:APR/91[28], *reviewed by* Robert Holcombe,
CWNEWS:JUN/90[4], *reviewed by* Terrence J. Winschel,
CWTI:JUN/90[20]

THE LINCOLN FAMILY, by Mark E. Neely Jr.,
CWNEWS:JUN/92[4], *reviewed by* Kale K. Phillips,
CWTI:DEC/95[38]

THE LINCOLN MURDER CONSPIRACIES, by William
Hanchett, CWTI:DEC/95[38]

THE LINCOLN NO ONE KNOWS, by Webb Garrison,
CWM:SEP/93[51], *reviewed by* Kemp P. Burpeau,
CWTI:SEP/94[18], *reviewed by* Lloyd Ostendorf

**THE LINCOLN PERSUASION: REMAKING AMERICAN
LIBERALISM,** by J. David Greenstone,
CWNEWS:MAY/95[33], *reviewed by* Allen C. Guelzo

**THE LINCOLN-DOUGLAS DEBATES: THE FIRST
COMPLETE, UNEXPURGATED TEXT,** (edited by) Harold
Holzer, B&G:JUN/94[34], *reviewed by* Scott W. Smith,
CWNEWS:JUL/94[25], *reviewed by* William F. Howard,
CWR:VOL3#2[105], *reviewed by* James Marten

LINCOLN AND BLACK FREEDOM, by LaWanda Cox,
CWNEWS:JUL/95[61], *reviewed by* Judy Yandoh

LINCOLN AND HIS GENERALS, by T. Harry Williams,
CWTI:DEC/95[38]

**LINCOLN AND THE ECONOMICS OF THE AMERICAN
DREAM,** by Gabor Boritt, CWTI:DEC/95[38]

LINCOLN AND THE MUSIC OF THE CIVIL WAR, by
Kenneth A. Bernard, AHI:JUN/68[51], *reviewed by* Robert D.
Hoffsommer

LINCOLN AND THE TOOLS OF WAR, by Robert W. Bruce,
CWNEWS:APR/91[4], *reviewed by* Gregory Urwin

**LINCOLN AND THE WAR DEMOCRATS: THE GRAND
EROSION OF CONSERVATIVE TRADITION,** by
Christopher Dell, AHI:JUN/76[50], *reviewed by* Lowell H.
Harrison

**LINCOLN AT GETTYSBURG: THE WORDS THAT
REMADE AMERICA,** by Garry Wills, CWNEWS:JAN/93[4],
reviewed by Dr. Allen C. Guelzo

LINCOLN COLLECTOR, by Jonathan Mann,
CWTI:DEC/95[38]

LINCOLN DAY BY DAY, (edited by) Earl Schenck Miers,
CWTI:DEC/95[38]

**LINCOLN FINDS A GENERAL. A MILITARY HISTORY OF
THE CIVIL WAR,** by Kenneth P. Williams,
CWM:FEB/95[42], *reviewed by* Gary W. Gallagher

LINCOLN IN AMERICAN MEMORY, by Merrill D. Peterson,
CWNEWS:JUN/95[33], *reviewed by* Spencer Gill

LINCOLN IN PHOTOGRAPHS, by Charles Hamilton,
CWTI:DEC/95[38]

LINCOLN MEMORIAL, by National Park Service,
AHI:OCT/87[10]

LINCOLN ON DEMOCRACY, (edited by) Mario M. Cuomo,
B&G:OCT/91[34], *reviewed by* John S. Peterson,
CWM:MAR/91[42], *reviewed by* William J. Miller,
CWNEWS:JUL/92[4], *reviewed by* Jock Baird

LINCOLN THE PRESIDENT, by James G. Randall,
CWTI:DEC/95[38]

**LINCOLN THE WAR PRESIDENT, THE GETTYSBURG
LECTURES,** (edited by) Gabor S. Boritt, B&G:FEB/94[36],
reviewed by John F. Marszalek

**LINCOLN VS DOUGLAS: THE GREAT DEBATES
CAMAPIGN,** by Richard A. Heckman, AHI:OCT/67[64]

LINCOLN'S GENERALS, (edited by) Gabor S. Boritt,
B&G:AUG/95[38], *reviewed by* Lawrence L. Hewitt,
CWM:AUG/95[45], *reviewed by* Gary W. Gallagher,
CWNEWS:AUG/95[33], *reviewed by* Willis R. Kocher,
CWTI:JUN/95[24]

LINCOLN'S HERNDON: A BIOGRAPHY, by David H.
Donald, CWTI:SEPT/89[28]

LINCOLN'S LOST SPEECH, by Elwell Crissey,
AHI:JUN/68[51], *reviewed by* Robert D. Hoffsommer

**LINCOLN'S LOYALISTS: UNION SOLDIERS FROM THE
CONFEDERACY,** by Richard N. Current, ACW:SEP/93[54],
reviewed by Richard F. Welch, B&G:APR/94[24], *reviewed by*
Earl J. Hess

LINCOLN'S PREPARATION FOR GREATNESS, by Paul
Simon, AHI:JUN/68[51], *reviewed by* Robert D. Hoffsommer

LINCOLN, DOUGLAS AND SLAVERY, by David Zarefsky,
CWNEWS:NOV/94[33], *reviewed by* Judy Yandoh

LINCOLN, LAND, AND LABOR, 1809-60, by Olivier Frayss'e,
CWM:DEC/95[10], *reviewed by* J. Jeffrey Cox

**LINCOLN, THE SOUTH, AND SLAVERY: THE POLITICAL
DIMENSION,** by Robert W. Johannsen, CWM:JAN/92[57],
reviewed by Gary W. Gallagher, CWNEWS:JUN/95[33],
reviewed by John L. Farber

**LINCOLN, THE WAR PRESIDENT: THE GETTYSBURG
LECTURES,** (edited by) Gabor S. Boritt, CWNEWS:JUL/93[5],
reviewed by Allen C. Guelzo

LINCOLN, by David Herbert Donald, CWTI:DEC/95[38]

LINCOLN: SPEECHES AND WRITINGS, by Don E.
Fehrenbacher, CWTI:APR/90[10], *reviewed by* Harold Holzer

**THE LION OF THE SOUTH: GENERAL THOMAS C.
HINDMAN,** by Diane Neal, B&G:JUN/94[34], *reviewed by*
Larry J. Daniel, CWM:APR/95[50], *reviewed by* Gary W.
Gallagher, CWNEWS:DEC/94[33], *reviewed by* Michael
Cavanaugh, CWR:VOL4#1[78], *reviewed by* Stephen D. Engle

**THE LONG ARM OF LEE OR THE HISTORY OF THE
ARTILLERY OF THE ARMY OF NORTHERN VIRGINIA,**
by Jennings C. Wise, CWNEWS:JUL/90[4], *reviewed by* Michael
Russert, CWM:FEB/95[42]564, CWNEWS:SEP/93[5], *reviewed
by* Brandon H. Beck

**THE LONG ROAD FOR HOME: THE CIVIL WAR
EXPERIENCES OF FOUR FARMBOY SOLDIERS OF
THE TWENTY-SEVENTH MASSACHUSETTS
REGIMENT OF VOLUNTEER INFANTRY AS TOLD BY
THEIR PERSONAL CORRESPONDENCE, 1861-1864,**
(edited by) Henry C. Lind, CWNEWS:JAN/94[5], *reviewed by*
Dr. Richard A. Sauers

THE LONG ROAD TO GETTYSBURG, by Jim Murphy,
CWNEWS:AUG/93[5], *reviewed by* Allen C. Guelzo

**LOOK TO THE EARTH: HISTORICAL ARCHAEOLOGY
AND THE AMERICAN CIVIL WAR,** (edited by) Clarence R.

Grier Jr., CWM:DEC/95[10], *reviewed by* Charles R. Norville, CWR:VOL4#3[37]

LOST LOVE: A TRUE STORY OF PASSION, MURDER, AND JUSTICE IN OLD NEW YORK, by George Cooper, CWNEWS:JAN/95[25], *reviewed by* DeAnne Blanton

LOST VICTORIES: THE MILITARY GENIUS OF STONEWALL JACKSON, by Kevin Alexander, CWM:MAY/93[51], *reviewed by* Brandon Beck, CWTI:SEP/93[26], *reviewed by* Edward D.C. Campbell

LOUISIANA NECKTIES: LOUISIANA RAILROADS IN THE CIVIL WAR, by Lawrence E. Estaville Jr., CWNEWS:APR/92[4], *reviewed by* Terrence J. Winschel

THE LOWER SHENANDOAH VALLEY IN THE CIVIL WAR: THE IMPACT OF WAR UPON THE CIVILIAN POPULATION AND UPON CIVIL INSTITUTIONS, by Edward H. Phillips, CWNEWS:AUG/94[33], *reviewed by* David F. Riggs

LOYAL MOUNTAIN TROOPERS: THE SECOND AND THIRD TENNESSEE CAVALRY IN THE CIVIL WAR, REMINISCENCES OF LIEUTENANT JOHN W. ANDES AND MAJOR WILL A. MCTEER, by John W. Andes, (edited by Charles S. McCammon), CWNEWS:NOV/93[5], *reviewed by* William L. Shea

LUCY BRECKINRIDGE OF GROVE HILL: THE JOURNAL OF A VIRGINIA GIRL, 1862-1864, by Lucy Breckinridge, (edited by Mary D. Robertson), CWNEWS:AUG/95[33], *reviewed by* DeAnne Blanton

THE LYON CAMPAIGN IN MISSOURI: BEING A HISTORY OF THE FIRST IOWA INFANTRY, by Eugene F. Ware, CWNEWS:JAN/92[4], *reviewed by* Robert D. Norris Jr., CWR:VOL1#4[77], *reviewed by* James Harwick Jr.

MAJOR GENERAL JAMES LAWSON KEMPER C.S.A.: THE CONFEDERACY'S FORGOTTEN SON, by Harold R. Woodward Jr., CWNEWS:APR/94[5], *reviewed by* Jeffry D. Wert

MAJOR GENERAL JOHN FREDERICK HARTRANFT, CITIZEN SOLDIER AND PENNSYLVANIA STATESMAN, by A.M. Gambone, CWNEWS:NOV/95[29], *reviewed by* Frank J. Piatek

MAKE ME A MAP OF THE VALLEY: THE CIVIL WAR JOURNAL OF STONEWALL JACKSON'S TOPOGRAPHER, by Jedediah Hotchkiss, CWM:FEB/95[42], *reviewed by* Gary W. Gallagher

THE MAN WHO TRIED TO BURN NEW YORK, by Nat Brandt, AHI:FEB/87[6]

MANUAL FOR ENGINEER TROOPS, by J.C. Duane, CWNEWS:NOV/92[4], *reviewed by* William Marvel

MANUAL OF MILITARY SURGERY, PREPARED FOR THE USE OF THE CONFEDERATE STATES ARMY BY ORDER OF THE SURGEON-GENERAL, CWNEWS:NOV/90[4], *reviewed by* Dr. Harris D. Riley

MANUSCRIPT RESOURCES FOR THE CIVIL WAR, (compiled by) Kim A. Scott, CWNEWS:JAN/92[4], *reviewed by* Michael Mullins

MAPPING FOR STONEWALL: THE CIVIL WAR SERVICE OF JED HOTCHKISS, by William J. Miller, B&G:DEC/94[28], *reviewed by* Archie P. McDonald, CWNEWS:FEB/94[5], *reviewed by* Blake A. Magner

MAPPING THE CIVIL WAR: FEATURING RARE MAPS FROM THE LIBRARY OF CONGRESS, by Christopher Nelson, B&G:OCT/93[24], *reviewed by* Paul Kallina, CWM:JUL/93[51], *reviewed by* Richard M. McMurry,

CWNEWS:OCT/92[4], *reviewed by* Blake Magner, CWNEWS:SEP/93[5], *reviewed by* Blake A. Magner

THE MARBLE MAN: ROBERT E. LEE AND HIS IMAGE IN AMERICAN SOCIETY, by Thomas L. Connelly, CWM:JUL/91[58], *reviewed by* Gary W. Gallagher

THE MARCH TO THE SEA AND BEYOND: SHERMAN'S TROOPS IN THE SAVANNAH AND CAROLINAS CAMPAIGNS, by Joseph T. Glatthaar, CWM:FEB/95[42], *reviewed by* Gary W. Gallagher

THE MARCH TO THE SEA, FRANKLIN AND NASHVILLE, by Jacob D. Cox, CWNEWS:NOV/91[4], *reviewed by* John F. Marszalek

THE MARCH TO THE SEA, by William R. Scaife, CWM:JAN/91[47], *reviewed by* Gary W. Gallagher

MARCHING THROUGH GEORGIA: THE STORY OF SOLDIERS AND CIVILIANS DURING SHERMAN'S CAMPAIGN, by Lee Kennett, CWTI:AUG/95[18], *reviewed by* Mark Grimsley

MARCHING TO COLD HARBOR: VICTORY & FAILURE, 1864, by R. Wayne Maney, B&G:JUN/95[30], *reviewed by* Robert E.L. Krick, CWNEWS:MAY/95[33], *reviewed by* Ethan S. Rafuse, CWR:VOL4#4[129], *reviewed by* Marshall Scott

MARGARET JUNKIN PRESTON: A BIOGRAPHY, by Mary P. Coulling, CWNEWS:SEP/94[33], *reviewed by* Linda G. Black, CWTI:MAR/94[12], *reviewed by* Wendy Hamand Venet

MARKETS AND PRODUCTION, VOLUME ONE. CONDITIONS OF SLAVE LIFE AND THE TRANSITION TO FREEDOM, VOLUME TWO, by Robert W. Fogel, CWNEWS:NOV/93[5], *reviewed by* Judy Yandoh

MARY CHESNUT'S CIVIL WAR, by C. Vann Woodward, AHI:SEP/82[8], *reviewed by* Joe Gray Taylor

MARY TODD LINCOLN: A BIOGRAPHY, by Jean H. Baker, AHI:FEB/88[8]

MATHEW BRADY: HIS LIFE AND PHOTOGRAPHS, by George Sullivan, CWNEWS:JUN/95[33]

MCCLELLAN'S OWN STORY, by George B. McClellan, CWM:JUN/95[6], *reviewed by* William J. Miller

MEADE OF GETTYSBURG, by Freeman Cleaves, CWM:DEC/94[7], *reviewed by* Gary W. Gallagher, CWNEWS:OCT/92[4], *reviewed by* Frank Piatek

MEADE'S HEADQUARTERS, 1863-1865: LETTERS OF COLONEL THEODORE LYMAN FROM THE WILDERNESS TO APPOMATTOX, by Theodore Lyman, (edited by George R. Agassiz), CWM:DEC/94[7], *reviewed by* Gary W. Gallagher

THE MEDICAL AND SURGICAL HISTORY OF THE WAR OF THE REBELLION. (1861-1865), by U.S. Surgeon General, CWM:MAY/91[38], *reviewed by* Gary W. Gallagher

MEDICAL HISTORIES OF CONFEDERATE GENERALS, by Jack D. Welsh, CWNEWS:NOV/95[29], *reviewed by* Harris D. Riley, M.D.

MEDICAL-MILITARY PORTRAITS OF UNION AND CONFEDERATE GENERALS, by Paul E. Steiner, CWM:MAY/91[38], *reviewed by* Gary W. Gallagher

THE MEMOIRS OF JOHN S. MOSBY, by John S. Mosby, (edited by Charles W. Russell), CWR:VOL1#3[94], *reviewed by* Theodore P. Savas

MEMOIRS OF A SWISS OFFICER IN THE AMERICAN CIVIL WAR, by Rudolf Aschmann, (edited by, Heinz K. Meier), CWNEWS:JAN/91[4], *reviewed by* Michael Mullins

MEMOIRS OF GENERAL W.T. SHERMAN, by William T. Sherman, AHI:JAN/91[8], CWM:AUG/95[8], *reviewed by* Gary

THE PAPERS OF JEFFERSON DAVIS: JANUARY 6, 1856-DECEMBER 28, 1860, VOL. 6, (edited by) Lynda L. Crist, CWNEWS:AUG/90[4], *reviewed by* Theodore P. Savas

THE PAPERS OF JEFFERSON DAVIS, VOL. 7, 1861, (edited by) Lynda L. Crist, B&G:DEC/93[24], *reviewed by* Judith L. Hallock, CWNEWS:DEC/92[4], *reviewed by* Theodore P. Savas

THE PAPERS OF JEFFERSON DAVIS, VOL. 8: 1862, (edited by) Lynda L. Crist, B&G:OCT/95[28], *reviewed by* Steve Davis, CWM:JUN/95[6], *reviewed by* Gary W. Gallagher, CWNEWS:DEC/95[29], *reviewed by* Theodore P. Savas

THE PAPERS OF ULYSSES S. GRANT. VOLUME 1: 1837-1861, by John Y. Simon, AHI:NOV/67[57], *reviewed by* Wilber S. Nye

PARKER'S VIRGINIA BATTERY, C.S.A., by Robert K. Krick, CWNEWS:APR/91[4], *reviewed by* Brandon Beck

PARTNERS IN COMMAND: THE RELATIONSHIPS BETWEEN LEADERS IN THE CIVIL WAR, by Joseph T. Glatthaar, CWTI:JUL/94[18], *reviewed by* Stephen D. Engle

THE PASSING OF THE ARMIES: AN ACCOUNT OF THE FINAL CAMPAIGN OF THE ARMY OF THE POTOMAC, BASED UPON PERSONAL RECOLLECTIONS, by Joshua L. Chamberlain, CWM:FEB/95[42]564, *reviewed by* Gary W. Gallagher

PATHS TO VICTORY: A HISTORY AND TOUR GUIDE OF THE STONES RIVER, CHICKAMAUGA, CHATTANOOGA, KNOXVILLE AND NASHVILLE CAMPAIGNS, by Jim Miles, CWNEWS:AUG/94[33], *reviewed by* Richard M. McMurry

PATRIOTISM FOR PROFIT: GEORGIA'S URBAN ENTERPRENEURS AND THE CONFEDERATE WAR EFFORT, by Mary A. DeCredico, CWNEWS:JUL/92[4], *reviewed by* Linda G. Black

PATRIOTS IN DISGUISE: WOMEN WARRIORS OF THE CIVIL WAR, by Richard Hall, ACW:JUL/94[58], *reviewed by* Michael D. Hull, B&G:JUN/94[34], *reviewed by* Lauren C. Burgess, CWNEWS:OCT/93[5], *reviewed by* Lauren C. Burgess, CWR:VOL3#2[105], *reviewed by* Anne J. Bailey

PAVING OVER THE PAST: A HISTORY AND GUIDE TO CIVIL WAR BATTLEFIELD PRESERVATION, by Georgia Boge, CWM:APR/94[51], *reviewed by* Chris Fordney, CWNEWS:MAY/94[5], *reviewed by* Blake A. Magner

PEA RIDGE: CIVIL WAR CAMPAIGN IN THE WEST, by William L. Shea, B&G:AUG/93[24], *reviewed by* Leo E. Huff, CWM:FEB/95[42], *reviewed by* Gary W. Gallagher, CWNEWS:DEC/94[33], *reviewed by* Robert D. Norris, CWR:VOL3#1[80], *reviewed by* Edward A. Hagerty

"PECOS BILL": A MILITARY BIOGRAPHY OF WILLIAM R. SHAFTER, by Paul Carlson, CWNEWS:APR/91[4], *reviewed by* Robert D. Norris

PEMBERTON, A BIOGRAPHY, by Michael B. Ballard, B&G:AUG/92[36], *reviewed by* Lawrence L. Hewitt, CWM:MAY/92[59], *reviewed by* Charles R. Norville, CWNEWS:AUG/92[4], *reviewed by* Terrence J. Winschell, CWR:VOL2#1[78], *reviewed by* Theodore P. Savas, CWTI:SEP/92[18], *reviewed by* Noah Andre Trudeau

THE PENINSULA CAMPAIGN OF 1862: YORKTOWN TO THE SEVEN DAYS, (edited by) William J. Miller, CWM:APR/95[50], *reviewed by* Gary W. Gallagher, CWNEWS:JUN/94[5], *reviewed by* Michael Russert, CWNEWS:AUG/95[33], *reviewed by* Ethan Rafuse

THE PENINSULA: MCCLELLAN'S CAMPAIGN OF 1862, by Alexander S. Webb, CWNEWS:MAY/91[4], *reviewed by* Richard A. Sauers

THE PERSONAL MEMOIRS OF JONATHAN THOMAS SCHARF OF THE FIRST MARYLAND ARTILLERY, by Jonathan T. Scharf, (edited by Tom Kelley), CWR:VOL3#3[92], *reviewed by* Brandon Beck

THE PERSONAL MEMOIRS OF JULIA DENT GRANT, by Julia Dent Grant, (edited by John Y. Simon), AHI:FEB/76[50], *reviewed by* Bell I. Wiley

PERSONAL AND HISTORICAL SKETCHES AND FACIAL HISTORY OF AND BY MEMBERS OF THE SEVENTH REGIMENT MICHIGAN VOLUNTEER CAVALRY 1862-1865, (complied by) William O. Lee, CWNEWS:JAN/92[4], *reviewed by* Barry Popchock

PERSONAL CIVIL WAR LETTERS OF GENERAL LAWRENCE SULLIVAN ROSS, by Lawrence S. Ross, (compiled by Perry W. Shelton), CWNEWS:JUL/95[61], *reviewed by* Jerry W. Holsworth

PERSONAL MEMOIRS OF PHILIP HENRY SHERIDAN, GENERAL, UNITED STATES ARMY, by Philip H. Sheridan, CWM:FEB/95[42], *reviewed by* Gary W. Gallagher

PERSONAL MEMOIRS OF U.S. GRANT, by Ulysses S. Grant, CWM:FEB/95[42], *reviewed by* Gary W. Gallagher

PERSONAL RECOLLECTIONS & OBSERVATIONS OF GENERAL NELSON A. MILES, by Nelson A. Miles, CWNEWS:DEC/94[33], *reviewed by* Norman E. Rourke

PERSONAL RECOLLECTIONS OF THE WAR OF 1861, by Charles A. Fuller, B&G:APR/91[28], *reviewed by* Mark Dunkelma, CWR:VOL4#1[78], *reviewed by* Michael Russert

PERSONAL REMINISCENCES OF GENERAL ROBERT E. LEE, by J. William Jones, CWNEWS:NOV/91[4], *reviewed by* Michael Pollcatti

PERSONAL/SELECTED LETTERS OF ULYSSES S. GRANT, by William S. McFeely, AHI:JAN/91[8]

THE PETERSBURG CAMPAIGN JUNE 1864-APRIL 1865, by John Horn, CWNEWS:APR/95[33], *reviewed by* Clint Johnson

THE PETERSBURG CAMPAIGN: THE BATTLE OF OLD MEN AND YOUNG BOYS, JUNE 9, 1864, by William G. Robertson, CWM:JAN/91[47], *reviewed by* Gary W. Gallagher

THE PETERSBURG CAMPAIGN: THE BATTLE OF THE CRATER: "THE HORRID PIT", JUNE 25-AUGUST 6, 1864, by Michael Cavanaugh, CWNEWS:JUL/90[4], *reviewed by* J. Tracy Power

THE PETERSBURG CAMPAIGN: THE DESTRUCTION OF THE WELDON RAILROAD (DEEP BOTTOM, GLOBE TAVERN, AND REAMS   TION, AUGUST 14-25, 1864, by John Horn, CWNEWS:JAN/92[4], *reviewed by* William F. Howard

PHIL SHERIDAN AND HIS ARMY, by Paul Andrew Hutton, AHI:SEP/85[10]

PICKETT'S CHARGE: EYEWITNESS ACCOUNTS, (edited by) Richard Rollins, CWNEWS:OCT/94[33], *reviewed by* Jeffry D. Wert

PIEDMONT FARMER: THE JOURNALS OF DAVID GOLIGHTLY HARRIS, 1855-1870, by David G. Harris (edited by Philip N. Racine), CWM:MAR/92[49], *reviewed by* Gary W. Gallagher

PIERCING THE HEARTLAND: A HISTORY AND TOUR GUIDE OF THE FORT DONELSON, SHILOH, AND PERRYVILLE CAMPAIGNS, by Jim Miles, CWNEWS:AUG/94[33], *reviewed by* Richard M. McMurry

THE PINKERTONS: THE DETECTIVE DYNASTY THAT MADE HISTORY, by James D. Horan, AHI:MAY/69[49], *reviewed by* J. E. Raymond

THE PLAIN PEOPLE OF THE CONFEDERACY, by Bell I. Wiley, CWM:OCT/95[10], *reviewed by* Gary W. Gallagher

PLOUGHSHARES INTO SWORDS: JOSIAH GORGAS AND CONFEDERATE ORDNANCE, by Frank E. Vandiver, CWM:FEB/95[42], *reviewed by* Gary W. Gallagher, CWR:VOL4#3[37], CWR:VOL4#4[129], *reviewed by* Archie P. McDonald

THE PLYMOUTH PILGRIMS: A HISTORY OF THE EIGHTY-FIFTH NEW YORK INFANTRY IN THE CIVIL WAR, by Wayne Mahood, B&G:APR/91[28], *reviewed by* E. A. Livingston, CWNEWS:AUG/90[4], *reviewed by* Frank Piatek

THE POETRY OF THE AMERICAN CIVIL WAR, (edited by) Lee Steinmetz, CWNEWS:NOV/93[5], *reviewed by* Linda G. Black

POLITICAL PARTIES AND AMERICAN POLITICAL DEVELOPMENT FROM THE AGE OF JACKSON TO THE AGE OF LINCOLN, by Michael F. Holt, CWNEWS:JUN/93[5], *reviewed by* John L. Farber

THE POLITICS OF UNION: NORTHERN POLITICS DURING THE CIVIL WAR, by James A. Rawley, CWNEWS:SEP/91[4], *reviewed by* Kemp Burpeau

PORTRAITS OF CONFLICT: A PHOTOGRAPHIC HISTORY OF LOUISIANA IN THE CIVIL WAR, by Bobby Roberts, CWNEWS:SEP/91[4], *reviewed by* Larry J. Daniel

PORTRAITS OF CONFLICT: A PHOTOGRAPHIC HISTORY OF MISSISSIPPI IN THE CIVIL WAR, by Bobby Roberts, CWM:APR/95[50], *reviewed by* Gary W. Gallagher, CWNEWS:JAN/94[5], *reviewed by* Larry J. Daniel

THE POWER THAT GOVERNS: THE EVOLUTION OF JUDICIAL ACTIVISM IN A MIDWESTERN STATE, 1840-1890, by Keith R. Schlesinger, CWNEWS:JUN/92[4], *reviewed by* Kemp Burpeau

PRELUDE TO CIVIL WAR: THE NULLIFICATION CONTROVERSY IN SOUTH CAROLINA, 1816-1836, by William W. Freehling, AHI:FEB/67[57], *reviewed by* Ralph Adams Brown

PRELUDE TO GREATNESS: LINCOLN IN THE 1850'S, by Don E. Fehrenbacher, CWTI:DEC/95[38]

THE PRESIDENCY OF ABRAHAM LINCOLN, by Philip S. Paludan, CWTI:MAR/95[14]

THE PRESIDENCY OF FRANKLIN PIERCE, by Larry Gara, CWM:JAN/92[57], *reviewed by* Gary W. Gallagher

PRESIDENT LINCOLN'S THIRD LARGEST CITY, BROOKLYN AND THE CIVIL WAR, by E.A. Livingston, CWNEWS:JUL/95[61], *reviewed by* Frank J. Piatek

THE PRESIDENT'S WIFE: MARY TODD LINCOLN, by Ishbel Ross, AHI:JAN/75[50], *reviewed by* Robert D. Hoffsommer

THE PRIVATE CIVIL WAR: POPULAR THOUGHT DURING THE SECTIONAL CONFLICT, by Randall C. Jimerson, CWNEWS:OCT/89[4], *reviewed by* William Howard

THE PROBLEM OF SLAVERY IN THE AGE OF REVOLUTION, 1770-1823, by David Brion Davis, AHI:MAY/76[48], *reviewed by* Bell I. Wiley

A POST OF HONOR: THE PRYOR LETTERS, 1861-63; LETTERS FROM CAPT. S.G. PRYOR, TWELFTH GEORGIA REGIMENT AND HIS WIFE, PENELOPE TYSON PRYOR, by Charles R. Pryor, CWM:FEB/95[42]564, *reviewed by* Gary W. Gallagher

PULLING THE TEMPLE DOWN: THE FIRE-EATERS AND THE DESTRUCTION OF THE UNION, by David S. Heidler, CWM:AUG/95[45], *reviewed by* Gary W. Gallagher, CWNEWS:SEP/95[33], *reviewed by* Stephen D. Engle

QUARTERMASTER GENERAL OF THE UNION ARMY: A BIOGRAPHY OF M.C. MEIGS, by Russell F. Weigley, CWM:FEB/95[42], *reviewed by* Gary W. Gallagher

R.E. LEE: A BIOGRAPHY, by Douglas S. Freeman, CWM:FEB/95[42], *reviewed by* Gary W. Gallagher, CWM:JUN/95[6], *reviewed by* William J. Miller

RACE OF THE SOIL: THE NINTH NEW HAMPSHIRE REGIMENT IN THE CIVIL WAR, by William Marvel, CWNEWS:MAY/89[4], *reviewed by* Harris D. Riley M.D.

THE RAGGED REBEL: A COMMON SOLDIER IN W.H. PARSON'S TEXAS CAVALRY, 1861-1865, by B. P. Gallaway, CWNEWS:OCT/89[4], *reviewed by* David F. Riggs

RAGGED AND SUBLIME: THE CIVIL WAR IN ARKANSAS, by Mark K. Christ, CWTI:JUN/95[24]

THE RAILROADS OF THE CONFEDERACY, by Robert C. Black, III, CWM:NOV/91[73], *reviewed by* Gary W. Gallagher

RALLY ROUND THE FLAG: CHICAGO AND THE CIVIL WAR, by Theodore J. Karamanski, CWNEWS:NOV/93[5], *reviewed by* Dale K. Phillips

RANKS OF HONOR: A REGIMENTAL HISTORY OF THE ELEVENTH ARKANSAS INFANTRY REGIMENT & POE'S CAVALRY BATTALION C.S.A. 1861, by Anthonyv Rushing, CWR:VOL1#3[94], *reviewed by* James Harwick Jr.

"...THE REAL WAR WILL NEVER GET IN THE BOOKS", SELECTIONS FROM WRITERS DURING THE CIVIL WAR (edited by) Louis P. Maser, CWM:AUG/94[9], *reviewed by* Charles Norville, CWR:VOL4#4[129], *reviewed by* Ron Calkins, CWNEWS:NOV/94[33], *reviewed by* Stehen D. Engle, CWTI:SEP/93[26]

REBEL RAIDER: THE LIFE OF GENERAL JOHN HUNT MORGAN, by James A. Ramage, CWM:FEB/95[42], *reviewed by* Gary W. Gallagher

REBEL SONS OF ERIN, A CIVIL WAR HISTORY OF THE TENTH TENNESSEE INFANTRY (IRISH), CONFEDERATE STATES VOLUNTEERS, by Ed Gleeson, CWNEWS:JUN/95[33], *reviewed by* Michael A. Cavanaugh, CWR:VOL4#3[89], *reviewed by* George Otott

REBEL VICTORY AT VICKSBURG, by Edwin C. Bearss, CWNEWS:JAN/91[4], *reviewed by* Terrence Winschel

REBEL WATCHDOG: THE CONFEDERATE STATES ARMY PROVOST GUARD, by Kenneth Radley, CWNEWS:JUL/90[4], *reviewed by* Michael Parrish

REBEL YELL AND YANKEE HURRAH: THE CIVIL WAR JOURNAL OF A MAINE VOLUNTEER, by John Haley, CWR:VOL4#3[1], *reviewed by* John Hennessy

REBEL, by Bernard Cornwell, CWNEWS:FEB/95[33], *reviewed by* Sarah W. Wiggins

REBELS FROM WEST POINT, by Gerard A. Patterson, AHI:APR/88[14]

REBELS ON THE RIO GRANDE: THE CIVIL WAR JOURNAL OF A.B. PETICOLAS, by A. B. Peticolas, (edited by Don E. Alberts), CWNEWS:AUG/94[33], *reviewed by* Norman E. Rourke

RECOLLECTIONS AND LETTERS OF GENERAL ROBERT E. LEE BY HIS SON, by Robert E. Lee, CWNEWS:MAY/89[4], *reviewed by* Michael Parrish

THE SINKING OF THE <u>USS CAIRO</u>, by John C. Wideman, CWM:APR/95[50], *reviewed by* Gary W. Gallagher, CWNEWS:FEB/94[5], *reviewed by* William Shea

SKETCHES FROM PRISON: A CONFEDERATE ARTIST'S RECORD OF LIFE AT POINT LOOKOUT PRISONER OF WAR CAMP, 1863-1865, by John J. Omenhausser, (edited by Ross M. Kimmel), CWNEWS:JUN/92[4], *reviewed by* Michael Mullins

THE SLAVE COMMUNITY: PLANTATION LIFE IN THE ANTEBELLUM SOUTH, by John W. Blassingame, AHI:JUN/80[6], *reviewed by* Larry Gara

SLAVERY ATTACKED: SOUTHERN SLAVES AND THEIR ALLIES, by Merton L. Dillon, CWM:JAN/92[57], *reviewed by* Gary W. Gallagher, CWNEWS:JUL/92[4], *reviewed by* Kemp Burpeau

SMITHSONIAN'S GREAT BATTLES OF THE CIVIL WAR, VOLUME IV, ACW:JUL/93[58]

SOLDERING IN THE ARMY OF TENNESSEE: A PORTRAIT OF LIFE IN A CONFEDERATE ARMY, by Larry J. Daniels, ACW:SEP/92[54], *reviewed by* Richard F. Welch

SOLDIER BOYS, by Daniel Panger, CWNEWS:MAY/89[4], *reviewed by* Dr. Allen Guelzo

SOLDIERING IN THE ARMY OF TENNESSEE: A PORTRAIT OF LIFE IN A CONFEDERATE ARMY, by Larry J. Daniel, B&G:AUG/92[36], *reviewed by* Steve Davis, CWNEWS:MAY/93[4], *reviewed by* Michael A. Cavanaugh, CWR:VOL2#1[78], *reviewed by* James Harwick Jr., CWTI:JUL/92[10], *reviewed by* George F. Skoch

SOLDIERING: THE CIVIL WAR DIARY OF RICE C. BULL, by Rice C. Bull, (edited by K. Jack Bauer), CWM:FEB/95[42]564, *reviewed by* Gary W. Gallagher

SOLDIERS BLUE AND GRAY, by James I. Robertson Jr., CWNEWS:SEP/89[8], *reviewed by* Ron Rago, CWTI:MAY/89[44], *reviewed by* Terry L. Jones

SONS OF OLD MONROE: A REGIMENTAL HISTORY OF PATRICK O'RORKE'S 140TH NEW YORK VOLUNTEER INFANTRY, by Brian A. Bennett, CWNEWS:APR/94[5], *reviewed by* Brian Pohanka

SOUL OF THE LION: A BIOGRAPHY OF GENERAL JOSHUA L. CHAMBERLAIN, by Willard M. Wallace, CWNEWS:NOV/92[4], *reviewed by* Mark A. Snell

THE SOUTH WAS RIGHT!, by James R. Kennedy, CWNEWS:OCT/94[33], *reviewed by* Richard McMurry

SOUTH GEORGIA REBELS: THE 26TH GEORGIA VOLUNTEER INFANTRY, by Alton J. Murray, CWNEWS:MAY/92[4], *reviewed by* Dale K. Phillips

THE SOUTH'S FINEST: THE FIRST MISSOURI CONFEDERATE BRIGADE FROM PEA RIDGE TO VICKSBURG, by Philip T. Tucker, CWM:APR/95[50], *reviewed by* Gary W. Gallagher, CWNEWS:DEC/94[33], *reviewed by* Robert D. Norris Jr., CWR:VOL4#1[78], *reviewed by* Marius Carriere

THE SOUTHERN HISTORICAL SOCIETY PAPERS, by J. William Jones, CWM:FEB/95[42], *reviewed by* Gary W. Gallagher

SOUTHERN BRONZE: CAPT. GARDEN'S (S.C.) ARTILLERY COMPANY DURING THE WAR BETWEEN THE STATES, by Glenn Dedmondt, CWNEWS:SEP/94[33], *reviewed by* Theodore P. Savas

SOUTHERN LOYALISTS IN THE CIVIL WAR: THE SOUTHERN CLAIMS, COMMISSION, by Gary B. Mills, CWNEWS:MAY/95[33], *reviewed by* Michael A. Cavanaugh, CWR:VOL4#3[37]

SOUTHERN NEGROES, 1861-1865, by Bell I. Wiley, CWM:OCT/95[10], *reviewed by* Gary W. Gallagher

SOUTHERN RAILROAD MAN: CONDUCTOR N.J. BELL'S RECOLLECTIONS OF THE CIVIL WAR ERA, by Nimrod J. Bell, (edited by James A. Ward), CWNEWS:OCT/95[33], *reviewed by* Kemp Burpeau, CWR:VOL4#4[129], *reviewed by* Arthur W. Bergeron

SOUTHERN REVENGE! CIVIL WAR HISTORY OF CHAMBERSBURG, PENNSYLVANIA, by Ted Alexander, CWNEWS:APR/91[4], *reviewed by* Steven J. Wright

SOUTHERN STORIES, by Drew Gilpin Faust, CWNEWS:DEC/95[29], *reviewed by* Judy Yandoh

SOUTHWEST VIRGINIA IN THE CIVIL WAR: THE BATTLES FOR SALTVILLE, by William Marvel, CWNEWS:DEC/93[5], *reviewed by* J. Tracy Power

SOUTHWEST VIRGINIA'S RAILROAD: MODERNIZATION AND THE SECTIONAL CRISIS, by Kenneth W. Noe, CWM:AUG/95[45], *reviewed by* Gary W. Gallagher

SPECTATOR OF AMERICA, by Edward Dicey, (edited by Herbert Mitgang), CWNEWS:MAY/91[4], *reviewed by* Mark Snell

SPIES & SPYMASTERS OF THE CIVIL WAR, by Donald E. Markle, CWTI:JAN/95[12], MH:DEC/94[70]

SPURS TO GLORY; THE STORY OF THE UNITED STATES CAVALRY, by James M. Merrill, AHI:FEB/67[57], *reviewed by* Ralph Adams Brown

THE SPY OF THE REBELLION, by Allan Pinkerton, CWNEWS:APR/91[4], *reviewed by* Frank Piatek

SQUALL ACROSS THE ATLANTIC: AMERICAN CIVIL WAR PRIZE CASES AND DIPLOMACY, by Stuart L. Bernath, AHI:JAN/75[50], *reviewed by* Jon M. Nielson

STATES RIGHTS GIST: A SOUTH CAROLINA GENERAL OF THE CIVIL WAR, by Walter B. Cisco, ACW:SEP/92[54], *reviewed by* Jon Guttman, B&G:OCT/92[30], *reviewed by* Christopher Losso, CWR:VOL2#2[169], *reviewed by* George E. Otott

STEPHEN ELLIOTT WELCH OF THE HAMPTON LEGION, by Stephen E. Welch, (edited by John M. Priest), CWM:APR/95[8], *reviewed by* Charles R. Norville

STILL MORE CONFEDERATE FACES, by D.A. Serrano, B&G:JUN/93[28], *reviewed by* Jai S. Cochrane, CWNEWS:MAY/93[4], *reviewed by* WIlliam F. Howard

STONES RIVER: BLOODY WINTER IN TENNESSEE, by James L. McDonough, ACW:MAR/91[54]

"STONEWALL" JACKSON AT FREDERICKSBURG: THE BATTLE OF PROSPECT HILL, DECEMBER 13, 1862 by Frank A. O'Reilly, CWM:FEB/95[7], *reviewed by* David A. Woodbury

STONEWALL JACKSON AND THE AMERICAN CIVIL WAR, by George F.R. Henderson, (edited by James A. Rawley), CWM:JAN/91[47], *reviewed by* Gary W. Gallagher, CWM:FEB/95[42], *reviewed by* Gary W. Gallagher, CWM:DEC/95[10], *reviewed by* Gary W. Gallagher

STONEWALL JACKSON AT CEDAR MOUNTAIN, by Robert K. Krick, ACW:JUL/91[50], *reviewed by* Kenneth P. Czech, CWM:JAN/91[47], *reviewed by* Gary W. Gallagher, CWM:FEB/95[42]564, *reviewed by* Gary W. Gallagher, CWNEWS:SEP/90[4], *reviewed by* Jeffry D. Wert, CWTI:SEP/90[12]

STONEWALL JACKSON'S SURGEON, HUNTER HOLMES MCGUIRE: A BIOGRAPHY, by Maurice F. Shaw, CWNEWS:JUL/94[25], *reviewed by* Michael A. Cavanaugh

STONEWALL JIM: A BIOGRAPHY OF GENERAL JAMES A. WALKER, C.S.A., by Willie W. Caldwell, CWNEWS:JUL/92[4], *reviewed by* Kemp Burpeau

STONEWALL: A BIOGRAPHY OF GENERAL THOMAS J. JACKSON, by Byron Farwell, ACW:NOV/93[58], *reviewed by* Michael D. Hull, CWM:JUL/93[51], *reviewed by* John Christian, CWNEWS:OCT/94[33], *reviewed by* Theodore P. Savas, CWTI:MAY/93[18], *reviewed by* George Skoch

THE STORY OF A CAVALRY REGIMENT: THE CAREER OF THE FOURTH IOWA VETERAN VOLUNTEERS, by William F. Scott, CWNEWS:JAN/94[5], *reviewed by* Gregory J.W. Urwin

THE STORY OF CAMP CHASE, by William H. Knauss, CWNEWS:JAN/92[4], *reviewed by* Frank J. Piatek

THE STORY OF OUR REGIMENT: A HISTORY OF THE 148TH PENNSYLVANIA VOLUNTEERS, (edited by) J.W. Muffly, CWR:VOL4#3[1], *reviewed by* Brian C. Pohanka, CWR:VOL4#3[37]

THE STORY OF THE 116TH REGIMENT PENNSYLVANIA INFANTRY, by St. Clair A. Mulholland, CWNEWS:JAN/92[4], *reviewed by* Dr. Allen C. Guelzo

THE STORY OF THE CONFEDERATE STATES ORDNANCE WORKS AT TYLER, TEXAS, 1861-1865, by William A. Albaugh III, CWNEWS:AUG/95[33], *reviewed by* Norman E. Rourke

THE STORY THE SOLDIERS WOULDN'T TELL—SEX IN THE CIVIL WAR, by Thomas P. Lowry, ACW:JAN/95[62], B&G:FEB/95[26], *reviewed by* Herbert M. Schiller, CWM:DEC/94[17], CWNEWS:APR/95[33], *reviewed by* Ted Alexander, CWR:VOL4#3[37]

STORY OF A CAVALRY REGIMENT: THE CAREER OF THE FOURTH IOWA VETERAN VOLUNTEERS, FROM KANSAS TO GEORGIA, 1861-1865, by William F. Scott, CWR:VOL3#1[80], *reviewed by* Leonne M. Hudson

STRAINED SISTERHOOD: GENDER AND CLASS IN THE BOSTON FEMALE ANTI-SLAVERY SOCIETY, by Debra G. Hansen, CWNEWS:SEP/94[33], *reviewed by* DeAnne Blanton

SUCH ARE THE TRIALS: THE CIVIL WAR DIARIES OF JACOB GANTZ, by Jacob Gantz, (edited by Kathleen Davis), CWNEWS:SEP/92[4], *reviewed by* Robert D. Norris Jr.

THE *SULTANA* TRAGEDY, by Jerry O. Potter, ACW:NOV/92[58], *reviewed by* Mike Haskew, B&G:APR/93[30], *reviewed by* William Marvel, CWNEWS:NOV/92[4], *reviewed by* Terrency J. Winschel, CWTI:JUL/92[10]

SUMTER: THE FIRST DAY OF THE CIVIL WAR, by Robert Henrickson, ACW:JAN/91[54], *reviewed by* Robert I. Alotta, B&G:JUN/91[22], *reviewed by* David R. Ruth, B&G:AUG/91[26], *reviewed by* David R. Ruth, CWNEWS:JUL/91[4], *reviewed by* William G. Roberts, CWTI:SEP/90[12], *reviewed by* Brian McGinty

THE SUPPLEMENT TO THE OFFICIAL RECORDS, VOLS. 1-3, (edited by) Janet B. Hewitt, B&G:FEB/95[26], *reviewed by* Steve Davis

SUPPLEMENT TO THE OFFICIAL RECORDS OF THE UNION AND CONFEDERATE ARMIES, (edited by) Janet Hewett, CWM:FEB/95[7], *reviewed by* Charles R. Norville, CWR:VOL4#3[37]

SYKES' REGULAR INFANTRY DIVISION, 1861-1864: A HISTORY OF REGULAR UNITED STATES INFANTRY OPERATIONS IN THE CIVIL WAR'S EASTERN THEATRE, by Timothy J. Reese, CWNEWS:JUL/91[4], *reviewed by* Richard M. McMurry, CWR:VOL1#3[94], *reviewed by* Colonel M.B. Halsey

SYMBOL, SWORD AND SHIELD: DEFENDING WASHINGTON DURING THE CIVIL WAR, by Benjamin F. Cooling III, CWNEWS:DEC/92[4], *reviewed by* Barry Popchock

TARA REVISITED: WOMEN, WAR, AND THE PLANTATION LEGEND, by Catherine Clinton, CWTI:AUG/95[18]

TECHNOLOGY AND WAR: FROM 2000 B.C. TO THE PRESENT, by Martin van Creveld, CWTI:MAY/89[44], *reviewed by* Richard Pindell

TED BARCLAY, LIBERTY HALL VOLUNTEERS: LETTERS FROM THE STONEWALL BRIGADE, by Ted Barclay, (edited by Charles W. Turner), B&G:DEC/92[26], *reviewed by* James I. Robertson, CWM:MAY/93[51], *reviewed by* John M. Priest, CWNEWS:AUG/93[5], *reviewed by* Frank J. Piatek, CWR:VOL2#4[346], *reviewed by* Brendon H. Beck

TENNESSEE'S BATTERED BRIGADIER: THE LIFE OF GENERAL JOSEPH B. PALMER, by Robert O. Neff, CWNEWS:APR/91[4], *reviewed by* Matthew Penrod, CWM:JAN/91[47], *reviewed by* Gary W. Gallagher, CWNEWS:SEP/91[4], *reviewed by* Steve Wright, CWTI:FEB/91[10]

TERRIBLE INNOCENCE, GENERAL SHERMAN AT WAR, by Mark Coburn, CWNEWS:JAN/94[5], *reviewed by* John F. Marszalek

A TEXAN IN SEARCH OF A FIGHT. BEING THE DIARY LETTERS OF A PRIVATE SOLDIER IN HOOD'S TEXAS BRIGADE, by John C. West, CWR:VOL4#3[37]

TEXAS DIVIDED: LOYALTY AND DISSENT IN THE LONE STAR STATE 1856-1874, by James Marten, CWM:MAR/92[49], *reviewed by* Gary W. Gallagher, CWNEWS:AUG/91[4], *reviewed by* T. Michael Parrish

TEXAS, THE DARK CORNER OF THE CONFEDERACY, by B.P. Gallaway, CWM:APR/95[8], *reviewed by* James A. Ramage, CWTI:JUN/95[24]

THAT DEVIL FORREST: LIFE OF GENERAL NATHAN BEDFORD FORREST, by John A. Wyeth, CWNEWS:JAN/91[4], *reviewed by* Theodore P. Savas

THAT REGIMENT OF HEROES, by Charles LaRocca, CWNEWS:OCT/93[5], *reviewed by* Michael Russert

THEIR TATTERED FLAGS, THE EPIC OF THE CONFEDERACY, by Frank E. Vandiver, AHI:JUL/70[50]

THEY FOLLOWED THE PLUME: THE STORY OF J.E.B. STUART AND HIS STAFF, by Robert J. Trout, ACW:MAR/94[58], *reviewed by* Jon Guttman, B&G:FEB/94[36], *reviewed by* John Hennessy, CWNEWS:MAY/94[5], *reviewed by* Ted Alexander

THEY SLEEP BENEATH THE MOCKINGBIRD: MISSISSIPPI BURIAL SITES AND BIOGRAPHIES OF CONFEDERATE GENERALS, by Harold Cross, CWR:VOL4#3[37]

THE THIRD DAY AT GETTYSBURG & BEYOND, by Gary W. Gallagher, B&G:APR/95[30], *reviewed by* Jeffry D. Wert, CWNEWS:FEB/95[33], *reviewed by* Michael Russert, CWR:VOL4#3[37], CWR:VOL4#3[89], *reviewed by* Michael A. Cavanaugh, CWTI:MAR/95[14], *reviewed by* Diane Treon

THE VIRGINIA CAMPAIGN OF 1864 AND 1865, by A.A. Humphreys, CWNEWS:JAN/91[4], *reviewed by* Michael J. Winey

VIRGINIA RAILROADS IN THE CIVIL WAR, by Angus J. Johnston II, CWM:NOV/91[73], *reviewed by* Gary W. Gallagher

VOICES FROM THE CIVIL WAR, by Richard Wheeler, ACW:SEP/91[54], *reviewed by* Albert Hemingway, AHI:JUL/77[50], *reviewed by* Bell I. Wiley, CWNEWS:JAN/92[4], *reviewed by* Michael Policatti

THE WAR AND LOUISA COUNTY 1861-1865, by Walbrook D. Swank, CWNEWS:OCT/92[4], *reviewed by* Michael Russert

THE WAR BETWEEN THE UNION AND THE CONFEDERACY AND ITS LOST OPPORTUNITIES WITH A HISTORY OF THE 15TH ALABAMA REGIMENT AND THE FORTY-EIGHT BATTLES IN WHICH IT WAS ENGAGED, by William C. Oates, CWR:VOL2#4[346], *reviewed by* Glenn LaFantasie

THE WAR OF THE REBELLION: A COMPILATION OF THE OFFICIAL RECORDS OF THE UNION AND CONFEDERATE ARMIES, by U.S. War Department, CWM:FEB/95[42], *reviewed by* Gary W. Gallagher

THE WAR REMINISCENCES OF MAJOR SILAS T. GRISAMORE, (edited by) Silas T. Grisamore, CWNEWS:DEC/93[5], *reviewed by* Richard M. McMurry

WAR AS VIEWED FROM THE RANKS, by William A. Keesy, CWNEWS:OCT/92[4], *reviewed by* Terrence J. Winschel

WAR DIARIES: THE 1861 KANAWHA VALLEY CAMPAIGN, by David L. Phillips, CWNEWS:AUG/92[4], *reviewed by* Michael Cavanaugh

WAR DIARY OF BREVET BRIGADIER GENERAL JOSEPH STOCKTON, FIRST LIEUTENANT, CAPTAIN, MAJOR AND LIEUTENANT COLONEL 72ND REGIMENT ILLINOIS INFANTRY VOLUNTEEERS (FIRST BOARD OF TRADE REGIMENT), by Joseph Stockton, CWNEWS:AUG/90[4], *reviewed by* Ron Rago

WAR IN KENTUCKY: FROM SHILOH TO PERRYVILLE, by James L. McDonough, ACW:SEP/95[62], *reviewed by* Kenneth P. Czech, B&G:AUG/95[38], *reviewed by* Steven E. Woodworth, CWR:VOL4#2[136], *reviewed by* Theodore P. Savas, CWR:VOL4#3[37]

WAR LETTERS AND DIARIES OF STEPHEN MINOT WELD, 1861-1865, by Stephen M. Weld, CWM:FEB/95[42], *reviewed by* Gary W. Gallagher

WAR OF ANOTHER KIND: A SOUTHERN COMMUNITY IN THE GREAT REBELLION, by Wayne K. Durrill, CWR:VOL4#4[129], *reviewed by* Nancy Smith

WAR YEARS WITH JEB STUART, by William W. Blackford, CWM:AUG/95[45], *reviewed by* Gary W. Gallagher, CWNEWS:AUG/94[33], *reviewed by* Jerry Holsworth

WARGAMMING IN HISTORY: THE AMERICAN CIVIL WAR, by Paul Stevenson, CWNEWS:AUG/92[4], *reviewed by* Dr. Martin G. Martin

WARSHIPS OF THE CIVIL WAR NAVIES, by Paul H. Silverstone, CWNEWS:JUL/91[4], *reviewed by* William F. Howard

THE WARTIME GENESIS OF FREE LABOR: THE UPPER SOUTH, (edited by) Ira Berlin, CWM:AUG/95[45], *reviewed by* Gary W. Gallagher

THE WARTIME PAPERS OF R.E. LEE, (edited by) Clifford Dowdey, CWM:JAN/91[47], *reviewed by* Gary W. Gallagher, CWM:JUL/91[58], *reviewed by* Gary W. Gallagher, CWM:JUN/95[6], *reviewed by* Gary W. Gallagher

WARTIME WASHINGTON: THE CIVIL WAR LETTERS OF ELIZABETH BLAIR LEE, (edited by) Virginia Jeans Laas, AHI:MAR/92[24], CWNEWS:APR/93[4], *reviewed by* Linda Black

WASHINGTON D.C., IN LINCOLN'S TIME, by Noah Brooks, (edited by Herbert Mitgang), CWNEWS:AUG/91[4], *reviewed by* Michael Policatti

WASTED VALOR: THE CONFEDERATE DEAD AT GETTYSBURG, by Gregory A. Coco, CWNEWS:APR/92[4], *reviewed by* Dr. David G. Martin

THE WAY IT WAS: A NOVEL OF THE CIVIL WAR, by G.R. Tredway, CWNEWS:SEP/95[33], *reviewed by* Blake A. Magner

WAY UP NORTH IN DIXIE: A BLACK FAMILY'S CLAIM TO THE CONFEDERATE ANTHEM, by Howard L. Sacks, CWTI:JAN/95[12]

WE NEED MEN: THE UNION DRAFT IN THE CIVIL WAR, by James W. Geary, B&G:DEC/91[30], *reviewed by* Frank J. Welcher, CWM:MAR/92[49], *reviewed by* Gary W. Gallagher, CWNEWS:JUL/92[4], *reviewed by* Michael Russert, CWTI:JUL/92[10], *reviewed by*

WEEP NOT FOR ME, DEAR MOTHER, by Eli Pinson Landers (edited by Elizabeth W. Robinson), B&G:DEC/92[26], *reviewed by* Garold L. Cole

WESTERNERS IN GRAY: THE MEN AND MISSIONS OF THE ELITE FIFTH MISSOURI INFANTRY REGIMENT, by Phillip T. Tucker, B&G:DEC/95[30], *reviewed by* Larry J. Daniel

WESTWARD THE TEXANS: THE CIVIL WAR JOURNAL OF PRIVATE WILLIAM RANDOLPH HOWELL, by William R. Howell, (edited by Jerry D. Thompson), CWM:MAR/92[49], *reviewed by* Gary W. Gallagher, CWNEWS:JUN/92[4], *reviewed by* Anne J. Bailey

WHAT THEY FOUGHT FOR, 1861-1865, by James McPherson, ACW:NOV/94[66], *reviewed by* Ken Bivin, CWNEWS:JUL/95[61], *reviewed by* Allen C. Guelzo, CWR:VOL4#1[78], *reviewed by* Glenn W. LaFantasie, CWR:VOL4#3[37], CWTI:SEP/94[18], *reviewed by* Herman M. Hattaway

WHEN THE GUNS ROARED, by Philip Van Doren Stern, AHI:JUN/66[59]

WHEN THIS CRUEL WAR IS OVER: THE CIVIL WAR LETTERS OF CHARLES HARVEY BREWSTER, by Charles H. Brewster, (edited by David W. Blight), CWNEWS:SEP/94[33], *reviewed by* William F. Howard, CWR:VOL3#4[68], *reviewed by* William A. Taylor

WHERE THEY LIE, THE STORY OF JEWISH SOLDIERS OF THE NORTH AND SOUTH WHOSE DEATHS OCCURRED DURING THE CIVIL WAR,, by Mel Young, ACW:JUL/91[50], *reviewed by* Nat C. Hughes Jr., CWNEWS:NOV/92[4], *reviewed by* Dr. David Martin

WHITE HOUSE OF THE CONFEDERACY, CWR:VOL3#3[92], *reviewed by* Eugene H. Berwanger

WHY THE CONFEDERACY LOST, by Gabor S. Boritt, B&G:OCT/92[30], *reviewed by* Steve Davis, CWNEWS:APR/93[4], *reviewed by* Michael Russert, CWR:VOL2#3[256], *reviewed by* Archie P. McDonald

WHY THE SOUTH LOST THE CIVIL WAR, by Richard E. Beringer, AHI:JAN/87[49], CWNEWS:AUG/92[4], *reviewed by* Michael Russert

THE WILDERNESS CAMPAIGN: MAY 1864, by John Cannan, CWNEWS:JUN/95[33], *reviewed by* Jock Baird

WILLIAM HENRY SEWARD, by Glyndon G. Van Deusen, AHI:FEB/68[57], *reviewed by* James I. Robertson

WILLIAM HENRY SEWARD: LINCOLN'S RIGHT HAND, by John M. Taylor, AHI:MAR/92[20], CWNEWS:OCT/92[4], *reviewed by* Gregory J.W. Urwin, CWTI:DEC/91[12]

WILLIAM HOWARD RUSSELL'S CIVIL WAR: PRIVATE DIARY AND LETTERS 1861-1862, by Martin Howard, (edited by Martin Crawford), CWNEWS:OCT/93[5], *reviewed by* Steven J. Wright

GENERAL JOHN H. WINDER, C.S.A., by Arch F. Blakey, CWM:MAY/91[34], *reviewed by* William J. Miller, CWNEWS:AUG/91[4], *reviewed by* John Marszalek

WINFIELD SCOTT HANCOCK: A SOLDIER'S LIFE, by David M. Jordan, CWNEWS:MAY/90[4], *reviewed by* Richard Sauers

WINSLOW HOMER: PAINTINGS OF THE CIVIL WAR, by Winslow Homer (edited by Marc Simpson), CWNEWS:JUL/91[4], *reviewed by* Anne J. Bailey

WITH A FLASH OF HIS SWORD, THE WRITINGS OF MAJOR HOLMAN S. MELCHER, 20TH MAINE INFANTRY, by Holman S. Melcher, (edited by William B. Styple), B&G:DEC/94[28], *reviewed by* Richard Rollins, CWNEWS:JUL/94[25], *reviewed by* Blake A. Magner

WITH FIRE AND SWORD, by S.H.M. Byers, B&G:APR/93[30], *reviewed by* Wiley Sword, CWNEWS:AUG/95[33], *reviewed by* Kevin J. Weddle

WITH GRANT & MEADE: FROM THE WILDERNESS TO APPOMATTOX, by Theodore Lyman, CWNEWS:DEC/95[29], *reviewed by* Kevin E. O'Brien, CWR:VOL4#2[136], *reviewed by* M. Jane Johansson

WITH MALICE TOWARD NONE: THE LIFE OF ABRAHAM LINCOLN, by Stephen B. Oates, AHI:AUG/77[49], CWTI:DEC/95[38]

WITH PORTER IN NORTH MISSOURI: A CHAPTER IN THE HISTORY OF THE WAR BETWEEN THE STATES, by Joseph A. Mudd, B&G:FEB/93[36], *reviewed by* Donal J. Stanton, CWNEWS:DEC/92[4], *reviewed by* Larry J. Daniel

WITHOUT CONSENT OF CONTRACT: THE RISE AND FALL OF AMERICAN SLAVERY — EVIDENCE AND METHODS (VOLUME IV), by Robert W. Fogel, CWNEWS:NOV/93[5], *reviewed by* Gregory J.W. Urwin

WITHOUT QUARTER: THE WICHITA EXPEDITION AND THE FIGHT ON CROOKED CREEK, by William Y. Chalfant, CWM:FEB/95[7], *reviewed by* William J. Miller, CWNEWS:APR/93[4], *reviewed by* Robert D. Norris Jr.

WITNESS TO AN ERA: THE LIFE AND PHOTOGRAPHS OF ALEXANDER GARDNER by D. Mark Katz, CWM:MAY/91[34], *reviewed by* William J. Miller, CWNEWS:OCT/92[4], *reviewed by* Jeffry D. Wert

WITNESS TO APPOMATTOX, by Richard Wheeler, CWNEWS:AUG/90[4], *reviewed by* Thomas E. Schott

WITNESS TO THE YOUNG REPUBLIC: A YANKEE'S JOURNAL, 1828-1870, by Benjamin B. French, (edited by Donald P. Cole), CWM:JAN/91[47], *reviewed by* Gary W. Gallagher

WOLVES FOR THE BLUE SOLDIERS: INDIAN SCOUTS AND AUXILIARIES WITH THE UNITED STATES ARMY, 1860-90, by Thomas Dunlay, CWNEWS:SEP/95[33], *reviewed by* Ted Alexander

WOMEN AT GETTYSBURG, 1863, by E.F. Conklin, CWNEWS:JUN/94[5], *reviewed by* DeAnne Blanton

WOMEN IN THE CIVIL WAR, by Mary E. Massey, CWNEWS:NOV/95[29], *reviewed by* DeAnne Blanton

THE WOUNDED RIVER: THE CIVIL WAR LETTERS OF JOHN VANCE LAUDERDALE, M.D., by John V. Lauderdale, (edited by Peter Josyph), CWM:APR/94[51], *reviewed by* Courtney B. Wilson, CWNEWS:FEB/94[5], *reviewed by* Anne J. Bailey

YANKEE DUTCHMAN: THE LIFE OF FRANZ SIGEL, by Stephen D. Engel, CWNEWS:APR/94[5], *reviewed by* Norman E. Rourke

YANKEE TIGERS: THROUGH THE CIVIL WAR WITH THE 125TH OHIO, by Ralsa C. Rice, CWNEWS:JAN/94[5], *reviewed by* Barry Popchock

YOURS IN LOVE: THE BIRMINGHAM CIVIL WAR LETTERS, by Theodore Birmingham, (edited by Zoe von Ende Lappin), CWNEWS:JAN/91[4]

ZOUAVES, THE FIRST AND THE BRAVEST, by Michael J. McAfee, CWNEWS:NOV/91[4], *reviewed by* Kathryn Jorgensen, CWNEWS:AUG/92[4], *reviewed by* Dr. Richard A. Sauers

AMERICAN HISTORY ILLUSTRATED MAGAZINE

By issue date, numerical sequence

BLUE & GRAY MAGAZINE
By issue date, numerical sequence

CIVIL WAR REGIMENTS: *A Journal of the American Civil War*

Volume number, numerical sequence

CIVIL WAR TIMES, ILLUSTRATED
Magazine
By issue date, numerical sequence

MARCH 1989, (Volume XXVIII, Number 1)

APRIL 1989, (Volume XXVIII, Number 2)

MAY 1989, (Volume XXVIII, Number 3)

SUMMER 1989, (Volume XXVIII, Number 4)

SEPTEMBER 1989, (Volume XXVIII, Number 5)

DECEMBER 1989, (Volume XXVIII, Number 6)

FEBRUARY 1990, (Volume XXVIII, Number 7)

MILITARY HISTORY MAGAZINE
By issue, numerical sequence